Collins
Thesaurus
A–Z

HarperCollins Publishers
Westerhill Road
Bishopbriggs
Glasgow
G64 2QT

Second Edition 2006

ISBN-10 0–00–722385–4
ISBN-13 978–0–00–722385–5

www.collins.co.uk

A catalogue record for this book is available from the British Library.

Designed by Mark Thomson

Typeset by Wordcraft

Printed in Italy by Legoprint S.P.A.

Acknowledgments
We would like to thank those authors and publishers who kindly gave permission for copyright material to be used in the Collins Word Web. We would also like to thank Times Newspapers Ltd for providing valuable data.

CONTENTS

EDITORIAL STAFF

EDITORS
Justin Crozier
Lorna Gilmour

COMPUTING SUPPORT
Thomas Callan
Nigel Rochford

FOR THE PUBLISHERS
Morven Dooner
Elaine Higgleton

ABOUT THE TYPE

This thesaurus is typeset in CollinsFedra, a special version of the Fedra family of types designed by Peter Bil'ak. CollinsFedra has been customized especially for Collins dictionaries and thesauruses; it includes both sans serif and serif versions, in several different weights. Its relatively large x-height and open 'eye', and its basis in the tradition of humanist letterforms, make CollinsFedra both familiar and easy to read at small sizes. It has been designed to use the minimum space without sacrificing legibility, as well as including a number of characters and signs that are specific to dictionary typography. Its companion phonetic type is the first of its kind to be drawn according to the same principles as the regular typeface, rather than assembled from rotated and reflected characters from other types.

Peter Bil'ak (b. 1973, Slovakia) is a graphic and type designer living in the Netherlands. He is the author of two books, *Illegibility* and *Transparency*. As well as the Fedra family, he has designed several other typefaces including Eureka. His typotheque.com website has become a focal point for research and debate around contemporary type design.

FOREWORD

The Collins Discovery Thesaurus is the the ideal reference for home, school, and the office. With a comprehensive range of alternatives for each entry, as well as a huge choice of opposites, the Discovery Thesaurus enables you to use words with precision and confidence.

Collins thesauruses have always been designed to give the user as much help as possible in finding the right word for every occasion. Collins pioneered the A–Z arrangement of main entry words, which lets you go straight to any word without having to resort to an index, just as if you were looking up a word in a dictionary. This arrangement is continued in the new Discovery Thesaurus, where it is combined with a clear, accessible layout, allowing easy access to the information you need.

Where appropriate, the entries include related words that have separate entries in the text, as well as opposites, enabling readers to find the words they need quickly and systematically. To reflect English's status as a truly global language, the Discovery Thesaurus contains words and phrases from all over the English-speaking world, with regional labels indicating where these terms are used. This new book also takes account of recent changes in the language, and includes up-to-the-minute terms like *cybersquatting, docu-soap, e-commerce, GMO, twenty-four-seven, webcam,* and *webcast.*

The World in Action supplement contains a wealth of important facts and figures covering geography, politics, and weights and measures, making the Discovery Thesaurus a useful all-round reference book, and the ideal companion to the Collins Discovery English Dictionary.

Main Entry Words

Main entry words are printed in bold type:

altogether

Parts of Speech

Parts of speech are shown in italics. Where a word has several senses for one part of speech, the senses are numbered:

altogether *adverb* **1**

Alternatives

The key synonym for each sense is given in small capitals, with other alternatives given in roman:

altogether *adverb* **1** ABSOLUTELY quite, completely, totally, perfectly,fully, thoroughly, wholly, utterly, downright, one hundred per cent (*informal*), undisputedly, lock, stock and barrel
2 COMPLETELY, all, fully, entirely, comprehensively, thoroughly, wholly, utterly, downright, one hundred per cent (*informal*), in every respect

Opposites

Opposites are indented with left-facing arrows:

<<OPPOSITE partially

Related words

Related words are indented with right-facing arrows:

>>RELATED WORD *prefix* circum-

Usage notes

Usage notes are shown in indented panels:

> The use of actress is now very much in decline, and women who workin the profession invariably prefer to be referred to as *actors*

ABBREVIATIONS USED IN THIS THESAURUS

AD	anno Domini	*med*	medicine
adj	adjective	*masc*	masculine
adv	adverb	*meteorol*	meteorology
anat	anatomy	*mil*	military
archit	architecture	*n*	noun
astrol	astrology	N	North
Aust	Australia(n)	*naut*	nautical
BC	before Christ	NW	Northwest
biol	biology	NZ	New Zealand
Brit	British	*obs*	obsolete
chem	chemistry	*offens*	offensive
C of E	Church of England	*orig*	originally
conj	conjunction	*path*	Pathology
derog	derogatory	*photog*	photography
dial	dialect	*pl*	plural
E	East	*prep*	preposition
eg	for example	*pron*	pronoun
Eng	English	*psychol*	psychology
esp	especially	®	trademark
etc	et cetera	RC	Roman Catholic
fem	feminine	*S*	South
foll	followed	*S Afr*	South Africa(n)
geom	geometry	*Scot*	Scottish
hist	history	*sing*	singular
hum	humorous	*US*	United States
inf	informal	*usu*	usually
interj	interjection	*v*	verb
lit	literary	W	West
masc	masculine	*zool*	zoology

aback *adverb* ▷▷ **taken aback** SURPRISED, thrown, shocked, stunned, confused, astonished, staggered, startled, bewildered, astounded, disconcerted, bowled over (*informal*), stupefied, floored (*informal*), knocked for six, dumbfounded, left open-mouthed, nonplussed, flabbergasted (*informal*)

abandon *verb* 1 LEAVE, strand, ditch, leave behind, walk out on, forsake, jilt, run out on, throw over, turn your back on, desert, dump, leave high and dry, leave in the lurch
2 STOP, drop, give up, halt, cease, cut out, pack in (*Brit informal*), discontinue, leave off, desist from
<< OPPOSITE continue
3 GIVE UP, resign from, yield, surrender, relinquish, renounce, waive, cede, forgo, abdicate
<< OPPOSITE keep
4 (takes *ship* as object) EVACUATE, quit, withdraw from, vacate, depart from
<< OPPOSITE maintain
▷ *noun* RECKLESSNESS, dash, wildness, wantonness, unrestraint, careless freedom
<< OPPOSITE restraint

abandoned *adjective* 1 UNOCCUPIED, empty, deserted, vacant, derelict, uninhabited
<< OPPOSITE occupied
2 DESERTED, dropped, rejected, neglected, stranded, ditched, discarded, relinquished, left, forsaken, cast off, jilted, cast aside, cast out, cast away
3 UNINHIBITED, wild, uncontrolled, unbridled, unrestrained, unconstrained
<< OPPOSITE inhibited

abandonment *noun* 1 DESERTION, leaving, forsaking, jilting
2 EVACUATION, leaving, quitting, departure, withdrawal
3 STOPPING, cessation, discontinuation
4 RENUNCIATION, giving up, surrender, waiver, abdication, cession, relinquishment

abate *verb* 1 DECREASE, decline, relax, ease, sink, fade, weaken, diminish, dwindle, lessen, slow, wane, subside, ebb, let up, slacken, attenuate, taper off
<< OPPOSITE increase
2 REDUCE, slow, relax, ease, relieve, moderate, weaken, dull, diminish, decrease, lessen, alleviate, quell, mitigate, attenuate
<< OPPOSITE increase

abatement *noun* 1 DECREASE, slowing, decline, easing, sinking, fading, weakening, relaxation, dwindling, lessening, waning, subsiding, ebbing, cessation, let-up, slackening, diminution, tapering off, attenuation
2 REDUCTION, slowing, relief, easing, weakening, dulling, decrease, lessening, cutback, quelling, moderation, remission, slackening, mitigation, diminution, curtailment, alleviation, attenuation, extenuation

abattoir *noun* SLAUGHTERHOUSE, shambles, butchery

abbey *noun* MONASTERY, convent, priory, cloister, nunnery, friary

abbreviate *verb* SHORTEN, reduce, contract, trim, cut, prune, summarize, compress, condense, abridge
<< OPPOSITE expand

abbreviated *adjective* SHORTENED, shorter, reduced, brief, potted, trimmed, pruned, cut, summarized, compressed, concise, condensed, abridged
<< OPPOSITE expanded

abbreviation *noun* SHORTENING, reduction, résumé, trimming, summary, contraction, compression, synopsis, précis, abridgment

abdicate *verb* 1 RESIGN, retire, quit, step down (*informal*)
2 GIVE UP, yield, hand over, surrender, relinquish, renounce, waive, vacate, cede, abjure
3 RENOUNCE, give up, abandon, surrender, relinquish, waive, forgo, abnegate

abdication *noun* 1 RESIGNATION, quitting, retirement, retiral (*chiefly Scot*)
2 GIVING UP, yielding, surrender, waiving, renunciation, cession, relinquishment, abjuration

abdomen *noun* STOMACH, guts (*slang*), belly, tummy (*informal*), midriff, midsection, makutu (NZ), puku (NZ)
>> RELATED WORD *adjective* abdominal

abdominal *adjective* GASTRIC, intestinal, visceral

abduct *verb* KIDNAP, seize, carry off, run off with, run away with, make off with, snatch (*slang*)

abduction *noun* KIDNAPPING, seizure, carrying off

aberrant *adjective* 1 ABNORMAL, odd, strange, extraordinary, curious, weird, peculiar, eccentric, queer, irregular, erratic, deviant, off-the-wall (*slang*), oddball (*informal*), anomalous, untypical, wacko (*slang*), outré, daggy (*Austral & NZ informal*)
2 DEPRAVED, corrupt, perverted, perverse, degenerate, deviant, debased, debauched

aberration *noun* ANOMALY, exception, defect, abnormality, inconsistency, deviation, quirk, peculiarity, divergence, departure, irregularity, incongruity

abet *verb* 1 HELP, aid, encourage, sustain, assist, uphold, back, second, incite, egg on, succour
2 ENCOURAGE, further, forward, promote, urge, boost, prompt, spur, foster, incite, connive at

abetting *noun* HELP, backing, support, aid, assistance, encouragement, abetment, abettal

abeyance *noun* ▷▷ **in abeyance** SHELVED, pending, on ice (*informal*), in cold storage (*informal*), hanging fire, suspended

abhor *verb* HATE, loathe, despise, detest, shrink from, shudder at, recoil from, be repelled by, have an aversion to, abominate, execrate, regard with repugnance *or* horror
<< OPPOSITE love

abhorrent *adjective* HATEFUL, hated, offensive, disgusting, horrible, revolting, obscene, distasteful, horrid, repellent, obnoxious, despicable, repulsive, heinous, odious, repugnant, loathsome, abominable, execrable, detestable

abide *verb* 1 TOLERATE, suffer, accept, bear, endure, brook, hack (*slang*), put up with, take, stand, stomach, thole (*Scot*)
2 LAST, continue, remain, survive, carry on, endure, persist, keep on
▷▷ **abide by something** OBEY, follow, agree to, carry out, observe, fulfil, stand by, act on, comply with, hold to, heed, submit to, conform to, keep to, adhere to, mind

abiding *adjective* ENDURING, lasting, continuing, remaining, surviving, permanent, constant, prevailing, persisting, persistent, eternal, tenacious, firm, fast, everlasting, unending, unchanging
<< OPPOSITE brief

ability *noun* 1 CAPABILITY, power, potential, facility, capacity, qualification, competence, proficiency, competency, potentiality
<< OPPOSITE inability
2 SKILL, talent, know-how (*informal*), gift, expertise, faculty, flair, competence, energy, accomplishment, knack, aptitude, proficiency, dexterity, cleverness, potentiality, adroitness, adeptness

abject *adjective* 1 WRETCHED, miserable, hopeless, dismal, outcast, pitiful, forlorn, deplorable, pitiable
2 SERVILE, humble, craven, cringing, fawning, submissive, grovelling, subservient, slavish, mean, low, obsequious
<< OPPOSITE dignified
3 DESPICABLE, base, degraded, worthless, vile, sordid, debased, reprehensible, contemptible, dishonourable, ignoble, detestable, scungy (*Austral & NZ*)

ablaze *adjective* 1 ON FIRE, burning, flaming, blazing, fiery, alight, aflame, afire
2 BRIGHT, brilliant, flashing, glowing, sparkling, illuminated, gleaming, radiant, luminous, incandescent, aglow
3 PASSIONATE, excited, stimulated, fierce, enthusiastic, aroused, animated, frenzied, fervent, impassioned, fervid

able *adjective* CAPABLE, experienced, fit, skilled, expert, powerful, masterly, effective, qualified, talented, gifted, efficient, clever, practised, accomplished, competent, skilful, adept, masterful, strong, proficient, adroit, highly endowed
<< OPPOSITE incapable

able-bodied *adjective* STRONG, firm, sound, fit, powerful, healthy, strapping, hardy, robust, vigorous, sturdy, hale, stout, staunch, hearty, lusty, right as rain (*Brit informal*), tough, capable, sturdy, Herculean, fighting fit, sinewy, fit as a fiddle
<< OPPOSITE weak

abnormal *adjective* UNUSUAL, different, odd, strange, surprising, extraordinary, remarkable, bizarre, unexpected, curious, weird, exceptional, peculiar, eccentric, unfamiliar, queer, irregular, phenomenal, uncommon, erratic, monstrous, singular, unnatural, deviant, unconventional, off-the-wall (*slang*), oddball (*informal*), out of the ordinary, left-field (*informal*), anomalous, atypical, aberrant, untypical, wacko (*slang*), outré, daggy (*Austral & NZ informal*)
<< OPPOSITE normal

abnormality *noun* 1 STRANGENESS, deviation, eccentricity, aberration, peculiarity, idiosyncrasy, irregularity, weirdness, singularity, oddness, waywardness, unorthodoxy, unexpectedness, queerness, unnaturalness, bizarreness, unusualness, extraordinariness, aberrance, atypicalness, uncommonness, untypicalness, curiousness
2 ANOMALY, flaw, rarity, deviation, oddity, aberration, exception, peculiarity, deformity, monstrosity, irregularity, malformation

abnormally *adverb* UNUSUALLY, oddly, strangely, extremely, exceptionally, extraordinarily, overly, excessively, peculiarly, particularly, bizarrely, disproportionately, singularly, fantastically, unnaturally, uncannily, inordinately, uncommonly, prodigiously, freakishly, atypically, subnormally, supernormally

abode *noun* HOME, house, quarters, lodging, pad (*slang*), residence, habitat, dwelling, habitation, domicile, dwelling place

abolish *verb* DO AWAY WITH, end, destroy, eliminate, shed, cancel, axe (*informal*), get rid of, ditch (*slang*), dissolve, junk (*informal*), suppress, overturn, throw out, discard, wipe out, overthrow, void, terminate, drop, trash (*slang*), repeal, eradicate, put an end to, quash, extinguish, dispense with, revoke, stamp out, obliterate, subvert, jettison, repudiate, annihilate, rescind, exterminate, invalidate, bring to an end, annul, nullify, blot out, expunge, abrogate, vitiate, extirpate, kennet (*Austral slang*), jeff (*Austral slang*)
<< OPPOSITE establish

abolition *noun* ERADICATION, ending, end, withdrawal, destruction, removal, overturning, wiping out, overthrow, voiding, extinction, repeal, elimination, cancellation, suppression, quashing, termination, stamping out, subversion, extermination, annihilation, blotting out, repudiation, erasure, annulment, obliteration, revocation, effacement, nullification, abrogation, rescission, extirpation, invalidation, vitiation, expunction

abominable *adjective* DETESTABLE, shocking, terrible, offensive, foul, disgusting, horrible, revolting, obscene, vile, horrid, repellent, atrocious, obnoxious, despicable, repulsive, base, heinous, hellish, odious, hateful, repugnant, reprehensible, loathsome, abhorrent, contemptible, villainous, nauseous, wretched, accursed, execrable, godawful (*slang*)
<< OPPOSITE pleasant

abomination *noun* 1 OUTRAGE, bête noire, horror, evil, shame, plague, curse, disgrace, crime, atrocity, torment, anathema, barbarism, bugbear
2 HATRED, hate, horror, disgust, dislike, loathing, distaste, animosity, aversion, revulsion, antagonism, antipathy, enmity, ill will, animus, abhorrence, repugnance, odium, detestation, execration

aboriginal *adjective* INDIGENOUS, first, earliest, original, primary, ancient, native, primitive, pristine, primordial, primeval, autochthonous

aborigine *noun* ORIGINAL INHABITANT, native, aboriginal, indigene

abort *verb* 1 TERMINATE (*a pregnancy*), miscarry
2 STOP, end, finish, check, arrest, halt, cease, bring *or* come to a halt *or* standstill, axe (*informal*), pull up, terminate, call off, break off, cut short, pack in (*Brit informal*), discontinue, desist

abortion *noun* 1 TERMINATION, feticide, aborticide, miscarriage, deliberate miscarriage
2 FAILURE, disappointment, fiasco, misadventure, vain effort
3 MONSTROSITY

abortive *adjective* FAILED, failing, useless, vain, unsuccessful, idle, ineffective, futile, fruitless, unproductive, ineffectual, miscarried, unavailing, bootless

abound *verb* BE PLENTIFUL, thrive, flourish, be numerous, proliferate, be abundant, be thick on the ground, superabound
▷▷ **abound with** *or* **in something** OVERFLOW WITH, be packed with, teem with, be crowded with, swell with, crawl with, swarm with, be jammed with, be infested with, be thronged with, luxuriate with

about *preposition* 1 REGARDING, on, re, concerning, touching, dealing with, respecting, referring to, relating to, concerned with, connected with, relative to, with respect to, as regards, anent (*Scot*)
2 AROUND, over, through, round, throughout, all over
3 NEAR, around, close to, bordering, nearby, beside, close by, adjacent to, just round the corner from, in the neighbourhood of, alongside of, contiguous to, within sniffing distance of (*informal*), at close quarters to, a hop, skip and a jump away from (*informal*)
▷ *adverb* 1 APPROXIMATELY, around, almost, nearing, nearly, approaching, close to, roughly, just about, more or less, in the region of, in the vicinity of, not far off
2 EVERYWHERE, around, all over, here and there, on all sides, in all directions, to and fro, from place to place, hither and thither
▷▷ **about to** ON THE POINT OF, ready to, intending to, on the verge *or* brink of

about-turn *noun* CHANGE OF DIRECTION, reverse, reversal, turnaround, U-turn, right

about (turn), about-face, volte-face, turnabout, paradigm shift
▷ *verb* CHANGE DIRECTION, reverse, about-face, volte-face, face the opposite direction, turn about *or* around, turn through 180 degrees, do *or* perform a U-turn *or* volte-face

above *preposition* 1 OVER, upon, beyond, on top of, exceeding, higher than, atop
<< OPPOSITE under
2 SENIOR TO, over, ahead of, in charge of, higher than, surpassing, superior to, more powerful than
<< OPPOSITE subordinate to
3 BEFORE, more than, rather than, beyond, instead of, sooner than, in preference to
▷ *adverb* OVERHEAD, upward, in the sky, on high, in heaven, atop, aloft, up above, skyward
▷ *adjective* PRECEDING, earlier, previous, prior, foregoing, aforementioned, aforesaid
>> RELATED WORDS *prefixes* super-, supra-, sur-

abrasion *noun* 1 (*Medical*) GRAZE, scratch, trauma (*Pathology*), scrape, scuff, chafe, surface injury
2 RUBBING, wear, scratching, scraping, grating, friction, scouring, attrition, corrosion, wearing down, erosion, scuffing, chafing, grinding down, wearing away, abrading

abrasive *adjective* 1 HARSH, cutting, biting, tough, sharp, severe, bitter, rough, hard, nasty, cruel, annoying, brutal, stern, irritating, unpleasant, grating, abusive, galling, unkind, hurtful, caustic, vitriolic, pitiless, unfeeling, comfortless
2 ROUGH, scratching, scraping, grating, scuffing, chafing, scratchy, frictional, erosive
▷ *noun* SCOURER, grinder, burnisher, scarifier, abradant

abreast *adverb* ALONGSIDE, level, beside, in a row, side by side, neck and neck, shoulder to shoulder
▷▷ **abreast of** *or* **with** INFORMED ABOUT, in touch with, familiar with, acquainted with, up to date with, knowledgeable about, conversant with, up to speed with (*informal*), in the picture about, *au courant* with, *au fait* with, keeping your finger on the pulse of

abridge *verb* SHORTEN, reduce, contract, trim, clip, diminish, decrease, abstract, digest, cut down, cut back, cut, prune, concentrate, lessen, summarize, compress, curtail, condense, abbreviate, truncate, epitomize, downsize, précis, synopsize (*US*)
<< OPPOSITE expand

abridged *adjective* SHORTENED, shorter, reduced, brief, potted (*informal*), trimmed, diminished, pruned, summarized, cut, compressed, curtailed, concise, condensed, abbreviated
<< OPPOSITE expanded

abroad *adverb* 1 OVERSEAS, out of the country, beyond the sea, in foreign lands
2 ABOUT, everywhere, circulating, at large, here and there, current, all over, in circulation

abrupt *adjective* 1 SUDDEN, unexpected, hurried, rapid, surprising, quick, swift, rash, precipitate, hasty, impulsive, headlong, unforeseen, unanticipated
<< OPPOSITE slow
2 CURT, direct, brief, sharp, rough, short, clipped, blunt, rude, tart, impatient, brisk, concise, snappy, terse, gruff, succinct, pithy, brusque, offhand, impolite, monosyllabic, ungracious, discourteous, uncivil, unceremonious, snappish
<< OPPOSITE polite
3 STEEP, sharp, sheer, sudden, precipitous
<< OPPOSITE gradual

abruptly *adverb* 1 SUDDENLY, short, unexpectedly, all of a sudden, hastily, precipitately, all at once, hurriedly
<< OPPOSITE gradually
2 CURTLY, bluntly, rudely, briskly, tersely, shortly, sharply, brusquely, gruffly, snappily
<< OPPOSITE politely

abscess *noun* BOIL, infection, swelling, blister, ulcer, inflammation, gathering, whitlow, blain, carbuncle, pustule, bubo, furuncle (*Pathology*), gumboil, parulis (*Pathology*)

abscond *verb* ESCAPE, flee, get away, bolt, fly, disappear, skip, run off, slip away, clear out, flit (*informal*), make off, break free *or* out, decamp, hook it (*slang*), do a runner (*slang*), steal away, sneak away, do a bunk (*Brit slang*), fly the coop (*US & Canad informal*), skedaddle (*informal*), take a powder (*US & Canad slang*), go on the lam (*US & Canad slang*), make your getaway, do a Skase (*Austral informal*), make *or* effect your escape

absence *noun* 1 TIME OFF, leave, break, vacation, recess, truancy, absenteeism, nonappearance, nonattendance
2 LACK, deficiency, deprivation, omission, scarcity, want, need, shortage, dearth, privation, unavailability, nonexistence

absent *adjective* 1 AWAY, missing, gone, lacking, elsewhere, unavailable, not present, truant, nonexistent, nonattendant
<< OPPOSITE present
2 ABSENT-MINDED, blank, unconscious, abstracted, vague, distracted, unaware, musing, vacant, preoccupied, empty, absorbed, bemused, oblivious, dreamy, daydreaming, faraway, unthinking, heedless, inattentive, unheeding
<< OPPOSITE alert
▷▷ **absent yourself** STAY AWAY, withdraw, depart, keep away, truant, abscond, play truant, slope off (*informal*), bunk off (*slang*),

remove yourself

absentee *noun* NONATTENDER, stay-at-home, truant, no-show, stayaway

absent-minded *adjective* FORGETFUL, absorbed, abstracted, vague, absent, distracted, unaware, musing, preoccupied, careless, bemused, oblivious, dreamy, faraway, engrossed, unthinking, neglectful, heedless, inattentive, unmindful, unheeding, apt to forget, in a brown study, ditzy *or* ditsy (*slang*)
<< OPPOSITE alert

absolute *adjective* **1** COMPLETE, total, perfect, entire, pure, sheer, utter, outright, thorough, downright, consummate, unqualified, full-on (*informal*), out-and-out, unadulterated, unmitigated, dyed-in-the-wool, thoroughgoing, unalloyed, unmixed, arrant, deep-dyed (*usually derogatory*)
2 SUPREME, sovereign, unlimited, ultimate, full, utmost, unconditional, unqualified, predominant, superlative, unrestricted, pre-eminent, unrestrained, tyrannical, peerless, unsurpassed, unquestionable, matchless, peremptory, unbounded
3 AUTOCRATIC, supreme, unlimited, autonomous, arbitrary, dictatorial, all-powerful, imperious, domineering, tyrannical, despotic, absolutist, tyrannous, autarchical
4 DEFINITE, sure, certain, positive, guaranteed, actual, assured, genuine, exact, precise, decisive, conclusive, unequivocal, unambiguous, infallible, categorical, unquestionable, dinkum (*Austral & NZ informal*), nailed-on (*slang*)

absolutely *adverb* **1** COMPLETELY, totally, perfectly, quite, fully, entirely, purely, altogether, thoroughly, wholly, utterly, consummately, every inch, to the hilt, a hundred per cent, one hundred per cent, unmitigatedly, lock, stock and barrel
<< OPPOSITE somewhat
2 DEFINITELY, surely, certainly, clearly, obviously, plainly, truly, precisely, exactly, genuinely, positively, decidedly, decisively, without doubt, unquestionably, undeniably, categorically, without question, unequivocally, conclusively, unambiguously, beyond any doubt, infallibly

absolution *noun* FORGIVENESS, release, freedom, liberation, discharge, amnesty, mercy, pardon, indulgence, exemption, acquittal, remission, vindication, deliverance, dispensation, exoneration, exculpation, shriving, condonation

absolve *verb* EXCUSE, free, clear, release, deliver, loose, forgive, discharge, liberate, pardon, exempt, acquit, vindicate, remit, let off, set free, exonerate, exculpate
<< OPPOSITE condemn

absorb *verb* **1** SOAK UP, drink in, devour, suck up, receive, digest, imbibe, ingest, osmose
2 ENGROSS, hold, involve, fill, arrest, fix, occupy, engage, fascinate, preoccupy, engulf, fill up, immerse, rivet, captivate, monopolize, enwrap

absorbed *adjective* ENGROSSED, lost, involved, fixed, concentrating, occupied, engaged, gripped, fascinated, caught up, intrigued, wrapped up, preoccupied, immersed, riveted, captivated, enthralled, rapt, up to your ears

absorbent *adjective* POROUS, receptive, imbibing, spongy, permeable, absorptive, blotting, penetrable, pervious, assimilative

absorbing *adjective* FASCINATING, interesting, engaging, gripping, arresting, compelling, intriguing, enticing, preoccupying, enchanting, seductive, riveting, captivating, alluring, bewitching, engrossing, spellbinding
<< OPPOSITE boring

absorption *noun* **1** SOAKING UP, consumption, digestion, sucking up, osmosis
2 IMMERSION, holding, involvement, concentration, occupation, engagement, fascination, preoccupation, intentness, captivation, raptness

abstain from *verb* REFRAIN FROM, avoid, decline, give up, stop, refuse, cease, do without, shun, renounce, eschew, leave off, keep from, forgo, withhold from, forbear, desist from, deny yourself, kick (*informal*)
<< OPPOSITE abandon yourself to

abstention *noun* **1** ABSTAINING, non-voting, refusal to vote
2 ABSTINENCE, refraining, avoidance, forbearance, eschewal, desistance, nonindulgence

abstinence *noun* ABSTENTION, continence, temperance, self-denial, self-restraint, forbearance, refraining, avoidance, moderation, sobriety, asceticism, teetotalism, abstemiousness, soberness
<< OPPOSITE self-indulgence

abstract *adjective* THEORETICAL, general, complex, academic, intellectual, subtle, profound, philosophical, speculative, unrealistic, conceptual, indefinite, deep, separate, occult, hypothetical, generalized, impractical, arcane, notional, abstruse, recondite, theoretic, conjectural, unpractical, nonconcrete
<< OPPOSITE actual
▷ *noun* SUMMARY, résumé, outline, extract, essence, summing-up, digest, epitome, rundown, condensation, compendium, synopsis, précis, recapitulation, review, abridgment

<< OPPOSITE expansion
▷ *verb* EXTRACT, draw, pull, remove, separate, withdraw, isolate, pull out, take out, take away, detach, dissociate, pluck out
<< OPPOSITE add

abstracted *adjective* PREOCCUPIED, withdrawn, remote, absorbed, intent, absent, distracted, unaware, wrapped up, bemused, immersed, oblivious, dreamy, daydreaming, faraway, engrossed, rapt, absent-minded, heedless, inattentive, distrait, woolgathering

abstraction *noun* 1 CONCEPT, thought, idea, view, theory, impression, formula, notion, hypothesis, generalization, theorem, generality
2 ABSENT-MINDEDNESS, musing, preoccupation, daydreaming, vagueness, remoteness, absence, inattention, dreaminess, obliviousness, absence of mind, pensiveness, woolgathering, distractedness, bemusedness

absurd *adjective* RIDICULOUS, crazy (*informal*), silly, incredible, outrageous, foolish, unbelievable, daft (*informal*), hilarious, ludicrous, meaningless, unreasonable, irrational, senseless, preposterous, laughable, funny, stupid, farcical, illogical, incongruous, comical, zany, idiotic, nonsensical, inane, dumb-ass (*slang*)
<< OPPOSITE sensible

absurdity *noun* RIDICULOUSNESS, nonsense, folly, stupidity, foolishness, silliness, idiocy, irrationality, incongruity, meaninglessness, daftness (*informal*), senselessness, illogicality, ludicrousness, unreasonableness, preposterousness, farcicality, craziness (*informal*), bêtise (*rare*), farcicalness, illogicalness

absurdly *adverb* RIDICULOUSLY, incredibly, unbelievably, foolishly, ludicrously, unreasonably, incongruously, laughably, irrationally, implausibly, preposterously, illogically, inanely, senselessly, idiotically, inconceivably, farcically

abundance *noun* 1 PLENTY, heap (*informal*), bounty, exuberance, profusion, plethora, affluence, fullness, opulence, plenitude, fruitfulness, copiousness, ampleness, cornucopia, plenteousness, plentifulness
<< OPPOSITE shortage
2 WEALTH, money, funds, capital, cash, riches, resources, assets, fortune, possessions, prosperity, big money, wad (*US & Canad slang*), affluence, big bucks (*informal, chiefly US*), opulence, megabucks (*US & Canad slang*), tidy sum (*informal*), lucre, pretty penny (*informal*), pelf, top whack (*informal*)

abundant *adjective* PLENTIFUL, full, rich, liberal, generous, lavish, ample, infinite, overflowing, exuberant, teeming, copious, inexhaustible, bountiful, luxuriant, profuse, rank, well-provided, well-supplied, bounteous, plenteous
<< OPPOSITE scarce

abundantly *adverb* PLENTIFULLY, greatly, freely, amply, richly, liberally, fully, thoroughly, substantially, lavishly, extensively, generously, profusely, copiously, exuberantly, in plentiful supply, luxuriantly, unstintingly, bountifully, bounteously, plenteously, in great *or* large numbers
<< OPPOSITE sparsely

abuse *noun* 1 MALTREATMENT, wrong, damage, injury, hurt, harm, spoiling, bullying, exploitation, oppression, imposition, mistreatment, manhandling, ill-treatment, rough handling
2 INSULTS, blame, slights, curses, put-downs, libel, censure, reproach, scolding, defamation, indignities, offence, tirade, derision, slander, rudeness, vilification, invective, swear words, opprobrium, insolence, upbraiding, aspersions, character assassination, disparagement, vituperation, castigation, contumely, revilement, traducement, calumniation
3 MISUSE, corruption, perversion, misapplication, misemployment, misusage
▷ *verb* 1 ILL-TREAT, wrong, damage, hurt, injure, harm, mar, oppress, maul, molest, impose upon, manhandle, rough up, brutalize, maltreat, handle roughly, knock about *or* around
<< OPPOSITE care for
2 INSULT, injure, offend, curse, put down, smear, libel, slate (*informal, chiefly Brit*), slag (off) (*slang*), malign, scold, swear at, disparage, castigate, revile, vilify, slander, defame, upbraid, slight, inveigh against, call names, traduce, calumniate, vituperate
<< OPPOSITE praise

abusive *adjective* 1 VIOLENT, wild, rough, cruel, savage, brutal, vicious, destructive, harmful, maddened, hurtful, unrestrained, impetuous, homicidal, intemperate, raging, furious, injurious, maniacal
<< OPPOSITE kind
2 INSULTING, offensive, rude, degrading, scathing, maligning, scolding, affronting, contemptuous, disparaging, castigating, reviling, vilifying, invective, scurrilous, defamatory, insolent, derisive, censorious, slighting, libellous, upbraiding, vituperative, reproachful, slanderous, traducing, opprobrious, calumniating, contumelious
<< OPPOSITE complimentary

abut *verb* ADJOIN, join, touch, border, neighbour, link to, attach to, combine with, connect with, couple with, communicate with, annex, meet, unite with, verge on, impinge, append, affix to

abysmal *adjective* DREADFUL, bad, terrible, awful, appalling, dismal, dire, ghastly, hideous, atrocious, godawful (*informal*)

abyss *noun* CHASM, gulf, split, crack, gap, pit, opening, breach, hollow, void, gorge, crater, cavity, ravine, cleft, fissure, crevasse, bottomless depth, abysm

academic *adjective* 1 SCHOLASTIC, school, university, college, educational, campus, collegiate

2 SCHOLARLY, learned, intellectual, literary, erudite, highbrow, studious, lettered

3 THEORETICAL, ideal, abstract, speculative, hypothetical, impractical, notional, conjectural

▷ *noun* SCHOLAR, intellectual, don, student, master, professor, fellow, pupil, lecturer, tutor, scholastic, bookworm, man of letters, egghead (*informal*), savant, academician, acca (*Austral slang*), bluestocking (*usually disparaging*), schoolman

academy *noun* COLLEGE, school, university, institution, institute, establishment, seminary, centre of learning, whare wananga (*NZ*)

accede to *verb* 1 AGREE TO, accept, grant, endorse, consent to, give in to, surrender to, yield to, concede to, acquiesce in, assent to, comply with, concur to

2 (takes *throne* as object) INHERIT, come to, assume, succeed, come into, attain, succeed to (*as heir*), enter upon, fall heir to

accelerate *verb* 1 INCREASE, grow, advance, extend, expand, build up, strengthen, raise, swell, intensify, enlarge, escalate, multiply, inflate, magnify, proliferate, snowball

<< OPPOSITE fall

2 EXPEDITE, press, forward, promote, spur, further, stimulate, hurry, step up (*informal*), speed up, facilitate, hasten, precipitate, quicken

<< OPPOSITE delay

3 SPEED UP, speed, advance, quicken, get under way, gather momentum, get moving, pick up speed, put your foot down (*informal*), open up the throttle, put on speed

<< OPPOSITE slow down

acceleration *noun* HASTENING, hurrying, stepping up (*informal*), expedition, speeding up, stimulation, advancement, promotion, spurring, quickening

accent *noun* PRONUNCIATION, tone, articulation, inflection, brogue, intonation, diction, modulation, elocution, enunciation, accentuation

▷ *verb* EMPHASIZE, stress, highlight, underline, bring home, underscore, accentuate, give emphasis to, call *or* draw attention to

accentuate *verb* EMPHASIZE, stress, highlight, accent, underline, bring home, underscore, foreground, give emphasis to, call *or* draw attention to

<< OPPOSITE minimize

accept *verb* 1 RECEIVE, take, gain, pick up, secure, collect, have, get, obtain, acquire

2 TAKE ON, try, begin, attempt, bear, assume, tackle, acknowledge, undertake, embark on, set about, commence, avow, enter upon

<< OPPOSITE reject

3 ACKNOWLEDGE, believe, allow, admit, adopt, approve, recognize, yield, concede, swallow (*informal*), buy (*slang*), affirm, profess, consent to, buy into (*slang*), cooperate with, take on board, accede, acquiesce, concur with

4 STAND, take, experience, suffer, bear, allow, weather, cope with, tolerate, sustain, put up with, wear (*Brit slang*), stomach, endure, undergo, brook, hack (*slang*), abide, withstand, bow to, yield to, countenance, like it or lump it (*informal*)

acceptability *noun* ADEQUACY, fitness, suitability, propriety, appropriateness, admissibility, permissibility, acceptableness, satisfactoriness

<< OPPOSITE unacceptability

acceptable *adjective* 1 SATISFACTORY, fair, all right, suitable, sufficient, good enough, standard, adequate, so-so (*informal*), tolerable, up to scratch (*informal*), passable, up to the mark

<< OPPOSITE unsatisfactory

2 PLEASANT, pleasing, welcome, satisfying, grateful, refreshing, delightful, gratifying, agreeable, pleasurable

acceptance *noun* 1 ACCEPTING, taking, receiving, obtaining, acquiring, reception, receipt

2 ACKNOWLEDGEMENT, agreement, belief, approval, recognition, admission, consent, consensus, adoption, affirmation, assent, credence, accession, approbation, concurrence, accedence, stamp *or* seal of approval

3 TAKING ON, admission, assumption, acknowledgement, undertaking, avowal

4 SUBMISSION, yielding, resignation, concession, compliance, deference, passivity, acquiescence

accepted *adjective* AGREED, received, common, standard, established, traditional, confirmed, regular, usual, approved, acknowledged, recognized, sanctioned, acceptable, universal, authorized, customary, agreed upon, time-honoured

<< OPPOSITE unconventional

access *noun* 1 ADMISSION, entry, passage, entrée, admittance, ingress

2 ENTRANCE, road, door, approach, entry, path, gate, opening, way in, passage, avenue, doorway, gateway, portal, passageway

accessibility *noun* 1 APPROACHABILITY, availability, readiness, nearness, handiness
2 AVAILABILITY, possibility, attainability, obtainability

accessible *adjective* HANDY, near, nearby, at hand, within reach, at your fingertips, reachable, achievable, get-at-able (*informal*), a hop, skip and a jump away
<< OPPOSITE inaccessible

accession *noun* ▷▷ **accession to** SUCCESSION TO, attainment of, inheritance of, elevation to, taking up of, assumption of, taking over of, taking on of

accessory *noun* 1 EXTRA, addition, supplement, convenience, attachment, add-on, component, extension, adjunct, appendage, appurtenance
2 ACCOMPLICE, partner, ally, associate (*in crime*), assistant, helper, colleague, collaborator, confederate, henchman, abettor
▷ *adjective* SUPPLEMENTARY, extra, additional, accompanying, secondary, subordinate, complementary, auxiliary, abetting, supplemental, contributory, ancillary

accident *noun* 1 CRASH, smash, wreck, collision, pile-up (*informal*), smash-up (*informal*)
2 MISFORTUNE, blow, disaster, tragedy, setback, calamity, mishap, misadventure, mischance, stroke of bad luck
3 CHANCE, fortune, luck, fate, hazard, coincidence, fluke, fortuity

accidental *adjective* 1 UNINTENTIONAL, unexpected, incidental, unforeseen, unintended, unplanned, unpremeditated
<< OPPOSITE deliberate
2 CHANCE, random, casual, unintentional, unintended, unplanned, fortuitous, inadvertent, serendipitous, unlooked-for, uncalculated, contingent

accidentally *adverb* UNINTENTIONALLY, casually, unexpectedly, incidentally, by accident, by chance, inadvertently, unwittingly, randomly, unconsciously, by mistake, haphazardly, fortuitously, adventitiously
<< OPPOSITE deliberately

acclaim *verb* PRAISE, celebrate, honour, cheer, admire, hail, applaud, compliment, salute, approve, congratulate, clap, pay tribute to, commend, exalt, laud, extol, crack up (*informal*), eulogize
▷ *noun* PRAISE, honour, celebration, approval, tribute, applause, cheering, clapping, ovation, accolades, plaudits, kudos, commendation, exaltation, approbation, acclamation, eulogizing, panegyric, encomium
<< OPPOSITE criticism

acclaimed *adjective* CELEBRATED, famous, acknowledged, praised, outstanding, distinguished, admired, renowned, noted, highly rated, eminent, revered, famed, illustrious, well received, much vaunted, highly esteemed, much touted, well thought of, lionized, highly thought of
<< OPPOSITE criticized

accolade *noun* 1 HONOUR, award, recognition, tribute
2 PRAISE, approval, acclaim, applause, compliment, homage, laud (*literary*), eulogy, congratulation, commendation, acclamation (*formal*), recognition, tribute, ovation, plaudit

accommodate *verb* 1 HOUSE, put up, take in, lodge, board, quarter, shelter, entertain, harbour, cater for, billet
2 HELP, support, aid, encourage, assist, befriend, cooperate with, abet, lend a hand to, lend a helping hand to, give a leg up to (*informal*)
3 ADAPT, match, fit, fashion, settle, alter, adjust, modify, compose, comply, accustom, reconcile, harmonize

accommodating *adjective* OBLIGING, willing, kind, friendly, helpful, polite, cooperative, agreeable, amiable, courteous, considerate, hospitable, unselfish, eager to please, complaisant
<< OPPOSITE unhelpful

accommodation *noun* 1 HOUSING, homes, houses, board, quartering, quarters, digs (*Brit informal*), shelter, sheltering, lodging(s), dwellings
2 ADAPTATION, change, settlement, compromise, composition, adjustment, transformation, reconciliation, compliance, modification, alteration, conformity

accompaniment *noun* 1 BACKING MUSIC, backing, support, obbligato
2 SUPPLEMENT, extra, addition, extension, companion, accessory, complement, decoration, frill, adjunct, appendage, adornment

accompany *verb* 1 GO WITH, lead, partner, protect, guide, attend, conduct, escort, shepherd, convoy, usher, chaperon
2 OCCUR WITH, belong to, come with, supplement, coincide with, join with, coexist with, go together with, follow, go cheek by jowl with

accompanying *adjective* ADDITIONAL, added, extra, related, associate, associated, joint, fellow, connected, attached, accessory, attendant, complementary, supplementary, supplemental, concurrent, concomitant, appended

accomplice *noun* PARTNER IN CRIME, ally,

associate, assistant, companion, accessory, comrade, helper, colleague, collaborator, confederate, henchman, coadjutor, abettor

accomplish *verb* REALIZE, produce, effect, finish, complete, manage, achieve, perform, carry out, conclude, fulfil, execute, bring about, attain, consummate, bring off (*informal*), do, effectuate

<< OPPOSITE fail

accomplished *adjective* SKILLED, able, professional, expert, masterly, talented, gifted, polished, practised, cultivated, skilful, adept, consummate, proficient

<< OPPOSITE unskilled

accomplishment *noun* 1 ACHIEVEMENT, feat, attainment, act, stroke, triumph, coup, exploit, deed

2 *often plural* TALENT, ability, skill, gift, achievement, craft, faculty, capability, forte, attainment, proficiency

3 ACCOMPLISHING, effecting, finishing, carrying out, achievement, conclusion, bringing about, execution, completion, realization, fulfilment, attainment, consummation

accord *noun* 1 TREATY, contract, agreement, arrangement, settlement, pact, deal (*informal*)

2 SYMPATHY, agreement, concert, harmony, accordance, unison, rapport, conformity, assent, unanimity, concurrence

<< OPPOSITE conflict

▷ *verb* GRANT, give, award, render, assign, present with, endow with, bestow on, confer on, vouchsafe, impart with

<< OPPOSITE refuse

▷▷ **accord with something** AGREE WITH, match, coincide with, fit with, square with, correspond with, conform with, concur with, tally with, be in tune with (*informal*), harmonize with, assent with

accordance *noun* ▷▷ **in accordance with** IN AGREEMENT WITH, consistent with, in harmony with, in concert with, in sympathy with, in conformity with, in assent with, in congruence with

accordingly *adverb* 1 CONSEQUENTLY, SO, thus, therefore, hence, subsequently, in consequence, ergo, as a result

2 APPROPRIATELY, correspondingly, properly, suitably, fitly

accost *verb* CONFRONT, challenge, address, stop, approach, oppose, halt, greet, hail, solicit (*as a prostitute*), buttonhole

account *noun* 1 DESCRIPTION, report, record, story, history, detail, statement, relation, version, tale, explanation, narrative, chronicle, portrayal, recital, depiction, narration

2 IMPORTANCE, standing, concern, value, note, benefit, use, profit, worth, weight, advantage, rank, import, honour, consequence, substance, merit, significance, distinction, esteem, usefulness, repute, momentousness

3 (*Commerce*) LEDGER, charge, bill, statement, balance, tally, invoice, computation

▷ *verb* CONSIDER, rate, value, judge, estimate, think, hold, believe, count, reckon, assess, weigh, calculate, esteem, deem, compute, gauge, appraise, regard as

▷▷ **account for something** 1 CONSTITUTE, make, make up, compose, comprise

2 EXPLAIN, excuse, justify, clarify, give a reason for, give an explanation for, illuminate, clear up, answer for, rationalize, elucidate

3 PUT OUT OF ACTION, kill, destroy, put paid to, incapacitate

▷▷ **on account of** BY REASON OF, because of, owing to, on the basis of, for the sake of, on the grounds of

accountability *noun* RESPONSIBILITY, liability, culpability, answerability, chargeability

accountable *adjective* ANSWERABLE, subject, responsible, obliged, liable, amenable, obligated, chargeable

accountant *noun* AUDITOR, book-keeper, bean counter (*informal*)

accounting *noun* ACCOUNTANCY, auditing, book-keeping

accoutrements *plural noun* PARAPHERNALIA, fittings, dress, material, clothing, stuff, equipment, tackle, gear, things, kit, outfit, trimmings, fixtures, array, decorations, baggage, apparatus, furnishings, trappings, garb, adornments, ornamentation, bells and whistles, impedimenta, appurtenances, equipage

accredit *verb* 1 APPROVE, support, back, commission, champion, favour, guarantee, promote, recommend, appoint, recognize, sanction, advocate, license, endorse, warrant, authorize, ratify, empower, certify, entrust, vouch for, depute

2 ATTRIBUTE, credit, assign, ascribe, trace to, put down to, lay at the door of

accredited *adjective* AUTHORIZED, official, commissioned, guaranteed, appointed, recognized, sanctioned, licensed, endorsed, empowered, certified, vouched for, deputed, deputized

accrue *verb* ACCUMULATE, issue, increase, grow, collect, gather, flow, build up, enlarge, follow, ensue, pile up, amass, spring up, stockpile

accumulate *verb* BUILD UP, increase, grow, be stored, collect, gather, pile up, amass, stockpile, hoard, accrue, cumulate

<< OPPOSITE disperse

accumulation *noun* 1 COLLECTION, increase, stock, store, mass, build-up, pile, stack, heap,

rick, stockpile, hoard
2 GROWTH, collection, gathering, build-up, aggregation, conglomeration, augmentation

accuracy *noun* EXACTNESS, precision, fidelity, authenticity, correctness, closeness, truth, verity, nicety, veracity, faithfulness, truthfulness, niceness, exactitude, strictness, meticulousness, carefulness, scrupulousness, preciseness, faultlessness, accurateness
<< OPPOSITE inaccuracy

accurate *adjective* 1 PRECISE, right, close, regular, correct, careful, strict, exact, faithful, explicit, authentic, spot-on, just, clear-cut, meticulous, truthful, faultless, scrupulous, unerring, veracious
<< OPPOSITE inaccurate
2 CORRECT, right, true, exact, faithful, spot-on (*Brit informal*), faultless, on the money (US)

accurately *adverb* 1 PRECISELY, rightly, correctly, closely, carefully, truly, properly, strictly, literally, exactly, faithfully, meticulously, to the letter, justly, scrupulously, truthfully, authentically, unerringly, faultlessly, veraciously
2 EXACTLY, rightly, closely, correctly, definitely, truly, properly, precisely, nicely, strictly, faithfully, explicitly, unequivocally, scrupulously, truthfully

accusation *noun* CHARGE, complaint, allegation, indictment, impeachment, recrimination, citation, denunciation, attribution, imputation, arraignment, incrimination

accuse *verb* 1 POINT A *or* THE FINGER AT, blame for, denounce, attribute to, hold responsible for, impute blame to
<< OPPOSITE exonerate
2 CHARGE WITH, indict for, impeach for, arraign for, cite, tax with, censure with, incriminate for, recriminate for
<< OPPOSITE absolve

accustom *verb* FAMILIARIZE, train, coach, discipline, adapt, instruct, make used, school, season, acquaint, inure, habituate, acclimatize, make conversant

accustomed *adjective* 1 USED, trained, familiar, disciplined, given to, adapted, acquainted, in the habit of, familiarized, seasoned, inured, habituated, exercised, acclimatized
<< OPPOSITE unaccustomed
2 USUAL, established, expected, general, common, standard, set, traditional, normal, fixed, regular, ordinary, familiar, conventional, routine, everyday, customary, habitual, wonted
<< OPPOSITE unusual

ace *noun* 1 (*Cards, Dice*) ONE, single point
2 (*informal*) EXPERT, star, champion, authority, winner, professional, master, pro (*informal*), specialist, genius, guru, buff (*informal*), wizard (*informal*), whizz (*informal*), virtuoso, connoisseur, hotshot (*informal*), past master, dab hand (*Brit informal*), maven (US)
▷ *adjective* (*informal*) GREAT, good, brilliant, mean (*slang*), fine, champion, expert, masterly, wonderful, excellent, cracking (*Brit informal*), outstanding, superb, fantastic (*informal*), tremendous (*informal*), marvellous (*informal*), terrific (*informal*), mega (*slang*), awesome (*slang*), dope (*slang*), admirable, virtuoso, first-rate, brill (*informal*), bitchin' (*US slang*), chillin' (*US slang*), booshit (*Austral slang*), exo (*Austral slang*), sik (*Austral slang*), ka pai (NZ), rad (*informal*), phat (*slang*), schmick (*Austral informal*)

acerbic *adjective* SHARP, cutting, biting, severe, acid, bitter, nasty, harsh, stern, rude, scathing, acrimonious, barbed, unkind, unfriendly, sarcastic, sardonic, caustic, churlish, vitriolic, trenchant, acrid, brusque, rancorous, mordant

ache *verb* 1 HURT, suffer, burn, pain, smart, sting, pound, throb, be tender, twinge, be sore
2 SUFFER, hurt, grieve, sorrow, agonize, be in pain, go through the mill (*informal*), mourn, feel wretched
▷ *noun* 1 PAIN, discomfort, suffering, hurt, smart, smarting, cramp, throb, throbbing, irritation, tenderness, pounding, spasm, pang, twinge, soreness, throe (*rare*)
2 ANGUISH, suffering, pain, torture, distress, grief, misery, mourning, torment, sorrow, woe, heartache, heartbreak

achievable *adjective* ATTAINABLE, obtainable, winnable, reachable, realizable, within your grasp, graspable, gettable, acquirable, possible, accessible, probable, feasible, practicable, accomplishable

achieve *verb* ACCOMPLISH, reach, fulfil, finish, complete, gain, perform, earn, do, get, win, carry out, realize, obtain, conclude, acquire, execute, bring about, attain, consummate, procure, bring off (*informal*), effectuate, put the tin lid on

achievement *noun* 1 ACCOMPLISHMENT, effort, feat, deed, stroke, triumph, coup, exploit, act, attainment, feather in your cap
2 FULFILMENT, effecting, performance, production, execution, implementation, completion, accomplishment, realization, attainment, acquirement, carrying out *or* through

achiever *noun* SUCCESS, winner, dynamo, high-flyer, doer, go-getter (*informal*), organizer, active person, overachiever, man *or* woman of action, wheeler-dealer (*informal*)

aching *adjective* 1 PAINFUL, suffering, hurting, tired, smarting, pounding, raw, tender, sore, throbbing, harrowing, inflamed, excruciating, agonizing

2 LONGING, anxious, eager, pining, hungering, craving, yearning, languishing, thirsting, ardent, avid, wishful, wistful, hankering, desirous

acid *adjective* 1 SOUR, sharp, tart, pungent, biting, acidic, acerbic, acrid, acetic, vinegary, acidulous, acidulated, vinegarish, acerb

<< OPPOSITE sweet

2 SHARP, cutting, biting, severe, bitter, harsh, stinging, scathing, acrimonious, barbed, pungent, hurtful, sarcastic, sardonic, caustic, vitriolic, acerbic, trenchant, mordant, mordacious

<< OPPOSITE kindly

acidity *noun* SOURNESS, bitterness, sharpness, pungency, tartness, acerbity, acridness, acidulousness, acridity, vinegariness, vinegarishness

acknowledge *verb* 1 ADMIT, own up, allow, accept, reveal, grant, declare, recognize, yield, concede, confess, disclose, affirm, profess, divulge, accede, acquiesce, 'fess up (*US slang*)

<< OPPOSITE deny

2 GREET, address, notice, recognize, salute, nod to, accost, tip your hat to

<< OPPOSITE snub

3 REPLY TO, answer, notice, recognize, respond to, come back to, react to, write back to, retort to

<< OPPOSITE ignore

acknowledged *adjective* ACCEPTED, admitted, established, confirmed, declared, approved, recognized, well-known, sanctioned, confessed, authorized, professed, accredited, agreed upon

acknowledgment *or* **acknowledgement** *noun* 1 RECOGNITION, allowing, understanding, yielding, profession, admission, awareness, acceptance, confession, realization, accession, acquiescence

2 GREETING, welcome, notice, recognition, reception, hail, hailing, salute, salutation

3 APPRECIATION, answer, thanks, credit, response, reply, reaction, recognition, gratitude, indebtedness, thankfulness, gratefulness

acme *noun* HEIGHT, top, crown, summit, peak, climax, crest, optimum, high point, pinnacle, culmination, zenith, apex, apogee, vertex

<< OPPOSITE depths

acolyte *noun* 1 FOLLOWER, fan, supporter, pupil, convert, believer, admirer, backer, partisan, disciple, devotee, worshipper, apostle, cohort (*chiefly US*), adherent, henchman, habitué, votary

2 ATTENDANT, assistant, follower, helper, altar boy

acquaint *verb* TELL, reveal, advise, inform, communicate, disclose, notify, enlighten, divulge, familiarize, apprise, let (someone) know

acquaintance *noun* 1 ASSOCIATE, contact, ally, colleague, comrade, confrère

<< OPPOSITE intimate

2 RELATIONSHIP, association, exchange, connection, intimacy, fellowship, familiarity, companionship, social contact, cognizance, conversance, conversancy

<< OPPOSITE unfamiliarity

acquainted *adjective* ▷▷ **acquainted with** FAMILIAR WITH, aware of, in on, experienced in, conscious of, informed of, alive to, privy to, knowledgeable about, versed in, conversant with, apprised of, cognizant of, up to speed with, *au fait* with

acquiesce *verb* SUBMIT, agree, accept, approve, yield, bend, surrender, consent, tolerate, comply, give in, conform, succumb, go along with, bow to, cave in (*informal*), concur, assent, capitulate, accede, play ball (*informal*), toe the line, hoist the white flag

<< OPPOSITE resist

acquiescence *noun* AGREEMENT, yielding, approval, acceptance, consent, harmony, giving in, submission, compliance, obedience, conformity, assent, accession, concord, concurrence

acquire *verb* GET, win, buy, receive, land, score (*slang*), gain, achieve, earn, pick up, bag, secure, collect, gather, realize, obtain, attain, amass, procure, come into possession of

<< OPPOSITE lose

acquisition *noun* 1 ACQUIRING, gaining, achievement, procurement, attainment, acquirement, obtainment

2 PURCHASE, buy, investment, property, gain, prize, asset, possession

acquisitive *adjective* GREEDY, grabbing, grasping, hungry, selfish, avid, predatory, rapacious, avaricious, desirous, covetous

<< OPPOSITE generous

acquit *verb* CLEAR, free, release, deliver, excuse, relieve, discharge, liberate, vindicate, exonerate, absolve, exculpate

<< OPPOSITE find guilty

▷▷ **acquit yourself** BEHAVE, bear yourself, conduct yourself, comport yourself

acquittal *noun* CLEARANCE, freeing, release, relief, liberation, discharge, pardon, setting free, vindication, deliverance, absolution, exoneration, exculpation

acrid *adjective* 1 PUNGENT, biting, strong, burning, sharp, acid, bitter, harsh, stinging, irritating, caustic, astringent, vitriolic, highly flavoured, acerb

2 HARSH, cutting, biting, sharp, bitter, nasty, acrimonious, caustic, vitriolic, trenchant, mordant, mordacious

acrimonious *adjective* BITTER, cutting, biting, sharp, severe, hostile, crabbed, sarcastic, embittered, caustic, petulant, spiteful, churlish, astringent, vitriolic, acerbic, trenchant, irascible, testy, censorious, rancorous, mordant, peevish, splenetic, mordacious
<< OPPOSITE good-tempered

acrimony *noun* BITTERNESS, harshness, rancour, ill will, virulence, sarcasm, pungency, asperity, tartness, astringency, irascibility, peevishness, acerbity, churlishness, trenchancy, mordancy
<< OPPOSITE goodwill

acrobat *noun* GYMNAST, balancer, tumbler, tightrope walker, rope walker, funambulist

across *preposition* 1 OVER, on the other *or* far side of, past, beyond
2 THROUGHOUT, over, all over, right through, all through, covering, straddling, everywhere in, through the whole of, from end to end of, over the length and breadth of
▷ *adverb* FROM SIDE TO SIDE, athwart, transversely, crossways *or* crosswise

across-the-board *adjective* GENERAL, full, complete, total, sweeping, broad, widespread, comprehensive, universal, blanket, thorough, wholesale, panoramic, indiscriminate, all-inclusive, wall-to-wall, all-embracing, overarching, all-encompassing, thoroughgoing, without exception *or* omission, one-size-fits-all
<< OPPOSITE limited

act *verb* 1 DO SOMETHING, perform, move, function, go about, conduct yourself, undertake something
2 PLAY, seem to be, pose as, pretend to be, posture as, imitate, sham, feign, characterize, enact, personify, impersonate, play the part of
3 PERFORM, mimic, mime
▷ *noun* 1 DEED, action, step, performance, operation, doing, move, blow, achievement, stroke, undertaking, exploit, execution, feat, accomplishment, exertion
2 PRETENCE, show, front, performance, display, attitude, pose, stance, fake, posture, façade, sham, veneer, counterfeit, feigning, affectation, dissimulation
3 LAW, bill, measure, resolution, decree, statute, ordinance, enactment, edict
4 PERFORMANCE, show, turn, production, routine, presentation, gig (*informal*), sketch
▷▷ **act for someone** STAND IN FOR, serve, represent, replace, substitute for, cover for, take the place of, fill in for, deputize for, function in place of
▷▷ **act on** *or* **upon something** 1 OBEY, follow, carry out, observe, embrace, execute, comply with, heed, conform to, adhere to, abide by, yield to, act upon, be ruled by, act in accordance with, do what is expected
2 AFFECT, change, influence, impact, transform, alter, modify
▷▷ **act up** MISBEHAVE, carry on, cause trouble, mess about, be naughty, horse around (*informal*), give trouble, give someone grief (*Brit & S African*), give bother

acting *noun* PERFORMANCE, playing, performing, theatre, dramatics, portraying, enacting, portrayal, impersonation, characterization, stagecraft
▷ *adjective* TEMPORARY, substitute, intervening, interim, provisional, surrogate, stopgap, pro tem

action *noun* 1 DEED, move, act, performance, blow, exercise, achievement, stroke, undertaking, exploit, feat, accomplishment, exertion
2 MEASURE, act, step, operation, manoeuvre
3 LAWSUIT, case, cause, trial, suit, argument, proceeding, dispute, contest, prosecution, litigation
4 ENERGY, activity, spirit, force, vitality, vigour, liveliness, vim
5 EFFECT, working, work, force, power, process, effort, operation, activity, movement, influence, functioning, motion, exertion
6 BATTLE, war, fight, fighting, conflict, clash, contest, encounter, combat, engagement, hostilities, warfare, fray, skirmish, sortie, affray

activate *verb* START, move, trigger (off), stimulate, turn on, set off, initiate, switch on, propel, rouse, prod, get going, mobilize, kick-start (*informal*), set in motion, impel, galvanize, set going, actuate
<< OPPOSITE stop

activation *noun* START, triggering, turning on, switching on, animation, arousal, initiation, mobilization, setting in motion, actuation

active *adjective* 1 BUSY, involved, occupied, engaged, tiring, lively, energetic, bustling, restless, on the move, strenuous, tireless, on the go (*informal*)
<< OPPOSITE sluggish
2 ENERGETIC, strong, spirited, quick, vital, alert, dynamic, lively, vigorous, potent, animated, vibrant, forceful, nimble, diligent, industrious, sprightly, vivacious, on the go (*informal*), alive and kicking, spry, full of beans (*informal*), bright-eyed and bushy-tailed (*informal*)
<< OPPOSITE inactive
3 IN OPERATION, working, live, running, moving, acting, functioning, stirring, at work, in business, in action, operative, in force, effectual, astir

activist *noun* MILITANT, partisan, organizer,

warrior

activity *noun* 1 ACTION, work, life, labour, movement, energy, exercise, spirit, enterprise, motion, bustle, animation, vigour, hustle, exertion, hurly-burly, liveliness, activeness

<< OPPOSITE inaction

2 PURSUIT, act, project, scheme, task, pleasure, interest, enterprise, undertaking, occupation, hobby, deed, endeavour, pastime, avocation

actor *or* **actress** *noun* PERFORMER, player, artiste, leading man *or* lady, Thespian, luvvie (*informal*), trouper, thesp (*informal*), play-actor, dramatic artist, tragedian *or* tragedienne

> The use of *actress* is now very much on the decline, and women who work in the profession invariably prefer to be referred to as *actors*

actual *adjective* 1 GENUINE, real, true, confirmed, authentic, verified, truthful, bona fide, dinkum (*Austral & NZ informal*)

<< OPPOSITE unreal

2 REAL, substantial, concrete, definite, tangible

<< OPPOSITE theoretical

> The words *actual* and *actually* are often used when speaking, but should only be used in writing where they add something to the meaning of a sentence. For example, in the sentence *he actually rather enjoyed the film*, the word *actually* is only needed if there was originally some doubt as to whether he would enjoy it

actuality *noun* 1 REALITY, truth, substance, verity, materiality, realness, substantiality, factuality, corporeality

2 FACT, truth, reality, verity

actually *adverb* REALLY, in fact, indeed, essentially, truly, literally, genuinely, in reality, in truth, in actuality, in point of fact, veritably, as a matter of fact ▷ see **actual**

acumen *noun* JUDGMENT, intelligence, perception, wisdom, insight, wit, ingenuity, sharpness, cleverness, keenness, shrewdness, discernment, perspicacity, sagacity, smartness, smarts (*slang, chiefly US*), astuteness, acuteness, perspicuity

acute *adjective* 1 SERIOUS, important, dangerous, critical, crucial, alarming, severe, grave, sudden, urgent, decisive

2 SHARP, shooting, powerful, violent, severe, intense, overwhelming, distressing, stabbing, cutting, fierce, piercing, racking, exquisite, poignant, harrowing, overpowering, shrill, excruciating

3 PERCEPTIVE, sharp, keen, smart, sensitive, clever, subtle, piercing, penetrating, discriminating, discerning, ingenious, astute, intuitive, canny, incisive, insightful, observant, perspicacious

<< OPPOSITE slow

adage *noun* SAYING, motto, maxim, proverb, dictum, precept, by-word, saw, axiom, aphorism, apophthegm

adamant *adjective* DETERMINED, firm, fixed, stiff, rigid, set, relentless, stubborn, uncompromising, insistent, resolute, inflexible, unrelenting, inexorable, unyielding, intransigent, immovable, unbending, obdurate, unshakable

<< OPPOSITE flexible

adapt *verb* 1 ADJUST, change, match, alter, modify, accommodate, comply, conform, reconcile, harmonize, familiarize, habituate, acclimatize

2 CONVERT, change, prepare, fit, fashion, make, shape, suit, qualify, transform, alter, modify, tailor, remodel, tweak (*informal*), metamorphose, customize

adaptability *noun* FLEXIBILITY, versatility, resilience, variability, convertibility, plasticity, malleability, pliability, changeability, pliancy, adjustability, compliancy, modifiability, adaptableness, alterability

adaptable *adjective* 1 FLEXIBLE, variable, versatile, resilient, easy-going, changeable, modifiable, conformable

2 ADJUSTABLE, flexible, compliant, malleable, pliant, plastic, modifiable, alterable

adaptation *noun* 1 ACCLIMATIZATION, naturalization, habituation, familiarization, accustomedness

2 CONVERSION, change, shift, variation, adjustment, transformation, modification, alteration, remodelling, reworking, refitting

add *verb* 1 COUNT UP, total, reckon, sum up, compute, add up, tot up

<< OPPOSITE take away

2 INCLUDE, attach, supplement, increase by, adjoin, annex, amplify, augment, affix, append, enlarge by

▷▷ **add to something** INCREASE, boost, expand, strengthen, enhance, step up (*informal*), intensify, raise, advance, spread, extend, heighten, enlarge, escalate, multiply, inflate, magnify, amplify, augment, proliferate

▷▷ **add up** 1 COUNT UP, add, total, count, reckon, calculate, sum up, compute, tally, tot up, add together

2 MAKE SENSE, hold up, be reasonable, ring true, be plausible, stand to reason, hold water, bear examination, bear investigation

▷▷ **add up to something** MEAN, reveal, indicate, imply, amount to, signify

addict *noun* 1 JUNKIE (*informal*), abuser, user (*informal*), druggie (*informal*), freak (*informal*), fiend (*informal*), mainliner (*slang*), smackhead

(*slang*), space cadet (*slang*), pill-popper (*informal*), head (*slang*), pothead (*slang*), dope-fiend (*slang*), cokehead (*slang*), acidhead (*slang*), hashhead (*slang*)
2 FAN, lover, nut (*slang*), follower, enthusiast, freak (*informal*), admirer, buff (*informal*), junkie (*informal*), devotee, fiend (*informal*), adherent, rooter (*US*), zealot, groupie (*slang*), aficionado
>> RELATED WORD *suffix* -holic

addicted *adjective* HOOKED, dependent
>> RELATED WORD *suffix* -holic

addiction *noun* 1 DEPENDENCE, need, habit, weakness, obsession, attachment, craving, vulnerability, subordination, enslavement, subservience, overreliance
2 *with* **to** LOVE OF, passion for, attachment to, fondness for, zeal for, fervour for, ardour for

addictive *adjective* HABIT-FORMING, compelling, compulsive, causing addiction *or* dependency, moreish *or* morish (*informal*)

addition *noun* 1 EXTRA, supplement, complement, adjunct, increase, gain, bonus, extension, accessory, additive, appendix, increment, appendage, addendum
2 INCLUSION, adding, increasing, extension, attachment, adjoining, insertion, incorporation, annexation, accession, affixing, augmentation
<< OPPOSITE removal
3 COUNTING UP, totalling, reckoning, summing up, adding up, computation, totting up, summation
<< OPPOSITE subtraction
▷▷ **in addition to** AS WELL AS, along with, on top of, besides, to boot, additionally, over and above, to say nothing of, into the bargain

additional *adjective* EXTRA, more, new, other, added, increased, further, fresh, spare, supplementary, auxiliary, ancillary, appended

additive *noun* ADDED INGREDIENT, artificial *or* synthetic ingredient, E number, extra, supplement

addled *adjective* CONFUSED, silly, foolish, at sea, bewildered, mixed-up, muddled, perplexed, flustered, befuddled

address *noun* 1 DIRECTION, label, inscription, superscription
2 LOCATION, home, place, house, point, position, situation, site, spot, venue, lodging, pad (*slang*), residence, dwelling, whereabouts, abode, locus, locale, domicile
3 SPEECH, talk, lecture, discourse, sermon, dissertation, harangue, homily, oration, spiel (*informal*), disquisition, korero (*NZ*)
▷ *verb* 1 GIVE A SPEECH TO, talk to, speak to, lecture, discourse, harangue, give a talk to, spout to, hold forth to, expound to, orate to, sermonize to
2 SPEAK TO, talk to, greet, hail, salute, invoke, communicate with, accost, approach, converse with, apostrophize
▷▷ **address yourself to something** CONCENTRATE ON, turn to, focus on, take up, look to, undertake, engage in, take care of, attend to, knuckle down to, devote yourself to, apply yourself to

adept *adjective* SKILFUL, able, skilled, expert, masterly, practised, accomplished, versed, masterful, proficient, adroit, dexterous
<< OPPOSITE unskilled
▷ *noun* EXPERT, master, genius, buff (*informal*), whizz (*informal*), hotshot (*informal*), rocket scientist (*informal, chiefly US*), dab hand (*Brit informal*), maven (*US*)

adequacy *noun* SUFFICIENCY, capability, competence, suitability, tolerability, fairness, commensurateness, requisiteness, satisfactoriness

adequate *adjective* 1 PASSABLE, acceptable, middling, average, fair, ordinary, moderate, satisfactory, competent, mediocre, so-so (*informal*), tolerable, up to scratch (*informal*), presentable, unexceptional
<< OPPOSITE inadequate
2 SUFFICIENT, enough, capable, suitable, requisite
<< OPPOSITE insufficient

adherent *noun* SUPPORTER, fan, advocate, follower, admirer, partisan, disciple, protagonist, devotee, henchman, hanger-on, upholder, sectary
<< OPPOSITE opponent
▷ *adjective* ADHERING, holding, sticking, clinging, sticky, tacky, adhesive, tenacious, glutinous, gummy, gluey, mucilaginous

adhere to *verb* 1 FOLLOW, keep, maintain, respect, observe, be true to, fulfil, obey, heed, keep to, abide by, be loyal to, mind, be constant to, be faithful to
2 BE FAITHFUL TO, follow, support, respect, observe, be true to, obey, be devoted to, be attached to, keep to, be loyal to
3 STICK TO, attach to, cling to, unite to, glue to, fix to, fasten to, hold fast to, paste to, cement to, cleave to, glue on to, stick fast to, cohere to

adhesion *noun* STICKING, grip, attachment, cohesion, coherence, adherence, adhesiveness

Adhesion is preferred when talking about sticking or holding fast in a physical sense and a useful alternative that could be used here is *sticking*. The word *adherence*, although close in meaning, would be the preferred word when talking about principles, rules and values

adhesive *noun* GLUE, cement, gum, paste, mucilage

▷ *adjective* STICKY, holding, sticking, attaching, clinging, adhering, tacky, cohesive, tenacious, glutinous, gummy, gluey, mucilaginous

ad hoc *adjective* MAKESHIFT, emergency, improvised, impromptu, expedient, stopgap, jury-rigged (*chiefly Nautical*)
<< OPPOSITE permanent

adjacent *adjective* ADJOINING, neighbouring, nearby, abutting
<< OPPOSITE far away

adjoin *verb* CONNECT WITH *or* TO, join, neighbour (on), link with, attach to, combine with, couple with, communicate with, touch on, border on, annex, approximate, unite with, verge on, impinge on, append, affix to, interconnect with

adjoining *adjective* CONNECTING, nearby, joined, joining, touching, bordering, neighbouring, next door, adjacent, interconnecting, abutting, contiguous

adjourn *verb* POSTPONE, delay, suspend, interrupt, put off, stay, defer, recess, discontinue, put on the back burner (*informal*), prorogue, take a rain check on (*US & Canad informal*)
<< OPPOSITE continue

adjournment *noun* POSTPONEMENT, delay, suspension, putting off, stay, recess, interruption, deferment, deferral, discontinuation, prorogation

adjudge *verb* JUDGE, determine, declare, decide, assign, pronounce, decree, apportion, adjudicate

adjudicate *verb* **1** DECIDE, judge, determine, settle, mediate, adjudge, arbitrate
2 JUDGE, referee, umpire

adjudication *noun* JUDGMENT, finding, ruling, decision, settlement, conclusion, verdict, determination, arbitration, pronouncement, adjudgment

adjudicator *noun* JUDGE, referee, umpire, umpie (*Austral slang*), arbiter, arbitrator, moderator

adjunct *noun* ADDITION, supplement, accessory, complement, auxiliary, add-on, appendage, addendum, appurtenance

adjust *verb* **1** ADAPT, change, settle, convert, alter, accommodate, dispose, get used, accustom, conform, reconcile, harmonize, acclimatize, familiarize yourself, attune
2 CHANGE, order, reform, fix, arrange, alter, adapt, revise, modify, set, regulate, amend, reconcile, remodel, redress, rectify, recast, customize, make conform
3 MODIFY, arrange, fix, tune (up), alter, adapt, remodel, tweak (*informal*), customize

adjustable *adjective* ALTERABLE, flexible, adaptable, malleable, movable, tractable, modifiable, mouldable

adjustment *noun* **1** ALTERATION, setting, change, ordering, fixing, arrangement, tuning, repair, conversion, modifying, adaptation, modification, remodelling, redress, refinement, rectification
2 ACCLIMATIZATION, settling in, orientation, familiarization, change, regulation, settlement, amendment, reconciliation, adaptation, accustoming, revision, modification, naturalization, acculturation, harmonization, habituation, acclimation, inurement

administer *verb* **1** MANAGE, run, control, rule, direct, handle, conduct, command, govern, oversee, supervise, preside over, be in charge of, superintend
2 DISPENSE, give, share, provide, apply, distribute, assign, allocate, allot, dole out, apportion, deal out
3 EXECUTE, do, give, provide, apply, perform, carry out, impose, realize, implement, enforce, render, discharge, enact, dispense, mete out, bring off

administration *noun* **1** MANAGEMENT, government, running, control, performance, handling, direction, conduct, application, command, provision, distribution, governing, administering, execution, overseeing, supervision, manipulation, governance, dispensation, superintendence
2 DIRECTORS, board, executive(s), bosses (*informal*), management, employers, directorate
3 GOVERNMENT, authority, executive, leadership, ministry, regime, governing body

administrative *adjective* MANAGERIAL, executive, management, directing, regulatory, governmental, organizational, supervisory, directorial, gubernatorial (*chiefly US*)

administrator *noun* MANAGER, head, official, director, officer, executive, minister, boss (*informal*), agent, governor, controller, supervisor, bureaucrat, superintendent, gaffer (*informal, chiefly Brit*), organizer, mandarin, functionary, overseer, baas (*S African*)

admirable *adjective* PRAISEWORTHY, good, great, fine, capital, noted, choice, champion, prime, select, wonderful, excellent, brilliant, rare, cracking (*Brit informal*), outstanding, valuable, superb, distinguished, superior, sterling, worthy, first-class, notable, sovereign, dope (*slang*), world-class, exquisite, exemplary, first-rate, superlative, commendable, top-notch (*informal*), brill (*informal*), laudable, meritorious, estimable, tiptop, A1 *or* A-one (*informal*), bitchin' (*US slang*), chillin' (*US slang*), booshit (*Austral slang*), exo (*Austral slang*), sik (*Austral slang*), ka pai (NZ), rad (*informal*), phat (*slang*), schmick (*Austral informal*)

<< OPPOSITE deplorable

admiration *noun* REGARD, surprise, wonder, respect, delight, pleasure, praise, approval, recognition, affection, esteem, appreciation, amazement, astonishment, reverence, deference, adoration, veneration, wonderment, approbation

admire *verb* 1 RESPECT, value, prize, honour, praise, appreciate, esteem, approve of, revere, venerate, take your hat off to, have a good *or* high opinion of, think highly of

<< OPPOSITE despise

2 ADORE, like, love, desire, take to, go for, fancy (*Brit informal*), treasure, worship, cherish, glorify, look up to, dote on, hold dear, be captivated by, have an eye for, find attractive, idolize, take a liking to, be infatuated with, be enamoured of, lavish affection on

3 MARVEL AT, look at, appreciate, delight in, gaze at, wonder at, be amazed by, take pleasure in, gape at, be awed by, goggle at, be filled with surprise by

admirer *noun* 1 FAN, supporter, follower, enthusiast, partisan, disciple, buff (*informal*), protagonist, devotee, worshipper, adherent, votary

2 SUITOR, lover, boyfriend, sweetheart, beau, wooer

admissible *adjective* PERMISSIBLE, allowed, permitted, acceptable, tolerated, tolerable, passable, allowable

<< OPPOSITE inadmissible

admission *noun* 1 ADMITTANCE, access, entry, introduction, entrance, acceptance, initiation, entrée, ingress

2 CONFESSION, admitting, profession, declaration, revelation, concession, allowance, disclosure, acknowledgement, affirmation, unburdening, avowal, divulgence, unbosoming

admit *verb* 1 CONFESS, own up, confide, profess, own up, come clean (*informal*), avow, come out of the closet, sing (*slang, chiefly US*), cough (*slang*), spill your guts (*slang*), 'fess up (*US slang*)

2 ALLOW, agree, accept, reveal, grant, declare, acknowledge, recognize, concede, disclose, affirm, divulge

<< OPPOSITE deny

3 LET IN, allow, receive, accept, introduce, take in, initiate, give access to, allow to enter

<< OPPOSITE keep out

admittance *noun* ACCESS, entry, way in, passage, entrance, reception, acceptance

admittedly *adverb* IT MUST BE ADMITTED, certainly, undeniably, it must be said, to be fair *or* honest, avowedly, it cannot be denied, it must be allowed, confessedly, it must be confessed, allowedly

admonish *verb* 1 REPRIMAND, caution, censure, rebuke, scold, berate, check, chide, tear into (*informal*), tell off (*informal*), reprove, upbraid, read the riot act to someone, carpet (*informal*), chew out (*US & Canad informal*), tear someone off a strip (*Brit informal*), give someone a rocket (*Brit & NZ informal*), slap someone on the wrist, rap someone over the knuckles

<< OPPOSITE praise

2 ADVISE, suggest, warn, urge, recommend, counsel, caution, prescribe, exhort, enjoin, forewarn

admonition *noun* REPRIMAND, warning, advice, counsel, caution, rebuke, reproach, scolding, berating, chiding, telling off (*informal*), upbraiding, reproof, remonstrance

ado *noun* FUSS, to-do, trouble, delay, bother, stir, confusion, excitement, disturbance, bustle, flurry, agitation, commotion, pother

adolescence *noun* TEENS, youth, minority, boyhood, girlhood, juvenescence

adolescent *adjective* 1 YOUNG, growing, junior, teenage, juvenile, youthful, childish, immature, boyish, undeveloped, girlish, puerile, in the springtime of life

2 TEENAGE, young, teen (*informal*), juvenile, youthful, immature

▷ *noun* TEENAGER, girl, boy, kid (*informal*), youth, lad, minor, young man, youngster, young woman, juvenile, young person, lass, young adult

adopt *verb* 1 TAKE ON, follow, support, choose, accept, maintain, assume, select, take over, approve, appropriate, take up, embrace, engage in, endorse, ratify, become involved in, espouse

2 TAKE IN, raise, nurse, mother, rear, foster, bring up, take care of

<< OPPOSITE abandon

adoption *noun* 1 FOSTERING, adopting, taking in, fosterage

2 EMBRACING, choice, taking on, taking up, support, taking over, selection, approval, following, assumption, maintenance, acceptance, endorsement, appropriation, ratification, approbation, espousal

adorable *adjective* LOVABLE, pleasing, appealing, dear, sweet, attractive, charming, precious, darling, fetching, delightful, cute, captivating, cutesy (*informal, chiefly US*)

<< OPPOSITE hateful

adoration *noun* LOVE, honour, worship, worshipping, esteem, admiration, reverence, estimation, exaltation, veneration, glorification, idolatry, idolization

adore *verb* LOVE, honour, admire, worship, esteem, cherish, bow to, revere, dote on, idolize

<< OPPOSITE hate

adoring *adjective* ADMIRING, loving, devoted, worshipping, fond, affectionate, ardent, doting, venerating, enamoured, reverential, reverent, idolizing, adulatory

<< OPPOSITE hating

adorn *verb* DECORATE, enhance, deck, trim, grace, array, enrich, garnish, ornament, embellish, emblazon, festoon, bedeck, beautify, engarland

adornment *noun* 1 DECORATION, trimming, supplement, accessory, ornament, frill, festoon, embellishment, frippery

2 BEAUTIFICATION, decorating, decoration, embellishment, ornamentation

adrift *adjective* 1 DRIFTING, afloat, cast off, unmoored, aweigh, unanchored

2 AIMLESS, goalless, directionless, purposeless

▷ *adverb* WRONG, astray, off course, amiss, off target, wide of the mark

adroit *adjective* SKILFUL, able, skilled, expert, bright (*informal*), clever, apt, cunning, ingenious, adept, deft, nimble, masterful, proficient, artful, quick-witted, dexterous

<< OPPOSITE unskilful

adulation *noun* EXTRAVAGANT FLATTERY, worship, fawning, sycophancy, fulsome praise, blandishment, bootlicking (*informal*), servile flattery

<< OPPOSITE ridicule

adult *noun* GROWN-UP, mature person, person of mature age, grown *or* grown-up person, man *or* woman

▷ *adjective* 1 FULLY GROWN, mature, grown-up, of age, ripe, fully fledged, fully developed, full grown

2 PORNOGRAPHIC, blue, dirty, offensive, sexy, erotic, porn (*informal*), obscene, taboo, filthy, indecent, sensual, hard-core, lewd, carnal, porno (*informal*), X-rated (*informal*), salacious, prurient, smutty

adulterer *or* **adulteress** *noun* CHEAT (*informal*), love rat (*slang*), love cheat (*slang*), fornicator

adulterous *adjective* UNFAITHFUL, cheating (*informal*), extramarital, fornicating, unchaste

adultery *noun* UNFAITHFULNESS, infidelity, cheating (*informal*), fornication, playing the field (*slang*), extramarital sex, playing away from home (*slang*), illicit sex, unchastity, extramarital relations, extracurricular sex (*informal*), extramarital congress, having an affair *or* a fling

<< OPPOSITE faithfulness

advance *verb* 1 PROGRESS, proceed, go ahead, move up, come forward, go forward, press on, gain ground, make inroads, make headway, make your way, cover ground, make strides, move onward

<< OPPOSITE retreat

2 ACCELERATE, speed, promote, hurry (up), step up (*informal*), hasten, precipitate, quicken, bring forward, push forward, expedite, send forward

3 IMPROVE, rise, grow, develop, reform, pick up, progress, thrive, upgrade, multiply, prosper, make strides

4 SUGGEST, offer, present, propose, allege, cite, advocate, submit, prescribe, put forward, proffer, adduce, offer as a suggestion

<< OPPOSITE withhold

5 LEND, loan, accommodate someone with, supply on credit

<< OPPOSITE withhold payment

▷ *noun* 1 CREDIT

2 DOWN PAYMENT, credit, fee, deposit, retainer, prepayment

3 LOAN, credit

4 INCREASE (*in price*)

5 ATTACK, charge, strike, rush, assault, raid, invasion, offensive, onslaught, advancement, foray, incursion, forward movement, onward movement

6 IMPROVEMENT, development, gain, growth, breakthrough, advancement, step, headway, inroads, betterment, furtherance, forward movement, amelioration, onward movement

▷ *modifier* PRIOR, early, previous, beforehand

▷▷ **in advance** BEFOREHAND, earlier, ahead, previously, in the lead, in the forefront

advanced *adjective* SOPHISTICATED, foremost, modern, revolutionary, up-to-date, higher, leading, recent, prime, forward, ahead, supreme, extreme, principal, progressive, paramount, state-of-the-art, avant-garde, precocious, pre-eminent, up-to-the-minute, ahead of the times

<< OPPOSITE backward

advancement *noun* 1 PROMOTION, rise, gain, growth, advance, progress, improvement, betterment, preferment, amelioration

2 PROGRESS, advance, headway, forward movement, onward movement

advantage *noun* 1 BENEFIT, use, start, help, service, aid, profit, favour, asset, assistance, blessing, utility, boon, ace in the hole, ace up your sleeve

<< OPPOSITE disadvantage

2 LEAD, control, edge, sway, dominance, superiority, upper hand, precedence, primacy, pre-eminence

3 SUPERIORITY, good, worth, gain, comfort, welfare, enjoyment, mileage (*informal*)

advantageous *adjective* 1 BENEFICIAL, useful, valuable, helpful, profitable, of service, convenient, worthwhile, expedient

<< OPPOSITE unfavourable

2 SUPERIOR, dominating, commanding, dominant, important, powerful, favourable, fortuitous

advent *noun* COMING, approach, appearance, arrival, entrance, onset, occurrence, visitation

adventure *noun* VENTURE, experience, chance, risk, incident, enterprise, speculation, undertaking, exploit, fling, hazard, occurrence, contingency, caper, escapade
▷ *verb* VENTURE, risk, brave, dare

adventurer *noun* 1 MERCENARY, rogue, gambler, speculator, opportunist, charlatan, fortune-hunter
2 VENTURER, hero, traveller, heroine, wanderer, voyager, daredevil, soldier of fortune, swashbuckler, knight-errant

adventurous *adjective* DARING, dangerous, enterprising, bold, risky, rash, have-a-go (*informal*), hazardous, reckless, audacious, intrepid, foolhardy, daredevil, headstrong, venturesome, adventuresome, temerarious (*rare*)
<< OPPOSITE cautious

adversary *noun* OPPONENT, rival, opposer, enemy, competitor, foe, contestant, antagonist
<< OPPOSITE ally

adverse *adjective* 1 HARMFUL, damaging, conflicting, dangerous, opposite, negative, destructive, detrimental, hurtful, antagonistic, injurious, inimical, inopportune, disadvantageous, unpropitious, inexpedient
<< OPPOSITE beneficial
2 UNFAVOURABLE, bad, threatening, hostile, unfortunate, unlucky, ominous, unfriendly, untimely, unsuited, ill-suited, inopportune, disadvantageous, unseasonable
3 NEGATIVE, opposing, reluctant, hostile, contrary, dissenting, unwilling, unfriendly, unsympathetic, ill-disposed

adversity *noun* HARDSHIP, trouble, distress, suffering, trial, disaster, reverse, misery, hard times, catastrophe, sorrow, woe, misfortune, bad luck, deep water, calamity, mishap, affliction, wretchedness, ill-fortune, ill-luck

advert *noun* (*Brit informal*) ADVERTISEMENT, bill, notice, display, commercial, ad (*informal*), announcement, promotion, publicity, poster, plug (*informal*), puff, circular, placard, blurb

advertise *verb* PUBLICIZE, promote, plug (*informal*), announce, publish, push (*informal*), display, declare, broadcast, advise, inform, praise, proclaim, puff, hype, notify, tout, flaunt, crack up (*informal*), promulgate, make known, apprise, beat the drum (*informal*), blazon, bring to public notice

advertisement *noun* ADVERT (*Brit informal*), bill, notice, display, commercial, ad (*informal*), announcement, promotion, publicity, poster, plug (*informal*), puff, circular, placard, blurb

advice *noun* 1 GUIDANCE, help, opinion, direction, suggestion, instruction, counsel, counselling, recommendation, injunction, admonition
2 INSTRUCTION, notification, view, information, warning, teaching, notice, word, intelligence

advisable *adjective* WISE, seemly, sound, suggested, fitting, fit, politic, recommended, appropriate, suitable, sensible, proper, profitable, desirable, apt, prudent, expedient, judicious
<< OPPOSITE unwise

advise *verb* 1 RECOMMEND, suggest, urge, counsel, advocate, caution, prescribe, commend, admonish, enjoin
2 NOTIFY, tell, report, announce, warn, declare, inform, acquaint, make known, apprise, let (someone) know

adviser *noun* COUNSELLOR, authority, teacher, coach, guide, lawyer, consultant, solicitor, counsel, aide, tutor, guru, mentor, helper, confidant, right-hand man

advisory *adjective* ADVISING, helping, recommending, counselling, consultative

advocacy *noun* RECOMMENDATION, support, defence, championing, backing, proposal, urging, promotion, campaigning for, upholding, encouragement, justification, argument for, advancement, pleading for, propagation, espousal, promulgation, boosterism, spokesmanship

advocate *verb* RECOMMEND, support, champion, encourage, propose, favour, defend, promote, urge, advise, justify, endorse, campaign for, prescribe, speak for, uphold, press for, argue for, commend, plead for, espouse, countenance, hold a brief for (*informal*)
<< OPPOSITE oppose
▷ *noun* 1 SUPPORTER, spokesman, champion, defender, speaker, pleader, campaigner, promoter, counsellor, backer, proponent, apostle, apologist, upholder, proposer
2 (*Law*) LAWYER, attorney, solicitor, counsel, barrister

aegis *noun* SUPPORT, backing, wing, favour, protection, shelter, sponsorship, patronage, advocacy, auspices, guardianship

aesthetic *adjective* ORNAMENTAL, artistic, pleasing, pretty, fancy, enhancing, decorative, tasteful, beautifying, nonfunctional

affable *adjective* FRIENDLY, kindly, civil, warm, pleasant, mild, obliging, benign, gracious, benevolent, good-humoured, amiable, courteous, amicable, cordial, sociable, genial, congenial, urbane, approachable, good-natured
<< OPPOSITE unfriendly

affair *noun* 1 MATTER, thing, business, question, issue, happening, concern, event, subject, project, activity, incident, proceeding, circumstance, episode, topic, undertaking, transaction, occurrence

2 RELATIONSHIP, romance, intrigue, fling, liaison, flirtation, amour, dalliance

affect[1] *verb* 1 INFLUENCE, involve, concern, impact, transform, alter, modify, change, manipulate, act on, sway, prevail over, bear upon, impinge upon
2 EMOTIONALLY MOVE, touch, upset, overcome, stir, disturb, perturb, impress on, tug at your heartstrings (*often facetious*) ▷ see **effect**

affect[2] *verb* PUT ON, assume, adopt, pretend, imitate, simulate, contrive, aspire to, sham, counterfeit, feign

affectation *noun* PRETENCE, show, posing, posturing, act, display, appearance, pose, façade, simulation, sham, pretension, veneer, artifice, mannerism, insincerity, pretentiousness, hokum (*slang, chiefly US & Canad*), artificiality, fakery, affectedness, assumed manners, false display, unnatural imitation

affected[1] *adjective* PRETENDED, artificial, contrived, put-on, assumed, mannered, studied, precious, stiff, simulated, mincing, sham, unnatural, pompous, pretentious, counterfeit, feigned, spurious, conceited, insincere, camp (*informal*), la-di-da (*informal*), arty-farty (*informal*), phoney *or* phony (*informal*)
<< OPPOSITE genuine

affected[2] *adjective* TOUCHED, influenced, concerned, troubled, damaged, hurt, injured, upset, impressed, stirred, altered, changed, distressed, stimulated, melted, impaired, afflicted, deeply moved
<< OPPOSITE untouched

affecting *adjective* EMOTIONALLY MOVING, touching, sad, pathetic, poignant, saddening, pitiful, pitiable, piteous

affection *noun* FONDNESS, liking, feeling, love, care, desire, passion, warmth, attachment, goodwill, devotion, kindness, inclination, tenderness, propensity, friendliness, amity, aroha (*NZ*)

affectionate *adjective* FOND, loving, kind, caring, warm, friendly, attached, devoted, tender, doting, warm-hearted
<< OPPOSITE cool

affiliate *verb* ASSOCIATE, unite, join, link, ally, combine, connect, incorporate, annex, confederate, amalgamate, band together

affiliated *adjective* ASSOCIATED, united, joined, linked, allied, connected, incorporated, confederated, amalgamated, federated, conjoined

affiliation *noun* ASSOCIATION, union, joining, league, relationship, connection, alliance, combination, coalition, merging, confederation, incorporation, amalgamation, banding together

affinity *noun* 1 ATTRACTION, liking, leaning, sympathy, inclination, rapport, fondness, partiality, aroha (*NZ*)
<< OPPOSITE hostility
2 SIMILARITY, relationship, relation, connection, alliance, correspondence, analogy, resemblance, closeness, likeness, compatibility, kinship
<< OPPOSITE difference

affirm *verb* 1 DECLARE, state, maintain, swear, assert, testify, pronounce, certify, attest, avow, aver, asseverate, avouch
<< OPPOSITE deny
2 CONFIRM, prove, sanction, endorse, ratify, verify, validate, bear out, substantiate, corroborate, authenticate
<< OPPOSITE refute

affirmation *noun* 1 DECLARATION, statement, assertion, oath, certification, pronouncement, avowal, asseveration, averment
2 CONFIRMATION, testimony, ratification, attestation, avouchment

affirmative *adjective* AGREEING, confirming, positive, approving, consenting, favourable, concurring, assenting, corroborative
<< OPPOSITE negative

affix *verb* ATTACH, add, join, stick on, bind, put on, tag, glue, paste, tack, fasten, annex, append, subjoin
<< OPPOSITE remove

afflict *verb* TORMENT, trouble, pain, hurt, wound, burden, distress, rack, try, plague, grieve, harass, ail, oppress, beset, smite

affliction *noun* MISFORTUNE, suffering, trouble, trial, disease, pain, distress, grief, misery, plague, curse, ordeal, sickness, torment, hardship, sorrow, woe, adversity, calamity, scourge, tribulation, wretchedness

affluence *noun* WEALTH, riches, plenty, fortune, prosperity, abundance, big money, exuberance, profusion, big bucks (*informal, chiefly US*), opulence, megabucks (*US & Canad slang*), pretty penny (*informal*), wad (*US & Canad slang*)

affluent *adjective* WEALTHY, rich, prosperous, loaded (*slang*), well-off, opulent, well-heeled (*informal*), well-to-do, moneyed
<< OPPOSITE poor

afford *verb* 1 HAVE THE MONEY FOR, manage, bear, pay for, spare, stand, stretch to
2 BEAR, stand, sustain, allow yourself
3 GIVE, offer, provide, produce, supply, grant, yield, render, furnish, bestow, impart

affordable *adjective* INEXPENSIVE, fair, cheap, reasonable, moderate, modest, low-price, low-cost, economical
<< OPPOSITE expensive

affront *verb* OFFEND, anger, provoke, outrage, insult, annoy, vex, displease, pique, put *or* get your back up, slight

▷ *noun* INSULT, wrong, injury, abuse, offence, slight, outrage, provocation, slur, indignity, slap in the face (*informal*), vexation

affronted *adjective* OFFENDED, cross, angry, upset, slighted, outraged, insulted, annoyed, stung, incensed, indignant, irate, miffed (*informal*), displeased, peeved (*informal*), piqued, tooshie (*Austral slang*)

afloat *adjective* 1 FLOATING, on the surface, buoyant, keeping your head above water, unsubmerged

<< OPPOSITE sunken

2 SOLVENT, in business, above water

<< OPPOSITE bankrupt

afoot *adjective* GOING ON, happening, current, operating, abroad, brewing, hatching, circulating, up (*informal*), about, in preparation, in progress, afloat, in the wind, on the go (*informal*), astir

afraid *adjective* 1 SCARED, frightened, nervous, anxious, terrified, shaken, alarmed, startled, suspicious, intimidated, fearful, cowardly, timid, apprehensive, petrified, panicky, panic-stricken, timorous, faint-hearted

<< OPPOSITE unafraid

2 RELUCTANT, slow, frightened, scared, unwilling, backward, hesitant, recalcitrant, loath, disinclined, unenthusiastic, indisposed

3 SORRY, apologetic, regretful, sad, distressed, unhappy

<< OPPOSITE pleased

afresh *adverb* AGAIN, newly, once again, once more, over again, anew

after *preposition* 1 AT THE END OF, following, subsequent to

<< OPPOSITE before

2 FOLLOWING, chasing, pursuing, on the hunt for, on the tail of (*informal*), on the track of

▷ *adverb* FOLLOWING, later, next, succeeding, afterwards, subsequently, thereafter

>> RELATED WORD *prefix* post-

aftereffect *noun usually plural* CONSEQUENCE, wake, trail, aftermath, hangover (*informal*), spin-off, repercussion, afterglow, aftershock, delayed response

aftermath *noun* EFFECTS, end, results, wake, consequences, outcome, sequel, end result, upshot, aftereffects

afterwards *or* **afterward** *adverb* LATER, after, then, after that, subsequently, thereafter, following that, at a later date *or* time

again *adverb* 1 ONCE MORE, another time, anew, afresh

2 ALSO, in addition, moreover, besides, furthermore

▷▷ **there again** *or* **then again** ON THE OTHER HAND, in contrast, on the contrary, conversely

against *preposition* 1 BESIDE, on, up against, in contact with, abutting, close up to

2 OPPOSED TO, anti (*informal*), opposing, counter, contra (*informal*), hostile to, in opposition to, averse to, opposite to, not in accord with

3 IN OPPOSITION TO, resisting, versus, counter to, in the opposite direction of

4 IN PREPARATION FOR, in case of, in anticipation of, in expectation of, in provision for

>> RELATED WORDS *prefixes* anti-, contra-, counter-

age *noun* 1 YEARS, days, generation, lifetime, stage of life, length of life, length of existence

2 OLD AGE, experience, maturity, completion, seniority, fullness, majority, maturation, senility, decline (*of life*), advancing years, declining years, senescence, full growth, matureness

<< OPPOSITE youth

3 TIME, day(s), period, generation, era, epoch

▷ *plural noun* (*informal*) A LONG TIME *or* WHILE, years, centuries, for ever (*informal*), aeons, donkey's years (*informal*), yonks (*informal*), a month of Sundays (*informal*), an age *or* eternity

▷ *verb* 1 GROW OLD, decline, weather, fade, deteriorate, wither

2 MATURE, season, condition, soften, mellow, ripen

aged *adjective* OLD, getting on, grey, ancient, antique, elderly, past it (*informal*), age-old, antiquated, hoary, superannuated, senescent, cobwebby

<< OPPOSITE young

ageing *or* **aging** *adjective* GROWING OLD *or* OLDER, declining, maturing, deteriorating, mellowing, in decline, senile, long in the tooth, senescent, getting on *or* past it (*informal*)

▷ *noun* GROWING OLD, decline, decay, deterioration, degeneration, maturation, senility, senescence

ageless *adjective* ETERNAL, enduring, abiding, perennial, timeless, immortal, unchanging, deathless, unfading

<< OPPOSITE momentary

agency *noun* 1 BUSINESS, company, office, firm, department, organization, enterprise, establishment, bureau

2 (*Old-fashioned*) MEDIUM, work, means, force, power, action, operation, activity, influence, vehicle, instrument, intervention, mechanism, efficiency, mediation, auspices, intercession, instrumentality

agenda *noun* PROGRAMME, list, plan, schedule, diary, calendar, timetable

agent *noun* 1 REPRESENTATIVE, deputy, substitute, advocate, rep (*informal*), broker, delegate, factor, negotiator, envoy, trustee, proxy, surrogate, go-between, emissary

2 AUTHOR, officer, worker, actor, vehicle,

instrument, operator, performer, operative, catalyst, executor, doer, perpetuator
3 FORCE, means, power, cause, instrument
aggravate *verb* 1 MAKE WORSE, exaggerate, intensify, worsen, heighten, exacerbate, magnify, inflame, increase, add insult to injury, fan the flames of
<< OPPOSITE improve
2 (*informal*) ANNOY, bother, provoke, needle (*informal*), irritate, tease, hassle (*informal*), gall, exasperate, nettle, pester, vex, irk, get under your skin (*informal*), get on your nerves (*informal*), nark (*Brit, Austral & NZ slang*), get up your nose (*informal*), be on your back (*slang*), rub (someone) up the wrong way (*informal*), get in your hair (*informal*), get on your wick (*Brit slang*), hack you off (*informal*)
<< OPPOSITE please
aggravating *adjective* 1 (*informal*) ANNOYING, provoking, irritating, teasing, galling, exasperating, vexing, irksome
2 WORSENING, exaggerating, intensifying, heightening, exacerbating, magnifying, inflaming
aggravation *noun* 1 (*informal*) ANNOYANCE, grief (*informal*), teasing, irritation, hassle (*informal*), provocation, gall, exasperation, vexation, irksomeness
2 WORSENING, heightening, inflaming, exaggeration, intensification, magnification, exacerbation
aggregate *noun* TOTAL, body, whole, amount, collection, mass, sum, combination, pile, mixture, bulk, lump, heap, accumulation, assemblage, agglomeration
▷ *adjective* COLLECTIVE, added, mixed, combined, collected, corporate, assembled, accumulated, composite, cumulative
▷ *verb* COMBINE, mix, collect, assemble, heap, accumulate, pile, amass
aggregation *noun* COLLECTION, body, mass, combination, pile, mixture, bulk, lump, heap, accumulation, assemblage, agglomeration
aggression *noun* 1 HOSTILITY, malice, antagonism, antipathy, aggressiveness, ill will, belligerence, destructiveness, malevolence, pugnacity
2 ATTACK, campaign, injury, assault, offence, raid, invasion, offensive, onslaught, foray, encroachment
aggressive *adjective* 1 HOSTILE, offensive, destructive, belligerent, unkind, unfriendly, malevolent, contrary, antagonistic, pugnacious, bellicose, quarrelsome, aggers (*Austral slang*), biffo (*Austral slang*), inimical, rancorous, ill-disposed
<< OPPOSITE friendly
2 FORCEFUL, powerful, convincing, effective, enterprising, dynamic, bold, militant, pushing, vigorous, energetic, persuasive, assertive, zealous, pushy (*informal*), in-your-face (*slang*)
<< OPPOSITE submissive
aggressor *noun* ATTACKER, assaulter, invader, assailant
aggrieved *adjective* HURT, wronged, injured, harmed, disturbed, distressed, unhappy, afflicted, saddened, woeful, peeved (*informal*), ill-used
aghast *adjective* HORRIFIED, shocked, amazed, stunned, appalled, astonished, startled, astounded, confounded, awestruck, horror-struck, thunder-struck
agile *adjective* 1 NIMBLE, active, quick, lively, swift, brisk, supple, sprightly, lithe, limber, spry, lissom(e)
<< OPPOSITE slow
2 ACUTE, sharp, quick, bright (*informal*), prompt, alert, clever, lively, nimble, quick-witted
agility *noun* 1 NIMBLENESS, activity, suppleness, quickness, swiftness, liveliness, briskness, litheness, sprightliness, spryness
2 ACUTENESS, sharpness, alertness, cleverness, quickness, liveliness, promptness, quick-wittedness, promptitude
agitate *verb* 1 STIR, beat, mix, shake, disturb, toss, rouse, churn
2 UPSET, worry, trouble, disturb, excite, alarm, stimulate, distract, rouse, ruffle, inflame, incite, unnerve, disconcert, disquiet, fluster, perturb, faze, work someone up, give someone grief (*Brit & S African*)
<< OPPOSITE calm
agitated *adjective* UPSET, worried, troubled, disturbed, shaken, excited, alarmed, nervous, anxious, distressed, rattled (*informal*), distracted, uneasy, unsettled, worked up, ruffled, unnerved, disconcerted, disquieted, edgy, flustered, perturbed, on edge, fazed, ill at ease, hot under the collar (*informal*), in a flap (*informal*), hot and bothered (*informal*), antsy (*informal*), angsty, all of a flutter (*informal*), discomposed
<< OPPOSITE calm
agitation *noun* 1 TURBULENCE, rocking, shaking, stirring, stir, tossing, disturbance, upheaval, churning, convulsion
2 TURMOIL, worry, trouble, upset, alarm, confusion, excitement, disturbance, distraction, upheaval, stimulation, flurry, outcry, clamour, arousal, ferment, disquiet, commotion, fluster, lather (*informal*), incitement, tumult, discomposure, tizzy, tizz *or* tiz-woz (*informal*)
agitator *noun* TROUBLEMAKER, revolutionary, inciter, firebrand, instigator, demagogue, rabble-rouser, agent provocateur, stirrer

(*informal*)

ago *adverb* PREVIOUSLY, back, before, since, earlier, formerly

Although *since* can be used as a synonym of *ago* in certain contexts, the use of *ago* and *since* together, as in *it's ten years ago since he wrote that novel*, is redundant. Instead, it would be correct to use *it is ten years since he wrote that novel*, or *it is ten years ago that he wrote that novel*

agonize *verb* SUFFER, labour, worry, struggle, strain, strive, writhe, be distressed, be in agony, go through the mill, be in anguish

agonized *adjective* TORTURED, suffering, wounded, distressed, racked, tormented, anguished, broken-hearted, grief-stricken, wretched

agonizing *adjective* PAINFUL, bitter, distressing, harrowing, heartbreaking, grievous, excruciating, hellish, heart-rending, gut-wrenching, torturous

agony *noun* SUFFERING, pain, distress, misery, torture, discomfort, torment, hardship, woe, anguish, pangs, affliction, throes

agrarian *adjective* AGRICULTURAL, country, land, farming, rural, rustic, agrestic

<< OPPOSITE urban

agree *verb* **1** CONCUR, engage, be as one, sympathize, assent, see eye to eye, be of the same opinion, be of the same mind

<< OPPOSITE disagree

2 CORRESPOND, match, accord, answer, fit, suit, square, coincide, tally, conform, chime, harmonize

▷▷ **agree on something** SHAKE HANDS ON, reach agreement on, settle on, negotiate, work out, arrive at, yield to, thrash out, accede to, concede to

▷▷ **agree to something** CONSENT TO, grant, approve, permit, accede to, assent to, acquiesce to, comply to, concur to

▷▷ **agree with someone** SUIT, get on with, be good for, befit

agreeable *adjective* **1** PLEASANT, pleasing, satisfying, acceptable, delightful, enjoyable, gratifying, pleasurable, congenial, to your liking, to your taste, likable *or* likeable

<< OPPOSITE unpleasant

2 FRIENDLY, nice, pleasant, sociable, affable, congenial, good-natured, likable *or* likeable

3 CONSENTING, willing, agreeing, approving, sympathetic, complying, responsive, concurring, amenable, in accord, well-disposed, acquiescent

agreed *adjective* SETTLED, given, established, guaranteed, fixed, arranged, definite, stipulated, predetermined

<< OPPOSITE indefinite

▷ *interjection* ALL RIGHT, done, settled, it's a bargain *or* deal, O.K. *or* okay (*informal*), you're on (*informal*), ka pai (NZ)

agreement *noun* **1** TREATY, contract, bond, arrangement, alliance, deal (*informal*), understanding, settlement, bargain, pact, compact, covenant, entente

2 CONCURRENCE, harmony, compliance, union, agreeing, concession, consent, unison, assent, concord, acquiescence

<< OPPOSITE disagreement

3 CORRESPONDENCE, agreeing, accord, similarity, consistency, analogy, accordance, correlation, affinity, conformity, compatibility, congruity, suitableness

<< OPPOSITE difference

agricultural *adjective* FARMING, country, rural, rustic, agrarian, agronomic, agronomical, agrestic

agriculture *noun* FARMING, culture, cultivation, husbandry, tillage, agronomy, agronomics

aground *adverb* BEACHED, grounded, stuck, shipwrecked, foundered, stranded, ashore, marooned, on the rocks, high and dry

ahead *adverb* **1** FORWARDS, in front, on, in advance, onwards, towards the front, frontwards

2 AT AN ADVANTAGE, in advance, in the lead

3 IN THE LEAD, winning, leading, at the head, to the fore, at an advantage

4 IN FRONT, before, in advance, onwards, in the lead, in the vanguard

aid *noun* **1** HELP, backing, support, benefit, favour, relief, promotion, assistance, encouragement, helping hand, succour

<< OPPOSITE hindrance

2 HELPER, supporter, assistant, aide, adjutant, aide-de-camp, second, abettor

▷ *verb* **1** HELP, second, support, serve, sustain, assist, relieve, avail, subsidize, abet, succour, be of service to, lend a hand to, give a leg up to (*informal*)

<< OPPOSITE hinder

2 PROMOTE, help, further, forward, encourage, favour, facilitate, pave the way for, expedite, smooth the path of, assist the progress of

aide *noun* ASSISTANT, supporter, deputy, attendant, helper, henchman, right-hand man, adjutant, second, helpmate, coadjutor (*rare*)

ail *verb* **1** (*Literary*) TROUBLE, worry, bother, distress, pain, upset, annoy, irritate, sicken, afflict, be the matter with

2 BE ILL, be sick, be unwell, feel unwell, be indisposed, be *or* feel off colour

ailing *adjective* **1** WEAK, failing, poor, flawed, unstable, feeble, unsatisfactory, deficient, unsound

2 ILL, suffering, poorly, diseased, sick, weak,

crook (*Austral & NZ informal*), feeble, invalid, debilitated, sickly, unwell, infirm, off colour, under the weather (*informal*), indisposed

ailment *noun* ILLNESS, disease, complaint, disorder, sickness, affliction, malady, infirmity, lurgy (*informal*)

aim *verb* 1 TRY FOR, want, seek, work for, plan for, strive, aspire to, wish for, have designs on, set your sights on
2 POINT, level, train, direct, sight, take aim (at)
▷ *noun* INTENTION, end, point, plan, course, mark, goal, design, target, wish, scheme, purpose, direction, desire, object, objective, ambition, intent, aspiration, Holy Grail (*informal*)

aimless *adjective* PURPOSELESS, random, stray, pointless, erratic, wayward, frivolous, chance, goalless, haphazard, vagrant, directionless, unguided, undirected
<< OPPOSITE purposeful

air *noun* 1 WIND, blast, breath, breeze, puff, whiff, draught, gust, waft, zephyr, air-current, current of air
2 ATMOSPHERE, sky, heavens, aerosphere
3 TUNE, song, theme, melody, strain, lay, aria
4 MANNER, feeling, effect, style, quality, character, bearing, appearance, look, aspect, atmosphere, tone, mood, impression, flavour, aura, ambience, demeanour, vibe (*slang*)
▷ *verb* 1 PUBLICIZE, tell, reveal, exhibit, communicate, voice, express, display, declare, expose, disclose, proclaim, utter, circulate, make public, divulge, disseminate, ventilate, make known, give vent to, take the wraps off
2 VENTILATE, expose, freshen, aerate
>> RELATED WORD *adjective* aerial

airborne *adjective* FLYING, floating, soaring, in the air, hovering, gliding, in flight, on the wing, wind-borne, volitant

aircraft *noun* PLANE, jet, aeroplane, airplane (*US & Canad*), airliner, kite (*Brit slang*), flying machine

airfield *noun* AIRPORT, airstrip, aerodrome, landing strip, air station, airdrome (US)

airily *adverb* LIGHT-HEARTEDLY, happily, blithely, gaily, animatedly, breezily, jauntily, buoyantly, high-spiritedly

airing *noun* 1 VENTILATION, drying, freshening, aeration
2 EXPOSURE, display, expression, publicity, vent, utterance, dissemination

airless *adjective* STUFFY, close, heavy, stifling, oppressive, stale, breathless, suffocating, sultry, muggy, unventilated
<< OPPOSITE airy

airplane *noun* (*US & Canad*) PLANE, aircraft, jet, aeroplane, airliner, kite (*Brit slang*), flying machine

airport *noun* AIRFIELD, aerodrome, airdrome (*US*)

airs *plural noun* AFFECTATION, arrogance, pretensions, pomposity, swank (*informal*), hauteur, haughtiness, superciliousness, affectedness

airy *adjective* 1 WELL-VENTILATED, open, light, fresh, spacious, windy, lofty, breezy, uncluttered, draughty, gusty, blowy
<< OPPOSITE stuffy
2 LIGHT-HEARTED, light, happy, gay, lively, cheerful, animated, merry, upbeat (*informal*), buoyant, graceful, cheery, genial, high-spirited, jaunty, chirpy (*informal*), sprightly, debonair, nonchalant, blithe, frolicsome
<< OPPOSITE gloomy
3 INSUBSTANTIAL, imaginary, visionary, flimsy, fanciful, ethereal, immaterial, illusory, wispy, weightless, incorporeal, vaporous
<< OPPOSITE real

aisle *noun* PASSAGEWAY, path, lane, passage, corridor, alley, gangway

ajar *adjective* OPEN, gaping, agape, partly open, unclosed

akin *adjective* ▷▷ **akin to** SIMILAR TO, like, related to, corresponding to, parallel to, comparable to, allied with, analogous to, affiliated with, of a piece with, kin to, cognate with, congenial with, connected with *or* to

alacrity *noun* EAGERNESS, enthusiasm, willingness, readiness, speed, zeal, gaiety, alertness, hilarity, cheerfulness, quickness, liveliness, briskness, promptness, avidity, joyousness, sprightliness
<< OPPOSITE reluctance

alarm *noun* 1 FEAR, horror, panic, anxiety, distress, terror, dread, dismay, fright, unease, apprehension, nervousness, consternation, trepidation, uneasiness
<< OPPOSITE calmness
2 DANGER SIGNAL, warning, bell, alert, siren, alarm bell, hooter, distress signal, tocsin
▷ *verb* FRIGHTEN, shock, scare, panic, distress, terrify, startle, rattle, dismay, daunt, unnerve, terrorize, put the wind up (*informal*), give (someone) a turn (*informal*), make (someone's) hair stand on end
<< OPPOSITE calm

alarmed *adjective* FRIGHTENED, troubled, shocked, scared, nervous, disturbed, anxious, distressed, terrified, startled, dismayed, uneasy, fearful, daunted, unnerved, apprehensive, in a panic
<< OPPOSITE calm

alarming *adjective* FRIGHTENING, shocking, scaring, disturbing, distressing, terrifying, appalling, startling, dreadful, horrifying, menacing, intimidating, dismaying, scary (*informal*), fearful, daunting, fearsome, unnerving, hair-raising, bloodcurdling

albeit *conjunction* EVEN THOUGH, though, although, even if, notwithstanding, tho' (*US poetic*)

album *noun* 1 RECORD, recording, CD, single, release, disc, waxing (*informal*), LP, vinyl, EP, forty-five, platter (*US slang*), seventy-eight, gramophone record, black disc
2 BOOK, collection, scrapbook

alchemy *noun* MAGIC, witchcraft, wizardry, sorcery, makutu (*NZ*)

alcohol *noun* 1 DRINK, spirits, liquor, intoxicant, juice (*informal*), booze (*informal*), the bottle (*informal*), grog (*informal, chiefly Austral & NZ*), the hard stuff (*informal*), strong drink, Dutch courage (*informal*), firewater, John Barleycorn, hooch *or* hootch (*informal, chiefly US & Canad*)
2 ETHANOL, ethyl alcohol
>> RELATED WORD *like* dipsomania

alcoholic *noun* DRUNKARD, drinker, drunk, boozer (*informal*), toper, soak (*slang*), lush (*slang*), sponge (*informal*), carouser, sot, tippler, wino (*informal*), inebriate, dipsomaniac, hard drinker, tosspot (*informal*), alky (*slang*), alko *or* alco (*Austral slang*)
▷ *adjective* INTOXICATING, hard, strong, stiff, brewed, fermented, distilled, vinous, inebriating, spirituous, inebriant

alcove *noun* RECESS, corner, bay, niche, bower, compartment, cubicle, nook, cubbyhole

alert *adjective* 1 ATTENTIVE, careful, awake, wary, vigilant, perceptive, watchful, ready, on the lookout, circumspect, observant, on guard, wide-awake, on your toes, on the watch, keeping a weather eye on, heedful
<< OPPOSITE careless
2 QUICK-WITTED, spirited, quick, bright, sharp, active, lively, brisk, on the ball (*informal*), nimble, agile, sprightly, bright-eyed and bushy-tailed (*informal*)
▷ *noun* WARNING, signal, alarm, siren
<< OPPOSITE all clear
▷ *verb* WARN, signal, inform, alarm, notify, tip off, forewarn
<< OPPOSITE lull

alertness *noun* WATCHFULNESS, vigilance, agility, wariness, quickness, liveliness, readiness, circumspection, attentiveness, spiritedness, briskness, nimbleness, perceptiveness, carefulness, sprightliness, promptitude, activeness, heedfulness

alias *noun* PSEUDONYM, pen name, assumed name, stage name, nom de guerre, nom de plume
▷ *adverb* ALSO KNOWN AS, otherwise, also called, otherwise known as, a.k.a. (*informal*)

alibi *noun* EXCUSE, reason, defence, explanation, plea, justification, pretext

alien *noun* FOREIGNER, incomer, immigrant, stranger, outsider, newcomer, asylum seeker, outlander
<< OPPOSITE citizen
▷ *adjective* 1 FOREIGN, outside, strange, imported, overseas, unknown, exotic, unfamiliar, not native, not naturalized
2 STRANGE, new, foreign, novel, remote, unknown, exotic, unfamiliar, estranged, outlandish, untried, unexplored
<< OPPOSITE similar
▷▷ **alien to** UNFAMILIAR TO, opposed to, contrary to, separated from, conflicting with, incompatible with, inappropriate to, repugnant to, adverse to

alienate *verb* ANTAGONIZE, anger, annoy, offend, irritate, hassle (*informal*), gall, repel, estrange, lose the affection of, disaffect, hack off (*informal*)

alienation *noun* ESTRANGEMENT, setting against, divorce, withdrawal, separation, turning away, indifference, breaking off, diversion, rupture, disaffection, remoteness

alight[1] *verb* 1 GET OFF, descend, get down, disembark, dismount
2 LAND, light, settle, come down, descend, perch, touch down, come to rest
<< OPPOSITE take off

alight[2] *adjective* 1 LIT UP, bright, brilliant, shining, illuminated, fiery
2 ON FIRE, ignited, set ablaze, lit, burning, aflame, blazing, flaming, flaring

align *verb* 1 ALLY, side, join, associate, affiliate, cooperate, sympathize
2 LINE UP, even, order, range, sequence, regulate, straighten, coordinate, even up, make parallel, arrange in line

alignment *noun* 1 ALLIANCE, union, association, agreement, sympathy, cooperation, affiliation
2 LINING UP, line, order, ranging, arrangement, evening, sequence, regulating, adjustment, coordination, straightening up, evening up

alike *adjective* SIMILAR, close, the same, equal, equivalent, uniform, parallel, resembling, identical, corresponding, akin, duplicate, analogous, homogeneous, of a piece, cut from the same cloth, like two peas in a pod
<< OPPOSITE different
▷ *adverb* SIMILARLY, identically, equally, uniformly, correspondingly, analogously
<< OPPOSITE differently

alive *adjective* 1 LIVING, breathing, animate, having life, subsisting, existing, functioning, alive and kicking, in the land of the living (*informal*)
<< OPPOSITE dead
2 IN EXISTENCE, existing, functioning, active, operative, in force, on-going, prevalent, existent, extant

<< OPPOSITE inoperative

3 LIVELY, spirited, active, vital, alert, eager, quick, awake, vigorous, cheerful, energetic, animated, brisk, agile, perky, chirpy (*informal*), sprightly, vivacious, full of life, spry, full of beans (*informal*), zestful

<< OPPOSITE dull

▷▷ **alive to** AWARE OF, sensitive to, susceptible to, alert to, eager for, awake to, cognizant of, sensible of

all *determiner* 1 THE WHOLE AMOUNT, everything, the whole, the total, the sum, the total amount, the aggregate, the totality, the sum total, the entirety, the entire amount, the complete amount

2 EVERY, each, every single, every one of, each and every

▷ *adjective* COMPLETE, greatest, full, total, perfect, entire, utter

▷ *adverb* COMPLETELY, totally, fully, entirely, absolutely, altogether, wholly, utterly

>> RELATED WORDS *prefixes* pan-, panto-

allay *verb* REDUCE, quiet, relax, ease, calm, smooth, relieve, check, moderate, dull, diminish, compose, soften, blunt, soothe, subdue, lessen, alleviate, appease, quell, mitigate, assuage, pacify, mollify

allegation *noun* CLAIM, charge, statement, profession, declaration, plea, accusation, assertion, affirmation, deposition, avowal, asseveration, averment

allege *verb* CLAIM, hold, charge, challenge, state, maintain, advance, declare, assert, uphold, put forward, affirm, profess, depose, avow, aver, asseverate

<< OPPOSITE deny

alleged *adjective* CLAIMED, supposed, declared, assumed, so-called, apparent, rumoured, stated, described, asserted, designated, presumed, affirmed, professed, reputed, hypothetical, putative, presupposed, averred, unproved

allegedly *adverb* SUPPOSEDLY, apparently, reportedly, by all accounts, reputedly, purportedly

allegiance *noun* LOYALTY, duty, obligation, devotion, fidelity, homage, obedience, adherence, constancy, faithfulness, troth (*archaic*), fealty

<< OPPOSITE disloyalty

allegorical *adjective* SYMBOLIC, figurative, symbolizing, emblematic, parabolic

allegory *noun* SYMBOL, story, tale, myth, symbolism, emblem, fable, parable, apologue

allergic *adjective* SENSITIVE, affected, susceptible, sensitized, hypersensitive

▷▷ **allergic to** (*informal*) AVERSE TO, opposed to, hostile to, loath to, disinclined to, antipathetic to

allergy *noun* 1 SENSITIVITY, reaction, susceptibility, antipathy, hypersensitivity, sensitiveness

2 (*informal*) DISLIKE, hatred, hostility, aversion, loathing, disgust, antipathy, animosity, displeasure, antagonism, distaste, enmity, opposition, repugnance, disinclination

alleviate *verb* EASE, reduce, relieve, moderate, smooth, dull, diminish, soften, check, blunt, soothe, subdue, lessen, lighten, quell, allay, mitigate, abate, slacken, assuage, quench, mollify, slake, palliate ▷ see **ameliorate**

alley *noun* PASSAGE, walk, lane, pathway, alleyway, passageway, backstreet

alliance *noun* UNION, league, association, agreement, marriage, connection, combination, coalition, treaty, partnership, federation, pact, compact, confederation, affinity, affiliation, confederacy, concordat

<< OPPOSITE division

allied *adjective* 1 UNITED, joined, linked, related, married, joint, combined, bound, integrated, unified, affiliated, leagued, confederate, amalgamated, cooperating, in league, hand in glove (*informal*), in cahoots (*US informal*)

2 CONNECTED, joined, linked, tied, related, associated, syndicated, affiliated, kindred

all-important *adjective* ESSENTIAL, central, significant, key, necessary, vital, critical, crucial, pivotal, momentous, consequential

allocate *verb* ASSIGN, grant, distribute, designate, set aside, earmark, give out, consign, allow, budget, allot, mete, share out, apportion, appropriate

allocation *noun* 1 ALLOWANCE, share, measure, grant, portion, quota, lot, ration, stint, stipend

2 ASSIGNMENT, allowance, rationing, allotment, apportionment, appropriation

allot *verb* ASSIGN, allocate, designate, set aside, earmark, mete, share out, apportion, budget, appropriate

allotment *noun* 1 PLOT, patch, tract, kitchen garden

2 ASSIGNMENT, share, measure, grant, allowance, portion, quota, lot, ration, allocation, stint, appropriation, stipend, apportionment

allotted *verb* ASSIGNED, given, allocated, designated, set aside, earmarked, apportioned

all-out *or* **all out** *adjective* TOTAL, full, complete, determined, supreme, maximum, outright, thorough, unlimited, full-scale, optimum, exhaustive, resolute, full-on (*informal*), unrestrained, unremitting, thoroughgoing, unstinted

<< OPPOSITE half-hearted

▷ *adverb* ENERGETICALLY, hard, strongly, sharply, heavily, severely, fiercely, vigorously, intensely, violently, powerfully, forcibly, forcefully, with all your might, with might and main

allow *verb* 1 PERMIT, approve, enable, sanction, endure, license, brook, endorse, warrant, tolerate, put up with (*informal*), authorize, stand, suffer, bear

<< OPPOSITE prohibit

2 LET, permit, sanction, authorize, license, tolerate, consent to, countenance, concede to, assent to, give leave to, give the green light for, give a blank cheque to

<< OPPOSITE forbid

3 GIVE, provide, grant, spare, devote, assign, allocate, set aside, deduct, earmark, remit, allot

4 ACKNOWLEDGE, accept, admit, grant, recognize, yield, concede, confess, acquiesce

▷▷ **allow for something** TAKE INTO ACCOUNT, consider, plan for, accommodate, provide for, arrange for, foresee, make provision for, make allowances for, make concessions for, keep in mind, set something aside for, take into consideration

allowable *adjective* PERMISSIBLE, all right, approved, appropriate, suitable, acceptable, tolerable, admissible, sufferable, sanctionable

allowance *noun* 1 PORTION, lot, share, amount, measure, grant, pension, subsidy, quota, allocation, stint, annuity, allotment, remittance, stipend, apportionment

2 POCKET MONEY, grant, fee, payment, consideration, ration, handout, remittance

3 CONCESSION, discount, reduction, repayment, deduction, rebate

alloy *noun* MIXTURE, combination, compound, blend, hybrid, composite, amalgam, meld, admixture

all right *adjective* 1 SATISFACTORY, O.K. *or* okay (*informal*), average, fair, sufficient, standard, acceptable, good enough, adequate, so-so (*informal*), up to scratch (*informal*), passable, up to standard, up to the mark, unobjectionable

<< OPPOSITE unsatisfactory

2 WELL, O.K. *or* okay (*informal*), strong, whole, sound, fit, safe, healthy, hale, unharmed, out of the woods, uninjured, unimpaired, up to par

<< OPPOSITE ill

▷ *adverb* SATISFACTORILY, O.K. *or* okay (*informal*), reasonably, well enough, adequately, suitably, acceptably, passably, unobjectionably ▷ see **alright**

allude to *verb* REFER TO, suggest, mention, speak of, imply, intimate, hint at, remark on, insinuate, touch upon ▷ see **elude**

allure *noun* ATTRACTIVENESS, appeal, charm, attraction, lure, temptation, glamour, persuasion, enchantment, enticement, seductiveness

▷ *verb* ATTRACT, persuade, charm, win over, tempt, lure, seduce, entice, enchant, lead on, coax, captivate, beguile, cajole, decoy, inveigle

alluring *adjective* ATTRACTIVE, fascinating, enchanting, seductive, tempting, sexy, intriguing, fetching, glamorous, captivating, beguiling, bewitching, come-hither

<< OPPOSITE unattractive

allusion *noun* REFERENCE, mention, suggestion, hint, implication, innuendo, intimation, insinuation, casual remark, indirect reference

ally *noun* PARTNER, friend, colleague, associate, mate, accessory, comrade, helper, collaborator, accomplice, confederate, co-worker, bedfellow, cobber (*Austral & NZ old-fashioned informal*), coadjutor, abettor, E hoa (*NZ*)

<< OPPOSITE opponent

▷▷ **ally yourself with something** *or* **someone** UNITE WITH, join, associate with, connect with, unify, league with, affiliate with, collaborate with, join forces with, confederate, band together with

almighty *adjective* 1 ALL-POWERFUL, supreme, absolute, unlimited, invincible, omnipotent

<< OPPOSITE powerless

2 (*informal*) GREAT, terrible, enormous, desperate, severe, intense, awful, loud, excessive

<< OPPOSITE slight

almost *adverb* NEARLY, about, approaching, close to, virtually, practically, roughly, all but, just about, not quite, on the brink of, not far from, approximately, well-nigh, as good as

alms *plural noun* (*Old-fashioned*) DONATION, relief, gift, charity, bounty, benefaction, koha (*NZ*)

aloft *adverb* 1 IN THE AIR, up, higher, above, overhead, in the sky, on high, high up, up above

2 UPWARD, skyward, heavenward

alone *adjective* 1 SOLITARY, isolated, sole, separate, apart, abandoned, detached, by yourself, unattended, unaccompanied, out on a limb, unescorted, on your tod (*slang*)

<< OPPOSITE accompanied

2 LONELY, abandoned, deserted, isolated, solitary, estranged, desolate, forsaken, forlorn, destitute, lonesome (*chiefly US & Canad*), friendless

▷ *adverb* 1 SOLELY, only, individually, singly, exclusively, uniquely

2 BY YOURSELF, independently, unaided, unaccompanied, without help, on your own, unassisted, without assistance, under your own steam

<< OPPOSITE with help

aloof *adjective* DISTANT, cold, reserved, cool, formal, remote, forbidding, detached, indifferent, chilly, unfriendly, unsympathetic, uninterested, haughty, unresponsive,

supercilious, unapproachable, unsociable, standoffish
<< OPPOSITE friendly

aloud *adverb* OUT LOUD, clearly, plainly, distinctly, audibly, intelligibly

alphabet *noun* LETTERS, script, writing system, syllabary

already *adverb* BEFORE NOW, before, previously, at present, by now, by then, even now, by this time, just now, by that time, heretofore, as of now

alright ▷ see **all right**

The single-word form *alright* is still considered by many people to be wrong or less acceptable than *all right*. This is borne out by the data in the Collins Word Web, which suggests that the two-word form is about twenty times commoner than the alternative spelling

also *adverb* AND, too, further, plus, along with, in addition, as well, moreover, besides, furthermore, what's more, on top of that, to boot, additionally, into the bargain, as well as

alter *verb* **1** MODIFY, change, reform, shift, vary, transform, adjust, adapt, revise, amend, diversify, remodel, tweak (*informal*), recast, reshape, metamorphose, transmute
2 CHANGE, turn, vary, transform, adjust, adapt, metamorphose

alteration *noun* **1** CHANGE, adjustment, shift, amendment, conversion, modification
2 ADJUSTMENT, change, amendment, variation, conversion, transformation, adaptation, difference, revision, modification, remodelling, reformation, diversification, metamorphosis, variance, reshaping, transmutation

altercation *noun* ARGUMENT, row, clash, disagreement, dispute, controversy, contention, quarrel, squabble, wrangle, bickering, discord, dissension

alternate *verb* **1** INTERCHANGE, change, alter, fluctuate, intersperse, take turns, oscillate, chop and change, follow one another, follow in turn
2 INTERSPERSE, interchange, exchange, swap, stagger, rotate
▷ *adjective* **1** ALTERNATING, interchanging, every other, rotating, every second, sequential
2 SUBSTITUTE, alternative, other, different, replacement, complementary
▷ *noun* (US) SUBSTITUTE, reserve, deputy, relief, replacement, stand-by, makeshift

alternating *adjective* INTERCHANGING, changing, shifting, swinging, rotating, fluctuating, occurring by turns, oscillating, vacillating, seesawing

alternative *noun* SUBSTITUTE, choice, other (*of two*), option, preference, recourse
▷ *adjective* DIFFERENT, other, substitute, alternate

alternatively *adverb* OR, instead, otherwise, on the other hand, if not, then again, as an alternative, by way of alternative, as another option

although *conjunction* THOUGH, while, even if, even though, whilst, albeit, despite the fact that, notwithstanding, even supposing, tho' (*US poetic*)

altitude *noun* HEIGHT, summit, peak, elevation, loftiness

altogether *adverb* **1** ABSOLUTELY, quite, completely, totally, perfectly, fully, thoroughly, wholly, utterly, downright, one hundred per cent (*informal*), undisputedly, lock, stock and barrel
2 COMPLETELY, all, fully, entirely, comprehensively, thoroughly, wholly, every inch, one hundred per cent (*informal*), in every respect
<< OPPOSITE partially
3 ON THE WHOLE, generally, mostly, in general, collectively, all things considered, on average, for the most part, all in all, on balance, in toto (*Latin*), as a whole
4 IN TOTAL, in all, all told, taken together, in sum, everything included, in toto (*Latin*)

The single-word form *altogether* should not be used as an alternative to *all together* because the meanings are very distinct. *Altogether* is an adverb meaning 'absolutely' or, in a different sense, ' in total'. *All together*, however, means 'all at the same time' or 'all in the same place'. The distinction can be seen in the following example: *altogether there were six or seven families sharing the flat's facilities* means ' in total', while *there were six or seven families all together in one flat*, means 'all crowded in together'

altruism *noun* SELFLESSNESS, charity, consideration, goodwill, generosity, self-sacrifice, philanthropy, benevolence, magnanimity, humanitarianism, unselfishness, beneficence, charitableness, greatheartedness, bigheartedness
<< OPPOSITE self-interest

altruistic *adjective* SELFLESS, generous, humanitarian, charitable, benevolent, considerate, self-sacrificing, philanthropic, unselfish, public-spirited
<< OPPOSITE self-interested

always *adverb* **1** HABITUALLY, regularly, every

time, inevitably, consistently, invariably, aye (*Scot*), perpetually, without exception, customarily, unfailingly, on every occasion, day in, day out
<< OPPOSITE seldom
2 FOREVER, for keeps, eternally, for all time, evermore, till the cows come home (*informal*), till Doomsday
3 CONTINUALLY, constantly, all the time, forever, repeatedly, aye (*Scot*), endlessly, persistently, eternally, perpetually, incessantly, interminably, unceasingly, everlastingly, in perpetuum (*Latin*)

amalgam *noun* COMBINATION, mixture, compound, blend, union, composite, fusion, alloy, amalgamation, meld, admixture

amalgamate *verb* COMBINE, unite, ally, compound, blend, incorporate, integrate, merge, fuse, mingle, alloy, coalesce, meld, commingle, intermix
<< OPPOSITE divide

amalgamation *noun* COMBINATION, union, joining, mixing, alliance, coalition, merger, mixture, compound, blend, integration, composite, fusion, mingling, alloy, amalgamating, incorporation, amalgam, meld, admixture, commingling

amass *verb* COLLECT, gather, assemble, compile, accumulate, aggregate, pile up, garner, hoard, scrape together, rake up, heap up

amateur *noun* NONPROFESSIONAL, outsider, layman, dilettante, layperson, non-specialist, dabbler

amateurish *adjective* UNPROFESSIONAL, amateur, crude, bungling, clumsy, inexpert, unaccomplished, unskilful
<< OPPOSITE professional

amaze *verb* ASTONISH, surprise, shock, stun, alarm, stagger, startle, bewilder, astound, daze, confound, stupefy, flabbergast, bowl someone over (*informal*), boggle someone's mind, dumbfound

amazement *noun* ASTONISHMENT, surprise, wonder, shock, confusion, admiration, awe, marvel, bewilderment, wonderment, perplexity, stupefaction

amazing *adjective* ASTONISHING, striking, surprising, brilliant, stunning, impressive, overwhelming, staggering, sensational (*informal*), bewildering, breathtaking, astounding, eye-opening, wondrous (*archaic* or *literary*), mind-boggling, jaw-dropping, stupefying

ambassador *noun* REPRESENTATIVE, minister, agent, deputy, diplomat, envoy, consul, attaché, emissary, legate, plenipotentiary

ambience *noun* ATMOSPHERE, feel, setting, air, quality, character, spirit, surroundings, tone, mood, impression, flavour, temper, tenor, aura, complexion, vibes (*slang*), vibrations (*slang*), milieu

ambiguity *noun* VAGUENESS, doubt, puzzle, uncertainty, obscurity, enigma, equivocation, inconclusiveness, indefiniteness, dubiety, dubiousness, tergiversation, indeterminateness, equivocality, doubtfulness, equivocacy

ambiguous *adjective* UNCLEAR, puzzling, uncertain, obscure, vague, doubtful, dubious, enigmatic, indefinite, inconclusive, cryptic, indeterminate, equivocal, Delphic, oracular, enigmatical, clear as mud (*informal*)
<< OPPOSITE clear

ambition *noun* 1 GOAL, end, hope, design, dream, target, aim, wish, purpose, desire, intention, objective, intent, aspiration, Holy Grail (*informal*)
2 ENTERPRISE, longing, drive, fire, spirit, desire, passion, enthusiasm, warmth, striving, initiative, aspiration, yearning, devotion, zeal, verve, zest, fervour, eagerness, gusto, hankering, get-up-and-go (*informal*), ardour, keenness, avidity, fervency

ambitious *adjective* 1 ENTERPRISING, spirited, keen, active, daring, eager, intent, enthusiastic, hopeful, striving, vigorous, aspiring, energetic, adventurous, avid, zealous, intrepid, resourceful, purposeful, desirous
<< OPPOSITE unambitious
2 DEMANDING, trying, hard, taxing, difficult, challenging, tough, severe, impressive, exhausting, exacting, bold, elaborate, formidable, energetic, strenuous, pretentious, arduous, grandiose, industrious
<< OPPOSITE modest

ambivalence *noun* INDECISION, doubt, opposition, conflict, uncertainty, contradiction, wavering, fluctuation, hesitancy, equivocation, vacillation, irresolution

ambivalent *adjective* UNDECIDED, mixed, conflicting, opposed, uncertain, doubtful, unsure, contradictory, wavering, unresolved, fluctuating, hesitant, inconclusive, debatable, equivocal, vacillating, warring, irresolute
<< OPPOSITE definite

amble *verb* STROLL, walk, wander, ramble, meander, saunter, dawdle, mosey (*informal*)

ambush *verb* TRAP, attack, surprise, deceive, dupe, ensnare, waylay, ambuscade, bushwhack (US)
▷ *noun* TRAP, snare, attack, lure, waylaying, ambuscade

ameliorate *verb* IMPROVE, better, benefit, reform, advance, promote, amend, elevate, raise, mend, mitigate, make better, assuage, meliorate

> *Ameliorate* is sometimes confused with *alleviate* but the words are not synonymous. *Ameliorate* comes ultimately from the Latin for 'better', and means 'to improve'. The nouns it typically goes with are *condition*, and *situation*. *Alleviate* means 'to lessen', and frequently occurs with *poverty*, *suffering*, *pain*, *symptoms*, and *effects*. Occasionally *ameliorate* is used with *effects* and *poverty* where the other verb may be more appropriate

amenable *adjective* RECEPTIVE, open, susceptible, responsive, agreeable, compliant, tractable, acquiescent, persuadable, able to be influenced

<< OPPOSITE stubborn

amend *verb* CHANGE, improve, reform, fix, correct, repair, edit, alter, enhance, update, revise, modify, remedy, rewrite, mend, rectify, tweak (*informal*), ameliorate, redraw

amendment *noun* 1 ADDITION, change, adjustment, attachment, adaptation, revision, modification, alteration, remodelling, reformation, clarification, adjunct, addendum

2 CHANGE, improvement, repair, edit, remedy, correction, revision, modification, alteration, mending, enhancement, reform, betterment, rectification, amelioration, emendation

amends *plural noun* (usually in *make amends*) COMPENSATION, apology, restoration, redress, reparation, indemnity, restitution, atonement, recompense, expiation, requital

amenity *noun* 1 FACILITY, service, advantage, comfort, convenience

2 REFINEMENT, politeness, affability, amiability, courtesy, mildness, pleasantness, suavity, agreeableness, complaisance

<< OPPOSITE rudeness

American *adjective* YANKEE *or* YANK, U.S.

▷ *noun* YANKEE *or* YANK, Yankee Doodle

amiable *adjective* PLEASANT, kind, kindly, pleasing, friendly, attractive, engaging, charming, obliging, delightful, cheerful, benign, winning, agreeable, good-humoured, lovable, sociable, genial, affable, congenial, winsome, good-natured, sweet-tempered, likable *or* likeable

<< OPPOSITE unfriendly

amicable *adjective* FRIENDLY, kindly, brotherly, civil, neighbourly, peaceful, polite, harmonious, good-humoured, amiable, courteous, cordial, sociable, fraternal, peaceable

<< OPPOSITE unfriendly

amid *or* **amidst** *preposition* 1 DURING, among, at a time of, in an atmosphere of

2 IN THE MIDDLE OF, among, surrounded by, amongst, in the midst of, in the thick of

amiss *adjective* WRONG, mistaken, confused, false, inappropriate, rotten, incorrect, faulty, inaccurate, unsuitable, improper, defective, out of order, awry, erroneous, untoward, fallacious

<< OPPOSITE right

▷▷ **take something amiss** TAKE AS AN INSULT, take wrongly, take as offensive, take out of turn

ammunition *noun* MUNITIONS, rounds, shot, shells, powder, explosives, cartridges, armaments, materiel, shot and shell

amnesty *noun* GENERAL PARDON, mercy, pardoning, immunity, forgiveness, reprieve, oblivion, remission (*of penalty*), clemency, dispensation, absolution, condonation

amok *or* **amuck** *adverb* ▷▷ **run amok** GO MAD, go wild, turn violent, go berserk, lose control, go insane, go into a frenzy

among *or* **amongst** *preposition* 1 IN THE MIDST OF, with, together with, in the middle of, amid, surrounded by, amidst, in the thick of

2 IN THE GROUP OF, one of, part of, included in, in the company of, in the class of, in the number of

3 BETWEEN, to

4 WITH ONE ANOTHER, mutually, by all of, by the whole of, by the joint action of

amoral *adjective* UNETHICAL, nonmoral, unvirtuous

> *Amoral* is sometimes confused with *immoral*. The *a-* at the beginning of the word means 'without' or 'lacking', so the word is properly used of people who have no moral code, or about places or situations where moral considerations do not apply: *the film was violent and amoral*. In contrast *immoral* should be used to talk about the breaking of moral rules, as in: *drug dealing is the most immoral and evil of all human activities*

amorous *adjective* LOVING, in love, tender, passionate, fond, erotic, affectionate, ardent, impassioned, doting, enamoured, lustful, attached, lovesick, amatory

<< OPPOSITE cold

amorphous *adjective* SHAPELESS, vague, irregular, nondescript, indeterminate, unstructured, nebulous, formless, inchoate, characterless, unformed, unshaped, unshapen

<< OPPOSITE definite

amount *noun* 1 QUANTITY, lot, measure, size, supply, mass, volume, capacity, extent, bulk,

number, magnitude, expanse
2 TOTAL, whole, mass, addition, sum, lot, extent, aggregate, entirety, totality, sum total
▷▷ **amount to something** **1** ADD UP TO, mean, total, equal, constitute, comprise, aggregate, purport, be equivalent to
2 COME TO, become, grow to, develop into, advance to, progress to, mature into

Although it is common to use a plural noun after *amount of*, for example in *the amount of people* and *the amount of goods*, this should be avoided. Preferred alternatives would be to use *quantity*, as in *the quantity of people*, or *number*, as in *the number of goods*

amour *noun* LOVE AFFAIR, relationship, affair, romance, intrigue, liaison, affaire de coeur (*French*)

ample *adjective* **1** PLENTY OF, great, rich, liberal, broad, generous, lavish, spacious, abounding, abundant, plentiful, expansive, copious, roomy, unrestricted, voluminous, capacious, profuse, commodious, plenteous
<< OPPOSITE insufficient
2 LARGE, great, big, full, wide, broad, extensive, generous, abundant, voluminous, bountiful

amplification *noun* **1** INCREASE, boosting, stretching, strengthening, expansion, extension, widening, raising, heightening, deepening, lengthening, enlargement, intensification, magnification, dilation, augmentation
2 EXPLANATION, development, expansion, supplementing, fleshing out, elaboration, rounding out, augmentation, expatiation

amplify *verb* **1** EXPAND, raise, extend, boost, stretch, strengthen, increase, widen, intensify, heighten, deepen, enlarge, lengthen, magnify, augment, dilate
<< OPPOSITE reduce
2 GO INTO DETAIL, develop, explain, expand, supplement, elaborate, augment, flesh out, round out, enlarge on, expatiate
<< OPPOSITE simplify

amplitude *noun* **1** EXTENT, reach, range, size, mass, sweep, dimension, bulk, scope, width, magnitude, compass, greatness, breadth, expanse, vastness, spaciousness, bigness, largeness, hugeness, capaciousness
2 FULLNESS, abundance, richness, plethora, profusion, completeness, plenitude, copiousness, ampleness

amply *adverb* FULLY, well, greatly, completely, richly, liberally, thoroughly, substantially, lavishly, extensively, generously, abundantly, profusely, copiously, plentifully, unstintingly, bountifully, without stinting, plenteously, capaciously
<< OPPOSITE insufficiently

amputate *verb* CUT OFF, remove, separate, sever, curtail, truncate, lop off

amuck ▷ see **amok**

amuse *verb* **1** ENTERTAIN, please, delight, charm, cheer, tickle, gratify, beguile, enliven, regale, gladden
<< OPPOSITE bore
2 OCCUPY, interest, involve, engage, entertain, absorb, divert, engross

amusement *noun* **1** ENJOYMENT, delight, entertainment, cheer, laughter, mirth, hilarity, merriment, gladdening, beguilement, regalement
<< OPPOSITE boredom
2 DIVERSION, interest, sport, pleasing, fun, pleasure, recreation, entertainment, gratification
3 PASTIME, game, sport, joke, entertainment, hobby, recreation, distraction, diversion, lark, prank

amusing *adjective* FUNNY, humorous, gratifying, laughable, farcical, comical, droll, interesting, pleasing, charming, cheering, entertaining, comic, pleasant, lively, diverting, delightful, enjoyable, cheerful, witty, merry, gladdening, facetious, jocular, rib-tickling, waggish
<< OPPOSITE boring

anaemic *adjective* **1** PALE, weak, dull, frail, feeble, wan, sickly, bloodless, colourless, infirm, pallid, ashen, characterless, enervated, like death warmed up (*informal*)
<< OPPOSITE rosy
2 WEAK, feeble

anaesthetic *noun* PAINKILLER, narcotic, sedative, opiate, anodyne, analgesic, soporific, stupefacient, stupefactive
▷ *adjective* PAIN-KILLING, dulling, numbing, narcotic, sedative, opiate, deadening, anodyne, analgesic, soporific, sleep-inducing, stupefacient, stupefactive

analogous *adjective* SIMILAR, like, related, equivalent, parallel, resembling, alike, corresponding, comparable, akin, homologous
<< OPPOSITE different

The correct word to use after *analogous* is *to*, not *with* – for example: *swimming has no event that is analogous to the 100 metres in athletics* (not *analogous with the 100 metres in athletics*)

analogy *noun* SIMILARITY, relation, comparison, parallel, correspondence, resemblance, correlation, likeness, equivalence, homology, similitude

analyse *verb* **1** EXAMINE, test, study, research, judge, estimate, survey, investigate, interpret, evaluate, inspect, work over

2 BREAK DOWN, consider, study, separate, divide, resolve, dissolve, dissect, think through, assay, anatomize

analysis *noun* 1 STUDY, reasoning, opinion, judgment, interpretation, evaluation, estimation, dissection
2 EXAMINATION, test, division, inquiry, investigation, resolution, interpretation, breakdown, scanning, separation, evaluation, scrutiny, sifting, anatomy, dissolution, dissection, assay, perusal, anatomization

analytic *or* **analytical** *adjective* RATIONAL, questioning, testing, detailed, searching, organized, exact, precise, logical, systematic, inquiring, diagnostic, investigative, dissecting, explanatory, discrete, inquisitive, interpretive, studious, interpretative, expository

anarchic *adjective* LAWLESS, rioting, confused, disordered, revolutionary, chaotic, rebellious, riotous, disorganized, misruled, ungoverned, misgoverned
<< OPPOSITE law-abiding

anarchist *noun* REVOLUTIONARY, rebel, terrorist, insurgent, nihilist

anarchy *noun* LAWLESSNESS, revolution, riot, disorder, confusion, chaos, rebellion, misrule, disorganization, misgovernment
<< OPPOSITE order

anathema *noun* ABOMINATION, bête noire, enemy, pariah, bane, bugbear

anatomy *noun* 1 STRUCTURE, build, make-up, frame, framework, composition
2 EXAMINATION, study, division, inquiry, investigation, analysis, dismemberment, dissection

ancestor *noun* FOREFATHER, predecessor, precursor, forerunner, forebear, antecedent, progenitor, tupuna *or* tipuna (NZ)
<< OPPOSITE descendant

ancestral *adjective* INHERITED, hereditary, patriarchal, antecedent, forefatherly, genealogical, lineal, ancestorial

ancestry *noun* ORIGIN, house, family, line, race, stock, blood, ancestors, descent, pedigree, extraction, lineage, forebears, antecedents, parentage, forefathers, genealogy, derivation, progenitors

anchor *noun* MOORING, hook (*Nautical*), bower (*Nautical*), kedge, drogue, sheet anchor
▷ *verb* 1 MOOR, harbour, dock, tie up, kedge
2 DOCK, moor, harbour, drop anchor, kedge, cast anchor, drop the hook, let go the anchor, lay anchor, come to anchor
3 SECURE, tie, fix, bind, chain, attach, bolt, fasten, affix

anchorage *noun* BERTH, haven, port, harbour, dock, quay, dockage, moorage, harbourage

ancient *adjective* 1 CLASSICAL, old, former, past, bygone, primordial, primeval, olden
2 VERY OLD, early, aged, antique, obsolete, archaic, age-old, bygone, antiquated, hoary, olden, superannuated, antediluvian, timeworn, old as the hills
3 OLD-FASHIONED, dated, outdated, obsolete, out of date, unfashionable, outmoded, passé
<< OPPOSITE up-to-date

ancillary *adjective* SUPPLEMENTARY, supporting, extra, additional, secondary, subsidiary, accessory, subordinate, auxiliary, contributory
<< OPPOSITE major

and *conjunction* 1 ALSO, including, along with, together with, in addition to, as well as
2 MOREOVER, plus, furthermore

The forms *try and do something* and *wait and do something* should only be used in informal or spoken English. In more formal writing, use *try to* and *wait to*, for example: *we must try to prevent this happening* (not *try and prevent*)

androgynous *adjective* HERMAPHRODITE, bisexual, androgyne, hermaphroditic, epicene

android *noun* (*Science fiction*) ROBOT, automaton, humanoid, cyborg, mechanical man, bionic man *or* woman

anecdote *noun* STORY, tale, sketch, short story, yarn, reminiscence, urban myth, urban legend

anew *adverb* AGAIN, once again, once more, over again, from the beginning, from scratch, another time, afresh

angel *noun* 1 DIVINE MESSENGER, spirit, cherub, archangel, seraph, spiritual being, guardian spirit
2 (*informal*) DEAR, ideal, beauty, saint, treasure, darling, dream, jewel, gem, paragon

angelic *adjective* 1 PURE, beautiful, lovely, innocent, entrancing, virtuous, saintly, adorable, beatific
2 HEAVENLY, celestial, ethereal, cherubic, seraphic
<< OPPOSITE demonic

anger *noun* RAGE, passion, outrage, temper, fury, resentment, irritation, wrath, indignation, annoyance, agitation, ire, antagonism, displeasure, exasperation, irritability, spleen, pique, ill temper, vehemence, vexation, high dudgeon, ill humour, choler
<< OPPOSITE calmness
▷ *verb* ENRAGE, provoke, outrage, annoy, offend, excite, irritate, infuriate, hassle (*informal*), aggravate (*informal*), incense, fret, gall, madden, exasperate, nettle, vex, affront, displease, rile, pique, get on someone's nerves (*informal*), antagonize, get someone's back up, put someone's back up, nark (*Brit, Austral*

& *NZ slang*), make someone's blood boil, get in someone's hair (*informal*), get someone's dander up (*informal*)
<< OPPOSITE soothe

angle *noun* 1 GRADIENT, bank, slope, incline, inclination
2 INTERSECTION, point, edge, corner, knee, bend, elbow, crook, crotch, nook, cusp
3 POINT OF VIEW, position, approach, direction, aspect, perspective, outlook, viewpoint, slant, standpoint, take (*informal*), side

angler *noun* FISHERMAN, fisher, piscator *or* piscatrix

angling *noun* FISHING

angry *adjective* FURIOUS, cross, heated, mad (*informal*), raging, provoked, outraged, annoyed, passionate, irritated, raving, hacked (off) (*US slang*), choked, infuriated, hot, incensed, enraged, ranting, exasperated, irritable, resentful, nettled, snappy, indignant, irate, tumultuous, displeased, uptight (*informal*), riled, up in arms, incandescent, ill-tempered, irascible, antagonized, waspish, piqued, hot under the collar (*informal*), on the warpath, hopping mad (*informal*), foaming at the mouth, choleric, splenetic, wrathful, at daggers drawn, in high dudgeon, as black as thunder, ireful, tooshie (*Austral slang*), off the air (*Austral slang*)
<< OPPOSITE calm

Some people feel it is more correct to talk about being *angry with* someone than being *angry at* them. In British English, *angry with* is still more common than *angry at*, but *angry at* is used more commonly in American English

angst *noun* ANXIETY, worry, distress, torment, unease, apprehension, agitation, malaise, perturbation, vexation, fretfulness, disquietude, inquietude
<< OPPOSITE peace of mind

anguish *noun* SUFFERING, pain, torture, distress, grief, misery, agony, torment, sorrow, woe, heartache, heartbreak, pang, throe

anguished *adjective* SUFFERING, wounded, tortured, distressed, tormented, afflicted, agonized, grief-stricken, wretched, brokenhearted

angular *adjective* SKINNY, spare, lean, gaunt, bony, lanky, scrawny, lank, rangy, rawboned, macilent (*rare*)

animal *noun* 1 CREATURE, beast, brute
2 BRUTE, devil, monster, savage, beast, bastard (*informal, offensive*), villain, barbarian, swine (*informal*), wild man
▷ *adjective* PHYSICAL, gross, fleshly, bodily, sensual, carnal, brutish, bestial
>> RELATED WORD *prefix* zoo-

animate *adjective* LIVING, live, moving, alive, breathing, alive and kicking
▷ *verb* ENLIVEN, encourage, excite, urge, inspire, stir, spark, move, fire, spur, stimulate, revive, activate, rouse, prod, quicken, incite, instigate, kick-start (*informal*), impel, energize, kindle, embolden, liven up, breathe life into, invigorate, gladden, gee up, vitalize, vivify, inspirit
<< OPPOSITE inhibit

animated *adjective* LIVELY, spirited, quick, excited, active, vital, dynamic, enthusiastic, passionate, vivid, vigorous, energetic, vibrant, brisk, buoyant, ardent, airy, fervent, zealous, elated, ebullient, sparky, sprightly, vivacious, gay, alive and kicking, full of beans (*informal*), zestful
<< OPPOSITE listless

animation *noun* LIVELINESS, life, action, activity, energy, spirit, passion, enthusiasm, excitement, pep, sparkle, vitality, vigour, zeal, verve, zest, fervour, high spirits, dynamism, buoyancy, elation, exhilaration, gaiety, ardour, vibrancy, brio, zing (*informal*), vivacity, ebullience, briskness, airiness, sprightliness, pizzazz *or* pizazz (*informal*)

animosity *noun* HOSTILITY, hate, hatred, resentment, bitterness, malice, antagonism, antipathy, enmity, acrimony, rancour, bad blood, ill will, animus, malevolence, virulence, malignity
<< OPPOSITE friendliness

animus *noun* ILL WILL, hate, hostility, hatred, resentment, bitterness, malice, animosity, antagonism, antipathy, enmity, acrimony, rancour, bad blood, malevolence, virulence, malignity

annals *plural noun* RECORDS, history, accounts, registers, journals, memorials, archives, chronicles

annex *verb* 1 SEIZE, take over, appropriate, acquire, occupy, conquer, expropriate, arrogate
2 JOIN, unite, add, connect, attach, tack, adjoin, fasten, affix, append, subjoin
<< OPPOSITE detach

annexation *noun* SEIZURE, takeover, occupation, conquest, appropriation, annexing, expropriation, arrogation

annexe *noun* 1 EXTENSION, wing, ell, supplementary building
2 APPENDIX, addition, supplement, attachment, adjunct, addendum, affixment

annihilate *verb* DESTROY, abolish, wipe out, erase, eradicate, extinguish, obliterate, liquidate, root out, exterminate, nullify, extirpate, wipe from the face of the earth, kennet (*Austral slang*), jeff (*Austral slang*)

annihilation *noun* DESTRUCTION, wiping out, abolition, extinction, extinguishing, liquidation, rooting out, extermination, eradication, erasure, obliteration, nullification, extirpation

anniversary *noun* JUBILEE, remembrance, commemoration

annotate *verb* MAKE NOTES ON, explain, note, illustrate, comment on, interpret, gloss, footnote, commentate, elucidate, make observations on

annotation *noun* NOTE, comment, explanation, observation, interpretation, illustration, commentary, gloss, footnote, exegesis, explication, elucidation

announce *verb* 1 MAKE KNOWN, tell, report, reveal, publish, declare, advertise, broadcast, disclose, intimate, proclaim, trumpet, make public, publicize, divulge, promulgate, propound, shout from the rooftops (*informal*)
<< OPPOSITE keep secret
2 BE A SIGN OF, signal, herald, warn of, signify, augur, harbinger, presage, foretell, portend, betoken

announcement *noun* 1 STATEMENT, communication, broadcast, explanation, publication, declaration, advertisement, testimony, disclosure, bulletin, communiqué, proclamation, utterance, intimation, promulgation, divulgence
2 DECLARATION, report, reporting, publication, revelation, disclosure, proclamation, intimation, promulgation, divulgence

announcer *noun* PRESENTER, newscaster, reporter, commentator, broadcaster, newsreader, master of ceremonies, anchor man, anchor

annoy *verb* IRRITATE, trouble, bore, anger, harry, bother, disturb, provoke, get (*informal*), bug (*informal*), needle (*informal*), plague, tease, harass, hassle (*informal*), aggravate (*informal*), badger, gall, madden, ruffle, exasperate, nettle, molest, pester, vex, displease, irk, bedevil, rile, peeve, get under your skin (*informal*), get on your nerves (*informal*), nark (*Brit, Austral & NZ slang*), get up your nose (*informal*), give someone grief (*Brit & S African*), make your blood boil, rub someone up the wrong way (*informal*), get your goat (*slang*), get in your hair (*informal*), get on your wick (*Brit slang*), get your dander up (*informal*), get your back up, incommode, put your back up, hack you off (*informal*)
<< OPPOSITE soothe

annoyance *noun* 1 IRRITATION, trouble, anger, bother, grief (*informal*), harassment, disturbance, hassle (*informal*), nuisance, provocation, displeasure, exasperation, aggravation, vexation, bedevilment
2 NUISANCE, bother, pain (*informal*), bind (*informal*), bore, drag (*informal*), plague, tease, pest, gall, pain in the neck (*informal*)

annoyed *adjective* IRRITATED, bothered, harassed, hassled (*informal*), aggravated (*informal*), maddened, ruffled, exasperated, nettled, vexed, miffed (*informal*), displeased, irked, riled, harried, peeved (*informal*), piqued, browned off (*informal*)

annoying *adjective* IRRITATING, boring, disturbing, provoking, teasing, harassing, aggravating, troublesome, galling, maddening, exasperating, displeasing, bedevilling, peeving (*informal*), irksome, bothersome, vexatious
<< OPPOSITE delightful

annual *adjective* 1 ONCE A YEAR, yearly
2 YEARLONG, yearly

annually *adverb* 1 ONCE A YEAR, yearly, each year, every year, per year, by the year, every twelve months, per annum, year after year
2 PER YEAR, yearly, each year, every year, by the year, per annum

annul *verb* INVALIDATE, reverse, cancel, abolish, void, repeal, recall, revoke, retract, negate, rescind, nullify, obviate, abrogate, countermand, declare *or* render null and void
<< OPPOSITE restore

anodyne *adjective* BLAND, dull, boring, insipid, unexciting, uninspiring, uninteresting, mind-numbing (*informal*)
▷ *noun* PAINKILLER, narcotic, palliative, analgesic, pain reliever

anoint *verb* 1 SMEAR, oil, rub, grease, spread over, daub, embrocate
2 CONSECRATE, bless, sanctify, hallow, anele (*archaic*)

anomalous *adjective* UNUSUAL, odd, rare, bizarre, exceptional, peculiar, eccentric, abnormal, irregular, inconsistent, off-the-wall (*slang*), incongruous, deviating, oddball (*informal*), atypical, aberrant, outré
<< OPPOSITE normal

anomaly *noun* IRREGULARITY, departure, exception, abnormality, rarity, inconsistency, deviation, eccentricity, oddity, aberration, peculiarity, incongruity

anon *adverb* (*Archaic* or *literary*) SOON, presently, shortly, promptly, before long, forthwith, betimes (*archaic*), erelong (*archaic* or *poetic*), in a couple of shakes (*informal*)

anonymity *noun* 1 NAMELESSNESS, innominateness
2 UNREMARKABILITY *or* UNREMARKABLENESS, characterlessness, unsingularity

anonymous *adjective* 1 UNNAMED, unknown, unidentified, nameless, unacknowledged, incognito, unauthenticated, innominate
<< OPPOSITE identified
2 UNSIGNED, uncredited, unattributed, unattested

<< OPPOSITE signed
3 NONDESCRIPT, impersonal, faceless, colourless, undistinguished, unexceptional, characterless

answer *verb* 1 REPLY, explain, respond, resolve, acknowledge, react, return, retort, rejoin, refute
<< OPPOSITE ask
2 SATISFY, meet, serve, fit, fill, suit, solve, fulfil, suffice, measure up to
▷ *noun* 1 REPLY, response, reaction, resolution, explanation, plea, comeback, retort, report, return, defence, acknowledgement, riposte, counterattack, refutation, rejoinder
<< OPPOSITE question
2 SOLUTION, resolution, explanation
3 REMEDY, solution, vindication
▷▷ **answer to someone** BE RESPONSIBLE TO, obey, work under, be ruled by, be managed by, be subordinate to, be accountable to, be answerable to

answerable *adjective* RESPONSIBLE FOR *or* TO, to blame for, liable for *or* to, accountable for *or* to, chargeable for, subject to

answer back *verb* BE IMPERTINENT, argue, dispute, disagree, retort, contradict, rebut, talk back, be cheeky

ant *noun*
>> RELATED WORD *habitation* ant hill

antagonism *noun* HOSTILITY, competition, opposition, conflict, rivalry, contention, friction, discord, antipathy, dissension
<< OPPOSITE friendship

antagonist *noun* OPPONENT, rival, opposer, enemy, competitor, contender, foe, adversary

antagonistic *adjective* HOSTILE, opposed, resistant, at odds, incompatible, set against, averse, unfriendly, at variance, inimical, antipathetic, ill-disposed

> A useful synonym for *antagonistic*, for example in *public opinion is antagonistic to nuclear energy*, is *averse*. However, this alternative should be used with care as a very common error is to confuse it with *adverse*. *Averse* is usually followed by *to* and is meant to convey a strong dislike or hostility towards something, normally expressed by a person or people. *Adverse* is wrong in this context and should be used in relation to conditions or results: *adverse road conditions*

antagonize *verb* ANNOY, anger, insult, offend, irritate, alienate, hassle (*informal*), aggravate (*informal*), gall, repel, estrange, get under your skin (*informal*), get on your nerves (*informal*), nark (*Brit, Austral & NZ slang*), get up your nose (*informal*), be on your back (*slang*), rub (you) up the wrong way (*informal*), disaffect, get in your hair (*informal*), get on your wick (*Brit slang*), hack you off (*informal*)
<< OPPOSITE pacify

antecedent *adjective* PRECEDING, earlier, former, previous, prior, preliminary, foregoing, anterior, precursory
<< OPPOSITE subsequent

anterior *adjective* 1 FRONT, forward, fore, frontward
2 EARLIER, former, previous, prior, preceding, introductory, foregoing, antecedent

anthem *noun* SONG OF PRAISE, carol, chant, hymn, psalm, paean, chorale, canticle

anthology *noun* COLLECTION, choice, selection, treasury, digest, compilation, garland, compendium, miscellany, analects

anticipate *verb* 1 EXPECT, predict, forecast, prepare for, look for, hope for, envisage, foresee, bank on, apprehend, foretell, think likely, count upon
2 AWAIT, look forward to, count the hours until

> The Collins Word Web reveals that the use of *anticipate* and *expect* as synonyms is well established. However, although both words relate to a person's knowledge of something that will happen in the future, there are subtle differences in meaning that should be understood when choosing which word to use. *Anticipate* means that someone foresees an event and has prepared for it, while *expect* means 'to regard something as probable', but does not necessarily suggest the state of being prepared. Similarly, using *foresee* as a synonym of *anticipate*, as in *they failed to foresee the vast explosion in commercial revenue which would follow*, is not entirely appropriate

anticipation *noun* EXPECTANCY, hope, expectation, apprehension, foresight, premonition, preconception, foretaste, prescience, forethought, presentiment

anticlimax *noun* DISAPPOINTMENT, letdown, comedown (*informal*), bathos
<< OPPOSITE climax

antics *plural noun* CLOWNING, tricks, stunts, mischief, larks, capers, pranks, frolics, escapades, foolishness, silliness, playfulness, skylarking, horseplay, buffoonery, tomfoolery, monkey tricks

antidote *noun* REMEDY, cure, preventive, corrective, neutralizer, nostrum, countermeasure, antitoxin, antivenin, counteragent

antipathy *noun* HOSTILITY, opposition, disgust, dislike, hatred, loathing, distaste, animosity, aversion, antagonism, enmity, rancour, bad blood, incompatibility, ill will, animus, repulsion, abhorrence, repugnance, odium, contrariety

<< OPPOSITE affinity

antiquated *adjective* OBSOLETE, old, aged, ancient, antique, old-fashioned, elderly, dated, past it (*informal*), out-of-date, archaic, outmoded, passé, old hat, hoary, superannuated, antediluvian, outworn, cobwebby, old as the hills

<< OPPOSITE up-to-date

antique *noun* PERIOD PIECE, relic, bygone, heirloom, collector's item, museum piece, object of virtu

▷ *adjective* 1 VINTAGE, classic, antiquarian, olden

2 OLD-FASHIONED, old, aged, ancient, remote, elderly, primitive, outdated, obsolete, archaic, bygone, primordial, primeval, immemorial, superannuated

antiquity *noun* 1 DISTANT PAST, ancient times, time immemorial, olden days

2 OLD AGE, age, oldness, ancientness, elderliness

antiseptic *adjective* HYGIENIC, clean, pure, sterile, sanitary, uncontaminated, unpolluted, germ-free, aseptic

<< OPPOSITE unhygienic

▷ *noun* DISINFECTANT, purifier, bactericide, germicide

antisocial *adjective* 1 UNSOCIABLE, reserved, retiring, withdrawn, alienated, unfriendly, uncommunicative, misanthropic, asocial

<< OPPOSITE sociable

2 DISRUPTIVE, disorderly, hostile, menacing, rebellious, belligerent, antagonistic, uncooperative

antithesis *noun* 1 OPPOSITE, contrast, reverse, contrary, converse, inverse, antipode

2 CONTRAST, opposition, contradiction, reversal, inversion, contrariety, contraposition

anxiety *noun* UNEASINESS, concern, care, worry, doubt, tension, alarm, distress, suspicion, angst, unease, apprehension, misgiving, suspense, nervousness, disquiet, trepidation, foreboding, restlessness, solicitude, perturbation, watchfulness, fretfulness, disquietude, apprehensiveness, dubiety

<< OPPOSITE confidence

anxious *adjective* 1 EAGER, keen, intent, yearning, impatient, itching, ardent, avid, expectant, desirous

<< OPPOSITE reluctant

2 UNEASY, concerned, worried, troubled, upset, careful, wired (*slang*), nervous, disturbed, distressed, uncomfortable, tense, fearful, unsettled, restless, neurotic, agitated, taut, disquieted, apprehensive, edgy, watchful, jittery (*informal*), perturbed, on edge, ill at ease, twitchy (*informal*), solicitous, overwrought, fretful, on tenterhooks, in suspense, hot and bothered, unquiet (*chiefly literary*), like a fish out of water, antsy (*informal*), angsty, on pins and needles, discomposed

<< OPPOSITE confident

apace *adverb* (*Literary*) QUICKLY, rapidly, swiftly, speedily, without delay, at full speed, expeditiously, posthaste, with dispatch

apart *adverb* 1 TO PIECES, to bits, asunder, into parts

2 AWAY FROM EACH OTHER, distant from each other

3 ASIDE, away, alone, independently, separately, singly, excluded, isolated, cut off, to one side, to yourself, by itself, aloof, to itself, by yourself, out on a limb

▷▷ **apart from** EXCEPT FOR, excepting, other than, excluding, besides, not including, aside from, but, save, bar, not counting

apartment *noun* 1 (US) FLAT, room, suite, compartment, penthouse, duplex (*US & Canad*), crib, bachelor apartment (*Canad*)

2 ROOMS, quarters, chambers, accommodation, living quarters

apathetic *adjective* UNINTERESTED, passive, indifferent, sluggish, unmoved, stoic, stoical, unconcerned, listless, cold, cool, impassive, unresponsive, phlegmatic, unfeeling, unemotional, torpid, emotionless, insensible

<< OPPOSITE interested

apathy *noun* LACK OF INTEREST, indifference, inertia, coolness, passivity, coldness, stoicism, nonchalance, torpor, phlegm, sluggishness, listlessness, unconcern, insensibility, unresponsiveness, impassivity, passiveness, impassibility, unfeelingness, emotionlessness, uninterestedness

<< OPPOSITE interest

ape *verb* IMITATE, copy, mirror, echo, mock, parrot, mimic, parody, caricature, affect, counterfeit

aperture *noun* OPENING, space, hole, crack, gap, rent, passage, breach, slot, vent, rift, slit, cleft, eye, chink, fissure, orifice, perforation, eyelet, interstice

apex *noun* 1 CULMINATION, top, crown, height, climax, highest point, zenith, apogee, acme

<< OPPOSITE depths

2 HIGHEST POINT, point, top, tip, summit, peak, crest, pinnacle, vertex

<< OPPOSITE lowest point

aphorism *noun* SAYING, maxim, gnome, adage, proverb, dictum, precept, axiom, apothegm, saw

aphrodisiac *noun* LOVE POTION, philtre

▷ *adjective* EROTIC *or* EROTICAL, exciting, stimulating, arousing, venereal
apiece *adverb* EACH, individually, separately, for each, to each, respectively, from each, severally
<< OPPOSITE all together
aplenty *adjective* IN PLENTY, to spare, galore, in abundance, in quantity, in profusion, à gogo (*informal*)
▷ *adverb* PLENTIFULLY, in abundance, abundantly, in quantity, in plenty, copiously, plenteously
aplomb *noun* SELF-POSSESSION, confidence, stability, self-confidence, composure, poise, coolness, calmness, equanimity, balance, self-assurance, sang-froid, level-headedness
<< OPPOSITE self-consciousness
apocalypse *noun* DESTRUCTION, holocaust, havoc, devastation, carnage, conflagration, cataclysm
apocryphal *adjective* DUBIOUS, legendary, doubtful, questionable, mythical, spurious, fictitious, unsubstantiated, equivocal, unverified, unauthenticated, uncanonical
<< OPPOSITE factual
apogee *noun* HIGHEST POINT, top, tip, crown, summit, height, peak, climax, crest, pinnacle, culmination, zenith, apex, acme, vertex
apologetic *adjective* REGRETFUL, sorry, rueful, contrite, remorseful, penitent
apologize *verb* SAY SORRY, express regret, ask forgiveness, make an apology, beg pardon, say you are sorry
apology *noun* REGRET, explanation, excuse, confession, extenuation
▷▷ **apology for something** *or* **someone** MOCKERY OF, excuse for, imitation of, caricature of, travesty of, poor substitute for
apostle *noun* **1** EVANGELIST, herald, missionary, preacher, messenger, proselytizer
2 SUPPORTER, champion, advocate, pioneer, proponent, propagandist, propagator
apotheosis *noun* DEIFICATION, elevation, exaltation, glorification, idealization, idolization
appal *verb* HORRIFY, shock, alarm, frighten, scare, terrify, outrage, disgust, dishearten, revolt, intimidate, dismay, daunt, sicken, astound, harrow, unnerve, petrify, scandalize, make your hair stand on end (*informal*)
appalled *adjective* HORRIFIED, shocked, stunned, alarmed, frightened, scared, terrified, outraged, dismayed, daunted, astounded, unnerved, disquieted, petrified, disheartened
appalling *adjective* **1** HORRIFYING, shocking, terrible, alarming, frightening, scaring, awful, terrifying, horrible, grim, dreadful, intimidating, dismaying, horrific, fearful, daunting, dire, astounding, ghastly, hideous, shameful, harrowing, vile, unnerving, petrifying, horrid, unspeakable, frightful, nightmarish, abominable, disheartening, godawful (*slang*), hellacious (*US slang*)
<< OPPOSITE reassuring
2 AWFUL, terrible, tremendous, distressing, horrible, dreadful, horrendous, ghastly, godawful (*slang*)
apparatus *noun* **1** ORGANIZATION, system, network, structure, bureaucracy, hierarchy, setup (*informal*), chain of command
2 EQUIPMENT, machine, tackle, gear, means, materials, device, tools, implements, mechanism, outfit, machinery, appliance, utensils, contraption (*informal*)
apparel *noun* (*Old-fashioned*) CLOTHING, dress, clothes, equipment, gear (*informal*), habit, outfit, costume, threads (*slang*), array (*poetic*), garments, robes, trappings, attire, garb, accoutrements, vestments, raiment (*archaic* or *poetic*), schmutter (*slang*), habiliments
apparent *adjective* **1** SEEMING, supposed, alleged, outward, exterior, superficial, ostensible, specious
<< OPPOSITE actual
2 OBVIOUS, marked, clear, plain, visible, bold, patent, evident, distinct, open, understandable, manifest, noticeable, blatant, conspicuous, overt, unmistakable, palpable, undeniable, discernible, salient, self-evident, indisputable, much in evidence, undisguised, unconcealed, indubitable, staring you in the face (*informal*), plain as the nose on your face
<< OPPOSITE unclear
apparently *adverb* SEEMINGLY, outwardly, ostensibly, speciously
apparition *noun* GHOST, spirit, shade (*literary*), phantom, spectre, spook (*informal*), wraith, chimera, revenant, visitant, eidolon, atua (*NZ*), kehua (*NZ*)
appeal *verb* PLEAD, call, ask, apply, refer, request, sue, lobby, pray, beg, petition, solicit, implore, beseech, entreat, importune, adjure, supplicate
<< OPPOSITE refuse
▷ *noun* **1** PLEA, call, application, request, prayer, petition, overture, invocation, solicitation, entreaty, supplication, suit, cry from the heart, adjuration
<< OPPOSITE refusal
2 ATTRACTION, charm, fascination, charisma, beauty, attractiveness, allure, magnetism, enchantment, seductiveness, interestingness, engagingness, pleasingness
<< OPPOSITE repulsiveness
▷▷ **appeal to someone** ATTRACT, interest, draw, please, invite, engage, charm, fascinate, tempt, lure, entice, enchant, captivate, allure, bewitch

appealing *adjective* ATTRACTIVE, inviting, engaging, charming, winning, desirable, endearing, alluring, winsome, prepossessing
<< OPPOSITE repellent

appear *verb* 1 SEEM, be clear, be obvious, be evident, look (like *or* as if), be apparent, be plain, be manifest, be patent
2 LOOK (LIKE *or* AS IF), seem, occur, look to be, come across as, strike you as
3 COME INTO VIEW, emerge, occur, attend, surface, come out, turn out, arise, turn up, be present, loom, show (*informal*), issue, develop, arrive, show up (*informal*), come to light, crop up (*informal*), materialize, come forth, come into sight, show your face
<< OPPOSITE disappear
4 COME INTO BEING, come out, be published, be developed, be created, be invented, become available, come into existence
5 PERFORM, play, act, enter, come on, take part, play a part, be exhibited, come onstage

appearance *noun* 1 LOOK, face, form, air, figure, image, looks, bearing, aspect, manner, expression, demeanour, mien (*literary*)
2 ARRIVAL, appearing, presence, turning up, introduction, showing up (*informal*), emergence, advent
3 IMPRESSION, air, front, image, illusion, guise, façade, pretence, veneer, semblance, outward show

appease *verb* 1 PACIFY, satisfy, calm, soothe, quiet, placate, mollify, conciliate
<< OPPOSITE anger
2 EASE, satisfy, calm, relieve, diminish, compose, quiet, blunt, soothe, subdue, lessen, alleviate, lull, quell, allay, mitigate, assuage, quench, tranquillize

appeasement *noun* 1 PACIFICATION, compromise, accommodation, concession, conciliation, acceding, propitiation, mollification, placation
2 EASING, relieving, satisfaction, softening, blunting, soothing, quieting, lessening, lulling, quelling, solace, quenching, mitigation, abatement, alleviation, assuagement, tranquillization

appellation *noun* (*Formal*) NAME, term, style, title, address, description, designation, epithet, sobriquet

append *verb* (*Formal*) ADD, attach, join, hang, adjoin, fasten, annex, tag on, affix, tack on, subjoin
<< OPPOSITE detach

appendage *noun* ATTACHMENT, addition, supplement, accessory, appendix, auxiliary, affix, ancillary, adjunct, annexe, addendum, appurtenance

appendix *noun* SUPPLEMENT, add-on, postscript, adjunct, appendage, addendum, addition, codicil

appetite *noun* 1 HUNGER
2 DESIRE, liking, longing, demand, taste, passion, stomach, hunger, willingness, relish, craving, yearning, inclination, zeal, zest, propensity, hankering, proclivity, appetence, appetency
<< OPPOSITE distaste

appetizer *noun* HORS D'OEUVRE, titbit, antipasto, canapé

applaud *verb* 1 CLAP, encourage, praise, cheer, hail, acclaim, laud, give (someone) a big hand
<< OPPOSITE boo
2 PRAISE, celebrate, approve, acclaim, compliment, salute, commend, extol, crack up (*informal*), big up (*slang, chiefly Caribbean*), eulogize
<< OPPOSITE criticize

applause *noun* OVATION, praise, cheering, cheers, approval, acclaim, clapping, accolade, big hand, commendation, hand-clapping, approbation, acclamation, eulogizing, plaudit

appliance *noun* DEVICE, machine, tool, instrument, implement, mechanism, apparatus, gadget, waldo

applicable *adjective* APPROPRIATE, fitting, fit, suited, useful, suitable, relevant, to the point, apt, pertinent, befitting, apposite, apropos, germane, to the purpose
<< OPPOSITE inappropriate

applicant *noun* CANDIDATE, entrant, claimant, suitor, petitioner, aspirant, inquirer, job-seeker, suppliant, postulant

application *noun* 1 REQUEST, claim, demand, appeal, suit, inquiry, plea, petition, requisition, solicitation
2 RELEVANCE, use, value, practice, bearing, exercise, purpose, function, appropriateness, aptness, pertinence, appositeness, germaneness
3 EFFORT, work, study, industry, labour, trouble, attention, struggle, pains, commitment, hard work, endeavour, dedication, toil, diligence, perseverance, travail (*literary*), attentiveness, assiduity, blood, sweat, and tears (*informal*)

apply *verb* 1 REQUEST, seek, appeal, put in, petition, inquire, solicit, claim, sue, requisition, make application
2 BE RELEVANT, concern, relate, refer, be fitting, be appropriate, be significant, fit, suit, pertain, be applicable, bear upon, appertain
3 USE, exercise, carry out, employ, engage, implement, practise, execute, assign, administer, exert, enact, utilize, bring to bear, put to use, bring into play
4 PUT ON, work in, cover with, lay on, paint on, anoint, spread on, rub in, smear on, shampoo in, bring into contact with

▷▷ **apply yourself** WORK HARD, concentrate, study, pay attention, try, commit yourself, buckle down (*informal*), be assiduous, devote yourself, be diligent, dedicate yourself, make an effort, address yourself, be industrious, persevere

appoint *verb* 1 ASSIGN, name, choose, commission, select, elect, install, delegate, nominate
<< OPPOSITE fire
2 DECIDE, set, choose, establish, determine, settle, fix, arrange, specify, assign, designate, allot
<< OPPOSITE cancel

appointed *adjective* 1 DECIDED, set, chosen, established, determined, settled, fixed, arranged, assigned, designated, allotted
2 ASSIGNED, named, chosen, commissioned, selected, elected, installed, delegated, nominated
3 EQUIPPED, provided, supplied, furnished, fitted out

appointment *noun* 1 SELECTION, naming, election, choosing, choice, commissioning, delegation, nomination, installation, assignment, allotment, designation
2 JOB, office, position, post, situation, place, station, employment, assignment, berth (*informal*)
3 MEETING, interview, date, session, arrangement, consultation, engagement, fixture, rendezvous, tryst (*archaic*), assignation
4 APPOINTEE, candidate, representative, delegate, nominee, office-holder

apportion *verb* DIVIDE, share, deal, distribute, assign, allocate, dispense, give out, allot, mete out, dole out, measure out, parcel out, ration out

apposite *adjective* APPROPRIATE, fitting, suited, suitable, relevant, proper, to the point, apt, applicable, pertinent, befitting, apropos, germane, to the purpose, appertaining
<< OPPOSITE inappropriate

appraisal *noun* 1 ASSESSMENT, opinion, estimate, judgment, evaluation, estimation, sizing up (*informal*), recce (*slang*)
2 VALUATION, pricing, rating, survey, reckoning, assay

appraise *verb* ASSESS, judge, review, estimate, survey, price, rate, value, evaluate, inspect, gauge, size up (*informal*), eye up, assay, recce (*slang*)

Appraise is sometimes used where *apprise* is meant: *both patients had been fully apprised* (not *appraised*) *of the situation*. This may well be due to the fact that *appraise* is considerably more common, and that people therefore tend to associate this meaning mistakenly with a word they know better

appreciable *adjective* SIGNIFICANT, marked, obvious, considerable, substantial, visible, evident, pronounced, definite, noticeable, clear-cut, discernible, measurable, material, recognizable, detectable, perceptible, distinguishable, ascertainable, perceivable
<< OPPOSITE insignificant

appreciably *adverb* SIGNIFICANTLY, obviously, definitely, considerably, substantially, evidently, visibly, markedly, noticeably, palpably, perceptively, measurably, recognizably, discernibly, detectably, distinguishably, perceivably, ascertainably

appreciate *verb* 1 ENJOY, like, value, regard, respect, prize, admire, treasure, esteem, relish, cherish, savour, rate highly
<< OPPOSITE scorn
2 BE AWARE OF, know, understand, estimate, realize, acknowledge, recognize, perceive, comprehend, take account of, be sensitive to, be conscious of, sympathize with, be alive to, be cognizant of
<< OPPOSITE be unaware of
3 BE GRATEFUL FOR, be obliged for, be thankful for, give thanks for, be indebted for, be in debt for, be appreciative of
<< OPPOSITE be ungrateful for
4 INCREASE, rise, grow, gain, improve, mount, enhance, soar, inflate
<< OPPOSITE fall

appreciation *noun* 1 ADMIRATION, liking, respect, assessment, esteem, relish, valuation, enjoyment, appraisal, estimation, responsiveness
2 GRATITUDE, thanks, recognition, obligation, acknowledgment, indebtedness, thankfulness, gratefulness
<< OPPOSITE ingratitude
3 AWARENESS, understanding, regard, knowledge, recognition, perception, sympathy, consciousness, sensitivity, realization, comprehension, familiarity, mindfulness, cognizance
<< OPPOSITE ignorance
4 INCREASE, rise, gain, growth, inflation, improvement, escalation, enhancement
<< OPPOSITE fall
5 REVIEW, report, notice, analysis, criticism, praise, assessment, recognition, tribute, evaluation, critique, acclamation

appreciative *adjective* 1 ENTHUSIASTIC, understanding, pleased, aware, sensitive, conscious, admiring, sympathetic, supportive, responsive, knowledgeable, respectful, mindful, perceptive, in the know (*informal*), cognizant, regardful
2 GRATEFUL, obliged, thankful, indebted, beholden

apprehend *verb* 1 ARREST, catch, lift (*slang*), nick (*slang, chiefly Brit*), capture, seize, run in

(*slang*), take, nail (*informal*), bust (*informal*), collar (*informal*), pinch (*informal*), nab (*informal*), take prisoner, feel your collar (*slang*)
<< OPPOSITE release
2 UNDERSTAND, know, think, believe, imagine, realize, recognize, appreciate, perceive, grasp, conceive, comprehend, get the message, get the picture
<< OPPOSITE be unaware of

apprehension *noun* 1 ANXIETY, concern, fear, worry, doubt, alarm, suspicion, dread, unease, mistrust, misgiving, disquiet, premonition, trepidation, foreboding, uneasiness, pins and needles, apprehensiveness
<< OPPOSITE confidence
2 ARREST, catching, capture, taking, seizure
<< OPPOSITE release
3 AWARENESS, understanding, knowledge, intelligence, ken, perception, grasp, comprehension
<< OPPOSITE incomprehension

apprehensive *adjective* ANXIOUS, concerned, worried, afraid, alarmed, nervous, suspicious, doubtful, uneasy, fearful, neurotic, disquieted, foreboding, twitchy (*informal*), mistrustful, antsy (*informal*)
<< OPPOSITE confident

apprentice *noun* TRAINEE, student, pupil, novice, beginner, learner, neophyte, tyro, probationer
<< OPPOSITE master

apprenticeship *noun* TRAINEESHIP, probation, studentship, novitiate *or* noviciate

apprise *verb* MAKE AWARE, tell, warn, advise, inform, communicate, notify, enlighten, acquaint, give notice, make cognizant ▷ see **appraise**

approach *verb* 1 MOVE TOWARDS, come to, reach, near, advance, catch up, meet, come close, gain on, converge on, come near, push forward, draw near, creep up on
2 MAKE A PROPOSAL TO, speak to, apply to, appeal to, proposition, solicit, sound out, make overtures to, make advances to, broach the matter with
3 SET ABOUT, tackle, undertake, embark on, get down to, launch into, begin work on, commence on, make a start on, enter upon
4 APPROXIMATE, touch, be like, compare with, resemble, come close to, border on, verge on, be comparable to, come near to
▷ *noun* 1 ADVANCE, coming, nearing, appearance, arrival, advent, drawing near
2 ACCESS, way, drive, road, passage, entrance, avenue, passageway
3 *often plural* PROPOSAL, offer, appeal, advance, application, invitation, proposition, overture
4 WAY, means, course, style, attitude, method, technique, manner, procedure, mode, modus operandi
5 APPROXIMATION, likeness, semblance

approachable *adjective* 1 FRIENDLY, open, cordial, sociable, affable, congenial
<< OPPOSITE unfriendly
2 ACCESSIBLE, attainable, reachable, get-at-able (*informal*), come-at-able (*informal*)
<< OPPOSITE inaccessible

appropriate *adjective* SUITABLE, right, fitting, fit, suited, correct, belonging, relevant, proper, to the point, in keeping, apt, applicable, pertinent, befitting, well-suited, well-timed, apposite, apropos, opportune, becoming, seemly, felicitous, germane, to the purpose, appurtenant, congruous
<< OPPOSITE unsuitable
▷ *verb* 1 SEIZE, take, claim, assume, take over, acquire, confiscate, annex, usurp, impound, pre-empt, commandeer, take possession of, expropriate, arrogate
<< OPPOSITE relinquish
2 ALLOCATE, allow, budget, devote, assign, designate, set aside, earmark, allot, share out, apportion
<< OPPOSITE withhold
3 STEAL, take, nick (*slang, chiefly Brit*), pocket, pinch (*informal*), pirate, poach, swipe (*slang*), lift (*informal*), heist (*US slang*), embezzle, blag (*slang*), pilfer, misappropriate, snitch (*slang*), purloin, filch, plagiarize, thieve, peculate

appropriateness *noun* SUITABILITY, fitness, relevance, correctness, felicity, rightness, applicability, timeliness, aptness, pertinence, fittingness, seemliness, appositeness, properness, germaneness, opportuneness, becomingness, congruousness, felicitousness, well-suitedness

appropriation *noun* 1 SETTING ASIDE, assignment, allocation, earmarking, allotment, apportionment
2 SEIZURE, taking, takeover, assumption, annexation, confiscation, commandeering, expropriation, pre-emption, usurpation, impoundment, arrogation

approval *noun* 1 CONSENT, agreement, sanction, licence, blessing, permission, recommendation, concession, confirmation, mandate, endorsement, leave, compliance, the go-ahead (*informal*), countenance, ratification, the green light, assent, authorization, validation, acquiescence, imprimatur, concurrence, O.K. *or* okay (*informal*)
2 FAVOUR, liking, regard, respect, praise, esteem, acclaim, appreciation, encouragement, admiration, applause, commendation, approbation, good opinion
<< OPPOSITE disapproval

approve *verb* AGREE TO, second, allow, pass,

accept, confirm, recommend, permit, sanction, advocate, bless, endorse, uphold, mandate, authorize, ratify, go along with, subscribe to, consent to, buy into (*informal*), validate, countenance, rubber stamp, accede to, give the go-ahead to (*informal*), give the green light to, assent to, concur in, O.K. *or* okay (*informal*)

<< OPPOSITE veto

▷▷ **approve of something** *or* **someone** FAVOUR, like, support, respect, praise, appreciate, agree with, admire, endorse, esteem, acclaim, applaud, commend, be pleased with, have a good opinion of, regard highly, think highly of

approving *adjective* FAVOURABLE, admiring, applauding, respectful, appreciative, commendatory, acclamatory

approximate *adjective* ROUGH, close, general, near, estimated, loose, vague, hazy, sketchy, amorphous, imprecise, inexact, almost exact, almost accurate

<< OPPOSITE exact

▷▷ **approximate to** RESEMBLE, reach, approach, touch, come close to, border on, come near, verge on

approximately *adverb* ALMOST, about, around, generally, nearly, close to, relatively, roughly, loosely, just about, more or less, in the region of, in the vicinity of, not far off, in the neighbourhood of

approximation *noun* GUESS, estimate, conjecture, estimation, guesswork, rough idea, rough calculation, ballpark figure (*informal*), ballpark estimate (*informal*)

a priori *adjective* DEDUCED, deductive, inferential

apron *noun* PINNY (*informal*), overall, pinafore

apropos *adjective* APPROPRIATE, right, seemly, fitting, fit, related, correct, belonging, suitable, relevant, proper, to the point, apt, applicable, pertinent, befitting, apposite, opportune, germane, to the purpose

▷▷ **apropos of** CONCERNING, about, re, regarding, respecting, on the subject of, in respect of, as to, with reference to, in re, in the matter of, as regards, in *or* with regard to

apt *adjective* 1 APPROPRIATE, timely, right, seemly, fitting, fit, related, correct, belonging, suitable, relevant, proper, to the point, applicable, pertinent, befitting, apposite, apropos, opportune, germane, to the purpose

<< OPPOSITE inappropriate

2 INCLINED, likely, ready, disposed, prone, liable, given, predisposed, of a mind

3 GIFTED, skilled, expert, quick, bright, talented, sharp, capable, smart, prompt, clever, intelligent, accomplished, ingenious, skilful, astute, adroit, teachable

<< OPPOSITE slow

aptitude *noun* GIFT, ability, talent, capacity, intelligence, leaning, bent, tendency, faculty, capability, flair, inclination, disposition, knack, propensity, proficiency, predilection, cleverness, proclivity, quickness, giftedness, proneness, aptness

arable *adjective* PRODUCTIVE, fertile, fruitful, fecund, cultivable, farmable, ploughable, tillable

arbiter *noun* 1 JUDGE, referee, umpire, umpie (*Austral slang*), arbitrator, adjudicator

2 AUTHORITY, expert, master, governor, ruler, dictator, controller, lord, pundit

arbitrary *adjective* 1 RANDOM, chance, optional, subjective, unreasonable, inconsistent, erratic, discretionary, personal, fanciful, wilful, whimsical, capricious

<< OPPOSITE logical

2 DICTATORIAL, absolute, unlimited, uncontrolled, autocratic, dogmatic, imperious, domineering, unrestrained, overbearing, tyrannical, summary, magisterial, despotic, high-handed, peremptory, tyrannous

arbitrate *verb* DECIDE, judge, determine, settle, referee, umpire, mediate, adjudicate, adjudge, pass judgment, sit in judgment

arbitration *noun* DECISION, settlement, judgment, determination, adjudication, arbitrament

arbitrator *noun* JUDGE, referee, umpire, umpie (*Austral slang*), arbiter, adjudicator

arc *noun* CURVE, bend, bow, arch, crescent, half-moon

arcade *noun* GALLERY, mall, cloister, portico, colonnade, covered walk, peristyle

arcane *adjective* MYSTERIOUS, secret, hidden, esoteric, occult, recondite, cabbalistic

arch[1] *noun* 1 ARCHWAY, curve, dome, span, vault

2 CURVE, bend, bow, crook, arc, hunch, sweep, hump, curvature, semicircle

▷ *verb* CURVE, bridge, bend, bow, span, arc

arch[2] *adjective* PLAYFUL, joking, teasing, humorous, sly, mischievous, saucy, tongue-in-cheek, jesting, jokey, pert, good-natured, roguish, frolicsome, waggish

archaic *adjective* 1 OLD, ancient, antique, primitive, bygone, olden (*archaic*)

<< OPPOSITE modern

2 OLD-FASHIONED, obsolete, out of date, antiquated, outmoded, passé, old hat, behind the times, superannuated

<< OPPOSITE up-to-date

arched *adjective* CURVED, domed, vaulted

archer *noun* BOWMAN (*archaic*), toxophilite (*formal*)

archetypal *or* **archetypical** *adjective* TYPICAL, standard, model, original, normal, classic, ideal, exemplary, paradigmatic, prototypal, prototypic *or* prototypical

archetype *noun* PRIME EXAMPLE, standard, model, original, pattern, classic, ideal, norm, form, prototype, paradigm, exemplar

architect *noun* 1 DESIGNER, planner, draughtsman, master builder
2 CREATOR, father, shaper, engineer, author, maker, designer, founder, deviser, planner, inventor, contriver, originator, prime mover, instigator, initiator

architecture *noun* 1 DESIGN, planning, building, construction, architectonics
2 CONSTRUCTION, design, style
3 STRUCTURE, design, shape, make-up, construction, framework, layout, anatomy

archive *noun* RECORD OFFICE, museum, registry, repository
▷ *plural noun* RECORDS, papers, accounts, rolls, documents, files, registers, deeds, chronicles, annals

arctic *adjective* (*informal*) FREEZING, cold, frozen, icy, chilly, frosty, glacial, frigid, gelid, frost-bound, cold as ice

Arctic *adjective* POLAR, far-northern, hyperborean

ardent *adjective* 1 ENTHUSIASTIC, keen, eager, avid, zealous, keen as mustard
<< OPPOSITE indifferent
2 PASSIONATE, warm, spirited, intense, flaming, fierce, fiery, hot, fervent, impassioned, ablaze, lusty, vehement, amorous, hot-blooded, warm-blooded, fervid
<< OPPOSITE cold

ardour *noun* 1 PASSION, feeling, fire, heat, spirit, intensity, warmth, devotion, fervour, vehemence, fierceness
2 ENTHUSIASM, zeal, eagerness, earnestness, keenness, avidity

arduous *adjective* DIFFICULT, trying, hard, tough, tiring, severe, painful, exhausting, punishing, harsh, taxing, heavy, steep, formidable, fatiguing, rigorous, troublesome, gruelling, strenuous, onerous, laborious, burdensome, backbreaking, toilsome
<< OPPOSITE easy

area *noun* 1 REGION, land, quarter, division, sector, district, stretch, territory, zone, plot, province, patch, neighbourhood, sphere, turf (*US slang*), realm, domain, tract, locality, neck of the woods (*informal*)
2 PART, section, sector, portion
3 RANGE, reach, size, sweep, extent, scope, sphere, domain, width, compass, breadth, parameters (*informal*), latitude, expanse, radius, ambit
4 REALM, part, department, field, province, arena, sphere, domain

arena *noun* 1 RING, ground, stage, field, theatre, bowl, pitch, stadium, enclosure, park (*US & Canad*), coliseum, amphitheatre
2 SCENE, world, area, stage, field, theatre, sector, territory, province, forum, scope, sphere, realm, domain

arguably *adverb* POSSIBLY, potentially, conceivably, plausibly, feasibly, questionably, debatably, deniably, disputably, contestably, controvertibly, dubitably, refutably

argue *verb* 1 QUARREL, fight, row, clash, dispute, disagree, feud, squabble, spar, wrangle, bicker, have an argument, cross swords, be at sixes and sevens, fight like cat and dog, go at it hammer and tongs, bandy words, altercate
2 DISCUSS, debate, dispute, thrash out, exchange views on, controvert
3 CLAIM, question, reason, challenge, insist, maintain, hold, allege, plead, assert, contend, uphold, profess, remonstrate, expostulate
4 DEMONSTRATE, show, suggest, display, indicate, imply, exhibit, denote, evince

argument *noun* 1 REASON, case, reasoning, ground(s), defence, excuse, logic, justification, rationale, polemic, dialectic, line of reasoning, argumentation
2 DEBATE, questioning, claim, row, discussion, dispute, controversy, pleading, plea, contention, assertion, polemic, altercation, remonstrance, expostulation, remonstration
3 QUARREL, fight, row, clash, dispute, controversy, disagreement, misunderstanding, feud, barney (*informal*), squabble, wrangle, bickering, difference of opinion, tiff, altercation
<< OPPOSITE agreement

argumentative *adjective* QUARRELSOME, contrary, contentious, belligerent, combative, opinionated, litigious, disputatious
<< OPPOSITE easy-going

arid *adjective* 1 DRY, desert, dried up, barren, sterile, torrid, parched, waterless, moistureless
<< OPPOSITE lush
2 BORING, dull, tedious, dreary, dry, tiresome, lifeless, colourless, uninteresting, flat, uninspired, vapid, spiritless, jejune, as dry as dust
<< OPPOSITE exciting

arise *verb* 1 HAPPEN, start, begin, follow, issue, result, appear, develop, emerge, occur, spring, set in, stem, originate, ensue, come about, commence, come to light, emanate, crop up (*informal*), come into being, materialize
2 (*Old-fashioned*) GET TO YOUR FEET, get up, rise, stand up, spring up, leap up
3 GET UP, wake up, awaken, get out of bed
4 ASCEND, rise, lift, mount, climb, tower, soar, move upward

aristocracy *noun* UPPER CLASS, elite, nobility, gentry, peerage, ruling class, patricians, upper

crust (*informal*), noblesse (*literary*), haut monde (*French*), patriciate, body of nobles
<< OPPOSITE commoners

aristocrat *noun* NOBLE, lord, lady, peer, patrician, grandee, nobleman, aristo (*informal*), childe (*archaic*), noblewoman, peeress

aristocratic *adjective* 1 UPPER-CLASS, lordly, titled, gentle (*archaic*), elite, gentlemanly, noble, patrician, blue-blooded, well-born, highborn
<< OPPOSITE common
2 REFINED, fine, polished, elegant, stylish, dignified, haughty, courtly, snobbish, well-bred
<< OPPOSITE vulgar

arm[1] *noun* 1 UPPER LIMB, limb, appendage
2 BRANCH, part, office, department, division, section, wing, sector, extension, detachment, offshoot, subdivision, subsection
3 AUTHORITY, might, force, power, strength, command, sway, potency

arm[2] *verb* 1 EQUIP, provide, supply, outfit, rig, array, furnish, issue with, deck out, accoutre
2 PROVIDE, prime, prepare, protect, guard, strengthen, outfit, equip, brace, fortify, forearm, make ready, gird your loins, jack up (*NZ*)
▷ *plural noun* WEAPONS, guns, firearms, weaponry, armaments, ordnance, munitions, instruments of war

armada *noun* FLEET, navy, squadron, flotilla

armaments *plural noun* WEAPONS, arms, guns, ammunition, weaponry, ordnance, munitions, materiel

armed *adjective* CARRYING WEAPONS, provided, prepared, supplied, ready, protected, guarded, strengthened, equipped, primed, arrayed, furnished, fortified, in arms, forearmed, fitted out, under arms, girded, rigged out, tooled up (*slang*), accoutred

armistice *noun* TRUCE, peace, ceasefire, suspension of hostilities

armour *noun* PROTECTION, covering, shield, sheathing, armour plate, chain mail, protective covering

armoured *adjective* PROTECTED, mailed, reinforced, toughened, bulletproof, armour-plated, steel-plated, ironclad, bombproof

armoury *or US* **armory** *noun* ARSENAL, magazine, ammunition dump, arms depot, ordnance depot

army *noun* 1 SOLDIERS, military, troops, armed force, legions, infantry, military force, land forces, land force, soldiery
2 VAST NUMBER, host, gang, mob, flock, array, legion, swarm, sea, pack, horde, multitude, throng

aroma *noun* SCENT, smell, perfume, fragrance, bouquet, savour, odour, redolence

aromatic *adjective* FRAGRANT, perfumed, spicy, savoury, pungent, balmy, redolent, sweet-smelling, sweet-scented, odoriferous
<< OPPOSITE smelly

around *preposition* 1 APPROXIMATELY, about, nearly, close to, roughly, just about, in the region of, circa (*used with dates*), in the vicinity of, not far off, in the neighbourhood of
2 SURROUNDING, about, enclosing, encompassing, framing, encircling, on all sides of, on every side of, environing
▷ *adverb* 1 EVERYWHERE, about, throughout, all over, here and there, on all sides, in all directions, to and fro
2 NEAR, close, nearby, handy, at hand, close by, close at hand
>> RELATED WORD *prefix* circum-

> In American English, *around* is used more often than *round* as an adverb and preposition, except in a few fixed phrases such as *all year round*. In British English, *round* is more commonly used as an adverb than *around*

arousal *noun* STIMULATION, movement, response, reaction, excitement, animation, stirring up, provocation, inflammation, agitation, exhilaration, incitement, enlivenment

arouse *verb* 1 STIMULATE, encourage, inspire, prompt, spark, spur, foster, provoke, rouse, stir up, inflame, incite, instigate, whip up, summon up, whet, kindle, foment, call forth
<< OPPOSITE quell
2 INFLAME, move, warm, excite, spur, provoke, animate, prod, stir up, agitate, quicken, enliven, goad, foment
3 AWAKEN, wake up, rouse, waken

arraign *verb* ACCUSE, charge, prosecute, denounce, indict, impeach, incriminate, call to account, take to task

arrange *verb* 1 PLAN, agree, prepare, determine, schedule, organize, construct, devise, contrive, fix up, jack up (*NZ informal*)
2 PUT IN ORDER, group, form, order, sort, class, position, range, file, rank, line up, organize, set out, sequence, exhibit, sort out (*informal*), array, classify, tidy, marshal, align, categorize, systematize, jack up (*NZ informal*)
<< OPPOSITE disorganize
3 ADAPT, score, orchestrate, harmonize, instrument

arrangement *noun* 1 *often plural* PLAN, planning, provision, preparation
2 AGREEMENT, contract, settlement, appointment, compromise, deal (*informal*), pact, compact, covenant
3 DISPLAY, grouping, system, order, ordering, design, ranging, structure, rank, organization,

exhibition, line-up, presentation, array, marshalling, classification, disposition, alignment, setup (*informal*)
4 ADAPTATION, score, version, interpretation, instrumentation, orchestration, harmonization

array *noun* 1 ARRANGEMENT, show, order, supply, display, collection, exhibition, line-up, mixture, parade, formation, presentation, spectacle, marshalling, muster, disposition
2 (*Poetic*) CLOTHING, dress, clothes, threads (*slang*), garments, apparel, attire, garb, finery, regalia, raiment (*archaic* or *poetic*), schmutter (*slang*)
▷ *verb* 1 ARRANGE, show, group, order, present, range, display, line up, sequence, parade, exhibit, unveil, dispose, draw up, marshal, lay out, muster, align, form up, place in order, set in line (*Military*)
2 DRESS, supply, clothe, wrap, deck, outfit, decorate, equip, robe, get ready, adorn, apparel (*archaic*), festoon, attire, fit out, garb, bedeck, caparison, accoutre

arrest *verb* 1 CAPTURE, catch, lift (*slang*), nick (*slang, chiefly Brit*), seize, run in (*slang*), nail (*informal*), bust (*informal*), collar (*informal*), take, detain, pinch (*informal*), nab (*informal*), apprehend, take prisoner, take into custody, lay hold of
<< OPPOSITE release
2 STOP, end, hold, limit, check, block, slow, delay, halt, stall, stay, interrupt, suppress, restrain, hamper, inhibit, hinder, obstruct, retard, impede
<< OPPOSITE speed up
3 FASCINATE, hold, involve, catch, occupy, engage, grip, absorb, entrance, intrigue, rivet, enthral, mesmerize, engross, spellbind
▷ *noun* 1 CAPTURE, bust (*informal*), detention, seizure, apprehension
<< OPPOSITE release
2 STOPPAGE, halt, suppression, obstruction, inhibition, blockage, hindrance
<< OPPOSITE acceleration

arresting *adjective* STRIKING, surprising, engaging, dramatic, stunning, impressive, extraordinary, outstanding, remarkable, noticeable, conspicuous, salient, jaw-dropping
<< OPPOSITE unremarkable

arrival *noun* 1 APPEARANCE, coming, arriving, entrance, advent, materialization
2 COMING, happening, taking place, dawn, emergence, occurrence, materialization
3 NEWCOMER, arriver, incomer, visitor, caller, entrant, comer, visitant

arrive *verb* 1 COME, appear, enter, turn up, show up (*informal*), materialize, draw near
<< OPPOSITE depart
2 OCCUR, happen, take place, ensue, transpire, fall, befall
3 (*informal*) SUCCEED, make it (*informal*), triumph, do well, thrive, flourish, be successful, make good, prosper, cut it (*informal*), reach the top, become famous, make the grade (*informal*), get to the top, crack it (*informal*), hit the jackpot (*informal*), turn out well, make your mark (*informal*), achieve recognition, do all right for yourself (*informal*)
▷▷ **arrive at something** REACH, make, get to, enter, land at, get as far as

arrogance *noun* CONCEIT, pride, swagger, pretension, presumption, bluster, hubris, pomposity, insolence, hauteur, pretentiousness, high-handedness, haughtiness, loftiness, imperiousness, pompousness, superciliousness, lordliness, conceitedness, contemptuousness, scornfulness, uppishness (*Brit informal*), disdainfulness, overweeningness
<< OPPOSITE modesty

arrogant *adjective* CONCEITED, lordly, assuming, proud, swaggering, pompous, pretentious, stuck up (*informal*), cocky, contemptuous, blustering, imperious, overbearing, haughty, scornful, puffed up, egotistical, disdainful, self-important, presumptuous, high-handed, insolent, supercilious, high and mighty (*informal*), overweening, immodest, swollen-headed, bigheaded (*informal*), uppish (*Brit informal*)
<< OPPOSITE modest

arrow *noun* 1 DART, flight, reed (*archaic*), bolt, shaft (*archaic*), quarrel
2 POINTER, indicator, marker

arsenal *noun* 1 STORE, stock, supply, magazine, stockpile
2 ARMOURY, storehouse, ammunition dump, arms depot, ordnance depot

art *noun* 1 ARTWORK, style of art, fine art, creativity
2 SKILL, knowledge, method, facility, craft, profession, expertise, competence, accomplishment, mastery, knack, ingenuity, finesse, aptitude, artistry, artifice (*archaic*), virtuosity, dexterity, cleverness, adroitness

artful *adjective* 1 CUNNING, designing, scheming, sharp, smart, clever, subtle, intriguing, tricky, shrewd, sly, wily, politic, crafty, foxy, deceitful
<< OPPOSITE straightforward
2 SKILFUL, masterly, smart, clever, subtle, ingenious, adept, resourceful, proficient, adroit, dexterous
<< OPPOSITE clumsy

article *noun* 1 FEATURE, story, paper, piece, item, creation, essay, composition, discourse, treatise

2 THING, piece, unit, item, object, device, tool, implement, commodity, gadget, utensil
3 CLAUSE, point, part, heading, head, matter, detail, piece, particular, division, section, item, passage, portion, paragraph, proviso

articulate *adjective* EXPRESSIVE, clear, effective, vocal, meaningful, understandable, coherent, persuasive, fluent, eloquent, lucid, comprehensible, communicative, intelligible
<< OPPOSITE incoherent
▷ *verb* 1 EXPRESS, say, tell, state, word, speak, declare, phrase, communicate, assert, pronounce, utter, couch, put across, enunciate, put into words, verbalize, asseverate
2 PRONOUNCE, say, talk, speak, voice, utter, enunciate, vocalize, enounce

articulation *noun* 1 EXPRESSION, delivery, pronunciation, saying, talking, voicing, speaking, utterance, diction, enunciation, vocalization, verbalization
2 VOICING, statement, expression, verbalization
3 JOINT, coupling, jointing, connection, hinge, juncture

artifice *noun* 1 CUNNING, scheming, trick, device, craft, tactic, manoeuvre, deception, hoax, expedient, ruse, guile, trickery, duplicity, subterfuge, stratagem, contrivance, chicanery, wile, craftiness, artfulness, slyness, machination
2 CLEVERNESS, skill, facility, invention, ingenuity, finesse, inventiveness, deftness, adroitness

artificial *adjective* 1 SYNTHETIC, manufactured, plastic, man-made, non-natural
2 INSINCERE, forced, affected, assumed, phoney *or* phony (*informal*), put on, false, pretended, hollow, contrived, unnatural, feigned, spurious, meretricious
<< OPPOSITE genuine
3 FAKE, mock, imitation, bogus, simulated, phoney *or* phony (*informal*), sham, pseudo (*informal*), fabricated, counterfeit, spurious, ersatz, specious
<< OPPOSITE authentic

artillery *noun* BIG GUNS, battery, cannon, ordnance, gunnery, cannonry

artisan *noun* CRAFTSMAN, technician, mechanic, journeyman, artificer, handicraftsman, skilled workman

artist *noun* CREATOR, master, maker, craftsman, artisan (*obsolete*), fine artist

artiste *noun* PERFORMER, player, entertainer, Thespian, trouper, play-actor

artistic *adjective* 1 CREATIVE, cultured, original, sensitive, sophisticated, refined, imaginative, aesthetic, discerning, eloquent, arty (*informal*)
<< OPPOSITE untalented
2 BEAUTIFUL, fine, pleasing, lovely, creative, elegant, stylish, cultivated, imaginative, decorative, aesthetic, exquisite, graceful, expressive, ornamental, tasteful
<< OPPOSITE unattractive

artistry *noun* SKILL, art, style, taste, talent, craft, genius, creativity, touch, flair, brilliance, sensibility, accomplishment, mastery, finesse, craftsmanship, proficiency, virtuosity, workmanship, artistic ability

artless *adjective* 1 NATURAL, simple, fair, frank, plain, pure, open, round, true, direct, genuine, humble, straightforward, sincere, honest, candid, unaffected, upfront (*informal*), unpretentious, unadorned, dinkum (*Austral & NZ informal*), guileless, uncontrived, undesigning
<< OPPOSITE artificial
2 UNSKILLED, awkward, crude, primitive, rude, bungling, incompetent, clumsy, inept, untalented, maladroit
<< OPPOSITE artful

arty *adjective* (*informal*) ARTISTIC, arty-farty (*informal*), arty-crafty (*informal*)

as *conjunction* 1 WHEN, while, just as, at the time that, during the time that
2 IN THE WAY THAT, like, in the manner that
3 SINCE, because, seeing that, considering that, on account of the fact that
▷ *preposition* IN THE ROLE OF, being, under the name of, in the character of
▷▷ **as for** *or* **to** WITH REGARD TO, about, re, concerning, regarding, respecting, relating to, with respect to, on the subject of, with reference to, in reference to, in the matter of, apropos of, as regards, anent (*Scot*)
▷▷ **as it were** IN A WAY, to some extent, so to speak, in a manner of speaking, so to say

ascend *verb* 1 CLIMB, scale, mount, go up
<< OPPOSITE go down
2 SLOPE UPWARDS, come up, rise up
<< OPPOSITE slope downwards
3 MOVE UP, rise, go up
<< OPPOSITE move down
4 FLOAT UP, rise, climb, tower, go up, take off, soar, lift off, fly up
<< OPPOSITE descend

ascendancy *or* **ascendence** *noun* INFLUENCE, power, control, rule, authority, command, reign, sovereignty, sway, dominance, domination, superiority, supremacy, mastery, dominion, upper hand, hegemony, prevalence, pre-eminence, predominance, rangatiratanga (*NZ*)
<< OPPOSITE inferiority

ascendant *or* **ascendent** *adjective* INFLUENTIAL, controlling, ruling, powerful, commanding, supreme, superior, dominant, prevailing, authoritative, predominant, uppermost, pre-eminent

▷▷ **in the ascendant** RISING, increasing, growing, powerful, mounting, climbing, dominating, commanding, supreme, dominant, influential, prevailing, flourishing, ascending, up-and-coming, on the rise, uppermost, on the way up

ascension *noun* 1 RISE, rising, mounting, climb, ascending, ascent, moving upwards
2 SUCCESSION, taking over, assumption, inheritance, elevation, entering upon

ascent *noun* 1 CLIMBING, scaling, mounting, climb, clambering, ascending, ascension
2 UPWARD SLOPE, rise, incline, ramp, gradient, rising ground, acclivity
3 RISE, rising, climb, ascension, upward movement

ascertain *verb* FIND OUT, learn, discover, determine, confirm, settle, identify, establish, fix, verify, make certain, suss (out) (*slang*), ferret out

ascetic *noun* RECLUSE, monk, nun, abstainer, hermit, anchorite, self-denier
<< OPPOSITE hedonist
▷ *adjective* SELF-DENYING, severe, plain, harsh, stern, rigorous, austere, Spartan, self-disciplined, celibate, puritanical, frugal, abstemious, abstinent
<< OPPOSITE self-indulgent

ascribe *verb* ATTRIBUTE, credit, refer, charge, assign, put down, set down, impute

> *Ascribe* is sometimes used where *subscribe* is meant: *I do not subscribe* (not *ascribe*) *to this view of music*

asexual *adjective* SEXLESS, neutral, neuter

ashamed *adjective* 1 EMBARRASSED, sorry, guilty, upset, distressed, shy, humbled, humiliated, blushing, self-conscious, red-faced, chagrined, flustered, mortified, sheepish, bashful, prudish, crestfallen, discomfited, remorseful, abashed, shamefaced, conscience-stricken, discountenanced
<< OPPOSITE proud
2 RELUCTANT, afraid, embarrassed, scared, unwilling, loath, disinclined

ashen *adjective* PALE, white, grey, wan, livid, pasty, leaden, colourless, pallid, anaemic, ashy, like death warmed up (*informal*)
<< OPPOSITE rosy

ashore *adverb* ON LAND, on the beach, on the shore, aground, to the shore, on dry land, shorewards, landwards

aside *adverb* TO ONE SIDE, away, alone, separately, apart, alongside, beside, out of the way, on one side, to the side, in isolation, in reserve, out of mind
▷ *noun* INTERPOLATION, remark, parenthesis, digression, interposition, confidential remark

ask *verb* 1 INQUIRE, question, quiz, query, interrogate
<< OPPOSITE answer
2 REQUEST, apply to, appeal to, plead with, demand, urge, sue, pray, beg, petition, crave, solicit, implore, enjoin, beseech, entreat, supplicate
3 INVITE, bid, summon

askance *adverb* 1 SUSPICIOUSLY, doubtfully, dubiously, sceptically, disapprovingly, distrustfully, mistrustfully
2 OUT OF THE CORNER OF YOUR EYE, sideways, indirectly, awry, obliquely, with a side glance

askew *adjective* CROOKED, awry, oblique, lopsided, off-centre, cockeyed (*informal*), skewwhiff (*Brit informal*)
<< OPPOSITE straight
▷ *adverb* CROOKEDLY, to one side, awry, obliquely, off-centre, aslant
<< OPPOSITE straight

asleep *adjective* SLEEPING, napping, dormant, crashed out (*slang*), dozing, slumbering, snoozing (*informal*), fast asleep, sound asleep, out for the count, dead to the world (*informal*), in a deep sleep

aspect *noun* 1 FEATURE, point, side, factor, angle, characteristic, facet
2 POSITION, view, situation, scene, bearing, direction, prospect, exposure, point of view, outlook
3 APPEARANCE, look, air, condition, quality, bearing, attitude, cast, manner, expression, countenance, demeanour, mien (*literary*)

aspirant *noun* CANDIDATE, applicant, hopeful, aspirer, seeker, suitor, postulant
▷ *adjective* HOPEFUL, longing, ambitious, eager, striving, aspiring, endeavouring, wishful

aspiration *noun* AIM, longing, end, plan, hope, goal, design, dream, wish, desire, object, intention, objective, ambition, craving, endeavour, yearning, eagerness, Holy Grail (*informal*), hankering

aspire to *verb* AIM FOR, desire, pursue, hope for, long for, crave, seek out, wish for, dream about, yearn for, hunger for, hanker after, be eager for, set your heart on, set your sights on, be ambitious for

aspiring *adjective* HOPEFUL, longing, would-be, ambitious, eager, striving, endeavouring, wannabe (*informal*), wishful, aspirant

ass *noun* 1 DONKEY, moke (*slang*), jennet
2 FOOL, dope (*informal*), jerk (*slang, chiefly US & Canad*), idiot, plank (*Brit slang*), berk (*Brit slang*), wally (*slang*), prat (*slang*), charlie (*Brit informal*), plonker (*slang*), coot, geek (*slang*), twit (*informal, chiefly Brit*), bonehead (*slang*), dunce, oaf, simpleton, airhead (*slang*), jackass, dipstick (*Brit slang*), gonzo (*slang*), schmuck (*US slang*), dork (*slang*), nitwit (*informal*), dolt, blockhead, ninny, divvy (*Brit slang*), pillock (*Brit

slang), halfwit, nincompoop, dweeb (*US slang*), putz (*US slang*), fathead (*informal*), weenie (*US informal*), eejit (*Scot & Irish*), dumb-ass (*slang*), numpty (*Scot informal*), doofus (*slang, chiefly US*), daftie (*informal*), nerd *or* nurd (*slang*), numbskull *or* numskull, twerp *or* twirp (*informal*), dorba *or* dorb (*Austral slang*), bogan (*Austral slang*)

>> RELATED WORD *adjective* asinine

>> RELATED WORD *male* jack

>> RELATED WORD *female* jenny

assail *verb* **1** CRITICIZE, abuse, blast, put down, malign, berate, revile, vilify, tear into (*informal*), diss (*slang, chiefly US*), impugn, go for the jugular, lambast(e)

2 ATTACK, charge, assault, invade, set about, beset, fall upon, set upon, lay into (*informal*), maltreat, belabour

assailant *noun* ATTACKER, assaulter, invader, aggressor, assailer

assassin *noun* MURDERER, killer, slayer, liquidator, executioner, hit man (*slang*), eliminator (*slang*), hatchet man (*slang*)

assassinate *verb* MURDER, kill, eliminate (*slang*), take out (*slang*), terminate, hit (*slang*), slay, blow away (*slang, chiefly US*), liquidate

assassination *noun* MURDER, killing, slaughter, purge, hit (*slang*), removal, elimination (*slang*), slaying, homicide, liquidation

assault *noun* ATTACK, campaign, strike, rush, storm, storming, raid, invasion, charge, offensive, onset, onslaught, foray, incursion, act of aggression, inroad

<< OPPOSITE defence

▷ *verb* STRIKE, attack, beat, knock, punch, belt (*informal*), bang, batter, clip (*informal*), slap, bash (*informal*), deck (*slang*), sock (*slang*), chin (*slang*), smack, thump, set about, lay one on (*slang*), clout (*informal*), cuff, flog, whack, lob, beset, clobber (*slang*), smite (*archaic*), wallop (*informal*), swat, fall upon, set upon, lay into (*informal*), tonk (*slang*), lambast(e), belabour, beat *or* knock seven bells out of (*informal*)

assay *verb* ANALYSE, examine, investigate, assess, weigh, evaluate, inspect, try, appraise

assemblage *noun* GROUP, company, meeting, body, crowd, collection, mass, gathering, rally, assembly, flock, congregation, accumulation, multitude, throng, hui (*NZ*), conclave, aggregation, convocation, runanga (*NZ*)

assemble *verb* **1** GATHER, meet, collect, rally, flock, accumulate, come together, muster, convene, congregate, foregather

<< OPPOSITE scatter

2 BRING TOGETHER, collect, gather, rally, summon, accumulate, round up, marshal, come together, muster, convene, amass, congregate, call together, foregather, convoke

3 PUT TOGETHER, make, join, set up, manufacture, build up, connect, construct, erect, piece together, fabricate, fit together

<< OPPOSITE take apart

assembly *noun* **1** GATHERING, group, meeting, body, council, conference, crowd, congress, audience, collection, mass, diet, rally, convention, flock, company, house, congregation, accumulation, multitude, throng, synod, hui (*NZ*), assemblage, conclave, aggregation, convocation, runanga (*NZ*)

2 PUTTING TOGETHER, joining, setting up, manufacture, construction, building up, connecting, erection, piecing together, fabrication, fitting together

assent *noun* AGREEMENT, accord, sanction, approval, permission, acceptance, consent, compliance, accession, acquiescence, concurrence

<< OPPOSITE refusal

▷▷ **assent to something** AGREE TO, allow, accept, grant, approve, permit, sanction, O.K., comply with, go along with, subscribe to, consent to, say yes to, accede to, fall in with, acquiesce in, concur with, give the green light to

assert *verb* **1** STATE, argue, maintain, declare, allege, swear, pronounce, contend, affirm, profess, attest, predicate, postulate, avow, aver, asseverate, avouch (*archaic*)

<< OPPOSITE deny

2 INSIST UPON, stress, defend, uphold, put forward, vindicate, press, stand up for

<< OPPOSITE retract

▷▷ **assert yourself** BE FORCEFUL, put your foot down (*informal*), put yourself forward, make your presence felt, exert your influence

assertion *noun* **1** STATEMENT, claim, allegation, profession, declaration, contention, affirmation, pronouncement, avowal, attestation, predication, asseveration

2 INSISTENCE, defence, stressing, maintenance, vindication

assertive *adjective* CONFIDENT, firm, demanding, decided, forward, can-do (*informal*), positive, aggressive, decisive, forceful, emphatic, insistent, feisty (*informal, chiefly US & Canad*), pushy (*informal*), in-your-face (*Brit slang*), dogmatic, strong-willed, domineering, overbearing, self-assured

<< OPPOSITE meek

assertiveness *noun* CONFIDENCE, insistence, aggressiveness, firmness, decisiveness, dogmatism, forcefulness, positiveness, pushiness (*informal*), forwardness, self-assuredness, decidedness, domineeringness

<< OPPOSITE meekness

assess *verb* **1** JUDGE, determine, estimate, fix, analyse, evaluate, rate, value, check out, compute, gauge, weigh up, appraise, size up

(*informal*), eye up
2 EVALUATE, rate, tax, value, demand, estimate, fix, impose, levy

assessment *noun* 1 JUDGMENT, analysis, determination, evaluation, valuation, appraisal, estimation, rating, opinion, estimate, computation
2 EVALUATION, rating, rate, charge, tax, demand, fee, duty, toll, levy, tariff, taxation, valuation, impost

asset *noun* BENEFIT, help, service, aid, advantage, strength, resource, attraction, blessing, boon, good point, strong point, ace in the hole, feather in your cap, ace up your sleeve
<< OPPOSITE disadvantage

assiduous *adjective* DILIGENT, constant, steady, hard-working, persistent, attentive, persevering, laborious, industrious, indefatigable, studious, unflagging, untiring, sedulous, unwearied
<< OPPOSITE lazy

assign *verb* 1 GIVE, set, grant, allocate, give out, consign, allot, apportion
2 ALLOCATE, give, determine, fix, appoint, distribute, earmark, mete
3 SELECT FOR, post, commission, elect, appoint, delegate, nominate, name, designate, choose for, stipulate for
4 ATTRIBUTE, credit, put down, set down, ascribe, accredit

assignment *noun* 1 TASK, work, job, charge, position, post, commission, exercise, responsibility, duty, mission, appointment, undertaking, occupation, chore
2 SELECTION, choice, option, appointment, delegation, nomination, designation
3 GIVING, issuing, grant, distribution, allocation, earmarking, allotment, designation, consignment, dealing out, assignation (*Law, chiefly Scot*), apportionment

assimilate *verb* 1 ADJUST, fit, adapt, accommodate, accustom, conform, mingle, blend in, become like, homogenize, acclimatize, intermix, become similar, acculturate
2 LEARN, absorb, take in, incorporate, digest, imbibe (*literary*), ingest

assist *verb* 1 HELP, back, support, further, benefit, aid, encourage, work with, work for, relieve, collaborate with, cooperate with, abet, expedite, succour, lend a hand to, lend a helping hand to, give a leg up to (*informal*)
2 FACILITATE, help, further, serve, aid, forward, promote, boost, ease, sustain, reinforce, speed up, pave the way for, make easy, expedite, oil the wheels of, smooth the path of, assist the progress of
<< OPPOSITE hinder

assistance *noun* HELP, backing, service, support, benefit, aid, relief, boost, promotion, cooperation, encouragement, collaboration, reinforcement, helping hand, sustenance, succour, furtherance, abetment
<< OPPOSITE hindrance

assistant *noun* HELPER, partner, ally, colleague, associate, supporter, deputy, subsidiary, aide, aider, second, accessory, attendant, backer, protagonist, collaborator, accomplice, confederate, auxiliary, henchman, right-hand man, adjutant, helpmate, coadjutor (*rare*), abettor, cooperator

associate *verb* 1 CONNECT, couple, league, link, mix, relate, pair, ally, identify, unite, join, combine, attach, affiliate, fasten, correlate, confederate, yoke, affix, lump together, cohere, mention in the same breath, conjoin, think of together
<< OPPOSITE separate
2 SOCIALIZE, mix, hang (*informal, chiefly US*), accompany, hang out (*informal*), run around (*informal*), mingle, be friends, befriend, consort, hang about, hobnob, fraternize
<< OPPOSITE avoid
▷ *noun* PARTNER, friend, ally, colleague, mate (*informal*), companion, comrade, affiliate, collaborator, confederate, co-worker, workmate, main man (*slang, chiefly US*), cobber (*Austral & NZ old-fashioned informal*), confrère, compeer, E hoa (NZ)

associated *adjective* CONNECTED, united, joined, leagued, linked, tied, related, allied, combined, involved, bound, syndicated, affiliated, correlated, confederated, yoked

association *noun* 1 GROUP, company, club, order, union, class, society, league, band, set, troop, pack, camp, collection, gathering, organization, circle, corporation, alliance, coalition, partnership, federation, bunch, formation, faction, cluster, syndicate, congregation, batch, confederation, cooperative, fraternity, affiliation, posse (*slang*), clique, confederacy, assemblage
2 FRIENDSHIP, relationship, link, tie, relations, bond, connection, partnership, attachment, intimacy, liaison, fellowship, affinity, familiarity, affiliation, companionship, comradeship, fraternization
3 CONNECTION, union, joining, linking, tie, mixing, relation, bond, pairing, combination, mixture, blend, identification, correlation, linkage, yoking, juxtaposition, lumping together, concomitance

assorted *adjective* VARIOUS, different, mixed, varied, diverse, diversified, miscellaneous, sundry, motley, variegated, manifold, heterogeneous
<< OPPOSITE similar

assortment *noun* VARIETY, choice, collection,

selection, mixture, diversity, array, jumble, medley, mixed bag (*informal*), potpourri, mélange (*French*), miscellany, mishmash, farrago, hotchpotch, salmagundi, pick 'n' mix

assuage *verb* **1** RELIEVE, ease, calm, moderate, temper, soothe, lessen, alleviate, lighten, allay, mitigate, quench, palliate

<< OPPOSITE increase

2 CALM, still, quiet, relax, satisfy, soften, soothe, appease, lull, pacify, mollify, tranquillize

<< OPPOSITE provoke

assume *verb* **1** PRESUME, think, believe, expect, accept, suppose, imagine, suspect, guess (*informal, chiefly US & Canad*), take it, fancy, take for granted, infer, conjecture, postulate, surmise, presuppose

<< OPPOSITE know

2 TAKE ON, begin, accept, manage, bear, handle, shoulder, take over, don, acquire, put on, take up, embrace, undertake, set about, attend to, take responsibility for, embark upon, enter upon

3 SIMULATE, affect, adopt, put on, imitate, mimic, sham, counterfeit, feign, impersonate

4 TAKE OVER, take, appropriate, acquire, seize, hijack, confiscate, wrest, usurp, lay claim to, pre-empt, commandeer, requisition, expropriate, arrogate

<< OPPOSITE give up

assumed *adjective* FALSE, affected, made-up, pretended, fake, imitation, bogus, simulated, sham, counterfeit, feigned, spurious, fictitious, make-believe, pseudonymous, phoney *or* phony (*informal*)

<< OPPOSITE real

assumption *noun* **1** PRESUMPTION, theory, opinion, belief, guess, expectation, fancy, suspicion, premise, acceptance, hypothesis, anticipation, inference, conjecture, surmise, supposition, presupposition, premiss, postulation

2 TAKING ON, managing, handling, shouldering, putting on, taking up, takeover, acquisition

3 SEIZURE, taking, takeover, acquisition, appropriation, wresting, confiscation, commandeering, expropriation, pre-empting, usurpation, arrogation

assurance *noun* **1** PROMISE, statement, guarantee, commitment, pledge, profession, vow, declaration, assertion, oath, affirmation, protestation, word, word of honour

<< OPPOSITE lie

2 CONFIDENCE, conviction, courage, certainty, self-confidence, poise, assertiveness, security, faith, coolness, nerve, aplomb, boldness, self-reliance, firmness, self-assurance, certitude, sureness, self-possession, positiveness, assuredness

<< OPPOSITE self-doubt

assure *verb* **1** CONVINCE, encourage, persuade, satisfy, comfort, prove to, reassure, soothe, hearten, embolden, win someone over, bring someone round

2 MAKE CERTAIN, ensure, confirm, guarantee, secure, make sure, complete, seal, clinch

3 PROMISE TO, pledge to, vow to, guarantee to, swear to, attest to, confirm to, certify to, affirm to, give your word to, declare confidently to

assured *adjective* **1** CONFIDENT, certain, positive, bold, poised, assertive, complacent, fearless, audacious, pushy (*informal*), brazen, self-confident, self-assured, self-possessed, overconfident, dauntless, sure of yourself

<< OPPOSITE self-conscious

2 CERTAIN, sure, ensured, confirmed, settled, guaranteed, fixed, secure, sealed, clinched, made certain, sound, in the bag (*slang*), dependable, beyond doubt, irrefutable, unquestionable, indubitable, nailed-on (*slang*)

<< OPPOSITE doubtful

astonish *verb* AMAZE, surprise, stun, stagger, bewilder, astound, daze, confound, stupefy, boggle the mind, dumbfound, flabbergast (*informal*)

astonished *adjective* AMAZED, surprised, staggered, bewildered, astounded, dazed, stunned, confounded, perplexed, gobsmacked (*informal*), dumbfounded, flabbergasted (*informal*), stupefied

astonishing *adjective* AMAZING, striking, surprising, brilliant, stunning, impressive, overwhelming, staggering, startling, sensational (*informal*), bewildering, breathtaking, astounding, eye-opening, wondrous (*archaic* or *literary*), jaw-dropping, stupefying

astonishment *noun* AMAZEMENT, surprise, wonder, confusion, awe, consternation, bewilderment, wonderment, stupefaction

astound *verb* AMAZE, surprise, overwhelm, astonish, stagger, bewilder, daze, confound, stupefy, stun, take your breath away, boggle the mind, dumbfound, flabbergast (*informal*)

astounding *adjective* AMAZING, striking, surprising, brilliant, impressive, astonishing, staggering, sensational (*informal*), bewildering, stunning, breathtaking, wondrous (*archaic* or *literary*), jaw-dropping, stupefying

astray *adjective* or *adverb* OFF THE RIGHT TRACK, adrift, off course, off the mark, amiss

▷▷ **lead someone astray** LEAD INTO SIN, lead into error, lead into bad ways, lead into wrong

astringent *adjective* **1** CONTRACTIVE, contractile, styptic

2 SEVERE, strict, exacting, harsh, grim, stern, hard, rigid, rigorous, stringent, austere, caustic, acerbic

astrology *noun* STARGAZING, astromancy, horoscopy

astronaut *noun* SPACE TRAVELLER, cosmonaut, spaceman, spacewoman, space pilot

astronomical *or* **astronomic** *adjective* HUGE, great, giant, massive, vast, enormous, immense, titanic, infinite, gigantic, monumental, colossal, boundless, galactic, Gargantuan, immeasurable

astute *adjective* INTELLIGENT, politic, bright, sharp, keen, calculating, clever, subtle, penetrating, knowing, shrewd, cunning, discerning, sly, on the ball (*informal*), canny, perceptive, wily, crafty, artful, insightful, foxy, adroit, sagacious

<< OPPOSITE stupid

asunder *adverb* or *adjective* (*Literary*) TO PIECES, apart, torn, rent, to bits, to shreds, in pieces, into pieces

asylum *noun* 1 (*Old-fashioned*) MENTAL HOSPITAL, hospital, institution, psychiatric hospital, madhouse (*informal*), funny farm (*facetious*), loony bin (*slang*), nuthouse (*slang*), rubber room (*US slang*), laughing academy (*US slang*)

2 REFUGE, security, haven, safety, protection, preserve, shelter, retreat, harbour, sanctuary

atheism *noun* NONBELIEF, disbelief, scepticism, infidelity, paganism, unbelief, freethinking, godlessness, irreligion, heathenism

atheist *noun* NONBELIEVER, pagan, sceptic, disbeliever, heathen, infidel, unbeliever, freethinker, irreligionist

athlete *noun* SPORTSPERSON, player, runner, competitor, contender, sportsman, contestant, gymnast, games player, sportswoman

athletic *adjective* FIT, strong, powerful, healthy, active, trim, strapping, robust, vigorous, energetic, muscular, sturdy, husky (*informal*), lusty, herculean, sinewy, brawny, able-bodied, well-proportioned

<< OPPOSITE feeble

athletics *plural noun* SPORTS, games, races, exercises, contests, sporting events, gymnastics, track and field events, games of strength

atmosphere *noun* 1 AIR, sky, heavens, aerosphere

2 FEELING, feel, air, quality, character, environment, spirit, surroundings, tone, mood, climate, flavour, aura, ambience, vibes (*slang*)

atom *noun* PARTICLE, bit, spot, trace, scrap, molecule, grain, dot, fragment, fraction, shred, crumb, mite, jot, speck, morsel, mote, whit, tittle, iota, scintilla (*rare*)

atone *verb* MAKE AMENDS, pay, do penance, make reparation, make redress

atonement *noun* AMENDS, payment, compensation, satisfaction, redress, reparation, restitution, penance, recompense, expiation, propitiation

atrocious *adjective* 1 (*informal*) SHOCKING, terrible, appalling, horrible, horrifying, grievous, execrable, detestable

<< OPPOSITE fine

2 CRUEL, savage, brutal, vicious, ruthless, infamous, monstrous, wicked, barbaric, inhuman, diabolical, heinous, flagrant, infernal, fiendish, villainous, nefarious, godawful (*slang*), hellacious (*US slang*)

<< OPPOSITE kind

atrocity *noun* 1 ACT OF CRUELTY, wrong, crime, horror, offence, evil, outrage, outrage, cruelty, brutality, obscenity, wrongdoing, enormity, monstrosity, transgression, abomination, barbarity, villainy

2 CRUELTY, wrong, horror, brutality, wrongdoing, enormity, savagery, ruthlessness, wickedness, inhumanity, infamy, transgression, barbarity, viciousness, villainy, baseness, monstrousness, heinousness, nefariousness, shockingness, atrociousness, fiendishness, barbarousness, grievousness, villainousness

atrophy *verb* 1 WASTE AWAY, waste, shrink, diminish, deteriorate, decay, dwindle, wither, wilt, degenerate, shrivel

2 DECLINE, waste, fade, shrink, diminish, deteriorate, dwindle, wither, wilt, degenerate, shrivel, waste away

▷ *noun* 1 WASTING AWAY, decline, wasting, decay, decaying, withering, deterioration, meltdown (*informal*), shrivelling, degeneration, diminution

2 WASTING, decline, decay, decaying, withering, deterioration, meltdown (*informal*), shrivelling, degeneration, diminution, wasting away

attach *verb* 1 AFFIX, stick, secure, bind, unite, add, join, couple, link, tie, fix, connect, lash, glue, adhere, fasten, annex, truss, yoke, append, make fast, cohere, subjoin

<< OPPOSITE detach

2 ASCRIBE, connect, attribute, assign, place, associate, lay on, accredit, invest with, impute

▷▷ **attach yourself to** *or* **be attached to something** JOIN, accompany, associate with, combine with, join forces with, latch on to, unite with, sign up with, become associated with, sign on with, affiliate yourself with

attached *adjective* SPOKEN FOR, married, partnered, engaged, accompanied

▷▷ **attached to** FOND OF, devoted to, affectionate towards, full of regard for

attachment *noun* 1 FONDNESS, liking, feeling, love, relationship, regard, bond, friendship, attraction, loyalty, affection, devotion, fidelity,

affinity, tenderness, reverence, predilection, possessiveness, partiality, aroha (NZ)
<< OPPOSITE aversion
2 ACCESSORY, fitting, extra, addition, component, extension, supplement, fixture, auxiliary, adaptor *or* adapter, supplementary part, add-on, adjunct, appendage, accoutrement, appurtenance

attack *verb* 1 ASSAULT, strike (at), mug, set about, ambush, assail, tear into, fall upon, set upon, lay into (*informal*)
<< OPPOSITE defend
2 INVADE, occupy, raid, infringe, charge, rush, storm, encroach
3 CRITICIZE, blame, abuse, blast, pan (*informal*), condemn, knock (*informal*), slam (*slang*), put down, slate (*informal*), have a go (at) (*informal*), censure, malign, berate, disparage, revile, vilify, tear into (*informal*), slag off (*Brit slang*), diss (*slang, chiefly* US), find fault with, impugn, go for the jugular, lambast(e), pick holes in, excoriate, bite someone's head off, snap someone's head off, pick to pieces
▷ *noun* 1 ASSAULT, charge, campaign, strike, rush, raid, invasion, offensive, aggression, blitz, onset, onslaught, foray, incursion, inroad
<< OPPOSITE defence
2 CRITICISM, panning (*informal*), slating (*informal*), censure, disapproval, slagging (*slang*), abuse, knocking (*informal*), bad press, vilification, denigration, calumny, character assassination, disparagement, impugnment
3 BOUT, fit, access, spell, stroke, seizure, spasm, convulsion, paroxysm

attacker *noun* ASSAILANT, assaulter, raider, intruder, invader, aggressor, mugger

attain *verb* 1 OBTAIN, get, win, reach, effect, land, score (*slang*), complete, gain, achieve, earn, secure, realize, acquire, fulfil, accomplish, grasp, reap, procure
2 REACH, achieve, realize, acquire, arrive at, accomplish

attainable *adjective* ACHIEVABLE, possible, likely, potential, accessible, probable, at hand, feasible, within reach, practicable, obtainable, reachable, realizable, graspable, gettable, procurable, accomplishable
<< OPPOSITE unattainable

attainment *noun* 1 ACHIEVEMENT, getting, winning, reaching, gaining, obtaining, acquisition, feat, completion, reaping, accomplishment, realization, fulfilment, arrival at, procurement, acquirement
2 SKILL, art, ability, talent, gift, achievement, capability, competence, accomplishment, mastery, proficiency

attempt *verb* TRY, seek, aim, struggle, tackle, take on, experiment, venture, undertake, essay, strive, endeavour, have a go at (*informal*), make an effort, make an attempt, have a crack at, have a shot at (*informal*), try your hand at, do your best to, jump through hoops (*informal*), have a stab at (*informal*), take the bit between your teeth
▷ *noun* 1 TRY, go (*informal*), shot (*informal*), effort, trial, bid, experiment, crack (*informal*), venture, undertaking, essay, stab (*informal*), endeavour
2 ATTACK, assault

attempted *adjective* TRIED, ventured, undertaken, endeavoured, assayed

attend *verb* 1 BE PRESENT, go to, visit, be at, be there, be here, frequent, haunt, appear at, turn up at, patronize, show up at (*informal*), show yourself, put in an appearance at, present yourself at
<< OPPOSITE be absent
2 PAY ATTENTION, listen, follow, hear, mark, mind, watch, note, regard, notice, observe, look on, heed, take to heart, pay heed, hearken (*archaic*)
<< OPPOSITE ignore
3 ESCORT, conduct, guard, shadow, accompany, companion, shepherd, convoy, usher, squire, chaperon
▷▷ **attend to someone** LOOK AFTER, help, mind, aid, tend, nurse, care for, take care of, minister to, administer to
▷▷ **attend to something** APPLY YOURSELF TO, concentrate on, look after, take care of, see to, get to work on, devote yourself to, occupy yourself with

attendance *noun* 1 PRESENCE, being there, attending, appearance
2 TURNOUT, audience, gate, congregation, house, crowd, throng, number present

attendant *noun* ASSISTANT, guide, guard, servant, companion, aide, escort, follower, steward, waiter, usher, warden, helper, auxiliary, custodian, page, menial, concierge, underling, lackey, chaperon, flunky
▷ *adjective* ACCOMPANYING, related, associated, accessory, consequent, resultant, concomitant

attention *noun* 1 THINKING, thought, mind, notice, consideration, concentration, observation, scrutiny, heed, deliberation, contemplation, thoughtfulness, attentiveness, intentness, heedfulness
2 CARE, support, concern, treatment, looking after, succour, ministration
3 AWARENESS, regard, notice, recognition, consideration, observation, consciousness
<< OPPOSITE inattention
▷ *plural noun* COURTESY, compliments, regard, respect, care, consideration, deference, politeness, civility, gallantry, mindfulness, assiduities
<< OPPOSITE discourtesy

attentive *adjective* 1 INTENT, listening, concentrating, careful, alert, awake, mindful, watchful, observant, studious, on your toes, heedful, regardful

<< OPPOSITE heedless

2 CONSIDERATE, kind, civil, devoted, helpful, obliging, accommodating, polite, thoughtful, gracious, conscientious, respectful, courteous, gallant

<< OPPOSITE neglectful

attenuate *verb* WEAKEN, reduce, contract, lower, diminish, decrease, dilute, lessen, sap, water down, adulterate, enfeeble, enervate, devaluate

attenuated *adjective* 1 SLENDER, extended, thinned, slimmed, refined, stretched out, lengthened, drawn out, spun out, elongated, rarefied

2 WEAKENED, reduced, contracted, lowered, diminished, decreased, dilute, diluted, lessened, devalued, sapped, watered down, adulterated, enfeebled, enervated

attest *verb* TESTIFY, show, prove, confirm, display, declare, witness, demonstrate, seal, swear, exhibit, warrant, assert, manifest, give evidence, invoke, ratify, affirm, certify, verify, bear out, substantiate, corroborate, bear witness, authenticate, vouch for, evince, aver, adjure

<< OPPOSITE disprove

attic *noun* LOFT, garret, roof space

attire *noun* CLOTHES, wear, dress, clothing, gear (*informal*), habit, uniform, outfit, costume, threads (*slang*), array (*poetic*), garments, robes, apparel, garb, accoutrements, raiment (*archaic or poetic*), vestment, schmutter (*slang*), habiliments

attitude *noun* 1 OPINION, thinking, feeling, thought, view, position, approach, belief, mood, perspective, point of view, stance, outlook, viewpoint, slant, frame of mind

2 MANNER, air, condition, bearing, aspect, carriage, disposition, demeanour, mien (*literary*)

3 POSITION, bearing, pose, stance, carriage, posture

attorney *noun* LAWYER, solicitor, counsel, advocate, barrister, counsellor, legal adviser

attract *verb* 1 ALLURE, interest, draw, invite, persuade, engage, charm, appeal to, fascinate, win over, tempt, lure (*informal*), induce, incline, seduce, entice, enchant, endear, lead on, coax, captivate, beguile, cajole, bewitch, decoy, inveigle, pull, catch (someone's) eye

<< OPPOSITE repel

2 PULL, draw, magnetize

attraction *noun* 1 APPEAL, interest, draw, pull (*informal*), come-on (*informal*), charm, incentive, invitation, lure, bait, temptation, fascination, attractiveness, allure, inducement, magnetism, enchantment, endearment, enticement, captivation, temptingness, pleasingness

2 PULL, draw, magnetism

attractive *adjective* 1 SEDUCTIVE, charming, tempting, interesting, pleasing, pretty, fair, beautiful, inviting, engaging, likable *or* likeable, lovely, winning, sexy (*informal*), pleasant, handsome, fetching, good-looking, glamorous, gorgeous, magnetic, cute, irresistible, enticing, provocative, captivating, beguiling, alluring, bonny, winsome, comely, prepossessing

<< OPPOSITE unattractive

2 APPEALING, pleasing, inviting, fascinating, tempting, enticing, agreeable, irresistible

<< OPPOSITE unappealing

attributable *adjective* ASCRIBABLE, accountable, applicable, traceable, explicable, assignable, imputable, blamable *or* blameable, placeable, referable *or* referrable

attribute *verb* ASCRIBE, apply, credit, blame, refer, trace, assign, charge, allocate, put down, set down, allot, impute

▷ *noun* QUALITY, point, mark, sign, note, feature, property, character, element, aspect, symbol, characteristic, indication, distinction, virtue, trait, hallmark, facet, quirk, peculiarity, idiosyncrasy

attribution *noun* ASCRIPTION, charge, credit, blame, assignment, attachment, placement, referral, assignation, imputation

attrition *noun* WEARING DOWN, harrying, weakening, harassment, thinning out, attenuation, debilitation

attuned *adjective* ACCUSTOMED, adjusted, coordinated, in tune, in harmony, in accord, harmonized, familiarized, acclimatized

atypical *adjective* UNUSUAL, exceptional, uncommon, singular, deviant, unconventional, unique, unorthodox, uncharacteristic, out of the ordinary, unrepresentative, out of keeping, uncustomary, nonconforming, unconforming

<< OPPOSITE normal

auburn *adjective* REDDISH-BROWN, tawny, russet, henna, rust-coloured, copper-coloured, chestnut-coloured, Titian red, nutbrown

audacious *adjective* 1 DARING, enterprising, brave, bold, risky, rash, adventurous, reckless, courageous, fearless, intrepid, valiant, daredevil, death-defying, dauntless, venturesome

<< OPPOSITE timid

2 CHEEKY, presumptuous, impertinent, insolent, impudent, forward, fresh (*informal*), assuming, rude, defiant, brazen, in-your-face (*Brit slang*), shameless, sassy (*US informal*), pert,

disrespectful
<< OPPOSITE tactful

audacity *noun* **1** DARING, nerve, courage, guts (*informal*), bravery, boldness, recklessness, face (*informal*), front, enterprise, valour, fearlessness, rashness, adventurousness, intrepidity, audaciousness, dauntlessness, venturesomeness
2 CHEEK, nerve, defiance, gall (*informal*), presumption, rudeness, chutzpah (*US & Canad informal*), insolence, impertinence, neck (*informal*), impudence, effrontery, brass neck (*Brit informal*), shamelessness, sassiness (*US informal*), forwardness, pertness, audaciousness, disrespectfulness

audible *adjective* CLEAR, distinct, discernible, detectable, perceptible, hearable
<< OPPOSITE inaudible

audience *noun* **1** SPECTATORS, company, house, crowd, gathering, gallery, assembly, viewers, listeners, patrons, congregation, turnout, onlookers, throng, assemblage
2 PUBLIC, market, following, fans, devotees, fanbase, aficionados
3 INTERVIEW, meeting, hearing, exchange, reception, consultation

audit (*Accounting*) *verb* INSPECT, check, review, balance, survey, examine, investigate, go through, assess, go over, evaluate, vet, verify, appraise, scrutinize, inquire into
▷ *noun* INSPECTION, check, checking, review, balancing, search, survey, investigation, examination, scan, scrutiny, supervision, surveillance, look-over, verification, once-over (*informal*), checkup, superintendence

augment *verb* INCREASE, grow, raise, extend, boost, expand, add to, build up, strengthen, enhance, reinforce, swell, intensify, heighten, enlarge, multiply, inflate, magnify, amplify, dilate
<< OPPOSITE diminish

augur *verb* BODE, promise, predict, herald, signify, foreshadow, prophesy, harbinger, presage, prefigure, portend, betoken, be an omen of

august *adjective* NOBLE, great, kingly, grand, excellent, imposing, impressive, superb, distinguished, magnificent, glorious, splendid, elevated, eminent, majestic, dignified, regal, stately, high-ranking, monumental, solemn, lofty, exalted

aura *noun* AIR, feeling, feel, quality, atmosphere, tone, suggestion, mood, scent, aroma, odour, ambience, vibes (*slang*), vibrations (*slang*), emanation

auspices *plural noun* SUPPORT, backing, control, charge, care, authority, championship, influence, protection, guidance, sponsorship, supervision, patronage, advocacy, countenance, aegis

auspicious *adjective* FAVOURABLE, timely, happy, promising, encouraging, bright, lucky, hopeful, fortunate, prosperous, rosy, opportune, propitious, felicitous
<< OPPOSITE unpromising

austere *adjective* **1** STERN, hard, serious, cold, severe, formal, grave, strict, exacting, harsh, stiff, forbidding, grim, rigorous, solemn, stringent, inflexible, unrelenting, unfeeling
<< OPPOSITE kindly
2 PLAIN, simple, severe, spare, harsh, stark, bleak, subdued, economical, Spartan, unadorned, unornamented
<< OPPOSITE luxurious
3 ASCETIC, strict, continent, exacting, rigid, sober, economical, solemn, Spartan, unrelenting, self-disciplined, puritanical, chaste, strait-laced, abstemious, self-denying, abstinent
<< OPPOSITE abandoned

austerity *noun* **1** PLAINNESS, economy, simplicity, severity, starkness, spareness, Spartanism
2 ASCETICISM, economy, rigidity, abstinence, self-discipline, chastity, sobriety, continence, puritanism, solemnity, self-denial, strictness, abstemiousness, chasteness, exactingness, Spartanism

authentic *adjective* **1** REAL, true, original, actual, pure, genuine, valid, faithful, undisputed, veritable, lawful, on the level (*informal*), bona fide, dinkum (*Austral & NZ informal*), pukka, the real McCoy, true-to-life
<< OPPOSITE fake
2 ACCURATE, true, certain, reliable, legitimate, authoritative, factual, truthful, dependable, trustworthy, veracious
<< OPPOSITE fictitious

authenticate *verb* **1** VERIFY, guarantee, warrant, authorize, certify, avouch
<< OPPOSITE invalidate
2 VOUCH FOR, confirm, endorse, validate, attest

authenticity *noun* **1** GENUINENESS, purity, realness, veritableness
2 ACCURACY, truth, certainty, validity, reliability, legitimacy, verity, actuality, faithfulness, truthfulness, dependability, trustworthiness, authoritativeness, factualness

author *noun* **1** WRITER, composer, novelist, hack, creator, columnist, scribbler, scribe, essayist, wordsmith, penpusher, littérateur, man *or* woman of letters
2 CREATOR, father, parent, mother, maker, producer, framer, designer, founder, architect, planner, inventor, mover, originator, prime mover, doer, initiator, begetter, fabricator

authoritarian *adjective* STRICT, severe, absolute,

harsh, rigid, autocratic, dictatorial, dogmatic, imperious, domineering, unyielding, tyrannical, disciplinarian, despotic, doctrinaire

<< OPPOSITE lenient

▷ *noun* DISCIPLINARIAN, dictator, tyrant, despot, autocrat, absolutist

authoritative *adjective* 1 COMMANDING, lordly, masterly, imposing, dominating, confident, decisive, imperative, assertive, autocratic, dictatorial, dogmatic, imperious, self-assured, peremptory

<< OPPOSITE timid

2 OFFICIAL, approved, sanctioned, legitimate, sovereign, authorized, commanding

<< OPPOSITE unofficial

3 RELIABLE, learned, sound, true, accurate, valid, scholarly, faithful, authentic, definitive, factual, truthful, veritable, dependable, trustworthy

<< OPPOSITE unreliable

authority *noun* 1 *usually plural* POWERS THAT BE, government, police, officials, the state, management, administration, the system, the Establishment, Big Brother (*informal*), officialdom

2 PREROGATIVE, right, influence, might, force, power, control, charge, rule, government, weight, strength, direction, command, licence, privilege, warrant, say-so, sway, domination, jurisdiction, supremacy, dominion, ascendancy, mana (*NZ*)

3 EXPERT, specialist, professional, master, ace (*informal*), scholar, guru, buff (*informal*), wizard, whizz (*informal*), virtuoso, connoisseur, arbiter, hotshot (*informal*), fundi (*S African*)

4 COMMAND, power, control, rule, management, direction, grasp, sway, domination, mastery, dominion

5 PERMISSION, leave, permit, sanction, licence, approval, go-ahead (*informal*), liberty, consent, warrant, say-so, tolerance, justification, green light, assent, authorization, dispensation, carte blanche, a blank cheque, sufferance

authorization *noun* PERMISSION, right, leave, power, authority, ability, strength, permit, sanction, licence, approval, warrant, say-so, credentials, a blank cheque

authorize *verb* 1 EMPOWER, commission, enable, entitle, mandate, accredit, give authority to

2 PERMIT, allow, suffer, grant, confirm, agree to, approve, sanction, endure, license, endorse, warrant, tolerate, ratify, consent to, countenance, accredit, vouch for, give leave, give the green light for, give a blank cheque to, give authority for

<< OPPOSITE forbid

authorized *adjective* OFFICIAL, commissioned, approved, licensed, ratified, signed and sealed

autobiography *noun* LIFE STORY, record, history, résumé, memoirs

autocracy *noun* DICTATORSHIP, tyranny, despotism, absolutism

autocrat *noun* DICTATOR, tyrant, despot, absolutist

autocratic *adjective* DICTATORIAL, absolute, unlimited, all-powerful, imperious, domineering, tyrannical, despotic, tyrannous

automatic *adjective* 1 MECHANICAL, robot, automated, mechanized, push-button, self-regulating, self-propelling, self-activating, self-moving, self-acting

<< OPPOSITE done by hand

2 INVOLUNTARY, natural, unconscious, mechanical, spontaneous, reflex, instinctive, instinctual, unwilled

<< OPPOSITE conscious

3 INEVITABLE, certain, necessary, assured, routine, unavoidable, inescapable

autonomous *adjective* SELF-RULING, free, independent, sovereign, self-sufficient, self-governing, self-determining

autonomy *noun* INDEPENDENCE, freedom, sovereignty, self-determination, self-government, self-rule, self-sufficiency, home rule, rangatiratanga (*NZ*)

<< OPPOSITE dependency

autopsy *noun* POSTMORTEM, dissection, postmortem examination, necropsy

auxiliary *adjective* 1 SUPPLEMENTARY, reserve, emergency, substitute, secondary, back-up, subsidiary, fall-back

2 SUPPORTING, helping, aiding, assisting, accessory, ancillary

<< OPPOSITE primary

▷ *noun* HELPER, partner, ally, associate, supporter, assistant, companion, accessory, subordinate, protagonist, accomplice, confederate, henchman

avail *noun* BENEFIT, use, help, good, service, aid, profit, advantage, purpose, assistance, utility, effectiveness, mileage (*informal*), usefulness, efficacy

▷▷ **avail yourself of something** MAKE USE OF, use, employ, exploit, take advantage of, profit from, make the most of, utilize, have recourse to, turn to account

availability *noun* ACCESSIBILITY, readiness, handiness, attainability, obtainability

available *adjective* ACCESSIBLE, ready, to hand, convenient, handy, vacant, on hand, at hand, free, applicable, to be had, achievable, obtainable, on tap (*informal*), attainable, at your fingertips, at your disposal, ready for use

<< OPPOSITE in use

avalanche *noun* 1 SNOW-SLIDE, landslide, landslip, snow-slip

2 LARGE AMOUNT, barrage, torrent, deluge, inundation

avant-garde *adjective* PROGRESSIVE, pioneering, way-out (*informal*), experimental, innovative, unconventional, far-out (*slang*), ground-breaking, innovatory

<< OPPOSITE conservative

avarice *noun* GREED, meanness, penny-pinching, parsimony, acquisitiveness, rapacity, cupidity, stinginess, covetousness, miserliness, greediness, niggardliness, graspingness, close-fistedness, penuriousness

<< OPPOSITE liberality

avenge *verb* GET REVENGE FOR, revenge, repay, retaliate for, take revenge for, hit back for, requite, pay (someone) back for, get even for (*informal*), even the score for, get your own back for, take vengeance for, take satisfaction for, pay (someone) back in his *or* her own coin for

In the past it was considered incorrect to use *avenge* with *yourself*, but this use is now acceptable and relatively common: *she was determined to avenge herself upon this monster*

avenue *noun* STREET, way, course, drive, road, pass, approach, channel, access, entry, route, path, passage, entrance, alley, pathway, boulevard, driveway, thoroughfare

average *noun* STANDARD, normal, usual, par, mode, mean, rule, medium, norm, run of the mill, midpoint

▷ *adjective* 1 USUAL, common, standard, general, normal, regular, ordinary, typical, commonplace, unexceptional

<< OPPOSITE unusual

2 MEAN, middle, medium, intermediate, median

<< OPPOSITE minimum

3 MEDIOCRE, fair, ordinary, moderate, pedestrian, indifferent, not bad, middling, insignificant, so-so (*informal*), banal, second-rate, middle-of-the-road, tolerable, run-of-the-mill, passable, undistinguished, uninspired, unexceptional, bog-standard (*Brit & Irish slang*), no great shakes (*informal*), fair to middling (*informal*)

▷ *verb* MAKE ON AVERAGE, be on average, even out to, do on average, balance out to

▷▷ **on average** USUALLY, generally, normally, typically, for the most part, as a rule

averse *adjective* OPPOSED, reluctant, hostile, unwilling, backward, unfavourable, loath, disinclined, inimical, indisposed, antipathetic, ill-disposed

<< OPPOSITE favourable

aversion *noun* HATRED, hate, horror, disgust, hostility, opposition, dislike, reluctance, loathing, distaste, animosity, revulsion, antipathy, repulsion, abhorrence, disinclination, repugnance, odium, detestation, indisposition

<< OPPOSITE love

avert *verb* 1 WARD OFF, avoid, prevent, frustrate, fend off, preclude, stave off, forestall

2 TURN AWAY, turn, turn aside

aviation *noun* FLYING, flight, aeronautics, powered flight

aviator *noun* PILOT, flyer, airman, airwoman, aeronaut

avid *adjective* 1 ENTHUSIASTIC, keen, devoted, intense, eager, passionate, ardent, fanatical, fervent, zealous, keen as mustard

<< OPPOSITE indifferent

2 INSATIABLE, hungry, greedy, thirsty, grasping, voracious, acquisitive, ravenous, rapacious, avaricious, covetous, athirst

avoid *verb* 1 PREVENT, stop, frustrate, hamper, foil, inhibit, head off, avert, thwart, intercept, hinder, obstruct, impede, ward off, stave off, forestall, defend against

2 REFRAIN FROM, bypass, dodge, eschew, escape, duck (out of) (*informal*), fight shy of, shirk from

3 KEEP AWAY FROM, dodge, shun, evade, steer clear of, sidestep, circumvent, bypass, body-swerve (*Scot*), give a wide berth to

avoidable *adjective* 1 PREVENTABLE, stoppable, avertible *or* avertable

<< OPPOSITE unpreventable

2 ESCAPABLE, evadable

<< OPPOSITE inevitable

avoidance *noun* 1 REFRAINING, dodging, shirking, eschewal

2 PREVENTION, safeguard, precaution, anticipation, thwarting, elimination, deterrence, forestalling, prophylaxis, preclusion, obviation

avow *verb* STATE, maintain, declare, allege, recognize, swear, assert, proclaim, affirm, profess, aver, asseverate

avowed *adjective* DECLARED, open, admitted, acknowledged, confessed, sworn, professed, self-proclaimed

await *verb* 1 WAIT FOR, expect, look for, look forward to, anticipate, stay for

2 BE IN STORE FOR, wait for, be ready for, lie in wait for, be in readiness for

awake *verb* 1 WAKE UP, come to, wake, stir, awaken, rouse

2 ALERT, excite, stimulate, provoke, revive, arouse, activate, awaken, fan, animate, stir up, incite, kick-start (*informal*), enliven, kindle, breathe life into, call forth, vivify

3 STIMULATE, excite, provoke, activate, alert, animate, fan, stir up, incite, kick-start (*informal*), enliven, kindle, breathe life into, call forth, vivify

▷ *adjective* 1 NOT SLEEPING, sleepless, wide-awake, aware, waking, conscious, aroused, awakened, restless, restive, wakeful, bright-eyed and bushy-tailed

<< OPPOSITE asleep

2 ALERT, aware, on the lookout, alive, attentive, on the alert, observant, watchful, on guard, on your toes, heedful, vigilant ▷ see **wake**

award *verb* 1 PRESENT WITH, give, grant, gift, distribute, render, assign, decree, hand out, confer, endow, bestow, allot, apportion, adjudge

2 GRANT, give, render, assign, decree, accord, confer, adjudge

▷ *noun* 1 GRANT, subsidy, scholarship, hand-out, endowment, stipend

2 PRIZE, gift, trophy, decoration, grant, bonsela (*S African*), koha (*NZ*)

3 (*Law*) SETTLEMENT, payment, compensation

aware *adjective* INFORMED, enlightened, knowledgeable, learned, expert, versed, up to date, in the picture, in the know (*informal*), erudite, well-read, au fait (*French*), in the loop, well-briefed, au courant (*French*), clued-up (*informal*)

<< OPPOSITE ignorant

▷▷ **aware of** KNOWING ABOUT, familiar with, conscious of, wise to (*slang*), alert to, mindful of, acquainted with, alive to, awake to, privy to, hip to (*slang*), appreciative of, attentive to, conversant with, apprised of, cognizant of, sensible of

awareness *noun* ▷▷ **awareness of** KNOWLEDGE OF, understanding of, appreciation of, recognition of, attention to, perception of, consciousness of, acquaintance with, enlightenment with, sensibility to, realization of, familiarity with, mindfulness of, cognizance of, sentience of

away *adjective* ABSENT, out, gone, elsewhere, abroad, not there, not here, not present, on vacation, not at home

▷ *adverb* 1 OFF, elsewhere, abroad, hence, from here

2 ASIDE, out of the way, to one side

3 AT A DISTANCE, far, apart, remote, isolated

4 CONTINUOUSLY, repeatedly, relentlessly, incessantly, interminably, unremittingly, uninterruptedly

awe *noun* WONDER, fear, respect, reverence, horror, terror, dread, admiration, amazement, astonishment, veneration

<< OPPOSITE contempt

▷ *verb* IMPRESS, amaze, stun, frighten, terrify, cow, astonish, horrify, intimidate, daunt

awed *adjective* IMPRESSED, shocked, amazed, afraid, stunned, frightened, terrified, cowed, astonished, horrified, intimidated, fearful, daunted, dumbfounded, wonder-struck

awe-inspiring *adjective* IMPRESSIVE, striking, wonderful, amazing, stunning (*informal*), magnificent, astonishing, intimidating, awesome, daunting, breathtaking, fearsome, wondrous (*archaic* or *literary*), jaw-dropping

<< OPPOSITE unimpressive

awesome *adjective* AWE-INSPIRING, striking, shocking, imposing, terrible, amazing, stunning, wonderful, alarming, impressive, frightening, awful, overwhelming, terrifying, magnificent, astonishing, horrible, dreadful, formidable, horrifying, intimidating, fearful, daunting, breathtaking, majestic, solemn, fearsome, wondrous (*archaic* or *literary*), redoubtable, jaw-dropping, stupefying

awestruck *or* **awe-stricken** *adjective* IMPRESSED, shocked, amazed, stunned, afraid, frightened, terrified, cowed, astonished, horrified, intimidated, fearful, awed, daunted, awe-inspired, dumbfounded, struck dumb, wonder-struck

awful *adjective* 1 DISGUSTING, terrible, tremendous, offensive, gross, nasty, foul, horrible, dreadful, unpleasant, revolting, stinking, sickening, hideous, vulgar, vile, distasteful, horrid, frightful, nauseating, odious, repugnant, loathsome, abominable, nauseous, detestable, godawful (*slang*), hellacious (*US slang*), festy (*Austral slang*), yucko (*Austral slang*)

2 BAD, poor, terrible, appalling, foul, rubbish (*slang*), dreadful, unpleasant, dire, horrendous, ghastly, from hell (*informal*), atrocious, deplorable, abysmal, frightful, hellacious (*US slang*)

<< OPPOSITE wonderful

3 SHOCKING, serious, alarming, distressing, dreadful, horrifying, horrific, hideous, harrowing, gruesome

4 UNWELL, poorly (*informal*), ill, terrible, sick, ugly, crook (*Austral & NZ informal*), unhealthy, unsightly, queasy, out of sorts (*informal*), off-colour, under the weather (*informal*), green about the gills

awfully *adverb* 1 (*informal*) VERY, extremely, terribly, exceptionally, quite, very much, seriously (*informal*), greatly, immensely, exceedingly, excessively, dreadfully

2 BADLY, woefully, dreadfully, inadequately, disgracefully, wretchedly, unforgivably, shoddily, reprehensibly, disreputably

awhile *adverb* FOR A WHILE, briefly, for a moment, for a short time, for a little while

> *Awhile*, written as a single word, is an adverb meaning 'for a period of time'. It can only be used with a verb, for example: *he stood awhile in thought*. It is quite commonly

written by mistake instead of the noun *a while*, meaning 'a period of time', so take care not to confuse the two parts of speech: *I thought about that for a while* (not *awhile*)

awkward *adjective* 1 EMBARRASSING, difficult, compromising, sensitive, embarrassed, painful, distressing, delicate, uncomfortable, tricky, trying, humiliating, unpleasant, sticky (*informal*), troublesome, perplexing, disconcerting, inconvenient, thorny, untimely, ill at ease, discomfiting, ticklish, inopportune, toe-curling (*slang*), barro (*Austral slang*), cringeworthy (*Brit informal*)
<< OPPOSITE comfortable
2 INCONVENIENT, difficult, troublesome, cumbersome, unwieldy, unmanageable, clunky (*informal*), unhandy
<< OPPOSITE convenient
3 CLUMSY, stiff, rude, blundering, coarse, bungling, lumbering, inept, unskilled, bumbling, unwieldy, ponderous, ungainly, gauche, gawky, uncouth, unrefined, artless, inelegant, uncoordinated, graceless, cack-handed (*informal*), unpolished, clownish, oafish, inexpert, maladroit, ill-bred, all thumbs, ungraceful, skill-less, unskilful, butterfingered (*informal*), unhandy, ham-fisted *or* ham-handed (*informal*), unco (*Austral slang*)
<< OPPOSITE graceful
4 UNCOOPERATIVE, trying, difficult, annoying, unpredictable, unreasonable, stubborn, troublesome, perverse, prickly, exasperating, irritable, intractable, vexing, unhelpful, touchy, obstinate, obstructive, bloody-minded (*Brit informal*), chippy (*informal*), vexatious, hard to handle, disobliging

awkwardness *noun* 1 CLUMSINESS, stiffness, rudeness, coarseness, ineptness, ill-breeding, artlessness, gaucheness, inelegance, gaucherie, gracelessness, oafishness, gawkiness, uncouthness, maladroitness, ungainliness, clownishness, inexpertness, uncoordination, unskilfulness, unskilledness
2 EMBARRASSMENT, difficulty, discomfort, delicacy, unpleasantness, inconvenience, stickiness (*informal*), painfulness, ticklishness, uphill (*S African*), thorniness, inopportuneness, perplexingness, untimeliness

awry *adverb* ASKEW, to one side, off course, out of line, obliquely, unevenly, off-centre, cockeyed (*informal*), out of true, crookedly, skew-whiff (*informal*)
▷ *adjective* ASKEW, twisted, crooked, to one side, uneven, off course, out of line, asymmetrical, off-centre, cockeyed (*informal*), misaligned, out of true, skew-whiff (*informal*)
▷ *adverb* or *adjective* WRONG, amiss

axe *noun* HATCHET, chopper, tomahawk, cleaver, adze
▷ *verb* 1 (*informal*) ABANDON, end, pull, eliminate, cancel, scrap, wind up, turn off (*informal*), relegate, cut back, terminate, dispense with, discontinue, pull the plug on
2 (*informal*) DISMISS, fire (*informal*), sack (*informal*), remove, get rid of, discharge, throw out, oust, give (someone) their marching orders, give the boot to (*slang*), give the bullet to (*Brit slang*), give the push to, kennet (*Austral slang*), jeff (*Austral slang*)
▷▷ **an axe to grind** PET SUBJECT, grievance, ulterior motive, private purpose, personal consideration, private ends
▷▷ **the axe** (*informal*) THE SACK (*informal*), dismissal, discharge, wind-up, the boot (*slang*), cancellation, cutback, termination, the chop (*slang*), the (old) heave-ho (*informal*), the order of the boot (*slang*)

axiom *noun* PRINCIPLE, fundamental, maxim, gnome, adage, postulate, dictum, precept, aphorism, truism, apophthegm

axis *noun* PIVOT, shaft, axle, spindle, centre line

axle *noun* SHAFT, pin, rod, axis, pivot, spindle, arbor, mandrel

azure *adjective* SKY BLUE, blue, clear blue, ultramarine, cerulean, sky-coloured

Bb

baas *noun* (*S African*) MASTER, bo (*informal*), chief, ruler, commander, head, overlord, overseer

babble *verb* 1 GABBLE, chatter, gush, spout, waffle (*informal, chiefly Brit*), splutter, gaggle, burble, prattle, gibber, rabbit on (*Brit informal*), jabber, prate, earbash (*Austral & NZ slang*)
2 GURGLE, lap, bubble, splash, murmur, ripple, burble, plash
▷ *noun* 1 GABBLE, chatter, burble, prattle, blabber
2 GIBBERISH, waffle (*informal, chiefly Brit*), drivel, twaddle

babe *noun* BABY, child, innocent, infant, bairn (*Scot & Northern English*), tacker (*Austral slang*), suckling, newborn child, babe in arms, nursling

baby *noun* CHILD, infant, babe, wean (*Scot*), little one, bairn (*Scot & Northern English*), suckling, newborn child, babe in arms, sprog (*slang*), neonate, rug rat (*US & Canad informal*), ankle biter (*Austral slang*), tacker (*Austral slang*)
▷ *adjective* SMALL, little, minute, tiny, mini, wee, miniature, dwarf, diminutive, petite, midget, teeny (*informal*), pocket-sized, undersized, teeny-weeny (*informal*), Lilliputian, teensy-weensy (*informal*), pygmy *or* pigmy
▷ *verb* SPOIL, pamper, cosset, coddle, pet, humour, indulge, spoon-feed, mollycoddle, overindulge, wrap up in cotton wool (*informal*)

back *noun* 1 SPINE, backbone, vertebrae, spinal column, vertebral column
2 REAR, back end
<< OPPOSITE front
3 REVERSE, rear, other side, wrong side, underside, flip side, verso
▷ *adjective* 1 REAR
<< OPPOSITE front
2 REARMOST, hind, hindmost
3 PREVIOUS, earlier, former, past, elapsed
<< OPPOSITE future
4 TAIL, end, rear, posterior
▷ *verb* 1 SUPPORT, help, second, aid, champion, encourage, favour, defend, promote, sanction, sustain, assist, advocate, endorse, side with, stand up for, espouse, stand behind, countenance, abet, stick up for (*informal*), take up the cudgels for
<< OPPOSITE oppose
2 SUBSIDIZE, help, support, finance, sponsor, assist, underwrite
▷▷ **back down** GIVE IN, collapse, withdraw, yield, concede, submit, surrender, comply, cave in (*informal*), capitulate, accede, admit defeat, back-pedal
▷▷ **back out** WITHDRAW, retire, give up, pull out, retreat, drop out, renege, cop out (*slang*), chicken out (*informal*), detach yourself
▷▷ **back someone up** SUPPORT, second, aid, assist, stand by, bolster
▷▷ **behind someone's back** SECRETLY, covertly, surreptitiously, furtively, conspiratorially, sneakily, deceitfully
>> RELATED WORD *adjective* dorsal

backbone *noun* 1 SPINAL COLUMN, spine, vertebrae, vertebral column
2 FOUNDATION, support, base, basis, mainstay, bedrock
3 STRENGTH OF CHARACTER, will, character, bottle (*Brit slang*), resolution, resolve, nerve, daring, courage, determination, guts, pluck, stamina, grit, bravery, fortitude, toughness, tenacity, willpower, mettle, boldness, firmness, spunk (*informal*), fearlessness, steadfastness, moral fibre, hardihood, dauntlessness

backer *noun* 1 SUPPORTER, second, ally, angel (*informal*), patron, promoter, subscriber, underwriter, helper, benefactor
2 ADVOCATE, supporter, patron, sponsor, promoter, protagonist

backfire *verb* FAIL, founder, flop (*informal*), rebound, fall through, fall flat, boomerang, miscarry, misfire, go belly-up (*slang*), turn out badly, meet with disaster

background *noun* 1 UPBRINGING, history, culture, environment, tradition,

circumstances, breeding, milieu
2 EXPERIENCE, grounding, education, preparation, qualifications, credentials
3 CIRCUMSTANCES, history, conditions, situation, atmosphere, environment, framework, ambience, milieu, frame of reference

backing *noun* 1 SUPPORT, seconding, championing, promotion, sanction, approval, blessing, encouragement, endorsement, patronage, accompaniment, advocacy, moral support, espousal
2 ASSISTANCE, support, help, funds, aid, grant, subsidy, sponsorship, patronage

backlash *noun* REACTION, response, resistance, resentment, retaliation, repercussion, counterblast, counteraction, retroaction

backlog *noun* BUILD-UP, stock, excess, accumulation, accretion

backside *noun* (*informal*) BUTTOCKS, behind (*informal*), seat, bottom, rear, tail (*informal*), cheeks (*informal*), butt (*US & Canad informal*), bum (*Brit slang*), buns (*US slang*), rump, rear end, posterior, haunches, hindquarters, derrière (*euphemistic*), tush, fundament, gluteus maximus (*Anatomy*), coit (*Austral slang*), nates (*technical name*), jacksy (*Brit slang*), keister *or* keester (*slang, chiefly US*)

backtrack *verb* 1 *often with* **on** RETRACT, withdraw, retreat, draw back, recant
2 RETRACE YOUR STEPS, go back, reverse, retreat, move back, back-pedal

backup *noun* 1 SUPPORT, backing, help, aid, reserves, assistance, reinforcement, auxiliaries
2 SUBSTITUTE, reserve, relief, stand-in, replacement, stand-by, understudy, second string, locum

backward *adjective* 1 REVERSE, inverted, inverse, back to front, rearward
<< OPPOSITE forward
2 UNDERDEVELOPED, undeveloped
3 SLOW, behind, stupid, retarded, deficient, underdeveloped, subnormal, half-witted, behindhand, slow-witted, intellectually handicapped (*Austral*)

backwardness *noun* 1 LACK OF DEVELOPMENT, underdevelopment
2 SLOWNESS, learning difficulties, underdevelopment, retardation, arrested development
<< OPPOSITE brightness

backwards *or* **backward** *adverb* TOWARDS THE REAR, behind you, in reverse, rearwards

backwoods *plural noun* STICKS (*informal*), outback, back country (*US*), back of beyond, backlands (*US*)

bacteria *plural noun* MICROORGANISMS, viruses, bugs (*slang*), germs, microbes, pathogens, bacilli

> *Bacteria* is a plural noun. It is therefore incorrect to talk about *a bacteria*, even though this is quite commonly heard, especially in the media. The correct singular is *a bacterium*

bad *adjective* 1 HARMFUL, damaging, dangerous, disastrous, destructive, unhealthy, detrimental, hurtful, ruinous, deleterious, injurious, disadvantageous
<< OPPOSITE beneficial
2 SEVERE, serious, terrible, acute, extreme, intense, painful, distressing, fierce, harsh
3 UNFAVOURABLE, troubling, distressing, unfortunate, grim, discouraging, unpleasant, gloomy, adverse
4 INFERIOR, poor, inadequate, pathetic, faulty, duff (*Brit informal*), unsatisfactory, mediocre, defective, second-class, deficient, imperfect, second-rate, shoddy, low-grade, erroneous, substandard, low-rent (*informal, chiefly US*), two-bit (*US & Canad slang*), crappy (*slang*), end-of-the-pier (*Brit informal*), poxy (*slang*), dime-a-dozen (*informal*), bush-league (*Austral & NZ informal*), tinhorn (*US slang*), half-pie (*NZ informal*), bodger *or* bodgie (*Austral slang*), strictly for the birds (*informal*)
<< OPPOSITE satisfactory
5 INCOMPETENT, poor, useless, incapable, unfit, inexpert
6 GRIM, severe, hard, tough
7 WICKED, criminal, evil, corrupt, worthless, base, vile, immoral, delinquent, sinful, depraved, debased, amoral, egregious, villainous, unprincipled, iniquitous, nefarious, dissolute, maleficent
<< OPPOSITE virtuous
8 NAUGHTY, defiant, perverse, wayward, mischievous, wicked, unruly, impish, undisciplined, roguish, disobedient
<< OPPOSITE well-behaved
9 GUILTY, sorry, ashamed, apologetic, rueful, sheepish, contrite, remorseful, regretful, shamefaced, conscience-stricken
10 ROTTEN, off, rank, sour, rancid, mouldy, fetid, putrid, festy (*Austral slang*)
▷▷ **not bad** (*informal*) O.K. *or* OKAY, fine, middling, average, fair, all right, acceptable, moderate, adequate, respectable, satisfactory, so-so, tolerable, passable, fair to middling (*informal*)

baddie *or* **baddy** *noun* (*informal*) VILLAIN, criminal, rogue, bad guy, scoundrel, miscreant, antihero, evildoer, wrong 'un (*Austral slang*)
<< OPPOSITE goodie *or* goody

badge *noun* 1 IMAGE, brand, stamp, identification, crest, emblem, insignia

2 MARK, sign, token

badger *verb* PESTER, worry, harry, bother, bug (*informal*), bully, plague, hound, get at, harass, nag, hassle (*informal*), chivvy, importune, bend someone's ear (*informal*), be on someone's back (*slang*)

>> RELATED WORD *habitation* set *or* sett

badly *adverb* 1 POORLY, incorrectly, carelessly, inadequately, erroneously, imperfectly, ineptly, shoddily, defectively, faultily

<< OPPOSITE well

2 SEVERELY, greatly, deeply, seriously, gravely, desperately, sorely, dangerously, intensely, painfully, acutely, exceedingly

3 UNFAVOURABLY, unsuccessfully

badness *noun* WICKEDNESS, wrong, evil, corruption, sin, impropriety, immorality, villainy, naughtiness, sinfulness, foulness, baseness, rottenness, vileness, shamefulness

<< OPPOSITE virtue

bad-tempered *adjective* IRRITABLE, cross, angry, tense, crabbed, fiery, grumbling, snarling, prickly, exasperated, edgy, snappy, sullen, touchy, surly, petulant, sulky, ill-tempered, irascible, cantankerous, tetchy, ratty (*Brit & NZ informal*), tooshie (*Austral slang*), testy, chippy (*informal*), fretful, grouchy (*informal*), querulous, peevish, crabby, huffy, dyspeptic, choleric, splenetic, crotchety (*informal*), oversensitive, snappish, ill-humoured, liverish, narky (*Brit slang*), out of humour

<< OPPOSITE good-tempered

baffle *verb* PUZZLE, beat (*slang*), amaze, confuse, stump, bewilder, astound, elude, confound, perplex, disconcert, mystify, flummox, boggle the mind of, dumbfound

<< OPPOSITE explain

baffling *adjective* PUZZLING, strange, confusing, weird, mysterious, unclear, bewildering, elusive, enigmatic, perplexing, incomprehensible, mystifying, inexplicable, unaccountable, unfathomable

<< OPPOSITE understandable

bag *noun* SACK, container, poke (*Scot*), sac, receptacle

▷ *verb* 1 GET, take, land, score (*slang*), gain, pick up, capture, acquire, get hold of, come by, procure, make sure of, win possession of

2 CATCH, get, kill, shoot, capture, acquire, trap

baggage *noun* LUGGAGE, things, cases, bags, equipment, gear, trunks, suitcases, belongings, paraphernalia, accoutrements, impedimenta

baggy *adjective* LOOSE, hanging, slack, loosened, bulging, not fitting, sagging, sloppy, floppy, billowing, roomy, slackened, ill-fitting, droopy, oversize, not tight

<< OPPOSITE tight

bail[1] *noun* (*Law*) SECURITY, bond, guarantee, pledge, warranty, surety, guaranty

▷▷ **bail out** ESCAPE, withdraw, get away, retreat, make your getaway, break free *or* out, make *or* effect your escape

▷▷ **bail something** *or* **someone out** (*informal*) SAVE, help, free, release, aid, deliver, recover, rescue, get out, relieve, liberate, salvage, set free, save the life of, extricate, save (someone's) bacon (*Brit informal*)

bail[2] *or* **bale** *verb* SCOOP, empty, dip, ladle, drain off

bait *noun* LURE, attraction, incentive, carrot (*informal*), temptation, bribe, magnet, snare, inducement, decoy, carrot and stick, enticement, allurement

▷ *verb* TEASE, provoke, annoy, irritate, guy (*informal*), bother, needle (*informal*), plague (*informal*), mock, rag, rib (*informal*), wind up (*Brit slang*), hound, torment, harass, ridicule, taunt, hassle (*informal*), aggravate (*informal*), badger, gall, persecute, pester, goad, irk, bedevil, take the mickey out of (*informal*), chaff, gibe, get on your nerves (*informal*), nark (*Brit, Austral & NZ slang*), be on your back (*slang*), get in your hair (*informal*), get *or* take a rise out of, hack you off (*informal*)

baked *adjective* DRY, desert, seared, dried up, scorched, barren, sterile, arid, torrid, desiccated, sun-baked, waterless, moistureless

bakkie *noun* (*S African*) TRUCK, pick-up, van, lorry, pick-up truck

balance *verb* 1 STABILIZE, level, steady

<< OPPOSITE overbalance

2 OFFSET, match, square, make up for, compensate for, counteract, neutralize, counterbalance, even up, equalize, counterpoise

3 WEIGH, consider, compare, estimate, contrast, assess, evaluate, set against, juxtapose

4 (*Accounting*) CALCULATE, rate, judge, total, determine, estimate, settle, count, square, reckon, work out, compute, gauge, tally

▷ *noun* 1 EQUILIBRIUM, stability, steadiness, evenness, equipoise, counterpoise

<< OPPOSITE instability

2 STABILITY, equanimity, constancy, steadiness

3 PARITY, equity, fairness, impartiality, equality, correspondence, equivalence

4 REMAINDER, rest, difference, surplus, residue

5 COMPOSURE, stability, restraint, self-control, poise, self-discipline, coolness, calmness, equanimity, self-restraint, steadiness, self-possession, self-mastery, strength of mind *or* will

balance sheet *noun* STATEMENT, report, account, budget, ledger, financial statement, credits and debits sheet

balcony *noun* 1 TERRACE, veranda
2 UPPER CIRCLE, gods, gallery
bald *adjective* 1 HAIRLESS, bare, shorn, clean-shaven, tonsured, depilated, glabrous (*Biology*), baldheaded, baldpated
2 PLAIN, direct, simple, straight, frank, severe, bare, straightforward, blunt, rude, outright, downright, forthright, unadorned, unvarnished, straight from the shoulder
balding *adjective* LOSING YOUR HAIR, receding, thin on top, becoming bald
baldness *noun* HAIRLESSNESS, alopecia (*Pathology*), baldheadedness, baldpatedness, glabrousness (*Biology*)
bale ▷ see **bail**[2]
baleful *adjective* MENACING, threatening, dangerous, frightening, evil, deadly, forbidding, intimidating, harmful, sinister, ominous, malignant, hurtful, vindictive, pernicious, mournful, malevolent, noxious, venomous, ruinous, intimidatory, minatory, maleficent, bodeful, louring *or* lowering, minacious
<< OPPOSITE friendly
balk *or* **baulk** *verb usually with* **at** RECOIL, resist, hesitate, dodge, falter, evade, shy away, flinch, quail, shirk, shrink, draw back, jib
<< OPPOSITE accept
ball *noun* 1 SPHERE, drop, globe, pellet, orb, globule, spheroid
2 PROJECTILE, shot, missile, bullet, ammunition, slug, pellet, grapeshot
ballast *noun* COUNTERBALANCE, balance, weight, stability, equilibrium, sandbag, counterweight, stabilizer
balloon *verb* EXPAND, rise, increase, extend, swell, blow up, enlarge, inflate, bulge, billow, dilate, be inflated, puff out, become larger, distend, bloat, grow rapidly
ballot *noun* VOTE, election, voting, poll, polling, referendum, show of hands
balm *noun* 1 OINTMENT, cream, lotion, salve, emollient, balsam, liniment, embrocation, unguent
2 COMFORT, support, relief, cheer, consolation, solace, palliative, anodyne, succour, restorative, curative
balmy *adjective* 1 MILD, warm, calm, moderate, pleasant, clement, tranquil, temperate, summery
<< OPPOSITE rough
2 ▷ see **barmy**
bamboozle *verb* (*informal*) 1 CHEAT, do (*informal*), kid (*informal*), skin (*slang*), trick, fool, take in (*informal*), con (*informal*), stiff, sting (*informal*), mislead, rip off (*slang*), thwart, deceive, fleece, hoax, defraud, dupe, beguile, gull (*archaic*), delude, swindle, stitch up (*slang*), victimize, hoodwink, double-cross (*informal*), diddle (*informal*), take for a ride (*informal*), do the dirty on (*Brit informal*), bilk, pull a fast one on (*informal*), cozen
2 PUZZLE, confuse, stump, baffle, bewilder, confound, perplex, mystify, befuddle, flummox, nonplus
ban *verb* 1 PROHIBIT, black, bar, block, restrict, veto, forbid, boycott, suppress, outlaw, banish, disallow, proscribe, debar, blackball, interdict
<< OPPOSITE permit
2 BAR, prohibit, exclude, forbid, disqualify, preclude, debar, declare ineligible
▷ *noun* PROHIBITION, block, restriction, veto, boycott, embargo, injunction, censorship, taboo, suppression, stoppage, disqualification, interdiction, interdict, proscription, disallowance, rahui (*NZ*), restraining order (*US Law*)
<< OPPOSITE permission
banal *adjective* UNORIGINAL, stock, ordinary, boring, tired, routine, dull, everyday, stereotypical, pedestrian, commonplace, mundane, tedious, vanilla (*slang*), dreary, stale, tiresome, monotonous, humdrum, threadbare, trite, unimaginative, uneventful, uninteresting, clichéd, old hat, mind-numbing, hackneyed, ho-hum (*informal*), vapid, repetitious, wearisome, platitudinous, cliché-ridden, unvaried
<< OPPOSITE original
banality *noun* 1 UNORIGINALITY, triviality, vapidity, triteness
2 CLICHÉ, commonplace, platitude, truism, bromide (*informal*), trite phrase
band[1] *noun* 1 ENSEMBLE, group, orchestra, combo
2 GANG, company, group, set, party, team, lot, club, body, association, crowd, troop, pack, camp, squad, crew (*informal*), assembly, mob, horde, troupe, posse (*informal*), clique, coterie, bevy
▷▷ **band together** UNITE, group, join, league, ally, associate, gather, pool, merge, consolidate, affiliate, collaborate, join forces, cooperate, confederate, pull together, join together, federate, close ranks, club together
band[2] *noun* 1 HEADBAND, tie, strip, ribbon, fillet
2 BANDAGE, tie, binding, strip, belt, strap, cord, swathe, fetter
bandage *noun* DRESSING, plaster, compress, gauze
▷ *verb* DRESS, cover, bind, swathe
bandit *noun* ROBBER, gunman, crook, outlaw, pirate, raider, gangster, plunderer, mugger (*informal*), hijacker, looter, highwayman, racketeer, desperado, marauder, brigand, freebooter, footpad
bandy *verb* EXCHANGE, trade, pass, throw, truck, swap, toss, shuffle, commute, interchange,

barter, reciprocate

bane *noun* PLAGUE, bête noire, trial, disaster, evil, ruin, burden, destruction, despair, misery, curse, pest, torment, woe, nuisance, downfall, calamity, scourge, affliction

<< OPPOSITE blessing

bang *noun* 1 EXPLOSION, report, shot, pop, clash, crack, blast, burst, boom, slam, discharge, thump, clap, thud, clang, peal, detonation

2 BLOW, hit, box, knock, stroke, punch, belt (*informal*), rap, bump, bash (*informal*), sock (*slang*), smack, thump, buffet, clout (*informal*), cuff, clump (*slang*), whack, wallop (*informal*), slosh (*Brit slang*), tonk (*informal*), clomp (*slang*)

▷ *verb* 1 RESOUND, beat, crash, burst, boom, echo, drum, explode, thunder, thump, throb, thud, clang

2 BUMP, knock, elbow, jostle

3 *often with* **on** HIT, pound, beat, strike, crash, knock, belt (*informal*), hammer, slam, rap, bump, bash (*informal*), thump, clatter, pummel, tonk (*informal*), beat *or* knock seven bells out of (*informal*)

▷ *adverb* EXACTLY, just, straight, square, squarely, precisely, slap, smack, plumb (*informal*)

banish *verb* 1 EXCLUDE, bar, ban, dismiss, expel, throw out, oust, drive away, eject, evict, shut out, ostracize

2 EXPEL, transport, exile, outlaw, deport, drive away, expatriate, excommunicate

<< OPPOSITE admit

3 GET RID OF, remove, eliminate, eradicate, shake off, dislodge, see the back of

banishment *noun* EXPULSION, exile, dismissal, removal, discharge, transportation, exclusion, deportation, eviction, ejection, extrusion, proscription, expatriation, debarment

banisters *plural noun* RAILING, rail, balustrade, handrail, balusters

bank¹ *noun* 1 FINANCIAL INSTITUTION, repository, depository

2 STORE, fund, stock, source, supply, reserve, pool, reservoir, accumulation, stockpile, hoard, storehouse

▷ *verb* DEPOSIT, keep, save

▷▷ **bank on something** RELY ON, trust (in), depend on, look to, believe in, count on, be sure of, lean on, be confident of, have confidence in, swear by, reckon on, repose trust in

bank² *noun* 1 SIDE, edge, margin, shore, brink, lakeside, waterside

2 MOUND, banking, rise, hill, mass, pile, heap, ridge, dune, embankment, knoll, hillock, kopje *or* koppie (*S African*)

▷ *verb* TILT, tip, pitch, heel, slope, incline, slant, cant, camber

bank³ *noun* ROW, group, line, train, range, series, file, rank, arrangement, sequence, succession, array, tier

bankrupt *adjective* INSOLVENT, broke (*informal*), spent, ruined, wiped out (*informal*), impoverished, beggared, in the red, on the rocks, destitute, gone bust (*informal*), in receivership, gone to the wall, in the hands of the receivers, on your uppers, in queer street

<< OPPOSITE solvent

bankruptcy *noun* INSOLVENCY, failure, crash, disaster, ruin, liquidation, indebtedness

banner *noun* 1 FLAG, standard, colours, jack, pennant, ensign, streamer, pennon

2 PLACARD

banquet *noun* FEAST, spread (*informal*), dinner, meal, entertainment, revel, blowout (*slang*), repast, slap-up meal (*Brit informal*), hakari (*NZ*)

banter *noun* JOKING, kidding (*informal*), ribbing (*informal*), teasing, jeering, mockery, derision, jesting, chaff, pleasantry, repartee, wordplay, badinage, chaffing, raillery, persiflage

▷ *verb* JOKE, kid (*informal*), rib (*informal*), tease, taunt, jeer, josh (*slang, chiefly US & Canad*), jest, take the mickey (*informal*), chaff

baptism *noun* 1 (*Christianity*) CHRISTENING, sprinkling, purification, immersion

2 INITIATION, beginning, debut, introduction, admission, dedication, inauguration, induction, inception, rite of passage, commencement, investiture, baptism of fire, instatement

baptize *verb* 1 (*Christianity*) CHRISTEN, cleanse, immerse, purify, besprinkle

2 INITIATE, admit, introduce, invest, recruit, enrol, induct, indoctrinate, instate

bar *noun* 1 PUBLIC HOUSE, pub (*informal, chiefly Brit*), counter, inn, local (*Brit informal*), lounge, saloon, tavern, canteen, watering hole (*facetious slang*), boozer (*Brit, Austral & NZ informal*), beer parlour (*Canad*), roadhouse, hostelry (*archaic* or *facetious*), alehouse (*archaic*), taproom

2 ROD, staff, stick, stake, rail, pole, paling, shaft, baton, mace, batten, palisade, crosspiece

3 OBSTACLE, block, barrier, hurdle, hitch, barricade, snag, deterrent, obstruction, stumbling block, impediment, hindrance, interdict

<< OPPOSITE aid

▷ *verb* 1 LOCK, block, secure, chain, attach, anchor, bolt, blockade, barricade, fortify, fasten, latch, obstruct, make firm, make fast

2 BLOCK, restrict, hold up, restrain, hamper, thwart, hinder, obstruct, impede, shut off

3 EXCLUDE, ban, forbid, prohibit, keep out of, disallow, shut out of, ostracize, debar, blackball, interdict, black

<< OPPOSITE admit

barb *noun* 1 POINT, spur, spike, thorn, bristle, quill, prickle, tine, prong
2 DIG, abuse, slight, insult, put-down, snub, sneer, scoff, rebuff, affront, slap in the face (*informal*), gibe, aspersion

barbarian *noun* 1 SAVAGE, monster, beast, brute, yahoo, swine, ogre, sadist
2 LOUT, hooligan, illiterate, vandal, yahoo, bigot, philistine, ned (*Scot slang*), hoon (*Austral & NZ*), cougan (*Austral slang*), scozza (*Austral slang*), bogan (*Austral slang*), ruffian, ignoramus, boor, lowbrow, vulgarian
▷ *adjective* UNCIVILIZED, wild, rough, savage, crude, primitive, vulgar, illiterate, barbaric, philistine, uneducated, unsophisticated, barbarous, boorish, uncouth, uncultivated, lowbrow, uncultured, unmannered
<< OPPOSITE civilized

barbaric *adjective* 1 BRUTAL, fierce, cruel, savage, crude, vicious, ruthless, coarse, vulgar, heartless, inhuman, merciless, bloodthirsty, remorseless, barbarous, pitiless, uncouth
2 UNCIVILIZED, wild, savage, primitive, rude, barbarian, barbarous
<< OPPOSITE civilized

barbarism *noun* CRUELTY, outrage, atrocity, brutality, savagery, ruthlessness, wickedness, inhumanity, barbarity, viciousness, coarseness, crudity, monstrousness, heinousness, fiendishness, barbarousness

barbarity *noun* 1 VICIOUSNESS, horror, cruelty, brutality, ferocity, savagery, ruthlessness, inhumanity
2 ATROCITY, cruelty, horror, inhumanity

barbarous *adjective* 1 UNCIVILIZED, wild, rough, gross, savage, primitive, rude, coarse, vulgar, barbarian, philistine, uneducated, brutish, unsophisticated, uncouth, uncultivated, unpolished, uncultured, unmannered
2 BRUTAL, cruel, savage, vicious, ruthless, ferocious, monstrous, barbaric, heartless, inhuman, merciless, remorseless, pitiless

barbed *adjective* 1 CUTTING, pointed, biting, critical, acid, hostile, nasty, harsh, savage, brutal, searing, withering, scathing, unkind, hurtful, belittling, sarcastic, caustic, scornful, vitriolic, trenchant, acrid, catty (*informal*), mordant, mordacious
2 SPIKED, pointed, toothed, hooked, notched, prickly, jagged, thorny, pronged, spiny, snaggy

bard *noun* (*Archaic*) POET, singer, rhymer, minstrel, lyricist, troubadour

bare *adjective* 1 NAKED, nude, stripped, exposed, uncovered, shorn, undressed, divested, denuded, in the raw (*informal*), disrobed, unclothed, buck naked (*slang*), unclad, scuddy (*slang*), without a stitch on (*informal*), in the bare scud (*slang*), naked as the day you were born (*informal*)
<< OPPOSITE dressed
2 SIMPLE, basic, severe, spare, stark, austere, spartan, unadorned, unfussy, unvarnished, unembellished, unornamented, unpatterned
<< OPPOSITE adorned
3 EMPTY, wanting, mean, lacking, deserted, vacant, void, scarce, barren, uninhabited, unoccupied, scanty, unfurnished
<< OPPOSITE full
4 PLAIN, hard, simple, cold, basic, essential, obvious, sheer, patent, evident, stark, manifest, bald, literal, overt, unembellished

barely *adverb* ONLY JUST, just, hardly, scarcely, at a push, almost not
<< OPPOSITE completely

bargain *noun* 1 GOOD BUY, discount purchase, good deal, good value, steal (*informal*), snip (*informal*), giveaway, cheap purchase
2 AGREEMENT, deal (*informal*), understanding, promise, contract, negotiation, arrangement, settlement, treaty, pledge, convention, transaction, engagement, pact, compact, covenant, stipulation
▷ *verb* 1 HAGGLE, deal, sell, trade, traffic, barter, drive a hard bargain
2 NEGOTIATE, deal, contract, mediate, covenant, stipulate, arbitrate, transact, cut a deal
▷▷ **bargain for** *or* **on something** ANTICIPATE, expect, look for, imagine, predict, plan for, forecast, hope for, contemplate, be prepared for, foresee, foretell, count upon

barge *noun* CANAL BOAT, lighter, narrow boat, scow, flatboat
▷▷ **barge in (on something** *or* **someone)** (*informal*) INTERRUPT, break in (on), muscle in (on) (*informal*), intrude (on), infringe (on), burst in (on), butt in (on), impose yourself (on), force your way in (on), elbow your way in (on)
▷▷ **barge into someone** BUMP INTO, drive into, press, push against, shoulder, thrust, elbow into, shove into, collide with, jostle with, cannon into

bark[1] *verb* 1 YAP, bay, howl, snarl, growl, yelp, woof
2 SHOUT, snap, yell, snarl, growl, bawl, bluster, raise your voice
▷ *noun* YAP, bay, howl, snarl, growl, yelp, woof

bark[2] *noun* COVERING, casing, cover, skin, protection, layer, crust, housing, cortex (*Anatomy, Botany*), rind, husk
▷ *verb* SCRAPE, skin, strip, rub, scratch, shave, graze, scuff, flay, abrade

barmy *or* **balmy** *adjective* (*Slang*) 1 STUPID, bizarre, foolish, silly, daft (*informal*), irresponsible, irrational, senseless, preposterous, impractical, idiotic, inane, fatuous, dumb-ass (*slang*)
2 INSANE, odd, crazy, stupid, silly, nuts (*slang*),

loony (*slang*), nutty (*slang*), goofy (*informal*), idiotic, loopy (*informal*), crackpot (*informal*), out to lunch (*informal*), dippy, out of your mind, gonzo (*slang*), doolally (*slang*), off your trolley (*slang*), round the twist (*Brit slang*), up the pole (*informal*), off your rocker (*slang*), off the air (*Austral slang*), wacko *or* whacko (*informal*), porangi (NZ)

<< OPPOSITE sane

baroque *adjective* ORNATE, fancy, bizarre, elegant, decorated, elaborate, extravagant, flamboyant, grotesque, convoluted, flowery, rococo, florid, bedecked, overelaborate, overdecorated

barrack *verb* (*informal*) HECKLE, abuse, mock, bait, criticize, boo, taunt, jeer, shout down, diss (*slang, chiefly US*)

barracks *plural noun* CAMP, quarters, garrison, encampment, billet, cantonment, casern

barrage *noun* 1 BOMBARDMENT, attack, bombing, assault, shelling, battery, volley, blitz, salvo, strafe, fusillade, cannonade, curtain of fire

2 TORRENT, attack, mass, storm, assault, burst, stream, hail, outburst, rain, spate, onslaught, deluge, plethora, profusion

barren *adjective* 1 DESOLATE, empty, desert, waste

2 UNPRODUCTIVE, dry, useless, fruitless, arid, unprofitable, unfruitful

<< OPPOSITE fertile

3 DULL, boring, commonplace, tedious, dreary, stale, lacklustre, monotonous, uninspiring, humdrum, uninteresting, vapid, unrewarding, as dry as dust

<< OPPOSITE interesting

4 (*Old-fashioned*) INFERTILE, sterile, childless, unproductive, nonproductive, infecund, unprolific

barricade *noun* BARRIER, wall, railing, fence, blockade, obstruction, rampart, fortification, bulwark, palisade, stockade

▷ *verb* BAR, block, defend, secure, lock, bolt, blockade, fortify, fasten, latch, obstruct

barrier *noun* BARRICADE, wall, bar, block, railing, fence, pale, boundary, obstacle, ditch, blockade, obstruction, rampart, bulwark, palisade, stockade

barter *verb* TRADE, sell, exchange, switch, traffic, bargain, swap, haggle, drive a hard bargain

base[1] *noun* 1 BOTTOM, floor, lowest part, deepest part

<< OPPOSITE top

2 SUPPORT, stand, foot, rest, bed, bottom, foundation, pedestal, groundwork

3 FOUNDATION, institution, organization, establishment, starting point

4 CENTRE, post, station, camp, settlement, headquarters

5 HOME, house, territory, pad (*slang*), residence, home ground, abode, stamping ground, dwelling place

6 ESSENCE, source, basis, concentrate, root, core, extract

▷ *verb* 1 GROUND, found, build, rest, establish, depend, root, construct, derive, hinge

2 PLACE, set, post, station, establish, fix, locate, install, garrison

base[2] *adjective* DISHONOURABLE, evil, corrupt, infamous, disgraceful, vulgar, shameful, vile, immoral, scandalous, wicked, sordid, abject, despicable, depraved, ignominious, disreputable, contemptible, villainous, ignoble, discreditable, scungy (*Austral & NZ*)

<< OPPOSITE honourable

baseless *adjective* UNFOUNDED, false, fabricated, unconfirmed, spurious, unjustified, unproven, unsubstantiated, groundless, unsupported, trumped up, without foundation, unjustifiable, uncorroborated, ungrounded, without basis

<< OPPOSITE well-founded

bash *verb* HIT, break, beat, strike, knock, smash, punch, belt (*informal*), crush, deck (*slang*), batter, slap, sock (*slang*), chin (*slang*), smack, thump, clout (*informal*), whack (*informal*), biff (*slang*), clobber (*slang*), wallop (*informal*), slosh (*Brit slang*), tonk (*informal*), lay one on (*slang*), beat *or* knock seven bells out of (*informal*)

bashful *adjective* SHY, reserved, retiring, nervous, modest, shrinking, blushing, constrained, timid, self-conscious, coy, reticent, self-effacing, diffident, sheepish, mousy, timorous, abashed, shamefaced, easily embarrassed, overmodest

<< OPPOSITE forward

basic *adjective* 1 FUNDAMENTAL, main, key, essential, primary, vital, principal, constitutional, cardinal, inherent, elementary, indispensable, innate, intrinsic, elemental, immanent

2 VITAL, needed, important, key, necessary, essential, primary, crucial, fundamental, elementary, indispensable, requisite

3 ESSENTIAL, central, key, vital, fundamental, underlying, indispensable

<< OPPOSITE secondary

4 MAIN, key, essential, primary

5 PLAIN, simple, classic, severe, straightforward, Spartan, uncluttered, unadorned, unfussy, bog-standard (*informal*), unembellished

▷ *plural noun* ESSENTIALS, facts, principles, fundamentals, practicalities, requisites, nuts and bolts (*informal*), hard facts, nitty-gritty (*informal*), rudiments, brass tacks (*informal*), necessaries

basically *adverb* ESSENTIALLY, firstly, mainly, mostly, principally, fundamentally, primarily, at heart, inherently, intrinsically, at bottom, in substance, au fond (*French*)

basis *noun* **1** ARRANGEMENT, way, system, footing, agreement
2 FOUNDATION, support, base, ground, footing, theory, bottom, principle, premise, groundwork, principal element, chief ingredient

bask *verb* LIE, relax, lounge, sprawl, loaf, lie about, swim in, sunbathe, recline, loll, laze, outspan (*S African*), warm yourself, toast yourself
▷▷ **bask in** ENJOY, relish, delight in, savour, revel in, wallow in, rejoice in, luxuriate in, indulge yourself in, take joy in, take pleasure in *or* from

bass *adjective* DEEP, low, resonant, sonorous, low-pitched, deep-toned

bastion *noun* STRONGHOLD, support, defence, rock, prop, refuge, fortress, mainstay, citadel, bulwark, tower of strength, fastness

batch *noun* GROUP, set, lot, crowd, pack, collection, quantity, bunch, accumulation, assortment, consignment, assemblage, aggregation

bath *noun* WASH, cleaning, washing, soaping, shower, soak, cleansing, scrub, scrubbing, bathe, shampoo, sponging, douse, douche, ablution
▷ *verb* CLEAN, wash, soap, shower, soak, cleanse, scrub, bathe, tub, sponge, rinse, douse, scrub down, lave (*archaic*)

bathe *verb* **1** SWIM
2 WASH, clean, bath, soap, shower, soak, cleanse, scrub, tub, sponge, rinse, scrub down, lave (*archaic*)
3 CLEANSE, clean, wash, soak, rinse
4 COVER, flood, steep, engulf, immerse, overrun, suffuse, wash over
▷ *noun* (*Brit*) SWIM, dip, dook (*Scot*)

bathroom *noun* LAVATORY, toilet, loo (*Brit informal*), washroom, can (*US & Canad slang*), john (*slang, chiefly US & Canad*), head(s) (*Nautical slang*), shower, convenience (*chiefly Brit*), bog (*slang*), bogger (*Austral slang*), brasco (*Austral slang*), privy, cloakroom (*Brit*), latrine, rest room, powder room, dunny (*Austral & NZ old-fashioned*), water closet, khazi (*slang*), comfort station (*US*), pissoir (*French*), Gents *or* Ladies, little boy's room *or* little girl's room (*informal*), (public) convenience, W.C.

baton *noun* STICK, club, staff, stake, pole, rod, crook, cane, mace, wand, truncheon, sceptre, mere (*NZ*), patu (*NZ*)

battalion *noun* COMPANY, army, force, team, host, division, troop, brigade, regiment, legion, contingent, squadron, military force, horde, multitude, throng

batten *verb usually with* **down** FASTEN, unite, fix, secure, lock, bind, chain, connect, attach, seal, tighten, anchor, bolt, clamp down, affix, nail down, make firm, make fast, fasten down

batter *verb* **1** BEAT, hit, strike, knock, assault, smash, punch, belt (*informal*), deck (*slang*), bang, bash (*informal*), lash, thrash, pound, lick (*informal*), buffet, flog, maul, pelt, clobber (*slang*), smite, wallop (*informal*), pummel, tonk (*informal*), cudgel, thwack, lambast(e), belabour, dash against, beat the living daylights out of, lay one on (*slang*), drub, beat *or* knock seven bells out of (*informal*)
2 DAMAGE, destroy, hurt, injure, harm, ruin, crush, mar, wreck, total (*slang*), shatter, weaken, bruise, demolish, shiver, trash (*slang*), maul, mutilate, mangle, mangulate (*Austral slang*), disfigure, deface, play (merry) hell with (*informal*)

battered *adjective* **1** BEATEN, injured, harmed, crushed, bruised, squashed, beat-up (*informal*), oppressed, manhandled, black-and-blue, ill-treated, maltreated
2 DAMAGED, broken-down, wrecked, beat-up (*informal*), ramshackle, dilapidated

battery *noun* **1** ARTILLERY, ordnance, gunnery, gun emplacement, cannonry
2 SERIES, set, course, chain, string, sequence, suite, succession
3 (*Criminal law*) BEATING, attack, assault, aggression, thumping, onslaught, physical violence

battle *noun* **1** FIGHT, war, attack, action, struggle, conflict, clash, set-to (*informal*), encounter, combat, scrap (*informal*), biffo (*Austral slang*), engagement, warfare, fray, duel, skirmish, head-to-head, tussle, scuffle, fracas, scrimmage, sparring match, bagarre (*French*), melee *or* mêlée, boilover (*Austral*)
<< OPPOSITE peace
2 CONFLICT, campaign, struggle, debate, clash, dispute, contest, controversy, disagreement, crusade, strife, head-to-head, agitation
3 CAMPAIGN, drive, movement, push, struggle
▷ *verb* **1** WRESTLE, war, fight, argue, dispute, contest, combat, contend, feud, grapple, agitate, clamour, scuffle, lock horns
2 STRUGGLE, work, labour, strain, strive, go for it (*informal*), toil, make every effort, go all out (*informal*), bend over backwards (*informal*), go for broke (*slang*), bust a gut (*informal*), give it your best shot (*informal*), break your neck (*informal*), exert yourself, make an all-out effort (*informal*), work like a Trojan, knock yourself out (*informal*), do your damnedest (*informal*), give it your all (*informal*), rupture yourself (*informal*)

battle cry *noun* **1** SLOGAN, motto, watchword,

catch phrase, tag-line, catchword, catchcry (*Austral*)
2 WAR CRY, rallying cry, war whoop

battlefield *noun* BATTLEGROUND, front, field, combat zone, field of battle

battleship *noun* WARSHIP, gunboat, man-of-war, ship of the line, capital ship

batty *adjective* CRAZY, odd, mad, eccentric, bats (*slang*), nuts (*slang*), barking (*slang*), peculiar, daft (*informal*), crackers (*Brit slang*), queer (*informal*), insane, lunatic, loony (*slang*), barmy (*slang*), off-the-wall (*slang*), touched, nutty (*slang*), potty (*Brit informal*), oddball (*informal*), off the rails, cracked (*slang*), bonkers (*slang, chiefly Brit*), cranky (*US, Canad & Irish informal*), dotty (*slang, chiefly Brit*), loopy (*informal*), crackpot (*informal*), out to lunch (*informal*), barking mad (*slang*), out of your mind, outré, gonzo (*slang*), screwy (*informal*), doolally (*slang*), off your trolley (*slang*), off the air (*Austral slang*), round the twist (*Brit slang*), up the pole (*informal*), off your rocker (*slang*), not the full shilling (*informal*), as daft as a brush (*informal, chiefly Brit*), wacko *or* whacko (*slang*), porangi (*NZ*), daggy (*Austral & NZ informal*)

bauble *noun* TRINKET, ornament, trifle, toy, plaything, bagatelle, gimcrack, gewgaw, knick-knack, bibelot, kickshaw

bawdy *adjective* RUDE, blue, dirty, gross, crude, erotic, obscene, coarse, filthy, indecent, vulgar, improper, steamy (*informal*), pornographic, raunchy (*US slang*), suggestive, racy, lewd, risqué, X-rated (*informal*), salacious, prurient, lascivious, smutty, lustful, lecherous, ribald, libidinous, licentious, indelicate, near the knuckle (*informal*), indecorous
<< OPPOSITE clean

bawl *verb* **1** SHOUT, call, scream, roar, yell, howl, bellow, bay, clamour, holler (*informal*), raise your voice, halloo, hollo, vociferate
2 CRY, weep, sob, wail, whine, whimper, whinge (*informal*), keen, greet (*Scot archaic*), squall, blubber, snivel, shed tears, yowl, mewl, howl your eyes out

bay¹ *noun* INLET, sound, gulf, entrance, creek, cove, fjord, arm (of the sea), bight, ingress, natural harbour, sea loch (*Scot*), firth *or* frith (*Scot*)

bay² *noun* RECESS, opening, corner, niche, compartment, nook, alcove, embrasure

bay³ *verb* HOWL, cry, roar (*used of hounds*), bark, lament, cry out, wail, growl, bellow, quest (*used of hounds*), bell, clamour, yelp
▷ *noun* CRY, bell, roar (*used of hounds*), bark, lament, howl, wail, growl, bellow, clamour, yelp
▷▷ **at bay** AWAY, off, at arm's length

bayonet *verb* STAB, cut, wound, knife, slash, pierce, run through, spear, transfix, impale, lacerate, stick

bazaar *noun* **1** MARKET, exchange, fair, marketplace, mart
2 FAIR, fête, gala, festival, garden party, bring-and-buy

be *verb* **1** BE ALIVE, live, exist, survive, breathe, last, be present, continue, endure, be living, be extant, happen
2 TAKE PLACE, happen, occur, arise, come about, transpire (*informal*), befall, come to pass

beach *noun* SHORE, coast, sands, margin, strand, seaside, shingle, lakeside, water's edge, lido, foreshore, seashore, plage, littoral, sea (*chiefly US*)

beached *adjective* STRANDED, grounded, abandoned, deserted, wrecked, ashore, marooned, aground, high and dry

beacon *noun* **1** SIGNAL, sign, rocket, beam, flare, bonfire, smoke signal, signal fire
2 LIGHTHOUSE, pharos, watchtower

bead *noun* DROP, tear, bubble, pearl, dot, drip, blob, droplet, globule, driblet
▷ *plural noun* NECKLACE, pearls, pendant, choker, necklet, chaplet

beady *adjective* BRIGHT, powerful, concentrated, sharp, intense, shining, glittering, gleaming, glinting

beak *noun* **1** BILL, nib, neb (*archaic* or *dialect*), mandible
2 (*Slang*) NOSE, snout, hooter (*slang*), snitch (*slang*), conk (*slang*), neb (*archaic* or *dialect*), proboscis, schnozzle (*slang, chiefly US*)

beam *verb* **1** SMILE, grin
2 TRANSMIT, show, air, broadcast, cable, send out, relay, televise, radio, emit, put on the air
3 RADIATE, flash, shine, glow, glitter, glare, gleam, emit light, give off light
▷ *noun* **1** RAY, bar, flash, stream, glow, radiation, streak, emission, shaft, gleam, glint, glimmer
2 RAFTER, support, timber, spar, plank, girder, joist
3 SMILE, grin

beaming *adjective* **1** SMILING, happy, grinning, pleasant, sunny, cheerful, cheery, joyful, chirpy (*informal*), light-hearted
2 RADIATING, bright, brilliant, flashing, shining, glowing, sparkling, glittering, gleaming, glimmering, radiant, glistening, scintillating, burnished, lustrous

bear *verb* **1** CARRY, take, move, bring, lift, transfer, conduct, transport, haul, transmit, convey, relay, tote (*informal*), hump (*Brit slang*), lug
<< OPPOSITE put down
2 SUPPORT, shoulder, sustain, endure, uphold, withstand, bear up under
<< OPPOSITE give up
3 DISPLAY, have, show, hold, carry, possess,

exhibit
4 SUFFER, feel, experience, go through, sustain, stomach, endure, undergo, admit, brook, hack (*slang*), abide, put up with (*informal*)
5 BRING YOURSELF TO, allow, accept, permit, endure, tolerate, hack (*informal*), countenance
6 PRODUCE, develop, generate, yield, bring forth
7 GIVE BIRTH TO, produce, deliver, breed, bring forth, beget
8 EXHIBIT, hold, maintain, entertain, harbour, cherish
9 CONDUCT, carry, move, deport
▷▷ **bear down on someone** ADVANCE ON, attack, approach, move towards, close in on, converge on, move in on, come near to, draw near to
▷▷ **bear down on something** *or* **someone** PRESS DOWN, push, strain, crush, compress, weigh down, encumber
▷▷ **bear on something** BE RELEVANT TO, involve, concern, affect, regard, refer to, be part of, relate to, belong to, apply to, be appropriate to, befit, pertain to, touch upon, appertain to
▷▷ **bear something out** SUPPORT, prove, confirm, justify, endorse, uphold, vindicate, validate, substantiate, corroborate, legitimize
▷▷ **bear with someone** BE PATIENT WITH, suffer, wait for, hold on (*informal*), stand by, tolerate, put up with (*informal*), make allowances for, hang fire

bearable *adjective* TOLERABLE, acceptable, sustainable, manageable, passable, admissible, supportable, endurable, sufferable
<< OPPOSITE intolerable

beard *noun* WHISKERS, bristles, stubble, five-o'clock shadow

bearded *adjective* UNSHAVEN, hairy, whiskered, stubbly, bushy, shaggy, hirsute, bristly, bewhiskered

bearer *noun* 1 AGENT, carrier, courier, herald, envoy, messenger, conveyor, emissary, harbinger
2 CARRIER, runner, servant, porter
3 PAYEE, beneficiary, consignee

bearing *noun* 1 *usually with* **on** *or* **upon** RELEVANCE, relation, application, connection, import, reference, significance, pertinence, appurtenance
<< OPPOSITE irrelevance
2 MANNER, attitude, conduct, appearance, aspect, presence, behaviour, tone, carriage, posture, demeanour, deportment, mien, air, comportment
3 (*Nautical*) POSITION, course, direction, point of compass
▷ *plural noun* WAY, course, position, situation, track, aim, direction, location, orientation, whereabouts

bearish *adjective* (*Stock Exchange*) FALLING, declining, slumping

beast *noun* 1 ANIMAL, creature, brute
2 BRUTE, monster, savage, barbarian, fiend, swine, ogre, ghoul, sadist

beastly *adjective* (*informal*) 1 UNPLEASANT, mean, terrible, awful, nasty, foul, rotten, horrid, disagreeable, irksome
<< OPPOSITE pleasant
2 (CRUEL, mean, nasty, harsh, savage, brutal, coarse, monstrous, malicious, insensitive, sadistic, unfriendly, unsympathetic, uncaring, spiteful, thoughtless, brutish, barbarous, unfeeling, inconsiderate, bestial, uncharitable, unchristian, hardhearted
<< OPPOSITE humane

beat *verb* 1 BATTER, break, hit, strike, knock, punch, belt (*informal*), whip, deck (*slang*), bruise, bash (*informal*), sock (*slang*), lash, chin (*slang*), pound, smack, thrash, cane, thump, lick (*informal*), buffet, clout (*informal*), flog, whack (*informal*), maul, clobber (*slang*), wallop (*informal*), tonk (*informal*), cudgel, thwack (*informal*), lambast(e), lay one on (*slang*), drub, beat *or* knock seven bells out of (*informal*)
2 POUND, strike, hammer, batter, thrash, pelt
3 THROB, pulse, tick, thump, tremble, pound, quake, quiver, vibrate, pulsate, palpitate
4 HIT, strike, bang
5 FLAP, thrash, flutter, agitate, wag, swish
6 DEFEAT, outdo, trounce, overcome, stuff (*slang*), master, tank (*slang*), crush, overwhelm, conquer, lick (*informal*), undo, subdue, excel, surpass, overpower, outstrip, clobber (*slang*), vanquish, outrun, subjugate, run rings around (*informal*), wipe the floor with (*informal*), knock spots off (*informal*), make mincemeat of (*informal*), pip at the post, outplay, blow out of the water (*slang*), put in the shade (*informal*), bring to their knees
▷ *noun* 1 THROB, pounding, pulse, thumping, vibration, pulsating, palpitation, pulsation
2 ROUTE, way, course, rounds, path, circuit
▷▷ **beat it** (*Slang*) GO AWAY, leave, depart, get lost (*informal*), shoo, exit, go to hell (*informal*), hook it (*slang*), scarper (*Brit slang*), pack your bags (*informal*), make tracks, hop it (*slang*), scram (*informal*), get on your bike (*Brit slang*), skedaddle (*informal*), sling your hook (*Brit slang*), vamoose (*slang, chiefly US*), voetsek (*S African offensive*), rack off (*Austral & NZ slang*)
▷▷ **beat someone up** (*informal*) ASSAULT, attack, batter, thrash, set about, do over (*Brit, Austral & NZ slang*), work over (*slang*), clobber (*slang*), assail, set upon, lay into (*informal*), put the boot in (*slang*), lambast(e), duff up (*Brit slang*), beat the living daylights out of (*informal*), knock

about *or* around, fill in (*Brit slang*), beat *or* knock seven bells out of (*informal*)

beaten *adjective* 1 WELL-TRODDEN, worn, trodden, trampled, well-used, much travelled
2 STIRRED, mixed, whipped, blended, whisked, frothy, foamy
3 SHAPED, worked, formed, stamped, hammered, forged
4 DEFEATED, overcome, frustrated, overwhelmed, cowed, thwarted, vanquished, disheartened

beating *noun* 1 THRASHING, hiding (*informal*), belting (*informal*), whipping (*slang*), slapping, tanning, lashing, smacking, caning, pasting (*slang*), flogging, drubbing, corporal punishment, chastisement
2 DEFEAT, ruin, overthrow, pasting (*slang*), conquest, rout, downfall

beau *noun* (*Chiefly US*) BOYFRIEND, man, guy (*informal*), date, lover, young man, steady, escort, admirer, fiancé, sweetheart, suitor, swain, toy boy, leman (*archaic*), fancy man (*slang*)

beautiful *adjective* ATTRACTIVE, pretty, lovely, stunning (*informal*), charming, tempting, pleasant, handsome, fetching, good-looking, gorgeous, fine, pleasing, fair, magnetic, delightful, cute, exquisite, enticing, seductive, graceful, captivating, appealing, radiant, alluring, drop-dead (*slang*), ravishing, bonny, winsome, comely, prepossessing
<< OPPOSITE ugly

beautify *verb* MAKE BEAUTIFUL, enhance, decorate, enrich, adorn, garnish, ornament, gild, embellish, grace, festoon, bedeck, glamorize

beauty *noun* 1 ATTRACTIVENESS, charm, grace, bloom, glamour, fairness, elegance, symmetry (*formal or literary*), allure, loveliness, handsomeness, pulchritude, comeliness, exquisiteness, seemliness
<< OPPOSITE ugliness
2 GOOD-LOOKER, looker (*informal, chiefly US*), lovely (*slang*), sensation, dazzler, belle, goddess, Venus, peach (*informal*), cracker (*slang*), wow (*slang, chiefly US*), dolly (*slang*), knockout (*informal*), heart-throb, stunner (*informal*), charmer, smasher (*informal*), humdinger (*slang*), glamour puss, beaut (*Austral & NZ slang*)
3 ADVANTAGE, good, use, benefit, profit, gain, asset, attraction, blessing, good thing, utility, excellence, boon
<< OPPOSITE disadvantage

becalmed *adjective* STILL, stuck, settled, stranded, motionless

because *conjunction* SINCE, as, in that
▷▷ **because of** AS A RESULT OF, on account of, by reason of, thanks to, owing to

The phrase *on account of* can provide a useful alternative to *because of* in writing. It occurs relatively infrequently in spoken language, where it is sometimes followed by a clause, as in *on account of I don't do drugs*. However, this use is considered nonstandard

beckon *verb* 1 GESTURE, sign, wave, indicate, signal, nod, motion, summon, gesticulate
2 LURE, call, draw, pull, attract, invite, tempt, entice, coax, allure

become *verb* 1 COME TO BE, develop into, be transformed into, grow into, change into, evolve into, alter to, mature into, metamorphose into, ripen into
2 SUIT, fit, enhance, flatter, ornament, embellish, grace, harmonize with, set off
▷▷ **become of something** *or* **someone** HAPPEN TO, befall, betide

becoming *adjective* 1 FLATTERING, pretty, attractive, enhancing, neat, graceful, tasteful, well-chosen, comely
<< OPPOSITE unflattering
2 APPROPRIATE, right, seemly, fitting, fit, correct, suitable, decent, proper, worthy, in keeping, compatible, befitting, decorous, comme il faut (*French*), congruous, meet (*archaic*)
<< OPPOSITE inappropriate

bed *noun* 1 BEDSTEAD, couch, berth, cot (*informal*), pallet, divan
2 PLOT, area, row, strip, patch, ground, land, garden, border
3 BOTTOM, ground, floor
4 BASE, footing, basis, bottom, foundation, underpinning, groundwork, bedrock, substructure, substratum
▷ *verb* FIX, set, found, base, plant, establish, settle, root, sink, insert, implant, embed
▷▷ **bed down** SLEEP, lie down, retire, turn in (*informal*), settle down, kip (*Brit slang*), hit the hay (*slang*)

bedclothes *plural noun* BEDDING, covers, sheets, blankets, linen, pillow, quilt, duvet, pillowcase, bed linen, coverlet, eiderdown

bedding *noun* BEDCLOTHES, covers, sheets, blankets, linen, pillow, quilt, duvet, pillowcase, bed linen, coverlet, eiderdown

bedeck *verb* DECORATE, grace, trim, array, enrich, adorn, garnish, ornament, embellish, festoon, beautify, bedight (*archaic*), bedizen (*archaic*), engarland

bedevil *verb* PLAGUE, worry, trouble, frustrate, torture, irritate, torment, harass, hassle (*informal*), aggravate (*informal*), afflict, pester, vex, irk

bedlam *noun* PANDEMONIUM, noise, confusion, chaos, turmoil, clamour, furore, uproar, commotion, rumpus, babel, tumult, hubbub, ruction (*informal*), hullabaloo, hue and cry, ruckus (*informal*)

bedraggled *adjective* MESSY, soiled, dirty, disordered, stained, dripping, muddied, muddy, drenched, ruffled, untidy, sodden, sullied, dishevelled, rumpled, unkempt, tousled, disarranged, disarrayed, daggy (*Austral & NZ informal*)

bedridden *adjective* CONFINED TO BED, confined, incapacitated, laid up (*informal*), flat on your back

bedrock *noun* 1 FIRST PRINCIPLE, rule, basis, basics, principle, essentials, roots, core, fundamentals, cornerstone, nuts and bolts (*informal*), sine qua non (*Latin*), rudiment
2 BOTTOM, bed, foundation, underpinning, rock bottom, substructure, substratum

bee *noun*
>> RELATED WORD *adjective* apian
>> RELATED WORDS *collective nouns* swarm, grist
>> RELATED WORDS *habitations* hive, apiary

beef *noun* (*Slang*) COMPLAINT, dispute, grievance, problem, grumble, criticism, objection, dissatisfaction, annoyance, grouse, gripe (*informal*), protestation, grouch (*informal*), remonstrance

beefy *adjective* (*informal*) BRAWNY, strong, powerful, athletic, strapping, robust, hefty (*informal*), muscular, sturdy, stalwart, bulky, burly, stocky, hulking, well-built, herculean, sinewy, thickset
<< OPPOSITE scrawny

beehive *noun* HIVE, colony, comb, swarm, honeycomb, apiary

beer *noun* ALE, brew, swipes (*Brit slang*), wallop (*Brit slang*), hop juice, amber fluid *or* nectar (*Austral informal*), tinnie *or* tinny (*Austral slang*)

beer parlour *noun* (*Canad*) TAVERN, inn, bar, pub (*informal, chiefly Brit*), public house, watering hole (*facetious slang*), boozer (*Brit, Austral & NZ informal*), beverage room (*Canad*), hostelry, alehouse (*archaic*), taproom

befall *verb* (*Archaic* or *literary*) HAPPEN TO, fall upon, occur in, take place in, ensue in, transpire in (*informal*), materialize in, come to pass in

befit *verb* BE APPROPRIATE FOR, become, suit, be fitting for, be suitable for, be seemly for, behove (*US*)

befitting *adjective* APPROPRIATE TO, right for, suitable for, fitting for, fit for, becoming to, seemly for, proper for, apposite to, meet (*archaic*)
<< OPPOSITE unsuitable for

before *preposition* 1 EARLIER THAN, ahead of, prior to, in advance of
<< OPPOSITE after
2 IN FRONT OF, ahead of, in advance of, to the fore of
3 IN THE PRESENCE OF, in front of
4 AHEAD OF, in front of, in advance of
▷ *adverb* 1 PREVIOUSLY, earlier, sooner, in advance, formerly
<< OPPOSITE after
2 IN THE PAST, earlier, once, previously, formerly, at one time, hitherto, beforehand, a while ago, heretofore, in days *or* years gone by
>> RELATED WORDS *prefixes* ante-, fore-, pre-

beforehand *adverb* IN ADVANCE, before, earlier, already, sooner, ahead, previously, in anticipation, before now, ahead of time

befriend *verb* MAKE FRIENDS WITH, back, help, support, benefit, aid, encourage, welcome, favour, advise, sustain, assist, stand by, uphold, side with, patronize, succour

befuddle *verb* CONFUSE, puzzle, baffle, bewilder, muddle, daze, perplex, mystify, disorient, faze, stupefy, flummox, bemuse, intoxicate
<< OPPOSITE make clear

befuddled *adjective* CONFUSED, upset, puzzled, baffled, at sea, bewildered, muddled, dazed, perplexed, taken aback, intoxicated, disorientated, disorganized, muzzy (*US informal*), groggy (*informal*), flummoxed, woozy (*informal*), at sixes and sevens, fuddled, inebriated, thrown off balance, discombobulated (*informal, chiefly US & Canad*), not with it (*informal*), not knowing if you are coming or going

beg *verb* 1 IMPLORE, plead with, beseech, desire, request, pray, petition, conjure, crave, solicit, entreat, importune, supplicate, go on bended knee to
2 SCROUNGE, bum (*informal*), blag (*slang*), touch (someone) for (*slang*), mooch (*slang*), cadge, forage for, hunt around (for), sponge on (someone) for, freeload (*slang*), seek charity, call for alms, solicit charity
<< OPPOSITE give
3 DODGE, avoid, get out of, duck (*informal*), hedge, parry, shun, evade, elude, fudge, fend off, eschew, flannel (*Brit informal*), sidestep, shirk, equivocate, body-swerve (*Scot*)

beget *verb* (*Old-fashioned*) 1 CAUSE, bring, produce, create, effect, lead to, occasion, result in, generate, provoke, induce, bring about, give rise to, precipitate, incite, engender
2 FATHER, breed, generate, sire, get, propagate, procreate

beggar *noun* TRAMP, bankrupt, bum (*informal*), derelict, drifter, down-and-out, pauper, vagrant, hobo (*chiefly US*), vagabond, bag lady

(*chiefly US*), dosser (*Brit slang*), derro (*Austral slang*), starveling
▷ *verb* DEFY, challenge, defeat, frustrate, foil, baffle, thwart, withstand, surpass, elude, repel

begin *verb* 1 START, commence, proceed
<< OPPOSITE stop
2 COMMENCE, start, initiate, embark on, set about, instigate, inaugurate, institute, make a beginning, set on foot
3 START TALKING, start, initiate, commence, begin business, get *or* start the ball rolling
4 COME INTO EXISTENCE, start, appear, emerge, spring, be born, arise, dawn, be developed, be created, originate, commence, be invented, become available, crop up (*informal*), come into being
5 EMERGE, start, spring, stem, derive, issue, originate
<< OPPOSITE end

beginner *noun* NOVICE, student, pupil, convert, recruit, amateur, initiate, newcomer, starter, trainee, apprentice, cub, fledgling, learner, freshman, neophyte, tyro, probationer, greenhorn (*informal*), novitiate, tenderfoot, proselyte
<< OPPOSITE expert

beginning *noun* 1 START, opening, break (*informal*), chance, source, opportunity, birth, origin, introduction, outset, starting point, onset, overture, initiation, inauguration, inception, commencement, opening move
<< OPPOSITE end
2 OUTSET, start, opening, birth, onset, prelude, preface, commencement, kickoff (*informal*)
3 *often plural* ORIGINS, family, beginnings, stock, birth, roots, heritage, descent, pedigree, extraction, ancestry, lineage, parentage, stirps

begrudge *verb* 1 RESENT, envy, grudge, be jealous of
2 BE BITTER ABOUT, object to, be angry about, give reluctantly, bear a grudge about, be in a huff about, give stingily, have hard feelings about

beguile *verb* 1 CHARM, please, attract, delight, occupy, cheer, fascinate, entertain, absorb, entrance, win over, amuse, divert, distract, enchant, captivate, solace, allure, bewitch, mesmerize, engross, enrapture, tickle the fancy of
2 FOOL, trick, take in, cheat, con (*informal*), mislead, impose on, deceive, dupe, gull (*archaic*), delude, bamboozle, hoodwink, take for a ride (*informal*), befool
<< OPPOSITE enlighten

beguiling *adjective* CHARMING, interesting, pleasing, attractive, engaging, lovely, entertaining, pleasant, intriguing, diverting, delightful, irresistible, enchanting, seductive, captivating, enthralling, winning, eye-catching, alluring, bewitching, delectable, winsome, likable *or* likeable

behalf *noun* 1 ▷▷ **on behalf of something** *or* **someone** *or* **on something** *or* **someone's behalf**
1 AS A REPRESENTATIVE OF, representing, in the name of, as a spokesperson for
2 FOR THE BENEFIT OF, for the sake of, in support of, on the side of, in the interests of, on account of, for the good of, in defence of, to the advantage of, for the profit of

> *On behalf of* is sometimes wrongly used as an alternative to *on the part of*. The distinction is that *on behalf of someone* means 'for someone's benefit' or 'representing someone', while *on the part of someone* can be roughly paraphrased as 'by someone'.

behave *verb* 1 ACT, react, conduct yourself, acquit yourself, comport yourself
2 *often reflexive* BE WELL-BEHAVED, be good, be polite, mind your manners, keep your nose clean, act correctly, act politely, conduct yourself properly
<< OPPOSITE misbehave

behaviour *noun* 1 CONDUCT, ways, actions, bearing, attitude, manner, manners, carriage, demeanour, deportment, mien (*literary*), comportment
2 ACTION, working, running, performance, operation, practice, conduct, functioning

behead *verb* DECAPITATE, execute, guillotine

behest *noun* ▷▷ **at someone's behest** AT SOMEONE'S COMMAND, by someone's order, at someone's demand, at someone's wish, by someone's decree, at someone's bidding, at someone's instruction, by someone's mandate, at someone's dictate, at someone's commandment

behind *preposition* 1 AT THE REAR OF, at the back of, at the heels of
2 AFTER, following
3 SUPPORTING, for, backing, on the side of, in agreement with
4 CAUSING, responsible for, the cause of, initiating, at the bottom of, to blame for, instigating
5 LATER THAN, after
▷ *adverb* 1 THE BACK, the rear
2 AFTER, next, following, afterwards, subsequently, in the wake (of)
<< OPPOSITE in advance of
3 BEHIND SCHEDULE, delayed, running late, behind time
<< OPPOSITE ahead
4 OVERDUE, in debt, in arrears, behindhand
▷ *noun* (*informal*) BOTTOM, seat, bum (*Brit slang*), butt (*US & Canad informal*), buns (*US*

slang), buttocks, rump, posterior, tail (*informal*), derrière (*euphemistic*), tush (*US slang*), jacksy (*Brit slang*)

behold *verb* (*Archaic* or *literary*) LOOK AT, see, view, eye, consider, study, watch, check, regard, survey, witness, clock (*Brit slang*), examine, observe, perceive, gaze, scan, contemplate, check out (*informal*), inspect, discern, eyeball (*slang*), scrutinize, recce (*slang*), get a load of (*informal*), take a gander at (*informal*), take a dekko at (*Brit slang*), feast your eyes upon

beholden *adjective* INDEBTED, bound, owing, grateful, obliged, in debt, obligated, under obligation

beige *noun* or *adjective* FAWN, coffee, cream, sand, neutral, mushroom, tan, biscuit, camel, buff, cinnamon, khaki, oatmeal, ecru, café au lait (*French*)

being *noun* 1 INDIVIDUAL, thing, body, animal, creature, human being, beast, mortal, living thing

2 LIFE, living, reality, animation, actuality

<< OPPOSITE nonexistence

3 SOUL, spirit, presence, substance, creature, essence, organism, entity

belated *adjective* LATE, delayed, overdue, late in the day, tardy, behind time, unpunctual, behindhand

belch *verb* 1 BURP, eructate, eruct

2 EMIT, discharge, erupt, send out, throw out, vent, vomit, issue, give out, gush, eject, diffuse, emanate, exude, give off, exhale, cast out, disgorge, give vent to, send forth, spew forth, breathe forth

beleaguered *adjective* 1 HARASSED, troubled, plagued, tormented, hassled (*informal*), aggravated (*informal*), badgered, persecuted, pestered, vexed, put upon

2 BESIEGED, surrounded, blockaded, encompassed, beset, encircled, assailed, hemmed in, hedged in, environed

belie *verb* 1 MISREPRESENT, disguise, conceal, distort, misinterpret, falsify, gloss over

2 DISPROVE, deny, expose, discredit, contradict, refute, repudiate, negate, invalidate, rebut, give the lie to, make a nonsense of, gainsay (*archaic* or *literary*), prove false, blow out of the water (*slang*), controvert, confute

belief *noun* 1 TRUST, confidence, conviction, reliance

<< OPPOSITE disbelief

2 FAITH, principles, doctrine, ideology, creed, dogma, tenet, credence, credo

3 OPINION, feeling, idea, view, theory, impression, assessment, notion, judgment, point of view, sentiment, persuasion, presumption

believable *adjective* CREDIBLE, possible, likely, acceptable, reliable, authentic, probable, plausible, imaginable, trustworthy, creditable

<< OPPOSITE unbelievable

believe *verb* 1 THINK, consider, judge, suppose, maintain, estimate, imagine, assume, gather, guess (*informal, chiefly US & Canad*), reckon, conclude, deem, speculate, presume, conjecture, postulate, surmise

2 ACCEPT, hold, buy (*slang*), trust, credit, depend on, rely on, swallow (*informal*), count on, buy into (*slang*), have faith in, swear by, be certain of, be convinced of, place confidence in, presume true, take as gospel, take on (*US*)

<< OPPOSITE disbelieve

▷▷ **believe in something** ADVOCATE, champion, approve of, swear by

believer *noun* FOLLOWER, supporter, convert, disciple, protagonist, devotee, worshipper, apostle, adherent, zealot, upholder, proselyte

<< OPPOSITE sceptic

belittle *verb* RUN DOWN, dismiss, diminish, put down, underestimate, discredit, ridicule, scorn, rubbish (*informal*), degrade, minimize, downgrade, undervalue, knock (*informal*), deride, malign, detract from, denigrate, scoff at, disparage, decry, sneer at, underrate, deprecate, depreciate, defame, derogate

<< OPPOSITE praise

belle *noun* BEAUTY, looker (*informal*), lovely, good-looker, goddess, Venus, peach (*informal*), cracker (*informal*), stunner (*informal*), charmer

bellicose *adjective* AGGRESSIVE, offensive, hostile, destructive, defiant, provocative, belligerent, combative, antagonistic, pugnacious, hawkish, warlike, quarrelsome, militaristic, sabre-rattling, jingoistic, warmongering

belligerence *noun* AGGRESSIVENESS, hostility, animosity, antagonism, destructiveness, pugnacity, combativeness, offensiveness, unfriendliness

belligerent *adjective* AGGRESSIVE, hostile, contentious, combative, unfriendly, antagonistic, pugnacious, argumentative, bellicose, quarrelsome, aggers (*Austral slang*), biffo (*Austral slang*), litigious

<< OPPOSITE friendly

▷ *noun* FIGHTER, battler, militant, contender, contestant, combatant, antagonist, warring nation, disputant

bellow *verb* SHOUT, call, cry (out), scream, roar, yell, howl, shriek, clamour, bawl, holler (*informal*)

▷ *noun* SHOUT, call, cry, scream, roar, yell, howl, shriek, bell, clamour, bawl

belly *noun* STOMACH, insides (*informal*), gut, abdomen, tummy, paunch, vitals, breadbasket (*slang*), potbelly, corporation (*informal*), puku (*NZ*)

belong *verb* GO WITH, fit into, be part of, relate

to, attach to, be connected with, pertain to, have as a proper place

belonging *noun* FELLOWSHIP, relationship, association, loyalty, acceptance, attachment, inclusion, affinity, rapport, affiliation, kinship

belongings *plural noun* POSSESSIONS, goods, things, effects, property, stuff, gear, paraphernalia, personal property, accoutrements, chattels, goods and chattels

beloved *adjective* DEAR, loved, valued, prized, dearest, sweet, admired, treasured, precious, darling, worshipped, adored, cherished, revered

below *preposition* 1 UNDER, underneath, lower than
2 LESS THAN, lower than
3 SUBORDINATE TO, subject to, inferior to, lesser than
▷ *adverb* 1 LOWER, down, under, beneath, underneath
2 BENEATH, following, at the end, underneath, at the bottom, further on

belt *noun* 1 WAISTBAND, band, sash, girdle, girth, cummerbund, cincture
2 CONVEYOR BELT, band, loop, fan belt, drive belt
3 (*Geography*) ZONE, area, region, section, sector, district, stretch, strip, layer, patch, portion, tract
▷▷ **below the belt** (*informal*) UNFAIR, foul, crooked (*informal*), cowardly, sly, fraudulent, unjust, dishonest, deceptive, unscrupulous, devious, unethical, sneaky, furtive, deceitful, surreptitious, dishonourable, unsporting, unsportsmanlike, underhanded, not playing the game (*informal*)

bemoan *verb* LAMENT, regret, complain about, rue, deplore, grieve for, weep for, bewail, cry over spilt milk, express sorrow about, moan over

bemused *adjective* PUZZLED, stunned, confused, stumped, baffled, at sea, bewildered, muddled, preoccupied, dazed, perplexed, mystified, engrossed, clueless, stupefied, nonplussed, absent-minded, flummoxed, half-drunk, fuddled

bench *noun* 1 SEAT, stall, pew
2 WORKTABLE, stand, table, counter, slab, trestle table, workbench
▷▷ **the bench** COURT, judge, judges, magistrate, magistrates, tribunal, judiciary, courtroom

benchmark *noun* REFERENCE POINT, gauge, yardstick, measure, level, example, standard, model, reference, par, criterion, norm, touchstone

bend *verb* 1 TWIST, turn, wind, lean, hook, bow, curve, arch, incline, arc, deflect, warp, buckle, coil, flex, stoop, veer, swerve, diverge, contort, inflect, incurvate
2 SUBMIT, yield, bow, surrender, give in, give way, cede, capitulate, resign yourself
3 FORCE, direct, influence, shape, persuade, compel, mould, sway
▷ *noun* CURVE, turn, corner, hook, twist, angle, bow, loop, arc, zigzag, camber

beneath *preposition* 1 UNDER, below, underneath, lower than
<< OPPOSITE over
2 INFERIOR TO, below
3 UNWORTHY OF, unfitting for, unsuitable for, inappropriate for, unbefitting
▷ *adverb* UNDERNEATH, below, in a lower place
>> RELATED WORD *prefix* sub-

benefactor *noun* SUPPORTER, friend, champion, defender, sponsor, angel (*informal*), patron, promoter, contributor, backer, helper, subsidizer, philanthropist, upholder, well-wisher

beneficial *adjective* FAVOURABLE, useful, valuable, helpful, profitable, benign, wholesome, advantageous, expedient, salutary, healthful, serviceable, salubrious, gainful
<< OPPOSITE harmful

beneficiary *noun* 1 RECIPIENT, receiver, payee, assignee, legatee
2 HEIR, inheritor

benefit *noun* 1 GOOD, use, help, profit, gain, favour, utility, boon, mileage (*informal*), avail
<< OPPOSITE harm
2 ADVANTAGE, interest, aid, gain, favour, assistance, betterment
▷ *verb* 1 PROFIT FROM, make the most of, gain from, do well out of, reap benefits from, turn to your advantage
2 HELP, serve, aid, profit, improve, advance, advantage, enhance, assist, avail
<< OPPOSITE harm

benevolence *noun* KINDNESS, understanding, charity, grace, sympathy, humanity, tolerance, goodness, goodwill, compassion, generosity, indulgence, decency, altruism, clemency, gentleness, philanthropy, magnanimity, fellow feeling, beneficence, kindliness, kind-heartedness, aroha (NZ)
<< OPPOSITE ill will

benevolent *adjective* KIND, good, kindly, understanding, caring, liberal, generous, obliging, sympathetic, humanitarian, charitable, benign, humane, compassionate, gracious, indulgent, amiable, amicable, lenient, cordial, considerate, affable, congenial, altruistic, philanthropic, bountiful, beneficent, well-disposed, kind-hearted, warm-hearted, bounteous, tender-hearted

benighted *adjective* UNCIVILIZED, crude,

primitive, backward, uncultivated, unenlightened

benign *adjective* 1 BENEVOLENT, kind, kindly, warm, liberal, friendly, generous, obliging, sympathetic, favourable, compassionate, gracious, amiable, genial, affable, complaisant

<< OPPOSITE unkind

2 (*Medical*) HARMLESS, innocent, superficial, innocuous, curable, inoffensive, not dangerous, remediable

<< OPPOSITE malignant

3 FAVOURABLE, good, encouraging, warm, moderate, beneficial, clement, advantageous, salutary, auspicious, propitious

<< OPPOSITE unfavourable

bent *adjective* 1 MISSHAPEN, twisted, angled, bowed, curved, arched, crooked, crippled, distorted, warped, deformed, tortuous, disfigured, out of shape

<< OPPOSITE straight

2 STOOPED, bowed, arched, hunched

▷ *noun* INCLINATION, ability, taste, facility, talent, leaning, tendency, preference, faculty, forte, flair, knack, penchant, bag (*slang*), propensity, aptitude, predisposition, predilection, proclivity, turn of mind

▷▷ **bent on** INTENT ON, set on, fixed on, predisposed to, resolved on, insistent on

bequeath *verb* 1 LEAVE, will, give, grant, commit, transmit, hand down, endow, bestow, entrust, leave to by will

2 GIVE, offer, accord, grant, afford, contribute, yield, lend, pass on, transmit, confer, bestow, impart

bequest *noun* LEGACY, gift, settlement, heritage, trust, endowment, estate, inheritance, dower, bestowal, koha (NZ)

berate *verb* SCOLD, rebuke, reprimand, reproach, blast, carpet (*informal*), put down, criticize, slate (*informal, chiefly Brit*), censure, castigate, revile, chide, harangue, tear into (*informal*), tell off (*informal*), rail at, read the riot act to, reprove, upbraid, slap on the wrist, lambast(e), bawl out (*informal*), excoriate, rap over the knuckles, chew out (*US & Canad informal*), tear (someone) off a strip (*Brit informal*), give a rocket (*Brit & NZ informal*), vituperate

<< OPPOSITE praise

bereavement *noun* LOSS, death, misfortune, deprivation, affliction, tribulation

bereft *adjective* ▷▷ **bereft of** DEPRIVED OF, without, minus, lacking in, devoid of, cut off from, parted from, sans (*archaic*), robbed of, empty of, denuded of

berg *noun* (*S African*) MOUNTAIN, peak, mount, height, ben (*Scot*), horn, ridge, fell (*Brit*), alp, pinnacle, elevation, eminence

berserk *adjective* CRAZY, wild, mad, frantic, ape (*slang*), insane, barro (*Austral slang*), off the air (*Austral slang*), porangi (NZ)

berth *noun* 1 BUNK, bed, cot (*Nautical*), hammock, billet

2 (*Nautical*) ANCHORAGE, haven, slip, port, harbour, dock, pier, wharf, quay

▷ *verb* (*Nautical*) ANCHOR, land, dock, moor, tie up, drop anchor

beseech *verb* BEG, ask, petition, call upon, plead with, solicit, implore, entreat, importune, adjure, supplicate

beset *verb* PLAGUE, trouble, embarrass, torture, haunt, torment, harass, afflict, badger, perplex, pester, vex, entangle, bedevil

besetting *adjective* CHRONIC, persistent, long-standing, prevalent, habitual, ingrained, deep-seated, incurable, deep-rooted, inveterate, incorrigible, ineradicable

beside *preposition* NEXT TO, near, close to, neighbouring, alongside, overlooking, next door to, adjacent to, at the side of, abreast of, cheek by jowl with

▷▷ **beside yourself** DISTRAUGHT, desperate, mad, distressed, frantic, frenzied, hysterical, insane, crazed, demented, unbalanced, uncontrolled, deranged, berserk, delirious, unhinged, very anxious, overwrought, apoplectic, out of your mind, at the end of your tether

> People occasionally confuse *beside* and *besides*. *Besides* is used for mentioning something that adds to what you have already said, for example: *I didn't feel like going and besides, I had nothing to wear*. *Beside* usually means *next to or at the side of something or someone*, for example: *he was standing beside me* (not *besides me*)

besides *preposition* APART FROM, barring, excepting, other than, excluding, as well (as), in addition to, over and above

▷ *adverb* ALSO, too, further, otherwise, in addition, as well, moreover, furthermore, what's more, into the bargain ▷ see **beside**

besiege *verb* 1 HARASS, worry, trouble, harry, bother, disturb, plague, hound, hassle (*informal*), badger, pester, importune, bend someone's ear (*informal*), give someone grief (*Brit & S African*), beleaguer

2 SURROUND, confine, enclose, blockade, encompass, beset, encircle, close in on, hem in, shut in, lay siege to, hedge in, environ, beleaguer, invest (*rare*)

besotted *adjective* INFATUATED, charmed, captivated, beguiled, doting, smitten, bewitched, bowled over (*informal*), spellbound, enamoured, hypnotized, swept off your feet

bespeak *verb* ENGAGE, solicit, prearrange, order beforehand

best *adjective* 1 FINEST, leading, chief, supreme, principal, first, foremost, superlative, pre-eminent, unsurpassed, most accomplished, most skilful, most excellent
2 MOST FITTING, right, most desirable, most apt, most advantageous, most correct
▷ *noun* UTMOST, most, greatest, hardest, highest endeavour
▷ *adverb* MOST HIGHLY, most fully, most deeply
▷▷ **the best** THE FINEST, the pick, the choice, the flower, the cream, the elite, the crème de la crème (*French*)

bestow *verb* PRESENT, give, accord, award, grant, commit, hand out, lavish, confer, endow, entrust, impart, allot, honour with, apportion
<< OPPOSITE obtain

bestseller *noun* SUCCESS, hit (*informal*), winner, smash (*informal*), belter (*slang*), sensation, blockbuster (*informal*), wow (*slang*), market leader, smash hit (*informal*), chart-topper (*informal*), runaway success, number one
<< OPPOSITE failure

bestselling *adjective* SUCCESSFUL, top, hit (*informal*), smash (*informal*), flourishing, lucrative, smash-hit (*informal*), chart-topping (*informal*), moneymaking, number one, highly successful

bet *verb* GAMBLE, chance, stake, venture, hazard, speculate, punt (*chiefly Brit*), wager, put money, risk money, pledge money, put your shirt
▷ *noun* GAMBLE, risk, stake, venture, pledge, speculation, hazard, flutter (*informal*), ante, punt, wager, long shot

betray *verb* 1 BE DISLOYAL TO, break with, grass on (*Brit slang*), dob in (*Austral slang*), double-cross (*informal*), stab in the back, be unfaithful to, sell down the river (*informal*), grass up (*slang*), shop (*slang, chiefly Brit*), put the finger on (*informal*), inform on *or* against
2 GIVE AWAY, tell, show, reveal, expose, disclose, uncover, manifest, divulge, blurt out, unmask, lay bare, tell on, let slip, evince

betrayal *noun* DISLOYALTY, sell-out (*informal*), deception, treason, treachery, trickery, duplicity, double-cross (*informal*), double-dealing, breach of trust, perfidy, unfaithfulness, falseness, inconstancy
<< OPPOSITE loyalty

better *adverb* 1 TO A GREATER DEGREE, more completely, more thoroughly
2 IN A MORE EXCELLENT MANNER, more effectively, more attractively, more advantageously, more competently, in a superior way
<< OPPOSITE worse
▷ *adjective* 1 WELL, stronger, improving, progressing, recovering, healthier, cured, mending, fitter, fully recovered, on the mend (*informal*), more healthy, less ill
<< OPPOSITE worse
2 SUPERIOR, finer, worthier, higher-quality, surpassing, preferable, more appropriate, more useful, more valuable, more suitable, more desirable, streets ahead, more fitting, more expert
<< OPPOSITE inferior
▷ *verb* 1 BEAT, top, exceed, excel, surpass, outstrip, outdo, improve on *or* upon, cap (*informal*)
2 IMPROVE, forward, reform, advance, promote, correct, amend, mend, rectify, augment, ameliorate, meliorate
▷▷ **get the better of someone** DEFEAT, beat, surpass, triumph over, outdo, trounce, outwit, best, subjugate, prevail over, outsmart (*informal*), get the upper hand over, score off, run rings around (*informal*), wipe the floor with (*informal*), make mincemeat of (*informal*), blow out of the water (*slang*)

betterment *noun* IMPROVEMENT, gain, advancement, enhancement, edification, amelioration, melioration

between *preposition* AMIDST, among, mid, in the middle of, betwixt
>> RELATED WORD *prefix* inter-

After *distribute* and words with a similar meaning, *among* should be used rather than *between*: *share out the sweets among the children* (not *between the children*, unless there are only two children)

beverage *noun* DRINK, liquid, liquor, refreshment, draught, bevvy (*dialect*), libation (*facetious*), thirst quencher, potable, potation

beverage room *noun* (*Canad*) TAVERN, inn, bar, pub (*informal, chiefly Brit*), public house, watering hole (*facetious slang*), boozer (*Brit, Austral & NZ informal*), beer parlour (*Canad*), hostelry, alehouse (*archaic*), taproom

bevy *noun* GROUP, company, set, party, band, crowd, troop, pack, collection, gathering, gang, bunch (*informal*), cluster, congregation, clump, troupe, posse (*slang*), clique, coterie, assemblage

beware *verb* 1 BE CAREFUL, look out, watch out, be wary, be cautious, take heed, guard against something
2 AVOID, mind, shun, refrain from, steer clear of, guard against

bewilder *verb* CONFOUND, surprise, stun, confuse, puzzle, baffle, mix up, daze, perplex, mystify, stupefy, befuddle, flummox, bemuse, dumbfound, nonplus, flabbergast (*informal*)

bewildered *adjective* CONFUSED, surprised, stunned, puzzled, uncertain, startled, baffled, at sea, awed, muddled, dizzy, dazed, perplexed, disconcerted, at a loss, mystified, taken aback, speechless, giddy, disorientated, bamboozled (*informal*), nonplussed, flummoxed, at sixes and sevens, thrown off balance, discombobulated (*informal, chiefly US & Canad*)

bewildering *adjective* CONFUSING, surprising, amazing, stunning, puzzling, astonishing, staggering, baffling, astounding, perplexing, mystifying, stupefying

bewitch *verb* ENCHANT, attract, charm, fascinate, absorb, entrance, captivate, beguile, allure, ravish, mesmerize, hypnotize, cast a spell on, enrapture, spellbind

<< OPPOSITE repulse

bewitched *adjective* ENCHANTED, charmed, transformed, fascinated, entranced, possessed, captivated, enthralled, beguiled, ravished, spellbound, mesmerized, enamoured, hypnotized, enraptured, under a spell

beyond *preposition* 1 ON THE OTHER SIDE OF, outwith (*Scot*)

2 AFTER, over, past, above

3 PAST, outwith (*Scot*)

4 EXCEPT FOR, but, save, apart from, other than, excluding, besides, aside from

5 EXCEEDING, surpassing, superior to, out of reach of

6 OUTSIDE, over, above, outwith (*Scot*)

bias *noun* 1 PREJUDICE, leaning, bent, tendency, inclination, penchant, intolerance, bigotry, propensity, favouritism, predisposition, nepotism, unfairness, predilection, proclivity, partiality, narrow-mindedness, proneness, one-sidedness

<< OPPOSITE impartiality

2 SLANT, cross, angle, diagonal line

▷ *verb* INFLUENCE, colour, weight, prejudice, distort, sway, warp, slant, predispose

biased *adjective* PREJUDICED, weighted, one-sided, partial, distorted, swayed, warped, slanted, embittered, predisposed, jaundiced

bicker *verb* QUARREL, fight, argue, row (*informal*), clash, dispute, scrap (*informal*), disagree, fall out (*informal*), squabble, spar, wrangle, cross swords, fight like cat and dog, go at it hammer and tongs, altercate

<< OPPOSITE agree

bid *noun* 1 ATTEMPT, try, effort, venture, undertaking, go (*informal*), shot (*informal*), stab (*informal*), crack (*informal*), endeavour

2 OFFER, price, attempt, amount, advance, proposal, sum, tender, proposition, submission

▷ *verb* 1 MAKE AN OFFER, offer, propose, submit, tender, proffer

2 WISH, say, call, tell, greet

3 TELL, call, ask, order, charge, require, direct, desire, invite, command, summon, instruct, solicit, enjoin

bidding *noun* 1 ORDER, call, charge, demand, request, command, instruction, invitation, canon, beck, injunction, summons, behest, beck and call

2 OFFER, proposal, auction, tender

big *adjective* 1 LARGE, great, huge, giant, massive, vast, enormous, considerable, substantial, extensive, immense, spacious, gigantic, monumental, mammoth, bulky, burly, colossal, stellar (*informal*), prodigious, hulking, ponderous, voluminous, elephantine, ginormous (*informal*), humongous *or* humungous (*US slang*), sizable *or* sizeable

<< OPPOSITE small

2 IMPORTANT, serious, significant, grave, urgent, paramount, big-time (*informal*), far-reaching, momentous, major league (*informal*), weighty

<< OPPOSITE unimportant

3 POWERFUL, important, prime, principal, prominent, dominant, influential, paramount, eminent, puissant, skookum (*Canad*)

4 GROWN-UP, adult, grown, mature, elder, full-grown

<< OPPOSITE young

5 GENEROUS, good, princely, noble, heroic, gracious, benevolent, disinterested, altruistic, unselfish, magnanimous, big-hearted

bighead *noun* (*informal*) BOASTER, know-all (*informal*), swaggerer, self-seeker, egomaniac, egotist, braggart, braggadocio, narcissist, swell-head (*informal*), blowhard (*informal*), self-admirer, figjam (*Austral slang*)

bigheaded *adjective* BOASTFUL, arrogant, swaggering, bragging, cocky, vaunting, conceited, puffed-up, bumptious, immodest, crowing, overconfident, vainglorious, swollen-headed, egotistic, full of yourself, too big for your boots *or* breeches

bigot *noun* FANATIC, racist, extremist, sectarian, maniac, fiend (*informal*), zealot, persecutor, dogmatist

bigoted *adjective* INTOLERANT, twisted, prejudiced, biased, warped, sectarian, dogmatic, opinionated, narrow-minded, obstinate, illiberal

<< OPPOSITE tolerant

bigotry *noun* INTOLERANCE, discrimination, racism, prejudice, bias, ignorance, injustice, sexism, unfairness, fanaticism, sectarianism, racialism, dogmatism, provincialism, narrow-mindedness, mindlessness, pig-ignorance (*slang*)

<< OPPOSITE tolerance

bigwig *noun* (*informal*) IMPORTANT PERSON, somebody, celebrity, heavyweight (*informal*), notable, big name, mogul, big gun (*informal*), dignitary, celeb (*informal*), big shot (*informal*),

personage, nob (*slang*), big cheese (*old-fashioned slang*), big noise (*informal*), big hitter (*informal*), heavy hitter (*informal*), panjandrum, notability, V.I.P.
<< OPPOSITE nonentity

bile *noun* BITTERNESS, anger, hostility, resentment, animosity, venom, irritability, spleen, acrimony, pique, nastiness, rancour, virulence, asperity, ill humour, irascibility, peevishness, churlishness

bill[1] *noun* **1** CHARGES, rate, costs, score, account, damage (*informal*), statement, reckoning, expense, tally, invoice, note of charge
2 ACT OF PARLIAMENT, measure, proposal, piece of legislation, projected law
3 LIST, listing, programme, card, schedule, agenda, catalogue, inventory, roster, syllabus
4 ADVERTISEMENT, notice, poster, leaflet, bulletin, circular, handout, placard, handbill, playbill
▷ *verb* **1** CHARGE, debit, invoice, send a statement to, send an invoice to
2 ADVERTISE, post, announce, push (*informal*), declare, promote, plug (*informal*), proclaim, tout, flaunt, publicize, crack up (*informal*), give advance notice of

bill[2] *noun* BEAK, nib, neb (*archaic* or *dialect*), mandible

billet *verb* QUARTER, post, station, locate, install, accommodate, berth, garrison
▷ *noun* QUARTERS, accommodation, lodging, barracks

billow *verb* SURGE, roll, expand, swell, balloon, belly, bulge, dilate, puff up, bloat
▷ *noun* SURGE, wave, flow, rush, flood, cloud, gush, deluge, upsurge, outpouring, uprush

bind *verb* **1** OBLIGE, make, force, require, engage, compel, prescribe, constrain, necessitate, impel, obligate
2 TIE, unite, join, stick, secure, attach, wrap, rope, knot, strap, lash, glue, tie up, hitch, paste, fasten, truss, make fast
<< OPPOSITE untie
3 RESTRICT, limit, handicap, confine, detain, restrain, hamper, inhibit, hinder, impede, hem in, keep within bounds *or* limits
4 FUSE, join, stick, bond, cement, adhere
5 BANDAGE, cover, dress, wrap, swathe, encase
▷ *noun* (*informal*) NUISANCE, inconvenience, hassle (*informal*), drag (*informal*), spot (*informal*), difficulty, bore, dilemma, pest, hot water (*informal*), uphill (*S African*), predicament, annoyance, quandary, pain in the neck (*informal*), pain in the backside, pain in the butt (*informal*)

binding *adjective* COMPULSORY, necessary, mandatory, imperative, obligatory, conclusive, irrevocable, unalterable, indissoluble
<< OPPOSITE optional

binge *noun* (*informal*) BOUT, session, spell, fling, feast, stint, spree, orgy, bender (*informal*), jag (*slang*), beano (*Brit slang*), blind (*slang*)

biography *noun* LIFE STORY, life, record, account, profile, memoir, CV, life history, curriculum vitae

bird *noun* FEATHERED FRIEND, fowl, songbird
>> RELATED WORD *adjective* avian
>> RELATED WORD *male* cock
>> RELATED WORD *female* hen
>> RELATED WORDS *young* chick, fledg(e)ling, nestling
>> RELATED WORDS *collective nouns* flock, flight
>> RELATED WORD *habitation* nest

birth *noun* **1** CHILDBIRTH, delivery, nativity, parturition
<< OPPOSITE death
2 BEGINNING, start, rise, source, origin, emergence, outset, genesis, initiation, inauguration, inception, commencement, fountainhead
3 ANCESTRY, line, race, stock, blood, background, breeding, strain, descent, pedigree, extraction, lineage, forebears, parentage, genealogy, derivation
>> RELATED WORD *adjective* natal

bisect *verb* CUT IN TWO, cross, separate, split, halve, cut across, intersect, cut in half, split down the middle, divide in two, bifurcate

bisexual *adjective* BI (*slang*), ambidextrous (*slang*), swinging both ways (*slang*), AC/DC (*slang*)

bit[1] *noun* **1** SLICE, segment, fragment, crumb, mouthful, small piece, morsel
2 PIECE, scrap, small piece
3 JOT, whit, tittle, iota
4 PART, moment, period
5 LITTLE WHILE, time, second, minute, moment, spell, instant, tick (*Brit informal*), jiffy (*informal*)

bit[2] *noun* CURB, check, brake, restraint, snaffle

bitchy *adjective* (*informal*) SPITEFUL, mean, nasty, cruel, vicious, malicious, barbed, vindictive, malevolent, venomous, snide, rancorous, catty (*informal*), backbiting, shrewish, ill-natured, vixenish, snarky (*informal*)
<< OPPOSITE nice

bite *verb* **1** NIP, cut, tear, wound, grip, snap, crush, rend, pierce, champ, pinch, chew, crunch, clamp, nibble, gnaw, masticate
2 EAT, burn, smart, sting, erode, tingle, eat away, corrode, wear away
▷ *noun* **1** SNACK, food, piece, taste, refreshment, mouthful, morsel, titbit, light meal
2 WOUND, sting, pinch, nip, prick
3 EDGE, interest, force, punch (*informal*), sting, zest, sharpness, keenness, pungency,

incisiveness, acuteness
4 KICK (*informal*), edge, punch (*informal*), spice, relish, zest, tang, sharpness, piquancy, pungency, spiciness

biting *adjective* 1 PIERCING, cutting, cold, sharp, freezing, frozen, bitter, raw, chill, harsh, penetrating, arctic, nipping, icy, blighting, chilly, wintry, gelid, cold as ice
2 SARCASTIC, cutting, sharp, severe, stinging, withering, scathing, acrimonious, incisive, virulent, caustic, vitriolic, trenchant, mordant, mordacious

bitter *adjective* 1 GRIEVOUS, hard, severe, distressing, fierce, harsh, cruel, savage, ruthless, dire, relentless, poignant, ferocious, galling, unrelenting, merciless, remorseless, gut-wrenching, vexatious, hard-hearted
<< OPPOSITE pleasant
2 RESENTFUL, hurt, wounded, angry, offended, sour, put out, sore, choked, crabbed, acrimonious, aggrieved, sullen, miffed (*informal*), embittered, begrudging, peeved (*informal*), piqued, rancorous
<< OPPOSITE happy
3 FREEZING, biting, severe, intense, raw, fierce, chill, stinging, penetrating, arctic, icy, polar, Siberian, glacial, wintry
<< OPPOSITE mild
4 SOUR, biting, sharp, acid, harsh, unpleasant, tart, astringent, acrid, unsweetened, vinegary, acidulated, acerb
<< OPPOSITE sweet

bitterly *adverb* 1 RESENTFULLY, sourly, sorely, tartly, grudgingly, sullenly, testily, acrimoniously, caustically, mordantly, irascibly
2 INTENSELY, freezing, severely, fiercely, icy, bitingly

bitterness *noun* 1 RESENTMENT, hurt, anger, hostility, indignation, animosity, venom, acrimony, pique, rancour, ill feeling, bad blood, ill will, umbrage, vexation, asperity
2 SOURNESS, acidity, sharpness, tartness, acerbity, vinegariness

bizarre *adjective* STRANGE, odd, unusual, extraordinary, fantastic, curious, weird, way-out (*informal*), peculiar, eccentric, abnormal, ludicrous, queer (*informal*), irregular, rum (*Brit slang*), uncommon, singular, grotesque, perplexing, uncanny, mystifying, off-the-wall (*slang*), outlandish, comical, oddball (*informal*), off the rails, zany, unaccountable, off-beat, left-field (*informal*), freakish, wacko (*slang*), outré, cockamamie (*slang, chiefly US*), daggy (*Austral & NZ informal*)
<< OPPOSITE normal

black *adjective* 1 DARK, raven, ebony, sable, jet, dusky, pitch-black, inky, swarthy, stygian, coal-black, pitchy, murky
<< OPPOSITE light
2 GLOOMY, sad, depressing, distressing, horrible, grim, bleak, hopeless, dismal, ominous, sombre, morbid, mournful, morose, lugubrious, joyless, funereal, doleful, cheerless
<< OPPOSITE happy
3 TERRIBLE, bad, devastating, tragic, fatal, unfortunate, dreadful, destructive, unlucky, harmful, adverse, dire, catastrophic, hapless, detrimental, untoward, ruinous, calamitous, cataclysmic, ill-starred, unpropitious, ill-fated, cataclysmal
4 WICKED, bad, evil, corrupt, vicious, immoral, depraved, debased, amoral, villainous, unprincipled, nefarious, dissolute, iniquitous, irreligious, impious, unrighteous
<< OPPOSITE good
5 ANGRY, cross, furious, hostile, sour, menacing, moody, resentful, glowering, sulky, baleful, louring *or* lowering
<< OPPOSITE happy
6 DIRTY, soiled, stained, filthy, muddy, blackened, grubby, dingy, grimy, sooty, mucky, scuzzy (*slang, chiefly US*), begrimed, festy (*Austral slang*), mud-encrusted, miry
<< OPPOSITE clean
▷▷ **black out** PASS OUT, drop, collapse, faint, swoon, lose consciousness, keel over (*informal*), flake out (*informal*), become unconscious
▷▷ **black something out** DARKEN, cover, shade, conceal, obscure, eclipse, dim, blacken, obfuscate, make dark, make darker, make dim
▷▷ **in the black** IN CREDIT, solid, solvent, in funds, financially sound, without debt, unindebted

> When referring to people with dark skin, the adjective *black* or *Black* is used. For people of the US whose origins lie in Africa, the preferred term is *African American*

blacken *verb* 1 DARKEN, deepen, grow black
2 MAKE DARK, shadow, shade, obscure, overshadow, make darker, make dim
3 DISCREDIT, stain, disgrace, smear, knock (*informal*), degrade, rubbish (*informal*), taint, tarnish, censure, slur, slag (off) (*slang*), malign, reproach, denigrate, disparage, decry, vilify, slander, sully, dishonour, defile, defame, bad-mouth (*slang, chiefly US & Canad*), traduce, bring into disrepute, smirch, calumniate

blacklist *verb* EXCLUDE, bar, ban, reject, rule out, veto, boycott, embargo, expel, vote against, preclude, disallow, repudiate, proscribe, ostracize, debar, blackball

black magic *noun* WITCHCRAFT, magic, witching, voodoo, the occult, wizardry, enchantment, sorcery, occultism, incantation, black art, witchery, necromancy, diabolism, sortilege, makutu (NZ)

blackmail *noun* THREAT, intimidation, ransom, compulsion, protection (*informal*), coercion, extortion, pay-off (*informal*), shakedown, hush money (*slang*), exaction
▷ *verb* THREATEN, force, squeeze, compel, exact, intimidate, wring, coerce, milk, wrest, dragoon, extort, bleed (*informal*), press-gang, hold to ransom

blackness *noun* DARKNESS, shade, gloom, dusk, obscurity, nightfall, murk, dimness, murkiness, duskiness, shadiness, melanism, swarthiness, inkiness, nigrescence, nigritude (*rare*)
<< OPPOSITE light

blackout *noun* **1** NONCOMMUNICATION, secrecy, censorship, suppression, radio silence
2 POWER CUT, power failure
3 UNCONSCIOUSNESS, collapse, faint, oblivion, swoon (*literary*), loss of consciousness, syncope (*Pathology*)

black sheep *noun* DISGRACE, rebel, maverick, outcast, renegade, dropout, prodigal, individualist, nonconformist, ne'er-do-well, reprobate, wastrel, bad egg (*old-fashioned informal*)

blame *verb* **1** HOLD RESPONSIBLE, accuse, denounce, indict, impeach, incriminate, impute, recriminate, point a *or* the finger at
<< OPPOSITE absolve
2 ATTRIBUTE TO, credit to, assign to, put down to, impute to
3 (used in negative constructions) CRITICIZE, charge, tax, blast, condemn, put down, disapprove of, censure, reproach, chide, admonish, tear into (*informal*), find fault with, reprove, upbraid, lambast(e), reprehend, express disapprobation of
<< OPPOSITE praise
▷ *noun* RESPONSIBILITY, liability, rap (*slang*), accountability, onus, culpability, answerability
<< OPPOSITE praise

blameless *adjective* INNOCENT, clear, clean, upright, stainless, honest, immaculate, impeccable, virtuous, faultless, squeaky-clean, unblemished, unsullied, uninvolved, unimpeachable, untarnished, above suspicion, irreproachable, guiltless, unspotted, unoffending
<< OPPOSITE guilty

blanch *verb* TURN PALE, fade, pale, drain, bleach, wan, whiten, go white, become pallid, become *or* grow white

bland *adjective* **1** DULL, boring, weak, plain, flat, commonplace, tedious, vanilla (*informal*), dreary, tiresome, monotonous, run-of-the-mill, uninspiring, humdrum, unimaginative, uninteresting, insipid, unexciting, ho-hum (*informal*), vapid, unstimulating, undistinctive
<< OPPOSITE exciting
2 TASTELESS, weak, watered-down, insipid, flavourless, thin, unstimulating, undistinctive

blank *adjective* **1** UNMARKED, white, clear, clean, empty, plain, bare, void, spotless, unfilled, uncompleted
<< OPPOSITE marked
2 EXPRESSIONLESS, empty, dull, vague, hollow, vacant, lifeless, deadpan, straight-faced, vacuous, impassive, inscrutable, inane, wooden, poker-faced (*informal*)
<< OPPOSITE expressive
3 PUZZLED, lost, confused, stumped, doubtful, baffled, stuck, at sea, bewildered, muddled, mixed up, confounded, perplexed, disconcerted, at a loss, mystified, clueless, dumbfounded, nonplussed, uncomprehending, flummoxed
4 ABSOLUTE, complete, total, utter, outright, thorough, downright, consummate, unqualified, out and out, unmitigated, unmixed
▷ *noun* **1** EMPTY SPACE, space, gap
2 VOID, vacuum, vacancy, emptiness, nothingness, vacuity, tabula rasa

blanket *noun* **1** COVER, rug, coverlet, afghan
2 COVERING, cover, bed, sheet, coating, coat, layer, film, carpet, cloak, mantle, thickness
▷ *verb* COAT, cover, hide, surround, cloud, mask, conceal, obscure, eclipse, cloak
▷ *adjective* COMPREHENSIVE, full, complete, wide, sweeping, broad, extensive, wide-ranging, thorough, inclusive, exhaustive, all-inclusive, all-embracing

blare *verb* BLAST, scream, boom, roar, thunder, trumpet, resound, hoot, toot, reverberate, sound out, honk, clang, peal

blarney *noun* FLATTERY, coaxing, exaggeration, fawning, adulation, wheedling, spiel, sweet talk (*informal*), flannel (*Brit informal*), soft soap (*informal*), sycophancy, servility, obsequiousness, cajolery, blandishment, fulsomeness, toadyism, overpraise, false praise, honeyed words

blasé *adjective* NONCHALANT, cool, bored, distant, regardless, detached, weary, indifferent, careless, lukewarm, glutted, jaded, unmoved, unconcerned, impervious, uncaring, uninterested, apathetic, offhand, world-weary, heedless, satiated, unexcited, surfeited, cloyed
<< OPPOSITE interested

blasphemous *adjective* IRREVERENT, cheeky (*informal*), contemptuous, profane, disrespectful, godless, ungodly, sacrilegious, irreligious, impious
<< OPPOSITE reverent

blasphemy *noun* IRREVERENCE, swearing, cursing, indignity (*to God*), desecration, sacrilege, profanity, impiety, profanation, execration, profaneness, impiousness

blast *noun* 1 EXPLOSION, crash, burst, discharge, blow-up, eruption, detonation
2 GUST, rush, storm, breeze, puff, gale, flurry, tempest, squall, strong breeze
3 BLARE, blow, scream, trumpet, wail, resound, clamour, hoot, toot, honk, clang, peal
▷ *verb* 1 BLOW UP, bomb, destroy, burst, ruin, break up, explode, shatter, demolish, rupture, dynamite, put paid to, blow sky-high
2 CRITICIZE, attack, put down, censure, berate, castigate, tear into (*informal*), flay, rail at, lambast(e), chew out (*US & Canad informal*)

blasted *adjective* (*Slang*) DAMNED (*chiefly US*), confounded, hateful, infernal, detestable

blastoff *noun* LAUNCH, launching, take off, discharge, projection, lift-off, propelling, sendoff

blatant *adjective* OBVIOUS, open, clear, plain, naked, sheer, patent, evident, pronounced, straightforward, outright, glaring, manifest, bald, transparent, noticeable, conspicuous, overt, unmistakable, flaunting, palpable, undeniable, brazen, flagrant, indisputable, ostentatious, unmitigated, cut-and-dried (*informal*), undisguised, obtrusive, unsubtle, unconcealed
<< OPPOSITE subtle

blaze *verb* 1 BURN, glow, flare, flicker, be on fire, go up in flames, be ablaze, fire, flash, flame
2 SHINE, flash, beam, glow, flare, glare, gleam, shimmer, radiate
3 FLARE UP, rage, boil, explode, fume, seethe, be livid, be incandescent
▷ *noun* 1 INFERNO, fire, flames, bonfire, combustion, conflagration
2 FLASH, glow, glitter, flare, glare, gleam, brilliance, radiance

bleach *verb* LIGHTEN, wash out, blanch, peroxide, whiten, blench, etiolate

bleak *adjective* 1 DISMAL, black, dark, depressing, grim, discouraging, gloomy, hopeless, dreary, sombre, unpromising, disheartening, joyless, cheerless, comfortless
<< OPPOSITE cheerful
2 EXPOSED, open, empty, raw, bare, stark, barren, desolate, gaunt, windswept, weather-beaten, unsheltered
<< OPPOSITE sheltered
3 STORMY, cold, severe, bitter, rough, harsh, chilly, windy, tempestuous, intemperate

bleary *adjective* DIM, blurred, fogged, murky, fuzzy, watery, misty, hazy, foggy, blurry, ill-defined, indistinct, rheumy

bleed *verb* 1 LOSE BLOOD, flow, weep, trickle, gush, exude, spurt, shed blood
2 BLEND, run, meet, unite, mix, combine, flow, fuse, mingle, converge, ooze, seep, amalgamate, meld, intermix
3 (*informal*) EXTORT, milk, squeeze, drain, exhaust, fleece

blemish *noun* 1 MARK, line, spot, scratch, bruise, scar, blur, defect, flaw, blot, smudge, imperfection, speck, blotch, disfigurement, pock, smirch
<< OPPOSITE perfection
2 DEFECT, fault, weakness, stain, disgrace, deficiency, shortcoming, taint, inadequacy, dishonour, demerit
▷ *verb* DISHONOUR, mark, damage, spot, injure, ruin, mar, spoil, stain, blur, disgrace, impair, taint, tarnish, blot, smudge, disfigure, sully, deface, blotch, besmirch, smirch
<< OPPOSITE enhance

blend *verb* 1 MIX, join, combine, compound, incorporate, merge, put together, fuse, unite, mingle, alloy, synthesize, amalgamate, interweave, coalesce, intermingle, meld, intermix, commingle, commix
2 GO WELL, match, fit, suit, go with, correspond, complement, coordinate, tone in, harmonize, cohere
3 COMBINE, mix, link, integrate, merge, put together, fuse, unite, synthesize, marry, amalgamate
▷ *noun* MIXTURE, cross, mix, combination, compound, brew, composite, union, fusion, synthesis, alloy, medley, concoction, amalgam, amalgamation, meld, mélange (*French*), conglomeration, admixture

bless *verb* 1 SANCTIFY, dedicate, ordain, exalt, anoint, consecrate, hallow, invoke happiness on
<< OPPOSITE curse
2 ENDOW, give to, provide for, grant for, favour, grace, bestow to
<< OPPOSITE afflict
3 PRAISE, thank, worship, glorify, magnify, exalt, extol, pay homage to, give thanks to

blessed *adjective* 1 ENDOWED, supplied, granted, favoured, lucky, fortunate, furnished, bestowed, jammy (*Brit slang*)
2 HAPPY, contented, glad, merry, heartening, joyous, joyful, blissful
3 HOLY, sacred, divine, adored, revered, hallowed, sanctified, beatified

blessing *noun* 1 BENEFIT, help, service, profit, gain, advantage, favour, gift, windfall, kindness, boon, good fortune, bounty, godsend, manna from heaven
<< OPPOSITE disadvantage
2 APPROVAL, backing, support, agreement, regard, favour, sanction, go-ahead (*informal*), permission, leave, consent, mandate, endorsement, green light, ratification, assent,

authorization, good wishes, acquiescence, approbation, concurrence, O.K. *or* okay (*informal*)
<< OPPOSITE disapproval
3 BENEDICTION, grace, dedication, thanksgiving, invocation, commendation, consecration, benison
<< OPPOSITE curse

blight *noun* 1 CURSE, suffering, evil, depression, corruption, distress, pollution, misery, plague, hardship, woe, misfortune, contamination, adversity, scourge, affliction, bane, wretchedness
<< OPPOSITE blessing
2 DISEASE, plague, pest, fungus, contamination, mildew, contagion, infestation, pestilence, canker, cancer
▷ *verb* FRUSTRATE, destroy, ruin, crush, mar, dash, wreck, spoil, crool *or* cruel (*Austral slang*), scar, undo, mess up, annihilate, nullify, put a damper on

blind *adjective* 1 SIGHTLESS, unsighted, unseeing, eyeless, visionless, stone-blind
<< OPPOSITE sighted
2 *usually followed by* **to** UNAWARE OF, unconscious of, deaf to, ignorant of, indifferent to, insensitive to, oblivious of, unconcerned about, inconsiderate of, neglectful of, heedless of, insensible of, unmindful of, disregardful of
<< OPPOSITE aware
3 UNQUESTIONING, prejudiced, wholesale, indiscriminate, uncritical, unreasoning, undiscriminating
4 HIDDEN, concealed, obscured, dim, unseen, tucked away
<< OPPOSITE open
5 DEAD-END, closed, dark, obstructed, leading nowhere, without exit
6 UNTHINKING, wild, violent, rash, reckless, irrational, hasty, senseless, mindless, uncontrollable, uncontrolled, unchecked, impetuous, intemperate, unconstrained ▷ see **disabled**

blinding *adjective* 1 BRIGHT, brilliant, intense, shining, glowing, blazing, dazzling, vivid, glaring, gleaming, beaming, effulgent, bedazzling
2 AMAZING, striking, surprising, stunning, impressive, astonishing, staggering, sensational (*informal*), breathtaking, wondrous (*archaic* or *literary*), jaw-dropping, gee-whizz (*slang*)

blindly *adverb* 1 THOUGHTLESSLY, carelessly, recklessly, indiscriminately, unreasonably, impulsively, senselessly, heedlessly, regardlessly
2 WILDLY, aimlessly, madly, frantically, confusedly

blink *verb* 1 FLUTTER, wink, bat
2 FLASH, flicker, sparkle, wink, shimmer, twinkle, glimmer, scintillate
▷▷ **on the blink** (*Slang*) NOT WORKING (PROPERLY), faulty, defective, playing up, out of action, malfunctioning, out of order, on the fritz (*US slang*)

blinkered *adjective* NARROW-MINDED, narrow, one-sided, prejudiced, biased, partial, discriminatory, parochial, constricted, insular, hidebound, one-eyed, lopsided
<< OPPOSITE broad-minded

bliss *noun* 1 JOY, ecstasy, euphoria, rapture, nirvana, felicity, gladness, blissfulness, delight, pleasure, heaven, satisfaction, happiness, paradise
<< OPPOSITE misery
2 BEATITUDE, ecstasy, exaltation, blessedness, felicity, holy joy

blissful *adjective* 1 DELIGHTFUL, pleasing, satisfying, heavenly (*informal*), enjoyable, gratifying, pleasurable
2 HAPPY, joyful, satisfied, ecstatic, joyous, euphoric, rapturous

blister *noun* SORE, boil, swelling, cyst, pimple, wen, blain, carbuncle, pustule, bleb, furuncle (*Pathology*)

blitz *noun* ATTACK, strike, assault, raid, offensive, onslaught, bombardment, bombing campaign, blitzkrieg

blizzard *noun* SNOWSTORM, storm, tempest

bloated *adjective* 1 PUFFED UP, swollen
<< OPPOSITE shrivelled
2 TOO FULL

blob *noun* DROP, ball, mass, pearl, lump, bead, dab, droplet, globule, glob, dewdrop

bloc *noun* GROUP, union, league, ring, alliance, coalition, axis, combine

block *noun* 1 PIECE, bar, square, mass, cake, brick, lump, chunk, cube, hunk, nugget, ingot
2 OBSTRUCTION, bar, barrier, obstacle, impediment, hindrance
▷ *verb* 1 OBSTRUCT, close, stop, cut off, plug, choke, clog, shut off, stop up, bung up (*informal*)
<< OPPOSITE clear
2 OBSCURE, bar, cut off, interrupt, obstruct, get in the way of, shut off
3 SHUT OFF, stop, bar, cut off, head off, hamper, obstruct, get in the way of

blockade *noun* STOPPAGE, block, barrier, restriction, obstacle, barricade, obstruction, impediment, hindrance, encirclement

blockage *noun* OBSTRUCTION, block, blocking, stoppage, impediment, occlusion

bloke *noun* (*informal*) MAN, person, individual, customer (*informal*), character (*informal*), guy (*informal*), fellow, punter (*informal*), chap, boy, bod (*informal*)

blonde *or* **blond** *adjective* 1 FAIR, light, light-coloured, flaxen

2 FAIR-HAIRED, golden-haired, tow-headed
blood *noun* 1 LIFEBLOOD, gore, vital fluid
2 FAMILY, relations, birth, descent, extraction, ancestry, lineage, kinship, kindred
▷▷ **bad blood** HOSTILITY, anger, offence, resentment, bitterness, animosity, antagonism, enmity, bad feeling, rancour, hard feelings, ill will, animus, dudgeon (*archaic*), disgruntlement, chip on your shoulder
bloodless *adjective* PALE, white, wan, sickly, pasty, colourless, pallid, anaemic, ashen, chalky, sallow, ashy, like death warmed up (*informal*)
bloodshed *noun* KILLING, murder, massacre, slaughter, slaying, carnage, butchery, blood-letting, blood bath
bloodthirsty *adjective* CRUEL, savage, brutal, vicious, ruthless, ferocious, murderous, heartless, inhuman, merciless, cut-throat, remorseless, warlike, barbarous, pitiless
bloody *adjective* 1 CRUEL, fierce, savage, brutal, vicious, ferocious, cut-throat, warlike, barbarous, sanguinary
2 BLOODSTAINED, raw, bleeding, blood-soaked, blood-spattered
bloody-minded *adjective* (*Brit informal*) DIFFICULT, contrary, annoying, awkward, unreasonable, stubborn, perverse, exasperating, intractable, unhelpful, obstructive, cussed (*informal*), uncooperative, disobliging
<< OPPOSITE helpful
bloom *noun* 1 FLOWER, bud, blossom
2 PRIME, flower, beauty, height, peak, flourishing, maturity, perfection, best days, heyday, zenith, full flowering
3 GLOW, flush, blush, freshness, lustre, radiance, rosiness
<< OPPOSITE pallor
▷ *verb* 1 FLOWER, blossom, open, bud
<< OPPOSITE wither
2 GROW, develop, wax
3 SUCCEED, flourish, thrive, prosper, fare well
<< OPPOSITE fail
blossom *noun* FLOWER, bloom, bud, efflorescence, floret
▷ *verb* 1 BLOOM, grow, develop, mature
2 SUCCEED, progress, thrive, flourish, prosper
3 FLOWER, bloom, bud
blot *noun* 1 DISGRACE, spot, fault, stain, scar, defect, flaw, taint, blemish, demerit, smirch, blot on your escutcheon
2 SPOT, mark, patch, smear, smudge, speck, blotch, splodge, stain
▷ *verb* SOAK UP, take up, absorb, dry up
▷▷ **blot something out** 1 OBLITERATE, hide, shadow, disguise, obscure, blur, eclipse, block out, efface, obfuscate
2 ERASE, cancel, excise, obliterate, expunge
blotch *noun* MARK, spot, patch, splash, stain, blot, smudge, blemish, splodge, smirch, smutch
blow[1] *verb* 1 MOVE, carry, drive, bear, sweep, fling, whisk, buffet, whirl, waft
2 BE CARRIED, hover, flutter, flit, flitter
3 EXHALE, breathe, pant, puff, breathe out, expel air
4 PLAY, sound, pipe, trumpet, blare, toot
▷▷ **blow over** DIE DOWN, end, pass, finish, cease, be forgotten, subside
▷▷ **blow someone away** 1 BOWL OVER, amaze, stun, stagger, astound, electrify (*informal*), stupefy, flabbergast
2 OPEN FIRE ON, kill, blast (*slang*), bring down, zap (*slang*), pick off, pump full of lead (*slang*)
▷▷ **blow something out** PUT OUT, extinguish, snuff out
▷▷ **blow something up** 1 EXPLODE, bomb, blast, dynamite, detonate, blow sky-high
2 INFLATE, pump up, fill, expand, swell, enlarge, puff up, distend
3 EXAGGERATE, heighten, enlarge on, inflate, embroider, magnify, amplify, overstate, embellish, blow out of (all) proportion, make a mountain out of a molehill, make a production out of, make a federal case of (*US informal*), hyperbolize
4 MAGNIFY, increase, extend, stretch, expand, widen, broaden, lengthen, amplify, elongate, dilate, make larger
▷▷ **blow up** 1 EXPLODE, burst, go off, shatter, erupt, detonate
2 (*informal*) LOSE YOUR TEMPER, rage, erupt, lose it (*informal*), crack up (*informal*), see red (*informal*), lose the plot (*informal*), become angry, go ballistic (*slang, chiefly US*), hit the roof (*informal*), blow a fuse (*slang, chiefly US*), fly off the handle (*informal*), become enraged, go off the deep end (*informal*), wig out (*slang*), go up the wall (*slang*), go crook (*Austral & NZ slang*), flip your lid (*slang*), blow your top
3 FLARE UP, widen, heighten, enlarge, broaden, magnify
▷▷ **blow your top** (*informal*) LOSE YOUR TEMPER, explode, blow up (*informal*), lose it (*informal*), see red (*informal*), lose the plot (*informal*), have a fit (*informal*), throw a tantrum, fly off the handle (*informal*), go spare (*Brit slang*), fly into a temper, flip your lid (*slang*), do your nut (*Brit slang*)
blow[2] *noun* 1 KNOCK, stroke, punch, belt (*informal*), bang, rap, bash (*informal*), sock (*slang*), smack, thump, buffet, clout (*informal*), whack (*informal*), wallop (*informal*), slosh (*Brit slang*), tonk (*informal*), clump (*slang*), clomp (*slang*)
2 SETBACK, shock, upset, disaster, reverse, disappointment, catastrophe, misfortune, jolt, bombshell, calamity, affliction, whammy

(*informal, chiefly US*), choker (*informal*), sucker punch, bummer (*slang*), bolt from the blue, comedown (*informal*)

blowout *noun* 1 (*Slang*) BINGE (*informal*), party, feast, rave (*Brit slang*), spree, beano (*Brit slang*), rave-up (*Brit slang*), carousal, carouse, hooley *or* hoolie (*chiefly Irish & NZ*)
2 PUNCTURE, burst, flat, flat tyre, flattie (NZ)

bludge *verb* (*Austral & NZ informal*) SLACK, skive (*Brit informal*), idle, shirk, gold-brick (*US slang*), bob off (*Brit slang*), scrimshank (*Brit Military slang*)

bludgeon *verb* 1 CLUB, batter, beat, strike, belt (*informal*), clobber (*slang*), pound, cosh (*Brit*), cudgel, beat *or* knock seven bells out of (*informal*)
2 BULLY, force, cow, intimidate, railroad (*informal*), hector, coerce, bulldoze (*informal*), dragoon, steamroller, browbeat, tyrannize
▷ *noun* CLUB, stick, baton, truncheon, cosh (*Brit*), cudgel, shillelagh, bastinado, mere (*NZ*), patu (*NZ*)

blue *adjective* 1 DEPRESSED, low, sad, unhappy, fed up, gloomy, dismal, melancholy, glum, dejected, despondent, downcast, down in the dumps (*informal*), down in the mouth, low-spirited, down-hearted
<< OPPOSITE happy
2 SMUTTY, dirty, naughty, obscene, indecent, vulgar, lewd, risqué, X-rated (*informal*), bawdy, near the knuckle (*informal*)
<< OPPOSITE respectable
▷ *plural noun* DEPRESSION, gloom, melancholy, unhappiness, despondency, the hump (*Brit informal*), dejection, moodiness, low spirits, the dumps (*informal*), doldrums, gloominess, glumness

blueprint *noun* 1 SCHEME, plan, design, system, idea, programme, proposal, strategy, pattern, suggestion, procedure, plot, draft, outline, sketch, proposition, prototype, layout, pilot scheme
2 PLAN, scheme, project, pattern, draft, outline, sketch, layout

bluff[1] *noun* DECEPTION, show, lie, fraud, fake, sham, pretence, deceit, bravado, bluster, humbug, subterfuge, feint, mere show
▷ *verb* DECEIVE, lie, trick, fool, pretend, cheat, con, fake, mislead, sham, dupe, feign, delude, humbug, bamboozle (*informal*), hoodwink, double-cross (*informal*), pull the wool over someone's eyes

bluff[2] *noun* PRECIPICE, bank, peak, cliff, ridge, crag, escarpment, promontory, scarp
▷ *adjective* HEARTY, open, frank, blunt, sincere, outspoken, honest, downright, cordial, genial, affable, ebullient, jovial, plain-spoken, good-natured, unreserved, back-slapping
<< OPPOSITE tactful

blunder *noun* MISTAKE, slip, fault, error, boob (*Brit slang*), oversight, gaffe, slip-up (*informal*), indiscretion, impropriety, howler (*informal*), bloomer (*Brit informal*), clanger (*informal*), faux pas, boo-boo (*informal*), gaucherie, barry *or* Barry Crocker (*Austral slang*)
<< OPPOSITE correctness
▷ *verb* 1 MAKE A MISTAKE, blow it (*slang*), err, slip up (*informal*), cock up (*Brit slang*), miscalculate, foul up, drop a clanger (*informal*), put your foot in it (*informal*), drop a brick (*Brit informal*), screw up (*informal*)
<< OPPOSITE be correct
2 STUMBLE, fall, reel, stagger, flounder, lurch, lose your balance

blunt *adjective* 1 FRANK, forthright, straightforward, explicit, rude, outspoken, bluff, downright, upfront (*informal*), trenchant, brusque, plain-spoken, tactless, impolite, discourteous, unpolished, uncivil, straight from the shoulder
<< OPPOSITE tactful
2 DULL, rounded, dulled, edgeless, unsharpened
<< OPPOSITE sharp
▷ *verb* DULL, weaken, soften, numb, dampen, water down, deaden, take the edge off
<< OPPOSITE stimulate

blur *noun* HAZE, confusion, fog, obscurity, dimness, cloudiness, blear, blurredness, indistinctness
▷ *verb* 1 BECOME INDISTINCT, soften, become vague, become hazy, become fuzzy
2 OBSCURE, make indistinct, mask, soften, muddy, obfuscate, make vague, befog, make hazy

blurred *adjective* INDISTINCT, faint, vague, unclear, dim, fuzzy, misty, hazy, foggy, blurry, out of focus, ill-defined, lacking definition

blush *verb* TURN RED, colour, burn, flame, glow, flush, crimson, redden, go red (as a beetroot), turn scarlet
<< OPPOSITE turn pale
▷ *noun* REDDENING, colour, glow, flush, pink tinge, rosiness, ruddiness, rosy tint

bluster *verb* BOAST, swagger, talk big (*slang*)
▷ *noun* HOT AIR, boasting, bluff, swagger, swaggering (*informal*), bravado, bombast

blustery *adjective* GUSTY, wild, violent, stormy, windy, tempestuous, inclement, squally, blusterous

board *noun* 1 PLANK, panel, timber, slat, piece of timber
2 COUNCIL, directors, committee, congress, ministry, advisers, panel, assembly, chamber, trustees, governing body, synod, directorate, quango, advisory group, conclave
3 MEALS, provisions, victuals, daily meals
▷ *verb* GET ON, enter, mount, embark, entrain,

embus, enplane
<< OPPOSITE get off
boast *verb* 1 BRAG, crow, vaunt, bluster, talk big (*slang*), blow your own trumpet, show off, be proud of, flaunt, congratulate yourself on, flatter yourself, pride yourself on, skite (*Austral & NZ informal*)
<< OPPOSITE cover up
2 POSSESS, offer, present, exhibit
▷ *noun* BRAGGING, vaunting, rodomontade (*literary*), gasconade (*rare*)
<< OPPOSITE disclaimer
boat *noun* VESSEL, ship, craft, barge (*informal*), barque (*poetic*)
▷▷ **in the same boat** IN THE SAME SITUATION, alike, even, together, equal, on a par, on equal *or* even terms, on the same *or* equal footing
▷▷ **miss the boat** MISS YOUR CHANCE *or* OPPORTUNITY, miss out, be too late, lose out, blow your chance (*informal*)
▷▷ **rock the boat** (*informal*) CAUSE TROUBLE, protest, object, dissent, make waves (*informal*), throw a spanner in the works, upset the apple cart
bob *verb* BOUNCE, duck, leap, hop, weave, skip, jerk, wobble, quiver, oscillate, waggle
▷▷ **bob up** SPRING UP, rise, appear, emerge, surface, pop up, jump up, bounce up
bode *verb* AUGUR, portend, threaten, predict, signify, foreshadow, presage, betoken, be an omen, forebode
bodily *adjective* PHYSICAL, material, actual, substantial, fleshly, tangible, corporal, carnal, corporeal
body *noun* 1 PHYSIQUE, build, form, figure, shape, make-up, frame, constitution
2 TORSO, trunk
3 CORPSE, dead body, remains, stiff (*slang*), relics, carcass, cadaver
4 ORGANIZATION, company, group, society, league, association, band, congress, institution, corporation, federation, outfit (*informal*), syndicate, bloc, confederation
5 MAIN PART, matter, material, mass, substance, bulk, essence
6 EXPANSE, mass, sweep
7 MASS, company, press, army, host, crowd, majority, assembly, mob, herd, swarm, horde, multitude, throng, bevy
8 CONSISTENCY, substance, texture, density, richness, firmness, solidity, viscosity
>> RELATED WORDS *adjectives* corporal, physical
boffin *noun* (*Brit informal*) EXPERT, authority, brain(s) (*informal*), intellectual, genius, guru, inventor, thinker, wizard, mastermind, intellect, egghead, wonk (*informal*), brainbox, bluestocking (*usually disparaging*), maven (*US*), fundi (*S African*)
bog *noun* MARSH, moss (*Scot & Northern English dialect*), swamp, slough, wetlands, fen, mire, quagmire, morass, marshland, peat bog, pakihi (*NZ*), muskeg (*Canad*)
▷▷ **bog something** *or* **someone down** HOLD UP, stick, delay, halt, stall, slow down, impede, slow up
bogey *noun* 1 BUGBEAR, bête noire, horror, nightmare, bugaboo
2 SPIRIT, ghost, phantom, spectre, spook (*informal*), apparition, imp, sprite, goblin, bogeyman, hobgoblin, eidolon, atua (*NZ*), kehua (*NZ*)
boggle *verb* CONFUSE, surprise, shock, amaze, stun, stagger, bewilder, astound, daze, confound, stupefy, dumbfound
bogus *adjective* FAKE, false, artificial, forged, dummy, imitation, sham, fraudulent, pseudo (*informal*), counterfeit, spurious, ersatz, phoney *or* phony (*informal*), assumed
<< OPPOSITE genuine
Bohemian *adjective often not cap.* UNCONVENTIONAL, alternative, artistic, exotic, way-out (*informal*), eccentric, avant-garde, off-the-wall (*slang*), unorthodox, arty (*informal*), oddball (*informal*), offbeat, left bank, nonconformist, outré
<< OPPOSITE conventional
▷ *noun often not cap.* NONCONFORMIST, rebel, radical, eccentric, maverick, hippy, dropout, individualist, beatnik, iconoclast
boil[1] *verb* 1 SIMMER, bubble, foam, churn, seethe, fizz, froth, effervesce
2 BE FURIOUS, storm, rage, rave, fume, be angry, crack up (*informal*), see red (*informal*), go ballistic (*slang, chiefly US*), be indignant, fulminate, foam at the mouth (*informal*), blow a fuse (*slang, chiefly US*), fly off the handle (*informal*), go off the deep end (*informal*), wig out (*slang*), go up the wall (*slang*)
▷▷ **boil something down** REDUCE, concentrate, precipitate (*Chemistry*), thicken, condense, decoct
boil[2] *noun* PUSTULE, gathering, swelling, blister, blain, carbuncle, furuncle (*Pathology*)
boisterous *adjective* 1 UNRULY, wild, disorderly, loud, noisy, wayward, rowdy, wilful, riotous, unrestrained, rollicking, impetuous, rumbustious, uproarious, obstreperous, clamorous
<< OPPOSITE self-controlled
2 STORMY, rough, raging, turbulent, tumultuous, tempestuous, blustery, gusty, squally
<< OPPOSITE calm
bold *adjective* 1 FEARLESS, enterprising, brave, daring, heroic, adventurous, courageous, gritty, gallant, gutsy (*slang*), audacious, intrepid, valiant, plucky, undaunted, unafraid,

unflinching, dauntless, lion-hearted, valorous
<< OPPOSITE timid
2 IMPUDENT, forward, fresh (*informal*), confident, rude, cheeky, brash, feisty (*informal, chiefly US & Canad*), saucy, pushy (*informal*), brazen, in-your-face (*Brit slang*), shameless, sassy (*US informal*), unabashed, pert, insolent, barefaced, spirited, forceful
<< OPPOSITE shy
3 BRIGHT, conspicuous, strong, striking, loud, prominent, lively, pronounced, colourful, vivid, flashy, eye-catching, salient, showy
<< OPPOSITE soft

bolster *verb* SUPPORT, help, aid, maintain, boost, strengthen, assist, prop, reinforce, hold up, cushion, brace, shore up, augment, buttress, buoy up, give a leg up to (*informal*)

bolt *noun* 1 PIN, rod, peg, rivet
2 BAR, catch, lock, latch, fastener, sliding bar
3 ARROW, missile, shaft, dart, projectile
4 DASH, race, flight, spring, rush, bound, sprint, dart, spurt
▷ *verb* 1 LOCK, close, bar, secure, fasten, latch
2 DASH, run, fly, spring, jump, rush, bound, leap, sprint, hurtle
3 GOBBLE, stuff, wolf, cram, gorge, devour, gulp, guzzle, swallow whole

bomb *noun* EXPLOSIVE, charge, mine, shell, missile, device, rocket, grenade, torpedo, bombshell, projectile
▷ *verb* BLOW UP, attack, destroy, assault, shell, blast, blitz, bombard, torpedo, open fire on, strafe, fire upon, blow sky-high

bombard *verb* 1 ATTACK, assault, batter, barrage, besiege, beset, assail
2 BOMB, shell, blast, blitz, open fire, strafe, fire upon

bombardment *noun* BOMBING, attack, fire, assault, shelling, blitz, barrage, flak, strafe, fusillade, cannonade

bombast *noun* POMPOSITY, ranting, bragging, hot air (*informal*), bluster, grandiosity, braggadocio, grandiloquence, rodomontade (*literary*), gasconade (*rare*), extravagant boasting, magniloquence

bombastic *adjective* GRANDILOQUENT, inflated, ranting, windy, high-flown, pompous, grandiose, histrionic, wordy, verbose, declamatory, fustian, magniloquent

bona fide *adjective* GENUINE, real, true, legal, actual, legitimate, authentic, honest, veritable, lawful, on the level (*informal*), kosher (*informal*), dinkum (*Austral & NZ informal*), the real McCoy
<< OPPOSITE bogus

bond *noun* 1 TIE, union, coupling, link, association, relation, connection, alliance, attachment, affinity, affiliation
2 FASTENING, band, tie, binding, chain, cord, shackle, fetter, manacle
3 AGREEMENT, word, promise, contract, guarantee, pledge, obligation, compact, covenant
▷ *verb* 1 FORM FRIENDSHIPS, connect
2 FIX, hold, bind, connect, glue, gum, fuse, stick, paste, fasten

bondage *noun* SLAVERY, imprisonment, captivity, confinement, yoke, duress, servitude, enslavement, subjugation, serfdom, subjection, vassalage, thraldom, enthralment

bonny *adjective* (*Scot & Northern English dialect*) BEAUTIFUL, pretty, fair, sweet, appealing, attractive, lovely, charming, handsome, good-looking, gorgeous, radiant, alluring, comely

bonus *noun* 1 EXTRA, benefit, commission, prize, gift, reward, premium, dividend, hand-out, perk (*Brit informal*), bounty, gratuity, honorarium
2 ADVANTAGE, benefit, gain, extra, plus, asset, perk (*Brit informal*), icing on the cake

bony *adjective* THIN, lean, skinny, angular, gaunt, skeletal, haggard, emaciated, scrawny, undernourished, cadaverous, rawboned, macilent (*rare*)

book *noun* 1 WORK, title, volume, publication, manual, paperback, textbook, tract, hardback, tome
2 NOTEBOOK, album, journal, diary, pad, record book, Filofax (*trademark*), notepad, exercise book, jotter, memorandum book
▷ *verb* RESERVE, schedule, engage, line up, organize, charter, arrange for, procure, make reservations
▷▷ **book in** REGISTER, enter, enrol

booking *noun* (*Chiefly Brit*) RESERVATION, date, appointment

bookish *adjective* STUDIOUS, learned, academic, intellectual, literary, scholarly, erudite, pedantic, well-read, donnish

booklet *noun* BROCHURE, leaflet, hand-out, pamphlet, folder, mailshot, handbill

boom *noun* 1 EXPANSION, increase, development, growth, advance, jump, boost, improvement, spurt, upsurge, upturn, upswing
<< OPPOSITE decline
2 BANG, report, shot, crash, clash, blast, burst, explosion, roar, thunder, rumble, clap, peal, detonation
▷ *verb* 1 INCREASE, flourish, grow, develop, succeed, expand, strengthen, do well, swell, thrive, intensify, prosper, burgeon, spurt
<< OPPOSITE fall
2 BANG, roll, crash, blast, echo, drum, explode, roar, thunder, rumble, resound, reverberate, peal

boomerang *verb* REBOUND, backfire, come

home to roost
boon *noun* 1 BENEFIT, advantage, blessing, godsend, gift
2 (*Archaic*) GIFT, present, grant, favour, donation, hand-out, gratuity, benefaction
boorish *adjective* LOUTISH, gross, crude, rude, hick (*informal, chiefly US & Canad*), coarse, vulgar, rustic, barbaric, churlish, uneducated, bearish, uncouth, unrefined, uncivilized, clownish, oafish, ill-bred, lubberly
<< OPPOSITE refined
boost *verb* INCREASE, develop, raise, expand, add to, build up, heighten, enlarge, inflate, magnify, amplify, augment, jack up
<< OPPOSITE decrease
▷ *noun* 1 RISE, increase, advance, jump, addition, improvement, expansion, upsurge, upturn, increment, upswing, upward turn
<< OPPOSITE fall
2 ENCOURAGEMENT, help
boot *verb* KICK, punt, put the boot in(to) (*slang*), drop-kick
▷▷ **boot someone out** (*informal*) DISMISS, sack (*informal*), expel, throw out, oust, relegate, kick out, eject, kiss off (*slang, chiefly US & Canad*), show someone the door, give someone the boot (*slang*), give someone their marching orders, give someone the bullet (*Brit slang*), give someone the bum's rush (*slang*), throw someone out on their ear (*informal*), give someone the heave *or* push (*informal*)
bootleg *adjective* ILLICIT, illegal, outlawed, pirate, unofficial, black-market, unlicensed, under-the-table, unauthorized, contraband, hooky (*slang*), under-the-counter
<< OPPOSITE official
booty *noun* PLUNDER, winnings, gains, haul, spoils, prey, loot, takings, pillage, swag (*slang*), boodle (*slang, chiefly US*)
booze *verb* (*informal*) DRINK, indulge, get drunk, tipple, imbibe, tope, carouse, bevvy (*dialect*), get plastered, drink like a fish, get soused, get tanked up (*informal*), go on a binge *or* bender (*informal*), hit the booze *or* bottle (*informal*)
boozer *noun* (*informal*) 1 PUB, local (*Brit informal*), bar (*informal, chiefly Brit*), inn, tavern, beer parlour (*Canad*), beverage room (*Canad*), public house, watering hole (*facetious slang*), roadhouse, hostelry, alehouse (*archaic*), taproom
2 DRINKER, toper, drunk, soak (*slang*), alcoholic, lush (*slang*), drunkard, sot, tippler, wino (*informal*), alko *or* alco (*Austral slang*), inebriate
border *noun* 1 FRONTIER, line, marches, limit, bounds, boundary, perimeter, borderline, borderland
2 EDGE, lip, margin, skirt, verge, rim, hem, brim, flange
▷ *verb* EDGE, bound, decorate, trim, fringe, rim, hem
▷▷ **border on something** COME CLOSE TO, approach, be like, resemble, be similar to, approximate, come near
borderline *adjective* MARGINAL, bordering, doubtful, peripheral, indefinite, indeterminate, equivocal, inexact, unclassifiable
bore¹ *verb* DRILL, mine, sink, tunnel, pierce, penetrate, burrow, puncture, perforate, gouge out
bore² *verb* TIRE, exhaust, annoy, fatigue, weary, wear out, jade, wear down, be tedious, pall on, send to sleep
<< OPPOSITE excite
▷ *noun* NUISANCE, pain (*informal*), drag (*informal*), headache (*informal*), yawn (*informal*), anorak (*informal*), pain in the neck (*informal*), dullard, dull person, tiresome person, wearisome talker
bored *adjective* FED UP, tired, hacked (off) (*US slang*), wearied, weary, uninterested, sick and tired (*informal*), listless, browned-off (*informal*), brassed off (*Brit slang*), ennuied, hoha (*NZ*)
boredom *noun* TEDIUM, apathy, doldrums, weariness, monotony, dullness, sameness, ennui, flatness, world-weariness, tediousness, irksomeness
<< OPPOSITE excitement
boring *adjective* UNINTERESTING, dull, tedious, stale, tiresome, monotonous, old, dead, flat, routine, humdrum, insipid, mind-numbing, unexciting, ho-hum (*informal*), repetitious, wearisome, unvaried
born *verb* BROUGHT INTO THIS WORLD, delivered

> This word is spelled without an *e*: *a new baby was born*. The word *borne*, spelled with an *e*, is the past participle of the verb *bear*: *he had borne his ordeal with great courage*, not *he had born his ordeal with great courage*

borrow *verb* 1 TAKE ON LOAN, touch (someone) for (*slang*), scrounge (*informal*), blag (*slang*), mooch (*slang*), cadge, use temporarily, take and return
<< OPPOSITE lend
2 STEAL, take, use, copy, adopt, appropriate, acquire, pinch (*informal*), pirate, poach, pilfer, filch, plagiarize
bosom *noun* 1 BREAST, chest, front, bust, teats, thorax
2 MIDST, centre, heart, protection, circle, shelter
3 HEART, feelings, spirit, soul, emotions, sympathies, sentiments, affections
▷ *adjective* INTIMATE, close, warm, dear, friendly, confidential, cherished, boon, very dear
boss *noun* MANAGER, head, leader, director,

chief, executive, owner, master, governor (*informal*), employer, administrator, supervisor, superintendent, gaffer (*informal, chiefly Brit*), foreman, overseer, kingpin, big cheese (*old-fashioned slang*), baas (*S African*), numero uno (*informal*), Mister Big (*slang, chiefly US*), sherang (*Austral & NZ*)

▷▷ **boss someone around** (*informal*) ORDER AROUND, dominate, bully, intimidate, oppress, dictate to, terrorize, put upon, push around (*slang*), browbeat, ride roughshod over, tyrannize, rule with an iron hand

bossy *adjective* (*informal*) DOMINEERING, lordly, arrogant, authoritarian, oppressive, hectoring, autocratic, dictatorial, coercive, imperious, overbearing, tyrannical, despotic, high-handed

botch *verb* SPOIL, mar, bungle, fumble, screw up (*informal*), mess up, cock up (*Brit slang*), mismanage, muff, make a nonsense of (*informal*), bodge (*informal*), make a pig's ear of (*informal*), flub (*US slang*), crool *or* cruel (*Austral slang*)

▷ *noun* MESS, failure, blunder, miscarriage, bungle, bungling, fumble, hash, cock-up (*Brit slang*), pig's ear (*informal*), pig's breakfast (*informal*)

bother *verb* 1 TROUBLE, concern, worry, upset, alarm, disturb, distress, annoy, dismay, gall, disconcert, vex, perturb, faze, put *or* get someone's back up

2 PESTER, plague, irritate, put out, harass, nag, hassle (*informal*), inconvenience, molest, breathe down someone's neck, get on your nerves (*informal*), nark (*Brit, Austral & NZ slang*), bend someone's ear (*informal*), give someone grief (*Brit & S African*), get on your wick (*Brit slang*)

<< OPPOSITE help

▷ *noun* TROUBLE, problem, worry, difficulty, strain, grief (*Brit & S African*), fuss, pest, irritation, hassle (*informal*), nuisance, flurry, uphill (*S African*), inconvenience, annoyance, aggravation, vexation

<< OPPOSITE help

bottleneck *noun* BLOCK, hold-up, obstacle, congestion, obstruction, impediment, blockage, snarl-up (*informal, chiefly Brit*), (traffic) jam

bottle shop *noun* (*Austral & NZ*) OFF-LICENCE (*Brit*), liquor store (*US & Canad*), bottle store (*S African*), package store (*US & Canad*), offie *or* offy (*Brit informal*)

bottle store *noun* (*S African*) OFF-LICENCE (*Brit*), liquor store (*US & Canad*), bottle shop (*Austral & NZ*), package store (*US & Canad*), offie *or* offy (*Brit informal*)

bottom *noun* 1 LOWEST PART, base, foot, bed, floor, basis, foundation, depths, support, pedestal, deepest part

<< OPPOSITE top

2 UNDERSIDE, sole, underneath, lower side

3 (*informal*) BUTTOCKS, behind (*informal*), rear, butt (*US & Canad informal*), bum (*Brit slang*), buns (*US slang*), backside, rump, seat, tail (*informal*), rear end, posterior, derrière (*euphemistic*), tush (*US slang*), fundament, jacksy (*Brit slang*)

▷ *adjective* LOWEST, last, base, ground, basement, undermost

<< OPPOSITE higher

bottomless *adjective* 1 UNLIMITED, endless, infinite, limitless, boundless, inexhaustible, immeasurable, unbounded, illimitable

2 DEEP, profound, yawning, boundless, unfathomable, immeasurable, fathomless, abyssal

bounce *verb* 1 REBOUND, return, thump, recoil, ricochet, spring back, resile

2 BOUND, spring, jump, leap, skip, caper, prance, gambol, jounce

3 (*Slang*) THROW OUT, fire (*informal*), turn out, expel, oust, relegate, kick out (*informal*), drive out, eject, evict, boot out (*informal*), show someone the door, give someone the bum's rush (*slang*), throw someone out on their ear (*informal*)

▷ *noun* 1 SPRINGINESS, give, spring, bound, rebound, resilience, elasticity, recoil

2 (*informal*) LIFE, go (*informal*), energy, pep, sparkle, zip (*informal*), vitality, animation, vigour, exuberance, dynamism, brio, vivacity, liveliness, vim (*slang*), lustiness, vivaciousness

bouncing *adjective* LIVELY, healthy, thriving, blooming, robust, vigorous, energetic, perky, sprightly, alive and kicking, fighting fit, full of beans (*informal*), fit as a fiddle (*informal*), bright-eyed and bushy-tailed

bouncy *adjective* 1 LIVELY, active, enthusiastic, energetic, bubbly, exuberant, irrepressible, ebullient, perky, chirpy (*informal*), sprightly, vivacious, effervescent, chipper (*informal*), full of beans (*informal*), zestful, full of pep (*informal*), bright-eyed and bushy-tailed

<< OPPOSITE listless

2 SPRINGY, flexible, elastic, resilient, rubbery, spongy

<< OPPOSITE flat

bound[1] *adjective* 1 COMPELLED, obliged, forced, committed, pledged, constrained, obligated, beholden, duty-bound

2 TIED, fixed, secured, attached, lashed, tied up, fastened, trussed, pinioned, made fast

3 CERTAIN, sure, fated, doomed, destined

bound[2] *verb* LEAP, bob, spring, jump, bounce, skip, vault, pounce

▷ *noun* LEAP, bob, spring, jump, bounce, hurdle, skip, vault, pounce, caper, prance, lope, frisk, gambol

bound[3] *verb* 1 SURROUND, confine, enclose, terminate, encircle, circumscribe, hem in, demarcate, delimit
2 LIMIT, fix, define, restrict, confine, restrain, circumscribe, demarcate, delimit
boundary *noun* 1 FRONTIER, edge, border, march, barrier, margin, brink
2 EDGES, limits, bounds, pale, confines, fringes, verges, precinct, extremities
3 DIVIDING LINE, borderline
boundless *adjective* UNLIMITED, vast, endless, immense, infinite, untold, limitless, unending, inexhaustible, incalculable, immeasurable, unbounded, unconfined, measureless, illimitable
<< OPPOSITE limited
bounds *plural noun* BOUNDARY, line, limit, edge, border, march, margin, pale, confine, fringe, verge, rim, perimeter, periphery
bountiful *adjective* 1 PLENTIFUL, generous, lavish, ample, prolific, abundant, exuberant, copious, luxuriant, bounteous, plenteous
2 GENEROUS, kind, princely, liberal, charitable, hospitable, prodigal, open-handed, unstinting, beneficent, bounteous, munificent, ungrudging
bounty *noun* 1 GENEROSITY, charity, assistance, kindness, philanthropy, benevolence, beneficence, liberality, almsgiving, open-handedness, largesse *or* largess
2 ABUNDANCE, plenty, exuberance, profusion, affluence, plenitude, copiousness, plenteousness
3 REWARD, present, grant, prize, payment, gift, compensation, bonus, premium, donation, recompense, gratuity, meed (*archaic*), largesse *or* largess, koha (*NZ*)
bouquet *noun* 1 BUNCH OF FLOWERS, spray, garland, wreath, posy, buttonhole, corsage, nosegay, boutonniere
2 AROMA, smell, scent, perfume, fragrance, savour, odour, redolence
bourgeois *adjective* MIDDLE-CLASS, traditional, conventional, materialistic, hidebound, Pooterish
bout *noun* 1 PERIOD, time, term, fit, session, stretch, spell, turn, patch, interval, stint
2 ROUND, run, course, series, session, cycle, sequence, stint, spree
3 FIGHT, match, battle, competition, struggle, contest, set-to, encounter, engagement, head-to-head, boxing match
bovine *adjective* DULL, heavy, slow, thick, stupid, dull, dense, sluggish, lifeless, inactive, inert, lethargic, dozy (*Brit informal*), listless, unresponsive, stolid, torpid, slothful
bow[1] *verb* BEND, bob, nod, incline, stoop, droop, genuflect, make obeisance
▷ *noun* BENDING, bob, nod, inclination, salaam, obeisance, kowtow, genuflection
▷▷ **bow out** GIVE UP, retire, withdraw, get out, resign, quit, pull out, step down (*informal*), back out, throw in the towel, cop out (*slang*), throw in the sponge, call it a day *or* night
▷▷ **bow to something** *or* **someone** GIVE IN TO, accept, comply with, succumb to, submit to, surrender to, yield to, defer to, concede to, acquiesce to, kowtow to
bow[2] *noun* (*Nautical*) PROW, head, stem, fore, beak
bowels *plural noun* 1 GUTS, insides (*informal*), intestines, innards (*informal*), entrails, viscera, vitals
2 DEPTHS, hold, middle, inside, deep, interior, core, belly, midst, remotest part, deepest part, furthest part, innermost part
bower *noun* ARBOUR, grotto, alcove, summerhouse, shady recess, leafy shelter
bowl[1] *noun* BASIN, plate, dish, vessel
bowl[2] *verb* 1 THROW, hurl, launch, cast, pitch, toss, fling, chuck (*informal*), lob (*informal*)
2 *often with* **along** DRIVE, shoot, speed, tear, barrel (along) (*informal, chiefly US & Canad*), trundle
▷▷ **bowl someone over** 1 KNOCK DOWN, fell, floor, deck (*slang*), overturn, overthrow, bring down
2 (*informal*) SURPRISE, amaze, stun, overwhelm, astonish, stagger, startle, astound, take (someone) aback, stupefy, strike (someone) dumb, throw off balance, sweep (someone) off their feet, dumbfound
box[1] *noun* CONTAINER, case, chest, trunk, pack, package, carton, casket, receptacle, ark (*dialect*), portmanteau, coffret, kist (*Scot & Northern English dialect*)
▷ *verb* PACK, package, wrap, encase, bundle up
▷▷ **box something** *or* **someone in** CONFINE, contain, surround, trap, restrict, isolate, cage, enclose, restrain, imprison, shut up, incarcerate, hem in, shut in, coop up
box[2] *verb* 1 FIGHT, spar, exchange blows
2 PUNCH, hit, strike, belt (*informal*), deck (*slang*), slap, sock (*slang*), buffet, clout (*informal*), cuff, whack (*informal*), wallop (*informal*), chin (*slang*), tonk (*informal*), thwack (*informal*), lay one on (*slang*)
boxer *noun* FIGHTER, pugilist, prizefighter, sparrer
boxing *noun* PRIZEFIGHTING, the ring, sparring, fisticuffs, the fight game (*informal*), pugilism
boy *noun* LAD, kid (*informal*), youth, fellow, youngster, chap (*informal*), schoolboy, junior, laddie (*Scot*), stripling
boycott *verb* EMBARGO, reject, snub, refrain from, spurn, blacklist, black, cold-shoulder, ostracize, blackball
<< OPPOSITE support

boyfriend *noun* SWEETHEART, man, lover, young man, steady, beloved, valentine, admirer, suitor, beau, date, swain, toy boy, truelove, leman (*archaic*), inamorato
boyish *adjective* YOUTHFUL, young, innocent, adolescent, juvenile, childish, immature
brace *verb* 1 STEADY, support, balance, secure, stabilize
2 SUPPORT, strengthen, steady, prop, reinforce, hold up, tighten, shove, bolster, fortify, buttress, shove up
▷ *noun* SUPPORT, stay, prop, bracer, bolster, bracket, reinforcement, strut, truss, buttress, stanchion
bracing *adjective* REFRESHING, fresh, cool, stimulating, reviving, lively, crisp, vigorous, rousing, brisk, uplifting, exhilarating, fortifying, chilly, rejuvenating, invigorating, energizing, healthful, restorative, tonic, rejuvenative
<< OPPOSITE tiring
brag *verb* BOAST, crow, swagger, vaunt, bluster, talk big (*slang*), blow your own trumpet, blow your own horn (*US & Canad*)
braid *verb* INTERWEAVE, weave, lace, intertwine, plait, entwine, twine, ravel, interlace
brain *noun* 1 CEREBRUM, mind, grey matter (*informal*)
2 (*informal*) INTELLECTUAL, genius, scholar, sage, pundit, mastermind, intellect, prodigy, highbrow, egghead (*informal*), brainbox, bluestocking (*usually disparaging*)
▷ *plural noun* INTELLIGENCE, mind, reason, understanding, sense, capacity, smarts (*slang, chiefly US*), wit, intellect, savvy (*slang*), nous (*Brit slang*), suss (*slang*), shrewdness, sagacity
>> RELATED WORD *adjective* cerebral
brainwashing *noun* INDOCTRINATION, conditioning, persuasion, re-education
brainwave *noun* IDEA, thought, bright idea, stroke of genius
brainy *adjective* (*informal*) INTELLIGENT, quick, bright, sharp, brilliant, acute, smart, alert, clever, rational, knowing, quick-witted
brake *noun* CONTROL, check, curb, restraint, constraint, rein
▷ *verb* SLOW, decelerate, reduce speed
branch *noun* 1 BOUGH, shoot, arm, spray, limb, sprig, offshoot, prong, ramification
2 OFFICE, department, unit, wing, chapter, bureau, local office
3 DIVISION, part, section, subdivision, subsection
4 DISCIPLINE, section, subdivision
▷▷ **branch out** EXPAND, diversify
brand *noun* 1 TRADEMARK
2 LABEL, mark, sign, stamp, symbol, logo, trademark, marker, hallmark, emblem
3 STIGMA, mark, stain, disgrace, taint, slur, blot, infamy, smirch
▷ *verb* 1 STIGMATIZE, mark, label, expose, denounce, disgrace, discredit, censure, pillory, defame
2 MARK, burn, label, stamp, scar
brandish *verb* WAVE, raise, display, shake, swing, exhibit, flourish, wield, flaunt
brash *adjective* BOLD, forward, rude, arrogant, cocky, pushy (*informal*), brazen, presumptuous, impertinent, insolent, impudent, bumptious, cocksure, overconfident, hubristic, full of yourself
<< OPPOSITE timid
brassy *adjective* 1 STRIDENT, loud, harsh, piercing, jarring, noisy, grating, raucous, blaring, shrill, jangling, dissonant, cacophonous
2 BRAZEN, forward, bold, brash, saucy, pushy (*informal*), pert, insolent, impudent, loud-mouthed, barefaced
3 FLASHY, loud, blatant, vulgar, gaudy, garish, jazzy (*informal*), showy, obtrusive
<< OPPOSITE discreet
brat *noun* YOUNGSTER, kid (*informal*), urchin, imp, rascal, spoilt child, devil, puppy (*informal*), cub, scallywag (*informal*), whippersnapper, guttersnipe
bravado *noun* SWAGGER, boast, boasting, swaggering, vaunting, bluster, swashbuckling, bombast, braggadocio, boastfulness, fanfaronade (*rare*)
brave *adjective* COURAGEOUS, daring, bold, heroic, adventurous, gritty, fearless, resolute, gallant, gutsy (*slang*), audacious, intrepid, valiant, plucky, undaunted, unafraid, unflinching, dauntless, lion-hearted, valorous
<< OPPOSITE timid
▷ *verb* CONFRONT, face, suffer, challenge, bear, tackle, dare, endure, defy, withstand, stand up to
<< OPPOSITE give in to
bravery *noun* COURAGE, nerve, daring, pluck, spirit, bottle (*Brit slang*), guts (*informal*), grit, fortitude, heroism, mettle, boldness, bravura, gallantry, valour, spunk (*informal*), hardiness, fearlessness, intrepidity, indomitability, hardihood, dauntlessness, doughtiness, pluckiness, lion-heartedness
<< OPPOSITE cowardice
bravo *interjection* CONGRATULATIONS, well done
bravura *noun* BRILLIANCE, energy, spirit, display, punch (*informal*), dash, animation, vigour, verve, panache, boldness, virtuosity, élan, exhibitionism, brio, ostentation
brawl *noun* FIGHT, battle, row (*informal*), clash, disorder, scrap (*informal*), fray, squabble, wrangle, skirmish, scuffle, punch-up (*Brit informal*), free-for-all (*informal*), fracas, altercation, rumpus, broil, tumult, affray

(*Law*), shindig (*informal*), donnybrook, ruckus (*informal*), scrimmage, shindy (*informal*), biffo (*Austral slang*), bagarre (*French*), melee *or* mêlée
▷ *verb* FIGHT, battle, scrap (*informal*), wrestle, wrangle, tussle, scuffle, go at it hammer and tongs, fight like Kilkenny cats, altercate

brawn *noun* MUSCLE, might, power, strength, muscles, beef (*informal*), flesh, vigour, robustness, muscularity, beefiness (*informal*), brawniness

bray *verb* 1 NEIGH, bellow, screech, heehaw
2 ROAR, trumpet, bellow, hoot
▷ *noun* 1 NEIGH, bellow, screech, heehaw
2 ROAR, cry, shout, bellow, screech, hoot, bawl, harsh sound

brazen *adjective* BOLD, forward, defiant, brash, saucy, audacious, pushy (*informal*), shameless, unabashed, pert, unashamed, insolent, impudent, immodest, barefaced, brassy (*informal*)
<< OPPOSITE shy
▷▷ **brazen it out** BE UNASHAMED, persevere, be defiant, confront something, be impenitent, outface, outstare

breach *noun* 1 NONOBSERVANCE, abuse, violation, infringement, trespass, disobedience, transgression, contravention, infraction, noncompliance
<< OPPOSITE compliance
2 DISAGREEMENT, difference, division, separation, falling-out (*informal*), quarrel, alienation, variance, severance, disaffection, schism, parting of the ways, estrangement, dissension
3 OPENING, crack, break, hole, split, gap, rent, rift, rupture, aperture, chasm, cleft, fissure

bread *noun* 1 FOOD, provisions, fare, necessities, subsistence, kai (*NZ informal*), nourishment, sustenance, victuals, nutriment, viands, aliment
2 (*Slang*) MONEY, funds, cash, finance, necessary (*informal*), silver, tin (*slang*), brass (*Northern English dialect*), dough (*slang*), dosh (*Brit & Austral slang*), needful (*informal*), shekels (*informal*), dibs (*slang*), ackers (*slang*), spondulicks (*slang*), rhino (*Brit slang*)

breadth *noun* 1 WIDTH, spread, beam, span, latitude, broadness, wideness
2 EXTENT, area, reach, range, measure, size, scale, spread, sweep, scope, magnitude, compass, expanse, vastness, amplitude, comprehensiveness, extensiveness

break *verb* 1 SHATTER, separate, destroy, split, divide, crack, snap, smash, crush, fragment, demolish, sever, trash (*slang*), disintegrate, splinter, smash to smithereens, shiver
<< OPPOSITE repair
2 FRACTURE, crack, smash
3 BURST, tear, split
4 DISOBEY, breach, defy, violate, disregard, flout, infringe, contravene, transgress, go counter to, infract (*Law*)
<< OPPOSITE obey
5 STOP, cut, check, suspend, interrupt, cut short, discontinue
6 DISTURB, interrupt
7 END, stop, cut, drop, give up, abandon, suspend, interrupt, terminate, put an end to, discontinue, pull the plug on
8 WEAKEN, undermine, cow, tame, subdue, demoralize, dispirit
9 RUIN, destroy, crush, humiliate, bring down, bankrupt, degrade, impoverish, demote, make bankrupt, bring to ruin
10 PAUSE, stop briefly, stop, rest, halt, cease, take a break, have a breather (*informal*)
11 INTERRUPT, stop, suspend
12 CUSHION, reduce, ease, moderate, diminish, temper, soften, lessen, alleviate, lighten
13 BE REVEALED, come out, be reported, be published, be announced, be made public, be proclaimed, be let out, be imparted, be divulged, come out in the wash
14 REVEAL, tell, announce, declare, disclose, proclaim, divulge, make known
15 BEAT, top, better, exceed, go beyond, excel, surpass, outstrip, outdo, cap (*informal*)
16 (always used of *dawn*) HAPPEN, appear, emerge, occur, erupt, burst out, come forth suddenly
▷ *noun* 1 FRACTURE, opening, tear, hole, split, crack, gap, rent, breach, rift, rupture, gash, cleft, fissure
2 INTERVAL, pause, recess, interlude, intermission, entr'acte
3 HOLIDAY, leave, vacation, time off, recess, awayday, schoolie (*Austral*), acumulated day off *or* ADO (*Austral*)
4 (*informal*) STROKE OF LUCK, chance, opportunity, advantage, fortune, opening
5 BREACH, split, dispute, separation, rift, rupture, alienation, disaffection, schism, estrangement
▷▷ **break away** GET AWAY, escape, flee, run away, break free, break loose, make your escape
▷▷ **break down** 1 STOP WORKING, stop, seize up, conk out (*informal*), go kaput (*informal*), go phut, cark it (*Austral & NZ slang*)
2 FAIL, collapse, fall through, be unsuccessful, come unstuck, run aground, come to grief, come a cropper (*informal*), turn out badly
3 BE OVERCOME, crack up (*informal*), go to pieces
▷▷ **break in** 1 BREAK AND ENTER, enter, gain access
2 INTERRUPT, intervene, interfere, intrude, burst in, interject, butt in, barge in, interpose, put your oar in, put your two cents in (*US slang*)
▷▷ **break off** STOP TALKING, pause, stumble,

falter, fumble, hem and haw *or* hum and haw
▷▷ **break out** 1 BEGIN, start, happen, occur, arise, set in, commence, spring up
2 ESCAPE, flee, bolt, burst out, get free, break loose, abscond, do a bunk (*Brit slang*), do a Skase (*Austral informal*)
3 ERUPT, gush, flare up, burst out, burst forth, pour forth
▷▷ **break someone in** INITIATE, train, accustom, habituate
▷▷ **break something in** PREPARE, condition, tame
▷▷ **break something off** DETACH, separate, divide, cut off, pull off, sever, part, remove, splinter, tear off, snap off
▷▷ **break something up** STOP, end, suspend, disrupt, dismantle, disperse, terminate, disband, diffuse
▷▷ **break through** SUCCEED, make it (*informal*), achieve, do well, flourish, cut it (*informal*), get to the top, crack it (*informal*), make your mark (*informal*), shine forth
▷▷ **break through something** PENETRATE, go through, get past, burst through
▷▷ **break up** 1 FINISH, be suspended, adjourn, recess
2 SPLIT UP, separate, part, divorce, end a relationship
3 SCATTER, separate, divide, dissolve
▷▷ **break with something** *or* **someone** SEPARATE FROM, drop (*informal*), reject, ditch (*slang*), renounce, depart from, break away from, part company with, repudiate, jilt

breakage *noun* BREAK, cut, tear, crack, rent, breach, fracture, rift, rupture, cleft, fissure

breakaway *adjective* REBEL, revolutionary, rebellious, dissenting, insurgent, seceding, secessionist, heretical, mutinous, insubordinate, insurrectionary, schismatic

breakdown *noun* 1 COLLAPSE, crackup (*informal*)
2 ANALYSIS, classification, dissection, categorization, detailed list, itemization

breaker *noun* WAVE, roller, comber, billow, white horse, whitecap

break-in *noun* BURGLARY, robbery, breaking and entering, home invasion (*Austral & NZ*)

breakneck *adjective* DANGEROUS, rapid, excessive, rash, reckless, precipitate, headlong, express

breakthrough *noun* DEVELOPMENT, advance, progress, improvement, discovery, find, finding, invention, step forward, leap forwards, turn of events, quantum leap

break-up *noun* 1 SEPARATION, split, divorce, breakdown, ending, parting, breaking, splitting, wind-up, rift, disintegration, dissolution, termination
2 DISSOLUTION, division, splitting, disintegration

breakwater *noun* SEA WALL, spur, mole, jetty, groyne

breast *noun* 1 HEART, feelings, thoughts, soul, being, emotions, core, sentiments, seat of the affections
2 BOSOM
>> RELATED WORD *adjective* mammary

breath *noun* 1 INHALATION, breathing, pant, gasp, gulp, wheeze, exhalation, respiration
2 GUST, sigh, puff, flutter, flurry, whiff, draught, waft, zephyr, slight movement, faint breeze
3 TRACE, suggestion, hint, whisper, suspicion, murmur, undertone, intimation
4 REST, breather
5 LIFE, energy, existence, vitality, animation, life force, lifeblood, mauri (*NZ*)

breathe *verb* 1 INHALE AND EXHALE, pant, gasp, puff, gulp, wheeze, respire, draw in breath
2 WHISPER, say, voice, express, sigh, utter, articulate, murmur
3 INSTIL, inspire, pass on, inject, impart, infuse, imbue

breather *noun* (*informal*) REST, break, halt, pause, recess, breathing space, breath of air

breathless *adjective* 1 OUT OF BREATH, winded, exhausted, panting, gasping, choking, gulping, wheezing, out of whack (*informal*), short-winded
2 EXCITED, anxious, curious, eager, enthusiastic, impatient, agog, on tenterhooks, in suspense

breathtaking *adjective* AMAZING, striking, exciting, brilliant, dramatic, stunning (*informal*), impressive, thrilling, overwhelming, magnificent, astonishing, sensational, awesome, wondrous (*archaic or literary*), awe-inspiring, jaw-dropping, heart-stirring

breed *noun* 1 VARIETY, race, stock, type, species, strain, pedigree
2 KIND, sort, type, variety, brand, stamp
▷ *verb* 1 REAR, tend, keep, raise, maintain, farm, look after, care for, bring up, nurture, nourish
2 REPRODUCE, multiply, propagate, procreate, produce offspring, bear young, bring forth young, generate offspring, beget offspring, develop
3 PRODUCE, cause, create, occasion, generate, bring about, arouse, originate, give rise to, stir up

breeding *noun* REFINEMENT, style, culture, taste, manners, polish, grace, courtesy, elegance, sophistication, delicacy, cultivation, politeness, civility, gentility, graciousness, urbanity, politesse

breeze *noun* LIGHT WIND, air, whiff, draught, gust, waft, zephyr, breath of wind, current of

air, puff of air, capful of wind
▷ *verb* SWEEP, move briskly, pass, trip, sail, hurry, sally, glide, flit

breezy *adjective* 1 CAREFREE, casual, lively, sparkling, sunny, informal, cheerful, animated, upbeat (*informal*), buoyant, airy, easy-going, genial, jaunty, chirpy (*informal*), sparky, sprightly, vivacious, debonair, blithe, free and easy, full of beans (*informal*), light, light-hearted
<< OPPOSITE serious
2 WINDY, fresh, airy, blustery, blowing, gusty, squally, blowy, blusterous
<< OPPOSITE calm

brevity *noun* 1 SHORTNESS, transience, impermanence, ephemerality, briefness, transitoriness
2 CONCISENESS, economy, crispness, concision, terseness, succinctness, curtness, pithiness
<< OPPOSITE wordiness

brew *verb* 1 BOIL, make, soak, steep, stew, infuse (*tea*)
2 MAKE, ferment, prepare by fermentation
3 START, develop, gather, foment
4 DEVELOP, form, gather, foment
▷ *noun* DRINK, preparation, mixture, blend, liquor, beverage, infusion, concoction, fermentation, distillation

bribe *noun* INDUCEMENT, incentive, pay-off (*informal*), graft (*informal*), sweetener (*slang*), kickback (US), sop, backhander (*slang*), enticement, hush money (*slang*), payola (*informal*), allurement, corrupting gift, reward for treachery
▷ *verb* BUY OFF, reward, pay off (*informal*), lure, corrupt, get at, square, suborn, grease the palm *or* hand of (*slang*), influence by gifts, oil the palm of (*slang*)

bribery *noun* CORRUPTION, graft (*informal*), inducement, buying off, payola (*informal*), crookedness (*informal*), palm-greasing (*slang*), subornation

bric-a-brac *noun* KNICK-KNACKS, ornaments, trinkets, baubles, curios, objets d'art (*French*), gewgaws, bibelots, kickshaws, objects of virtu

bridal *adjective* MATRIMONIAL, marriage, wedding, marital, bride's, nuptial, conjugal, spousal, connubial, hymeneal

bride *noun* WIFE, newly-wed, marriage partner, wifey (*informal*)

bridegroom *noun* HUSBAND, groom, newly-wed, marriage partner

bridge *noun* 1 ARCH, span, viaduct, flyover, overpass
2 LINK, tie, bond, connection
▷ *verb* 1 SPAN, cross, go over, cross over, traverse, reach across, extend across, arch over
2 RECONCILE, unite, resolve

bridle *noun* REIN, curb, control, check, restraint, trammels
▷ *verb* 1 GET ANGRY, draw (yourself) up, bristle, seethe, see red, be infuriated, rear up, be indignant, be maddened, raise your hackles, get your dander up (*slang*), get your back up
2 CURB, control, master, govern, moderate, restrain, rein, subdue, repress, constrain, keep in check, check, keep a tight rein on, keep on a string

brief *adjective* 1 SHORT, fast, quick, temporary, fleeting, swift, short-lived, little, hasty, momentary, ephemeral, quickie (*informal*), transitory
<< OPPOSITE long
2 CONCISE, short, limited, to the point, crisp, compressed, terse, curt, laconic, succinct, clipped, pithy, thumbnail, monosyllabic
<< OPPOSITE long
3 CURT, short, sharp, blunt, abrupt, brusque
▷ *verb* INFORM, prime, prepare, advise, fill in (*informal*), instruct, clue in (*informal*), gen up (*Brit informal*), put in the picture (*informal*), give a rundown, keep posted, give the gen (*Brit informal*)
▷ *noun* 1 SUMMARY, résumé, outline, sketch, abstract, summing-up, digest, epitome, rundown, synopsis, précis, recapitulation, abridgment
2 CASE, defence, argument, data, contention

briefing *noun* 1 CONFERENCE, meeting, priming
2 INSTRUCTIONS, information, priming, directions, instruction, preparation, guidance, preamble, rundown

briefly *adverb* 1 QUICKLY, shortly, precisely, casually, temporarily, abruptly, hastily, briskly, momentarily, hurriedly, curtly, summarily, fleetingly, cursorily
2 IN OUTLINE, in brief, in passing, in a nutshell, concisely, in a few words

brigade *noun* 1 CORPS, company, force, unit, division, troop, squad, crew, team, outfit, regiment, contingent, squadron, detachment
2 GROUP, party, body, band, camp, squad, organization, crew, bunch (*informal*)

bright *adjective* 1 VIVID, rich, brilliant, intense, glowing, colourful, highly-coloured
2 SHINING, flashing, beaming, glowing, blazing, sparkling, glittering, dazzling, illuminated, gleaming, shimmering, twinkling, radiant, luminous, glistening, resplendent, scintillating, lustrous, lambent, effulgent
3 (*informal*) INTELLIGENT, smart, clever, knowing, thinking, quick, aware, sharp, keen, acute, alert, rational, penetrating, enlightened, apt, astute, brainy, wide-awake, clear-headed, perspicacious, quick-witted
<< OPPOSITE stupid
4 (*informal*) CLEVER, brilliant, smart, sensible,

cunning, ingenious, inventive, canny
5 CHEERFUL, happy, glad, lively, jolly, merry, upbeat (*informal*), joyous, joyful, genial, chirpy (*informal*), sparky, vivacious, full of beans (*informal*), gay, light-hearted
6 PROMISING, good, encouraging, excellent, golden, optimistic, hopeful, favourable, prosperous, rosy, auspicious, propitious, palmy
7 SUNNY, clear, fair, pleasant, clement, lucid, cloudless, unclouded, sunlit
<< OPPOSITE cloudy

brighten *verb* 1 CHEER UP, rally, take heart, perk up, buck up (*informal*), become cheerful
<< OPPOSITE become gloomy
2 LIGHT UP, shine, glow, gleam, clear up, lighten, enliven
<< OPPOSITE dim
3 ENLIVEN, animate, make brighter, vitalize
4 BECOME BRIGHTER, light up, glow, gleam, clear up

brightness *noun* 1 VIVIDNESS, intensity, brilliance, splendour, resplendence
2 (*informal*) INTELLIGENCE, intellect, brains (*informal*), awareness, sharpness, alertness, cleverness, quickness, acuity, brain power, smarts (*slang, chiefly US*), smartness

brilliance *or* **brilliancy** *noun* 1 CLEVERNESS, talent, wisdom, distinction, genius, excellence, greatness, aptitude, inventiveness, acuity, giftedness, braininess
<< OPPOSITE stupidity
2 BRIGHTNESS, blaze, intensity, sparkle, glitter, dazzle, gleam, sheen, lustre, radiance, luminosity, vividness, resplendence, effulgence, refulgence
<< OPPOSITE darkness
3 SPLENDOUR, glamour, grandeur, magnificence, éclat, gorgeousness, illustriousness, pizzazz *or* pizazz (*informal*), gilt

brilliant *adjective* 1 INTELLIGENT, sharp, intellectual, alert, clever, quick, acute, profound, rational, penetrating, discerning, inventive, astute, brainy, perspicacious, quick-witted
<< OPPOSITE stupid
2 EXPERT, masterly, talented, gifted, accomplished
<< OPPOSITE untalented
3 SPLENDID, grand, famous, celebrated, rare, supreme, outstanding, remarkable, superb, magnificent, sterling, glorious, exceptional, notable, renowned, heroic, admirable, eminent, sublime, illustrious
4 BRIGHT, shining, intense, sparkling, glittering, dazzling, vivid, radiant, luminous, ablaze, resplendent, scintillating, lustrous, coruscating, refulgent, lambent
<< OPPOSITE dark

brim *noun* RIM, edge, border, lip, margin, verge, brink, flange
▷ *verb* 1 BE FULL, spill, well over, run over, overflow, spill over, brim over
2 FILL, well over, fill up, overflow

brine *noun* SALT WATER, saline solution, pickling solution

bring *verb* 1 FETCH, take, carry, bear, transfer, deliver, transport, import, convey
2 TAKE, guide, conduct, accompany, escort, usher
3 CAUSE, produce, create, effect, occasion, result in, contribute to, inflict, wreak, engender
4 MAKE, force, influence, convince, persuade, prompt, compel, induce, move, dispose, sway, prevail on *or* upon
▷▷ **bring someone up** REAR, raise, support, train, develop, teach, nurse, breed, foster, educate, care for, nurture
▷▷ **bring something about** CAUSE, produce, create, effect, manage, achieve, occasion, realize, generate, accomplish, give rise to, make happen, effectuate, bring to pass
▷▷ **bring something down** 1 OVERTURN, reduce, undermine, overthrow, abase
2 REDUCE, cut, drop, lower, slash, decrease
3 CUT DOWN, level, fell, hew, lop, raze
4 DEMOLISH, level, destroy, dismantle, flatten, knock down, pull down, tear down, bulldoze, raze, kennet (*Austral slang*), jeff (*Austral slang*)
▷▷ **bring something in** 1 INTRODUCE, start, found, launch, establish, set up, institute, organize, pioneer, initiate, usher in, inaugurate
2 PRODUCE, return, net, realize, generate, be worth, yield, gross, fetch, accrue
▷▷ **bring something off** ACCOMPLISH, achieve, perform, carry out, succeed, execute, discharge, pull off, carry off, bring to pass
▷▷ **bring something up** MENTION, raise, introduce, point out, refer to, allude to, broach, call attention to, speak about *or* of

brink *noun* EDGE, point, limit, border, lip, margin, boundary, skirt, frontier, fringe, verge, threshold, rim, brim

brio *noun* ENERGY, spirit, enthusiasm, dash, pep, zip (*informal*), animation, vigour, verve, zest, panache, gusto, get-up-and-go (*informal*), élan, vivacity, liveliness

brisk *adjective* 1 QUICK, lively, energetic, active, vigorous, animated, bustling, speedy, nimble, agile, sprightly, vivacious, spry
<< OPPOSITE slow
2 SHORT, sharp, brief, blunt, rude, tart, abrupt, no-nonsense, terse, gruff, pithy, brusque, offhand, monosyllabic, ungracious, uncivil, snappish
3 INVIGORATING, fresh, biting, sharp, keen,

stimulating, crisp, bracing, refreshing, exhilarating, nippy
<< OPPOSITE tiring

briskly *adverb* 1 QUICKLY, smartly, promptly, rapidly, readily, actively, efficiently, vigorously, energetically, pronto (*informal*), nimbly, posthaste
2 RAPIDLY, quickly, apace, pdq (*slang*)
3 BRUSQUELY, firmly, decisively, incisively

bristle *noun* HAIR, spine, thorn, whisker, barb, stubble, prickle
▷ *verb* 1 STAND UP, rise, prickle, stand on end, horripilate
2 BE ANGRY, rage, seethe, flare up, bridle, see red, be infuriated, spit (*informal*), go ballistic (*slang, chiefly US*), be maddened, wig out (*slang*), get your dander up (*slang*)
3 ABOUND, crawl, be alive, hum, swarm, teem, be thick

Briton *noun* BRIT. (*informal*), limey (*US & Canad slang*), Britisher, pommy *or* pom (*Austral & NZ slang*), Anglo-Saxon

brittle *adjective* 1 FRAGILE, delicate, crisp, crumbling, frail, crumbly, breakable, shivery, friable, frangible, shatterable
<< OPPOSITE tough
2 TENSE, nervous, edgy, stiff, wired (*slang*), irritable, curt

broach *verb* 1 BRING UP, approach, introduce, mention, speak of, talk of, open up, hint at, touch on, raise the subject of
2 OPEN, crack, pierce, puncture, uncork

broad *adjective* 1 WIDE, large, ample, generous, expansive
2 LARGE, huge, comfortable, vast, extensive, ample, spacious, expansive, roomy, voluminous, capacious, uncrowded, commodious, beamy (*of a ship*), sizable *or* sizeable
<< OPPOSITE narrow
3 FULL, general, comprehensive, complete, wide, global, catholic, sweeping, extensive, wide-ranging, umbrella, thorough, unlimited, inclusive, far-reaching, exhaustive, all-inclusive, all-embracing, overarching, encyclopedic
4 UNIVERSAL, general, common, wide, sweeping, worldwide, widespread, wide-ranging, far-reaching
5 GENERAL, loose, vague, approximate, indefinite, ill-defined, inexact, nonspecific, unspecific, undetailed
6 CLEAR, open, full, plain
7 VULGAR, blue, dirty, gross, crude, rude, naughty, coarse, indecent, improper, suggestive, risqué, boorish, uncouth, unrefined, ribald, indelicate, near the knuckle (*informal*), indecorous, unmannerly

broadcast *noun* TRANSMISSION, show, programme, telecast
▷ *verb* 1 TRANSMIT, show, send, air, radio, cable, beam, send out, relay, televise, disseminate, put on the air
2 MAKE PUBLIC, report, announce, publish, spread, advertise, proclaim, circulate, disseminate, promulgate, shout from the rooftops (*informal*)

broaden *verb* EXPAND, increase, develop, spread, extend, stretch, open up, swell, supplement, widen, enlarge, augment
<< OPPOSITE restrict

broadly *adverb* 1 WIDELY, greatly, hugely, vastly, extensively, expansively
2 GENERALLY, commonly, widely, universally, popularly
<< OPPOSITE narrowly

broadside *noun* ATTACK, criticism, censure, swipe, denunciation, diatribe, philippic

brochure *noun* BOOKLET, advertisement, leaflet, hand-out, circular, pamphlet, folder, mailshot, handbill

broekies *plural noun* (*S African informal*) UNDERPANTS, pants, briefs, drawers, knickers, panties, boxer shorts, Y-fronts (*trademark*), underdaks (*Austral slang*)

broke *adjective* (*informal*) PENNILESS, short, ruined, bust (*informal*), bankrupt, impoverished, in the red, cleaned out (*slang*), insolvent, down and out, skint (*Brit slang*), strapped for cash (*informal*), dirt-poor (*informal*), flat broke (*informal*), penurious, on your uppers, stony-broke (*Brit slang*), in queer street, without two pennies to rub together (*informal*), without a penny to your name
<< OPPOSITE rich

broken *adjective* 1 INTERRUPTED, disturbed, incomplete, erratic, disconnected, intermittent, fragmentary, spasmodic, discontinuous
2 IMPERFECT, halting, hesitating, stammering, disjointed
3 SMASHED, destroyed, burst, shattered, fragmented, fractured, demolished, severed, ruptured, rent, separated, shivered
4 DEFECTIVE, not working, ruined, imperfect, out of order, not functioning, on the blink (*slang*), on its last legs, kaput (*informal*)
5 VIOLATED, forgotten, ignored, disregarded, not kept, infringed, retracted, disobeyed, dishonoured, transgressed, traduced
6 DEFEATED, beaten, crushed, humbled, crippled, tamed, subdued, oppressed, overpowered, vanquished, demoralized, browbeaten

broken-down *adjective* NOT IN WORKING ORDER, old, worn out, out of order, dilapidated, not functioning, out of commission, on the blink (*slang*), inoperative, kaput (*informal*), in

disrepair, on the fritz (*US slang*)
brokenhearted *adjective* HEARTBROKEN, devastated, disappointed, despairing, miserable, choked, desolate, mournful, prostrated, grief-stricken, sorrowful, wretched, disconsolate, inconsolable, crestfallen, down in the dumps (*informal*), heart-sick
broker *noun* DEALER, marketer, agent, trader, supplier, merchant, entrepreneur, negotiator, chandler, mediator, intermediary, wholesaler, middleman, factor, purveyor, go-between, tradesman, merchandiser
bronze *adjective* REDDISH-BROWN, copper, tan, rust, chestnut, brownish, copper-coloured, yellowish-brown, reddish-tan, metallic brown
brood *noun* 1 OFFSPRING, young, issue, breed, infants, clutch, hatch, litter, chicks, progeny
2 CHILDREN, family, offspring, progeny, nearest and dearest, flesh and blood, ainga (NZ)
▷ *verb* THINK, obsess, muse, ponder, fret, meditate, agonize, mull over, mope, ruminate, eat your heart out, dwell upon, repine
brook¹ *noun* STREAM, burn (*Scot & Northern English*), rivulet, gill (*dialect*), beck, watercourse, rill, streamlet, runnel (*literary*)
brook² *verb* TOLERATE, stand, allow, suffer, accept, bear, stomach, endure, swallow, hack (*slang*), abide, put up with (*informal*), withstand, countenance, support, thole (*dialect*)
brothel *noun* WHOREHOUSE, red-light district, bordello, cathouse (*US slang*), house of ill repute, knocking shop (*slang*), bawdy house (*archaic*), house of prostitution, bagnio, house of ill fame, stews (*archaic*)
brother *noun* 1 MALE SIBLING
2 COMRADE, partner, colleague, associate, mate, pal (*informal*), companion, cock (*Brit informal*), chum (*informal*), fellow member, confrère, compeer
3 MONK, cleric, friar, monastic, religious, regular
>> RELATED WORD *adjective* fraternal
brotherhood *noun* 1 FELLOWSHIP, kinship, companionship, comradeship, friendliness, camaraderie, brotherliness
2 ASSOCIATION, order, union, community, society, league, alliance, clan, guild, fraternity, clique, coterie
brotherly *adjective* FRATERNAL, friendly, neighbourly, sympathetic, affectionate, benevolent, kind, amicable, altruistic, philanthropic
brow *noun* 1 FOREHEAD, temple
2 TOP, summit, peak, edge, tip, crown, verge, brink, rim, crest, brim
brown *adjective* 1 BRUNETTE, dark, bay, coffee, chocolate, brick, toasted, ginger, rust, chestnut, hazel, dun, auburn, tawny, umber, donkey brown, fuscous
2 TANNED, browned, bronze, bronzed, tan, dusky, sunburnt
▷ *verb* FRY, cook, grill, sear, sauté
browse *verb* 1 SKIM, scan, glance at, survey, look through, look round, dip into, leaf through, peruse, flip through, examine cursorily
2 GRAZE, eat, feed, crop, pasture, nibble
bruise *noun* DISCOLORATION, mark, injury, trauma (*Pathology*), blemish, black mark, contusion, black-and-blue mark
▷ *verb* 1 HURT, injure, mark, blacken
2 DAMAGE, mark, mar, blemish, discolour
3 INJURE, hurt, pain, wound, slight, insult, sting, offend, grieve, displease, rile, pique
bruiser *noun* (*informal*) TOUGH, heavy (*slang*), rough (*informal*), bully, thug, gorilla (*informal*), hard man, rowdy, tough guy, hoodlum, bully boy, ruffian, roughneck (*slang*)
brunt *noun* FULL FORCE, force, pressure, violence, shock, stress, impact, strain, burden, thrust
brush¹ *noun* 1 BROOM, sweeper, besom
2 CONFLICT, fight, clash, set-to (*informal*), scrap (*informal*), confrontation, skirmish, tussle, fracas, spot of bother (*informal*), slight engagement
3 ENCOUNTER, meeting, confrontation, rendezvous
▷ *verb* 1 CLEAN, wash, polish, buff
2 TOUCH, come into contact with, sweep, kiss, stroke, glance, flick, scrape, graze, caress
▷▷ **brush someone off** (*Slang*) IGNORE, cut, reject, dismiss, slight, blank (*slang*), put down, snub, disregard, scorn, disdain, spurn, rebuff, repudiate, disown, cold-shoulder, kiss off (*slang, chiefly US & Canad*), send to Coventry
▷▷ **brush something aside** DISMISS, ignore, discount, override, disregard, sweep aside, have no time for, kiss off (*slang, chiefly US & Canad*)
▷▷ **brush something up** *or* **brush up on something** REVISE, study, go over, cram, polish up, read up on, relearn, bone up on (*informal*), refresh your memory
brush² *noun* SHRUBS, bushes, scrub, underwood, undergrowth, thicket, copse, brushwood
brusque *adjective* CURT, short, sharp, blunt, tart, abrupt, hasty, terse, surly, gruff, impolite, monosyllabic, discourteous, unmannerly
<< OPPOSITE polite
brutal *adjective* 1 CRUEL, harsh, savage, grim, vicious, ruthless, ferocious, callous, sadistic, heartless, atrocious, inhuman, merciless, cold-blooded, inhumane, brutish,

bloodthirsty, remorseless, barbarous, pitiless, uncivilized, hard-hearted
<< OPPOSITE kind
2 HARSH, tough, severe, rough, rude, indifferent, insensitive, callous, merciless, unconcerned, uncaring, gruff, bearish, tactless, unfeeling, impolite, uncivil, unmannerly
<< OPPOSITE sensitive

brutality *noun* CRUELTY, atrocity, ferocity, savagery, ruthlessness, barbarism, inhumanity, barbarity, viciousness, brutishness, bloodthirstiness, savageness

brutally *adverb* CRUELLY, fiercely, savagely, ruthlessly, viciously, mercilessly, ferociously, remorselessly, in cold blood, callously, murderously, pitilessly, heartlessly, inhumanly, barbarously, brutishly, barbarically, hardheartedly

brute *noun* 1 SAVAGE, devil, monster, beast, barbarian, fiend, swine, ogre, ghoul, sadist
2 BEAST, animal, creature, wild animal
▷ *adjective* PHYSICAL, bodily, mindless, instinctive, senseless, unthinking

brutish *adjective* COARSE, stupid, gross, cruel, savage, crude, vulgar, barbarian, crass, boorish, uncouth, loutish, subhuman, swinish

bubble *noun* AIR BALL, drop, bead, blister, blob, droplet, globule, vesicle
▷ *verb* 1 BOIL, seethe
2 FOAM, fizz, froth, churn, agitate, percolate, effervesce
3 GURGLE, splash, murmur, trickle, ripple, babble, trill, burble, lap, purl, plash

bubbly *adjective* 1 LIVELY, happy, excited, animated, merry, bouncy, elated, sparky, alive and kicking, full of beans (*informal*)
2 FROTHY, sparkling, fizzy, effervescent, carbonated, foamy, sudsy, lathery

buccaneer *noun* PIRATE, privateer, corsair, freebooter, sea-rover

buckle *noun* FASTENER, catch, clip, clasp, hasp
▷ *verb* 1 FASTEN, close, secure, hook, clasp
2 DISTORT, bend, warp, crumple, contort
3 COLLAPSE, bend, twist, fold, give way, subside, cave in, crumple
▷▷ **buckle down** (*informal*) APPLY YOURSELF, set to, fall to, pitch in, get busy, get cracking (*informal*), exert yourself, put your shoulder to the wheel

bud *noun* SHOOT, branch, sprout, twig, sprig, offshoot, scion
▷ *verb* DEVELOP, grow, shoot, sprout, burgeon, burst forth, pullulate

budding *adjective* DEVELOPING, beginning, growing, promising, potential, burgeoning, fledgling, embryonic

buddy *noun* (*Chiefly US & Canad*) FRIEND, mate (*informal*), pal, companion, comrade, chum (*informal*), crony, main man (*slang, chiefly US*), homeboy (*slang, chiefly US*), cobber (*Austral & NZ old-fashioned informal*), E hoa (*NZ*)

budge *verb* 1 YIELD, change, bend, concede, surrender, comply, give way, capitulate
2 PERSUADE, influence, convince, sway
3 MOVE, roll, slide, stir, give way, change position
4 DISLODGE, move, push, roll, remove, transfer, shift, slide, stir, propel

budget *noun* ALLOWANCE, means, funds, income, finances, resources, allocation
▷ *verb* PLAN, estimate, allocate, cost, ration, apportion, cost out

buff[1] *adjective* FAWN, cream, tan, beige, yellowish, ecru, straw-coloured, sand-coloured, yellowish-brown, biscuit-coloured, camel-coloured, oatmeal-coloured
▷ *verb* POLISH, clean, smooth, brush, shine, rub, wax, brighten, burnish
▷▷ **in the buff** NAKED, bare, nude, in the raw (*informal*), unclothed, in the altogether (*informal*), buck naked (*slang*), unclad, in your birthday suit (*informal*), scuddy (*slang*), without a stitch on (*informal*), with bare skin, in the bare scud (*slang*)

buff[2] *noun* (*informal*) EXPERT, fan, addict, enthusiast, freak (*informal*), admirer, whizz (*informal*), devotee, connoisseur, fiend (*informal*), grandmaster, hotshot (*informal*), aficionado, wonk (*informal*), maven (*US*), fundi (*S African*)

buffer *noun* SAFEGUARD, screen, shield, cushion, intermediary, bulwark

buffet[1] *noun* 1 SMORGASBORD, counter, cold table
2 SNACK BAR, café, cafeteria, brasserie, salad bar, refreshment counter

buffet[2] *verb* KNOCK, push, bang, rap, slap, bump, smack, shove, thump, cuff, jolt, wallop (*informal*), box

buffoon *noun* CLOWN, fool, comic, comedian, wag, joker, jester, dag (*NZ informal*), harlequin, droll, silly billy (*informal*), joculator *or* (*fem.*) joculatrix

bug *noun* 1 (*informal*) ILLNESS, disease, complaint, virus, infection, disorder, disability, sickness, ailment, malaise, affliction, malady, lurgy (*informal*)
2 FAULT, failing, virus, error, defect, flaw, blemish, imperfection, glitch, gremlin
3 (*informal*) MANIA, passion, rage, obsession, craze, fad, thing (*informal*)
▷ *verb* 1 TAP, eavesdrop, listen in on, wiretap
2 (*informal*) ANNOY, bother, disturb, needle (*informal*), plague, irritate, harass, hassle (*informal*), aggravate (*informal*), badger, gall,

nettle, pester, vex, irk, get under your skin (*informal*), get on your nerves (*informal*), nark (*Brit, Austral & NZ slang*), get up your nose (*informal*), be on your back (*slang*), get in your hair (*informal*), get on your wick (*Brit slang*), hack you off (*informal*)

build *verb* 1 CONSTRUCT, make, raise, put up, assemble, erect, fabricate, form
<< OPPOSITE demolish
2 ESTABLISH, start, begin, found, base, set up, institute, constitute, initiate, originate, formulate, inaugurate
<< OPPOSITE finish
3 DEVELOP, increase, improve, extend, strengthen, intensify, enlarge, amplify, augment
<< OPPOSITE decrease
▷ *noun* PHYSIQUE, form, body, figure, shape, structure, frame
▷▷ **build something up** INCREASE, develop, improve, extend, expand, add to, strengthen, enhance, reinforce, intensify, heighten, fortify, amplify, augment

building *noun* STRUCTURE, house, construction, dwelling, erection, edifice, domicile, pile

build-up *noun* 1 INCREASE, development, growth, expansion, accumulation, enlargement, escalation, upsurge, intensification, augmentation
2 ACCUMULATION, accretion
3 HYPE, promotion, publicity, plug (*informal*), puff, razzmatazz (*slang*), brouhaha, ballyhoo (*informal*)

built-in *adjective* ESSENTIAL, integral, included, incorporated, inherent, implicit, in-built, intrinsic, inseparable, immanent

bulbous *adjective* BULGING, rounded, swelling, swollen, bloated, convex

bulge *verb* 1 SWELL OUT, project, expand, swell, stand out, stick out, protrude, puff out, distend, bag
2 STICK OUT, stand out, protrude
▷ *noun* 1 LUMP, swelling, bump, projection, hump, protuberance, protrusion
<< OPPOSITE hollow
2 INCREASE, rise, boost, surge, intensification

bulk *noun* 1 SIZE, volume, dimensions, magnitude, substance, vastness, amplitude, immensity, bigness, largeness, massiveness
2 WEIGHT, size, mass, heaviness, poundage, portliness
3 MAJORITY, mass, most, body, quantity, best part, major part, lion's share, better part, generality, preponderance, main part, plurality, nearly all, greater number
▷▷ **bulk large** BE IMPORTANT, dominate, loom, stand out, loom large, carry weight, preponderate, threaten

> The use of a plural noun after *bulk*, as in sense 3, although common, is considered by some to be incorrect and should be avoided. This usage is most commonly encountered, according to the *Collins Word Web*, when referring to *funds* and *profits*: *the bulk of our profits stem from the sale of beer*. The synonyms *majority* and *most* would work better in this context

bulky *adjective* LARGE, big, huge, heavy, massive, enormous, substantial, immense, mega (*slang*), very large, mammoth, colossal, cumbersome, weighty, hulking, unwieldy, ponderous, voluminous, unmanageable, elephantine, massy, ginormous (*informal*), humongous *or* humungous (*US slang*)
<< OPPOSITE small

bulldoze *verb* 1 DEMOLISH, level, destroy, flatten, knock down, tear down, raze, kennet (*Austral slang*), jeff (*Austral slang*)
2 (*informal*) PUSH, force, drive, thrust, shove, propel
3 (*informal*) FORCE, bully, intimidate, railroad (*informal*), cow, hector, coerce, dragoon, browbeat, put the screws on

bullet *noun* PROJECTILE, ball, shot, missile, slug, pellet

bulletin *noun* REPORT, account, statement, message, communication, announcement, dispatch, communiqué, notification, news flash

bully *noun* PERSECUTOR, tough, oppressor, tormentor, bully boy, browbeater, coercer, ruffian, intimidator
▷ *verb* 1 PERSECUTE, intimidate, torment, hound, oppress, pick on, victimize, terrorize, push around (*slang*), ill-treat, ride roughshod over, maltreat, tyrannize, overbear
2 FORCE, coerce, railroad (*informal*), bulldoze (*informal*), dragoon, pressurize, browbeat, cow, hector, press-gang, domineer, bullyrag

bulwark *noun* 1 FORTIFICATION, defence, bastion, buttress, rampart, redoubt, outwork
2 DEFENCE, support, safeguard, security, guard, buffer, mainstay

bumbling *adjective* CLUMSY, awkward, blundering, bungling, incompetent, inefficient, lumbering, inept, maladroit, unco (*Austral slang*)
<< OPPOSITE efficient

bump *verb* 1 KNOCK, hit, strike, crash, smash, slam, bang
2 JERK, shake, bounce, rattle, jar, jog, lurch, jolt, jostle, jounce
▷ *noun* 1 KNOCK, hit, blow, shock, impact, rap, collision, thump

2 THUD, crash, knock, smash, bang, smack, thump, clump, wallop (*informal*), clunk, clonk
3 LUMP, swelling, bulge, hump, node, nodule, protuberance, contusion
▷▷ **bump into someone** (*informal*) MEET, encounter, come across, run into, run across, meet up with, chance upon, happen upon, light upon
▷▷ **bump someone off** (*Slang*) MURDER, kill, assassinate, remove, do in (*slang*), eliminate, take out (*slang*), wipe out (*informal*), dispatch, finish off, do away with, blow away (*slang, chiefly US*), knock off (*slang*), liquidate, rub out (*US slang*)

bumper *adjective* EXCEPTIONAL, excellent, exo (*Austral slang*), massive, unusual, mega (*slang*), jumbo (*informal*), abundant, whacking (*informal, chiefly Brit*), spanking (*informal*), whopping (*informal*), bountiful

bumpy *adjective* 1 UNEVEN, rough, pitted, irregular, rutted, lumpy, potholed, knobby
2 JOLTING, jarring, bouncy, choppy, jerky, bone-breaking, jolty

bunch *noun* 1 (*informal*) GROUP, band, crowd, party, team, troop, gathering, crew (*informal*), gang, knot, mob, flock, swarm, multitude, posse (*informal*), bevy
2 BOUQUET, spray, sheaf
3 CLUSTER, clump
▷▷ **bunch together** *or* **up** GROUP, crowd, mass, collect, assemble, cluster, flock, herd, huddle, congregate

bundle *noun* BUNCH, group, collection, mass, pile, quantity, stack, heap, rick, batch, accumulation, assortment
▷ *verb* PUSH, thrust, shove, throw, rush, hurry, hasten, jostle, hustle
▷▷ **bundle someone up** WRAP UP, swathe, muffle up, clothe warmly
▷▷ **bundle something up** PACKAGE, tie, pack, bind, wrap, tie up, bale, fasten, truss, tie together, palletize

bungle *verb* MESS UP, blow (*slang*), ruin, spoil, blunder, fudge, screw up (*informal*), botch, cock up (*Brit slang*), miscalculate, make a mess of, mismanage, muff, foul up, make a nonsense of (*informal*), bodge (*informal*), make a pig's ear of (*informal*), flub (*US slang*), crool *or* cruel (*Austral slang*), louse up (*slang*)
<< OPPOSITE accomplish

bungling *adjective* INCOMPETENT, blundering, awkward, clumsy, inept, botching, cack-handed (*informal*), maladroit, ham-handed (*informal*), unskilful, ham-fisted (*informal*), unco (*Austral slang*)

bunk[1] *noun* ▷▷ **do a bunk** (*Brit slang*) RUN AWAY, flee, bolt, clear out (*informal*), beat it (*slang*), abscond, decamp, do a runner (*slang*), run for it (*informal*), cut and run (*informal*), scram (*informal*), fly the coop (*US & Canad informal*), skedaddle (*informal*), take a powder (*US & Canad slang*), take it on the lam (*US & Canad slang*), do a Skase (*Austral informal*)

bunk[2] *or* **bunkum** *noun* (*informal*) NONSENSE, rubbish, rot, crap (*slang*), garbage (*informal*), trash, hot air (*informal*), tosh (*slang, chiefly Brit*), bilge (*informal*), twaddle, tripe (*informal*), guff (*slang*), havers (*Scot*), moonshine, baloney (*informal*), hogwash, bizzo (*Austral slang*), bull's wool (*Austral & NZ slang*), hokum (*slang, chiefly US & Canad*), piffle (*informal*), tomfoolery, poppycock (*informal*), balderdash, bosh (*informal*), eyewash (*informal*), kak (*S African taboo slang*), stuff and nonsense, hooey (*slang*), tommyrot, horsefeathers (*US slang*), tarradiddle

buoy *noun* FLOAT, guide, signal, marker, beacon
▷▷ **buoy someone up** ENCOURAGE, support, boost, cheer, sustain, hearten, cheer up, keep afloat, gee up

buoyancy *noun* 1 FLOATABILITY, lightness, weightlessness
2 CHEERFULNESS, bounce (*informal*), pep, animation, good humour, high spirits, zing (*informal*), liveliness, spiritedness, cheeriness, sunniness

buoyant *adjective* 1 CHEERFUL, happy, bright, lively, sunny, animated, upbeat (*informal*), joyful, carefree, bouncy, breezy, genial, jaunty, chirpy (*informal*), sparky, vivacious, debonair, blithe, full of beans (*informal*), peppy (*informal*), light-hearted
<< OPPOSITE gloomy
2 FLOATING, light, floatable

burden *noun* 1 TROUBLE, care, worry, trial, weight, responsibility, stress, strain, anxiety, sorrow, grievance, affliction, onus, albatross, millstone, encumbrance
2 LOAD, weight, cargo, freight, bale, consignment, encumbrance
▷ *verb* WEIGH DOWN, worry, load, tax, strain, bother, overwhelm, handicap, oppress, inconvenience, overload, saddle with, encumber, trammel, incommode
>> RELATED WORD *adjective* onerous

burdensome *adjective* TROUBLESOME, trying, taxing, difficult, heavy, crushing, exacting, oppressive, weighty, onerous, irksome

bureau *noun* 1 AGENCY
2 OFFICE, department, section, branch, station, unit, division, subdivision
3 DESK, writing desk

bureaucracy *noun* 1 GOVERNMENT, officials, authorities, administration, ministry, the system, civil service, directorate, officialdom, corridors of power
2 RED TAPE, regulations, officialdom, officialese, bumbledom

bureaucrat *noun* OFFICIAL, minister, officer,

administrator, civil servant, public servant, functionary, apparatchik, office-holder, mandarin

burglar *noun* HOUSEBREAKER, thief, robber, pilferer, filcher, cat burglar, sneak thief, picklock

burglary *noun* BREAKING AND ENTERING, housebreaking, break-in, home invasion (*Austral* & NZ)

burial *noun* FUNERAL, interment, burying, obsequies, entombment, inhumation, exequies, sepulture

burial ground *noun* GRAVEYARD, cemetery, churchyard, necropolis, God's acre

burlesque *noun* PARODY, mockery, satire, caricature, send-up (*Brit informal*), spoof (*informal*), travesty, takeoff (*informal*)
▷ *adjective* SATIRICAL, comic, mocking, mock, farcical, travestying, ironical, parodic, mock-heroic, caricatural, hudibrastic

burly *adjective* BRAWNY, strong, powerful, big, strapping, hefty, muscular, sturdy, stout, bulky, stocky, hulking, beefy (*informal*), well-built, thickset
<< OPPOSITE scrawny

burn *verb* 1 BE ON FIRE, blaze, be ablaze, smoke, flame, glow, flare, flicker, go up in flames
2 SET ON FIRE, light, ignite, kindle, incinerate, reduce to ashes
3 SCORCH, toast, sear, char, singe, brand
4 STING, hurt, smart, tingle, bite, pain
5 BE PASSIONATE, blaze, be excited, be aroused, be inflamed
6 SEETHE, fume, be angry, simmer, smoulder

burning *adjective* 1 INTENSE, passionate, earnest, eager, frantic, frenzied, ardent, fervent, impassioned, zealous, vehement, all-consuming, fervid
<< OPPOSITE mild
2 CRUCIAL, important, pressing, significant, essential, vital, critical, acute, compelling, urgent

burnish *verb* POLISH, shine, buff, brighten, rub up, furbish
<< OPPOSITE scuff

burrow *noun* HOLE, shelter, tunnel, den, lair, retreat
▷ *verb* 1 DIG, tunnel, excavate
2 DELVE, search, dig, probe, ferret, rummage, forage, fossick (*Austral* & NZ)

burst *verb* 1 EXPLODE, blow up, break, split, crack, shatter, fragment, shiver, disintegrate, puncture, rupture
2 RUSH, run, break, break out, erupt, spout, gush forth
3 BARGE, charge, rush, shove
▷ *noun* 1 RUSH, surge, fit, outbreak, outburst, spate, gush, torrent, eruption, spurt, outpouring
2 EXPLOSION, crack, blast, blasting, bang, discharge

bury *verb* 1 INTER, lay to rest, entomb, sepulchre, consign to the grave, inearth, inhume, inurn
<< OPPOSITE dig up
2 HIDE, cover, conceal, stash (*informal*), secrete, cache, stow away
<< OPPOSITE uncover
3 SINK, embed, immerse, enfold
4 FORGET, draw a veil over, think no more of, put in the past, not give another thought to
5 ENGROSS, involve, occupy, interest, busy, engage, absorb, preoccupy, immerse

bush *noun* SHRUB, plant, hedge, thicket, shrubbery
▷▷ **the bush** THE WILDS, brush, scrub, woodland, backwoods, back country (*US*), scrubland, backlands (*US*)

bushy *adjective* THICK, bristling, spreading, rough, stiff, fuzzy, fluffy, unruly, shaggy, wiry, luxuriant, bristly

busily *adverb* ACTIVELY, briskly, intently, earnestly, strenuously, speedily, purposefully, diligently, energetically, assiduously, industriously

business *noun* 1 TRADE, selling, trading, industry, manufacturing, commerce, dealings, merchandising
2 ESTABLISHMENT, company, firm, concern, organization, corporation, venture, enterprise
3 PROFESSION, work, calling, job, line, trade, career, function, employment, craft, occupation, pursuit, vocation, métier
4 MATTER, issue, subject, point, problem, question, responsibility, task, duty, function, topic, assignment
5 CONCERN, affair

businesslike *adjective* EFFICIENT, professional, practical, regular, correct, organized, routine, thorough, systematic, orderly, matter-of-fact, methodical, well-ordered, workaday
<< OPPOSITE inefficient

businessman *or* **businesswoman** *noun* EXECUTIVE, director, manager, merchant, capitalist, administrator, entrepreneur, tycoon, industrialist, financier, tradesman, homme d'affaires (*French*)

bust[1] *noun* BOSOM, breasts, chest, front

bust[2] (*informal*) *verb* 1 BREAK, smash, split, burst, shatter, fracture, rupture, break into fragments
2 ARREST, catch, lift (*slang*), raid, cop (*slang*), nail (*informal*), collar (*informal*), nab (*informal*), feel your collar (*slang*)
▷ *noun* ARREST, capture, raid, cop (*slang*)
▷▷ **go bust** GO BANKRUPT, fail, break, be ruined, become insolvent

bustle *verb* HURRY, tear, rush, dash, scramble,

fuss, flutter, beetle, hasten, scuttle, scurry, scamper
<< OPPOSITE idle
▷ *noun* ACTIVITY, to-do, stir, excitement, hurry, fuss, flurry, haste, agitation, commotion, ado, tumult, hurly-burly, pother
<< OPPOSITE inactivity

bustling *adjective* BUSY, full, crowded, rushing, active, stirring, lively, buzzing, energetic, humming, swarming, thronged, hustling, teeming, astir

busy *adjective* 1 ACTIVE, brisk, diligent, industrious, assiduous, rushed off your feet
<< OPPOSITE idle
2 OCCUPIED WITH, working, engaged in, on duty, employed in, hard at work, engrossed in, in harness, on active service
<< OPPOSITE unoccupied
3 HECTIC, full, active, tiring, exacting, energetic, strenuous, on the go (*informal*)
▷▷ **busy yourself** OCCUPY YOURSELF, be engrossed, immerse yourself, involve yourself, amuse yourself, absorb yourself, employ yourself, engage yourself, keep busy *or* occupied

but *conjunction* HOWEVER, still, yet, nevertheless
▷ *preposition* EXCEPT (FOR), save, bar, barring, excepting, excluding, with the exception of
▷ *adverb* ONLY, just, simply, merely

butcher *noun* MURDERER, killer, slaughterer, slayer, destroyer, liquidator, executioner, cut-throat, exterminator
▷ *verb* 1 SLAUGHTER, prepare, carve, cut up, dress, cut, clean, joint
2 KILL, slaughter, massacre, destroy, cut down, assassinate, slay, liquidate, exterminate, put to the sword
3 MESS UP, destroy, ruin, wreck, spoil, mutilate, botch, bodge (*informal*)

butchery *noun* SLAUGHTER, killing, murder, massacre, bloodshed, carnage, mass murder, blood-letting, blood bath

butt[1] *noun* 1 END, handle, shaft, stock, shank, hilt, haft
2 STUB, end, base, foot, tip, tail, leftover, fag end (*informal*)

butt[2] *noun* TARGET, victim, object, point, mark, subject, dupe, laughing stock, Aunt Sally

butt[3] *verb* KNOCK, push, bump, punch, buck, thrust, ram, shove, poke, buffet, prod, jab, bunt
▷▷ **butt in** 1 INTERFERE, meddle, intrude, heckle, barge in (*informal*), stick your nose in, put your oar in
2 INTERRUPT, cut in, break in, chip in (*informal*), put your two cents in (*US slang*)

butt[4] *noun* CASK, drum, barrel, cylinder

butter *noun* ▷▷ **butter someone up** FLATTER, coax, cajole, pander to, blarney, wheedle, suck up to (*informal*), soft-soap, fawn on *or* upon

butterfly *noun*
>> RELATED WORDS *young* caterpillar, chrysalis *or* chrysalid
>> RELATED WORD *enthusiast* lepidopterist

buttocks *noun* BOTTOM, behind (*informal*), bum (*Brit slang*), backside (*informal*), seat, rear, tail (*informal*), butt (*US & Canad informal*), buns (*US slang*), rump, posterior, haunches, hindquarters, derrière (*euphemistic*), tush (*US slang*), fundament, gluteus maximus (*Anatomy*), jacksy (*Brit slang*)

buttonhole *verb* DETAIN, catch, grab, intercept, accost, waylay, take aside

buttress *noun* SUPPORT, shore, prop, brace, pier, reinforcement, strut, mainstay, stanchion, stay, abutment
▷ *verb* SUPPORT, sustain, strengthen, shore, prop, reinforce, back up, brace, uphold, bolster, prop up, shore up, augment

buxom *adjective* PLUMP, ample, voluptuous, busty, well-rounded, curvaceous, comely, bosomy, full-bosomed
<< OPPOSITE slender

buy *verb* PURCHASE, get, score (*slang*), secure, pay for, obtain, acquire, invest in, shop for, procure
<< OPPOSITE sell
▷ *noun* PURCHASE, deal, bargain, acquisition, steal (*informal*), snip (*informal*), giveaway
▷▷ **buy someone off** BRIBE, square, fix (*informal*), pay off (*informal*), lure, corrupt, get at, suborn, grease someone's palm (*slang*), influence by gifts, oil the palm of (*slang*)

buzz *verb* HUM, whizz, drone, whir
▷ *noun* 1 HUM, buzzing, murmur, drone, whir, bombilation *or* bombination (*literary*)
2 GOSSIP, news, report, latest (*informal*), word, scandal, rumour, whisper, dirt (*US slang*), gen (*Brit informal*), hearsay, scuttlebutt (*US slang*), goss (*informal*)

by *preposition* 1 THROUGH, under the aegis of, through the agency of
2 VIA, over, by way of
3 NEAR, past, along, close to, closest to, neighbouring, next to, beside, nearest to, adjoining, adjacent to
▷ *adverb* NEARBY, close, handy, at hand, within reach
▷▷ **by and by** PRESENTLY, shortly, soon, eventually, one day, before long, in a while, anon, in the course of time, erelong (*archaic or poetic*)

bygone *adjective* PAST, former, previous, lost, forgotten, ancient, of old, one-time, departed, extinct, gone by, erstwhile, antiquated, of yore, olden, past recall, sunk in oblivion
<< OPPOSITE future

bypass *verb* 1 GET ROUND, avoid, evade, circumvent, outmanoeuvre, body-swerve (*Scot*)

2 GO ROUND, skirt, circumvent, depart from, deviate from, pass round, detour round
<< OPPOSITE cross

bystander *noun* ONLOOKER, passer-by, spectator, witness, observer, viewer, looker-on, watcher, eyewitness
<< OPPOSITE participant

byword *noun* SAYING, slogan, motto, maxim, gnome, adage, proverb, epithet, dictum, precept, aphorism, saw, apophthegm

Cc

cab *noun* TAXI, minicab, taxicab, hackney, hackney carriage
cabal *noun* **1** CLIQUE, set, party, league, camp, coalition, faction, caucus, junta, coterie, schism, confederacy, conclave
2 PLOT, scheme, intrigue, conspiracy, machination
cabin *noun* **1** ROOM, berth, quarters, compartment, deckhouse
2 HUT, shed, cottage, lodge, cot (*archaic*), shack, chalet, shanty, hovel, bothy, whare (*NZ*)
cabinet *noun* CUPBOARD, case, locker, dresser, closet, press, chiffonier
Cabinet *noun* COUNCIL, committee, administration, ministry, assembly, board
cache *noun* STORE, fund, supply, reserve, treasury, accumulation, stockpile, hoard, stash (*informal*)
cackle *verb* LAUGH, giggle, chuckle
▷ *noun* LAUGH, giggle, chuckle
cacophony *noun* DISCORD, racket, din, dissonance, disharmony, stridency
cad *noun* (*Old-fashioned, informal*) SCOUNDREL (*slang*), rat (*informal*), bounder (*Brit old-fashioned slang*), cur, knave, rotter (*slang, chiefly Brit*), heel, scumbag (*slang*), churl, dastard (*archaic*), wrong 'un (*Austral slang*)
cadence *noun* **1** INTONATION, accent, inflection, modulation
2 RHYTHM, beat, measure (*Prosody*), metre, pulse, throb, tempo, swing, lilt
café *noun* SNACK BAR, restaurant, cafeteria, coffee shop, brasserie, coffee bar, tearoom, lunchroom, eatery *or* eaterie
cage *noun* ENCLOSURE, pen, coop, hutch, pound, corral (*US*)
▷ *verb* SHUT UP, confine, restrain, imprison, lock up, mew, incarcerate, fence in, impound, coop up, immure, pound
cagey *or* **cagy** *adjective* (*informal*) GUARDED, reserved, careful, cautious, restrained, wary, discreet, shrewd, wily, reticent, noncommittal, chary
<< OPPOSITE careless
cajole *verb* PERSUADE, tempt, lure, flatter, manoeuvre, seduce, entice, coax, beguile, wheedle, sweet-talk (*informal*), inveigle
cake *noun* BLOCK, bar, slab, lump, cube, loaf, mass
▷ *verb* SOLIDIFY, dry, consolidate, harden, thicken, congeal, coagulate, ossify, encrust
calamitous *adjective* DISASTROUS, terrible, devastating, tragic, fatal, deadly, dreadful, dire, catastrophic, woeful, ruinous, cataclysmic
<< OPPOSITE fortunate
calamity *noun* DISASTER, tragedy, ruin, distress, reversal of fortune, hardship, catastrophe, woe, misfortune, downfall, adversity, scourge, mishap, affliction, trial, tribulation, misadventure, cataclysm, wretchedness, mischance
<< OPPOSITE benefit
calculate *verb* **1** WORK OUT, value, judge, determine, estimate, count, reckon, weigh, consider, compute, rate, gauge, enumerate, figure
2 PLAN, design, aim, intend, frame, arrange, formulate, contrive
calculated *adjective* DELIBERATE, planned, considered, studied, intended, intentional, designed, aimed, purposeful, premeditated
<< OPPOSITE unplanned
calculating *adjective* SCHEMING, designing, sharp, shrewd, cunning, contriving, sly, canny, devious, manipulative, crafty, Machiavellian
<< OPPOSITE direct
calculation *noun* **1** COMPUTATION, working out, reckoning, figuring, estimate, forecast, judgment, estimation, result, answer
2 PLANNING, intention, deliberation, foresight, contrivance, forethought, circumspection, premeditation
calibrate *verb* MEASURE, gauge
calibre *or US* **caliber** *noun* **1** WORTH, quality, ability, talent, gifts, capacity, merit,

distinction, faculty, endowment, stature
2 DIAMETER, bore, gauge, measure
call *verb* 1 NAME, entitle, dub, designate, term, style, label, describe as, christen, denominate
2 CONSIDER, think, judge, estimate, describe as, refer to as, regard as
3 CRY, announce, shout, scream, proclaim, yell, cry out, whoop
<< OPPOSITE whisper
4 PHONE, contact, telephone, ring (up) (*informal, chiefly Brit*), give (someone) a bell (*Brit slang*)
5 HAIL, address, summon, contact, halloo
6 SUMMON, gather, invite, rally, assemble, muster, convene, convoke, collect
<< OPPOSITE dismiss
7 WAKEN, arouse, awaken, rouse
▷ *noun* 1 VISIT
2 REQUEST, order, demand, appeal, notice, command, announcement, invitation, plea, summons, supplication
3 (usually used in a negative construction) NEED, cause, reason, grounds, occasion, excuse, justification, claim
4 ATTRACTION, draw, pull (*informal*), appeal, lure, attractiveness, allure, magnetism
5 CRY, shout, scream, yell, whoop
<< OPPOSITE whisper
▷▷ **call for someone** FETCH, pick up, collect, uplift (*Scot*)
▷▷ **call for something** 1 DEMAND, order, request, insist on, cry out for
2 REQUIRE, need, involve, demand, occasion, entail, necessitate
▷▷ **call on someone** 1 REQUEST, ask, bid, invite, appeal to, summon, invoke, call upon, entreat, supplicate
2 VISIT, look up, drop in on, look in on, see
▷▷ **call someone up** 1 TELEPHONE, phone, ring (*chiefly Brit*), buzz (*informal*), dial, call up, give someone a ring (*informal, chiefly Brit*), put a call through to, give someone a call, give someone a buzz (*informal*), give someone a bell (*Brit slang*), give someone a tinkle (*Brit informal*), get on the blower to (*informal*)
2 ENLIST, draft, recruit, muster
calling *noun* PROFESSION, work, business, line, trade, career, mission, employment, province, occupation, pursuit, vocation, walk of life, life's work, métier
callous *adjective* HEARTLESS, cold, harsh, hardened, indifferent, insensitive, hard-boiled (*informal*), unsympathetic, uncaring, soulless, hard-bitten, unfeeling, obdurate, case-hardened, hardhearted
<< OPPOSITE compassionate
callousness *noun* HEARTLESSNESS, insensitivity, hardness, coldness, harshness, obduracy, soullessness, hardheartedness, obdurateness
callow *adjective* INEXPERIENCED, juvenile, naïve, immature, raw, untried, green, unsophisticated, puerile, guileless, jejune, unfledged
calm *adjective* 1 COOL, relaxed, composed, sedate, undisturbed, collected, unmoved, dispassionate, unfazed (*informal*), impassive, unflappable (*informal*), unruffled, unemotional, self-possessed, imperturbable, equable, keeping your cool, unexcited, unexcitable, as cool as a cucumber
<< OPPOSITE excited
2 STILL, quiet, smooth, peaceful, mild, serene, tranquil, placid, halcyon, balmy, restful, windless, pacific
<< OPPOSITE rough
▷ *noun* 1 PEACEFULNESS, peace, serenity, calmness
2 STILLNESS, peace, quiet, hush, serenity, tranquillity, repose, calmness, peacefulness
3 PEACE, calmness
<< OPPOSITE disturbance
▷ *verb* 1 SOOTHE, settle, quiet, relax, appease, still, allay, assuage, quieten
<< OPPOSITE excite
2 PLACATE, hush, pacify, mollify
<< OPPOSITE aggravate
calmly *adverb* COOLLY, casually, sedately, serenely, nonchalantly, impassively, dispassionately, placidly, unflinchingly, equably, imperturbably, tranquilly, composedly, collectedly, self-possessedly
camaraderie *noun* COMRADESHIP, fellowship, brotherhood, companionship, togetherness, esprit de corps, good-fellowship, companionability
camouflage *noun* 1 PROTECTIVE COLOURING, mimicry, false appearance, deceptive markings
2 DISGUISE, front, cover, screen, blind, mask, cloak, guise, masquerade, subterfuge, concealment
▷ *verb* DISGUISE, cover, screen, hide, mask, conceal, obscure, veil, cloak, obfuscate
<< OPPOSITE reveal
camp[1] *noun* 1 CAMP SITE, tents, encampment, camping ground
2 BIVOUAC, cantonment (*Military*)
camp[2] *adjective* (*informal*) 1 EFFEMINATE, campy (*informal*), camped up (*informal*), poncy (*slang*)
2 AFFECTED, mannered, artificial, posturing, ostentatious, campy (*informal*), camped up (*informal*)
campaign *noun* 1 DRIVE, appeal, movement, push (*informal*), offensive, crusade
2 OPERATION, drive, attack, movement, push, offensive, expedition, crusade, jihad
campaigner *noun* DEMONSTRATOR, champion,

advocate, activist, reformer, crusader
canal *noun* WATERWAY, channel, passage, conduit, duct, watercourse
cancel *verb* 1 CALL OFF, drop, abandon, forget about
2 ANNUL, abolish, repeal, abort, quash, do away with, revoke, repudiate, rescind, obviate, abrogate, countermand, eliminate
▷▷ **cancel something out** COUNTERBALANCE, offset, make up for, compensate for, redeem, neutralize, nullify, obviate, balance out
cancellation *noun* 1 ABANDONMENT, abandoning
2 ANNULMENT, abolition, repeal, elimination, quashing, revocation
cancer *noun* 1 GROWTH, tumour, carcinoma (*Pathology*), malignancy
2 EVIL, corruption, rot, sickness, blight, pestilence, canker
>> RELATED WORD *prefix* carcino-
candid *adjective* 1 HONEST, just, open, truthful, fair, plain, straightforward, blunt, sincere, outspoken, downright, impartial, forthright, upfront (*informal*), unequivocal, unbiased, guileless, unprejudiced, free, round, frank
<< OPPOSITE diplomatic
2 INFORMAL, impromptu, uncontrived, unposed
candidate *noun* CONTENDER, competitor, applicant, nominee, entrant, claimant, contestant, suitor, aspirant, possibility, runner
candour *noun* HONESTY, simplicity, fairness, sincerity, impartiality, frankness, directness, truthfulness, outspokenness, forthrightness, straightforwardness, ingenuousness, artlessness, guilelessness, openness, unequivocalness, naïveté
<< OPPOSITE dishonesty
cannabis *noun* MARIJUANA, pot (*slang*), dope (*slang*), hash (*slang*), blow (*slang*), smoke (*informal*), stuff (*slang*), leaf (*slang*), tea (*US slang*), grass (*slang*), chronic (*US slang*), weed (*slang*), hemp, gage (*US dated slang*), hashish, mary jane (*US slang*), ganja, bhang, kif, sinsemilla, dagga (*S African*), charas
cannon *noun* GUN, big gun, artillery piece, field gun, mortar
canny *adjective* SHREWD, knowing, sharp, acute, careful, wise, clever, subtle, cautious, prudent, astute, on the ball (*informal*), artful, judicious, circumspect, perspicacious, sagacious, worldly-wise
<< OPPOSITE inept
canon *noun* 1 RULE, standard, principle, regulation, formula, criterion, dictate, statute, yardstick, precept
2 LIST, index, catalogue, syllabus, roll
canopy *noun* AWNING, covering, shade, shelter, sunshade
cant[1] *noun* 1 HYPOCRISY, pretence, lip service, humbug, insincerity, pretentiousness, sanctimoniousness, pious platitudes, affected piety, sham holiness
2 JARGON, slang, vernacular, patter, lingo, argot
cant[2] *verb* TILT, angle, slope, incline, slant, bevel, rise
cantankerous *adjective* BAD-TEMPERED, contrary, perverse, irritable, crusty, grumpy, disagreeable, cranky (*US, Canad & Irish informal*), irascible, tetchy, ratty (*Brit & NZ informal*), testy, quarrelsome, waspish, grouchy (*informal*), peevish, crabby, choleric, crotchety (*informal*), ill-humoured, captious, difficult
<< OPPOSITE cheerful
canter *verb* JOG, lope
▷ *noun* JOG, lope, easy gait, dogtrot
canvass *verb* 1 CAMPAIGN, solicit votes, electioneer
2 POLL, study, examine, investigate, analyse, scan, inspect, sift, scrutinize
canyon *noun* GORGE, pass, gulf, valley, clough (*dialect*), gully, ravine, defile, gulch (*US & Canad*), coulee (*US*)
cap *verb* 1 (*informal*) BEAT, top, better, exceed, eclipse, lick (*informal*), surpass, transcend, outstrip, outdo, run rings around (*informal*), put in the shade, overtop
2 TOP, cover, crown
capability *noun* ABILITY, means, power, potential, facility, capacity, qualification(s), faculty, competence, proficiency, wherewithal, potentiality
<< OPPOSITE inability
capable *adjective* 1 ABLE, fitted, suited, adapted, adequate
<< OPPOSITE incapable
2 ACCOMPLISHED, experienced, masterly, qualified, talented, gifted, efficient, clever, intelligent, competent, apt, skilful, adept, proficient
<< OPPOSITE incompetent
capacious *adjective* SPACIOUS, wide, broad, vast, substantial, comprehensive, extensive, generous, ample, expansive, roomy, voluminous, commodious, sizable *or* sizeable
<< OPPOSITE limited
capacity *noun* 1 ABILITY, power, strength, facility, gift, intelligence, efficiency, genius, faculty, capability, forte, readiness, aptitude, aptness, competence *or* competency
2 SIZE, room, range, space, volume, extent, dimensions, scope, magnitude, compass, amplitude
3 FUNCTION, position, role, post, appointment, province, sphere, service, office
cape *noun* HEADLAND, point, head, peninsula, ness (*archaic*), promontory

caper *verb* DANCE, trip, spring, jump, bound, leap, bounce, hop, skip, romp, frolic, cavort, frisk, gambol
▷ *noun* ESCAPADE, sport, stunt, mischief, lark (*informal*), prank, jest, practical joke, high jinks, antics, jape, shenanigan (*informal*)

capital *noun* MONEY, funds, stock, investment(s), property, cash, finance, finances, financing, resources, assets, wealth, principal, means, wherewithal
▷ *adjective* (*Old-fashioned*) FIRST-RATE, fine, excellent, superb, sterling, splendid, world-class

capitalism *noun* PRIVATE ENTERPRISE, free enterprise, private ownership, laissez faire *or* laisser faire

capitalize *verb* SELL, put up for sale, trade, dispose of
▷▷ **capitalize on something** TAKE ADVANTAGE OF, exploit, benefit from, profit from, make the most of, gain from, cash in on (*informal*)

capitulate *verb* GIVE IN, yield, concede, submit, surrender, comply, give up, come to terms, succumb, cave in (*informal*), relent
<< OPPOSITE resist

capitulation *noun* SURRENDER, yielding, submission, cave-in (*informal*)

caprice *noun* WHIM, notion, impulse, freak, fad, quirk, vagary, whimsy, humour, fancy, fickleness, inconstancy, fitfulness, changeableness

capricious *adjective* UNPREDICTABLE, variable, unstable, inconsistent, erratic, quirky, fickle, impulsive, mercurial, freakish, fitful, inconstant
<< OPPOSITE consistent

capsize *verb* OVERTURN, turn over, invert, tip over, keel over, turn turtle, upset

capsule *noun* **1** PILL, tablet, lozenge, bolus
2 (*Botany*) POD, case, shell, vessel, sheath, receptacle, seed case

captain *noun* **1** LEADER, boss, master, skipper, chieftain, head, number one (*informal*), chief
2 COMMANDER, officer, skipper, (senior) pilot

captivate *verb* CHARM, attract, fascinate, absorb, entrance, dazzle, seduce, enchant, enthral, beguile, allure, bewitch, ravish, enslave, mesmerize, ensnare, hypnotize, enrapture, sweep off your feet, enamour, infatuate
<< OPPOSITE repel

captive *adjective* CONFINED, caged, imprisoned, locked up, enslaved, incarcerated, ensnared, subjugated, penned, restricted
▷ *noun* PRISONER, hostage, convict, prisoner of war, detainee, internee

captivity *noun* CONFINEMENT, custody, detention, imprisonment, incarceration, internment, durance (*archaic*), restraint

captor *noun* JAILER *or* GAOLER, guard, keeper, custodian

capture *verb* CATCH, arrest, take, bag, secure, seize, nail (*informal*), collar (*informal*), nab (*informal*), apprehend, lift (*slang*), take prisoner, take into custody, feel your collar (*slang*)
<< OPPOSITE release
▷ *noun* ARREST, catching, trapping, imprisonment, seizure, apprehension, taking, taking captive

car *noun* **1** VEHICLE, motor, wheels (*informal*), auto (*US*), automobile, jalopy (*informal*), motorcar, machine
2 (*US & Canad*) (RAILWAY) CARRIAGE, coach, cable car, dining car, sleeping car, buffet car, van

carcass *noun* **1** BODY, remains, corpse, skeleton, dead body, cadaver (*Medical*)
2 REMAINS, shell, framework, debris, remnants, hulk

cardinal *adjective* PRINCIPAL, first, highest, greatest, leading, important, chief, main, prime, central, key, essential, primary, fundamental, paramount, foremost, pre-eminent
<< OPPOSITE secondary

care *verb* BE CONCERNED, mind, bother, be interested, be bothered, give a damn, concern yourself
▷ *noun* **1** CUSTODY, keeping, control, charge, management, protection, supervision, guardianship, safekeeping, ministration
2 CAUTION, attention, regard, pains, consideration, heed, prudence, vigilance, forethought, circumspection, watchfulness, meticulousness, carefulness
<< OPPOSITE carelessness
3 WORRY, concern, pressure, trouble, responsibility, stress, burden, anxiety, hardship, woe, disquiet, affliction, tribulation, perplexity, vexation
<< OPPOSITE pleasure
▷▷ **care for someone** **1** LOOK AFTER, mind, tend, attend, nurse, minister to, watch over
2 LOVE, desire, be fond of, want, prize, find congenial
▷▷ **care for something** *or* **someone** LIKE, enjoy, take to, relish, be fond of, be keen on, be partial to
▷▷ **take care of something** *or* **someone** **1** LOOK AFTER, mind, watch, protect, tend, nurse, care for, provide for
2 DEAL WITH, manage, cope with, see to, handle

career *noun* **1** OCCUPATION, calling, employment, pursuit, vocation, livelihood, life's work
2 PROGRESS, course, path, procedure, passage
▷ *verb* RUSH, race, speed, tear, dash, barrel (along) (*informal, chiefly US & Canad*), bolt, hurtle,

burn rubber (*informal*)

carefree *adjective* UNTROUBLED, happy, cheerful, careless, buoyant, airy, radiant, easy-going, cheery, breezy, halcyon, sunny, jaunty, chirpy (*informal*), happy-go-lucky, blithe, insouciant, light-hearted
<< OPPOSITE unhappy

careful *adjective* 1 CAUTIOUS, painstaking, scrupulous, fastidious, circumspect, punctilious, chary, heedful, thoughtful, discreet
<< OPPOSITE careless
2 THOROUGH, full, particular, accurate, precise, intensive, in-depth, meticulous, conscientious, attentive, exhaustive, painstaking, scrupulous, assiduous
<< OPPOSITE casual
3 PRUDENT, sparing, economical, canny, provident, frugal, thrifty

careless *adjective* 1 SLAPDASH, irresponsible, sloppy (*informal*), cavalier, offhand, neglectful, slipshod, lackadaisical, inattentive
<< OPPOSITE careful
2 NEGLIGENT, hasty, unconcerned, cursory, perfunctory, thoughtless, indiscreet, unthinking, forgetful, absent-minded, inconsiderate, heedless, remiss, incautious, unmindful
<< OPPOSITE careful
3 NONCHALANT, casual, offhand, artless, unstudied
<< OPPOSITE careful

carelessness *noun* NEGLIGENCE, neglect, omission, indiscretion, inaccuracy, irresponsibility, slackness, inattention, sloppiness (*informal*), laxity, thoughtlessness, laxness, remissness

caress *noun* STROKE, pat, kiss, embrace, hug, cuddle, fondling
▷ *verb* STROKE, cuddle, fondle, pet, embrace, hug, nuzzle, neck (*informal*), kiss

caretaker *noun* WARDEN, keeper, porter, superintendent, curator, custodian, watchman, janitor, concierge
▷ *adjective* TEMPORARY, holding, short-term, interim

cargo *noun* LOAD, goods, contents, shipment, freight, merchandise, baggage, ware, consignment, tonnage, lading

caricature *noun* PARODY, cartoon, distortion, satire, send-up (*Brit informal*), travesty, takeoff (*informal*), lampoon, burlesque, mimicry, farce
▷ *verb* PARODY, take off (*informal*), mock, distort, ridicule, mimic, send up (*Brit informal*), lampoon, burlesque, satirize

caring *adjective* COMPASSIONATE, loving, kindly, warm, soft, sensitive, tender, sympathetic, responsive, receptive, considerate, warmhearted, tenderhearted, softhearted, touchy-feely (*informal*)

carnage *noun* SLAUGHTER, murder, massacre, holocaust, havoc, bloodshed, shambles, mass murder, butchery, blood bath

carnal *adjective* SEXUAL, animal, sexy (*informal*), fleshly, erotic, sensual, randy (*informal, chiefly Brit*), steamy (*informal*), raunchy (*slang*), sensuous, voluptuous, lewd, wanton, amorous, salacious, prurient, impure, lascivious, lustful, lecherous, libidinous, licentious, unchaste

carnival *noun* FESTIVAL, fair, fête, celebration, gala, jubilee, jamboree, Mardi Gras, revelry, merrymaking, fiesta, holiday

carol *noun* SONG, noël, hymn, Christmas song, canticle

carouse *verb* DRINK, booze (*informal*), revel, imbibe, quaff, pub-crawl (*informal, chiefly Brit*), bevvy (*dialect*), make merry, bend the elbow (*informal*), roister

carp *verb* FIND FAULT, complain, beef (*slang*), criticize, nag, censure, reproach, quibble, cavil, pick holes, kvetch (*US slang*)
<< OPPOSITE praise

carpenter *noun* JOINER, cabinet-maker, woodworker

carping *adjective* FAULT-FINDING, critical, nagging, picky (*informal*), nit-picking (*informal*), hard to please, cavilling, captious

carriage *noun* 1 VEHICLE, coach, trap, gig, cab, wagon, hackney, conveyance
2 TRANSPORTATION, transport, delivery, conveying, freight, conveyance, carrying
3 BEARING, posture, gait, deportment, air

carry *verb* 1 CONVEY, take, move, bring, bear, lift, transfer, conduct, transport, haul, transmit, fetch, relay, cart, tote (*informal*), hump (*Brit slang*), lug
2 TRANSPORT, take, transfer, transmit
3 SUPPORT, stand, bear, maintain, shoulder, sustain, hold up, suffer, uphold, bolster, underpin
4 TRANSMIT, transfer, spread, pass on
5 PUBLISH, include, release, display, print, broadcast, communicate, disseminate, give
6 WIN, gain, secure, capture, accomplish
▷▷ **carry on** 1 CONTINUE, last, endure, persist, keep going, persevere
2 (*informal*) MAKE A FUSS, act up (*informal*), misbehave, create (*slang*), raise Cain
▷▷ **carry something on** ENGAGE IN, conduct, carry out, undertake, embark on, enter into
▷▷ **carry something out** PERFORM, effect, achieve, realize, implement, fulfil, accomplish, execute, discharge, consummate, carry through

carry-on *noun* (*informal, chiefly Brit*) FUSS, disturbance, racket, fracas, commotion, rumpus, tumult, hubbub, shindy (*informal*)

carton *noun* BOX, case, pack, package, container

cartoon *noun* 1 DRAWING, parody, satire, caricature, comic strip, takeoff (*informal*), lampoon, sketch
2 ANIMATION, animated film, animated cartoon

cartridge *noun* 1 SHELL, round, charge
2 CONTAINER, case, magazine, cassette, cylinder, capsule

carve *verb* 1 SCULPT, form, cut, chip, sculpture, whittle, chisel, hew, fashion
2 ETCH, engrave, inscribe, fashion, slash

carving *noun* SCULPTURE

cascade *noun* WATERFALL, falls, torrent, flood, shower, fountain, avalanche, deluge, downpour, outpouring, cataract
▷ *verb* FLOW, fall, flood, pour, plunge, surge, spill, tumble, descend, overflow, gush, teem, pitch

case[1] *noun* 1 SITUATION, event, circumstance(s), state, position, condition, context, dilemma, plight, contingency, predicament
2 INSTANCE, example, occasion, specimen, occurrence
3 (*Law*) LAWSUIT, process, trial, suit, proceedings, dispute, cause, action

case[2] *noun* 1 CABINET, box, chest, holder
2 CONTAINER, compact, capsule, carton, cartridge, canister, casket, receptacle
3 SUITCASE, bag, grip, trunk, holdall, portmanteau, valise
4 CRATE, box
5 COVERING, casing, cover, shell, wrapping, jacket, envelope, capsule, folder, sheath, wrapper, integument

cash *noun* MONEY, change, funds, notes, ready (*informal*), the necessary (*informal*), resources, currency, silver, bread (*slang*), coin, tin (*slang*), brass (*Northern English dialect*), dough (*slang*), rhino (*Brit slang*), banknotes, bullion, dosh (*Brit & Austral slang*), wherewithal, coinage, needful (*informal*), specie, shekels (*informal*), dibs (*slang*), ready money, ackers (*slang*), spondulicks (*slang*)

cashier[1] *noun* TELLER, accountant, clerk, treasurer, bank clerk, purser, bursar, banker

cashier[2] *verb* DISMISS, discharge, expel, cast off, drum out, give the boot to (*slang*)

casing *noun* COVERING, case, cover, shell, container, integument

cask *noun* BARREL, drum, cylinder, keg

casket *noun* BOX, case, chest, coffer, ark (*dialect*), jewel box, kist (*Scot & Northern English dialect*)

cast *noun* 1 ACTORS, company, players, characters, troupe, dramatis personae
2 TYPE, turn, sort, kind, style, stamp
▷ *verb* 1 CHOOSE, name, pick, select, appoint, assign, allot
2 BESTOW, give, level, accord, direct, confer
3 GIVE OUT, spread, deposit, shed, distribute, scatter, emit, radiate, bestow, diffuse
4 THROW, project, launch, pitch, shed, shy, toss, thrust, hurl, fling, chuck (*informal*), sling, lob, impel, drive, drop
5 MOULD, set, found, form, model, shape
▷▷ **cast someone down** DISCOURAGE, depress, desolate, dishearten, dispirit, deject

caste *noun* CLASS, order, race, station, rank, status, stratum, social order, lineage

castigate *verb* REPRIMAND, blast, carpet (*informal*), put down, criticize, lash, slate (*informal, chiefly Brit*), censure, rebuke, scold, berate, dress down (*informal*), chastise, chasten, tear into (*informal*), diss (*slang, chiefly US*), read the riot act, slap on the wrist, lambast(e), bawl (someone) out (*informal*), excoriate, rap over the knuckles, haul over the coals (*informal*), chew out (*US & Canad informal*), tear (someone) off a strip (*Brit informal*), give a rocket (*Brit & NZ informal*)

cast-iron *adjective* CERTAIN, established, settled, guaranteed, fixed, definite, copper-bottomed, idiot-proof, nailed-on (*slang*)

castle *noun* FORTRESS, keep, palace, tower, peel, chateau, stronghold, citadel, fastness

castrate *verb* NEUTER, unman, emasculate, geld

casual *adjective* 1 CARELESS, relaxed, informal, indifferent, unconcerned, apathetic, blasé, offhand, nonchalant, insouciant, lackadaisical
<< OPPOSITE serious
2 CHANCE, unexpected, random, accidental, incidental, unforeseen, unintentional, fortuitous (*informal*), serendipitous, unpremeditated
<< OPPOSITE planned
3 INFORMAL, leisure, sporty, non-dressy
<< OPPOSITE formal

casualty *noun* 1 FATALITY, death, loss, wounded
2 VICTIM, sufferer

cat *noun* FELINE, pussy (*informal*), moggy (*slang*), puss (*informal*), ballarat (*Austral informal*), tabby
>> RELATED WORD *adjective* feline
>> RELATED WORD *male* tom
>> RELATED WORD *female* tabby
>> RELATED WORD *young* kitten

cataclysm *noun* DISASTER, collapse, catastrophe, upheaval, debacle, devastation, calamity

cataclysmic *adjective* DISASTROUS, devastating, catastrophic, calamitous

catalogue *or US* **catalog** *noun* LIST, record, schedule, index, register, directory, inventory, gazetteer
▷ *verb* LIST, file, index, register, classify, inventory, tabulate, alphabetize

catapult *noun* SLING, slingshot (US), trebuchet,

ballista
▷ *verb* SHOOT, pitch, plunge, toss, hurl, propel, hurtle, heave
cataract *noun* 1 (*Medical*) OPACITY (*of the eye*)
2 WATERFALL, falls, rapids, cascade, torrent, deluge, downpour, Niagara
catastrophe *noun* DISASTER, tragedy, calamity, meltdown (*informal*), cataclysm, trouble, trial, blow, failure, reverse, misfortune, devastation, adversity, mishap, affliction, whammy (*informal, chiefly US*), bummer (*slang*), mischance, fiasco
catastrophic *adjective* DISASTROUS, devastating, tragic, calamitous, cataclysmic
catch *verb* 1 CAPTURE, arrest, trap, seize, nail (*informal*), nab (*informal*), snare, lift (*slang*), apprehend, ensnare, entrap, feel your collar (*slang*)
<< OPPOSITE free
2 TRAP, capture, snare, entangle, ensnare, entrap
3 SEIZE, get, grab, snatch
4 GRAB, take, grip, seize, grasp, clutch, lay hold of
<< OPPOSITE release
5 DISCOVER, surprise, find out, expose, detect, catch in the act, take unawares
6 CONTRACT, get, develop, suffer from, incur, succumb to, go down with
<< OPPOSITE escape
▷ *noun* 1 FASTENER, hook, clip, bolt, latch, clasp, hasp, hook and eye, snib (*Scot*), sneck (*dialect, chiefly Scot & Northern English*)
2 (*informal*) DRAWBACK, trick, trap, disadvantage, hitch, snag, stumbling block, fly in the ointment
<< OPPOSITE advantage
▷▷ **catch on** 1 (*informal*) UNDERSTAND, see, find out, grasp, see through, comprehend, twig (*Brit informal*), get the picture, see the light of day
2 BECOME POPULAR, take off, become trendy, come into fashion
catchcry *noun* (*Austral*) CATCHPHRASE, slogan, saying, quotation, motto
catching *adjective* INFECTIOUS, contagious, transferable, communicable, infective, transmittable
<< OPPOSITE non-infectious
catch phrase *noun* SLOGAN, saying, quotation, motto, catchcry (*Austral*)
catchy *adjective* MEMORABLE, haunting, unforgettable, captivating
categorical *adjective* ABSOLUTE, direct, express, positive, explicit, unconditional, emphatic, downright, unequivocal, unqualified, unambiguous, unreserved
<< OPPOSITE vague
category *noun* CLASS, grouping, heading, head, order, sort, list, department, type, division, section, rank, grade, classification
cater *verb* ▷▷ **cater for something** *or* **someone** 1 PROVIDE FOR, supply, provision, purvey, victual
2 TAKE INTO ACCOUNT, consider, bear in mind, make allowance for, have regard for
▷▷ **cater to something** *or* **someone** INDULGE, spoil, minister to, pamper, gratify, pander to, coddle, mollycoddle
catharsis *noun* RELEASE, cleansing, purging, purification
catholic *adjective* WIDE, general, liberal, global, varied, comprehensive, universal, world-wide, tolerant, eclectic, all-inclusive, ecumenical, all-embracing, broad-minded, unbigoted, unsectarian
<< OPPOSITE limited
cattle *plural noun* cows, stock, beasts, livestock, bovines
>> RELATED WORD *adjective* bovine
>> RELATED WORDS *collective nouns* drove, herd
caucus *noun* GROUP, division, section, camp, sector, lobby, bloc, contingent, pressure group, junta, public-interest group (*US & Canad*)
cause *noun* 1 ORIGIN, source, agency, spring, agent, maker, producer, root, beginning, creator, genesis, originator, prime mover, mainspring
<< OPPOSITE result
2 REASON, call, need, grounds, basis, incentive, motive, motivation, justification, inducement
3 AIM, movement, purpose, principle, object, ideal, enterprise, end
▷ *verb* PRODUCE, begin, create, effect, lead to, occasion, result in, generate, provoke, compel, motivate, induce, bring about, give rise to, precipitate, incite, engender
<< OPPOSITE prevent
caustic *adjective* 1 BURNING, corrosive, corroding, astringent, vitriolic, acrid
2 SARCASTIC, biting, keen, cutting, severe, stinging, scathing, acrimonious, pungent, vitriolic, trenchant, mordant
<< OPPOSITE kind
caution *noun* 1 CARE, discretion, heed, prudence, vigilance, alertness, forethought, circumspection, watchfulness, belt and braces, carefulness, heedfulness
<< OPPOSITE carelessness
2 REPRIMAND, warning, injunction, admonition
▷ *verb* 1 WARN, urge, advise, alert, tip off, forewarn, put you on your guard
2 REPRIMAND, warn, admonish, give an injunction to
cautious *adjective* CAREFUL, guarded, alert, wary, discreet, tentative, prudent, vigilant, watchful, judicious, circumspect, cagey (*informal*), on your toes, chary, belt-and-braces,

keeping a weather eye on
<< OPPOSITE careless
cautiously *adverb* CAREFULLY, alertly, discreetly, tentatively, warily, prudently, judiciously, guardedly, circumspectly, watchfully, vigilantly, cagily (*informal*), mindfully
cavalcade *noun* PARADE, train, procession, march-past
cavalier *adjective* OFFHAND, lordly, arrogant, lofty, curt, condescending, haughty, scornful, disdainful, insolent, supercilious
cavalry *noun* HORSEMEN, horse, mounted troops
<< OPPOSITE infantrymen
cave *noun* HOLLOW, cavern, grotto, den, cavity
caveat *noun* WARNING, caution, admonition, qualification, proviso, reservation, condition
cavern *noun* CAVE, hollow, grotto, underground chamber
cavernous *adjective* VAST, wide, huge, enormous, extensive, immense, spacious, expansive, capacious, commodious
cavity *noun* HOLLOW, hole, gap, pit, dent, crater
cavort *verb* FROLIC, sport, romp, caper, prance, frisk, gambol
cease *verb* 1 STOP, end, finish, be over, come to an end, peter out, die away
<< OPPOSITE start
2 DISCONTINUE, end, stop, fail, finish, give up, conclude, suspend, halt, terminate, break off, refrain, leave off, give over (*informal*), bring to an end, desist, belay (*Nautical*)
<< OPPOSITE begin
ceaseless *adjective* CONTINUAL, constant, endless, continuous, eternal, perennial, perpetual, never-ending, interminable, incessant, everlasting, unending, unremitting, nonstop, untiring
<< OPPOSITE occasional
cede *verb* SURRENDER, grant, transfer, abandon, yield, concede, hand over, relinquish, renounce, make over, abdicate
celebrate *verb* 1 REJOICE, party, enjoy yourself, carouse, live it up (*informal*), whoop it up (*informal*), make merry, paint the town red (*informal*), go on a spree, put the flags out, roister, kill the fatted calf
2 COMMEMORATE, honour, observe, toast, drink to, keep
3 PERFORM, observe, preside over, officiate at, solemnize
4 PRAISE, honour, commend (*informal*), glorify, publicize, exalt, laud, extol, eulogize
celebrated *adjective* RENOWNED, popular, famous, outstanding, distinguished, well-known, prominent, glorious, acclaimed, notable, eminent, revered, famed, illustrious, pre-eminent, lionized
<< OPPOSITE unknown
celebration *noun* 1 PARTY, festival, gala, jubilee, festivity, rave (*Brit slang*), beano (*Brit slang*), revelry, red-letter day, rave-up (*Brit slang*), merrymaking, carousal, -fest (*in combination*), hooley *or* hoolie (*chiefly Irish & NZ*)
2 COMMEMORATION, honouring, remembrance
3 PERFORMANCE, observance, solemnization
celebrity *noun* 1 PERSONALITY, name, star, superstar, big name, dignitary, luminary, bigwig (*informal*), celeb (*informal*), face (*informal*), big shot (*informal*), personage, megastar (*informal*), V.I.P.
<< OPPOSITE nobody
2 FAME, reputation, honour, glory, popularity, distinction, prestige, prominence, stardom, renown, pre-eminence, repute, éclat, notability
<< OPPOSITE obscurity
celestial *adjective* 1 ASTRONOMICAL, planetary, stellar, astral, extraterrestrial
2 HEAVENLY, spiritual, divine, eternal, sublime, immortal, supernatural, astral, ethereal, angelic, godlike, seraphic
celibacy *noun* CHASTITY, purity, virginity, continence, singleness
celibate *adjective* CHASTE, single, pure, virgin, continent
cell *noun* 1 ROOM, chamber, lock-up, compartment, cavity, cubicle, dungeon, stall
2 UNIT, group, section, core, nucleus, caucus, coterie
cement *noun* 1 MORTAR, plaster, paste
2 SEALANT, glue, gum, adhesive, binder
▷ *verb* STICK, join, bond, attach, seal, glue, plaster, gum, weld, solder
cemetery *noun* GRAVEYARD, churchyard, burial ground, necropolis, God's acre
censor *verb* EXPURGATE, cut, blue-pencil, bowdlerize
censorship *noun* EXPURGATION, blue pencil, purgation, bowdlerization *or* bowdlerisation, sanitization *or* sanitisation
censure *verb* CRITICIZE, blame, abuse, condemn, carpet (*informal*), denounce, put down, slate (*informal, chiefly US*), rebuke, reprimand, reproach, scold, berate, castigate, chide, tear into (*informal*), diss (*slang, chiefly US*), blast, read (someone) the riot act, reprove, upbraid, slap (someone) on the wrist, lambast(e), bawl (someone) out (*informal*), excoriate, rap (someone) over the knuckles, chew (someone) out (*US & Canad informal*), tear (someone) off a strip (*Brit informal*), give (someone) a rocket (*Brit & NZ informal*), reprehend
<< OPPOSITE applaud
▷ *noun* DISAPPROVAL, criticism, blame, condemnation, rebuke, reprimand, reproach, dressing down (*informal*), stick (*slang*), stricture,

reproof, castigation, obloquy, remonstrance
<< OPPOSITE approval

central *adjective* **1** INNER, middle, mid, interior
<< OPPOSITE outer
2 MAIN, chief, key, essential, primary, principal, fundamental, focal
<< OPPOSITE minor

centralize *verb* UNIFY, concentrate, incorporate, compact, streamline, converge, condense, amalgamate, rationalize

centre *noun* MIDDLE, heart, focus, core, nucleus, hub, pivot, kernel, crux, bull's-eye, midpoint
<< OPPOSITE edge
▷▷ **centre on something** *or* **someone** FOCUS, concentrate, cluster, revolve, converge

centrepiece *noun* FOCUS, highlight, hub, star

ceremonial *adjective* FORMAL, public, official, ritual, stately, solemn, liturgical, courtly, ritualistic
<< OPPOSITE informal
▷ *noun* RITUAL, ceremony, rite, formality, solemnity

ceremony *noun* **1** RITUAL, service, rite, observance, commemoration, solemnities
2 FORMALITY, ceremonial, propriety, decorum, formal courtesy

certain *adjective* **1** SURE, convinced, positive, confident, satisfied, assured, free from doubt
<< OPPOSITE unsure
2 BOUND, sure, fated, destined
<< OPPOSITE unlikely
3 INEVITABLE, unavoidable, inescapable, inexorable, ineluctable
4 KNOWN, true, positive, plain, ascertained, unmistakable, conclusive, undoubted, unequivocal, undeniable, irrefutable, unquestionable, incontrovertible, indubitable, nailed-on (*slang*)
<< OPPOSITE doubtful
5 FIXED, decided, established, settled, definite
<< OPPOSITE indefinite
6 PARTICULAR, special, individual, specific

certainly *adverb* DEFINITELY, surely, truly, absolutely, undoubtedly, positively, decidedly, without doubt, unquestionably, undeniably, without question, unequivocally, indisputably, assuredly, indubitably, doubtlessly, come hell or high water, irrefutably

certainty *noun* **1** CONFIDENCE, trust, faith, conviction, assurance, certitude, sureness, positiveness
<< OPPOSITE doubt
2 INEVITABILITY
<< OPPOSITE uncertainty
3 FACT, truth, reality, sure thing (*informal*), surety, banker

certificate *noun* DOCUMENT, licence, warrant, voucher, diploma, testimonial, authorization, credential(s)

certify *verb* CONFIRM, show, declare, guarantee, witness, assure, endorse, testify, notify, verify, ascertain, validate, attest, corroborate, avow, authenticate, vouch for, aver

cessation *noun* CEASING, ending, break, halt, halting, pause, suspension, interruption, respite, standstill, stoppage, termination, let-up (*informal*), remission, abeyance, discontinuance, stay

chafe *verb* **1** RUB, scratch, scrape, rasp, abrade
2 BE ANNOYED, rage, fume, be angry, fret, be offended, be irritated, be incensed, be impatient, be exasperated, be inflamed, be ruffled, be vexed, be narked (*Brit, Austral & NZ slang*)

chaff *noun* HUSKS, remains, refuse, waste, hulls, rubbish, trash, dregs

chagrin *noun* ANNOYANCE, embarrassment, humiliation, dissatisfaction, disquiet, displeasure, mortification, discomfiture, vexation, discomposure
▷ *verb* ANNOY, embarrass, humiliate, disquiet, vex, displease, mortify, discomfit, dissatisfy, discompose

chain *noun* **1** TETHER, coupling, link, bond, shackle, fetter, manacle
2 SERIES, set, train, string, sequence, succession, progression, concatenation
▷ *verb* BIND, confine, restrain, handcuff, shackle, tether, fetter, manacle

chairman *or* **chairwoman** *noun* **1** DIRECTOR, president, chief, executive, chairperson
2 MASTER OF CEREMONIES, spokesman, chair, speaker, MC, chairperson

> The general trend of nonsexist language is to find a term which can apply to both sexes equally, as in the use of *actor* to refer to both men and women. *Chairman* can seem inappropriate when applied to a woman, while *chairwoman* specifies gender, and so, as the entry above illustrates, the terms *chair* and *chairperson* are often preferred as alternatives

chalk up *verb* (*informal*) **1** SCORE, win, gain, achieve, accumulate, attain
2 RECORD, mark, enter, credit, register, log, tally

challenge *noun* **1** DARE, provocation, summons to contest, wero (*NZ*)
2 TEST, trial, opposition, confrontation, defiance, ultimatum, face-off (*slang*)
▷ *verb* **1** DISPUTE, question, tackle, confront, defy, object to, disagree with, take issue with, impugn
2 DARE, invite, provoke, defy, summon, call out, throw down the gauntlet
3 TEST, try, tax

4 QUESTION, interrogate, accost

chamber *noun* 1 HALL, room
2 COUNCIL, assembly, legislature, legislative body
3 ROOM, bedroom, apartment, enclosure, cubicle
4 COMPARTMENT, hollow, cavity

champion *noun* 1 WINNER, hero, victor, conqueror, title holder, warrior
2 DEFENDER, guardian, patron, backer, protector, upholder, vindicator
▷ *verb* SUPPORT, back, defend, promote, advocate, fight for, uphold, espouse, stick up for (*informal*)

chance *noun* 1 PROBABILITY, odds, possibility, prospect, liability, likelihood
<< OPPOSITE certainty
2 OPPORTUNITY, opening, occasion, time, scope, window
3 ACCIDENT, fortune, luck, fate, destiny, coincidence, misfortune, providence
<< OPPOSITE design
4 RISK, speculation, gamble, hazard
▷ *adjective* ACCIDENTAL, random, casual, incidental, unforeseen, unintentional, fortuitous, inadvertent, serendipitous, unforeseeable, unlooked-for
<< OPPOSITE planned
▷ *verb* 1 HAPPEN
2 RISK, try, stake, venture, gamble, hazard, wager
>> RELATED WORD *adjective* fortuitous

change *noun* 1 ALTERATION, innovation, transformation, modification, mutation, metamorphosis, permutation, transmutation, difference, revolution, transition
2 VARIETY, break (*informal*), departure, variation, novelty, diversion, whole new ball game (*informal*)
<< OPPOSITE monotony
3 EXCHANGE, trade, conversion, swap, substitution, interchange
▷ *verb* 1 ALTER, reform, transform, adjust, moderate, revise, modify, remodel, reorganize, restyle, convert
<< OPPOSITE keep
2 SHIFT, vary, transform, alter, modify, diversify, fluctuate, mutate, metamorphose, transmute
<< OPPOSITE stay
3 EXCHANGE, trade, replace, substitute, swap, interchange

changeable *adjective* VARIABLE, shifting, mobile, uncertain, volatile, unsettled, unpredictable, versatile, unstable, irregular, erratic, wavering, uneven, unreliable, fickle, temperamental, whimsical, mercurial, capricious, unsteady, protean, vacillating, fitful, mutable, inconstant
<< OPPOSITE constant

channel *noun* 1 MEANS, way, course, approach, medium, route, path, avenue
2 STRAIT, sound, route, passage, canal, waterway, main
3 DUCT, chamber, artery, groove, gutter, furrow, conduit
▷ *verb* DIRECT, guide, conduct, transmit, convey

chant *noun* SONG, carol, chorus, melody, psalm
▷ *verb* SING, chorus, recite, intone, carol

chaos *noun* DISORDER, confusion, mayhem, anarchy, lawlessness, pandemonium, entropy, bedlam, tumult, disorganization
<< OPPOSITE orderliness

chaotic *adjective* DISORDERED, confused, uncontrolled, anarchic, tumultuous, lawless, riotous, topsy-turvy, disorganized, purposeless

chap *noun* (*informal*) FELLOW, man, person, individual, type, sort, customer (*informal*), character, guy (*informal*), bloke (*Brit informal*), cove (*slang*), dude (*US & Canad informal*)

chapter *noun* 1 SECTION, part, stage, division, episode, topic, segment, instalment
2 PERIOD, time, stage, phase

char *verb* SCORCH, sear, singe

character *noun* 1 PERSONALITY, nature, make-up, cast, constitution, bent, attributes, temper, temperament, complexion, disposition, individuality, marked traits
2 NATURE, kind, quality, constitution, calibre
3 (*informal*) PERSON, sort, individual, type, guy (*informal*), fellow
4 REPUTATION, honour, integrity, good name, rectitude
5 ROLE, part, persona
6 ECCENTRIC, card (*informal*), original, nut (*slang*), flake (*slang, chiefly US*), oddity, oddball (*informal*), odd bod (*informal*), queer fish (*Brit informal*), wacko *or* whacko (*informal*)
7 SYMBOL, mark, sign, letter, figure, type, device, logo, emblem, rune, cipher, hieroglyph

characteristic *noun* FEATURE, mark, quality, property, attribute, faculty, trait, quirk, peculiarity, idiosyncrasy
▷ *adjective* TYPICAL, special, individual, specific, representative, distinguishing, distinctive, peculiar, singular, idiosyncratic, symptomatic
<< OPPOSITE rare

characterize *verb* DISTINGUISH, mark, identify, brand, inform, stamp, typify

charade *noun* PRETENCE, farce, parody, pantomime, fake

charge *verb* 1 ACCUSE, indict, impeach, incriminate, arraign
<< OPPOSITE acquit
2 ATTACK, assault, assail
<< OPPOSITE retreat

3 RUSH, storm, stampede
4 FILL, load, instil, suffuse, lade
▷ *noun* 1 PRICE, rate, cost, amount, payment, expense, toll, expenditure, outlay, damage (*informal*)
2 ACCUSATION, allegation, indictment, imputation
<< OPPOSITE acquittal
3 CARE, trust, responsibility, custody, safekeeping
4 DUTY, office, concern, responsibility, remit
5 WARD, pupil, protégé, dependant
6 ATTACK, rush, assault, onset, onslaught, stampede, sortie
<< OPPOSITE retreat

charisma *noun* CHARM, appeal, personality, attraction, lure, allure, magnetism, force of personality

charismatic *adjective* CHARMING, appealing, attractive, influential, magnetic, enticing, alluring

charitable *adjective* 1 BENEVOLENT, liberal, generous, lavish, philanthropic, bountiful, beneficent
<< OPPOSITE mean
2 KIND, understanding, forgiving, sympathetic, favourable, tolerant, indulgent, lenient, considerate, magnanimous, broad-minded
<< OPPOSITE unkind

charity *noun* 1 CHARITABLE ORGANIZATION, fund, movement, trust, endowment
2 DONATIONS, help, relief, gift, contributions, assistance, hand-out, philanthropy, alms-giving, benefaction, largesse *or* largess, koha (NZ)
<< OPPOSITE meanness
3 KINDNESS, love, pity, humanity, affection, goodness, goodwill, compassion, generosity, indulgence, bounty, altruism, benevolence, fellow feeling, bountifulness, tenderheartedness, aroha (NZ)
<< OPPOSITE ill will

charlatan *noun* FRAUD, cheat, fake, sham, pretender, quack, con man (*informal*), impostor, fraudster, swindler, mountebank, grifter (*slang, chiefly US & Canad*), phoney *or* phony (*informal*), rorter (*Austral slang*), rogue trader

charm *noun* 1 ATTRACTION, appeal, fascination, allure, magnetism, desirability, allurement
<< OPPOSITE repulsiveness
2 TRINKET
3 TALISMAN, amulet, lucky piece, good-luck piece, fetish
4 SPELL, magic, enchantment, sorcery, makutu (NZ)
▷ *verb* 1 ATTRACT, win, please, delight, fascinate, absorb, entrance, win over, enchant, captivate, beguile, allure, bewitch, ravish, mesmerize, enrapture, enamour
<< OPPOSITE repel
2 PERSUADE, seduce, coax, beguile, cajole, sweet-talk (*informal*)

charming *adjective* ATTRACTIVE, pleasing, appealing, engaging, lovely, winning, pleasant, fetching, delightful, cute, irresistible, seductive, captivating, eye-catching, bewitching, delectable, winsome, likable *or* likeable
<< OPPOSITE unpleasant

chart *noun* TABLE, diagram, blueprint, graph, tabulation, plan, map
▷ *verb* 1 PLOT, map out, delineate, sketch, draft, graph, tabulate
2 MONITOR, follow, record, note, document, register, trace, outline, log, graph, tabulate

charter *noun* 1 DOCUMENT, right, contract, bond, permit, licence, concession, privilege, franchise, deed, prerogative, indenture
2 CONSTITUTION, laws, rules, code
▷ *verb* 1 HIRE, commission, employ, rent, lease
2 AUTHORIZE, permit, sanction, entitle, license, empower, give authority

chase *verb* 1 PURSUE, follow, track, hunt, run after, course
2 DRIVE AWAY, drive, expel, hound, send away, send packing, put to flight
3 (*informal*) RUSH, run, race, shoot, fly, speed, dash, sprint, bolt, dart, hotfoot
▷ *noun* PURSUIT, race, hunt, hunting

chasm *noun* 1 GULF, opening, crack, gap, rent, hollow, void, gorge, crater, cavity, abyss, ravine, cleft, fissure, crevasse
2 GAP, division, gulf, split, breach, rift, alienation, hiatus

chassis *noun* FRAME, framework, fuselage, bodywork, substructure

chaste *adjective* 1 PURE, moral, decent, innocent, immaculate, wholesome, virtuous, virginal, unsullied, uncontaminated, undefiled, incorrupt
<< OPPOSITE promiscuous
2 SIMPLE, quiet, elegant, modest, refined, restrained, austere, unaffected, decorous

chasten *verb* SUBDUE, discipline, cow, curb, humble, soften, humiliate, tame, afflict, repress, put in your place

chastise *verb* SCOLD, blame, correct, discipline, lecture, carpet (*informal*), nag, censure, rebuke, reprimand, reproach, berate, tick (someone) off (*informal*), castigate, chide, tell off (*informal*), find fault with, remonstrate with, bring (someone) to book, take (someone) to task, reprove, upbraid, bawl (someone) out (*informal*), give (someone) a talking-to (*informal*), haul (someone) over the coals (*informal*), chew (someone) out (*US & Canad informal*), give (someone) a dressing-down, give (someone) a

rocket (*Brit & NZ informal*), give (someone) a row
<< OPPOSITE praise
chastity *noun* PURITY, virtue, innocence, modesty, virginity, celibacy, continence, maidenhood
<< OPPOSITE promiscuity
chat *verb* TALK, gossip, jaw (*slang*), natter, blather, schmooze (*slang*), blether (*Scot*), shoot the breeze (*US slang*), chew the rag *or* fat (*slang*)
▷ *noun* TALK, tête-à-tête, conversation, gossip, heart-to-heart, natter, blather, schmooze (*slang*), blether (*Scot*), chinwag (*Brit informal*), confab (*informal*), craic (*Irish informal*), korero (*NZ*)
chatter *verb* PRATTLE, chat, rabbit on (*Brit informal*), babble, gab (*informal*), natter, tattle, jabber, blather, schmooze (*slang*), blether (*Scot*), run off at the mouth (*US slang*), prate, gossip
▷ *noun* PRATTLE, chat, rabbit (*Brit informal*), gossip, babble, twaddle, gab (*informal*), natter, tattle, jabber, blather, blether (*Scot*)
chatty *adjective* TALKATIVE, informal, effusive, garrulous, gabby (*informal*), gossipy, newsy (*informal*)
<< OPPOSITE quiet
cheap *adjective* **1** INEXPENSIVE, sale, economy, reduced, keen, reasonable, bargain, low-priced, low-cost, cut-price, economical, cheapo (*informal*)
<< OPPOSITE expensive
2 INFERIOR, poor, worthless, second-rate, shoddy, tawdry, tatty, trashy, substandard, low-rent (*informal, chiefly US*), two-bit (*US & Canad slang*), crappy (*slang*), two a penny, rubbishy, dime-a-dozen (*informal*), tinhorn (*US slang*), bodger *or* bodgie (*Austral slang*)
<< OPPOSITE good
3 (*informal*) DESPICABLE, mean, low, base, vulgar, sordid, contemptible, scurvy, scungy (*Austral & NZ*)
<< OPPOSITE decent
cheapen *verb* DEGRADE, lower, discredit, devalue, demean, belittle, depreciate, debase, derogate
cheat *verb* **1** DECEIVE, skin (*slang*), trick, fool, take in (*informal*), con (*informal*), stiff (*slang*), sting (*informal*), mislead, rip off (*slang*), fleece, hoax, defraud, dupe, beguile, gull (*archaic*), do (*informal*), swindle, stitch up (*slang*), victimize, bamboozle (*informal*), hoodwink, double-cross (*informal*), diddle (*informal*), take for a ride (*informal*), bilk, pull a fast one on (*informal*), screw (*informal*), finagle (*informal*)
2 FOIL, check, defeat, prevent, frustrate, deprive, baffle, thwart
▷ *noun* DECEIVER, sharper, cheater, shark, charlatan, trickster, con man (*informal*), impostor, fraudster, double-crosser (*informal*), swindler, grifter (*slang, chiefly US & Canad*), rorter (*Austral slang*), chiseller (*informal*), rogue trader
check *verb* **1** *often with* **out** EXAMINE, test, study, look at, research, note, confirm, investigate, monitor, probe, tick, vet, inspect, look over, verify, work over, scrutinize, make sure of, inquire into, take a dekko at (*Brit slang*)
<< OPPOSITE overlook
2 STOP, control, limit, arrest, delay, halt, curb, bar, restrain, inhibit, rein, thwart, hinder, repress, obstruct, retard, impede, bridle, stem the flow of, nip in the bud, put a spoke in someone's wheel
<< OPPOSITE further
▷ *noun* **1** EXAMINATION, test, research, investigation, inspection, scrutiny, once-over (*informal*)
2 CONTROL, limitation, restraint, constraint, rein, obstacle, curb, obstruction, stoppage, inhibition, impediment, hindrance, damper
cheek *noun* (*informal*) IMPUDENCE, face (*informal*), front, nerve, sauce (*informal*), gall (*informal*), disrespect, audacity, neck (*informal*), lip (*slang*), temerity, chutzpah (*US & Canad informal*), insolence, impertinence, effrontery, brass neck (*Brit informal*), brazenness, sassiness (*US informal*)
cheeky *adjective* IMPUDENT, rude, forward, fresh (*informal*), insulting, saucy, audacious, sassy (*US informal*), pert, disrespectful, impertinent, insolent, lippy (*US & Canad slang*)
<< OPPOSITE respectful
cheer *verb* **1** APPLAUD, hail, acclaim, clap, hurrah
<< OPPOSITE boo
2 HEARTEN, encourage, warm, comfort, elevate, animate, console, uplift, brighten, exhilarate, solace, enliven, cheer up, buoy up, gladden, elate, inspirit
<< OPPOSITE dishearten
▷ *noun* **1** APPLAUSE, ovation
2 CHEERFULNESS, comfort, joy, optimism, animation, glee, solace, buoyancy, mirth, gaiety, merriment, liveliness, gladness, hopefulness, merry-making
▷▷ **cheer someone up** COMFORT, encourage, brighten, hearten, enliven, gladden, gee up, jolly along (*informal*)
▷▷ **cheer up** TAKE HEART, rally, perk up, buck up (*informal*)
cheerful *adjective* **1** HAPPY, bright, contented, glad, optimistic, bucked (*informal*), enthusiastic, sparkling, gay, sunny, jolly, animated, merry, upbeat (*informal*), buoyant, hearty, cheery, joyful, jovial, genial, jaunty, chirpy (*informal*), sprightly, blithe, light-hearted
<< OPPOSITE sad
2 PLEASANT, bright, sunny, gay, enlivening

<< OPPOSITE gloomy

cheerfulness *noun* HAPPINESS, good humour, exuberance, high spirits, buoyancy, gaiety, good cheer, gladness, geniality, light-heartedness, jauntiness, joyousness

cheery *adjective* CHEERFUL, happy, pleasant, lively, sunny, upbeat (*informal*), good-humoured, carefree, breezy, genial, chirpy (*informal*), jovial, full of beans (*informal*)

chemical *noun* COMPOUND, drug, substance, synthetic substance, potion

chemist *noun* PHARMACIST, apothecary (*obsolete*), pharmacologist, dispenser

cherish *verb* **1** CLING TO, prize, treasure, hold dear, cleave to

<< OPPOSITE despise

2 CARE FOR, love, support, comfort, look after, shelter, treasure, nurture, cosset, hold dear

<< OPPOSITE neglect

3 HARBOUR, nurse, sustain, foster, entertain

chest *noun* **1** BREAST, front

2 BOX, case, trunk, crate, coffer, ark (*dialect*), casket, strongbox

>> RELATED WORD *adjective* pectoral

chew *verb* MUNCH, bite, grind, champ, crunch, gnaw, chomp, masticate

▷▷ **chew something over** CONSIDER, weigh up, ponder, mull (over), meditate on, reflect upon, muse on, ruminate, deliberate upon

chewy *adjective* TOUGH, fibrous, leathery, as tough as old boots

chic *adjective* STYLISH, smart, elegant, fashionable, trendy (*Brit informal*), up-to-date, modish, à la mode, voguish (*informal*), schmick (*Austral informal*)

<< OPPOSITE unfashionable

chide *verb* SCOLD, blame, lecture, carpet (*informal*), put down, criticize, slate (*informal, chiefly Brit*), censure, rebuke, reprimand, reproach, berate, tick (someone) off (*informal*), admonish, tear into (*informal*), blast, tell (someone) off (*informal*), find fault with, diss (*slang, chiefly US*), read (someone) the riot act, reprove, upbraid, slap (someone) on the wrist, lambast(e), bawl (someone) out (*informal*), rap (someone) over the knuckles, chew (someone) out (*US & Canad informal*), tear (someone) off a strip (*Brit informal*), give (someone) a rocket (*Brit & NZ informal*), reprehend, give (someone) a row (*Scot informal*)

chief *noun* HEAD, leader, director, manager, lord, boss (*informal*), captain, master, governor, commander, principal, superior, ruler, superintendent, chieftain, ringleader, baas (*S African*), ariki (*NZ*), sherang (*Austral & NZ*)

<< OPPOSITE subordinate

▷ *adjective* PRIMARY, highest, leading, main, prime, capital, central, key, essential, premier, supreme, most important, outstanding, principal, prevailing, cardinal, paramount, big-time (*informal*), foremost, major league (*informal*), predominant, uppermost, pre-eminent, especial

<< OPPOSITE minor

chiefly *adverb* **1** ESPECIALLY, essentially, principally, primarily, above all

2 MAINLY, largely, usually, mostly, in general, on the whole, predominantly, in the main

child *noun* **1** YOUNGSTER, baby, kid (*informal*), minor, infant, babe, juvenile, toddler, tot, wean (*Scot*), little one, brat, bairn (*Scot*), suckling, nipper (*informal*), chit, babe in arms, sprog (*slang*), munchkin (*informal, chiefly US*), rug rat (*slang*), nursling, littlie (*Austral informal*), ankle-biter (*Austral slang*), tacker (*Austral slang*)

2 OFFSPRING, issue, descendant, progeny

>> RELATED WORD *adjective* filial

>> RELATED WORD *prefix* paedo-

childbirth *noun* CHILD-BEARING, labour, delivery, lying-in, confinement, parturition

>> RELATED WORDS *adjectives* natal, obstetric

childhood *noun* YOUTH, minority, infancy, schooldays, immaturity, boyhood *or* girlhood

childish *adjective* **1** YOUTHFUL, young, boyish *or* girlish

2 IMMATURE, silly, juvenile, foolish, trifling, frivolous, infantile, puerile

<< OPPOSITE mature

childlike *adjective* INNOCENT, trusting, simple, naive, credulous, artless, ingenuous, guileless, unfeigned, trustful

chill *verb* **1** COOL, refrigerate, freeze

2 DISHEARTEN, depress, discourage, dismay, dampen, deject

▷ *noun* **1** COLDNESS, bite, nip, sharpness, coolness, rawness, crispness, frigidity

2 SHIVER, frisson, goose pimples, goose flesh

▷ *adjective* CHILLY, biting, sharp, freezing, raw, bleak, chilly, wintry, frigid, parky (*Brit informal*)

chilly *adjective* **1** COOL, fresh, sharp, crisp, penetrating, brisk, breezy, draughty, nippy, parky (*Brit informal*), blowy

<< OPPOSITE warm

2 UNFRIENDLY, hostile, unsympathetic, frigid, unresponsive, unwelcoming, cold as ice

<< OPPOSITE friendly

chime *verb* RING

▷ *noun* SOUND, boom, toll, jingle, dong, tinkle, clang, peal

chimera *noun* ILLUSION, dream, fantasy, delusion, spectre, snare, hallucination, figment, ignis fatuus, will-o'-the-wisp

china[1] *noun* POTTERY, ceramics, ware, porcelain, crockery, tableware, service

china[2] *noun* (*Brit & S African informal*) FRIEND, pal, mate (*informal*), buddy (*informal*), companion, best friend, intimate, cock (*Brit informal*), close friend, comrade, chum (*informal*), crony, main man (*slang, chiefly US*), soul mate, homeboy (*slang, chiefly US*), cobber (*Austral & NZ old-fashioned informal*), bosom friend, boon companion, E hoa (*NZ*)

chink *noun* OPENING, crack, gap, rift, aperture, cleft, crevice, fissure, cranny

chip *noun* **1** FRAGMENT, scrap, shaving, flake, paring, wafer, sliver, shard
2 SCRATCH, nick, flaw, notch, dent
3 COUNTER, disc, token
▷ *verb* **1** NICK, damage, gash
2 CHISEL, whittle
▷▷ **chip in** (*informal*) **1** CONTRIBUTE, pay, donate, subscribe, go Dutch (*informal*)
2 INTERPOSE, put in, interrupt, interject, butt in, put your oar in

chirp *verb* CHIRRUP, pipe, peep, warble, twitter, cheep, tweet

chirpy *adjective* (*informal*) CHEERFUL, happy, bright, enthusiastic, lively, sparkling, sunny, jolly, animated, buoyant, radiant, jaunty, sprightly, in high spirits, blithe, full of beans (*informal*), light-hearted

chivalry *noun* **1** COURTESY, politeness, gallantry, courtliness, gentlemanliness
2 KNIGHT-ERRANTRY, knighthood, gallantry, courtliness

choice *noun* **1** RANGE, variety, selection, assortment
2 SELECTION, preference, election, pick
3 OPTION, say, alternative
▷ *adjective* BEST, bad (*slang*), special, prime, nice, prize, select, excellent, elect, crucial (*slang*), exclusive, elite, superior, exquisite, def (*slang*), booshit (*Austral slang*), exo (*Austral slang*), sik (*Austral slang*), hand-picked, dainty, rad (*informal*), phat (*slang*), schmick (*Austral informal*)

choke *verb* **1** SUFFOCATE, stifle, smother, overpower, asphyxiate
2 STRANGLE, throttle, asphyxiate
3 BLOCK, dam, clog, obstruct, bung, constrict, occlude, congest, close, stop, bar

choose *verb* **1** PICK, take, prefer, select, elect, adopt, opt for, designate, single out, espouse, settle on, fix on, cherry-pick, settle upon, predestine
<< OPPOSITE reject
2 WISH, want, desire, see fit

choosy *adjective* (*informal*) FUSSY, particular, exacting, discriminating, selective, fastidious, picky (*informal*), finicky, faddy
<< OPPOSITE indiscriminating

chop *verb* CUT, fell, axe, slash, hack, sever, shear, cleave, hew, lop, truncate
▷▷ **chop something up** CUT UP, divide, fragment, cube, dice, mince
▷▷ **the chop** (*Brit & Austral slang*) THE SACK, sacking (*informal*), dismissal, the boot (*slang*), your cards (*informal*), the axe (*informal*), termination, the (old) heave-ho (*informal*), the order of the boot (*slang*)

choppy *adjective* ROUGH, broken, ruffled, tempestuous, blustery, squally
<< OPPOSITE calm

chore *noun* TASK, job, duty, burden, hassle (*informal*), fag (*informal*), errand, no picnic

chortle *verb* CHUCKLE, laugh, cackle, guffaw
▷ *noun* CHUCKLE, laugh, cackle, guffaw

chorus *noun* **1** REFRAIN, response, strain, burden
2 CHOIR, singers, ensemble, vocalists, choristers
▷▷ **in chorus** IN UNISON, as one, all together, in concert, in harmony, in accord, with one voice

christen *verb* **1** BAPTIZE, name
2 NAME, call, term, style, title, dub, designate

Christmas *noun* THE FESTIVE SEASON, Noël, Xmas (*informal*), Yule (*archaic*), Yuletide (*archaic*)

chronic *adjective* **1** PERSISTENT, constant, continual, deep-seated, incurable, deep-rooted, ineradicable
2 (*informal*) DREADFUL, awful, appalling, atrocious, abysmal

chronicle *verb* RECORD, tell, report, enter, relate, register, recount, set down, narrate, put on record
▷ *noun* RECORD, story, history, account, register, journal, diary, narrative, annals

chronicler *noun* RECORDER, reporter, historian, narrator, scribe, diarist, annalist

chronological *adjective* SEQUENTIAL, ordered, historical, progressive, consecutive, in sequence
<< OPPOSITE random

chubby *adjective* PLUMP, stout, fleshy, tubby, flabby, portly, buxom, roly-poly, rotund, round, podgy
<< OPPOSITE skinny

chuck *verb* (*informal*) **1** THROW, cast, pitch, shy, toss, hurl, fling, sling, heave
2 *often with* **away** *or* **out** THROW OUT, dump (*informal*), scrap, get rid of, bin (*informal*), ditch (*slang*), junk (*informal*), discard, dispose of, dispense with, jettison
3 GIVE UP *or* OVER, leave, stop, abandon, cease, resign from, pack in, jack in
4 (*US, Austral & NZ informal*) VOMIT, throw up (*informal*), spew, heave (*slang*), puke (*slang*), barf (*US slang*), chunder (*slang, chiefly Austral*), upchuck (*US slang*), do a technicolour yawn, toss your cookies (*US slang*)

chuckle *verb* LAUGH, giggle, snigger, chortle, titter
▷ *noun* LAUGH, giggle, snigger, chortle, titter

chum *noun* (*informal*) FRIEND, mate (*informal*), pal (*informal*), companion, cock (*Brit informal*), comrade, crony, main man (*slang, chiefly US*),

cobber (*Austral & NZ old-fashioned informal*), E hoa (*NZ*)
chummy *adjective* (*informal*) FRIENDLY, close, thick (*informal*), pally (*informal*), intimate, affectionate, buddy-buddy (*slang, chiefly US & Canad*), palsy-walsy (*informal*), matey *or* maty (*Brit informal*)
chunk *noun* PIECE, block, mass, portion, lump, slab, hunk, nugget, wad, dollop (*informal*), wodge (*Brit informal*)
chunky *adjective* THICKSET, stocky, beefy (*informal*), stubby, dumpy
church *noun* CHAPEL, temple, cathedral, kirk (*Scot*), minster, tabernacle, place of worship, house of God
>> RELATED WORD *adjective* ecclesiastical
churlish *adjective* RUDE, harsh, vulgar, sullen, surly, morose, brusque, ill-tempered, boorish, uncouth, impolite, loutish, oafish, uncivil, unmannerly
<< OPPOSITE polite
churn *verb* 1 STIR UP, beat, disturb, swirl, agitate
2 SWIRL, boil, toss, foam, seethe, froth
cigarette *noun* FAG (*Brit slang*), smoke, gasper (*slang*), ciggy (*informal*), coffin nail (*slang*), cancer stick (*slang*)
cinema *noun* 1 PICTURES, movies, picture-house, flicks (*slang*)
2 FILMS, pictures, movies, the big screen (*informal*), motion pictures, the silver screen
cipher *noun* 1 CODE, coded message, cryptogram
2 NOBODY, nonentity
circa *preposition* APPROXIMATELY, about, around, roughly, in the region of, round about
circle *noun* 1 RING, round, band, disc, loop, hoop, cordon, perimeter, halo
2 GROUP, company, set, school, club, order, class, society, crowd, assembly, fellowship, fraternity, clique, coterie
3 SPHERE, world, area, range, field, scene, orbit, realm, milieu
▷ *verb* 1 GO ROUND, ring, surround, belt, curve, enclose, encompass, compass, envelop, encircle, circumscribe, hem in, gird, circumnavigate, enwreath
2 WHEEL, spiral, revolve, rotate, whirl, pivot
circuit *noun* 1 COURSE, round, tour, track, route, journey
2 RACETRACK, course, track, racecourse
3 LAP, round, tour, revolution, orbit, perambulation
circuitous *adjective* 1 INDIRECT, winding, rambling, roundabout, meandering, tortuous, labyrinthine
<< OPPOSITE direct
2 OBLIQUE, indirect
circular *adjective* 1 ROUND, ring-shaped, discoid
2 CIRCUITOUS, cyclical, orbital
▷ *noun* ADVERTISEMENT, notice, ad (*informal*), announcement, advert (*Brit informal*), press release
circulate *verb* 1 SPREAD, issue, publish, broadcast, distribute, diffuse, publicize, propagate, disseminate, promulgate, make known
2 FLOW, revolve, rotate, radiate
circulation *noun* 1 DISTRIBUTION, currency, readership
2 BLOODSTREAM, blood flow
3 FLOW, circling, motion, rotation
4 SPREAD, distribution, transmission, dissemination
circumference *noun* EDGE, limits, border, bounds, outline, boundary, fringe, verge, rim, perimeter, periphery, extremity
circumscribe *verb* RESTRICT, limit, define, confine, restrain, delineate, hem in, demarcate, delimit, straiten
circumspect *adjective* CAUTIOUS, politic, guarded, careful, wary, discriminating, discreet, sage, prudent, canny, attentive, vigilant, watchful, judicious, observant, sagacious, heedful
<< OPPOSITE rash
circumstance *noun* 1 *usually plural* SITUATION, condition, scenario, contingency, state of affairs, lie of the land
2 *usually plural* DETAIL, fact, event, particular, respect, factor
3 *usually plural* SITUATION, state, means, position, station, resources, status, lifestyle
4 CHANCE, the times, accident, fortune, luck, fate, destiny, misfortune, providence
circumstantial *adjective* 1 INDIRECT, contingent, incidental, inferential, presumptive, conjectural, founded on circumstances
2 DETAILED, particular, specific
circumvent *verb* 1 (*Formal*) EVADE, bypass, elude, steer clear of, sidestep
2 OUTWIT, trick, mislead, thwart, deceive, dupe, beguile, outflank, hoodwink
cistern *noun* TANK, vat, basin, reservoir, sink
citadel *noun* FORTRESS, keep, tower, stronghold, bastion, fortification, fastness
citation *noun* 1 COMMENDATION, award, mention
2 QUOTATION, quote, reference, passage, illustration, excerpt
cite *verb* 1 QUOTE, name, evidence, advance, mention, extract, specify, allude to, enumerate, adduce
2 (*Law*) SUMMON, call, subpoena
citizen *noun* INHABITANT, resident, dweller, ratepayer, denizen, subject, freeman, burgher, townsman

>> RELATED WORD *adjective* civil

city *noun* TOWN, metropolis, municipality, conurbation, megalopolis

>> RELATED WORD *adjective* civic

civic *adjective* PUBLIC, community, borough, municipal, communal, local

civil *adjective* 1 CIVIC, home, political, domestic, interior, municipal

<< OPPOSITE state

2 POLITE, obliging, accommodating, civilized, courteous, considerate, affable, courtly, well-bred, complaisant, well-mannered

<< OPPOSITE rude

civility *noun* POLITENESS, consideration, courtesy, tact, good manners, graciousness, cordiality, affability, amiability, complaisance, courteousness

civilization *noun* 1 SOCIETY, people, community, nation, polity

2 CULTURE, development, education, progress, enlightenment, sophistication, advancement, cultivation, refinement

civilize *verb* CULTIVATE, improve, polish, educate, refine, tame, enlighten, humanize, sophisticate

civilized *adjective* 1 CULTURED, educated, sophisticated, enlightened, humane

<< OPPOSITE primitive

2 POLITE, mannerly, tolerant, gracious, courteous, affable, well-behaved, well-mannered

clad *adjective* DRESSED, clothed, arrayed, draped, fitted out, decked out, attired, rigged out (*informal*), covered

claim *verb* 1 ASSERT, insist, maintain, allege, uphold, profess, hold

2 TAKE, receive, pick up, collect, lay claim to

3 DEMAND, call for, ask for, insist on

▷ *noun* 1 ASSERTION, statement, allegation, declaration, contention, pretension, affirmation, protestation

2 DEMAND, application, request, petition, call

3 RIGHT, title, entitlement

claimant *noun* APPLICANT, pretender, petitioner, supplicant, suppliant

clairvoyant *adjective* PSYCHIC, visionary, prophetic, prescient, telepathic, fey, second-sighted, extrasensory, oracular, sibylline

▷ *noun* PSYCHIC, diviner, prophet, visionary, oracle, seer, augur, fortune-teller, soothsayer, sibyl, prophetess, telepath

clamber *verb* CLIMB, scale, scramble, claw, shin, scrabble

clammy *adjective* 1 MOIST, sweating, damp, sticky, sweaty, slimy

2 DAMP, humid, dank, muggy, close

clamour *noun* NOISE, shouting, racket, outcry, din, uproar, agitation, blare, commotion, babel, hubbub, brouhaha, hullabaloo, shout

clamp *noun* VICE, press, grip, bracket, fastener

▷ *verb* FASTEN, fix, secure, clinch, brace, make fast

clan *noun* 1 FAMILY, house, group, order, race, society, band, tribe, sept, fraternity, brotherhood, sodality, ainga (NZ), ngai *or* ngati (NZ)

2 GROUP, set, crowd, circle, crew (*informal*), gang, faction, coterie, schism, cabal

clandestine *adjective* SECRET, private, hidden, underground, concealed, closet, covert, sly, furtive, underhand, surreptitious, stealthy, cloak-and-dagger, under-the-counter

clang *verb* RING, toll, resound, chime, reverberate, jangle, clank, bong, clash

▷ *noun* RINGING, clash, jangle, knell, clank, reverberation, ding-dong, clangour

clap *verb* 1 APPLAUD, cheer, acclaim, give (someone) a big hand

<< OPPOSITE boo

2 STRIKE, pat, punch, bang, thrust, slap, whack, wallop (*informal*), thwack

clarification *noun* EXPLANATION, interpretation, exposition, illumination, simplification, elucidation

clarify *verb* 1 EXPLAIN, resolve, interpret, illuminate, clear up, simplify, make plain, elucidate, explicate, clear the air about, throw *or* shed light on

2 REFINE, cleanse, purify

clarity *noun* 1 CLEARNESS, precision, simplicity, transparency, lucidity, explicitness, intelligibility, obviousness, straightforwardness, comprehensibility

<< OPPOSITE obscurity

2 TRANSPARENCY, clearness

<< OPPOSITE cloudiness

clash *verb* 1 CONFLICT, grapple, wrangle, lock horns, cross swords, war, feud, quarrel

2 DISAGREE, conflict, vary, counter, differ, depart, contradict, diverge, deviate, run counter to, be dissimilar, be discordant

3 NOT GO, jar, not match, be discordant

4 CRASH, bang, rattle, jar, clatter, jangle, clang, clank

▷ *noun* 1 CONFLICT, fight, brush, confrontation, collision, showdown (*informal*), boilover (*Austral*)

2 DISAGREEMENT, difference, division, argument, dispute, dissent, difference of opinion

clasp *verb* GRASP, hold, press, grip, seize, squeeze, embrace, clutch, hug, enfold

▷ *noun* 1 GRASP, hold, grip, embrace, hug

2 FASTENING, catch, grip, hook, snap, pin, clip, buckle, brooch, fastener, hasp, press stud

class *noun* 1 GROUP, grouping, set, order, league, division, rank, caste, status, sphere

2 TYPE, set, sort, kind, collection, species,

grade, category, stamp, genre, classification, denomination, genus
▷ *verb* CLASSIFY, group, rate, rank, brand, label, grade, designate, categorize, codify ▷ see **family**
classic *adjective* 1 TYPICAL, standard, model, regular, usual, ideal, characteristic, definitive, archetypal, exemplary, quintessential, time-honoured, paradigmatic, dinki-di (*Austral informal*)
2 MASTERLY, best, finest, master, world-class, consummate, first-rate
  << OPPOSITE second-rate
3 LASTING, enduring, abiding, immortal, undying, ageless, deathless
▷ *noun* STANDARD, masterpiece, prototype, paradigm, exemplar, masterwork, model
classification *noun* 1 CATEGORIZATION, grading, cataloguing, taxonomy, codification, sorting, analysis, arrangement
2 CLASS, grouping, heading, head, order, sort, list, department, type, division, section, rank, grade
classify *verb* CATEGORIZE, sort, file, rank, arrange, grade, catalogue, codify, pigeonhole, tabulate, systematize
classy *adjective* (*informal*) HIGH-CLASS, select, exclusive, superior, elegant, stylish, posh (*informal, chiefly Brit*), swish (*informal, chiefly Brit*), up-market, urbane, swanky (*informal*), top-drawer, ritzy (*slang*), high-toned, schmick (*Austral informal*)
clause *noun* SECTION, condition, article, item, chapter, rider, provision, passage, point, part, heading, paragraph, specification, proviso, stipulation
claw *noun* 1 NAIL, talon
2 PINCER, nipper
▷ *verb* SCRATCH, tear, dig, rip, scrape, graze, maul, scrabble, mangle, mangulate (*Austral slang*), lacerate
clean *adjective* 1 HYGIENIC, natural, fresh, sterile, pure, purified, antiseptic, sterilized, unadulterated, uncontaminated, unpolluted, decontaminated
  << OPPOSITE contaminated
2 SPOTLESS, fresh, washed, immaculate, laundered, impeccable, flawless, sanitary, faultless, squeaky-clean, hygienic, unblemished, unsullied, unstained, unsoiled, unspotted
  << OPPOSITE dirty
3 MORAL, good, pure, decent, innocent, respectable, upright, honourable, impeccable, exemplary, virtuous, chaste, undefiled
  << OPPOSITE immoral
4 COMPLETE, final, whole, total, perfect, entire, decisive, thorough, conclusive, unimpaired
5 NEAT, simple, elegant, trim, delicate, tidy, graceful, uncluttered
  << OPPOSITE untidy
▷ *verb* CLEANSE, wash, bath, sweep, dust, wipe, vacuum, scrub, sponge, rinse, mop, launder, scour, purify, do up, swab, disinfect, deodorize, sanitize
  << OPPOSITE dirty
clean-cut *adjective* NEAT, trim, tidy, chiselled
cleanliness *noun* CLEANNESS, purity, freshness, whiteness, sterility, spotlessness
cleanse *verb* 1 PURIFY, clear, purge
2 ABSOLVE, clear, purge, purify
3 CLEAN, wash, scrub, rinse, scour
cleanser *noun* DETERGENT, soap, solvent, disinfectant, soap powder, purifier, scourer, wash
clear *adjective* 1 COMPREHENSIBLE, explicit, articulate, understandable, coherent, lucid, user-friendly, intelligible
  << OPPOSITE confused
2 DISTINCT, audible, perceptible
  << OPPOSITE indistinct
3 OBVIOUS, plain, apparent, bold, patent, evident, distinct, pronounced, definite, manifest, blatant, conspicuous, unmistakable, express, palpable, unequivocal, recognizable, unambiguous, unquestionable, cut-and-dried (*informal*), incontrovertible
  << OPPOSITE ambiguous
4 CERTAIN, sure, convinced, positive, satisfied, resolved, explicit, definite, decided
  << OPPOSITE confused
5 TRANSPARENT, see-through, translucent, crystalline, glassy, limpid, pellucid
  << OPPOSITE opaque
6 UNOBSTRUCTED, open, free, empty, unhindered, unimpeded, unhampered
  << OPPOSITE blocked
7 BRIGHT, fine, fair, shining, sunny, luminous, halcyon, cloudless, undimmed, light, unclouded
  << OPPOSITE cloudy
8 UNTROUBLED, clean, pure, innocent, stainless, immaculate, unblemished, untarnished, guiltless, sinless, undefiled
▷ *verb* 1 UNBLOCK, unclog, free, loosen, extricate, disengage, open, disentangle
2 REMOVE, clean, wipe, cleanse, tidy (up), sweep away
3 BRIGHTEN, break up, lighten
4 PASS OVER, jump, leap, vault, miss
5 ABSOLVE, acquit, vindicate, exonerate
  << OPPOSITE blame
▷▷ **clear out** (*informal*) GO AWAY, leave, retire, withdraw, depart, beat it (*slang*), decamp, hook it (*slang*), slope off, pack your bags (*informal*), make tracks, take yourself off, make yourself scarce, rack off (*Austral & NZ slang*)
▷▷ **clear something out** 1 EMPTY, sort, tidy up

2 GET RID OF, remove, dump, dispose of, throw away *or* out
▷▷ **clear something up** 1 TIDY (UP), order, straighten, rearrange, put in order
2 SOLVE, explain, resolve, clarify, unravel, straighten out, elucidate
clearance *noun* 1 EVACUATION, emptying, withdrawal, removal, eviction, depopulation
2 PERMISSION, consent, endorsement, green light, authorization, blank cheque, go-ahead (*informal*), leave, sanction, O.K. *or* okay (*informal*)
3 SPACE, gap, margin, allowance, headroom
clear-cut *adjective* STRAIGHTFORWARD, specific, plain, precise, black-and-white, explicit, definite, unequivocal, unambiguous, cut-and-dried (*informal*)
clearing *noun* GLADE, space, dell
clearly *adverb* 1 OBVIOUSLY, undoubtedly, evidently, distinctly, markedly, overtly, undeniably, beyond doubt, incontrovertibly, incontestably, openly
2 LEGIBLY, distinctly
3 AUDIBLY, distinctly, intelligibly, comprehensibly
cleave *verb* SPLIT, open, divide, crack, slice, rend, sever, part, hew, tear asunder, sunder
cleft *noun* OPENING, break, crack, gap, rent, breach, fracture, rift, chink, crevice, fissure, cranny
clemency *noun* MERCY, pity, humanity, compassion, kindness, forgiveness, indulgence, leniency, forbearance, quarter
clement *adjective* MILD, fine, fair, calm, temperate, balmy
clergy *noun* PRIESTHOOD, ministry, clerics, clergymen, churchmen, the cloth, holy orders, ecclesiastics
>> RELATED WORDS *adjectives* clerical, pastoral
clergyman *noun* MINISTER, priest, vicar, parson, reverend (*informal*), rabbi, pastor, chaplain, cleric, rector, curate, father, churchman, padre, man of God, man of the cloth, divine
clerical *adjective* 1 ADMINISTRATIVE, office, bureaucratic, secretarial, book-keeping, stenographic
2 ECCLESIASTICAL, priestly, pastoral, sacerdotal
clever *adjective* 1 INTELLIGENT, quick, bright, talented, gifted, keen, capable, smart, sensible, rational, witty, apt, discerning, knowledgeable, astute, brainy (*informal*), quick-witted, sagacious, knowing, deep, expert
<< OPPOSITE stupid
2 SHREWD, bright, cunning, ingenious, inventive, astute, resourceful, canny
<< OPPOSITE unimaginative
3 SKILFUL, able, talented, gifted, capable, inventive, adroit, dexterous
<< OPPOSITE inept
cleverness *noun* 1 INTELLIGENCE, sense, brains, wit, brightness, nous (*Brit slang*), suss (*slang*), quickness, gumption (*Brit informal*), sagacity, smartness, astuteness, quick wits, smarts (*slang, chiefly US*)
2 SHREWDNESS, sharpness, resourcefulness, canniness
3 DEXTERITY, ability, talent, gift, flair, ingenuity, adroitness
cliché *noun* PLATITUDE, stereotype, commonplace, banality, truism, bromide, old saw, hackneyed phrase, chestnut (*informal*)
click *noun* SNAP, beat, tick, clack
▷ *verb* 1 SNAP, beat, tick, clack
2 (*informal*) BECOME CLEAR, come home (to), make sense, fall into place
3 (*Slang*) GET ON, be compatible, hit it off (*informal*), be on the same wavelength, get on like a house on fire (*informal*), take to each other, feel a rapport
client *noun* CUSTOMER, consumer, buyer, patron, shopper, habitué, patient
clientele *noun* CUSTOMERS, market, business, following, trade, regulars, clients, patronage
cliff *noun* ROCK FACE, overhang, crag, precipice, escarpment, face, scar, bluff
climactic *adjective* CRUCIAL, central, critical, peak, decisive, paramount, pivotal

> *Climatic* is sometimes wrongly used where *climactic* is meant. *Climatic* should be used to talk about things relating to climate; *climactic* is used to describe something which forms a climax: *the climactic moment of the* Revolution

climate *noun* 1 WEATHER, country, region, temperature, clime
2 ATMOSPHERE, environment, spirit, surroundings, tone, mood, trend, flavour, feeling, tendency, temper, ambience, vibes (*slang*)
climax *noun* CULMINATION, head, top, summit, height, highlight, peak, pay-off (*informal*), crest, high point, zenith, apogee, high spot (*informal*), acme, ne plus ultra (*Latin*)
▷ *verb* CULMINATE, end, finish, conclude, peak, come to a head
climb *verb* 1 ASCEND, scale, mount, go up, clamber, shin up
2 CLAMBER, descend, scramble, dismount
3 RISE, go up, soar, ascend, fly up
▷▷ **climb down** BACK DOWN, withdraw, yield, concede, retreat, surrender, give in, cave in (*informal*), retract, admit defeat, back-pedal, eat your words, eat crow (*US informal*)
clinch *verb* 1 SECURE, close, confirm, conclude, seal, verify, sew up (*informal*), set the seal on
2 SETTLE, decide, determine, tip the balance

cling *verb* 1 CLUTCH, grip, embrace, grasp, hug, hold on to, clasp
2 STICK TO, attach to, adhere to, fasten to, twine round
▷▷ **cling to something** ADHERE TO, maintain, stand by, cherish, abide by, be true to, be loyal to, be faithful to, cleave to

clinical *adjective* UNEMOTIONAL, cold, scientific, objective, detached, analytic, impersonal, antiseptic, disinterested, dispassionate, emotionless

clip[1] *verb* 1 TRIM, cut, crop, dock, prune, shorten, shear, cut short, snip, pare
2 (*informal*) SMACK, strike, box, knock, punch, belt (*informal*), thump, clout (*informal*), cuff, whack, wallop (*informal*), skelp (*dialect*)
▷ *noun* 1 (*informal*) SMACK, strike, box, knock, punch, belt (*informal*), thump, clout (*informal*), cuff, whack, wallop (*informal*), skelp (*dialect*)
2 (*informal*) SPEED, rate, pace, gallop, lick (*informal*), velocity

clip[2] *verb* ATTACH, fix, secure, connect, pin, staple, fasten, affix, hold

clipping *noun* CUTTING, passage, extract, excerpt, piece, article

clique *noun* GROUP, set, crowd, pack, circle, crew (*informal*), gang, faction, mob, clan, posse (*informal*), coterie, schism, cabal

cloak *noun* 1 CAPE, coat, wrap, mantle
2 COVERING, layer, blanket, shroud
3 DISGUISE, front, cover, screen, blind, mask, shield, cover-up, façade, pretext, smoke screen
▷ *verb* 1 COVER, coat, wrap, blanket, shroud, envelop
2 HIDE, cover, screen, mask, disguise, conceal, obscure, veil, camouflage

clobber[1] *verb* (*Slang*) BATTER, beat, assault, smash, bash (*informal*), lash, thrash, pound, beat up (*informal*), wallop (*informal*), pummel, rough up (*informal*), lambast(e), belabour, duff up (*informal*), beat *or* knock seven bells out of (*informal*)

clobber[2] *noun* (*Brit slang*) BELONGINGS, things, effects, property, stuff, gear, possessions, paraphernalia, accoutrements, chattels

clog *verb* OBSTRUCT, block, jam, hamper, hinder, impede, bung, stop up, dam up, occlude, congest

cloistered *adjective* SHELTERED, protected, restricted, shielded, confined, insulated, secluded, reclusive, shut off, sequestered, withdrawn, cloistral
<< OPPOSITE public

close[1] *verb* 1 SHUT, lock, push to, fasten, secure
<< OPPOSITE open
2 SHUT DOWN, finish, cease, discontinue
3 WIND UP, finish, axe (*informal*), shut down, terminate, discontinue, mothball
4 BLOCK UP, bar, seal, shut up
<< OPPOSITE open
5 END, finish, complete, conclude, wind up, culminate, terminate
<< OPPOSITE begin
6 CLINCH, confirm, secure, conclude, seal, verify, sew up (*informal*), set the seal on
7 COME TOGETHER, join, connect
<< OPPOSITE separate
▷ *noun* END, ending, finish, conclusion, completion, finale, culmination, denouement

close[2] *adjective* 1 NEAR, neighbouring, nearby, handy, adjacent, adjoining, hard by, just round the corner, within striking distance (*informal*), cheek by jowl, proximate, within spitting distance (*informal*), within sniffing distance, a hop, skip and a jump away
<< OPPOSITE far
2 INTIMATE, loving, friendly, familiar, thick (*informal*), attached, devoted, confidential, inseparable, dear
<< OPPOSITE distant
3 NOTICEABLE, marked, strong, distinct, pronounced
4 CAREFUL, detailed, searching, concentrated, keen, intense, minute, alert, intent, thorough, rigorous, attentive, painstaking, assiduous
5 EVEN, level, neck and neck, fifty-fifty (*informal*), evenly matched, equally balanced
6 IMMINENT, near, approaching, impending, at hand, upcoming, nigh, just round the corner
<< OPPOSITE far away
7 STIFLING, confined, oppressive, stale, suffocating, stuffy, humid, sweltering, airless, muggy, unventilated, heavy, thick
<< OPPOSITE airy
8 ACCURATE, strict, exact, precise, faithful, literal, conscientious

closed *adjective* 1 SHUT, locked, sealed, fastened
<< OPPOSITE open
2 SHUT DOWN, out of business, out of service
3 EXCLUSIVE, select, restricted
4 FINISHED, over, ended, decided, settled, concluded, resolved, terminated

closet *noun* (*US*) CUPBOARD, cabinet, recess, cubicle, cubbyhole
▷ *adjective* SECRET, private, hidden, unknown, concealed, covert, unrevealed

closure *noun* CLOSING, end, finish, conclusion, stoppage, termination, cessation

clot *verb* CONGEAL, thicken, curdle, coalesce, jell, coagulate

cloth *noun* FABRIC, material, textiles, dry goods, stuff

clothe *verb* DRESS, outfit, rig, array, robe, drape, get ready, swathe, apparel, attire, fit out, garb, doll up (*slang*), accoutre, cover, deck
<< OPPOSITE undress

clothes *plural noun* CLOTHING, wear, dress, gear

(*informal*), habits, get-up (*informal*), outfit, costume, threads (*slang*), wardrobe, ensemble, garments, duds (*informal*), apparel, clobber (*Brit slang*), attire, garb, togs (*informal*), vestments, glad rags (*informal*), raiment (*archaic or poetic*), rigout (*informal*)

clothing *noun* CLOTHES, wear, dress, gear (*informal*), habits, get-up (*informal*), outfit, costume, threads (*slang*), wardrobe, ensemble, garments, duds (*informal*), apparel, clobber (*Brit slang*), attire, garb, togs (*informal*), vestments, glad rags (*informal*), raiment (*archaic* or *poetic*), rigout (*informal*)

cloud *noun* **1** MIST, fog, haze, obscurity, vapour, nebula, murk, darkness, gloom
2 BILLOW, mass, shower, puff
▷ *verb* **1** CONFUSE, obscure, distort, impair, muddle, disorient
2 DARKEN, dim, be overshadowed, be overcast

cloudy *adjective* **1** DULL, dark, dim, gloomy, dismal, sombre, overcast, leaden, sunless, louring *or* lowering
<< OPPOSITE clear
2 OPAQUE, muddy, murky
3 VAGUE, confused, obscure, blurred, unclear, hazy, indistinct
<< OPPOSITE plain

clout (*informal*) *verb* HIT, strike, punch, deck (*slang*), slap, sock (*slang*), chin (*slang*), smack, thump, cuff, clobber (*slang*), wallop (*informal*), box, wham, lay one on (*slang*), skelp (*dialect*)
▷ *noun* **1** THUMP, blow, crack, punch, slap, sock (*slang*), cuff, wallop (*informal*), skelp (*dialect*)
2 INFLUENCE, power, standing, authority, pull, weight, bottom, prestige, mana (*NZ*)

cloven *adjective* SPLIT, divided, cleft, bisected

clown *noun* **1** COMEDIAN, fool, harlequin, jester, buffoon, pierrot, dolt
2 JOKER, comic, prankster
3 FOOL, dope (*informal*), jerk (*slang, chiefly US & Canad*), idiot, ass, berk (*Brit slang*), prat (*slang*), moron, twit (*informal, chiefly Brit*), imbecile (*informal*), ignoramus, jackass, dolt, blockhead, ninny, putz (*US slang*), eejit (*Scot & Irish*), doofus (*slang, chiefly US*), dorba *or* dorb (*Austral slang*), bogan (*Austral slang*), lamebrain (*informal*), numbskull *or* numskull
▷ *verb usually with* **around** PLAY THE FOOL, mess about, jest, act the fool, act the goat, play the goat

cloying *adjective* **1** SICKLY, nauseating, icky (*informal*), treacly, oversweet, excessive
2 OVER-SENTIMENTAL, sickly, nauseating, mushy, twee, slushy, mawkish, icky (*informal*), treacly, oversweet

club *noun* **1** ASSOCIATION, company, group, union, society, circle, lodge, guild, fraternity, set, order, sodality
2 STICK, bat, bludgeon, truncheon, cosh (*Brit*), cudgel
▷ *verb* BEAT, strike, hammer, batter, bash, clout (*informal*), bludgeon, clobber (*slang*), pummel, cosh (*Brit*), beat *or* knock seven bells out of (*informal*)

clue *noun* INDICATION, lead, sign, evidence, tip, suggestion, trace, hint, suspicion, pointer, tip-off, inkling, intimation

clueless *adjective* STUPID, thick, dull, naive, dim, dense, dumb (*informal*), simple-minded, dozy (*Brit informal*), simple, slow, witless, dopey (*informal*), moronic, unintelligent, half-witted, slow on the uptake (*informal*)

clump *noun* CLUSTER, group, bunch, bundle, shock
▷ *verb* STOMP, stamp, stump, thump, lumber, tramp, plod, thud, clomp

clumsiness *noun* INSENSITIVITY, heavy-handedness, tactlessness, gaucheness, lack of tact, uncouthness
<< OPPOSITE sensitivity

clumsy *adjective* **1** AWKWARD, blundering, bungling, lumbering, inept, bumbling, ponderous, ungainly, gauche, accident-prone, gawky, heavy, uncoordinated, cack-handed (*informal*), inexpert, maladroit, ham-handed (*informal*), like a bull in a china shop, klutzy (*US & Canad slang*), unskilful, butterfingered (*informal*), ham-fisted (*informal*), unco (*Austral slang*)
<< OPPOSITE skilful
2 UNWIELDY, ill-shaped, unhandy, clunky (*informal*)

cluster *noun* GATHERING, group, collection, bunch, knot, clump, assemblage
▷ *verb* GATHER, group, collect, bunch, assemble, flock, huddle

clutch *verb* **1** HOLD, grip, embrace, grasp, cling to, clasp
2 SEIZE, catch, grab, grasp, snatch
▷ *plural noun* POWER, hands, control, grip, possession, grasp, custody, sway, keeping, claws

clutter *noun* UNTIDINESS, mess, disorder, confusion, litter, muddle, disarray, jumble, hotchpotch
<< OPPOSITE order
▷ *verb* LITTER, scatter, strew, mess up
<< OPPOSITE tidy

cluttered *adjective* UNTIDY, confused, disordered, littered, messy, muddled, jumbled, disarrayed

coach *noun* **1** INSTRUCTOR, teacher, trainer, tutor, handler
2 BUS, charabanc
▷ *verb* INSTRUCT, train, prepare, exercise, drill, tutor, cram

coalesce *verb* BLEND, unite, mix, combine, incorporate, integrate, merge, consolidate, come together, fuse, amalgamate, meld, cohere

coalition *noun* ALLIANCE, union, league, association, combination, merger, integration, compact, conjunction, bloc, confederation, fusion, affiliation, amalgam, amalgamation, confederacy

coarse *adjective* 1 ROUGH, crude, unfinished, homespun, impure, unrefined, rough-hewn, unprocessed, unpolished, coarse-grained, unpurified

<< OPPOSITE smooth

2 VULGAR, offensive, rude, indecent, improper, raunchy (*slang*), earthy, foul-mouthed, bawdy, impure, smutty, impolite, ribald, immodest, indelicate

3 LOUTISH, rough, brutish, boorish, uncivil

<< OPPOSITE well-mannered

coast *noun* SHORE, border, beach, strand, seaside, coastline, seaboard

▷ *verb* CRUISE, sail, drift, taxi, glide, freewheel

>> RELATED WORD *adjective* littoral

coat *noun* 1 FUR, hair, skin, hide, wool, fleece, pelt

2 LAYER, covering, coating, overlay

▷ *verb* COVER, spread, plaster, smear

coating *noun* LAYER, covering, finish, skin, sheet, coat, dusting, blanket, membrane, glaze, film, varnish, veneer, patina, lamination

coat of arms *noun* HERALDRY, crest, insignia, escutcheon, blazonry

coax *verb* PERSUADE, cajole, talk into, wheedle, sweet-talk (*informal*), prevail upon, inveigle, soft-soap (*informal*), twist (someone's) arm, flatter, entice, beguile, allure

<< OPPOSITE bully

cobber *noun* (*Austral & NZ old-fashioned informal*) FRIEND, pal, mate (*informal*), buddy (*informal*), china (*Brit & S African informal*), best friend, intimate, cock (*Brit informal*), close friend, comrade, chum (*informal*), crony, alter ego, main man (*slang, chiefly US*), soul mate, homeboy (*slang, chiefly US*), bosom friend, boon companion, E hoa (NZ)

cock *noun* COCKEREL, rooster, chanticleer

▷ *verb* RAISE, prick up, perk up

cocktail *noun* MIXTURE, combination, compound, blend, concoction, mix, amalgamation, admixture

cocky[1] *adjective* OVERCONFIDENT, arrogant, brash, swaggering, conceited, egotistical, cocksure, swollen-headed, vain, full of yourself

<< OPPOSITE modest

cocky[2] *or* **cockie** *noun* (*Austral & NZ informal*) FARMER, smallholder, crofter (*Scot*), grazier, agriculturalist, rancher, husbandman

cocoon *verb* 1 WRAP, swathe, envelop, swaddle, pad

2 PROTECT, shelter, cushion, insulate, screen

coddle *verb* PAMPER, spoil, indulge, cosset, baby, nurse, pet, wet-nurse (*informal*), mollycoddle

code *noun* 1 PRINCIPLES, rules, manners, custom, convention, ethics, maxim, etiquette, system, kawa (NZ), tikanga (NZ)

2 CIPHER, cryptograph

codify *verb* SYSTEMATIZE, catalogue, classify, summarize, tabulate, collect, organize

coerce *verb* FORCE, compel, bully, intimidate, railroad (*informal*), constrain, bulldoze (*informal*), dragoon, pressurize, browbeat, press-gang, twist (someone's) arm (*informal*), drive

coercion *noun* FORCE, pressure, threats, bullying, constraint, intimidation, compulsion, duress, browbeating, strong-arm tactics (*informal*)

cogent *adjective* CONVINCING, strong, powerful, effective, compelling, urgent, influential, potent, irresistible, compulsive, forceful, conclusive, weighty, forcible

cognition *noun* PERCEPTION, reasoning, understanding, intelligence, awareness, insight, comprehension, apprehension, discernment

coherence *noun* CONSISTENCY, rationality, concordance, consonance, congruity, union, agreement, connection, unity, correspondence

coherent *adjective* 1 CONSISTENT, reasoned, organized, rational, logical, meaningful, systematic, orderly

<< OPPOSITE inconsistent

2 ARTICULATE, lucid, comprehensible, intelligible

<< OPPOSITE unintelligible

cohort *noun* GROUP, set, band, contingent, batch

coil *verb* 1 WIND, twist, curl, loop, spiral, twine

2 CURL, wind, twist, snake, loop, entwine, twine, wreathe, convolute

coin *noun* MONEY, change, cash, silver, copper, dosh (*Brit & Austral slang*), specie, kembla (*Austral slang*)

▷ *verb* INVENT, create, make up, frame, forge, conceive, originate, formulate, fabricate, think up

>> RELATED WORD *enthusiast* numismatist

coincide *verb* 1 OCCUR SIMULTANEOUSLY, coexist, synchronize, be concurrent

2 AGREE, match, accord, square, correspond, tally, concur, harmonize

<< OPPOSITE disagree

coincidence *noun* CHANCE, accident, luck, fluke, eventuality, stroke of luck, happy accident, fortuity

coincidental *adjective* ACCIDENTAL, unintentional, unintended, unplanned, fortuitous, fluky (*informal*), chance, casual

<< OPPOSITE deliberate

cold *adjective* 1 CHILLY, biting, freezing, bitter, raw, chill, harsh, bleak, arctic, icy, frosty, wintry, frigid, inclement, parky (*Brit informal*), cool
<< OPPOSITE hot
2 FREEZING, frozen, chilled, numb, chilly, shivery, benumbed, frozen to the marrow
3 DISTANT, reserved, indifferent, aloof, glacial, cold-blooded, apathetic, frigid, unresponsive, unfeeling, passionless, undemonstrative, standoffish
<< OPPOSITE emotional
4 UNFRIENDLY, indifferent, stony, lukewarm, glacial, unmoved, unsympathetic, apathetic, frigid, inhospitable, unresponsive
<< OPPOSITE friendly
▷ *noun* COLDNESS, chill, frigidity, chilliness, frostiness, iciness

cold-blooded *adjective* CALLOUS, cruel, savage, brutal, ruthless, steely, heartless, inhuman, merciless, unmoved, dispassionate, barbarous, pitiless, unfeeling, unemotional, stony-hearted
<< OPPOSITE caring

collaborate *verb* 1 WORK TOGETHER, team up, join forces, cooperate, play ball (*informal*), participate
2 CONSPIRE, cooperate, collude, fraternize

collaboration *noun* 1 TEAMWORK, partnership, cooperation, association, alliance, concert
2 CONSPIRING, cooperation, collusion, fraternization

collaborator *noun* 1 CO-WORKER, partner, colleague, associate, team mate, confederate
2 TRAITOR, turncoat, quisling, collaborationist, fraternizer

collapse *verb* 1 FALL DOWN, fall, give way, subside, cave in, crumple, fall apart at the seams
2 FAIL, fold, founder, break down, fall through, come to nothing, go belly-up (*informal*)
3 FAINT, break down, pass out, black out, swoon (*literary*), crack up (*informal*), keel over (*informal*), flake out (*informal*)
▷ *noun* 1 FALLING DOWN, ruin, falling apart, cave-in, disintegration, subsidence
2 FAILURE, slump, breakdown, flop, downfall
3 FAINT, breakdown, blackout, prostration

collar *verb* (*informal*) SEIZE, catch, arrest, appropriate, grab, capture, nail (*informal*), nab (*informal*), apprehend, lay hands on

collate *verb* COLLECT, gather, organize, assemble, compose, adduce, systematize

collateral *noun* SECURITY, guarantee, deposit, assurance, surety, pledge

colleague *noun* FELLOW WORKER, partner, ally, associate, assistant, team-mate, companion, comrade, helper, collaborator, confederate, auxiliary, workmate, confrère

collect *verb* 1 GATHER, save, assemble, heap, accumulate, aggregate, amass, stockpile, hoard
<< OPPOSITE scatter
2 RAISE, secure, gather, obtain, acquire, muster, solicit
3 ASSEMBLE, meet, rally, cluster, come together, convene, converge, congregate, flock together
<< OPPOSITE disperse

collected *adjective* CALM, together (*slang*), cool, confident, composed, poised, serene, sedate, self-controlled, unfazed (*informal*), unperturbed, unruffled, self-possessed, keeping your cool, unperturbable, as cool as a cucumber
<< OPPOSITE nervous

collection *noun* 1 ACCUMULATION, set, store, mass, pile, heap, stockpile, hoard, congeries
2 COMPILATION, accumulation, anthology
3 GROUP, company, crowd, gathering, assembly, cluster, congregation, assortment, assemblage
4 GATHERING, acquisition, accumulation
5 CONTRIBUTION, donation, alms
6 OFFERING, offertory

collective *adjective* 1 JOINT, united, shared, common, combined, corporate, concerted, unified, cooperative
<< OPPOSITE individual
2 COMBINED, aggregate, composite, cumulative
<< OPPOSITE separate

collide *verb* 1 CRASH, clash, meet head-on, come into collision
2 CONFLICT, clash, be incompatible, be at variance

collision *noun* 1 CRASH, impact, accident, smash, bump, pile-up (*informal*), prang (*informal*)
2 CONFLICT, opposition, clash, clashing, encounter, disagreement, incompatibility

colloquial *adjective* INFORMAL, familiar, everyday, vernacular, conversational, demotic, idiomatic

collude *verb* CONSPIRE, scheme, plot, intrigue, collaborate, contrive, abet, connive, be in cahoots (*informal*), machinate

collusion *noun* CONSPIRACY, intrigue, deceit, complicity, connivance, secret understanding

colonist *noun* SETTLER, immigrant, pioneer, colonial, homesteader (*US*), colonizer, frontiersman

colonize *verb* SETTLE, populate, put down roots in, people, pioneer, open up

colonnade *noun* CLOISTERS, arcade, portico, covered walk

colony *noun* SETTLEMENT, territory, province, possession, dependency, outpost, dominion, satellite state, community

colossal *adjective* HUGE, massive, vast, enormous, immense, titanic, gigantic, monumental, monstrous, mammoth, mountainous, stellar (*informal*), prodigious, gargantuan, herculean, elephantine, humongous *or* humungous (*US slang*)
<< OPPOSITE tiny

colour *or US* **color** *noun* **1** HUE, tone, shade, tint, tinge, tincture, colourway
2 PAINT, stain, dye, tint, pigment, tincture, coloration, colourwash, colorant
3 LIVELINESS, life, interest, excitement, animation, zest
▷ *plural noun* **1** FLAG, standard, banner, emblem, ensign
2 NATURE, quality, character, aspect, personality, stamp, traits, temperament
▷ *verb* **1** BLUSH, flush, crimson, redden, go crimson, burn, go as red as a beetroot
2 INFLUENCE, affect, prejudice, distort, pervert, taint, slant
3 EXAGGERATE, disguise, embroider, misrepresent, falsify, gloss over

colourful *adjective* **1** BRIGHT, rich, brilliant, intense, vivid, vibrant, psychedelic, motley, variegated, jazzy (*informal*), multicoloured, Day-glo (*trademark*), kaleidoscopic
<< OPPOSITE drab
2 INTERESTING, rich, unusual, stimulating, graphic, lively, distinctive, vivid, picturesque, characterful
<< OPPOSITE boring

colourless *adjective* **1** UNCOLOURED, faded, neutral, bleached, washed out, achromatic
2 ASHEN, washed out, wan, sickly, anaemic
<< OPPOSITE radiant
3 UNINTERESTING, dull, tame, dreary, drab, lacklustre, vacuous, insipid, vapid, characterless, unmemorable
<< OPPOSITE interesting

column *noun* **1** PILLAR, support, post, shaft, upright, obelisk
2 LINE, train, row, file, rank, string, queue, procession, cavalcade

columnist *noun* JOURNALIST, correspondent, editor, reporter, critic, reviewer, gossip columnist, journo (*slang*)

coma *noun* UNCONSCIOUSNESS, trance, oblivion, lethargy, stupor, torpor, insensibility

comatose *adjective* **1** UNCONSCIOUS, in a coma, out cold, insensible
2 INERT, stupefied, out cold, somnolent, torpid, insensible, dead to the world (*informal*), drugged

comb *verb* **1** UNTANGLE, arrange, groom, dress
2 SEARCH, hunt through, sweep, rake, sift, scour, rummage, ransack, forage, fossick (*Austral & NZ*), go through with a fine-tooth comb

combat *noun* FIGHT, war, action, battle, conflict, engagement, warfare, skirmish
<< OPPOSITE peace
▷ *verb* FIGHT, battle against, oppose, contest, engage, cope with, resist, defy, withstand, struggle against, contend with, do battle with, strive against
<< OPPOSITE support

combatant *noun* FIGHTER, soldier, warrior, contender, gladiator, belligerent, antagonist, fighting man, serviceman *or* servicewoman
▷ *adjective* FIGHTING, warring, battling, conflicting, opposing, contending, belligerent, combative

combative *adjective* AGGRESSIVE, militant, contentious, belligerent, antagonistic, pugnacious, warlike, bellicose, truculent, quarrelsome
<< OPPOSITE nonaggressive

combination *noun* **1** MIXTURE, mix, compound, blend, composite, amalgam, amalgamation, meld, coalescence
2 ASSOCIATION, union, alliance, coalition, merger, federation, consortium, unification, syndicate, confederation, cartel, confederacy, cabal

combine *verb* **1** AMALGAMATE, marry, mix, bond, bind, compound, blend, incorporate, integrate, merge, put together, fuse, synthesize
<< OPPOSITE separate
2 JOIN TOGETHER, link, connect, integrate, merge, fuse, amalgamate, meld
3 UNITE, associate, team up, unify, get together, collaborate, join forces, cooperate, join together, pool resources
<< OPPOSITE split up

combustible *adjective* FLAMMABLE, explosive, incendiary, inflammable

come *verb* **1** APPROACH, near, advance, move towards, draw near
2 ARRIVE, move, appear, enter, turn up (*informal*), show up (*informal*), materialize
3 REACH, extend
4 HAPPEN, fall, occur, take place, come about, come to pass
5 BE AVAILABLE, be made, be offered, be produced, be on offer
▷▷ **come about** HAPPEN, result, occur, take place, arise, transpire (*informal*), befall, come to pass
▷▷ **come across as something** *or* **someone** SEEM, look, seem to be, appear to be, give the impression of being
▷▷ **come across someone** MEET, encounter, run into, bump into (*informal*)
▷▷ **come across something** FIND, discover, notice, unearth, stumble upon, hit upon, chance upon, happen upon, light upon

▷▷ **come at someone** ATTACK, charge, rush, go for, assault, fly at, assail, fall upon, rush at

▷▷ **come back** RETURN, reappear, re-enter

▷▷ **come between someone** SEPARATE, part, divide, alienate, estrange, set at odds

▷▷ **come by something** GET, win, land, score (*slang*), secure, obtain, acquire, get hold of, procure, take possession of

▷▷ **come down** 1 DECREASE, fall, drop, reduce, go down, diminish, lessen, become lower

2 FALL, descend

▷▷ **come down on someone** REPRIMAND, blast, carpet (*informal*), put down, criticize, jump on (*informal*), rebuke, dress (someone) down (*informal*), tear into (*informal*), diss (*slang, chiefly US*), read (someone) the riot act, lambast(e), bawl (someone) out (*informal*), rap (someone) over the knuckles, chew (someone) out (*US & Canad informal*), tear (someone) off a strip (*Brit informal*), give (someone) a rocket (*Brit & NZ informal*)

▷▷ **come down on something** (with one or other side of an argument as object) DECIDE ON, choose, favour

▷▷ **come down to something** AMOUNT TO, boil down to

▷▷ **come down with something** (with illness as object) CATCH, get, take, contract, fall victim to, fall ill, be stricken with, take sick, sicken with

▷▷ **come forward** VOLUNTEER, step forward, present yourself, offer your services

▷▷ **come from something** 1 BE FROM, originate, hail from, be a native of

2 BE OBTAINED, be from, issue, emerge, flow, arise, originate, emanate

▷▷ **come in** 1 ARRIVE, enter, appear, show up (*informal*), cross the threshold

2 FINISH

▷▷ **come in for something** (with criticism or blame as object) RECEIVE, get, suffer, endure, be subjected to, bear the brunt of, be the object of

▷▷ **come into something** (with money or property as object) INHERIT, be left, acquire, succeed to, be bequeathed, fall heir to

▷▷ **come off** (*informal*) SUCCEED, work out, be successful, pan out (*informal*), turn out well

▷▷ **come on** 1 PROGRESS, develop, improve, advance, proceed, make headway

2 BEGIN, appear, take place

▷▷ **come out** 1 BE PUBLISHED, appear, be released, be issued, be launched

2 BE REVEALED, emerge, be reported, be announced, become apparent, come to light, be divulged

3 TURN OUT, result, end up, work out, pan out (*informal*)

▷▷ **come out with something** SAY, speak, utter, let out

▷▷ **come round** *or* **around** 1 CALL, visit, drop in, stop by, pop in

2 CHANGE YOUR OPINION, yield, concede, mellow, relent, accede, acquiesce

3 REGAIN CONSCIOUSNESS, come to, recover, rally, revive

▷▷ **come through** SUCCEED, triumph, prevail, make the grade (*informal*)

▷▷ **come through something** (with a negative or bad experience as object) SURVIVE, overcome, endure, withstand, weather, pull through

▷▷ **come to** REVIVE, recover, rally, come round, regain consciousness

▷▷ **come to something** AMOUNT TO, total, add up to

▷▷ **come up** HAPPEN, occur, arise, turn up, spring up, crop up

▷▷ **come up to something** MEASURE UP TO, meet, match, approach, rival, equal, compare with, resemble, admit of comparison with, stand *or* bear comparison with

▷▷ **come up with something** PRODUCE, offer, provide, present, suggest, advance, propose, submit, furnish

comeback *noun* 1 (*informal*) RETURN, revival, rebound, resurgence, rally, recovery, triumph

2 RESPONSE, reply, retort, retaliation, riposte, rejoinder

comedian *noun* COMIC, laugh (*informal*), wit, clown, funny man, humorist, wag, joker, jester, dag (*NZ informal*), card (*informal*)

comedy *noun* 1 LIGHT ENTERTAINMENT, sitcom (*informal*), soap opera (*slang*), soapie *or* soapy (*Austral*)

<< OPPOSITE tragedy

2 HUMOUR, fun, joking, farce, jesting, slapstick, wisecracking, hilarity, witticisms, facetiousness, chaffing

<< OPPOSITE seriousness

comfort *noun* 1 EASE, luxury, wellbeing, opulence

2 CONSOLATION, cheer, encouragement, succour, help, support, aid, relief, ease, compensation, alleviation

<< OPPOSITE annoyance

▷ *verb* CONSOLE, encourage, ease, cheer, strengthen, relieve, reassure, soothe, hearten, solace, assuage, gladden, commiserate with

<< OPPOSITE distress

comfortable *adjective* 1 LOOSE-FITTING, loose, adequate, ample, snug, roomy, commodious

<< OPPOSITE tight-fitting

2 PLEASANT, homely, easy, relaxing, delightful, enjoyable, cosy, agreeable, restful

<< OPPOSITE unpleasant

3 AT EASE, happy, at home, contented, relaxed, serene

<< OPPOSITE uncomfortable

4 (*informal*) WELL-OFF, prosperous, affluent, well-to-do, comfortably-off, in clover (*informal*)

comforting *adjective* CONSOLING, encouraging, cheering, reassuring, soothing, heart-warming, inspiriting

<< OPPOSITE upsetting

comic *adjective* FUNNY, amusing, witty, humorous, farcical, comical, light, joking, droll, facetious, jocular, waggish

<< OPPOSITE sad

▷ *noun* COMEDIAN, funny man, humorist, wit, clown, wag, jester, dag (*NZ informal*), buffoon

comical *adjective* FUNNY, entertaining, comic, silly, amusing, ridiculous, diverting, absurd, hilarious, ludicrous, humorous, priceless, laughable, farcical, whimsical, zany, droll, risible, side-splitting

coming *adjective* 1 APPROACHING, next, future, near, due, forthcoming, imminent, in store, impending, at hand, upcoming, on the cards, in the wind, nigh, just round the corner

2 UP-AND-COMING, future, promising, aspiring

▷ *noun* ARRIVAL, approach, advent, accession

command *verb* 1 ORDER, tell, charge, demand, require, direct, bid, compel, enjoin

<< OPPOSITE beg

2 HAVE AUTHORITY OVER, lead, head, control, rule, manage, handle, dominate, govern, administer, supervise, be in charge of, reign over

<< OPPOSITE be subordinate to

▷ *noun* 1 ORDER, demand, direction, instruction, requirement, decree, bidding, mandate, canon, directive, injunction, fiat, ultimatum, commandment, edict, behest, precept

2 DOMINATION, control, rule, grasp, sway, mastery, dominion, upper hand, power, government

3 MANAGEMENT, power, control, charge, authority, direction, supervision

commandeer *verb* SEIZE, appropriate, hijack, confiscate, requisition, sequester, expropriate, sequestrate

commander *noun* LEADER, director, chief, officer, boss, head, captain, bass (*S African*), ruler, commander-in-chief, commanding officer, C in C, C.O., sherang (*Austral* & *NZ*)

commanding *adjective* 1 DOMINANT, controlling, dominating, superior, decisive, advantageous

2 AUTHORITATIVE, imposing, impressive, compelling, assertive, forceful, autocratic, peremptory

<< OPPOSITE unassertive

commemorate *verb* CELEBRATE, remember, honour, recognize, salute, pay tribute to, immortalize, memorialize

<< OPPOSITE ignore

commemoration *noun* 1 CEREMONY, tribute, memorial service, testimonial

2 REMEMBRANCE, honour, tribute

commemorative *adjective* MEMORIAL, celebratory

commence *verb* 1 EMBARK ON, start, open, begin, initiate, originate, instigate, inaugurate, enter upon

<< OPPOSITE stop

2 START, open, begin, go ahead

<< OPPOSITE end

commencement *noun* BEGINNING, start, opening, launch, birth, origin, dawn, outset, onset, initiation, inauguration, inception, embarkation

commend *verb* 1 PRAISE, acclaim, applaud, compliment, extol, approve, big up (*slang, chiefly Caribbean*), eulogize, speak highly of

<< OPPOSITE criticize

2 RECOMMEND, suggest, approve, advocate, endorse, vouch for, put in a good word for

commendable *adjective* PRAISEWORTHY, deserving, worthy, admirable, exemplary, creditable, laudable, meritorious, estimable

commendation *noun* PRAISE, credit, approval, acclaim, encouragement, Brownie points, approbation, acclamation, good opinion, panegyric, encomium

commensurate *adjective* 1 EQUIVALENT, consistent, corresponding, comparable, compatible, in accord, proportionate, coextensive

2 APPROPRIATE, fitting, fit, due, sufficient, adequate

comment *verb* 1 REMARK, say, note, mention, point out, observe, utter, opine, interpose

2 *usually with* **on** REMARK ON, explain, talk about, discuss, speak about, say something about, allude to, elucidate, make a comment on

▷ *noun* 1 REMARK, statement, observation

2 NOTE, criticism, explanation, illustration, commentary, exposition, annotation, elucidation

commentary *noun* 1 NARRATION, report, review, explanation, description, voice-over

2 ANALYSIS, notes, review, critique, treatise

commentator *noun* 1 REPORTER, special correspondent, sportscaster, commenter

2 CRITIC, interpreter, annotator

commercial *adjective* 1 MERCANTILE, business, trade, trading, sales

2 PROFITABLE, popular, in demand, marketable, saleable

3 MATERIALISTIC, mercenary, profit-making, venal, monetary, exploited, pecuniary

commiserate *verb often with* **with** SYMPATHIZE, pity, feel for, console, condole

commission *verb* APPOINT, order, contract, select, engage, delegate, nominate, authorize, empower, depute
▷ *noun* 1 DUTY, authority, trust, charge, task, function, mission, employment, appointment, warrant, mandate, errand
2 FEE, cut, compensation, percentage, allowance, royalties, brokerage, rake-off (*slang*)
3 COMMITTEE, board, representatives, commissioners, delegation, deputation, body of commissioners
commit *verb* 1 DO, perform, carry out, execute, enact, perpetrate
2 GIVE, deliver, engage, deposit, hand over, commend, entrust, consign
<< OPPOSITE withhold
3 PUT IN CUSTODY, confine, imprison, consign
<< OPPOSITE release
▷▷ **commit yourself to something** PLEDGE TO, promise to, bind yourself to, make yourself liable for, obligate yourself to
commitment *noun* 1 DEDICATION, loyalty, devotion, adherence
<< OPPOSITE indecisiveness
2 RESPONSIBILITY, tie, duty, obligation, liability, engagement
3 PLEDGE, promise, guarantee, undertaking, vow, assurance, word
<< OPPOSITE disavowal
committee *noun* GROUP, commission, panel, delegation, subcommittee, deputation ▷ see **family**
commodity *noun usually plural* GOODS, produce, stock, products, merchandise, wares
common *adjective* 1 USUAL, standard, daily, regular, ordinary, familiar, plain, conventional, routine, frequent, everyday, customary, commonplace, vanilla (*slang*), habitual, run-of-the-mill, humdrum, stock, workaday, bog-standard (*Brit & Irish slang*), a dime a dozen
<< OPPOSITE rare
2 POPULAR, general, accepted, standard, routine, widespread, universal, prevailing, prevalent
3 SHARED, collective
4 ORDINARY, average, simple, typical, undistinguished, dinki-di (*Austral informal*)
<< OPPOSITE important
5 VULGAR, low, inferior, coarse, plebeian
<< OPPOSITE refined
6 COLLECTIVE, public, community, social, communal
<< OPPOSITE personal
commonplace *adjective* EVERYDAY, common, ordinary, widespread, pedestrian, customary, mundane, vanilla (*slang*), banal, run-of-the-mill, humdrum, dime-a-dozen (*informal*)
<< OPPOSITE rare
▷ *noun* CLICHÉ, platitude, banality, truism
common sense *noun* GOOD SENSE, sound judgment, level-headedness, practicality, prudence, nous (*Brit slang*), soundness, reasonableness, gumption (*Brit informal*), horse sense, native intelligence, mother wit, smarts (*slang, chiefly US*), wit
common-sense *adjective* SENSIBLE, sound, practical, reasonable, realistic, shrewd, down-to-earth, matter-of-fact, sane, astute, judicious, level-headed, hard-headed
<< OPPOSITE foolish
commotion *noun* DISTURBANCE, to-do, riot, disorder, excitement, fuss, turmoil, racket, upheaval, bustle, furore, uproar, ferment, agitation, ado, rumpus, tumult, hubbub, hurly-burly, brouhaha, hullabaloo, hue and cry
communal *adjective* 1 COMMUNITY, neighbourhood
2 PUBLIC, shared, general, joint, collective, communistic
<< OPPOSITE private
commune *noun* COMMUNITY, collective, cooperative, kibbutz
commune with *verb* 1 CONTEMPLATE, ponder, reflect on, muse on, meditate on
2 TALK TO, communicate with, discuss with, confer with, converse with, discourse with, parley with
communicable *adjective* INFECTIOUS, catching, contagious, transferable, transmittable
communicate *verb* 1 CONTACT, talk, speak, phone, correspond, make contact, be in touch, ring up (*informal, chiefly Brit*), be in contact, get in contact
2 MAKE KNOWN, report, announce, reveal, publish, declare, spread, disclose, pass on, proclaim, transmit, convey, impart, divulge, disseminate
<< OPPOSITE keep secret
3 PASS ON, transfer, spread, transmit
communication *noun* 1 CONTACT, conversation, correspondence, intercourse, link, relations, connection
2 PASSING ON, spread, circulation, transmission, disclosure, imparting, dissemination, conveyance
3 MESSAGE, news, report, word, information, statement, intelligence, announcement, disclosure, dispatch
▷ *plural noun* CONNECTIONS, travel, links, transport, routes
communicative *adjective* TALKATIVE, open, frank, forthcoming, outgoing, informative, candid, expansive, chatty, voluble, loquacious, unreserved
<< OPPOSITE reserved

communion *noun* AFFINITY, accord, agreement, unity, sympathy, harmony, intercourse, fellowship, communing, closeness, rapport, converse, togetherness, concord

Communion *noun* (*Christianity*) EUCHARIST, Mass, Sacrament, Lord's Supper

communiqué *noun* ANNOUNCEMENT, report, bulletin, dispatch, news flash, official communication

communism *noun usually cap.* SOCIALISM, Marxism, Stalinism, collectivism, Bolshevism, Marxism-Leninism, state socialism, Maoism, Trotskyism, Eurocommunism, Titoism

communist *noun often cap.* SOCIALIST, Red (*informal*), Marxist, Bolshevik, collectivist

community *noun* 1 SOCIETY, people, public, association, population, residents, commonwealth, general public, populace, body politic, state, company
2 DISTRICT, area, quarter, region, sector, parish, neighbourhood, vicinity, locality, locale, neck of the woods (*informal*)

commute *verb* 1 TRAVEL
2 (*Law*) REDUCE, cut, modify, shorten, alleviate, curtail, remit, mitigate

commuter *noun* DAILY TRAVELLER, passenger, suburbanite

compact[1] *adjective* 1 CLOSELY PACKED, firm, solid, thick, dense, compressed, condensed, impenetrable, impermeable, pressed together
<< OPPOSITE loose
2 CONCISE, brief, to the point, succinct, terse, laconic, pithy, epigrammatic, pointed
<< OPPOSITE lengthy
▷ *verb* PACK CLOSELY, stuff, cram, compress, condense, tamp
<< OPPOSITE loosen

compact[2] *noun* AGREEMENT, deal, understanding, contract, bond, arrangement, alliance, treaty, bargain, pact, covenant, entente, concordat

companion *noun* 1 FRIEND, partner, ally, colleague, associate, mate (*informal*), gossip (*archaic*), buddy (*informal*), comrade, accomplice, crony, confederate, consort, main man (*slang, chiefly* US), homeboy (*slang, chiefly* US), cobber (*Austral & NZ old-fashioned informal*)
2 ASSISTANT, aide, escort, attendant
3 COMPLEMENT, match, fellow, mate, twin, counterpart

companionship *noun* FELLOWSHIP, company, friendship, fraternity, rapport, camaraderie, togetherness, comradeship, amity, esprit de corps, conviviality

company *noun* 1 BUSINESS, firm, association, corporation, partnership, establishment, syndicate, house, concern
2 GROUP, troupe, set, community, league, band, crowd, camp, collection, gathering, circle, crew, assembly, convention, ensemble, throng, coterie, bevy, assemblage, party, body
3 TROOP, unit, squad, team
4 COMPANIONSHIP, society, presence, fellowship
5 GUESTS, party, visitors, callers

comparable *adjective* 1 EQUAL, equivalent, on a par, tantamount, a match, proportionate, commensurate, as good
<< OPPOSITE unequal
2 SIMILAR, related, alike, corresponding, akin, analogous, of a piece, cognate, cut from the same cloth

comparative *adjective* RELATIVE, qualified, by comparison, approximate

compare *verb* CONTRAST, balance, weigh, set against, collate, juxtapose
▷▷ **compare to something** LIKEN TO, parallel, identify with, equate to, correlate to, mention in the same breath as
▷▷ **compare with something** BE AS GOOD AS, match, approach, equal, compete with, come up to, vie, be on a par with, be the equal of, approximate to, hold a candle to, bear comparison, be in the same class as

comparison *noun* 1 CONTRAST, distinction, differentiation, juxtaposition, collation
2 SIMILARITY, analogy, resemblance, correlation, likeness, comparability

compartment *noun* 1 SECTION, carriage, berth
2 BAY, chamber, booth, locker, niche, cubicle, alcove, pigeonhole, cubbyhole, cell
3 CATEGORY, area, department, division, section, subdivision

compass *noun* RANGE, field, area, reach, scope, sphere, limit, stretch, bound, extent, zone, boundary, realm

compassion *noun* SYMPATHY, understanding, charity, pity, humanity, mercy, heart, quarter, sorrow, kindness, tenderness, condolence, clemency, commiseration, fellow feeling, soft-heartedness, tender-heartedness, aroha (*NZ*)
<< OPPOSITE indifference

compassionate *adjective* SYMPATHETIC, kindly, understanding, tender, pitying, humanitarian, charitable, humane, indulgent, benevolent, lenient, merciful, kind-hearted, tender-hearted
<< OPPOSITE uncaring

compatibility *noun* 1 AGREEMENT, consistency, accordance, affinity, conformity, concord, congruity, accord
2 LIKE-MINDEDNESS, harmony, empathy, rapport, single-mindedness, amity, sympathy, congeniality

compatible *adjective* 1 CONSISTENT, in keeping, consonant, congenial, congruent, reconcilable, congruous, accordant, agreeable
<< OPPOSITE inappropriate
2 LIKE-MINDED, harmonious, in harmony, in

accord, of one mind, of the same mind, en rapport (*French*)
<< OPPOSITE incompatible

compatriot *noun* FELLOW COUNTRYMAN, countryman, fellow citizen

compel *verb* FORCE, make, urge, enforce, railroad (*informal*), drive, oblige, constrain, hustle (*slang*), necessitate, coerce, bulldoze (*informal*), impel, dragoon

compelling *adjective* 1 CONVINCING, telling, powerful, forceful, conclusive, weighty, cogent, irrefutable
2 FASCINATING, gripping, irresistible, enchanting, enthralling, hypnotic, spellbinding, mesmeric
<< OPPOSITE boring

compendium *noun* COLLECTION, summary, abstract, digest, compilation, epitome, synopsis, précis

compensate *verb* 1 RECOMPENSE, repay, refund, reimburse, indemnify, make restitution, requite, remunerate, satisfy, make good
2 MAKE AMENDS FOR, make up for, atone for, pay for, do penance for, cancel out, make reparation for, make redress for
3 BALANCE, cancel (out), offset, make up for, redress, counteract, neutralize, counterbalance

compensation *noun* 1 REPARATION, damages, payment, recompense, indemnification, offset, remuneration, indemnity, restitution, reimbursement, requital
2 RECOMPENSE, amends, reparation, restitution, atonement

compete *verb* 1 CONTEND, fight, rival, vie, challenge, struggle, contest, strive, pit yourself against
2 TAKE PART, participate, be in the running, be a competitor, be a contestant, play

competence *noun* 1 ABILITY, skill, talent, capacity, expertise, proficiency, competency, capability
<< OPPOSITE incompetence
2 FITNESS, suitability, adequacy, appropriateness
<< OPPOSITE inadequacy

competent *adjective* 1 ABLE, skilled, capable, clever, endowed, proficient
<< OPPOSITE incompetent
2 FIT, qualified, equal, appropriate, suitable, sufficient, adequate
<< OPPOSITE unqualified

competition *noun* 1 RIVALRY, opposition, struggle, contest, contention, strife, one-upmanship (*informal*)
2 OPPOSITION, field, rivals, challengers
3 CONTEST, event, championship, tournament, head-to-head

competitive *adjective* 1 CUT-THROAT, aggressive, fierce, ruthless, relentless, antagonistic, dog-eat-dog
2 AMBITIOUS, pushing, opposing, aggressive, vying, contentious, combative

competitor *noun* 1 RIVAL, competition, opposition, adversary, antagonist
2 CONTESTANT, participant, contender, challenger, entrant, player, opponent

compilation *noun* COLLECTION, treasury, accumulation, anthology, assortment, assemblage

compile *verb* PUT TOGETHER, collect, gather, organize, accumulate, marshal, garner, amass, cull, anthologize

complacency *noun* SMUGNESS, satisfaction, gratification, contentment, self-congratulation, self-satisfaction

complacent *adjective* SMUG, self-satisfied, pleased with yourself, resting on your laurels, pleased, contented, satisfied, gratified, serene, unconcerned, self-righteous, self-assured, self-contented
<< OPPOSITE insecure

complain *verb* FIND FAULT, moan, grumble, whinge (*informal*), beef (*slang*), carp, fuss, bitch (*slang*), groan, grieve, lament, whine, growl, deplore, grouse, gripe (*informal*), bemoan, bleat, put the boot in (*slang*), bewail, kick up a fuss (*informal*), grouch (*informal*), bellyache (*slang*), kvetch (*US slang*)

complaint *noun* 1 PROTEST, accusation, objection, grievance, remonstrance, charge
2 GRUMBLE, criticism, beef (*slang*), moan, bitch (*slang*), lament, grievance, wail, dissatisfaction, annoyance, grouse, gripe (*informal*), grouch (*informal*), plaint, fault-finding
3 DISORDER, problem, trouble, disease, upset, illness, sickness, ailment, affliction, malady, indisposition

complement *verb* ENHANCE, complete, improve, boost, crown, add to, set off, heighten, augment, round off
▷ *noun* 1 ACCOMPANIMENT, companion, accessory, completion, finishing touch, rounding-off, adjunct, supplement
2 TOTAL, capacity, quota, aggregate, contingent, entirety

> This is sometimes confused with *compliment* but the two words have very different meanings. As the synonyms show, the verb form of *complement* means 'to enhance' and 'to complete' something. In contrast, common synonyms of *compliment* as a verb are *praise*, *commend*, and *flatter*

complementary *adjective* MATCHING, companion, corresponding, compatible, reciprocal, interrelating, interdependent, harmonizing

<< OPPOSITE incompatible

complete *adjective* 1 TOTAL, perfect, absolute, utter, outright, thorough, consummate, out-and-out, unmitigated, dyed-in-the-wool, thoroughgoing, deep-dyed (*usually derogatory*)

2 WHOLE, full, entire

<< OPPOSITE partial

3 ENTIRE, full, whole, intact, unbroken, faultless, undivided, unimpaired

<< OPPOSITE incomplete

4 UNABRIDGED, full, entire

5 FINISHED, done, ended, completed, achieved, concluded, fulfilled, accomplished

<< OPPOSITE unfinished

▷ *verb* 1 PERFECT, accomplish, finish off, round off, crown, cap

<< OPPOSITE spoil

2 FINISH, conclude, fulfil, accomplish, do, end, close, achieve, perform, settle, realize, execute, discharge, wrap up (*informal*), terminate, finalize

<< OPPOSITE start

completely *adverb* TOTALLY, entirely, wholly, utterly, quite, perfectly, fully, solidly, absolutely, altogether, thoroughly, in full, every inch, en masse, heart and soul, a hundred per cent, one hundred per cent, from beginning to end, down to the ground, root and branch, in toto (*Latin*), from A to Z, hook, line and sinker, lock, stock and barrel

completion *noun* FINISHING, end, close, conclusion, accomplishment, realization, fulfilment, culmination, attainment, fruition, consummation, finalization

complex *adjective* 1 COMPOUND, compounded, multiple, composite, manifold, heterogeneous, multifarious

2 COMPLICATED, difficult, involved, mixed, elaborate, tangled, mingled, intricate, tortuous, convoluted, knotty, labyrinthine, circuitous

<< OPPOSITE simple

▷ *noun* 1 STRUCTURE, system, scheme, network, organization, aggregate, composite, synthesis

2 (*informal*) OBSESSION, preoccupation, phobia, fixation, fixed idea, idée fixe (*French*)

> Although *complex* and *complicated* are close in meaning, care should be taken when using one as a synonym of the other. *Complex* should be used to say that something consists of several parts rather than that it is difficult to understand, analyse, or deal with, which is what *complicated* inherently means. In the following real example a clear distinction is made between the two words: *the British benefits system is phenomenally complex and is administered by a complicated range of agencies*

complexion *noun* 1 SKIN, colour, colouring, hue, skin tone, pigmentation

2 NATURE, character, make-up, cast, stamp, disposition

complexity *noun* COMPLICATION, involvement, intricacy, entanglement, convolution

compliance *noun* 1 CONFORMITY, agreement, obedience, assent, observance, concurrence

<< OPPOSITE disobedience

2 SUBMISSIVENESS, yielding, submission, obedience, deference, passivity, acquiescence, complaisance, consent

<< OPPOSITE defiance

compliant *adjective* OBEDIENT, willing, accepting, yielding, obliging, accommodating, passive, cooperative, agreeable, submissive, conformist, deferential, acquiescent, complaisant, conformable

complicate *verb* MAKE DIFFICULT, confuse, muddle, embroil, entangle, make intricate, involve

<< OPPOSITE simplify

complicated *adjective* 1 INVOLVED, difficult, puzzling, troublesome, problematic, perplexing

<< OPPOSITE simple

2 COMPLEX, involved, elaborate, intricate, Byzantine

<< OPPOSITE understandable

3 (*of attitudes, etc*) CONVOLUTED, labyrinthine

▷ see **complex**

complication *noun* 1 PROBLEM, difficulty, obstacle, drawback, snag, uphill (*S African*), stumbling block, aggravation

2 COMPLEXITY, combination, mixture, web, confusion, intricacy, entanglement

complicity *noun* COLLUSION, conspiracy, collaboration, connivance, abetment

compliment *noun* PRAISE, honour, tribute, courtesy, admiration, bouquet, flattery, eulogy

<< OPPOSITE criticism

▷ *plural noun* 1 GREETINGS, regards, respects, good wishes, salutation

<< OPPOSITE insult

2 CONGRATULATIONS, praise, commendation

▷ *verb* PRAISE, flatter, salute, congratulate, pay tribute to, commend, laud, extol, crack up (*informal*), pat on the back, sing the praises of, wax lyrical about, big up (*slang, chiefly Caribbean*), speak highly of

<< OPPOSITE criticize

> *Compliment* is sometimes confused with *complement*

complimentary *adjective* 1 FLATTERING, approving, appreciative, congratulatory, eulogistic, commendatory
<< OPPOSITE critical
2 FREE, donated, courtesy, honorary, free of charge, on the house, gratuitous, gratis
comply *verb* OBEY, follow, respect, agree to, satisfy, observe, fulfil, submit to, conform to, adhere to, abide by, consent to, yield to, defer to, accede to, act in accordance with, perform, acquiesce with
<< OPPOSITE defy
component *noun* PART, piece, unit, item, element, ingredient, constituent
▷ *adjective* CONSTITUENT, composing, inherent, intrinsic
compose *verb* 1 PUT TOGETHER, make up, constitute, comprise, make, build, form, fashion, construct, compound
<< OPPOSITE destroy
2 CREATE, write, produce, imagine, frame, invent, devise, contrive
3 ARRANGE, make up, construct, put together, order, organize
▷▷ **compose yourself** CALM YOURSELF, be still, control yourself, settle yourself, collect yourself, pull yourself together
composed *adjective* CALM, together (*slang*), cool, collected, relaxed, confident, poised, at ease, laid-back (*informal*), serene, tranquil, sedate, self-controlled, level-headed, unfazed (*informal*), unflappable, unruffled, self-possessed, imperturbable, unworried, keeping your cool, as cool as a cucumber
<< OPPOSITE agitated
composite *adjective* COMPOUND, mixed, combined, complex, blended, conglomerate, synthesized
▷ *noun* COMPOUND, blend, conglomerate, fusion, synthesis, amalgam, meld
composition *noun* 1 DESIGN, form, structure, make-up, organization, arrangement, constitution, formation, layout, configuration
2 CREATION, work, piece, production, opus, masterpiece, chef-d'oeuvre (*French*)
3 ESSAY, writing, study, exercise, treatise, literary work
4 ARRANGEMENT, balance, proportion, harmony, symmetry, concord, consonance, placing
5 PRODUCTION, creation, making, fashioning, formation, putting together, invention, compilation, formulation
compost *noun* FERTILIZER, mulch, humus
composure *noun* CALMNESS, calm, poise, self-possession, cool (*slang*), ease, dignity, serenity, tranquillity, coolness, aplomb, equanimity, self-assurance, sang-froid, placidity, sedateness
<< OPPOSITE agitation

compound *noun* COMBINATION, mixture, blend, composite, conglomerate, fusion, synthesis, alloy, medley, amalgam, meld, composition
<< OPPOSITE element
▷ *adjective* COMPLEX, multiple, composite, conglomerate, intricate, not simple
<< OPPOSITE simple
▷ *verb* 1 INTENSIFY, add to, complicate, worsen, heighten, exacerbate, aggravate, magnify, augment, add insult to injury
<< OPPOSITE lessen
2 COMBINE, unite, mix, blend, fuse, mingle, synthesize, concoct, amalgamate, coalesce, intermingle, meld
<< OPPOSITE divide
comprehend *verb* UNDERSTAND, see, take in, perceive, grasp, conceive, make out, discern, assimilate, see the light, fathom, apprehend, get the hang of (*informal*), get the picture, know
<< OPPOSITE misunderstand
comprehensible *adjective* UNDERSTANDABLE, clear, plain, explicit, coherent, user-friendly, intelligible
comprehension *noun* UNDERSTANDING, grasp, conception, realization, sense, knowledge, intelligence, judgment, perception, discernment
<< OPPOSITE incomprehension
comprehensive *adjective* BROAD, full, complete, wide, catholic, sweeping, extensive, blanket, umbrella, thorough, inclusive, exhaustive, all-inclusive, all-embracing, overarching, encyclopedic
<< OPPOSITE limited
compress *verb* 1 SQUEEZE, crush, squash, constrict, press, crowd, wedge, cram
2 CONDENSE, contract, concentrate, compact, shorten, summarize, abbreviate
compressed *adjective* 1 SQUEEZED, concentrated, compact, compacted, consolidated, squashed, flattened, constricted
2 REDUCED, compacted, shortened, abridged
compression *noun* SQUEEZING, pressing, crushing, consolidation, condensation, constriction
comprise *verb* 1 BE COMPOSED OF, include, contain, consist of, take in, embrace, encompass, comprehend
2 MAKE UP, form, constitute, compose

> The use of *of* after *comprise* should be avoided: *the library comprises* (not *comprises of*) *6,500,000 books and manuscripts*. *Consist*, however, should be followed by *of* when used in this way: *Her crew consisted of children from Devon and Cornwall*

compromise *noun* GIVE-AND-TAKE, agreement, settlement, accommodation, concession, adjustment, trade-off, middle ground, half

measures
<< OPPOSITE disagreement
▷ *verb* **1** MEET HALFWAY, concede, make concessions, give and take, strike a balance, strike a happy medium, go fifty-fifty (*informal*)
<< OPPOSITE disagree
2 UNDERMINE, expose, embarrass, weaken, prejudice, endanger, discredit, implicate, jeopardize, dishonour, imperil
<< OPPOSITE support

compulsion *noun* **1** URGE, need, obsession, necessity, preoccupation, drive
2 FORCE, pressure, obligation, constraint, urgency, coercion, duress, demand

compulsive *adjective* **1** OBSESSIVE, confirmed, chronic, persistent, addictive, uncontrollable, incurable, inveterate, incorrigible
2 FASCINATING, gripping, absorbing, compelling, captivating, enthralling, hypnotic, engrossing, spellbinding
3 IRRESISTIBLE, overwhelming, compelling, urgent, neurotic, besetting, uncontrollable, driving

compulsory *adjective* OBLIGATORY, forced, required, binding, mandatory, imperative, requisite, de rigueur (*French*)
<< OPPOSITE voluntary

compute *verb* CALCULATE, rate, figure, total, measure, estimate, count, reckon, sum, figure out, add up, tally, enumerate

comrade *noun* COMPANION, friend, partner, ally, colleague, associate, fellow, mate (*informal*), pal (*informal*), buddy (*informal*), compatriot, crony, confederate, co-worker, main man (*slang, chiefly US*), homeboy (*slang, chiefly US*), cobber (*Austral & NZ old-fashioned informal*), compeer

comradeship *noun* FELLOWSHIP, solidarity, fraternity, brotherhood, companionship, camaraderie, kotahitanga (*NZ*)

con (*informal*) *verb* SWINDLE, trick, cheat, rip off (*slang*), kid (*informal*), skin (*slang*), stiff (*slang*), mislead, deceive, hoax, defraud, dupe, gull (*archaic*), rook (*slang*), humbug, bamboozle (*informal*), hoodwink, double-cross (*informal*), diddle (*informal*), take for a ride (*informal*), inveigle, do the dirty on (*Brit informal*), bilk, sell a pup, pull a fast one on (*informal*)
▷ *noun* SWINDLE, trick, fraud, deception, scam (*slang*), sting (*informal*), bluff, fastie (*Austral slang*)

concave *adjective* HOLLOW, cupped, depressed, scooped, hollowed, excavated, sunken, indented
<< OPPOSITE convex

conceal *verb* **1** HIDE, bury, stash (*informal*), secrete, cover, screen, disguise, obscure, camouflage
<< OPPOSITE reveal
2 KEEP SECRET, hide, disguise, mask, suppress, veil, dissemble, draw a veil over, keep dark, keep under your hat
<< OPPOSITE show

concealed *adjective* HIDDEN, covered, secret, screened, masked, obscured, covert, unseen, tucked away, secreted, under wraps, inconspicuous

concealment *noun* **1** COVER, hiding, camouflage, hiding place
2 COVER-UP, disguise, keeping secret
<< OPPOSITE disclosure

concede *verb* **1** ADMIT, allow, accept, acknowledge, own, grant, confess
<< OPPOSITE deny
2 GIVE UP, yield, hand over, surrender, relinquish, cede
<< OPPOSITE conquer

conceit *noun* **1** SELF-IMPORTANCE, vanity, arrogance, complacency, pride, swagger, narcissism, egotism, self-love, amour-propre, vainglory
2 (*Archaic*) IMAGE, idea, concept, metaphor, imagery, figure of speech, trope

conceited *adjective* SELF-IMPORTANT, vain, arrogant, stuck up (*informal*), cocky, narcissistic, puffed up, egotistical, overweening, immodest, vainglorious, swollen-headed, bigheaded (*informal*), full of yourself, too big for your boots *or* breeches
<< OPPOSITE modest

conceivable *adjective* IMAGINABLE, possible, credible, believable, thinkable
<< OPPOSITE inconceivable

conceive *verb* **1** IMAGINE, envisage, comprehend, visualize, think, believe, suppose, fancy, appreciate, grasp, apprehend
2 THINK UP, form, produce, create, develop, design, project, purpose, devise, formulate, contrive
3 BECOME PREGNANT, get pregnant, become impregnated

concentrate *verb* **1** FOCUS YOUR ATTENTION, focus, pay attention, be engrossed, apply yourself
<< OPPOSITE pay no attention
2 FOCUS, centre, converge, bring to bear
3 GATHER, collect, cluster, accumulate, congregate
<< OPPOSITE scatter

concentrated *adjective* **1** CONDENSED, rich, undiluted, reduced, evaporated, thickened, boiled down
2 INTENSE, hard, deep, intensive, all-out (*informal*)

concentration *noun* **1** ATTENTION, application, absorption, single-mindedness, intentness
<< OPPOSITE inattention
2 FOCUSING, centring, consolidation, convergence, bringing to bear, intensification, centralization

3 CONVERGENCE, collection, mass, cluster, accumulation, aggregation
<< OPPOSITE scattering

concept *noun* IDEA, view, image, theory, impression, notion, conception, hypothesis, abstraction, conceptualization

conception *noun* 1 UNDERSTANDING, idea, picture, impression, perception, clue, appreciation, comprehension, inkling
2 IDEA, plan, design, image, concept, notion
3 IMPREGNATION, insemination, fertilization, germination
4 ORIGIN, beginning, launching, birth, formation, invention, outset, initiation, inception

concern *noun* 1 ANXIETY, fear, worry, distress, unease, apprehension, misgiving, disquiet
2 WORRY, care, anxiety
3 AFFAIR, issue, matter, consideration
4 CARE, interest, regard, consideration, solicitude, attentiveness
5 BUSINESS, job, charge, matter, department, field, affair, responsibility, task, mission, pigeon (*informal*)
6 COMPANY, house, business, firm, organization, corporation, enterprise, establishment
7 IMPORTANCE, interest, bearing, relevance
▷ *verb* 1 WORRY, trouble, bother, disturb, distress, disquiet, perturb, make uneasy, make anxious
2 BE ABOUT, cover, deal with, go into, relate to, have to do with
3 BE RELEVANT TO, involve, affect, regard, apply to, bear on, have something to do with, pertain to, interest, touch

concerned *adjective* 1 INVOLVED, interested, active, mixed up, implicated, privy to
2 WORRIED, troubled, upset, bothered, disturbed, anxious, distressed, uneasy
<< OPPOSITE indifferent
3 CARING, attentive, solicitous

concerning *preposition* REGARDING, about, re, touching, respecting, relating to, on the subject of, as to, with reference to, in the matter of, apropos of, as regards

concert ▷▷ **in concert** TOGETHER, jointly, unanimously, in unison, in league, in collaboration, shoulder to shoulder, concertedly

concerted *adjective* COORDINATED, united, joint, combined, collaborative
<< OPPOSITE separate

concession *noun* 1 COMPROMISE, agreement, settlement, accommodation, adjustment, trade-off, give-and-take, half measures
2 PRIVILEGE, right, permit, licence, franchise, entitlement, indulgence, prerogative
3 REDUCTION, saving, grant, discount, allowance
4 SURRENDER, yielding, conceding, renunciation, relinquishment

conciliation *noun* PACIFICATION, reconciliation, disarming, appeasement, propitiation, mollification, soothing, placation

conciliatory *adjective* PACIFYING, pacific, disarming, appeasing, mollifying, peaceable, placatory, soothing

concise *adjective* BRIEF, short, to the point, compact, summary, compressed, condensed, terse, laconic, succinct, pithy, synoptic, epigrammatic, compendious
<< OPPOSITE rambling

conclave *noun* (SECRET *or* PRIVATE) MEETING, council, conference, congress, session, cabinet, assembly, parley, runanga (NZ)

conclude *verb* 1 DECIDE, judge, establish, suppose, determine, assume, gather, reckon (*informal*), work out, infer, deduce, surmise
2 COME TO AN END, end, close, finish, wind up, draw to a close
<< OPPOSITE begin
3 BRING TO AN END, end, close, finish, complete, wind up, terminate, round off
<< OPPOSITE begin
4 ACCOMPLISH, effect, settle, bring about, fix, carry out, resolve, clinch, pull off, bring off (*informal*)

conclusion *noun* 1 DECISION, agreement, opinion, settlement, resolution, conviction, verdict, judgment, deduction, inference
2 END, ending, close, finish, completion, finale, termination, bitter end, result
3 OUTCOME, result, upshot, consequence, sequel, culmination, end result, issue
▷▷ **in conclusion** FINALLY, lastly, in closing, to sum up

conclusive *adjective* DECISIVE, final, convincing, clinching, definite, definitive, irrefutable, unanswerable, unarguable, ultimate
<< OPPOSITE inconclusive

concoct *verb* MAKE UP, design, prepare, manufacture, plot, invent, devise, brew, hatch, formulate, contrive, fabricate, think up, cook up (*informal*), trump up, project

concoction *noun* MIXTURE, preparation, compound, brew, combination, creation, blend

concord *noun* TREATY, agreement, convention, compact, protocol, entente, concordat

concourse *noun* CROWD, collection, gathering, assembly, crush, multitude, throng, convergence, hui (NZ), assemblage, meeting, runanga (NZ)

concrete *noun* CEMENT (*not in technical usage*)
▷ *adjective* 1 SPECIFIC, precise, explicit, definite, clear-cut, unequivocal, unambiguous

<< OPPOSITE vague
2 REAL, material, actual, substantial, sensible, tangible, factual
<< OPPOSITE abstract

concubine *noun* (*Old-fashioned*) MISTRESS, courtesan, kept woman

concur *verb* AGREE, accord, approve, assent, accede, acquiesce

concurrent *adjective* SIMULTANEOUS, coexisting, concomitant, contemporaneous, coincident, synchronous, concerted

concussion *noun* 1 SHOCK, brain injury
2 IMPACT, crash, shaking, clash, jarring, collision, jolt, jolting

condemn *verb* 1 DENOUNCE, damn, criticize, disapprove, censure, reprove, upbraid, excoriate, reprehend, blame
<< OPPOSITE approve
2 SENTENCE, convict, damn, doom, pass sentence on
<< OPPOSITE acquit

condemnation *noun* DENUNCIATION, blame, censure, disapproval, reproach, stricture, reproof, denouncement

condensation *noun* 1 DISTILLATION, precipitation, liquefaction
2 ABRIDGMENT, summary, abstract, digest, contraction, synopsis, précis, encapsulation

condense *verb* 1 ABRIDGE, contract, concentrate, compact, shorten, summarize, compress, encapsulate, abbreviate, epitomize, précis
<< OPPOSITE expand
2 CONCENTRATE, reduce, precipitate (*Chemistry*), thicken, boil down, solidify, coagulate
<< OPPOSITE dilute

condensed *adjective* 1 ABRIDGED, concentrated, compressed, potted, shortened, summarized, slimmed-down, encapsulated
2 CONCENTRATED, reduced, thickened, boiled down, precipitated (*Chemistry*)

condescend *verb* 1 PATRONIZE, talk down to, treat like a child, treat as inferior, treat condescendingly
2 DEIGN, see fit, lower yourself, be courteous enough, bend, submit, stoop, unbend (*informal*), vouchsafe, come down off your high horse (*informal*), humble *or* demean yourself

condescending *adjective* PATRONIZING, lordly, superior, lofty, snooty (*informal*), snobbish, disdainful, supercilious, toffee-nosed (*slang, chiefly Brit*), on your high horse (*informal*)

condescension *noun* PATRONIZING ATTITUDE, superiority, disdain, haughtiness, loftiness, superciliousness, lordliness, airs

condition *noun* 1 STATE, order, shape, nick (*Brit informal*), trim
2 SITUATION, state, position, status, circumstances, plight, status quo (*Latin*), case, predicament
3 REQUIREMENT, terms, rider, provision, restriction, qualification, limitation, modification, requisite, prerequisite, proviso, stipulation, rule, demand
4 HEALTH, shape, fitness, trim, form, kilter, state of health, fettle, order
5 AILMENT, problem, complaint, weakness, malady, infirmity
▷ *plural noun* CIRCUMSTANCES, situation, environment, surroundings, way of life, milieu
▷ *verb* TRAIN, teach, educate, adapt, accustom, inure, habituate

conditional *adjective* DEPENDENT, limited, qualified, contingent, provisional, with reservations
<< OPPOSITE unconditional

conditioning *noun* TRAINING, education, teaching, accustoming, habituation

condom *noun* SHEATH, safe (*US & Canad slang*), rubber (*US slang*), blob (*Brit slang*), scumbag (*US slang*), Frenchie (*slang*), flunky (*slang*), French letter (*slang*), rubber johnny (*Brit slang*), French tickler (*slang*)

condone *verb* OVERLOOK, excuse, forgive, pardon, disregard, turn a blind eye to, wink at, look the other way, make allowance for, let pass
<< OPPOSITE condemn

conducive *adjective* FAVOURABLE, helpful, productive, contributory, calculated to produce, leading, tending

conduct *verb* 1 CARRY OUT, run, control, manage, direct, handle, organize, govern, regulate, administer, supervise, preside over
2 ACCOMPANY, lead, escort, guide, attend, steer, convey, usher, pilot
▷ *noun* 1 MANAGEMENT, running, control, handling, administration, direction, leadership, organization, guidance, supervision
2 BEHAVIOUR, ways, bearing, attitude, manners, carriage, demeanour, deportment, mien (*literary*), comportment
▷▷ **conduct yourself** BEHAVE YOURSELF, act, carry yourself, acquit yourself, deport yourself, comport yourself

conduit *noun* PASSAGE, channel, tube, pipe, canal, duct, main

confederacy *noun* UNION, league, alliance, coalition, federation, compact, confederation, covenant, bund

confederate *noun* ASSOCIATE, partner, ally, colleague, accessory, accomplice, abettor
▷ *adjective* ALLIED, federal, associated, combined, federated, in alliance

confer *verb* 1 DISCUSS, talk, consult, deliberate, discourse, converse, parley

2 GRANT, give, present, accord, award, hand out, bestow, vouchsafe

conference *noun* MEETING, congress, discussion, convention, forum, consultation, seminar, symposium, hui (NZ), convocation, colloquium

confess *verb* 1 ADMIT, acknowledge, disclose, confide, own up, come clean (*informal*), divulge, blurt out, come out of the closet, make a clean breast of, get (something) off your chest (*informal*), spill your guts (*slang*), 'fess up (US), sing (*slang, chiefly US*)

<< OPPOSITE cover up

2 DECLARE, own up, allow, prove, reveal, grant, confirm, concede, assert, manifest, affirm, profess, attest, evince, aver

confession *noun* ADMISSION, revelation, disclosure, acknowledgment, avowal, divulgence, exposure, unbosoming

confidant *or* **confidante** *noun* CLOSE FRIEND, familiar, intimate, crony, alter ego, bosom friend

confide *verb* TELL, admit, reveal, confess, whisper, disclose, impart, divulge, breathe

confidence *noun* 1 TRUST, belief, faith, dependence, reliance, credence

<< OPPOSITE distrust

2 SELF-ASSURANCE, courage, assurance, aplomb, boldness, self-reliance, self-possession, nerve

<< OPPOSITE shyness

3 SECRET

▷▷ **in confidence** IN SECRECY, privately, confidentially, between you and me (and the gatepost), (just) between ourselves

confident *adjective* 1 CERTAIN, sure, convinced, positive, secure, satisfied, counting on

<< OPPOSITE unsure

2 SELF-ASSURED, positive, assured, bold, self-confident, self-reliant, self-possessed, sure of yourself, can-do (*informal*)

<< OPPOSITE insecure

confidential *adjective* 1 SECRET, private, intimate, classified, privy, off the record, hush-hush (*informal*)

2 SECRETIVE, low, soft, hushed

confidentially *adverb* IN SECRET, privately, personally, behind closed doors, in confidence, in camera, between ourselves, sub rosa

configuration *noun* ARRANGEMENT, form, shape, cast, outline, contour, conformation, figure

confine *verb* 1 IMPRISON, enclose, shut up, intern, incarcerate, circumscribe, hem in, immure, keep, cage

2 RESTRICT, limit

▷ *plural noun* LIMITS, bounds, boundaries, compass, precincts, circumference, edge, pale

confined *adjective* RESTRICTED, small, limited, narrow, enclosed, cramped

confinement *noun* 1 IMPRISONMENT, custody, detention, incarceration, internment, porridge (*slang*)

2 CHILDBIRTH, labour, travail, childbed, accouchement (*French*), time

confirm *verb* 1 PROVE, support, establish, back up, verify, validate, bear out, substantiate, corroborate, authenticate

2 RATIFY, establish, approve, sanction, endorse, authorize, certify, validate, authenticate

3 STRENGTHEN, establish, settle, fix, secure, assure, reinforce, clinch, verify, fortify

confirmation *noun* 1 PROOF, evidence, testimony, verification, ratification, validation, corroboration, authentication, substantiation

<< OPPOSITE repudiation

2 AFFIRMATION, approval, acceptance, endorsement, ratification, assent, agreement

<< OPPOSITE disapproval

confirmed *adjective* LONG-ESTABLISHED, seasoned, rooted, chronic, hardened, habitual, ingrained, inveterate, inured, dyed-in-the-wool

confiscate *verb* SEIZE, appropriate, impound, commandeer, sequester, expropriate

<< OPPOSITE give back

confiscation *noun* SEIZURE, appropriation, impounding, forfeiture, expropriation, sequestration, takeover

conflagration *noun* FIRE, blaze, holocaust, inferno, wildfire

conflict *noun* 1 DISPUTE, difference, opposition, hostility, disagreement, friction, strife, fighting, antagonism, variance, discord, bad blood, dissension, divided loyalties

<< OPPOSITE agreement

2 STRUGGLE, battle, clash, strife

3 BATTLE, war, fight, clash, contest, set-to (*informal*), encounter, combat, engagement, warfare, collision, contention, strife, head-to-head, fracas, boilover (*Austral*)

<< OPPOSITE peace

▷ *verb* BE INCOMPATIBLE, clash, differ, disagree, contend, strive, collide, be at variance

<< OPPOSITE agree

conflicting *adjective* INCOMPATIBLE, opposed, opposing, clashing, contrary, contradictory, inconsistent, paradoxical, discordant

<< OPPOSITE agreeing

conform *verb* 1 FIT IN, follow, yield, adjust, adapt, comply, obey, fall in, toe the line, follow the crowd, run with the pack, follow convention

2 *with* **with** FULFIL, meet, match, suit, satisfy, agree with, obey, abide by, accord with, square with, correspond with, tally with, harmonize

with
conformation *noun* SHAPE, build, form, structure, arrangement, outline, framework, anatomy, configuration
conformist *noun* TRADITIONALIST, conservative, reactionary, Babbitt (*US*), stickler, yes man, stick-in-the-mud (*informal*), conventionalist
conformity *noun* 1 COMPLIANCE, agreement, accordance, observance, conformance, obedience
2 CONVENTIONALITY, compliance, allegiance, orthodoxy, observance, traditionalism, Babbittry (*US*)
confound *verb* 1 BEWILDER, baffle, amaze, confuse, astonish, startle, mix up, astound, perplex, surprise, mystify, flummox, boggle the mind, be all Greek to (*informal*), dumbfound, nonplus, flabbergast (*informal*)
2 DISPROVE, contradict, refute, negate, destroy, ruin, overwhelm, explode, overthrow, demolish, annihilate, give the lie to, make a nonsense of, prove false, blow out of the water (*slang*), controvert, confute
confront *verb* 1 TACKLE, deal with, cope with, brave, beard, face up to, meet head-on
2 TROUBLE, face, afflict, perplex, perturb, bedevil
3 CHALLENGE, face, oppose, tackle, encounter, defy, call out, stand up to, come face to face with, accost, face off (*slang*)
<< OPPOSITE evade
confrontation *noun* CONFLICT, fight, crisis, contest, set-to (*informal*), encounter, showdown (*informal*), head-to-head, face-off (*slang*), boilover (*Austral*)
confuse *verb* 1 MIX UP WITH, take for, mistake for, muddle with
2 BEWILDER, puzzle, baffle, perplex, mystify, fluster, faze, flummox, bemuse, be all Greek to (*informal*), nonplus
3 OBSCURE, cloud, complicate, muddle, darken, make more difficult, muddy the waters
confused *adjective* 1 BEWILDERED, puzzled, baffled, at sea, muddled, dazed, perplexed, at a loss, taken aback, disorientated, muzzy (*US informal*), nonplussed, flummoxed, at sixes and sevens, thrown off balance, discombobulated (*informal, chiefly US & Canad*), not with it (*informal*), not knowing if you are coming or going
<< OPPOSITE enlightened
2 DISORDERLY, disordered, chaotic, mixed up, jumbled, untidy, out of order, in disarray, topsy-turvy, disorganized, higgledy-piggledy (*informal*), at sixes and sevens, disarranged, disarrayed
<< OPPOSITE tidy
confusing *adjective* BEWILDERING, complicated, puzzling, misleading, unclear, baffling, muddling, contradictory, ambiguous, inconsistent, perplexing, clear as mud (*informal*)
<< OPPOSITE clear
confusion *noun* 1 BEWILDERMENT, doubt, uncertainty, puzzlement, perplexity, mystification, bafflement, perturbation
<< OPPOSITE enlightenment
2 DISORDER, chaos, turmoil, upheaval, muddle, bustle, shambles, disarray, commotion, disorganization, disarrangement
<< OPPOSITE order
3 PUZZLEMENT, bewilderment, perplexity, bafflement, mystification, perturbation
congeal *verb* THICKEN, set, freeze, harden, clot, stiffen, condense, solidify, curdle, jell, coagulate
congenial *adjective* PLEASANT, kindly, pleasing, friendly, agreeable, cordial, sociable, genial, affable, convivial, companionable, favourable, complaisant
congenital *adjective* 1 INBORN, innate, inherent, hereditary, natural, constitutional, inherited, inbred
2 (*informal*) COMPLETE, confirmed, chronic, utter, hardened, thorough, habitual, incurable, inveterate, incorrigible, deep-dyed (*usually derogatory*)
congested *adjective* 1 PACKED (OUT), crowded, overcrowded, teeming
2 CLOGGED, jammed, blocked-up, overfilled, stuffed, packed, crammed, overflowing, stuffed-up
<< OPPOSITE clear
congestion *noun* OVERCROWDING, crowding, mass, jam, clogging, bottleneck, snarl-up (*informal, chiefly Brit*)
conglomerate *noun* CORPORATION, multinational, corporate body, business, association, consortium, aggregate, agglomerate
congratulate *verb* COMPLIMENT, pat on the back, wish joy to
congratulations *plural noun* GOOD WISHES, greetings, compliments, best wishes, pat on the back, felicitations
▷ *interjection* GOOD WISHES, greetings, compliments, best wishes, felicitations
congregate *verb* COME TOGETHER, meet, mass, collect, gather, concentrate, rally, assemble, flock, muster, convene, converge, throng, rendezvous, foregather, convoke
<< OPPOSITE disperse
congregation *noun* PARISHIONERS, host, brethren, crowd, assembly, parish, flock, fellowship, multitude, throng, laity, flock
congress *noun* 1 MEETING, council, conference, diet, assembly, convention, conclave, legislative assembly, convocation, hui (*NZ*),

runanga (NZ)
2 LEGISLATURE, house, council, parliament, representatives, delegates, quango, legislative assembly, chamber of deputies, House of Representatives (NZ)

conical *or* **conic** *adjective* CONE-SHAPED, pointed, tapered, tapering, pyramidal, funnel-shaped

conjecture *noun* GUESS, theory, fancy, notion, speculation, assumption, hypothesis, inference, presumption, surmise, theorizing, guesswork, supposition, shot in the dark, guesstimate (*informal*)
▷ *verb* GUESS, speculate, surmise, theorize, suppose, imagine, assume, fancy, infer, hypothesize

conjunction *noun* COMBINATION, union, joining, association, coincidence, juxtaposition, concurrence

conjure *verb* 1 PRODUCE, generate, bring about, give rise to, make, create, effect, produce as if by magic
2 *often with* **up** SUMMON UP, raise, invoke, rouse, call upon
▷▷ **conjure something up** BRING TO MIND, recall, evoke, recreate, recollect, produce as if by magic

conjuring *noun* MAGIC, juggling, trickery, sleight of hand

connect *verb* 1 LINK, join, couple, attach, fasten, affix, unite
<< OPPOSITE separate
2 ASSOCIATE, unite, join, couple, league, link, mix, relate, pair, ally, identify, combine, affiliate, correlate, confederate, lump together, mention in the same breath, think of together

connected *adjective* LINKED, united, joined, coupled, related, allied, associated, combined, bracketed, affiliated, akin, banded together

connection *noun* 1 ASSOCIATION, relationship, link, relation, bond, correspondence, relevance, tie-in, correlation, interrelation
2 COMMUNICATION, alliance, commerce, attachment, intercourse, liaison, affinity, affiliation, union
3 LINK, coupling, junction, fastening, tie
4 CONTACT, friend, relation, ally, associate, relative, acquaintance, kin, kindred, kinsman, kith
5 CONTEXT, relation, reference, frame of reference

connivance *noun* COLLUSION, intrigue, conspiring, complicity, abetting, tacit consent, abetment

connive *verb* CONSPIRE, scheme, plot, intrigue, collude

connoisseur *noun* EXPERT, authority, judge, specialist, buff (*informal*), devotee, whiz (*informal*), arbiter, aficionado, savant, maven (US), appreciator, cognoscente, fundi (*S African*)

connotation *noun* IMPLICATION, colouring, association, suggestion, significance, nuance, undertone

connote *verb* IMPLY, suggest, indicate, intimate, signify, hint at, betoken, involve

conquer *verb* 1 SEIZE, obtain, acquire, occupy, overrun, annex, win
2 DEFEAT, overcome, overthrow, beat, stuff (*slang*), master, tank (*slang*), triumph, crush, humble, lick (*informal*), undo, subdue, rout, overpower, quell, get the better of, clobber (*slang*), vanquish, subjugate, prevail over, checkmate, run rings around (*informal*), wipe the floor with (*informal*), make mincemeat of (*informal*), put in their place, blow out of the water (*slang*), bring to their knees
<< OPPOSITE lose to
3 OVERCOME, beat, defeat, master, rise above, overpower, get the better of, surmount, best

conqueror *noun* WINNER, champion, master, victor, conquistador, lord

conquest *noun* 1 TAKEOVER, coup, acquisition, invasion, occupation, appropriation, annexation, subjugation, subjection
2 DEFEAT, victory, triumph, overthrow, pasting (*slang*), rout, mastery, vanquishment
3 SEDUCTION
4 CATCH, prize, supporter, acquisition, follower, admirer, worshipper, adherent, fan, feather in your cap

conscience *noun* 1 PRINCIPLES, scruples, moral sense, sense of right and wrong, still small voice
2 GUILT, shame, regret, remorse, contrition, self-reproach, self-condemnation
▷▷ **in all conscience** IN FAIRNESS, rightly, certainly, fairly, truly, honestly, in truth, assuredly

conscientious *adjective* THOROUGH, particular, careful, exact, faithful, meticulous, painstaking, diligent, punctilious
<< OPPOSITE careless

conscious *adjective* 1 *often with* **of** AWARE OF, wise to (*slang*), alert to, responsive to, cognizant of, sensible of, clued-up on (*informal*), percipient of
<< OPPOSITE unaware
2 DELIBERATE, knowing, reasoning, studied, responsible, calculated, rational, reflective, self-conscious, intentional, wilful, premeditated
<< OPPOSITE unintentional
3 AWAKE, wide-awake, sentient, alive
<< OPPOSITE asleep

consciousness *noun* AWARENESS, understanding, knowledge, recognition, enlightenment, sensibility, realization, apprehension

consecrate *verb* SANCTIFY, dedicate, ordain, exalt, venerate, set apart, hallow, devote

consecutive *adjective* SUCCESSIVE, running, following, succeeding, in turn, uninterrupted, chronological, sequential, in sequence, seriatim

consensus *noun* AGREEMENT, general agreement, unanimity, common consent, unity, harmony, assent, concord, concurrence, kotahitanga (NZ)

> The original meaning of the word *consensus* is *a collective opinion*. Because the concept of 'opinion' is contained within this word, a few people argue that the phrase *a consensus of opinion* is incorrect and should be avoided. However, this common use of the word is unlikely to jar with the majority of speakers

consent *noun* AGREEMENT, sanction, approval, go-ahead (*informal*), permission, compliance, green light, assent, acquiescence, concurrence, O.K. *or* okay (*informal*)
<< OPPOSITE refusal
▷ *verb* AGREE, approve, yield, permit, comply, concur, assent, accede, acquiesce, play ball (*informal*)
<< OPPOSITE refuse

consequence *noun* **1** RESULT, effect, outcome, repercussion, end, issue, event, sequel, end result, upshot
2 IMPORTANCE, interest, concern, moment, value, account, note, weight, import, significance, portent
3 STATUS, standing, bottom, rank, distinction, eminence, repute, notability
▷▷ **in consequence** CONSEQUENTLY, as a result, so, then, thus, therefore, hence, accordingly, for that reason, thence, ergo

consequent *adjective* FOLLOWING, resulting, subsequent, successive, ensuing, resultant, sequential

consequential *adjective* **1** RESULTING, subsequent, successive, ensuing, indirect, consequent, resultant, sequential, following
2 IMPORTANT, serious, significant, grave, far-reaching, momentous, weighty, eventful

consequently *adverb* AS A RESULT, thus, therefore, necessarily, hence, subsequently, accordingly, for that reason, thence, ergo

conservation *noun* **1** PRESERVATION, saving, protection, maintenance, custody, safeguarding, upkeep, guardianship, safekeeping
2 ECONOMY, saving, thrift, husbandry, careful management, thriftiness

conservative *adjective* TRADITIONAL, guarded, quiet, conventional, moderate, cautious, sober, reactionary, die-hard, middle-of-the-road, hidebound
<< OPPOSITE radical
▷ *noun* TRADITIONALIST, moderate, reactionary, die-hard, middle-of-the-roader, stick-in-the-mud (*informal*)
<< OPPOSITE radical

Conservative *adjective* TORY, Republican (US), right-wing
▷ *noun* TORY, Republican (US), right-winger

conservatory *noun* GREENHOUSE, hothouse, glasshouse

conserve *verb* **1** SAVE, husband, take care of, hoard, store up, go easy on, use sparingly
<< OPPOSITE waste
2 PROTECT, keep, save, preserve

consider *verb* **1** THINK, see, believe, rate, judge, suppose, deem, view as, look upon, regard as, hold to be, adjudge
2 THINK ABOUT, study, reflect on, examine, weigh, contemplate, deliberate, muse, ponder, revolve, meditate, work over, mull over, eye up, ruminate, chew over, cogitate, turn over in your mind
3 BEAR IN MIND, remember, regard, respect, think about, care for, take into account, reckon with, take into consideration, make allowance for, keep in view

considerable *adjective* LARGE, goodly, much, great, marked, comfortable, substantial, reasonable, tidy, lavish, ample, noticeable, abundant, plentiful, tolerable, appreciable, sizable *or* sizeable
<< OPPOSITE small

considerably *adverb* GREATLY, very much, seriously (*informal*), significantly, remarkably, substantially, markedly, noticeably, appreciably

considerate *adjective* THOUGHTFUL, kind, kindly, concerned, obliging, attentive, mindful, unselfish, solicitous
<< OPPOSITE inconsiderate

consideration *noun* **1** THOUGHT, study, review, attention, regard, analysis, examination, reflection, scrutiny, deliberation, contemplation, perusal, cogitation
2 THOUGHTFULNESS, concern, respect, kindness, friendliness, tact, solicitude, kindliness, considerateness
3 FACTOR, point, issue, concern, element, aspect, determinant
4 PAYMENT, fee, reward, remuneration, recompense, perquisite, tip
▷▷ **take something into consideration** BEAR IN MIND, consider, remember, think about, weigh, take into account, make allowance for, keep in view

considering *preposition* TAKING INTO ACCOUNT,

in the light of, bearing in mind, in view of, keeping in mind, taking into consideration
▷ *adverb* (*informal*) ALL THINGS CONSIDERED, all in all, taking everything into consideration, taking everything into account

consign *verb* 1 PUT AWAY, commit, deposit, relegate
2 DELIVER, ship, transfer, transmit, convey

consignment *noun* SHIPMENT, delivery, batch, goods

consist *verb* ▷▷ **consist in something** LIE IN, involve, reside in, be expressed by, subsist in, be found *or* contained in
▷▷ **consist of something** BE MADE UP OF, include, contain, incorporate, amount to, comprise, be composed of

consistency *noun* 1 AGREEMENT, harmony, correspondence, accordance, regularity, coherence, compatibility, uniformity, constancy, steadiness, steadfastness, evenness, congruity
2 TEXTURE, density, thickness, firmness, viscosity, compactness

consistent *adjective* 1 STEADY, even, regular, stable, constant, persistent, dependable, unchanging, true to type, undeviating
<< OPPOSITE erratic
2 COMPATIBLE, agreeing, in keeping, harmonious, in harmony, consonant, in accord, congruent, congruous, accordant
<< OPPOSITE incompatible
3 COHERENT, logical, compatible, harmonious, consonant, all of a piece
<< OPPOSITE contradictory

consolation *noun* COMFORT, help, support, relief, ease, cheer, encouragement, solace, succour, alleviation, assuagement

console *verb* COMFORT, cheer, relieve, soothe, support, encourage, calm, solace, assuage, succour, express sympathy for
<< OPPOSITE distress

consolidate *verb* 1 STRENGTHEN, secure, reinforce, cement, fortify, stabilize
2 COMBINE, unite, join, marry, merge, unify, amalgamate, federate, conjoin

consolidation *noun* 1 STRENGTHENING, reinforcement, fortification, stabilization
2 COMBINATION, union, association, alliance, merger, federation, amalgamation

consort *verb* ASSOCIATE WITH, mix with, mingle with, hang with (*informal, chiefly US*), go around with, keep company with, fraternize with, hang about, around *or* out with
▷ *noun* SPOUSE, wife, husband, partner, associate, fellow, companion, significant other (*US informal*), wahine (*NZ*), wifey (*informal*)

conspicuous *adjective* OBVIOUS, clear, apparent, visible, patent, evident, manifest, noticeable, blatant, discernible, salient, perceptible, easily seen
<< OPPOSITE inconspicuous

conspiracy *noun* PLOT, scheme, intrigue, collusion, confederacy, cabal, frame-up (*slang*), machination, league

conspirator *noun* PLOTTER, intriguer, conspirer, traitor, schemer

conspire *verb* 1 PLOT, scheme, intrigue, devise, manoeuvre, contrive, machinate, plan, hatch treason
2 WORK TOGETHER, combine, contribute, cooperate, concur, tend, conduce

constancy *noun* 1 STEADINESS, stability, regularity, uniformity, perseverance, firmness, permanence
2 FAITHFULNESS, loyalty, devotion, fidelity, dependability, trustworthiness, steadfastness

constant *adjective* 1 CONTINUOUS, sustained, endless, persistent, eternal, relentless, perpetual, continual, never-ending, habitual, uninterrupted, interminable, unrelenting, incessant, everlasting, ceaseless, unremitting, nonstop
<< OPPOSITE occasional
2 UNCHANGING, even, fixed, regular, permanent, stable, steady, uniform, continual, unbroken, immutable, immovable, invariable, unalterable, unvarying, firm
<< OPPOSITE changing
3 FAITHFUL, true, devoted, loyal, stalwart, staunch, dependable, trustworthy, trusty, steadfast, unfailing, tried-and-true
<< OPPOSITE undependable

constantly *adverb* CONTINUOUSLY, always, all the time, invariably, continually, aye (*Scot*), endlessly, relentlessly, persistently, perpetually, night and day, incessantly, nonstop, interminably, everlastingly, morning, noon and night
<< OPPOSITE occasionally

consternation *noun* DISMAY, shock, alarm, horror, panic, anxiety, distress, confusion, terror, dread, fright, amazement, fear, bewilderment, trepidation

constituent *noun* 1 VOTER, elector, member of the electorate
2 COMPONENT, element, ingredient, part, unit, factor, principle
▷ *adjective* COMPONENT, basic, essential, integral, elemental

constitute *verb* 1 REPRESENT, be, consist of, embody, exemplify, be equivalent to
2 MAKE UP, make, form, compose, comprise
3 SET UP, found, name, create, commission, establish, appoint, delegate, nominate, enact, authorize, empower, ordain, depute

constitution *noun* 1 STATE OF HEALTH, build, body, make-up, frame, physique, physical condition

2 STRUCTURE, form, nature, make-up, organization, establishment, formation, composition, character, temper, temperament, disposition

constitutional *adjective* LEGITIMATE, official, legal, chartered, statutory, vested

constrain *verb* 1 RESTRICT, confine, curb, restrain, rein, constrict, hem in, straiten, check, chain

2 FORCE, pressure, urge, bind, compel, oblige, necessitate, coerce, impel, pressurize, drive

constraint *noun* 1 RESTRICTION, limitation, curb, rein, deterrent, hindrance, damper, check

2 FORCE, pressure, necessity, restraint, compulsion, coercion

3 REPRESSION, reservation, embarrassment, restraint, inhibition, timidity, diffidence, bashfulness

constrict *verb* 1 SQUEEZE, contract, narrow, restrict, shrink, tighten, pinch, choke, cramp, strangle, compress, strangulate

2 LIMIT, restrict, confine, curb, inhibit, delimit, straiten

constriction *noun* TIGHTNESS, pressure, narrowing, reduction, squeezing, restriction, constraint, cramp, compression, blockage, limitation, impediment, stricture

construct *verb* 1 BUILD, make, form, create, design, raise, establish, set up, fashion, shape, engineer, frame, manufacture, put up, assemble, put together, erect, fabricate

<< OPPOSITE demolish

2 CREATE, make, form, set up, organize, compose, put together, formulate

construction *noun* 1 BUILDING, assembly, creation, formation, composition, erection, fabrication

2 STRUCTURE, building, edifice, form, figure, shape

3 (*Formal*) INTERPRETATION, meaning, reading, sense, explanation, rendering, take (*informal, chiefly US*), inference

constructive *adjective* HELPFUL, positive, useful, practical, valuable, productive

<< OPPOSITE unproductive

construe *verb* INTERPRET, take, read, explain

consult *verb* 1 ASK, refer to, turn to, interrogate, take counsel, ask advice of, pick (someone's) brains, question

2 CONFER, talk, debate, deliberate, commune, compare notes, consider

3 REFER TO, check in, look in

consultant *noun* SPECIALIST, adviser, counsellor, authority

consultation *noun* 1 DISCUSSION, talk, council, conference, dialogue

2 MEETING, interview, session, appointment, examination, deliberation, hearing

consume *verb* 1 EAT, swallow, devour, put away, gobble (up), eat up, guzzle, polish off (*informal*)

2 USE UP, use, spend, waste, employ, absorb, drain, exhaust, deplete, squander, utilize, dissipate, expend, eat up, fritter away

3 DESTROY, devastate, demolish, ravage, annihilate, lay waste

4 *often passive* OBSESS, dominate, absorb, preoccupy, devour, eat up, monopolize, engross

consumer *noun* BUYER, customer, user, shopper, purchaser

consuming *adjective* OVERWHELMING, gripping, absorbing, compelling, devouring, engrossing, immoderate

consummate *adjective* 1 SKILLED, perfect, supreme, polished, superb, practised, accomplished, matchless

2 COMPLETE, total, supreme, extreme, ultimate, absolute, utter, conspicuous, unqualified, deep-dyed (*usually derogatory*)

▷ *verb* COMPLETE, finish, achieve, conclude, perform, perfect, carry out, crown, fulfil, end, accomplish, effectuate, put the tin lid on

<< OPPOSITE initiate

consummation *noun* COMPLETION, end, achievement, perfection, realization, fulfilment, culmination

consumption *noun* 1 USING UP, use, loss, waste, drain, consuming, expenditure, exhaustion, depletion, utilization, dissipation

2 (*Old-fashioned*) TUBERCULOSIS, atrophy, T.B., emaciation

contact *noun* 1 COMMUNICATION, link, association, connection, correspondence, intercourse

2 TOUCH, contiguity

3 CONNECTION, colleague, associate, liaison, acquaintance, confederate

▷ *verb* GET *or* BE IN TOUCH WITH, call, reach, approach, phone, ring (up) (*informal, chiefly Brit*), write to, speak to, communicate with, get hold of, touch base with (*US & Canad informal*)

contagion *noun* SPREAD, spreading, communication, passage, proliferation, diffusion, transference, dissemination, dispersal, transmittal

contagious *adjective* INFECTIOUS, catching, spreading, epidemic, communicable, transmissible

contain *verb* 1 HOLD, incorporate, accommodate, enclose, have capacity for

2 INCLUDE, consist of, embrace, comprise, embody, comprehend

3 RESTRAIN, control, hold in, curb, suppress, hold back, stifle, repress, keep a tight rein on

container *noun* HOLDER, vessel, repository, receptacle

contaminate *verb* POLLUTE, infect, stain, corrupt, taint, sully, defile, adulterate, befoul, soil

<< OPPOSITE purify

contaminated *adjective* POLLUTED, dirtied, poisoned, infected, stained, corrupted, tainted, sullied, defiled, soiled, adulterated

contamination *noun* POLLUTION, dirtying, infection, corruption, poisoning, decay, taint, filth, impurity, contagion, adulteration, foulness, defilement

contemplate *verb* 1 CONSIDER, plan, think of, propose, intend, envisage, foresee, have in view *or* in mind

2 THINK ABOUT, consider, ponder, mull over, reflect upon, ruminate (upon), meditate on, brood over, muse over, deliberate over, revolve *or* turn over in your mind

3 LOOK AT, examine, observe, check out (*informal*), inspect, gaze at, behold, eye up, view, study, regard, survey, stare at, scrutinize, eye

contemplation *noun* 1 THOUGHT, consideration, reflection, musing, meditation, pondering, deliberation, reverie, rumination, cogitation

2 OBSERVATION, viewing, looking at, survey, examination, inspection, scrutiny, gazing at

contemplative *adjective* THOUGHTFUL, reflective, introspective, rapt, meditative, pensive, ruminative, in a brown study, intent, musing, deep *or* lost in thought

contemporary *adjective* 1 MODERN, latest, recent, current, with it (*informal*), trendy (*Brit informal*), up-to-date, present-day, in fashion, up-to-the-minute, à la mode, newfangled, happening (*informal*), present, ultramodern

<< OPPOSITE old-fashioned

2 COEXISTING, concurrent, contemporaneous, synchronous, coexistent

▷ *noun* PEER, fellow, equal

> Since *contemporary* can mean either 'of the present period' or 'of the same period', it is best to avoid it where ambiguity might arise, as in *a production of Othello in contemporary dress*. A synonym such as *modern* or *present-day* would clarify if the first sense were being used, while a specific term, such as *Elizabethan*, would be appropriate for the second sense

contempt *noun* SCORN, disdain, mockery, derision, disrespect, disregard

<< OPPOSITE respect

contemptible *adjective* DESPICABLE, mean, low, base, cheap, worthless, shameful, shabby, vile, degenerate, low-down (*informal*), paltry, pitiful, abject, ignominious, measly, scurvy, detestable, odious

<< OPPOSITE admirable

contemptuous *adjective* SCORNFUL, insulting, arrogant, withering, sneering, cavalier, condescending, haughty, disdainful, insolent, derisive, supercilious, high and mighty, on your high horse (*informal*)

<< OPPOSITE respectful

contend *verb* 1 ARGUE, hold, maintain, allege, assert, affirm, avow, aver

2 COMPETE, fight, struggle, clash, contest, strive, vie, grapple, jostle, skirmish

contender *noun* COMPETITOR, rival, candidate, applicant, hopeful, contestant, aspirant

content[1] *noun* 1 SUBJECT MATTER, ideas, matter, material, theme, text, substance, essence, gist

2 AMOUNT, measure, size, load, volume, capacity

▷ *plural noun* 1 CONSTITUENTS, elements, load, ingredients

2 SUBJECTS, chapters, themes, topics, subject matter, divisions

content[2] *adjective* SATISFIED, happy, pleased, contented, comfortable, fulfilled, at ease, gratified, agreeable, willing to accept

▷ *noun* SATISFACTION, peace, ease, pleasure, comfort, peace of mind, gratification, contentment

▷▷ **content yourself with something** SATISFY YOURSELF WITH, be happy with, be satisfied with, be content with

contented *adjective* SATISFIED, happy, pleased, content, comfortable, glad, cheerful, at ease, thankful, gratified, serene, at peace

<< OPPOSITE discontented

contention *noun* 1 ASSERTION, claim, stand, idea, view, position, opinion, argument, belief, allegation, profession, declaration, thesis, affirmation

2 DISPUTE, hostility, disagreement, feuding, strife, wrangling, discord, enmity, dissension

contentious *adjective* ARGUMENTATIVE, wrangling, perverse, bickering, combative, pugnacious, quarrelsome, litigious, querulous, cavilling, disputatious, factious, captious

contentment *noun* SATISFACTION, peace, content, ease, pleasure, comfort, happiness, fulfilment, gratification, serenity, equanimity, gladness, repletion, contentedness

<< OPPOSITE discontent

contest *noun* 1 COMPETITION, game, match, trial, tournament, head-to-head

2 STRUGGLE, fight, battle, debate, conflict, dispute, encounter, controversy, combat, discord

▷ *verb* 1 COMPETE IN, take part in, fight in, go in for, contend for, vie in

2 OPPOSE, question, challenge, argue, debate, dispute, object to, litigate, call in *or* into question

contestant *noun* COMPETITOR, candidate,

participant, contender, entrant, player, aspirant

context *noun* 1 CIRCUMSTANCES, times, conditions, situation, ambience
2 FRAME OF REFERENCE, background, framework, relation, connection

contingency *noun* POSSIBILITY, happening, chance, event, incident, accident, emergency, uncertainty, eventuality, juncture

contingent *noun* GROUP, detachment, deputation, set, body, section, bunch (*informal*), quota, batch
▷ *adjective* CHANCE, random, casual, uncertain, accidental, haphazard, fortuitous
▷▷ **contingent on** DEPENDENT ON, subject to, controlled by, conditional on

continual *adjective* 1 CONSTANT, endless, continuous, eternal, perpetual, uninterrupted, interminable, incessant, everlasting, unremitting, unceasing
<< OPPOSITE erratic
2 FREQUENT, regular, repeated, repetitive, recurrent, oft-repeated
<< OPPOSITE occasional

continually *adverb* 1 CONSTANTLY, always, all the time, forever, aye (*Scot*), endlessly, eternally, incessantly, nonstop, interminably, everlastingly
2 REPEATEDLY, often, frequently, many times, over and over, again and again, time and (time) again, persistently, time after time, many a time and oft (*archaic* or *poetic*)

continuance *noun* PERPETUATION, lasting, carrying on, keeping up, endurance, continuation, prolongation

continuation *noun* 1 CONTINUING, lasting, carrying on, maintenance, keeping up, endurance, perpetuation, prolongation
2 ADDITION, extension, supplement, sequel, resumption, postscript

continue *verb* 1 KEEP ON, go on, maintain, pursue, sustain, carry on, stick to, keep up, prolong, persist in, keep at, persevere, stick at, press on with
<< OPPOSITE stop
2 GO ON, advance, progress, proceed, carry on, keep going
3 RESUME, return to, take up again, proceed, carry on, recommence, pick up where you left off
<< OPPOSITE stop
4 REMAIN, last, stay, rest, survive, carry on, live on, endure, stay on, persist, abide
<< OPPOSITE quit

continuing *adjective* LASTING, sustained, enduring, ongoing, in progress

continuity *noun* COHESION, flow, connection, sequence, succession, progression, wholeness, interrelationship

continuous *adjective* CONSTANT, continued, extended, prolonged, unbroken, uninterrupted, unceasing
<< OPPOSITE occasional

contort *verb* TWIST, knot, distort, warp, deform, misshape

contortion *noun* TWIST, distortion, deformity, convolution, bend, knot, warp

contour *noun* OUTLINE, profile, lines, form, figure, shape, relief, curve, silhouette

contraband *adjective* SMUGGLED, illegal, illicit, black-market, hot (*informal*), banned, forbidden, prohibited, unlawful, bootleg, bootlegged, interdicted

contract *noun* AGREEMENT, deal (*informal*), commission, commitment, arrangement, understanding, settlement, treaty, bargain, convention, engagement, pact, compact, covenant, bond, stipulation, concordat
▷ *verb* 1 AGREE, arrange, negotiate, engage, pledge, bargain, undertake, come to terms, shake hands, covenant, make a deal, commit yourself, enter into an agreement
<< OPPOSITE refuse
2 CONSTRICT, confine, tighten, shorten, wither, compress, condense, shrivel
3 TIGHTEN, narrow, knit, purse, shorten, pucker
<< OPPOSITE stretch
4 LESSEN, reduce, shrink, diminish, decrease, dwindle
<< OPPOSITE increase
5 CATCH, get, develop, acquire, incur, be infected with, go down with, be afflicted with
<< OPPOSITE avoid

contraction *noun* 1 TIGHTENING, narrowing, tensing, shortening, drawing in, constricting, shrinkage
2 ABBREVIATION, reduction, shortening, compression, diminution, constriction, elision

contradict *verb* 1 DISPUTE, deny, challenge, belie, fly in the face of, make a nonsense of, be at variance with
2 NEGATE, deny, oppose, counter, contravene, rebut, impugn, controvert
<< OPPOSITE confirm

contradiction *noun* 1 CONFLICT, inconsistency, contravention, incongruity, confutation
2 NEGATION, opposite, denial, antithesis

contradictory *adjective* INCONSISTENT, conflicting, opposed, opposite, contrary, incompatible, paradoxical, irreconcilable, antithetical, discrepant

contraption *noun* (*informal*) DEVICE, instrument, mechanism, apparatus, gadget, contrivance, rig

contrary *adjective* 1 OPPOSITE, different, opposed, clashing, counter, reverse, differing,

adverse, contradictory, inconsistent, diametrically opposed, antithetical
<< OPPOSITE in agreement
2 PERVERSE, difficult, awkward, wayward, intractable, wilful, obstinate, cussed (*informal*), stroppy (*Brit slang*), cantankerous, disobliging, unaccommodating, thrawn (*Scot & Northern English dialect*)
<< OPPOSITE cooperative
▷ *noun* OPPOSITE, reverse, converse, antithesis
▷▷ **on the contrary** QUITE THE OPPOSITE *or* REVERSE, on the other hand, in contrast, conversely

contrast *noun* DIFFERENCE, opposition, comparison, distinction, foil, disparity, differentiation, divergence, dissimilarity, contrariety
▷ *verb* 1 DIFFERENTIATE, compare, oppose, distinguish, set in opposition
2 DIFFER, be contrary, be distinct, be at variance, be dissimilar

contravene *verb* 1 (*Formal*) BREAK, violate, go against, infringe, disobey, transgress
2 CONFLICT WITH, cross, oppose, interfere with, thwart, contradict, hinder, go against, refute, counteract

contravention *noun* 1 BREACH, violation, infringement, trespass, disobedience, transgression, infraction
2 CONFLICT, interference, contradiction, hindrance, rebuttal, refutation, disputation, counteraction

contribute *verb* GIVE, provide, supply, donate, furnish, subscribe, chip in (*informal*), bestow
▷▷ **contribute to something** BE PARTLY RESPONSIBLE FOR, lead to, be instrumental in, be conducive to, conduce to, help

contribution *noun* GIFT, offering, grant, donation, input, subscription, bestowal, koha (NZ)

contributor *noun* 1 DONOR, supporter, patron, subscriber, backer, bestower, giver
2 WRITER, correspondent, reporter, journalist, freelance, freelancer, journo (*slang*)

contrite *adjective* SORRY, humble, chastened, sorrowful, repentant, remorseful, regretful, penitent, conscience-stricken, in sackcloth and ashes

contrition *noun* REGRET, sorrow, remorse, repentance, compunction, penitence, self-reproach

contrivance *noun* 1 DEVICE, machine, equipment, gear, instrument, implement, mechanism, invention, appliance, apparatus, gadget, contraption
2 STRATAGEM, plan, design, measure, scheme, trick, plot, dodge, expedient, ruse, artifice, machination

contrive *verb* 1 DEVISE, plan, fabricate, create, design, scheme, engineer, frame, manufacture, plot, construct, invent, improvise, concoct, wangle (*informal*)
2 MANAGE, succeed, arrange, manoeuvre

contrived *adjective* FORCED, planned, laboured, strained, artificial, elaborate, unnatural, overdone, recherché
<< OPPOSITE natural

control *noun* 1 POWER, government, rule, authority, management, direction, command, discipline, guidance, supervision, jurisdiction, supremacy, mastery, superintendence, charge
2 RESTRAINT, check, regulation, brake, limitation, curb
3 SELF-DISCIPLINE, cool, calmness, self-restraint, restraint, coolness, self-mastery, self-command
4 SWITCH, instrument, button, dial, lever, knob
▷ *plural noun* INSTRUMENTS, dash, dials, console, dashboard, control panel
▷ *verb* 1 HAVE POWER OVER, lead, rule, manage, boss (*informal*), direct, handle, conduct, dominate, command, pilot, govern, steer, administer, oversee, supervise, manipulate, call the shots, call the tune, reign over, keep a tight rein on, have charge of, superintend, have (someone) in your pocket, keep (someone) on a string
2 LIMIT, restrict, curb, delimit
3 RESTRAIN, limit, check, contain, master, curb, hold back, subdue, repress, constrain, bridle, rein in

controversial *adjective* DISPUTED, contended, contentious, at issue, debatable, polemic, under discussion, open to question, disputable

controversy *noun* ARGUMENT, debate, row, discussion, dispute, contention, quarrel, squabble, strife, wrangle, wrangling, polemic, altercation, dissension

conundrum *noun* PUZZLE, problem, riddle, enigma, teaser, poser, brain-teaser (*informal*)

convalesce *verb* RECOVER, rest, rally, rehabilitate, recuperate, improve

convalescence *noun* RECOVERY, rehabilitation, recuperation, return to health, improvement

convalescent *adjective* RECOVERING, getting better, recuperating, on the mend, improving, mending

convene *verb* 1 CALL, gather, assemble, summon, bring together, muster, convoke
2 MEET, gather, rally, assemble, come together, muster, congregate

convenience *noun* 1 BENEFIT, good, interest, advantage
2 SUITABILITY, fitness, appropriateness, opportuneness
3 USEFULNESS, utility, serviceability,

handiness
<< OPPOSITE uselessness
4 ACCESSIBILITY, availability, nearness, handiness
5 APPLIANCE, facility, comfort, amenity, labour-saving device, help
▷▷ **at your convenience** AT A SUITABLE TIME, at your leisure, in your own time, whenever you like, in your spare time, in a spare moment

convenient *adjective* 1 SUITABLE, fitting, fit, handy, satisfactory
2 USEFUL, practical, handy, serviceable, labour-saving
<< OPPOSITE useless
3 NEARBY, available, accessible, handy, at hand, within reach, close at hand, just round the corner
<< OPPOSITE inaccessible
4 APPROPRIATE, timely, suited, suitable, beneficial, well-timed, opportune, seasonable, helpful

convent *noun* NUNNERY, religious community, religious house

convention *noun* 1 CUSTOM, practice, tradition, code, usage, protocol, formality, etiquette, propriety, kawa (*NZ*), tikanga (*NZ*), rule
2 AGREEMENT, contract, treaty, bargain, pact, compact, protocol, stipulation, concordat
3 ASSEMBLY, meeting, council, conference, congress, convocation, hui (*NZ*), runanga (*NZ*)

conventional *adjective* 1 PROPER, conservative, correct, formal, respectable, bourgeois, genteel, staid, conformist, decorous, Pooterish
2 ORDINARY, standard, normal, regular, usual, vanilla (*slang*), habitual, bog-standard (*Brit & Irish slang*), common
3 TRADITIONAL, accepted, prevailing, orthodox, customary, prevalent, hidebound, wonted
4 UNORIGINAL, routine, stereotyped, pedestrian, commonplace, banal, prosaic, run-of-the-mill, hackneyed, vanilla (*slang*)
<< OPPOSITE unconventional

converge *verb* COME TOGETHER, meet, join, combine, gather, merge, coincide, mingle, intersect
▷▷ **converge on something** CLOSE IN ON, arrive at, move towards, home in on, come together at

convergence *noun* MEETING, junction, intersection, confluence, concentration, blending, merging, coincidence, conjunction, mingling, concurrence, conflux

conversation *noun* TALK, exchange, discussion, dialogue, tête-à-tête, conference, communication, chat, gossip, intercourse, discourse, communion, converse, powwow, colloquy, chinwag (*Brit informal*), confabulation, confab (*informal*), craic (*Irish informal*), korero (*NZ*)
>> RELATED WORD *adjective* colloquial

conversational *adjective* CHATTY, informal, communicative, colloquial

converse[1] *verb* TALK, speak, chat, communicate, discourse, confer, commune, exchange views, shoot the breeze (*slang, chiefly US & Canad*)

converse[2] *noun* OPPOSITE, reverse, contrary, other side of the coin, obverse, antithesis
▷ *adjective* OPPOSITE, counter, reverse, contrary

conversion *noun* 1 CHANGE, transformation, metamorphosis, transfiguration, transmutation, transmogrification (*jocular*)
2 ADAPTATION, reconstruction, modification, alteration, remodelling, reorganization
3 REFORMATION, rebirth, change of heart, proselytization

convert *verb* 1 CHANGE, turn, transform, alter, metamorphose, transpose, transmute, transmogrify (*jocular*)
2 ADAPT, modify, remodel, reorganize, customize, restyle
3 REFORM, save, convince, proselytize, bring to God
▷ *noun* NEOPHYTE, disciple, proselyte, catechumen

convertible *adjective* CHANGEABLE, interchangeable, exchangeable, adjustable, adaptable

convex *adjective* ROUNDED, bulging, protuberant, gibbous, outcurved
<< OPPOSITE concave

convey *verb* 1 COMMUNICATE, impart, reveal, relate, disclose, make known, tell
2 CARRY, transport, move, bring, support, bear, conduct, transmit, fetch

conveyance *noun* 1 (*Old-fashioned*) VEHICLE, transport
2 TRANSPORTATION, movement, transfer, transport, transmission, carriage, transference

convict *verb* FIND GUILTY, sentence, condemn, imprison, pronounce guilty
▷ *noun* PRISONER, criminal, con (*slang*), lag (*slang*), villain, felon, jailbird, malefactor

conviction *noun* 1 BELIEF, view, opinion, principle, faith, persuasion, creed, tenet, kaupapa (*NZ*)
2 CERTAINTY, confidence, assurance, fervour, firmness, earnestness, certitude

convince *verb* 1 ASSURE, persuade, satisfy, prove to, reassure
2 PERSUADE, induce, coax, talk into, prevail upon, inveigle, twist (someone's) arm, bring round to the idea of

The use of *convince* to talk about persuading someone to do something is considered by many British speakers to be wrong or unacceptable. It would be preferable to use an alternative such as *persuade* or *talk into*

convincing *adjective* PERSUASIVE, credible, conclusive, incontrovertible, telling, likely, powerful, impressive, probable, plausible, cogent
<< OPPOSITE unconvincing

convivial *adjective* SOCIABLE, friendly, lively, cheerful, jolly, merry, festive, hearty, genial, fun-loving, jovial, back-slapping, gay, partyish (*informal*)

convocation *noun* (*Formal*) MEETING, congress, convention, synod, diet, assembly, concourse, council, assemblage, conclave, hui (NZ), runanga (NZ)

convoy *verb* ESCORT, conduct, accompany, shepherd, protect, attend, guard, pilot, usher

convulse *verb* 1 SHAKE, twist, agitate, contort
2 TWIST, contort, work

convulsion *noun* 1 SPASM, fit, shaking, seizure, contraction, tremor, cramp, contortion, paroxysm
2 UPHEAVAL, disturbance, furore, turbulence, agitation, commotion, tumult

cool *adjective* 1 COLD, chilled, chilling, refreshing, chilly, nippy
<< OPPOSITE warm
2 CALM, together (*slang*), collected, relaxed, composed, laid-back (*informal*), serene, sedate, self-controlled, placid, level-headed, dispassionate, unfazed (*informal*), unruffled, unemotional, self-possessed, imperturbable, unexcited
<< OPPOSITE agitated
3 UNFRIENDLY, reserved, distant, indifferent, aloof, lukewarm, unconcerned, uninterested, frigid, unresponsive, offhand, unenthusiastic, uncommunicative, unwelcoming, standoffish
<< OPPOSITE friendly
4 UNENTHUSIASTIC, indifferent, lukewarm, uninterested, apathetic, unresponsive, unwelcoming
5 (*informal*) FASHIONABLE, with it (*informal*), hip (*slang*), stylish, trendy (*Brit informal*), chic, up-to-date, urbane, up-to-the-minute, voguish (*informal*), trendsetting, schmick (*Austral informal*)
6 IMPUDENT, bold, cheeky, audacious, brazen, shameless, presumptuous, impertinent
▷ *verb* 1 LOSE HEAT, cool off
<< OPPOSITE warm (up)
2 MAKE COOL, freeze, chill, refrigerate, cool off
<< OPPOSITE warm (up)
3 CALM (DOWN), lessen, abate
4 LESSEN, calm (down), quiet, moderate, temper, dampen, allay, abate, assuage
▷ *noun* 1 COLDNESS, chill, coolness
2 (*Slang*) CALMNESS, control, temper, composure, self-control, poise, self-discipline, self-possession

coolness *noun* 1 COLDNESS, freshness, chilliness, nippiness
<< OPPOSITE warmness
2 CALMNESS, control, composure, self-control, self-discipline, self-possession, level-headedness, imperturbability, sedateness, placidness
<< OPPOSITE agitation
3 UNFRIENDLINESS, reserve, distance, indifference, apathy, remoteness, aloofness, frigidity, unconcern, unresponsiveness, frostiness, offhandedness
<< OPPOSITE friendliness
4 IMPUDENCE, audacity, boldness, insolence, impertinence, shamelessness, cheekiness, brazenness, presumptuousness, audaciousness

coop *noun* PEN, pound, box, cage, enclosure, hutch, corral (*chiefly US & Canad*)
▷▷ **coop someone up** CONFINE, imprison, shut up, impound, pound, pen, cage, immure

cooperate *verb* 1 WORK TOGETHER, collaborate, coordinate, join forces, conspire, concur, pull together, pool resources, combine your efforts
<< OPPOSITE conflict
2 HELP, contribute to, assist, go along with, aid, pitch in, abet, play ball (with) (*informal*), lend a helping hand
<< OPPOSITE oppose

cooperation *noun* 1 TEAMWORK, concert, unity, collaboration, give-and-take, combined effort, esprit de corps, concurrence, kotahitanga (NZ)
<< OPPOSITE opposition
2 HELP, assistance, participation, responsiveness, helpfulness
<< OPPOSITE hindrance

cooperative *adjective* 1 SHARED, united, joint, combined, concerted, collective, unified, coordinated, collaborative
2 HELPFUL, obliging, accommodating, supportive, responsive, onside (*informal*)

coordinate *verb* 1 ORGANIZE, synchronize, integrate, bring together, mesh, correlate, systematize
2 MATCH, blend, harmonize
▷▷ **coordinate with** GO WITH, match, blend with, harmonize with

cope *verb* MANAGE, get by (*informal*), struggle through, rise to the occasion, survive, carry on, make out (*informal*), make the grade, hold your own
▷▷ **cope with something** DEAL WITH, handle, struggle with, grapple with, wrestle with, contend with, tangle with, tussle with, weather

copious *adjective* ABUNDANT, liberal, generous, lavish, full, rich, extensive, ample, overflowing, plentiful, exuberant,

bountiful, luxuriant, profuse, bounteous, superabundant, plenteous
cop out *verb* (*Slang*) AVOID, dodge, abandon, withdraw from, desert, quit, skip, renounce, revoke, renege, skive (*Brit slang*), bludge (*Austral & NZ informal*)
cop-out *noun* (*Slang*) PRETENCE, dodge, pretext, fraud, alibi
copulate *verb* HAVE INTERCOURSE, have sex
copy *noun* REPRODUCTION, duplicate, photocopy, carbon copy, image, print, fax, representation, fake, replica, imitation, forgery, counterfeit, Xerox (*trademark*), transcription, likeness, replication, facsimile, Photostat (*trademark*)
<< OPPOSITE original
▷ *verb* 1 REPRODUCE, replicate, duplicate, photocopy, transcribe, counterfeit, Xerox (*trademark*), Photostat (*trademark*)
<< OPPOSITE create
2 IMITATE, act like, emulate, behave like, follow, repeat, mirror, echo, parrot, ape, mimic, simulate, follow suit, follow the example of
cord *noun* ROPE, line, string, twine
cordial *adjective* 1 WARM, welcoming, friendly, cheerful, affectionate, hearty, agreeable, sociable, genial, affable, congenial, warm-hearted
<< OPPOSITE unfriendly
2 WHOLEHEARTED, earnest, sincere, heartfelt
cordon *noun* CHAIN, line, ring, barrier, picket line
▷▷ **cordon something off** SURROUND, isolate, close off, fence off, separate, enclose, picket, encircle
core *noun* 1 CENTRE
2 HEART, essence, nucleus, kernel, crux, gist, nub, pith
corner *noun* 1 ANGLE, joint, crook
2 BEND, curve
3 SPACE, hole, niche, recess, cavity, hideaway, nook, cranny, hide-out, hidey-hole (*informal*)
4 TIGHT SPOT, predicament, tricky situation, spot (*informal*), hole (*informal*), hot water (*informal*), pickle (*informal*)
▷ *verb* 1 TRAP, catch, run to earth, bring to bay
2 (usually with *market* as object) MONOPOLIZE, take over, dominate, control, hog (*slang*), engross, exercise *or* have a monopoly of
cornerstone *noun* BASIS, key, premise, starting point, bedrock
corny *adjective* (*Slang*) 1 UNORIGINAL, banal, trite, hackneyed, dull, old-fashioned, stereotyped, commonplace, feeble, stale, old hat
2 SENTIMENTAL, mushy (*informal*), maudlin, slushy (*informal*), mawkish, schmaltzy (*slang*)
corollary *noun* CONSEQUENCE, result, effect, outcome, sequel, end result, upshot
corporal *adjective* BODILY, physical, fleshly, anatomical, carnal, corporeal (*archaic*), material
corporate *adjective* COLLECTIVE, collaborative, united, shared, allied, joint, combined, pooled, merged, communal
corporation *noun* 1 BUSINESS, company, concern, firm, society, association, organization, enterprise, establishment, corporate body
2 TOWN COUNCIL, council, municipal authorities, civic authorities
corps *noun* TEAM, unit, regiment, detachment, company, body, band, division, troop, squad, crew, contingent, squadron
corpse *noun* BODY, remains, carcass, cadaver, stiff (*slang*)
corpus *noun* COLLECTION, body, whole, compilation, entirety, oeuvre (*French*), complete works
corral *verb* (*US & Canad*) ENCLOSE, confine, cage, fence in, impound, pen in, coop up
correct *adjective* 1 ACCURATE, right, true, exact, precise, flawless, faultless, on the right lines, O.K. *or* okay (*informal*)
<< OPPOSITE inaccurate
2 RIGHT, standard, regular, appropriate, acceptable, strict, proper, precise
3 PROPER, seemly, standard, fitting, diplomatic, kosher (*informal*)
<< OPPOSITE inappropriate
▷ *verb* 1 RECTIFY, remedy, redress, right, improve, reform, cure, adjust, regulate, amend, set the record straight, emend
<< OPPOSITE spoil
2 REBUKE, discipline, reprimand, chide, admonish, chastise, chasten, reprove, punish
<< OPPOSITE praise
correction *noun* 1 RECTIFICATION, improvement, amendment, adjustment, modification, alteration, emendation
2 PUNISHMENT, discipline, reformation, admonition, chastisement, reproof, castigation
corrective *adjective* 1 REMEDIAL, therapeutic, palliative, restorative, rehabilitative
2 DISCIPLINARY, punitive, penal, reformatory
correctly *adverb* RIGHTLY, right, perfectly, properly, precisely, accurately, aright
correctness *noun* 1 TRUTH, accuracy, precision, exactitude, exactness, faultlessness
2 DECORUM, propriety, good manners, civility, good breeding, bon ton (*French*)
correlate *verb* 1 CORRESPOND, parallel, be connected, equate, tie in, match
2 CONNECT, compare, associate, tie in, coordinate, match
correlation *noun* CORRESPONDENCE, link,

relation, connection, equivalence
correspond *verb* 1 BE CONSISTENT, match, agree, accord, fit, square, coincide, complement, be related, tally, conform, correlate, dovetail, harmonize
<< OPPOSITE differ
2 COMMUNICATE, write, keep in touch, exchange letters
correspondence *noun* 1 COMMUNICATION, writing, contact
2 LETTERS, post, mail
3 RELATION, match, agreement, fitness, comparison, harmony, coincidence, similarity, analogy, correlation, conformity, comparability, concurrence, congruity
correspondent *noun* 1 REPORTER, journalist, contributor, special correspondent, journo (*slang*), hack
2 LETTER WRITER, pen friend *or* pen pal
corresponding *adjective* EQUIVALENT, matching, similar, related, correspondent, identical, complementary, synonymous, reciprocal, analogous, interrelated, correlative
corridor *noun* PASSAGE, alley, aisle, hallway, passageway
corroborate *verb* SUPPORT, establish, confirm, document, sustain, back up, endorse, ratify, validate, bear out, substantiate, authenticate
<< OPPOSITE contradict
corrode *verb* EAT AWAY, waste, consume, corrupt, deteriorate, erode, rust, gnaw, oxidize
corrosive *adjective* CORRODING, wasting, caustic, vitriolic, acrid, erosive
corrugated *adjective* FURROWED, channelled, ridged, grooved, wrinkled, creased, fluted, rumpled, puckered, crinkled
corrupt *adjective* 1 DISHONEST, bent (*slang*), crooked (*informal*), rotten, shady (*informal*), fraudulent, unscrupulous, unethical, venal, unprincipled
<< OPPOSITE honest
2 DEPRAVED, abandoned, vicious, degenerate, debased, demoralized, profligate, dishonoured, defiled, dissolute
3 DISTORTED, doctored, altered, falsified
▷ *verb* 1 BRIBE, square, fix (*informal*), buy off, suborn, grease (someone's) palm (*slang*)
2 DEPRAVE, pervert, subvert, debase, demoralize, debauch
<< OPPOSITE reform
3 DISTORT, doctor, tamper with
corruption *noun* 1 DISHONESTY, fraud, fiddling (*informal*), graft (*informal*), bribery, extortion, profiteering, breach of trust, venality, shady dealings (*informal*), shadiness
2 DEPRAVITY, vice, evil, degradation, perversion, decadence, impurity, wickedness, degeneration, immorality, iniquity, profligacy, viciousness, sinfulness, turpitude, baseness
3 DISTORTION, doctoring, falsification
corset *noun* GIRDLE, bodice, foundation garment, panty girdle, stays (*rare*)
cortege *noun* PROCESSION, train, entourage, cavalcade, retinue, suite
cosmetic *adjective* SUPERFICIAL, surface, touching-up, nonessential
cosmic *adjective* 1 EXTRATERRESTRIAL, stellar
2 UNIVERSAL, general, omnipresent, all-embracing, overarching
3 VAST, huge, immense, infinite, grandiose, limitless, measureless
cosmonaut *noun* ASTRONAUT, spaceman, space pilot, space cadet
cosmopolitan *adjective* SOPHISTICATED, worldly, cultured, refined, cultivated, urbane, well-travelled, worldly-wise
<< OPPOSITE unsophisticated
cosmos *noun* UNIVERSE, world, creation, macrocosm
cosset *verb* PAMPER, baby, pet, coddle, mollycoddle, wrap up in cotton wool (*informal*)
cost *noun* 1 PRICE, worth, expense, rate, charge, figure, damage (*informal*), amount, payment, expenditure, outlay
2 LOSS, suffering, damage, injury, penalty, hurt, expense, harm, sacrifice, deprivation, detriment
▷ *plural noun* EXPENSES, spending, expenditure, overheads, outgoings, outlay, budget
▷ *verb* 1 SELL AT, come to, set (someone) back (*informal*), be priced at, command a price of
2 LOSE, deprive of, cheat of
▷▷ **at all costs** NO MATTER WHAT, regardless, whatever happens, at any price, come what may, without fail
costly *adjective* 1 EXPENSIVE, dear, stiff, excessive, steep (*informal*), highly-priced, exorbitant, extortionate
<< OPPOSITE inexpensive
2 SPLENDID, rich, valuable, precious, gorgeous, lavish, luxurious, sumptuous, priceless, opulent
3 DAMAGING, disastrous, harmful, catastrophic, loss-making, ruinous, deleterious
costume *noun* OUTFIT, dress, clothing, get-up (*informal*), uniform, ensemble, robes, livery, apparel, attire, garb, national dress
cosy *adjective* 1 COMFORTABLE, homely, warm, intimate, snug, comfy (*informal*), sheltered
2 SNUG, warm, secure, comfortable, sheltered, comfy (*informal*), tucked up, cuddled up, snuggled down
3 INTIMATE, friendly, informal
coterie *noun* CLIQUE, group, set, camp, circle, gang, outfit (*informal*), posse (*informal*), cabal
cottage *noun* CABIN, lodge, hut, shack, chalet, but-and-ben (*Scot*), cot, whare (*NZ*)

couch *noun* SOFA, bed, chesterfield, ottoman, settee, divan, chaise longue, day bed
▷ *verb* EXPRESS, word, frame, phrase, utter, set forth

cough *verb* CLEAR YOUR THROAT, bark, hawk, hack, hem
▷ *noun* FROG *or* TICKLE IN YOUR THROAT, bark, hack
▷▷ **cough up** (*informal*) FORK OUT, deliver, hand over, surrender, come across (*informal*), shell out (*informal*), ante up (*informal, chiefly US*)

council *noun* **1** COMMITTEE, governing body, board, panel, quango
2 GOVERNING BODY, house, parliament, congress, cabinet, ministry, diet, panel, assembly, chamber, convention, synod, conclave, convocation, conference, runanga (NZ)

counsel *noun* **1** ADVICE, information, warning, direction, suggestion, recommendation, caution, guidance, admonition
2 LEGAL ADVISER, lawyer, attorney, solicitor, advocate, barrister
▷ *verb* ADVISE, recommend, advocate, prescribe, warn, urge, caution, instruct, exhort, admonish

count *verb* **1** *often with* **up** ADD (UP), total, reckon (up), tot up, score, check, estimate, calculate, compute, tally, number, enumerate, cast up
2 MATTER, be important, cut any ice (*informal*), carry weight, tell, rate, weigh, signify, enter into consideration
3 CONSIDER, judge, regard, deem, think of, rate, esteem, look upon, impute
4 INCLUDE, number among, take into account *or* consideration
▷ *noun* CALCULATION, poll, reckoning, sum, tally, numbering, computation, enumeration
▷▷ **count on** *or* **upon something** *or* **someone** DEPEND ON, trust, rely on, bank on, take for granted, lean on, reckon on, take on trust, believe in, pin your faith on
▷▷ **count someone out** (*informal*) LEAVE OUT, except, exclude, disregard, pass over, leave out of account

countenance *noun* (*Literary*) FACE, features, expression, look, appearance, aspect, visage, mien, physiognomy
▷ *verb* TOLERATE, sanction, endorse, condone, support, encourage, approve, endure, brook, stand for (*informal*), hack (*slang*), put up with (*informal*)

counter *verb* **1** OPPOSE, meet, block, resist, offset, parry, deflect, repel, rebuff, fend off, counteract, ward off, stave off, repulse, obviate, hold at bay
2 RETALIATE, return, answer, reply, respond, come back, retort, hit back, rejoin, strike back
<< OPPOSITE yield
▷ *adverb* OPPOSITE TO, against, versus, conversely, in defiance of, at variance with, contrarily, contrariwise
<< OPPOSITE in accordance with
▷ *adjective* OPPOSING, conflicting, opposed, contrasting, opposite, contrary, adverse, contradictory, obverse, against
<< OPPOSITE similar

counteract *verb* **1** ACT AGAINST, check, defeat, prevent, oppose, resist, frustrate, foil, thwart, hinder, cross
2 OFFSET, negate, neutralize, invalidate, counterbalance, annul, obviate, countervail

counterbalance *verb* OFFSET, balance out, compensate for, make up for, counterpoise, countervail

counterfeit *adjective* FAKE, copied, false, forged, imitation, bogus, simulated, sham, fraudulent, feigned, spurious, ersatz, phoney *or* phony (*informal*), pseud *or* pseudo (*informal*)
<< OPPOSITE genuine
▷ *noun* FAKE, copy, reproduction, imitation, sham, forgery, phoney *or* phony (*informal*), fraud
<< OPPOSITE the real thing
▷ *verb* FAKE, copy, forge, imitate, simulate, sham, fabricate, feign

counterpart *noun* OPPOSITE NUMBER, equal, twin, equivalent, peer, match, fellow, mate

countless *adjective* INNUMERABLE, legion, infinite, myriad, untold, limitless, incalculable, immeasurable, numberless, uncounted, multitudinous, endless, measureless
<< OPPOSITE limited

country *noun* **1** NATION, state, land, commonwealth, kingdom, realm, sovereign state, people
2 PEOPLE, community, nation, society, citizens, voters, inhabitants, grass roots, electors, populace, citizenry, public
3 COUNTRYSIDE, rural areas, provinces, outdoors, sticks (*informal*), farmland, outback (*Austral* & *NZ*), the middle of nowhere, green belt, wide open spaces (*informal*), backwoods, back country (*US*), the back of beyond, bush (*NZ* & *S African*), backlands (*US*), boondocks (*US slang*)
<< OPPOSITE town
4 TERRITORY, part, land, region, terrain
5 NATIVE LAND, nationality, homeland, motherland, fatherland, patria (*Latin*), Hawaiki (NZ), Godzone (*Austral informal*)
▷ *adjective* RURAL, pastoral, rustic, agrarian, bucolic, Arcadian
<< OPPOSITE urban
>> RELATED WORDS *adjectives* pastoral, rural

countryman *noun* **1** COMPATRIOT, fellow citizen

2 YOKEL, farmer, peasant, provincial, hick (*informal, chiefly US & Canad*), rustic, swain, hillbilly, bucolic, country dweller, hayseed (*US & Canad informal*), clodhopper (*informal*), cockie (NZ), (country) bumpkin

countryside *noun* COUNTRY, rural areas, outdoors, farmland, outback (*Austral & NZ*), green belt, wide open spaces (*informal*), sticks (*informal*)

county *noun* PROVINCE, district, shire
▷ *adjective* (*informal*) UPPER-CLASS, upper-crust (*informal*), tweedy, plummy (*informal*), green-wellie, huntin', shootin', and fishin' (*informal*)

coup *noun* MASTERSTROKE, feat, stunt, action, stroke, exploit, manoeuvre, deed, accomplishment, tour de force (*French*), stratagem, stroke of genius

coup d'état *noun* OVERTHROW, takeover, coup, rebellion, putsch, seizure of power, palace revolution

couple *noun* PAIR, two, brace, span (*of horses or oxen*), duo, twain (*archaic*), twosome
▷▷ **couple something to something** LINK TO, connect to, pair with, unite with, join to, hitch to, buckle to, clasp to, yoke to, conjoin to

coupon *noun* SLIP, ticket, certificate, token, voucher, card, detachable portion

courage *noun* BRAVERY, nerve, fortitude, boldness, bottle (*Brit slang*), resolution, daring, guts (*informal*), pluck, grit, heroism, mettle, firmness, gallantry, valour, spunk (*informal*), fearlessness, intrepidity
<< OPPOSITE cowardice

courageous *adjective* BRAVE, daring, bold, plucky, hardy, heroic, gritty, stalwart, fearless, resolute, gallant, audacious, intrepid, valiant, indomitable, dauntless, ballsy (*taboo slang*), lion-hearted, valorous, stouthearted
<< OPPOSITE cowardly

courier *noun* 1 MESSENGER, runner, carrier, bearer, herald, envoy, emissary
2 GUIDE, representative, escort, conductor, chaperon, cicerone, dragoman

course *noun* 1 ROUTE, way, line, road, track, channel, direction, path, passage, trail, orbit, tack, trajectory
2 PROCEDURE, plan, policy, programme, method, conduct, behaviour, manner, mode, regimen
3 PROGRESSION, order, unfolding, development, movement, advance, progress, flow, sequence, succession, continuity, advancement, furtherance, march
4 CLASSES, course of study, programme, schedule, lectures, curriculum, studies
5 RACECOURSE, race, circuit, cinder track, lap
6 PERIOD, time, duration, term, passing, sweep, passage, lapse
▷ *verb* 1 RUN, flow, stream, gush, race, speed, surge, dash, tumble, scud, move apace
2 HUNT, follow, chase, pursue
▷▷ **in due course** IN TIME, finally, eventually, in the end, sooner or later, in the course of time
▷▷ **of course** NATURALLY, certainly, obviously, definitely, undoubtedly, needless to say, without a doubt, indubitably

court *noun* 1 LAW COURT, bar, bench, tribunal, court of justice, seat of judgment
2 PALACE, hall, castle, manor
3 ROYAL HOUSEHOLD, train, suite, attendants, entourage, retinue, cortege
▷ *verb* 1 CULTIVATE, seek, flatter, solicit, pander to, curry favour with, fawn upon
2 INVITE, seek, attract, prompt, provoke, bring about, incite
3 WOO, go (out) with, go steady with (*informal*), date, chase, pursue, take out, make love to, run after, walk out with, keep company with, pay court to, set your cap at, pay your addresses to

courteous *adjective* POLITE, civil, respectful, mannerly, polished, refined, gracious, gallant, affable, urbane, courtly, well-bred, well-mannered
<< OPPOSITE discourteous

courtesan *noun* (*History*) MISTRESS, prostitute, whore, call girl, working girl (*facetious slang*), kept woman, harlot, paramour, scarlet woman, fille de joie (*French*)

courtesy *noun* 1 POLITENESS, grace, good manners, civility, gallantry, good breeding, graciousness, affability, urbanity, courtliness
2 FAVOUR, consideration, generosity, kindness, indulgence, benevolence

courtier *noun* ATTENDANT, follower, squire, train-bearer

courtly *adjective* CEREMONIOUS, civil, formal, obliging, refined, polite, dignified, stately, aristocratic, gallant, affable, urbane, decorous, chivalrous, highbred

courtship *noun* WOOING, courting, suit, romance, engagement, keeping company

courtyard *noun* YARD, square, piazza, quadrangle, area, plaza, enclosure, cloister, quad (*informal*), peristyle

cove *noun* BAY, sound, creek, inlet, bayou, firth *or* frith (*Scot*), anchorage

covenant *noun* 1 PROMISE, contract, agreement, commitment, arrangement, treaty, pledge, bargain, convention, pact, compact, concordat, trust
2 (*Law*) DEED, contract, bond

cover *verb* 1 CONCEAL, cover up, screen, hide, shade, curtain, mask, disguise, obscure, hood, veil, cloak, shroud, camouflage, enshroud
<< OPPOSITE reveal
2 CLOTHE, invest, dress, wrap, envelop
<< OPPOSITE uncover
3 OVERLAY, blanket, eclipse, mantle, canopy,

overspread, layer
4 COAT, cake, plaster, smear, envelop, spread, encase, daub, overspread
5 SUBMERGE, flood, engulf, overrun, wash over
6 TRAVEL OVER, cross, traverse, pass through *or* over, range
7 PROTECT, guard, defend, shelter, shield, watch over
8 INSURE, compensate, provide for, offset, balance, make good, make up for, take account of, counterbalance
9 DEAL WITH, refer to, provide for, take account of, include, involve, contain, embrace, incorporate, comprise, embody, encompass, comprehend
<< OPPOSITE exclude
10 CONSIDER, deal with, examine, investigate, detail, describe, survey, refer to, tell of, recount
11 REPORT ON, write about, commentate on, give an account of, relate, tell of, narrate, write up
12 PAY FOR, fund, provide for, offset, be enough for
▷ *noun* 1 PROTECTION, shelter, shield, refuge, defence, woods, guard, sanctuary, camouflage, hiding place, undergrowth, concealment
2 INSURANCE, payment, protection, compensation, indemnity, reimbursement
3 COVERING, case, top, cap, coating, envelope, lid, canopy, sheath, wrapper, awning
4 BEDCLOTHES, bedding, sheet, blanket, quilt, duvet, eiderdown
5 JACKET, case, binding, wrapper
6 DISGUISE, front, screen, mask, cover-up, veil, cloak, façade, pretence, pretext, window-dressing, smoke screen
▷▷ **cover for someone** STAND IN FOR, take over for, substitute for, relieve, double for, fill in for, hold the fort for (*informal*)
▷▷ **cover something up** CONCEAL, hide, suppress, repress, keep secret, whitewash (*informal*), hush up, sweep under the carpet, draw a veil over, keep silent about, cover your tracks, keep dark, feign ignorance about, keep under your hat (*informal*)

coverage *noun* REPORTING, treatment, analysis, description, reportage

covering *noun* COVER, coating, casing, wrapping, layer, blanket
▷ *adjective* EXPLANATORY, accompanying, introductory, descriptive

covert *adjective* SECRET, private, hidden, disguised, concealed, veiled, sly, clandestine, underhand, unsuspected, surreptitious, stealthy

cover-up *noun* CONCEALMENT, conspiracy, whitewash (*informal*), complicity, front, smoke screen

covet *verb* LONG FOR, desire, fancy (*informal*), envy, crave, aspire to, yearn for, thirst for, begrudge, hanker after, lust after, set your heart on, have your eye on, would give your eyeteeth for

cow *verb* INTIMIDATE, daunt, frighten, scare, bully, dismay, awe, subdue, unnerve, overawe, terrorize, browbeat, psych out (*informal*), dishearten

coward *noun* WIMP, chicken (*slang*), scaredy-cat (*informal*), sneak, pussy (*slang, chiefly US*), yellow-belly (*slang*)

cowardice *noun* FAINT-HEARTEDNESS, weakness, softness, fearfulness, pusillanimity, spinelessness, timorousness

cowardly *adjective* FAINT-HEARTED, scared, spineless, gutless (*informal*), base, soft, yellow (*informal*), weak, chicken (*slang*), shrinking, fearful, craven, abject, dastardly, timorous, weak-kneed (*informal*), pusillanimous, chicken-hearted, lily-livered, white-livered, sookie (*NZ*)
<< OPPOSITE brave

cowboy *noun* COWHAND, drover, herder, rancher, stockman, cattleman, herdsman, gaucho (*S American*), buckaroo (*US*), ranchero (*US*), cowpuncher (*US informal*), broncobuster (*US*), wrangler (*US*)

cower *verb* CRINGE, shrink, tremble, crouch, flinch, quail, draw back, grovel

coy *adjective* 1 MODEST, retiring, shy, shrinking, arch, timid, self-effacing, demure, flirtatious, bashful, prudish, skittish, coquettish, kittenish, overmodest
<< OPPOSITE bold
2 UNCOMMUNICATIVE, mum, secretive, reserved, quiet, silent, evasive, taciturn, unforthcoming, tight-lipped, close-lipped

crack *verb* 1 SPLIT, break, burst, snap, fracture, splinter, craze, rive
2 SNAP, ring, crash, burst, explode, crackle, pop, detonate
3 (*informal*) HIT, clip (*informal*), slap, smack, thump, buffet, clout (*informal*), cuff, whack, wallop (*informal*), chop
4 BREAK, cleave
5 SOLVE, work out, resolve, interpret, clarify, clear up, fathom, decipher, suss (out) (*slang*), get to the bottom of, disentangle, elucidate, get the answer to
6 BREAK DOWN, collapse, yield, give in, give way, succumb, lose control, be overcome, go to pieces
▷ *noun* 1 BREAK, chink, gap, breach, fracture, rift, cleft, crevice, fissure, cranny, interstice
2 SPLIT, break, chip, breach, fracture, rupture, cleft
3 SNAP, pop, crash, burst, explosion, clap, report
4 (*informal*) BLOW, slap, smack, thump, buffet, clout (*informal*), cuff, whack, wallop (*informal*),

clip (*informal*)
5 (*informal*) ATTEMPT, go (*informal*), try, shot, opportunity, stab (*informal*)
6 (*informal*) JOKE, dig, insult, gag (*informal*), quip, jibe, wisecrack, witticism, funny remark, smart-alecky remark
▷ *adjective* (*Slang*) FIRST-CLASS, choice, excellent, ace, elite, superior, world-class, first-rate, hand-picked
▷▷ **crack up** (*informal*) 1 HAVE A BREAKDOWN, collapse, break down, go crazy (*informal*), go berserk, freak out (*informal*), go to pieces, go ape (*slang*), fly off the handle (*informal*), come apart at the seams (*informal*), throw a wobbly (*slang*), go off the deep end (*informal*), go out of your mind, flip your lid (*slang*), go off your rocker (*slang*), go off your head (*slang*)
2 BURST OUT LAUGHING, laugh, fall about (laughing), guffaw, roar with laughter, be in stitches, split your sides

crackdown *noun* CLAMPDOWN, crushing, repression, suppression

cracked *adjective* 1 BROKEN, damaged, split, chipped, flawed, faulty, crazed, defective, imperfect, fissured
2 (*informal*) CRAZY, nuts (*slang*), eccentric, nutty (*slang*), touched, bats (*slang* or *informal*), daft (*informal*), batty (*slang*), insane, loony (*slang*), off-the-wall (*slang*), oddball (*informal*), loopy (*informal*), crackpot (*informal*), out to lunch (*informal*), round the bend (*slang*), out of your mind, gonzo (*slang*), doolally (*slang*), off your trolley (*slang*), off the air (*Austral slang*), round the twist (*Brit slang*), up the pole (*informal*), off your rocker (*slang*), crackbrained, off your head *or* nut (*slang*), wacko *or* whacko (*informal*), porangi (*NZ*), daggy (*Austral & NZ informal*)

cradle *noun* 1 CRIB, cot, Moses basket, bassinet
2 BIRTHPLACE, beginning, source, spring, origin, fount, fountainhead, wellspring
▷ *verb* HOLD, support, rock, nurse, nestle

craft *noun* 1 VESSEL, boat, ship, plane, aircraft, spacecraft, barque
2 OCCUPATION, work, calling, business, line, trade, employment, pursuit, vocation, handiwork, handicraft
3 SKILL, art, ability, technique, know-how (*informal*), expertise, knack, aptitude, artistry, dexterity, workmanship
4 CUNNING, ingenuity, guile, cleverness, scheme, subtlety, deceit, ruse, artifice, trickery, wiles, duplicity, subterfuge, contrivance, shrewdness, artfulness

craftsman *noun* SKILLED WORKER, artisan, master, maker, wright, technician, artificer, smith

craftsmanship *noun* WORKMANSHIP, technique, expertise, mastery, artistry

crafty *adjective* CUNNING, scheming, sly, devious, knowing, designing, sharp, calculating, subtle, tricky, shrewd, astute, fraudulent, canny, wily, insidious, artful, foxy, deceitful, duplicitous, tricksy, guileful
<< OPPOSITE open

crag *noun* ROCK, peak, bluff, pinnacle, tor, aiguille

craggy *adjective* ROCKY, broken, rough, rugged, uneven, jagged, stony, precipitous, jaggy (*Scot*)

cram *verb* 1 STUFF, force, jam, ram, shove, compress, compact
2 PACK, fill, stuff
3 SQUEEZE, press, crowd, pack, crush, pack in, fill to overflowing, overfill, overcrowd
4 STUDY, revise, swot, bone up (*informal*), grind, swot up, mug up (*slang*)

cramp[1] *noun* SPASM, pain, ache, contraction, pang, stiffness, stitch, convulsion, twinge, crick, shooting pain

cramp[2] *verb* RESTRICT, hamper, inhibit, hinder, check, handicap, confine, hamstring, constrain, obstruct, impede, shackle, circumscribe, encumber

cramped *adjective* RESTRICTED, confined, overcrowded, crowded, packed, narrow, squeezed, uncomfortable, awkward, closed in, congested, circumscribed, jammed in, hemmed in
<< OPPOSITE spacious

crank *noun* (*informal*) ECCENTRIC, freak (*informal*), oddball (*informal*), weirdo *or* weirdie (*informal*), case (*informal*), character (*informal*), nut (*slang*), flake (*slang, chiefly US*), screwball (*slang, chiefly US & Canad*), odd fish (*informal*), kook (*US & Canad informal*), queer fish (*Brit informal*), rum customer (*Brit slang*), wacko *or* whacko (*informal*)

cranky *adjective* (*US, Canad & Irish informal*) ECCENTRIC, wacky (*slang*), oddball (*informal*), freakish, odd, strange, funny (*informal*), bizarre, peculiar, queer (*informal*), rum (*Brit slang*), quirky, idiosyncratic, off-the-wall (*slang*), freaky (*slang*), outré, wacko *or* whacko (*informal*), daggy (*Austral & NZ informal*)

cranny *noun* CREVICE, opening, hole, crack, gap, breach, rift, nook, cleft, chink, fissure, interstice

crash *noun* 1 COLLISION, accident, smash, wreck, prang (*informal*), bump, pile-up (*informal*), smash-up
2 SMASH, clash, boom, smashing, bang, thunder, thump, racket, din, clatter, clattering, thud, clang
3 COLLAPSE, failure, depression, ruin, bankruptcy, downfall
▷ *verb* 1 FALL, pitch, plunge, sprawl, topple, lurch, hurtle, come a cropper (*informal*), overbalance, fall headlong
2 PLUNGE, hurtle, precipitate yourself
3 SMASH, break, break up, shatter, fragment,

fracture, shiver, disintegrate, splinter, dash to pieces
4 COLLAPSE, fail, go under, be ruined, go bust (*informal*), fold up, go broke (*informal*), go to the wall, go belly up (*informal*), smash, fold
▷ *adjective* INTENSIVE, concentrated, immediate, urgent, round-the-clock, emergency
▷▷ **crash into** COLLIDE WITH, hit, bump into, bang into, run into, drive into, plough into, hurtle into

crass *adjective* INSENSITIVE, stupid, gross, blundering, dense, coarse, witless, boorish, obtuse, unrefined, asinine, indelicate, oafish, lumpish, doltish
<< OPPOSITE sensitive

crate *noun* CONTAINER, case, box, packing case, tea chest
▷ *verb* BOX, pack, enclose, pack up, encase, case

crater *noun* HOLLOW, hole, depression, dip, cavity, shell hole

crave *verb* 1 LONG FOR, yearn for, hanker after, be dying for, want, need, require, desire, fancy (*informal*), hope for, cry out for (*informal*), thirst for, pine for, lust after, pant for, sigh for, set your heart on, hunger after, eat your heart out over, would give your eyeteeth for
2 BEG, ask for, seek, petition, pray for, plead for, solicit, implore, beseech, entreat, supplicate

craven *adjective* COWARDLY, weak, scared, fearful, abject, dastardly, mean-spirited, timorous, pusillanimous, chicken-hearted, yellow (*informal*), lily-livered

craving *noun* LONGING, hope, desire, urge, yen (*informal*), hunger, appetite, ache, lust, yearning, thirst, hankering

crawl *verb* 1 CREEP, slither, go on all fours, move on hands and knees, inch, drag, wriggle, writhe, move at a snail's pace, worm your way, advance slowly, pull *or* drag yourself along
<< OPPOSITE run
2 GROVEL, creep, cringe, humble yourself, abase yourself
▷▷ **be crawling with something** BE FULL OF, teem with, be alive with, swarm with, be overrun with (*slang*), be lousy with
▷▷ **crawl to someone** FAWN ON, pander to, suck up to (*slang*), toady to, truckle to, lick someone's boots (*slang*)

craze *noun* FAD, thing, fashion, trend, passion, rage, enthusiasm, mode, vogue, novelty, preoccupation, mania, infatuation, the latest thing (*informal*)

crazed *adjective* MAD, crazy, raving, insane, lunatic, demented, unbalanced, deranged, berserk, unhinged, berko (*Austral slang*), off the air (*Austral slang*), porangi (NZ)

crazy *adjective* 1 STRANGE, odd, bizarre, fantastic, silly, weird, ridiculous, outrageous, peculiar, eccentric, rum (*Brit slang*), oddball (*informal*), cockamamie (*slang, chiefly US*), wacko *or* whacko (*informal*), off the air (*Austral slang*), porangi (NZ), daggy (*Austral & NZ informal*)
<< OPPOSITE normal
2 (*informal*) RIDICULOUS, wild, absurd, inappropriate, foolish, ludicrous, irresponsible, unrealistic, unwise, senseless, preposterous, potty (*Brit informal*), short-sighted, unworkable, foolhardy, idiotic, nonsensical, half-baked (*informal*), inane, fatuous, ill-conceived, quixotic, imprudent, impracticable, cockeyed (*informal*), cockamamie (*slang, chiefly US*), porangi (NZ)
<< OPPOSITE sensible
3 INSANE, mad, unbalanced, deranged, touched, cracked (*slang*), mental (*slang*), nuts (*slang*), barking (*slang*), daft (*informal*), batty (*slang*), crazed, lunatic, demented, cuckoo (*informal*), barmy (*slang*), off-the-wall (*slang*), off the air (*Austral slang*), nutty (*slang*), potty (*Brit informal*), berserk, delirious, bonkers (*slang, chiefly Brit*), idiotic, unhinged, loopy (*informal*), crackpot (*informal*), out to lunch (*informal*), round the bend (*slang*), barking mad (*slang*), out of your mind, maniacal, not all there (*informal*), doolally (*slang*), off your head (*slang*), off your trolley (*slang*), round the twist (*Brit slang*), up the pole (*informal*), of unsound mind, not right in the head, off your rocker (*slang*), not the full shilling (*informal*), a bit lacking upstairs (*informal*), as daft as a brush (*informal, chiefly Brit*), mad as a hatter, mad as a March hare, nutty as a fruitcake (*slang*), porangi (NZ)
<< OPPOSITE sane
4 FANATICAL, wild (*informal*), mad, devoted, enthusiastic, passionate, hysterical, ardent, very keen, zealous, smitten, infatuated, enamoured
<< OPPOSITE uninterested ▷ see **mad**

creak *verb* SQUEAK, grind, scrape, groan, grate, screech, squeal, scratch, rasp

creaky *adjective* SQUEAKY, creaking, squeaking, unoiled, grating, rusty, rasping, raspy

cream *noun* 1 LOTION, ointment, oil, essence, cosmetic, paste, emulsion, salve, liniment, unguent
2 BEST, elite, prime, pick, flower, crème de la crème (*French*)
▷ *adjective* OFF-WHITE, ivory, yellowish-white

creamy *adjective* 1 MILKY, buttery
2 SMOOTH, soft, creamed, lush, oily, velvety, rich

crease *noun* 1 FOLD, ruck, line, tuck, ridge, groove, pucker, corrugation
2 WRINKLE, line, crow's-foot
▷ *verb* 1 CRUMPLE, rumple, pucker, crinkle, fold, ridge, double up, crimp, ruck up, corrugate

2 WRINKLE, crumple, screw up

create *verb* 1 CAUSE, lead to, occasion, bring about
2 MAKE, form, produce, develop, design, generate, invent, coin, compose, devise, initiate, hatch, originate, formulate, give birth to, spawn, dream up (*informal*), concoct, beget, give life to, bring into being *or* existence
<< OPPOSITE destroy
3 APPOINT, make, found, establish, set up, invest, install, constitute

creation *noun* 1 UNIVERSE, world, life, nature, cosmos, natural world, living world, all living things
2 INVENTION, production, concept, achievement, brainchild (*informal*), concoction, handiwork, pièce de résistance (*French*), magnum opus, chef-d'oeuvre (*French*)
3 MAKING, generation, formation, conception, genesis
4 SETTING UP, development, production, institution, foundation, constitution, establishment, formation, laying down, inception, origination

creative *adjective* IMAGINATIVE, gifted, artistic, inventive, original, inspired, clever, productive, fertile, ingenious, visionary

creativity *noun* IMAGINATION, talent, inspiration, productivity, fertility, ingenuity, originality, inventiveness, cleverness, fecundity

creator *noun* 1 MAKER, father, author, framer, designer, architect, inventor, originator, initiator, begetter
2 *usually with cap.* GOD, Maker

creature *noun* 1 LIVING THING, being, animal, beast, brute, critter (*US dialect*), quadruped, dumb animal, lower animal
2 PERSON, man, woman, individual, character, fellow, soul, human being, mortal, body
3 MINION, tool, instrument (*informal*), puppet, cohort (*chiefly US*), dependant, retainer, hanger-on, lackey

credence *noun* 1 CREDIBILITY, credit, plausibility, believability
2 BELIEF, trust, confidence, faith, acceptance, assurance, certainty, dependence, reliance

credentials *plural noun* 1 QUALIFICATIONS, ability, skill, capacity, fitness, attribute, capability, endowment(s), accomplishment, eligibility, aptitude, suitability
2 CERTIFICATION, document, reference(s), papers, title, card, licence, recommendation, passport, warrant, voucher, deed, testament, diploma, testimonial, authorization, missive, letters of credence, attestation, letter of recommendation *or* introduction

credibility *noun* BELIEVABILITY, reliability, plausibility, trustworthiness, tenability

credible *adjective* 1 BELIEVABLE, possible, likely, reasonable, probable, plausible, conceivable, imaginable, tenable, verisimilar
<< OPPOSITE unbelievable
2 RELIABLE, honest, dependable, trustworthy, sincere, trusty
<< OPPOSITE unreliable

credit *noun* 1 PRAISE, honour, recognition, glory, thanks, approval, fame, tribute, merit, acclaim, acknowledgment, kudos, commendation, Brownie points
2 SOURCE OF SATISFACTION *or* PRIDE, asset, honour, feather in your cap
3 PRESTIGE, reputation, standing, position, character, influence, regard, status, esteem, clout (*informal*), good name, estimation, repute
4 BELIEF, trust, confidence, faith, reliance, credence
▷ *verb* BELIEVE, rely on, have faith in, trust, buy (*slang*), accept, depend on, swallow (*informal*), fall for, bank on
▷▷ **credit someone with something** ATTRIBUTE TO, assign to, ascribe to, accredit to, impute to, chalk up to (*informal*)
▷▷ **credit something to someone** ATTRIBUTE TO, ascribe to, accredit to, impute to, chalk up to (*informal*)
▷▷ **on credit** ON ACCOUNT, by instalments, on tick (*informal*), on hire-purchase, on the slate (*informal*), by deferred payment, on (the) H.P.

creditable *adjective* PRAISEWORTHY, worthy, respectable, admirable, honourable, exemplary, reputable, commendable, laudable, meritorious, estimable

credulity *noun* GULLIBILITY, naïveté *or* naivety, blind faith, credulousness

creed *noun* BELIEF, principles, profession (*of faith*), doctrine, canon, persuasion, dogma, tenet, credo, catechism, articles of faith

creek *noun* 1 INLET, bay, cove, bight, firth *or* frith (*Scot*)
2 (*US, Canad, Austral & NZ*) STREAM, brook, tributary, bayou, rivulet, watercourse, streamlet, runnel

creep *verb* 1 CRAWL, worm, wriggle, squirm, slither, writhe, drag yourself, edge, inch, crawl on all fours
2 SNEAK, steal, tiptoe, slink, skulk
▷ *noun* (*Slang*) BOOTLICKER (*informal*), sneak, sycophant, crawler (*slang*), toady
▷▷ **give someone the creeps** (*informal*) DISGUST, frighten, scare, repel, repulse, make your hair stand on end, make you squirm

creeper *noun* CLIMBING PLANT, runner, vine (*chiefly US*), climber, rambler, trailing plant

creepy *adjective* (*informal*) DISTURBING, threatening, frightening, terrifying, weird, forbidding, horrible, menacing, unpleasant, scary (*informal*), sinister, ominous, eerie,

macabre, nightmarish, hair-raising, awful
crescent *noun* MENISCUS, sickle, new moon, half-moon, old moon, sickle-shape
crest *noun* 1 TOP, summit, peak, ridge, highest point, pinnacle, apex, head, crown, height
2 TUFT, crown, comb, plume, mane, tassel, topknot, cockscomb
3 EMBLEM, badge, symbol, insignia, charge, bearings, device
crestfallen *adjective* DISAPPOINTED, depressed, discouraged, dejected, despondent, downcast, disheartened, disconsolate, downhearted, sick as a parrot (*informal*), choked
<< OPPOSITE elated
crevice *noun* GAP, opening, hole, split, crack, rent, fracture, rift, slit, cleft, chink, fissure, cranny, interstice
crew *noun* 1 (SHIP'S) COMPANY, hands, (ship's) complement
2 TEAM, company, party, squad, gang, corps, working party, posse
3 (*informal*) CROWD, set, lot, bunch (*informal*), band, troop, pack, camp, gang, mob, herd, swarm, company, horde, posse (*informal*), assemblage
crib *noun* 1 CRADLE, bed, cot, bassinet, Moses basket
2 (*informal*) TRANSLATION, notes, key, trot (*US slang*)
3 MANGER, box, stall, rack, bunker
▷ *verb* (*informal*) COPY, cheat, pirate, pilfer, purloin, plagiarize, pass off as your own work
crick (*informal*) *noun* SPASM, cramp, convulsion, twinge
▷ *verb* RICK, jar, wrench
crime *noun* 1 OFFENCE, job (*informal*), wrong, fault, outrage, atrocity, violation, trespass, felony, misdemeanour, misdeed, transgression, unlawful act
2 LAWBREAKING, corruption, delinquency, illegality, wrong, vice, sin, guilt, misconduct, wrongdoing, wickedness, iniquity, villainy, unrighteousness, malefaction
criminal *noun* LAWBREAKER, convict, con (*slang*), offender, crook (*informal*), lag (*slang*), villain, culprit, sinner, delinquent, felon, con man (*informal*), rorter (*Austral slang*), jailbird, malefactor, evildoer, transgressor, skelm (*S African*), rogue trader
▷ *adjective* 1 UNLAWFUL, illicit, lawless, wrong, illegal, corrupt, crooked (*informal*), vicious, immoral, wicked, culpable, under-the-table, villainous, nefarious, iniquitous, indictable, felonious, bent (*slang*)
<< OPPOSITE lawful
2 (*informal*) DISGRACEFUL, ridiculous, foolish, senseless, scandalous, preposterous, deplorable
criminality *noun* ILLEGALITY, crime, corruption, delinquency, wrongdoing, lawlessness, wickedness, depravity, culpability, villainy, sinfulness, turpitude
cringe *verb* 1 SHRINK, flinch, quail, recoil, start, shy, tremble, quiver, cower, draw back, blench
2 WINCE, squirm, writhe
crinkle *noun* CREASE, wrinkle, crumple, ruffle, twist, fold, curl, rumple, pucker, crimp
cripple *verb* 1 DISABLE, paralyse, lame, debilitate, mutilate, maim, incapacitate, enfeeble, weaken, hamstring
2 DAMAGE, destroy, ruin, bring to a standstill, halt, spoil, cramp, impair, put paid to, vitiate, put out of action
<< OPPOSITE help
crippled *adjective* DISABLED, handicapped, challenged, paralysed, lame, deformed, incapacitated, bedridden, housebound, enfeebled ▷ see **disabled**
crisis *noun* 1 EMERGENCY, plight, catastrophe, predicament, pass, trouble, disaster, mess, dilemma, strait, deep water, meltdown (*informal*), extremity, quandary, dire straits, exigency, critical situation
2 CRITICAL POINT, climax, point of no return, height, confrontation, crunch (*informal*), turning point, culmination, crux, moment of truth, climacteric, tipping point
crisp *adjective* 1 FIRM, crunchy, crispy, crumbly, fresh, brittle, unwilted
<< OPPOSITE soft
2 BRACING, fresh, refreshing, brisk, invigorating
<< OPPOSITE warm
3 CLEAN, smart, trim, neat, tidy, orderly, spruce, snappy, clean-cut, well-groomed, well-pressed
4 BRIEF, clear, short, tart, incisive, terse, succinct, pithy, brusque
criterion *noun* STANDARD, test, rule, measure, principle, proof, par, norm, canon, gauge, yardstick, touchstone, bench mark

> The word *criteria* is the plural of *criterion* and it is incorrect to use it as an alternative singular form; *these criteria are not valid* is correct, and so is *this criterion is not valid*, but not *this criteria is not valid*

critic *noun* 1 JUDGE, authority, expert, analyst, commentator, pundit, reviewer, connoisseur, arbiter, expositor
2 FAULT-FINDER, attacker, detractor, knocker (*informal*)
critical *adjective* 1 CRUCIAL, decisive, momentous, deciding, pressing, serious, vital, psychological, urgent, all-important, pivotal, high-priority, now or never
<< OPPOSITE unimportant
2 GRAVE, serious, dangerous, acute, risky, hairy

(*slang*), precarious, perilous
<< OPPOSITE safe
3 DISPARAGING, disapproving, scathing, derogatory, nit-picking (*informal*), censorious, cavilling, fault-finding, captious, carping, niggling
<< OPPOSITE complimentary
4 ANALYTICAL, penetrating, discriminating, discerning, diagnostic, perceptive, judicious, accurate, precise
<< OPPOSITE undiscriminating

criticism *noun* 1 FAULT-FINDING, censure, disapproval, disparagement, stick (*slang*), knocking (*informal*), panning (*informal*), slamming (*slang*), slating (*informal*), flak (*informal*), slagging (*slang*), strictures, bad press, denigration, brickbats (*informal*), character assassination, critical remarks, animadversion
2 ANALYSIS, review, notice, assessment, judgment, commentary, evaluation, appreciation, appraisal, critique, elucidation

criticize *verb* FIND FAULT WITH, censure, disapprove of, knock (*informal*), blast, pan (*informal*), condemn, slam (*slang*), carp, put down, slate (*informal*), have a go (at) (*informal*), disparage, tear into (*informal*), diss (*slang, chiefly US*), nag at, lambast(e), pick holes in, pick (someone *or* something) to pieces, give (someone *or* something) a bad press, pass strictures upon
<< OPPOSITE praise

critique *noun* ESSAY, review, analysis, assessment, examination, commentary, appraisal, treatise

croak *verb* 1 GRUNT, squawk, caw
2 RASP, gasp, grunt, wheeze, utter *or* speak harshly, utter *or* speak huskily, utter *or* speak throatily
3 (*Slang*) DIE, expire, pass away, perish, buy it (*US slang*), check out (*US slang*), kick it (*slang*), go belly-up (*slang*), peg out (*informal*), kick the bucket (*informal*), buy the farm (*US slang*), peg it (*informal*), cark it (*Austral & NZ slang*), pop your clogs (*informal*), hop the twig (*informal*)

crone *noun* OLD WOMAN, witch, hag, old bag (*derogatory slang*), old bat (*slang*), kuia (*NZ*)

crony *noun* FRIEND, china (*Brit slang*), colleague, associate, mate (*informal*), pal (*informal*), companion, cock (*Brit informal*), buddy (*informal*), comrade, chum (*informal*), accomplice, ally, sidekick (*slang*), main man (*slang, chiefly US*), homeboy (*slang, chiefly US*), cobber (*Austral & NZ old-fashioned informal*)

crook *noun* (*informal*) CRIMINAL, rogue, cheat, thief, shark, lag (*slang*), villain, robber, racketeer, fraudster, swindler, knave (*archaic*), grifter (*slang, chiefly US & Canad*), chiseller (*informal*), skelm (*S African*)
▷ *verb* BEND, hook, angle, bow, curve, curl, cock, flex
▷ *adjective* (*Austral & NZ informal*) ILL, sick, poorly (*informal*), funny (*informal*), weak, ailing, queer, frail, feeble, unhealthy, seedy (*informal*), sickly, unwell, laid up (*informal*), queasy, infirm, out of sorts (*informal*), dicky (*Brit informal*), nauseous, off-colour, under the weather (*informal*), at death's door, indisposed, peaky, on the sick list (*informal*), green about the gills
▷▷ **go (off) crook** (*Austral & NZ informal*) LOSE YOUR TEMPER, be furious, rage, go mad, lose it (*informal*), seethe, crack up (*informal*), see red (*informal*), lose the plot (*informal*), go ballistic (*slang, chiefly US*), blow a fuse (*slang, chiefly US*), fly off the handle (*informal*), be incandescent, go off the deep end (*informal*), throw a fit (*informal*), wig out (*slang*), go up the wall (*slang*), blow your top, lose your rag (*slang*), be beside yourself, flip your lid (*slang*)

crooked *adjective* 1 BENT, twisted, bowed, curved, irregular, warped, deviating, out of shape, misshapen
<< OPPOSITE straight
2 DEFORMED, crippled, distorted, disfigured
3 AT AN ANGLE, angled, tilted, to one side, uneven, slanted, slanting, squint, awry, lopsided, askew, asymmetric, off-centre, skewwhiff (*Brit informal*), unsymmetrical
4 (*informal*) DISHONEST, criminal, illegal, corrupt, dubious, questionable, unlawful, shady (*informal*), fraudulent, unscrupulous, under-the-table, bent (*slang*), shifty, deceitful, underhand, unprincipled, dishonourable, nefarious, knavish
<< OPPOSITE honest

croon *verb* 1 SING, warble
2 SAY SOFTLY, breathe, hum, purr

crop *noun* YIELD, produce, gathering, fruits, harvest, vintage, reaping, season's growth
▷ *verb* 1 HARVEST, pick, collect, gather, bring in, reap, bring home, garner, mow
2 GRAZE, eat, browse, feed on, nibble
3 CUT, reduce, trim, clip, dock, prune, shorten, shear, snip, pare, lop
▷▷ **crop up** (*informal*) HAPPEN, appear, emerge, occur, arise, turn up, spring up

cross *verb* 1 GO ACROSS, pass over, traverse, cut across, move across, travel across
2 SPAN, bridge, ford, go across, extend over
3 INTERSECT, meet, intertwine, crisscross
4 OPPOSE, interfere with, hinder, obstruct, deny, block, resist, frustrate, foil, thwart, impede
5 INTERBREED, mix, blend, cross-pollinate, crossbreed, hybridize, cross-fertilize, intercross
▷ *noun* 1 CRUCIFIX
2 TROUBLE, worry, trial, load, burden,

grief, misery, woe, misfortune, affliction, tribulation
3 MIXTURE, combination, blend, amalgam, amalgamation
4 CROSSBREED, hybrid
▷ *adjective* ANGRY, impatient, irritable, annoyed, put out, hacked (off) (*informal*), crusty, snappy, grumpy, vexed, sullen, surly, fractious, petulant, disagreeable, short, churlish, peeved (*informal*), ill-tempered, irascible, cantankerous, tetchy, ratty (*Brit & NZ informal*), tooshie (*Austral slang*), testy, fretful, waspish, in a bad mood, grouchy (*informal*), querulous, shirty (*slang, chiefly Brit*), peevish, splenetic, crotchety (*informal*), snappish, ill-humoured, captious, pettish, out of humour, hoha (NZ)
<< OPPOSITE good-humoured
▷▷ **cross something out** *or* **off** STRIKE OFF *or* OUT, eliminate, cancel, delete, blue-pencil, score off *or* out

cross-examine *verb* QUESTION, grill (*informal*), quiz, interrogate, catechize, pump

crotch *noun* GROIN, lap, crutch

crouch *verb* BEND DOWN, kneel, squat, stoop, bow, duck, hunch

crow *verb* GLOAT, triumph, boast, swagger, brag, vaunt, bluster, exult, blow your own trumpet

crowd *noun* 1 MULTITUDE, mass, assembly, throng, company, press, army, host, pack, mob, flock, herd, swarm, horde, rabble, concourse, bevy
2 GROUP, set, lot, circle, gang, bunch (*informal*), clique
3 AUDIENCE, spectators, house, gate, attendance
▷ *verb* 1 FLOCK, press, push, mass, collect, gather, stream, surge, cluster, muster, huddle, swarm, throng, congregate, foregather
2 SQUEEZE, pack, pile, bundle, cram
3 CONGEST, pack, cram
4 (*informal*) JOSTLE, batter, butt, push, elbow, shove
▷▷ **the crowd** THE MASSES, the people, the public, the mob, the rank and file, the populace, the rabble, the proletariat, the hoi polloi, the riffraff, the vulgar herd

crowded *adjective* PACKED, full, busy, mobbed, cramped, swarming, overflowing, thronged, teeming, congested, populous, jam-packed, crushed

crown *noun* 1 CORONET, tiara, diadem, circlet, coronal (*poetic*), chaplet
2 LAUREL WREATH, trophy, distinction, prize, honour, garland, laurels, wreath, kudos
3 HIGH POINT, head, top, tip, summit, crest, pinnacle, apex
▷ *verb* 1 INSTALL, invest, honour, dignify, ordain, inaugurate
2 TOP, cap, be on top of, surmount
3 CAP, finish, complete, perfect, fulfil, consummate, round off, put the finishing touch to, put the tin lid on, be the climax *or* culmination of
4 (*Slang*) STRIKE, belt (*informal*), bash, hit over the head, box, punch, cuff, biff (*slang*), wallop
▷▷ **the Crown** 1 MONARCH, ruler, sovereign, rex (*Latin*), emperor *or* empress, king *or* queen
2 MONARCHY, sovereignty, royalty

crucial *adjective* 1 (*informal*) VITAL, important, pressing, essential, urgent, momentous, high-priority
2 CRITICAL, central, key, psychological, decisive, pivotal, now or never

crucify *verb* 1 EXECUTE, put to death, nail to a cross
2 (*Slang*) PAN (*informal*), rubbish (*informal*), ridicule, slag (off) (*slang*), lampoon, wipe the floor with (*informal*), tear to pieces
3 TORTURE, rack, torment, harrow

crude *adjective* 1 ROUGH, undeveloped, basic, outline, unfinished, makeshift, sketchy, unformed
2 SIMPLE, rudimentary, basic, primitive, coarse, clumsy, rough-and-ready, rough-hewn
3 VULGAR, dirty, rude, obscene, coarse, indecent, crass, tasteless, lewd, X-rated (*informal*), boorish, smutty, uncouth, gross
<< OPPOSITE tasteful
4 UNREFINED, natural, raw, unprocessed, unpolished, unprepared
<< OPPOSITE processed

crudely *adverb* 1 ROUGHLY, basically, sketchily
2 SIMPLY, roughly, basically, coarsely, clumsily
3 VULGARLY, rudely, coarsely, crassly, indecently, obscenely, lewdly, impolitely, tastelessly

cruel *adjective* 1 BRUTAL, ruthless, callous, sadistic, inhumane, hard, fell (*archaic*), severe, harsh, savage, grim, vicious, relentless, murderous, monstrous, unnatural, unkind, heartless, atrocious, inhuman, merciless, cold-blooded, malevolent, hellish, depraved, spiteful, brutish, bloodthirsty, remorseless, barbarous, pitiless, unfeeling, hard-hearted, stony-hearted
<< OPPOSITE kind
2 BITTER, severe, painful, ruthless, traumatic, grievous, unrelenting, merciless, pitiless

cruelly *adverb* 1 BRUTALLY, severely, savagely, viciously, mercilessly, in cold blood, callously, monstrously, unmercifully, sadistically, pitilessly, spitefully, heartlessly, barbarously
2 BITTERLY, deeply, severely, mortally, painfully, ruthlessly, mercilessly, grievously, pitilessly, traumatically

cruelty *noun* BRUTALITY, spite, severity, savagery, ruthlessness, sadism, depravity, harshness, inhumanity, barbarity, callousness, viciousness, bestiality, heartlessness, spitefulness, bloodthirstiness, mercilessness, fiendishness, hardheartedness

cruise *noun* SAIL, voyage, boat trip, sea trip
▷ *verb* 1 SAIL, coast, voyage
2 TRAVEL ALONG, coast, drift, keep a steady pace

crumb *noun* 1 BIT, grain, particle, fragment, shred, speck, sliver, morsel
2 MORSEL, scrap, atom, shred, mite, snippet, sliver, soupçon (*French*)

crumble *verb* 1 DISINTEGRATE, collapse, break up, deteriorate, decay, fall apart, perish, degenerate, decompose, tumble down, moulder, go to pieces
2 CRUSH, fragment, crumb, pulverize, pound, grind, powder, granulate
3 COLLAPSE, break down, deteriorate, decay, fall apart, degenerate, go to pieces, go to wrack and ruin

crummy *adjective* (*Slang*) SECOND-RATE, cheap, inferior, substandard, poor, pants (*informal*), miserable, rotten (*informal*), duff (*Brit informal*), lousy (*slang*), shoddy, trashy, low-rent (*informal, chiefly US*), for the birds (*informal*), third-rate, contemptible, two-bit (*US & Canad slang*), crappy (*slang*), rubbishy, poxy (*slang*), dime-a-dozen (*informal*), bodger *or* bodgie (*Austral slang*), bush-league (*Austral & NZ informal*), tinhorn (*US slang*), of a sort *or* of sorts, strictly for the birds (*informal*)

crumple *verb* 1 CRUSH, squash, screw up, scrumple
2 CREASE, wrinkle, rumple, ruffle, pucker
3 COLLAPSE, sink, go down, fall
4 BREAK DOWN, fall, collapse, give way, cave in, go to pieces
5 SCREW UP, pucker

crunch *verb* CHOMP, champ, munch, masticate, chew noisily, grind
▷▷ **the crunch** (*informal*) CRITICAL POINT, test, crisis, emergency, crux, moment of truth, hour of decision

crusade *noun* 1 CAMPAIGN, drive, movement, cause, push
2 HOLY WAR, jihad
▷ *verb* CAMPAIGN, fight, push, struggle, lobby, agitate, work

crusader *noun* CAMPAIGNER, champion, advocate, activist, reformer

crush *verb* 1 SQUASH, pound, break, smash, squeeze, crumble, crunch, mash, compress, press, crumple, pulverize
2 CREASE, wrinkle, crumple, rumple, scrumple, ruffle
3 OVERCOME, overwhelm, put down, subdue, overpower, quash, quell, extinguish, stamp out, vanquish, conquer
4 DEMORALIZE, depress, devastate, discourage, humble, put down (*slang*), humiliate, squash, flatten, deflate, mortify, psych out (*informal*), dishearten, dispirit, deject
5 SQUEEZE, press, embrace, hug, enfold
▷ *noun* CROWD, mob, horde, throng, press, pack, mass, jam, herd, huddle, swarm, multitude, rabble

crust *noun* LAYER, covering, coating, incrustation, film, outside, skin, surface, shell, coat, caking, scab, concretion

crusty *adjective* 1 CRISPY, well-baked, crisp, well-done, brittle, friable, hard, short
2 IRRITABLE, short, cross, prickly, touchy, curt, surly, gruff, brusque, cantankerous, tetchy, ratty (*Brit & NZ informal*), testy, chippy (*informal*), short-tempered, peevish, crabby, choleric, splenetic, ill-humoured, captious, snappish *or* snappy

crux *noun* CRUCIAL POINT, heart, core, essence, nub, decisive point

cry *verb* 1 WEEP, sob, bawl, shed tears, keen, greet (*Scot archaic*), wail, whine, whimper, whinge (*informal*), blubber, snivel, yowl, howl your eyes out
<< OPPOSITE laugh
2 SHOUT, call, scream, roar, hail, yell, howl, call out, exclaim, shriek, bellow, whoop, screech, bawl, holler (*informal*), ejaculate, sing out, halloo, vociferate
<< OPPOSITE whisper
3 ANNOUNCE, hawk, advertise, proclaim, bark (*informal*), trumpet, shout from the rooftops (*informal*)
▷ *noun* 1 WEEP, greet (*Scot archaic*), sob, howl, bawl, blubber, snivel
2 SHOUT, call, scream, roar, yell, howl, shriek, bellow, whoop, screech, hoot, ejaculation, bawl, holler (*informal*), exclamation, squawk, yelp, yoo-hoo
3 WEEPING, sobbing, blubbering, snivelling
▷▷ **cry off** (*informal*) BACK OUT, withdraw, quit, cop out (*slang*), beg off, excuse yourself

crypt *noun* VAULT, tomb, catacomb

cryptic *adjective* MYSTERIOUS, dark, coded, puzzling, obscure, vague, veiled, ambiguous, enigmatic, perplexing, arcane, equivocal, abstruse, Delphic, oracular

crystallize *verb* HARDEN, solidify, coalesce, form crystals

cub *noun* YOUNG, baby, offspring, whelp
>> RELATED WORD *collective noun* litter

cuddle *verb* 1 HUG, embrace, clasp, fondle, cosset
2 PET, hug, canoodle (*slang*), bill and coo
▷▷ **cuddle up** SNUGGLE, nestle

cuddly *adjective* SOFT, plump, buxom, curvaceous, warm

cue *noun* SIGNAL, sign, nod, hint, prompt, reminder, suggestion

cuff[1] *noun* ▷▷ **off the cuff** (*informal*) 1

IMPROMPTU, spontaneous, improvised, offhand, unrehearsed, extempore
2 WITHOUT PREPARATION, spontaneously, impromptu, offhand, on the spur of the moment, ad lib, extempore, off the top of your head

cuff² *noun* SMACK, blow, knock, punch, thump, box, belt (*informal*), rap, slap, clout (*informal*), whack, biff (*slang*)

cul-de-sac *noun* DEAD END, blind alley

cull *verb* SELECT, collect, gather, amass, choose, pick, pick up, pluck, glean, cherry-pick

culminate *verb* END UP, end, close, finish, conclude, wind up, climax, terminate, come to a head, come to a climax, rise to a crescendo

culmination *noun* CLIMAX, conclusion, completion, finale, consummation

culpability *noun* FAULT, blame, responsibility, liability, accountability

culpable *adjective* BLAMEWORTHY, wrong, guilty, to blame, liable, in the wrong, at fault, sinful, answerable, found wanting, reprehensible
<< OPPOSITE blameless

culprit *noun* OFFENDER, criminal, villain, sinner, delinquent, felon, person responsible, guilty party, wrongdoer, miscreant, evildoer, transgressor

cult *noun* 1 SECT, following, body, faction, party, school, church, faith, religion, denomination, clique, hauhau (NZ)
2 CRAZE, fashion, trend, fad
3 OBSESSION, worship, admiration, devotion, reverence, veneration, idolization

cultivate *verb* 1 FARM, work, plant, tend, till, harvest, plough, bring under cultivation
2 DEVELOP, establish, acquire, foster, devote yourself to, pursue
3 COURT, associate with, seek out, run after, consort with, butter up, dance attendance upon, seek someone's company *or* friendship, take trouble *or* pains with
4 FOSTER, further, forward, encourage
5 IMPROVE, better, train, discipline, polish, refine, elevate, enrich, civilize

cultivated *adjective* REFINED, cultured, advanced, polished, educated, sophisticated, accomplished, discriminating, enlightened, discerning, civilized, genteel, well-educated, urbane, erudite, well-bred

cultivation *noun* 1 FARMING, working, gardening, tilling, ploughing, husbandry, agronomy
2 GROWING, planting, production, farming
3 DEVELOPMENT, fostering, pursuit, devotion to
4 PROMOTION, support, encouragement, nurture, patronage, advancement, advocacy, enhancement, furtherance
5 REFINEMENT, letters, learning, education, culture, taste, breeding, manners, polish, discrimination, civilization, enlightenment, sophistication, good taste, civility, gentility, discernment

cultural *adjective* 1 ETHNIC, national, native, folk, racial
2 ARTISTIC, educational, elevating, aesthetic, enriching, broadening, enlightening, developmental, civilizing, edifying, educative

culture *noun* 1 THE ARTS
2 CIVILIZATION, society, customs, way of life
3 LIFESTYLE, habit, way of life, mores
4 REFINEMENT, education, breeding, polish, enlightenment, accomplishment, sophistication, good taste, erudition, gentility, urbanity

cultured *adjective* REFINED, advanced, polished, intellectual, educated, sophisticated, accomplished, scholarly, enlightened, knowledgeable, well-informed, genteel, urbane, erudite, highbrow, well-bred, well-read
<< OPPOSITE uneducated

culvert *noun* DRAIN, channel, gutter, conduit, watercourse

cumbersome *adjective* 1 AWKWARD, heavy, hefty (*informal*), clumsy, bulky, weighty, impractical, inconvenient, burdensome, unmanageable, clunky (*informal*)
<< OPPOSITE easy to use
2 INEFFICIENT, unwieldy, badly organized
<< OPPOSITE efficient

cumulative *adjective* COLLECTIVE, increasing, aggregate, amassed, accruing, snowballing, accumulative

cunning *adjective* 1 CRAFTY, sly, devious, artful, sharp, subtle, tricky, shrewd, astute, canny, wily, Machiavellian, shifty, foxy, guileful
<< OPPOSITE frank
2 INGENIOUS, subtle, imaginative, shrewd, sly, astute, devious, artful, Machiavellian
3 SKILFUL, clever, deft, adroit, dexterous
<< OPPOSITE clumsy
▷ *noun* 1 CRAFTINESS, guile, trickery, shrewdness, deviousness, artfulness, slyness, wiliness
<< OPPOSITE candour
2 SKILL, art, ability, craft, subtlety, ingenuity, finesse, artifice, dexterity, cleverness, deftness, astuteness, adroitness
<< OPPOSITE clumsiness

cup *noun* 1 MUG, goblet, chalice, teacup, beaker, demitasse, bowl
2 TROPHY

cupboard *noun* CABINET, closet, locker, press

curative *adjective* RESTORATIVE, healing, therapeutic, tonic, corrective, medicinal, remedial, salutary, healthful, health-giving

curb *verb* RESTRAIN, control, check, contain,

restrict, moderate, suppress, inhibit, subdue, hinder, repress, constrain, retard, impede, stem the flow of, keep a tight rein on
▷ *noun* RESTRAINT, control, check, brake, limitation, rein, deterrent, bridle

curdle *verb* CONGEAL, clot, thicken, condense, turn sour, solidify, coagulate
<< OPPOSITE dissolve

cure *verb* **1** MAKE BETTER, correct, heal, relieve, remedy, mend, rehabilitate, help, ease
2 RESTORE TO HEALTH, restore, heal
3 PRESERVE, smoke, dry, salt, pickle, kipper
▷ *noun* REMEDY, treatment, medicine, healing, antidote, corrective, panacea, restorative, nostrum

cure-all *noun* PANACEA, elixir, nostrum, elixir vitae (*Latin*)

curio *noun* COLLECTOR'S ITEM, antique, trinket, knick-knack, bibelot

curiosity *noun* **1** INQUISITIVENESS, interest, prying, snooping (*informal*), nosiness (*informal*)
2 ODDITY, wonder, sight, phenomenon, spectacle, freak, marvel, novelty, rarity
3 COLLECTOR'S ITEM, trinket, curio, knick-knack, objet d'art (*French*), bibelot

curious *adjective* **1** INQUISITIVE, interested, questioning, searching, inquiring, peering, puzzled, peeping, meddling, prying, snoopy (*informal*), nosy (*informal*)
<< OPPOSITE uninterested
2 STRANGE, unusual, bizarre, odd, novel, wonderful, rare, unique, extraordinary, puzzling, unexpected, exotic, mysterious, marvellous, peculiar, queer (*informal*), rum (*Brit slang*), singular, unconventional, quaint, unorthodox
<< OPPOSITE ordinary

curl *noun* **1** RINGLET, lock
2 TWIST, spiral, coil, kink, whorl, curlicue
▷ *verb* **1** CRIMP, wave, perm, frizz
2 TWIRL, turn, bend, twist, curve, loop, spiral, coil, meander, writhe, corkscrew, wreathe
3 WIND, entwine, twine

curly *adjective* WAVY, waved, curled, curling, fuzzy, kinky, permed, corkscrew, crimped, frizzy

currency *noun* **1** MONEY, coinage, legal tender, medium of exchange, bills, notes, coins
2 ACCEPTANCE, exposure, popularity, circulation, vogue, prevalence

current *noun* **1** FLOW, course, undertow, jet, stream, tide, progression, river, tideway
2 DRAUGHT, flow, breeze, puff
3 MOOD, feeling, spirit, atmosphere, trend, tendency, drift, inclination, vibe (*slang*), undercurrent
▷ *adjective* **1** PRESENT, fashionable, ongoing, up-to-date, in, now (*informal*), happening (*informal*), contemporary, in the news, sexy (*informal*), trendy (*Brit informal*), topical, present-day, in fashion, in vogue, up-to-the-minute
<< OPPOSITE out-of-date
2 PREVALENT, general, common, accepted, popular, widespread, in the air, prevailing, circulating, going around, customary, rife, in circulation

curse *verb* **1** SWEAR, cuss (*informal*), blaspheme, use bad language, turn the air blue (*informal*), be foul-mouthed, take the Lord's name in vain
2 ABUSE, damn, scold, swear at, revile, vilify, fulminate, execrate, vituperate, imprecate
3 PUT A CURSE ON, damn, doom, jinx, excommunicate, execrate, put a jinx on, accurse, imprecate, anathematize
4 AFFLICT, trouble, burden
▷ *noun* **1** OATH, obscenity, blasphemy, expletive, profanity, imprecation, swearword
2 MALEDICTION, jinx, anathema, hoodoo (*informal*), evil eye, excommunication, imprecation, execration
3 AFFLICTION, evil, plague, scourge, cross, trouble, disaster, burden, ordeal, torment, hardship, misfortune, calamity, tribulation, bane, vexation

cursed *adjective* UNDER A CURSE, damned, doomed, jinxed, bedevilled, fey (*Scot*), star-crossed, accursed, ill-fated

cursory *adjective* BRIEF, passing, rapid, casual, summary, slight, hurried, careless, superficial, hasty, perfunctory, desultory, offhand, slapdash

curt *adjective* TERSE, short, brief, sharp, summary, blunt, rude, tart, abrupt, gruff, brusque, offhand, ungracious, uncivil, unceremonious, snappish

curtail *verb* REDUCE, cut, diminish, decrease, dock, cut back, shorten, lessen, cut short, pare down, retrench

curtain *noun* HANGING, drape (*chiefly US*), portière
▷▷ **curtain something off** CONCEAL, screen, hide, veil, drape, shroud, shut off

curvaceous *adjective* (*informal*) SHAPELY, voluptuous, curvy, busty, well-rounded, buxom, full-figures, bosomy, well-stacked (*Brit slang*), Rubenesque

curvature *noun* CURVING, bend, curve, arching, arc

curve *noun* BEND, turn, loop, arc, curvature, camber
▷ *verb* BEND, turn, wind, twist, bow, arch, snake, arc, coil, swerve
>> RELATED WORD *adjective* sinuous

curved *adjective* BENT, rounded, sweeping, twisted, bowed, arched, arced, humped, serpentine, sinuous, twisty

cushion *noun* PILLOW, pad, bolster, headrest, beanbag, scatter cushion, hassock

▷ *verb* 1 PROTECT, support, bolster, cradle, buttress
2 SOFTEN, dampen, muffle, mitigate, deaden, suppress, stifle

cushy *adjective* (*informal*) EASY, soft, comfortable, undemanding, jammy (*Brit slang*)

custodian *noun* KEEPER, guardian, superintendent, warden, caretaker, curator, protector, warder, watchman, overseer

custody *noun* 1 CARE, charge, protection, supervision, preservation, auspices, aegis, tutelage, guardianship, safekeeping, keeping, trusteeship, custodianship
2 IMPRISONMENT, detention, confinement, incarceration

custom *noun* 1 TRADITION, practice, convention, ritual, form, policy, rule, style, fashion, usage, formality, etiquette, observance, praxis, unwritten law, kaupapa (*NZ*)
2 HABIT, way, practice, manner, procedure, routine, mode, wont
3 CUSTOMERS, business, trade, patronage

customarily *adverb* USUALLY, generally, commonly, regularly, normally, traditionally, ordinarily, habitually, in the ordinary way, as a rule

customary *adjective* 1 USUAL, general, common, accepted, established, traditional, normal, ordinary, familiar, acknowledged, conventional, routine, everyday
<< OPPOSITE unusual
2 ACCUSTOMED, regular, usual, habitual, wonted

customer *noun* CLIENT, consumer, regular (*informal*), buyer, patron, shopper, purchaser, habitué

customs *plural noun* IMPORT CHARGES, tax, duty, toll, tariff

cut *verb* 1 SLIT, saw, score, nick, slice, slash, pierce, hack, penetrate, notch
2 CHOP, split, divide, slice, segment, dissect, cleave, part
3 CARVE, slice
4 SEVER, cut in two, sunder
5 SHAPE, carve, engrave, chisel, form, score, fashion, chip, sculpture, whittle, sculpt, inscribe, hew
6 SLASH, nick, wound, lance, gash, lacerate, incise
7 CLIP, mow, trim, dock, prune, snip, pare, lop
8 TRIM, shave, hack, snip
9 REDUCE, lower, slim (down), diminish, slash, decrease, cut back, rationalize, ease up on, downsize, kennet (*Austral slang*), jeff (*Austral slang*)
<< OPPOSITE increase
10 ABRIDGE, edit, shorten, curtail, condense, abbreviate, précis
<< OPPOSITE extend
11 DELETE, take out, expurgate
12 HURT, wound, upset, sting, grieve, pain, hurt someone's feelings
13 (*informal*) IGNORE, avoid, slight, blank (*slang*), snub, spurn, freeze (someone) out (*informal*), cold-shoulder, turn your back on, send to Coventry, look straight through (someone)
<< OPPOSITE greet
14 CROSS, interrupt, intersect, bisect
▷ *noun* 1 INCISION, nick, rent, stroke, rip, slash, groove, slit, snip
2 GASH, nick, wound, slash, graze, laceration
3 REDUCTION, fall, lowering, slash, decrease, cutback, diminution
4 (*informal*) SHARE, piece, slice, percentage, portion, kickback (*chiefly US*), rake-off (*slang*)
5 STYLE, look, form, fashion, shape, mode, configuration

▷▷ **a cut above something** *or* **someone** (*informal*) SUPERIOR TO, better than, more efficient than, more reliable than, streets ahead of, more useful than, more capable than, more competent than

▷▷ **be cut out for something** BE SUITED FOR, be designed for, be fitted for, be suitable for, be adapted for, be equipped for, be adequate for, be eligible for, be competent for, be qualified for

▷▷ **cut in** INTERRUPT, break in, butt in, interpose

▷▷ **cut someone down to size** MAKE (SOMEONE) LOOK SMALL, humble, humiliate, bring (someone) low, take (someone) down a peg (*informal*), abash, crush, put (someone) in their place, take the wind out of (someone's) sails

▷▷ **cut someone off** 1 SEPARATE, isolate, sever, keep apart
2 INTERRUPT, stop, break in, butt in, interpose
3 DISINHERIT, renounce, disown

▷▷ **cut someone out** (*informal*) EXCLUDE, eliminate, oust, displace, supersede, supplant

▷▷ **cut someone up** SLASH, injure, wound, knife, lacerate

▷▷ **cut something back** 1 REDUCE, check, lower, slash, decrease, curb, lessen, economize, downsize, retrench, draw *or* pull in your horns (*informal*), kennet (*Austral slang*), jeff (*Austral slang*)
2 TRIM, prune, shorten

▷▷ **cut something down** 1 REDUCE, moderate, decrease, lessen, lower
2 FELL, level, hew, lop

▷▷ **cut something off** DISCONTINUE, disconnect, suspend, halt, obstruct, bring to an end

▷▷ **cut something out** 1 REMOVE, extract, censor, delete, edit out
2 STOP, cease, refrain from, pack in, kick

(*informal*), give up, sever

▷▷ **be cut up** BE UPSET, be disturbed, be distressed, be stricken, be agitated, be heartbroken, be desolated, be dejected, be wretched

▷▷ **cut something up** CHOP, divide, slice, carve, dice, mince

cutback *noun* REDUCTION, cut, retrenchment, economy, decrease, lessening

cute *adjective* APPEALING, sweet, attractive, engaging, charming, delightful, lovable, winsome, winning, cutesy (*informal, chiefly US*)

cut-price *adjective* CHEAP, sale, reduced, bargain, cut-rate (*chiefly US*), cheapo (*informal*)

cut-throat *adjective* **1** COMPETITIVE, fierce, ruthless, relentless, unprincipled, dog-eat-dog
2 MURDEROUS, violent, bloody, cruel, savage, ferocious, bloodthirsty, barbarous, homicidal, thuggish, death-dealing

cutting *adjective* **1** HURTFUL, wounding, severe, acid, bitter, malicious, scathing, acrimonious, barbed, sarcastic, sardonic, caustic, vitriolic, trenchant, pointed
<< OPPOSITE kind
2 PIERCING, biting, sharp, keen, bitter, raw, chilling, stinging, penetrating, numbing
<< OPPOSITE pleasant

cycle *noun* SERIES OF EVENTS, round (*of years*), circle, revolution, rotation

cyclone *noun* TYPHOON, hurricane, tornado, whirlwind, tempest, twister (*US informal*), storm

cynic *noun* SCEPTIC, doubter, pessimist, misanthrope, misanthropist, scoffer

cynical *adjective* **1** SCEPTICAL, mocking, ironic, sneering, pessimistic, scoffing, contemptuous, sarcastic, sardonic, scornful, distrustful, derisive, misanthropic
<< OPPOSITE trusting
2 UNBELIEVING, sceptical, disillusioned, pessimistic, disbelieving, mistrustful
<< OPPOSITE optimistic

cynicism *noun* **1** SCEPTICISM, pessimism, sarcasm, misanthropy, sardonicism
2 DISBELIEF, doubt, scepticism, mistrust

cyst *noun* SAC, growth, blister, wen, vesicle

Dd

dab *verb* 1 PAT, touch, tap, wipe, blot, swab
2 APPLY, daub, stipple
▷ *noun* 1 SPOT, bit, drop, pat, fleck, smudge, speck, dollop (*informal*), smidgen *or* smidgin (*informal, chiefly US & Canad*)
2 TOUCH, stroke, flick, smudge

dabble *verb usually with* **in** *or* **with** PLAY (AT *or* WITH), potter, tinker (with), trifle (with), dip into, dally (with)

daft *adjective* (*informal, chiefly Brit*) 1 STUPID, simple, crazy, silly, absurd, foolish, giddy, goofy, idiotic, inane, loopy (*informal*), witless, crackpot (*informal*), out to lunch (*informal*), dopey (*informal*), scatty (*Brit informal*), asinine, gonzo (*slang*), doolally (*slang*), off your head (*informal*), off your trolley (*slang*), up the pole (*informal*), dumb-ass (*slang*), wacko *or* whacko (*slang*), off the air (*Austral slang*)
2 CRAZY, mad, mental (*slang*), touched, nuts (*slang*), barking (*slang*), crackers (*Brit slang*), insane, lunatic, demented, nutty (*slang*), deranged, unhinged, round the bend (*Brit slang*), barking mad (*slang*), not right in the head, not the full shilling (*informal*), off the air (*Austral slang*), porangi (NZ)
▷▷ **daft about** ENTHUSIASTIC ABOUT, mad about, crazy about (*informal*), doting on, besotted with, sweet on, nuts about (*slang*), potty about (*Brit informal*), infatuated by, dotty about (*slang, chiefly Brit*), nutty about (*informal*)

dag *noun* (*NZ informal*) JOKER, comic, wag, wit, comedian, clown, kidder (*informal*), jester, humorist, prankster
▷▷ **rattle your dags** (*NZ informal*) HURRY UP, get a move on, step on it (*informal*), get your skates on (*informal*), make haste

dagga *noun* (*S African*) CANNABIS, marijuana, pot (*slang*), dope (*slang*), hash (*slang*), black (*slang*), blow (*slang*), smoke (*informal*), stuff (*slang*), leaf (*slang*), tea (*US slang*), grass (*slang*), chronic (*US slang*), weed (*slang*), hemp, gage (*US dated slang*), hashish, mary jane (*US slang*), ganja, bhang, kif, wacky baccy (*slang*), sinsemilla, charas

dagger *noun* KNIFE, bayonet, dirk, stiletto, poniard, skean
▷▷ **at daggers drawn** ON BAD TERMS, at odds, at war, at loggerheads, up in arms, at enmity
▷▷ **look daggers at someone** GLARE, frown, scowl, glower, look black, lour *or* lower

daggy *adjective* (*Austral & NZ informal*) 1 UNTIDY, unkempt, dishevelled, tousled, disordered, messy, ruffled, scruffy, rumpled, bedraggled, ratty (*informal*), straggly, windblown, disarranged, mussed up (*informal*)
2 ECCENTRIC, odd, strange, bizarre, weird, peculiar, abnormal, queer (*informal*), irregular, uncommon, quirky, singular, unconventional, idiosyncratic, off-the-wall (*slang*), outlandish, whimsical, rum (*Brit slang*), capricious, anomalous, freakish, aberrant, wacko (*slang*), outré

daily *adjective* 1 EVERYDAY, regular, circadian (*Biology*), diurnal, quotidian
2 DAY-TO-DAY, common, ordinary, routine, everyday, commonplace, quotidian
▷ *adverb* EVERY DAY, day by day, day after day, once a day, per diem

dainty *adjective* 1 DELICATE, pretty, charming, fine, elegant, neat, exquisite, graceful, petite
<< OPPOSITE clumsy
2 DELECTABLE, choice, delicious, tender, tasty, savoury, palatable, toothsome
3 PARTICULAR, nice, refined, fussy, scrupulous, fastidious, choosy, picky (*informal*), finicky, finical

dais *noun* PLATFORM, stage, podium, rostrum, estrade

dale *noun* VALLEY, glen, vale, dell, dingle, strath (*Scot*), coomb

dalliance *noun* (*Old-fashioned*) DABBLING, playing, toying, trifling

dally *verb* WASTE TIME, delay, fool (about *or* around), linger, hang about, loiter, while away, dawdle, fritter away, procrastinate, tarry, dilly-dally (*informal*), drag your feet *or* heels
<< OPPOSITE hurry (up)

▷▷ **dally with someone** FLIRT WITH, tease, lead on, toy with, play around with, fool (about *or* around) with, trifle with, play fast and loose with (*informal*), frivol with (*informal*)

dam *noun* BARRIER, wall, barrage, obstruction, embankment, hindrance

▷ *verb* BLOCK UP, block, hold in, restrict, check, confine, choke, hold back, barricade, obstruct

damage *noun* **1** DESTRUCTION, harm, loss, injury, suffering, hurt, ruin, crushing, wrecking, shattering, devastation, detriment, mutilation, impairment, annihilation, ruination

<< OPPOSITE improvement

2 (*informal*) COST, price, charge, rate, bill, figure, amount, total, payment, expense, outlay

▷ *plural noun* (*Law*) COMPENSATION, fine, payment, satisfaction, amends, reparation, indemnity, restitution, reimbursement, atonement, recompense, indemnification, meed (*archaic*), requital

▷ *verb* SPOIL, hurt, injure, smash, harm, ruin, crush, devastate, mar, wreck, shatter, weaken, gut, demolish, undo, trash (*slang*), total (*slang*), impair, ravage, mutilate, annihilate, incapacitate, raze, deface, play (merry) hell with (*informal*)

<< OPPOSITE fix

damaging *adjective* HARMFUL, detrimental, hurtful, ruinous, prejudicial, deleterious, injurious, disadvantageous

<< OPPOSITE helpful

dame *noun* **1** *with cap.* LADY, baroness, dowager, grande dame (*French*), noblewoman, peeress

2 (*Slang, chiefly US & Canad*) WOMAN, girl, lady, female, bird (*slang*), maiden (*archaic*), miss, chick (*slang*), maid (*archaic*), gal (*slang*), lass, lassie (*informal*), wench (*facetious*), charlie (*Austral slang*), chook (*Austral slang*), wahine (*NZ*)

damn *verb* CRITICIZE, condemn, blast, pan (*informal*), slam (*slang*), denounce, put down, slate (*informal*), censure, castigate, tear into (*informal*), diss (*slang, chiefly US*), inveigh against, lambast(e), excoriate, denunciate

<< OPPOSITE praise

▷▷ **not give a damn** (*informal*) NOT CARE, not mind, be indifferent, not give a hoot, not care a jot, not give two hoots, not care a whit, not care a brass farthing, not give a tinker's curse *or* damn (*slang*)

damnation *noun* (*Theology*) CONDEMNATION, damning, sending to hell, consigning to perdition

damned *adjective* (*Slang*) INFERNAL, accursed, detestable, revolting, infamous, confounded, despicable, abhorred, hateful, loathsome, abominable, freaking (*slang, chiefly US*)

damning *adjective* INCRIMINATING, implicating, condemnatory, dooming, accusatorial, damnatory, implicative

damp *adjective* MOIST, wet, dripping, soggy, humid, sodden, dank, sopping, clammy, dewy, muggy, drizzly, vaporous

<< OPPOSITE dry

▷ *noun* MOISTURE, liquid, humidity, drizzle, dew, dampness, wetness, dankness, clamminess, mugginess

<< OPPOSITE dryness

▷ *verb* MOISTEN, wet, soak, dampen, lick, moisturize, humidify

▷▷ **damp something down** CURB, reduce, check, cool, moderate, dash, chill, dull, diminish, discourage, restrain, inhibit, stifle, allay, deaden, pour cold water on

dampen *verb* **1** REDUCE, check, moderate, dash, dull, restrain, deter, stifle, lessen, smother, muffle, deaden

2 MOISTEN, wet, spray, make damp, bedew, besprinkle

damper *noun* DISCOURAGEMENT, cloud, chill, curb, restraint, gloom, cold water (*informal*), pall

dampness *noun* MOISTNESS, damp, moisture, humidity, wetness, sogginess, dankness, clamminess, mugginess

<< OPPOSITE dryness

dance *verb* **1** PRANCE, rock, trip, swing, spin, hop, skip, sway, whirl, caper, jig, frolic, cavort, gambol, bob up and down, cut a rug (*informal*)

2 CAPER, trip, spring, jump, bound, leap, bounce, hop, skip, romp, frolic, cavort, gambol

▷ *noun* BALL, social, hop (*informal*), disco, knees-up (*Brit informal*), discotheque, dancing party, B and S (*Austral informal*)

dancer *noun* BALLERINA, hoofer (*slang*), Terpsichorean

dandy *noun* FOP, beau, swell (*informal*), blood (*rare*), buck (*archaic*), blade (*archaic*), peacock, dude (*US & Canad informal*), toff (*Brit slang*), macaroni (*obsolete*), man about town, popinjay, coxcomb

▷ *adjective* (*informal*) EXCELLENT, great, fine, capital, splendid, first-rate

danger *noun* **1** JEOPARDY, vulnerability, insecurity, precariousness, endangerment

2 HAZARD, risk, threat, menace, peril, pitfall

dangerous *adjective* PERILOUS, threatening, risky, hazardous, exposed, alarming, vulnerable, nasty, ugly, menacing, insecure, hairy (*slang*), unsafe, precarious, treacherous, breakneck, parlous (*archaic*), fraught with danger, chancy (*informal*), unchancy (*Scot*)

<< OPPOSITE safe

dangerously *adverb* PERILOUSLY, alarmingly, carelessly, precariously, recklessly, daringly, riskily, harmfully, hazardously, unsafely, unsecurely

dangle *verb* **1** HANG, swing, trail, sway, flap,

hang down, depend
2 OFFER, flourish, brandish, flaunt, tempt someone with, lure someone with, entice someone with, tantalize someone with

dangling *adjective* HANGING, swinging, loose, trailing, swaying, disconnected, drooping, unconnected

dank *adjective* DAMP, dripping, moist, soggy, clammy, dewy

dapper *adjective* (only ever used with reference to *men*, not *women*) NEAT, nice, smart, trim, stylish, spruce, dainty, natty (*informal*), well-groomed, well turned out, trig (*archaic* or *dialect*), soigné
<< OPPOSITE untidy

dappled *adjective* MOTTLED, spotted, speckled, pied, flecked, variegated, checkered, freckled, stippled, piebald, brindled

dare *verb* 1 RISK DOING, venture, presume, make bold (*archaic*), hazard doing, brave doing
2 CHALLENGE, provoke, defy, taunt, goad, throw down the gauntlet

daredevil *noun* ADVENTURER, show-off (*informal*), madcap, desperado, exhibitionist, stunt man, hot dog (*chiefly US*), adrenalin junky (*slang*)
▷ *adjective* DARING, bold, adventurous, reckless, audacious, madcap, death-defying

daring *adjective* BRAVE, bold, adventurous, rash, have-a-go (*informal*), reckless, fearless, audacious, intrepid, impulsive, valiant, plucky, game (*informal*), daredevil, venturesome, (as) game as Ned Kelly (*Austral slang*)
<< OPPOSITE timid
▷ *noun* BRAVERY, nerve (*informal*), courage, face (*informal*), spirit, bottle (*Brit slang*), guts (*informal*), pluck, grit, audacity, boldness, temerity, derring-do (*archaic*), spunk (*informal*), fearlessness, rashness, intrepidity
<< OPPOSITE timidity

dark *adjective* 1 DIM, murky, shady, shadowy, grey, cloudy, dingy, overcast, dusky, unlit, pitch-black, indistinct, poorly lit, sunless, tenebrous, darksome (*literary*), pitchy, unilluminated
2 BLACK, brunette, ebony, dark-skinned, sable, dusky, swarthy
<< OPPOSITE fair
3 EVIL, foul, horrible, sinister, infamous, vile, satanic, wicked, atrocious, sinful, hellish, infernal, nefarious, damnable
4 SECRET, deep, hidden, mysterious, concealed, obscure, mystic, enigmatic, puzzling, occult, arcane, cryptic, abstruse, recondite, Delphic
5 GLOOMY, sad, grim, miserable, low, bleak, moody, dismal, pessimistic, melancholy, sombre, morbid, glum, mournful, morose, joyless, doleful, cheerless
<< OPPOSITE cheerful
6 ANGRY, threatening, forbidding, frowning, ominous, dour, scowling, sullen, glum, glowering, sulky
▷ *noun* 1 DARKNESS, shadows, gloom, dusk, obscurity, murk, dimness, semi-darkness, murkiness
2 NIGHT, twilight, evening, evo (*Austral slang*), dusk, night-time, nightfall

darken *verb* 1 CLOUD, shadow, shade, obscure, eclipse, dim, deepen, overshadow, blacken, becloud
<< OPPOSITE brighten
2 MAKE DARK, shade, blacken, make darker, deepen
3 BECOME GLOOMY, blacken, become angry, look black, go crook (*Austral & NZ slang*), grow troubled
<< OPPOSITE become cheerful
4 SADDEN, upset, cloud, blacken, cast a pall over, cast a gloom upon

darkness *noun* DARK, shadows, shade, gloom, obscurity, blackness, murk, dimness, murkiness, duskiness, shadiness

darling *noun* 1 BELOVED, love, dear, dearest, angel, treasure, precious, loved one, sweetheart, sweetie, truelove, dear one
2 FAVOURITE, pet, spoilt child, apple of your eye, blue-eyed boy, fair-haired boy (*US*)
▷ *adjective* 1 BELOVED, dear, dearest, sweet, treasured, precious, adored, cherished, revered
2 ADORABLE, sweet, attractive, lovely, charming, cute, enchanting, captivating

darn *verb* MEND, repair, patch, stitch, sew up, cobble up
▷ *noun* MEND, patch, reinforcement, invisible repair

dart *verb* DASH, run, race, shoot, fly, speed, spring, tear, rush, bound, flash, hurry, sprint, bolt, hasten, whizz, haste, flit, scoot

dash *verb* 1 RUSH, run, race, shoot, fly, career, speed, spring, tear, bound, hurry, barrel (along) (*informal, chiefly US & Canad*), sprint, bolt, dart, hasten, scurry, haste, stampede, burn rubber (*informal*), make haste, hotfoot
<< OPPOSITE dawdle
2 THROW, cast, pitch, slam, toss, hurl, fling, chuck (*informal*), propel, project, sling, lob (*informal*)
3 CRASH, break, smash, shatter, shiver, splinter
4 DISAPPOINT, ruin, frustrate, spoil, foil, undo, thwart, dampen, confound, crool *or* cruel (*Austral slang*)
▷ *noun* 1 RUSH, run, race, sprint, bolt, dart, spurt, sortie
2 DROP, little, bit, shot (*informal*), touch, spot, suggestion, trace, hint, pinch, sprinkling, tot, trickle, nip, tinge, soupçon (*French*)
<< OPPOSITE lot

3 STYLE, spirit, flair, flourish, vigour, verve, panache, élan, brio, vivacity

dashing *adjective* (*Old-fashioned*) STYLISH, smart, elegant, dazzling, flamboyant, sporty, swish (*informal, chiefly Brit*), urbane, jaunty, dapper, showy

dastardly *adjective* (*Old-fashioned*) DESPICABLE, mean, low, base, sneaking, cowardly, craven, vile, abject, sneaky, contemptible, underhand, weak-kneed (*informal*), faint-hearted, spiritless, recreant (*archaic*), caitiff (*archaic*), niddering (*archaic*)

data *noun* 1 DETAILS, facts, figures, materials, documents, intelligence, statistics, gen (*Brit informal*), dope (*informal*), info (*informal*)
2 (*Computing*) INFORMATION, input

From a historical point of view only, the word *data* is a plural. In fact, in many cases it is not clear from context if it is being used as a singular or plural, so there is no issue: *when next needed the data can be accessed very quickly*. When it is necessary to specify, the preferred usage nowadays in general language is to treat it as singular, as in: *this data is useful to the government in the planning of housing services*. There are rather more examples in the Collins Word Web of *these data* than *this data*, with a marked preference for the plural in academic and scientific writing. As regards *data is* versus *data are*, the preference for the plural form overall is even more marked in that kind of writing. When speaking, however, it is best to opt for treating the word as singular, except in precise scientific contexts. The singular form *datum* is comparatively rare in the sense of a single item of data

date *noun* 1 TIME, stage, period
2 APPOINTMENT, meeting, arrangement, commitment, engagement, rendezvous, tryst, assignation
3 PARTNER, escort, friend, steady (*informal*)
▷ *verb* 1 PUT A DATE ON, determine the date of, assign a date to, fix the period of
2 BECOME DATED, become old-fashioned, obsolesce
▷▷ **date from** *or* **date back to** (with a *time* or *date* as object) COME FROM, belong to, originate in, exist from, bear a date of
▷▷ **to date** UP TO NOW, yet, so far, until now, now, as yet, thus far, up to this point, up to the present

dated *adjective* OLD-FASHIONED, outdated, out of date, obsolete, archaic, unfashionable, antiquated, outmoded, passé, out, old hat, untrendy (*Brit informal*), démodé (*French*), out of the ark (*informal*)
<< OPPOSITE modern

daub *verb* SMEAR, dirty, splatter, stain, spatter, sully, deface, smirch, begrime, besmear, bedaub, paint, coat, stain, plaster, slap on (*informal*)
▷ *noun* SMEAR, spot, stain, blot, blotch, splodge, splotch, smirch

daughter *noun* 1 FEMALE CHILD, girl
2 DESCENDANT, girl
>> RELATED WORD *adjective* filial

daunt *verb* DISCOURAGE, alarm, shake, frighten, scare, terrify, cow, intimidate, deter, dismay, put off, subdue, overawe, frighten off, dishearten, dispirit
<< OPPOSITE reassure

daunted *adjective* INTIMIDATED, alarmed, shaken, frightened, overcome, cowed, discouraged, deterred, dismayed, put off, disillusioned, unnerved, demoralized, dispirited, downcast

daunting *adjective* INTIMIDATING, alarming, frightening, discouraging, awesome, unnerving, disconcerting, demoralizing, off-putting (*Brit informal*), disheartening
<< OPPOSITE reassuring

dawdle *verb* 1 WASTE TIME, potter, trail, lag, idle, loaf, hang about, dally, loiter, dilly-dally (*informal*), drag your feet *or* heels
<< OPPOSITE hurry
2 LINGER, idle, dally, take your time, procrastinate, drag your feet *or* heels

dawn *noun* 1 DAYBREAK, morning, sunrise, dawning, daylight, aurora (*poetic*), crack of dawn, sunup, cockcrow, dayspring (*poetic*)
2 (*Literary*) BEGINNING, start, birth, rise, origin, dawning, unfolding, emergence, outset, onset, advent, genesis, inception
▷ *verb* 1 BEGIN, start, open, rise, develop, emerge, unfold, originate
2 GROW LIGHT, break, brighten, lighten
▷▷ **dawn on** *or* **upon someone** HIT, strike, occur to, register (*informal*), become apparent, come to mind, cross your mind, come into your head, flash across your mind

day *noun* 1 TWENTY-FOUR HOURS, working day
2 DAYTIME, daylight, daylight hours
3 DATE, particular day
4 TIME, age, era, prime, period, generation, heyday, epoch
▷▷ **call it a day** STOP, finish, cease, pack up (*informal*), leave off, knock off (*informal*), desist, pack it in (*slang*), shut up shop, jack it in, chuck it in (*informal*), give up *or* over
▷▷ **day after day** CONTINUALLY, regularly,

relentlessly, persistently, incessantly, nonstop, unremittingly, monotonously, unfalteringly
▷▷ **day by day** GRADUALLY, slowly, progressively, daily, steadily, bit by bit, little by little, by degrees
>> RELATED WORD *adjective* diurnal
daybreak *noun* DAWN, morning, sunrise, first light, crack of dawn, break of day, sunup, cockcrow, dayspring (*poetic*)
daydream *noun* FANTASY, dream, imagining, fancy, reverie, figment of the imagination WISH, pipe dream, fond hope, castle in the air *or* in Spain
▷ *verb* FANTASIZE, dream, imagine, envision, stargaze
daylight *noun* 1 SUNLIGHT, sunshine, light of day
2 DAYTIME, broad daylight, daylight hours
day-to-day *adjective* EVERYDAY, regular, usual, routine, accustomed, customary, habitual, run-of-the-mill, wonted
daze *verb* 1 STUN, shock, paralyse, numb, stupefy, benumb
2 CONFUSE, surprise, amaze, blind, astonish, stagger, startle, dazzle, bewilder, astound, perplex, flummox, dumbfound, nonplus, flabbergast (*informal*), befog
▷ *noun* (usually used in the phrase *in a daze*) SHOCK, confusion, distraction, trance, bewilderment, stupor, trancelike state
dazed *adjective* SHOCKED, stunned, confused, staggered, baffled, at sea, bewildered, muddled, numbed, dizzy, bemused, perplexed, disorientated, flabbergasted (*informal*), dopey (*slang*), groggy (*informal*), stupefied, nonplussed, light-headed, flummoxed, punch-drunk, woozy (*informal*), fuddled
dazzle *verb* 1 IMPRESS, amaze, fascinate, overwhelm, astonish, awe, overpower, bowl over (*informal*), overawe, hypnotize, stupefy, take your breath away, strike dumb
2 BLIND, confuse, daze, bedazzle
▷ *noun* SPLENDOUR, sparkle, glitter, flash, brilliance, magnificence, razzmatazz (*slang*), razzle-dazzle (*slang*), éclat
dazzling *adjective* SPLENDID, brilliant, stunning, superb, divine, glorious, sparkling, glittering, sensational (*informal*), sublime, virtuoso, drop-dead (*slang*), ravishing, scintillating
<< OPPOSITE ordinary
dead *adjective* 1 DECEASED, gone, departed, late, perished, extinct, defunct, passed away, pushing up (the) daisies
<< OPPOSITE alive
2 INANIMATE, still, barren, sterile, stagnant, lifeless, inert, uninhabited
3 BORING, dull, dreary, flat, plain, stale, tasteless, humdrum, uninteresting, insipid, ho-hum (*informal*), vapid, dead-and-alive
4 NOT WORKING, useless, inactive, inoperative
<< OPPOSITE working
5 OBSOLETE, old, antique, discarded, extinct, archaic, disused
6 SPIRITLESS, cold, dull, wooden, glazed, indifferent, callous, lukewarm, inhuman, unsympathetic, apathetic, frigid, glassy, unresponsive, unfeeling, torpid
<< OPPOSITE lively
7 NUMB, frozen, paralysed, insensitive, inert, deadened, immobilized, unfeeling, torpid, insensible, benumbed
8 (usually used of *centre, silence,* or *stop*) TOTAL, complete, perfect, entire, absolute, utter, outright, thorough, downright, unqualified
9 (*informal*) EXHAUSTED, tired, worn out, spent, wasted, done in (*informal*), all in (*slang*), drained, wiped out (*informal*), sapped, knackered (*slang*), prostrated, clapped out (*Brit, Austral & NZ informal*), tired out, ready to drop, dog-tired (*informal*), zonked (*slang*), dead tired, dead beat (*informal*), shagged out (*Brit slang*), worn to a frazzle (*informal*), on your last legs (*informal*), creamcrackered (*Brit slang*)
▷ *noun* MIDDLE, heart, depth, thick, midst
▷ *adverb* EXACTLY, quite, completely, totally, directly, perfectly, fully, entirely, absolutely, thoroughly, wholly, utterly, consummately, wholeheartedly, unconditionally, to the hilt, one hundred per cent, unmitigatedly
deadbeat *noun* (*informal, chiefly US & Canad*) LAYABOUT, bum (*informal*), waster, lounger, piker (*Austral & NZ slang*), sponge (*informal*), parasite, drone, loafer, slacker (*informal*), scrounger (*informal*), skiver (*Brit slang*), idler, freeloader (*slang*), good-for-nothing, sponger (*informal*), wastrel, bludger (*Austral & NZ informal*), cadger, quandong (*Austral slang*)
deaden *verb* 1 REDUCE, dull, diminish, check, weaken, cushion, damp, suppress, blunt, paralyse, impair, numb, lessen, alleviate, smother, dampen, anaesthetize, benumb
2 SUPPRESS, reduce, dull, diminish, cushion, damp, mute, stifle, hush, lessen, smother, dampen, muffle, quieten
deadline *noun* TIME LIMIT, cutoff point, target date *or* time, limit
deadlock *noun* 1 IMPASSE, stalemate, standstill, halt, cessation, gridlock, standoff, full stop
2 TIE, draw, stalemate, impasse, standstill, gridlock, standoff, dead heat
deadly *adjective* 1 LETHAL, fatal, deathly, dangerous, devastating, destructive, mortal, murderous, poisonous, malignant, virulent, pernicious, noxious, venomous, baleful, death-dealing, baneful
2 (*informal*) BORING, dull, tedious, flat, monotonous, uninteresting, mind-numbing,

unexciting, ho-hum (*informal*), wearisome, as dry as dust
3 DEATHLY, white, pale, ghostly, ghastly, wan, pasty, colourless, pallid, anaemic, ashen, sallow, whitish, cadaverous, waxen, ashy, deathlike, wheyfaced

deadpan *adjective* EXPRESSIONLESS, empty, blank, wooden, straight-faced, vacuous, impassive, inscrutable, poker-faced, inexpressive

deaf *adjective* 1 HARD OF HEARING, without hearing, stone deaf
2 OBLIVIOUS, indifferent, unmoved, unconcerned, unsympathetic, impervious, unresponsive, heedless, unhearing ▷ see **disabled**

deafen *verb* MAKE DEAF, split *or* burst the eardrums

deafening *adjective* EAR-SPLITTING, intense, piercing, ringing, booming, overpowering, resounding, dinning, thunderous, ear-piercing

deal *noun* 1 (*informal*) AGREEMENT, understanding, contract, business, negotiation, arrangement, bargain, transaction, pact
2 AMOUNT, quantity, measure, degree, mass, volume, share, portion, bulk
▷▷ **deal in something** SELL, trade in, stock, traffic in, buy and sell
▷▷ **deal something out** DISTRIBUTE, give, administer, share, divide, assign, allocate, dispense, bestow, allot, mete out, dole out, apportion
▷▷ **deal with something** BE CONCERNED WITH, involve, concern, touch, regard, apply to, bear on, pertain to, be relevant to, treat of
▷▷ **deal with something** *or* **someone**
1 HANDLE, manage, treat, cope with, take care of, see to, attend to, get to grips with, come to grips with
2 BEHAVE TOWARDS, act towards, conduct yourself towards

dealer *noun* TRADER, marketer, merchant, supplier, wholesaler, purveyor, tradesman, merchandiser

dealings *plural noun* BUSINESS, selling, trading, trade, traffic, truck, bargaining, commerce, transactions, business relations

dear *adjective* 1 BELOVED, close, valued, favourite, respected, prized, dearest, sweet, treasured, precious, darling, intimate, esteemed, cherished, revered
<< OPPOSITE hated
2 EXPENSIVE, costly, high-priced, excessive, pricey (*informal*), at a premium, overpriced, exorbitant
<< OPPOSITE cheap
▷ *noun* DARLING, love, dearest, sweet, angel, treasure, precious, beloved, loved one, sweetheart, truelove

dearly *adverb* 1 VERY MUCH, greatly, extremely, profoundly
2 AT GREAT COST, dear, at a high price, at a heavy cost

dearth *noun* LACK, want, need, absence, poverty, shortage, deficiency, famine, inadequacy, scarcity, paucity, insufficiency, sparsity, scantiness, exiguousness

death *noun* 1 DYING, demise, bereavement, end, passing, release, loss, departure, curtains (*informal*), cessation, expiration, decease, quietus
<< OPPOSITE birth
2 DESTRUCTION, ending, finish, ruin, wiping out, undoing, extinction, elimination, downfall, extermination, annihilation, obliteration, ruination
<< OPPOSITE beginning
3 *sometimes capital* THE GRIM REAPER, the Dark Angel
>> RELATED WORDS *adjectives* fatal, lethal, mortal

deathly *adjective* 1 DEATHLIKE, white, pale, ghastly, wan, gaunt, haggard, bloodless, pallid, ashen, sallow, cadaverous, ashy, like death warmed up (*informal*)
2 FATAL, terminal, deadly, terrible, destructive, lethal, mortal, malignant, incurable, pernicious

debacle *or* **débâcle** *noun* DISASTER, catastrophe, fiasco

debar *verb* BAR, exclude, prohibit, black, stop, keep out, preclude, shut out, blackball, interdict, refuse admission to

debase *verb* 1 (*Formal*) CORRUPT, contaminate, devalue, pollute, impair, taint, depreciate, defile, adulterate, vitiate, bastardize
<< OPPOSITE purify
2 DEGRADE, reduce, lower, shame, humble, disgrace, humiliate, demean, drag down, dishonour, cheapen, abase
<< OPPOSITE exalt

debased *adjective* 1 CORRUPT, devalued, reduced, lowered, mixed, contaminated, polluted, depreciated, impure, adulterated
2 DEGRADED, corrupt, fallen, low, base, abandoned, perverted, vile, sordid, depraved, debauched, scungy (*Austral & NZ*)
<< OPPOSITE virtuous

debatable *adjective* DOUBTFUL, uncertain, dubious, controversial, unsettled, questionable, undecided, borderline, in dispute, moot, arguable, iffy (*informal*), open to question, disputable

debate *noun* DISCUSSION, talk, argument, dispute, analysis, conversation, consideration, controversy, dialogue, contention,

deliberation, polemic, altercation, disputation
▷ *verb* 1 DISCUSS, question, talk about, argue about, dispute, examine, contest, deliberate, contend, wrangle, thrash out, controvert
2 CONSIDER, reflect, think about, weigh, contemplate, deliberate, ponder, revolve, mull over, ruminate, give thought to, cogitate, meditate upon

debauched *adjective* CORRUPT, abandoned, perverted, degraded, degenerate, immoral, dissipated, sleazy, depraved, wanton, debased, profligate, dissolute, licentious, pervy (*slang*)

debauchery *noun* DEPRAVITY, excess, lust, revel, indulgence, orgy, incontinence, gluttony, dissipation, licentiousness, intemperance, overindulgence, lewdness, dissoluteness, carousal

debilitate *verb* WEAKEN, exhaust, wear out, sap, incapacitate, prostrate, enfeeble, enervate, devitalize
<< OPPOSITE invigorate

debilitating *adjective* WEAKENING, tiring, exhausting, draining, fatiguing, wearing, sapping, incapacitating, enervating, enfeebling, devitalizing
<< OPPOSITE invigorating

debonair *adjective* ELEGANT, charming, dashing, smooth, refined, courteous, affable, suave, urbane, well-bred

debrief *verb* INTERROGATE, question, examine, probe, quiz, cross-examine

debris *noun* REMAINS, bits, pieces, waste, ruins, wreck, rubbish, fragments, litter, rubble, wreckage, brash, detritus, dross

debt *noun* DEBIT, bill, score, due, duty, commitment, obligation, liability, arrears
▷▷ **in debt** OWING, liable, accountable, in the red (*informal*), in arrears, beholden, in hock (*informal, chiefly US*)

debtor *noun* BORROWER, mortgagor

debunk *verb* (*informal*) EXPOSE, show up, mock, ridicule, puncture, deflate, disparage, lampoon, cut down to size

debut *noun* 1 ENTRANCE, beginning, launch, launching, introduction, first appearance, inauguration
2 PRESENTATION, coming out, introduction, first appearance, launching, initiation

decadence *noun* DEGENERATION, decline, corruption, fall, decay, deterioration, dissolution, perversion, dissipation, debasement, retrogression

decadent *adjective* DEGENERATE, abandoned, corrupt, degraded, immoral, self-indulgent, depraved, debased, debauched, dissolute
<< OPPOSITE moral

decamp *verb* MAKE OFF, fly, escape, desert, flee, bolt, run away, flit (*informal*), abscond, hook it (*slang*), sneak off, do a runner (*slang*), scarper (*Brit slang*), steal away, do a bunk (*Brit slang*), fly the coop (*US & Canad informal*), skedaddle (*informal*), hightail it (*informal, chiefly US*), take a powder (*US & Canad slang*), take it on the lam (*US & Canad slang*), do a Skase (*Austral informal*)

decant *verb* (*Formal*) TRANSFER, tap, drain, pour out, draw off, let flow

decapitate *verb* BEHEAD, execute, guillotine

decay *verb* 1 ROT, break down, disintegrate, spoil, crumble, deteriorate, perish, degenerate, fester, decompose, mortify, moulder, go bad, putrefy
2 DECLINE, sink, break down, diminish, dissolve, crumble, deteriorate, fall off, dwindle, lessen, wane, disintegrate, degenerate
<< OPPOSITE grow
▷ *noun* 1 ROT, rotting, deterioration, corruption, mould, blight, perishing, disintegration, corrosion, decomposition, gangrene, mortification, canker, caries, putrefaction, putrescence, cariosity, putridity
2 DECLINE, collapse, deterioration, failing, fading, decadence, degeneration, degeneracy
<< OPPOSITE growth

decayed *adjective* ROTTEN, bad, decaying, wasted, spoiled, perished, festering, decomposed, corroded, unsound, putrid, putrefied, putrescent, carrion, carious

decaying *adjective* ROTTING, deteriorating, disintegrating, crumbling, perishing, wasting away, wearing away, gangrenous, putrefacient

deceased *adjective* DEAD, late, departed, lost, gone, expired, defunct, lifeless, pushing up daisies (*informal*)

deceit *noun* LYING, fraud, cheating, deception, hypocrisy, cunning, pretence, treachery, dishonesty, guile, artifice, trickery, misrepresentation, duplicity, subterfuge, feint, double-dealing, chicanery, wile, dissimulation, craftiness, imposture, fraudulence, slyness, deceitfulness, underhandedness
<< OPPOSITE honesty

deceitful *adjective* DISHONEST, false, deceiving, fraudulent, treacherous, deceptive, hypocritical, counterfeit, crafty, sneaky, illusory, two-faced, disingenuous, untrustworthy, underhand, insincere, double-dealing, duplicitous, fallacious, guileful, knavish (*archaic*)

deceive *verb* TAKE IN, trick, fool (*informal*), cheat, con (*informal*), kid (*informal*), stiff (*slang*), sting (*informal*), mislead, betray, lead (someone) on (*informal*), hoax, dupe, beguile, delude, swindle, outwit, ensnare, bamboozle (*informal*), hoodwink, entrap, double-cross (*informal*), take (someone) for a ride (*informal*), pull a fast one on (*slang*), cozen, pull the wool over (someone's) eyes

decency *noun* 1 PROPRIETY, correctness, decorum, fitness, good form, respectability, etiquette, appropriateness, seemliness
2 COURTESY, grace, politeness, good manners, civility, good breeding, graciousness, urbanity, courteousness, gallantness

decent *adjective* 1 SATISFACTORY, average, fair, all right, reasonable, suitable, sufficient, acceptable, good enough, adequate, competent, ample, tolerable, up to scratch, passable, up to standard, up to the mark
<< OPPOSITE unsatisfactory
2 PROPER, becoming, seemly, fitting, fit, appropriate, suitable, respectable, befitting, decorous, comme il faut (*French*)
<< OPPOSITE improper
3 (*informal*) GOOD, kind, friendly, neighbourly, generous, helpful, obliging, accommodating, sympathetic, comradely, benign, gracious, benevolent, courteous, amiable, amicable, sociable, genial, peaceable, companionable, well-disposed
4 RESPECTABLE, nice, pure, proper, modest, polite, chaste, presentable, decorous

deception *noun* 1 TRICKERY, fraud, deceit, hypocrisy, cunning, treachery, guile, duplicity, insincerity, legerdemain, dissimulation, craftiness, fraudulence, deceitfulness, deceptiveness
<< OPPOSITE honesty
2 TRICK, lie, fraud, cheat, bluff, sham, snare, hoax, decoy, ruse, artifice, subterfuge, canard, feint, stratagem, porky (*Brit slang*), pork pie (*Brit slang*), wile, hokum (*slang, chiefly US & Canad*), leg-pull (*Brit informal*), imposture, snow job (*slang, chiefly US & Canad*), fastie (*Austral slang*)

deceptive *adjective* 1 MISLEADING, false, fake, mock, ambiguous, unreliable, spurious, illusory, specious, fallacious, delusive
2 DISHONEST, deceiving, fraudulent, treacherous, hypocritical, crafty, sneaky, two-faced, disingenuous, deceitful, untrustworthy, underhand, insincere, duplicitous, guileful

decide *verb* 1 MAKE A DECISION, make up your mind, reach *or* come to a decision, end, choose, determine, purpose, elect, conclude, commit yourself, come to a conclusion
<< OPPOSITE hesitate
2 RESOLVE, answer, determine, settle, conclude, decree, clear up, ordain, adjudicate, adjudge, arbitrate
3 SETTLE, determine, conclude, resolve

decided *adjective* 1 DEFINITE, certain, positive, absolute, distinct, pronounced, clear-cut, undisputed, unequivocal, undeniable, unambiguous, indisputable, categorical, unquestionable
<< OPPOSITE doubtful
2 DETERMINED, firm, decisive, assertive, emphatic, resolute, strong-willed, unhesitating, unfaltering
<< OPPOSITE irresolute

decidedly *adverb* DEFINITELY, clearly, certainly, absolutely, positively, distinctly, downright, decisively, unequivocally, unmistakably

deciding *adjective* DETERMINING, chief, prime, significant, critical, crucial, principal, influential, decisive, conclusive

decimate *verb* DESTROY, devastate, wipe out, ravage, eradicate, annihilate, put paid to, lay waste, wreak havoc on

> This word, which comes from Latin, originally referred to the slaughtering of one in ten soldiers, a practice of the army of Ancient Rome. In current language, however, the meaning of the word has broadened and it is now used not only to describe the destruction of people and animals, but also of institutions: *overseas visitors will stay away in droves, decimating the tourist industry*. The synonym *destroy* is an appropriate alternative

decipher *verb* 1 DECODE, crack, solve, understand, explain, reveal, figure out (*informal*), unravel, suss (out) (*slang*)
2 FIGURE OUT, read, understand, interpret (*informal*), make out, unravel, deduce, construe, suss (out) (*slang*)

decision *noun* 1 JUDGMENT, finding, ruling, order, result, sentence, settlement, resolution, conclusion, outcome, verdict, decree, arbitration
2 DECISIVENESS, purpose, resolution, resolve, determination, firmness, forcefulness, purposefulness, resoluteness, strength of mind *or* will

decisive *adjective* 1 CRUCIAL, significant, critical, final, positive, absolute, influential, definite, definitive, momentous, conclusive, fateful
<< OPPOSITE uncertain
2 RESOLUTE, decided, firm, determined, forceful, uncompromising, incisive, trenchant, strong-minded
<< OPPOSITE indecisive

deck *verb* DECORATE, dress, trim, clothe, grace, array, garland, adorn, ornament, embellish, apparel (*archaic*), festoon, attire, bedeck, beautify, bedight (*archaic*), bedizen (*archaic*), engarland
▷▷ **deck someone** *or* **something out** DRESS UP, doll up (*slang*), prettify, trick out, rig out, pretty up, prink, tog up *or* out

declaim *verb* SPEAK, lecture, proclaim, recite,

rant, harangue, hold forth, spiel (*informal*), orate, perorate
▷▷ **declaim against something** *or* **someone** PROTEST AGAINST, attack, rail at *or* against, denounce, decry, inveigh against
declaration *noun* 1 ANNOUNCEMENT, proclamation, decree, notice, manifesto, notification, edict, pronouncement, promulgation, pronunciamento
2 AFFIRMATION, profession, assertion, revelation, disclosure, acknowledgment, protestation, avowal, averment
3 STATEMENT, testimony, deposition, attestation
declare *verb* 1 STATE, claim, announce, voice, express, maintain, confirm, assert, proclaim, pronounce, utter, notify, affirm, profess, avow, aver, asseverate
2 TESTIFY, state, witness, swear, assert, affirm, certify, attest, bear witness, vouch, give testimony, asseverate
3 MAKE KNOWN, tell, reveal, show, broadcast, confess, communicate, disclose, convey, manifest, make public
decline *verb* 1 FALL, fail, drop, contract, lower, sink, flag, fade, shrink, diminish, decrease, slow down, fall off, dwindle, lessen, wane, ebb, slacken
<< OPPOSITE rise
2 DETERIORATE, fade, weaken, pine, decay, worsen, lapse, languish, degenerate, droop
<< OPPOSITE improve
3 REFUSE, reject, turn down, avoid, deny, spurn, abstain, forgo, send your regrets, say 'no'
<< OPPOSITE accept
▷ *noun* 1 DEPRESSION, recession, slump, falling off, downturn, dwindling, lessening, diminution, abatement
<< OPPOSITE rise
2 DETERIORATION, fall, failing, slump, weakening, decay, worsening, descent, downturn, disintegration, degeneration, atrophy, decrepitude, retrogression, enfeeblement
<< OPPOSITE improvement
decode *verb* 1 DECIPHER, crack, work out, solve, interpret, unscramble, decrypt, descramble
<< OPPOSITE encode
2 UNDERSTAND, explain, interpret, make sense of, construe, decipher, elucidate, throw light on, explicate
decompose *verb* 1 ROT, spoil, corrupt, crumble, decay, perish, fester, corrode, moulder, go bad, putrefy
2 BREAK DOWN, break up, crumble, deteriorate, fall apart, disintegrate, degenerate
decomposition *noun* ROT, corruption, decay, rotting, perishing, mortification, putrefaction, putrescence, putridity
decor *or* **décor** *noun* DECORATION, colour scheme, ornamentation, furnishing style
decorate *verb* 1 ADORN, deck, trim, embroider, garnish, ornament, embellish, festoon, bedeck, beautify, grace, engarland
2 DO UP, paper, paint, wallpaper, renovate (*informal*), furbish
3 PIN A MEDAL ON, cite, confer an honour on *or* upon
decoration *noun* 1 ADORNMENT, trimming, garnishing, enhancement, elaboration, embellishment, ornamentation, beautification
2 ORNAMENT, trimmings, garnish, frill, scroll, spangle, festoon, trinket, bauble, flounce, arabesque, curlicue, furbelow, falderal, cartouch(e)
3 MEDAL, award, order, star, colours, ribbon, badge, emblem, garter
decorative *adjective* ORNAMENTAL, fancy, pretty, attractive, enhancing, adorning, for show, embellishing, showy, beautifying, nonfunctional, arty-crafty
decorum *noun* PROPRIETY, decency, etiquette, breeding, protocol, respectability, politeness, good manners, good grace, gentility, deportment, courtliness, politesse, punctilio, seemliness
<< OPPOSITE impropriety
decoy *noun* LURE, attraction, bait, trap, inducement, enticement, ensnarement
decrease *verb* 1 DROP, decline, lessen, contract, lower, ease, shrink, diminish, fall off, dwindle, wane, subside, abate, peter out, slacken
2 REDUCE, cut, lower, contract, depress, moderate, weaken, diminish, turn down, slow down, cut down, shorten, dilute, impair, lessen, curtail, wind down, abate, tone down, truncate, abridge, downsize
<< OPPOSITE increase
▷ *noun* LESSENING, decline, reduction, loss, falling off, downturn, dwindling, contraction, ebb, cutback, subsidence, curtailment, shrinkage, diminution, abatement
<< OPPOSITE growth
decree *noun* 1 LAW, order, ruling, act, demand, command, regulation, mandate, canon, statute, covenant, ordinance, proclamation, enactment, edict, dictum, precept
2 JUDGMENT, finding, order, result, ruling, decision, award, conclusion, verdict, arbitration
▷ *verb* ORDER, rule, command, decide, demand, establish, determine, proclaim, dictate, prescribe, pronounce, lay down, enact, ordain
decrepit *adjective* 1 RUINED, broken-down, battered, crumbling, run-down, deteriorated, decaying, beat-up (*informal*), shabby, worn-out,

ramshackle, dilapidated, antiquated, rickety, weather-beaten, tumbledown

2 WEAK, aged, frail, wasted, fragile, crippled, feeble, past it, debilitated, incapacitated, infirm, superannuated, doddering

decry *verb* CONDEMN, blame, abuse, blast, denounce, put down, criticize, run down, discredit, censure, detract, denigrate, belittle, disparage, rail against, depreciate, tear into (*informal*), diss (*slang, chiefly US*), lambast(e), traduce, excoriate, derogate, cry down, asperse

dedicate *verb* 1 DEVOTE, give, apply, commit, concern, occupy, pledge, surrender, give over

2 OFFER, address, assign, inscribe

3 CONSECRATE, bless, sanctify, set apart, hallow

dedicated *adjective* COMMITTED, devoted, sworn, enthusiastic, single-minded, zealous, purposeful, given over to, wholehearted

<< OPPOSITE indifferent

dedication *noun* 1 COMMITMENT, loyalty, devotion, allegiance, adherence, single-mindedness, faithfulness, wholeheartedness, devotedness

<< OPPOSITE indifference

2 INSCRIPTION, message, address

deduce *verb* WORK OUT, reason, understand, gather, conclude, derive, infer, glean

deduct *verb* SUBTRACT, remove, take off, withdraw, take out, take from, take away, reduce by, knock off (*informal*), decrease by

<< OPPOSITE add

deduction *noun* 1 CONCLUSION, finding, verdict, judgment, assumption, inference, corollary

2 REASONING, thinking, thought, reason, analysis, logic, cogitation, ratiocination

3 DISCOUNT, reduction, cut, concession, allowance, decrease, rebate, diminution

4 SUBTRACTION, reduction, allowance, concession

deed *noun* 1 ACTION, act, performance, achievement, exploit, feat

2 (*Law*) DOCUMENT, title, contract, title deed, indenture

deem *verb* CONSIDER, think, believe, hold, account, judge, suppose, regard, estimate, imagine, reckon, esteem, conceive

deep *adjective* 1 BIG, wide, broad, profound, yawning, cavernous, bottomless, unfathomable, fathomless, abyssal

<< OPPOSITE shallow

2 INTENSE, great, serious (*informal*), acute, extreme, grave, profound, heartfelt, unqualified, abject, deeply felt, heartrending

<< OPPOSITE superficial

3 SOUND, peaceful, profound, unbroken, undisturbed, untroubled

4 *with* **in** ABSORBED IN, lost in, gripped by, intent on, preoccupied with, carried away by, immersed in, engrossed in, rapt by

5 WISE, learned, searching, keen, critical, acute, profound, penetrating, discriminating, shrewd, discerning, astute, perceptive, incisive, perspicacious, sagacious

<< OPPOSITE simple

6 DARK, strong, rich, warm, intense, vivid

<< OPPOSITE light

7 LOW, booming, bass, full, mellow, resonant, sonorous, mellifluous, dulcet, low-pitched, full-toned

<< OPPOSITE high

8 ASTUTE, knowing, clever, designing, scheming, sharp, smart, intelligent, discriminating, shrewd, cunning, discerning, canny, devious, perceptive, insidious, artful, far-sighted, far-seeing, perspicacious, sagacious

<< OPPOSITE simple

9 SECRET, hidden, unknown, mysterious, concealed, obscure, abstract, veiled, esoteric, mystifying, impenetrable, arcane, abstruse, recondite

▷ *noun* MIDDLE, heart, midst, dead, thick, culmination

▷ *adverb* 1 FAR, a long way, a good way, miles, deeply, far down, a great distance

2 LATE, far

▷▷ **the deep** (*Poetic*) THE OCEAN, the sea, the waves, the main, the drink (*informal*), the high seas, the briny (*informal*)

deepen *verb* 1 INTENSIFY, increase, grow, strengthen, reinforce, escalate, magnify, augment

2 DIG OUT, excavate, scoop out, hollow out, scrape out

deeply *adverb* THOROUGHLY, completely, seriously, sadly, severely, gravely, profoundly, intensely, to the heart, passionately, acutely, to the core, feelingly, movingly, distressingly, to the quick, affectingly

deep-rooted *or* **deep-seated** *adjective* FIXED, confirmed, rooted, settled, entrenched, ingrained, inveterate, dyed-in-the-wool, ineradicable

<< OPPOSITE superficial

deface *verb* VANDALIZE, damage, destroy, total (*slang*), injure, mar, spoil, trash (*slang*), impair, tarnish, obliterate, mutilate, deform, blemish, disfigure, sully

de facto *adverb* IN FACT, really, actually, in effect, in reality

▷ *adjective* ACTUAL, real, existing

defamation *noun* SLANDER, smear, libel, scandal, slur, vilification, opprobrium, denigration, calumny, character assassination, disparagement, obloquy, aspersion, traducement

defamatory *adjective* SLANDEROUS, insulting, abusive, denigrating, disparaging, vilifying, derogatory, injurious, libellous, vituperative, calumnious, contumelious

defame *verb* SLANDER, smear, libel, discredit, knock (*informal*), rubbish (*informal*), disgrace, blacken, slag (off) (*slang*), detract, malign, denigrate, disparage, vilify, dishonour, stigmatize, bad-mouth (*slang, chiefly US & Canad*), besmirch, traduce, cast aspersions on, speak evil of, cast a slur on, calumniate, vituperate, asperse

default *noun* 1 (usually in phrase *by default* or *in default of*) FAILURE, want, lack, fault, absence, neglect, defect, deficiency, lapse, omission, dereliction

2 NONPAYMENT, evasion

▷ *verb* FAIL TO PAY, dodge, evade, rat (*informal*), neglect, levant (*Brit*), welch *or* welsh (*slang*)

defeat *verb* 1 BEAT, crush, overwhelm, conquer, stuff (*slang*), master, worst, tank (*slang*), overthrow, lick (*informal*), undo, subdue, rout, overpower, quell, trounce, clobber (*slang*), vanquish, repulse, subjugate, run rings around (*informal*), wipe the floor with (*informal*), make mincemeat of (*informal*), pip at the post, outplay, blow out of the water (*slang*)

<< OPPOSITE surrender

2 FRUSTRATE, foil, thwart, ruin, baffle, confound, balk, get the better of, forestall, stymie

▷ *noun* 1 CONQUEST, beating, overthrow, pasting (*slang*), rout, debacle, trouncing, repulse, vanquishment

<< OPPOSITE victory

2 FRUSTRATION, failure, reverse, disappointment, setback, thwarting

defeated *adjective* BEATEN, crushed, conquered, worsted, routed, overcome, overwhelmed, thrashed, licked (*informal*), thwarted, overpowered, balked, trounced, vanquished, checkmated, bested

<< OPPOSITE victorious

defeatist *noun* PESSIMIST, sceptic, scoffer, doubter, quitter, prophet of doom, yielder

▷ *adjective* PESSIMISTIC, resigned, despairing, hopeless, foreboding, despondent, fatalistic

defecate *verb* EXCRETE, eliminate, discharge, evacuate (*Physiology*), dump (*slang, chiefly US*), pass a motion, move the bowels, empty the bowels, open the bowels, egest, void excrement

defect *noun* DEFICIENCY, want, failing, lack, mistake, fault, error, absence, weakness, flaw, shortcoming, inadequacy, imperfection, frailty, foible

▷ *verb* DESERT, rebel, quit, revolt, change sides, apostatize, tergiversate

defection *noun* DESERTION, revolt, rebellion, abandonment, dereliction, backsliding, apostasy

defective *adjective* 1 FAULTY, broken, not working, flawed, imperfect, out of order, on the blink (*slang*)

<< OPPOSITE perfect

2 DEFICIENT, lacking, short, inadequate, insufficient, incomplete, scant

<< OPPOSITE adequate

defector *noun* DESERTER, renegade, turncoat, apostate, recreant (*archaic*), runagate (*archaic*), tergiversator

defence *or US* **defense** *noun* 1 PROTECTION, cover, security, guard, shelter, refuge, resistance, safeguard, immunity

2 ARMAMENTS, weapons

3 ARGUMENT, explanation, excuse, plea, apology, justification, vindication, rationalization, apologia, exoneration, exculpation, extenuation

4 PLEA (*Law*), case, claim, pleading, declaration, testimony, denial, alibi, vindication, rebuttal

▷ *plural noun* SHIELD, barricade, fortification, bastion, buttress, rampart, bulwark, fastness, fortified pa (*NZ*)

defenceless *or US* **defenseless** *adjective* HELPLESS, exposed, vulnerable, naked, endangered, powerless, wide open, unarmed, unprotected, unguarded

<< OPPOSITE safe

defend *verb* 1 PROTECT, cover, guard, screen, secure, preserve, look after, shelter, shield, harbour, safeguard, fortify, ward off, watch over, stick up for (*informal*), keep safe, give sanctuary

2 SUPPORT, champion, justify, maintain, sustain, plead for, endorse, assert, stand by, uphold, vindicate, stand up for, espouse, speak up for, stick up for (*informal*)

defendant *noun* ACCUSED, respondent, appellant, litigant, prisoner at the bar

defender *noun* 1 SUPPORTER, champion, advocate, sponsor, follower, patron, apologist, upholder, vindicator

2 PROTECTOR, guard, guardian, escort, bodyguard, guardian angel

defensible *adjective* JUSTIFIABLE, right, sound, reasonable, acceptable, sensible, valid, legitimate, plausible, permissible, well-founded, tenable, excusable, pardonable, vindicable

<< OPPOSITE unjustifiable

defensive *adjective* 1 PROTECTIVE, defending, opposing, safeguarding, watchful, on the defensive, on guard

2 OVERSENSITIVE, uptight (*informal*)

defensively *adverb* IN SELF-DEFENCE, in defence, suspiciously, on the defensive

defer[1] *verb* POSTPONE, delay, put off, suspend,

shelve, set aside, adjourn, hold over, procrastinate, put on ice (*informal*), put on the back burner (*informal*), protract, take a rain check on (*US & Canad informal*), prorogue

defer² *with* **to** COMPLY WITH, give way to, submit to, bow to, give in to, yield to, accede to, capitulate to

deference *noun* 1 RESPECT, regard, consideration, attention, honour, esteem, courtesy, homage, reverence, politeness, civility, veneration, thoughtfulness
<< OPPOSITE disrespect
2 OBEDIENCE, yielding, submission, compliance, capitulation, acquiescence, obeisance, complaisance
<< OPPOSITE disobedience

deferential *adjective* RESPECTFUL, civil, polite, courteous, considerate, obedient, submissive, dutiful, ingratiating, reverential, obsequious, complaisant, obeisant, regardful

defiance *noun* RESISTANCE, challenge, opposition, confrontation, contempt, disregard, provocation, disobedience, insolence, insubordination, rebelliousness, recalcitrance, contumacy
<< OPPOSITE obedience

defiant *adjective* RESISTING, challenging, rebellious, daring, aggressive, bold, provocative, audacious, recalcitrant, antagonistic, insolent, mutinous, disobedient, refractory, insubordinate, contumacious
<< OPPOSITE obedient

deficiency *noun* 1 LACK, want, deficit, absence, shortage, deprivation, inadequacy, scarcity, dearth, privation, insufficiency, scantiness
<< OPPOSITE sufficiency
2 FAILING, fault, weakness, defect, flaw, drawback, shortcoming, imperfection, frailty, demerit

deficient *adjective* 1 LACKING, wanting, needing, short, inadequate, insufficient, scarce, scant, meagre, skimpy, scanty, exiguous
2 UNSATISFACTORY, weak, flawed, inferior, impaired, faulty, incomplete, defective, imperfect

deficit *noun* SHORTFALL, shortage, deficiency, loss, default, arrears

defile *verb* 1 DEGRADE, stain, disgrace, sully, debase, dishonour, besmirch, smirch
2 DESECRATE, violate, contaminate, abuse, pollute, profane, dishonour, despoil, treat sacrilegiously
3 DIRTY, soil, contaminate, smear, pollute, taint, tarnish, make foul, smirch, befoul

define *verb* 1 MARK OUT, outline, limit, bound, delineate, circumscribe, demarcate, delimit
2 DESCRIBE, interpret, characterize, explain, spell out, expound
3 ESTABLISH, detail, determine, specify, designate

definite *adjective* 1 SPECIFIC, exact, precise, clear, particular, express, determined, fixed, black-and-white, explicit, clear-cut, cut-and-dried (*informal*), clearly defined
<< OPPOSITE vague
2 CLEAR, explicit, black-and-white, clear-cut, unequivocal, unambiguous, guaranteed, cut-and-dried (*informal*)
3 NOTICEABLE, marked, clear, decided, striking, noted, particular, obvious, dramatic, considerable, remarkable, apparent, evident, distinct, notable, manifest, conspicuous
4 CERTAIN, decided, sure, settled, convinced, positive, confident, assured
<< OPPOSITE uncertain

Definite and *definitive* should be carefully distinguished. *Definite* indicates precision and firmness, as in *a definite decision*. *Definitive* includes these senses but also indicates conclusiveness. *A definite answer* indicates a clear and firm answer to a particular question; *a definitive answer* implies an authoritative resolution of a complex question

definitely *adverb* CERTAINLY, clearly, obviously, surely, easily, plainly, absolutely, positively, decidedly, needless to say, without doubt, unquestionably, undeniably, categorically, without question, unequivocally, unmistakably, far and away, without fail, beyond any doubt, indubitably, come hell or high water (*informal*)

definition *noun* 1 DESCRIPTION, interpretation, explanation, clarification, exposition, explication, elucidation, statement of meaning
2 SHARPNESS, focus, clarity, contrast, precision, distinctness

definitive *adjective* 1 FINAL, convincing, absolute, clinching, decisive, definite, conclusive, irrefutable
2 AUTHORITATIVE, greatest, ultimate, reliable, most significant, exhaustive, superlative, mother of all (*informal*) ▷ see **definite**

deflate *verb* 1 HUMILIATE, humble, squash, put down (*slang*), disconcert, chasten, mortify, dispirit
2 PUNCTURE, flatten, empty
<< OPPOSITE inflate
3 COLLAPSE, go down, contract, empty, shrink, void, flatten
<< OPPOSITE expand
4 (*Economics*) REDUCE, depress, decrease, diminish, devalue, depreciate

deflect *verb* TURN ASIDE, turn, bend, twist, sidetrack

deflection *noun* DEVIATION, bending, veering, swerving, divergence, turning aside, refraction, declination

deform *verb* 1 DISFIGURE, twist, injure, cripple, ruin, mar, spoil, mutilate, maim, deface
2 DISTORT, twist, warp, buckle, mangle, contort, gnarl, misshape, malform

deformation *noun* DISTORTION, warping, contortion, malformation, disfiguration, misshapenness

deformed *adjective* DISTORTED, bent, twisted, crooked, crippled, warped, maimed, marred, mangled, disfigured, misshapen, malformed, misbegotten

deformity *noun* 1 ABNORMALITY, defect, malformation, disfigurement
2 DISTORTION, irregularity, misshapenness, misproportion

defraud *verb* CHEAT, rob, con (*informal*), do (*slang*), skin (*slang*), stiff (*slang*), rip off (*slang*), fleece, swindle, stitch up (*slang*), rook (*slang*), diddle (*informal*), bilk, gyp (*slang*), pull a fast one on (*informal*), cozen

defray *verb* (used with *costs* or *expenses* as object) PAY, meet, cover, clear, settle, discharge

deft *adjective* SKILFUL, able, expert, clever, neat, handy, adept, nimble, proficient, agile, adroit, dexterous
<< OPPOSITE clumsy

defunct *adjective* 1 DEAD, extinct, gone, departed, expired, deceased, bygone, nonexistent
2 NOT FUNCTIONING, obsolete, out of commission, inoperative

defuse *verb* 1 CALM, settle, cool, contain, smooth, stabilize, damp down, take the heat *or* sting out of
<< OPPOSITE aggravate
2 DEACTIVATE, disable, disarm, make safe
<< OPPOSITE activate ▷ see **diffuse**

defy *verb* 1 RESIST, oppose, confront, face, brave, beard, disregard, stand up to, spurn, flout, disobey, hold out against, put up a fight against, hurl defiance at, contemn
2 CHALLENGE, dare, provoke
3 FOIL, defeat, escape, frustrate, be beyond, baffle, thwart, elude, confound

degenerate *verb* DECLINE, slip, sink, decrease, deteriorate, worsen, rot, decay, lapse, fall off, regress, go to pot, retrogress
▷ *adjective* DEPRAVED, base, corrupt, fallen, low, perverted, degraded, degenerated, immoral, decadent, debased, debauched, dissolute, pervy (*slang*)

degeneration *noun* DETERIORATION, decline, dissolution, descent, regression, dissipation, degeneracy, debasement

degradation *noun* 1 DISGRACE, shame, humiliation, discredit, ignominy, dishonour, mortification
2 DETERIORATION, decline, decadence, degeneration, perversion, degeneracy, debasement, abasement

degrade *verb* 1 DEMEAN, disgrace, humiliate, injure, shame, corrupt, humble, discredit, pervert, debase, dishonour, cheapen
<< OPPOSITE ennoble
2 DEMOTE, reduce, lower, downgrade, depose, cashier
<< OPPOSITE promote

degraded *adjective* 1 HUMILIATED, embarrassed, shamed, mortified, debased, discomfited, abased
2 CORRUPT, low, base, abandoned, vicious, vile, sordid, decadent, despicable, depraved, debased, profligate, disreputable, debauched, dissolute, scungy (*Austral & NZ*)

degrading *adjective* DEMEANING, lowering, humiliating, disgraceful, shameful, unworthy, debasing, undignified, contemptible, cheapening, dishonourable, infra dig (*informal*)

degree *noun* 1 AMOUNT, measure, rate, stage, extent, grade, proportion, gradation
2 (*Archaic*) RANK, order, standing, level, class, position, station, status, grade, caste, nobility, echelon
▷▷ **by degrees** LITTLE BY LITTLE, slowly, gradually, moderately, gently, piecemeal, bit by bit, imperceptibly, inch by inch, unhurriedly

dehydrate *verb* DRY, evaporate, parch, desiccate, exsiccate

deign *verb* CONDESCEND, consent, stoop, see fit, think fit, lower yourself, deem it worthy

deity *noun* GOD, goddess, immortal, divinity, godhead, divine being, supreme being, celestial being, atua (NZ)

dejected *adjective* DOWNHEARTED, down, low, blue, sad, depressed, miserable, gloomy, dismal, melancholy, glum, despondent, downcast, morose, disheartened, wretched, disconsolate, crestfallen, doleful, down in the dumps (*informal*), cast down, sick as a parrot (*informal*), woebegone, low-spirited
<< OPPOSITE cheerful

delay *verb* 1 PUT OFF, suspend, postpone, stall, shelve, prolong, defer, hold over, temporize, put on the back burner (*informal*), protract, take a rain check on (*US & Canad informal*)
2 HOLD UP, detain, hold back, stop, arrest, halt, hinder, obstruct, retard, impede, bog down, set back, slow up
<< OPPOSITE speed (up)
3 LINGER, lag, loiter, dawdle, tarry, dilly-dally (*informal*), drag your feet *or* heels (*informal*)
▷ *noun* 1 HOLD-UP, wait, check, setback,

interruption, obstruction, stoppage, impediment, hindrance
2 DAWDLING, lingering, loitering, procrastination, tarrying, dilly-dallying (*informal*)

delectable *adjective* 1 DELICIOUS, tasty, luscious, inviting, satisfying, pleasant, delightful, enjoyable, lush, enticing, gratifying, dainty, yummy (*slang*), scrumptious (*informal*), appetizing, toothsome, lekker (*S African slang*), yummo (*Austral slang*)
<< OPPOSITE disgusting
2 CHARMING, pleasant, delightful, agreeable, adorable

delegate *noun* REPRESENTATIVE, agent, deputy, ambassador, commissioner, envoy, proxy, depute (*Scot*), legate, spokesman *or* spokeswoman
▷ *verb* 1 ENTRUST, transfer, hand over, give, pass on, assign, relegate, consign, devolve
2 APPOINT, commission, select, contract, engage, nominate, designate, mandate, authorize, empower, accredit, depute

delegation *noun* 1 DEPUTATION, envoys, contingent, commission, embassy, legation
2 COMMISSIONING, relegation, assignment, devolution, committal, deputizing, entrustment

delete *verb* REMOVE, cancel, cut out, erase, edit, excise, strike out, obliterate, efface, blot out, cross out, expunge, dele, rub out, edit out, blue-pencil

deliberate *adjective* 1 INTENTIONAL, meant, planned, considered, studied, designed, intended, conscious, calculated, thoughtful, wilful, purposeful, premeditated, prearranged, done on purpose
<< OPPOSITE accidental
2 CAREFUL, measured, slow, cautious, wary, thoughtful, prudent, circumspect, methodical, unhurried, heedful
<< OPPOSITE hurried
▷ *verb* CONSIDER, think, ponder, discuss, debate, reflect, consult, weigh, meditate, mull over, ruminate, cogitate

deliberately *adverb* INTENTIONALLY, on purpose, consciously, emphatically, knowingly, resolutely, pointedly, determinedly, wilfully, by design, studiously, in cold blood, wittingly, calculatingly

deliberation *noun* 1 CONSIDERATION, thought, reflection, study, speculation, calculation, meditation, forethought, circumspection, cogitation
2 *usually plural* DISCUSSION, talk, conference, exchange, debate, analysis, conversation, dialogue, consultation, seminar, symposium, colloquy, confabulation

delicacy *noun* 1 FRAGILITY, frailty, brittleness, flimsiness, frailness, frangibility
2 DAINTINESS, charm, grace, elegance, neatness, prettiness, slenderness, exquisiteness
3 DIFFICULTY, sensitivity, stickiness (*informal*), precariousness, critical nature, touchiness, ticklishness
4 SENSITIVITY, understanding, consideration, judgment, perception, diplomacy, discretion, skill, finesse, tact, thoughtfulness, savoir-faire, adroitness, sensitiveness
5 TREAT, luxury, goody, savoury, dainty, morsel, titbit, choice item, juicy bit, bonne bouche (*French*)
6 LIGHTNESS, accuracy, precision, elegance, sensibility, purity, subtlety, refinement, finesse, nicety, fineness, exquisiteness

delicate *adjective* 1 FINE, detailed, elegant, exquisite, graceful
2 SUBTLE, fine, nice, soft, delicious, faint, refined, muted, subdued, pastel, understated, dainty
<< OPPOSITE bright
3 FRAGILE, weak, frail, brittle, tender, flimsy, dainty, breakable, frangible
<< OPPOSITE strong
4 DIFFICULT, critical, sensitive, complicated, sticky (*informal*), problematic, precarious, thorny, touchy, knotty, ticklish
5 SKILLED, accurate, precise, deft
6 FASTIDIOUS, nice, critical, pure, Victorian, proper, refined, discriminating, stuffy, scrupulous, prim, puritanical, squeamish, prudish, prissy (*informal*), strait-laced, schoolmarmish (*Brit informal*), old-maidish (*informal*)
<< OPPOSITE crude
7 DIPLOMATIC, sensitive, careful, subtle, thoughtful, discreet, prudent, considerate, judicious, tactful
<< OPPOSITE insensitive

delicately *adverb* 1 FINELY, lightly, subtly, softly, carefully, precisely, elegantly, gracefully, deftly, exquisitely, skilfully, daintily
2 TACTFULLY, carefully, subtly, discreetly, thoughtfully, diplomatically, sensitively, prudently, judiciously, considerately

delicious *adjective* 1 DELECTABLE, tasty, luscious, choice, savoury, palatable, dainty, mouthwatering, yummy (*slang*), scrumptious (*informal*), appetizing, toothsome, ambrosial, lekker (*S African slang*), nectareous, yummo (*Austral slang*)
<< OPPOSITE unpleasant
2 DELIGHTFUL, pleasing, charming, heavenly, thrilling, entertaining, pleasant, enjoyable, exquisite, captivating, agreeable, pleasurable, rapturous, delectable

delight *verb* PLEASE, satisfy, content, thrill,

charm, cheer, amuse, divert, enchant, rejoice, gratify, ravish, gladden, give pleasure to, tickle pink (*informal*)
<< OPPOSITE displease
▷ *noun* PLEASURE, joy, satisfaction, comfort, happiness, ecstasy, enjoyment, bliss, felicity, glee, gratification, rapture, gladness
<< OPPOSITE displeasure
▷▷ **delight in** *or* **take (a) delight in something** *or* **someone** LIKE, love, enjoy, appreciate, relish, indulge in, savour, revel in, take pleasure in, glory in, luxuriate in

delighted *adjective* PLEASED, happy, charmed, thrilled, enchanted, ecstatic, captivated, jubilant, joyous, elated, over the moon (*informal*), overjoyed, rapt, gladdened, cock-a-hoop, blissed out, in seventh heaven, sent, stoked (*Austral & NZ informal*)

delightful *adjective* PLEASANT, pleasing, charming, engaging, heavenly, thrilling, fascinating, entertaining, amusing, enjoyable, enchanting, captivating, gratifying, agreeable, pleasurable, ravishing, rapturous
<< OPPOSITE unpleasant

delineate *verb* OUTLINE, describe, draw, picture, paint, chart, trace, portray, sketch, render, depict, characterize, map out

delinquency *noun* CRIME, misconduct, wrongdoing, fault, offence, misdemeanour, misdeed, misbehaviour, villainy, lawbreaking

delinquent *noun* CRIMINAL, offender, villain, culprit, young offender, wrongdoer, juvenile delinquent, miscreant, malefactor, lawbreaker

delirious *adjective* 1 MAD, crazy, raving, insane, demented, deranged, incoherent, unhinged, light-headed
<< OPPOSITE rational
2 ECSTATIC, wild, excited, frantic, frenzied, hysterical, carried away, blissed out, beside yourself, sent, Corybantic
<< OPPOSITE calm

delirium *noun* 1 MADNESS, raving, insanity, lunacy, derangement
2 FRENZY, passion, rage, fever, fury, ecstasy, hysteria

deliver *verb* 1 BRING, carry, bear, transport, distribute, convey, cart
2 *sometimes with* **over** *or* **up** HAND OVER, present, commit, give up, yield, surrender, turn over, relinquish, make over
3 GIVE, read, present, announce, publish, declare, proclaim, pronounce, utter, give forth
4 STRIKE, give, deal, launch, throw, direct, aim, administer, inflict
5 RELEASE, free, save, rescue, loose, discharge, liberate, acquit, redeem, ransom, emancipate

deliverance *noun* RELEASE, rescue, liberation, salvation, redemption, ransom, emancipation

delivery *noun* 1 HANDING OVER, transfer, distribution, transmission, dispatch, consignment, conveyance, transmittal
2 CONSIGNMENT, goods, shipment, batch
3 SPEECH, speaking, expression, pronunciation, utterance, articulation, intonation, diction, elocution, enunciation, vocalization
4 CHILDBIRTH, labour, confinement, parturition

delude *verb* DECEIVE, kid (*informal*), fool, trick, take in (*informal*), cheat, con (*informal*), mislead, impose on, hoax, dupe, beguile, gull (*archaic*), bamboozle (*informal*), hoodwink, take someone for a ride (*informal*), pull the wool over someone's eyes, lead someone up the garden path (*informal*), cozen, misguide

deluge *noun* 1 RUSH, flood, avalanche, barrage, spate, torrent
2 FLOOD, spate, overflowing, torrent, downpour, cataclysm, inundation
▷ *verb* 1 OVERWHELM, swamp, engulf, overload, overrun, inundate
2 FLOOD, drown, swamp, submerge, soak, drench, inundate, douse

delusion *noun* MISCONCEPTION, mistaken idea, misapprehension, fancy, illusion, deception, hallucination, fallacy, self-deception, false impression, phantasm, misbelief

deluxe *or* **de luxe** *adjective* LUXURIOUS, grand, select, special, expensive, rich, exclusive, superior, elegant, costly, splendid, gorgeous, sumptuous, plush (*informal*), opulent, palatial, splendiferous (*facetious*)

delve *verb* 1 RESEARCH, investigate, explore, examine, probe, look into, burrow into, dig into
2 RUMMAGE, search, look, burrow, ransack, forage, dig, fossick (*Austral & NZ*)

demagogue *noun* AGITATOR, firebrand, haranguer, rabble-rouser, soapbox orator

demand *verb* 1 REQUEST, ask (for), order, expect, claim, seek, call for, insist on, exact, appeal for, solicit
2 CHALLENGE, ask, question, inquire
3 REQUIRE, take, want, need, involve, call for, entail, necessitate, cry out for
<< OPPOSITE provide
▷ *noun* 1 REQUEST, order, charge, bidding
2 NEED, want, call, market, claim, requirement, necessity
▷▷ **in demand** SOUGHT AFTER, needed, popular, favoured, requested, in favour, fashionable, well-liked, in vogue, like gold dust

demanding *adjective* DIFFICULT, trying, hard, taxing, wearing, challenging, tough, exhausting, exacting, exigent
<< OPPOSITE easy

demarcation *noun* 1 LIMIT, bound, margin,

boundary, confine, enclosure, pale
2 DELIMITATION, division, distinction, separation, differentiation
demean *verb* DEGRADE, lower, debase, humble, abase
▷▷ **demean yourself** LOWER YOURSELF, humiliate yourself, humble yourself, debase yourself, downgrade yourself, abase yourself, belittle yourself, degrade yourself
demeanour *or US* **demeanor** *noun*
1 BEHAVIOUR, conduct, manner
2 BEARING, air, manner, carriage, deportment, mien, comportment
demented *adjective* MAD, crazy, foolish, daft (*informal*), frenzied, distraught, manic, insane, crazed, lunatic, unbalanced, deranged, idiotic, unhinged, dotty (*slang, chiefly Brit*), loopy (*informal*), crackpot (*informal*), out to lunch (*informal*), barking mad (*slang*), barking (*slang*), maniacal, gonzo (*slang*), doolally (*slang*), off your trolley (*slang*), up the pole (*informal*), non compos mentis (*Latin*), not the full shilling (*informal*), crackbrained, wacko *or* whacko (*slang*), off the air (*Austral slang*), porangi (NZ)
<< OPPOSITE sane
demise *noun* 1 FAILURE, end, fall, defeat, collapse, ruin, breakdown, overthrow, downfall, dissolution, termination
2 (*Euphemistic*) DEATH, end, dying, passing, departure, expiration, decease
democracy *noun* SELF-GOVERNMENT, republic, commonwealth, representative government, government by the people
Democrat *noun* LEFT-WINGER
democratic *adjective* SELF-GOVERNING, popular, republican, representative, autonomous, populist, egalitarian
demolish *verb* 1 KNOCK DOWN, level, destroy, ruin, overthrow, dismantle, flatten, trash (*slang*), total (*slang*), tear down, bulldoze, raze, pulverize
<< OPPOSITE build
2 DESTROY, wreck, overturn, overthrow, undo, blow out of the water (*slang*)
3 (*Facetious*) DEVOUR, eat, consume, swallow, bolt, gorge, put away, gobble up, guzzle, polish off (*informal*), gulp down, wolf down, pig out on (*slang*)
demolition *noun* KNOCKING DOWN, levelling, destruction, explosion, wrecking, tearing down, bulldozing, razing
demon *noun* 1 EVIL SPIRIT, devil, fiend, goblin, ghoul, malignant spirit, atua (NZ), wairua (NZ)
2 WIZARD, master, ace (*informal*), addict, fanatic, fiend
3 MONSTER, beast, villain, rogue, barbarian, brute, ogre
demoniac, demonic *or* **demoniacal** *adjective*
1 DEVILISH, satanic, diabolical, hellish, infernal, fiendish, diabolic
2 FRENZIED, mad, furious, frantic, hectic, manic, crazed, frenetic, maniacal, like one possessed
demonstrable *adjective* PROVABLE, obvious, evident, certain, positive, unmistakable, palpable, undeniable, self-evident, verifiable, irrefutable, incontrovertible, axiomatic, indubitable, attestable, evincible
demonstrate *verb* 1 PROVE, show, establish, indicate, make clear, manifest, evidence, testify to, evince, show clearly
2 SHOW, evidence, express, display, indicate, exhibit, manifest, make clear *or* plain
3 MARCH, protest, rally, object, parade, picket, say no to, remonstrate, take up the cudgels, express disapproval, hikoi (NZ)
4 DESCRIBE, show, explain, teach, illustrate
demonstration *noun* 1 MARCH, protest, rally, sit-in, parade, procession, demo (*informal*), picket, mass lobby, hikoi (NZ)
2 DISPLAY, show, performance, explanation, description, presentation, demo (*informal*), exposition
3 INDICATION, proof, testimony, confirmation, affirmation, validation, substantiation, attestation
4 EXHIBITION, display, expression, illustration
demoralize *verb* DISHEARTEN, undermine, discourage, shake, depress, weaken, rattle (*informal*), daunt, unnerve, disconcert, psych out (*informal*), dispirit, deject
<< OPPOSITE encourage
demoralized *adjective* DISHEARTENED, undermined, discouraged, broken, depressed, crushed, weakened, subdued, unnerved, unmanned, dispirited, downcast, sick as a parrot (*informal*)
demoralizing *adjective* DISHEARTENING, discouraging, depressing, crushing, disappointing, daunting, dampening, dispiriting
<< OPPOSITE encouraging
demote *verb* DOWNGRADE, relegate, degrade, kick downstairs (*slang*), declass, disrate (*Naval*), lower in rank
<< OPPOSITE promote
demur *verb* OBJECT, refuse, protest, doubt, dispute, pause, disagree, hesitate, waver, balk, take exception, cavil
▷ *noun* (always used in a negative construction) OBJECTION, protest, dissent, hesitation, misgiving, qualm, scruple, compunction, demurral, demurrer
demure *adjective* (usually used of a young woman) SHY, reserved, modest, retiring, reticent, unassuming, diffident, decorous
<< OPPOSITE brazen

den *noun* **1** LAIR, hole, shelter, cave, haunt, cavern, hide-out
2 (*Chiefly US*) STUDY, retreat, sanctuary, hideaway, cloister, sanctum, cubbyhole, snuggery

denial *noun* **1** NEGATION, dismissal, contradiction, dissent, disclaimer, retraction, repudiation, disavowal, adjuration
<< OPPOSITE admission
2 REFUSAL, veto, rejection, prohibition, rebuff, repulse

denigrate *verb* DISPARAGE, run down, slag (off) (*slang*), knock (*informal*), rubbish (*informal*), blacken, malign, belittle, decry, revile, vilify, slander, defame, bad-mouth (*slang, chiefly US & Canad*), besmirch, impugn, calumniate, asperse
<< OPPOSITE praise

denizen *noun* INHABITANT, resident, citizen, occupant, dweller

denomination *noun* **1** RELIGIOUS GROUP, belief, sect, persuasion, creed, school, hauhau (NZ)
2 UNIT, value, size, grade

denote *verb* INDICATE, show, mean, mark, express, import, imply, designate, signify, typify, betoken

denouement *or* **dénouement** *noun* OUTCOME, end, result, consequence, resolution, conclusion, end result, upshot

denounce *verb* **1** CONDEMN, attack, censure, decry, castigate, revile, vilify, proscribe, stigmatize, impugn, excoriate, declaim against
2 REPORT, dob in (*Austral slang*)

dense *adjective* **1** THICK, close, heavy, solid, substantial, compact, compressed, condensed, impenetrable, close-knit, thickset
<< OPPOSITE thin
2 HEAVY, thick, substantial, opaque, impenetrable
3 (*informal*) STUPID, slow, thick, dull, dumb (*informal*), crass, dozy (*Brit informal*), dozy (*Brit informal*), stolid, dopey (*informal*), moronic, obtuse, brainless, blockheaded, braindead (*informal*), dumb-ass (*informal*), dead from the neck up (*informal*), thickheaded, blockish, dim-witted (*informal*), slow-witted, thick-witted
<< OPPOSITE bright

density *noun* **1** TIGHTNESS, closeness, thickness, compactness, impenetrability, denseness, crowdedness
2 MASS, body, bulk, consistency, solidity

dent *noun* HOLLOW, chip, indentation, depression, impression, pit, dip, crater, ding (*Austral & NZ dated informal*), dimple, concavity
▷ *verb* MAKE A DENT IN, press in, gouge, depress, hollow, imprint, push in, dint, make concave

denude *verb* STRIP, expose, bare, uncover, divest, lay bare

denunciation *noun* **1** CONDEMNATION, criticism, accusation, censure, stick (*slang*), invective, character assassination, stigmatization, castigation, obloquy, denouncement, fulmination
2 IMPLICATION, accusation, indictment, incrimination, denouncement, inculpation

deny *verb* **1** CONTRADICT, oppose, counter, disagree with, rebuff, negate, rebut, refute, gainsay (*archaic or literary*)
<< OPPOSITE admit
2 RENOUNCE, reject, discard, revoke, retract, repudiate, renege, disown, rebut, disavow, recant, disclaim, abjure, abnegate, refuse to acknowledge *or* recognize
3 REFUSE, decline, forbid, reject, rule out, veto, turn down, prohibit, withhold, preclude, disallow, negate, begrudge, interdict
<< OPPOSITE permit

deodorant *noun* **1** ANTIPERSPIRANT, deodorizer
2 DEODORIZER, disinfectant, air freshener, fumigant

depart *verb* **1** LEAVE, go, withdraw, retire, disappear, quit, retreat, exit, go away, vanish, absent (yourself), start out, migrate, set forth, take (your) leave, decamp, hook it (*slang*), slope off, pack your bags (*informal*), make tracks, rack off (*Austral & NZ slang*)
<< OPPOSITE arrive
2 DEVIATE, vary, differ, stray, veer, swerve, diverge, digress, turn aside
3 (*Chiefly US*) RESIGN, leave, quit, step down (*informal*), give in your notice, call it a day *or* night, vacate your post

departed *adjective* (*Euphemistic*) DEAD, late, deceased, expired, perished

department *noun* **1** SECTION, office, unit, station, division, branch, bureau, subdivision
2 (*informal*) AREA, line, responsibility, function, province, sphere, realm, domain, speciality

departure *noun* **1** LEAVING, going, retirement, withdrawal, exit, going away, removal, exodus, leave-taking
<< OPPOSITE arrival
2 RETIREMENT, going, withdrawal, exit, going away, removal
3 SHIFT, change, difference, variation, innovation, novelty, veering, deviation, branching out, divergence, digression

dependable *adjective* RELIABLE, sure, responsible, steady, faithful, staunch, reputable, trustworthy, trusty, unfailing
<< OPPOSITE undependable

dependant *noun* RELATIVE, rellie (*Austral slang*), child, minor, subordinate, cohort (*chiefly US*), protégé, henchman, retainer, hanger-on, minion, vassal

Dependant is the generally accepted correct spelling in British usage for the noun and always refers to people: *if you are single and have no dependants*. The adjective should be spelt *dependent*: *tax allowance for dependent* (not *dependant*) *children*. American usage spells both adjective and noun with an *e* in the last syllable

dependence *or sometimes US* **dependance** *noun* RELIANCE, trust, hope, confidence, belief, faith, expectation, assurance

dependency *or sometimes US* **dependancy** *noun* 1 OVERRELIANCE, attachment
2 ADDICTION, dependence, craving, need, habit, obsession, enslavement, overreliance

dependent *or sometimes US* **dependant** *adjective* 1 RELIANT, vulnerable, helpless, powerless, weak, defenceless
<< OPPOSITE independent
2 DETERMINED BY, depending on, subject to, influenced by, relative to, liable to, conditional on, contingent on
▷▷ **dependent on** *or* **upon** RELIANT ON, relying on, counting on ▷ see **dependant**

depend on *verb* 1 BE DETERMINED BY, be based on, be subject to, hang on, rest on, revolve around, hinge on, be subordinate to, be contingent on
2 COUNT ON, turn to, trust in, bank on, lean on, rely upon, confide in, build upon, calculate on, reckon on

depict *verb* 1 ILLUSTRATE, portray, picture, paint, outline, draw, sketch, render, reproduce, sculpt, delineate, limn
2 DESCRIBE, present, represent, detail, outline, sketch, characterize

depiction *noun* 1 PICTURE, drawing, image, outline, illustration, sketch, likeness, delineation
2 REPRESENTATION, description, portrait, illustration, sketch, portrayal

deplete *verb* USE UP, reduce, drain, exhaust, consume, empty, decrease, evacuate, lessen, impoverish, expend
<< OPPOSITE increase

depleted *adjective* USED (UP), drained, exhausted, consumed, spent, reduced, emptied, weakened, decreased, lessened, worn out, depreciated

depletion *noun* USING UP, reduction, drain, consumption, lowering, decrease, expenditure, deficiency, dwindling, lessening, exhaustion, diminution

deplorable *adjective* 1 TERRIBLE, distressing, dreadful, sad, unfortunate, disastrous, miserable, dire, melancholy, heartbreaking, grievous, regrettable, lamentable, calamitous, wretched, pitiable
<< OPPOSITE excellent
2 DISGRACEFUL, shameful, scandalous, reprehensible, disreputable, dishonourable, execrable, blameworthy, opprobrious
<< OPPOSITE admirable

deplore *verb* 1 DISAPPROVE OF, condemn, object to, denounce, censure, abhor, deprecate, take a dim view of, excoriate
2 LAMENT, regret, mourn, rue, bemoan, grieve for, bewail, sorrow over

deploy *verb* (used of troops or military resources) USE, station, set up, position, arrange, set out, dispose, utilize, spread out, distribute

deployment *noun* (used of troops or military resources) USE, stationing, spread, organization, arrangement, positioning, disposition, setup, utilization

deport *verb* EXPEL, exile, throw out, oust, banish, expatriate, extradite, evict, send packing, show you the door

deportation *noun* EXPULSION, exile, removal, transportation, exclusion, extradition, eviction, ejection, banishment, expatriation, debarment

depose *verb* OUST, dismiss, displace, degrade, downgrade, cashier, demote, dethrone, remove from office

deposit *verb* 1 PUT, place, lay, drop, settle
2 STORE, keep, put, bank, save, lodge, entrust, consign, hoard, stash (*informal*), lock away, put in storage
▷ *noun* 1 DOWN PAYMENT, security, stake, pledge, warranty, instalment, retainer, part payment
2 ACCUMULATION, growth, mass, build-up, layer
3 SEDIMENT, grounds, residue, lees, precipitate, deposition, silt, dregs, alluvium, settlings

deposition *noun* 1 (*Law*) SWORN STATEMENT, evidence, testimony, declaration, affidavit
2 REMOVAL, dismissal, ousting, toppling, expulsion, displacement, unseating, dethronement

depository *noun* STOREHOUSE, store, warehouse, depot, repository, safe-deposit box

depot *noun* 1 ARSENAL, warehouse, storehouse, repository, depository, dump
2 (*US & Canad*) BUS STATION, station, garage, terminus

deprave *verb* CORRUPT, pervert, degrade, seduce, subvert, debase, demoralize, debauch, brutalize, lead astray, vitiate

depraved *adjective* CORRUPT, abandoned, perverted, evil, vicious, degraded, vile, degenerate, immoral, wicked, shameless,

sinful, lewd, debased, profligate, debauched, lascivious, dissolute, licentious, pervy (*slang*)
<< OPPOSITE moral

depravity *noun* CORRUPTION, vice, evil, criminality, wickedness, immorality, iniquity, profligacy, debauchery, viciousness, degeneracy, sinfulness, debasement, turpitude, baseness, depravation, vitiation

deprecate *verb* DISPARAGE, criticize, run down, discredit, scorn, deride, detract, malign, denigrate, belittle, vilify, depreciate, knock (*informal*), diss (*slang, chiefly US*), bad-mouth (*slang, chiefly US & Canad*), lambast(e) ▷ see **depreciate**

depreciate *verb* 1 DECREASE, reduce, lessen, devalue, deflate, lower in value, devaluate
<< OPPOSITE augment
2 LOSE VALUE, devalue, devaluate
<< OPPOSITE appreciate

The word *depreciate* is not synonymous with *deprecate*. *Depreciate* means 'to reduce or decline in value or price' while *deprecate* means 'to express disapproval of'

depreciation *noun* DEVALUATION, fall, drop, depression, slump, deflation

depress *verb* 1 SADDEN, upset, distress, chill, discourage, grieve, daunt, oppress, desolate, weigh down, cast down, bring tears to your eyes, make sad, dishearten, dispirit, make your heart bleed, aggrieve, deject, make despondent, cast a gloom upon
<< OPPOSITE cheer
2 LOWER, cut, reduce, diminish, decrease, impair, lessen
<< OPPOSITE raise
3 DEVALUE, depreciate, cheapen, devaluate
4 PRESS DOWN, push, squeeze, lower, flatten, compress, push down, bear down on

depressed *adjective* 1 SAD, down, low, blue, unhappy, discouraged, fed up, moody, gloomy, pessimistic, melancholy, sombre, glum, mournful, dejected, despondent, dispirited, downcast, morose, disconsolate, crestfallen, doleful, downhearted, heavy-hearted, down in the dumps (*informal*), cheerless, woebegone, down in the mouth (*informal*), low-spirited
2 POVERTY-STRICKEN, poor, deprived, distressed, disadvantaged, run-down, impoverished, needy, destitute, down at heel
3 LOWERED, devalued, weakened, impaired, depreciated, cheapened
4 SUNKEN, hollow, recessed, set back, indented, concave

depressing *adjective* BLEAK, black, sad, distressing, discouraging, gloomy, daunting, hopeless, dismal, melancholy, dreary, harrowing, saddening, sombre, heartbreaking, dispiriting, disheartening, funereal, dejecting

depression *noun* 1 DESPAIR, misery, sadness, dumps (*informal*), the blues, melancholy, unhappiness, hopelessness, despondency, the hump (*Brit informal*), bleakness, melancholia, dejection, wretchedness, low spirits, gloominess, dolefulness, cheerlessness, downheartedness
2 RECESSION, slump, economic decline, stagnation, inactivity, hard *or* bad times
3 HOLLOW, pit, dip, bowl, valley, sink, impression, dent, sag, cavity, excavation, indentation, dimple, concavity

deprivation *noun* 1 LACK, denial, withdrawal, removal, expropriation, divestment, dispossession, deprival
2 WANT, need, hardship, suffering, distress, disadvantage, oppression, detriment, privation, destitution

deprive *verb* DISPOSSESS, rob, strip, divest, expropriate, despoil, bereave

deprived *adjective* POOR, disadvantaged, needy, in need, lacking, bereft, destitute, in want, denuded, down at heel, necessitous
<< OPPOSITE prosperous

depth *noun* 1 DEEPNESS, drop, measure, extent, profundity, profoundness
2 STRENGTH, intensity, seriousness, severity, extremity, keenness, intenseness
3 INSIGHT, intelligence, wisdom, penetration, profundity, acuity, discernment, perspicacity, sagacity, astuteness, profoundness, perspicuity
<< OPPOSITE superficiality
4 BREADTH, degree, magnitude, amplitude
5 INTENSITY, strength, warmth, richness, brightness, vibrancy, vividness
6 COMPLEXITY, intricacy, elaboration, obscurity, abstruseness, reconditeness
▷ *plural noun* 1 DEEPEST PART, middle, midst, remotest part, furthest part, innermost part
2 MOST INTENSE PART, pit, void, abyss, chasm, deepest part, furthest part, bottomless depth

deputy *noun* SUBSTITUTE, representative, ambassador, agent, commissioner, delegate, lieutenant, proxy, surrogate, second-in-command, nuncio, legate, vicegerent, number two
▷ *modifier* ASSISTANT, subordinate, depute (*Scot*)

deranged *adjective* MAD, crazy, insane, distracted, frantic, frenzied, irrational, maddened, crazed, lunatic, demented, unbalanced, berserk, delirious, unhinged, loopy (*informal*), crackpot (*informal*), out to lunch (*informal*), barking mad (*slang*), barking (*slang*), gonzo (*slang*), doolally (*slang*), off your trolley (*slang*), up the pole (*informal*), not the full shilling (*informal*), wacko *or* whacko (*slang*),

berko (*Austral slang*), off the air (*Austral slang*), porangi (NZ)
<< OPPOSITE sane

derelict *adjective* 1 ABANDONED, deserted, ruined, neglected, discarded, forsaken, dilapidated
2 (only used with *duty*) NEGLIGENT, slack, irresponsible, careless, lax, remiss
▷ *noun* TRAMP, bum (*informal*), outcast, drifter, down-and-out, vagrant, hobo (*chiefly US*), vagabond, bag lady, dosser (*Brit slang*), derro (*Austral slang*)

dereliction *noun* 1 ABANDONMENT, desertion, renunciation, relinquishment
2 (only used with *duty*) NEGLIGENCE, failure, neglect, evasion, delinquency, abdication, faithlessness, nonperformance, remissness

deride *verb* MOCK, ridicule, scorn, knock (*informal*), insult, taunt, sneer, jeer, disdain, scoff, detract, flout, disparage, chaff, gibe, pooh-pooh, contemn

derision *noun* MOCKERY, laughter, contempt, ridicule, scorn, insult, sneering, disdain, scoffing, disrespect, denigration, disparagement, contumely, raillery

derisory *adjective* RIDICULOUS, insulting, outrageous, ludicrous, preposterous, laughable, contemptible

derivation *noun* ORIGIN, source, basis, beginning, root, foundation, descent, ancestry, genealogy, etymology

derivative *adjective* UNORIGINAL, copied, second-hand, rehashed, imitative, plagiarized, uninventive, plagiaristic
<< OPPOSITE original
▷ *noun* BY-PRODUCT, spin-off, offshoot, descendant, derivation, outgrowth

derive *verb* OBTAIN, get, receive, draw, gain, collect, gather, extract, elicit, glean, procure
▷▷ **derive from something** COME FROM, stem from, arise from, flow from, spring from, emanate from, proceed from, descend from, issue from, originate from

derogatory *adjective* DISPARAGING, damaging, offensive, slighting, detracting, belittling, unfavourable, unflattering, dishonouring, defamatory, injurious, discreditable, uncomplimentary, depreciative
<< OPPOSITE complimentary

descend *verb* 1 FALL, drop, sink, go down, plunge, dive, tumble, plummet, subside, move down
<< OPPOSITE rise
2 GO DOWN, come down, walk down, move down, climb down
3 SLOPE, dip, incline, slant, gravitate
▷▷ **be descended from** ORIGINATE FROM, derive from, spring from, proceed from, issue from
▷▷ **descend on something** *or* **someone** ATTACK, assault, raid, invade, swoop, pounce, assail, arrive, come in force
▷▷ **descend to something** LOWER YOURSELF TO, stoop to, condescend to, abase yourself by

descendant *noun* SUCCESSOR, child, issue, son, daughter, heir, offspring, progeny, scion, inheritor
<< OPPOSITE ancestor

descent *noun* 1 FALL, drop, plunge, coming down, swoop
2 SLOPE, drop, dip, incline, slant, declination, declivity
3 DECLINE, deterioration, degradation, decadence, degeneration, debasement
4 ORIGIN, extraction, ancestry, lineage, family tree, parentage, heredity, genealogy, derivation

describe *verb* 1 RELATE, tell, report, present, detail, explain, express, illustrate, specify, chronicle, recount, recite, impart, narrate, set forth, give an account of
2 PORTRAY, depict, characterize, define, sketch
3 TRACE, draw, outline, mark out, delineate

description *noun* 1 ACCOUNT, report, explanation, representation, sketch, narrative, portrayal, depiction, narration, characterization, delineation
2 CALLING, naming, branding, labelling, dubbing, designation
3 KIND, sort, type, order, class, variety, brand, species, breed, category, kidney, genre, genus, ilk

descriptive *adjective* GRAPHIC, vivid, expressive, picturesque, detailed, explanatory, pictorial, illustrative, depictive

desecrate *verb* PROFANE, dishonour, defile, violate, contaminate, pollute, pervert, despoil, blaspheme, commit sacrilege
<< OPPOSITE revere

desert[1] *noun* WILDERNESS, waste, wilds, wasteland
▷ *adjective* BARREN, dry, waste, wild, empty, bare, lonely, solitary, desolate, arid, unproductive, infertile, uninhabited, uncultivated, unfruitful, untilled

desert[2] *verb* 1 ABANDON, leave, give up, quit (*informal*), withdraw from, move out of, relinquish, renounce, vacate, forsake, go away from, leave empty, relinquish possession of
2 LEAVE, abandon, strand, betray, maroon, walk out on (*informal*), forsake, jilt, run out on (*informal*), throw over, leave stranded, leave high and dry, leave (someone) in the lurch
<< OPPOSITE take care of
3 ABSCOND, defect, decamp, go over the hill (*Military slang*)

deserted *adjective* 1 EMPTY, abandoned, desolate, neglected, lonely, vacant, derelict, bereft, unoccupied, godforsaken

2 ABANDONED, neglected, forsaken, lonely, forlorn, cast off, left stranded, left in the lurch, unfriended

deserter *noun* DEFECTOR, runaway, fugitive, traitor, renegade, truant, escapee, absconder, apostate

desertion *noun* 1 ABANDONMENT, betrayal, forsaking, dereliction, relinquishment
2 DEFECTION, apostasy
3 ABSCONDING, flight, escape (*informal*), evasion, truancy

deserts ▷▷ **just deserts** DUE, payment, reward, punishment, right, return, retribution, recompense, come-uppance (*slang*), meed (*archaic*), requital, guerdon (*poetic*)

deserve *verb* MERIT, warrant, be entitled to, have a right to, win, rate, earn, justify, be worthy of, have a claim to

deserved *adjective* WELL-EARNED, just, right, meet (*archaic*), fitting, due, fair, earned, appropriate, justified, suitable, merited, proper, warranted, rightful, justifiable, condign

deservedly *adverb* RIGHTLY, fittingly, fairly, appropriately, properly, duly, justifiably, justly, by rights, rightfully, according to your due, condignly
<< OPPOSITE undeservedly

deserving *adjective* WORTHY, righteous, commendable, laudable, praiseworthy, meritorious, estimable
<< OPPOSITE undeserving

design *verb* 1 PLAN, describe, draw, draft, trace, outline, invent, devise, sketch, formulate, contrive, think out, delineate
2 CREATE, make, plan, project, fashion, scheme, propose, invent, devise, tailor, draw up, conceive, originate, contrive, fabricate, think up
3 INTEND, mean, plan, aim, purpose
▷ *noun* 1 PATTERN, form, figure, style, shape, organization, arrangement, construction, motif, configuration
2 PLAN, drawing, model, scheme, draft, outline, sketch, blueprint, delineation
3 INTENTION, end, point, aim, goal, target, purpose, object, objective, intent

designate *verb* 1 NAME, call, term, style, label, entitle, dub, nominate, christen
2 SPECIFY, describe, indicate, define, characterize, stipulate, denote
3 CHOOSE, reserve, select, label, flag, assign, allocate, set aside
4 APPOINT, name, choose, commission, select, elect, delegate, nominate, assign, depute

designation *noun* 1 NAME, title, label, description, denomination, epithet
2 APPOINTMENT, specification, classification
3 ELECTION, choice, selection, appointment, nomination

designer *noun* 1 COUTURIER, stylist
2 PRODUCER, architect, deviser, creator, planner, inventor, artificer, originator

designing *adjective* SCHEMING, plotting, intriguing, crooked (*informal*), shrewd, conspiring, cunning, sly, astute, treacherous, unscrupulous, devious, wily, crafty, artful, conniving, Machiavellian, deceitful

desirability *noun* WORTH, value, benefit, profit, advantage, merit, usefulness

desirable *adjective* 1 ADVANTAGEOUS, useful, valuable, helpful, profitable, of service, convenient, worthwhile, beneficial, preferable, advisable
<< OPPOSITE disadvantageous
2 POPULAR
<< OPPOSITE unpopular
3 ATTRACTIVE, appealing, beautiful, winning, interesting, pleasing, pretty, fair, inviting, engaging, lovely, charming, fascinating, sexy (*informal*), handsome, fetching, good-looking, eligible, glamorous, gorgeous, magnetic, cute, enticing, seductive, captivating, alluring, adorable, bonny, winsome, comely
<< OPPOSITE unattractive

desire *verb* 1 WANT, long for, crave, fancy, hope for, ache for, covet, aspire to, wish for, yearn for, thirst for, hanker after, set your heart on, desiderate
2 (*Formal*) REQUEST, ask, petition, solicit, entreat, importune
▷ *noun* 1 WISH, want, longing, need, hope, urge, yen (*informal*), hunger, appetite, aspiration, ache, craving, yearning, inclination, thirst, hankering
2 LUST, passion, libido, appetite, lechery, carnality, lasciviousness, concupiscence, randiness (*informal, chiefly Brit*), lustfulness

desired *adjective* REQUIRED, necessary, correct, appropriate, right, expected, fitting, particular, express, accurate, proper, exact

desist *verb* STOP, cease, refrain from, end, kick (*informal*), give up, suspend, break off, abstain, discontinue, leave off, have done with, give over (*informal*), forbear, belay (*Nautical*)

desolate *adjective* 1 UNINHABITED, deserted, bare, waste, wild, ruined, bleak, solitary, barren, dreary, godforsaken, unfrequented
<< OPPOSITE inhabited
2 MISERABLE, depressed, lonely, lonesome (*chiefly US & Canad*), gloomy, dismal, melancholy, forlorn, bereft, dejected, despondent, downcast, wretched, disconsolate, down in the dumps (*informal*), cheerless, comfortless, companionless
<< OPPOSITE happy
▷ *verb* 1 DEJECT, depress, distress, discourage, dismay, grieve, daunt, dishearten

<< OPPOSITE cheer
2 DESTROY, ruin, devastate, ravage, lay low, lay waste, despoil, depopulate
desolation *noun* **1** MISERY, distress, despair, gloom, sadness, woe, anguish, melancholy, unhappiness, dejection, wretchedness, gloominess
2 BLEAKNESS, isolation, loneliness, solitude, wildness, barrenness, solitariness, forlornness, desolateness
3 RUIN, destruction, havoc, devastation, ruination
despair *verb* LOSE HOPE, give up, lose heart, be despondent, be dejected
▷ *noun* DESPONDENCY, depression, misery, gloom, desperation, anguish, melancholy, hopelessness, dejection, wretchedness, disheartenment
despairing *adjective* HOPELESS, desperate, depressed, anxious, miserable, frantic, dismal, suicidal, melancholy, dejected, broken-hearted, despondent, downcast, grief-stricken, wretched, disconsolate, inconsolable, down in the dumps (*informal*), at the end of your tether
despatch ▷ see **dispatch**
desperado *noun* CRIMINAL, thug, outlaw, villain, gangster, gunman, bandit, mugger (*informal*), cut-throat, hoodlum (*chiefly US*), ruffian, heavy (*slang*), lawbreaker, skelm (*S African*)
desperate *adjective* **1** HOPELESS, despairing, in despair, forlorn, abject, dejected, despondent, demoralized, wretched, disconsolate, inconsolable, downhearted, at the end of your tether
2 GRAVE, great, pressing, serious, critical, acute, severe, extreme, urgent, dire, drastic, very grave
3 LAST-DITCH, dangerous, daring, determined, wild, violent, furious, risky, frantic, rash, hazardous, precipitate, hasty, audacious, madcap, foolhardy, headstrong, impetuous, death-defying
desperately *adverb* GRAVELY, badly, seriously, severely, dangerously, perilously
desperation *noun* **1** MISERY, worry, trouble, pain, anxiety, torture, despair, agony, sorrow, distraction, anguish, unhappiness, heartache, hopelessness, despondency
2 RECKLESSNESS, madness, defiance, frenzy, impetuosity, rashness, foolhardiness, heedlessness
despicable *adjective* CONTEMPTIBLE, mean, low, base, cheap, infamous, degrading, worthless, disgraceful, shameful, vile, sordid, pitiful, abject, hateful, reprehensible, ignominious, disreputable, wretched, scurvy, detestable, scungy (*Austral & NZ*), beyond contempt
<< OPPOSITE admirable
despise *verb* LOOK DOWN ON, loathe, scorn, disdain, spurn, undervalue, deride, detest, revile, abhor, have a down on (*informal*), contemn
<< OPPOSITE admire
despite *preposition* IN SPITE OF, in the face of, regardless of, even with, notwithstanding, in defiance of, in the teeth of, undeterred by, in contempt of
despondency *noun* DEJECTION, depression, despair, misery, gloom, sadness, desperation, melancholy, hopelessness, the hump (*Brit informal*), discouragement, wretchedness, low spirits, disconsolateness, dispiritedness, downheartedness
despondent *adjective* DEJECTED, sad, depressed, down, low, blue, despairing, discouraged, miserable, gloomy, hopeless, dismal, melancholy, in despair, glum, dispirited, downcast, morose, disheartened, sorrowful, wretched, disconsolate, doleful, downhearted, down in the dumps (*informal*), sick as a parrot (*informal*), woebegone, low-spirited
<< OPPOSITE cheerful
despot *noun* TYRANT, dictator, oppressor, autocrat, monocrat
despotic *adjective* TYRANNICAL, authoritarian, dictatorial, absolute, arrogant, oppressive, autocratic, imperious, domineering, monocratic
despotism *noun* TYRANNY, dictatorship, oppression, totalitarianism, autocracy, absolutism, autarchy, monocracy
dessert *noun* PUDDING, sweet (*informal*), afters (*Brit informal*), second course, last course, sweet course
destination *noun* STOP, station, haven, harbour, resting-place, terminus, journey's end, landing-place
destined *adjective* FATED, meant, intended, designed, certain, bound, doomed, ordained, predestined, foreordained
▷▷ **destined for** BOUND FOR, booked for, directed towards, scheduled for, routed for, heading for, assigned to, en route to, on the road to
destiny *noun* **1** FATE, fortune, lot, portion, doom, nemesis, divine decree
2 *usually cap.* FORTUNE, chance, karma, providence, kismet, predestination, divine will
destitute *adjective* PENNILESS, poor, impoverished, distressed, needy, on the rocks, insolvent, poverty-stricken, down and out, indigent, impecunious, dirt-poor (*informal*), on the breadline (*informal*), flat broke (*informal*), short, penurious, on your uppers, necessitous, in queer street (*informal*), moneyless, without

two pennies to rub together (*informal*)
▷▷ **destitute of** LACKING, wanting, without, in need of, deprived of, devoid of, bereft of, empty of, drained of, deficient in, depleted in

destroy *verb* 1 RUIN, smash, crush, waste, devastate, break down, wreck, shatter, gut, wipe out, dispatch, dismantle, demolish, trash (*slang*), total (*slang*), ravage, slay, eradicate, torpedo, extinguish, desolate, annihilate, put paid to, raze, blow to bits, extirpate, blow sky-high
2 SLAUGHTER, kill, exterminate

destruction *noun* 1 RUIN, havoc, wreckage, crushing, wrecking, shattering, undoing, demolition, devastation, annihilation, ruination
2 MASSACRE, overwhelming, slaughter, overthrow, extinction, end, downfall, liquidation, obliteration, extermination, eradication
3 SLAUGHTER

destructive *adjective* 1 DEVASTATING, fatal, deadly, lethal, harmful, damaging, catastrophic, detrimental, hurtful, pernicious, noxious, ruinous, calamitous, cataclysmic, baleful, deleterious, injurious, baneful, maleficent
2 NEGATIVE, hostile, discouraging, undermining, contrary, vicious, adverse, discrediting, disparaging, antagonistic, derogatory

desultory *adjective* RANDOM, vague, irregular, loose, rambling, inconsistent, erratic, disconnected, haphazard, cursory, aimless, off and on, fitful, spasmodic, discursive, unsystematic, inconstant, maundering, unmethodical

detach *verb* 1 SEPARATE, free, remove, divide, isolate, cut off, sever, loosen, segregate, disconnect, tear off, disengage, disentangle, unfasten, disunite, uncouple, unhitch, disjoin, unbridle
<< OPPOSITE attach
2 FREE, remove, separate, isolate, cut off, segregate, disengage

detached *adjective* 1 OBJECTIVE, neutral, impartial, reserved, aloof, impersonal, disinterested, unbiased, dispassionate, uncommitted, uninvolved, unprejudiced
<< OPPOSITE subjective
2 SEPARATE, free, severed, disconnected, loosened, discrete, unconnected, undivided, disjoined

detachment *noun* 1 INDIFFERENCE, fairness, neutrality, objectivity, impartiality, coolness, remoteness, nonchalance, aloofness, unconcern, disinterestedness, nonpartisanship
2 (*Military*) UNIT, party, force, body, detail, squad, patrol, task force

detail *noun* 1 POINT, fact, feature, particular, respect, factor, count, item, instance, element, aspect, specific, component, facet, technicality
2 FINE POINT, part, particular, nicety, minutiae, triviality
3 (*Military*) PARTY, force, body, duty, squad, assignment, fatigue, detachment
▷ *verb* 1 LIST, describe, relate, catalogue, portray, specify, depict, recount, rehearse, recite, narrate, delineate, enumerate, itemize, tabulate, particularize
2 APPOINT, name, choose, commission, select, elect, delegate, nominate, assign, allocate, charge
▷▷ **in detail** COMPREHENSIVELY, completely, fully, thoroughly, extensively, inside out, exhaustively, point by point, item by item

detailed *adjective* 1 COMPREHENSIVE, full, complete, minute, particular, specific, extensive, exact, thorough, meticulous, exhaustive, all-embracing, itemized, encyclopedic, blow-by-blow, particularized
<< OPPOSITE brief
2 COMPLICATED, involved, complex, fancy, elaborate, intricate, meticulous, convoluted

detain *verb* 1 HOLD, arrest, confine, restrain, imprison, intern, take prisoner, take into custody, hold in custody
2 DELAY, keep, stop, hold up, hamper, hinder, retard, impede, keep back, slow up *or* down

detect *verb* 1 DISCOVER, find, reveal, catch, expose, disclose, uncover, track down, unmask
2 NOTICE, see, spot, catch, note, identify, observe, remark, recognize, distinguish, perceive, scent, discern, ascertain, descry

detection *noun* DISCOVERY, exposure, uncovering, tracking down, unearthing, unmasking, ferreting out

detective *noun* INVESTIGATOR, cop (*slang*), copper (*slang*), dick (*slang, chiefly US*), constable, tec (*slang*), private eye, sleuth (*informal*), private investigator, gumshoe (*US slang*), bizzy (*slang*), C.I.D. man

detention *noun* IMPRISONMENT, custody, restraint, keeping in, quarantine, confinement, porridge (*slang*), incarceration
<< OPPOSITE release

deter *verb* 1 DISCOURAGE, inhibit, put off, frighten, intimidate, daunt, hinder, dissuade, talk out of
2 PREVENT, stop, check, curb, damp, restrain, prohibit, hinder, debar

detergent *noun* CLEANER, cleanser
▷ *adjective* CLEANSING, cleaning, purifying, abstergent, detersive

deteriorate *verb* 1 DECLINE, worsen, degenerate, slump, degrade, depreciate, go downhill, go to the dogs (*informal*), go to pot

<< OPPOSITE improve
2 DISINTEGRATE, decay, spoil, fade, break down, weaken, crumble, fall apart, ebb, decompose, wear away, retrogress

deterioration *noun* 1 DECLINE, fall, drop, slump, worsening, downturn, depreciation, degradation, degeneration, debasement, retrogression, vitiation, dégringolade (*French*)
2 DISINTEGRATION, corrosion, atrophy

determination *noun* 1 RESOLUTION, purpose, resolve, drive, energy, conviction, courage, dedication, backbone, fortitude, persistence, tenacity, perseverance, willpower, boldness, firmness, staying power, stubbornness, constancy, single-mindedness, earnestness, obstinacy, steadfastness, doggedness, relentlessness, resoluteness, indomitability, staunchness
<< OPPOSITE indecision
2 DECISION, ruling, settlement, resolution, resolve, conclusion, verdict, judgment

determine *verb* 1 AFFECT, control, decide, rule, condition, direct, influence, shape, govern, regulate, ordain
2 SETTLE, learn, establish, discover, check, find out, work out, detect, certify, verify, ascertain
3 DECIDE ON, choose, establish, purpose, fix, elect, resolve
4 DECIDE, purpose, conclude, resolve, make up your mind

determined *adjective* RESOLUTE, firm, dogged, fixed, constant, bold, intent, persistent, relentless, stalwart, persevering, single-minded, purposeful, tenacious, undaunted, strong-willed, steadfast, unwavering, immovable, unflinching, strong-minded

determining *adjective* DECIDING, important, settling, essential, critical, crucial, decisive, final, definitive, conclusive

deterrent *noun* DISCOURAGEMENT, obstacle, curb, restraint, impediment, check, hindrance, disincentive, defensive measures, determent
<< OPPOSITE incentive

detest *verb* HATE, loathe, despise, abhor, be hostile to, recoil from, be repelled by, have an aversion to, abominate, dislike intensely, execrate, feel aversion towards, feel disgust towards, feel hostility towards, feel repugnance towards
<< OPPOSITE love

dethrone *verb* DEPOSE, overthrow, oust, unseat, uncrown

detonate *verb* SET OFF, trigger, explode, discharge, blow up, touch off

detonation *noun* EXPLOSION, blast, bang, report, boom, discharge, fulmination

detour *noun* DIVERSION, bypass, deviation, circuitous route, roundabout way, indirect course

detract from *verb* 1 LESSEN, reduce, diminish, lower, take away from, derogate, devaluate
<< OPPOSITE enhance
2 DIVERT, shift, distract, deflect, draw *or* lead away from

> *Detract* is sometimes wrongly used where *distract* is meant: *a noise distracted* (not *detracted*) *my attention*

detractor *noun* SLANDERER, belittler, disparager, defamer, traducer, muckraker, scandalmonger, denigrator, backbiter, derogator (*rare*)

detriment *noun* DAMAGE, loss, harm, injury, hurt, prejudice, disadvantage, impairment, disservice

detrimental *adjective* DAMAGING, destructive, harmful, adverse, pernicious, unfavourable, prejudicial, baleful, deleterious, injurious, inimical, disadvantageous
<< OPPOSITE beneficial

devastate *verb* 1 DESTROY, waste, ruin, sack, wreck, spoil, demolish, trash (*slang*), level, total (*slang*), ravage, plunder, desolate, pillage, raze, lay waste, despoil
2 (*informal*) SHATTER, overwhelm, confound, floor (*informal*)

devastating *adjective* 1 DESTRUCTIVE, damaging, catastrophic, harmful, detrimental, pernicious, ruinous, calamitous, cataclysmic, deleterious, injurious, maleficent
2 TRAUMATIC, shocking, upsetting, disturbing, painful, scarring
3 SAVAGE, cutting, overwhelming, withering, overpowering, satirical, incisive, sardonic, caustic, vitriolic, trenchant, mordant

devastation *noun* DESTRUCTION, ruin, havoc, ravages, demolition, plunder, pillage, desolation, depredation, ruination, spoliation

develop *verb* 1 GROW, advance, progress, mature, evolve, flourish, blossom, ripen
2 RESULT, follow, arise, issue, happen, spring, stem, derive, break out, ensue, come about, be a direct result of
3 ESTABLISH, set up, promote, generate, undertake, initiate, embark on, cultivate, instigate, inaugurate, set in motion
4 FORM, start, begin, contract, establish, pick up, breed, acquire, generate, foster, originate
5 EXPAND, extend, work out, elaborate, unfold, enlarge, broaden, amplify, augment, dilate upon

development *noun* 1 GROWTH, increase, growing, advance, progress, spread, expansion, extension, evolution, widening, maturing, unfolding, unravelling, advancement, progression, thickening, enlargement

2 ESTABLISHMENT, forming, generation, institution, invention, initiation, inauguration, instigation, origination
3 EVENT, change, happening, issue, result, situation, incident, circumstance, improvement, outcome, phenomenon, evolution, unfolding, occurrence, upshot, turn of events, evolvement

deviant *adjective* PERVERTED, sick (*informal*), twisted, bent (*slang*), abnormal, queer (*informal* or *derogatory*), warped, perverse, wayward, kinky (*slang*), devious, deviate, freaky (*slang*), aberrant, pervy (*slang*), sicko (*informal*)
<< OPPOSITE normal
▷ *noun* PERVERT, freak, queer (*informal* or *derogatory*), misfit, sicko (*informal*), odd type

deviate *verb* DIFFER, vary, depart, part, turn, bend, drift, wander, stray, veer, swerve, meander, diverge, digress, turn aside

deviation *noun* DEPARTURE, change, variation, shift, alteration, discrepancy, inconsistency, disparity, aberration, variance, divergence, fluctuation, irregularity, digression

device *noun* 1 GADGET, machine, tool, instrument, implement, invention, appliance, apparatus, gimmick, utensil, contraption, contrivance, waldo, gizmo *or* gismo (*slang, chiefly US & Canad*)
2 PLOY, scheme, strategy, plan, design, project, shift, trick, manoeuvre, stunt, dodge, expedient, ruse, artifice, gambit, stratagem, wile

devil *noun* 1 EVIL SPIRIT, demon, fiend, ghoul, hellhound, atua (*NZ*), wairua (*NZ*)
2 BRUTE, monster, savage, beast, villain, rogue, barbarian, fiend, terror, swine, ogre
3 PERSON, individual, soul, creature, thing, human being, beggar
4 SCAMP, monkey (*informal*), rogue, imp, rascal, tyke (*informal*), scoundrel, scallywag (*informal*), mischief-maker, whippersnapper, toerag (*slang*), pickle (*Brit informal*), nointer (*Austral slang*)
▷▷ **the Devil** SATAN, Lucifer, Prince of Darkness, Old One, Deuce, Old Gentleman (*informal*), Lord of the Flies, Old Harry (*informal*), Mephistopheles, Evil One, Beelzebub, Old Nick (*informal*), Mephisto, Belial, Clootie (*Scot*), deil (*Scot*), Apollyon, Old Scratch (*informal*), Foul Fiend, Wicked One, archfiend, Old Hornie (*informal*), Abbadon

devilish *adjective* 1 FIENDISH, diabolical, wicked, satanic, atrocious, hellish, infernal, accursed, execrable, detestable, damnable, diabolic
2 DIFFICULT, involved, complex, complicated, baffling, intricate, perplexing, thorny, knotty, problematical, ticklish

devious *adjective* 1 SLY, scheming, calculating, tricky, crooked (*informal*), indirect, treacherous, dishonest, wily, insidious, evasive, deceitful, underhand, insincere, surreptitious, double-dealing, not straightforward
<< OPPOSITE straightforward
2 INDIRECT, roundabout, wandering, crooked, rambling, tortuous, deviating, circuitous, excursive
<< OPPOSITE direct

devise *verb* WORK OUT, plan, form, design, imagine, frame, arrange, plot, construct, invent, conceive, formulate, contrive, dream up, concoct, think up

devoid *adjective with* **of** LACKING IN, without, free from, wanting in, sans (*archaic*), bereft of, empty of, deficient in, denuded of, barren of

devolution *noun* TRANSFER OF POWER, decentralization, distribution of power, surrender of power, relinquishment of power

devolve *verb with* **on, upon, to,** *etc.* TRANSFER, entrust, consign, depute

devote *verb* DEDICATE, give, commit, apply, reserve, pledge, surrender, assign, allot, give over, consecrate, set apart

devoted *adjective* DEDICATED, loving, committed, concerned, caring, true, constant, loyal, faithful, fond, ardent, staunch, devout, steadfast
<< OPPOSITE disloyal

devotee *noun* 1 ENTHUSIAST, fan, supporter, follower, addict, admirer, buff (*informal*), fanatic, adherent, aficionado
2 FOLLOWER, student, supporter, pupil, convert, believer, partisan, disciple, learner, apostle, adherent, votary, proselyte, catechumen

devotion *noun* 1 LOVE, passion, affection, intensity, attachment, zeal, fondness, fervour, adoration, ardour, earnestness
2 DEDICATION, commitment, loyalty, allegiance, fidelity, adherence, constancy, faithfulness
<< OPPOSITE indifference
3 WORSHIP, reverence, spirituality, holiness, piety, sanctity, adoration, godliness, religiousness, devoutness
<< OPPOSITE irreverence
▷ *plural noun* PRAYERS, religious observance, church service, divine office

devotional *adjective* RELIGIOUS, spiritual, holy, sacred, devout, pious, reverential

devour *verb* 1 EAT, consume, swallow, bolt, dispatch, cram, stuff, wolf, gorge, gulp, gobble, guzzle, polish off (*informal*), pig out on (*slang*)
2 ENJOY, go through, absorb, appreciate, take in, relish, drink in, delight in, revel in, be preoccupied with, feast on, be engrossed by, read compulsively *or* voraciously

devouring *adjective* OVERWHELMING, powerful,

intense, flaming, consuming, excessive, passionate, insatiable

devout *adjective* 1 RELIGIOUS, godly, pious, pure, holy, orthodox, saintly, reverent, prayerful
<< OPPOSITE irreverent
2 SINCERE, serious, deep, earnest, genuine, devoted, intense, passionate, profound, ardent, fervent, heartfelt, zealous, dinkum (*Austral & NZ informal*)
<< OPPOSITE indifferent

dexterity *noun* 1 SKILL, expertise, mastery, touch, facility, craft, knack, finesse, artistry, proficiency, smoothness, neatness, deftness, nimbleness, adroitness, effortlessness, handiness
<< OPPOSITE incompetence
2 CLEVERNESS, art, ability, ingenuity, readiness, aptitude, adroitness, aptness, expertness, skilfulness

diabolical *adjective* 1 (*informal*) DREADFUL, shocking, terrible, appalling, nasty, tricky, unpleasant, outrageous, vile, excruciating, atrocious, abysmal, damnable
2 WICKED, cruel, savage, monstrous, malicious, satanic, from hell (*informal*), malignant, unspeakable, inhuman, implacable, malevolent, hellish, devilish, infernal, fiendish, ungodly, black-hearted, demoniac, hellacious (*US slang*)

diagnose *verb* IDENTIFY, determine, recognize, distinguish, interpret, pronounce, pinpoint

diagnosis *noun* 1 IDENTIFICATION, discovery, recognition, detection
2 OPINION, conclusion, interpretation, pronouncement

diagnostic *adjective* SYMPTOMATIC, particular, distinguishing, distinctive, peculiar, indicative, idiosyncratic, recognizable, demonstrative

diagonal *adjective* SLANTING, angled, oblique, cross, crosswise, crossways, cater-cornered (*US informal*), cornerways

diagonally *adverb* ASLANT, obliquely, on the cross, at an angle, crosswise, on the bias, cornerwise

diagram *noun* PLAN, figure, drawing, chart, outline, representation, sketch, layout, graph

dialect *noun* LANGUAGE, speech, tongue, jargon, idiom, vernacular, brogue, lingo (*informal*), patois, provincialism, localism

dialectic *noun* DEBATE, reasoning, discussion, logic, contention, polemics, disputation, argumentation, ratiocination

dialogue *noun* 1 DISCUSSION, conference, exchange, debate, confabulation
2 CONVERSATION, discussion, communication, discourse, converse, colloquy, confabulation, duologue, interlocution
3 SCRIPT, conversation, lines, spoken part

diametrically *adverb* COMPLETELY, totally, entirely, absolutely, utterly

diarrhoea *or US* **diarrhea** *noun* THE RUNS, the trots (*informal*), dysentery, looseness, the skits (*informal*), Montezuma's revenge (*informal*), gippy tummy, holiday tummy, Spanish tummy, the skitters (*informal*)

diary *noun* 1 JOURNAL, chronicle, day-to-day account
2 ENGAGEMENT BOOK, Filofax (*trademark*), appointment book

diatribe *noun* TIRADE, abuse, criticism, denunciation, reviling, stricture, harangue, invective, vituperation, stream of abuse, verbal onslaught, philippic

dicey *adjective* (*informal, chiefly Brit*) DANGEROUS, difficult, tricky, risky, hairy (*slang*), ticklish, chancy (*informal*)

dichotomy *noun* DIVISION, split, separation, disjunction

dicky *adjective* (*Brit informal*) WEAK, queer (*informal*), shaky, unreliable, unsteady, unsound, fluttery

dictate *verb* SPEAK, say, utter, read out
▷ *noun* 1 COMMAND, order, decree, word, demand, direction, requirement, bidding, mandate, injunction, statute, fiat, ultimatum, ordinance, edict, behest
2 PRINCIPLE, law, rule, standard, code, criterion, ethic, canon, maxim, dictum, precept, axiom, moral law
▷▷ **dictate to someone** ORDER (ABOUT), direct, lay down the law to, pronounce to

dictator *noun* ABSOLUTE RULER, tyrant, despot, oppressor, autocrat, absolutist, martinet

dictatorial *adjective* 1 ABSOLUTE, unlimited, totalitarian, autocratic, unrestricted, tyrannical, despotic
<< OPPOSITE democratic
2 DOMINEERING, authoritarian, oppressive, bossy (*informal*), imperious, overbearing, magisterial, iron-handed, dogmatical
<< OPPOSITE servile

dictatorship *noun* ABSOLUTE RULE, tyranny, totalitarianism, authoritarianism, reign of terror, despotism, autocracy, absolutism

diction *noun* PRONUNCIATION, speech, articulation, delivery, fluency, inflection, intonation, elocution, enunciation

dictionary *noun* WORDBOOK, vocabulary, glossary, encyclopedia, lexicon, concordance

dictum *noun* 1 SAYING, saw, maxim, adage, proverb, precept, axiom, gnome
2 DECREE, order, demand, statement, command, dictate, canon, fiat, edict, pronouncement

didactic *adjective* 1 INSTRUCTIVE, educational, enlightening, moral, edifying, homiletic, preceptive

2 PEDANTIC, academic, formal, pompous, schoolmasterly, erudite, bookish, abstruse, moralizing, priggish, pedagogic

die *verb* 1 PASS AWAY, depart, expire, perish, buy it (*US slang*), check out (*US slang*), kick it (*slang*), croak (*slang*), give up the ghost, go belly-up (*slang*), snuff it (*slang*), peg out (*informal*), kick the bucket (*slang*), buy the farm (*US slang*), peg it (*informal*), decease, cark it (*Austral & NZ slang*), pop your clogs (*informal*), breathe your last, hop the twig (*slang*)

<< OPPOSITE live

2 STOP, fail, halt, break down, run down, stop working, peter out, fizzle out, lose power, seize up, conk out (*informal*), go kaput (*informal*), go phut, fade out *or* away

3 DWINDLE, end, decline, pass, disappear, sink, fade, weaken, diminish, vanish, decrease, decay, lapse, wither, wilt, lessen, wane, subside, ebb, die down, die out, abate, peter out, die away, grow less

<< OPPOSITE increase

▷▷ **be dying for something** LONG FOR, want, desire, crave, yearn for, hunger for, pine for, hanker after, be eager for, ache for, swoon over, languish for, set your heart on

▷▷ **be dying of something** (*informal*) BE OVERCOME WITH, succumb to, collapse with

die-hard *or* **diehard** *noun* REACTIONARY, fanatic, zealot, intransigent, stick-in-the-mud (*informal*), old fogey, ultraconservative

diet[1] *noun* 1 FOOD, provisions, fare, rations, subsistence, kai (*NZ informal*), nourishment, sustenance, victuals, commons, edibles, comestibles, nutriment, viands, aliment

2 FAST, regime, abstinence, regimen, dietary regime

▷ *verb* SLIM, fast, lose weight, abstain, eat sparingly

<< OPPOSITE overindulge

diet[2] *noun often cap.* COUNCIL, meeting, parliament, sitting, congress, chamber, convention, legislature, legislative assembly

dieter *noun* SLIMMER, weight watcher, calorie counter, faster, reducer

differ *verb* 1 BE DISSIMILAR, contradict, contrast with, vary, counter, belie, depart from, diverge, negate, fly in the face of, run counter to, be distinct, stand apart, make a nonsense of, be at variance with

<< OPPOSITE accord

2 DISAGREE, clash, dispute, dissent

<< OPPOSITE agree

difference *noun* 1 DISSIMILARITY, contrast, variation, change, variety, exception, distinction, diversity, alteration, discrepancy, disparity, deviation, differentiation, peculiarity, divergence, singularity, particularity, distinctness, unlikeness

<< OPPOSITE similarity

2 REMAINDER, rest, balance, remains, excess

3 DISAGREEMENT, conflict, argument, row, clash, dispute, set-to (*informal*), controversy, contention, quarrel, strife, wrangle, tiff, contretemps, discordance, contrariety

<< OPPOSITE agreement

different *adjective* 1 DISSIMILAR, opposed, contrasting, changed, clashing, unlike, altered, diverse, at odds, inconsistent, disparate, deviating, divergent, at variance, discrepant, streets apart

2 VARIOUS, some, many, several, varied, numerous, diverse, divers (*archaic*), assorted, miscellaneous, sundry, manifold, multifarious

3 UNUSUAL, unique, special, strange, rare, extraordinary, bizarre, distinctive, something else, peculiar, uncommon, singular, unconventional, out of the ordinary, left-field (*informal*), atypical

4 OTHER, another, separate, individual, distinct, discrete

On the whole, *different from* is preferable to *different to* and *different than*, both of which are considered unacceptable by some people. *Different to* is often heard in British English, but is thought by some people to be incorrect; and *different than*, though acceptable in American English, is often regarded as unacceptable in British English. This makes *different from* the safest option: *this result is only slightly different from that obtained in the US* – or you can rephrase the sentence: *this result differs only slightly from that obtained in the US*

differential *adjective* DISTINCTIVE, distinguishing, discriminative, diacritical

▷ *noun* DIFFERENCE, discrepancy, disparity, amount of difference

differentiate *verb* 1 DISTINGUISH, separate, discriminate, contrast, discern, mark off, make a distinction, tell apart, set off *or* apart

2 MAKE DIFFERENT, separate, distinguish, characterize, single out, segregate, individualize, mark off, set apart, set off *or* apart

3 BECOME DIFFERENT, change, convert, transform, alter, adapt, modify

differently *adverb* DISSIMILARLY, otherwise, in another way, in contrary fashion

<< OPPOSITE similarly

difficult *adjective* 1 HARD, tough, taxing, demanding, challenging, painful, exacting, formidable, uphill, strenuous, problematic, arduous, onerous, laborious, burdensome,

wearisome, no picnic (*informal*), toilsome, like getting blood out of a stone
<< OPPOSITE easy
2 PROBLEMATICAL, involved, complex, complicated, delicate, obscure, abstract, baffling, intricate, perplexing, thorny, knotty, abstruse, ticklish, enigmatical
<< OPPOSITE simple
3 TROUBLESOME, trying, awkward, demanding, rigid, stubborn, perverse, fussy, tiresome, intractable, fastidious, fractious, unyielding, obstinate, intransigent, unmanageable, unbending, uncooperative, hard to please, refractory, obstreperous, pig-headed, bull-headed, unaccommodating, unamenable
<< OPPOSITE cooperative
4 TOUGH, trying, hard, dark, grim, straitened, full of hardship
<< OPPOSITE easy

difficulty *noun* 1 PROBLEM, trouble, obstacle, hurdle, dilemma, hazard, complication, hassle (*informal*), snag, uphill (*S African*), predicament, pitfall, stumbling block, impediment, hindrance, tribulation, quandary, can of worms (*informal*), point at issue, disputed point
2 HARDSHIP, labour, pain, strain, awkwardness, painfulness, strenuousness, arduousness, laboriousness

diffident *adjective* SHY, reserved, withdrawn, reluctant, modest, shrinking, doubtful, backward, unsure, insecure, constrained, timid, self-conscious, hesitant, meek, unassuming, unobtrusive, self-effacing, sheepish, bashful, timorous, unassertive

diffuse *verb* SPREAD, distribute, scatter, circulate, disperse, dispense, dispel, dissipate, propagate, disseminate
▷ *adjective* 1 SPREAD-OUT, scattered, dispersed, unconcentrated
<< OPPOSITE concentrated
2 RAMBLING, loose, vague, meandering, waffling (*informal*), long-winded, wordy, discursive, verbose, prolix, maundering, digressive, diffusive, circumlocutory
<< OPPOSITE concise

> This word is quite commonly misused instead of *defuse*, when talking about calming down a situation. However, the words are very different in meaning and should never be used as alternatives to each other

diffusion *noun* SPREADING, distribution, scattering, circulation, expansion, propagation, dissemination, dispersal, dispersion, dissipation

dig *verb* 1 HOLLOW OUT, mine, pierce, quarry, excavate, gouge, scoop out
2 DELVE, tunnel, burrow, grub
3 TURN OVER, till, break up, hoe
4 SEARCH, hunt, root, delve, forage, dig down, fossick (*Austral & NZ*)
5 POKE, drive, push, stick, punch, stab, thrust, shove, prod, jab
6 (*informal*) LIKE, enjoy, go for, appreciate, groove (*dated slang*), delight in, be fond of, be keen on, be partial to
7 (*informal*) UNDERSTAND, follow
▷ *noun* 1 CUTTING REMARK, crack (*slang*), insult, taunt, sneer, jeer, quip, barb, wisecrack (*informal*), gibe
2 POKE, thrust, butt, nudge, prod, jab, punch
▷▷ **dig in** (*informal*) BEGIN *or* START EATING, tuck in (*informal*)

digest *verb* 1 INGEST, absorb, incorporate, dissolve, assimilate
2 TAKE IN, master, absorb, grasp, drink in, soak up, devour, assimilate
▷ *noun* SUMMARY, résumé, abstract, epitome, condensation, compendium, synopsis, précis, abridgment

digestion *noun* INGESTION, absorption, incorporation, assimilation
>> RELATED WORD *adjective* peptic

digit *noun* FINGER, toe

dignified *adjective* DISTINGUISHED, august, reserved, imposing, formal, grave, noble, upright, stately, solemn, lofty, exalted, decorous
<< OPPOSITE undignified

dignify *verb* DISTINGUISH, honour, grace, raise, advance, promote, elevate, glorify, exalt, ennoble, aggrandize

dignitary *noun* PUBLIC FIGURE, worthy, notable, high-up (*informal*), bigwig (*informal*), celeb (*informal*), personage, pillar of society, pillar of the church, notability, pillar of the state, V.I.P.

dignity *noun* 1 DECORUM, breeding, gravity, majesty, grandeur, respectability, nobility, propriety, solemnity, gentility, courtliness, loftiness, stateliness
2 SELF-IMPORTANCE, pride, self-esteem, self-respect, self-regard, self-possession, amour-propre (*French*)

digress *verb* WANDER, drift, stray, depart, ramble, meander, diverge, deviate, turn aside, be diffuse, expatiate, go off at a tangent, get off the point *or* subject

dilapidated *adjective* RUINED, fallen in, broken-down, battered, neglected, crumbling, run-down, decayed, decaying, falling apart, beat-up (*informal*), shaky, shabby, worn-out, ramshackle, in ruins, rickety, decrepit, tumbledown, uncared for, gone to rack and ruin

dilate *verb* ENLARGE, extend, stretch, expand,

swell, widen, broaden, puff out, distend
<< OPPOSITE contract
dilemma *noun* PREDICAMENT, problem, difficulty, spot (*informal*), fix (*informal*), mess, puzzle, jam (*informal*), embarrassment, plight, strait, pickle (*informal*), how-do-you-do (*informal*), quandary, perplexity, tight corner *or* spot
▷▷ **on the horns of a dilemma** BETWEEN THE DEVIL AND THE DEEP BLUE SEA, between a rock and a hard place (*informal*), between Scylla and Charybdis

The use of *dilemma* to refer to a problem that seems incapable of solution is considered by some people to be incorrect. To avoid this misuse of the word, an appropriate alternative such as *predicament* could be used

dilettante *noun* AMATEUR, aesthete, dabbler, trifler, nonprofessional
diligence *noun* APPLICATION, industry, care, activity, attention, perseverance, earnestness, attentiveness, assiduity, intentness, assiduousness, laboriousness, heedfulness, sedulousness
diligent *adjective* HARD-WORKING, careful, conscientious, earnest, active, busy, persistent, attentive, persevering, tireless, painstaking, laborious, industrious, indefatigable, studious, assiduous, sedulous
<< OPPOSITE indifferent
dilute *verb* 1 WATER DOWN, thin (out), weaken, adulterate, make thinner, cut (*informal*)
<< OPPOSITE condense
2 REDUCE, weaken, diminish, temper, decrease, lessen, diffuse, mitigate, attenuate
<< OPPOSITE intensify
diluted *adjective* WATERED DOWN, thinned, weak, weakened, dilute, watery, adulterated, cut (*informal*), wishy-washy (*informal*)
dim *adjective* 1 DULL, weak, pale, muted, subdued, feeble, murky, opaque, dingy, subfusc
2 POORLY LIT, dark, gloomy, murky, shady, shadowy, dusky, crepuscular, darkish, tenebrous, unilluminated, caliginous (*archaic*)
3 CLOUDY, grey, gloomy, dismal, overcast, leaden
<< OPPOSITE bright
4 UNCLEAR, obscured, faint, blurred, fuzzy, shadowy, hazy, indistinguishable, bleary, undefined, out of focus, ill-defined, indistinct, indiscernible
<< OPPOSITE distinct
5 OBSCURE, remote, vague, confused, shadowy, imperfect, hazy, intangible, indistinct
6 UNFAVOURABLE, bad, black, depressing, discouraging, gloomy, dismal, sombre, unpromising, dispiriting, disheartening
7 (*informal*) STUPID, slow, thick, dull, dense, dumb (*informal*), daft (*informal*), dozy (*Brit informal*), obtuse, unintelligent, asinine, slow on the uptake (*informal*), braindead (*informal*), doltish
<< OPPOSITE bright
▷ *verb* 1 TURN DOWN, lower, fade, dull, bedim
2 GROW *or* BECOME FAINT, fade, dull, grow *or* become dim
3 DARKEN, dull, cloud over
dimension *noun* 1 ASPECT, side, feature, angle, facet
2 EXTENT, size, magnitude, importance, scope, greatness, amplitude, largeness
▷ *plural noun* PROPORTIONS, range, size, scale, measure, volume, capacity, bulk, measurement, amplitude, bigness
diminish *verb* 1 DECREASE, decline, lessen, contract, weaken, shrink, dwindle, wane, recede, subside, ebb, taper, die out, fade away, abate, peter out
<< OPPOSITE grow
2 REDUCE, cut, decrease, lessen, contract, lower, weaken, curtail, abate, retrench
<< OPPOSITE increase
3 BELITTLE, scorn, devalue, undervalue, deride, demean, denigrate, scoff at, disparage, decry, sneer at, underrate, deprecate, depreciate, cheapen, derogate
diminution *noun* 1 DECREASE, decline, lessening, weakening, decay, contraction, abatement
2 REDUCTION, cut, decrease, weakening, deduction, contraction, lessening, cutback, retrenchment, abatement, curtailment
diminutive *adjective* SMALL, little, tiny, minute, pocket(-sized), mini, wee, miniature, petite, midget, undersized, teeny-weeny, Lilliputian, bantam, teensy-weensy, pygmy *or* pigmy
<< OPPOSITE giant
din *noun* NOISE, row, racket, crash, clash, shout, outcry, clamour, clatter, uproar, commotion, pandemonium, babel, hubbub, hullabaloo, clangour
<< OPPOSITE silence
dine *verb* EAT, lunch, feast, sup, chow down (*slang*)
▷▷ **dine on** *or* **off something** EAT, consume, feed on
dingy *adjective* DISCOLOURED, soiled, dirty, shabby, faded, seedy, grimy
dinkum *adjective* (*Austral & NZ informal*) GENUINE, honest, natural, frank, sincere, candid, upfront (*informal*), artless, guileless
dinky *adjective* (*Brit informal*) CUTE, small, neat, mini, trim, miniature, petite, dainty, natty (*informal*), cutesy (*informal, chiefly US*)
dinner *noun* 1 MEAL, main meal, spread (*informal*), repast, blowout (*slang*), collation,

refection
2 BANQUET, feast, blowout (*slang*), repast, beanfeast (*Brit informal*), carousal, hakari (*NZ*)

dinosaur *noun* FUDDY-DUDDY, anachronism, dodo (*informal*), stick-in-the-mud (*informal*), antique (*informal*), fossil (*informal*), relic (*informal*), back number (*informal*)

dint ▷▷ **by dint of** BY MEANS OF, using, by virtue of, by force of

diocese *noun* BISHOPRIC, see

dip *verb* 1 PLUNGE, immerse, bathe, duck, rinse, douse, dunk, souse
2 DROP (DOWN), set, fall, lower, disappear, sink, fade, slump, descend, tilt, subside, sag, droop
3 SLOPE, drop (down), descend, fall, decline, pitch, sink, incline, drop away
▷ *noun* 1 PLUNGE, ducking, soaking, drenching, immersion, douche, submersion
2 NOD, drop, lowering, slump, sag
3 HOLLOW, hole, depression, pit, basin, dent, trough, indentation, concavity
4 MIXTURE, solution, preparation, suspension, infusion, concoction, dilution
▷▷ **dip into something** 1 SAMPLE, try, skim, play at, glance at, run over, browse, dabble, peruse, surf (*Computing*)
2 DRAW UPON, use, employ, extract, take from, make use of, fall back on, reach into, have recourse to

diplomacy *noun* 1 STATESMANSHIP, statecraft, international negotiation
2 TACT, skill, sensitivity, craft, discretion, subtlety, delicacy, finesse, savoir-faire, artfulness
<< OPPOSITE tactlessness

diplomat *noun* OFFICIAL, ambassador, envoy, statesman, consul, attaché, emissary, chargé d'affaires

diplomatic *adjective* 1 CONSULAR, official, foreign-office, ambassadorial, foreign-politic
2 TACTFUL, politic, sensitive, subtle, delicate, polite, discreet, prudent, adept, considerate, judicious, treating with kid gloves
<< OPPOSITE tactless

dire *adjective* DESPERATE, pressing, crying, critical, terrible, crucial, alarming, extreme, awful, appalling, urgent, cruel, horrible, disastrous, grim, dreadful, gloomy, fearful, dismal, drastic, catastrophic, ominous, horrid, woeful, ruinous, calamitous, cataclysmic, portentous, godawful (*slang*), exigent, bodeful

direct *verb* 1 AIM, point, turn, level, train, focus, fix, cast
2 GUIDE, show, lead, point the way, point in the direction of
3 CONTROL, run, manage, lead, rule, guide, handle, conduct, advise, govern, regulate, administer, oversee, supervise, dispose, preside over, mastermind, call the shots, call the tune, superintend
4 ORDER, command, instruct, charge, demand, require, bid, enjoin, adjure
5 ADDRESS, send, mail, route, label, superscribe
▷ *adjective* 1 QUICKEST, shortest
2 STRAIGHT, through
<< OPPOSITE circuitous
3 FIRST-HAND, personal, immediate
<< OPPOSITE indirect
4 CLEAR, specific, plain, absolute, distinct, definite, explicit, downright, point-blank, unequivocal, unqualified, unambiguous, categorical
<< OPPOSITE ambiguous
5 STRAIGHTFORWARD, open, straight, frank, blunt, sincere, outspoken, honest, matter-of-fact, downright, candid, forthright, truthful, upfront (*informal*), man-to-man, plain-spoken
<< OPPOSITE indirect
6 VERBATIM, exact, word-for-word, strict, accurate, faithful, letter-for-letter
▷ *adverb* NON-STOP, straight

direction *noun* 1 WAY, course, line, road, track, bearing, route, path
2 TENDENCY, bent, current, trend, leaning, drift, bias, orientation, tack, tenor, proclivity
3 MANAGEMENT, government, control, charge, administration, leadership, command, guidance, supervision, governance, oversight, superintendence

directions *plural noun* INSTRUCTIONS, rules, information, plan, briefing, regulations, recommendations, indication, guidelines, guidance

directive *noun* ORDER, ruling, regulation, charge, notice, command, instruction, dictate, decree, mandate, canon, injunction, imperative, fiat, ordinance, edict

directly *adverb* 1 STRAIGHT, unswervingly, without deviation, by the shortest route, in a beeline
2 IMMEDIATELY, promptly, instantly, right away, straightaway, speedily, instantaneously, pronto (*informal*), pdq (*slang*)
3 AT ONCE, presently, soon, quickly, as soon as possible, in a second, straightaway, forthwith, posthaste
4 HONESTLY, openly, frankly, plainly, face-to-face, overtly, point-blank, unequivocally, truthfully, candidly, unreservedly, straightforwardly, straight from the shoulder (*informal*), without prevarication

directness *noun* HONESTY, candour, frankness, sincerity, plain speaking, bluntness, outspokenness, forthrightness, straightforwardness

director *noun* CONTROLLER, head, leader, manager, chief, executive, chairman, boss (*informal*), producer, governor, principal, administrator, supervisor, organizer, baas (*S African*), helmer, sherang (*Austral* & *NZ*)

dirge *noun* LAMENT, requiem, elegy, death march, threnody, dead march, funeral song, coronach (*Scot* & *Irish*)

dirt *noun* **1** FILTH, muck, grime, dust, mud, stain, tarnish, smudge, mire, impurity, slob (*Irish*), crud (*slang*), grot (*slang*)
2 SOIL, ground, earth, clay, turf, clod, loam, loam

dirty *adjective* **1** FILTHY, soiled, grubby, nasty, foul, muddy, polluted, messy, sullied, grimy, unclean, mucky, grotty (*slang*), grungy (*slang, chiefly US* & *Canad*), scuzzy (*slang, chiefly US*), begrimed, festy (*Austral slang*)
<< OPPOSITE clean
2 DISHONEST, illegal, unfair, cheating, corrupt, crooked, deceiving, fraudulent, treacherous, deceptive, unscrupulous, crafty, deceitful, double-dealing, unsporting, knavish (*archaic*)
<< OPPOSITE honest
3 OBSCENE, rude, coarse, indecent, blue, offensive, gross, filthy, vulgar, pornographic, sleazy, suggestive, lewd, risqué, X-rated (*informal*), bawdy, salacious, smutty, off-colour, unwholesome
<< OPPOSITE decent
4 DESPICABLE, mean, low, base, cheap, nasty, cowardly, beggarly, worthless, shameful, shabby, vile, sordid, low-down (*informal*), abject, squalid, ignominious, contemptible, wretched, scurvy, detestable, scungy (*Austral* & *NZ*)
▷ *verb* SOIL, foul, stain, spoil, smear, muddy, pollute, blacken, mess up, smudge, sully, defile, smirch, begrime
<< OPPOSITE clean

disability *noun* HANDICAP, affliction, disorder, defect, impairment, disablement, infirmity

disable *verb* HANDICAP, weaken, cripple, damage, hamstring, paralyse, impair, debilitate, incapacitate, prostrate, unman, immobilize, put out of action, enfeeble, render inoperative, render *hors de combat*

disabled *adjective* DIFFERENTLY ABLED, physically challenged, handicapped, challenged, weakened, crippled, paralysed, lame, mutilated, maimed, incapacitated, infirm, bedridden
<< OPPOSITE able-bodied

> Referring to people with disabilities as *the disabled* can cause offence and should be avoided. Instead, refer to them as people *with disabilities* or *who are physically challenged*, or, possibly, *disabled people* or *differently abled people*. In general, the terms used for disabilities or medical conditions should be avoided as collective nouns for people who have them – so, for example, instead of *the blind*, it is preferable to refer to *sightless people*, *vision-impaired people*, or *partially-sighted people*, depending on the degree of their condition

disabuse *verb* (usually in phrase *disabuse someone of an idea or notion*) ENLIGHTEN, correct, set right, open the eyes of, set straight, shatter (someone's) illusions, free from error, undeceive

disadvantage *noun* **1** DRAWBACK, trouble, burden, weakness, handicap, liability, minus (*informal*), flaw, hardship, nuisance, snag, inconvenience, downside, impediment, hindrance, privation, weak point, fly in the ointment (*informal*)
<< OPPOSITE advantage
2 HARM, loss, damage, injury, hurt, prejudice, detriment, disservice
<< OPPOSITE benefit
▷▷ **at a disadvantage** EXPOSED, vulnerable, wide open, unprotected, defenceless, open to attack, assailable

disadvantaged *adjective* DEPRIVED, struggling, impoverished, discriminated against, underprivileged

disaffected *adjective* ALIENATED, resentful, discontented, hostile, estranged, dissatisfied, rebellious, antagonistic, disloyal, seditious, mutinous, uncompliant, unsubmissive

disaffection *noun* ALIENATION, resentment, discontent, hostility, dislike, disagreement, dissatisfaction, animosity, aversion, antagonism, antipathy, disloyalty, estrangement, ill will, repugnance, unfriendliness

disagree *verb* **1** DIFFER (IN OPINION), argue, debate, clash, dispute, contest, fall out (*informal*), contend, dissent, quarrel, wrangle, bicker, take issue with, have words (*informal*), cross swords, be at sixes and sevens
<< OPPOSITE agree
2 *with* **with** MAKE ILL, upset, sicken, trouble, hurt, bother, distress, discomfort, nauseate, be injurious to
▷▷ **disagree with something** *or* **someone** OPPOSE, object to, dissent from

disagreeable *adjective* **1** NASTY, offensive, disgusting, unpleasant, distasteful, horrid, repellent, unsavoury, obnoxious, unpalatable, displeasing, repulsive, objectionable, repugnant, uninviting, yucky *or* yukky (*slang*), yucko (*Austral slang*)
<< OPPOSITE pleasant
2 ILL-NATURED, difficult, nasty, cross, contrary, unpleasant, rude, irritable, unfriendly, bad-

tempered, surly, churlish, brusque, tetchy, ratty (*Brit & NZ informal*), peevish, ungracious, disobliging, unlikable *or* unlikeable
<< OPPOSITE good-natured

disagreement *noun* ARGUMENT, row, difference, division, debate, conflict, clash, dispute, falling out, misunderstanding, dissent, quarrel, squabble, strife, wrangle, discord, tiff, altercation
<< OPPOSITE agreement

disallow *verb* REJECT, refuse, ban, dismiss, cancel, veto, forbid, embargo, prohibit, rebuff, repudiate, disown, proscribe, disavow, disclaim, abjure

disappear *verb* 1 VANISH, recede, drop out of sight, vanish off the face of the earth, evanesce, be lost to view *or* sight
<< OPPOSITE appear
2 PASS, wane, ebb, fade away
3 FLEE, bolt, run away, fly, escape, split (*slang*), retire, withdraw, take off (*informal*), get away, vanish, depart, go, make off, abscond, take flight, do a runner (*slang*), scarper (*Brit slang*), slope off, cut and run (*informal*), beat a hasty retreat, make your escape, make your getaway
4 BE LOST, be taken, be stolen, go missing, be mislaid
5 CEASE, end, fade, vanish, dissolve, expire, evaporate, perish, die out, pass away, cease to exist, melt away, leave no trace, cease to be known

disappearance *noun* 1 VANISHING, going, passing, disappearing, fading, melting, eclipse, evaporation, evanescence
2 FLIGHT, departure, desertion, disappearing trick
3 LOSS, losing, mislaying

disappoint *verb* 1 LET DOWN, dismay, fail, dash, disillusion, sadden, vex, chagrin, dishearten, disenchant, dissatisfy, disgruntle
2 FRUSTRATE, foil, thwart, defeat, baffle, balk

disappointed *adjective* LET DOWN, upset, distressed, discouraged, depressed, choked, disillusioned, discontented, dejected, disheartened, disgruntled, dissatisfied, downcast, saddened, disenchanted, despondent, downhearted, cast down
<< OPPOSITE satisfied

disappointing *adjective* UNSATISFACTORY, inadequate, discouraging, sorry, upsetting, sad, depressing, unhappy, unexpected, pathetic, inferior, insufficient, lame, disconcerting, second-rate, unworthy, not much cop (*Brit slang*)

disappointment *noun* 1 REGRET, distress, discontent, dissatisfaction, disillusionment, displeasure, chagrin, disenchantment, dejection, despondency, discouragement, mortification, unfulfilment
2 LETDOWN, blow, disaster, failure, setback, fiasco, misfortune, calamity, whammy (*informal, chiefly US*), choker (*informal*), washout (*informal*)
3 FRUSTRATION, failure, ill-success

disapproval *noun* DISPLEASURE, criticism, objection, condemnation, dissatisfaction, censure, reproach, denunciation, deprecation, disapprobation, stick (*slang*)

disapprove *verb* 1 CONDEMN, object to, dislike, censure, deplore, deprecate, frown on, take exception to, take a dim view of, find unacceptable, have a down on (*informal*), discountenance, look down your nose at (*informal*), raise an *or* your eyebrow at
<< OPPOSITE approve
2 TURN DOWN, reject, veto, set aside, spurn, disallow
<< OPPOSITE endorse

disapproving *adjective* CRITICAL, discouraging, frowning, disparaging, censorious, reproachful, deprecatory, condemnatory, denunciatory, disapprobatory
<< OPPOSITE approving

disarm *verb* 1 DEMILITARIZE, disband, demobilize, deactivate
2 WIN OVER, persuade

disarmament *noun* ARMS REDUCTION, demobilization, arms limitation, demilitarization, de-escalation

disarming *adjective* CHARMING, winning, irresistible, persuasive, likable *or* likeable

disarray *noun* 1 CONFUSION, upset, disorder, indiscipline, disunity, disharmony, disorganization, unruliness, discomposure, disorderliness
<< OPPOSITE order
2 UNTIDINESS, state, mess, chaos, tangle, mix-up, muddle, clutter, shambles, jumble, hotchpotch, hodgepodge (*US*), dishevelment, pig's breakfast (*informal*)
<< OPPOSITE tidiness

disaster *noun* 1 CATASTROPHE, trouble, blow, accident, stroke, reverse, tragedy, ruin, misfortune, adversity, calamity, mishap, whammy (*informal, chiefly US*), misadventure, cataclysm, act of God, bummer (*slang*), ruination, mischance
2 FAILURE, mess, flop (*informal*), catastrophe, rout, debacle, cock-up (*Brit slang*), washout (*informal*)

disastrous *adjective* 1 TERRIBLE, devastating, tragic, fatal, unfortunate, dreadful, destructive, unlucky, harmful, adverse, dire, catastrophic, detrimental, untoward, ruinous, calamitous, cataclysmic, ill-starred, unpropitious, ill-fated, cataclysmal
2 UNSUCCESSFUL, devastating, tragic, calamitous, cataclysmic

disavow *verb* DENY, reject, contradict, retract, repudiate, disown, rebut, disclaim, forswear, gainsay (*archaic* or *literary*), abjure

disband *verb* **1** DISMISS, separate, break up, scatter, dissolve, let go, disperse, send home, demobilize

2 BREAK UP, separate, scatter, disperse, part company, go (their) separate ways

disbelief *noun* SCEPTICISM, doubt, distrust, mistrust, incredulity, unbelief, dubiety

<< OPPOSITE belief

disbelieve *verb* DOUBT, reject, discount, suspect, discredit, not accept, mistrust, not buy (*slang*), repudiate, scoff at, not credit, not swallow (*informal*), give no credence to

disburse *verb* PAY OUT, spend, lay out, fork out (*slang*), expend, shell out (*informal*)

> *Disburse* is sometimes wrongly used where *disperse* is meant: *the police used water cannons to disperse* (not *disburse*) *the crowd*

disbursement *noun* PAYMENT, spending, expenditure, disposal, outlay

disc *noun* **1** CIRCLE, plate, saucer, discus

2 (*Old-fashioned*) RECORD, vinyl, gramophone record, phonograph record (*US & Canad*), platter (*US slang*)

> In British English, the spelling *disc* is generally preferred, except when using the word in its computer senses, where *disk* is preferred. In US English, the spelling *disk* is used for all senses.

discard *verb* GET RID OF, drop, remove, throw away *or* out, reject, abandon, dump (*informal*), shed, scrap, axe (*informal*), ditch (*slang*), junk (*informal*), chuck (*informal*), dispose of, relinquish, dispense with, jettison, repudiate, cast aside

<< OPPOSITE keep

discern *verb* SEE, perceive, make out, notice, observe, recognize, behold, catch sight of, suss (out) (*slang*), espy, descry

discernible *adjective* CLEAR, obvious, apparent, plain, visible, distinct, noticeable, recognizable, detectable, observable, perceptible, distinguishable, appreciable, discoverable

discerning *adjective* DISCRIMINATING, knowing, sharp, critical, acute, sensitive, wise, intelligent, subtle, piercing, penetrating, shrewd, ingenious, astute, perceptive, judicious, clear-sighted, percipient, perspicacious, sagacious

discharge *verb* **1** RELEASE, free, clear, liberate, pardon, let go, acquit, allow to go, set free, exonerate, absolve

2 DISMISS, sack (*informal*), fire (*informal*), remove, expel, discard, oust, eject, cashier, give (someone) the boot (*slang*), give (someone) the sack (*informal*), kennet (*Austral slang*), jeff (*Austral slang*)

3 CARRY OUT, perform, fulfil, accomplish, do, effect, realize, observe, implement, execute, carry through

4 PAY, meet, clear, settle, square (up), honour, satisfy, relieve, liquidate

5 POUR FORTH, release, empty, leak, emit, dispense, void, gush, ooze, exude, give off, excrete, disembogue

6 FIRE, shoot, set off, explode, let off, detonate, let loose (*informal*)

▷ *noun* **1** RELEASE, liberation, clearance, pardon, acquittal, remittance, exoneration

2 DISMISSAL, notice, removal, the boot (*slang*), expulsion, the sack (*informal*), the push (*slang*), marching orders (*informal*), ejection, demobilization, kiss-off (*slang, chiefly US & Canad*), the bum's rush (*slang*), the (old) heave-ho (*informal*), the order of the boot (*slang*), congé, your books *or* cards (*informal*)

3 EMISSION, flow, ooze, secretion, excretion, pus, seepage, suppuration

4 FIRING, report, shot, blast, burst, explosion, discharging, volley, salvo, detonation, fusillade

5 CARRYING OUT, performance, achievement, execution, accomplishment, fulfilment, observance

disciple *noun* **1** APOSTLE

2 FOLLOWER, student, supporter, pupil, convert, believer, partisan, devotee, apostle, adherent, proselyte, votary, catechumen

<< OPPOSITE teacher

disciplinarian *noun* AUTHORITARIAN, tyrant, despot, stickler, taskmaster, martinet, drill sergeant, strict teacher, hard master

discipline *noun* **1** CONTROL, rule, authority, direction, regulation, supervision, orderliness, strictness

2 SELF-CONTROL, control, restraint, self-discipline, coolness, cool, willpower, calmness, self-restraint, orderliness, self-mastery, strength of mind *or* will

3 TRAINING, practice, exercise, method, regulation, drill, regimen

4 FIELD OF STUDY, area, subject, theme, topic, course, curriculum, speciality, subject matter, branch of knowledge, field of inquiry *or* reference

▷ *verb* **1** PUNISH, correct, reprimand, castigate, chastise, chasten, penalize, bring to book, reprove

2 TRAIN, control, govern, check, educate, regulate, instruct, restrain

disclaim *verb* **1** DENY, decline, reject, disallow, retract, repudiate, renege, rebut, disavow, abnegate, disaffirm

2 RENOUNCE, reject, abandon, relinquish, disown, abdicate, forswear, abjure
disclaimer *noun* DENIAL, rejection, renunciation, retraction, repudiation, disavowal, abjuration
disclose *verb* 1 MAKE KNOWN, tell, reveal, publish, relate, broadcast, leak, confess, communicate, unveil, utter, make public, impart, divulge, out (*informal*), let slip, spill the beans about (*informal*), blow wide open (*slang*), get off your chest (*informal*), spill your guts about (*slang*)
<< OPPOSITE keep secret
2 SHOW, reveal, expose, discover, exhibit, unveil, uncover, lay bare, bring to light, take the wraps off
<< OPPOSITE hide
disclosure *noun* 1 REVELATION, exposé, announcement, publication, leak, admission, declaration, confession, acknowledgment
2 UNCOVERING, publication, exposure, revelation, divulgence
discolour *or US* **discolor** *verb* 1 MARK, soil, mar, fade, stain, streak, tinge
2 STAIN, fade, streak, rust, tarnish
discoloured *or US* **discolored** *adjective* STAINED, tainted, tarnished, faded, pale, washed out, wan, blotched, besmirched, foxed, etiolated
discomfort *noun* 1 PAIN, suffering, hurt, smarting, ache, throbbing, irritation, tenderness, pang, malaise, twinge, soreness
<< OPPOSITE comfort
2 UNEASINESS, worry, anxiety, doubt, alarm, distress, suspicion, apprehension, misgiving, nervousness, disquiet, agitation, qualms, trepidation, perturbation, apprehensiveness, dubiety, inquietude
<< OPPOSITE reassurance
3 INCONVENIENCE, trouble, difficulty, bother, hardship, irritation, hassle (*informal*), nuisance, uphill (*S African*), annoyance, awkwardness, unpleasantness, vexation
▷ *verb* MAKE UNCOMFORTABLE, worry, trouble, shake, alarm, disturb, distress, unsettle, ruffle, unnerve, disquiet, perturb, discomfit, discompose
<< OPPOSITE reassure
disconcert *verb* DISTURB, worry, trouble, upset, confuse, rattle (*informal*), baffle, put off, unsettle, bewilder, shake up (*informal*), undo, flurry, agitate, ruffle, perplex, unnerve, unbalance, take aback, fluster, perturb, faze, flummox, throw off balance, nonplus, abash, discompose, put out of countenance
disconcerted *adjective* DISTURBED, worried, troubled, thrown (*informal*), upset, confused, embarrassed, annoyed, rattled (*informal*), distracted, at sea, unsettled, bewildered, shook up (*informal*), flurried, ruffled, taken aback, flustered, perturbed, fazed, nonplussed, flummoxed, caught off balance, out of countenance
disconcerting *adjective* DISTURBING, upsetting, alarming, confusing, embarrassing, awkward, distracting, dismaying, baffling, bewildering, perplexing, off-putting (*Brit informal*), bothersome
disconnect *verb* 1 CUT OFF
2 DETACH, separate, part, divide, sever, disengage, take apart, uncouple
disconnected *adjective* 1 UNRELATED
2 CONFUSED, mixed-up, rambling, irrational, jumbled, unintelligible, illogical, incoherent, disjointed, garbled, uncoordinated
disconsolate *adjective* 1 INCONSOLABLE, crushed, despairing, miserable, hopeless, heartbroken, desolate, forlorn, woeful, grief-stricken, wretched
2 SAD, low, unhappy, miserable, gloomy, dismal, melancholy, forlorn, woeful, dejected, wretched, down in the dumps (*informal*)
discontent *noun* DISSATISFACTION, unhappiness, displeasure, regret, envy, restlessness, uneasiness, vexation, discontentment, fretfulness
discontented *adjective* DISSATISFIED, complaining, unhappy, miserable, fed up, disgruntled, disaffected, vexed, displeased, fretful, cheesed off (*Brit slang*), brassed off (*Brit slang*), with a chip on your shoulder (*informal*)
<< OPPOSITE satisfied
discontinue *verb* STOP, end, finish, drop, kick (*informal*), give up, abandon, suspend, quit, halt, pause, cease, axe (*informal*), interrupt, terminate, break off, put an end to, refrain from, leave off, pull the plug on, belay (*Nautical*)
discontinued *adjective* STOPPED, ended, finished, abandoned, halted, terminated, no longer made, given up *or* over
discontinuity *noun* LACK OF UNITY, disconnection, incoherence, disunion, lack of coherence, disjointedness, disconnectedness
discord *noun* DISAGREEMENT, division, conflict, difference, opposition, row, clashing, dispute, contention, friction, strife, wrangling, variance, disunity, dissension, incompatibility, discordance, lack of concord
<< OPPOSITE agreement
discordant *adjective* 1 DISAGREEING, conflicting, clashing, different, opposite, contrary, at odds, contradictory, inconsistent, incompatible, incongruous, divergent
2 HARSH, jarring, grating, strident, shrill, jangling, dissonant, cacophonous, inharmonious, unmelodious
discount *verb* 1 MARK DOWN, reduce, lower
2 DISREGARD, reject, ignore, overlook,

discard, set aside, dispel, pass over, repudiate, disbelieve, brush off (*slang*), lay aside, pooh-pooh
▷ *noun* DEDUCTION, cut, reduction, concession, allowance, rebate, cut price

discourage *verb* 1 DISHEARTEN, daunt, deter, crush, put off, depress, cow, dash, intimidate, dismay, unnerve, unman, overawe, demoralize, cast down, put a damper on, psych out (*informal*), dispirit, deject
<< OPPOSITE hearten
2 PUT OFF, deter, prevent, dissuade, talk out of, discountenance
<< OPPOSITE encourage

discouraged *adjective* PUT OFF, deterred, daunted, dashed, dismayed, pessimistic, dispirited, downcast, disheartened, crestfallen, sick as a parrot (*informal*)

discouragement *noun* 1 DETERRENT, opposition, obstacle, curb, check, setback, restraint, constraint, impediment, hindrance, damper, disincentive
2 DEPRESSION, disappointment, despair, pessimism, hopelessness, despondency, loss of confidence, dejection, discomfiture, low spirits, downheartedness

discouraging *adjective* DISHEARTENING, disappointing, depressing, daunting, dampening, unfavourable, off-putting (*Brit informal*), dispiriting, unpropitious

discourse *noun* 1 CONVERSATION, talk, discussion, speech, communication, chat, dialogue, converse
2 SPEECH, talk, address, essay, lecture, sermon, treatise, dissertation, homily, oration, disquisition, whaikorero (NZ)

discover *verb* 1 FIND OUT, see, learn, reveal, spot, determine, notice, realize, recognize, perceive, detect, disclose, uncover, discern, ascertain, suss (out) (*slang*), get wise to (*informal*)
2 FIND, come across, uncover, unearth, turn up, dig up, come upon, bring to light, light upon
3 INVENT, design, pioneer, devise, originate, contrive, conceive of

discoverer *noun* 1 EXPLORER, pioneer
2 INVENTOR, author, originator, initiator

discovery *noun* 1 FINDING OUT, news, announcement, revelation, disclosure, realization
2 INVENTION, launch, institution, introduction, pioneering, innovation, initiation, inauguration, induction, coinage, origination
3 BREAKTHROUGH, find, finding, development, advance, leap, coup, invention, step forward, godsend, quantum leap
4 FINDING, turning up, locating, revelation, uncovering, disclosure, detection, espial

discredit *verb* 1 DISGRACE, blame, shame, smear, stain, humiliate, degrade, taint, slur, detract from, disparage, vilify, slander, sully, dishonour, stigmatize, defame, bring into disrepute, bring shame upon
<< OPPOSITE honour
2 DISPUTE, question, challenge, deny, reject, discount, distrust, mistrust, repudiate, cast doubt on *or* upon, disbelieve, pooh-pooh
▷ *noun* DISGRACE, scandal, shame, disrepute, smear, stigma, censure, slur, ignominy, dishonour, imputation, odium, ill-repute, aspersion
<< OPPOSITE honour

discredited *adjective* REJECTED, exposed, exploded, discarded, obsolete, refuted, debunked, outworn

discreet *adjective* TACTFUL, diplomatic, politic, reserved, guarded, careful, sensible, cautious, wary, discerning, prudent, considerate, judicious, circumspect, sagacious
<< OPPOSITE tactless
▷ see **discrete**

discrepancy *noun* DISAGREEMENT, difference, variation, conflict, contradiction, inconsistency, disparity, variance, divergence, dissonance, incongruity, dissimilarity, discordance, contrariety

discrete *adjective* SEPARATE, individual, distinct, detached, disconnected, unattached, discontinuous

> This word is quite often used by mistake where *discreet* is intended: *reading is a set of discrete skills; she was discreet* (not *discrete*) *about the affair*

discretion *noun* 1 TACT, care, consideration, judgment, caution, diplomacy, good sense, prudence, acumen, wariness, discernment, circumspection, sagacity, carefulness, judiciousness, heedfulness
<< OPPOSITE tactlessness
2 CHOICE, will, wish, liking, mind, option, pleasure, preference, inclination, disposition, predilection, volition

discretionary *adjective* OPTIONAL, arbitrary (*Law*), unrestricted, elective, open to choice, nonmandatory

discriminate *verb* DIFFERENTIATE, distinguish, discern, separate, assess, evaluate, tell the difference, draw a distinction
▷▷ **discriminate against someone** TREAT DIFFERENTLY, single out, victimize, disfavour, treat as inferior, show bias against, show prejudice against

discriminating *adjective* DISCERNING, particular, keen, critical, acute, sensitive, refined, cultivated, selective, astute, tasteful, fastidious

<< OPPOSITE undiscriminating

discrimination *noun* 1 PREJUDICE, bias, injustice, intolerance, bigotry, favouritism, unfairness, inequity
2 DISCERNMENT, taste, judgment, perception, insight, penetration, subtlety, refinement, acumen, keenness, sagacity, acuteness, clearness

discriminatory *adjective* PREJUDICED, biased, partial, weighted, favouring, one-sided, partisan, unjust, preferential, prejudicial, inequitable

discuss *verb* TALK ABOUT, consider, debate, review, go into, examine, argue about, thrash out, ventilate, reason about, exchange views on, deliberate about, weigh up the pros and cons of, converse about, confer about

discussion *noun* 1 TALK, debate, argument, conference, exchange, review, conversation, consideration, dialogue, consultation, seminar, discourse, deliberation, symposium, colloquy, confabulation, korero (NZ)
2 EXAMINATION, investigation, analysis, scrutiny, dissection

disdain *noun* CONTEMPT, dislike, scorn, arrogance, indifference, sneering, derision, hauteur, snobbishness, contumely, haughtiness, superciliousness
▷ *verb* SCORN, reject, despise, slight, disregard, spurn, undervalue, deride, look down on, belittle, sneer at, pooh-pooh, contemn, look down your nose at (*informal*), misprize

disdainful *adjective* CONTEMPTUOUS, scornful, arrogant, superior, proud, sneering, aloof, haughty, derisive, supercilious, high and mighty (*informal*), hoity-toity (*informal*), turning up your nose (at), on your high horse (*informal*), looking down your nose (at)

disease *noun* 1 ILLNESS, condition, complaint, upset, infection, disorder, sickness, ailment, affliction, malady, infirmity, indisposition, lurgy (*informal*)
2 EVIL, disorder, plague, curse, cancer, blight, contamination, scourge, affliction, bane, contagion, malady, canker

diseased *adjective* UNHEALTHY, sick, infected, rotten, ailing, tainted, sickly, unwell, crook (*Austral & NZ informal*), unsound, unwholesome

disembark *verb* LAND, get off, alight, arrive, step out, go ashore

disembodied *adjective* GHOSTLY, phantom, spectral

disenchanted *adjective* DISILLUSIONED, disappointed, soured, cynical, indifferent, sick, let down, blasé, jaundiced, undeceived

disenchantment *noun* DISILLUSIONMENT, disappointment, disillusion, rude awakening

disengage *verb* 1 RELEASE, free, separate, ease, liberate, loosen, set free, extricate, untie, disentangle, unloose, unbridle
2 DETACH, withdraw

disengaged *adjective* UNCONNECTED, separate, apart, detached, unattached

disengagement *noun* DISCONNECTION, withdrawal, separation, detachment, disentanglement

disentangle *verb* 1 RESOLVE, clear (up), work out, sort out, clarify, simplify
2 FREE, separate, loose, detach, sever, disconnect, extricate, disengage
3 UNTANGLE, unravel, untwist, unsnarl

disfigure *verb* 1 DAMAGE, scar, mutilate, maim, injure, wound, deform
2 MAR, distort, blemish, deface, make ugly, disfeature

disgorge *verb* EMIT, discharge, send out, expel, throw out, vent, throw up, eject, spout, spew, belch, send forth

disgrace *noun* 1 SHAME, contempt, discredit, degradation, disrepute, ignominy, dishonour, infamy, opprobrium, odium, disfavour, obloquy, disesteem
<< OPPOSITE honour
2 SCANDAL, stain, stigma, blot, blemish
▷ *verb* SHAME, stain, humiliate, discredit, degrade, taint, sully, dishonour, stigmatize, defame, abase, bring shame upon
<< OPPOSITE honour

disgraced *adjective* SHAMED, humiliated, discredited, branded, degraded, mortified, in disgrace, dishonoured, stigmatized, under a cloud, in the doghouse (*informal*)

disgraceful *adjective* SHAMEFUL, shocking, scandalous, mean, low, infamous, degrading, unworthy, ignominious, disreputable, contemptible, dishonourable, detestable, discreditable, blameworthy, opprobrious

disgruntled *adjective* DISCONTENTED, dissatisfied, annoyed, irritated, put out, hacked (off) (*US slang*), grumpy, vexed, sullen, displeased, petulant, sulky, peeved, malcontent, testy, peevish, huffy, cheesed off (*Brit slang*), hoha (NZ)

disguise *verb* HIDE, cover, conceal, screen, mask, suppress, withhold, veil, cloak, shroud, camouflage, keep secret, hush up, draw a veil over, keep dark, keep under your hat
▷ *noun* COSTUME, get-up (*informal*), mask, camouflage, false appearance

disguised *adjective* 1 IN DISGUISE, masked, camouflaged, undercover, incognito, unrecognizable
2 FALSE, assumed, pretend, artificial, forged, fake, mock, imitation, sham, pseudo (*informal*), counterfeit, feigned, phoney *or* phony (*informal*)

disgust *verb* 1 SICKEN, outrage, offend, revolt, put off, repel, nauseate, gross out (*US slang*), turn your stomach, fill with loathing, cause

aversion
<< OPPOSITE delight
2 OUTRAGE, shock, anger, hurt, fury, resentment, wrath, indignation

disgusted *adjective* 1 OUTRAGED, appalled, offended, sickened, scandalized
2 SICKENED, repelled, repulsed, nauseated

disgusting *adjective* 1 SICKENING, foul, revolting, gross, repellent, nauseating, repugnant, loathsome, festy (*Austral slang*), yucko (*Austral slang*)
2 APPALLING, shocking, awful, offensive, dreadful, horrifying

dish *noun* 1 BOWL, plate, platter, salver
2 FOOD, fare, recipe
▷▷ **dish something out** (*informal*) DISTRIBUTE, assign, allocate, designate, set aside, hand out, earmark, inflict, mete out, dole out, share out, apportion
▷▷ **dish something up** SERVE UP, serve, produce, present, hand out, ladle out, spoon out

disharmony *noun* DISCORD, conflict, clash, friction, discordance, disaccord, inharmoniousness

disheartened *adjective* DISCOURAGED, depressed, crushed, dismayed, choked, daunted, dejected, dispirited, downcast, crestfallen, downhearted, sick as a parrot (*informal*)

dishevelled *or US* **disheveled** *adjective* UNTIDY, disordered, messy, ruffled, rumpled, bedraggled, unkempt, tousled, hanging loose, blowsy, uncombed, disarranged, disarrayed, frowzy, daggy (*Austral & NZ informal*)
<< OPPOSITE tidy

dishonest *adjective* DECEITFUL, corrupt, crooked (*informal*), designing, lying, bent (*slang*), false, unfair, cheating, deceiving, shady (*informal*), fraudulent, treacherous, deceptive, unscrupulous, crafty, swindling, disreputable, untrustworthy, double-dealing, unprincipled, mendacious, perfidious, untruthful, guileful, knavish (*archaic*)
<< OPPOSITE honest

dishonesty *noun* DECEIT, fraud, corruption, cheating, graft (*informal*), treachery, trickery, criminality, duplicity, falsehood, chicanery, falsity, sharp practice, perfidy, mendacity, fraudulence, crookedness, wiliness, unscrupulousness, improbity

dishonour *or US* **dishonor** *verb* DISGRACE, shame, discredit, corrupt, degrade, blacken, sully, debase, debauch, defame, abase
<< OPPOSITE respect
▷ *noun* DISGRACE, scandal, shame, discredit, degradation, disrepute, reproach, ignominy, infamy, opprobrium, odium, disfavour, abasement, obloquy
<< OPPOSITE honour

disillusion *verb* SHATTER THE ILLUSIONS OF, disabuse, bring down to earth, open the eyes of, disenchant, undeceive

disillusioned *adjective* DISENCHANTED, disappointed, enlightened, indifferent, disabused, sadder and wiser, undeceived

disillusionment *noun* DISENCHANTMENT, disappointment, disillusion, enlightenment, rude awakening, lost innocence

disincentive *noun* DISCOURAGEMENT, deterrent, impediment, damper, dissuasion, determent

disinclined *adjective* RELUCTANT, unwilling, averse, opposed, resistant, hesitant, balking, loath, not in the mood, indisposed, antipathetic

disinfect *verb* STERILIZE, purify, decontaminate, clean, cleanse, fumigate, deodorize, sanitize
<< OPPOSITE contaminate

disinfectant *noun* ANTISEPTIC, sterilizer, germicide, sanitizer

disintegrate *verb* BREAK UP, crumble, fall apart, separate, shatter, splinter, break apart, fall to pieces, go to pieces, disunite

disinterest *noun* INDIFFERENCE, apathy, lack of interest, disregard, detachment, absence of feeling

disinterested *adjective* 1 IMPARTIAL, objective, neutral, detached, equitable, impersonal, unbiased, even-handed, unselfish, uninvolved, unprejudiced, free from self-interest
<< OPPOSITE biased
2 INDIFFERENT, apathetic, uninterested

> *Disinterested* is now so commonly used to mean 'not interested' that to avoid ambiguity it is often advisable to replace it by a synonym when the meaning intended is 'impartial, unbiased'. In the Collins Word Web about 10% of the examples of the word occur followed by *in*, and overall about a third of examples are of this usage

disjointed *adjective* 1 INCOHERENT, confused, disordered, rambling, disconnected, unconnected, loose, aimless, fitful, spasmodic
2 DISCONNECTED, separated, divided, split, displaced, dislocated, disunited

dislike *verb* HATE, object to, loathe, despise, shun, scorn, disapprove of, detest, abhor, recoil from, take a dim view of, be repelled by, be averse to, disfavour, have an aversion to, abominate, have a down on (*informal*), disrelish, have no taste *or* stomach for, not be able to bear *or* abide *or* stand
<< OPPOSITE like
▷ *noun* HATRED, disgust, hostility, loathing,

disapproval, distaste, animosity, aversion, antagonism, displeasure, antipathy, enmity, animus, disinclination, repugnance, odium, detestation, disapprobation
<< OPPOSITE liking

dislocate *verb* 1 PUT OUT OF JOINT, disconnect, disengage, unhinge, disunite, disjoint, disarticulate
2 DISRUPT, disturb, disorder

dislocation *noun* 1 DISRUPTION, disorder, disturbance, disarray, disorganization
2 PUTTING OUT OF JOINT, unhinging, disengagement, disconnection, disarticulation

dislodge *verb* 1 DISPLACE, remove, disturb, dig out, uproot, extricate, disentangle, knock loose
2 OUST, remove, expel, throw out, displace, topple, force out, eject, depose, unseat

disloyal *adjective* TREACHEROUS, false, unfaithful, subversive, two-faced, faithless, untrustworthy, perfidious, apostate, traitorous
<< OPPOSITE loyal

disloyalty *noun* TREACHERY, infidelity, breach of trust, double-dealing, falsity, perfidy, unfaithfulness, falseness, betrayal of trust, inconstancy, deceitfulness, breaking of faith, Punic faith

dismal *adjective* 1 BAD, awful, dreadful, rotten (*informal*), terrible, poor, dire, duff (*Brit informal*), abysmal, frightful, godawful (*slang*)
2 SAD, gloomy, melancholy, black, dark, depressing, discouraging, bleak, dreary, sombre, forlorn, despondent, lugubrious, sorrowful, wretched, funereal, cheerless, dolorous
<< OPPOSITE happy
3 GLOOMY, depressing, dull, dreary, lugubrious, cheerless
<< OPPOSITE cheerful

dismantle *verb* TAKE APART, strip, demolish, raze, disassemble, unrig, take to pieces *or* bits

dismay *verb* 1 ALARM, frighten, scare, panic, distress, terrify, appal, startle, horrify, paralyse, unnerve, put the wind up (someone) (*informal*), give (someone) a turn (*informal*), affright, fill (someone) with consternation
2 DISAPPOINT, upset, sadden, dash, discourage, put off, daunt, disillusion, let down, vex, chagrin, dishearten, dispirit, disenchant, disgruntle
▷ *noun* 1 ALARM, fear, horror, panic, anxiety, distress, terror, dread, fright, unease, apprehension, nervousness, agitation, consternation, trepidation, uneasiness
2 DISAPPOINTMENT, upset, distress, frustration, dissatisfaction, disillusionment, chagrin, disenchantment, discouragement, mortification

dismember *verb* CUT INTO PIECES, divide, rend, sever, mutilate, dissect, dislocate, amputate, disjoint, anatomize, dislimb

dismiss *verb* 1 REJECT, disregard, spurn, repudiate, pooh-pooh
2 BANISH, drop, dispel, shelve, discard, set aside, eradicate, cast out, lay aside, put out of your mind
3 SACK, fire (*informal*), remove (*informal*), axe (*informal*), discharge, oust, lay off, kick out (*informal*), cashier, send packing (*informal*), give notice to, kiss off (*slang, chiefly US & Canad*), give (someone) their marching orders, give (someone) the push (*informal*), give (someone) the elbow, give the boot to (*slang*), give the bullet to (*Brit slang*), kennet (*Austral slang*), jeff (*Austral slang*)
4 LET GO, free, release, discharge, dissolve, liberate, disperse, disband, send away

dismissal *noun* THE SACK, removal, discharge, notice, the boot (*slang*), expulsion (*informal*), the push (*slang*), marching orders (*informal*), kiss-off (*slang, chiefly US & Canad*), the bum's rush (*slang*), the (old) heave-ho (*informal*), the order of the boot (*slang*), your books *or* cards (*informal*)

dismount *verb* GET OFF, descend, get down, alight, light

disobedience *noun* DEFIANCE, mutiny, indiscipline, revolt, insubordination, waywardness, infraction, recalcitrance, noncompliance, unruliness, nonobservance

disobey *verb* 1 DEFY, ignore, rebel, resist, disregard, refuse to obey, dig your heels in (*informal*), go counter to
2 INFRINGE, defy, refuse to obey, flout, violate, contravene, overstep, transgress, go counter to

disorder *noun* 1 ILLNESS, disease, complaint, condition, sickness, ailment, affliction, malady, infirmity, indisposition
2 UNTIDINESS, mess, confusion, chaos, muddle, state, clutter, shambles, disarray, jumble, irregularity, disorganization, hotchpotch, derangement, hodgepodge (*US*), pig's breakfast (*informal*), disorderliness
3 DISTURBANCE, fight, riot, turmoil, unrest, quarrel, upheaval, brawl, clamour, uproar, turbulence, fracas, commotion, rumpus, tumult, hubbub, shindig (*informal*), hullabaloo, scrimmage, unruliness, shindy (*informal*), bagarre (*French*), biffo (*Austral slang*)

disorderly *adjective* 1 UNTIDY, confused, chaotic, messy, irregular, jumbled, indiscriminate, shambolic (*informal*), disorganized, higgledy-piggledy (*informal*), unsystematic
<< OPPOSITE tidy
2 UNRULY, disruptive, rowdy, turbulent, unlawful, stormy, rebellious, boisterous,

tumultuous, lawless, riotous, unmanageable, ungovernable, refractory, obstreperous, indisciplined

disorganized *adjective* MUDDLED, confused, disordered, shuffled, chaotic, jumbled, haphazard, unorganized, unsystematic, unmethodical

disorientate *or* **disorient** *verb* CONFUSE, upset, perplex, dislocate, cause to lose your bearings

disorientated *or* **disoriented** *adjective* CONFUSED, lost, unsettled, bewildered, mixed up, perplexed, all at sea

disown *verb* DENY, reject, abandon, renounce, disallow, retract, repudiate, cast off, rebut, disavow, disclaim, abnegate, refuse to acknowledge *or* recognize

disparage *verb* RUN DOWN, dismiss, put down, criticize, underestimate, discredit, ridicule, scorn, minimize, disdain, undervalue, deride, slag (off) (*slang*), knock (*informal*), blast, rubbish (*informal*), malign, detract from, denigrate, belittle, decry, underrate, vilify, slander, deprecate, depreciate, tear into (*informal*), diss (*slang, chiefly US*), defame, bad-mouth (*slang, chiefly US & Canad*), lambast(e), traduce, derogate, asperse

disparaging *adjective* CONTEMPTUOUS, damaging, critical, slighting, offensive, insulting, abusive, scathing, dismissive, belittling, unfavourable, derogatory, unflattering, scornful, disdainful, defamatory, derisive, libellous, slanderous, deprecatory, uncomplimentary, fault-finding, contumelious

<< OPPOSITE complimentary

disparate *adjective* DIFFERENT, contrasting, unlike, contrary, distinct, diverse, at odds, dissimilar, discordant, at variance, discrepant

disparity *noun* DIFFERENCE, gap, inequality, distinction, imbalance, discrepancy, incongruity, unevenness, dissimilarity, disproportion, unlikeness, dissimilitude

dispassionate *adjective* 1 UNEMOTIONAL, cool, collected, calm, moderate, composed, sober, serene, unmoved, temperate, unfazed (*informal*), unruffled, imperturbable, unexcited, unexcitable

<< OPPOSITE emotional

2 OBJECTIVE, fair, neutral, detached, indifferent, impartial, impersonal, disinterested, unbiased, uninvolved, unprejudiced

<< OPPOSITE biased

dispatch *or* **despatch** *verb* 1 SEND, transmit, forward, express, communicate, consign, remit

2 KILL, murder, destroy, do in (*slang*), eliminate (*slang*), take out (*slang*), execute, butcher, slaughter, assassinate, slay, finish off, put an end to, do away with, blow away (*slang, chiefly US*), liquidate, annihilate, exterminate, take (someone's) life, bump off (*slang*)

3 CARRY OUT, perform, fulfil, effect, finish, achieve, settle, dismiss, conclude, accomplish, execute, discharge, dispose of, expedite, make short work of (*informal*)

▷ *noun* 1 MESSAGE, news, report, story, letter, account, piece, item, document, communication, instruction, bulletin, communiqué, missive

2 SPEED, haste, promptness, alacrity, rapidity, quickness, swiftness, briskness, expedition, celerity, promptitude, precipitateness

dispel *verb* DRIVE AWAY, dismiss, eliminate, resolve, scatter, expel, disperse, banish, rout, allay, dissipate, chase away

dispensation *noun* 1 EXEMPTION, licence, exception, permission, privilege, relaxation, immunity, relief, indulgence, reprieve, remission

2 DISTRIBUTION, supplying, dealing out, appointment, endowment, allotment, consignment, disbursement, apportionment, bestowal, conferment

dispense *verb* 1 DISTRIBUTE, assign, allocate, allot, mete out, dole out, share out, apportion, deal out, disburse

2 PREPARE, measure, supply, mix

3 ADMINISTER, direct, operate, carry out, implement, undertake, enforce, execute, apply, discharge

4 EXEMPT, except, excuse, release, relieve, reprieve, let off (*informal*), exonerate

▷▷ **dispense with something** *or* **someone** 1 DO AWAY WITH, ignore, give up, cancel, abolish, omit, disregard, pass over, brush aside, forgo, render needless

2 DO WITHOUT, get rid of, dispose of, relinquish, shake off

dispersal *noun* 1 SCATTERING, spread, distribution, dissemination, dissipation

2 SPREAD, broadcast, circulation, diffusion, dissemination

disperse *verb* 1 SCATTER, spread, distribute, circulate, strew, diffuse, dissipate, disseminate, throw about

2 BREAK UP, separate, dismiss, disappear, send off, vanish, scatter, dissolve, rout, dispel, disband, part company, demobilize, go (their) separate ways

<< OPPOSITE gather

3 DISSOLVE, disappear, vanish, evaporate, break up, dissipate, melt away, evanesce ▷ see **disburse**

dispirited *adjective* DISHEARTENED, depressed, discouraged, down, low, sad, gloomy, glum, dejected, in the doldrums, despondent, downcast, morose, crestfallen, sick as a parrot

(*informal*)

dispiriting *adjective* DISHEARTENING, disappointing, depressing, crushing, discouraging, daunting, sickening, saddening, demoralizing
<< OPPOSITE reassuring

displace *verb* 1 REPLACE, succeed, take over from, supersede, oust, usurp, supplant, take the place of, crowd out, fill *or* step into (someone's) boots
2 FORCE OUT, turn out, expel, throw out, oust, unsettle, kick out (*informal*), eject, evict, dislodge, boot out (*informal*), dispossess, turf out (*informal*)
3 MOVE, shift, disturb, budge, misplace, disarrange, derange
4 REMOVE, fire (*informal*), dismiss, sack (*informal*), discharge, oust, depose, cashier, dethrone, remove from office

display *verb* 1 SHOW, present, exhibit, unveil, open to view, take the wraps off, put on view
<< OPPOSITE conceal
2 EXPOSE, show, reveal, bare, exhibit, uncover, lay bare, expose to view
3 DEMONSTRATE, show, reveal, register, expose, disclose, betray, manifest, divulge, make known, evidence, evince
4 SHOW OFF, parade, exhibit, sport (*informal*), flash (*informal*), boast, flourish, brandish, flaunt, vaunt, make a (great) show of, disport, make an exhibition of
▷ *noun* 1 PROOF, exhibition, demonstration, evidence, expression, exposure, illustration, revelation, testimony, confirmation, manifestation, affirmation, substantiation
2 EXHIBITION, show, demonstration, presentation, showing, array, expo (*informal*), exposition
3 OSTENTATION, show, dash, flourish, fanfare, pomp
4 SHOW, exhibition, demonstration, parade, spectacle, pageant, pageantry

displease *verb* ANNOY, upset, anger, provoke, offend, irritate, put out, hassle (*informal*), aggravate (*informal*), incense, gall, exasperate, nettle, vex, irk, rile, pique, nark (*Brit, Austral & NZ slang*), dissatisfy, put your back up, hack you off (*informal*)

displeasure *noun* ANNOYANCE, anger, resentment, irritation, offence, dislike, wrath, dissatisfaction, disapproval, indignation, distaste, pique, vexation, disgruntlement, disfavour, disapprobation
<< OPPOSITE satisfaction

disposable *adjective* 1 THROWAWAY, paper, nonreturnable
2 AVAILABLE, expendable, free for use, consumable, spendable, at your service

disposal *noun* THROWING AWAY, dumping (*informal*), scrapping, removal, discarding, clearance, jettisoning, ejection, riddance, relinquishment
▷▷ **at your disposal** AVAILABLE, ready, to hand, accessible, convenient, handy, on hand, at hand, obtainable, on tap, expendable, at your fingertips, at your service, free for use, ready for use, consumable, spendable

dispose *verb* 1 ARRANGE, put, place, group, set, order, stand, range, settle, fix, rank, distribute, array
2 LEAD, move, condition, influence, prompt, tempt, adapt, motivate, bias, induce, incline, predispose, actuate
▷▷ **dispose of someone** KILL, murder, destroy, do in (*slang*), take out (*slang*), execute, slaughter, dispatch, assassinate, slay, do away with, knock off (*slang*), liquidate, neutralize, exterminate, take (someone's) life, bump off (*slang*), wipe from the face of the earth (*informal*)
▷▷ **dispose of something** 1 GET RID OF, destroy, dump (*informal*), scrap, bin (*informal*), junk (*informal*), chuck (*informal*), discard, unload, dispense with, jettison, get shot of, throw out *or* away
2 DEAL WITH, manage, treat, handle, settle, cope with, take care of, see to, finish with, attend to, get to grips with
3 GIVE, give up, part with, bestow, transfer, make over

disposed *adjective* INCLINED, given, likely, subject, ready, prone, liable, apt, predisposed, tending towards, of a mind to

disposition *noun* 1 CHARACTER, nature, spirit, make-up, constitution, temper, temperament
2 TENDENCY, inclination, propensity, habit, leaning, bent, bias, readiness, predisposition, proclivity, proneness
3 (*Archaic*) ARRANGEMENT, grouping, ordering, organization, distribution, disposal, placement

dispossess *verb* STRIP, deprive

dispossessed *adjective* DESTITUTE, landless

disproportionate *adjective* EXCESSIVE, too much, unreasonable, uneven, unequal, unbalanced, out of proportion, inordinate, incommensurate

disprove *verb* PROVE FALSE, discredit, refute, contradict, negate, invalidate, rebut, give the lie to, make a nonsense of, blow out of the water (*slang*), controvert, confute
<< OPPOSITE prove

dispute *verb* 1 CONTEST, question, challenge, deny, doubt, oppose, object to, contradict, rebut, impugn, controvert, call in *or* into question
2 ARGUE, fight, clash, row, disagree, fall out (*informal*), contend, feud, quarrel, brawl,

squabble, spar, wrangle, bicker, have an argument, cross swords, be at sixes and sevens, fight like cat and dog, go at it hammer and tongs, altercate
▷ *noun* 1 DISAGREEMENT, conflict, argument, falling out, dissent, friction, strife, discord, altercation
2 ARGUMENT, row, clash, controversy, disturbance, contention, feud, quarrel, brawl, squabble, wrangle, difference of opinion, tiff, dissension, shindig (*informal*), shindy (*informal*), bagarre (*French*)

disqualification *noun* BAN, exclusion, elimination, rejection, ineligibility, debarment, disenablement, disentitlement

disqualified *adjective* ELIMINATED, knocked out, out of the running, debarred, ineligible

disqualify *verb* BAN, rule out, prohibit, preclude, debar, declare ineligible, disentitle

disquiet *noun* UNEASINESS, concern, fear, worry, alarm, anxiety, distress, unrest, angst, nervousness, trepidation, foreboding, restlessness, fretfulness, disquietude
▷ *verb* MAKE UNEASY, concern, worry, trouble, upset, bother, disturb, distress, annoy, plague, unsettle, harass, hassle (*informal*), agitate, vex, perturb, discompose, incommode

disquieting *adjective* WORRYING, troubling, upsetting, disturbing, distressing, annoying, irritating, unsettling, harrowing, unnerving, disconcerting, vexing, perturbing, bothersome

disregard *verb* IGNORE, discount, take no notice of, overlook, neglect, pass over, turn a blind eye to, disobey, laugh off, make light of, pay no attention to, pay no heed to, leave out of account, brush aside *or* away
<< OPPOSITE pay attention to
▷ *noun* IGNORING, neglect, contempt, indifference, negligence, disdain, disrespect, heedlessness

disrepair *noun* DILAPIDATION, collapse, decay, deterioration, ruination
▷▷ **in disrepair** OUT OF ORDER, broken, decayed, worn-out, decrepit, not functioning, out of commission, on the blink (*slang*), bust (*informal*), kaput (*informal*)

disreputable *adjective* DISCREDITABLE, mean, low, base, shocking, disorderly, notorious, vicious, infamous, disgraceful, shameful, vile, shady (*informal*), scandalous, ignominious, contemptible, louche, unprincipled, dishonourable, opprobrious
<< OPPOSITE respectable

disrepute *noun* DISCREDIT, shame, disgrace, unpopularity, ignominy, dishonour, infamy, disfavour, ill repute, obloquy, ill favour, disesteem

disrespect *noun* CONTEMPT, cheek, disregard, rudeness, lack of respect, irreverence, insolence, impertinence, impudence, discourtesy, incivility, impoliteness, lese-majesty, unmannerliness
<< OPPOSITE respect

disrespectful *adjective* CONTEMPTUOUS, insulting, rude, cheeky, irreverent, bad-mannered, impertinent, insolent, impolite, impudent, discourteous, uncivil, ill-bred

disrupt *verb* 1 INTERRUPT, stop, upset, hold up, interfere with, unsettle, obstruct, cut short, intrude on, break up *or* into
2 DISTURB, upset, confuse, disorder, spoil, unsettle, agitate, disorganize, disarrange, derange, throw into disorder

disruption *noun* DISTURBANCE, disorder, confusion, interference, disarray, interruption, stoppage, disorderliness

disruptive *adjective* DISTURBING, upsetting, disorderly, unsettling, troublesome, unruly, obstreperous, troublemaking
<< OPPOSITE well-behaved

dissatisfaction *noun* DISCONTENT, frustration, resentment, regret, distress, disappointment, dismay, irritation, unhappiness, annoyance, displeasure, exasperation, chagrin

dissatisfied *adjective* DISCONTENTED, frustrated, unhappy, disappointed, fed up, disgruntled, not satisfied, unfulfilled, displeased, unsatisfied, ungratified
<< OPPOSITE satisfied

dissect *verb* 1 CUT UP *or* APART, dismember, lay open, anatomize
2 ANALYSE, study, investigate, research, explore, break down, inspect, scrutinize

dissection *noun* 1 CUTTING UP, anatomy, autopsy, dismemberment, postmortem (examination), necropsy, anatomization
2 ANALYSIS, examination, breakdown, research, investigation, inspection, scrutiny

disseminate *verb* SPREAD, publish, broadcast, distribute, scatter, proclaim, circulate, sow, disperse, diffuse, publicize, dissipate, propagate, promulgate

dissemination *noun* SPREAD, publishing, broadcasting, publication, distribution, circulation, diffusion, propagation, promulgation

dissension *noun* DISAGREEMENT, conflict, dissent, dispute, contention, quarrelling, friction, strife, discord, discordance, conflict of opinion

dissent *noun* DISAGREEMENT, opposition, protest, resistance, refusal, objection, discord, demur, dissension, dissidence, nonconformity, remonstrance
▷▷ **dissent from something** DISAGREE WITH, object to, protest against, refuse to accept
<< OPPOSITE assent

dissenter *noun* OBJECTOR, dissident,

nonconformist, protestant, disputant

dissenting *adjective* DISAGREEING, protesting, opposing, conflicting, differing, dissident

dissertation *noun* THESIS, essay, discourse, critique, exposition, treatise, disquisition

disservice *noun* WRONG, injury, harm, injustice, disfavour, unkindness, bad turn, ill turn

<< OPPOSITE good turn

dissident *adjective* DISSENTING, disagreeing, nonconformist, heterodox, schismatic, dissentient

▷ *noun* PROTESTER, rebel, dissenter, demonstrator, agitator, recusant, protest marcher

dissimilar *adjective* DIFFERENT, unlike, various, varied, diverse, assorted, unrelated, disparate, miscellaneous, sundry, divergent, manifold, heterogeneous, mismatched, multifarious, not similar, not alike, not capable of comparison

<< OPPOSITE alike

dissipate *verb* DISAPPEAR, fade, vanish, dissolve, disperse, evaporate, diffuse, melt away, evanesce

dissipated *adjective* 1 DEBAUCHED, abandoned, self-indulgent, profligate, intemperate, dissolute, rakish

2 SQUANDERED, spent, wasted, exhausted, consumed, scattered

dissociate *or* **disassociate** *verb* SEPARATE, distance, divorce, isolate, detach, segregate, disconnect, set apart

▷▷ **dissociate yourself from something** *or* **someone** BREAK AWAY FROM, part company with, break off relations with

dissociation *noun* SEPARATION, break, division, distancing, divorce, isolation, segregation, detachment, severance, disengagement, disconnection, disunion

dissolution *noun* 1 ENDING, end, finish, conclusion, suspension, dismissal, termination, adjournment, disbandment, discontinuation

<< OPPOSITE union

2 BREAKING UP, parting, divorce, separation, disintegration

dissolve *verb* 1 MELT, soften, thaw, flux, liquefy, deliquesce

2 END, dismiss, suspend, axe (*informal*), break up, wind up, overthrow, terminate, discontinue, dismantle, disband, disunite

3 DISAPPEAR, fade, vanish, break down, crumble, disperse, dwindle, evaporate, disintegrate, perish, diffuse, dissipate, decompose, melt away, waste away, evanesce

▷▷ **dissolve into** *or* **in something** (with *tears* or *laughter* as object) BREAK INTO, burst into, give way to, launch into

dissonance *or* **dissonancy** *noun* DISCORDANCE, discord, jangle, cacophony, jarring, harshness, lack of harmony, unmelodiousness

distance *noun* 1 SPACE, length, extent, range, stretch, gap, interval, separation, span, width

2 REMOTENESS

3 ALOOFNESS, reserve, detachment, restraint, indifference, stiffness, coolness, coldness, remoteness, frigidity, uninvolvement, standoffishness

▷▷ **go the distance** FINISH, stay the course, complete, see through, bring to an end

▷▷ **in the distance** FAR OFF, far away, the horizon, afar, yonder

distant *adjective* 1 FAR-OFF, far, remote, removed, abroad, out-of-the-way, far-flung, faraway, outlying, afar

<< OPPOSITE close

2 REMOTE, slight

3 RESERVED, cold, withdrawn, cool, formal, remote, stiff, restrained, detached, indifferent, aloof, unfriendly, reticent, haughty, unapproachable, standoffish

<< OPPOSITE friendly

4 FARAWAY, blank, abstracted, vague, absorbed, distracted, unaware, musing, vacant, preoccupied, bemused, oblivious, dreamy, daydreaming, absent-minded, inattentive

distaste *noun* DISLIKE, horror, disgust, loathing, aversion, revulsion, displeasure, antipathy, abhorrence, disinclination, repugnance, odium, disfavour, detestation, disrelish

distasteful *adjective* UNPLEASANT, offensive, obscene, undesirable, unsavoury, obnoxious, unpalatable, displeasing, repulsive, objectionable, disagreeable, repugnant, loathsome, abhorrent, nauseous, uninviting

<< OPPOSITE enjoyable

distil *verb* 1 PURIFY, refine, evaporate, condense, sublimate, vaporize

2 EXTRACT, express, squeeze, obtain, take out, draw out, separate out, press out

distillation *noun* ESSENCE, extract, elixir, spirit, quintessence

distinct *adjective* 1 DIFFERENT, individual, separate, disconnected, discrete, dissimilar, unconnected, unattached

<< OPPOSITE similar

2 STRIKING, sharp, dramatic, stunning (*informal*), outstanding, bold, noticeable, well-defined

3 DEFINITE, marked, clear, decided, obvious, sharp, plain, apparent, patent, evident, black-and-white, manifest, noticeable, conspicuous, clear-cut, unmistakable, palpable, recognizable, unambiguous, observable, perceptible, appreciable

<< OPPOSITE vague

distinction *noun* 1 DIFFERENCE, contrast, variation, differential, discrepancy, disparity, deviation, differentiation, fine line, distinctness, dissimilarity
2 EXCELLENCE, note, quality, worth, account, rank, reputation, importance, consequence, fame, celebrity, merit, superiority, prominence, greatness, eminence, renown, repute
3 FEATURE, quality, characteristic, name, mark, individuality, peculiarity, singularity, distinctiveness, particularity
4 MERIT, credit, honour, integrity, excellence, righteousness, rectitude, uprightness

distinctive *adjective* CHARACTERISTIC, special, individual, specific, unique, typical, extraordinary, distinguishing, peculiar, singular, idiosyncratic
<< OPPOSITE ordinary

distinctly *adverb* 1 DEFINITELY, clearly, obviously, sharply, plainly, patently, manifestly, decidedly, markedly, noticeably, unmistakably, palpably
2 CLEARLY, plainly, precisely

distinguish *verb* 1 DIFFERENTIATE, determine, separate, discriminate, decide, judge, discern, ascertain, tell the difference, make a distinction, tell apart, tell between
2 CHARACTERIZE, mark, separate, single out, individualize, set apart
3 MAKE OUT, recognize, perceive, know, see, tell, pick out, discern

distinguishable *adjective* 1 RECOGNIZABLE, noticeable, conspicuous, discernible, obvious, evident, manifest, perceptible, well-marked
2 CONSPICUOUS, clear, strong, bright, plain, bold, pronounced, colourful, vivid, eye-catching, salient

distinguished *adjective* EMINENT, great, important, noted, famous, celebrated, well-known, prominent, esteemed, acclaimed, notable, renowned, prestigious, elevated, big-time (*informal*), famed, conspicuous, illustrious, major league (*informal*)
<< OPPOSITE unknown

distinguishing *adjective* CHARACTERISTIC, marked, distinctive, typical, peculiar, differentiating, individualistic

distort *verb* 1 MISREPRESENT, twist, bias, disguise, pervert, slant, colour, misinterpret, falsify, garble
2 DEFORM, bend, twist, warp, buckle, mangle, mangulate (*Austral slang*), disfigure, contort, gnarl, misshape, malform

distorted *adjective* DEFORMED, bent, twisted, crooked, irregular, warped, buckled, disfigured, contorted, misshapen

distortion *noun* 1 MISREPRESENTATION, bias, slant, perversion, falsification, colouring
2 DEFORMITY, bend, twist, warp, buckle, contortion, malformation, crookedness, twistedness

distract *verb* 1 DIVERT, sidetrack, draw away, turn aside, lead astray, lead away
2 AMUSE, occupy, entertain, beguile, engross
3 AGITATE, trouble, disturb, confuse, puzzle, torment, bewilder, madden, confound, perplex, disconcert, derange, discompose ▷ see **detract**

distracted *adjective* 1 AGITATED, troubled, confused, puzzled, at sea, bewildered, bemused, confounded, perplexed, flustered, in a flap (*informal*)
2 FRANTIC, wild, mad, crazy, desperate, raving, frenzied, distraught, insane, deranged, grief-stricken, overwrought, at the end of your tether

distraction *noun* 1 DISTURBANCE, interference, diversion, interruption
2 ENTERTAINMENT, recreation, amusement, diversion, pastime, divertissement, beguilement
3 FRENZY, desperation, mania, insanity, delirium, derangement

distraught *adjective* FRANTIC, wild, desperate, mad, anxious, distressed, raving, distracted, hysterical, worked-up, agitated, crazed, overwrought, out of your mind, at the end of your tether, wrought-up, beside yourself

distress *verb* UPSET, worry, trouble, pain, wound, bother, disturb, dismay, grieve, torment, harass, afflict, harrow, agitate, sadden, perplex, disconcert, agonize, fluster, perturb, faze, throw (someone) off balance
▷ *noun* 1 SUFFERING, pain, worry, anxiety, torture, grief, misery, agony, sadness, discomfort, torment, sorrow, woe, anguish, heartache, affliction, desolation, wretchedness
2 NEED, suffering, trouble, trial, difficulties, poverty, misery, hard times, hardship, straits, misfortune, adversity, calamity, affliction, privation, destitution, ill-fortune, ill-luck, indigence

distressed *adjective* 1 UPSET, worried, troubled, anxious, distracted, tormented, distraught, afflicted, agitated, saddened, wretched
2 POVERTY-STRICKEN, poor, impoverished, needy, destitute, indigent, down at heel, straitened, penurious

distressing *adjective* UPSETTING, worrying, disturbing, painful, affecting, sad, afflicting, harrowing, grievous, hurtful, lamentable, heart-breaking, nerve-racking, gut-wrenching, distressful

distribute *verb* 1 HAND OUT, dispense, give out, dish out (*informal*), disseminate, deal out, disburse, pass round

2 CIRCULATE, deliver, convey
3 SHARE, give, deal, divide, assign, administer, allocate, dispose, dispense, allot, mete out, dole out, apportion, measure out
4 SPREAD, scatter, disperse, diffuse, disseminate, strew

distribution *noun* 1 DELIVERY, mailing, transport, transportation, handling
2 (*Economics*) SHARING, division, assignment, rationing, allocation, partition, allotment, dispensation, apportionment
3 SPREADING, circulation, diffusion, scattering, propagation, dissemination, dispersal, dispersion
4 SPREAD, organization, arrangement, location, placement, disposition

district *noun* AREA, community, region, sector, quarter, ward, parish, neighbourhood, vicinity, locality, locale, neck of the woods (*informal*)

distrust *verb* SUSPECT, doubt, discredit, be wary of, wonder about, mistrust, disbelieve, be suspicious of, be sceptical of, misbelieve
<< OPPOSITE trust
▷ *noun* SUSPICION, question, doubt, disbelief, scepticism, mistrust, misgiving, qualm, wariness, lack of faith, dubiety
<< OPPOSITE trust

distrustful *adjective* SUSPICIOUS, doubting, wary, cynical, doubtful, sceptical, uneasy, dubious, distrusting, disbelieving, leery (*slang*), mistrustful, chary

disturb *verb* 1 INTERRUPT, trouble, bother, startle, plague, disrupt, put out, interfere with, rouse, hassle, inconvenience, pester, intrude on, butt in on
2 UPSET, concern, worry, trouble, shake, excite, alarm, confuse, distress, distract, dismay, unsettle, agitate, ruffle, confound, unnerve, vex, fluster, perturb, derange, discompose
<< OPPOSITE calm
3 MUDDLE, disorder, mix up, mess up, disorganize, jumble up, disarrange, muss (*US & Canad*)

disturbance *noun* 1 DISORDER, bother (*informal*), turmoil, riot, upheaval, fray, brawl, uproar, agitation, fracas, commotion, rumpus, tumult, hubbub, shindig (*informal*), ruction (*informal*), ruckus (*informal*), shindy (*informal*)
2 UPSET, bother, disorder, confusion, distraction, intrusion, interruption, annoyance, agitation, hindrance, perturbation, derangement
3 PROBLEM, upset, disorder, trouble

disturbed *adjective* 1 (*Psychiatry*) UNBALANCED, troubled, disordered, unstable, neurotic, upset, deranged, unsound, maladjusted
<< OPPOSITE balanced
2 WORRIED, concerned, troubled, upset, bothered, nervous, anxious, uneasy
<< OPPOSITE calm

disturbing *adjective* WORRYING, troubling, upsetting, alarming, frightening, distressing, startling, discouraging, dismaying, unsettling, harrowing, agitating, disconcerting, disquieting, perturbing

ditch *noun* CHANNEL, drain, trench, dyke, furrow, gully, moat, watercourse
▷ *verb* 1 (*Slang*) GET RID OF, dump (*informal*), scrap, discard, dispose of, dispense with, jettison, throw out *or* overboard
2 (*Slang*) LEAVE, drop, abandon, dump (*informal*), axe (*informal*), get rid of, bin (*informal*), chuck (*informal*), forsake, jilt

dither (*Chiefly Brit*) *verb* VACILLATE, hesitate, waver, haver, falter, hum and haw, faff about (*Brit informal*), shillyshally (*informal*), swither (*Scot*)
<< OPPOSITE decide
▷ *noun* FLUTTER, flap (*informal*), fluster, bother, stew (*informal*), twitter (*informal*), tizzy (*informal*), pother, tiz-woz (*informal*)

diva *noun* SINGER, opera singer, prima donna

dive *verb* 1 PLUNGE, drop, jump, pitch, leap, duck, dip, descend, plummet
2 GO UNDERWATER, submerge
3 NOSE-DIVE, fall, plunge, crash, pitch, swoop, plummet
▷ *noun* 1 PLUNGE, spring, jump, leap, dash, header (*informal*), swoop, lunge, nose dive
2 (*Slang*) SLEAZY BAR, joint (*slang*), honky-tonk (*US slang*)

diverge *verb* 1 SEPARATE, part, split, branch, divide, fork, divaricate
2 CONFLICT, differ, disagree, dissent, be at odds, be at variance
3 DEVIATE, depart, stray, wander, meander, turn aside

divergence *noun* DIFFERENCE, varying, departure, disparity, deviation, separation

divergent *adjective* DIFFERENT, conflicting, differing, disagreeing, diverse, separate, varying, variant, diverging, dissimilar, deviating

> Some people dislike the use of *divergent* in this sense, preferring synonyms such as *different* or *differing*

diverse *adjective* 1 VARIOUS, mixed, varied, diversified, assorted, miscellaneous, several, sundry, motley, manifold, heterogeneous, of every description
2 DIFFERENT, contrasting, unlike, varying, differing, separate, distinct, disparate, discrete, dissimilar, divergent, discrepant

diversify *verb* VARY, change, expand, transform, alter, spread out, branch out

diversion *noun* 1 DISTRACTION, deviation,

deflection, digression
2 PASTIME, play, game, sport, delight, pleasure, entertainment, hobby, relaxation, recreation, enjoyment, distraction, amusement, gratification, divertissement, beguilement
3 (*Chiefly Brit*) DETOUR, deviation, circuitous route, roundabout way, indirect course
4 (*Chiefly Brit*) DEVIATION, departure, straying, divergence, digression

diversity *noun* 1 DIFFERENCE, diversification, variety, divergence, multiplicity, heterogeneity, variegation, diverseness
2 RANGE, variety, scope, sphere

divert *verb* 1 REDIRECT, switch, avert, deflect, deviate, sidetrack, turn aside
2 DISTRACT, shift, deflect, detract, sidetrack, lead astray, draw *or* lead away
3 ENTERTAIN, delight, amuse, please, charm, gratify, beguile, regale

diverting *adjective* ENTERTAINING, amusing, enjoyable, fun, pleasant, humorous, beguiling

divest *verb* 1 DEPRIVE, strip, dispossess, despoil
2 STRIP, remove, take off, undress, denude, disrobe, unclothe

divide *verb* 1 SEPARATE, part, split, cut (up), sever, shear, segregate, cleave, subdivide, bisect, sunder
<< OPPOSITE join
2 SHARE, distribute, allocate, portion, dispense, allot, mete, dole out, apportion, deal out, measure out, divvy (up) (*informal*)
3 SPLIT, break up, alienate, embroil, come between, disunite, estrange, sow dissension, cause to disagree, set at variance *or* odds, set *or* pit against one another
▷▷ **divide something up** GROUP, sort, separate, arrange, grade, classify, categorize

dividend *noun* BONUS, share, cut (*informal*), gain, extra, plus, portion, divvy (*informal*)

divination *noun* PREDICTION, divining, prophecy, presage, foretelling, clairvoyance, fortune-telling, prognostication, augury, soothsaying, sortilege

divine *adjective* 1 HEAVENLY, spiritual, holy, immortal, supernatural, celestial, angelic, superhuman, godlike, cherubic, seraphic, supernal (*literary*), paradisaical
2 SACRED, religious, holy, spiritual, blessed, revered, venerable, hallowed, consecrated, sanctified
3 (*informal*) WONDERFUL, perfect, beautiful, excellent, lovely, stunning (*informal*), glorious, marvellous, splendid, gorgeous, delightful, exquisite, radiant, superlative, ravishing
▷ *noun* PRIEST, minister, vicar, reverend, pastor, cleric, clergyman, curate, churchman, padre (*informal*), holy man, man of God, man of the cloth, ecclesiastic, father confessor
▷ *verb* 1 GUESS, understand, suppose, suspect, perceive, discern, infer, deduce, apprehend, conjecture, surmise, foretell, intuit, prognosticate
2 DOWSE (*for water or minerals*)

divinity *noun* 1 THEOLOGY, religion, religious studies
2 GODLINESS, holiness, sanctity, godhead, divine nature, godhood
3 DEITY, spirit, genius, guardian spirit, daemon, god *or* goddess, atua (NZ)

division *noun* 1 SEPARATION, dividing, splitting up, detaching, partition, cutting up, bisection
2 SHARING, sharing, distribution, assignment, rationing, allocation, allotment, apportionment
3 DISAGREEMENT, split, breach, feud, rift, rupture, abyss, chasm, variance, discord, difference of opinion, estrangement, disunion
<< OPPOSITE unity
4 DIVIDING LINE, border, boundary, divide, partition, demarcation, divider
5 DEPARTMENT, group, head, sector, branch, subdivision
6 PART, bit, piece, section, sector, class, category, segment, portion, fraction, compartment

divisive *adjective* DISRUPTIVE, unsettling, alienating, troublesome, controversial, contentious

divorce *noun* 1 SEPARATION, split, break-up, parting, split-up, rift, dissolution, severance, estrangement, annulment, decree nisi, disunion
2 BREACH, break, split, falling-out (*informal*), disagreement, feud, rift, bust-up (*informal*), rupture, abyss, chasm, schism, estrangement
▷ *verb* 1 SPLIT UP, separate, part company, annul your marriage, dissolve your marriage
2 SEPARATE, divide, isolate, detach, distance, sever, disconnect, dissociate, set apart, disunite, sunder

divulge *verb* MAKE KNOWN, tell, reveal, publish, declare, expose, leak, confess, exhibit, communicate, spill (*informal*), disclose, proclaim, betray, uncover, impart, promulgate, let slip, blow wide open (*slang*), get off your chest (*informal*), out (*informal*), spill your guts about (*slang*)
<< OPPOSITE keep secret

dizzy *adjective* 1 GIDDY, faint, light-headed, swimming, reeling, staggering, shaky, wobbly, off balance, unsteady, vertiginous, woozy (*informal*), weak at the knees
2 CONFUSED, dazzled, at sea, bewildered, muddled, bemused, dazed, disorientated, befuddled, light-headed, punch-drunk, fuddled
3 (*informal*) SCATTERBRAINED, silly, foolish, frivolous, giddy, capricious, forgetful,

flighty, light-headed, scatty (*Brit informal*), empty-headed, bird-brained (*informal*), featherbrained, ditzy *or* ditsy (*slang*)
4 STEEP, towering, soaring, lofty, sky-high, vertiginous

do *verb* 1 PERFORM, work, achieve, carry out, produce, effect, complete, conclude, undertake, accomplish, execute, discharge, pull off, transact
2 BEHAVE, act, conduct yourself, deport yourself, bear yourself, acquit yourself
3 MAKE, prepare, fix, arrange, look after, organize, be responsible for, see to, get ready, make ready
4 SOLVE, work out, resolve, figure out, decode, decipher, puzzle out
5 GET ON, manage, fare, proceed, make out, prosper, get along
6 PRESENT, give, show, act, produce, stage, perform, mount, put on
7 BE ADEQUATE, be enough, be sufficient, answer, serve, suit, content, satisfy, suffice, be of use, pass muster, cut the mustard, fill the bill (*informal*), meet requirements
8 (*informal*) CHEAT, trick, con (*informal*), skin (*slang*), stiff (*slang*), deceive, fleece, hoax, defraud, dupe, swindle, diddle (*informal*), take (someone) for a ride (*informal*), pull a fast one on (*informal*), cozen
9 PRODUCE, make, create, develop, manufacture, construct, invent, fabricate
10 (*informal*) VISIT, tour in *or* around, look at, cover, explore, take in (*informal*), stop in, journey through *or* around, travel in *or* around
▷ *noun* (*informal, chiefly Brit & NZ*) PARTY, gathering, function, social, event, affair, at-home, occasion, celebration, reception, bash (*informal*), rave (*Brit slang*), get-together (*informal*), festivity, knees-up (*Brit informal*), beano (*Brit slang*), social gathering, shindig (*informal*), soirée, rave-up (*Brit slang*), hooley *or* hoolie (*chiefly Irish & NZ*)
▷▷ **do away with someone** KILL, murder, do in (*slang*), destroy, take out (*slang*), dispatch, slay, blow away (*slang, chiefly US*), knock off (*slang*), liquidate, exterminate, take (someone's) life, bump off (*slang*)
▷▷ **do away with something** GET RID OF, remove, eliminate, axe (*informal*), abolish, junk (*informal*), pull, chuck (*informal*), discard, put an end to, dispense with, discontinue, put paid to, pull the plug on
▷▷ **do's and don'ts** (*informal*) RULES, code, regulations, standards, instructions, customs, convention, usage, protocol, formalities, etiquette, p's and q's, good *or* proper behaviour
▷▷ **do someone in** (*Slang*) 1 KILL, murder, destroy, eliminate (*slang*), take out (*slang*), execute, butcher, slaughter, dispatch, assassinate, slay, do away with, blow away (*slang, chiefly US*), knock off (*slang*), liquidate, annihilate, neutralize, take (someone's) life, bump off (*slang*)
2 EXHAUST, tire, drain, shatter (*informal*), weaken, fatigue, weary, fag (*informal*), sap, wear out, tire out, knacker (*slang*)
▷▷ **do without something** *or* **someone** MANAGE WITHOUT, give up, dispense with, forgo, kick (*informal*), sacrifice, abstain from, get along without

docile *adjective* OBEDIENT, manageable, compliant, amenable, submissive, pliant, tractable, biddable, ductile, teachable (*rare*)
<< OPPOSITE difficult

dock¹ *noun* PORT, haven, harbour, pier, wharf, quay, waterfront, anchorage
▷ *verb* 1 MOOR, land, anchor, put in, tie up, berth, drop anchor
2 (*of spacecraft*) LINK UP, unite, join, couple, rendezvous, hook up

dock² *verb* 1 CUT, reduce, decrease, diminish, lessen
<< OPPOSITE increase
2 DEDUCT, subtract
3 CUT OFF, crop, clip, shorten, curtail, cut short

docket *noun* 1 (*Chiefly Brit*) LABEL, bill, ticket, certificate, tag, voucher, tab, receipt, tally, chit, chitty, counterfoil
2 (*US law*) FILE, index, register

doctor *noun* PHYSICIAN, medic (*informal*), general practitioner, medical practitioner, G.P.
▷ *verb* 1 CHANGE, alter, interfere with, disguise, pervert, fudge, tamper with, tinker with, misrepresent, falsify, meddle with, mess about with
2 ADD TO, spike, cut, mix something with something, dilute, water down, adulterate

doctrinaire *adjective* 1 DOGMATIC, rigid, fanatical, inflexible
2 IMPRACTICAL, theoretical, speculative, ideological, unrealistic, hypothetical, unpragmatic

doctrine *noun* TEACHING, principle, belief, opinion, article, concept, conviction, canon, creed, dogma, tenet, precept, article of faith, kaupapa (*NZ*)

document *noun* PAPER, form, certificate, report, record, testimonial, authorization, legal form
▷ *verb* SUPPORT, back up, certify, verify, detail, instance, validate, substantiate, corroborate, authenticate, give weight to, particularize

doddle *noun* (*Brit informal*) PIECE OF CAKE (*informal*), picnic (*informal*), child's play (*informal*), pushover (*slang* or *informal*), no sweat (*slang*), cinch (*slang*), cakewalk (*informal*), money for old rope, bludge (*Austral & NZ informal*)

dodge *verb* 1 DUCK, dart, swerve, sidestep,

shoot, shift, turn aside, body-swerve (*Scot*)
2 EVADE, avoid, escape, get away from, elude, body-swerve (*Scot*), slip through the net of
3 AVOID, hedge, parry, get out of, evade, shirk
▷ *noun* TRICK, scheme, ploy, trap, device, fraud, con (*slang*), manoeuvre, deception, scam (*slang*), gimmick, hoax, wheeze (*Brit slang*), deceit, ruse, artifice, subterfuge, canard, feint, stratagem, contrivance, machination, fastie (*Austral slang*)

dodgy *adjective* 1 (*Brit, Austral & NZ informal*) NASTY, offensive, unpleasant, revolting, distasteful, repellent, unsavoury, obnoxious, repulsive, objectionable, repugnant, shonky (*Austral & NZ informal*)
2 (*Brit, Austral & NZ informal*) RISKY, difficult, tricky, dangerous, delicate, uncertain, problematic(al), unreliable, dicky (*Brit informal*), dicey (*informal, chiefly Brit*), ticklish, chancy (*informal*), shonky (*Austral & NZ informal*)

doer *noun* ACHIEVER, organizer, powerhouse (*slang*), dynamo, live wire (*slang*), go-getter (*informal*), active person, wheeler-dealer (*informal*)

doff *verb* 1 TIP, raise, remove, lift, take off
2 TAKE OFF, remove, shed, discard, throw off, cast off, slip out of, slip off

dog *noun* 1 HOUND, canine, bitch, puppy, pup, mongrel, tyke, mutt (*slang*), pooch (*slang*), cur, man's best friend, kuri *or* goorie (*NZ*), brak (*S African*)
2 (*informal*) SCOUNDREL, villain, cur, heel (*slang*), knave (*archaic*), blackguard
▷ *verb* 1 PLAGUE, follow, trouble, haunt, hound, torment, afflict
2 PURSUE, follow, track, chase, shadow, harry, tail (*informal*), trail, hound, stalk, go after, give chase to
▷▷ **dog-eat-dog** RUTHLESS, fierce, vicious, ferocious, cut-throat, with no holds barred
>> RELATED WORD *adjective* canine
>> RELATED WORD *female* bitch
>> RELATED WORDS *young* pup, puppy

dogged *adjective* DETERMINED, steady, persistent, stubborn, firm, staunch, persevering, resolute, single-minded, tenacious, steadfast, unyielding, obstinate, indefatigable, immovable, stiff-necked, unshakable, unflagging, pertinacious
<< OPPOSITE irresolute

dogma *noun* DOCTRINE, teachings, principle, opinion, article, belief, creed, tenet, precept, credo, article of faith, kaupapa (*NZ*)

dogmatic *adjective* 1 OPINIONATED, arrogant, assertive, arbitrary, emphatic, downright, dictatorial, imperious, overbearing, categorical, magisterial, doctrinaire, obdurate, peremptory
2 DOCTRINAL, authoritative, categorical, canonical, oracular, ex cathedra

doing *noun* 1 CARRYING OUT *or* THROUGH, performance, execution, implementation
2 HANDIWORK, act, action, achievement, exploit, deed

doings *plural noun* DEEDS, actions, exploits, concerns, events, affairs, happenings, proceedings, transactions, dealings, goings-on (*informal*)

doldrums ▷▷ **the doldrums** BLUES, depression, dumps (*informal*), gloom, boredom, apathy, inertia, stagnation, inactivity, tedium, dullness, the hump (*Brit informal*), ennui, torpor, lassitude, listlessness

dole *noun* SHARE, grant, gift, allowance, portion, donation, quota, parcel, handout, modicum, pittance, alms, gratuity, koha (*NZ*)
▷▷ **dole something out** GIVE OUT, share, deal out, distribute, divide, assign, administer, allocate, hand out, dispense, allot, mete, apportion

dollop *noun* 1 LUMP, blob
2 HELPING, serving, portion, scoop, gob

dolphin *noun*
>> RELATED WORD *collective noun* school

domain *noun* AREA, field, department, discipline, sphere, realm, speciality

domestic *adjective* 1 HOME, internal, native, indigenous, not foreign
2 HOUSEHOLD, home, family, private, domiciliary
3 HOME-LOVING, homely, housewifely, stay-at-home, domesticated
4 DOMESTICATED, trained, tame, house, pet, house-trained
▷ *noun* SERVANT, help, maid, woman (*informal*), daily, char (*informal*), charwoman, daily help

domesticate *or sometimes US* **domesticize** *verb*
1 TAME, break, train, house-train, gentle
2 NATURALIZE, accustom, familiarize, habituate, acclimatize

domesticated *adjective* 1 TAME, broken (in), tamed
<< OPPOSITE wild
2 HOME-LOVING, homely, domestic, housewifely, house-trained (*jocular*)

domesticity *noun* HOME LIFE, housekeeping, domestication, homemaking, housewifery, home-lovingness

dominance *noun* CONTROL, government, power, rule, authority, command, sway, domination, supremacy, mastery, ascendancy, paramountcy

dominant *adjective* 1 MAIN, chief, primary, outstanding, principal, prominent, influential, prevailing, paramount, prevalent, predominant, pre-eminent
<< OPPOSITE minor
2 CONTROLLING, leading, ruling, commanding, supreme, governing, superior, presiding,

authoritative, ascendant

dominate *verb* 1 CONTROL, lead, rule, direct, master, govern, monopolize, tyrannize, have the upper hand over, lead by the nose (*informal*), overbear, have the whip hand over, domineer, keep under your thumb, have the upper hand (in), rule the roost (in)
2 TOWER ABOVE, overlook, survey, stand over, loom over, stand head and shoulders above, bestride

domination *noun* CONTROL, power, rule, authority, influence, command, sway, dictatorship, repression, oppression, suppression, supremacy, mastery, tyranny, ascendancy, subordination, despotism, subjection

domineering *adjective* OVERBEARING, arrogant, authoritarian, oppressive, autocratic, masterful, dictatorial, coercive, bossy (*informal*), imperious, tyrannical, magisterial, despotic, high-handed, iron-handed
<< OPPOSITE submissive

dominion *noun* 1 CONTROL, government, power, rule, authority, command, sovereignty, sway, domination, jurisdiction, supremacy, mastery, ascendancy, mana (*NZ*)
2 KINGDOM, territory, province, country, region, empire, patch, turf (*US slang*), realm, domain

don *verb* PUT ON, get into, dress in, pull on, change into, get dressed in, clothe yourself in, slip on *or* into

donate *verb* GIVE, present, contribute, grant, commit, gift, hand out, subscribe, endow, chip in (*informal*), bestow, entrust, impart, bequeath, make a gift of

donation *noun* CONTRIBUTION, gift, subscription, offering, present, grant, hand-out, boon, alms, stipend, gratuity, benefaction, largesse *or* largess, koha (*NZ*)

done *interjection* AGREED, you're on (*informal*), O.K. *or* okay (*informal*), it's a bargain, it's a deal, ka pai (*NZ*)
▷ *adjective* 1 FINISHED, completed, accomplished, over, through, ended, perfected, realized, concluded, executed, terminated, consummated, in the can (*informal*)
2 COOKED, ready, cooked enough, cooked to a turn, cooked sufficiently
3 ACCEPTABLE, proper, conventional, protocol, de rigueur (*French*)
▷▷ **done for** (*informal*) FINISHED, lost, beaten, defeated, destroyed, ruined, broken, dashed, wrecked, doomed, foiled, undone
▷▷ **done in** *or* **up** (*informal*) EXHAUSTED, bushed (*informal*), all in (*slang*), worn out, dead (*informal*), knackered (*slang*), clapped out (*Austral & NZ informal*), tired out, ready to drop, dog-tired (*informal*), zonked (*slang*), dead beat (*informal*), fagged out (*informal*), worn to a frazzle (*informal*), on your last legs, creamcrackered (*Brit slang*)
▷▷ **have** *or* **be done with something** *or* **someone** BE THROUGH WITH, give up, be finished with, throw over, wash your hands of, end relations with

donor *noun* GIVER, contributor, benefactor, philanthropist, grantor (*Law*), donator, almsgiver
<< OPPOSITE recipient

doom *noun* DESTRUCTION, ruin, catastrophe, death, downfall
▷ *verb* CONDEMN, sentence, consign, foreordain, destine, predestine, preordain

doomed *adjective* HOPELESS, condemned, ill-fated, fated, unhappy, unfortunate, cursed, unlucky, blighted, hapless, bedevilled, luckless, ill-starred, star-crossed, ill-omened

door *noun* OPENING, entry, entrance, exit, doorway, ingress, egress
▷▷ **out of doors** IN THE OPEN AIR, outside, outdoors, out, alfresco
▷▷ **show someone the door** THROW OUT, remove, eject, evict, turn out, bounce (*slang*), oust, drive out, boot out (*informal*), ask to leave, show out, throw out on your ear (*informal*)

do-or-die *adjective* DESPERATE, risky, hazardous, going for broke, win-or-bust, death-or-glory, kill-or-cure

dope *noun* 1 (*Slang*) DRUGS, narcotics, opiates, dadah (*Austral slang*)
2 (*informal*) IDIOT, fool, jerk (*slang, chiefly US & Canad*), plank (*Brit slang*), charlie (*Brit informal*), berk (*Brit slang*), wally (*slang*), prat (*slang*), plonker (*slang*), coot, geek (*slang*), twit (*informal, chiefly Brit*), dunce, oaf, simpleton, dimwit (*informal*), dipstick (*Brit slang*), gonzo (*slang*), schmuck (*US slang*), dork (*slang*), nitwit (*informal*), dolt, blockhead, divvy (*Brit slang*), pillock (*Brit slang*), dweeb (*US slang*), putz (*US slang*), fathead (*informal*), eejit (*Scot & Irish*), dumb-ass (*slang*), numpty (*Scot informal*), lamebrain (*informal*), nerd *or* nurd (*slang*), numbskull *or* numskull, dorba *or* dorb (*Austral slang*), bogan (*Austral slang*)
3 (*informal*) INFORMATION, facts, details, material, news, intelligence, gen (*Brit informal*), info (*informal*), inside information, lowdown (*informal*)
▷ *verb* DRUG, doctor, knock out, inject, sedate, stupefy, anaesthetize, narcotize

dopey *or* **dopy** *adjective* (*informal*) 1 DROWSY, dazed, groggy (*informal*), drugged, muzzy, stupefied, half-asleep, woozy (*informal*)
2 STUPID, simple, slow, thick, silly, foolish, dense, dumb (*informal*), senseless, goofy (*informal*), idiotic, dozy (*Brit informal*), asinine,

dumb-ass (*slang*)

dormant *adjective* LATENT, inactive, lurking, quiescent, unrealized, unexpressed, inoperative

dorp *noun* (*S African*) TOWN, village, settlement, municipality, kainga *or* kaika (NZ)

dose *noun* 1 (*Medical*) MEASURE, amount, allowance, portion, prescription, ration, draught, dosage, potion
2 QUANTITY, measure, supply, portion

dot *noun* SPOT, point, mark, circle, atom, dab, mite, fleck, jot, speck, full stop, speckle, mote, iota
▷ *verb* SPOT, stud, fleck, speckle
▷▷ **on the dot** ON TIME, promptly, precisely, exactly (*informal*), to the minute, on the button (*informal*), punctually

dote *with* **on** *or* **upon** *verb* ADORE, prize, treasure, admire, hold dear, idolize, lavish affection on

doting *adjective* ADORING, devoted, fond, foolish, indulgent, lovesick

dotty *adjective* (*Slang, chiefly Brit*) CRAZY, touched, peculiar, eccentric, batty (*slang*), off-the-wall (*slang*), potty (*Brit informal*), oddball (*informal*), loopy (*informal*), crackpot (*informal*), out to lunch (*informal*), outré, doolally (*slang*), off your trolley (*slang*), up the pole (*informal*), wacko *or* whacko (*slang*), off the air (*Austral slang*), porangi (NZ), daggy (*Austral & NZ informal*)

double *adjective* 1 MATCHING, coupled, doubled, paired, twin, duplicate, in pairs, binate (*Botany*)
2 DECEITFUL, false, fraudulent, deceiving, treacherous, dishonest, deceptive, hypocritical, counterfeit, two-faced, disingenuous, insincere, double-dealing, duplicitous, perfidious, knavish (*archaic*), Janus-faced
3 DUAL, enigmatic, cryptic, twofold, Delphic, enigmatical
▷ *noun* TWIN, lookalike, spitting image, copy, fellow, mate, counterpart, clone, replica, ringer (*slang*), impersonator (*informal*), dead ringer (*slang*), Doppelgänger, duplicate
▷ *verb* 1 MULTIPLY BY TWO, duplicate, increase twofold, repeat, enlarge, magnify
2 FOLD UP *or* OVER
3 *with* **as** FUNCTION AS, serve as
▷▷ **at** *or* **on the double** AT ONCE, now, immediately, directly, quickly, promptly, right now, straight away, right away, briskly, without delay, pronto (*informal*), at full speed, in double-quick time, this instant, this very minute, pdq (*slang*), posthaste, tout de suite (*French*)

double-cross *verb* BETRAY, trick, cheat, mislead, two-time (*informal*), defraud, swindle, hoodwink, sell down the river (*informal*), cozen

doubly *adverb* TWICE AS, in two ways, twofold, as much again, in double measure

doubt *noun* 1 UNCERTAINTY, confusion, hesitation, dilemma, scepticism, misgiving, suspense, indecision, bewilderment, lack of confidence, hesitancy, perplexity, vacillation, lack of conviction, irresolution, dubiety
<< OPPOSITE certainty
2 SUSPICION, scepticism, distrust, fear, apprehension, mistrust, misgivings, disquiet, qualms, incredulity, lack of faith
<< OPPOSITE belief
▷ *verb* 1 BE UNCERTAIN, be sceptical, be dubious
2 WAVER, hesitate, vacillate, sway, fluctuate, dither (*chiefly Brit*), haver, oscillate, chop and change, blow hot and cold (*informal*), keep changing your mind, shillyshally (*informal*), be irresolute *or* indecisive, swither (*Scot*)
3 DISBELIEVE, question, suspect, query, distrust, mistrust, lack confidence in, misgive
<< OPPOSITE believe
▷▷ **no doubt** CERTAINLY, surely, probably, admittedly, doubtless, assuredly, doubtlessly

> In affirmative sentences, *whether* was in the past the only word considered acceptable for linking the verb *doubt* to a following clause, for example *I doubt whether he will come*. Nowadays, *doubt if* and *doubt that* are both considered acceptable alternatives to *doubt whether*. In negative sentences, use *that* after *doubt*, for example *I don't doubt that he is telling the truth*. The old-fashioned form *not doubt but that*, as in *I do not doubt but that he is telling the truth*, is now rarely used and sounds very stiff and formal

doubter *noun* SCEPTIC, questioner, disbeliever, agnostic, unbeliever, doubting Thomas

doubtful *adjective* 1 UNLIKELY, unclear, dubious, unsettled, dodgy (*Brit, Austral & NZ informal*), questionable, ambiguous, improbable, indefinite, unconfirmed, inconclusive, debatable, indeterminate, iffy (*informal*), equivocal, inexact
<< OPPOSITE certain
2 UNSURE, uncertain, hesitant, suspicious, hesitating, sceptical, unsettled, tentative, wavering, unresolved, perplexed, undecided, unconvinced, vacillating, leery (*slang*), distrustful, in two minds (*informal*), irresolute
<< OPPOSITE certain
3 QUESTIONABLE, suspect, suspicious, crooked, dubious, dodgy (*Brit, Austral & NZ informal*), slippery, shady (*informal*), unscrupulous, fishy (*informal*), shifty, disreputable, untrustworthy, shonky (*Austral & NZ informal*)

> In the past, *whether* was the only word considered acceptable for linking the adjective *doubtful* in

the sense of 'improbable' to a following clause, for example *it is doubtful whether he will come*. Nowadays, however, *doubtful if* and *doubtful that* are also considered acceptable

doubtless *adverb* PROBABLY, presumably, most likely

doughty *adjective* (*Old-fashioned*) INTREPID, brave, daring, bold, hardy, heroic, courageous, gritty, fearless, resolute, gallant, valiant, redoubtable, dauntless, valorous, stouthearted

dour *adjective* GLOOMY, forbidding, grim, sour, dismal, dreary, sullen, unfriendly, morose
<< OPPOSITE cheery

douse *or* **dowse** *verb* 1 PUT OUT, smother, blow out, extinguish, snuff (out)
2 DRENCH, soak, steep, saturate, duck, submerge, immerse, dunk, souse, plunge into water

dovetail *verb* CORRESPOND, match, agree, accord, coincide, tally, conform, harmonize

dowdy *adjective* FRUMPY, old-fashioned, shabby, drab, tacky (*US informal*), unfashionable, dingy, frumpish, ill-dressed, frowzy
<< OPPOSITE chic

down *adjective* DEPRESSED, low, sad, blue, unhappy, discouraged, miserable, fed up, dismal, pessimistic, melancholy, glum, dejected, despondent, dispirited, downcast, morose, disheartened, crestfallen, downhearted, down in the dumps (*informal*), sick as a parrot (*informal*), low-spirited
▷ *verb* 1 (*informal*) SWALLOW, drink (down), drain, gulp (down), put away (*informal*), toss off
2 BRING DOWN, fell, knock down, throw, trip, floor, tackle, deck (*slang*), overthrow, prostrate

down-and-out *adjective* DESTITUTE, ruined, impoverished, derelict, penniless, dirt-poor (*informal*), flat broke (*informal*), on your uppers (*informal*), without two pennies to rub together (*informal*)
▷ *noun* TRAMP, bum (*informal*), beggar, derelict, outcast, pauper, vagrant, vagabond, bag lady, dosser (*Brit slang*), derro (*Austral slang*)

downbeat *adjective* (*informal*) 1 LOW-KEY, muted, subdued, sober, sombre
2 GLOOMY, negative, depressed, pessimistic, unfavourable
<< OPPOSITE cheerful

downcast *adjective* DEJECTED, sad, depressed, unhappy, disappointed, discouraged, miserable, dismayed, choked, daunted, dismal, despondent, dispirited, disheartened, disconsolate, crestfallen, down in the dumps (*informal*), cheerless, sick as a parrot (*informal*)
<< OPPOSITE cheerful

downfall *noun* RUIN, fall, destruction, collapse, breakdown, disgrace, overthrow, descent, undoing, comeuppance (*slang*), comedown

downgrade *verb* 1 DEMOTE, degrade, take down a peg (*informal*), lower *or* reduce in rank
<< OPPOSITE promote
2 RUN DOWN, denigrate, disparage, detract from, decry

down-market *adjective* SECOND-RATE, cheap, inferior, tacky (*informal*), shoddy, low-grade, tawdry, low-quality, two-bit (*US & Canad slang*), cheap and nasty (*informal*), lowbrow, bush-league (*Austral & NZ informal*), bodger *or* bodgie (*Austral slang*)
<< OPPOSITE first-rate

downpour *noun* RAINSTORM, flood, deluge, torrential rain, cloudburst, inundation

downright *adjective* COMPLETE, absolute, utter, total, positive, clear, plain, simple, explicit, outright, blatant, unequivocal, unqualified, out-and-out, categorical, undisguised, thoroughgoing, arrant, deep-dyed (*usually derogatory*)

downside *noun* DRAWBACK, disadvantage, snag, problem, trouble, minus (*informal*), flip side, other side of the coin (*informal*), bad *or* weak point
<< OPPOSITE benefit

down-to-earth *adjective* SENSIBLE, practical, realistic, common-sense, matter-of-fact, sane, no-nonsense, hard-headed, unsentimental, plain-spoken

downtrodden *adjective* OPPRESSED, abused, exploited, subservient, subjugated, tyrannized

downward *adjective* DESCENDING, declining, heading down, earthward

doze *verb* NAP, sleep, slumber, nod, kip (*Brit slang*), snooze (*informal*), catnap, drowse, sleep lightly, zizz (*Brit informal*)
▷ *noun* NAP, kip (*Brit slang*), snooze (*informal*), siesta, little sleep, catnap, forty winks (*informal*), shuteye (*slang*), zizz (*Brit informal*)

dozy *adjective* (*Brit informal*) STUPID, simple, slow, silly, daft (*informal*), senseless, goofy (*informal*), witless, not all there, slow-witted

drab *adjective* DULL, grey, gloomy, dismal, dreary, shabby, sombre, lacklustre, flat, dingy, colourless, uninspired, vapid, cheerless
<< OPPOSITE bright

Draconian *adjective sometimes not cap.* SEVERE, hard, harsh, stern, drastic, stringent, punitive, austere, pitiless

draft *noun* 1 OUTLINE, plan, sketch, version, rough, abstract, delineation, preliminary form
2 MONEY ORDER, bill (of exchange), cheque, postal order
▷ *verb* OUTLINE, write, plan, produce, create, design, draw, frame, compose, devise, sketch,

draw up, formulate, contrive, delineate

drag *verb* 1 PULL, draw, haul, trail, tow, tug, jerk, yank, hale, lug
2 LAG, trail, linger, loiter, straggle, dawdle, hang back, tarry, draggle
3 GO SLOWLY, inch, creep, crawl, advance slowly
▷ *noun* (*informal*) NUISANCE, pain (*informal*), bore, bother, pest, hassle (*informal*), inconvenience, annoyance, pain in the neck, pain in the backside, pain in the butt (*informal*)
▷▷ **drag on** LAST, continue, carry on, remain, endure, persist, linger, abide
▷▷ **drag yourself** GO SLOWLY, creep, crawl, inch, shuffle, shamble, limp along, move at a snail's pace, advance slowly

dragoon *verb* FORCE, drive, compel, bully, intimidate, railroad (*informal*), constrain, coerce, impel, strong-arm (*informal*), browbeat

drain *noun* 1 SEWER, channel, pipe, sink, outlet, ditch, trench, conduit, duct, culvert, watercourse
2 REDUCTION, strain, drag, expenditure, exhaustion, sapping, depletion
▷ *verb* 1 REMOVE, draw, empty, withdraw, milk, tap, pump, bleed, evacuate
2 EMPTY
3 FLOW OUT, leak, discharge, trickle, ooze, seep, exude, well out, effuse
4 DRINK UP, swallow, finish, put away (*informal*), quaff, gulp down
5 EXHAUST, tire, wear out, strain, weaken, fatigue, weary, debilitate, prostrate, tax, tire out, enfeeble, enervate
6 CONSUME, waste, exhaust, empty, deplete, use up, sap, dissipate, swallow up
▷▷ **down the drain** GONE, lost, wasted, ruined, gone for good

drainage *noun* SEWERAGE, waste, sewage

dram *noun* MEASURE, shot (*informal*), drop, glass, tot, slug, snort (*slang*), snifter (*informal*)

drama *noun* 1 PLAY, show, stage show, stage play, dramatization, theatrical piece
2 THEATRE, acting, dramatic art, stagecraft, dramaturgy, Thespian art
3 EXCITEMENT, crisis, dramatics, spectacle, turmoil, histrionics, theatrics

dramatic *adjective* 1 EXCITING, emotional, thrilling, tense, startling, sensational, breathtaking, electrifying, melodramatic, climactic, high-octane (*informal*), shock-horror (*facetious*), suspenseful
2 THEATRICAL, Thespian, dramaturgical, dramaturgic
3 EXPRESSIVE
4 POWERFUL, striking, stunning (*informal*), impressive, effective, vivid, jaw-dropping
<< OPPOSITE ordinary

dramatist *noun* PLAYWRIGHT, screenwriter, scriptwriter, dramaturge

dramatize *or* **dramatise** *verb* EXAGGERATE, overdo, overstate, lay it on (thick) (*slang*), play-act, play to the gallery, make a performance of

drape *verb* 1 COVER, wrap, fold, array, adorn, swathe
2 HANG, drop, dangle, suspend, lean, droop, let fall

drastic *adjective* EXTREME, strong, radical, desperate, severe, harsh, dire, forceful

draught *or US* **draft** *noun* 1 BREEZE, current, movement, flow, puff, influx, gust, current of air
2 DRINK

draw *verb* 1 SKETCH, design, outline, trace, portray, paint, depict, mark out, map out, delineate
2 PULL, drag, haul, tow, tug
3 INHALE, breathe in, pull, inspire, suck, respire
4 EXTRACT, take, remove, drain
5 CHOOSE, pick, select, take, single out
6 DEDUCE, make, get, take, derive, infer
7 ATTRACT, engage
8 ENTICE, bring in
▷ *noun* 1 TIE, deadlock, stalemate, impasse, dead heat
2 (*informal*) APPEAL, interest, pull (*informal*), charm, attraction, lure, temptation, fascination, attractiveness, allure, magnetism, enchantment, enticement, captivation, temptingness
▷▷ **draw back** RECOIL, withdraw, retreat, shrink, falter, back off, shy away, flinch, retract, quail, start back
▷▷ **draw on** *or* **upon something** MAKE USE OF, use, employ, rely on, exploit, extract, take from, fall back on, have recourse to
▷▷ **draw something out** STRETCH OUT, extend, lengthen, elongate, attenuate
▷▷ **draw something up** DRAFT, write, produce, create, prepare, frame, compose, devise, formulate, contrive
▷▷ **draw up** HALT, stop, pull up, stop short, come to a stop

drawback *noun* DISADVANTAGE, trouble, difficulty, fault, handicap, obstacle, defect, deficiency, flaw, hitch, nuisance, snag, downside, stumbling block, impediment, detriment, imperfection, hindrance, fly in the ointment (*informal*)
<< OPPOSITE advantage

drawing *noun* PICTURE, illustration, representation, cartoon, sketch, portrayal, depiction, study, outline, delineation

drawl *verb* SPEAK *or* SAY SLOWLY

drawn *adjective* TENSE, worn, strained, stressed, tired, pinched, fatigued, harassed, fraught, sapped, harrowed, haggard

dread *verb* FEAR, shrink from, cringe at the thought of, quail from, shudder to think about, have cold feet about (*informal*), anticipate with horror, tremble to think about
▷ *noun* FEAR, alarm, horror, terror, dismay, fright, apprehension, consternation, trepidation, apprehensiveness, affright

dreadful *adjective* 1 TERRIBLE, shocking, awful, alarming, distressing, appalling, tragic, horrible, formidable, fearful, dire, horrendous, hideous, monstrous, from hell (*informal*), grievous, atrocious, frightful, godawful (*slang*), hellacious (*US slang*)
2 SERIOUS, terrible, awful, appalling, horrendous, monstrous, unspeakable, abysmal
3 AWFUL, terrible, horrendous, frightful

dream *noun* 1 VISION, illusion, delusion, hallucination, reverie
2 AMBITION, wish, fantasy, desire, Holy Grail (*informal*), pipe dream
3 DAYDREAM
4 DELIGHT, pleasure, joy, beauty, treasure, gem, marvel, pearler (*Austral slang*), beaut (*Austral & NZ slang*)
▷ *verb* 1 HAVE DREAMS, hallucinate
2 DAYDREAM, stargaze, build castles in the air *or* in Spain
▷▷ **dream of something** *or* **someone** DAYDREAM ABOUT, fantasize about
▷▷ **dream something up** INVENT, create, imagine, devise, hatch, contrive, concoct, think up, cook up (*informal*), spin

dreamer *noun* IDEALIST, visionary, daydreamer, utopian, theorizer, fantasizer, romancer, Don Quixote, escapist, Walter Mitty, fantasist, fantast

dreamy *adjective* 1 VAGUE, abstracted, absent, musing, preoccupied, daydreaming, faraway, pensive, in a reverie, with your head in the clouds
2 RELAXING, calming, romantic, gentle, soothing, lulling
3 IMPRACTICAL, vague, imaginary, speculative, visionary, fanciful, quixotic, dreamlike, airy-fairy
<< OPPOSITE realistic

dreary *adjective* 1 DULL, boring, tedious, routine, drab, tiresome, lifeless, monotonous, humdrum, colourless, uneventful, uninteresting, mind-numbing, ho-hum (*informal*), wearisome, as dry as dust
<< OPPOSITE exciting
2 DISMAL, depressing, bleak, sad, lonely, gloomy, solitary, melancholy, sombre, forlorn, glum, mournful, lonesome (*chiefly US & Canad*), downcast, sorrowful, wretched, joyless, funereal, doleful, cheerless, drear, comfortless

dredge up *verb* (*informal*) DIG UP, raise, rake up, discover, uncover, draw up, unearth, drag up, fish up

dregs *plural noun* SEDIMENT, grounds, lees, waste, deposit, trash, residue, scum, dross, residuum, scourings, draff
▷▷ **the dregs** (*Brit informal*) SCUM, outcasts, rabble, down-and-outs, good-for-nothings, riffraff, canaille (*French*), ragtag and bobtail

drench *verb* SOAK, flood, wet, duck, drown, steep, swamp, saturate, inundate, souse, imbrue

dress *noun* 1 FROCK, gown, garment, robe
2 CLOTHING, clothes, gear (*informal*), costume, threads (*slang*), garments, apparel, attire, garb, togs, raiment (*archaic* or *poetic*), vestment, schmutter (*slang*), habiliment
▷ *verb* 1 PUT ON CLOTHES, don clothes, slip on *or* into something
<< OPPOSITE undress
2 CLOTHE
3 BANDAGE, treat, plaster, bind up
4 DECORATE, deck, adorn, trim, array, drape, ornament, embellish, festoon, bedeck, furbish, rig out
5 ARRANGE, do (up), groom, set, prepare, comb (out), get ready
▷▷ **dress someone down** (*informal*) REPRIMAND, rebuke, scold, berate, castigate, tear into (*informal*), tell off (*informal*), read the riot act, reprove, upbraid, slap on the wrist, carpet (*informal*), bawl out (*informal*), rap over the knuckles, haul over the coals, chew out (*US & Canad informal*), tear (someone) off a strip (*Brit informal*), give a rocket (*Brit & NZ informal*)
▷▷ **dress up** 1 PUT ON FANCY DRESS, wear a costume, disguise yourself
2 DRESS FORMALLY, dress for dinner, doll yourself up (*slang*), put on your best bib and tucker (*informal*), put on your glad rags (*informal*)

dressmaker *noun* SEAMSTRESS, tailor, couturier, sewing woman, modiste

dribble *verb* 1 RUN, drip, trickle, drop, leak, ooze, seep, fall in drops
2 DROOL, drivel, slaver, slobber, drip saliva

drift *verb* 1 FLOAT, go (aimlessly), bob, coast, slip, sail, slide, glide, meander, waft, be carried along, move gently
2 WANDER, stroll, stray, roam, meander, rove, range, straggle, traipse (*informal*), stravaig (*Scot & Northern English dialect*), peregrinate
3 STRAY, wander, roam, meander, digress, get sidetracked, go off at a tangent, get off the point
4 PILE UP, gather, accumulate, amass, bank up
▷ *noun* 1 PILE, bank, mass, heap, mound, accumulation
2 MEANING, point, gist, aim, direction, object, import, intention, implication, tendency, significance, thrust, tenor, purport

drifter *noun* WANDERER, bum (*informal*), tramp, itinerant, vagrant, hobo (*US*), vagabond, rolling stone, bag lady (*chiefly US*), derro (*Austral slang*)

drill *noun* **1** BIT, borer, gimlet, rotary tool, boring tool
2 TRAINING, exercise, discipline, instruction, preparation, repetition
3 (*informal*) PRACTICE
▷ *verb* **1** BORE, pierce, penetrate, sink in, puncture, perforate
2 TRAIN, coach, teach, exercise, discipline, practise, instruct, rehearse

drink *verb* **1** SWALLOW, drain, sip, suck, gulp, sup, swig (*informal*), swill, guzzle, imbibe, quaff, partake of, toss off
2 BOOZE (*informal*), tipple, tope, hit the bottle (*informal*), bevvy (*dialect*), bend the elbow (*informal*), go on a binge *or* bender (*informal*)
▷ *noun* **1** GLASS, cup, swallow, sip, draught, gulp, swig (*informal*), taste, tipple, snifter (*informal*), noggin
2 BEVERAGE, refreshment, potion, liquid, thirst quencher
3 ALCOHOL, booze (*informal*), liquor, spirits, the bottle (*informal*), Dutch courage, hooch *or* hootch (*informal, chiefly US & Canad*)
▷▷ **drink something in** ABSORB, take in, digest, pay attention to, soak up, devour, assimilate, be fascinated by, imbibe
▷▷ **drink to something** TOAST, salute, pledge the health of
▷▷ **the drink** (*informal*) THE SEA, the main, the deep, the ocean, the briny (*informal*)

drinker *noun* ALCOHOLIC, drunk, boozer (*informal*), soak (*slang*), lush (*slang*), toper, sponge (*informal*), guzzler, drunkard, sot, tippler, wino (*informal*), inebriate, dipsomaniac, bibber, alko *or* alco (*Austral slang*)

drip *verb* DROP, splash, sprinkle, trickle, dribble, exude, drizzle, plop
▷ *noun* **1** DROP, bead, trickle, dribble, droplet, globule, pearl, driblet
2 (*informal*) WEAKLING, wet (*Brit informal*), weed (*informal*), softie (*informal*), mummy's boy (*informal*), namby-pamby, ninny, milksop

drive *verb* **1** GO (BY CAR), ride (by car), motor, travel by car
2 OPERATE, manage, direct, guide, handle, steer
3 PUSH, propel
4 THRUST, push, sink, dig, hammer, plunge, stab, ram
5 HERD, urge, impel
6 FORCE, press, prompt, spur, compel, motivate, oblige, railroad (*informal*), prod, constrain, prick, coerce, goad, impel, dragoon, actuate
7 WORK, overwork, overburden
▷ *noun* **1** RUN, ride, trip, journey, spin (*informal*), hurl (*Scot*), outing, excursion, jaunt
2 INITIATIVE, push (*informal*), energy, enterprise, ambition, pep, motivation, zip (*informal*), vigour, get-up-and-go (*informal*)
3 CAMPAIGN, push (*informal*), crusade, action, effort, appeal, advance, surge
▷▷ **drive at something** (*informal*) MEAN, suggest, intend, refer to, imply, intimate, get at, hint at, have in mind, allude to, insinuate

drivel *verb* BABBLE, ramble, waffle (*informal, chiefly Brit*), gab (*informal*), gas (*informal*), maunder, blether, prate
▷ *noun* NONSENSE, rubbish, garbage (*informal*), rot, crap (*slang*), trash, bunk (*informal*), blah (*slang*), hot air (*informal*), tosh (*slang, chiefly Brit*), waffle (*informal, chiefly Brit*), prating, pap, bilge (*informal*), twaddle, tripe (*informal*), dross, gibberish, guff (*slang*), moonshine, hogwash, hokum (*slang, chiefly US & Canad*), piffle (*informal*), poppycock (*informal*), balderdash, bosh (*informal*), eyewash (*informal*), tommyrot, horsefeathers (*US slang*), bunkum *or* buncombe (*chiefly US*), bizzo (*Austral slang*), bull's wool (*Austral & NZ slang*)

drizzle *noun* FINE RAIN, Scotch mist, smir (*Scot*)
▷ *verb* RAIN, shower, spit, spray, sprinkle, mizzle (*dialect*), spot *or* spit with rain

droll *adjective* AMUSING, odd, funny, entertaining, comic, ridiculous, diverting, eccentric, ludicrous, humorous, quaint, off-the-wall (*slang*), laughable, farcical, whimsical, comical, oddball (*informal*), risible, jocular, clownish, waggish

drone[1] *noun* PARASITE, skiver (*Brit slang*), idler, lounger, leech, loafer, couch potato (*slang*), scrounger (*informal*), sponger (*informal*), sluggard, bludger (*Austral & NZ informal*), quandong (*Austral slang*)

drone[2] *verb* **1** HUM, buzz, vibrate, purr, whirr, thrum
2 *often with* **on** SPEAK MONOTONOUSLY, drawl, chant, spout, intone, talk interminably
▷ *noun* HUM, buzz, purr, vibration, whirr, whirring, thrum

droning *adjective* MONOTONOUS, boring, tedious, drawling, soporific

drool *verb* **1** DRIVEL, dribble, salivate, slaver, slobber, water at the mouth
2 *often with* **over** GLOAT OVER, pet, gush, make much of, rave about (*informal*), dote on, slobber over

droop *verb* SAG, drop, hang (down), sink, bend, dangle, fall down

droopy *adjective* SAGGING, limp, wilting, stooped, floppy, drooping, languid, flabby, languorous, pendulous, lassitudinous

drop *verb* **1** FALL, lower, decline, diminish
2 *often with* **away** DECLINE, fall, sink

3 PLUNGE, fall, dive, tumble, descend, plummet
4 DRIP, trickle, dribble, fall in drops
5 SINK, fall, descend, droop
6 SET DOWN, leave, deposit, unload, let off
7 QUIT, give up, abandon, cease, axe (*informal*), kick (*informal*), terminate, relinquish, remit, discontinue, forsake
8 ABANDON, desert, forsake, repudiate, leave, jilt, throw over
▷ *noun* 1 DECREASE, fall, cut, lowering, decline, reduction, slump, fall-off, downturn, deterioration, cutback, diminution, decrement
2 DROPLET, bead, globule, bubble, pearl, drip, driblet
3 DASH, shot (*informal*), spot, taste, trace, pinch, sip, tot, trickle, nip, dab, mouthful
4 FALL, plunge, descent, abyss, chasm, precipice
▷▷ **drop in** (*informal*) VISIT, call, stop, turn up, look up, call in, look in, pop in (*informal*)
▷▷ **drop off** (*informal*) 1 FALL ASLEEP, nod (off), doze (off), snooze (*informal*), catnap, drowse, have forty winks (*informal*)
2 DECREASE, lower, decline, shrink, diminish, fall off, dwindle, lessen, wane, subside, slacken
▷▷ **drop out** LEAVE, stop, give up, withdraw, quit, pull out, back out, renege, throw in the towel, cop out (*slang*), fall by the wayside
▷▷ **drop out of something** DISCONTINUE, give up, abandon, quit, cease, terminate, forsake
▷▷ **drop someone off** SET DOWN, leave, deliver, let off, allow to alight

droppings *plural noun* EXCREMENT, stool, manure, dung, faeces, guano, excreta, doo-doo (*informal*), ordure, kak (*S African taboo slang*)

dross 1 RUBBISH, remains, refuse, lees, waste, debris, dregs
2 NONSENSE, garbage (*chiefly US*), drivel, twaddle, pants (*slang*), rot, crap (*slang*), trash, hot air (*informal*), tosh (*slang, chiefly Brit*), pap, bilge (*informal*), tripe (*informal*), gibberish, guff (*slang*), havers (*Scot*), moonshine, claptrap (*informal*), hogwash, hokum (*slang, chiefly US & Canad*), codswallop (*Brit slang*), piffle (*informal*), poppycock (*informal*), balderdash, bosh (*informal*), wack (*US slang*), eyewash (*informal*), stuff and nonsense, flapdoodle (*slang*), tommyrot, horsefeathers (*US slang*), bunkum *or* buncombe (*chiefly US*), bizzo (*Austral slang*), bull's wool (*Austral & NZ slang*)

drought *noun* 1 WATER SHORTAGE, dryness, dry weather, dry spell, aridity, drouth (*Scot*), parchedness
<< OPPOSITE flood
2 SHORTAGE, lack, deficit, deficiency, want, need, shortfall, scarcity, dearth, insufficiency
<< OPPOSITE abundance

drove *noun often plural* HERD, company, crowds, collection, gathering, mob, flocks, swarm, horde, multitude, throng

drown *verb* 1 GO DOWN, go under
2 DRENCH, flood, soak, steep, swamp, saturate, engulf, submerge, immerse, inundate, deluge
3 *often with* **out** OVERWHELM, overcome, wipe out, overpower, obliterate, swallow up

drowsiness *noun* SLEEPINESS, tiredness, lethargy, torpor, sluggishness, languor, somnolence, heavy eyelids, doziness, torpidity
<< OPPOSITE wakefulness

drowsy *adjective* 1 SLEEPY, tired, lethargic, heavy, nodding, dazed, dozy, comatose, dopey (*slang*), half asleep, somnolent, torpid
<< OPPOSITE awake
2 PEACEFUL, quiet, sleepy, soothing, lulling, dreamy, restful, soporific

drubbing *noun* BEATING, defeat, hammering (*informal*), pounding, whipping, thrashing, licking (*informal*), pasting (*slang*), flogging, trouncing, clobbering (*slang*), walloping (*informal*), pummelling

drudge *noun* MENIAL, worker, servant, slave, toiler, dogsbody (*informal*), plodder, factotum, scullion (*archaic*), skivvy (*chiefly Brit*), maid *or* man of all work

drudgery *noun* LABOUR, grind (*informal*), sweat (*informal*), hard work, slavery, chore, fag (*informal*), toil, slog, donkey-work, sweated labour, menial labour, skivvying (*Brit*)

drug *noun* 1 MEDICATION, medicine, remedy, physic, medicament
2 DOPE (*slang*), narcotic (*slang*), stimulant, opiate, dadah (*Austral slang*)
▷ *verb* KNOCK OUT, dope (*slang*), numb, deaden, stupefy, anaesthetize
>> RELATED WORD *combining form* pharmaco-

drug addict *noun* JUNKIE (*informal*), tripper (*informal*), crack-head (*informal*), acid head (*informal*), dope-fiend (*slang*), hop-head (*informal*), head (*informal*)

drugged *adjective* STONED, high (*informal*), flying (*slang*), bombed (*slang*), tripping (*informal or slang*), wasted (*slang*), smashed (*slang*), wrecked (*slang*), turned on (*slang*), out of it (*slang*), doped (*slang*), under the influence (*informal*), on a trip (*informal*), spaced out (*slang*), comatose, stupefied, out of your mind (*slang*), zonked (*slang*), out to it (*Austral & NZ slang*)

drum *verb* POUND, beat, tap, rap, lash, thrash, tattoo, throb, pulsate, reverberate
▷▷ **drum something into someone** DRIVE, hammer, instil, din, harp on about
▷▷ **drum something up** SEEK, attract, request, ask for, obtain, bid for, petition, round up, solicit, canvass

drunk *adjective* INTOXICATED, loaded (*slang, chiefly US & Canad*), tight (*informal*), canned (*slang*), flying (*slang*), bombed (*slang*), stoned (*slang*), wasted (*slang*), smashed (*slang*), steaming (*slang*), wrecked (*slang*), soaked (*informal*), out of it (*slang*), plastered (*slang*), drunken, blitzed (*slang*), lit up (*slang*), merry (*Brit informal*), stewed (*slang*), pickled (*informal*), bladdered (*slang*), under the influence (*informal*), sloshed (*slang*), tipsy, maudlin, well-oiled (*slang*), legless (*informal*), paralytic (*informal*), tired and emotional (*euphemistic*), steamboats (*Scot slang*), tiddly (*slang, chiefly Brit*), zonked (*slang*), blotto (*slang*), fuddled, inebriated, out to it (*Austral & NZ slang*), sottish, tanked up (*slang*), bacchic, half seas over (*informal*), bevvied (*dialect*), babalas (*S African*), fu' (*Scot*), pie-eyed (*slang*)
▷ *noun* DRUNKARD, alcoholic, lush (*slang*), boozer (*informal*), toper, sot, soak (*slang*), wino (*informal*), inebriate, alko *or* alco (*Austral slang*)

drunkard *noun* DRUNK, alcoholic, soak (*slang*), drinker, lush (*slang*), carouser, sot, tippler, toper, wino (*informal*), dipsomaniac, alko *or* alco (*Austral slang*)

drunken *adjective* **1** INTOXICATED, smashed (*slang*), drunk, flying (*slang*), bombed (*slang*), wasted (*slang*), steaming (*slang*), wrecked (*slang*), out of it (*slang*), boozing (*informal*), blitzed (*slang*), lit up (*slang*), bladdered (*slang*), under the influence (*informal*), tippling, toping, red-nosed, legless (*informal*), paralytic (*informal*), steamboats (*Scot slang*), zonked (*slang*), bibulous, blotto (*slang*), inebriate, out to it (*Austral & NZ slang*), sottish, bevvied (*dialect*), (gin-)sodden
2 BOOZY, dissipated (*informal*), riotous, debauched, dionysian, orgiastic, bacchanalian, bacchic, saturnalian

drunkenness *noun* INTOXICATION, alcoholism, intemperance, inebriation, dipsomania, tipsiness, insobriety, bibulousness, sottishness

dry *adjective* **1** DEHYDRATED, dried-up, arid, torrid, parched, desiccated, waterless, juiceless, sapless, moistureless
<< OPPOSITE wet
2 DRIED, crisp, withered, brittle, shrivelled, crispy, parched, desiccated, sun-baked
3 THIRSTY, parched
4 SARCASTIC, cutting, sharp, keen, cynical, low-key, sly, sardonic, deadpan, droll, ironical, quietly humorous
5 DULL, boring, tedious, commonplace, dreary, tiresome, monotonous, run-of-the-mill, humdrum, unimaginative, uninteresting, mind-numbing, ho-hum (*informal*)
<< OPPOSITE interesting
6 PLAIN, simple, bare, basic, pure, stark, unembellished
▷ *verb* **1** DRAIN, make dry
2 *often with* **out** DEHYDRATE, make dry, desiccate, sear, parch, dehumidify
<< OPPOSITE wet
▷▷ **dry out** *or* **up** BECOME DRY, harden, wither, mummify, shrivel up, wizen

dryness *noun* **1** ARIDITY, drought, dehydration, aridness, dehumidification, waterlessness, moisturelessness, parchedness
2 THIRSTINESS, thirst, parchedness

dual *adjective* TWOFOLD, double, twin, matched, coupled, paired, duplicate, binary, duplex

duality *noun* DUALISM, dichotomy, polarity, doubleness, biformity, duplexity

dub *verb* NAME, call, term, style, label, nickname, designate, christen, denominate

dubious *adjective* **1** SUSPECT, suspicious, crooked, dodgy (*Brit, Austral & NZ informal*), questionable, unreliable, shady (*informal*), unscrupulous, fishy (*informal*), disreputable, untrustworthy, undependable
<< OPPOSITE trustworthy
2 UNSURE, uncertain, suspicious, hesitating, doubtful, sceptical, tentative, wavering, hesitant, undecided, unconvinced, iffy (*informal*), leery (*slang*), distrustful, in two minds (*informal*)
<< OPPOSITE sure
3 DOUBTFUL, questionable, ambiguous, debatable, moot, arguable, equivocal, open to question, disputable

duck *verb* **1** BOB, drop, lower, bend, bow, dodge, crouch, stoop
2 (*informal*) DODGE, avoid, escape, evade, elude, sidestep, circumvent, shirk, body-swerve (*Scot*)
3 DUNK, wet, plunge, dip, submerge, immerse, douse, souse

duct *noun* PIPE, channel, passage, tube, canal, funnel, conduit

dud (*informal*) *noun* FAILURE, flop (*informal*), washout (*informal*), clinker (*slang, chiefly US*), clunker (*informal*)
▷ *adjective* FAULTY, broken, failed, damaged, bust (*informal*), not working, useless, flawed, impaired, duff (*Brit informal*), worthless, defective, imperfect, malfunctioning, out of order, unsound, not functioning, valueless, on the blink, inoperative, kaput (*informal*)

due *adjective* **1** EXPECTED, scheduled, expected to arrive
2 FITTING, deserved, appropriate, just, right, becoming, fit, justified, suitable, merited, proper, obligatory, rightful, requisite, well-earned, bounden
3 PAYABLE, outstanding, owed, owing, unpaid, in arrears
▷ *noun* RIGHT(S), privilege, deserts, merits, prerogative, comeuppance (*informal*)

▷ *adverb* DIRECTLY, dead, straight, exactly, undeviatingly

> For years people have been debating the use of *due to* in the sense 'because of'. Purists claimed that a sentence such as *the late arrival of the 10.15 train from Guildford is due to snow on the lines* was correct, while *the trains are running late due to snow on the lines* was incorrect. Their reasoning was that as an adjective, *due* should modify a noun, as it does in the first sentence (the train's late *arrival* was *due to* the snow); but in the second sentence there is no specific noun that the word *due* can be said to modify. Few people nowadays would object strongly to the use of *due* in the second sentence, but if you want to avoid any possibility of this, you may find it preferable to replace it with an alternative that is not the subject of debate, such as *because of*

duel *noun* 1 SINGLE COMBAT, affair of honour
2 CONTEST, fight, competition, clash, encounter, engagement, rivalry
▷ *verb* FIGHT, struggle, clash, compete, contest, contend, vie with, lock horns

dues *plural noun* MEMBERSHIP FEE, charges, fee, contribution, levy

duff *adjective* (*Brit, Austral & NZ informal*) BAD, poor, useless, pathetic, inferior, worthless, unsatisfactory, defective, deficient, imperfect, substandard, low-rent (*informal, chiefly US*), poxy (*slang*), pants (*informal*), bodger *or* bodgie (*Austral slang*)

duffer *noun* (*informal*) CLOT, blunderer (*Brit informal*), booby, clod, oaf, bungler, galoot (*slang, chiefly US*), lubber, lummox (*informal*)

dulcet *adjective* SWEET, pleasing, musical, charming, pleasant, honeyed, delightful, soothing, agreeable, harmonious, melodious, mellifluous, euphonious, mellifluent

dull *adjective* 1 BORING, tedious, dreary, flat, dry, plain, commonplace, tiresome, monotonous, prosaic, run-of-the-mill, humdrum, unimaginative, dozy, uninteresting, mind-numbing, ho-hum (*informal*), vapid, as dry as dust
<< OPPOSITE exciting
2 LIFELESS, dead, heavy, slow, indifferent, sluggish, insensitive, apathetic, listless, unresponsive, passionless, insensible
<< OPPOSITE lively
3 DRAB, faded, muted, subdued, feeble, murky, sombre, toned-down, subfusc
4 CLOUDY, dim, gloomy, dismal, overcast, leaden, turbid
<< OPPOSITE bright
5 MUTED, faint, suppressed, subdued, stifled, indistinct
6 BLUNT, dulled, blunted, not keen, not sharp, edgeless, unsharpened
<< OPPOSITE sharp
▷ *verb* 1 RELIEVE, blunt, lessen, moderate, soften, alleviate, allay, mitigate, assuage, take the edge off, palliate
2 CLOUD OVER, darken, grow dim, become cloudy
3 DAMPEN, reduce, check, depress, moderate, discourage, stifle, lessen, smother, sadden, dishearten, dispirit, deject

dullness *noun* 1 TEDIOUSNESS, monotony, banality, flatness, dreariness, vapidity, insipidity
<< OPPOSITE interest
2 STUPIDITY, thickness, slowness, dimness, obtuseness, doziness (*Brit informal*), dim-wittedness, dopiness (*slang*)
<< OPPOSITE intelligence
3 DRABNESS, greyness, dimness, gloominess, dinginess, colourlessness
<< OPPOSITE brilliance

duly *adverb* 1 PROPERLY, fittingly, correctly, appropriately, accordingly, suitably, deservedly, rightfully, decorously, befittingly
2 ON TIME, promptly, in good time, punctually, at the proper time

dumb *adjective* 1 UNABLE TO SPEAK, mute
<< OPPOSITE articulate
2 SILENT, mute, speechless, inarticulate, tongue-tied, wordless, voiceless, soundless, at a loss for words, mum
3 (*informal*) STUPID, thick, dull, foolish, dense, dozy (*Brit informal*), dim, obtuse, unintelligent, asinine, braindead (*informal*), dim-witted (*informal*)
<< OPPOSITE clever

dumbfounded *adjective* AMAZED, stunned, astonished, confused, overcome, overwhelmed, staggered, thrown, startled, at sea, dumb, bewildered, astounded, breathless, confounded, taken aback, speechless, bowled over (*informal*), gobsmacked (*Brit slang*), flabbergasted (*informal*), nonplussed, lost for words, flummoxed, thunderstruck, knocked sideways (*informal*), knocked for six (*informal*)

dummy *noun* 1 MODEL, figure, mannequin, form, manikin, lay figure
2 IMITATION, copy, duplicate, sham, counterfeit, replica
3 (*Slang*) FOOL, jerk (*slang, chiefly US & Canad*), idiot, plank (*Brit slang*), charlie (*Brit informal*), berk (*Brit slang*), wally (*slang*), prat (*slang*), plonker (*slang*), coot, geek (*slang*), dunce, oaf, simpleton, dullard, dimwit (*informal*),

dipstick (*Brit slang*), gonzo (*slang*), schmuck (*US slang*), dork (*slang*), nitwit (*informal*), dolt, blockhead, divvy (*Brit slang*), pillock (*Brit slang*), dweeb (*US slang*), fathead (*informal*), weenie (*US informal*), eejit (*Scot & Irish*), dumb-ass (*slang*), numpty (*Scot informal*), doofus (*slang, chiefly US*), lamebrain (*informal*), nerd *or* nurd (*slang*), numbskull *or* numskull, dorba *or* dorb (*Austral slang*), bogan (*Austral slang*)
▷ *modifier* IMITATION, false, fake, artificial, mock, bogus, simulated, sham, phoney *or* phony (*informal*)

dummy run *noun* PRACTICE, trial, dry run

dump *verb* 1 DROP, deposit, throw down, let fall, fling down
2 GET RID OF, tip, discharge, dispose of, unload, jettison, empty out, coup (*Scot*), throw away *or* out
3 SCRAP, axe (*informal*), get rid of, abolish, junk (*informal*), put an end to, discontinue, jettison, put paid to
▷ *noun* 1 RUBBISH TIP, tip, junkyard, rubbish heap, refuse heap
2 (*informal*) PIGSTY, hole (*informal*), joint (*slang*), slum, shack, shanty, hovel

dumps *plural noun* ▷▷ **down in the dumps** DOWN, low, blue, sad, unhappy, low-spirited, discouraged, fed up, moody, pessimistic, melancholy, glum, dejected, despondent, dispirited, downcast, morose, crestfallen, downhearted

dumpy *adjective* PODGY, homely, short, plump, squat, stout, chunky, chubby, tubby, roly-poly, pudgy, squab, fubsy (*archaic* or *dialect*)

dunce *noun* SIMPLETON, moron, duffer (*informal*), bonehead (*slang*), loon (*informal*), goose (*informal*), ass, donkey, oaf, dullard, dimwit (*informal*), ignoramus, nitwit (*informal*), dolt, blockhead, halfwit, nincompoop, fathead (*informal*), dunderhead, lamebrain (*informal*), thickhead, numbskull *or* numskull

dungeon *noun* PRISON, cell, cage, vault, lockup, oubliette, calaboose (*US informal*), donjon, boob (*Austral slang*)

dunny *noun* (*Austral & NZ old-fashioned informal*) TOILET, lavatory, bathroom, loo (*Brit informal*), W.C., bog (*slang*), Gents *or* Ladies, can (*US & Canad slang*), john (*slang, chiefly US & Canad*), head(s) (*Nautical slang*), throne (*informal*), closet, privy, cloakroom (*Brit*), urinal, latrine, washroom, powder room, crapper (*taboo slang*), water closet, khazi (*slang*), pissoir (*French*), little boy's room *or* little girl's room (*informal*), (public) convenience, bogger (*Austral slang*), brasco (*Austral slang*)

dupe *noun* VICTIM, mug (*Brit slang*), sucker (*slang*), pigeon (*slang*), sap (*slang*), gull, pushover (*slang*), fall guy (*informal*), simpleton
▷ *verb* DECEIVE, trick, cheat, con (*informal*), kid (*informal*), rip off (*slang*), hoax, defraud, beguile, gull (*archaic*), delude, swindle, outwit, bamboozle (*informal*), hoodwink, take for a ride (*informal*), pull a fast one on (*informal*), cozen

duplicate *adjective* IDENTICAL, matched, matching, twin, corresponding, twofold
▷ *noun* 1 COPY, facsimile
2 PHOTOCOPY, copy, reproduction, replica, Xerox (*trademark*), carbon copy, Photostat (*trademark*)
▷ *verb* 1 REPEAT, reproduce, echo, copy, clone, replicate
2 COPY, photocopy, Xerox (*trademark*), Photostat (*trademark*)

duplicity *noun* DECEIT, fraud, deception, hypocrisy, dishonesty, guile, artifice, falsehood, double-dealing, chicanery, perfidy, dissimulation
<< OPPOSITE honesty

durable *adjective* 1 HARD-WEARING, strong, tough, sound, substantial, reliable, resistant, sturdy, long-lasting
<< OPPOSITE fragile
2 ENDURING, lasting, permanent, continuing, firm, fast, fixed, constant, abiding, dependable, unwavering, unfaltering

duration *noun* LENGTH, time, period, term, stretch, extent, spell, span, time frame, timeline

duress *noun* (usually in phrase *under duress*) PRESSURE, threat, constraint, compulsion, coercion

dusk *noun* 1 TWILIGHT, evening, evo (*Austral slang*), nightfall, sunset, dark, sundown, eventide, gloaming (*Scot poetic*)
<< OPPOSITE dawn
2 (*Poetic*) SHADE, darkness, gloom, obscurity, murk, shadowiness

dusky *adjective* 1 DIM, twilight, shady, shadowy, gloomy, murky, cloudy, overcast, crepuscular, darkish, twilit, tenebrous, caliginous (*archaic*)
2 DARK, swarthy, dark-complexioned

dust *noun* 1 GRIME, grit, powder, powdery dirt
2 EARTH, ground, soil, dirt
3 PARTICLES, fine fragments
▷ *verb* SPRINKLE, cover, powder, spread, spray, scatter, sift, dredge

dusty *adjective* 1 DIRTY, grubby, unclean, unswept, undusted
2 POWDERY, sandy, chalky, crumbly, granular, friable

dutiful *adjective* CONSCIENTIOUS, devoted, obedient, respectful, compliant, submissive, docile, deferential, reverential, filial, punctilious, duteous (*archaic*)
<< OPPOSITE disrespectful

duty *noun* 1 RESPONSIBILITY, job, task, work, calling, business, service, office, charge, role,

function, mission, province, obligation, assignment, pigeon (*informal*), onus
2 TAX, customs, toll, levy, tariff, excise, due, impost
▷▷ **off duty** OFF WORK, off, free, on holiday, at leisure
▷▷ **on duty** AT WORK, busy, engaged, on active service

dwarf *noun* GNOME, midget, Lilliputian, Tom Thumb, munchkin (*informal, chiefly US*), homunculus, manikin, hop-o'-my-thumb, pygmy *or* pigmy
▷ *modifier* MINIATURE, small, baby, tiny, pocket, dwarfed, diminutive, petite, bonsai, pint-sized, undersized, teeny-weeny, Lilliputian, teensy-weensy
▷ *verb* **1** TOWER ABOVE *or* OVER, dominate, overlook, stand over, loom over, stand head and shoulders above
2 ECLIPSE, tower above *or* over, put in the shade, diminish

dwell *verb* (*Formal* or *literary*) LIVE, stay, reside, rest, quarter, settle, lodge, abide, hang out (*informal*), sojourn, establish yourself
▷▷ **dwell on** *or* **upon something** GO ON ABOUT, emphasize (*informal*), elaborate on, linger over, harp on about, be engrossed in, expatiate on, continue to think about, tarry over

dwelling *noun* (*Formal* or *literary*) HOME, house, residence, abode, quarters, establishment, lodging, pad (*slang*), habitation, domicile, dwelling house, whare (*NZ*)

dwindle *verb* LESSEN, fall, decline, contract, sink, fade, weaken, shrink, diminish, decrease, decay, wither, wane, subside, ebb, die down, die out, abate, shrivel, peter out, die away, waste away, taper off, grow less
<< OPPOSITE increase

dye *noun* COLOURING, colour, pigment, stain, tint, tinge, colorant
▷ *verb* COLOUR, stain, tint, tinge, pigment, tincture

dying *adjective* **1** NEAR DEATH, going, failing, fading, doomed, expiring, ebbing, near the end, moribund, fading fast, in extremis (*Latin*), at death's door, not long for this world, on your deathbed, breathing your last
2 FINAL, last, parting, departing
3 FAILING, declining, sinking, foundering, diminishing, decreasing, dwindling, subsiding

dynamic *adjective* ENERGETIC, spirited, powerful, active, vital, driving, electric, go-ahead, lively, magnetic, vigorous, animated, high-powered, forceful, go-getting (*informal*), tireless, indefatigable, high-octane (*informal*), zippy (*informal*), full of beans (*informal*)
<< OPPOSITE apathetic

dynamism *noun* ENERGY, go (*informal*), drive, push (*informal*), initiative, enterprise, pep, zip (*informal*), vigour, zap (*slang*), get-up-and-go (*informal*), brio, liveliness, forcefulness

dynasty *noun* EMPIRE, house, rule, regime, sovereignty

Ee

each *adjective* EVERY, every single
▷ *pronoun* EVERY ONE, all, each one, each and every one, one and all
▷ *adverb* APIECE, individually, singly, for each, to each, respectively, per person, from each, per head, per capita

Each is a singular pronoun and should be used with a singular verb – for example, *each of the candidates was interviewed separately* (not *were interviewed separately*)

eager *adjective* **1** *often with* **to** *or* **for** ANXIOUS, keen, raring, hungry, intent, yearning, impatient, itching, thirsty, zealous
<< OPPOSITE unenthusiastic
2 KEEN, interested, earnest, intense, enthusiastic, passionate, ardent, avid (*informal*), fervent, zealous, fervid, keen as mustard, bright-eyed and bushy-tailed (*informal*)
<< OPPOSITE uninterested

eagerness *noun* **1** LONGING, anxiety, hunger, yearning, zeal, impatience, impetuosity, avidity
2 PASSION, interest, enthusiasm, intensity, fervour, ardour, earnestness, keenness, heartiness, thirst, intentness

ear *noun* **1** SENSITIVITY, taste, discrimination, appreciation, musical perception
2 ATTENTION, hearing, regard, notice, consideration, observation, awareness, heed
▷▷ **lend an ear** LISTEN, pay attention, heed, take notice, pay heed, hearken (*archaic*), give ear
>> RELATED WORD *adjective* aural

early *adverb* **1** IN GOOD TIME, beforehand, ahead of schedule, in advance, with time to spare, betimes (*archaic*)
<< OPPOSITE late
2 TOO SOON, before the usual time, prematurely, ahead of time
<< OPPOSITE late
▷ *adjective* **1** FIRST, opening, earliest, initial, introductory
2 PREMATURE, forward, advanced, untimely, unseasonable
<< OPPOSITE belated
3 PRIMITIVE, first, earliest, young, original, undeveloped, primordial, primeval
<< OPPOSITE developed

earmark *verb* **1** SET ASIDE, reserve, label, flag, tag, allocate, designate, mark out, keep back
2 MARK OUT, identify, designate

earn *verb* **1** BE PAID, make, get, receive, draw, gain, net, collect, bring in, gross, procure, clear, get paid, take home
2 DESERVE, win, gain, attain, justify, merit, warrant, be entitled to, reap, be worthy of

earnest *adjective* **1** SERIOUS, keen, grave, intense, steady, dedicated, eager, enthusiastic, passionate, sincere, thoughtful, solemn, ardent, fervent, impassioned, zealous, staid, keen as mustard
<< OPPOSITE frivolous
2 DETERMINED, firm, dogged, constant, urgent, intent, persistent, ardent, persevering, resolute, heartfelt, zealous, vehement, wholehearted
<< OPPOSITE half-hearted

earnestness *noun* **1** SERIOUSNESS, resolution, passion, enthusiasm, warmth, gravity, urgency, zeal, sincerity, fervour, eagerness, ardour, keenness
2 DETERMINATION, resolve, urgency, zeal, ardour, vehemence

earnings *plural noun* INCOME, pay, wages, revenue, reward, proceeds, salary, receipts, return, remuneration, takings, stipend, take-home pay, emolument, gross pay, net pay

earth *noun* **1** WORLD, planet, globe, sphere, orb, earthly sphere, terrestrial sphere
2 GROUND, land, dry land, terra firma
3 SOIL, ground, land, dust, mould, clay, dirt, turf, sod, silt, topsoil, clod, loam
>> RELATED WORD *adjective* terrestrial

earthenware *noun* CROCKERY, pots, ceramics,

pottery, terracotta, crocks, faience, maiolica

earthly *adjective* 1 WORLDLY, material, physical, secular, mortal, mundane, terrestrial, temporal, human, materialistic, profane, telluric, sublunary, non-spiritual, tellurian, terrene

<< OPPOSITE spiritual

2 SENSUAL, worldly, base, physical, gross, low, fleshly, bodily, vile, sordid, carnal

3 (*informal*) POSSIBLE, likely, practical, feasible, conceivable, imaginable

earthy *adjective* 1 CRUDE, coarse, raunchy (*slang*), lusty, bawdy, ribald

2 CLAYLIKE, soil-like

ease *noun* 1 STRAIGHTFORWARDNESS, simplicity, readiness

2 COMFORT, luxury, leisure, relaxation, prosperity, affluence, rest, repose, restfulness

<< OPPOSITE hardship

3 PEACE OF MIND, peace, content, quiet, comfort, happiness, enjoyment, serenity, tranquillity, contentment, calmness, quietude

<< OPPOSITE agitation

4 NATURALNESS, informality, freedom, liberty, unaffectedness, unconstraint, unreservedness, relaxedness

<< OPPOSITE awkwardness

▷ *verb* 1 RELIEVE, calm, moderate, soothe, lessen, alleviate, appease, lighten, lower, allay, relax, still, mitigate, assuage, pacify, mollify, tranquillize, palliate

<< OPPOSITE aggravate

2 *often with* **off** *or* **up** REDUCE, moderate, weaken, diminish, decrease, slow down, dwindle, lessen, die down, abate, slacken, grow less, de-escalate

3 MOVE CAREFULLY, edge, guide, slip, inch, slide, creep, squeeze, steer, manoeuvre

4 FACILITATE, further, aid, forward, smooth, assist, speed up, simplify, make easier, expedite, lessen the labour of

<< OPPOSITE hinder

easily *adverb* 1 WITHOUT A DOUBT, clearly, surely, certainly, obviously, definitely, plainly, absolutely, undoubtedly, unquestionably, undeniably, unequivocally, far and away, indisputably, beyond question, indubitably, doubtlessly

2 WITHOUT DIFFICULTY, smoothly, readily, comfortably, effortlessly, simply, with ease, straightforwardly, without trouble, standing on your head, with your eyes closed *or* shut

easy *adjective* 1 SIMPLE, straightforward, no trouble, not difficult, effortless, painless, clear, light, uncomplicated, child's play (*informal*), plain sailing, undemanding, a pushover (*slang*), a piece of cake (*informal*), no bother, a bed of roses, easy-peasy (*slang*)

<< OPPOSITE hard

2 UNTROUBLED, contented, relaxed, satisfied, calm, peaceful, serene, tranquil, quiet, undisturbed, unworried

3 RELAXED, friendly, open, natural, pleasant, casual, informal, laid-back (*informal*), graceful, gracious, unaffected, easy-going, affable, unpretentious, unforced, undemanding, unconstrained, unceremonious

<< OPPOSITE stiff

4 CAREFREE, comfortable, leisurely, trouble-free, untroubled, cushy (*informal*)

<< OPPOSITE difficult

5 TOLERANT, light, liberal, soft, flexible, mild, laid-back (*informal*), indulgent, easy-going, lenient, permissive, unoppressive

<< OPPOSITE strict

6 (*informal*) ACCOMMODATING, yielding, manageable, easy-going, compliant, amenable, submissive, docile, pliant, tractable, biddable

<< OPPOSITE difficult

7 VULNERABLE, soft, naive, susceptible, gullible, exploitable

8 LEISURELY, relaxed, comfortable, moderate, unhurried, undemanding

easy-going *adjective* RELAXED, easy, liberal, calm, flexible, mild, casual, tolerant, laid-back (*informal*), indulgent, serene, lenient, carefree, placid, unconcerned, amenable, permissive, happy-go-lucky, unhurried, nonchalant, insouciant, even-tempered, easy-peasy (*slang*)

<< OPPOSITE tense

eat *verb* 1 CONSUME, swallow, chew, scoff (*slang*), devour, munch, tuck into (*informal*), put away, gobble, polish off (*informal*), wolf down

2 HAVE A MEAL, lunch, breakfast, dine, snack, feed, graze (*informal*), have lunch, have dinner, have breakfast, nosh (*slang*), take food, have supper, break bread, chow down (*slang*), take nourishment

eavesdrop *verb* LISTEN IN, spy, overhear, bug (*informal*), pry, tap in, snoop (*informal*), earwig (*informal*)

ebb *verb* 1 FLOW BACK, go out, withdraw, sink, retreat, fall back, wane, recede, fall away

2 DECLINE, drop, sink, flag, weaken, shrink, diminish, decrease, deteriorate, decay, dwindle, lessen, subside, degenerate, fall away, fade away, abate, peter out, slacken

▷ *noun* FLOWING BACK, going out, withdrawal, retreat, wane, waning, regression, low water, low tide, ebb tide, outgoing tide, falling tide, receding tide

ebony *adjective* BLACK, dark, jet, raven, sable, pitch-black, jet-black, inky, swarthy, coal-black

ebullient *adjective* EXUBERANT, excited, enthusiastic, buoyant, exhilarated, elated, irrepressible, vivacious, effervescent, effusive, in high spirits, zestful

eccentric *adjective* ODD, strange, bizarre, weird, peculiar, abnormal, queer (*informal*), irregular, uncommon, quirky, singular, unconventional, idiosyncratic, off-the-wall (*slang*), outlandish, whimsical, rum (*Brit slang*), capricious, anomalous, freakish, aberrant, wacko (*slang*), outré, daggy (*Austral & NZ informal*)
<< OPPOSITE normal
▷ *noun* CRANK (*informal*), character (*informal*), nut (*slang*), freak (*informal*), flake (*slang, chiefly US*), oddity, oddball (*informal*), loose cannon, nonconformist, wacko (*slang*), case (*informal*), screwball (*slang, chiefly US & Canad*), card (*informal*), odd fish (*informal*), kook (*US & Canad informal*), queer fish (*Brit informal*), rum customer (*Brit slang*), weirdo *or* weirdie (*informal*)

eccentricity *noun* 1 ODDITY, peculiarity, strangeness, irregularity, weirdness, singularity, oddness, waywardness, nonconformity, capriciousness, unconventionality, queerness (*informal*), bizarreness, whimsicality, freakishness, outlandishness
2 FOIBLE, anomaly, abnormality, quirk, oddity, aberration, peculiarity, idiosyncrasy

ecclesiastical *adjective* CLERICAL, religious, church, churchly, priestly, spiritual, holy, divine, pastoral, sacerdotal

echelon *noun* LEVEL, place, office, position, step, degree, rank, grade, tier, rung

echo *noun* 1 REVERBERATION, ringing, repetition, answer, resonance, resounding
2 COPY, reflection, clone, reproduction, imitation, duplicate, double, reiteration
3 REMINDER, suggestion, trace, hint, recollection, vestige, evocation, intimation
▷ *verb* 1 REVERBERATE, repeat, resound, ring, resonate
2 RECALL, reflect, copy, mirror, resemble, reproduce, parrot, imitate, reiterate, ape

eclectic *adjective* DIVERSE, general, broad, varied, comprehensive, extensive, wide-ranging, selective, diversified, manifold, heterogeneous, catholic, all-embracing, liberal, many-sided, multifarious, dilettantish

eclipse *noun* 1 OBSCURING, covering, blocking, shading, dimming, extinction, darkening, blotting out, occultation
2 DECLINE, fall, loss, failure, weakening, deterioration, degeneration, diminution
▷ *verb* 1 SURPASS, exceed, overshadow, excel, transcend, outdo, outclass, outshine, leave *or* put in the shade (*informal*)
2 OBSCURE, cover, block, cloud, conceal, dim, veil, darken, shroud, extinguish, blot out

economic *adjective* 1 FINANCIAL, business, trade, industrial, commercial, mercantile
2 MONETARY, financial, material, fiscal, budgetary, bread-and-butter (*informal*), pecuniary
3 (*Brit*) PROFITABLE, successful, commercial, rewarding, productive, lucrative, worthwhile, viable, solvent, cost-effective, money-making, profit-making, remunerative
4 (*informal*) ECONOMICAL, fair, cheap, reasonable, modest, low-priced, inexpensive

economical *adjective* 1 ECONOMIC, fair, cheap, reasonable, modest, low-priced, inexpensive
<< OPPOSITE expensive
2 THRIFTY, sparing, careful, prudent, provident, frugal, parsimonious, scrimping, economizing
<< OPPOSITE extravagant
3 EFFICIENT, sparing, cost-effective, money-saving, time-saving, work-saving, unwasteful
<< OPPOSITE wasteful

economics *noun* FINANCE, commerce, the dismal science

economy *noun* 1 FINANCIAL SYSTEM, financial state
2 THRIFT, saving, restraint, prudence, providence, husbandry, retrenchment, frugality, parsimony, thriftiness, sparingness

ecstasy *noun* RAPTURE, delight, joy, enthusiasm, frenzy, bliss, trance, euphoria, fervour, elation, rhapsody, exaltation, transport, ravishment
<< OPPOSITE agony

ecstatic *adjective* RAPTUROUS, entranced, enthusiastic, frenzied, joyous, fervent, joyful, elated, over the moon (*informal*), overjoyed, blissful, delirious, euphoric, enraptured, on cloud nine (*informal*), cock-a-hoop, blissed out, transported, rhapsodic, sent, walking on air, in seventh heaven, floating on air, in exaltation, in transports of delight, stoked (*Austral & NZ informal*)

ecumenical, oecumenical, ecumenic *or* **oecumenic** *adjective* UNIFYING, universal, non-denominational, non-sectarian, general

eddy *noun* SWIRL, whirlpool, vortex, undertow, tideway, counter-current, counterflow
▷ *verb* SWIRL, turn, roll, spin, twist, surge, revolve, whirl, billow

edge *noun* 1 BORDER, side, line, limit, bound, lip, margin, outline, boundary, fringe, verge, brink, threshold, rim, brim, perimeter, contour, periphery, flange
2 VERGE, point, brink, threshold
3 ADVANTAGE, lead, dominance, superiority, upper hand, head start, ascendancy, whip hand
4 POWER, interest, force, bite, effectiveness, animation, zest, incisiveness, powerful quality
5 SHARPNESS, point, sting, urgency, bitterness,

keenness, pungency, acuteness
▷ *verb* 1 INCH, ease, creep, worm, slink, steal, sidle, work, move slowly
2 BORDER, shape, bind, trim, fringe, rim, hem, pipe
▷▷ **on edge** TENSE, excited, wired (*slang*), nervous, eager, impatient, irritable, apprehensive, edgy, uptight (*informal*), ill at ease, twitchy (*informal*), tetchy, on tenterhooks, keyed up, antsy (*informal*), adrenalized

edgy *adjective* NERVOUS, wired (*slang*), anxious, tense, neurotic, irritable, touchy, uptight (*informal*), on edge, nervy (*Brit informal*), ill at ease, restive, twitchy (*informal*), irascible, tetchy, chippy (*informal*), on tenterhooks, keyed up, antsy (*informal*), on pins and needles, adrenalized

edible *adjective* SAFE TO EAT, harmless, wholesome, palatable, digestible, eatable, comestible (*rare*), fit to eat, good
<< OPPOSITE inedible

edict *noun* DECREE, law, act, order, ruling, demand, command, regulation, dictate, mandate, canon, manifesto, injunction, statute, fiat, ordinance, proclamation, enactment, dictum, pronouncement, ukase (*rare*), pronunciamento

edifice *noun* BUILDING, house, structure, construction, pile, erection, habitation

edify *verb* INSTRUCT, school, teach, inform, guide, improve, educate, nurture, elevate, enlighten, uplift

edifying *adjective* INSTRUCTIVE, improving, inspiring, elevating, enlightening, uplifting, instructional

edit *verb* 1 REVISE, check, improve, correct, polish, adapt, rewrite, censor, condense, annotate, rephrase, redraft, copy-edit, emend, prepare for publication, redact
2 PUT TOGETHER, select, arrange, organize, assemble, compose, rearrange, reorder
3 BE IN CHARGE OF, control, direct, be responsible for, be the editor of

edition *noun* 1 PRINTING, publication
2 COPY, impression, number
3 VERSION, volume, issue
4 PROGRAMME (*TV, Radio*)

educate *verb* TEACH, school, train, coach, develop, improve, exercise, inform, discipline, rear, foster, mature, drill, tutor, instruct, cultivate, enlighten, civilize, edify, indoctrinate

educated *adjective* 1 CULTURED, lettered, intellectual, learned, informed, experienced, polished, literary, sophisticated, refined, cultivated, enlightened, knowledgeable, civilized, tasteful, urbane, erudite, well-bred
<< OPPOSITE uncultured
2 TAUGHT, schooled, coached, informed, tutored, instructed, nurtured, well-informed, well-read, well-taught
<< OPPOSITE uneducated

education *noun* 1 TEACHING, schooling, training, development, coaching, improvement, discipline, instruction, drilling, tutoring, nurture, tuition, enlightenment, erudition, indoctrination, edification
2 LEARNING, schooling, culture, breeding, scholarship, civilization, cultivation, refinement

educational *adjective* 1 ACADEMIC, school, learning, teaching, scholastic, pedagogical, pedagogic
2 INSTRUCTIVE, useful, cultural, illuminating, enlightening, informative, instructional, didactic, edifying, educative, heuristic

educator *noun* TEACHER, professor, lecturer, don, coach, guide, fellow, trainer, tutor, instructor, mentor, schoolteacher, pedagogue, edifier, educationalist *or* educationist, schoolmaster *or* schoolmistress, master *or* mistress

eerie *adjective* UNCANNY, strange, frightening, ghostly, weird, mysterious, scary (*informal*), sinister, uneasy, fearful, awesome, unearthly, supernatural, unnatural, spooky (*informal*), creepy (*informal*), spectral, eldritch (*poetic*), preternatural

efface *verb* OBLITERATE, remove, destroy, cancel, wipe out, erase, eradicate, excise, delete, annihilate, raze, blot out, cross out, expunge, rub out, extirpate

effect *noun* 1 RESULT, consequence, conclusion, outcome, event, issue, aftermath, fruit, end result, upshot
2 IMPRESSION, feeling, impact, influence
3 PURPOSE, meaning, impression, sense, import, drift, intent, essence, thread, tenor, purport
4 IMPLEMENTATION, force, action, performance, operation, enforcement, execution
▷ *verb* BRING ABOUT, make, cause, produce, create, complete, achieve, perform, carry out, fulfil, accomplish, execute, initiate, give rise to, consummate, actuate, effectuate
▷▷ **in effect** IN FACT, really, actually, essentially, virtually, effectively, in reality, in truth, as good as, in actual fact, to all intents and purposes, in all but name, in actuality, for practical purposes
▷▷ **put, bring** *or* **carry into effect** IMPLEMENT, perform, carry out, fulfil, enforce, execute, bring about, put into action, put into operation, bring into force
▷▷ **take effect** PRODUCE RESULTS, work, begin,

come into force, become operative

> It is quite common for the verb *effect* to be mistakenly used where *affect* is intended. *Effect* is relatively uncommon and rather formal, and is a synonym of 'bring about'. Conversely, the noun *effect* is quite often mistakenly written with an initial *a*. The following are correct: *the group is still recovering from the effects of the recession; they really are powerless to effect any change*. The next two examples are incorrect: *the full affects of the shutdown won't be felt for several more days; men whose lack of hair doesn't effect their self-esteem*.

effective *adjective* 1 EFFICIENT, successful, useful, active, capable, valuable, helpful, adequate, productive, operative, competent, serviceable, efficacious, effectual
<< OPPOSITE ineffective
2 POWERFUL, strong, convincing, persuasive, telling, impressive, compelling, potent, forceful, striking, emphatic, weighty, forcible, cogent
<< OPPOSITE weak
3 VIRTUAL, essential, practical, implied, implicit, tacit, unacknowledged
4 IN OPERATION, official, current, legal, real, active, actual, in effect, valid, operative, in force, in execution
<< OPPOSITE inoperative

effectiveness *noun* POWER, effect, efficiency, success, strength, capability, use, validity, usefulness, potency, efficacy, fruitfulness, productiveness

effects *plural noun* BELONGINGS, goods, things, property, stuff, gear, furniture, possessions, trappings, paraphernalia, personal property, accoutrements, chattels, movables

effeminate *adjective* WOMANLY, affected, camp (*informal*), soft, weak, feminine, unmanly, sissy, effete, foppish, womanish, wussy (*slang*), womanlike, poofy (*slang*), wimpish *or* wimpy (*informal*)
<< OPPOSITE manly

effervescent *adjective* 1 FIZZY, bubbling, sparkling, bubbly, foaming, fizzing, fermenting, frothing, frothy, aerated, carbonated, foamy, gassy
<< OPPOSITE still
2 LIVELY, excited, dynamic, enthusiastic, sparkling, energetic, animated, merry, buoyant, exhilarated, bubbly, exuberant, high-spirited, irrepressible, ebullient, chirpy, vital, scintillating, vivacious, zingy (*informal*)
<< OPPOSITE dull

effete *adjective* WEAK, cowardly, feeble, ineffectual, decrepit, spineless, enfeebled, weak-kneed (*informal*), enervated, overrefined, chicken-hearted, wimpish *or* wimpy (*informal*)

efficacy *noun* EFFECTIVENESS, efficiency, power, value, success, strength, virtue, vigour, use, usefulness, potency, fruitfulness, productiveness, efficaciousness

efficiency *noun* 1 EFFECTIVENESS, power, economy, productivity, organization, efficacy, cost-effectiveness, orderliness
2 COMPETENCE, ability, skill, expertise, capability, readiness, professionalism, proficiency, adeptness, skilfulness

efficient *adjective* 1 EFFECTIVE, successful, structured, productive, powerful, systematic, streamlined, cost-effective, methodical, well-organized, well-planned, labour-saving, effectual
<< OPPOSITE inefficient
2 COMPETENT, able, professional, capable, organized, productive, skilful, adept, ready, proficient, businesslike, well-organized, workmanlike
<< OPPOSITE incompetent

effigy *noun* LIKENESS, figure, image, model, guy, carving, representation, statue, icon, idol, dummy, statuette

effluent *noun* WASTE, discharge, flow, emission, sewage, pollutant, outpouring, outflow, exhalation, issue, emanation, liquid waste, efflux, effluvium, effluence

effort *noun* 1 ATTEMPT, try, endeavour, shot (*informal*), bid, essay, go (*informal*), stab (*informal*)
2 EXERTION, work, labour, trouble, force, energy, struggle, stress, application, strain, striving, graft, toil, hard graft, travail (*literary*), elbow grease (*facetious*), blood, sweat, and tears (*informal*)
3 ACHIEVEMENT, act, performance, product, job, production, creation, feat, deed, accomplishment, attainment

effortless *adjective* 1 EASY, simple, flowing, smooth, graceful, painless, uncomplicated, trouble-free, facile, undemanding, easy-peasy (*slang*), untroublesome, unexacting
<< OPPOSITE difficult
2 NATURAL, simple, spontaneous, instinctive, intuitive

effusive *adjective* DEMONSTRATIVE, enthusiastic, lavish, extravagant, overflowing, gushing, exuberant, expansive, ebullient, free-flowing, unrestrained, talkative, fulsome, profuse, unreserved

egg *noun* OVUM, gamete, germ cell
▷▷ **egg someone on** INCITE, push, encourage, urge, prompt, spur, provoke, prod, goad, exhort

egocentric *adjective* SELF-CENTRED, vain, selfish, narcissistic, self-absorbed, egotistical, inward-looking, self-important, self-obsessed, self-seeking, egoistic, egoistical

egotism *or* **egoism** *noun* SELF-CENTREDNESS, self-esteem, vanity, superiority, self-interest, selfishness, narcissism, self-importance, self-regard, self-love, self-seeking, self-absorption, self-obsession, egocentricity, egomania, self-praise, vainglory, self-conceit, self-admiration, conceitedness

ejaculate *verb* 1 HAVE AN ORGASM, climax, emit semen

2 DISCHARGE, release, emit, shoot out, eject, spurt

3 (*Literary*) EXCLAIM, declare, shout, call out, cry out, burst out, blurt out

ejaculation *noun* DISCHARGE, release, emission, ejection

eject *verb* 1 THROW OUT, remove, turn out, expel (*slang*), exile, oust, banish, deport, drive out, evict, boot out (*informal*), force to leave, chuck out (*informal*), bounce, turf out (*informal*), give the bum's rush (*slang*), show someone the door, throw someone out on their ear (*informal*)

2 DISMISS, sack (*informal*), fire (*informal*), remove, get rid of, discharge, expel, throw out, oust, kick out (*informal*), kennet (*Austral slang*), jeff (*Austral slang*)

3 DISCHARGE, expel, emit, give off

4 BAIL OUT, escape, get out

ejection *noun* 1 EXPULSION, removal, ouster (*Law*), deportation, eviction, banishment, exile

2 DISMISSAL, sacking (*informal*), firing (*informal*), removal, discharge, the boot (*slang*), expulsion, the sack (*informal*), dislodgement

3 EMISSION, throwing out, expulsion, spouting, casting out, disgorgement

eke out *verb* BE SPARING WITH, stretch out, be economical with, economize on, husband, be frugal with

▷▷ **eke out a living** SUPPORT YOURSELF, survive, get by, make ends meet, scrimp, save, scrimp and save

elaborate *adjective* 1 COMPLICATED, detailed, studied, laboured, perfected, complex, careful, exact, precise, thorough, intricate, skilful, painstaking

2 ORNATE, detailed, involved, complex, fancy, complicated, decorated, extravagant, intricate, baroque, ornamented, fussy, embellished, showy, ostentatious, florid

<< OPPOSITE plain

▷ *verb* 1 DEVELOP, improve, enhance, polish, complicate, decorate, refine, garnish, ornament, flesh out

2 *usually with* **on** *or* **upon** EXPAND UPON, extend upon, enlarge on, amplify upon, embellish, flesh out, add detail to

<< OPPOSITE simplify

élan *noun* STYLE, spirit, dash, flair, animation, vigour, verve, zest, panache, esprit, brio, vivacity, impetuosity

elapse *verb* PASS, go, go by, lapse, pass by, slip away, roll on, slip by, roll by, glide by

elastic *adjective* 1 FLEXIBLE, yielding, supple, rubbery, pliable, plastic, springy, pliant, tensile, stretchy, ductile, stretchable

<< OPPOSITE rigid

2 ADAPTABLE, yielding, variable, flexible, accommodating, tolerant, adjustable, supple, complaisant

<< OPPOSITE inflexible

elasticity *noun* 1 FLEXIBILITY, suppleness, plasticity, give (*informal*), pliability, ductility, springiness, pliancy, stretchiness, rubberiness

2 ADAPTABILITY, accommodation, flexibility, tolerance, variability, suppleness, complaisance, adjustability, compliantness

elated *adjective* JOYFUL, excited, delighted, proud, cheered, thrilled, elevated, animated, roused, exhilarated, ecstatic, jubilant, joyous, over the moon (*informal*), overjoyed, blissful, euphoric, rapt, gleeful, sent, puffed up, exultant, in high spirits, on cloud nine (*informal*), cock-a-hoop, blissed out, in seventh heaven, floating *or* walking on air, stoked (*Austral & NZ informal*)

<< OPPOSITE dejected

elation *noun* JOY, delight, thrill, excitement, ecstasy, bliss, euphoria, glee, rapture, high spirits, exhilaration, jubilation, exaltation, exultation, joyfulness, joyousness

elbow *noun* JOINT, turn, corner, bend, angle, curve

▷ *verb* PUSH, force, crowd, shoulder, knock, bump, shove, nudge, jostle, hustle

▷▷ **at your elbow** WITHIN REACH, near, to hand, handy, at hand, close by

elder *adjective* OLDER, first, senior, first-born, earlier born

▷ *noun* 1 OLDER PERSON, senior

2 (*Presbyterianism*) CHURCH OFFICIAL, leader, office bearer, presbyter

elect *verb* 1 VOTE FOR, choose, pick, determine, select, appoint, opt for, designate, pick out, settle on, decide upon

2 CHOOSE, decide, prefer, select, opt

▷ *adjective* 1 SELECTED, chosen, picked, choice, preferred, select, elite, hand-picked

2 FUTURE, to-be, coming, next, appointed, designate, prospective

election *noun* 1 VOTE, poll, ballot, determination, referendum, franchise, plebiscite, show of hands

2 APPOINTMENT, choosing, picking, choice, selection

elector *noun* VOTER, chooser, selector, constituent, member of the electorate, member of a constituency, enfranchised person

electric *adjective* 1 ELECTRIC-POWERED,

powered, cordless, battery-operated, electrically-charged, mains-operated
2 CHARGED, exciting, stirring, thrilling, stimulating, dynamic, tense, rousing, electrifying, adrenalized

electrify *verb* 1 THRILL, shock, excite, amaze, stir, stimulate, astonish, startle, arouse, animate, rouse, astound, jolt, fire, galvanize, take your breath away
<< OPPOSITE bore
2 WIRE UP, wire, supply electricity to, convert to electricity

elegance *noun* STYLE, taste, beauty, grace, dignity, sophistication, grandeur, refinement, polish, gentility, sumptuousness, courtliness, gracefulness, tastefulness, exquisiteness

elegant *adjective* 1 STYLISH, fine, beautiful, sophisticated, delicate, artistic, handsome, fashionable, refined, cultivated, chic, luxurious, exquisite, nice, discerning, graceful, polished, sumptuous, genteel, choice, tasteful, urbane, courtly, modish, comely, à la mode, schmick (*Austral informal*)
<< OPPOSITE inelegant
2 INGENIOUS, simple, effective, appropriate, clever, neat, apt

elegiac *adjective* (*Literary*) LAMENTING, sad, melancholy, nostalgic, mournful, plaintive, melancholic, sorrowful, funereal, valedictory, keening, dirgeful, threnodial, threnodic

elegy *noun* LAMENT, requiem, dirge, plaint (*archaic*), threnody, keen, funeral song, coronach (*Scot & Irish*), funeral poem

element *noun* 1 COMPONENT, part, feature, unit, section, factor, principle, aspect, foundation, ingredient, constituent, subdivision
2 GROUP, faction, clique, set, party, circle
3 TRACE, suggestion, hint, dash, suspicion, tinge, smattering, soupçon
▷ *plural noun* WEATHER CONDITIONS, climate, the weather, wind and rain, atmospheric conditions, powers of nature, atmospheric forces
▷▷ **in your element** IN A SITUATION YOU ENJOY, in your natural environment, in familiar surroundings

elemental *adjective* 1 PRIMAL, original, primitive, primordial
2 ATMOSPHERIC, natural, meteorological

elementary *adjective* 1 BASIC, essential, primary, initial, fundamental, introductory, preparatory, rudimentary, elemental, bog-standard (*informal*)
<< OPPOSITE advanced
2 SIMPLE, clear, easy, plain, straightforward, rudimentary, uncomplicated, facile, undemanding, unexacting
<< OPPOSITE complicated

elevate *verb* 1 PROMOTE, raise, advance, upgrade, exalt, kick upstairs (*informal*), aggrandize, give advancement to
2 INCREASE, lift, raise, step up, intensify, move up, hoist, raise high
3 RAISE, lift, heighten, uplift, hoist, lift up, raise up, hike up, upraise
4 CHEER, raise, excite, boost, animate, rouse, uplift, brighten, exhilarate, hearten, lift up, perk up, buoy up, gladden, elate

elevated *adjective* 1 EXALTED, high, important, august, grand, superior, noble, dignified, high-ranking, lofty
2 HIGH-MINDED, high, fine, grand, noble, inflated, dignified, sublime, lofty, high-flown, pompous, exalted, bombastic
<< OPPOSITE humble
3 RAISED, high, lifted up, upraised

elevation *noun* 1 SIDE, back, face, front, aspect
2 ALTITUDE, height
3 PROMOTION, upgrading, advancement, exaltation, preferment, aggrandizement
4 RISE, hill, mountain, height, mound, berg (*S African*), high ground, higher ground, eminence, hillock, rising ground, acclivity

elicit *verb* 1 BRING ABOUT, cause, derive, bring out, evoke, give rise to, draw out, bring forth, bring to light, call forth
2 OBTAIN, extract, exact, evoke, wrest, draw out, extort, educe

eligible *adjective* 1 ENTITLED, fit, qualified, suited, suitable
<< OPPOSITE ineligible
2 AVAILABLE, free, single, unmarried, unattached

eliminate *verb* 1 REMOVE, end, stop, withdraw, get rid of, abolish, cut out, dispose of, terminate, banish, eradicate, put an end to, do away with, dispense with, stamp out, exterminate, get shot of, wipe from the face of the earth
2 KNOCK OUT, drop, reject, exclude, axe (*informal*), get rid of, expel, leave out, throw out, omit, put out, eject
3 (*Slang*) MURDER, kill, do in (*slang*), take out (*slang*), terminate, slay, blow away (*slang, chiefly US*), liquidate, annihilate, exterminate, bump off (*slang*), rub out (*US slang*), waste (*informal*)

elite *noun* ARISTOCRACY, best, pick, elect, cream, upper class, nobility, gentry, high society, crème de la crème (*French*), flower, nonpareil
<< OPPOSITE rabble
▷ *adjective* LEADING, best, finest, pick, choice, selected, elect, crack (*slang*), supreme, exclusive, privileged, first-class, foremost, first-rate, pre-eminent, most excellent

elitist *adjective* SNOBBISH, exclusive, superior, arrogant, selective, pretentious, stuck-up (*informal*), patronizing, condescending, snooty (*informal*), uppity, high and mighty (*informal*), hoity-toity (*informal*), high-hat (*informal, chiefly US*), uppish (*Brit informal*)

elixir *noun* 1 PANACEA, cure-all, nostrum, sovereign remedy
2 SYRUP, essence, solution, concentrate, mixture, extract, potion, distillation, tincture, distillate

elliptical *adjective* OBLIQUE, concentrated, obscure, compact, indirect, ambiguous, concise, condensed, terse, cryptic, laconic, abstruse, recondite

elongate *verb* LENGTHEN, extend, stretch (out), make longer

elongated *adjective* EXTENDED, long, stretched

elope *verb* RUN AWAY, leave, escape, disappear, bolt, run off, slip away, abscond, decamp, sneak off, steal away, do a bunk (*informal*)

eloquence *noun* 1 FLUENCY, effectiveness, oratory, expressiveness, persuasiveness, forcefulness, gracefulness, powerfulness, whaikorero (NZ)
2 EXPRESSIVENESS, significance, meaningfulness, pointedness

eloquent *adjective* 1 SILVER-TONGUED, moving, powerful, effective, stirring, articulate, persuasive, graceful, forceful, fluent, expressive, well-expressed
<< OPPOSITE inarticulate
2 EXPRESSIVE, telling, pointed, revealing, significant, pregnant, vivid, meaningful, indicative, suggestive

elsewhere *adverb* IN *or* TO ANOTHER PLACE, away, abroad, hence (*archaic*), somewhere else, not here, in other places, in *or* to a different place

elucidate *verb* CLARIFY, explain, illustrate, interpret, make clear, unfold, illuminate, spell out, clear up, gloss, expound, make plain, annotate, explicate, shed *or* throw light upon

elude *verb* 1 EVADE, escape, lose, avoid, flee, duck (*informal*), dodge, get away from, shake off, run away from, circumvent, outrun, body-swerve (*Scot*)
2 ESCAPE, baffle, frustrate, puzzle, stump, foil, be beyond (someone), thwart, confound

> *Elude* is sometimes wrongly used where *allude* is meant: *he was alluding* (not *eluding*) *to his previous visit to the city*.

elusive *adjective* 1 DIFFICULT TO CATCH, tricky, slippery, difficult to find, evasive, shifty
2 INDEFINABLE, puzzling, fleeting, subtle, baffling, indefinite, transient, intangible, indescribable, transitory, indistinct

> The spelling of *elusive*, as in *a shy, elusive character*, should be noted. This adjective derives from the verb *elude*, and should not be confused with the rare word *illusive* meaning 'not real' or 'based on illusion'.

emaciated *adjective* SKELETAL, thin, weak, lean, pinched, skinny, wasted, gaunt, bony, haggard, atrophied, scrawny, attenuate, attenuated, undernourished, scraggy, half-starved, cadaverous, macilent (*rare*)

emanate *verb* 1 GIVE OUT, send out, emit, radiate, exude, issue, give off, exhale, send forth
2 *often with* **from** FLOW, emerge, spring, proceed, arise, stem, derive, originate, issue, come forth

emancipate *verb* FREE, release, liberate, set free, deliver, discharge, let out, let loose, untie, unchain, enfranchise, unshackle, disencumber, unfetter, unbridle, disenthral, manumit
<< OPPOSITE enslave

emancipation *noun* LIBERATION, freedom, freeing, release, liberty, discharge, liberating, setting free, letting loose, untying, deliverance, unchaining, manumission, enfranchisement, unshackling, unfettering
<< OPPOSITE slavery

emasculate *verb* WEAKEN, soften, cripple, impoverish, debilitate, reduce the power of, enfeeble, make feeble, enervate, deprive of force

embalm *verb* PRESERVE, lay out, mummify

embargo *noun* BAN, bar, block, barrier, restriction, boycott, restraint, check, prohibition, moratorium, stoppage, impediment, blockage, hindrance, interdiction, interdict, proscription, rahui (NZ)
▷ *verb* BLOCK, stop, bar, ban, restrict, boycott, check, prohibit, impede, blacklist, proscribe, ostracize, debar, interdict

embark *verb* GO ABOARD, climb aboard, board ship, step aboard, go on board, take ship
<< OPPOSITE get off
▷▷ **embark on something** BEGIN, start, launch, enter, engage, take up, set out, undertake, initiate, set about, plunge into, commence, broach

embarrass *verb* SHAME, distress, show up (*informal*), humiliate, disconcert, chagrin, fluster, mortify, faze, discomfit, make uncomfortable, make awkward, discountenance, nonplus, abash, discompose, make ashamed, put out of countenance

embarrassed *adjective* ASHAMED, upset, shamed, uncomfortable, shown-up, awkward, abashed, humiliated, uneasy, unsettled, self-conscious, thrown, disconcerted, red-faced, chagrined, flustered, mortified, sheepish, discomfited, discountenanced, caught with egg on your face, not knowing where to put yourself, put out of countenance

embarrassing *adjective* HUMILIATING, upsetting, compromising, shaming, distressing, delicate, uncomfortable, awkward, tricky, sensitive, troublesome, shameful, disconcerting, touchy, mortifying, discomfiting, toe-curling (*slang*), cringe-making (*Brit informal*), cringeworthy (*Brit informal*), barro (*Austral slang*)

embarrassment *noun* 1 SHAME, distress, showing up (*informal*), humiliation, discomfort, unease, chagrin, self-consciousness, awkwardness, mortification, discomfiture, bashfulness, discomposure
2 PROBLEM, difficulty, nuisance, source of trouble, thorn in your flesh
3 PREDICAMENT, problem, difficulty (*informal*), mess, jam (*informal*), plight, scrape (*informal*), pickle (*informal*)

embed *or* **imbed** *verb often with* **in** FIX, set, plant, root, sink, lodge, insert, implant, drive in, dig in, hammer in, ram in

embellish *verb* 1 DECORATE, enhance, adorn, dress, grace, deck, trim, dress up, enrich, garnish, ornament, gild, festoon, bedeck, tart up (*slang*), beautify
2 ELABORATE, colour, exaggerate, dress up, embroider, varnish

embellishment *noun* 1 DECORATION, garnishing, ornament, gilding, enhancement, enrichment, adornment, ornamentation, trimming, beautification
2 ELABORATION, exaggeration, embroidery

ember *noun usually plural* CINDERS, ashes, residue, live coals

embezzle *verb* MISAPPROPRIATE, steal, appropriate, rob, pocket, nick (*slang, chiefly Brit*), pinch (*informal*), rip off (*slang*), siphon off, pilfer, purloin, filch, help yourself to, thieve, defalcate (*Law*), peculate

embezzlement *noun* MISAPPROPRIATION, stealing, robbing, fraud, pocketing, theft, robbery, nicking (*slang, chiefly Brit*), pinching (*informal*), appropriation, siphoning off, thieving, pilfering, larceny, purloining, filching, pilferage, peculation, defalcation (*Law*)

embittered *adjective* RESENTFUL, angry, acid, bitter, sour, soured, alienated, disillusioned, disaffected, venomous, rancorous, at daggers drawn (*informal*), nursing a grudge, with a chip on your shoulder (*informal*)

emblazon *verb* DECORATE, show, display, present, colour, paint, illuminate, adorn, ornament, embellish, blazon

emblem *noun* 1 CREST, mark, design, image, figure, seal, shield, badge, insignia, coat of arms, heraldic device, sigil (*rare*)
2 REPRESENTATION, symbol, mark, sign, type, token

emblematic *or* **emblematical** *adjective* 1 SYMBOLIC, significant, figurative, allegorical
2 CHARACTERISTIC, representative, typical, symptomatic

embodiment *noun* PERSONIFICATION, example, model, type, ideal, expression, symbol, representation, manifestation, realization, incarnation, paradigm, epitome, incorporation, paragon, perfect example, exemplar, quintessence, actualization, exemplification, reification

embody *verb* 1 PERSONIFY, represent, express, realize, incorporate, stand for, manifest, exemplify, symbolize, typify, incarnate, actualize, reify, concretize
2 *often with* **in** INCORPORATE, include, contain, combine, collect, concentrate, organize, take in, integrate, consolidate, bring together, encompass, comprehend, codify, systematize

embolden *verb* ENCOURAGE, cheer, stir, strengthen, nerve, stimulate, reassure, fire, animate, rouse, inflame, hearten, invigorate, gee up, make brave, give courage, vitalize, inspirit

embrace *verb* 1 HUG, hold, cuddle, seize, squeeze, grasp, clasp, envelop, encircle, enfold, canoodle (*slang*), take *or* hold in your arms
2 ACCEPT, support, receive, welcome, adopt, grab, take up, seize, make use of, espouse, take on board, welcome with open arms, avail yourself of, receive enthusiastically
3 INCLUDE, involve, cover, deal with, contain, take in, incorporate, comprise, enclose, provide for, take into account, embody, encompass, comprehend, subsume
▷ *noun* HUG, hold, cuddle, squeeze, clinch (*slang*), clasp, canoodle (*slang*)

embroil *verb* INVOLVE, complicate, mix up, implicate, entangle, mire, ensnare, encumber, enmesh

embryo *noun* 1 FETUS, unborn child, fertilized egg
2 GERM, beginning, source, root, seed, nucleus, rudiment

embryonic *or* **embryonal** *adjective* RUDIMENTARY, early, beginning, primary, budding, fledgling, immature, seminal, nascent, undeveloped, incipient, inchoate, unformed, germinal
<< OPPOSITE advanced

emerge *verb* 1 COME OUT, appear, come up, surface, rise, proceed, arise, turn up, spring up, emanate, materialize, issue, come into view, come forth, become visible, manifest yourself
<< OPPOSITE withdraw
2 BECOME APPARENT, develop, come out, turn up, become known, come to light, crop up, transpire, materialize, become evident, come out in the wash

emergence *noun* 1 COMING, development, arrival, surfacing, rise, appearance, arising,

turning up, issue, dawn, advent, emanation, materialization
2 DISCLOSURE, publishing, broadcasting, broadcast, publication, declaration, revelation, becoming known, becoming apparent, coming to light, becoming evident

emergency *noun* CRISIS, danger, difficulty, accident, disaster, necessity, pinch, plight, scrape (*informal*), strait, catastrophe, predicament, calamity, extremity, quandary, exigency, critical situation, urgent situation
▷ *adjective* 1 URGENT, crisis, immediate
2 ALTERNATIVE, extra, additional, substitute, replacement, temporary, makeshift, stopgap

emergent *adjective* DEVELOPING, coming, beginning, rising, appearing, budding, burgeoning, fledgling, nascent, incipient

emigrate *verb* MOVE ABROAD, move, relocate, migrate, remove, resettle, leave your country

emigration *noun* DEPARTURE, removal, migration, exodus, relocation, resettlement

eminence *noun* 1 PROMINENCE, reputation, importance, fame, celebrity, distinction, note, esteem, rank, dignity, prestige, superiority, greatness, renown, pre-eminence, repute, notability, illustriousness
2 HIGH GROUND, bank, rise, hill, summit, height, mound, elevation, knoll, hillock, kopje *or* koppie (*S African*)

eminent *adjective* PROMINENT, high, great, important, noted, respected, grand, famous, celebrated, outstanding, distinguished, well-known, superior, esteemed, notable, renowned, prestigious, elevated, paramount, big-time (*informal*), foremost, high-ranking, conspicuous, illustrious, major league (*informal*), exalted, noteworthy, pre-eminent
<< OPPOSITE unknown

emissary *noun* ENVOY, agent, deputy, representative, ambassador, diplomat, delegate, courier, herald, messenger, consul, attaché, go-between, legate

emission *noun* GIVING OFF *or* OUT, release, shedding, leak, radiation, discharge, transmission, venting, issue, diffusion, utterance, ejaculation, outflow, issuance, ejection, exhalation, emanation, exudation

emit *verb* 1 GIVE OFF, release, shed, leak, transmit, discharge, send out, throw out, vent, issue, give out, radiate, eject, pour out, diffuse, emanate, exude, exhale, breathe out, cast out, give vent to, send forth
<< OPPOSITE absorb
2 UTTER, produce, voice, give out, let out

emotion *noun* 1 FEELING, spirit, soul, passion, excitement, sensation, sentiment, agitation, fervour, ardour, vehemence, perturbation
2 INSTINCT, sentiment, sensibility, intuition, tenderness, gut feeling, soft-heartedness

emotional *adjective* 1 PSYCHOLOGICAL, private, personal, hidden, spiritual, inner
2 MOVING, touching, affecting, exciting, stirring, thrilling, sentimental, poignant, emotive, heart-rending, heart-warming, tear-jerking (*informal*)
3 EMOTIVE, sensitive, controversial, delicate, contentious, heated, inflammatory, touchy
4 PASSIONATE, enthusiastic, sentimental, fiery, feeling, susceptible, responsive, ardent, fervent, zealous, temperamental, excitable, demonstrative, hot-blooded, fervid, touchy-feely (*informal*)
<< OPPOSITE dispassionate

Although *emotive* can be used as a synonym of *emotional*, there are differences in meaning that should first be understood. *Emotional* is the more general and neutral word for referring to anything to do with the emotions and emotional states. *Emotive* has the more restricted meaning of 'tending to arouse emotion', and is often associated with issues, subjects, language, and words. However, since *emotional* can also mean 'arousing emotion', with certain nouns it is possible to use either word, depending on the slant one wishes to give: *an emotive/emotional appeal on behalf of the disadvantaged young.*

emotive *adjective* 1 SENSITIVE, controversial, delicate, contentious, inflammatory, touchy
2 MOVING, touching, affecting, emotional, exciting, stirring, thrilling, sentimental, poignant, heart-rending, heart-warming, tear-jerking (*informal*)

empathize ▷▷ **empathize with** IDENTIFY WITH, understand, relate to, feel for, sympathize with, have a rapport with, feel at one with, be on the same wavelength as

emphasis *noun* 1 IMPORTANCE, attention, weight, significance, stress, strength, priority, moment, intensity, insistence, prominence, underscoring, pre-eminence
2 STRESS, accent, accentuation, force, weight

emphasize *verb* 1 HIGHLIGHT, stress, insist, underline, draw attention to, dwell on, underscore, weight, play up, make a point of, give priority to, press home, give prominence to, prioritize
<< OPPOSITE minimize
2 STRESS, accent, accentuate, lay stress on, put the accent on

emphatic *adjective* 1 FORCEFUL, decided, certain, direct, earnest, positive, absolute, distinct, definite, vigorous, energetic,

unmistakable, insistent, unequivocal, vehement, forcible, categorical
<< OPPOSITE hesitant
2 SIGNIFICANT, marked, strong, striking, powerful, telling, storming (*informal*), impressive, pronounced, decisive, resounding, momentous, conclusive
<< OPPOSITE insignificant

empire *noun* 1 KINGDOM, territory, province, federation, commonwealth, realm, domain, imperium (*rare*)
2 ORGANIZATION, company, business, firm, concern, corporation, consortium, syndicate, multinational, conglomeration
>> RELATED WORD *adjective* imperial

empirical *adjective* FIRST-HAND, direct, observed, practical, actual, experimental, pragmatic, factual, experiential
<< OPPOSITE hypothetical

employ *verb* 1 HIRE, commission, appoint, take on, retain, engage, recruit, sign up, enlist, enrol, have on the payroll
2 USE, apply, exercise, exert, make use of, utilize, ply, bring to bear, put to use, bring into play, avail yourself of
3 SPEND, fill, occupy, involve, engage, take up, make use of, use up

employed *adjective* 1 WORKING, in work, having a job, in employment, in a job, earning your living
<< OPPOSITE out of work
2 BUSY, active, occupied, engaged, hard at work, in harness, rushed off your feet
<< OPPOSITE idle

employee *or US* **employe** *noun* WORKER, labourer, workman, staff member, member of staff, hand, wage-earner, white-collar worker, blue-collar worker, hired hand, job-holder, member of the workforce

employer *noun* 1 BOSS (*informal*), manager, head, leader, director, chief, executive, owner, owner, master, chief executive, governor (*informal*), skipper, managing director, administrator, patron, supervisor, superintendent, gaffer (*informal, chiefly Brit*), foreman, proprietor, manageress, overseer, kingpin, honcho (*informal*), big cheese (*slang* or *old-fashioned*), baas (*S African*), numero uno (*informal*), Mister Big (*slang, chiefly US*), sherang (*Austral* & *NZ*)
2 COMPANY, business, firm, organization, establishment, outfit (*informal*)

employment *noun* 1 JOB, work, business, position, trade, post, situation, employ, calling, profession, occupation, pursuit, vocation, métier
2 TAKING ON, commissioning, appointing, hire, hiring, retaining, engaging, appointment, recruiting, engagement, recruitment, enlisting, enrolling, enlistment
3 USE, application, exertion, exercise, utilization

emporium *noun* (*Old-fashioned*) SHOP, market, store, supermarket, outlet, warehouse, department store, mart, boutique, bazaar, retail outlet, superstore, hypermarket

empower *verb* 1 AUTHORIZE, allow, commission, qualify, permit, sanction, entitle, delegate, license, warrant, give power to, give authority to, invest with power
2 ENABLE, equip, emancipate, give means to, enfranchise

emptiness *noun* 1 FUTILITY, banality, worthlessness, hollowness, pointlessness, meaninglessness, barrenness, senselessness, aimlessness, purposelessness, unsatisfactoriness, valuelessness
2 MEANINGLESSNESS, vanity, banality, frivolity, idleness, unreality, silliness, triviality, ineffectiveness, cheapness, insincerity, worthlessness, hollowness, inanity, unsubstantiality, trivialness, vainness
3 VOID, gap, vacuum, empty space, nothingness, blank space, free space, vacuity
4 BARENESS, waste, desolation, destitution, blankness, barrenness, desertedness, vacantness
5 BLANKNESS, vacancy, vacuity, impassivity, vacuousness, expressionlessness, stoniness, unintelligence, absentness, vacantness

empty *adjective* 1 BARE, clear, abandoned, deserted, vacant, free, void, desolate, destitute, uninhabited, unoccupied, waste, unfurnished, untenanted, without contents
<< OPPOSITE full
2 MEANINGLESS, cheap, hollow, vain, idle, trivial, ineffective, futile, insubstantial, insincere
3 WORTHLESS, meaningless, hollow, pointless, unsatisfactory, futile, unreal, senseless, frivolous, fruitless, aimless, inane, valueless, purposeless, otiose, bootless
<< OPPOSITE meaningful
4 BLANK, absent, vacant, stony, deadpan, vacuous, impassive, expressionless, unintelligent
▷ *verb* 1 CLEAR, drain, gut, void, unload, pour out, unpack, unburden, remove the contents of
<< OPPOSITE fill
2 EXHAUST, consume the contents of, void, deplete, use up
<< OPPOSITE replenish
3 EVACUATE, clear, vacate

emulate *verb* IMITATE, follow, copy, mirror, echo, mimic, take after, follow in the footsteps of, follow the example of, take a leaf out of someone's book, model yourself on

emulation *noun* IMITATION, following, copying, mirroring, reproduction, mimicry

enable *verb* 1 ALLOW, permit, facilitate, empower, give someone the opportunity, give someone the means
<< OPPOSITE prevent
2 AUTHORIZE, allow, commission, permit, qualify, sanction, entitle, license, warrant, empower, give someone the right
<< OPPOSITE stop

enact *verb* 1 ESTABLISH, order, pass, command, approve, sanction, proclaim, decree, authorize, ratify, ordain, validate, legislate, make law
2 PERFORM, play, act, present, stage, represent, put on, portray, depict, act out, play the part of, appear as *or* in, personate

enactment *or* **enaction** *noun* 1 PASSING, legislation, sanction, approval, establishment, proclamation, ratification, authorization, validation, making law
2 DECREE, order, law, act, ruling, bill, measure, command, legislation, regulation, resolution, dictate, canon, statute, ordinance, commandment, edict, bylaw
3 PORTRAYAL, staging, performance, playing, acting, performing, representation, depiction, play-acting, personation

enamoured ▷▷ **enamoured with** IN LOVE WITH, taken with, charmed by, fascinated by, entranced by, fond of, enchanted by, captivated by, enthralled by, smitten with, besotted with, bewitched by, crazy about (*informal*), infatuated with, enraptured by, wild about (*informal*), swept off your feet by, nuts on *or* about (*slang*)

encampment *noun* CAMP, base, post, station, quarters, campsite, bivouac, camping ground, cantonment

encapsulate *or* **incapsulate** *verb* SUM UP, digest, summarize, compress, condense, abbreviate, epitomize, abridge, précis

enchant *verb* FASCINATE, delight, charm, entrance, dazzle, captivate, enthral, beguile, bewitch, ravish, mesmerize, hypnotize, cast a spell on, enrapture, enamour, spellbind

enchanting *adjective* DELIGHTFUL, fascinating, appealing, attractive, lovely, charming, entrancing, pleasant, endearing, captivating, alluring, bewitching, ravishing, winsome, Orphean

enchantment *noun* 1 CHARM, fascination, delight, beauty, joy, attraction, bliss, allure, transport, rapture, mesmerism, ravishment, captivation, beguilement, allurement
2 SPELL, magic, charm, witchcraft, voodoo, wizardry, sorcery, occultism, incantation, necromancy, conjuration, makutu (NZ)

encircle *verb* SURROUND, ring, circle, enclose, encompass, compass, envelop, girdle, circumscribe, hem in, enfold, environ, gird in, begird (*poetic*), enwreath

enclose *or* **inclose** *verb* 1 SURROUND, cover, circle, bound, wrap, fence, pound, pen, hedge, confine, close in, encompass, wall in, encircle, encase, fence in, impound, circumscribe, hem in, shut in, environ
2 SEND WITH, include, put in, insert

encompass *verb* 1 INCLUDE, hold, involve, cover, admit, deal with, contain, take in, embrace, incorporate, comprise, embody, comprehend, subsume
2 SURROUND, circle, enclose, close in, envelop, encircle, fence in, ring, girdle, circumscribe, hem in, shut in, environ, enwreath

encounter *verb* 1 EXPERIENCE, meet, face, suffer, have, go through, sustain, endure, undergo, run into, live through
2 MEET, confront, come across, run into (*informal*), bump into (*informal*), run across, come upon, chance upon, meet by chance, happen on *or* upon
3 BATTLE WITH, attack, fight, oppose, engage with, confront, combat, clash with, contend with, strive against, struggle with, grapple with, face off (*slang*), do battle with, cross swords with, come into conflict with, meet head on
▷ *noun* 1 MEETING, brush, confrontation, rendezvous, chance meeting
2 BATTLE, fight, action, conflict, clash, dispute, contest, set-to (*informal*), run-in (*informal*), combat, confrontation, engagement, collision, skirmish, head-to-head, face-off (*slang*)

encourage *verb* 1 INSPIRE, comfort, rally, cheer, stimulate, reassure, animate, console, rouse, hearten, cheer up, embolden, buoy up, pep up, boost someone's morale, give hope to, buck up (*informal*), gee up, lift the spirits of, give confidence to, inspirit
<< OPPOSITE discourage
2 URGE, persuade, prompt, spur, coax, incite, egg on, abet
<< OPPOSITE dissuade
3 PROMOTE, back, help, support, increase, further, aid, forward, advance, favour, boost, strengthen, foster, advocate, stimulate, endorse, commend, succour
<< OPPOSITE prevent

encouragement *noun* 1 INSPIRATION, help, support, aid, favour, comfort, comforting, cheer, cheering, consolation, reassurance, morale boosting, succour
2 URGING, prompting, stimulus, persuasion, coaxing, egging on, incitement
3 PROMOTION, backing, support, boost, endorsement, stimulation, advocacy,

furtherance

encouraging *adjective* PROMISING, good, bright, comforting, cheering, stimulating, reassuring, hopeful, satisfactory, cheerful, favourable, rosy, heartening, auspicious, propitious

<< OPPOSITE discouraging

encroach *verb often with* **on** *or* **upon** INTRUDE, invade, trespass, infringe, usurp, impinge, trench, overstep, make inroads, impose yourself

encroachment *noun* INTRUSION, invasion, violation, infringement, trespass, incursion, usurpation, inroad, impingement

encumber *verb* 1 BURDEN, load, embarrass, saddle, oppress, obstruct, retard, weigh down
2 HAMPER, restrict, handicap, slow down, cramp, inhibit, clog, hinder, inconvenience, overload, impede, weigh down, trammel, incommode

encyclopedic *or* **encyclopaedic** *adjective* COMPREHENSIVE, full, complete, vast, universal, wide-ranging, thorough, in-depth, exhaustive, all-inclusive, all-embracing, all-encompassing, thoroughgoing

end *noun* 1 CLOSE, ending, finish, expiry, expiration

<< OPPOSITE beginning

2 CONCLUSION, ending, climax, completion, finale, culmination, denouement, consummation

<< OPPOSITE start

3 FINISH, close, stop, resolution, conclusion, closure, wind-up, completion, termination, cessation
4 EXTREMITY, limit, edge, border, bound, extent, extreme, margin, boundary, terminus
5 TIP, point, head, peak, extremity
6 PURPOSE, point, reason, goal, design, target, aim, object, mission, intention, objective, drift, intent, aspiration
7 OUTCOME, result, consequence, resolution, conclusion, completion, issue, sequel, end result, attainment, upshot, consummation
8 DEATH, dying, ruin, destruction, passing on, doom, demise, extinction, dissolution, passing away, extermination, annihilation, expiration, ruination
9 REMNANT, butt, bit, stub, scrap, fragment, stump, remainder, leftover, tail end, oddment, tag end
▷ *verb* 1 STOP, finish, complete, resolve, halt, cease, axe (*informal*), dissolve, wind up, terminate, call off, discontinue, put paid to, bring to an end, pull the plug on, call a halt to, nip in the bud, belay (*Nautical*)

<< OPPOSITE start

2 FINISH, close, conclude, wind up, culminate, terminate, come to an end, draw to a close

<< OPPOSITE begin

3 DESTROY, take, kill, abolish, put an end to, do away with, extinguish, annihilate, exterminate, put to death
▷▷ **end up** 1 FINISH UP, stop, wind up, come to a halt, fetch up (*informal*)
2 TURN OUT TO BE, finish as, finish up, pan out as (*informal*), become eventually

>> RELATED WORDS *adjectives* final, terminal, ultimate

endanger *verb* PUT AT RISK, risk, threaten, compromise, hazard, jeopardize, imperil, put in danger, expose to danger

<< OPPOSITE save

endear *verb* ATTRACT, draw, bind, engage, charm, attach, win, incline, captivate

endearing *adjective* ATTRACTIVE, winning, pleasing, appealing, sweet, engaging, charming, pleasant, cute, enticing, captivating, lovable, alluring, adorable, winsome, cutesy (*informal, chiefly US*)

endeavour (*Formal*) *verb* TRY, labour, attempt, aim, struggle, venture, undertake, essay, strive, aspire, have a go, go for it (*informal*), make an effort, have a shot (*informal*), have a crack (*informal*), take pains, bend over backwards (*informal*), do your best, go for broke (*slang*), bust a gut (*informal*), give it your best shot (*informal*), jump through hoops (*informal*), have a stab (*informal*), break your neck (*informal*), make an all-out effort (*informal*), knock yourself out (*informal*), do your damnedest (*informal*), give it your all (*informal*), rupture yourself (*informal*)
▷ *noun* ATTEMPT, try, shot (*informal*), effort, trial, go (*informal*), aim, bid, crack (*informal*), venture, enterprise, undertaking, essay, stab (*informal*)

ended *adjective* FINISHED, done, over, through, closed, past, complete, done with, settled, all over (bar the shouting), no more, concluded, accomplished, wrapped-up (*informal*), at an end, finis

ending *noun* FINISH, end, close, resolution, conclusion, summing up, wind-up, completion, finale, termination, culmination, cessation, denouement, last part, consummation

<< OPPOSITE start

endless *adjective* 1 ETERNAL, constant, infinite, perpetual, continual, immortal, unbroken, unlimited, uninterrupted, limitless, interminable, incessant, boundless, everlasting, unending, ceaseless, inexhaustible, undying, unceasing, unbounded, measureless, unfading

<< OPPOSITE temporary

2 INTERMINABLE, constant, persistent, perpetual, never-ending, incessant, monotonous, overlong
3 CONTINUOUS, unbroken, uninterrupted,

undivided, without end

endorse *or* **indorse** *verb* 1 APPROVE, back, support, champion, favour, promote, recommend, sanction, sustain, advocate, warrant, prescribe, uphold, authorize, ratify, affirm, approve of, subscribe to, espouse, vouch for, throw your weight behind
2 SIGN, initial, countersign, sign on the back of, superscribe, undersign

endorsement *or* **indorsement** *noun* APPROVAL, backing, support, championing, favour, promotion, sanction, recommendation, acceptance, agreement, warrant, confirmation, upholding, subscription, fiat, advocacy, affirmation, ratification, authorization, seal of approval, approbation, espousal, O.K. *or* okay (*informal*)

endow *verb* 1 FINANCE, fund, pay for, award, grant, invest in, confer, settle on, bestow, make over, bequeath, purvey, donate money to
2 IMBUE, steep, bathe, saturate, pervade, instil, infuse, permeate, impregnate, inculcate

endowed *adjective usually with* **with** PROVIDED, favoured, graced, blessed, supplied, furnished, enriched

endowment *noun* 1 PROVISION, fund, funding, award, income, grant, gift, contribution, revenue, subsidy, presentation, donation, legacy, hand-out, boon, bequest, stipend, bestowal, benefaction, largesse *or* largess, koha (NZ)
2 *usually plural* TALENT, power, feature, quality, ability, gift, capacity, characteristic, attribute, qualification, genius, faculty, capability, flair, aptitude

endurance *noun* 1 STAYING POWER, strength, resolution, resignation, determination, patience, submission, stamina, fortitude, persistence, tenacity, perseverance, toleration, sufferance, doggedness, stickability (*informal*), pertinacity
2 PERMANENCE, stability, continuity, duration, continuation, longevity, durability, continuance, immutability, lastingness

endure *verb* 1 EXPERIENCE, suffer, bear, weather, meet, go through, encounter, cope with, sustain, brave, undergo, withstand, live through, thole (*Scot*)
2 PUT UP WITH, stand, suffer, bear, allow, accept, stick (*slang*), take (*informal*), permit, stomach, swallow, brook, tolerate, hack (*slang*), abide, submit to, countenance, stick out (*informal*), take patiently
3 LAST, live, continue, remain, stay, hold, stand, go on, survive, live on, prevail, persist, abide, be durable, wear well

enduring *adjective* LONG-LASTING, lasting, living, continuing, remaining, firm, surviving, permanent, constant, steady, prevailing, persisting, abiding, perennial, durable, immortal, steadfast, unwavering, immovable, imperishable, unfaltering
<< OPPOSITE brief

enemy *noun* FOE, rival, opponent, the opposition, competitor, the other side, adversary, antagonist
<< OPPOSITE friend
>> RELATED WORD *adjective* inimical

energetic *adjective* 1 FORCEFUL, strong, determined, powerful, storming (*informal*), active, aggressive, dynamic, vigorous, potent, hard-hitting, high-powered, strenuous, punchy (*informal*), forcible, high-octane (*informal*)
2 LIVELY, spirited, active, dynamic, vigorous, animated, brisk, tireless, bouncy, indefatigable, alive and kicking, zippy (*informal*), full of beans (*informal*), bright-eyed and bushy-tailed (*informal*)
<< OPPOSITE lethargic
3 STRENUOUS, hard, taxing, demanding, tough, exhausting, vigorous, arduous

energize *or* **energise** *verb* 1 MOTIVATE, stimulate, drive, stir, activate, animate, enthuse, quicken, enliven, galvanize, liven up, pep up, invigorate, vitalize, inspirit
2 STIMULATE, operate, trigger, turn on, start up, activate, switch on, kick-start, electrify, actuate

energy *noun* 1 STRENGTH, might, force, power, activity, intensity, stamina, exertion, forcefulness
2 LIVELINESS, life, drive, fire, spirit, determination, pep, go (*informal*), zip (*informal*), vitality, animation, vigour, verve, zest, resilience, get-up-and-go (*informal*), élan, brio, vivacity, vim (*slang*)
3 POWER

enfold *or* **infold** *verb* 1 WRAP, surround, enclose, wrap up, encompass, shroud, immerse, swathe, envelop, sheathe, enwrap
2 EMBRACE, hold, fold, hug, cuddle, clasp

enforce *verb* 1 CARRY OUT, apply, implement, fulfil, execute, administer, put into effect, put into action, put into operation, put in force
2 IMPOSE, force, require, urge, insist on, compel, exact, oblige, constrain, coerce

enforced *adjective* IMPOSED, required, necessary, compelled, dictated, prescribed, compulsory, mandatory, constrained, ordained, obligatory, unavoidable, involuntary

enforcement *noun* 1 ADMINISTRATION, carrying out, application, prosecution, execution, implementation, reinforcement, fulfilment
2 IMPOSITION, requirement, obligation, insistence, exaction

engage *verb* 1 PARTICIPATE IN, join in, take part in, undertake, practise, embark on, enter into, become involved in, set about, partake of
2 CAPTIVATE, win, draw, catch, arrest, fix, attract, capture, charm, attach, fascinate, enchant, allure, enamour
3 OCCUPY, involve, draw, busy, grip, absorb, tie up, preoccupy, immerse, engross
4 EMPLOY, commission, appoint, take on, hire, retain, recruit, enlist, enrol, put on the payroll
<< OPPOSITE dismiss
5 BOOK, reserve, secure, hire, rent, charter, lease, prearrange
6 INTERLOCK, join, interact, mesh, interconnect, dovetail
7 SET GOING, apply, trigger, activate, switch on, energize, bring into operation
8 (*Military*) BEGIN BATTLE WITH, attack, take on, encounter, combat, fall on, battle with, meet, fight with, assail, face off (*slang*), wage war on, join battle with, give battle to, come to close quarters with

engaged *adjective* 1 OCCUPIED, working, involved, committed, employed, busy, absorbed, tied up, preoccupied, engrossed
2 BETROTHED, promised, pledged, affianced, promised in marriage
<< OPPOSITE unattached
3 IN USE, busy, tied up, unavailable
<< OPPOSITE free

engagement *noun* 1 APPOINTMENT, meeting, interview, date, commitment, arrangement, rendezvous
2 BETROTHAL, marriage contract, troth (*archaic*), agreement to marry
3 BATTLE, fight, conflict, action, struggle, clash, contest, encounter, combat, confrontation, skirmish, face-off (*slang*)
4 PARTICIPATION, joining, taking part, involvement
5 JOB, work, post, situation, commission, employment, appointment, gig (*informal*), stint

engaging *adjective* CHARMING, interesting, pleasing, appealing, attractive, lovely, fascinating, entertaining, winning, pleasant, fetching (*informal*), delightful, cute, enchanting, captivating, agreeable, lovable, winsome, cutesy (*informal, chiefly US*), likable *or* likeable
<< OPPOSITE unpleasant

engender *verb* PRODUCE, make, cause, create, lead to, occasion, excite, result in, breed, generate, provoke, induce, bring about, arouse, give rise to, precipitate, incite, instigate, foment, beget

engine *noun* MACHINE, motor, mechanism, generator, dynamo

engineer *noun* 1 DESIGNER, producer, architect, developer, deviser, creator, planner, inventor, stylist, artificer, originator, couturier
2 WORKER, specialist, operator, practitioner, operative, driver, conductor, technician, handler, skilled employee
▷ *verb* 1 DESIGN, plan, create, construct, devise, originate
2 BRING ABOUT, plan, control, cause, effect, manage, set up (*informal*), scheme, arrange, plot, manoeuvre, encompass, mastermind, orchestrate, contrive, concoct, wangle (*informal*), finagle (*informal*)

engrave *verb* CARVE, cut, etch, inscribe, chisel, incise, chase, enchase (*rare*), grave (*archaic*)

engraved *adjective* FIXED, set, printed, impressed, lodged, embedded, imprinted, etched, ingrained, infixed

engraving *noun* 1 PRINT, block, impression, carving, etching, inscription, plate, woodcut, dry point
2 CUTTING, carving, etching, inscribing, chiselling, inscription, chasing, dry point, enchasing (*rare*)

engrossed *adjective* ABSORBED, lost, involved, occupied, deep, engaged, gripped, fascinated, caught up, intrigued, intent, preoccupied, immersed, riveted, captivated, enthralled, rapt

engrossing *adjective* ABSORBING, interesting, arresting, engaging, gripping, fascinating, compelling, intriguing, riveting, captivating, enthralling

engulf *or* **ingulf** *verb* 1 IMMERSE, bury, flood (out), plunge, consume, drown, swamp, encompass, submerge, overrun, inundate, deluge, envelop, swallow up
2 OVERWHELM, overcome, crush, absorb, swamp, engross

enhance *verb* IMPROVE, better, increase, raise, lift, boost, add to, strengthen, reinforce, swell, intensify, heighten, elevate, magnify, augment, exalt, embellish, ameliorate
<< OPPOSITE reduce

enhancement *noun* IMPROVEMENT, strengthening, heightening, enrichment, increment, embellishment, boost, betterment, augmentation, amelioration

enigma *noun* MYSTERY, problem, puzzle, riddle, paradox, conundrum, teaser

enigmatic *or* **enigmatical** *adjective* MYSTERIOUS, puzzling, obscure, baffling, ambiguous, perplexing, incomprehensible, mystifying, inexplicable, unintelligible, paradoxical, cryptic, inscrutable, unfathomable, indecipherable, recondite, Delphic, oracular, sphinxlike
<< OPPOSITE straightforward

enjoin *verb* 1 ORDER, charge, warn, urge, require, direct, bid, command, advise, counsel, prescribe, instruct, call upon
2 (*Law*) PROHIBIT, bar, ban, forbid, restrain,

preclude, disallow, proscribe, interdict, place an injunction on

enjoy *verb* 1 TAKE PLEASURE IN *or* FROM, like, love, appreciate, relish, delight in, revel in, be pleased with, be fond of, be keen on, rejoice in, be entertained by, find pleasure in, find satisfaction in, take joy in
<< OPPOSITE hate
2 HAVE, use, own, experience, possess, have the benefit of, reap the benefits of, have the use of, be blessed *or* favoured with
▷▷ **enjoy yourself** HAVE A GOOD TIME, be happy, have fun, have a field day (*informal*), have a ball (*informal*), live life to the full, make merry, let your hair down

enjoyable *adjective* PLEASURABLE, good, great, fine, pleasing, nice, satisfying, lovely, entertaining, pleasant, amusing, delicious, delightful, gratifying, agreeable, delectable, to your liking
<< OPPOSITE unpleasant

enjoyment *noun* 1 PLEASURE, liking, fun, delight, entertainment, joy, satisfaction, happiness, relish, recreation, amusement, indulgence, diversion, zest, gratification, gusto, gladness, delectation, beer and skittles (*informal*)
2 BENEFIT, use, advantage, favour, possession, blessing

enlarge *verb* 1 EXPAND, increase, extend, add to, build up, widen, intensify, blow up (*informal*), heighten, broaden, inflate, lengthen, magnify, amplify, augment, make bigger, elongate, make larger
<< OPPOSITE reduce
2 GROW, increase, extend, stretch, expand, swell, wax, multiply, inflate, lengthen, diffuse, elongate, dilate, become bigger, puff up, grow larger, grow bigger, become larger, distend, bloat
▷▷ **enlarge on something** EXPAND ON, develop, add to, fill out, elaborate on, flesh out, expatiate on, give further details about

enlighten *verb* INFORM, tell, teach, advise, counsel, educate, instruct, illuminate, make aware, edify, apprise, let know, cause to understand

enlightened *adjective* INFORMED, aware, liberal, reasonable, educated, sophisticated, refined, cultivated, open-minded, knowledgeable, literate, broad-minded
<< OPPOSITE ignorant

enlightenment *noun* UNDERSTANDING, information, learning, education, teaching, knowledge, instruction, awareness, wisdom, insight, literacy, sophistication, comprehension, cultivation, refinement, open-mindedness, edification, broad-mindedness

enlist *verb* 1 JOIN UP, join, enter (into), register, volunteer, sign up, enrol
2 OBTAIN, get, gain, secure, engage, procure

enliven *verb* CHEER UP, excite, inspire, cheer, spark, enhance, stimulate, wake up, animate, fire, rouse, brighten, exhilarate, quicken, hearten, perk up, liven up, buoy up, pep up, invigorate, gladden, vitalize, vivify, inspirit, make more exciting, make more lively
<< OPPOSITE subdue

en masse *adverb* ALL TOGETHER, together, as one, as a whole, ensemble, as a group, in a group, all at once, in a mass, as a body, in a body

enmity *noun* HOSTILITY, hate, spite, hatred, bitterness, friction, malice, animosity, aversion, venom, antagonism, antipathy, acrimony, rancour, bad blood, ill will, animus, malevolence, malignity
<< OPPOSITE friendship

ennoble *verb* 1 DIGNIFY, honour, enhance, elevate, magnify, raise, glorify, exalt, aggrandize
2 RAISE TO THE PEERAGE, kick upstairs (*informal*), make noble

ennui *noun* (*Literary*) BOREDOM, dissatisfaction, tiredness, the doldrums, lethargy, tedium, lassitude, listlessness

enormity *noun* 1 (*informal*) HUGENESS, extent, magnitude, greatness, vastness, immensity, massiveness, enormousness, extensiveness
2 WICKEDNESS, disgrace, atrocity, depravity, viciousness, villainy, turpitude, outrageousness, baseness, vileness, evilness, monstrousness, heinousness, nefariousness, atrociousness
3 ATROCITY, crime, horror, evil, outrage, disgrace, monstrosity, abomination, barbarity, villainy

enormous *adjective* HUGE, massive, vast, extensive, tremendous, gross, excessive, immense, titanic, jumbo (*informal*), gigantic, monstrous, mammoth, colossal, mountainous, stellar (*informal*), prodigious, gargantuan, elephantine, astronomic, ginormous (*informal*), Brobdingnagian, humongous *or* humungous (*US slang*)
<< OPPOSITE tiny

enough *adjective* SUFFICIENT, adequate, ample, abundant, as much as you need, as much as is necessary
▷ *pronoun* SUFFICIENCY, plenty, sufficient, abundance, adequacy, right amount, ample supply
▷ *adverb* SUFFICIENTLY, amply, fairly, moderately, reasonably, adequately, satisfactorily, abundantly, tolerably, passably

enquire ▷ see **inquire**

enquiry ▷ see **inquiry**

enrage *verb* ANGER, provoke, irritate, infuriate, aggravate (*informal*), incense, gall, madden, inflame, exasperate, incite, antagonize, make you angry, nark (*Brit, Austral & NZ slang*), make your blood boil, get your back up, make you see red (*informal*), put your back up
<< OPPOSITE calm
enraged *adjective* FURIOUS, cross, wild, angry, angered, mad (*informal*), raging, irritated, fuming, choked, infuriated, aggravated (*informal*), incensed, inflamed, exasperated, very angry, irate, livid (*informal*), incandescent, on the warpath, fit to be tied (*slang*), boiling mad, raging mad, tooshie (*Austral slang*), off the air (*Austral slang*)
enraptured *adjective* ENCHANTED, delighted, charmed, fascinated, absorbed, entranced, captivated, transported, enthralled, beguiled, bewitched, ravished, spellbound, enamoured
enrich *verb* 1 ENHANCE, develop, improve, boost, supplement, refine, cultivate, heighten, endow, augment, ameliorate, aggrandize
2 MAKE RICH, make wealthy, make affluent, make prosperous, make well-off
enrol *or US* **enroll** *verb* 1 ENLIST, register, be accepted, be admitted, join up, matriculate, put your name down for, sign up *or* on
2 RECRUIT, take on, engage, enlist
enrolment *or US* **enrollment** *noun* ENLISTMENT, admission, acceptance, engagement, registration, recruitment, matriculation, signing on *or* up
en route *adverb* ON *or* ALONG THE WAY, travelling, on the road, in transit, on the journey
ensemble *noun* 1 GROUP, company, band, troupe, cast, orchestra, chorus, supporting cast
2 COLLECTION, set, body, whole, total, sum, combination, entity, aggregate, entirety, totality, assemblage, conglomeration
3 OUTFIT, suit, get-up (*informal*), costume
enshrine *verb* PRESERVE, protect, treasure, cherish, revere, exalt, consecrate, embalm, sanctify, hallow, apotheosize
ensign *noun* FLAG, standard, colours, banner, badge, pennant, streamer, jack, pennon
enslave *verb* SUBJUGATE, bind, dominate, trap, suppress, enthral, yoke, tyrannize, sell into slavery, reduce to slavery, enchain
ensnare *verb* TRAP, catch, capture, seize, snarl, embroil, net, snare, entangle, entrap, enmesh
ensue *verb* FOLLOW, result, develop, succeed, proceed, arise, stem, derive, come after, issue, befall, flow, come next, come to pass (*archaic*), supervene, be consequent on, turn out *or* up
<< OPPOSITE come first
ensure *or especially US* **insure** *verb* 1 MAKE CERTAIN, guarantee, secure, make sure, confirm, warrant, certify
2 PROTECT, defend, secure, safeguard, guard, make safe
entail *verb* INVOLVE, require, cause, produce, demand, lead to, call for, occasion, need, impose, result in, bring about, give rise to, encompass, necessitate
entangle *verb* 1 TANGLE, catch, trap, twist, knot, mat, mix up, snag, snarl, snare, jumble, ravel, trammel, enmesh
<< OPPOSITE disentangle
2 EMBROIL, involve, complicate, mix up, muddle, implicate, bog down, enmesh
entanglement *noun* BECOMING ENTANGLED, mix-up, becoming enmeshed, becoming ensnared, becoming jumbled, entrapment, snarl-up (*informal, chiefly Brit*), ensnarement
enter *verb* 1 COME *or* GO IN *or* INTO, arrive, set foot in somewhere, cross the threshold of somewhere, make an entrance
<< OPPOSITE exit
2 PENETRATE, get in, insert into, pierce, pass into, perforate
3 JOIN, start work at, begin work at, sign up for, enrol in, become a member of, enlist in, commit yourself to
<< OPPOSITE leave
4 PARTICIPATE IN, join (in), be involved in, get involved in, play a part in, partake in, associate yourself with, start to be in
5 BEGIN, start, take up, move into, set about, commence, set out on, embark upon
6 COMPETE IN, contest, take part in, join in, fight, sign up for, go in for
7 RECORD, note, register, log, list, write down, take down, inscribe, set down, put in writing
8 SUBMIT, offer, present, table, register, lodge, tender, put forward, proffer
enterprise *noun* 1 FIRM, company, business, concern, operation, organization, establishment, commercial undertaking
2 VENTURE, operation, project, adventure, undertaking, programme, pursuit, endeavour
3 INITIATIVE, energy, spirit, resource, daring, enthusiasm, push (*informal*), imagination, drive, pep, readiness, vigour, zeal, ingenuity, originality, eagerness, audacity, boldness, get-up-and-go (*informal*), alertness, resourcefulness, gumption (*informal*), adventurousness, imaginativeness
enterprising *adjective* RESOURCEFUL, original, spirited, keen, active, daring, alert, eager, bold, enthusiastic, vigorous, imaginative, energetic, adventurous, ingenious, up-and-coming, audacious, zealous, intrepid, venturesome
entertain *verb* 1 AMUSE, interest, please, delight, occupy, charm, enthral, cheer, divert, recreate (*rare*), regale, give pleasure to
2 SHOW HOSPITALITY TO, receive, accommodate, treat, put up, lodge, be host to, have company

of, invite round, ask round, invite to a meal, ask for a meal
3 CONSIDER, support, maintain, imagine, think about, hold, foster, harbour, contemplate, conceive of, ponder, cherish, bear in mind, keep in mind, think over, muse over, give thought to, cogitate on, allow yourself to consider

entertaining *adjective* ENJOYABLE, interesting, pleasing, funny, charming, cheering, pleasant, amusing, diverting, delightful, witty, humorous, pleasurable, recreative (*rare*)

entertainment *noun* 1 ENJOYMENT, fun, pleasure, leisure, satisfaction, relaxation, recreation, enjoyment, distraction, amusement, diversion
2 PASTIME, show, sport, performance, play, treat, presentation, leisure activity, beer and skittles

enthral *or US* **enthrall** *verb* ENGROSS, charm, grip, fascinate, absorb, entrance, intrigue, enchant, rivet, captivate, beguile, ravish, mesmerize, hypnotize, enrapture, hold spellbound, spellbind

enthralling *adjective* ENGROSSING, charming, gripping, fascinating, entrancing, compelling, intriguing, compulsive, enchanting, riveting, captivating, beguiling, mesmerizing, hypnotizing, spellbinding

enthusiasm *noun* 1 KEENNESS, interest, passion, excitement, warmth, motivation, relish, devotion, zeal, zest, fervour, eagerness, ardour, vehemence, earnestness, zing (*informal*), avidity
2 INTEREST, passion, rage, hobby, obsession, craze, fad (*informal*), mania, hobbyhorse

enthusiast *noun* FAN, supporter, lover, follower, addict, freak (*informal*), admirer, buff (*informal*), fanatic, devotee, fiend (*informal*), adherent, zealot, aficionado

enthusiastic *adjective* KEEN, earnest, spirited, committed, excited, devoted, warm, eager, lively, passionate, vigorous, ardent, hearty, exuberant, avid, fervent, zealous, ebullient, vehement, wholehearted, full of beans (*informal*), fervid, keen as mustard, bright-eyed and bushy-tailed (*informal*)
<< OPPOSITE apathetic

entice *verb* LURE, attract, invite, persuade, draw, tempt, induce, seduce, lead on, coax, beguile, allure, cajole, decoy, wheedle, prevail on, inveigle, dangle a carrot in front of

enticing *adjective* ATTRACTIVE, appealing, inviting, charming, fascinating, tempting, intriguing, irresistible, persuasive, seductive, captivating, beguiling, alluring
<< OPPOSITE unattractive

entire *adjective* 1 CONTINUOUS, unified, unbroken, uninterrupted, undivided
2 WHOLE, full, complete, total
3 ABSOLUTE, full, total, utter, outright, thorough, unqualified, unrestricted, undiminished, unmitigated, unreserved
4 INTACT, whole, perfect, unmarked, unbroken, sound, unharmed, undamaged, without a scratch, unmarred

entirely *adverb* 1 COMPLETELY, totally, perfectly, absolutely, fully, altogether, thoroughly, wholly, utterly, every inch, without exception, unreservedly, in every respect, without reservation, lock, stock and barrel
<< OPPOSITE partly
2 ONLY, exclusively, solely

entirety *noun* WHOLE, total, sum, unity, aggregate, totality

entitle *verb* 1 GIVE THE RIGHT TO, allow, enable, permit, sanction, license, qualify for, warrant, authorize, empower, enfranchise, make eligible
2 CALL, name, title, term, style, label, dub, designate, characterize, christen, give the title of, denominate

entity *noun* 1 THING, being, body, individual, object, presence, existence, substance, quantity, creature, organism
2 ESSENTIAL NATURE, being, existence, essence, quintessence, real nature, quiddity (*Philosophy*)

entomb *verb* BURY, inter, lay to rest, sepulchre, place in a tomb, inhume, inurn

entourage *noun* RETINUE, company, following, staff, court, train, suite, escort, cortege

entrails *plural noun* INTESTINES, insides (*informal*), guts, bowels, offal, internal organs, innards (*informal*), vital organs, viscera

entrance[1] *noun* 1 WAY IN, opening, door, approach, access, entry, gate, passage, avenue, doorway, portal, inlet, ingress, means of access
<< OPPOSITE exit
2 APPEARANCE, coming in, entry, arrival, introduction, ingress
<< OPPOSITE exit
3 ADMISSION, access, entry, entrée, admittance, permission to enter, ingress, right of entry

entrance[2] *verb* 1 ENCHANT, delight, charm, absorb, fascinate, dazzle, captivate, transport, enthral, beguile, bewitch, ravish, gladden, enrapture, spellbind
<< OPPOSITE bore
2 MESMERIZE, bewitch, hypnotize, put a spell on, cast a spell on, put in a trance

entrant *noun* 1 NEWCOMER, novice, initiate, beginner, trainee, apprentice, convert, new member, fresher, neophyte, tyro, probationer
2 COMPETITOR, player, candidate, entry, participant, applicant, contender, contestant

entrap *noun* TRICK, lure, seduce, entice, deceive, implicate, lead on, embroil, beguile,

allure, entangle, ensnare, inveigle, set a trap for, enmesh
▷ *verb* CATCH, net, capture, trap, snare, entangle, ensnare

entreaty *noun* PLEA, appeal, suit, request, prayer, petition, exhortation, solicitation, supplication, importunity, earnest request

entrench *or* **intrench** *verb* FIX, set, establish, plant, seat, settle, root, install, lodge, anchor, implant, embed, dig in, ensconce, ingrain

entrenched *or* **intrenched** *adjective* FIXED, set, firm, rooted, well-established, ingrained, deep-seated, deep-rooted, indelible, unshakeable *or* unshakable, ineradicable

entrepreneur *noun* BUSINESSMAN *or* BUSINESSWOMAN, tycoon, director, executive, contractor, industrialist, financier, speculator, magnate, impresario, business executive

entrust *or* **intrust** *verb* 1 GIVE CUSTODY OF, trust, deliver, commit, delegate, hand over, turn over, confide, commend, consign
2 *usually with* **with** ASSIGN, charge, trust, invest, authorize

entry *noun* 1 ADMISSION, access, entrance, admittance, entrée, permission to enter, right of entry
2 COMING IN, entering, appearance, arrival, entrance
<< OPPOSITE exit
3 INTRODUCTION, presentation, initiation, inauguration, induction, debut, investiture
4 RECORD, listing, account, note, minute, statement, item, registration, memo, memorandum, jotting
5 COMPETITOR, player, attempt, effort, candidate, participant, challenger, submission, entrant, contestant
6 WAY IN, opening, door, approach, access, gate, passage, entrance, avenue, doorway, portal, inlet, passageway, ingress, means of access

entwine *or* **intwine** *verb* TWIST, surround, embrace, weave, knit, braid, encircle, wind, intertwine, interweave, plait, twine, ravel, interlace, entwist (*archaic*)
<< OPPOSITE disentangle

enumerate *verb* 1 LIST, tell, name, detail, relate, mention, quote, cite, specify, spell out, recount, recite, itemize, recapitulate
2 COUNT, calculate, sum up, total, reckon, compute, add up, tally, number

enunciate *verb* 1 PRONOUNCE, say, speak, voice, sound, utter, articulate, vocalize, enounce (*formal*)
2 STATE, declare, proclaim, pronounce, publish, promulgate, propound

envelop *verb* ENCLOSE, cover, hide, surround, wrap around, embrace, blanket, conceal, obscure, veil, encompass, engulf, cloak, shroud, swathe, encircle, encase, swaddle, sheathe, enfold, enwrap

envelope *noun* WRAPPING, casing, case, covering, cover, skin, shell, coating, jacket, sleeve, sheath, wrapper

enviable *adjective* DESIRABLE, favoured, privileged, fortunate, lucky, blessed, advantageous, to die for (*informal*), much to be desired, covetable
<< OPPOSITE undesirable

envious *adjective* COVETOUS, jealous, grudging, malicious, resentful, green-eyed, begrudging, spiteful, jaundiced, green with envy

environment *noun* 1 SURROUNDINGS, setting, conditions, situation, medium, scene, circumstances, territory, background, atmosphere, context, habitat, domain, milieu, locale
2 (*Ecology*) HABITAT, home, surroundings, territory, terrain, locality, natural home

environmental *adjective* ECOLOGICAL, green

environmentalist *noun* CONSERVATIONIST, ecologist, green, friend of the earth

environs *plural noun* SURROUNDING AREA, surroundings, district, suburbs, neighbourhood, outskirts, precincts, vicinity, locality, purlieus

envisage *verb* 1 IMAGINE, contemplate, conceive (of), visualize, picture, fancy, think up, conceptualize
2 FORESEE, see, expect, predict, anticipate, envision

envision *verb* CONCEIVE OF, expect, imagine, predict, anticipate, see, contemplate, envisage, foresee, visualize

envoy *noun* 1 AMBASSADOR, minister, diplomat, emissary, legate, plenipotentiary
2 MESSENGER, agent, deputy, representative, delegate, courier, intermediary, emissary

envy *noun* COVETOUSNESS, spite, hatred, resentment, jealousy, bitterness, malice, ill will, malignity, resentfulness, enviousness (*informal*)
▷ *verb* 1 BE JEALOUS (OF), resent, begrudge, be envious (of)
2 COVET, desire, crave, aspire to, yearn for, hanker after

ephemeral *adjective* TRANSIENT, short, passing, brief, temporary, fleeting, short-lived, fugitive, flitting, momentary, transitory, evanescent, impermanent, fugacious
<< OPPOSITE eternal

epidemic *adjective* WIDESPREAD, wide-ranging, general, sweeping, prevailing, rampant, prevalent, rife, pandemic
▷ *noun* 1 OUTBREAK, plague, growth, spread, scourge, contagion
2 SPATE, plague, outbreak, wave, rash, eruption, upsurge

epilogue *noun* CONCLUSION, postscript, coda, afterword, concluding speech
<< OPPOSITE prologue

episode *noun* 1 EVENT, experience, happening, matter, affair, incident, circumstance, adventure, business, occurrence, escapade
2 INSTALMENT, part, act, scene, section, chapter, passage

episodic *or* **episodical** *adjective* 1 IRREGULAR, occasional, sporadic, intermittent
2 RAMBLING, irregular, disconnected, anecdotal, disjointed, wandering, discursive, digressive

epistle *noun* LETTER, note, message, communication, missive

epitaph *noun* 1 COMMEMORATION, elegy, obituary
2 INSCRIPTION, engraving

epithet *noun* NAME, title, description, tag, nickname, designation, appellation, sobriquet, moniker *or* monicker (*slang*), obscenity, blasphemy, swear word, imprecation

epitome *noun* PERSONIFICATION, essence, embodiment, type, representation, norm, archetype, exemplar, typical example, quintessence

epitomize *or* **epitomise** *verb* TYPIFY, represent, illustrate, embody, exemplify, symbolize, personify, incarnate

epoch *noun* ERA, time, age, period, date, aeon

equal *adjective* 1 *often with* **to** *or* **with** IDENTICAL, the same, matched, matching, like, equivalent, uniform, alike, corresponding, tantamount, one and the same, proportionate, commensurate
<< OPPOSITE unequal
2 FAIR, just, impartial, egalitarian, unbiased, even-handed, equable
<< OPPOSITE unfair
3 EVEN, balanced, fifty-fifty (*informal*), evenly matched, evenly balanced, evenly proportioned
<< OPPOSITE uneven
4 *with* **to** CAPABLE OF, adequate for
▷ *noun* MATCH, equivalent, fellow, twin, mate, peer, parallel, counterpart, compeer
▷ *verb* 1 AMOUNT TO, make, come to, total, balance with, agree with, level with, parallel, tie with, equate with, correspond to, be equal to, square with, be tantamount to, equalize, tally with, be level with, be even with
<< OPPOSITE be unequal to
2 BE EQUAL TO, match, reach, rival, come up to, be level with, be even with
3 BE AS GOOD AS, match, compare with, equate with, measure up to, be as great as

equality *noun* 1 FAIRNESS, equal opportunity, equal treatment, egalitarianism, fair treatment, justness
<< OPPOSITE inequality
2 SAMENESS, balance, identity, similarity, correspondence, parity, likeness, uniformity, equivalence, evenness, coequality, equatability
<< OPPOSITE disparity

equalize *or* **equalise** *verb* 1 MAKE EQUAL, match, level, balance, square, equal, smooth, equate, standardize, even out, even up, regularize, make level
2 DRAW LEVEL, level the score, square the score, make the score level

equanimity *noun* COMPOSURE, peace, calm, poise, serenity, tranquillity, coolness, aplomb, calmness, phlegm, steadiness, presence of mind, sang-froid, self-possession, placidity, level-headedness, imperturbability

equate *verb* 1 IDENTIFY, associate, connect, compare, relate, mention in the same breath, think of in connection with, think of together
2 MAKE EQUAL, match, balance, square, even up, equalize

equation *noun* EQUATING, match, agreement, balancing, pairing, comparison, parallel, equality, correspondence, likeness, equivalence, equalization

equestrian *adjective* RIDING, mounted, horse riding

equilibrium *noun* 1 STABILITY, balance, symmetry, steadiness, evenness, equipoise, counterpoise
2 COMPOSURE, calm, stability, poise, serenity, coolness, calmness, equanimity, steadiness, self-possession, collectedness

equip *verb* 1 SUPPLY, provide, stock, dress, outfit, arm, rig, array, furnish, endow, attire, fit out, deck out, kit out, fit up, accoutre
2 PREPARE, qualify, educate, get ready, endow

equipment *noun* APPARATUS, stock, supplies, material, stuff, tackle, gear, tools, provisions, kit, rig, baggage, paraphernalia, accoutrements, appurtenances, equipage

equitable *adjective* EVEN-HANDED, just, right, fair, due, reasonable, proper, honest, impartial, rightful, unbiased, dispassionate, proportionate, unprejudiced, nondiscriminatory

equity *noun* FAIRNESS, justice, integrity, honesty, fair play, righteousness, impartiality, rectitude, reasonableness, even-handedness, fair-mindedness, uprightness, equitableness
<< OPPOSITE unfairness

equivalence *or* **equivalency** *noun* EQUALITY, correspondence, agreement, similarity, identity, parallel, match, parity, conformity, likeness, sameness, parallelism, evenness, synonymy, alikeness, interchangeableness

equivalent *adjective* EQUAL, even, same,

comparable, parallel, identical, alike, corresponding, correspondent, synonymous, of a kind, tantamount, interchangeable, of a piece with, commensurate, homologous
<< OPPOSITE different
▷ *noun* EQUAL, counterpart, correspondent, twin, peer, parallel, match, opposite number

equivocal *adjective* AMBIGUOUS, uncertain, misleading, obscure, suspicious, vague, doubtful, dubious, questionable, ambivalent, indefinite, evasive, oblique, indeterminate, prevaricating, oracular
<< OPPOSITE clear

era *noun* AGE, time, period, stage, date, generation, cycle, epoch, aeon, day *or* days

eradicate *verb* WIPE OUT, eliminate, remove, destroy, get rid of, abolish, erase, excise, extinguish, stamp out, obliterate, uproot, weed out, annihilate, put paid to, root out, efface, exterminate, expunge, extirpate, wipe from the face of the earth

eradication *noun* WIPING OUT, abolition, destruction, elimination, removal, extinction, extermination, annihilation, erasure, obliteration, effacement, extirpation, expunction

erase *verb* 1 DELETE, cancel out, wipe out, remove, eradicate, excise, obliterate, efface, blot out, expunge
2 RUB OUT, remove, wipe out, delete, scratch out

erect *adjective* UPRIGHT, raised, straight, standing, stiff, firm, rigid, vertical, elevated, perpendicular, pricked-up
<< OPPOSITE bent
▷ *verb* 1 BUILD, raise, set up, lift, pitch, mount, stand up, rear, construct, put up, assemble, put together, elevate
<< OPPOSITE demolish
2 FOUND, establish, form, create, set up, institute, organize, put up, initiate

erection *noun* 1 HARD-ON (*slang*), erect penis
2 BUILDING, setting-up, manufacture, construction, assembly, creation, establishment, elevation, fabrication

ergo *conjunction* THEREFORE, so, then, thus, hence, consequently, accordingly, for that reason, in consequence

erode *verb* 1 DISINTEGRATE, crumble, deteriorate, corrode, break up, grind down, waste away, wear down *or* away
2 DESTROY, consume, spoil, crumble, eat away, corrode, break up, grind down, abrade, wear down *or* away
3 WEAKEN, destroy, undermine, diminish, impair, lessen, wear away

erosion *noun* 1 DISINTEGRATION, deterioration, corrosion, corrasion, wearing down *or* away, grinding down
2 DETERIORATION, wearing, undermining, destruction, consumption, weakening, spoiling, attrition, eating away, abrasion, grinding down, wearing down *or* away

erotic *adjective* SEXUAL, sexy (*informal*), crude, explicit, rousing, sensual, seductive, vulgar, stimulating, steamy (*informal*), suggestive, aphrodisiac, voluptuous, carnal, titillating, bawdy, lustful, sexually arousing, erogenous, amatory

err *verb* 1 MAKE A MISTAKE, mistake, go wrong, blunder, slip up (*informal*), misjudge, be incorrect, be inaccurate, miscalculate, go astray, be in error, put your foot in it (*informal*), misapprehend, blot your copybook (*informal*), drop a brick *or* clanger (*informal*)
2 SIN, fall, offend, lapse, trespass, do wrong, deviate, misbehave, go astray, transgress, be out of order, blot your copybook (*informal*)

errand *noun* JOB, charge, commission, message, task, mission

errant *adjective* SINNING, offending, straying, wayward, deviant, erring, aberrant

erratic *adjective* UNPREDICTABLE, variable, unstable, irregular, shifting, eccentric, abnormal, inconsistent, uneven, unreliable, wayward, capricious, desultory, changeable, aberrant, fitful, inconstant
<< OPPOSITE regular

erroneous *adjective* INCORRECT, wrong, mistaken, false, flawed, faulty, inaccurate, untrue, invalid, unfounded, spurious, amiss, unsound, wide of the mark, inexact, fallacious
<< OPPOSITE correct

error *noun* MISTAKE, slip, fault, blunder, flaw, boob (*Brit slang*), delusion, oversight, misconception, fallacy, inaccuracy, howler (*informal*), bloomer (*Brit informal*), boner (*slang*), miscalculation, misapprehension, solecism, erratum, barry *or* Barry Crocker (*Austral slang*)

ersatz *adjective* ARTIFICIAL, substitute, pretend, fake, imitation, synthetic, bogus, simulated, sham, counterfeit, spurious, phoney *or* phony (*informal*)

erstwhile *adjective* FORMER, old, late, previous, once, past, ex (*informal*), one-time, sometime, bygone, quondam

erudite *adjective* LEARNED, lettered, cultured, educated, scholarly, cultivated, knowledgeable, literate, well-educated, well-read
<< OPPOSITE uneducated

erudition *noun* LEARNING, education, knowledge, scholarship, letters, lore, academic knowledge

erupt *verb* 1 EXPLODE, blow up, flare up, emit lava
2 GUSH, burst out, be ejected, burst forth, pour forth, belch forth, spew forth *or* out

3 START, break out, begin, explode, flare up, burst out, boil over
4 (*Medical*) BREAK OUT, appear, flare up

eruption *noun* 1 EXPLOSION, discharge, outburst, venting, ejection
2 FLARE-UP, outbreak, sally
3 (*Medical*) INFLAMMATION, outbreak, rash, flare-up

escalate *verb* 1 GROW, increase, extend, intensify, expand, surge, be increased, mount, heighten
<< OPPOSITE decrease
2 INCREASE, develop, extend, intensify, expand, build up, step up, heighten, enlarge, magnify, amplify
<< OPPOSITE lessen

escalation *noun* INCREASE, rise, build-up, expansion, heightening, developing, acceleration, upsurge, intensification, amplification

escapade *noun* ADVENTURE, fling, stunt, romp, trick, scrape (*informal*), spree, mischief, lark (*informal*), caper, prank, antic

escape *verb* 1 GET AWAY, flee, take off, fly, bolt, skip, slip away, abscond, decamp, hook it (*slang*), do a runner (*slang*), do a bunk (*Brit slang*), fly the coop (*US & Canad informal*), make a break for it, slip through your fingers, skedaddle (*informal*), take a powder (*US & Canad slang*), make your getaway, take it on the lam (*US & Canad slang*), break free *or* out, make *or* effect your escape, run away *or* off, do a Skase (*Austral informal*)
2 AVOID, miss, evade, dodge, shun, elude, duck, steer clear of, circumvent, body-swerve (*Scot*)
3 BE FORGOTTEN BY, be beyond (someone), baffle, elude, puzzle, stump
4 *usually with* **from** LEAK OUT, flow out, drain away, discharge, gush out, emanate, seep out, exude, spurt out, spill out, pour forth
▷ *noun* 1 GETAWAY, break, flight, break-out, bolt, decampment
2 AVOIDANCE, evasion, circumvention, elusion
3 RELAXATION, relief, recreation, distraction, diversion, pastime
4 LEAK, emission, discharge, outpouring, gush, spurt, outflow, leakage, drain, seepage, issue, emanation, efflux, effluence, outpour

eschew *verb* AVOID, give up, abandon, have nothing to do with, shun, elude, renounce, refrain from, forgo, abstain from, fight shy of, forswear, abjure, kick (*informal*), swear off, give a wide berth to, keep *or* steer clear of

escort *noun* 1 GUARD, protection, safeguard, bodyguard, company, train, convoy, entourage, retinue, cortege
2 COMPANION, partner, attendant, guide, squire (*rare*), protector, beau, chaperon
▷ *verb* ACCOMPANY, lead, partner, conduct, guide, guard, shepherd, convoy, usher, squire, hold (someone's) hand, chaperon

esoteric *adjective* OBSCURE, private, secret, hidden, inner, mysterious, mystical, mystic, occult, arcane, cryptic, inscrutable, abstruse, recondite, cabbalistic

especially *adverb* 1 NOTABLY, largely, chiefly, mainly, mostly, principally, strikingly, conspicuously, outstandingly
2 VERY, specially, particularly, signally, extremely, remarkably, unusually, exceptionally, extraordinarily, markedly, supremely, uncommonly
3 PARTICULARLY, expressly, exclusively, precisely, specifically, uniquely, peculiarly, singularly

espionage *noun* SPYING, intelligence, surveillance, counter-intelligence, undercover work

espouse *verb* SUPPORT, back, champion, promote, maintain, defend, adopt, take up, advocate, embrace, uphold, stand up for

espy *verb* CATCH SIGHT OF, see, discover, spot, notice, sight, observe, spy, perceive, detect, glimpse, make out, discern, behold, catch a glimpse of, descry

essay *noun* 1 COMPOSITION, study, paper, article, piece, assignment, discourse, tract, treatise, dissertation, disquisition
2 (*Formal*) ATTEMPT, go (*informal*), try, effort, shot (*informal*), trial, struggle, bid, test, experiment, crack (*informal*), venture, undertaking, stab (*informal*), endeavour, exertion
▷ *verb* (*Formal*) ATTEMPT, try, test, take on, undertake, strive for, endeavour, have a go at, try out, have a shot at (*informal*), have a crack at (*informal*), have a bash at (*informal*)

essence *noun* 1 FUNDAMENTAL NATURE, nature, being, life, meaning, heart, spirit, principle, soul, core, substance, significance, entity, bottom line, essential part, kernel, crux, lifeblood, pith, quintessence, basic characteristic, quiddity
2 CONCENTRATE, spirits, extract, elixir, tincture, distillate
▷▷ **in essence** ESSENTIALLY, materially, virtually, basically, fundamentally, in effect, substantially, in the main, to all intents and purposes, in substance
▷▷ **of the essence** VITALLY IMPORTANT, essential, vital, critical, crucial, key, indispensable, of the utmost importance

essential *adjective* 1 VITAL, important, needed, necessary, critical, crucial, key, indispensable, requisite, vitally important, must-have
<< OPPOSITE unimportant
2 FUNDAMENTAL, main, basic, radical, key, principal, constitutional, cardinal, inherent, elementary, innate, intrinsic, elemental,

immanent
<< OPPOSITE secondary
3 CONCENTRATED, extracted, refined, volatile, rectified, distilled
▷ *noun* PREREQUISITE, principle, fundamental, necessity, must, basic, requisite, vital part, sine qua non (*Latin*), rudiment, must-have
establish *verb* 1 SET UP, found, start, create, institute, organize, install, constitute, inaugurate
2 PROVE, show, confirm, demonstrate, ratify, certify, verify, validate, substantiate, corroborate, authenticate
3 SECURE, form, base, ground, plant, settle, fix, root, implant, entrench, ensconce, put down roots
establishment *noun* 1 CREATION, founding, setting up, foundation, institution, organization, formation, installation, inauguration, enactment
2 ORGANIZATION, company, business, firm, house, concern, operation, structure, institution, institute, corporation, enterprise, outfit (*informal*), premises, setup (*informal*)
3 OFFICE, house, building, plant, quarters, factory
Establishment *noun* ▷▷ **the Establishment** THE AUTHORITIES, the system, the powers that be, the ruling class, the established order, institutionalized authority
estate *noun* 1 LANDS, property, area, grounds, domain, manor, holdings, demesne, homestead (*US & Canad*)
2 (*Chiefly Brit*) AREA, centre, park, development, site, zone, plot
3 (*Law*) PROPERTY, capital, assets, fortune, goods, effects, wealth, possessions, belongings
esteem *verb* RESPECT, admire, think highly of, like, love, value, prize, honour, treasure, cherish, revere, reverence, be fond of, venerate, regard highly, take off your hat to
▷ *noun* RESPECT, regard, honour, consideration, admiration, reverence, estimation, veneration
estimate *verb* 1 CALCULATE ROUGHLY, value, guess, judge, reckon, assess, evaluate, gauge, number, appraise
2 THINK, believe, consider, rate, judge, hold, rank, guess, reckon, assess, conjecture, surmise
▷ *noun* 1 APPROXIMATE CALCULATION, guess, reckoning, assessment, judgment, evaluation, valuation, appraisal, educated guess, guesstimate (*informal*), rough calculation, ballpark figure (*informal*), approximate cost, approximate price, ballpark estimate (*informal*), appraisement
2 ASSESSMENT, opinion, belief, appraisal, evaluation, conjecture, appraisement, judgment, estimation, surmise
estimation *noun* 1 OPINION, view, regard, belief, honour, credit, consideration, judgment, esteem, evaluation, admiration, reverence, veneration, good opinion, considered opinion
2 ESTIMATE, reckoning, assessment, appreciation, valuation, appraisal, guesstimate (*informal*), ballpark figure (*informal*)
estrangement *noun* ALIENATION, parting, division, split, withdrawal, break-up, breach, hostility, separation, withholding, disaffection, disunity, dissociation, antagonization
estuary *noun* INLET, mouth, creek, firth, fjord
et cetera *or* **etcetera** *adverb* AND SO ON, and so forth, etc.

The literal meaning of the Latin phrase *et cetera* is 'and other things'. The use of *and* in a list ending with *et cetera*, as in *we bought bread, cheese, butter, and et cetera*, is therefore redundant. Nor is there ever any need to repeat the phrase *et cetera* for emphasis at the end of a list. Such repetition, as in *he bought paper, ink, notebooks, et cetera, et cetera* is very informal and should not be used in writing or formal speaking

etch *verb* 1 ENGRAVE, cut, impress, stamp, carve, imprint, inscribe, furrow, incise, ingrain
2 CORRODE, eat into, burn into
etching *noun* PRINT, impression, carving, engraving, imprint, inscription
eternal *adjective* 1 EVERLASTING, lasting, permanent, enduring, endless, perennial, perpetual, timeless, immortal, unending, unchanging, immutable, indestructible, undying, without end, unceasing, imperishable, deathless, sempiternal (*literary*)
<< OPPOSITE transitory
2 INTERMINABLE, constant, endless, abiding, infinite, continual, immortal, never-ending, everlasting, ceaseless, unremitting, deathless
<< OPPOSITE occasional
eternity *noun* 1 THE AFTERLIFE, heaven, paradise, the next world, the hereafter
2 PERPETUITY, immortality, infinity, timelessness, endlessness, infinitude, time without end
3 AGES, years, an age, centuries, for ever (*informal*), aeons, donkey's years (*informal*), yonks (*informal*), a month of Sundays (*informal*), a long time *or* while, an age *or* eternity
ethereal *adjective* 1 INSUBSTANTIAL, light, fairy, aerial, airy, intangible, rarefied, impalpable
2 SPIRITUAL, heavenly, unearthly, sublime, celestial, unworldly, empyreal
ethical *adjective* 1 MORAL, behavioural

2 RIGHT, morally right, morally acceptable, good, just, fitting, fair, responsible, principled, correct, decent, proper, upright, honourable, honest, righteous, virtuous
<< OPPOSITE unethical

ethics *plural noun* MORAL CODE, standards, principles, morals, conscience, morality, moral values, moral principles, moral philosophy, rules of conduct, moral beliefs, tikanga (*NZ*)

ethnic *or* **ethnical** *adjective* CULTURAL, national, traditional, native, folk, racial, genetic, indigenous

ethos *noun* SPIRIT, character, attitude, beliefs, ethic, tenor, disposition

etiquette *noun* GOOD *or* PROPER BEHAVIOUR, manners, rules, code, customs, convention, courtesy, usage, protocol, formalities, propriety, politeness, good manners, decorum, civility, politesse, p's and q's, polite behaviour, kawa (*NZ*), tikanga (*NZ*)

eulogy *noun* PRAISE, tribute, acclaim, compliment, applause, accolade, paean, commendation, exaltation, glorification, acclamation, panegyric, encomium, plaudit, laudation

euphoria *noun* ELATION, joy, ecstasy, bliss, glee, rapture, high spirits, exhilaration, jubilation, intoxication, transport, exaltation, joyousness
<< OPPOSITE despondency

evacuate *verb* 1 REMOVE, clear, withdraw, expel, move out, send to a safe place
2 ABANDON, leave, clear, desert, quit, depart (from), withdraw from, pull out of, move out of, relinquish, vacate, forsake, decamp from

evacuation *noun* 1 REMOVAL, departure, withdrawal, clearance, flight, expulsion, exodus
2 ABANDONMENT, withdrawal from, pulling out, moving out, clearance from, vacation from

evade *verb* 1 AVOID, escape, dodge, get away from, shun, elude, eschew, steer clear of, sidestep, circumvent, duck, shirk, slip through the net of, escape the clutches of, body-swerve (*Scot*)
<< OPPOSITE face
2 AVOID ANSWERING, parry, circumvent, fend off, balk, cop out of (*slang*), fence, fudge, hedge, prevaricate, flannel (*Brit informal*), beat about the bush about, equivocate

evaluate *verb* ASSESS, rate, value, judge, estimate, rank, reckon, weigh, calculate, gauge, weigh up, appraise, size up (*informal*), assay

evaluation *noun* ASSESSMENT, rating, judgment, calculation, valuation, appraisal, estimation

evangelical (*Christianity*) *adjective* CRUSADING, converting, missionary, zealous, revivalist, proselytizing, propagandizing

evaporate *verb* 1 DISAPPEAR, vaporize, dematerialize, evanesce, melt, vanish, dissolve, disperse, dry up, dispel, dissipate, fade away, melt away
2 DRY UP, dry, dehydrate, vaporize, desiccate
3 FADE AWAY, disappear, fade, melt, vanish, dissolve, disperse, dissipate, melt away

evaporation *noun* 1 VAPORIZATION, vanishing, disappearance, dispelling, dissolution, fading away, melting away, dispersal, dissipation, evanescence, dematerialization
2 DRYING UP, drying, dehydration, desiccation, vaporization

evasion *noun* 1 AVOIDANCE, escape, dodging, shirking, cop-out (*slang*), circumvention, elusion
2 DECEPTION, shuffling, cunning, fudging, pretext, ruse, artifice, trickery, subterfuge, equivocation, prevarication, sophistry, evasiveness, obliqueness, sophism

evasive *adjective* 1 DECEPTIVE, misleading, indirect, cunning, slippery, tricky, shuffling, devious, oblique, shifty, cagey (*informal*), deceitful, dissembling, prevaricating, equivocating, sophistical, casuistic, casuistical
<< OPPOSITE straightforward
2 AVOIDING, escaping, circumventing

eve *noun* 1 NIGHT BEFORE, day before, vigil
2 BRINK, point, edge, verge, threshold

even *adjective* 1 REGULAR, stable, constant, steady, smooth, uniform, unbroken, uninterrupted, unwavering, unvarying, metrical
<< OPPOSITE variable
2 LEVEL, straight, flat, plane, smooth, true, steady, uniform, parallel, flush, horizontal, plumb
<< OPPOSITE uneven
3 EQUAL, like, the same, matching, similar, uniform, parallel, identical, comparable, commensurate, coequal
<< OPPOSITE unequal
4 EQUALLY MATCHED, level, tied, drawn, on a par, neck and neck, fifty-fifty (*informal*), equalized, all square, equally balanced
<< OPPOSITE ill-matched
5 SQUARE, quits, on the same level, on an equal footing
6 CALM, stable, steady, composed, peaceful, serene, cool, tranquil, well-balanced, placid, undisturbed, unruffled, imperturbable, equable, even-tempered, unexcitable, equanimous
<< OPPOSITE excitable
7 FAIR, just, balanced, equitable, impartial, disinterested, unbiased, dispassionate, fair

and square, unprejudiced
<< OPPOSITE unfair
▷ *adverb* 1 DESPITE, in spite of, disregarding, notwithstanding, in spite of the fact that, regardless of the fact that
2 ALL THE MORE, much, still, yet, to a greater extent, to a greater degree
▷▷ **even as** WHILE, just as, whilst, at the time that, at the same time as, exactly as, during the time that
▷▷ **even so** NEVERTHELESS, still, however, yet, despite that, in spite of (that), nonetheless, all the same, notwithstanding that, be that as it may
▷▷ **even something out** MAKE *or* BECOME LEVEL, align, level, square, smooth, steady, flatten, stabilize, balance out, regularize
▷▷ **even something up** EQUALIZE, match, balance, equal
▷▷ **get even (with)** (*informal*) PAY BACK, repay, reciprocate, even the score, requite, get your own back, settle the score, take vengeance, take an eye for an eye, be revenged *or* revenge yourself, give tit for tat, pay (someone) back in their own coin, return like for like

even-handed *adjective* FAIR, just, balanced, equitable, impartial, disinterested, unbiased, fair and square, unprejudiced

evening *noun* DUSK (*archaic*), night, sunset, twilight, sundown, eve, vesper (*archaic*), eventide (*archaic* or *poetic*), gloaming (*Scot poetic*), e'en (*archaic* or *poetic*), close of day, crepuscule, even, evo (*Austral slang*)

event *noun* 1 INCIDENT, happening, experience, matter, affair, occasion, proceeding, fact, business, circumstance, episode, adventure, milestone, occurrence, escapade
2 COMPETITION, game, tournament, contest, bout
▷▷ **in any event** *or* **at all events** WHATEVER HAPPENS, regardless, in any case, no matter what, at any rate, come what may
▷▷ **in the event of** IN THE EVENTUALITY OF, in the situation of, in the likelihood of

eventful *adjective* EXCITING, active, busy, dramatic, remarkable, historic, full, lively, memorable, notable, momentous, fateful, noteworthy, consequential
<< OPPOSITE dull

eventual *adjective* FINAL, later, resulting, future, overall, concluding, ultimate, prospective, ensuing, consequent

eventuality *noun* POSSIBILITY, event, likelihood, probability, case, chance, contingency

eventually *adverb* IN THE END, finally, one day, after all, some time, ultimately, at the end of the day, in the long run, sooner or later, some day, when all is said and done, in the fullness of time, in the course of time

ever *adverb* 1 AT ANY TIME, at all, in any case, at any point, by any chance, on any occasion, at any period
2 ALWAYS, for ever, at all times, relentlessly, eternally, evermore, unceasingly, to the end of time, everlastingly, unendingly, aye (*Scot*)
3 CONSTANTLY, continually, endlessly, perpetually, incessantly, unceasingly, unendingly

everlasting *adjective* 1 ETERNAL, endless, abiding, infinite, perpetual, timeless, immortal, never-ending, indestructible, undying, imperishable, deathless
<< OPPOSITE transitory
2 CONTINUAL, constant, endless, continuous, never-ending, interminable, incessant, ceaseless, unremitting, unceasing

every *adjective* EACH, each and every, every single

everybody *pronoun* EVERYONE, each one, the whole world, each person, every person, all and sundry, one and all ▷ see **everyone**

everyday *adjective* 1 DAILY, day-to-day, diurnal, quotidian
<< OPPOSITE occasional
2 ORDINARY, common, usual, familiar, conventional, routine, dull, stock, accustomed, customary, commonplace, mundane, vanilla (*slang*), banal, habitual, run-of-the-mill, unimaginative, workaday, unexceptional, bog-standard (*Brit & Irish slang*), common or garden (*informal*), dime-a-dozen (*informal*), wonted
<< OPPOSITE unusual

everyone *pronoun* EVERYBODY, each one, the whole world, each person, every person, all and sundry, one and all

> *Everyone* and *everybody* are interchangeable, and can be used as synonyms of each other in any context. Care should be taken, however, to distinguish between *everyone* as a single word and *every one* as two words, the latter form correctly being used to refer to each individual person or thing in a particular group: *every one of them is wrong*

everything *pronoun* ALL, the whole, the total, the lot, the sum, the whole lot, the aggregate, the entirety, each thing, the whole caboodle (*informal*), the whole kit and caboodle (*informal*)

everywhere *adverb* 1 ALL OVER, all around, the world over, high and low, in each place, in every nook and cranny, far and wide *or* near, to *or* in every place
2 ALL AROUND, all over, in each place, in every nook and cranny, ubiquitously, far and wide *or* near, to *or* in every place

evict *verb* EXPEL, remove, turn out, put out, throw out, oust, kick out (*informal*), eject, dislodge, boot out (*informal*), force to leave, dispossess, chuck out (*informal*), show the door (to), turf out (*informal*), throw on to the streets

eviction *noun* EXPULSION, removal, clearance, ouster (*Law*), ejection, dispossession, dislodgement

evidence *noun* **1** PROOF, grounds, data, demonstration, confirmation, verification, corroboration, authentication, substantiation
2 SIGN(s), mark, suggestion, trace, indication, token, manifestation
3 (*Law*) TESTIMONY, statement, witness, declaration, submission, affirmation, deposition, avowal, attestation, averment
▷ *verb* SHOW, prove, reveal, display, indicate, witness, demonstrate, exhibit, manifest, signify, denote, testify to, evince

evident *adjective* OBVIOUS, clear, plain, apparent, visible, patent, manifest, tangible, noticeable, blatant, conspicuous, unmistakable, palpable, salient, indisputable, perceptible, incontrovertible, incontestable, plain as the nose on your face
<< OPPOSITE hidden

evidently *adverb* **1** OBVIOUSLY, clearly, plainly, patently, undoubtedly, manifestly, doubtless, without question, unmistakably, indisputably, doubtlessly, incontrovertibly, incontestably
2 APPARENTLY, it seems, seemingly, outwardly, it would seem, ostensibly, so it seems, to all appearances

evil *adjective* **1** WICKED, bad, wrong, corrupt, vicious, vile, malicious, base, immoral, malignant, sinful, unholy, malevolent, heinous, depraved, villainous, nefarious, iniquitous, reprobate, maleficent
2 HARMFUL, painful, disastrous, destructive, dire, catastrophic, mischievous, detrimental, hurtful, woeful, pernicious, ruinous, sorrowful, deleterious, injurious, baneful (*archaic*)
3 DEMONIC, satanic, diabolical, hellish, devilish, infernal, fiendish
4 OFFENSIVE, nasty, foul, unpleasant, vile, noxious, disagreeable, putrid, pestilential, mephitic
5 UNFORTUNATE, unlucky, unfavourable, ruinous, calamitous, inauspicious
▷ *noun* **1** WICKEDNESS, bad, wrong, vice, corruption, sin, wrongdoing, depravity, immorality, iniquity, badness, viciousness, villainy, sinfulness, turpitude, baseness, malignity, heinousness, maleficence
2 HARM, suffering, pain, hurt, misery, sorrow, woe
3 ACT OF CRUELTY, crime, ill, horror, outrage, cruelty, brutality, misfortune, mischief, affliction, monstrosity, abomination, barbarity, villainy

evince *verb* (*Formal*) SHOW, evidence, reveal, establish, express, display, indicate, demonstrate, exhibit, make clear, manifest, signify, attest, bespeak, betoken, make evident

evoke *verb* **1** AROUSE, cause, excite, stimulate, induce, awaken, give rise to, stir up, rekindle, summon up
<< OPPOSITE suppress
2 PROVOKE, produce, elicit, call to mind, call forth, educe (*rare*)

evolution *noun* **1** (*Biology*) RISE, development, adaptation, natural selection, Darwinism, survival of the fittest, evolvement
2 DEVELOPMENT, growth, advance, progress, working out, expansion, extension, unfolding, progression, enlargement, maturation, unrolling

evolve *verb* **1** DEVELOP, metamorphose, adapt yourself
2 GROW, develop, advance, progress, mature
3 WORK OUT, develop, progress, expand, elaborate, unfold, enlarge, unroll

exacerbate *verb* IRRITATE, excite, provoke, infuriate, aggravate (*informal*), enrage, madden, inflame, exasperate, vex, embitter, add insult to injury, fan the flames of, envenom

exact *adjective* **1** ACCURATE, very, correct, true, particular, right, express, specific, careful, precise, identical, authentic, faithful, explicit, definite, literal, unequivocal, faultless, on the money (*US*), unerring, veracious
<< OPPOSITE approximate
2 METICULOUS, severe, careful, strict, exacting, precise, rigorous, painstaking, scrupulous, methodical, orderly, punctilious
▷ *verb* **1** DEMAND, claim, require, call for, force, impose, command, squeeze, extract, compel, wring, wrest, insist upon, extort
2 INFLICT, apply, impose, administer, mete out, deal out

exacting *adjective* **1** DEMANDING, hard, taxing, difficult, tough, painstaking
<< OPPOSITE easy
2 STRICT, severe, harsh, stern, rigid, rigorous, stringent, oppressive, imperious, unsparing

exactly *adverb* **1** ACCURATELY, correctly, definitely, truly, precisely, strictly, literally, faithfully, explicitly, rigorously, unequivocally, scrupulously, truthfully, methodically, unerringly, faultlessly, veraciously
2 PRECISELY, just, expressly, prompt (*informal*), specifically, bang on (*informal*), to the letter, on the button (*informal*)
▷ *sentence substitute* PRECISELY, yes, quite, of course, certainly, indeed, truly, that's right,

absolutely, spot-on (*Brit informal*), just so, quite so, ya (*S African*), as you say, you got it (*informal*), assuredly, yebo (*S African informal*)
▷▷ **not exactly** (*Ironical*) NOT AT ALL, hardly, not really, not quite, certainly not, by no means, in no way, not by any means, in no manner

exaggerate *verb* OVERSTATE, emphasize, enlarge, inflate, embroider, magnify, overdo, amplify, exalt, embellish, overestimate, overemphasize, pile it on about (*informal*), blow up out of all proportion, lay it on thick about (*informal*), lay it on with a trowel about (*informal*), make a production (out) of (*informal*), make a federal case of (*US informal*), hyperbolize

exaggerated *adjective* OVERSTATED, extreme, excessive, over the top (*informal*), inflated, extravagant, overdone, tall (*informal*), amplified, hyped, pretentious, exalted, overestimated, overblown, fulsome, hyperbolic, highly coloured, O.T.T. (*slang*)

exaggeration *noun* OVERSTATEMENT, inflation, emphasis, excess, enlargement, pretension, extravagance, hyperbole, magnification, amplification, embellishment, exaltation, pretentiousness, overemphasis, overestimation
<< OPPOSITE understatement

exalt *verb* **1** PRAISE, acclaim, applaud, pay tribute to, bless, worship, magnify (*archaic*), glorify, reverence, laud, extol, crack up (*informal*), pay homage to, idolize, apotheosize, set on a pedestal
2 UPLIFT, raise, lift, excite, delight, inspire, thrill, stimulate, arouse, heighten, elevate, animate, exhilarate, electrify, fire the imagination of, fill with joy, elate, inspirit

exaltation *noun* **1** ELATION, delight, joy, excitement, inspiration, ecstasy, stimulation, bliss, transport, animation, elevation, rapture, exhilaration, jubilation, exultation, joyousness
2 PRAISE, tribute, worship, acclaim, applause, glory, blessing, homage, reverence, magnification, apotheosis, glorification, acclamation, panegyric, idolization, extolment, lionization, laudation

exalted *adjective* **1** HIGH-RANKING, high, grand, honoured, intellectual, noble, prestigious, august, elevated, eminent, dignified, lofty
2 NOBLE, ideal, superior, elevated, intellectual, uplifting, sublime, lofty, high-minded
3 ELATED, excited, inspired, stimulated, elevated, animated, uplifted, transported, exhilarated, ecstatic, jubilant, joyous, joyful, over the moon (*informal*), blissful, rapturous, exultant, in high spirits, on cloud nine (*informal*), cock-a-hoop, in seventh heaven, inspirited, stoked (*Austral & NZ informal*)

examination *noun* **1** (*Medical*) CHECKUP, analysis, going-over (*informal*), exploration, health check, check, medical, once-over (*informal*)
2 EXAM, test, research, paper, investigation, practical, assessment, quiz, evaluation, oral, appraisal, catechism

examine *verb* **1** INSPECT, test, consider, study, check, research, review, survey, investigate, explore, probe, analyse, scan, vet, check out, ponder, look over, look at, sift through, work over, pore over, appraise, scrutinize, peruse, take stock of, assay, recce (*slang*), look at carefully, go over *or* through
2 (*Medical*) CHECK, analyse, check over
3 (*Education*) TEST, question, assess, quiz, evaluate, appraise, catechize
4 (*Law*) QUESTION, quiz, interrogate, cross-examine, grill (*informal*), give the third degree to (*informal*)

example *noun* **1** INSTANCE, specimen, case, sample, illustration, case in point, particular case, particular instance, typical case, exemplification, representative case
2 ILLUSTRATION, model, ideal, standard, norm, precedent, pattern, prototype, paradigm, archetype, paragon, exemplar
3 WARNING, lesson, caution, deterrent, admonition
▷▷ **for example** AS AN ILLUSTRATION, like, such as, for instance, to illustrate, by way of illustration, exempli gratia (*Latin*), e.g., to cite an instance

exasperate *verb* IRRITATE, anger, provoke, annoy, rouse, infuriate, hassle (*informal*), exacerbate, aggravate (*informal*), incense, enrage, gall, madden, inflame, bug (*informal*), nettle, get to (*informal*), vex, embitter, irk, rile (*informal*), pique, rankle, peeve (*informal*), needle (*informal*), get on your nerves (*informal*), try the patience of, nark (*Brit, Austral & NZ slang*), get in your hair (*informal*), get on your wick (*Brit slang*), hack you off (*informal*)
<< OPPOSITE calm

exasperating *adjective* IRRITATING, provoking, annoying, infuriating, aggravating (*informal*), galling, maddening, vexing, irksome, enough to drive you up the wall (*informal*), enough to try the patience of a saint

exasperation *noun* IRRITATION, anger, rage, fury, wrath, provocation, passion, annoyance, ire (*literary*), pique, aggravation (*informal*), vexation, exacerbation

excavate *verb* **1** DIG UP, mine, dig, tunnel, scoop, cut, hollow, trench, burrow, quarry, delve, gouge
2 UNEARTH, expose, uncover, dig out, exhume, lay bare, bring to light, bring to the surface, disinter

excavation *noun* HOLE, mine, pit, ditch, shaft,

cutting, cut, hollow, trench, burrow, quarry, dig, trough, cavity, dugout, diggings

exceed *verb* 1 SURPASS, better, pass, eclipse, beat, cap (*informal*), top, be over, be more than, overtake, go beyond, excel, transcend, be greater than, outstrip, outdo, outreach, be larger than, outshine, surmount, be superior to, outrun, run rings around (*informal*), outdistance, knock spots off (*informal*), put in the shade (*informal*)
2 GO OVER THE LIMIT OF, go beyond, overstep, go beyond the bounds of

exceeding *adjective* EXTRAORDINARY, great, huge, vast, enormous, superior, excessive, exceptional, surpassing, superlative, pre-eminent, streets ahead

exceedingly *adverb* EXTREMELY, very, highly, greatly, especially, hugely, seriously (*informal*), vastly, unusually, enormously, exceptionally, extraordinarily, excessively, superlatively, inordinately, to a fault, to the nth degree, surpassingly

excel *verb* BE SUPERIOR TO, better, pass, eclipse, beat, top, cap (*informal*), exceed, go beyond, surpass, transcend, outdo, outshine, surmount, run rings around (*informal*), put in the shade (*informal*), outrival
▷▷ **excel in** *or* **at something** BE GOOD AT, be master of, predominate in, shine at, be proficient in, show talent in, be skilful at, have (something) down to a fine art, be talented at

excellence *noun* HIGH QUALITY, worth, merit, distinction, virtue, goodness, perfection, superiority, purity, greatness, supremacy, eminence, virtuosity, transcendence, pre-eminence, fineness

excellent *adjective* OUTSTANDING, good, great, fine, prime, capital, noted, choice, champion, cool (*informal*), select, brilliant, very good, cracking (*Brit informal*), crucial (*slang*), mean (*slang*), superb, distinguished, fantastic, magnificent, superior, sterling, worthy, first-class, marvellous, exceptional, terrific, splendid, notable, mega (*slang*), topping (*Brit slang*), sovereign, dope (*slang*), world-class, exquisite, admirable, exemplary, wicked (*slang*), first-rate, def (*slang*), superlative, top-notch (*informal*), brill (*informal*), pre-eminent, meritorious, estimable, tiptop, bodacious (*slang, chiefly US*), boffo (*slang*), jim-dandy (*slang*), A1 *or* A-one (*informal*), bitchin' (*US slang*), chillin' (*US slang*), booshit (*Austral slang*), exo (*Austral slang*), sik (*Austral slang*), rad (*informal*), phat (*slang*), schmick (*Austral informal*)
<< OPPOSITE terrible

except *preposition often with* **for** APART FROM, but for, saving, bar, barring, excepting, other than, excluding, omitting, with the exception of, aside from, save (*archaic*), not counting, exclusive of
▷ *verb* EXCLUDE, rule out, leave out, omit, disregard, pass over

exception *noun* SPECIAL CASE, departure, freak, anomaly, inconsistency, deviation, quirk, oddity, peculiarity, irregularity
▷▷ **take exception** *usually with* **to** OBJECT TO, disagree with, take offence at, take umbrage at, be resentful of, be offended at, demur at, quibble at

exceptional *adjective* 1 REMARKABLE, special, excellent, extraordinary, outstanding, superior, first-class, marvellous, notable, phenomenal, first-rate, prodigious, unsurpassed, one in a million, bodacious (*slang, chiefly US*), unexcelled
<< OPPOSITE average
2 UNUSUAL, special, odd, strange, rare, extraordinary, unprecedented, peculiar, abnormal, irregular, uncommon, inconsistent, singular, deviant, anomalous, atypical, aberrant
<< OPPOSITE ordinary

excerpt *noun* EXTRACT, part, piece, section, selection, passage, portion, fragment, quotation, citation, pericope
▷ *verb* EXTRACT, take, select, quote, cite, pick out, cull

excess *noun* 1 SURFEIT, surplus, overdose, overflow, overload, plethora, glut, overabundance, superabundance, superfluity
<< OPPOSITE shortage
2 OVERINDULGENCE, extravagance, profligacy, debauchery, dissipation, intemperance, indulgence, prodigality, extreme behaviour, immoral behaviour, dissoluteness, immoderation, exorbitance, unrestraint
<< OPPOSITE moderation
▷ *adjective* SPARE, remaining, extra, additional, surplus, unwanted, redundant, residual, leftover, superfluous, unneeded

excessive *adjective* 1 IMMODERATE, too much, enormous, extreme, exaggerated, over the top (*slang*), extravagant, needless, unreasonable, disproportionate, undue, uncontrolled, superfluous, prodigal, unrestrained, profligate, inordinate, fulsome, intemperate, unconscionable, overmuch, O.T.T. (*slang*)
2 INORDINATE, unfair, unreasonable, disproportionate, undue, unwarranted, exorbitant, over the odds, extortionate, immoderate

exchange *verb* INTERCHANGE, change, trade, switch, swap, truck, barter, reciprocate, bandy, give to each other, give to one another
▷ *noun* 1 CONVERSATION, talk, word, discussion, chat, dialogue, natter, powwow
2 INTERCHANGE, dealing, trade, switch, swap, traffic, trafficking, truck, swapping,

substitution, barter, bartering, reciprocity, tit for tat, quid pro quo
3 MARKET, money market, Bourse

excise[1] *noun* TAX, duty, customs, toll, levy, tariff, surcharge, impost

excise[2] *verb* 1 DELETE, cut, remove, erase, destroy, eradicate, strike out, exterminate, cross out, expunge, extirpate, wipe from the face of the earth
2 CUT OFF *or* OUT *or* AWAY, remove, take out, extract

excitable *adjective* NERVOUS, emotional, violent, sensitive, tense, passionate, volatile, hasty, edgy, temperamental, touchy, mercurial, uptight (*informal*), irascible, testy, hot-headed, chippy (*informal*), hot-tempered, quick-tempered, highly strung, adrenalized
<< OPPOSITE calm

excite *verb* 1 THRILL, inspire, stir, stimulate, provoke, awaken, animate, move, fire, rouse, exhilarate, agitate, quicken, inflame, enliven, galvanize, foment
2 AROUSE, stimulate, provoke, evoke, rouse, stir up, fire, elicit, work up, incite, instigate, whet, kindle, waken
3 TITILLATE, thrill, stimulate, turn on (*slang*), arouse, get going (*informal*), electrify

excited *adjective* 1 THRILLED, stirred, stimulated, enthusiastic, high (*informal*), moved, wild, aroused, awakened, animated, roused, tumultuous, aflame
2 AGITATED, worried, stressed, alarmed, nervous, disturbed, tense, flurried, worked up, feverish, overwrought, hot and bothered (*informal*), discomposed, adrenalized

excitement *noun* 1 EXHILARATION, action, activity, passion, heat, thrill, adventure, enthusiasm, fever, warmth, flurry, animation, furore, ferment, agitation, commotion, elation, ado, tumult, perturbation, discomposure
2 PLEASURE, thrill, sensation, stimulation, tingle, kick (*informal*)

exciting *adjective* 1 STIMULATING, inspiring, dramatic, gripping, stirring, thrilling, moving, sensational, rousing, exhilarating, electrifying, intoxicating, rip-roaring (*informal*)
<< OPPOSITE boring
2 TITILLATING, stimulating, sexy (*informal*), arousing, erotic, provocative

exclaim *verb* CRY OUT, call, declare, cry, shout, proclaim, yell, utter, call out, ejaculate, vociferate

exclamation *noun* CRY, call, shout, yell, outcry, utterance, ejaculation, expletive, interjection, vociferation

exclude *verb* 1 KEEP OUT, bar, ban, veto, refuse, forbid, boycott, embargo, prohibit, disallow, shut out, proscribe, black, refuse to admit, ostracize, debar, blackball, interdict, prevent from entering
<< OPPOSITE let in
2 OMIT, reject, eliminate, rule out, miss out, leave out, preclude, repudiate
<< OPPOSITE include
3 ELIMINATE, reject, ignore, rule out, except, leave out, set aside, omit, pass over, not count, repudiate, count out

exclusion *noun* 1 BAN, bar, veto, refusal, boycott, embargo, prohibition, disqualification, interdict, proscription, debarment, preclusion, forbiddance, nonadmission
2 ELIMINATION, exception, missing out, rejection, leaving out, omission, repudiation

exclusive *adjective* 1 SELECT, fashionable, stylish, private, limited, choice, narrow, closed, restricted, elegant, posh (*informal, chiefly Brit*), chic, selfish, classy (*slang*), restrictive, aristocratic, high-class, swish (*informal, chiefly Brit*), up-market, snobbish, top-drawer, ritzy (*slang*), high-toned, clannish, discriminative, cliquish
<< OPPOSITE unrestricted
2 SOLE, only, full, whole, single, private, complete, total, entire, unique, absolute, undivided, unshared
<< OPPOSITE shared
3 ENTIRE, full, whole, complete, total, absolute, undivided
4 LIMITED, unique, restricted, confined, peculiar
▷▷ **exclusive of** EXCEPT FOR, excepting, excluding, ruling out, not including, omitting, not counting, leaving aside, debarring

excommunicate *verb* (*RC Church*) EXPEL, ban, remove, exclude, denounce, banish, eject, repudiate, proscribe, cast out, unchurch, anathematize

excrement *noun* FAECES, dung, stool, droppings, motion, mess (*especially of a domestic animal*), defecation, excreta, ordure, kak (*S African taboo slang*), night soil

excrete *verb* DEFECATE, discharge, expel, evacuate, eliminate, void, eject, exude, egest

excruciating *adjective* AGONIZING, acute, severe, extreme, burning, violent, intense, piercing, racking, searing, tormenting, exquisite, harrowing, unbearable, insufferable, torturous, unendurable

excursion *noun* TRIP, airing, tour, journey, outing, expedition, ramble, day trip, jaunt, pleasure trip

excuse *verb* 1 JUSTIFY, explain, defend, vindicate, condone, mitigate, apologize for, make excuses for
<< OPPOSITE blame
2 FORGIVE, pardon, overlook, tolerate,

indulge, acquit, pass over, turn a blind eye to, exonerate, absolve, bear with, wink at, make allowances for, extenuate, exculpate
3 FREE, relieve, liberate, exempt, release, spare, discharge, let off, absolve
<< OPPOSITE convict
▷ *noun* 1 JUSTIFICATION, reason, explanation, defence, grounds, plea, apology, pretext, vindication, mitigation, mitigating circumstances, extenuation
<< OPPOSITE accusation
2 PRETEXT, evasion, pretence, cover-up, expedient, get-out, cop-out (*slang*), subterfuge
3 (*informal*) POOR SUBSTITUTE, apology, mockery, travesty

execute *verb* 1 PUT TO DEATH, kill, shoot, hang, behead, decapitate, guillotine, electrocute
2 CARRY OUT, effect, finish, complete, achieve, realize, do, implement, fulfil, enforce, accomplish, render, discharge, administer, prosecute, enact, consummate, put into effect, bring off
3 PERFORM, do, carry out, accomplish

execution *noun* 1 KILLING, hanging, the death penalty, the rope, capital punishment, beheading, the electric chair, the guillotine, the noose, the scaffold, electrocution, decapitation, the firing squad, necktie party (*informal*)
2 CARRYING OUT, performance, operation, administration, achievement, effect, prosecution, rendering, discharge, enforcement, implementation, completion, accomplishment, realization, enactment, bringing off, consummation
3 PERFORMANCE, style, delivery, manner, technique, mode, presentation, rendition

executioner *noun* HANGMAN, firing squad, headsman, public executioner, Jack Ketch

executive *noun* 1 ADMINISTRATOR, official, director, manager, chairman, managing director, controller, chief executive officer, senior manager, chairwoman, chairperson
2 ADMINISTRATION, government, directors, management, leadership, hierarchy, directorate
▷ *adjective* ADMINISTRATIVE, controlling, directing, governing, regulating, decision-making, managerial

exemplar *noun* 1 MODEL, example, standard, ideal, criterion, paradigm, epitome, paragon
2 EXAMPLE, instance, illustration, type, specimen, prototype, typical example, representative example, exemplification

exemplary *adjective* 1 IDEAL, good, fine, model, excellent, sterling, admirable, honourable, commendable, laudable, praiseworthy, meritorious, estimable, punctilious
2 TYPICAL, representative, characteristic, illustrative
3 WARNING, harsh, cautionary, admonitory, monitory

exemplify *verb* SHOW, represent, display, demonstrate, instance, illustrate, exhibit, depict, manifest, evidence, embody, serve as an example of

exempt *verb* GRANT IMMUNITY, free, except, excuse, release, spare, relieve, discharge, liberate, let off, exonerate, absolve
▷ *adjective* IMMUNE, free, excepted, excused, released, spared, clear, discharged, liberated, not subject to, absolved, not liable to
<< OPPOSITE liable

exemption *noun* IMMUNITY, freedom, privilege, relief, exception, discharge, release, dispensation, absolution, exoneration

exercise *verb* 1 PUT TO USE, use, apply, employ, practise, exert, enjoy, wield, utilize, bring to bear, avail yourself of
2 TRAIN, work out, practise, drill, keep fit, inure, do exercises
3 WORRY, concern, occupy, try, trouble, pain, disturb, burden, distress, preoccupy, agitate, perplex, vex, perturb
▷ *noun* 1 USE, practice, application, operation, employment, discharge, implementation, enjoyment, accomplishment, fulfilment, exertion, utilization
2 EXERTION, training, activity, action, work, labour, effort, movement, discipline, toil, physical activity
3 (*Military*) MANOEUVRE, campaign, operation, movement, deployment
4 TASK, problem, lesson, assignment, work, schooling, practice, schoolwork

exert *verb* APPLY, use, exercise, employ, wield, make use of, utilize, expend, bring to bear, put forth, bring into play
▷▷ **exert yourself** MAKE AN EFFORT, work, labour, struggle, strain, strive, endeavour, go for it (*informal*), try hard, toil, bend over backwards (*informal*), do your best, go for broke (*slang*), bust a gut (*informal*), spare no effort, make a great effort, give it your best shot (*informal*), break your neck (*informal*), apply yourself, put yourself out, make an all-out effort (*informal*), get your finger out (*Brit informal*), pull your finger out (*Brit informal*), knock yourself out (*informal*), do your damnedest (*informal*), give it your all (*informal*), rupture yourself (*informal*)

exertion *noun* 1 EFFORT, action, exercise, struggle, industry, labour, trial, pains, stretch, strain, endeavour, toil, travail (*literary*), elbow grease (*facetious*)
2 USE, exercise, application, employment, bringing to bear, utilization

exhale *verb* GIVE OFF, emit, steam, discharge,

send out, evaporate, issue, eject, emanate

exhaust *verb* 1 TIRE OUT, tire, fatigue, drain, disable, weaken, cripple, weary, sap, wear out, debilitate, prostrate, enfeeble, make tired, enervate
2 USE UP, spend, finish, consume, waste, go through, run through, deplete, squander, dissipate, expend

exhausted *adjective* 1 WORN OUT, tired out, drained, spent, beat (*slang*), bushed (*informal*), dead (*informal*), wasted, done in (*informal*), weak, all in (*slang*), disabled, crippled, fatigued, wiped out (*informal*), sapped, debilitated, jaded, knackered (*slang*), prostrated, clapped out (*Brit, Austral & NZ informal*), effete, enfeebled, enervated, ready to drop, dog-tired (*informal*), zonked (*slang*), dead tired, dead beat (*informal*), shagged out (*Brit slang*), fagged out (*informal*), worn to a frazzle (*informal*), on your last legs (*informal*), creamcrackered (*Brit slang*), out on your feet (*informal*)
<< OPPOSITE invigorated
2 USED UP, consumed, spent, finished, gone, depleted, dissipated, expended, at an end
<< OPPOSITE replenished

exhausting *adjective* TIRING, hard, testing, taxing, difficult, draining, punishing, crippling, fatiguing, wearying, gruelling, sapping, debilitating, strenuous, arduous, laborious, enervating, backbreaking

exhaustion *noun* 1 TIREDNESS, fatigue, weariness, lassitude, feebleness, prostration, debilitation, enervation
2 DEPLETION, emptying, consumption, using up

exhaustive *adjective* THOROUGH, detailed, complete, full, total, sweeping, comprehensive, extensive, intensive, full-scale, in-depth, far-reaching, all-inclusive, all-embracing, encyclopedic, thoroughgoing
<< OPPOSITE superficial

exhibit *verb* 1 SHOW, reveal, display, demonstrate, air, evidence, express, indicate, disclose, manifest, evince, make clear *or* plain
2 DISPLAY, show, present, set out, parade, unveil, flaunt, put on view
▷ *noun* OBJECT, piece, model, article, illustration

exhibition *noun* 1 SHOW, display, exhibit, showing, fair, representation, presentation, spectacle, showcase, expo (*informal*), exposition
2 DISPLAY, show, performance, demonstration, airing, revelation, manifestation

exhilarate *verb* EXCITE, delight, cheer, thrill, stimulate, animate, exalt, lift, enliven, invigorate, gladden, elate, inspirit, pep *or* perk up

exhilarating *adjective* EXCITING, thrilling, stimulating, breathtaking, cheering, exalting, enlivening, invigorating, gladdening, vitalizing, exhilarant

exhilaration *noun* EXCITEMENT, delight, joy, happiness, animation, high spirits, elation, mirth, gaiety, hilarity, exaltation, cheerfulness, vivacity, liveliness, gladness, joyfulness, sprightliness, gleefulness
<< OPPOSITE depression

exhort *verb* (*Formal*) URGE, warn, encourage, advise, bid, persuade, prompt, spur, press, counsel, caution, call upon, incite, goad, admonish, enjoin, beseech, entreat

exhortation *noun* (*Formal*) URGING, warning, advice, counsel, lecture, caution, bidding, encouragement, sermon, persuasion, goading, incitement, admonition, beseeching, entreaty, clarion call, enjoinder (*rare*)

exhume *verb* DIG UP, unearth, disinter, unbury, disentomb
<< OPPOSITE bury

exile *noun* 1 BANISHMENT, expulsion, deportation, eviction, separation, ostracism, proscription, expatriation
2 EXPATRIATE, refugee, outcast, émigré, deportee
▷ *verb* BANISH, expel, throw out, deport, oust, drive out, eject, expatriate, proscribe, cast out, ostracize

exiled *adjective* BANISHED, deported, expatriate, outcast, refugee, ostracized, expat

exist *verb* 1 LIVE, be present, be living, last, survive, breathe, endure, be in existence, be, be extant, have breath
2 OCCUR, happen, stand, remain, obtain, be present, prevail, abide
3 SURVIVE, stay alive, make ends meet, subsist, eke out a living, scrape by, scrimp and save, support yourself, keep your head above water, get along *or* by

Although *be extant* is given as a synonym of *exist*, according to some, *extant* should properly only be used where there is a connotation of survival, often against all odds: *the oldest extant document dates from 1492*. Using *extant* where the phrase *in existence* can be substituted, would in this view be incorrect: *in existence* (not *extant*) *for nearly 15 years, they have been consistently one of the finest rock bands on the planet*. In practice, however, the distinct meanings of the two phrases often overlap: *these beasts, the largest primates on the planet and the greatest of the great apes, are man's closest living relatives and the only extant primates with which we share close physical characteristics*.

existence *noun* 1 REALITY, being, life, survival, duration, endurance, continuation, subsistence, actuality, continuance
2 LIFE, situation, way of life, life style
3 CREATION, life, the world, reality, the human condition, this mortal coil

existent *adjective* IN EXISTENCE, living, existing, surviving, around, standing, remaining, present, current, alive, enduring, prevailing, abiding, to the fore (*Scot*), extant

existing *adjective* IN EXISTENCE, living, present, surviving, remaining, available, alive, in operation, extant, alive and kicking
<< OPPOSITE gone

exit *noun* 1 WAY OUT, door, gate, outlet, doorway, vent, gateway, escape route, passage out, egress
<< OPPOSITE entry
2 DEPARTURE, withdrawal, retreat, farewell, going, retirement, goodbye, exodus, evacuation, decamping, leave-taking, adieu
▷ *verb* DEPART, leave, go out, withdraw, retire, quit, retreat, go away, say goodbye, bid farewell, make tracks, take your leave, go offstage (*Theatre*)
<< OPPOSITE enter

exodus *noun* DEPARTURE, withdrawal, retreat, leaving, flight, retirement, exit, migration, evacuation

exonerate *verb* ACQUIT, clear, excuse, pardon, justify, discharge, vindicate, absolve, exculpate

exorbitant *adjective* EXCESSIVE, high, expensive, extreme, ridiculous, outrageous, extravagant, unreasonable, undue, preposterous, unwarranted, inordinate, extortionate, unconscionable, immoderate
<< OPPOSITE reasonable

exorcise *or* **exorcize** *verb* 1 DRIVE OUT, expel, cast out, adjure
2 PURIFY, free, cleanse

exorcism *noun* 1 DRIVING OUT, expulsion, deliverance, casting out, adjuration
2 PURIFICATION, freeing, cleansing

exotic *adjective* 1 UNUSUAL, different, striking, strange, extraordinary, bizarre, fascinating, curious, mysterious, colourful, glamorous, peculiar, unfamiliar, outlandish
<< OPPOSITE ordinary
2 FOREIGN, alien, tropical, external, extraneous, naturalized, extrinsic, not native

expand *verb* 1 GET BIGGER, increase, grow, extend, swell, widen, blow up, wax, heighten, enlarge, multiply, inflate, thicken, fill out, lengthen, fatten, dilate, become bigger, puff up, become larger, distend
<< OPPOSITE contract
2 MAKE BIGGER, increase, develop, extend, widen, blow up, heighten, enlarge, multiply, broaden, inflate, thicken, fill out, lengthen, magnify, amplify, augment, dilate, make larger, distend, bloat, protract
<< OPPOSITE reduce
3 SPREAD (OUT), open (out), stretch (out), unfold, unravel, diffuse, unfurl, unroll, outspread
▷▷ **expand on something** GO INTO DETAIL ABOUT, embellish, elaborate on, develop, flesh out, expound on, enlarge on, expatiate on, add detail to

expanse *noun* AREA, range, field, space, stretch, sweep, extent, plain, tract, breadth

expansion *noun* 1 INCREASE, development, growth, spread, diffusion, magnification, multiplication, amplification, augmentation
2 ENLARGEMENT, inflation, increase, growth, swelling, unfolding, expanse, unfurling, opening out, distension

expansive *adjective* 1 WIDE, broad, extensive, spacious, sweeping
2 COMPREHENSIVE, extensive, broad, wide, widespread, wide-ranging, thorough, inclusive, far-reaching, voluminous, all-embracing
3 TALKATIVE, open, friendly, outgoing, free, easy, warm, sociable, genial, affable, communicative, effusive, garrulous, loquacious, unreserved

expatriate *adjective* EXILED, refugee, banished, emigrant, émigré, expat
▷ *noun* EXILE, refugee, emigrant, émigré

expect *verb* 1 THINK, believe, suppose, assume, trust, imagine, reckon, forecast, calculate, presume, foresee, conjecture, surmise, think likely
2 ANTICIPATE, look forward to, predict, envisage, await, hope for, contemplate, bargain for, look ahead to
3 REQUIRE, demand, want, wish, look for, call for, ask for, hope for, insist on, count on, rely upon

expectancy *noun* 1 LIKELIHOOD, prospect, tendency, outlook, probability
2 EXPECTATION, hope, anticipation, waiting, belief, looking forward, assumption, prediction, probability, suspense, presumption, conjecture, surmise, supposition

expectant *adjective* 1 EXPECTING, excited, anticipating, anxious, ready, awaiting, eager, hopeful, apprehensive, watchful, in suspense
2 PREGNANT, expecting (*informal*), gravid, enceinte

expectation *noun* 1 *usually plural* PROJECTION, supposition, assumption, calculation, belief, forecast, assurance, likelihood, probability, presumption, conjecture, surmise, presupposition

2 ANTICIPATION, hope, possibility, prospect, chance, fear, promise, looking forward, excitement, prediction, outlook, expectancy, apprehension, suspense
3 *usually plural* REQUIREMENT, demand, want, wish, insistence, reliance

expected *adjective* ANTICIPATED, wanted, promised, looked-for, predicted, forecast, awaited, hoped-for, counted on, long-awaited

expecting *adjective (informal)* PREGNANT, with child, expectant, in the club (*Brit slang*), in the family way (*informal*), gravid, enceinte

expediency *or* **expedience** *noun* SUITABILITY, benefit, fitness, utility, effectiveness, convenience, profitability, practicality, usefulness, prudence, pragmatism, propriety, desirability, appropriateness, utilitarianism, helpfulness, advisability, aptness, judiciousness, properness, meetness, advantageousness

expedient *adjective* ADVANTAGEOUS, effective, useful, profitable, fit, politic, appropriate, practical, suitable, helpful, proper, convenient, desirable, worthwhile, beneficial, pragmatic, prudent, advisable, utilitarian, judicious, opportune
<< OPPOSITE unwise
▷ *noun* MEANS, measure, scheme, method, resource, resort, device, manoeuvre, expediency, stratagem, contrivance, stopgap

expedite *verb* SPEED (UP), forward, promote, advance, press, urge, rush, assist, hurry, accelerate, dispatch, facilitate, hasten, precipitate, quicken
<< OPPOSITE hold up

expedition *noun* 1 JOURNEY, exploration, mission, voyage, tour, enterprise, undertaking, quest, trek
2 TEAM, crew, party, group, company, travellers, explorers, voyagers, wayfarers
3 TRIP, tour, outing, excursion, jaunt

expel *verb* 1 THROW OUT, exclude, ban, bar, dismiss, discharge, relegate, kick out (*informal*), ask to leave, send packing, turf out (*informal*), black, debar, drum out, blackball, give the bum's rush (*slang*), show you the door, throw out on your ear (*informal*)
<< OPPOSITE let in
2 BANISH, exile, oust, deport, expatriate, evict, force to leave, proscribe
<< OPPOSITE take in
3 DRIVE OUT, discharge, throw out, force out, let out, eject, issue, dislodge, spew, belch, cast out

expend *verb* 1 USE (UP), employ, go through (*informal*), exhaust, consume, dissipate
2 SPEND, pay out, lay out (*informal*), fork out (*slang*), shell out, disburse

expendable *adjective* DISPENSABLE, unnecessary, unimportant, replaceable, nonessential, inessential
<< OPPOSITE indispensable

expenditure *noun* 1 SPENDING, payment, expense, outgoings, cost, charge, outlay, disbursement
2 CONSUMPTION, use, using, application, output

expense *noun* COST, charge, expenditure, payment, spending, output, toll, consumption, outlay, disbursement
▷▷ **at the expense of** WITH THE SACRIFICE OF, with the loss of, at the cost of, at the price of

expensive *adjective* COSTLY, high-priced, lavish, extravagant, rich, dear, stiff, excessive, steep (*informal*), pricey, overpriced, exorbitant
<< OPPOSITE cheap

experience *noun* 1 KNOWLEDGE, understanding, practice, skill, evidence, trial, contact, expertise, know-how (*informal*), proof, involvement, exposure, observation, participation, familiarity, practical knowledge
2 EVENT, affair, incident, happening, test, trial, encounter, episode, adventure, ordeal, occurrence
▷ *verb* UNDERGO, have, know, feel, try, meet, face, suffer, taste, go through, observe, sample, encounter, sustain, perceive, endure, participate in, run into, live through, behold, come up against, apprehend, become familiar with

experienced *adjective* 1 KNOWLEDGEABLE, trained, professional, skilled, tried, tested, seasoned, expert, master, qualified, familiar, capable, veteran, practised, accomplished, competent, skilful, adept, well-versed
<< OPPOSITE inexperienced
2 WORLDLY-WISE, knowing, worldly, wise, mature, sophisticated

experiment *noun* 1 TEST, trial, investigation, examination, venture, procedure, demonstration, observation, try-out, assay, trial run, scientific test, dummy run
2 RESEARCH, investigation, analysis, observation, research and development, experimentation, trial and error
▷ *verb* TEST, investigate, trial, research, try, examine, pilot, sample, verify, put to the test, assay

experimental *adjective* 1 TEST, trial, pilot, preliminary, provisional, tentative, speculative, empirical, exploratory, trial-and-error, fact-finding, probationary
2 INNOVATIVE, new, original, radical, creative, ingenious, avant-garde, inventive, ground-breaking

expert *noun* SPECIALIST, authority, professional, master, pro (*informal*), ace (*informal*), genius, guru, pundit, buff (*informal*), wizard,

adept, whizz (*informal*), maestro, virtuoso, connoisseur, hotshot (*informal*), past master, dab hand (*Brit informal*), wonk (*informal*), maven (*US*), fundi (*S African*)
<< OPPOSITE amateur
▷ *adjective* SKILFUL, trained, experienced, able, professional, skilled, master, masterly, qualified, talented, outstanding, clever, practised, accomplished, handy, competent, apt, adept, knowledgeable, virtuoso, deft, proficient, facile, adroit, dexterous
<< OPPOSITE unskilled

expertise *noun* SKILL, knowledge, know-how (*informal*), facility, grip, craft, judgment, grasp, mastery, knack, proficiency, dexterity, cleverness, deftness, adroitness, aptness, expertness, knowing inside out, ableness, masterliness, skilfulness

expiration *noun* EXPIRY, end, finish, conclusion, close, termination, cessation

expire *verb* 1 BECOME INVALID, end, finish, conclude, close, stop, run out, cease, lapse, terminate, come to an end, be no longer valid
2 DIE, decease, depart, buy it (*US slang*), check out (*US slang*), perish, kick it (*slang*), croak (*slang*), go belly-up (*slang*), snuff it (*informal*), peg out (*informal*), kick the bucket (*informal*), peg it (*informal*), depart this life, meet your maker, cark it (*Austral & NZ slang*), pop your clogs (*informal*), pass away *or* on

expiry *noun* EXPIRATION, ending, end, conclusion, close, demise, lapsing, lapse, termination, cessation

explain *verb* 1 MAKE CLEAR *or* PLAIN, describe, demonstrate, illustrate, teach, define, solve, resolve, interpret, disclose, unfold, clarify, clear up, simplify, expound, elucidate, put into words, throw light on, explicate (*formal*), give the details of
2 ACCOUNT FOR, excuse, justify, give a reason for, give an explanation for

explanation *noun* 1 REASON, meaning, cause, sense, answer, account, excuse, motive, justification, vindication, mitigation, the why and wherefore
2 DESCRIPTION, report, definition, demonstration, teaching, resolution, interpretation, illustration, clarification, exposition, simplification, explication, elucidation

explanatory *or* **explanative** *adjective* DESCRIPTIVE, interpretive, illustrative, interpretative, demonstrative, justifying, expository, illuminative, elucidatory, explicative

explicit *adjective* 1 CLEAR, obvious, specific, direct, certain, express, plain, absolute, exact, precise, straightforward, definite, overt, unequivocal, unqualified, unambiguous, categorical
<< OPPOSITE vague
2 FRANK, direct, open, specific, positive, plain, patent, graphic, distinct, outspoken, upfront (*informal*), unambiguous, unrestricted, unrestrained, uncensored, unreserved
<< OPPOSITE indirect

explode *verb* 1 BLOW UP, erupt, burst, go off, shatter, shiver
2 DETONATE, set off, discharge, let off
3 LOSE YOUR TEMPER, rage, erupt, blow up (*informal*), lose it (*informal*), crack up (*informal*), see red (*informal*), lose the plot (*informal*), become angry, have a fit (*informal*), go ballistic (*slang, chiefly US*), hit the roof (*informal*), throw a tantrum, blow a fuse (*slang, chiefly US*), go berserk (*slang*), go mad (*slang*), fly off the handle (*informal*), go spare (*Brit slang*), become enraged, go off the deep end (*informal*), go up the wall (*slang*), blow your top (*informal*), go crook (*Austral & NZ slang*), fly into a temper, flip your lid (*slang*), do your nut (*Brit slang*)
4 INCREASE, grow, develop, extend, advance, shoot up, soar, boost, expand, build up, swell, step up (*informal*), escalate, multiply, proliferate, snowball, aggrandize
5 DISPROVE, discredit, refute, belie, demolish, repudiate, put paid to, invalidate, debunk, prove impossible, prove wrong, give the lie to, blow out of the water (*slang*)

exploit *noun* FEAT, act, achievement, enterprise, adventure, stunt, deed, accomplishment, attainment, escapade
▷ *verb* 1 TAKE ADVANTAGE OF, abuse, use, manipulate, milk, misuse, dump on (*slang, chiefly US*), ill-treat, play on *or* upon
2 MAKE THE BEST USE OF, use, make use of, utilize, cash in on (*informal*), capitalize on, put to use, make capital out of, use to advantage, use to good advantage, live off the backs of, turn to account, profit by *or* from

exploitation *noun* 1 MISUSE, abuse, manipulation, imposition, using, ill-treatment
2 CAPITALIZATION, utilization, using to good advantage, trading upon

exploration *noun* 1 EXPEDITION, tour, trip, survey, travel, journey, reconnaissance, recce (*slang*)
2 INVESTIGATION, study, research, survey, search, inquiry, analysis, examination, probe, inspection, scrutiny, once-over (*informal*)

exploratory *adjective* INVESTIGATIVE, trial, searching, probing, experimental, analytic, fact-finding

explore *verb* 1 TRAVEL AROUND, tour, survey, scout, traverse, range over, recce (*slang*), reconnoitre, case (*slang*), have *or* take a look around

2 INVESTIGATE, consider, research, survey, search, prospect, examine, probe, analyse, look into, inspect, work over, scrutinize, inquire into

explosion *noun* 1 BLAST, crack, burst, bang, discharge, report, blowing up, outburst, clap, detonation
2 INCREASE, rise, development, growth, boost, expansion, enlargement, escalation, upturn
3 OUTBURST, fit, storm, attack, surge, flare-up, eruption, paroxysm
4 OUTBREAK, flare-up, eruption, upsurge

explosive *adjective* 1 UNSTABLE, dangerous, volatile, hazardous, unsafe, perilous, combustible, inflammable
2 DANGEROUS, worrying, strained, anxious, charged, ugly, tense, hazardous, stressful, perilous, nerve-racking, overwrought
3 FIERY, violent, volatile, stormy, touchy, vehement, chippy (*informal*)
▷ *noun* BOMB, mine, shell, missile, rocket, grenade, charge, torpedo, incendiary

exponent *noun* 1 ADVOCATE, champion, supporter, defender, spokesman, spokeswoman, promoter, backer, spokesperson, proponent, propagandist, upholder
2 PERFORMER, player, interpreter, presenter, executant

expose *verb* 1 UNCOVER, show, reveal, display, exhibit, present, unveil, manifest, lay bare, take the wraps off, put on view
<< OPPOSITE hide
2 REVEAL, disclose, uncover, air, detect, betray, show up, denounce, unearth, let out, divulge, unmask, lay bare, make known, bring to light, out (*informal*), smoke out, blow wide open (*slang*)
<< OPPOSITE keep secret
3 MAKE VULNERABLE, subject, leave open, lay open
▷▷ **expose someone to something** INTRODUCE TO, acquaint with, bring into contact with, familiarize with, make familiar with, make conversant with

exposé *noun* EXPOSURE, revelation, uncovering, disclosure, divulgence

exposed *adjective* 1 UNCONCEALED, revealed, bare, exhibited, unveiled, shown, uncovered, on display, on show, on view, laid bare, made manifest
2 UNSHELTERED, open, unprotected, open to the elements
3 VULNERABLE, open, subject, in danger, liable, susceptible, wide open, left open, laid bare, in peril, laid open

exposition *noun* 1 EXPLANATION, account, description, interpretation, illustration, presentation, commentary, critique, exegesis, explication, elucidation
2 EXHIBITION, show, fair, display, demonstration, presentation, expo (*informal*)

exposure *noun* 1 VULNERABILITY, subjection, susceptibility, laying open
2 HYPOTHERMIA, frostbite, extreme cold, intense cold
3 REVELATION, exposé, uncovering, disclosure, airing, manifestation, detection, divulging, denunciation, unmasking, divulgence
4 PUBLICITY, promotion, attention, advertising, plugging (*informal*), propaganda, hype, pushing, media hype
5 UNCOVERING, showing, display, exhibition, baring, revelation, presentation, unveiling, manifestation
6 CONTACT, experience, awareness, acquaintance, familiarity

expound *verb* EXPLAIN, describe, illustrate, interpret, unfold, spell out, set forth, elucidate, explicate (*formal*)

express *verb* 1 STATE, communicate, convey, articulate, say, tell, put, word, speak, voice, declare, phrase, assert, pronounce, utter, couch, put across, enunciate, put into words, give voice to, verbalize, asseverate
2 SHOW, indicate, exhibit, demonstrate, reveal, disclose, intimate, convey, testify to, depict, designate, manifest, embody, signify, symbolize, denote, divulge, bespeak, make known, evince
▷ *adjective* 1 EXPLICIT, clear, direct, precise, pointed, certain, plain, accurate, exact, distinct, definite, outright, unambiguous, categorical
2 SPECIFIC, exclusive, particular, sole, special, deliberate, singular, clear-cut, especial
3 FAST, direct, quick, rapid, priority, prompt, swift, high-speed, speedy, quickie (*informal*), nonstop, expeditious

expression *noun* 1 STATEMENT, declaration, announcement, communication, mention, assertion, utterance, articulation, pronouncement, enunciation, verbalization, asseveration
2 INDICATION, demonstration, exhibition, display, showing, show, sign, symbol, representation, token, manifestation, embodiment
3 LOOK, countenance, face, air, appearance, aspect, mien (*literary*)
4 INTONATION, style, delivery, phrasing, emphasis, execution, diction
5 PHRASE, saying, word, wording, term, language, speech, remark, maxim, idiom, adage, choice of words, turn of phrase, phraseology, locution, set phrase

expressionless *adjective* BLANK, empty, deadpan, straight-faced, wooden, dull, vacuous, inscrutable, poker-faced (*informal*)

expressive *adjective* 1 VIVID, strong, striking, telling, moving, lively, sympathetic, energetic, poignant, emphatic, eloquent, forcible
<< OPPOSITE impassive
2 *with* **of** MEANINGFUL, indicative, suggestive, demonstrative, revealing, significant, allusive

expressly *adverb* 1 EXPLICITLY, clearly, plainly, absolutely, positively, definitely, outright, manifestly, distinctly, decidedly, categorically, pointedly, unequivocally, unmistakably, in no uncertain terms, unambiguously
2 SPECIFICALLY, specially, especially, particularly, purposely, exclusively, precisely, solely, exactly, deliberately, intentionally, on purpose

expropriate *verb* (*Formal*) SEIZE, take, appropriate, confiscate, assume, take over, take away, commandeer, requisition, arrogate

expropriation *noun* (*Formal*) SEIZURE, takeover, impounding, confiscation, commandeering, requisitioning, sequestration, disseisin (*Law*)

expulsion *noun* 1 EJECTION, exclusion, dismissal, removal, exile, discharge, eviction, banishment, extrusion, proscription, expatriation, debarment, dislodgment
2 DISCHARGE, emptying, emission, voiding, spewing, secretion, excretion, ejection, seepage, suppuration

expunge *verb* (*Formal*) ERASE, remove, destroy, abolish, cancel, get rid of, wipe out, eradicate, excise, delete, extinguish, strike out, obliterate, annihilate, efface, exterminate, annul, raze, blot out, extirpate

exquisite *adjective* 1 BEAUTIFUL, elegant, graceful, pleasing, attractive, lovely, charming, comely
<< OPPOSITE unattractive
2 FINE, beautiful, lovely, elegant, precious, delicate, dainty
3 INTENSE, acute, severe, sharp, keen, extreme, piercing, poignant, excruciating
4 REFINED, cultivated, discriminating, sensitive, polished, selective, discerning, impeccable, meticulous, consummate, appreciative, fastidious
5 EXCELLENT, fine, outstanding, superb, choice, perfect, select, delicious, divine, splendid, admirable, consummate, flawless, superlative, incomparable, peerless, matchless
<< OPPOSITE imperfect

extant *adjective* IN EXISTENCE, existing, remaining, surviving, living, existent, subsisting, undestroyed

> Used carefully, the word *extant* describes something that has survived, often against all odds. It therefore carries a slightly more specific meaning than *in existence*, and should not be considered as being automatically interchangeable with this phrase. For example, you might say *the oldest extant document dates from 1492*; but *in existence* (not *extant*) *for 15 years, they are still one of the most successful bands in the world*. In many contexts, however, these ideas overlap, leaving the writer to decide whether *extant* or *in existence* best expresses the intended meaning

extend *verb* 1 SPREAD OUT, reach, stretch, continue, carry on
2 STRETCH, stretch out, spread out, unfurl, straighten out, unroll
3 LAST, continue, go on, stretch, carry on
4 PROTRUDE, project, stand out, bulge, stick out, hang, overhang, jut out
5 REACH, spread, go as far as
6 WIDEN, increase, develop, expand, spread, add to, enhance, supplement, enlarge, broaden, diversify, amplify, augment
<< OPPOSITE reduce
7 MAKE LONGER, prolong, lengthen, draw out, spin out, elongate, drag out, protract
<< OPPOSITE shorten
8 OFFER, give, hold out, present, grant, advance, yield, reach out, confer, stretch out, stick out, bestow, impart, proffer, put forth
<< OPPOSITE withdraw

extended *adjective* 1 LENGTHENED, long, prolonged, protracted, stretched out, drawn-out, unfurled, elongated, unrolled
2 BROAD, wide, expanded, extensive, widespread, comprehensive, large-scale, enlarged, far-reaching
3 OUTSTRETCHED, conferred, stretched out, proffered

extension *noun* 1 ANNEXE, wing, addition, supplement, branch, appendix, add-on, adjunct, appendage, ell, addendum
2 LENGTHENING, extra time, continuation, postponement, prolongation, additional period of time, protraction
3 DEVELOPMENT, expansion, widening, increase, stretching, broadening, continuation, enlargement, diversification, amplification, elongation, augmentation

extensive *adjective* 1 LARGE, considerable, substantial, spacious, wide, sweeping, broad, expansive, capacious, commodious
<< OPPOSITE confined
2 COMPREHENSIVE, complete, thorough, lengthy, long, wide, wholesale, pervasive, protracted, all-inclusive
<< OPPOSITE restricted
3 GREAT, large, huge, extended, vast,

widespread, comprehensive, universal, large-scale, far-reaching, prevalent, far-flung, all-inclusive, voluminous, humongous *or* humungous (*US slang*)
<< OPPOSITE limited

extent *noun* 1 MAGNITUDE, amount, degree, scale, level, measure, stretch, quantity, bulk, duration, expanse, amplitude
2 SIZE, area, range, length, reach, bounds, sweep, sphere, width, compass, breadth, ambit

exterior *noun* OUTSIDE, face, surface, covering, finish, skin, appearance, aspect, shell, coating, façade, outside surface
▷ *adjective* OUTER, outside, external, surface, outward, superficial, outermost
<< OPPOSITE inner

exterminate *verb* DESTROY, kill, eliminate, abolish, eradicate, annihilate, extirpate

extermination *noun* DESTRUCTION, murder, massacre, slaughter, killing, wiping out, genocide, elimination, mass murder, annihilation, eradication, extirpation

external *adjective* 1 OUTER, outside, surface, apparent, visible, outward, exterior, superficial, outermost
<< OPPOSITE internal
2 FOREIGN, international, alien, exotic, exterior, extraneous, extrinsic
<< OPPOSITE domestic
3 OUTSIDE, visiting, independent, extramural
<< OPPOSITE inside

extinct *adjective* 1 DEAD, lost, gone, vanished, defunct
<< OPPOSITE living
2 INACTIVE, extinguished, doused, out, snuffed out, quenched

extinction *noun* DYING OUT, death, destruction, abolition, oblivion, extermination, annihilation, eradication, obliteration, excision, extirpation

extinguish *verb* 1 PUT OUT, stifle, smother, blow out, douse, snuff out, quench
2 DESTROY, end, kill, remove, eliminate, obscure, abolish, suppress, wipe out, erase, eradicate, annihilate, put paid to, exterminate, expunge, extirpate

extol *verb* PRAISE, acclaim, applaud, pay tribute to, celebrate, commend, magnify (*archaic*), glorify, exalt, laud, crack up (*informal*), sing the praises of, eulogize, cry up, panegyrize

extort *verb* EXTRACT, force, squeeze, exact, bully, bleed (*informal*), blackmail, wring, coerce, wrest

extortion *noun* BLACKMAIL, force, oppression, compulsion, coercion, shakedown (*US slang*), rapacity, exaction

extortionate *adjective* EXORBITANT, excessive, outrageous, unreasonable, inflated, extravagant, preposterous, sky-high, inordinate, immoderate
<< OPPOSITE reasonable

extra *adjective* 1 ADDITIONAL, more, new, other, added, further, fresh, accessory, supplementary, auxiliary, add-on, supplemental, ancillary
<< OPPOSITE vital
2 SURPLUS, excess, reserve, spare, unnecessary, redundant, needless, unused, leftover, superfluous, extraneous, unneeded, inessential, supernumerary, supererogatory
▷ *noun* ADDITION, bonus, supplement, accessory, complement, add-on, affix, adjunct, appendage, addendum, supernumerary, appurtenance
<< OPPOSITE necessity
▷ *adverb* 1 IN ADDITION, additionally, over and above
2 EXCEPTIONALLY, very, specially, especially, particularly, extremely, remarkably, unusually, extraordinarily, uncommonly

extract *verb* 1 OBTAIN, take out, distil, squeeze out, draw out, express, separate out, press out
2 TAKE OUT, draw, pull, remove, withdraw, pull out, bring out
3 PULL OUT, remove, take out, draw, uproot, pluck out, extirpate
4 ELICIT, get, obtain, force, draw, gather, derive, exact, bring out, evoke, reap, wring, glean, coerce, wrest
5 SELECT, quote, cite, abstract, choose, cut out, reproduce, cull, copy out
▷ *noun* 1 PASSAGE, selection, excerpt, cutting, clipping, abstract, quotation, citation
2 ESSENCE, solution, concentrate, juice, distillation, decoction, distillate

> People sometimes use *extract* where *extricate* would be better. Although both words can refer to a physical act of removal from a place, *extract* has a more general sense than *extricate*. *Extricate* has additional overtones of 'difficulty', and is most commonly used with reference to getting a person – particularly *yourself* – out of a situation. So, for example, you might say *he will find it difficult to extricate himself* (not *extract himself*) *from this situation*

extraction *noun* 1 ORIGIN, family, ancestry, descent, race, stock, blood, birth, pedigree, lineage, parentage, derivation
2 TAKING OUT, drawing, pulling, withdrawal, removal, uprooting, extirpation
3 DISTILLATION, separation, derivation

extraneous *adjective* 1 NONESSENTIAL, unnecessary, extra, additional, redundant,

needless, peripheral, supplementary, incidental, superfluous, unneeded, inessential, adventitious, unessential
2 IRRELEVANT, inappropriate, unrelated, unconnected, immaterial, beside the point, impertinent, inadmissible, off the subject, inapplicable, inapt, inapposite

extraordinary *adjective* 1 REMARKABLE, special, wonderful, outstanding, rare, amazing, fantastic, astonishing, marvellous, exceptional, notable, serious (*informal*), phenomenal, singular, wondrous (*archaic* or *literary*), out of this world (*informal*), extremely good
<< OPPOSITE unremarkable
2 UNUSUAL, surprising, odd, strange, unique, remarkable, bizarre, curious, weird, unprecedented, peculiar, unfamiliar, uncommon, unheard-of, unwonted
<< OPPOSITE ordinary

extravagance *noun* 1 OVERSPENDING, squandering, profusion, profligacy, wastefulness, waste, lavishness, prodigality, improvidence
2 LUXURY, treat, indulgence, extra, frill, nonessential
3 EXCESS, folly, exaggeration, absurdity, recklessness, wildness, dissipation, outrageousness, unreasonableness, preposterousness, immoderation, exorbitance, unrestraint

extravagant *adjective* 1 WASTEFUL, excessive, lavish, prodigal, profligate, spendthrift, imprudent, improvident
<< OPPOSITE economical
2 OVERPRICED, expensive, costly
3 EXORBITANT, excessive, steep (*informal*), unreasonable, inordinate, extortionate
<< OPPOSITE reasonable
4 EXCESSIVE, exaggerated, outrageous, wild, fantastic, absurd, foolish, over the top (*slang*), unreasonable, preposterous, fanciful, unrestrained, inordinate, outré, immoderate, O.T.T. (*slang*)
<< OPPOSITE moderate
5 SHOWY, elaborate, flamboyant, impressive, fancy, flashy, ornate, pretentious, grandiose, gaudy, garish, ostentatious
<< OPPOSITE restrained

extravaganza *noun* SPECTACULAR, show, spectacle, display, pageant, flight of fancy

extreme *adjective* 1 GREAT, high, highest, greatest, worst, supreme, acute, severe, maximum, intense, ultimate, utmost, mother of all (*informal*), uttermost
<< OPPOSITE mild
2 SEVERE, radical, strict, harsh, stern, rigid, dire, drastic, uncompromising, unbending
3 RADICAL, unusual, excessive, exceptional, exaggerated, outrageous, over the top (*slang*), unreasonable, uncommon, unconventional, fanatical, zealous, out-and-out, inordinate, egregious, intemperate, immoderate, O.T.T. (*slang*)
<< OPPOSITE moderate
4 FARTHEST, furthest, far, final, last, ultimate, remotest, terminal, utmost, far-off, faraway, outermost, most distant, uttermost
<< OPPOSITE nearest
▷ *noun* LIMIT, end, edge, opposite, pole, ultimate, boundary, antithesis, extremity, acme

extremely *adverb* VERY, highly, greatly, particularly, severely, terribly, ultra, utterly, unusually, exceptionally, extraordinarily, intensely, tremendously, markedly, awfully (*informal*), acutely, exceedingly, excessively, inordinately, uncommonly, to a fault, to the nth degree, to *or* in the extreme

extremist *noun* RADICAL, activist, militant, enthusiast, fanatic, devotee, die-hard, bigot, zealot, energumen
▷ *adjective* EXTREME, wild, mad, enthusiastic, passionate, frenzied, obsessive, fanatical, fervent, zealous, bigoted, rabid, immoderate, overenthusiastic

extremity *noun* 1 LIMIT, end, edge, border, top, tip, bound, minimum, extreme, maximum, pole, margin, boundary, terminal, frontier, verge, brink, rim, brim, pinnacle, termination, nadir, zenith, apex, terminus, apogee, farthest point, furthest point, acme
2 DEPTH, height, excess, climax, consummation, acuteness
3 CRISIS, trouble, emergency, disaster, setback, pinch, plight, hardship, adversity, dire straits, exigency, extreme suffering
▷ *plural noun* HANDS AND FEET, limbs, fingers and toes

extricate *verb* 1 WITHDRAW, relieve, free, clear, deliver, liberate, wriggle out of, get (someone) off the hook (*slang*), disembarrass
2 FREE, clear, release, remove, rescue, get out, disengage, disentangle ▷ see **extract**

extrovert *or* **extravert** (*Psychology*) *noun* OUTGOING PERSON, mingler, socializer, mixer, life and soul of the party
<< OPPOSITE introvert
▷ *adjective* SOCIABLE, social, lively, outgoing, hearty, exuberant, amiable, gregarious
<< OPPOSITE introverted

exuberance *noun* 1 HIGH SPIRITS, energy, enthusiasm, vitality, life, spirit, excitement, pep, animation, vigour, zest, eagerness, buoyancy, exhilaration, cheerfulness, brio, vivacity, ebullience, liveliness, effervescence, sprightliness
2 LUXURIANCE, abundance, richness,

profusion, plenitude, lushness, superabundance, lavishness, rankness, copiousness

exuberant *adjective* 1 HIGH-SPIRITED, spirited, enthusiastic, lively, excited, eager, sparkling, vigorous, cheerful, energetic, animated, upbeat (*informal*), buoyant, exhilarated, elated, ebullient, chirpy (*informal*), sprightly, vivacious, effervescent, full of life, full of beans (*informal*), zestful

<< OPPOSITE subdued

2 LUXURIANT, rich, lavish, abundant, lush, overflowing, plentiful, teeming, copious, profuse, superabundant, plenteous

3 FULSOME, excessive, exaggerated, lavish, overdone, superfluous, prodigal, effusive

exude *verb* 1 RADIATE, show, display, exhibit, manifest, emanate

2 EMIT, leak, discharge, ooze, emanate, issue, secrete, excrete

3 SEEP, leak, sweat, bleed, weep, trickle, ooze, emanate, issue, filter through, well forth

exult *verb* 1 BE JOYFUL, be delighted, rejoice, be overjoyed, celebrate, be elated, be jubilant, jump for joy, make merry, be in high spirits, jubilate

2 *often with* **over** REVEL, glory in, boast, crow, taunt, brag, vaunt, drool, gloat, take delight in

exultant *adjective* JOYFUL, delighted, flushed, triumphant, revelling, rejoicing, jubilant, joyous, transported, elated, over the moon (*informal*), overjoyed, rapt, gleeful, exulting, cock-a-hoop, stoked (*Austral & NZ informal*)

eye *noun* 1 EYEBALL, optic (*informal*), peeper (*slang*), orb (*poetic*), organ of vision, organ of sight

2 *often plural* EYESIGHT, sight, vision, observation, perception, ability to see, range of vision, power of seeing

3 APPRECIATION, taste, recognition, judgment, discrimination, perception, discernment

4 OBSERVANCE, observation, supervision, surveillance, attention, notice, inspection, heed, vigil, watch, lookout, vigilance, alertness, watchfulness

5 CENTRE, heart, middle, mid, core, nucleus

▷ *verb* LOOK AT, view, study, watch, check, regard, survey, clock (*Brit slang*), observe, stare at, scan, contemplate, check out (*informal*), inspect, glance at, gaze at, behold (*archaic* or *literary*), eyeball (*slang*), scrutinize, peruse, get a load of (*informal*), take a dekko at (*Brit slang*), have *or* take a look at

▷▷ **an eye for an eye** RETALIATION, justice, revenge, vengeance, reprisal, retribution, requital, lex talionis

▷▷ **turn a blind eye to** *or* **close your eyes to** IGNORE, reject, overlook, disregard, pass over, take no notice of, be oblivious to, pay no attention to, turn your back on, turn a deaf ear to, bury your head in the sand

▷▷ **eye something** *or* **someone up** OGLE, leer at, make eyes at, give (someone) the (glad) eye

▷▷ **see eye to eye (with)** AGREE (WITH), accord (with), get on (with), fall in (with), coincide (with), go along (with), subscribe (to), be united (with), concur (with), harmonize (with), speak the same language (as), be on the same wavelength (as), be of the same mind (as), be in unison (with)

▷▷ **set, clap** *or* **lay eyes on someone** SEE, meet, notice, observe, encounter, come across, run into, behold

▷▷ **up to your eyes (in)** VERY BUSY (WITH), overwhelmed (with), caught up (in), inundated (by), wrapped up (in), engaged (in), flooded out (by), fully occupied (with), up to here (with), up to your elbows (in)

>> RELATED WORDS *adjectives* ocular, ophthalmic, optic

eye-catching *adjective* STRIKING, arresting, attractive, dramatic, spectacular, captivating, showy

eyesight *noun* VISION, sight, observation, perception, ability to see, range of vision, power of seeing, power of sight

eyesore *noun* MESS, blight, blot, blemish, sight (*informal*), horror, disgrace, atrocity, ugliness, monstrosity, disfigurement

eyewitness *noun* OBSERVER, witness, spectator, looker-on, viewer, passer-by, watcher, onlooker, bystander

Ff

fable *noun* 1 LEGEND, myth, parable, allegory, story, tale, apologue
2 FICTION, lie, fantasy, myth, romance, invention, yarn (*informal*), fabrication, falsehood, fib, figment, untruth, fairy story (*informal*), urban myth, white lie, tall story (*informal*), urban legend
<< OPPOSITE fact
fabled *adjective* LEGENDARY, fictional, famed, mythical, storied, famous, fabulous
fabric *noun* 1 CLOTH, material, stuff, textile, web
2 FRAMEWORK, structure, make-up, organization, frame, foundations, construction, constitution, infrastructure
3 STRUCTURE, foundations, construction, framework, infrastructure
fabricate *verb* 1 MAKE UP, invent, concoct, falsify, form, coin, devise, forge, fake, feign, trump up
2 MANUFACTURE, make, build, form, fashion, shape, frame, construct, assemble, erect
fabrication *noun* 1 FORGERY, lie, fiction, myth, fake, invention, fable, concoction, falsehood, figment, untruth, porky (*Brit slang*), fairy story (*informal*), pork pie (*Brit slang*), cock-and-bull story (*informal*)
2 MANUFACTURE, production, construction, assembly, erection, assemblage, building
fabulous *adjective* 1 (*informal*) WONDERFUL, excellent, brilliant, superb, spectacular, fantastic (*informal*), marvellous, sensational (*informal*), first-rate, brill (*informal*), magic (*informal*), out-of-this-world (*informal*)
<< OPPOSITE ordinary
2 ASTOUNDING, amazing, extraordinary, remarkable, incredible, astonishing, legendary, immense, unbelievable, breathtaking, phenomenal, inconceivable
3 LEGENDARY, imaginary, mythical, fictitious, made-up, fantastic, invented, unreal, mythological, apocryphal
façade *noun* 1 FRONT, face, exterior, frontage
2 SHOW, front, appearance, mask, exterior, guise, pretence, veneer, semblance
face *noun* 1 COUNTENANCE, features, kisser (*slang*), profile, dial (*Brit slang*), mug (*slang*), visage, physiognomy, lineaments, phiz *or* phizog (*slang*)
2 EXPRESSION, look, air, appearance, aspect, countenance
3 SIDE, front, cover, outside, surface, aspect, exterior, right side, elevation, facet, vertical surface
4 (*informal*) IMPUDENCE, front, confidence, audacity, nerve, neck (*informal*), sauce (*informal*), cheek (*informal*), assurance, gall (*informal*), presumption, boldness, chutzpah (*US & Canad informal*), sass (*US & Canad informal*), effrontery, brass neck (*Brit informal*), sassiness (*US informal*)
▷ *verb* 1 *often with* **to, towards,** *or* **on** LOOK ONTO, overlook, be opposite, look out on, front onto, give towards *or* onto
2 CONFRONT, meet, encounter, deal with, oppose, tackle, cope with, experience, brave, defy, come up against, be confronted by, face off (*slang*)
▷▷ **face up to** ACCEPT, deal with, tackle, acknowledge, cope with, confront, come to terms with, meet head-on, reconcile yourself to
▷▷ **make** *or* **pull a face at someone** SCOWL, frown, pout, grimace, smirk, moue (*French*)
▷▷ **on the face of it** TO ALL APPEARANCES, apparently, seemingly, outwardly, at first sight, at face value, to the eye
▷▷ **show your face** TURN UP, come, appear, be seen, show up (*informal*), put in *or* make an appearance, approach
faceless *adjective* IMPERSONAL, remote, unknown, unidentified, anonymous
face-lift *noun* 1 RENOVATION, improvement, restoration, refurbishing, modernization, redecoration
2 COSMETIC SURGERY, plastic surgery
facet *noun* 1 ASPECT, part, face, side, phase,

angle
2 FACE, side, surface, plane, slant
facile *adjective* 1 SUPERFICIAL, shallow, slick, glib, hasty, cursory
2 EFFORTLESS, easy, simple, quick, ready, smooth, skilful, adept, fluent, uncomplicated, proficient, adroit, dexterous, light
<< OPPOSITE difficult
facilitate *verb* FURTHER, help, forward, promote, ease, speed up, pave the way for, make easy, expedite, oil the wheels of, smooth the path of, assist the progress of
<< OPPOSITE hinder
facility *noun* 1 *often plural* AMENITY, means, aid, opportunity, advantage, resource, equipment, provision, convenience, appliance
2 OPPORTUNITY, possibility, convenience
3 ABILITY, skill, talent, gift, craft, efficiency, knack, fluency, proficiency, dexterity, quickness, adroitness, expertness, skilfulness
4 EASE, readiness, fluency, smoothness, effortlessness
<< OPPOSITE difficulty
facsimile *noun* COPY, print, carbon, reproduction, replica, transcript, duplicate, photocopy, Xerox (*trademark*), carbon copy, Photostat (*trademark*), fax
fact *noun* 1 TRUTH, reality, gospel (truth), certainty, verity, actuality, naked truth
<< OPPOSITE fiction
2 DETAIL, point, feature, particular, item, specific, circumstance
3 (usually in phrase *after* or *before the fact*) (*Criminal law*) EVENT, happening, act, performance, incident, deed, occurrence, fait accompli (*French*)
▷ *plural noun* INFORMATION, details, data, the score (*informal*), gen (*Brit informal*), info (*informal*), the whole story, ins and outs, the lowdown (*informal*)
▷▷ **as a matter of fact** *or* **in fact** *or* **in point of fact** ACTUALLY, really, indeed, truly, in reality, in truth, to tell the truth, in actual fact, in point of fact
faction *noun* 1 GROUP, set, party, division, section, camp, sector, minority, combination, coalition, gang, lobby, bloc, contingent, pressure group, caucus, junta, clique, coterie, schism, confederacy, splinter group, cabal, ginger group, public-interest group (*US & Canad*)
2 DISSENSION, division, conflict, rebellion, disagreement, friction, strife, turbulence, variance, discord, infighting, disunity, sedition, tumult, disharmony, divisiveness
<< OPPOSITE agreement
factor *noun* ELEMENT, thing, point, part, cause, influence, item, aspect, circumstance, characteristic, consideration, component, determinant

In strict usage, *factor* should only be used to refer to something which contributes to a result. It should not be used to refer to a part of something, such as a plan or arrangement; more appropriate alternatives to *factor* in this sense are words such as *component* or *element*

factory *noun* WORKS, plant, mill, workshop, assembly line, shop floor, manufactory (*obsolete*)
factual *adjective* TRUE, objective, authentic, unbiased, close, real, sure, correct, genuine, accurate, exact, precise, faithful, credible, matter-of-fact, literal, veritable, circumstantial, unadorned, dinkum (*Austral & NZ informal*), true-to-life
<< OPPOSITE fictitious
faculty *noun* 1 ABILITY, power, skill, facility, talent, gift, capacity, bent, capability, readiness, knack, propensity, aptitude, dexterity, cleverness, adroitness, turn
<< OPPOSITE failing
2 DEPARTMENT, school, discipline, profession, branch of learning
3 TEACHING STAFF, staff, teachers, professors, lecturers (*chiefly US*)
4 POWER, reason, sense, intelligence, mental ability, physical ability
fad *noun* CRAZE, fashion, trend, fancy, rage, mode, vogue, whim, mania, affectation
fade *verb* 1 BECOME PALE, dull, dim, bleach, wash out, blanch, discolour, blench, lose colour, lose lustre, decolour
2 MAKE PALE, dull, dim, bleach, wash out, blanch, discolour, decolour
3 GROW DIM, dim, fade away, become less loud
4 *usually with* **away** *or* **out** DWINDLE, disappear, vanish, melt away, fall, fail, decline, flag, dissolve, dim, disperse, wither, wilt, wane, perish, ebb, languish, die out, droop, shrivel, die away, waste away, vanish into thin air, become unimportant, evanesce, etiolate
faded *adjective* DISCOLOURED, pale, bleached, washed out, dull, dim, indistinct, etiolated, lustreless
fading *adjective* DECLINING, dying, disappearing, vanishing, decreasing, on the decline
faeces *or esp US* **feces** *plural noun* EXCREMENT, stools, excreta, bodily waste, dung, droppings, ordure
fail *verb* 1 BE UNSUCCESSFUL, founder, fall flat, come to nothing, fall, miss, go down, break down, flop (*informal*), be defeated, fall short, fall through, fall short of, fizzle out (*informal*), come unstuck, run aground, miscarry, be in vain,

misfire, fall by the wayside, go astray, come to grief, come a cropper (*informal*), bite the dust, go up in smoke, go belly-up (*slang*), come to naught, lay an egg (*slang, chiefly US & Canad*), go by the board, not make the grade (*informal*), go down like a lead balloon (*informal*), turn out badly, fall flat on your face, meet with disaster, be found lacking *or* wanting

<< OPPOSITE succeed

2 DISAPPOINT, abandon, desert, neglect, omit, let down, forsake, turn your back on, be disloyal to, break your word, forget

3 STOP WORKING, stop, die, give up, break down, cease, stall, cut out, malfunction, conk out (*informal*), go on the blink (*informal*), go phut

4 WITHER, perish, sag, droop, waste away, shrivel up

5 GO BANKRUPT, crash, collapse, fold (*informal*), close down, go under, go bust (*informal*), go out of business, be wound up, go broke (*informal*), go to the wall, go into receivership, go into liquidation, become insolvent, smash

6 DECLINE, fade, weaken, deteriorate, dwindle, sicken, degenerate, fall apart at the seams, be on your last legs (*informal*)

7 GIVE OUT, disappear, fade, dim, dwindle, wane, gutter, languish, peter out, die away, grow dim, sink

▷▷ **without fail** WITHOUT EXCEPTION, regularly, constantly, invariably, religiously, unfailingly, conscientiously, like clockwork, punctually, dependably

failing *noun* SHORTCOMING, failure, fault, error, weakness, defect, deficiency, lapse, flaw, miscarriage, drawback, misfortune, blemish, imperfection, frailty, foible, blind spot

<< OPPOSITE strength

▷ *preposition* IN THE ABSENCE OF, lacking, in default of

failure *noun* 1 LACK OF SUCCESS, defeat, collapse, abortion, wreck, frustration, breakdown, overthrow, miscarriage, fiasco, downfall

<< OPPOSITE success

2 LOSER, disappointment, no-good, flop (*informal*), write-off, incompetent, no-hoper (*chiefly Austral*), dud (*informal*), clinker (*slang, chiefly US*), black sheep, washout (*informal*), clunker (*informal*), dead duck (*slang*), ne'er-do-well, nonstarter

3 NEGLIGENCE, neglect, deficiency, default, shortcoming, omission, oversight, dereliction, nonperformance, nonobservance, nonsuccess, remissness

<< OPPOSITE observance

4 BREAKDOWN, stalling, cutting out, malfunction, crash, disruption, stoppage, mishap, conking out (*informal*)

5 FAILING, deterioration, decay, loss, decline

6 BANKRUPTCY, crash, collapse, ruin, folding (*informal*), closure, winding up, downfall, going under, liquidation, insolvency

<< OPPOSITE prosperity

faint *adjective* 1 DIM, low, light, soft, thin, faded, whispered, distant, dull, delicate, vague, unclear, muted, subdued, faltering, hushed, bleached, feeble, indefinite, muffled, hazy, ill-defined, indistinct

<< OPPOSITE clear

2 SLIGHT, weak, feeble, unenthusiastic, remote, slim, vague, slender

3 TIMID, weak, feeble, lame, unconvincing, unenthusiastic, timorous, faint-hearted, spiritless, half-hearted, lily-livered

<< OPPOSITE brave

4 DIZZY, giddy, light-headed, vertiginous, weak, exhausted, fatigued, faltering, wobbly, drooping, languid, lethargic, muzzy, woozy (*informal*), weak at the knees, enervated

<< OPPOSITE energetic

▷ *verb* PASS OUT, black out, lose consciousness, keel over (*informal*), fail, go out, collapse, fade, weaken, languish, swoon (*literary*), flake out (*informal*)

▷ *noun* BLACKOUT, collapse, coma, swoon (*literary*), unconsciousness, syncope (*Pathology*)

faintly *adverb* 1 SLIGHTLY, rather, a little, somewhat, dimly

2 SOFTLY, weakly, feebly, in a whisper, indistinctly, unclearly

fair[1] *adjective* 1 UNBIASED, impartial, even-handed, unprejudiced, just, clean, square, equal, objective, reasonable, proper, legitimate, upright, honourable, honest, equitable, lawful, trustworthy, on the level (*informal*), disinterested, dispassionate, above board, according to the rules

<< OPPOSITE unfair

2 RESPECTABLE, middling, average, reasonable, decent, acceptable, moderate, adequate, satisfactory, not bad, mediocre, so-so (*informal*), tolerable, passable, O.K. *or* okay (*informal*), all right

3 LIGHT, golden, blonde, blond, yellowish, fair-haired, light-coloured, flaxen-haired, towheaded, tow-haired

4 LIGHT-COMPLEXIONED, white, pale

5 FINE, clear, dry, bright, pleasant, sunny, favourable, clement, cloudless, unclouded, sunshiny

6 BEAUTIFUL, pretty, attractive, lovely, handsome, good-looking, bonny, comely, beauteous, well-favoured

<< OPPOSITE ugly

▷▷ **fair and square** HONESTLY, straight, legally, on the level (*informal*), by the book, lawfully, above board, according to the rules, without cheating

fair[2] *noun* 1 CARNIVAL, fête, gala, bazaar

2 EXHIBITION, show, market, festival, mart, expo (*informal*), exposition

fairly *adverb* 1 EQUITABLY, objectively, legitimately, honestly, justly, lawfully, without prejudice, dispassionately, impartially, even-handedly, without bias
2 MODERATELY, rather, quite, somewhat, reasonably, adequately, pretty well, tolerably, passably
3 POSITIVELY, really, simply, absolutely, in a manner of speaking, veritably
4 DESERVEDLY, objectively, honestly, justifiably, justly, impartially, equitably, without fear or favour, properly

fair-minded *adjective* IMPARTIAL, just, fair, reasonable, open-minded, disinterested, unbiased, even-handed, unprejudiced

fairness *noun* IMPARTIALITY, justice, equity, legitimacy, decency, disinterestedness, uprightness, rightfulness, equitableness

fairy *noun* SPRITE, elf, brownie, hob, pixie, puck, imp, leprechaun, peri, Robin Goodfellow

fairy tale *or* **fairy story** *noun* 1 FOLK TALE, romance, traditional story
2 LIE, fantasy, fiction, invention, fabrication, untruth, porky (*Brit slang*), pork pie (*Brit slang*), urban myth, tall story, urban legend, cock-and-bull story (*informal*)

faith *noun* 1 CONFIDENCE, trust, credit, conviction, assurance, dependence, reliance, credence
<< OPPOSITE distrust
2 RELIGION, church, belief, persuasion, creed, communion, denomination, dogma
<< OPPOSITE agnosticism

faithful *adjective* 1 LOYAL, true, committed, constant, attached, devoted, dedicated, reliable, staunch, truthful, dependable, trusty, steadfast, unwavering, true-blue, immovable, unswerving
<< OPPOSITE disloyal
2 ACCURATE, just, close, true, strict, exact, precise
▷▷ **the faithful** BELIEVERS, brethren, followers, congregation, adherents, the elect, communicants

faithfulness *noun* LOYALTY, devotion, fidelity, constancy, dependability, trustworthiness, fealty, adherence

faithless *adjective* DISLOYAL, unreliable, unfaithful, untrustworthy, doubting, false, untrue, treacherous, dishonest, fickle, perfidious, untruthful, traitorous, unbelieving, inconstant, false-hearted, recreant (*archaic*)

fake *verb* 1 FORGE, copy, reproduce, fabricate, counterfeit, falsify
2 SHAM, affect, assume, put on, pretend, simulate, feign, go through the motions of
▷ *noun* 1 FORGERY, copy, fraud, reproduction, dummy, imitation, hoax, counterfeit
2 CHARLATAN, deceiver, sham, quack, mountebank, phoney *or* phony (*informal*)
▷ *adjective* ARTIFICIAL, false, forged, counterfeit, affected, assumed, put-on, pretend (*informal*), mock, imitation, sham, pseudo (*informal*), feigned, pinchbeck, phoney *or* phony (*informal*)
<< OPPOSITE genuine

fall *verb* 1 DROP, plunge, tumble, plummet, trip, settle, crash, collapse, pitch, sink, go down, come down, dive, stumble, descend, topple, subside, cascade, trip over, drop down, nose-dive, come a cropper (*informal*), keel over, go head over heels
<< OPPOSITE rise
2 DECREASE, drop, decline, go down, flag, slump, diminish, fall off, dwindle, lessen, subside, ebb, abate, depreciate, become lower
<< OPPOSITE increase
3 BE OVERTHROWN, be taken, surrender, succumb, yield, submit, give way, capitulate, be conquered, give in *or* up, pass into enemy hands
<< OPPOSITE triumph
4 BE KILLED, die, be lost, perish, be slain, be a casualty, meet your end
<< OPPOSITE survive
5 OCCUR, happen, come about, chance, take place, fall out, befall, come to pass
▷ *noun* 1 DROP, slip, plunge, dive, spill, tumble, descent, plummet, nose dive
2 DECREASE, drop, lowering, decline, reduction, slump, dip, falling off, dwindling, lessening, diminution, cut
3 COLLAPSE, defeat, surrender, downfall, death, failure, ruin, resignation, destruction, overthrow, submission, capitulation
4 SLOPE, incline, descent, downgrade, slant, declivity
▷ *plural noun* WATERFALL, rapids, cascade, cataract, linn (*Scot*), force (*Northern English dialect*)
▷▷ **fall apart** 1 BREAK UP, crumble, disintegrate, fall to bits, go to seed, come apart at the seams, break into pieces, go *or* come to pieces, shatter
2 BREAK DOWN, dissolve, disperse, disband, lose cohesion
3 GO TO PIECES, break down, crack up (*informal*), have a breakdown, crumble
▷▷ **fall away** 1 SLOPE, drop, go down, incline, incline downwards
2 DECREASE, drop, diminish, fall off, dwindle, lessen
▷▷ **fall back** RETREAT, retire, withdraw, move back, recede, pull back, back off, recoil, draw back

▷▷ **fall back on something** *or* **someone** RESORT TO, have recourse to, employ, turn to, make use of, call upon, press into service

▷▷ **fall behind** 1 LAG, trail, be left behind, drop back, get left behind, lose your place
2 BE IN ARREARS, be late, not keep up

▷▷ **fall down** *often with* **on** (*informal*) FAIL, disappoint, go wrong, fall short, fail to make the grade, prove unsuccessful

▷▷ **fall for someone** FALL IN LOVE WITH, become infatuated with, be smitten by, be swept off your feet by, desire, fancy (*Brit informal*), succumb to the charms of, lose your head over

▷▷ **fall for something** BE FOOLED BY, be deceived by, be taken in by, be duped by, buy (*slang*), accept, swallow (*informal*), take on board, give credence to

▷▷ **fall in** COLLAPSE, sink, cave in, crash in, fall to the ground, fall apart at the seams, come down about your ears

▷▷ **fall in with someone** *often with* **with** MAKE FRIENDS WITH, go around with, become friendly with, hang about with (*informal*)

▷▷ **fall in with something** GO ALONG WITH, support, accept, agree with, comply with, submit to, yield to, buy into (*informal*), cooperate with, assent, take on board, concur with

▷▷ **fall off** 1 TUMBLE, topple, plummet, be unseated, come a cropper *or* purler (*informal*), take a fall *or* tumble
2 DECREASE, drop, reduce, decline, fade, slump, weaken, shrink, diminish, dwindle, lessen, wane, subside, fall away, peter out, slacken, tail off (*informal*), ebb away, go down *or* downhill

▷▷ **fall on** *or* **upon something** *or* **someone** ATTACK, assault, snatch, assail, tear into (*informal*), lay into, descend upon, pitch into (*informal*), belabour, let fly at, set upon *or* about

▷▷ **fall out** (*informal*) ARGUE, fight, row, clash, differ, disagree, quarrel, squabble, have a row, have words, come to blows, cross swords, altercate

▷▷ **fall short** *often with* **of** BE LACKING, miss, fail, disappoint, be wanting, be inadequate, be deficient, fall down on (*informal*), prove inadequate, not come up to expectations *or* scratch (*informal*)

▷▷ **fall through** FAIL, be unsuccessful, come to nothing, fizzle out (*informal*), miscarry, go awry, go by the board

▷▷ **fall to someone** BE THE RESPONSIBILITY OF, be up to, come down to, devolve upon

▷▷ **fall to something** BEGIN, start, set to, set about, commence, apply yourself to

fallacy *noun* ERROR, mistake, illusion, flaw, deception, delusion, inconsistency, misconception, deceit, falsehood, untruth, misapprehension, sophistry, casuistry, sophism, faultiness

fallen *adjective* 1 KILLED, lost, dead, slaughtered, slain, perished
2 DISHONOURED, lost, loose, shamed, ruined, disgraced, immoral, sinful, unchaste

fallible *adjective* IMPERFECT, weak, uncertain, ignorant, mortal, frail, erring, prone to error
<< OPPOSITE infallible

fallout *noun* CONSEQUENCES, results, effects, outcome, repercussions, upshot

fallow *adjective* 1 UNCULTIVATED, unused, undeveloped, unplanted, untilled
2 INACTIVE, resting, idle, dormant, inert

false *adjective* 1 INCORRECT, wrong, mistaken, misleading, faulty, inaccurate, invalid, improper, unfounded, erroneous, inexact
<< OPPOSITE correct
2 UNTRUE, fraudulent, unreal, concocted, fictitious, trumped up, fallacious, untruthful, truthless
<< OPPOSITE true
3 ARTIFICIAL, forged, fake, mock, reproduction, synthetic, replica, imitation, bogus, simulated, sham, pseudo (*informal*), counterfeit, feigned, spurious, ersatz, pretended
<< OPPOSITE real
4 TREACHEROUS, lying, deceiving, unreliable, two-timing (*informal*), dishonest, deceptive, hypocritical, unfaithful, two-faced, disloyal, unsound, deceitful, faithless, untrustworthy, insincere, double-dealing, dishonourable, duplicitous, mendacious, perfidious, treasonable, traitorous, inconstant, delusive, false-hearted
<< OPPOSITE loyal

falsehood *noun* 1 UNTRUTHFULNESS, deception, deceit, dishonesty, prevarication, mendacity, dissimulation, perjury, inveracity (*rare*)
2 LIE, story, fiction, fabrication, fib, untruth, porky (*Brit slang*), pork pie (*Brit slang*), misstatement

falsify *verb* ALTER, forge, fake, tamper with, doctor, cook (*slang*), distort, pervert, belie, counterfeit, misrepresent, garble, misstate

falter *verb* 1 HESITATE, delay, waver, vacillate, break
<< OPPOSITE persevere
2 TUMBLE, shake, tremble, totter
3 STUTTER, pause, stumble, hesitate, stammer, speak haltingly

faltering *adjective* HESITANT, broken, weak, uncertain, stumbling, tentative, stammering, timid, irresolute

fame *noun* PROMINENCE, glory, celebrity, stardom, name, credit, reputation, honour, prestige, stature, eminence, renown, repute, public esteem, illustriousness

<< OPPOSITE obscurity

famed *adjective* RENOWNED, celebrated, recognized, well-known, acclaimed, widely-known

familiar *adjective* 1 WELL-KNOWN, household, everyday, recognized, common, stock, domestic, repeated, ordinary, conventional, routine, frequent, accustomed, customary, mundane, recognizable, common or garden (*informal*)

<< OPPOSITE unfamiliar

2 FRIENDLY, close, dear, intimate, confidential, amicable, chummy (*informal*), buddy-buddy (*slang, chiefly US & Canad*), palsy-walsy (*informal*)

<< OPPOSITE formal

3 RELAXED, open, easy, friendly, free, near, comfortable, intimate, casual, informal, amicable, cordial, free-and-easy, unreserved, unconstrained, unceremonious, hail-fellow-well-met

4 DISRESPECTFUL, forward, bold, presuming, intrusive, presumptuous, impudent, overfamiliar, overfree

▷▷ **familiar with** ACQUAINTED WITH, aware of, introduced to, conscious of, at home with, no stranger to, informed about, abreast of, knowledgeable about, versed in, well up in, proficient in, conversant with, on speaking terms with, in the know about, *au courant* with, *au fait* with

familiarity *noun* 1 ACQUAINTANCE, experience, understanding, knowledge, awareness, grasp, acquaintanceship

<< OPPOSITE unfamiliarity

2 FRIENDLINESS, friendship, intimacy, closeness, freedom, ease, openness, fellowship, informality, sociability, naturalness, absence of reserve, unceremoniousness

<< OPPOSITE formality

3 DISRESPECT, forwardness, overfamiliarity, liberties, liberty, cheek, presumption, boldness

<< OPPOSITE respect

familiarize *or* **familiarise** *verb* ACCUSTOM, instruct, habituate, make used to, school, season, train, prime, coach, get to know (about), inure, bring into common use, make conversant

family *noun* 1 RELATIONS, people, children, issue, relatives, household, folk (*informal*), offspring, descendants, brood, kin, nuclear family, progeny, kindred, next of kin, kinsmen, ménage, kith and kin, your nearest and dearest, kinsfolk, your own flesh and blood, ainga (*NZ*), rellies (*Austral slang*)

2 CHILDREN, kids (*informal*), offspring, little ones, munchkins (*informal, chiefly US*), littlies (*Austral informal*)

3 ANCESTORS, forebears, parentage, forefathers, house, line, race, blood, birth, strain, tribe, sept, clan, descent, dynasty, pedigree, extraction, ancestry, lineage, genealogy, line of descent, stemma, stirps

4 SPECIES, group, class, system, order, kind, network, genre, classification, subdivision, subclass

>> RELATED WORD *adjective* familial

Some careful writers insist that a singular verb should always be used with collective nouns such as *government, team, family, committee,* and *class*, for example: *the class is doing a project on Vikings; the company is mounting a big sales campaign*. In British usage, however, a plural verb is often used with a collective noun, especially where the emphasis is on a collection of individual objects or people rather than a group regarded as a unit: *the family are all on holiday*. The most important thing to remember is never to treat the same collective noun as both singular and plural in the same sentence: *the family is well and sends its best wishes* or *the family are well and send their best wishes*, but not *the family is well and send their best wishes*

family tree *noun* LINEAGE, genealogy, line of descent, ancestral tree, line, descent, pedigree, extraction, ancestry, blood line, stemma, stirps, whakapapa (NZ)

famine *noun* HUNGER, want, starvation, deprivation, scarcity, dearth, destitution

famous *adjective* WELL-KNOWN, celebrated, acclaimed, notable, noted, excellent, signal, honoured, remarkable, distinguished, prominent, glorious, legendary, renowned, eminent, conspicuous, illustrious, much-publicized, lionized, far-famed

<< OPPOSITE unknown

fan[1] *noun* BLOWER, ventilator, air conditioner, vane, punkah (*in India*), blade, propeller

▷ *verb* 1 BLOW, cool, refresh, air-condition, ventilate, air-cool, winnow (*rare*)

2 STIMULATE, increase, excite, provoke, arouse, rouse, stir up, work up, agitate, whip up, add fuel to the flames, impassion, enkindle

3 *often with* **out** SPREAD OUT, spread, lay out, disperse, unfurl, open out, space out

fan[2] *noun* 1 SUPPORTER, lover, follower, enthusiast, admirer, groupie (*slang*), rooter (US)

2 DEVOTEE, addict, freak (*informal*), buff (*informal*), fiend (*informal*), adherent, zealot, aficionado

fanatic *noun* EXTREMIST, activist, militant, addict, enthusiast, buff (*informal*), visionary, devotee, bigot, zealot, energumen

fanatical *adjective* OBSESSIVE, burning, wild, mad, extreme, enthusiastic, passionate, frenzied, visionary, fervent, zealous, bigoted, rabid, immoderate, overenthusiastic

fanaticism *noun* IMMODERATION, enthusiasm, madness, devotion, dedication, zeal, bigotry, extremism, infatuation, single-mindedness, zealotry, obsessiveness, monomania, overenthusiasm

fancier *noun* EXPERT, amateur, breeder, connoisseur, aficionado

fanciful *adjective* UNREAL, wild, ideal, romantic, fantastic, curious, fabulous, imaginative, imaginary, poetic, extravagant, visionary, fairy-tale, mythical, whimsical, capricious, chimerical

<< OPPOSITE unimaginative

fancy *adjective* 1 ELABORATE, decorated, decorative, extravagant, intricate, baroque, ornamented, ornamental, ornate, elegant, fanciful, embellished

<< OPPOSITE plain

2 EXPENSIVE, high-quality, classy, flashy, swish (*informal*), showy, ostentatious

▷ *noun* 1 WHIM, thought, idea, desire, urge, notion, humour, impulse, inclination, caprice

2 DELUSION, dream, vision, fantasy, nightmare, daydream, chimera, phantasm

▷ *verb* 1 (*informal*) WISH FOR, want, desire, would like, hope for, dream of, relish, long for, crave, be attracted to, yearn for, thirst for, hanker after, have a yen for

2 (*Brit informal*) BE ATTRACTED TO, find attractive, desire, lust after, like, prefer, favour, take to, go for, be captivated by, have an eye for, have a thing about (*informal*), have eyes for, take a liking to

3 SUPPOSE, think, believe, imagine, guess (*informal, chiefly US & Canad*), reckon, conceive, infer, conjecture, surmise, think likely, be inclined to think

▷▷ **fancy yourself** THINK YOU ARE GOD'S GIFT, have a high opinion of yourself, think you are the cat's whiskers

▷▷ **take a fancy to something** *or* **someone** START LIKING, like, want, be fond of, hanker after, have a partiality for

fanfare *noun* TRUMPET CALL, flourish, trump (*archaic*), tucket (*archaic*), fanfaronade

fang *noun* TOOTH, tusk

fantasize *or* **fantasise** *verb* DAYDREAM, imagine, invent, romance, envision, hallucinate, see visions, live in a dream world, build castles in the air, give free rein to the imagination

fantastic *adjective* 1 (*informal*) WONDERFUL, great, excellent, very good, mean (*slang*), topping (*Brit slang*), cracking (*Brit informal*), crucial (*slang*), smashing (*informal*), superb, tremendous (*informal*), magnificent, marvellous, terrific (*informal*), sensational (*informal*), mega (*slang*), awesome (*slang*), dope (*slang*), world-class, first-rate, def (*slang*), brill (*informal*), out of this world (*informal*), boffo (*slang*), jim-dandy (*slang*), bitchin' (*US slang*), chillin' (*US slang*), booshit (*Austral slang*), exo (*Austral slang*), sik (*Austral slang*), rad (*informal*), phat (*slang*), schmick (*Austral informal*)

<< OPPOSITE ordinary

2 (*informal*) ENORMOUS, great, huge, vast, severe, extreme, overwhelming, tremendous, immense

3 STRANGE, bizarre, weird, exotic, peculiar, imaginative, queer, grotesque, quaint, unreal, fanciful, outlandish, whimsical, freakish, chimerical, phantasmagorical

4 IMPLAUSIBLE, unlikely, incredible, absurd, irrational, preposterous, capricious, cock-and-bull (*informal*), cockamamie (*slang, chiefly US*), mad

fantasy *or* **phantasy** *noun* 1 DAYDREAM, dream, wish, fancy, delusion, reverie, flight of fancy, pipe dream

2 IMAGINATION, fancy, invention, creativity, originality

far *adverb* 1 A LONG WAY, miles, deep, a good way, afar, a great distance

2 MUCH, greatly, very much, extremely, significantly, considerably, decidedly, markedly, incomparably

▷ *adjective often with* **off** REMOTE, distant, far-flung, faraway, long, removed, out-of-the-way, far-off, far-removed, outlying, off the beaten track

<< OPPOSITE near

▷▷ **by far** *or* **far and away** VERY MUCH, easily, immeasurably, by a long way, incomparably, to a great degree, by a long shot, by a long chalk (*informal*), by a great amount

▷▷ **far and wide** EXTENSIVELY, everywhere, worldwide, far and near, widely, broadly, in all places, in every nook and cranny, here, there and everywhere

▷▷ **far from** NOT AT ALL, not, by no means, absolutely not

▷▷ **so far** 1 UP TO A POINT, to a certain extent, to a limited extent

2 UP TO NOW, to date, until now, thus far, up to the present

faraway *adjective* 1 DISTANT, far, remote, far-off, far-removed, far-flung, outlying, beyond the horizon

2 DREAMY, lost, distant, abstracted, vague, absent

farce *noun* 1 COMEDY, satire, slapstick, burlesque, buffoonery, broad comedy

2 MOCKERY, joke, nonsense, parody, shambles,

sham, absurdity, travesty, ridiculousness

farcical *adjective* 1 LUDICROUS, ridiculous, diverting, absurd, preposterous, laughable, nonsensical, derisory, risible
2 COMIC, funny, amusing, slapstick, droll, custard-pie

fare *noun* 1 CHARGE, price, ticket price, transport cost, ticket money, passage money
2 FOOD, meals, diet, provisions, board, commons, table, feed, menu, rations, tack (*informal*), kai (*NZ informal*), nourishment, sustenance, victuals, nosebag (*slang*), nutriment, vittles (*obsolete* or *dialect*), eatables
3 PASSENGER, customer, pick-up (*informal*), traveller
▷ *verb* 1 GET ON, do, manage, make out, prosper, get along
2 *used impersonally* HAPPEN, go, turn out, proceed, pan out (*informal*)

farewell *interjection* GOODBYE, bye (*informal*), so long, see you, take care, good morning, bye-bye (*informal*), good day, all the best, good night, good evening, good afternoon, see you later, ciao (*Italian*), have a nice day (*US*), adieu (*French*), au revoir (*French*), be seeing you, auf Wiedersehen (*German*), adios (*Spanish*), mind how you go, haere ra (*NZ*)
▷ *noun* GOODBYE, parting, departure, leave-taking, adieu, valediction, sendoff (*informal*), adieux *or* adieus

far-fetched *adjective* UNCONVINCING, unlikely, strained, fantastic, incredible, doubtful, unbelievable, dubious, unrealistic, improbable, unnatural, preposterous, implausible, hard to swallow (*informal*), cock-and-bull (*informal*)
<< OPPOSITE believable

farm *noun* SMALLHOLDING, holding, ranch (*chiefly US & Canad*), farmstead, land, station (*Austral & NZ*), acres, vineyard, plantation, croft (*Scot*), grange, homestead, acreage
▷ *verb* CULTIVATE, work, plant, operate, till the soil, grow crops on, bring under cultivation, keep animals on, practise husbandry

farmer *noun* AGRICULTURIST, yeoman, smallholder, crofter (*Scot*), grazier, agriculturalist, rancher, agronomist, husbandman, cockie *or* cocky (*Austral & NZ informal*)

farming *noun* AGRICULTURE, cultivation, husbandry, land management, agronomy, tilling

far-out *adjective* STRANGE, wild, unusual, bizarre, weird, avant-garde, unconventional, off-the-wall (*slang*), outlandish, outré, advanced

far-reaching *adjective* EXTENSIVE, important, significant, sweeping, broad, widespread, pervasive, momentous

far-sighted *adjective* PRUDENT, acute, wise, cautious, sage, shrewd, discerning, canny, provident, judicious, prescient, far-seeing, politic

farther

> *Farther, farthest, further,* and *furthest* can all be used to refer to literal distance, but *further* and *furthest* are used for figurative senses denoting greater or additional amount, time, etc.: *further to my letter*. *Further* and *furthest* are also preferred for figurative distance

farthest ▷ see **farther**

fascinate *verb* ENTRANCE, delight, charm, absorb, intrigue, enchant, rivet, captivate, enthral, beguile, allure, bewitch, ravish, transfix, mesmerize, hypnotize, engross, enrapture, interest greatly, enamour, hold spellbound, spellbind, infatuate
<< OPPOSITE bore

fascinated *adjective* ENTRANCED, charmed, absorbed, very interested, captivated, hooked on, enthralled, beguiled, smitten, bewitched, engrossed, spellbound, infatuated, hypnotized, under a spell

fascinating *adjective* CAPTIVATING, engaging, gripping, compelling, intriguing, very interesting, irresistible, enticing, enchanting, seductive, riveting, alluring, bewitching, ravishing, engrossing
<< OPPOSITE boring

fascination *noun* ATTRACTION, pull, spell, magic, charm, lure, glamour, allure, magnetism, enchantment, sorcery

Fascism *noun sometimes not cap.* AUTHORITARIANISM, dictatorship, totalitarianism, despotism, autocracy, absolutism, Hitlerism

fashion *noun* 1 STYLE, look, trend, rage, custom, convention, mode, vogue, usage, craze, fad, latest style, prevailing taste, latest
2 METHOD, way, style, approach, manner, mode
▷ *verb* 1 MAKE, shape, cast, construct, work, form, create, design, manufacture, forge, mould, contrive, fabricate
2 FIT, adapt, tailor, suit, adjust, accommodate
▷▷ **after a fashion** TO SOME EXTENT, somehow, in a way, moderately, to a certain extent, to a degree, somehow or other, in a manner of speaking

fashionable *adjective* POPULAR, in fashion, trendy (*Brit informal*), cool (*slang*), in (*informal*), latest, happening (*informal*), current, modern, with it (*informal*), usual, smart, hip (*slang*), prevailing, stylish, chic, up-to-date, customary, genteel, in vogue, all the rage, up-to-the-minute, modish, à la mode, voguish

(*informal*), trendsetting, all the go (*informal*), schmick (*Austral informal*)
<< OPPOSITE unfashionable

fast[1] *adjective* 1 QUICK, flying, winged, rapid, fleet, hurried, accelerated, swift, speedy, brisk, hasty, nimble, mercurial, sprightly, nippy (*Brit informal*)
<< OPPOSITE slow
2 FIXED, firm, sound, stuck, secure, tight, jammed, fortified, fastened, impregnable, immovable
<< OPPOSITE unstable
3 DISSIPATED, wild, exciting, loose, extravagant, reckless, immoral, promiscuous, giddy, self-indulgent, wanton, profligate, impure, intemperate, dissolute, rakish, licentious, gadabout (*informal*)
4 CLOSE, lasting, firm, permanent, constant, devoted, loyal, faithful, stalwart, staunch, steadfast, unwavering
▷ *adverb* 1 QUICKLY, rapidly, swiftly, hastily, hurriedly, speedily, presto, apace, in haste, like a shot (*informal*), at full speed, hell for leather (*informal*), like lightning, hotfoot, like a flash, at a rate of knots, like the clappers (*Brit informal*), like a bat out of hell (*slang*), pdq (*slang*), like nobody's business (*informal*), posthaste, like greased lightning (*informal*), with all haste
<< OPPOSITE slowly
2 FIRMLY, staunchly, resolutely, steadfastly, determinedly, unwaveringly, unchangeably
3 SECURELY, firmly, tightly, fixedly
4 FIXEDLY, firmly, soundly, deeply, securely, tightly
5 RECKLESSLY, wildly, loosely, extravagantly, promiscuously, rakishly, intemperately

fast[2] *verb* GO HUNGRY, abstain, go without food, deny yourself, practise abstention, refrain from food *or* eating
▷ *noun* FASTING, diet, abstinence

fasten *verb* 1 SECURE, close, lock, chain, seal, bolt, do up
2 TIE, bind, lace, tie up
3 FIX, join, link, connect, grip, attach, anchor, affix, make firm, make fast
4 *often with* **on** *or* **upon** CONCENTRATE, focus, fix
5 DIRECT, aim, focus, fix, concentrate, bend, rivet

fastening *noun* TIE, union, coupling, link, linking, bond, joint, binding, connection, attachment, junction, zip, fusion, clasp, concatenation, ligature, affixation

fastidious *adjective* PARTICULAR, meticulous, fussy, overdelicate, difficult, nice, critical, discriminating, dainty, squeamish, choosy, picky (*informal*), hard to please, finicky, punctilious, pernickety, hypercritical, overnice
<< OPPOSITE careless

fat *noun* FATNESS, flesh, bulk, obesity, cellulite, weight problem, flab, blubber, paunch, fatty tissue, adipose tissue, corpulence, beef (*informal*)
▷ *adjective* 1 OVERWEIGHT, large, heavy, plump, gross, stout, obese, fleshy, beefy (*informal*), tubby, portly, roly-poly, rotund, podgy, corpulent, elephantine, broad in the beam (*informal*), solid
<< OPPOSITE thin
2 LARGE, rich, substantial, thriving, flourishing, profitable, productive, lucrative, fertile, lush, prosperous, affluent, fruitful, cushy (*slang*), jammy (*Brit slang*), remunerative
<< OPPOSITE scanty
3 FATTY, greasy, lipid, adipose, oleaginous, suety, oily
<< OPPOSITE lean
▷▷ **a fat chance** (*Slang*) NO CHANCE, (a) slim chance, very little chance, not much chance

fatal *adjective* 1 DISASTROUS, devastating, crippling, lethal, catastrophic, ruinous, calamitous, baleful, baneful
<< OPPOSITE minor
2 DECISIVE, final, determining, critical, crucial, fateful
3 LETHAL, deadly, mortal, causing death, final, killing, terminal, destructive, malignant, incurable, pernicious
<< OPPOSITE harmless

fatalism *noun* RESIGNATION, acceptance, passivity, determinism, stoicism, necessitarianism, predestinarianism

fatality *noun* CASUALTY, death, loss, victim

fate *noun* 1 DESTINY, chance, fortune, luck, the stars, weird (*archaic*), providence, nemesis, kismet, predestination, divine will
2 FORTUNE, destiny, lot, portion, cup, horoscope
3 OUTCOME, future, destiny, end, issue, upshot
4 DOWNFALL, end, death, ruin, destruction, doom, demise

fated *adjective* DESTINED, doomed, predestined, preordained, foreordained, pre-elected

fateful *adjective* 1 CRUCIAL, important, significant, critical, decisive, momentous, portentous
<< OPPOSITE unimportant
2 DISASTROUS, fatal, deadly, destructive, lethal, ominous, ruinous

father *noun* 1 DADDY (*informal*), dad (*informal*), male parent, patriarch, pop (*US informal*), governor (*informal*), old man (*Brit informal*), pa (*informal*), old boy (*informal*), papa (*old-fashioned informal*), sire, pater, biological father, foster father, begetter, paterfamilias, birth father
2 FOUNDER, author, maker, architect, creator, inventor, originator, prime mover, initiator
3 *often plural* FOREFATHER, predecessor,

ancestor, forebear, progenitor, tupuna *or* tipuna (NZ)
4 *usually plural* LEADER, senator, elder, patron, patriarch, guiding light, city father, kaumatua (NZ)
▷ *verb* 1 SIRE, parent, conceive, bring to life, beget, procreate, bring into being, give life to, get
2 ORIGINATE, found, create, establish, author, institute, invent, engender
>> RELATED WORD *adjective* paternal

Father *noun* PRIEST, minister, vicar, parson, pastor, cleric, churchman, padre (*informal*), confessor, abbé, curé, man of God

fatherland *noun* HOMELAND, motherland, old country, native land, land of your birth, land of your fathers, whenua (NZ), Godzone (*Austral informal*)

fatherly *adjective* PATERNAL, kind, kindly, tender, protective, supportive, benign, affectionate, indulgent, patriarchal, benevolent, forbearing

fathom *verb* UNDERSTAND, grasp, comprehend, interpret, get to the bottom of

fatigue *noun* TIREDNESS, lethargy, weariness, ennui, heaviness, debility, languor, listlessness, overtiredness
<< OPPOSITE freshness
▷ *verb* TIRE, exhaust, weaken, weary, drain, fag (out) (*informal*), whack (*Brit informal*), wear out, jade, take it out of (*informal*), poop (*informal*), tire out, knacker (*slang*), drain of energy, overtire
<< OPPOSITE refresh

fatigued *adjective* TIRED, exhausted, weary, tired out, bushed (*informal*), wasted, all in (*slang*), fagged (out) (*informal*), whacked (*Brit informal*), jaded, knackered (*slang*), clapped out (*Austral & NZ informal*), overtired, zonked (*slang*), dead beat (*informal*), jiggered (*informal*), on your last legs, creamcrackered (*Brit informal*)

fatten *verb* 1 GROW FAT, spread, expand, swell, thrive, broaden, thicken, put on weight, gain weight, coarsen, become fat, become fatter
2 FEED UP, feed, stuff, build up, cram, nourish, distend, bloat, overfeed

fatty *adjective* GREASY, fat, creamy, oily, adipose, oleaginous, suety, rich

fatuous *adjective* FOOLISH, stupid, silly, dull, absurd, dense, ludicrous, lunatic, mindless, idiotic, vacuous, inane, witless, puerile, moronic, brainless, asinine, weak-minded, dumb-ass (*slang*)

faucet *noun* (*US & Canad*) TAP, spout, spigot, stopcock, valve

fault *noun* 1 RESPONSIBILITY, liability, guilt, accountability, culpability
2 MISTAKE, slip, error, offence, blunder, lapse, negligence, omission, boob (*Brit slang*), oversight, slip-up, indiscretion, inaccuracy, howler (*informal*), glitch (*informal*), error of judgment, boo-boo (*informal*), barry *or* Barry Crocker (*Austral slang*)
3 FAILING, lack, weakness, defect, deficiency, flaw, drawback, shortcoming, snag, blemish, imperfection, Achilles heel, weak point, infirmity, demerit
<< OPPOSITE strength
▷ *verb* CRITICIZE, blame, complain, condemn, moan about, censure, hold (someone) responsible, hold (someone) accountable, find fault with, call to account, impugn, find lacking, hold (someone) to blame
▷▷ **at fault** GUILTY, responsible, to blame, accountable, in the wrong, culpable, answerable, blamable
▷▷ **find fault with something** *or* **someone** CRITICIZE, complain about, whinge about (*informal*), whine about (*informal*), quibble, diss (*slang, chiefly US*), carp at, take to task, pick holes in, grouse about (*informal*), haul over the coals (*informal*), pull to pieces
▷▷ **to a fault** EXCESSIVELY, overly (*US*), unduly, ridiculously, in the extreme, needlessly, out of all proportion, preposterously, overmuch, immoderately

faultless *adjective* FLAWLESS, model, perfect, classic, correct, accurate, faithful, impeccable, exemplary, foolproof, unblemished

faulty *adjective* 1 DEFECTIVE, damaged, not working, malfunctioning, broken, bad, flawed, impaired, imperfect, blemished, out of order, on the blink
2 INCORRECT, wrong, flawed, inaccurate, bad, weak, invalid, erroneous, unsound, imprecise, fallacious

faux pas *noun* GAFFE, blunder, indiscretion, impropriety, bloomer (*Brit informal*), boob (*Brit slang*), clanger (*informal*), solecism, breach of etiquette, gaucherie

favour *or US* **favor** *noun* 1 APPROVAL, grace, esteem, goodwill, kindness, friendliness, commendation, partiality, approbation, kind regard
<< OPPOSITE disapproval
2 FAVOURITISM, preference, bias, nepotism, preferential treatment, partisanship, jobs for the boys (*informal*), partiality, one-sidedness
3 SUPPORT, backing, aid, championship, promotion, assistance, patronage, espousal, good opinion
4 GOOD TURN, service, benefit, courtesy, kindness, indulgence, boon, good deed, kind act, obligement (*Scot archaic*)
<< OPPOSITE wrong
5 MEMENTO, present, gift, token, souvenir, keepsake, love-token
▷ *verb* 1 PREFER, opt for, like better, incline towards, choose, pick, desire, select, elect,

adopt, go for, fancy, single out, plump for, be partial to
<< OPPOSITE object to
2 INDULGE, reward, spoil, esteem, side with, pamper, befriend, be partial to, smile upon, pull strings for (*informal*), have in your good books, treat with partiality, value
3 SUPPORT, like, back, choose, champion, encourage, approve, fancy, advocate, opt for, subscribe to, commend, stand up for, espouse, be in favour of, countenance, patronize
<< OPPOSITE oppose
4 HELP, benefit, aid, advance, promote, assist, accommodate, facilitate, abet, succour, do a kindness to
5 OBLIGE, please, honour, accommodate, benefit
▷▷ **in favour of** FOR, backing, supporting, behind, pro, all for (*informal*), on the side of, right behind

favourable *or US* **favorable** *adjective* 1 POSITIVE, kind, understanding, encouraging, welcoming, friendly, approving, praising, reassuring, enthusiastic, sympathetic, benign, commending, complimentary, agreeable, amicable, well-disposed, commendatory
<< OPPOSITE disapproving
2 AFFIRMATIVE, agreeing, confirming, positive, assenting, corroborative
3 ADVANTAGEOUS, timely, good, promising, fit, encouraging, fair, appropriate, suitable, helpful, hopeful, convenient, beneficial, auspicious, opportune, propitious
<< OPPOSITE disadvantageous

favourably *or US* **favorably** *adverb* 1 POSITIVELY, well, enthusiastically, helpfully, graciously, approvingly, agreeably, with approval, without prejudice, genially, with approbation, in a kindly manner, with cordiality
2 ADVANTAGEOUSLY, well, fortunately, conveniently, profitably, to your advantage, auspiciously, opportunely

favourite *or US* **favorite** *adjective* PREFERRED, favoured, best-loved, most-liked, special, choice, dearest, pet, esteemed, fave (*informal*)
▷ *noun* DARLING, pet, preference, blue-eyed boy (*informal*), pick, choice, dear, beloved, idol, fave (*informal*), teacher's pet, the apple of your eye

favouritism *or US* **favoritism** *noun* BIAS, preference, nepotism, preferential treatment, partisanship, jobs for the boys (*informal*), partiality, one-sidedness
<< OPPOSITE impartiality

fawn[1] *adjective* BEIGE, neutral, buff, yellowish-brown, greyish-brown

fawn[2] *verb usually with* **on** *or* **upon** INGRATIATE YOURSELF, court, flatter, pander to, creep, crawl, kneel, cringe, grovel, curry favour, toady, pay court, kowtow, bow and scrape, dance attendance, truckle, be obsequious, be servile, lick (someone's) boots

fawning *adjective* OBSEQUIOUS, crawling, flattering, cringing, abject, grovelling, prostrate, deferential, sycophantic, servile, slavish, bowing and scraping, bootlicking (*informal*)

fear *noun* 1 DREAD, horror, panic, terror, dismay, awe, fright, tremors, qualms, consternation, alarm, trepidation, timidity, fearfulness, blue funk (*informal*), apprehensiveness, cravenness
2 BUGBEAR, bête noire, horror, nightmare, anxiety, terror, dread, spectre, phobia, bogey, thing (*informal*)
3 ANXIETY, concern, worry, doubt, nerves (*informal*), distress, suspicion, willies (*informal*), creeps (*informal*), butterflies (*informal*), funk (*informal*), angst, unease, apprehension, misgiving(s), nervousness, agitation, foreboding(s), uneasiness, solicitude, blue funk (*informal*), heebie-jeebies (*informal*), collywobbles (*informal*), disquietude
4 AWE, wonder, respect, worship, dread, reverence, veneration
▷ *verb* 1 BE AFRAID OF, dread, be scared of, be frightened of, shudder at, be fearful of, be apprehensive about, tremble at, be terrified by, have a horror of, take fright at, have a phobia about, have qualms about, live in dread of, be in a blue funk about (*informal*), have butterflies in your stomach about (*informal*), shake in your shoes about
2 REVERE, respect, reverence, venerate, stand in awe of
3 REGRET, feel, suspect, have a feeling, have a hunch, have a sneaking suspicion, have a funny feeling
▷▷ **fear for something** *or* **someone** WORRY ABOUT, be concerned about, be anxious about, tremble for, be distressed about, feel concern for, be disquieted over

fearful *adjective* 1 SCARED, afraid, alarmed, frightened, nervous, terrified, apprehensive, petrified, jittery (*informal*)
<< OPPOSITE unafraid
2 TIMID, afraid, frightened, scared, alarmed, wired (*slang*), nervous, anxious, shrinking, tense, intimidated, uneasy, neurotic, hesitant, apprehensive, jittery (*informal*), panicky, nervy (*Brit informal*), diffident, jumpy, timorous, pusillanimous, faint-hearted
<< OPPOSITE brave
3 (*informal*) FRIGHTFUL, shocking, terrible, awful, distressing, appalling, horrible, grim, dreadful, horrific, dire, horrendous, ghastly, hideous, monstrous, harrowing, gruesome,

grievous, unspeakable, atrocious, hair-raising, hellacious (*US slang*)

fearfully *adverb* 1 NERVOUSLY, uneasily, timidly, apprehensively, diffidently, in fear and trembling, timorously, with bated breath, with many misgivings *or* forebodings, with your heart in your mouth
2 (*informal*) VERY, terribly, horribly, tremendously, awfully, exceedingly, excessively, dreadfully, frightfully

fearless *adjective* INTREPID, confident, brave, daring, bold, heroic, courageous, gallant, gutsy (*slang*), valiant, plucky, game (*informal*), doughty, undaunted, indomitable, unabashed, unafraid, unflinching, dauntless, lion-hearted, valorous, (as) game as Ned Kelly (*Austral slang*)

fearsome *adjective* FORMIDABLE, alarming, frightening, awful, terrifying, appalling, horrifying, menacing, dismaying, awesome, daunting, horrendous, unnerving, hair-raising, awe-inspiring, baleful, hellacious (*US slang*)

feasibility *noun* POSSIBILITY, viability, usefulness, expediency, practicability, workability

feasible *adjective* PRACTICABLE, possible, reasonable, viable, workable, achievable, attainable, realizable, likely
<< OPPOSITE impracticable

feast *noun* 1 BANQUET, repast, spread (*informal*), dinner, entertainment, barbecue, revel, junket, beano (*Brit slang*), blowout (*slang*), carouse, slap-up meal (*Brit informal*), beanfeast (*Brit informal*), jollification, carousal, festive board, treat, hakari (*NZ*)
2 FESTIVAL, holiday, fête, celebration, holy day, red-letter day, religious festival, saint's day, -fest, gala day
3 TREAT, delight, pleasure, enjoyment, gratification, cornucopia
▷ *verb* EAT YOUR FILL, wine and dine, overindulge, eat to your heart's content, stuff yourself, consume, indulge, gorge, devour, pig out (*slang*), stuff your face (*slang*), fare sumptuously, gormandize
▷▷ **feast your eyes on something** LOOK AT WITH DELIGHT, gaze at, devour with your eyes

feat *noun* ACCOMPLISHMENT, act, performance, achievement, enterprise, undertaking, exploit, deed, attainment, feather in your cap

feather *noun* PLUME

feathery *adjective* DOWNY, soft, feathered, fluffy, plumed, wispy, plumy, plumate *or* plumose (*Botany, Zoology*), light

feature *noun* 1 ASPECT, quality, characteristic, attribute, point, mark, property, factor, trait, hallmark, facet, peculiarity
2 ARTICLE, report, story, piece, comment, item, column
3 HIGHLIGHT, draw, attraction, innovation, speciality, specialty, main item, crowd puller (*informal*), special attraction, special
▷ *plural noun* FACE, countenance, physiognomy, lineament
▷ *verb* 1 SPOTLIGHT, present, promote, set off, emphasize, play up, accentuate, foreground, call attention to, give prominence to, give the full works (*slang*)
2 STAR, appear, headline, participate, play a part

febrile *adjective* (*Formal*) FEVERISH, hot, fevered, flushed, fiery, inflamed, delirious, pyretic (*Medical*)

feckless *adjective* IRRESPONSIBLE, useless, hopeless, incompetent, feeble, worthless, futile, ineffectual, aimless, good-for-nothing, shiftless, weak

federation *noun* UNION, league, association, alliance, combination, coalition, partnership, consortium, syndicate, confederation, amalgamation, confederacy, entente, Bund (*German*), copartnership, federacy

fed up *adjective* CHEESED OFF, down, depressed, bored, tired, annoyed, hacked (off) (*US slang*), weary, gloomy, blue, dismal, discontented, dissatisfied, glum, sick and tired (*informal*), browned-off (*informal*), down in the mouth (*informal*), brassed off (*Brit slang*), hoha (*NZ*)

fee *noun* CHARGE, pay, price, cost, bill, account, payment, wage, reward, hire, salary, compensation, toll, remuneration, recompense, emolument, honorarium, meed (*archaic*)

feeble *adjective* 1 WEAK, failing, exhausted, weakened, delicate, faint, powerless, frail, debilitated, sickly, languid, puny, weedy (*informal*), infirm, effete, enfeebled, doddering, enervated, etiolated, shilpit (*Scot*)
<< OPPOSITE strong
2 INADEQUATE, weak, pathetic, insufficient, incompetent, ineffective, inefficient, lame, insignificant, ineffectual, indecisive
3 UNCONVINCING, poor, thin, weak, slight, tame, pathetic, lame, flimsy, paltry, flat
<< OPPOSITE effective

feed *verb* 1 CATER FOR, provide for, nourish, provide with food, supply, sustain, nurture, cook for, wine and dine, victual, provision
2 GRAZE, eat, browse, pasture
3 EAT, drink milk, take nourishment
4 SUPPLY, take, send, carry, convey, impart
5 DISCLOSE, give, tell, reveal, supply, communicate, pass on, impart, divulge, make known
6 ENCOURAGE, boost, fuel, strengthen, foster, minister to, bolster, fortify, augment, make stronger

▷ *noun* 1 FOOD, fodder, forage, silage, provender, pasturage
2 (*informal*) MEAL, spread (*informal*), dinner, lunch, tea, breakfast, feast, supper, tuck-in (*informal*), nosh (*slang*), repast, nosh-up (*Brit slang*)
▷▷ **feed on something** LIVE ON, depend on, devour, exist on, partake of, subsist on

feel *verb* 1 EXPERIENCE, suffer, bear, go through, endure, undergo, have a sensation of, have
2 TOUCH, handle, manipulate, run your hands over, finger, stroke, paw, maul, caress, fondle
3 BE AWARE OF, have a sensation of, be sensible of, enjoy
4 PERCEIVE, sense, detect, discern, know, experience, notice, observe
5 GROPE, explore, fumble, sound
6 SENSE, be aware, be convinced, have a feeling, have the impression, intuit, have a hunch, feel in your bones
7 BELIEVE, consider, judge, deem, think, hold, be of the opinion that
8 SEEM, appear, strike you as
9 NOTICE, note, observe, perceive, detect, discern
▷ *noun* 1 TEXTURE, finish, touch, surface, surface quality
2 IMPRESSION, feeling, air, sense, quality, atmosphere, mood, aura, ambience, vibes (*slang*)
▷▷ **feel for someone** FEEL COMPASSION FOR, pity, feel sorry for, sympathize with, be moved by, be sorry for, empathize, commiserate with, bleed for, feel sympathy for, condole with
▷▷ **feel like something** WANT, desire, would like, fancy, wish for, could do with, feel the need for, feel inclined, feel up to, have the inclination for

feeler ▷▷ **put out feelers** APPROACH, probe, test of the waters, overture, trial, launch a trial balloon

feeling *noun* 1 EMOTION, sentiment
2 OPINION, view, attitude, belief, point of view, instinct, inclination
3 PASSION, heat, emotion, intensity, warmth, sentimentality
4 ARDOUR, love, care, affection, warmth, tenderness, fondness, fervour
5 SYMPATHY, understanding, concern, pity, appreciation, sensitivity, compassion, sorrow, sensibility, empathy, fellow feeling
6 SENSATION, sense, impression, awareness
7 SENSE OF TOUCH, sense, perception, sensation, feel, touch
8 IMPRESSION, idea, sense, notion, suspicion, consciousness, hunch, apprehension, inkling, presentiment
9 ATMOSPHERE, mood, aura, ambience, feel, air, quality, vibes (*slang*)
▷ *plural noun* EMOTIONS, ego, self-esteem, sensibilities, susceptibilities, sensitivities
▷▷ **bad feeling** HOSTILITY, anger, dislike, resentment, bitterness, distrust, enmity, ill feeling, ill will, upset

feign *verb* PRETEND, affect, assume, put on, devise, forge, fake, imitate, simulate, sham, act, fabricate, counterfeit, give the appearance of, dissemble, make a show of

feigned *adjective* PRETENDED, affected, assumed, false, artificial, fake, imitation, simulated, sham, pseudo (*informal*), fabricated, counterfeit, spurious, ersatz, insincere

feint *noun* BLUFF, manoeuvre, dodge, mock attack, play, blind, distraction, pretence, expedient, ruse, artifice, gambit, subterfuge, stratagem, wile

feisty *adjective* (*informal*) FIERY, spirited, bold, plucky, vivacious, (as) game as Ned Kelly (*Austral slang*)

felicity *noun* 1 HAPPINESS, joy, ecstasy, bliss, delectation, blessedness, blissfulness
2 APTNESS, grace, effectiveness, suitability, propriety, appropriateness, applicability, becomingness, suitableness

feline *adjective* 1 CATLIKE, leonine
2 GRACEFUL, flowing, smooth, elegant, sleek, slinky, sinuous, stealthy

fell *verb* 1 CUT DOWN, cut, level, demolish, flatten, knock down, hew, raze
2 KNOCK DOWN, floor, flatten, strike down, prostrate, deck (*slang*)

fellow *noun* 1 (*Old-fashioned*) MAN, boy, person, individual, customer (*informal*), character, guy (*informal*), bloke (*Brit informal*), punter (*informal*), chap (*informal*)
2 ASSOCIATE, colleague, peer, co-worker, member, friend, partner, equal, companion, comrade, crony, compeer
▷ *modifier* co-, similar, related, allied, associate, associated, affiliated, akin, like

fellowship *noun* 1 SOCIETY, club, league, association, organization, guild, fraternity, brotherhood, sisterhood, order, sodality
2 CAMARADERIE, intimacy, communion, familiarity, brotherhood, companionship, sociability, amity, kindliness, fraternization, companionability, intercourse

feminine *adjective* 1 WOMANLY, pretty, soft, gentle, tender, modest, delicate, graceful, girlie, girlish, ladylike
<< OPPOSITE masculine
2 EFFEMINATE, camp (*informal*), weak, unmanly, effete, womanish, unmasculine

femininity *noun* WOMANLINESS, delicacy, softness, womanhood, gentleness, girlishness, feminineness, muliebrity

fen *noun* MARSH, moss (*Scot*), swamp, bog, slough, quagmire, holm (*dialect*), morass, pakihi (NZ), muskeg (*Canad*)

fence *noun* BARRIER, wall, defence, guard, railings, paling, shield, hedge, barricade, hedgerow, rampart, palisade, stockade, barbed wire

▷ *verb with* **in** *or* **off** ENCLOSE, surround, bound, hedge, pound, protect, separate, guard, defend, secure, pen, restrict, confine, fortify, encircle, coop, impound, circumscribe

▷▷ **sit on the fence** BE UNCOMMITTED, be uncertain, be undecided, vacillate, be in two minds, blow hot and cold (*informal*), be irresolute, avoid committing yourself

fend ▷▷ **fend for yourself** LOOK AFTER YOURSELF, support yourself, sustain yourself, take care of yourself, provide for yourself, make do, make provision for yourself, shift for yourself

▷▷ **fend something** *or* **someone off** 1 DEFLECT, resist, parry, avert, ward off, stave off, turn aside, hold *or* keep at bay

2 BEAT OFF, resist, parry, avert, deflect, repel, drive back, ward off, stave off, repulse, keep off, turn aside, hold *or* keep at bay

feral *adjective* 1 WILD, untamed, uncultivated, undomesticated, unbroken

2 SAVAGE, fierce, brutal, ferocious, fell, wild, vicious, bestial

ferment *noun* COMMOTION, turmoil, unrest, turbulence, trouble, heat, excitement, glow, fever, disruption, frenzy, stew, furore, uproar, agitation, tumult, hubbub, brouhaha, imbroglio, state of unrest

<< OPPOSITE tranquillity

▷ *verb* 1 BREW, froth, concoct, effervesce, work, rise, heat, boil, bubble, foam, seethe, leaven

2 STIR UP, excite, provoke, rouse, agitate, inflame, incite

ferocious *adjective* 1 FIERCE, violent, savage, ravening, predatory, feral, rapacious, wild

<< OPPOSITE gentle

2 CRUEL, bitter, brutal, vicious, ruthless, relentless, barbaric, merciless, brutish, bloodthirsty, barbarous, pitiless, tigerish

ferocity *noun* SAVAGERY, violence, cruelty, brutality, ruthlessness, inhumanity, wildness, barbarity, viciousness, fierceness, rapacity, bloodthirstiness, savageness, ferociousness

ferry *noun* FERRY BOAT, boat, ship, passenger boat, packet boat, packet

▷ *verb* TRANSPORT, bring, carry, ship, take, run, shuttle, convey, chauffeur

fertile *adjective* PRODUCTIVE, rich, flowering, lush, fat, yielding, prolific, abundant, plentiful, fruitful, teeming, luxuriant, generative, fecund, fruit-bearing, flowing with milk and honey, plenteous

<< OPPOSITE barren

fertility *noun* FRUITFULNESS, abundance, richness, fecundity, luxuriance, productiveness

fertilization *or* **fertilisation** *noun* INSEMINATION, propagation, procreation, implantation, pollination, impregnation

fertilize *or* **fertilise** *verb* 1 INSEMINATE, impregnate, pollinate, make pregnant, fructify, make fruitful, fecundate

2 ENRICH, feed, compost, manure, mulch, top-dress, dress, fertigate (*Austral*)

fertilizer *or* **fertiliser** *noun* COMPOST, muck, manure, dung, guano, marl, bone meal, dressing

fervent *adjective* ARDENT, earnest, enthusiastic, fervid, passionate, warm, excited, emotional, intense, flaming, eager, animated, fiery, ecstatic, devout, heartfelt, impassioned, zealous, vehement, perfervid (*literary*)

<< OPPOSITE apathetic

> Care should be taken when using *fervid* as an alternative to *fervent*. Although both come from the same root and share the meaning 'intense, ardent', *fervent* has largely positive connotations, and is associated with hopes, wishes, and beliefs, or admirers, supporters, and fans. Apart from being used less often than *fervent*, *fervid* is chiefly negative: *in the fervid politics of New York city*. *A fervent kiss* from an admirer would probably be welcome; a *fervid* one would not

fervour *or US* **fervor** *noun* ARDOUR, passion, enthusiasm, excitement, intensity, warmth, animation, zeal, eagerness, vehemence, earnestness, fervency

fester *verb* 1 INTENSIFY, gall, smoulder, chafe, irk, rankle, aggravate

2 PUTREFY, decay, become infected, become inflamed, suppurate, ulcerate, maturate, gather

festering *adjective* SEPTIC, infected, poisonous, inflamed, pussy, suppurating, ulcerated, purulent, maturating, gathering

festival *noun* 1 CELEBRATION, fair, carnival, gala, treat, fête, entertainment, jubilee, fiesta, festivities, jamboree, -fest, field day

2 HOLY DAY, holiday, feast, commemoration, feast day, red-letter day, saint's day, fiesta, fête, anniversary

festive *adjective* CELEBRATORY, happy, holiday, carnival, jolly, merry, gala, hearty, jubilant, cheery, joyous, joyful, jovial, convivial, gleeful, back-slapping, Christmassy, mirthful, sportive, light-hearted, festal, gay

<< OPPOSITE mournful

festivity *noun* 1 MERRYMAKING, fun, pleasure, amusement, mirth, gaiety, merriment, revelry, conviviality, joviality, joyfulness,

jollification, sport
2 *often plural* CELEBRATION, party, festival, entertainment, rave (*Brit slang*), beano (*Brit slang*), fun and games, rave-up (*Brit slang*), jollification, festive event, carousal, festive proceedings, hooley *or* hoolie (*chiefly Irish & NZ*)
festoon *noun* DECORATION, garland, swathe, wreath, swag, lei, chaplet
▷ *verb* DECORATE, deck, array, drape, garland, swathe, bedeck, wreathe, beribbon, engarland, hang
fetch *verb* 1 BRING, pick up, collect, go and get, get, carry, deliver, conduct, transport, go for, obtain, escort, convey, retrieve
2 SELL FOR, make, raise, earn, realize, go for, yield, bring in
▷▷ **fetch up** (*informal*) END UP, reach, arrive, turn up, come, stop, land, halt, finish up
fetching *adjective* (*informal*) ATTRACTIVE, sweet, charming, enchanting, fascinating, intriguing, cute, enticing, captivating, alluring, winsome
fête *or* **fete** *noun* FAIR, festival, gala, bazaar, garden party, sale of work
▷ *verb* ENTERTAIN, welcome, honour, make much of, wine and dine, hold a reception for (someone), lionize, bring out the red carpet for (someone), kill the fatted calf for (someone), treat
fetish *noun* 1 FIXATION, obsession, mania, thing (*informal*), idée fixe (*French*)
2 TALISMAN, amulet, cult object
fetter *plural noun* 1 RESTRAINTS, checks, curbs, constraints, captivity, obstructions, bondage, hindrances
2 CHAINS, bonds, irons, shackles, manacles, leg irons, gyves (*archaic*), bilboes
▷ *verb* 1 RESTRICT, bind, confine, curb, restrain, hamstring, hamper, encumber, clip someone's wings, trammel, straiten
2 CHAIN, tie, tie up, shackle, hobble, hold captive, manacle, gyve (*archaic*), put a straitjacket on
feud *noun* HOSTILITY, row, conflict, argument, faction, falling out, disagreement, rivalry, contention, quarrel, grudge, strife, bickering, vendetta, discord, enmity, broil, bad blood, estrangement, dissension
▷ *verb* QUARREL, row, clash, dispute, fall out, contend, brawl, war, squabble, duel, bicker, be at odds, be at daggers drawn
fever *noun* 1 AGUE, high temperature, feverishness, pyrexia (*Medical*)
2 EXCITEMENT, heat, passion, intensity, flush, turmoil, ecstasy, frenzy, ferment, agitation, fervour, restlessness, delirium
>> RELATED WORD *adjective* febrile
fevered *adjective* FRANTIC, excited, desperate, distracted, frenzied, impatient, obsessive, restless, agitated, frenetic, overwrought
feverish *or* **fevorous** *adjective* 1 FRANTIC, excited, desperate, distracted, frenzied, impatient, obsessive, restless, agitated, frenetic, overwrought
<< OPPOSITE calm
2 HOT, burning, flaming, fevered, flushed, hectic, inflamed, febrile, pyretic (*Medical*)
few *adjective* NOT MANY, one or two, hardly any, scarcely any, rare, thin, scattered, insufficient, scarce, scant, meagre, negligible, sporadic, sparse, infrequent, scanty, inconsiderable
<< OPPOSITE many
▷ *pronoun* A SMALL NUMBER, a handful, a sprinkling, a scattering, some, scarcely any
▷▷ **few and far between** SCARCE, rare, unusual, scattered, irregular, uncommon, in short supply, hard to come by, infrequent, thin on the ground, widely spaced, seldom met with
fiancé *or* **fiancée** *noun* HUSBAND- *or* WIFE-TO-BE, intended, betrothed, prospective spouse, future husband *or* wife
fiasco *noun* FLOP, failure, disaster, ruin, mess (*informal*), catastrophe, rout, debacle, cock-up (*Brit slang*), washout (*informal*)
fib *noun* LIE, story, fiction, untruth, whopper (*informal*), porky (*Brit slang*), pork pie (*Brit slang*), white lie, prevarication
fibre *or* *US* **fiber** *noun* THREAD, strand, filament, tendril, pile, texture, staple, wisp, fibril
▷▷ **moral fibre** STRENGTH OF CHARACTER, strength, resolution, resolve, stamina, backbone, toughness
fickle *adjective* CAPRICIOUS, variable, volatile, unpredictable, unstable, unfaithful, temperamental, mercurial, unsteady, faithless, changeable, quicksilver, vacillating, fitful, flighty, blowing hot and cold, mutable, irresolute, inconstant
<< OPPOSITE constant
fiction *noun* 1 TALE, story, novel, legend, myth, romance, fable, storytelling, narration, creative writing, work of imagination
2 IMAGINATION, fancy, fantasy, creativity
3 LIE, fancy, fantasy, invention, improvisation, fabrication, concoction, falsehood, untruth, porky (*Brit slang*), pork pie (*Brit slang*), urban myth, tall story, urban legend, cock and bull story (*informal*), figment of the imagination
fictional *adjective* IMAGINARY, made-up, invented, legendary, unreal, nonexistent
fictitious *adjective* 1 FALSE, made-up, bogus, untrue, non-existent, fabricated, counterfeit, feigned, spurious, apocryphal
<< OPPOSITE true
2 IMAGINARY, imagined, made-up, assumed, invented, artificial, improvised, mythical, unreal, fanciful, make-believe
fiddle *noun* 1 (*Brit informal*) FRAUD, racket,

scam (*slang*), piece of sharp practice, fix, sting (*informal*), graft (*informal*), swindle, wangle (*informal*)
2 (*informal*) VIOLIN
▷ *verb* (*informal*) 1 *often with* **with** FIDGET, play, finger, toy, tamper, trifle, mess about *or* around
2 *often with* **with** TINKER, adjust, interfere, mess about *or* around
3 CHEAT, cook (*informal*), fix, manoeuvre (*informal*), graft (*informal*), diddle (*informal*), wangle (*informal*), gerrymander, finagle (*informal*)

fiddling *adjective* TRIVIAL, small, petty, trifling, insignificant, unimportant, pettifogging, futile

fidelity *noun* 1 LOYALTY, faith, integrity, devotion, allegiance, constancy, faithfulness, dependability, trustworthiness, troth (*archaic*), fealty, staunchness, devotedness, lealty (*archaic, Scot*), true-heartedness
<< OPPOSITE disloyalty
2 ACCURACY, precision, correspondence, closeness, adherence, faithfulness, exactitude, exactness, scrupulousness, preciseness
<< OPPOSITE inaccuracy

fidget *verb* MOVE RESTLESSLY, fiddle (*informal*), bustle, twitch, fret, squirm, chafe, jiggle, jitter (*informal*), be like a cat on hot bricks (*informal*), worry

field *noun* 1 MEADOW, land, green, lea (*poetic*), pasture, mead (*archaic*), greensward (*archaic* or *literary*)
2 SPECIALITY, line, area, department, environment, territory, discipline, province, pale, confines, sphere, domain, specialty, sphere of influence, purview, metier, sphere of activity, bailiwick, sphere of interest, sphere of study
3 LINE, reach, range, limits, bounds, sweep, scope
4 COMPETITORS, competition, candidates, runners, applicants, entrants, contestants
▷ *verb* 1 (*informal*) DEAL WITH, answer, handle, respond to, reply to, deflect, turn aside
2 (*Sport*) RETRIEVE, return, stop, catch, pick up

fiend *noun* 1 BRUTE, monster, savage, beast, degenerate, barbarian, ogre, ghoul
2 (*informal*) ENTHUSIAST, fan, addict, freak (*informal*), fanatic, maniac, energumen
3 DEMON, devil, evil spirit, hellhound, atua (NZ)

fiendish *adjective* 1 (*informal*) DIFFICULT, involved, complex, puzzling, baffling, intricate, thorny, knotty
2 WICKED, cruel, savage, monstrous, malicious, satanic, malignant, unspeakable, atrocious, inhuman, diabolical, implacable, malevolent, hellish, devilish, infernal, accursed, ungodly, black-hearted, demoniac

fierce *adjective* 1 FEROCIOUS, wild, dangerous, cruel, savage, brutal, aggressive, menacing, vicious, fiery, murderous, uncontrollable, feral, untamed, barbarous, fell (*archaic*), threatening, baleful, truculent, tigerish, aggers (*Austral slang*), biffo (*Austral slang*)
<< OPPOSITE gentle
2 INTENSE, strong, keen, passionate, relentless, cut-throat
3 STORMY, strong, powerful, violent, intense, raging, furious, howling, uncontrollable, boisterous, tumultuous, tempestuous, blustery, inclement
<< OPPOSITE tranquil

fiercely *adverb* FEROCIOUSLY, savagely, passionately, furiously, viciously, menacingly, tooth and nail, in a frenzy, like cat and dog, frenziedly, tigerishly, with no holds barred, tempestuously, with bared teeth, uncontrolledly

fiery *adjective* 1 BURNING, flaming, glowing, blazing, on fire, red-hot, ablaze, in flames, aflame, afire
2 EXCITABLE, violent, fierce, passionate, irritable, impetuous, irascible, peppery, hot-headed, choleric

fiesta *noun* CARNIVAL, party, holiday, fair, fête, festival, celebration, feast, revel, jubilee, festivity, jamboree, Mardi Gras, revelry, Saturnalia, saint's day, merrymaking, carousal, bacchanal *or* bacchanalia, gala

fight *verb* 1 OPPOSE, campaign against, dispute, contest, resist, defy, contend, withstand, stand up to, take issue with, make a stand against
2 STRIVE, battle, push, struggle, contend
3 BATTLE, assault, combat, war with, go to war, do battle, wage war, take up arms, bear arms against, engage in hostilities, carry on war, engage
4 ENGAGE IN, conduct, wage, pursue, carry on
5 TAKE THE FIELD, cross swords, taste battle
6 BRAWL, clash, scrap (*informal*), exchange blows, struggle, row, tilt, wrestle, feud, grapple, tussle, joust, come to blows, lock horns, fight like Kilkenny cats
7 BOX, spar with, exchange blows with
▷ *noun* 1 BATTLE, campaign, movement, struggle
2 CONFLICT, war, action, clash, contest, encounter, brush, combat, engagement, hostilities, skirmish, passage of arms
3 BRAWL, set-to (*informal*), riot, scrap (*informal*), confrontation, rumble (*US & NZ slang*), fray, duel, skirmish, head-to-head, tussle, scuffle, free-for-all (*informal*), fracas, altercation, dogfight, joust, dissension, affray (*Law*), shindig (*informal*), scrimmage, sparring match, exchange of blows, shindy (*informal*), melee *or* mêlée, biffo (*Austral slang*), boilover (*Austral*)

4 ROW, argument, dispute, quarrel, squabble
5 MATCH, contest, bout, battle, competition, struggle, set-to, encounter, engagement, head-to-head, boxing match
6 RESISTANCE, spirit, pluck, militancy, mettle, belligerence, will to resist, gameness, pluckiness
▷▷ **fight shy of something** AVOID, shun, steer clear of, duck out of (*informal*), keep at arm's length, hang back from, keep aloof from

fighter *noun* 1 COMBATANT, battler, militant, contender, contestant, belligerent, antagonist, disputant
2 BOXER, wrestler, bruiser (*informal*), pugilist, prize fighter
3 SOLDIER, warrior, fighting man, man-at-arms

figment *noun* INVENTION, production, fancy, creation, fiction, fable, improvisation, fabrication, falsehood

figurative *adjective* SYMBOLICAL, representative, abstract, allegorical, typical, tropical (*Rhetoric*), imaginative, ornate, descriptive, fanciful, pictorial, metaphorical, flowery, florid, poetical, emblematical
<< OPPOSITE literal

figure *noun* 1 DIGIT, character, symbol, number, numeral, cipher
2 OUTLINE, form, shape, shadow, profile, silhouette
3 SHAPE, build, body, frame, proportions, chassis (*slang*), torso, physique
4 PERSONAGE, force, face (*informal*), leader, person, individual, character, presence, somebody, personality, celebrity, worthy, notable, big name, dignitary, notability
5 DIAGRAM, drawing, picture, illustration, representation, sketch, emblem
6 DESIGN, shape, pattern, device, motif, depiction
7 PRICE, cost, value, amount, total, sum
▷ *verb* 1 (*informal*) MAKE SENSE, follow, be expected, add up, go without saying, seem reasonable
2 *usually with* **in** FEATURE, act, appear, contribute to, be included, be mentioned, play a part, be featured, have a place in, be conspicuous
3 CALCULATE, work out, compute, tot up, add, total, count, reckon, sum, tally
▷▷ **figure on something** (*US, Canad & NZ informal*) PLAN ON, depend on, rely on, count on, bargain on
▷▷ **figure something out** (*informal*) CALCULATE, reckon, work out, compute
▷▷ **figure something** *or* **someone out** UNDERSTAND, make out, fathom, make head or tail of (*informal*), see, solve, resolve, comprehend, make sense of, decipher, think through, suss (out) (*slang*)

figurehead *noun* NOMINAL HEAD, leader in name only, titular head, front man, name, token, dummy, puppet, mouthpiece, cipher, nonentity, straw man (*chiefly US*), man of straw

figure of speech *noun* EXPRESSION, image, turn of phrase, trope

filament *noun* STRAND, string, wire, fibre, thread, staple, wisp, cilium (*Biology, Zoology*), fibril, pile

file[1] *noun* 1 FOLDER, case, portfolio, binder
2 DOSSIER, record, information, data, documents, case history, report, case
3 LINE, row, chain, string, column, queue, procession
▷ *verb* 1 ARRANGE, order, classify, put in place, slot in (*informal*), categorize, pigeonhole, put in order
2 REGISTER, record, enter, log, put on record
3 MARCH, troop, parade, walk in line, walk behind one another

file[2] *verb* SMOOTH, shape, polish, rub, refine, scrape, rasp, burnish, rub down, abrade

filibuster *noun* OBSTRUCTION, delay, postponement, hindrance, procrastination
▷ *verb* OBSTRUCT, prevent, delay, put off, hinder, play for time, procrastinate

filigree *noun* WIREWORK, lace, lattice, tracery, lacework

fill *verb* 1 TOP UP, fill up, make full, become full, brim over
2 SWELL, expand, inflate, become bloated, extend, balloon, fatten
3 PACK, crowd, squeeze, cram, throng
4 STOCK, supply, store, pack, load, furnish, replenish
5 PLUG, close, stop, seal, cork, bung, block up, stop up
6 SATURATE, charge, pervade, permeate, imbue, impregnate, suffuse, overspread
7 FULFIL, hold, perform, carry out, occupy, take up, execute, discharge, officiate
8 *often with* **up** SATISFY, stuff, gorge, glut, satiate, sate
▷▷ **fill in for someone** REPLACE, represent, substitute for, cover for, take over from, act for, stand in for, sub for, deputize for
▷▷ **fill someone in** (*informal*) INFORM, acquaint, advise of, apprise of, bring up to date with, update with, put wise to (*slang*), give the facts *or* background of
▷▷ **fill something in** COMPLETE, answer, fill up, fill out (*US*)
▷▷ **your fill** SUFFICIENT, enough, plenty, ample, all you want, a sufficiency

filling *noun* STUFFING, padding, filler, wadding, inside, insides, contents, innards (*informal*)
▷ *adjective* SATISFYING, heavy, square, substantial, ample

fillip *noun* BOOST, push, spur, spice, incentive, stimulus, prod, zest, goad

film *noun* 1 MOVIE, picture, flick (*slang*), motion picture
2 CINEMA, the movies
3 LAYER, covering, cover, skin, coating, coat, dusting, tissue, membrane, scum, gauze, integument, pellicle
4 HAZE, cloud, blur, mist, veil, opacity, haziness, mistiness
▷ *verb* 1 PHOTOGRAPH, record, shoot, video, videotape, take
2 ADAPT FOR THE SCREEN, make into a film
>> RELATED WORD *adjective* cinematic

filter *noun* SIEVE, mesh, gauze, strainer, membrane, riddle, sifter
▷ *verb* 1 TRICKLE, leach, seep, percolate, well, escape, leak, penetrate, ooze, dribble, exude
2 *with* **through** PURIFY, treat, strain, refine, riddle, sift, sieve, winnow, filtrate, screen

filth *noun* 1 DIRT, refuse, pollution, muck, garbage, sewage, contamination, dung, sludge, squalor, grime, faeces, slime, excrement, nastiness, carrion, excreta, crud (*slang*), foulness, putrefaction, ordure, defilement, grot (*slang*), filthiness, uncleanness, putrescence, foul matter
2 OBSCENITY, corruption, pornography, indecency, impurity, vulgarity, smut, vileness, dirty-mindedness

filthy *adjective* 1 DIRTY, nasty, foul, polluted, vile, squalid, slimy, unclean, putrid, faecal, scummy, scuzzy (*slang, chiefly US*), feculent, festy (*Austral slang*)
2 GRIMY, black, muddy, smoky, blackened, grubby, sooty, unwashed, mucky, scuzzy (*slang, chiefly US*), begrimed, mud-encrusted, miry, festy (*Austral slang*)
3 OBSCENE, foul, corrupt, coarse, indecent, pornographic, suggestive, lewd, depraved, foul-mouthed, X-rated (*informal*), bawdy, impure, smutty, licentious, dirty-minded
4 DESPICABLE, mean, low, base, offensive, vicious, vile, contemptible, scurvy

final *adjective* 1 LAST, latest, end, closing, finishing, concluding, ultimate, terminal, last-minute, eventual, terminating
<< OPPOSITE first
2 IRREVOCABLE, absolute, decisive, definitive, decided, finished, settled, definite, conclusive, irrefutable, incontrovertible, unalterable, determinate

finale *noun* CLIMAX, ending, close, conclusion, culmination, denouement, last part, epilogue, last act, crowning glory, finis
<< OPPOSITE opening

finality *noun* CONCLUSIVENESS, resolution, decisiveness, certitude, definiteness, irrevocability, inevitableness, unavoidability, decidedness

finalize *or* **finalise** *verb* COMPLETE, settle, conclude, tie up, decide, agree, work out, clinch, wrap up (*informal*), shake hands, sew up (*informal*), complete the arrangements for

finally *adverb* 1 EVENTUALLY, at last, in the end, ultimately, at the last, at the end of the day, in the long run, at length, at the last moment, at long last, when all is said and done, in the fullness of time, after a long time
2 LASTLY, in the end, ultimately
3 IN CONCLUSION, lastly, in closing, to conclude, to sum up, in summary
4 CONCLUSIVELY, for good, permanently, for ever, completely, definitely, once and for all, decisively, convincingly, inexorably, irrevocably, for all time, inescapably, beyond the shadow of a doubt

finance *noun* ECONOMICS, business, money, banking, accounts, investment, commerce, financial affairs, money management
▷ *plural noun* RESOURCES, money, funds, capital, cash, affairs, budgeting, assets, cash flow, financial affairs, money management, wherewithal, financial condition
▷ *verb* FUND, back, support, pay for, guarantee, float, invest in, underwrite, endow, subsidize, bankroll (*US*), set up in business, provide security for, provide money for

financial *adjective* ECONOMIC, business, money, budgeting, budgetary, commercial, monetary, fiscal, pecuniary

find *verb* 1 DISCOVER, turn up, uncover, unearth, spot, expose, come up with, locate, detect, come across, track down, catch sight of, stumble upon, hit upon, espy, ferret out, chance upon, light upon, put your finger on, lay your hand on, run to ground, run to earth, descry
<< OPPOSITE lose
2 REGAIN, recover, get back, retrieve, repossess
3 OBTAIN, get, come by, procure, win, gain, achieve, earn, acquire, attain
4 ENCOUNTER, meet, recognize
5 OBSERVE, learn, note, discover, notice, realize, remark, come up with, arrive at, perceive, detect, become aware of, experience, ascertain
6 FEEL, have, experience, sense, obtain, know
7 PROVIDE, supply, contribute, furnish, cough up (*informal*), purvey, be responsible for, bring
▷ *noun* DISCOVERY, catch, asset, bargain, acquisition, good buy
▷▷ **find someone out** DETECT, catch, unmask, rumble (*Brit informal*), reveal, expose, disclose, uncover, suss (out) (*slang*), bring to light
▷▷ **find something out** LEARN, discover, realize, observe, perceive, detect, become aware, come to know, note

finding *noun* (*Law*) JUDGMENT, ruling, decision, award, conclusion, verdict, recommendation, decree, pronouncement

fine[1] *adjective* 1 EXCELLENT, good, great, striking, choice, beautiful, masterly, select, rare, very good, supreme, impressive, outstanding, magnificent, superior, accomplished, sterling, first-class, divine, exceptional, splendid, world-class, exquisite, admirable, skilful, ornate, first-rate, showy
<< OPPOSITE poor
2 SATISFACTORY, good, all right, suitable, acceptable, convenient, agreeable, hunky-dory (*informal*), fair, O.K. *or* okay (*informal*)
3 THIN, small, light, narrow, wispy
4 DELICATE, light, thin, sheer, lightweight, flimsy, wispy, gossamer, diaphanous, gauzy, chiffony
<< OPPOSITE coarse
5 STYLISH, expensive, elegant, refined, tasteful, quality, schmick (*Austral informal*)
6 EXQUISITE, delicate, fragile, dainty
7 MINUTE, exact, precise, nice
8 KEEN, minute, nice, quick, sharp, critical, acute, sensitive, subtle, precise, refined, discriminating, tenuous, fastidious, hairsplitting
9 BRILLIANT, quick, keen, alert, clever, intelligent, penetrating, astute
10 SHARP, keen, polished, honed, razor-sharp, cutting
11 GOOD-LOOKING, striking, pretty, attractive, lovely, smart, handsome, stylish, bonny, well-favoured
12 SUNNY, clear, fair, dry, bright, pleasant, clement, balmy, cloudless
<< OPPOSITE cloudy
13 PURE, clear, refined, unadulterated, unalloyed, unpolluted, solid, sterling

fine[2] *noun* PENALTY, damages, punishment, forfeit, financial penalty, amercement (*obsolete*)
▷ *verb* PENALIZE, charge, punish

finery *noun* SPLENDOUR, trappings, frippery, glad rags (*informal*), gear (*informal*), decorations, ornaments, trinkets, Sunday best, gewgaws, showiness, best bib and tucker (*informal*)

finesse *noun* 1 SKILL, style, know-how (*informal*), polish, craft, sophistication, cleverness, quickness, adroitness, adeptness
2 DIPLOMACY, discretion, subtlety, delicacy, tact, savoir-faire, artfulness, adeptness
▷ *verb* MANOEUVRE, steer, manipulate, bluff

finger *verb* TOUCH, feel, handle, play with, manipulate, paw (*informal*), maul, toy with, fiddle with (*informal*), meddle with, play about with
▷▷ **put your finger on something** IDENTIFY, place, remember, discover, indicate, recall, find out, locate, pin down, bring to mind, hit upon, hit the nail on the head
>> RELATED WORD *adjective* digital

finish *verb* 1 STOP, close, complete, achieve, conclude, cease, accomplish, execute, discharge, culminate, wrap up (*informal*), terminate, round off, bring to a close *or* conclusion
<< OPPOSITE start
2 GET DONE, complete, put the finishing touch(es) to, finalize, do, deal with, settle, conclude, fulfil, carry through, get out of the way, make short work of
3 END, stop, conclude, wind up, terminate
4 CONSUME, dispose of, devour, polish off, drink, eat, drain, get through, dispatch, deplete
5 USE UP, use, spend, empty, exhaust, expend
6 COAT, polish, stain, texture, wax, varnish, gild, veneer, lacquer, smooth off, face
7 *often with* **off** DESTROY, defeat, overcome, bring down, best, worst, ruin, get rid of, dispose of, rout, put an end to, overpower, annihilate, put paid to, move in for the kill, drive to the wall, administer *or* give the coup de grâce
8 *often with* **off** KILL, murder, destroy, do in (*slang*), take out (*slang*), massacre, butcher, slaughter, dispatch, slay, eradicate, do away with, blow away (*slang, chiefly US*), knock off (*slang*), annihilate, exterminate, take (someone's) life, bump off (*slang*)
▷ *noun* 1 END, ending, close, closing, conclusion, run-in, winding up (*informal*), wind-up, completion, finale, termination, culmination, cessation, last stage(s), denouement, finalization
<< OPPOSITE beginning
2 SURFACE, appearance, polish, shine, grain, texture, glaze, veneer, lacquer, lustre, smoothness, patina

finished *adjective* 1 OVER, done, completed, achieved, through, ended, closed, full, final, complete, in the past, concluded, shut, accomplished, executed, tied up, wrapped up (*informal*), terminated, sewn up (*informal*), finalized, over and done with
<< OPPOSITE begun
2 RUINED, done for (*informal*), doomed, bankrupt, through, lost, gone, defeated, devastated, wrecked, wiped out, undone, washed up (*informal, chiefly US*), wound up, liquidated

finite *adjective* LIMITED, bounded, restricted, demarcated, conditioned, circumscribed, delimited, terminable, subject to limitations
<< OPPOSITE infinite

fire *noun* 1 FLAMES, blaze, combustion, inferno, conflagration, holocaust

2 PASSION, force, light, energy, heat, spirit, enthusiasm, excitement, dash, intensity, sparkle, life, vitality, animation, vigour, zeal, splendour, verve, fervour, eagerness, dynamism, lustre, radiance, virtuosity, élan, ardour, brio, vivacity, impetuosity, burning passion, scintillation, fervency, pizzazz *or* pizazz (*informal*)
3 BOMBARDMENT, shooting, firing, shelling, hail, volley, barrage, gunfire, sniping, flak, salvo, fusillade, cannonade
▷ *verb* 1 LET OFF, shoot, launch, shell, loose, set off, discharge, hurl, eject, detonate, let loose (*informal*), touch off
2 SHOOT, explode, discharge, detonate, pull the trigger
3 (*informal*) DISMISS, sack (*informal*), get rid of, discharge, lay off, make redundant, cashier, give notice, show the door, give the boot (*slang*), kiss off (*slang, chiefly US & Canad*), give the push, give the bullet (*Brit slang*), give marching orders, give someone their cards, give the sack to (*informal*), kennet (*Austral slang*), jeff (*Austral slang*)
4 INSPIRE, excite, stir, stimulate, motivate, irritate, arouse, awaken, animate, rouse, stir up, quicken, inflame, incite, electrify, enliven, spur on, galvanize, inspirit, impassion
5 SET FIRE TO, torch, ignite, set on fire, kindle, set alight, set ablaze, put a match to, set aflame, enkindle, light
▷▷ **on fire** 1 BURNING, flaming, blazing, alight, ablaze, in flames, aflame, fiery
2 ARDENT, excited, inspired, eager, enthusiastic, passionate, fervent
>> RELATED WORD *like* pyromania

firearm *noun* GUN, weapon, handgun, revolver, shooter (*slang*), piece (*slang*), rod (*slang*), pistol, heater (*US slang*)

firebrand *noun* RABBLE-ROUSER, activist, incendiary, fomenter, instigator, agitator, demagogue, tub-thumper, soapbox orator

fireworks *plural noun* 1 PYROTECHNICS, illuminations, feux d'artifice
2 (*informal*) TROUBLE, row, storm, rage, temper, wax (*informal, chiefly Brit*), uproar, hysterics, paroxysms, fit of rage

firm[1] *adjective* 1 HARD, solid, compact, dense, set, concentrated, stiff, compacted, rigid, compressed, inflexible, solidified, unyielding, congealed, inelastic, jelled, close-grained, jellified
<< OPPOSITE soft
2 SECURE, strong, fixed, secured, rooted, stable, steady, anchored, braced, robust, cemented, fast, sturdy, embedded, fastened, riveted, taut, stationary, motionless, immovable, unmoving, unshakeable, unfluctuating
<< OPPOSITE unstable
3 STRONG, close, tight, steady
4 STRICT, unwavering, unswerving, unshakeable, constant, stalwart, resolute, inflexible, steadfast, unyielding, immovable, unflinching, unbending, obdurate, unalterable, unfaltering
5 DETERMINED, true, settled, fixed, resolved, strict, definite, set on, adamant, stalwart, staunch, resolute, inflexible, steadfast, unyielding, unwavering, immovable, unflinching, unswerving, unbending, obdurate, unshakeable, unalterable, unshaken, unfaltering
<< OPPOSITE wavering
6 DEFINITE, hard, clear, confirmed, settled, fixed, hard-and-fast, cut-and-dried (*informal*)

firm[2] *noun* COMPANY, business, concern, association, organization, house, corporation, venture, enterprise, partnership, establishment, undertaking, outfit (*informal*), consortium, conglomerate

firmament *noun* SKY, skies, heaven, heavens, the blue, vault, welkin (*archaic*), empyrean (*poetic*), vault of heaven, rangi (NZ)

firmly *adverb* 1 SECURELY, safely, tightly
2 IMMOVABLY, securely, steadily, like a rock, unflinchingly, enduringly, motionlessly, unshakeably
3 STEADILY, securely, tightly, unflinchingly
4 RESOLUTELY, strictly, staunchly, steadfastly, determinedly, through thick and thin, with decision, with a rod of iron, definitely, unwaveringly, unchangeably

firmness *noun* 1 HARDNESS, resistance, density, rigidity, stiffness, solidity, inflexibility, compactness, fixedness, inelasticity
2 STEADINESS, tension, stability, tightness, soundness, tautness, tensile strength, immovability
3 STRENGTH, tightness, steadiness
4 RESOLVE, resolution, constancy, inflexibility, steadfastness, obduracy, strictness, strength of will, fixity, fixedness, staunchness

first *adjective* 1 EARLIEST, initial, opening, introductory, original, maiden, primitive, primordial, primeval, pristine
2 TOP, best, winning, premier
3 ELEMENTARY, key, basic, primary, fundamental, cardinal, rudimentary, elemental
4 FOREMOST, highest, greatest, leading, head, ruling, chief, prime, supreme, principal, paramount, overriding, pre-eminent
▷ *noun* 1 NOVELTY, innovation, originality, new experience
2 *usually in phrase* **from the first** START, beginning, outset, the very beginning, introduction, starting point, inception, commencement, the word 'go' (*informal*)

▷ *adverb* TO BEGIN WITH, firstly, initially, at the beginning, in the first place, beforehand, to start with, at the outset, before all else

first class *or* **first-class** *adjective* EXCELLENT, great, very good, superb, topping (*Brit slang*), top, tops (*slang*), bad (*slang*), prime, capital, choice, champion, cool (*informal*), brilliant, crack (*slang*), mean (*slang*), cracking (*Brit informal*), crucial (*slang*), outstanding, premium, ace (*informal*), marvellous, exceptional, mega (*slang*), sovereign, dope (*slang*), world-class, blue-chip, top-flight, top-class, five-star, exemplary, wicked (*slang*), first-rate, def (*slang*), superlative, second to none, top-notch (*informal*), brill (*informal*), top-drawer, matchless, tiptop, boffo (*slang*), jim-dandy (*slang*), twenty-four carat, A1 *or* A-one (*informal*), bitchin' (*US slang*), chillin' (*US slang*), booshit (*Austral slang*), exo (*Austral slang*), sik (*Austral slang*), rad (*informal*), phat (*slang*), schmick (*Austral informal*)

<< OPPOSITE terrible

first-hand *adjective* DIRECT, personal, immediate, face-to-face, straight from the horse's mouth

▷▷ **at first hand** DIRECTLY, personally, immediately, face-to-face, straight from the horse's mouth

first-rate (*informal*) *adjective* EXCELLENT, outstanding, first class, exceptional, mean (*slang*), topping (*Brit slang*), top, tops (*slang*), prime, cool (*informal*), crack (*slang*), cracking (*Brit informal*), crucial (*slang*), exclusive, superb, mega (*slang*), sovereign, dope (*slang*), world-class, admirable, wicked (*slang*), def (*slang*), superlative, second to none, top-notch (*informal*), brill (*informal*), tiptop, bodacious (*slang, chiefly US*), boffo (*slang*), jim-dandy (*slang*), A1 *or* A-one (*informal*), bitchin' (*US slang*), chillin' (*US slang*), booshit (*Austral slang*), exo (*Austral slang*), sik (*Austral slang*), rad (*informal*), phat (*slang*), schmick (*Austral informal*)

fiscal *adjective* FINANCIAL, money, economic, monetary, budgetary, pecuniary, tax

fish *verb* **1** ANGLE, net, cast, trawl

2 LOOK (FOR), search, delve, ferret, rummage, fossick (*Austral & NZ*)

▷▷ **fish for something** SEEK, look for, angle for, try to get, hope for, hunt for, hint at, elicit, solicit, invite, search for

▷▷ **fish something out** *verb* PULL OUT, produce, take out, extract, bring out, extricate, haul out, find

>> RELATED WORDS *adjectives* piscine, ichthyoid

>> RELATED WORD *young* fry

>> RELATED WORD *collective noun* shoal

fishy *adjective* **1** FISHLIKE, piscine, piscatorial, piscatory

2 (*informal*) SUSPICIOUS, odd, suspect, unlikely, funny (*informal*), doubtful, dubious, dodgy (*Brit, Austral & NZ informal*), queer, rum (*Brit slang*), questionable, improbable, implausible, cock-and-bull (*informal*), shonky (*Austral & NZ informal*)

fission *noun* SPLITTING, parting, breaking, division, rending, rupture, cleavage, schism, scission

fissure *noun* CRACK, opening, hole, split, gap, rent, fault, breach, break, fracture, rift, slit, rupture, cleavage, cleft, chink, crevice, cranny, interstice

fit[1] *verb* **1** ADAPT, fashion, shape, arrange, alter, adjust, modify, tweak (*informal*), customize

2 PLACE, position, insert

3 ATTACH, join, connect, interlock

4 SUIT, meet, match, belong to, agree with, go with, conform to, correspond to, accord with, be appropriate to, concur with, tally with, dovetail with, be consonant with

5 EQUIP, provide, arm, prepare, outfit, accommodate, fit out, kit out, rig out, accoutre

▷ *adjective* **1** APPROPRIATE, qualified, suitable, competent, right, becoming, meet (*archaic*), seemly, trained, able, prepared, fitting, fitted, ready, skilled, correct, deserving, capable, adapted, proper, equipped, good enough, adequate, worthy, convenient, apt, well-suited, expedient, apposite

<< OPPOSITE inappropriate

2 HEALTHY, strong, robust, sturdy, well, trim, strapping, hale, in good shape, in good condition, in good health, toned up, as right as rain, in good trim, able-bodied

<< OPPOSITE unfit

fit[2] *noun* **1** (*Pathology*) SEIZURE, attack, bout, spasm, convulsion, paroxysm

2 BOUT, burst, outbreak, outburst, spell

▷▷ **have a fit** (*informal*) GO MAD, explode, blow up (*informal*), lose it (*informal*), see red (*informal*), lose the plot (*informal*), throw a tantrum, fly off the handle (*informal*), go spare (*Brit slang*), blow your top (*informal*), fly into a temper, flip your lid (*slang*), do your nut (*Brit slang*)

▷▷ **in** *or* **by fits and starts** SPASMODICALLY, sporadically, erratically, fitfully, on and off, irregularly, intermittently, off and on, unsystematically

fitful *adjective* IRREGULAR, broken, disturbed, erratic, variable, flickering, unstable, uneven, fluctuating, sporadic, intermittent, impulsive, haphazard, desultory, spasmodic, inconstant

<< OPPOSITE regular

fitfully *adverb* IRREGULARLY, on and off, intermittently, sporadically, off and on, erratically, in fits and starts, spasmodically, in snatches, desultorily, by fits and starts, interruptedly

fitness *noun* 1 APPROPRIATENESS, qualifications, adaptation, competence, readiness, eligibility, suitability, propriety, preparedness, applicability, aptness, pertinence, seemliness
2 HEALTH, strength, good health, vigour, good condition, wellness, robustness

fitted *adjective* BUILT-IN, permanent

fitting *adjective* APPROPRIATE, suitable, proper, apt, right, becoming, meet (*archaic*), seemly, correct, decent, desirable, apposite, decorous, comme il faut (*French*)
<< OPPOSITE unsuitable
▷ *noun* ACCESSORY, part, piece, unit, connection, component, attachment
▷ *plural noun* FURNISHINGS, extras, equipment, fixtures, appointments, furniture, trimmings, accessories, conveniences, accoutrements, bells and whistles, fitments, appurtenances

fix *verb* 1 PLACE, join, stick, attach, set, position, couple, plant, link, establish, tie, settle, secure, bind, root, connect, locate, pin, install, anchor, glue, cement, implant, embed, fasten, make fast
2 *often with* **up** DECIDE, set, name, choose, limit, establish, determine, settle, appoint, arrange, define, conclude, resolve, arrive at, specify, agree on
3 *often with* **up** ARRANGE, organize, sort out, see to, make arrangements for
4 REPAIR, mend, service, sort, correct, restore, adjust, regulate, see to, overhaul, patch up, get working, put right, put to rights
5 FOCUS, direct at, level at, fasten on, rivet on
6 (*informal*) RIG, set up (*informal*), influence, manipulate, bribe, manoeuvre, fiddle (*informal*), pull strings (*informal*)
7 STABILIZE, set, consolidate, harden, thicken, stiffen, solidify, congeal, rigidify
▷ *noun* (*informal*) MESS, spot (*informal*), corner, hole (*slang*), difficulty, jam (*informal*), dilemma, embarrassment, plight, hot water (*informal*), pickle (*informal*), uphill (*S African*), predicament, difficult situation, quandary, tight spot, ticklish situation
▷▷ **fix someone up** *often with* **with** PROVIDE, supply, accommodate, bring about, furnish, lay on, arrange for
▷▷ **fix something up** ARRANGE, plan, settle, fix, organize, sort out, agree on, make arrangements for

fixated *adjective* OBSESSED, fascinated, preoccupied, captivated, attached, devoted, absorbed, caught up in, single-minded, smitten, taken up with, besotted, wrapped up in, engrossed, spellbound, infatuated, mesmerized, hypnotized, hung up on (*slang*), monomaniacal, prepossessed
<< OPPOSITE uninterested

fixation *noun* OBSESSION, complex, addiction, hang-up (*informal*), preoccupation, mania, infatuation, idée fixe (*French*), thing (*informal*)

fixed *adjective* 1 INFLEXIBLE, set, steady, resolute, unwavering, unflinching, unblinking, unbending, undeviating
<< OPPOSITE wavering
2 IMMOVABLE, set, established, secure, rooted, permanent, attached, anchored, rigid, made fast
<< OPPOSITE mobile
3 AGREED, set, planned, decided, established, settled, arranged, resolved, specified, definite
4 (*informal*) RIGGED, framed, put-up, manipulated, packed

fizz *verb* 1 BUBBLE, froth, fizzle, effervesce, produce bubbles
2 SPUTTER, buzz, sparkle, hiss, crackle

fizzle *verb* (*informal*) *often with* **out** DIE AWAY, fail, collapse, fold (*informal*), abort, fall through, peter out, come to nothing, miss the mark, end in disappointment

fizzy *adjective* BUBBLY, bubbling, sparkling, effervescent, carbonated, gassy

flab *noun* FAT, flesh, flabbiness, fleshiness, weight, beef (*informal*), heaviness, slackness, plumpness, loose flesh

flabbergasted *adjective* ASTONISHED, amazed, stunned, overcome, overwhelmed, staggered, astounded, dazed, confounded, disconcerted, speechless, bowled over (*informal*), gobsmacked (*Brit slang*), dumbfounded, nonplussed, lost for words, struck dumb, abashed, rendered speechless

flabby *adjective* 1 LIMP, hanging, loose, slack, unfit, sagging, sloppy, baggy, floppy, lax, drooping, flaccid, pendulous, toneless, yielding
<< OPPOSITE firm
2 WEAK, ineffective, feeble, impotent, wasteful, ineffectual, disorganized, spineless, effete, boneless, nerveless, enervated, wussy (*slang*), wimpish *or* wimpy (*informal*)

flaccid *adjective* LIMP, soft, weak, loose, slack, lax, drooping, flabby, nerveless

flag[1] *noun* BANNER, standard, colours, jack, pennant, ensign, streamer, pennon, banderole, gonfalon
▷ *verb* 1 MARK, identify, indicate, label, tab, pick out, note, docket
2 *often with* **down** HAIL, stop, signal, salute, wave down

flag[2] *verb* WEAKEN, fall, die, fail, decline, sink, fade, slump, pine, faint, weary, fall off, succumb, falter, wilt, wane, ebb, sag, languish, abate, droop, peter out, taper off, feel the pace, lose your strength

flagging *adjective* WEAKENING, failing,

declining, waning, giving up, tiring, sinking, fading, decreasing, slowing down, deteriorating, wearying, faltering, wilting, ebbing

flagrant *adjective* OUTRAGEOUS, open, blatant, barefaced, shocking, crying, enormous, awful, bold, dreadful, notorious, glaring, infamous, scandalous, flaunting, atrocious, brazen, shameless, out-and-out, heinous, ostentatious, egregious, undisguised, immodest, arrant, flagitious

<< OPPOSITE slight

flagstone *noun* PAVING STONE, flag, slab, block

flail *verb* THRASH, beat, windmill, thresh

flair *noun* 1 ABILITY, feel, talent, gift, genius, faculty, accomplishment, mastery, knack, aptitude

2 (*informal*) STYLE, taste, dash, chic, elegance, panache, discernment, stylishness

flak (*informal*) *noun* CRITICISM, stick (*slang*), opposition, abuse, complaints, hostility, condemnation, censure, disapproval, bad press, denigration, brickbats (*informal*), disparagement, fault-finding, disapprobation

flake *noun* CHIP, scale, layer, peeling, shaving, disk, wafer, sliver, lamina, squama (*Biology*)

▷ *verb* CHIP, scale (off), peel (off), blister, desquamate

flamboyance *noun* SHOWINESS, show, style, dash, sparkle, chic, flair, verve, swagger, extravagance, panache, pomp, glitz (*informal*), élan, bravura, swank (*informal*), theatricality, exhibitionism, brio, ostentation, stylishness, flashiness, flamboyancy, floridity, pizzazz *or* pizazz (*informal*)

<< OPPOSITE restraint

flamboyant *adjective* 1 CAMP (*informal*), dashing, theatrical, swashbuckling

2 SHOWY, rich, elaborate, over the top (*informal*), extravagant, baroque, ornate, ostentatious, rococo

3 COLOURFUL, striking, exciting, brilliant, glamorous, stylish, dazzling, glitzy (*slang*), showy, florid

flame *noun* 1 FIRE, light, spark, glow, blaze, brightness, inferno

2 PASSION, fire, enthusiasm, intensity, affection, warmth, fervour, ardour, keenness, fervency

3 (*informal*) SWEETHEART, partner, lover, girlfriend, boyfriend, beloved, heart-throb (*Brit*), beau, ladylove

▷ *verb* BURN, flash, shine, glow, blaze, flare, glare

flaming *adjective* 1 BURNING, blazing, fiery, ignited, red, brilliant, raging, glowing, red-hot, ablaze, in flames, afire

2 INTENSE, angry, raging, impassioned, hot, aroused, vivid, frenzied, ardent, scintillating, vehement

flammable *adjective* COMBUSTIBLE, incendiary, inflammable, ignitable

> *Flammable* and *inflammable* are interchangeable when used of the properties of materials. *Flammable* is, however, often preferred for warning labels as there is less likelihood of misunderstanding (*inflammable* being sometimes taken to mean *not flammable*). *Inflammable* is preferred in figurative contexts: *this could prove to be an inflammable situation*

flank *noun* 1 SIDE, quarter, hip, thigh, loin, haunch, ham

2 WING, side, sector, aspect

▷ *verb* BORDER, line, wall, screen, edge, circle, bound, skirt, fringe, book-end

flannel (*Brit informal*) *noun* WAFFLE, flattery, blarney, sweet talk (*US informal*), baloney (*informal*), equivocation, hedging, prevarication, weasel words (*informal, chiefly US*), soft soap (*informal*)

▷ *verb* PREVARICATE, hedge, flatter, waffle (*informal, chiefly Brit*), blarney, sweet-talk (*informal*), soft-soap (*informal*), equivocate, butter up, pull the wool over (someone's) eyes

flap *verb* 1 FLUTTER, wave, swing, swish, flail

2 BEAT, wave, thrash, flutter, agitate, wag, vibrate, shake, thresh

3 (*informal*) PANIC, fuss, dither (*chiefly Brit*)

▷ *noun* 1 COVER, covering, tail, fold, skirt, tab, overlap, fly, apron, lapel, lappet

2 FLUTTER, beating, waving, shaking, swinging, bang, banging, swish

3 (*informal*) PANIC, state (*informal*), agitation, commotion, sweat (*informal*), stew (*informal*), dither (*chiefly Brit*), fluster, twitter (*informal*), tizzy (*informal*)

flare *verb* 1 BLAZE, flame, dazzle, glare, flicker, flutter, waver, burn up

2 WIDEN, spread, broaden, spread out, dilate, splay

▷ *noun* 1 FLAME, burst, flash, blaze, dazzle, glare, flicker

▷▷ **flare up** 1 BURN, explode, blaze, be on fire, go up in flames, be alight, flame (*informal*)

2 LOSE YOUR TEMPER, explode, lose it (*informal*), lose control, lose the plot (*informal*), throw a tantrum, fly off the handle (*informal*), lose your cool (*informal*), blow your top (*informal*), fly into a temper

flash *noun* 1 BLAZE, ray, burst, spark, beam, sparkle, streak, flare, dazzle, shaft, glare, gleam, flicker, shimmer, twinkle, scintillation, coruscation

2 BURST, show, sign, touch, display, rush, demonstration, surge, outbreak, outburst,

manifestation
3 *usually in phrase* **in a flash** MOMENT, second, instant, split second, trice, jiffy (*informal*), the twinkling of an eye, a twinkling, two shakes of a lamb's tail (*informal*), the bat of an eye (*informal*)
▷ *verb* 1 BLAZE, shine, beam, sparkle, glitter, flare, glare, gleam, light up, flicker, shimmer, twinkle, glint, glisten, scintillate, coruscate
2 SPEED, race, shoot, fly, tear, sweep, dash, barrel (along) (*informal, chiefly US & Canad*), whistle, sprint, bolt, streak, dart, zoom, burn rubber (*informal*)
3 (*informal*) SHOW QUICKLY, display, expose, exhibit, flourish, show off, flaunt
▷ *adjective* (*informal*) OSTENTATIOUS, smart, glamorous, trendy, showy, cheap

flashy *adjective* SHOWY, loud, over the top (*informal*), flamboyant, brash, tacky (*informal*), flaunting, glitzy (*slang*), tasteless, naff (*Brit slang*), gaudy, garish, jazzy (*informal*), tawdry, ostentatious, snazzy (*informal*), glittery, meretricious, cheap and nasty, in poor taste, tinselly
<< OPPOSITE plain

flat[1] *adjective* 1 EVEN, level, levelled, plane, smooth, uniform, horizontal, unbroken, planar
<< OPPOSITE uneven
2 HORIZONTAL, prone, outstretched, reclining, prostrate, laid low, supine, recumbent, lying full length
<< OPPOSITE upright
3 PUNCTURED, collapsed, burst, blown out, deflated, empty
4 USED UP, finished, empty, drained, expired
5 ABSOLUTE, firm, direct, straight, positive, fixed, plain, final, explicit, definite, outright, unconditional, downright, unmistakable, unequivocal, unqualified, out-and-out, categorical, peremptory
6 DULL, dead, empty, boring, depressing, pointless, tedious, stale, lacklustre, tiresome, lifeless, monotonous, uninteresting, insipid, unexciting, spiritless
<< OPPOSITE exciting
7 WITHOUT ENERGY, empty, weak, tired, depressed, drained, weary, worn out, dispirited, downhearted, tired out
8 MONOTONOUS, boring, uniform, dull, tedious, droning, tiresome, unchanging, colourless, toneless, samey (*informal*), uninflected, unvaried
▷ *noun often plural* PLAIN, strand, shallow, marsh, swamp, shoal, lowland, mud flat
▷ *adverb* COMPLETELY, directly, absolutely, categorically, precisely, exactly, utterly, outright, point blank, unequivocally
▷▷ **flat out** (*informal*) AT FULL SPEED, all out, to the full, hell for leather (*informal*), as hard as possible, at full tilt, at full gallop, posthaste, for all you are worth, under full steam

flat[2] *noun* APARTMENT, rooms, quarters, digs, suite, penthouse, living quarters, duplex (*US & Canad*), bachelor apartment (*Canad*)

flatly *adverb* ABSOLUTELY, completely, positively, categorically, unequivocally, unhesitatingly

flatten *verb* 1 *sometimes with* **out** LEVEL, roll, plaster, squash, compress, trample, iron out, even out, smooth off
2 *sometimes with* **out** DESTROY, level, ruin, demolish, knock down, pull down, tear down, throw down, bulldoze, raze, remove, kennet (*Austral slang*), jeff (*Austral slang*)
3 (*informal*) KNOCK DOWN, fell, floor, deck (*slang*), bowl over, prostrate, knock off your feet
4 (*informal*) CRUSH, beat, defeat, trounce, master, worst, overwhelm, conquer, lick (*informal*), undo, subdue, rout, overpower, quell, clobber (*slang*), vanquish, run rings around (*informal*), wipe the floor with (*informal*), make mincemeat of (*informal*), blow out of the water (*slang*)

flatter *verb* 1 PRAISE, compliment, pander to, sweet-talk (*informal*), court, humour, puff, flannel (*Brit informal*), fawn, cajole, lay it on (thick) (*slang*), wheedle, inveigle, soft-soap (*informal*), butter up, blandish
2 SUIT, become, enhance, set off, embellish, do something for, show to advantage

flattering *adjective* 1 BECOMING, kind, effective, enhancing, well-chosen
<< OPPOSITE unflattering
2 INGRATIATING, complimentary, gratifying, fawning, sugary, fulsome, laudatory, adulatory, honeyed, honey-tongued
<< OPPOSITE uncomplimentary

flattery *noun* OBSEQUIOUSNESS, fawning, adulation, sweet-talk (*informal*), flannel (*Brit informal*), blarney, soft-soap (*informal*), sycophancy, servility, cajolery, blandishment, fulsomeness, toadyism, false praise, honeyed words

flatulence *noun* WIND, borborygmus (*Medical*), eructation

flaunt *verb* SHOW OFF, display, boast, parade, exhibit, flourish, brandish, vaunt, make a (great) show of, sport (*informal*), disport, make an exhibition of, flash about

> *Flaunt* is sometimes wrongly used where *flout* is meant: *they must be prevented from flouting* (not *flaunting*) *the law*

flavour *or* (*US*) **flavor** *noun* 1 TASTE, seasoning, flavouring, savour, extract, essence, relish, smack, aroma, odour, zest, tang, zing (*informal*), piquancy, tastiness
<< OPPOSITE blandness

2 QUALITY, feeling, feel, style, property, touch, character, aspect, tone, suggestion, stamp, essence, tinge, soupçon (*French*)

▷ *verb* SEASON, spice, add flavour to, enrich, infuse, imbue, pep up, leaven, ginger up, lace

flavouring *or* (*US*) **flavoring** *noun* ESSENCE, extract, zest, tincture, spirit

flaw *noun* 1 WEAKNESS, failing, defect, weak spot, spot, fault, scar, blemish, imperfection, speck, disfigurement, chink in your armour

2 CRACK, break, split, breach, tear, rent, fracture, rift, cleft, crevice, fissure, scission

flawed *adjective* 1 DAMAGED, defective, imperfect, blemished, broken, cracked, chipped, faulty

2 ERRONEOUS, incorrect, inaccurate, invalid, wrong, mistaken, false, faulty, untrue, unfounded, spurious, amiss, unsound, wide of the mark, inexact, fallacious

flawless *adjective* PERFECT, impeccable, faultless, spotless, unblemished, unsullied

flay *verb* 1 SKIN, strip, peel, scrape, excoriate, remove the skin from

2 UPBRAID, slam (*slang*), castigate, revile, tear into (*informal*), diss (*slang, chiefly US*), excoriate, tear a strip off, execrate, pull to pieces (*informal*), give a tongue-lashing, criticize severely

fleck *noun* MARK, speck, streak, spot, dot, pinpoint, speckle

▷ *verb* SPECKLE, mark, spot, dust, dot, streak, dapple, stipple, mottle, variegate, bespeckle, besprinkle

fledgling *or* **fledgeling** *noun* CHICK, nestling, young bird

flee *verb* RUN AWAY, leave, escape, bolt, fly, avoid, split (*slang*), take off (*informal*), get away, vanish, depart, run off, shun, make off, abscond, decamp, take flight, hook it (*slang*), do a runner (*slang*), scarper (*Brit slang*), slope off, cut and run (*informal*), make a run for it, beat a hasty retreat, turn tail, fly the coop (*US & Canad informal*), make a quick exit, skedaddle (*informal*), make yourself scarce (*informal*), take a powder (*US & Canad slang*), make your escape, make your getaway, take it on the lam (*US & Canad slang*), take to your heels

fleece *noun* WOOL, hair, coat, fur, coat of wool

▷ *verb* CHEAT, skin (*slang*), steal, rob, con (*informal*), rifle, stiff (*slang*), soak (*US & Canad slang*), bleed (*informal*), rip off (*slang*), plunder, defraud, overcharge, swindle, rook (*slang*), diddle (*informal*), take for a ride (*informal*), despoil, take to the cleaners (*slang*), sell a pup, cozen, mulct

fleet[1] *noun* NAVY, vessels, task force, squadron, warships, flotilla, armada, naval force, sea power, argosy

fleet[2] *adjective* SWIFT, flying, fast, quick, winged, rapid, speedy, nimble, mercurial, meteoric, nimble-footed

fleeting *adjective* MOMENTARY, short, passing, flying, brief, temporary, short-lived, fugitive, transient, flitting, ephemeral, transitory, evanescent, fugacious, here today, gone tomorrow

<< OPPOSITE lasting

flesh *noun* 1 FAT, muscle, beef (*informal*), tissue, body, brawn

2 (*informal*) FATNESS, fat, adipose tissue, corpulence, weight

3 MEAT, food

4 PHYSICAL NATURE, sensuality, physicality, carnality, body, human nature, flesh and blood, animality, sinful nature

▷▷ **your own flesh and blood** FAMILY, blood, relations, relatives, kin, kindred, kith and kin, blood relations, kinsfolk, ainga (*NZ*), rellies (*Austral slang*)

>> RELATED WORD *adjective* carnal

fleshy *adjective* PLUMP, fat, chubby, obese, hefty, overweight, ample, stout, chunky, meaty, beefy (*informal*), tubby, podgy, brawny, corpulent, well-padded

flex *verb* BEND, contract, stretch, angle, curve, tighten, crook, move

flexibility *noun* 1 ELASTICITY, pliability, springiness, pliancy, tensility, give (*informal*)

2 ADAPTABILITY, openness, versatility, adjustability

3 COMPLAISANCE, accommodation, give and take, amenability

flexible *adjective* 1 PLIABLE, plastic, yielding, elastic, supple, lithe, limber, springy, willowy, pliant, tensile, stretchy, whippy, lissom(e), ductile, bendable, mouldable

<< OPPOSITE rigid

2 ADAPTABLE, open, variable, adjustable, discretionary

<< OPPOSITE inflexible

3 COMPLIANT, accommodating, manageable, amenable, docile, tractable, biddable, complaisant, responsive, gentle

<< OPPOSITE unyielding

flick *verb* 1 JERK, pull, tug, lurch, jolt

2 STRIKE, tap, jab, remove quickly, hit, touch, stroke, rap, flip, peck, whisk, dab, fillip

▷ *noun* TAP, touch, sweep, stroke, rap, flip, peck, whisk, jab

▷▷ **flick through something** BROWSE, glance at, skim, leaf through, flip through, thumb through, skip through

flicker *verb* 1 TWINKLE, flash, sparkle, flare, shimmer, gutter, glimmer

2 FLUTTER, waver, quiver, vibrate

▷ *noun* 1 GLIMMER, flash, spark, flare, gleam

2 TRACE, drop, breath, spark, atom, glimmer, vestige, iota

flier ▷ see **flyer**
flight¹ *noun* 1 JOURNEY, trip, voyage
2 AVIATION, flying, air transport, aeronautics, aerial navigation
3 FLYING, winging, mounting, soaring, ability to fly
4 FLOCK, group, unit, cloud, formation, squadron, swarm, flying group
flight² *noun* ESCAPE, fleeing, departure, retreat, exit, running away, exodus, getaway, absconding
▷▷ **put to flight** DRIVE OFF, scatter, disperse, rout, stampede, scare off, send packing, chase off
▷▷ **take (to) flight** RUN AWAY *or* OFF, flee, bolt, abscond, decamp, do a runner (*slang*), turn tail, do a bunk (*Brit slang*), fly the coop (*US & Canad informal*), beat a retreat, light out (*informal*), skedaddle (*informal*), make a hasty retreat, take a powder (*US & Canad slang*), withdraw hastily, take it on the lam (*US & Canad slang*), do a Skase (*Austral informal*)
flighty *adjective* FRIVOLOUS, wild, volatile, unstable, irresponsible, dizzy, fickle, unbalanced, impulsive, mercurial, giddy, capricious, unsteady, thoughtless, changeable, impetuous, skittish, light-headed, harebrained, scatterbrained, ditzy *or* ditsy (*slang*)
flimsy *adjective* 1 FRAGILE, weak, slight, delicate, shallow, shaky, frail, superficial, makeshift, rickety, insubstantial, gimcrack, unsubstantial
<< OPPOSITE sturdy
2 THIN, light, sheer, transparent, chiffon, gossamer, gauzy
3 UNCONVINCING, poor, thin, weak, inadequate, pathetic, transparent, trivial, feeble, unsatisfactory, frivolous, tenuous, implausible
flinch *verb* 1 WINCE, start, duck, shrink, cringe, quail, recoil, cower, blench
2 *often with* **from** SHY AWAY, shrink, withdraw, flee, retreat, back off, swerve, shirk, draw back, baulk
fling *verb* THROW, toss, hurl, chuck (*informal*), launch, cast, pitch, send, shy, jerk, propel, sling, precipitate, lob (*informal*), catapult, heave, let fly
▷ *noun* 1 BINGE, good time, bash, bit of fun, party, rave (*Brit slang*), spree, indulgence (*informal*), beano (*Brit slang*), night on the town, rave-up (*Brit slang*), hooley *or* hoolie (*chiefly Irish & NZ*)
2 TRY, go (*informal*), attempt, shot (*informal*), trial, crack (*informal*), venture, gamble, stab (*informal*), bash (*informal*), whirl (*informal*)
flip *verb* 1 FLICK, switch, snap, jerk
2 SPIN, turn, overturn, turn over, roll over, twist
3 TOSS, throw, cast, pitch, flick, fling, sling
▷ *noun* TOSS, throw, cast, pitch, spin, snap, twist, flick, jerk
flippant *adjective* FRIVOLOUS, rude, cheeky, irreverent, flip (*informal*), superficial, saucy, glib, pert, disrespectful, offhand, impertinent, impudent
<< OPPOSITE serious
flirt *verb* 1 CHAT UP, lead on (*informal*), dally with, make advances at, make eyes at, coquet, philander, make sheep's eyes at
2 *usually with* **with** TOY WITH, consider, entertain, play with, dabble in, trifle with, give a thought to, expose yourself to
▷ *noun* TEASE, philanderer, coquette, heart-breaker, wanton, trifler
flirtation *noun* TEASING, philandering, dalliance, coquetry, toying, intrigue, trifling
flirtatious *adjective* TEASING, flirty, coquettish, amorous, come-on (*informal*), arch, enticing, provocative, coy, come-hither, sportive
flit *verb* FLY, dash, dart, skim, pass, speed, wing, flash, fleet, whisk, flutter
float *verb* 1 GLIDE, sail, drift, move gently, bob, coast, slide, be carried, slip along
2 BE BUOYANT, stay afloat, be *or* lie on the surface, rest on water, hang, hover, poise, displace water
<< OPPOSITE sink
3 LAUNCH, offer, sell, set up, promote, get going, push off
<< OPPOSITE dissolve
floating *adjective* 1 UNCOMMITTED, wavering, undecided, indecisive, vacillating, sitting on the fence (*informal*), unaffiliated, independent
2 FREE, wandering, variable, fluctuating, unattached, migratory, movable, unfixed
flock *noun* 1 HERD, group, flight, drove, colony, gaggle, skein
2 CROWD, company, group, host, collection, mass, gathering, assembly, convoy, herd, congregation, horde, multitude, throng, bevy
▷ *verb* 1 STREAM, crowd, mass, swarm, throng
2 GATHER, group, crowd, mass, collect, assemble, herd, huddle, converge, throng, congregate, troop
flog *verb* BEAT, whip, lash, thrash, whack, scourge, hit hard, trounce, castigate, chastise, flay, lambast(e), flagellate, punish severely, beat *or* knock seven bells out of (*informal*)
flogging *noun* BEATING, hiding (*informal*), whipping, lashing, thrashing, caning, scourging, trouncing, flagellation, horsewhipping
flood *noun* 1 DELUGE, downpour, flash flood, inundation, tide, overflow, torrent, spate, freshet
2 TORRENT, flow, rush, stream, tide,

abundance, multitude, glut, outpouring, profusion
3 SERIES, stream, avalanche, barrage, spate, torrent
4 OUTPOURING, rush, stream, surge, torrent
▷ *verb* 1 IMMERSE, swamp, submerge, inundate, deluge, drown, cover with water
2 POUR OVER, swamp, run over, overflow, inundate, brim over
3 ENGULF, flow into, rush into, sweep into, overwhelm, surge into, swarm into, pour into, gush into
4 SATURATE, fill, choke, swamp, glut, oversupply, overfill
5 STREAM, flow, rush, pour, surge
>> RELATED WORDS *adjectives* fluvial, diluvial

floor *noun* 1 GROUND
2 STOREY, level, stage, tier
▷ *verb* 1 (*informal*) DISCONCERT, stump, baffle, confound, beat, throw (*informal*), defeat, puzzle, conquer, overthrow, bewilder, perplex, bowl over (*informal*), faze, discomfit, bring up short, dumbfound, nonplus
2 KNOCK DOWN, fell, knock over, prostrate, deck (*slang*)

flop *verb* 1 SLUMP, fall, drop, collapse, sink, tumble, topple
2 HANG DOWN, hang, dangle, sag, droop, hang limply
3 (*informal*) FAIL, close, bomb (*US & Canad slang*), fold (*informal*), founder, fall short, fall flat, come to nothing, come unstuck, misfire, go belly-up (*slang*), go down like a lead balloon (*informal*)
<< OPPOSITE succeed
▷ *noun* (*informal*) FAILURE, disaster, loser, fiasco, debacle, washout (*informal*), cockup (*Brit slang*), nonstarter
<< OPPOSITE success

floppy *adjective* DROOPY, soft, loose, hanging, limp, flapping, sagging, baggy, flip-flop, flaccid, pendulous

floral *adjective* FLOWERY, flower-patterned

florid *adjective* 1 FLOWERY, high-flown, figurative, grandiloquent, euphuistic
2 ORNATE, busy, flamboyant, baroque, fussy, embellished, flowery, overelaborate
<< OPPOSITE plain
3 FLUSHED, ruddy, rubicund, high-coloured, high-complexioned, blowsy
<< OPPOSITE pale

flotsam *noun* 1 DEBRIS, rubbish, wreckage, detritus, jetsam
2 RUBBISH, sweepings, debris, junk, odds and ends

flounce *verb often with* **out**, **away**, **out**, *etc.* BOUNCE, storm, stamp, go quickly, throw, spring, toss, fling, jerk

flounder *verb* 1 FALTER, struggle, stall, slow down, run into trouble, come unstuck (*informal*), be in difficulties, hit a bad patch
2 DITHER, struggle, blunder, be confused, falter, be in the dark, be out of your depth
3 STRUGGLE, toss, thrash, plunge, stumble, tumble, muddle, fumble, grope, wallow

> *Flounder* is sometimes wrongly used where *founder* is meant: *the project foundered* (not *floundered*) *because of lack of funds*

flourish *verb* 1 THRIVE, increase, develop, advance, progress, boom, bloom, blossom, prosper, burgeon
<< OPPOSITE fail
2 SUCCEED, do well, be successful, move ahead, get ahead, go places (*informal*), go great guns (*slang*), go up in the world
3 GROW, thrive, develop, flower, succeed, get on, bloom, blossom, prosper, bear fruit, be vigorous, be in your prime
4 WAVE, brandish, sweep, swish, display, shake, swing, wield, flutter, wag, flaunt, vaunt, twirl
▷ *noun* 1 WAVE, sweep, brandish, swish, shaking, swing, dash, brandishing, twirling, twirl, showy gesture
2 SHOW, display, parade, fanfare
3 CURLICUE, sweep, decoration, swirl, plume, embellishment, ornamentation

flourishing *adjective* THRIVING, successful, doing well, blooming, mushrooming, prospering, rampant, burgeoning, on a roll, going places, going strong, in the pink, in top form, on the up and up (*informal*)

flout *verb* DEFY, scorn, spurn, scoff at, outrage, insult, mock, scout (*archaic*), ridicule, taunt, deride, sneer at, jeer at, laugh in the face of, show contempt for, gibe at, treat with disdain
<< OPPOSITE respect
▷ see **flaunt**

flow *verb* 1 RUN, course, rush, sweep, move, issue, pass, roll, flood, pour, slide, proceed, stream, run out, surge, spill, go along, circulate, swirl, glide, ripple, cascade, whirl, overflow, gush, inundate, deluge, spurt, teem, spew, squirt, purl, well forth
2 POUR, move, sweep, flood, stream, overflow
3 ISSUE, follow, result, emerge, spring, pour, proceed, arise, derive, ensue, emanate
▷ *noun* 1 STREAM, current, movement, motion, course, issue, flood, drift, tide, spate, gush, flux, outpouring, outflow, undertow, tideway
2 OUTPOURING, flood, stream, succession, train, plenty, abundance, deluge, plethora, outflow, effusion, emanation

flower *noun* 1 BLOOM, blossom, efflorescence
2 ELITE, best, prime, finest, pick, choice, cream, height, crème de la crème (*French*),

choicest part
3 HEIGHT, prime, peak, vigour, freshness, greatest *or* finest point
▷ *verb* 1 BLOOM, open, mature, flourish, unfold, blossom, burgeon, effloresce
2 BLOSSOM, grow, develop, progress, mature, thrive, flourish, bloom, bud, prosper
>> RELATED WORD *adjective* floral
>> RELATED WORD *prefix* antho-

flowering *adjective* BLOOMING, in flower, in bloom, in blossom, out, open, ready, blossoming, florescent, abloom

flowery *adjective* 1 FLORAL, flower-patterned
2 ORNATE, fancy, rhetorical, high-flown, embellished, figurative, florid, overwrought, euphuistic, baroque
<< OPPOSITE plain

flowing *adjective* 1 STREAMING, rushing, gushing, teeming, falling, full, rolling, sweeping, flooded, fluid, prolific, abundant, overrun, brimming over
2 SLEEK, smooth, fluid, unbroken, uninterrupted
3 FLUENT, easy, natural, continuous, effortless, uninterrupted, free-flowing, cursive, rich

fluctuate *verb* 1 CHANGE, swing, vary, alter, hesitate, alternate, waver, veer, rise and fall, go up and down, ebb and flow, seesaw
2 SHIFT, undulate, oscillate, vacillate

fluctuation *noun* CHANGE, shift, swing, variation, instability, alteration, wavering, oscillation, alternation, vacillation, unsteadiness, inconstancy

fluency *noun* EASE, control, facility, command, assurance, readiness, smoothness, slickness, glibness, volubility, articulateness

fluent *adjective* EFFORTLESS, natural, articulate, well-versed, glib, facile, voluble, smooth-spoken

fluff *noun* FUZZ, down, pile, dust, fibre, threads, nap, lint, oose (*Scot*), dustball
▷ *verb* (*informal*) MESS UP, spoil, bungle, screw up (*informal*), cock up (*Brit slang*), foul up (*informal*), make a nonsense of, be unsuccessful in, make a mess off, muddle, crool *or* cruel (*Austral slang*)

fluffy *adjective* SOFT, fuzzy, feathery, downy, fleecy, flossy

fluid *noun* LIQUID, solution, juice, liquor, sap
▷ *adjective* 1 CHANGEABLE, mobile, flexible, volatile, unstable, adjustable, fluctuating, indefinite, shifting, floating, adaptable, mercurial, protean, mutable
<< OPPOSITE fixed
2 LIQUID, running, flowing, watery, molten, melted, runny, liquefied, in solution, aqueous
<< OPPOSITE solid

fluke *noun* STROKE OF LUCK, accident, coincidence, chance occurrence, chance, stroke, blessing, freak, windfall, quirk, lucky break, serendipity, quirk of fate, fortuity, break

flunk (*informal, US & Canad*) *verb* FAIL, screw up (*informal*), flop in (*informal*), plough (*Brit slang*), be unsuccessful in, not make the grade at (*informal*), not come up to scratch in (*informal*), not come up to the mark in (*informal*)

flurry *noun* 1 COMMOTION, stir, bustle, flutter, to-do, excitement, hurry, fuss, disturbance, flap, whirl, furore, ferment, agitation, fluster, ado, tumult
2 BURST, spell, bout, outbreak, spurt
3 GUST, shower, gale, swirl, squall, storm

flush[1] *verb* 1 BLUSH, colour, burn, flame, glow, crimson, redden, suffuse, turn red, go red, colour up, go as red as a beetroot
2 CLEANSE, wash out, swab, rinse out, flood, drench, syringe, swill, hose down, douche
3 EXPEL, drive, eject, dislodge
▷ *noun* 1 BLUSH, colour, glow, reddening, redness, rosiness
2 BLOOM, glow, vigour, freshness

flush[2] *adjective* 1 LEVEL, even, true, flat, square, plane
2 (*informal*) WEALTHY, rich, rolling (*slang*), well-off, in the money (*informal*), in funds, well-heeled (*informal*), replete, moneyed, well-supplied
3 AFFLUENT, liberal, generous, lavish, abundant, overflowing, plentiful, prodigal, full
▷ *adverb* LEVEL, even, touching, squarely, in contact, hard (against)

flush[3] *verb often with* **out** DRIVE OUT, force, dislodge, put to flight, start, discover, disturb, uncover, rouse

flushed *adjective* 1 *often with* **with** EXHILARATED, excited, aroused, elated, high (*informal*), inspired, thrilled, animated, enthused, intoxicated, stoked (*Austral & NZ informal*)
2 BLUSHING, red, hot, burning, embarrassed, glowing, rosy, crimson, feverish, ruddy, rubicund

fluster *verb* UPSET, bother, disturb, ruffle, heat, excite, confuse, hurry, rattle (*informal*), bustle, hassle (*informal*), flurry, agitate, confound, unnerve, perturb, throw off balance, make nervous

fluted *adjective* (*Architecture*) GROOVED, channelled, furrowed, corrugated

flutter *verb* 1 BEAT, bat, flap, tremble, shiver, flicker, ripple, waver, fluctuate, agitate, ruffle, quiver, vibrate, palpitate
2 FLIT, hover, flitter
▷ *noun* 1 TREMOR, tremble, shiver, shudder, palpitation
2 VIBRATION, twitching, quiver, quivering
3 AGITATION, state (*informal*), confusion, excitement, flap (*informal*), tremble, flurry,

dither (*chiefly Brit*), commotion, fluster, tumult, perturbation, state of nervous excitement

flux *noun* 1 INSTABILITY, change, transition, unrest, modification, alteration, mutation, fluctuation, mutability
2 FLOW, movement, motion, fluidity

fly[1] *verb* 1 TAKE WING, soar, glide, take to the air, wing, mount, sail, hover, flutter, flit
2 PILOT, control, operate, steer, manoeuvre, navigate, be at the controls, aviate
3 AIRLIFT, send by plane, take by plane, take in an aircraft
4 FLUTTER, wave, float, flap
5 DISPLAY, show, flourish, brandish
6 RUSH, race, shoot, career, speed, tear, dash, hurry, barrel (along) (*informal, chiefly US & Canad*), sprint, bolt, dart, zoom, hare (*Brit informal*), hasten, whizz (*informal*), scoot, scamper, burn rubber (*informal*), be off like a shot (*informal*)
7 PASS SWIFTLY, pass, glide, slip away, roll on, flit, elapse, run its course, go quickly
8 LEAVE, disappear, get away, depart, run, escape, flee, take off, run from, shun, clear out (*informal*), light out (*informal*), abscond, decamp, take flight, do a runner (*slang*), run for it, cut and run (*informal*), fly the coop (*US & Canad informal*), beat a retreat, make a quick exit, make a getaway, show a clean pair of heels, skedaddle (*informal*), hightail (*informal, chiefly US*), take a powder (*US & Canad slang*), hasten away, make your escape, take it on the lam (*US & Canad slang*), take to your heels
▷▷ **let fly** (*informal*) LOSE YOUR TEMPER, lash out, burst forth, keep nothing back, give free rein, let (someone) have it
▷▷ **let something fly** THROW, launch, cast, hurl, shoot, fire, fling, chuck (*informal*), sling, lob (*informal*), hurtle, let off, heave

fly[2] *noun* ▷▷ **fly in the ointment** PROBLEM, difficulty, rub, flaw, hitch, drawback, snag, small problem

fly[3] *adjective* (*Slang, chiefly Brit*) CUNNING, knowing, sharp, smart, careful, shrewd, astute, on the ball (*informal*), canny, wide-awake, nobody's fool, not born yesterday

flyer *or* **flier** *noun* 1 (*Old-fashioned*) PILOT, aeronaut, airman *or* airwoman, aviator *or* aviatrix
2 AIR TRAVELLER, air passenger
3 HANDBILL, bill, notice, leaf, release, literature (*informal*), leaflet, advert (*Brit informal*), circular, booklet, pamphlet, handout, throwaway (*US*), promotional material, publicity material
4 (*informal*) JUMP, spring, bound, leap, hurdle, vault, jeté, flying *or* running jump

flying *adjective* 1 AIRBORNE, waving, winging, floating, streaming, soaring, in the air, hovering, flapping, gliding, fluttering, wind-borne, volitant
2 FAST, running, express, speedy, winged, mobile, rapid, fleet, mercurial
3 HURRIED, brief, rushed, fleeting, short-lived, hasty, transitory, fugacious

foam *noun* FROTH, spray, bubbles, lather, suds, spume, head
▷ *verb* BUBBLE, boil, fizz, froth, lather, effervesce

fob ▷▷ **fob someone off** PUT OFF, deceive, appease, flannel (*Brit informal*), give (someone) the run-around (*informal*), stall, equivocate with
▷▷ **fob something off on someone** PASS OFF, dump, get rid of, inflict, unload, foist, palm off

focus *noun* 1 CENTRE, focal point, central point, core, bull's eye, centre of attraction, centre of activity, cynosure
2 FOCAL POINT, heart, target, headquarters, hub, meeting place
▷ *verb* 1 *often with* **on** CONCENTRATE, centre, spotlight, zero in on (*informal*), meet, join, direct, aim, pinpoint, converge, rivet, bring to bear, zoom in
2 FIX, train, direct, aim

fodder *noun* FEED, food, rations, tack (*informal*), foodstuff, kai (*NZ informal*), forage, victuals, provender, vittles (*obsolete* or *dialect*)

foe *noun* (*Formal or literary*) ENEMY, rival, opponent, adversary, antagonist, foeman (*archaic*)
<< OPPOSITE friend

fog *noun* 1 MIST, gloom, haze, smog, murk, miasma, murkiness, peasouper (*informal*)
2 STUPOR, confusion, trance, daze, haze, disorientation
▷ *verb* 1 MIST OVER *or* UP, cloud over, steam up, become misty
2 DAZE, cloud, dim, muddle, blind, confuse, obscure, bewilder, darken, perplex, stupefy, befuddle, muddy the waters, obfuscate, blear, becloud, bedim

foggy *adjective* 1 MISTY, grey, murky, cloudy, obscure, blurred, dim, hazy, nebulous, indistinct, soupy, smoggy, vaporous, brumous (*rare*)
<< OPPOSITE clear
2 UNCLEAR, confused, clouded, stupid, obscure, vague, dim, bewildered, muddled, dazed, cloudy, stupefied, indistinct, befuddled, dark
<< OPPOSITE sharp

foible *noun* IDIOSYNCRASY, failing, fault, weakness, defect, quirk, imperfection, peculiarity, weak point, infirmity

foil[1] *verb* THWART, stop, check, defeat, disappoint, counter, frustrate, hamper, baffle, elude, balk, circumvent, outwit, nullify, checkmate, nip in the bud, put a spoke in (someone's) wheel (*Brit*)

foil² *noun* COMPLEMENT, setting, relief, contrast, background, antithesis

foist ▷▷ **foist something on** *or* **upon someone** FORCE

fold *verb* **1** BEND, double, gather, tuck, overlap, crease, pleat, intertwine, double over, turn under

2 *often with* **up** (*informal*) GO BANKRUPT, close, fail, crash, collapse, founder, shut down, go under, be ruined, go bust (*informal*), go to the wall, go belly-up (*slang*)

3 *with* **in** WRAP, envelop, entwine, enfold

4 *often with* **up** *or* **in** WRAP UP, wrap, enclose, envelop, do up, enfold

▷ *noun* CREASE, turn, gather, bend, layer, overlap, wrinkle, pleat, ruffle, furrow, knife-edge, double thickness, folded portion

folder *noun* FILE, portfolio, envelope, dossier, binder

folk *noun* **1** PEOPLE, persons, humans, individuals, men and women, human beings, humanity, inhabitants, mankind, mortals

2 *usually plural* (*informal*) FAMILY, parents, relations, relatives, tribe, clan, kin, kindred, ainga (*NZ*), rellies (*Austral slang*)

follow *verb* **1** ACCOMPANY, attend, escort, come after, go behind, tag along behind, bring up the rear, come behind, come *or* go with, tread on the heels of

2 PURSUE, track, dog, hunt, chase, shadow, tail (*informal*), trail, hound, stalk, run after

<< OPPOSITE avoid

3 COME AFTER, go after, come next

<< OPPOSITE precede

4 RESULT, issue, develop, spring, flow, proceed, arise, ensue, emanate, be consequent, supervene

5 OBEY, observe, comply with, adhere to, mind, watch, note, regard, stick to, heed, conform to, keep to, pay attention to, be guided by, act according to, act in accordance with, give allegiance to

<< OPPOSITE ignore

6 COPY, imitate, emulate, mimic, model, adopt, live up to, take a leaf out of someone's book, take as an example, pattern yourself upon

7 SUCCEED, replace, come after, take over from, come next, supersede, supplant, take the place of, step into the shoes of

8 UNDERSTAND, get, see, catch, realize, appreciate, take in, grasp, catch on (*informal*), keep up with, comprehend, fathom, get the hang of (*informal*), get the picture

9 KEEP UP WITH, support, be interested in, cultivate, be devoted to, be a fan of, keep abreast of, be a devotee *or* supporter of

▷▷ **follow something through** COMPLETE, conclude, pursue, see through, consummate, bring to a conclusion

follower *noun* **1** SUPPORTER, fan, representative, convert, believer, admirer, backer, partisan, disciple, protagonist, devotee, worshipper, apostle, pupil, cohort (*chiefly US*), adherent, henchman, groupie (*slang*), habitué, votary

<< OPPOSITE leader

2 ATTENDANT, assistant, companion, helper, sidekick (*slang*), henchman, retainer (*History*), hanger-on, minion, lackey

<< OPPOSITE opponent

following *adjective* **1** NEXT, subsequent, successive, ensuing, coming, later, succeeding, specified, consequent, consequential

2 COMING, about to be mentioned

▷ *noun* SUPPORTERS, backing, public, support, train, fans, audience, circle, suite, patronage, clientele, entourage, coterie, retinue

folly *noun* FOOLISHNESS, bêtise (*rare*), nonsense, madness, stupidity, absurdity, indiscretion, lunacy, recklessness, silliness, idiocy, irrationality, imprudence, rashness, imbecility, fatuity, preposterousness, daftness (*informal*), desipience

<< OPPOSITE wisdom

foment *verb* STIR UP, raise, encourage, promote, excite, spur, foster, stimulate, provoke, brew, arouse, rouse, agitate, quicken, incite, instigate, whip up, goad, abet, sow the seeds of, fan the flames

> Both *foment* and *ferment* can be used to talk about stirring up trouble: *he was accused of fomenting/fermenting unrest*. Only *ferment* can be used intransitively or as a noun: *his anger continued to ferment* (not *foment*); *rural areas were unaffected by the ferment in the cities*

fond *adjective* **1** LOVING, caring, warm, devoted, tender, adoring, affectionate, indulgent, doting, amorous

<< OPPOSITE indifferent

2 UNREALISTIC, empty, naive, vain, foolish, deluded, indiscreet, credulous, overoptimistic, delusive, delusory, absurd

<< OPPOSITE sensible

▷▷ **fond of 1** ATTACHED TO, in love with, keen on, attracted to, having a soft spot for, enamoured of

2 KEEN ON, into (*informal*), hooked on, partial to, having a soft spot for, having a taste for, addicted to, having a liking for, predisposed towards, having a fancy for

fondle *verb* CARESS, pet, cuddle, touch gently, pat, stroke, dandle

fondly *adverb* **1** LOVINGLY, tenderly, affectionately, amorously, dearly, possessively, with affection, indulgently, adoringly

2 UNREALISTICALLY, stupidly, vainly, foolishly,

naively, credulously

fondness *noun* 1 DEVOTION, love, affection, warmth, attachment, kindness, tenderness, care, aroha (*NZ*)
<< OPPOSITE dislike
2 LIKING, love, taste, fancy, attraction, weakness, preference, attachment, penchant, susceptibility, predisposition, soft spot, predilection, partiality

food *noun* NOURISHMENT, cooking, provisions, fare, board, commons, table, eats (*slang*), stores, feed, diet, meat, bread, menu, tuck (*informal*), tucker (*Austral & NZ informal*), rations, nutrition, cuisine, tack (*informal*), refreshment, scoff (*slang*), nibbles, grub (*slang*), foodstuffs, subsistence, kai (*NZ informal*), larder, chow (*informal*), sustenance, nosh (*slang*), daily bread, victuals, edibles, comestibles, provender, nosebag (*slang*), pabulum (*rare*), nutriment, vittles (*obsolete* or *dialect*), viands, aliment, eatables (*slang*), survival rations
>> RELATED WORD *adjective* alimentary
>> RELATED WORD *noun* gastronomy

fool *noun* 1 SIMPLETON, idiot, mug (*Brit slang*), berk (*Brit slang*), charlie (*Brit informal*), silly, goose (*informal*), dope (*informal*), jerk (*slang, chiefly US & Canad*), dummy (*slang*), ass (*US & Canad taboo slang*), clot (*Brit informal*), plank (*Brit slang*), sap (*slang*), wally (*slang*), illiterate, prat (*slang*), plonker (*slang*), coot, moron, nit (*informal*), git (*Brit slang*), geek (*slang*), twit (*informal, chiefly Brit*), bonehead (*slang*), chump (*informal*), dunce, imbecile (*informal*), loon, clod, cretin, oaf, bozo (*US slang*), dullard, dimwit (*informal*), ignoramus, dumbo (*slang*), jackass, dipstick (*Brit slang*), gonzo (*slang*), schmuck (*US slang*), dork (*slang*), nitwit (*informal*), dolt, blockhead, ninny, divvy (*Brit slang*), bird-brain (*informal*), pillock (*Brit slang*), halfwit, nincompoop, dweeb (*US slang*), putz (*US slang*), fathead (*informal*), weenie (*US informal*), schlep (*US slang*), eejit (*Scot & Irish*), dumb-ass (*slang*), pea-brain (*slang*), dunderhead, numpty (*Scot informal*), doofus (*slang, chiefly US*), lamebrain (*informal*), mooncalf, thickhead, clodpate (*archaic*), nerd *or* nurd (*slang*), numbskull *or* numskull, twerp *or* twirp (*informal*), dorba *or* dorb (*Austral slang*), bogan (*Austral slang*)
<< OPPOSITE genius
2 DUPE, butt, mug (*Brit slang*), sucker (*slang*), gull (*archaic*), stooge (*slang*), laughing stock, pushover (*informal*), fall guy (*informal*), chump (*informal*), greenhorn (*informal*), easy mark (*informal*)
3 JESTER, comic, clown, harlequin, motley, buffoon, pierrot, court jester, punchinello, joculator *or (fem.)* joculatrix, merry-andrew
▷ *verb* DECEIVE, cheat, mislead, delude, kid (*informal*), trick, take in, con (*informal*), stiff (*slang*), have (someone) on, bluff, hoax, dupe, beguile, gull (*archaic*), swindle, make a fool of, bamboozle, hoodwink, take for a ride (*informal*), put one over on (*informal*), play a trick on, pull a fast one on (*informal*)
▷▷ **fool around with something** (*informal*) PLAY AROUND WITH, play with, tamper with, toy with, mess around with, meddle with, trifle with, fiddle around with (*informal*), monkey around with

foolhardy *adjective* RASH, risky, irresponsible, reckless, precipitate, unwise, impulsive, madcap, impetuous, hot-headed, imprudent, incautious, venturesome, venturous, temerarious
<< OPPOSITE cautious

foolish *adjective* 1 UNWISE, silly, absurd, rash, unreasonable, senseless, short-sighted, ill-advised, foolhardy, nonsensical, inane, indiscreet, ill-judged, ill-considered, imprudent, unintelligent, asinine, injudicious, incautious
<< OPPOSITE sensible
2 SILLY, stupid, mad, daft (*informal*), simple, weak, crazy, ridiculous, dumb (*informal*), ludicrous, senseless, barmy (*slang*), potty (*Brit informal*), goofy (*informal*), idiotic, half-baked (*informal*), dotty (*slang*), inane, fatuous, loopy (*informal*), witless, crackpot (*informal*), moronic, brainless, half-witted, imbecilic, off your head (*informal*), braindead (*informal*), harebrained, as daft as a brush (*informal, chiefly Brit*), dumb-ass (*slang*), doltish

foolishly *adverb* UNWISELY, stupidly, mistakenly, absurdly, like a fool, idiotically, incautiously, imprudently, ill-advisedly, indiscreetly, short-sightedly, injudiciously, without due consideration

foolishness *noun* 1 STUPIDITY, irresponsibility, recklessness, idiocy, weakness, absurdity, indiscretion, silliness, inanity, imprudence, rashness, foolhardiness, folly, bêtise (*rare*)
2 NONSENSE, carrying-on (*informal, chiefly Brit*), rubbish, trash, bunk (*informal*), claptrap (*informal*), rigmarole, foolery, bunkum *or* buncombe (*chiefly US*)

foolproof *adjective* INFALLIBLE, certain, safe, guaranteed, never-failing, unassailable, sure-fire (*informal*), unbreakable

footing *noun* 1 BASIS, foundation, foothold, base position, ground, settlement, establishment, installation, groundwork
2 RELATIONSHIP, terms, position, basis, state, standing, condition, relations, rank, status, grade
3 FOOTHOLD, hold, grip, toehold, support

footpath *noun* (*Austral & NZ*) PAVEMENT, sidewalk (*US & Canad*)

footstep *noun* 1 STEP, tread, footfall

2 FOOTPRINT, mark, track, trace, outline, imprint, indentation, footmark

footwear *noun* FOOTGEAR, boots, shoes, slippers, sandals

forage *noun* (*for cattle, etc*) FODDER, food, feed, foodstuffs, provender
▷ *verb* SEARCH, hunt, scavenge, cast about, seek, explore, raid, scour, plunder, look round, rummage, ransack, scrounge (*informal*), fossick (*Austral* & NZ)

foray *noun* RAID, sally, incursion, inroad, attack, assault, invasion, swoop, reconnaissance, sortie, irruption

forbearance *noun* 1 PATIENCE, resignation, restraint, tolerance, indulgence, long-suffering, moderation, self-control, leniency, temperance, mildness, lenity, longanimity (*rare*)
<< OPPOSITE impatience
2 ABSTINENCE, refraining, avoidance

forbid *verb* PROHIBIT, ban, disallow, proscribe, exclude, rule out, veto, outlaw, inhibit, hinder, preclude, make illegal, debar, interdict
<< OPPOSITE permit

> Traditionally, it has been considered more correct to talk about *forbidding someone to do something*, rather than *forbidding someone from doing something*. Recently, however, the *from* option has become generally more acceptable, so that *he was forbidden to come in* and *he was forbidden from coming in* may both now be considered correct

forbidden *adjective* PROHIBITED, banned, vetoed, outlawed, taboo, out of bounds, proscribed, verboten (*German*)

forbidding *adjective* THREATENING, severe, frightening, hostile, grim, menacing, sinister, daunting, ominous, unfriendly, foreboding, baleful, bodeful
<< OPPOSITE inviting

force *noun* 1 COMPULSION, pressure, violence, enforcement, constraint, oppression, coercion, duress, arm-twisting (*informal*)
2 POWER, might, pressure, energy, stress, strength, impact, muscle, momentum, impulse, stimulus, vigour, potency, dynamism, life
<< OPPOSITE weakness
3 INFLUENCE, power, effect, authority, weight, strength, punch (*informal*), significance, effectiveness, validity, efficacy, soundness, persuasiveness, cogency, bite
4 INTENSITY, vigour, vehemence, fierceness, drive, emphasis, persistence
5 ARMY, unit, division, corps, company, body, host, troop, squad, patrol, regiment, battalion, legion, squadron, detachment
▷ *verb* 1 COMPEL, make, drive, press, pressure, urge, overcome, oblige, railroad (*informal*), constrain, necessitate, coerce, impel, strong-arm (*informal*), dragoon, pressurize, press-gang, put the squeeze on (*informal*), obligate, twist (someone's) arm, put the screws on (*informal*), bring pressure to bear upon
2 IMPOSE, foist
3 PUSH, thrust, propel
4 BREAK OPEN, blast, wrench, prise, wrest, use violence on
5 EXTORT, drag, exact, wring
<< OPPOSITE coax
▷▷ **in force** 1 VALID, working, current, effective, binding, operative, operational, in operation, on the statute book
2 IN GREAT NUMBERS, all together, in full strength

forced *adjective* 1 COMPULSORY, enforced, slave, unwilling, mandatory, obligatory, involuntary, conscripted
<< OPPOSITE voluntary
2 FALSE, affected, strained, wooden, stiff, artificial, contrived, unnatural, insincere, laboured
<< OPPOSITE natural

forceful *adjective* 1 DYNAMIC, powerful, vigorous, potent, assertive
<< OPPOSITE weak
2 POWERFUL, strong, convincing, effective, compelling, persuasive, weighty, pithy, cogent, telling

forcible *adjective* 1 VIOLENT, armed, aggressive, compulsory, drastic, coercive
2 COMPELLING, strong, powerful, effective, active, impressive, efficient, valid, mighty, potent, energetic, forceful, weighty, cogent

forcibly *adverb* BY FORCE, compulsorily, under protest, against your will, under compulsion, by main force, willy-nilly

forebear *or* **forbear** *noun* ANCESTOR, father, predecessor, forerunner, forefather, progenitor, tupuna *or* tipuna (NZ)

foreboding *noun* 1 DREAD, fear, anxiety, chill, unease, apprehension, misgiving, premonition, presentiment, apprehensiveness
2 OMEN, warning, prediction, portent, sign, token, foreshadowing, presage, prognostication, augury, foretoken

forecast *verb* PREDICT, anticipate, foresee, foretell, call, plan, estimate, calculate, divine, prophesy, augur, forewarn, prognosticate, vaticinate (*rare*)
▷ *noun* PREDICTION, projection, anticipation, prognosis, planning, guess, outlook, prophecy, foresight, conjecture, forewarning, forethought

forefather *noun* ANCESTOR, father, predecessor,

forerunner, forebear, progenitor, procreator, primogenitor, tupuna *or* tipuna (*NZ*)
forefront *noun* LEAD, centre, front, fore, spearhead, prominence, vanguard, foreground, leading position, van
forego ▷ see **forgo**
foregoing *adjective* PRECEDING, former, above, previous, prior, antecedent, anterior, just mentioned, previously stated
foreground *noun* 1 FRONT, focus, forefront
2 PROMINENCE, limelight, fore, forefront
foreign *adjective* 1 ALIEN, overseas, exotic, unknown, outside, strange, imported, borrowed, remote, distant, external, unfamiliar, far off, outlandish, beyond your ken
<< OPPOSITE native
2 UNASSIMILABLE, external, extraneous, outside
3 UNCHARACTERISTIC, inappropriate, unrelated, incongruous, inapposite, irrelevant
foreigner *noun* ALIEN, incomer, immigrant, non-native, stranger, newcomer, settler, outlander
>> RELATED WORD *fear* xenophobia
foremost *adjective* LEADING, best, first, highest, front, chief, prime, primary, supreme, initial, most important, principal, paramount, inaugural, pre-eminent, headmost
forerunner *noun* 1 OMEN, sign, indication, token, premonition, portent, augury, prognostic, foretoken, harbinger
2 PRECURSOR, predecessor, ancestor, prototype, forebear, progenitor, herald
foresee *verb* PREDICT, forecast, anticipate, envisage, prophesy, foretell, forebode, vaticinate (*rare*), divine
foreshadow *verb* PREDICT, suggest, promise, indicate, signal, imply, bode, prophesy, augur, presage, prefigure, portend, betoken, adumbrate, forebode
foresight *noun* FORETHOUGHT, prudence, circumspection, far-sightedness, care, provision, caution, precaution, anticipation, preparedness, prescience, premeditation, prevision (*rare*)
<< OPPOSITE hindsight
forestall *verb* PREVENT, stop, frustrate, anticipate, head off, parry, thwart, intercept, hinder, preclude, balk, circumvent, obviate, nip in the bud, provide against
forestry *noun* WOODCRAFT, silviculture, arboriculture, dendrology (*Botany*), woodmanship
foretaste *noun* SAMPLE, example, indication, preview, trailer, prelude, whiff, foretoken, warning
foretell *verb* PREDICT, forecast, prophesy, portend, call, signify, bode, foreshadow, augur, presage, forewarn, prognosticate, adumbrate, forebode, foreshow, soothsay, vaticinate (*rare*)
forever or for ever *adverb* 1 EVERMORE, always, ever, for good, for keeps, for all time, in perpetuity, for good and all (*informal*), till the cows come home (*informal*), world without end, till the end of time, till Doomsday
2 CONSTANTLY, always, all the time, continually, endlessly, persistently, eternally, perpetually, incessantly, interminably, unremittingly, everlastingly

> *Forever* and *for ever* can both be used to say that something is without end. For all other meanings, *forever* is the preferred form

forewarn *verb* ALERT, advise, caution, tip off, apprise, give fair warning, put on guard, put on the qui vive
foreword *noun* INTRODUCTION, preliminary, preface, preamble, prologue, prolegomenon
forfeit *noun* PENALTY, fine, damages, forfeiture, loss, mulct, amercement (*obsolete*)
▷ *verb* RELINQUISH, lose, give up, surrender, renounce, be deprived of, say goodbye to, be stripped of
forfeiture *noun* LOSS, giving up, surrender, forfeiting, confiscation, sequestration (*Law*), relinquishment
forge *verb* 1 FORM, build, create, establish, set up, fashion, shape, frame, construct, invent, devise, mould, contrive, fabricate, hammer out, make, work
2 FAKE, copy, reproduce, imitate, counterfeit, feign, falsify, coin
3 CREATE, make, work, found, form, model, fashion, shape, cast, turn out, construct, devise, mould, contrive, fabricate, hammer out, beat into shape
forged *adjective* 1 FAKE, copy, false, counterfeit, pretend, artificial, mock, pirated, reproduction, synthetic, imitation, bogus, simulated, duplicate, quasi, sham, fraudulent, pseudo, fabricated, copycat (*informal*), falsified, ersatz, unoriginal, ungenuine, phony *or* phoney (*informal*)
<< OPPOSITE genuine
2 FORMED, worked, founded, modelled, fashioned, shaped, cast, framed, stamped, crafted, moulded, minted, hammered out, beat out, beaten into shape
forger *noun* COUNTERFEITER, copier, copyist, falsifier, coiner
forgery *noun* 1 FALSIFICATION, faking, pirating, counterfeiting, fraudulence, fraudulent imitation, coining
2 FAKE, imitation, sham, counterfeit, falsification, phoney *or* phony (*informal*)
forget *verb* 1 FAIL TO REMEMBER, not remember, not recollect, let slip from the memory, fail to

bring to mind
<< OPPOSITE remember
2 NEGLECT, overlook, omit, not remember, be remiss, fail to remember
3 LEAVE BEHIND, lose, lose sight of, mislay
4 DISMISS FROM YOUR MIND, ignore, overlook, stop thinking about, let bygones be bygones, consign to oblivion, put out of your mind

forgetful *adjective* ABSENT-MINDED, vague, careless, neglectful, oblivious, lax, negligent, dreamy, slapdash, heedless, slipshod, inattentive, unmindful, apt to forget, having a memory like a sieve
<< OPPOSITE mindful

forgetfulness *noun* ABSENT-MINDEDNESS, oblivion, inattention, carelessness, abstraction, laxity, laxness, dreaminess, obliviousness, lapse of memory, heedlessness, woolgathering

forgive *verb* EXCUSE, pardon, bear no malice towards, not hold something against, understand, acquit, condone, remit, let off (*informal*), turn a blind eye to, exonerate, absolve, bury the hatchet, let bygones be bygones, turn a deaf ear to, accept (someone's) apology
<< OPPOSITE blame

forgiveness *noun* PARDON, mercy, absolution, exoneration, overlooking, amnesty, acquittal, remission, condonation

forgiving *adjective* LENIENT, tolerant, compassionate, clement, patient, mild, humane, gracious, long-suffering, merciful, magnanimous, forbearing, willing to forgive, soft-hearted

forgo *or* **forego** *verb* GIVE UP, sacrifice, surrender, do without, kick (*informal*), abandon, resign, yield, relinquish, renounce, waive, say goodbye to, cede, abjure, leave alone *or* out

fork *verb* BRANCH, part, separate, split, divide, diverge, subdivide, branch off, go separate ways, bifurcate

forked *adjective* BRANCHING, split, branched, divided, angled, pronged, zigzag, tined, Y-shaped, bifurcate(d)

forlorn *adjective* 1 MISERABLE, helpless, pathetic, pitiful, lost, forgotten, abandoned, unhappy, lonely, lonesome (*chiefly US & Canad*), homeless, forsaken, bereft, destitute, wretched, disconsolate, friendless, down in the dumps (*informal*), pitiable, cheerless, woebegone, comfortless
<< OPPOSITE cheerful
2 ABANDONED, deserted, ruined, bleak, dreary, desolate, godforsaken, waste
3 HOPELESS, useless, vain, pointless, futile, no-win, unattainable, impracticable, unachievable, impossible, not having a prayer

form *noun* 1 TYPE, sort, kind, variety, way, system, order, class, style, practice, method, species, manner, stamp, description
2 SHAPE, formation, configuration, construction, cut, model, fashion, structure, pattern, cast, appearance, stamp, mould
3 STRUCTURE, plan, order, organization, arrangement, construction, proportion, format, framework, harmony, symmetry, orderliness
4 BUILD, being, body, figure, shape, frame, outline, anatomy, silhouette, physique, person
5 CONDITION, health, shape, nick (*informal*), fitness, trim, good condition, good spirits, fettle
6 DOCUMENT, paper, sheet, questionnaire, application
7 PROCEDURE, behaviour, manners, etiquette, use, rule, conduct, ceremony, custom, convention, ritual, done thing, usage, protocol, formality, wont, right practice, kawa (*NZ*), tikanga (*NZ*)
8 (*Education, chiefly Brit*) CLASS, year, set, rank, grade, stream
9 MODE, character, shape, appearance, arrangement, manifestation, guise, semblance, design
▷ *verb* 1 ARRANGE, combine, line up, organize, assemble, dispose, draw up
2 MAKE, produce, model, fashion, build, create, shape, manufacture, stamp, construct, assemble, forge, mould, fabricate
3 CONSTITUTE, make up, compose, comprise, serve as, make
4 ESTABLISH, start, found, launch, set up, invent, devise, put together, bring about, contrive
5 TAKE SHAPE, grow, develop, materialize, rise, appear, settle, show up (*informal*), accumulate, come into being, crystallize, become visible
6 DRAW UP, design, devise, formulate, plan, pattern, frame, organize, think up
7 DEVELOP, pick up, acquire, cultivate, contract, get into (*informal*)
8 TRAIN, develop, shape, mould, school, teach, guide, discipline, rear, educate, bring up, instruct

formal *adjective* 1 SERIOUS, stiff, detached, aloof, official, reserved, correct, conventional, remote, exact, precise, starched, prim, unbending, punctilious, ceremonious
<< OPPOSITE informal
2 OFFICIAL, express, explicit, authorized, set, legal, fixed, regular, approved, strict, endorsed, prescribed, rigid, certified, solemn, lawful, methodical, pro forma (*Latin*)
3 CEREMONIAL, traditional, solemn, ritualistic, dressy
4 CONVENTIONAL, established, traditional

formality *noun* 1 CORRECTNESS, seriousness,

decorum, ceremoniousness, protocol, etiquette, politesse, p's and q's, punctilio
2 CONVENTION, form, conventionality, matter of form, procedure, ceremony, custom, gesture, ritual, rite

format *noun* ARRANGEMENT, form, style, make-up, look, plan, design, type, appearance, construction, presentation, layout

formation *noun* 1 ESTABLISHMENT, founding, forming, setting up, starting, production, generation, organization, manufacture, constitution
2 DEVELOPMENT, shaping, constitution, evolution, moulding, composition, compilation, accumulation, genesis, crystallization
3 ARRANGEMENT, grouping, figure, design, structure, pattern, rank, organization, array, disposition, configuration

formative *adjective* 1 DEVELOPMENTAL, sensitive, susceptible, impressionable, malleable, pliant, mouldable
2 INFLUENTIAL, determinative, controlling, important, shaping, significant, moulding, decisive, developmental

former *adjective* 1 PREVIOUS, one-time, erstwhile, ex-, late, earlier, prior, sometime, foregoing, antecedent, anterior, quondam, whilom (*archaic*), ci-devant (*French*)
<< OPPOSITE current
2 PAST, earlier, long ago, bygone, old, ancient, departed, old-time, long gone, of yore
<< OPPOSITE present
3 AFOREMENTIONED, above, first mentioned, aforesaid, preceding, foregoing

formerly *adverb* PREVIOUSLY, earlier, in the past, at one time, before, lately, once, already, heretofore, aforetime (*archaic*)

formidable *adjective* 1 DIFFICULT, taxing, challenging, overwhelming, staggering, daunting, mammoth, colossal, arduous, very great, onerous, toilsome
<< OPPOSITE easy
2 IMPRESSIVE, great, powerful, tremendous, mighty, terrific, awesome, invincible, indomitable, redoubtable, puissant
3 INTIMIDATING, threatening, dangerous, terrifying, appalling, horrible, dreadful, menacing, dismaying, fearful, daunting, frightful, baleful, shocking
<< OPPOSITE encouraging

formula *noun* 1 METHOD, plan, policy, rule, principle, procedure, recipe, prescription, blueprint, precept, modus operandi, way
2 FORM OF WORDS, code, phrase, formulary, set expression
3 MIXTURE, preparation, compound, composition, concoction, tincture, medicine

formulate *verb* 1 DEVISE, plan, develop, prepare, work out, invent, evolve, coin, forge, draw up, originate, map out
2 EXPRESS, detail, frame, define, specify, articulate, set down, codify, put into words, systematize, particularize, give form to

forsake *verb* 1 DESERT, leave, abandon, quit, strand, jettison, repudiate, cast off, disown, jilt, throw over, leave in the lurch
2 GIVE UP, set aside, relinquish, forgo, kick (*informal*), yield, surrender, renounce, have done with, stop using, abdicate, stop having, turn your back on, forswear
3 ABANDON, leave, go away from, take your leave of

forsaken *adjective* 1 ABANDONED, ignored, lonely, lonesome (*chiefly US & Canad*), stranded, ditched, left behind, marooned, outcast, forlorn, cast off, jilted, friendless, left in the lurch
2 DESERTED, abandoned, isolated, solitary, desolate, forlorn, destitute, disowned, godforsaken

fort *noun* FORTRESS, keep, station, camp, tower, castle, garrison, stronghold, citadel, fortification, redoubt, fastness, blockhouse, fortified pa (*NZ*)
▷▷ **hold the fort** (*informal*) TAKE RESPONSIBILITY, cover, stand in, carry on, take over the reins, maintain the status quo, deputize, keep things moving, keep things on an even keel

forte *noun* SPECIALITY, strength, talent, strong point, métier, long suit (*informal*), gift
<< OPPOSITE weak point

forth *adverb* (*Formal* or *old-fashioned*) 1 FORWARD, out, away, ahead, onward, outward
2 OUT, into the open, out of concealment

forthcoming *adjective* 1 APPROACHING, coming, expected, future, imminent, prospective, impending, upcoming
2 AVAILABLE, ready, accessible, at hand, in evidence, obtainable, on tap (*informal*)
3 COMMUNICATIVE, open, free, informative, expansive, sociable, chatty, talkative, unreserved

forthright *adjective* OUTSPOKEN, open, direct, frank, straightforward, blunt, downright, candid, upfront (*informal*), plain-spoken, straight from the shoulder (*informal*)
<< OPPOSITE secretive

forthwith *adverb* IMMEDIATELY, directly, instantly, at once, right away, straightaway, without delay, tout de suite (*French*), quickly

fortification *noun* 1 REINFORCEMENT, protecting, securing, protection, strengthening, reinforcing, embattlement
2 DEFENCE, keep, protection, castle, fort, fortress, stronghold, bastion, citadel, bulwark, fastness, fortified pa (*NZ*)
3 STRENGTHENING, supplementing,

reinforcement

fortify *verb* 1 PROTECT, defend, secure, strengthen, reinforce, support, brace, garrison, shore up, augment, buttress, make stronger, embattle

2 STRENGTHEN, add alcohol to

3 SUSTAIN, encourage, confirm, cheer, strengthen, reassure, brace, stiffen, hearten, embolden, invigorate

<< OPPOSITE dishearten

fortitude *noun* COURAGE, strength, resolution, determination, guts (*informal*), patience, pluck, grit, endurance, bravery, backbone, perseverance, firmness, staying power, valour, fearlessness, strength of mind, intrepidity, hardihood, dauntlessness, stoutheartedness

fortress *noun* CASTLE, fort, stronghold, citadel, redoubt, fastness, fortified pa (*NZ*)

fortuitous *adjective* 1 CHANCE, lucky, random, casual, contingent, accidental, arbitrary, incidental, unforeseen, unplanned

2 LUCKY, happy, fortunate, serendipitous, providential, fluky (*informal*)

fortunate *adjective* 1 LUCKY, happy, favoured, bright, golden, rosy, on a roll, jammy (*Brit slang*), in luck, having a charmed life, born with a silver spoon in your mouth

<< OPPOSITE unfortunate

2 PROVIDENTIAL, auspicious, fortuitous, felicitous, timely, promising, encouraging, helpful, profitable, convenient, favourable, advantageous, expedient, opportune, propitious

fortunately *adverb* LUCKILY, happily, as luck would have it, providentially, by good luck, by a happy chance

fortune *noun* 1 LARGE SUM OF MONEY, bomb (*Brit slang*), packet (*slang*), bundle (*slang*), big money, big bucks (*informal, chiefly US*), megabucks (*US & Canad slang*), an arm and a leg (*informal*), king's ransom, pretty penny (*informal*), top whack (*informal*)

2 WEALTH, means, property, riches, resources, assets, pile (*informal*), possessions, treasure, prosperity, mint, gold mine, wad (*US & Canad slang*), affluence, opulence, tidy sum (*informal*)

<< OPPOSITE poverty

3 LUCK, accident, fluke (*informal*), stroke of luck, serendipity, hap (*archaic*), twist of fate, run of luck

4 CHANCE, fate, destiny, providence, the stars, Lady Luck, kismet, fortuity

5 *often plural* DESTINY, life, lot, experiences, history, condition, success, means, circumstances, expectation, adventures

forum *noun* 1 MEETING, conference, assembly, meeting place, court, body, council, parliament, congress, gathering, diet, senate, rally, convention, tribunal (*archaic* or *literary*), seminar, get-together (*informal*), congregation, caucus (*chiefly US & Canad*), synod, convergence, symposium, hui (*NZ*), moot, assemblage, conclave, convocation, consistory (*in various Churches*), ecclesia (*in Church use*), colloquium, folkmoot (*in medieval England*), runanga (*NZ*)

2 PUBLIC SQUARE, court, square, chamber, platform, arena, pulpit, meeting place, amphitheatre, stage, rostrum, agora (*in ancient Greece*)

forward *adjective* 1 LEADING, first, head, front, advance, foremost, fore

2 FUTURE, early, advanced, progressive, premature, prospective, onward, forward-looking

3 PRESUMPTUOUS, confident, familiar, bold, fresh (*informal*), assuming, presuming, cheeky, brash, pushy (*informal*), brazen, shameless, sassy (*US informal*), pert, impertinent, impudent, bare-faced, overweening, immodest, brass-necked (*Brit informal*), overfamiliar, brazen-faced, overassertive

<< OPPOSITE shy

▷ *adverb* INTO THE OPEN, out, to light, to the front, to the surface, into consideration, into view, into prominence

▷ *verb* 1 FURTHER, back, help, support, aid, encourage, speed, advance, favour, promote, foster, assist, hurry, hasten, expedite

<< OPPOSITE retard

2 SEND ON, send, post, pass on, ship, route, transmit, dispatch, freight, redirect

forwards *or* **forward** *adverb* 1 FORTH, on, ahead, onwards

<< OPPOSITE backward(s)

2 ON, onward, onwards

fossick *verb* (*Austral & NZ*) SEARCH, hunt, explore, ferret, check, forage, rummage

foster *verb* 1 BRING UP, mother, raise, nurse, look after, rear, care for, take care of, nurture

2 DEVELOP, support, further, encourage, feed, promote, stimulate, uphold, nurture, cultivate, foment

<< OPPOSITE suppress

3 CHERISH, sustain, entertain, harbour, accommodate, nourish

foul *adjective* 1 DIRTY, rank, offensive, nasty, disgusting, unpleasant, revolting, contaminated, rotten, polluted, stinking, filthy, tainted, grubby, repellent, squalid, repulsive, sullied, grimy, nauseating, loathsome, unclean, impure, grotty (*slang*), fetid, grungy (*slang, chiefly US & Canad*), putrid, malodorous, noisome, scuzzy (*slang, chiefly US*), mephitic, olid, yucky *or* yukky (*slang*), festy (*Austral slang*), yucko (*Austral slang*)

<< OPPOSITE clean

2 OBSCENE, crude, indecent, foul-mouthed, low, blue, dirty, gross, abusive, coarse,

filthy, vulgar, lewd, profane, blasphemous, scurrilous, smutty, scatological
3 STORMY, bad, wild, rough, wet, rainy, murky, foggy, disagreeable, blustery
4 UNFAIR, illegal, dirty, crooked, shady (*informal*), fraudulent, unjust, dishonest, unscrupulous, underhand, inequitable, unsportsmanlike
5 OFFENSIVE, bad, base, wrong, evil, notorious, corrupt, vicious, infamous, disgraceful, shameful, vile, immoral, scandalous, wicked, sinful, despicable, heinous, hateful, abhorrent, egregious, abominable, dishonourable, nefarious, iniquitous, detestable
<< OPPOSITE admirable
▷ *verb* 1 DIRTY, soil, stain, contaminate, smear, pollute, taint, sully, defile, besmirch, smirch, begrime, besmear
<< OPPOSITE clean
2 CLOG, block, jam, choke
3 ENTANGLE, catch, twist, snarl, ensnare, tangle up
▷▷ **foul something up** BUNGLE, spoil, botch, mess up, cock up (*Brit slang*), make a mess of, mismanage, make a nonsense of, muck up (*slang*), bodge (*informal*), make a pig's ear of (*informal*), put a spanner in the works (*Brit informal*), flub (*US slang*), crool *or* cruel (*Austral slang*)

foul play *noun* CRIME, fraud, corruption, deception, treachery, criminal activity, duplicity, dirty work, double-dealing, skulduggery, chicanery, villainy, sharp practice, perfidy, roguery, dishonest behaviour

found *verb* 1 ESTABLISH, start, set up, begin, create, institute, organize, construct, constitute, originate, endow, inaugurate, bring into being
2 ERECT, build, construct, raise, settle

foundation *noun* 1 BASIS, heart, root, mainstay, beginning, support, ground, rest, key, principle, fundamental, premise, starting point, principal element
2 *often plural* SUBSTRUCTURE, underpinning, groundwork, bedrock, base, footing, bottom
3 SETTING UP, institution, instituting, organization, settlement, establishment, initiating, originating, starting, endowment, inauguration

founded ▷▷ **founded on** BASED ON, built on, rooted in, grounded on, established on

founder[1] *noun* INITIATOR, father, establisher, author, maker, framer, designer, architect, builder, creator, beginner, generator, inventor, organizer, patriarch, benefactor, originator, constructor, institutor

founder[2] *verb* 1 FAIL, collapse, break down, abort, fall through, be unsuccessful, come to nothing, come unstuck, miscarry, misfire, fall by the wayside, come to grief, bite the dust, go belly-up (*slang*), go down like a lead balloon (*informal*)
2 SINK, go down, be lost, submerge, capsize, go to the bottom

> *Founder* is sometimes wrongly used where *flounder* is meant: *this unexpected turn of events left him floundering* (not *foundering*)

fountain *noun* 1 FONT, spring, reservoir, spout, fount, water feature, well
2 JET, stream, spray, gush
3 SOURCE, fount, wellspring, wellhead, beginning, rise, cause, origin, genesis, commencement, derivation, fountainhead

fowl *noun* POULTRY
>> RELATED WORD *male* cock
>> RELATED WORD *female* hen

foxy *adjective* CRAFTY, knowing, sharp, tricky, shrewd, cunning, sly, astute, canny, devious, wily, artful, guileful

foyer *noun* ENTRANCE HALL, lobby, reception area, vestibule, anteroom, antechamber

fracas *noun* BRAWL, fight, trouble, row, riot, disturbance, quarrel, uproar, skirmish, scuffle, free-for-all (*informal*), rumpus, aggro (*slang*), affray (*Law*), shindig (*informal*), donnybrook, scrimmage, shindy (*informal*), bagarre (*French*), melee *or* mêlée, biffo (*Austral slang*)

fraction *noun* 1 BIT, little bit, mite, jot, tiny amount, iota, scintilla
2 PERCENTAGE, share, cut, division, section, proportion, slice, ratio, portion, quota, subdivision, moiety
3 FRAGMENT, part, piece, section, sector, selection, segment

fractious *adjective* IRRITABLE, cross, awkward, unruly, touchy, recalcitrant, petulant, tetchy, ratty (*Brit & NZ informal*), testy, chippy (*informal*), fretful, grouchy (*informal*), querulous, peevish, refractory, crabby, captious, froward (*archaic*), pettish
<< OPPOSITE affable

fracture *noun* 1 BREAK, split, crack
2 CLEFT, opening, split, crack, gap, rent, breach, rift, rupture, crevice, fissure, schism
▷ *verb* 1 BREAK, crack
2 SPLIT, separate, divide, rend, fragment, splinter, rupture

fragile *adjective* 1 UNSTABLE, weak, vulnerable, delicate, uncertain, insecure, precarious, flimsy
2 FINE, weak, delicate, frail, feeble, brittle, flimsy, dainty, easily broken, breakable, frangible
<< OPPOSITE durable
3 UNWELL, poorly, weak, delicate, crook (*Austral & NZ informal*), shaky, frail, feeble, sickly,

unsteady, infirm

fragility *noun* WEAKNESS, delicacy, frailty, infirmity, feebleness, brittleness, frangibility

fragment *noun* PIECE, part, bit, scrap, particle, portion, fraction, shiver, shred, remnant, speck, sliver, wisp, morsel, oddment, chip
▷ *verb* 1 BREAK, split, shatter, crumble, shiver, disintegrate, splinter, come apart, break into pieces, come to pieces
<< OPPOSITE fuse
2 BREAK UP, divide, split up, disunite

fragmentary *adjective* INCOMPLETE, broken, scattered, partial, disconnected, discrete, sketchy, piecemeal, incoherent, scrappy, disjointed, bitty, unsystematic

fragrance *or* **fragrancy** *noun* 1 SCENT, smell, perfume, bouquet, aroma, balm, sweet smell, sweet odour, redolence, fragrancy
<< OPPOSITE stink
2 PERFUME, scent, cologne, eau de toilette, eau de Cologne, toilet water, Cologne water

fragrant *adjective* AROMATIC, perfumed, balmy, redolent, sweet-smelling, sweet-scented, odorous, ambrosial, odoriferous
<< OPPOSITE stinking

frail *adjective* 1 FEEBLE, weak, puny, decrepit, infirm
<< OPPOSITE strong
2 FLIMSY, weak, vulnerable, delicate, fragile, brittle, unsound, wispy, insubstantial, breakable, frangible, slight

frailty *noun* 1 WEAKNESS, susceptibility, fallibility, peccability
<< OPPOSITE strength
2 INFIRMITY, poor health, feebleness, puniness, frailness
3 FAULT, failing, vice, weakness, defect, deficiency, flaw, shortcoming, blemish, imperfection, foible, weak point, peccadillo, chink in your armour
<< OPPOSITE strong point

frame *noun* 1 MOUNTING, setting, surround, mount
2 CASING, framework, structure, shell, system, form, construction, fabric, skeleton, chassis
3 PHYSIQUE, build, form, body, figure, skeleton, anatomy, carcass, morphology
▷ *verb* 1 MOUNT, case, enclose
2 SURROUND, ring, enclose, close in, encompass, envelop, encircle, fence in, hem in
3 DEVISE, plan, form, shape, institute, draft, compose, sketch, forge, put together, conceive, hatch, draw up, formulate, contrive, map out, concoct, cook up, block out
▷▷ **frame of mind** MOOD, state, spirit, attitude, humour, temper, outlook, disposition, mind-set, fettle

framework *noun* 1 SYSTEM, plan, order, scheme, arrangement, fabric, schema, frame of reference, the bare bones
2 STRUCTURE, body, frame, foundation, shell, fabric, skeleton

franchise *noun* 1 AUTHORIZATION, right, permit, licence, charter, privilege, prerogative
2 VOTE, voting rights, suffrage

frank *adjective* 1 CANDID, open, free, round, direct, plain, straightforward, blunt, outright, sincere, outspoken, honest, downright, truthful, forthright, upfront (*informal*), unrestricted, plain-spoken, unreserved, artless, ingenuous, straight from the shoulder (*informal*)
<< OPPOSITE secretive
2 UNCONCEALED, open, undisguised, dinkum (*Austral & NZ informal*)

frankly *adverb* 1 HONESTLY, sincerely, in truth, candidly, to tell you the truth, to be frank, to be honest
2 OPENLY, freely, directly, straight, plainly, bluntly, overtly, candidly, without reserve, straight from the shoulder

frankness *noun* OUTSPOKENNESS, openness, candour, truthfulness, plain speaking, bluntness, forthrightness, laying it on the line, ingenuousness, absence of reserve

frantic *adjective* 1 FRENZIED, wild, mad, raging, furious, raving, distracted, distraught, berserk, uptight (*informal*), overwrought, at the end of your tether, beside yourself, at your wits' end, berko (*Austral slang*)
<< OPPOSITE calm
2 HECTIC, desperate, frenzied, fraught (*informal*), frenetic

fraternity *noun* 1 COMPANIONSHIP, fellowship, brotherhood, kinship, camaraderie, comradeship
2 CIRCLE, company, set, order, clan, guild
3 (*US & Canad*) BROTHERHOOD, club, union, society, league, association, sodality

fraud *noun* 1 DECEPTION, deceit, treachery, swindling, guile, trickery, duplicity, double-dealing, chicanery, sharp practice, imposture, fraudulence, spuriousness
<< OPPOSITE honesty
2 SCAM, craft, cheat, sting (*informal*), deception (*slang*), artifice, humbug, canard, stratagems, chicane
3 HOAX, trick, cheat, con (*informal*), deception, sham, spoof (*informal*), prank, swindle, ruse, practical joke, joke, fast one (*informal*), imposture, fastie (*Austral slang*)
4 (*informal*) IMPOSTOR, cheat, fake, bluffer, sham, hoax, hoaxer, forgery, counterfeit, pretender, charlatan, quack, fraudster, swindler, mountebank, grifter (*slang, chiefly US & Canad*), double-dealer, phoney *or* phony (*informal*)

fraudulent *adjective* DECEITFUL, false, crooked

(*informal*), untrue, sham, treacherous, dishonest, deceptive, counterfeit, spurious, crafty, swindling, double-dealing, duplicitous, knavish, phoney *or* phony (*informal*), criminal
<< OPPOSITE genuine

fraught *adjective* 1 (*informal*) TENSE, trying, difficult, distressing, tricky, emotionally charged
2 *usually with* **with** AGITATED, wired (*slang*), anxious, distressed, tense, distracted, emotive, uptight (*informal*), emotionally charged, strung-up, on tenterhooks, hag-ridden, adrenalized
▷▷ **fraught with** FILLED WITH, full of, charged with, accompanied by, attended by, stuffed with, laden with, heavy with, bristling with, replete with, abounding with

fray[1] *noun* FIGHT, battle, row, conflict, clash, set-to (*informal*), riot, combat, disturbance, rumble (*US & NZ slang*), quarrel, brawl, skirmish, scuffle, rumpus, broil, affray (*Law*), shindig (*informal*), donnybrook, battle royal, ruckus (*informal*), scrimmage, shindy (*informal*), bagarre (*French*), melee *or* mêlée, biffo (*Austral slang*), boilover (*Austral*)

fray[2] *verb* WEAR THIN, wear, rub, fret, wear out, chafe, wear away, become threadbare

frayed *adjective* 1 WORN, ragged, worn out, tattered, threadbare, worn thin, out at elbows
2 STRAINED, stressed, tense, edgy, uptight (*informal*), frazzled

freak *modifier* ABNORMAL, chance, unusual, unexpected, exceptional, unpredictable, queer, erratic, unparalleled, unforeseen, fortuitous, unaccountable, atypical, aberrant, fluky (*informal*), odd, bizarre
▷ *noun* 1 (*informal*) ENTHUSIAST, fan, nut (*slang*), addict, buff (*informal*), fanatic, devotee, fiend (*informal*), aficionado
2 ABERRATION, eccentric, anomaly, abnormality, sport (*Biology*), monster, mutant, oddity, monstrosity, malformation, rara avis (*Latin*), queer fish (*Brit informal*), teratism
3 (*informal*) WEIRDO *or* WEIRDIE (*informal*), eccentric, oddity, case (*informal*), character (*informal*), nut (*slang*), flake (*slang, chiefly US*), oddball (*informal*), nonconformist, screwball (*slang, chiefly US & Canad*), odd fish (*informal*), kook (*US & Canad informal*), queer fish (*Brit informal*)

freakish *adjective* ODD, strange, fantastic, weird, abnormal, monstrous, grotesque, unnatural, unconventional, outlandish, freaky (*slang*), aberrant, outré, malformed, preternatural, teratoid (*Biology*)

freaky *adjective* WEIRD, odd, wild, strange, crazy, bizarre, abnormal, queer, rum (*Brit slang*), unconventional, far-out (*slang*), freakish

free *adjective* 1 COMPLIMENTARY, for free (*informal*), for nothing, unpaid, for love, free of charge, on the house, without charge, gratuitous, at no cost, gratis, buckshee (*Brit slang*)
2 ALLOWED, permitted, unrestricted, unimpeded, open, clear, able, loose, unattached, unregulated, disengaged, untrammelled, unobstructed, unhampered, unengaged
3 AT LIBERTY, loose, liberated, at large, off the hook (*slang*), on the loose
<< OPPOSITE confined
4 INDEPENDENT, unfettered, unrestrained, uncommitted, footloose, unconstrained, unengaged, not tied down
5 AVAILABLE, extra, empty, spare, vacant, unused, uninhabited, unoccupied, untaken
6 *often with* **of** *or* **with** GENEROUS, willing, liberal, eager, lavish, charitable, hospitable, prodigal, bountiful, open-handed, unstinting, unsparing, bounteous, munificent, big (*informal*)
<< OPPOSITE mean
7 AUTONOMOUS, independent, democratic, sovereign, self-ruling, self-governing, emancipated, self-determining, autarchic
8 RELAXED, open, easy, forward, natural, frank, liberal, familiar, loose, casual, informal, spontaneous, laid-back (*informal*), easy-going (*informal*), lax, uninhibited, unforced, free and easy, unbidden, unconstrained, unceremonious
<< OPPOSITE formal
▷ *adverb* FREELY, easily, loosely, smoothly, idly
▷ *verb* 1 *often with* **of** *or* **from** CLEAR, deliver, disengage, cut loose, release, rescue, rid, relieve, exempt, undo, redeem, ransom, extricate, unburden, unshackle
2 RELEASE, liberate, let out, set free, deliver, loose, discharge, unleash, let go, untie, emancipate, unchain, turn loose, uncage, set at liberty, unfetter, disenthrall, unbridle, manumit
<< OPPOSITE confine
3 DISENTANGLE, extricate, disengage, detach, separate, loose, unfold, unravel, disconnect, untangle, untwist, unsnarl
▷▷ **free and easy** RELAXED, liberal, casual, informal, tolerant, laid-back (*informal*), easy-going, lax, lenient, uninhibited, unceremonious
▷▷ **free of** *or* **from** UNAFFECTED BY, without, above, lacking (in), beyond, clear of, devoid of, exempt from, immune to, sans (*archaic*), safe from, untouched by, deficient in, unencumbered by, not liable to

freedom *noun* 1 INDEPENDENCE, democracy, sovereignty, autonomy, self-determination, emancipation, self-government, home rule,

autarchy, rangatiratanga (*NZ*)
2 LIBERTY, release, discharge, emancipation, deliverance, manumission
<< OPPOSITE captivity
3 *usually with* **from** EXEMPTION, release, relief, privilege, immunity, impunity
4 LICENCE, latitude, a free hand, free rein, play, power, range, opportunity, ability, facility, scope, flexibility, discretion, leeway, carte blanche, blank cheque, elbowroom
<< OPPOSITE restriction
5 OPENNESS, ease, directness, naturalness, abandon, familiarity, candour, frankness, informality, casualness, ingenuousness, lack of restraint *or* reserve, unconstraint
<< OPPOSITE restraint

free-for-all *noun* (*informal*) FIGHT, row, riot, brawl, fracas, affray (*Law*), dust-up (*informal*), shindig (*informal*), donnybrook, scrimmage, shindy (*informal*), bagarre (*French*), melee *or* mêlée, biffo (*Austral slang*)

freely *adverb* 1 ABUNDANTLY, liberally, lavishly, like water, extravagantly, copiously, unstintingly, with a free hand, bountifully, open-handedly, amply
2 OPENLY, frankly, plainly, candidly, unreservedly, straightforwardly, without reserve
3 WILLINGLY, readily, voluntarily, spontaneously, without prompting, of your own free will, of your own accord
4 EASILY, cleanly, loosely, smoothly, readily
5 WITHOUT RESTRAINT, voluntarily, willingly, unchallenged, as you please, without being forced, without let or hindrance

freeway *noun* (*US & Austral*) MOTORWAY (*Brit*), autobahn (*German*), autoroute (*French*), autostrada (*Italian*)

freewheel *verb* COAST, drift, glide, relax your efforts, rest on your oars, float

freeze *verb* 1 ICE OVER *or* UP, harden, stiffen, solidify, congeal, become solid, glaciate
2 CHILL, benumb
3 FIX, hold, limit, hold up, peg
4 SUSPEND, stop, shelve, curb, cut short, discontinue

freezing *adjective* (*informal*) 1 ICY, biting, bitter, raw, chill, chilled, penetrating, arctic, numbing, polar, Siberian, frosty, glacial, wintry, parky (*Brit informal*), cold as ice, frost-bound, cutting
2 FROZEN, chilled, numb, chilly, very cold, shivery, benumbed, frozen to the marrow

freight *noun* 1 TRANSPORTATION, traffic, delivery, carriage, shipment, haulage, conveyance, transport
2 CARGO, goods, contents, load, lading, delivery, burden, haul, bulk, shipment, merchandise, bales, consignment, payload, tonnage

French *adjective* GALLIC
>> RELATED WORDS *combining forms* Franco-, Gallo-

frenetic *adjective* FRANTIC, wild, excited, crazy, frenzied, distraught, obsessive, fanatical, demented, unbalanced, overwrought, maniacal

frenzied *adjective* UNCONTROLLED, wild, excited, mad, crazy, furious, frantic, distraught, hysterical, agitated, frenetic, feverish, rabid, maniacal

frenzy *noun* 1 FIT, burst, bout, outburst, spasm, convulsion, paroxysm
2 FURY, transport, passion, rage, madness, turmoil, distraction, seizure, hysteria, mania, insanity, agitation, aberration, lunacy, delirium, paroxysm, derangement
<< OPPOSITE calm

frequency *noun* RECURRENCE, repetition, constancy, periodicity, commonness, frequentness, prevalence

frequent *adjective* COMMON, repeated, usual, familiar, constant, everyday, persistent, reiterated, recurring, customary, continual, recurrent, habitual, incessant
<< OPPOSITE infrequent
▷ *verb* VISIT, attend, haunt, be found at, patronize, hang out at (*informal*), visit often, go to regularly, be a regular customer of
<< OPPOSITE keep away

frequently *adverb* OFTEN, commonly, repeatedly, many times, very often, oft (*archaic* or *poetic*), over and over again, habitually, customarily, oftentimes (*archaic*), not infrequently, many a time, much
<< OPPOSITE infrequently

fresh *adjective* 1 ADDITIONAL, more, new, other, added, further, extra, renewed, supplementary, auxiliary
2 NATURAL, raw, crude, unsalted, unprocessed, uncured, unpreserved, undried, green
<< OPPOSITE preserved
3 NEW, original, novel, unusual, latest, different, recent, modern, up-to-date, this season's, unconventional, unorthodox, ground-breaking, left-field (*informal*), new-fangled, modernistic
<< OPPOSITE old
4 INVIGORATING, clear, clean, bright, sweet, pure, stiff, crisp, sparkling, bracing, refreshing, brisk, spanking, unpolluted
<< OPPOSITE stale
5 COOL, cold, refreshing, brisk, chilly, nippy
6 VIVID, bright, verdant, undimmed, unfaded
<< OPPOSITE old
7 ROSY, clear, fair, bright, healthy, glowing, hardy, blooming, wholesome, ruddy, florid, dewy, good

<< OPPOSITE pallid

8 LIVELY, rested, bright, keen, vital, restored, alert, bouncing, revived, refreshed, vigorous, energetic, sprightly, invigorated, spry, chipper (*informal*), full of beans (*informal*), like a new man, full of vim and vigour (*informal*), unwearied, bright-eyed and bushy-tailed (*informal*)

<< OPPOSITE weary

9 INEXPERIENCED, new, young, green, natural, raw, youthful, unqualified, callow, untrained, untried, artless, uncultivated, wet behind the ears

<< OPPOSITE experienced

10 (*informal*) CHEEKY (*informal*), bold, brazen, impertinent, forward, familiar, flip (*informal*), saucy, audacious, sassy (*US informal*), pert, disrespectful, presumptuous, insolent, impudent, smart-alecky (*informal*)

<< OPPOSITE well-mannered

freshen *verb* REFRESH, restore, rouse, enliven, revitalize, spruce up, liven up, freshen up, titivate

freshness *noun* 1 NOVELTY, creativity, originality, inventiveness, newness, innovativeness

2 CLEANNESS, shine, glow, bloom, sparkle, vigour, brightness, wholesomeness, clearness, dewiness

fret *verb* 1 WORRY, anguish, brood, agonize, obsess, lose sleep, upset yourself, distress yourself

2 ANNOY, trouble, bother, disturb, distress, provoke, irritate, grieve, torment, harass, nag, gall, agitate, ruffle, nettle, vex, goad, chagrin, irk, rile, pique, peeve (*informal*), rankle with

friction *noun* 1 CONFLICT, opposition, hostility, resentment, disagreement, rivalry, discontent, wrangling, bickering, animosity, antagonism, discord, bad feeling, bad blood, dissension, incompatibility, disharmony, dispute

2 RESISTANCE, rubbing, scraping, grating, irritation, erosion, fretting, attrition, rasping, chafing, abrasion, wearing away

3 RUBBING, scraping, grating, fretting, rasping, chafing, abrasion

friend *noun* 1 COMPANION, pal, mate (*informal*), buddy (*informal*), partner, china (*Brit & S African informal*), familiar, best friend, intimate, cock (*Brit informal*), close friend, comrade, chum (*informal*), crony, alter ego, confidant, playmate, confidante, main man (*slang, chiefly US*), soul mate, homeboy (*slang, chiefly US*), cobber (*Austral & NZ*), E hoa (*NZ old-fashioned informal*), bosom friend, boon companion, Achates

<< OPPOSITE foe

2 SUPPORTER, ally, associate, sponsor, advocate, patron, backer, partisan, protagonist, benefactor, adherent, well-wisher

friendliness *noun* AMIABILITY, warmth, sociability, conviviality, neighbourliness, affability, geniality, kindliness, congeniality, companionability, mateyness *or* matiness (*Brit informal*), open arms

friendly *adjective* 1 AMIABLE, kind, kindly, welcoming, warm, neighbourly, thick (*informal*), attached, pally (*informal*), helpful, sympathetic, fond, outgoing, comradely, confiding, affectionate, receptive, benevolent, attentive, sociable, genial, affable, fraternal, good, close, on good terms, chummy (*informal*), peaceable, companionable, clubby, well-disposed, buddy-buddy (*slang, chiefly US & Canad*), palsy-walsy (*informal*), matey *or* maty (*Brit informal*), on visiting terms

2 AMICABLE, warm, familiar, pleasant, intimate, informal, benign, conciliatory, cordial, congenial, convivial

<< OPPOSITE unfriendly

friendship *noun* 1 ATTACHMENT, relationship, bond, alliance, link, association, tie

2 FRIENDLINESS, affection, harmony, goodwill, intimacy, affinity, familiarity, closeness, rapport, fondness, companionship, concord, benevolence, comradeship, amity, good-fellowship

<< OPPOSITE unfriendliness

3 CLOSENESS, love, regard, affection, intimacy, fondness, companionship, comradeship

fright *noun* 1 FEAR, shock, alarm, horror, panic, terror, dread, dismay, quaking, apprehension, consternation, trepidation, cold sweat, fear and trembling, (blue) funk (*informal*)

<< OPPOSITE courage

2 SCARE, start, turn, surprise, shock, jolt, the creeps (*informal*), the shivers, the willies (*slang*), the heebie-jeebies (*slang*)

3 (*informal*) SIGHT (*informal*), mess (*informal*), eyesore, scarecrow, frump

frighten *verb* SCARE, shock, alarm, terrify, cow, appal, startle, intimidate, dismay, daunt, unnerve, petrify, unman, terrorize, scare (someone) stiff, put the wind up (someone) (*informal*), scare the living daylights out of (someone) (*informal*), make your hair stand on end (*informal*), get the wind up, make your blood run cold, throw into a panic, affright (*archaic*), freeze your blood, make (someone) jump out of his skin (*informal*), throw into a fright

<< OPPOSITE reassure

frightened *adjective* AFRAID, alarmed, scared, terrified, shocked, frozen, cowed, startled, dismayed, unnerved, petrified, flustered, panicky, terrorized, in a panic, scared stiff, in a cold sweat, abashed, terror-stricken, affrighted (*archaic*), in fear and trepidation, numb with fear

frightening *adjective* TERRIFYING, shocking, alarming, appalling, startling, dreadful, horrifying, menacing, intimidating, dismaying, scary (*informal*), fearful, daunting, fearsome, unnerving, spooky (*informal*), hair-raising, baleful, spine-chilling, bloodcurdling

frightful *adjective* 1 TERRIBLE, shocking, alarming, awful, appalling, horrible, grim, terrifying, dreadful, dread, fearful, traumatic, dire, horrendous, ghastly, hideous, harrowing, gruesome, unnerving, lurid, from hell (*informal*), grisly, macabre, petrifying, horrid, unspeakable, godawful (*slang*), hellacious (*US slang*)

<< OPPOSITE pleasant

2 DREADFUL, great, terrible, extreme, awful, annoying, unpleasant, disagreeable, insufferable

<< OPPOSITE slight

frigid *adjective* 1 FREEZING, cold, frozen, icy, chill, arctic, Siberian, frosty, cool, glacial, wintry, gelid, frost-bound, hyperboreal

<< OPPOSITE hot

2 CHILLY, formal, stiff, forbidding, rigid, passive, icy, austere, aloof, lifeless, repellent, unresponsive, unfeeling, unbending, unapproachable, passionless, unloving, cold as ice, cold-hearted

<< OPPOSITE warm

frill *noun* 1 RUFFLE, gathering, tuck, ruff, flounce, ruche, ruching, furbelow, purfle

2 *often plural* TRIMMINGS, extras, additions, fuss, jazz (*slang*), dressing up, decoration(s), bits and pieces, icing on the cake, finery, embellishments, affectation(s), ornamentation, ostentation, frippery, bells and whistles, tomfoolery, gewgaws, superfluities, fanciness, frilliness, fandangles

frilly *adjective* RUFFLED, fancy, lacy, frothy, ruched, flouncy

fringe *noun* 1 BORDER, edging, edge, binding, trimming, hem, frill, tassel, flounce

2 EDGE, limits, border, margin, march, marches, outskirts, perimeter, periphery, borderline

▷ *modifier* UNOFFICIAL, alternative, radical, innovative, avant-garde, unconventional, unorthodox

▷ *verb* BORDER, edge, surround, bound, skirt, trim, enclose, flank

fringed *adjective* 1 BORDERED, edged, befringed

2 EDGED, bordered, margined, outlined

frisk *verb* 1 (*informal*) SEARCH, check, inspect, run over, shake down (*US slang*), body-search

2 FROLIC, play, sport, dance, trip, jump, bounce, hop, skip, romp, caper, prance, cavort, gambol, rollick, curvet

frisky *adjective* LIVELY, spirited, romping, playful, bouncy, high-spirited, rollicking, in high spirits, full of beans (*informal*), coltish, kittenish, frolicsome, ludic (*literary*), sportive, full of joie de vivre

<< OPPOSITE sedate

fritter *verb usually with* **away** SQUANDER, waste, run through, dissipate, misspend, idle away, fool away, spend like water

frivolous *adjective* 1 FLIPPANT, foolish, dizzy, superficial, silly, flip (*informal*), juvenile, idle, childish, giddy, puerile, flighty, ill-considered, empty-headed, light-hearted, nonserious, light-minded, ditzy *or* ditsy (*slang*)

<< OPPOSITE serious

2 TRIVIAL, petty, trifling, unimportant, light, minor, shallow, pointless, extravagant, peripheral, niggling, paltry, impractical, nickel-and-dime (*US slang*), footling (*informal*)

<< OPPOSITE important

frivolousness *or* **frivolity** *noun* FLIPPANCY, fun, nonsense, folly, trifling, lightness, jest, gaiety, silliness, triviality, superficiality, levity, shallowness, childishness, giddiness, flummery, light-heartedness, puerility, flightiness, frivolousness

<< OPPOSITE seriousness

frizzy *adjective* TIGHT-CURLED, crisp, corrugated, wiry, crimped, frizzed

frog *noun*

>> RELATED WORD *young* tadpole

frolic *noun* MERRIMENT, sport, fun, amusement, gaiety, fun and games, skylarking (*informal*), high jinks, drollery

▷ *verb* PLAY, romp, lark, caper, cavort, frisk, gambol, make merry, rollick, cut capers, sport

front *noun* 1 HEAD, start, lead, beginning, top, fore, forefront

2 EXTERIOR, facing, face, façade, frontage, anterior, obverse, forepart

3 FOREGROUND, fore, forefront, nearest part

4 (*Military*) FRONT LINE, trenches, vanguard, firing line, van

5 APPEARANCE, show, face, air, bearing, aspect, manner, expression, exterior, countenance, demeanour, mien

6 (*informal*) DISGUISE, cover, blind, mask, cover-up, cloak, façade, pretext

▷ *adjective* 1 FOREMOST, at the front

<< OPPOSITE back

2 LEADING, first, lead, head, foremost, topmost, headmost

▷ *verb often with* **on** *or* **onto** FACE ONTO, overlook, look out on, have a view of, look over *or* onto

frontier *noun* BORDER, limit, edge, bound, boundary, confines, verge, perimeter, borderline, dividing line, borderland, marches

frost *noun* HOARFROST, freeze, freeze-up, Jack Frost, rime

frosty *adjective* 1 COLD, frozen, icy, chilly,

wintry, parky (*Brit informal*)
2 ICY, ice-capped, icicled, hoar (*rare*), rimy
3 UNFRIENDLY, discouraging, icy, frigid, off-putting (*Brit informal*), unenthusiastic, unwelcoming, standoffish, cold as ice

froth *noun* FOAM, head, bubbles, lather, suds, spume, effervescence, scum
▷ *verb* FIZZ, foam, come to a head, lather, bubble over, effervesce

frothy *adjective* 1 FOAMY, foaming, bubbly, effervescent, sudsy, spumous, spumescent, spumy
2 TRIVIAL, light, empty, slight, unnecessary, vain, petty, trifling, frivolous, frilly, unsubstantial

frown *verb* GLARE, scowl, glower, make a face, look daggers, knit your brows, give a dirty look, lour *or* lower
▷ *noun* SCOWL, glare, glower, dirty look
▷▷ **frown on** DISAPPROVE OF, dislike, discourage, take a dim view of, look askance at, discountenance, view with disfavour, not take kindly to, show disapproval *or* displeasure

frozen *adjective* 1 ICY, hard, solid, frosted, arctic, ice-covered, icebound
2 CHILLED, cold, iced, refrigerated, ice-cold
3 ICE-COLD, freezing, numb, very cold, frigid, frozen stiff, chilled to the marrow
4 MOTIONLESS, rooted, petrified, stock-still, turned to stone, stopped dead in your tracks
5 FIXED, held, stopped, limited, suspended, pegged (*of prices*)

frugal *adjective* 1 THRIFTY, sparing, careful, prudent, provident, parsimonious, abstemious, penny-wise, saving, cheeseparing
<< OPPOSITE wasteful
2 MEAGRE, economical, niggardly

fruit *noun* 1 (*Botany*) PRODUCE, crop, yield, harvest
2 *often plural* RESULT, reward, outcome, end result, return, effect, benefit, profit, advantage, consequence

fruitful *adjective* 1 USEFUL, successful, effective, rewarding, profitable, productive, worthwhile, beneficial, advantageous, well-spent, gainful
<< OPPOSITE useless
2 FERTILE, fecund, fructiferous
<< OPPOSITE barren
3 PRODUCTIVE, prolific, abundant, plentiful, rich, flush, spawning, copious, profuse, plenteous

fruition *noun* FULFILMENT, maturity, completion, perfection, enjoyment, realization, attainment, maturation, consummation, ripeness, actualization, materialization

fruitless *adjective* USELESS, vain, unsuccessful, in vain, pointless, futile, unproductive, abortive, to no avail, ineffectual, unprofitable, to no effect, unavailing, unfruitful, profitless, bootless
<< OPPOSITE fruitful

fruity *adjective* 1 RICH, full, mellow
2 RESONANT, full, deep, rich, vibrant, mellow
3 (*informal, chiefly Brit*) RISQUÉ, indecent, suggestive, racy, blue, hot, sexy, ripe, spicy (*informal*), vulgar, juicy, titillating, bawdy, salacious, smutty, indelicate, near the knuckle (*informal*)

frumpy *or* **frumpish** *adjective* DOWDY, dated, dreary, out of date, drab, unfashionable, dingy, mumsy, badly-dressed

frustrate *verb* 1 DISCOURAGE, anger, depress, annoy, infuriate, exasperate, dishearten, dissatisfy
<< OPPOSITE encourage
2 THWART, stop, check, block, defeat, disappoint, counter, confront, spoil, foil, baffle, inhibit, hobble, balk, circumvent, forestall, neutralize, stymie, nullify, render null and void, crool *or* cruel (*Austral slang*)
<< OPPOSITE further

frustrated *adjective* DISAPPOINTED, discouraged, infuriated, discontented, exasperated, resentful, embittered, irked, disheartened, carrying a chip on your shoulder (*informal*)

frustration *noun* 1 ANNOYANCE, disappointment, resentment, irritation, grievance, dissatisfaction, exasperation, vexation
2 OBSTRUCTION, blocking, curbing, foiling, failure, spoiling, thwarting, contravention, circumvention, nonfulfilment, nonsuccess

fudge *verb* MISREPRESENT, avoid, dodge, evade, hedge, stall, fake, flannel (*Brit informal*), patch up, falsify, equivocate

fuel *noun* 1 NOURISHMENT, food, kai (*NZ informal*), sustenance
2 INCITEMENT, encouragement, ammunition, provocation, food, material, incentive, fodder
▷ *verb* INFLAME, power, charge, fire, fan, encourage, feed, boost, sustain, stimulate, nourish, incite, whip up, stoke up

fugitive *noun* RUNAWAY, refugee, deserter, escapee, runagate (*archaic*)

fulfil *or US* **fullfil** *verb* 1 CARRY OUT, perform, execute, discharge, keep, effect, finish, complete, achieve, conclude, accomplish, bring to completion
<< OPPOSITE neglect
2 ACHIEVE, realize, satisfy, attain, consummate, bring to fruition, perfect
3 SATISFY, please, content, cheer, refresh, gratify, make happy
4 COMPLY WITH, meet, fill, satisfy, observe, obey, conform to, answer

fulfilment *or US* **fullfilment** *noun* ACHIEVEMENT, effecting, implementation, carrying out *or* through, end, crowning, discharge, discharging, completion, perfection, accomplishment, realization, attainment, observance, consummation

full *adjective* 1 FILLED, stocked, brimming, replete, complete, entire, loaded, sufficient, intact, gorged, saturated, bursting at the seams, brimful

2 CRAMMED, crowded, packed, crushed, jammed, in use, congested, chock-full, chock-a-block

<< OPPOSITE empty

3 OCCUPIED, taken, in use, unavailable

4 SATIATED, satisfied, having had enough, replete, sated

5 EXTENSIVE, detailed, complete, broad, generous, adequate, ample, abundant, plentiful, copious, plenary, plenteous

<< OPPOSITE incomplete

6 COMPREHENSIVE, complete, thorough, exhaustive, all-inclusive, all-embracing, unabridged

7 ROUNDED, strong, rich, powerful, intense, pungent

8 PLUMP, rounded, voluptuous, shapely, well-rounded, buxom, curvaceous

9 VOLUMINOUS, large, loose, baggy, billowing, puffy, capacious, loose-fitting, balloon-like

<< OPPOSITE tight

10 (*Music*) RICH, strong, deep, loud, distinct, resonant, sonorous, clear

<< OPPOSITE thin

▷▷ **in full** COMPLETELY, fully, in total, without exception, in its entirety, in toto (*Latin*)

▷▷ **to the full** THOROUGHLY, completely, fully, entirely, to the limit, without reservation, to the utmost

full-blooded *adjective* WHOLEHEARTED, full, complete, sweeping, thorough, uncompromising, exhaustive, all-embracing

full-blown *adjective* 1 FULLY DEVELOPED, total, full-scale, fully fledged, full, whole, developed, complete, advanced, entire, full-sized, fully grown, fully formed

<< OPPOSITE undeveloped

2 IN FULL BLOOM, full, flowering, unfolded, blossoming, opened out

full-bodied *adjective* RICH, strong, heavy, heady, mellow, fruity, redolent, full-flavoured, well-matured

fullness *or US* **fulness** *noun* 1 PLENTY, glut, saturation, sufficiency, profusion, satiety, repletion, copiousness, ampleness, adequateness

2 COMPLETENESS, wealth, entirety, totality, wholeness, vastness, plenitude, comprehensiveness, broadness, extensiveness

3 ROUNDNESS, voluptuousness, curvaceousness, swelling, enlargement, dilation, distension, tumescence

4 (*Music*) RICHNESS, strength, resonance, loudness, clearness

full-scale *adjective* MAJOR, extensive, wide-ranging, all-out, sweeping, comprehensive, proper, thorough, in-depth, exhaustive, all-encompassing, thoroughgoing, full-dress

fully *adverb* 1 COMPLETELY, totally, perfectly, entirely, absolutely, altogether, thoroughly, intimately, wholly, positively, utterly, every inch, heart and soul, to the hilt, one hundred per cent, in all respects, from first to last, lock, stock and barrel

2 IN ALL RESPECTS, completely, totally, entirely, altogether, thoroughly, wholly

3 ADEQUATELY, amply, comprehensively, sufficiently, enough, satisfactorily, abundantly, plentifully

4 AT LEAST, quite, without (any) exaggeration, without a word of a lie (*informal*)

fully-fledged *or* **full-fledged** *adjective* EXPERIENCED, trained, senior, professional, qualified, mature, proficient, time-served

fulsome *adjective* EXTRAVAGANT, excessive, over the top, sickening, overdone, fawning, nauseating, inordinate, ingratiating, cloying, insincere, saccharine, sycophantic, unctuous, smarmy (*Brit informal*), immoderate, adulatory, gross

> In journalism, *fulsome* is often used simply to mean 'extremely complimentary' or 'full, rich, or abundant'. In other kinds of writing, however, this word should only be used if you intend to suggest negative overtones of excess or insincerity

fumble *verb* 1 *often with* **for** *or* **with** GROPE, flounder, paw (*informal*), scrabble, feel around

2 BUNGLE, spoil, botch, mess up, cock up (*Brit slang*), mishandle, mismanage, muff, make a hash of (*informal*), make a nonsense of, bodge (*informal*), misfield, crool *or* cruel (*Austral slang*)

fume *verb* RAGE, boil, seethe, see red (*informal*), storm, rave, rant, smoulder, crack up (*informal*), go ballistic (*slang, chiefly US*), champ at the bit (*informal*), blow a fuse (*slang, chiefly US*), fly off the handle (*informal*), get hot under the collar (*informal*), go off the deep end (*informal*), wig out (*slang*), go up the wall (*slang*), get steamed up about (*slang*)

▷ *noun* 1 *often plural* SMOKE, gas, exhaust, pollution, haze, vapour, smog, miasma, exhalation, effluvium

2 STENCH, stink, whiff (*Brit slang*), reek, pong (*Brit informal*), foul smell, niff (*Brit slang*), malodour, mephitis, fetor, noisomeness

fuming *adjective* FURIOUS, angry, raging, choked, roused, incensed, enraged, seething, up in arms, incandescent, in a rage, on the warpath (*informal*), foaming at the mouth, at boiling point (*informal*), all steamed up (*slang*), tooshie (*Austral slang*)

fun *noun* 1 AMUSEMENT, sport, treat, pleasure, entertainment, cheer, good time, recreation, enjoyment, romp, distraction, diversion, frolic, junketing, merriment, whoopee (*informal*), high jinks, living it up, jollity, beer and skittles (*informal*), merrymaking, jollification

2 JOKING, clowning, merriment, playfulness, play, game, sport, nonsense, teasing, jesting, skylarking (*informal*), horseplay, buffoonery, tomfoolery, jocularity, foolery

3 ENJOYMENT, pleasure, joy, cheer, mirth, gaiety

<< OPPOSITE gloom

▷ *modifier* ENJOYABLE, entertaining, pleasant, amusing, lively, diverting, witty, convivial

▷▷ **for** *or* **in fun** FOR A JOKE, tongue in cheek, jokingly, playfully, for a laugh, mischievously, in jest, teasingly, with a straight face, facetiously, light-heartedly, roguishly, with a gleam *or* twinkle in your eye

▷▷ **make fun of something** *or* **someone** MOCK, tease, ridicule, poke fun at, take off, rag, rib (*informal*), laugh at, taunt, mimic, parody, deride, send up (*Brit informal*), scoff at, sneer at, lampoon, make a fool of, pour scorn on, take the mickey out of (*Brit informal*), satirize, pull someone's leg, hold up to ridicule, make a monkey of, make sport of, make the butt of, make game of

function *noun* 1 PURPOSE, business, job, concern, use, part, office, charge, role, post, operation, situation, activity, exercise, responsibility, task, duty, mission, employment, capacity, province, occupation, raison d'être (*French*)

2 RECEPTION, party, affair, gathering, bash (*informal*), lig (*Brit slang*), social occasion, soiree, do (*informal*)

▷ *verb* 1 WORK, run, operate, perform, be in business, be in running order, be in operation *or* action, go

2 *with* **as** ACT, serve, operate, perform, behave, officiate, act the part of, do duty, have the role of, be in commission, be in operation *or* action, serve your turn

functional *adjective* 1 PRACTICAL, utility, utilitarian, serviceable, hard-wearing, useful

2 WORKING, operative, operational, in working order, going, prepared, ready, viable, up and running, workable, usable

functionary *noun* OFFICER, official, dignitary, office holder, office bearer, employee

fund *noun* 1 RESERVE, stock, supply, store, collection, pool, foundation, endowment, tontine

2 STORE, stock, source, supply, mine, reserve, treasury, vein, reservoir, accumulation, hoard, repository

▷ *verb* FINANCE, back, support, pay for, promote, float, endow, subsidize, stake, capitalize, provide money for, put up the money for

fundamental *adjective* 1 CENTRAL, first, most important, prime, key, necessary, basic, essential, primary, vital, radical, principal, cardinal, integral, indispensable, intrinsic

<< OPPOSITE incidental

2 BASIC, essential, underlying, organic, profound, elementary, rudimentary

fundamentally *adverb* 1 BASICALLY, at heart, at bottom

2 ESSENTIALLY, radically, basically, primarily, profoundly, intrinsically

fundi *noun* (*S African*) EXPERT, authority, specialist, professional, master, pro (*informal*), ace (*informal*), genius, guru, pundit, buff (*informal*), maestro, virtuoso, boffin (*Brit informal*), hotshot (*informal*), past master, dab hand (*Brit informal*), wonk (*informal*), maven (*US*)

funds *plural noun* MONEY, capital, cash, finance, means, savings, necessary (*informal*), resources, assets, silver, bread (*slang*), wealth, tin (*slang*), brass (*Northern English dialect*), dough (*slang*), rhino (*Brit slang*), the ready (*informal*), dosh (*Brit & Austral slang*), hard cash, the wherewithal, needful (*informal*), shekels (*informal*), dibs (*slang*), ready money, ackers (*slang*), spondulicks (*slang*)

funeral *noun* BURIAL, committal, laying to rest, cremation, interment, obsequies, entombment, inhumation

funereal *adjective* GLOOMY, dark, sad, grave, depressing, dismal, lamenting, solemn, dreary, sombre, woeful, mournful, lugubrious, sepulchral, dirge-like, deathlike

funk *verb* CHICKEN OUT OF, dodge, recoil from, take fright, flinch from, duck out of (*informal*), turn tail (*informal*)

funnel *verb* 1 CONDUCT, direct, channel, convey, move, pass, pour, filter

2 CHANNEL, direct, pour, filter, convey

funny *adjective* 1 HUMOROUS, amusing, comical, entertaining, killing (*informal*), rich, comic, silly, ridiculous, diverting, absurd, jolly, witty, hilarious, ludicrous, laughable, farcical, slapstick, riotous, droll, risible, facetious, jocular, side-splitting, waggish, jocose

<< OPPOSITE unfunny

2 COMIC, comical, a scream, a card (*informal*), a caution (*informal*)

3 PECULIAR, odd, strange, unusual, remarkable, bizarre, puzzling, curious, weird,

mysterious, suspicious, dubious, queer, rum (*Brit slang*), quirky, perplexing
4 (*informal*) ILL, poorly (*informal*), queasy, sick, odd, crook (*Austral & NZ informal*), ailing, queer, unhealthy, seedy (*informal*), unwell, out of sorts (*informal*), off-colour (*informal*), under the weather (*informal*)

furious *adjective* 1 ANGRY, mad, raging, boiling, fuming, choked, frantic, frenzied, infuriated, incensed, enraged, maddened, inflamed, very angry, cross, livid (*informal*), up in arms, incandescent, on the warpath (*informal*), foaming at the mouth, wrathful, in high dudgeon, wroth (*archaic*), fit to be tied (*slang*), beside yourself, tooshie (*Austral slang*)
<< OPPOSITE pleased
2 VIOLENT, wild, intense, fierce, savage, turbulent, stormy, agitated, boisterous, tumultuous, vehement, unrestrained, tempestuous, impetuous, ungovernable

furnish *verb* 1 DECORATE, fit, fit out, appoint, provide, stock, supply, store, provision, outfit, equip, fit up, purvey
2 SUPPLY, give, offer, provide, present, reveal, grant, afford, hand out, endow, bestow

furniture *noun* HOUSEHOLD GOODS, furnishings, fittings, house fittings, goods, things (*informal*), effects, equipment, appointments, possessions, appliances, chattels, movable property, movables

furore *or US* **furor** *noun* COMMOTION, to-do, stir, excitement, fury, disturbance, flap (*informal*), outburst, frenzy, outcry, uproar, brouhaha, hullabaloo

furrow *noun* 1 GROOVE, line, channel, hollow, trench, seam, crease, fluting, rut, corrugation
2 WRINKLE, line, crease, crinkle, crow's-foot, gather, fold, crumple, rumple, pucker, corrugation
▷ *verb* WRINKLE, knit, draw together, crease, seam, flute, corrugate

further *adverb* IN ADDITION, moreover, besides, furthermore, also, yet, on top of, what's more, to boot, additionally, over and above, as well as, into the bargain
▷ *adjective* ADDITIONAL, more, new, other, extra, fresh, supplementary
▷ *verb* PROMOTE, help, develop, aid, forward, champion, push, encourage, speed, advance, work for, foster, contribute to, assist, plug (*informal*), facilitate, pave the way for, hasten, patronize, expedite, succour, lend support to
<< OPPOSITE hinder
▷ see **farther**

furthermore *adverb* MOREOVER, further, in addition, besides, too, as well, not to mention, what's more, to boot, additionally, into the bargain

furthest *adjective* MOST DISTANT, extreme, ultimate, remotest, outermost, uttermost, furthermost, outmost ▷ see **farthest**

furtive *adjective* SLY, secret, hidden, sneaking, covert, cloaked, behind someone's back, secretive, clandestine, sneaky, under-the-table, slinking, conspiratorial, skulking, underhand, surreptitious, stealthy
<< OPPOSITE open

fury *noun* 1 ANGER, passion, rage, madness, frenzy, wrath, ire, red mist (*informal*), impetuosity
<< OPPOSITE calmness
2 VIOLENCE, force, power, intensity, severity, turbulence, ferocity, savagery, vehemence, fierceness, tempestuousness
<< OPPOSITE peace

fuse *verb* 1 JOIN, unite, combine, blend, integrate, merge, put together, dissolve, amalgamate, federate, coalesce, intermingle, meld, run together, commingle, intermix, agglutinate
<< OPPOSITE separate
2 BOND, join, stick, melt, weld, smelt, solder

fusion *noun* MERGING, uniting, union, merger, federation, mixture, blend, blending, integration, synthesis, amalgamation, coalescence, commingling, commixture

fuss *noun* 1 COMMOTION, to-do, worry, upset, bother, stir, confusion, excitement, hurry, flap (*informal*), bustle, flutter, flurry, agitation, fidget, fluster, ado, hue and cry, palaver, storm in a teacup (*Brit*), pother
2 BOTHER, trouble, struggle, hassle (*informal*), nuisance, inconvenience, hindrance
3 COMPLAINT, row, protest, objection, trouble, display, argument, difficulty, upset, bother, unrest, hassle (*informal*), squabble, furore, altercation
▷ *verb* WORRY, flap (*informal*), bustle, fret, niggle, fidget, chafe, take pains, make a meal of (*informal*), be agitated, labour over, get worked up, get in a stew (*informal*), make a thing of (*informal*)

fussy *adjective* 1 PARTICULAR, difficult, exacting, discriminating, fastidious, dainty, squeamish, choosy (*informal*), picky (*informal*), nit-picking (*informal*), hard to please, finicky, pernickety, faddish, faddy, old-maidish, old womanish, overparticular
2 OVERELABORATE, busy, cluttered, rococo, overdecorated, overembellished

futile *adjective* 1 USELESS, vain, unsuccessful, pointless, empty, hollow, in vain, worthless, barren, sterile, fruitless, forlorn, unproductive, abortive, to no avail, ineffectual, unprofitable, valueless, unavailing, otiose, profitless, nugatory, without rhyme or reason, bootless
<< OPPOSITE useful

2 TRIVIAL, pointless, trifling, unimportant
<< OPPOSITE important

futility *noun* **1** USELESSNESS, ineffectiveness, pointlessness, fruitlessness, emptiness, hollowness, spitting in the wind, bootlessness
2 TRIVIALITY, vanity, pointlessness, unimportance

future *noun* **1** TIME TO COME, hereafter, what lies ahead
2 PROSPECT, expectation, outlook
▷ *adjective* FORTHCOMING, to be, coming, later, expected, approaching, to come, succeeding, fated, ultimate, subsequent, destined, prospective, eventual, ensuing, impending, unborn, in the offing
<< OPPOSITE past

fuzz *noun* FLUFF, down, hair, pile, fibre, nap, floss, lint

fuzzy *adjective* **1** FRIZZY, fluffy, woolly, downy, flossy, down-covered, linty, napped
2 INDISTINCT, faint, blurred, vague, distorted, unclear, shadowy, bleary, unfocused, out of focus, ill-defined
<< OPPOSITE distinct

Gg

gadget *noun* DEVICE, thing, appliance, machine, tool, implement, invention, instrument, novelty, apparatus, gimmick, utensil, contraption (*informal*), gizmo (*slang, chiefly US & Canad*), contrivance

gaffe *noun* BLUNDER, mistake, error, indiscretion, lapse, boob (*Brit slang*), slip-up (*informal*), slip, howler, bloomer (*informal*), clanger (*informal*), faux pas, boo-boo (*informal*), solecism, gaucherie, barry *or* Barry Crocker (*Austral slang*)

gag[1] *noun* MUZZLE, tie, restraint
▷ *verb* 1 SUPPRESS, silence, subdue, muffle, curb, stifle, muzzle, quieten
2 RETCH, choke, heave

gag[2] *noun* (*informal*) JOKE, crack (*slang*), funny (*informal*), quip, pun, jest, wisecrack (*informal*), sally, witticism

gaiety *noun* 1 CHEERFULNESS, glee, good humour, buoyancy, happiness, animation, exuberance, high spirits, elation, exhilaration, hilarity, merriment, joie de vivre (*French*), good cheer, vivacity, jollity, liveliness, gladness, effervescence, light-heartedness, joyousness
<< OPPOSITE misery
2 MERRYMAKING, celebration, revels, festivity, fun, mirth, revelry, conviviality, jollification, carousal

gaily *adverb* 1 CHEERFULLY, happily, gleefully, brightly, blithely, merrily, joyfully, cheerily, jauntily, light-heartedly, chirpily (*informal*)
2 COLOURFULLY, brightly, vividly, flamboyantly, gaudily, brilliantly, flashily, showily

gain *verb* 1 ACQUIRE, get, receive, achieve, earn, pick up, win, secure, collect, gather, obtain, build up, attain, glean, procure
2 PROFIT, make, earn, get, win, clear, land, score (*slang*), achieve, net, bag, secure, collect, gather, realize, obtain, capture, acquire, bring in, harvest, attain, reap, glean, procure
<< OPPOSITE lose
3 PUT ON, increase in, gather, build up
4 ATTAIN, earn, get, achieve, win, reach, get to, secure, obtain, acquire, arrive at, procure
▷ *noun* 1 RISE, increase, growth, advance, improvement, upsurge, upturn, increment, upswing
2 PROFIT, income, earnings, proceeds, winnings, return, produce, benefit, advantage, yield, dividend, acquisition, attainment, lucre, emolument
<< OPPOSITE loss
▷ *plural noun* PROFITS, earnings, revenue, proceeds, winnings, takings, pickings, booty
▷▷ **gain on something** *or* **someone** GET NEARER TO, close in on, approach, catch up with, narrow the gap on

gainful *adjective* PROFITABLE, rewarding, productive, lucrative, paying, useful, valuable, worthwhile, beneficial, fruitful, advantageous, expedient, remunerative, moneymaking

gainsay *verb* DENY, dispute, disagree with, contradict, contravene, rebut, controvert
<< OPPOSITE confirm

gait *noun* WALK, step, bearing, pace, stride, carriage, tread, manner of walking

gala *noun* FESTIVAL, party, fête, celebration, carnival, festivity, pageant, jamboree
▷ *adjective* FESTIVE, merry, joyous, joyful, celebratory, convivial, gay, festal

galaxy *noun* STAR SYSTEM, solar system, nebula
>> RELATED WORD *adjective* galactic

gale *noun* 1 STORM, hurricane, tornado, cyclone, whirlwind, blast, gust, typhoon, tempest, squall
2 (*informal*) OUTBURST, scream, roar, fit, storm, shout, burst, explosion, outbreak, howl, shriek, eruption, peal, paroxysm

gall[1] *verb* ANNOY, provoke, irritate, aggravate (*informal*), get (*informal*), trouble, bother, disturb, plague, madden, ruffle, exasperate, nettle, vex, displease, irk, rile (*informal*), peeve (*informal*), get under your skin (*informal*), get on your nerves (*informal*), nark (*Brit, Austral & NZ slang*), get up your nose (*informal*), make your blood boil, rub up the wrong way, get on your wick (*Brit slang*), get your back up, put your back up, hack you off (*informal*)

gall² *noun* GROWTH, lump, excrescence

gallant *adjective* 1 BRAVE, daring, bold, heroic, courageous, dashing, noble, manly, gritty, fearless, intrepid, valiant, plucky, doughty, dauntless, lion-hearted, valorous, manful, mettlesome

<< OPPOSITE cowardly

2 COURTEOUS, mannerly, gentlemanly, polite, gracious, attentive, courtly, chivalrous

<< OPPOSITE discourteous

gallantry *noun* 1 BRAVERY, spirit, daring, courage, nerve, guts (*informal*), pluck, grit, heroism, mettle, boldness, manliness, valour, derring-do (*archaic*), fearlessness, intrepidity, valiance, courageousness, dauntlessness, doughtiness

<< OPPOSITE cowardice

2 COURTESY, politeness, chivalry, attentiveness, graciousness, courtliness, gentlemanliness, courteousness

<< OPPOSITE discourtesy

galling *adjective* ANNOYING, provoking, irritating, aggravating (*informal*), disturbing, humiliating, maddening, exasperating, vexing, displeasing, rankling, irksome, vexatious, nettlesome

gallop *verb* 1 RUN, race, shoot, career, speed, bolt, stampede

2 DASH, run, race, shoot, fly, career, speed, tear, rush, barrel (along) (*informal, chiefly US & Canad*), sprint, dart, zoom

galore *adverb* IN ABUNDANCE, everywhere, to spare, all over the place, aplenty, in great numbers, in profusion, in great quantity, à gogo (*informal*)

galvanize *verb* STIMULATE, encourage, inspire, prompt, move, fire, shock, excite, wake, stir, spur, provoke, startle, arouse, awaken, rouse, prod, jolt, kick-start, electrify, goad, impel, invigorate

gamble *noun* 1 RISK, chance, venture, lottery, speculation, uncertainty, leap in the dark

<< OPPOSITE certainty

2 BET, flutter (*informal*), punt (*chiefly Brit*), wager

▷ *verb* 1 *often with* **on** TAKE A CHANCE, back, speculate, take the plunge, stick your neck out (*informal*), put your faith *or* trust in

2 RISK, chance, stake, venture, hazard, wager

3 BET, play, game, stake, speculate, back, punt, wager, put money on, have a flutter (*informal*), try your luck, put your shirt on, lay *or* make a bet

game¹ *noun* 1 PASTIME, sport, activity, entertainment, recreation, distraction, amusement, diversion

<< OPPOSITE job

2 MATCH, meeting, event, competition, tournament, clash, contest, round, head-to-head

3 AMUSEMENT, joke, entertainment, diversion, lark

4 ACTIVITY, business, line, situation, proceeding, enterprise, undertaking, occupation, pursuit

5 WILD ANIMALS *or* BIRDS, prey, quarry

6 SCHEME, plan, design, strategy, trick, plot, tactic, manoeuvre, dodge, ploy, scam, stratagem, fastie (*Austral slang*)

▷ *adjective* 1 WILLING, prepared, ready, keen, eager, interested, inclined, disposed, up for it (*informal*), desirous

2 BRAVE, courageous, dogged, spirited, daring, bold, persistent, gritty, fearless, feisty (*informal, chiefly US & Canad*), persevering, intrepid, valiant, plucky, unflinching, dauntless, (as) game as Ned Kelly (*Austral slang*)

<< OPPOSITE cowardly

game² *adjective* LAME, injured, disabled, crippled, defective, bad, maimed, deformed, gammy (*Brit slang*)

gamut *noun* RANGE, series, collection, variety, lot, field, scale, sweep, catalogue, scope, compass, assortment

gang *noun* GROUP, crowd, pack, company, party, lot, band, crew (*informal*), bunch, mob, horde

gangster *noun* HOODLUM (*chiefly US*), crook (*informal*), thug, bandit, heavy (*slang*), tough, hood (*US slang*), robber, gang member, mobster (*US slang*), racketeer, desperado, ruffian, brigand, wise guy (*US*), tsotsi (*S African*)

gaol ▷ see **jail**

gap *noun* 1 OPENING, space, hole, break, split, divide, crack, rent, breach, slot, vent, rift, aperture, cleft, chink, crevice, fissure, cranny, perforation, interstice

2 INTERVAL, pause, recess, interruption, respite, lull, interlude, breathing space, hiatus, intermission, lacuna, entr'acte

3 DIFFERENCE, gulf, contrast, disagreement, discrepancy, inconsistency, disparity, divergence

gape *verb* 1 STARE, wonder, goggle, gawp (*Brit slang*), gawk

2 OPEN, split, crack, yawn

gaping *adjective* WIDE, great, open, broad, vast, yawning, wide open, cavernous

garb *noun* CLOTHES, dress, clothing, gear (*slang*), wear, habit, get-up (*informal*), uniform, outfit, costume, threads (*slang*), array, ensemble, garments, robes, duds (*informal*), apparel, clobber (*Brit slang*), attire, togs (*informal*), vestments, raiment (*archaic*), rigout (*informal*)

garbage *noun* 1 JUNK, rubbish, litter, trash (*chiefly US*), refuse, waste, sweepings, scraps, debris, muck, filth, swill, slops, offal, detritus, dross, odds and ends, flotsam and jetsam, grot (*slang*), leavings, dreck (*slang, chiefly US*), scourings, offscourings

2 NONSENSE, rot, crap (*slang*), trash, hot air (*informal*), tosh (*informal*), pap, bilge (*informal*), drivel, twaddle, tripe (*informal*), gibberish, guff (*slang*), moonshine, claptrap (*informal*), hogwash, hokum (*slang, chiefly US & Canad*), codswallop (*Brit slang*), piffle (*informal*), poppycock (*informal*), balderdash, bosh (*informal*), eyewash (*informal*), kak (*S African slang*), stuff and nonsense, bunkum *or* buncombe (*chiefly US*), bizzo (*Austral slang*), bull's wool (*Austral & NZ slang*)

garbled *adjective* JUMBLED, confused, distorted, mixed up, muddled, incomprehensible, unintelligible

garden *noun* GROUNDS, park, plot, patch, lawn, allotment, yard (*US & Canad*), forest park (*NZ*)

>> RELATED WORD *adjective* horticultural

gargantuan *adjective* HUGE, big, large, giant, massive, towering, vast, enormous, extensive, tremendous, immense, mega (*slang*), titanic, jumbo (*informal*), gigantic, monumental, monstrous, mammoth, colossal, mountainous, prodigious, stupendous, elephantine, ginormous (*informal*), Brobdingnagian, humongous *or* humungous (*US slang*)

<< OPPOSITE tiny

Some people think that *gargantuan* should only be used to describe things connected with food: *a gargantuan meal*; *his gargantuan appetite*. Nevertheless, the word is now widely used as a synonym of *colossal* or *massive*

garish *adjective* GAUDY, bright, glaring, vulgar, brilliant, flash (*informal*), loud, brash, tacky (*informal*), flashy, tasteless, naff (*Brit slang*), jazzy (*informal*), tawdry, showy, brassy, raffish

<< OPPOSITE dull

garland *noun* WREATH, band, bays, crown, honours, loop, laurels, festoon, coronet, coronal, chaplet

▷ *verb* ADORN, crown, deck, festoon, wreathe

garment *noun often plural* CLOTHES, wear, dress, clothing, gear (*slang*), habit, get-up (*informal*), uniform, outfit, costume, threads (*slang*), array, robes, duds (*informal*), apparel, clobber (*Brit slang*), attire, garb, togs, vestments, articles of clothing, raiment (*archaic*), rigout (*informal*), habiliment

garnish *noun* DECORATION, ornament, embellishment, adornment, ornamentation, trimming, trim

▷ *verb* DECORATE, adorn, ornament, embellish, deck, festoon, trim, bedeck

<< OPPOSITE strip

garrison *noun* 1 TROOPS, group, unit, section, command, armed force, detachment

2 FORT, fortress, camp, base, post, station, stronghold, fortification, encampment, fortified pa (*NZ*)

▷ *verb* STATION, position, post, mount, install, assign, put on duty

garrulous *adjective* 1 TALKATIVE, gossiping, chattering, babbling, gushing, chatty, long-winded, effusive, gabby (*informal*), prattling, voluble, gossipy, loquacious, verbose, mouthy

<< OPPOSITE taciturn

2 RAMBLING, lengthy, diffuse, long-winded, wordy, discursive, windy, overlong, verbose, prolix, prosy

<< OPPOSITE concise

gas *noun* 1 FUMES, vapour

2 (*US, Canad & NZ*) PETROL, gasoline (*trademark*)

gash *noun* CUT, tear, split, wound, rent, slash, slit, gouge, incision, laceration

▷ *verb* CUT, tear, split, wound, rend, slash, slit, gouge, lacerate

gasp *verb* PANT, blow, puff, choke, gulp, fight for breath, catch your breath

▷ *noun* PANT, puff, gulp, intake of breath, sharp intake of breath

gate *noun* BARRIER, opening, door, access, port (*Scot*), entrance, exit, gateway, portal, egress

gather *verb* 1 CONGREGATE, assemble, get together, collect, group, meet, mass, rally, flock, come together, muster, convene, converge, rendezvous, foregather

<< OPPOSITE scatter

2 ASSEMBLE, group, collect, round up, marshal, bring together, muster, convene, call together

<< OPPOSITE disperse

3 COLLECT, assemble, accumulate, round up, mass, heap, marshal, bring together, muster, pile up, garner, amass, stockpile, hoard, stack up

4 PICK, harvest, pluck, reap, garner, glean

5 BUILD UP, rise, increase, grow, develop, expand, swell, intensify, wax, heighten, deepen, enlarge, thicken

6 UNDERSTAND, believe, hear, learn, assume, take it, conclude, presume, be informed, infer, deduce, surmise, be led to believe

7 FOLD, tuck, pleat, ruffle, pucker, shirr

gathering *noun* ASSEMBLY, group, crowd, meeting, conference, company, party, congress, mass, rally, convention, knot, flock, get-together (*informal*), congregation, muster, turnout, multitude, throng, hui (*NZ*), concourse, assemblage, conclave, convocation, runanga (*NZ*)

gauche *adjective* AWKWARD, clumsy, inept, unsophisticated, inelegant, graceless, unpolished, uncultured, maladroit, ill-bred, ill-mannered, lacking in social graces

<< OPPOSITE sophisticated

gaudy *adjective* GARISH, bright, glaring, vulgar, brilliant, flash (*informal*), loud, brash, tacky (*informal*), flashy, tasteless, jazzy (*informal*), tawdry, showy, gay, ostentatious, raffish

<< OPPOSITE dull

gauge *verb* **1** MEASURE, calculate, evaluate, value, size, determine, count, weigh, compute, ascertain, quantify

2 JUDGE, estimate, guess, assess, evaluate, rate, appraise, reckon, adjudge

▷ *noun* METER, indicator, dial, measuring instrument

gaunt *adjective* **1** THIN, lean, skinny, skeletal, wasted, drawn, spare, pinched, angular, bony, lanky, haggard, emaciated, scrawny, skin and bone, scraggy, cadaverous, rawboned

<< OPPOSITE plump

2 BLEAK, bare, harsh, forbidding, grim, stark, dismal, dreary, desolate, forlorn

<< OPPOSITE inviting

gawky *adjective* AWKWARD, clumsy, lumbering, ungainly, gauche, uncouth, loutish, graceless, clownish, oafish, maladroit, lumpish, ungraceful, unco (*Austral slang*)

<< OPPOSITE graceful

gay *adjective* **1** HOMOSEXUAL, camp (*informal*), lesbian, pink (*informal*), queer (*informal* or *derogatory*), same-sex, sapphic, moffie (*S African slang*)

2 CHEERFUL, happy, bright, glad, lively, sparkling, sunny, jolly, animated, merry, upbeat (*informal*), buoyant, cheery, joyous, joyful, carefree, jaunty, chirpy (*informal*), vivacious, jovial, gleeful, debonair, blithe, insouciant, full of beans (*informal*), light-hearted

<< OPPOSITE sad

3 COLOURFUL, rich, bright, brilliant, vivid, flamboyant, flashy, gaudy, garish, showy

<< OPPOSITE drab

▷ *noun* HOMOSEXUAL, lesbian, fairy (*slang*), queer (*informal* or *derogatory*), faggot (*slang, chiefly US & Canad*), auntie *or* aunty (*Austral slang*), lily (*Austral slang*)

<< OPPOSITE heterosexual

By far the most common and up-to-date use of the word *gay* is in reference to being homosexual. Other senses of the word have become uncommon and dated

gaze *verb* STARE, look, view, watch, regard, contemplate, gape, eyeball (*slang*), ogle, look fixedly

▷ *noun* STARE, look, fixed look

gazette *noun* NEWSPAPER, paper, journal, organ, periodical, news-sheet

g'day *or* **gidday** *interjection* (*Austral & NZ*) HELLO, hi (*informal*), greetings, how do you do?, good morning, good evening, good afternoon, welcome, kia ora (*NZ*)

gear *noun* **1** MECHANISM, works, action, gearing, machinery, cogs, cogwheels, gearwheels

2 EQUIPMENT, supplies, tackle, tools, instruments, outfit, rigging, rig, accessories, apparatus, trappings, paraphernalia, accoutrements, appurtenances, equipage

3 POSSESSIONS, things, effects, stuff, kit, luggage, baggage, belongings, paraphernalia, personal property, chattels

4 CLOTHING, wear, dress, clothes, habit, outfit, costume, threads (*slang*), array, garments, apparel, attire, garb, togs, rigout

▷ *verb with* **to** *or* **towards** EQUIP, fit, suit, adjust, adapt, rig, tailor

gem *noun* **1** PRECIOUS STONE, jewel, stone, semiprecious stone

2 TREASURE, pick, prize, jewel, flower, pearl, masterpiece, paragon, humdinger (*slang*), taonga (*NZ*)

genealogy *noun* ANCESTRY, descent, pedigree, line, origin, extraction, lineage, family tree, parentage, derivation, blood line

general *adjective* **1** WIDESPREAD, accepted, popular, public, common, broad, extensive, universal, prevailing, prevalent

<< OPPOSITE individual

2 OVERALL, complete, total, global, comprehensive, blanket, inclusive, all-embracing, overarching

<< OPPOSITE restricted

3 UNIVERSAL, overall, widespread, collective, across-the-board, all-inclusive

<< OPPOSITE exceptional

4 VAGUE, broad, loose, blanket, sweeping, unclear, inaccurate, approximate, woolly, indefinite, hazy, imprecise, ill-defined, inexact, unspecific, undetailed

<< OPPOSITE specific

generality *noun* **1** GENERALIZATION, abstraction, sweeping statement, vague notion, loose statement

2 IMPRECISENESS, vagueness, looseness, lack of detail, inexactitude, woolliness, indefiniteness, approximateness, inexactness, lack of preciseness

generally *adverb* **1** BROADLY, mainly, mostly, principally, on the whole, predominantly, in the main, for the most part

2 USUALLY, commonly, typically, regularly, normally, on average, on the whole, for the most part, almost always, in most cases, by and large, ordinarily, as a rule, habitually, conventionally, customarily

<< OPPOSITE occasionally

3 COMMONLY, widely, publicly, universally, extensively, popularly, conventionally,

customarily
<< OPPOSITE individually
generate *verb* PRODUCE, create, make, form, cause, initiate, bring about, originate, give rise to, engender, whip up
<< OPPOSITE end
generation *noun* 1 AGE GROUP, peer group
2 AGE, period, era, time, days, lifetime, span, epoch
generic *adjective* COLLECTIVE, general, common, wide, sweeping, comprehensive, universal, blanket, inclusive, all-encompassing
<< OPPOSITE specific
generosity *noun* 1 LIBERALITY, charity, bounty, munificence, beneficence, largesse *or* largess
2 MAGNANIMITY, goodness, kindness, benevolence, selflessness, charity, unselfishness, high-mindedness, nobleness
generous *adjective* 1 LIBERAL, lavish, free, charitable, free-handed, hospitable, prodigal, bountiful, open-handed, unstinting, beneficent, princely, bounteous, munificent, ungrudging
<< OPPOSITE mean
2 MAGNANIMOUS, kind, noble, benevolent, good, big, high-minded, unselfish, big-hearted, ungrudging
3 PLENTIFUL, lavish, ample, abundant, full, rich, liberal, overflowing, copious, bountiful, unstinting, profuse, bounteous (*literary*), plenteous
<< OPPOSITE meagre
genesis *noun* BEGINNING, source, root, origin, start, generation, birth, creation, dawn, formation, outset, starting point, engendering, inception, commencement, propagation
<< OPPOSITE end
genial *adjective* FRIENDLY, kind, kindly, pleasant, warm, cheerful, jolly, hearty, agreeable, cheery, amiable, cordial, affable, congenial, jovial, convivial, good-natured, warm-hearted
<< OPPOSITE unfriendly
genitals *plural noun* SEX ORGANS, privates, loins, genitalia, private parts, reproductive organs, pudenda
>> RELATED WORD *adjective* venereal
genius *noun* 1 BRILLIANCE, ability, talent, capacity, gift, bent, faculty, excellence, endowment, flair, inclination, knack, propensity, aptitude, cleverness, creative power
2 MASTER, expert, mastermind, brain (*informal*), buff (*informal*), intellect (*informal*), adept, maestro, virtuoso, whiz (*informal*), hotshot (*informal*), rocket scientist (*informal, chiefly US*), wonk (*informal*), brainbox, maven (*US*), master-hand, fundi (*S African*)
<< OPPOSITE dunce
genre *noun* TYPE, group, school, form, order, sort, kind, class, style, character, fashion, brand, species, category, stamp, classification, genus, subdivision
genteel *adjective* REFINED, cultured, mannerly, elegant, formal, gentlemanly, respectable, polite, cultivated, courteous, courtly, well-bred, ladylike, well-mannered
<< OPPOSITE unmannerly
gentility *noun* 1 REFINEMENT, culture, breeding, courtesy, elegance, formality, respectability, cultivation, politeness, good manners, courtliness
2 BLUE BLOOD, high birth, rank, good family, good breeding, gentle birth
gentle *adjective* 1 KIND, loving, kindly, peaceful, soft, quiet, pacific, tender, mild, benign, humane, compassionate, amiable, meek, lenient, placid, merciful, kind-hearted, sweet-tempered, tender-hearted
<< OPPOSITE unkind
2 SLOW, easy, slight, deliberate, moderate, gradual, imperceptible
3 MODERATE, low, light, easy, soft, calm, slight, mild, soothing, clement, temperate, balmy
<< OPPOSITE violent
gentlemanly *adjective* CHIVALROUS, mannerly, obliging, refined, polite, civil, cultivated, courteous, gallant, genteel, suave, well-bred, well-mannered
gentleness *noun* TENDERNESS, compassion, kindness, consideration, sympathy, sweetness, softness, mildness, kindliness
gentry *noun* NOBILITY, lords, elite, nobles, upper class, aristocracy, peerage, ruling class, patricians, upper crust (*informal*), gentility, gentlefolk
genuine *adjective* 1 AUTHENTIC, real, original, actual, sound, true, pure, sterling, valid, legitimate, honest, veritable, bona fide, dinkum (*Austral & NZ informal*), the real McCoy
<< OPPOSITE counterfeit
2 HEARTFELT, sincere, honest, earnest, real, true, frank, unaffected, wholehearted, unadulterated, unalloyed, unfeigned
<< OPPOSITE affected
3 SINCERE, straightforward, honest, natural, frank, candid, upfront (*informal*), dinkum (*Austral & NZ informal*), artless, guileless
<< OPPOSITE hypocritical
genus *noun* TYPE, sort, kind, group, set, order, race, class, breed, category, genre, classification
germ *noun* 1 MICROBE, virus, bug (*informal*), bacterium, bacillus, microorganism
2 BEGINNING, root, seed, origin, spark, bud, embryo, rudiment
germinate *verb* SPROUT, grow, shoot, develop,

generate, swell, bud, vegetate

gestation *noun* INCUBATION, development, growth, pregnancy, evolution, ripening, maturation

gesticulate *verb* SIGNAL, sign, wave, indicate, motion, gesture, beckon, make a sign

gesture *noun* SIGN, action, signal, motion, indication, gesticulation
▷ *verb* SIGNAL, sign, wave, indicate, motion, beckon, gesticulate

get *verb* 1 BECOME, grow, turn, wax, come to be
2 PERSUADE, convince, win over, induce, influence, sway, entice, coax, incite, impel, talk into, wheedle, prevail upon
3 ARRIVE, come, reach, make it (*informal*)
4 MANAGE, fix, succeed, arrange, contrive, wangle (*informal*)
5 (*informal*) ANNOY, upset, anger, bother, disturb, trouble, bug (*informal*), irritate, aggravate (*informal*), gall, madden, exasperate, nettle, vex, irk, rile, pique, get on your nerves (*informal*), nark (*Brit, Austral & NZ slang*), get up your nose (*informal*), give someone grief (*Brit & S African*), make your blood boil, get your goat (*slang*), get on your wick (*Brit slang*), get your back up, hack you off (*informal*)
6 OBTAIN, receive, gain, acquire, win, land, score (*slang*), achieve, net, pick up, bag, secure, attain, reap, get hold of, come by, glean, procure, get your hands on, come into possession of
7 FETCH, bring, collect
8 UNDERSTAND, follow, catch, see, notice, realize, appreciate, be aware of, take in, perceive, grasp, comprehend, fathom, apprehend, suss (out) (*slang*), get the hang of (*informal*), get your head round
9 CATCH, develop, contract, succumb to, fall victim to, go down with, come down with, become infected with, be afflicted with, be smitten by
10 ARREST, catch, grab, capture, trap, seize, take, nail (*informal*), collar (*informal*), nab (*informal*), apprehend, take prisoner, take into custody, lay hold of
11 CONTACT, reach, communicate with, get hold of, get in touch with
12 PUZZLE, confuse, baffle, bewilder, confound, perplex, mystify, stump, beat (*slang*), flummox, nonplus
13 (*informal*) MOVE, touch, affect, excite, stir, stimulate, arouse, have an impact on, have an effect on, tug at (someone's) heartstrings (*often facetious*)
▷▷ **get across something** CROSS, negotiate, pass over, traverse, ford
▷▷ **get at someone** 1 CRITICIZE, attack, blame, put down, knock (*informal*), carp, have a go (at) (*informal*), taunt, nag, hassle (*informal*), pick on, disparage, diss (*slang, chiefly US*), find fault with, put the boot into (*slang*), nark (*Brit, Austral & NZ slang*), be on your back (*slang*)
2 CORRUPT, influence, bribe, tamper with, buy off, fix (*informal*), suborn
▷▷ **get at something** 1 REACH, touch, grasp, get (a) hold of, stretch to *verb*
2 FIND OUT, get, learn, reach, reveal, discover, acquire, detect, uncover, attain, get hold of, gain access to, come to grips with
3 IMPLY, mean, suggest, hint, intimate, lead up to, insinuate
▷▷ **get away** ESCAPE, leave, disappear, flee, depart, fly, slip away, abscond, decamp, hook it (*slang*), do a runner (*slang*), slope off, do a bunk (*Brit slang*), fly the coop (*US & Canad informal*), skedaddle (*informal*), take a powder (*US & Canad slang*), make good your escape, make your getaway, take it on the lam (*US & Canad slang*), break free *or* out, run away *or* off, do a Skase (*Austral informal*)
▷▷ **get back** RETURN, arrive home, come back *or* home
▷▷ **get back at someone** RETALIATE, pay (someone) back, hit back at, take revenge on, get even with, strike back at, even the score with, exact retribution on, get your own back on, make reprisal with, be avenged on, settle the score with, give (someone) a taste of his *or* her own medicine, give tit for tat, take *or* wreak vengeance on
▷▷ **get by** MANAGE, survive, cope, fare, get through, exist, make out, get along, make do, subsist, muddle through, keep your head above water, make both ends meet
▷▷ **get in** ARRIVE, come in, appear, land
▷▷ **get off** 1 BE ABSOLVED, be acquitted, escape punishment, walk (*slang, chiefly US*)
2 LEAVE, go, move, take off (*informal*), depart, slope off, make tracks, set out *or* off
3 DESCEND, leave, exit, step down, alight, disembark, dismount
▷▷ **get on** 1 BE FRIENDLY, agree, get along, concur, be compatible, hit it off (*informal*), harmonize, be on good terms
2 PROGRESS, manage, cope, fare, advance, succeed, make out (*informal*), prosper, cut it (*informal*), get along
3 BOARD, enter, mount, climb, embark, ascend
▷▷ **get out** LEAVE, escape, withdraw, quit, take off (*informal*), exit, go, break out, go away, depart, evacuate, vacate, clear out (*informal*), abscond, decamp, hook it (*slang*), free yourself, do a bunk (*Brit slang*), extricate yourself, sling your hook (*Brit slang*), rack off (*Austral & NZ slang*), do a Skase (*Austral informal*)
▷▷ **get out of something** AVOID, dodge, evade, escape, shirk, body-swerve (*Scot*)
▷▷ **get over something** 1 RECOVER FROM,

survive, get better from, come round, bounce back, mend, get well, recuperate, turn the corner, pull through, get back on your feet, feel yourself again, regain your health *or* strength
2 OVERCOME, deal with, solve, resolve, defeat, master, lick (*informal*), shake off, rise above, get the better of, surmount
3 CROSS, pass, pass over, traverse, get across, move across, ford, go across
▷▷ **get round someone** (*informal*) WIN OVER, persuade, charm, influence, convince, convert, sway, coax, cajole, wheedle, prevail upon, bring round, talk round
▷▷ **get round something** OVERCOME, deal with, solve, resolve, defeat, master, bypass, lick (*informal*), shake off, rise above, get the better of, circumvent, surmount
▷▷ **get something across** COMMUNICATE, publish, spread, pass on, transmit, convey, impart, get (something) through, disseminate, bring home, make known, put over, make clear *or* understood
▷▷ **get something back** REGAIN, recover, retrieve, take back, recoup, repossess
▷▷ **get something over** COMMUNICATE, spread, pass on, convey, impart, make known, get *or* put across, make clear *or* understood
▷▷ **get together** MEET, unite, join, collect, gather, rally, assemble, muster, convene, converge, congregate
▷▷ **get up** ARISE, stand (up), rise, get to your feet

getaway *noun* ESCAPE, break, flight, break-out, decampment

get-together *noun* GATHERING, party, celebration, reception, meeting, social, function, bash (*informal*), rave (*Brit slang*), festivity, do (*informal*), knees-up (*Brit informal*), beano (*Brit slang*), social gathering, shindig (*informal*), soirée, rave-up (*Brit slang*), hooley *or* hoolie (*chiefly Irish & NZ*)

ghastly *adjective* HORRIBLE, shocking, terrible, awful, grim, dreadful, horrendous, hideous, from hell (*informal*), horrid (*informal*), repulsive, frightful, loathsome, godawful (*slang*)
<< OPPOSITE lovely

ghost *noun* **1** SPIRIT, soul, phantom, spectre, spook (*informal*), apparition, wraith, shade (*literary*), phantasm, atua (*NZ*), kehua (*NZ*), wairua (*NZ*)
2 TRACE, shadow, suggestion, hint, suspicion, glimmer, semblance
>> RELATED WORD *adjective* spectral

ghostly *adjective* UNEARTHLY, weird, phantom, eerie, supernatural, uncanny, spooky (*informal*), spectral, eldritch (*poetic*), phantasmal

ghoulish *adjective* MACABRE, sick (*informal*), disgusting, hideous, gruesome, grisly, horrid, morbid, unwholesome

giant *adjective* HUGE, great, large, vast, enormous, extensive, tremendous, immense, titanic, jumbo (*informal*), gigantic, monumental, monstrous, mammoth, colossal, mountainous, stellar (*informal*), prodigious, stupendous, gargantuan, elephantine, ginormous (*informal*), Brobdingnagian, humongous *or* humungous (*US slang*)
<< OPPOSITE tiny
▷ *noun* OGRE, monster, titan, colossus, leviathan, behemoth

gibber *verb* GABBLE, chatter, babble, waffle (*informal, chiefly Brit*), prattle, jabber, blab, rabbit on (*Brit informal*), blather, blabber, earbash (*Austral & NZ slang*)

gibberish *noun* NONSENSE, crap (*slang*), garbage (*informal*), hot air (*informal*), tosh (*slang, chiefly Brit*), babble, pap, bilge (*informal*), drivel, twaddle, tripe (*informal*), guff (*slang*), prattle, mumbo jumbo, moonshine, jabber, gabble, gobbledegook (*informal*), hogwash, hokum (*slang, chiefly US & Canad*), blather, double talk, piffle (*informal*), all Greek (*informal*), poppycock (*informal*), balderdash, bosh (*informal*), yammer (*informal*), eyewash (*informal*), tommyrot, horsefeathers (*US slang*), bunkum *or* buncombe (*chiefly US*), bizzo (*Austral slang*), bull's wool (*Austral & NZ slang*)

gibe ▷ see **jibe**

giddy *adjective* **1** DIZZY, reeling, faint, unsteady, light-headed, vertiginous
2 FLIGHTY, silly, volatile, irresponsible, reckless, dizzy, careless, frivolous, impulsive, capricious, thoughtless, impetuous, skittish, heedless, scatterbrained, ditzy *or* ditsy (*slang*)
<< OPPOSITE serious

gift *noun* **1** DONATION, offering, present, contribution, grant, legacy, hand-out, endowment, boon, bequest, gratuity, prezzie (*informal*), bonsela (*S African*), largesse *or* largess, koha (*NZ*)
2 TALENT, ability, capacity, genius, power, bent, faculty, capability, forte, flair, knack, aptitude

gifted *adjective* TALENTED, able, skilled, expert, masterly, brilliant, capable, clever, accomplished, proficient, adroit
<< OPPOSITE talentless

gigantic *adjective* HUGE, great, large, giant, massive, vast, enormous, extensive, tremendous, immense, titanic, jumbo (*informal*), monumental, monstrous, mammoth, colossal, mountainous, stellar (*informal*), prodigious, stupendous, gargantuan, herculean, elephantine, ginormous (*informal*), Brobdingnagian, humongous *or* humungous (*US slang*)
<< OPPOSITE tiny

giggle *verb* LAUGH, chuckle, snigger, chortle,

titter, twitter, tee-hee

▷ *noun* LAUGH, chuckle, snigger, chortle, titter, twitter

gimmick *noun* STUNT, trick, device, scheme, manoeuvre, dodge, ploy, gambit, stratagem, contrivance

gingerly *adverb* CAUTIOUSLY, carefully, reluctantly, suspiciously, tentatively, warily, hesitantly, timidly, circumspectly, cagily (*informal*), charily

<< OPPOSITE carelessly

gird *verb* **1** GIRDLE, bind, belt

2 SURROUND, ring, pen, enclose, encompass, encircle, hem in, enfold, engird

3 PREPARE, ready, steel, brace, fortify, make *or* get ready

girdle *noun* BELT, band, sash, waistband, cummerbund

▷ *verb* SURROUND, ring, bound, enclose, encompass, hem, encircle, fence in, gird

girl *noun* FEMALE CHILD, schoolgirl, lass, lassie (*informal*), miss, maiden (*archaic*), maid (*archaic*)

girth *noun* SIZE, measure, proportions, dimensions, bulk, measurement(s), circumference

gist *noun* ESSENCE, meaning, point, idea, sense, import, core, substance, drift, significance, nub, pith, quintessence

give *verb* **1** PERFORM, do, carry out, execute

2 COMMUNICATE, announce, publish, transmit, pronounce, utter, emit, issue, be a source of, impart

3 PRODUCE, make, cause, occasion, engender

4 PRESENT, contribute, donate, provide, supply, award, grant, deliver, commit, administer, furnish, confer, bestow, entrust, consign, make over, hand over *or* out

<< OPPOSITE take

5 COLLAPSE, fall, break, sink, bend

6 CONCEDE, allow, grant

7 SURRENDER, yield, devote, hand over, relinquish, part with, cede

8 DEMONSTRATE, show, offer, provide, evidence, display, indicate, manifest, set forth

▷▷ **give in** ADMIT DEFEAT, yield, concede, collapse, quit, submit, surrender, comply, succumb, cave in (*informal*), capitulate

▷▷ **give something away** REVEAL, expose, leak, disclose, betray, uncover, let out, divulge, let slip, let the cat out of the bag (*informal*)

▷▷ **give something off** *or* **out** EMIT, produce, release, discharge, send out, throw out, vent, exude, exhale

▷▷ **give something out** **1** DISTRIBUTE, issue, deliver, circulate, hand out, dispense, dole out, pass round

2 MAKE KNOWN, announce, publish, broadcast, communicate, transmit, utter, notify, impart, disseminate, shout from the rooftops (*informal*)

▷▷ **give something up** **1** ABANDON, stop, quit, kick (*informal*), cease, cut out, renounce, leave off, say goodbye to, desist, kiss (something) goodbye, forswear

2 QUIT, leave, resign, step down from (*informal*)

3 HAND OVER, yield, surrender, relinquish, waive

given *adjective* **1** SPECIFIED, particular, specific, designated, stated, predetermined

2 INCLINED, addicted, disposed, prone, liable

glacial *adjective* **1** ICY, biting, cold, freezing, frozen, bitter, raw, chill, piercing, arctic, polar, chilly, frosty, wintry

2 UNFRIENDLY, hostile, cold, icy, frosty, antagonistic, frigid, inimical

glad *adjective* **1** HAPPY, pleased, delighted, contented, cheerful, gratified, joyful, overjoyed, chuffed (*slang*), gleeful

<< OPPOSITE unhappy

2 (*Archaic*) PLEASING, happy, cheering, pleasant, delightful, cheerful, merry, gratifying, cheery, joyous, felicitous

gladly *adverb* **1** HAPPILY, cheerfully, gleefully, merrily, gaily, joyfully, joyously, jovially

2 WILLINGLY, freely, happily, readily, cheerfully, with pleasure, with (a) good grace

<< OPPOSITE reluctantly

glamorous *adjective* **1** ATTRACTIVE, beautiful, lovely, charming, entrancing, elegant, dazzling, enchanting, captivating, alluring, bewitching

<< OPPOSITE unglamorous

2 EXCITING, glittering, prestigious, glossy, glitzy (*slang*)

<< OPPOSITE unglamorous

glamour *noun* **1** CHARM, appeal, beauty, attraction, fascination, allure, magnetism, enchantment, bewitchment

2 EXCITEMENT, magic, thrill, romance, prestige, glitz (*slang*)

glance *verb* **1** PEEK, look, view, check, clock (*Brit informal*), gaze, glimpse, check out (*informal*), peep, take a dekko at (*Brit slang*)

<< OPPOSITE scrutinize

2 *with* **over, through,** *etc.* SCAN, browse, dip into, leaf through, flip through, thumb through, skim through, riffle through, run over *or* through, surf (*Computing*)

▷ *noun* PEEK, look, glimpse, peep, squint, butcher's (*Brit slang*), quick look, gander (*informal*), brief look, dekko (*slang*), shufti (*Brit slang*)

<< OPPOSITE good look

Care should be taken not to confuse *glance* and *glimpse*: *he caught a glimpse* (not *glance*) *of her making her way through the crowd; he gave a quick glance* (not *glimpse*) *at his watch*. A *glance* is a deliberate action, while a *glimpse* seems opportunistic

glare *verb* **1** SCOWL, frown, glower, look

daggers, stare angrily, give a dirty look, lour *or* lower
2 DAZZLE, blaze, flare, flame
▷ *noun* 1 SCOWL, frown, glower, dirty look, black look, angry stare, lour *or* lower
2 DAZZLE, glow, blaze, flare, flame, brilliance
glaring *adjective* OBVIOUS, open, outstanding, patent, visible, gross, outrageous, manifest, blatant, conspicuous, overt, audacious, flagrant, rank, egregious, unconcealed
<< OPPOSITE inconspicuous
glassy *adjective* 1 SMOOTH, clear, slick, shiny, glossy, transparent, slippery
2 EXPRESSIONLESS, cold, fixed, empty, dull, blank, glazed, vacant, dazed, lifeless
glaze *noun* COAT, finish, polish, shine, gloss, varnish, enamel, lacquer, lustre, patina
▷ *verb* COAT, polish, gloss, varnish, enamel, lacquer, burnish, furbish
gleam *verb* SHINE, flash, glow, sparkle, glitter, flare, shimmer, glint, glimmer, glisten, scintillate
▷ *noun* 1 GLIMMER, flash, beam, glow, sparkle
2 TRACE, ray, suggestion, hint, flicker, glimmer, inkling
gleaming *adjective* SHINING, bright, brilliant, glowing, sparkling, glimmering, glistening, scintillating, burnished, lustrous
<< OPPOSITE dull
glean *verb* GATHER, learn, pick up, collect, harvest, accumulate, reap, garner, amass, cull
glee *noun* DELIGHT, joy, triumph, exuberance, elation, exhilaration, mirth, hilarity, merriment, exultation, gladness, joyfulness, joyousness
<< OPPOSITE gloom
gleeful *adjective* DELIGHTED, happy, pleased, cheerful, merry, triumphant, gratified, exuberant, jubilant, joyous, joyful, elated, overjoyed, chirpy (*informal*), exultant, cock-a-hoop, mirthful, stoked (*Austral & NZ informal*)
glib *adjective* SMOOTH, easy, ready, quick, slick, plausible, slippery, fluent, suave, artful, insincere, fast-talking, smooth-tongued
<< OPPOSITE sincere
glide *verb* SLIP, sail, slide, skim
glimmer *verb* GLEAM, shine, glow, sparkle, glitter, blink, flicker, shimmer, twinkle, glisten
▷ *noun* 1 GLOW, ray, sparkle, gleam, blink, flicker, shimmer, twinkle
2 TRACE, ray, suggestion, hint, grain, gleam, flicker, inkling
glimpse *noun* LOOK, sighting, sight, glance, peep, peek, squint, butcher's (*Brit slang*), quick look, gander (*informal*), brief view, shufti (*Brit slang*)
▷ *verb* CATCH SIGHT OF, spot, sight, view, clock (*Brit informal*), spy, espy
glint *verb* GLEAM, flash, shine, sparkle, glitter, twinkle, glimmer
▷ *noun* GLEAM, flash, shine, sparkle, glitter, twinkle, twinkling, glimmer
glisten *verb* GLEAM, flash, shine, sparkle, glitter, shimmer, twinkle, glint, glimmer, scintillate
glitch *noun* PROBLEM, difficulty, fault, flaw, bug (*informal*), hitch, snag, uphill (*S African*), interruption, blip, malfunction, kink, gremlin, fly in the ointment
glitter *verb* SHINE, flash, sparkle, flare, glare, gleam, shimmer, twinkle, glint, glimmer, glisten, scintillate
▷ *noun* 1 GLAMOUR, show, display, gilt, splendour, tinsel, pageantry, gaudiness, showiness
2 SPARKLE, flash, shine, beam, glare, gleam, brilliance, sheen, shimmer, brightness, lustre, radiance, scintillation
gloat *verb* RELISH, triumph, glory, crow, revel in, vaunt, drool, exult, rub your hands
global *adjective* 1 WORLDWIDE, world, international, universal, planetary
2 COMPREHENSIVE, general, total, thorough, unlimited, exhaustive, all-inclusive, all-encompassing, encyclopedic, unbounded
<< OPPOSITE limited
globe *noun* PLANET, world, earth, sphere, orb
gloom *noun* 1 DARKNESS, dark, shadow, cloud, shade, twilight, dusk, obscurity, blackness, dullness, murk, dimness, murkiness, cloudiness, gloominess, duskiness
<< OPPOSITE light
2 DEPRESSION, despair, misery, sadness, sorrow, blues, woe, melancholy, unhappiness, desolation, despondency, dejection, low spirits, downheartedness
<< OPPOSITE happiness
gloomy *adjective* 1 DARK, dull, dim, dismal, black, grey, obscure, murky, dreary, sombre, shadowy, overcast, dusky
<< OPPOSITE light
2 MISERABLE, down, sad, dismal, low, blue, pessimistic, melancholy, glum, dejected, despondent, dispirited, downcast, joyless, downhearted, down in the dumps (*informal*), cheerless, down in the mouth, in low spirits
<< OPPOSITE happy
3 DEPRESSING, bad, dismal, dreary, black, saddening, sombre, dispiriting, disheartening, funereal, cheerless, comfortless
glorify *verb* 1 PRAISE, celebrate, magnify, laud, extol, crack up (*informal*), eulogize, sing *or* sound the praises of
<< OPPOSITE condemn
2 WORSHIP, honour, bless, adore, revere, exalt, pay homage to, venerate, sanctify, immortalize

<< OPPOSITE dishonour
3 ENHANCE, raise, elevate, adorn, dignify, magnify, augment, lift up, ennoble, add lustre to, aggrandize
<< OPPOSITE degrade

glorious *adjective* 1 SPLENDID, beautiful, bright, brilliant, shining, superb, divine, gorgeous, dazzling, radiant, resplendent, splendiferous (*facetious*)
<< OPPOSITE dull
2 DELIGHTFUL, fine, wonderful, excellent, heavenly (*informal*), marvellous, splendid, gorgeous, pleasurable, splendiferous (*facetious*)
3 ILLUSTRIOUS, famous, celebrated, distinguished, noted, grand, excellent, honoured, magnificent, noble, renowned, elevated, eminent, triumphant, majestic, famed, sublime
<< OPPOSITE ordinary

glory *noun* 1 HONOUR, praise, fame, celebrity, distinction, acclaim, prestige, immortality, eminence, kudos, renown, exaltation, illustriousness
<< OPPOSITE shame
2 SPLENDOUR, majesty, greatness, grandeur, nobility, pomp, magnificence, pageantry, éclat, sublimity
3 BEAUTY, brilliance, lustre, radiance, gorgeousness, resplendence
4 WORSHIP, praise, blessing, gratitude, thanksgiving, homage, adoration, veneration
▷ *verb* TRIUMPH, boast, relish, revel, crow, drool, gloat, exult, take delight, pride yourself

gloss[1] *noun* 1 SHINE, gleam, sheen, polish, brilliance, varnish, brightness, veneer, lustre, burnish, patina
2 FAÇADE, show, front, surface, appearance, mask, semblance

gloss[2] *noun* INTERPRETATION, comment, note, explanation, commentary, translation, footnote, elucidation
▷ *verb* INTERPRET, explain, comment, translate, construe, annotate, elucidate

glossy *adjective* SHINY, polished, shining, glazed, bright, brilliant, smooth, sleek, silky, burnished, glassy, silken, lustrous
<< OPPOSITE dull

glow *noun* 1 LIGHT, gleam, splendour, glimmer, brilliance, brightness, radiance, luminosity, vividness, incandescence, phosphorescence
<< OPPOSITE dullness
2 COLOUR, bloom, flush, blush, reddening, rosiness
<< OPPOSITE pallor
▷ *verb* 1 SHINE, burn, gleam, brighten, glimmer, smoulder
2 BE PINK, colour, flush, blush
3 BE SUFFUSED, thrill, radiate, tingle

glower *verb* SCOWL, glare, frown, look daggers, give a dirty look, lour *or* lower
▷ *noun* SCOWL, glare, frown, dirty look, black look, angry stare, lour *or* lower

glowing *adjective* 1 COMPLIMENTARY, enthusiastic, rave (*informal*), ecstatic, rhapsodic, laudatory, adulatory
<< OPPOSITE scathing
2 BRIGHT, vivid, vibrant, rich, warm, radiant, luminous
<< OPPOSITE dull

glue *noun* ADHESIVE, cement, gum, paste
▷ *verb* STICK, fix, seal, cement, gum, paste, affix

glum *adjective* GLOOMY, miserable, dismal, down, low, melancholy, dejected, downcast, morose, doleful, downhearted, down in the dumps (*informal*), down in the mouth, in low spirits
<< OPPOSITE cheerful

glut *noun* SURFEIT, excess, surplus, plethora, saturation, oversupply, overabundance, superabundance
<< OPPOSITE scarcity
▷ *verb* 1 SATURATE, flood, choke, clog, overload, inundate, deluge, oversupply
2 OVERFILL, fill, stuff, cram, satiate

glutinous *adjective* STICKY, adhesive, cohesive, gooey, viscous, gummy, gluey, viscid

glutton *noun* GOURMAND, gorger, gannet (*slang*), gobbler, pig (*informal*)

gluttonous *adjective* GREEDY, insatiable, voracious, ravenous, rapacious, piggish, hoggish

gluttony *noun* GREED, rapacity, voracity, greediness, voraciousness, piggishness

gnarled *adjective* 1 TWISTED, knotted, contorted, knotty
2 WRINKLED, rough, rugged, leathery

gnaw *verb* 1 BITE, chew, nibble, munch
2 DISTRESS, worry, trouble, harry, haunt, plague, nag, fret
3 ERODE, consume, devour, eat away *or* into, wear away *or* down

go *verb* 1 MOVE, travel, advance, journey, proceed, pass, fare (*archaic*), set off
<< OPPOSITE stay
2 LEAVE, withdraw, depart, move out, decamp, slope off, make tracks
3 LEAD, run, reach, spread, extend, stretch, connect, span, give access
4 ELAPSE, pass, flow, fly by, expire, lapse, slip away
5 BE GIVEN, be spent, be awarded, be allotted
6 DIE, perish, pass away, buy it (*US slang*), expire, check out (*US slang*), kick it (*slang*), croak (*slang*), give up the ghost, snuff it (*informal*), peg out (*informal*), kick the bucket (*slang*), peg it (*informal*), cark it (*Austral & NZ slang*), pop your clogs (*informal*)

7 PROCEED, develop, turn out, work out, fare, fall out, pan out (*informal*)
8 FUNCTION, work, run, move, operate, perform
<< OPPOSITE fail
9 MATCH, blend, correspond, fit, suit, chime, harmonize
10 SERVE, help, tend
▷ *noun* 1 ATTEMPT, try, effort, bid, shot (*informal*), crack (*informal*), essay, stab (*informal*), whirl (*informal*), whack (*informal*)
2 TURN, shot (*informal*), spell, stint
3 (*informal*) ENERGY, life, drive, spirit, pep, vitality, vigour, verve, force, get-up-and-go (*informal*), oomph (*informal*), brio, vivacity
▷▷ **go about something** 1 TACKLE, begin, approach, undertake, set about
2 ENGAGE IN, perform, conduct, pursue, practise, ply, carry on with, apply yourself to, busy *or* occupy yourself with
▷▷ **go along with something** AGREE, follow, cooperate, concur, assent, acquiesce
▷▷ **go at something** SET ABOUT, start, begin, tackle, set to, get down to, wade into, get to work on, make a start on, get cracking on (*informal*), address yourself to, get weaving on (*informal*)
▷▷ **go away** LEAVE, withdraw, exit, depart, move out, go to hell (*informal*), decamp, hook it (*slang*), slope off, pack your bags (*informal*), make tracks, get on your bike (*Brit slang*), bog off (*Brit slang*), sling your hook (*Brit slang*), rack off (*Austral & NZ slang*)
▷▷ **go back** RETURN
▷▷ **go back on something** REPUDIATE, break, forsake, retract, renege on, desert, back out of, change your mind about
▷▷ **go by** PASS, proceed, elapse, flow on, move onward
▷▷ **go by something** OBEY, follow, adopt, observe, comply with, heed, submit to, be guided by, take as guide
▷▷ **go down** 1 FALL, drop, decline, slump, decrease, fall off, dwindle, lessen, ebb, depreciate, become lower
2 SET, sink
3 SINK, founder, go under, be submerged
▷▷ **go for someone** 1 PREFER, like, choose, favour, admire, be attracted to, be fond of, hold with
2 ATTACK, assault, assail, spring upon, rush upon, launch yourself at, set about *or* upon
3 SCOLD, attack, blast, criticize, flame (*informal*), put down, tear into (*informal*), diss (*slang, chiefly US*), impugn, lambast(e)
▷▷ **go in for something** PARTICIPATE IN, pursue, take part in, undertake, embrace, practise, engage in
▷▷ **go into something** 1 INVESTIGATE, consider, study, research, discuss, review, examine, pursue, probe, analyse, look into, delve into, work over, scrutinize, inquire into
2 ENTER, begin, participate in
▷▷ **go off** 1 DEPART, leave, quit, go away, move out, decamp, hook it (*slang*), slope off, pack your bags (*informal*), rack off (*Austral & NZ slang*)
2 EXPLODE, fire, blow up, detonate
3 SOUND, ring, toll, chime, peal
4 TAKE PLACE, happen, occur, come off (*informal*), come about
5 (*informal*) GO BAD, turn, spoil, rot, go stale
▷▷ **go on** 1 HAPPEN, occur, take place
2 CONTINUE, last, stay, proceed, carry on, keep going
3 *often with* **about** RAMBLE ON, carry on, chatter, waffle (*informal, chiefly Brit*), witter (on) (*informal*), rabbit on (*Brit informal*), prattle, blether, earbash (*Austral & NZ slang*)
▷▷ **go on doing something** *or* **go on with something** CONTINUE, pursue, proceed, carry on, stick to, persist, keep on, keep at, persevere, stick at
▷▷ **go out** 1 SEE SOMEONE, court, date (*informal, chiefly US*), woo, go steady (*informal*), be romantically involved with *verb*
2 BE EXTINGUISHED, die out, fade out
▷▷ **go over something** 1 EXAMINE, study, review, revise, inspect, work over
2 REHEARSE, read, scan, reiterate, skim over, peruse
▷▷ **go through something** 1 SUFFER, experience, bear, endure, brave, undergo, tolerate, withstand
2 SEARCH, look through, rummage through, rifle through, hunt through, fossick through (*Austral & NZ*), ferret about in
3 EXAMINE, check, search, explore, look through, work over
4 USE UP, exhaust, consume, squander
▷▷ **go through with something** CARRY ON, continue, pursue, keep on, persevere
▷▷ **go together** 1 HARMONIZE, match, agree, accord, fit, make a pair
2 (*informal*) GO OUT, court, date (*informal, chiefly US*), go steady (*informal*)
▷▷ **go under** 1 FAIL, die, sink, go down, fold (*informal*), founder, succumb, go bankrupt
2 SINK, go down, founder, submerge
▷▷ **go up** INCREASE, rise, mount, soar, get higher
▷▷ **go with something** MATCH, suit, blend, correspond with, agree with, fit, complement, harmonize
▷▷ **go without something** BE DEPRIVED OF, want, lack, be denied, do without, abstain, go short, deny yourself
▷▷ **no go** IMPOSSIBLE, not on (*informal*), vain, hopeless, futile

goad *verb* URGE, drive, prompt, spur, stimulate,

provoke, arouse, propel, prod, prick, incite, instigate, egg on, exhort, impel
▷ *noun* INCENTIVE, urge, spur, motivation, pressure, stimulus, stimulation, impetus, incitement

go-ahead *noun* (*informal*) PERMISSION, consent, green light, assent, leave, authorization, O.K. *or* okay (*informal*)
▷ *adjective* ENTERPRISING, pioneering, ambitious, progressive, go-getting (*informal*), up-and-coming

goal *noun* AIM, end, target, purpose, object, intention, objective, ambition, destination, Holy Grail (*informal*)

goat *noun*
>> RELATED WORD *adjective* caprine
>> RELATED WORDS *male* billy, buck
>> RELATED WORD *female* nanny
>> RELATED WORDS *young* kid, yeanling
>> RELATED WORDS *collective nouns* herd, tribe

gob *noun* PIECE, lump, chunk, hunk, nugget, blob, wad, clod, wodge (*Brit informal*)

gobble *verb* DEVOUR, swallow, gulp, guzzle, wolf, bolt, cram in, gorge on, pig out on (*slang*), stuff yourself with

go-between *noun* INTERMEDIARY, agent, medium, broker, factor, dealer, liaison, mediator, middleman

god *noun* DEITY, immortal, divinity, divine being, supreme being, atua (*NZ*)

godforsaken *adjective* DESOLATE, abandoned, deserted, remote, neglected, lonely, bleak, gloomy, backward, dismal, dreary, forlorn, wretched

godless *adjective* WICKED, depraved, profane, unprincipled, atheistic, ungodly, irreligious, impious, unrighteous

godlike *adjective* DIVINE, heavenly, celestial, superhuman

godly *adjective* DEVOUT, religious, holy, righteous, pious, good, saintly, god-fearing

godsend *noun* BLESSING, help, benefit, asset, boon

gogga *noun* (*S African*) INSECT, bug, creepy-crawly (*Brit informal*)

goggle *verb* STARE, gape, gawp (*slang*), gawk

going-over *noun* **1** EXAMINATION, study, check, review, survey, investigation, analysis, inspection, scrutiny, perusal
2 THRASHING, attack, beating, whipping, thumping, pasting (*slang*), buffeting, drubbing (*informal*)
3 DRESSING-DOWN, talking-to (*informal*), lecture, rebuke, reprimand, scolding, chiding, tongue-lashing, chastisement, castigation

golden *adjective* **1** YELLOW, bright, brilliant, blonde, blond, flaxen
<< OPPOSITE dark
2 SUCCESSFUL, glorious, prosperous, best, rich, flourishing, halcyon
<< OPPOSITE worst
3 PROMISING, excellent, valuable, favourable, advantageous, auspicious, opportune, propitious
<< OPPOSITE unfavourable

gone *adjective* **1** MISSING, lost, away, vanished, absent, astray
2 USED UP, spent, finished, consumed
3 PAST, over, ended, finished, elapsed

good *adjective* **1** EXCELLENT, great, fine, pleasing, capital, choice, crucial (*slang*), acceptable, pleasant, worthy, first-class, divine, splendid, satisfactory, superb, enjoyable, awesome (*slang*), dope (*slang*), world-class, admirable, agreeable, super (*informal*), pleasurable, wicked (*slang*), bad (*slang*), first-rate, tiptop, bitchin' (*US slang*), booshit (*Austral slang*), exo (*Austral slang*), sik (*Austral slang*), rad (*informal*), phat (*slang*), schmick (*Austral informal*)
<< OPPOSITE bad
2 PROFICIENT, able, skilled, capable, expert, talented, efficient, clever, accomplished, reliable, first-class, satisfactory, competent, thorough, adept, first-rate, adroit, dexterous
<< OPPOSITE bad
3 BENEFICIAL, useful, healthy, helpful, favourable, wholesome, advantageous, salutary, salubrious
<< OPPOSITE harmful
4 HONOURABLE, moral, worthy, ethical, upright, admirable, honest, righteous, exemplary, right, virtuous, trustworthy, altruistic, praiseworthy, estimable
<< OPPOSITE bad
5 WELL-BEHAVED, seemly, mannerly, proper, polite, orderly, obedient, dutiful, decorous, well-mannered
<< OPPOSITE naughty
6 KIND, kindly, friendly, obliging, charitable, humane, gracious, benevolent, merciful, beneficent, well-disposed, kind-hearted
<< OPPOSITE unkind
7 TRUE, real, genuine, proper, reliable, dependable, sound, trustworthy, dinkum (*Austral & NZ informal*)
8 FULL, long, whole, complete, entire, solid, extensive
<< OPPOSITE scant
9 CONSIDERABLE, large, substantial, sufficient, adequate, ample
10 VALID, convincing, compelling, legitimate, authentic, persuasive, sound, bona fide
<< OPPOSITE invalid
11 BEST, newest, special, finest, nicest, smartest, fancy, most valuable, most precious
12 EDIBLE, untainted, uncorrupted, eatable, fit to eat

<< OPPOSITE bad
13 CONVENIENT, timely, fitting, fit, appropriate, suitable, well-timed, opportune
<< OPPOSITE inconvenient
▷ *noun* 1 BENEFIT, interest, gain, advantage, use, service, profit, welfare, behalf, usefulness, wellbeing
<< OPPOSITE disadvantage
2 VIRTUE, goodness, righteousness, worth, merit, excellence, morality, probity, rectitude, uprightness
<< OPPOSITE evil
▷▷ **for good** PERMANENTLY, finally, for ever, once and for all, irrevocably, never to return, sine die (*Latin*)
goodbye *noun* FAREWELL, parting, leave-taking
▷ *interjection* FAREWELL, see you, see you later, ciao (*Italian*), cheerio, adieu, ta-ta, au revoir (*French*), auf Wiedersehen (*German*), adios (*Spanish*), haere ra (*NZ*)
good-humoured *adjective* GENIAL, happy, pleasant, cheerful, amiable, affable, congenial, good-tempered
good-looking *adjective* ATTRACTIVE, pretty, fair, beautiful, lovely, handsome, gorgeous, bonny, personable, comely, well-favoured
good-natured *adjective* AMIABLE, kind, kindly, friendly, generous, helpful, obliging, tolerant, agreeable, benevolent, good-hearted, magnanimous, well-disposed, warm-hearted
goodness *noun* 1 VIRTUE, honour, merit, integrity, morality, honesty, righteousness, probity, rectitude, uprightness
<< OPPOSITE badness
2 EXCELLENCE, value, quality, worth, merit, superiority
3 NUTRITION, benefit, advantage, nourishment, wholesomeness, salubriousness
4 KINDNESS, charity, humanity, goodwill, mercy, compassion, generosity, friendliness, benevolence, graciousness, beneficence, kindliness, humaneness, kind-heartedness
goods *plural noun* 1 MERCHANDISE, stock, products, stuff, commodities, wares
2 PROPERTY, things, effects, gear, furniture, movables, possessions, furnishings, belongings, trappings, paraphernalia, chattels, appurtenances
goodwill *noun* FRIENDLINESS, favour, friendship, benevolence, amity, kindliness
gooey *adjective* 1 STICKY, soft, tacky, viscous, glutinous, gummy, icky (*informal*), gluey, gloopy, gungy
2 SENTIMENTAL, romantic, sloppy, soppy, maudlin, syrupy (*informal*), slushy (*informal*), mawkish, tear-jerking (*informal*), icky (*informal*)
gore[1] *noun* BLOOD, slaughter, bloodshed, carnage, butchery
gore[2] *verb* PIERCE, wound, stab, spit, transfix, impale
gorge *noun* RAVINE, canyon, pass, clough (*dialect*), chasm, cleft, fissure, defile, gulch (*US & Canad*)
▷ *verb* 1 OVEREAT, bolt, devour, gobble, wolf, swallow, gulp, guzzle, pig out (*slang*)
2 *usually reflexive* STUFF, fill, feed, cram, glut, surfeit, satiate, sate
gorgeous *adjective* 1 MAGNIFICENT, grand, beautiful, superb, spectacular, splendid, glittering, dazzling, luxurious, sumptuous, opulent
<< OPPOSITE shabby
2 (*informal*) BEAUTIFUL, attractive, lovely, stunning (*informal*), elegant, handsome, good-looking, exquisite, drop-dead (*slang*), ravishing
<< OPPOSITE dull
gory *adjective* 1 GRISLY, bloody, murderous, bloodthirsty
2 BLOODY, bloodstained, blood-soaked
gospel *noun* 1 DOCTRINE, news, teachings, message, revelation, creed, credo, tidings
2 TRUTH, fact, certainty, the last word, verity
gossip *noun* 1 IDLE TALK, scandal, hearsay, tittle-tattle, buzz, dirt (*US slang*), goss (*informal*), jaw (*slang*), gen (*Brit informal*), small talk, chitchat, blether, scuttlebutt (*US slang*), chinwag (*Brit informal*)
2 BUSYBODY, babbler, prattler, chatterbox (*informal*), blether, chatterer, scandalmonger, gossipmonger, tattletale (*chiefly US & Canad*)
▷ *verb* CHAT, chatter, blather, schmooze (*slang*), jaw (*slang*), dish the dirt (*informal*), blether, shoot the breeze (*slang, chiefly US*), chew the fat *or* rag (*slang*)
gouge *verb* SCOOP, cut, score, dig (out), scratch, hollow (out), claw, chisel, gash, incise
▷ *noun* GASH, cut, scratch, hollow, score, scoop, notch, groove, trench, furrow, incision
gourmet *noun* CONNOISSEUR, foodie (*informal*), bon vivant (*French*), epicure, gastronome
govern *verb* 1 RULE, lead, control, command, manage, direct, guide, handle, conduct, order, reign over, administer, oversee, supervise, be in power over, call the shots, call the tune, hold sway over, superintend
2 DETERMINE, decide, guide, rule, influence, underlie, sway
3 RESTRAIN, control, check, contain, master, discipline, regulate, curb, inhibit, tame, subdue, get the better of, bridle, hold in check, keep a tight rein on
government *noun* 1 ADMINISTRATION, executive, ministry, regime, governing body, powers-that-be
2 RULE, state, law, authority, administration, sovereignty, governance, dominion, polity, statecraft ▷ see **family**
governmental *adjective* ADMINISTRATIVE, state,

political, official, executive, ministerial, sovereign, bureaucratic

governor *noun* LEADER, administrator, ruler, head, minister, director, manager, chief, officer, executive, boss (*informal*), commander, controller, supervisor, superintendent, mandarin, comptroller, functionary, overseer, baas (*S African*)

>> RELATED WORD *adjective* gubernatorial

gown *noun* DRESS, costume, garment, robe, frock, garb, habit

grab *verb* SNATCH, catch, seize, capture, bag, grip, grasp, clutch, snap up, pluck, latch on to, catch *or* take hold of

grace *noun* 1 ELEGANCE, finesse, poise, ease, polish, refinement, fluency, suppleness, gracefulness

<< OPPOSITE ungainliness

2 MANNERS, decency, cultivation, etiquette, breeding, consideration, propriety, tact, decorum, mannerliness

<< OPPOSITE bad manners

3 INDULGENCE, mercy, pardon, compassion, quarter, charity, forgiveness, reprieve, clemency, leniency

4 BENEVOLENCE, favour, goodness, goodwill, generosity, kindness, beneficence, kindliness

<< OPPOSITE ill will

5 PRAYER, thanks, blessing, thanksgiving, benediction

6 FAVOUR, regard, respect, approval, esteem, approbation, good opinion

<< OPPOSITE disfavour

▷ *verb* 1 ADORN, enhance, decorate, enrich, set off, garnish, ornament, deck, embellish, bedeck, beautify

2 HONOUR, favour, distinguish, elevate, dignify, glorify

<< OPPOSITE insult

graceful *adjective* ELEGANT, easy, flowing, smooth, fine, pleasing, beautiful, agile, symmetrical, gracile (*rare*)

<< OPPOSITE inelegant

graceless *adjective* 1 INELEGANT, forced, awkward, clumsy, ungainly, unco (*Austral slang*)

2 ILL-MANNERED, crude, rude, coarse, vulgar, rough, improper, shameless, unsophisticated, gauche, barbarous, boorish, gawky, uncouth, loutish, indecorous, unmannerly

gracious *adjective* COURTEOUS, polite, civil, accommodating, kind, kindly, pleasing, friendly, obliging, amiable, cordial, hospitable, courtly, chivalrous, well-mannered

<< OPPOSITE ungracious

grade *verb* CLASSIFY, rate, order, class, group, sort, value, range, rank, brand, arrange, evaluate

▷ *noun* 1 CLASS, condition, quality, brand

2 MARK, degree, place, order

3 LEVEL, position, rank, group, order, class, stage, step, station, category, rung, echelon

▷▷ **make the grade** (*informal*) SUCCEED, measure up, win through, pass muster, come up to scratch (*informal*), come through with flying colours, prove acceptable, measure up to expectations

gradient *noun* SLOPE, hill, rise, grade, incline, bank

gradual *adjective* STEADY, even, slow, regular, gentle, moderate, progressive, piecemeal, unhurried

<< OPPOSITE sudden

gradually *adverb* STEADILY, slowly, moderately, progressively, gently, step by step, evenly, piecemeal, bit by bit, little by little, by degrees, piece by piece, unhurriedly, drop by drop

graduate *verb* 1 MARK OFF, grade, proportion, regulate, gauge, calibrate, measure out

2 CLASSIFY, rank, grade, group, order, sort, range, arrange, sequence

graft[1] *noun* SHOOT, bud, implant, sprout, splice, scion

▷ *verb* JOIN, insert, transplant, implant, splice, affix

graft[2] (*informal*) *noun* LABOUR, work, industry, effort, struggle, sweat, toil, slog, exertion, blood, sweat, and tears (*informal*)

▷ *verb* WORK, labour, struggle, sweat (*informal*), grind (*informal*), slave, strive, toil, drudge

grain *noun* 1 SEED, kernel, grist

2 CEREAL, corn

3 BIT, piece, trace, spark, scrap, suspicion, molecule, particle, fragment, atom, ounce, crumb, mite, jot, speck, morsel, granule, modicum, mote, whit, iota

4 TEXTURE, pattern, surface, fibre, weave, nap

grammar *noun* SYNTAX, rules of language

grammatical *adjective* SYNTACTIC, linguistic

grand *adjective* 1 IMPRESSIVE, great, large, magnificent, striking, fine, princely, imposing, superb, glorious, noble, splendid, gorgeous, luxurious, eminent, majestic, regal, stately, monumental, sublime, sumptuous, grandiose, opulent, palatial, ostentatious, splendiferous (*facetious*)

<< OPPOSITE unimposing

2 AMBITIOUS, great, glorious, lofty, grandiose, exalted, ostentatious

3 SUPERIOR, great, lordly, noble, elevated, eminent, majestic, dignified, stately, lofty, august, illustrious, pompous, pretentious, haughty

4 EXCELLENT, great (*informal*), fine, wonderful, very good, brilliant, outstanding, smashing (*informal*), superb, first-class, divine, marvellous (*informal*), terrific (*informal*), splendid, awesome (*slang*), world-class,

admirable, super (*informal*), first-rate, splendiferous (*facetious*)
<< OPPOSITE bad
5 CHIEF, highest, lead, leading, head, main, supreme, principal, big-time (*informal*), major league (*informal*), pre-eminent
<< OPPOSITE inferior

grandeur *noun* SPLENDOUR, glory, majesty, nobility, pomp, state, magnificence, sumptuousness, sublimity, stateliness

grandiose *adjective* 1 PRETENTIOUS, ambitious, extravagant, flamboyant, high-flown, pompous, showy, ostentatious, bombastic
<< OPPOSITE unpretentious
2 IMPOSING, grand, impressive, magnificent, majestic, stately, monumental, lofty
<< OPPOSITE humble

grant *noun* AWARD, allowance, donation, endowment, gift, concession, subsidy, hand-out, allocation, bounty, allotment, bequest, stipend
▷ *verb* 1 GIVE, allow, present, award, accord, permit, assign, allocate, hand out, confer on, bestow on, impart on, allot, vouchsafe
2 ACCEPT, allow, admit, acknowledge, concede, cede, accede

granule *noun* GRAIN, scrap, molecule, particle, fragment, atom, crumb, jot, speck, iota

graphic *adjective* 1 VIVID, clear, detailed, striking, telling, explicit, picturesque, forceful, expressive, descriptive, illustrative, well-drawn
<< OPPOSITE vague
2 PICTORIAL, seen, drawn, visible, visual, representational, illustrative, diagrammatic
<< OPPOSITE impressionistic

grapple *verb* 1 DEAL, tackle, cope, face, fight, battle, struggle, take on, engage, encounter, confront, combat, contend, wrestle, tussle, get to grips, do battle, address yourself to
2 STRUGGLE, fight, combat, wrestle, battle, clash, contend, strive, tussle, scuffle, come to grips

grasp *verb* 1 GRIP, hold, catch, grab, seize, snatch, clutch, clinch, clasp, lay *or* take hold of
2 UNDERSTAND, realize, take in, get, see, follow, catch on, comprehend, get the message about, get the picture about, catch *or* get the drift of
▷ *noun* 1 GRIP, hold, possession, embrace, clutches, clasp
2 UNDERSTANDING, knowledge, grip, perception, awareness, realization, mastery, comprehension
3 REACH, power, control, range, sweep, capacity, scope, sway, compass, mastery

grasping *adjective* GREEDY, acquisitive, rapacious, mean, selfish, stingy, penny-pinching (*informal*), venal, miserly, avaricious, niggardly, covetous, tightfisted, close-fisted, snoep (*S African informal*)
<< OPPOSITE generous

grate *verb* 1 SHRED, mince, pulverize
2 SCRAPE, grind, rub, scratch, creak, rasp
▷▷ **grate on someone** *or* **grate on someone's nerves** ANNOY, irritate, aggravate (*informal*), gall, exasperate, nettle, jar, vex, chafe, irk, rankle, peeve, get under your skin (*informal*), get up your nose (*informal*), get on your nerves (*informal*), nark (*Brit, Austral & NZ slang*), set your teeth on edge, get on your wick (*Brit slang*), rub you up the wrong way, hack you off (*informal*)

grateful *adjective* THANKFUL, obliged, in (someone's) debt, indebted, appreciative, beholden

gratification *noun* 1 SATISFACTION, delight, pleasure, joy, thrill, relish, enjoyment, glee, kick *or* kicks (*informal*)
<< OPPOSITE disappointment
2 INDULGENCE, satisfaction, fulfilment
<< OPPOSITE denial

gratify *verb* PLEASE, delight, satisfy, thrill, give pleasure, gladden

grating[1] *noun* GRILLE, grid, grate, lattice, trellis, gridiron

grating[2] *adjective* IRRITATING, grinding, harsh, annoying, jarring, unpleasant, scraping, raucous, strident, squeaky, rasping, discordant, disagreeable, irksome
<< OPPOSITE pleasing

gratitude *noun* THANKFULNESS, thanks, recognition, obligation, appreciation, indebtedness, sense of obligation, gratefulness
<< OPPOSITE ingratitude

gratuitous *adjective* UNJUSTIFIED, unnecessary, needless, unfounded, unwarranted, superfluous, wanton, unprovoked, groundless, baseless, uncalled-for, unmerited, causeless
<< OPPOSITE justifiable

gratuity *noun* TIP, present, gift, reward, bonus, donation, boon, bounty, recompense, perquisite, baksheesh, benefaction, pourboire (*French*), bonsela (*S African*), largesse *or* largess

grave[1] *noun* TOMB, vault, crypt, mausoleum, sepulchre, pit, last resting place, burying place
>> RELATED WORD *adjective* sepulchral

grave[2] *adjective* 1 SERIOUS, important, significant, critical, pressing, threatening, dangerous, vital, crucial, acute, severe, urgent, hazardous, life-and-death, momentous, perilous, weighty, leaden, of great consequence
<< OPPOSITE trifling
2 SOLEMN, sober, gloomy, dull, thoughtful, subdued, sombre, dour, grim-faced, long-faced, unsmiling
<< OPPOSITE carefree

graveyard *noun* CEMETERY, churchyard, burial ground, charnel house, necropolis, boneyard

(*informal*), God's acre (*literary*)
gravitas *noun* SERIOUSNESS, gravity, solemnity
gravitate *verb with* **to** *or* **towards** BE DRAWN, move, tend, lean, be pulled, incline, be attracted, be influenced
gravity *noun* 1 SERIOUSNESS, importance, consequence, significance, urgency, severity, acuteness, moment, weightiness, momentousness, perilousness, hazardousness
<< OPPOSITE triviality
2 SOLEMNITY, gloom, seriousness, gravitas, thoughtfulness, grimness
<< OPPOSITE frivolity
graze[1] *verb* FEED, crop, browse, pasture
graze[2] *verb* 1 SCRATCH, skin, bark, scrape, chafe, abrade
2 TOUCH, brush, rub, scrape, shave, skim, kiss, glance off
▷ *noun* SCRATCH, scrape, abrasion
greasy *adjective* 1 FATTY, slick, slippery, oily, slimy, oleaginous
2 SYCOPHANTIC, fawning, grovelling, ingratiating, smooth, slick, oily, unctuous, smarmy (*Brit informal*), toadying
great *adjective* 1 LARGE, big, huge, vast, enormous, extensive, tremendous, immense, gigantic, mammoth, bulky, colossal, prodigious, stupendous, voluminous, elephantine, ginormous (*informal*), humongous *or* humungous (*US slang*)
<< OPPOSITE small
2 EXTREME, considerable, excessive, high, decided, pronounced, extravagant, prodigious, inordinate
3 MAJOR, lead, leading, chief, main, capital, grand, primary, principal, prominent, superior, paramount, big-time (*informal*), major league (*informal*)
4 IMPORTANT, serious, significant, critical, crucial, heavy, grave, momentous, weighty, consequential
<< OPPOSITE unimportant
5 FAMOUS, celebrated, outstanding, excellent, remarkable, distinguished, prominent, glorious, notable, renowned, eminent, famed, illustrious, exalted, noteworthy
6 EXPERT, skilled, talented, skilful, good, able, masterly, crack (*slang*), superb, world-class, adept, stellar (*informal*), superlative, proficient, adroit
<< OPPOSITE unskilled
7 (*informal*) EXCELLENT, good, fine, wonderful, mean (*slang*), topping (*Brit slang*), cracking (*Brit informal*), superb, fantastic (*informal*), tremendous (*informal*), marvellous (*informal*), terrific (*informal*), mega (*slang*), sovereign, awesome (*slang*), dope (*slang*), admirable, first-rate, def (*informal*), brill (*informal*), boffo (*slang*), bitchin', chillin' (*US slang*), booshit (*Austral slang*), exo (*Austral slang*), sik (*Austral slang*), rad (*informal*), phat (*slang*), schmick (*Austral informal*)
<< OPPOSITE poor
8 VERY, really, particularly, truly, extremely, awfully (*informal*), exceedingly
9 ENTHUSIASTIC, keen, active, devoted, zealous
greatly *adverb* VERY MUCH, much, hugely, vastly, extremely, highly, seriously (*informal*), notably, considerably, remarkably, enormously, immensely, tremendously, markedly, powerfully, exceedingly, mightily, abundantly, by much, by leaps and bounds, to the nth degree
greatness *noun* 1 GRANDEUR, glory, majesty, splendour, power, pomp, magnificence
2 FAME, glory, celebrity, distinction, eminence, note, lustre, renown, illustriousness
greed *or* **greediness** *noun* 1 GLUTTONY, voracity, insatiableness, ravenousness
2 AVARICE, longing, desire, hunger, craving, eagerness, selfishness, acquisitiveness, rapacity, cupidity, covetousness, insatiableness
<< OPPOSITE generosity
greedy *adjective* 1 GLUTTONOUS, insatiable, voracious, ravenous, piggish, hoggish
2 AVARICIOUS, grasping, selfish, insatiable, acquisitive, rapacious, materialistic, desirous, covetous
<< OPPOSITE generous
Greek *adjective* HELLENIC
▷ *noun* HELLENE
green *adjective* 1 VERDANT, leafy, grassy
2 ECOLOGICAL, conservationist, environment-friendly, ecologically sound, eco-friendly, ozone-friendly, non-polluting
3 UNRIPE, fresh, raw, immature
4 INEXPERIENCED, new, innocent, raw, naive, ignorant, immature, gullible, callow, untrained, unsophisticated, credulous, ingenuous, unpolished, wet behind the ears (*informal*)
5 JEALOUS, grudging, resentful, envious, covetous
6 NAUSEOUS, ill, sick, pale, unhealthy, wan, under the weather
▷ *noun* 1 *with capital* ENVIRONMENTALIST, conservationist
2 LAWN, common, turf, sward, grassplot
>> RELATED WORD *adjective* verdant
green light *noun* AUTHORIZATION, sanction, approval, go-ahead (*informal*), blessing, permission, confirmation, clearance, imprimatur, O.K. *or* okay (*informal*)
greet *verb* 1 SALUTE, hail, nod to, say hello to, address, accost, tip your hat to
2 WELCOME, meet, receive, karanga (NZ), mihi (NZ)
3 RECEIVE, take, respond to, react to

greeting *noun* WELCOME, reception, hail, salute, address, salutation, hongi (NZ), kia ora (NZ)
▷ *plural noun* BEST WISHES, regards, respects, compliments, good wishes, salutations

gregarious *adjective* OUTGOING, friendly, social, cordial, sociable, affable, convivial, companionable
<< OPPOSITE unsociable

grey *adjective* 1 DULL, dark, dim, gloomy, cloudy, murky, drab, misty, foggy, overcast, sunless
2 BORING, dull, anonymous, faceless, colourless, nondescript, characterless
3 OLD, aged, ancient, mature, elderly, venerable, hoary
4 PALE, wan, livid, bloodless, colourless, pallid, ashen, like death warmed up (*informal*)
5 AMBIGUOUS, uncertain, neutral, unclear, debatable

gridlock *noun* 1 TRAFFIC JAM
2 DEADLOCK, halt, stalemate, impasse, standstill, full stop

grief *noun* SADNESS, suffering, pain, regret, distress, misery, agony, mourning, sorrow, woe, anguish, remorse, bereavement, heartache, heartbreak, mournfulness
<< OPPOSITE joy
▷▷ **come to grief** (*informal*) FAIL, founder, break down, come unstuck, miscarry, fall flat on your face, meet with disaster

grievance *noun* COMPLAINT, protest, beef (*slang*), gripe (*informal*), axe to grind, chip on your shoulder (*informal*)

grieve *verb* 1 MOURN, suffer, weep, ache, lament, sorrow, wail
2 SADDEN, hurt, injure, distress, wound, crush, pain, afflict, upset, agonize, break the heart of, make your heart bleed
<< OPPOSITE gladden

grievous *adjective* 1 DEPLORABLE, shocking, appalling, dreadful, outrageous, glaring, intolerable, monstrous, shameful, unbearable, atrocious, heinous, lamentable, egregious
<< OPPOSITE pleasant
2 SEVERE, damaging, heavy, wounding, grave, painful, distressing, dreadful, harmful, calamitous, injurious
<< OPPOSITE mild

grim *adjective* TERRIBLE, shocking, severe, harsh, forbidding, horrible, formidable, sinister, ghastly, hideous, gruesome (*slang*), grisly, horrid, frightful, godawful

grimace *verb* SCOWL, frown, sneer, wince, lour *or* lower, make a face *or* faces
▷ *noun* SCOWL, frown, sneer, wince, face, wry face

grime *noun* DIRT, filth, soot, smut, grot (*slang*)

grimy *adjective* DIRTY, polluted, filthy, soiled, foul, grubby, sooty, unclean, grotty (*slang*), smutty, scuzzy (*slang*), begrimed, festy (*Austral slang*)

grind *verb* 1 CRUSH, mill, powder, grate, pulverize, pound, kibble, abrade, granulate
2 PRESS, push, crush, jam, mash, force down
3 GRATE, scrape, grit, gnash
4 SHARPEN, file, polish, sand, smooth, whet
▷ *noun* (*informal*) HARD WORK, labour, effort, task, sweat (*informal*), chore, toil, drudgery
▷▷ **grind someone down** OPPRESS, suppress, harass, subdue, hound, bring down, plague, persecute, subjugate, trample underfoot, tyrannize (over)

grip *verb* 1 GRASP, hold, catch, seize, clutch, clasp, latch on to, take hold of
2 ENGROSS, fascinate, absorb, entrance, hold, catch up, compel, rivet, enthral, mesmerize, spellbind
▷ *noun* 1 CLASP, hold, grasp, handclasp (*US*)
2 CONTROL, rule, influence, command, power, possession, sway, dominance, domination, mastery
3 HOLD, purchase, friction, traction
4 UNDERSTANDING, sense, command, perception, awareness, grasp, appreciation, mastery, comprehension, discernment
▷▷ **come** *or* **get to grips with something** TACKLE, deal with, handle, take on, meet, encounter, cope with, confront, undertake, grasp, face up to, grapple with, close with, contend with

gripe (*informal*) *verb* COMPLAIN, moan, groan, grumble, beef (*slang*), carp, bitch (*slang*), nag, whine, grouse, bleat, grouch (*informal*), bellyache (*slang*), kvetch (*US slang*)
▷ *noun* COMPLAINT, protest, objection, beef (*slang*), moan, grumble, grievance, grouse, grouch (*informal*)

gripping *adjective* FASCINATING, exciting, thrilling, entrancing, compelling, compulsive, riveting, enthralling, engrossing, spellbinding, unputdownable (*informal*)

grisly *adjective* GRUESOME, shocking, terrible, awful, terrifying, appalling, horrible, grim, dreadful, sickening, ghastly, hideous, macabre, horrid, frightful, abominable, hellacious (*US slang*)
<< OPPOSITE pleasant

> Note the spelling of *grisly* (as in *a grisly murder*). It should be carefully distinguished from the word *grizzly* (as in *a grizzly bear*), which means 'greyish in colour'

grit *noun* 1 GRAVEL, sand, dust, pebbles
2 COURAGE, spirit, resolution, determination, nerve, guts (*informal*), pluck, backbone, fortitude, toughness, tenacity, perseverance, mettle, doggedness, hardihood
▷ *verb* CLENCH, grind, grate, gnash

gritty *adjective* 1 ROUGH, sandy, dusty, abrasive, rasping, grainy, gravelly, granular
2 COURAGEOUS, game, dogged, determined, tough, spirited, brave, hardy, feisty (*informal, chiefly US & Canad*), resolute, tenacious, plucky, steadfast, mettlesome, (as) game as Ned Kelly (*Austral slang*)

grizzle *verb* WHINE, fret, whimper, whinge (*informal*), snivel, girn (*Scot*)

grizzled *adjective* GREY, greying, grey-haired, grizzly, hoary, grey-headed

groan *verb* 1 MOAN, cry, sigh
2 (*informal*) COMPLAIN, object, moan, grumble, gripe (*informal*), beef (*slang*), carp, bitch (*slang*), lament, whine, grouse, bemoan, whinge (*informal*), grouch (*informal*), bellyache (*slang*)
▷ *noun* 1 MOAN, cry, sigh, whine
2 (*informal*) COMPLAINT, protest, objection, grumble, beef (*slang*), grouse, gripe (*informal*), grouch (*informal*)

groggy *adjective* DIZZY, faint, stunned, confused, reeling, shaky, dazed, wobbly, weak, unsteady, muzzy, stupefied, befuddled, punch-drunk, woozy (*informal*)

groom *noun* 1 STABLEMAN, stableboy, hostler *or* ostler (*archaic*)
2 NEWLY-WED, husband, bridegroom, marriage partner
▷ *verb* 1 BRUSH, clean, tend, rub down, curry
2 SMARTEN UP, dress, clean, turn out, get up (*informal*), tidy, preen, spruce up, primp, gussy up (*slang, chiefly US*)
3 TRAIN, prime, prepare, coach, ready, educate, drill, nurture, make ready

groove *noun* INDENTATION, cut, hollow, score, channel, trench, flute, gutter, trough, furrow, rut

grope *verb* FEEL, search, fumble, flounder, fish, finger, scrabble, cast about, fossick (*Austral & NZ*)

gross *adjective* 1 FLAGRANT, obvious, glaring, blatant, serious, shocking, rank, plain, sheer, utter, outrageous, manifest, shameful, downright, grievous, unqualified, heinous, egregious, unmitigated, arrant
<< OPPOSITE qualified
2 VULGAR, offensive, crude, rude, obscene, low, coarse, indecent, improper, unseemly, lewd, X-rated (*informal*), impure, smutty, ribald, indelicate
<< OPPOSITE decent
3 COARSE, crass, tasteless, unsophisticated, ignorant, insensitive, callous, boorish, unfeeling, unrefined, uncultured, undiscriminating, imperceptive
<< OPPOSITE cultivated
4 FAT, obese, overweight, great, big, large, heavy, massive, dense, bulky, hulking, corpulent, lumpish
<< OPPOSITE slim
5 TOTAL, whole, entire, aggregate, before tax, before deductions
<< OPPOSITE net
▷ *verb* EARN, make, take, bring in, rake in (*informal*)

grotesque *adjective* 1 UNNATURAL, bizarre, weird, odd, strange, fantastic, distorted, fanciful, deformed, outlandish, whimsical, freakish, misshapen, malformed
<< OPPOSITE natural
2 ABSURD, ridiculous, ludicrous, preposterous, incongruous
<< OPPOSITE natural

grouch *verb* COMPLAIN, moan, grumble, beef (*slang*), carp, bitch (*slang*), whine, grouse, gripe (*informal*), whinge (*informal*), bleat, find fault, bellyache (*slang*), kvetch (*US slang*)
▷ *noun* 1 MOANER, complainer, grumbler, whiner, grouser, malcontent, curmudgeon, crosspatch (*informal*), crab (*informal*), faultfinder
2 COMPLAINT, protest, objection, grievance, moan, grumble, beef (*slang*), grouse, gripe (*informal*)

grouchy *adjective* BAD-TEMPERED, cross, irritable, grumpy, discontented, grumbling, surly, petulant, sulky, ill-tempered, irascible, cantankerous, tetchy, ratty (*Brit & NZ informal*), testy, querulous, peevish, huffy, liverish

ground *noun* 1 EARTH, land, dry land, terra firma
2 ARENA, pitch, stadium, park (*informal*), field, enclosure
▷ *plural noun* 1 ESTATE, holding, land, fields, gardens, property, district, territory, domain
2 REASON, cause, basis, argument, call, base, occasion, foundation, excuse, premise, motive, justification, rationale, inducement
3 DREGS, lees, deposit, sediment
▷ *verb* 1 BASE, found, establish, set, settle, fix
2 INSTRUCT, train, prepare, coach, teach, inform, initiate, tutor, acquaint with, familiarize with

groundless *adjective* BASELESS, false, unfounded, unjustified, unproven, empty, unauthorized, unsubstantiated, unsupported, uncorroborated
<< OPPOSITE well-founded

groundwork *noun* PRELIMINARIES, basis, foundation, base, footing, preparation, fundamentals, cornerstone, underpinnings, spadework

group *noun* 1 CROWD, company, party, band, troop, pack, gathering, gang, bunch, congregation, posse (*slang*), bevy, assemblage
2 CLUSTER, formation, clump, aggregation
▷ *verb* 1 ARRANGE, order, sort, class, range, gather, organize, assemble, put together, classify, marshal, bracket, assort

2 UNITE, associate, gather, cluster, get together, congregate, band together

grouse *verb* COMPLAIN, moan, grumble, gripe (*informal*), beef (*slang*), carp, bitch (*slang*), whine, whinge (*informal*), bleat, find fault, grouch (*informal*), bellyache (*slang*), kvetch (*US slang*)
▷ *noun* COMPLAINT, protest, objection, moan, grievance, grumble, gripe (*informal*), beef (*slang*), grouch (*informal*)

grove *noun* WOOD, woodland, plantation, covert, thicket, copse, brake, coppice, spinney

grovel *verb* HUMBLE YOURSELF, creep, crawl, flatter, fawn, pander, cower, toady, kowtow, bow and scrape, lick someone's boots, demean yourself, abase yourself
<< OPPOSITE hold your head high

grow *verb* 1 DEVELOP, fill out, get bigger, get taller
<< OPPOSITE shrink
2 GET BIGGER, spread, swell, extend, stretch, expand, widen, enlarge, multiply, thicken
3 SPRING UP, shoot up, develop, flourish, sprout, germinate, vegetate
4 CULTIVATE, produce, raise, farm, breed, nurture, propagate
5 BECOME, get, turn, come to be
6 ORIGINATE, spring, arise, stem, issue
7 IMPROVE, advance, progress, succeed, expand, thrive, flourish, prosper

grown-up *noun* ADULT, man, woman
▷ *adjective* MATURE, adult, of age, fully-grown

growth *noun* 1 INCREASE, development, expansion, extension, growing, heightening, proliferation, enlargement, multiplication
<< OPPOSITE decline
2 PROGRESS, success, improvement, expansion, advance, prosperity, advancement
<< OPPOSITE failure
3 VEGETATION, development, production, sprouting, germination, shooting
4 (*Medical*) TUMOUR, cancer, swelling, lump, carcinoma (*Pathology*), sarcoma (*Medical*), excrescence

grub *noun* 1 LARVA, maggot, caterpillar
2 (*Slang*) FOOD, feed, rations, tack (*informal*), eats (*slang*), kai (*NZ informal*), sustenance, nosh (*slang*), victuals, nosebag (*slang*), vittles (*obsolete or dialect*)
▷ *verb* 1 SEARCH, hunt, scour, ferret, rummage, forage, fossick (*Austral & NZ*)
2 DIG, search, root (*informal*), probe, burrow, rootle (*Brit*)

grubby *adjective* DIRTY, soiled, filthy, squalid, messy, shabby, seedy, scruffy, sordid, untidy, grimy, unwashed, unkempt, mucky, smutty, grungy (*slang, chiefly US & Canad*), slovenly, manky (*Scot dialect*), scuzzy (*slang*), scungy (*Austral & NZ*), frowzy, besmeared, festy (*Austral slang*)

grudge *noun* RESENTMENT, bitterness, grievance, malice, hate, spite, dislike, animosity, aversion, venom, antipathy, enmity, rancour, hard feelings, ill will, animus, malevolence
<< OPPOSITE goodwill
▷ *verb* RESENT, mind, envy, covet, begrudge
<< OPPOSITE welcome

gruelling *adjective* EXHAUSTING, demanding, difficult, tiring, trying, hard, taxing, grinding, severe, crushing, fierce, punishing, harsh, stiff, brutal, fatiguing, strenuous, arduous, laborious, backbreaking
<< OPPOSITE easy

gruesome *adjective* HORRIFIC, shocking, terrible, awful, horrible, grim, horrifying, fearful, obscene, horrendous, ghastly, hideous, from hell (*informal*), grisly, macabre, horrid, repulsive, repugnant, loathsome, abominable, spine-chilling, hellacious (*US slang*)
<< OPPOSITE pleasant

gruff *adjective* 1 HOARSE, rough, harsh, rasping, husky, low, croaking, throaty, guttural
<< OPPOSITE mellifluous
2 SURLY, rough, rude, grumpy, blunt, crabbed, crusty, sullen, bad-tempered, curt, churlish, brusque, impolite, grouchy (*informal*), ungracious, discourteous, uncivil, ill-humoured, unmannerly, ill-natured
<< OPPOSITE polite

grumble *verb* 1 COMPLAIN, moan, gripe (*informal*), whinge (*informal*), beef (*slang*), carp, bitch (*slang*), whine, grouse, bleat, grouch (*informal*), bellyache (*slang*), kvetch (*US slang*), repine
2 RUMBLE, growl, gurgle
▷ *noun* 1 COMPLAINT, protest, objection, moan, grievance, grouse, gripe (*informal*), grouch (*informal*), beef (*slang*)
2 RUMBLE, growl, gurgle

grumpy *adjective* IRRITABLE, cross, bad-tempered, grumbling, crabbed, edgy, surly, petulant, ill-tempered, cantankerous, tetchy, ratty (*Brit & NZ informal*), testy, grouchy (*informal*), querulous, peevish, huffy, crotchety (*informal*), liverish

guarantee *verb* 1 ENSURE, secure, assure, warrant, insure, make certain
2 PROMISE, pledge, undertake, swear
▷ *noun* 1 PROMISE, word, pledge, undertaking, assurance, certainty, covenant, word of honour
2 WARRANTY, contract, bond, guaranty

guarantor *noun* UNDERWRITER, guarantee, supporter, sponsor, backer, surety, warrantor

guard *verb* PROTECT, watch, defend, secure, police, mind, cover, screen, preserve, shelter, shield, patrol, oversee, safeguard, watch over
▷ *noun* 1 SENTRY, warder, warden, custodian, watch, patrol, lookout, watchman, sentinel

2 ESCORT, patrol, convoy
3 SHIELD, security, defence, screen, protection, pad, safeguard, bumper, buffer, rampart, bulwark
▷▷ **off (your) guard** UNPREPARED, napping, unwary, unready, with your defences down
▷▷ **on (your) guard** VIGILANT, cautious, wary, prepared, ready, alert, watchful, on the lookout, circumspect, on the alert, on the qui vive
>> RELATED WORD *adjective* custodial

guarded *adjective* CAUTIOUS, reserved, careful, suspicious, restrained, wary, discreet, prudent, reticent, circumspect, cagey (*informal*), leery (*slang*), noncommittal

guardian *noun* KEEPER, champion, defender, guard, trustee, warden, curator, protector, warder, custodian, preserver

guerrilla *noun* FREEDOM FIGHTER, partisan, irregular, underground fighter, member of the underground *or* resistance

guess *verb* 1 ESTIMATE, predict, work out, speculate, fathom, conjecture, postulate, surmise, hazard a guess, hypothesize
<< OPPOSITE know
2 SUPPOSE, think, believe, suspect, judge, imagine, reckon, fancy, conjecture, dare say
▷ *noun* 1 ESTIMATE, reckoning, speculation, judgment, hypothesis, conjecture, surmise, shot in the dark, ballpark figure (*informal*)
<< OPPOSITE certainty
2 SUPPOSITION, feeling, idea, theory, notion, suspicion, hypothesis

guesswork *noun* SPECULATION, theory, presumption, conjecture, estimation, surmise, supposition

guest *noun* VISITOR, company, caller, manu(w)hiri (NZ)

guff *noun* (*informal*) NONSENSE, rubbish, rot, crap (*slang*), garbage (*informal*), trash, hot air (*informal*), tosh (*slang, chiefly Brit*), pap, bilge (*informal*), humbug, drivel, tripe (*informal*), moonshine, hogwash, hokum (*slang, chiefly US & Canad*), piffle (*informal*), poppycock (*informal*), balderdash, bosh (*informal*), eyewash (*informal*), kak (*S African taboo slang*), empty talk, tommyrot, horsefeathers (*US slang*), bunkum *or* buncombe (*chiefly US*), bizzo (*Austral slang*), bull's wool (*Austral & NZ slang*)

guidance *noun* ADVICE, direction, leadership, instruction, government, help, control, management, teaching, counsel, counselling, auspices

guide *noun* 1 HANDBOOK, manual, guidebook, instructions, catalogue
2 DIRECTORY, street map
3 ESCORT, leader, controller, attendant, usher, chaperon, torchbearer, dragoman
4 POINTER, sign, signal, mark, key, clue, landmark, marker, beacon, signpost, guiding light, lodestar
5 MODEL, example, standard, ideal, master, inspiration, criterion, paradigm, exemplar, lodestar
▷ *verb* 1 LEAD, direct, escort, conduct, pilot, accompany, steer, shepherd, convoy, usher, show the way
2 STEER, control, manage, direct, handle, command, manoeuvre
3 SUPERVISE, train, rule, teach, influence, advise, counsel, govern, educate, regulate, instruct, oversee, sway, superintend

guild *noun* SOCIETY, union, league, association, company, club, order, organization, corporation, lodge, fellowship, fraternity, brotherhood

guile *noun* CUNNING, craft, deception, deceit, trickery, duplicity, cleverness, art, gamesmanship (*informal*), craftiness, artfulness, slyness, trickiness, wiliness
<< OPPOSITE honesty

guilt *noun* 1 SHAME, regret, remorse, contrition, guilty conscience, bad conscience, self-reproach, self-condemnation, guiltiness
<< OPPOSITE pride
2 CULPABILITY, blame, responsibility, misconduct, delinquency, criminality, wickedness, iniquity, sinfulness, blameworthiness, guiltiness
<< OPPOSITE innocence

guilty *adjective* 1 ASHAMED, sorry, rueful, sheepish, contrite, remorseful, regretful, shamefaced, hangdog, conscience-stricken
<< OPPOSITE proud
2 CULPABLE, responsible, convicted, to blame, offending, erring, at fault, reprehensible, iniquitous, felonious, blameworthy
<< OPPOSITE innocent

guise *noun* 1 FORM, appearance, dress, fashion, shape, aspect, mode, semblance
2 PRETENCE, show, mask, disguise, face, front, aspect, façade, semblance

gulch *noun* (*US & Canad*) RAVINE, canyon, defile, gorge, gully, pass

gulf *noun* 1 BAY, bight, sea inlet
2 CHASM, opening, split, gap, rent, breach, separation, void, rift, abyss, cleft

gullible *adjective* TRUSTING, innocent, naive, unsuspecting, green, simple, silly, foolish, unsophisticated, credulous, born yesterday, wet behind the ears (*informal*), easily taken in, unsceptical, as green as grass
<< OPPOSITE suspicious

gully *noun* RAVINE, canyon, gorge, chasm, channel, fissure, defile, watercourse

gulp *verb* 1 SWALLOW, bolt, devour, gobble, knock back (*informal*), wolf, swig (*informal*),

swill, guzzle, quaff
2 GASP, swallow, choke
▷ *noun* SWALLOW, draught, mouthful, swig (*informal*)

gum *noun* GLUE, adhesive, resin, cement, paste
▷ *verb* STICK, glue, affix, cement, paste, clog

gun *noun* FIREARM, shooter (*slang*), piece (*slang*), rod (*slang*), heater (*US slang*), handgun

gunman *noun* ARMED MAN, hit man (*slang*), gunslinger (*US slang*)

gurgle *verb* RIPPLE, lap, bubble, splash, murmur, babble, burble, purl, plash
▷ *noun* BURBLE, chuckle, ripple, babble

guru *noun* **1** AUTHORITY, expert, leader, master, pundit, arbiter, Svengali, torchbearer, fundi (*S African*)
2 TEACHER, mentor, sage, master, tutor, mahatma, guiding light, swami, maharishi

gush *verb* **1** FLOW, run, rush, flood, pour, jet, burst, stream, cascade, issue, spurt, spout
2 ENTHUSE, rave, spout, overstate, rhapsodize, effuse
▷ *noun* STREAM, flow, rush, flood, jet, burst, issue, outburst, cascade, torrent, spurt, spout, outflow

gust *noun* **1** BLAST, blow, rush, breeze, puff, gale, flurry, squall
2 SURGE, fit, storm, burst, explosion, gale, outburst, eruption, paroxysm
▷ *verb* BLOW, blast, puff, squall

gusto *noun* RELISH, enthusiasm, appetite, appreciation, liking, delight, pleasure, enjoyment, savour, zeal, verve, zest, fervour, exhilaration, brio, zing (*informal*)
<< OPPOSITE apathy

gusty *adjective* WINDY, stormy, breezy, blustering, tempestuous, blustery, inclement, squally, blowy

gut *noun* (*informal*) PAUNCH, belly, spare tyre (*Brit slang*), potbelly, puku (*NZ*)
▷ *verb* **1** DISEMBOWEL, draw, dress, clean, eviscerate
2 RAVAGE, strip, empty, sack, rifle, plunder, clean out, ransack, pillage, despoil
▷ *adjective* INSTINCTIVE, natural, basic, emotional, spontaneous, innate, intuitive, involuntary, heartfelt, deep-seated, unthinking
>> RELATED WORD *technical name* viscera
>> RELATED WORD *adjective* visceral

guts *plural noun* **1** INTESTINES, insides (*informal*), stomach, belly, bowels, inwards, innards (*informal*), entrails
2 (*informal*) COURAGE, spirit, nerve, daring, pluck, grit, backbone, willpower, bottle (*slang*), audacity, mettle, boldness, spunk (*informal*), forcefulness, hardihood

gutsy *adjective* BRAVE, determined, spirited, bold, have-a-go (*informal*), courageous, gritty, staunch, feisty (*informal, chiefly US & Canad*), game (*informal*), resolute, gallant, plucky, indomitable, mettlesome, (as) game as Ned Kelly (*Austral slang*)

gutter *noun* DRAIN, channel, tube, pipe, ditch, trench, trough, conduit, duct, sluice

guy *noun* (*informal*) MAN, person, fellow, lad, cat (*dated slang*), bloke (*Brit informal*), chap

guzzle *verb* DEVOUR, drink, bolt, wolf, cram, gorge, gobble, knock back (*informal*), swill, quaff, tope, pig out on (*slang*), stuff yourself with

Gypsy or **Gipsy** *noun* TRAVELLER, roamer, wanderer, Bohemian, rover, rambler, nomad, vagrant, Romany, vagabond

gyrate *verb* ROTATE, circle, spin, spiral, revolve, whirl, twirl, pirouette

Hh

habit *noun* 1 MANNERISM, custom, way, practice, manner, characteristic, tendency, quirk, propensity, foible, proclivity
2 CUSTOM, rule, practice, tradition, routine, convention, mode, usage, wont, second nature
3 ADDICTION, weakness, obsession, dependence, compulsion, fixation
4 DRESS, costume, garment, apparel, garb, habiliment, riding dress

habitat *noun* HOME, environment, surroundings, element, territory, domain, terrain, locality, home ground, abode, habitation, natural home

habitation *noun* 1 OCCUPATION, living in, residence, tenancy, occupancy, residency, inhabitance, inhabitancy
2 (*Formal*) DWELLING, home, house, residence, quarters, lodging, pad (*slang*), abode, living quarters, domicile, dwelling house

habitual *adjective* 1 CUSTOMARY, normal, usual, common, standard, natural, traditional, fixed, regular, ordinary, familiar, routine, accustomed, wonted
<< OPPOSITE unusual
2 PERSISTENT, established, confirmed, constant, frequent, chronic, hardened, recurrent, ingrained, inveterate
<< OPPOSITE occasional

hack[1] *verb* 1 CUT, chop, slash, mutilate, mangle, mangulate (*Austral slang*), gash, hew, lacerate
2 (*informal*) COUGH, bark, wheeze, rasp
▷ *noun* (*informal*) COUGH, bark, wheeze, rasp

hack[2] *noun* 1 REPORTER, writer, correspondent, journalist, scribbler, contributor, literary hack, penny-a-liner, Grub Street writer
2 YES-MAN, lackey, toady, flunky
▷ *adjective* UNORIGINAL, pedestrian, mediocre, poor, tired, stereotyped, banal, undistinguished, uninspired

hackles ▷▷ **raise someone's hackles** *or* **make someone's hackles rise** ANGER, annoy, infuriate, cause resentment, rub someone up the wrong way, make someone see red (*informal*), get someone's dander up (*slang*), hack you off (*informal*)

hackneyed *adjective* CLICHÉD, stock, tired, common, stereotyped, pedestrian, played out (*informal*), commonplace, worn-out, stale, overworked, banal, run-of-the-mill, threadbare, trite, unoriginal, timeworn
<< OPPOSITE original

Hades *noun* UNDERWORLD, hell, nether regions, lower world, infernal regions, realm of Pluto, (the) inferno

hag *noun* WITCH, virago, shrew, vixen, crone, fury, harridan, beldam (*archaic*), termagant

haggard *adjective* GAUNT, wasted, drawn, thin, pinched, wrinkled, ghastly, wan, emaciated, shrunken, careworn, hollow-eyed
<< OPPOSITE robust

haggle *verb* 1 BARGAIN, barter, beat down, drive a hard bargain, dicker (*chiefly US*), chaffer, palter, higgle
2 WRANGLE, dispute, quarrel, squabble, bicker

hail[1] *noun* 1 HAILSTONES, sleet, hailstorm, frozen rain
2 SHOWER, rain, storm, battery, volley, barrage, bombardment, pelting, downpour, salvo, broadside
▷ *verb* 1 RAIN, shower, pelt
2 BATTER, rain, barrage, bombard, pelt, rain down on, beat down upon

hail[2] *verb* 1 ACCLAIM, honour, acknowledge, cheer, applaud, glorify, exalt
<< OPPOSITE condemn
2 SALUTE, call, greet, address, welcome, speak to, shout to, say hello to, accost, sing out, halloo
<< OPPOSITE snub
3 FLAG DOWN, summon, signal to, wave down
▷▷ **hail from somewhere** COME FROM, be born in, originate in, be a native of, have your roots in

hair *noun* LOCKS, mane, tresses, shock, mop, head of hair
▷▷ **let your hair down** LET YOURSELF GO,

relax, chill out (*slang, chiefly US*), let off steam (*informal*), let it all hang out (*informal*), mellow out (*informal*), veg out (*slang, chiefly US*), outspan (*S African*)
▷▷ **not turn a hair** REMAIN CALM, keep your cool (*slang*), not bat an eyelid, keep your hair on (*Brit informal*)
▷▷ **split hairs** QUIBBLE, find fault, cavil, overrefine, pettifog

hairdresser *noun* STYLIST, barber, coiffeur *or* coiffeuse, friseur

hair-raising *adjective* FRIGHTENING, shocking, alarming, thrilling, exciting, terrifying, startling, horrifying, scary, breathtaking, creepy, petrifying, spine-chilling, bloodcurdling

hairstyle *noun* HAIRCUT, hairdo, coiffure, cut, style

hairy *adjective* **1** SHAGGY, woolly, furry, stubbly, bushy, bearded, unshaven, hirsute, fleecy, bewhiskered, pileous (*Biology*), pilose (*Biology*)
2 (*Slang*) DANGEROUS, scary, risky, unpredictable, hazardous, perilous

halcyon *adjective* **1** HAPPY, golden, flourishing, prosperous, carefree, palmy
2 PEACEFUL, still, quiet, calm, gentle, mild, serene, tranquil, placid, pacific, undisturbed, unruffled

hale *adjective* (*Old-fashioned*) HEALTHY, well, strong, sound, fit, flourishing, blooming, robust, vigorous, hearty, in the pink, in fine fettle, right as rain (*Brit informal*), able-bodied

half *noun* FIFTY PER CENT, equal part
▷ *adjective* PARTIAL, limited, fractional, divided, moderate, halved, incomplete
▷ *adverb* PARTIALLY, partly, incompletely, slightly, all but, barely, in part, inadequately, after a fashion, pretty nearly
>> RELATED WORDS *prefixes* bi-, hemi-, demi-, semi-

half-baked *adjective* (*informal*) STUPID, impractical, crazy, silly, foolish, senseless, short-sighted, inane, loopy (*informal*), ill-conceived, crackpot (*informal*), ill-judged, brainless, unformed, poorly planned, harebrained, dumb-ass (*slang*), unthought out *or* through

half-hearted *adjective* UNENTHUSIASTIC, indifferent, apathetic, cool, neutral, passive, lacklustre, lukewarm, uninterested, perfunctory, listless, spiritless
<< OPPOSITE enthusiastic

halfway *adverb* **1** MIDWAY, to the midpoint, to *or* in the middle
2 (*informal*) PARTIALLY, partly, moderately, rather, nearly
▷ *adjective* MIDWAY, middle, mid, central, intermediate, equidistant
▷▷ **meet someone halfway** COMPROMISE, accommodate, come to terms, reach a compromise, strike a balance, trade off with, find the middle ground

hall *noun* **1** PASSAGE, lobby, corridor, hallway, foyer, entry, passageway, entrance hall, vestibule
2 MEETING PLACE, chamber, auditorium, concert hall, assembly room

hallmark *noun* **1** TRADEMARK, indication, badge, emblem, sure sign, telltale sign
2 (*Brit*) MARK, sign, device, stamp, seal, symbol, signet, authentication

hallowed *adjective* SANCTIFIED, holy, blessed, sacred, honoured, dedicated, revered, consecrated, sacrosanct, inviolable, beatified

hallucinate *verb* IMAGINE, trip (*informal*), envision, daydream, fantasize, freak out (*informal*), have hallucinations

hallucination *noun* ILLUSION, dream, vision, fantasy, delusion, mirage, apparition, phantasmagoria, figment of the imagination

hallucinogenic *adjective* PSYCHEDELIC, mind-blowing (*informal*), psychoactive, hallucinatory, psychotropic, mind-expanding

halo *noun* RING OF LIGHT, aura, corona, radiance, nimbus, halation (*Photography*), aureole *or* aureola

halt *verb* **1** STOP, draw up, pull up, break off, stand still, wait, rest, call it a day, belay (*Nautical*)
<< OPPOSITE continue
2 COME TO AN END, stop, cease
3 HOLD BACK, end, check, block, arrest, stem, curb, terminate, obstruct, staunch, cut short, impede, bring to an end, stem the flow, nip in the bud
<< OPPOSITE aid
▷ *noun* STOP, end, close, break, stand, arrest, pause, interruption, impasse, standstill, stoppage, termination
<< OPPOSITE continuation

halting *adjective* FALTERING, stumbling, awkward, hesitant, laboured, stammering, imperfect, stuttering

halve *verb* **1** CUT IN HALF, reduce by fifty per cent, decrease by fifty per cent, lessen by fifty per cent
2 SPLIT IN TWO, cut in half, bisect, divide in two, share equally, divide equally

hammer *verb* **1** HIT, drive, knock, beat, strike, tap, bang
2 *often with* **into** IMPRESS UPON, repeat, drive home, drum into, grind into, din into, drub into
3 (*informal*) DEFEAT, beat, thrash, stuff (*slang*), master, worst, tank (*slang*), lick (*informal*), slate (*informal*), trounce, clobber (*slang*), run rings around (*informal*), wipe the floor with (*informal*), blow out of the water (*slang*), drub

▷▷ **hammer away at something** WORK, keep on, persevere, grind, persist, stick at, plug away (*informal*), drudge, pound away, peg away (*chiefly Brit*), beaver away (*Brit informal*)

hamper *verb* HINDER, handicap, hold up, prevent, restrict, frustrate, curb, slow down, restrain, hamstring, interfere with, cramp, thwart, obstruct, impede, hobble, fetter, encumber, trammel

<< OPPOSITE help

hamstring *verb* THWART, stop, block, prevent, ruin, frustrate, handicap, curb, foil, obstruct, impede, balk, fetter

hamstrung *adjective* INCAPACITATED, disabled, crippled, helpless, paralysed, at a loss, hors de combat (*French*)

hand *noun* **1** PALM, fist, paw (*informal*), mitt (*slang*), hook, meathook (*slang*)
2 INFLUENCE, part, share, agency, direction, participation
3 ASSISTANCE, help, aid, support, helping hand
4 WORKER, employee, labourer, workman, operative, craftsman, artisan, hired man, hireling
5 ROUND OF APPLAUSE, clap, ovation, big hand
6 WRITING, script, handwriting, calligraphy, longhand, penmanship, chirography
▷ *verb* **1** GIVE, pass, hand over, present to, deliver
2 HELP, guide, conduct, lead, aid, assist, convey

▷▷ **at** *or* **on hand** WITHIN REACH, nearby, handy, close, available, ready, on tap (*informal*), at your fingertips

▷▷ **hand in glove** IN ASSOCIATION, in partnership, in league, in collaboration, in cooperation, in cahoots (*informal*)

▷▷ **hand over fist** SWIFTLY, easily, steadily, by leaps and bounds

▷▷ **hand something down** PASS ON *or* DOWN, pass, transfer, bequeath, will, give, grant, gift, endow

▷▷ **hand something on** PASS ON *or* DOWN, pass, transfer, bequeath, will, give, grant, relinquish

▷▷ **hand something** *or* **someone over 1** GIVE, present, deliver, donate
2 TURN OVER, release, transfer, deliver, yield, surrender

▷▷ **hands down** EASILY, effortlessly, with ease, comfortably, without difficulty, with no trouble, standing on your head, with one hand tied behind your back, with no contest, with your eyes closed *or* shut

▷▷ **in hand 1** IN RESERVE, ready, put by, available for use
2 UNDER CONTROL, in order, receiving attention

▷▷ **lay hands on someone 1** ATTACK, assault, set on, beat up, work over (*slang*), lay into (*informal*)
2 BLESS (*Christianity*), confirm, ordain, consecrate

▷▷ **lay hands on something** GET HOLD OF, get, obtain, gain, grab, acquire, seize, grasp

>> RELATED WORD *adjective* manual

handbook *noun* GUIDEBOOK, guide, manual, instruction book, Baedeker, vade mecum

handcuff *verb* SHACKLE, secure, restrain, fetter, manacle
▷ *plural noun* SHACKLES, cuffs (*informal*), fetters, manacles, bracelets (*slang*)

handful *noun* FEW, sprinkling, small amount, small quantity, smattering, small number

<< OPPOSITE a lot

handgun *noun* PISTOL, automatic, revolver, shooter (*informal*), piece (*US slang*), rod (*US slang*), derringer

handicap *noun* **1** DISABILITY, defect, impairment, physical abnormality
2 DISADVANTAGE, block, barrier, restriction, obstacle, limitation, hazard, drawback, shortcoming, stumbling block, impediment, albatross, hindrance, millstone, encumbrance

<< OPPOSITE advantage

3 ADVANTAGE, penalty, head start
▷ *verb* HINDER, limit, restrict, burden, hamstring, hamper, hold back, retard, impede, hobble, encumber, place at a disadvantage

<< OPPOSITE help

handicraft *noun* SKILL, art, craft, handiwork

handily *adverb* **1** CONVENIENTLY, readily, suitably, helpfully, advantageously, accessibly
2 SKILFULLY, expertly, cleverly, deftly, adroitly, capably, proficiently, dexterously

handiwork *noun* CREATION, product, production, achievement, result, design, invention, artefact, handicraft, handwork

handkerchief *noun* HANKY (*informal*), tissue, mouchoir, snot rag (*slang*), nose rag (*slang*)

handle *noun* GRIP, knob, hilt, haft, stock, handgrip, helve
▷ *verb* **1** MANAGE, deal with, tackle, cope with
2 DEAL WITH, manage, take care of, administer, conduct, supervise
3 CONTROL, manage, direct, operate, guide, use, steer, manipulate, manoeuvre, wield
4 HOLD, feel, touch, pick up, finger, grasp, poke, paw (*informal*), maul, fondle
5 DEAL IN, market, sell, trade in, carry, stock, traffic in
6 DISCUSS, report, treat, review, tackle, examine, discourse on

▷▷ **fly off the handle** (*informal*) LOSE YOUR TEMPER, explode, lose it (*informal*), lose the plot (*informal*), let fly (*informal*), go ballistic (*slang, chiefly US*), fly into a rage, have a tantrum, wig out (*slang*), lose your cool (*slang*), blow your top, flip your lid (*slang*), hit *or* go through the roof (*informal*)

handling *noun* MANAGEMENT, running, treatment, approach, administration, conduct, manipulation

hand-out *noun* **1** *often plural* CHARITY, dole, alms, pogey (*Canad*)
2 PRESS RELEASE, bulletin, circular, mailshot
3 LEAFLET, literature (*informal*), bulletin, flyer, pamphlet, printed matter
4 GIVEAWAY, freebie (*informal*), free gift, free sample

hand-picked *adjective* SELECTED, chosen, choice, select, elect, elite, recherché
<< OPPOSITE random

handsome *adjective* **1** GOOD-LOOKING, attractive, gorgeous, fine, stunning, elegant, personable, nice-looking, dishy (*informal, chiefly Brit*), comely, fanciable, well-proportioned
<< OPPOSITE ugly
2 GENEROUS, large, princely, liberal, considerable, lavish, ample, abundant, plentiful, bountiful, sizable *or* sizeable
<< OPPOSITE mean

handsomely *adverb* GENEROUSLY, amply, richly, liberally, lavishly, abundantly, plentifully, bountifully, munificently

handwriting *noun* WRITING, hand, script, fist, scrawl, calligraphy, longhand, penmanship, chirography
>> RELATED WORD *noun* graphology

handy *adjective* **1** USEFUL, practical, helpful, neat, convenient, easy to use, manageable, user-friendly, serviceable
<< OPPOSITE useless
2 CONVENIENT, close, near, available, nearby, accessible, on hand, at hand, within reach, just round the corner, at your fingertips
<< OPPOSITE inconvenient
3 SKILFUL, skilled, expert, clever, adept, ready, deft, nimble, proficient, adroit, dexterous
<< OPPOSITE unskilled

handyman *noun* ODD-JOBMAN, jack-of-all-trades, handy Andy (*informal*), DIY expert

hang *verb* **1** DANGLE, swing, suspend, be pendent
2 LOWER, suspend, dangle, let down, let droop
3 LEAN, incline, loll, bend forward, bow, bend downward
4 DROOP, drop, dangle, trail, sag
5 DECORATE, cover, fix, attach, deck, furnish, drape, fasten
6 EXECUTE, lynch, string up (*informal*), gibbet, send to the gallows
7 HOVER, float, drift, linger, remain
▷▷ **get the hang of something** GRASP, understand, learn, master, comprehend, catch on to, acquire the technique of, get the knack *or* technique of
▷▷ **hang about** *or* **around** LOITER, frequent, haunt, linger, roam, loaf, waste time, dally, dawdle, skulk, tarry, dilly-dally (*informal*)
▷▷ **hang around with someone** ASSOCIATE WITH, go around with, mix with, hang with (*informal, chiefly US*), hang out with (*informal*)
▷▷ **hang back** BE RELUCTANT, hesitate, hold back, recoil, demur, be backward
▷▷ **hang fire** PUT OFF, delay, stall, be slow, vacillate, hang back, procrastinate
▷▷ **hang on** (*informal*) **1** WAIT, stop, hold on, hold the line, remain
2 CONTINUE, remain, go on, carry on, endure, hold on, persist, hold out, persevere, stay the course
3 GRASP, grip, clutch, cling, hold fast
▷▷ **hang on** *or* **upon something 1** DEPEND ON, turn on, rest on, be subject to, hinge on, be determined by, be dependent on, be conditional on, be contingent on
2 LISTEN ATTENTIVELY TO, pay attention to, be rapt, give ear to

hanger-on *noun* PARASITE, follower, cohort (*chiefly US*), leech, dependant, minion, lackey, sycophant, freeloader (*slang*), sponger (*informal*), ligger (*slang*), quandong (*Austral slang*)

hanging *adjective* SUSPENDED, swinging, dangling, loose, flopping, flapping, floppy, drooping, unattached, unsupported, pendent

hang-out *noun* HAUNT, joint (*slang*), resort, dive (*slang*), den

hangover *noun* AFTEREFFECTS, morning after (*informal*), head (*informal*), crapulence

hang-up *noun* (*informal*) PREOCCUPATION, thing (*informal*), problem, block, difficulty, obsession, mania, inhibition, phobia, fixation

hank *noun* COIL, roll, length, bunch, piece, loop, clump, skein

hanker after *or* **for** *verb* DESIRE, want, long for, hope for, crave, covet, wish for, yearn for, pine for, lust after, eat your heart out, ache for, yen for (*informal*), itch for, set your heart on, hunger for *or* after, thirst for *or* after

hankering *noun* DESIRE, longing, wish, hope, urge, yen (*informal*), pining, hunger, ache, craving, yearning, itch, thirst

haphazard *adjective* **1** UNSYSTEMATIC, disorderly, disorganized, casual, careless, indiscriminate, aimless, slapdash, slipshod, hit or miss (*informal*), unmethodical
<< OPPOSITE systematic
2 RANDOM, chance, accidental, arbitrary, fluky (*informal*)
<< OPPOSITE planned

hapless *adjective* UNLUCKY, unfortunate, cursed, unhappy, miserable, jinxed, luckless, wretched, ill-starred, ill-fated

happen *verb* **1** OCCUR, take place, come about,

follow, result, appear, develop, arise, come off (*informal*), ensue, crop up (*informal*), transpire (*informal*), materialize, present itself, come to pass, see the light of day, eventuate
2 CHANCE, turn out (*informal*), have the fortune to be
3 BEFALL, overtake, become of, betide
▷▷ **happen on** *or* **upon something** FIND, encounter, run into, come upon, turn up, stumble on, hit upon, chance upon, light upon, blunder on, discover unexpectedly

happening *noun* EVENT, incident, occasion, case, experience, chance, affair, scene, accident, proceeding, episode, adventure, phenomenon, occurrence, escapade

happily *adverb* 1 LUCKILY, fortunately, providentially, favourably, auspiciously, opportunely, propitiously, seasonably
2 JOYFULLY, cheerfully, gleefully, blithely, merrily, gaily, joyously, delightedly
3 WILLINGLY, freely, gladly, enthusiastically, heartily, with pleasure, contentedly, lief (*rare*)

happiness *noun* PLEASURE, delight, joy, cheer, satisfaction, prosperity, ecstasy, enjoyment, bliss, felicity, exuberance, contentment, wellbeing, high spirits, elation, gaiety, jubilation, merriment, cheerfulness, gladness, beatitude, cheeriness, blessedness, light-heartedness
<< OPPOSITE unhappiness

happy *adjective* 1 PLEASED, delighted, content, contented, thrilled, glad, blessed, blest, sunny, cheerful, jolly, merry, ecstatic, gratified, jubilant, joyous, joyful, elated, over the moon (*informal*), overjoyed, blissful, rapt, blithe, on cloud nine (*informal*), cock-a-hoop, walking on air (*informal*), floating on air, stoked (*Austral & NZ informal*)
2 CONTENTED, blessed, blest, joyful, blissful, blithe
<< OPPOSITE sad
3 FORTUNATE, lucky, timely, appropriate, convenient, favourable, auspicious, propitious, apt, befitting, advantageous, well-timed, opportune, felicitous, seasonable
<< OPPOSITE unfortunate

happy-go-lucky *adjective* CAREFREE, casual, easy-going, irresponsible, unconcerned, untroubled, nonchalant, blithe, heedless, insouciant, devil-may-care, improvident, light-hearted
<< OPPOSITE serious

harangue *verb* RANT AT, address, lecture, exhort, preach to, declaim, hold forth, spout at (*informal*)
▷ *noun* RANT, address, speech, lecture, tirade, polemic, broadside, diatribe, homily, exhortation, oration, spiel (*informal*), declamation, philippic

harass *verb* ANNOY, trouble, bother, worry, harry, disturb, devil (*informal*), plague, bait, hound, torment, hassle (*informal*), badger, persecute, exasperate, pester, vex, breathe down someone's neck, chivvy (*Brit*), give someone grief (*Brit & S African*), be on your back (*slang*), beleaguer

harassed *adjective* HASSLED, worried, troubled, strained, harried, under pressure, plagued, tormented, distraught (*informal*), vexed, under stress, careworn

harassment *noun* HASSLE, trouble, bother, grief (*informal*), torment, irritation, persecution (*informal*), nuisance, badgering, annoyance, pestering, aggravation (*informal*), molestation, vexation, bedevilment

harbinger *noun* (*Literary*) SIGN, indication, herald, messenger, omen, precursor, forerunner, portent, foretoken

harbour *noun* 1 PORT, haven, dock, mooring, marina, pier, wharf, anchorage, jetty, pontoon, slipway
2 SANCTUARY, haven, shelter, retreat, asylum, refuge, oasis, covert, safe haven, sanctum
▷ *verb* 1 HOLD, bear, maintain, nurse, retain, foster, entertain, nurture, cling to, cherish, brood over
2 SHELTER, protect, hide, relieve, lodge, shield, conceal, secrete, provide refuge, give asylum to

hard *adjective* 1 TOUGH, strong, firm, solid, stiff, compact, rigid, resistant, dense, compressed, stony, impenetrable, inflexible, unyielding, rocklike
<< OPPOSITE soft
2 DIFFICULT, involved, complex, complicated, puzzling, tangled, baffling, intricate, perplexing, impenetrable, thorny, knotty, unfathomable, ticklish
<< OPPOSITE easy
3 EXHAUSTING, tough, exacting, formidable, fatiguing, wearying, rigorous, uphill, gruelling, strenuous, arduous, laborious, burdensome, Herculean, backbreaking, toilsome
<< OPPOSITE easy
4 FORCEFUL, strong, powerful, driving, heavy, sharp, violent, smart, tremendous, fierce, vigorous, hefty
5 HARSH, severe, strict, cold, exacting, cruel, grim, stern, ruthless, stubborn, unjust, callous, unkind, unrelenting, implacable, unsympathetic, pitiless, unfeeling, obdurate, unsparing, affectless, hardhearted
<< OPPOSITE kind
6 GRIM, dark, painful, distressing, harsh, disastrous, unpleasant, intolerable, grievous, disagreeable, calamitous
7 DEFINITE, reliable, verified, cold, plain, actual, bare, undeniable, indisputable,

verifiable, unquestionable, unvarnished
▷ *adverb* 1 STRENUOUSLY, steadily, persistently, earnestly, determinedly, doggedly, diligently, energetically, assiduously, industriously, untiringly
2 INTENTLY, closely, carefully, sharply, keenly
3 FORCEFULLY, strongly, heavily, sharply, severely, fiercely, vigorously, intensely, violently, powerfully, forcibly, with all your might, with might and main
<< OPPOSITE softly
4 WITH DIFFICULTY, painfully, laboriously

hard-bitten *adjective* (*informal*) TOUGH, realistic, cynical, practical, shrewd, down-to-earth, matter-of-fact, hard-nosed (*informal*), hard-headed, unsentimental, hard-boiled (*informal*), case-hardened, badass (*slang, chiefly US*)
<< OPPOSITE idealistic

hard-boiled *adjective* (*informal*) TOUGH, practical, realistic, cynical, shrewd, down-to-earth, matter-of-fact, hard-nosed (*informal*), hard-headed, hard-bitten (*informal*), unsentimental, case-hardened, badass (*slang, chiefly US*)
<< OPPOSITE idealistic

hard-core *adjective* 1 DYED-IN-THE-WOOL, extreme, dedicated, rigid, staunch, die-hard, steadfast, obstinate, intransigent
2 EXPLICIT, obscene, pornographic, X-rated (*informal*)

harden *verb* 1 SOLIDIFY, set, freeze, cake, bake, clot, thicken, stiffen, crystallize, congeal, coagulate, anneal
2 ACCUSTOM, season, toughen, train, brutalize, inure, habituate, case-harden
3 REINFORCE, strengthen, fortify, steel, nerve, brace, toughen, buttress, gird, indurate

hardened *adjective* 1 HABITUAL, set, fixed, chronic, shameless, inveterate, incorrigible, reprobate, irredeemable, badass (*slang, chiefly US*)
<< OPPOSITE occasional
2 SEASONED, experienced, accustomed, toughened, inured, habituated
<< OPPOSITE naive

hard-headed *adjective* SHREWD, tough, practical, cool, sensible, realistic, pragmatic, astute, hard-boiled (*informal*), hard-bitten, level-headed, unsentimental, badass (*slang, chiefly US*)
<< OPPOSITE idealistic

hard-hearted *adjective* UNSYMPATHETIC, hard, cold, cruel, indifferent, insensitive, callous, stony, unkind, heartless, inhuman, merciless, intolerant, uncaring, pitiless, unfeeling, unforgiving, hard as nails, affectless
<< OPPOSITE kind

hardly *adverb* 1 BARELY, only just, scarcely, just, faintly, with difficulty, infrequently, with effort, at a push (*Brit informal*), almost not
<< OPPOSITE completely
2 ONLY JUST, just, only, barely, not quite, scarcely
3 NOT AT ALL, not, no way, by no means ▷ see **scarcely**

hard-nosed *adjective* (*informal*) TOUGH, practical, realistic, shrewd, pragmatic, down-to-earth, hardline, uncompromising, businesslike, hard-headed, unsentimental, badass (*slang, chiefly US*)

hard-pressed *adjective* 1 UNDER PRESSURE, pushed (*informal*), harried, in difficulties, up against it (*informal*), with your back to the wall
2 PUSHED (*informal*), in difficulties, up against it (*informal*)

hardship *noun* SUFFERING, want, need, trouble, trial, difficulty, burden, misery, torment, oppression, persecution, grievance, misfortune, austerity, adversity, calamity, affliction, tribulation, privation, destitution
<< OPPOSITE ease

hard up *adjective* POOR, broke (*informal*), short, bust (*informal*), bankrupt, impoverished, in the red (*informal*), cleaned out (*slang*), penniless, out of pocket, down and out, skint (*Brit slang*), strapped for cash (*informal*), impecunious, dirt-poor (*informal*), on the breadline, flat broke (*informal*), on your uppers (*informal*), in queer street, without two pennies to rub together (*informal*), short of cash *or* funds
<< OPPOSITE wealthy

hardy *adjective* 1 STRONG, tough, robust, sound, fit, healthy, vigorous, rugged, sturdy, hale, stout, stalwart, hearty, lusty, in fine fettle
<< OPPOSITE frail
2 COURAGEOUS, brave, daring, bold, heroic, manly, gritty, feisty (*informal, chiefly US & Canad*), resolute, intrepid, valiant, plucky, valorous, stouthearted
<< OPPOSITE feeble

hare *noun*
>> RELATED WORD *adjective* leporine
>> RELATED WORD *male* buck
>> RELATED WORD *female* doe
>> RELATED WORD *young* leveret
>> RELATED WORDS *habitations* down, husk

harem *noun* WOMEN'S QUARTERS, seraglio, zenana (*in eastern countries*), gynaeceum (*in ancient Greece*)

hark *verb* LISTEN, attend, pay attention, hearken (*archaic*), give ear, hear, mark, notice, give heed
▷▷ **hark back to something** 1 RECALL, recollect, call to mind, cause you to remember, cause you to recollect
2 RETURN TO, remember, recall, revert to, look back to, think back to, recollect, regress to

harlot *noun* (*Literary*) PROSTITUTE, tart (*informal*), whore, slag (*Brit slang*), pro (*slang*), tramp (*slang*), call girl, working girl (*facetious slang*), slapper (*Brit slang*), hussy, streetwalker, loose woman, fallen woman, scrubber (*Brit & Austral slang*), strumpet

harm *verb* 1 INJURE, hurt, wound, abuse, molest, ill-treat, maltreat, lay a finger on, ill-use
<< OPPOSITE heal
2 DAMAGE, hurt, ruin, mar, spoil, impair, blemish
▷ *noun* 1 INJURY, suffering, damage, ill, hurt, distress
2 DAMAGE, loss, ill, hurt, misfortune, mischief, detriment, impairment, disservice
<< OPPOSITE good
3 SIN, wrong, evil, wickedness, immorality, iniquity, sinfulness, vice
<< OPPOSITE goodness

harmful *adjective* DAMAGING, dangerous, negative, evil, destructive, hazardous, unhealthy, detrimental, hurtful, pernicious, noxious, baleful, deleterious, injurious, unwholesome, disadvantageous, baneful, maleficent
<< OPPOSITE harmless

harmless *adjective* 1 SAFE, benign, wholesome, innocuous, not dangerous, nontoxic, innoxious
<< OPPOSITE dangerous
2 INOFFENSIVE, innocent, innocuous, gentle, tame, unobjectionable

harmonious *adjective* 1 FRIENDLY, amicable, cordial, sympathetic, compatible, agreeable, in harmony, in unison, fraternal, congenial, in accord, concordant, of one mind, en rapport (*French*)
<< OPPOSITE unfriendly
2 COMPATIBLE, matching, coordinated, correspondent, agreeable, consistent, consonant, congruous
<< OPPOSITE incompatible
3 MELODIOUS, musical, harmonic, harmonizing, tuneful, concordant, mellifluous, dulcet, sweet-sounding, euphonious, euphonic, symphonious (*literary*)
<< OPPOSITE discordant

harmonize *verb* 1 MATCH, accord, suit, blend, correspond, tally, chime, coordinate, go together, tone in, cohere, attune, be of one mind, be in unison
2 COORDINATE, match, agree, blend, tally, reconcile, attune

harmony *noun* 1 ACCORD, order, understanding, peace, agreement, friendship, unity, sympathy, consensus, cooperation, goodwill, rapport, conformity, compatibility, assent, unanimity, concord, amity, amicability, like-mindedness
<< OPPOSITE conflict
2 TUNE, melody, unison, tunefulness, euphony, melodiousness
<< OPPOSITE discord
3 BALANCE, consistency, fitness, correspondence, coordination, symmetry, compatibility, suitability, concord, parallelism, consonance, congruity
<< OPPOSITE incongruity

harness *verb* 1 EXPLOIT, control, channel, apply, employ, utilize, mobilize, make productive, turn to account, render useful
2 PUT IN HARNESS, couple, saddle, yoke, hitch up
▷ *noun* EQUIPMENT, tackle, gear, tack, trappings
▷▷ **in harness** 1 WORKING, together, in a team
2 AT WORK, working, employed, active, busy, in action

harp *verb* GO ON, reiterate, dwell on, labour, press, repeat, rub in

harried *adjective* HARASSED, worried, troubled, bothered, anxious, distressed, plagued, tormented, hassled (*informal*), agitated, beset, hard-pressed, hag-ridden

harrowing *adjective* DISTRESSING, disturbing, alarming, frightening, painful, terrifying, chilling, traumatic, tormenting, heartbreaking, excruciating, agonizing, nerve-racking, heart-rending, gut-wrenching

harry *verb* PESTER, trouble, bother, disturb, worry, annoy, plague, tease, torment, harass, hassle (*informal*), badger, persecute, molest, vex, bedevil, breathe down someone's neck, chivvy, give someone grief (*Brit & S African*), be on your back (*slang*), get in your hair (*informal*)

harsh *adjective* 1 SEVERE, hard, tough, grim, stark, stringent, austere, Spartan, inhospitable, comfortless
2 BLEAK, cold, freezing, severe, bitter, icy
3 CRUEL, savage, brutal, ruthless, relentless, unrelenting, barbarous, pitiless
4 HARD, sharp, severe, bitter, cruel, stern, unpleasant, abusive, unkind, pitiless, unfeeling
<< OPPOSITE kind
5 DRASTIC, hard, severe, stringent, punitive, austere, Draconian, punitory
6 RAUCOUS, rough, jarring, grating, strident, rasping, discordant, croaking, guttural, dissonant, unmelodious
<< OPPOSITE soft

harshly *adverb* SEVERELY, roughly, cruelly, strictly, grimly, sternly, brutally

harshness *noun* BITTERNESS, acrimony, ill-temper, sourness, asperity, acerbity

harvest *noun* 1 HARVESTING, picking, gathering, collecting, reaping, harvest-time
2 CROP, yield, year's growth, produce
▷ *verb* 1 GATHER, pick, collect, bring in, pluck,

reap
2 COLLECT, get, gain, earn, obtain, acquire, accumulate, garner, amass

hash *noun* ▷▷ **make a hash of** (*informal*) MESS UP, muddle, bungle, botch, cock up (*Brit slang*), mishandle, mismanage, make a nonsense of (*informal*), bodge (*informal*), make a pig's ear of (*informal*), flub (*US slang*)

hassle (*informal*) *noun* TROUBLE, problem, difficulty, upset, bother, grief (*informal*), trial, struggle, uphill (*S African*), inconvenience
▷ *verb* BOTHER, bug (*informal*), annoy, harry, hound, harass, badger, pester, get on your nerves (*informal*), be on your back (*slang*), get in your hair (*informal*), breath down someone's neck

hassled *adjective* BOTHERED, pressured, worried, stressed, under pressure, hounded, uptight, browbeaten, hunted, hot and bothered

haste *noun* SPEED, rapidity, urgency, expedition, dispatch, velocity, alacrity, quickness, swiftness, briskness, nimbleness, fleetness, celerity, promptitude, rapidness
<< OPPOSITE slowness

hasten *verb* 1 HURRY (UP), speed (up), advance, urge, step up (*informal*), accelerate, press, dispatch, precipitate, quicken, push forward, expedite
<< OPPOSITE slow down
2 RUSH, run, race, fly, speed, tear (along), dash, hurry (up), barrel (along) (*informal, chiefly US & Canad*), sprint, bolt, beetle, scuttle, scurry, haste, burn rubber (*informal*), step on it (*informal*), make haste, get your skates on (*informal*)
<< OPPOSITE dawdle

hastily *adverb* 1 QUICKLY, fast, rapidly, promptly, straightaway, speedily, apace, pronto (*informal*), double-quick, hotfoot, pdq (*slang*), posthaste
2 HURRIEDLY, rashly, precipitately, recklessly, too quickly, on the spur of the moment, impulsively, impetuously, heedlessly

hasty *adjective* 1 SPEEDY, fast, quick, prompt, rapid, fleet, hurried, urgent, swift, brisk, expeditious
<< OPPOSITE leisurely
2 BRIEF, short, quick, passing, rushed, fleeting, superficial, cursory, perfunctory, transitory
<< OPPOSITE long
3 RASH, premature, reckless, precipitate, impulsive, headlong, foolhardy, thoughtless, impetuous, indiscreet, imprudent, heedless, incautious, unduly quick
<< OPPOSITE cautious

hatch *verb* 1 INCUBATE, breed, sit on, brood, bring forth
2 DEVISE, plan, design, project, scheme, manufacture, plot, invent, put together, conceive, brew, formulate, contrive, dream up (*informal*), concoct, think up, cook up (*informal*), trump up

hatchet *noun* AXE, machete, tomahawk, cleaver

hate *verb* 1 DETEST, loathe, despise, dislike, be sick of, abhor, be hostile to, recoil from, be repelled by, have an aversion to, abominate, not be able to bear, execrate
<< OPPOSITE love
2 DISLIKE, detest, shrink from, recoil from, have no stomach for, not be able to bear
<< OPPOSITE like
3 BE UNWILLING, regret, be reluctant, hesitate, be sorry, be loath, feel disinclined
▷ *noun* DISLIKE, hostility, hatred, loathing, animosity, aversion, antagonism, antipathy, enmity, abomination, animus, abhorrence, odium, detestation, execration
<< OPPOSITE love

hateful *adjective* HORRIBLE, despicable, offensive, foul, disgusting, forbidding, revolting, obscene, vile, repellent, obnoxious, repulsive, heinous, odious, repugnant, loathsome, abhorrent, abominable, execrable, detestable
<< OPPOSITE pleasant

hatred *noun* HATE, dislike, animosity, aversion, revulsion, antagonism, antipathy, enmity, abomination, ill will, animus, repugnance, odium, detestation, execration
<< OPPOSITE love

haughty *adjective* PROUD, arrogant, lofty, high, stuck-up (*informal*), contemptuous, conceited, imperious, snooty (*informal*), scornful, snobbish, disdainful, supercilious, high and mighty (*informal*), overweening, hoity-toity (*informal*), on your high horse (*informal*), uppish (*Brit informal*)
<< OPPOSITE humble

haul *verb* 1 DRAG, draw, pull, hale, heave
2 PULL, trail, convey, tow, move, carry, transport, tug, cart, hump (*Brit slang*), lug
▷ *noun* YIELD, gain, spoils, find, catch, harvest, loot, takings, booty

haunt *verb* 1 PLAGUE, trouble, obsess, torment, come back to, possess, stay with, recur, beset, prey on, weigh on
2 VISIT, hang around *or* about, frequent, linger in, resort to, patronize, repair to, spend time in, loiter in, be a regular in
3 APPEAR IN, materialize in
▷ *noun* MEETING PLACE, resort, hangout (*informal*), den, rendezvous, stamping ground, gathering place

haunted *adjective* 1 POSSESSED, ghostly, cursed, eerie, spooky (*informal*), jinxed
2 PREOCCUPIED, worried, troubled, plagued, obsessed, tormented

haunting *adjective* EVOCATIVE, poignant, unforgettable, indelible

have *verb* 1 OWN, keep, possess, hold, retain, occupy, boast, be the owner of
2 GET, obtain, take, receive, accept, gain, secure, acquire, procure, take receipt of
3 SUFFER, experience, undergo, sustain, endure, be suffering from
4 GIVE BIRTH TO, bear, deliver, bring forth, beget, bring into the world
5 PUT UP WITH (*informal*), allow, permit, consider, think about, entertain, tolerate
6 EXPERIENCE, go through, undergo, meet with, come across, run into, be faced with
▷▷ **have had it** (*informal*) BE EXHAUSTED, be knackered (*Brit informal*), be finished, be pooped (*US slang*)
▷▷ **have someone on** TEASE, kid (*informal*), wind up (*Brit slang*), trick, deceive, take the mickey out of (*informal*), pull someone's leg, play a joke on, jerk *or* yank someone's chain (*informal*)
▷▷ **have something on** 1 WEAR, be wearing, be dressed in, be clothed in, be attired in
2 HAVE SOMETHING PLANNED, be committed to, be engaged to, have something on the agenda
▷▷ **have to** 1 *with* **to** MUST, should, be forced, ought, be obliged, be bound, have got to, be compelled
2 HAVE GOT TO, must

haven *noun* 1 SANCTUARY, shelter, retreat, asylum, refuge, oasis, sanctum
2 HARBOUR, port, anchorage, road (*Nautical*)

havoc *noun* 1 DEVASTATION, damage, destruction, waste, ruin, wreck, slaughter, ravages, carnage, desolation, rack and ruin, despoliation
2 (*informal*) DISORDER, confusion, chaos, disruption, mayhem, shambles
▷▷ **play havoc with something** WRECK, destroy, devastate, disrupt, demolish, disorganize, bring into chaos

hawk *verb* PEDDLE, market, sell, push, traffic, tout (*informal*), vend

hawker *noun* PEDLAR, tout, vendor, travelling salesman, crier, huckster, barrow boy (*Brit*), door-to-door salesman

haywire *adjective* 1 OUT OF ORDER, out of commission, on the blink (*slang*), on the fritz (*slang*)
2 (*of people*) CRAZY, wild, mad, potty (*Brit informal*), berserk, bonkers (*slang, chiefly Brit*), loopy (*informal*), mad as a hatter, berko (*Austral slang*), off the air (*Austral slang*), porangi (*NZ*)

hazard *noun* DANGER, risk, threat, problem, menace, peril, jeopardy, pitfall, endangerment, imperilment
▷ *verb* JEOPARDIZE, risk, endanger, threaten, expose, imperil, put in jeopardy
▷▷ **hazard a guess** GUESS, conjecture, suppose, speculate, presume, take a guess

hazardous *adjective* DANGEROUS, risky, difficult, uncertain, unpredictable, insecure, hairy (*slang*), unsafe, precarious, perilous, parlous (*archaic* or *humorous*), dicey (*informal, chiefly Brit*), fraught with danger, chancy (*informal*)
<< OPPOSITE safe

haze *noun* MIST, film, cloud, steam, fog, obscurity, vapour, smog, dimness, smokiness

hazy *adjective* 1 MISTY, faint, dim, dull, obscure, veiled, smoky, cloudy, foggy, overcast, blurry, nebulous
<< OPPOSITE bright
2 VAGUE, uncertain, unclear, muddled, fuzzy, indefinite, loose, muzzy, nebulous, ill-defined, indistinct
<< OPPOSITE clear

head *noun* 1 SKULL, crown, pate, bean (*US & Canad slang*), nut (*slang*), loaf (*slang*), cranium, conk (*slang*), noggin, noddle (*informal, chiefly Brit*)
2 MIND, reasoning, understanding, thought, sense, brain, brains (*informal*), intelligence, wisdom, wits, common sense, loaf (*Brit informal*), intellect, rationality, grey matter, brainpower, mental capacity
3 ABILITY, mind, talent, capacity, faculty, flair, mentality, aptitude
4 FRONT, beginning, top, first place, fore, forefront
5 FOREFRONT, cutting edge, vanguard, van
6 TOP, crown, summit, height, peak, crest, pinnacle, apex, vertex
7 (*informal*) HEAD TEACHER, principal, headmaster *or* headmistress
8 LEADER, president, director, manager, chief, boss (*informal*), captain, master, premier, commander, principal, supervisor, superintendent, chieftain, sherang (*Austral & NZ*)
9 CLIMAX, crisis, turning point, culmination, end, conclusion, tipping point
10 SOURCE, start, beginning, rise, origin, commencement, well head
11 (*Geography*) HEADLAND, point, cape, promontory, foreland
▷ *adjective* CHIEF, main, leading, first, highest, front, prime, premier, supreme, principal, arch, foremost, pre-eminent, topmost
▷ *verb* 1 LEAD, precede, be the leader of, be *or* go first, be *or* go at the front of, lead the way
2 TOP, lead, crown, cap
3 BE IN CHARGE OF, run, manage, lead, control, rule, direct, guide, command, govern, supervise
▷▷ **go to your head** 1 INTOXICATE, befuddle, inebriate, addle, stupefy, fuddle, put (someone) under the table (*informal*)
2 MAKE SOMEONE CONCEITED, puff someone

up, make someone full of themselves
▷▷ **head for something** *or* **someone** MAKE FOR, aim for, set off for, go to, turn to, set out for, make a beeline for, start towards, steer for
▷▷ **head over heels** COMPLETELY, thoroughly, utterly, intensely, wholeheartedly, uncontrollably
▷▷ **head someone off** INTERCEPT, divert, deflect, cut someone off, interpose, block someone off
▷▷ **head something off** PREVENT, stop, avert, parry, fend off, ward off, forestall
▷▷ **put your heads together** (*informal*) CONSULT, confer, discuss, deliberate, talk (something) over, powwow, confab (*informal*), confabulate
>> RELATED WORDS *adjectives* capital, cephalic

headache *noun* **1** MIGRAINE, head (*informal*), neuralgia, cephalalgia (*Medical*)
2 (*informal*) PROBLEM, worry, trouble, bother, nuisance, inconvenience, bane, vexation

headfirst *or* **head first** *adverb* **1** HEADLONG, head foremost
2 RECKLESSLY, rashly, hastily, precipitately, without thinking, carelessly, heedlessly, without forethought

heading *noun* **1** TITLE, name, caption, headline, rubric
2 CATEGORY, class, section, division

headland *noun* PROMONTORY, point, head, cape, cliff, bluff, mull (*Scot*), foreland, bill

headlong *adverb* **1** HASTILY, hurriedly, helter-skelter, pell-mell, heedlessly
2 HEADFIRST, head-on, headforemost
3 RASHLY, wildly, hastily, precipitately, head first, thoughtlessly, impetuously, heedlessly, without forethought
▷ *adjective* HASTY, reckless, precipitate, dangerous, impulsive, thoughtless, breakneck, impetuous, inconsiderate

headmaster *or* **headmistress** *noun* PRINCIPAL, head, head teacher, rector

> The general trend of nonsexist language is to find a term which can apply to both sexes equally, as in the use of *actor* to refer to both men and women. This being so, *head teacher* is usually preferable to the gender-specific terms *headmaster* and *headmistress*

headstrong *adjective* STUBBORN, wilful, obstinate, contrary, perverse, unruly, intractable, stiff-necked, ungovernable, self-willed, pig-headed, mulish, froward (*archaic*)
<< OPPOSITE manageable

headway *noun* PROGRESS, ground, inroads, strides

heady *adjective* **1** EXCITING, thrilling, stimulating, exhilarating, overwhelming, intoxicating
2 INTOXICATING, strong, potent, inebriating, spirituous

heal *verb* **1** *sometimes with* **up** MEND, get better, get well, cure, regenerate, show improvement
2 CURE, restore, mend, make better, remedy, make good, make well
<< OPPOSITE injure
3 PATCH UP, settle, reconcile, put right, harmonize, conciliate

healing *adjective* RESTORING, medicinal, therapeutic, remedial, restorative, curative, analeptic, sanative

health *noun* **1** CONDITION, state, form, shape, tone, constitution, fettle
2 WELLBEING, strength, fitness, vigour, good condition, wellness, soundness, robustness, healthiness, salubrity, haleness
<< OPPOSITE illness
3 STATE, condition, shape

healthful *adjective* HEALTHY, beneficial, good for you, bracing, nourishing, wholesome, nutritious, invigorating, salutary, salubrious, health-giving

healthy *adjective* **1** WELL, sound, fit, strong, active, flourishing, hardy, blooming, robust, vigorous, sturdy, hale, hearty, in good shape (*informal*), in good condition, in the pink, alive and kicking, fighting fit, in fine form, in fine fettle, hale and hearty, fit as a fiddle (*informal*), right as rain (*Brit informal*), physically fit, in fine feather
<< OPPOSITE ill
2 WHOLESOME, beneficial, nourishing, good for you, nutritious, salutary, hygienic, healthful, salubrious, health-giving
<< OPPOSITE unwholesome
3 INVIGORATING, bracing, beneficial, good for you, salutary, healthful, salubrious

heap *noun* **1** PILE, lot, collection, store, mountain, mass, stack, rick, mound, accumulation, stockpile, hoard, aggregation
2 *often plural* (*informal*) A LOT, lots (*informal*), plenty, masses, load(s) (*informal*), ocean(s), great deal, quantities, tons, stack(s), lashings (*Brit informal*), abundance, oodles (*informal*)
▷ *verb sometimes with* **up** PILE, store, collect, gather, stack, accumulate, mound, amass, stockpile, hoard, bank
▷▷ **heap something on someone** LOAD WITH, burden with, confer on, assign to, bestow on, shower upon

hear *verb* **1** OVERHEAR, catch, detect
2 LISTEN TO, heed, attend to, eavesdrop on, listen in to, give attention to, hearken to (*archaic*), hark to, be all ears for (*informal*)
3 (*Law*) TRY, judge, examine, investigate
4 LEARN, discover, find out, understand, pick up, gather, be informed, ascertain, be told of,

get wind of (*informal*), hear tell (*dialect*)

hearing *noun* 1 SENSE OF HEARING, auditory perception, ear, aural faculty
2 INQUIRY, trial, investigation, industrial tribunal
3 CHANCE TO SPEAK, interview, audience, audition
4 EARSHOT, reach, range, hearing distance, auditory range
>> RELATED WORD *adjective* audio

hearsay *noun* RUMOUR, talk, gossip, report, buzz, dirt (*US slang*), goss (*informal*), word of mouth, tittle-tattle, talk of the town, scuttlebutt (*slang, chiefly US*), idle talk, mere talk, on dit (*French*)

heart *noun* 1 EMOTIONS, feelings, sentiments, love, affection
2 NATURE, character, soul, constitution, essence, temperament, inclination, disposition
3 TENDERNESS, feeling(s), love, understanding, concern, sympathy, pity, humanity, affection, compassion, kindness, empathy, benevolence, concern for others
4 ROOT, core, essence, centre, nucleus, marrow, hub, kernel, crux, gist, central part, nitty-gritty (*informal*), nub, pith, quintessence
5 COURAGE, will, spirit, mind, purpose, bottle (*Brit informal*), resolution, resolve, nerve, stomach, enthusiasm, determination, guts (*informal*), spine, pluck, bravery, backbone, fortitude, mettle, boldness, spunk (*informal*)
▷▷ **by heart** FROM *or* BY MEMORY, verbatim, word for word, pat, word-perfect, by rote, off by heart, off pat, parrot-fashion (*informal*)
▷▷ **from (the bottom of) your heart** DEEPLY, heartily, fervently, heart and soul, devoutly, with all your heart
▷▷ **take heart** BE ENCOURAGED, be comforted, cheer up, perk up, brighten up, be heartened, buck up (*informal*), derive comfort
>> RELATED WORD *adjective* cardiac

heartache *noun* SORROW, suffering, pain, torture, distress, despair, grief, agony, torment, bitterness, anguish, remorse, heartbreak, affliction, heartsickness

heartbreak *noun* GRIEF, suffering, pain, despair, misery, sorrow, anguish, desolation

heartbreaking *adjective* SAD, distressing, tragic, bitter, poignant, harrowing, desolating, grievous, pitiful, agonizing, heart-rending, gut-wrenching
<< OPPOSITE happy

hearten *verb* ENCOURAGE, inspire, cheer, comfort, assure, stimulate, reassure, animate, console, rouse, incite, embolden, buoy up, buck up (*informal*), raise someone's spirits, revivify, gee up, inspirit

heartfelt *adjective* SINCERE, deep, earnest, warm, genuine, profound, honest, ardent, devout, hearty, fervent, cordial, wholehearted, dinkum (*Austral & NZ informal*), unfeigned
<< OPPOSITE insincere

heartily *adverb* 1 SINCERELY, feelingly, deeply, warmly, genuinely, profoundly, cordially, unfeignedly
2 ENTHUSIASTICALLY, vigorously, eagerly, resolutely, earnestly, zealously
3 THOROUGHLY, very, completely, totally, absolutely

heartless *adjective* CRUEL, hard, callous, cold, harsh, brutal, unkind, inhuman, merciless, cold-blooded, uncaring, pitiless, unfeeling, cold-hearted, affectless, hardhearted
<< OPPOSITE compassionate

heart-rending *adjective* MOVING, sad, distressing, affecting, tragic, pathetic, poignant, harrowing, heartbreaking, pitiful, gut-wrenching, piteous

heart-to-heart *adjective* INTIMATE, honest, candid, open, personal, sincere, truthful, unreserved
▷ *noun* TÊTE-À-TÊTE, cosy chat, one-to-one, private conversation, private chat

heart-warming *adjective* MOVING, touching, affecting, pleasing, encouraging, warming, rewarding, satisfying, cheering, gratifying, heartening

hearty *adjective* 1 FRIENDLY, genial, warm, generous, eager, enthusiastic, ardent, cordial, affable, ebullient, jovial, effusive, unreserved, back-slapping
<< OPPOSITE cool
2 WHOLEHEARTED, sincere, heartfelt, real, true, earnest, genuine, honest, unfeigned
<< OPPOSITE insincere
3 SUBSTANTIAL, filling, ample, square, solid, nourishing, sizable *or* sizeable
4 HEALTHY, well, strong, sound, active, hardy, robust, vigorous, energetic, hale, alive and kicking, right as rain (*Brit informal*)
<< OPPOSITE frail

heat *verb* 1 *sometimes with* **up** WARM (UP), cook, boil, roast, reheat, make hot
<< OPPOSITE chill
2 INTENSIFY, increase, heighten, deepen, escalate
▷ *noun* 1 WARMTH, hotness, temperature, swelter, sultriness, fieriness, torridity, warmness, calefaction
<< OPPOSITE cold
2 HOT WEATHER, warmth, closeness, high temperature, heatwave, warm weather, hot climate, hot spell, mugginess
3 PASSION, excitement, intensity, violence, fever, fury, warmth, zeal, agitation, fervour, ardour, vehemence, earnestness, impetuosity
<< OPPOSITE calmness

▷▷ **heat up** WARM UP, get hotter, become hot, rise in temperature, become warm, grow hot

>> RELATED WORD *adjective* thermal

heated *adjective* 1 IMPASSIONED, intense, spirited, excited, angry, violent, bitter, raging, furious, fierce, lively, passionate, animated, frenzied, fiery, stormy, vehement, tempestuous

<< OPPOSITE calm

2 WOUND UP, worked up, keyed up, het up (*informal*)

heathen *noun* 1 PAGAN, infidel, unbeliever, idolater, idolatress

2 BARBARIAN, savage, philistine, oaf, ignoramus, boor

▷ *adjective* 1 PAGAN, infidel, godless, irreligious, idolatrous, heathenish

2 UNCIVILIZED, savage, primitive, barbaric, brutish, unenlightened, uncultured

heave *verb* 1 LIFT, raise, pull (up), drag (up), haul (up), tug, lever, hoist, heft (*informal*)

2 THROW, fling, toss, send, cast, pitch, hurl, sling

3 SURGE, rise, swell, billow

4 VOMIT, be sick, throw up (*informal*), chuck (up) (*slang, chiefly US*), chuck (*Austral & NZ informal*), gag, spew, retch, barf (*US slang*), chunder (*slang, chiefly Austral*), upchuck (*US slang*), do a technicolour yawn (*slang*), toss your cookies (*US slang*)

5 BREATHE, sigh, puff, groan, sob, breathe heavily, suspire (*archaic*), utter wearily

heaven *noun* 1 PARADISE, next world, hereafter, nirvana (*Buddhism, Hinduism*), bliss, Zion (*Christianity*), Valhalla (*Norse myth*), Happy Valley, happy hunting ground (*Native American legend*), life to come, life everlasting, abode of God, Elysium *or* Elysian fields (*Greek myth*)

2 (*informal*) HAPPINESS, paradise, ecstasy, bliss, felicity, utopia, contentment, rapture, enchantment, dreamland, seventh heaven, transport, sheer bliss

▷▷ **the heavens** (*Old-fashioned*) SKY, ether, firmament, celestial sphere, welkin (*archaic*), empyrean (*poetic*)

heavenly *adjective* 1 CELESTIAL, holy, divine, blessed, blest, immortal, supernatural, angelic, extraterrestrial, superhuman, godlike, beatific, cherubic, seraphic, supernal (*literary*), empyrean (*poetic*), paradisaical

<< OPPOSITE earthly

2 (*informal*) WONDERFUL, lovely, delightful, beautiful, entrancing, divine (*informal*), glorious, exquisite, sublime, alluring, blissful, ravishing, rapturous

<< OPPOSITE awful

heavily *adverb* 1 EXCESSIVELY, to excess, very much, a great deal, frequently, considerably, copiously, without restraint, immoderately, intemperately

2 DENSELY, closely, thickly, compactly

3 HARD, clumsily, awkwardly, weightily

heaviness *noun* 1 WEIGHT, gravity, ponderousness, heftiness

2 SADNESS, depression, gloom, seriousness, melancholy, despondency, dejection, gloominess, glumness

heavy *adjective* 1 WEIGHTY, large, massive, hefty, bulky, ponderous

<< OPPOSITE light

2 INTENSIVE, severe, serious, concentrated, fierce, excessive, relentless

3 CONSIDERABLE, large, huge, substantial, abundant, copious, profuse

<< OPPOSITE slight

4 ONEROUS, hard, difficult, severe, harsh, tedious, intolerable, oppressive, grievous, burdensome, wearisome, vexatious

<< OPPOSITE easy

5 SLUGGISH, slow, dull, wooden, stupid, inactive, inert, apathetic, drowsy, listless, indolent, torpid

<< OPPOSITE alert

6 HARD, demanding, difficult, physical, strenuous, laborious

7 OVERCAST, dull, gloomy, cloudy, leaden, louring *or* lowering

8 SAD, depressed, gloomy, grieving, melancholy, dejected, despondent, downcast, sorrowful, disconsolate, crestfallen

<< OPPOSITE happy

9 SERIOUS, grave, solemn, difficult, deep, complex, profound, weighty

<< OPPOSITE trivial

heavy-handed *adjective* 1 OPPRESSIVE, harsh, Draconian, autocratic, domineering, overbearing

2 CLUMSY, awkward, bungling, inept, graceless, inexpert, maladroit, ham-handed (*informal*), like a bull in a china shop (*informal*), ham-fisted (*informal*)

<< OPPOSITE skilful

heckle *verb* JEER, interrupt, shout down, disrupt, bait, barrack (*informal*), boo, taunt, pester

hectic *adjective* FRANTIC, chaotic, frenzied, heated, wild, excited, furious, fevered, animated, turbulent, flurrying, frenetic, boisterous, feverish, tumultuous, flustering, riotous, rumbustious

<< OPPOSITE peaceful

hector *verb* BULLY, harass, browbeat, worry, threaten, menace, intimidate, ride roughshod over, bullyrag

hedge *noun* GUARD, cover, protection, compensation, shield, safeguard, counterbalance, insurance cover

▷ *verb* 1 PREVARICATE, evade, sidestep, duck,

dodge, flannel (*Brit informal*), waffle (*informal, chiefly Brit*), quibble, beg the question, pussyfoot (*informal*), equivocate, temporize, be noncommittal

2 ENCLOSE, edge, border, surround, fence

▷▷ **hedge against something** PROTECT, insure, guard, safeguard, shield, cover, fortify

▷▷ **hedge someone in** HAMPER, restrict, handicap, hamstring, hinder, hem in

▷▷ **hedge something in** SURROUND, enclose, encompass, encircle, ring, fence in, girdle, hem in

▷▷ **hedge something** *or* **someone about** RESTRICT, confine, hinder, hem in, hem around, hem about

hedonism *noun* PLEASURE-SEEKING, gratification, sensuality, self-indulgence, dolce vita, pursuit of pleasure, luxuriousness, sensualism, sybaritism, epicureanism, epicurism

hedonistic *adjective* PLEASURE-SEEKING, self-indulgent, luxurious, voluptuous, sybaritic, epicurean, bacchanalian

heed *verb* PAY ATTENTION TO, listen to, take notice of, follow, mark, mind, consider, note, regard, attend, observe, obey, bear in mind, be guided by, take to heart, give ear to

<< OPPOSITE ignore

▷ *noun* THOUGHT, care, mind, note, attention, regard, respect, notice, consideration, watchfulness

<< OPPOSITE disregard

heedless *adjective* CARELESS, reckless, negligent, rash, precipitate, oblivious, foolhardy, thoughtless, unthinking, imprudent, neglectful, inattentive, incautious, unmindful, unobservant

<< OPPOSITE careful

heel *noun* 1 END, stump, remainder, crust, rump, stub

2 (*Slang*) SWINE, cad (*Brit informal*), scoundrel, scally (*Northwest English dialect*), bounder (*Brit old-fashioned slang*), rotter (*slang, chiefly Brit*), scumbag (*slang*), blackguard, wrong 'un (*Austral slang*)

▷▷ **take to your heels** FLEE, escape, run away *or* off, take flight, hook it (*slang*), turn tail, show a clean pair of heels, skedaddle (*informal*), vamoose (*slang, chiefly US*)

hefty *adjective* (*informal*) 1 BIG, strong, massive, strapping, robust, muscular, burly, husky (*informal*), hulking, beefy (*informal*), brawny

<< OPPOSITE small

2 FORCEFUL, heavy, powerful, vigorous (*slang*)

<< OPPOSITE gentle

3 HEAVY, large, massive, substantial, tremendous, awkward, ample, bulky, colossal, cumbersome, weighty, unwieldy, ponderous

<< OPPOSITE light

4 LARGE, massive, substantial, excessive, inflated, sizeable, astronomical (*informal*), extortionate

height *noun* 1 TALLNESS, stature, highness, loftiness

<< OPPOSITE shortness

2 ALTITUDE, measurement, highness, elevation, tallness

<< OPPOSITE depth

3 PEAK, top, hill, mountain, crown, summit, crest, pinnacle, elevation, apex, apogee, vertex

<< OPPOSITE valley

4 CULMINATION, climax, zenith, limit, maximum, ultimate, extremity, uttermost, ne plus ultra (*Latin*), utmost degree

<< OPPOSITE low point

>> RELATED WORD *fear* acrophobia

heighten *verb* INTENSIFY, increase, add to, improve, strengthen, enhance, sharpen, aggravate, magnify, amplify, augment

heinous *adjective* SHOCKING, evil, monstrous, grave, awful, vicious, outrageous, revolting, infamous, hideous, unspeakable, atrocious, flagrant, odious, hateful, abhorrent, abominable, villainous, nefarious, iniquitous, execrable

heir *noun* SUCCESSOR, beneficiary, inheritor, heiress (*fem*), scion, next in line, inheritress *or* inheritrix (*fem*)

hell *noun* 1 THE UNDERWORLD, the abyss, Hades (*Greek myth*), hellfire, the inferno, fire and brimstone, the bottomless pit, Gehenna (*New Testament, Judaism*), the nether world, the lower world, Tartarus (*Greek myth*), the infernal regions, the bad fire (*informal*), Acheron (*Greek myth*), Abaddon, the abode of the damned

2 (*informal*) TORMENT, suffering, agony, trial, nightmare, misery, ordeal, anguish, affliction, martyrdom, wretchedness

▷▷ **hell for leather** HEADLONG, speedily, quickly, swiftly, hurriedly, at the double, full-tilt, pell-mell, hotfoot, at a rate of knots, like a bat out of hell (*slang*), posthaste

hellbent *adjective* (*informal*) INTENT, set, determined, settled, fixed, resolved, bent

hellish *adjective* 1 (*informal*) ATROCIOUS, terrible, dreadful, cruel, vicious, monstrous, wicked, inhuman, barbarous, abominable, nefarious, accursed, execrable, detestable

<< OPPOSITE wonderful

2 DEVILISH, fiendish, diabolical, infernal, damned, damnable, demoniacal

hello *interjection* HI (*informal*), greetings, how do you do?, good morning, good evening, good afternoon, welcome, kia ora (*NZ*), gidday *or* g'day (*Austral & NZ*)

helm *noun* (*Nautical*) TILLER, wheel, rudder, steering gear

▷▷ **at the helm** IN CHARGE, in control, in

command, directing, at the wheel, in the saddle, in the driving seat

help *verb* 1 *sometimes with* **out** AID, back, support, second, encourage, promote, assist, relieve, stand by, befriend, cooperate with, abet, lend a hand, succour, lend a helping hand, give someone a leg up (*informal*)

<< OPPOSITE hinder

2 IMPROVE, ease, heal, cure, relieve, remedy, facilitate, alleviate, mitigate, ameliorate

<< OPPOSITE make worse

3 ASSIST, aid, support, give a leg up (*informal*)

4 RESIST, refrain from, avoid, control, prevent, withstand, eschew, keep from, abstain from, forbear

▷ *noun* 1 ASSISTANCE, aid, support, service, advice, promotion, guidance, cooperation, helping hand

<< OPPOSITE hindrance

2 REMEDY, cure, relief, corrective, balm, salve, succour, restorative

3 ASSISTANT, hand, worker, employee, helper

helper *noun* ASSISTANT, partner, ally, colleague, supporter, mate, deputy, second, subsidiary, aide, aider, attendant, collaborator, auxiliary, henchman, right-hand man, adjutant, helpmate, coadjutor, abettor

helpful *adjective* 1 COOPERATIVE, accommodating, kind, caring, friendly, neighbourly, sympathetic, supportive, benevolent, considerate, beneficent

2 USEFUL, practical, productive, profitable, constructive, serviceable

3 BENEFICIAL, advantageous, expedient, favourable

helpfulness *noun* 1 COOPERATION, kindness, support, assistance, sympathy, friendliness, rallying round, neighbourliness, good neighbourliness

2 USEFULNESS, benefit, advantage

helping *noun* PORTION, serving, ration, piece, dollop (*informal*), plateful

helpless *adjective* 1 VULNERABLE, exposed, unprotected, defenceless, abandoned, dependent, stranded, wide open, forlorn, destitute

<< OPPOSITE invulnerable

2 POWERLESS, weak, disabled, incapable, challenged, paralysed, incompetent, unfit, feeble, debilitated, impotent, infirm

<< OPPOSITE powerful

helplessness *noun* VULNERABILITY, weakness, impotence, powerlessness, disability, infirmity, feebleness, forlornness, defencelessness

helter-skelter *adjective* HAPHAZARD, confused, disordered, random, muddled, jumbled, topsy-turvy, hit-or-miss, higgledy-piggledy (*informal*)

▷ *adverb* WILDLY, rashly, anyhow, headlong, recklessly, carelessly, pell-mell

hem *noun* EDGE, border, margin, trimming, fringe

▷▷ **hem something** *or* **someone in**

1 SURROUND, edge, border, skirt, confine, enclose, shut in, hedge in, environ

2 RESTRICT, confine, beset, circumscribe

hence *adverb* THEREFORE, thus, consequently, for this reason, in consequence, ergo, on that account

henceforth *adverb* FROM NOW ON, in the future, hereafter, hence, hereinafter, from this day forward

henchman *noun* ATTENDANT, supporter, heavy (*slang*), associate, aide, follower, subordinate, bodyguard, minder (*slang*), crony, sidekick (*slang*), cohort (*chiefly US*), right-hand man, minion, satellite, myrmidon

henpecked *adjective* DOMINATED, subjugated, browbeaten, subject, bullied, timid, cringing, meek, treated like dirt, led by the nose, tied to someone's apron strings

<< OPPOSITE domineering

herald *verb* 1 INDICATE, promise, precede, pave the way, usher in, harbinger, presage, portend, foretoken

2 ANNOUNCE, publish, advertise, proclaim, broadcast, trumpet, publicize

▷ *noun* 1 (*Often literary*) FORERUNNER, sign, signal, indication, token, omen, precursor, harbinger

2 MESSENGER, courier, proclaimer, announcer, crier, town crier, bearer of tidings

herculean *adjective* 1 ARDUOUS, hard, demanding, difficult, heavy, tough, exhausting, formidable, gruelling, strenuous, prodigious, onerous, laborious, toilsome

2 STRONG, muscular, powerful, athletic, strapping, mighty, rugged, sturdy, stalwart, husky (*informal*), sinewy, brawny

herd *noun* 1 FLOCK, crowd, collection, mass, drove, crush, mob, swarm, horde, multitude, throng, assemblage, press

2 (*Often disparaging*) MOB, the masses, rabble, populace, the hoi polloi, the plebs, riffraff

▷ *verb* 1 LEAD, drive, force, direct, guide, shepherd

2 DRIVE, lead, force, guide, shepherd

hereafter *adverb* IN FUTURE, after this, from now on, henceforth, henceforward, hence

▷▷ **the hereafter** AFTERLIFE, next world, life after death, future life, the beyond

hereditary *adjective* 1 GENETIC, inborn, inbred, transmissible, inheritable

2 (*Law*) INHERITED, handed down, passed down, willed, family, traditional, transmitted, ancestral, bequeathed, patrimonial

heredity *noun* GENETICS, inheritance, genetic make-up, congenital traits

heresy *noun* UNORTHODOXY, apostasy, dissidence, impiety, revisionism, iconoclasm, heterodoxy

heretic *noun* NONCONFORMIST, dissident, separatist, sectarian, renegade, revisionist, dissenter, apostate, schismatic

heretical *adjective* 1 CONTROVERSIAL, unorthodox, revisionist, freethinking
2 UNORTHODOX, revisionist, iconoclastic, heterodox, impious, idolatrous, schismatic, freethinking

heritage *noun* INHERITANCE, legacy, birthright, lot, share, estate, tradition, portion, endowment, bequest, patrimony

hermit *noun* RECLUSE, monk, loner (*informal*), solitary, anchorite, anchoress, stylite, eremite

hero *noun* 1 PROTAGONIST, leading man, lead actor, male lead, principal male character
2 STAR, champion, celebrity, victor, superstar, great man, heart-throb (*Brit*), conqueror, exemplar, celeb (*informal*), megastar (*informal*), popular figure, man of the hour
3 IDOL, favourite, pin-up (*slang*), fave (*informal*)

heroic *adjective* 1 COURAGEOUS, brave, daring, bold, fearless, gallant, intrepid, valiant, doughty, undaunted, dauntless, lion-hearted, valorous, stouthearted
<< OPPOSITE cowardly
2 LEGENDARY, classical, mythological, Homeric
3 EPIC, grand, classic, extravagant, exaggerated, elevated, inflated, high-flown, grandiose
<< OPPOSITE simple

heroine *noun* 1 PROTAGONIST, leading lady, diva, prima donna, female lead, lead actress, principal female character
2 STAR, celebrity, goddess, celeb (*informal*), megastar (*informal*), woman of the hour
3 IDOL, favourite, pin-up (*slang*), fave (*informal*)

> Note that the word *heroine*, meaning 'a female hero', has an *e* at the end. The drug *heroin* is spelled without a final *e*

heroism *noun* BRAVERY, daring, courage, spirit, fortitude, boldness, gallantry, valour, fearlessness, intrepidity, courageousness

hero-worship *noun* ADMIRATION, idolization, adulation, adoration, veneration, idealization, putting on a pedestal

hesitant *adjective* UNCERTAIN, reluctant, shy, halting, doubtful, sceptical, unsure, hesitating, wavering, timid, diffident, lacking confidence, vacillating, hanging back, irresolute, half-hearted
<< OPPOSITE confident

hesitate *verb* 1 WAVER, delay, pause, haver (*Brit*), wait, doubt, falter, be uncertain, dither (*chiefly Brit*), vacillate, equivocate, temporize, hum and haw, shillyshally (*informal*), swither (*Scot dialect*)
<< OPPOSITE be decisive
2 BE RELUCTANT, be unwilling, shrink from, think twice, boggle, scruple, demur, hang back, be disinclined, balk *or* baulk
<< OPPOSITE be determined

hesitation *noun* 1 DELAY, pausing, uncertainty, stalling, dithering, indecision, hesitancy, doubt, vacillation, temporizing, shilly-shallying, irresolution, hemming and hawing, dubiety
2 RELUCTANCE, reservation(s), misgiving(s), ambivalence, qualm(s), unwillingness, scruple(s), compunction, demurral

heterogeneous *adjective* VARIED, different, mixed, contrasting, unlike, diverse, diversified, assorted, unrelated, disparate, miscellaneous, motley, incongruous, dissimilar, divergent, manifold, discrepant

hew *verb* 1 CUT, chop, axe, hack, split, lop
2 (*Old-fashioned*) CARVE, make, form, fashion, shape, model, sculpture, sculpt

heyday *noun* PRIME, time, day, flowering, pink, bloom, high point, zenith, salad days, prime of life

hiatus *noun* PAUSE, break, interval, space, gap, breach, blank, lapse, interruption, respite, chasm, discontinuity, lacuna, entr'acte

hibernate *verb* SLEEP, lie dormant, winter, overwinter, vegetate, remain torpid, sleep snug

hidden *adjective* 1 SECRET, veiled, dark, mysterious, obscure, mystical, mystic, shrouded, occult, latent, cryptic, hermetic, ulterior, abstruse, recondite, hermetical
2 CONCEALED, covered, secret, covert, unseen, clandestine, secreted, under wraps, unrevealed

hide[1] *verb* 1 CONCEAL, stash (*informal*), secrete, cache, put out of sight
<< OPPOSITE display
2 GO INTO HIDING, take cover, keep out of sight, hole up, lie low, go underground, go to ground, go to earth
3 KEEP SECRET, suppress, withhold, keep quiet about, hush up, draw a veil over, keep dark, keep under your hat
<< OPPOSITE disclose
4 OBSCURE, cover, screen, bury, shelter, mask, disguise, conceal, eclipse, veil, cloak, shroud, camouflage, blot out
<< OPPOSITE reveal

hide[2] *noun* SKIN, fell, leather, pelt

hideaway *noun* HIDING PLACE, haven, retreat, refuge, sanctuary, hide-out, nest, sequestered nook

hidebound *adjective* CONVENTIONAL, set, rigid, narrow, puritan, narrow-minded, strait-laced,

brassbound, ultraconservative, set in your ways
<< OPPOSITE broad-minded

hideous *adjective* **1** UGLY, revolting, ghastly, monstrous, grotesque, gruesome, grisly, unsightly, repulsive
<< OPPOSITE beautiful
2 TERRIFYING, shocking, terrible, awful, appalling, disgusting, horrible, dreadful, horrific, obscene, sickening, horrendous, macabre, horrid, odious, loathsome, abominable, detestable, godawful (*slang*)

hide-out *noun* HIDING PLACE, shelter, den, hideaway, lair, secret place

hiding *noun* (*informal*) BEATING, whipping, thrashing, tanning (*slang*), caning, licking (*informal*), flogging, spanking, walloping (*informal*), drubbing, lathering (*informal*), whaling, larruping (*Brit dialect*)

hierarchy *noun* GRADING, ranking, social order, pecking order, class system, social stratum

higgledy-piggledy (*informal*) *adjective* HAPHAZARD, muddled, jumbled, indiscriminate, topsy-turvy, helter-skelter, pell-mell
▷ *adverb* HAPHAZARDLY, all over the place, anyhow, topsy-turvy, helter-skelter, all over the shop (*informal*), pell-mell, confusedly, any old how

high *adjective* **1** TALL, towering, soaring, steep, elevated, lofty
<< OPPOSITE short
2 EXTREME, great, acute, severe, extraordinary, excessive
<< OPPOSITE low
3 STRONG, violent, extreme, blustery, squally, sharp
4 EXPENSIVE, dear, steep (*informal*), costly, stiff, high-priced, exorbitant
5 IMPORTANT, leading, ruling, chief, powerful, significant, distinguished, prominent, superior, influential, notable, big-time (*informal*), eminent, major league (*informal*), exalted, consequential, skookum (*Canad*)
<< OPPOSITE lowly
6 NOTABLE, important, leading, famous, significant, celebrated, distinguished, renowned, eminent, pre-eminent
7 HIGH-PITCHED, piercing, shrill, penetrating, treble, soprano, strident, sharp, acute, piping
<< OPPOSITE deep
8 CHEERFUL, excited, merry, exhilarated, exuberant, joyful, bouncy (*informal*), boisterous, elated, light-hearted, stoked (*Austral & NZ informal*)
<< OPPOSITE dejected
9 (*informal*) INTOXICATED, stoned (*slang*), spaced out (*slang*), tripping (*informal*), turned on (*slang*), on a trip (*informal*), delirious, euphoric, freaked out (*informal*), hyped up (*slang*), inebriated
10 LUXURIOUS, rich, grand, lavish, extravagant, opulent, hedonistic
▷ *adverb* WAY UP, aloft, far up, to a great height
▷ *noun* **1** PEAK, height, top, summit, crest, record level, apex
2 (*informal*) INTOXICATION, trip (*informal*), euphoria, delirium, ecstasy
▷▷ **high and dry** ABANDONED, stranded, helpless, forsaken, bereft, destitute, in the lurch
▷▷ **high and mighty** (*informal*) SELF-IMPORTANT, superior, arrogant, stuck-up (*informal*), conceited, imperious, overbearing, haughty, snobbish, disdainful

highbrow (*Often disparaging*) *adjective* INTELLECTUAL, cultured, sophisticated, deep, cultivated, brainy (*informal*), highbrowed, bookish
<< OPPOSITE unintellectual
▷ *noun* INTELLECTUAL, scholar, egghead (*informal*), brain (*informal*), mastermind, Brahmin (*US*), aesthete, savant, brainbox (*slang*)
<< OPPOSITE philistine

high-class *adjective* HIGH-QUALITY, top (*slang*), choice, select, exclusive, elite, superior, posh (*informal, chiefly Brit*), classy (*slang*), top-flight, upper-class, swish (*informal, chiefly Brit*), first-rate, up-market, top-drawer, ritzy (*slang*), tip-top, high-toned, A1 *or* A-one (*informal*)
<< OPPOSITE inferior

higher-up *noun* (*informal*) SUPERIOR, senior, manager, director, executive, boss, gaffer (*informal, chiefly Brit*), baas (*S African*), sherang (*Austral & NZ*)

high-flown *adjective* EXTRAVAGANT, elaborate, pretentious, exaggerated, inflated, lofty, grandiose, overblown, florid, high-falutin (*informal*), arty-farty (*informal*), magniloquent
<< OPPOSITE straightforward

high-handed *adjective* DICTATORIAL, domineering, overbearing, arbitrary, oppressive, autocratic, bossy (*informal*), imperious, tyrannical, despotic, peremptory

highlight *verb* EMPHASIZE, stress, accent, feature, set off, show up, underline, spotlight, play up, accentuate, foreground, focus attention on, call attention to, give prominence to, bring to the fore
<< OPPOSITE play down
▷ *noun* HIGH POINT, peak, climax, feature, focus, best part, focal point, main feature, high spot, memorable part
<< OPPOSITE low point

highly *adverb* **1** EXTREMELY, very, greatly, seriously (*informal*), vastly, exceptionally, extraordinarily, immensely, decidedly, tremendously, supremely, eminently

2 FAVOURABLY, well, warmly, enthusiastically, approvingly, appreciatively

highly-strung *adjective* NERVOUS, stressed, tense, sensitive, wired (*slang*), restless, neurotic, taut, edgy, temperamental, excitable, nervy (*Brit informal*), twitchy (*informal*), on tenterhooks, easily upset, on pins and needles, adrenalized

<< OPPOSITE relaxed

high-minded *adjective* PRINCIPLED, moral, worthy, noble, good, fair, pure, ethical, upright, elevated, honourable, righteous, idealistic, virtuous, magnanimous

<< OPPOSITE dishonourable

high-powered *adjective* DYNAMIC, driving, powerful, enterprising, effective, go-ahead, aggressive, vigorous, energetic, forceful, fast-track, go-getting (*informal*), high-octane (*informal*), highly capable

high-pressure *adjective* (*informal*) FORCEFUL, aggressive, compelling, intensive, persistent, persuasive, high-powered, insistent, bludgeoning, pushy (*informal*), in-your-face (*slang*), coercive, importunate

high-spirited *adjective* LIVELY, spirited, vivacious, vital, daring, dashing, bold, energetic, animated, vibrant, exuberant, bouncy, boisterous, fun-loving, ebullient, sparky, effervescent, alive and kicking, full of life, spunky (*informal*), full of beans (*informal*), frolicsome, mettlesome

hijack *or* **highjack** *verb* SEIZE, take over, commandeer, expropriate, skyjack

hike *noun* WALK, march, trek, ramble, tramp, traipse, journey on foot

▷ *verb* WALK, march, trek, ramble, tramp, leg it (*informal*), back-pack, hoof it (*slang*)

▷▷ **hike something up** HITCH UP, raise, lift, pull up, jack up

hiker *noun* WALKER, rambler, backpacker, wayfarer, hillwalker

hilarious *adjective* 1 FUNNY, entertaining, amusing, hysterical, humorous, exhilarating, comical, side-splitting

2 MERRY, uproarious, happy, gay, noisy, jolly, joyous, joyful, jovial, rollicking, convivial, mirthful

<< OPPOSITE serious

hilarity *noun* MERRIMENT, high spirits, mirth, gaiety, laughter, amusement, glee, exuberance, exhilaration, cheerfulness, jollity, levity, conviviality, joviality, boisterousness, joyousness, jollification

hill *noun* 1 MOUNT, down (*archaic*), fell, height, mound, prominence, elevation, eminence, hilltop, tor, knoll, hillock, brae (*Scot*), kopje *or* koppie (*S African*)

2 SLOPE, incline, gradient, rise, climb, brae (*Scot*), acclivity

hilly *adjective* MOUNTAINOUS, rolling, steep, undulating

hilt *noun* HANDLE, grip, haft, handgrip, helve

▷▷ **to the hilt** (*informal*) FULLY, completely, totally, entirely, wholly

hind *adjective* BACK, rear, hinder, posterior, caudal (*Anatomy*)

hinder *verb* OBSTRUCT, stop, check, block, prevent, arrest, delay, oppose, frustrate, handicap, interrupt, slow down, deter, hamstring, hamper, thwart, retard, impede, hobble, stymie, encumber, throw a spanner in the works, trammel, hold up *or* back

<< OPPOSITE help

hindrance *noun* OBSTACLE, check, bar, block, difficulty, drag, barrier, restriction, handicap, limitation, hazard, restraint, hitch, drawback, snag, deterrent, interruption, obstruction, stoppage, stumbling block, impediment, encumbrance, trammel

<< OPPOSITE help

hinge on *verb* DEPEND ON, be subject to, hang on, turn on, rest on, revolve around, be contingent on, pivot on

hint *noun* 1 CLUE, mention, suggestion, implication, indication, reminder, tip-off, pointer, allusion, innuendo, inkling, intimation, insinuation, word to the wise

2 ADVICE, help, tip(s), suggestion(s), pointer(s)

3 TRACE, touch, suggestion, taste, breath, dash, whisper, suspicion, tinge, whiff, speck, undertone, soupçon (*French*)

▷ *verb sometimes with* **at** SUGGEST, mention, indicate, imply, intimate, tip off, let it be known, insinuate, allude to the fact, tip the wink (*informal*)

hip *adjective* (*Slang*) TRENDY (*Brit informal*), with it, fashionable, in, aware, informed, wise (*slang*), clued-up (*informal*)

hippy *or* **hippie** *noun* FLOWER CHILD, bohemian, dropout, free spirit, beatnik, basketweaver (*Austral derogatory slang*)

hire *verb* 1 EMPLOY, commission, take on, engage, appoint, sign up, enlist

2 RENT, charter, lease, let, engage

▷ *noun* 1 RENTAL, hiring, rent, lease

2 CHARGE, rental, price, cost, fee

hirsute *adjective* (*Formal*) HAIRY, bearded, shaggy, unshaven, bristly, bewhiskered, hispid (*Biology*)

hiss *verb* 1 WHISTLE, wheeze, rasp, whiz, whirr, sibilate

2 JEER, mock, ridicule, deride, decry, revile

▷ *noun* FIZZ, buzz, hissing, fizzing, sibilance, sibilation

historian *noun* CHRONICLER, recorder, biographer, antiquarian, historiographer, annalist, chronologist

historic *adjective* SIGNIFICANT, notable,

momentous, famous, celebrated, extraordinary, outstanding, remarkable, ground-breaking, consequential, red-letter, epoch-making
<< OPPOSITE unimportant

Although *historic* and *historical* are similarly spelt they are very different in meaning and should not be used interchangeably. A distinction is usually made between *historic*, which means 'important' or 'significant', and *historical*, which means 'pertaining to history': *a historic decision*; *a historical perspective*

historical *adjective* FACTUAL, real, documented, actual, authentic, chronicled, attested, archival, verifiable
<< OPPOSITE contemporary ▷ see **historic**

history *noun* **1** THE PAST, the old days, antiquity, yesterday, the good old days, yesteryear, ancient history, olden days, days of old, days of yore, bygone times
2 CHRONICLE, record, story, account, relation, narrative, saga, recital, narration, annals, recapitulation

histrionic *adjective* THEATRICAL, affected, dramatic, forced, camp (*informal*), actorly, artificial, unnatural, melodramatic, actressy
▷ *plural noun* DRAMATICS, scene, tantrums, performance, temperament, theatricality, staginess, hissy fit (*informal*)

hit *verb* **1** STRIKE, beat, knock, punch, belt (*informal*), deck (*slang*), bang, batter, clip (*informal*), slap, bash (*informal*), sock (*slang*), chin (*slang*), smack, thump, clout (*informal*), cuff, flog, whack, clobber (*slang*), smite (*archaic*), wallop (*informal*), swat, lay one on (*slang*), beat *or* knock seven bells out of (*informal*)
2 COLLIDE WITH, run into, bump into, clash with, smash into, crash against, bang into, meet head-on
3 AFFECT, damage, harm, ruin, devastate, overwhelm, touch, impact on, impinge on, leave a mark on, make an impact *or* impression on
4 REACH, strike, gain, achieve, secure, arrive at, accomplish, attain
▷ *noun* **1** SHOT, blow, impact, collision
2 BLOW, knock, stroke, belt (*informal*), rap, slap, bump, smack, clout (*informal*), cuff, swipe (*informal*), wallop (*informal*)
3 SUCCESS, winner, triumph, smash (*informal*), sensation, sellout, smasheroo (*informal*)
▷▷ **hit it off** (*informal*) GET ON (WELL) WITH, take to, click (*slang*), warm to, be on good terms, get on like a house on fire (*informal*)
▷▷ **hit on** *or* **upon something** THINK UP, discover, arrive at, guess, realize, invent, come upon, stumble on, chance upon, light upon, strike upon
▷▷ **hit out at someone** ATTACK, condemn, denounce, lash out, castigate, rail against, assail, inveigh against, strike out at

hit-and-miss *or* **hit-or-miss** *adjective* HAPHAZARD, random, uneven, casual, indiscriminate, cursory, perfunctory, aimless, disorganized, undirected, scattershot
<< OPPOSITE systematic

hitch *noun* PROBLEM, catch, trouble, check, difficulty, delay, hold-up, obstacle, hazard, drawback, hassle (*informal*), snag, uphill (*S African*), stoppage, mishap, impediment, hindrance
▷ *verb* **1** (*informal*) HITCHHIKE, thumb a lift
2 FASTEN, join, attach, unite, couple, tie, connect, harness, tether, yoke, make fast
▷▷ **hitch something up** PULL UP, tug, jerk, yank, hoick

hither *adverb* (*Old-fashioned*) HERE, over here, to this place, close, closer, near, nearer, nigh (*archaic*)

hitherto *adverb* (*Formal*) PREVIOUSLY, so far, until now, thus far, up to now, till now, heretofore

hive *noun* **1** COLONY, swarm
2 CENTRE, hub, powerhouse (*slang*)

hoard *verb* SAVE, store, collect, gather, treasure, accumulate, garner, amass, stockpile, buy up, put away, hive, cache, lay up, put by, stash away (*informal*)
▷ *noun* STORE, fund, supply, reserve, mass, pile, heap, fall-back, accumulation, stockpile, stash, cache, treasure-trove

hoarse *adjective* ROUGH, harsh, husky, grating, growling, raucous, rasping, gruff, throaty, gravelly, guttural, croaky
<< OPPOSITE clear

hoary *adjective* **1** OLD, aged, ancient, antique, venerable, antiquated
2 WHITE-HAIRED, white, grey, silvery, frosty, grey-haired, grizzled, hoar

hoax *noun* TRICK, joke, fraud, con (*informal*), deception, spoof (*informal*), prank, swindle, ruse, practical joke, canard, fast one (*informal*), imposture, fastie (*Austral slang*)
▷ *verb* DECEIVE, trick, fool, take in (*informal*), con (*slang*), wind up (*Brit slang*), kid (*informal*), bluff, dupe, gull (*archaic*), delude, swindle, bamboozle (*informal*), gammon (*Brit informal*), hoodwink, take (someone) for a ride (*informal*), befool, hornswoggle (*slang*)

hobble *verb* **1** LIMP, stagger, stumble, shuffle, falter, shamble, totter, dodder, halt
2 RESTRICT, hamstring, shackle, fetter

hobby *noun* PASTIME, relaxation, leisure pursuit, sideline, diversion, avocation, favourite occupation, (leisure) activity

hobnob *verb* SOCIALIZE, mix, associate, hang out (*informal*), mingle, consort, hang about, keep company, fraternize

hog *verb* (*Slang*) MONOPOLIZE, dominate, tie up, corner, corner the market in, be a dog in the manger

hoist *verb* RAISE, lift, erect, elevate, heave, upraise
▷ *noun* LIFT, crane, elevator, winch, tackle

hold *verb* 1 CARRY, keep, grip, grasp, cling to, clasp
2 SUPPORT, take, bear, shoulder, sustain, prop, brace
<< OPPOSITE give way
3 EMBRACE, grasp, clutch, hug, squeeze, cradle, clasp, enfold
4 RESTRAIN, constrain, check, bind, curb, hamper, hinder
<< OPPOSITE release
5 DETAIN, arrest, confine, imprison, impound, pound, hold in custody, put in jail
<< OPPOSITE release
6 ACCOMMODATE, take, contain, seat, comprise, have a capacity for
7 CONSIDER, think, believe, view, judge, regard, maintain, assume, reckon, esteem, deem, presume, entertain the idea
<< OPPOSITE deny
8 OCCUPY, have, fill, maintain, retain, possess, hold down (*informal*)
9 CONDUCT, convene, have, call, run, celebrate, carry on, assemble, preside over, officiate at, solemnize
<< OPPOSITE cancel
10 *sometimes with* **up** CONTINUE, last, remain, stay, wear, resist, endure, persist, persevere
11 APPLY, exist, be the case, stand up, operate, be in force, remain true, hold good, remain valid
▷ *noun* 1 GRIP, grasp, clutch, clasp
2 FOOTHOLD, footing, purchase, leverage, vantage, anchorage
3 CONTROL, authority, influence, pull (*informal*), sway, dominance, clout (*informal*), mastery, dominion, ascendancy, mana (NZ)
▷▷ **hold back** DESIST, forbear, hesitate, stop yourself, restrain yourself, refrain from doing something
▷▷ **hold forth** SPEAK, go on, discourse, lecture, preach, spout (*informal*), harangue, declaim, spiel (*informal*), descant, orate, speechify, korero (NZ)
▷▷ **hold off** PUT OFF, delay, postpone, defer, avoid, refrain, keep from
▷▷ **hold on** (*informal*) WAIT (A MINUTE), hang on (*informal*), sit tight (*informal*), hold your horses (*informal*), just a moment *or* second
▷▷ **hold onto something** *or* **someone** 1 GRAB, hold, grip, clutch, cling to
2 RETAIN, keep, hang onto, not give away, keep possession of
▷▷ **hold out** LAST, continue, carry on, endure, hang on, persist, persevere, stay the course, stand fast
▷▷ **hold out against something** *or* **someone** WITHSTAND, resist, fend off, keep at bay, fight
▷▷ **hold someone back** HINDER, prevent, restrain, check, hamstring, hamper, inhibit, thwart, obstruct, impede
▷▷ **hold someone up** DELAY, slow down, hinder, stop, detain, retard, impede, set back
▷▷ **hold something back** 1 RESTRAIN, check, curb, control, suppress, rein (in), repress, stem the flow of
2 WITHHOLD, hold in, suppress, stifle, repress, keep the lid on (*informal*), keep back
▷▷ **hold something out** OFFER, give, present, extend, proffer
▷▷ **hold something over** POSTPONE, delay, suspend, put off, defer, adjourn, waive, take a rain check on (*US & Canad informal*)
▷▷ **hold something up** 1 DISPLAY, show, exhibit, flourish, show off, hold aloft, present
2 SUPPORT, prop, brace, bolster, sustain, shore up, buttress, jack up
3 ROB, mug (*informal*), stick up (*slang, chiefly US*), waylay
▷▷ **hold something** *or* **someone off** FEND OFF, repel, rebuff, stave off, repulse, keep off
▷▷ **hold up** LAST, survive, endure, bear up, wear
▷▷ **hold with something** APPROVE OF, be in favour of, support, subscribe to, countenance, agree to *or* with, take kindly to

holder *noun* 1 OWNER, bearer, possessor, keeper, purchaser, occupant, proprietor, custodian, incumbent
2 CASE, cover, container, sheath, receptacle, housing

holding *noun often plural* PROPERTY, securities, investments, resources, estate, assets, possessions, stocks and shares, land interests

hold-up *noun* 1 ROBBERY, theft, mugging (*informal*), stick-up (*slang, chiefly US*)
2 DELAY, wait, hitch, trouble, difficulty, setback, snag, traffic jam, obstruction, stoppage, bottleneck

hole *noun* 1 CAVITY, depression, pit, hollow, pocket, chamber, cave, shaft, cavern, excavation
2 OPENING, split, crack, break, tear, gap, rent, breach, outlet, vent, puncture, aperture, fissure, orifice, perforation
3 BURROW, nest, den, earth, shelter, retreat, covert, lair
4 FAULT, error, flaw, defect, loophole, discrepancy, inconsistency, fallacy
5 (*informal*) HOVEL, dump (*informal*), dive (*slang*), slum, joint (*slang*)

6 (*informal*) PREDICAMENT, spot (*informal*), fix (*informal*), mess, jam (*informal*), dilemma, scrape (*informal*), tangle, hot water (*informal*), quandary, tight spot, imbroglio

▷▷ **hole up** HIDE, shelter, take refuge, go into hiding, take cover, go to earth

holiday *noun* 1 VACATION, leave, break, time off, recess, away day, schoolie (*Austral*), accumulated day off *or* ADO (*Austral*)

2 FESTIVAL, bank holiday, festivity, public holiday, fête, celebration, anniversary, feast, red-letter day, name day, saint's day, gala

holiness *noun* SANCTITY, spirituality, sacredness, purity, divinity, righteousness, piety, godliness, saintliness, blessedness, religiousness, devoutness, virtuousness

holler (*informal*) *verb sometimes with* **out** YELL, call, cry, shout, cheer, roar, hail, bellow, whoop, clamour, bawl, hurrah, halloo, huzzah (*archaic*)

▷ *noun* YELL, call, cry, shout, cheer, roar, hail, bellow, whoop, clamour, bawl, hurrah, halloo, huzzah (*archaic*)

hollow *adjective* 1 EMPTY, vacant, void, unfilled, not solid

<< OPPOSITE solid

2 SUNKEN, depressed, cavernous, indented, concave, deep-set

<< OPPOSITE rounded

3 WORTHLESS, empty, useless, vain, meaningless, pointless, futile, fruitless, specious, Pyrrhic, unavailing

<< OPPOSITE meaningful

4 INSINCERE, false, artificial, cynical, hypocritical, hollow-hearted

5 DULL, low, deep, flat, rumbling, muted, muffled, expressionless, sepulchral, toneless, reverberant

<< OPPOSITE vibrant

▷ *noun* 1 CAVITY, cup, hole, bowl, depression, pit, cave, den, basin, dent, crater, trough, cavern, excavation, indentation, dimple, concavity

<< OPPOSITE mound

2 VALLEY, dale, glen, dell, dingle

<< OPPOSITE hill

▷ *verb often followed by* **out** SCOOP OUT, dig out, excavate, gouge out, channel, groove, furrow

holocaust *noun* 1 DEVASTATION, destruction, carnage, genocide, inferno, annihilation, conflagration

2 GENOCIDE, massacre, carnage, mass murder, annihilation, pogrom

holy *adjective* 1 SACRED, blessed, hallowed, dedicated, venerable, consecrated, venerated, sacrosanct, sanctified

<< OPPOSITE unsanctified

2 DEVOUT, godly, religious, pure, divine, faithful, righteous, pious, virtuous, hallowed, saintly, god-fearing

<< OPPOSITE sinful

homage *noun* 1 RESPECT, honour, worship, esteem, admiration, awe, devotion, reverence, duty, deference, adulation, adoration

<< OPPOSITE contempt

2 ALLEGIANCE, service, tribute, loyalty, devotion, fidelity, faithfulness, obeisance, troth (*archaic*), fealty

home *noun* 1 DWELLING, house, residence, abode, habitation, pad (*slang*), domicile, dwelling place

2 BIRTHPLACE, household, homeland, home town, homestead, native land, Godzone (*Austral informal*)

3 TERRITORY, environment, habitat, range, element, haunt, home ground, abode, habitation, stamping ground

▷ *adjective* DOMESTIC, national, local, central, internal, native, inland

▷▷ **at home** 1 IN, present, available

2 AT EASE, relaxed, comfortable, content, at peace

▷▷ **at home in, on,** *or* **with** FAMILIAR WITH, experienced in, skilled in, proficient in, conversant with, au fait with, knowledgeable of, well-versed in

▷▷ **bring something home to someone** MAKE CLEAR, emphasize, drive home, press home, impress upon ▷ see **hone**

homeland *noun* NATIVE LAND, birthplace, motherland, fatherland, country of origin, mother country, Godzone (*Austral informal*)

homeless *adjective* DESTITUTE, exiled, displaced, dispossessed, unsettled, outcast, abandoned, down-and-out

homely *adjective* 1 COMFORTABLE, welcoming, friendly, domestic, familiar, informal, cosy, comfy (*informal*), homespun, downhome (*slang, chiefly US*), homelike, homy

2 PLAIN, simple, natural, ordinary, modest, everyday, down-to-earth, unaffected, unassuming, unpretentious, unfussy

<< OPPOSITE elaborate

3 (*US*) UNATTRACTIVE, plain, ugly, not striking, unprepossessing, not beautiful, no oil painting (*informal*), ill-favoured

homespun *adjective* UNSOPHISTICATED, homely, plain, rough, rude, coarse, home-made, rustic, artless, inelegant, unpolished

homicidal *adjective* MURDEROUS, deadly, lethal, maniacal, death-dealing

homicide *noun* MURDER, killing, manslaughter, slaying, bloodshed

homily *noun* SERMON, talk, address, speech, lecture, preaching, discourse, oration, declamation

homogeneous *or* **homogenous** *adjective* UNIFORM, similar, consistent, identical, alike, comparable, akin, analogous, kindred,

unvarying, cognate
<< OPPOSITE diverse

homosexual *adjective* GAY, lesbian, queer (*informal* or *derogatory*), camp (*informal*), pink (*informal*), same-sex, homoerotic, sapphic, moffie (*S African slang*)
▷ *noun* GAY, lesbian, queer (*informal* or *derogatory*), moffie (*S African slang*), auntie *or* aunty (*Austral slang*), lily (*Austral slang*)
>> RELATED WORD *fear* homophobia

homy *or* **homey** *adjective* (*Chiefly US*) HOMELY, comfortable, welcoming, domestic, friendly, familiar, cosy, comfy (*informal*), homespun, downhome (*slang, chiefly US*), homelike

hone *verb* **1** IMPROVE, better, polish, enhance, upgrade, refine, sharpen, augment, help
2 SHARPEN, point, grind, edge, file, polish, whet, strop

Hone is sometimes wrongly used where *home* is meant: *this device makes it easier to home in on* (not *hone in on*) *the target*

honest *adjective* **1** TRUSTWORTHY, decent, upright, reliable, ethical, honourable, conscientious, reputable, truthful, virtuous, law-abiding, trusty, scrupulous, high-minded, veracious
<< OPPOSITE dishonest
2 OPEN, direct, frank, plain, straightforward, outright, sincere, candid, forthright, upfront (*informal*), undisguised, round, ingenuous, unfeigned
<< OPPOSITE secretive
3 GENUINE, real, true, straight, fair, proper, authentic, equitable, impartial, on the level (*informal*), bona fide, dinkum (*Austral & NZ informal*), above board, fair and square, on the up and up, honest to goodness
<< OPPOSITE false

honestly *adverb* **1** ETHICALLY, legitimately, legally, in good faith, on the level (*informal*), lawfully, honourably, by fair means, with clean hands
2 FRANKLY, plainly, candidly, straight (out), truthfully, to your face, in plain English, in all sincerity

honesty *noun* **1** INTEGRITY, honour, virtue, morality, fidelity, probity, rectitude, veracity, faithfulness, truthfulness, trustworthiness, straightness, incorruptibility, scrupulousness, uprightness, reputability
2 FRANKNESS, openness, sincerity, candour, bluntness, outspokenness, genuineness, plainness, straightforwardness

honeyed *adjective* **1** FLATTERING, sweet, soothing, enticing, mellow, seductive, agreeable, sweetened, cajoling, alluring, melodious, unctuous, dulcet
2 (*Poetic*) SWEET, sweetened, luscious, sugary, syrupy, toothsome

honorary *adjective* NOMINAL, unofficial, titular, ex officio, honoris causa (*Latin*), in name *or* title only

honour *noun* **1** INTEGRITY, principles, morality, honesty, goodness, fairness, decency, righteousness, probity, rectitude, trustworthiness, uprightness
<< OPPOSITE dishonour
2 PRESTIGE, credit, reputation, glory, fame, distinction, esteem, dignity, elevation, eminence, renown, repute, high standing
<< OPPOSITE disgrace
3 REPUTATION, standing, prestige, image, status, stature, good name, kudos, cachet
4 ACCLAIM, regard, respect, praise, recognition, compliments, homage, accolades, reverence, deference, adoration, commendation, veneration
<< OPPOSITE contempt
5 PRIVILEGE, credit, favour, pleasure, compliment, source of pride *or* satisfaction
6 (*Old-fashioned*) VIRGINITY, virtue, innocence, purity, modesty, chastity
▷ *verb* **1** ACCLAIM, celebrate, praise, decorate, compliment, commemorate, dignify, commend, glorify, exalt, laud, lionize
2 RESPECT, value, esteem, prize, appreciate, admire, worship, adore, revere, glorify, reverence, exalt, venerate, hallow
<< OPPOSITE scorn
3 FULFIL, keep, carry out, observe, discharge, live up to, be true to, be as good as (*informal*), be faithful to
4 PAY, take, accept, clear, pass, cash, credit, acknowledge
<< OPPOSITE refuse

honourable *adjective* **1** PRINCIPLED, moral, ethical, just, true, fair, upright, honest, virtuous, trustworthy, trusty, high-minded, upstanding
2 PROPER, right, respectable, righteous, virtuous, creditable
3 PRESTIGIOUS, great, noble, noted, distinguished, notable, renowned, eminent, illustrious, venerable

hoodoo *noun* (*informal*) JINX, curse, bad luck, voodoo, nemesis, hex (*US & Canad informal*), evil eye, evil star

hoodwink *verb* DECEIVE, trick, fool, cheat, con (*informal*), kid (*informal*), mislead, hoax, dupe, gull (*archaic*), delude, swindle, rook (*slang*), bamboozle (*informal*), take for a ride (*informal*), lead up the garden path (*informal*), sell a pup, pull a fast one on (*informal*), cozen, befool

hook *noun* FASTENER, catch, link, lock, holder, peg, clasp, hasp
▷ *verb* **1** FASTEN, fix, secure, catch, clasp, hasp
2 CATCH, land, trap, entrap

▷▷ **by hook or by crook** BY ANY MEANS, somehow, somehow or other, someway, by fair means or foul
▷▷ **hook, line, and sinker** (*informal*) COMPLETELY, totally, entirely, thoroughly, wholly, utterly, through and through, lock, stock and barrel
▷▷ **off the hook** (*informal*) LET OFF, cleared, acquitted, vindicated, in the clear, exonerated, under no obligation, allowed to walk (*slang, chiefly US*)

hooked *adjective* 1 BENT, curved, beaked, aquiline, beaky, hook-shaped, hamate (*rare*), hooklike, falcate (*Biology*), unciform (*Anatomy, etc*), uncinate (*Biology*)
2 (*informal*) OBSESSED, addicted, taken, devoted, turned on (*slang*), enamoured
3 (*informal*) ADDICTED, dependent, using (*informal*), having a habit

hooligan *noun* DELINQUENT, tough, vandal, casual, ned (*Scot slang*), rowdy, hoon (*Austral & NZ*), hoodlum (*chiefly US*), ruffian, lager lout, yob *or* yobbo (*Brit slang*), cougan (*Austral slang*), scozza (*Austral slang*), bogan (*Austral slang*)

hooliganism *noun* DELINQUENCY, violence, disorder, vandalism, rowdiness, loutishness, yobbishness

hoop *noun* RING, band, loop, wheel, round, girdle, circlet

hoot *noun* 1 CRY, shout, howl, scream, shriek, whoop
2 TOOT, beep, honk
3 JEER, yell, boo, catcall
4 (*informal*) LAUGH, scream (*informal*), caution (*informal*), card (*informal*)
▷ *verb* 1 JEER, boo, howl, yell, catcall
2 CRY, call, screech, tu-whit tu-whoo
3 TOOT, sound, blast, blare, beep, honk
4 SHOUT, cry, yell, scream, shriek, whoop

hop *verb* JUMP, spring, bound, leap, skip, vault, caper
▷ *noun* JUMP, step, spring, bound, leap, bounce, skip, vault

hope *verb* BELIEVE, expect, trust, rely, look forward to, anticipate, contemplate, count on, foresee, keep your fingers crossed, cross your fingers
▷ *noun* BELIEF, confidence, expectation, longing, dream, desire, faith, ambition, assumption, anticipation, expectancy, light at the end of the tunnel
<< OPPOSITE despair

hopeful *adjective* 1 OPTIMISTIC, confident, assured, looking forward to, anticipating, buoyant, sanguine, expectant
<< OPPOSITE despairing
2 PROMISING, encouraging, bright, reassuring, cheerful, rosy, heartening, auspicious, propitious
<< OPPOSITE unpromising

hopefully *adverb* 1 OPTIMISTICALLY, confidently, expectantly, with anticipation, sanguinely
2 (*informal*) IT IS HOPED, probably, all being well, God willing, conceivably, feasibly, expectedly

> Some people object to the use of *hopefully* as a synonym for the phrase 'it is hoped that' in a sentence such as *hopefully I'll be able to attend the meeting*. This use of the adverb first appeared in America in the 1960s, but it has rapidly established itself elsewhere. There are really no strong grounds for objecting to it, since we accept other sentence adverbials that fulfil a similar function, for example *unfortunately*, which means 'it is unfortunate that' in a sentence such as *unfortunately I won't be able to attend the meeting*

hopeless *adjective* 1 PESSIMISTIC, desperate, despairing, forlorn, in despair, abject, dejected, despondent, demoralized, defeatist, disconsolate, downhearted
<< OPPOSITE hopeful
2 IMPOSSIBLE, pointless, futile, useless, vain, forlorn, no-win, unattainable, impracticable, unachievable, not having a prayer
3 (*informal*) NO GOOD, inadequate, useless (*informal*), poor, pants (*informal*), pathetic, inferior, incompetent, ineffectual
4 INCURABLE, irreversible, irreparable, lost, helpless, irremediable, past remedy, remediless
<< OPPOSITE curable

hopelessly *adverb* 1 WITHOUT HOPE, desperately, in despair, despairingly, irredeemably, irremediably, beyond all hope
2 COMPLETELY, totally, extremely, desperately, terribly, utterly, tremendously, awfully, impossibly, frightfully

horde *noun* CROWD, mob, swarm, press, host, band, troop, pack, crew, drove, gang, multitude, throng

horizon *noun* 1 SKYLINE, view, vista, field *or* range of vision
2 SCOPE, perspective, range, prospect, stretch, ken, sphere, realm, compass, ambit, purview

horizontal *adjective* LEVEL, flat, plane, parallel, supine

horny *adjective* (*informal*) AROUSED, excited, turned on (*slang*), randy (*informal, chiefly Brit*), raunchy (*slang*), amorous, lustful

horrible *adjective* 1 (*informal*) DREADFUL, terrible, awful, nasty, cruel, beastly (*informal*), mean, unpleasant, ghastly (*informal*), unkind, horrid, disagreeable
<< OPPOSITE wonderful

2 TERRIBLE, awful, appalling, terrifying, shocking, grim, dreadful, revolting, fearful, obscene, ghastly, hideous, shameful, gruesome, from hell (*informal*), grisly, horrid, repulsive, frightful, heinous, loathsome, abhorrent, abominable, hellacious (*US slang*)

horrid *adjective* (*informal*) 1 UNPLEASANT, terrible, awful, offensive, nasty, disgusting, horrible, dreadful, obscene, disagreeable, yucky *or* yukky (*slang*), yucko (*Austral slang*)
2 NASTY, dreadful, horrible, mean, unkind, cruel, beastly (*informal*)

horrific *adjective* HORRIFYING, shocking, appalling, frightening, awful, terrifying, grim, dreadful, horrendous, ghastly, from hell (*informal*), grisly, frightful, hellacious (*US slang*)

horrify *verb* 1 TERRIFY, alarm, frighten, scare, intimidate, petrify, terrorize, put the wind up (*informal*), gross out (*US slang*), make your hair stand on end, affright
<< OPPOSITE comfort
2 SHOCK, appal, disgust, dismay, sicken, outrage
<< OPPOSITE delight

horror *noun* 1 TERROR, fear, alarm, panic, dread, dismay, awe, fright, apprehension, consternation, trepidation
2 HATRED, disgust, loathing, aversion, revulsion, antipathy, abomination, abhorrence, repugnance, odium, detestation
<< OPPOSITE love

horse *noun* NAG, mount, mare, colt, filly, stallion, gelding, jade, pony, yearling, steed (*archaic* or *literary*), dobbin, moke (*Austral slang*), hobby (*archaic* or *dialect*), yarraman *or* yarramin (*Austral*), gee-gee (*slang*), cuddy *or* cuddie (*dialect, chiefly Scot*), studhorse *or* stud
▷▷ **horse around** *or* **about** (*informal*) PLAY AROUND *or* ABOUT, fool about *or* around, clown, misbehave, play the fool, roughhouse (*slang*), play the goat, monkey about *or* around, indulge in horseplay, lark about *or* around
>> RELATED WORDS *adjectives* equestrian, equine, horsey
>> RELATED WORD *noun* equitation
>> RELATED WORD *male* stallion
>> RELATED WORD *female* mare
>> RELATED WORDS *young* foal, colt, filly
>> RELATED WORD *like* hippomania
>> RELATED WORD *fear* hippophobia

horseman *noun* RIDER, equestrian

hospitable *adjective* WELCOMING, kind, friendly, liberal, generous, gracious, amicable, cordial, sociable, genial, bountiful
<< OPPOSITE inhospitable

hospitality *noun* WELCOME, warmth, kindness, friendliness, sociability, conviviality, neighbourliness, cordiality, heartiness, hospitableness

host[1] *or* **hostess** *noun* 1 MASTER OF CEREMONIES, proprietor, innkeeper, landlord *or* landlady
2 PRESENTER, compere (*Brit*), anchorman *or* anchorwoman
▷ *verb* PRESENT, introduce, compere (*Brit*), front (*informal*)

host[2] *noun* 1 MULTITUDE, lot, load (*informal*), wealth, array, myriad, great quantity, large number
2 CROWD, army, pack, drove, mob, herd, legion, swarm, horde, throng

hostage *noun* CAPTIVE, prisoner, pledge, pawn, security, surety

hostile *adjective* 1 ANTAGONISTIC, anti (*informal*), opposed, opposite, contrary, inimical, ill-disposed
2 UNFRIENDLY, belligerent, antagonistic, unkind, malevolent, warlike, bellicose, inimical, rancorous, ill-disposed
<< OPPOSITE friendly
3 INHOSPITABLE, adverse, alien, uncongenial, unsympathetic, unwelcoming, unpropitious
<< OPPOSITE hospitable

hostility *noun* 1 UNFRIENDLINESS, hatred, animosity, spite, bitterness, malice, venom, antagonism, enmity, abhorrence, malevolence, detestation
<< OPPOSITE friendliness
2 OPPOSITION, resentment, antipathy, aversion, antagonism, ill feeling, bad blood, ill-will, animus
<< OPPOSITE approval
▷ *plural noun* WARFARE, war, fighting, conflict, combat, armed conflict, state of war
<< OPPOSITE peace

hot *adjective* 1 HEATED, burning, boiling, steaming, flaming, roasting, searing, blistering, fiery, scorching, scalding, piping hot
2 WARM, close, stifling, humid, torrid, sultry, sweltering, balmy, muggy
<< OPPOSITE cold
3 SPICY, pungent, peppery, piquant, biting, sharp, acrid
<< OPPOSITE mild
4 INTENSE, passionate, heated, spirited, excited, fierce, lively, animated, ardent, inflamed, fervent, impassioned, fervid
5 NEW, latest, fresh, recent, up to date, just out, up to the minute, bang up to date (*informal*), hot off the press
<< OPPOSITE old
6 POPULAR, hip, fashionable, cool, in demand, sought-after, must-see, in vogue
<< OPPOSITE unpopular
7 FIERCE, intense, strong, keen, competitive, cut-throat
8 FIERY, violent, raging, passionate, stormy,

touchy, vehement, impetuous, irascible
<< OPPOSITE calm
hot air *noun* EMPTY TALK, rant, guff (*slang*), bombast, wind, gas (*informal*), verbiage, claptrap (*informal*), blather, bunkum (*chiefly US*), blether, bosh (*informal*), tall talk (*informal*)
hotbed *noun* BREEDING GROUND, nest, den
hot-headed *adjective* VOLATILE, rash, fiery, reckless, precipitate, hasty, unruly, foolhardy, impetuous, hot-tempered, quick-tempered
hothouse *noun* GREENHOUSE, conservatory, glasshouse, orangery
hotly *adverb* 1 FIERCELY, passionately, angrily, vehemently, indignantly, with indignation, heatedly, impetuously
2 CLOSELY, enthusiastically, eagerly, with enthusiasm, hotfoot
hound *verb* 1 HARASS, harry, bother, provoke, annoy, torment, hassle (*informal*), prod, badger, persecute, pester, goad, keep after
2 FORCE, drive, pressure, push, chase, railroad (*informal*), propel, impel, pressurize
>> RELATED WORD *collective noun* pack
house *noun* 1 HOME, residence, dwelling, building, pad (*slang*), homestead, edifice, abode, habitation, domicile, whare (NZ)
2 HOUSEHOLD, family, ménage
3 FIRM, company, business, concern, organization, partnership, establishment, outfit (*informal*)
4 ASSEMBLY, parliament, Commons, legislative body
5 RESTAURANT, inn, hotel, pub (*Brit informal*), tavern, public house, hostelry
6 DYNASTY, line, race, tribe, clan, ancestry, lineage, family tree, kindred
▷ *verb* 1 ACCOMMODATE, board, quarter, take in, put up, lodge, harbour, billet, domicile
2 CONTAIN, keep, hold, cover, store, protect, shelter
3 TAKE, accommodate, sleep, provide shelter for, give a bed to
▷▷ **on the house** FREE, for free (*informal*), for nothing, free of charge, gratis, without expense
household *noun* FAMILY, home, house, ménage, family circle, ainga (NZ)
▷ *modifier* DOMESTIC, family, domiciliary
householder *noun* OCCUPANT, resident, tenant, proprietor, homeowner, freeholder, leaseholder
housekeeping *noun* HOUSEHOLD MANAGEMENT, homemaking (US), home economy, housewifery, housecraft
housing *noun* 1 ACCOMMODATION, homes, houses, dwellings, domiciles
2 CASE, casing, covering, cover, shell, jacket, holder, container, capsule, sheath, encasement
hovel *noun* HUT, hole, shed, cabin, den, slum, shack, shanty, whare (NZ)
hover *verb* 1 FLOAT, fly, hang, drift, be suspended, flutter, poise
2 LINGER, loiter, wait nearby, hang about *or* around (*informal*)
3 WAVER, alternate, fluctuate, haver (*Brit*), falter, dither (*chiefly Brit*), oscillate, vacillate, seesaw, swither (*Scot dialect*)
however *adverb* BUT, nevertheless, still, though, yet, even though, on the other hand, nonetheless, notwithstanding, anyhow, be that as it may
howl *verb* 1 BAY, cry, bark, yelp, quest (*used of hounds*)
2 CRY, shout, scream, roar, weep, yell, cry out, wail, shriek, bellow, bawl, yelp
▷ *noun* 1 BAYING, cry, bay, bark, barking, yelp, yelping, yowl
2 CRY, scream, roar, bay, wail, outcry, shriek, bellow, clamour, hoot, bawl, yelp, yowl
howler *noun* (*informal*) MISTAKE, error, blunder, boob (*Brit slang*), bloomer (*Brit informal*), clanger (*informal*), malapropism, schoolboy howler, booboo (*informal*), barry *or* Barry Crocker (*Austral slang*)
hub *noun* CENTRE, heart, focus, core, middle, focal point, pivot, nerve centre
hubbub *noun* 1 NOISE, racket, din, uproar, cacophony, pandemonium, babel, tumult, hurly-burly
2 HUE AND CRY, confusion, disturbance, riot, disorder, clamour, rumpus, bedlam, brouhaha, ruction (*informal*), hullabaloo, ruckus (*informal*)
hubris *noun* PRIDE, vanity, arrogance, conceit, self-importance, haughtiness, conceitedness
huddle *verb* 1 CURL UP, crouch, hunch up, nestle, snuggle, make yourself small
2 CROWD, press, gather, collect, squeeze, cluster, flock, herd, throng
▷ *noun* 1 CROWD, mass, bunch, cluster, heap, muddle, jumble
2 (*informal*) DISCUSSION, conference, meeting, hui (NZ), powwow, confab (*informal*), korero (NZ)
hue *noun* 1 COLOUR, tone, shade, dye, tint, tinge, tincture
2 ASPECT, light, cast, complexion
huff *noun* SULK, temper, bad mood, passion, rage, pet, pique, foulie (*Austral slang*)
hug *verb* 1 EMBRACE, hold (onto), cuddle, squeeze, cling, clasp, enfold, hold close, take in your arms
2 FOLLOW CLOSELY, keep close, stay near, cling to, follow the course of
▷ *noun* EMBRACE, squeeze, bear hug, clinch (*slang*), clasp
huge *adjective* ENORMOUS, great, giant, large, massive, vast, extensive, tremendous,

immense, mega (*slang*), titanic, jumbo (*informal*), gigantic, monumental, mammoth, bulky, colossal, mountainous, stellar (*informal*), prodigious, stupendous, gargantuan, elephantine, ginormous (*informal*), Brobdingnagian, humongous *or* humungous (*US slang*)
<< OPPOSITE tiny
hugely *adverb* IMMENSELY, enormously, massively, prodigiously, monumentally, stupendously
hui *noun* (NZ) MEETING, gathering, assembly, meet, conference, congress, session, rally, convention, get-together (*informal*), reunion, congregation, conclave, convocation, powwow
hulk *noun* WRECK, shell, hull, shipwreck, frame
hulking *adjective* UNGAINLY, massive, lumbering, gross, awkward, clumsy, bulky, cumbersome, overgrown, unwieldy, ponderous, clunky (*informal*), oafish, lumpish, lubberly, unco (*Austral slang*)
hull *noun* 1 FRAMEWORK, casing, body, covering, frame, skeleton
2 HUSK, skin, shell, peel, pod, rind, shuck
▷ *verb* TRIM, peel, skin, shell, husk, shuck
hum *verb* 1 DRONE, buzz, murmur, throb, vibrate, purr, croon, thrum, whir
2 (*informal*) BE BUSY, buzz, bustle, move, stir, pulse, be active, vibrate, pulsate
human *adjective* 1 MORTAL, anthropoid, manlike
<< OPPOSITE nonhuman
2 KIND, natural, vulnerable, kindly, understandable, humane, compassionate, considerate, approachable
<< OPPOSITE inhuman
▷ *noun* HUMAN BEING, person, individual, body, creature, mortal, man *or* woman
<< OPPOSITE nonhuman
>> RELATED WORD *combining form* anthropo-
humane *adjective* KIND, compassionate, good, kindly, understanding, gentle, forgiving, tender, mild, sympathetic, charitable, benign, clement, benevolent, lenient, merciful, good-natured, forbearing, kind-hearted
<< OPPOSITE cruel
humanitarian *adjective* 1 COMPASSIONATE, charitable, humane, benevolent, altruistic, beneficent
2 CHARITABLE, philanthropic, public-spirited
▷ *noun* PHILANTHROPIST, benefactor, Good Samaritan, altruist
humanity *noun* 1 THE HUMAN RACE, man, mankind, people, men, mortals, humankind, Homo sapiens
2 HUMAN NATURE, mortality, humanness
3 KINDNESS, charity, compassion, understanding, sympathy, mercy, tolerance, tenderness, philanthropy, benevolence, fellow feeling, benignity, brotherly love, kind-heartedness
▷ *plural noun* ARTS, liberal arts, classics, classical studies, literae humaniores
humble *adjective* 1 MODEST, meek, unassuming, unpretentious, submissive, self-effacing, unostentatious
<< OPPOSITE proud
2 LOWLY, common, poor, mean, low, simple, ordinary, modest, obscure, commonplace, insignificant, unimportant, unpretentious, undistinguished, plebeian, low-born
<< OPPOSITE distinguished
▷ *verb* HUMILIATE, shame, disgrace, break, reduce, lower, sink, crush, put down (*slang*), bring down, subdue, degrade, demean, chagrin, chasten, mortify, debase, put (someone) in their place, abase, take (someone) down a peg (*informal*), abash
<< OPPOSITE exalt
humbly *adverb* MEEKLY, modestly, respectfully, cap in hand, diffidently, deferentially, submissively, unassumingly, obsequiously, subserviently, on bended knee, servilely
humbug *noun* NONSENSE, rubbish, trash, hypocrisy, cant, baloney (*informal*), claptrap (*informal*), quackery, eyewash (*informal*), charlatanry
humdrum *adjective* DULL, ordinary, boring, routine, commonplace, mundane, tedious, dreary, banal, tiresome, monotonous, uneventful, uninteresting, mind-numbing, ho-hum (*informal*), repetitious, wearisome, unvaried
<< OPPOSITE exciting
humid *adjective* DAMP, sticky, moist, wet, steamy, sultry, dank, clammy, muggy
<< OPPOSITE dry
humidity *noun* DAMP, moisture, dampness, wetness, moistness, sogginess, dankness, clamminess, mugginess, humidness
humiliate *verb* EMBARRASS, shame, humble, crush, disgrace, put down, subdue, degrade, chagrin, chasten, mortify, debase, discomfit, bring low, put (someone) in their place, take the wind out of someone's sails, abase, take down a peg (*informal*), abash, make (someone) eat humble pie
<< OPPOSITE honour
humiliating *adjective* EMBARRASSING, shaming, humbling, mortifying, crushing, disgracing, degrading, ignominious, toe-curling (*slang*), cringe-making (*Brit informal*), cringeworthy (*Brit informal*), barro (*Austral slang*)
humiliation *noun* EMBARRASSMENT, shame, disgrace, humbling, put-down, degradation, affront, indignity, chagrin, ignominy, dishonour, mortification, loss of face,

abasement, self-abasement

humility *noun* MODESTY, diffidence, meekness, submissiveness, servility, self-abasement, humbleness, lowliness, unpretentiousness, lack of pride
<< OPPOSITE pride

humorist *noun* COMEDIAN, comic, wit, eccentric, wag, joker, card (*informal*), jester, dag (*NZ informal*), funny man

humorous *adjective* FUNNY, comic, amusing, entertaining, witty, merry, hilarious, ludicrous, laughable, farcical, whimsical, comical, droll, facetious, jocular, side-splitting, waggish, jocose
<< OPPOSITE serious

humour *noun* **1** COMEDY, funniness, fun, amusement, funny side, jocularity, facetiousness, ludicrousness, drollery, comical aspect
<< OPPOSITE seriousness
2 MOOD, spirits, temper, disposition, frame of mind
3 JOKING, jokes, comedy, wit, gags (*informal*), farce, jesting, jests, wisecracks (*informal*), witticisms, wittiness
▷ *verb* INDULGE, accommodate, go along with, spoil, flatter, pamper, gratify, pander to, mollify, cosset, fawn on
<< OPPOSITE oppose

humourless *adjective* SERIOUS, intense, solemn, straight, dry, dour, unfunny, po-faced, unsmiling, heavy-going, unamused, unamusing

hump *noun* LUMP, bump, projection, bulge, mound, hunch, knob, protuberance, protrusion
▷ *verb* (*informal*) CARRY, lug, heave, hoist, shoulder

hunch *noun* FEELING, idea, impression, suspicion, intuition, premonition, inkling, presentiment
▷ *verb* CROUCH, bend, stoop, curve, arch, huddle, draw in, squat, hump

hunger *noun* **1** APPETITE, emptiness, voracity, hungriness, ravenousness
2 STARVATION, famine, malnutrition, undernourishment
3 DESIRE, appetite, craving, yen (*informal*), ache, lust, yearning, itch, thirst, greediness
▷▷ **hunger for** *or* **after something** WANT, desire, crave, hope for, long for, wish for, yearn for, pine for, hanker after, ache for, thirst after, itch after

hungry *adjective* **1** STARVING, ravenous, famished, starved, empty, hollow, voracious, peckish (*informal, chiefly Brit*), famishing
2 EAGER, keen, craving, yearning, greedy, avid, desirous, covetous, athirst

hunk *noun* LUMP, piece, chunk, block, mass, wedge, slab, nugget, wodge (*Brit informal*), gobbet

hunt *verb* STALK, track, chase, pursue, trail, hound, gun for
▷ *noun* SEARCH, hunting, investigation, chase, pursuit, quest
▷▷ **hunt for something** *or* **someone** SEARCH FOR, look for, try to find, seek for, forage for, rummage for, scour for, look high and low, fossick for (*Austral & NZ*), go in quest of, ferret about for

hunted *adjective* HARASSED, desperate, harried, tormented, stricken, distraught, persecuted, terror-stricken

hunter *noun* HUNTSMAN *or* HUNTRESS, Diana, Herne, Orion, Nimrod, jaeger (*rare*), Artemis, sportsman *or* sportswoman

hurdle *noun* **1** OBSTACLE, block, difficulty, barrier, handicap, hazard, complication, snag, uphill (*S African*), obstruction, stumbling block, impediment, hindrance
2 FENCE, wall, hedge, block, barrier, barricade

hurl *verb* THROW, fling, chuck (*informal*), send, fire, project, launch, cast, pitch, shy, toss, propel, sling, heave, let fly (with)

hurly-burly *noun* COMMOTION, confusion, chaos, turmoil, disorder, upheaval, furore, uproar, turbulence, pandemonium, bedlam, tumult, hubbub, brouhaha
<< OPPOSITE order

hurricane *noun* STORM, gale, tornado, cyclone, typhoon, tempest, twister (*US informal*), windstorm, willy-willy (*Austral*)

hurried *adjective* **1** HASTY, quick, brief, rushed, short, swift, speedy, precipitate, quickie (*informal*), breakneck
2 RUSHED, perfunctory, hectic, speedy, superficial, hasty, cursory, slapdash

hurriedly *adverb* HASTILY, quickly, briskly, speedily, in a rush, at the double, hurry-scurry

hurry *verb* **1** RUSH, fly, dash, barrel (along) (*informal, chiefly US & Canad*), scurry, scoot, burn rubber (*informal*)
<< OPPOSITE dawdle
2 MAKE HASTE, rush, lose no time, get a move on (*informal*), step on it (*informal*), get your skates on (*informal*)
3 *sometimes with* **up** SPEED (UP), accelerate, hasten, quicken, hustle, urge, push on, goad, expedite
<< OPPOSITE slow down
▷ *noun* RUSH, haste, speed, urgency, bustle, flurry, commotion, precipitation, quickness, celerity, promptitude
<< OPPOSITE slowness

hurt *verb* **1** INJURE, damage, wound, cut, disable, bruise, scrape, impair, gash
<< OPPOSITE heal
2 ACHE, be sore, be painful, burn, smart, sting,

throb, be tender
3 HARM, injure, molest, ill-treat, maltreat, lay a finger on
4 UPSET, distress, pain, wound, annoy, sting, grieve, afflict, sadden, cut to the quick, aggrieve
▷ *noun* 1 DISTRESS, suffering, pain, grief, misery, agony, sadness, sorrow, woe, anguish, heartache, wretchedness
<< OPPOSITE happiness
2 HARM, trouble, damage, wrong, loss, injury, misfortune, mischief, affliction
▷ *adjective* 1 INJURED, wounded, damaged, harmed, cut, scratched, bruised, scarred, scraped, grazed
<< OPPOSITE healed
2 UPSET, pained, injured, wounded, sad, crushed, offended, aggrieved, miffed (*informal*), rueful, piqued, tooshie (*Austral slang*)
<< OPPOSITE calmed

hurtful *adjective* UNKIND, upsetting, distressing, mean, cutting, damaging, wounding, nasty, cruel, destructive, harmful, malicious, mischievous, detrimental, pernicious, spiteful, prejudicial, injurious, disadvantageous, maleficent

hurtle *verb* RUSH, charge, race, shoot, fly, speed, tear, crash, plunge, barrel (along) (*informal, chiefly US & Canad*), scramble, spurt, stampede, scoot, burn rubber (*informal*), rush headlong, go hell for leather (*informal*)

husband *noun* PARTNER, man (*informal*), spouse, hubby (*informal*), mate, old man (*informal*), bridegroom, significant other (*US informal*), better half (*humorous*)
▷ *verb* CONSERVE, budget, use sparingly, save, store, hoard, economize on, use economically, manage thriftily
<< OPPOSITE squander

husbandry *noun* 1 FARMING, agriculture, cultivation, land management, tillage, agronomy
2 THRIFT, economy, good housekeeping, frugality, careful management

hush *verb* QUIETEN, still, silence, suppress, mute, muzzle, shush
▷ *noun* QUIET, silence, calm, still (*poetic*), peace, tranquillity, stillness, peacefulness
▷▷ **hush something up** COVER UP, conceal, suppress, sit on (*informal*), squash, smother, keep secret, sweep under the carpet (*informal*), draw a veil over, keep dark

hush-hush *adjective* (*informal*) SECRET, confidential, classified, top-secret, restricted, under wraps

husk *noun* RIND, shell, hull, covering, bark, chaff, shuck

husky *adjective* 1 HOARSE, rough, harsh, raucous, rasping, croaking, gruff, throaty, guttural, croaky
2 (*informal*) MUSCULAR, powerful, strapping, rugged, hefty, burly, stocky, beefy (*informal*), brawny, thickset

hustle *verb* 1 JOSTLE, force, push, crowd, rush, hurry, thrust, elbow, shove, jog, bustle, impel
2 HURRY, hasten, get a move on (*informal*)

hut *noun* 1 CABIN, shack, shanty, hovel, whare (*NZ*)
2 SHED, outhouse, lean-to, lockup

hybrid *noun* 1 CROSSBREED, cross, mixture, compound, composite, mule, amalgam, mongrel, half-breed, half-blood
2 MIXTURE, compound, composite, amalgam

hygiene *noun* CLEANLINESS, sanitation, disinfection, sterility, sanitary measures, hygienics

hygienic *adjective* CLEAN, healthy, sanitary, pure, sterile, salutary, disinfected, germ-free, aseptic
<< OPPOSITE dirty

hymn *noun* 1 RELIGIOUS SONG, song of praise, carol, chant, anthem, psalm, paean, canticle, doxology
2 SONG OF PRAISE, anthem, paean

hype *noun* PUBLICITY, promotion, build-up, plugging (*informal*), puffing, racket, razzmatazz (*slang*), brouhaha, ballyhoo (*informal*)

hyperbole *noun* EXAGGERATION, hype (*informal*), overstatement, enlargement, magnification, amplification

hypnotic *adjective* MESMERIC, soothing, narcotic, opiate, soporific, sleep-inducing, somniferous

hypnotize *verb* 1 MESMERIZE, put in a trance, put to sleep
2 FASCINATE, absorb, entrance, magnetize, spellbind

hypochondriac *noun* NEUROTIC, valetudinarian

hypocrisy *noun* INSINCERITY, pretence, deceit, deception, cant, duplicity, dissembling, falsity, imposture, sanctimoniousness, phoniness (*informal*), deceitfulness, pharisaism, speciousness, two-facedness, phariseeism
<< OPPOSITE sincerity

hypocrite *noun* FRAUD, deceiver, pretender, charlatan, impostor, pharisee, dissembler, Tartuffe, Pecksniff, Holy Willie, whited sepulchre, phoney *or* phony (*informal*)

hypocritical *adjective* INSINCERE, false, fraudulent, hollow, deceptive, spurious, two-faced, deceitful, sanctimonious, specious, duplicitous, dissembling, canting, Janus-faced, pharisaical, phoney *or* phony (*informal*)

hypodermic *noun* SYRINGE, needle, works (*slang*)

hypothesis *noun* THEORY, premise,

proposition, assumption, thesis, postulate, supposition, premiss

hypothetical *adjective* THEORETICAL, supposed, academic, assumed, imaginary, speculative, putative, conjectural
<< OPPOSITE real

hysteria *noun* FRENZY, panic, madness, agitation, delirium, hysterics, unreason

hysterical *adjective* **1** FRENZIED, mad, frantic, raving, distracted, distraught, crazed, uncontrollable, berserk, overwrought, convulsive, beside yourself, berko (*Austral slang*)
<< OPPOSITE calm
2 (*informal*) HILARIOUS, uproarious, side-splitting, farcical, comical, wildly funny
<< OPPOSITE serious

Ii

ice ▷▷ **break the ice** KICK OFF (*informal*), lead the way, take the plunge (*informal*), make a start, begin a relationship, initiate the proceedings, start *or* set the ball rolling (*informal*)
▷▷ **skate on thin ice** BE AT RISK, be vulnerable, be unsafe, be in jeopardy, be out on a limb, be open to attack, be sticking your neck out (*informal*)

icy *adjective* 1 COLD, freezing, bitter, biting, raw, chill, chilling, arctic, chilly, frosty, glacial, ice-cold, frozen over, frost-bound
<< OPPOSITE hot
2 SLIPPERY, glassy, slippy (*informal* or *dialect*), like a sheet of glass, rimy
3 UNFRIENDLY, cold, distant, hostile, forbidding, indifferent, aloof, stony, steely, frosty, glacial, frigid, unwelcoming
<< OPPOSITE friendly

idea *noun* 1 PLAN, scheme, proposal, design, theory, strategy, method, solution, suggestion, recommendation, proposition
2 NOTION, thought, view, understanding, teaching, opinion, belief, conclusion, hypothesis, impression, conviction, judgment, interpretation, sentiment, doctrine, conception, viewpoint
3 IMPRESSION, estimate, guess, hint, notion, clue, conjecture, surmise, inkling, approximation, intimation, ballpark figure
4 UNDERSTANDING, thought, view, sense, opinion, concept, impression, judgment, perception, conception, abstraction, estimation
5 INTENTION, aim, purpose, object, end, plan, reason, goal, design, objective, motive

It is usually considered correct to say that someone has *the idea of doing something*, rather than *the idea to do something*. For example, you would say *he had the idea of taking a holiday*, not *he had the idea to take a holiday*

ideal *noun* 1 *often plural* PRINCIPLE, standard, ideology, morals, conviction, integrity, scruples, probity, moral value, rectitude, sense of duty, sense of honour, uprightness
2 EPITOME, standard, dream, pattern, perfection, last word, paragon, nonpareil, standard of perfection
3 MODEL, example, criterion, prototype, paradigm, archetype, exemplar
▷ *adjective* 1 PERFECT, best, model, classic, supreme, ultimate, archetypal, exemplary, consummate, optimal, quintessential
<< OPPOSITE imperfect
2 IMAGINARY, impractical, Utopian, romantic, fantastic, fabulous, poetic, visionary, fairy-tale, mythical, unreal, fanciful, unattainable, ivory-towered, imagal (*Psychoanalysis*)
<< OPPOSITE actual
3 HYPOTHETICAL, academic, intellectual, abstract, theoretical, speculative, conceptual, metaphysical, transcendental, notional

idealist *noun* ROMANTIC, visionary, dreamer, Utopian

idealistic *adjective* PERFECTIONIST, romantic, optimistic, visionary, Utopian, quixotic, impracticable, starry-eyed
<< OPPOSITE realistic

idealize *verb* ROMANTICIZE, glorify, exalt, worship, magnify, ennoble, deify, put on a pedestal, apotheosize

ideally *adverb* IN A PERFECT WORLD, in theory, preferably, if possible, all things being equal, under the best of circumstances, if you had your way, in a Utopia

identical *adjective* ALIKE, like, the same, matching, equal, twin, equivalent, corresponding, duplicate, synonymous, indistinguishable, analogous, interchangeable, a dead ringer (*slang*), the dead spit (*informal*), like two peas in a pod
<< OPPOSITE different

identifiable *adjective* RECOGNIZABLE, noticeable, known, unmistakable, discernible, detectable, distinguishable, ascertainable

identification *noun* 1 DISCOVERY, recognition, determining, establishment, diagnosis, confirmation, detection, divination
2 RECOGNITION, naming, labelling, distinguishing, cataloguing, classifying, confirmation, pinpointing, establishment of identity
3 CONNECTION, relationship, link, association, tie, partnership, affinity, familiarity, interconnection, interrelation
4 UNDERSTANDING, relationship, involvement, unity, sympathy, empathy, rapport, fellow feeling
5 ID, papers, credentials, licence, warrant, identity card, proof of identity, letters of introduction

identify *verb* 1 RECOGNIZE, place, name, remember, spot, label, flag, catalogue, tag, diagnose, classify, make out, pinpoint, recollect, put your finger on (*informal*)
2 ESTABLISH, spot, confirm, finger (*informal, chiefly US*), demonstrate, pick out, single out, certify, verify, validate, mark out, substantiate, corroborate
▷▷ **identify something** *or* **someone with something** *or* **someone** EQUATE WITH, associate with, think of in connection with, put in the same category as
▷▷ **identify with someone** RELATE TO, understand, respond to, feel for, ally with, empathize with, speak the same language as, put yourself in the place *or* shoes of, see through another's eyes, be on the same wavelength as

identity *noun* INDIVIDUALITY, self, character, personality, existence, distinction, originality, peculiarity, uniqueness, oneness, singularity, separateness, distinctiveness, selfhood, particularity

ideology *noun* BELIEF(s), ideas, principles, ideals, opinion, philosophy, doctrine, creed, dogma, tenets, world view, credence, articles of faith, Weltanschauung (*German*)

idiocy *noun* FOOLISHNESS, insanity, lunacy, tomfoolery, inanity, imbecility, senselessness, cretinism, fatuity, abject stupidity, asininity, fatuousness
<< OPPOSITE wisdom

idiom *noun* 1 PHRASE, expression, turn of phrase, locution, set phrase
2 LANGUAGE, talk, style, usage, jargon, vernacular, parlance, mode of expression

idiosyncrasy *noun* PECULIARITY, habit, characteristic, quirk, eccentricity, oddity, mannerism, affectation, trick, singularity, personal trait

idiosyncratic *adjective* DISTINCTIVE, special, individual, typical, distinguishing, distinct, peculiar, individualistic

idiot *noun* FOOL, jerk (*slang, chiefly US & Canad*), ass, plank (*Brit slang*), charlie (*Brit informal*), berk (*Brit slang*), wally (*slang*), prat (*slang*), plonker (*slang*), moron, geek (*slang*), twit (*informal, chiefly Brit*), chump, imbecile, cretin, oaf, simpleton, airhead (*slang*), dimwit (*informal*), dipstick (*Brit slang*), gonzo (*slang*), schmuck (*US slang*), dork (*slang*), nitwit (*informal*), blockhead, divvy (*Brit slang*), pillock (*Brit slang*), halfwit, nincompoop, dweeb (*US slang*), putz (*US slang*), eejit (*Scot & Irish*), dumb-ass (*slang*), dunderhead, numpty (*Scot informal*), doofus (*slang, chiefly US*), lamebrain (*informal*), mooncalf, nerd *or* nurd (*slang*), numbskull *or* numskull, galah (*Austral & NZ informal*), dorba *or* dorb (*Austral slang*), bogan (*Austral slang*)

idiotic *adjective* FOOLISH, crazy, stupid, dumb (*informal*), daft (*informal*), insane, lunatic, senseless, foolhardy, inane, fatuous, loopy (*informal*), crackpot (*informal*), moronic, imbecile, unintelligent, asinine, imbecilic, braindead (*informal*), harebrained, dumb-ass (*slang*), halfwitted
<< OPPOSITE wise

idle *adjective* 1 UNOCCUPIED, unemployed, redundant, jobless, out of work, out of action, inactive, at leisure, between jobs, unwaged, at a loose end
<< OPPOSITE occupied
2 UNUSED, stationary, inactive, out of order, ticking over, gathering dust, mothballed, out of service, out of action *or* operation
3 LAZY, slow, slack, sluggish, lax, negligent, inactive, inert, lethargic, indolent, lackadaisical, good-for-nothing, remiss, workshy, slothful, shiftless
<< OPPOSITE busy
4 USELESS, vain, pointless, hopeless, unsuccessful, ineffective, worthless, futile, fruitless, unproductive, abortive, ineffectual, groundless, of no use, valueless, disadvantageous, unavailing, otiose, of no avail, profitless, bootless
<< OPPOSITE useful
5 TRIVIAL, superficial, insignificant, frivolous, silly, unnecessary, irrelevant, foolish, unhelpful, flippant, puerile, flighty, ill-considered, empty-headed, nugatory
<< OPPOSITE meaningful
▷ *verb often with* **away** FRITTER, while, waste, fool, lounge, potter, loaf, dally, loiter, dawdle, laze

idleness *noun* 1 INACTIVITY, unemployment, leisure, inaction, time on your hands
2 LOAFING, inertia, sloth, pottering, trifling, laziness, time-wasting, lazing, torpor, sluggishness, skiving (*Brit slang*), vegetating, dilly-dallying (*informal*), shiftlessness

idly *adverb* LAZILY, casually, passively, languidly,

unthinkingly, sluggishly, languorously, lethargically, apathetically, indolently, inertly, lackadaisically, inactively, shiftlessly, slothfully
<< OPPOSITE energetically

idol *noun* 1 HERO, superstar, pin-up, favourite, pet, darling, beloved (*slang*), fave (*informal*)
2 GRAVEN IMAGE, god, image, deity, pagan symbol

idolize *verb* WORSHIP, love, adore, admire, revere, glorify, exalt, look up to, venerate, hero-worship, deify, bow down before, dote upon, apotheosize, worship to excess

idyllic *adjective* HEAVENLY, idealized, ideal, charming, peaceful, pastoral, picturesque, rustic, Utopian, halcyon, out of this world, unspoiled, arcadian

if *conjunction* 1 PROVIDED, assuming, given that, providing, allowing, admitting, supposing, granting, in case, presuming, on the assumption that, on condition that, as long as
2 WHEN, whenever, every time, any time
3 WHETHER
▷ *noun* DOUBT, condition, uncertainty, provision, constraint, hesitation, vagueness, stipulation

iffy *adjective* UNCERTAIN, doubtful, unpredictable, conditional, undecided, up in the air, problematical, chancy (*informal*), in the lap of the gods

ignite *verb* 1 CATCH FIRE, burn, burst into flames, fire, inflame, flare up, take fire
2 SET FIRE TO, light, set alight, torch, kindle, touch off, put a match to (*informal*)

ignoble *adjective* 1 DISHONOURABLE, low, base, mean, petty, infamous, degraded, craven, disgraceful, shabby, vile, degenerate, abject, unworthy, shameless, despicable, heinous, dastardly, contemptible, wretched
2 LOWLY, mean, low, base, common, peasant, vulgar, plebeian, humble, lowborn (*rare*), baseborn (*archaic*)

ignominious *adjective* HUMILIATING, disgraceful, shameful, sorry, scandalous, abject, despicable, mortifying, undignified, disreputable, dishonourable, inglorious, discreditable, indecorous
<< OPPOSITE honourable

ignominy *noun* DISGRACE, shame, humiliation, contempt, discredit, stigma, disrepute, dishonour, infamy, mortification, bad odour
<< OPPOSITE honour

ignorance *noun* 1 LACK OF EDUCATION, stupidity, foolishness, blindness, illiteracy, benightedness, unenlightenment, unintelligence, mental darkness
<< OPPOSITE knowledge
2 *with* **of** UNAWARENESS OF, inexperience of, unfamiliarity with, innocence of, unconsciousness of, greenness about, oblivion about, nescience of (*literary*)

ignorant *adjective* 1 UNEDUCATED, unaware, naive, green, illiterate, inexperienced, innocent, untrained, unlearned, unread, untutored, uncultivated, wet behind the ears (*informal*), unlettered, untaught, unknowledgeable, uncomprehending, unscholarly, as green as grass
<< OPPOSITE educated
2 INSENSITIVE, gross, crude, rude, shallow, superficial, crass
3 *with* **of** UNINFORMED OF, unaware of, oblivious to, blind to, innocent of, in the dark about, unconscious of, unschooled in, out of the loop of, inexperienced of, uninitiated about, unknowing of, unenlightened about
<< OPPOSITE informed

ignore *verb* 1 PAY NO ATTENTION TO, neglect, disregard, slight, overlook, scorn, spurn, rebuff, take no notice of, be oblivious to
<< OPPOSITE pay attention to
2 OVERLOOK, discount, disregard, reject, neglect, shrug off, pass over, brush aside, turn a blind eye to, turn a deaf ear to, shut your eyes to
3 SNUB, cut (*informal*), slight, blank (*slang*), rebuff, cold-shoulder, turn your back on, give (someone) the cold shoulder, send (someone) to Coventry, give (someone) the brush-off

ilk *noun* TYPE, sort, kind, class, style, character, variety, brand, breed, stamp, description, kidney, disposition

> Some people object to the use of the phrase *of that ilk* to mean 'of that type or class', claiming that it arises from a misunderstanding of the original Scottish expression. The Scottish phrase *of that ilk* has a very specific meaning, indicating that the person mentioned is laird of an estate with the same name as his family, for example *Moncrieff of that ilk* (that is, 'Moncrieff, laird of Moncrieff estate'). The more general use is, however, well established and is now generally regarded as acceptable

ill *adjective* 1 UNWELL, sick, poorly (*informal*), diseased, funny (*informal*), weak, crook (*Austral & NZ slang*), ailing, queer, frail, feeble, unhealthy, seedy (*informal*), sickly, laid up (*informal*), queasy, infirm, out of sorts (*informal*), dicky (*Brit informal*), nauseous, off-colour, under the weather (*informal*), at death's door, indisposed, peaky, on the sick list (*informal*), valetudinarian, green about the gills, not up to snuff (*informal*)

<< OPPOSITE healthy
2 HARMFUL, bad, damaging, evil, foul, unfortunate, destructive, unlucky, vile, detrimental, hurtful, pernicious, noxious, ruinous, deleterious, injurious, iniquitous, disadvantageous, maleficent
<< OPPOSITE favourable
3 HOSTILE, malicious, acrimonious, cross, harsh, adverse, belligerent, unkind, hurtful, unfriendly, malevolent, antagonistic, hateful, bellicose, cantankerous, inimical, rancorous, ill-disposed
<< OPPOSITE kind
4 BAD, threatening, disturbing, menacing, unlucky, sinister, gloomy, dire, ominous, unhealthy, unfavourable, foreboding, unpromising, inauspicious, unwholesome, unpropitious, bodeful
▷ *noun* 1 PROBLEM, trouble, suffering, worry, trial, injury, pain, hurt, strain, harm, distress, misery, hardship, woe, misfortune, affliction, tribulation, unpleasantness
2 HARM, suffering, damage, hurt, evil, destruction, grief, trauma, anguish, mischief, malice
<< OPPOSITE good
▷ *adverb* 1 BADLY, unfortunately, unfavourably, inauspiciously
2 HARDLY, barely, scarcely, just, only just, by no means, at a push
<< OPPOSITE well
3 ILLEGALLY, criminally, unlawfully, fraudulently, dishonestly, illicitly, illegitimately, unscrupulously, foully
4 INSUFFICIENTLY, badly, poorly, inadequately, imperfectly, deficiently

ill-advised *adjective* MISGUIDED, inappropriate, foolish, rash, reckless, unwise, short-sighted, unseemly, foolhardy, thoughtless, indiscreet, ill-judged, ill-considered, imprudent, wrong-headed, injudicious, incautious, impolitic, overhasty
<< OPPOSITE wise

ill at ease *adjective* UNCOMFORTABLE, nervous, tense, strange, wired (*slang*), disturbed, anxious, awkward, uneasy, unsettled, faltering, unsure, restless, out of place, neurotic, self-conscious, hesitant, disquieted, edgy, on edge, twitchy (*informal*), on tenterhooks, fidgety, unquiet, like a fish out of water, antsy (*informal*), unrelaxed, on pins and needles (*informal*)
<< OPPOSITE comfortable

ill-considered *adjective* UNWISE, rash, imprudent, careless, precipitate, hasty, heedless, injudicious, improvident, overhasty

ill-defined *adjective* UNCLEAR, vague, indistinct, blurred, dim, fuzzy, shadowy, woolly, nebulous
<< OPPOSITE clear

illegal *adjective* UNLAWFUL, banned, forbidden, prohibited, criminal, outlawed, unofficial, illicit, unconstitutional, lawless, wrongful, off limits, unlicensed, under-the-table, unauthorized, proscribed, under-the-counter, actionable (*Law*), felonious
<< OPPOSITE legal

illegality *noun* CRIME, wrong, felony, criminality, lawlessness, illegitimacy, wrongness, unlawfulness, illicitness

illegible *adjective* INDECIPHERABLE, unreadable, faint, crabbed, scrawled, hieroglyphic, hard to make out, undecipherable, obscure
<< OPPOSITE legible

illegitimacy *noun* 1 BASTARDY, bastardism
2 ILLEGALITY, unconstitutionality, unlawfulness, illicitness, irregularity

illegitimate *adjective* 1 BORN OUT OF WEDLOCK, natural, bastard, love, misbegotten (*literary*), baseborn (*archaic*)
2 UNLAWFUL, illegal, illicit, improper, unconstitutional, under-the-table, unauthorized, unsanctioned
<< OPPOSITE legal
3 INVALID, incorrect, illogical, spurious, unsound

ill-fated *adjective* DOOMED, unfortunate, unlucky, unhappy, blighted, hapless, luckless, ill-starred, star-crossed, ill-omened

ill feeling *noun* HOSTILITY, resentment, bitterness, offence, indignation, animosity, antagonism, enmity, rancour, bad blood, hard feelings, ill will, animus, dudgeon (*archaic*), chip on your shoulder
<< OPPOSITE goodwill

illiberal *adjective* INTOLERANT, prejudiced, bigoted, narrow-minded, small-minded, reactionary, hidebound, uncharitable, ungenerous
<< OPPOSITE tolerant

illicit *adjective* 1 ILLEGAL, criminal, prohibited, unlawful, black-market, illegitimate, off limits, unlicensed, unauthorized, bootleg, contraband, felonious
<< OPPOSITE legal
2 FORBIDDEN, improper, immoral, wrong, guilty, clandestine, furtive

illiteracy *noun* LACK OF EDUCATION, ignorance, benightedness, illiterateness

illiterate *adjective* UNEDUCATED, ignorant, unlettered, unable to read and write, analphabetic
<< OPPOSITE educated

ill-judged *adjective* MISGUIDED, foolish, rash, unwise, short-sighted, ill-advised, ill-considered, wrong-headed, injudicious, overhasty

ill-mannered *adjective* RUDE, impolite, discourteous, coarse, churlish, boorish,

insolent, uncouth, loutish, uncivil, ill-bred, badly behaved, ill-behaved, unmannerly
<< OPPOSITE polite

illness *noun* SICKNESS, ill health, malaise, attack, disease, complaint, infection, disorder, bug (*informal*), disability, ailment, affliction, poor health, malady, infirmity, indisposition, lurgy (*informal*)

illogical *adjective* IRRATIONAL, absurd, unreasonable, meaningless, incorrect, faulty, inconsistent, invalid, senseless, spurious, inconclusive, unsound, unscientific, specious, fallacious, sophistical
<< OPPOSITE logical

ill-tempered *adjective* CROSS, irritable, grumpy, irascible, sharp, annoyed, impatient, touchy, bad-tempered, curt, spiteful, tetchy, ratty (*Brit & NZ informal*), testy, chippy (*informal*), choleric, ill-humoured, liverish
<< OPPOSITE good-natured

ill-treat *verb* ABUSE, injure, harm, wrong, damage, harry, harass, misuse, oppress, dump on (*slang, chiefly US*), mishandle, maltreat, ill-use, handle roughly, knock about *or* around

ill-treatment *noun* ABUSE, harm, mistreatment, damage, injury, misuse, ill-use, rough handling

illuminate *verb* **1** LIGHT UP, light, brighten, irradiate, illumine (*literary*)
<< OPPOSITE darken
2 EXPLAIN, interpret, make clear, clarify, clear up, enlighten, shed light on, elucidate, explicate, give insight into
<< OPPOSITE obscure
3 DECORATE, illustrate, adorn, ornament

illuminating *adjective* INFORMATIVE, revealing, enlightening, helpful, explanatory, instructive
<< OPPOSITE confusing

illumination *noun* **1** LIGHT, lighting, lights, ray, beam, lighting up, brightening, brightness, radiance
2 ENLIGHTENMENT, understanding, insight, perception, awareness, revelation, inspiration, clarification, edification
▷ *plural noun* (*chiefly Brit*) LIGHTS, decorations, fairy lights

illusion *noun* **1** DELUSION, misconception, misapprehension, fancy, deception, fallacy, self-deception, false impression, false belief, misbelief
2 FALSE IMPRESSION, feeling, appearance, impression, fancy, deception, imitation, sham, pretence, semblance, fallacy
<< OPPOSITE reality
3 FANTASY, vision, hallucination, trick, spectre, mirage, semblance, daydream, apparition, chimera, figment of the imagination, phantasm, ignis fatuus, will-o'-the-wisp

illusory *or* **illusive** *adjective* UNREAL, false, misleading, untrue, seeming, mistaken, apparent, sham, deceptive, deceitful, hallucinatory, fallacious, chimerical, delusive
<< OPPOSITE real

illustrate *verb* **1** DEMONSTRATE, show, exhibit, emphasize, exemplify, explicate
2 EXPLAIN, describe, interpret, sum up, make clear, clarify, summarize, bring home, point up, make plain, elucidate
3 ADORN, ornament, embellish

illustrated *adjective* PICTURED, decorated, illuminated, embellished, pictorial, with illustrations

illustration *noun* **1** EXAMPLE, case, instance, sample, explanation, demonstration, interpretation, specimen, analogy, clarification, case in point, exemplar, elucidation, exemplification
2 PICTURE, drawing, painting, image, print, plate, figure, portrait, representation, sketch, decoration, portrayal, likeness, adornment

illustrative *adjective* **1** REPRESENTATIVE, typical, descriptive, explanatory, interpretive, expository, explicatory, illustrational
2 PICTORIAL, graphic, diagrammatic, delineative

illustrious *adjective* FAMOUS, great, noted, celebrated, signal, brilliant, remarkable, distinguished, prominent, glorious, noble, splendid, notable, renowned, eminent, famed, exalted
<< OPPOSITE obscure

ill will *noun* HOSTILITY, spite, dislike, hatred, envy, resentment, grudge, malice, animosity, aversion, venom, antagonism, antipathy, enmity, acrimony, rancour, bad blood, hard feelings, animus, malevolence, unfriendliness
<< OPPOSITE goodwill

image *noun* **1** THOUGHT, idea, vision, concept, impression, perception, conception, mental picture, conceptualization
2 FIGURE OF SPEECH, metaphor, simile, conceit, trope
3 REFLECTION, appearance, likeness, mirror image
4 FIGURE, idol, icon, fetish, talisman
5 REPLICA, copy, reproduction, counterpart, spit (*informal, chiefly Brit*), clone, facsimile, spitting image (*informal*), similitude, Doppelgänger, (dead) ringer (*slang*), double
6 PICTURE, photo, photograph, representation, reproduction, snapshot

imaginable *adjective* POSSIBLE, conceivable, likely, credible, plausible, believable, under the sun, comprehensible, thinkable, within the bounds of possibility, supposable
<< OPPOSITE unimaginable

imaginary *adjective* FICTIONAL, made-up, invented, supposed, imagined, assumed, ideal, fancied, legendary, visionary, shadowy, unreal, hypothetical, fanciful, fictitious, mythological, illusory, nonexistent, dreamlike, hallucinatory, illusive, chimerical, unsubstantial, phantasmal, suppositious, imagal (*Psychoanalysis*)
<< OPPOSITE real

imagination *noun* 1 CREATIVITY, vision, invention, ingenuity, enterprise, insight, inspiration, wit, originality, inventiveness, resourcefulness
2 MIND'S EYE, fancy

imaginative *adjective* CREATIVE, original, inspired, enterprising, fantastic, clever, stimulating, vivid, ingenious, visionary, inventive, fanciful, dreamy, whimsical, poetical
<< OPPOSITE unimaginative

imagine *verb* 1 ENVISAGE, see, picture, plan, create, project, think of, scheme, frame, invent, devise, conjure up, envision, visualize, dream up (*informal*), think up, conceive of, conceptualize, fantasize about, see in the mind's eye, form a mental picture of
2 BELIEVE, think, suppose, assume, suspect, gather, guess (*informal, chiefly US & Canad*), realize, take it, reckon, fancy, deem, speculate, presume, take for granted, infer, deduce, apprehend, conjecture, surmise

imbalance *noun* UNEVENNESS, bias, inequality, unfairness, partiality, disproportion, lopsidedness, top-heaviness, lack of proportion

imbibe *verb* (*Formal*) 1 DRINK, consume, knock back (*informal*), sink (*informal*), swallow, suck, swig (*informal*), quaff
2 ABSORB, receive, take in, gain, gather, acquire, assimilate, ingest

imbue *verb* INSTIL, infuse, steep, bathe, saturate, pervade, permeate, impregnate, inculcate

imitate *verb* 1 COPY, follow, repeat, echo, emulate, ape, simulate, mirror, follow suit, duplicate, counterfeit, follow in the footsteps of, take a leaf out of (someone's) book
2 DO AN IMPRESSION OF, take off (*informal*), mimic, do (*informal*), affect, copy, mock, parody, caricature, send up (*Brit informal*), spoof (*informal*), impersonate, burlesque, personate

imitation *noun* 1 REPLICA, fake, reproduction, sham, forgery, carbon copy (*informal*), counterfeit, counterfeiting, likeness, duplication
2 COPYING, echoing, resemblance, aping, simulation, mimicry
3 IMPRESSION, parody, mockery, takeoff (*informal*), impersonation
▷ *adjective* ARTIFICIAL, mock, reproduction, dummy, synthetic, man-made, simulated, sham, pseudo (*informal*), ersatz, repro, phoney *or* phony (*informal*)
<< OPPOSITE real

imitator *noun* IMPERSONATOR, mimic, impressionist, copycat, echo, follower, parrot (*informal*), copier, carbon copy (*informal*)

immaculate *adjective* 1 CLEAN, impeccable, spotless, trim, neat, spruce, squeaky-clean, spick-and-span, neat as a new pin
<< OPPOSITE dirty
2 PURE, perfect, innocent, impeccable, virtuous, flawless, faultless, squeaky-clean, guiltless, above reproach, sinless, incorrupt
<< OPPOSITE corrupt
3 PERFECT, flawless, impeccable, stainless, faultless, unblemished, unsullied, uncontaminated, unpolluted, untarnished, unexceptionable, undefiled
<< OPPOSITE tainted

immaterial *adjective* IRRELEVANT, insignificant, unimportant, unnecessary, trivial, trifling, inconsequential, extraneous, inconsiderable, of no importance, of no consequence, inessential, a matter of indifference, of little account, inapposite
<< OPPOSITE significant

immature *adjective* 1 YOUNG, adolescent, undeveloped, green, raw, premature, unfinished, imperfect, untimely, unripe, unformed, unseasonable, unfledged
2 CHILDISH, juvenile, infantile, puerile, callow, babyish, wet behind the ears (*informal*), jejune
<< OPPOSITE adult

immaturity *noun* 1 RAWNESS, imperfection, greenness, unpreparedness, unripeness
2 CHILDISHNESS, puerility, callowness, juvenility, babyishness

immeasurable *adjective* INCALCULABLE, vast, immense, endless, unlimited, infinite, limitless, boundless, bottomless, inexhaustible, unfathomable, unbounded, inestimable, measureless, illimitable
<< OPPOSITE finite

immediate *adjective* 1 INSTANT, prompt, instantaneous, quick, on-the-spot, split-second
<< OPPOSITE later
2 CURRENT, present, pressing, existing, actual, urgent, on hand, extant
3 NEAREST, next, direct, close, near, adjacent, contiguous, proximate
<< OPPOSITE far

immediately *adverb* AT ONCE, now, instantly, straight away, directly, promptly, right now, right away, there and then, speedily, without delay, without hesitation, instantaneously, forthwith, pronto (*informal*), unhesitatingly, this instant, on the nail, this very minute, posthaste, tout de suite (*French*), before you could say Jack Robinson (*informal*)

immemorial *adjective* AGE-OLD, ancient, long-standing, traditional, fixed, rooted, archaic, time-honoured, of yore, olden (*archaic*)

immense *adjective* HUGE, great, massive, vast, large, giant, enormous, extensive, tremendous, mega (*slang*), titanic, infinite, jumbo (*informal*), very big, gigantic, monumental, monstrous, mammoth, colossal, mountainous, stellar (*informal*), prodigious, interminable, stupendous, king-size, king-sized, immeasurable, elephantine, ginormous (*informal*), Brobdingnagian, illimitable, humongous *or* humungous (*US slang*)

<< OPPOSITE tiny

immerse *verb* **1** ENGROSS, involve, absorb, busy, occupy, engage

2 PLUNGE, dip, submerge, sink, duck, bathe, douse, dunk, submerse

immersed *adjective* ENGROSSED, involved, absorbed, deep, busy, occupied, taken up, buried, consumed, wrapped up, bound up, rapt, spellbound, mesmerized, in a brown study

immersion *noun* **1** INVOLVEMENT, concentration, preoccupation, absorption

2 DIPPING, submerging, plunging, ducking, dousing, dunking

immigrant *noun* SETTLER, incomer, alien, stranger, outsider, newcomer, migrant, emigrant

imminent *adjective* NEAR, coming, close, approaching, threatening, gathering, on the way, in the air, forthcoming, looming, menacing, brewing, impending, at hand, upcoming, on the cards, on the horizon, in the pipeline, nigh (*archaic*), in the offing, fast-approaching, just round the corner, near-at-hand

<< OPPOSITE remote

immobile *adjective* MOTIONLESS, still, stationary, fixed, rooted, frozen, stable, halted, stiff, rigid, static, riveted, lifeless, inert, at rest, inanimate, immovable, immobilized, at a standstill, unmoving, stock-still, like a statue, immotile

<< OPPOSITE mobile

immobility *noun* STILLNESS, firmness, steadiness, stability, fixity, inertness, immovability, motionlessness, absence of movement

immobilize *verb* PARALYSE, stop, freeze, halt, disable, cripple, lay up (*informal*), bring to a standstill, put out of action, render inoperative

immoral *adjective* WICKED, bad, wrong, abandoned, evil, corrupt, vicious, obscene, indecent, vile, degenerate, dishonest, pornographic, sinful, unethical, lewd, depraved, impure, debauched, unprincipled, nefarious, dissolute, iniquitous, reprobate, licentious, of easy virtue, unchaste

<< OPPOSITE moral ▷ see **amoral**

immorality *noun* WICKEDNESS, wrong, vice, evil, corruption, sin, depravity, iniquity, debauchery, badness, licentiousness, turpitude, dissoluteness

<< OPPOSITE morality

immortal *adjective* **1** TIMELESS, eternal, everlasting, lasting, traditional, classic, constant, enduring, persistent, abiding, perennial, ageless, unfading

<< OPPOSITE ephemeral

2 UNDYING, eternal, perpetual, indestructible, death-defying, imperishable, deathless

<< OPPOSITE mortal

▷ *noun* **1** HERO, genius, paragon, great

2 GOD, goddess, deity, Olympian, divine being, immortal being, atua (NZ)

immortality *noun* **1** ETERNITY, perpetuity, everlasting life, timelessness, incorruptibility, indestructibility, endlessness, deathlessness

2 FAME, glory, celebrity, greatness, renown, glorification, gloriousness

immovable *adjective* **1** FIXED, set, fast, firm, stuck, secure, rooted, stable, jammed, stationary, immutable, unbudgeable

2 INFLEXIBLE, adamant, resolute, steadfast, constant, unyielding, unwavering, impassive, obdurate, unshakable, unchangeable, unshaken, stony-hearted, unimpressionable

<< OPPOSITE flexible

immune ▷▷ **immune from** EXEMPT FROM, free from, let off (*informal*), not subject to, not liable to

▷▷ **immune to** **1** RESISTANT TO, free from, protected from, safe from, not open to, spared from, secure against, invulnerable to, insusceptible to

2 UNAFFECTED BY, not affected by, invulnerable to, insusceptible to

immunity *noun* **1** EXEMPTION, amnesty, indemnity, release, freedom, liberty, privilege, prerogative, invulnerability, exoneration

2 *with* **to** RESISTANCE, protection, resilience, inoculation, immunization

<< OPPOSITE susceptibility

immunize *verb* VACCINATE, inoculate, protect, safeguard

immutable *adjective* UNCHANGING, fixed, permanent, stable, constant, enduring, abiding, perpetual, inflexible, steadfast, sacrosanct, immovable, ageless, invariable, unalterable, unchangeable, changeless

imp *noun* **1** DEMON, devil, sprite

2 RASCAL, rogue, brat, urchin, minx, scamp, pickle (*Brit informal*), gamin, nointer (*Austral slang*)

impact *noun* 1 EFFECT, influence, consequences, impression, repercussions, ramifications
2 COLLISION, force, contact, shock, crash, knock, stroke, smash, bump, thump, jolt
▷ *verb* HIT, strike, crash, clash, crush, ram, smack, collide

impair *verb* WORSEN, reduce, damage, injure, harm, mar, undermine, weaken, spoil, diminish, decrease, blunt, deteriorate, lessen, hinder, debilitate, vitiate, enfeeble, enervate
<< OPPOSITE improve

impaired *adjective* DAMAGED, flawed, faulty, defective, imperfect, unsound

impale *verb* PIERCE, stick, run through, spike, lance, spear, skewer, spit, transfix

impart *verb* 1 COMMUNICATE, pass on, convey, tell, reveal, discover, relate, disclose, divulge, make known
2 GIVE, accord, lend, bestow, offer, grant, afford, contribute, yield, confer

impartial *adjective* NEUTRAL, objective, detached, just, fair, equal, open-minded, equitable, disinterested, unbiased, even-handed, nonpartisan, unprejudiced, without fear or favour, nondiscriminating
<< OPPOSITE unfair

impartiality *noun* NEUTRALITY, equity, fairness, equality, detachment, objectivity, disinterest, open-mindedness, even-handedness, disinterestedness, dispassion, nonpartisanship, lack of bias
<< OPPOSITE unfairness

impassable *adjective* BLOCKED, closed, obstructed, impenetrable, unnavigable

impasse *noun* DEADLOCK, stalemate, standstill, dead end, standoff, blind alley (*informal*)

impassioned *adjective* INTENSE, heated, passionate, warm, excited, inspired, violent, stirring, flaming, furious, glowing, blazing, vivid, animated, rousing, fiery, worked up, ardent, inflamed, fervent, ablaze, vehement, fervid
<< OPPOSITE cool

impassive *adjective* UNEMOTIONAL, unmoved, emotionless, reserved, cool, calm, composed, indifferent, self-contained, serene, callous, aloof, stoical, unconcerned, apathetic, dispassionate, unfazed (*informal*), inscrutable, stolid, unruffled, phlegmatic, unfeeling, poker-faced (*informal*), imperturbable, insensible, impassible (*rare*), unexcitable, insusceptible, unimpressible

impatience *noun* 1 IRRITABILITY, shortness, edginess, intolerance, quick temper, snappiness, irritableness
<< OPPOSITE patience
2 EAGERNESS, longing, enthusiasm, hunger, yearning, thirst, zeal, fervour, ardour, vehemence, earnestness, keenness, impetuosity, heartiness, avidity, intentness, greediness
3 HASTE, hurry, impetuosity, rashness, hastiness

impatient *adjective* 1 CROSS, tense, annoyed, irritated, prickly, edgy, touchy, bad-tempered, intolerant, petulant, ill-tempered, cantankerous, ratty (*Brit & NZ informal*), chippy (*informal*), hot-tempered, quick-tempered, crotchety (*informal*), ill-humoured, narky (*Brit slang*), out of humour
2 IRRITABLE, fiery, abrupt, hasty, snappy, indignant, curt, vehement, brusque, irascible, testy
<< OPPOSITE easy-going
3 EAGER, longing, keen, hot, earnest, raring, anxious, hungry, intent, enthusiastic, yearning, greedy, restless, ardent, avid, fervent, zealous, chafing, vehement, fretful, straining at the leash, fervid, keen as mustard, like a cat on hot bricks (*informal*), athirst
<< OPPOSITE calm

impeach *verb* CHARGE, accuse, prosecute, blame, denounce, indict, censure, bring to trial, arraign

impeachment *noun* ACCUSATION, prosecution, indictment, arraignment

impeccable *adjective* FAULTLESS, perfect, pure, exact, precise, exquisite, stainless, immaculate, flawless, squeaky-clean, unerring, unblemished, unimpeachable, irreproachable, sinless, incorrupt
<< OPPOSITE flawed

impede *verb* HINDER, stop, slow (down), check, bar, block, delay, hold up, brake, disrupt, curb, restrain, hamper, thwart, clog, obstruct, retard, encumber, cumber, throw a spanner in the works of (*Brit informal*)
<< OPPOSITE help

impediment *noun* OBSTACLE, barrier, check, bar, block, difficulty, hazard, curb, snag, obstruction, stumbling block, hindrance, encumbrance, fly in the ointment, millstone around your neck
<< OPPOSITE aid

impel *verb* FORCE, move, compel, drive, require, push, influence, urge, inspire, prompt, spur, stimulate, motivate, oblige, induce, prod, constrain, incite, instigate, goad, actuate
<< OPPOSITE discourage

impending *adjective* LOOMING, coming, approaching, near, nearing, threatening, forthcoming, brewing, imminent, hovering, upcoming, on the horizon, in the pipeline, in the offing

impenetrable *adjective* 1 IMPASSABLE, solid, impervious, thick, dense, hermetic, impermeable, inviolable, unpierceable
<< OPPOSITE passable
2 INCOMPREHENSIBLE, obscure, baffling, dark, hidden, mysterious, enigmatic, arcane, inexplicable, unintelligible, inscrutable, unfathomable, indiscernible, cabbalistic, enigmatical
<< OPPOSITE understandable

imperative *adjective* URGENT, essential, pressing, vital, crucial, compulsory, indispensable, obligatory, exigent
<< OPPOSITE unnecessary

imperceptible *adjective* UNDETECTABLE, slight, subtle, small, minute, fine, tiny, faint, invisible, gradual, shadowy, microscopic, indistinguishable, inaudible, infinitesimal, teeny-weeny, unnoticeable, insensible, impalpable, indiscernible, teensy-weensy, inappreciable
<< OPPOSITE perceptible

imperceptibly *adverb* INVISIBLY, slowly, subtly, little by little, unobtrusively, unseen, by a hair's-breadth, unnoticeably, indiscernibly, inappreciably

imperfect *adjective* FLAWED, impaired, faulty, broken, limited, damaged, partial, unfinished, incomplete, defective, patchy, immature, deficient, rudimentary, sketchy, undeveloped, inexact
<< OPPOSITE perfect

imperfection *noun* 1 BLEMISH, fault, defect, flaw, stain
2 FAULT, failing, weakness, defect, deficiency, flaw, shortcoming, inadequacy, frailty, foible, weak point
3 INCOMPLETENESS, deficiency, inadequacy, frailty, insufficiency
<< OPPOSITE perfection

imperial *adjective* ROYAL, regal, kingly, queenly, princely, sovereign, majestic, monarchial, monarchal

imperil *verb* ENDANGER, risk, hazard, jeopardize
<< OPPOSITE protect

imperious *adjective* DOMINEERING, dictatorial, bossy (*informal*), haughty, lordly, commanding, arrogant, authoritative, autocratic, overbearing, tyrannical, magisterial, despotic, high-handed, overweening, tyrannous

impermanent *adjective* TEMPORARY, passing, brief, fleeting, elusive, mortal, short-lived, flying, fugitive, transient, momentary, ephemeral, transitory, perishable, fly-by-night (*informal*), evanescent, inconstant, fugacious, here today, gone tomorrow (*informal*)

impersonal *adjective* 1 INHUMAN, cold, remote, bureaucratic
2 DETACHED, neutral, dispassionate, cold, formal, aloof, businesslike
<< OPPOSITE intimate

impersonate *verb* 1 IMITATE, pose as (*informal*), masquerade as, enact, ape, act out, pass yourself off as
2 MIMIC, take off (*informal*), do (*informal*), ape, parody, caricature, do an impression of, personate

impersonation *noun* IMITATION, impression, parody, caricature, takeoff (*informal*), mimicry

impertinent *adjective* 1 RUDE, forward, cheeky (*informal*), saucy (*informal*), fresh (*informal*), bold, flip (*informal*), brazen, sassy (*US informal*), pert, disrespectful, presumptuous, insolent, impolite, impudent, lippy (*US & Canad slang*), discourteous, uncivil, unmannerly
<< OPPOSITE polite
2 INAPPROPRIATE, irrelevant, incongruous, inapplicable
<< OPPOSITE appropriate

imperturbable *adjective* CALM, cool, collected, composed, complacent, serene, tranquil, sedate, undisturbed, unmoved, stoic, stoical, unfazed (*informal*), unflappable (*informal*), unruffled, self-possessed, nerveless, unexcitable, equanimous
<< OPPOSITE agitated

impervious *adjective* 1 UNAFFECTED, immune, unmoved, closed, untouched, proof, invulnerable, unreceptive, unswayable
2 RESISTANT, sealed, impenetrable, invulnerable, impassable, hermetic, impermeable, imperviable

impetuous *adjective* RASH, hasty, impulsive, violent, furious, fierce, eager, passionate, spontaneous, precipitate, ardent, impassioned, headlong, unplanned, unbridled, vehement, unrestrained, spur-of-the-moment, unthinking, unpremeditated, unreflecting
<< OPPOSITE cautious

impetus *noun* 1 INCENTIVE, push, spur, motivation, impulse, stimulus, catalyst, goad, impulsion
2 FORCE, power, energy, momentum

impinge ▷▷ **impinge on** *or* **upon something** INVADE, violate, encroach on, trespass on, infringe on, make inroads on, obtrude on
▷▷ **impinge on** *or* **upon something** *or* **someone** AFFECT, influence, relate to, impact on, touch, touch upon, have a bearing on, bear upon

impish *adjective* MISCHIEVOUS, devilish, roguish, rascally, elfin, puckish, waggish, sportive, prankish

implacable *adjective* RUTHLESS, cruel, relentless, uncompromising, intractable, inflexible, unrelenting, merciless, unforgiving, inexorable, unyielding,

remorseless, pitiless, unbending, unappeasable
<< OPPOSITE merciful

implant *verb* **1** INSERT, place, plant, fix, root, sow, graft, embed, ingraft
2 INSTIL, sow, infuse, inculcate, infix

implausible *adjective* IMPROBABLE, unlikely, weak, incredible, unbelievable, dubious, suspect, unreasonable, flimsy, unconvincing, far-fetched, cock-and-bull (*informal*)

implement *verb* CARRY OUT, effect, carry through, complete, apply, perform, realize, fulfil, enforce, execute, discharge, bring about, enact, put into action *or* effect
<< OPPOSITE hinder
▷ *noun* TOOL, machine, device, instrument, appliance, apparatus, gadget, utensil, contraption, contrivance, agent

implementation *noun* CARRYING OUT, effecting, execution, performance, performing, discharge, enforcement, accomplishment, realization, fulfilment

implicate *verb* INCRIMINATE, involve, compromise, embroil, entangle, inculpate
<< OPPOSITE dissociate
▷▷ **implicate something** *or* **someone in something** INVOLVE IN, associate with, connect with, tie up with

implicated *adjective* INVOLVED, suspected, incriminated, under suspicion

implication *noun* **1** SUGGESTION, hint, inference, meaning, conclusion, significance, presumption, overtone, innuendo, intimation, insinuation, signification
2 INVOLVEMENT, association, connection, incrimination, entanglement
3 CONSEQUENCE, result, development, ramification, complication, upshot

implicit *adjective* **1** IMPLIED, understood, suggested, hinted at, taken for granted, unspoken, inferred, tacit, undeclared, insinuated, unstated, unsaid, unexpressed
<< OPPOSITE explicit
2 INHERENT, contained, underlying, intrinsic, latent, ingrained, inbuilt
3 ABSOLUTE, full, complete, total, firm, fixed, entire, constant, utter, outright, consummate, unqualified, out-and-out, steadfast, wholehearted, unadulterated, unreserved, unshakable, unshaken, unhesitating

implicitly *adverb* ABSOLUTELY, completely, utterly, unconditionally, unreservedly, firmly, unhesitatingly, without reservation

implied *adjective* SUGGESTED, inherent, indirect, hinted at, implicit, unspoken, tacit, undeclared, insinuated, unstated, unexpressed

implore *verb* BEG, beseech, entreat, conjure, plead with, solicit, pray to, importune, crave of, supplicate, go on bended knee to

imply *verb* **1** SUGGEST, hint, insinuate, indicate, signal, intimate, signify, connote, give (someone) to understand
2 INVOLVE, mean, entail, include, require, indicate, import, point to, signify, denote, presuppose, betoken ▷ see **infer**

impolite *adjective* BAD-MANNERED, rude, disrespectful, rough, churlish, boorish, insolent, uncouth, unrefined, loutish, ungentlemanly, ungracious, discourteous, indelicate, uncivil, unladylike, indecorous, ungallant, ill-bred, unmannerly, ill-mannered
<< OPPOSITE polite

import *verb* BRING IN, buy in, ship in, land, introduce
▷ *noun* (*Formal*) **1** SIGNIFICANCE, concern, value, worth, weight, consequence, substance, moment, magnitude, usefulness, momentousness
2 MEANING, implication, significance, sense, message, bearing, intention, explanation, substance, drift, interpretation, thrust, purport, upshot, gist, signification

importance *noun* **1** SIGNIFICANCE, interest, concern, matter, moment, value, worth, weight, import, consequence, substance, relevance, usefulness, momentousness
2 PRESTIGE, standing, status, rule, authority, influence, distinction, esteem, prominence, supremacy, mastery, dominion, eminence, ascendancy, pre-eminence, mana (*NZ*)

important *adjective* **1** SIGNIFICANT, critical, substantial, grave, urgent, serious, material, signal, primary, meaningful, far-reaching, momentous, seminal, weighty, of substance, salient, noteworthy
<< OPPOSITE unimportant
2 *often with* **to** VALUED, loved, prized, dear, essential, valuable, of interest, treasured, precious, esteemed, cherished, of concern, highly regarded
3 POWERFUL, leading, prominent, commanding, supreme, outstanding, high-level, dominant, influential, notable, big-time (*informal*), foremost, eminent, high-ranking, authoritative, major league (*informal*), of note, noteworthy, pre-eminent, skookum (*Canad*)

impose ▷▷ **impose on someone** INTRUDE ON, exploit, take advantage of, use, trouble, abuse, bother, encroach on, horn in (*informal*), trespass on, gate-crash (*informal*), take liberties with, butt in on, presume upon, force yourself on, obtrude on
▷▷ **impose something on** *or* **upon someone** **1** LEVY, apply, introduce, put, place, set, charge, establish, lay, fix, institute, exact, decree, ordain
2 INFLICT, force, enforce, visit, press, apply,

thrust, dictate, saddle (someone) with, foist

imposing *adjective* IMPRESSIVE, striking, grand, august, powerful, effective, commanding, awesome, majestic, dignified, stately, forcible
<< OPPOSITE unimposing

imposition *noun* 1 APPLICATION, introduction, levying, decree, laying on
2 INTRUSION, liberty, presumption, cheek (*informal*), encroachment
3 CHARGE, tax, duty, burden, levy

impossibility *noun* HOPELESSNESS, inability, impracticability, inconceivability

impossible *adjective* 1 NOT POSSIBLE, out of the question, impracticable, unfeasible, beyond the bounds of possibility
2 UNACHIEVABLE, hopeless, out of the question, vain, unthinkable, inconceivable, far-fetched, unworkable, implausible, unattainable, unobtainable, beyond you, not to be thought of
<< OPPOSITE possible
3 ABSURD, crazy (*informal*), ridiculous, unacceptable, outrageous, ludicrous, unreasonable, unsuitable, intolerable, preposterous, laughable, farcical, illogical, insoluble, unanswerable, inadmissible, ungovernable

impostor *noun* FRAUD, cheat, fake, impersonator, rogue, deceiver, sham, pretender, hypocrite, charlatan, quack, trickster, knave (*archaic*), phoney *or* phony (*informal*)

impotence *noun* POWERLESSNESS, inability, helplessness, weakness, disability, incompetence, inadequacy, paralysis, inefficiency, frailty, incapacity, infirmity, ineffectiveness, uselessness, feebleness, enervation, inefficacy
<< OPPOSITE powerfulness

impotent *adjective* POWERLESS, weak, helpless, unable, disabled, incapable, paralysed, frail, incompetent, ineffective, feeble, incapacitated, unmanned, infirm, emasculate, nerveless, enervated
<< OPPOSITE powerful

impoverish *verb* 1 BANKRUPT, ruin, beggar, break, pauperize
2 DEPLETE, drain, exhaust, diminish, use up, sap, wear out, reduce

impoverished *adjective* 1 POOR, needy, destitute, ruined, distressed, bankrupt, poverty-stricken, indigent, impecunious, straitened, penurious, necessitous, in reduced *or* straitened circumstances
<< OPPOSITE rich
2 DEPLETED, spent, reduced, empty, drained, exhausted, played out, worn out, denuded

impracticable *adjective* UNFEASIBLE, impossible, out of the question, unworkable, unattainable, unachievable
<< OPPOSITE practicable

impractical *adjective* 1 UNWORKABLE, impracticable, unrealistic, inoperable, impossible, unserviceable, nonviable
<< OPPOSITE practical
2 IDEALISTIC, wild, romantic, unrealistic, visionary, unbusinesslike, starry-eyed
<< OPPOSITE realistic

imprecise *adjective* INDEFINITE, estimated, rough, vague, loose, careless, ambiguous, inaccurate, sloppy (*informal*), woolly, hazy, indeterminate, wide of the mark, equivocal, ill-defined, inexact, inexplicit, blurred round the edges
<< OPPOSITE precise

impregnable *adjective* INVULNERABLE, strong, secure, unbeatable, invincible, impenetrable, unassailable, indestructible, immovable, unshakable, unconquerable
<< OPPOSITE vulnerable

impregnate *verb* 1 SATURATE, soak, steep, fill, seep, pervade, infuse, permeate, imbue, suffuse, percolate, imbrue (*rare*)
2 INSEMINATE, fertilize, make pregnant, fructify, fecundate, get with child

impress *verb* EXCITE, move, strike, touch, affect, influence, inspire, grab (*informal*), amaze, overcome, stir, overwhelm, astonish, dazzle, sway, awe, overawe, make an impression on
▷▷ **impress something on** *or* **upon someone** STRESS, bring home to, instil in, drum into, knock into, emphasize to, fix in, inculcate in, ingrain in

impression *noun* 1 IDEA, feeling, thought, sense, opinion, view, assessment, judgment, reaction, belief, concept, fancy, notion, conviction, suspicion, hunch, apprehension, inkling, funny feeling (*informal*)
2 EFFECT, influence, impact, sway
3 IMITATION, parody, impersonation, mockery, send-up (*Brit informal*), takeoff (*informal*)
4 MARK, imprint, stamp, stamping, depression, outline, hollow, dent, impress, indentation
▷▷ **make an impression** CAUSE A STIR, stand out, make an impact, be conspicuous, find favour, make a hit (*informal*), arouse comment, excite notice

impressionable *adjective* SUGGESTIBLE, vulnerable, susceptible, open, sensitive, responsive, receptive, gullible, ingenuous
<< OPPOSITE blasé

impressive *adjective* GRAND, striking, splendid, good, great (*informal*), fine, affecting, powerful, exciting, wonderful, excellent, dramatic, outstanding, stirring, superb, first-class, marvellous (*informal*), terrific (*informal*), awesome, world-class, admirable, first-rate,

forcible
<< OPPOSITE unimpressive

imprint *noun* MARK, print, impression, stamp, indentation
▷ *verb* ENGRAVE, print, stamp, impress, etch, emboss

imprison *verb* JAIL, confine, detain, lock up, constrain, put away, intern, incarcerate, send down (*informal*), send to prison, impound, put under lock and key, immure
<< OPPOSITE free

imprisoned *adjective* JAILED, confined, locked up, inside (*slang*), in jail, captive, behind bars, put away, interned, incarcerated, in irons, under lock and key, immured

imprisonment *noun* CONFINEMENT, custody, detention, captivity, incarceration, internment, duress

improbable *adjective* **1** DOUBTFUL, unlikely, uncertain, unbelievable, dubious, questionable, fanciful, far-fetched, implausible
<< OPPOSITE probable
2 UNCONVINCING, weak, unbelievable, preposterous
<< OPPOSITE convincing

impromptu *adjective* SPONTANEOUS, improvised, unprepared, off-the-cuff (*informal*), offhand, ad-lib, unscripted, unrehearsed, unpremeditated, extempore, unstudied, extemporaneous, extemporized
<< OPPOSITE rehearsed

improper *adjective* **1** INAPPROPRIATE, unfit, unsuitable, out of place, unwarranted, incongruous, unsuited, ill-timed, uncalled-for, inopportune, inapplicable, unseasonable, inapt, infelicitous, inapposite, malapropos
<< OPPOSITE appropriate
2 INDECENT, vulgar, suggestive, unseemly, untoward, risqué, smutty, unbecoming, unfitting, impolite, off-colour, indelicate, indecorous
<< OPPOSITE decent
3 INCORRECT, wrong, inaccurate, false, irregular, erroneous

impropriety *noun* **1** INDECENCY, vulgarity, immodesty, bad taste, incongruity, unsuitability, indecorum
<< OPPOSITE propriety
2 LAPSE, mistake, slip, blunder, gaffe, bloomer (*Brit informal*), faux pas, solecism, gaucherie

improve *verb* **1** ENHANCE, better, add to, upgrade, amend, mend, augment, embellish, touch up, ameliorate, polish up
<< OPPOSITE worsen
2 GET BETTER, pick up, look up (*informal*), develop, advance, perk up, take a turn for the better (*informal*)
3 RECUPERATE, recover, rally, mend, make progress, turn the corner, gain ground, gain strength, convalesce, be on the mend, grow better, make strides, take on a new lease of life (*informal*)

improvement *noun* **1** ENHANCEMENT, increase, gain, boost, amendment, correction, heightening, advancement, enrichment, face-lift, embellishment, betterment, rectification, augmentation, amelioration
2 ADVANCE, development, progress, recovery, reformation, upswing, furtherance

improvisation *noun* **1** INVENTION, spontaneity, ad-libbing, extemporizing
2 AD-LIB

improvise *verb* **1** DEVISE, contrive, make do, concoct, throw together
2 AD-LIB, invent, vamp, busk, wing it (*informal*), play it by ear (*informal*), extemporize, speak off the cuff (*informal*)

improvised *adjective* UNPREPARED, spontaneous, makeshift, spur-of-the-moment, off-the-cuff (*informal*), ad-lib, unrehearsed, extempore, extemporaneous, extemporized

imprudent *adjective* UNWISE, foolish, rash, irresponsible, reckless, careless, ill-advised, foolhardy, indiscreet, unthinking, ill-judged, ill-considered, inconsiderate, heedless, injudicious, incautious, improvident, impolitic, overhasty, temerarious
<< OPPOSITE prudent

impudence *noun* BOLDNESS, nerve (*informal*), cheek (*informal*), face (*informal*), front, neck (*informal*), gall (*informal*), lip (*slang*), presumption, audacity, rudeness, chutzpah (*US & Canad informal*), insolence, impertinence, effrontery, brass neck (*Brit informal*), shamelessness, sauciness, brazenness, sassiness (*US informal*), pertness, bumptiousness

impudent *adjective* BOLD, rude, cheeky (*informal*), forward, fresh (*informal*), saucy (*informal*), cocky (*informal*), audacious, brazen, shameless, sassy (*US informal*), pert, presumptuous, impertinent, insolent, lippy (*US & Canad slang*), bumptious, immodest, bold-faced
<< OPPOSITE polite

impulse *noun* **1** URGE, longing, desire, drive, wish, fancy, notion, yen (*informal*), instinct, yearning, inclination, itch, whim, compulsion, caprice
2 FORCE, pressure, push, movement, surge, motive, thrust, momentum, stimulus, catalyst, impetus
▷▷ **on impulse** IMPULSIVELY, of your own accord, freely, voluntarily, instinctively, impromptu, off the cuff (*informal*), in the heat of the moment, off your own bat, quite

unprompted

impulsive *adjective* INSTINCTIVE, emotional, unpredictable, quick, passionate, rash, spontaneous, precipitate, intuitive, hasty, headlong, impetuous, devil-may-care, unconsidered, unpremeditated
<< OPPOSITE cautious

impunity *noun* IMMUNITY, freedom, licence, permission, liberty, security, exemption, dispensation, nonliability

impure *adjective* 1 UNREFINED, mixed, alloyed, debased, adulterated, admixed
2 IMMORAL, corrupt, obscene, indecent, gross, coarse, lewd, carnal, X-rated (*informal*), salacious, unclean, prurient, lascivious, smutty, lustful, ribald, immodest, licentious, indelicate, unchaste
<< OPPOSITE moral
3 UNCLEAN, dirty, foul, infected, contaminated, polluted, filthy, tainted, sullied, defiled, unwholesome, vitiated, festy (*Austral slang*)
<< OPPOSITE clean

impurity *noun* 1 *often plural* DIRT, pollutant, scum, grime, contaminant, dross, bits, foreign body, foreign matter
2 CONTAMINATION, infection, pollution, taint, filth, foulness, defilement, dirtiness, uncleanness, befoulment
3 IMMORALITY, corruption, obscenity, indecency, vulgarity, prurience, coarseness, licentiousness, immodesty, carnality, lewdness, grossness, salaciousness, lasciviousness, unchastity, smuttiness

impute *verb* ATTRIBUTE, assign, ascribe, credit, refer, accredit

inaccessible *adjective* OUT-OF-REACH, remote, out-of-the-way, unattainable, impassable, unreachable, unapproachable, un-get-at-able (*informal*)
<< OPPOSITE accessible

inaccuracy *noun* 1 IMPRECISION, unreliability, incorrectness, unfaithfulness, erroneousness, inexactness
2 ERROR, mistake, slip, fault, defect, blunder, lapse, boob (*Brit slang*), literal (*Printing*), howler (*informal*), miscalculation, typo (*informal, Printing*), erratum, corrigendum, barry *or* Barry Crocker (*Austral slang*)

inaccurate *adjective* INCORRECT, wrong, mistaken, wild, faulty, careless, unreliable, defective, unfaithful, erroneous, unsound, imprecise, wide of the mark, out, inexact, off-base (*US & Canad informal*), off-beam (*informal*), discrepant, way off-beam (*informal*)
<< OPPOSITE accurate

inaction *noun* INACTIVITY, inertia, idleness, immobility, torpor, dormancy, torpidity

inactive *adjective* 1 UNUSED, idle, dormant, latent, inert, immobile, mothballed, out of service, inoperative, abeyant
<< OPPOSITE used
2 IDLE, unemployed, out of work, jobless, unoccupied, kicking your heels
<< OPPOSITE employed
3 LAZY, passive, slow, quiet, dull, low-key (*informal*), sluggish, lethargic, sedentary, indolent, somnolent, torpid, slothful
<< OPPOSITE active

inactivity *noun* IMMOBILITY, unemployment, inaction, passivity, hibernation, dormancy
<< OPPOSITE mobility

inadequacy *noun* 1 SHORTAGE, poverty, dearth, paucity, insufficiency, incompleteness, meagreness, skimpiness, scantiness, inadequateness
2 INCOMPETENCE, inability, deficiency, incapacity, ineffectiveness, incompetency, unfitness, inefficacy, defectiveness, inaptness, faultiness, unsuitableness
3 SHORTCOMING, failing, lack, weakness, shortage, defect, imperfection

inadequate *adjective* 1 INSUFFICIENT, short, scarce, meagre, poor, lacking, incomplete, scant, sparse, skimpy, sketchy, insubstantial, scanty, niggardly, incommensurate
<< OPPOSITE adequate
2 INCAPABLE, incompetent, pathetic, faulty, unfitted, defective, unequal, deficient, imperfect, unqualified, not up to scratch (*informal*), inapt
<< OPPOSITE capable

inadequately *adverb* INSUFFICIENTLY, poorly, thinly, sparsely, scantily, imperfectly, sketchily, skimpily, meagrely

inadvertent *adjective* UNINTENTIONAL, accidental, unintended, chance, careless, negligent, unwitting, unplanned, thoughtless, unthinking, heedless, unpremeditated, unheeding

inadvertently *adverb* UNINTENTIONALLY, accidentally, by accident, mistakenly, unwittingly, by mistake, involuntarily
<< OPPOSITE deliberately

inalienable *adjective* SACROSANCT, absolute, unassailable, inherent, entailed (*Law*), non-negotiable, inviolable, nontransferable, untransferable

inane *adjective* SENSELESS, stupid, silly, empty, daft (*informal*), worthless, futile, trifling, frivolous, mindless, goofy (*informal*), idiotic, vacuous, fatuous, puerile, vapid, unintelligent, asinine, imbecilic, devoid of intelligence
<< OPPOSITE sensible

inanimate *adjective* LIFELESS, inert, dead, cold, extinct, defunct, inactive, soulless, quiescent, spiritless, insensate, insentient

<< OPPOSITE animate
inaugural *adjective* FIRST, opening, initial, maiden, introductory, dedicatory
inaugurate *verb* 1 INVEST, install, induct, instate
2 OPEN, commission, dedicate, ordain
3 LAUNCH, begin, introduce, institute, set up, kick off (*informal*), initiate, originate, commence, get under way, usher in, set in motion
inauguration *noun* 1 INVESTITURE, installation, induction
2 OPENING, launch, birth, inception, commencement
3 LAUNCH, launching, setting up, institution, initiation
inborn *adjective* NATURAL, inherited, inherent, hereditary, instinctive, innate, intuitive, ingrained, congenital, inbred, native, immanent, in your blood, connate
inbred *adjective* INNATE, natural, constitutional, native, ingrained, inherent, deep-seated, immanent
inbuilt *adjective* INTEGRAL, built-in, incorporated, component
incalculable *adjective* VAST, enormous, immense, countless, infinite, innumerable, untold, limitless, boundless, inestimable, numberless, uncountable, measureless, without number, incomputable
incandescent *adjective* GLOWING, brilliant, shining, red-hot, radiant, luminous, white-hot, Day-Glo, phosphorescent
incantation *noun* CHANT, spell, charm, formula, invocation, hex (*US & Canad informal*), abracadabra, conjuration
incapacitate *verb* DISABLE, cripple, paralyse, scupper (*Brit slang*), prostrate, immobilize, put someone out of action (*informal*), lay someone up (*informal*)
incapacitated *adjective* DISABLED, challenged, unfit, out of action (*informal*), laid up (*informal*), immobilized, indisposed, hors de combat (*French*)
incapacity *noun* INABILITY, weakness, inadequacy, impotence, powerlessness, ineffectiveness, feebleness, incompetency, unfitness, incapability
incarcerate *verb* IMPRISON, confine, detain, lock up, restrict, restrain, intern, send down (*Brit*), impound, coop up, throw in jail, put under lock and key, immure, jail *or* gaol
incarceration *noun* CONFINEMENT, restraint, imprisonment, detention, captivity, bondage, internment
incarnate *adjective* 1 PERSONIFIED, embodied, typified
2 MADE FLESH, in the flesh, in human form, in bodily form
incarnation *noun* EMBODIMENT, manifestation, epitome, type, impersonation, personification, avatar, exemplification, bodily form
incendiary *adjective* INFLAMMATORY, provocative, subversive, seditious, rabble-rousing, dissentious
incense[1] *noun* PERFUME, scent, fragrance, bouquet, aroma, balm, redolence
incense[2] *verb* ANGER, infuriate, enrage, excite, provoke, irritate, gall, madden, inflame, exasperate, rile (*informal*), raise the hackles of, nark (*Brit, Austral & NZ slang*), make your blood boil (*informal*), rub you up the wrong way, make your hackles rise, get your hackles up, make you see red (*informal*)
incensed *adjective* ANGRY, mad (*informal*), furious, cross, fuming, choked, infuriated, enraged, maddened, exasperated, indignant, irate, up in arms, incandescent, steamed up (*slang*), hot under the collar (*informal*), on the warpath (*informal*), wrathful, ireful (*literary*), tooshie (*Austral slang*), off the air (*Austral slang*)
incentive *noun* INDUCEMENT, motive, encouragement, urge, come-on (*informal*), spur, lure, bait, motivation, carrot (*informal*), impulse, stimulus, impetus, stimulant, goad, incitement, enticement
<< OPPOSITE disincentive
inception *noun* BEGINNING, start, rise, birth, origin, dawn, outset, initiation, inauguration, commencement, kickoff (*informal*)
<< OPPOSITE end
incessant *adjective* CONSTANT, endless, continuous, persistent, eternal, relentless, perpetual, continual, unbroken, never-ending, interminable, unrelenting, everlasting, unending, ceaseless, unremitting, nonstop, unceasing
<< OPPOSITE intermittent
incessantly *adverb* ALL THE TIME, constantly, continually, endlessly, persistently, eternally, perpetually, nonstop, ceaselessly, without a break, interminably, everlastingly
incidence *noun* PREVALENCE, frequency, occurrence, rate, amount, degree, extent
incident *noun* 1 DISTURBANCE, scene, clash, disorder, confrontation, brawl, uproar, skirmish, mishap, fracas, commotion, contretemps
2 HAPPENING, event, affair, business, fact, matter, occasion, circumstance, episode, occurrence, escapade
3 ADVENTURE, drama, excitement, crisis, spectacle, theatrics
incidental *adjective* 1 SECONDARY, subsidiary, subordinate, minor, occasional, ancillary, nonessential
<< OPPOSITE essential
2 ACCOMPANYING, related, attendant,

contingent, contributory, concomitant

incidentally *adverb* 1 BY THE WAY, in passing, en passant, parenthetically, by the bye
2 ACCIDENTALLY, casually, by chance, coincidentally, fortuitously, by happenstance

incinerate *verb* 1 BURN UP, carbonize
2 CREMATE, burn up, reduce to ashes, consume by fire

incipient *adjective* BEGINNING, starting, developing, originating, commencing, embryonic, nascent, inchoate, inceptive

incision *noun* CUT, opening, slash, notch, slit, gash

incisive *adjective* PENETRATING, sharp, keen, acute, piercing, trenchant, perspicacious
<< OPPOSITE dull

incite *verb* PROVOKE, encourage, drive, excite, prompt, urge, spur, stimulate, set on, animate, rouse, prod, stir up, inflame, instigate, whip up, egg on, goad, impel, foment, put up to, agitate for *or* against
<< OPPOSITE discourage

incitement *noun* PROVOCATION, prompting, encouragement, spur, motive, motivation, impulse, stimulus, impetus, agitation, inducement, goad, instigation, clarion call

inclination *noun* 1 DESIRE, longing, wish, need, aspiration, craving, yearning, hankering
2 TENDENCY, liking, taste, turn, fancy, leaning, bent, stomach, prejudice, bias, affection, thirst, disposition, penchant, fondness, propensity, aptitude, predisposition, predilection, proclivity, partiality, turn of mind, proneness
<< OPPOSITE aversion
3 BOW, bending, nod, bowing

incline *verb* 1 PREDISPOSE, influence, tend, persuade, prejudice, bias, sway, turn, dispose
2 BEND, lower, nod, bow, stoop, nutate (*rare*)
▷ *noun* SLOPE, rise, dip, grade, descent, ramp, ascent, gradient, declivity, acclivity

inclined *adjective* 1 DISPOSED, given, prone, likely, subject, liable, apt, predisposed, tending towards
2 WILLING, minded, ready, disposed, of a mind (*informal*)

inclose ▷ see **enclose**

include *verb* 1 CONTAIN, involve, incorporate, cover, consist of, take in, embrace, comprise, take into account, embody, encompass, comprehend, subsume
<< OPPOSITE exclude
2 COUNT, introduce, make a part of, number among
3 ADD, enter, put in, insert

including *preposition* CONTAINING, with, counting, plus, together with, as well as, inclusive of

inclusion *noun* ADDITION, incorporation, introduction, insertion
<< OPPOSITE exclusion

inclusive *adjective* COMPREHENSIVE, full, overall, general, global, sweeping, all-in, blanket, umbrella, across-the-board, all-together, catch-all (*chiefly US*), all-embracing, overarching, in toto (*Latin*)
<< OPPOSITE limited

incognito *adjective* IN DISGUISE, unknown, disguised, unrecognized, under an assumed name

incoherent *adjective* UNINTELLIGIBLE, wild, confused, disordered, wandering, muddled, rambling, inconsistent, jumbled, stammering, disconnected, stuttering, unconnected, disjointed, inarticulate, uncoordinated
<< OPPOSITE coherent

income *noun* REVENUE, gains, earnings, means, pay, interest, returns, profits, wages, rewards, yield, proceeds, salary, receipts, takings

incoming *adjective* 1 ARRIVING, landing, approaching, entering, returning, homeward
<< OPPOSITE departing
2 NEW, next, succeeding, elected, elect

incomparable *adjective* UNEQUALLED, supreme, unparalleled, paramount, superlative, transcendent, unrivalled, inimitable, unmatched, peerless, matchless, beyond compare

incompatibility *noun* INCONSISTENCY, conflict, discrepancy, antagonism, incongruity, irreconcilability, disparateness, uncongeniality

incompatible *adjective* INCONSISTENT, conflicting, contradictory, unsuitable, disparate, incongruous, discordant, antagonistic, irreconcilable, unsuited, mismatched, discrepant, uncongenial, antipathetic, ill-assorted, inconsonant
<< OPPOSITE compatible

incompetence *noun* INEPTITUDE, inability, inadequacy, incapacity, ineffectiveness, uselessness, insufficiency, ineptness, incompetency, unfitness, incapability, skill-lessness

incompetent *adjective* INEPT, useless, incapable, unable, cowboy (*informal*), floundering, bungling, unfit, unfitted, ineffectual, incapacitated, inexpert, skill-less, unskilful
<< OPPOSITE competent

incomplete *adjective* UNFINISHED, partial, insufficient, wanting, short, lacking, undone, defective, deficient, imperfect, undeveloped, fragmentary, unaccomplished, unexecuted, half-pie (*NZ informal*)
<< OPPOSITE complete

incomprehensible *adjective* 1 UNINTELLIGIBLE

<< OPPOSITE comprehensible
2 OBSCURE, puzzling, mysterious, baffling, enigmatic, perplexing, opaque, impenetrable, inscrutable, unfathomable, above your head, beyond comprehension, all Greek to you (*informal*), beyond your grasp
<< OPPOSITE understandable

inconceivable *adjective* UNIMAGINABLE, impossible, incredible, staggering (*informal*), unbelievable, unthinkable, out of the question, incomprehensible, unheard-of, mind-boggling (*informal*), beyond belief, unknowable, not to be thought of
<< OPPOSITE conceivable

inconclusive *adjective* UNCERTAIN, vague, ambiguous, open, indecisive, unsettled, undecided, unconvincing, up in the air (*informal*), indeterminate

incongruity *noun* INAPPROPRIATENESS, discrepancy, inconsistency, disparity, incompatibility, unsuitability, inaptness, inharmoniousness

incongruous *adjective* INAPPROPRIATE, absurd, out of place, conflicting, contrary, contradictory, inconsistent, unsuitable, improper, incompatible, discordant, incoherent, extraneous, unsuited, unbecoming, out of keeping, inapt, disconsonant
<< OPPOSITE appropriate

inconsequential *adjective* UNIMPORTANT, trivial, insignificant, minor, petty, trifling, negligible, paltry, immaterial, measly, inconsiderable, nickel-and-dime (*US slang*), of no significance

inconsiderable *adjective* INSIGNIFICANT, small, slight, light, minor, petty, trivial, trifling, negligible, unimportant, small-time (*informal*), inconsequential, exiguous

inconsiderate *adjective* SELFISH, rude, insensitive, self-centred, careless, unkind, intolerant, thoughtless, unthinking, tactless, uncharitable, ungracious, indelicate
<< OPPOSITE considerate

inconsistency *noun* 1 UNRELIABILITY, instability, unpredictability, fickleness, unsteadiness
2 INCOMPATIBILITY, paradox, discrepancy, disparity, disagreement, variance, divergence, incongruity, contrariety, inconsonance

inconsistent *adjective* 1 CHANGEABLE, variable, unpredictable, unstable, irregular, erratic, uneven, fickle, capricious, unsteady, inconstant
<< OPPOSITE consistent
2 INCOMPATIBLE, conflicting, contrary, at odds, contradictory, in conflict, incongruous, discordant, incoherent, out of step, irreconcilable, at variance, discrepant, inconstant
<< OPPOSITE compatible

inconsolable *adjective* HEARTBROKEN, devastated, despairing, desolate, wretched, heartsick, brokenhearted, sick at heart, prostrate with grief

inconspicuous *adjective* 1 UNOBTRUSIVE, hidden, unnoticeable, retiring, quiet, ordinary, plain, muted, camouflaged, insignificant, unassuming, unostentatious
<< OPPOSITE noticeable
2 PLAIN, ordinary, modest, unobtrusive, unnoticeable

incontrovertible *adjective* INDISPUTABLE, sure, certain, established, positive, undeniable, irrefutable, unquestionable, unshakable, beyond dispute, incontestable, indubitable, nailed-on (*slang*)

inconvenience *noun* 1 TROUBLE, difficulty, bother, upset, fuss, disadvantage, disturbance, disruption, drawback, hassle (*informal*), nuisance, downside, annoyance, hindrance, awkwardness, vexation, uphill (*S African*)
2 AWKWARDNESS, unfitness, unwieldiness, cumbersomeness, unhandiness, unsuitableness, untimeliness
▷ *verb* TROUBLE, bother, disturb, upset, disrupt, put (someone) out, hassle (*informal*), irk, discommode, give (someone) bother *or* trouble, make (someone) go out of his way, put (someone) to trouble

inconvenient *adjective* 1 TROUBLESOME, annoying, awkward, embarrassing, disturbing, unsuitable, tiresome, untimely, bothersome, vexatious, inopportune, disadvantageous, unseasonable
<< OPPOSITE convenient
2 DIFFICULT, awkward, unmanageable, cumbersome, unwieldy, unhandy

incorporate *verb* 1 INCLUDE, contain, take in, embrace, integrate, embody, encompass, assimilate, comprise of
2 INTEGRATE, include, absorb, unite, merge, accommodate, knit, fuse, assimilate, amalgamate, subsume, coalesce, harmonize, meld
3 BLEND, mix, combine, compound, consolidate, fuse, mingle, meld

incorporation *noun* MERGER, federation, blend, integration, unifying, inclusion, fusion, absorption, assimilation, amalgamation, coalescence

incorrect *adjective* FALSE, wrong, mistaken, flawed, faulty, unfitting, inaccurate, untrue, improper, erroneous, out, wide of the mark (*informal*), specious, inexact, off-base (*US & Canad informal*), off-beam (*informal*), way off-beam (*informal*)
<< OPPOSITE correct

incorrigible *adjective* INCURABLE, hardened, hopeless, intractable, inveterate, unreformed, irredeemable

increase *verb* 1 RAISE, extend, boost, expand, develop, advance, add to, strengthen, enhance, step up (*informal*), widen, prolong, intensify, heighten, elevate, enlarge, multiply, inflate, magnify, amplify, augment, aggrandize

<< OPPOSITE decrease

2 GROW, develop, spread, mount, expand, build up, swell, wax, enlarge, escalate, multiply, fill out, get bigger, proliferate, snowball, dilate

<< OPPOSITE shrink

▷ *noun* GROWTH, rise, boost, development, gain, addition, expansion, extension, heightening, proliferation, enlargement, escalation, upsurge, upturn, increment, intensification, augmentation, aggrandizement

▷▷ **on the increase** GROWING, increasing, spreading, expanding, escalating, multiplying, developing, on the rise, proliferating

increasingly *adverb* PROGRESSIVELY, more and more, to an increasing extent, continuously more

incredible *adjective* 1 (*informal*) AMAZING, great, wonderful, brilliant, stunning, extraordinary, overwhelming, ace (*informal*), astonishing, staggering, marvellous, sensational (*informal*), mega (*slang*), breathtaking, astounding, far-out (*slang*), prodigious, awe-inspiring, superhuman, rad (*informal*)

2 UNBELIEVABLE, impossible, absurd, unthinkable, questionable, improbable, inconceivable, preposterous, unconvincing, unimaginable, outlandish, far-fetched, implausible, beyond belief, cock-and-bull (*informal*), not able to hold water

incredulity *noun* DISBELIEF, doubt, scepticism, distrust, unbelief

incredulous *adjective* DISBELIEVING, doubting, sceptical, suspicious, doubtful, dubious, unconvinced, distrustful, mistrustful, unbelieving

<< OPPOSITE credulous

increment *noun* INCREASE, gain, addition, supplement, step up, advancement, enlargement, accretion, accrual, augmentation, accruement

incriminate *verb* IMPLICATE, involve, accuse, blame, indict, point the finger at (*informal*), stigmatize, arraign, blacken the name of, inculpate

incumbent *noun* HOLDER, keeper, bearer, custodian

▷ *adjective* (*Formal*) OBLIGATORY, required, necessary, essential, binding, compulsory, mandatory, imperative

incur *verb* SUSTAIN, experience, suffer, gain, earn, collect, meet with, provoke, run up, induce, arouse, expose yourself to, lay yourself open to, bring upon yourself

incurable *adjective* 1 FATAL, terminal, inoperable, irrecoverable, irremediable, remediless

2 INCORRIGIBLE, hopeless, inveterate, dyed-in-the-wool

incursion *noun* FORAY, raid, invasion, penetration, infiltration, inroad, irruption

indebted *adjective* GRATEFUL, obliged, in debt, obligated, beholden, under an obligation

indecency *noun* OBSCENITY, impurity, lewdness, impropriety, pornography, vulgarity, coarseness, crudity, licentiousness, foulness, outrageousness, immodesty, grossness, vileness, bawdiness, unseemliness, indelicacy, smuttiness, indecorum

<< OPPOSITE decency

indecent *adjective* 1 OBSCENE, lewd, dirty, blue, offensive, outrageous, inappropriate, rude, gross, foul, crude, coarse, filthy, vile, improper, pornographic, salacious, impure, smutty, immodest, licentious, scatological, indelicate

<< OPPOSITE decent

2 UNBECOMING, unsuitable, vulgar, improper, tasteless, unseemly, undignified, disreputable, unrefined, discreditable, indelicate, indecorous, unbefitting

<< OPPOSITE proper

indecision *noun* HESITATION, doubt, uncertainty, wavering, ambivalence, dithering (*chiefly Brit*), hesitancy, indecisiveness, vacillation, shilly-shallying (*informal*), irresolution

indecisive *adjective* 1 HESITATING, uncertain, wavering, doubtful, faltering, tentative, undecided, dithering (*chiefly Brit*), vacillating, in two minds (*informal*), undetermined, pussyfooting (*informal*), irresolute

<< OPPOSITE decisive

2 INCONCLUSIVE, unclear, undecided, indefinite, indeterminate

<< OPPOSITE conclusive

indeed *adverb* 1 CERTAINLY, yes, definitely, surely, truly, absolutely, undoubtedly, positively, decidedly, without doubt, undeniably, without question, unequivocally, indisputably, assuredly, doubtlessly

2 REALLY, actually, in fact, certainly, undoubtedly, genuinely, in reality, to be sure, in truth, categorically, verily (*archaic*), in actuality, in point of fact, veritably

indefatigable *adjective* TIRELESS, dogged, persevering, patient, relentless, diligent, inexhaustible, unremitting, assiduous, unflagging, untiring, sedulous, pertinacious, unwearying, unwearied

indefensible *adjective* UNFORGIVABLE, wrong, inexcusable, unjustifiable, untenable, unpardonable, insupportable, unwarrantable
<< OPPOSITE defensible

indefinite *adjective* 1 UNCERTAIN, general, vague, unclear, unsettled, loose, unlimited, evasive, indeterminate, imprecise, undefined, equivocal, ill-defined, indistinct, undetermined, inexact, unfixed, oracular
<< OPPOSITE settled
2 UNCLEAR, unknown, uncertain, obscure, doubtful, ambiguous, indeterminate, imprecise, undefined, ill-defined, indistinct, undetermined, inexact, unfixed
<< OPPOSITE specific

indefinitely *adverb* ENDLESSLY, continually, for ever, ad infinitum, sine die (*Latin*), till the cows come home (*informal*)

indelible *adjective* PERMANENT, lasting, enduring, ingrained, indestructible, ineradicable, ineffaceable, inexpungible, inextirpable
<< OPPOSITE temporary

indemnify *verb* 1 INSURE, protect, guarantee, secure, endorse, underwrite
2 COMPENSATE, pay, reimburse, satisfy, repair, repay, requite, remunerate

indemnity *noun* 1 INSURANCE, security, guarantee, protection
2 COMPENSATION, remuneration, reparation, satisfaction, redress, restitution, reimbursement, requital
3 (*Law*) EXEMPTION, immunity, impunity, privilege

indent *verb* 1 NOTCH, cut, score, mark, nick, pink, scallop, dint, serrate
2 ORDER, request, ask for, requisition

indentation *noun* NOTCH, cut, nick, depression, pit, dip, bash (*informal*), hollow, dent, jag, dimple

independence *noun* FREEDOM, liberty, autonomy, separation, sovereignty, self-determination, self-government, self-rule, self-sufficiency, self-reliance, home rule, autarchy, rangatiratanga (NZ)
<< OPPOSITE subjugation

independent *adjective* 1 SEPARATE, unrelated, unconnected, unattached, uncontrolled, unconstrained
<< OPPOSITE controlled
2 SELF-SUFFICIENT, free, liberated, unconventional, self-contained, individualistic, unaided, self-reliant, self-supporting
3 SELF-GOVERNING, free, autonomous, separated, liberated, sovereign, self-determining, nonaligned, decontrolled, autarchic
<< OPPOSITE subject

independently *adverb* SEPARATELY, alone, solo, on your own, by yourself, unaided, individually, autonomously, under your own steam

indescribable *adjective* UNUTTERABLE, indefinable, beyond words, ineffable, inexpressible, beyond description, incommunicable, beggaring description

indestructible *adjective* PERMANENT, durable, unbreakable, lasting, enduring, abiding, immortal, everlasting, indelible, incorruptible, imperishable, indissoluble, unfading, nonperishable
<< OPPOSITE breakable

indeterminate *adjective* UNCERTAIN, indefinite, unspecified, vague, inconclusive, imprecise, undefined, undetermined, inexact, unfixed, unstipulated
<< OPPOSITE fixed

index *noun* INDICATION, guide, sign, mark, note, evidence, signal, symptom, hint, clue, token

indicate *verb* 1 SHOW, suggest, reveal, display, signal, demonstrate, point to, imply, disclose, manifest, signify, denote, bespeak, make known, be symptomatic of, evince, betoken
2 IMPLY, suggest, hint, intimate, signify, insinuate, give someone to understand
3 POINT TO, point out, specify, gesture towards, designate
4 REGISTER, show, record, mark, read, express, display, demonstrate

indication *noun* SIGN, mark, evidence, warning, note, signal, suggestion, symptom, hint, clue, manifestation, omen, inkling, portent, intimation, forewarning, wake-up call

indicative *adjective* SUGGESTIVE, significant, symptomatic, pointing to, exhibitive, indicatory, indicial

indicator *noun* SIGN, mark, measure, guide, display, index, signal, symbol, meter, gauge, marker, benchmark, pointer, signpost, barometer

indict *verb* CHARGE, accuse, prosecute, summon, impeach, arraign, serve with a summons

indictment *noun* CHARGE, allegation, prosecution, accusation, impeachment, summons, arraignment

indifference *noun* 1 DISREGARD, apathy, lack of interest, negligence, detachment, coolness, carelessness, coldness, nonchalance, callousness, aloofness, inattention, unconcern, absence of feeling, heedlessness
<< OPPOSITE concern
2 IRRELEVANCE, insignificance, triviality, unimportance

indifferent *adjective* 1 UNCONCERNED, distant, detached, cold, cool, regardless, careless, callous, aloof, unimpressed, unmoved, unsympathetic, impervious, uncaring, uninterested, apathetic, unresponsive, heedless, inattentive

<< OPPOSITE concerned

2 MEDIOCRE, middling, average, fair, ordinary, moderate, insignificant, unimportant, so-so (*informal*), immaterial, passable, undistinguished, uninspired, of no consequence, no great shakes (*informal*), half-pie (*NZ informal*)

<< OPPOSITE excellent

indigenous *adjective* NATIVE, original, aboriginal, home-grown, autochthonous

indigent *adjective* (*Formal*) DESTITUTE, poor, impoverished, needy, penniless, poverty-stricken, down and out, in want, down at heel (*informal*), impecunious, dirt-poor, straitened, on the breadline, short, flat broke (*informal*), penurious, necessitous

<< OPPOSITE wealthy

indigestion *noun* UPSET STOMACH, heartburn, dyspepsia, dyspepsy

indignant *adjective* RESENTFUL, angry, mad (*informal*), heated, provoked, furious, annoyed, hacked (off) (*US slang*), sore (*informal*), fuming (*informal*), choked, incensed, disgruntled, exasperated, irate, livid (*informal*), seeing red (*informal*), miffed (*informal*), riled, up in arms (*informal*), peeved (*informal*), in a huff, hot under the collar (*informal*), huffy (*informal*), wrathful, narked (*Brit, Austral & NZ slang*), in high dudgeon, tooshie (*Austral slang*), off the air (*Austral slang*)

indignation *noun* RESENTMENT, anger, rage, fury, wrath, ire (*literary*), exasperation, pique, umbrage, righteous anger

indignity *noun* HUMILIATION, abuse, outrage, injury, slight, insult, snub, reproach, affront, disrespect, dishonour, opprobrium, obloquy, contumely

indirect *adjective* 1 RELATED, accompanying, secondary, subsidiary, contingent, collateral, incidental, unintended, ancillary, concomitant

2 CIRCUITOUS, winding, roundabout, curving, wandering, rambling, deviant, meandering, tortuous, zigzag, long-drawn-out, circumlocutory

<< OPPOSITE direct

indirectly *adverb* 1 BY IMPLICATION, in a roundabout way, circumlocutorily

2 OBLIQUELY, in a roundabout way, evasively, not in so many words, circuitously, periphrastically

indiscreet *adjective* TACTLESS, foolish, rash, reckless, unwise, hasty, ill-advised, unthinking, ill-judged, ill-considered, imprudent, heedless, injudicious, incautious, undiplomatic, impolitic

<< OPPOSITE discreet

indiscretion *noun* 1 FOLLY, foolishness, recklessness, imprudence, rashness, tactlessness, gaucherie

2 MISTAKE, slip, error, lapse, folly, boob (*Brit slang*), gaffe, bloomer (*Brit informal*), faux pas, barry *or* Barry Crocker (*Austral slang*)

indiscriminate *adjective* RANDOM, general, wholesale, mixed, sweeping, confused, chaotic, careless, mingled, jumbled, miscellaneous, promiscuous, motley, haphazard, uncritical, aimless, desultory, hit or miss (*informal*), higgledy-piggledy (*informal*), undiscriminating, unsystematic, unselective, undistinguishable, unmethodical, scattershot

<< OPPOSITE systematic

indispensable *adjective* ESSENTIAL, necessary, needed, key, vital, crucial, imperative, requisite, needful, must-have

<< OPPOSITE dispensable

indistinct *adjective* 1 UNCLEAR, confused, obscure, faint, blurred, vague, doubtful, ambiguous, fuzzy, shadowy, indefinite, misty, hazy, unintelligible, indistinguishable, indeterminate, bleary, undefined, out of focus, ill-defined, indiscernible

<< OPPOSITE distinct

2 MUFFLED, confused, faint, dim, weak, indistinguishable, indiscernible

indistinguishable *adjective* IDENTICAL, the same, cut from the same cloth, like as two peas in a pod (*informal*)

individual *adjective* 1 SEPARATE, single, independent, isolated, lone, solitary, discrete

<< OPPOSITE collective

2 UNIQUE, special, fresh, novel, exclusive, distinct, singular, idiosyncratic, unorthodox

<< OPPOSITE conventional

▷ *noun* PERSON, being, human, party, body (*informal*), type, unit, character, soul, creature, human being, mortal, personage, living soul

individualism *noun* INDEPENDENCE, self-interest, originality, self-reliance, egoism, egocentricity, self-direction, freethinking

individualist *noun* MAVERICK, nonconformist, independent, original, loner, lone wolf, freethinker

individuality *noun* CHARACTER, personality, uniqueness, distinction, distinctiveness, originality, peculiarity, singularity, separateness, discreteness

individually *adverb* SEPARATELY, independently, singly, one by one, one at a time, severally

indoctrinate *verb* BRAINWASH, school, train, teach, drill, initiate, instruct, imbue

indoctrination *noun* BRAINWASHING, schooling, training, instruction, drilling, inculcation

indomitable *adjective* INVINCIBLE, resolute,

steadfast, set, staunch, unbeatable, unyielding, unflinching, unconquerable, untameable
<< OPPOSITE weak

indorse ▷ see **endorse**

indorsement ▷ see **endorsement**

induce *verb* 1 CAUSE, produce, create, begin, effect, lead to, occasion, generate, provoke, motivate, set off, bring about, give rise to, precipitate, incite, instigate, engender, set in motion
<< OPPOSITE prevent
2 PERSUADE, encourage, influence, get, move, press, draw, convince, urge, prompt, sway, entice, coax, incite, impel, talk someone into, prevail upon, actuate
<< OPPOSITE dissuade

inducement *noun* INCENTIVE, motive, cause, influence, reward, come-on (*informal*), spur, consideration, attraction, lure, bait, carrot (*informal*), encouragement, impulse, stimulus, incitement, clarion call

induct *verb* INSTALL, admit, introduce, allow, swear, initiate, inaugurate

induction *noun* INSTALLATION, institution, introduction, initiation, inauguration, investiture

indulge *verb* 1 GRATIFY, satisfy, fulfil, feed, give way to, yield to, cater to, pander to, regale, gladden, satiate
2 SPOIL, pamper, cosset, baby, favour, humour, give in to, coddle, spoon-feed, mollycoddle, fawn on, overindulge
▷▷ **indulge yourself** TREAT YOURSELF, splash out, spoil yourself, luxuriate in something, overindulge yourself

indulgence *noun* 1 LUXURY, treat, extravagance, favour, privilege
2 LENIENCY, pampering, spoiling, kindness, fondness, permissiveness, partiality
3 INTEMPERANCE, excess, extravagance, debauchery, dissipation, overindulgence, prodigality, immoderation, dissoluteness, intemperateness
<< OPPOSITE temperance
4 GRATIFICATION, satisfaction, fulfilment, appeasement, satiation

indulgent *adjective* LENIENT, liberal, kind, kindly, understanding, gentle, tender, mild, fond, favourable, tolerant, gratifying, easy-going, compliant, permissive, forbearing
<< OPPOSITE strict

industrialist *noun* CAPITALIST, tycoon, magnate, boss, producer, manufacturer, baron, financier, captain of industry, big businessman

industrious *adjective* HARD-WORKING, diligent, active, busy, steady, productive, energetic, conscientious, tireless, zealous, laborious, assiduous, sedulous
<< OPPOSITE lazy

industry *noun* 1 BUSINESS, production, manufacturing, trade, trading, commerce, commercial enterprise
2 TRADE, world, business, service, line, field, craft, profession, occupation
3 DILIGENCE, effort, labour, hard work, trouble, activity, application, striving, endeavour, toil, vigour, zeal, persistence, assiduity, tirelessness

ineffable *adjective* INDESCRIBABLE, unspeakable, indefinable, beyond words, unutterable, inexpressible, incommunicable

ineffective *adjective* 1 UNPRODUCTIVE, useless, futile, vain, unsuccessful, pointless, fruitless, to no avail, ineffectual, unprofitable, to no effect, unavailing, unfruitful, profitless, bootless, inefficacious
<< OPPOSITE effective
2 INEFFICIENT, inadequate, useless, poor, weak, pathetic, powerless, unfit, feeble, worthless, inept, impotent, ineffectual

ineffectual *adjective* 1 UNPRODUCTIVE, useless, ineffective, vain, unsuccessful, pointless, futile, fruitless, to no avail, unprofitable, to no effect, unavailing, unfruitful, profitless, bootless, inefficacious
2 INEFFICIENT, useless, powerless, poor, weak, inadequate, pathetic, unfit, ineffective, feeble, worthless, inept, impotent

inefficiency *noun* INCOMPETENCE, slackness, sloppiness, disorganization, carelessness

inefficient *adjective* 1 WASTEFUL, uneconomical, profligate, ruinous, improvident, unthrifty, inefficacious
2 INCOMPETENT, incapable, inept, weak, bungling, feeble, sloppy, ineffectual, disorganized, slipshod, inexpert
<< OPPOSITE efficient

ineligible *adjective* UNQUALIFIED, ruled out, unacceptable, disqualified, incompetent (*Law*), unfit, unfitted, unsuitable, undesirable, objectionable, unequipped

inept *adjective* 1 INCOMPETENT, bungling, clumsy, cowboy (*informal*), awkward, bumbling, gauche, cack-handed (*informal*), inexpert, maladroit, unskilful, unhandy, unworkmanlike
<< OPPOSITE competent
2 UNSUITABLE, inappropriate, out of place, ridiculous, absurd, meaningless, pointless, unfit, improper, inapt, infelicitous, malapropos
<< OPPOSITE appropriate

ineptitude *noun* INCOMPETENCE, inefficiency, inability, incapacity, clumsiness, unfitness, gaucheness, inexpertness, unhandiness

inequality *noun* DISPARITY, prejudice, difference, bias, diversity, irregularity, unevenness, lack of balance, disproportion, imparity, preferentiality

inert *adjective* INACTIVE, still, motionless, dead, passive, slack, static, dormant, lifeless, leaden, immobile, inanimate, unresponsive, unmoving, quiescent, torpid, unreactive, slumberous (*chiefly poetic*)
<< OPPOSITE moving

inertia *noun* INACTIVITY, apathy, lethargy, passivity, stillness, laziness, sloth, idleness, stupor, drowsiness, dullness, immobility, torpor, sluggishness, indolence, lassitude, languor, listlessness, deadness, unresponsiveness
<< OPPOSITE activity

inescapable *adjective* UNAVOIDABLE, inevitable, certain, sure, fated, destined, inexorable, ineluctable, ineludible (*rare*)

inevitable *adjective* UNAVOIDABLE, inescapable, inexorable, sure, certain, necessary, settled, fixed, assured, fated, decreed, destined, ordained, predetermined, predestined, preordained, ineluctable, unpreventable
<< OPPOSITE avoidable

inevitably *adverb* UNAVOIDABLY, naturally, necessarily, surely, certainly, as a result, automatically, consequently, of necessity, perforce, inescapably, as a necessary consequence

inexcusable *adjective* UNFORGIVABLE, indefensible, unjustifiable, outrageous, unpardonable, unwarrantable, inexpiable
<< OPPOSITE excusable

inexhaustible *adjective* 1 ENDLESS, infinite, never-ending, limitless, boundless, bottomless, unbounded, measureless, illimitable
<< OPPOSITE limited
2 TIRELESS, undaunted, indefatigable, unfailing, unflagging, untiring, unwearying, unwearied
<< OPPOSITE tiring

inexorable *adjective* UNRELENTING, relentless, implacable, hard, severe, harsh, cruel, adamant, inescapable, inflexible, merciless, unyielding, immovable, remorseless, pitiless, unbending, obdurate, ineluctable, unappeasable
<< OPPOSITE relenting

inexorably *adverb* RELENTLESSLY, inevitably, irresistibly, remorselessly, implacably, unrelentingly

inexpensive *adjective* CHEAP, reasonable, low-priced, budget, bargain, modest, low-cost, economical
<< OPPOSITE expensive

inexperience *noun* UNFAMILIARITY, ignorance, newness, rawness, greenness, callowness, unexpertness

inexperienced *adjective* NEW, unskilled, untrained, green, fresh, amateur, raw, unfamiliar, unused, callow, immature, unaccustomed, untried, unschooled, wet behind the ears (*informal*), unacquainted, unseasoned, unpractised, unversed, unfledged
<< OPPOSITE experienced

inexplicable *adjective* UNACCOUNTABLE, strange, mysterious, baffling, enigmatic, incomprehensible, mystifying, unintelligible, insoluble, inscrutable, unfathomable, beyond comprehension
<< OPPOSITE explicable

inextricably *adverb* INSEPARABLY, totally, intricately, irretrievably, indissolubly, indistinguishably

infallibility *noun* 1 SUPREMACY, perfection, omniscience, impeccability, faultlessness, irrefutability, unerringness
2 RELIABILITY, safety, dependability, trustworthiness, sureness

infallible *adjective* 1 PERFECT, impeccable, faultless, unerring, omniscient, unimpeachable
<< OPPOSITE fallible
2 SURE, certain, reliable, unbeatable, dependable, trustworthy, foolproof, sure-fire (*informal*), unfailing
<< OPPOSITE unreliable

infamous *adjective* NOTORIOUS, base, shocking, outrageous, disgraceful, monstrous, shameful, vile, scandalous, wicked, atrocious, heinous, odious, hateful, loathsome, ignominious, disreputable, egregious, abominable, villainous, dishonourable, nefarious, iniquitous, detestable, opprobrious, ill-famed, flagitious
<< OPPOSITE esteemed

infamy *noun* NOTORIETY, scandal, shame, disgrace, atrocity, discredit, stigma, disrepute, ignominy, dishonour, abomination, opprobrium, villainy, odium, outrageousness, obloquy

infancy *noun* 1 EARLY CHILDHOOD, babyhood
2 BEGINNINGS, start, birth, roots, seeds, origins, dawn, early stages, emergence, outset, cradle, inception
<< OPPOSITE end

infant *noun* BABY, child, babe, toddler, tot, wean (*Scot*), little one, bairn (*Scot*), suckling, newborn child, babe in arms, sprog (*slang*), munchkin (*informal, chiefly US*), neonate, rug rat (*slang*), littlie (*Austral informal*), ankle-biter (*Austral slang*), tacker (*Austral slang*)
▷ *adjective* EARLY, new, developing, young, growing, initial, dawning, fledgling, newborn, immature, embryonic, emergent, nascent, unfledged

infantile *adjective* CHILDISH, immature, puerile, babyish, young, weak
<< OPPOSITE mature

infatuated *adjective* OBSESSED, fascinated, captivated, possessed, carried away, inflamed, beguiled, smitten (*informal*), besotted, bewitched, intoxicated, crazy about (*informal*), spellbound, enamoured, enraptured, under the spell of, head over heels in love with, swept off your feet

infatuation *noun* OBSESSION, thing (*informal*), passion, crush (*informal*), madness, folly, fixation, foolishness

infect *verb* **1** CONTAMINATE, transmit disease to, spread disease to *or* among
2 POLLUTE, dirty, poison, foul, corrupt, contaminate, taint, defile, vitiate
3 AFFECT, move, touch, influence, upset, overcome, stir, disturb

infection *noun* DISEASE, condition, complaint, illness, virus, disorder, corruption, poison, pollution, contamination, contagion, defilement, septicity

infectious *adjective* CATCHING, spreading, contagious, communicable, poisoning, corrupting, contaminating, polluting, virulent, defiling, infective, vitiating, pestilential, transmittable

infer *verb* DEDUCE, understand, gather, conclude, derive, presume, conjecture, surmise, read between the lines, put two and two together

> The use of *infer* to mean *imply* is becoming more and more common in both speech and writing. There is nevertheless a useful distinction between the two which many people would be in favour of maintaining. To *infer* means 'to deduce', and is used in the construction 'to infer something from something': *I inferred from what she said that she had not been well*. To *imply* means 'to suggest, to insinuate' and is normally followed by a clause: *are you implying that I was responsible for the mistake?*

inference *noun* DEDUCTION, conclusion, assumption, reading, consequence, presumption, conjecture, surmise, corollary

inferior *adjective* **1** LOWER, junior, minor, secondary, subsidiary, lesser, humble, subordinate, lowly, less important, menial
<< OPPOSITE superior
2 SUBSTANDARD, bad, poor, mean, worse, poorer, pants (*informal*), flawed, rotten, dire, indifferent, duff (*Brit informal*), mediocre, second-class, deficient, imperfect, second-rate, shoddy, low-grade, unsound, downmarket, low-rent (*informal, chiefly US*), for the birds (*informal*), wretched, two-bit (*US & Canad slang*), crappy (*slang*), no great shakes (*informal*), poxy (*slang*), dime-a-dozen (*informal*), bush-league (*Austral & NZ informal*), not much cop (*Brit slang*), tinhorn (*US slang*), half-pie (*NZ informal*), of a sort *or* of sorts, strictly for the birds (*informal*), bodger *or* bodgie (*Austral slang*)
<< OPPOSITE excellent
▷ *noun* UNDERLING, junior, subordinate, lesser, menial, minion

inferiority *noun* SUBSERVIENCE, subordination, lowliness, servitude, abasement, inferior status *or* standing
<< OPPOSITE superiority

infernal *adjective* **1** (*informal*) DAMNED, malevolent, hellish, devilish, accursed, damnable
2 HELLISH, lower, underworld, nether, Stygian, Hadean, Plutonian, chthonian, Tartarean (*literary*)
<< OPPOSITE heavenly

infertile *adjective* **1** STERILE, barren, infecund
2 BARREN, unproductive, nonproductive, unfruitful, infecund
<< OPPOSITE fertile

infertility *noun* STERILITY, barrenness, unproductiveness, unfruitfulness, infecundity

infest *verb* OVERRUN, flood, invade, penetrate, ravage, swarm, throng, beset, permeate

infested *adjective* OVERRUN, plagued, crawling, swarming, ridden, alive, ravaged, lousy (*slang*), beset, pervaded, teeming

infidel *noun* UNBELIEVER, sceptic, atheist, heretic, agnostic, heathen, nonconformist, freethinker, nonbeliever

infidelity *noun* UNFAITHFULNESS, cheating (*informal*), adultery, betrayal, duplicity, disloyalty, bad faith, perfidy, falseness, faithlessness, false-heartedness

infiltrate *verb* PENETRATE, pervade, permeate, creep in, percolate, filter through to, make inroads into, sneak into (*informal*), insinuate yourself, work *or* worm your way into

infinite *adjective* **1** VAST, enormous, immense, wide, countless, innumerable, untold, stupendous, incalculable, immeasurable, inestimable, numberless, uncounted, measureless, uncalculable
2 ENORMOUS, total, supreme, absolute, all-embracing, unbounded
3 LIMITLESS, endless, unlimited, eternal, perpetual, never-ending, interminable, boundless, everlasting, bottomless, unending, inexhaustible, immeasurable, without end, unbounded, numberless, measureless, illimitable, without number

<< OPPOSITE finite
infinity *noun* ETERNITY, vastness, immensity, perpetuity, endlessness, infinitude, boundlessness
infirm *adjective* 1 FRAIL, weak, feeble, failing, ailing, debilitated, decrepit, enfeebled, doddery, doddering
<< OPPOSITE robust
2 IRRESOLUTE, weak, faltering, unstable, shaky, insecure, wavering, wobbly, indecisive, unsound, vacillating
inflame *verb* 1 ENRAGE, stimulate, provoke, fire, heat, excite, anger, arouse, rouse, infuriate, ignite, incense, madden, agitate, kindle, rile, foment, intoxicate, make your blood boil, impassion
<< OPPOSITE calm
2 AGGRAVATE, increase, intensify, worsen, exacerbate, fan
inflamed *adjective* SWOLLEN, sore, red, hot, angry, infected, fevered, festering, chafing, septic
inflammable *adjective* FLAMMABLE, explosive, volatile, incendiary, combustible ▷ see **flammable**
inflammation *noun* SWELLING, soreness, burning, heat, sore, rash, tenderness, redness, painfulness
inflammatory *adjective* PROVOCATIVE, incendiary, explosive, fiery, inflaming, insurgent, anarchic, rabid, riotous, intemperate, seditious, rabble-rousing, demagogic, like a red rag to a bull, instigative
inflate *verb* 1 BLOW UP, pump up, swell, balloon, dilate, distend, aerate, bloat, puff up *or* out
<< OPPOSITE deflate
2 INCREASE, boost, expand, enlarge, escalate, amplify
<< OPPOSITE diminish
3 EXAGGERATE, embroider, embellish, emphasize, enlarge, magnify, overdo, amplify, exalt, overstate, overestimate, overemphasize, blow out of all proportion, aggrandize, hyperbolize
inflated *adjective* EXAGGERATED, excessive, swollen, amplified, hyped, exalted, overblown
inflation *noun* INCREASE, expansion, extension, swelling, escalation, enlargement, intensification
inflection *noun* 1 INTONATION, stress, emphasis, beat, measure, rhythm, cadence, modulation, accentuation
2 (*Grammar*) CONJUGATION, declension
inflexibility *noun* OBSTINACY, persistence, intransigence, obduracy, fixity, steeliness
inflexible *adjective* 1 FIXED, set, established, rooted, rigid, immovable, unadaptable
2 OBSTINATE, strict, relentless, firm, fixed, iron, adamant, rigorous, stubborn, stringent, uncompromising, resolute, steely, intractable, inexorable, implacable, steadfast, hard and fast, unyielding, immutable, immovable, unbending, obdurate, stiff-necked, dyed-in-the-wool, unchangeable, brassbound, set in your ways
<< OPPOSITE flexible
3 STIFF, hard, rigid, hardened, taut, inelastic, nonflexible
<< OPPOSITE pliable
inflict *verb* IMPOSE, exact, administer, visit, apply, deliver, levy, wreak, mete *or* deal out
influence *noun* 1 CONTROL, power, authority, direction, command, domination, supremacy, mastery, ascendancy, mana (NZ)
2 POWER, force, authority, pull (*informal*), weight, strength, connections, importance, prestige, clout (*informal*), leverage, good offices
3 SPELL, hold, power, rule, weight, magic, sway, allure, magnetism, enchantment
▷ *verb* 1 AFFECT, have an effect on, have an impact on, control, concern, direct, guide, impact on, modify, bear upon, impinge upon, act *or* work upon
2 PERSUADE, move, prompt, urge, counsel, induce, incline, dispose, arouse, sway, rouse, entice, coax, incite, instigate, predispose, impel, prevail upon
3 CARRY WEIGHT WITH, cut any ice with (*informal*), pull strings with (*informal*), bring pressure to bear upon, make yourself felt with
influential *adjective* 1 IMPORTANT, powerful, moving, telling, leading, strong, guiding, inspiring, prestigious, meaningful, potent, persuasive, authoritative, momentous, weighty
<< OPPOSITE unimportant
2 INSTRUMENTAL, important, significant, controlling, guiding, effective, crucial, persuasive, forcible, efficacious
influx *noun* ARRIVAL, flow, rush, invasion, convergence, inflow, incursion, inundation, inrush
infold ▷ see **enfold**
inform *verb* 1 TELL, advise, let someone know, notify, brief, instruct, enlighten, acquaint, leak to, communicate to, fill someone in, keep someone posted, apprise, clue someone in (*informal*), put someone in the picture (*informal*), tip someone off, send word to, give someone to understand, make someone conversant (with)
2 INFUSE, characterize, permeate, animate, saturate, typify, imbue, suffuse
▷▷ **inform on someone** BETRAY, report, denounce, shop (*slang, chiefly Brit*), peach (*slang*), give someone away, incriminate, tell on (*informal*), blow the whistle on (*informal*), grass on (*Brit slang*), double-cross (*informal*), rat

on (*informal*), spill the beans on (*informal*), stab someone in the back, nark (*Brit, Austral & NZ slang*), blab about, squeal on (*slang*), snitch on (*slang*), put the finger on (*informal*), sell someone down the river (*informal*), blow the gaff on (*Brit slang*), tell all on, inculpate, dob someone in (*Austral & NZ slang*)

informal *adjective* 1 NATURAL, relaxed, casual, familiar, unofficial, laid-back, easy-going, colloquial, unconstrained, unceremonious
2 RELAXED, easy, comfortable, simple, natural, casual, cosy, laid-back (*informal*), mellow, leisurely, easy-going
<< OPPOSITE formal
3 CASUAL, comfortable, leisure, everyday, simple
4 UNOFFICIAL, irregular, unconstrained, unceremonious
<< OPPOSITE official

informality *noun* FAMILIARITY, naturalness, casualness, ease, relaxation, simplicity, lack of ceremony

information *noun* FACTS, details, material, news, latest (*informal*), report, word, message, notice, advice, knowledge, data, intelligence, instruction, counsel, the score (*informal*), gen (*Brit informal*), dope (*informal*), info (*informal*), inside story, blurb, lowdown (*informal*), tidings, drum (*Austral informal*)

informative *adjective* INSTRUCTIVE, revealing, educational, forthcoming, illuminating, enlightening, chatty, communicative, edifying, gossipy, newsy

informed *adjective* KNOWLEDGEABLE, up to date, enlightened, learned, primed, posted, expert, briefed, familiar, versed, acquainted, in the picture, up, abreast, in the know (*informal*), erudite, well-read, conversant, au fait (*French*), in the loop, genned up (*Brit informal*), au courant (*French*), keeping your finger on the pulse

informer *noun* BETRAYER, grass (*Brit slang*), sneak, squealer (*slang*), Judas, accuser, stool pigeon, nark (*Brit, Austral & NZ slang*), fizgig (*Austral slang*)

infrequent *adjective* OCCASIONAL, rare, uncommon, unusual, sporadic, few and far between, once in a blue moon
<< OPPOSITE frequent

infringe *verb* BREAK, violate, contravene, disobey, transgress
▷▷ **infringe on** *or* **upon** INTRUDE ON, compromise, undermine, limit, weaken, diminish, disrupt, curb, encroach on, trespass on

infringement *noun* CONTRAVENTION, breach, violation, trespass, transgression, infraction, noncompliance, nonobservance

infuriate *verb* ENRAGE, anger, provoke, irritate, incense, gall, madden, exasperate, rile, nark (*Brit, Austral & NZ slang*), be like a red rag to a bull, make your blood boil, get your goat (*slang*), make your hackles rise, raise your hackles, get your back up, make you see red (*informal*), put your back up
<< OPPOSITE soothe

infuriating *adjective* ANNOYING, irritating, aggravating (*informal*), provoking, galling, maddening, exasperating, irksome, vexatious, pestilential

infuse *verb* BREW, soak, steep, saturate, immerse, macerate

ingenious *adjective* CREATIVE, original, brilliant, clever, masterly, bright, subtle, fertile, shrewd, inventive, skilful, crafty, resourceful, adroit, dexterous
<< OPPOSITE unimaginative

ingenuity *noun* ORIGINALITY, genius, inventiveness, skill, gift, faculty, flair, knack, sharpness, cleverness, resourcefulness, shrewdness, adroitness, ingeniousness
<< OPPOSITE dullness

ingrained *or* **engrained** *adjective* FIXED, rooted, deep-seated, fundamental, constitutional, inherent, hereditary, in the blood, intrinsic, deep-rooted, indelible, inveterate, inborn, inbred, inbuilt, ineradicable, brassbound

ingratiate *verb* ▷▷ **ingratiate yourself with someone** GET ON THE RIGHT SIDE OF, court, win over, flatter, pander to, crawl to, play up to, get in with, suck up to (*informal*), curry favour with, grovel to, keep someone sweet, lick someone's boots, fawn to, toady to, seek someone's favour, rub someone up the right way (*informal*), be a yes man to, insinuate yourself with

ingratiating *adjective* SYCOPHANTIC, servile, obsequious, crawling, humble, flattering, fawning, unctuous, toadying, bootlicking (*informal*), timeserving

ingredient *noun* COMPONENT, part, element, feature, piece, unit, item, aspect, attribute, constituent

inhabit *verb* LIVE IN, people, occupy, populate, reside in, tenant, lodge in, dwell in, colonize, take up residence in, abide in, make your home in

inhabitant *noun* OCCUPANT, resident, citizen, local, native, tenant, inmate, dweller, occupier, denizen, indigene, indweller

inhabited *adjective* POPULATED, peopled, occupied, held, developed, settled, tenanted, colonized

inhalation *noun* BREATHING, breath, inspiration, inhaling

inhale *verb* BREATHE IN, gasp, draw in, suck in, respire
<< OPPOSITE exhale

inherent *adjective* INTRINSIC, natural, basic, central, essential, native, fundamental,

underlying, hereditary, instinctive, innate, ingrained, elemental, congenital, inborn, inbred, inbuilt, immanent, connate
<< OPPOSITE extraneous
inherit *verb* BE LEFT, come into, be willed, accede to, succeed to, be bequeathed, fall heir to
inheritance *noun* LEGACY, estate, heritage, provision, endowment, bequest, birthright, patrimony
inheritor *noun* HEIR, successor, recipient, beneficiary, legatee
inhibit *verb* 1 HINDER, stop, prevent, check, bar, arrest, frustrate, curb, restrain, constrain, obstruct, impede, bridle, stem the flow of, throw a spanner in the works of, hold back *or* in
<< OPPOSITE further
2 PREVENT, stop, bar, frustrate, forbid, prohibit, debar
<< OPPOSITE allow
inhibited *adjective* SHY, reserved, guarded, withdrawn, frustrated, subdued, repressed, constrained, self-conscious, reticent, uptight (*informal*)
<< OPPOSITE uninhibited
inhibition *noun* 1 SHYNESS, reserve, restraint, hang-up (*informal*), modesty, nervousness, reticence, self-consciousness, timidity, diffidence, bashfulness, mental blockage, timidness
2 OBSTACLE, check, bar, block, barrier, restriction, hazard, restraint, hitch, drawback, snag, deterrent, obstruction, stumbling block, impediment, hindrance, encumbrance, interdict
inhospitable *adjective* 1 BLEAK, empty, bare, hostile, lonely, forbidding, barren, sterile, desolate, unfavourable, uninhabitable, godforsaken
2 UNFRIENDLY, unwelcoming, uncongenial, cool, unkind, xenophobic, ungenerous, unsociable, unreceptive
<< OPPOSITE hospitable
inhuman *adjective* CRUEL, savage, brutal, vicious, ruthless, barbaric, heartless, merciless, diabolical, cold-blooded, remorseless, barbarous, fiendish, pitiless, unfeeling, bestial
<< OPPOSITE humane
inhumane *adjective* CRUEL, savage, brutal, severe, harsh, grim, unkind, heartless, atrocious, unsympathetic, hellish, depraved, barbarous, pitiless, unfeeling, uncompassionate
inhumanity *noun* CRUELTY, atrocity, brutality, ruthlessness, barbarism, viciousness, heartlessness, unkindness, brutishness, cold-bloodedness, pitilessness, cold-heartedness, hardheartedness
inimical *adjective* HOSTILE, opposed, contrary, destructive, harmful, adverse, hurtful, unfriendly, unfavourable, antagonistic, injurious, unwelcoming, ill-disposed
<< OPPOSITE helpful
inimitable *adjective* UNIQUE, unparalleled, unrivalled, incomparable, supreme, consummate, unmatched, peerless, unequalled, matchless, unsurpassable, nonpareil, unexampled
iniquity *noun* WICKEDNESS, wrong, crime, evil, sin, offence, injustice, wrongdoing, misdeed, infamy, abomination, sinfulness, baseness, unrighteousness, heinousness, evildoing
<< OPPOSITE goodness
initial *adjective* OPENING, first, early, earliest, beginning, primary, maiden, inaugural, commencing, introductory, embryonic, incipient, inchoate, inceptive
<< OPPOSITE final
initially *adverb* AT FIRST, first, firstly, originally, primarily, at the start, in the first place, to begin with, at the outset, in the beginning, in the early stages, at *or* in the beginning
initiate *verb* 1 BEGIN, start, open, launch, establish, institute, pioneer, kick off (*informal*), bring about, embark on, originate, set about, get under way, instigate, kick-start, inaugurate, set in motion, trigger off, lay the foundations of, commence on, set going, break the ice on, set the ball rolling on
2 INTRODUCE, admit, enlist, enrol, launch, establish, invest, recruit, induct, instate
▷ *noun* NOVICE, member, pupil, convert, amateur, newcomer, beginner, trainee, apprentice, entrant, learner, neophyte, tyro, probationer, novitiate, proselyte
▷▷ **initiate someone into something** INSTRUCT IN, train in, coach in, acquaint with, drill in, make aware of, teach about, tutor in, indoctrinate, prime in, familiarize with
initiation *noun* 1 INTRODUCTION, installation, inauguration, inception, commencement
2 ENTRANCE, debut, introduction, admission, inauguration, induction, inception, enrolment, investiture, baptism of fire, instatement
initiative *noun* 1 ADVANTAGE, start, lead, upper hand
2 ENTERPRISE, drive, push (*informal*), energy, spirit, resource, leadership, ambition, daring, enthusiasm, pep, vigour, zeal, originality, eagerness, dynamism, boldness, inventiveness, get-up-and-go (*informal*), resourcefulness, gumption (*informal*), adventurousness
inject *verb* 1 VACCINATE, shoot (*informal*), administer, jab (*informal*), shoot up (*informal*),

mainline (*informal*), inoculate
2 INTRODUCE, bring in, insert, instil, infuse, breathe, interject

injection *noun* 1 VACCINATION, shot (*informal*), jab (*informal*), dose, vaccine, booster, immunization, inoculation
2 INTRODUCTION, investment, insertion, advancement, dose, infusion, interjection

injunction *noun* ORDER, ruling, command, instruction, dictate, mandate, precept, exhortation, admonition

injure *verb* 1 HURT, wound, harm, break, damage, smash, crush, mar, disable, shatter, bruise, impair, mutilate, maim, mangle, mangulate (*Austral slang*), incapacitate
2 DAMAGE, harm, ruin, wreck, weaken, spoil, impair, crool *or* cruel (*Austral slang*)
3 UNDERMINE, damage, mar, blight, tarnish, blacken, besmirch, vitiate

injured *adjective* 1 HURT, damaged, wounded, broken, cut, crushed, disabled, challenged, weakened, bruised, scarred, crook (*Austral & NZ slang*), fractured, lamed, mutilated, maimed, mangled
2 WRONGED, abused, harmed, insulted, offended, tainted, tarnished, blackened, maligned, vilified, mistreated, dishonoured, defamed, ill-treated, maltreated, ill-used
3 UPSET, hurt, wounded, troubled, bothered, undermined, distressed, unhappy, stung, put out, grieved, hassled (*informal*), disgruntled, displeased, reproachful, cut to the quick

injurious *adjective* HARMFUL, bad, damaging, corrupting, destructive, adverse, unhealthy, detrimental, hurtful, pernicious, noxious, ruinous, deleterious, iniquitous, disadvantageous, baneful (*archaic*), maleficent, unconducive

injury *noun* 1 WOUND, cut, damage, slash, trauma (*Pathology*), sore, gash, lesion, abrasion, laceration
2 HARM, suffering, damage, ill, hurt, disability, misfortune, affliction, impairment, disfigurement
3 WRONG, abuse, offence, insult, injustice, grievance, affront, detriment, disservice

injustice *noun* 1 UNFAIRNESS, discrimination, prejudice, bias, inequality, oppression, intolerance, bigotry, favouritism, inequity, chauvinism, iniquity, partisanship, partiality, narrow-mindedness, one-sidedness, unlawfulness, unjustness
  << OPPOSITE justice
2 WRONG, injury, crime, abuse, error, offence, sin, grievance, infringement, trespass, misdeed, transgression, infraction, bad *or* evil deed

inkling *noun* SUSPICION, idea, hint, suggestion, notion, indication, whisper, clue, conception, glimmering, intimation, faintest *or* foggiest idea

inland *adjective* INTERIOR, internal, upcountry

inlet *noun* BAY, creek, cove, passage, entrance, fjord, bight, ingress, sea loch (*Scot*), arm of the sea, firth *or* frith (*Scot*)

innards *plural noun* 1 INTESTINES, insides (*informal*), guts, entrails, viscera, vitals
2 WORKS, mechanism, guts (*informal*)

innate *adjective* INBORN, natural, inherent, essential, native, constitutional, inherited, indigenous, instinctive, intuitive, intrinsic, ingrained, congenital, inbred, immanent, in your blood, connate
  << OPPOSITE acquired

inner *adjective* 1 INSIDE, internal, interior, inward
  << OPPOSITE outer
2 CENTRAL, middle, internal, interior
3 INTIMATE, close, personal, near, private, friendly, confidential, cherished, bosom
4 HIDDEN, deep, secret, underlying, obscure, repressed, esoteric, unrevealed
  << OPPOSITE obvious

innkeeper *noun* PUBLICAN, hotelier, mine host, host *or* hostess, landlord *or* landlady

innocence *noun* 1 NAIVETÉ, simplicity, inexperience, freshness, credulity, gullibility, ingenuousness, artlessness, unworldliness, guilelessness, credulousness, simpleness, trustfulness, unsophistication, naiveness
  << OPPOSITE worldliness
2 BLAMELESSNESS, righteousness, clean hands, uprightness, sinlessness, irreproachability, guiltlessness
  << OPPOSITE guilt
3 CHASTITY, virtue, purity, modesty, virginity, celibacy, continence, maidenhood, stainlessness
4 IGNORANCE, oblivion, lack of knowledge, inexperience, unfamiliarity, greenness, unawareness, nescience (*literary*)

innocent *adjective* 1 NOT GUILTY, in the clear, blameless, clear, clean, honest, faultless, squeaky-clean, uninvolved, irreproachable, guiltless, unoffending
  << OPPOSITE guilty
2 NAIVE, open, trusting, simple, natural, frank, confiding, candid, unaffected, childlike, gullible, unpretentious, unsophisticated, unworldly, credulous, artless, ingenuous, guileless, wet behind the ears (*informal*), unsuspicious
  << OPPOSITE worldly
3 HARMLESS, innocuous, inoffensive, well-meant, unobjectionable, unmalicious, well-intentioned
  << OPPOSITE malicious
4 PURE, stainless, immaculate, moral, virgin,

decent, upright, impeccable, righteous, pristine, wholesome, spotless, demure, chaste, unblemished, virginal, unsullied, sinless, incorrupt
<< OPPOSITE impure
▷ *noun* CHILD, novice, greenhorn (*informal*), babe in arms (*informal*), ingénue *or (masc.)* ingénu
▷▷ **innocent of** FREE FROM, clear of, unaware of, ignorant of, untouched by, unfamiliar with, empty of, lacking, unacquainted with, nescient of

innocuous *adjective* HARMLESS, safe, innocent, inoffensive, innoxious

innovation *noun* 1 CHANGE, revolution, departure, introduction, variation, transformation, upheaval, alteration
2 NEWNESS, novelty, originality, freshness, modernism, modernization, uniqueness

innovative *adjective* NOVEL, new, original, different, fresh, unusual, unfamiliar, uncommon, inventive, singular, ground-breaking, left-field (*informal*), transformational, variational

innovator *noun* MODERNIZER, introducer, inventor, changer, transformer

innuendo *noun* INSINUATION, suggestion, hint, implication, whisper, overtone, intimation, imputation, aspersion

innumerable *adjective* COUNTLESS, many, numerous, infinite, myriad, untold, incalculable, numberless, unnumbered, multitudinous, beyond number
<< OPPOSITE limited

inordinate *adjective* EXCESSIVE, unreasonable, disproportionate, extravagant, undue, preposterous, unwarranted, exorbitant, unrestrained, intemperate, unconscionable, immoderate
<< OPPOSITE moderate

inorganic *adjective* ARTIFICIAL, chemical, man-made, mineral

inquest *noun* INQUIRY, investigation, probe, inquisition

inquire *or* **enquire** *verb* ASK, question, query, quiz, seek information of, request information of
▷▷ **inquire into** INVESTIGATE, study, examine, consider, research, search, explore, look into, inspect, probe into, scrutinize, make inquiries into

inquiry *or* **enquiry** *noun* 1 QUESTION, query, investigation
2 INVESTIGATION, hearing, study, review, search, survey, analysis, examination, probe, inspection, exploration, scrutiny, inquest
3 RESEARCH, investigation, analysis, examination, inspection, exploration, scrutiny, interrogation

inquisition *noun* INVESTIGATION, questioning, examination, inquiry, grilling (*informal*), quizzing, inquest, cross-examination, third degree (*informal*)

inquisitive *adjective* CURIOUS, questioning, inquiring, peering, probing, intrusive, prying, snooping (*informal*), scrutinizing, snoopy (*informal*), nosy (*informal*), nosy-parkering (*informal*)
<< OPPOSITE uninterested

insane *adjective* 1 MAD, crazy, nuts (*slang*), cracked (*slang*), mental (*slang*), barking (*slang*), crackers (*Brit slang*), mentally ill, crazed, demented, cuckoo (*informal*), deranged, loopy (*informal*), round the bend (*informal*), barking mad (*slang*), out of your mind, gaga (*informal*), screwy (*informal*), doolally (*slang*), off your trolley (*slang*), round the twist (*informal*), of unsound mind, not right in the head, non compos mentis (*Latin*), off your rocker (*slang*), not the full shilling (*informal*), mentally disordered, off the air (*Austral slang*), porangi (NZ)
<< OPPOSITE sane
2 STUPID, foolish, daft (*informal*), bizarre, irresponsible, irrational, lunatic, senseless, preposterous, impractical, idiotic, inane, fatuous, dumb-ass (*slang*)
<< OPPOSITE reasonable ▷ see **mad**

insanity *noun* 1 MADNESS, mental illness, dementia, aberration, mental disorder, delirium, craziness, mental derangement, psychiatric disorder, psychiatric illness
<< OPPOSITE sanity
2 STUPIDITY, folly, lunacy, irresponsibility, senselessness, preposterousness
<< OPPOSITE sense

> The word *insane* has a specific legal use, as in *insane and unfit to plead*. The word *insanity*, however, is not acceptable in general mental health contexts, and many of its synonyms, for example *mental derangement*, are also considered inappropriate or offensive. Acceptable terms are *psychiatric disorder* or *psychiatric illness*

insatiable *adjective* UNQUENCHABLE, greedy, voracious, ravenous, rapacious, intemperate, gluttonous, unappeasable, insatiate, quenchless, edacious
<< OPPOSITE satiable

inscribe *verb* 1 CARVE, cut, etch, engrave, impress, imprint
2 DEDICATE, sign, address

inscription *noun* ENGRAVING, words, lettering, label, legend, saying

inscrutable *adjective* 1 ENIGMATIC, blank, impenetrable, deadpan, unreadable, poker-

faced (*informal*), sphinxlike
<< OPPOSITE transparent
2 MYSTERIOUS, incomprehensible, inexplicable, hidden, unintelligible, unfathomable, unexplainable, undiscoverable
<< OPPOSITE comprehensible

insect *noun* BUG, creepy-crawly (*Brit informal*), gogga (*S African informal*)
>> RELATED WORD *adjective* entomic
>> RELATED WORD *collective noun* swarm

insecure *adjective* 1 UNCONFIDENT, worried, anxious, afraid, shy, uncertain, unsure, timid, self-conscious, hesitant, meek, self-effacing, diffident, unassertive
<< OPPOSITE confident
2 UNSAFE, dangerous, exposed, vulnerable, hazardous, wide-open, perilous, unprotected, defenceless, unguarded, open to attack, unshielded, ill-protected
<< OPPOSITE safe
3 UNRELIABLE, unstable, unsafe, precarious, unsteady, unsound
<< OPPOSITE secure UNRELIABLE

insecurity *noun* 1 ANXIETY, fear, worry, uncertainty, unsureness
<< OPPOSITE confidence
2 VULNERABILITY, risk, danger, weakness, uncertainty, hazard, peril, defencelessness
<< OPPOSITE safety
3 INSTABILITY, uncertainty, unreliability, precariousness, weakness, shakiness, unsteadiness, dubiety, frailness
<< OPPOSITE stability

insensitive *adjective* UNFEELING, indifferent, unconcerned, uncaring, tough, hardened, callous, crass, unresponsive, thick-skinned, obtuse, tactless, imperceptive, unsusceptible
<< OPPOSITE sensitive
▷▷ **insensitive to** UNAFFECTED BY, immune to, impervious to, dead to, unmoved by, proof against

inseparable *adjective* 1 DEVOTED, close, intimate, bosom
2 INDIVISIBLE, inalienable, conjoined, indissoluble, inseverable

insert *verb* PUT, place, set, position, work in, slip, slide, slot, thrust, stick in, wedge, tuck in

insertion *noun* 1 INCLUSION, introduction, interpolation
2 INSERT, addition, inclusion, supplement, implant, inset

inside *noun* INTERIOR, contents, core, nucleus, inner part, inner side
▷ *plural noun* (*informal*) STOMACH, gut, guts, belly, bowels, internal organs, innards (*informal*), entrails, viscera, vitals
▷ *adjective* 1 INNER, internal, interior, inward, innermost
<< OPPOSITE outside
2 CONFIDENTIAL, private, secret, internal, exclusive, restricted, privileged, classified
▷ *adverb* INDOORS, in, within, under cover

insidious *adjective* STEALTHY, subtle, cunning, designing, smooth, tricky, crooked, sneaking, slick, sly, treacherous, deceptive, wily, crafty, artful, disingenuous, Machiavellian, deceitful, surreptitious, duplicitous, guileful
<< OPPOSITE straightforward

insight *noun* 1 INTELLIGENCE, understanding, perception, sense, knowledge, vision, judgment, awareness, grasp, appreciation, intuition, penetration, comprehension, acumen, discernment, perspicacity
2 *with* **into** UNDERSTANDING, perception, awareness, experience, description, introduction, observation, judgment, revelation, comprehension, intuitiveness

insightful *adjective* PERCEPTIVE, shrewd, discerning, understanding, wise, penetrating, knowledgeable, astute, observant, perspicacious, sagacious

insignia *noun* BADGE, symbol, decoration, crest, earmark, emblem, ensign, distinguishing mark

insignificance *noun* UNIMPORTANCE, irrelevance, triviality, pettiness, worthlessness, meaninglessness, inconsequence, immateriality, paltriness, negligibility
<< OPPOSITE importance

insignificant *adjective* UNIMPORTANT, minor, irrelevant, petty, trivial, meaningless, trifling, meagre, negligible, flimsy, paltry, immaterial, inconsequential, nondescript, measly, scanty, inconsiderable, of no consequence, nonessential, small potatoes, nickel-and-dime (*US slang*), of no account, nugatory, unsubstantial, not worth mentioning, of no moment
<< OPPOSITE important

insincere *adjective* DECEITFUL, lying, false, pretended, hollow, untrue, dishonest, deceptive, devious, hypocritical, unfaithful, evasive, two-faced, disingenuous, faithless, double-dealing, duplicitous, dissembling, mendacious, perfidious, untruthful, dissimulating, Janus-faced
<< OPPOSITE sincere

insinuate *verb* IMPLY, suggest, hint, indicate, intimate, allude

insipid *adjective* 1 TASTELESS, bland, flavourless, watered down, watery, wishy-washy (*informal*), unappetizing, savourless
<< OPPOSITE tasty
2 BLAND, boring, dull, flat, dry, weak, stupid, limp, tame, pointless, tedious, stale, drab, banal, tiresome, lifeless, prosaic, trite, unimaginative, colourless, uninteresting,

anaemic, wishy-washy (*informal*), ho-hum (*informal*), vapid, wearisome, characterless, spiritless, jejune, prosy
<< OPPOSITE exciting

insist *verb* 1 PERSIST, press (someone), be firm, stand firm, stand your ground, lay down the law, put your foot down (*informal*), not take no for an answer, brook no refusal, take *or* make a stand
2 DEMAND, order, urge, require, command, dictate, entreat
3 ASSERT, state, maintain, hold, claim, declare, repeat, vow, swear, contend, affirm, reiterate, profess, avow, aver, asseverate

insistence *noun* 1 DEMAND, urging, command, pressing, dictate, entreaty, importunity, insistency
2 ASSERTION, claim, statement, declaration, contention, persistence, affirmation, pronouncement, reiteration, avowal, attestation

insistent *adjective* 1 EMPHATIC, persistent, demanding, pressing, dogged, urgent, forceful, persevering, unrelenting, peremptory, importunate, exigent
2 PERSISTENT, repeated, constant, repetitive, incessant, unremitting

insolence *noun* RUDENESS, cheek (*informal*), disrespect, front, abuse, sauce (*informal*), gall (*informal*), audacity, boldness, chutzpah (*US & Canad informal*), insubordination, impertinence, impudence, effrontery, backchat (*informal*), incivility, sassiness (*US informal*), pertness, contemptuousness
<< OPPOSITE politeness

insolent *adjective* RUDE, cheeky, impertinent, fresh (*informal*), bold, insulting, abusive, saucy, contemptuous, pert, impudent, uncivil, insubordinate, brazen-faced
<< OPPOSITE polite

insoluble *adjective* INEXPLICABLE, mysterious, baffling, obscure, mystifying, impenetrable, unaccountable, unfathomable, indecipherable, unsolvable
<< OPPOSITE explicable

insolvency *noun* BANKRUPTCY, failure, ruin, liquidation

insolvent *adjective* BANKRUPT, ruined, on the rocks (*informal*), broke (*informal*), failed, gone bust (*informal*), in receivership, gone to the wall, in the hands of the receivers, in queer street (*informal*)

insomnia *noun* SLEEPLESSNESS, restlessness, wakefulness

insouciance *noun* NONCHALANCE, light-heartedness, jauntiness, airiness, breeziness, carefreeness

inspect *verb* 1 EXAMINE, check, look at, view, eye, survey, observe, scan, check out (*informal*), look over, eyeball (*slang*), scrutinize, give (something *or* someone) the once-over (*informal*), take a dekko at (*Brit slang*), go over *or* through
2 CHECK, examine, investigate, study, look at, research, search, survey, assess, probe, audit, vet, oversee, supervise, check out (*informal*), look over, work over, superintend, give (something *or* someone) the once-over (*informal*), go over *or* through

inspection *noun* 1 EXAMINATION, investigation, scrutiny, scan, look-over, once-over (*informal*)
2 CHECK, search, investigation, review, survey, examination, scan, scrutiny, supervision, surveillance, look-over, once-over (*informal*), checkup, recce (*slang*), superintendence

inspector *noun* EXAMINER, investigator, supervisor, monitor, superintendent, auditor, censor, surveyor, scrutinizer, checker, overseer, scrutineer

inspiration *noun* 1 IMAGINATION, creativity, ingenuity, talent, insight, genius, productivity, fertility, stimulation, originality, inventiveness, cleverness, fecundity, imaginativeness
2 MOTIVATION, example, influence, model, boost, spur, incentive, revelation, encouragement, stimulus, catalyst, stimulation, inducement, incitement, instigation, afflatus
<< OPPOSITE deterrent
3 INFLUENCE, spur, stimulus, muse

inspire *verb* 1 MOTIVATE, move, cause, stimulate, encourage, influence, persuade, spur, be responsible for, animate, rouse, instil, infuse, hearten, enliven, imbue, spark off, energize, galvanize, gee up, inspirit, fire *or* touch the imagination of
<< OPPOSITE discourage
2 GIVE RISE TO, cause, produce, result in, prompt, stir, spawn, engender

inspired *adjective* 1 BRILLIANT, wonderful, impressive, exciting, outstanding, thrilling, memorable, dazzling, enthralling, superlative, of genius
2 STIMULATED, possessed, aroused, uplifted, exhilarated, stirred up, enthused, exalted, elated, galvanized

inspiring *adjective* UPLIFTING, encouraging, exciting, moving, affecting, stirring, stimulating, rousing, exhilarating, heartening
<< OPPOSITE uninspiring

instability *noun* 1 UNCERTAINTY, insecurity, weakness, imbalance, vulnerability, wavering, volatility, unpredictability, restlessness, fluidity, fluctuation, disequilibrium, transience, impermanence, precariousness, mutability, shakiness, unsteadiness,

inconstancy
<< OPPOSITE stability
2 IMBALANCE, weakness, volatility, variability, frailty, unpredictability, oscillation, vacillation, capriciousness, unsteadiness, flightiness, fitfulness, changeableness

install *verb* 1 SET UP, put in, place, position, station, establish, lay, fix, locate, lodge
2 INSTITUTE, establish, introduce, invest, ordain, inaugurate, induct, instate
3 SETTLE, position, plant, establish, lodge, ensconce

installation *noun* 1 SETTING UP, fitting, instalment, placing, positioning, establishment
2 APPOINTMENT, ordination, inauguration, induction, investiture, instatement
3 (*Military*) BASE, centre, post, station, camp, settlement, establishment, headquarters

instalment *noun* 1 PAYMENT, repayment, part payment
2 PART, section, chapter, episode, portion, division

instance *noun* 1 EXAMPLE, case, occurrence, occasion, sample, illustration, precedent, case in point, exemplification
2 INSISTENCE, demand, urging, pressure, stress, application, request, prompting, impulse, behest, incitement, instigation, solicitation, entreaty, importunity
▷ *verb* NAME, mention, identify, point out, advance, quote, finger (*informal, chiefly US*), refer to, point to, cite, specify, invoke, allude to, adduce, namedrop

instant *noun* 1 MOMENT, second, minute, shake (*informal*), flash, tick (*Brit informal*), no time, twinkling, split second, jiffy (*informal*), trice, twinkling of an eye (*informal*), two shakes (*informal*), two shakes of a lamb's tail (*informal*), bat of an eye (*informal*)
2 TIME, point, hour, moment, stage, occasion, phase, juncture
▷ *adjective* 1 IMMEDIATE, prompt, instantaneous, direct, quick, urgent, on-the-spot, split-second
2 READY-MADE, fast, convenience, ready-mixed, ready-cooked, precooked

instantaneous *adjective* IMMEDIATE, prompt, instant, direct, on-the-spot

instantaneously *adverb* IMMEDIATELY, instantly, at once, straight away, promptly, on the spot, forthwith, in the same breath, then and there, pronto (*informal*), in the twinkling of an eye (*informal*), on the instant, in a fraction of a second, posthaste, quick as lightning, in the bat of an eye (*informal*)

instantly *adverb* IMMEDIATELY, at once, straight away, now, directly, on the spot, right away, there and then, without delay, instantaneously, forthwith, this minute, pronto (*informal*), posthaste, instanter (*Law*), tout de suite (*French*)

instead *adverb* RATHER, alternatively, preferably, in preference, in lieu, on second thoughts
▷▷ **instead of** IN PLACE OF, rather than, in preference to, in lieu of, in contrast with, as an alternative *or* equivalent to

instigate *verb* PROVOKE, start, encourage, move, influence, prompt, trigger, spur, stimulate, set off, initiate, bring about, rouse, prod, stir up, get going, incite, kick-start, whip up, impel, kindle, foment, actuate
<< OPPOSITE suppress

instigation *noun* PROMPTING, urging, bidding, incentive, encouragement, behest, incitement

instigator *noun* RINGLEADER, inciter, motivator, leader, spur, goad, troublemaker, incendiary, firebrand, prime mover, fomenter, agitator, stirrer (*informal*), mischief-maker

instil *or* **instill** *verb* INTRODUCE, implant, engender, infuse, imbue, impress, insinuate, sow the seeds, inculcate, engraft, infix

instinct *noun* 1 NATURAL INCLINATION, feeling, urge, talent, tendency, faculty, inclination, intuition, knack, aptitude, predisposition, sixth sense, proclivity, gut reaction (*informal*), second sight
2 TALENT, skill, gift, capacity, bent, genius, faculty, knack, aptitude
3 INTUITION, feeling, impulse, gut feeling (*informal*), sixth sense

instinctive *adjective* NATURAL, inborn, automatic, unconscious, mechanical, native, inherent, spontaneous, reflex, innate, intuitive, subconscious, involuntary, visceral, unthinking, instinctual, unlearned, unpremeditated, intuitional
<< OPPOSITE acquired

instinctively *adverb* INTUITIVELY, naturally, automatically, without thinking, involuntarily, by instinct, in your bones

institute *noun* ESTABLISHMENT, body, centre, school, university, society, association, college, institution, organization, foundation, academy, guild, conservatory, fellowship, seminary, seat of learning
▷ *verb* ESTABLISH, start, begin, found, launch, set up, introduce, settle, fix, invest, organize, install, pioneer, constitute, initiate, originate, enact, commence, inaugurate, set in motion, bring into being, put into operation
<< OPPOSITE end

institution *noun* 1 ESTABLISHMENT, body, centre, school, university, society, association, college, institute, organization, foundation, academy, guild, conservatory, fellowship, seminary, seat of learning

2 CUSTOM, practice, tradition, law, rule, procedure, convention, ritual, fixture, rite
3 CREATION, introduction, establishment, investment, debut, foundation, formation, installation, initiation, inauguration, enactment, inception, commencement, investiture

institutional *adjective* CONVENTIONAL, accepted, established, formal, establishment (*informal*), organized, routine, orthodox, bureaucratic, procedural, societal

instruct *verb* 1 ORDER, tell, direct, charge, bid, command, mandate, enjoin
2 TEACH, school, train, direct, coach, guide, discipline, educate, drill, tutor, enlighten, give lessons in
3 TELL, advise, inform, counsel, notify, brief, acquaint, apprise

instruction *noun* 1 ORDER, ruling, command, rule, demand, direction, regulation, dictate, decree, mandate, directive, injunction, behest
2 TEACHING, schooling, training, classes, grounding, education, coaching, lesson(s), discipline, preparation, drilling, guidance, tutoring, tuition, enlightenment, apprenticeship, tutorials, tutelage
▷ *plural noun* INFORMATION, rules, advice, directions, recommendations, guidance, specifications

instructive *adjective* INFORMATIVE, revealing, useful, educational, helpful, illuminating, enlightening, instructional, cautionary, didactic, edifying

instructor *noun* TEACHER, coach, guide, adviser, trainer, demonstrator, tutor, guru, mentor, educator, pedagogue, preceptor (*rare*), master *or* mistress, schoolmaster *or* schoolmistress

instrument *noun* 1 TOOL, device, implement, mechanism, appliance, apparatus, gadget, utensil, contraption (*informal*), contrivance, waldo
2 AGENT, means, force, cause, medium, agency, factor, channel, vehicle, mechanism, organ
3 (*informal*) PUPPET, tool, pawn, toy, creature, dupe, stooge (*slang*), plaything, cat's-paw

instrumental *adjective* ACTIVE, involved, influential, useful, helpful, conducive, contributory, of help *or* service

insubstantial *adjective* 1 FLIMSY, thin, weak, slight, frail, feeble, tenuous
<< OPPOSITE substantial
2 IMAGINARY, unreal, fanciful, immaterial, ephemeral, illusory, incorporeal, chimerical

insufferable *adjective* UNBEARABLE, impossible, intolerable, dreadful, outrageous, unspeakable, detestable, insupportable, unendurable, past bearing, more than flesh and blood can stand, enough to test the patience of a saint, enough to try the patience of Job
<< OPPOSITE bearable

insufficient *adjective* INADEQUATE, incomplete, scant, meagre, short, sparse, deficient, lacking, unqualified, insubstantial, incommensurate
<< OPPOSITE ample

insular *adjective* NARROW-MINDED, prejudiced, provincial, closed, limited, narrow, petty, parochial, blinkered, circumscribed, inward-looking, illiberal, parish-pump
<< OPPOSITE broad-minded

insulate *verb* ISOLATE, protect, screen, defend, shelter, shield, cut off, cushion, cocoon, close off, sequester, wrap up in cotton wool

insult *verb* OFFEND, abuse, injure, wound, slight, outrage, put down, humiliate, libel, snub, slag (off) (*slang*), malign, affront, denigrate, disparage, revile, slander, displease, defame, hurt (someone's) feelings, call names, give offence to
<< OPPOSITE praise
▷ *noun* 1 JIBE, slight, put-down, abuse, snub, barb, affront, indignity, contumely, abusive remark, aspersion
2 OFFENCE, slight, outrage, snub, slur, affront, rudeness, slap in the face (*informal*), kick in the teeth (*informal*), insolence, aspersion

insulting *adjective* OFFENSIVE, rude, abusive, slighting, degrading, affronting, contemptuous, disparaging, scurrilous, insolent
<< OPPOSITE complimentary

insuperable *adjective* INSURMOUNTABLE, invincible, impassable, unconquerable
<< OPPOSITE surmountable

insurance *noun* 1 ASSURANCE, cover, security, protection, coverage, safeguard, indemnity, indemnification
2 PROTECTION, security, guarantee, provision, shelter, safeguard, warranty

insure *verb* 1 ASSURE, cover, protect, guarantee, warrant, underwrite, indemnify
2 PROTECT, cover, safeguard

insurgent *noun* REBEL, revolutionary, revolter, rioter, resister, mutineer, revolutionist, insurrectionist
▷ *adjective* REBELLIOUS, revolutionary, mutinous, revolting, riotous, seditious, disobedient, insubordinate, insurrectionary

insurmountable *adjective* INSUPERABLE, impossible, overwhelming, hopeless, invincible, impassable, unconquerable

insurrection *noun* REBELLION, rising, revolution, riot, coup, revolt, uprising, mutiny, insurgency, putsch, sedition

intact *adjective* UNDAMAGED, whole, complete,

sound, perfect, entire, virgin, untouched, unscathed, unbroken, flawless, unhurt, faultless, unharmed, uninjured, unimpaired, undefiled, all in one piece, together, scatheless, unviolated

<< OPPOSITE damaged

intangible *adjective* ABSTRACT, vague, invisible, dim, elusive, shadowy, airy, unreal, indefinite, ethereal, evanescent, incorporeal, impalpable, unsubstantial

integral *adjective* 1 ESSENTIAL, basic, fundamental, necessary, component, constituent, indispensable, intrinsic, requisite, elemental

<< OPPOSITE inessential

2 WHOLE, full, complete, entire, intact, undivided

<< OPPOSITE partial

integrate *verb* JOIN, unite, combine, blend, incorporate, merge, accommodate, knit, fuse, mesh, assimilate, amalgamate, coalesce, harmonize, meld, intermix

<< OPPOSITE separate

integrity *noun* 1 HONESTY, principle, honour, virtue, goodness, morality, purity, righteousness, probity, rectitude, truthfulness, trustworthiness, incorruptibility, uprightness, scrupulousness, reputability

<< OPPOSITE dishonesty

2 UNITY, unification, cohesion, coherence, wholeness, soundness, completeness

<< OPPOSITE fragility

intellect *noun* 1 INTELLIGENCE, mind, reason, understanding, sense, brains (*informal*), judgment

2 (*informal*) THINKER, intellectual, genius, mind, brain (*informal*), intelligence, rocket scientist (*informal, chiefly US*), egghead (*informal*)

intellectual *adjective* SCHOLARLY, learned, academic, lettered, intelligent, rational, cerebral, erudite, scholastic, highbrow, well-read, studious, bookish

<< OPPOSITE stupid

▷ *noun* ACADEMIC, expert, genius, thinker, master, brain (*informal*), mastermind, maestro, highbrow, rocket scientist (*informal, chiefly US*), egghead (*informal*), brainbox, bluestocking (*usually disparaging*), master-hand, fundi (*S African*), acca (*Austral slang*)

<< OPPOSITE idiot

intelligence *noun* 1 INTELLECT, understanding, brains (*informal*), mind, reason, sense, knowledge, capacity, smarts (*slang, chiefly US*), judgment, wit, perception, awareness, insight, penetration, comprehension, brightness, aptitude, acumen, nous (*Brit slang*), alertness, cleverness, quickness, discernment, grey matter (*informal*), brain power

<< OPPOSITE stupidity

2 INFORMATION, news, facts, report, findings, word, notice, advice, knowledge, data, disclosure, gen (*Brit informal*), tip-off, low-down (*informal*), notification

<< OPPOSITE misinformation

intelligent *adjective* CLEVER, bright, smart, knowing, quick, sharp, acute, alert, rational, penetrating, enlightened, apt, discerning, knowledgeable, astute, well-informed, brainy (*informal*), perspicacious, quick-witted, sagacious

<< OPPOSITE stupid

intelligentsia *noun* INTELLECTUALS, highbrows, literati, masterminds, the learned, eggheads (*informal*), illuminati

intelligible *adjective* UNDERSTANDABLE, clear, distinct, lucid, comprehensible

<< OPPOSITE unintelligible

intemperate *adjective* EXCESSIVE, extreme, over the top (*slang*), wild, violent, severe, passionate, extravagant, uncontrollable, self-indulgent, unbridled, prodigal, unrestrained, tempestuous, profligate, inordinate, incontinent, ungovernable, immoderate, O.T.T. (*slang*)

<< OPPOSITE temperate

intend *verb* 1 PLAN, mean, aim, determine, scheme, propose, purpose, contemplate, envisage, foresee, be resolved *or* determined, have in mind *or* view

2 *often with* **for** DESTINE, mean, design, earmark, consign, aim, mark out, set apart

intended *adjective* PLANNED, proposed

▷ *noun* (*informal*) BETROTHED, fiancé *or* fiancée, future wife *or* husband, husband- *or* wife-to-be

intense *adjective* 1 EXTREME, great, severe, fierce, serious (*informal*), deep, powerful, concentrated, supreme, acute, harsh, excessive, profound, exquisite, drastic, forceful, protracted, unqualified, agonizing, mother of all (*informal*)

<< OPPOSITE mild

2 FIERCE, close, tough

3 PASSIONATE, burning, earnest, emotional, keen, flaming, consuming, fierce, eager, enthusiastic, heightened, energetic, animated, ardent, fanatical, fervent, heartfelt, impassioned, vehement, forcible, fervid

<< OPPOSITE indifferent

> *Intense* is sometimes wrongly used where *intensive* is meant: *the land is under intensive* (not *intense*) *cultivation*. *Intensely* is sometimes wrongly used where *intently* is meant: *he listened intently* (not *intensely*)

intensely *adverb* 1 VERY, highly, extremely, greatly, strongly, severely, terribly, ultra, utterly, unusually, exceptionally,

extraordinarily, markedly, awfully (*informal*), acutely, exceedingly, excessively, inordinately, uncommonly, to the nth degree, to *or* in the extreme
2 DEEPLY, seriously (*informal*), profoundly, passionately

Intensely is sometimes wrongly used where *intently* is meant: *he listened intently* (not *intensely*)

intensify *verb* 1 INCREASE, boost, raise, extend, concentrate, add to, strengthen, enhance, compound, reinforce, step up (*informal*), emphasize, widen, heighten, sharpen, magnify, amplify, augment, redouble
<< OPPOSITE decrease
2 ESCALATE, increase, extend, widen, heighten, deepen, quicken
intensity *noun* 1 FORCE, power, strength, severity, extremity, fierceness
2 PASSION, emotion, fervour, force, power, fire, energy, strength, depth, concentration, excess, severity, vigour, potency, extremity, fanaticism, ardour, vehemence, earnestness, keenness, fierceness, fervency, intenseness
intensive *adjective* CONCENTRATED, thorough, exhaustive, full, demanding, detailed, complete, serious, concerted, comprehensive, vigorous, all-out, in-depth, strenuous, painstaking, all-embracing, assiduous, thoroughgoing ▷ see **intense**
intent *adjective* ABSORBED, focused, fixed, earnest, committed, concentrated, occupied, fascinated, steady, alert, wrapped up, preoccupied, enthralled, attentive, watchful, engrossed, steadfast, rapt, enrapt
<< OPPOSITE indifferent
▷ *noun* INTENTION, aim, purpose, meaning, end, plan, goal, design, target, object, resolution, resolve, objective, ambition, aspiration
<< OPPOSITE chance
▷▷ **intent on something** SET ON, committed to, eager to, bent on, fixated on, hellbent on (*informal*), insistent about, determined about, resolute about, inflexible about, resolved about
▷▷ **to all intents and purposes** IN EFFECT, essentially, effectively, really, actually, in fact, virtually, in reality, in truth, in actuality, for practical purposes
intention *noun* AIM, plan, idea, goal, end, design, target, wish, scheme, purpose, object, objective, determination, intent
intentional *adjective* DELIBERATE, meant, planned, studied, designed, purposed, intended, calculated, wilful, premeditated, prearranged, done on purpose, preconcerted
<< OPPOSITE unintentional
intentionally *adverb* DELIBERATELY, on purpose, wilfully, by design, designedly
intently *adverb* ATTENTIVELY, closely, hard, keenly, steadily, fixedly, searchingly, watchfully ▷ see **intensely**
inter *verb* BURY, lay to rest, entomb, sepulchre, consign to the grave, inhume, inurn
intercede *verb* MEDIATE, speak, plead, intervene, arbitrate, advocate, interpose
intercept *verb* CATCH, take, stop, check, block, arrest, seize, cut off, interrupt, head off, deflect, obstruct
interchange *noun* EXCHANGE, give and take, alternation, reciprocation
▷ *verb* EXCHANGE, switch, swap, alternate, trade, barter, reciprocate, bandy
interchangeable *adjective* IDENTICAL, the same, equivalent, synonymous, reciprocal, exchangeable, transposable, commutable
intercourse *noun* 1 SEXUAL INTERCOURSE, sex (*informal*), lovemaking, the other (*informal*), congress, screwing (*taboo slang*), intimacy, shagging (*Brit taboo slang*), sexual relations, sexual act, nookie (*slang*), copulation, coitus, carnal knowledge, intimate relations, rumpy-pumpy (*slang*), legover (*slang*), coition, rumpo (*slang*)
2 CONTACT, relationships, communication, association, relations, trade, traffic, connection, truck, commerce, dealings, correspondence, communion, converse, intercommunication
interest *noun* 1 IMPORTANCE, concern, significance, moment, note, weight, import, consequence, substance, relevance, momentousness
<< OPPOSITE insignificance
2 ATTENTION, regard, curiosity, notice, suspicion, scrutiny, heed, absorption, attentiveness, inquisitiveness, engrossment
<< OPPOSITE disregard
3 *often plural* HOBBY, activity, pursuit, entertainment, relaxation, recreation, amusement, preoccupation, diversion, pastime, leisure activity
4 *often plural* ADVANTAGE, good, benefit, profit, gain, boot (*dialect*)
5 *often plural* BUSINESS, concern, matter, affair
6 STAKE, investment
▷ *verb* 1 AROUSE YOUR CURIOSITY, engage, appeal to, fascinate, move, involve, touch, affect, attract, grip, entertain, absorb, intrigue, amuse, divert, rivet, captivate, catch your eye, hold your attention, engross
<< OPPOSITE bore
2 *with* **in** SELL, persuade to buy
▷▷ **in the interest(s) of** FOR THE SAKE OF, on behalf of, on the part of, to the advantage of
interested *adjective* 1 CURIOUS, into (*informal*), moved, affected, attracted, excited, drawn,

keen, gripped, fascinated, stimulated, intent, responsive, riveted, captivated, attentive
<< OPPOSITE uninterested
2 INVOLVED, concerned, affected, prejudiced, biased, partial, partisan, implicated, predisposed

interesting *adjective* INTRIGUING, fascinating, absorbing, pleasing, appealing, attractive, engaging, unusual, gripping, stirring, entertaining, entrancing, stimulating, curious, compelling, amusing, compulsive, riveting, captivating, enthralling, beguiling, thought-provoking, engrossing, spellbinding
<< OPPOSITE uninteresting

interface *noun* CONNECTION, link, boundary, border, frontier
▷ *verb* CONNECT, couple, link, combine, join together

interfere *verb* MEDDLE, intervene, intrude, butt in, get involved, tamper, pry, encroach, intercede, stick your nose in (*informal*), stick your oar in (*informal*), poke your nose in (*informal*), intermeddle, put your two cents in (*US slang*)
▷▷ **interfere with something** *or* **someone** CONFLICT WITH, affect, get in the way of, check, block, clash, frustrate, handicap, hamper, disrupt, cramp, inhibit, thwart, hinder, obstruct, impede, baulk, trammel, be a drag upon (*informal*)

interference *noun* INTRUSION, intervention, meddling, opposition, conflict, obstruction, prying, impedance, meddlesomeness, intermeddling

interfering *adjective* MEDDLING, intrusive, prying, obtrusive, meddlesome, interruptive

interim *adjective* TEMPORARY, provisional, makeshift, acting, passing, intervening, caretaker, improvised, transient, stopgap, pro tem
▷ *noun* INTERVAL, meanwhile, meantime, respite, interregnum, entr'acte

interior *noun* **1** INSIDE, centre, heart, middle, contents, depths, core, belly, nucleus, bowels, bosom, innards (*informal*)
2 (*Geography*) HEARTLAND, centre, hinterland, upcountry
▷ *adjective* **1** INSIDE, internal, inner
<< OPPOSITE exterior
2 MENTAL, emotional, psychological, private, personal, secret, hidden, spiritual, intimate, inner, inward, instinctive, impulsive
3 DOMESTIC, home, national, civil, internal

interject *verb* INTERRUPT WITH, put in, interpose, introduce, throw in, interpolate

interjection *noun* EXCLAMATION, cry, ejaculation, interpolation, interposition

interloper *noun* TRESPASSER, intruder, gate-crasher (*informal*), uninvited guest, meddler, unwanted visitor, intermeddler

interlude *noun* INTERVAL, break, spell, stop, rest, halt, episode, pause, respite, stoppage, breathing space, hiatus, intermission, entr'acte

intermediary *noun* MEDIATOR, agent, middleman, broker, entrepreneur, go-between

intermediate *adjective* MIDDLE, mid, halfway, in-between (*informal*), midway, intervening, transitional, intermediary, median, interposed

interminable *adjective* ENDLESS, long, never-ending, dragging, unlimited, infinite, perpetual, protracted, limitless, boundless, everlasting, ceaseless, long-winded, long-drawn-out, immeasurable, wearisome, unbounded
<< OPPOSITE limited

intermission *noun* INTERVAL, break, pause, stop, rest, suspension, recess, interruption, respite, lull, stoppage, interlude, cessation, let-up (*informal*), breathing space, entr'acte

intermittent *adjective* PERIODIC, broken, occasional, recurring, irregular, punctuated, sporadic, recurrent, stop-go (*informal*), fitful, spasmodic, discontinuous
<< OPPOSITE continuous

intern *verb* IMPRISON, hold, confine, detain, hold in custody

internal *adjective* **1** DOMESTIC, home, national, local, civic, in-house, intramural
2 INNER, inside, interior
<< OPPOSITE external
3 EMOTIONAL, mental, private, secret, subjective
<< OPPOSITE revealed

international *adjective* GLOBAL, world, worldwide, universal, cosmopolitan, planetary, intercontinental

Internet *noun* ▷▷ **the Internet** THE INFORMATION SUPERHIGHWAY, the net (*informal*), the web (*informal*), the World Wide Web, cyberspace

interplay *noun* INTERACTION, give-and-take, reciprocity, reciprocation, meshing

interpret *verb* **1** TAKE, understand, read, explain, regard, construe
2 TRANSLATE, convert, paraphrase, adapt, transliterate
3 EXPLAIN, define, clarify, spell out, make sense of, decode, decipher, expound, elucidate, throw light on, explicate
4 UNDERSTAND, read, explain, crack, solve, figure out (*informal*), comprehend, decode, deduce, decipher, suss out (*slang*)
5 PORTRAY, present, perform, render, depict, enact, act out

interpretation *noun* **1** EXPLANATION, meaning, reading, understanding, sense, analysis,

construction, exposition, explication, elucidation, signification
2 PERFORMANCE, portrayal, presentation, rendering, reading, execution, rendition, depiction
3 READING, study, review, version, analysis, explanation, examination, diagnosis, evaluation, exposition, exegesis, explication, elucidation
interpreter *noun* TRANSLATOR, linguist, metaphrast, paraphrast
interrogate *verb* QUESTION, ask, examine, investigate, pump, grill (*informal*), quiz, cross-examine, cross-question, put the screws on (*informal*), catechize, give (someone) the third degree (*informal*)
interrogation *noun* QUESTIONING, inquiry, examination, probing, grilling (*informal*), cross-examination, inquisition, third degree (*informal*), cross-questioning
interrupt *verb* 1 INTRUDE, disturb, intervene, interfere (with), break in, heckle, butt in, barge in (*informal*), break (someone's) train of thought
2 SUSPEND, break, stop, end, cut, stay, check, delay, cease, cut off, postpone, shelve, put off, defer, break off, adjourn, cut short, discontinue
interruption *noun* 1 DISRUPTION, break, halt, obstacle, disturbance, hitch, intrusion, obstruction, impediment, hindrance
2 STOPPAGE, stop, pause, suspension, cessation, severance, hiatus, disconnection, discontinuance
intersect *verb* CROSS, meet, cut, divide, cut across, bisect, crisscross
intersection *noun* JUNCTION, crossing, crossroads
intersperse *verb* SCATTER, sprinkle, intermix, pepper, interlard, bestrew
interval *noun* 1 PERIOD, time, spell, term, season, space, stretch, pause, span
2 BREAK, interlude, intermission, rest, gap, pause, respite, lull, entr'acte
3 DELAY, wait, gap, interim, hold-up, meanwhile, meantime, stoppage, hiatus
4 STRETCH, area, space, distance, gap
intervene *verb* 1 STEP IN (*informal*), interfere, mediate, intrude, intercede, arbitrate, interpose, take a hand (*informal*)
2 INTERRUPT, involve yourself, put your oar in, interpose yourself, put your two cents in (*US slang*)
3 HAPPEN, occur, take place, follow, succeed, arise, ensue, befall, materialize, come to pass, supervene
intervention *noun* MEDIATION, involvement, interference, intrusion, arbitration, conciliation, intercession, interposition, agency
interview *noun* 1 MEETING, examination, evaluation, oral (examination), interrogation
2 AUDIENCE, talk, conference, exchange, dialogue, consultation, press conference
▷ *verb* 1 EXAMINE, talk to, sound out
2 QUESTION, interrogate, examine, investigate, ask, pump, grill (*informal*), quiz, cross-examine, cross-question, put the screws on (*informal*), catechize, give (someone) the third degree (*informal*)
interviewer *noun* QUESTIONER, reporter, investigator, examiner, interrogator, interlocutor
intestinal *adjective* ABDOMINAL, visceral, duodenal, gut (*informal*), inner, coeliac, stomachic
intestine *noun usu pl* GUTS, insides (*informal*), bowels, internal organs, innards (*informal*), entrails, vitals
>> RELATED WORD *technical name* viscera
intimacy *noun* FAMILIARITY, closeness, understanding, confidence, confidentiality, fraternization
<< OPPOSITE aloofness
intimate[1] *adjective* 1 CLOSE, dear, loving, near, warm, friendly, familiar, thick (*informal*), devoted, confidential, cherished, bosom, inseparable, nearest and dearest
<< OPPOSITE distant
2 PRIVATE, personal, confidential, special, individual, particular, secret, exclusive, privy
<< OPPOSITE public
3 DETAILED, minute, full, experienced, personal, deep, particular, specific, immediate, comprehensive, exact, elaborate, profound, penetrating, thorough, in-depth, intricate, first-hand, exhaustive
4 COSY, relaxed, friendly, informal, harmonious, snug, comfy (*informal*), warm
▷ *noun* FRIEND, close friend, buddy (*informal*), mate (*informal*), pal, comrade, chum (*informal*), mucker (*Brit slang*), crony, main man (*slang, chiefly US*), china (*Brit slang*), homeboy (*slang, chiefly US*), cobber (*Austral & NZ old-fashioned informal*), bosom friend, familiar, confidant *or* confidante, (constant) companion, E hoa (NZ)
<< OPPOSITE stranger
intimate[2] *verb* 1 SUGGEST, indicate, hint, imply, warn, allude, let it be known, insinuate, give (someone) to understand, drop a hint, tip (someone) the wink (*Brit informal*)
2 ANNOUNCE, state, declare, communicate, impart, make known
intimately *adverb* 1 CLOSELY, very well, personally, warmly, familiarly, tenderly, affectionately, confidentially, confidingly
2 FULLY, very well, thoroughly, in detail, inside out, to the core, through and through

intimation *noun* 1 HINT, warning, suggestion, indication, allusion, inkling, insinuation
2 ANNOUNCEMENT, notice, communication, declaration

intimidate *verb* FRIGHTEN, pressure, threaten, alarm, scare, terrify, cow, bully, plague, menace, hound, awe, daunt, harass, subdue, oppress, persecute, lean on (*informal*), coerce, overawe, scare off (*informal*), terrorize, pressurize, browbeat, twist someone's arm (*informal*), tyrannize, dishearten, dispirit, affright (*archaic*), domineer

intimidation *noun* BULLYING, pressure, threat(s), menaces, coercion, arm-twisting (*informal*), browbeating, terrorization

intonation *noun* 1 TONE, inflection, cadence, modulation, accentuation
2 INCANTATION, spell, charm, formula, chant, invocation, hex (*US & Canad informal*), conjuration

intone *verb* CHANT, sing, recite, croon, intonate

intoxicating *adjective* 1 ALCOHOLIC, strong, intoxicant, spirituous, inebriant
2 EXCITING, thrilling, stimulating, sexy (*informal*), heady, exhilarating

intoxication *noun* 1 DRUNKENNESS, inebriation, tipsiness, inebriety, insobriety
2 EXCITEMENT, euphoria, elation, exhilaration, infatuation, delirium, exaltation

intractable *adjective* DIFFICULT, contrary, awkward, wild, stubborn, perverse, wayward, unruly, uncontrollable, wilful, incurable, fractious, unyielding, obstinate, intransigent, headstrong, unmanageable, undisciplined, cantankerous, unbending, obdurate, uncooperative, stiff-necked, ungovernable, self-willed, refractory, pig-headed, bull-headed

intransigent *adjective* UNCOMPROMISING, intractable, tough, stubborn, hardline, tenacious, unyielding, obstinate, immovable, unbending, obdurate, stiff-necked, inflexible, unbudgeable
<< OPPOSITE compliant

intrenched ▷ see **entrenched**

intrepid *adjective* FEARLESS, brave, daring, bold, heroic, game (*informal*), have-a-go (*informal*), courageous, stalwart, resolute, gallant, audacious, valiant, plucky, doughty, undaunted, unafraid, unflinching, nerveless, dauntless, lion-hearted, valorous, stouthearted, (as) game as Ned Kelly (*Austral slang*)
<< OPPOSITE fearful

intricacy *noun* COMPLEXITY, involvement, complication, elaborateness, obscurity, entanglement, convolutions, involution, intricateness, knottiness

intricate *adjective* COMPLICATED, involved, complex, difficult, fancy, sophisticated, elaborate, obscure, tangled, baroque, perplexing, tortuous, Byzantine, convoluted, rococo, knotty, labyrinthine, daedal (*literary*)
<< OPPOSITE simple

intrigue *noun* 1 PLOT, scheme, conspiracy, manoeuvre, manipulation, collusion, ruse, trickery, cabal, stratagem, double-dealing, chicanery, sharp practice, wile, knavery, machination
2 AFFAIR, romance, intimacy, liaison, amour
▷ *verb* 1 INTEREST, fascinate, arouse the curiosity of, attract, charm, rivet, titillate, pique, tickle your fancy
2 PLOT, scheme, manoeuvre, conspire, connive, machinate

intriguing *adjective* INTERESTING, fascinating, absorbing, exciting, engaging, gripping, stirring, stimulating, curious, compelling, amusing, diverting, provocative, beguiling, thought-provoking, titillating, engrossing, tantalizing

intrinsic *adjective* ESSENTIAL, real, true, central, natural, basic, radical, native, genuine, fundamental, constitutional, built-in, underlying, inherent, elemental, congenital, inborn, inbred
<< OPPOSITE extrinsic

intrinsically *adverb* ESSENTIALLY, basically, fundamentally, constitutionally, as such, in itself, at heart, by definition, per se

introduce *verb* 1 BRING IN, establish, set up, start, begin, found, develop, launch, institute, organize, pioneer, initiate, originate, commence, get going, instigate, phase in, usher in, inaugurate, set in motion, bring into being
2 PRESENT, acquaint, make known, familiarize, do the honours, make the introductions
3 ANNOUNCE, present, open, launch, precede, lead into, preface, lead off
4 SUGGEST, offer, air, table, advance, propose, recommend, float, submit, bring up, put forward, set forth, ventilate, broach, moot
5 ADD, insert, inject, throw in (*informal*), infuse, interpose, interpolate

introduction *noun* 1 LAUNCH, institution, establishment, start, opening, beginning, pioneering, presentation, initiation, inauguration, induction, commencement, instigation
<< OPPOSITE elimination
2 OPENING, prelude, preface, lead-in, preliminaries, overture, preamble, foreword, prologue, intro (*informal*), commencement, opening remarks, proem, opening passage, prolegomena, prolegomenon, exordium
<< OPPOSITE conclusion

3 INSERTION, addition, injection, interpolation
<< OPPOSITE extraction

introductory *adjective* 1 PRELIMINARY, elementary, first, early, initial, inaugural, preparatory, initiatory, prefatory, precursory
<< OPPOSITE concluding
2 STARTING, opening, initial, early

introspection *noun* SELF-EXAMINATION, brooding, self-analysis, navel-gazing (*slang*), introversion, heart-searching

introspective *adjective* INWARD-LOOKING, introverted, brooding, contemplative, meditative, subjective, pensive, inner-directed

introverted *adjective* INTROSPECTIVE, withdrawn, inward-looking, self-contained, self-centred, indrawn, inner-directed

intrude *verb* BUTT IN, encroach, push in, obtrude, thrust yourself in *or* forward, put your two cents in (*US slang*)
▷▷ **intrude on something** *or* **someone**
1 INTERFERE WITH, interrupt, impinge on, encroach on, meddle with, infringe on
2 TRESPASS ON, invade, infringe on, obtrude on

intruder *noun* TRESPASSER, burglar, invader, squatter, prowler, interloper, infiltrator, gate-crasher (*informal*)

intrusion *noun* 1 INTERRUPTION, interference, infringement, trespass, encroachment
2 INVASION, breach, infringement, infiltration, encroachment, infraction, usurpation

intrusive *adjective* 1 INTERFERING, disturbing, invasive, unwanted, presumptuous, uncalled-for, importunate
2 PUSHY (*informal*), forward, interfering, unwanted, impertinent, nosy (*informal*), officious, meddlesome

intrust ▷ see **entrust**

intuition *noun* 1 INSTINCT, perception, insight, sixth sense, discernment
2 FEELING, idea, impression, suspicion, premonition, inkling, presentiment

intuitive *adjective* INSTINCTIVE, spontaneous, innate, involuntary, instinctual, untaught, unreflecting

intuitively *adverb* INSTINCTIVELY, automatically, spontaneously, involuntarily, innately, instinctually

inundate *verb* 1 OVERWHELM, flood, swamp, engulf, overflow, overrun, glut
2 FLOOD, engulf, submerge, drown, overflow, immerse, deluge

invade *verb* 1 ATTACK, storm, assault, capture, occupy, seize, raid, overwhelm, violate, conquer, overrun, annex, march into, assail, descend upon, infringe on, burst in on, make inroads on
2 INFEST, swarm, overrun, flood, infect, ravage, beset, pervade, permeate, overspread

invader *noun* ATTACKER, raider, plunderer, aggressor, looter, trespasser

invalid¹ *noun* PATIENT, sufferer, convalescent, valetudinarian
▷ *adjective* DISABLED, challenged, ill, sick, poorly (*informal*), weak, ailing, frail, feeble, sickly, infirm, bedridden, valetudinarian

invalid² *adjective* 1 NULL AND VOID, void, worthless, untrue, null, not binding, inoperative, nugatory
<< OPPOSITE valid
2 UNFOUNDED, false, untrue, illogical, irrational, unsound, unscientific, baseless, fallacious, ill-founded
<< OPPOSITE sound

invalidate *verb* NULLIFY, cancel, annul, undermine, weaken, overthrow, undo, quash, overrule, rescind, abrogate, render null and void
<< OPPOSITE validate

invalidity *noun* FALSITY, fallacy, unsoundness, inconsistency, irrationality, illogicality, speciousness, sophism, fallaciousness

invaluable *adjective* PRECIOUS, valuable, priceless, costly, inestimable, beyond price, worth your *or* its weight in gold
<< OPPOSITE worthless

invariably *adverb* ALWAYS, regularly, constantly, every time, inevitably, repeatedly, consistently, ever, continually, aye (*Scot*), eternally, habitually, perpetually, without exception, customarily, unfailingly, on every occasion, unceasingly, day in, day out

invasion *noun* 1 ATTACK, assault, capture, takeover, raid, offensive, occupation, conquering, seizure, onslaught, foray, appropriation, sortie, annexation, incursion, expropriation, inroad, irruption, arrogation
2 INTRUSION, breach, violation, disturbance, disruption, infringement, overstepping, infiltration, encroachment, infraction, usurpation

invective *noun* ABUSE, censure, tirade, reproach, berating, denunciation, diatribe, vilification, tongue-lashing, billingsgate, vituperation, castigation, obloquy, contumely, philippic(s), revilement

invent *verb* 1 CREATE, make, produce, develop, design, discover, imagine, manufacture, generate, come up with (*informal*), coin, devise, conceive, originate, formulate, spawn, contrive, improvise, dream up (*informal*), concoct, think up
2 MAKE UP, devise, concoct, forge, fake, fabricate, feign, falsify, cook up (*informal*), trump up

invention *noun* 1 CREATION, machine, device, design, development, instrument, discovery, innovation, gadget, brainchild (*informal*),

contraption, contrivance
2 DEVELOPMENT, design, production, setting up, foundation, construction, constitution, creation, discovery, introduction, establishment, pioneering, formation, innovation, conception, masterminding, formulation, inception, contrivance, origination
3 FICTION, story, fantasy, lie, yarn, fabrication, concoction, falsehood, fib (*informal*), untruth, urban myth, prevarication, tall story (*informal*), urban legend, figment *or* product of (someone's) imagination
4 CREATIVITY, vision, imagination, initiative, enterprise, inspiration, genius, brilliance, ingenuity, originality, inventiveness, resourcefulness, creativeness, ingeniousness, imaginativeness

inventive *adjective* CREATIVE, original, innovative, imaginative, gifted, inspired, fertile, ingenious, ground-breaking, resourceful
<< OPPOSITE uninspired

inventor *noun* CREATOR, father, maker, author, framer, designer, architect, coiner, originator

inventory *noun* LIST, record, catalogue, listing, account, roll, file, schedule, register, description, log, directory, tally, roster, stock book

inverse *adjective* 1 OPPOSITE, reverse, reversed, contrary, inverted, converse, transposed
2 REVERSE, opposite, reversed, inverted, transposed

inversion *noun* REVERSAL, opposite, antithesis, transposition, contrary, contrariety, contraposition, transposal, antipode

invert *verb* OVERTURN, upturn, turn upside down, upset, reverse, capsize, transpose, introvert, turn inside out, turn turtle, invaginate (*Pathology*), overset, intussuscept (*Pathology*)

invest *verb* 1 SPEND, expend, advance, venture, put in, devote, lay out, sink in, use up, plough in
2 CHARGE, fill, steep, saturate, endow, pervade, infuse, imbue, suffuse, endue
3 EMPOWER, provide, charge, sanction, license, authorize, vest
4 INSTALL, establish, ordain, crown, inaugurate, anoint, consecrate, adopt, induct, enthrone, instate
▷▷ **invest in something** BUY, get, purchase, score (*slang*), pay for, obtain, acquire, procure

investigate *verb* EXAMINE, study, research, consider, go into, explore, search for, analyse, look into, inspect, look over, sift, probe into, work over, scrutinize, inquire into, make inquiries about, enquire into

investigation *noun* EXAMINATION, study, inquiry, hearing, research, review, search, survey, analysis, probe, inspection, exploration, scrutiny, inquest, fact finding, recce (*slang*)

investigative *adjective* FACT-FINDING, researching, investigating, research, inspecting

investigator *noun* EXAMINER, researcher, inspector, monitor, detective, analyser, explorer, reviewer, scrutinizer, checker, inquirer, scrutineer

investment *noun* 1 INVESTING, backing, funding, financing, contribution, speculation, transaction, expenditure, outlay
2 STAKE, interest, share, concern, portion, ante (*informal*)
3 BUY, asset, acquisition, venture, risk, speculation, gamble

inveterate *adjective* 1 CHRONIC, confirmed, incurable, hardened, established, long-standing, hard-core, habitual, obstinate, incorrigible, dyed-in-the-wool, ineradicable, deep-dyed (*usually derogatory*)
2 DEEP-ROOTED, entrenched, ingrained, deep-seated, incurable, established
3 STAUNCH, long-standing, dyed-in-the-wool, deep-dyed (*usually derogatory*)

invidious *adjective* UNDESIRABLE, unpleasant, hateful, thankless
<< OPPOSITE pleasant

invigorating *adjective* REFRESHING, stimulating, bracing, fresh, tonic, uplifting, exhilarating, rejuvenating, energizing, healthful, restorative, salubrious, rejuvenative

invincible *adjective* UNBEATABLE, unassailable, indomitable, unyielding, indestructible, impregnable, insuperable, invulnerable, unconquerable, unsurmountable
<< OPPOSITE vulnerable

invisible *adjective* 1 UNSEEN, imperceptible, indiscernible, unseeable, unperceivable
<< OPPOSITE visible
2 HIDDEN, concealed, obscured, secret, disguised, inconspicuous, unobserved, unnoticeable, inappreciable

invitation *noun* 1 REQUEST, call, invite (*informal*), bidding, summons
2 INDUCEMENT, come-on (*informal*), temptation, challenge, provocation, open door, overture, incitement, enticement, allurement

invite *verb* 1 ASK, bid, summon, request the pleasure of (someone's) company
2 REQUEST, seek, look for, call for, ask for, bid for, appeal for, petition, solicit
3 ENCOURAGE, attract, cause, draw, lead to, court, ask for (*informal*), generate, foster, tempt, provoke, induce, bring on, solicit, engender, allure, call forth, leave the door open to

inviting *adjective* TEMPTING, appealing,

attractive, pleasing, welcoming, warm, engaging, fascinating, intriguing, magnetic, delightful, enticing, seductive, captivating, beguiling, alluring, mouthwatering
<< OPPOSITE uninviting

invocation *noun* 1 APPEAL, request, petition, beseeching, solicitation, entreaty
2 PRAYER, chant, supplication, orison, karakia (NZ)

invoke *verb* 1 APPLY, use, implement, call in, initiate, resort to, put into effect
2 CALL UPON, appeal to, pray to, petition, conjure, solicit, beseech, entreat, adjure, supplicate

involuntary *adjective* UNINTENTIONAL, automatic, unconscious, spontaneous, reflex, instinctive, uncontrolled, unthinking, instinctual, blind, unconditioned
<< OPPOSITE voluntary

involve *verb* 1 ENTAIL, mean, demand, require, call for, occasion, result in, imply, give rise to, encompass, necessitate
2 INCLUDE, contain, take in, embrace, cover, incorporate, draw in, comprise of, number among
3 IMPLICATE, tangle, mix up, embroil, link, entangle, incriminate, mire, stitch up (*slang*), enmesh, inculpate (*formal*)
4 CONCERN, draw in, associate, connect, bear on

involved *adjective* COMPLICATED, complex, intricate, hard, difficult, confused, confusing, sophisticated, elaborate, tangled, bewildering, jumbled, entangled, tortuous, Byzantine, convoluted, knotty, unfathomable, labyrinthine
<< OPPOSITE straightforward

involvement *noun* CONNECTION, interest, relationship, concern, association, commitment, friendship, attachment

invulnerable *adjective* SAFE, secure, invincible, impenetrable, unassailable, indestructible, insusceptible
<< OPPOSITE vulnerable

inward *adjective* 1 INCOMING, entering, penetrating, inbound, inflowing, ingoing, inpouring
2 INTERNAL, inner, private, personal, inside, secret, hidden, interior, confidential, privy, innermost, inmost
<< OPPOSITE outward

inwardly *adverb* PRIVATELY, secretly, to yourself, within, inside, at heart, deep down, in your head, in your inmost heart

iota *noun* BIT, particle, atom, trace, hint, scrap, grain, mite, jot, speck, whit, tittle

irascible *adjective* BAD-TEMPERED, cross, irritable, crabbed, touchy, cantankerous, peppery, tetchy, ratty (*Brit & NZ informal*), testy, chippy (*informal*), short-tempered, hot-tempered, quick-tempered, choleric, narky (*Brit slang*)

irate *adjective* ANGRY, cross, furious, angered, mad (*informal*), provoked, annoyed, irritated, fuming (*informal*), choked, infuriated, incensed, enraged, worked up, exasperated, indignant, livid, riled, up in arms, incandescent, hacked off (*US slang*), piqued, hot under the collar (*informal*), wrathful, fit to be tied (*slang*), as black as thunder, tooshie (*Austral slang*), off the air (*Austral slang*)

ire *noun Literary* ANGER, rage, fury, wrath, passion, indignation, annoyance, displeasure, exasperation, choler

Ireland *noun* HIBERNIA (*Latin*)

iridescent *adjective* SHIMMERING, pearly, opalescent, shot, opaline, prismatic, rainbow-coloured, polychromatic, nacreous

Irish *adjective* HIBERNIAN, green

irk *verb* IRRITATE, annoy, aggravate (*informal*), provoke, bug (*informal*), put out (*informal*), gall, ruffle, nettle, vex, rile, peeve (*informal*), get on your nerves (*informal*), nark (*Brit, Austral & NZ slang*), miff (*informal*), be on your back (*slang*), get in your hair (*informal*), rub you up the wrong way (*informal*), put your nose out of joint (*informal*), get your back up, put your back up, hack you off (*informal*)

irksome *adjective* IRRITATING, trying, annoying, aggravating, troublesome, unwelcome, exasperating, tiresome, vexing, disagreeable, burdensome, wearisome, bothersome, vexatious
<< OPPOSITE pleasant

iron *modifier* FERROUS, ferric, irony
▷ *adjective* INFLEXIBLE, hard, strong, tough, steel, rigid, adamant, unconditional, steely, implacable, indomitable, unyielding, immovable, unbreakable, unbending, obdurate
<< OPPOSITE weak
▷▷ **iron something out** SETTLE, resolve, sort out, eliminate, get rid of, reconcile, clear up, simplify, unravel, erase, eradicate, put right, straighten out, harmonize, expedite, smooth over
>> RELATED WORDS *adjectives* ferric, ferrous
>> RELATED WORD *combining form* ferro-

ironic *or* **ironical** *adjective* 1 SARCASTIC, dry, sharp, acid, bitter, stinging, mocking, sneering, scoffing, wry, scathing, satirical, tongue-in-cheek, sardonic, caustic, double-edged, acerbic, trenchant, mordant, mordacious
2 PARADOXICAL, absurd, contradictory, puzzling, baffling, ambiguous, inconsistent, confounding, enigmatic, illogical,

incongruous
irons *plural noun* CHAINS, shackles, fetters, manacles, bonds
irony *noun* 1 SARCASM, mockery, ridicule, bitterness, scorn, satire, cynicism, derision, causticity, mordancy
2 PARADOX, ambiguity, absurdity, incongruity, contrariness
irrational *adjective* 1 ILLOGICAL, crazy, silly, absurd, foolish, unreasonable, unwise, preposterous, idiotic, nonsensical, unsound, unthinking, injudicious, unreasoning
<< OPPOSITE rational
2 SENSELESS, wild, crazy, unstable, insane, mindless, demented, aberrant, brainless, off the air (*Austral slang*)
irrationality *noun* SENSELESSNESS, madness, insanity, absurdity, lunacy, lack of judgment, illogicality, unreasonableness, preposterousness, unsoundness, brainlessness
irreconcilable *adjective* 1 IMPLACABLE, uncompromising, inflexible, inexorable, intransigent, unappeasable
2 INCOMPATIBLE, conflicting, opposed, inconsistent, incongruous, diametrically opposed
irrefutable *adjective* UNDENIABLE, sure, certain, irresistible, invincible, unassailable, indisputable, unanswerable, unquestionable, incontrovertible, beyond question, incontestable, indubitable, apodictic, irrefragable
irregular *adjective* 1 VARIABLE, inconsistent, erratic, shifting, occasional, random, casual, shaky, wavering, uneven, fluctuating, eccentric, patchy, sporadic, intermittent, haphazard, unsteady, desultory, fitful, spasmodic, unsystematic, inconstant, nonuniform, unmethodical, scattershot
<< OPPOSITE steady
2 UNEVEN, broken, rough, twisted, twisting, curving, pitted, ragged, crooked, unequal, jagged, bumpy, lumpy, serpentine, contorted, lopsided, craggy, indented, asymmetrical, serrated, holey, unsymmetrical
<< OPPOSITE even
3 INAPPROPRIATE, unconventional, improper, unethical, odd, unusual, extraordinary, disorderly, exceptional, peculiar, unofficial, abnormal, queer, rum (*Brit slang*), back-door, unsuitable, unorthodox, out-of-order, unprofessional, anomalous
4 UNOFFICIAL, underground, guerrilla, volunteer, resistance, partisan, rogue, paramilitary, mercenary
irregularity *noun* 1 INCONSISTENCY, randomness, disorganization, unsteadiness, unpunctuality, haphazardness, disorderliness, lack of method, desultoriness
2 UNEVENNESS, deformity, asymmetry, crookedness, contortion, patchiness, lopsidedness, raggedness, lack of symmetry, spottiness, jaggedness
3 MALPRACTICE, anomaly, breach, abnormality, deviation, oddity, aberration, malfunction, peculiarity, singularity, unorthodoxy, unconventionality
irregularly *adverb* ERRATICALLY, occasionally, now and again, intermittently, off and on, anyhow, unevenly, fitfully, haphazardly, eccentrically, spasmodically, jerkily, in snatches, out of sequence, by fits and starts, disconnectedly, unmethodically, unpunctually
irrelevance *or* **irrelevancy** *noun* INAPPROPRIATENESS, inapplicability, inaptness, unconnectedness, pointlessness, non sequitur, inconsequence, extraneousness, inappositeness
<< OPPOSITE relevance
irrelevant *adjective* UNCONNECTED, unrelated, unimportant, inappropriate, peripheral, insignificant, negligible, immaterial, extraneous, beside the point, impertinent, neither here nor there, inapplicable, inapt, inapposite, inconsequent
<< OPPOSITE relevant
irreparable *adjective* BEYOND REPAIR, irreversible, incurable, irretrievable, irrecoverable, irremediable
irreplaceable *adjective* INDISPENSABLE, unique, invaluable, priceless
irrepressible *adjective* UNSTOPPABLE, buoyant, uncontrollable, boisterous, ebullient, effervescent, unmanageable, unquenchable, bubbling over, uncontainable, unrestrainable, insuppressible
irresistible *adjective* 1 OVERWHELMING, compelling, overpowering, urgent, potent, imperative, compulsive, uncontrollable, overmastering
2 SEDUCTIVE, inviting, tempting, enticing, provocative, fascinating, enchanting, captivating, beguiling, alluring, bewitching, ravishing
3 INESCAPABLE, inevitable, unavoidable, sure, certain, fated, destined, inexorable, ineluctable
irrespective of *preposition* DESPITE, in spite of, regardless of, discounting, notwithstanding, without reference to, without regard to
irresponsible *adjective* THOUGHTLESS, reckless, careless, wild, unreliable, giddy, untrustworthy, flighty, ill-considered, good-for-nothing, shiftless, harebrained, undependable, harum-scarum, scatterbrained, featherbrained
<< OPPOSITE responsible

irreverence *noun* DISRESPECT, cheek (*informal*), impertinence, sauce (*informal*), mockery, derision, lack of respect, impudence, flippancy, cheekiness (*informal*)

irreverent *adjective* DISRESPECTFUL, cheeky (*informal*), impertinent, fresh (*informal*), mocking, flip (*informal*), saucy, contemptuous, tongue-in-cheek, sassy (*US informal*), flippant, iconoclastic, derisive, impudent

<< OPPOSITE reverent

irreversible *adjective* IRREVOCABLE, incurable, irreparable, final, unalterable

irrevocable *adjective* FIXED, settled, irreversible, fated, predetermined, immutable, invariable, irretrievable, predestined, unalterable, unchangeable, changeless, irremediable, unreversible

irrigate *verb* WATER, wet, moisten, flood, inundate, fertigate (*Austral*)

irritability *noun* BAD TEMPER, impatience, ill humour, prickliness, tetchiness, irascibility, peevishness, testiness, touchiness

<< OPPOSITE good humour

irritable *adjective* BAD-TEMPERED, cross, snappy, hot, tense, crabbed, fiery, snarling, prickly, exasperated, edgy, touchy, petulant, ill-tempered, irascible, cantankerous, tetchy, ratty (*Brit & NZ informal*), testy, chippy (*informal*), fretful, peevish, crabby, dyspeptic, choleric, crotchety (*informal*), oversensitive, snappish, ill-humoured, narky (*Brit slang*), out of humour

<< OPPOSITE even-tempered

irritate *verb* **1** ANNOY, anger, bother, provoke, offend, needle (*informal*), harass, infuriate, aggravate (*informal*), incense, fret, enrage, gall, ruffle, inflame, exasperate, nettle, pester, vex, irk, pique, rankle with, get under your skin (*informal*), get on your nerves (*informal*), nark (*Brit, Austral & NZ slang*), drive you up the wall (*slang*), rub you up the wrong way (*informal*), get your goat (*slang*), try your patience, get in your hair (*informal*), get on your wick (*informal*), get your dander up (*informal*), raise your hackles, get your back up, get your hackles up, put your back up, hack you off (*informal*)

<< OPPOSITE placate

2 INFLAME, pain, rub, scratch, scrape, grate, graze, fret, gall, chafe, abrade

irritated *adjective* ANNOYED, cross, angry, bothered, put out, hacked (off) (*US slang*), harassed, impatient, ruffled, exasperated, irritable, nettled, vexed, displeased, flustered, peeved (*informal*), piqued, out of humour, tooshie (*Austral slang*), hoha (*NZ*)

irritating *adjective* ANNOYING, trying, provoking, infuriating, upsetting, disturbing, nagging, aggravating (*informal*), troublesome, galling, maddening, disquieting, displeasing, worrisome, irksome, vexatious, pestilential

<< OPPOSITE pleasing

irritation *noun* **1** ANNOYANCE, anger, fury, resentment, wrath, gall, indignation, impatience, displeasure, exasperation, chagrin, irritability, ill temper, shortness, vexation, ill humour, testiness, crossness, snappiness, infuriation

<< OPPOSITE pleasure

2 NUISANCE, annoyance, irritant, pain (*informal*), drag (*informal*), bother, plague, menace, tease, pest, hassle, provocation, gall, goad, aggravation (*informal*), pain in the neck (*informal*), thorn in your flesh

island *noun* ISLE, inch (*Scot & Irish*), atoll, holm (*dialect*), islet, ait *or* eyot (*dialect*), cay *or* key

>> RELATED WORD *adjective* insular

isolate *verb* **1** SEPARATE, break up, cut off, detach, split up, insulate, segregate, disconnect, divorce, sequester, set apart, disunite, estrange

2 QUARANTINE, separate, exclude, cut off, detach, keep in solitude

isolated *adjective* REMOTE, far, distant, lonely, out-of-the-way, hidden, retired, far-off, secluded, inaccessible, faraway, outlying, in the middle of nowhere, off the beaten track, backwoods, godforsaken, incommunicado, unfrequented

isolation *noun* SEPARATION, withdrawal, loneliness, segregation, detachment, quarantine, solitude, exile, self-sufficiency, seclusion, remoteness, disconnection, insularity

issue *noun* **1** TOPIC, point, matter, problem, business, case, question, concern, subject, affair, argument, theme, controversy, can of worms (*informal*)

2 POINT, question, concern, bone of contention, matter of contention, point in question

3 EDITION, printing, copy, impression, publication, number, instalment, imprint, version

4 CHILDREN, young, offspring, babies, kids (*informal*), seed (*chiefly biblical*), successors, heirs, descendants, progeny, scions

<< OPPOSITE parent

5 DISTRIBUTION, issuing, supply, supplying, delivery, publication, circulation, sending out, dissemination, dispersal, issuance

▷ *verb* **1** GIVE OUT, release, publish, announce, deliver, spread, broadcast, distribute, communicate, proclaim, put out, circulate, emit, impart, disseminate, promulgate, put in circulation

2 EMERGE, come out, proceed, rise, spring, flow, arise, stem, originate, emanate, exude, come forth, be a consequence of

▷▷ **at issue** UNDER DISCUSSION, in question, in

dispute, under consideration, to be decided, for debate

▷▷ **take issue with something** *or* **someone** DISAGREE WITH, question, challenge, oppose, dispute, object to, argue with, take exception to, raise an objection to

itch *verb* **1** PRICKLE, tickle, tingle, crawl
2 LONG, ache, crave, burn, pine, pant, hunger, lust, yearn, hanker
▷ *noun* **1** IRRITATION, tingling, prickling, itchiness
2 DESIRE, longing, craving, passion, yen (*informal*), hunger, lust, yearning, hankering, restlessness

itchy *adjective* IMPATIENT, eager, restless, unsettled, edgy, restive, fidgety

item *noun* **1** ARTICLE, thing, object, piece, unit, component
2 MATTER, point, issue, case, question, concern, detail, subject, feature, particular, affair, aspect, entry, theme, consideration, topic
3 REPORT, story, piece, account, note, feature, notice, article, paragraph, bulletin, dispatch, communiqué, write-up

itemize *verb* LIST, record, detail, count, document, instance, set out, specify, inventory, number, enumerate, particularize

itinerant *adjective* WANDERING, travelling, journeying, unsettled, Gypsy, roaming, roving, nomadic, migratory, vagrant, peripatetic, vagabond, ambulatory, wayfaring
<< OPPOSITE settled

itinerary *noun* SCHEDULE, line, programme, tour, route, journey, circuit, timetable

ivory tower *noun* SECLUSION, remoteness, unreality, retreat, refuge, cloister, sanctum, splendid isolation, world of your own

jab *verb* POKE, dig, punch, thrust, tap, stab, nudge, prod, lunge
▷ *noun* POKE, dig, punch, thrust, tap, stab, nudge, prod, lunge

jacket *noun* COVERING, casing, case, cover, skin, shell, coat, wrapping, envelope, capsule, folder, sheath, wrapper, encasement, housing

jackpot *noun* PRIZE, winnings, award, pool, reward, pot, kitty, bonanza, pot of gold at the end of the rainbow

jack up *verb* **1** HOIST, raise, elevate, winch up, lift, rear, uplift, lift up, heave, haul up, hike up, upraise
2 INCREASE, raise, put up, augment, advance, boost, expand, add to, enhance, step up (*informal*), intensify, enlarge, escalate, inflate, amplify

jaded *adjective* **1** TIRED, bored, weary, worn out, done in (*informal*), clapped out (*Brit, Austral & NZ informal*), spent, drained, exhausted, shattered, dulled, fatigued, fed up, wearied, fagged (out) (*informal*), sapped, uninterested, listless, tired-out, enervated, zonked (*slang*), over-tired, ennuied, hoha (NZ)
<< OPPOSITE fresh
2 SATIATED, sated, surfeited, cloyed, gorged, glutted

jagged *adjective* UNEVEN, pointed, craggy, broken, toothed, rough, ragged, ridged, spiked, notched, barbed, cleft, indented, serrated, snaggy, denticulate
<< OPPOSITE rounded

jail *or* **gaol** *noun* PRISON, penitentiary (US), jailhouse (*Southern US*), penal institution, can (*slang*), inside, cooler (*slang*), confinement, dungeon, clink (*slang*), glasshouse (*Military informal*), brig (*chiefly US*), borstal, calaboose (*US informal*), choky (*slang*), pound, nick (*Brit slang*), stir (*slang*), jug (*slang*), slammer (*slang*), lockup, reformatory, quod (*slang*), poky *or* pokey (*US & Canad slang*), boob (*Austral slang*)
▷ *verb* IMPRISON, confine, detain, lock up, constrain, put away, intern, incarcerate, send down, send to prison, impound, put under lock and key, immure

jailbird *or* **gaolbird** *noun* PRISONER, convict, con (*slang*), lag (*slang*), trusty, felon, malefactor, ticket-of-leave man (*Historical*)

jailer *or* **gaoler** *noun* GUARD, keeper, warden, screw (*slang*), captor, warder, turnkey (*archaic*)

jam *noun* **1** TAILBACK, queue, hold-up, bottleneck, snarl-up, line, chain, congestion, obstruction, stoppage, gridlock
2 (*informal*) PREDICAMENT, tight spot, scrape (*informal*), corner, state, situation, trouble, spot (*informal*), hole (*slang*), fix (*informal*), bind, emergency, mess, dilemma, pinch, plight, strait, hot water, pickle (*informal*), deep water, quandary
▷ *verb* **1** PACK, force, press, stuff, squeeze, compact, ram, wedge, cram, compress
2 CROWD, cram, throng, crush, press, mass, surge, flock, swarm, congregate
3 CONGEST, block, clog, stick, halt, stall, obstruct

jamboree *noun* FESTIVAL, party, fête, celebration, blast (*US slang*), rave (*Brit slang*), carnival, spree, jubilee, festivity, beano (*Brit slang*), merriment, revelry, carouse, rave-up (*Brit slang*), carousal, frolic, hooley *or* hoolie (*chiefly Irish & NZ*)

jangle *verb* RATTLE, ring, clash, clatter, chime, ping, vibrate, jingle, ding, clank
▷ *noun* CLASH, clang, cacophony, reverberation, rattle, jar, racket, din, dissonance, clangour
<< OPPOSITE quiet

janitor *noun* CARETAKER, porter, custodian, concierge, doorkeeper

jar[1] *noun* POT, container, flask, receptacle, vessel, drum, vase, jug, pitcher, urn, crock, canister, repository, decanter, carafe, flagon

jar[2] *verb* **1** *usually with* **on** IRRITATE, grind, clash, annoy, offend, rattle, gall, nettle, jangle, irk, grate on, get on your nerves (*informal*), nark (*Brit, Austral & NZ slang*), discompose
2 *sometimes with* **with** CLASH, conflict, contrast,

differ, disagree, interfere, contend, collide, oppose
3 JOLT, rock, shake, disturb, bump, rattle, grate, agitate, vibrate, rasp, convulse
jargon *noun* PARLANCE, slang, idiom, patter, tongue, usage, dialect, cant, lingo (*informal*), patois, argot
jaundiced *adjective* CYNICAL, bitter, hostile, prejudiced, biased, suspicious, partial, jealous, distorted, sceptical, resentful, envious, bigoted, spiteful, preconceived
<< OPPOSITE optimistic
jaunt *noun* OUTING, tour, trip, stroll, expedition, excursion, ramble, promenade, airing
jaunty *adjective* 1 SPRIGHTLY, buoyant, carefree, high-spirited, gay, lively, airy, breezy, perky, sparky, self-confident
<< OPPOSITE serious
2 SMART, trim, gay, dapper, spruce, showy
jaw *plural noun* OPENING, gates, entrance, aperture, mouth, abyss, maw, orifice, ingress
▷ *verb* (*Slang*) TALK, chat, rabbit (on) (*Brit informal*), gossip, chatter, spout, babble, natter, schmooze (*slang*), shoot the breeze (*US slang*), run off at the mouth (*slang*), chew the fat *or* rag (*slang*)
>> RELATED WORDS *technical names* maxilla (upper), mandible (lower)
jealous *adjective* 1 SUSPICIOUS, suspecting, guarded, protective, wary, doubtful, sceptical, attentive, anxious, apprehensive, vigilant, watchful, zealous, possessive, solicitous, distrustful, mistrustful, unbelieving
<< OPPOSITE trusting
2 ENVIOUS, grudging, resentful, begrudging, green, intolerant, green-eyed, invidious, green with envy, desirous, covetous, emulous
<< OPPOSITE satisfied
jealousy *noun* SUSPICION, distrust, mistrust, possessiveness, doubt, spite, resentment, wariness, ill-will, dubiety
jeer *verb* MOCK, hector, deride, heckle, knock (*informal*), barrack, ridicule, taunt, sneer, scoff, banter, flout, gibe, cock a snook at (*Brit*), contemn (*formal*)
<< OPPOSITE cheer
▷ *noun* MOCKERY, abuse, ridicule, taunt, sneer, hiss, boo, scoff, hoot, derision, gibe, catcall, obloquy, aspersion
<< OPPOSITE applause
jeopardize *verb* ENDANGER, threaten, put at risk, put in jeopardy, risk, expose, gamble, hazard, menace, imperil, put on the line
jeopardy *noun* DANGER, risk, peril, vulnerability, venture, exposure, liability, hazard, insecurity, pitfall, precariousness, endangerment
jerk *verb* JOLT, bang, bump, lurch, shake
▷ *noun* LURCH, movement, thrust, twitch, jolt, throw
jerky *adjective* BUMPY, rough, jolting, jumpy, shaky, bouncy, uncontrolled, twitchy, fitful, spasmodic, convulsive, tremulous
<< OPPOSITE smooth
jest *noun* JOKE, play, crack (*slang*), sally, gag (*informal*), quip, josh (*slang, chiefly US & Canad*), banter, hoax, prank, wisecrack (*informal*), pleasantry, witticism, jape, bon mot
▷ *verb* JOKE, kid (*informal*), mock, tease, sneer, jeer, quip, josh (*slang, chiefly US & Canad*), scoff, banter, deride, chaff, gibe
jester *noun* FOOL, clown, harlequin, zany, madcap, prankster, buffoon, pantaloon, mummer
jet *noun* STREAM, current, spring, flow, rush, flood, burst, spray, fountain, cascade, gush, spurt, spout, squirt
▷ *verb* 1 FLY, wing, cruise, soar, zoom
2 STREAM, course, issue, shoot, flow, rush, surge, spill, gush, emanated, spout, spew, squirt
jet-black *adjective* BLACK, jet, raven, ebony, sable, pitch-black, inky, coal-black
jet-setting *adjective* FASHIONABLE, rich, sophisticated, trendy (*Brit informal*), cosmopolitan, well-off, high-society, ritzy (*slang*), trendsetting
jettison *verb* 1 ABANDON, reject, desert, dump, shed, scrap, throw out, discard, throw away, relinquish, forsake, slough off, throw on the scrapheap
2 EXPEL, dump, unload, throw overboard, eject, heave
jetty *noun* PIER, dock, wharf, mole, quay, breakwater, groyne
jewel *noun* 1 GEMSTONE, gem, precious stone, brilliant, ornament, trinket, sparkler (*informal*), rock (*slang*)
2 TREASURE, wonder, prize, darling, pearl, gem, paragon, pride and joy, taonga (*NZ*)
jewellery *noun* JEWELS, treasure, gems, trinkets, precious stones, ornaments, finery, regalia
jibe *or* **gibe** *noun* JEER, sneer, dig (*informal*), crack, taunt, snide remark
▷ *verb* JEER, mock, sneer, taunt
jig *verb* SKIP, bob, prance, jiggle, shake, bounce, twitch, wobble, caper, wiggle, jounce
jiggle *verb* 1 SHAKE, jerk, agitate, joggle
2 JERK, bounce, jog, fidget, shake, twitch, wiggle, jig, shimmy, joggle
jilt *verb* REJECT, drop, disappoint, abandon, desert, ditch (*slang*), betray, discard, deceive, forsake, throw over, coquette, leave (someone) in the lurch
jingle *verb* RING, rattle, clatter, chime, jangle, tinkle, clink, clank, tintinnabulate
▷ *noun* 1 RATTLE, ringing, tinkle, clang, clink,

reverberation, clangour
2 SONG, tune, melody, ditty, chorus, slogan, verse, limerick, refrain, doggerel

jinx *noun* CURSE, plague, voodoo, nemesis, black magic, hoodoo (*informal*), hex (*US & Canad informal*), evil eye
▷ *verb* CURSE, bewitch, hex (*US & Canad informal*)

jitters *plural noun* NERVES, anxiety, butterflies (in your stomach) (*informal*), nervousness, the shakes (*informal*), fidgets, cold feet (*informal*), the willies (*informal*), tenseness, heebie-jeebies (*slang*)

jittery *adjective* NERVOUS, anxious, jumpy, twitchy (*informal*), wired (*slang*), trembling, shaky, neurotic, agitated, quivering, hyper (*informal*), fidgety, antsy (*informal*)
<< OPPOSITE calm

job *noun* **1** POSITION, post, function, capacity, work, posting, calling, place, business, office, trade, field, career, situation, activity, employment, appointment, craft, profession, occupation, placement, vocation, livelihood, métier
2 TASK, concern, duty, charge, work, business, role, operation, affair, responsibility, function, contribution, venture, enterprise, undertaking, pursuit, assignment, stint, chore, errand

jobless *adjective* UNEMPLOYED, redundant, out of work, on the dole (*Brit informal*), inactive, out of a job, unoccupied, idle

jockey *verb* MANOEUVRE, manage, engineer, negotiate, trim, manipulate, cajole, insinuate, wheedle, finagle (*informal*)

jog *verb* **1** RUN, trot, canter, lope, dogtrot
2 NUDGE, push, shake, prod
3 STIMULATE, remind, prompt, stir, arouse, activate, nudge, prod

join *verb* **1** ENROL IN, enter, sign up for, become a member of, enlist in
2 CONNECT, unite, couple, link, marry, tie, combine, attach, knit, cement, adhere, fasten, annex, add, splice, yoke, append
<< OPPOSITE detach
3 MEET, touch, border, extend, butt, adjoin, conjoin, reach
<< OPPOSITE part

joint *adjective* SHARED, mutual, collective, communal, united, joined, allied, combined, corporate, concerted, consolidated, cooperative, reciprocal, collaborative
▷ *noun* JUNCTION, union, link, connection, knot, brace, bracket, seam, hinge, weld, linkage, intersection, node, articulation, nexus
>> RELATED WORD *adjective* articular

jointly *adverb* COLLECTIVELY, together, in conjunction, as one, in common, mutually, in partnership, in league, unitedly
<< OPPOSITE separately

joke *noun* **1** JEST, gag (*informal*), wisecrack (*informal*), witticism, crack (*informal*), sally, quip, josh (*slang, chiefly US & Canad*), pun, quirk, one-liner (*informal*), jape
2 LAUGH, jest, fun, josh (*slang, chiefly US & Canad*), lark, sport, frolic, whimsy, jape
3 PRANK, trick, practical joke, lark (*informal*), caper, frolic, escapade, antic, jape
4 LAUGHING STOCK, butt, clown, buffoon, simpleton
▷ *verb* JEST, kid (*informal*), fool, mock, wind up (*Brit slang*), tease, ridicule, taunt, quip, josh (*slang, chiefly US & Canad*), banter, deride, frolic, chaff, gambol, play the fool, play a trick

joker *noun* COMEDIAN, comic, wit, clown, wag, kidder (*informal*), jester, prankster, buffoon, trickster, humorist

jokey *adjective* PLAYFUL, funny, amusing, teasing, humorous, mischievous, jesting, wisecracking, droll, facetious, waggish, prankish, nonserious
<< OPPOSITE humourless

jolly *adjective* HAPPY, bright, funny, lively, hopeful, sunny, cheerful, merry, vibrant, hilarious, festive, upbeat (*informal*), bubbly, gay, airy, playful, exuberant, jubilant, cheery, good-humoured, joyous, joyful, carefree, breezy, genial, ebullient, chirpy (*informal*), sprightly, jovial, convivial, effervescent, frolicsome, ludic (*literary*), mirthful, sportive, light-hearted, jocund, gladsome (*archaic*), blithesome
<< OPPOSITE miserable

jolt *verb* **1** JERK, push, shake, knock, jar, shove, jog, jostle
2 SURPRISE, upset, stun, disturb, astonish, stagger, startle, perturb, discompose
▷ *noun* **1** JERK, start, jump, shake, bump, jar, jog, lurch, quiver
2 SURPRISE, blow, shock, setback, reversal, bombshell, thunderbolt, whammy (*informal, chiefly US*), bolt from the blue

jostle *verb* PUSH, press, crowd, shake, squeeze, thrust, butt, elbow, bump, scramble, shove, jog, jolt, throng, hustle, joggle

jot *verb* *usually with* **down** NOTE DOWN, record, list, note, register, tally, scribble
▷ *noun* BIT, detail, ace, scrap, grain, particle, atom, fraction, trifle, mite, tad (*informal, chiefly US*), speck, morsel, whit, tittle, iota, scintilla, smidgen *or* smidgin (*informal, chiefly US & Canad*)

journal *noun* **1** MAGAZINE, record, review, register, publication, bulletin, chronicle, gazette, periodical, zine (*informal*)
2 NEWSPAPER, paper, daily, weekly, monthly, tabloid
3 DIARY, record, history, log, notebook, chronicle, annals, yearbook, commonplace

book, daybook
journalist *noun* REPORTER, writer, correspondent, newsman *or* newswoman, stringer, commentator, broadcaster, hack (*derogatory*), columnist, contributor, scribe (*informal*), pressman, journo (*slang*), newshound (*informal*), newspaperman *or* newspaperwoman
journey *noun* 1 TRIP, drive, tour, flight, excursion, progress, cruise, passage, trek, outing, expedition, voyage, ramble, jaunt, peregrination, travel
2 PROGRESS, passage, voyage, pilgrimage, odyssey
▷ *verb* TRAVEL, go, move, walk, fly, range, cross, tour, progress, proceed, fare, wander, trek, voyage, roam, ramble, traverse, rove, wend, go walkabout (*Austral*), peregrinate
jovial *adjective* CHEERFUL, happy, jolly, animated, glad, merry, hilarious, buoyant, airy, jubilant, cheery, cordial, convivial, blithe, gay, mirthful, jocund, jocose
<< OPPOSITE solemn
joy *noun* 1 DELIGHT, pleasure, triumph, satisfaction, happiness, ecstasy, enjoyment, bliss, transport, euphoria, festivity, felicity, glee, exuberance, rapture, elation, exhilaration, radiance, gaiety, jubilation, hilarity, exaltation, ebullience, exultation, gladness, joyfulness, ravishment
<< OPPOSITE sorrow
2 TREASURE, wonder, treat, prize, delight, pride, charm, thrill
joyful *adjective* 1 PLEASING, satisfying, engaging, charming, delightful, enjoyable, gratifying, agreeable, pleasurable
2 DELIGHTED, happy, satisfied, glad, jolly, merry, gratified, pleased, jubilant, elated, over the moon (*informal*), jovial, rapt, enraptured, on cloud nine (*informal*), cock-a-hoop, floating on air, light-hearted, jocund, gladsome (*archaic*), blithesome, stoked (*Austral & NZ informal*)
joyless *adjective* UNHAPPY, sad, depressing, miserable, gloomy, dismal, dreary, dejected, dispirited, downcast, down in the dumps (*informal*), cheerless
joyous *adjective* JOYFUL, cheerful, merry, festive, heartening, rapturous, blithe
jubilant *adjective* OVERJOYED, excited, thrilled, glad, triumphant, rejoicing, exuberant, joyous, elated, over the moon (*informal*), euphoric, triumphal, enraptured, exultant, cock-a-hoop, rhapsodic, stoked (*Austral & NZ informal*)
<< OPPOSITE downcast
jubilation *noun* JOY, triumph, celebration, excitement, ecstasy, jubilee, festivity, elation, jamboree, exultation
jubilee *noun* CELEBRATION, holiday, fête, festival, carnival, festivity, gala
judge *noun* 1 MAGISTRATE, justice, beak (*Brit slang*), His, Her *or* Your Honour
2 REFEREE, expert, specialist, umpire, umpie (*Austral slang*), mediator, examiner, connoisseur, assessor, arbiter, appraiser, arbitrator, moderator, adjudicator, evaluator, authority
3 CRITIC, assessor, arbiter, appraiser, evaluator
▷ *verb* 1 ADJUDICATE, referee, umpire, mediate, officiate, adjudge, arbitrate
2 EVALUATE, rate, consider, appreciate, view, class, value, review, rank, examine, esteem, criticize, ascertain, surmise
3 ESTIMATE, guess, assess, calculate, evaluate, gauge, appraise
4 FIND, rule, pass, pronounce, decree, adjudge
>> RELATED WORD *adjective* judicial
judgment *noun* 1 OPINION, view, estimate, belief, assessment, conviction, diagnosis, valuation, deduction, appraisal
2 VERDICT, finding, result, ruling, decision, sentence, conclusion, determination, decree, order, arbitration, adjudication, pronouncement
3 SENSE, common sense, good sense, judiciousness, reason, understanding, taste, intelligence, smarts (*slang, chiefly US*), discrimination, perception, awareness, wisdom, wit, penetration, prudence, sharpness, acumen, shrewdness, discernment, perspicacity, sagacity, astuteness, percipience
judgmental *adjective* CONDEMNATORY, self-righteous, censorious, pharisaic, critical
judicial *adjective* LEGAL, official, judiciary, juridical
judicious *adjective* SENSIBLE, considered, reasonable, discerning, sound, politic, acute, informed, diplomatic, careful, wise, cautious, rational, sober, discriminating, thoughtful, discreet, sage, enlightened, shrewd, prudent, sane, skilful, astute, expedient, circumspect, well-advised, well-judged, sagacious, sapient
<< OPPOSITE injudicious
jug *noun* CONTAINER, pitcher, urn, carafe, creamer (*US & Canad*), vessel, jar, crock, ewer
juggle *verb* MANIPULATE, change, doctor (*informal*), fix (*informal*), alter, modify, disguise, manoeuvre, tamper with, misrepresent, falsify
juice *noun* 1 LIQUID, extract, fluid, liquor, sap, nectar
2 SECRETION, serum
juicy *adjective* 1 MOIST, lush, watery, succulent, sappy
2 INTERESTING, colourful, sensational, vivid, provocative, spicy (*informal*), suggestive, racy, risqué
jumble *noun* MUDDLE, mixture, mess, disorder,

confusion, chaos, litter, clutter, disarray, medley, mélange (*French*), miscellany, mishmash, farrago, hotchpotch (*US*), hodgepodge, gallimaufry, pig's breakfast (*informal*), disarrangement
▷ *verb* MIX, mistake, confuse, disorder, shuffle, tangle, muddle, confound, entangle, ravel, disorganize, disarrange, dishevel

jumbo *adjective* GIANT, large, huge, immense, mega (*informal*), gigantic, oversized, elephantine, ginormous (*informal*), humongous *or* humungous (*US slang*)
<< OPPOSITE tiny

jump *verb* 1 LEAP, dance, spring, bound, bounce, hop, skip, caper, prance, gambol
2 VAULT, clear, hurdle, go over, sail over, hop over
3 SPRING, bound, leap, bounce
4 RECOIL, start, jolt, flinch, shake, jerk, quake, shudder, twitch, wince
5 INCREASE, rise, climb, escalate, gain, advance, boost, mount, soar, surge, spiral, hike, ascend
6 MISS, avoid, skip, omit, evade, digress
▷ *noun* 1 LEAP, spring, skip, bound, buck, hop, vault, caper
2 RISE, increase, escalation, upswing, advance, boost, elevation, upsurge, upturn, increment, augmentation
3 JOLT, start, movement, shock, shake, jar, jerk, lurch, twitch, swerve, spasm
4 HURDLE, gate, barrier, fence, obstacle, barricade, rail

jumped-up *adjective* (*informal*) CONCEITED, arrogant, pompous, stuck-up, cocky, overbearing, puffed up, presumptuous, insolent, immodest, toffee-nosed, self-opinionated, too big for your boots *or* breeches

jumper *noun* SWEATER, top, jersey, cardigan, woolly, pullover

jumpy *adjective* NERVOUS, anxious, tense, shaky, restless, neurotic, agitated, hyper (*informal*), apprehensive, jittery (*informal*), on edge, twitchy (*informal*), fidgety, timorous, antsy (*informal*), wired (*slang*)
<< OPPOSITE calm

juncture *noun* MOMENT, time, point, crisis, occasion, emergency, strait, contingency, predicament, crux, exigency, conjuncture

junior *adjective* 1 MINOR, lower, secondary, lesser, subordinate, inferior
2 YOUNGER
<< OPPOSITE senior

junk *noun* RUBBISH, refuse, waste, scrap, litter, debris, crap (*slang*), garbage (*chiefly US*), trash, clutter, rummage, dross, odds and ends, oddments, flotsam and jetsam, leavings, dreck (*slang, chiefly US*)

junkie *or* **junky** *noun* (*informal*) ADDICT, user, drug addict, druggie (*informal*), head (*slang*), freak (*informal*), mainliner (*slang*), smackhead (*slang*), pill-popper (*slang*), pothead (*slang*), cokehead (*slang*), acidhead (*slang*), hashhead (*slang*), weedhead (*slang*)

junta *noun* CABAL, council, faction, league, set, party, ring, camp, crew, combination, assembly, gang, clique, coterie, schism, confederacy, convocation

jurisdiction *noun* 1 AUTHORITY, say, power, control, rule, influence, command, sway, dominion, prerogative, mana (*NZ*)
2 RANGE, area, field, district, bounds, zone, province, circuit, scope, orbit, sphere, compass, dominion

just *adverb* 1 RECENTLY, lately, only now
2 MERELY, but, only, simply, solely, no more than, nothing but
3 BARELY, hardly, only just, scarcely, at most, by a whisker, at a push, by the skin of your teeth
4 EXACTLY, really, quite, completely, totally, perfectly, entirely, truly, absolutely, precisely, altogether, positively
▷ *adjective* 1 FAIR, good, legitimate, honourable, right, square, pure, decent, upright, honest, equitable, righteous, conscientious, impartial, virtuous, lawful, blameless, unbiased, fair-minded, unprejudiced
<< OPPOSITE unfair
2 FITTING, due, correct, deserved, appropriate, justified, reasonable, suitable, decent, sensible, merited, proper, legitimate, desirable, apt, rightful, well-deserved, condign
<< OPPOSITE inappropriate
▷▷ **just about** PRACTICALLY, almost, nearly, close to, virtually, all but, not quite, well-nigh

The expression *just exactly* is considered to be poor style because, since both words mean the same thing, only one or the other is needed. Use *just* – *it's just what they want* – or *exactly* – *it's exactly what they want*, but not both together

justice *noun* 1 FAIRNESS, equity, integrity, honesty, decency, impartiality, rectitude, reasonableness, uprightness, justness, rightfulness, right
<< OPPOSITE injustice
2 JUSTNESS, fairness, legitimacy, reasonableness, right, integrity, honesty, legality, rectitude, rightfulness
3 JUDGE, magistrate, beak (*Brit slang*), His, Her *or* Your Honour

justifiable *adjective* REASONABLE, right, sound, fit, acceptable, sensible, proper,

valid, legitimate, understandable, lawful, well-founded, defensible, tenable, excusable, warrantable, vindicable
  << OPPOSITE indefensible

justification *noun* REASON, grounds, defence, basis, excuse, approval, plea, warrant, apology, rationale, vindication, rationalization, absolution, exoneration, explanation, exculpation, extenuation

justify *verb* EXPLAIN, support, warrant, bear out, legitimize, establish, maintain, confirm, defend, approve, excuse, sustain, uphold, acquit, vindicate, validate, substantiate, exonerate, legalize, absolve, exculpate

justly *adverb* JUSTIFIABLY, rightly, correctly, properly, legitimately, rightfully, with good reason, lawfully

jut *verb* STICK OUT, project, extend, protrude, poke, bulge, overhang, impend

juvenile *noun* CHILD, youth, minor, girl, boy, teenager, infant, adolescent
  << OPPOSITE adult
▷ *adjective* **1** YOUNG, junior, adolescent, youthful, immature
  << OPPOSITE adult
2 IMMATURE, childish, infantile, puerile, young, youthful, inexperienced, boyish, callow, undeveloped, unsophisticated, girlish, babyish, jejune

juxtaposition *noun* PROXIMITY, adjacency, contact, closeness, vicinity, nearness, contiguity, propinquity

kai *noun* (*NZ informal*) FOOD, grub (*slang*), provisions, fare, board, commons, eats (*slang*), feed, diet, meat, bread, tuck (*informal*), tucker (*Austral & NZ informal*), rations, nutrition, tack (*informal*), refreshment, scoff (*slang*), nibbles, foodstuffs, nourishment, chow (*informal*), sustenance, nosh (*slang*), daily bread, victuals, edibles, comestibles, provender, nosebag (*slang*), pabulum (*rare*), nutriment, vittles (*obsolete* or *dialect*), viands, aliment, eatables (*slang*)

kak *noun* (*S African taboo*) 1 FAECES, excrement, stool, muck, manure, dung, droppings, waste matter
2 RUBBISH, nonsense, garbage (*informal*), rot, crap (*taboo slang*), drivel, tripe (*informal*), claptrap (*informal*), poppycock (*informal*), pants, bizzo (*Austral slang*), bull's wool (*Austral & NZ slang*)

kaleidoscopic *adjective* 1 MANY-COLOURED, multi-coloured, harlequin, psychedelic, motley, variegated, prismatic, varicoloured
2 CHANGEABLE, shifting, varied, mobile, variable, fluid, uncertain, volatile, unpredictable, unstable, fluctuating, indefinite, unsteady, protean, mutable, impermanent, inconstant
3 COMPLICATED, complex, confused, confusing, disordered, puzzling, unclear, baffling, bewildering, chaotic, muddled, intricate, jumbled, convoluted, disorganized, disarranged

kamikaze *modifier* SELF-DESTRUCTIVE, suicidal, foolhardy

keel over *verb* 1 (*informal*) COLLAPSE, faint, pass out, black out (*informal*), swoon (*literary*)
2 CAPSIZE, list, upset, founder, overturn, turn over, lean over, tip over, topple over, turn turtle

keen[1] *adjective* 1 EAGER, earnest, spirited, devoted, intense, fierce, enthusiastic, passionate, ardent, avid, fervent, impassioned, zealous, ebullient, wholehearted, fervid, bright-eyed and bushy-tailed (*informal*)
<< OPPOSITE unenthusiastic
2 EARNEST, fierce, intense, vehement, burning, flaming, consuming, eager, passionate, heightened, energetic, ardent, fanatical, fervent, impassioned, fervid
3 SHARP, satirical, incisive, trenchant, pointed, cutting, biting, edged, acute, acid, stinging, piercing, penetrating, searing, tart, withering, scathing, pungent, sarcastic, sardonic, caustic, astringent, vitriolic, acerbic, mordant, razor-like, finely honed
<< OPPOSITE dull
4 PERCEPTIVE, quick, sharp, brilliant, acute, smart, wise, clever, subtle, piercing, penetrating, discriminating, shrewd, discerning, ingenious, astute, intuitive, canny, incisive, insightful, observant, perspicacious, sapient
<< OPPOSITE obtuse
5 PENETRATING, clear, powerful, sharp, acute, sensitive, piercing, discerning, perceptive, observant
6 INTENSE, strong, fierce, relentless, cut-throat

keen[2] *verb* LAMENT, cry, weep, sob, mourn, grieve, howl, sorrow, wail, whine, whimper, bewail

keep *verb* 1 *usually with* **from** PREVENT, hold back, deter, inhibit, block, stall, restrain, hamstring, hamper, withhold, hinder, retard, impede, shackle, keep back
2 *sometimes with* **on** CONTINUE, go on, carry on, persist in, persevere in, remain
3 HOLD ON TO, maintain, retain, keep possession of, save, preserve, nurture, cherish, conserve
<< OPPOSITE lose
4 STORE, put, place, house, hold, deposit, pile, stack, heap, amass, stow
5 CARRY, stock, have, hold, sell, supply, handle, trade in, deal in
6 COMPLY WITH, carry out, honour, fulfil, hold, follow, mind, respect, observe, respond to, embrace, execute, obey, heed, conform to,

adhere to, abide by, act upon
<< OPPOSITE disregard
7 SUPPORT, maintain, sustain, provide for, mind, fund, board, finance, feed, look after, foster, shelter, care for, take care of, nurture, safeguard, cherish, nourish, subsidize
8 RAISE, own, maintain, tend, farm, breed, look after, rear, care for, bring up, nurture, nourish
9 MANAGE, run, administer, be in charge (of), rule, direct, handle, govern, oversee, supervise, preside over, superintend
10 DELAY, detain, hinder, impede, stop, limit, check, arrest, curb, constrain, obstruct, retard, set back
<< OPPOSITE release
11 ASSOCIATE WITH, mix with, mingle with, hang out with (*informal*), hang with (*informal, chiefly US*), be friends with, consort with, run around with (*informal*), hobnob with, socialize with, hang about with, fraternize with
▷ *noun* 1 BOARD, food, maintenance, upkeep, means, living, support, nurture, livelihood, subsistence, kai (*NZ informal*), nourishment, sustenance
2 TOWER, castle, stronghold, dungeon, citadel, fastness, donjon
▷▷ **keep at it** PERSIST, continue, carry on, keep going, stick with it, stay with it, be steadfast, grind it out, persevere, remain with it
▷▷ **keep something back** 1 HOLD BACK, hold, save, set aside, husband, store, retain, preserve, hang on to, conserve, stockpile, hoard, lay up, put by
2 SUPPRESS, hide, reserve, conceal, restrain, cover up, withhold, stifle, censor, repress, smother, muffle, muzzle, keep something under your hat
3 RESTRAIN, control, limit, check, delay, restrict, curb, prohibit, withhold, hold back, constrain, retard, keep a tight rein on
▷▷ **keep something up** 1 CONTINUE, make, maintain, carry on, persist in, persevere with
2 MAINTAIN, sustain, uphold, perpetuate, retain, preserve, prolong
▷▷ **keep up** KEEP PACE, match, compete, contend, emulate, persevere

keeper *noun* CURATOR, guardian, steward, superintendent, attendant, caretaker, overseer, preserver

keeping *noun* CARE, keep, charge, trust, protection, possession, maintenance, custody, patronage, guardianship, safekeeping
▷▷ **in keeping with** IN AGREEMENT WITH, consistent with, in harmony with, in accord with, in compliance with, in conformity with, in balance with, in correspondence with, in proportion with, in congruity with, in observance with

keepsake *noun* SOUVENIR, symbol, token, reminder, relic, remembrance, emblem, memento, favour

keg *noun* BARREL, drum, vat, cask, firkin, tun, hogshead

ken ▷▷ **beyond someone's ken** BEYOND THE KNOWLEDGE OF, beyond the comprehension of, beyond the understanding of, beyond the acquaintance of, beyond the awareness of, beyond the cognizance of

kernel *noun* ESSENCE, core, substance, gist, grain, marrow, germ, nub, pith

key *noun* 1 OPENER, door key, latchkey
2 ANSWER, means, secret, solution, path, formula, passage, clue, cue, pointer, sign
▷ *modifier* ESSENTIAL, leading, major, main, important, chief, necessary, basic, vital, crucial, principal, fundamental, decisive, indispensable, pivotal, must-have
<< OPPOSITE minor

keynote *noun* HEART, centre, theme, core, substance, essence, marrow, kernel, gist, pith

keystone *noun* BASIS, principle, core, crux, ground, source, spring, root, motive, cornerstone, lynchpin, mainspring, fundament, quoin

kia ora *interjection* (NZ) HELLO, hi (*informal*), greetings, gidday *or* g'day (*Austral* & *NZ*), how do you do?, good morning, good evening, good afternoon, welcome

kick *verb* 1 BOOT, strike, knock, punt, put the boot in(to) (*slang*)
2 (*informal*) GIVE UP, break, stop, abandon, quit, cease, eschew, leave off, desist from, end
▷ *noun* 1 (*informal*) THRILL, glow, buzz (*slang*), tingle, high (*slang*), sensation
2 (*informal*) PUNGENCY, force, power, edge, strength, snap (*informal*), punch, intensity, pep, sparkle, vitality, verve, zest, potency, tang, piquancy
▷▷ **kick someone out** (*informal*) DISMISS, remove, reject, get rid of, discharge, expel, oust, eject, evict, toss out, give the boot (*slang*), sack (*informal*), kiss off (*slang, chiefly US* & *Canad*), give (someone) their marching orders, give the push, give the bum's rush (*slang*), show you the door, throw you out on your ear (*informal*), kennet (*Austral slang*), jeff (*Austral slang*)
▷▷ **kick something off** (*informal*) BEGIN, start, open, commence, launch, initiate, get under way, kick-start, get on the road

kickback *noun* BRIBE, payoff, backhander (*slang*), enticement, share, cut (*informal*), payment, gift, reward, incentive, graft (*informal*), sweetener (*slang*), inducement, sop, recompense, hush money (*slang*), payola (*informal*), allurement

kick-off *noun* (*informal*) START, opening, beginning, commencement, outset, starting point, inception

kid[1] *noun* (*informal*) CHILD, girl, boy, baby, lad, teenager, youngster, infant, adolescent, juvenile, toddler, tot, lass, wean, little one, bairn, stripling, sprog (*slang*), munchkin (*informal, chiefly US*), rug rat (*US & Canad informal*), littlie (*Austral informal*), ankle-biter (*Austral slang*), tacker (*Austral slang*)

kid[2] *verb* TEASE, joke, trick, fool, pretend, mock, rag (*Brit*), wind up (*Brit slang*), ridicule, hoax, beguile, gull (*archaic*), delude, jest, bamboozle, hoodwink, cozen, jerk *or* yank someone's chain (*informal*)

kidnap *verb* ABDUCT, remove, steal, capture, seize, snatch (*slang*), hijack, run off with, run away with, make off with, hold to ransom

kill *verb* **1** SLAY, murder, execute, slaughter, destroy, waste (*informal*), do in (*slang*), take out (*slang*), massacre, butcher, wipe out (*informal*), dispatch, cut down, erase, assassinate, eradicate, whack (*informal*), do away with, blow away (*slang, chiefly US*), obliterate, knock off (*slang*), liquidate, decimate, annihilate, neutralize, exterminate, croak, mow down, take (someone's) life, bump off (*slang*), extirpate, wipe from the face of the earth (*informal*)
2 (*informal*) DESTROY, defeat, crush, scotch, still, stop, total (*slang*), ruin, halt, cancel, wreck, shatter, veto, suppress, dismantle, stifle, trash (*slang*), ravage, eradicate, smother, quash, quell, extinguish, annihilate, put paid to

killer *noun* MURDERER, slaughterer, slayer, hit man (*slang*), butcher, gunman, assassin, destroyer, liquidator, terminator, executioner, exterminator

killing *noun* MURDER, massacre, slaughter, execution, dispatch, manslaughter, elimination, slaying, homicide, bloodshed, carnage, fatality, liquidation, extermination, annihilation, eradication, butchery, necktie party (*informal*)
▷ *adjective* **1** (*informal*) TIRING, hard, testing, taxing, difficult, draining, exhausting, punishing, crippling, fatiguing, gruelling, sapping, debilitating, strenuous, arduous, laborious, enervating, backbreaking
2 DEADLY, deathly, dangerous, fatal, destructive, lethal, mortal, murderous, death-dealing
▷▷ **make a killing** (*informal*) PROFIT, gain, clean up (*informal*), be lucky, be successful, make a fortune, strike it rich (*informal*), make a bomb (*slang*), rake it in (*informal*), have a windfall

killjoy *noun* SPOILSPORT, dampener, damper, wet blanket (*informal*)

kin *noun* FAMILY, people, relations, relatives, connections, kindred, kinsmen, kith, kinsfolk, ainga (*NZ*), rellies (*Austral slang*)

kind[1] *adjective* CONSIDERATE, good, loving, kindly, understanding, concerned, friendly, neighbourly, gentle, generous, mild, obliging, sympathetic, charitable, thoughtful, benign, humane, affectionate, compassionate, clement, gracious, indulgent, benevolent, attentive, amiable, courteous, amicable, lenient, cordial, congenial, philanthropic, unselfish, propitious, beneficent, kind-hearted, bounteous, tender-hearted
<< OPPOSITE unkind

kind[2] *noun* **1** CLASS, sort, type, variety, brand, grade, category, genre, classification, league
2 SORT, set, type, ilk, family, race, species, breed, genus
3 NATURE, sort, type, manner, style, quality, character, make-up, habit, stamp, description, mould, essence, temperament, persuasion, calibre, disposition

It is common in informal speech to combine singular and plural in sentences like *children enjoy those kind of stories*. However, this is not acceptable in careful writing, where the plural must be used consistently: *children enjoy those kinds of stories*

kind-hearted *adjective* SYMPATHETIC, kind, generous, helpful, tender, humane, compassionate, gracious, amicable, considerate, altruistic, good-natured, tender-hearted
<< OPPOSITE hard-hearted

kindle *verb* **1** AROUSE, excite, inspire, stir, thrill, stimulate, provoke, induce, awaken, animate, rouse, sharpen, inflame, incite, foment, bestir, enkindle
2 LIGHT, start, ignite, fire, spark, torch, inflame, set fire to, set a match to
<< OPPOSITE extinguish

kindly *adjective* BENEVOLENT, kind, caring, nice, warm, gentle, helpful, pleasant, mild, sympathetic, beneficial, polite, favourable, benign, humane, compassionate, hearty, cordial, considerate, genial, affable, good-natured, beneficent, well-disposed, kind-hearted, warm-hearted
<< OPPOSITE cruel
▷ *adverb* BENEVOLENTLY, politely, generously, thoughtfully, tenderly, lovingly, cordially, affectionately, helpfully, graciously, obligingly, agreeably, indulgently, selflessly, unselfishly, compassionately, considerately
<< OPPOSITE unkindly

kindness *noun* **1** GOODWILL, understanding, charity, grace, humanity, affection, patience, tolerance, goodness, compassion, hospitality, generosity, indulgence, decency, tenderness, clemency, gentleness, philanthropy,

benevolence, magnanimity, fellow-feeling, amiability, beneficence, kindliness
<< OPPOSITE malice
2 GOOD DEED, help, service, aid, favour, assistance, bounty, benefaction

kindred *noun* FAMILY, relations, relatives, connections, flesh, kin, lineage, kinsmen, kinsfolk, ainga (*NZ*), rellies (*Austral slang*)
▷ *adjective* 1 SIMILAR, like, related, allied, corresponding, affiliated, akin, kin, cognate, matching
2 LIKE-MINDED, similar, compatible, understanding, similar, friendly, sympathetic, responsive, agreeable, in tune, congenial, like, companionable

king *noun* RULER, monarch, sovereign, crowned head, leader, lord, prince, Crown, emperor, majesty, head of state, consort, His Majesty, overlord
>> RELATED WORDS *adjectives* royal, regal, monarchical

kingdom *noun* 1 COUNTRY, state, nation, land, division, territory, province, empire, commonwealth, realm, domain, tract, dominion, sovereign state
2 DOMAIN, territory, province, realm, area, department, field, zone, arena, sphere

kink *noun* 1 TWIST, bend, wrinkle, knot, tangle, coil, corkscrew, entanglement, crimp, frizz
2 QUIRK, eccentricity, foible, idiosyncrasy, whim, fetish, vagary, singularity, crotchet
3 FLAW, difficulty, defect, complication, tangle, knot, hitch, imperfection

kinky *adjective* 1 (*Slang*) PERVERTED, warped, deviant, unnatural, degenerated, unsavoury, unhealthy, depraved, licentious, pervy (*slang*)
2 (*informal*) WEIRD, odd, strange, bizarre, peculiar, eccentric, queer, quirky, unconventional, off-the-wall (*slang*), outlandish, oddball (*informal*), wacko (*slang*), outré
3 TWISTED, curled, curly, frizzy, tangled, coiled, crimped, frizzled

kinship *noun* 1 RELATIONSHIP, kin, family ties, consanguinity, ties of blood, blood relationship
2 SIMILARITY, relationship, association, bearing, connection, alliance, correspondence, affinity

kinsman *or* **kinswoman** *noun* RELATIVE, relation, blood relative, fellow tribesman, fellow clansman, rellie (*Austral slang*)

kiosk *noun* BOOTH, stand, counter, stall, newsstand, bookstall

kiss *verb* 1 PECK (*informal*), osculate, snog (*Brit slang*), neck (*informal*), smooch (*informal*), canoodle (*slang*)
2 BRUSH, touch, shave, scrape, graze, caress, glance off, stroke
▷ *noun* PECK (*informal*), snog (*Brit slang*), smacker (*slang*), smooch (*informal*), French kiss, osculation

kit *noun* 1 EQUIPMENT, supplies, materials, tackle, tools, instruments, provisions, implements, rig, apparatus, trappings, utensils, paraphernalia, accoutrements, appurtenances
2 GEAR, things, effects, dress, clothes, clothing, stuff, equipment, uniform, outfit, rig, costume, garments, baggage, equipage
▷▷ **kit something** *or* **someone out** *or* **up** EQUIP, fit, supply, provide with, arm, stock, outfit, costume, furnish, fix up, fit out, deck out, accoutre

kitchen *noun* COOKHOUSE, galley, kitchenette, scullery

knack *noun* SKILL, art, ability, facility, talent, gift, capacity, trick, bent, craft, genius, expertise, forte, flair, competence, ingenuity, propensity, aptitude, dexterity, cleverness, quickness, adroitness, expertness, handiness, skilfulness
<< OPPOSITE ineptitude

knackered *adjective* (*Brit slang*) 1 EXHAUSTED, worn out, tired out, drained, beat (*slang*), done in (*informal*), all in (*slang*), debilitated, prostrated, enervated, ready to drop, dog-tired (*informal*), zonked (*slang*), dead tired, dead beat (*slang*)
2 BROKEN, not working, out of order, not functioning, done in (*informal*), ruined, worn out, on the blink (*slang*), on its last legs

knavish *adjective* (*Archaic*) DISHONEST, tricky, fraudulent, deceptive, unscrupulous, rascally, scoundrelly, deceitful, villainous, unprincipled, dishonourable, roguish
<< OPPOSITE honourable

knead *verb* SQUEEZE, work, massage, manipulate, form, press, shape, stroke, blend, rub, mould

kneel *verb* GENUFLECT, bow, stoop, curtsy *or* curtsey, bow down, kowtow, get down on your knees, make obeisance

knell *noun* RING, sound, toll, chime, clang, peal

knickers *plural noun* UNDERWEAR, smalls, briefs, drawers, panties, bloomers

knife *noun* BLADE, carver, cutter, cutting tool
▷ *verb* CUT, wound, stab, slash, thrust, gore, pierce, spear, jab, bayonet, impale, lacerate

knit *verb* 1 JOIN, unite, link, tie, bond, ally, combine, secure, bind, connect, merge, weave, fasten, meld
2 HEAL, unite, join, link, bind, connect, loop, mend, fasten, intertwine, interlace
3 FURROW, tighten, knot, wrinkle, crease, screw up, pucker, scrunch up

knob *noun* BALL, stud, nub, protuberance, boss, bunch, swell, knot, bulk, lump, bump, projection, snag, hump, protrusion, knurl

knock *verb* 1 BANG, beat, strike, tap, rap, bash (*informal*), thump, buffet, pummel
2 HIT, strike, punch, belt (*informal*), deck (*slang*), slap, chin (*slang*), smack, thump, clap, cuff, smite (*archaic*), thwack, lay one on (*slang*), beat *or* knock seven bells out of (*informal*)
3 (*informal*) CRITICIZE, condemn, put down, run down, abuse, blast, pan (*informal*), slam (*slang*), slate (*informal*), have a go (at) (*informal*), censure, slag (off) (*slang*), denigrate, belittle, disparage, deprecate, diss (*slang, chiefly US*), find fault with, carp at, lambast(e), pick holes in, cast aspersions on, cavil at, pick to pieces, give (someone *or* something) a bad press
▷ *noun* 1 KNOCKING, pounding, beating, tap, hammering, bang, banging, rap, thump, thud
2 BANG, blow, impact, jar, collision, jolt, smash
3 BLOW, hit, punch, crack, belt (*informal*), clip, slap, bash, smack, thump, clout (*informal*), cuff, box
4 (*informal*) SETBACK, check, defeat, blow, upset, reverse, disappointment, hold-up, hitch, reversal, misfortune, rebuff, whammy (*informal, chiefly US*), bummer (*slang*)
▷▷ **knock about** *or* **around** WANDER, travel, roam, rove, range, drift, stray, ramble, straggle, traipse, go walkabout (*Austral*), stravaig (*Scot & Northern English dialect*)
▷▷ **knock about** *or* **around with someone** MIX WITH, associate with, mingle with, hang out with (*informal*), hang with (*informal, chiefly US*), be friends with, consort with, run around with (*informal*), hobnob with, socialize with, accompany, hang about with, fraternize with
▷▷ **knock off** (*informal*) STOP WORK, get out, conclude, shut down, terminate, call it a day (*informal*), finish work, clock off, clock out
▷▷ **knock someone about** *or* **around** HIT, attack, beat, strike, damage, abuse, hurt, injure, wound, assault, harm, batter, slap, bruise, thrash, beat up (*informal*), buffet, maul, work over (*slang*), clobber (*slang*), mistreat, manhandle, maltreat, lambast(e), slap around (*informal*), beat *or* knock seven bells out of (*informal*)
▷▷ **knock someone down** RUN OVER, hit, run down, knock over, mow down
▷▷ **knock someone off** (*Slang*) KILL, murder, do in (*slang*), slaughter, destroy, waste (*informal*), take out (*slang*), execute, massacre, butcher, wipe out (*informal*), dispatch, cut down, erase, assassinate, slay, eradicate, whack (*informal*), do away with, blow away (*slang, chiefly US*), obliterate, liquidate, decimate, annihilate, neutralize, exterminate, croak, mow down, take (someone's) life, bump off (*slang*), extirpate, wipe from the face of the earth (*informal*)
▷▷ **knock someone out** 1 FLOOR, knock unconscious, knock senseless, render unconscious, level, stun, daze
2 ELIMINATE, beat, defeat, trounce, vanquish
3 (*informal*) IMPRESS, move, strike, touch, affect, influence, excite, inspire, grab (*informal*), stir, overwhelm, sway, make an impression on
▷▷ **knock something down** DEMOLISH, destroy, flatten, tear down, level, total (*slang*), fell, ruin, dismantle, trash (*slang*), bulldoze, raze, pulverize, kennet (*Austral slang*), jeff (*Austral slang*)
▷▷ **knock something off** 1 (*Slang*) STEAL, take, nick (*slang, chiefly Brit*), thieve, rob, pinch, cabbage (*Brit slang*), blag (*slang*), pilfer, purloin, filch
2 REMOVE, take away, deduct, debit, subtract

knockabout *adjective* BOISTEROUS, riotous, rollicking, rough-and-tumble, rumbustious, rambunctious (*informal*), harum-scarum, farcical, slapstick

knockout *noun* 1 KILLER BLOW, coup de grâce (*French*), kayo (*slang*), KO *or* K.O. (*slang*)
2 (*informal*) SUCCESS, hit, winner, triumph, smash, sensation, smash hit, stunner (*informal*), smasheroo (*informal*)
<< OPPOSITE failure

knoll HILLOCK

knot *noun* 1 CONNECTION, tie, bond, joint, bow, loop, braid, splice, rosette, ligature
2 GROUP, company, set, band, crowd, pack, squad, circle, crew (*informal*), gang, mob, clique, assemblage
▷ *verb* TIE, secure, bind, complicate, weave, loop, knit, tether, entangle

knotty *adjective* 1 PUZZLING, hard, difficult, complex, complicated, tricky, baffling, intricate, troublesome, perplexing, mystifying, thorny, problematical
2 KNOTTED, rough, rugged, bumpy, gnarled, knobby, nodular

know *verb* 1 HAVE KNOWLEDGE OF, see, understand, recognize, perceive, be aware of, be conscious of
2 BE ACQUAINTED WITH, recognize, associate with, be familiar with, be friends with, be friendly with, have knowledge of, have dealings with, socialize with, fraternize with, be pals with
<< OPPOSITE be unfamiliar with
3 *sometimes with* **about** *or* **of** BE FAMILIAR WITH, experience, understand, ken (*Scot*), comprehend, fathom, apprehend, have knowledge of, be acquainted with, feel certain of, have dealings in, be versed in
<< OPPOSITE be ignorant of
4 RECOGNIZE, remember, identify, recall, place, spot, notice, distinguish, perceive, make out, discern, differentiate, recollect

know-all *noun* (*informal*) SMART ALECK, wise guy (*informal*), smarty (*informal*), clever-clogs (*informal*), clever Dick (*informal*), smarty-pants (*informal*), smartarse (*slang*), wiseacre, smarty-boots (*informal*)

know-how *noun* (*informal*) EXPERTISE, experience, ability, skill, knowledge, facility, talent, command, craft, grasp, faculty, capability, flair, knack, ingenuity, aptitude, proficiency, dexterity, cleverness, deftness, savoir-faire, adroitness, ableness

knowing *adjective* MEANINGFUL, significant, expressive, eloquent, enigmatic, suggestive

knowingly *adverb* DELIBERATELY, purposely, consciously, intentionally, on purpose, wilfully, wittingly

knowledge *noun* **1** UNDERSTANDING, sense, intelligence, judgment, perception, awareness, insight, grasp, appreciation, penetration, comprehension, discernment **2** LEARNING, schooling, education, science, intelligence, instruction, wisdom, scholarship, tuition, enlightenment, erudition
  << OPPOSITE ignorance
3 CONSCIOUSNESS, recognition, awareness, apprehension, cognition, discernment
  << OPPOSITE unawareness
4 ACQUAINTANCE, information, notice, intimacy, familiarity, cognizance
  << OPPOSITE unfamiliarity

knowledgeable *adjective* **1** WELL-INFORMED, acquainted, conversant, au fait (*French*), experienced, understanding, aware, familiar, conscious, in the know (*informal*), cognizant, in the loop, au courant (*French*), clued-up (*informal*) **2** INTELLIGENT, lettered, learned, educated, scholarly, erudite

known *adjective* FAMOUS, well-known, celebrated, popular, common, admitted, noted, published, obvious, familiar, acknowledged, recognized, plain, confessed, patent, manifest, avowed
  << OPPOSITE unknown

koppie *or* **kopje** *noun* (*S African*) HILL, down (*archaic*), fell, mount, height, mound, prominence, elevation, eminence, hilltop, tor, knoll, hillock, brae (*Scot*)

kudos *noun* PRESTIGE, regard, honour, praise, glory, fame, distinction, esteem, acclaim, applause, plaudits, renown, repute, notability, laudation

L l

label *noun* 1 TAG, ticket, tab, marker, flag, tally, sticker, docket (*chiefly Brit*)
2 EPITHET, description, classification, characterization
3 BRAND, company, mark, trademark, brand name, trade name
▷ *verb* 1 TAG, mark, stamp, ticket, flag, tab, tally, sticker, docket (*chiefly Brit*)
2 BRAND, classify, describe, class, call, name, identify, define, designate, characterize, categorize, pigeonhole

laborious *adjective* 1 HARD, difficult, tiring, exhausting, wearing, tough, fatiguing, uphill, strenuous, arduous, tiresome, onerous, burdensome, herculean, wearisome, backbreaking, toilsome
<< OPPOSITE easy
2 INDUSTRIOUS, hard-working, diligent, tireless, persevering, painstaking, indefatigable, assiduous, unflagging, sedulous
3 (*of literary style, etc*) FORCED, laboured, strained, ponderous, not fluent
<< OPPOSITE natural

labour *noun* 1 TOIL, effort, industry, grind (*informal*), pains, sweat (*informal*), slog (*informal*), exertion, drudgery, travail, donkey-work
<< OPPOSITE leisure
2 WORKERS, employees, workforce, labourers, hands, workmen
3 WORK, effort, employment, toil, industry
4 CHILDBIRTH, birth, delivery, contractions, pains, throes, travail, labour pains, parturition
5 CHORE, job, task, undertaking
▷ *verb* 1 WORK, toil, strive, work hard, grind (*informal*), sweat (*informal*), slave, endeavour, plod away, drudge, travail, slog away (*informal*), exert yourself, peg along *or* away (*chiefly Brit*), plug along *or* away (*informal*)
<< OPPOSITE rest
2 STRUGGLE, work, strain, work hard, strive, go for it (*informal*), grapple, toil, make an effort, make every effort, do your best, exert yourself, work like a Trojan
3 OVEREMPHASIZE, stress, elaborate, exaggerate, strain, dwell on, overdo, go on about, make a production (out) of (*informal*), make a federal case of (*US informal*)
4 *usually with* **under** BE DISADVANTAGED BY, suffer from, be a victim of, be burdened by

Labour *adjective* LEFT-WING, Democrat (*US*)

laboured *adjective* 1 DIFFICULT, forced, strained, heavy, awkward
2 CONTRIVED, studied, affected, awkward, unnatural, overdone, ponderous, overwrought

labourer *noun* WORKER, workman, working man, manual worker, hand, blue-collar worker, drudge, unskilled worker, navvy (*Brit informal*), labouring man

labyrinth *noun* MAZE, jungle, tangle, coil, snarl, entanglement

labyrinthine *adjective* MAZELIKE, winding, tangled, intricate, tortuous, convoluted, mazy

lace *noun* 1 NETTING, net, filigree, tatting, meshwork, openwork
2 CORD, tie, string, lacing, thong, shoelace, bootlace
▷ *verb* 1 FASTEN, tie, tie up, do up, secure, bind, close, attach, thread
2 MIX, drug, doctor, add to, spike, contaminate, fortify, adulterate
3 INTERTWINE, interweave, entwine, twine, interlink

lacerate *verb* 1 TEAR, cut, wound, rend, rip, slash, claw, maim, mangle, mangulate (*Austral slang*), gash, jag
2 HURT, wound, rend, torture, distress, torment, afflict, harrow

laceration *noun* CUT, injury, tear, wound, rent, rip, slash, trauma (*Pathology*), gash, mutilation

lack *noun* SHORTAGE, want, absence, deficiency, need, shortcoming, deprivation, inadequacy, scarcity, dearth, privation, shortness, destitution, insufficiency, scantiness
<< OPPOSITE abundance
▷ *verb* MISS, want, need, require, not have, be

without, be short of, be in need of, be deficient in
<< OPPOSITE have

lackey *noun* HANGER-ON, fawner, pawn, attendant, tool, instrument, parasite, cohort (*chiefly US*), valet, menial, minion, footman, sycophant, yes-man, manservant, toady, flunky, flatterer, varlet (*archaic*)

lacking *adjective* DEFICIENT, wanting, needing, missing, inadequate, minus (*informal*), flawed, impaired, sans (*archaic*)

lacklustre *adjective* FLAT, boring, dull, dim, dry, muted, sombre, drab, lifeless, prosaic, leaden, unimaginative, uninspired, unexciting, vapid, lustreless

laconic *adjective* TERSE, short, brief, clipped, to the point, crisp, compact, concise, curt, succinct, pithy, monosyllabic, sententious
<< OPPOSITE long-winded

lacy *adjective* FILIGREE, open, fine, sheer, delicate, frilly, gossamer, gauzy, net-like, lace-like, meshy

lad *noun* BOY, kid (*informal*), guy (*informal*), youth, fellow, youngster, chap (*informal*), juvenile, shaver (*informal*), nipper (*informal*), laddie (*Scot*), stripling

laden *adjective* LOADED, burdened, hampered, weighted, full, charged, taxed, oppressed, fraught, weighed down, encumbered

lady *noun* 1 GENTLEWOMAN, duchess, noble, dame, baroness, countess, aristocrat, viscountess, noblewoman, peeress
2 WOMAN, female, girl, miss, maiden (*archaic*), maid (*archaic*), lass, damsel, lassie (*informal*), charlie (*Austral slang*), chook (*Austral slang*), wahine (NZ)

ladylike *adjective* REFINED, cultured, sophisticated, elegant, proper, modest, respectable, polite, genteel, courtly, well-bred, decorous
<< OPPOSITE unladylike

lag *verb* 1 HANG BACK, delay, drag (behind), trail, linger, be behind, idle, saunter, loiter, straggle, dawdle, tarry, drag your feet (*informal*)
2 DROP, fail, diminish, decrease, flag, fall off, wane, ebb, slacken, lose strength

laggard *noun* STRAGGLER, lounger, lingerer, piker (*Austral & NZ slang*), snail, saunterer, loafer, loiterer, dawdler, skiver (*Brit slang*), idler, slowcoach (*Brit informal*), sluggard, bludger (*Austral & NZ informal*), slowpoke (*US & Canad informal*)

laid-back *adjective* RELAXED, calm, casual, together (*slang*), at ease, easy-going, unflappable (*informal*), unhurried, free and easy, easy-peasy (*slang*)
<< OPPOSITE tense

lair *noun* 1 NEST, den, hole, burrow, resting place
2 HIDE-OUT (*informal*), retreat, refuge, den, sanctuary

laissez faire *or* **laisser faire** *noun* NONINTERVENTION, free trade, individualism, free enterprise, live and let live

lake *noun* POND, pool, reservoir, loch (*Scot*), lagoon, mere, lough (*Irish*), tarn

lame *adjective* 1 DISABLED, handicapped, crippled, limping, defective, hobbling, game, halt (*archaic*)
2 UNCONVINCING, poor, pathetic, inadequate, thin, weak, insufficient, feeble, unsatisfactory, flimsy

lament *verb* BEMOAN, grieve, mourn, weep over, complain about, regret, wail about, deplore, bewail
▷ *noun* 1 COMPLAINT, moaning, moan, keening, wail, wailing, lamentation, plaint, ululation
2 DIRGE, requiem, elegy, threnody, monody, coronach (*Scot & Irish*)

lamentable *adjective* 1 REGRETTABLE, distressing, tragic, unfortunate, harrowing, grievous, woeful, deplorable, mournful, sorrowful, gut-wrenching
2 DISAPPOINTING, poor, miserable, unsatisfactory, mean, low quality, meagre, pitiful, wretched, not much cop (*Brit slang*)

lamentation *noun* SORROW, grief, weeping, mourning, moan, grieving, sobbing, keening, lament, wailing, dirge, plaint, ululation

laminated *adjective* COVERED, coated, overlaid, veneered, faced

lampoon *verb* RIDICULE, mock, mimic, parody, caricature, send up (*Brit informal*), take off (*informal*), make fun of, squib, burlesque, satirize, pasquinade
▷ *noun* SATIRE, parody, caricature, send-up (*Brit informal*), takeoff (*informal*), skit, squib, burlesque, pasquinade

land *noun* 1 GROUND, earth, dry land, terra firma
2 SOIL, ground, earth, clay, dirt, sod, loam
3 COUNTRYSIDE, farming, farmland, rural districts
4 (*Law*) PROPERTY, grounds, estate, acres, real estate, realty, acreage, real property, homestead (*US & Canad*)
5 COUNTRY, nation, region, state, district, territory, province, kingdom, realm, tract, motherland, fatherland
▷ *verb* 1 ARRIVE, dock, put down, moor, berth, alight, touch down, disembark, come to rest, debark
2 (*informal*) GAIN, get, win, score (*slang*), secure, obtain, acquire
▷▷ **land up** END UP, arrive, turn up, wind up, finish up, fetch up (*informal*)
>> RELATED WORD *adjective* terrestrial

landing *noun* 1 COMING IN, arrival, touchdown, disembarkation, disembarkment
2 PLATFORM, jetty, quayside, landing stage
landlord *noun* 1 OWNER, landowner, proprietor, freeholder, lessor, landholder
2 INNKEEPER, host, hotelier, hotel-keeper
landmark *noun* 1 FEATURE, spectacle, monument
2 MILESTONE, turning point, watershed, critical point, tipping point
3 BOUNDARY MARKER, cairn, benchmark, signpost, milepost
landscape *noun* SCENERY, country, view, land, scene, prospect, countryside, outlook, terrain, panorama, vista
landslide *noun* LANDSLIP, avalanche, rockfall
lane *noun* ROAD, street, track, path, strip, way, passage, trail, pathway, footpath, passageway, thoroughfare
language *noun* 1 TONGUE, speech, vocabulary, dialect, idiom, vernacular, patter, lingo (*informal*), patois, lingua franca
2 SPEECH, communication, expression, speaking, talk, talking, conversation, discourse, interchange, utterance, parlance, vocalization, verbalization
3 STYLE, wording, expression, phrasing, vocabulary, usage, parlance, diction, phraseology
languid *adjective* INACTIVE, lazy, indifferent, lethargic, weary, sluggish, inert, uninterested, listless, unenthusiastic, languorous, lackadaisical, torpid, spiritless
<< OPPOSITE energetic
languish *verb* 1 DECLINE, waste away, fade away, wither away, flag, weaken, wilt, sicken
<< OPPOSITE flourish
2 (*Literary*) WASTE AWAY, suffer, rot, be abandoned, be neglected, be disregarded
<< OPPOSITE thrive
3 *often with* **for** PINE, want, long, desire, sigh, hunger, yearn, hanker, eat your heart out over, suspire
languishing *adjective* FADING, failing, declining, flagging, sinking, weakening, deteriorating, withering, wilting, sickening, drooping, droopy, wasting away
lank *adjective* 1 LIMP, lifeless, long, dull, straggling, lustreless
2 THIN, lean, slim, slender, skinny, spare, gaunt, lanky, emaciated, scrawny, attenuated, scraggy, rawboned
lanky *adjective* GANGLING, thin, tall, spare, angular, gaunt, bony, weedy (*informal*), scrawny, rangy, scraggy, rawboned, loose-jointed
<< OPPOSITE chubby
lap[1] *noun* CIRCUIT, course, round, tour, leg, distance, stretch, circle, orbit, loop
lap[2] *verb* 1 RIPPLE, wash, splash, slap, swish, gurgle, slosh, purl, plash
2 DRINK, sip, lick, swallow, gulp, sup
▷▷ **lap something up** RELISH, like, enjoy, appreciate, delight in, savour, revel in, wallow in, accept eagerly
lapse *noun* 1 DECLINE, fall, drop, descent, deterioration, relapse, backsliding
2 MISTAKE, failing, fault, failure, error, slip, negligence, omission, oversight, indiscretion
3 INTERVAL, break, gap, passage, pause, interruption, lull, breathing space, intermission
▷ *verb* 1 SLIP, fall, decline, sink, drop, slide, deteriorate, degenerate
2 END, stop, run out, expire, terminate, become obsolete, become void
lapsed *adjective* 1 EXPIRED, ended, finished, run out, invalid, out of date, discontinued, unrenewed
2 BACKSLIDING, uncommitted, lacking faith, nonpractising
large *adjective* 1 BIG, great, huge, heavy, giant, massive, vast, enormous, tall, considerable, substantial, strapping, immense (*informal*), hefty, gigantic, monumental, bulky, chunky, burly, colossal, hulking, goodly, man-size, brawny, elephantine, thickset, ginormous (*informal*), humongous *or* humungous (*US slang*), sizable *or* sizeable
<< OPPOSITE small
2 MASSIVE, great, big, huge, giant, vast, enormous, considerable, substantial, immense, tidy (*informal*), jumbo (*informal*), gigantic, monumental, mammoth, colossal, gargantuan, stellar (*informal*), king-size, ginormous (*informal*), humongous *or* humungous (*US slang*), sizable *or* sizeable
<< OPPOSITE small
3 PLENTIFUL, full, grand, liberal, sweeping, broad, comprehensive, extensive, generous, lavish, ample, spacious, abundant, grandiose, copious, roomy, bountiful, capacious, profuse
<< OPPOSITE scanty
▷▷ **at large** 1 IN GENERAL, generally, chiefly, mainly, as a whole, in the main
2 FREE, roaming, on the run, fugitive, at liberty, on the loose, unchained, unconfined
▷▷ **by and large** ON THE WHOLE, generally, mostly, in general, all things considered, predominantly, in the main, for the most part, all in all, as a rule, taking everything into consideration
largely *adverb* MAINLY, generally, chiefly, widely, mostly, principally, primarily, considerably, predominantly, extensively, by and large, as a rule, to a large extent, to a great extent
large-scale *adjective* WIDE-RANGING, global,

sweeping, broad, wide, vast, extensive, wholesale, far-reaching

largesse *or* **largess** *noun* 1 GENEROSITY, charity, bounty, philanthropy, munificence, liberality, alms-giving, benefaction, open-handedness
2 GIFT, present, grant, donation, endowment, bounty, bequest

lark (*informal*) *noun* PRANK, game, fun, fling, romp, spree, revel, mischief, caper, frolic, escapade, skylark, gambol, antic, jape, rollick
▷▷ **lark about** FOOL AROUND, play around, romp around, have fun, caper, frolic, cavort, gambol, muck around, make mischief, lark around, rollick, cut capers

lascivious *adjective* 1 LUSTFUL, sensual, immoral, randy (*informal, chiefly Brit*), horny (*slang*), voluptuous, lewd, wanton, salacious, prurient, lecherous, libidinous, licentious, unchaste
2 BAWDY, dirty, offensive, crude, obscene, coarse, indecent, blue, vulgar, immoral, pornographic, suggestive, X-rated (*informal*), scurrilous, smutty, ribald

lash[1] *verb* 1 POUND, beat, strike, hammer, drum, smack (*dialect*)
2 CENSURE, attack, blast, put down, criticize, slate (*informal, chiefly Brit*), ridicule, scold, berate, castigate, lampoon, tear into (*informal*), flay, upbraid, satirize, lambast(e), belabour
3 WHIP, beat, thrash, birch, flog, lam (*slang*), scourge, chastise, lambast(e), flagellate, horsewhip
▷ *noun* BLOW, hit, strike, stroke, stripe, swipe (*informal*)

lash[2] *verb* FASTEN, join, tie, secure, bind, rope, strap, make fast

lass *noun* GIRL, young woman, miss, bird (*slang*), maiden, chick (*slang*), maid, damsel, colleen (*Irish*), lassie (*informal*), wench (*facetious*), charlie (*Austral slang*), chook (*Austral slang*)

last[1] *adjective* 1 MOST RECENT, latest, previous
2 HINDMOST, furthest, final, at the end, remotest, furthest behind, most distant, rearmost, aftermost
<< OPPOSITE foremost
3 FINAL, closing, concluding, ultimate, utmost
<< OPPOSITE first
▷ *adverb* IN *or* AT THE END, after, behind, in the rear, bringing up the rear
▷ *noun* END, ending, close, finish, conclusion, completion, finale, termination
▷▷ **at last** FINALLY, eventually, in the end, ultimately, at the end of the day, at length, at long last, in conclusion, in the fullness of time
▷▷ **the last word** 1 FINAL DECISION, final say, final statement, conclusive comment
2 LEADING, best, first, highest, finest, cream, supreme, elite, first-class, foremost, first-rate, superlative, pre-eminent, unsurpassed, crème de la crème (*French*), most excellent

Since *last* can mean either *after all others* or *most recent*, it is better to avoid using this word where ambiguity might arise, as in *her last novel*. *Final* or *latest* should be used as alternatives in such contexts to avoid any possible confusion

last[2] *verb* CONTINUE, keep, remain, survive, wear, carry on, endure, hold on, persist, keep on, hold out, abide
<< OPPOSITE end

last-ditch *adjective* FINAL, frantic, desperate, struggling, straining, heroic, all-out (*informal*)

lasting *adjective* CONTINUING, long-term, permanent, enduring, remaining, eternal, abiding, long-standing, perennial, lifelong, durable, perpetual, long-lasting, deep-rooted, indelible, unending, undying, unceasing
<< OPPOSITE passing

lastly *conjunction* FINALLY, to conclude, at last, in the end, ultimately, all in all, to sum up, in conclusion

latch *noun* FASTENING, catch, bar, lock, hook, bolt, clamp, hasp, sneck (*dialect*)
▷ *verb* FASTEN, bar, secure, lock, bolt, make fast, sneck (*dialect*)

late *adjective* 1 OVERDUE, delayed, last-minute, belated, tardy, behind time, unpunctual, behindhand
<< OPPOSITE early
2 DEAD, deceased, departed, passed on, old, former, previous, preceding, defunct
<< OPPOSITE alive
3 RECENT, new, advanced, fresh
<< OPPOSITE old
▷ *adverb* BEHIND TIME, belatedly, tardily, behindhand, dilatorily, unpunctually
<< OPPOSITE early

lately *adverb* RECENTLY, of late, just now, in recent times, not long ago, latterly

lateness *noun* DELAY, late date, retardation, tardiness, unpunctuality, belatedness, advanced hour

latent *adjective* HIDDEN, secret, concealed, invisible, lurking, veiled, inherent, unseen, dormant, undeveloped, quiescent, immanent, unrealized, unexpressed
<< OPPOSITE obvious

later *adverb* AFTERWARDS, after, next, eventually, in time, subsequently, later on, thereafter, in a while, in due course, at a later date, by and by, at a later time
▷ *adjective* SUBSEQUENT, next, following, ensuing

lateral *adjective* SIDEWAYS, side, flanking, edgeways, sideward

latest *adjective* UP-TO-DATE, current, fresh,

newest, happening (*informal*), modern, most recent, up-to-the-minute

lather *noun* **1** FROTH, soap, bubbles, foam, suds, soapsuds
2 (*informal*) FLUSTER, state (*informal*), sweat, fever, fuss, flap (*informal*), stew (*informal*), dither (*chiefly Brit*), twitter (*informal*), tizzy (*informal*), pother
▷ *verb* FROTH, soap, foam

latitude *noun* SCOPE, liberty, indulgence, freedom, play, room, space, licence, leeway, laxity, elbowroom, unrestrictedness

latter *noun* SECOND, last, last-mentioned, second-mentioned
▷ *adjective* LAST, later, latest, ending, closing, final, concluding
<< OPPOSITE earlier

The latter should only be used to specify the second of two items, for example in *if I had to choose between the hovercraft and the ferry, I would opt for the latter*. Where there are three or more items, the last can be referred to as *the last-named*, but not *the latter*

latterly *adverb* RECENTLY, lately, of late, hitherto

lattice *noun* GRID, network, web, grating, mesh, grille, trellis, fretwork, tracery, latticework, openwork, reticulation

laud *verb* (*Literary*) PRAISE, celebrate, honour, acclaim, approve, magnify (*archaic*), glorify, extol, sing *or* sound the praises of

laudable *adjective* PRAISEWORTHY, excellent, worthy, admirable, of note, commendable, creditable, meritorious, estimable
<< OPPOSITE blameworthy

laugh *verb* CHUCKLE, giggle, snigger, crack up (*informal*), cackle, chortle, guffaw, titter, roar, bust a gut (*informal*), be convulsed (*informal*), be in stitches, crease up (*informal*), split your sides, be rolling in the aisles (*informal*)
▷ *noun* **1** CHORTLE, giggle, chuckle, snigger, guffaw, titter, belly laugh, roar, shriek
2 (*informal*) JOKE, scream (*informal*), hoot (*informal*), lark, prank
3 (*informal*) CLOWN, character (*informal*), scream (*informal*), comic, caution (*informal*), wit, comedian, entertainer, card (*informal*), wag, joker, hoot (*informal*), humorist
▷▷ **laugh at something** *or* **someone** MAKE FUN OF, mock, tease, ridicule, taunt, jeer, deride, scoff at, belittle, lampoon, take the mickey out of (*informal*), pour scorn on, make a mock of
▷▷ **laugh something off** DISREGARD, ignore, dismiss, overlook, shrug off, minimize, brush aside, make light of, pooh-pooh

laughable *adjective* **1** RIDICULOUS, absurd, ludicrous, preposterous, farcical, nonsensical, derisory, risible, derisive, worthy of scorn
2 FUNNY, amusing, hilarious, humorous, diverting, comical, droll, mirthful

laughing stock *noun* FIGURE OF FUN, target, victim, butt, fair game, Aunt Sally (*Brit*), everybody's fool

laughter *noun* **1** CHUCKLING, laughing, giggling, chortling, guffawing, tittering, cachinnation
2 AMUSEMENT, entertainment, humour, glee, fun, mirth, hilarity, merriment

launch *verb* **1** PROPEL, fire, dispatch, discharge, project, send off, set in motion, send into orbit
2 BEGIN, start, open, initiate, introduce, found, set up, originate, commence, get under way, instigate, inaugurate, embark upon
▷ *noun* **1** PROPELLING, projection, sendoff
2 BEGINNING, start, introduction, initiation, opening, founding, setting-up, inauguration, commencement, instigation
▷▷ **launch into something** START ENTHUSIASTICALLY, begin, initiate, embark on, instigate, inaugurate, embark upon

launder *verb* **1** WASH, clean, dry-clean, tub, wash and iron, wash and press
2 PROCESS, doctor, manipulate

laurel ▷▷ **rest on your laurels** SIT BACK, relax, take it easy, relax your efforts

lavatory *noun* TOILET, bathroom, loo (*Brit informal*), bog (*slang*), can (*US & Canad slang*), john (*slang, chiefly US & Canad*), head(s) (*Nautical slang*), throne (*informal*), closet, privy, cloakroom (*Brit*), urinal, latrine, washroom, powder room, ablutions (*Military informal*), crapper (*taboo slang*), water closet, khazi (*slang*), pissoir (*French*), Gents *or* Ladies, little boy's room *or* little girl's room (*informal*), (public) convenience, W.C., dunny (*Austral & NZ old-fashioned informal*), bogger (*Austral slang*), brasco (*Austral slang*)

lavish *adjective* **1** GRAND, magnificent, splendid, lush, abundant, sumptuous, exuberant, opulent, copious, luxuriant, profuse
<< OPPOSITE stingy
2 EXTRAVAGANT, wild, excessive, exaggerated, unreasonable, wasteful, prodigal, unrestrained, intemperate, immoderate, improvident, thriftless
<< OPPOSITE thrifty
3 GENEROUS, free, liberal, bountiful, effusive, open-handed, unstinting, munificent
<< OPPOSITE stingy
▷ *verb* SHOWER, pour, heap, deluge, dissipate
<< OPPOSITE stint

law *noun* **1** CONSTITUTION, code, legislation, charter, jurisprudence
2 STATUTE, act, bill, rule, demand, order, command, code, regulation, resolution,

decree, canon, covenant, ordinance, commandment, enactment, edict
3 PRINCIPLE, standard, code, formula, criterion, canon, precept, axiom, kaupapa (NZ)
4 THE LEGAL PROFESSION, the bar, barristers
▷▷ **lay down the law** BE DOGMATIC, call the shots (*informal*), pontificate, rule the roost, crack the whip, boss around, dogmatize, order about *or* around
>> RELATED WORDS *adjectives* legal, judicial

law-abiding *adjective* OBEDIENT, good, peaceful, honourable, orderly, honest, lawful, compliant, dutiful, peaceable

lawful *adjective* LEGAL, constitutional, just, proper, valid, warranted, legitimate, authorized, rightful, permissible, legalized, allowable, licit
<< OPPOSITE unlawful

lawless *adjective* DISORDERLY, wild, unruly, rebellious, chaotic, reckless, insurgent, anarchic, riotous, unrestrained, seditious, mutinous, insubordinate, ungoverned
<< OPPOSITE law-abiding

lawlessness *noun* ANARCHY, disorder, chaos, reign of terror, mob rule, mobocracy, ochlocracy

lawsuit *noun* CASE, cause, action, trial, suit, argument, proceedings, dispute, contest, prosecution, legal action, indictment, litigation, industrial tribunal, legal proceedings

lawyer *noun* LEGAL ADVISER, attorney, solicitor, counsel, advocate, barrister, counsellor, legal representative

lax *adjective* SLACK, casual, careless, sloppy (*informal*), easy-going, negligent, lenient, slapdash, neglectful, slipshod, remiss, easy-peasy (*slang*), overindulgent
<< OPPOSITE strict

laxative *noun* PURGATIVE, salts, purge, cathartic, physic (*rare*), aperient

lay[1] *verb* 1 PLACE, put, set, spread, plant, establish, settle, leave, deposit, put down, set down, posit
2 DEVISE, plan, design, prepare, work out, plot, hatch, contrive, concoct
3 PRODUCE, bear, deposit
4 ARRANGE, prepare, make, organize, position, locate, set out, devise, put together, dispose, draw up
5 ATTRIBUTE, charge, assign, allocate, allot, ascribe, impute
6 PUT FORWARD, offer, present, advance, lodge, submit, bring forward
7 BET, stake, venture, gamble, chance, risk, hazard, wager, give odds
▷▷ **lay into someone** (*informal*) ATTACK, hit, set about, hit out at, assail, tear into, pitch into (*informal*), go for the jugular, lambast(e), belabour, lash into, let fly at
▷▷ **lay off** (*informal*) STOP, give up, quit, cut it out, leave alone, pack in, abstain, leave off, give over (*informal*), let up, get off someone's back (*informal*), give it a rest (*informal*)
▷▷ **lay someone off** DISMISS, fire (*informal*), release, drop, sack (*informal*), pay off, discharge, oust, let go, make redundant, give notice to, give the boot to (*slang*), give the sack to (*informal*), give someone their cards, kennet (*Austral slang*), jeff (*Austral slang*)
▷▷ **lay someone out** (*informal*) KNOCK OUT, fell, floor, knock unconscious, knock for six, kayo (*slang*)
▷▷ **lay someone up** (*informal*) CONFINE (TO BED), hospitalize, incapacitate
▷▷ **lay something aside** ABANDON, reject, dismiss, postpone, shelve, put off, renounce, put aside, cast aside
▷▷ **lay something bare** REVEAL, show, expose, disclose, unveil, divulge
▷▷ **lay something down** 1 STIPULATE, state, establish, prescribe, assume, formulate, affirm, ordain, set down, postulate
2 SACRIFICE, give up, yield, surrender, turn over, relinquish
▷▷ **lay something in** STORE (UP), collect, build up, accumulate, buy in, amass, stockpile, hoard, stock up, heap up
▷▷ **lay something on** PROVIDE, prepare, supply, organize, give, cater (for), furnish, purvey
▷▷ **lay something out** 1 ARRANGE, order, design, display, exhibit, put out, spread out
2 (*informal*) SPEND, pay, invest, fork out (*slang*), expend, shell out (*informal*), disburse

In standard English, the verb *to lay* (meaning 'to put something somewhere') always needs an object, for example *the Queen laid a wreath*. By contrast, the verb *to lie* is always used without an object, for example *he was just lying there*

lay[2] *adjective* 1 NONCLERICAL, secular, non-ordained, laic, laical
2 NONSPECIALIST, amateur, unqualified, untrained, inexpert, nonprofessional

layer *noun* 1 COVERING, film, cover, sheet, coating, coat, blanket, mantle
2 TIER, level, seam, stratum

layman *noun* NONPROFESSIONAL, amateur, outsider, lay person, non-expert, nonspecialist

lay-off *noun* UNEMPLOYMENT, firing (*informal*), sacking (*informal*), dismissal, discharge

layout *noun* ARRANGEMENT, design, draft, outline, format, plan, formation, geography

laze *verb* 1 IDLE, lounge, hang around, loaf, stand around, loll
2 *often with* **away** KILL TIME, waste time, fritter

away, pass time, while away the hours, veg out (*slang, chiefly US*), fool away

laziness *noun* IDLENESS, negligence, inactivity, slowness, sloth, sluggishness, slackness, indolence, tardiness, dilatoriness, slothfulness, do-nothingness, faineance

lazy *adjective* **1** IDLE, inactive, indolent, slack, negligent, inert, remiss, workshy, slothful, shiftless
<< OPPOSITE industrious
2 LETHARGIC, languorous, slow-moving, languid, sleepy, sluggish, drowsy, somnolent, torpid
<< OPPOSITE quick

leach *verb* EXTRACT, strain, drain, filter, seep, percolate, filtrate, lixiviate (*Chemistry*)

lead *verb* **1** GO IN FRONT (OF), head, be in front (of), be at the head (of), walk in front (of)
2 GUIDE, conduct, steer, escort, precede, usher, pilot, show the way
3 CONNECT TO, link, open onto
4 BE AHEAD (OF), be first, exceed, be winning, excel, surpass, come first, transcend, outstrip, outdo, blaze a trail
5 COMMAND, rule, govern, preside over, head, control, manage, direct, supervise, be in charge of, head up
6 LIVE, have, spend, experience, pass, undergo
7 RESULT IN, cause, produce, contribute, generate, bring about, bring on, give rise to, conduce
8 CAUSE, prompt, persuade, move, draw, influence, motivate, prevail, induce, incline, dispose
▷ *noun* **1** FIRST PLACE, winning position, primary position, vanguard, van
2 ADVANTAGE, start, advance, edge, margin, winning margin
3 EXAMPLE, direction, leadership, guidance, model, pattern
4 CLUE, tip, suggestion, trace, hint, guide, indication, pointer, tip-off
5 LEADING ROLE, principal, protagonist, title role, star part, principal part
6 LEASH, line, cord, rein, tether
▷ *adjective* MAIN, prime, top, leading, first, head, chief, premier, primary, most important, principal, foremost
▷▷ **lead off** BEGIN, start, open, set out, kick off (*informal*), initiate, commence, get going, get under way, inaugurate, start the ball rolling (*informal*)
▷▷ **lead someone on** ENTICE, tempt, lure, mislead, draw on, seduce, deceive, beguile, delude, hoodwink, inveigle, string along (*informal*)
▷▷ **lead up to something** INTRODUCE, approach, prepare for, intimate, pave the way for, prepare the way, make advances, make overtures, work round to

leaden *adjective* **1** GREY, dingy, overcast, sombre, lacklustre, dark grey, greyish, lustreless, louring *or* lowering
2 LABOURED, wooden, stiff, sluggish, plodding, stilted, humdrum
3 LIFELESS, dull, gloomy, dismal, dreary, languid, listless, spiritless
4 HEAVY, lead, crushing, oppressive, cumbersome, inert, onerous, burdensome

leader *noun* PRINCIPAL, president, head, chief, boss (*informal*), director, manager, chairman, captain, chair, premier, governor, commander, superior, ruler, conductor, controller, counsellor, supervisor, superintendent, big name, big gun (*informal*), chairwoman, chieftain, bigwig (*informal*), ringleader, chairperson, big shot (*informal*), overseer, big cheese (*slang* or *old-fashioned*), big noise (*informal*), big hitter (*informal*), baas (*S African*), torchbearer, number one, sherang (*Austral* & *NZ*)
<< OPPOSITE follower

leadership *noun* **1** AUTHORITY, control, influence, command, premiership, captaincy, governance, headship, superintendency
2 GUIDANCE, government, authority, management, administration, direction, supervision, domination, directorship, superintendency

leading *adjective* PRINCIPAL, top, major, main, first, highest, greatest, ruling, chief, prime, key, primary, supreme, most important, outstanding, governing, superior, dominant, foremost, pre-eminent, unsurpassed, number one
<< OPPOSITE minor

leaf *noun* **1** FROND, flag, needle, pad, blade, bract, cotyledon, foliole
2 PAGE, sheet, folio
▷▷ **leaf through something** (with *book, magazine* etc. as object) SKIM, glance through, scan, browse, look through, dip into, flick through, flip through, thumb through, riffle through
▷▷ **turn over a new leaf** REFORM, change, improve, amend, make a fresh start, begin anew, change your ways, mend your ways

leaflet *noun* BOOKLET, notice, advert (*Brit informal*), brochure, bill, circular, flyer, tract, pamphlet, handout, mailshot, handbill

leafy *adjective* GREEN, leaved, leafed, shaded, shady, summery, verdant, bosky (*literary*), springlike, in foliage

league *noun* **1** ASSOCIATION, union, alliance, coalition, group, order, band, corporation, combination, partnership, federation, compact, consortium, guild, confederation, fellowship, fraternity, confederacy

2 CLASS, group, level, category, ability group
▷▷ **in league with someone** COLLABORATING WITH, leagued with, allied with, conspiring with, working together with, in cooperation with, in cahoots with (*informal*), hand in glove with

leak *verb* 1 ESCAPE, pass, spill, release, discharge, drip, trickle, ooze, seep, exude, percolate
2 DISCLOSE, tell, reveal, pass on, give away, make public, divulge, let slip, make known, spill the beans (*informal*), blab (*informal*), let the cat out of the bag, blow wide open (*slang*)
▷ *noun* 1 LEAKAGE, leaking, discharge, drip, oozing, seepage, percolation
2 HOLE, opening, crack, puncture, aperture, chink, crevice, fissure, perforation
3 DISCLOSURE, exposé, exposure, admission, revelation, uncovering, betrayal, unearthing, divulgence

leaky *adjective* LEAKING, split, cracked, punctured, porous, waterlogged, perforated, holey, not watertight

lean[1] *verb* 1 BEND, tip, slope, incline, tilt, heel, slant
2 REST, prop, be supported, recline, repose
3 TEND, prefer, favour, incline, be prone to, gravitate, be disposed to, have a propensity to
▷▷ **lean on someone** DEPEND ON, trust, rely on, cling to, count on, confide in, have faith in

lean[2] *adjective* THIN, slim, slender, skinny, angular, trim, spare, gaunt, bony, lanky, wiry, emaciated, scrawny, svelte, lank, rangy, scraggy, macilent (*rare*)
<< OPPOSITE fat

leaning *noun* TENDENCY, liking for, bias, inclination, taste, bent, disposition, penchant, propensity, aptitude, predilection, proclivity, partiality, proneness

leap *verb* 1 JUMP, spring, bound, bounce, hop, skip, caper, cavort, frisk, gambol
2 VAULT, clear, jump, bound, spring
▷ *noun* 1 JUMP, spring, bound, hop, skip, vault, caper, frisk
2 RISE, change, increase, soaring, surge, escalation, upsurge, upswing
▷▷ **leap at something** ACCEPT EAGERLY, seize on, jump at

learn *verb* 1 MASTER, grasp, acquire, pick up, take in, attain, become able, familiarize yourself with
2 DISCOVER, hear, understand, gain knowledge, find out about, become aware, discern, ascertain, come to know, suss (out) (*slang*)
3 MEMORIZE, commit to memory, learn by heart, learn by rote, get (something) word-perfect, learn parrot-fashion, get off pat, con (*archaic*)

learned *adjective* SCHOLARLY, experienced, lettered, cultured, skilled, expert, academic, intellectual, versed, literate, well-informed, erudite, highbrow, well-read
<< OPPOSITE uneducated

learner *noun* STUDENT, pupil, scholar, novice, beginner, trainee, apprentice, disciple, neophyte, tyro
<< OPPOSITE expert

learning *noun* KNOWLEDGE, study, education, schooling, research, scholarship, tuition, enlightenment

lease *verb* HIRE, rent, let, loan, charter, rent out, hire out

leash *noun* 1 LEAD, line, restraint, cord, rein, tether
2 RESTRAINT, hold, control, check, curb
▷ *verb* TETHER, control, secure, restrain, tie up, hold back, fasten

least *adjective* SMALLEST, meanest, fewest, minutest, lowest, tiniest, minimum, slightest, minimal
▷▷ **at least** AT THE MINIMUM, at the very least, not less than

leathery *adjective* TOUGH, hard, rough, hardened, rugged, wrinkled, durable, leathern (*archaic*), coriaceous, leatherlike

leave[1] *verb* 1 DEPART FROM, withdraw from, go from, escape from, desert, quit, flee, exit, pull out of, retire from, move out of, disappear from, run away from, forsake, flit (*informal*), set out from, go away from, hook it (*slang*), pack your bags (*informal*), make tracks, abscond from, decamp from, sling your hook (*Brit slang*), slope off from, take your leave of, do a bunk from (*Brit slang*), take yourself off from (*informal*)
<< OPPOSITE arrive
2 QUIT, give up, get out of, resign from, drop out of
3 GIVE UP, abandon, desert, dump (*informal*), drop, surrender, ditch (*informal*), chuck (*informal*), discard, relinquish, renounce, jilt (*informal*), cast aside, forbear, leave in the lurch
<< OPPOSITE stay with
4 ENTRUST, commit, delegate, refer, hand over, assign, consign, allot, cede, give over
5 BEQUEATH, will, transfer, endow, transmit, confer, hand down, devise (*Law*), demise
6 FORGET, lay down, leave behind, mislay
7 CAUSE, produce, result in, generate, deposit
▷▷ **leave off something** STOP, end, finish, give up, cease, halt, break off, refrain from, abstain from, discontinue, knock off (*informal*), give over (*informal*), kick (*informal*), desist, keep off, belay (*Nautical*)
▷▷ **leave something** *or* **someone out** OMIT, exclude, miss out, forget, except, reject, ignore, overlook, neglect, skip, disregard, bar, cast aside, count out

leave² *noun* **1** HOLIDAY, break, vacation, time off, sabbatical, leave of absence, furlough, schoolie (*Austral*), accumulated day off *or* ADO (*Austral*)
2 PERMISSION, freedom, sanction, liberty, concession, consent, allowance, warrant, authorization, dispensation
<< OPPOSITE refusal
3 DEPARTURE, parting, withdrawal, goodbye, farewell, retirement, leave-taking, adieu, valediction
<< OPPOSITE arrival

leave-taking *noun* DEPARTURE, going, leaving, parting, goodbye, farewell, valediction, sendoff (*informal*)

lecherous *adjective* LUSTFUL, randy (*informal, chiefly Brit*), raunchy (*slang*), lewd, wanton, carnal, salacious, prurient, lascivious, libidinous, licentious, lubricious (*literary*), concupiscent, goatish (*archaic* or *literary*), unchaste, ruttish
<< OPPOSITE puritanical

lechery *noun* LUSTFULNESS, lust, licentiousness, salaciousness, sensuality, profligacy, debauchery, prurience, womanizing, carnality, lewdness, wantonness, lasciviousness, libertinism, concupiscence, randiness (*informal, chiefly Brit*), leching (*informal*), rakishness, lubricity, libidinousness, lecherousness

lecture *noun* **1** TALK, address, speech, lesson, instruction, presentation, discourse, sermon, exposition, harangue, oration, disquisition
2 TELLING-OFF (*informal*), rebuke, reprimand, talking-to (*informal*), heat (*slang, chiefly US & Canad*), going-over (*informal*), wigging (*Brit slang*), censure, scolding, chiding, dressing-down (*informal*), reproof, castigation
▷ *verb* **1** TALK, speak, teach, address, discourse, spout, expound, harangue, give a talk, hold forth, expatiate
2 TELL OFF (*informal*), berate, scold, reprimand, carpet (*informal*), censure, castigate, chide, admonish, tear into (*informal*), read someone the riot act, reprove, bawl someone out (*informal*), chew someone out (*US & Canad informal*), tear someone off a strip (*Brit informal*), give someone a rocket (*Brit & NZ informal*), give someone a talking-to (*informal*), give someone a dressing-down (*informal*), give someone a telling-off (*informal*)

ledge *noun* SHELF, step, ridge, projection, mantle, sill

lee *noun* SHELTER, cover, screen, protection, shadow, shade, shield, refuge

leech *noun* PARASITE, hanger-on, sycophant, freeloader (*slang*), sponger (*informal*), ligger (*slang*), bloodsucker (*informal*), quandong (*Austral slang*)

leer *verb* GRIN, eye, stare, wink, squint, goggle, smirk, drool, gloat, ogle
▷ *noun* GRIN, stare, wink, squint, smirk, drool, gloat, ogle

leery *adjective* (*Slang*) WARY, cautious, uncertain, suspicious, doubting, careful, shy, sceptical, dubious, unsure, distrustful, on your guard, chary

lees *plural noun* SEDIMENT, grounds, refuse, deposit, precipitate, dregs, settlings

leeway *noun* ROOM, play, space, margin, scope, latitude, elbowroom

left *adjective* **1** LEFT-HAND, port, larboard (*Nautical*)
2 (*of politics*) SOCIALIST, liberal, radical, progressive, left-wing, leftist
>> RELATED WORDS *adjectives* sinister, sinistral

leftover *noun* REMNANT, leaving, remains, scrap, oddment
▷ *adjective* SURPLUS, remaining, extra, excess, unwanted, unused, uneaten

left-wing *adjective* SOCIALIST, communist, red (*informal*), radical, leftist, liberal, revolutionary, militant, Marxist, Bolshevik, Leninist, collectivist, Trotskyite

left-winger *noun* SOCIALIST, communist, red (*informal*), radical, revolutionary, militant, Marxist, Bolshevik, Leninist, Trotskyite

leg *noun* **1** LIMB, member, shank, lower limb, pin (*informal*), stump (*informal*)
2 SUPPORT, prop, brace, upright
3 STAGE, part, section, stretch, lap, segment, portion
▷▷ **leg it** (*informal*) RUN, walk, escape, flee, hurry, run away, make off, make tracks, hotfoot, go on foot, skedaddle (*informal*)
▷▷ **not have a leg to stand on** (*informal*) HAVE NO BASIS, be vulnerable, be undermined, be invalid, be illogical, be defenceless, lack support, be full of holes
▷▷ **on its** *or* **your last legs** WORN OUT, dying, failing, exhausted, giving up the ghost, at death's door, about to collapse, about to fail, about to break down
▷▷ **pull someone's leg** (*informal*) TEASE, joke, trick, fool, kid (*informal*), have (someone) on, rag, rib (*informal*), wind up (*Brit slang*), deceive, hoax, make fun of, poke fun at, twit, chaff, lead someone up the garden path, jerk *or* yank someone's chain (*informal*)
▷▷ **shake a leg** (*informal*) HURRY, rush, move it, hasten, get cracking (*informal*), get a move on (*informal*), look lively (*informal*), stir your stumps (*informal*)
▷▷ **stretch your legs** TAKE A WALK, exercise, stroll, promenade, move about, go for a walk, take the air

legacy *noun* BEQUEST, inheritance,

endowment, gift, estate, devise (*Law*), heirloom

legal *adjective* **1** JUDICIAL, judiciary, forensic, juridical, jurisdictive
2 LAWFUL, allowed, sanctioned, constitutional, proper, valid, legitimate, authorized, rightful, permissible, legalized, allowable, within the law, licit

legalistic *adjective* HAIRSPLITTING, narrow, strict, contentious, literal, narrow-minded, polemical, litigious, disputatious

legality *noun* LAWFULNESS, validity, legitimacy, accordance with the law, permissibility, rightfulness, admissibleness

legalize *or* **legalise** *verb* PERMIT, allow, approve, sanction, license, legitimate, authorize, validate, legitimize, make legal, decriminalize

legal tender *noun* CURRENCY, money, medium, payment, specie

legend *noun* **1** MYTH, story, tale, fiction, narrative, saga, fable, folk tale, urban myth, urban legend, folk story
2 CELEBRITY, star, phenomenon, genius, spectacle, wonder, big name, marvel, prodigy, luminary, celeb (*informal*), megastar (*informal*)
3 INSCRIPTION, title, caption, device, device, motto, rubric

legendary *adjective* **1** FAMOUS, celebrated, well-known, acclaimed, renowned, famed, immortal, illustrious
<< OPPOSITE unknown
2 MYTHICAL, fabled, traditional, romantic, fabulous, fanciful, fictitious, storybook, apocryphal
<< OPPOSITE factual

legible *adjective* READABLE, clear, plain, bold, neat, distinct, easy to read, easily read, decipherable

legion *noun* **1** ARMY, company, force, division, troop, brigade
2 MULTITUDE, host, mass, drove, number, horde, myriad, throng
▷ *adjective* VERY MANY, numerous, countless, myriad, numberless, multitudinous

legislate *verb* MAKE LAWS, establish laws, prescribe, enact laws, pass laws, ordain, codify laws, put laws in force

legislation *noun* **1** LAW, act, ruling, rule, bill, measure, regulation, charter, statute
2 LAWMAKING, regulation, prescription, enactment, codification

legislative *adjective* LAW-MAKING, parliamentary, congressional, judicial, ordaining, law-giving, juridical, jurisdictive

legislator *noun* LAWMAKER, parliamentarian, lawgiver

legislature *noun* PARLIAMENT, house, congress, diet, senate, assembly, chamber, law-making body

legitimate *adjective* **1** LAWFUL, real, true, legal, acknowledged, sanctioned, genuine, proper, authentic, statutory, authorized, rightful, kosher (*informal*), dinkum (*Austral & NZ informal*), legit (*slang*), licit
<< OPPOSITE unlawful
2 REASONABLE, just, correct, sensible, valid, warranted, logical, justifiable, well-founded, admissible
<< OPPOSITE unreasonable
▷ *verb* LEGITIMIZE, allow, permit, sanction, authorize, legalize, give the green light to, legitimatize, pronounce lawful

legitimize *or* **legitimise** *verb* LEGALIZE, permit, sanction, legitimate, authorize, give the green light to, pronounce lawful

leisure *noun* SPARE, free, rest, holiday, quiet, ease, retirement, relaxation, vacation, recreation, time off, breathing space, spare moments
<< OPPOSITE work
▷▷ **at one's leisure** IN YOUR OWN (GOOD) TIME, in due course, at your convenience, unhurriedly, when it suits you, without hurry, at an unhurried pace, when you get round to it (*informal*)

leisurely *adjective* UNHURRIED, relaxed, slow, easy, comfortable, gentle, lazy, laid-back (*informal*), restful
<< OPPOSITE hurried
▷ *adverb* UNHURRIEDLY, slowly, easily, comfortably, lazily, at your leisure, at your convenience, lingeringly, indolently, without haste
<< OPPOSITE hurriedly

lekker *adjective* (*S African slang*) DELICIOUS, tasty, luscious, choice, savoury, palatable, dainty, delectable, mouthwatering, yummy (*slang*), scrumptious (*informal*), appetizing, toothsome, ambrosial, yummo (*Austral slang*)

lemon *noun*
>> RELATED WORDS *adjectives* citric, citrine, citrous

lend *verb* **1** LOAN, advance, sub (*Brit informal*), accommodate one with
2 GIVE, provide, add, present, supply, grant, afford, contribute, hand out, furnish, confer, bestow, impart
▷▷ **lend itself to something** BE APPROPRIATE FOR, suit, be suitable for, fit, be appropriate to, be adaptable to, present opportunities of, be serviceable for

length *noun* **1** DISTANCE, reach, measure, extent, span, longitude
2 DURATION, term, period, space, stretch, span, expanse
3 PIECE, measure, section, segment, portion
4 LENGTHINESS, extent, elongation, wordiness, verbosity, prolixity, long-windedness,

extensiveness, protractedness
▷▷ **at length** 1 AT LAST, finally, eventually, in time, in the end, at long last
2 FOR A LONG TIME, completely, fully, thoroughly, for hours, in detail, for ages, in depth, to the full, exhaustively, interminably
lengthen *verb* 1 EXTEND, continue, increase, stretch, expand, elongate, make longer
<< OPPOSITE shorten
2 PROTRACT, extend, prolong, draw out, spin out, make longer
<< OPPOSITE cut down
lengthy *adjective* 1 PROTRACTED, long, prolonged, very long, tedious, lengthened, diffuse, drawn-out, interminable, long-winded, long-drawn-out, overlong, verbose, prolix
2 VERY LONG, rambling, interminable, long-winded, wordy, discursive, extended, overlong, verbose, prolix
<< OPPOSITE brief
leniency *or* **lenience** *noun* MERCY, compassion, clemency, quarter, pity, tolerance, indulgence, tenderness, moderation, gentleness, forbearance, mildness, lenity
lenient *adjective* MERCIFUL, sparing, gentle, forgiving, kind, tender, mild, tolerant, compassionate, clement, indulgent, forbearing
<< OPPOSITE severe
leper *noun* OUTCAST, reject, untouchable, pariah, lazar (*archaic*)
lesbian *adjective* HOMOSEXUAL, gay, les (*slang*), butch (*slang*), sapphic, lesbo (*slang*), tribadic
▷ *noun* LEZZIE (*slang*), les (*slang*), butch (*slang*), lesbo (*slang*)
lesion *noun* INJURY, hurt, wound, bruise, trauma (*Pathology*), sore, impairment, abrasion, contusion
less *adjective* SMALLER, shorter, slighter, not so much
▷ *adverb* TO A SMALLER EXTENT, little, barely, not much, not so much, meagrely
▷ *preposition* MINUS, without, lacking, excepting, subtracting

Less should not be confused with *fewer*. *Less* refers strictly only to quantity and not to number: *there is less water than before*. *Fewer* means smaller in number: *there are fewer people than before*

lessen *verb* 1 REDUCE, lower, diminish, decrease, relax, ease, narrow, moderate, weaken, erode, impair, degrade, minimize, curtail, lighten, wind down, abridge, de-escalate
<< OPPOSITE increase
2 GROW LESS, diminish, decrease, contract, ease, weaken, shrink, slow down, dwindle, lighten, wind down, die down, abate, slacken
lesser *adjective* LOWER, slighter, secondary, subsidiary, subordinate, inferior, less important
<< OPPOSITE greater
lesson *noun* 1 CLASS, schooling, period, teaching, coaching, session, instruction, lecture, seminar, tutoring, tutorial
2 EXAMPLE, warning, model, message, moral, deterrent, precept, exemplar
3 EXERCISE, reading, practice, task, lecture, drill, assignment, homework, recitation
4 BIBLE READING, reading, text, Bible passage, Scripture passage
let *verb* 1 ENABLE, make, allow, cause, grant, permit
2 ALLOW, grant, permit, warrant, authorize, give the go-ahead, give permission, suffer (*archaic*), give the green light, give leave, give the O.K. *or* okay (*informal*)
3 LEASE, hire, rent, rent out, hire out, sublease
▷▷ **let on** (*informal*) 1 REVEAL, disclose, say, tell, admit, give away, divulge, let slip, make known, let the cat out of the bag (*informal*)
2 PRETEND, make out, feign, simulate, affect, profess, counterfeit, make believe, dissemble, dissimulate
▷▷ **let someone down** DISAPPOINT, fail, abandon, desert, disillusion, fall short, leave stranded, leave in the lurch, disenchant, dissatisfy
▷▷ **let someone off** (*informal*) EXCUSE, release, discharge, pardon, spare, forgive, exempt, dispense, exonerate, absolve, grant an amnesty to
▷▷ **let something down** DEFLATE, empty, exhaust, flatten, puncture
▷▷ **let something off** 1 FIRE, explode, set off, discharge, detonate
2 EMIT, release, leak, exude, give off
▷▷ **let something out** 1 RELEASE, discharge
2 EMIT, make, produce, give vent to
3 REVEAL, tell, make known, let slip, leak, disclose, betray, let fall, take the wraps off
▷▷ **let something** *or* **someone in** ADMIT, include, receive, welcome, greet, take in, incorporate, give access to, allow to enter
▷▷ **let up** STOP, diminish, decrease, subside, relax, ease (up), moderate, lessen, abate, slacken
letdown *noun* DISAPPOINTMENT, disillusionment, frustration, anticlimax, setback, washout (*informal*), comedown (*informal*), disgruntlement
lethal *adjective* DEADLY, terminal, fatal, deathly, dangerous, devastating, destructive, mortal, murderous, poisonous, virulent, pernicious, noxious, baneful
<< OPPOSITE harmless

lethargic *adjective* SLUGGISH, slow, lazy, sleepy, heavy, dull, indifferent, debilitated, inactive, inert, languid, apathetic, drowsy, listless, comatose, stupefied, unenthusiastic, somnolent, torpid, slothful, enervated, unenergetic
<< OPPOSITE energetic

lethargy *noun* SLUGGISHNESS, inertia, inaction, slowness, indifference, apathy, sloth, stupor, drowsiness, dullness, torpor, sleepiness, lassitude, languor, listlessness, torpidity, hebetude (*rare*)
<< OPPOSITE energy

letter *noun* 1 MESSAGE, line, answer, note, reply, communication, dispatch, acknowledgment, billet (*archaic*), missive, epistle
2 CHARACTER, mark, sign, symbol
▷▷ **to the letter** PRECISELY, strictly, literally, exactly, faithfully, accurately, word for word, punctiliously
>> RELATED WORD *adjective* epistolatory

letters *plural noun* LEARNING, education, culture, literature, humanities, scholarship, erudition, belles-lettres

let-up *noun* (*informal*) LESSENING, break, pause, interval, recess, respite, lull, cessation, remission, breathing space, slackening, abatement

level *noun* 1 POSITION, standard, degree, grade, standing, stage, rank, status
2 HEIGHT, altitude, elevation, vertical position
3 FLAT SURFACE, plane, horizontal
▷ *adjective* 1 EQUAL, in line, aligned, balanced, on a line, at the same height
2 HORIZONTAL, even, flat, plane, smooth, uniform, as flat as a pancake
<< OPPOSITE slanted
3 EVEN, tied, equal, drawn, neck and neck, all square, level pegging
▷ *verb* 1 EQUALIZE, balance, even up
2 DESTROY, devastate, wreck, demolish, flatten, knock down, pull down, tear down, bulldoze, raze, lay waste to, kennet (*Austral slang*), jeff (*Austral slang*)
<< OPPOSITE build
3 DIRECT, point, turn, train, aim, focus, beam
4 FLATTEN, plane, smooth, make flat, even off *or* out
▷▷ **level with someone** (*informal*) BE HONEST, be open, be frank, come clean (*informal*), be straightforward, be up front (*slang*), be above board, keep nothing back
▷▷ **on the level** (*informal*) HONEST, genuine, sincere, open, straight, fair, square, straightforward, up front (*slang*), dinkum (*Austral & NZ informal*), above board

level-headed *adjective* CALM, balanced, reasonable, composed, together (*slang*), cool, collected, steady, sensible, sane, dependable, unflappable (*informal*), self-possessed, even-tempered

lever *noun* HANDLE, bar, crowbar, jemmy, handspike
▷ *verb* PRISE, move, force, raise, pry (*US*), jemmy

leverage *noun* 1 INFLUENCE, authority, pull (*informal*), weight, rank, clout (*informal*), purchasing power, ascendancy
2 FORCE, hold, pull, strength, grip, grasp

leviathan *noun* MONSTER, whale, mammoth, Titan, hulk, colossus, behemoth

levy *noun* TAX, fee, toll, tariff, duty, assessment, excise, imposition, impost, exaction
▷ *verb* IMPOSE, charge, tax, collect, gather, demand, exact

lewd *adjective* INDECENT, obscene, vulgar, dirty, blue, loose, vile, pornographic, wicked, wanton, X-rated (*informal*), profligate, bawdy, salacious, impure, lascivious, smutty, lustful, libidinous, licentious, unchaste

lexicon *noun* VOCABULARY, dictionary, glossary, word list, wordbook

liabilities *plural noun* DEBTS, expenditure, debit, arrears, obligations, accounts payable

liability *noun* 1 DISADVANTAGE, burden, drawback, inconvenience, drag, handicap, minus (*informal*), nuisance, impediment, albatross, hindrance, millstone, encumbrance
2 RESPONSIBILITY, accountability, culpability, obligation, onus, answerability

liable *adjective* 1 LIKELY, tending, inclined, disposed, prone, apt
2 VULNERABLE, subject, exposed, prone, susceptible, open, at risk of
3 RESPONSIBLE, accountable, amenable, answerable, bound, obligated, chargeable

> In the past, it was considered incorrect to use *liable* to mean 'probable' or 'likely', as in *it's liable to happen soon*. However, this usage is now generally considered acceptable

liaise *verb* COMMUNICATE, link up, connect, intermediate, mediate, interchange, hook up, keep contact

liaison *noun* 1 CONTACT, communication, connection, interchange
2 INTERMEDIARY, contact, hook-up, go-between
3 AFFAIR, romance, intrigue, fling, love affair, amour, entanglement, illicit romance

liar *noun* FALSIFIER, storyteller (*informal*), perjurer, fibber, fabricator, prevaricator

libel *noun* DEFAMATION, slander, misrepresentation, denigration, smear, calumny, vituperation, obloquy, aspersion
▷ *verb* DEFAME, smear, slur, blacken, malign, denigrate, revile, vilify, slander, traduce,

derogate, calumniate, drag (someone's) name through the mud

liberal *adjective* 1 TOLERANT, enlightened, open-minded, permissive, advanced, catholic, humanitarian, right-on (*informal*), indulgent, easy-going, unbiased, high-minded, broad-minded, unprejudiced, unbigoted, politically correct *or* PC

<< OPPOSITE intolerant

2 PROGRESSIVE, radical, reformist, libertarian, advanced, right-on (*informal*), forward-looking, humanistic, free-thinking, latitudinarian, politically correct *or* PC

<< OPPOSITE conservative

3 ABUNDANT, generous, handsome, lavish, ample, rich, plentiful, copious, bountiful, profuse, munificent

<< OPPOSITE limited

4 GENEROUS, kind, charitable, extravagant, free-handed, prodigal, altruistic, open-hearted, bountiful, magnanimous, open-handed, unstinting, beneficent, bounteous

<< OPPOSITE stingy

5 FLEXIBLE, general, broad, rough, free, loose, lenient, not close, inexact, not strict, not literal

<< OPPOSITE strict

liberalism *noun* PROGRESSIVISM, radicalism, humanitarianism, libertarianism, freethinking, latitudinarianism

liberalize *verb* RELAX, ease, moderate, modify, stretch, soften, broaden, loosen, mitigate, slacken, ameliorate

liberate *verb* FREE, release, rescue, save, deliver, discharge, redeem, let out, set free, let loose, untie, emancipate, unchain, unbind, manumit

<< OPPOSITE imprison

liberator *noun* DELIVERER, saviour, rescuer, redeemer, freer, emancipator, manumitter

liberty *noun* 1 INDEPENDENCE, sovereignty, liberation, autonomy, immunity, self-determination, emancipation, self-government, self-rule

2 FREEDOM, liberation, redemption, emancipation, deliverance, manumission, enfranchisement, unshackling, unfettering

<< OPPOSITE restraint

▷▷ **at liberty** 1 FREE, escaped, unlimited, at large, not confined, untied, on the loose, unchained, unbound

2 ABLE, free, allowed, permitted, entitled, authorized

▷▷ **take liberties** *or* **a liberty** NOT SHOW ENOUGH RESPECT, show disrespect, act presumptuously, behave too familiarly, behave impertinently

libretto *noun* WORDS, book, lines, text, script, lyrics

licence *noun* 1 CERTIFICATE, document, permit, charter, warrant

2 PERMISSION, the right, authority, leave, sanction, liberty, privilege, immunity, entitlement, exemption, prerogative, authorization, dispensation, a free hand, carte blanche, blank cheque

<< OPPOSITE denial

3 FREEDOM, creativity, latitude, independence, liberty, deviation, leeway, free rein, looseness

<< OPPOSITE restraint

4 LAXITY, abandon, disorder, excess, indulgence, anarchy, lawlessness, impropriety, irresponsibility, profligacy, licentiousness, unruliness, immoderation

<< OPPOSITE moderation

license *verb* PERMIT, commission, enable, sanction, allow, entitle, warrant, authorize, empower, certify, accredit, give a blank cheque to

<< OPPOSITE forbid

lick *verb* 1 TASTE, lap, tongue, touch, wash, brush

2 (*informal*) BEAT, defeat, overcome, best, top, stuff (*slang*), tank (*slang*), undo, rout, excel, surpass, outstrip, outdo, trounce, clobber (*slang*), vanquish, run rings around (*informal*), wipe the floor with (*informal*), blow out of the water (*slang*)

3 (*of flames*) FLICKER, touch, flick, dart, ripple, ignite, play over, kindle

▷ *noun* 1 DAB, little, bit, touch, taste, sample, stroke, brush, speck

2 (*informal*) PACE, rate, speed, clip (*informal*)

licking *noun* THRASHING, beating, hiding (*informal*), whipping, tanning (*slang*), flogging, spanking, drubbing

lie[1] *noun* FALSEHOOD, deceit, fabrication, fib, fiction, invention, deception, untruth, porky (*Brit slang*), pork pie (*Brit slang*), white lie, falsification, prevarication, falsity, mendacity

▷ *verb* FIB, fabricate, invent, misrepresent, falsify, tell a lie, prevaricate, perjure, not tell the truth, equivocate, dissimulate, tell untruths, not speak the truth, say something untrue, forswear yourself

▷▷ **give the lie to something** DISPROVE, expose, discredit, contradict, refute, negate, invalidate, rebut, make a nonsense of, prove false, controvert, confute

>> RELATED WORD *adjective* mendacious

lie[2] *verb* 1 RECLINE, rest, lounge, couch, sprawl, stretch out, be prone, loll, repose, be prostrate, be supine, be recumbent

2 BE PLACED, be, rest, exist, extend, be situated

3 BE SITUATED, sit, be located, be positioned

4 *usually with* **in** EXIST, be present, consist, dwell, reside, pertain, inhere

5 BE BURIED, remain, rest, be, be found, belong, be located, be interred, be entombed

6 *usually with* **on** *or* **upon** WEIGH, press, rest, burden, oppress

liege *noun* FEUDAL LORD, master, superior, sovereign, chieftain, overlord, seigneur, suzerain

lieu ▷▷ **in lieu of** INSTEAD OF, in place of

life *noun* 1 BEING, existence, breath, entity, vitality, animation, viability, sentience
2 LIVING THINGS, creatures, wildlife, organisms, living beings
3 EXISTENCE, being, lifetime, time, days, course, span, duration, continuance
4 WAY OF LIFE, situation, conduct, behaviour, life style
5 LIVELINESS, activity, energy, spirit, go (*informal*), pep, sparkle, vitality, animation, vigour, verve, zest, high spirits, get-up-and-go (*informal*), oomph (*informal*), brio, vivacity
6 BIOGRAPHY, story, history, career, profile, confessions, autobiography, memoirs, life story
7 SPIRIT, heart, soul, essence, core, lifeblood, moving spirit, vital spark, animating spirit, élan vital (*French*)
8 PERSON, human, individual, soul, human being, mortal
>> RELATED WORDS *adjectives* animate, vital

lifeblood *noun* ANIMATING FORCE, life, heart, inspiration, guts (*informal*), essence, stimulus, driving force, vital spark

lifeless *adjective* 1 DEAD, unconscious, extinct, deceased, cold, defunct, inert, inanimate, comatose, out cold, out for the count, insensible, in a faint, insensate, dead to the world (*informal*)
<< OPPOSITE alive
2 BARREN, empty, desert, bare, waste, sterile, unproductive, uninhabited
3 DULL, cold, flat, hollow, heavy, slow, wooden, stiff, passive, static, pointless, sluggish, lacklustre, lethargic, colourless, listless, torpid, spiritless
<< OPPOSITE lively

lifelike *adjective* REALISTIC, faithful, authentic, natural, exact, graphic, vivid, photographic, true-to-life, undistorted

lifelong *adjective* LONG-LASTING, enduring, lasting, permanent, constant, lifetime, for life, persistent, long-standing, perennial, deep-rooted, for all your life

lifetime *noun* EXISTENCE, time, day(s), course, period, span, life span, your natural life, all your born days

lift *verb* 1 RAISE, pick up, hoist, draw up, elevate, uplift, heave up, buoy up, raise high, bear aloft, upheave, upraise
<< OPPOSITE lower
2 REVOKE, end, remove, withdraw, stop, relax, cancel, terminate, rescind, annul, countermand
<< OPPOSITE impose
3 EXALT, raise, improve, advance, promote, boost, enhance, upgrade, elevate, dignify, cheer up, perk up, ameliorate, buoy up
<< OPPOSITE depress
4 DISAPPEAR, clear, vanish, disperse, dissipate, rise, be dispelled
5 (*informal*) STEAL, take, copy, appropriate, nick (*slang, chiefly Brit*), pocket, pinch (*informal*), pirate, cabbage (*Brit slang*), crib (*informal*), half-inch (*old-fashioned slang*), blag (*slang*), pilfer, purloin, plagiarize, thieve
▷ *noun* 1 BOOST, encouragement, stimulus, reassurance, uplift, pick-me-up, fillip, shot in the arm (*informal*), gee-up
<< OPPOSITE blow
2 ELEVATOR (*chiefly US*), hoist, paternoster
3 RIDE, run, drive, transport, hitch (*informal*), car ride
▷▷ **lift off** TAKE OFF, be launched, blast off, take to the air

light[1] *noun* 1 BRIGHTNESS, illumination, luminosity, luminescence, ray of light, flash of light, shining, glow, blaze, sparkle, glare, gleam, brilliance, glint, lustre, radiance, incandescence, phosphorescence, scintillation, effulgence, lambency, refulgence
<< OPPOSITE dark
2 LAMP, bulb, torch, candle, flare, beacon, lighthouse, lantern, taper
3 MATCH, spark, flame, lighter
4 ASPECT, approach, attitude, context, angle, point of view, interpretation, viewpoint, slant, standpoint, vantage point
5 UNDERSTANDING, knowledge, awareness, insight, information, explanation, illustration, enlightenment, comprehension, illumination, elucidation
<< OPPOSITE mystery
6 DAYBREAK, morning, dawn, sun, sunrise, sunshine, sunlight, daylight, daytime, sunbeam, morn (*poetic*), cockcrow, broad day
▷ *adjective* 1 BRIGHT, brilliant, shining, glowing, sunny, illuminated, luminous, well-lighted, well-lit, lustrous, aglow, well-illuminated
<< OPPOSITE dark
2 PALE, fair, faded, blonde, blond, bleached, pastel, light-coloured, whitish, light-toned, light-hued
<< OPPOSITE dark
▷ *verb* 1 ILLUMINATE, light up, brighten, lighten, put on, turn on, clarify, switch on, floodlight, irradiate, illumine, flood with light
<< OPPOSITE darken
2 IGNITE, inflame, fire, torch, kindle, touch off, set alight, set a match to

<< OPPOSITE put out
▷▷ **bring something to light** REVEAL, expose, unveil, show, discover, disclose, show up, uncover, unearth, lay bare
▷▷ **come to light** BE REVEALED, appear, come out, turn up, be discovered, become known, become apparent, be disclosed, transpire
▷▷ **in the light of something** CONSIDERING, because of, taking into account, bearing in mind, in view of, taking into consideration, with knowledge of
▷▷ **light up** 1 CHEER, shine, blaze, sparkle, animate, brighten, lighten, irradiate
2 SHINE, flash, beam, blaze, sparkle, flare, glare, gleam, flicker

light² *adjective* 1 INSUBSTANTIAL, thin, delicate, lightweight, easy, slight, portable, buoyant, airy, flimsy, underweight, not heavy, transportable, lightsome, imponderous
<< OPPOSITE heavy
2 WEAK, soft, gentle, moderate, slight, mild, faint, indistinct
<< OPPOSITE strong
3 CRUMBLY, loose, sandy, porous, spongy, friable
<< OPPOSITE hard
4 DIGESTIBLE, small, restricted, modest, frugal, not rich, not heavy
<< OPPOSITE substantial
5 UNDEMANDING, easy, simple, moderate, manageable, effortless, cushy (*informal*), untaxing, unexacting
<< OPPOSITE strenuous
6 INSIGNIFICANT, small, minute, tiny, slight, petty, trivial, trifling, inconsequential, inconsiderable, unsubstantial
<< OPPOSITE serious
7 LIGHT-HEARTED, pleasing, funny, entertaining, amusing, diverting, witty, trivial, superficial, humorous, gay, trifling, frivolous, unserious
<< OPPOSITE serious
8 CAREFREE, happy, bright, lively, sunny, cheerful, animated, merry, gay, airy, frivolous, cheery, untroubled, blithe, light-hearted
9 NIMBLE, graceful, airy, deft, agile, sprightly, lithe, limber, lissom, light-footed, sylphlike
<< OPPOSITE clumsy
10 DIZZY, reeling, faint, volatile, giddy, unsteady, light-headed
▷▷ **light on** *or* **upon something** 1 SETTLE, land, perch, alight
2 COME ACROSS, find, discover, encounter, stumble on, hit upon, happen upon
▷▷ **light out** (US) RUN AWAY, escape, depart, make off, abscond, quit, do a runner (*slang*), scarper (*Brit slang*), do a bunk (*Brit slang*), fly the coop (*US & Canad informal*), skedaddle (*informal*), take a powder (*US & Canad slang*), take it on the lam (*US & Canad slang*), do a Skase (*Austral informal*)

lighten¹ *verb* BRIGHTEN, flash, shine, illuminate, gleam, light up, irradiate, become light, make bright

lighten² *verb* 1 EASE, relieve, alleviate, allay, reduce, facilitate, lessen, mitigate, assuage
<< OPPOSITE intensify
2 CHEER, lift, revive, brighten, hearten, perk up, buoy up, gladden, elate
<< OPPOSITE depress
3 MAKE LIGHTER, ease, disburden, reduce in weight

light-headed *adjective* 1 FAINT, dizzy, hazy, giddy, delirious, unsteady, vertiginous, woozy (*informal*)
2 FRIVOLOUS, silly, shallow, foolish, superficial, trifling, inane, flippant, flighty, bird-brained (*informal*), featherbrained, rattlebrained (*slang*)

light-hearted *adjective* CAREFREE, happy, bright, glad, sunny, cheerful, jolly, merry, upbeat (*informal*), playful, joyous, joyful, genial, chirpy (*informal*), jovial, untroubled, gleeful, happy-go-lucky, gay, effervescent, blithe, insouciant, frolicsome, ludic (*literary*), jocund, blithesome (*literary*)
<< OPPOSITE gloomy

lightly *adverb* 1 MODERATELY, thinly, slightly, sparsely, sparingly
<< OPPOSITE heavily
2 GENTLY, softly, slightly, faintly, delicately, gingerly, airily, timidly
<< OPPOSITE forcefully
3 CARELESSLY, indifferently, breezily, thoughtlessly, flippantly, frivolously, heedlessly, slightingly
<< OPPOSITE seriously
4 EASILY, simply, readily, effortlessly, unthinkingly, without thought, flippantly, heedlessly
<< OPPOSITE with difficulty

lightweight *adjective* 1 THIN, fine, delicate, sheer, flimsy, gossamer, diaphanous, filmy, unsubstantial
2 UNIMPORTANT, shallow, trivial, insignificant, slight, petty, worthless, trifling, flimsy, paltry, inconsequential, undemanding, insubstantial, nickel-and-dime (*US slang*), of no account
<< OPPOSITE significant

like¹ *adjective* SIMILAR TO, same as, allied to, equivalent to, parallel to, resembling, identical to, alike, corresponding to, comparable to, akin to, approximating, analogous to, cognate to
<< OPPOSITE different
▷ *noun* EQUAL, equivalent, parallel, match, twin, counterpart

<< OPPOSITE opposite

The use of *like* to mean 'such as' was in the past considered undesirable in formal writing, but has now become acceptable, for example in *I enjoy team sports like football and rugby*. However, the common use of *look like* and *seem like* to mean 'look or seem as if' is thought by many people to be incorrect or nonstandard. You might say *it looks as if* (or *as though*) *he's coming*, but it is still wise to avoid *it looks like he's coming*, particularly in formal or written contexts

like[2] *verb* 1 ENJOY, love, adore (*informal*), delight in, go for, dig (*slang*), relish, savour, revel in, be fond of, be keen on, be partial to, have a preference for, have a weakness for
<< OPPOSITE dislike
2 ADMIRE, approve of, appreciate, prize, take to, esteem, cherish, hold dear, take a shine to (*informal*), think well of
<< OPPOSITE dislike
3 WISH, want, choose, prefer, desire, select, fancy, care, feel inclined
▷ *noun usually plural* LIKING, favourite, preference, cup of tea (*informal*), predilection, partiality

likelihood *noun* PROBABILITY, chance, possibility, prospect, liability, good chance, strong possibility, reasonableness, likeliness

likely *adjective* 1 INCLINED, disposed, prone, liable, tending, apt
2 PROBABLE, expected, anticipated, odds-on, on the cards, to be expected
3 PLAUSIBLE, possible, reasonable, credible, feasible, believable, verisimilar
4 APPROPRIATE, promising, pleasing, fit, fair, favourite, qualified, suitable, acceptable, proper, hopeful, agreeable, up-and-coming, befitting
▷ *adverb* PROBABLY, no doubt, presumably, in all probability, like enough (*informal*), doubtlessly, like as not (*informal*)

When using *likely* as an adverb, it is usual to precede it by another, intensifying, adverb such as *very* or *most*, for example *it will most likely rain*. The use of *likely* as an adverb without an intensifier, for example *it will likely rain*, is considered nonstandard in British English, though it is common in colloquial US English

like-minded *adjective* AGREEING, compatible, harmonious, in harmony, unanimous, in accord, of one mind, of the same mind, en rapport (*French*)

liken *verb* COMPARE, match, relate, parallel, equate, juxtapose, mention in the same breath, set beside

likeness *noun* 1 RESEMBLANCE, similarity, correspondence, affinity, similitude
2 PORTRAIT, study, picture, model, image, photograph, copy, counterpart, representation, reproduction, replica, depiction, facsimile, effigy, delineation
3 APPEARANCE, form, guise, semblance

likewise *adverb* 1 ALSO, too, as well, further, in addition, moreover, besides, furthermore
2 SIMILARLY, the same, in the same way, in similar fashion, in like manner

liking *noun* FONDNESS, love, taste, desire, bent, stomach, attraction, weakness, tendency, preference, bias, affection, appreciation, inclination, thirst, affinity, penchant, propensity, soft spot, predilection, partiality, proneness
<< OPPOSITE dislike

lilt *noun* RHYTHM, intonation, cadence, beat, pitch, swing, sway

limb *noun* 1 PART, member, arm, leg, wing, extension, extremity, appendage
2 BRANCH, spur, projection, offshoot, bough

limber *adjective* PLIANT, flexible, supple, agile, plastic, graceful, elastic, lithe, pliable, lissom(e), loose-jointed, loose-limbed
▷▷ **limber up** LOOSEN UP, prepare, exercise, warm up, get ready

limelight *noun* PUBLICITY, recognition, fame, the spotlight, attention, prominence, stardom, public eye, public notice, glare of publicity

limit *noun* 1 END, bound, ultimate, deadline, utmost, breaking point, termination, extremity, greatest extent, the bitter end, end point, cutoff point, furthest bound
2 BOUNDARY, end, edge, border, extent, pale, confines, frontier, precinct, perimeter, periphery
3 LIMITATION, maximum, restriction, ceiling, restraint
▷ *verb* RESTRICT, control, check, fix, bound, confine, specify, curb, restrain, ration, hinder, circumscribe, hem in, demarcate, delimit, put a brake on, keep within limits, straiten
▷▷ **the limit** (*informal*) THE END, it (*informal*), enough, the last straw, the straw that broke the camel's back

limitation *noun* 1 RESTRICTION, control, check, block, curb, restraint, constraint, obstruction, impediment
2 WEAKNESS, failing, qualification, reservation, defect, disadvantage, flaw, drawback, shortcoming, snag, imperfection

limited *adjective* 1 RESTRICTED, controlled,

fixed, defined, checked, bounded, confined, curbed, hampered, constrained, finite, circumscribed
<< OPPOSITE unlimited
2 NARROW, little, small, restricted, slight, inadequate, minimal, insufficient, unsatisfactory, scant

limitless *adjective* INFINITE, endless, unlimited, never-ending, vast, immense, countless, untold, boundless, unending, inexhaustible, undefined, immeasurable, unbounded, numberless, measureless, illimitable, uncalculable

limp[1] *verb* HOBBLE, stagger, stumble, shuffle, halt (*archaic*), hop, falter, shamble, totter, dodder, hirple (*Scot*)
▷ *noun* LAMENESS, hobble, hirple (*Scot*)

limp[2] *adjective* 1 FLOPPY, soft, relaxed, loose, flexible, slack, lax, drooping, flabby, limber, pliable, flaccid
<< OPPOSITE stiff
2 WEAK, tired, exhausted, worn out, spent, debilitated, lethargic, enervated
<< OPPOSITE strong

limpid *adjective* 1 CLEAR, bright, pure, transparent, translucent, crystal-clear, crystalline, pellucid
2 UNDERSTANDABLE, clear, lucid, unambiguous, comprehensible, intelligible, perspicuous

line[1] *noun* 1 STROKE, mark, rule, score, bar, band, channel, dash, scratch, slash, underline, streak, stripe, groove
2 WRINKLE, mark, crease, furrow, crow's foot
3 ROW, queue, rank, file, series, column, sequence, convoy, procession, crocodile (*Brit*)
4 STRING, cable, wire, strand, rope, thread, cord, filament, wisp
5 TRAJECTORY, way, course, track, channel, direction, route, path, axis
6 OUTLINE, shape, figure, style, cut, features, appearance, profile, silhouette, configuration, contour
7 BOUNDARY, mark, limit, edge, border, frontier, partition, borderline, demarcation
8 (*Military*) FORMATION, front, position, front line, trenches, firing line
9 APPROACH, policy, position, way, course, practice, scheme, method, technique, procedure, tactic, avenue, ideology, course of action
10 OCCUPATION, work, calling, interest, business, job, area, trade, department, field, career, activity, bag (*slang*), employment, province, profession, pursuit, forte, vocation, specialization
11 LINEAGE, family, breed, succession, race, stock, strain, descent, ancestry, parentage
12 NOTE, message, letter, memo, report, word, card, e-mail, postcard
▷ *verb* 1 BORDER, edge, bound, fringe, rank, skirt, verge, rim
2 MARK, draw, crease, furrow, cut, rule, score, trace, underline, inscribe
▷▷ **draw the line at something** OBJECT TO, prohibit, stop short at, set a limit at, put your foot down over
▷▷ **in line** IN ACCORD, in agreement, in harmony, in step, in conformity
▷▷ **in line for** DUE FOR, being considered for, a candidate for, shortlisted for, in the running for, on the short list for, next in succession to
▷▷ **line something up** 1 ALIGN, order, range, arrange, sequence, array, regiment, dispose, marshal, straighten, straighten up, put in a line
2 PREPARE, schedule, organize, secure, obtain, come up with, assemble, get together, lay on, procure, jack up (*NZ informal*)
▷▷ **line up** QUEUE UP, file, fall in, form a queue, form ranks

line[2] *verb* FILL, face, cover, reinforce, encase, inlay, interline, ceil

lineage *noun* DESCENT, family, line, succession, house, stock, birth, breed, pedigree, extraction, ancestry, forebears, progeny, heredity, forefathers, genealogy

lined *adjective* 1 WRINKLED, worn, furrowed, wizened
2 RULED, feint

lines *plural noun* PRINCIPLE, plan, example, model, pattern, procedure, convention

line-up *noun* ARRANGEMENT, team, row, selection, array

linger *verb* 1 CONTINUE, last, remain, stay, carry on, endure, persist, abide
2 HANG ON, last, survive, cling to life, die slowly
3 STAY, remain, stop, wait, delay, lag, hang around, idle, dally, loiter, take your time, wait around, dawdle, hang in the air, procrastinate, tarry, drag your feet *or* heels

lingering *adjective* SLOW, prolonged, protracted, long-drawn-out, remaining, dragging, persistent

lingo *noun* (*informal*) LANGUAGE, jargon, dialect, talk, speech, tongue, idiom, vernacular, patter, cant, patois, argot

link *noun* 1 CONNECTION, relationship, association, tie-up, affinity, affiliation, vinculum
2 RELATIONSHIP, association, tie, bond, connection, attachment, liaison, affinity, affiliation
3 COMPONENT, part, piece, division, element, constituent
▷ *verb* 1 ASSOCIATE, relate, identify, connect, bracket

2 CONNECT, join, unite, couple, tie, bind, attach, fasten, yoke
<< OPPOSITE separate

lion *noun* HERO, champion, fighter, warrior, conqueror, lionheart, brave person
>> RELATED WORD *adjective* leonine
>> RELATED WORD *female* lioness
>> RELATED WORD *young* cub
>> RELATED WORDS *collective nouns* pride, troop

lip *noun* **1** EDGE, rim, brim, margin, brink, flange
2 (*Slang*) IMPUDENCE, rudeness, insolence, impertinence, sauce (*informal*), cheek (*informal*), effrontery, backchat (*informal*), brass neck (*informal*)
▷▷ **smack** *or* **lick your lips** GLOAT, drool, slaver
>> RELATED WORD *adjective* labial

liquefy *verb* MELT, dissolve, thaw, liquidize, run, fuse, flux, deliquesce

liquid *noun* FLUID, solution, juice, liquor, sap
▷ *adjective* **1** FLUID, running, flowing, wet, melted, thawed, watery, molten, runny, liquefied, aqueous
2 CLEAR, bright, brilliant, shining, transparent, translucent, limpid
3 SMOOTH, clear, soft, flowing, sweet, pure, melting, fluent, melodious, mellifluous, dulcet, mellifluent
4 (*of assets*) CONVERTIBLE, disposable, negotiable, realizable

liquidate *verb* **1** DISSOLVE, cancel, abolish, terminate, annul
2 CONVERT TO CASH, cash, realize, sell off, sell up
3 KILL, murder, remove, destroy, do in (*slang*), silence, eliminate, take out (*slang*), get rid of, wipe out (*informal*), dispatch, finish off, do away with, blow away (*slang, chiefly US*), annihilate, exterminate, bump off (*slang*), rub out (*US slang*)

liquor *noun* **1** ALCOHOL, drink, spirits, booze (*informal*), grog, hard stuff (*informal*), strong drink, Dutch courage (*informal*), intoxicant, juice (*informal*), hooch *or* hootch (*informal, chiefly US & Canad*)
2 JUICE, stock, liquid, extract, gravy, infusion, broth

list[1] *noun* INVENTORY, record, listing, series, roll, file, schedule, index, register, catalogue, directory, tally, invoice, syllabus, tabulation, leet (*Scot*)
▷ *verb* ITEMIZE, record, note, enter, file, schedule, index, register, catalogue, write down, enrol, set down, enumerate, note down, tabulate

list[2] *verb* LEAN, tip, heel, incline, tilt, cant, heel over, careen
▷ *noun* TILT, leaning, slant, cant

listen *verb* **1** HEAR, attend, pay attention, hark, be attentive, be all ears, lend an ear, hearken (*archaic*), prick up your ears, give ear, keep your ears open, pin back your ears (*informal*)
2 PAY ATTENTION, observe, obey, mind, concentrate, heed, take notice, take note of, take heed of, do as you are told, give heed to

listless *adjective* LANGUID, sluggish, lifeless, lethargic, heavy, limp, vacant, indifferent, languishing, inert, apathetic, lymphatic, impassive, supine, indolent, torpid, inattentive, enervated, spiritless, mopish
<< OPPOSITE energetic

litany *noun* **1** RECITAL, list, tale, catalogue, account, repetition, refrain, recitation, enumeration
2 PRAYER, petition, invocation, supplication, set words

literacy *noun* EDUCATION, learning, knowledge, scholarship, cultivation, proficiency, articulacy, ability to read and write, articulateness

literal *adjective* **1** EXACT, close, strict, accurate, faithful, verbatim, word for word
2 UNIMAGINATIVE, boring, dull, down-to-earth, matter-of-fact, factual, prosaic, colourless, uninspired, prosy
3 ACTUAL, real, true, simple, plain, genuine, gospel, bona fide, unvarnished, unexaggerated

literally *adverb* EXACTLY, really, closely, actually, simply, plainly, truly, precisely, strictly, faithfully, to the letter, verbatim, word for word

literary *adjective* WELL-READ, lettered, learned, formal, intellectual, scholarly, literate, erudite, bookish

literate *adjective* EDUCATED, lettered, learned, cultured, informed, scholarly, cultivated, knowledgeable, well-informed, erudite, well-read

literature *noun* **1** WRITINGS, letters, compositions, lore, creative writing, written works, belles-lettres
2 (*informal*) INFORMATION, publicity, leaflet, brochure, circular, pamphlet, handout, mailshot, handbill

lithe *adjective* SUPPLE, flexible, agile, limber, pliable, pliant, lissom(e), loose-jointed, loose-limbed

litigant *noun* CLAIMANT, party, plaintiff, contestant, litigator, disputant

litigation *noun* LAWSUIT, case, action, process, disputing, prosecution, contending

litigious *adjective* CONTENTIOUS, belligerent, argumentative, quarrelsome, disputatious

litter *noun* **1** RUBBISH, refuse, waste, fragments, junk, debris, shreds, garbage (*chiefly US*), trash, muck, detritus, grot (*slang*)
2 JUMBLE, mess, disorder, confusion, scatter,

tangle, muddle, clutter, disarray, untidiness
3 BROOD, family, young, offspring, progeny
4 BEDDING, couch, mulch, floor cover, straw-bed
5 STRETCHER, palanquin
▷ *verb* 1 CLUTTER, mess up, clutter up, be scattered about, disorder, disarrange, derange, muss (*US & Canad*)
2 SCATTER, spread, shower, strew

little *adjective* 1 NOT MUCH, small, insufficient, scant, meagre, sparse, skimpy, measly, hardly any
<< OPPOSITE ample
2 SMALL, minute, short, tiny, mini, wee, compact, miniature, dwarf, slender, diminutive, petite, dainty, elfin, bijou, infinitesimal, teeny-weeny, Lilliputian, munchkin (*informal, chiefly US*), teensy-weensy, pygmy *or* pigmy
<< OPPOSITE big
3 YOUNG, small, junior, infant, immature, undeveloped, babyish
4 UNIMPORTANT, minor, petty, trivial, trifling, insignificant, negligible, paltry, inconsiderable
<< OPPOSITE important
5 MEAN, base, cheap, petty, narrow-minded, small-minded, illiberal
▷ *adverb* 1 HARDLY, barely, not quite, not much, only just, scarcely
<< OPPOSITE much
2 RARELY, seldom, scarcely, not often, infrequently, hardly ever
<< OPPOSITE always
▷ *noun* BIT, touch, spot, trace, hint, dash, particle, fragment, pinch, small amount, dab, trifle, tad (*informal, chiefly US*), snippet, speck, modicum
<< OPPOSITE lot
▷▷ **a little** TO A SMALL EXTENT, slightly, to some extent, to a certain extent, to a small degree

liturgical *adjective* CEREMONIAL, ritual, solemn, sacramental, formal, eucharistic

liturgy *noun* CEREMONY, service, ritual, services, celebration, formula, worship, rite, sacrament, form of worship

live[1] *verb* 1 DWELL, board, settle, lodge, occupy, abide, inhabit, hang out (*informal*), stay (*chiefly Scot*), reside, have as your home, have your home in
2 EXIST, last, prevail, be, have being, breathe, persist, be alive, have life, draw breath, remain alive
3 SURVIVE, remain alive, feed yourself, get along, make a living, earn a living, make ends meet, subsist, eke out a living, support yourself, maintain yourself
4 THRIVE, be happy, flourish, prosper, have fun, enjoy life, enjoy yourself, luxuriate, live life to the full, make the most of life

live[2] *adjective* 1 LIVING, alive, breathing, animate, existent, vital, quick (*archaic*)
2 ACTIVE, connected, switched on, unexploded
3 TOPICAL, important, pressing, current, hot, burning, active, vital, controversial, unsettled, prevalent, pertinent
▷▷ **live wire** (*informal*) DYNAMO, hustler (*US & Canad slang*), ball of fire (*informal*), life and soul of the party, go-getter (*informal*), self-starter

livelihood *noun* OCCUPATION, work, employment, means, living, job, maintenance, subsistence, bread and butter (*informal*), sustenance, (means of) support, (source of) income

lively *adjective* 1 ANIMATED, spirited, quick, keen, active, alert, dynamic, sparkling, vigorous, cheerful, energetic, outgoing, merry, upbeat (*informal*), brisk, bubbly, nimble, agile, perky, chirpy (*informal*), sparky, sprightly, vivacious, frisky, gay, alive and kicking, spry, chipper (*informal*), blithe, full of beans (*informal*), frolicsome, full of pep (*informal*), blithesome, bright-eyed and bushy-tailed
<< OPPOSITE dull
2 BUSY, crowded, stirring, buzzing, bustling, moving, eventful
<< OPPOSITE slow
3 VIVID, strong, striking, bright, exciting, stimulating, bold, colourful, refreshing, forceful, racy, invigorating
<< OPPOSITE dull
4 ENTHUSIASTIC, strong, keen, stimulating, eager, formidable, vigorous, animated, weighty

liven up *verb* 1 STIR, brighten, hot up (*informal*), cheer up, perk up, buck up (*informal*)
2 CHEER UP, animate, rouse, enliven, perk up, brighten up, pep up, buck up (*informal*), put life into, vitalize, vivify

livery *noun* COSTUME, dress, clothing, suit, uniform, attire, garb, regalia, vestments, raiment (*archaic* or *poetic*)

livid *adjective* 1 (*informal*) ANGRY, cross, furious, outraged, mad (*informal*), boiling, fuming, choked, infuriated, incensed, enraged, exasperated, indignant, incandescent, hot under the collar (*informal*), fit to be tied (*slang*), beside yourself, as black as thunder, tooshie (*Austral slang*), off the air (*Austral slang*)
<< OPPOSITE delighted
2 DISCOLOURED, angry, purple, bruised, black-and-blue, contused

living *noun* 1 LIVELIHOOD, work, job, maintenance, occupation, subsistence, bread and butter (*informal*), sustenance, (means of) support, (source of) income
2 LIFESTYLE, ways, situation, conduct, behaviour, customs, lifestyle, way of life,

mode of living
▷ *adjective* 1 ALIVE, existing, moving, active, vital, breathing, lively, vigorous, animated, animate, alive and kicking, in the land of the living (*informal*), quick (*archaic*)
<< OPPOSITE dead
2 CURRENT, continuing, present, developing, active, contemporary, persisting, ongoing, operative, in use, extant
<< OPPOSITE obsolete

load *verb* 1 FILL, stuff, pack, pile, stack, heap, cram, freight, lade
2 MAKE READY, charge, prime, prepare to fire
▷ *noun* 1 CARGO, lading, delivery, haul, shipment, batch, freight, bale, consignment
2 OPPRESSION, charge, pressure, worry, trouble, weight, responsibility, burden, affliction, onus, albatross, millstone, encumbrance, incubus
▷▷ **load someone down** BURDEN, worry, trouble, hamper, oppress, weigh down, saddle with, encumber, snow under

loaded *adjective* 1 LADEN, full, charged, filled, weighted, burdened, freighted
2 CHARGED, armed, primed, at the ready, ready to shoot *or* fire
3 TRICKY, charged, sensitive, delicate, manipulative, emotive, insidious, artful, prejudicial, tendentious
4 BIASED, weighted, rigged, distorted
5 (*Slang*) RICH, wealthy, affluent, well off, rolling (*slang*), flush (*informal*), well-heeled (*informal*), well-to-do, moneyed

loaf[1] *noun* 1 LUMP, block, cake, cube, slab
2 (*Slang*) HEAD, mind, sense, common sense, block (*informal*), nous (*Brit slang*), chump (*Brit slang*), gumption (*Brit informal*), noddle (*informal, chiefly Brit*)

loaf[2] *verb* IDLE, hang around, take it easy, lie around, loiter, loll, laze, lounge around, veg out (*slang, chiefly US*), be indolent

loafer *noun* IDLER, lounger, bum (*informal*), piker (*Austral & NZ slang*), drone (*Brit*), shirker, couch potato (*slang*), time-waster, layabout, skiver (*Brit slang*), ne'er-do-well, wastrel, bludger (*Austral & NZ informal*), lazybones (*informal*)

loan *noun* ADVANCE, credit, mortgage, accommodation, allowance, touch (*slang*), overdraft
▷ *verb* LEND, allow, credit, advance, accommodate, let out

loath *or* **loth** *adjective* UNWILLING, against, opposed, counter, resisting, reluctant, backward, averse, disinclined, indisposed
<< OPPOSITE willing

loathe *verb* HATE, dislike, despise, detest, abhor, abominate, have a strong aversion to, find disgusting, execrate, feel repugnance towards, not be able to bear *or* abide

loathing *noun* HATRED, hate, horror, disgust, aversion, revulsion, antipathy, abomination, repulsion, abhorrence, repugnance, odium, detestation, execration

loathsome *adjective* HATEFUL, offensive, nasty, disgusting, horrible, revolting, obscene, vile, obnoxious, repulsive, nauseating, odious, repugnant, abhorrent, abominable, execrable, detestable, yucky *or* yukky (*slang*), yucko (*Austral slang*)
<< OPPOSITE delightful

lob *verb* THROW, launch, toss, hurl, lift, pitch, shy (*informal*), fling, loft

lobby *verb* CAMPAIGN, press, pressure, push, influence, promote, urge, persuade, appeal, petition, pull strings (*Brit informal*), exert influence, bring pressure to bear, solicit votes
▷ *noun* 1 PRESSURE GROUP, group, camp, faction, lobbyists, interest group, special-interest group, ginger group, public-interest group (*US & Canad*)
2 CORRIDOR, hall, passage, entrance, porch, hallway, foyer, passageway, entrance hall, vestibule

lobola *noun* (*S African*) DOWRY, portion, marriage settlement, dot (*archaic*)

local *adjective* 1 COMMUNITY, district, regional, provincial, parish, neighbourhood, small-town (*chiefly US*), parochial, parish pump
2 CONFINED, limited, narrow, restricted
▷ *noun* RESIDENT, native, inhabitant, character (*informal*), local yokel (*disparaging*)

locale *noun* SITE, place, setting, position, spot, scene, location, venue, locality, locus

locality *noun* 1 NEIGHBOURHOOD, area, region, district, vicinity, neck of the woods (*informal*)
2 SITE, place, setting, position, spot, scene, location, locale

localize *verb* RESTRICT, limit, contain, concentrate, confine, restrain, circumscribe, delimit

locate *verb* 1 FIND, discover, detect, come across, track down, pinpoint, unearth, pin down, lay your hands on, run to earth *or* ground
2 PLACE, put, set, position, seat, site, establish, settle, fix, situate

location *noun* PLACE, point, setting, position, situation, spot, venue, whereabouts, locus, locale

lock[1] *verb* 1 FASTEN, close, secure, shut, bar, seal, bolt, latch, sneck (*dialect*)
2 UNITE, join, link, engage, mesh, clench, entangle, interlock, entwine
3 EMBRACE, press, grasp, clutch, hug, enclose, grapple, clasp, encircle
▷ *noun* FASTENING, catch, bolt, clasp, padlock
▷▷ **lock someone out** SHUT OUT, bar, ban, exclude, keep out, debar, refuse admittance to

▷▷ **lock someone up** IMPRISON, jail, confine, cage, detain, shut up, incarcerate, send down (*informal*), send to prison, put behind bars

lock² *noun* STRAND, curl, tuft, tress, ringlet

lodge *noun* 1 CABIN, house, shelter, cottage, hut, chalet, gatehouse, hunting lodge
2 SOCIETY, group, club, association, section, wing, chapter, branch, assemblage
▷ *verb* 1 REGISTER, put, place, set, lay, enter, file, deposit, submit, put on record
2 STAY, room, stop, board, reside, sojourn
3 ACCOMMODATE, house, shelter, put up, entertain, harbour, quarter, billet
4 STICK, remain, catch, implant, come to rest, become fixed, imbed

lodger *noun* TENANT, roomer, guest, resident, boarder, paying guest

lodging *noun often plural* ACCOMMODATION, rooms, boarding, apartments, quarters, digs (*Brit informal*), shelter, residence, dwelling, abode, habitation, bachelor apartment (*Canad*)

lofty *adjective* 1 NOBLE, grand, distinguished, superior, imposing, renowned, elevated, majestic, dignified, stately, sublime, illustrious, exalted
<< OPPOSITE humble
2 HIGH, raised, towering, tall, soaring, elevated, sky-high
<< OPPOSITE low
3 HAUGHTY, lordly, proud, arrogant, patronizing, condescending, snooty (*informal*), disdainful, supercilious, high and mighty (*informal*), toffee-nosed (*slang, chiefly Brit*)
<< OPPOSITE modest

log *noun* 1 STUMP, block, branch, chunk, trunk, bole, piece of timber
2 RECORD, listing, account, register, journal, chart, diary, tally, logbook, daybook
▷ *verb* RECORD, report, enter, book, note, register, chart, put down, tally, set down, make a note of

loggerhead ▷▷ **at loggerheads** QUARRELLING, opposed, feuding, at odds, estranged, in dispute, at each other's throats, at daggers drawn, at enmity

logic *noun* 1 SCIENCE OF REASONING, deduction, dialectics, argumentation, ratiocination, syllogistic reasoning
2 CONNECTION, rationale, coherence, relationship, link, chain of thought
3 REASON, reasoning, sense, good reason, good sense, sound judgment

logical *adjective* 1 RATIONAL, clear, reasoned, reasonable, sound, relevant, consistent, valid, coherent, pertinent, well-organized, cogent, well-reasoned, deducible
<< OPPOSITE illogical
2 REASONABLE, obvious, sensible, most likely, natural, necessary, wise, plausible, judicious
<< OPPOSITE unlikely

logistics *noun* ORGANIZATION, management, strategy, engineering, plans, masterminding, coordination, orchestration

loiter *verb* LINGER, idle, loaf, saunter, delay, stroll, lag, dally, loll, dawdle, skulk, dilly-dally (*informal*), hang about *or* around

loll *verb* 1 LOUNGE, relax, lean, slump, flop, sprawl, loaf, slouch, recline, outspan (*S African*)
2 DROOP, drop, hang, flop, flap, dangle, sag, hang loosely

lone *adjective* 1 SOLITARY, single, separate, one, only, sole, by yourself, unaccompanied
2 ISOLATED, deserted, remote, secluded, lonesome (*chiefly US & Canad*), godforsaken

loneliness *noun* SOLITUDE, isolation, desolation, seclusion, aloneness, dreariness, solitariness, forlornness, lonesomeness (*chiefly US & Canad*), desertedness

lonely *adjective* 1 SOLITARY, alone, isolated, abandoned, lone, withdrawn, single, estranged, outcast, forsaken, forlorn, destitute, by yourself, lonesome (*chiefly US & Canad*), friendless, companionless
<< OPPOSITE accompanied
2 DESOLATE, deserted, remote, isolated, solitary, out-of-the-way, secluded, uninhabited, sequestered, off the beaten track (*informal*), godforsaken, unfrequented
<< OPPOSITE crowded

loner *noun* (*informal*) INDIVIDUALIST, outsider, solitary, maverick, hermit, recluse, misanthrope, lone wolf

lonesome *adjective* (*Chiefly US & Canad*) LONELY, deserted, isolated, lone, gloomy, dreary, desolate, forlorn, friendless, cheerless, companionless

long¹ *adjective* 1 ELONGATED, extended, stretched, expanded, extensive, lengthy, far-reaching, spread out
<< OPPOSITE short
2 PROLONGED, slow, dragging, sustained, lengthy, lingering, protracted, interminable, spun out, long-drawn-out
<< OPPOSITE brief

long² *verb* DESIRE, want, wish, burn, dream of, pine, hunger, ache, lust, crave, yearn, covet, itch, hanker, set your heart on, eat your heart out over

long-drawn-out *adjective* PROLONGED, marathon, lengthy, protracted, interminable, spun out, dragged out, overlong, overextended

longing *noun* DESIRE, hope, wish, burning, urge, ambition, hunger, yen (*informal*), hungering, aspiration, ache, craving, yearning, coveting, itch, thirst, hankering
<< OPPOSITE indifference
▷ *adjective* YEARNING, anxious, eager, burning, hungry, pining, craving, languishing, ardent,

avid, wishful, wistful, desirous
<< OPPOSITE indifferent
long-lived *adjective* LONG-LASTING, enduring, full of years, old as Methuselah, longevous
long-standing *adjective* ESTABLISHED, fixed, enduring, abiding, long-lasting, long-lived, long-established, time-honoured
long-suffering *adjective* UNCOMPLAINING, patient, resigned, forgiving, tolerant, easy-going, stoical, forbearing
long-winded *adjective* RAMBLING, prolonged, lengthy, tedious, diffuse, tiresome, wordy, long-drawn-out, garrulous, discursive, repetitious, overlong, verbose, prolix
<< OPPOSITE brief
look *verb* 1 SEE, view, consider, watch, eye, study, check, regard, survey, clock (*Brit slang*), examine, observe, stare, glance, gaze, scan, check out (*informal*), inspect, gape, peep, behold (*archaic*), goggle, eyeball (*slang*), scrutinize, ogle, gawp (*Brit slang*), gawk, recce (*slang*), get a load of (*informal*), take a gander at (*informal*), rubberneck (*slang*), take a dekko at (*Brit slang*), feast your eyes upon
2 SEARCH, seek, hunt, forage, fossick (*Austral & NZ*)
3 CONSIDER, contemplate
4 FACE, overlook, front on, give onto
5 HOPE, expect, await, anticipate, reckon on
6 SEEM, appear, display, seem to be, look like, exhibit, manifest, strike you as
▷ *noun* 1 GLIMPSE, view, glance, observation, review, survey, sight, examination, gaze, inspection, peek, squint (*informal*), butcher's (*Brit slang*), gander (*informal*), once-over (*informal*), recce (*slang*), eyeful (*informal*), look-see (*slang*), shufti (*Brit slang*)
2 APPEARANCE, effect, bearing, face, air, style, fashion, cast, aspect, manner, expression, impression, complexion, guise, countenance, semblance, demeanour, mien (*literary*)
▷▷ **look after something** *or* **someone** TAKE CARE OF, mind, watch, protect, tend, guard, nurse, care for, supervise, sit with, attend to, keep an eye on, take charge of
▷▷ **look down on** *or* **upon someone** DISDAIN, despise, scorn, sneer at, spurn, hold in contempt, treat with contempt, turn your nose up (at) (*informal*), contemn (*formal*), look down your nose at (*informal*), misprize
▷▷ **look forward to something** ANTICIPATE, expect, look for, wait for, await, hope for, long for, count on, count the days until, set your heart on
▷▷ **look out for something** BE CAREFUL OF, beware, watch out for, pay attention to, be wary of, be alert to, be vigilant about, keep an eye out for, be on guard for, keep your eyes open for, keep your eyes peeled for, keep your eyes skinned for, be on the qui vive for
▷▷ **look over something** EXAMINE, view, check, monitor, scan, check out (*informal*), inspect, look through, eyeball (*slang*), work over, flick through, peruse, cast an eye over, take a dekko at (*Brit slang*)
▷▷ **look someone up** VISIT, call on, go to see, pay a visit to, drop in on (*informal*), look in on
▷▷ **look something up** RESEARCH, find, search for, hunt for, track down, seek out
▷▷ **look up** IMPROVE, develop, advance, pick up, progress, come along, get better, shape up (*informal*), perk up, ameliorate, show improvement
▷▷ **look up to someone** RESPECT, honour, admire, esteem, revere, defer to, have a high opinion of, regard highly, think highly of
lookalike *noun* DOUBLE, twin, clone, replica, spit (*informal, chiefly Brit*), ringer (*slang*), spitting image (*informal*), dead ringer (*slang*), living image, exact match, spit and image (*informal*)
lookout *noun* 1 WATCHMAN, guard, sentry, sentinel, vedette (*Military*)
2 WATCH, guard, vigil, qui vive
3 WATCHTOWER, post, tower, beacon, observatory, citadel, observation post
4 (*informal*) CONCERN, business, worry, funeral (*informal*), pigeon (*Brit informal*)
loom *verb* 1 APPEAR, emerge, hover, take shape, threaten, bulk, menace, come into view, become visible
2 OVERHANG, rise, mount, dominate, tower, soar, overshadow, hang over, rise up, overtop
loop *noun* CURVE, ring, circle, bend, twist, curl, spiral, hoop, coil, loophole, twirl, kink, noose, whorl, eyelet, convolution
▷ *verb* TWIST, turn, join, roll, circle, connect, bend, fold, knot, curl, spiral, coil, braid, encircle, wind round, curve round
loophole *noun* LET-OUT, escape, excuse, plea, avoidance, evasion, pretence, pretext, subterfuge, means of escape
loose *adjective* 1 FREE, detached, insecure, unfettered, released, floating, wobbly, unsecured, unrestricted, untied, unattached, movable, unfastened, unbound, unconfined
2 SLACK, easy, hanging, relaxed, loosened, not fitting, sloppy, baggy, slackened, loose-fitting, not tight
<< OPPOSITE tight
3 (*Old-fashioned*) PROMISCUOUS, fast, abandoned, immoral, dissipated, lewd, wanton, profligate, disreputable, debauched, dissolute, libertine, licentious, unchaste
<< OPPOSITE chaste
4 VAGUE, random, inaccurate, disordered, rambling, diffuse, indefinite, disconnected, imprecise, ill-defined, indistinct, inexact
<< OPPOSITE precise

▷ *verb* FREE, release, ease, liberate, detach, unleash, let go, undo, loosen, disconnect, set free, slacken, untie, disengage, unfasten, unbind, unloose, unbridle
<< OPPOSITE fasten

loosen *verb* UNTIE, undo, release, separate, detach, let out, unstick, slacken, unbind, work free, work loose, unloose
▷▷ **loosen up** RELAX, chill (*slang*), soften, unwind, go easy (*informal*), lighten up (*slang*), hang loose, outspan (*S African*), ease up *or* off

loot *verb* PLUNDER, rob, raid, sack, rifle, ravage, ransack, pillage, despoil
▷ *noun* PLUNDER, goods, prize, haul, spoils, booty, swag (*slang*)

lop *verb* CUT, crop, chop, trim, clip, dock, hack, detach, prune, shorten, sever, curtail, truncate

lope *verb* STRIDE, spring, bound, gallop, canter, lollop

lopsided *adjective* CROOKED, one-sided, tilting, warped, uneven, unequal, disproportionate, squint, unbalanced, off balance, awry, askew, out of shape, asymmetrical, cockeyed, out of true, skewwhiff (*Brit informal*)

lord *noun* 1 PEER, nobleman, count, duke, gentleman, earl, noble, baron, aristocrat, viscount, childe (*archaic*)
2 RULER, leader, chief, king, prince, master, governor, commander, superior, monarch, sovereign, liege, overlord, potentate, seigneur
▷▷ **lord it over someone** BOSS AROUND *or* ABOUT (*informal*), order around, threaten, bully, menace, intimidate, hector, bluster, browbeat, ride roughshod over, pull rank on, tyrannize, put on airs, be overbearing, act big (*slang*), overbear, play the lord, domineer
▷▷ **the Lord** *or* **Our Lord** JESUS CHRIST, God, Christ, Messiah, Jehovah, the Almighty, the Galilean, the Good Shepherd, the Nazarene

lore *noun* TRADITIONS, sayings, experience, saws, teaching, beliefs, wisdom, doctrine, mythos, folk-wisdom, traditional wisdom

lose *verb* 1 BE DEFEATED, be beaten, lose out, be worsted, come to grief, come a cropper (*informal*), be the loser, suffer defeat, get the worst of, take a licking (*informal*)
2 MISLAY, miss, drop, forget, displace, be deprived of, fail to keep, lose track of, suffer the loss of, misplace
3 FORFEIT, miss, fail, yield, default, be deprived of, pass up (*informal*), lose out on (*informal*)
4 WASTE, consume, squander, drain, exhaust, lavish, deplete, use up, dissipate, expend, misspend
5 STRAY FROM, miss, confuse, wander from
6 ESCAPE FROM, pass, leave behind, evade, lap, duck, dodge, shake off, elude, slip away from, outstrip, throw off, outrun, outdistance, give someone the slip

loser *noun* FAILURE, flop (*informal*), underdog, also-ran, no-hoper (*Austral slang*), dud (*informal*), lemon (*slang*), clinker (*slang, chiefly US*), washout (*informal*), non-achiever

loss *noun* 1 LOSING, waste, disappearance, deprivation, squandering, drain, forfeiture
<< OPPOSITE gain
2 *sometimes plural* DEFICIT, debt, deficiency, debit, depletion, shrinkage, losings
<< OPPOSITE gain
3 DAMAGE, cost, injury, hurt, harm, disadvantage, detriment, impairment
<< OPPOSITE advantage
▷ *plural noun* CASUALTIES, dead, victims, death toll, fatalities, number killed, number wounded
▷▷ **at a loss** CONFUSED, puzzled, baffled, bewildered, stuck (*informal*), helpless, stumped, perplexed, mystified, nonplussed, at your wits' end

lost *adjective* 1 MISSING, missed, disappeared, vanished, strayed, wayward, forfeited, misplaced, mislaid
2 BEWILDERED, confused, puzzled, baffled, helpless, ignorant, perplexed, mystified, clueless (*slang*)
3 WASTED, consumed, neglected, misused, squandered, forfeited, dissipated, misdirected, frittered away, misspent, misapplied
4 GONE, finished, destroyed, vanished, extinct, defunct, died out
5 PAST, former, gone, dead, forgotten, lapsed, extinct, obsolete, out-of-date, bygone, unremembered
6 ENGROSSED, taken up, absorbed, entranced, abstracted, absent, distracted, preoccupied, immersed, dreamy, rapt, spellbound
7 FALLEN, corrupt, depraved, wanton, abandoned, damned, profligate, dissolute, licentious, unchaste, irreclaimable

lot *noun* 1 BUNCH (*informal*), group, crowd, crew, set, band, quantity, assortment, consignment
2 DESTINY, situation, circumstances, fortune, chance, accident, fate, portion, doom, hazard, plight
3 SHARE, group, set, piece, collection, portion, parcel, batch
▷▷ **a lot** *or* **lots** 1 PLENTY, scores, masses (*informal*), load(s) (*informal*), ocean(s), wealth, piles (*informal*), a great deal, quantities, stack(s), heap(s), a good deal, a large amount, abundance, reams (*informal*), oodles (*informal*)
2 OFTEN, regularly, a great deal, frequently, a good deal
▷▷ **draw lots** CHOOSE, pick, select, toss up, draw straws (*informal*), throw dice, spin a coin
▷▷ **throw in your lot with someone** JOIN WITH, support, join forces with, make common cause

with, align yourself with, ally *or* align yourself with, join fortunes with

loth ▷ see **loath**

lotion *noun* CREAM, solution, balm, salve, liniment, embrocation

lottery *noun* **1** RAFFLE, draw, lotto (*Brit, NZ & S African*), sweepstake
2 GAMBLE, chance, risk, venture, hazard, toss-up (*informal*)

loud *adjective* **1** NOISY, strong, booming, roaring, piercing, thundering, forte (*Music*), turbulent, resounding, deafening, thunderous, rowdy, blaring, strident, boisterous, tumultuous, vociferous, vehement, sonorous, ear-splitting, obstreperous, stentorian, clamorous, ear-piercing, high-sounding
<< OPPOSITE quiet
2 GARISH, bold, glaring, flamboyant, vulgar, brash, tacky (*informal*), flashy, lurid, tasteless, naff (*Brit slang*), gaudy, tawdry, showy, ostentatious, brassy
<< OPPOSITE sombre
3 LOUD-MOUTHED, offensive, crude, coarse, vulgar, brash, crass, raucous, brazen (*informal*)
<< OPPOSITE quiet

loudly *adverb* NOISILY, vigorously, vehemently, vociferously, uproariously, lustily, shrilly, fortissimo (*Music*), at full volume, deafeningly, at the top of your voice, clamorously

lounge *verb* RELAX, pass time, hang out (*informal*), idle, loaf, potter, sprawl, lie about, waste time, recline, take it easy, saunter, loiter, loll, dawdle, laze, kill time, make yourself at home, veg out (*slang, chiefly US*), outspan (*S African*), fritter time away
▷ *noun* SITTING ROOM, living room, parlour, drawing room, front room, reception room, television room

louring *or* **lowering** *adjective* **1** DARKENING, threatening, forbidding, menacing, black, heavy, dark, grey, clouded, gloomy, ominous, cloudy, overcast, foreboding
2 GLOWERING, forbidding, grim, frowning, brooding, scowling, sullen, surly

lousy *adjective* (*Slang*) **1** INFERIOR, bad, poor, terrible, awful, no good, miserable, rotten (*informal*), duff, second-rate, shoddy, low-rent (*informal, chiefly US*), for the birds (*informal*), two-bit (*US & Canad slang*), slovenly, poxy (*slang*), dime-a-dozen (*informal*), bush-league (*Austral & NZ informal*), not much cop (*Brit slang*), tinhorn (*US slang*), of a sort *or* of sorts, strictly for the birds (*informal*), bodger *or* bodgie (*Austral slang*)
2 MEAN, low, base, dirty, vicious, rotten (*informal*), vile, despicable, hateful, contemptible
3 *with* **with** WELL-SUPPLIED WITH, rolling in (*slang*), not short of, amply supplied with

lout *noun* OAF, boor, bear, ned (*Scot slang*), yahoo, hoon (*Austral & NZ slang*), clod, bumpkin, gawk, dolt, churl, lubber, lummox (*informal*), clumsy idiot, yob *or* yobbo (*Brit slang*), cougan (*Austral slang*), scozza (*Austral slang*), bogan (*Austral slang*)

lovable *or* **loveable** *adjective* ENDEARING, attractive, engaging, charming, winning, pleasing, sweet, lovely, fetching (*informal*), delightful, cute, enchanting, captivating, cuddly, amiable, adorable, winsome, likable *or* likeable
<< OPPOSITE detestable

love *verb* **1** ADORE, care for, treasure, cherish, prize, worship, be devoted to, be attached to, be in love with, dote on, hold dear, think the world of, idolize, feel affection for, have affection for, adulate
<< OPPOSITE hate
2 ENJOY, like, desire, fancy, appreciate, relish, delight in, savour, take pleasure in, have a soft spot for, be partial to, have a weakness for
<< OPPOSITE dislike
3 CUDDLE, neck (*informal*), kiss, pet, embrace, caress, fondle, canoodle (*slang*)
▷ *noun* **1** PASSION, liking, regard, friendship, affection, warmth, attachment, intimacy, devotion, tenderness, fondness, rapture, adulation, adoration, infatuation, ardour, endearment, aroha (*NZ*), amity
<< OPPOSITE hatred
2 *with* **of** LIKING FOR, taste for, delight in, bent for, weakness for, relish for, enjoyment, devotion to, penchant for, inclination for, zest for, fondness for, soft spot for, partiality to
3 BELOVED, dear, dearest, sweet, lover, angel, darling, honey, loved one, sweetheart, truelove, dear one, leman (*archaic*), inamorata *or* inamorato
<< OPPOSITE enemy
4 SYMPATHY, understanding, heart, charity, pity, humanity, warmth, mercy, sorrow, kindness, tenderness, friendliness, condolence, commiseration, fellow feeling, soft-heartedness, tender-heartedness, aroha (*NZ*)
▷▷ **fall in love with someone** LOSE YOUR HEART TO, fall for, be taken with, take a shine to (*informal*), become infatuated with, fall head over heels in love with, be swept off your feet by, bestow your affections on
▷▷ **for love** WITHOUT PAYMENT, freely, for nothing, free of charge, gratis, pleasurably
▷▷ **for love or money** BY ANY MEANS, ever, under any conditions
▷▷ **in love** ENAMOURED, charmed, captivated, smitten, wild (*informal*), mad (*informal*), crazy (*informal*), enthralled, besotted, infatuated, enraptured
▷▷ **make love** HAVE SEXUAL INTERCOURSE, have

sex, go to bed, sleep together, do it (*informal*), mate, have sexual relations, have it off (*slang*), have it away (*slang*)

>> RELATED WORD *adjective* amatory

love affair *noun* ROMANCE, relationship, affair, intrigue, liaison, amour, affaire de coeur (*French*)

loveless *adjective* 1 UNLOVING, hard, cold, icy, insensitive, unfriendly, heartless, frigid, unresponsive, unfeeling, cold-hearted

2 UNLOVED, disliked, forsaken, lovelorn, friendless, unappreciated, unvalued, uncherished

lovelorn *adjective* LOVESICK, mooning, slighted, pining, yearning, languishing, spurned, jilted, moping, unrequited, crossed in love

lovely *adjective* 1 BEAUTIFUL, appealing, attractive, charming, winning, pretty, sweet, handsome, good-looking, exquisite, admirable, enchanting, graceful, captivating, amiable, adorable, comely

<< OPPOSITE ugly

2 WONDERFUL, pleasing, nice, pleasant, engaging, marvellous, delightful, enjoyable, gratifying, agreeable

<< OPPOSITE horrible

lovemaking *noun* SEXUAL INTERCOURSE, intercourse, intimacy, sexual relations, the other (*informal*), mating, nookie (*slang*), copulation, coitus, act of love, carnal knowledge, rumpy-pumpy (*slang*), coition, sexual union *or* congress, rumpo (*slang*)

lover *noun* SWEETHEART, beloved, loved one, beau, flame (*informal*), mistress, admirer, suitor, swain (*archaic*), woman friend, lady friend, man friend, toy boy, paramour, leman (*archaic*), fancy bit (*slang*), boyfriend *or* girlfriend, fancy man *or* fancy woman (*slang*), fiancé *or* fiancée, inamorata *or* inamorato

loving *adjective* 1 AFFECTIONATE, kind, warm, dear, friendly, devoted, tender, fond, ardent, cordial, doting, amorous, solicitous, demonstrative, warm-hearted

<< OPPOSITE cruel

2 TENDER, kind, caring, warm, gentle, sympathetic, considerate

low¹ *adjective* 1 SMALL, little, short, stunted, squat, fubsy (*archaic* or *dialect*)

<< OPPOSITE tall

2 LOW-LYING, deep, depressed, shallow, subsided, sunken, ground-level

<< OPPOSITE high

3 INEXPENSIVE, cheap, reasonable, bargain, moderate, modest, cut-price, economical, bargain-basement

4 MEAGRE, little, small, reduced, depleted, scant, trifling, insignificant, sparse, paltry, measly

<< OPPOSITE significant

5 INFERIOR, bad, poor, inadequate, pathetic, worthless, unsatisfactory, mediocre, deficient, second-rate, shoddy, low-grade, puny, substandard, low-rent (*informal, chiefly US*), half-pie (*NZ informal*), bodger *or* bodgie (*Austral slang*)

6 QUIET, soft, gentle, whispered, muted, subdued, hushed, muffled

<< OPPOSITE loud

7 DEJECTED, down, blue, sad, depressed, unhappy, miserable, fed up, moody, gloomy, dismal, forlorn, glum, despondent, downcast, morose, disheartened, downhearted, down in the dumps (*informal*), sick as a parrot (*informal*), cheesed off (*informal*), brassed off (*Brit slang*)

<< OPPOSITE happy

8 COARSE, common, rough, gross, crude, rude, obscene, disgraceful, vulgar, undignified, disreputable, unbecoming, unrefined, dishonourable, ill-bred

9 CONTEMPTIBLE, mean, base, nasty, cowardly, degraded, vulgar, vile, sordid, abject, unworthy, despicable, depraved, menial, reprehensible, dastardly, scurvy, servile, unprincipled, dishonourable, ignoble

<< OPPOSITE honourable

10 LOWLY, poor, simple, plain, peasant, obscure, humble, meek, unpretentious, plebeian, lowborn

11 ILL, weak, exhausted, frail, dying, reduced, sinking, stricken, feeble, debilitated, prostrate

<< OPPOSITE strong

▷▷ **lie low** HIDE, lurk, hole up, hide away, keep a low profile, hide out, go underground, skulk, go into hiding, take cover, keep out of sight, go to earth, conceal yourself

low² *verb* MOO, bellow

low-down *noun* (*informal*) INFORMATION, intelligence, info (*informal*), inside story, gen (*Brit informal*), dope (*informal*)

▷ *adjective* MEAN, low, base, cheap (*informal*), nasty, ugly, despicable, reprehensible, contemptible, underhand, scurvy

lower *adjective* 1 SUBORDINATE, under, smaller, junior, minor, secondary, lesser, low-level, inferior, second-class

2 REDUCED, cut, diminished, decreased, lessened, curtailed, pared down

<< OPPOSITE increased

▷ *verb* 1 DROP, sink, depress, let down, submerge, take down, let fall, make lower

<< OPPOSITE raise

2 LESSEN, cut, reduce, moderate, diminish, slash, decrease, prune, minimize, curtail, abate

<< OPPOSITE increase

3 DEMEAN, humble, disgrace, humiliate, degrade, devalue, downgrade, belittle, condescend, debase, deign, abase

4 QUIETEN, soften, hush, tone down
lowering ▷ see **louring**
low-key *adjective* SUBDUED, quiet, restrained, muted, played down, understated, muffled, toned down, low-pitched
lowly *adjective* 1 LOWBORN, obscure, subordinate, inferior, mean, proletarian, ignoble, plebeian
2 UNPRETENTIOUS, common, poor, average, simple, ordinary, plain, modest, homespun
low-tech *adjective* UNSOPHISTICATED, simple, basic, elementary
<< OPPOSITE high-tech *or* hi-tech
loyal *adjective* FAITHFUL, true, devoted, dependable, constant, attached, patriotic, staunch, trustworthy, trusty, steadfast, dutiful, unwavering, true-blue, immovable, unswerving, tried and true, true-hearted
<< OPPOSITE disloyal
loyalty *noun* FAITHFULNESS, commitment, devotion, allegiance, reliability, fidelity, homage, patriotism, obedience, constancy, dependability, trustworthiness, steadfastness, troth (*archaic*), fealty, staunchness, trueness, trustiness, true-heartedness
lozenge *noun* TABLET, pastille, troche, cough drop, jujube
lubricate *verb* OIL, grease, smear, smooth the way, oil the wheels, make smooth, make slippery
lucid *adjective* 1 CLEAR, obvious, plain, evident, distinct, explicit, transparent, clear-cut, crystal clear, comprehensible, intelligible, limpid, pellucid
<< OPPOSITE vague
2 CLEAR-HEADED, sound, reasonable, sensible, rational, sober, all there, sane, compos mentis (*Latin*), in your right mind
<< OPPOSITE confused
luck *noun* 1 GOOD FORTUNE, success, advantage, prosperity, break (*informal*), stroke of luck, blessing, windfall, good luck, fluke, godsend, serendipity
2 FORTUNE, lot, stars, chance, accident, fate, hazard, destiny, hap (*archaic*), twist of fate, fortuity
luckily *adverb* FORTUNATELY, happily, by chance, as luck would have it, fortuitously, opportunely, as it chanced
luckless *adjective* UNLUCKY, unfortunate, unsuccessful, hapless, unhappy, disastrous, cursed, hopeless, jinxed, calamitous, ill-starred, star-crossed, unpropitious, ill-fated
lucky *adjective* 1 FORTUNATE, successful, favoured, charmed, blessed, prosperous, jammy (*Brit slang*), serendipitous
<< OPPOSITE unlucky
2 FORTUITOUS, timely, fortunate, auspicious, opportune, propitious, providential, adventitious
<< OPPOSITE unlucky
lucrative *adjective* PROFITABLE, rewarding, productive, fruitful, paying, high-income, well-paid, money-making, advantageous, gainful, remunerative
ludicrous *adjective* RIDICULOUS, crazy, absurd, preposterous, odd, funny, comic, silly, laughable, farcical, outlandish, incongruous, comical, zany, nonsensical, droll, burlesque, cockamamie (*slang, chiefly US*)
<< OPPOSITE sensible
lug *verb* DRAG, carry, pull, haul, tow, yank, hump (*Brit slang*), heave
luggage *noun* BAGGAGE, things, cases, bags, gear, trunks, suitcases, paraphernalia, impedimenta
lugubrious *adjective* GLOOMY, serious, sad, dismal, melancholy, dreary, sombre, woeful, mournful, morose, sorrowful, funereal, doleful, woebegone, dirgelike
lukewarm *adjective* 1 TEPID, warm, blood-warm
2 HALF-HEARTED, cold, cool, indifferent, unconcerned, uninterested, apathetic, unresponsive, phlegmatic, unenthusiastic, laodicean
lull *noun* RESPITE, pause, quiet, silence, calm, hush, tranquillity, stillness, let-up (*informal*), calmness
▷ *verb* CALM, soothe, subdue, still, quiet, compose, hush, quell, allay, pacify, lullaby, tranquillize, rock to sleep
lullaby *noun* CRADLESONG, berceuse
lumber¹ *verb* (*Brit informal*) BURDEN, land, load, saddle, impose upon, encumber
▷ *noun* (*Brit*) JUNK, refuse, rubbish, discards, trash, clutter, jumble, white elephants, castoffs, trumpery
lumber² *verb* PLOD, shuffle, shamble, trudge, stump, clump, waddle, trundle, lump along
lumbering *adjective* AWKWARD, heavy, blundering, bumbling, hulking, unwieldy, ponderous, ungainly, elephantine, heavy-footed, lubberly
luminary *noun* CELEBRITY, star, expert, somebody, lion, worthy, notable, big name, dignitary, leading light, celeb (*informal*), personage, megastar (*informal*), fundi (*S African*), V.I.P.
luminous *adjective* BRIGHT, lighted, lit, brilliant, shining, glowing, vivid, illuminated, radiant, resplendent, lustrous, luminescent
lump¹ *noun* 1 PIECE, group, ball, spot, block, mass, cake, bunch, cluster, chunk, wedge, dab, hunk, nugget, gob, clod, gobbet
2 SWELLING, growth, bump, tumour, bulge, hump, protuberance, protrusion, tumescence
▷ *verb* GROUP, throw, mass, combine, collect, unite, pool, bunch, consolidate, aggregate,

batch, conglomerate, coalesce, agglutinate

lump² *verb* ▷▷**lump it** PUT UP WITH IT, take it, stand it, bear it, suffer it, hack it (*slang*), tolerate it, endure it, brook it

lumpy *adjective* BUMPY, clotted, uneven, knobbly, grainy, curdled, granular, full of lumps

lunacy *noun* **1** FOOLISHNESS, madness, folly, stupidity, absurdity, aberration, idiocy, craziness, tomfoolery, imbecility, foolhardiness, senselessness

<< OPPOSITE sense

2 INSANITY, madness, mania, dementia, psychosis, idiocy, derangement

<< OPPOSITE sanity

lunatic *noun* MADMAN, maniac, psychopath, nut (*slang*), loony (*slang*), nutter (*Brit slang*), nutcase (*slang*), headcase (*informal*), headbanger (*informal*)

▷ *adjective* MAD, crazy, insane, irrational, nuts (*slang*), barking (*slang*), daft, demented, barmy (*slang*), deranged, bonkers (*slang, chiefly Brit*), unhinged, loopy (*informal*), crackpot (*informal*), out to lunch (*informal*), barking mad (*slang*), maniacal, gonzo (*slang*), up the pole (*informal*), crackbrained, wacko *or* whacko (*informal*), off the air (*Austral slang*) ▷ see **mad**

lunge *verb* POUNCE, charge, bound, dive, leap, plunge, dash, thrust, poke, jab

▷ *noun* THRUST, charge, pounce, pass, spring, swing, jab, swipe (*informal*)

lurch *verb* **1** TILT, roll, pitch, list, rock, lean, heel

2 STAGGER, reel, stumble, weave, sway, totter

lure *verb* TEMPT, draw, attract, invite, trick, seduce, entice, beckon, lead on, allure, decoy, ensnare, inveigle

▷ *noun* TEMPTATION, attraction, incentive, bait, carrot (*informal*), magnet, inducement, decoy, enticement, siren song, allurement

lurid *adjective* **1** SENSATIONAL, shocking, disgusting, graphic, violent, savage, startling, grim, exaggerated, revolting, explicit, vivid, ghastly, gruesome, grisly, macabre, melodramatic, yellow (*of journalism*), gory, unrestrained, shock-horror (*facetious*)

<< OPPOSITE mild

2 GLARING, bright, bloody, intense, flaming, vivid, fiery, livid, sanguine, glowering, overbright

<< OPPOSITE pale

lurk *verb* HIDE, sneak, crouch, prowl, snoop, lie in wait, slink, skulk, conceal yourself, move with stealth, go furtively

luscious *adjective* **1** SEXY, attractive, arousing, erotic, inviting, provocative, seductive, cuddly, sensuous, alluring, voluptuous, kissable, beddable

2 DELICIOUS, sweet, juicy, rich, honeyed, savoury, succulent, palatable, mouth-watering, delectable, yummy (*slang*), scrumptious (*informal*), appetizing, toothsome, yummo (*Austral slang*)

lush *adjective* **1** ABUNDANT, green, flourishing, lavish, dense, prolific, rank, teeming, overgrown, verdant

2 LUXURIOUS, grand, elaborate, lavish, extravagant, sumptuous, plush (*informal*), ornate, opulent, palatial, ritzy (*slang*)

3 SUCCULENT, fresh, tender, ripe, juicy

lust *noun* **1** LECHERY, sensuality, licentiousness, carnality, the hots (*slang*), libido, lewdness, wantonness, salaciousness, lasciviousness, concupiscence, randiness (*informal, chiefly Brit*), pruriency

2 DESIRE, longing, passion, appetite, craving, greed, thirst, cupidity, covetousness, avidity, appetence

▷▷**lust for** *or* **after someone** DESIRE, want, crave, need, yearn for, covet, slaver over, lech after (*informal*), be consumed with desire for, hunger for *or* after

▷▷**lust for** *or* **after something** DESIRE, crave, yearn for, covet

lustful *adjective* LASCIVIOUS, sexy (*informal*), passionate, erotic, craving, sensual, randy (*informal, chiefly Brit*), raunchy (*slang*), horny (*slang*), hankering, lewd, wanton, carnal, prurient, lecherous, hot-blooded, libidinous, licentious, concupiscent, unchaste

lustre *noun* **1** SPARKLE, shine, glow, glitter, dazzle, gleam, gloss, brilliance, sheen, shimmer, glint, brightness, radiance, burnish, resplendence, lambency, luminousness

2 GLORY, honour, fame, distinction, prestige, renown, illustriousness

lustrous *adjective* SHINING, bright, glowing, sparkling, dazzling, shiny, gleaming, glossy, shimmering, radiant, luminous, glistening, burnished

lusty *adjective* VIGOROUS, strong, powerful, healthy, strapping, robust, rugged, energetic, sturdy, hale, stout, stalwart, hearty, virile, red-blooded (*informal*), brawny

luxuriant *adjective* **1** LUSH, rich, dense, abundant, excessive, thriving, flourishing, rank, productive, lavish, ample, fertile, prolific, overflowing, plentiful, exuberant, fruitful, teeming, copious, prodigal, riotous, profuse, fecund, superabundant, plenteous

<< OPPOSITE sparse

2 ELABORATE, fancy, decorated, extravagant, flamboyant, baroque, sumptuous, ornate, festooned, flowery, rococo, florid, corinthian

<< OPPOSITE plain ▷ see **luxurious**

luxuriate *verb* **1** ENJOY, delight, indulge, relish, revel, bask, wallow

2 LIVE IN LUXURY, take it easy, live the life of Riley, have the time of your life, be in clover

luxurious *adjective* 1 SUMPTUOUS, expensive, comfortable, magnificent, costly, splendid, lavish, plush (*informal*), opulent, ritzy (*slang*), de luxe, well-appointed
2 SELF-INDULGENT, pleasure-loving, sensual, pampered, voluptuous, sybaritic, epicurean
<< OPPOSITE austere

Luxurious is sometimes wrongly used where *luxuriant* is meant: *he had a luxuriant* (not *luxurious*) *moustache; the walls were covered with a luxuriant growth of wisteria*

luxury *noun* 1 OPULENCE, splendour, richness, extravagance, affluence, hedonism, a bed of roses, voluptuousness, the life of Riley, sumptuousness
<< OPPOSITE poverty
2 EXTRAVAGANCE, treat, extra, indulgence, frill, nonessential
<< OPPOSITE necessity
3 PLEASURE, delight, comfort, satisfaction, enjoyment, bliss, indulgence, gratification, wellbeing
<< OPPOSITE discomfort

lyric *adjective* 1 (*of poetry*) SONGLIKE, musical, lyrical, expressive, melodic
2 (*of a voice*) MELODIC, clear, clear, light, flowing, graceful, mellifluous, dulcet

lyrical *adjective* ENTHUSIASTIC, emotional, inspired, poetic, carried away, ecstatic, expressive, impassioned, rapturous, effusive, rhapsodic

Mm

macabre *adjective* GRUESOME, grim, ghastly, frightening, ghostly, weird, dreadful, unearthly, hideous, eerie, grisly, horrid, morbid, frightful, ghoulish
<< OPPOSITE delightful

Machiavellian *adjective* SCHEMING, cynical, shrewd, cunning, designing, intriguing, sly, astute, unscrupulous, wily, opportunist, crafty, artful, amoral, foxy, deceitful, underhand, double-dealing, perfidious

machine *noun* **1** APPLIANCE, device, apparatus, engine, tool, instrument, mechanism, gadget, contraption, gizmo (*informal*), contrivance
2 SYSTEM, agency, structure, organization, machinery, setup (*informal*)

machinery *noun* **1** EQUIPMENT, gear, instruments, apparatus, works, technology, tackle, tools, mechanism(s), gadgetry
2 ADMINISTRATION, system, organization, agency, machine, structure, channels, procedure

macho *adjective* MANLY, masculine, butch (*slang*), chauvinist, virile, he-man

mad *adjective* **1** INSANE, mental (*slang*), crazy (*informal*), nuts (*slang*), bananas (*slang*), barking (*slang*), raving, distracted, frantic, frenzied, unstable, crackers (*Brit slang*), batty (*slang*), crazed, lunatic, loony (*slang*), psychotic, demented, cuckoo (*informal*), unbalanced, barmy (*slang*), nutty (*slang*), deranged, delirious, rabid, bonkers (*slang, chiefly Brit*), flaky (*US slang*), unhinged, loopy (*informal*), crackpot (*informal*), out to lunch (*informal*), round the bend (*Brit slang*), aberrant, barking mad (*slang*), out of your mind, gonzo (*slang*), screwy (*informal*), doolally (*slang*), off your head (*slang*), off your trolley (*slang*), round the twist (*Brit slang*), up the pole (*informal*), of unsound mind, as daft as a brush (*informal, chiefly Brit*), having lost your marbles (*informal*), not right in the head, non compos mentis (*Latin*), off your rocker (*slang*), not the full shilling (*informal*), off your nut (*slang*), off your chump (*slang*), wacko or whacko (*informal*), off the air (*Austral slang*)
<< OPPOSITE sane
2 FOOLISH, absurd, wild, stupid, daft (*informal*), ludicrous, unreasonable, irrational, unsafe, senseless, preposterous, foolhardy, nonsensical, unsound, inane, imprudent, asinine
<< OPPOSITE sensible
3 (*informal*) ANGRY, cross, furious, irritated, fuming, choked, infuriated, raging, ape (*slang*), incensed, enraged, exasperated, irate, livid (*informal*), berserk, seeing red (*informal*), incandescent, wrathful, fit to be tied (*slang*), in a wax (*informal, chiefly Brit*), berko (*Austral slang*), tooshie (*Austral slang*), off the air (*Austral slang*)
<< OPPOSITE calm
4 *usually with* **about** ENTHUSIASTIC, wild, crazy (*informal*), nuts (*slang*), keen, hooked, devoted, in love with, fond, daft (*informal*), ardent, fanatical, avid, impassioned, zealous, infatuated, dotty (*slang, chiefly Brit*), enamoured
<< OPPOSITE nonchalant
5 FRENZIED, wild, excited, energetic, abandoned, agitated, frenetic, uncontrolled, boisterous, full-on (*informal*), ebullient, gay, riotous, unrestrained

> *Mad* is often used in informal speech to describe behaviour that is wild or unpredictable, or a person who is behaving in such a way. Care should be taken with this word and with all its synonyms, since many of them can cause great offence. In particular, it is important to avoid the loose use of clinical terms such as *psychotic* unless you are referring seriously to specific psychiatric disorders. In contexts where psychiatric disorders are being discussed, you should avoid labelling people with the name of their condition. For example,

instead of describing someone as *psychotic*, you would say they were *having a psychotic episode*; similarly, you would say that someone is *affected by depression*, rather than labelling them *a depressive*. Note that some people also object to the phrase *suffer from* in this context, as in *he suffers from paranoia*, preferring more neutral verbs such as *experience* or *be affected by*. Also avoid using old-fashioned words such as *insane*, *demented*, and *lunatic* with reference to psychiatric disorders. In all contexts, informal and judgmental words such as *mental* and *loony* are to be avoided

madcap *adjective* RECKLESS, rash, impulsive, ill-advised, wild, crazy, foolhardy, thoughtless, crackpot (*informal*), hot-headed, imprudent, heedless, hare-brained
▷ *noun* DAREDEVIL, tearaway, wild man, hothead

madden *verb* INFURIATE, irritate, incense, enrage, upset, provoke, annoy, aggravate (*informal*), gall, craze, inflame, exasperate, vex, unhinge, drive you crazy, nark (*Brit, Austral & NZ slang*), drive you round the bend (*Brit slang*), make your blood boil, drive you to distraction (*informal*), get your goat (*slang*), drive you round the twist (*Brit slang*), get your dander up (*informal*), make your hackles rise, raise your hackles, drive you off your head (*slang*), drive you out of your mind, get your back up, get your hackles up, make you see red (*informal*), put your back up, hack you off (*informal*)
<< OPPOSITE calm

made-up *adjective* 1 PAINTED, powdered, rouged, done up
2 FALSE, invented, imaginary, fictional, untrue, mythical, unreal, fabricated, make-believe, trumped-up, specious

madly *adverb* 1 (*informal*) PASSIONATELY, wildly, desperately, intensely, exceedingly, extremely, excessively, to distraction, devotedly
2 FOOLISHLY, wildly, absurdly, ludicrously, unreasonably, irrationally, senselessly, nonsensically
3 ENERGETICALLY, quickly, wildly, rapidly, hastily, furiously, excitedly, hurriedly, recklessly, speedily, like mad (*informal*), hell for leather, like lightning, hotfoot, like the clappers (*Brit informal*), like nobody's business (*informal*), like greased lightning (*informal*)
4 INSANELY, frantically, hysterically, crazily, deliriously, distractedly, rabidly, frenziedly, dementedly

madman *or* **madwoman** *noun* LUNATIC, psycho (*slang*), maniac, loony (*slang*), nut (*slang*), psychotic, psychopath, nutter (*Brit slang*), nutcase (*slang*), headcase (*informal*), mental case (*slang*), headbanger (*informal*) ▷ see **mad**

madness *noun* 1 INSANITY, mental illness, delusion, mania, dementia, distraction, aberration, psychosis, lunacy, craziness, derangement, psychopathy
2 FOOLISHNESS, nonsense, folly, absurdity, idiocy, wildness, daftness (*informal*), foolhardiness, preposterousness
3 FRENZY, riot, furore, uproar, abandon, excitement, agitation, intoxication, unrestraint

maelstrom *noun* 1 WHIRLPOOL, swirl, eddy, vortex, Charybdis (*literary*)
2 TURMOIL, disorder, confusion, chaos, upheaval, uproar, pandemonium, bedlam, tumult

maestro *noun* MASTER, expert, genius, virtuoso, wonk (*informal*), fundi (*S African*)

magazine *noun* JOURNAL, paper, publication, supplement, rag (*informal*), issue, glossy (*informal*), pamphlet, periodical, fanzine (*informal*)

magic *noun* 1 SORCERY, wizardry, witchcraft, enchantment, occultism, black art, spells, necromancy, sortilege, theurgy
2 CONJURING, illusion, trickery, sleight of hand, hocus-pocus, jiggery-pokery (*informal, chiefly Brit*), legerdemain, prestidigitation, jugglery
3 CHARM, power, glamour, fascination, magnetism, enchantment, allurement
▷ *adjective* MIRACULOUS, entrancing, charming, fascinating, marvellous, magical, magnetic, enchanting, bewitching, spellbinding, sorcerous

magician *noun* 1 CONJUROR, illusionist, prestidigitator
2 SORCERER, witch, wizard, illusionist, warlock, necromancer, thaumaturge (*rare*), theurgist, archimage (*rare*), enchanter *or* enchantress
3 MIRACLE-WORKER, genius, marvel, wizard, virtuoso, wonder-worker, spellbinder

magisterial *adjective* AUTHORITATIVE, lordly, commanding, masterful, imperious
<< OPPOSITE subservient

magistrate *noun* JUDGE, justice, provost (*Scot*), bailie (*Scot*), justice of the peace, J.P.
>> RELATED WORD *adjective* magisterial

magnanimous *adjective* GENEROUS, kind, noble, selfless, big, free, kindly, handsome, charitable, high-minded, bountiful, unselfish, open-handed, big-hearted, unstinting, beneficent, great-hearted, munificent, ungrudging
<< OPPOSITE petty

magnate *noun* TYCOON, leader, chief, fat cat

(*slang, chiefly US*), baron, notable, mogul, bigwig (*informal*), grandee, big shot (*informal*), captain of industry, big wheel (*slang*), big cheese (*slang* or *old-fashioned*), plutocrat, big noise (*informal*), big hitter (*informal*), magnifico, heavy hitter (*informal*), nabob (*informal*), Mister Big (*slang, chiefly US*), V.I.P.

magnetic *adjective* ATTRACTIVE, irresistible, seductive, captivating, charming, fascinating, entrancing, charismatic, enchanting, hypnotic, alluring, mesmerizing
<< OPPOSITE repulsive

magnetism *noun* CHARM, appeal, attraction, power, draw, pull, spell, magic, fascination, charisma, attractiveness, allure, enchantment, hypnotism, drawing power, seductiveness, mesmerism, captivatingness

magnification *noun* 1 ENLARGEMENT, increase, inflation, boost, expansion, blow-up (*informal*), intensification, amplification, dilation, augmentation
2 EXAGGERATION, build-up, heightening, deepening, enhancement, aggrandizement

magnificence *noun* SPLENDOUR, glory, majesty, grandeur, brilliance, nobility, gorgeousness, sumptuousness, sublimity, resplendence

magnificent *adjective* 1 SPLENDID, striking, grand, impressive, august, rich, princely, imposing, elegant, divine (*informal*), glorious, noble, gorgeous, lavish, elevated, luxurious, majestic, regal, stately, sublime, sumptuous, grandiose, exalted, opulent, transcendent, resplendent, splendiferous (*facetious*)
<< OPPOSITE ordinary
2 BRILLIANT, fine, excellent, outstanding, superb, superior, splendid

magnify *verb* 1 ENLARGE, increase, boost, expand, intensify, blow up (*informal*), heighten, amplify, augment, dilate
<< OPPOSITE reduce
2 MAKE WORSE, exaggerate, intensify, worsen, heighten, deepen, exacerbate, aggravate, increase, inflame, fan the flames of
3 EXAGGERATE, overdo, overstate, build up, enhance, blow up, inflate, overestimate, dramatize, overrate, overplay, overemphasize, blow up out of all proportion, aggrandize, make a production (out) of (*informal*), make a federal case of (*US informal*)
<< OPPOSITE understate

magnitude *noun* 1 IMPORTANCE, consequence, significance, mark, moment, note, weight, proportion, dimension, greatness, grandeur, eminence
<< OPPOSITE unimportance
2 IMMENSITY, size, extent, enormity, strength, volume, vastness, bigness, largeness, hugeness
<< OPPOSITE smallness
3 INTENSITY, measure, capacity, amplitude

maid *noun* 1 SERVANT, chambermaid, housemaid, menial, handmaiden (*archaic*), maidservant, female servant, domestic (*archaic*), parlourmaid, serving-maid
2 (*Archaic* or *Literary*) GIRL, maiden, lass, miss, nymph (*poetic*), damsel, lassie (*informal*), wench

maiden *noun* (*Archaic* or *Literary*) GIRL, maid, lass, damsel, miss, virgin, nymph (*poetic*), lassie (*informal*), wench
▷ *modifier* 1 FIRST, initial, inaugural, introductory, initiatory
2 UNMARRIED, pure, virgin, intact, chaste, virginal, unwed, undefiled

mail *noun* 1 LETTERS, post, packages, parcels, correspondence
2 POSTAL SERVICE, post, postal system
▷ *verb* 1 POST, send, forward, dispatch, send by mail *or* post
2 E-MAIL, send, forward

maim *verb* CRIPPLE, hurt, injure, wound, mar, disable, hamstring, impair, lame, mutilate, mangle, incapacitate, put out of action, mangulate (*Austral slang*)

main *adjective* CHIEF, leading, major, prime, head, special, central, particular, necessary, essential, premier, primary, vital, critical, crucial, supreme, outstanding, principal, cardinal, paramount, foremost, predominant, pre-eminent, must-have
<< OPPOSITE minor
▷ *plural noun* 1 PIPELINE, channel, pipe, conduit, duct
2 CABLE, line, electricity supply, mains supply
▷▷ **in the main** ON THE WHOLE, generally, mainly, mostly, in general, for the most part

mainly *adverb* CHIEFLY, mostly, largely, generally, usually, principally, in general, primarily, above all, substantially, on the whole, predominantly, in the main, for the most part, most of all, first and foremost, to the greatest extent

mainstay *noun* PILLAR, backbone, bulwark, prop, anchor, buttress, lynchpin, chief support

mainstream *adjective* CONVENTIONAL, general, established, received, accepted, central, current, core, prevailing, orthodox
<< OPPOSITE unconventional

maintain *verb* 1 CONTINUE, retain, preserve, sustain, carry on, keep, keep up, prolong, uphold, nurture, conserve, perpetuate
<< OPPOSITE end
2 ASSERT, state, hold, claim, insist, declare, allege, contend, affirm, profess, avow, aver, asseverate
<< OPPOSITE disavow
3 LOOK AFTER, care for, take care of, finance, conserve, keep in good condition

maintenance *noun* 1 UPKEEP, keeping, care,

supply, repairs, provision, conservation, nurture, preservation
2 ALLOWANCE, living, support, keep, food, livelihood, subsistence, upkeep, sustenance, alimony, aliment
3 CONTINUATION, carrying-on, continuance, support, perpetuation, prolongation, sustainment, retainment

majestic *adjective* GRAND, magnificent, impressive, superb, kingly, royal, august, princely, imposing, imperial, noble, splendid, elevated, awesome, dignified, regal, stately, monumental, sublime, lofty, pompous, grandiose, exalted, splendiferous (*facetious*)
<< OPPOSITE modest

majesty *noun* GRANDEUR, glory, splendour, magnificence, dignity, nobility, sublimity, loftiness, impressiveness, awesomeness, exaltedness
<< OPPOSITE triviality

major *adjective* 1 IMPORTANT, vital, critical, significant, great, serious, radical, crucial, outstanding, grave, extensive, notable, weighty, pre-eminent
2 MAIN, higher, greater, bigger, lead, leading, head, larger, better, chief, senior, supreme, superior, elder, uppermost
<< OPPOSITE minor

majority *noun* 1 MOST, more, mass, bulk, best part, better part, lion's share, preponderance, plurality, greater number
2 ADULTHOOD, maturity, age of consent, seniority, manhood *or* womanhood

> *The majority of* should always refer to a countable number of things or people. If you are talking about an amount or quantity, rather than a countable number, use *most of*, as in *most of the harvest was saved* (not *the majority of the harvest was saved*)

make *verb* 1 PRODUCE, cause, create, effect, lead to, occasion, generate, bring about, give rise to, engender, beget
2 PERFORM, do, act out, effect, carry out, engage in, execute, prosecute
3 FORCE, cause, press, compel, drive, require, oblige, induce, railroad (*informal*), constrain, coerce, impel, dragoon, pressurize, prevail upon
4 APPOINT, name, select, elect, invest, install, nominate, assign, designate, hire as, cast as, employ as, ordain, vote in as, recruit as, engage as, enlist as
5 CREATE, build, produce, manufacture, form, model, fashion, shape, frame, construct, assemble, compose, forge, mould, put together, originate, fabricate
6 ENACT, form, pass, establish, fix, institute, frame, devise, lay down, draw up
7 EARN, get, gain, net, win, clear, secure, realize, obtain, acquire, bring in, take in, fetch
8 AMOUNT TO, total, constitute, add up to, count as, tot up to (*informal*)
9 GET TO, reach, catch, arrive at, meet, arrive in time for
10 CALCULATE, judge, estimate, determine, think, suppose, reckon, work out, compute, gauge, count up, put a figure on
▷ *noun* BRAND, sort, style, model, build, form, mark, kind, type, variety, construction, marque
▷▷ **make as if** PRETEND, affect, give the impression that, feign, feint, make a show of, act as if *or* though
▷▷ **make away** *or* **off with something** STEAL, nick (*slang, chiefly Brit*), pinch (*informal*), nab (*informal*), carry off, swipe (*slang*), knock off (*slang*), pilfer, cart off (*slang*), purloin, filch
▷▷ **make believe** PRETEND, play, enact, feign, play-act, act as if *or* though
▷▷ **make do** MANAGE, cope, improvise, muddle through, get along *or* by, scrape along *or* by
▷▷ **make for something** 1 HEAD FOR, aim for, head towards, set out for, be bound for, make a beeline for, steer (a course) for, proceed towards
2 CONTRIBUTE TO, produce, further, forward, advance, promote, foster, facilitate, be conducive to
▷▷ **make it** (*informal*) 1 SUCCEED, be successful, prosper, be a success, arrive (*informal*), get on, make good, cut it (*informal*), get ahead, make the grade (*informal*), crack it (*informal*), make it big, get somewhere, distinguish yourself
2 GET BETTER, survive, recover, rally, come through, pull through
▷▷ **make off** FLEE, clear out (*informal*), abscond, fly, bolt, decamp, hook it (*slang*), do a runner (*slang*), run for it (*informal*), slope off, cut and run (*informal*), beat a hasty retreat, fly the coop (*US & Canad informal*), make away, skedaddle (*informal*), take a powder (*US & Canad slang*), take to your heels, run away *or* off
▷▷ **make out** FARE, manage, do, succeed, cope, get on, proceed, thrive, prosper
▷▷ **make something out** 1 SEE, observe, distinguish, perceive, recognize, detect, glimpse, pick out, discern, catch sight of, espy, descry
2 UNDERSTAND, see, work out, grasp, perceive, follow, realize, comprehend, fathom, decipher, suss (out) (*slang*), get the drift of
3 WRITE OUT, complete, draft, draw up, inscribe, fill in *or* out
4 PRETEND, claim, suggest, maintain, declare, allege, hint, imply, intimate, assert, insinuate, let on, make as if

5 PROVE, show, describe, represent, demonstrate, justify

▷▷ **make something up** INVENT, create, construct, compose, write, frame, manufacture, coin, devise, hatch, originate, formulate, dream up, fabricate, concoct, cook up (*informal*), trump up

▷▷ **make up** SETTLE YOUR DIFFERENCES, shake hands, make peace, bury the hatchet, call it quits, forgive and forget, mend fences, become reconciled, declare a truce, be friends again

▷▷ **make up for something** COMPENSATE FOR, redress, make amends for, atone for, balance out, offset, expiate, requite, make reparation for, make recompense for

▷▷ **make up something** 1 FORM, account for, constitute, compose, comprise

2 COMPLETE, meet, supply, fill, round off

▷▷ **make up to someone** (*informal*) FLIRT WITH, be all over, come on to, chase after, court, pursue, woo, run after, chat up (*informal*), curry favour with, make overtures to, make eyes at

make-believe *noun* FANTASY, imagination, pretence, charade, unreality, dream, play-acting

<< OPPOSITE reality

▷ *adjective* IMAGINARY, dream, imagined, made-up, fantasy, pretend, pretended, mock, sham, unreal, fantasized

<< OPPOSITE real

maker *noun* MANUFACTURER, producer, builder, constructor, fabricator

Maker *noun* GOD, Creator, Prime Mover

makeshift *adjective* TEMPORARY, provisional, make-do, substitute, jury (*chiefly Nautical*), expedient, rough and ready, stopgap

make-up *noun* 1 COSMETICS, paint (*informal*), powder, face (*informal*), greasepaint (*Theatre*), war paint (*informal*), maquillage (*French*)

2 NATURE, character, constitution, temperament, make, build, figure, stamp, temper, disposition, frame of mind, cast of mind

3 STRUCTURE, organization, arrangement, form, construction, assembly, constitution, format, formation, composition, configuration

making *noun* CREATION, production, manufacture, construction, assembly, forging, composition, fabrication

▷ *plural noun* BEGINNINGS, qualities, potential, stuff, basics, materials, capacity, ingredients, essence, capability, potentiality

▷▷ **in the making** BUDDING, potential, up and coming, emergent, coming, growing, developing, promising, burgeoning, nascent, incipient

malady *noun* DISEASE, complaint, illness, disorder, sickness, ailment, affliction, infirmity, ill, indisposition, lurgy (*informal*)

malaise *noun* UNEASE, illness, depression, anxiety, weakness, sickness, discomfort, melancholy, angst, disquiet, doldrums, lassitude, enervation

malcontent *noun* TROUBLEMAKER, rebel, complainer, grumbler, grouser, agitator, stirrer (*informal*), mischief-maker, grouch (*informal*), fault-finder

▷ *adjective* DISCONTENTED, unhappy, disgruntled, dissatisfied, disgusted, rebellious, resentful, disaffected, restive, unsatisfied, ill-disposed, factious

male *adjective* MASCULINE, manly, macho, virile, manlike, manful

<< OPPOSITE female

malevolent *adjective* SPITEFUL, hostile, vicious, malicious, malign, malignant, vindictive, pernicious, vengeful, hateful (*archaic*), baleful, rancorous, evil-minded, maleficent, ill-natured

<< OPPOSITE benevolent

malfunction *verb* BREAK DOWN, fail, go wrong, play up (*Brit informal*), stop working, be defective, conk out (*informal*), develop a fault

▷ *noun* FAULT, failure, breakdown, defect, flaw, impairment, glitch

malice *noun* SPITE, animosity, enmity, hate, hatred, bitterness, venom, spleen, rancour, bad blood, ill will, animus, malevolence, vindictiveness, evil intent, malignity, spitefulness, vengefulness, maliciousness

malicious *adjective* SPITEFUL, malevolent, malignant, vicious, bitter, resentful, pernicious, vengeful, bitchy (*informal*), hateful, baleful, injurious, rancorous, catty (*informal*), shrewish, ill-disposed, evil-minded, ill-natured

<< OPPOSITE benevolent

malign *verb* DISPARAGE, abuse, run down, libel, knock (*informal*), injure, rubbish (*informal*), smear, blacken (someone's name), slag (off) (*slang*), denigrate, revile, vilify, slander, defame, bad-mouth (*slang, chiefly US & Canad*), traduce, speak ill of, derogate, do a hatchet job on (*informal*), calumniate, asperse

<< OPPOSITE praise

▷ *adjective* EVIL, bad, destructive, harmful, hostile, vicious, malignant, wicked, hurtful, pernicious, malevolent, baleful, deleterious, injurious, baneful, maleficent

<< OPPOSITE good

malignant *adjective* 1 (*Medical*) UNCONTROLLABLE, dangerous, evil, fatal, deadly, cancerous, virulent, irremediable

2 HOSTILE, harmful, bitter, vicious, destructive, malicious, malign, hurtful, pernicious, malevolent, spiteful, baleful, injurious, inimical, maleficent, of evil intent

<< OPPOSITE benign

malleable *adjective* 1 MANAGEABLE, adaptable, compliant, impressionable, pliable, tractable, biddable, governable, like putty in your hands

2 WORKABLE, soft, plastic, tensile, ductile

malpractice *noun* MISCONDUCT, abuse, negligence, mismanagement, misbehaviour, dereliction

mammoth *adjective* COLOSSAL, huge, giant, massive, vast, enormous, mighty, immense, titanic, jumbo (*informal*), gigantic, monumental, mountainous, stellar (*informal*), prodigious, stupendous, gargantuan, elephantine, ginormous (*informal*), Brobdingnagian, humongous *or* humungous (*US slang*)

<< OPPOSITE tiny

man *noun* 1 MALE, guy (*informal*), fellow (*informal*), gentleman, bloke (*Brit informal*), chap (*Brit informal*), dude (*US informal*), geezer (*informal*), adult male

2 HUMAN, human being, body, person, individual, adult, being, somebody, soul, personage

3 MANKIND, humanity, people, mortals, human race, humankind, Homo sapiens

4 PARTNER, boy, husband, lover, mate, boyfriend, old man, groom, spouse, sweetheart, beau, significant other (US)

▷ *verb* STAFF, people, fill, crew, occupy, garrison, furnish with men

▷▷ **to a man** WITHOUT EXCEPTION, as one, every one, unanimously, each and every one, one and all, bar none

>> RELATED WORDS *adjectives* anthropic, anthropoid, anthropoidal

mana *noun* (NZ) AUTHORITY, influence, power, might, force, weight, strength, domination, sway, standing, status, importance, esteem, stature, eminence

manacle *noun* HANDCUFF, bond, chain, shackle, tie, iron, fetter, gyve (*archaic*)

▷ *verb* HANDCUFF, bind, confine, restrain, check, chain, curb, hamper, inhibit, constrain, shackle, fetter, tie someone's hands, put in chains, clap *or* put in irons

manage *verb* 1 BE IN CHARGE OF, run, handle, rule, direct, conduct, command, govern, administer, oversee, supervise, preside over, be head of, call the shots in, superintend, call the tune in

2 ORGANIZE, use, handle, govern, regulate

3 COPE, survive, shift, succeed, get on, carry on, fare, get through, make out, cut it (*informal*), get along, make do, get by (*informal*), crack it (*informal*), muddle through

4 PERFORM, do, deal with, achieve, carry out, undertake, cope with, accomplish, contrive, finish off, bring about *or* off

5 CONTROL, influence, guide, handle, master, dominate, manipulate

6 STEER, operate, pilot

manageable *adjective* EASY, convenient, handy, user-friendly, wieldy

<< OPPOSITE difficult

management *noun* 1 ADMINISTRATION, control, rule, government, running, charge, care, operation, handling, direction, conduct, command, guidance, supervision, manipulation, governance, superintendence

2 DIRECTORS, board, executive(s), bosses (*informal*), administration, employers, directorate

manager *noun* SUPERVISOR, head, director, executive, boss (*informal*), governor, administrator, conductor, controller, superintendent, gaffer (*informal, chiefly Brit*), proprietor, organizer, comptroller, overseer, baas (*S African*), sherang (*Austral & NZ*)

mandate *noun* COMMAND, order, charge, authority, commission, sanction, instruction, warrant, decree, bidding, canon, directive, injunction, fiat, edict, authorization, precept

mandatory *adjective* COMPULSORY, required, binding, obligatory, requisite

<< OPPOSITE optional

manfully *adverb* BRAVELY, boldly, vigorously, stoutly, hard, strongly, desperately, courageously, stalwartly, powerfully, resolutely, determinedly, heroically, valiantly, nobly, gallantly, like the devil, to the best of your ability, like a Trojan, intrepidly, like one possessed, with might and main

mangle *verb* CRUSH, mutilate, maim, deform, cut, total (*slang*), tear, destroy, ruin, mar, rend, wreck, spoil, butcher, cripple, hack, distort, trash (*slang*), maul, disfigure, lacerate, mangulate (*Austral slang*)

manhandle *verb* 1 ROUGH UP, pull, push, paw (*informal*), maul, handle roughly, knock about *or* around

2 HAUL, carry, pull, push, lift, manoeuvre, tug, shove, hump (*Brit slang*), heave

manhood *noun* MANLINESS, masculinity, spirit, strength, resolution, courage, determination, maturity, bravery, fortitude, mettle, firmness, virility, valour, hardihood, manfulness

mania *noun* 1 OBSESSION, passion, thing (*informal*), desire, rage, enthusiasm, craving, preoccupation, craze, fad (*informal*), fetish, fixation, partiality

2 MADNESS, disorder, frenzy, insanity, dementia, aberration, lunacy, delirium, craziness, derangement

maniac *noun* 1 MADMAN *or* MADWOMAN, psycho (*slang*), lunatic, loony (*slang*), psychopath, nutter (*Brit slang*), nutcase (*slang*), headcase (*informal*), headbanger (*informal*)

2 FANATIC, fan, enthusiast, freak (*informal*), fiend (*informal*)

manifest *adjective* OBVIOUS, apparent, patent, evident, open, clear, plain, visible, bold, distinct, glaring, noticeable, blatant, conspicuous, unmistakable, palpable, salient

<< OPPOSITE concealed

▷ *verb* DISPLAY, show, reveal, establish, express, prove, declare, demonstrate, expose, exhibit, set forth, make plain, evince

<< OPPOSITE conceal

manifestation *noun* 1 SIGN, symptom, indication, mark, example, evidence, instance, proof, token, testimony

2 DISPLAY, show, exhibition, expression, demonstration, appearance, exposure, revelation, disclosure, materialization

manifold *adjective* (*Formal*) NUMEROUS, many, various, varied, multiple, diverse, multiplied, diversified, abundant, assorted, copious, multifarious, multitudinous, multifold

manipulate *verb* 1 INFLUENCE, control, direct, guide, conduct, negotiate, exploit, steer, manoeuvre, do a number on (*chiefly US*), twist around your little finger

2 WORK, use, operate, handle, employ, wield

mankind *noun* PEOPLE, man, humanity, human race, humankind, Homo sapiens

Some people object to the use of *mankind* to refer to all human beings on the grounds that it is sexist. A preferable term is *humankind*, which refers to both men and women

manliness *noun* VIRILITY, masculinity, manhood, machismo, courage, bravery, vigour, heroism, mettle, boldness, firmness, valour, fearlessness, intrepidity, hardihood

manly *adjective* VIRILE, male, masculine, macho, strong, powerful, brave, daring, bold, strapping, hardy, heroic, robust, vigorous, muscular, courageous, fearless, butch (*slang*), resolute, gallant, valiant, well-built, red-blooded (*informal*), dauntless, stout-hearted, valorous, manful

<< OPPOSITE effeminate

man-made *adjective* ARTIFICIAL, manufactured, plastic (*slang*), mock, synthetic, ersatz

manner *noun* 1 STYLE, way, fashion, method, means, form, process, approach, practice, procedure, habit, custom, routine, mode, genre, tack, tenor, usage, wont

2 BEHAVIOUR, look, air, bearing, conduct, appearance, aspect, presence, tone, demeanour, deportment, mien (*literary*), comportment

3 TYPE, form, sort, kind, nature, variety, brand, breed, category

▷ *plural noun* 1 CONDUCT, bearing, behaviour, breeding, carriage, demeanour, deportment, comportment

2 POLITENESS, courtesy, etiquette, refinement, polish, decorum, p's and q's

3 PROTOCOL, ceremony, customs, formalities, good form, proprieties, the done thing, social graces, politesse

mannered *adjective* AFFECTED, put-on, posed, artificial, pseudo (*informal*), pretentious, stilted, arty-farty (*informal*)

<< OPPOSITE natural

mannerism *noun* HABIT, characteristic, trait, quirk, peculiarity, foible, idiosyncrasy

manoeuvre *verb* 1 STEER, direct, guide, pilot, work, move, drive, handle, negotiate, jockey, manipulate, navigate

2 SCHEME, plot, plan, intrigue, wangle (*informal*), machinate

3 MANIPULATE, arrange, organize, devise, manage, set up, engineer, fix, orchestrate, contrive, stage-manage

▷ *noun* 1 STRATAGEM, move, plan, action, movement, scheme, trick, plot, tactic, intrigue, dodge, ploy, ruse, artifice, subterfuge, machination

2 *often plural* MOVEMENT, operation, exercise, deployment, war game

mansion *noun* RESIDENCE, manor, hall, villa, dwelling, abode, habitation, seat

mantle *noun* 1 COVERING, cover, screen, cloud, curtain, envelope, blanket, veil, shroud, canopy, pall

2 (*Archaic*) CLOAK, wrap, cape, hood, shawl

▷ *verb* COVER, hide, blanket, cloud, wrap, screen, mask, disguise, veil, cloak, shroud, envelop, overspread

manual *adjective* 1 PHYSICAL, human, done by hand

2 HAND-OPERATED, hand, non-automatic

▷ *noun* HANDBOOK, guide, instructions, bible, guidebook, workbook

manufacture *verb* 1 MAKE, build, produce, construct, form, create, process, shape, turn out, assemble, compose, forge, mould, put together, fabricate, mass-produce

2 CONCOCT, make up, invent, devise, hatch, fabricate, think up, cook up (*informal*), trump up

▷ *noun* MAKING, production, construction, assembly, creation, produce, fabrication, mass-production

manufacturer *noun* MAKER, producer, builder, creator, industrialist, factory-owner, constructor, fabricator

manure *noun* COMPOST, muck, fertilizer, dung, droppings, excrement, ordure

many *adjective* NUMEROUS, various, varied, countless, abundant, myriad, innumerable, sundry, copious, manifold, umpteen (*informal*),

profuse, multifarious, multitudinous, multifold, divers (*archaic*)
▷ *pronoun* A LOT, lots (*informal*), plenty, a mass, scores, piles (*informal*), tons (*informal*), heaps (*informal*), large numbers, a multitude, umpteen (*informal*), a horde, a thousand and one, a gazillion (*informal*)
▷▷ **the many** THE MASSES, the people, the crowd, the majority, the rank and file, the multitude, (the) hoi polloi

mar *verb* 1 HARM, damage, hurt, spoil, stain, blight, taint, tarnish, blot, sully, vitiate, put a damper on
2 RUIN, injure, spoil, scar, flaw, impair, mutilate, detract from, maim, deform, blemish, mangle, disfigure, deface
<< OPPOSITE improve

marauder *noun* RAIDER, outlaw, bandit, pirate, robber, ravager, plunderer, pillager, buccaneer, brigand, corsair, sea wolf, freebooter, reiver (*dialect*)

march *verb* 1 PARADE, walk, file, pace, stride, tread, tramp, swagger, footslog
2 WALK, strut, storm, sweep, stride, stalk, flounce
▷ *noun* 1 WALK, trek, hike, tramp, slog, yomp (*Brit informal*), routemarch
2 DEMONSTRATION, parade, procession, demo (*informal*)
3 PROGRESS, development, advance, evolution, progression

margin *noun* 1 ROOM, space, surplus, allowance, scope, play, compass, latitude, leeway, extra room, elbowroom
2 EDGE, side, limit, border, bound, boundary, confine, verge, brink, rim, brim, perimeter, periphery

marginal *adjective* 1 INSIGNIFICANT, small, low, minor, slight, minimal, negligible
2 BORDERLINE, bordering, on the edge, peripheral

marijuana *noun* CANNABIS, pot (*slang*), weed (*slang*), dope (*slang*), blow (*slang*), smoke (*informal*), stuff (*slang*), leaf (*slang*), tea (*US slang*), grass (*slang*), chronic (*US slang*), hemp, hash (*slang*), gage (*US dated slang*), hashish, mary jane (*US slang*), ganja, bhang, kif, wacky baccy (*slang*), sinsemilla, dagga (*S African*), charas

marine *adjective* NAUTICAL, sea, maritime, oceanic, naval, saltwater, seafaring, ocean-going, seagoing, pelagic, thalassic

mariner *noun* SAILOR, seaman, sea dog, seafarer, hand, salt, tar, navigator, gob (*US slang*), matelot (*slang, chiefly Brit*), Jack Tar, seafaring man, bluejacket

marital *adjective* MATRIMONIAL, married, wedded, nuptial, conjugal, spousal, connubial

maritime *adjective* 1 NAUTICAL, marine, naval, sea, oceanic, seafaring
2 COASTAL, seaside, littoral

mark *noun* 1 SPOT, stain, streak, smudge, line, nick, impression, scratch, bruise, scar, dent, blot, blemish, blotch, pock, splotch, smirch
2 CHARACTERISTIC, feature, symptom, standard, quality, measure, stamp, par, attribute, criterion, norm, trait, badge, hallmark, yardstick, peculiarity
3 INDICATION, sign, note, evidence, symbol, proof, token
4 BRAND, impression, label, stamp, print, device, flag, seal, symbol, token, earmark, emblem, insignia, signet
5 IMPRESSION, effect, influence, impact, trace, imprint, vestiges
6 TARGET, goal, aim, purpose, end, object, objective
▷ *verb* 1 SCAR, scratch, dent, imprint, nick, brand, impress, stain, bruise, streak, blot, smudge, blemish, blotch, splotch, smirch
2 LABEL, identify, brand, flag, stamp, characterize
3 GRADE, correct, assess, evaluate, appraise
4 DISTINGUISH, show, illustrate, exemplify, denote, evince, betoken
5 OBSERVE, mind, note, regard, notice, attend to, pay attention to, pay heed to, hearken to (*archaic*)
▷▷ **make your mark** SUCCEED, make it (*informal*), make good, prosper, be a success, achieve recognition, get on in the world, make something of yourself, find a place in the sun, make a success of yourself

marked *adjective* NOTICEABLE, clear, decided, striking, noted, obvious, signal, dramatic, considerable, outstanding, remarkable, apparent, prominent, patent, evident, distinct, pronounced, notable, manifest, blatant, conspicuous, salient
<< OPPOSITE imperceptible

markedly *adverb* NOTICEABLY, greatly, clearly, obviously, seriously (*informal*), signally, patently, notably, considerably, remarkably, evidently, manifestly, distinctly, decidedly, strikingly, conspicuously, to a great extent, outstandingly

market *noun* FAIR, mart, bazaar, souk (*Arabic*)
▷ *verb* SELL, promote, retail, peddle, vend, offer for sale

marketable *adjective* SOUGHT AFTER, wanted, in demand, saleable, merchantable, vendible

marksman *or* **markswoman** *noun* SHARPSHOOTER, good shot, crack shot (*informal*), dead shot (*informal*), deadeye (*informal, chiefly US*)

maroon *verb* ABANDON, leave, desert, strand, leave high and dry (*informal*), cast away, cast ashore

marriage *noun* 1 WEDDING, match, nuptials, wedlock, wedding ceremony, matrimony,

espousal, nuptial rites
2 UNION, coupling, link, association, alliance, merger, confederation, amalgamation
>> RELATED WORDS *adjectives* conjugal, connubial, marital, nuptial

married *adjective* 1 WEDDED, one, united, joined, wed, hitched (*slang*), spliced (*informal*)
2 MARITAL, wifely, husbandly, nuptial, matrimonial, conjugal, spousal, connubial

marry *verb* 1 TIE THE KNOT (*informal*), wed, take the plunge (*informal*), walk down the aisle (*informal*), get hitched (*slang*), get spliced (*informal*), become man and wife, plight your troth (*old-fashioned*)
2 UNITE, match, join, link, tie, bond, ally, merge, knit, unify, splice, yoke

marsh *noun* SWAMP, moss (*Scot & Northern English dialect*), bog, slough, fen, quagmire, morass, muskeg (*Canad*)

marshal *verb* 1 CONDUCT, take, lead, guide, steer, escort, shepherd, usher
2 ARRANGE, group, order, collect, gather, line up, organize, assemble, deploy, array, dispose, draw up, muster, align

martial *adjective* MILITARY, soldierly, brave, heroic, belligerent, warlike, bellicose

martyrdom *noun* PERSECUTION, suffering, torture, agony, ordeal, torment, anguish
<< OPPOSITE bliss

marvel *verb* BE AMAZED, wonder, gaze, gape, goggle, be awed, be filled with surprise
▷ *noun* 1 WONDER, phenomenon, miracle, portent
2 GENIUS, whizz (*informal*), prodigy

marvellous *adjective* EXCELLENT, great (*informal*), mean (*slang*), topping (*Brit slang*), wonderful, brilliant, bad (*slang*), cracking (*Brit informal*), amazing, crucial (*slang*), extraordinary, remarkable, smashing (*informal*), superb, spectacular, fantastic (*informal*), magnificent, astonishing, fabulous (*informal*), divine (*informal*), glorious, terrific (*informal*), splendid, sensational (*informal*), mega (*slang*), sovereign, awesome (*slang*), breathtaking, phenomenal, astounding, singular, miraculous, colossal, super (*informal*), wicked (*informal*), def (*slang*), prodigious, wondrous (*archaic* or *literary*), brill (*informal*), stupendous, jaw-dropping, bodacious (*slang, chiefly US*), boffo (*slang*), jim-dandy (*slang*), chillin' (*US slang*), booshit (*Austral slang*), exo (*Austral slang*), sik (*Austral slang*), rad (*informal*), phat (*slang*), schmick (*Austral informal*)
<< OPPOSITE terrible

masculine *adjective* 1 MALE, manly, mannish, manlike, virile, manful
2 STRONG, powerful, bold, brave, strapping, hardy, robust, vigorous, muscular, macho, butch (*slang*), resolute, gallant, well-built, red-blooded (*informal*), stout-hearted

mask *noun* 1 DISGUISE, visor, vizard (*archaic*), stocking mask, false face, domino (*rare*)
2 FAÇADE, disguise, show, front, cover, screen, blind, cover-up, veil, cloak, guise, camouflage, veneer, semblance, concealment
▷ *verb* DISGUISE, hide, conceal, obscure, cover (up), screen, blanket, veil, cloak, mantle, camouflage, enshroud

masquerade *verb* POSE, pretend to be, impersonate, profess to be, pass yourself off, simulate, disguise yourself
▷ *noun* 1 PRETENCE, disguise, deception, front (*informal*), cover, screen, put-on (*slang*), mask, cover-up, cloak, guise, subterfuge, dissimulation, imposture
2 MASKED BALL, revel, mummery, fancy dress party, costume ball, masked party

mass *noun* 1 LOT, collection, load, combination, pile, quantity, bunch, stack, heap, rick, batch, accumulation, stockpile, assemblage, aggregation, conglomeration
2 PIECE, block, lump, chunk, hunk, concretion
3 MAJORITY, body, bulk, best part, greater part, almost all, lion's share, preponderance
4 CROWD, group, body, pack, lot, army, host, band, troop, drove, crush, bunch (*informal*), mob, flock, herd, number, horde, multitude, throng, rabble, assemblage
5 SIZE, matter, weight, extent, dimensions, bulk, magnitude, greatness
▷ *adjective* LARGE-SCALE, general, popular, widespread, extensive, universal, wholesale, indiscriminate, pandemic
▷ *verb* GATHER, assemble, accumulate, collect, rally, mob, muster, swarm, amass, throng, congregate, foregather
▷▷ **the masses** THE MULTITUDE, the crowd, the mob, the common people, the great unwashed (*derogatory*), the hoi polloi, the commonalty

massacre *noun* SLAUGHTER, killing, murder, holocaust, carnage, extermination, annihilation, butchery, mass slaughter, blood bath
▷ *verb* SLAUGHTER, kill, murder, butcher, take out (*slang*), wipe out, slay, blow away (*slang, chiefly US*), annihilate, exterminate, mow down, cut to pieces

massage *noun* RUB-DOWN, rubbing, manipulation, kneading, reflexology, shiatsu, acupressure, chiropractic treatment, palpation
▷ *verb* 1 RUB DOWN, rub, manipulate, knead, pummel, palpate
2 MANIPULATE, alter, distort, doctor, cook (*informal*), fix (*informal*), rig, fiddle (*informal*), tamper with, tinker with, misrepresent, fiddle with, falsify

massive *adjective* HUGE, great, big, heavy,

imposing, vast, enormous, solid, impressive, substantial, extensive, monster, immense, hefty, titanic, gigantic, monumental, whacking (*informal*), mammoth, bulky, colossal, whopping (*informal*), weighty, stellar (*informal*), hulking, ponderous, gargantuan, elephantine, ginormous (*informal*), humongous *or* humungous (*US slang*)

<< OPPOSITE tiny

master *noun* 1 LORD, ruler, commander, chief, director, manager, boss (*informal*), head, owner, captain, governor, employer, principal, skipper (*informal*), controller, superintendent, overlord, overseer, baas (*S African*)

<< OPPOSITE servant

2 EXPERT, maestro, pro (*informal*), ace (*informal*), genius, wizard, adept, virtuoso, grandmaster, doyen, past master, dab hand (*Brit informal*), wonk (*informal*), maven (US), fundi (*S African*)

<< OPPOSITE amateur

3 TEACHER, tutor, instructor, schoolmaster, pedagogue, preceptor

<< OPPOSITE student

▷ *adjective* MAIN, principal, chief, prime, grand, great, foremost, predominant

<< OPPOSITE lesser

▷ *verb* 1 LEARN, understand, pick up, acquire, grasp, get the hang of (*informal*), become proficient in, know inside out, know backwards

2 OVERCOME, defeat, suppress, conquer, check, curb, tame, lick (*informal*), subdue, overpower, quash, quell, triumph over, bridle, vanquish, subjugate

<< OPPOSITE give in to

3 CONTROL, manage, direct, dominate, rule, command, govern, regulate

masterful *adjective* 1 SKILFUL, skilled, expert, finished, fine, masterly, excellent, crack (*informal*), supreme, clever, superior, world-class, exquisite, adept, consummate, first-rate, deft, superlative, adroit, dexterous

<< OPPOSITE unskilled

2 DOMINEERING, authoritative, dictatorial, bossy (*informal*), arrogant, imperious, overbearing, tyrannical, magisterial, despotic, high-handed, peremptory, overweening, self-willed

<< OPPOSITE meek

> In current usage there is a lot of overlap between the meanings of *masterful* and *masterly*. According to some, the first should only be used where there is a connotation of power and domination, the second where the connotations are of great skill. Nevertheless, as the Collins Word Web shows, the majority of uses of *masterful* these days relate to the second meaning, as in *musically, it was a masterful display of the folk singer's art*. Anyone wishing to observe the distinction would use only *masterly* in the context just given, and *masterful* in contexts such as: *his need to be masterful with women was extreme; Alec was so masterful that he surprised himself*

masterly *adjective* SKILFUL, skilled, expert, finished, fine, excellent, crack (*informal*), supreme, clever, superior, world-class, exquisite, adept, consummate, first-rate, superlative, masterful, adroit, dexterous ▷ see **masterful**

mastermind *verb* PLAN, manage, direct, organize, devise, conceive, be the brains behind (*informal*)

▷ *noun* ORGANIZER, director, manager, authority, engineer, brain(s) (*informal*), architect, genius, planner, intellect, virtuoso, rocket scientist (*informal, chiefly US*), brainbox

masterpiece *noun* CLASSIC, tour de force (*French*), pièce de résistance (*French*), magnum opus, master work, jewel, chef-d'oeuvre (*French*)

mastery *noun* 1 UNDERSTANDING, knowledge, comprehension, ability, skill, know-how, command, grip, grasp, expertise, prowess, familiarity, attainment, finesse, proficiency, virtuosity, dexterity, cleverness, deftness, acquirement

2 CONTROL, authority, command, rule, victory, triumph, sway, domination, superiority, conquest, supremacy, dominion, upper hand, ascendancy, pre-eminence, mana (NZ), whip hand

masturbation *noun* SELF-ABUSE, onanism, playing with yourself (*slang*), autoeroticism

match *noun* 1 GAME, test, competition, trial, tie, contest, fixture, bout, head-to-head

2 COMPANION, mate, equal, equivalent, counterpart, fellow, complement

3 REPLICA, double, copy, twin, equal, spit (*informal, chiefly Brit*), duplicate, lookalike, ringer (*slang*), spitting image (*informal*), dead ringer (*slang*), spit and image (*informal*)

4 MARRIAGE, union, couple, pair, pairing, item (*informal*), alliance, combination, partnership, duet, affiliation

5 EQUAL, rival, equivalent, peer, competitor, counterpart

▷ *verb* 1 CORRESPOND WITH, suit, go with, complement, fit with, accompany, team with, blend with, tone with, harmonize with, coordinate with

2 TAILOR, fit, suit, adapt

3 CORRESPOND, agree, accord, square, coincide,

tally, conform, match up, be compatible, harmonize, be consonant
4 PAIR, unite, join, couple, link, marry, ally, combine, mate, yoke
5 RIVAL, equal, compete with, compare with, emulate, contend with, measure up to
▷▷ **match something** *or* **someone against something** *or* **someone** PIT AGAINST, set against, play off against, put in opposition to
matching *adjective* IDENTICAL, like, same, double, paired, equal, toning, twin, equivalent, parallel, corresponding, comparable, duplicate, coordinating, analogous
<< OPPOSITE different
matchless *adjective* UNEQUALLED, unique, unparalleled, unrivalled, perfect, supreme, exquisite, consummate, superlative, inimitable, incomparable, unmatched, peerless, unsurpassed
<< OPPOSITE average
mate *noun* 1 (*informal*) FRIEND, pal (*informal*), companion, buddy (*informal*), china (*Brit slang*), cock (*Brit informal*), comrade, chum (*informal*), mucker (*Brit informal*), crony, main man (*slang, chiefly US*), homeboy (*slang, chiefly US*), cobber (*Austral & NZ old-fashioned informal*), E hoa (NZ)
2 PARTNER, lover, companion, spouse, consort, significant other (*US informal*), better half (*humorous*), helpmeet, husband *or* wife
3 DOUBLE, match, fellow, twin, counterpart, companion
4 ASSISTANT, subordinate, apprentice, helper, accomplice, sidekick (*informal*)
5 COLLEAGUE, associate, companion, co-worker, fellow-worker, compeer
▷ *verb* 1 PAIR, couple, breed, copulate
2 MARRY, match, wed, get married, shack up (*informal*)
3 JOIN, match, couple, pair, yoke
material *noun* 1 SUBSTANCE, body, matter, stuff, elements, constituents
2 CLOTH, stuff, fabric, textile
3 INFORMATION, work, details, facts, notes, evidence, particulars, data, info (*informal*), subject matter, documentation
▷ *adjective* 1 PHYSICAL, worldly, solid, substantial, concrete, fleshly, bodily, tangible, palpable, corporeal, nonspiritual
2 RELEVANT, important, significant, essential, vital, key, serious, grave, meaningful, applicable, indispensable, momentous, weighty, pertinent, consequential, apposite, apropos, germane
materialize *verb* 1 OCCUR, happen, take place, turn up, come about, take shape, come into being, come to pass
2 APPEAR, arrive, emerge, surface, turn up, loom, show up (*informal*), pop up (*informal*), put in an appearance
materially *adverb* SIGNIFICANTLY, much, greatly, considerably, essentially, seriously, gravely, substantially
<< OPPOSITE insignificantly
maternal *adjective* MOTHERLY, protective, nurturing, maternalistic
maternity *noun* MOTHERHOOD, parenthood, motherliness
matey *adjective* (*Brit informal*) FRIENDLY, intimate, comradely, thick (*informal*), pally (*informal*), amiable, sociable, chummy (*informal*), free-and-easy, companionable, clubby, buddy-buddy (*slang, chiefly US & Canad*), hail-fellow-well-met, palsy-walsy (*informal*)
matrimonial *adjective* MARITAL, married, wedding, wedded, nuptial, conjugal, spousal, connubial, hymeneal
matrimony *noun* MARRIAGE, nuptials, wedlock, wedding ceremony, marital rites
matted *adjective* TANGLED, knotted, unkempt, knotty, tousled, ratty, uncombed
matter *noun* 1 SITUATION, thing, issue, concern, business, question, event, subject, affair, incident, proceeding, episode, topic, transaction, occurrence
2 SUBSTANCE, material, body, stuff
3 CONTENT, sense, subject, argument, text, substance, burden, thesis, purport, gist, pith
4 (*Medical*) PUS, discharge, secretion, suppuration, purulence
5 IMPORTANCE, interest, moment, note, weight, import, consequence, significance
▷ *verb* BE IMPORTANT, make a difference, count, be relevant, make any difference, mean anything, have influence, carry weight, cut any ice (*informal*), be of consequence, be of account
matter-of-fact *adjective* UNSENTIMENTAL, flat, dry, plain, dull, sober, down-to-earth, mundane, lifeless, prosaic, deadpan, unimaginative, unvarnished, emotionless, unembellished
mature *verb* DEVELOP, grow up, bloom, blossom, come of age, become adult, age, reach adulthood, maturate
▷ *adjective* 1 MATURED, seasoned, ripe, mellow, ripened
2 GROWN-UP, adult, grown, of age, full-blown, fully fledged, fully developed, full-grown
<< OPPOSITE immature
maturity *noun* 1 ADULTHOOD, majority, completion, puberty, coming of age, fullness, full bloom, full growth, pubescence, manhood *or* womanhood
<< OPPOSITE immaturity
2 RIPENESS, perfection, maturation
maudlin *adjective* SENTIMENTAL, tearful, mushy (*informal*), soppy (*Brit informal*), weepy (*informal*),

slushy (*informal*), mawkish, lachrymose, icky (*informal*), overemotional

maul *verb* 1 MANGLE, claw, lacerate, tear, mangulate (*Austral slang*)
2 ILL-TREAT, beat, abuse, batter, thrash, beat up (*informal*), molest, work over (*slang*), pummel, manhandle, rough up, handle roughly, knock about *or* around, beat *or* knock seven bells out of (*informal*)

maverick *noun* REBEL, radical, dissenter, individualist, protester, eccentric, heretic, nonconformist, iconoclast, dissentient
<< OPPOSITE traditionalist
▷ *adjective* REBEL, radical, dissenting, individualistic, eccentric, heretical, iconoclastic, nonconformist

maw *noun* MOUTH, crop, throat, jaws, gullet, craw

maxim *noun* SAYING, motto, adage, proverb, rule, saw, gnome, dictum, axiom, aphorism, byword, apophthegm

maximum *adjective* GREATEST, highest, supreme, paramount, utmost, most, maximal, topmost
<< OPPOSITE minimal
▷ *noun* TOP, most, peak, ceiling, crest, utmost, upper limit, uttermost
<< OPPOSITE minimum

maybe *adverb* PERHAPS, possibly, it could be, conceivably, perchance (*archaic*), mayhap (*archaic*), peradventure (*archaic*)

mayhem *noun* CHAOS, trouble, violence, disorder, destruction, confusion, havoc, fracas, commotion

maze *noun* WEB, puzzle, confusion, tangle, snarl, mesh, labyrinth, imbroglio, convolutions, complex network

meadow *noun* FIELD, pasture, grassland, ley, lea (*poetic*)

meagre *adjective* INSUBSTANTIAL, little, small, poor, spare, slight, inadequate, pathetic, slender, scant, sparse, deficient, paltry, skimpy, puny, measly, scanty, exiguous, scrimpy

mean[1] *verb* 1 SIGNIFY, say, suggest, indicate, represent, express, stand for, convey, spell out, purport, symbolize, denote, connote, betoken
2 IMPLY, suggest, intend, indicate, refer to, intimate, get at (*informal*), hint at, have in mind, drive at (*informal*), allude to, insinuate
3 PRESAGE, promise, herald, foreshadow, augur, foretell, portend, betoken, adumbrate
4 RESULT IN, cause, produce, effect, lead to, involve, bring about, give rise to, entail, engender, necessitate
5 INTEND, want, plan, expect, design, aim, wish, think, propose, purpose, desire, set out, contemplate, aspire, have plans, have in mind
6 DESTINE, make, design, suit, fate, predestine, preordain

In standard British English, *mean* should not be followed by *for* when expressing intention. *I didn't mean this to happen* is acceptable, but not *I didn't mean for this to happen*

mean[2] *adjective* 1 MISERLY, stingy, parsimonious, niggardly, close (*informal*), near (*informal*), tight, selfish, beggarly, mercenary, skimpy, penny-pinching, ungenerous, penurious, tight-fisted, mingy (*Brit informal*), snoep (*S African informal*)
<< OPPOSITE generous
2 DISHONOURABLE, base, petty, degraded, disgraceful, shameful, shabby, vile, degenerate, callous, sordid, abject, despicable, narrow-minded, contemptible, wretched, scurvy, ignoble, hard-hearted, scungy (*Austral & NZ*), low-minded
<< OPPOSITE honourable
3 (*informal*) MALICIOUS, hostile, nasty, sour, unpleasant, rude, unfriendly, bad-tempered, disagreeable, churlish, ill-tempered, cantankerous
<< OPPOSITE kind
4 SHABBY, poor, miserable, run-down, beggarly, seedy, scruffy, sordid, paltry, squalid, tawdry, low-rent (*informal, chiefly US*), contemptible, wretched, down-at-heel, grungy (*slang, chiefly US*), scuzzy (*slang, chiefly US*)
<< OPPOSITE superb
5 LOWLY, low, common, ordinary, modest, base, obscure, humble, inferior, vulgar, menial, proletarian, undistinguished, servile, ignoble, plebeian, lowborn, baseborn (*archaic*)
<< OPPOSITE noble

mean[3] *noun* AVERAGE, middle, balance, norm, median, midpoint
▷ *adjective* AVERAGE, middle, middling, standard, medium, normal, intermediate, median, medial

meander *verb* 1 WIND, turn, snake, zigzag
2 WANDER, stroll, stray, ramble, stravaig (*Scot & Northern English dialect*)
▷ *noun* CURVE, bend, turn, twist, loop, coil, zigzag

meandering *adjective* WINDING, wandering, snaking, tortuous, convoluted, serpentine, circuitous
<< OPPOSITE straight

meaning *noun* 1 SIGNIFICANCE, message, explanation, substance, value, import, implication, drift, interpretation, essence, purport, connotation, upshot, gist, signification
2 DEFINITION, sense, interpretation, explication, elucidation, denotation
3 PURPOSE, point, end, idea, goal, design, aim, object, intention

4 FORCE, use, point, effect, value, worth, consequence, thrust, validity, usefulness, efficacy
▷ *adjective* EXPRESSIVE, meaningful, pointed, revealing, significant, speaking, pregnant, suggestive, telltale

meaningful *adjective* 1 SIGNIFICANT, important, serious, material, useful, relevant, valid, worthwhile, purposeful
<< OPPOSITE trivial
2 EXPRESSIVE, suggestive, meaning, pointed, speaking, pregnant

meaningless *adjective* NONSENSICAL, senseless, inconsequential, inane, insubstantial
<< OPPOSITE worthwhile

meanness *noun* 1 MISERLINESS, parsimony, stinginess, tight-fistedness, niggardliness, selfishness, minginess (*Brit informal*), penuriousness
2 PETTINESS, degradation, degeneracy, wretchedness, narrow-mindedness, shabbiness, baseness, vileness, sordidness, shamefulness, scurviness, abjectness, low-mindedness, ignobility, despicableness, disgracefulness, dishonourableness
3 MALICE, hostility, bad temper, rudeness, nastiness, unpleasantness, ill temper, sourness, unfriendliness, maliciousness, cantankerousness, churlishness, disagreeableness
4 SHABBINESS, squalor, insignificance, pettiness, wretchedness, seediness, tawdriness, sordidness, scruffiness, humbleness, poorness, paltriness, beggarliness, contemptibleness

means *plural noun* 1 METHOD, way, course, process, medium, measure, agency, channel, instrument, avenue, mode, expedient
2 MONEY, funds, capital, property, riches, income, resources, estate, fortune, wealth, substance, affluence, wherewithal
▷▷ **by all means** CERTAINLY, surely, of course, definitely, absolutely, positively, doubtlessly
▷▷ **by means of** BY WAY OF, using, through, via, utilizing, with the aid of, by dint of
▷▷ **by no means** IN NO WAY, no way, not at all, definitely not, not in the least, on no account, not in the slightest, not the least bit, absolutely not

meantime *or* **meanwhile** *adverb* AT THE SAME TIME, in the meantime, simultaneously, for the present, concurrently, in the meanwhile

meanwhile *or* **meantime** *adverb* FOR NOW, in the meantime, for the moment, in the interim, for then, in the interval, in the meanwhile, in the intervening time

measly *adjective* (*informal*) MEAGRE, miserable, pathetic, paltry, mean, poor, petty, beggarly, pitiful, skimpy, puny, stingy, contemptible, scanty, miserly, niggardly, ungenerous, mingy (*Brit informal*), snoep (*S African informal*)

measurable *adjective* 1 PERCEPTIBLE, material, significant, distinct, palpable, discernible, detectable
2 QUANTIFIABLE, material, quantitative, assessable, determinable, computable, gaugeable, mensurable

measure *verb* QUANTIFY, rate, judge, determine, value, size, estimate, survey, assess, weigh, calculate, evaluate, compute, gauge, mark out, appraise, calibrate
▷ *noun* 1 QUANTITY, share, amount, degree, reach, range, size, capacity, extent, proportion, allowance, portion, scope, quota, ration, magnitude, allotment, amplitude
2 STANDARD, example, model, test, par, criterion, norm, benchmark, barometer, yardstick, touchstone, litmus test
3 ACTION, act, step, procedure, means, course, control, proceeding, initiative, manoeuvre, legal action, deed, expedient
4 GAUGE, rule, scale, metre, ruler, yardstick
5 LAW, act, bill, legislation, resolution, statute, enactment
▷▷ **for good measure** IN ADDITION, as well, besides, to boot, as an extra, into the bargain, as a bonus
▷▷ **measure up** COME UP TO STANDARD, be fit, be adequate, be capable, be suitable, make the grade (*informal*), be suited, be satisfactory, come up to scratch (*informal*), cut the mustard (*US slang*), fulfil the expectations, fit *or* fill the bill
▷▷ **measure up to something** *or* **someone** ACHIEVE, meet, match, rival, equal, compare to, come up to, be equal to, vie with, be on a level with

measured *adjective* 1 STEADY, even, slow, regular, dignified, stately, solemn, leisurely, sedate, unhurried
2 CONSIDERED, planned, reasoned, studied, calculated, deliberate, sober, premeditated, well-thought-out
3 QUANTIFIED, standard, exact, regulated, precise, gauged, verified, predetermined, modulated

measurement *noun* 1 SIZE, length, dimension, area, amount, weight, volume, capacity, extent, height, depth, width, magnitude, amplitude
2 CALCULATION, assessment, evaluation, estimation, survey, judgment, valuation, appraisal, computation, calibration, mensuration, metage

meat *noun* 1 FOOD, provisions, nourishment, sustenance, eats (*slang*), fare, flesh, rations, grub (*slang*), subsistence, kai (*NZ informal*), chow (*informal*), nosh (*slang*), victuals, comestibles, provender, nutriment, viands

2 GIST, point, heart, core, substance, essence, nucleus, marrow, kernel, nub, pith

meaty *adjective* 1 SUBSTANTIAL, rich, nourishing, hearty

2 BRAWNY, muscular, heavy, solid, strapping, sturdy, burly, husky (*informal*), fleshy, beefy (*informal*), heavily built

3 INTERESTING, rich, significant, substantial, profound, meaningful, pithy

mechanical *adjective* 1 AUTOMATIC, automated, mechanized, power-driven, motor-driven, machine-driven

<< OPPOSITE manual

2 UNTHINKING, routine, automatic, matter-of-fact, cold, unconscious, instinctive, lacklustre, involuntary, impersonal, habitual, cursory, perfunctory, unfeeling, machine-like, emotionless, spiritless

<< OPPOSITE conscious

mechanism *noun* 1 WORKINGS, motor, gears, works, action, components, machinery, innards (*informal*)

2 PROCESS, workings, way, means, system, performance, operation, medium, agency, method, functioning, technique, procedure, execution, methodology

3 MACHINE, system, structure, device, tool, instrument, appliance, apparatus, contrivance

meddle *verb* INTERFERE, intervene, tamper, intrude, pry, butt in, interpose, stick your nose in (*informal*), put your oar in, intermeddle, put your two cents in (*US slang*)

mediate *verb* INTERVENE, moderate, step in (*informal*), intercede, settle, referee, resolve, umpire, reconcile, arbitrate, interpose, conciliate, make peace, restore harmony, act as middleman, bring to terms, bring to an agreement

mediation *noun* ARBITRATION, intervention, reconciliation, conciliation, good offices, intercession, interposition

mediator *noun* NEGOTIATOR, arbitrator, judge, referee, advocate, umpire, intermediary, middleman, arbiter, peacemaker, go-between, moderator, interceder, honest broker

medicinal *adjective* THERAPEUTIC, medical, healing, remedial, restorative, curative, analeptic, roborant, sanative

medicine *noun* REMEDY, drug, cure, prescription, medication, nostrum, physic, medicament

medieval *adjective* (*informal*) OLD-FASHIONED, antique, primitive, obsolete, out-of-date, archaic, prehistoric, antiquated, anachronistic, antediluvian, unenlightened, out of the ark

mediocre *adjective* SECOND-RATE, average, ordinary, indifferent, middling, pedestrian, inferior, commonplace, vanilla (*slang*), insignificant, so-so (*informal*), banal, tolerable, run-of-the-mill, passable, undistinguished, uninspired, bog-standard (*Brit & Irish slang*), no great shakes (*informal*), half-pie (*NZ informal*), fair to middling (*informal*)

<< OPPOSITE excellent

mediocrity *noun* 1 INSIGNIFICANCE, indifference, inferiority, meanness, ordinariness, unimportance, poorness

2 NONENTITY, nobody, lightweight (*informal*), second-rater, cipher

meditate *verb* REFLECT, think, consider, contemplate, deliberate, muse, ponder, ruminate, cogitate, be in a brown study

▷▷ **meditate on something** CONSIDER, study, contemplate, ponder, reflect on, mull over, think over, chew over, deliberate on, weigh, turn something over in your mind

meditation *noun* REFLECTION, thought, concentration, study, musing, pondering, contemplation, reverie, ruminating, rumination, cogitation, cerebration, a brown study

meditative *adjective* REFLECTIVE, thoughtful, contemplative, studious, pensive, deliberative, ruminative, cogitative

medium *adjective* AVERAGE, mean, middle, middling, fair, intermediate, midway, mediocre, median, medial

<< OPPOSITE extraordinary

▷ *noun* 1 SPIRITUALIST, seer, clairvoyant, fortune teller, spiritist, channeller

2 MIDDLE, mean, centre, average, compromise, middle ground, middle way, midpoint, middle course, middle path

medley *noun* MIXTURE, confusion, jumble, assortment, patchwork, pastiche, mixed bag (*informal*), potpourri, mélange (*French*), miscellany, mishmash, farrago, hotchpotch, hodgepodge, salmagundi, olio, gallimaufry, omnium-gatherum

meek *adjective* 1 SUBMISSIVE, soft, yielding, gentle, peaceful, modest, mild, patient, humble, timid, long-suffering, compliant, unassuming, unpretentious, docile, deferential, forbearing, acquiescent

<< OPPOSITE overbearing

2 SPINELESS, weak, tame, boneless, weak-kneed (*informal*), spiritless, unresisting, wussy (*slang*), wimpish *or* wimpy (*informal*)

meet *verb* 1 ENCOUNTER, come across, run into, happen on, find, contact, confront, bump into (*informal*), run across, chance on, come face to face with

<< OPPOSITE avoid

2 GATHER, collect, assemble, get together, rally, come together, muster, convene, congregate, foregather

<< OPPOSITE disperse

3 FULFIL, match (up to), answer, perform, handle, carry out, equal, satisfy, cope with, discharge, comply with, come up to, conform to, gratify, measure up to
<< OPPOSITE fall short of
4 EXPERIENCE, face, suffer, bear, go through, encounter, endure, undergo
5 CONVERGE, unite, join, cross, touch, connect, come together, link up, adjoin, intersect, abut
<< OPPOSITE diverge

meeting *noun* 1 CONFERENCE, gathering, assembly, meet, congress, session, rally, convention, get-together (*informal*), reunion, congregation, hui (NZ), conclave, convocation, powwow
2 ENCOUNTER, introduction, confrontation, engagement, rendezvous, tryst, assignation
3 CONVERGENCE, union, crossing, conjunction, junction, intersection, concourse, confluence

melancholy *adjective* SAD, down, depressed, unhappy, low, blue, miserable, moody, gloomy, dismal, sombre, woeful, glum, mournful, dejected, despondent, dispirited, melancholic, downcast, lugubrious, pensive, sorrowful, disconsolate, joyless, doleful, downhearted, heavy-hearted, down in the dumps (*informal*), woebegone, down in the mouth, low-spirited
<< OPPOSITE happy
▷ *noun* SADNESS, depression, misery, gloom, sorrow, woe, blues, unhappiness, despondency, the hump (*Brit informal*), dejection, low spirits, gloominess, pensiveness
<< OPPOSITE happiness

melee *or* **mêlée** *noun* FIGHT, fray, brawl, skirmish, tussle, scuffle, free-for-all (*informal*), fracas, set-to (*informal*), rumpus, broil, affray (*Law*), shindig (*informal*), donnybrook, ruction (*informal*), battle royal, ruckus (*informal*), scrimmage, stramash (*Scot*), shindy (*informal*), bagarre (*French*), biffo (*Austral slang*)

mellow *adjective* 1 TUNEFUL, full, rich, soft, melodious, mellifluous, dulcet, well-tuned, euphonic
2 FULL-FLAVOURED, rounded, rich, sweet, smooth, delicate, juicy
3 RIPE, perfect, mature, ripened, well-matured
<< OPPOSITE unripe
4 RELAXED, happy, cheerful, jolly, elevated, merry (*Brit informal*), expansive, cordial, genial, jovial
▷ *verb* 1 RELAX, improve, settle, calm, mature, soften, sweeten
2 SEASON, develop, improve, perfect, ripen

melodramatic *adjective* THEATRICAL, actorly, extravagant, histrionic, sensational, hammy (*informal*), actressy, stagy, overemotional, overdramatic

melody *noun* 1 TUNE, song, theme, refrain, air, music, strain, descant
2 TUNEFULNESS, music, harmony, musicality, euphony, melodiousness

melt *verb* 1 DISSOLVE, run, soften, fuse, thaw, diffuse, flux, defrost, liquefy, unfreeze, deliquesce
2 *often with* **away** DISAPPEAR, fade, vanish, dissolve, disperse, evaporate, evanesce
3 SOFTEN, touch, relax, disarm, mollify

member *noun* REPRESENTATIVE, associate, supporter, fellow, subscriber, comrade, disciple

membership *noun* 1 PARTICIPATION, belonging, fellowship, enrolment
2 MEMBERS, body, associates, fellows

memento *noun* SOUVENIR, trophy, memorial, token, reminder, relic, remembrance, keepsake

memoir *noun* ACCOUNT, life, record, register, journal, essay, biography, narrative, monograph

memoirs *plural noun* AUTOBIOGRAPHY, diary, life story, life, experiences, memories, journals, recollections, reminiscences

memorable *adjective* NOTEWORTHY, celebrated, impressive, historic, important, special, striking, famous, significant, signal, extraordinary, remarkable, distinguished, haunting, notable, timeless, unforgettable, momentous, illustrious, catchy, indelible, unfading
<< OPPOSITE forgettable

memorandum *noun* NOTE, minute, message, communication, reminder, memo, jotting

memorial *noun* 1 MONUMENT, cairn, shrine, plaque, cenotaph
2 PETITION, address, statement, memorandum
▷ *adjective* COMMEMORATIVE, remembrance, monumental

memorize *verb* REMEMBER, learn, commit to memory, learn by heart, learn by rote, get by heart, con (*archaic*)

memory *noun* 1 RECALL, mind, retention, ability to remember, powers of recall, powers of retention
2 RECOLLECTION, reminder, reminiscence, impression, echo, remembrance
3 COMMEMORATION, respect, honour, recognition, tribute, remembrance, observance

menace *noun* 1 DANGER, risk, threat, hazard, peril, jeopardy
2 (*informal*) NUISANCE, plague, pest, annoyance, troublemaker, mischief-maker
3 THREAT, warning, intimidation, ill-omen, ominousness, commination
▷ *verb* BULLY, threaten, intimidate, terrorize, alarm, frighten, scare, browbeat, utter threats to

menacing *adjective* THREATENING, dangerous, alarming, frightening, forbidding, looming, intimidating, ominous, baleful, intimidatory, minatory, bodeful, louring *or* lowering, minacious
<< OPPOSITE encouraging

mend *verb* 1 REPAIR, fix, restore, renew, patch up, renovate, refit, retouch
2 DARN, repair, patch, stitch, sew
3 HEAL, improve, recover, cure, remedy, get better, be all right, be cured, recuperate, pull through, convalesce
4 IMPROVE, better, reform, correct, revise, amend, rectify, ameliorate, emend
▷▷ **on the mend** CONVALESCENT, improving, recovering, getting better, recuperating, convalescing

menial *adjective* LOW-STATUS, degrading, lowly, unskilled, low, base, sorry, boring, routine, dull, humble, mean, vile, demeaning, fawning, abject, grovelling, humdrum, subservient, ignominious, sycophantic, servile, slavish, ignoble, obsequious
<< OPPOSITE high
▷ *noun* SERVANT, domestic, attendant, lackey, labourer, serf, underling, drudge, vassal (*archaic*), dogsbody (*informal*), flunky, skivvy (*chiefly Brit*), varlet (*archaic*)
<< OPPOSITE master

menstruation *noun* PERIOD, menstrual cycle, menses, courses (*Physiology*), flow (*informal*), monthly (*informal*), the curse (*informal*), catamenia (*Physiology*)

mental *adjective* 1 INTELLECTUAL, rational, theoretical, cognitive, brain, conceptual, cerebral
2 (*Slang*) INSANE, mad, disturbed, unstable, mentally ill, lunatic, psychotic, unbalanced, deranged, round the bend (*Brit slang*), as daft as a brush (*informal, chiefly Brit*), not right in the head

mentality *noun* ATTITUDE, character, personality, psychology, make-up, outlook, disposition, way of thinking, frame of mind, turn of mind, cast of mind

mentally *adverb* PSYCHOLOGICALLY, intellectually, rationally, inwardly, subjectively

mention *verb* REFER TO, point out, acknowledge, bring up, state, report, reveal, declare, cite, communicate, disclose, intimate, tell of, recount, hint at, impart, allude to, divulge, broach, call attention to, make known, touch upon, adduce, speak about *or* of
▷ *noun* 1 *often with* **of** REFERENCE, announcement, observation, indication, remark, notification, allusion
2 ACKNOWLEDGMENT, recognition, tribute, citation, honourable mention
▷▷ **not to mention** TO SAY NOTHING OF, besides, not counting, as well as

mentor *noun* GUIDE, teacher, coach, adviser, tutor, instructor, counsellor, guru

menu *noun* BILL OF FARE, tariff (*chiefly Brit*), set menu, table d'hôte, carte du jour (*French*)

mercantile *adjective* 1 COMMERCIAL, business, trade, trading, merchant
2 PROFIT-MAKING, money-orientated

mercenary *noun* HIRELING, freelance (*History*), soldier of fortune, condottiere (*History*), free companion (*History*)
▷ *adjective* 1 GREEDY, grasping, acquisitive, venal, avaricious, covetous, money-grubbing (*informal*), bribable
<< OPPOSITE generous
2 HIRED, paid, bought, venal

merchandise *noun* GOODS, produce, stock, products, truck, commodities, staples, wares, stock in trade, vendibles
▷ *verb* TRADE, market, sell, retail, distribute, deal in, buy and sell, traffic in, vend, do business in

merchant *noun* TRADESMAN, dealer, trader, broker, retailer, supplier, seller, salesman, vendor, shopkeeper, trafficker, wholesaler, purveyor

merciful *adjective* COMPASSIONATE, forgiving, sympathetic, kind, liberal, soft, sparing, generous, mild, pitying, humane, clement, gracious, lenient, beneficent, forbearing, tender-hearted, benignant
<< OPPOSITE merciless

merciless *adjective* CRUEL, ruthless, hard, severe, harsh, relentless, callous, heartless, unforgiving, fell (*archaic*), inexorable, implacable, unsympathetic, inhumane, barbarous, pitiless, unfeeling, unsparing, hard-hearted, unmerciful, unappeasable, unpitying

mercurial *adjective* CAPRICIOUS, volatile, unpredictable, erratic, variable, unstable, fickle, temperamental, impulsive, irrepressible, changeable, quicksilver, flighty, inconstant
<< OPPOSITE consistent

mercy *noun* 1 COMPASSION, charity, pity, forgiveness, quarter, favour, grace, kindness, clemency, leniency, benevolence, forbearance
<< OPPOSITE cruelty
2 BLESSING, relief, boon, godsend, piece of luck, benison (*archaic*)
▷▷ **at the mercy of something** *or* **someone**
1 DEFENCELESS AGAINST, subject to, open to, exposed to, vulnerable to, threatened by, susceptible to, prey to, an easy target for, naked before, unprotected against
2 IN THE POWER OF, under the control of, in the clutches of, under the heel of

mere *adjective* 1 SIMPLE, merely, no more than, nothing more than, just, common, plain, pure, pure and simple, unadulterated, unmitigated, unmixed
2 BARE, slender, trifling, meagre, just, only, basic, no more than, minimal, scant, paltry, skimpy, scanty

merge *verb* 1 COMBINE, blend, fuse, amalgamate, unite, join, mix, consolidate, mingle, converge, coalesce, melt into, meld, intermix
<< OPPOSITE separate
2 JOIN, unite, combine, consolidate, fuse
<< OPPOSITE separate
3 MELT, blend, incorporate, mingle, tone with, be swallowed up by, become lost in

merger *noun* UNION, fusion, consolidation, amalgamation, combination, coalition, incorporation

merit *noun* ADVANTAGE, value, quality, worth, strength, asset, virtue, good point, strong point, worthiness
▷ *verb* DESERVE, warrant, be entitled to, earn, incur, have a right to, be worthy of, have a claim to

merited *adjective* DESERVED, justified, warranted, just, earned, appropriate, entitled, rightful, condign, rightly due

merriment *noun* FUN, amusement, glee, mirth, sport, laughter, festivity, frolic, gaiety, hilarity, revelry, jollity, levity, liveliness, conviviality, joviality, jocularity, merrymaking

merry *adjective* 1 CHEERFUL, happy, upbeat (*informal*), carefree, glad, jolly, festive, joyous, joyful, genial, fun-loving, chirpy (*informal*), vivacious, rollicking, convivial, gleeful, blithe, frolicsome, mirthful, sportive, light-hearted, jocund, gay, blithesome
<< OPPOSITE gloomy
2 (*Brit informal*) TIPSY, happy, elevated (*informal*), mellow, tiddly (*slang, chiefly Brit*), squiffy (*Brit informal*)
▷▷ **make merry** HAVE FUN, celebrate, revel, have a good time, feast, frolic, enjoy yourself, carouse, make whoopee (*informal*)

mesh *noun* 1 NET, netting, network, web, tracery
2 TRAP, web, tangle, toils, snare, entanglement
▷ *verb* 1 ENGAGE, combine, connect, knit, come together, coordinate, interlock, dovetail, fit together, harmonize
2 ENTANGLE, catch, net, trap, tangle, snare, ensnare, enmesh

mesmerize *verb* ENTRANCE, fascinate, absorb, captivate, grip, enthral, hypnotize, magnetize, hold spellbound, spellbind

mess *noun* 1 UNTIDINESS, disorder, confusion, chaos, turmoil, litter, clutter, disarray, jumble, disorganization, grot (*slang*), dirtiness
2 SHAMBLES, botch, hash, cock-up (*Brit slang*), state, bodge (*informal*), pig's breakfast (*informal*)
3 DIFFICULTY, dilemma, plight, spot (*informal*), hole (*informal*), fix (*informal*), jam (*informal*), hot water (*informal*), stew (*informal*), mix-up, muddle, pickle (*informal*), uphill (*S African*), predicament, deep water, perplexity, tight spot, imbroglio, fine kettle of fish (*informal*)
▷▷ **mess about** *or* **around** 1 POTTER ABOUT, dabble, amuse yourself, footle (*informal*), fool about *or* around, muck about *or* around (*informal*), play about *or* around
2 MEDDLE, play, interfere, toy, fiddle (*informal*), tamper, tinker, trifle, fool about *or* around
▷▷ **mess something up** 1 BOTCH, bungle, make a hash of (*informal*), make a nonsense of, make a pig's ear of (*informal*), cock something up (*Brit slang*), muck something up (*Brit slang*), muddle something up
2 DIRTY, foul, litter, pollute, clutter, besmirch, disarrange, befoul, dishevel
▷▷ **mess with something** *or* **someone** INTERFERE WITH, play with, fiddle with (*informal*), tamper with, tinker with, meddle with

message *noun* 1 COMMUNICATION, note, bulletin, word, letter, notice, memo, dispatch, memorandum, communiqué, missive, intimation, tidings
2 POINT, meaning, idea, moral, theme, import, purport
▷▷ **get the message** UNDERSTAND, see, get it, catch on (*informal*), comprehend, twig (*Brit informal*), get the point, take the hint

messenger *noun* COURIER, agent, runner, carrier, herald, envoy, bearer, go-between, emissary, harbinger, delivery boy, errand boy

messy *adjective* 1 DISORGANIZED, sloppy (*informal*), untidy, slovenly
2 DIRTY, grubby, grimy, scuzzy (*slang, chiefly US*)
3 UNTIDY, disordered, littered, chaotic, muddled, cluttered, shambolic, disorganized, daggy (*Austral & NZ informal*)
<< OPPOSITE tidy
4 DISHEVELLED, ruffled, untidy, rumpled, bedraggled, unkempt, tousled, uncombed, daggy (*Austral & NZ informal*)
5 CONFUSING, difficult, complex, confused, tangled, chaotic, tortuous

metamorphose *verb* TRANSFORM, change, alter, remake, convert, remodel, mutate, reshape, be reborn, transmute, transfigure, transmogrify (*jocular*), transubstantiate

metamorphosis *noun* TRANSFORMATION, conversion, alteration, change, mutation, rebirth, changeover, transfiguration, transmutation, transubstantiation, transmogrification (*jocular*)

metaphor *noun* FIGURE OF SPEECH, image, symbol, analogy, emblem, conceit (*literary*), allegory, trope, figurative expression

metaphorical *adjective* FIGURATIVE, symbolic, emblematic, allegorical, emblematical, tropical (*Rhetoric*)

metaphysical *adjective* **1** ABSTRACT, intellectual, theoretical, deep, basic, essential, ideal, fundamental, universal, profound, philosophical, speculative, high-flown, esoteric, transcendental, abstruse, recondite, oversubtle

2 SUPERNATURAL, spiritual, unreal, intangible, immaterial, incorporeal, impalpable, unsubstantial

meteoric *adjective* SPECTACULAR, sudden, overnight, rapid, fast, brief, brilliant, flashing, fleeting, swift, dazzling, speedy, transient, momentary, ephemeral

<< OPPOSITE gradual

mete out *verb* DISTRIBUTE, portion, assign, administer, ration, dispense, allot, dole out, share out, apportion, deal out, measure out, parcel out, divide out

method *noun* **1** MANNER, process, approach, technique, way, plan, course, system, form, rule, programme, style, practice, fashion, scheme, arrangement, procedure, routine, mode, modus operandi

2 ORDERLINESS, planning, order, system, form, design, structure, purpose, pattern, organization, regularity

methodical *adjective* ORDERLY, planned, ordered, structured, regular, disciplined, organized, efficient, precise, neat, deliberate, tidy, systematic, meticulous, painstaking, businesslike, well-regulated

<< OPPOSITE haphazard

meticulous *adjective* THOROUGH, detailed, particular, strict, exact, precise, microscopic, fussy, painstaking, perfectionist, scrupulous, fastidious, punctilious

<< OPPOSITE careless

metropolis *noun* CITY, town, capital, big city, municipality, conurbation, megalopolis

mettle *noun* **1** COURAGE, spirit, resolution, resolve, life, heart, fire, bottle (*Brit slang*), nerve, daring, guts (*informal*), pluck, grit, bravery, fortitude, vigour, boldness, gallantry, ardour, valour, spunk (*informal*), indomitability, hardihood, gameness

2 CHARACTER, quality, nature, make-up, stamp, temper, kidney, temperament, calibre, disposition

microbe *noun* MICROORGANISM, virus, bug (*informal*), germ, bacterium, bacillus

microscopic *adjective* TINY, minute, invisible, negligible, minuscule, imperceptible, infinitesimal, teeny-weeny, teensy-weensy

<< OPPOSITE huge

midday *noun* NOON, twelve o'clock, noonday, noontime, twelve noon, noontide

middle *noun* **1** CENTRE, heart, inside, thick, core, midst, nucleus, hub, halfway point, midpoint, midsection

2 WAIST, gut, belly, tummy (*informal*), waistline, midriff, paunch, midsection

▷ *adjective* **1** CENTRAL, medium, inside, mid, intervening, inner, halfway, intermediate, median, medial

2 INTERMEDIATE, inside, intervening, inner

middle-class *adjective* BOURGEOIS, traditional, conventional, suburban, petit-bourgeois

middleman *noun* INTERMEDIARY, broker, entrepreneur, distributor, go-between

middling *adjective* **1** MEDIOCRE, all right, indifferent, so-so (*informal*), unremarkable, tolerable, run-of-the-mill, passable, serviceable, unexceptional, half-pie (*NZ informal*), O.K. *or* okay (*informal*)

2 MODERATE, medium, average, fair, ordinary, modest, adequate, bog-standard (*Brit & Irish slang*)

midget *noun* DWARF, shrimp (*informal*), gnome, Tom Thumb, munchkin (*informal, chiefly US*), homunculus, manikin, homuncule, pygmy *or* pigmy

▷ *adjective* **1** BABY, small, tiny, miniature, dwarf, teeny-weeny, teensy-weensy

2 DIMINUTIVE, little, pocket-sized, Lilliputian, dwarfish, pygmy *or* pigmy

midnight *noun* TWELVE O'CLOCK, middle of the night, dead of night, twelve o'clock at night, the witching hour

midst *noun* MIDDLE, centre, heart, interior, thick, depths, core, hub, bosom

▷▷ **in the midst of 1** DURING, in the middle of, amidst

2 AMONG, in the middle of, surrounded by, amidst, in the thick of, enveloped by

midway *adverb* HALFWAY, in the middle of, part-way, equidistant, at the midpoint, betwixt and between

miffed *adjective* UPSET, hurt, annoyed, offended, irritated, put out, hacked (off) (*US slang*), resentful, nettled, aggrieved, vexed, displeased, irked, in a huff, piqued, narked (*Brit, Austral & NZ slang*), tooshie (*Austral slang*)

might *noun* POWER, force, energy, ability, strength, capacity, efficiency, capability, sway, clout (*informal*), vigour, prowess, potency, efficacy, valour, puissance

mightily *adverb* **1** VERY, highly, greatly, hugely, very much, seriously (*informal*), extremely, intensely, decidedly, exceedingly

2 POWERFULLY, vigorously, strongly, forcefully, energetically, with all your strength, with all your might and main

mighty *adjective* 1 POWERFUL, strong, strapping, robust, hardy, vigorous, potent, sturdy, stout, forceful, stalwart, doughty, lusty, indomitable, manful, puissant
<< OPPOSITE weak
2 GREAT, large, huge, grand, massive, towering, vast, enormous, tremendous, immense, titanic, gigantic, monumental, bulky, colossal, stellar (*informal*), prodigious, stupendous, elephantine, ginormous (*informal*), humongous *or* humungous (*US slang*)
<< OPPOSITE tiny

migrant *noun* WANDERER, immigrant, traveller, gypsy, tinker, rover, transient, nomad, emigrant, itinerant, drifter, vagrant
▷ *adjective* ITINERANT, wandering, drifting, roving, travelling, shifting, immigrant, gypsy, transient, nomadic, migratory, vagrant

migrate *verb* MOVE, travel, journey, wander, shift, drift, trek, voyage, roam, emigrate, rove

migration *noun* WANDERING, journey, voyage, travel, movement, shift, trek, emigration, roving

migratory *adjective* NOMADIC, travelling, wandering, migrant, itinerant, unsettled, shifting, gypsy, roving, transient, vagrant, peripatetic

mild *adjective* 1 GENTLE, kind, easy, soft, pacific, calm, moderate, forgiving, tender, pleasant, mellow, compassionate, indulgent, serene, easy-going, amiable, meek, placid, docile, merciful, peaceable, forbearing, equable, easy-oasy (*slang*)
<< OPPOSITE harsh
2 TEMPERATE, warm, calm, moderate, clement, tranquil, balmy
<< OPPOSITE cold
3 BLAND, thin, smooth, tasteless, insipid, flavourless
4 SOOTHING, mollifying, emollient, demulcent, lenitive

milieu *noun* SURROUNDINGS, setting, scene, environment, element, background, location, sphere, locale, mise en scène (*French*)

militant *adjective* AGGRESSIVE, warring, fighting, active, combating, contending, vigorous, assertive, in arms, embattled, belligerent, combative
<< OPPOSITE peaceful
▷ *noun* ACTIVIST, radical, fighter, partisan, belligerent, combatant

military *adjective* WARLIKE, armed, soldierly, martial, soldierlike
▷▷ **the military** THE ARMED FORCES, the forces, the services, the army

militate ▷▷ **militate against something** COUNTERACT, conflict with, contend with, count against, oppose, counter, resist, be detrimental to, weigh against, tell against
▷ see **mitigate**

militia *noun* RESERVE(s), National Guard (*US*), Territorial Army (*Brit*), yeomanry (*History*), fencibles (*History*), trainband (*History*)

milk *verb* EXPLOIT, use, pump, squeeze, drain, take advantage of, bleed, impose on, wring, fleece, suck dry
>> RELATED WORDS *adjectives* lactic, lacteal

milky *adjective* WHITE, clouded, opaque, cloudy, alabaster, whitish, milk-white

mill *noun* 1 GRINDER, crusher, quern
2 FACTORY, works, shop, plant, workshop, foundry
▷ *verb* GRIND, pound, press, crush, powder, grate, pulverize, granulate, comminute
▷▷ **mill about** *or* **around** SWARM, crowd, stream, surge, seethe, throng

millstone *noun* BURDEN, weight, load, albatross, drag, affliction, dead weight, encumbrance

mime *noun* DUMB SHOW, gesture, pantomime, mummery
▷ *verb* ACT OUT, represent, gesture, simulate, pantomime

mimic *verb* 1 IMITATE, do (*informal*), take off (*informal*), ape, parody, caricature, impersonate
2 RESEMBLE, look like, mirror, echo, simulate, take on the appearance of
▷ *noun* IMITATOR, impressionist, copycat (*informal*), impersonator, caricaturist, parodist, parrot

mimicry *noun* IMITATION, impression, impersonation, copying, imitating, mimicking, parody, caricature, mockery, burlesque, apery

mince *verb* 1 CUT, grind, crumble, dice, hash, chop up
2 POSTURE, pose, ponce (*slang*), attitudinize
3 TONE DOWN, spare, moderate, weaken, diminish, soften, hold back, extenuate, palliate, euphemize

mincing *adjective* AFFECTED, nice, camp (*informal*), precious, pretentious, dainty, sissy, effeminate, foppish, poncy (*slang*), arty-farty (*informal*), lah-di-dah (*informal*), niminy-piminy

mind *noun* 1 BRAIN, head, imagination, psyche, subconscious
2 MEMORY, recollection, remembrance, powers of recollection
3 ATTENTION, thinking, thoughts, concentration
4 INTELLIGENCE, reason, reasoning, understanding, sense, spirit, brain(s) (*informal*), wits, mentality, intellect, grey matter (*informal*), ratiocination
5 THINKER, academic, intellectual, genius, brain (*informal*), scholar, sage, intellect, rocket scientist (*informal, chiefly US*), brainbox, acca

(*Austral slang*)
6 INTENTION, will, wish, desire, urge, fancy, purpose, leaning, bent, notion, tendency, inclination, disposition
7 SANITY, reason, senses, judgment, wits, marbles (*informal*), rationality, mental balance
▷ *verb* 1 TAKE OFFENCE AT, dislike, care about, object to, resent, disapprove of, be bothered by, look askance at, be affronted by
2 BE CAREFUL, watch, take care, be wary, be cautious, be on your guard
3 BE SURE, ensure, make sure, be careful, make certain
4 LOOK AFTER, watch, protect, tend, guard, take care of, attend to, keep an eye on, have *or* take charge of
5 PAY ATTENTION TO, follow, mark, watch, note, regard, respect, notice, attend to, listen to, observe, comply with, obey, heed, adhere to, take heed of, pay heed to
▷▷ **in** *or* **of two minds** UNDECIDED, uncertain, unsure, wavering, hesitant, dithering (*chiefly Brit*), vacillating, swithering (*Scot*), shillyshallying (*informal*)
▷▷ **make up your mind** DECIDE, choose, determine, resolve, reach a decision, come to a decision
▷▷ **mind out** BE CAREFUL, watch out, take care, look out, beware, pay attention, keep your eyes open, be on your guard
>> RELATED WORD *adjective* mental

mindful *adjective* *with* **of** AWARE, careful, conscious, alert, sensible, wary, thoughtful, attentive, respectful, watchful, alive to, cognizant, chary, heedful, regardful
<< OPPOSITE heedless

mindless *adjective* 1 UNTHINKING, gratuitous, thoughtless, careless, oblivious, brutish, inane, witless, heedless, unmindful, dumb-ass (*slang*)
<< OPPOSITE reasoning
2 UNINTELLIGENT, stupid, foolish, careless, negligent, idiotic, thoughtless, inane, witless, forgetful, moronic, obtuse, neglectful, asinine, imbecilic, braindead (*informal*), dumb-ass (*slang*), dead from the neck up (*informal*)
3 MECHANICAL, automatic, monotonous, mind-numbing, brainless

mind's eye ▷▷ **in your mind's eye** IN YOUR IMAGINATION, in your head, in your mind

mine *noun* 1 PIT, deposit, shaft, vein, colliery, excavation, coalfield, lode
2 SOURCE, store, fund, stock, supply, reserve, treasury, wealth, abundance, hoard
▷ *verb* 1 DIG UP, extract, quarry, unearth, delve, excavate, hew, dig for
2 LAY MINES IN *or* UNDER, sow with mines

miner *noun* COALMINER, pitman (*Brit*), collier (*Brit*)

mingle *verb* 1 MIX, combine, blend, merge, unite, join, marry, compound, alloy, interweave, coalesce, intermingle, meld, commingle, intermix, admix
<< OPPOSITE separate
2 ASSOCIATE, circulate, hang out (*informal*), consort, socialize, rub shoulders (*informal*), hobnob, fraternize, hang about *or* around
<< OPPOSITE dissociate

miniature *adjective* SMALL, little, minute, baby, reduced, tiny, pocket, toy, mini, wee, dwarf, scaled-down, diminutive, minuscule, midget, teeny-weeny, Lilliputian, teensy-weensy, pygmy *or* pigmy
<< OPPOSITE giant

minimal *adjective* MINIMUM, smallest, least, slightest, token, nominal, negligible, least possible, littlest

minimize *verb* 1 REDUCE, decrease, shrink, diminish, prune, curtail, attenuate, downsize, miniaturize
<< OPPOSITE increase
2 PLAY DOWN, discount, underestimate, belittle, disparage, decry, underrate, deprecate, depreciate, make light *or* little of
<< OPPOSITE praise

minimum *adjective* LOWEST, smallest, least, slightest, minimal, least possible, littlest
<< OPPOSITE maximum
▷ *noun* LOWEST, least, depth, slightest, lowest level, nadir, bottom level

minion *noun* FOLLOWER, henchman, underling, lackey, favourite, pet, creature, darling, parasite, cohort (*chiefly US*), dependant, hanger-on, sycophant, yes man, toady, hireling, flunky, flatterer, lickspittle, bootlicker (*informal*)

minister *noun* 1 OFFICIAL, ambassador, diplomat, delegate, executive, administrator, envoy, cabinet member, office-holder, plenipotentiary
2 CLERGYMAN, priest, divine, vicar, parson, preacher, pastor, chaplain, cleric, rector, curate, churchman, padre (*informal*), ecclesiastic
▷▷ **minister to** ATTEND TO, serve, tend to, answer to, accommodate, take care of, cater to, pander to, administer to, be solicitous of

ministry *noun* 1 DEPARTMENT, office, bureau, government department
2 ADMINISTRATION, government, council, cabinet
3 THE PRIESTHOOD, the church, the cloth, the pulpit, holy orders

minor *adjective* SMALL, lesser, subordinate, smaller, light, slight, secondary, petty, inferior, trivial, trifling, insignificant, negligible, unimportant, paltry, inconsequential, inconsiderable, nickel-and-dime (*US slang*)

<< OPPOSITE major

minstrel *noun* MUSICIAN, singer, harper, bard, troubadour, songstress, jongleur

mint *verb* 1 MAKE, produce, strike, cast, stamp, punch, coin
2 INVENT, produce, fashion, make up, construct, coin, devise, forge, fabricate, think up
▷ *noun* FORTUNE, million, bomb (*Brit slang*), pile (*informal*), packet (*slang*), bundle (*slang*), heap (*informal*), King's ransom, top whack (*informal*)
▷ *adjective* PERFECT, excellent, first-class, brand-new, fresh, unmarked, undamaged, unblemished, untarnished

minuscule *adjective* TINY, little, minute, fine, very small, miniature, microscopic, diminutive, infinitesimal, teeny-weeny, Lilliputian, teensy-weensy

minute[1] *noun* 1 SIXTY SECONDS, sixtieth of an hour
2 MOMENT, second, bit, shake (*informal*), flash, instant, tick (*Brit informal*), sec (*informal*), short time, little while, jiffy (*informal*), trice
▷▷ **up to the minute** LATEST, in, newest, now (*informal*), with it (*informal*), smart, stylish, trendiest, trendy (*Brit informal*), vogue, up to date, modish, (most) fashionable, schmick (*Austral informal*)

minute[2] *adjective* 1 SMALL, little, tiny, miniature, slender, fine, microscopic, diminutive, minuscule, infinitesimal, teeny-weeny, Lilliputian, teensy-weensy
<< OPPOSITE huge
2 NEGLIGIBLE, slight, petty, trivial, trifling, unimportant, paltry, puny, piddling (*informal*), inconsiderable, picayune (*US*)
<< OPPOSITE significant
3 PRECISE, close, detailed, critical, exact, meticulous, exhaustive, painstaking, punctilious
<< OPPOSITE imprecise

minutely *adverb* PRECISELY, closely, exactly, in detail, critically, meticulously, painstakingly, exhaustively, with a fine-tooth comb

minutes *plural noun* RECORD, notes, proceedings, transactions, transcript, memorandum

minutiae *plural noun* DETAILS, particulars, subtleties, trifles, trivia, niceties, finer points, ins and outs

miracle *noun* WONDER, phenomenon, sensation, marvel, amazing achievement, astonishing feat

miraculous *adjective* WONDERFUL, amazing, extraordinary, incredible, astonishing, marvellous, magical, unbelievable, phenomenal, astounding, inexplicable, wondrous (*archaic* or *literary*), unaccountable, superhuman
<< OPPOSITE ordinary

mirage *noun* ILLUSION, vision, hallucination, pipe dream, chimera, optical illusion, phantasm

mire *noun* 1 MUD, dirt, muck, ooze, sludge, slime, slob (*Irish*), gloop (*informal*), grot (*slang*)
2 SWAMP, marsh, bog, fen, quagmire, morass, wetland, pakihi (*NZ*), muskeg (*Canad*)
▷ *verb* 1 SOIL, dirty, muddy, besmirch, begrime, bespatter
2 ENTANGLE, involve, mix up, catch up, bog down, tangle up, enmesh

mirror *noun* LOOKING-GLASS, glass (*Brit*), reflector, speculum
▷ *verb* REFLECT, show, follow, match, represent, copy, repeat, echo, parallel, depict, reproduce, emulate

mirror image *noun* REFLECTION, double, image, copy, twin, representation, clone, replica, likeness, spitting image (*informal*), dead ringer (*informal*), exact likeness

mirth *noun* MERRIMENT, amusement, fun, pleasure, laughter, rejoicing, festivity, glee, frolic, sport, gaiety, hilarity, cheerfulness, revelry, jollity, levity, gladness, joviality, jocularity, merrymaking, joyousness

misadventure *noun* MISFORTUNE, accident, disaster, failure, reverse, setback, catastrophe, debacle, bad luck, calamity, mishap, bad break (*informal*), ill fortune, ill luck, mischance

misapprehension *noun* MISUNDERSTANDING, mistake, error, delusion, misconception, fallacy, misreading, false impression, misinterpretation, false belief, misconstruction, wrong idea *or* impression

misappropriate *verb* STEAL, embezzle, pocket, misuse, swindle, misspend, misapply, defalcate (*Law*)

misbehave *verb* BE NAUGHTY, be bad, act up (*informal*), muck about (*Brit slang*), get up to mischief (*informal*), carry on (*informal*), be insubordinate
<< OPPOSITE behave

misbehaviour *noun* MISCONDUCT, mischief, misdemeanour, shenanigans (*informal*), impropriety, acting up (*informal*), bad behaviour, misdeeds, rudeness, indiscipline, insubordination, naughtiness, monkey business (*informal*), incivility

miscalculate *verb* 1 MISJUDGE, get something wrong, underestimate, underrate, overestimate, overrate
2 CALCULATE WRONGLY, blunder, make a mistake, get it wrong, err, slip up

miscarriage *noun* 1 SPONTANEOUS ABORTION, still birth
2 FAILURE, error, breakdown, mismanagement, undoing, thwarting, mishap, botch (*informal*), perversion, misfire,

mischance, nonsuccess

miscarry *verb* **1** HAVE A MISCARRIAGE, lose your baby, have a spontaneous abortion
2 FAIL, go wrong, fall through, come to nothing, misfire, go astray, go awry, come to grief, go amiss, go pear-shaped (*informal*), gang agley (*Scot*)

miscellaneous *adjective* MIXED, various, varied, diverse, confused, diversified, mingled, assorted, jumbled, sundry, motley, indiscriminate, manifold, heterogeneous, multifarious, multiform

mischief *noun* **1** MISBEHAVIOUR, trouble, naughtiness, pranks, shenanigans (*informal*), monkey business (*informal*), waywardness, devilment, impishness, roguishness, roguery
2 HARM, trouble, damage, injury, hurt, evil, disadvantage, disruption, misfortune, detriment

mischievous *adjective* **1** NAUGHTY, bad, troublesome, wayward, exasperating, playful, rascally, impish, roguish, vexatious, puckish, frolicsome, arch, ludic (*literary*), sportive, badly behaved
2 MALICIOUS, damaging, vicious, destructive, harmful, troublesome, malignant, detrimental, hurtful, pernicious, spiteful, deleterious, injurious

misconception *noun* DELUSION, error, misunderstanding, fallacy, misapprehension, mistaken belief, wrong idea, wrong end of the stick, misconstruction

misconduct *noun* IMMORALITY, wrongdoing, mismanagement, malpractice, misdemeanour, delinquency, impropriety, transgression, misbehaviour, dereliction, naughtiness, malfeasance (*Law*), unethical behaviour, malversation (*rare*)

misconstrue *verb* MISINTERPRET, misunderstand, misjudge, misread, mistake, misapprehend, get a false impression of, misconceive, mistranslate, get your lines crossed about, make a wrong interpretation of

misdeed *noun often plural* OFFENCE, wrong, crime, fault, sin, misconduct, trespass, misdemeanour, transgression, villainy

misdemeanour *noun* OFFENCE, misconduct, infringement, trespass, misdeed, transgression, misbehaviour, peccadillo

miserable *adjective* **1** SAD, down, low, depressed, distressed, gloomy, dismal, afflicted, melancholy, heartbroken, desolate, forlorn, mournful, dejected, broken-hearted, despondent, downcast, sorrowful, wretched, disconsolate, crestfallen, doleful, down in the dumps (*informal*), woebegone, down in the mouth (*informal*)
<< OPPOSITE happy
2 PATHETIC, low, sorry, disgraceful, mean, shameful, shabby, abject, despicable, deplorable, lamentable, contemptible, scurvy, pitiable, detestable, piteous
<< OPPOSITE respectable

miserly *adjective* MEAN, stingy, penny-pinching (*informal*), parsimonious, close, near, grasping, beggarly, illiberal, avaricious, niggardly, ungenerous, covetous, penurious, tightfisted, close-fisted, mingy (*Brit informal*), snoep (*S African informal*)
<< OPPOSITE generous

misery *noun* **1** UNHAPPINESS, distress, despair, grief, suffering, depression, torture, agony, gloom, sadness, discomfort, torment, hardship, sorrow, woe, anguish, melancholy, desolation, wretchedness
<< OPPOSITE happiness
2 POVERTY, want, need, squalor, privation, penury, destitution, wretchedness, sordidness, indigence
<< OPPOSITE luxury
3 (*Brit informal*) MOANER, pessimist, killjoy, spoilsport, grouch (*informal*), prophet of doom, wet blanket (*informal*), sourpuss (*informal*), wowser (*Austral & NZ slang*)
4 MISFORTUNE, trouble, trial, disaster, load, burden, curse, ordeal, hardship, catastrophe, sorrow, woe, calamity, affliction, tribulation, bitter pill (*informal*)

misfire *verb* FAIL, go wrong, fall through, miscarry, go pear-shaped (*informal*), fail to go off, go phut (*informal*)

misfit *noun* NONCONFORMIST, eccentric, flake (*slang, chiefly US*), oddball (*informal*), fish out of water (*informal*), square peg (in a round hole) (*informal*)

misfortune *noun* **1** *often plural* BAD LUCK, adversity, hard luck, ill luck, infelicity, evil fortune, bad trot (*Austral slang*)
2 MISHAP, loss, trouble, trial, blow, failure, accident, disaster, reverse, tragedy, harm, misery, setback, hardship, calamity, affliction, tribulation, whammy (*informal, chiefly US*), misadventure, bummer (*slang*), mischance, stroke of bad luck, evil chance
<< OPPOSITE good luck

misgiving *noun* UNEASE, worry, doubt, anxiety, suspicion, uncertainty, reservation, hesitation, distrust, apprehension, qualm, trepidation, scruple, dubiety

misguided *adjective* UNWISE, mistaken, foolish, misled, misplaced, deluded, ill-advised, imprudent, injudicious, labouring under a delusion *or* misapprehension

mishandle *verb* MISMANAGE, bungle, botch, mess up (*informal*), screw (up) (*informal*), make a mess of, muff, make a hash of (*informal*), make a nonsense of, bodge (*informal*), flub (*US slang*)

mishap *noun* ACCIDENT, disaster, misfortune,

stroke of bad luck, adversity, calamity, misadventure, contretemps, mischance, infelicity, evil chance, evil fortune

misinform *verb* MISLEAD, deceive, misdirect, misguide, give someone a bum steer (*informal, chiefly US*)

misinterpret *verb* MISUNDERSTAND, mistake, distort, misrepresent, misjudge, falsify, pervert, misread, misconstrue, get wrong, misapprehend, misconceive

misjudge *verb* MISCALCULATE, be wrong about, underestimate, underrate, overestimate, overrate, get the wrong idea about

mislay *verb* LOSE, misplace, miss, be unable to find, lose track of, be unable to put *or* lay your hand on, forget the whereabouts of

mislead *verb* DECEIVE, fool, delude, take someone in (*informal*), bluff, beguile, misdirect, misinform, hoodwink, lead someone astray, pull the wool over someone's eyes (*informal*), take someone for a ride (*informal*), misguide, give someone a bum steer (*informal, chiefly US*)

misleading *adjective* CONFUSING, false, ambiguous, deceptive, spurious, evasive, disingenuous, tricky (*informal*), deceitful, specious, delusive, delusory, sophistical, casuistical, unstraightforward
<< OPPOSITE straightforward

mismatched *adjective* INCOMPATIBLE, clashing, irregular, disparate, incongruous, discordant, unsuited, ill-assorted, unreconcilable, misallied

misquote *verb* MISREPRESENT, twist, distort, pervert, muddle, mangle, falsify, garble, misreport, misstate, quote *or* take out of context

misrepresent *verb* DISTORT, disguise, pervert, belie, twist, misinterpret, falsify, garble, misstate

miss[1] *verb* 1 FAIL TO NOTICE, mistake, overlook, pass over
2 MISUNDERSTAND, fail to appreciate
3 LONG FOR, wish for, yearn for, want, need, hunger for, pine for, long to see, ache for, feel the loss of, regret the absence of
4 BE LATE FOR, fail to catch *or* get
5 NOT GO TO, skip, cut, omit, be absent from, fail to attend, skive off (*informal*), play truant from, bludge (*Austral & NZ informal*), absent yourself from
6 AVOID, beat, escape, skirt, duck, cheat, bypass, dodge, evade, get round, elude, steer clear of, sidestep, circumvent, find a way round, give a wide berth to
▷ *noun* MISTAKE, failure, fault, error, blunder, omission, oversight

miss[2] *noun* GIRL, maiden, maid, schoolgirl, young lady, lass, damsel, spinster, lassie (*informal*)

misshapen *adjective* DEFORMED, twisted, crippled, distorted, ugly, crooked, warped, grotesque, wry, unsightly, contorted, ungainly, malformed, ill-made, unshapely, ill-proportioned

missile *noun* PROJECTILE, weapon, shell, rocket

missing *adjective* LOST, misplaced, not present, gone, left behind, astray, unaccounted for, mislaid, nowhere to be found

mission *noun* 1 ASSIGNMENT, job, labour, operation, work, commission, trip, message (*Scot*), task, undertaking, expedition, chore, errand
2 TASK, work, calling, business, job, office, charge, goal, operation, commission, trust, aim, purpose, duty, undertaking, pursuit, quest, assignment, vocation, errand

missionary *noun* EVANGELIST, preacher, apostle, converter, propagandist, proselytizer

missive *noun* LETTER, report, note, message, communication, dispatch, memorandum, epistle

mist *noun* FOG, cloud, steam, spray, film, haze, vapour, drizzle, smog, dew, condensation, haar (*Eastern Brit*), smur *or* smir (*Scot*)
▷▷ **mist over** *or* **up** STEAM (UP), cloud, obscure, blur, fog, film, blear, becloud, befog

mistake *noun* 1 ERROR, blunder, oversight, slip, misunderstanding, boob (*Brit slang*), misconception, gaffe (*informal*), slip-up (*informal*), bloomer (*Brit informal*), clanger (*informal*), miscalculation, error of judgment, faux pas, false move, boo-boo (*informal*), barry *or* Barry Crocker (*Austral slang*)
2 OVERSIGHT, error, slip, inaccuracy, fault, slip-up (*informal*), howler (*informal*), goof, solecism, erratum, barry *or* Barry Crocker (*Austral slang*)
▷ *verb* MISUNDERSTAND, misinterpret, misjudge, misread, misconstrue, get wrong, misapprehend, misconceive
▷▷ **mistake something** *or* **someone for something** *or* **someone** CONFUSE WITH, accept as, take for, mix up with, misinterpret as, confound with

mistaken *adjective* 1 WRONG, incorrect, misled, in the wrong, misguided, off the mark, off target, wide of the mark, misinformed, off base (*US & Canad informal*), barking up the wrong tree (*informal*), off beam (*informal*), getting the wrong end of the stick (*informal*), way off beam (*informal*), labouring under a misapprehension
<< OPPOSITE correct
2 INACCURATE, false, inappropriate, faulty, unfounded, erroneous, unsound, fallacious
<< OPPOSITE accurate

mistakenly *adverb* INCORRECTLY, wrongly, falsely, by mistake, inappropriately, erroneously, in error, inaccurately, misguidedly, fallaciously

mistimed *adjective* INOPPORTUNE, badly timed, inconvenient, untimely, ill-timed, unseasonable, unsynchronized

mistreat *verb* ABUSE, injure, harm, molest, misuse, maul, manhandle, wrong, rough up, ill-treat, brutalize, maltreat, ill-use, handle roughly, knock about *or* around

mistreatment *noun* ABUSE, ill-treatment, maltreatment, injury, harm, misuse, mauling, manhandling, roughing up, molestation, unkindness, rough handling, brutalization, ill-usage

mistress *noun* LOVER, girlfriend, concubine, kept woman, paramour, floozy (*slang*), fancy woman (*slang*), inamorata, doxy (*archaic*), fancy bit (*slang*), ladylove (*rare*)

mistrust *noun* SUSPICION, scepticism, distrust, doubt, uncertainty, apprehension, misgiving, wariness, dubiety

▷ *verb* BE WARY OF, suspect, beware, distrust, apprehend, have doubts about

misty *adjective* FOGGY, unclear, murky, fuzzy, obscure, blurred, vague, dim, opaque, cloudy, hazy, overcast, bleary, nebulous, indistinct

<< OPPOSITE clear

misunderstand *verb* 1 MISINTERPRET, misread, get the wrong idea (about), mistake, misjudge, misconstrue, mishear, misapprehend, be at cross-purposes with, misconceive

2 MISS THE POINT, get the wrong end of the stick, get your wires crossed, get your lines crossed

misunderstanding *noun* 1 MISTAKE, error, mix-up, misconception, misreading, misapprehension, false impression, misinterpretation, misjudgment, wrong idea, misconstruction

2 DISAGREEMENT, difference, conflict, argument, difficulty, breach, falling-out (*informal*), quarrel, rift, squabble, rupture, variance, discord, dissension

misunderstood *adjective* MISJUDGED, misinterpreted, misread, misconstrued, unrecognized, misheard, unappreciated

misuse *noun* 1 WASTE, embezzlement, squandering, dissipation, fraudulent use, misemployment, misusage

2 ABUSE, corruption, exploitation

3 ILLEGAL USE, abuse, misapplication, wrong use

4 PERVERSION, distortion, desecration, profanation

5 MISAPPLICATION, solecism, malapropism, catachresis

6 MISTREATMENT, abuse, harm, exploitation, injury, manhandling, ill-treatment, maltreatment, rough handling, inhumane treatment, cruel treatment, ill-usage

▷ *verb* 1 ABUSE, misapply, misemploy, prostitute

2 WASTE, squander, dissipate, embezzle, misappropriate

3 MISTREAT, abuse, injure, harm, exploit, wrong, molest, manhandle, ill-treat, brutalize, maltreat, ill-use, handle roughly

<< OPPOSITE cherish

4 PROFANE, corrupt, desecrate, pervert

mitigate *verb* EASE, moderate, soften, check, quiet, calm, weaken, dull, diminish, temper, blunt, soothe, subdue, lessen, appease, lighten, remit, allay, placate, abate, tone down, assuage, pacify, mollify, take the edge off, extenuate, tranquillize, palliate, reduce the force of

<< OPPOSITE intensify

Mitigate is sometimes wrongly used where *militate* is meant: *his behaviour militates* (not *mitigates*) *against his chances of promotion*

mitigation *noun* 1 EXTENUATION, explanation, excuse

2 RELIEF, moderation, allaying, remission, diminution, abatement, alleviation, easement, extenuation, mollification, palliation, assuagement

mix *verb* 1 BLEND, combine, merge, unite, join, cross, compound, incorporate, put together, fuse, mingle, jumble, alloy, amalgamate, interweave, coalesce, intermingle, meld, commingle, commix

2 SOCIALIZE, associate, hang out (*informal*), mingle, circulate, come together, consort, hobnob, fraternize, rub elbows (*informal*)

3 *often with* **up** COMBINE, marry, blend, integrate, amalgamate, coalesce, meld, commix

▷ *noun* MIXTURE, combination, blend, fusion, compound, jumble, assortment, alloy, medley, concoction, amalgam, mixed bag (*informal*), meld, melange, miscellany

▷▷ **mix someone up** BEWILDER, upset, confuse, disturb, puzzle, muddle, perplex, unnerve, fluster, throw into confusion

▷▷ **mix someone up in something** *usually passive* ENTANGLE, involve, implicate, embroil, rope in

▷▷ **mix something up** 1 CONFUSE, scramble, muddle, confound

2 BLEND, beat, mix, stir, fold

mixed *adjective* 1 UNCERTAIN, conflicting, confused, doubtful, unsure, muddled, contradictory, ambivalent, indecisive, equivocal

2 VARIED, diverse, different, differing, diversified, cosmopolitan, assorted, jumbled, disparate, miscellaneous, motley, haphazard, manifold, heterogeneous

<< OPPOSITE homogeneous

3 COMBINED, blended, fused, alloyed, united, compound, incorporated, composite, mingled, amalgamated
<< OPPOSITE pure

mixed-up *adjective* CONFUSED, disturbed, puzzled, bewildered, at sea, upset, distraught, muddled, perplexed, maladjusted

mixture *noun* 1 BLEND, mix, variety, fusion, assortment, combine, brew, jumble, medley, concoction, amalgam, amalgamation, mixed bag (*informal*), meld, potpourri, mélange (*French*), miscellany, conglomeration, hotchpotch, admixture, salmagundi
2 COMPOSITE, union, compound, alloy
3 CROSS, combination, blend, association
4 CONCOCTION, union, compound, blend, brew, composite, amalgam, conglomeration

mix-up *noun* CONFUSION, mistake, misunderstanding, mess, tangle, muddle, jumble, fankle (*Scot*)

moan *verb* 1 GROAN, sigh, sob, whine, keen, lament, deplore, bemoan, bewail
2 (*informal*) GRUMBLE, complain, groan, whine, beef (*slang*), carp, bitch (*slang*), grouse, gripe (*informal*), whinge (*informal*), bleat, moan and groan, grouch (*informal*)
▷ *noun* 1 GROAN, sigh, sob, lament, wail, grunt, whine, lamentation
2 (*informal*) COMPLAINT, protest, grumble, beef (*slang*), bitch (*slang*), whine, grouse, gripe (*informal*), grouch (*informal*), kvetch (*US slang*)

mob *noun* 1 CROWD, pack, collection, mass, body, press, host, gathering, drove, gang, flock, herd, swarm, horde, multitude, throng, assemblage
2 MASSES, rabble, hoi polloi, scum, great unwashed (*informal or derogatory*), riffraff, canaille (*French*), commonalty
3 GANG, company, group, set, lot, troop, crew (*informal*)
▷ *verb* 1 SURROUND, besiege, overrun, jostle, fall on, set upon, crowd around, swarm around
2 CROWD INTO, fill, crowd, pack, jam, cram into, fill to overflowing

mobile *adjective* 1 MOVABLE, moving, travelling, wandering, portable, locomotive, itinerant, peripatetic, ambulatory, motile
2 CHANGEABLE, meaning, animated, expressive, eloquent, suggestive, ever-changing

mobilize *verb* 1 RALLY, organize, stimulate, excite, prompt, marshal, activate, awaken, animate, muster, foment, put in motion
2 DEPLOY, prepare, ready, rally, assemble, call up, marshal, muster, call to arms, get *or* make ready

mock *verb* LAUGH AT, insult, tease, ridicule, taunt, scorn, sneer, scoff, deride, flout, make fun of, wind someone up (*Brit slang*), poke fun at, chaff, take the mickey out of (*informal*), jeer at, show contempt for, make a monkey out of, laugh to scorn
<< OPPOSITE respect
▷ *adjective* IMITATION, pretended, artificial, forged, fake, false, faked, dummy, bogus, sham, fraudulent, pseudo (*informal*), counterfeit, feigned, spurious, ersatz, phoney *or* phony (*informal*)
<< OPPOSITE genuine
▷ *noun* LAUGHING STOCK, fool, dupe, sport, travesty, jest, Aunt Sally (*Brit*)

mockery *noun* 1 DERISION, contempt, ridicule, scorn, jeering, disdain, scoffing, disrespect, gibes, contumely
2 FARCE, laughing stock, joke, apology (*informal*), letdown

mocking *adjective* SCORNFUL, insulting, taunting, scoffing, satirical, contemptuous, irreverent, sarcastic, sardonic, derisory, disrespectful, disdainful, derisive, satiric, contumelious

mode *noun* 1 METHOD, way, plan, course, system, form, state, process, condition, style, approach, quality, practice, fashion, technique, manner, procedure, custom, vein
2 FASHION, style, trend, rage, vogue, look, craze

model *noun* 1 REPRESENTATION, image, copy, miniature, dummy, replica, imitation, duplicate, lookalike, facsimile, mock-up
2 PATTERN, example, design, standard, type, original, ideal, mould, norm, gauge, prototype, paradigm, archetype, exemplar, lodestar
3 VERSION, form, kind, design, style, type, variety, stamp, mode, configuration
4 SITTER, subject, poser
5 MANNEQUIN, supermodel, fashion model, clothes horse (*informal*)
▷ *modifier* 1 IMITATION, copy, toy, miniature, dummy, duplicate, facsimile
2 IDEAL, perfect, impeccable, exemplary, consummate, flawless, faultless
<< OPPOSITE imperfect
3 ARCHETYPAL, standard, typical, illustrative, paradigmatic
▷ *verb* 1 BASE, shape, plan, found, pattern, mould
2 SHOW OFF (*informal*), wear, display, sport
3 SHAPE, form, design, fashion, cast, stamp, carve, mould, sculpt

moderate *adjective* 1 MILD, reasonable, controlled, limited, cool, calm, steady, modest, restrained, deliberate, sober, middle-of-the-road, temperate, judicious, peaceable, equable
<< OPPOSITE extreme
2 AVERAGE, middling, medium, fair, ordinary, indifferent, mediocre, so-so (*informal*), passable, unexceptional, fairish, half-pie (NZ

informal), fair to middling (*informal*)
▷ *verb* 1 SOFTEN, control, calm, temper, regulate, quiet, diminish, decrease, curb, restrain, tame, subdue, play down, lessen, repress, mitigate, tone down, pacify, modulate, soft-pedal (*informal*)
2 LESSEN, relax, ease, wane, abate
<< OPPOSITE intensify
3 ARBITRATE, judge, chair, referee, preside, mediate, take the chair

moderation *noun* RESTRAINT, justice, fairness, composure, coolness, temperance, calmness, equanimity, reasonableness, mildness, justness, judiciousness, sedateness, moderateness
▷▷ **in moderation** MODERATELY, within reason, within limits, within bounds, in moderate quantities

modern *adjective* 1 CURRENT, present, contemporary, recent, late, present-day, latter-day
2 UP-TO-DATE, latest, fresh, new, novel, with it (*informal*), up-to-the-minute, newfangled, neoteric (*rare*)
<< OPPOSITE old-fashioned

modernity *noun* NOVELTY, currency, innovation, freshness, newness, contemporaneity, recentness

modernize *verb* UPDATE, renew, revamp, remake, renovate, remodel, rejuvenate, make over, face-lift, bring up to date, rebrand

modest *adjective* 1 MODERATE, small, limited, fair, ordinary, middling, meagre, frugal, scanty, unexceptional
2 UNPRETENTIOUS, simple, reserved, retiring, quiet, shy, humble, discreet, blushing, self-conscious, coy, meek, reticent, unassuming, self-effacing, demure, diffident, bashful

modesty *noun* RESERVE, decency, humility, shyness, propriety, reticence, timidity, diffidence, quietness, coyness, self-effacement, meekness, lack of pretension, bashfulness, humbleness, unpretentiousness, demureness, unobtrusiveness, discreetness
<< OPPOSITE conceit

modicum *noun* LITTLE, bit, drop, touch, inch, scrap, dash, grain, particle, fragment, atom, pinch, ounce, shred, small amount, crumb, tinge, mite, tad (*informal, chiefly US*), speck, iota

modification *noun* CHANGE, restriction, variation, qualification, adjustment, revision, alteration, mutation, reformation, refinement, modulation

modify *verb* 1 CHANGE, reform, vary, convert, transform, alter, adjust, adapt, revise, remodel, rework, tweak (*informal*), reorganize, recast, reshape, redo, refashion
2 TONE DOWN, limit, reduce, lower, qualify, relax, ease, restrict, moderate, temper, soften, restrain, lessen, abate

modish *adjective* FASHIONABLE, current, smart, stylish, trendy (*Brit informal*), in, now (*informal*), with it (*informal*), contemporary, hip (*slang*), vogue, chic, all the rage, up-to-the-minute, à la mode, voguish, schmick (*Austral informal*)

modulate *verb* ADJUST, balance, vary, tone, tune, regulate, harmonize, inflect, attune

modus operandi *noun* PROCEDURE, way, system, process, operation, practice, method, technique, praxis

mogul *noun* TYCOON, lord, baron, notable, magnate, big gun (*informal*), big shot (*informal*), personage, nob (*slang, chiefly Brit*), potentate, big wheel (*slang*), big cheese (*slang* or *old-fashioned*), big noise (*informal*), big hitter (*informal*), heavy hitter (*informal*), nabob (*informal*), bashaw, V.I.P.

moist *adjective* DAMP, wet, dripping, rainy, soggy, humid, dank, clammy, dewy, not dry, drizzly, dampish, wettish

moisten *verb* DAMPEN, water, wet, soak, damp, moisturize, humidify, bedew

moisture *noun* DAMP, water, liquid, sweat, humidity, dew, perspiration, dampness, wetness, dankness, wateriness

molecule *noun* PARTICLE, atom, mite, jot, speck, mote, iota

molest *verb* 1 ABUSE, attack, hurt, injure, harm, interfere with, assail, accost, manhandle, ill-treat, maltreat
2 ANNOY, worry, upset, harry, bother, disturb, bug (*informal*), plague, irritate, tease, torment, harass, afflict, badger, persecute, beset, hector, pester, vex

mollify *verb* PACIFY, quiet, calm, compose, soothe, appease, quell, sweeten, placate, conciliate, propitiate

mom *noun* (*US & Canad*) MUM, mother, ma

moment *noun* 1 INSTANT, second, minute, flash, shake (*informal*), tick (*Brit informal*), no time, twinkling, split second, jiffy (*informal*), trice, two shakes (*informal*), two shakes of a lamb's tail (*informal*), bat of an eye (*informal*)
2 TIME, point, stage, instant, point in time, hour, juncture
3 IMPORTANCE, concern, value, worth, weight, import, consequence, substance, significance, gravity, seriousness, weightiness

momentarily *adverb* BRIEFLY, for a moment, temporarily, for a second, for a minute, for a short time, for an instant, for a little while, for a short while, for the nonce

momentary *adjective* SHORT-LIVED, short, brief, temporary, passing, quick, fleeting, hasty, transitory
<< OPPOSITE lasting

momentous *adjective* SIGNIFICANT, important, serious, vital, critical, crucial, grave, historic, decisive, pivotal, fateful, weighty,

consequential, of moment, earth-shaking (*informal*)
<< OPPOSITE unimportant

momentum *noun* IMPETUS, force, power, drive, push, energy, strength, thrust, propulsion

monarch *noun* RULER, king *or* queen, sovereign, tsar, potentate, crowned head, emperor *or* empress, prince *or* princess

monarchy *noun* 1 SOVEREIGNTY, despotism, autocracy, kingship, absolutism, royalism, monocracy
2 KINGDOM, empire, realm, principality

monastery *noun* ABBEY, house, convent, priory, cloister, religious community, nunnery, friary

monastic *adjective* MONKISH, secluded, cloistered, reclusive, withdrawn, austere, celibate, contemplative, ascetic, sequestered, hermit-like, conventual, cenobitic, coenobitic, cloistral, eremitic, monachal

monetary *adjective* FINANCIAL, money, economic, capital, cash, fiscal, budgetary, pecuniary

money *noun* CASH, funds, capital, currency, hard cash, green (*slang*), readies (*informal*), riches, necessary (*informal*), silver, bread (*slang*), coin, tin (*slang*), brass (*Northern English dialect*), loot (*informal*), dough (*slang*), the ready (*informal*), banknotes, dosh (*Brit & Austral slang*), lolly (*Brit slang*), the wherewithal, legal tender, megabucks (*US & Canad slang*), needful (*informal*), specie, shekels (*informal*), dibs (*slang*), filthy lucre (*facetious*), moolah (*slang*), ackers (*slang*), gelt (*slang, chiefly US*), spondulicks (*slang*), pelf (*contemptuous*), mazuma (*slang, chiefly US*), kembla (*Austral slang*)
▷▷ **in the money** (*informal*) RICH, wealthy, prosperous, affluent, rolling (*slang*), loaded (*slang*), flush (*informal*), well-off, well-heeled (*informal*), well-to-do, on Easy Street (*informal*), in clover (*informal*)
>> RELATED WORD *adjective* pecuniary

moneyed *or* **monied** *adjective* RICH, loaded (*slang*), wealthy, flush (*informal*), prosperous, affluent, well-off, well-heeled (*informal*), well-to-do

moneymaking *adjective* PROFITABLE, successful, lucrative, gainful, paying, thriving, remunerative

mongrel *noun* HYBRID, cross, half-breed, crossbreed, mixed breed, bigener (*Biology*)
▷ *adjective* HALF-BREED, hybrid, crossbred, of mixed breed

monitor *verb* CHECK, follow, record, watch, survey, observe, scan, oversee, supervise, keep an eye on, keep track of, keep tabs on
▷ *noun* 1 GUIDE, observer, supervisor, overseer, invigilator
2 PREFECT (*Brit*), head girl, head boy, senior boy, senior girl

monk *noun* (*Loosely*) FRIAR, brother, religious, novice, monastic, oblate
>> RELATED WORD *adjective* monastic

monkey *noun* 1 SIMIAN, ape, primate, jackanapes (*archaic*)
2 RASCAL, horror, devil, rogue, imp, tyke, scallywag, mischief maker, scamp, nointer (*Austral slang*)
>> RELATED WORD *adjective* simian
>> RELATED WORD *collective noun* troop

monolithic *adjective* HUGE, giant, massive, imposing, solid, substantial, gigantic, monumental, colossal, impenetrable, intractable, immovable

monologue *noun* SPEECH, lecture, sermon, harangue, soliloquy, oration, spiel (*informal*)

monopolize *verb* 1 CONTROL, corner, take over, dominate, exercise *or* have a monopoly of
2 KEEP TO YOURSELF, corner, hog (*slang*), engross

monotonous *adjective* 1 TEDIOUS, boring, dull, repetitive, uniform, all the same, plodding, tiresome, humdrum, unchanging, colourless, mind-numbing, soporific, ho-hum (*informal*), repetitious, wearisome, samey (*informal*), unvaried
<< OPPOSITE interesting
2 TONELESS, flat, uniform, droning, unchanging, uninflected
<< OPPOSITE animated

monotony *noun* TEDIUM, routine, boredom, dullness, sameness, uniformity, flatness, repetitiveness, tediousness, repetitiousness, colourlessness, tiresomeness

monster *noun* 1 GIANT, mammoth, titan, colossus, monstrosity, leviathan, behemoth
2 BRUTE, devil, savage, beast, demon, villain, barbarian, fiend, ogre, ghoul, bogeyman

monstrosity *noun* 1 FREAK, horror, monster, mutant, ogre, lusus naturae, miscreation, teratism
2 HIDEOUSNESS, horror, evil, atrocity, abnormality, obscenity, dreadfulness, frightfulness, heinousness, hellishness, loathsomeness

monstrous *adjective* 1 OUTRAGEOUS, shocking, evil, horrifying, vicious, foul, cruel, infamous, intolerable, disgraceful, scandalous, atrocious, inhuman, diabolical, heinous, odious, loathsome, devilish, egregious, fiendish, villainous
<< OPPOSITE decent
2 HUGE, giant, massive, great, towering, vast, enormous, tremendous, immense, titanic, gigantic, mammoth, colossal, stellar (*informal*), prodigious, stupendous, gargantuan, elephantine, ginormous (*informal*), humongous *or* humungous (*US slang*)
<< OPPOSITE tiny

3 UNNATURAL, terrible, horrible, dreadful, abnormal, obscene, horrendous, hideous, grotesque, gruesome, frightful, hellish, freakish, fiendish, miscreated
<< OPPOSITE normal

month *noun* FOUR WEEKS, thirty days, moon

monument *noun* 1 MEMORIAL, cairn, statue, pillar, marker, shrine, tombstone, mausoleum, commemoration, headstone, gravestone, obelisk, cenotaph
2 TESTAMENT, record, witness, token, reminder, remembrance, memento

monumental *adjective* 1 IMPORTANT, classic, significant, outstanding, lasting, enormous, historic, enduring, memorable, awesome, majestic, immortal, unforgettable, prodigious, stupendous, awe-inspiring, epoch-making
<< OPPOSITE unimportant
2 (*informal*) IMMENSE, great, massive, terrible, tremendous, horrible, staggering, catastrophic, gigantic, colossal, whopping (*informal*), indefensible, unforgivable, egregious
<< OPPOSITE tiny
3 COMMEMORATIVE, memorial, monolithic, statuary, funerary

mood *noun* 1 STATE OF MIND, spirit, humour, temper, vein, tenor, disposition, frame of mind
2 DEPRESSION, sulk, bad temper, blues, dumps (*informal*), wax (*informal, chiefly Brit*), melancholy, doldrums, the hump (*Brit informal*), bate (*Brit slang*), fit of pique, low spirits, the sulks, grumps (*informal*), foulie (*Austral slang*)
▷▷ **in the mood** INCLINED, willing, interested, minded, keen, eager, disposed towards, in the (right) frame of mind, favourable towards

moody *adjective* 1 CHANGEABLE, volatile, unpredictable, unstable, erratic, fickle, temperamental, impulsive, mercurial, capricious, unsteady, fitful, flighty, faddish, inconstant
<< OPPOSITE stable
2 SULKY, cross, wounded, angry, offended, irritable, crabbed, crusty, temperamental, touchy, curt, petulant, ill-tempered, irascible, cantankerous, tetchy, testy, chippy (*informal*), in a huff, short-tempered, waspish, piqued, crabby, huffy, splenetic, crotchety (*informal*), ill-humoured, huffish, tooshie (*Austral slang*)
<< OPPOSITE cheerful
3 GLOOMY, sad, miserable, melancholy, frowning, dismal, dour, sullen, glum, introspective, in the doldrums, out of sorts (*informal*), downcast, morose, lugubrious, pensive, broody, crestfallen, doleful, down in the dumps (*informal*), saturnine, down in the mouth (*informal*), mopish, mopy
<< OPPOSITE cheerful
4 SAD, gloomy, melancholy, sombre

moon *noun* SATELLITE
▷ *verb* IDLE, drift, loaf, languish, waste time, daydream, mope, mooch (*Brit slang*)
>> RELATED WORD *adjective* lunar

moor[1] *noun* MOORLAND, fell (*Brit*), heath, muir (*Scot*)

moor[2] *verb* TIE UP, fix, secure, anchor, dock, lash, berth, fasten, make fast

moot *verb* BRING UP, propose, suggest, introduce, put forward, ventilate, broach
▷ *adjective* DEBATABLE, open, controversial, doubtful, unsettled, unresolved, undecided, at issue, arguable, open to debate, contestable, disputable

mop *noun* 1 SQUEEGEE, sponge, swab
2 MANE, shock, mass, tangle, mat, thatch
▷ *verb* CLEAN, wash, wipe, sponge, swab, squeegee
▷▷ **mop something up** 1 CLEAN UP, wash, sponge, mop, soak up, swab, wipe up, sop up
2 (*Military*) FINISH OFF, clear, account for, eliminate, round up, clean out, neutralize, pacify

mope *verb* BROOD, moon, pine, hang around, idle, fret, pout, languish, waste time, sulk, be gloomy, eat your heart out, be apathetic, be dejected, be down in the mouth (*informal*), have a long face, wear a long face, go about like a half-shut knife (*informal*)

moral *adjective* 1 ETHICAL, social, behavioural
2 PSYCHOLOGICAL, emotional, mental
3 GOOD, just, right, principled, pure, decent, innocent, proper, noble, ethical, upright, honourable, honest, righteous, virtuous, blameless, high-minded, chaste, upstanding, meritorious, incorruptible
<< OPPOSITE immoral
▷ *noun* LESSON, meaning, point, message, teaching, import, significance, precept
▷ *plural noun* MORALITY, standards, conduct, principles, behaviour, manners, habits, ethics, integrity, mores, scruples

morale *noun* CONFIDENCE, heart, spirit, temper, self-esteem, team spirit, mettle, esprit de corps

morality *noun* 1 VIRTUE, justice, principles, morals, honour, integrity, goodness, honesty, decency, fair play, righteousness, good behaviour, propriety, chastity, probity, rectitude, rightness, uprightness
2 ETHICS, conduct, principles, ideals, morals, manners, habits, philosophy, mores, moral code
3 RIGHTS AND WRONGS, ethics, ethicality

morass *noun* 1 MESS, confusion, chaos, jam (*informal*), tangle, mix-up, muddle, quagmire
2 MARSH, swamp, bog, slough, fen, moss (*Scot & Northern English dialect*), quagmire, marshland, muskeg (*Canad*)

moratorium *noun* POSTPONEMENT, stay, freeze,

halt, suspension, respite, standstill

morbid *adjective* **1** GRUESOME, sick, dreadful, ghastly, hideous, unhealthy, grisly, macabre, horrid, ghoulish, unwholesome
2 GLOOMY, brooding, pessimistic, melancholy, sombre, grim, glum, lugubrious, funereal, low-spirited
<< OPPOSITE cheerful
3 DISEASED, sick, infected, deadly, ailing, unhealthy, malignant, sickly, pathological, unsound
<< OPPOSITE healthy

more *determiner* EXTRA, additional, spare, new, other, added, further, fresh, new-found, supplementary
▷ *adverb* **1** TO A GREATER EXTENT, longer, better, further, some more
2 MOREOVER, also, in addition, besides, furthermore, what's more, on top of that, to boot, into the bargain, over and above that
▷ see **most**

moreover *adverb* FURTHERMORE, also, further, in addition, too, as well, besides, likewise, what is more, to boot, additionally, into the bargain, withal (*literary*)

moribund *adjective* DECLINING, weak, waning, standing still, stagnant, stagnating, on the way out, at a standstill, obsolescent, on its last legs, forceless

morning *noun* **1** BEFORE NOON, forenoon, morn (*poetic*), a.m.
2 DAWN, sunrise, morrow (*archaic*), first light, daybreak, break of day

moron *noun* FOOL, idiot, dummy (*slang*), berk (*Brit slang*), charlie (*Brit informal*), tosser (*Brit slang*), dope (*informal*), jerk (*slang, chiefly US & Canad*), ass, plank (*Brit slang*), wally (*slang*), prat (*slang*), plonker (*slang*), coot, geek (*slang*), twit (*informal, chiefly Brit*), bonehead (*slang*), chump, dunce, imbecile, cretin, oaf, simpleton, airhead (*slang*), dimwit (*informal*), dipstick (*Brit slang*), gonzo (*slang*), schmuck (*US slang*), dork (*slang*), nitwit (*informal*), dolt, blockhead, divvy (*Brit slang*), pillock (*Brit slang*), halfwit, dweeb (*US slang*), putz (*US slang*), fathead (*informal*), weenie (*US informal*), eejit (*Scot & Irish*), dumb-ass (*slang*), dunderhead, numpty (*Scot informal*), doofus (*slang, chiefly US*), lamebrain (*informal*), mental defective, thickhead, muttonhead (*slang*), nerd *or* nurd (*slang*), numbskull *or* numskull, dorba *or* dorb (*Austral slang*), bogan (*Austral slang*)

moronic *adjective* IDIOTIC, simple, foolish, mindless, thick, stupid, daft (*informal*), retarded, gormless (*Brit informal*), brainless, cretinous, unintelligent, dimwitted (*informal*), asinine, imbecilic, braindead (*informal*), mentally defective, dumb-ass (*slang*), doltish, dead from the neck up (*informal*), halfwitted, muttonheaded (*slang*)

morose *adjective* SULLEN, miserable, moody, gloomy, down, low, cross, blue, depressed, sour, crabbed, pessimistic, perverse, melancholy, dour, crusty, glum, surly, mournful, gruff, churlish, sulky, taciturn, ill-tempered, in a bad mood, grouchy (*informal*), down in the dumps (*informal*), crabby, saturnine, ill-humoured, ill-natured
<< OPPOSITE cheerful

morsel *noun* PIECE, bite, bit, slice, scrap, part, grain, taste, segment, fragment, fraction, snack, crumb, nibble, mouthful, tad (*informal, chiefly US*), titbit, soupçon (*French*)

mortal *adjective* **1** HUMAN, worldly, passing, earthly, fleshly, temporal, transient, ephemeral, perishable, corporeal, impermanent, sublunary
2 FATAL, killing, terminal, deadly, destructive, lethal, murderous, death-dealing
3 UNRELENTING, bitter, sworn, deadly, relentless, to the death, implacable, out-and-out, irreconcilable, remorseless
4 GREAT, serious, terrible, enormous, severe, extreme, grave, intense, awful, dire, agonizing
▷ *noun* HUMAN BEING, being, man, woman, body, person, human, individual, earthling

mortality *noun* **1** HUMANITY, transience, impermanence, ephemerality, temporality, corporeality, impermanency
2 DEATH, dying, fatality, loss of life

mortified *adjective* HUMILIATED, embarrassed, shamed, crushed, annoyed, humbled, horrified, put down, put out (*informal*), ashamed, confounded, deflated, vexed, affronted, displeased, chagrined, chastened, discomfited, abashed, put to shame, rendered speechless, made to eat humble pie (*informal*), given a showing-up (*informal*)

mortify *verb* **1** HUMILIATE, disappoint, embarrass, shame, crush, annoy, humble, deflate, vex, affront, displease, chagrin, discomfit, abase, put someone to shame, abash
2 DISCIPLINE, control, deny, subdue, chasten, abase

mortuary *noun* MORGUE, funeral home (*US*), funeral parlour

most *pronoun* NEARLY ALL, the majority, the mass, almost all, the bulk, the lion's share, the preponderance

More and *most* should be distinguished when used in comparisons. *More* applies to cases involving two people, objects, etc., *most* to cases involving three or more: *John is the more intelligent of the two; he is the most intelligent of the students*

mostly *adverb* 1 MAINLY, largely, chiefly, principally, primarily, above all, on the whole, predominantly, for the most part, almost entirely
2 GENERALLY, usually, on the whole, most often, as a rule, customarily
mote *noun* SPECK, spot, grain, particle, fragment, atom, mite
moth *noun*
>> RELATED WORD *young* caterpillar
>> RELATED WORD *enthusiast* lepidopterist
mother *noun* FEMALE PARENT, mum (*Brit informal*), ma (*informal*), mater, dam, old woman (*informal*), mom (*US & Canad*), mummy (*Brit informal*), old lady (*informal*), foster mother, birth mother, biological mother
▷ *verb* 1 GIVE BIRTH TO, produce, bear, bring forth, drop
2 NURTURE, raise, protect, tend, nurse, rear, care for, cherish
▷ *modifier* NATIVE, natural, innate, inborn, connate
>> RELATED WORD *adjective* maternal
motherly *adjective* MATERNAL, loving, kind, caring, warm, comforting, sheltering, gentle, tender, protective, fond, affectionate
motif *noun* 1 DESIGN, form, shape, decoration, ornament
2 THEME, idea, subject, concept, leitmotif
motion *noun* 1 MOVEMENT, action, mobility, passing, travel, progress, flow, passage, locomotion, motility, kinesics
2 GESTURE, sign, wave, signal, gesticulation
3 PROPOSAL, suggestion, recommendation, proposition, submission
▷ *verb* GESTURE, direct, wave, signal, nod, beckon, gesticulate
▷▷ **in motion** 1 IN PROGRESS, going on, under way, afoot, on the go (*informal*)
2 MOVING, going, working, travelling, functioning, under way, operational, on the move (*informal*)
>> RELATED WORD *adjective* kinetic
motionless *adjective* STILL, static, stationary, standing, fixed, frozen, calm, halted, paralysed, lifeless, inert, unmoved, transfixed, at rest, immobile, inanimate, at a standstill, unmoving, stock-still
<< OPPOSITE moving
motivate *verb* 1 INSPIRE, drive, stimulate, provoke, lead, move, cause, prompt, stir, trigger, set off, induce, arouse, prod, get going, instigate, impel, actuate, give incentive to, inspirit
2 STIMULATE, drive, inspire, stir, arouse, get going, galvanize, incentivize
motivation *noun* 1 INCENTIVE, inspiration, motive, stimulus, reason, spur, impulse, persuasion, inducement, incitement, instigation, carrot and stick
2 INSPIRATION, drive, desire, ambition, hunger, interest
motive *noun* REASON, motivation, cause, ground(s), design, influence, purpose, object, intention, spur, incentive, inspiration, stimulus, rationale, inducement, incitement, mainspring, the why and wherefore
▷ *adjective* MOVING, driving, motivating, operative, activating, impelling
motley *adjective* MISCELLANEOUS, mixed, varied, diversified, mingled, unlike, assorted, disparate, dissimilar, heterogeneous
<< OPPOSITE homogeneous
mottled *adjective* BLOTCHY, spotted, pied, streaked, marbled, flecked, variegated, chequered, speckled, freckled, dappled, tabby, stippled, piebald, brindled
motto *noun* SAYING, slogan, maxim, rule, cry, formula, gnome, adage, proverb, dictum, precept, byword, watchword, tag-line
mould[1] *noun* 1 CAST, form, die, shape, pattern, stamp, matrix
2 DESIGN, line, style, fashion, build, form, cut, kind, shape, structure, pattern, brand, frame, construction, stamp, format, configuration
3 NATURE, character, sort, kind, quality, type, stamp, kidney, calibre, ilk
▷ *verb* 1 SHAPE, make, work, form, create, model, fashion, cast, stamp, construct, carve, forge, sculpt
2 INFLUENCE, make, form, control, direct, affect, shape
mould[2] *noun* FUNGUS, blight, mildew, mustiness, mouldiness
moulder *verb* DECAY, waste, break down, crumble, rot, disintegrate, perish, decompose
mouldy *adjective* STALE, spoiled, rotting, decaying, bad, rotten, blighted, musty, fusty, mildewed
mound *noun* 1 HEAP, bing (*Scot*), pile, drift, stack, rick
2 HILL, bank, rise, dune, embankment, knoll, hillock, kopje *or* koppie (*S African*)
3 (*Archaeology*) BARROW, tumulus
4 EARTHWORK, rampart, bulwark, motte (*History*)
mount *verb* 1 (*Military*) LAUNCH, stage, prepare, deliver, set in motion
2 INCREASE, build, grow, swell, intensify, escalate, multiply
<< OPPOSITE decrease
3 ACCUMULATE, increase, collect, gather, build up, pile up, amass, cumulate
4 ASCEND, scale, climb (up), go up, clamber up, make your way up
<< OPPOSITE descend
5 GET (UP) ON, jump on, straddle, climb onto, climb up on, hop on to, bestride, get on the

back of, get astride
<< OPPOSITE get off
6 DISPLAY, set, frame, set off
7 FIT, place, set, position, set up, fix, secure, attach, install, erect, put in place, put in position, emplace
8 PRESENT, display, stage, prepare, put on, organize, get up (*informal*), exhibit, put on display
▷ *noun* 1 HORSE, steed (*literary*)
2 BACKING, setting, support, stand, base, mounting, frame, fixture, foil

mountain *noun* 1 PEAK, mount, height, ben (*Scot*), horn, ridge, fell (*Brit*), berg (*S African*), alp, pinnacle, elevation, Munro, eminence
2 HEAP, mass, masses, pile, a great deal, ton, stack, abundance, mound, profusion, shedload (*Brit informal*)

mountainous *adjective* 1 HIGH, towering, soaring, steep, rocky, highland, alpine, upland
2 HUGE, great, enormous, mighty, immense, daunting, gigantic, monumental, mammoth, prodigious, hulking, ponderous
<< OPPOSITE tiny

mourn *verb* 1 *often with* **for** GRIEVE FOR, miss, lament, keen for, weep for, sorrow for, wail for, wear black for
2 BEMOAN, rue, deplore, bewail

mournful *adjective* 1 DISMAL, sad, unhappy, miserable, gloomy, grieving, melancholy, sombre, heartbroken, desolate, woeful, rueful, heavy, downcast, grief-stricken, lugubrious, disconsolate, joyless, funereal, heavy-hearted, down in the dumps (*informal*), cheerless, brokenhearted
<< OPPOSITE happy
2 SAD, distressing, unhappy, tragic, painful, afflicting, melancholy, harrowing, grievous, woeful, deplorable, lamentable, plaintive, calamitous, sorrowful, piteous
<< OPPOSITE cheerful

mourning *noun* 1 GRIEVING, grief, bereavement, weeping, woe, lamentation, keening
2 BLACK, weeds, sackcloth and ashes, widow's weeds

mouth *noun* 1 LIPS, trap (*slang*), chops (*slang*), jaws, gob (*slang, esp Brit*), maw, yap (*slang*), cakehole (*Brit slang*)
2 ENTRANCE, opening, gateway, cavity, door, aperture, crevice, orifice
3 OPENING, lip, rim
4 INLET, outlet, estuary, firth, outfall, debouchment
5 (*informal*) BOASTING, gas (*informal*), bragging, hot air (*slang*), braggadocio, idle talk, empty talk
>> RELATED WORDS *adjectives* oral, oscular

mouthful *noun* TASTE, little, bite, bit, drop, sample, swallow, sip, sup, spoonful, morsel, forkful

mouthpiece *noun* 1 SPOKESPERSON, agent, representative, delegate, spokesman *or* spokeswoman
2 PUBLICATION, journal, organ, periodical

movable *adjective* PORTABLE, mobile, transferable, detachable, not fixed, transportable, portative

move *verb* 1 TRANSFER, change, carry, transport, switch, shift, transpose
2 GO, walk, march, advance, progress, shift, proceed, stir, budge, make a move, change position
3 RELOCATE, leave, remove, quit, go away, migrate, emigrate, move house, flit (*Scot & Northern English dialect*), decamp, up sticks (*Brit informal*), pack your bags (*informal*), change residence
4 DRIVE, lead, cause, influence, persuade, push, shift, inspire, prompt, stimulate, motivate, induce, shove, activate, propel, rouse, prod, incite, impel, set going
<< OPPOSITE discourage
5 TOUCH, affect, excite, impress, stir, agitate, disquiet, make an impression on, tug at your heartstrings (*often facetious*)
6 PROPOSE, suggest, urge, recommend, request, advocate, submit, put forward
▷ *noun* 1 ACTION, act, step, movement, shift, motion, manoeuvre, deed
2 PLOY, action, measure, step, initiative, stroke, tactic, manoeuvre, deed, tack, ruse, gambit, stratagem
3 TRANSFER, posting, shift, removal, migration, relocation, flit (*Scot & Northern English dialect*), flitting (*Scot & Northern English dialect*), change of address
4 TURN, go, play, chance, shot (*informal*), opportunity
▷▷ **get a move on** SPEED UP, hurry (up), get going, get moving, get cracking (*informal*), step on it (*informal*), make haste, shake a leg (*informal*), get your skates on (*informal*), stir yourself
▷▷ **on the move** 1 IN TRANSIT, moving, travelling, journeying, on the road (*informal*), under way, voyaging, on the run, in motion, on the wing
2 ACTIVE, moving, developing, advancing, progressing, succeeding, stirring, going forward, astir

movement *noun* 1 GROUP, party, organization, grouping, front, camp, faction
2 CAMPAIGN, drive, push, crusade
3 MOVE, act, action, operation, motion, gesture, manoeuvre
4 ACTIVITY, moving, stirring, bustle, agitation
5 ADVANCE, progress, flow, progression

6 TRANSFER, transportation, displacement
7 TREND, flow, swing, current, tendency
8 DEVELOPMENT, change, shift, variation, fluctuation
9 PROGRESSION, advance, progress, breakthrough
10 (*Music*) SECTION, part, division, passage

movie *noun* FILM, picture, feature, flick (*slang*), motion picture, moving picture (US)
▷▷ **the movies** THE CINEMA, a film, the pictures (*informal*), the flicks (*slang*), the silver screen (*informal*)

moving *adjective* 1 EMOTIONAL, touching, affecting, exciting, inspiring, stirring, arousing, poignant, emotive, impelling
<< OPPOSITE unemotional
2 MOBILE, running, active, going, operational, in motion, driving, kinetic, movable, motile, unfixed
<< OPPOSITE stationary
3 MOTIVATING, stimulating, dynamic, propelling, inspirational, impelling, stimulative

mow *verb* CUT, crop, trim, shear, scythe
▷▷ **mow something** *or* **someone down** MASSACRE, butcher, slaughter, cut down, shoot down, blow away (*slang, chiefly US*), cut to pieces

much *adverb* 1 GREATLY, a lot, considerably, decidedly, exceedingly, appreciably
<< OPPOSITE hardly
2 OFTEN, a lot, regularly, routinely, a great deal, frequently, many times, habitually, on many occasions, customarily
▷ *adjective* GREAT, a lot of, plenty of, considerable, substantial, piles of (*informal*), ample, abundant, copious, oodles of (*informal*), plenteous, sizable *or* sizeable amount, shedful (*slang*)
<< OPPOSITE little
▷ *pronoun* A LOT, plenty, a great deal, lots (*informal*), masses (*informal*), loads (*informal*), tons (*informal*), heaps (*informal*), a good deal, an appreciable amount
<< OPPOSITE little

muck *noun* 1 DIRT, mud, filth, crap (*taboo slang*), sewage, ooze, scum, sludge, mire, slime, slob (*Irish*), gunk (*informal*), gunge (*informal*), crud (*slang*), kak (*S African taboo*), grot (*slang*)
2 MANURE, crap (*taboo slang*), dung, ordure
▷▷ **muck something up** RUIN, bungle, botch, make a mess of, blow (*slang*), mar, spoil, muff, make a nonsense of, bodge (*informal*), make a pig's ear of (*informal*), flub (*US slang*), make a muck of (*slang*), mess something up, screw something up (*informal*), cock something up (*Brit slang*), crool *or* cruel (*Austral slang*)

mucky *adjective* DIRTY, soiled, muddy, filthy, messy, grimy, mud-caked, bespattered, begrimed, festy (*Austral slang*)

mud *noun* DIRT, clay, ooze, silt, sludge, mire, slime, slob (*Irish*), gloop (*informal*)

muddle *noun* CONFUSION, mess, disorder, chaos, plight, tangle, mix-up, clutter, disarray, daze, predicament, jumble, ravel, perplexity, disorganization, hotchpotch, hodgepodge (US), pig's breakfast (*informal*), fankle (*Scot*)
▷ *verb* 1 JUMBLE, confuse, disorder, scramble, tangle, mix up, make a mess of
2 CONFUSE, bewilder, daze, confound, perplex, disorient, stupefy, befuddle
▷▷ **muddle along** *or* **through** SCRAPE BY, make it, manage, cope, get along, get by (*informal*), manage somehow

muddled *adjective* 1 INCOHERENT, confused, loose, vague, unclear, woolly, muddleheaded
<< OPPOSITE clear
2 BEWILDERED, confused, at sea, dazed, perplexed, disoriented, stupefied, befuddled
3 JUMBLED, confused, disordered, scrambled, tangled, chaotic, messy, mixed-up, disorganized, higgledy-piggledy (*informal*), disarrayed
<< OPPOSITE orderly

muddy *adjective* 1 BOGGY, swampy, marshy, miry, quaggy
2 DIRTY, soiled, grimy, mucky, mud-caked, bespattered, clarty (*Scot & Northern English dialect*)
3 DULL, flat, blurred, unclear, smoky, washed-out, dingy, lustreless
4 CLOUDY, dirty, foul, opaque, impure, turbid
5 CONFUSED, vague, unclear, muddled, fuzzy, woolly, hazy, indistinct
▷ *verb* SMEAR, soil, dirty, smirch, begrime, bespatter

muffle *verb* 1 DEADEN, suppress, gag, stifle, silence, dull, soften, hush, muzzle, quieten
2 *often with* **up** WRAP UP, cover, disguise, conceal, cloak, shroud, swathe, envelop, swaddle

muffled *adjective* INDISTINCT, suppressed, subdued, dull, faint, dim, muted, strangled, stifled

mug[1] *noun* CUP, pot, jug, beaker, tankard, stein, flagon, toby jug

mug[2] *noun* 1 (*Slang*) FACE, features, countenance, visage, clock (*Brit slang*), kisser (*slang*), dial (*slang*), mush (*Brit slang*), puss (*slang*), phiz *or* phizog (*Brit slang*)
2 (*Brit*) FOOL, innocent, sucker (*slang*), charlie (*Brit informal*), gull (*archaic*), chump (*informal*), simpleton, putz (*US slang*), weenie (*US informal*), muggins (*Brit slang*), easy *or* soft touch (*slang*), dorba *or* dorb (*Austral slang*), bogan (*Austral slang*)
▷ *verb* (*informal*) ATTACK, assault, beat up, rob, steam (*informal*), hold up, do over (*Brit, Austral & NZ slang*), work over (*slang*), assail, lay into (*informal*), put the boot in (*slang*), duff up (*Brit slang*), set about *or* upon, beat *or* knock seven

bells out of (*informal*)
▷▷ **mug up (on) something** STUDY, cram (*informal*), bone up on (*informal*), swot up on (*Brit informal*), get up (*informal*)

mull over *verb* PONDER, consider, study, think about, examine, review, weigh, contemplate, reflect on, think over, muse on, meditate on, ruminate on, deliberate on, turn something over in your mind

multiple *adjective* MANY, several, various, numerous, collective, sundry, manifold, multitudinous

multiplicity *noun* NUMBER, lot, host, mass, variety, load (*informal*), pile (*informal*), ton, stack, diversity, heap (*informal*), array, abundance, myriad, profusion

multiply *verb* 1 INCREASE, extend, expand, spread, build up, accumulate, augment, proliferate
<< OPPOSITE decrease
2 REPRODUCE, breed, propagate

multitude *noun* 1 GREAT NUMBER, lot, host, collection, army, sea, mass, assembly, legion, horde, myriad, concourse, assemblage
2 CROWD, host, mass, mob, congregation, swarm, sea, horde, throng, great number
3 PUBLIC, mob, herd, populace, rabble, proletariat, common people, hoi polloi, commonalty

mum *adjective* SILENT, quiet, dumb, mute, secretive, uncommunicative, unforthcoming, tight-lipped, closemouthed

mumbo jumbo *noun* 1 GIBBERISH, nonsense, jargon, humbug, cant, Greek (*informal*), claptrap (*informal*), gobbledegook (*informal*), rigmarole, double talk
2 SUPERSTITION, magic, ritual, hocus-pocus

munch *verb* CHEW, champ, crunch, chomp, scrunch, masticate

mundane *adjective* 1 ORDINARY, routine, commonplace, banal, everyday, day-to-day, vanilla (*slang*), prosaic, humdrum, workaday
<< OPPOSITE extraordinary
2 EARTHLY, worldly, human, material, fleshly, secular, mortal, terrestrial, temporal, sublunary
<< OPPOSITE spiritual

municipal *adjective* CIVIC, city, public, local, community, council, town, district, urban, metropolitan, borough

municipality *noun* TOWN, city, district, borough, township, burgh (*Scot*), urban community, dorp (*S African*)

murder *noun* 1 KILLING, homicide, massacre, assassination, slaying, bloodshed, carnage, butchery
2 (*informal*) AGONY, misery, hell (*informal*)
▷ *verb* 1 KILL, massacre, slaughter, assassinate, hit (*slang*), destroy, waste (*informal*), do in (*informal*), eliminate (*slang*), take out (*slang*), butcher, dispatch, slay, blow away (*slang, chiefly US*), bump off (*slang*), rub out (*US slang*), take the life of, do to death
2 RUIN, destroy, mar, spoil, butcher, mangle
3 (*informal*) BEAT DECISIVELY, thrash, stuff (*slang*), cream (*slang, chiefly US*), tank (*slang*), hammer (*informal*), slaughter, lick (*informal*), wipe the floor with (*informal*), make mincemeat of (*informal*), blow someone out of the water (*slang*), drub, defeat someone utterly

murderer *noun* KILLER, assassin, slayer, butcher, slaughterer, cut-throat, hit man (*slang*)

murderous *adjective* 1 DEADLY, savage, brutal, destructive, fell (*archaic*), bloody, devastating, cruel, lethal, withering, ferocious, cut-throat, bloodthirsty, barbarous, internecine, death-dealing, sanguinary
2 (*informal*) UNPLEASANT, difficult, dangerous, exhausting, sapping, harrowing, strenuous, arduous, hellish (*informal*), killing (*informal*)

murky *adjective* 1 DARK, gloomy, dismal, grey, dull, obscure, dim, dreary, cloudy, misty, impenetrable, foggy, overcast, dusky, nebulous, cheerless
<< OPPOSITE bright
2 OBSCURE, dark, cloudy, impenetrable

murmur *verb* MUMBLE, whisper, mutter, drone, purr, babble, speak in an undertone
▷ *noun* 1 WHISPER, whispering, mutter, mumble, drone, purr, babble, undertone
2 COMPLAINT, word, moan (*informal*), grumble, beef (*slang*), grouse, gripe (*informal*)

muscle *noun* 1 TENDON, sinew, muscle tissue, thew
2 STRENGTH, might, force, power, weight, stamina, potency, brawn, sturdiness
▷▷ **muscle in** (*informal*) IMPOSE YOURSELF, encroach, butt in, force your way in, elbow your way in

muscular *adjective* STRONG, powerful, athletic, strapping, robust, vigorous, sturdy, stalwart, husky (*informal*), beefy (*informal*), lusty, sinewy, muscle-bound, brawny, powerfully built, thickset, well-knit

muse *verb* PONDER, consider, reflect, contemplate, think, weigh up, deliberate, speculate, brood, meditate, mull over, think over, ruminate, cogitate, be lost in thought, be in a brown study

mush *noun* 1 PULP, paste, mash, purée, pap, slush, goo (*informal*)
2 (*informal*) SENTIMENTALITY, corn (*informal*), slush (*informal*), schmaltz (*slang*), mawkishness

mushroom *verb* EXPAND, increase, spread, boom, flourish, sprout, burgeon, spring up, shoot up, proliferate, luxuriate, grow rapidly

mushy *adjective* 1 SOFT, squidgy (*informal*),

slushy, squashy, squelchy, pulpy, doughy, pappy, semi-liquid, paste-like, semi-solid
2 (*informal*) SENTIMENTAL, wet (*Brit informal*), sloppy (*informal*), corny (*slang*), sugary, maudlin, weepy, saccharine, syrupy, slushy (*informal*), mawkish, schmaltzy (*slang*), icky (*informal*), three-hankie (*informal*)

musical *adjective* MELODIOUS, lyrical, harmonious, melodic, lilting, tuneful, dulcet, sweet-sounding, euphonious, euphonic
<< OPPOSITE discordant

musing *noun* THINKING, reflection, meditation, abstraction, contemplation, introspection, reverie, dreaming, day-dreaming, rumination, navel gazing (*slang*), absent-mindedness, cogitation, brown study, cerebration, woolgathering

muskeg *noun* (*Canad*) SWAMP, bog, marsh, quagmire, moss (*Scot & Northern English dialect*), slough, fen, mire, morass, everglade(s) (*US*), pakihi (*NZ*)

muss (*US & Canad*) *verb* MESS (UP), disarrange, dishevel, ruffle, rumple, make untidy, tumble

must[1] *noun* NECESSITY, essential, requirement, duty, fundamental, obligation, imperative, requisite, prerequisite, sine qua non (*Latin*), necessary thing, must-have

must[2] *noun* MOULD, rot, decay, mildew, mustiness, fustiness, fetor, mouldiness

muster *verb* 1 SUMMON UP, collect, call up, marshal
2 RALLY, group, gather, assemble, round up, marshal, mobilize, call together
3 ASSEMBLE, meet, come together, convene, congregate, convoke
▷ *noun* ASSEMBLY, meeting, collection, gathering, rally, convention, congregation, roundup, mobilization, hui (*NZ*), concourse, assemblage, convocation, runanga (*NZ*)
▷▷ **pass muster** BE ACCEPTABLE, qualify, measure up, make the grade, fill the bill (*informal*), be *or* come up to scratch

musty *adjective* STALE, stuffy, airless, decayed, smelly, dank, mouldy, fusty, mildewed, frowsty, mildewy

mutation *noun* 1 ANOMALY, variation, deviant, freak of nature
2 CHANGE, variation, evolution, transformation, modification, alteration, deviation, metamorphosis, transfiguration

mute *adjective* 1 CLOSE-MOUTHED, silent, taciturn, tongue-tied, tight-lipped, unspeaking
2 SILENT, dumb, unspoken, tacit, wordless, voiceless, unvoiced
3 DUMB, speechless, voiceless, unspeaking, aphasic, aphonic
▷ *verb* 1 TONE DOWN, lower, moderate, subdue, dampen, soft-pedal
2 MUFFLE, subdue, moderate, lower, turn down, soften, dampen, tone down, deaden

mutilate *verb* 1 MAIM, damage, injure, disable, butcher, cripple, hack, lame, cut up, mangle, mangulate (*Austral slang*), dismember, disfigure, lacerate, cut to pieces
2 DISTORT, cut, damage, mar, spoil, butcher, hack, censor, adulterate, expurgate, bowdlerize

mutiny *noun* REBELLION, revolt, uprising, insurrection, rising, strike, revolution, riot, resistance, disobedience, insubordination, refusal to obey orders
▷ *verb* REBEL, revolt, rise up, disobey, strike, resist, defy authority, refuse to obey orders, be insubordinate

mutt *noun* (*Slang*) 1 MONGREL, dog, hound, tyke, pooch (*informal*), cur
2 FOOL, idiot, berk (*Brit slang*), moron, charlie (*Brit informal*), jerk (*slang, chiefly US & Canad*), plank (*Brit slang*), wally (*slang*), prat (*slang*), plonker (*slang*), coot, geek (*slang*), twit (*informal, chiefly Brit*), imbecile (*informal*), ignoramus, dipstick (*Brit slang*), gonzo (*slang*), schmuck (*US slang*), dork (*slang*), dolt, divvy (*Brit slang*), pillock (*Brit slang*), dweeb (*US slang*), putz (*US slang*), weenie (*US informal*), eejit (*Scot & Irish*), dumb-ass (*slang*), dunderhead, numpty (*Scot informal*), doofus (*slang, chiefly US*), thickhead, nerd *or* nurd (*slang*), numbskull *or* numskull, dorba *or* dorb (*Austral slang*), bogan (*Austral slang*)

mutter *verb* GRUMBLE, complain, murmur, rumble, whine, mumble, grouse, bleat, grouch (*informal*), talk under your breath

mutual *adjective* SHARED, common, joint, interactive, returned, communal, reciprocal, interchangeable, reciprocated, correlative, requited

> *Mutual* is sometimes used, as in *a mutual friend*, to mean 'common to or shared by two or more people'. This use has sometimes been frowned on in the past because it does not reflect the two-way relationship contained in the origins of the word, which comes from Latin *mutuus* meaning 'reciprocal'. However, this usage is very common and is now generally regarded as acceptable

muzzle *noun* 1 JAWS, mouth, nose, snout
2 GAG, guard, restraint
▷ *verb* SUPPRESS, silence, curb, restrain, choke, gag, stifle, censor

myopic *adjective* 1 NARROW-MINDED, short-sighted, narrow, unimaginative, small-minded, unadventurous, near-sighted
2 SHORT-SIGHTED, near-sighted, as blind as a

bat (*informal*)

myriad *noun* MULTITUDE, millions, scores, host, thousands, army, sea, mountain, flood, a million, a thousand, swarm, horde
▷ *adjective* INNUMERABLE, countless, untold, incalculable, immeasurable, a thousand and one, multitudinous

mysterious *adjective* 1 STRANGE, unknown, puzzling, curious, secret, hidden, weird, concealed, obscure, baffling, veiled, mystical, perplexing, uncanny, incomprehensible, mystifying, impenetrable, arcane, inexplicable, cryptic, insoluble, unfathomable, abstruse, recondite
<< OPPOSITE clear
2 SECRETIVE, enigmatic, evasive, discreet, covert, reticent, furtive, inscrutable, non-committal, surreptitious, cloak-and-dagger, sphinx-like

mystery *noun* 1 PUZZLE, problem, question, secret, riddle, enigma, conundrum, teaser, poser (*informal*), closed book
2 SECRECY, uncertainty, obscurity, mystique, darkness, ambiguity, ambiguousness

mystical *or* **mystic** *adjective* SUPERNATURAL, mysterious, transcendental, esoteric, occult, arcane, metaphysical, paranormal, inscrutable, otherworldly, abstruse, cabalistic, preternatural, nonrational

mystify *verb* PUZZLE, confuse, baffle, bewilder, beat (*slang*), escape, stump, elude, confound, perplex, bamboozle (*informal*), flummox, be all Greek to (*informal*), nonplus, befog

mystique *noun* FASCINATION, spell, magic, charm, glamour, awe, charisma

myth *noun* 1 LEGEND, story, tradition, fiction, saga, fable, parable, allegory, fairy story, folk tale, urban myth, urban legend
2 ILLUSION, story, fancy, fantasy, imagination, invention, delusion, superstition, fabrication, falsehood, figment, tall story, cock and bull story (*informal*)

mythical *adjective* 1 LEGENDARY, storied, fabulous, imaginary, fairy-tale, fabled, mythological, storybook, allegorical, folkloric, chimerical
2 IMAGINARY, made-up, fantasy, invented, pretended, untrue, unreal, fabricated, fanciful, fictitious, make-believe, nonexistent

mythological *adjective* LEGENDARY, fabulous, fabled, traditional, invented, heroic, imaginary, mythical, mythic, folkloric

mythology *noun* LEGEND, myths, folklore, stories, tradition, lore, folk tales, mythos

nab *verb* CATCH, arrest, apprehend, seize, lift (*slang*), nick (*slang, chiefly Brit*), grab, capture, nail (*informal*), collar (*informal*), snatch, catch in the act, feel your collar (*slang*)

nadir *noun* BOTTOM, depths, lowest point, rock bottom, all-time low

<< OPPOSITE height

naff *adjective* (*Brit slang*) BAD, poor, inferior, worthless, pants (*slang*), duff (*Brit informal*), shabby, second-rate, shoddy, low-grade, low-quality, trashy, substandard, for the birds (*informal*), crappy (*slang*), valueless, rubbishy, poxy (*slang*), strictly for the birds (*informal*), twopenny-halfpenny, bodger *or* bodgie (*Austral slang*)

<< OPPOSITE excellent

nag[1] *verb* SCOLD, harass, badger, pester, worry, harry, plague, hassle (*informal*), vex, berate, breathe down someone's neck, upbraid, chivvy, bend someone's ear (*informal*), be on your back (*slang*), henpeck

▷ *noun* SCOLD, complainer, grumbler, virago, shrew, tartar, moaner, harpy, harridan, termagant, fault-finder

nag[2] *noun often derog* HORSE, hack, jade, plug

nagging *adjective* 1 CONTINUOUS, persistent, continual, niggling, repeated, constant, endless, relentless, perpetual, never-ending, interminable, unrelenting, incessant, unremitting

2 SCOLDING, complaining, critical, sharp-tongued, shrewish

nail *noun* 1 TACK, spike, rivet, hobnail, brad (*technical*)

2 FINGERNAIL, toenail, talon, thumbnail, claw

▷ *verb* 1 FASTEN, fix, secure, attach, pin, hammer, tack

2 (*informal*) CATCH, arrest, capture, apprehend, lift (*slang*), trap, nab (*informal*), snare, ensnare, entrap, feel your collar (*slang*)

naive, naïve *or* **naïf** *adjective* GULLIBLE, trusting, credulous, unsuspicious, green, simple, innocent, childlike, callow, unsophisticated, unworldly, artless, ingenuous, guileless, wet behind the ears (*informal*), jejune, as green as grass

<< OPPOSITE worldly

naivety, naiveté *or* **naïveté** *noun* GULLIBILITY, innocence, simplicity, inexperience, credulity, ingenuousness, artlessness, guilelessness, callowness

naked *adjective* 1 NUDE, stripped, exposed, bare, uncovered, undressed, in the raw (*informal*), starkers (*informal*), stark-naked, unclothed, in the buff (*informal*), in the altogether (*informal*), buck naked (*slang*), undraped, in your birthday suit (*informal*), scuddy (*slang*), without a stitch on (*informal*), in the bare scud (*slang*), naked as the day you were born (*informal*)

<< OPPOSITE dressed

2 UNDISGUISED, open, simple, plain, patent, evident, stark, manifest, blatant, overt, unmistakable, unqualified, unadorned, unvarnished, unconcealed

<< OPPOSITE disguised

nakedness *noun* 1 NUDITY, undress, bareness, deshabille

2 STARKNESS, simplicity, openness, plainness

name *noun* 1 TITLE, nickname, designation, appellation, term, handle (*slang*), denomination, epithet, sobriquet, cognomen, moniker *or* monicker (*slang*)

2 REPUTATION, character, honour, fame, distinction, esteem, eminence, renown, repute, note

▷ *verb* 1 CALL, christen, baptize, dub, term, style, label, entitle, denominate

2 NOMINATE, choose, commission, mention, identify, select, appoint, specify, designate

>> RELATED WORD *adjective* nominal

named *adjective* 1 CALLED, christened, known as, dubbed, termed, styled, labelled, entitled, denominated, baptized

2 NOMINATED, chosen, picked, commissioned, mentioned, identified, selected, appointed, cited, specified, designated, singled out

nameless *adjective* 1 UNNAMED, unknown, obscure, anonymous, unheard-of, undistinguished, untitled
2 ANONYMOUS, unknown, unnamed, incognito
3 HORRIBLE, unspeakable, indescribable, abominable, ineffable, unutterable, inexpressible

namely *adverb* SPECIFICALLY, that is to say, to wit, i.e., viz.

nap[1] *verb* SLEEP, rest, nod, drop off (*informal*), doze, kip (*Brit slang*), snooze (*informal*), nod off (*informal*), catnap, drowse, zizz (*Brit informal*)
▷ *noun* SLEEP, rest, kip (*Brit slang*), siesta, catnap, forty winks (*informal*), shuteye (*slang*), zizz (*Brit informal*)

nap[2] *noun* PILE, down, fibre, weave, shag, grain

napkin *noun* SERVIETTE, cloth

narcissism *or* **narcism** *noun* EGOTISM, vanity, self-love, self-admiration

narcotic *noun* DRUG, anaesthetic, painkiller, sedative, opiate, tranquillizer, anodyne, analgesic
▷ *adjective* SEDATIVE, calming, dulling, numbing, hypnotic, analgesic, stupefying, soporific, painkilling

narrate *verb* TELL, recount, report, detail, describe, relate, unfold, chronicle, recite, set forth

narration *noun* 1 STORYTELLING, telling, reading, relation, explanation, description
2 ACCOUNT, explanation, description, recital, voice-over (*in film*)

narrative *noun* STORY, report, history, detail, account, statement, tale, chronicle

narrator *noun* STORYTELLER, writer, author, reporter, commentator, chronicler, reciter, raconteur

narrow *adjective* 1 THIN, fine, slim, pinched, slender, tapering, attenuated
<< OPPOSITE broad
2 LIMITED, restricted, confined, tight, close, near, cramped, meagre, constricted, circumscribed, scanty, straitened, incapacious
<< OPPOSITE wide
3 INSULAR, prejudiced, biased, partial, reactionary, puritan, bigoted, dogmatic, intolerant, narrow-minded, small-minded, illiberal
<< OPPOSITE broad-minded
4 EXCLUSIVE, limited, select, restricted, confined
▷ *verb* 1 *often with* **down** RESTRICT, limit, reduce, diminish, constrict, circumscribe, straiten
2 GET NARROWER, taper, shrink, tighten, constrict

narrowly *adverb* 1 JUST, barely, only just, scarcely, by the skin of your teeth, by a whisker *or* hair's-breadth
2 CLOSELY, keenly, carefully, intently, intensely, fixedly, searchingly

narrow-minded *adjective* INTOLERANT, conservative, prejudiced, biased, provincial, petty, reactionary, parochial, short-sighted, bigoted, insular, opinionated, small-minded, hidebound, illiberal, strait-laced
<< OPPOSITE broad-minded

narrows *plural noun* CHANNEL, sound, gulf, passage, straits

nastiness *noun* 1 SPITE, malice, venom, unpleasantness, meanness, bitchiness (*slang*), offensiveness, spitefulness
2 OBSCENITY, porn (*informal*), pornography, indecency, licentiousness, ribaldry, smuttiness

nasty *adjective* 1 UNPLEASANT, ugly, disagreeable
<< OPPOSITE pleasant
2 SPITEFUL, mean, offensive, annoying, vicious, unpleasant, abusive, vile, malicious, bad-tempered, despicable, disagreeable
<< OPPOSITE pleasant
3 DISGUSTING, unpleasant, dirty, offensive, foul, horrible, polluted, filthy, sickening, vile, distasteful, repellent, obnoxious, objectionable, disagreeable, nauseating, odious, repugnant, loathsome, grotty (*slang*), malodorous, noisome, unappetizing, yucky *or* yukky (*slang*), festy (*Austral slang*), yucko (*Austral slang*)
4 SERIOUS, bad, dangerous, critical, severe, painful
5 OBSCENE, blue, gross, foul, indecent, pornographic, lewd, impure, lascivious, smutty, ribald, licentious
<< OPPOSITE clean

nation *noun* 1 COUNTRY, state, commonwealth, realm
2 PUBLIC, people, community, society, population

national *adjective* 1 NATIONWIDE, state, public, civil, widespread, governmental, countrywide
2 ETHNIC, social
▷ *noun* CITIZEN, subject, resident, native, inhabitant

nationalism *noun* PATRIOTISM, loyalty to your country, chauvinism, jingoism, nationality, allegiance, fealty

nationalistic *adjective* PATRIOTIC, xenophobic, chauvinistic, jingoistic, loyal to your country

nationality *noun* 1 CITIZENSHIP, birth
2 RACE, nation, ethnic group

nationwide *adjective* NATIONAL, general, widespread, countrywide, overall

native *adjective* 1 INDIGENOUS, local, aboriginal (*often offensive*)
2 MOTHER, indigenous, vernacular

3 DOMESTIC, local, indigenous, home-made, home-grown, home
▷ *noun usually with* **of** INHABITANT, national, resident, citizen, countryman, aborigine (*often offensive*), dweller

Nativity *noun* BIRTH OF CHRIST, manger scene

natter (*Chiefly Brit informal*) *verb* GOSSIP, talk, rabbit (on) (*Brit informal*), jaw (*slang*), chatter, witter (*informal*), prattle, jabber, gabble, blather, blether, shoot the breeze (*informal*), run off at the mouth (*slang*), prate, talk idly, chew the fat *or* rag (*slang*), earbash (*Austral & NZ slang*)
▷ *noun* GOSSIP, talk, conversation, chat, jaw (*slang*), craic (*Irish informal*), gab (*informal*), prattle, jabber, gabble, palaver, blather, chitchat, blether, chinwag (*Brit informal*), gabfest (*informal, chiefly US & Canad*), confabulation

natty *adjective* SMART, sharp, dashing, elegant, trim, neat, fashionable, stylish, trendy (*Brit informal*), chic, spruce, well-dressed, dapper, snazzy (*informal*), well-turned-out, crucial (*slang*), schmick (*Austral informal*)

natural *adjective* 1 LOGICAL, reasonable, valid, legitimate
2 NORMAL, common, regular, usual, ordinary, typical, everyday
<< OPPOSITE abnormal
3 INNATE, native, characteristic, indigenous, inherent, instinctive, intuitive, congenital, inborn, immanent, in your blood, essential
4 UNAFFECTED, open, frank, genuine, spontaneous, candid, unpretentious, unsophisticated, dinkum (*Austral & NZ informal*), artless, ingenuous, real, simple, unstudied
<< OPPOSITE affected
5 PURE, plain, organic, whole, unrefined, unbleached, unpolished, unmixed
<< OPPOSITE processed

naturalism *noun* REALISM, authenticity, plausibility, verisimilitude, factualism

naturalist *noun* BIOLOGIST, ecologist, botanist, zoologist

naturalistic *adjective* 1 REALISTIC, photographic, kitchen sink, representational, lifelike, warts and all (*informal*), true-to-life, vérité, factualistic
2 LIFELIKE, realistic, real-life, true-to-life

naturally *adverb* 1 OF COURSE, certainly, as a matter of course, as anticipated
2 TYPICALLY, simply, normally, spontaneously, customarily

nature *noun* 1 CREATION, world, earth, environment, universe, cosmos, natural world
2 FLORA AND FAUNA, country, landscape, countryside, scenery, natural history
3 QUALITY, character, make-up, constitution, attributes, essence, traits, complexion, features
4 TEMPERAMENT, character, personality, disposition, outlook, mood, humour, temper
5 KIND, sort, style, type, variety, species, category, description

naughty *adjective* 1 DISOBEDIENT, bad, mischievous, badly behaved, wayward, playful, wicked, sinful, fractious, impish, roguish, refractory
<< OPPOSITE good
2 OBSCENE, blue, vulgar, improper, lewd, risqué, X-rated (*informal*), bawdy, smutty, off-colour, ribald
<< OPPOSITE clean

nausea *noun* 1 SICKNESS, vomiting, retching, squeamishness, queasiness, biliousness
2 DISGUST, loathing, aversion, revulsion, abhorrence, repugnance, odium

nauseate *verb* 1 SICKEN, turn your stomach
2 DISGUST, offend, horrify, revolt, repel, repulse, gross out (*US slang*)

nauseous *adjective* 1 SICK, crook (*Austral & NZ informal*)
2 SICKENING, offensive, disgusting, revolting, distasteful, repulsive, nauseating, repugnant, loathsome, abhorrent, detestable, yucky *or* yukky (*slang*), yucko (*Austral slang*)

nautical *adjective* MARITIME, marine, yachting, naval, seafaring, seagoing

naval *adjective* NAUTICAL, marine, maritime

navel *noun* 1 BELLYBUTTON (*informal*)
2 CENTRE, middle, hub, central point
>> RELATED WORD *technical name* umbilicus
>> RELATED WORD *adjective* umbilical

navigate *verb* 1 STEER, drive, direct, guide, handle, pilot, sail, skipper, manoeuvre
2 MANOEUVRE, drive, direct, guide, handle, pilot
3 PLOT A COURSE, sail, find your way, plan a course
4 SAIL, cruise, manoeuvre, voyage

navigation *noun* SAILING, cruising, steering, voyaging, seamanship, helmsmanship

navigator *noun* HELMSMAN, pilot, seaman, mariner

navy *noun* FLEET, warships, flotilla, armada

near *adjective* 1 CLOSE, bordering, neighbouring, nearby, beside, adjacent, adjoining, close by, at close quarters, just round the corner, contiguous, proximate, within sniffing distance (*informal*), a hop, skip and a jump away (*informal*)
<< OPPOSITE far
2 IMMINENT, forthcoming, approaching, looming, impending, upcoming, on the cards (*informal*), nigh, in the offing, near-at-hand, next
<< OPPOSITE far-off
3 INTIMATE, close, related, allied, familiar,

connected, attached, akin
<< OPPOSITE distant
4 (*informal*) MEAN, stingy, parsimonious, miserly, niggardly, ungenerous, tightfisted, close-fisted

nearby *adjective* NEIGHBOURING, adjacent, adjoining
▷ *adverb* CLOSE AT HAND, within reach, not far away, at close quarters, just round the corner, proximate, within sniffing distance (*informal*)

nearing *adjective* APPROACHING, coming, advancing, imminent, impending, upcoming

nearly *adverb* 1 PRACTICALLY, about, almost, virtually, all but, just about, not quite, as good as, well-nigh
2 ALMOST, about, approaching, roughly, just about, approximately

neat *adjective* 1 TIDY, nice, straight, trim, orderly, spruce, uncluttered, shipshape, spick-and-span
<< OPPOSITE untidy
2 METHODICAL, tidy, systematic, fastidious
<< OPPOSITE disorganized
3 SMART, trim, tidy, spruce, dapper, natty (*informal*), well-groomed, well-turned-out
4 GRACEFUL, elegant, adept, nimble, agile, adroit, efficient
<< OPPOSITE clumsy
5 CLEVER, efficient, handy, apt, well-judged
<< OPPOSITE inefficient
6 (*Chiefly US & Canad slang*) COOL, great (*informal*), excellent, brilliant, cracking (*Brit informal*), smashing (*informal*), superb, fantastic (*informal*), tremendous, ace (*informal*), fabulous (*informal*), marvellous, terrific, awesome (*slang*), mean (*slang*), super (*informal*), brill (*informal*), bodacious (*slang, chiefly US*), boffo (*slang*), chillin' (*US slang*), booshit (*Austral slang*), exo (*Austral slang*), sik (*Austral slang*), rad (*informal*), phat (*slang*), schmick (*Austral informal*)
<< OPPOSITE terrible
7 (*of alcoholic drinks*) UNDILUTED, straight, pure, unmixed

neatly *adverb* 1 TIDILY, nicely, smartly, systematically, methodically, fastidiously
2 SMARTLY, elegantly, stylishly, tidily, nattily
3 GRACEFULLY, expertly, efficiently, adeptly, skilfully, nimbly, adroitly, dexterously, agilely
4 CLEVERLY, precisely, accurately, efficiently, aptly, elegantly

neatness *noun* 1 ORDER, organization, harmony, tidiness, orderliness
2 TIDINESS, niceness, orderliness, smartness, fastidiousness, trimness, spruceness
3 GRACE, skill, efficiency, expertise, precision, elegance, agility, dexterity, deftness, nimbleness, adroitness, adeptness, daintiness, gracefulness, preciseness, skilfulness
4 CLEVERNESS, efficiency, precision, elegance, aptness

nebulous *adjective* 1 VAGUE, confused, uncertain, obscure, unclear, ambiguous, indefinite, hazy, indeterminate, imprecise, indistinct
2 (*Rare*) OBSCURE, vague, dim, murky, shadowy, cloudy, misty, hazy, amorphous, indeterminate, shapeless, indistinct, unformed

necessarily *adverb* 1 AUTOMATICALLY, naturally, definitely, undoubtedly, accordingly, by definition, of course, certainly
2 INEVITABLY, of necessity, unavoidably, perforce, incontrovertibly, nolens volens (*Latin*)

necessary *adjective* 1 NEEDED, required, essential, vital, compulsory, mandatory, imperative, indispensable, obligatory, requisite, de rigueur (*French*), needful, must-have
<< OPPOSITE unnecessary
2 INEVITABLE, certain, unavoidable, inescapable
<< OPPOSITE avoidable

necessitate *verb* COMPEL, force, demand, require, call for, oblige, entail, constrain, impel, make necessary

necessity *noun* 1 NEED, demand, requirement, exigency, indispensability, needfulness
2 ESSENTIAL, need, necessary, requirement, fundamental, requisite, prerequisite, sine qua non (*Latin*), desideratum, want, must-have
3 INEVITABILITY, certainty
4 POVERTY, need, privation, penury, destitution, extremity, indigence
5 REQUIREMENT, essential, need, fundamental

necropolis *noun* CEMETERY, graveyard, churchyard, burial ground

need *verb* 1 WANT, miss, require, lack, have to have, demand
2 REQUIRE, want, demand, call for, entail, necessitate, have occasion to *or* for
3 HAVE TO, be obliged to
▷ *noun* 1 REQUIREMENT, demand, essential, necessity, requisite, desideratum, must-have
2 NECESSITY, call, demand, requirement, obligation
3 EMERGENCY, want, necessity, urgency, exigency
4 POVERTY, deprivation, destitution, neediness, distress, extremity, privation, penury, indigence, impecuniousness

needed *adjective* NECESSARY, wanted, required, lacked, called for, desired

needle *verb* IRRITATE, provoke, annoy, sting, bait, harass, taunt, nag, hassle (*informal*), aggravate (*informal*), prod, gall, ruffle, spur, prick, nettle, goad, irk, rile, get under your skin (*informal*), get on your nerves (*informal*), nark (*Brit, Austral & NZ slang*), hack you off (*informal*), get in your hair (*informal*)

needless *adjective* UNNECESSARY, excessive, pointless, gratuitous, useless, unwanted, redundant, superfluous, groundless, expendable, uncalled-for, dispensable, nonessential, undesired
<< OPPOSITE essential

needlework *noun* EMBROIDERY, tailoring, stitching, sewing, needlecraft

needy *adjective* POOR, deprived, disadvantaged, impoverished, penniless, destitute, poverty-stricken, underprivileged, indigent, down at heel (*informal*), impecunious, dirt-poor, on the breadline (*informal*)
<< OPPOSITE wealthy

negate *verb* 1 INVALIDATE, reverse, cancel, wipe out, void, repeal, revoke, retract, rescind, neutralize, annul, nullify, obviate, abrogate, countermand
2 DENY, oppose, contradict, refute, disallow, disprove, rebut, gainsay (*archaic* or *literary*)
<< OPPOSITE confirm

negation *noun* 1 OPPOSITE, reverse, contrary, contradiction, converse, antithesis, inverse, antonym
2 DENIAL, refusal, rejection, contradiction, renunciation, repudiation, disavowal, veto

negative *adjective* 1 NEUTRALIZING, invalidating, annulling, nullifying, counteractive
2 PESSIMISTIC, cynical, unwilling, gloomy, antagonistic, jaundiced, uncooperative, contrary
<< OPPOSITE optimistic
3 DISSENTING, contradictory, refusing, denying, rejecting, opposing, resisting, contrary
<< OPPOSITE assenting
▷ *noun* DENIAL, no, refusal, rejection, contradiction

neglect *verb* 1 DISREGARD, ignore, leave alone, turn your back on, fail to look after
<< OPPOSITE look after
2 SHIRK, forget, overlook, omit, evade, pass over, skimp, procrastinate over, let slide, be remiss in *or* about
3 FAIL, forget, omit
▷ *noun* 1 NEGLIGENCE, inattention, unconcern
<< OPPOSITE care
2 SHIRKING, failure, oversight, carelessness, dereliction, forgetfulness, slackness, laxity, laxness, slovenliness, remissness

neglected *adjective* 1 UNCARED-FOR, abandoned, underestimated, disregarded, undervalued, unappreciated
2 RUN DOWN, derelict, overgrown, uncared-for

negligence *noun* CARELESSNESS, failure, neglect, disregard, shortcoming, omission, oversight, dereliction, forgetfulness, slackness, inattention, laxity, thoughtlessness, laxness, inadvertence, inattentiveness, heedlessness, remissness

negligent *adjective* CARELESS, slack, thoughtless, unthinking, forgetful, slapdash, neglectful, heedless, slipshod, inattentive, remiss, unmindful, disregardful
<< OPPOSITE careful

negligible *adjective* INSIGNIFICANT, small, minute, minor, petty, trivial, trifling, unimportant, inconsequential, imperceptible, nickel-and-dime (*US slang*)
<< OPPOSITE significant

negotiable *adjective* 1 DEBATABLE, flexible, unsettled, undecided, open to discussion, discussable *or* discussible
2 VALID, transferable, transactional

negotiate *verb* 1 BARGAIN, deal, contract, discuss, debate, consult, confer, mediate, hold talks, arbitrate, cut a deal, conciliate, parley, discuss terms
2 ARRANGE, manage, settle, work out, bring about, transact
3 GET ROUND, clear, pass, cross, pass through, get over, get past, surmount

negotiation *noun* 1 BARGAINING, debate, discussion, transaction, dialogue, mediation, arbitration, wheeling and dealing (*informal*)
2 ARRANGEMENT, management, settlement, working out, transaction, bringing about

negotiator *noun* MEDIATOR, ambassador, diplomat, delegate, intermediary, arbitrator, moderator, honest broker

neighbourhood *or US* **neighborhood** *noun*
1 DISTRICT, community, quarter, region, surroundings, locality, locale
2 VICINITY, confines, proximity, precincts, environs, purlieus

neighbouring *or US* **neighboring** *adjective* NEARBY, next, near, bordering, surrounding, connecting, adjacent, adjoining, abutting, contiguous, nearest
<< OPPOSITE remote

neighbourly *or US* **neighborly** *adjective* HELPFUL, kind, social, civil, friendly, obliging, harmonious, amiable, considerate, sociable, genial, hospitable, companionable, well-disposed

Nemesis *sometimes not cap. noun* RETRIBUTION, fate, destruction, destiny, vengeance

neophyte *noun* (*Formal*) NOVICE, student, pupil, recruit, amateur, beginner, trainee, apprentice, disciple, learner, tyro, probationer, novitiate, proselyte, catechumen

nepotism *noun* FAVOURITISM, bias, patronage, preferential treatment, partiality

nerd *or* **nurd** *noun* (*Slang*) 1 BORE, obsessive, anorak (*informal*), geek (*informal*), trainspotter

(*informal*), dork (*slang*), wonk (*informal*)
2 FOOL, weed, drip (*informal*), sap (*slang*), wally (*slang*), sucker (*slang*), wimp (*informal*), booby, prat (*slang*), plonker (*slang*), twit (*informal, chiefly Brit*), simpleton, dipstick (*Brit slang*), schmuck (*US slang*), divvy (*Brit slang*), putz (*US slang*), wuss (*slang*), eejit (*Scot & Irish*), dumb-ass (*slang*), doofus (*slang, chiefly US*), dorba *or* dorb (*Austral slang*), bogan (*Austral slang*)

nerve *noun* 1 BRAVERY, courage, spirit, bottle (*Brit slang*), resolution, daring, determination, guts (*informal*), pluck, grit, fortitude, vigour, coolness, balls (*taboo slang*), mettle, firmness, spunk (*informal*), fearlessness, steadfastness, intrepidity, hardihood, gameness
2 (*informal*) IMPUDENCE, face (*informal*), front, neck (*informal*), sauce (*informal*), cheek (*informal*), brass (*informal*), gall, audacity, boldness, temerity, chutzpah (*US & Canad informal*), insolence, impertinence, effrontery, brass neck (*Brit informal*), brazenness, sassiness (*US slang*)
▷ *plural noun* (*informal*) TENSION, stress, strain, anxiety, butterflies (in your stomach) (*informal*), nervousness, cold feet (*informal*), heebie-jeebies (*slang*), worry
▷▷ **nerve yourself** BRACE YOURSELF, prepare yourself, steel yourself, fortify yourself, gear yourself up, gee yourself up
>> RELATED WORD *technical name* neuron *or* neurone
>> RELATED WORD *adjective* neural

nerve-racking *or* **nerve-wracking** *adjective* TENSE, trying, difficult, worrying, frightening, distressing, daunting, harassing, stressful, harrowing, gut-wrenching

nervous *adjective often with* **of** APPREHENSIVE, anxious, uneasy, edgy, worried, wired (*slang*), tense, fearful, shaky, hysterical, neurotic, agitated, ruffled, timid, hyper (*informal*), jittery (*informal*), uptight (*informal*), flustered, on edge, excitable, nervy (*Brit informal*), jumpy, twitchy (*informal*), fidgety, timorous, highly strung, antsy (*informal*), toey (*Austral slang*), adrenalized
<< OPPOSITE calm

nervous breakdown *noun* COLLAPSE, breakdown, crack-up (*informal*), neurasthenia (*obsolete*), nervous disorder

nervousness *noun* ANXIETY, stress, tension, strain, unease, disquiet, agitation, trepidation, timidity, excitability, perturbation, edginess, worry, jumpiness, antsiness (*informal*)

nervy *adjective* (*Brit informal*) ANXIOUS, nervous, tense, agitated, wired (*slang*), restless, jittery (*informal*), on edge, excitable, jumpy, twitchy (*informal*), fidgety, adrenalized

nest *noun* 1 REFUGE, resort, retreat, haunt, den, hideaway
2 HOTBED, den, breeding-ground

nest egg *noun* SAVINGS, fund(s), store, reserve, deposit, fall-back, cache

nestle *verb often with* **up** *or* **down** SNUGGLE, cuddle, huddle, curl up, nuzzle

nestling *noun* CHICK, fledgling, baby bird

net[1] *noun* MESH, netting, network, web, lattice, lacework, openwork
▷ *verb* CATCH, bag, capture, trap, nab (*informal*), entangle, ensnare, enmesh

net[2] *or* **nett** *adjective* 1 AFTER TAXES, final, clear, take-home
2 FINAL, closing, ultimate, eventual, conclusive
▷ *verb* EARN, make, clear, gain, realize, bring in, accumulate, reap

nether *adjective* LOWER, bottom, beneath, underground, inferior, basal

nettle *verb* IRRITATE, provoke, annoy, gall, sting, aggravate (*informal*), incense, ruffle, exasperate, vex, goad, pique, get on your nerves (*informal*), nark (*Brit, Austral & NZ slang*), hack you off (*informal*)

network *noun* 1 WEB, system, arrangement, grid, mesh, lattice, circuitry, nexus, plexus, interconnection, net
2 MAZE, warren, labyrinth

neurosis *noun* OBSESSION, instability, mental illness, abnormality, phobia, derangement, mental disturbance, psychological *or* emotional disorder

neurotic *adjective* UNSTABLE, nervous, disturbed, anxious, abnormal, obsessive, compulsive, manic, unhealthy, hyper (*informal*), twitchy (*informal*), overwrought, maladjusted
<< OPPOSITE rational

neuter *verb* CASTRATE, doctor (*informal*), emasculate, spay, dress, fix (*informal*), geld

neutral *adjective* 1 UNBIASED, impartial, disinterested, even-handed, dispassionate, sitting on the fence, uninvolved, noncommittal, nonpartisan, unprejudiced, nonaligned, unaligned, noncombatant, nonbelligerent
<< OPPOSITE biased
2 EXPRESSIONLESS, dull, blank, deadpan, toneless
3 UNCONTROVERSIAL *or* NONCONTROVERSIAL, safe, inoffensive
4 COLOURLESS, achromatic

neutrality *noun* IMPARTIALITY, detachment, noninterference, nonpartisanship, noninvolvement, nonalignment, noninterventionism

neutralize *or* **neutralise** *verb* COUNTERACT, cancel, offset, undo, compensate for, negate, invalidate, counterbalance, nullify

never *adverb* 1 AT NO TIME, not once, not ever

<< OPPOSITE always

2 UNDER NO CIRCUMSTANCES, no way, not at all, on no account, not on your life (*informal*), not on your nelly (*Brit slang*), not for love nor money (*informal*), not ever

> *Never* is sometimes used in informal speech and writing as an emphatic form of *not*, with simple past tenses of certain verbs: *I never said that* – and in very informal speech as a denial in place of *did not*: *he says I hit him, but I never.* These uses of *never* should be avoided in careful writing

never-never *noun* (*Brit informal*) HIRE-PURCHASE (*Brit*), H.P. (*Brit*)

nevertheless *adverb* EVEN SO, still, however, yet, regardless, nonetheless, notwithstanding, in spite of that, (even) though, but

new *adjective* 1 MODERN, recent, contemporary, up-to-date, latest, happening (*informal*), different, current, advanced, original, fresh, novel, topical, state-of-the-art, ground-breaking, modish, newfangled, modernistic, ultramodern, all-singing, all-dancing

<< OPPOSITE old-fashioned

2 BRAND NEW, unused

3 EXTRA, more, added, new-found, supplementary

4 UNFAMILIAR, unaccustomed, strange, unknown

5 RENEWED, changed, improved, restored, altered, rejuvenated, revitalized

newcomer *noun* 1 NEW ARRIVAL, incomer, immigrant, stranger, foreigner, alien, settler

2 BEGINNER, stranger, outsider, novice, new arrival, parvenu, Johnny-come-lately (*informal*)

newly *adverb* RECENTLY, just, lately, freshly, anew, latterly

newness *noun* NOVELTY, innovation, originality, freshness, strangeness, unfamiliarity

>> RELATED WORD *combining form* neo-

>> RELATED WORD *fear* neophobia

news *noun* INFORMATION, latest (*informal*), report, word, story, release, account, statement, advice, exposé, intelligence, scandal, rumour, leak, revelation, buzz, gossip, dirt (*US slang*), goss (*informal*), disclosure, bulletin, dispatch, gen (*Brit informal*), communiqué, hearsay, tidings, news flash, scuttlebutt (*US slang*)

newsworthy *adjective* INTERESTING, important, arresting, significant, remarkable, notable, sensational, noteworthy

next *adjective* 1 FOLLOWING, later, succeeding, subsequent

2 ADJACENT, closest, nearest, neighbouring, adjoining

▷ *adverb* AFTERWARDS, then, later, following, subsequently, thereafter

nexus *noun* CONNECTION, link, tie, bond, junction, joining

nibble *verb often with* **at** BITE, eat, peck, pick at, nip, munch, gnaw

▷ *noun* SNACK, bite, taste, peck, crumb, morsel, titbit, soupçon (*French*)

nice *adjective* 1 PLEASANT, delightful, agreeable, good, attractive, charming, pleasurable, enjoyable

<< OPPOSITE unpleasant

2 KIND, helpful, obliging, considerate

<< OPPOSITE unkind

3 LIKABLE *or* LIKEABLE, friendly, engaging, charming, pleasant, agreeable, amiable, prepossessing

4 POLITE, cultured, refined, courteous, genteel, well-bred, well-mannered

<< OPPOSITE vulgar

5 PRECISE, fine, careful, strict, accurate, exact, exacting, subtle, delicate, discriminating, rigorous, meticulous, scrupulous, fastidious

<< OPPOSITE vague

nicely *adverb* 1 PLEASANTLY, well, delightfully, attractively, charmingly, agreeably, pleasingly, acceptably, pleasurably

<< OPPOSITE unpleasantly

2 KINDLY, politely, thoughtfully, amiably, courteously

3 PRECISELY, exactly, accurately, finely, carefully, strictly, subtly, delicately, meticulously, rigorously, scrupulously

<< OPPOSITE carelessly

4 SATISFACTORILY, well, adequately, acceptably, passably

nicety *noun* FINE POINT, distinction, subtlety, nuance, refinement, minutiae

niche *noun* 1 RECESS, opening, corner, hollow, nook, alcove

2 POSITION, calling, place, slot (*informal*), vocation, pigeonhole (*informal*)

nick *noun* CUT, mark, scratch, score, chip, scar, notch, dent, snick

▷ *verb* 1 (*Slang, Chiefly Brit*) STEAL, pinch (*informal*), swipe (*slang*), pilfer, snitch (*slang*)

2 CUT, mark, score, damage, chip, scratch, scar, notch, dent, snick

nickname *noun* PET NAME, label, diminutive, epithet, sobriquet, familiar name, moniker *or* monicker (*slang*), handle (*slang*)

nifty *adjective* (*informal*) 1 SLICK, excellent, sharp, smart, clever, neat, stylish, schmick (*Austral informal*)

2 AGILE, quick, swift, skilful, deft

niggle *verb* 1 BOTHER, concern, worry, trouble, disturb, rankle

2 CRITICIZE, provoke, annoy, plague, irritate, hassle (*informal*), badger, find fault with, nag

at, cavil, be on your back (*slang*)
▷ *noun* COMPLAINT, moan, grievance, grumble, beef (*slang*), bitch (*slang*), lament, grouse, gripe (*informal*), grouch (*informal*)

niggling *adjective* 1 IRRITATING, troubling, persistent, bothersome
2 PETTY, minor, trifling, insignificant, unimportant, fussy, quibbling, picky (*informal*), piddling (*informal*), nit-picking (*informal*), finicky, pettifogging

nigh *adverb* ALMOST, about, nearly, close to, practically, approximately
▷ *adjective* NEAR, next, close, imminent, impending, at hand, upcoming

night *noun* DARKNESS, dark, night-time, dead of night, night watches, hours of darkness
>> RELATED WORD *adjective* nocturnal

nightfall *noun* EVENING, sunset, twilight, dusk, sundown, eventide, gloaming (*Scot poetic*), eve (*archaic*), evo (*Austral slang*)
<< OPPOSITE daybreak

nightly *adjective* NOCTURNAL, night-time
▷ *adverb* EVERY NIGHT, nights (*informal*), each night, night after night

nightmare *noun* 1 BAD DREAM, hallucination, night terror
2 ORDEAL, trial, hell, horror, torture, torment, tribulation, purgatory, hell on earth

nightmarish *adjective* TERRIFYING, frightening, disturbing, appalling, horrible, horrific, ghastly, hideous, harrowing, frightful

nihilism *noun* NEGATIVITY, rejection, denial, scepticism, cynicism, pessimism, renunciation, atheism, repudiation, agnosticism, unbelief, abnegation

nil *noun* 1 NOTHING, love, zero, zip (*US slang*)
2 ZERO, nothing, none, naught, zilch (*slang*), zip (*US slang*)

nimble *adjective* 1 AGILE, active, lively, deft, proficient, sprightly, nippy (*Brit informal*), spry, dexterous
<< OPPOSITE clumsy
2 ALERT, ready, bright (*informal*), sharp, keen, active, smart, quick-witted

nimbus *noun* HALO, atmosphere, glow, aura, ambience, corona, irradiation, aureole

nip¹ *verb* 1 *with* **along, up, out** (*Brit informal*) POP, go, run, rush, dash
2 BITE, snap, nibble
3 PINCH, catch, grip, squeeze, clip, compress, tweak
▷▷ **nip something in the bud** THWART, check, frustrate

nip² *noun* DRAM, shot (*informal*), drop, taste, finger, swallow, portion, peg (*Brit*), sip, draught, sup, mouthful, snifter (*informal*), soupçon (*French*)

nipper *noun* 1 (*informal, Chiefly Brit & Austral*) CHILD, girl, boy, baby, kid (*informal*), infant, tot, little one, sprog (*slang*), munchkin (*informal, chiefly US*), rug rat (*slang*), littlie (*Austral informal*), ankle-biter (*Austral slang*), tacker (*Austral slang*)
2 PINCER, claw

nipple *noun* TEAT, breast, udder, tit, pap, papilla, mamilla

nippy *adjective* 1 CHILLY, biting, parky (*Brit informal*)
2 (*Brit informal*) FAST (*informal*), quick, speedy
3 (*Brit informal*) AGILE, fast, quick, active, lively, nimble, sprightly, spry

nirvana *noun* (*Buddhism & Hinduism*) PARADISE, peace, joy, bliss, serenity, tranquillity

nitty-gritty *noun* (*informal*) BASICS, facts, reality, essentials, core, fundamentals, substance, essence, bottom line, crux, gist, nuts and bolts, heart of the matter, ins and outs, brass tacks (*informal*)

no *sentence substitute* NOT AT ALL, certainly not, of course not, absolutely not, never, no way, nay
<< OPPOSITE yes
▷ *noun* 1 REFUSAL, rejection, denial, negation, veto
<< OPPOSITE consent
2 OBJECTOR, protester, dissident, dissenter

nob *noun* (*Slang, chiefly Brit*) ARISTOCRAT, fat cat (*slang, chiefly US*), toff (*Brit slang*), bigwig (*informal*), celeb (*informal*), big shot (*informal*), big hitter (*informal*), aristo (*informal*), heavy hitter (*informal*), nabob (*informal*), V.I.P.

nobble *verb* (*Brit slang*) 1 INFLUENCE, square, win over, pay off (*informal*), corrupt, intimidate, bribe, get at, buy off, suborn, grease the palm *or* hand of (*slang*)
2 DISABLE, handicap, weaken, incapacitate
3 THWART, check, defeat, frustrate, snooker, foil, baffle, balk, prevent

nobility *noun* 1 ARISTOCRACY, lords, elite, nobles, upper class, peerage, ruling class, patricians, high society
2 DIGNITY, majesty, greatness, grandeur, magnificence, stateliness, nobleness
3 INTEGRITY, honour, virtue, goodness, honesty, righteousness, probity, rectitude, worthiness, incorruptibility, uprightness

noble *adjective* 1 WORTHY, generous, upright, honourable, virtuous, magnanimous
<< OPPOSITE despicable
2 DIGNIFIED, great, august, imposing, impressive, distinguished, magnificent, splendid, stately
<< OPPOSITE lowly
3 ARISTOCRATIC, lordly, titled, gentle (*archaic*), patrician, blue-blooded, highborn
<< OPPOSITE humble
▷ *noun* LORD, peer, aristocrat, nobleman, aristo (*informal*)
<< OPPOSITE commoner

nobody *pronoun* NO-ONE

▷ *noun* NONENTITY, nothing (*informal*), lightweight (*informal*), zero, cipher
<< OPPOSITE celebrity

nocturnal *adjective* NIGHTLY, night, of the night, night-time

nod *verb* 1 AGREE, concur, assent, show agreement
2 INCLINE, bob, bow, duck, dip
3 SIGNAL, indicate, motion, gesture
4 SALUTE, acknowledge
▷ *noun* 1 SIGNAL, sign, motion, gesture, indication
2 SALUTE, greeting, acknowledgment

node *noun* NODULE, growth, swelling, knot, lump, bump, bud, knob, protuberance

noise *noun* SOUND, talk, row, racket, outcry, clamour, din, clatter, uproar, babble, blare, fracas, commotion, pandemonium, rumpus, cry, tumult, hubbub
<< OPPOSITE silence

noisy *adjective* 1 ROWDY, chattering, strident, boisterous, vociferous, riotous, uproarious, obstreperous, clamorous
<< OPPOSITE quiet
2 LOUD, piercing, deafening, tumultuous, ear-splitting, cacophonous, clamorous
<< OPPOSITE quiet

nomad *noun* WANDERER, migrant, rover, rambler, itinerant, drifter, vagabond

nomadic *adjective* WANDERING, travelling, roaming, migrant, roving, itinerant, migratory, vagrant, peripatetic

nomenclature *noun* TERMINOLOGY, vocabulary, classification, taxonomy, phraseology, locution

nominal *adjective* 1 TITULAR, formal, purported, in name only, supposed, so-called, pretended, theoretical, professed, ostensible
2 TOKEN, small, symbolic, minimal, trivial, trifling, insignificant, inconsiderable

nominate *verb* 1 PROPOSE, suggest, recommend, submit, put forward
2 APPOINT, name, choose, commission, select, elect, assign, designate, empower

nomination *noun* 1 PROPOSAL, suggestion, recommendation
2 APPOINTMENT, election, selection, designation, choice

nominee *noun* CANDIDATE, applicant, entrant, contestant, aspirant, runner

nonaligned *adjective* NEUTRAL, impartial, uninvolved, nonpartisan, noncombatant, nonbelligerent

nonchalance *noun* INDIFFERENCE, insouciance, detachment, unconcern, cool (*slang*), calm, apathy, composure, carelessness, equanimity, casualness, sang-froid, self-possession, dispassion, imperturbability

nonchalant *adjective* INDIFFERENT, cool, calm, casual, detached, careless, laid-back (*informal*), airy, unconcerned, apathetic, dispassionate, unfazed (*informal*), unperturbed, blasé, offhand, unemotional, insouciant, imperturbable
<< OPPOSITE concerned

noncommittal *adjective* EVASIVE, politic, reserved, guarded, careful, cautious, neutral, vague, wary, discreet, tentative, ambiguous, indefinite, circumspect, tactful, equivocal, temporizing, unrevealing

nonconformist *noun* DISSENTER, rebel, radical, protester, eccentric, maverick, heretic, individualist, iconoclast, dissentient
<< OPPOSITE traditionalist

nondescript *adjective* UNDISTINGUISHED, ordinary, dull, commonplace, unremarkable, run-of-the-mill, uninspiring, indeterminate, uninteresting, featureless, insipid, unexceptional, common or garden (*informal*), mousy, characterless, unmemorable, vanilla (*informal*), nothing to write home about
<< OPPOSITE distinctive

none *pronoun* 1 NOT ANY, nothing, zero, not one, nil, no part, not a bit, zilch (*slang, chiefly US & Canad*), diddly (*US slang*)
2 NO-ONE, nobody, not one

nonentity *noun* NOBODY, lightweight (*informal*), mediocrity, cipher, small fry, unimportant person

nonetheless *sentence connector* NEVERTHELESS, however, yet, even so, despite that, in spite of that

nonevent *noun* FLOP (*informal*), failure, disappointment, fiasco, dud (*informal*), washout, clunker (*informal*)

nonexistent *adjective* IMAGINARY, imagined, fancied, fictional, mythical, unreal, hypothetical, illusory, insubstantial, hallucinatory
<< OPPOSITE real

nonplussed *adjective* TAKEN ABACK, stunned, confused, embarrassed, puzzled, astonished, stumped, dismayed, baffled, bewildered, astounded, confounded, perplexed, disconcerted, mystified, fazed, dumbfounded, discomfited, flummoxed, discountenanced

nonsense *noun* 1 RUBBISH, hot air (*informal*), waffle (*informal, chiefly Brit*), twaddle, pants (*slang*), rot, crap (*slang*), garbage (*informal*), trash, bunk (*informal*), tosh (*slang, chiefly Brit*), rhubarb, pap, foolishness, bilge (*informal*), drivel, tripe (*informal*), gibberish, guff (*slang*), bombast, moonshine, claptrap (*informal*), hogwash, hokum (*slang, chiefly US & Canad*), blather, double Dutch (*Brit informal*), piffle (*informal*), poppycock (*informal*), balderdash, bosh (*informal*), eyewash (*informal*), stuff and nonsense, tommyrot, horsefeathers (*US slang*),

bunkum *or* buncombe (*chiefly US*), bizzo (*Austral slang*), bull's wool (*Austral & NZ slang*)
<< OPPOSITE sense
2 IDIOCY, folly, stupidity, absurdity, silliness, inanity, senselessness, ridiculousness, ludicrousness, fatuity
nonsensical *adjective* SENSELESS, crazy, silly, ridiculous, absurd, foolish, ludicrous, meaningless, irrational, incomprehensible, inane, asinine, cockamamie (*slang, chiefly US*)
nonstarter *noun* DEAD LOSS, dud (*informal*), washout (*informal*), no-hoper (*informal*), turkey (*informal*), lemon (*informal*), loser, waste of space *or* time
nonstop *adjective* CONTINUOUS, constant, relentless, uninterrupted, steady, endless, unbroken, interminable, incessant, unending, ceaseless, unremitting, unfaltering
<< OPPOSITE occasional
▷ *adverb* CONTINUOUSLY, constantly, steadily, endlessly, relentlessly, perpetually, incessantly, without stopping, ceaselessly, interminably, unremittingly, uninterruptedly, unendingly, unfalteringly, unbrokenly
nook *noun* NICHE, corner, recess, cavity, crevice, alcove, cranny, inglenook (*Brit*), cubbyhole, opening
noon *noun* MIDDAY, high noon, noonday, noontime, twelve noon, noontide
norm *noun* STANDARD, rule, model, pattern, mean, type, measure, average, par, criterion, benchmark, yardstick
normal *adjective* 1 USUAL, common, standard, average, natural, regular, ordinary, acknowledged, typical, conventional, routine, accustomed, habitual, run-of-the-mill
<< OPPOSITE unusual
2 SANE, reasonable, rational, lucid, well-adjusted, compos mentis (*Latin*), in your right mind, mentally sound, in possession of all your faculties
normality *or US* **normalcy** *noun* 1 REGULARITY, order, routine, ordinariness, naturalness, conventionality, usualness
2 SANITY, reason, balance, rationality, lucidity
normally *adverb* 1 USUALLY, generally, commonly, regularly, typically, ordinarily, as a rule, habitually
2 AS USUAL, naturally, properly, conventionally, in the usual way
normative *adjective* STANDARDIZING, controlling, regulating, prescriptive, normalizing, regularizing
north *adjective* NORTHERN, polar, arctic, boreal, northerly
▷ *adverb* NORTHWARD(S), in a northerly direction
North Star *noun* POLE STAR, Polaris, lodestar
nose *noun* SNOUT, bill, beak, hooter (*slang*), snitch (*slang*), conk (*slang*), neb (*archaic* or *dialect*), proboscis, schnozzle (*slang, chiefly US*)
▷ *verb* EASE FORWARD, push, edge, shove, nudge
>> RELATED WORDS *adjectives* nasal, rhinal
nose dive *noun* 1 DROP, plunge, dive, plummet, sharp fall
2 (*informal*) SHARP FALL, plunge, drop, dive, plummet
▷ *verb* 1 DROP, plunge, dive, plummet, fall sharply
2 (*informal*) FALL SHARPLY, drop, plunge, dive, plummet
nosh (*Slang*) *noun* 1 FOOD, eats (*slang*), fare, grub (*slang*), feed, tack (*informal*), scoff (*slang*), kai (*NZ informal*), chow (*informal*), sustenance, victuals, comestibles, nosebag (*slang*), vittles (*obsolete* or *dialect*), viands
2 MEAL, repast
▷ *verb* EAT, consume, scoff (*slang*), devour, feed on, munch, gobble, partake of, wolf down
nostalgia *noun* REMINISCENCE, longing, regret, pining, yearning, remembrance, homesickness, wistfulness
nostalgic *adjective* SENTIMENTAL, longing, emotional, homesick, wistful, maudlin, regretful
notable *adjective* 1 REMARKABLE, marked, striking, unusual, extraordinary, outstanding, evident, pronounced, memorable, noticeable, uncommon, conspicuous, salient, noteworthy
<< OPPOSITE imperceptible
2 PROMINENT, famous, celebrated, distinguished, well-known, notorious, renowned, eminent, pre-eminent
<< OPPOSITE unknown
▷ *noun* CELEBRITY, worthy, big name, dignitary, luminary, celeb (*informal*), personage, megastar (*informal*), notability, V.I.P.
notably *adverb* REMARKABLY, unusually, distinctly, extraordinarily, markedly, noticeably, strikingly, conspicuously, singularly, outstandingly, uncommonly, pre-eminently, signally
notation *noun* 1 SIGNS, system, characters, code, symbols, script
2 NOTE, record, noting, jotting
notch *noun* 1 (*informal*) LEVEL, step, degree, grade, cut (*informal*)
2 CUT, nick, incision, indentation, mark, score, cleft
▷ *verb* CUT, mark, score, nick, scratch, indent
note *noun* 1 MESSAGE, letter, communication, memo, memorandum, epistle
2 RECORD, reminder, memo, memorandum, jotting, minute
3 ANNOTATION, comment, remark, gloss
4 DOCUMENT, form, record, certificate

5 SYMBOL, mark, sign, indication, token
6 TONE, touch, trace, hint, sound
▷ *verb* 1 NOTICE, see, observe, perceive
2 BEAR IN MIND, be aware, take into account
3 MENTION, record, mark, indicate, register, remark
4 WRITE DOWN, record, scribble, take down, set down, jot down, put in writing, put down in black and white
▷▷ **of note** 1 FAMOUS, prestigious, eminent, renowned, of standing, of character, of reputation, of consequence, celebrated
2 IMPORTANT, consequential, significant, of distinction
▷▷ **take note of something** *or* **someone** NOTICE, note, regard, observe, heed, pay attention to

notebook *noun* NOTEPAD, record book, exercise book, jotter, journal, diary, Filofax (*trademark*), memorandum book

noted *adjective* FAMOUS, celebrated, recognized, distinguished, well-known, prominent, notorious, acclaimed, notable, renowned, eminent, conspicuous, illustrious
<< OPPOSITE unknown

noteworthy *adjective* REMARKABLE, interesting, important, significant, extraordinary, outstanding, exceptional, notable
<< OPPOSITE ordinary

nothing *pronoun* 1 NOUGHT, zero, nil, naught, not a thing, zilch (*slang*), sod all (*slang*), damn all (*slang*), zip (*US slang*)
2 A TRIFLE, no big deal, a mere bagatelle
3 VOID, emptiness, nothingness, nullity, nonexistence
▷ *noun* (*informal*) NOBODY, cipher, nonentity

nothingness *noun* 1 OBLIVION, nullity, nonexistence, nonbeing
2 INSIGNIFICANCE, triviality, worthlessness, meaninglessness, unimportance

notice *noun* 1 SIGN, advertisement, poster, placard, warning, bill
2 NOTIFICATION, warning, advice, intimation, news, communication, intelligence, announcement, instruction, advance warning, wake-up call
3 REVIEW, comment, criticism, evaluation, critique, critical assessment
4 ATTENTION, interest, note, regard, consideration, observation, scrutiny, heed, cognizance
<< OPPOSITE oversight
5 (*Chiefly Brit*) THE SACK (*informal*), dismissal, discharge, the boot (*slang*), the push (*slang*), marching orders (*informal*), the (old) heave-ho (*informal*), your books *or* cards (*informal*)
▷ *verb* OBSERVE, see, mind, note, spot, remark, distinguish, perceive, detect, heed, discern, behold (*archaic* or *literary*), mark, eyeball (*slang*)
<< OPPOSITE overlook

noticeable *adjective* OBVIOUS, clear, striking, plain, bold, evident, distinct, manifest, conspicuous, unmistakable, salient, observable, perceptible, appreciable

notification *noun* ANNOUNCEMENT, declaration, notice, statement, telling, information, warning, message, advice, intelligence, publication, notifying

notify *verb* INFORM, tell, advise, alert to, announce, warn, acquaint with, make known to, apprise of

notion *noun* 1 IDEA, view, opinion, belief, concept, impression, judgment, sentiment, conception, apprehension, inkling, mental image *or* picture, picture
2 WHIM, wish, desire, fancy, impulse, inclination, caprice

notional *adjective* HYPOTHETICAL, ideal, abstract, theoretical, imaginary, speculative, conceptual, unreal, fanciful
<< OPPOSITE actual

notoriety *noun* INFAMY, discredit, disrepute, dishonour, bad reputation, opprobrium, ill repute, obloquy

notorious *adjective* INFAMOUS, disreputable, opprobrious

notoriously *adverb* INFAMOUSLY, disreputably

notwithstanding *preposition* DESPITE, in spite of, regardless of
▷ *sentence connector* NEVERTHELESS, however, though, nonetheless

nought *or* (*Archaic* or *literary*) **naught, ought** *or* **aught** *noun* 1 ZERO, nothing, nil
2 NOTHING, zip (*US slang*), slang, nothingness, nada, zilch, sod all (*slang*), damn all (*slang*)

nourish *verb* 1 FEED, supply, sustain, nurture
2 ENCOURAGE, support, maintain, promote, sustain, foster, cultivate

nourishing *adjective* NUTRITIOUS, beneficial, wholesome, healthful, health-giving, nutritive

nourishment *noun* FOOD, nutrition, sustenance, nutriment, tack (*informal*), kai (*NZ informal*), victuals, vittles (*obsolete* or *dialect*)

novel[1] *noun* STORY, tale, fiction, romance, narrative

novel[2] *adjective* NEW, different, original, fresh, unusual, innovative, uncommon, singular, ground-breaking, left-field (*informal*)
<< OPPOSITE ordinary

novelist *noun* AUTHOR, writer

novelty *noun* 1 NEWNESS, originality, freshness, innovation, surprise, uniqueness, strangeness, unfamiliarity
2 CURIOSITY, marvel, rarity, oddity, wonder
3 TRINKET, souvenir, memento, bauble, bagatelle, gimcrack, trifle, gewgaw, knick-knack

novice *noun* BEGINNER, pupil, amateur,

newcomer, trainee, apprentice, learner, neophyte, tyro, probationer, proselyte
<< OPPOSITE expert

now *adverb* 1 NOWADAYS, at the moment, these days
2 IMMEDIATELY, presently (*Scot & US*), promptly, instantly, at once, straightaway
▷▷ **now and then** *or* **again** OCCASIONALLY, sometimes, at times, from time to time, on and off, on occasion, once in a while, intermittently, infrequently, sporadically

nowadays *adverb* NOW, today, at the moment, these days, in this day and age

noxious *adjective* HARMFUL, deadly, poisonous, unhealthy, hurtful, pernicious, injurious, unwholesome, noisome, pestilential, insalubrious, foul
<< OPPOSITE harmless

nuance *noun* SUBTLETY, degree, distinction, graduation, refinement, nicety, gradation

nub *noun* GIST, point, heart, core, essence, nucleus, kernel, crux, pith

nubile *adjective* ATTRACTIVE, sexy (*informal*), desirable, ripe (*informal*), marriageable

nucleus *noun* CENTRE, heart, focus, basis, core, pivot, kernel, nub

nude *adjective* NAKED, stripped, exposed, bare, uncovered, undressed, stark-naked, in the raw (*informal*), disrobed, starkers (*informal*), unclothed, in the buff (*informal*), au naturel (*French*), in the altogether (*informal*), buck naked (*slang*), unclad, undraped, in your birthday suit (*informal*), scuddy (*slang*), without a stitch on (*informal*), in the bare scud (*slang*), naked as the day you were born (*informal*)
<< OPPOSITE dressed

nudge *verb* 1 PUSH, touch, dig, jog, prod, elbow, shove, poke
2 PROMPT, influence, urge, persuade, spur, prod, coax, prevail upon
▷ *noun* 1 PUSH, touch, dig, elbow, bump, shove, poke, jog, prod
2 PROMPTING, push, encouragement, prod

nudity *noun* NAKEDNESS, undress, nudism, bareness, deshabille

nugget *noun* LUMP, piece, mass, chunk, clump, hunk

nuisance *noun* TROUBLE, problem, trial, bore, drag (*informal*), bother, plague, pest, irritation, hassle (*informal*), inconvenience, annoyance, pain (*informal*), pain in the neck (*informal*), pain in the backside (*informal*), pain in the butt (*informal*)
<< OPPOSITE benefit

null ▷▷ **null and void** INVALID, useless, void, worthless, ineffectual, valueless, inoperative

nullify *verb* 1 INVALIDATE, quash, revoke, render null and void, abolish, void, repeal, rescind, annul, abrogate
<< OPPOSITE validate
2 CANCEL OUT, counteract, negate, neutralize, obviate, countervail, bring to naught

numb *adjective* 1 UNFEELING, dead, frozen, paralysed, insensitive, deadened, immobilized, torpid, insensible
<< OPPOSITE sensitive
2 STUPEFIED, deadened, unfeeling, insensible
▷ *verb* 1 STUN, knock out, paralyse, daze, stupefy
2 DEADEN, freeze, dull, paralyse, immobilize, benumb

number *noun* 1 NUMERAL, figure, character, digit, integer
2 AMOUNT, quantity, collection, total, count, sum, aggregate
<< OPPOSITE shortage
3 CROWD, horde, multitude, throng
4 GROUP, company, set, band, crowd, gang, coterie
5 ISSUE, copy, edition, imprint, printing
▷ *verb* 1 AMOUNT TO, come to, total, add up to
2 CALCULATE, account, reckon, compute, enumerate
<< OPPOSITE guess
3 INCLUDE, count

numbered *adjective* 1 RECKONED, totalled, counted
2 LIMITED, restricted, limited in number

numbness *noun* 1 DEADNESS, paralysis, insensitivity, dullness, torpor, insensibility
2 TORPOR, deadness, dullness, stupefaction

numeral *noun* NUMBER, figure, digit, character, symbol, cipher, integer

numerous *adjective* MANY, several, countless, lots, abundant, plentiful, innumerable, copious, manifold, umpteen (*informal*), profuse, thick on the ground
<< OPPOSITE few

nuptial *adjective* MARITAL, wedding, wedded, bridal, matrimonial, conjugal, connubial, hymeneal (*poetic*)

nuptials *plural noun sometimes singular* WEDDING, marriage, matrimony, espousal (*archaic*)

nurse *verb* 1 LOOK AFTER, treat, tend, care for, take care of, minister to
2 HARBOUR, have, maintain, preserve, entertain, cherish, keep alive
3 BREAST-FEED, feed, nurture, nourish, suckle, wet-nurse

nursery *noun* CRÈCHE, kindergarten, playgroup, play-centre (*NZ*)

nurture *noun* UPBRINGING, training, education, instruction, rearing, development
▷ *verb* BRING UP, raise, look after, rear, care for, develop
<< OPPOSITE neglect

nut *noun* 1 KERNEL, stone, seed, pip
2 (*Slang*) MADMAN, eccentric, flake (*slang, chiefly*

US), psycho (*slang*), crank (*informal*), lunatic, maniac, loony (*slang*), nutter (*Brit slang*), oddball (*informal*), crackpot (*informal*), wacko (*slang*), nutcase (*slang*), headcase (*informal*)
3 (*Slang*) HEAD, skull, noggin

nutrition *noun* FOOD, nourishment, sustenance, nutriment

nutritious *adjective* NOURISHING, beneficial, wholesome, healthful, health-giving, nutritive

nuts *adjective* (*Slang*) INSANE, mad, crazy (*informal*), bananas (*slang*), barking (*slang*), eccentric, batty (*slang*), psycho (*slang*), irrational, loony (*slang*), demented, nutty (*slang*), deranged, loopy (*informal*), out to lunch (*informal*), barking mad (*slang*), gonzo (*slang*), doolally (*slang*), off your trolley (*slang*), up the pole (*informal*), as daft as a brush (*informal, chiefly Brit*), not the full shilling (*informal*), wacko *or* whacko (*informal*), off the air (*Austral slang*)
▷▷ **nuts and bolts** (*informal*) ESSENTIALS, basics, fundamentals, nitty-gritty (*informal*), practicalities, ins and outs, details

nuzzle *verb* SNUGGLE, cuddle, nudge, burrow, nestle

nymph *noun* 1 (*Mythology*) SYLPH, dryad, naiad, hamadryad, Oceanid (*Greek myth*), oread
2 (*Chiefly poetic*) GIRL, lass, maiden, maid, damsel

Oo

oasis *noun* 1 WATERING HOLE
2 HAVEN, retreat, refuge, sanctuary, island, resting place, sanctum

oath *noun* 1 PROMISE, bond, pledge, vow, word, compact, covenant, affirmation, sworn statement, avowal, word of honour
2 SWEAR WORD, curse, obscenity, blasphemy, expletive, four-letter word, cuss (*informal*), profanity, strong language, imprecation, malediction

obedience *noun* COMPLIANCE, yielding, submission, respect, conformity, reverence, deference, observance, subservience, submissiveness, docility, complaisance, tractability, dutifulness, conformability
<< OPPOSITE disobedience

obedient *adjective* SUBMISSIVE, yielding, compliant, under control, respectful, law-abiding, well-trained, amenable, docile, dutiful, subservient, deferential, tractable, acquiescent, biddable, accommodating, passive, meek, ingratiating, malleable, pliant, unresisting, bootlicking (*informal*), obeisant, duteous
<< OPPOSITE disobedient

obese *adjective* FAT, overweight, heavy, solid, gross, plump, stout, fleshy, beefy (*informal*), tubby, portly, outsize, roly-poly, rotund, podgy, corpulent, elephantine, paunchy, well-upholstered (*informal*), Falstaffian
<< OPPOSITE thin

obesity *or* **obeseness** *noun* FATNESS, flab, heaviness, a weight problem, grossness, corpulence, beef (*informal*), embonpoint (*French*), rotundity, fleshiness, stoutness, portliness, bulkiness, podginess, tubbiness
<< OPPOSITE thinness

obey *verb* 1 SUBMIT TO, surrender (to), give way to, succumb to, bow to, give in to, yield to, serve, cave in to (*informal*), take orders from, do what you are told by
<< OPPOSITE disobey
2 SUBMIT, yield, surrender, give in, give way, succumb, cave in, toe the line, knuckle under (*informal*), do what is expected, come to heel, get into line
3 CARRY OUT, follow, perform, respond to, implement, fulfil, execute, discharge, act upon, carry through
<< OPPOSITE disregard
4 ABIDE BY, keep, follow, comply with, observe, mind, embrace, hold to, heed, conform to, keep to, adhere to, be ruled by

object[1] *noun* 1 THING, article, device, body, item, implement, entity, gadget, contrivance
2 PURPOSE, aim, end, point, plan, idea, reason, goal, design, target, principle, function, intention, objective, intent, motive, end in view, end purpose, the why and wherefore
3 TARGET, victim, focus, butt, recipient

object[2] *verb* 1 *often with* **to** PROTEST AGAINST, oppose, say no to, kick against (*informal*), argue against, draw the line at, take exception to, raise objections to, cry out against, complain against, take up the cudgels against, expostulate against
<< OPPOSITE accept
2 DISAGREE, demur, remonstrate, expostulate, express disapproval
<< OPPOSITE agree

objection *noun* PROTEST, opposition, complaint, doubt, exception, dissent, outcry, censure, disapproval, niggle (*informal*), protestation, scruple, demur, formal complaint, counter-argument, cavil, remonstrance, demurral
<< OPPOSITE agreement

objectionable *adjective* OFFENSIVE, annoying, irritating, unacceptable, unpleasant, rude, intolerable, undesirable, distasteful, obnoxious, deplorable, displeasing, unseemly, disagreeable, repugnant, abhorrent, beyond the pale, insufferable, detestable, discourteous, uncivil, unmannerly, exceptionable, dislikable *or* dislikeable
<< OPPOSITE pleasant

objective *adjective* 1 FACTUAL, real, circumstantial
2 UNBIASED, detached, just, fair, judicial, open-minded, equitable, impartial, impersonal, disinterested, even-handed, dispassionate, unemotional, uninvolved, unprejudiced, uncoloured
<< OPPOSITE subjective
▷ *noun* PURPOSE, aim, goal, end, plan, hope, idea, design, target, wish, scheme, desire, object, intention, ambition, aspiration, Holy Grail (*informal*), end in view, why and wherefore

objectively *adverb* IMPARTIALLY, neutrally, fairly, justly, without prejudice, dispassionately, with an open mind, equitably, without fear or favour, even-handedly, without bias, disinterestedly, with objectivity *or* impartiality

objectivity *noun* IMPARTIALITY, detachment, neutrality, equity, fairness, disinterest, open-mindedness, even-handedness, impersonality, disinterestedness, dispassion, nonpartisanship, lack of bias, equitableness
<< OPPOSITE subjectivity

obligation *noun* 1 DUTY, compulsion
2 TASK, job, duty, work, calling, business, charge, role, function, mission, province, assignment, pigeon (*informal*), chore
3 RESPONSIBILITY, duty, liability, accountability, culpability, answerability, accountableness

obligatory *adjective* 1 COMPULSORY, required, necessary, essential, binding, enforced, mandatory, imperative, unavoidable, requisite, coercive, de rigueur (*French*)
<< OPPOSITE optional
2 CUSTOMARY, regular, usual, popular, normal, familiar, conventional, fashionable, bog-standard (*Brit & Irish slang*)

oblige *verb* 1 COMPEL, make, force, require, bind, railroad (*informal*), constrain, necessitate, coerce, impel, dragoon, obligate
2 HELP, assist, serve, benefit, please, favour, humour, accommodate, indulge, gratify, do someone a service, put yourself out for, do (someone) a favour *or* a kindness, meet the wants *or* needs of
<< OPPOSITE bother

obliged *adjective* 1 FORCED, required, bound, compelled, obligated, duty-bound, under an obligation, under compulsion, without any option
2 GRATEFUL, in (someone's) debt, thankful, indebted, appreciative, beholden

obliging *adjective* ACCOMMODATING, kind, helpful, willing, civil, friendly, polite, cooperative, agreeable, amiable, courteous, considerate, hospitable, unselfish, good-natured, eager to please, complaisant
<< OPPOSITE unhelpful

oblique *adjective* 1 INDIRECT, implied, roundabout, backhanded, evasive, elliptical, circuitous, circumlocutory, inexplicit, periphrastic
<< OPPOSITE direct
2 SLANTING, angled, sloped, sloping, inclined, tilted, tilting, slanted, diagonal, at an angle, asymmetrical, canted, aslant, slantwise, atilt, cater-cornered (*US informal*)
3 SIDELONG, sideways, covert, indirect, furtive, surreptitious

obliquely *adverb* 1 INDIRECTLY, evasively, not in so many words, circuitously, in a roundabout manner *or* way
2 AT AN ANGLE, sideways, diagonally, sidelong, aslant, slantwise, aslope

obliterate *verb* 1 DESTROY, eliminate, devastate, waste, wreck, wipe out, demolish, ravage, eradicate, desolate, annihilate, put paid to, raze, blow to bits, extirpate, blow sky-high, destroy root and branch, kennet (*Austral slang*), jeff (*Austral slang*), wipe from *or* off the face of the earth
<< OPPOSITE create
2 ERADICATE, remove, eliminate, cancel, get rid of, wipe out, erase, excise, delete, extinguish, root out, efface, blot out, expunge, extirpate

oblivion *noun* NEGLECT, anonymity, insignificance, obscurity, limbo, nothingness, unimportance

oblivious *adjective usually with* **of** *or* **to** UNAWARE, unconscious, ignorant, regardless, careless, negligent, blind to, unaffected by, impervious to, forgetful, deaf to, unconcerned about, neglectful, heedless, inattentive, insensible, unmindful, unobservant, disregardful, incognizant
<< OPPOSITE aware

> It was formerly considered incorrect to use *oblivious* and *unaware* as synonyms, but this use is now acceptable. When employed with this meaning, *oblivious* should be followed either by *to* or *of*, *to* being much the commoner

obnoxious *adjective* LOATHSOME, offensive, nasty, foul, disgusting, unpleasant, revolting, obscene, sickening, vile, horrid, repellent, repulsive, objectionable, disagreeable, nauseating, odious, hateful, repugnant, reprehensible, abhorrent, abominable, insufferable, execrable, detestable, hateable, dislikable *or* dislikeable, yucky *or* yukky (*slang*), yucko (*Austral slang*)
<< OPPOSITE pleasant

obscene *adjective* 1 INDECENT, dirty, offensive, gross, foul, coarse, filthy, vile, improper, immoral, pornographic, suggestive, blue, loose, shameless, lewd, depraved, X-rated (*informal*), bawdy, salacious, prurient, impure, lascivious, smutty, ribald, unwholesome, scabrous, immodest, licentious, indelicate, unchaste

<< OPPOSITE decent

2 OFFENSIVE, shocking, evil, disgusting, outrageous, revolting, sickening, vile, wicked, repellent, atrocious, obnoxious, heinous, nauseating, odious, loathsome, abominable, detestable

obscenity *noun* 1 INDECENCY, pornography, impurity, impropriety, vulgarity, smut, prurience, coarseness, crudity, licentiousness, foulness, outrageousness, blueness, immodesty, suggestiveness, lewdness, dirtiness, grossness, vileness, filthiness, bawdiness, unseemliness, indelicacy, smuttiness, salacity

<< OPPOSITE decency

2 SWEAR WORD, curse, oath, expletive, four-letter word, cuss (*informal*), profanity, vulgarism

obscure *adjective* 1 UNKNOWN, minor, little-known, humble, unfamiliar, out-of-the-way, unseen, lowly, unimportant, unheard-of, unsung, nameless, undistinguished, inconspicuous, unnoted, unhonoured, unrenowned

<< OPPOSITE famous

2 ABSTRUSE, involved, complex, confusing, puzzling, subtle, mysterious, deep, vague, unclear, doubtful, mystical, intricate, ambiguous, enigmatic, esoteric, perplexing, occult, opaque, incomprehensible, arcane, cryptic, unfathomable, recondite, clear as mud (*informal*)

<< OPPOSITE straightforward

3 UNCLEAR, hidden, uncertain, confused, mysterious, concealed, doubtful, indefinite, indeterminate

<< OPPOSITE well-known

4 INDISTINCT, vague, blurred, dark, clouded, faint, dim, gloomy, veiled, murky, fuzzy, shadowy, cloudy, misty, hazy, indistinguishable, indeterminate, dusky, undefined, out of focus, ill-defined, obfuscated, indiscernible, tenebrous

<< OPPOSITE clear

▷ *verb* 1 OBSTRUCT, hinder, block out

2 HIDE, cover (up), screen, mask, disguise, conceal, veil, cloak, shroud, camouflage, envelop, encase, enshroud

<< OPPOSITE expose

obscurity *noun* 1 INSIGNIFICANCE, oblivion, unimportance, non-recognition, inconsequence, lowliness, inconspicuousness, namelessness, ingloriousness

2 VAGUENESS, complexity, ambiguity, intricacy, incomprehensibility, inexactitude, woolliness, abstruseness, impreciseness, impenetrableness, reconditeness, lack of preciseness

<< OPPOSITE clarity

3 DARKNESS, dark, shadows, shade, gloom, haze, blackness, murk, dimness, murkiness, haziness, duskiness, shadiness, shadowiness, indistinctness

observable *adjective* NOTICEABLE, clear, obvious, open, striking, apparent, visible, patent, evident, distinct, manifest, blatant, conspicuous, unmistakable, discernible, salient, recognizable, detectable, perceptible, appreciable, perceivable

observance *noun* 1 *with* **of** CARRYING OUT OF, attention to, performance of, respect for, notice of, honouring of, observation of, compliance with, adherence to, fulfilment of, discharge of, obedience to, keeping of, heeding of, conformity to

<< OPPOSITE disregard for

2 CEREMONY, rite, procedure, service, form, act, practice, tradition, celebration, custom, ritual, formality, ceremonial, ordinance, liturgy

observant *adjective* 1 ATTENTIVE, quick, alert, perceptive, concentrating, careful, vigilant, mindful, watchful, wide-awake, sharp-eyed, eagle-eyed, keen-eyed, on your toes, heedful

<< OPPOSITE unobservant

2 DEVOUT, godly, holy, orthodox, pious, obedient, reverent

observation *noun* 1 WATCHING, study, survey, review, notice, investigation, monitoring, attention, consideration, examination, inspection, scrutiny, surveillance, contemplation, cognition, perusal

2 COMMENT, finding, thought, note, statement, opinion, remark, explanation, reflection, exposition, utterance, pronouncement, annotation, elucidation, obiter dictum

3 REMARK, thought, comment, statement, opinion, reflection, assertion, utterance, animadversion

4 *with* **of** OBSERVANCE OF, attention to, compliance with, notice of, honouring of, adherence to, fulfilment of, discharge of, heeding of, carrying out of

observe *verb* 1 WATCH, study, view, look at, note, check, regard, survey, monitor, contemplate, check out (*informal*), look on, keep an eye on (*informal*), gaze at, pay attention to, keep track of, scrutinize, keep tabs on (*informal*), recce (*slang*), keep under observation, watch like a hawk, take a dekko at (*Brit slang*)

2 NOTICE, see, note, mark, discover, spot,

regard, witness, clock (*Brit slang*), distinguish, perceive, detect, discern, behold (*archaic* or *literary*), eye, eyeball (*slang*), peer at, espy, get a load of (*informal*)
3 REMARK, say, comment, state, note, reflect, mention, declare, opine, pass comment, animadvert
4 COMPLY WITH, keep, follow, mind, respect, perform, carry out, honour, fulfil, discharge, obey, heed, conform to, adhere to, abide by
<< OPPOSITE disregard

observer *noun* 1 WITNESS, viewer, spectator, looker-on, watcher, onlooker, eyewitness, bystander, spotter, fly on the wall, beholder
2 COMMENTATOR, commenter, reporter, special correspondent
3 MONITOR, inspector, watchdog, supervisor, overseer, scrutineer

obsess *verb* PREOCCUPY, dominate, grip, absorb, possess, consume, rule, haunt, plague, hound, torment, bedevil, monopolize, be on your mind, engross, prey on your mind, be uppermost in your thoughts

obsessed *adjective often with* **with** *or* **by** ABSORBED, dominated, gripped, caught up, haunted, distracted, hung up (*slang*), preoccupied, immersed, beset, in the grip, infatuated, fixated, having a one-track mind
<< OPPOSITE indifferent

obsession *noun* PREOCCUPATION, thing (*informal*), complex, enthusiasm, addiction, hang-up (*informal*), mania, phobia, fetish, fixation, infatuation, ruling passion, pet subject, hobbyhorse, idée fixe (*French*), bee in your bonnet (*informal*)

obsessive *adjective* COMPULSIVE, fixed, gripping, consuming, haunting, tormenting, irresistible, neurotic, besetting, uncontrollable, obsessional

obsolete *adjective* OUTDATED, old, passé, ancient, antique, old-fashioned, dated, discarded, extinct, past it, out of date, archaic, disused, out of fashion, out, antiquated, anachronistic, outmoded, musty, old hat, behind the times, superannuated, antediluvian, outworn, démodé (*French*), out of the ark (*informal*), vieux jeu (*French*)
<< OPPOSITE up-to-date

obstacle *noun* 1 OBSTRUCTION, block, barrier, hurdle, hazard, snag, impediment, blockage, hindrance
2 HINDRANCE, check, bar, block, difficulty, barrier, handicap, hurdle, hitch, drawback, snag, deterrent, uphill (*S African*), obstruction, stumbling block, impediment
<< OPPOSITE help

obstinacy *noun* STUBBORNNESS, persistence, tenacity, perseverance, resolution, intransigence, firmness, single-mindedness, inflexibility, obduracy, doggedness, relentlessness, wilfulness, resoluteness, pig-headedness, pertinacity, tenaciousness, mulishness
<< OPPOSITE flexibility

obstinate *adjective* STUBBORN, dogged, determined, persistent, firm, perverse, intractable, inflexible, wilful, tenacious, recalcitrant, steadfast, unyielding, opinionated, intransigent, immovable, headstrong, unmanageable, cussed, strong-minded, unbending, obdurate, stiff-necked, unshakable, self-willed, refractory, pig-headed, bull-headed, mulish, contumacious, pertinacious
<< OPPOSITE flexible

obstruct *verb* 1 BLOCK, close, bar, cut off, plug, choke, clog, barricade, shut off, stop up, bung up (*informal*)
2 HOLD UP, stop, check, bar, block, prevent, arrest, restrict, interrupt, slow down, hamstring, interfere with, hamper, inhibit, clog, hinder, retard, impede, get in the way of, bring to a standstill, cumber
3 IMPEDE, prevent, frustrate, hold up, slow down, hamstring, interfere with, hamper, hold back, thwart, hinder, retard, get in the way of, trammel, cumber
<< OPPOSITE help
4 OBSCURE, screen, cut off, cover, hide, mask, shield

obstruction *noun* 1 OBSTACLE, bar, block, difficulty, barrier, hazard, barricade, snag, impediment, hindrance
2 BLOCKAGE, stoppage, occlusion
3 HINDRANCE, stop, check, bar, block, difficulty, barrier, restriction, handicap, obstacle, restraint, deterrent, stumbling block, impediment, trammel
<< OPPOSITE help

obstructive *adjective* UNHELPFUL, difficult, awkward, blocking, delaying, contrary, stalling, inhibiting, restrictive, hindering, uncooperative, disobliging, unaccommodating
<< OPPOSITE helpful

obtain *verb* 1 GET, gain, acquire, land, net, pick up, bag, secure, get hold of, come by, procure, get your hands on, score (*slang*), come into possession of
<< OPPOSITE lose
2 ACHIEVE, get, gain, realize, accomplish, attain
3 (*Formal*) PREVAIL, hold, stand, exist, be the case, abound, predominate, be in force, be current, be prevalent

obtainable *adjective* 1 AVAILABLE, to be had, procurable
2 ATTAINABLE, accessible, achievable, at

your fingertips, at your disposal, reachable, realizable, gettable, accomplishable

obtuse *adjective* STUPID, simple, slow, thick, dull, dim, dense, dumb (*informal*), sluggish, retarded, simple-minded, dozy (*Brit informal*), witless, stolid, dopey (*informal*), moronic, brainless, uncomprehending, cretinous, unintelligent, half-witted, slow on the uptake (*informal*), braindead (*informal*), dumb-ass (*informal*), doltish, dead from the neck up (*informal*), boneheaded (*slang*), thickheaded, dull-witted, imperceptive, slow-witted, muttonheaded (*slang*), thick as mince (*Scot informal*), woodenheaded (*informal*)
<< OPPOSITE clever

obviate *verb* (*Formal*) AVERT, avoid, remove, prevent, counter, do away with, preclude, counteract, ward off, stave off, forestall, render unnecessary

obvious *adjective* CLEAR, open, plain, apparent, visible, bold, patent, evident, distinct, pronounced, straightforward, explicit, manifest, transparent, noticeable, blatant, conspicuous, overt, unmistakable, palpable, unequivocal, undeniable, salient, recognizable, unambiguous, self-evident, indisputable, perceptible, much in evidence, unquestionable, open-and-shut, cut-and-dried (*informal*), undisguised, incontrovertible, self-explanatory, unsubtle, unconcealed, clear as a bell, staring you in the face (*informal*), right under your nose (*informal*), sticking out a mile (*informal*), plain as the nose on your face (*informal*)
<< OPPOSITE unclear

obviously *adverb* 1 CLEARLY, of course, certainly, needless to say, without doubt, assuredly
2 PLAINLY, patently, undoubtedly, evidently, manifestly, markedly, without doubt, unquestionably, undeniably, beyond doubt, palpably, indubitably, incontrovertibly, irrefutably, incontestably

occasion *noun* 1 TIME, moment, point, stage, incident, instance, occurrence, juncture
2 FUNCTION, event, affair, do (*informal*), happening, experience, gathering, celebration, occurrence, social occasion
3 OPPORTUNITY, chance, time, opening, window
4 REASON, cause, call, ground(s), basis, excuse, incentive, motive, warrant, justification, provocation, inducement
▷ *verb* (*Formal*) CAUSE, begin, produce, create, effect, lead to, inspire, result in, generate, prompt, provoke, induce, bring about, originate, evoke, give rise to, precipitate, elicit, incite, engender

occasional *adjective* INFREQUENT, odd, rare, casual, irregular, sporadic, intermittent, few and far between, desultory, periodic
<< OPPOSITE constant

occasionally *adverb* SOMETIMES, at times, from time to time, on and off, now and then, irregularly, on occasion, now and again, periodically, once in a while, every so often, at intervals, off and on, (every) now and then
<< OPPOSITE constantly

occult *adjective* SUPERNATURAL, dark, magical, mysterious, psychic, mystical, mystic, unearthly, unnatural, esoteric, uncanny, arcane, paranormal, abstruse, recondite, preternatural, cabbalistic, supranatural
▷▷ **the occult** MAGIC, witchcraft, sorcery, wizardry, enchantment, occultism, black art, necromancy, theurgy

occultism *noun* BLACK MAGIC, magic, witchcraft, wizardry, sorcery, the black arts, necromancy, diabolism, theurgy, supernaturalism

occupancy *noun* OCCUPATION, use, residence, holding, term, possession, tenure, tenancy, habitation, inhabitancy

occupant *noun* OCCUPIER, resident, tenant, user, holder, inmate, inhabitant, incumbent, dweller, denizen, addressee, lessee, indweller

occupation *noun* 1 JOB, work, calling, business, line (of work), office, trade, position, post, career, situation, activity, employment, craft, profession, pursuit, vocation, livelihood, walk of life
2 HOBBY, pastime, diversion, relaxation, sideline, leisure pursuit, (leisure) activity
3 INVASION, seizure, conquest, incursion, subjugation, foreign rule
4 OCCUPANCY, use, residence, holding, control, possession, tenure, tenancy, habitation, inhabitancy

occupied *adjective* 1 IN USE, taken, full, engaged, unavailable
2 INHABITED, peopled, lived-in, settled, tenanted
<< OPPOSITE uninhabited
3 BUSY, engaged, employed, working, active, tied up (*informal*), engrossed, hard at work, in harness, hard at it (*informal*), rushed off your feet

occupy *verb* 1 INHABIT, own, live in, stay in (*Scot*), be established in, dwell in, be in residence in, establish yourself in, ensconce yourself in, tenant, reside in, lodge in, take up residence in, make your home, abide in
<< OPPOSITE vacate
2 INVADE, take over, capture, seize, conquer, keep, hold, garrison, overrun, annex, take possession of, colonize
<< OPPOSITE withdraw

3 HOLD, control, dominate, possess
4 TAKE UP, consume, tie up, use up, monopolize, keep busy *or* occupied
5 *often passive* ENGAGE, interest, involve, employ, busy, entertain, absorb, amuse, divert, preoccupy, immerse, hold the attention of, engross, keep busy *or* occupied
6 FILL, take up, cover, fill up, utilize, pervade, permeate, extend over

occur *verb* 1 HAPPEN, take place, come about, follow, result, chance, arise, turn up (*informal*), come off (*informal*), ensue, crop up (*informal*), transpire (*informal*), befall, materialize, come to pass (*archaic*), betide, eventuate
2 EXIST, appear, be found, develop, obtain, turn up, be present, be met with, manifest itself, present itself, show itself
▷▷ **occur to someone** COME TO MIND, strike someone, dawn on someone, come to you, spring to mind, cross someone's mind, present itself to someone, enter someone's head, offer itself to someone, suggest itself to someone

> It is usually regarded as incorrect to talk of pre-arranged events *occurring* or *happening*. For this meaning a synonym such as *take place* would be more appropriate: *the wedding took place* (not *occurred* or *happened*) *in the afternoon*

occurrence *noun* 1 INCIDENT, happening, event, fact, matter, affair, proceeding, circumstance, episode, adventure, phenomenon, transaction
2 EXISTENCE, instance, appearance, manifestation, materialization

odd *adjective* 1 PECULIAR, strange, unusual, different, funny, extraordinary, bizarre, weird, exceptional, eccentric, abnormal, queer, rum (*Brit slang*), deviant, unconventional, far-out (*slang*), quaint, kinky (*informal*), off-the-wall (*slang*), outlandish, whimsical, oddball (*informal*), out of the ordinary, offbeat, left-field (*informal*), freakish, freaky (*slang*), wacko (*slang*), outré, daggy (*Austral & NZ informal*)
2 UNUSUAL, different, strange, rare, funny (*slang*), extraordinary, remarkable, bizarre, fantastic, curious, weird, exceptional, peculiar, abnormal, queer, irregular, uncommon, singular, uncanny, outlandish, out of the ordinary, freakish, atypical, freaky
<< OPPOSITE normal
3 OCCASIONAL, various, varied, random, casual, seasonal, irregular, periodic, miscellaneous, sundry, incidental, intermittent, infrequent
<< OPPOSITE regular
4 SPARE, remaining, extra, surplus, single, lone, solitary, uneven, leftover, unmatched, unpaired
<< OPPOSITE matched
▷▷ **odd man** *or* **odd one out** MISFIT, exception, outsider, freak, eccentric, maverick, oddball (*informal*), nonconformist, fish out of water (*informal*), square peg in a round hole (*informal*)

oddity *noun* 1 MISFIT, eccentric, crank (*informal*), nut (*slang*), maverick, flake (*slang, chiefly US*), oddball (*informal*), loose cannon, nonconformist, odd man out, wacko (*slang*), screwball (*slang, chiefly US & Canad*), card (*informal*), fish out of water, square peg (in a round hole) (*informal*), odd fish (*Brit informal*), odd bird (*informal*), rara avis, weirdo *or* weirdie (*informal*)
2 STRANGENESS, abnormality, peculiarity, eccentricity, weirdness, singularity, incongruity, oddness, unconventionality, queerness, unnaturalness, bizarreness, freakishness, extraordinariness, outlandishness
3 IRREGULARITY, phenomenon, anomaly, freak, abnormality, rarity, quirk, eccentricity, kink, peculiarity, idiosyncrasy, singularity, unorthodoxy, unconventionality

odds *plural noun* PROBABILITY, chances, likelihood
▷▷ **at odds** 1 IN CONFLICT, arguing, quarrelling, in opposition to, at loggerheads, in disagreement, at daggers drawn, on bad terms
2 AT VARIANCE, conflicting, contrary to, at odds, out of line, out of step, at sixes and sevens (*informal*), not in keeping, out of harmony
▷▷ **odds and ends** SCRAPS, bits, pieces, remains, rubbish, fragments, litter, debris, shreds, remnants, bits and pieces, bric-a-brac, bits and bobs, oddments, odds and sods, leavings, miscellanea, sundry *or* miscellaneous items

odious *adjective* OFFENSIVE, nasty, foul, disgusting, horrible, unpleasant, revolting, obscene, sickening, vile, horrid, repellent, unsavoury, obnoxious, unpalatable, repulsive, disagreeable, nauseating, hateful, repugnant, loathsome, abhorrent, abominable, execrable, detestable, yucky *or* yukky (*slang*), yucko (*Austral slang*)
<< OPPOSITE delightful

odour *or US* **odor** *noun* 1 SMELL, scent, perfume, fragrance, stink, bouquet, aroma, whiff, stench, pong (*Brit informal*), niff (*Brit slang*), redolence, malodour, fetor
2 ATMOSPHERE, feeling, air, quality, spirit, tone, climate, flavour, aura, vibe (*slang*)

Odyssey *noun often not cap.* JOURNEY, tour, trip, passage, quest, trek, expedition, voyage, crusade, excursion, pilgrimage, jaunt, peregrination

of *preposition* ABOUT, on, concerning, regarding,

with respect to, as regards

> *Of* is sometimes used instead of *have* in phrases such as *should have*, *could have*, and *might have*. This is because, when people are speaking, they often drop the *h* at the beginning of *have*, making the word's pronunciation very similar to that of *of*. Using *of* in this way is, however, regarded as nonstandard, and in writing it should definitely be avoided

off *adverb* 1 AWAY, out, apart, elsewhere, aside, hence, from here
2 ABSENT, gone, unavailable, not present, inoperative, nonattendant
▷ *adjective* 1 CANCELLED, abandoned, postponed, shelved
2 BAD, rotten, rancid, mouldy, high, turned, spoiled, sour, decayed, decomposed, putrid
3 UNACCEPTABLE, poor, unsatisfactory, disappointing, inadequate, second-rate, shoddy, displeasing, below par, mortifying, substandard, disheartening
▷▷ **off and on** OCCASIONALLY, sometimes, at times, from time to time, on and off, now and then, irregularly, on occasion, now and again, periodically, once in a while, every so often, intermittently, at intervals, sporadically, every once in a while, (every) now and again

offbeat *adjective* UNUSUAL, odd, strange, novel, extraordinary, bizarre, weird, way-out (*informal*), eccentric, queer, rum (*Brit slang*), uncommon, Bohemian, unconventional, far-out (*slang*), idiosyncratic, kinky (*informal*), off-the-wall (*slang*), unorthodox, oddball (*informal*), out of the ordinary, left-field (*informal*), freaky (*slang*), wacko (*slang*), outré, daggy (*Austral & NZ informal*)
<< OPPOSITE conventional

offence *or US* **offense** *noun* 1 CRIME, wrong, sin, lapse, fault, violation, wrongdoing, trespass, felony, misdemeanour, delinquency, misdeed, transgression, peccadillo, unlawful act, breach of conduct
2 OUTRAGE, shock, anger, trouble, bother, grief (*informal*), resentment, irritation, hassle (*informal*), wrath, indignation, annoyance, ire (*literary*), displeasure, pique, aggravation, hard feelings, umbrage, vexation, wounded feelings
3 INSULT, injury, slight, hurt, harm, outrage, put-down (*slang*), injustice, snub, affront, indignity, displeasure, rudeness, slap in the face (*informal*), insolence
▷▷ **take offence** BE OFFENDED, resent, be upset, be outraged, be put out (*informal*), be miffed (*informal*), be displeased, take umbrage, be disgruntled, be affronted, be piqued, take the needle (*informal*), get riled, take the huff, go into a huff, be huffy

offend *verb* 1 DISTRESS, upset, outrage, pain, wound, slight, provoke, insult, annoy, irritate, put down, dismay, snub, aggravate (*informal*), gall, agitate, ruffle, disconcert, vex, affront, displease, rile, pique, give offence, hurt (someone's) feelings, nark (*Brit, Austral & NZ slang*), cut to the quick, miff (*informal*), tread on (someone's) toes (*informal*), put (someone's) nose out of joint, put (someone's) back up, disgruntle, get (someone's) goat (*slang*), hack you off (*informal*)
<< OPPOSITE please
2 DISGUST, revolt, turn (someone) off (*informal*), put off, sicken, repel, repulse, nauseate, gross out (*US slang*), make (someone) sick, turn your stomach, be disagreeable to, fill with loathing
3 BREAK THE LAW, sin, err, do wrong, fall, fall from grace, go astray

offended *adjective* UPSET, pained, hurt, bothered, disturbed, distressed, outraged, stung, put out (*informal*), grieved, disgruntled, agitated, ruffled, resentful, affronted, miffed (*informal*), displeased, in a huff, piqued, huffy, tooshie (*Austral slang*)

offender *noun* CRIMINAL, convict, con (*slang*), crook, lag (*slang*), villain, culprit, sinner, delinquent, felon, jailbird, wrongdoer, miscreant, malefactor, evildoer, transgressor, lawbreaker

offensive *adjective* 1 INSULTING, rude, abusive, embarrassing, slighting, annoying, irritating, degrading, affronting, contemptuous, disparaging, displeasing, objectionable, disrespectful, scurrilous, detestable, discourteous, uncivil, unmannerly
<< OPPOSITE respectful
2 DISGUSTING, gross, nasty, foul, unpleasant, revolting, stinking, sickening, vile, repellent, unsavoury, obnoxious, unpalatable, objectionable, disagreeable, nauseating, odious, repugnant, loathsome, abominable, grotty (*slang*), detestable, noisome, yucky *or* yukky (*slang*), festy (*Austral slang*), yucko (*Austral slang*)
<< OPPOSITE pleasant
3 ATTACKING, threatening, aggressive, striking, hostile, invading, combative
<< OPPOSITE defensive
▷ *noun* ATTACK, charge, campaign, strike, push (*informal*), rush, assault, raid, drive, invasion, onslaught, foray, incursion

offer *verb* 1 PRESENT WITH, give, hand, hold out to
2 PROVIDE, present, furnish, make available, afford, place at (someone's) disposal
<< OPPOSITE withhold
3 VOLUNTEER, come forward, offer your

services, be at (someone's) service
4 PROPOSE, suggest, advance, extend, submit, put forward, put forth
5 GIVE, show, bring, provide, render, impart
6 PUT UP FOR SALE, sell, put on the market, put under the hammer
7 BID, submit, propose, extend, tender, proffer
▷ *noun* 1 PROPOSAL, suggestion, proposition, submission, attempt, endeavour, overture
2 BID, tender, bidding price

offering *noun* 1 CONTRIBUTION, gift, donation, present, subscription, hand-out, stipend, widow's mite
2 SACRIFICE, tribute, libation, burnt offering, oblation (*in religious contexts*)

offhand *adjective* CASUAL, informal, indifferent, careless, abrupt, cavalier, aloof, unconcerned, curt, uninterested, glib, cursory, couldn't-care-less, apathetic, perfunctory, blasé, brusque, take-it-or-leave-it (*informal*), nonchalant, lackadaisical, unceremonious, offhanded
<< OPPOSITE attentive
▷ *adverb* OFF THE CUFF (*informal*), spontaneously, impromptu, just like that (*informal*), ad lib, extempore, off the top of your head (*informal*), without preparation, extemporaneously

office *noun* 1 PLACE OF WORK, workplace, base, workroom, place of business
2 BRANCH, department, division, section, wing, subdivision, subsection
3 POST, place, role, work, business, service, charge, situation, commission, station, responsibility, duty, function, employment, capacity, appointment, occupation
▷ *plural noun* SUPPORT, help, backing, aid, favour, assistance, intervention, recommendation, patronage, mediation, advocacy, auspices, aegis, moral support, intercession, espousal

officer *noun* 1 OFFICIAL, executive, agent, representative, bureaucrat, public servant, appointee, dignitary, functionary, office-holder, office bearer
2 POLICE OFFICER, detective, PC, police constable, police man, police woman

official *adjective* 1 AUTHORIZED, approved, formal, sanctioned, licensed, proper, endorsed, warranted, legitimate, authentic, ratified, certified, authoritative, accredited, bona fide, signed and sealed, ex officio, ex cathedra, straight from the horse's mouth (*informal*)
<< OPPOSITE unofficial
2 FORMAL, prescribed, bureaucratic, ceremonial, solemn, ritualistic
▷ *noun* OFFICER, executive, agent, representative, bureaucrat, public servant, appointee, dignitary, functionary, office-holder, office bearer

officiate *verb* 1 PRESIDE, conduct, celebrate
2 SUPERINTEND, supervise, be in charge, run, control, serve, manage, direct, handle, chair, look after, overlook, oversee, preside, take charge, adjudicate, emcee (*informal*)

offing ▷▷ **in the offing** IMMINENT, coming, close, near, coming up, gathering, on the way, in the air, forthcoming, looming, brewing, hovering, impending, at hand, upcoming, on the cards, on the horizon, in the wings, in the pipeline, nigh (*archaic*), in prospect, close at hand, fast-approaching, in the immediate future, just round the corner

off-key *adjective* CACOPHONOUS, harsh, jarring, grating, shrill, jangling, discordant, dissonant, inharmonious, unmelodious

off-load *verb* GET RID OF, shift, dump, dispose of, unload, dispense with, jettison, foist, see the back of, palm off

off-putting *adjective* (*informal*) DISCOURAGING, upsetting, disturbing, frustrating, nasty, formidable, intimidating, dismaying, unsettling, daunting, dampening, unnerving, disconcerting, unfavourable, dispiriting, discomfiting

offset *verb* CANCEL OUT, balance, set off, make up for, compensate for, redeem, counteract, neutralize, counterbalance, nullify, obviate, balance out, counterpoise, countervail

offshoot *noun* BY-PRODUCT, development, product, branch, supplement, complement, spin-off, auxiliary, adjunct, appendage, outgrowth, appurtenance

offspring *noun* 1 CHILD, baby, kid (*informal*), youngster, infant, successor, babe, toddler, heir, issue, tot, descendant, wean (*Scot*), little one, brat, bairn (*Scot*), nipper (*informal*), chit, scion, babe in arms (*informal*), sprog (*slang*), munchkin (*informal, chiefly US*), rug rat (*slang*), littlie (*Austral informal*), ankle-biter (*Austral slang*), tacker (*Austral slang*)
<< OPPOSITE parent
2 CHILDREN, kids (*informal*), young, family, issue, stock, seed (*chiefly biblical*), fry, successors, heirs, spawn, descendants, brood, posterity, lineage, progeny, scions

often *adverb* FREQUENTLY, much, generally, commonly, repeatedly, again and again, very often, oft (*archaic* or *poetic*), over and over again, time and again, habitually, time after time, customarily, oftentimes (*archaic*), not infrequently, many a time, ofttimes (*archaic*)
<< OPPOSITE never

ogle *verb* LEER AT, stare at, eye up (*informal*), gawp at (*Brit slang*), give the once-over (*informal*), make sheep's eyes at (*informal*), give the glad eye (*informal*), lech *or* letch after (*informal*)

ogre *noun* 1 FIEND, monster, beast, villain, brute, bogeyman
2 MONSTER, giant, devil, beast, demon, bogey,

spectre, fiend, ghoul, bogeyman, bugbear

oil *noun* 1 LUBRICANT, grease, lubrication, fuel oil
2 LOTION, cream, balm, salve, liniment, embrocation, solution
▷ *verb* LUBRICATE, grease, make slippery

oily *adjective* 1 GREASY, slick, slimy, fatty, slippery, oleaginous, smeary
2 SYCOPHANTIC, smooth, flattering, slick, plausible, hypocritical, fawning, grovelling, glib, ingratiating, fulsome, deferential, servile, unctuous, obsequious, smarmy (*Brit informal*), mealy-mouthed, toadying

ointment *noun* SALVE, dressing, cream, lotion, balm, lubricant, emollient, liniment, embrocation, unguent, cerate

O.K. *or* **okay** *sentence substitute* ALL RIGHT, right, yes, agreed, very good, roger, very well, ya (*S African*), righto (*Brit informal*), okey-dokey (*informal*), yebo (*S African informal*)
▷ *adjective* (*informal*) 1 ALL RIGHT, fine, fitting, fair, in order, correct, approved, permitted, suitable, acceptable, convenient, allowable
<< OPPOSITE unacceptable
2 FINE, good, average, middling, fair, all right, acceptable, adequate, satisfactory, not bad (*informal*), so-so (*informal*), tolerable, up to scratch (*informal*), passable, unobjectionable
<< OPPOSITE unsatisfactory
3 WELL, all right, safe, sound, healthy, hale, unharmed, uninjured, unimpaired
▷ *verb* APPROVE, allow, pass, agree to, permit, sanction, second, endorse, authorize, ratify, go along with, consent to, validate, countenance, give the go-ahead, rubber-stamp (*informal*), say yes to, give the green light, assent to, give the thumbs up (*informal*), concur in, give your consent to, give your blessing to
▷ *noun* AUTHORIZATION, agreement, sanction, licence, approval, go-ahead (*informal*), blessing, permission, consent, say-so (*informal*), confirmation, mandate, endorsement, green light, ratification, assent, seal of approval, approbation

old *adjective* 1 AGED, elderly, ancient, getting on, grey, mature, past it (*informal*), venerable, patriarchal, grey-haired, antiquated, over the hill (*informal*), senile, grizzled, decrepit, hoary, senescent, advanced in years, full of years, past your prime
<< OPPOSITE young
2 TUMBLEDOWN, ruined, crumbling, decayed, shaky, disintegrating, worn-out, done, tottering, ramshackle, rickety, decrepit, falling to pieces
3 WORN, ragged, shabby, frayed, cast-off, tattered, tatty, threadbare
4 OUT OF DATE, old-fashioned, dated, passé, antique, outdated, obsolete, archaic, unfashionable, antiquated, outmoded, behind the times, superannuated, out of style, antediluvian, out of the ark (*informal*), démodé (*French*)
<< OPPOSITE up-to-date
5 FORMER, earlier, past, previous, prior, one-time, erstwhile, late, quondam, whilom (*archaic*), ex-
6 LONG-STANDING, established, fixed, enduring, abiding, long-lasting, long-established, time-honoured
7 EARLY, ancient, original, remote, of old, antique, aboriginal, primitive, archaic, gone by, bygone, undeveloped, primordial, primeval, immemorial, of yore, olden (*archaic*), pristine
8 STALE, common, commonplace, worn-out, banal, threadbare, trite, old hat, insipid, hackneyed, overused, repetitious, unoriginal, platitudinous, cliché-ridden, timeworn
9 LONG-ESTABLISHED, seasoned, experienced, tried, tested, trained, professional, skilled, expert, master, qualified, familiar, capable, veteran, practised, accomplished, vintage, versed, hardened, competent, skilful, adept, knowledgeable, age-old, of long standing, well-versed
10 CUSTOMARY, established, traditional, conventional, historic, long-established, time-honoured, of long standing ▷ see **senile**

old-fashioned *adjective* 1 OUT OF DATE, ancient, dated, outdated, unfashionable, antiquated, outmoded, passé, old hat, behind the times, fusty, out of style, démodé (*French*), out of the ark (*informal*), not with it (*informal*), (old-)fogeyish
<< OPPOSITE up-to-date
2 OLDFANGLED, square (*informal*), outdated, old, past, dead, past it (*informal*), obsolete, old-time, archaic, unfashionable, superannuated, obsolescent, out of the ark (*informal*)

old man *noun* 1 SENIOR CITIZEN, grandfather (*slang*), patriarch, old age pensioner, old person, old-timer (*US*), elder, elder statesman, wrinkly (*informal*), old codger (*informal*), old stager, greybeard, coffin-dodger (*slang*), oldster (*informal*), O.A.P. (*Brit*), koro (*NZ*)
2 (*informal*) FATHER, pop (*informal*), dad (*informal*), daddy (*informal*), pa (*informal*), old boy (*informal*), papa (*old-fashioned informal*), pater, paterfamilias
3 MANAGER, boss (*informal*), supervisor, governor (*informal*), ganger, superintendent, gaffer (*informal*), foreman, overseer, baas (*S African*) ▷ see **old person**

old person *noun* SENIOR CITIZEN, senior, retired person, old age pensioner, elder, pensioner (*slang*), coffin-dodger (*slang*), elderly person,

O.A.P. (*Brit*)

While not as offensive as *coffin-dodger* and some of the other synonyms listed here, phrases such as *old man*, *old woman*, *old person*, and *elderly person* may still cause offence. It is better to use *senior citizen* or *senior*

old-time *adjective* OLD-FASHIONED, traditional, vintage, ancient, antique, old-style, bygone

old-world *adjective* TRADITIONAL, old-fashioned, picturesque, quaint, archaic, gentlemanly, courteous, gallant, courtly, chivalrous, ceremonious

Olympian *adjective* MAJESTIC, kingly, regal, royal, august, grand, princely, imperial, glorious, noble, splendid, elevated, awesome, dignified, regal, stately, sublime, lofty, pompous, grandiose, exalted, rarefied, godlike

omen *noun* PORTENT, sign, warning, threat, indication, foreshadowing, foreboding, harbinger, presage, forewarning, writing on the wall, prognostication, augury, prognostic, foretoken

ominous *adjective* THREATENING, menacing, sinister, dark, forbidding, grim, fateful, foreboding, unpromising, portentous, baleful, inauspicious, premonitory, unpropitious, minatory, bodeful

<< OPPOSITE promising

omission *noun* 1 EXCLUSION, removal, leaving out, elimination, deletion, excision, noninclusion

<< OPPOSITE inclusion

2 FAILURE, neglect, default, negligence, oversight, carelessness, dereliction, forgetfulness, slackness, laxity, laxness, slovenliness, neglectfulness, remissness

3 GAP, space, blank, exclusion, lacuna

omit *verb* 1 LEAVE OUT, miss (out), drop, exclude, eliminate, skip, give (something) a miss (*informal*)

<< OPPOSITE include

2 FORGET, fail, overlook, neglect, pass over, lose sight of, leave (something) undone, let (something) slide

omnipotence *noun* SUPREMACY, sovereignty, dominance, domination, mastery, primacy, ascendancy, pre-eminence, predominance, invincibility, supreme power, absolute rule, undisputed sway

<< OPPOSITE powerlessness

omnipotent *adjective* ALMIGHTY, supreme, invincible, all-powerful

<< OPPOSITE powerless

once *adverb* 1 ON ONE OCCASION, one time, one single time

2 AT ONE TIME, in the past, previously, formerly, long ago, in the old days, once upon a time, in times past, in times gone by

▷ *conjunction* AS SOON AS, when, after, the moment, immediately, the instant

▷▷ **at once** 1 IMMEDIATELY, now, right now, straight away, directly, promptly, instantly, right away, without delay, without hesitation, forthwith, this (very) minute, pronto (*informal*), this instant, straightway (*archaic*), posthaste, tout de suite (*French*)

2 SIMULTANEOUSLY, together, at the same time, all together, in concert, in unison, concurrently, in the same breath, in chorus, at *or* in one go (*informal*)

▷▷ **once and for all** FOR THE LAST TIME, finally, completely, for good, positively, permanently, for ever, decisively, inexorably, conclusively, irrevocably, for all time, inescapably, with finality, beyond the shadow of a doubt

▷▷ **once in a while** OCCASIONALLY, sometimes, at times, from time to time, on and off, irregularly, on occasion, now and again, periodically, every now and then, every so often, at intervals, off and on

oncoming *adjective* 1 APPROACHING, advancing, looming, onrushing

2 FORTHCOMING, coming, approaching, expected, threatening, advancing, gathering, imminent, impending, upcoming, fast-approaching

one-horse *adjective* (*informal*) (only used to describe *towns*) SMALL, slow, quiet, minor, obscure, sleepy, unimportant, small-time (*informal*), backwoods, tinpot (*Brit informal*)

onerous *adjective* TRYING, hard, taxing, demanding, difficult, heavy, responsible, grave, crushing, exhausting, exacting, formidable, troublesome, oppressive, weighty, laborious, burdensome, irksome, backbreaking, exigent

<< OPPOSITE easy

one-sided *adjective* 1 UNEQUAL, unfair, uneven, unjust, unbalanced, lopsided, inequitable, ill-matched

<< OPPOSITE equal

2 BIASED, prejudiced, weighted, twisted, coloured, unfair, partial, distorted, partisan, warped, slanted, unjust, discriminatory, lopsided

<< OPPOSITE unbiased

one-time *adjective* FORMER, previous, prior, sometime, late, erstwhile, quondam, ci-devant (*French*), ex-

ongoing *adjective* IN PROGRESS, current, growing, developing, advancing, progressing, evolving, unfolding, unfinished, extant

onlooker *noun* SPECTATOR, witness, observer, viewer, looker-on, watcher, eyewitness, bystander

only *adjective* SOLE, one, single, individual,

exclusive, unique, lone, solitary, one and only
▷ *adverb* 1 JUST, simply, purely, merely, no more than, nothing but, but, at most, at a push
2 HARDLY, just, barely, only just, scarcely, at most, at a push
3 EXCLUSIVELY, entirely, purely, solely

onset *noun* BEGINNING, start, rise, birth, kick-off (*informal*), outbreak, starting point, inception, commencement
<< OPPOSITE end

onslaught *noun* ATTACK, charge, campaign, strike, rush, assault, raid, invasion, offensive, blitz, onset, foray, incursion, onrush, inroad
<< OPPOSITE retreat

onus *noun* BURDEN, weight, responsibility, worry, task, stress, load, obligation, liability

onwards *or* **onward** *adverb* FORWARD, on, forwards, ahead, beyond, in front, forth

ooze[1] *verb* 1 SEEP, well, drop, escape, strain, leak, drain, sweat, filter, bleed, weep, drip, trickle, leach, dribble, percolate
2 EMIT, release, leak, sweat, bleed, discharge, drip, leach, give out, dribble, exude, give off, excrete, overflow with, pour forth
3 EXUDE, emit, radiate, display, exhibit, manifest, emanate, overflow with

ooze[2] *noun* MUD, clay, dirt, muck, silt, sludge, mire, slime, slob (*Irish*), gloop (*informal*), alluvium

opaque *adjective* 1 CLOUDY, clouded, dull, dim, muddied, muddy, murky, hazy, filmy, turbid, lustreless
<< OPPOSITE clear
2 INCOMPREHENSIBLE, obscure, unclear, difficult, puzzling, baffling, enigmatic, perplexing, impenetrable, unintelligible, cryptic, unfathomable, abstruse, obfuscated, beyond comprehension
<< OPPOSITE lucid

open *adjective* 1 UNCLOSED, unlocked, ajar, unfastened, yawning, gaping, unlatched, unbolted, partly open, unbarred, off the latch
<< OPPOSITE closed
2 UNSEALED, unstoppered
<< OPPOSITE unopened
3 EXTENDED, expanded, unfolded, stretched out, spread out, unfurled, straightened out, unrolled
<< OPPOSITE shut
4 FRANK, direct, natural, plain, innocent, straightforward, sincere, transparent, honest, candid, truthful, upfront (*informal*), plain-spoken, above board, unreserved, artless, ingenuous, guileless, straight from the shoulder (*informal*)
<< OPPOSITE sly
5 OBVIOUS, clear, frank, plain, apparent, visible, patent, evident, distinct, pronounced, manifest, transparent, noticeable, blatant, conspicuous, downright, overt, unmistakable, palpable, recognizable, avowed, flagrant, perceptible, much in evidence, undisguised, unsubtle, barefaced, unconcealed
<< OPPOSITE hidden
6 RECEPTIVE, welcoming, sympathetic, responsive, amenable
7 SUSCEPTIBLE, subject, exposed, vulnerable, in danger, disposed, liable, wide open, unprotected, at the mercy of, left open, laid bare, an easy target for, undefended, laid open, defenceless against, unfortified
<< OPPOSITE defended
8 UNRESOLVED, unsettled, undecided, debatable, up in the air, moot, arguable, yet to be decided
9 CLEAR, free, passable, uncluttered, unhindered, unimpeded, navigable, unobstructed, unhampered
<< OPPOSITE obstructed
10 UNENCLOSED, wide, rolling, sweeping, exposed, extensive, bare, spacious, wide-open, undeveloped, uncrowded, unfenced, not built-up, unsheltered
<< OPPOSITE enclosed
11 UNDONE, gaping, unbuttoned, unzipped, agape, unfastened
<< OPPOSITE fastened
12 AVAILABLE, to hand, accessible, handy, vacant, on hand, obtainable, attainable, at your fingertips, at your disposal
13 GENERAL, public, free, catholic, broad, universal, blanket, unconditional, across-the-board, unqualified, all-inclusive, unrestricted, overarching, free to all, nondiscriminatory, one-size-fits-all
<< OPPOSITE restricted
14 VACANT, free, available, empty, up for grabs (*informal*), unoccupied, unfilled, unengaged
15 GENEROUS, kind, liberal, charitable, benevolent, prodigal, bountiful, open-handed, unstinting, beneficent, bounteous, munificent, ungrudging
16 GAPPY, loose, lacy, porous, honeycombed, spongy, filigree, fretted, holey, openwork
▷ *verb* 1 UNFASTEN, unlock, unclasp, throw wide, unbar, unclose
<< OPPOSITE close
2 UNWRAP, uncover, undo, unravel, untie, unstrap, unseal, unlace
<< OPPOSITE wrap
3 UNCORK, crack (open)
4 UNFOLD, spread (out), expand, stretch out, unfurl, unroll
<< OPPOSITE fold
5 CLEAR, unblock
<< OPPOSITE block
6 UNDO, loosen, unbutton, unfasten

<< OPPOSITE fasten
7 BEGIN BUSINESS
8 START, begin, launch, trigger, kick off (*informal*), initiate, commence, get going, instigate, kick-start, inaugurate, set in motion, get (something) off the ground (*informal*), enter upon
<< OPPOSITE end
9 BEGIN, start, commence
<< OPPOSITE end

open-air *modifier* OUTDOOR, outside, out-of-door(s), alfresco

open-and-shut *adjective* STRAIGHTFORWARD, simple, obvious, routine, clear-cut, foregone, noncontroversial

opening *adjective* FIRST, early, earliest, beginning, premier, primary, initial, maiden, inaugural, commencing, introductory, initiatory
▷ *noun* 1 BEGINNING, start, launch, launching, birth, dawn, outset, starting point, onset, overture, initiation, inauguration, inception, commencement, kickoff (*informal*), opening move
<< OPPOSITE ending
2 HOLE, break, space, tear, split, crack, gap, rent, breach, slot, outlet, vent, puncture, rupture, aperture, cleft, chink, fissure, orifice, perforation, interstice
<< OPPOSITE blockage
3 OPPORTUNITY, chance, break (*informal*), time, place, moment, window, occasion, look-in (*informal*)
4 JOB, position, post, situation, opportunity, vacancy

openly *adverb* 1 FRANKLY, plainly, in public, honestly, face to face, overtly, candidly, unreservedly, unhesitatingly, forthrightly, straight from the shoulder (*informal*)
<< OPPOSITE privately
2 BLATANTLY, publicly, brazenly, unashamedly, shamelessly, in full view, flagrantly, unabashedly, wantonly, undisguisedly, without pretence
<< OPPOSITE secretly

open-minded *adjective* UNPREJUDICED, liberal, free, balanced, catholic, broad, objective, reasonable, enlightened, tolerant, impartial, receptive, unbiased, even-handed, dispassionate, fair-minded, broad-minded, undogmatic
<< OPPOSITE narrow-minded

openness *noun* FRANKNESS, honesty, truthfulness, naturalness, bluntness, forthrightness, ingenuousness, artlessness, guilelessness, candidness, freeness, open-heartedness, absence of reserve, candour *or (U.S.)* candor, sincerity *or* sincereness, unreservedness

operate *verb* 1 MANAGE, run, direct, handle, govern, oversee, supervise, preside over, be in charge of, call the shots in, superintend, call the tune in
2 FUNCTION, work, act, be in business, be in action
3 RUN, work, use, control, drive, manoeuvre
4 WORK, go, run, perform, function
<< OPPOSITE break down
5 PERFORM SURGERY, carry out surgery, put someone under the knife (*informal*)

operation *noun* 1 UNDERTAKING, process, affair, organization, proceeding, procedure, coordination
2 MANOEUVRE, campaign, movement, exercise, assault, deployment
3 BUSINESS, concern, firm, organization, corporation, venture, enterprise
4 SURGERY, surgical operation, surgical intervention
5 PERFORMANCE, working, running, action, movement, functioning, motion, manipulation
6 EFFECT, force, activity, agency, influence, impact, effectiveness, instrumentality
▷▷ **in operation** IN ACTION, current, effective, going, functioning, active, in effect, in business, operative, in force

operational *adjective* WORKING, going, running, ready, functioning, operative, viable, functional, up and running, workable, usable, in working order
<< OPPOSITE inoperative

operative *adjective* 1 IN FORCE, current, effective, standing, functioning, active, efficient, in effect, in business, operational, functional, in operation, workable, serviceable
<< OPPOSITE inoperative
2 RELEVANT, important, key, fitting, significant, appropriate, crucial, influential, apt, applicable, indicative, pertinent, apposite, germane
▷ *noun* 1 WORKER, hand, employee, mechanic, labourer, workman, artisan, machinist, working man *or* working woman
2 (*US & Canad*) SPY, secret agent, double agent, secret service agent, undercover agent, mole, foreign agent, fifth columnist, nark (*Brit, Austral & NZ slang*)

operator *noun* 1 WORKER, hand, driver, mechanic, operative, conductor, technician, handler, skilled employee
2 CONTRACTOR, dealer, trader, administrator
3 (*informal*) MANIPULATOR, worker, mover, Machiavellian, mover and shaker, machinator, wheeler-dealer (*informal*), wirepuller

opiate *noun* NARCOTIC, drug, downer (*slang*), painkiller, sedative, tranquillizer, bromide, anodyne, analgesic, soporific, pacifier, nepenthe

opine *verb* (*Formal*) SUGGEST, say, think, believe, judge, suppose, declare, conclude, venture, volunteer, imply, intimate, presume, conjecture, surmise, ween (*poetic*), give as your opinion

opinion *noun* **1** BELIEF, feeling, view, idea, theory, notion, conviction, point of view, sentiment, viewpoint, persuasion, conjecture
2 ESTIMATION, view, impression, assessment, judgment, evaluation, conception, appraisal, considered opinion
▷▷ **be of the opinion** BELIEVE, think, hold, consider, judge, suppose, maintain, imagine, guess (*informal, chiefly US & Canad*), reckon, conclude, be convinced, speculate, presume, conjecture, postulate, surmise, be under the impression
▷▷ **matter of opinion** DEBATABLE POINT, debatable, open question, open to question, moot point, open for discussion, matter of judgment

opinionated *adjective* DOGMATIC, prejudiced, biased, arrogant, adamant, stubborn, assertive, uncompromising, single-minded, inflexible, bigoted, dictatorial, imperious, overbearing, obstinate, doctrinaire, obdurate, cocksure, pig-headed, self-assertive, bull-headed
<< OPPOSITE open-minded

opponent *noun* **1** ADVERSARY, rival, enemy, the opposition, competitor, challenger, foe, contestant, antagonist
<< OPPOSITE ally
2 OPPOSER, dissident, objector, dissentient, disputant
<< OPPOSITE supporter

opportune *adjective* (*Formal*) TIMELY, fitting, fit, welcome, lucky, appropriate, suitable, happy, proper, convenient, fortunate, favourable, apt, advantageous, auspicious, fortuitous, well-timed, propitious, heaven-sent, felicitous, providential, seasonable, falling into your lap
<< OPPOSITE inopportune

opportunism *noun* EXPEDIENCY, convenience, exploitation, realism, manipulation, pragmatism, capitalization, realpolitik, utilitarianism, making hay while the sun shines (*informal*), striking while the iron is hot (*informal*), unscrupulousness, Machiavellianism

opportunity *noun* CHANCE, opening, time, turn, hour, break (*informal*), moment, window, possibility, occasion, slot, scope, look-in (*informal*)

oppose *verb* BE AGAINST, fight (against), check, bar, block, prevent, take on, counter, contest, resist, confront, face, combat, defy, thwart, contradict, withstand, stand up to, hinder, struggle against, obstruct, fly in the face of, take issue with, be hostile to, counterattack, speak (out) against, be in opposition to, be in defiance of, strive against, set your face against, take *or* make a stand against
<< OPPOSITE support

opposed *adjective* **1** *with* **to** AGAINST, anti (*informal*), hostile, adverse, contra (*informal*), in opposition, averse, antagonistic, inimical, (dead) set against
2 CONTRARY, opposite, conflicting, opposing, clashing, counter, adverse, contradictory, in opposition, incompatible, antithetical, antipathetic, dissentient

opposing *adjective* **1** CONFLICTING, different, opposed, contrasting, opposite, differing, contrary, contradictory, incompatible, irreconcilable
2 RIVAL, warring, conflicting, clashing, competing, enemy, opposite, hostile, combatant, antagonistic, antipathetic

opposite *adjective* **1** FACING, other, opposing
2 DIFFERENT, conflicting, opposed, contrasted, contrasting, unlike, differing, contrary, diverse, adverse, at odds, contradictory, inconsistent, dissimilar, divergent, irreconcilable, at variance, poles apart, diametrically opposed, antithetical, streets apart
<< OPPOSITE alike
3 RIVAL, conflicting, opposed, opposing, competing, hostile, antagonistic, inimical
▷ *preposition often with* **to** FACING, face to face with, across from, eyeball to eyeball with (*informal*)
▷ *noun* REVERSE, contrary, converse, antithesis, the other extreme, contradiction, inverse, the other side of the coin (*informal*), obverse

opposition *noun* **1** HOSTILITY, resistance, resentment, disapproval, obstruction, animosity, aversion, antagonism, antipathy, obstructiveness, counteraction, contrariety
<< OPPOSITE support
2 OPPONENT(s), competition, rival(s), enemy, competitor(s), other side, challenger(s), foe, contestant(s), antagonist(s)

oppress *verb* **1** SUBJUGATE, abuse, suppress, wrong, master, overcome, crush, overwhelm, put down, subdue, overpower, persecute, rule over, enslave, maltreat, hold sway over, trample underfoot, bring someone to heel, tyrannize over, rule with an iron hand, bring someone under the yoke
<< OPPOSITE liberate
2 DEPRESS, burden, discourage, torment, daunt, harass, afflict, sadden, vex, weigh down, dishearten, cast someone down, dispirit, take the heart out of, deject, lie *or*

weigh heavy upon, make someone despondent

oppressed *adjective* DOWNTRODDEN, abused, exploited, subject, burdened, distressed, slave, disadvantaged, helpless, misused, enslaved, prostrate, underprivileged, subservient, subjugated, browbeaten, maltreated, tyrannized, henpecked

<< OPPOSITE liberated

oppression *noun* PERSECUTION, control, suffering, abuse, injury, injustice, cruelty, domination, repression, brutality, suppression, severity, tyranny, authoritarianism, harshness, despotism, ill-treatment, subjugation, subjection, maltreatment

<< OPPOSITE justice

oppressive *adjective* 1 TYRANNICAL, severe, harsh, heavy, overwhelming, cruel, brutal, authoritarian, unjust, repressive, Draconian, autocratic, inhuman, dictatorial, coercive, imperious, domineering, overbearing, burdensome, despotic, high-handed, peremptory, overweening, tyrannous

<< OPPOSITE merciful

2 STIFLING, close, heavy, sticky, overpowering, suffocating, stuffy, humid, torrid, sultry, airless, muggy

oppressor *noun* PERSECUTOR, tyrant, bully, scourge, tormentor, despot, autocrat, taskmaster, iron hand, slave-driver, harrier, intimidator, subjugator

opt *verb* CHOOSE, decide, prefer, select, elect, see fit, make a selection

<< OPPOSITE reject

▷▷ **opt for something** *or* **someone** CHOOSE, pick, select, take, adopt, go for, designate, decide on, single out, espouse, fix on, plump for, settle upon, exercise your discretion in favour of

optimistic *adjective* 1 HOPEFUL, positive, confident, encouraged, can-do (*informal*), bright, assured, cheerful, rosy, buoyant, idealistic, Utopian, sanguine, expectant, looking on the bright side, buoyed up, disposed to take a favourable view, seeing through rose-coloured spectacles

<< OPPOSITE pessimistic

2 ENCOURAGING, promising, bright, good, cheering, reassuring, satisfactory, rosy, heartening, auspicious, propitious

<< OPPOSITE discouraging

optimum *adjective* IDEAL, best, highest, finest, choicest, perfect, supreme, peak, outstanding, first-class, foremost, first-rate, flawless, superlative, pre-eminent, most excellent, A1 *or* A-one (*informal*), most favourable *or* advantageous

<< OPPOSITE worst

option *noun* CHOICE, alternative, selection, preference, freedom of choice, power to choose, election

optional *adjective* VOLUNTARY, open, discretionary, possible, extra, elective, up to the individual, noncompulsory

<< OPPOSITE compulsory

opulence *or* **opulency** *noun* 1 LUXURY, riches, wealth, splendour, prosperity, richness, affluence, voluptuousness, lavishness, sumptuousness, luxuriance

2 WEALTH, means, riches (*informal*), capital, resources, assets, fortune, substance, prosperity, affluence, easy circumstances, prosperousness

<< OPPOSITE poverty

opulent *adjective* 1 LUXURIOUS, expensive, magnificent, costly, splendid, lavish, sumptuous, plush (*informal*), ritzy (*slang*), de luxe, well-appointed

2 RICH, wealthy, prosperous, propertied, loaded (*slang*), flush (*informal*), affluent, well-off, well-heeled (*informal*), well-to-do, moneyed, filthy rich, stinking rich (*informal*), made of money (*informal*)

<< OPPOSITE poor

opus *noun* WORK, piece, production, creation, composition, work of art, brainchild, oeuvre (*French*)

oracle *noun* 1 PROPHET, diviner, sage, seer, clairvoyant, augur, soothsayer, sibyl, prophesier

2 PROPHECY, vision, revelation, forecast, prediction, divination, prognostication, augury, divine utterance

oral *adjective* SPOKEN, vocal, verbal, unwritten, viva voce

oration *noun* SPEECH, talk, address, lecture, discourse, harangue, homily, spiel (*informal*), disquisition, declamation, whaikorero (*NZ*)

orator *noun* PUBLIC SPEAKER, speaker, lecturer, spokesperson, declaimer, rhetorician, Cicero, spieler (*informal*), word-spinner, spokesman *or* spokeswoman

oratory *noun* RHETORIC, eloquence, public speaking, speech-making, expressiveness, fluency, a way with words, declamation, speechifying, grandiloquence, spieling (*informal*), whaikorero (*NZ*)

orb *noun* SPHERE, ball, circle, globe, round

orbit *noun* 1 PATH, course, track, cycle, circle, revolution, passage, rotation, trajectory, sweep, ellipse, circumgyration

2 SPHERE OF INFLUENCE, reach, range, influence, province, scope, sphere, domain, compass, ambit

▷ *verb* CIRCLE, ring, go round, compass, revolve around, encircle, circumscribe, gird, circumnavigate

orchestrate *verb* 1 ORGANIZE, plan, run, set

up, arrange, be responsible for, put together, see to (*informal*), marshal, coordinate, concert, stage-manage
2 SCORE, set, arrange, adapt

ordain *verb* 1 APPOINT, call, name, commission, select, elect, invest, install, nominate, anoint, consecrate, frock
2 (*Formal*) ORDER, will, rule, demand, require, direct, establish, command, dictate, prescribe, pronounce, lay down, decree, instruct, enact, legislate, enjoin
3 PREDESTINE, fate, intend, mark out, predetermine, foreordain, destine, preordain

ordeal *noun* HARDSHIP, trial, difficulty, test, labour, suffering, trouble(s), nightmare, burden, torture, misery, agony, torment, anguish, toil, affliction, tribulation(s), baptism of fire
<< OPPOSITE pleasure

order *verb* 1 COMMAND, instruct, direct, charge, demand, require, bid, compel, enjoin, adjure
<< OPPOSITE forbid
2 DECREE, rule, demand, establish, prescribe, pronounce, ordain
<< OPPOSITE ban
3 REQUEST, ask (for), book, demand, seek, call for, reserve, engage, apply for, contract for, solicit, requisition, put in for, send away for
4 ARRANGE, group, sort, class, position, range, file, rank, line up, organize, set out, sequence, catalogue, sort out, classify, array, dispose, tidy, marshal, lay out, tabulate, systematize, neaten, put in order, set in order, put to rights
<< OPPOSITE disarrange
▷ *noun* 1 INSTRUCTION, ruling, demand, direction, command, say-so (*informal*), dictate, decree, mandate, directive, injunction, behest, stipulation
2 REQUEST, booking, demand, commission, application, reservation, requisition
3 SEQUENCE, grouping, ordering, line, series, structure, chain, arrangement, line-up, succession, disposal, array, placement, classification, layout, progression, disposition, setup (*informal*), categorization, codification
4 ORGANIZATION, system, method, plan, pattern, arrangement, harmony, symmetry, regularity, propriety, neatness, tidiness, orderliness
<< OPPOSITE chaos
5 PEACE, control, law, quiet, calm, discipline, law and order, tranquillity, peacefulness, lawfulness
6 SOCIETY, company, group, club, union, community, league, association, institute, organization, circle, corporation, lodge, guild, sect, fellowship, fraternity, brotherhood, sisterhood, sodality
7 CLASS, set, rank, degree, grade, sphere, caste
8 (*Biology*) KIND, group, class, family, form, sort, type, variety, cast, species, breed, strain, category, tribe, genre, classification, genus, ilk, subdivision, subclass, taxonomic group
▷▷ **in order** 1 TIDY, ordered, neat, arranged, trim, orderly, spruce, well-kept, well-ordered, shipshape, spick-and-span, trig (*archaic* or *dialect*), in apple-pie order (*informal*)
2 APPROPRIATE, right, fitting, seemly, called for, correct, suitable, acceptable, proper, to the point, apt, applicable, pertinent, befitting, well-suited, well-timed, apposite, germane, to the purpose, meet (*archaic*), O.K. *or* okay (*informal*)
▷▷ **out of order** 1 NOT WORKING, broken, broken-down, ruined, bust (*informal*), defective, wonky (*Brit slang*), not functioning, out of commission, on the blink (*slang*), on its last legs, inoperative, kaput (*informal*), in disrepair, gone haywire (*informal*), nonfunctional, on the fritz (*US slang*), gone phut (*informal*), U.S. (*informal*)
2 IMPROPER, wrong, unsuitable, not done, not on (*informal*), unfitting, vulgar, out of place, unseemly, untoward, unbecoming, impolite, off-colour, out of turn, uncalled-for, not cricket (*informal*), indelicate, indecorous

orderly *adjective* 1 WELL-BEHAVED, controlled, disciplined, quiet, restrained, law-abiding, nonviolent, peaceable, decorous
<< OPPOSITE disorderly
2 WELL-ORGANIZED, ordered, regular, in order, organized, trim, precise, neat, tidy, systematic, businesslike, methodical, well-kept, shipshape, systematized, well-regulated, in apple-pie order (*informal*)
<< OPPOSITE disorganized

ordinance *noun* RULE, order, law, ruling, standard, guide, direction, principle, command, regulation, guideline, criterion, decree, canon, statute, fiat, edict, dictum, precept

ordinarily *adverb* USUALLY, generally, normally, commonly, regularly, routinely, in general, as a rule, habitually, customarily, in the usual way, as is usual, as is the custom, in the general run (of things)
<< OPPOSITE seldom

ordinary *adjective* 1 USUAL, standard, normal, common, established, settled, regular, familiar, household, typical, conventional, routine, stock, everyday, prevailing, accustomed, customary, habitual, quotidian, wonted
2 COMMONPLACE, plain, modest, humble, stereotyped, pedestrian, mundane, vanilla (*slang*), stale, banal, unremarkable, prosaic, run-of-the-mill, humdrum, homespun,

uninteresting, workaday, common or garden (*informal*), unmemorable
3 AVERAGE, middling, fair, indifferent, not bad, mediocre, so-so (*informal*), unremarkable, tolerable, run-of-the-mill, passable, undistinguished, uninspired, unexceptional, bog-standard (*Brit & Irish slang*), no great shakes (*informal*), dime-a-dozen (*informal*)
<< OPPOSITE extraordinary
▷▷ **out of the ordinary** UNUSUAL, different, odd, important, special, striking, surprising, significant, strange, exciting, rare, impressive, extraordinary, outstanding, remarkable, bizarre, distinguished, unexpected, curious, exceptional, notable, unfamiliar, abnormal, queer, uncommon, singular, unconventional, noteworthy, atypical

ordnance *noun* WEAPONS, arms, guns, artillery, cannon, firearms, weaponry, big guns, armaments, munitions, materiel, instruments of war

organ *noun* 1 BODY PART, part of the body, member, element, biological structure
2 NEWSPAPER, paper, medium, voice, agency, channel, vehicle, journal, publication, rag (*informal*), gazette, periodical, mouthpiece

organic *adjective* 1 NATURAL, biological, living, live, vital, animate, biotic
2 SYSTEMATIC, ordered, structured, organized, integrated, orderly, standardized, methodical, well-ordered, systematized
3 INTEGRAL, fundamental, constitutional, structural, inherent, innate, immanent

organism *noun* CREATURE, being, thing, body, animal, structure, beast, entity, living thing, critter (*US dialect*)

organization *or* **organisation** *noun* 1 GROUP, company, party, body, concern, league, association, band, institution, gathering, circle, corporation, federation, outfit (*informal*), faction, consortium, syndicate, combine, congregation, confederation
2 MANAGEMENT, running, planning, making, control, operation, handling, structuring, administration, direction, regulation, construction, organizing, supervision, governance, formulation, coordination, methodology, superintendence
3 STRUCTURE, grouping, plan, system, form, design, method, pattern, make-up, arrangement, construction, constitution, format, formation, framework, composition, chemistry, configuration, conformation, interrelation of parts

organize *or* **organise** *verb* 1 ARRANGE, run, plan, form, prepare, establish, set up, shape, schedule, frame, look after, be responsible for, construct, constitute, devise, put together, take care of, see to (*informal*), get together, marshal, contrive, get going, coordinate, fix up, straighten out, lay the foundations of, lick into shape, jack up (*NZ informal*)
<< OPPOSITE disrupt
2 PUT IN ORDER, arrange, group, list, file, index, catalogue, classify, codify, pigeonhole, tabulate, inventory, systematize, dispose
<< OPPOSITE muddle

orgasm *noun* CLIMAX, coming (*taboo slang*), pleasure, the big O (*informal*), (sexual) satisfaction

orgy *noun* 1 PARTY, celebration, rave (*Brit slang*), revel, festivity, bender (*informal*), debauch, revelry, carouse, Saturnalia, bacchanal, rave-up (*Brit slang*), bacchanalia, carousal, hooley *or* hoolie (*chiefly Irish & NZ*)
2 SPREE, fit, spell, run, session, excess, bout, indulgence, binge (*informal*), splurge, surfeit, overindulgence

orient *or* **orientate** *verb* ADJUST, settle, adapt, tune, convert, alter, compose, accommodate, accustom, reconcile, align, harmonize, familiarize, acclimatize, find your feet (*informal*)
▷▷ **orient yourself** GET YOUR BEARINGS, get the lie of the land, establish your location

orientation *noun* 1 INCLINATION, tendency, bias, leaning, bent, disposition, predisposition, predilection, proclivity, partiality, turn of mind
2 INDUCTION, introduction, breaking in, adjustment, settling in, adaptation, initiation, assimilation, familiarization, acclimatization
3 POSITION, situation, location, site, bearings, direction, arrangement, whereabouts, disposition, coordination

orifice *noun* OPENING, space, hole, split, mouth, gap, rent, breach, vent, pore, rupture, aperture, cleft, chink, fissure, perforation, interstice

origin *noun* 1 BEGINNING, start, birth, source, launch, foundation, creation, dawning, early stages, emergence, outset, starting point, onset, genesis, initiation, inauguration, inception, font (*poetic*), commencement, fountain, fount, origination, fountainhead, mainspring
<< OPPOSITE end
2 ROOT, source, basis, beginnings, base, cause, spring, roots, seed, foundation, nucleus, germ, provenance, derivation, wellspring, fons et origo (*Latin*)
3 ANCESTRY, family, race, beginnings, stock, blood, birth, heritage, ancestors, descent, pedigree, extraction, lineage, forebears, antecedents, parentage, forefathers, genealogy, derivation, progenitors, stirps

original *adjective* 1 FIRST, earliest, early, initial, aboriginal, primitive, pristine, primordial, primeval, autochthonous

2 INITIAL, first, starting, opening, primary, inaugural, commencing, introductory
<< OPPOSITE final
3 AUTHENTIC, real, actual, genuine, legitimate, first generation, bona fide, the real McCoy
<< OPPOSITE copied
4 NEW, fresh, novel, different, unusual, unknown, unprecedented, innovative, unfamiliar, unconventional, seminal, ground-breaking, untried, innovatory, newfangled
<< OPPOSITE unoriginal
5 CREATIVE, inspired, imaginative, artistic, fertile, ingenious, visionary, inventive, resourceful
▷ *noun* **1** PROTOTYPE, master, pattern
<< OPPOSITE copy
2 CHARACTER, eccentric, case (*informal*), card (*informal*), nut (*slang*), flake (*slang, chiefly US*), anomaly, oddity, oddball (*informal*), nonconformist, wacko (*slang*), odd bod (*informal*), queer fish (*Brit informal*), weirdo *or* weirdie (*informal*)

originality *noun* NOVELTY, imagination, creativity, innovation, new ideas, individuality, ingenuity, freshness, uniqueness, boldness, inventiveness, cleverness, resourcefulness, break with tradition, newness, unfamiliarity, creative spirit, unorthodoxy, unconventionality, creativeness, innovativeness, imaginativeness
<< OPPOSITE conventionality

originally *adverb* INITIALLY, first, firstly, at first, primarily, at the start, in the first place, to begin with, at the outset, in the beginning, in the early stages

originate *verb* **1** BEGIN, start, emerge, come, issue, happen, rise, appear, spring, flow, be born, proceed, arise, dawn, stem, derive, commence, emanate, crop up (*informal*), come into being, come into existence
<< OPPOSITE end
2 INVENT, produce, create, form, develop, design, launch, set up, introduce, imagine, institute, generate, come up with (*informal*), pioneer, evolve, devise, initiate, conceive, bring about, formulate, give birth to, contrive, improvise, dream up (*informal*), inaugurate, think up, set in motion

originator *noun* CREATOR, father *or* mother, founder, author, maker, framer, designer, architect, pioneer, generator, inventor, innovator, prime mover, initiator, begetter

ornament *noun* **1** DECORATION, trimming, accessory, garnish, frill, festoon, trinket, bauble, flounce, gewgaw, knick-knack, furbelow, falderal
2 EMBELLISHMENT, trimming, decoration, embroidery, elaboration, adornment, ornamentation
▷ *verb* DECORATE, trim, adorn, enhance, deck, array, dress up, enrich, brighten, garnish, gild, do up (*informal*), embellish, emblazon, festoon, bedeck, beautify, prettify, bedizen (*archaic*), engarland

ornamental *adjective* DECORATIVE, pretty, attractive, fancy, enhancing, for show, embellishing, showy, beautifying, nonfunctional

ornamentation *noun* DECORATION, trimming, frills, garnishing, embroidery, enrichment, elaboration, embellishment, adornment, beautification, ornateness

ornate *adjective* ELABORATE, fancy, decorated, detailed, beautiful, complex, busy, complicated, elegant, extravagant, baroque, ornamented, fussy, flowery, showy, ostentatious, rococo, florid, bedecked, overelaborate, high-wrought, aureate
<< OPPOSITE plain

orthodox *adjective* **1** ESTABLISHED, official, accepted, received, common, popular, traditional, normal, regular, usual, ordinary, approved, familiar, acknowledged, conventional, routine, customary, well-established, kosher (*informal*)
<< OPPOSITE unorthodox
2 CONFORMIST, conservative, traditional, strict, devout, observant, doctrinal
<< OPPOSITE nonconformist

orthodoxy *noun* **1** DOCTRINE, teaching, opinion, principle, belief, convention, canon, creed, dogma, tenet, precept, article of faith
2 CONFORMITY, received wisdom, traditionalism, inflexibility, conformism, conventionality
<< OPPOSITE nonconformity

oscillate *verb* **1** FLUCTUATE, swing, vary, sway, waver, veer, rise and fall, vibrate, undulate, go up and down, seesaw
2 WAVER, change, swing, shift, vary, sway, alternate, veer, ebb and flow, vacillate, seesaw
<< OPPOSITE settle

oscillation *noun* **1** FLUCTUATION, swing, variation, instability, imbalance, wavering, volatility, variability, unpredictability, seesawing, disequilibrium, capriciousness, mutability, inconstancy, changeableness
2 WAVERING, swing, shift, swaying, alteration, veering, seesawing, vacillation

ostensible *adjective* APPARENT, seeming, supposed, alleged, so-called, pretended, exhibited, manifest, outward, superficial, professed, purported, avowed, specious

ostensibly *adverb* APPARENTLY, seemingly, supposedly, outwardly, on the surface, on the face of it, superficially, to all intents and purposes, professedly, speciously, for the ostensible purpose of

ostentatious *adjective* PRETENTIOUS, extravagant, flamboyant, flash (*informal*), loud, dashing, inflated, conspicuous, vulgar, brash, high-flown, flashy, pompous, flaunted, flaunting, grandiose, crass, gaudy, showy, swanky (*informal*), snobbish, puffed up, specious, boastful, obtrusive, highfalutin (*informal*), arty-farty (*informal*), magniloquent
<< OPPOSITE modest

ostracism *noun* EXCLUSION, boycott, isolation, exile, rejection, expulsion, avoidance, cold-shouldering, renunciation, banishment
<< OPPOSITE acceptance

other *determiner* **1** ADDITIONAL, more, further, new, added, extra, fresh, spare, supplementary, auxiliary
2 DIFFERENT, alternative, contrasting, distinct, diverse, dissimilar, separate, alternative, substitute, alternate, unrelated, variant
3 REMAINING, left-over, residual, extant

otherwise *sentence connector* OR ELSE, or, if not, or then
▷ *adverb* **1** APART FROM THAT, in other ways, in (all) other respects
2 DIFFERENTLY, any other way, in another way, contrarily, contrastingly, in contrary fashion

ounce *noun* SHRED, bit, drop, trace, scrap, grain, particle, fragment, atom, crumb, snippet, speck, whit, iota

oust *verb* EXPEL, turn out, dismiss, exclude, exile, discharge, throw out, relegate, displace, topple, banish, eject, depose, evict, dislodge, unseat, dispossess, send packing, turf out (*informal*), disinherit, drum out, show someone the door, give someone the bum's rush (*slang*), throw out on your ear (*informal*)

out *adjective* **1** NOT IN, away, elsewhere, outside, gone, abroad, from home, absent, not here, not there, not at home
2 EXTINGUISHED, ended, finished, dead, cold, exhausted, expired, used up, doused, at an end
<< OPPOSITE alight
3 IN BLOOM, opening, open, flowering, blooming, in flower, in full bloom
4 AVAILABLE, on sale, in the shops, at hand, to be had, purchasable, procurable
5 NOT ALLOWED, banned, forbidden, ruled out, vetoed, not on (*informal*), unacceptable, prohibited, taboo, verboten (*German*)
<< OPPOSITE allowed
6 OUT OF DATE, dead, square (*informal*), old-fashioned, dated, outdated, unfashionable, antiquated, outmoded, passé, old hat, behind the times, out of style, démodé (*French*), not with it (*informal*)
<< OPPOSITE fashionable
7 INACCURATE, wrong, incorrect, faulty, off the mark, erroneous, off target, wide of the mark
<< OPPOSITE accurate
8 REVEALED, exposed, common knowledge, public knowledge, (out) in the open
<< OPPOSITE kept secret
▷ *verb* EXPOSE, uncover, unmask

out-and-out *adjective* ABSOLUTE, complete, total, perfect, sheer, utter, outright, thorough, downright, consummate, unqualified, unmitigated, dyed-in-the-wool, thoroughgoing, unalloyed, arrant, deep-dyed (*usually derogatory*)

outbreak *noun* **1** ERUPTION, burst, explosion, epidemic, rash, outburst, flare-up, flash, spasm, upsurge
2 ONSET, beginning, outset, opening, dawn, commencement

outburst *noun* **1** EXPLOSION, surge, outbreak, eruption, flare-up
2 FIT, storm, attack, gush, flare-up, eruption, spasm, outpouring, paroxysm

outcast *noun* PARIAH, exile, outlaw, undesirable, untouchable, leper, vagabond, wretch, persona non grata (*Latin*)

outclass *verb* SURPASS, top, beat, cap (*informal*), exceed, eclipse, overshadow, excel, transcend, outstrip, outdo, outshine, leave standing (*informal*), tower above, go one better than (*informal*), be a cut above (*informal*), run rings around (*informal*), outdistance, outrank, put in the shade, leave in the shade

outcome *noun* RESULT, end, consequence, conclusion, end result, payoff (*informal*), upshot

outcry *noun* PROTEST, complaint, objection, cry, dissent, outburst, disapproval, clamour, uproar, commotion, protestation, exclamation, formal complaint, hue and cry, hullaballoo, demurral

outdated *adjective* OLD-FASHIONED, dated, obsolete, out of date, passé, antique, archaic, unfashionable, antiquated, outmoded, behind the times, out of style, obsolescent, démodé (*French*), out of the ark (*informal*), oldfangled
<< OPPOSITE modern

outdo *verb* SURPASS, best, top, beat, overcome, exceed, eclipse, overshadow, excel, transcend, outstrip, get the better of, outclass, outshine, tower above, outsmart (*informal*), outmanoeuvre, go one better than (*informal*), run rings around (*informal*), outfox, outdistance, be one up on, score points off, put in the shade, outjockey

outdoor *adjective* OPEN-AIR, outside, out-of-door(s), alfresco
<< OPPOSITE indoor

outer *adjective* **1** EXTERNAL, outside, outward, exterior, exposed, outermost
<< OPPOSITE inner
2 SURFACE, external, outward, exterior, superficial
3 OUTLYING, remote, distant, provincial, out-

of-the-way, peripheral, far-flung
<< OPPOSITE central

outfit *noun* 1 COSTUME, dress, clothes, clothing, suit, gear (*informal*), get-up (*informal*), kit, ensemble, apparel, attire, garb, togs (*informal*), threads (*slang*), schmutter (*slang*), rigout (*informal*)
2 (*informal*) GROUP, company, team, set, party, firm, association, unit, crowd, squad, organization, crew, gang, corps, setup (*informal*), galère (*French*)
▷ *verb* 1 EQUIP, stock, supply, turn out, appoint, provision, furnish, fit out, deck out, kit out, fit up, accoutre
2 DRESS, clothe, attire, deck out, kit out, rig out

outfitter *noun* (*Old-fashioned*) CLOTHIER, tailor, couturier, dressmaker, seamstress, haberdasher (*US*), costumier, garment maker, modiste

outflow *noun* 1 STREAM, issue, flow, rush, emergence, spate, deluge, outpouring, effusion, emanation, efflux
2 DISCHARGE, flow, jet, cascade, ebb, gush, drainage, torrent, deluge, spurt, spout, outpouring, outfall, efflux, effluence, debouchment

outgoing *adjective* 1 LEAVING, last, former, past, previous, retiring, withdrawing, prior, departing, erstwhile, late, ex-
<< OPPOSITE incoming
2 SOCIABLE, open, social, warm, friendly, accessible, expansive, cordial, genial, affable, extrovert, approachable, gregarious, communicative, convivial, demonstrative, unreserved, companionable
<< OPPOSITE reserved

outgoings *plural noun* EXPENSES, costs, payments, expenditure, overheads, outlay

outgrowth *noun* 1 PRODUCT, result, development, fruit, consequence, outcome, legacy, emergence, derivative, spin-off, by-product, end result, offshoot, upshot
2 OFFSHOOT, shoot, branch, limb, projection, sprout, node, outcrop, appendage, scion, protuberance, excrescence

outing *noun* JOURNEY, run, trip, tour, expedition, excursion, spin (*informal*), ramble, jaunt, pleasure trip

outlandish *adjective* STRANGE, odd, extraordinary, wonderful, funny, bizarre, fantastic, astonishing, curious, weird, foreign, alien, exotic, exceptional, peculiar, eccentric, abnormal, out-of-the-way, queer, irregular, singular, grotesque, far-out (*slang*), unheard-of, preposterous, off-the-wall (*slang*), left-field (*informal*), freakish, barbarous, outré, daggy (*Austral & NZ informal*)
<< OPPOSITE normal

outlast *verb* OUTLIVE, survive, live after, outstay, live on after, endure beyond, outwear, remain alive after

outlaw *noun* BANDIT, criminal, thief, crook, robber, fugitive, outcast, delinquent, felon, highwayman, desperado, marauder, brigand, lawbreaker, footpad (*archaic*)
▷ *verb* 1 BAN, bar, veto, forbid, condemn, exclude, embargo, suppress, prohibit, banish, disallow, proscribe, make illegal, interdict
<< OPPOSITE legalise
2 BANISH, excommunicate, ostracize, put a price on (someone's) head

outlay *noun* EXPENDITURE, cost, spending, charge, investment, payment, expense(s), outgoings, disbursement

outlet *noun* 1 SHOP, store, supermarket, market, mart, boutique, emporium, hypermarket
2 CHANNEL, release, medium, avenue, vent, conduit, safety valve, means of expression
3 PIPE, opening, channel, passage, tube, exit, canal, way out, funnel, conduit, duct, orifice, egress

outline *noun* 1 SUMMARY, review, résumé, abstract, summing-up, digest, rundown, compendium, main features, synopsis, rough idea, précis, bare facts, thumbnail sketch, recapitulation, abridgment
2 DRAFT, plan, drawing, frame, tracing, rough, framework, sketch, skeleton, layout, delineation, preliminary form
3 SHAPE, lines, form, figure, profile, silhouette, configuration, contour(s), delineation, lineament(s)
▷ *verb* 1 SUMMARIZE, review, draft, plan, trace, sketch (in), sum up, encapsulate, delineate, rough out, adumbrate
2 SILHOUETTE, etch, delineate

outlive *verb* SURVIVE, outlast, live on after, endure beyond, remain alive after

outlook *noun* 1 ATTITUDE, views, opinion, position, approach, mood, perspective, point of view, stance, viewpoint, disposition, standpoint, frame of mind
2 PROSPECT(s), future, expectations, forecast, prediction, projection, probability, prognosis
3 VIEW, prospect, scene, aspect, perspective, panorama, vista

outlying *adjective* REMOTE, isolated, distant, outer, provincial, out-of-the-way, peripheral, far-off, secluded, far-flung, faraway, in the middle of nowhere, off the beaten track, backwoods, godforsaken

outmanoeuvre *or US* **outmaneuver** *verb* OUTWIT, outdo, get the better of, circumvent, outflank, outsmart (*informal*), steal a march on (*informal*), put one over on (*informal*), outfox, run rings round (*informal*), outthink, outgeneral, outjockey

outmoded *adjective* OLD-FASHIONED, passé, dated, out, dead, square (*informal*), ancient, antique, outdated, obsolete, out-of-date, old-time, archaic, unfashionable, superseded, bygone, antiquated, anachronistic, olden (*archaic*), behind the times, superannuated, fossilized, out of style, antediluvian, outworn, obsolescent, démodé (*French*), out of the ark (*informal*), not with it (*informal*), oldfangled
<< OPPOSITE modern

out of date *adjective* 1 OLD-FASHIONED, ancient, dated, discarded, extinct, outdated, stale, obsolete, démodé (*French*), archaic, unfashionable, superseded, antiquated, outmoded, passé, old hat, behind the times, superannuated, out of style, outworn, obsolescent, out of the ark (*informal*), oldfangled
<< OPPOSITE modern
2 INVALID, expired, lapsed, void, superseded, elapsed, null and void

out of the way *adjective* 1 REMOTE, far, distant, isolated, lonely, obscure, far-off, secluded, inaccessible, far-flung, faraway, outlying, in the middle of nowhere, off the beaten track, backwoods, godforsaken, unfrequented
<< OPPOSITE nearby
2 UNUSUAL, surprising, odd, strange, extraordinary, remarkable, bizarre, unexpected, curious, exceptional, notable, peculiar, abnormal, queer, uncommon, singular, unconventional, outlandish, out of the ordinary, left-field (*informal*), atypical

outpouring *noun* OUTBURST, storm, stream, explosion, surge, outbreak, deluge, eruption, spasm, paroxysm, effusion, issue

output *noun* PRODUCTION, manufacture, manufacturing, yield, productivity, outturn (*rare*)

outrage *noun* 1 INDIGNATION, shock, anger, rage, fury, hurt, resentment, scorn, wrath, ire (*literary*), exasperation, umbrage, righteous anger
2 ATROCITY, crime, horror, evil, cruelty, brutality, enormity, barbarism, inhumanity, abomination, barbarity, villainy, act of cruelty
▷ *verb* OFFEND, shock, upset, pain, wound, provoke, insult, infuriate, incense, gall, madden, vex, affront, displease, rile, scandalize, give offence, nark (*Brit, Austral & NZ slang*), cut to the quick, make your blood boil, put your nose out of joint, put your back up, disgruntle

outrageous *adjective* 1 ATROCIOUS, shocking, terrible, violent, offensive, appalling, cruel, savage, horrible, beastly, horrifying, vicious, ruthless, infamous, disgraceful, scandalous, wicked, barbaric, unspeakable, inhuman, diabolical, heinous, flagrant, egregious, abominable, infernal, fiendish, villainous, nefarious, iniquitous, execrable, godawful (*slang*), hellacious (*US slang*)
<< OPPOSITE mild
2 UNREASONABLE, unfair, excessive, steep (*informal*), shocking, over the top (*slang*), extravagant, too great, scandalous, preposterous, unwarranted, exorbitant, extortionate, immoderate, O.T.T. (*slang*)
<< OPPOSITE reasonable

outright *adjective* 1 ABSOLUTE, complete, total, direct, perfect, pure, sheer, utter, thorough, wholesale, unconditional, downright, consummate, unqualified, undeniable, out-and-out, unadulterated, unmitigated, thoroughgoing, unalloyed, arrant, deep-dyed (*usually derogatory*)
2 DEFINITE, clear, certain, straight, flat, absolute, black-and-white, decisive, straightforward, clear-cut, unmistakable, unequivocal, unqualified, unambiguous, cut-and-dried (*informal*), incontrovertible, uncontestable
▷ *adverb* 1 OPENLY, frankly, plainly, face to face, explicitly, overtly, candidly, unreservedly, unhesitatingly, forthrightly, straight from the shoulder (*informal*)
2 ABSOLUTELY, completely, totally, fully, entirely, thoroughly, wholly, utterly, to the full, without hesitation, to the hilt, one hundred per cent, straightforwardly, without restraint, unmitigatedly, lock, stock and barrel
3 INSTANTLY, immediately, at once, straight away, cleanly, on the spot, right away, there and then, instantaneously

outset *noun* BEGINNING, start, opening, early days, starting point, onset, inauguration, inception, commencement, kickoff (*informal*)
<< OPPOSITE finish

outside *adjective* 1 EXTERNAL, outer, exterior, surface, extreme, outdoor, outward, superficial, extraneous, outermost, extramural
<< OPPOSITE inner
2 REMOTE, small, unlikely, slight, slim, poor, distant, faint, marginal, doubtful, dubious, slender, meagre, negligible, inconsiderable
▷ *adverb* OUTDOORS, out, out of the house, out-of-doors
▷ *noun* EXTERIOR, face, front, covering, skin, surface, shell, coating, finish, façade, topside

> The use of *outside of* and *inside of*, although fairly common, is generally thought to be incorrect or nonstandard: *She waits outside* (not *outside of*) *the school*.

outsider *noun* STRANGER, incomer, visitor, foreigner, alien, newcomer, intruder, new arrival, unknown, interloper, odd one out, nonmember, outlander

outsize *adjective* 1 HUGE, great, large, giant, massive, enormous, monster, immense, mega (*slang*), jumbo (*informal*), gigantic, monumental, mammoth, bulky, colossal, mountainous, oversized, stupendous, gargantuan, elephantine, ginormous (*informal*), Brobdingnagian, humongous *or* humungous (*US slang*)

<< OPPOSITE tiny

2 EXTRA-LARGE, large, generous, ample, roomy

outskirts *plural noun* EDGE, borders, boundary, suburbs, fringe, perimeter, vicinity, periphery, suburbia, environs, purlieus, faubourgs

outsmart *verb* (*informal*) OUTWIT, trick, take in (*informal*), cheat, deceive, defraud, dupe, gull (*archaic*), get the better of, swindle, circumvent, outperform, make a fool of (*informal*), outmanoeuvre, go one better than (*informal*), put one over on (*informal*), outfox, run rings round (*informal*), pull a fast one on (*informal*), outthink, outjockey

outspan *verb* (*S African*) RELAX, chill out (*slang, chiefly US*), take it easy, loosen up, laze, lighten up (*slang*), put your feet up, hang loose (*slang*), let yourself go (*informal*), let your hair down (*informal*), mellow out (*informal*), make yourself at home

outspoken *adjective* FORTHRIGHT, open, free, direct, frank, straightforward, blunt, explicit, downright, candid, upfront (*informal*), unequivocal, undisguised, plain-spoken, unreserved, unconcealed, unceremonious, free-spoken, straight from the shoulder (*informal*), undissembling

<< OPPOSITE reserved

outstanding *adjective* 1 EXCELLENT, good, great, important, special, fine, noted, champion, celebrated, brilliant, impressive, superb, distinguished, well-known, prominent, superior, first-class, exceptional, notable, world-class, exquisite, admirable, eminent, exemplary, first-rate, stellar (*informal*), superlative, top-notch (*informal*), mean (*slang*), pre-eminent, meritorious, estimable, tiptop, A1 *or* A-one (*informal*), booshit (*Austral slang*), exo (*Austral slang*), sik (*Austral slang*), rad (*informal*), phat (*slang*), schmick (*Austral informal*)

<< OPPOSITE mediocre

2 CONSPICUOUS, marked, striking, arresting, signal, remarkable, memorable, notable, eye-catching, salient, noteworthy

3 UNPAID, remaining, due, owing, ongoing, pending, payable, unsettled, unresolved, uncollected

4 UNDONE, left, not done, omitted, unfinished, incomplete, passed over, unfulfilled, not completed, unperformed, unattended to

outstrip *verb* 1 EXCEED, eclipse, overtake, top, cap (*informal*), go beyond, surpass, outdo

2 SURPASS (*informal*), beat, leave behind, eclipse, overtake, best, top, better, overshadow, outdo, outclass, outperform, outshine, leave standing (*informal*), tower above, get ahead of, go one better than (*informal*), run rings around, knock spots off (*informal*), put in the shade

3 OUTDISTANCE, shake off, outrun, outpace

outward *adjective* APPARENT, seeming, outside, surface, external, outer, superficial, ostensible

<< OPPOSITE inward

outwardly *adverb* APPARENTLY, externally, seemingly, it seems that, on the surface, it appears that, ostensibly, on the face of it, superficially, to the eye, to all intents and purposes, to all appearances, as far as you can see, professedly

outweigh *verb* OVERRIDE, cancel (out), eclipse, offset, make up for, compensate for, redeem, supersede, neutralize, counterbalance, nullify, take precedence over, prevail over, obviate, balance out, preponderate, outbalance

outwit *verb* OUTSMART (*informal*), get the better of, circumvent, outperform, outmanoeuvre, go one better than (*informal*), put one over on (*informal*), outfox, run rings round (*informal*), pull a fast one on (*informal*), outthink, outjockey

oval *adjective* ELLIPTICAL, egg-shaped, ovoid, ovate, ellipsoidal, oviform

ovation *noun* APPLAUSE, hand, cheering, cheers, praise, tribute, acclaim, clapping, accolade, plaudits, big hand, commendation, hand-clapping, acclamation, laudation

<< OPPOSITE derision

over *preposition* 1 ABOVE, on top of, atop

2 ON TOP OF, on, across, upon

3 ACROSS, past, (looking) onto

4 MORE THAN, above, exceeding, in excess of, upwards of

5 ABOUT, regarding, relating to, with respect to, re, concerning, apropos of, anent (*Scot*)

▷ *adverb* 1 ABOVE, overhead, in the sky, on high, aloft, up above

2 EXTRA, more, other, further, beyond, additional, in addition, surplus, in excess, left over, unused, supplementary, auxiliary

▷ *adjective* FINISHED, by, done (with), through, ended, closed, past, completed, complete, gone, in the past, settled, concluded, accomplished, wrapped up (*informal*), bygone, at an end, ancient history (*informal*), over and done with

▷▷ **over and above** IN ADDITION TO, added to, on top of, besides, plus, let alone, not to mention, as well as, over and beyond

▷▷ **over and over (again)** REPEATEDLY, frequently, again and again, often, many times, time and (time) again, time after time, ad nauseam

>> RELATED WORDS *prefixes* hyper-, super-, supra-, sur-

overall *adjective* TOTAL, full, whole, general, complete, long-term, entire, global, comprehensive, gross, blanket, umbrella, long-range, inclusive, all-embracing, overarching

▷ *adverb* IN GENERAL, generally, mostly, all things considered, on average, in (the) large, on the whole, predominantly, in the main, in the long term, by and large, all in all, on balance, generally speaking, taking everything into consideration

overawed *adjective* INTIMIDATED, threatened, alarmed, frightened, scared, terrified, cowed, put off, daunted, unnerved

overbearing *adjective* DOMINEERING, lordly, superior, arrogant, authoritarian, oppressive, autocratic, masterful, dictatorial, coercive, bossy (*informal*), imperious, haughty, tyrannical, magisterial, despotic, high-handed, peremptory, supercilious, officious, overweening, iron-handed

<< OPPOSITE submissive

overblown *adjective* 1 EXCESSIVE, exaggerated, over the top (*slang*), too much, inflated, extravagant, overdone, disproportionate, undue, fulsome, intemperate, immoderate, O.T.T. (*slang*)

2 INFLATED, rhetorical, high-flown, pompous, pretentious, flowery, florid, turgid, bombastic, windy, grandiloquent, fustian, magniloquent, aureate, euphuistic

overcast *adjective* CLOUDY, grey, dull, threatening, dark, clouded, dim, gloomy, dismal, murky, dreary, leaden, clouded over, sunless, louring *or* lowering

<< OPPOSITE bright

overcharge *verb* CHEAT, con (*informal*), do (*slang*), skin (*slang*), stiff (*slang*), sting (*informal*), rip off (*slang*), fleece, defraud, surcharge, swindle, stitch up (*slang*), rook (*slang*), short-change, diddle (*informal*), take for a ride (*informal*), cozen

overcome *verb* 1 DEFEAT, beat, conquer, master, tank (*slang*), crush, overwhelm, overthrow, lick (*informal*), undo, subdue, rout, overpower, quell, triumph over, best, get the better of, trounce, worst, clobber (*slang*), stuff (*slang*), vanquish, surmount, subjugate, prevail over, wipe the floor with (*informal*), make mincemeat of (*informal*), blow (someone) out of the water (*slang*), come out on top of (*informal*), bring (someone) to their knees (*informal*), render incapable, render powerless, be victorious over, render helpless

2 CONQUER, beat, master, survive, weather, curb, suppress, subdue, rise above, quell, triumph over, get the better of, vanquish

overdo *verb* EXAGGERATE, overstate, overuse, overplay, do to death (*informal*), belabour, carry *or* take too far, make a production (out) of (*informal*), lay (something) on thick (*informal*)

<< OPPOSITE minimize

▷▷ **overdo it** OVERWORK, go too far, go overboard, strain *or* overstrain yourself, burn the midnight oil, burn the candle at both ends (*informal*), wear yourself out, bite off more than you can chew, have too many irons in the fire, overtire yourself, drive yourself too far, overburden yourself, overload yourself, overtax your strength, work your fingers to the bone

overdone *adjective* 1 OVERCOOKED, burnt, spoiled, dried up, charred, burnt to a crisp *or* cinder

2 EXCESSIVE, too much, unfair, unnecessary, exaggerated, over the top (*slang*), needless, unreasonable, disproportionate, undue, hyped, preposterous, inordinate, fulsome, immoderate, overelaborate, beyond all bounds, O.T.T. (*slang*)

<< OPPOSITE minimized

overdue *adjective* 1 DELAYED, belated, late, late in the day, long delayed, behind schedule, tardy, not before time (*informal*), behind time, unpunctual, behindhand

<< OPPOSITE early

2 UNPAID, owing

overflow *verb* 1 SPILL OVER, discharge, well over, run over, pour over, pour out, bubble over, brim over, surge over, slop over, teem over

2 FLOOD, swamp, submerge, cover, drown, soak, immerse, inundate, deluge, pour over

▷ *noun* 1 FLOOD, flooding, spill, discharge, spilling over, inundation

2 SURPLUS, extra, excess, overspill, inundation, overabundance, additional people *or* things

overflowing *adjective* FULL, abounding, swarming, rife, plentiful, thronged, teeming, copious, bountiful, profuse, brimful, overfull, superabundant

<< OPPOSITE deficient

overhang *verb* PROJECT (OVER), extend (over), loom (over), stand out (over), bulge (over), stick out (over), protrude (over), jut (over), impend (over)

overhaul *verb* 1 CHECK, service, maintain, examine, restore, tune (up), repair, go over, inspect, fine tune, do up (*informal*), re-examine, recondition

2 OVERTAKE, pass, leave behind, catch up with, get past, outstrip, get ahead of, draw level with, outdistance

▷ *noun* CHECK, service, examination, going-over (*informal*), inspection, once-over (*informal*), checkup, reconditioning

overhead *adjective* RAISED, suspended, elevated, aerial, overhanging

▷ *adverb* ABOVE, in the sky, on high, aloft, up above
<< OPPOSITE underneath

overheads *plural noun* RUNNING COSTS, expenses, outgoings, operating costs, oncosts

overjoyed *adjective* DELIGHTED, happy, pleased, thrilled, ecstatic, jubilant, joyous, joyful, elated, over the moon (*informal*), euphoric, rapturous, rapt, only too happy, gladdened, on cloud nine (*informal*), transported, cock-a-hoop, blissed out, in raptures, tickled pink (*informal*), deliriously happy, in seventh heaven, floating on air, stoked (*Austral & NZ informal*)
<< OPPOSITE heartbroken

overlay *verb* COVER, coat, blanket, adorn, mantle, ornament, envelop, veneer, encase, inlay, superimpose, laminate, overspread
▷ *noun* COVERING, casing, wrapping, decoration, veneer, adornment, ornamentation, appliqué

overlook *verb* **1** LOOK OVER *or* OUT ON, have a view of, command a view of, front on to, give upon, afford a view of
2 MISS, forget, neglect, omit, disregard, pass over, fail to notice, leave undone, slip up on, leave out of consideration
<< OPPOSITE notice
3 IGNORE, excuse, forgive, pardon, disregard, condone, turn a blind eye to, wink at, blink at, make allowances for, let someone off with, let pass, let ride, discount, pass over, take no notice of, be oblivious to, pay no attention to, turn a deaf ear to, shut your eyes to

overly *adverb* TOO, very, extremely, exceedingly, unduly, excessively, unreasonably, inordinately, immoderately, over-

overpower *verb* **1** OVERCOME, master, overwhelm, overthrow, subdue, quell, get the better of, subjugate, prevail over, immobilize, bring (someone) to their knees (*informal*), render incapable, render powerless, render helpless, get the upper hand over
2 BEAT, defeat, tank (*slang*), crush, lick (*informal*), triumph over, best, clobber (*slang*), stuff (*slang*), vanquish, be victorious (over), wipe the floor with (*informal*), make mincemeat of (*informal*), worst
3 OVERWHELM, overcome, bowl over (*informal*), stagger

overpowering *adjective* **1** OVERWHELMING, powerful, extreme, compelling, irresistible, breathtaking, compulsive, invincible, uncontrollable
2 STRONG, marked, powerful, distinct, sickening, unbearable, suffocating, unmistakable, nauseating
3 FORCEFUL, powerful, overwhelming, dynamic, compelling, persuasive, overbearing

overrate *verb* OVERESTIMATE, glorify, overvalue, oversell, make too much of, rate too highly, assess too highly, overpraise, exaggerate the worth of, overprize, think *or* expect too much of, think too highly of, attach too much importance to

override *verb* **1** OUTWEIGH, overcome, eclipse, supersede, take precedence over, prevail over, outbalance
2 OVERRULE, reverse, cancel, overturn, set aside, repeal, quash, revoke, disallow, rescind, upset, rule against, invalidate, annul, nullify, ride roughshod over, outvote, countermand, trample underfoot, make null and void
3 IGNORE, reject, discount, overlook, set aside, disregard, pass over, take no notice of, take no account of, pay no attention to, turn a deaf ear to

overriding *adjective* MAJOR, chief, main, prime, predominant, leading, controlling, final, ruling, determining, primary, supreme, principal, ultimate, dominant, compelling, prevailing, cardinal, sovereign, paramount, prevalent, pivotal, top-priority, overruling, preponderant, number one
<< OPPOSITE minor

overrule *verb* REVERSE, alter, cancel, recall, discount, overturn, set aside, override, repeal, quash, revoke, disallow, rescind, rule against, invalidate, annul, nullify, outvote, countermand, make null and void
<< OPPOSITE approve

overrun *verb* **1** OVERWHELM, attack, assault, occupy, raid, invade, penetrate, swamp, rout, assail, descend upon, run riot over
2 SPREAD OVER, overwhelm, choke, swamp, overflow, infest, inundate, permeate, spread like wildfire, swarm over, surge over, overgrow
3 EXCEED, go beyond, surpass, overshoot, outrun, run over *or* on

overseer *noun* SUPERVISOR, manager, chief, boss (*informal*), master, inspector, superior, administrator, steward, superintendent, gaffer (*informal, chiefly Brit*), foreman, super (*informal*), baas (*S African*)

overshadow *verb* **1** SPOIL, ruin, mar, wreck, scar, blight, crool *or* cruel (*Austral slang*), mess up, take the edge off, put a damper on, cast a gloom upon, take the pleasure *or* enjoyment out of
2 OUTSHINE, eclipse, surpass, dwarf, rise above, take precedence over, tower above, steal the limelight from, leave *or* put in the shade, render insignificant by comparison, throw into the shade
3 SHADE, cloud, eclipse, darken, overcast, adumbrate

oversight *noun* **1** MISTAKE, error, slip, fault, misunderstanding, blunder, lapse, omission, boob (*Brit slang*), gaffe, slip-up (*informal*),

delinquency, inaccuracy, carelessness, howler (*informal*), goof (*informal*), bloomer (*Brit informal*), clanger (*informal*), miscalculation, error of judgment, faux pas, inattention, laxity, boo-boo (*informal*), erratum, barry *or* Barry Crocker (*Austral slang*)
2 SUPERVISION, keeping, control, charge, care, management, handling, administration, direction, custody, stewardship, superintendence

overt *adjective* OPEN, obvious, plain, public, clear, apparent, visible, patent, evident, manifest, noticeable, blatant, downright, avowed, flagrant, observable, undisguised, barefaced, unconcealed
<< OPPOSITE hidden

overtake *verb* 1 PASS, leave behind, overhaul, catch up with, get past, draw level with, outdistance, go by *or* past
2 OUTDO, top, exceed, eclipse, surpass, outstrip, get the better of, outclass, outshine, best, go one better than (*informal*), outdistance, be one up on
3 BEFALL, hit, happen to, come upon, take by surprise, catch off guard, catch unawares, catch unprepared
4 ENGULF, overwhelm, hit, strike, consume, swamp, envelop, swallow up

overthrow *verb* DEFEAT, beat, master, overcome, crush, overwhelm, conquer, bring down, oust, lick (*informal*), topple, subdue, rout, overpower, do away with, depose, trounce, unseat, vanquish, subjugate, dethrone
<< OPPOSITE uphold
▷ *noun* DOWNFALL, end, fall, defeat, collapse, ruin, destruction, breakdown, ousting, undoing, rout, suppression, displacement, subversion, deposition, unseating, subjugation, dispossession, disestablishment, dethronement
<< OPPOSITE preservation

overtone *noun often plural* CONNOTATION, association, suggestion, sense, hint, flavour, implication, significance, nuance, colouring, innuendo, undercurrent, intimation

overture *noun* (*Music*) PRELUDE, opening, introduction, introductory movement
<< OPPOSITE finale

overtures *plural noun* APPROACH, offer, advance, proposal, appeal, invitation, tender, proposition, opening move, conciliatory move
<< OPPOSITE rejection

overturn *verb* 1 TIP OVER, spill, topple, upturn, capsize, upend, keel over, overbalance
2 KNOCK OVER *or* DOWN, upset, upturn, tip over, upend
3 REVERSE, change, alter, cancel, abolish, overthrow, set aside, repeal, quash, revoke, overrule, override, negate, rescind, invalidate, annul, nullify, obviate, countermand, declare null and void, overset
4 OVERTHROW, defeat, destroy, overcome, crush, bring down, oust, topple, do away with, depose, unseat, dethrone

overweight *adjective* FAT, heavy, stout, huge, massive, solid, gross, hefty, ample, plump, bulky, chunky, chubby, obese, fleshy, beefy (*informal*), tubby (*informal*), portly, outsize, buxom, roly-poly, rotund, podgy, corpulent, elephantine, well-padded (*informal*), well-upholstered (*informal*), broad in the beam (*informal*), on the plump side
<< OPPOSITE underweight

overwhelm *verb* 1 OVERCOME, overpower, devastate, stagger, get the better of, bowl (someone) over (*informal*), prostrate, knock (someone) for six (*informal*), render (someone) speechless, render (someone) incapable, render (someone) powerless, render (someone) helpless, sweep (someone) off his *or* her feet, take (someone's) breath away
2 DESTROY, beat, defeat, overcome, smash, crush, massacre, conquer, wipe out, overthrow, knock out, lick (*informal*), subdue, rout, eradicate, overpower, quell, annihilate, put paid to, vanquish, subjugate, immobilize, make mincemeat of (*informal*), cut to pieces
3 SWAMP, bury, flood, crush, engulf, submerge, beset, inundate, deluge, snow under

overwhelming *adjective* 1 OVERPOWERING, strong, powerful, towering, vast, stunning, extreme, crushing, devastating, shattering, compelling, irresistible, breathtaking, compulsive, forceful, unbearable, uncontrollable
<< OPPOSITE negligible
2 VAST, huge, massive, enormous, tremendous, immense, very large, astronomic, humongous *or* humungous (*US slang*)
<< OPPOSITE insignificant

overwork *verb* 1 WEAR YOURSELF OUT, burn the midnight oil, burn the candle at both ends, bite off more than you can chew, strain yourself, overstrain yourself, work your fingers to the bone, overtire yourself, drive yourself too far, overburden yourself, overload yourself, overtax yourself
2 EXPLOIT, exhaust, fatigue, weary, oppress, wear out, prostrate, overtax, drive into the ground, be a slave-driver *or* hard taskmaster to

overwrought *adjective* 1 DISTRAUGHT, upset, excited, desperate, wired (*slang*), anxious, distressed, tense, distracted, frantic, in a state, hysterical, wound up (*informal*), worked up (*informal*), agitated, uptight (*informal*), on edge, strung out (*informal*), out of your mind, keyed up, overexcited, in a tizzy (*informal*), at the end of your tether, wrought-up, beside yourself, in a twitter (*informal*), tooshie (*Austral slang*), adrenalized

<< OPPOSITE calm

2 OVERELABORATE, contrived, overdone, flamboyant, baroque, high-flown, ornate, fussy, flowery, busy, rococo, florid, grandiloquent, euphuistic, overembellished, overornate

owe *verb* BE IN DEBT (TO), be in arrears (to), be overdrawn (by), be beholden to, be under an obligation to, be obligated *or* indebted (to)

owing *adjective* UNPAID, due, outstanding, owed, payable, unsettled, overdue

▷▷ **owing to** BECAUSE OF, thanks to, as a result of, on account of, by reason of

own *determiner* PERSONAL, special, private, individual, particular, exclusive

▷ *verb* POSSESS, have, keep, hold, enjoy, retain, be responsible for, be in possession of, have to your name

▷▷ **hold your own** KEEP GOING, compete, get on, get along, stand your ground, keep your head above water, keep your end up, maintain your position

▷▷ **on your own** **1** ALONE, by yourself, all alone, unaccompanied, on your tod (*Brit slang*) **2** INDEPENDENTLY, alone, singly, single-handedly, by yourself, unaided, without help, unassisted, left to your own devices, under your own steam, off your own bat, by your own efforts, (standing) on your own two feet

owner *noun* POSSESSOR, holder, proprietor, freeholder, titleholder, proprietress, proprietrix, landlord *or* landlady, master *or* mistress, deed holder

ownership *noun* POSSESSION, occupation, tenure, dominion, occupancy, proprietorship, proprietary rights, right of possession

pace *noun* 1 SPEED, rate, momentum, tempo, progress, motion, clip (*informal*), lick (*informal*), velocity
2 STEP, walk, stride, tread, gait
3 FOOTSTEP, step, stride
▷ *verb* STRIDE, walk, pound, patrol, walk up and down, march up and down, walk back and forth

pacific *adjective* 1 NONAGGRESSIVE, pacifist, nonviolent, friendly, gentle, mild, peace-loving, peaceable, dovish, nonbelligerent, dovelike
<< OPPOSITE aggressive
2 PEACEMAKING, diplomatic, appeasing, conciliatory, placatory, propitiatory, irenic, pacificatory

pacifist *noun* PEACE LOVER, dove, conscientious objector, peacenik (*informal*), conchie (*informal*), peacemonger, satyagrahi (*rare*), passive resister

pacify *verb* CALM (DOWN), appease, placate, still, content, quiet, moderate, compose, soften, soothe, allay, assuage, make peace with, mollify, ameliorate, conciliate, propitiate, tranquillize, smooth someone's ruffled feathers, clear the air with, restore harmony to

pack *verb* 1 PACKAGE, load, store, bundle, batch, stow
2 CRAM, charge, crowd, press, fill, stuff, jam, compact, mob, ram, wedge, compress, throng, tamp
▷ *noun* 1 PACKET, box, package, carton
2 BUNDLE, kit, parcel, load, burden, bale, rucksack, truss, knapsack, back pack, kitbag, fardel (*archaic*)
3 GROUP, crowd, collection, company, set, lot, band, troop, crew, drove, gang, deck, bunch, mob, flock, herd, assemblage
▷▷ **pack someone off** SEND AWAY, dismiss, send packing (*informal*), bundle out, hustle out
▷▷ **pack something in** 1 (*Brit & NZ informal*) RESIGN FROM, leave, give up, quit (*informal*), chuck (*informal*), jack in (*informal*)
2 STOP, give up, kick (*informal*), cease, chuck (*informal*), leave off, jack in, desist from
▷▷ **pack something up** 1 PUT AWAY, store, tidy up
2 (*informal*) STOP, finish, give up, pack in (*Brit informal*), call it a day (*informal*), call it a night (*informal*)
▷▷ **pack up** BREAK DOWN, stop, fail, stall, give out, conk out (*informal*)
▷▷ **send someone packing** (*informal*) SEND SOMEONE AWAY, dismiss, discharge, give someone the bird (*informal*), give someone the brushoff (*slang*), send someone about his *or* her business, send someone away with a flea in his *or* her ear (*informal*)

package *noun* 1 PARCEL, box, container, packet, carton
2 COLLECTION, lot, unit, combination, compilation
▷ *verb* PACK, box, wrap up, parcel (up), batch

packaging *noun* WRAPPING, casing, covering, cover, box, packing, wrapper

packed *adjective* FILLED, full, crowded, jammed, crammed, swarming, overflowing, overloaded, seething, congested, jam-packed, chock-full, bursting at the seams, cram-full, brimful, chock-a-block, packed like sardines, hoatching (*Scot*), loaded *or* full to the gunwales
<< OPPOSITE empty

packet *noun* 1 CONTAINER, box, package, wrapping, poke (*dialect*), carton, wrapper
2 PACKAGE, parcel
3 (*Slang*) A FORTUNE, lot(s), pot(s) (*informal*), a bomb (*Brit slang*), a pile (*informal*), big money, a bundle (*slang*), big bucks (*informal, chiefly US*), a small fortune, a mint, a wad (*US & Canad slang*), megabucks (*US & Canad slang*), an arm and a leg (*informal*), a bob or two (*Brit informal*), a tidy sum (*informal*), a king's ransom (*informal*), a pretty penny (*informal*), top whack (*informal*)

pact *noun* AGREEMENT, contract, alliance, treaty, deal, understanding, league, bond, arrangement, bargain, convention, compact, protocol, covenant, concord, concordat

pad[1] *noun* 1 WAD, dressing, pack, padding, compress, wadding
2 CUSHION, filling, stuffing, pillow, bolster, upholstery
3 NOTEPAD, block, tablet, notebook, jotter, writing pad
4 (*Slang*) HOME, flat, apartment, place, room, quarters, hang-out (*informal*), bachelor apartment (*Canad*)
5 PAW, foot, sole
▷ *verb* PACK, line, fill, protect, shape, stuff, cushion
▷▷ **pad something out** LENGTHEN, stretch, elaborate, inflate, fill out, amplify, augment, spin out, flesh out, eke out, protract

pad[2] *verb* SNEAK, creep, steal, pussyfoot (*informal*), go barefoot

padding *noun* 1 FILLING, stuffing, packing, wadding
2 WAFFLE (*informal, chiefly Brit*), hot air (*informal*), verbiage, wordiness, verbosity, prolixity

paddle[1] *noun* OAR, sweep, scull
▷ *verb* ROW, pull, scull

paddle[2] *verb* WADE, splash (about), slop, plash

paddy *noun* (*Brit slang*) TEMPER, tantrum, bad mood, passion, rage, pet, fit of pique, fit of temper, foulie (*Austral slang*), hissy fit (*informal*)

paean *or (sometimes) US* **pean** *noun* (*Literary*) EULOGY, tribute, panegyric, hymn of praise, encomium

pagan *noun* HEATHEN, infidel, unbeliever, polytheist, idolater
▷ *adjective* HEATHEN, infidel, irreligious, polytheistic, idolatrous, heathenish

page[1] *noun* 1 FOLIO, side, leaf, sheet
2 PERIOD, chapter, phase, era, episode, time, point, event, stage, incident, epoch

page[2] *noun* 1 ATTENDANT, bellboy (*US*), pageboy, footboy
2 SERVANT, attendant, squire, pageboy, footboy
▷ *verb* CALL, seek, summon, call out for, send for

pageant *noun* SHOW, display, parade, ritual, spectacle, procession, extravaganza, tableau

pageantry *noun* SPECTACLE, show, display, drama, parade, splash (*informal*), state, glitter, glamour, grandeur, splendour, extravagance, pomp, magnificence, theatricality, showiness

pain *noun* 1 SUFFERING, discomfort, trouble, hurt, irritation, tenderness, soreness
2 ACHE, smarting, stinging, aching, cramp, cramp, throb, throbbing, spasm, pang, twinge, shooting pain
3 SORROW, suffering, torture, distress, despair, grief, misery, agony, sadness, torment, hardship, bitterness, woe, anguish, heartache, affliction, tribulation, desolation, wretchedness
▷ *plural noun* TROUBLE, labour, effort, industry, care, bother, diligence, special attention, assiduousness
▷ *verb* 1 DISTRESS, worry, hurt, wound, torture, grieve, torment, afflict, sadden, disquiet, vex, agonize, cut to the quick, aggrieve
2 HURT, chafe, cause pain to, cause discomfort to

pained *adjective* DISTRESSED, worried, hurt, injured, wounded, upset, unhappy, stung, offended, aggrieved, anguished, miffed (*informal*), reproachful

painful *adjective* 1 SORE, hurting, smarting, aching, raw, tender, throbbing, inflamed, excruciating
<< OPPOSITE painless
2 DISTRESSING, unpleasant, harrowing, saddening, grievous, distasteful, agonizing, disagreeable, afflictive
<< OPPOSITE pleasant
3 DIFFICULT, arduous, trying, hard, severe, troublesome, laborious, vexatious
<< OPPOSITE easy
4 (*informal*) TERRIBLE, awful, dreadful, dire, excruciating, abysmal, gut-wrenching, godawful, extremely bad

painfully *adverb* DISTRESSINGLY, clearly, sadly, unfortunately, markedly, excessively, alarmingly, woefully, dreadfully, deplorably

painkiller *noun* ANALGESIC, drug, remedy, anaesthetic, sedative, palliative, anodyne

painless *adjective* 1 PAIN-FREE, without pain
2 SIMPLE, easy, fast, quick, no trouble, effortless, trouble-free

painstaking *adjective* THOROUGH, careful, meticulous, earnest, exacting, strenuous, conscientious, persevering, diligent, scrupulous, industrious, assiduous, thoroughgoing, punctilious, sedulous
<< OPPOSITE careless

paint *noun* COLOURING, colour, stain, dye, tint, pigment, emulsion
▷ *verb* 1 COLOUR, cover, coat, decorate, stain, whitewash, daub, distemper, apply paint to
2 DEPICT, draw, portray, figure, picture, represent, sketch, delineate, catch a likeness
3 DESCRIBE, capture, portray, depict, evoke, recount, bring to life, make you see, conjure up a vision, put graphically, tell vividly
▷▷ **paint the town red** (*informal*) CELEBRATE, revel, carouse, live it up (*informal*), make merry, make whoopee (*informal*), go on a binge (*informal*), go on a spree, go on the town

pair *noun* 1 SET, match, combination, doublet, matched set, two of a kind
2 COUPLE, brace, duo, twosome
▷ *verb often with* **off** TEAM, match (up), join, couple, marry, wed, twin, put together,

bracket, yoke, pair off

> Like other collective nouns, *pair* takes a singular or a plural verb according to whether it is seen as a unit or as a collection of two things: *the pair are said to dislike each other; a pair of good shoes is essential*

pal *noun* (*informal*) FRIEND, companion, mate (*informal*), buddy (*informal*), comrade, chum (*informal*), crony, cock (*Brit informal*), main man (*slang, chiefly US*), homeboy (*slang, chiefly US*), cobber (*Austral & NZ old-fashioned informal*), boon companion, E hoa (*NZ*)

palatable *adjective* 1 DELICIOUS, tasty, luscious, savoury, delectable, mouthwatering, appetizing, toothsome, yummo (*Austral slang*)
<< OPPOSITE unpalatable
2 ACCEPTABLE, pleasant, agreeable, fair, attractive, satisfactory, enjoyable

palate *noun* TASTE, heart, stomach, appetite

> This word is occasionally confused with *palette*: *I have a sweet palate* (not *palette*)

palatial *adjective* MAGNIFICENT, grand, imposing, splendid, gorgeous, luxurious, spacious, majestic, regal, stately, sumptuous, plush (*informal*), illustrious, grandiose, opulent, de luxe, splendiferous (*facetious*)

pale[1] *adjective* 1 LIGHT, soft, faded, subtle, muted, bleached, pastel, light-coloured
2 DIM, weak, faint, feeble, thin, wan, watery
3 WHITE, pasty, bleached, washed-out, wan, bloodless, colourless, pallid, anaemic, ashen, sallow, whitish, ashy, like death warmed up (*informal*)
<< OPPOSITE rosy-cheeked
4 POOR, weak, inadequate, pathetic, feeble
▷ *verb* 1 FADE, dull, diminish, decrease, dim, lessen, grow dull, lose lustre
2 BECOME PALE, blanch, whiten, go white, lose colour

pale[2] *noun* POST, stake, paling, upright, picket, slat, palisade
▷▷ **beyond the pale** UNACCEPTABLE, not done, forbidden, irregular, indecent, unsuitable, improper, barbaric, unspeakable, out of line, unseemly, inadmissible

pall[1] *noun* 1 CLOUD, shadow, veil, mantle, shroud
2 GLOOM, damp, dismay, melancholy, damper, check

pall[2] *verb often with* **on** BECOME BORING, become dull, become tedious, become tiresome, jade, cloy, become wearisome

pallid *adjective* PALE, wan, pasty, colourless, anaemic, ashen, sallow, whitish, cadaverous, waxen, ashy, like death warmed up (*informal*), wheyfaced

pallor *noun* PALENESS, whiteness, lack of colour, wanness, bloodlessness, ashen hue, pallidness

palm *noun* HAND, hook, paw (*informal*), mitt (*slang*), meathook (*slang*)
▷▷ **in the palm of your hand** IN YOUR POWER, in your control, in your clutches, at your mercy
▷▷ **palm someone off** FOB OFF, dismiss, disregard, pooh-pooh (*informal*)
▷▷ **palm something off on someone** FOIST ON, force upon, impose upon, pass off, thrust upon, unload upon

palpable *adjective* OBVIOUS, apparent, patent, clear, plain, visible, evident, manifest, open, blatant, conspicuous, unmistakable, salient

paltry *adjective* 1 MEAGRE, petty, trivial, trifling, beggarly, derisory, measly, piddling (*informal*), inconsiderable
<< OPPOSITE considerable
2 INSIGNIFICANT, trivial, worthless, unimportant, small, low, base, minor, slight, petty, trifling, Mickey Mouse (*slang*), piddling (*informal*), toytown (*slang*), poxy (*slang*), nickel-and-dime (*US slang*), picayune (*US*), twopenny-halfpenny (*Brit informal*)
<< OPPOSITE important

pamper *verb* SPOIL, indulge, gratify, baby, pet, humour, pander to, fondle, cosset, coddle, mollycoddle, wait on (someone) hand and foot, cater to someone's every whim

pamphlet *noun* BOOKLET, leaflet, brochure, circular, tract, folder

pan[1] *noun* POT, vessel, container, saucepan
▷ *verb* 1 (*informal*) CRITICIZE, knock, blast, hammer (*Brit informal*), slam (*slang*), rubbish (*informal*), roast (*informal*), put down, slate (*informal*), censure, slag (off) (*slang*), tear into (*informal*), flay, lambast(e), throw brickbats at (*informal*)
2 SIFT OUT, look for, wash, search for
▷▷ **pan out** (*informal*) WORK OUT, happen, result, come out, turn out, culminate, come to pass (*archaic*), eventuate

pan[2] *verb* MOVE ALONG *or* ACROSS, follow, track, sweep, scan, traverse, swing across

panacea *noun* CURE-ALL, elixir, nostrum, heal-all, sovereign remedy, universal cure

panache *noun* STYLE, spirit, dash, flair, verve, swagger, flourish, élan, flamboyance, brio

pandemonium *noun* UPROAR, confusion, chaos, turmoil, racket, clamour, din, commotion, rumpus, bedlam, babel, tumult, hubbub, ruction (*informal*), hullabaloo, hue and cry, ruckus (*informal*)
<< OPPOSITE order

pander ▷▷ **pander to something** *or* **someone** INDULGE, please, satisfy, gratify, cater to, play up to (*informal*), fawn on

pang *noun* 1 PAIN, stab, sting, stitch, ache, wrench, prick, spasm, twinge, throe (*rare*)
2 TWINGE, stab, prick, spasm, qualm, gnawing

panic *noun* FEAR, alarm, horror, terror, anxiety, dismay, hysteria, fright, agitation, consternation, trepidation, a flap (*informal*)
▷ *verb* 1 GO TO PIECES, overreact, become hysterical, have kittens (*informal*), lose your nerve, be terror-stricken, lose your bottle (*Brit slang*)
2 ALARM, scare, terrify, startle, unnerve

panicky *adjective* FRIGHTENED, worried, afraid, nervous, distressed, fearful, frantic, frenzied, hysterical, worked up, windy (*slang*), agitated, jittery (*informal*), in a flap (*informal*), antsy (*informal*), in a tizzy (*informal*)
<< OPPOSITE calm

panic-stricken *or* **panic-struck** *adjective* FRIGHTENED, alarmed, scared, terrified, startled, horrified, fearful, frenzied, hysterical, agitated, unnerved, petrified, aghast, panicky, scared stiff, in a cold sweat (*informal*), frightened to death, terror-stricken, horror-stricken, frightened out of your wits

panoply *noun* 1 ARRAY, range, display, collection
2 TRAPPINGS, show, dress, get-up (*informal*), turnout, attire, garb, insignia, regalia, raiment (*archaic* or *poetic*)

panorama *noun* 1 VIEW, prospect, scenery, vista, bird's-eye view, scenic view
2 SURVEY, perspective, overview, overall picture

panoramic *adjective* 1 WIDE, overall, extensive, scenic, bird's-eye
2 COMPREHENSIVE, general, extensive, sweeping, inclusive, far-reaching, all-embracing

pant *verb* PUFF, blow, breathe, gasp, throb, wheeze, huff, heave, palpitate
▷ *noun* GASP, puff, wheeze, huff
▷▷ **pant for something** LONG FOR, want, desire, crave for, covet, yearn for, thirst for, hunger for, pine for, hanker after, ache for, sigh for, set your heart on, eat your heart out over, suspire for (*archaic* or *poetic*)

panting *adjective* 1 OUT OF BREATH, winded, gasping, puffed, puffing, breathless, puffed out, short of breath, out of puff, out of whack (*informal*)
2 EAGER, raring, anxious, impatient, champing at the bit (*informal*), all agog

pants *plural noun* 1 (*Brit*) UNDERPANTS, briefs, drawers, knickers, panties, boxer shorts, Y-fronts (*trademark*), broekies (*S African*), underdaks (*Austral slang*)
2 (US) TROUSERS, slacks

pap *noun* RUBBISH, trash, trivia, drivel

paper *noun* 1 NEWSPAPER, news, daily, journal, organ, rag (*informal*), tabloid, gazette, broadsheet
2 ESSAY, study, article, analysis, script, composition, assignment, thesis, critique, treatise, dissertation, monograph
3 EXAMINATION, test, exam
4 REPORT, study, survey, inquiry
▷ *plural noun* LETTERS, records, documents, file, diaries, archive, paperwork, dossier
2 DOCUMENTS, records, certificates, identification, deeds, identity papers, I.D. (*informal*)
▷ *verb* WALLPAPER, line, hang, paste up, cover with paper
▷▷ **on paper** 1 IN WRITING, written down, on (the) record, in print, in black and white
2 IN THEORY, ideally, theoretically, in the abstract

parable *noun* LESSON, story, fable, allegory, moral tale, exemplum

parade *noun* 1 PROCESSION, march, ceremony, pageant, train, review, column, spectacle, tattoo, motorcade, cavalcade, cortège
2 SHOW, display, exhibition, spectacle, array
▷ *verb* 1 MARCH, process, file, promenade
2 FLAUNT, show, display, exhibit, show off (*informal*), air, draw attention to, brandish, vaunt, make a show of
3 STRUT, show off (*informal*), swagger, swank

paradigm *noun* MODEL, example, original, pattern, ideal, norm, prototype, archetype, exemplar

paradise *noun* 1 HEAVEN, Promised Land, Zion (*Christianity*), Happy Valley (*Islam*), City of God, Elysian fields, garden of delights, divine abode, heavenly kingdom
2 GARDEN OF EDEN, Eden
3 BLISS, delight, heaven, felicity, utopia, seventh heaven

paradox *noun* CONTRADICTION, mystery, puzzle, ambiguity, anomaly, inconsistency, enigma, oddity, absurdity

paradoxical *adjective* CONTRADICTORY, inconsistent, impossible, puzzling, absurd, baffling, riddling, ambiguous, improbable, confounding, enigmatic, illogical, equivocal, oracular

paragon *noun* MODEL, standard, pattern, ideal, criterion, norm, jewel, masterpiece, prototype, paradigm, archetype, epitome, exemplar, apotheosis, quintessence, nonesuch (*archaic*), nonpareil, best *or* greatest thing since sliced bread (*informal*), cynosure

paragraph *noun* SECTION, part, notice, item, passage, clause, portion, subdivision

parallel *noun* 1 EQUIVALENT, counterpart, match, equal, twin, complement, duplicate, analogue, likeness, corollary
<< OPPOSITE opposite
2 SIMILARITY, correspondence, correlation, comparison, analogy, resemblance, likeness, parallelism

<< OPPOSITE difference
▷ *verb* 1 CORRESPOND TO, compare with, agree with, complement, conform to, be alike, chime with, correlate to
<< OPPOSITE differ from
2 MATCH, equal, duplicate, keep pace (with), measure up to
▷ *adjective* 1 MATCHING, correspondent, corresponding, like, similar, uniform, resembling, complementary, akin, analogous
<< OPPOSITE different
2 EQUIDISTANT, alongside, aligned, side by side, coextensive
<< OPPOSITE divergent

paralyse *verb* 1 DISABLE, cripple, lame, debilitate, incapacitate
2 FREEZE, stun, numb, petrify, transfix, stupefy, halt, stop dead, immobilize, anaesthetize, benumb
3 IMMOBILIZE, freeze, halt, disable, cripple, arrest, incapacitate, bring to a standstill

paralysis *noun* 1 IMMOBILITY, palsy, paresis (*Pathology*)
2 STANDSTILL, breakdown, stoppage, shutdown, halt, stagnation, inactivity

parameter *noun usually plural* (*informal*) LIMIT, constant, restriction, guideline, criterion, framework, limitation, specification

paramount *adjective* PRINCIPAL, prime, first, chief, main, capital, primary, supreme, outstanding, superior, dominant, cardinal, foremost, eminent, predominant, pre-eminent
<< OPPOSITE secondary

paranoid *adjective* 1 (*informal*) SUSPICIOUS, worried, nervous, fearful, apprehensive, antsy (*informal*)
2 OBSESSIVE, disturbed, unstable, manic, neurotic, mentally ill, psychotic, deluded, paranoiac

paraphernalia *noun* EQUIPMENT, things, effects, material, stuff, tackle, gear, baggage, apparatus, belongings, clobber (*Brit slang*), accoutrements, impedimenta, appurtenances, equipage

paraphrase *verb* REWORD, interpret, render, restate, rehash, rephrase, express in other words *or* your own words
▷ *noun* REWORDING, version, interpretation, rendering, translation, rendition, rehash, restatement, rephrasing

parasite *noun* SPONGER (*informal*), sponge (*informal*), drone (*Brit*), leech, hanger-on, scrounger (*informal*), bloodsucker (*informal*), cadger, quandong (*Austral slang*)

parasitic *or* **parasitical** *adjective* SCROUNGING (*informal*), sponging (*informal*), cadging, bloodsucking (*informal*), leechlike

parcel *noun* 1 PACKAGE, case, box, pack, packet, bundle, carton
2 PLOT, area, property, section, patch, tract, allotment, piece of land
3 GROUP, crowd, pack, company, lot, band, collection, crew, gang, bunch, batch
▷ *verb often with* **up** WRAP, pack, package, tie up, do up, gift-wrap, box up, fasten together
▷▷ **parcel something out** DISTRIBUTE, divide, portion, allocate, split up, dispense, allot, carve up, mete out, dole out, share out, apportion, deal out

parched *adjective* 1 DRIED OUT *or* UP, dry, withered, scorched, arid, torrid, shrivelled, dehydrated, waterless
2 THIRSTY, dry, dehydrated, drouthy (*Scot*)

pardon *verb* ACQUIT, free, release, liberate, reprieve, remit, amnesty, let off (*informal*), exonerate, absolve, exculpate
<< OPPOSITE punish
▷ *noun* 1 FORGIVENESS, mercy, indulgence, absolution, grace
<< OPPOSITE condemnation
2 ACQUITTAL, release, discharge, amnesty, reprieve, remission, exoneration
<< OPPOSITE punishment
▷▷ **pardon me** FORGIVE ME, excuse me

pare *verb* 1 PEEL, cut, skin, trim, clip, shave
2 CUT BACK, cut, reduce, crop, decrease, dock, prune, shear, lop, retrench

parent *noun* 1 FATHER *or* MOTHER, sire, progenitor, begetter, procreator, old (*Austral & NZ informal*), oldie (*Austral informal*), patriarch
2 SOURCE, cause, author, root, origin, architect, creator, prototype, forerunner, originator, wellspring

parentage *noun* FAMILY, birth, origin, descent, line, race, stock, pedigree, extraction, ancestry, lineage, paternity, derivation

parenthood *noun* FATHERHOOD *or* MOTHERHOOD, parenting, rearing, bringing up, nurturing, upbringing, child rearing, baby *or* child care, fathering *or* mothering

pariah *noun* OUTCAST, exile, outlaw, undesirable, untouchable, leper, unperson

parings *plural noun* PEELINGS, skins, slices, clippings, peel, fragments, shavings, shreds, flakes, rind, snippets, slivers

parish *noun* 1 DISTRICT, community
2 COMMUNITY, fold, flock, church, congregation, parishioners, churchgoers
>> RELATED WORD *adjective* parochial

parity *noun* EQUALITY, correspondence, consistency, equivalence, quits (*informal*), par, unity, similarity, likeness, uniformity, equal terms, sameness, parallelism, congruity

park *noun* 1 RECREATION GROUND, garden, playground, pleasure garden, playpark, domain (*NZ*), forest park (*NZ*)
2 PARKLAND, grounds, estate, lawns,

woodland, grassland
3 FIELD, pitch, playing field
▷ *verb* 1 LEAVE, stop, station, position
2 PUT (DOWN), leave, place, stick, deposit, dump, shove, plonk (*informal*)

parlance *noun* LANGUAGE, talk, speech, tongue, jargon, idiom, lingo (*informal*), phraseology, manner of speaking

parliament *noun* 1 ASSEMBLY, council, congress, senate, convention, legislature, talking shop (*informal*), convocation
2 SITTING, diet
3 *with cap.* HOUSES OF PARLIAMENT, the House, Westminster, Mother of Parliaments, the House of Commons and the House of Lords, House of Representatives (NZ)

parliamentary *adjective* GOVERNMENTAL, congressional, legislative, law-making, law-giving, deliberative

parlour *or US* **parlor** *noun* 1 (*Old-fashioned*) SITTING ROOM, lounge, living room, drawing room, front room, reception room, best room
2 ESTABLISHMENT, shop, store, salon

parlous *adjective* (*Archaic or humorous*) DANGEROUS, difficult, desperate, risky, dire, hazardous, hairy (*slang*), perilous, chancy (*informal*)

parochial *adjective* PROVINCIAL, narrow, insular, limited, restricted, petty, narrow-minded, inward-looking, small-minded, parish-pump
<< OPPOSITE cosmopolitan

parody *noun* 1 TAKEOFF (*informal*), imitation, satire, caricature, send-up (*Brit informal*), spoof (*informal*), lampoon, skit, burlesque
2 TRAVESTY, farce, caricature, mockery, apology for
▷ *verb* TAKE OFF (*informal*), mimic, caricature, send up (*Brit informal*), spoof (*informal*), travesty, lampoon, poke fun at, burlesque, satirize, do a takeoff of (*informal*)

paroxysm *noun* OUTBURST, attack, fit, seizure, flare-up (*informal*), eruption, spasm, convulsion

parrot *verb* REPEAT, echo, imitate, copy, reiterate, mimic

parry *verb* 1 EVADE, avoid, fence off, dodge, duck (*informal*), shun, sidestep, circumvent, fight shy of
2 WARD OFF, block, deflect, repel, rebuff, fend off, stave off, repulse, hold at bay

parsimonious *adjective* MEAN, stingy, penny-pinching (*informal*), miserly, near (*informal*), saving, sparing, grasping, miserable, stinting, frugal, niggardly, penurious, tightfisted, close-fisted, mingy (*Brit informal*), cheeseparing, skinflinty, snoep (*S African informal*)
<< OPPOSITE extravagant

parson *noun* CLERGYMAN, minister, priest, vicar, divine, incumbent, reverend (*informal*), preacher, pastor, cleric, rector, curate, churchman, man of God, man of the cloth, ecclesiastic

part *noun* 1 PIECE, share, proportion, percentage, lot, bit, section, sector, slice, scrap, particle, segment, portion, fragment, lump, fraction, chunk, wedge
<< OPPOSITE entirety
2 *often plural* REGION, area, district, territory, neighbourhood, quarter, vicinity, neck of the woods (*informal*), airt (*Scot*)
3 COMPONENT, bit, piece, unit, element, ingredient, constituent, module
4 BRANCH, department, division, office, section, wing, subdivision, subsection
5 ORGAN, member, limb
6 (*Theatre*) ROLE, representation, persona, portrayal, depiction, character part
7 (*Theatre*) LINES, words, script, dialogue
8 DUTY, say, place, work, role, hand, business, share, charge, responsibility, task, function, capacity, involvement, participation
9 SIDE, behalf
▷ *verb* 1 DIVIDE, separate, break, tear, split, rend, detach, sever, disconnect, cleave, come apart, disunite, disjoin
<< OPPOSITE join
2 PART COMPANY, separate, break up, split up, say goodbye, go (their) separate ways
<< OPPOSITE meet
▷▷ **for the most part** MAINLY, largely, generally, chiefly, mostly, principally, on the whole, in the main
▷▷ **in good part** GOOD-NATUREDLY, well, cheerfully, cordially, without offence
▷▷ **in part** PARTLY, a little, somewhat, slightly, partially, to some degree, to a certain extent, in some measure
▷▷ **on the part of** BY, in, from, made by, carried out by
▷▷ **part with something** GIVE UP, abandon, yield, sacrifice, surrender, discard, relinquish, renounce, let go of, forgo
▷▷ **take part in** PARTICIPATE IN, be involved in, join in, play a part in, be instrumental in, have a hand in, partake in, take a hand in, associate yourself with, put your twopence-worth in

partake ▷▷ **partake in something** PARTICIPATE IN, share in, take part in, engage in, enter into
▷▷ **partake of something** 1 CONSUME, take, share, receive, eat
2 DISPLAY, exhibit, evoke, hint at, be characterized by

> The phrase *partake of* is sometimes inappropriately used as if it were a synonym of *eat* or *drink*. In strict usage, you can only *partake of* food or drink which is available for several people to share

partial *adjective* 1 INCOMPLETE, limited, unfinished, imperfect, fragmentary, uncompleted

<< OPPOSITE complete

2 BIASED, prejudiced, discriminatory, partisan, influenced, unfair, one-sided, unjust, predisposed, tendentious

<< OPPOSITE unbiased

partially *adverb* PARTLY, somewhat, moderately, in part, halfway, piecemeal, not wholly, fractionally, incompletely, to a certain extent *or* degree ▷ see **partly**

participant *noun* PARTICIPATOR, party, member, player, associate, shareholder, contributor, stakeholder, partaker

participate *verb* TAKE PART, be involved, engage, perform, join, enter, partake, have a hand, get in on the act, be a party to, be a participant

<< OPPOSITE refrain from

participation *noun* TAKING PART, contribution, partnership, involvement, assistance, sharing in, joining in, partaking

particle *noun* BIT, piece, scrap, grain, molecule, atom, shred, crumb, mite, jot, speck, mote, whit, tittle, iota

particular *adjective* 1 SPECIFIC, special, express, exact, precise, distinct, peculiar

<< OPPOSITE general

2 SPECIAL, exceptional, notable, uncommon, marked, unusual, remarkable, singular, noteworthy, especial

3 FUSSY, demanding, critical, exacting, discriminating, meticulous, fastidious, dainty, choosy (*informal*), picky (*informal*), finicky, pernickety (*informal*), overnice

<< OPPOSITE indiscriminate

4 DETAILED, minute, precise, thorough, selective, painstaking, circumstantial, itemized, blow-by-blow

▷ *noun usually plural* DETAIL, fact, feature, item, circumstance, specification

▷▷ **in particular** ESPECIALLY, particularly, expressly, specifically, exactly, distinctly

particularly *adverb* 1 SPECIFICALLY, expressly, explicitly, especially, in particular, distinctly

2 ESPECIALLY, surprisingly, notably, unusually, exceptionally, decidedly, markedly, peculiarly, singularly, outstandingly, uncommonly

parting *noun* 1 FAREWELL, departure, goodbye, leave-taking, adieu, valediction

2 DIVISION, breaking, split, separation, rift, partition, detachment, rupture, divergence

▷ *modifier* FAREWELL, last, final, departing, valedictory

partisan *adjective* 1 PREJUDICED, one-sided, biased, partial, sectarian, factional, tendentious

<< OPPOSITE unbiased

2 UNDERGROUND, resistance, guerrilla, irregular

▷ *noun* 1 SUPPORTER, champion, follower, backer, disciple, stalwart, devotee, adherent, upholder, votary

<< OPPOSITE opponent

2 UNDERGROUND FIGHTER, guerrilla, irregular, freedom fighter, resistance fighter

partition *noun* 1 SCREEN, wall, barrier, divider, room divider

2 DIVISION, splitting, dividing, separation, segregation, severance

▷ *verb* 1 SEPARATE, screen, divide, fence off, wall off

2 DIVIDE, separate, segment, split up, share, section, portion, cut up, apportion, subdivide, parcel out

partly *adverb* PARTIALLY, relatively, somewhat, slightly, in part, halfway, not fully, in some measure, incompletely, up to a certain point, to a certain degree *or* extent

<< OPPOSITE completely

> *Partly* and *partially* are to some extent interchangeable, but *partly* should be used when referring to a part or parts of something: *the building is partly* (not *partially*) *made of stone*, while *partially* is preferred for the meaning *to some extent: his mother is partially* (not *partly*) *sighted*

partner *noun* 1 SPOUSE, consort, bedfellow, significant other (*US informal*), mate, better half (*Brit informal*), helpmate, husband *or* wife

2 COMPANION, collaborator, accomplice, ally, colleague, associate, mate, team-mate, participant, comrade, confederate, bedfellow, copartner

3 ASSOCIATE, colleague, collaborator, copartner

partnership *noun* 1 COOPERATION, association, alliance, sharing, union, connection, participation, copartnership

2 COMPANY, firm, corporation, house, interest, society, conglomerate, cooperative

party *noun* 1 FACTION, association, alliance, grouping, set, side, league, camp, combination, coalition, clique, coterie, schism, confederacy, cabal

2 GET-TOGETHER (*informal*), celebration, do (*informal*), social, at-home, gathering, function, reception, bash (*informal*), rave (*Brit slang*), festivity, knees-up (*Brit informal*), beano (*Brit slang*), social gathering, shindig (*informal*), soirée, rave-up (*Brit slang*), hooley *or* hoolie (*chiefly Irish & NZ*)

3 GROUP, team, band, company, body, unit, squad, gathering, crew, gang, bunch (*informal*), detachment (*Military*)

4 (*Law*) LITIGANT, defendant, participant, contractor (*Law*), plaintiff

pass *verb* **1** GO BY *or* PAST, overtake, drive past, lap, leave behind, pull ahead of
<< OPPOSITE stop
2 GO, move, travel, roll, progress, flow, proceed, move onwards
3 RUN, move, stroke
4 GIVE, hand, send, throw, exchange, transfer, deliver, toss, transmit, convey, chuck (*informal*), let someone have
5 BE LEFT, come, be bequeathed, be inherited by
6 KICK, hit, loft, head, lob
7 ELAPSE, progress, go by, lapse, wear on, go past, tick by
8 END, go, die, disappear, fade, cease, vanish, dissolve, expire, terminate, dwindle, evaporate, wane, ebb, melt away, blow over
9 SPEND, use (up), kill, fill, waste, employ, occupy, devote, beguile, while away
10 EXCEED, beat, overtake, go beyond, excel, surpass, transcend, outstrip, outdo, surmount
11 BE SUCCESSFUL (IN), qualify (in), succeed (in), graduate (in), get through, do, pass muster (in), come up to scratch (in) (*informal*), gain a pass (in)
<< OPPOSITE fail
12 APPROVE, accept, establish, adopt, sanction, decree, enact, authorize, ratify, ordain, validate, legislate (for)
<< OPPOSITE ban
13 PRONOUNCE, deliver, issue, set forth
14 UTTER, speak, voice, express, declare
15 DISCHARGE, release, expel, evacuate, emit, let out, eliminate (*rare*)
▷ *noun* **1** LICENCE, ticket, permit, permission, passport, warrant, identification, identity card, authorization
2 GAP, route, canyon, col, gorge, ravine, defile
3 PREDICAMENT, condition, situation, state, stage, pinch, plight, straits, state of affairs, juncture
▷▷ **make a pass at someone** MAKE ADVANCES TO, proposition, hit on (*US & Canad slang*), come on to (*informal*), make a play for (*informal*), make an approach to, make sexual overtures to
▷▷ **pass as** *or* **for something** *or* **someone** BE MISTAKEN FOR, be taken for, impersonate, be accepted as, be regarded as
▷▷ **pass away** *or* **on** (*Euphemistic*) DIE, pass on, depart (this life), buy it (*US slang*), expire, check out (*US slang*), pass over, kick it (*slang*), croak (*slang*), go belly-up (*slang*), snuff it (*informal*), peg out (*informal*), kick the bucket (*slang*), buy the farm (*US slang*), peg it (*informal*), decease, shuffle off this mortal coil, cark it (*Austral & NZ informal*), pop your clogs (*informal*)
▷▷ **pass off 1** TAKE PLACE, happen, occur, turn out, go down (*US & Canad*), be completed, go off, fall out, be finished, pan out
2 COME TO AN END, disappear, vanish, die away, fade out *or* away
▷▷ **pass out** (*informal*) FAINT, drop, black out (*informal*), swoon (*literary*), lose consciousness, keel over (*informal*), flake out (*informal*), become unconscious
▷▷ **pass someone over** OVERLOOK, ignore, discount, pass by, disregard, not consider, take no notice of, not take into consideration, pay no attention to
▷▷ **pass something out** HAND OUT, distribute, dole out, deal out
▷▷ **pass something over** DISREGARD, forget, ignore, skip, omit, pass by, not dwell on
▷▷ **pass something** *or* **someone off as something** *or* **someone** MISREPRESENT, palm something *or* someone off, falsely represent, disguise something *or* someone, dress something *or* someone up
▷▷ **pass something up** (*informal*) MISS, ignore, let slip, refuse, decline, reject, neglect, forgo, abstain from, let (something) go by, give (something) a miss (*informal*)

> The past participle of *pass* is sometimes wrongly spelt *past*: *the time for recriminations has passed* (not *past*)

passable *adjective* **1** ADEQUATE, middling, average, fair, all right, ordinary, acceptable, moderate, fair enough, mediocre, so-so (*informal*), tolerable, not too bad, allowable, presentable, admissible, unexceptional, half-pie (*NZ informal*)
<< OPPOSITE unsatisfactory
2 CLEAR, open, navigable, unobstructed, traversable, crossable
<< OPPOSITE impassable

passage *noun* **1** CORRIDOR, hallway, passageway, hall, lobby, entrance, exit, doorway, aisle, entrance hall, vestibule
2 ALLEY, way, opening, close (*Brit*), course, road, channel, route, path, lane, avenue, thoroughfare
3 EXTRACT, reading, piece, section, sentence, text, clause, excerpt, paragraph, verse, quotation
4 MOVEMENT, passing, advance, progress, flow, motion, transit, progression
5 TRANSITION, change, move, development, progress, shift, conversion, progression, metamorphosis
6 ESTABLISHMENT, passing, legislation, sanction, approval, acceptance, adoption, ratification, enactment, authorization, validation, legalization
7 JOURNEY, crossing, tour, trip, trek, voyage
8 SAFE-CONDUCT, right to travel, freedom to travel, permission to travel, authorization to travel

passageway *noun* CORRIDOR, passage,

hallway, hall, lane, lobby, entrance, exit, alley, aisle, wynd (*Scot*)

passé *adjective* OUT-OF-DATE, old-fashioned, dated, outdated, obsolete, unfashionable, antiquated, outmoded, old hat, outworn, démodé (*French*)

passenger *noun* TRAVELLER, rider, fare, commuter, hitchhiker, pillion rider, fare payer

passer-by *noun* BYSTANDER, witness, observer, viewer, spectator, looker-on, watcher, onlooker, eyewitness

passing *adjective* 1 MOMENTARY, fleeting, short-lived, transient, ephemeral, short, brief, temporary, transitory, evanescent, fugacious (*rare*)
2 SUPERFICIAL, short, quick, slight, glancing, casual, summary, shallow, hasty, cursory, perfunctory, desultory
▷ *noun* 1 END, finish, loss, vanishing, disappearance, termination, dying out, expiry, expiration
2 DEATH, demise, decease, passing on *or* away
▷▷ **in passing** INCIDENTALLY, on the way, by the way, accidentally, en passant, by the bye

passion *noun* 1 LOVE, desire, affection, lust, the hots (*slang*), attachment, itch, fondness, adoration, infatuation, ardour, keenness, concupiscence
2 EMOTION, feeling, fire, heat, spirit, transport, joy, excitement, intensity, warmth, animation, zeal, zest, fervour, eagerness, rapture, ardour
<< OPPOSITE indifference
3 MANIA, fancy, enthusiasm, obsession, bug (*informal*), craving, fascination, craze, infatuation
4 RAGE, fit, storm, anger, fury, resentment, outburst, frenzy, wrath, indignation, flare-up (*informal*), ire, vehemence, paroxysm

passionate *adjective* 1 EMOTIONAL, excited, eager, enthusiastic, animated, strong, warm, wild, intense, flaming, fierce, frenzied, ardent, fervent, heartfelt, impassioned, zealous, impulsive, vehement, impetuous, fervid
<< OPPOSITE unemotional
2 LOVING, erotic, hot, sexy (*informal*), aroused, sensual, ardent, steamy (*informal*), wanton, amorous, lustful, desirous
<< OPPOSITE cold

passionately *adverb* 1 EMOTIONALLY, eagerly, enthusiastically, vehemently, excitedly, strongly, warmly, wildly, fiercely, intensely, fervently, impulsively, ardently, zealously, animatedly, with all your heart, frenziedly, impetuously, fervidly
<< OPPOSITE unemotionally
2 LOVINGLY, with passion, erotically, ardently, sexily (*informal*), sensually, lustfully, amorously, steamily (*informal*), libidinously, desirously
<< OPPOSITE coldly

passive *adjective* 1 SUBMISSIVE, resigned, compliant, receptive, lifeless, docile, nonviolent, quiescent, acquiescent, unassertive, unresisting
<< OPPOSITE spirited
2 INACTIVE, inert, uninvolved, non-participating
<< OPPOSITE active

password *noun* WATCHWORD, key word, magic word (*informal*), open sesame

past *noun* 1 FORMER TIMES, history, long ago, antiquity, the good old days, yesteryear (*literary*), times past, the old times, days gone by, the olden days, days of yore
<< OPPOSITE future
2 BACKGROUND, life, experience, history, past life, life story, career to date
▷ *adjective* 1 FORMER, late, early, recent, previous, ancient, prior, long-ago, preceding, foregoing, erstwhile, bygone, olden
<< OPPOSITE future
2 PREVIOUS, former, one-time, sometime, erstwhile, quondam, ex-
3 LAST, recent, previous, preceding
4 OVER, done, ended, spent, finished, completed, gone, forgotten, accomplished, extinct, elapsed, over and done with
▷ *preposition* 1 AFTER, beyond, later than, over, outside, farther than, in excess of, subsequent to
2 BY, across, in front of
▷ *adverb* ON, by, along

> The past participle of *pass* is sometimes wrongly spelt *past*: *the time for recrimination has passed* (not *past*)

paste *noun* 1 ADHESIVE, glue, cement, gum, mucilage
2 PURÉE, pâté, spread
▷ *verb* STICK, fix, glue, cement, gum, fasten

pastel *adjective* PALE, light, soft, delicate, muted, soft-hued
<< OPPOSITE bright

pastiche *noun* 1 MEDLEY, mixture, blend, motley, mélange (*French*), miscellany, farrago, hotchpotch, gallimaufry
2 PARODY, take-off, imitation

pastime *noun* ACTIVITY, game, sport, entertainment, leisure, hobby, relaxation, recreation, distraction, amusement, diversion

pastor *noun* CLERGYMAN, minister, priest, vicar, divine, parson, rector, curate, churchman, ecclesiastic

pastoral *adjective* 1 ECCLESIASTICAL, priestly, ministerial, clerical
2 RUSTIC, country, simple, rural, idyllic, bucolic, Arcadian, georgic (*literary*), agrestic

pasture *noun* GRASSLAND, grass, meadow,

grazing, lea (*poetic*), grazing land, pasturage, shieling (*Scot*)

pasty *adjective* PALE, unhealthy, wan, sickly, pallid, anaemic, sallow, like death warmed up (*informal*), wheyfaced

pat[1] *verb* STROKE, touch, tap, pet, slap, dab, caress, fondle

▷ *noun* **1** TAP, stroke, slap, clap, dab, light blow

2 LUMP, cake, portion, dab, small piece

pat[2] *adjective* GLIB, easy, ready, smooth, automatic, slick, simplistic, facile

▷▷ **off pat** PERFECTLY, precisely, exactly, flawlessly, faultlessly

patch *noun* **1** SPOT, bit, stretch, scrap, shred, small piece

2 PLOT, area, ground, land, tract

3 REINFORCEMENT, piece of fabric, piece of cloth, piece of material, piece sewn on

▷ *verb* **1** *often with* **up** SEW (UP), mend, repair, reinforce, stitch (up)

2 *often with* **up** MEND, cover, fix, reinforce

▷▷ **patch things up** SETTLE, make friends, placate, bury the hatchet, conciliate, settle differences, smooth something over

patchwork *noun* MIXTURE, confusion, jumble, medley, hash, pastiche, mishmash, hotchpotch

patchy *adjective* **1** UNEVEN, irregular, variegated, spotty, mottled, dappled

<< OPPOSITE even

2 IRREGULAR, varying, variable, random, erratic, uneven, sketchy, fitful, bitty, inconstant, scattershot

<< OPPOSITE constant

patent *noun* COPYRIGHT, licence, franchise, registered trademark

▷ *adjective* OBVIOUS, apparent, evident, blatant, open, clear, glaring, manifest, transparent, conspicuous, downright, unmistakable, palpable, unequivocal, flagrant, indisputable, unconcealed

paternal *adjective* **1** FATHERLY, concerned, protective, benevolent, vigilant, solicitous, fatherlike

2 PATRILINEAL, patrimonial

paternity *noun* FATHERHOOD, fathership (*rare*)

path *noun* **1** WAY, road, walk, track, trail, avenue, pathway, footpath, walkway (*chiefly US*), towpath, footway, berm (*NZ*)

2 ROUTE, way, course, direction, passage

3 COURSE, way, road, track, route, procedure

pathetic *adjective* **1** SAD, moving, touching, affecting, distressing, tender, melting, poignant, harrowing, heartbreaking, plaintive, heart-rending, gut-wrenching, pitiable

<< OPPOSITE funny

2 INADEQUATE, useless, feeble, poor, sorry, wet (*Brit informal*), pants (*informal*), miserable, petty, worthless, meagre, pitiful, woeful, deplorable, lamentable, trashy, measly, crummy (*slang*), crappy (*slang*), rubbishy, poxy (*slang*)

pathfinder *noun* PIONEER, guide, scout, explorer, discoverer, trailblazer

pathos *noun* SADNESS, poignancy, plaintiveness, pitifulness, pitiableness

patience *noun* **1** FORBEARANCE, tolerance, composure, serenity, cool (*slang*), restraint, calmness, equanimity, toleration, sufferance, even temper, imperturbability

<< OPPOSITE impatience

2 ENDURANCE, resignation, submission, fortitude, persistence, long-suffering, perseverance, stoicism, constancy

patient *noun* SICK PERSON, case, sufferer, invalid

▷ *adjective* **1** FORBEARING, understanding, forgiving, mild, accommodating, tolerant, indulgent, lenient, even-tempered

<< OPPOSITE impatient

2 LONG-SUFFERING, resigned, calm, enduring, quiet, composed, persistent, philosophical, serene, persevering, stoical, submissive, self possessed, uncomplaining, untiring

patois *noun* **1** DIALECT, vernacular

2 JARGON, slang, vernacular, patter, cant, lingo (*informal*), argot

patriarch *noun* FATHER, old man, elder, grandfather, sire, paterfamilias, greybeard

patrician *noun* ARISTOCRAT, peer, noble, nobleman, aristo (*informal*)

▷ *adjective* ARISTOCRATIC, noble, lordly, high-class, blue-blooded, highborn

patriot *noun* NATIONALIST, loyalist, chauvinist, flag-waver (*informal*), lover of your country

patriotic *adjective* NATIONALISTIC, loyal, flag-waving (*informal*), chauvinistic, jingoistic

patriotism *noun* NATIONALISM, loyalty, flag-waving (*informal*), jingoism, love of your country

patrol *verb* POLICE, guard, keep watch (on), pound, range (over), cruise, inspect, safeguard, make the rounds (of), keep guard (on), walk *or* pound the beat (of)

▷ *noun* GUARD, watch, garrison, watchman, sentinel, patrolman

patron *noun* **1** SUPPORTER, friend, champion, defender, sponsor, guardian, angel (*informal*), advocate, backer, helper, protagonist, protector, benefactor, philanthropist

2 CUSTOMER, client, buyer, frequenter, shopper, habitué

patronage *noun* SUPPORT, promotion, sponsorship, backing, help, aid, championship, assistance, encouragement, espousal, benefaction

patronize *verb* **1** TALK DOWN TO, look down on, treat as inferior, treat like a child, be lofty

with, treat condescendingly
2 SUPPORT, promote, sponsor, back, help, fund, maintain, foster, assist, subscribe to, befriend
3 BE A CUSTOMER *or* CLIENT OF, deal with, frequent, buy from, trade with, shop at, do business with
patronizing *adjective* CONDESCENDING, superior, stooping, lofty, gracious, contemptuous, haughty, snobbish, disdainful, supercilious, toffee-nosed (*slang, chiefly Brit*)
<< OPPOSITE respectful
patter[1] *verb* TAP, beat, pat, pelt, spatter, rat-a-tat, pitter-patter, pitapat
▷ *noun* TAPPING, pattering, pitter-patter, pitapat
patter[2] *noun* 1 SPIEL (*informal*), line, pitch, monologue
2 CHATTER, prattle, nattering, jabber, gabble, yak (*slang*)
3 JARGON, slang, vernacular, cant, lingo (*informal*), patois, argot
pattern *noun* 1 ORDER, plan, system, method, arrangement, sequence, orderliness
2 DESIGN, arrangement, motif, figure, device, decoration, ornament, decorative design
3 PLAN, design, original, guide, instructions, diagram, stencil, template
4 MODEL, example, standard, original, guide, par, criterion, norm, prototype, paradigm, archetype, paragon, exemplar, cynosure
paucity *noun* (*Formal*) SCARCITY, lack, poverty, shortage, deficiency, rarity, dearth, smallness, insufficiency, slenderness, sparseness, slightness, sparsity, meagreness, paltriness, scantiness
paunch *noun* BELLY, beer-belly (*informal*), spread (*informal*), corporation (*informal*), pot, spare tyre (*Brit slang*), middle-age spread (*informal*), potbelly, large abdomen, puku (NZ)
pauper *noun* DOWN-AND-OUT, have-not, bankrupt, beggar, insolvent, indigent, poor person, mendicant
pause *verb* STOP BRIEFLY, delay, hesitate, break, wait, rest, halt, cease, interrupt, deliberate, waver, take a break, discontinue, desist, have a breather (*informal*)
<< OPPOSITE continue
▷ *noun* STOP, break, delay, interval, hesitation, stay, wait, rest, gap, halt, interruption, respite, lull, stoppage, interlude, cessation, let-up (*informal*), breathing space, breather (*informal*), intermission, discontinuance, entr'acte, caesura
<< OPPOSITE continuance
pave *verb* COVER, floor, surface, flag, concrete, tile, tar, asphalt, macadamize
paw *verb* (*informal*) MANHANDLE, grab, maul, molest, handle roughly
pawn[1] *verb* HOCK (*informal, chiefly US*), pop (*Brit informal*), stake, mortgage, deposit, pledge, hazard, wager
pawn[2] *noun* TOOL, instrument, toy, creature, puppet, dupe, stooge (*slang*), plaything, cat's-paw
pay *verb* 1 REWARD, compensate, reimburse, recompense, requite, remunerate
2 SPEND, offer, give, fork out (*informal*), remit, cough up (*informal*), shell out (*informal*)
3 SETTLE, meet, clear, foot, honour, discharge, liquidate, square up
4 BRING IN, earn, return, net, yield
5 BE PROFITABLE, make money, make a return, provide a living, be remunerative
6 BENEFIT, serve, repay, be worthwhile, be advantageous
7 GIVE, extend, present with, grant, render, hand out, bestow, proffer
▷ *noun* WAGES, income, payment, earnings, fee, reward, hire, salary, compensation, allowance, remuneration, takings, reimbursement, hand-outs, recompense, stipend, emolument, meed (*archaic*)
▷▷ **pay off** SUCCEED, work, be successful, be effective, be profitable
▷▷ **pay someone back** GET EVEN WITH (*informal*), punish, repay, retaliate, hit back at, reciprocate, recompense, get revenge on, settle a score with, get your own back on, revenge yourself on, avenge yourself for
▷▷ **pay someone off** 1 (*informal*) BRIBE, corrupt, oil (*informal*), get at, buy off, suborn, grease the palm of (*slang*)
2 DISMISS, fire, sack (*informal*), discharge, let go, lay off, kennet (*Austral slang*), jeff (*Austral slang*)
▷▷ **pay something back** REPAY, return, square, refund, reimburse, settle up
▷▷ **pay something off** SETTLE, clear, square, discharge, liquidate, pay in full
▷▷ **pay something out** SPEND, lay out (*informal*), expend, cough up (*informal*), shell out (*informal*), disburse, fork out *or* over *or* up (*slang*)
▷▷ **pay up** PAY, fork out (*informal*), stump up (*Brit informal*), make payment, pay in full, settle up, come up with the money
payable *adjective* DUE, outstanding, owed, owing, mature, to be paid, obligatory, receivable
payment *noun* 1 REMITTANCE, advance, deposit, premium, portion, instalment
2 SETTLEMENT, paying, discharge, outlay, remittance, defrayal
3 WAGES, fee, reward, hire, remuneration
payoff *noun* 1 BRIBE, incentive, cut (*informal*), payment, sweetener (*informal*), bung (*Brit informal*), inducement, kick-back (*informal*), backhander (*informal*), hush money (*informal*)
2 SETTLEMENT, payment, reward, payout, recompense

3 (*informal*) OUTCOME, result, consequence, conclusion, climax, finale, culmination, the crunch (*informal*), upshot, moment of truth, clincher (*informal*), punch line

peace *noun* 1 TRUCE, ceasefire, treaty, armistice, pacification, conciliation, cessation of hostilities
<< OPPOSITE war
2 STILLNESS, rest, quiet, silence, calm, hush, tranquillity, seclusion, repose, calmness, peacefulness, quietude, restfulness
3 SERENITY, calm, relaxation, composure, contentment, repose, equanimity, peacefulness, placidity, harmoniousness
4 HARMONY, accord, agreement, concord, amity

peaceable *adjective* PEACE-LOVING, friendly, gentle, peaceful, mild, conciliatory, amiable, pacific, amicable, placid, inoffensive, dovish, unwarlike, nonbelligerent

peaceful *adjective* 1 AT PEACE, friendly, harmonious, amicable, cordial, nonviolent, without hostility, free from strife, on friendly *or* good terms
<< OPPOSITE hostile
2 PEACE-LOVING, conciliatory, peaceable, placatory, irenic, pacific, unwarlike
<< OPPOSITE belligerent
3 CALM, still, quiet, gentle, pleasant, soothing, tranquil, placid, restful
<< OPPOSITE agitated
4 SERENE, placid, undisturbed, untroubled, unruffled

peacemaker *noun* MEDIATOR, appeaser, arbitrator, conciliator, pacifier, peacemonger

peak *noun* 1 HIGH POINT, crown, climax, culmination, zenith, maximum point, apogee, acme, ne plus ultra (*Latin*)
2 POINT, top, tip, summit, brow, crest, pinnacle, apex, aiguille
▷ *verb* CULMINATE, climax, come to a head, be at its height, reach its highest point, reach the zenith

peal *verb* RING, sound, toll, resound, chime, resonate, tintinnabulate
▷ *noun* 1 RING, sound, ringing, clamour, chime, clang, carillon, tintinnabulation
2 CLAP, sound, crash, blast, roar, rumble, resounding, reverberation
3 ROAR, fit, shout, scream, gale, howl, shriek, hoot

pearly *adjective* 1 IRIDESCENT, mother-of-pearl, opalescent, nacreous, margaric, margaritic
2 IVORY, creamy, milky, silvery

peasant *noun* 1 RUSTIC, countryman, hind (*obsolete*), swain (*archaic*), son of the soil, churl (*archaic*)
2 (*informal*) BOOR, provincial, hick (*informal, chiefly US & Canad*), lout, yokel, country bumpkin, hayseed (*US & Canad informal*), churl

peck *verb* 1 PICK, bite, hit, strike, tap, poke, jab, prick, nibble
2 KISS, plant a kiss on, give someone a smacker, give someone a peck *or* kiss
▷ *noun* KISS, smacker, osculation (*rare*)

peculiar *adjective* 1 ODD, strange, unusual, bizarre, funny, extraordinary, curious, weird, exceptional, eccentric, abnormal, out-of-the-way, queer, uncommon, singular, unconventional, far-out (*slang*), quaint, off-the-wall (*slang*), outlandish, offbeat, freakish, wacko (*slang*), outré, daggy (*Austral & NZ informal*)
<< OPPOSITE ordinary
2 SPECIAL, private, individual, personal, particular, unique, characteristic, distinguishing, distinct, idiosyncratic
<< OPPOSITE common
3 *with* **to** SPECIFIC TO, restricted to, appropriate to, endemic to

peculiarity *noun* 1 ODDITY, abnormality, eccentricity, weirdness, queerness, bizarreness, freakishness
2 QUIRK, caprice, mannerism, whimsy, foible, idiosyncrasy, odd trait
3 CHARACTERISTIC, mark, feature, quality, property, attribute, trait, speciality, singularity, distinctiveness, particularity

pecuniary *adjective* MONETARY, economic, financial, capital, commercial, fiscal, budgetary

pedantic *adjective* 1 HAIRSPLITTING, particular, formal, precise, fussy, picky (*informal*), nit-picking (*informal*), punctilious, priggish, pedagogic, overnice
2 ACADEMIC, pompous, schoolmasterly, stilted, erudite, scholastic, didactic, bookish, abstruse, donnish, sententious

peddle *verb* SELL, trade, push (*informal*), market, hawk, flog (*slang*), vend, huckster, sell door to door

peddler *or* **pedlar** *noun* SELLER, vendor, hawker, duffer (*dialect*), huckster, door-to-door salesman, cheap-jack (*informal*), colporteur

pedestal *noun* SUPPORT, stand, base, foot, mounting, foundation, pier, plinth, dado (*Architecture*)
▷▷ **put someone on a pedestal** WORSHIP, dignify, glorify, exalt, idealize, ennoble, deify, apotheosize

pedestrian *noun* WALKER, foot-traveller, footslogger
<< OPPOSITE driver
▷ *adjective* DULL, flat, ordinary, boring, commonplace, mundane, mediocre, plodding, banal, prosaic, run-of-the-mill, humdrum, unimaginative, uninteresting, uninspired, ho-hum (*informal*), no great shakes (*informal*),

half-pie (*NZ informal*)
<< OPPOSITE exciting

pedigree *modifier* PUREBRED, thoroughbred, full-blooded
▷ *noun* LINEAGE, family, line, race, stock, blood, breed, heritage, descent, extraction, ancestry, family tree, genealogy, derivation

pedlar ▷ see **peddler**

peek *verb* GLANCE, look, peer, spy, take a look, peep, eyeball (*slang*), sneak a look, keek (*Scot*), snatch a glimpse, take *or* have a gander (*informal*)
▷ *noun* GLANCE, look, glimpse, blink, peep, butcher's (*Brit slang*), gander (*informal*), look-see (*slang*), shufti (*Brit slang*), keek (*Scot*)

peel *noun* RIND, skin, peeling, epicarp, exocarp
▷ *verb* SKIN, scale, strip, pare, shuck, flake off, decorticate (*rare*), take the skin *or* rind off

peep *verb* 1 PEEK, look, peer, spy, eyeball (*slang*), sneak a look, steal a look, keek (*Scot*), look surreptitiously, look from hiding
2 APPEAR BRIEFLY, emerge, pop up, spring up, issue from, peer out, peek from, show partially
▷ *noun* LOOK, glimpse, peek, butcher's (*Brit slang*), gander (*informal*), look-see (*slang*), shufti (*Brit slang*), keek (*Scot*)

peer[1] *noun* 1 NOBLE, lord, count, duke, earl, baron, aristocrat, viscount, marquess, marquis, nobleman, aristo (*informal*)
2 EQUAL, like, match, fellow, contemporary, coequal, compeer

peer[2] *verb* SQUINT, look, spy, gaze, scan, inspect, peep, peek, snoop, scrutinize, look closely

peerage *noun* ARISTOCRACY, peers, nobility, lords and ladies, titled classes

peerless *adjective* UNEQUALLED, excellent, unique, outstanding, unparalleled, superlative, unrivalled, second to none, incomparable, unmatched, unsurpassed, matchless, beyond compare, nonpareil
<< OPPOSITE mediocre

peeved *adjective* IRRITATED, upset, annoyed, put out, hacked off (*US slang*), sore, galled, exasperated, nettled, vexed, irked, riled, piqued, tooshie (*Austral slang*)

peg *noun* PIN, spike, rivet, skewer, dowel, spigot
▷ *verb* 1 FASTEN, join, fix, secure, attach, make fast
2 FIX, set, control, limit, freeze

pejorative *adjective* DEROGATORY, negative, slighting, unpleasant, belittling, disparaging, debasing, deprecatory, uncomplimentary, depreciatory, detractive, detractory

pelt[1] *verb* 1 SHOWER, beat, strike, pepper, batter, thrash, bombard, wallop (*informal*), assail, pummel, hurl at, cast at, belabour, sling at
2 POUR, teem, rain hard, bucket down (*informal*), rain cats and dogs (*informal*)
3 RUSH, charge, shoot, career, speed, tear, belt (*slang*), dash, hurry, barrel (along) (*informal, chiefly US & Canad*), whizz (*informal*), stampede, run fast, burn rubber (*informal*)

pelt[2] *noun* COAT, fell, skin, hide

pen[1] *verb* WRITE (DOWN), draft, compose, pencil, draw up, scribble, take down, inscribe, scrawl, jot down, dash off, commit to paper

pen[2] *noun* ENCLOSURE, pound, fold, cage, coop, hutch, corral (*chiefly US & Canad*), sty
▷ *verb* ENCLOSE, confine, cage, pound, mew (up), fence in, impound, hem in, coop up, hedge in, shut up *or* in

penal *adjective* DISCIPLINARY, punitive, corrective, penalizing, retributive

penalize *verb* 1 PUNISH, discipline, correct, handicap, award a penalty against (*Sport*), impose a penalty on
2 PUT AT A DISADVANTAGE, handicap, cause to suffer, unfairly disadvantage, inflict a handicap on

penalty *noun* PUNISHMENT, price, fine, handicap, forfeit, retribution, forfeiture

penance *noun* ATONEMENT, punishment, penalty, reparation, expiation, sackcloth and ashes, self-punishment, self-mortification

penchant *noun* LIKING, taste, tendency, turn, leaning, bent, bias, inclination, affinity, disposition, fondness, propensity, predisposition, predilection, proclivity, partiality, proneness

pending *adjective* 1 UNDECIDED, unsettled, in the balance, up in the air, undetermined
2 FORTHCOMING, imminent, prospective, impending, in the wind, in the offing
▷ *preposition* AWAITING, until, waiting for, till

penetrate *verb* 1 PIERCE, enter, go through, bore, probe, stab, prick, perforate, impale
2 PERVADE, enter, permeate, filter through, suffuse, seep through, get in through, percolate through
3 INFILTRATE, enter, get in to, make inroads into, sneak in to (*informal*), work *or* worm your way into
4 GRASP, understand, work out, figure out (*informal*), unravel, discern, comprehend, fathom, decipher, suss (out) (*slang*), get to the bottom of

penetrating *adjective* 1 SHARP, harsh, piercing, carrying, piping, loud, intrusive, strident, shrill, high-pitched, ear-splitting
<< OPPOSITE sweet
2 PUNGENT, biting, strong, powerful, sharp, heady, pervasive, aromatic
3 PIERCING, cutting, biting, sharp, freezing, fierce, stinging, frosty, bitterly cold, artic
4 INTELLIGENT, quick, sharp, keen, critical, acute, profound, discriminating, shrewd, discerning, astute, perceptive, incisive, sharp-witted, perspicacious, sagacious

<< OPPOSITE dull
5 PERCEPTIVE, searching, sharp, keen, alert, probing, discerning
<< OPPOSITE unperceptive

penetration *noun* 1 PIERCING, entry, entrance, invasion, puncturing, incision, perforation
2 ENTRY, entrance, inroad

pennant *noun* FLAG, jack, banner, ensign, streamer, burgee (*Nautical*), pennon, banderole

penniless *adjective* POOR, broke (*informal*), bankrupt, impoverished, short, ruined, strapped (*slang*), needy, cleaned out (*slang*), destitute, poverty-stricken, down and out, skint (*Brit slang*), indigent, down at heel, impecunious, dirt-poor (*informal*), on the breadline, flat broke (*informal*), penurious, on your uppers, stony-broke (*Brit slang*), necessitous, in queer street, moneyless, without two pennies to rub together (*informal*), without a penny to your name
<< OPPOSITE rich

penny-pinching *adjective* MEAN, close, near (*informal*), frugal, stingy, scrimping, miserly, niggardly, tightfisted, Scrooge-like, mingy (*Brit informal*), cheeseparing, snoep (*S African informal*)
<< OPPOSITE generous

pension *noun* ALLOWANCE, benefit, welfare, annuity, superannuation

pensioner *noun* SENIOR CITIZEN, retired person, retiree (*US*), old-age pensioner, O.A.P.

pensive *adjective* THOUGHTFUL, serious, sad, blue (*informal*), grave, sober, musing, preoccupied, melancholy, solemn, reflective, dreamy, wistful, mournful, contemplative, meditative, sorrowful, ruminative, in a brown study (*informal*), cogitative
<< OPPOSITE carefree

pent-up *adjective* SUPPRESSED, checked, curbed, inhibited, held back, stifled, repressed, smothered, constrained, bridled, bottled up

penury *noun* POVERTY, want, need, privation, destitution, straitened circumstances, beggary, indigence, pauperism

people *plural noun* 1 PERSONS, humans, individuals, folk (*informal*), men and women, human beings, humanity, mankind, mortals, the human race, Homo sapiens
2 THE PUBLIC, the crowd, the masses, the general public, the mob, the herd, the grass roots, the rank and file, the multitude, the populace, the proletariat, the rabble, the plebs, the proles (*derogatory slang, chiefly Brit*), the commonalty, (the) hoi polloi
3 NATION, public, community, subjects, population, residents, citizens, folk, inhabitants, electors, populace, tax payers, citizenry, (general) public
4 RACE, tribe, ethnic group
5 FAMILY, parents, relations, relatives, folk, folks (*informal*), clan, kin, next of kin, kinsmen, nearest and dearest, kith and kin, your own flesh and blood, rellies (*Austral slang*)
▷ *verb* INHABIT, occupy, settle, populate, colonize

pep *noun* ENERGY, life, spirit, zip (*informal*), vitality, animation, vigour, verve, high spirits, gusto, get-up-and-go (*informal*), brio, vivacity, liveliness, vim (*slang*)
▷▷ **pep something** *or* **someone up** ENLIVEN, inspire, stimulate, animate, exhilarate, quicken, invigorate, jazz up (*informal*), vitalize, vivify

pepper *noun* SEASONING, flavour, spice
▷ *verb* 1 PELT, hit, shower, scatter, blitz, riddle, rake, bombard, assail, strafe, rain down on
2 SPRINKLE, spot, scatter, dot, stud, fleck, intersperse, speck, spatter, freckle, stipple, bespatter

peppery *adjective* HOT, fiery, spicy, pungent, highly seasoned, piquant
<< OPPOSITE mild

perceive *verb* 1 SEE, notice, note, identify, discover, spot, observe, remark, recognize, distinguish, glimpse, make out, pick out, discern, behold, catch sight of, espy, descry
2 UNDERSTAND, sense, gather, get (*informal*), know, see, feel, learn, realize, conclude, appreciate, grasp, comprehend, get the message about, deduce, apprehend, suss (out) (*slang*), get the picture about
3 CONSIDER, believe, judge, suppose, rate, deem, adjudge

perceptible *adjective* NOTICEABLE, clear, obvious, apparent, visible, evident, distinct, tangible, blatant, conspicuous, palpable, discernible, recognizable, detectable, observable, appreciable, perceivable
<< OPPOSITE imperceptible

perception *noun* 1 AWARENESS, understanding, sense, impression, feeling, idea, taste, notion, recognition, observation, consciousness, grasp, sensation, conception, apprehension
2 UNDERSTANDING, intelligence, observation, discrimination, insight, sharpness, cleverness, keenness, shrewdness, acuity, discernment, perspicacity, astuteness, incisiveness, perceptiveness, quick-wittedness, perspicuity

perceptive *adjective* OBSERVANT, acute, intelligent, discerning, quick, aware, sharp, sensitive, alert, penetrating, discriminating, shrewd, responsive, astute, intuitive, insightful, percipient, perspicacious
<< OPPOSITE obtuse

perch *verb* 1 SIT, rest, balance, settle
2 PLACE, put, rest, balance
3 LAND, alight, roost

▷ *noun* RESTING PLACE, post, branch, pole, roost

percolate *verb* 1 PENETRATE, filter, seep, pervade, permeate, transfuse
2 FILTER, brew, perk (*informal*)
3 SEEP, strain, drain, filter, penetrate, drip, leach, ooze, pervade, permeate, filtrate

perennial *adjective* CONTINUAL, lasting, continuing, permanent, constant, enduring, chronic, persistent, abiding, lifelong, perpetual, recurrent, never-ending, incessant, unchanging, inveterate

perfect *adjective* 1 FAULTLESS, correct, pure, accurate, faithful, impeccable, exemplary, flawless, foolproof, blameless
<< OPPOSITE deficient
2 EXCELLENT, ideal, supreme, superb, splendid, sublime, superlative
3 IMMACULATE, impeccable, flawless, spotless, unblemished, untarnished, unmarred
<< OPPOSITE flawed
4 COMPLETE, absolute, sheer, utter, consummate, out-and-out, unadulterated, unmitigated, unalloyed
<< OPPOSITE partial
5 EXACT, true, accurate, precise, right, close, correct, strict, faithful, spot-on (*Brit informal*), on the money (*US*), unerring
▷ *verb* IMPROVE, develop, polish, elaborate, refine, cultivate, hone
<< OPPOSITE mar

For most of its meanings, the adjective *perfect* describes an absolute state, so that something either is or is not *perfect*, and cannot be referred to in terms of degree – thus, one thing should not be described as *more perfect* or *less perfect* than another thing. However, when *perfect* is used in the sense of 'excellent in all respects', *more* and *most* are acceptable, for example *the next day the weather was even more perfect*

perfection *noun* 1 EXCELLENCE, integrity, superiority, purity, wholeness, sublimity, exquisiteness, faultlessness, flawlessness, perfectness, immaculateness
2 THE IDEAL, the crown, the last word, one in a million (*informal*), a paragon, the crème de la crème, the acme, a nonpareil, the beau idéal
3 ACCOMPLISHMENT, achieving, achievement, polishing, evolution, refining, completion, realization, fulfilment, consummation

perfectionist *noun* STICKLER, purist, formalist, precisionist, precisian

perfectly *adverb* 1 COMPLETELY, totally, entirely, absolutely, quite, fully, altogether, thoroughly, wholly, utterly, consummately, every inch
<< OPPOSITE partially
2 FLAWLESSLY, ideally, wonderfully, superbly, admirably, supremely, to perfection, exquisitely, superlatively, impeccably, like a dream, faultlessly
<< OPPOSITE badly

perforate *verb* PIERCE, hole, bore, punch, drill, penetrate, puncture, honeycomb

perform *verb* 1 DO, achieve, carry out, effect, complete, satisfy, observe, fulfil, accomplish, execute, bring about, pull off, act out, transact
2 FULFIL, carry out, execute, discharge
3 PRESENT, act (out), stage, play, produce, represent, put on, render, depict, enact, appear as
4 APPEAR ON STAGE, act

performance *noun* 1 PRESENTATION, playing, acting (out), staging, production, exhibition, interpretation, representation, rendering, portrayal, rendition
2 SHOW, appearance, concert, gig (*informal*), recital
3 WORK, acts, conduct, exploits, feats
4 FUNCTIONING, running, operation, working, action, behaviour, capacity, efficiency, capabilities
5 CARRYING OUT, practice, achievement, discharge, execution, completion, accomplishment, fulfilment, consummation
6 (*informal*) CARRY-ON (*informal, chiefly Brit*), business, to-do, act, scene, display, bother, fuss, pantomime (*informal, chiefly Brit*), song and dance (*informal*), palaver, rigmarole, pother

performer *noun* ARTISTE, player, Thespian, trouper, play-actor, actor *or* actress

perfume *noun* 1 FRAGRANCE, scent, essence, incense, cologne, eau de toilette, eau de cologne, attar
2 SCENT, smell, fragrance, bouquet, aroma, odour, sweetness, niff (*Brit slang*), redolence, balminess

perfunctory *adjective* OFFHAND, routine, wooden, automatic, stereotyped, mechanical, indifferent, careless, superficial, negligent, sketchy, unconcerned, cursory, unthinking, slovenly, heedless, slipshod, inattentive
<< OPPOSITE thorough

perhaps *adverb* MAYBE, possibly, it may be, it is possible (that), conceivably, as the case may be, perchance (*archaic*), feasibly, for all you know, happen (*Northern English dialect*)

peril *noun* 1 DANGER, risk, threat, hazard, menace, jeopardy, perilousness
2 *often plural* PITFALL, problem, risk, hazard
<< OPPOSITE safety

perilous *adjective* DANGEROUS, threatening, exposed, vulnerable, risky, unsure, hazardous, hairy (*slang*), unsafe, precarious, parlous (*archaic*), fraught with danger, chancy (*informal*)

perimeter *noun* BOUNDARY, edge, border,

bounds, limit, margin, confines, periphery, borderline, circumference, ambit
<< OPPOSITE centre

period *noun* 1 TIME, term, season, space, run, stretch, spell, phase, patch (*Brit informal*), interval, span
2 AGE, generation, years, time, days, term, stage, date, cycle, era, epoch, aeon

periodic *adjective* RECURRENT, regular, repeated, occasional, periodical, seasonal, cyclical, sporadic, intermittent, every so often, infrequent, cyclic, every once in a while, spasmodic, at fixed intervals

periodical *noun* PUBLICATION, paper, review, magazine, journal, weekly, monthly, organ, serial, quarterly, zine (*informal*)
▷ *adjective* RECURRENT, regular, repeated, occasional, seasonal, cyclical, sporadic, intermittent, every so often, infrequent, cyclic, every once in a while, spasmodic, at fixed intervals

peripheral *adjective* 1 SECONDARY, beside the point, minor, marginal, irrelevant, superficial, unimportant, incidental, tangential, inessential
2 OUTERMOST, outside, external, outer, exterior, borderline, perimetric

periphery *noun* BOUNDARY, edge, border, skirt, fringe, verge, brink, outskirts, rim, hem, brim, perimeter, circumference, outer edge, ambit

perish *verb* 1 DIE, be killed, be lost, expire, pass away, lose your life, decease, cark it (*Austral & NZ slang*)
2 BE DESTROYED, fall, decline, collapse, disappear, vanish, go under
3 ROT, waste away, break down, decay, wither, disintegrate, decompose, moulder

perishable *adjective* SHORT-LIVED, biodegradable, easily spoilt, decomposable, liable to rot
<< OPPOSITE non-perishable

perjury *noun* LYING UNDER OATH, false statement, forswearing, bearing false witness, giving false testimony, false oath, oath breaking, false swearing, violation of an oath, wilful falsehood

perk *noun* (*Brit informal*) BONUS, benefit, extra, plus, dividend, icing on the cake, fringe benefit, perquisite

perk up *verb* CHEER UP, recover, rally, revive, look up, brighten, take heart, recuperate, buck up (*informal*)
▷▷ **perk something** *or* **someone up** LIVEN UP, revive, cheer up, pep up

perky *adjective* LIVELY, spirited, bright, sunny, cheerful, animated, upbeat (*informal*), buoyant, bubbly, cheery, bouncy, genial, jaunty, chirpy (*informal*), sprightly, vivacious, in fine fettle, full of beans (*informal*), gay, bright-eyed and bushy-tailed (*informal*)

permanence *noun* CONTINUITY, survival, stability, duration, endurance, immortality, durability, finality, perpetuity, constancy, continuance, dependability, permanency, fixity, indestructibility, fixedness, lastingness, perdurability (*rare*)

permanent *adjective* 1 LASTING, fixed, constant, enduring, persistent, eternal, abiding, perennial, durable, perpetual, everlasting, unchanging, immutable, indestructible, immovable, invariable, imperishable, unfading
<< OPPOSITE temporary
2 LONG-TERM, established, secure, stable, steady, long-lasting
<< OPPOSITE temporary

permanently *adverb* FOR EVER, constantly, continually, always, invariably, perennially, persistently, eternally, perpetually, steadfastly, indelibly, in perpetuity, enduringly, unwaveringly, immutably, lastingly, immovably, abidingly, unchangingly, unfadingly
<< OPPOSITE temporarily

permeable *adjective* PENETRABLE, porous, absorbent, spongy, absorptive, pervious

permeate *verb* 1 INFILTRATE, fill, pass through, pervade, filter through, spread through, diffuse throughout
2 PERVADE, saturate, charge, fill, pass through, penetrate, infiltrate, imbue, filter through, spread through, impregnate, seep through, percolate, soak through, diffuse throughout

permissible *adjective* PERMITTED, acceptable, legitimate, legal, all right, sanctioned, proper, authorized, lawful, allowable, kosher (*informal*), admissible, legit (*slang*), licit, O.K. *or* okay (*informal*)
<< OPPOSITE forbidden

permission *noun* AUTHORIZATION, sanction, licence, approval, leave, freedom, permit, go-ahead (*informal*), liberty, consent, allowance, tolerance, green light, assent, dispensation, carte blanche, blank cheque, sufferance
<< OPPOSITE prohibition

permissive *adjective* TOLERANT, liberal, open-minded, indulgent, easy-going, free, lax, lenient, forbearing, acquiescent, latitudinarian, easy-oasy (*slang*)
<< OPPOSITE strict

permit *verb* 1 ALLOW, admit, grant, sanction, let, suffer, agree to, entitle, endure, license, endorse, warrant, tolerate, authorize, empower, consent to, give the green light to, give leave *or* permission
<< OPPOSITE forbid
2 ENABLE, let, allow, cause
▷ *noun* LICENCE, pass, document, certificate,

passport, visa, warrant, authorization
<< OPPOSITE prohibition

permutation *noun* TRANSFORMATION, change, shift, variation, modification, alteration, mutation, transmutation, transposition

pernicious *adjective* (*Formal*) WICKED, bad, damaging, dangerous, evil, offensive, fatal, deadly, destructive, harmful, poisonous, malicious, malign, malignant, detrimental, hurtful, malevolent, noxious, venomous, ruinous, baleful, deleterious, injurious, noisome, baneful (*archaic*), pestilent, maleficent

perpendicular *adjective* 1 UPRIGHT, straight, vertical, plumb, on end
2 AT RIGHT ANGLES, at 90 degrees

perpetrate *verb* COMMIT, do, perform, carry out, effect, be responsible for, execute, inflict, bring about, enact, wreak

> *Perpetrate* and *perpetuate* are sometimes confused: *he must answer for the crimes he has perpetrated* (not *perpetuated*); *the book helped to perpetuate* (not *perpetrate*) *some of the myths surrounding his early life*

perpetual *adjective* 1 EVERLASTING, permanent, endless, eternal, lasting, enduring, abiding, perennial, infinite, immortal, never-ending, unending, unchanging, undying, sempiternal (*literary*)
<< OPPOSITE temporary
2 CONTINUAL, repeated, constant, endless, continuous, persistent, perennial, recurrent, never-ending, uninterrupted, interminable, incessant, ceaseless, unremitting, unfailing, unceasing
<< OPPOSITE brief

perpetuate *verb* MAINTAIN, preserve, sustain, keep up, keep going, continue, keep alive, immortalize, eternalize
<< OPPOSITE end ▷ see **perpetrate**

perplex *verb* PUZZLE, confuse, stump, baffle, bewilder, muddle, confound, beset, mystify, faze, befuddle, flummox, bemuse, dumbfound, nonplus, mix you up

perplexing *adjective* PUZZLING, complex, confusing, complicated, involved, hard, taxing, difficult, strange, weird, mysterious, baffling, bewildering, intricate, enigmatic, mystifying, inexplicable, thorny, paradoxical, unaccountable, knotty, labyrinthine

perplexity *noun* 1 PUZZLEMENT, confusion, bewilderment, incomprehension, bafflement, mystification, stupefaction
2 *usually plural* COMPLEXITY, difficulty, mystery, involvement, puzzle, paradox, obscurity, enigma, intricacy, inextricability

per se *adverb* IN ITSELF, essentially, as such, in essence, by itself, of itself, by definition, intrinsically, by its very nature

persecute *verb* 1 VICTIMIZE, hunt, injure, pursue, torture, hound, torment, martyr, oppress, pick on, molest, ill-treat, maltreat
<< OPPOSITE mollycoddle
2 HARASS, bother, annoy, bait, tease, worry, hassle (*informal*), badger, pester, vex, be on your back (*slang*)
<< OPPOSITE leave alone

perseverance *noun* PERSISTENCE, resolution, determination, dedication, stamina, endurance, tenacity, diligence, constancy, steadfastness, doggedness, purposefulness, pertinacity, indefatigability, sedulity

persevere *verb* KEEP GOING, continue, go on, carry on, endure, hold on (*informal*), hang on, persist, stand firm, plug away (*informal*), hold fast, remain firm, stay the course, keep your hand in, pursue your goal, be determined *or* resolved, keep on *or* at, stick at *or* to
<< OPPOSITE give up

persist *verb* 1 CONTINUE, last, remain, carry on, endure, keep up, linger, abide
2 PERSEVERE, continue, go on, carry on, hold on (*informal*), keep on, keep going, press on, not give up, stand firm, soldier on (*informal*), stay the course, plough on, be resolute, stick to your guns (*informal*), show determination

persistence *noun* DETERMINATION, resolution, pluck, stamina, grit, endurance, tenacity, diligence, perseverance, constancy, steadfastness, doggedness, pertinacity, indefatigability, tirelessness

persistent *adjective* 1 CONTINUOUS, constant, relentless, lasting, repeated, endless, perpetual, continual, never-ending, interminable, unrelenting, incessant, unremitting
<< OPPOSITE occasional
2 DETERMINED, dogged, fixed, steady, enduring, stubborn, persevering, resolute, tireless, tenacious, steadfast, obstinate, indefatigable, immovable, assiduous, obdurate, stiff-necked, unflagging, pertinacious
<< OPPOSITE irresolute

person *noun* INDIVIDUAL, being, body, human, soul, creature, human being, mortal, living soul, man *or* woman
▷▷ **in person** 1 PERSONALLY, yourself
2 IN THE FLESH, actually, physically, bodily

persona *noun* PERSONALITY, part, face, front, role, character, mask, façade, public face, assumed role

personable *adjective* PLEASANT, pleasing, nice, attractive, charming, handsome, good-looking, winning, agreeable, amiable, affable, presentable, likable *or* likeable
<< OPPOSITE unpleasant

personage *noun* PERSONALITY, celebrity, big name, somebody, worthy, notable, public figure, dignitary, luminary, celeb (*informal*), big shot (*informal*), megastar (*informal*), big noise (*informal*), well-known person, V.I.P.

personal *adjective* 1 OWN, special, private, individual, particular, peculiar, privy
2 INDIVIDUAL, special, particular, exclusive
3 PRIVATE, intimate, confidential
4 OFFENSIVE, critical, slighting, nasty, insulting, rude, belittling, disparaging, derogatory, disrespectful, pejorative
5 PHYSICAL, intimate, bodily, corporal, corporeal

personality *noun* 1 NATURE, character, make-up, identity, temper, traits, temperament, psyche, disposition, individuality
2 CHARACTER, charm, attraction, charisma, attractiveness, dynamism, magnetism, pleasantness, likableness *or* likeableness
3 CELEBRITY, star, big name, notable, household name, famous name, celeb (*informal*), personage, megastar (*informal*), well-known face, well-known person

personalized *adjective* CUSTOMIZED, special, private, individual, distinctive, tailor-made, individualized, monogrammed

personally *adverb* 1 IN YOUR OPINION, for yourself, in your book, for your part, from your own viewpoint, in your own view
2 BY YOURSELF, alone, independently, solely, on your own, in person, in the flesh
3 INDIVIDUALLY, specially, subjectively, individualistically
4 PRIVATELY, in private, off the record

personification *noun* EMBODIMENT, image, representation, recreation, portrayal, incarnation, likeness, semblance, epitome

personify *verb* EMBODY, represent, express, mirror, exemplify, symbolize, typify, incarnate, image (*rare*), epitomize, body forth

personnel *noun* EMPLOYEES, people, members, staff, workers, men and women, workforce, human resources, helpers, liveware

perspective *noun* 1 OUTLOOK, attitude, context, angle, overview, way of looking, frame of reference, broad view
2 OBJECTIVITY, proportion, relation, relativity, relative importance
3 VIEW, scene, prospect, outlook, panorama, vista

perspiration *noun* SWEAT, moisture, wetness, exudation

perspire *verb* SWEAT, glow, swelter, drip with sweat, break out in a sweat, pour with sweat, secrete sweat, be damp *or* wet *or* soaked with sweat, exude sweat

persuade *verb* 1 TALK (SOMEONE) INTO, urge, advise, prompt, influence, counsel, win (someone) over, induce, sway, entice, coax, incite, prevail upon, inveigle, bring (someone) round (*informal*), twist (someone's) arm, argue (someone) into
<< OPPOSITE dissuade
2 CAUSE, prompt, lead, move, influence, motivate, induce, incline, dispose, impel, actuate
3 CONVINCE, satisfy, assure, prove to, convert to, cause to believe

persuasion *noun* 1 URGING, influencing, conversion, inducement, exhortation, wheedling, enticement, cajolery, blandishment, inveiglement
2 BELIEF, views, opinion, party, school, side, camp, faith, conviction, faction, cult, sect, creed, denomination, tenet, school of thought, credo, firm belief, certitude, fixed opinion

persuasive *adjective* CONVINCING, telling, effective, winning, moving, sound, touching, impressive, compelling, influential, valid, inducing, logical, credible, plausible, forceful, eloquent, weighty, impelling, cogent
<< OPPOSITE unconvincing

pertain to *verb* RELATE TO, concern, refer to, regard, be part of, belong to, apply to, bear on, befit, be relevant to, be appropriate to, appertain to

pertinent *adjective* RELEVANT, fitting, fit, material, appropriate, pat, suitable, proper, to the point, apt, applicable, apposite, apropos, admissible, germane, to the purpose, ad rem (*Latin*)
<< OPPOSITE irrelevant

perturb *verb* DISTURB, worry, trouble, upset, alarm, bother, unsettle, agitate, ruffle, unnerve, disconcert, disquiet, vex, fluster, faze, discountenance, discompose

perturbed *adjective* DISTURBED, worried, troubled, shaken, upset, alarmed, nervous, anxious, uncomfortable, uneasy, fearful, restless, flurried, agitated, disconcerted, disquieted, flustered, ill at ease, antsy (*informal*)
<< OPPOSITE relaxed

peruse *verb* READ, study, scan, check, examine, inspect, browse, look through, eyeball (*slang*), work over, scrutinize, run your eye over, surf (*Computing*)

pervade *verb* SPREAD THROUGH, fill, affect, penetrate, infuse, permeate, imbue, suffuse, percolate, extend through, diffuse through, overspread

pervasive *adjective* WIDESPREAD, general, common, extensive, universal, prevalent, ubiquitous, rife, pervading, permeating, inescapable, omnipresent

perverse *adjective* 1 STUBBORN, contrary, unreasonable, dogged, contradictory, troublesome, rebellious, wayward,

delinquent, intractable, wilful, unyielding, obstinate, intransigent, headstrong, unmanageable, cussed (*informal*), obdurate, stiff-necked, disobedient, wrong-headed, refractory, pig-headed, miscreant, mulish, cross-grained, contumacious
<< OPPOSITE cooperative
2 ILL-NATURED, cross, surly, petulant, crabbed, fractious, spiteful, churlish, ill-tempered, stroppy (*Brit slang*), cantankerous, peevish, shrewish
<< OPPOSITE good-natured
3 ABNORMAL, incorrect, unhealthy, improper, deviant, depraved

perversion *noun* 1 DEVIATION, vice, abnormality, aberration, kink (*Brit informal*), wickedness, depravity, immorality, debauchery, unnaturalness, kinkiness (*slang*), vitiation
2 DISTORTION, twisting, corruption, misuse, misrepresentation, misinterpretation, falsification

perversity *noun* CONTRARINESS, intransigence, obduracy, waywardness, contradictoriness, wrong-headedness, refractoriness, contumacy, contradictiveness, frowardness (*archaic*)

pervert *verb* 1 DISTORT, abuse, twist, misuse, warp, misinterpret, misrepresent, falsify, misconstrue
2 CORRUPT, degrade, subvert, deprave, debase, desecrate, debauch, lead astray
▷ *noun* DEVIANT, degenerate, sicko (*informal*), sleazeball (*slang*), debauchee, weirdo *or* weirdie (*informal*)

perverted *adjective* UNNATURAL, sick, corrupt, distorted, abnormal, evil, twisted, impaired, warped, misguided, unhealthy, immoral, deviant, wicked, kinky (*slang*), depraved, debased, debauched, aberrant, vitiated, pervy (*slang*), sicko (*slang*)

pessimism *noun* GLOOMINESS, depression, despair, gloom, cynicism, melancholy, hopelessness, despondency, dejection, glumness

pessimist *noun* DEFEATIST, cynic, melancholic, worrier, killjoy, prophet of doom, misanthrope, wet blanket (*informal*), gloom merchant (*informal*), doomster

pessimistic *adjective* GLOOMY, dark, despairing, bleak, resigned, sad, depressed, cynical, hopeless, melancholy, glum, dejected, foreboding, despondent, morose, fatalistic, distrustful, downhearted, misanthropic
<< OPPOSITE optimistic

pest *noun* 1 INFECTION, bug, insect, plague, epidemic, blight, scourge, bane, pestilence, gogga (*S African informal*)
2 NUISANCE, bore, trial, pain (*informal*), drag (*informal*), bother, irritation, gall, annoyance, bane, pain in the neck (*informal*), vexation, thorn in your flesh

pester *verb* ANNOY, worry, bother, disturb, bug (*informal*), plague, torment, get at, harass, nag, hassle (*informal*), harry, aggravate (*informal*), fret, badger, pick on, irk, bedevil, chivvy, get on your nerves (*informal*), bend someone's ear (*informal*), drive you up the wall (*slang*), be on your back (*slang*), get in your hair (*informal*)

pestilence *noun* PLAGUE, epidemic, visitation, pandemic

pet *adjective* 1 FAVOURITE, chosen, special, personal, particular, prized, preferred, favoured, dearest, cherished, fave (*informal*), dear to your heart
2 TAME, trained, domestic, house, domesticated, house-trained (*Brit*), house-broken
▷ *noun* FAVOURITE, treasure, darling, jewel, idol, fave (*informal*), apple of your eye, blue-eyed boy *or* girl (*Brit informal*)
▷ *verb* 1 FONDLE, pat, stroke, caress
2 PAMPER, spoil, indulge, cosset, baby, dote on, coddle, mollycoddle, wrap in cotton wool
3 (*informal*) CUDDLE, kiss, snog (*Brit slang*), smooch (*informal*), neck (*informal*), canoodle (*slang*)

peter out *verb* DIE OUT, stop, fail, run out, fade, dwindle, evaporate, wane, give out, ebb, come to nothing, run dry, taper off

petite *adjective* SMALL, little, slight, delicate, dainty, dinky (*Brit informal*), elfin

petition *noun* 1 APPEAL, round robin, list of signatures
2 ENTREATY, appeal, address, suit, application, request, prayer, plea, invocation, solicitation, supplication
▷ *verb* APPEAL, press, plead, call (upon), ask, urge, sue, pray, beg, crave, solicit, beseech, entreat, adjure, supplicate

petrified *adjective* 1 TERRIFIED, horrified, shocked, frozen, stunned, appalled, numb, dazed, speechless, aghast, dumbfounded, stupefied, scared stiff, terror-stricken
2 FOSSILIZED, ossified, rocklike

petrify *verb* 1 TERRIFY, horrify, amaze, astonish, stun, appal, paralyse, astound, confound, transfix, stupefy, immobilize, dumbfound
2 FOSSILIZE, set, harden, solidify, ossify, turn to stone, calcify

petty *adjective* 1 TRIVIAL, inferior, insignificant, little, small, slight, trifling, negligible, unimportant, paltry, measly (*informal*), contemptible, piddling (*informal*), inconsiderable, inessential, nickel-and-dime (*US slang*)
<< OPPOSITE important
2 SMALL-MINDED, mean, cheap, grudging,

shabby, spiteful, stingy, ungenerous, mean-minded
<< OPPOSITE broad-minded
3 MINOR, lower, junior, secondary, lesser, subordinate, inferior

petulance *noun* SULKINESS, bad temper, irritability, spleen, pique, sullenness, ill-humour, peevishness, querulousness, crabbiness, waspishness, pettishness

petulant *adjective* SULKY, cross, moody, sour, crabbed, impatient, pouting, perverse, irritable, crusty, sullen, bad-tempered, ratty (*Brit & NZ informal*), fretful, waspish, querulous, peevish, ungracious, cavilling, huffy, fault-finding, snappish, ill-humoured, captious
<< OPPOSITE good-natured

phantom *noun* SPECTRE, ghost, spirit, shade (*literary*), spook (*informal*), apparition, wraith, revenant, phantasm

phase *noun* STAGE, time, state, point, position, step, development, condition, period, chapter, aspect, juncture
▷▷ **phase something in** INTRODUCE, incorporate, ease in, start
▷▷ **phase something out** ELIMINATE, close, pull, remove, replace, withdraw, pull out, axe (*informal*), wind up, run down, terminate, wind down, ease off, taper off, deactivate, dispose of gradually

phenomenal *adjective* EXTRAORDINARY, outstanding, remarkable, fantastic, unique, unusual, marvellous, exceptional, notable, sensational, uncommon, singular, miraculous, stellar (*informal*), prodigious, unparalleled, wondrous (*archaic* or *literary*)
<< OPPOSITE unremarkable

phenomenon *noun* 1 OCCURRENCE, happening, fact, event, incident, circumstance, episode
2 WONDER, sensation, spectacle, sight, exception, miracle, marvel, prodigy, rarity, nonpareil

Although *phenomena* is often treated as a singular, this is not grammatically correct. *Phenomenon* is the singular form of this word, and *phenomena* the plural; so *several new phenomena were recorded in his notes* is correct, but *that is an interesting phenomena* is not

philanthropic *adjective* HUMANITARIAN, generous, charitable, benevolent, kind, humane, gracious, altruistic, public-spirited, beneficent, kind-hearted, munificent, almsgiving, benignant
<< OPPOSITE selfish

philanthropist *noun* HUMANITARIAN, patron, benefactor, giver, donor, contributor, altruist, almsgiver

philanthropy *noun* HUMANITARIANISM, charity, generosity, patronage, bounty, altruism, benevolence, munificence, beneficence, liberality, public-spiritedness, benignity, almsgiving, brotherly love, charitableness, kind-heartedness, generousness, open-handedness, largesse *or* largess

Philistine *sometimes not cap noun* BOOR, barbarian, yahoo, lout, bourgeois, hoon (*Austral & NZ*), ignoramus, lowbrow, vulgarian, cougan (*Austral slang*), scozza (*Austral slang*), bogan (*Austral slang*)
▷ *adjective* UNCULTURED, ignorant, crass, tasteless, bourgeois, uneducated, boorish, unrefined, uncultivated, anti-intellectual, lowbrow, inartistic

philosopher *noun* THINKER, theorist, sage, wise man, logician, metaphysician, dialectician, seeker after truth

philosophical *or* **philosophic** *adjective* 1 THEORETICAL, abstract, learned, wise, rational, logical, thoughtful, erudite, sagacious
<< OPPOSITE practical
2 STOICAL, calm, composed, patient, cool, collected, resigned, serene, tranquil, sedate, impassive, unruffled, imperturbable
<< OPPOSITE emotional

philosophy *noun* 1 THOUGHT, reason, knowledge, thinking, reasoning, wisdom, logic, metaphysics
2 OUTLOOK, values, principles, convictions, thinking, beliefs, doctrine, ideology, viewpoint, tenets, world view, basic idea, attitude to life, Weltanschauung (*German*)

phlegmatic *adjective* UNEMOTIONAL, indifferent, cold, heavy, dull, sluggish, matter-of-fact, placid, stoical, lethargic, bovine, apathetic, frigid, lymphatic, listless, impassive, stolid, unfeeling, undemonstrative
<< OPPOSITE emotional

phobia *noun* FEAR, horror, terror, thing (*informal*), obsession, dislike, dread, hatred, loathing, distaste, revulsion, aversion, repulsion, irrational fear, detestation, overwhelming anxiety
<< OPPOSITE liking

phone *noun* 1 TELEPHONE, blower (*informal*), dog and bone (*slang*)
2 CALL, ring (*informal, chiefly Brit*), bell (*Brit slang*), buzz (*informal*), tinkle (*Brit informal*)
▷ *verb* CALL, telephone, ring (up) (*informal, chiefly Brit*), give someone a call, give someone a ring (*informal, chiefly Brit*), make a call, give someone a buzz (*informal*), give someone a bell (*Brit slang*), give someone a tinkle (*Brit informal*), get on the blower (*informal*)

phoney (*informal*) *adjective* 1 FAKE, affected, assumed, trick, put-on, false, forged, imitation, sham, pseudo (*informal*), counterfeit, feigned, spurious

<< OPPOSITE genuine
2 BOGUS, false, fake, pseudo (*informal*), ersatz
▷ *noun* 1 FAKER, fraud, fake, pretender, humbug, impostor, pseud (*informal*)
2 FAKE, sham, forgery, counterfeit

photograph *noun* PICTURE, photo (*informal*), shot, image, print, slide, snap (*informal*), snapshot, transparency, likeness
▷ *verb* TAKE A PICTURE OF, record, film, shoot, snap (*informal*), take (someone's) picture, capture on film, get a shot of

photographic *adjective* 1 PICTORIAL, visual, graphic, cinematic, filmic
2 ACCURATE, minute, detailed, exact, precise, faithful, retentive

phrase *noun* EXPRESSION, saying, remark, motto, construction, tag, quotation, maxim, idiom, utterance, adage, dictum, way of speaking, group of words, locution
▷ *verb* EXPRESS, say, word, put, term, present, voice, frame, communicate, convey, utter, couch, formulate, put into words

physical *adjective* 1 CORPORAL, fleshly, bodily, carnal, somatic, corporeal
2 EARTHLY, fleshly, mortal, incarnate, unspiritual
3 MATERIAL, real, substantial, natural, solid, visible, sensible, tangible, palpable

physician *noun* DOCTOR, specialist, doc (*informal*), healer, medic (*informal*), general practitioner, medical practitioner, medico (*informal*), doctor of medicine, sawbones (*slang*), G.P., M.D.

physique *noun* BUILD, form, body, figure, shape, structure, make-up, frame, constitution

pick *verb* 1 SELECT, choose, identify, elect, nominate, sort out, specify, opt for, single out, mark out, plump for, hand-pick, decide upon, cherry-pick, fix upon, settle on *or* upon, sift out
<< OPPOSITE reject
2 GATHER, cut, pull, collect, take in, harvest, pluck, garner, cull
3 PROVOKE, start, cause, stir up, incite, instigate, foment
4 OPEN, force, crack (*informal*), break into, break open, prise open, jemmy (*informal*)
▷ *noun* 1 CHOICE, decision, choosing, option, selection, preference
2 BEST, prime, finest, tops (*slang*), choicest, flower, prize, elect, pride, elite, cream, jewel in the crown, crème de la crème (*French*)
▷▷ **pick at something** NIBBLE (AT), peck at, have no appetite for, play *or* toy with, push round the plate, eat listlessly
▷▷ **pick on someone** 1 TORMENT, bully, bait, tease, get at (*informal*), badger, persecute, hector, goad, victimize, have it in for (*informal*), tyrannize, have a down on (*informal*)
2 CHOOSE, select, prefer, elect, single out, fix on, settle upon
▷▷ **pick someone up** ARREST, nick (*slang, chiefly Brit*), bust (*informal*), do (*slang*), lift (*slang*), run in (*slang*), nail (*informal*), collar (*informal*), pinch (*informal*), pull in (*Brit slang*), nab (*informal*), apprehend, take someone into custody, feel your collar (*slang*)
▷▷ **pick something up** 1 LEARN, master, acquire, get the hang of (*informal*), become proficient in
2 OBTAIN, get, find, buy, score (*slang*), discover, purchase, acquire, locate, come across, come by, unearth, garner, stumble across, chance upon, happen upon
▷▷ **pick something** *or* **someone out**
1 IDENTIFY, notice, recognize, distinguish, perceive, discriminate, make something *or* someone out, tell something *or* someone apart, single something *or* someone out
2 SELECT, choose, decide on, take, sort out, opt for, cull, plump for, hand-pick
▷▷ **pick something** *or* **someone up** 1 LIFT, raise, gather, take up, grasp, uplift, hoist
2 COLLECT, get, call for, go for, go to get, fetch, uplift (*Scot*), go and get, give someone a lift *or* a ride
▷▷ **pick up** 1 IMPROVE, recover, rally, get better, bounce back, make progress, make a comeback (*informal*), perk up, turn the corner, gain ground, take a turn for the better, be on the road to recovery
2 RECOVER, improve, rally, get better, mend, perk up, turn the corner, be on the mend, take a turn for the better
▷▷ **pick your way** TREAD CAREFULLY, work through, move cautiously, walk tentatively, find *or* make your way

picket *verb* BLOCKADE, boycott, demonstrate outside
▷ *noun* 1 DEMONSTRATION, strike, blockade
2 PROTESTER, demonstrator, picketer, flying picket
3 LOOKOUT, watch, guard, patrol, scout, spotter, sentry, sentinel, vedette (*Military*)
4 STAKE, post, pale, paling, peg, upright, palisade, stanchion

pickings *plural noun* PROFITS, returns, rewards, earnings, yield, proceeds, spoils, loot, plunder, gravy (*slang*), booty, ill-gotten gains

pickle *verb* PRESERVE, marinade, keep, cure, steep
▷ *noun* 1 CHUTNEY, relish, piccalilli
2 (*informal*) PREDICAMENT, spot (*informal*), fix (*informal*), difficulty, bind (*informal*), jam (*informal*), dilemma, scrape (*informal*), hot water (*informal*), uphill (*S African*), quandary, tight spot

pick-me-up *noun* (*informal*) TONIC, drink, pick-up (*slang*), bracer (*informal*), refreshment, stimulant, shot in the arm (*informal*), restorative

pick-up *noun* IMPROVEMENT, recovery, rise, gain, rally, strengthening, revival, upturn, change for the better, upswing

picky *adjective* (*informal*) FUSSY, particular, critical, carping, fastidious, dainty, choosy, finicky, cavilling, pernickety (*informal*), fault-finding, captious

picnic *noun* 1 EXCURSION, fête champêtre (*French*), barbecue, barbie (*informal*), cookout (*US & Canad*), alfresco meal, déjèuner sur l'herbe (*French*), clambake (*US & Canad*), outdoor meal, outing
2 (*informal*) (In this sense, the construction is always negative) WALKOVER (*informal*), breeze (*US & Canad informal*), pushover (*slang*), snap (*informal*), child's play (*informal*), piece of cake (*Brit informal*), cinch (*slang*), cakewalk (*informal*), duck soup (*US slang*)

pictorial *adjective* GRAPHIC, striking, illustrated, vivid, picturesque, expressive, scenic, representational

picture *noun* 1 REPRESENTATION, drawing, painting, portrait, image, print, illustration, sketch, portrayal, engraving, likeness, effigy, delineation, similitude
2 PHOTOGRAPH, photo, still, shot, image, print, frame, slide, snap, exposure, portrait, snapshot, transparency, enlargement
3 FILM, movie (*US informal*), flick (*slang*), feature film, motion picture
4 IDEA, vision, concept, impression, notion, visualization, mental picture, mental image
5 DESCRIPTION, impression, explanation, report, account, image, sketch, depiction, re-creation
6 PERSONIFICATION, model, embodiment, soul, essence, archetype, epitome, perfect example, exemplar, quintessence, living example
▷ *verb* 1 IMAGINE, see, envision, visualize, conceive of, fantasize about, conjure up an image of, see in the mind's eye
2 REPRESENT, show, describe, draw, paint, illustrate, portray, sketch, render, depict, delineate
3 SHOW, photograph, capture on film
>> RELATED WORD *adjective* pictorial

picturesque *adjective* 1 INTERESTING, pretty, beautiful, attractive, charming, scenic, quaint
<< OPPOSITE unattractive
2 VIVID, striking, graphic, colourful, memorable
<< OPPOSITE dull

piddling *adjective* (*informal*) TRIVIAL, little, petty, worthless, insignificant, pants (*informal*), useless, fiddling, trifling, unimportant, paltry, Mickey Mouse (*slang*), puny, derisory, measly (*informal*), crappy (*slang*), toytown (*slang*), piffling, poxy (*slang*), nickel-and-dime (*US slang*)
<< OPPOSITE significant

piece *noun* 1 BIT, section, slice, part, share, division, block, length, quantity, scrap, segment, portion, fragment, fraction, chunk, wedge, shred, slab, mouthful, morsel, wodge (*Brit informal*)
2 COMPONENT, part, section, bit, unit, segment, constituent, module
3 INSTANCE, case, example, sample, specimen, occurrence
4 ITEM, report, story, bit (*informal*), study, production, review, article
5 COMPOSITION, work, production, opus
6 WORK OF ART, work, creation
7 SHARE, cut (*informal*), slice, percentage, quantity, portion, quota, fraction, allotment, subdivision
▷▷ **go** *or* **fall to pieces** BREAK DOWN, fall apart, disintegrate, lose control, crumple, crack up (*informal*), have a breakdown, lose your head
▷▷ **of a piece (with)** LIKE, the same (as), similar (to), consistent (with), identical (to), analogous (to), of the same kind (as)

piecemeal *adjective* UNSYSTEMATIC, interrupted, partial, patchy, intermittent, spotty, fragmentary
▷ *adverb* BIT BY BIT, slowly, gradually, partially, intermittently, at intervals, little by little, fitfully, by degrees, by fits and starts

pied *adjective* VARIEGATED, spotted, streaked, irregular, flecked, motley, mottled, dappled, multicoloured, piebald, parti-coloured, varicoloured

pier *noun* 1 JETTY, wharf, quay, promenade, landing place
2 PILLAR, support, post, column, pile, piling, upright, buttress

pierce *verb* 1 PENETRATE, stab, spike, enter, bore, probe, drill, run through, lance, puncture, prick, transfix, stick into, perforate, impale
2 HURT, cut, wound, strike, touch, affect, pain, move, excite, stir, thrill, sting, rouse, cut to the quick

piercing *adjective* 1 (*of sound*) PENETRATING, sharp, loud, shattering, shrill, high-pitched, ear-splitting
<< OPPOSITE low
2 PERCEPTIVE, searching, aware, bright (*informal*), sharp, keen, alert, probing, penetrating, shrewd, perspicacious, quick-witted
<< OPPOSITE unperceptive
3 SHARP, shooting, powerful, acute, severe, intense, painful, stabbing, fierce, racking, exquisite, excruciating, agonizing
4 (*of weather*) COLD, biting, keen, freezing, bitter, raw, arctic, nipping, numbing, frosty,

wintry, nippy

piety *noun* HOLINESS, duty, faith, religion, grace, devotion, reverence, sanctity, veneration, godliness, devoutness, dutifulness, piousness

pig *noun* **1** HOG, sow, boar, piggy, swine, grunter, piglet, porker, shoat
2 (*informal*) SLOB, hog (*informal*), guzzler (*slang*), glutton, gannet (*informal*), sloven, greedy guts (*slang*)
3 (*informal*) BRUTE, monster, scoundrel, animal, beast, rogue, swine, rotter, boor
>> RELATED WORD *adjective* porcine
>> RELATED WORD *male* boar
>> RELATED WORD *female* sow
>> RELATED WORD *young* piglet
>> RELATED WORD *collective noun* litter
>> RELATED WORD *habitation* sty

pigeon *noun* SQUAB, bird, dove, culver (*archaic*)
>> RELATED WORD *young* squab
>> RELATED WORDS *collective nouns* flock, flight

pigment *noun* COLOUR, colouring, paint, stain, dye, tint, tincture, colouring matter, colorant, dyestuff

piker *noun* (*Austral & NZ slang*) SLACKER, shirker, skiver (*Brit slang*), loafer, layabout, idler, passenger, do-nothing, dodger, good-for-nothing, bludger (*Austral & NZ informal*), gold brick (*US slang*), scrimshanker (*Brit Military slang*)

pile[1] *noun* **1** HEAP, collection, mountain, mass, stack, rick, mound, accumulation, stockpile, hoard, assortment, assemblage
2 (*informal*) *often plural* LOT(s), mountain(s), load(s) (*informal*), oceans, wealth, great deal, stack(s), abundance, large quantity, oodles (*informal*), shedload (*Brit informal*)
3 MANSION, building, residence, manor, country house, seat, big house, stately home, manor house
4 (*informal*) FORTUNE, bomb (*Brit slang*), pot, packet (*slang*), mint, big money, wad (*US & Canad slang*), big bucks (*informal, chiefly US*), megabucks (*US & Canad slang*), tidy sum (*informal*), pretty penny (*informal*), top whack (*informal*)
▷ *verb* **1** LOAD, stuff, pack, stack, charge, heap, cram, lade
2 CROWD, pack, charge, rush, climb, flood, stream, crush, squeeze, jam, flock, shove
▷▷ **pile something up** **1** GATHER (UP), collect, assemble, stack (up), mass, heap (up), load up
2 COLLECT, accumulate, gather in, pull in, amass, hoard, stack up, store up, heap up
▷▷ **pile up** ACCUMULATE, collect, gather (up), build up, amass

pile[2] *noun* FOUNDATION, support, post, column, piling, beam, upright, pier, pillar

pile[3] *noun* NAP, fibre, down, hair, surface, fur, plush, shag, filament

piles *plural noun* HAEMORRHOIDS

pile-up *noun* (*informal*) COLLISION, crash, accident, smash, smash-up (*informal*), multiple collision

pilfer *verb* STEAL, take, rob, lift (*informal*), nick (*slang, chiefly Brit*), appropriate, rifle, pinch (*informal*), swipe (*slang*), embezzle, blag (*slang*), walk off with, snitch (*slang*), purloin, filch, snaffle (*Brit informal*), thieve

pilgrim *noun* TRAVELLER, crusader, wanderer, devotee, palmer, haji (*Islam*), wayfarer

pilgrimage *noun* JOURNEY, tour, trip, mission, expedition, crusade, excursion, hajj (*Islam*)

pill *noun* TABLET, capsule, pellet, bolus, pilule
▷▷ **a bitter pill (to swallow)** TRIAL, pain (*informal*), bore, drag (*informal*), pest, nuisance, pain in the neck (*informal*)

pillage *verb* PLUNDER, strip, sack, rob, raid, spoil (*archaic*), rifle, loot, ravage, ransack, despoil, maraud, reive (*dialect*), depredate (*rare*), freeboot, spoliate
▷ *noun* PLUNDERING, sacking, robbery, plunder, sack, devastation, marauding, depredation, rapine, spoliation

pillar *noun* **1** SUPPORT, post, column, piling, prop, shaft, upright, pier, obelisk, stanchion, pilaster
2 SUPPORTER, leader, rock, worthy, mainstay, leading light (*informal*), tower of strength, upholder, torchbearer

pillory *verb* RIDICULE, denounce, stigmatize, brand, lash, show someone up, expose someone to ridicule, cast a slur on, heap *or* pour scorn on, hold someone up to shame

pilot *noun* **1** AIRMAN, captain, flyer, aviator, aeronaut
2 HELMSMAN, guide, navigator, leader, director, conductor, coxswain, steersman
▷ *verb* **1** FLY, control, operate, be at the controls of
2 NAVIGATE, drive, manage, direct, guide, handle, conduct, steer
3 DIRECT, lead, manage, conduct, steer
▷ *modifier* TRIAL, test, model, sample, experimental

pimp *noun* PROCURER, go-between, bawd (*archaic*), white-slaver, pander, panderer, whoremaster (*archaic*)
▷ *verb* PROCURE, sell, tout, solicit, live off immoral earnings

pimple *noun* SPOT, boil, swelling, pustule, zit (*slang*), papule (*Pathology*), plook (*Scot*)

pin *noun* **1** TACK, nail, needle, safety pin
2 PEG, rod, brace, bolt
▷ *verb* **1** FASTEN, stick, attach, join, fix, secure, nail, clip, staple, tack, affix
2 HOLD FAST, hold down, press, restrain, constrain, immobilize, pinion

▷▷ **pin someone down** FORCE, pressure, compel, put pressure on, pressurize, nail someone down, make someone commit themselves
▷▷ **pin something down** 1 DETERMINE, identify, locate, name, specify, designate, pinpoint, home in on
2 TRAP, confine, constrain, bind, squash, tie down, nail down, immobilize

pinch *verb* 1 NIP, press, squeeze, grasp, compress, tweak
2 HURT, crush, squeeze, pain, confine, cramp, chafe
3 (*Brit informal*) STEAL, rob, snatch, lift (*informal*), nick (*slang, chiefly Brit*), swipe (*slang*), knock off (*slang*), blag (*slang*), pilfer, snitch (*slang*), purloin, filch, snaffle (*Brit informal*)
▷ *noun* 1 NIP, squeeze, tweak
2 DASH, bit, taste, mite, jot, speck, small quantity, smidgen (*informal*), soupçon (*French*)
3 EMERGENCY, crisis, difficulty, plight, scrape (*informal*), strait, uphill (*S African*), predicament, extremity, hardship

pinched *adjective* THIN, starved, worn, drawn, gaunt, haggard, careworn, peaky
<< OPPOSITE plump

pine *verb* WASTE, decline, weaken, sicken, sink, flag, fade, decay, dwindle, wither, wilt, languish, droop
▷▷ **pine for something** *or* **someone** 1 LONG FOR, ache for, crave, yearn for, sigh for, carry a torch for, eat your heart out over, suspire for (*archaic* or *poetic*)
2 HANKER AFTER, crave, covet, wish for, yearn for, thirst for, hunger for, lust after

pink *adjective* ROSY, rose, salmon, flushed, reddish, flesh coloured, roseate

pinnacle *noun* 1 SUMMIT, top, height, peak, eminence
2 HEIGHT, top, crown, crest, meridian, zenith, apex, apogee, acme, vertex

pinpoint *verb* 1 IDENTIFY, discover, spot, define, distinguish, put your finger on
2 LOCATE, find, spot, identify, home in on, zero in on, get a fix on

pint *noun* (*Brit informal*) BEER, jar (*Brit informal*), jug (*Brit informal*), ale

pint-sized *adjective* (*informal*) SMALL, little, tiny, wee, pocket-sized, miniature, diminutive, midget, teeny-weeny, teensy-weensy, pygmy *or* pigmy

pioneer *noun* 1 FOUNDER, leader, developer, innovator, founding father, trailblazer
2 SETTLER, explorer, colonist, colonizer, frontiersman
▷ *verb* DEVELOP, create, launch, establish, start, prepare, discover, institute, invent, open up, initiate, originate, take the lead on, instigate, map out, show the way on, lay the groundwork on

pious *adjective* 1 RELIGIOUS, godly, devoted, spiritual, holy, dedicated, righteous, devout, saintly, God-fearing, reverent
<< OPPOSITE irreligious
2 SELF-RIGHTEOUS, hypocritical, sanctimonious, goody-goody, unctuous, holier-than-thou, pietistic, religiose
<< OPPOSITE humble

pipe *noun* 1 TUBE, drain, canal, pipeline, line, main, passage, cylinder, hose, conduit, duct, conveyor
2 CLAY (PIPE), briar, calabash (*rare*), meerschaum, hookah (*rare*)
3 WHISTLE, horn, recorder, fife, flute, wind instrument, penny whistle
▷ *verb* CONVEY, channel, supply, conduct, bring in, transmit, siphon
▷▷ **pipe down** (*informal*) BE QUIET, shut up (*informal*), hush, stop talking, quieten down, shush, button it (*slang*), belt up (*slang*), shut your mouth, hold your tongue, put a sock in it (*Brit slang*), button your lip (*slang*)
▷▷ **pipe up** SPEAK, volunteer, speak up, have your say, raise your voice, make yourself heard, put your oar in

pipe dream *noun* DAYDREAM, dream, notion, fantasy, delusion, vagary, reverie, chimera, castle in the air

pipeline *noun* TUBE, passage, pipe, line, conduit, duct, conveyor
▷▷ **in the pipeline** ON THE WAY, expected, coming, close, near, being prepared, anticipated, forthcoming, under way, brewing, imminent, in preparation, in production, in process, in the offing

piquant *adjective* 1 SPICY, biting, sharp, stinging, tart, savoury, pungent, tangy, highly-seasoned, peppery, zesty, with a kick (*informal*), acerb
<< OPPOSITE mild
2 INTERESTING, spirited, stimulating, lively, sparkling, provocative, salty, racy, scintillating
<< OPPOSITE dull

pique *noun* RESENTMENT, offence, irritation, annoyance, huff, displeasure, umbrage, hurt feelings, vexation, wounded pride
▷ *verb* 1 AROUSE, excite, stir, spur, stimulate, provoke, rouse, goad, whet, kindle, galvanize
2 DISPLEASE, wound, provoke, annoy, get (*informal*), sting, offend, irritate, put out, incense, gall, nettle, vex, affront, mortify, irk, rile, peeve (*informal*), nark (*Brit, Austral & NZ slang*), put someone's nose out of joint (*informal*), miff (*informal*), hack off (*informal*)

piracy *noun* 1 ROBBERY, stealing, theft, hijacking, infringement, buccaneering, rapine, freebooting
2 ILLEGAL COPYING, bootlegging, plagiarism,

copyright infringement, illegal reproduction

pirate *noun* BUCCANEER, raider, rover, filibuster, marauder, corsair, sea wolf, freebooter, sea robber, sea rover
▷ *verb* COPY, steal, reproduce, bootleg, lift (*informal*), appropriate, borrow, poach, crib (*informal*), plagiarize

pirouette *noun* SPIN, turn, whirl, pivot, twirl
▷ *verb* SPIN, turn, whirl, pivot, twirl

pit *noun* 1 COAL MINE, mine, shaft, colliery, mine shaft
2 HOLE, gulf, depression, hollow, trench, crater, trough, cavity, abyss, chasm, excavation, pothole
▷ *verb* SCAR, mark, hole, nick, notch, dent, gouge, indent, dint, pockmark
▷▷ **pit something** *or* **someone against something** *or* **someone** SET AGAINST, oppose, match against, measure against, put in competition with, put in opposition to

pitch *noun* 1 SPORTS FIELD, ground, stadium, arena, park, field of play
2 TONE, sound, key, frequency, timbre, modulation
3 LEVEL, point, degree, summit, extent, height, intensity, high point
4 TALK, line, patter, spiel (*informal*)
▷ *verb* 1 THROW, launch, cast, toss, hurl, fling, chuck (*informal*), sling, lob (*informal*), bung (*Brit slang*), heave
2 FALL, drop, plunge, dive, stagger, tumble, topple, plummet, fall headlong, (take a) nosedive
3 SET UP, place, station, locate, raise, plant, settle, fix, put up, erect
4 TOSS (ABOUT), roll, plunge, flounder, lurch, wallow, welter, make heavy weather
▷▷ **pitch in** HELP, contribute, participate, join in, cooperate, chip in (*informal*), get stuck in (*Brit informal*), lend a hand, muck in (*Brit informal*), do your bit, lend a helping hand

pitch-black *or* **pitch-dark** *adjective* DARK, black, jet, raven, ebony, sable, unlit, jet-black, inky, Stygian, pitchy, unilluminated

pitfall *noun usually plural* DANGER, difficulty, peril, catch, trap, hazard, drawback, snag, uphill (*S African*), banana skin (*informal*)

pithy *adjective* SUCCINCT, pointed, short, brief, to the point, compact, meaningful, forceful, expressive, concise, terse, laconic, trenchant, cogent, epigrammatic, finely honed
<< OPPOSITE long-winded

pitiful *adjective* 1 PATHETIC, distressing, miserable, harrowing, heartbreaking, grievous, sad, woeful, deplorable, lamentable, heart-rending, gut-wrenching, wretched, pitiable, piteous
<< OPPOSITE funny
2 INADEQUATE, mean, low, miserable, dismal, beggarly, shabby, insignificant, paltry, despicable, measly, contemptible
<< OPPOSITE adequate
3 WORTHLESS, base, sorry, vile, abject, scurvy
<< OPPOSITE admirable

pitiless *adjective* MERCILESS, ruthless, heartless, harsh, cruel, brutal, relentless, callous, inhuman, inexorable, implacable, unsympathetic, cold-blooded, uncaring, unfeeling, cold-hearted, unmerciful, hardhearted
<< OPPOSITE merciful

pittance *noun* PEANUTS (*slang*), trifle, modicum, drop, mite, chicken feed (*slang*), slave wages, small allowance

pitted *adjective* SCARRED, marked, rough, scratched, dented, riddled, blemished, potholed, indented, eaten away, holey, pockmarked, rutty

pity *noun* 1 COMPASSION, understanding, charity, sympathy, distress, sadness, sorrow, kindness, tenderness, condolence, commiseration, fellow feeling
<< OPPOSITE mercilessness
2 SHAME, crime (*informal*), sin (*informal*), misfortune, bad luck, sad thing, bummer (*slang*), crying shame, source of regret
3 MERCY, kindness, clemency, leniency, forbearance, quarter
▷ *verb* FEEL SORRY FOR, feel for, sympathize with, grieve for, weep for, take pity on, empathize with, bleed for, commiserate with, have compassion for, condole with
▷▷ **take pity on something** *or* **someone** HAVE MERCY ON, spare, forgive, pity, pardon, reprieve, show mercy to, feel compassion for, put out of your misery, relent against

pivot *noun* 1 HUB, centre, heart, hinge, focal point, kingpin
2 AXIS, swivel, axle, spindle, fulcrum
▷ *verb* TURN, spin, revolve, rotate, swivel, twirl

pivotal *adjective* CRUCIAL, central, determining, vital, critical, decisive, focal, climactic

pixie *noun* ELF, fairy, brownie, sprite, peri

placard *noun* NOTICE, bill, advertisement, poster, sticker, public notice, affiche (*French*)

placate *verb* CALM, satisfy, humour, soothe, appease, assuage, pacify, mollify, win someone over, conciliate, propitiate

place *noun* 1 SPOT, point, position, site, area, situation, station, location, venue, whereabouts, locus
2 REGION, city, town, quarter, village, district, neighbourhood, hamlet, vicinity, locality, locale, dorp (*S African*)
3 POSITION, point, spot, location
4 SPACE, position, seat, chair
5 SITUATION, position, circumstances, shoes (*informal*)

6 JOB, position, post, situation, office, employment, appointment, berth (*informal*), billet (*informal*)
7 HOME, house, room, property, seat, flat, apartment, accommodation, pad (*slang*), residence, mansion, dwelling, manor, abode, domicile, bachelor apartment (*Canad*)
8 (In this context, the construction is always negative) DUTY, right, job, charge, concern, role, affair, responsibility, task, function, prerogative
▷ *verb* 1 LAY (DOWN), leave, put (down), set (down), stand, sit, position, rest, plant, station, establish, stick (*informal*), settle, fix, arrange, lean, deposit, locate, set out, install, prop, dispose, situate, stow, bung (*Brit slang*), plonk (*informal*), array
2 PUT, lay, set, invest, pin
3 CLASSIFY, class, group, put, order, sort, rank, arrange, grade, assign, categorize
4 ENTRUST TO, give to, assign to, appoint to, allocate to, find a home for
5 IDENTIFY, remember, recognize, pin someone down, put your finger on, put a name to, set someone in context
▷▷ **in place of** INSTEAD OF, rather than, in exchange for, as an alternative to, taking the place of, in lieu of, as a substitute for, as a replacement for
▷▷ **know your place** KNOW YOUR RANK, know your standing, know your position, know your footing, know your station, know your status, know your grade, know your niche
▷▷ **put someone in their place** HUMBLE, humiliate, deflate, crush, mortify, take the wind out of someone's sails, cut someone down to size (*informal*), take someone down a peg (*informal*), make someone eat humble pie, bring someone down to size (*informal*), make someone swallow their pride, settle someone's hash (*informal*)
▷▷ **take place** HAPPEN, occur, go on, go down (*US & Canad*), arise, come about, crop up, transpire (*informal*), befall, materialize, come to pass (*archaic*), betide

placement *noun* 1 POSITIONING, stationing, arrangement, location, ordering, distribution, locating, installation, deployment, disposition, emplacement
2 APPOINTMENT, employment, engagement, assignment

placid *adjective* 1 CALM, cool, quiet, peaceful, even, collected, gentle, mild, composed, serene, tranquil, undisturbed, unmoved, untroubled, unfazed (*informal*), unruffled, self-possessed, imperturbable, equable, even-tempered, unexcitable
<< OPPOSITE excitable
2 STILL, quiet, calm, peaceful, serene, tranquil, undisturbed, halcyon, unruffled
<< OPPOSITE rough

plagiarism *noun* COPYING, borrowing, theft, appropriation, infringement, piracy, lifting (*informal*), cribbing (*informal*)

plague *noun* 1 DISEASE, infection, epidemic, contagion, pandemic, pestilence, lurgy (*informal*)
2 INFESTATION, invasion, epidemic, influx, host, swarm, multitude
3 (*informal*) BANE, trial, cancer, evil, curse, torment, blight, calamity, scourge, affliction
4 (*informal*) NUISANCE, problem, pain (*informal*), bother, pest, hassle (*informal*), annoyance, irritant, aggravation (*informal*), vexation, thorn in your flesh
▷ *verb* 1 TORMENT, trouble, pain, torture, haunt, afflict
2 PESTER, trouble, bother, disturb, annoy, tease, harry, harass, hassle, fret, badger, persecute, molest, vex, bedevil, get on your nerves (*informal*), give someone grief (*Brit & S African*), be on your back (*slang*), get in your hair (*informal*)

plain *adjective* 1 UNADORNED, simple, basic, severe, pure, bare, modest, stark, restrained, muted, discreet, austere, spartan, unfussy, unvarnished, unembellished, unornamented, unpatterned
<< OPPOSITE ornate
2 CLEAR, obvious, patent, evident, apparent, visible, distinct, understandable, manifest, transparent, overt, unmistakable, lucid, unambiguous, comprehensible, legible
<< OPPOSITE hidden
3 STRAIGHTFORWARD, open, direct, frank, bold, blunt, sincere, outspoken, honest, downright, candid, forthright, upfront (*informal*), artless, ingenuous, guileless
<< OPPOSITE roundabout
4 UGLY, ordinary, unattractive, homely (*US & Canad*), not striking, unlovely, unprepossessing, not beautiful, no oil painting (*informal*), ill-favoured, unalluring
<< OPPOSITE attractive
5 ORDINARY, homely, common, simple, modest, everyday, commonplace, lowly, unaffected, unpretentious, frugal, workaday
<< OPPOSITE sophisticated
▷ *noun* FLATLAND, plateau, prairie, grassland, mesa, lowland, steppe, open country, pampas, tableland, veld, llano

plain-spoken *adjective* BLUNT, direct, frank, straightforward, open, explicit, outright, outspoken, downright, candid, forthright, upfront (*informal*), unequivocal
<< OPPOSITE tactful

plaintive *adjective* SORROWFUL, sad, pathetic, melancholy, grievous, pitiful, woeful, wistful, mournful, heart-rending, rueful, grief-stricken, disconsolate, doleful, woebegone, piteous

plan *noun* 1 SCHEME, system, design, idea, programme, project, proposal, strategy, method, suggestion, procedure, plot, device, scenario, proposition, contrivance
2 DIAGRAM, map, drawing, chart, illustration, representation, sketch, blueprint, layout, delineation, scale drawing
▷ *verb* 1 DEVISE, arrange, prepare, scheme, frame, plot, draft, organize, outline, invent, formulate, contrive, think out, concoct
2 INTEND, aim, mean, propose, purpose, contemplate, envisage, foresee
3 DESIGN, outline, draw up a plan of

plane *noun* 1 AEROPLANE, aircraft, jet, airliner, jumbo jet
2 FLAT SURFACE, the flat, horizontal, level surface
3 LEVEL, position, stage, footing, condition, standard, degree, rung, stratum, echelon
▷ *adjective* LEVEL, even, flat, regular, plain, smooth, uniform, flush, horizontal
▷ *verb* SKIM, sail, skate, glide

plant[1] *noun* FLOWER, bush, vegetable, herb, weed, shrub
▷ *verb* 1 SOW, scatter, set out, transplant, implant, put in the ground
2 SEED, sow, implant
3 PLACE, put, set, settle, fix
4 HIDE, put, place, conceal
5 PUT, place, establish, found, fix, institute, root, lodge, insert, sow the seeds of, imbed
>> RELATED WORD *like* florimania

plant[2] *noun* 1 FACTORY, works, shop, yard, mill, foundry
2 MACHINERY, equipment, gear, apparatus

plaque *noun* PLATE, panel, medal, tablet, badge, slab, brooch, medallion, cartouch(e)

plaster *noun* 1 MORTAR, stucco, gypsum, plaster of Paris, gesso
2 BANDAGE, dressing, sticking plaster, Elastoplast (*trademark*), adhesive plaster
▷ *verb* COVER, spread, coat, smear, overlay, daub, besmear, bedaub

plastic *adjective* 1 (*Slang*) FALSE, artificial, synthetic, superficial, sham, pseudo (*informal*), spurious, specious, meretricious, phoney *or* phony (*informal*)
<< OPPOSITE natural
2 PLIANT, soft, flexible, supple, pliable, tensile, ductile, mouldable, fictile
<< OPPOSITE rigid

plate *noun* 1 PLATTER, dish, dinner plate, salver, trencher (*archaic*)
2 HELPING, course, serving, dish, portion, platter, plateful
3 LAYER, panel, sheet, slab
4 ILLUSTRATION, picture, photograph, print, engraving, lithograph
▷ *verb* COAT, gild, laminate, face, cover, silver, nickel, overlay, electroplate, anodize, platinize

plateau *noun* 1 UPLAND, table, highland, mesa, tableland
2 LEVELLING OFF, level, stage, stability

platform *noun* 1 STAGE, stand, podium, rostrum, dais, soapbox
2 POLICY, programme, principle, objective(s), manifesto, tenet(s), party line

platitude *noun* CLICHÉ, stereotype, commonplace, banality, truism, bromide, verbiage, inanity, trite remark, hackneyed saying

Platonic *adjective often not cap* NONPHYSICAL, ideal, intellectual, spiritual, idealistic, transcendent

platoon *noun* SQUAD, company, group, team, outfit (*informal*), patrol, squadron

platter *noun* PLATE, dish, tray, charger, salver, trencher (*archaic*)

plaudits *plural noun* APPROVAL, acclaim, applause, praise, clapping, ovation, kudos, congratulation, round of applause, commendation, approbation, acclamation

plausible *adjective* 1 BELIEVABLE, possible, likely, reasonable, credible, probable, persuasive, conceivable, tenable, colourable, verisimilar
<< OPPOSITE unbelievable
2 GLIB, smooth, specious, smooth-talking, smooth-tongued, fair-spoken

play *verb* 1 AMUSE YOURSELF, have fun, frolic, sport, fool, romp, revel, trifle, caper, frisk, gambol, entertain yourself, engage in games
2 TAKE PART IN, be involved in, engage in, participate in, compete in, be in a team for
3 COMPETE AGAINST, challenge, take on, rival, oppose, vie with, contend against
4 PERFORM, carry out, execute
5 ACT, portray, represent, perform, impersonate, act the part of, take the part of, personate
6 PERFORM ON, strum, make music on
7 *often with* **about** *or* **around** FOOL AROUND, toy, fiddle, trifle, mess around, take something lightly
▷ *noun* 1 AMUSEMENT, pleasure, leisure, games, sport, fun, entertainment, relaxation, a good time, recreation, enjoyment, romping, larks, capering, frolicking, junketing, fun and games, revelry, skylarking, living it up (*informal*), gambolling, horseplay, merrymaking, me-time
2 DRAMA, show, performance, piece, comedy, entertainment, tragedy, farce, soap opera, soapie *or* soapie (*Austral slang*), pantomime, stage show, television drama, radio play,

masque, dramatic piece
▷▷ **in play** IN *or* FOR FUN, for sport, for a joke, for a lark (*informal*), as a prank, for a jest
▷▷ **play around** PHILANDER, have an affair, carry on (*informal*), fool around, dally, sleep around (*informal*), womanize, play away from home (*informal*)
▷▷ **play at something** PRETEND TO BE, pose as, impersonate, make like (*US & Canad informal*), profess to be, assume the role of, give the appearance of, masquerade as, pass yourself off as
▷▷ **play on *or* upon something** TAKE ADVANTAGE OF, abuse, exploit, impose on, trade on, misuse, milk, make use of, utilize, profit by, capitalize on, turn to your account
▷▷ **play something down** MINIMIZE, make light of, gloss over, talk down, underrate, underplay, pooh-pooh (*informal*), soft-pedal (*informal*), make little of, set no store by
▷▷ **play something up** EMPHASIZE, highlight, underline, magnify, stress, accentuate, point up, call attention to, turn the spotlight on, bring to the fore
▷▷ **play up** (*Brit informal*) 1 HURT, be painful, bother you, trouble you, be sore, pain you, give you trouble, give you gyp (*Brit & NZ slang*)
2 MALFUNCTION, not work properly, be on the blink (*slang*), be wonky (*Brit slang*)
3 BE AWKWARD, misbehave, give trouble, be disobedient, give someone grief (*Brit & S African*), be stroppy (*Brit slang*), be bolshie (*Brit informal*)
▷▷ **play up to someone** (*informal*) BUTTER UP, flatter, pander to, crawl to, get in with, suck up to (*informal*), curry favour with, toady, fawn over, keep someone sweet, bootlick (*informal*), ingratiate yourself to

playboy *noun* WOMANIZER, philanderer, rake, socialite, man about town, pleasure seeker, lady-killer (*informal*), roué, lover boy (*slang*), ladies' man

player *noun* 1 SPORTSMAN *or* SPORTSWOMAN, competitor, participant, contestant, team member
2 MUSICIAN, artist, performer, virtuoso, instrumentalist, music maker
3 PERFORMER, entertainer, Thespian, trouper, actor *or* actress

playful *adjective* 1 JOKING, humorous, jokey, arch, teasing, coy, tongue-in-cheek, jesting, flirtatious, good-natured, roguish, waggish
2 LIVELY, spirited, cheerful, merry, mischievous, joyous, sprightly, vivacious, rollicking, impish, frisky, puckish, coltish, kittenish, frolicsome, ludic (*literary*), sportive, gay, larkish (*informal*)
<< OPPOSITE sedate

playmate *noun* FRIEND, companion, comrade, chum (*informal*), pal (*informal*), cobber (*Austral & NZ old-fashioned informal*), playfellow

plaything *noun* TOY, amusement, game, pastime, trifle, trinket, bauble, gimcrack, gewgaw

playwright *noun* DRAMATIST, scriptwriter, tragedian, dramaturge, dramaturgist

plea *noun* 1 APPEAL, request, suit, prayer, begging, petition, overture, entreaty, intercession, supplication
2 (*Law*) SUIT, cause, action, allegation
3 EXCUSE, claim, defence, explanation, justification, pretext, vindication, extenuation

plead *verb* 1 APPEAL, ask, request, beg, petition, crave, solicit, implore, beseech, entreat, importune, supplicate
2 ALLEGE, claim, argue, maintain, assert, put forward, adduce, use as an excuse

pleasant *adjective* 1 PLEASING, nice, welcome, satisfying, fine, lovely, acceptable, amusing, refreshing, delightful, enjoyable, gratifying, agreeable, pleasurable, delectable, lekker (*S African slang*)
<< OPPOSITE horrible
2 FRIENDLY, nice, agreeable, likable *or* likeable, engaging, charming, cheerful, cheery, good-humoured, amiable, genial, affable, congenial
<< OPPOSITE disagreeable

pleasantry *noun usually plural* COMMENT, remark, casual remark, polite remark

please *verb* DELIGHT, entertain, humour, amuse, suit, content, satisfy, charm, cheer, indulge, tickle, gratify, gladden, give pleasure to, tickle someone pink (*informal*)
<< OPPOSITE annoy

pleased *adjective* HAPPY, delighted, contented, satisfied, thrilled, glad, tickled, gratified, over the moon (*informal*), chuffed (*Brit slang*), euphoric, rapt, in high spirits, tickled pink (*informal*), pleased as punch (*informal*)

pleasing *adjective* 1 ENJOYABLE, satisfying, attractive, charming, entertaining, delightful, gratifying, agreeable, pleasurable
<< OPPOSITE unpleasant
2 LIKABLE *or* LIKEABLE, attractive, engaging, charming, winning, entertaining, amusing, delightful, polite, agreeable, amiable
<< OPPOSITE disagreeable

pleasurable *adjective* ENJOYABLE, pleasant, diverting, good, nice, welcome, fun, lovely, entertaining, delightful, gratifying, agreeable, congenial

pleasure *noun* 1 HAPPINESS, delight, satisfaction, enjoyment, bliss, gratification, contentment, gladness, delectation
<< OPPOSITE displeasure

2 AMUSEMENT, joy, recreation, diversion, solace, jollies (*slang*), beer and skittles (*informal*)
<< OPPOSITE duty
3 WISH, choice, desire, will, mind, option, preference, inclination

pledge *noun* 1 PROMISE, vow, assurance, word, undertaking, warrant, oath, covenant, word of honour
2 GUARANTEE, security, deposit, bail, bond, collateral, earnest, pawn, gage, surety
▷ *verb* 1 PROMISE, vow, vouch, swear, contract, engage, undertake, give your word, give your word of honour, give your oath
2 BIND, guarantee, mortgage, engage, gage (*archaic*)

plenary *adjective* 1 (*of assemblies, councils, etc*) FULL, open, general, whole, complete, entire
2 COMPLETE, full, sweeping, absolute, thorough, unlimited, unconditional, unqualified, unrestricted

plentiful *adjective* 1 ABUNDANT, liberal, generous, lavish, complete, ample, infinite, overflowing, copious, inexhaustible, bountiful, profuse, thick on the ground, bounteous (*literary*), plenteous
<< OPPOSITE scarce
2 PRODUCTIVE, bumper, fertile, prolific, fruitful, luxuriant, plenteous

plenty *noun* 1 ABUNDANCE, wealth, luxury, prosperity, fertility, profusion, affluence, opulence, plenitude, fruitfulness, copiousness, plenteousness, plentifulness
2 *usually with* **of** LOTS OF (*informal*), enough, a great deal of, masses of, quantities of, piles of (*informal*), mountains of, a good deal of, stacks of, heaps of (*informal*), a mass of, a volume of, an abundance of, a plethora of, a quantity of, a fund of, oodles of (*informal*), a store of, a mine of, a sufficiency of

plethora *noun* EXCESS, surplus, glut, profusion, surfeit, overabundance, superabundance, superfluity
<< OPPOSITE shortage

pliable *adjective* 1 FLEXIBLE, plastic, supple, lithe, limber, malleable, pliant, tensile, bendy, ductile, bendable
<< OPPOSITE rigid
2 COMPLIANT, susceptible, responsive, manageable, receptive, yielding, adaptable, docile, impressionable, easily led, pliant, tractable, persuadable, influenceable, like putty in your hands
<< OPPOSITE stubborn

plight *noun* DIFFICULTY, condition, state, situation, trouble, circumstances, dilemma, straits, predicament, extremity, perplexity

plod *verb* 1 TRUDGE, drag, tread, clump, lumber, tramp, stomp (*informal*), slog
2 SLOG AWAY, labour, grind away (*informal*), toil, grub, persevere, soldier on, plough through, plug away (*informal*), drudge, peg away

plot[1] *noun* 1 PLAN, scheme, intrigue, conspiracy, cabal, stratagem, machination, covin (*Law*)
2 STORY, action, subject, theme, outline, scenario, narrative, thread, story line
▷ *verb* 1 PLAN, scheme, conspire, intrigue, manoeuvre, contrive, collude, cabal, hatch a plot, machinate
2 DEVISE, design, project, lay, imagine, frame, conceive, brew, hatch, contrive, concoct, cook up (*informal*)
3 CHART, mark, draw, map, draft, locate, calculate, outline, compute

plot[2] *noun* PATCH, lot, area, ground, parcel, tract, allotment

plotter *noun* CONSPIRATOR, architect, intriguer, planner, conspirer, strategist, conniver, Machiavellian, schemer, cabalist

plough *verb* TURN OVER, dig, till, ridge, cultivate, furrow, break ground
▷▷ **plough into something** *or* **someone** PLUNGE INTO, crash into, smash into, career into, shove into, hurtle into, bulldoze into
▷▷ **plough through something** FORGE, cut, drive, press, push, plunge, surge, stagger, wade, flounder, trudge, plod

ploy *noun* TACTIC, move, trick, device, game, scheme, manoeuvre, dodge, ruse, gambit, subterfuge, stratagem, contrivance, wile

pluck *verb* 1 PULL OUT *or* OFF, pick, draw, collect, gather, harvest
2 TUG, catch, snatch, clutch, jerk, yank, tweak, pull at
3 STRUM, pick, finger, twang, thrum, plunk
▷ *noun* COURAGE, nerve, heart, spirit, bottle (*Brit slang*), resolution, determination, guts (*informal*), grit, bravery, backbone, mettle, boldness, spunk (*informal*), intrepidity, hardihood

plucky *adjective* COURAGEOUS, spirited, brave, daring, bold, game, hardy, heroic, gritty, feisty (*informal, chiefly US & Canad*), gutsy (*slang*), intrepid, valiant, doughty, undaunted, unflinching, spunky (*informal*), ballsy (*taboo slang*), mettlesome, (as) game as Ned Kelly (*Austral slang*)
<< OPPOSITE cowardly

plug *noun* 1 STOPPER, cork, bung, spigot, stopple
2 (*informal*) MENTION, advertisement, advert (*Brit informal*), push, promotion, publicity, puff, hype, good word
▷ *verb* 1 SEAL, close, stop, fill, cover, block, stuff, pack, cork, choke, stopper, bung, stop up, stopple
2 (*informal*) MENTION, push, promote, publicize, advertise, build up, puff, hype, write up

▷▷ **plug away** *(informal)* SLOG AWAY, labour, toil away, grind away *(informal)*, peg away, plod away, drudge away

plum *modifier* CHOICE, prize, first-class

plumb *verb* DELVE INTO, measure, explore, probe, sound out, search, go into, penetrate, gauge, unravel, fathom
▷ *adverb* EXACTLY, precisely, bang, slap, spot-on *(Brit informal)*

plume *noun* FEATHER, crest, quill, pinion, aigrette

plummet *verb* 1 DROP, fall, crash, nose-dive, descend rapidly
2 PLUNGE, fall, drop, crash, tumble, swoop, stoop, nose-dive, descend rapidly

plummy *adjective (of a voice)* DEEP, posh *(informal, chiefly Brit)*, refined, upper-class, fruity, resonant

plump¹ *adjective* CHUBBY, fat, stout, full, round, burly, obese, fleshy, beefy *(informal)*, tubby, portly, buxom, dumpy, roly-poly, well-covered, rotund, podgy, corpulent, well-upholstered *(informal)*
<< OPPOSITE scrawny

plump² *verb* FLOP, fall, drop, sink, dump, slump
▷▷ **plump for something** *or* **someone** CHOOSE, favour, go for, back, support, opt for, side with, come down in favour of

plunder *verb* 1 LOOT, strip, sack, rob, raid, devastate, spoil, rifle, ravage, ransack, pillage, despoil
2 STEAL, rob, take, nick *(informal)*, pinch *(informal)*, embezzle, pilfer, thieve
▷ *noun* 1 PILLAGE, sacking, robbery, marauding, rapine, spoliation
2 LOOT, spoils, prey, booty, swag *(slang)*, ill-gotten gains

plunge *verb* 1 DESCEND, fall, drop, crash, pitch, sink, go down, dive, tumble, plummet, nose-dive
2 HURTLE, charge, career, jump, tear, rush, dive, dash, swoop, lurch
3 SUBMERGE, sink, duck, dip, immerse, douse, dunk
4 THROW, cast, pitch, propel
5 FALL STEEPLY, drop, crash *(informal)*, go down, slump, plummet, take a nosedive *(informal)*
▷ *noun* 1 FALL, crash *(informal)*, slump, drop, tumble
2 DIVE, jump, duck, swoop, descent, immersion, submersion

plurality *noun* MULTIPLICITY, variety, diversity, profusion, numerousness

plus *preposition* AND, with, added to, coupled with, with the addition of
▷ *noun (informal)* ADVANTAGE, benefit, asset, gain, extra, bonus, perk *(Brit informal)*, good point, icing on the cake
▷ *adjective* ADDITIONAL, added, extra, positive, supplementary, add-on

When you have a sentence with more than one subject linked by *and*, this makes the subject plural and means it should take a plural verb: *the doctor and all the nurses were* (not *was*) *waiting for the patient*. However, where the subjects are linked by *plus*, *together with*, or *along with*, the number of the verb remains just as it would have been if the extra subjects had not been mentioned. Therefore you would say *the doctor, together with all the nurses, was* (not *were*) *waiting for the patient*

plush *adjective* LUXURIOUS, luxury, costly, lavish, rich, sumptuous, opulent, palatial, ritzy *(slang)*, de luxe
<< OPPOSITE cheap

ply¹ *verb* 1 PROVIDE, supply, shower, lavish, regale
2 BOMBARD, press, harass, besiege, beset, assail, importune
3 WORK AT, follow, exercise, pursue, carry on, practise
4 TRAVEL, go, ferry, shuttle
5 USE, handle, employ, swing, manipulate, wield, utilize

ply² *noun* THICKNESS, leaf, sheet, layer, fold, strand

poach *verb* 1 STEAL, rob, plunder, hunt *or* fish illegally
2 TAKE, steal, appropriate, snatch *(informal)*, nab *(informal)*, purloin

pocket *noun* POUCH, bag, sack, hollow, compartment, receptacle
▷ *modifier* SMALL, compact, miniature, portable, little, potted *(informal)*, concise, pint-size(d) *(informal)*, abridged
▷ *verb* STEAL, take, lift *(informal)*, appropriate, pilfer, purloin, filch, help yourself to, snaffle *(Brit informal)*

pod *noun* SHELL, case, hull, husk, shuck

podium *noun* PLATFORM, stand, stage, rostrum, dais

poem *noun* VERSE, song, lyric, rhyme, sonnet, ode, verse composition

poet *noun* BARD, rhymer, lyricist, lyric poet, versifier, maker *(archaic)*, elegist

poetic *adjective* 1 FIGURATIVE, creative, lyric, symbolic, lyrical, rhythmic, rhythmical, songlike
2 LYRICAL, lyric, rhythmic, elegiac, rhythmical, metrical

poetry *noun* VERSE, poems, rhyme, rhyming, poesy *(archaic)*, verse composition, metrical composition

po-faced *adjective* HUMOURLESS, disapproving,

solemn, prim, puritanical, narrow-minded, stolid, prudish, strait-laced

pogey *noun* (*Canad*) BENEFITS, the dole (*Brit & Austral*), welfare, social security, unemployment benefit, state benefit, allowance

poignancy *noun* SADNESS, emotion, sentiment, intensity, feeling, tenderness, pathos, emotionalism, plaintiveness, evocativeness, piteousness

poignant *adjective* MOVING, touching, affecting, upsetting, sad, bitter, intense, painful, distressing, pathetic, harrowing, heartbreaking, agonizing, heart-rending, gut-wrenching

point *noun* **1** ESSENCE, meaning, subject, question, matter, heart, theme, import, text, core, burden, drift, thrust, proposition, marrow, crux, gist, main idea, nub, pith
2 PURPOSE, aim, object, use, end, reason, goal, design, intention, objective, utility, intent, motive, usefulness
3 ASPECT, detail, feature, side, quality, property, particular, respect, item, instance, characteristic, topic, attribute, trait, facet, peculiarity, nicety
4 PLACE, area, position, station, site, spot, location, locality, locale
5 MOMENT, time, stage, period, phase, instant, juncture, moment in time, very minute
6 STAGE, level, position, condition, degree, pitch, circumstance, extent
7 END, tip, sharp end, top, spur, spike, apex, nib, tine, prong
8 SCORE, tally, mark
9 HEADLAND, head, bill, cape, ness (*archaic*), promontory, foreland
10 PINPOINT, mark, spot, dot, fleck, speck
▷ *verb* **1** *usually followed by* **at** *or* **to** AIM, level, train, direct
2 FACE, look, direct
▷▷ **beside the point** IRRELEVANT, inappropriate, pointless, peripheral, unimportant, incidental, unconnected, immaterial, inconsequential, nothing to do with it, extraneous, neither here nor there, off the subject, inapplicable, not to the point, inapposite, without connection, inconsequent, not pertinent, not germane, not to the purpose
▷▷ **point at** *or* **to something** *or* **someone** INDICATE, show, signal, point to, point out, specify, designate, gesture towards
▷▷ **point of view 1** OPINION, view, attitude, belief, feeling, thought, idea, approach, judgment, sentiment, viewpoint, way of thinking, way of looking at it
2 PERSPECTIVE, side, position, stance, stand, angle, outlook, orientation, viewpoint, slant, standpoint, frame of reference
▷▷ **point something up** EMPHASIZE, stress, highlight, underline, make clear, accent, spotlight, draw attention to, underscore, play up, accentuate, foreground, focus attention on, give prominence to, turn the spotlight on, bring to the fore, put emphasis on
▷▷ **point something** *or* **someone out**
1 IDENTIFY, show, point to, indicate, finger (*informal, chiefly US*), single out, call attention to, draw attention to
2 ALLUDE TO, reveal, mention, identify, indicate, bring up, specify, call attention to, draw attention to
▷▷ **point to something 1** DENOTE, reveal, indicate, show, suggest, evidence, signal, signify, be evidence of, bespeak (*literary*)
2 REFER TO, mention, indicate, specify, single out, touch on, call attention to
▷▷ **to the point** RELEVANT, appropriate, apt, pointed, short, fitting, material, related, brief, suitable, applicable, pertinent, terse, pithy, apposite, apropos, germane

point-blank *adjective* DIRECT, plain, blunt, explicit, abrupt, express, downright, categorical, unreserved, straight-from-the-shoulder
▷ *adverb* DIRECTLY, openly, straight, frankly, plainly, bluntly, explicitly, overtly, candidly, brusquely, straightforwardly, forthrightly

pointed *adjective* **1** SHARP, edged, acute, barbed
2 CUTTING, telling, biting, sharp, keen, acute, accurate, penetrating, pertinent, incisive, trenchant

pointer *noun* **1** HINT, tip, suggestion, warning, recommendation, caution, piece of information, piece of advice
2 INDICATOR, hand, guide, needle, arrow

pointless *adjective* SENSELESS, meaningless, futile, fruitless, unproductive, stupid, silly, useless, absurd, irrelevant, in vain, worthless, ineffectual, unprofitable, nonsensical, aimless, inane, unavailing, without rhyme or reason
<< OPPOSITE worthwhile

poise *noun* **1** COMPOSURE, cool (*slang*), presence, assurance, dignity, equilibrium, serenity, coolness, aplomb, calmness, equanimity, presence of mind, sang-froid, savoir-faire, self-possession
2 GRACE, balance, equilibrium, elegance

poised *adjective* **1** READY, waiting, prepared, standing by, on the brink, in the wings, all set
2 COMPOSED, calm, together (*informal*), collected, dignified, graceful, serene, suave, urbane, self-confident, unfazed (*informal*), debonair, unruffled, nonchalant, self-possessed
<< OPPOSITE agitated

poison *noun* 1 TOXIN, venom, bane (*archaic*)
2 CONTAMINATION, corruption, contagion, cancer, virus, blight, bane, malignancy, miasma, canker
▷ *verb* 1 MURDER, kill, give someone poison, administer poison to
2 CONTAMINATE, foul, infect, spoil, pollute, blight, taint, adulterate, envenom, befoul
3 CORRUPT, colour, undermine, bias, sour, pervert, warp, taint, subvert, embitter, deprave, defile, jaundice, vitiate, envenom

poisonous *adjective* 1 TOXIC, fatal, deadly, lethal, mortal, virulent, noxious, venomous, baneful (*archaic*), mephitic
2 EVIL, vicious, malicious, corrupting, pernicious, baleful, baneful (*archaic*), pestiferous

poke *verb* 1 JAB, hit, push, stick, dig, punch, stab, thrust, butt, elbow, shove, nudge, prod
2 PROTRUDE, stick, thrust, jut
▷ *noun* JAB, hit, dig, punch, thrust, butt, nudge, prod

polar *adjective* OPPOSITE, opposed, contrary, contradictory, antagonistic, antithetical, diametric, antipodal

polarity *noun* OPPOSITION, contradiction, paradox, ambivalence, dichotomy, duality, contrariety

pole[1] *noun* ROD, post, support, staff, standard, bar, stick, stake, paling, shaft, upright, pillar, mast, picket, spar, stave

pole[2] *noun* EXTREMITY, limit, terminus, antipode
▷▷ **poles apart** AT OPPOSITE EXTREMES, incompatible, irreconcilable, worlds apart, miles apart, like chalk and cheese (*Brit*), like night and day, widely separated, completely different, at opposite ends of the earth

polemic *noun* ARGUMENT, attack, debate, dispute, controversy, rant, tirade, diatribe, invective, philippic (*rare*)

polemics *noun* DISPUTE, debate, argument, discussion, controversy, contention, wrangling, disputation, argumentation

police *noun* THE LAW (*informal*), police force, constabulary, fuzz (*slang*), law enforcement agency, boys in blue (*informal*), the Old Bill (*slang*), rozzers (*slang*)
▷ *verb* 1 CONTROL, patrol, guard, watch, protect, regulate, keep the peace, keep in order
2 MONITOR, check, observe, oversee, supervise

police officer *noun* COP (*slang*), officer, pig (*offensive slang*), bobby (*informal*), copper (*slang*), constable, peeler (*Irish & Brit obsolete slang*), gendarme (*slang*), fuzz (*slang*), woodentop (*slang*), bizzy (*informal*), flatfoot (*slang*), rozzer (*slang*), policeman *or* policewoman

policy *noun* 1 PROCEDURE, plan, action, programme, practice, scheme, theory, code, custom, stratagem
2 LINE, rules, approach, guideline, protocol

polish *noun* 1 VARNISH, wax, glaze, lacquer, japan
2 SHEEN, finish, sparkle, glaze, gloss, brilliance, brightness, veneer, lustre, smoothness
3 STYLE, class (*informal*), finish, breeding, grace, elegance, refinement, finesse, urbanity, suavity, politesse
▷ *verb* 1 SHINE, wax, clean, smooth, rub, buff, brighten, burnish, furbish
2 *often with up* PERFECT, improve, enhance, refine, finish, correct, cultivate, brush up, touch up, emend
▷▷ **polish someone off** ELIMINATE, take out (*slang*), get rid of, dispose of, do away with, blow away (*slang, chiefly US*), beat someone once and for all
▷▷ **polish something off** (*informal*) FINISH, down, shift (*informal*), wolf, consume, put away, eat up, swill

polished *adjective* 1 ELEGANT, sophisticated, refined, polite, cultivated, civilized, genteel, suave, finished, urbane, courtly, well-bred
<< OPPOSITE unsophisticated
2 ACCOMPLISHED, professional, masterly, fine, expert, outstanding, skilful, adept, impeccable, flawless, superlative, faultless
<< OPPOSITE amateurish
3 SHINING, bright, smooth, gleaming, glossy, slippery, burnished, glassy, furbished
<< OPPOSITE dull

polite *adjective* 1 MANNERLY, civil, courteous, affable, obliging, gracious, respectful, well-behaved, deferential, complaisant, well-mannered
<< OPPOSITE rude
2 REFINED, cultured, civilized, polished, sophisticated, elegant, genteel, urbane, courtly, well-bred
<< OPPOSITE uncultured

politeness *noun* COURTESY, decency, correctness, etiquette, deference, grace, civility, graciousness, common courtesy, complaisance, courteousness, respectfulness, mannerliness, obligingness

politic *adjective* WISE, diplomatic, sensible, discreet, prudent, advisable, expedient, judicious, tactful, sagacious, in your best interests

political *adjective* 1 GOVERNMENTAL, government, state, parliamentary, constitutional, administrative, legislative, civic, ministerial, policy-making, party political
2 FACTIONAL, party, militant, partisan

politician *noun* STATESMAN *or* STATESWOMAN, representative, senator (*US*), congressman

(US), Member of Parliament, legislator, public servant, congresswoman (US), politico (*informal, chiefly US*), lawmaker, office bearer, M.P., elected offical

politics *noun* 1 AFFAIRS OF STATE, government, government policy, public affairs, civics
2 POLITICAL BELIEFS, party politics, political allegiances, political leanings, political sympathies
3 POLITICAL SCIENCE, polity, statesmanship, civics, statecraft
4 POWER STRUGGLE, machinations, opportunism, realpolitik, Machiavellianism

poll *noun* 1 SURVEY, figures, count, sampling, returns, ballot, tally, census, canvass, Gallup Poll, (public) opinion poll
2 ELECTION, vote, voting, referendum, ballot, plebiscite
▷ *verb* 1 QUESTION, interview, survey, sample, ballot, canvass
2 GAIN, return, record, register, tally

pollute *verb* 1 CONTAMINATE, dirty, mar, poison, soil, foul, infect, spoil, stain, taint, adulterate, make filthy, smirch, befoul
<< OPPOSITE decontaminate
2 DEFILE, violate, corrupt, sully, deprave, debase, profane, desecrate, dishonour, debauch, besmirch
<< OPPOSITE honour

pollution *noun* 1 CONTAMINATION, dirtying, corruption, taint, adulteration, foulness, defilement, uncleanness, vitiation
2 WASTE, poisons, dirt, impurities

pomp *noun* 1 CEREMONY, grandeur, splendour, state, show, display, parade, flourish, pageant, magnificence, solemnity, pageantry, ostentation, éclat
2 SHOW, pomposity, grandiosity, vainglory

pompous *adjective* 1 SELF-IMPORTANT, affected, arrogant, pretentious, bloated, grandiose, imperious, showy, overbearing, ostentatious, puffed up, portentous, magisterial, supercilious, pontifical, vainglorious
<< OPPOSITE unpretentious
2 GRANDILOQUENT, high-flown, inflated, windy, overblown, turgid, bombastic, boastful, flatulent, arty-farty (*informal*), fustian, orotund, magniloquent
<< OPPOSITE simple

pond *noun* POOL, tarn, small lake, fish pond, duck pond, millpond, lochan (*Scot*), dew pond

ponder *verb* THINK ABOUT, consider, study, reflect on, examine, weigh up, contemplate, deliberate about, muse on, brood on, meditate on, mull over, puzzle over, ruminate on, give thought to, cogitate on, rack your brains about, excogitate

ponderous *adjective* 1 DULL, laboured, pedestrian, dreary, heavy, tedious, plodding, tiresome, lifeless, stilted, stodgy, pedantic, long-winded, verbose, prolix
2 CLUMSY, awkward, lumbering, laborious, graceless, elephantine, heavy-footed, unco (*Austral slang*)
<< OPPOSITE graceful

pontificate *verb* EXPOUND, preach, sound off, pronounce, declaim, lay down the law, hold forth, dogmatize, pontify

pool[1] *noun* 1 SWIMMING POOL, lido, swimming bath(s) (*Brit*), bathing pool (*archaic*)
2 POND, lake, mere, tarn
3 PUDDLE, drop, patch, splash

pool[2] *noun* 1 SUPPLY, reserve, fall-back
2 KITTY, bank, fund, stock, store, pot, jackpot, stockpile, hoard, cache
▷ *verb* COMBINE, share, merge, put together, amalgamate, lump together, join forces on

poor *adjective* 1 IMPOVERISHED, broke (*informal*), badly off, hard up (*informal*), short, in need, needy, on the rocks, penniless, destitute, poverty-stricken, down and out, skint (*Brit slang*), in want, indigent, down at heel, impecunious, dirt-poor (*informal*), on the breadline, flat broke (*informal*), penurious, on your uppers, stony-broke (*Brit slang*), necessitous, in queer street, without two pennies to rub together (*informal*), on your beam-ends
<< OPPOSITE rich
2 UNFORTUNATE, pathetic, miserable, unlucky, hapless, pitiful, luckless, wretched, ill-starred, pitiable, ill-fated
<< OPPOSITE fortunate
3 INFERIOR, unsatisfactory, mediocre, second-rate, sorry, weak, pants (*informal*), rotten (*informal*), faulty, feeble, worthless, shabby, shoddy, low-grade, below par, substandard, low-rent (*informal*), crappy (*slang*), valueless, no great shakes (*informal*), rubbishy, poxy (*slang*), not much cop (*Brit slang*), half-pie (*NZ informal*), bodger *or* bodgie (*Austral slang*)
<< OPPOSITE excellent
4 MEAGRE, inadequate, insufficient, reduced, lacking, slight, miserable, pathetic, incomplete, scant, sparse, deficient, skimpy, measly, scanty, pitiable, niggardly, straitened, exiguous
<< OPPOSITE ample
5 UNPRODUCTIVE, barren, fruitless, bad, bare, exhausted, depleted, impoverished, sterile, infertile, unfruitful
<< OPPOSITE productive

poorly *adverb* BADLY, incompetently, inadequately, crudely, inferiorly, unsuccessfully, insufficiently, shabbily, unsatisfactorily, inexpertly
<< OPPOSITE well
▷ *adjective* (*informal*) ILL, sick, ailing, unwell,

crook (*Austral & NZ informal*), seedy (*informal*), below par, out of sorts, off colour, under the weather (*informal*), indisposed, feeling rotten (*informal*)
<< OPPOSITE healthy

pop *noun* 1 (*informal*) SOFT DRINK, ginger (*Scot*), soda (*US & Canad*), fizzy drink, cool drink (*S African*)
2 BANG, report, crack, noise, burst, explosion
▷ *verb* 1 BURST, crack, snap, bang, explode, report, go off (with a bang)
2 PROTRUDE, bulge, stick out
3 PUT, insert, push, stick, slip, thrust, tuck, shove
4 (*informal*) *often with* **in, out,** *etc.* CALL, visit, appear, drop in (*informal*), leave quickly, come *or* go suddenly, nip in *or* out (*Brit informal*)

pope *noun* HOLY FATHER, pontiff, His Holiness, Bishop of Rome, Vicar of Christ
>> RELATED WORD *adjective* papal

populace *noun* PEOPLE, crowd, masses, mob, inhabitants, general public, multitude, throng, rabble, hoi polloi, Joe Public (*slang*), Joe Six-Pack (*US slang*), commonalty

popular *adjective* 1 WELL-LIKED, liked, favoured, celebrated, in, accepted, favourite, famous, approved, in favour, fashionable, in demand, sought-after, fave (*informal*)
<< OPPOSITE unpopular
2 COMMON, general, standard, widespread, prevailing, stock, current, public, conventional, universal, prevalent, ubiquitous
<< OPPOSITE rare

popularity *noun* 1 FAVOUR, fame, esteem, acclaim, regard, reputation, approval, recognition, celebrity, vogue, adoration, renown, repute, idolization, lionization
2 CURRENCY, acceptance, circulation, vogue, prevalence

popularize *verb* 1 MAKE SOMETHING POPULAR, spread the word about, disseminate, universalize, give mass appeal to
2 SIMPLIFY, make available to all, give currency to, give mass appeal to

popularly *adverb* GENERALLY, commonly, widely, usually, regularly, universally, traditionally, ordinarily, conventionally, customarily

populate *verb* 1 INHABIT, people, live in, occupy, reside in, dwell in (*formal*)
2 SETTLE, people, occupy, pioneer, colonize

population *noun* INHABITANTS, people, community, society, residents, natives, folk, occupants, populace, denizens, citizenry

populous *adjective* POPULATED, crowded, packed, swarming, thronged, teeming, heavily populated, overpopulated

pore[1] *noun* OPENING, hole, outlet, orifice, stoma

pore[2] *verb* 1 *followed by* **over** STUDY, read, examine, go over, scrutinize, peruse
2 *followed by* **over, on** *or* **upon** CONTEMPLATE, ponder, brood, dwell on, work over▷ see **pour**

pornographic *adjective* OBSCENE, erotic, indecent, blue, dirty, offensive, rude, sexy, filthy, lewd, risqué, X-rated (*informal*), salacious, prurient, smutty

pornography *noun* OBSCENITY, porn (*informal*), erotica, dirt, filth, indecency, porno (*informal*), smut

porous *adjective* PERMEABLE, absorbent, spongy, absorptive, penetrable, pervious
<< OPPOSITE impermeable

port *noun* HARBOUR, haven, anchorage, seaport, roadstead

portable *adjective* LIGHT, compact, convenient, handy, lightweight, manageable, movable, easily carried, portative

portal *noun* (*Literary*) DOORWAY, door, entry, way in, entrance, gateway, entrance way

portent *noun* OMEN, sign, warning, threat, indication, premonition, foreshadowing, foreboding, harbinger, presage, forewarning, prognostication, augury, presentiment, prognostic

portentous *adjective* 1 POMPOUS, solemn, ponderous, self-important, pontifical
2 SIGNIFICANT, alarming, sinister, ominous, important, threatening, crucial, forbidding, menacing, momentous, fateful, minatory, bodeful

porter[1] *noun* BAGGAGE ATTENDANT, carrier, bearer, baggage-carrier

porter[2] *noun* (*Chiefly Brit*) DOORMAN, caretaker, janitor, concierge, gatekeeper

portion *noun* 1 PART, bit, piece, section, scrap, segment, fragment, fraction, chunk, wedge, hunk, morsel
2 HELPING, serving, piece, plateful
3 SHARE, division, allowance, lot, measure, quantity, quota, ration, allocation, allotment

portly *adjective* STOUT, fat, overweight, plump, large, heavy, ample, bulky, burly, obese, fleshy, beefy (*informal*), tubby (*informal*), rotund, corpulent

portrait *noun* 1 PICTURE, painting, image, photograph, representation, sketch, likeness, portraiture
2 DESCRIPTION, account, profile, biography, portrayal, depiction, vignette, characterization, thumbnail sketch

portray *verb* 1 PLAY, take the role of, act the part of, represent, personate (*rare*)
2 DESCRIBE, present, depict, evoke, delineate, put in words
3 REPRESENT, draw, paint, illustrate, sketch, figure, picture, render, depict, delineate
4 CHARACTERIZE, describe, represent, depict, paint a mental picture of

portrayal *noun* 1 PERFORMANCE, interpretation, enacting, take (*informal, chiefly US*), acting, impersonation, performance as, characterization, personation (*rare*)
2 DEPICTION, picture, representation, sketch, rendering, delineation
3 DESCRIPTION, account, representation
4 CHARACTERIZATION, representation, depiction

pose *verb* 1 PRESENT, cause, produce, create, lead to, result in, constitute, give rise to
2 ASK, state, advance, put, set, submit, put forward, posit, propound
3 POSITION YOURSELF, sit, model, strike a pose, arrange yourself
4 PUT ON AIRS, affect, posture, show off (*informal*), strike an attitude, attitudinize
▷ *noun* 1 POSTURE, position, bearing, attitude, stance, mien (*literary*)
2 ACT, role, façade, air, front, posturing, pretence, masquerade, mannerism, affectation, attitudinizing
▷▷ **pose as something** *or* **someone** IMPERSONATE, pretend to be, sham, feign, profess to be, masquerade as, pass yourself off as

poser[1] *noun* PUZZLE, problem, question, riddle, enigma, conundrum, teaser, tough one, vexed question, brain-teaser (*informal*), knotty point

poser[2] *noun* SHOW-OFF (*informal*), poseur, posturer, masquerader, hot dog (*chiefly US*), impostor, exhibitionist, self-publicist, mannerist, attitudinizer

posh *adjective* (*informal, chiefly Brit*) 1 SMART, grand, exclusive, luxury, elegant, fashionable, stylish, luxurious, classy (*slang*), swish (*informal, chiefly Brit*), up-market, swanky (*informal*), ritzy (*slang*), schmick (*Austral informal*)
2 UPPER-CLASS, high-class, top-drawer, plummy, high-toned, la-di-da (*informal*)

posit *verb* PUT FORWARD, advance, submit, state, assume, assert, presume, predicate, postulate, propound

position *noun* 1 LOCATION, place, point, area, post, situation, station, site, spot, bearings, reference, orientation, whereabouts, locality, locale
2 POSTURE, attitude, arrangement, pose, stance, disposition
3 STATUS, place, standing, class, footing, station, rank, reputation, importance, consequence, prestige, caste, stature, eminence, repute
4 JOB, place, post, opening, office, role, situation, duty, function, employment, capacity, occupation, berth (*informal*), billet (*informal*)
5 PLACE, standing, rank, status
6 SITUATION, state, condition, set of circumstances, plight, strait(s), predicament
7 ATTITUDE, view, perspective, point of view, standing, opinion, belief, angle, stance, outlook, posture, viewpoint, slant, way of thinking, standpoint
▷ *verb* PLACE, put, set, stand, stick (*informal*), settle, fix, arrange, locate, sequence, array, dispose, lay out

positive *adjective* 1 BENEFICIAL, effective, useful, practical, helpful, progressive, productive, worthwhile, constructive, pragmatic, efficacious
<< OPPOSITE harmful
2 CERTAIN, sure, convinced, confident, satisfied, assured, free from doubt
<< OPPOSITE uncertain
3 DEFINITE, real, clear, firm, certain, direct, express, actual, absolute, concrete, decisive, explicit, affirmative, clear-cut, unmistakable, conclusive, unequivocal, indisputable, categorical, incontrovertible, nailed-on (*slang*)
<< OPPOSITE inconclusive
4 (*informal*) ABSOLUTE, complete, perfect, right (*Brit informal*), real, total, rank, sheer, utter, thorough, downright, consummate, veritable, unqualified, out-and-out, unmitigated, thoroughgoing, unalloyed

positively *adverb* 1 DEFINITELY, surely, firmly, certainly, absolutely, emphatically, unquestionably, undeniably, categorically, unequivocally, unmistakably, with certainty, assuredly, without qualification
2 REALLY, completely, simply, plain (*informal*), absolutely, thoroughly, utterly, downright

possess *verb* 1 OWN, have, hold, be in possession of, be the owner of, have in your possession, have to your name
2 BE ENDOWED WITH, have, enjoy, benefit from, be born with, be blessed with, be possessed of, be gifted with
3 CONTROL, influence, dominate, consume, obsess, bedevil, mesmerize, eat someone up, fixate, put under a spell
4 SEIZE, hold, control, dominate, occupy, haunt, take someone over, bewitch, take possession of, have power over, have mastery over

possessed *adjective* CRAZED, haunted, cursed, obsessed, raving, frenzied, consumed, enchanted, maddened, demented, frenetic, berserk, bewitched, bedevilled, under a spell, hag-ridden

possession *noun* 1 OWNERSHIP, control, custody, hold, hands, tenure, occupancy, proprietorship
2 PROVINCE, territory, colony, dominion, protectorate
▷ *plural noun* PROPERTY, things, effects, estate, assets, wealth, belongings, chattels, goods and

chattels

possessive *adjective* 1 JEALOUS, controlling, dominating, domineering, proprietorial, overprotective
2 SELFISH, grasping, acquisitive

possibility *noun* 1 FEASIBILITY, likelihood, plausibility, potentiality, practicability, workableness
2 LIKELIHOOD, chance, risk, odds, prospect, liability, hazard, probability
3 *often plural* POTENTIAL, promise, prospects, talent, capabilities, potentiality

possible *adjective* 1 FEASIBLE, viable, workable, achievable, within reach, on (*informal*), practicable, attainable, doable, realizable
<< OPPOSITE unfeasible
2 LIKELY, potential, anticipated, probable, odds-on, on the cards
<< OPPOSITE improbable
3 CONCEIVABLE, likely, credible, plausible, hypothetical, imaginable, believable, thinkable
<< OPPOSITE inconceivable
4 ASPIRING, would-be, promising, hopeful, prospective, wannabe (*informal*)

> Although it is very common to talk about something's being *very possible* or *more possible*, many people object to such uses, claiming that *possible* describes an absolute state, and therefore something can only be either *possible* or *not possible*. If you want to refer to different degrees of probability, a word such as *likely* or *easy* may be more appropriate than *possible*, for example *it is very likely that he will resign* (not *very possible*)

possibly *adverb* 1 PERHAPS, maybe, God willing, perchance (*archaic*), mayhap (*archaic*), peradventure (*archaic*), haply (*archaic*)
2 AT ALL, in any way, conceivably, by any means, under any circumstances, by any chance

post¹ *noun* SUPPORT, stake, pole, stock, standard, column, pale, shaft, upright, pillar, picket, palisade, newel
▷ *verb* PUT UP, announce, publish, display, advertise, proclaim, publicize, promulgate, affix, stick something up, make something known, pin something up

post² *noun* 1 JOB, place, office, position, situation, employment, appointment, assignment, berth (*informal*), billet (*informal*)
2 POSITION, place, base, beat, station
▷ *verb* STATION, assign, put, place, position, establish, locate, situate, put on duty

post³ *noun* 1 MAIL, collection, delivery, postal service, snail mail (*informal*)
2 CORRESPONDENCE, letters, cards, mail
▷ *verb* SEND (OFF), forward, mail, get off, transmit, dispatch, consign
▷▷ **keep someone posted** NOTIFY, brief, advise, inform, report to, keep someone informed, keep someone up to date, apprise, fill someone in on (*informal*)

poster *noun* NOTICE, bill, announcement, advertisement, sticker, placard, public notice, affiche (*French*)

posterior *noun* BOTTOM, behind (*informal*), bum (*Brit slang*), seat, rear, tail (*informal*), butt (*US & Canad informal*), buns (*US slang*), buttocks, backside, rump, rear end, derrière (*euphemistic*), tush (*US slang*), fundament, jacksy (*Brit slang*)
▷ *adjective* REAR, back, hinder, hind

posterity *noun* THE FUTURE, future generations, succeeding generations

postpone *verb* PUT OFF, delay, suspend, adjourn, table, shelve, defer, put back, hold over, put on ice (*informal*), put on the back burner (*informal*), take a rain check on (*US & Canad informal*)
<< OPPOSITE go ahead with

postponement *noun* DELAY, stay, suspension, moratorium, respite, adjournment, deferment, deferral

postscript *noun* P.S., addition, supplement, appendix, afterthought, afterword

postulate *verb* (*Formal*) PRESUPPOSE, suppose, advance, propose, assume, put forward, take for granted, predicate, theorize, posit, hypothesize

posture *noun* 1 BEARING, set, position, attitude, pose, stance, carriage, disposition, mien (*literary*)
2 ATTITUDE, feeling, mood, point of view, stance, outlook, inclination, disposition, standpoint, frame of mind
▷ *verb* SHOW OFF (*informal*), pose, affect, hot-dog (*chiefly US*), make a show, put on airs, try to attract attention, attitudinize, do something for effect

posy *noun* BOUQUET, spray, buttonhole, corsage, nosegay, boutonniere

pot *noun* 1 CONTAINER, bowl, pan, vessel, basin, vase, jug, cauldron, urn, utensil, crock, skillet
2 JACKPOT, bank, prize, stakes, purse
3 KITTY, funds, pool
4 PAUNCH, beer belly *or* gut (*informal*), spread (*informal*), corporation (*informal*), gut, bulge, spare tyre (*Brit slang*), potbelly

pot-bellied *adjective* FAT, overweight, bloated, obese, distended, corpulent, paunchy

pot belly *noun* PAUNCH, beer belly *or* gut (*informal*), spread (*informal*), corporation (*informal*), pot, gut, spare tyre (*Brit slang*), middle-age spread (*informal*), puku (NZ)

potency *noun* 1 INFLUENCE, might, force,

control, authority, energy, potential, strength, capacity, mana (NZ)
2 PERSUASIVENESS, force, strength, muscle, effectiveness, sway, forcefulness, cogency, impressiveness
3 POWER, force, strength, effectiveness, efficacy
4 VIGOUR, puissance

potent *adjective* 1 POWERFUL, commanding, dynamic, dominant, influential, authoritative
2 PERSUASIVE, telling, convincing, effective, impressive, compelling, forceful, cogent
<< OPPOSITE unconvincing
3 STRONG, powerful, mighty, vigorous, forceful, efficacious, puissant
<< OPPOSITE weak

potentate *noun* RULER, king, prince, emperor, monarch, sovereign, mogul, overlord

potential *adjective* 1 POSSIBLE, future, likely, promising, budding, embryonic, undeveloped, unrealized, probable
2 HIDDEN, possible, inherent, dormant, latent
▷ *noun* ABILITY, possibilities, capacity, capability, the makings, what it takes (*informal*), aptitude, wherewithal, potentiality

potion *noun* CONCOCTION, mixture, brew, tonic, cup, dose, draught, elixir, philtre

potter *verb usually with* **around** *or* **about** MESS ABOUT, fiddle (*informal*), tinker, dabble, fritter, footle (*informal*), poke along, fribble

pottery *noun* CERAMICS, terracotta, crockery, earthenware, stoneware

potty *adjective* (*Brit informal*) CRAZY, eccentric, crackers (*Brit slang*), barmy (*slang*), touched, soft (*informal*), silly, foolish, daft (*informal*), off-the-wall (*slang*), oddball (*informal*), off the rails, dotty (*slang, chiefly Brit*), loopy (*informal*), crackpot (*informal*), out to lunch (*informal*), dippy (*slang*), gonzo (*slang*), doolally (*slang*), off your trolley (*slang*), up the pole (*informal*), off your chump (*slang*), wacko *or* whacko (*informal*), off the air (*Austral slang*), porangi (NZ), daggy (*Austral & NZ informal*)

pouch *noun* BAG, pocket, sack, container, purse, poke (*dialect*)

pounce *verb often followed by* **on** *or* **upon** ATTACK, strike, jump, leap, swoop

pound[1] *noun* ENCLOSURE, yard, pen, compound, kennels, corral (*chiefly US & Canad*)

pound[2] *verb* 1 *sometimes with* **on** BEAT, strike, hammer, batter, thrash, thump, pelt, clobber (*slang*), pummel, belabour, beat *or* knock seven bells out of (*informal*), beat the living daylights out of
2 CRUSH, powder, bruise, bray (*dialect*), pulverize
3 PULSATE, beat, pulse, throb, palpitate, pitapat
4 *often with* **out** THUMP, beat, hammer, bang
5 STOMP, tramp, march, thunder (*informal*), clomp

pour *verb* 1 LET FLOW, spill, splash, dribble, drizzle, slop (*informal*), slosh (*informal*), decant
2 FLOW, stream, run, course, rush, emit, cascade, gush, spout, spew
3 RAIN, sheet, pelt (down), teem, bucket down (*informal*), rain cats and dogs (*informal*), come down in torrents, rain hard *or* heavily
4 STREAM, crowd, flood, swarm, gush, throng, teem

> The spelling of *pour* (as in *she poured cream on her strudel*) should be carefully distinguished from that of *pore over or through* (as in *she pored over the manuscript*)

pout *verb* SULK, glower, mope, look sullen, purse your lips, look petulant, pull a long face, lour *or* lower, make a moue, turn down the corners of your mouth
▷ *noun* SULLEN LOOK, glower, long face, moue (*French*)

poverty *noun* 1 PENNILESSNESS, want, need, distress, necessity, hardship, insolvency, privation, penury, destitution, hand-to-mouth existence, beggary, indigence, pauperism, necessitousness
<< OPPOSITE wealth
2 SCARCITY, lack, absence, want, deficit, shortage, deficiency, inadequacy, dearth, paucity, insufficiency, sparsity
<< OPPOSITE abundance
3 BARRENNESS, deficiency, infertility, sterility, aridity, bareness, poorness, meagreness, unfruitfulness
<< OPPOSITE fertility

poverty-stricken *adjective* PENNILESS, broke (*informal*), bankrupt, impoverished, short, poor, distressed, beggared, needy, destitute, down and out, skint (*Brit slang*), indigent, down at heel, impecunious, dirt-poor (*informal*), on the breadline, flat broke (*informal*), penurious, on your uppers, stony-broke (*Brit slang*), in queer street, without two pennies to rub together (*informal*), on your beam-ends

powder *noun* DUST, pounce (*rare*), talc, fine grains, loose particles
▷ *verb* 1 DUST, cover, scatter, sprinkle, strew, dredge
2 GRIND, crush, pound, pestle, pulverize, granulate

powdery *adjective* FINE, dry, sandy, dusty, loose, crumbling, grainy, chalky, crumbly, granular, pulverized, friable

power *noun* 1 CONTROL, authority, influence, command, sovereignty, sway, dominance, domination, supremacy, mastery, dominion, ascendancy, mana (NZ)
2 ABILITY, capacity, faculty, property, potential, capability, competence, competency

<< OPPOSITE inability

3 AUTHORITY, right, licence, privilege, warrant, prerogative, authorization

4 STRENGTH, might, energy, weight, muscle, vigour, potency, brawn

<< OPPOSITE weakness

5 FORCEFULNESS, force, strength, punch (*informal*), intensity, potency, eloquence, persuasiveness, cogency, powerfulness

powerful *adjective* 1 INFLUENTIAL, dominant, controlling, commanding, supreme, prevailing, sovereign, authoritative, puissant, skookum (*Canad*)

<< OPPOSITE powerless

2 STRONG, strapping, mighty, robust, vigorous, potent, energetic, sturdy, stalwart

<< OPPOSITE weak

3 PERSUASIVE, convincing, effective, telling, moving, striking, storming, dramatic, impressive, compelling, authoritative, forceful, weighty, forcible, cogent, effectual

powerfully *adverb* STRONGLY, hard, vigorously, forcibly, forcefully, mightily, with might and main

powerless *adjective* 1 DEFENCELESS, vulnerable, dependent, subject, tied, ineffective, unarmed, disenfranchised, over a barrel (*informal*), disfranchised

2 WEAK, disabled, helpless, incapable, paralysed, frail, feeble, debilitated, impotent, ineffectual, incapacitated, prostrate, infirm, etiolated

<< OPPOSITE strong

practicable *adjective* FEASIBLE, possible, viable, workable, achievable, attainable, doable, within the realm of possibility, performable

<< OPPOSITE unfeasible ▷ see **practical**

practical *adjective* 1 FUNCTIONAL, efficient, realistic, pragmatic

<< OPPOSITE impractical

2 EMPIRICAL, real, applied, actual, hands-on, in the field, experimental, factual

<< OPPOSITE theoretical

3 SENSIBLE, ordinary, realistic, down-to-earth, mundane, matter-of-fact, no-nonsense, businesslike, hard-headed, workaday

<< OPPOSITE impractical

4 FEASIBLE, possible, sound, viable, constructive, workable, practicable, doable

<< OPPOSITE impractical

5 USEFUL, ordinary, appropriate, sensible, everyday, functional, utilitarian, serviceable

6 SKILLED, working, seasoned, trained, experienced, qualified, veteran, efficient, accomplished, proficient

<< OPPOSITE inexperienced

A distinction is usually made between *practical* and *practicable*. *Practical* refers to a person, idea, project, etc., as being more concerned with or relevant to practice than theory: *he is a very practical person; the idea had no practical application*. *Practicable* refers to a project or idea as being capable of being done or put into effect: *the plan was expensive, yet practicable*

practically *adverb* 1 ALMOST, nearly, close to, essentially, virtually, basically, fundamentally, all but, just about, in effect, very nearly, to all intents and purposes, well-nigh

2 SENSIBLY, reasonably, matter-of-factly, realistically, rationally, pragmatically, with common sense, unsentimentally

practice *noun* 1 CUSTOM, use, way, system, rule, method, tradition, habit, routine, mode, usage, wont, praxis, usual procedure, tikanga (*NZ*)

2 TRAINING, study, exercise, work-out, discipline, preparation, drill, rehearsal, repetition

3 PROFESSION, work, business, career, occupation, pursuit, vocation

4 BUSINESS, company, office, firm, enterprise, partnership, outfit (*informal*)

5 USE, experience, action, effect, operation, application, enactment

practise *verb* 1 REHEARSE, study, prepare, perfect, repeat, go through, polish, go over, refine, run through

2 DO, train, exercise, work out, drill, warm up, keep your hand in

3 CARRY OUT, follow, apply, perform, observe, engage in, live up to, put into practice

4 WORK AT, pursue, carry on, undertake, specialize in, ply your trade

practised *adjective* SKILLED, trained, experienced, seasoned, able, expert, qualified, accomplished, versed, proficient

<< OPPOSITE inexperienced

pragmatic *adjective* PRACTICAL, efficient, sensible, realistic, down-to-earth, matter-of-fact, utilitarian, businesslike, hard-headed

<< OPPOSITE idealistic

praise *verb* 1 ACCLAIM, approve of, honour, cheer, admire, applaud, compliment, congratulate, pay tribute to, laud, extol, sing the praises of, pat someone on the back, cry someone up, big someone up (*slang, chiefly Caribbean*), eulogize, take your hat off to, crack someone up (*informal*)

<< OPPOSITE criticize

2 GIVE THANKS TO, bless, worship, adore, magnify (*archaic*), glorify, exalt, pay homage to

▷ *noun* 1 APPROVAL, acclaim, applause, cheering, tribute, compliment, congratulations, ovation, accolade, good word, kudos, eulogy, commendation, approbation,

acclamation, panegyric, encomium, plaudit, laudation
<< OPPOSITE criticism
2 THANKS, glory, worship, devotion, homage, adoration

prance *verb* 1 DANCE, bound, leap, trip, spring, jump, skip, romp, caper, cavort, frisk, gambol, cut a rug (*informal*)
2 STRUT, parade, stalk, show off (*informal*), swagger, swank (*informal*)

prank *noun* TRICK, lark (*informal*), caper, frolic, escapade, practical joke, skylarking (*informal*), antic, jape

prattle *verb* CHATTER, babble, waffle (*informal, chiefly Brit*), run on, rabbit on (*Brit informal*), witter on (*informal*), patter, drivel, clack, twitter, jabber, gabble, rattle on, blather, blether, run off at the mouth (*slang*), earbash (*Austral & NZ slang*)
▷ *noun* CHATTER, talk, babble, waffle (*informal*), rambling, wittering (*informal*), prating, drivel, jabber, gabble, blather, blether

pray *verb* 1 SAY YOUR PRAYERS, offer a prayer, recite the rosary
2 BEG, ask, plead, petition, urge, request, sue, crave, invoke, call upon, cry, solicit, implore, beseech, entreat, importune, adjure, supplicate

prayer *noun* 1 SUPPLICATION, devotion, communion
2 ORISON, litany, invocation, intercession
3 PLEA, appeal, suit, request, petition, entreaty, supplication

preach *verb* 1 *often with* **to** DELIVER A SERMON, address, exhort, evangelize, preach a sermon, orate
2 URGE, teach, champion, recommend, advise, counsel, advocate, exhort

preacher *noun* CLERGYMAN, minister, parson, missionary, evangelist, revivalist

preamble *noun* INTRODUCTION, prelude, preface, foreword, overture, opening move, proem, prolegomenon, exordium, opening statement *or* remarks

precarious *adjective* 1 INSECURE, dangerous, uncertain, tricky, risky, doubtful, dubious, unsettled, dodgy (*Brit, Austral & NZ informal*), unstable, unsure, hazardous, shaky, hairy (*slang*), perilous, touch and go, dicey (*informal, chiefly Brit*), chancy (*informal*), built on sand, shonky (*Austral & NZ informal*)
<< OPPOSITE secure
2 DANGEROUS, unstable, shaky, slippery, insecure, unsafe, unreliable, unsteady
<< OPPOSITE stable

precaution *noun* SAFEGUARD, insurance, protection, provision, safety measure, preventative measure, belt and braces (*informal*)

precede *verb* 1 GO BEFORE, introduce, herald, pave the way for, usher in, antedate, antecede, forerun
2 GO AHEAD OF, lead, head, go before, take precedence
3 PREFACE, introduce, go before, launch, prefix

precedence *noun* PRIORITY, lead, rank, preference, superiority, supremacy, seniority, primacy, pre-eminence, antecedence

precedent *noun* INSTANCE, example, authority, standard, model, pattern, criterion, prototype, paradigm, antecedent, exemplar, previous example

preceding *adjective* 1 PREVIOUS, earlier, former, above, foregoing, aforementioned, anterior, aforesaid
2 PAST, earlier, former, prior, foregoing

precept *noun* 1 RULE, order, law, direction, principle, command, regulation, instruction, decree, mandate, canon, statute, ordinance, commandment, behest, dictum
2 MAXIM, saying, rule, principle, guideline, motto, dictum, axiom, byword

precinct *noun* AREA, quarter, section, sector, district, zone
▷ *plural noun* DISTRICT, limits, region, borders, bounds, boundaries, confines, neighbourhood, milieu, surrounding area, environs, purlieus

precious *adjective* 1 VALUABLE, expensive, rare, fine, choice, prized, dear, costly, high-priced, exquisite, invaluable, priceless, recherché, inestimable
<< OPPOSITE worthless
2 LOVED, valued, favourite, prized, dear, dearest, treasured, darling, beloved, adored, cherished, fave (*informal*), idolized, worth your *or* its weight in gold
3 AFFECTED, artificial, fastidious, twee (*Brit informal*), chichi, overrefined, overnice

precipice *noun* CLIFF, crag, rock face, cliff face, height, brink, bluff, sheer drop, steep cliff, scarp

precipitate *verb* 1 QUICKEN, trigger, accelerate, further, press, advance, hurry, dispatch, speed up, bring on, hasten, push forward, expedite
2 THROW, launch, cast, discharge, hurl, fling, let fly, send forth
▷ *adjective* 1 HASTY, hurried, frantic, rash, reckless, impulsive, madcap, ill-advised, precipitous, impetuous, indiscreet, heedless, harum-scarum
2 SUDDEN, quick, brief, rushing, violent, plunging, rapid, unexpected, swift, abrupt, without warning, headlong, breakneck

precipitous *adjective* 1 SHEER, high, steep, dizzy, abrupt, perpendicular, falling sharply
2 HASTY, sudden, hurried, precipitate, abrupt, harum-scarum

Some people think the use of *precipitous* to mean 'hasty' is incorrect, and that *precipitate* should be used instead

precise *adjective* 1 EXACT, specific, actual, particular, express, fixed, correct, absolute, accurate, explicit, definite, clear-cut, literal, unequivocal
<< OPPOSITE vague
2 STRICT, particular, exact, nice, formal, careful, stiff, rigid, meticulous, inflexible, scrupulous, fastidious, prim, puritanical, finicky, punctilious, ceremonious
<< OPPOSITE inexact

precisely *adverb* 1 EXACTLY, bang on, squarely, correctly, absolutely, strictly, accurately, plumb (*informal*), slap on (*informal*), square on, on the dot, smack on (*informal*)
2 JUST SO, yes, absolutely, exactly, quite so, you bet (*informal*), without a doubt, on the button (*informal*), indubitably
3 JUST, entirely, absolutely, altogether, exactly, in all respects
4 WORD FOR WORD, literally, exactly, to the letter, neither more nor less

precision *noun* EXACTNESS, care, accuracy, fidelity, correctness, rigour, nicety, particularity, exactitude, meticulousness, definiteness, dotting the i's and crossing the t's, preciseness

preclude *verb* 1 RULE OUT, put a stop to, obviate, make impossible, make impracticable
2 PREVENT, stop, check, exclude, restrain, prohibit, inhibit, hinder, forestall, debar

precocious *adjective* ADVANCED, developed, forward, quick, bright, smart
<< OPPOSITE backward

preconceived *adjective* PRESUMED, premature, predetermined, presupposed, prejudged, forejudged

preconception *noun* PRECONCEIVED IDEA *or* NOTION, notion, prejudice, bias, presumption, predisposition, presupposition, prepossession

precondition *noun* NECESSITY, essential, requirement, prerequisite, must, sine qua non (*Latin*), must-have

precursor *noun* 1 FORERUNNER, pioneer, predecessor, forebear, antecedent, originator
2 HERALD, usher, messenger, vanguard, forerunner, harbinger

predatory *adjective* 1 HUNTING, ravening, carnivorous, rapacious, raptorial, predacious
2 PLUNDERING, ravaging, pillaging, marauding, thieving, despoiling
3 RAPACIOUS, greedy, voracious, vulturous, vulturine

predecessor *noun* 1 PREVIOUS JOB HOLDER, precursor, forerunner, antecedent, former job holder, prior job holder
2 ANCESTOR, forebear, antecedent, forefather, tupuna *or* tipuna (*NZ*)

predetermined *adjective* 1 FATED, predestined, preordained, meant, doomed, foreordained, pre-elected, predestinated
2 PREARRANGED, set, agreed, set up, settled, fixed, cut and dried (*informal*), preplanned, decided beforehand, arranged in advance

predicament *noun* FIX (*informal*), state, situation, spot (*informal*), corner, hole (*slang*), emergency, mess, jam (*informal*), dilemma, pinch, plight, scrape (*informal*), hot water (*informal*), pickle (*informal*), how-do-you-do (*informal*), quandary, tight spot

predict *verb* FORETELL, forecast, divine, foresee, prophesy, call, augur, presage, portend, prognosticate, forebode, soothsay, vaticinate (*rare*)

predictable *adjective* LIKELY, expected, sure, certain, anticipated, reliable, foreseen, on the cards, foreseeable, sure-fire (*informal*), calculable
<< OPPOSITE unpredictable

prediction *noun* PROPHECY, forecast, prognosis, divination, prognostication, augury, soothsaying, sortilege

predilection *noun* LIKING, love, taste, weakness, fancy, leaning, tendency, preference, bias, inclination, penchant, fondness, propensity, predisposition, proclivity, partiality, proneness

predispose *verb* INCLINE, influence, prepare, prompt, lead, prime, affect, prejudice, bias, induce, dispose, sway, make you of a mind to

predisposed *adjective* 1 INCLINED, willing, given, minded, ready, agreeable, amenable
2 SUSCEPTIBLE, subject, prone, liable

predisposition *noun* 1 INCLINATION, tendency, disposition, bent, bias, willingness, likelihood, penchant, propensity, predilection, proclivity, potentiality, proneness
2 SUSCEPTIBILITY, tendency, proneness

predominance *noun* 1 PREVALENCE, weight, preponderance, greater number
2 DOMINANCE, hold, control, edge, leadership, sway, supremacy, mastery, dominion, upper hand, ascendancy, paramountcy

predominant *adjective* 1 MAIN, chief, prevailing, notable, paramount, prevalent, preponderant
2 PRINCIPAL, leading, important, prime, controlling, ruling, chief, capital, primary, supreme, prominent, superior, dominant, sovereign, top-priority, ascendant
<< OPPOSITE minor

predominantly *adverb* MAINLY, largely, chiefly, mostly, generally, principally, primarily, on the whole, in the main, for the most part, to a great extent, preponderantly

predominate *verb* 1 BE IN THE MAJORITY, dominate, prevail, stand out, be predominant, be most noticeable, preponderate
2 PREVAIL, rule, reign, hold sway, get the upper

hand, carry weight

pre-eminence *noun* SUPERIORITY, distinction, excellence, supremacy, prestige, prominence, transcendence, renown, predominance, paramountcy

pre-eminent *adjective* OUTSTANDING, supreme, paramount, chief, excellent, distinguished, superior, renowned, foremost, consummate, predominant, transcendent, unrivalled, incomparable, peerless, unsurpassed, unequalled, matchless

preen *verb* 1 *often reflexive* SMARTEN, admire, dress up, doll up (*slang*), trim, array, deck out, spruce up, prettify, primp, trig (*archaic* or *dialect*), titivate, prink

2 (*of birds*) CLEAN, smooth, groom, tidy, plume

▷▷ **preen yourself** PRIDE YOURSELF, congratulate yourself, give yourself a pat on the back, pique yourself, plume yourself

preface *noun* INTRODUCTION, preliminary, prelude, preamble, foreword, prologue, proem, prolegomenon, exordium

▷ *verb* INTRODUCE, precede, open, begin, launch, lead up to, prefix

prefer *verb* 1 LIKE BETTER, favour, go for, pick, select, adopt, fancy, opt for, single out, plump for, incline towards, be partial to

2 CHOOSE, elect, opt for, pick, wish, desire, would rather, would sooner, incline towards

> Normally, *to* (not *than*) is used after *prefer* and *preferable*. Therefore, you would say *I prefer skating to skiing*, and *a small income is preferable to no income at all*. However, when expressing a preference between two activities stated as infinitive verbs, for example *to skate* and *to ski*, use *than*, as in *I prefer to skate than to ski*

preferable *adjective* BETTER, best, chosen, choice, preferred, recommended, favoured, superior, worthier, more suitable, more desirable, more eligible

<< OPPOSITE undesirable ▷ see **prefer**

> Since *preferable* already means 'more desirable', it is better when writing not to say something is *more preferable* or *most preferable*

preferably *adverb* IDEALLY, if possible, rather, sooner, much rather, by choice, much sooner, as a matter of choice, in *or* for preference

preference *noun* 1 LIKING, wish, taste, desire, bag (*slang*), leaning, bent, bias, cup of tea (*informal*), inclination, penchant, fondness, predisposition, predilection, proclivity, partiality

2 FIRST CHOICE, choice, favourite, election, pick, option, selection, top of the list, fave (*informal*)

3 PRIORITY, first place, precedence, advantage, favouritism, pride of place, favoured treatment

preferential *adjective* PRIVILEGED, favoured, superior, better, special, partial, partisan, advantageous

prefigure *verb* FORESHADOW, suggest, indicate, intimate, presage, portend, shadow forth, adumbrate, foretoken

pregnancy *noun* GESTATION, gravidity

>> RELATED WORDS *adjectives* antenatal, postnatal, maternity

pregnant *adjective* 1 EXPECTANT, expecting (*informal*), with child, in the club (*Brit slang*), in the family way (*informal*), gravid, preggers (*Brit informal*), enceinte, in the pudding club (*slang*), big *or* heavy with child

2 MEANINGFUL, pointed, charged, significant, telling, loaded, expressive, eloquent, weighty, suggestive

3 *with* **with** FULL OF, rich in, fraught with, teeming with, replete with, abounding in, abundant in, fecund with

prehistoric *adjective* EARLIEST, early, primitive, primordial, primeval

prejudice *noun* 1 DISCRIMINATION, racism, injustice, sexism, intolerance, bigotry, unfairness, chauvinism, narrow-mindedness

2 BIAS, preconception, partiality, preconceived notion, warp, jaundiced eye, prejudgment

3 HARM, damage, hurt, disadvantage, loss, mischief, detriment, impairment

▷ *verb* 1 BIAS, influence, colour, poison, distort, sway, warp, slant, predispose, jaundice, prepossess

2 HARM, damage, hurt, injure, mar, undermine, spoil, impair, hinder, crool *or* cruel (*Austral slang*)

prejudiced *adjective* BIASED, influenced, unfair, one-sided, conditioned, partial, partisan, discriminatory, bigoted, intolerant, opinionated, narrow-minded, jaundiced, prepossessed

<< OPPOSITE unbiased

prejudicial *adjective* HARMFUL, damaging, undermining, detrimental, hurtful, unfavourable, counterproductive, deleterious, injurious, inimical, disadvantageous

preliminary *adjective* 1 FIRST, opening, trial, initial, test, pilot, prior, introductory, preparatory, exploratory, initiatory, prefatory, precursory

2 QUALIFYING, eliminating

▷ *noun* INTRODUCTION, opening, beginning, foundation, start, preparation, first round, prelude, preface, overture, initiation, preamble, groundwork, prelims

prelude *noun* 1 INTRODUCTION, beginning, preparation, preliminary, start, commencement, curtain-raiser

2 OVERTURE, opening, introduction, introductory movement

premature *adjective* 1 EARLY, untimely, before time, unseasonable
2 HASTY, rash, too soon, precipitate, impulsive, untimely, ill-considered, jumping the gun, ill-timed, inopportune, overhasty
3 PRETERM, prem (*informal*), preemie (*US & Canad informal*)

prematurely *adverb* 1 TOO EARLY, too soon, before your time, preterm
2 OVERHASTILY, rashly, too soon, precipitately, too hastily, half-cocked, at half-cock

premeditated *adjective* PLANNED, calculated, deliberate, considered, studied, intended, conscious, contrived, intentional, wilful, aforethought, prepense
<< OPPOSITE unplanned

premier *noun* HEAD OF GOVERNMENT, prime minister, chancellor, chief minister, P.M.
▷ *adjective* CHIEF, leading, top, first, highest, head, main, prime, primary, principal, arch, foremost

premiere *noun* FIRST NIGHT, opening, debut, first showing, first performance

premise *noun* ASSUMPTION, proposition, thesis, ground, argument, hypothesis, assertion, postulate, supposition, presupposition, postulation

premises *plural noun* BUILDING(S), place, office, property, site, establishment

premium *noun* 1 FEE, charge, payment, instalment
2 SURCHARGE, extra charge, additional fee *or* charge
3 BONUS, reward, prize, percentage (*informal*), perk (*Brit informal*), boon, bounty, remuneration, recompense, perquisite
▷▷ **at a premium** IN GREAT DEMAND, valuable, expensive, rare, costly, scarce, in short supply, hard to come by, like gold dust, beyond your means, not to be had for love or money

premonition *noun* FEELING, idea, intuition, suspicion, hunch, apprehension, misgiving, foreboding, funny feeling (*informal*), presentiment, feeling in your bones

preoccupation *noun* 1 OBSESSION, concern, hang-up (*informal*), fixation, pet subject, hobbyhorse, idée fixe (*French*), bee in your bonnet
2 ABSORPTION, musing, oblivion, abstraction, daydreaming, immersion, reverie, absent-mindedness, brown study, inattentiveness, absence of mind, pensiveness, engrossment, prepossession, woolgathering

preoccupied *adjective* 1 ABSORBED, taken up, caught up, lost, intent, wrapped up, immersed, engrossed, rapt
2 LOST IN THOUGHT, abstracted, distracted, unaware, oblivious, faraway, absent-minded, heedless, distrait, in a brown study

preparation *noun* 1 GROUNDWORK, development, preparing, arranging, devising, getting ready, thinking-up, putting in order
2 READINESS, expectation, provision, safeguard, precaution, anticipation, foresight, preparedness, alertness
3 *usually plural* ARRANGEMENT, plan, measure, provision
4 MIXTURE, cream, medicine, compound, composition, lotion, concoction, amalgam, ointment, tincture

preparatory *adjective* INTRODUCTORY, preliminary, opening, basic, primary, elementary, prefatory, preparative
▷▷ **preparatory to** BEFORE, prior to, in preparation for, in advance of, in anticipation of

prepare *verb* 1 MAKE *or* GET READY, arrange, draw up, form, fashion, get up (*informal*), construct, assemble, contrive, put together, make provision, put in order, jack up (*NZ informal*)
2 EQUIP, fit, adapt, adjust, outfit, furnish, fit out, accoutre
3 TRAIN, guide, prime, direct, coach, brief, discipline, groom, put someone in the picture
4 MAKE, cook, put together, get, produce, assemble, muster, concoct, fix up, dish up, rustle up (*informal*)
5 GET READY, plan, anticipate, make provision, lay the groundwork, make preparations, arrange things, get everything set
6 PRACTISE, get ready, train, exercise, warm up, get into shape

prepared *adjective* 1 WILLING, minded, able, ready, inclined, disposed, in the mood, predisposed, of a mind
2 READY, set, all set
3 FIT, primed, in order, arranged, in readiness, all systems go (*informal*)

preparedness *noun* READINESS, order, preparation, fitness, alertness

preponderance *noun* 1 PREDOMINANCE, instance, dominance, prevalence
2 GREATER PART, mass, bulk, weight, lion's share, greater numbers, extensiveness
3 DOMINATION, power, sway, superiority, supremacy, dominion, ascendancy

preposterous *adjective* RIDICULOUS, bizarre, incredible, outrageous, shocking, impossible, extreme, crazy, excessive, absurd, foolish, ludicrous, extravagant, unthinkable, unreasonable, insane, irrational, monstrous, senseless, out of the question, laughable, exorbitant, nonsensical, risible, asinine, cockamamie (*slang, chiefly US*)

prerequisite *noun* REQUIREMENT, must,

essential, necessity, condition, qualification, imperative, precondition, requisite, sine qua non (*Latin*), must-have
▷ *adjective* REQUIRED, necessary, essential, called for, vital, mandatory, imperative, indispensable, obligatory, requisite, of the essence, needful

prerogative *noun* RIGHT, choice, claim, authority, title, due, advantage, sanction, liberty, privilege, immunity, exemption, birthright, droit, perquisite

presage *verb* PORTEND, point to, warn of, signify, omen, bode, foreshadow, augur, betoken, adumbrate, forebode, foretoken
▷ *noun* OMEN, sign, warning, forecast, prediction, prophecy, portent, harbinger, intimation, forewarning, prognostication, augury, prognostic, auspice

prescient *adjective* FORESIGHTED, psychic, prophetic, divining, discerning, perceptive, clairvoyant, far-sighted, divinatory, mantic

prescribe *verb* 1 SPECIFY, order, direct, stipulate, write a prescription for
2 ORDAIN, set, order, establish, rule, require, fix, recommend, impose, appoint, command, define, dictate, assign, lay down, decree, stipulate, enjoin

prescription *noun* 1 INSTRUCTION, direction, formula, script (*informal*), recipe
2 MEDICINE, drug, treatment, preparation, cure, mixture, dose, remedy

prescriptive *adjective* DICTATORIAL, rigid, authoritarian, legislating, dogmatic, didactic, preceptive

presence *noun* 1 BEING, existence, company, residence, attendance, showing up, companionship, occupancy, habitation, inhabitance
2 PROXIMITY, closeness, vicinity, nearness, neighbourhood, immediate circle, propinquity
3 PERSONALITY, bearing, appearance, aspect, air, ease, carriage, aura, poise, demeanour, self-assurance, mien (*literary*), comportment
4 SPIRIT, ghost, manifestation, spectre, apparition, shade (*literary*), wraith, supernatural being, revenant, eidolon, atua (*NZ*), wairua (*NZ*)
▷▷ **presence of mind** LEVEL-HEADEDNESS, assurance, composure, poise, cool (*slang*), wits, countenance, coolness, aplomb, alertness, calmness, equanimity, self-assurance, phlegm, quickness, sang-froid, self-possession, unflappability (*informal*), imperturbability, quick-wittedness, self-command, collectedness

present[1] *adjective* 1 CURRENT, existing, immediate, contemporary, instant, present-day, existent, extant
2 HERE, there, near, available, ready, nearby, accounted for, to hand, at hand, in attendance
<< OPPOSITE absent
3 IN EXISTENCE, existing, existent, extant
▷▷ **at present** JUST NOW, now, presently, currently, at the moment, right now, nowadays, at this time, at the present time, in this day and age
▷▷ **for the present** FOR NOW, for a while, in the meantime, temporarily, for the moment, for the time being, provisionally, not for long, for the nonce
▷▷ **the present** NOW, today, the time being, here and now, this day and age, the present moment

present[2] *noun* GIFT, offering, grant, favour, donation, hand-out, endowment, boon, bounty, gratuity, prezzie (*informal*), benefaction, bonsela (*S African*), koha (*NZ*), largesse *or* largess
▷ *verb* 1 GIVE, award, hand over, offer, grant, donate, hand out, furnish, confer, bestow, entrust, proffer, put at someone's disposal
2 PUT FORWARD, offer, suggest, raise, state, produce, introduce, advance, relate, declare, extend, pose, submit, tender, hold out, recount, expound, proffer, adduce
3 PUT ON, stage, perform, give, show, mount, render, put before the public
4 LAUNCH, display, demonstrate, parade, exhibit, unveil
5 INTRODUCE, make known, acquaint someone with

presentable *adjective* 1 TIDY, elegant, well groomed, becoming, trim, spruce, dapper, natty (*informal*), smartly dressed, fit to be seen
<< OPPOSITE unpresentable
2 SATISFACTORY, suitable, decent, acceptable, proper, good enough, respectable, not bad (*informal*), tolerable, passable, O.K. *or* okay (*informal*)
<< OPPOSITE unsatisfactory

presentation *noun* 1 GIVING, award, offering, donation, investiture, bestowal, conferral
2 APPEARANCE, look, display, packaging, arrangement, layout delivery
3 PERFORMANCE, staging, production, show, arrangement, representation, portrayal, rendition

present-day *adjective* CURRENT, modern, present, recent, contemporary, up-to-date, latter-day, newfangled

presently *adverb* 1 AT PRESENT, currently, now, today, these days, nowadays, at the present time, in this day and age, at the minute (*Brit informal*)
2 SOON, shortly, directly, before long, momentarily (*US & Canad*), in a moment, in a minute, pretty soon (*informal*), anon (*archaic*), by and by, in a short while, in a jiffy (*informal*), erelong (*archaic* or *poetic*)

preservation *noun* 1 UPHOLDING, keeping, support, security, defence, maintenance, perpetuation
2 PROTECTION, safety, maintenance, conservation, salvation, safeguarding, safekeeping
3 STORAGE, smoking, drying, bottling, freezing, curing, chilling, candying, pickling, conserving, tinning

preserve *verb* 1 MAINTAIN, keep, continue, retain, sustain, keep up, prolong, uphold, conserve, perpetuate, keep alive
<< OPPOSITE end
2 PROTECT, keep, save, maintain, guard, defend, secure, shelter, shield, care for, safeguard, conserve
<< OPPOSITE attack
3 KEEP, save, store, can, dry, bottle, salt, cure, candy, pickle, conserve
▷ *noun* 1 *often plural* JAM, jelly, conserve, marmalade, confection, sweetmeat, confiture
2 AREA, department, field, territory, province, arena, orbit, sphere, realm, domain, specialism
3 RESERVE, reservation, sanctuary, game reserve

preside *verb* OFFICIATE, chair, moderate, be chairperson
▷▷ **preside over something** *or* **someone** RUN, lead, head, control, manage, direct, conduct, govern, administer, supervise, be at the head of, be in authority

press *verb* 1 PUSH (DOWN), depress, lean on, bear down, press down, force down
2 PUSH, squeeze, jam, thrust, ram, wedge, shove
3 HUG, squeeze, embrace, clasp, crush, encircle, enfold, hold close, fold in your arms
4 URGE, force, beg, petition, sue, enforce, insist on, compel, constrain, exhort, implore, enjoin, pressurize, entreat, importune, supplicate
5 PLEAD, present, lodge, submit, tender, advance insistently
6 IRON, finish, steam, smooth, flatten, put the creases in
7 COMPRESS, grind, reduce, mill, crush, pound, squeeze, tread, pulp, mash, trample, condense, pulverize, tamp, macerate
8 CROWD, push, gather, rush, surge, mill, hurry, cluster, flock, herd, swarm, hasten, seethe, throng
▷▷ **the press** 1 NEWSPAPERS, the papers, journalism, news media, Fleet Street, fourth estate
2 JOURNALISTS, correspondents, reporters, photographers, columnists, pressmen, newsmen, journos (*slang*), gentlemen of the press

pressing *adjective* URGENT, serious, burning, vital, crucial, imperative, important, constraining, high-priority, now or never, importunate, exigent
<< OPPOSITE unimportant

pressure *noun* 1 FORCE, crushing, squeezing, compressing, weight, compression, heaviness
2 POWER, influence, force, obligation, constraint, sway, compulsion, coercion
3 STRESS, demands, difficulty, strain, press, heat, load, burden, distress, hurry, urgency, hassle (*informal*), uphill (*S African*), adversity, affliction, exigency

pressurize *verb* FORCE, drive, compel, intimidate, coerce, dragoon, breathe down someone's neck, browbeat, press-gang, twist someone's arm (*informal*), turn on the heat (*informal*), put the screws on (*slang*)

prestige *noun* STATUS, standing, authority, influence, credit, regard, weight, reputation, honour, importance, fame, celebrity, distinction, esteem, stature, eminence, kudos, cachet, renown, Brownie points, mana (NZ)

prestigious *adjective* CELEBRATED, respected, prominent, great, important, imposing, impressive, influential, esteemed, notable, renowned, eminent, illustrious, reputable, exalted
<< OPPOSITE unknown

presumably *adverb* IT WOULD SEEM, probably, likely, apparently, most likely, seemingly, doubtless, on the face of it, in all probability, in all likelihood, doubtlessly

presume *verb* 1 BELIEVE, think, suppose, assume, guess (*informal, chiefly US & Canad*), take it, take for granted, infer, conjecture, postulate, surmise, posit, presuppose
2 DARE, venture, undertake, go so far as, have the audacity, take the liberty, make bold, make so bold as
▷▷ **presume on something** *or* **someone** DEPEND ON, rely on, exploit, take advantage of, count on, bank on, take liberties with, trust in *or* to

presumption *noun* 1 ASSUMPTION, opinion, belief, guess, hypothesis, anticipation, conjecture, surmise, supposition, presupposition, premiss
2 CHEEK (*informal*), front, neck (*informal*), nerve (*informal*), assurance, brass (*informal*), gall (*informal*), audacity, boldness, temerity, chutzpah (*US & Canad informal*), insolence, impudence, effrontery, brass neck (*Brit informal*), sassiness (*US informal*), presumptuousness, forwardness

presumptuous *adjective* PUSHY (*informal*), forward, bold, arrogant, presuming, rash, audacious, conceited, foolhardy, insolent, overweening, overconfident, overfamiliar, bigheaded (*informal*), uppish (*Brit informal*), too

big for your boots
 << OPPOSITE shy
presuppose *verb* PRESUME, consider, accept, suppose, assume, take it, imply, take for granted, postulate, posit, take as read
presupposition *noun* ASSUMPTION, theory, belief, premise, hypothesis, presumption, preconception, supposition, preconceived idea
pretence *noun* 1 DECEPTION, invention, sham, fabrication, acting, faking, simulation, deceit, feigning, charade, make-believe, trickery, falsehood, subterfuge, fakery
 << OPPOSITE candour
2 SHOW, posturing, artifice, affectation, display, appearance, posing, façade, veneer, pretentiousness, hokum (*slang, chiefly US & Canad*)
 << OPPOSITE reality
3 PRETEXT, claim, excuse, show, cover, mask, veil, cloak, guise, façade, masquerade, semblance, ruse, garb, wile
pretend *verb* 1 FEIGN, affect, assume, allege, put on, fake, make out, simulate, profess, sham, counterfeit, falsify, impersonate, dissemble, dissimulate, pass yourself off as
2 MAKE BELIEVE, suppose, imagine, play, act, make up, play the part of
3 LAY CLAIM, claim, allege, aspire, profess, purport
pretended *adjective* FEIGNED, alleged, so-called, phoney *or* phony (*informal*), false, pretend (*informal*), fake, imaginary, bogus, professed, sham, purported, pseudo (*informal*), counterfeit, spurious, fictitious, avowed, ostensible
pretender *noun* CLAIMANT, claimer, aspirant
pretension *noun* 1 AFFECTATION, hypocrisy, conceit, show, airs, vanity, snobbery, pomposity, self-importance, ostentation, pretentiousness, snobbishness, vainglory, showiness
2 *usually plural* ASPIRATION, claim, demand, profession, assumption, assertion, pretence
pretentious *adjective* AFFECTED, mannered, exaggerated, pompous, assuming, hollow, inflated, extravagant, high-flown, flaunting, grandiose, conceited, showy, ostentatious, snobbish, puffed up, bombastic, specious, grandiloquent, vainglorious, high-sounding, highfalutin (*informal*), overambitious, arty-farty (*informal*), magniloquent
 << OPPOSITE unpretentious
pretext *noun* GUISE, excuse, veil, show, cover, appearance, device, mask, ploy, cloak, simulation, pretence, semblance, ruse, red herring, alleged reason
pretty *adjective* 1 ATTRACTIVE, appealing, beautiful, sweet, lovely, charming, fair, fetching, good-looking, cute, graceful, bonny, personable, comely, prepossessing
 << OPPOSITE plain
2 PLEASANT, fine, pleasing, nice, elegant, trim, delicate, neat, tasteful, dainty, bijou
▷ *adverb* (*informal*) FAIRLY, rather, quite, kind of (*informal*), somewhat, moderately, reasonably
prevail *verb* 1 WIN, succeed, triumph, overcome, overrule, be victorious, carry the day, prove superior, gain mastery
2 BE WIDESPREAD, abound, predominate, be current, be prevalent, preponderate, exist generally
▷▷ **prevail on** *or* **upon someone** PERSUADE, influence, convince, prompt, win over, induce, incline, dispose, sway, talk into, bring round
prevailing *adjective* 1 WIDESPREAD, general, established, popular, common, set, current, usual, ordinary, fashionable, in style, customary, prevalent, in vogue
2 PREDOMINATING, ruling, main, existing, principal
prevalence *noun* COMMONNESS, frequency, regularity, currency, universality, ubiquity, common occurrence, pervasiveness, extensiveness, widespread presence, rampancy, rifeness
prevalent *adjective* COMMON, accepted, established, popular, general, current, usual, widespread, extensive, universal, frequent, everyday, rampant, customary, commonplace, ubiquitous, rife, habitual
 << OPPOSITE rare
prevent *verb* STOP, avoid, frustrate, restrain, check, bar, block, anticipate, hamper, foil, inhibit, head off, avert, thwart, intercept, hinder, obstruct, preclude, impede, counteract, ward off, balk, stave off, forestall, defend against, obviate, nip in the bud
 << OPPOSITE help
prevention *noun* ELIMINATION, safeguard, precaution, anticipation, thwarting, avoidance, deterrence, forestalling, prophylaxis, preclusion, obviation
preventive *or* **preventative** *adjective* 1 PRECAUTIONARY, protective, hampering, hindering, deterrent, impeding, pre-emptive, obstructive, inhibitory
2 PROPHYLACTIC, protective, precautionary, counteractive

In all contexts, *preventive* is commoner than, and generally used in preference to, *preventative*

preview *noun* SAMPLE, sneak preview, trailer, sampler, taster, foretaste, advance showing
▷ *verb* SAMPLE, taste, give a foretaste of
previous *adjective* 1 EARLIER, former, past, prior, one-time, preceding, sometime, erstwhile, antecedent, anterior, quondam, ex-
 << OPPOSITE later

2 PRECEDING, past, prior, foregoing

previously *adverb* BEFORE, earlier, once, in the past, formerly, back then, until now, at one time, hitherto, beforehand, a while ago, heretofore, in days *or* years gone by

prey *noun* 1 QUARRY, game, kill
2 VICTIM, target, mark, mug (*Brit slang*), dupe, fall guy (*informal*)
▷▷ **prey on something** *or* **someone** 1 HUNT, live off, eat, seize, devour, feed upon
2 VICTIMIZE, bully, intimidate, exploit, take advantage of, bleed (*informal*), blackmail, terrorize
3 WORRY, trouble, burden, distress, haunt, hang over, oppress, weigh down, weigh heavily

price *noun* 1 COST, value, rate, charge, bill, figure, worth, damage (*informal*), amount, estimate, fee, payment, expense, assessment, expenditure, valuation, face value, outlay, asking price
2 CONSEQUENCES, penalty, cost, result, sacrifice, toll, forfeit
3 REWARD, bounty, compensation, premium, recompense
▷ *verb* EVALUATE, value, estimate, rate, cost, assess, put a price on
▷▷ **at any price** WHATEVER THE COST, regardless, no matter what the cost, anyhow, cost what it may, expense no object

priceless *adjective* VALUABLE, expensive, precious, invaluable, rich, prized, dear, rare, treasured, costly, cherished, incomparable, irreplaceable, incalculable, inestimable, beyond price, worth a king's ransom, worth your *or* its weight in gold
<< OPPOSITE worthless

pricey *or* **pricy** *adjective* EXPENSIVE, dear, steep (*informal*), costly, high-priced, exorbitant, over the odds (*Brit informal*), extortionate

prick *verb* 1 PIERCE, stab, puncture, bore, pink, punch, lance, jab, perforate, impale
2 MOVE, trouble, touch, pain, wound, distress, grieve
▷ *noun* 1 PANG, smart, sting, spasm, gnawing, twinge, prickle
2 PUNCTURE, cut, hole, wound, gash, perforation, pinhole
▷▷ **prick up** RAISE, point, rise, stand erect

prickle *verb* 1 TINGLE, smart, sting, twitch, itch
2 PRICK, stick into, nick, jab
▷ *noun* 1 TINGLING, smart, chill, tickle, tingle, pins and needles (*informal*), goose bumps, goose flesh
2 SPIKE, point, spur, needle, spine, thorn, barb

prickly *adjective* 1 SPINY, barbed, thorny, bristly, brambly, briery
2 ITCHY, sharp, smarting, stinging, crawling, pricking, tingling, scratchy, prickling
3 IRRITABLE, edgy, grumpy, touchy, bad-tempered, fractious, petulant, stroppy (*Brit slang*), cantankerous, tetchy, ratty (*Brit & NZ informal*), chippy (*informal*), waspish, shirty (*slang, chiefly Brit*), peevish, snappish, liverish, pettish
4 DIFFICULT, complicated, tricky, trying, involved, intricate, troublesome, thorny, knotty, ticklish

pride *noun* 1 SATISFACTION, achievement, fulfilment, delight, content, pleasure, joy, gratification
2 SELF-RESPECT, honour, ego, dignity, self-esteem, self-image, self-worth, amour-propre (*French*)
3 CONCEIT, vanity, arrogance, pretension, presumption, snobbery, morgue (*French*), hubris, smugness, self-importance, egotism, self-love, hauteur, pretentiousness, haughtiness, loftiness, vainglory, superciliousness, bigheadedness (*informal*)
<< OPPOSITE humility
4 ELITE, pick, best, choice, flower, prize, cream, glory, boast, treasure, jewel, gem, pride and joy
▷▷ **pride yourself on something** BE PROUD OF, revel in, boast of, glory in, vaunt, take pride in, brag about, crow about, exult in, congratulate yourself on, flatter yourself that, pique yourself on, plume yourself on

priest *noun* CLERGYMAN, minister, father, divine, vicar, pastor, cleric, curate, churchman, padre (*informal*), holy man, man of God, man of the cloth, ecclesiastic, father confessor

priestly *adjective* ECCLESIASTIC, pastoral, clerical, canonical, hieratic, sacerdotal, priestlike

prim *adjective* PRUDISH, particular, formal, proper, precise, stiff, fussy, fastidious, puritanical, demure, starchy (*informal*), prissy (*informal*), strait-laced, priggish, schoolmarmish (*Brit informal*), old-maidish (*informal*), niminy-piminy
<< OPPOSITE liberal

primacy *noun* SUPREMACY, leadership, command, dominance, superiority, dominion, ascendancy, pre-eminence

prima donna *noun* DIVA, star, leading lady, female lead

primal *adjective* 1 BASIC, prime, central, first, highest, greatest, major, chief, main, most important, principal, paramount
2 EARLIEST, prime, original, primary, first, initial, primitive, pristine, primordial

primarily *adverb* 1 CHIEFLY, largely, generally, mainly, especially, essentially, mostly, basically, principally, fundamentally, above all, on the whole, for the most part
2 AT FIRST, originally, initially, in the first

place, in the beginning, first and foremost, at *or* from the start

primary *adjective* 1 CHIEF, leading, main, best, first, highest, greatest, top, prime, capital, principal, dominant, cardinal, paramount
<< OPPOSITE subordinate
2 BASIC, essential, radical, fundamental, ultimate, underlying, elemental, bog-standard (*informal*)
<< OPPOSITE secondary

prime *adjective* 1 MAIN, leading, chief, central, major, ruling, key, senior, primary, supreme, principal, ultimate, cardinal, paramount, overriding, foremost, predominant, pre-eminent, number-one (*informal*)
2 BEST, top, select, highest, capital, quality, choice, selected, excellent, superior, first-class, first-rate, grade-A
3 FUNDAMENTAL, original, basic, primary, underlying
▷ *noun* PEAK, flower, bloom, maturity, height, perfection, best days, heyday, zenith, full flowering
▷ *verb* 1 INFORM, tell, train, coach, brief, fill in (*informal*), groom (*informal*), notify, clue in (*informal*), gen up (*Brit informal*), give someone the lowdown, clue up (*informal*)
2 PREPARE, set up, load, equip, get ready, make ready

primeval *or* **primaeval** *adjective* 1 EARLIEST, old, original, ancient, primitive, first, early, pristine, primal, prehistoric, primordial
2 PRIMAL, primitive, natural, basic, inherited, inherent, hereditary, instinctive, innate, congenital, primordial, inborn, inbred

primitive *adjective* 1 UNCIVILIZED, savage, barbarian, barbaric, undeveloped, uncultivated
<< OPPOSITE civilized
2 EARLY, first, earliest, original, primary, elementary, pristine, primordial, primeval
<< OPPOSITE modern
3 SIMPLE, naive, childlike, untrained, undeveloped, unsophisticated, untutored
<< OPPOSITE sophisticated
4 CRUDE, simple, rough, rude, rudimentary, unrefined
<< OPPOSITE elaborate

primordial *adjective* 1 PRIMEVAL, primitive, first, earliest, pristine, primal, prehistoric
2 FUNDAMENTAL, original, basic, radical, elemental

prince *noun* RULER, lord, monarch, sovereign, crown prince, liege, potentate, prince regent, crowned head, dynast

princely *adjective* 1 SUBSTANTIAL, considerable, goodly, large, huge, massive, enormous, tidy (*informal*), whopping (great) (*informal*), sizable *or* sizeable
2 REGAL, royal, imposing, magnificent, august, grand, imperial, noble, sovereign, majestic, dignified, stately, lofty, high-born

princess *noun* RULER, lady, monarch, sovereign, liege, crowned head, crowned princess, dynast, princess regent

principal *adjective* MAIN, leading, chief, prime, first, highest, controlling, strongest, capital, key, essential, primary, most important, dominant, arch, cardinal, paramount, foremost, pre-eminent
<< OPPOSITE minor
▷ *noun* 1 HEADMASTER *or* HEADMISTRESS, head (*informal*), director, dean, head teacher, rector, master *or* mistress
2 BOSS, head, leader, director, chief (*informal*), master, ruler, superintendent, baas (*S African*), sherang (*Austral* & *NZ*)
3 STAR, lead, leader, prima ballerina, first violin, leading man *or* lady, coryphée
4 CAPITAL, money, assets, working capital, capital funds ▷ see **principle**

principally *adverb* MAINLY, largely, chiefly, especially, particularly, mostly, primarily, above all, predominantly, in the main, for the most part, first and foremost

principle *noun* 1 MORALS, standards, ideals, honour, virtue, ethics, integrity, conscience, morality, decency, scruples, probity, rectitude, moral standards, sense of duty, moral law, sense of honour, uprightness, kaupapa (*NZ*)
2 BELIEF, rule, standard, attitude, code, notion, criterion, ethic, doctrine, canon, creed, maxim, dogma, tenet, dictum, credo, axiom
3 RULE, idea, law, theory, basis, truth, concept, formula, fundamental, assumption, essence, proposition, verity, golden rule, precept
▷▷ **in principle** 1 IN GENERAL, generally, all things considered, on the whole, in the main, by and large, in essence, all in all, on balance
2 IN THEORY, ideally, on paper, theoretically, in an ideal world, en principe (*French*)

> *Principle* and *principal* are often confused: *the principal* (not *principle*) *reason for his departure; the plan was approved in principle* (not *principal*)

principled *adjective* MORAL, ethical, upright, honourable, just, correct, decent, righteous, conscientious, virtuous, scrupulous, right-minded, high-minded

print *verb* 1 RUN OFF, publish, copy, reproduce, issue, engrave, go to press, put to bed (*informal*)
2 PUBLISH, release, circulate, issue, disseminate
3 MARK, impress, stamp, imprint
▷ *noun* 1 PHOTOGRAPH, photo, snap
2 PICTURE, plate, etching, engraving, lithograph, woodcut, linocut
3 COPY, photo (*informal*), picture, reproduction,

replica
4 TYPE, lettering, letters, characters, face, font (*chiefly US*), fount, typeface
▷▷ **in print** 1 PUBLISHED, printed, on the streets, on paper, in black and white, out
2 AVAILABLE, current, on the market, in the shops, on the shelves, obtainable
▷▷ **out of print** UNAVAILABLE, unobtainable, no longer published, o.p.

prior *adjective* EARLIER, previous, former, preceding, foregoing, antecedent, aforementioned, pre-existing, anterior, pre-existent
▷▷ **prior to** BEFORE, preceding, earlier than, in advance of, previous to

priority *noun* 1 PRIME CONCERN, first concern, primary issue, most pressing matter
2 PRECEDENCE, preference, greater importance, primacy, predominance
3 SUPREMACY, rank, the lead, superiority, precedence, prerogative, seniority, right of way, pre-eminence

priory *noun* MONASTERY, abbey, convent, cloister, nunnery, religious house

prise ▷ see **prize**3

prison *noun* JAIL, confinement, can (*slang*), pound, nick (*Brit slang*), stir (*slang*), cooler (*slang*), jug (*slang*), dungeon, clink (*slang*), glasshouse (*Military informal*), gaol, penitentiary (*US*), slammer (*slang*), lockup, quod (*slang*), penal institution, calaboose (*US informal*), choky (*slang*), poky *or* pokey (*US & Canad slang*), boob (*Austral slang*)

prisoner *noun* 1 CONVICT, con (*slang*), lag (*slang*), jailbird
2 CAPTIVE, hostage, detainee, internee

prissy *adjective* PRIM, precious, fussy, fastidious, squeamish, prudish, finicky, strait-laced, schoolmarmish (*Brit informal*), old-maidish (*informal*), niminy-piminy, overnice, prim and proper

pristine *adjective* NEW, pure, virgin, immaculate, untouched, unspoiled, virginal, unsullied, uncorrupted, undefiled

The use of *pristine* to mean 'fresh, clean, and unspoiled' used to be considered incorrect by some people, but it is now generally accepted

privacy *noun* SECLUSION, isolation, solitude, retirement, retreat, separateness, sequestration, privateness

private *adjective* 1 NONPUBLIC, independent, commercial, privatised, private-enterprise, denationalized
2 EXCLUSIVE, individual, privately owned, own, special, particular, reserved
<< OPPOSITE public
3 SECRET, confidential, covert, inside, closet, unofficial, privy (*archaic*), clandestine, off the record, hush-hush (*informal*), in camera
<< OPPOSITE public
4 PERSONAL, individual, secret, intimate, undisclosed, unspoken, innermost, unvoiced
5 SECLUDED, secret, separate, isolated, concealed, retired, sequestered, not overlooked
<< OPPOSITE busy
6 SOLITARY, reserved, retiring, withdrawn, discreet, secretive, self-contained, reclusive, reticent, insular, introvert, uncommunicative
<< OPPOSITE sociable
▷ *noun* ENLISTED MAN (*US*), tommy (*Brit informal*), private soldier, Tommy Atkins (*Brit informal*), squaddie *or* squaddy (*Brit slang*)
▷▷ **in private** IN SECRET, privately, personally, behind closed doors, in camera, between ourselves, confidentially

privation *noun* (*Formal*) WANT, poverty, need, suffering, loss, lack, distress, misery, necessity, hardship, penury, destitution, neediness, indigence

privilege *noun* RIGHT, benefit, due, advantage, claim, freedom, sanction, liberty, concession, franchise, entitlement, prerogative, birthright

privileged *adjective* 1 SPECIAL, powerful, advantaged, favoured, ruling, honoured, entitled, elite, indulged
2 CONFIDENTIAL, special, inside, exceptional, privy, off the record, not for publication

privy *noun* (*Obsolete*) LAVATORY, closet, bog (*slang*), latrine, outside toilet, earth closet, pissoir (*French*), bogger (*Austral slang*), brasco (*Austral slang*)
▷ *adjective with* **to** INFORMED OF, aware of, in on, wise to (*slang*), hip to (*slang*), in the loop, apprised of, cognizant of, in the know about (*informal*)

prize[1] *noun* 1 REWARD, cup, award, honour, premium, medal, trophy, accolade
2 WINNINGS, haul, jackpot, stakes, purse, windfall
3 GOAL, hope, gain, aim, desire, ambition, conquest, Holy Grail (*informal*)
▷ *modifier* CHAMPION, best, winning, top, outstanding, award-winning, first-rate, top-notch (*informal*)

prize[2] *verb* VALUE, appreciate, treasure, esteem, cherish, hold dear, regard highly, set store by

prize3 *or* **prise** *verb* 1 FORCE, pull, lever
2 DRAG, force, draw, wring, extort

probability *noun* 1 LIKELIHOOD, prospect, chance, odds, expectation, liability, presumption, likeliness
2 CHANCE, odds, possibility, likelihood

probable *adjective* LIKELY, possible, apparent, reasonable to think, most likely, presumed, credible, plausible, feasible, odds-on, on the

cards, presumable
<< OPPOSITE unlikely
probably *adverb* LIKELY, perhaps, maybe, possibly, presumably, most likely, doubtless, in all probability, in all likelihood, perchance (*archaic*), as likely as not
probation *noun* TRIAL PERIOD, test, trial, examination, apprenticeship, initiation, novitiate
probe *verb* 1 *often with* **into** EXAMINE, research, go into, investigate, explore, test, sound, search, look into, query, verify, sift, analyze, dissect, delve into, work over, scrutinize
2 EXPLORE, examine, poke, prod, feel around
▷ *noun* INVESTIGATION, study, research, inquiry, analysis, examination, exploration, scrutiny, inquest, scrutinization
probity *noun* (*Formal*) INTEGRITY, worth, justice, honour, equity, virtue, goodness, morality, honesty, fairness, fidelity, sincerity, righteousness, rectitude, truthfulness, trustworthiness, uprightness
problem *noun* 1 DIFFICULTY, trouble, dispute, plight, obstacle, dilemma, headache (*informal*), disagreement, complication, predicament, quandary
2 PUZZLE, question, riddle, enigma, conundrum, teaser, poser, brain-teaser (*informal*)
▷ *modifier* DIFFICULT, disturbed, troublesome, unruly, delinquent, uncontrollable, intractable, recalcitrant, intransigent, unmanageable, disobedient, ungovernable, refractory, maladjusted
problematic *adjective* TRICKY, puzzling, uncertain, doubtful, dubious, unsettled, questionable, enigmatic, debatable, moot, problematical, chancy (*informal*), open to doubt
<< OPPOSITE clear
procedure *noun* METHOD, policy, process, course, system, form, action, step, performance, operation, practice, scheme, strategy, conduct, formula, custom, routine, transaction, plan of action, modus operandi
proceed *verb* 1 BEGIN, go ahead, get going, make a start, get under way, set something in motion
2 CONTINUE, go on, progress, carry on, go ahead, get on, press on
<< OPPOSITE discontinue
3 GO ON, continue, advance, progress, carry on, go ahead, move on, move forward, press on, push on, make your way
<< OPPOSITE stop
4 ARISE, come, follow, issue, result, spring, flow, stem, derive, originate, ensue, emanate
proceeding *noun* ACTION, process, procedure, move, act, step, measure, venture, undertaking, deed, occurrence, course of action
proceeds *plural noun* INCOME, profit, revenue, returns, produce, products, gain, earnings, yield, receipts, takings
process *noun* 1 PROCEDURE, means, course, system, action, performance, operation, measure, proceeding, manner, transaction, mode, course of action
2 DEVELOPMENT, growth, progress, course, stage, step, movement, advance, formation, evolution, unfolding, progression
3 METHOD, system, practice, technique, procedure
4 (*Law*) ACTION, case, trial, suit
▷ *verb* 1 PREPARE, treat, convert, transform, alter, refine
2 HANDLE, manage, action, deal with, fulfil, take care of, dispose of
procession *noun* PARADE, train, march, file, column, motorcade, cavalcade, cortege
proclaim *verb* 1 ANNOUNCE, declare, advertise, show, publish, indicate, blaze (abroad), herald, circulate, trumpet, affirm, give out, profess, promulgate, make known, enunciate, blazon (abroad), shout from the housetops (*informal*)
<< OPPOSITE keep secret
2 PRONOUNCE, announce, declare
proclamation *noun* 1 DECLARATION, notice, announcement, decree, manifesto, edict, pronouncement, pronunciamento
2 PUBLISHING, broadcasting, announcement, publication, declaration, notification, pronouncement, promulgation
proclivity *noun* (*Formal*) TENDENCY, liking, leaning, inclination, bent, weakness, bias, disposition, penchant, propensity, kink, predisposition, predilection, partiality, proneness, liableness
procrastinate *verb* DELAY, stall, postpone, prolong, put off, defer, adjourn, retard, dally, play for time, gain time, temporize, play a waiting game, protract, drag your feet (*informal*), be dilatory
<< OPPOSITE hurry (up)
procrastination *noun* DELAY, hesitation, slowness, slackness, dilatoriness, temporization *or* temporisation
procure *verb* OBTAIN, get, find, buy, win, land, score (*slang*), gain, earn, pick up, purchase, secure, appropriate, acquire, manage to get, get hold of, come by, lay hands on
prod *verb* 1 POKE, push, dig, shove, propel, nudge, jab, prick
2 PROMPT, move, urge, motivate, spur, stimulate, rouse, stir up, incite, egg on, goad, impel, put a bomb under (*informal*)
▷ *noun* 1 POKE, push, boost, dig, elbow, shove, nudge, jab
2 PROMPT, boost, signal, cue, reminder,

stimulus
3 GOAD, stick, spur, poker

prodigal *adjective* 1 EXTRAVAGANT, excessive, reckless, squandering, wasteful, wanton, profligate, spendthrift, intemperate, immoderate, improvident
<< OPPOSITE thrifty
2 *often with* **of** LAVISH, bountiful, unstinting, unsparing, bounteous, profuse
<< OPPOSITE generous

prodigious *adjective* 1 HUGE, giant, massive, vast, enormous, tremendous, immense, gigantic, monumental, monstrous, mammoth, colossal, stellar (*informal*), stupendous, inordinate, immeasurable
<< OPPOSITE tiny
2 WONDERFUL, striking, amazing, unusual, dramatic, impressive, extraordinary, remarkable, fantastic (*informal*), fabulous, staggering, marvellous, startling, exceptional, abnormal, phenomenal, astounding, miraculous, stupendous, flabbergasting (*informal*)
<< OPPOSITE ordinary

prodigy *noun* GENIUS, talent, wizard, mastermind, whizz (*informal*), whizz kid (*informal*), wunderkind, brainbox, child genius, wonder child, up-and-comer (*informal*)

produce *verb* 1 CAUSE, lead to, result in, effect, occasion, generate, trigger, make for, provoke, set off, induce, bring about, give rise to, engender
2 MAKE, build, create, develop, turn out, manufacture, construct, invent, assemble, put together, originate, fabricate, mass-produce
3 CREATE, develop, write, turn out, compose, originate, churn out (*informal*)
4 YIELD, provide, grow, bear, give, supply, afford, render, furnish
5 BRING FORTH, bear, deliver, breed, give birth to, beget, bring into the world
6 SHOW, provide, present, advance, demonstrate, offer, come up with, exhibit, put forward, furnish, bring forward, set forth, bring to light
7 DISPLAY, show, present, proffer
8 PRESENT, stage, direct, put on, do, show, mount, exhibit, put before the public
▷ *noun* FRUIT AND VEGETABLES, goods, food, products, crops, yield, harvest, greengrocery (*Brit*)

producer *noun* 1 DIRECTOR, promoter, impresario, régisseur (*French*)
2 MAKER, manufacturer, builder, creator, fabricator
3 GROWER, farmer

product *noun* 1 GOODS, produce, production, creation, commodity, invention, merchandise, artefact, concoction
2 RESULT, fruit, consequence, yield, returns, issue, effect, outcome, legacy, spin-off, end result, offshoot, upshot

production *noun* 1 PRODUCING, making, manufacture, manufacturing, construction, assembly, preparation, formation, fabrication, origination
2 CREATION, development, fashioning, composition, origination
3 MANAGEMENT, administration, direction
4 PRESENTATION, staging, mounting

productive *adjective* 1 FERTILE, rich, producing, prolific, plentiful, fruitful, teeming, generative, fecund
<< OPPOSITE barren
2 CREATIVE, dynamic, vigorous, energetic, inventive
3 USEFUL, rewarding, valuable, profitable, effective, worthwhile, beneficial, constructive, gratifying, fruitful, advantageous, gainful
<< OPPOSITE useless

productivity *noun* OUTPUT, production, capacity, yield, efficiency, mass production, work rate, productive capacity, productiveness

profane *adjective* 1 SACRILEGIOUS, wicked, irreverent, sinful, disrespectful, heathen, impure, godless, ungodly, irreligious, impious, idolatrous
<< OPPOSITE religious
2 CRUDE, foul, obscene, abusive, coarse, filthy, vulgar, blasphemous
3 SECULAR, lay, temporal, unholy, worldly, unconsecrated, unhallowed, unsanctified
▷ *verb* DESECRATE, violate, abuse, prostitute, contaminate, pollute, pervert, misuse, debase, defile, vitiate, commit sacrilege

profess *verb* 1 CLAIM, allege, pretend, fake, make out, sham, purport, feign, act as if, let on, dissemble
2 STATE, admit, announce, maintain, own, confirm, declare, acknowledge, confess, assert, proclaim, affirm, certify, avow, vouch, aver, asseverate

professed *adjective* 1 SUPPOSED, would-be, alleged, so-called, apparent, pretended, purported, self-styled, ostensible, soi-disant (*French*)
2 DECLARED, confirmed, confessed, proclaimed, certified, self-confessed, avowed, self-acknowledged

profession *noun* OCCUPATION, calling, business, career, employment, line, office, position, sphere, vocation, walk of life, line of work, métier

professional *adjective* 1 QUALIFIED, trained, skilled, white-collar
2 EXPERT, experienced, finished, skilled, masterly, efficient, crack (*slang*), polished,

practised, ace (*informal*), accomplished, slick, competent, adept, proficient
<< OPPOSITE amateurish
▷ *noun* EXPERT, authority, master, pro (*informal*), specialist, guru, buff (*informal*), wizard, adept, whizz (*informal*), maestro, virtuoso, hotshot (*informal*), past master, dab hand (*Brit informal*), wonk (*informal*), maven (*US*), fundi (*S African*)

professor *noun* DON (*Brit*), fellow (*Brit*), prof (*informal*), head of faculty

proffer *verb* 1 OFFER, hand over, present, extend, hold out
2 SUGGEST, propose, volunteer, submit, tender, propound

proficiency *noun* SKILL, ability, know-how (*informal*), talent, facility, craft, expertise, competence, accomplishment, mastery, knack, aptitude, dexterity, expertness, skilfulness

proficient *adjective* SKILLED, trained, experienced, qualified, able, expert, masterly, talented, gifted, capable, efficient, clever, accomplished, versed, competent, apt, skilful, adept, conversant
<< OPPOSITE unskilled

profile *noun* 1 OUTLINE, lines, form, figure, shape, silhouette, contour, side view
2 BIOGRAPHY, sketch, vignette, characterization, thumbnail sketch, character sketch
3 ANALYSIS, study, table, review, survey, chart, examination, diagram, graph

profit *noun* 1 *often plural* EARNINGS, winnings, return, revenue, gain, boot (*dialect*), yield, proceeds, percentage (*informal*), surplus, receipts, bottom line, takings, emoluments
<< OPPOSITE loss
2 BENEFIT, good, use, interest, value, gain, advantage, advancement, mileage (*informal*), avail
<< OPPOSITE disadvantage
▷ *verb* 1 MAKE MONEY, clear up, gain, earn, clean up (*informal*), rake in (*informal*), make a killing (*informal*), make a good thing of (*informal*)
2 BENEFIT, help, serve, aid, gain, promote, contribute to, avail, be of advantage to

profitable *adjective* 1 MONEY-MAKING, lucrative, paying, commercial, rewarding, worthwhile, cost-effective, fruitful, gainful, remunerative
2 BENEFICIAL, useful, rewarding, valuable, productive, worthwhile, fruitful, advantageous, expedient, serviceable
<< OPPOSITE useless

profligacy *noun* EXTRAVAGANCE, excess, squandering, waste, recklessness, wastefulness, lavishness, prodigality, improvidence

profligate *adjective* EXTRAVAGANT, reckless, squandering, wasteful, prodigal, spendthrift, immoderate, improvident

profound *adjective* 1 SINCERE, acute, intense, great, keen, extreme, hearty, heartfelt, abject, deeply felt, heartrending
<< OPPOSITE insincere
2 WISE, learned, serious, deep, skilled, subtle, penetrating, philosophical, thoughtful, sage, discerning, weighty, insightful, erudite, abstruse, recondite, sagacious
<< OPPOSITE uninformed
3 COMPLETE, intense, absolute, serious (*informal*), total, extreme, pronounced, utter, consummate, unqualified, out-and-out
<< OPPOSITE slight
4 RADICAL, extensive, thorough, far-reaching, exhaustive, thoroughgoing

profoundly *adverb* GREATLY, very, deeply, seriously, keenly, extremely, thoroughly, sincerely, intensely, acutely, heartily, to the core, abjectly, to the nth degree, from the bottom of your heart

profundity *noun* INSIGHT, intelligence, depth, wisdom, learning, penetration, acumen, erudition, acuity, perspicacity, sagacity, perceptiveness, perspicuity

profuse *adjective* 1 PLENTIFUL, ample, prolific, abundant, overflowing, teeming, copious, bountiful, luxuriant
<< OPPOSITE sparse
2 EXTRAVAGANT, liberal, generous, excessive, lavish, exuberant, prodigal, fulsome, open-handed, unstinting, immoderate
<< OPPOSITE moderate

profusion *noun* ABUNDANCE, wealth, excess, quantity, surplus, riot, multitude, bounty, plethora, exuberance, glut, extravagance, cornucopia, oversupply, plenitude, superabundance, superfluity, lavishness, luxuriance, prodigality, copiousness

progenitor *noun* 1 ANCESTOR, parent, forebear, forefather, begetter, procreator, primogenitor
2 ORIGINATOR, source, predecessor, precursor, forerunner, antecedent, instigator

progeny *noun* 1 CHILDREN, family, young, issue, offspring, descendants
2 RACE, stock, breed, posterity (*archaic*), seed (*chiefly biblical*), lineage, scions

prognosis *noun* FORECAST, prediction, diagnosis, expectation, speculation, projection, surmise, prognostication

programme *noun* 1 PLAN, scheme, strategy, procedure, project, plan of action
2 SCHEDULE, plan, agenda, timetable, listing, list, line-up, calendar, order
3 COURSE, curriculum, syllabus
4 SHOW, performance, production, broadcast, episode, presentation, transmission, telecast
▷ *verb* 1 SCHEDULE, plan, timetable, book, bill, list, design, arrange, work out, line up,

organize, lay on, formulate, map out, itemize, prearrange
2 SET, fix

progress *noun* **1** DEVELOPMENT, increase, growth, advance, gain, improvement, promotion, breakthrough, step forward, advancement, progression, headway, betterment, amelioration
<< OPPOSITE regression
2 MOVEMENT FORWARD, passage, advancement, progression, course, advance, headway, onward movement
<< OPPOSITE movement backward
▷ *verb* **1** MOVE ON, continue, travel, advance, proceed, go forward, gain ground, forge ahead, make inroads (into), make headway, make your way, cover ground, make strides, gather way
<< OPPOSITE move back
2 DEVELOP, improve, advance, better, increase, grow, gain, get on, come on, mature, blossom, ameliorate
<< OPPOSITE get behind
▷▷ **in progress** GOING ON, happening, continuing, being done, occurring, taking place, proceeding, under way, ongoing, being performed, in operation

progression *noun* **1** PROGRESS, advance, advancement, gain, headway, furtherance, movement forward
2 SEQUENCE, course, order, series, chain, cycle, string, succession

progressive *adjective* **1** ENLIGHTENED, liberal, modern, advanced, radical, enterprising, go-ahead, revolutionary, dynamic, avant-garde, reformist, up-and-coming, forward-looking
2 GROWING, continuing, increasing, developing, advancing, accelerating, ongoing, continuous, intensifying, escalating

prohibit *verb* **1** FORBID, ban, rule out, veto, outlaw, disallow, proscribe, debar, interdict
<< OPPOSITE permit
2 PREVENT, restrict, rule out, stop, hamper, hinder, constrain, obstruct, preclude, impede, make impossible
<< OPPOSITE allow

prohibited *adjective* FORBIDDEN, barred, banned, illegal, not allowed, vetoed, taboo, off limits, proscribed, verboten (*German*)

prohibition *noun* BAN, boycott, embargo, bar, veto, prevention, exclusion, injunction, disqualification, interdiction, interdict, proscription, disallowance, forbiddance, restraining order (*US Law*)

prohibitive *adjective* **1** EXORBITANT, excessive, steep (*informal*), high-priced, preposterous, sky-high, extortionate, beyond your means
2 PROHIBITING, forbidding, restraining, restrictive, repressive, suppressive, proscriptive

project *noun* **1** SCHEME, plan, job, idea, design, programme, campaign, operation, activity, proposal, venture, enterprise, undertaking, occupation, proposition, plan of action
2 ASSIGNMENT, task, homework, piece of research
▷ *verb* **1** FORECAST, expect, estimate, predict, reckon, calculate, gauge, extrapolate, predetermine
2 PLAN, propose, design, scheme, purpose, frame, draft, outline, devise, contemplate, contrive, map out
3 LAUNCH, shoot, throw, cast, transmit, discharge, hurl, fling, propel
4 STICK OUT, extend, stand out, bulge, beetle, protrude, overhang, jut

projectile *noun* MISSILE, shell, bullet, rocket

projection *noun* FORECAST, estimate, reckoning, prediction, calculation, estimation, computation, extrapolation

proletarian *adjective* WORKING-CLASS, common, cloth-cap (*informal*), plebeian, blue-singlet (*Austral slang*)
▷ *noun* WORKER, commoner, Joe Bloggs (*Brit informal*), pleb, plebeian, prole (*derogatory slang, chiefly Brit*)

proletariat *noun* WORKING CLASS, the masses, lower classes, commoners, the herd, wage-earners, lower orders, the common people, hoi polloi, plebs, the rabble, the great unwashed (*derogatory*), labouring classes, proles (*derogatory slang, chiefly Brit*), commonalty
<< OPPOSITE ruling class

proliferate *verb* INCREASE, expand, breed, mushroom, escalate, multiply, burgeon, snowball, run riot, grow rapidly

proliferation *noun* MULTIPLICATION, increase, spread, build-up, concentration, expansion, extension, step-up (*informal*), escalation, intensification

prolific *adjective* **1** PRODUCTIVE, creative, fertile, inventive, copious
2 FRUITFUL, fertile, abundant, rich, rank, teeming, bountiful, luxuriant, generative, profuse, fecund
<< OPPOSITE unproductive

prologue *noun* INTRODUCTION, preliminary, prelude, preface, preamble, foreword, proem, exordium

prolong *verb* LENGTHEN, continue, perpetuate, draw out, extend, delay, stretch out, carry on, spin out, drag out, make longer, protract
<< OPPOSITE shorten

promenade *noun* **1** WALKWAY, parade, boulevard, prom, esplanade, public walk
2 STROLL, walk, turn, airing, constitutional, saunter
▷ *verb* **1** STROLL, walk, saunter, take a walk,

perambulate, stretch your legs
2 PARADE, strut, swagger, flaunt

prominence *noun* 1 FAME, name, standing, rank, reputation, importance, celebrity, distinction, prestige, greatness, eminence, pre-eminence, notability, outstandingness
2 CONSPICUOUSNESS, weight, precedence, top billing, specialness, salience, markedness
3 PROTRUSION, swelling, projection, bulge, jutting, protuberance

prominent *adjective* 1 FAMOUS, leading, top, chief, important, main, noted, popular, respected, celebrated, outstanding, distinguished, well-known, notable, renowned, big-time (*informal*), foremost, eminent, major league (*informal*), pre-eminent, well-thought-of
<< OPPOSITE unknown
2 NOTICEABLE, striking, obvious, outstanding, remarkable, pronounced, blatant, conspicuous, to the fore, unmistakable, eye-catching, salient, in the foreground, easily seen, obtrusive
<< OPPOSITE inconspicuous
3 JUTTING, projecting, standing out, bulging, hanging over, protruding, protuberant, protrusive
<< OPPOSITE indented

promiscuity *noun* LICENTIOUSNESS, profligacy, sleeping around (*informal*), permissiveness, abandon, incontinence, depravity, immorality, debauchery, laxity, dissipation, looseness, amorality, lechery, laxness, wantonness, libertinism, promiscuousness

promiscuous *adjective* LICENTIOUS, wanton, profligate, debauched, fast, wild, abandoned, loose, immoral, lax, dissipated, unbridled, dissolute, libertine, of easy virtue, unchaste
<< OPPOSITE chaste

promise *verb* 1 GUARANTEE, pledge, vow, swear, contract, assure, undertake, warrant, plight, stipulate, vouch, take an oath, give an undertaking, cross your heart, give your word
2 SEEM LIKELY, look like, hint at, show signs of, bespeak, augur, betoken, lead you to expect, hold out hopes of, give hope of, bid fair, hold a probability of
▷ *noun* 1 GUARANTEE, word, bond, vow, commitment, pledge, undertaking, assurance, engagement, compact, oath, covenant, word of honour
2 POTENTIAL, ability, talent, capacity, capability, flair, aptitude

promising *adjective* 1 ENCOURAGING, likely, bright, reassuring, hopeful, favourable, rosy, auspicious, propitious, full of promise
<< OPPOSITE unpromising
2 TALENTED, able, gifted, rising, likely, up-and-coming

promontory *noun* POINT, cape, head, spur, ness (*archaic*), headland, foreland

promote *verb* 1 HELP, back, support, further, develop, aid, forward, champion, encourage, advance, work for, urge, boost, recommend, sponsor, foster, contribute to, assist, advocate, stimulate, endorse, prescribe, speak for, nurture, push for, espouse, popularize, gee up
<< OPPOSITE impede
2 ADVERTISE, sell, hype, publicize, push, plug (*informal*), puff, call attention to, beat the drum for (*informal*)
3 RAISE, upgrade, elevate, honour, dignify, exalt, kick upstairs (*informal*), aggrandize
<< OPPOSITE demote

promoter *noun* 1 ORGANIZER, arranger, entrepreneur, impresario
2 SUPPORTER, champion, advocate, campaigner, helper, proponent, stalwart, mainstay, upholder

promotion *noun* 1 RISE, upgrading, move up, advancement, elevation, exaltation, preferment, aggrandizement, ennoblement
2 PUBLICITY, advertising, hype, pushing, plugging (*informal*), propaganda, advertising campaign, hard sell, media hype, ballyhoo (*informal*), puffery (*informal*), boosterism
3 ENCOURAGEMENT, backing, support, development, progress, boosting, advancement, advocacy, cultivation, espousal, furtherance, boosterism

prompt *verb* 1 CAUSE, move, inspire, stimulate, occasion, urge, spur, provoke, motivate, induce, evoke, give rise to, elicit, incite, instigate, impel, call forth
<< OPPOSITE discourage
2 REMIND, assist, cue, help out, prod, jog the memory, refresh the memory
▷ *adjective* 1 IMMEDIATE, quick, rapid, instant, timely, early, swift, on time, speedy, instantaneous, punctual, pdq (*slang*), unhesitating
<< OPPOSITE slow
2 QUICK, ready, efficient, eager, willing, smart, alert, brisk, responsive, expeditious
<< OPPOSITE inefficient
▷ *adverb* (*informal*) EXACTLY, sharp, promptly, on the dot, punctually
▷ *noun* REMINDER, hint, cue, help, spur, stimulus, jog, prod, jolt

promptly *adverb* 1 IMMEDIATELY, instantly, swiftly, directly, quickly, at once, speedily, by return, pronto (*informal*), unhesitatingly, hotfoot, pdq (*slang*), posthaste
2 PUNCTUALLY, on time, spot on (*informal*), bang on (*informal*), on the dot, on the button (US), on the nail

promulgate *verb* 1 MAKE KNOWN, issue, announce, publish, spread, promote,

advertise, broadcast, communicate, proclaim, circulate, notify, make public, disseminate
2 MAKE OFFICIAL, pass, declare, decree

prone *adjective* 1 LIABLE, given, subject, inclined, tending, bent, disposed, susceptible, apt, predisposed
<< OPPOSITE disinclined
2 FACE DOWN, flat, lying down, horizontal, prostrate, recumbent, procumbent
<< OPPOSITE face up

pronounce *verb* 1 SAY, speak, voice, stress, sound, utter, articulate, enunciate, vocalize
2 DECLARE, announce, judge, deliver, assert, proclaim, decree, affirm

pronounced *adjective* NOTICEABLE, clear, decided, strong, marked, striking, obvious, broad, evident, distinct, definite, conspicuous, unmistakable, salient
<< OPPOSITE imperceptible

pronouncement *noun* ANNOUNCEMENT, statement, declaration, judgment, decree, manifesto, proclamation, notification, edict, dictum, promulgation, pronunciamento

pronunciation *noun* INTONATION, accent, speech, stress, articulation, inflection, diction, elocution, enunciation, accentuation

The *-un-* in *pronunciation* should be written and pronounced in the same way as the *-un-* in *unkind*. It is incorrect to add an *o* after the *u* to make this word look and sound more like *pronounce*

proof *noun* 1 EVIDENCE, demonstration, testimony, confirmation, verification, certification, corroboration, authentication, substantiation, attestation
2 (*Printing*) TRIAL PRINT, pull, slip, galley, page proof, galley proof, trial impression
▷ *adjective* IMPERVIOUS, strong, tight, resistant, impenetrable, repellent

prop *verb* 1 LEAN, place, set, stand, position, rest, lay, balance, steady
2 *often with* **up** SUPPORT, maintain, sustain, shore, hold up, brace, uphold, bolster, truss, buttress
▷ *noun* 1 SUPPORT, stay, brace, mainstay, truss, buttress, stanchion
2 MAINSTAY, support, sustainer, anchor, backbone, cornerstone, upholder
3 SUBSIDIZE, support, fund, finance, maintain, underwrite, shore up, buttress, bolster up

propaganda *noun* INFORMATION, advertising, promotion, publicity, hype, brainwashing, disinformation, ballyhoo (*informal*), agitprop, newspeak, boosterism

propagandist *noun* PUBLICIST, advocate, promoter, proponent, evangelist, proselytizer, pamphleteer, indoctrinator

propagate *verb* 1 SPREAD, publish, promote, broadcast, proclaim, transmit, circulate, diffuse, publicize, disseminate, promulgate, make known
<< OPPOSITE suppress
2 PRODUCE, generate, engender, increase
3 REPRODUCE, breed, multiply, proliferate, beget, procreate

propagation *noun* 1 SPREADING, spread, promotion, communication, distribution, circulation, transmission, diffusion, dissemination, promulgation
2 REPRODUCTION, generation, breeding, increase, proliferation, multiplication, procreation

propel *verb* 1 DRIVE, launch, start, force, send, shoot, push, thrust, shove, set in motion
<< OPPOSITE stop
2 IMPEL, drive, push, prompt, spur, motivate
<< OPPOSITE hold back

propensity *noun* TENDENCY, leaning, weakness, inclination, bent, liability, bias, disposition, penchant, susceptibility, predisposition, proclivity, proneness, aptness

proper *adjective* 1 REAL, actual, genuine, true, bona fide, kosher (*informal*), dinkum (*Austral & NZ informal*)
2 CORRECT, accepted, established, appropriate, right, formal, conventional, accurate, exact, precise, legitimate, orthodox, apt
<< OPPOSITE improper
3 POLITE, right, becoming, seemly, fitting, fit, mannerly, suitable, decent, gentlemanly, refined, respectable, befitting, genteel, de rigueur (*French*), ladylike, meet (*archaic*), decorous, punctilious, comme il faut (*French*)
<< OPPOSITE unseemly
4 CHARACTERISTIC, own, special, individual, personal, particular, specific, peculiar, respective

properly *adverb* 1 CORRECTLY, rightly, fittingly, appropriately, legitimately, accurately, suitably, aptly, deservedly, as intended, in the true sense, in the accepted *or* approved manner
<< OPPOSITE incorrectly
2 POLITELY, respectfully, ethically, decently, respectably, decorously, punctiliously
<< OPPOSITE badly

property *noun* 1 POSSESSIONS, goods, means, effects, holdings, capital, riches, resources, estate, assets, wealth, belongings, chattels
2 LAND, holding, title, estate, acres, real estate, freehold, realty, real property
3 QUALITY, feature, characteristic, mark, ability, attribute, virtue, trait, hallmark, peculiarity, idiosyncrasy

prophecy *noun* 1 PREDICTION, forecast, revelation, prognosis, foretelling, prognostication, augury, sortilege, vaticination (*rare*)

2 SECOND SIGHT, divination, augury, telling the future, soothsaying

prophesy *verb* PREDICT, forecast, divine, foresee, augur, presage, foretell, forewarn, prognosticate, soothsay, vaticinate (*rare*)

prophet *or* **prophetess** *noun* SOOTHSAYER, forecaster, diviner, oracle, seer, clairvoyant, augur, sibyl, prognosticator, prophesier

prophetic *adjective* PREDICTIVE, foreshadowing, presaging, prescient, divinatory, oracular, sibylline, prognostic, mantic, vatic (*rare*), augural, fatidic (*rare*)

propitious *adjective* FAVOURABLE, timely, promising, encouraging, bright, lucky, fortunate, prosperous, rosy, advantageous, auspicious, opportune, full of promise

proponent *noun* SUPPORTER, friend, champion, defender, advocate, patron, enthusiast, subscriber, backer, partisan, exponent, apologist, upholder, vindicator, spokesman *or* spokeswoman

proportion *noun* 1 PART, share, cut (*informal*), amount, measure, division, percentage, segment, quota, fraction

2 RELATIVE AMOUNT, relationship, distribution, ratio

3 BALANCE, agreement, harmony, correspondence, symmetry, concord, congruity

▷ *plural noun* DIMENSIONS, size, volume, capacity, extent, range, bulk, scope, measurements, magnitude, breadth, expanse, amplitude

proportional *or* **proportionate** *adjective* CORRESPONDENT, equivalent, corresponding, even, balanced, consistent, comparable, compatible, equitable, in proportion, analogous, commensurate

<< OPPOSITE disproportionate

proposal *noun* SUGGESTION, plan, programme, scheme, offer, terms, design, project, bid, motion, recommendation, tender, presentation, proposition, overture

propose *verb* 1 PUT FORWARD, present, suggest, advance, come up with, submit, tender, proffer, propound

2 INTEND, mean, plan, aim, design, scheme, purpose, have in mind, have every intention

3 NOMINATE, name, present, introduce, invite, recommend, put up

4 OFFER MARRIAGE, pop the question (*informal*), ask for someone's hand (in marriage), pay suit

proposition *noun* 1 TASK, problem, activity, job, affair, venture, undertaking

2 THEORY, idea, argument, concept, thesis, hypothesis, theorem, premiss, postulation

3 PROPOSAL, plan, suggestion, scheme, bid, motion, recommendation

4 ADVANCE, pass (*informal*), proposal, overture, improper suggestion, come-on (*informal*)

▷ *verb* MAKE A PASS AT, solicit, accost, make an indecent proposal to, make an improper suggestion to

propound *verb* PUT FORWARD, present, advance, propose, advocate, submit, suggest, lay down, contend, postulate, set forth

proprietor *or* **proprietress** *noun* OWNER, landowner, freeholder, possessor, titleholder, deed holder, landlord *or* landlady

propriety *noun* 1 DECORUM, manners, courtesy, protocol, good form, decency, breeding, delicacy, modesty, respectability, etiquette, refinement, politeness, good manners, rectitude, punctilio, seemliness

<< OPPOSITE indecorum

2 CORRECTNESS, fitness, appropriateness, rightness, aptness, seemliness, suitableness

▷▷ **the proprieties** ETIQUETTE, the niceties, the civilities, the amenities, the done thing, the social graces, the rules of conduct, the social conventions, social code, accepted conduct, kawa (*NZ*), tikanga (*NZ*)

propulsion *noun* POWER, pressure, push, thrust, momentum, impulse, impetus, motive power, impulsion, propelling force

prosaic *adjective* DULL, ordinary, boring, routine, flat, dry, everyday, tame, pedestrian, commonplace, mundane, matter-of-fact, stale, banal, uninspiring, humdrum, trite, unimaginative, hackneyed, workaday, vapid

<< OPPOSITE exciting

proscribe *verb* 1 PROHIBIT, ban, forbid, boycott, embargo, interdict

<< OPPOSITE permit

2 CONDEMN, reject, damn, denounce, censure

3 OUTLAW, exclude, exile, expel, banish, deport, expatriate, excommunicate, ostracize, blackball, attaint (*archaic*)

prosecute *verb* 1 (*Law*) TAKE SOMEONE TO COURT, try, sue, summon, indict, do (*slang*), arraign, seek redress, put someone on trial, litigate, bring suit against, bring someone to trial, put someone in the dock, bring action against, prefer charges against

2 CONDUCT, continue, manage, direct, pursue, work at, carry on, practise, engage in, discharge, persist in, see through, follow through, persevere, carry through

prospect *noun* 1 LIKELIHOOD, chance, possibility, plan, hope, promise, proposal, odds, expectation, probability, anticipation, presumption

2 IDEA, thought, outlook, contemplation

3 VIEW, perspective, landscape, scene, sight, vision, outlook, spectacle, panorama, vista

▷ *plural noun* POSSIBILITIES, openings, chances, future, potential, expectations, outlook, scope

▷ *verb* LOOK, search, seek, survey, explore, drill, go after, dowse

prospective *adjective* 1 POTENTIAL, possible, to come, about to be, upcoming, soon-to-be
2 EXPECTED, coming, future, approaching, likely, looked-for, intended, awaited, hoped-for, anticipated, forthcoming, imminent, destined, eventual, on the cards

prospectus *noun* CATALOGUE, plan, list, programme, announcement, outline, brochure, handbook, syllabus, synopsis, conspectus

prosper *verb* SUCCEED, advance, progress, thrive, make it (*informal*), flower, get on, do well, flourish, bloom, make good, be fortunate, grow rich, fare well

prosperity *noun* SUCCESS, riches, plenty, ease, fortune, wealth, boom, luxury, well-being, good times, good fortune, the good life, affluence, life of luxury, life of Riley (*informal*), prosperousness
<< OPPOSITE poverty

prosperous *adjective* 1 WEALTHY, rich, affluent, well-off, in the money (*informal*), blooming, opulent, well-heeled (*informal*), well-to-do, moneyed, in clover (*informal*)
<< OPPOSITE poor
2 SUCCESSFUL, booming, thriving, flourishing, doing well, prospering, on a roll, on the up and up (*Brit*), palmy
<< OPPOSITE unsuccessful

prostitute *noun* WHORE, hooker (*US slang*), pro (*slang*), brass (*slang*), tart (*informal*), hustler (*US & Canad slang*), moll (*slang*), call girl, courtesan, working girl (*facetious slang*), harlot, streetwalker, camp follower, loose woman, fallen woman, scrubber (*Brit & Austral slang*), strumpet, trollop, white slave, bawd (*archaic*), cocotte, fille de joie (*French*)
▷ *verb* CHEAPEN, sell out, pervert, degrade, devalue, squander, demean, debase, profane, misapply

prostitution *noun* HARLOTRY, the game (*slang*), vice, the oldest profession, whoredom, streetwalking, harlot's trade, Mrs. Warren's profession

prostrate *adjective* 1 PRONE, fallen, flat, horizontal, abject, bowed low, kowtowing, procumbent
2 EXHAUSTED, overcome, depressed, drained, spent, worn out, desolate, dejected, inconsolable, at a low ebb, fagged out (*informal*)
3 HELPLESS, overwhelmed, disarmed, paralysed, powerless, reduced, impotent, defenceless, brought to your knees
▷ *verb* EXHAUST, tire, drain, fatigue, weary, sap, wear out, fag out (*informal*)
▷▷ **prostrate yourself** BOW DOWN, submit, kneel, cringe, grovel, fall at someone's feet, bow, kowtow, bend the knee, abase yourself, cast yourself, fall on your knees

protagonist *noun* 1 SUPPORTER, leader, champion, advocate, exponent, mainstay, prime mover, standard-bearer, moving spirit, torchbearer
2 LEADING CHARACTER, lead, principal, central character, hero *or* heroine

protean *adjective* CHANGEABLE, variable, volatile, versatile, temperamental, ever-changing, mercurial, many-sided, mutable, polymorphous, multiform

protect *verb* KEEP SOMEONE SAFE, defend, keep, support, save, guard, secure, preserve, look after, foster, shelter, shield, care for, harbour, safeguard, watch over, stick up for (*informal*), cover up for, chaperon, give someone sanctuary, take someone under your wing, mount *or* stand guard over
<< OPPOSITE endanger

protection *noun* 1 SAFETY, charge, care, defence, protecting, security, guarding, custody, safeguard, preservation, aegis, guardianship, safekeeping
2 SAFEGUARD, cover, guard, shelter, screen, barrier, shield, refuge, buffer, bulwark
3 ARMOUR, cover, screen, barrier, shelter, shield, bulwark

protective *adjective* 1 PROTECTING, covering, sheltering, shielding, safeguarding, insulating
2 CARING, defensive, motherly, fatherly, warm, careful, maternal, vigilant, watchful, paternal, possessive

protector *noun* 1 DEFENDER, champion, guard, guardian, counsel, advocate, patron, safeguard, bodyguard, benefactor, guardian angel, tower of strength, knight in shining armour
2 GUARD, screen, protection, shield, pad, cushion, buffer

protégé *or* **protégée** *noun* CHARGE, student, pupil, ward, discovery, dependant

protest *verb* 1 OBJECT, demonstrate, oppose, complain, disagree, cry out, disapprove, say no to, demur, take exception, remonstrate, kick against (*informal*), expostulate, take up the cudgels, express disapproval
2 ASSERT, argue, insist, maintain, declare, vow, testify, contend, affirm, profess, attest, avow, asseverate
▷ *noun* 1 DEMONSTRATION, march, rally, sit-in, demo (*informal*), hikoi (*NZ*)
2 OBJECTION, complaint, declaration, dissent, outcry, disapproval, protestation, demur, formal complaint, remonstrance, demurral

protestation *noun* (*Formal*) DECLARATION, pledge, vow, oath, profession, affirmation, avowal, asseveration

protester *noun* 1 DEMONSTRATOR, rebel, dissident, dissenter, agitator, picketers,

protest marcher
2 OBJECTOR, opposer, complainer, opponent, dissident, dissenter

protocol *noun* 1 CODE OF BEHAVIOUR, manners, courtesies, conventions, customs, formalities, good form, etiquette, propriety, decorum, rules of conduct, politesse, p's and q's
2 AGREEMENT, contract, treaty, convention, pact, compact, covenant, concordat

prototype *noun* ORIGINAL, model, precedent, first, example, standard, paradigm, archetype, mock-up

protracted *adjective* EXTENDED, long, prolonged, lengthy, time-consuming, never-ending, drawn-out, interminable, spun out, dragged out, long-drawn-out, overlong

protrude *verb* STICK OUT, start (from), point, project, pop (*of eyes*), extend, come through, stand out, bulge, shoot out, jut, stick out like a sore thumb, obtrude

proud *adjective* 1 SATISFIED, pleased, content, contented, honoured, thrilled, glad, gratified, joyful, appreciative, well-pleased
<< OPPOSITE dissatisfied
2 GLORIOUS, rewarding, memorable, pleasing, satisfying, illustrious, gratifying, exalted, red-letter
3 DISTINGUISHED, great, grand, imposing, magnificent, noble, august, splendid, eminent, majestic, stately, illustrious
<< OPPOSITE lowly
4 CONCEITED, vain, arrogant, stuck-up (*informal*), lordly, imperious, narcissistic, overbearing, snooty (*informal*), haughty, snobbish, egotistical, self-satisfied, disdainful, self-important, presumptuous, boastful, supercilious, high and mighty (*informal*), toffee-nosed (*slang, chiefly Brit*), too big for your boots *or* breeches
<< OPPOSITE humble

prove *verb* 1 TURN OUT, come out, end up, be found to be
2 VERIFY, establish, determine, show, evidence, confirm, demonstrate, justify, ascertain, bear out, attest, substantiate, corroborate, authenticate, evince, show clearly
<< OPPOSITE disprove

proven *adjective* ESTABLISHED, accepted, proved, confirmed, tried, tested, checked, reliable, valid, definite, authentic, certified, verified, attested, undoubted, dependable, trustworthy

provenance *noun* ORIGIN, source, birthplace, derivation

proverb *noun* SAYING, saw, maxim, gnome, adage, dictum, aphorism, byword, apophthegm

proverbial *adjective* CONVENTIONAL, accepted, traditional, famous, acknowledged, typical, well-known, legendary, notorious, customary, famed, archetypal, time-honoured, self-evident, unquestioned, axiomatic

provide *verb* 1 SUPPLY, give, contribute, provision, distribute, outfit, equip, accommodate, donate, furnish, dispense, part with, fork out (*informal*), stock up, cater to, purvey
<< OPPOSITE withhold
2 GIVE, bring, add, produce, present, serve, afford, yield, lend, render, impart
3 STIPULATE, state, require, determine, specify, lay down
▷▷ **provide for someone** SUPPORT, look after, care for, keep, maintain, sustain, take care of, fend for
▷▷ **provide for something** TAKE PRECAUTIONS AGAINST, plan for, prepare for, anticipate, arrange for, get ready for, make plans for, make arrangements for, plan ahead for, take measures against, forearm for

providence *noun* FATE, fortune, destiny, God's will, divine intervention, predestination

provider *noun* 1 SUPPLIER, giver, source, donor, benefactor
2 BREADWINNER, supporter, earner, mainstay, wage earner

providing *or* **provided** *conjunction often with* **that** ON CONDITION THAT, if, subject to, given that, on the assumption that, in the event that, with the proviso that, contingent upon, with the understanding that, as long as, if and only if, upon these terms

province *noun* 1 REGION, section, county, district, territory, zone, patch, colony, domain, dependency, tract
2 AREA, business, concern, responsibility, part, line, charge, role, post, department, field, duty, function, employment, capacity, orbit, sphere, turf (*US slang*), pigeon (*Brit informal*)

provincial *adjective* 1 REGIONAL, state, local, county, district, territorial, parochial
2 RURAL, country, local, home-grown, rustic, homespun, hick (*informal, chiefly US & Canad*), backwoods
<< OPPOSITE urban
3 PAROCHIAL, insular, narrow-minded, unsophisticated, limited, narrow, small-town (*chiefly US*), uninformed, inward-looking, small-minded, parish-pump, upcountry
<< OPPOSITE cosmopolitan
▷ *noun* YOKEL, hick (*informal, chiefly US & Canad*), rustic, country cousin, hayseed (*US & Canad informal*)

provision *noun* 1 SUPPLYING, giving, providing, supply, delivery, distribution, catering, presentation, equipping, furnishing, allocation, fitting out, purveying, accoutrement
2 ARRANGEMENT, plan, planning, preparation,

precaution, contingency, prearrangement
3 FACILITIES, services, funds, resources, means, opportunities, arrangements, assistance, concession(s), allowance(s), amenities
4 CONDITION, term, agreement, requirement, demand, rider, restriction, qualification, clause, reservation, specification, caveat, proviso, stipulation
▷ *plural noun* FOOD, supplies, stores, feed, fare, rations, eats (*slang*), groceries, tack (*informal*), grub (*slang*), foodstuff, kai (*NZ informal*), sustenance, victuals, edibles, comestibles, provender, nosebag (*slang*), vittles (*obsolete* or *dialect*), viands, eatables

provisional *adjective* 1 TEMPORARY, interim, transitional, stopgap, pro tem
<< OPPOSITE permanent
2 CONDITIONAL, limited, qualified, contingent, tentative, provisory
<< OPPOSITE definite

proviso *noun* CONDITION, requirement, provision, strings, rider, restriction, qualification, clause, reservation, limitation, stipulation

provocation *noun* 1 CAUSE, reason, grounds, motivation, justification, stimulus, inducement, incitement, instigation, casus belli (*Latin*)
2 OFFENCE, challenge, insult, taunt, injury, dare, grievance, annoyance, affront, indignity, red rag, vexation

provocative *adjective* 1 OFFENSIVE, provoking, insulting, challenging, disturbing, stimulating, annoying, outrageous, aggravating (*informal*), incensing, galling, goading
2 SUGGESTIVE, tempting, stimulating, exciting, inviting, sexy (*informal*), arousing, erotic, seductive, alluring, tantalizing

provoke *verb* 1 ANGER, insult, annoy, offend, irritate, infuriate, hassle (*informal*), aggravate (*informal*), incense, enrage, gall, put someone out, madden, exasperate, vex, affront, chafe, irk, rile, pique, get on someone's nerves (*informal*), get someone's back up, put someone's back up, try someone's patience, nark (*Brit, Austral & NZ slang*), make someone's blood boil, get in someone's hair (*informal*), rub someone up the wrong way, hack someone off (*informal*)
<< OPPOSITE pacify
2 ROUSE, cause, produce, lead to, move, fire, promote, occasion, excite, inspire, generate, prompt, stir, stimulate, motivate, induce, bring about, evoke, give rise to, precipitate, elicit, inflame, incite, instigate, kindle, foment, call forth, draw forth, bring on *or* down
<< OPPOSITE curb

prowess *noun* 1 SKILL, ability, talent, expertise, facility, command, genius, excellence, accomplishment, mastery, attainment, aptitude, dexterity, adroitness, adeptness, expertness
<< OPPOSITE inability
2 BRAVERY, daring, courage, heroism, mettle, boldness, gallantry, valour, fearlessness, intrepidity, hardihood, valiance, dauntlessness, doughtiness
<< OPPOSITE cowardice

prowl *verb* MOVE STEALTHILY, hunt, patrol, range, steal, cruise, stalk, sneak, lurk, roam, rove, scavenge, slink, skulk, nose around

proximity *noun* NEARNESS, closeness, vicinity, neighbourhood, juxtaposition, contiguity, propinquity, adjacency

proxy *noun* REPRESENTATIVE, agent, deputy, substitute, factor, attorney, delegate, surrogate

prudence *noun* 1 CAUTION, care, discretion, vigilance, wariness, circumspection, canniness, heedfulness
2 WISDOM, common sense, good sense, good judgment, sagacity, judiciousness
3 THRIFT, economy, planning, saving, precaution, foresight, providence, preparedness, good management, husbandry, frugality, forethought, economizing, far-sightedness, careful budgeting

prudent *adjective* 1 CAUTIOUS, careful, wary, discreet, canny, vigilant, circumspect
<< OPPOSITE careless
2 WISE, politic, sensible, sage, shrewd, discerning, judicious, sagacious
<< OPPOSITE unwise
3 THRIFTY, economical, sparing, careful, canny, provident, frugal, far-sighted
<< OPPOSITE extravagant

prudish *adjective* PRIM, formal, proper, stuffy, puritanical, demure, squeamish, narrow-minded, starchy (*informal*), prissy (*informal*), strait-laced, Victorian, priggish, schoolmarmish (*Brit informal*), old-maidish (*informal*), niminy-piminy, overmodest, overnice
<< OPPOSITE broad-minded

prune *verb* 1 CUT, trim, clip, dock, shape, cut back, shorten, snip, lop, pare down
2 REDUCE, cut, cut back, trim, cut down, pare down, make reductions in

prurient *adjective* 1 LECHEROUS, longing, lewd, salacious, lascivious, itching, hankering, voyeuristic, lustful, libidinous, desirous, concupiscent
2 INDECENT, dirty, erotic, obscene, steamy (*informal*), pornographic, X-rated (*informal*), salacious, smutty

pry *verb* BE INQUISITIVE, peer, interfere, poke,

peep, meddle, intrude, snoop (*informal*), nose into, be nosy (*informal*), be a busybody, ferret about, poke your nose in *or* into (*informal*)

prying *adjective* INQUISITIVE, spying, curious, interfering, meddling, intrusive, eavesdropping, snooping (*informal*), snoopy (*informal*), impertinent, nosy (*informal*), meddlesome

psalm *noun* HYMN, carol, chant, paean, song of praise

pseudonym *noun* FALSE NAME, alias, incognito, stage name, pen name, assumed name, nom de guerre, nom de plume, professional name

psyche *noun* SOUL, mind, self, spirit, personality, individuality, subconscious, true being, anima, essential nature, pneuma (*Philosophy*), innermost self, inner man, wairua (*NZ*)

psychedelic *adjective* 1 HALLUCINOGENIC, mind-blowing (*informal*), psychoactive, hallucinatory, mind-bending (*informal*), psychotropic, mind-expanding, consciousness-expanding, psychotomimetic
2 MULTICOLOURED, wild, crazy, freaky (*slang*), kaleidoscopic

psychiatrist *noun* PSYCHOTHERAPIST, analyst, therapist, psychologist, shrink (*slang*), psychoanalyst, psychoanalyser, headshrinker (*slang*)

psychic *adjective* 1 SUPERNATURAL, mystic, occult, clairvoyant, telepathic, extrasensory, preternatural, telekinetic
2 MYSTICAL, spiritual, magical, other-worldly, paranormal, preternatural
3 PSYCHOLOGICAL, emotional, mental, spiritual, inner, psychiatric, cognitive, psychogenic
▷ *noun* CLAIRVOYANT, fortune teller

psychological *adjective* 1 MENTAL, emotional, intellectual, inner, cognitive, cerebral
2 IMAGINARY, psychosomatic, unconscious, subconscious, subjective, irrational, unreal, all in the mind

psychology *noun* 1 BEHAVIOURISM, study of personality, science of mind
2 (*informal*) WAY OF THINKING, attitude, behaviour, temperament, mentality, thought processes, mental processes, what makes you tick, mental make-up

psychopath *noun* MADMAN, lunatic, maniac, psychotic, nutter (*Brit slang*), nutcase (*slang*), sociopath, headcase (*informal*), mental case (*slang*), headbanger (*informal*), insane person ▷ see **mad**

psychotic *adjective* MAD, mental (*slang*), insane, lunatic, demented, unbalanced, deranged, psychopathic, round the bend (*Brit slang*), certifiable, off your head (*slang*), off your trolley (*slang*), not right in the head, non compos mentis (*Latin*), off your rocker (*slang*), off your chump
▷ *noun* LUNATIC, maniac, psychopath, nut (*slang*), psycho (*slang*), loony (*slang*), nutter (*Brit slang*), nutcase (*slang*), headcase (*informal*), mental case (*slang*), headbanger (*informal*) ▷ see **mad**

pub *or* **public house** *noun* TAVERN, bar, inn, local (*Brit informal*), saloon, watering hole (*facetious slang*), boozer (*Brit, Austral & NZ informal*), beer parlour (*Canad*), beverage room (*Canad*), roadhouse, hostelry (*archaic* or *facetious*), alehouse (*archaic*), taproom

puberty *noun* ADOLESCENCE, teenage, teens, young adulthood, pubescence, awkward age, juvenescence

public *noun* PEOPLE, society, country, population, masses, community, nation, everyone, citizens, voters, electorate, multitude, populace, hoi polloi, Joe Public (*slang*), Joe Six-Pack (*US slang*), commonalty
▷ *adjective* 1 CIVIC, government, state, national, local, official, community, social, federal, civil, constitutional, municipal
2 GENERAL, popular, national, shared, common, widespread, universal, collective
3 OPEN, community, accessible, communal, open to the public, unrestricted, free to all, not private
<< OPPOSITE private
4 WELL-KNOWN, leading, important, respected, famous, celebrated, recognized, distinguished, prominent, influential, notable, renowned, eminent, famed, noteworthy, in the public eye
5 KNOWN, published, exposed, open, obvious, acknowledged, recognized, plain, patent, notorious, overt, in circulation
<< OPPOSITE secret

publication *noun* 1 PAMPHLET, book, newspaper, magazine, issue, title, leaflet, brochure, booklet, paperback, hardback, periodical, zine (*informal*), handbill
2 ANNOUNCEMENT, publishing, broadcasting, reporting, airing, appearance, declaration, advertisement, disclosure, proclamation, notification, dissemination, promulgation

publicity *noun* 1 ADVERTISING, press, promotion, hype, boost, build-up, plug (*informal*), puff, ballyhoo (*informal*), puffery (*informal*), boosterism
2 ATTENTION, exposure, fame, celebrity, fuss, public interest, limelight, notoriety, media attention, renown, public notice

publicize *verb* 1 ADVERTISE, promote, plug (*informal*), hype, push, spotlight, puff, play up, write up, spread about, beat the drum for (*informal*), give publicity to, bring to public notice
2 MAKE KNOWN, report, reveal, publish,

broadcast, leak, disclose, proclaim, circulate, make public, divulge
<< OPPOSITE keep secret
public-spirited *adjective* ALTRUISTIC, generous, humanitarian, charitable, philanthropic, unselfish, community-minded
publish *verb* 1 PUT OUT, issue, produce, print, bring out
2 ANNOUNCE, reveal, declare, spread, advertise, broadcast, leak, distribute, communicate, disclose, proclaim, circulate, impart, publicize, divulge, promulgate, shout from the rooftops (*informal*), blow wide open (*slang*)
pucker *verb* WRINKLE, tighten, purse, pout, contract, gather, knit, crease, compress, crumple, ruffle, furrow, screw up, crinkle, draw together, ruck up, ruckle
▷ *noun* WRINKLE, fold, crease, crumple, ruck, crinkle, ruckle
pudding *noun* DESSERT, afters (*Brit informal*), sweet, pud (*informal*), second course, last course
puerile *adjective* CHILDISH, juvenile, naive, weak, silly, ridiculous, foolish, petty, trivial, irresponsible, immature, infantile, inane, babyish, jejune
<< OPPOSITE mature
puff *verb* 1 SMOKE, draw, drag (*slang*), suck, inhale, pull at *or* on
2 BREATHE HEAVILY, pant, exhale, blow, gasp, gulp, wheeze, fight for breath, puff and pant
3 PROMOTE, push, plug (*informal*), hype, publicize, advertise, praise, crack up (*informal*), big up (*slang, chiefly Caribbean*), overpraise
▷ *noun* 1 DRAG (*slang*), pull, smoke
2 BLAST, breath, flurry, whiff, draught, gust, emanation
3 ADVERTISEMENT, ad (*informal*), promotion, plug (*informal*), good word, commendation, sales talk, favourable mention, piece of publicity
▷▷ **puff out** *or* **up** SWELL, expand, enlarge, inflate, dilate, distend, bloat
puffy *adjective* SWOLLEN, enlarged, inflated, inflamed, bloated, puffed up, distended
pugnacious *adjective* AGGRESSIVE, contentious, irritable, belligerent, combative, petulant, antagonistic, argumentative, bellicose, irascible, quarrelsome, hot-tempered, choleric, disputatious, aggers (*Austral slang*), biffo (*Austral slang*)
<< OPPOSITE peaceful
puke *verb* (*Slang*) VOMIT, be sick, throw up (*informal*), spew, heave, regurgitate, disgorge, retch, be nauseated, chuck (*Austral & NZ informal*), barf (*US slang*), chunder (*slang, chiefly Austral*), upchuck (*US slang*), do a technicolour yawn (*slang*), toss your cookies (*US slang*)
pull *verb* 1 DRAW, haul, drag, trail, tow, tug, jerk, yank, prise, wrench, lug, wrest
<< OPPOSITE push
2 EXTRACT, pick, remove, gather, take out, weed, pluck, cull, uproot, draw out
<< OPPOSITE insert
3 (*informal*) ATTRACT, draw, bring in, tempt, lure, interest, entice, pull in, magnetize
<< OPPOSITE repel
4 STRAIN, tear, stretch, rend, rip, wrench, dislocate, sprain
▷ *noun* 1 TUG, jerk, yank, twitch, heave
<< OPPOSITE shove
2 ATTRACTION, appeal, lure, fascination, force, draw, influence, magnetism, enchantment, drawing power, enticement, allurement
3 FORCE, exertion, magnetism, forcefulness
4 PUFF, drag (*slang*), inhalation
5 (*informal*) INFLUENCE, power, authority, say, standing, weight, advantage, muscle, sway, prestige, clout (*informal*), leverage, kai (*NZ informal*)
▷▷ **pull a fast one on someone** (*informal*) TRICK, cheat, con (*informal*), take advantage of, deceive, defraud, swindle, bamboozle (*informal*), hoodwink, take for a ride (*informal*), put one over on (*informal*)
▷▷ **pull in** DRAW IN, stop, park, arrive, come in, halt, draw up, pull over, come to a halt
▷▷ **pull out (of)** 1 WITHDRAW, retire from, abandon, quit, step down from, back out, bow out, stop participating in
2 LEAVE, abandon, get out, quit, retreat from, depart, evacuate
▷▷ **pull someone in** (*Brit slang*) ARREST, nail (*informal*), bust (*informal*), lift (*slang*), run in (*slang*), collar (*informal*), pinch (*informal*), nab (*informal*), take someone into custody, feel someone's collar (*slang*)
▷▷ **pull someone up** REPRIMAND, lecture, rebuke, reproach, carpet (*informal*), censure, scold, berate, castigate, admonish, chastise, tear into (*informal*), read the riot act to, tell someone off (*informal*), reprove, upbraid, take someone to task, tick someone off (*informal*), read someone the riot act, bawl someone out (*informal*), dress someone down (*informal*), lambaste, give someone an earful, chew someone out (*US & Canad informal*), tear someone off a strip (*Brit informal*), haul someone over the coals, give someone a dressing down, give someone a rocket (*Brit & NZ informal*), slap someone on the wrist, rap someone over the knuckles
▷▷ **pull something apart** *or* **to pieces**
1 DISMANTLE, strip down, disassemble, take something apart, break something up, take something to bits
2 CRITICIZE, attack, blast, pan (*informal*), slam (*slang*), put down, run down, slate (*informal*), tear into (*informal*), lay into (*informal*), flay, diss

(*slang, chiefly US*), find fault with, lambast(e), pick holes in
▷▷ **pull something down** DEMOLISH, level, destroy, dismantle, remove, flatten, knock down, take down, tear down, bulldoze, raze, lay waste, raze to the ground, kennet (*Austral slang*), jeff (*Austral slang*)
▷▷ **pull something in** 1 ATTRACT, draw, pull, bring in, lure
2 EARN, make, clear, gain, net, collect, be paid, pocket, bring in, gross, take home, rake in
▷▷ **pull something off** 1 (*informal*) SUCCEED IN, manage, establish, effect, complete, achieve, engineer, carry out, crack (*informal*), fulfil, accomplish, execute, discharge, clinch, bring about, carry off, perpetrate, bring off
2 REMOVE, detach, rip off, tear off, doff, wrench off
▷▷ **pull something out** PRODUCE, draw, bring out, draw out
▷▷ **pull something up** UPROOT, raise, lift, weed, dig up, dig out, rip up
▷▷ **pull through** SURVIVE, improve, recover, rally, come through, get better, be all right, recuperate, turn the corner, pull round, get well again
▷▷ **pull up** STOP, park, halt, arrive, brake, draw up, come to a halt, reach a standstill
▷▷ **pull yourself together** (*informal*) GET A GRIP ON YOURSELF, recover, get over it, buck up (*informal*), snap out of it (*informal*), get your act together, regain your composure

pulp *noun* 1 PASTE, mash, pap, mush, semisolid, pomace, semiliquid
2 FLESH, meat, marrow, soft part
▷ *modifier* CHEAP, sensational, lurid, mushy (*informal*), trashy, rubbishy
▷ *verb* CRUSH, squash, mash, pulverize

pulsate *verb* THROB, pound, beat, hammer, pulse, tick, thump, quiver, vibrate, thud, palpitate

pulse *noun* BEAT, rhythm, vibration, beating, stroke, throb, throbbing, oscillation, pulsation
▷ *verb* BEAT, tick, throb, vibrate, pulsate

pummel *verb* BEAT, punch, pound, strike, knock, belt (*informal*), hammer, bang, batter, thump, clobber (*slang*), lambast(e), beat the living daylights out of, rain blows upon, beat *or* knock seven bells out of (*informal*)

pump *verb* 1 DRIVE OUT, empty, drain, force out, bail out, siphon, draw off
2 SUPPLY, send, pour, inject
3 INTERROGATE, probe, quiz, cross-examine, grill (*informal*), worm out of, give someone the third degree, question closely
▷▷ **pump something up** INFLATE, blow up, fill up, dilate, puff up, aerate

pun *noun* PLAY ON WORDS, quip, double entendre, witticism, paronomasia (*Rhetoric*), equivoque

punch[1] *verb* HIT, strike, box, smash, belt (*informal*), slam, plug (*slang*), bash (*informal*), sock (*slang*), clout (*informal*), slug, swipe (*informal*), biff (*slang*), bop (*informal*), wallop (*informal*), pummel
▷ *noun* 1 BLOW, hit, knock, bash (*informal*), plug (*slang*), sock (*slang*), thump, clout (*informal*), jab, swipe (*informal*), biff (*slang*), bop (*informal*), wallop (*informal*)
2 (*informal*) EFFECTIVENESS, force, bite, impact, point, drive, vigour, verve, forcefulness

punch[2] *verb* PIERCE, cut, bore, drill, pink, stamp, puncture, prick, perforate

punch-up *noun* (*Brit informal*) FIGHT, row, argument, set-to (*informal*), scrap (*informal*), brawl, free-for-all (*informal*), dust-up (*informal*), shindig (*informal*), battle royal, stand-up fight (*informal*), dingdong, shindy (*informal*), bagarre (*French*), biffo (*Austral slang*)

punchy *adjective* (*informal*) EFFECTIVE, spirited, dynamic, lively, storming (*informal*), aggressive, vigorous, forceful, incisive, in-your-face (*slang*)

punctual *adjective* ON TIME, timely, early, prompt, strict, exact, precise, in good time, on the dot, seasonable
<< OPPOSITE late

punctuality *noun* PROMPTNESS, readiness, regularity, promptitude

punctuate *verb* INTERRUPT, break, pepper, sprinkle, intersperse, interject

puncture *noun* 1 FLAT TYRE, flat, flattie (*NZ*)
2 HOLE, opening, break, cut, nick, leak, slit, rupture, perforation
▷ *verb* 1 PIERCE, cut, nick, penetrate, prick, rupture, perforate, impale, bore a hole
2 DEFLATE, go down, go flat
3 HUMBLE, discourage, disillusion, flatten, deflate, take down a peg (*informal*)

pundit *noun* EXPERT, guru, maestro, buff (*informal*), wonk (*informal*), fundi (*S African*), one of the cognoscenti, (self-appointed) expert *or* authority

pungent *adjective* 1 STRONG, hot, spicy, seasoned, sharp, acid, bitter, stinging, sour, tart, aromatic, tangy, acrid, peppery, piquant, highly flavoured, acerb
<< OPPOSITE mild
2 CUTTING, pointed, biting, acute, telling, sharp, keen, stinging, piercing, penetrating, poignant, stringent, scathing, acrimonious, barbed, incisive, sarcastic, caustic, vitriolic, trenchant, mordant, mordacious
<< OPPOSITE dull

punish *verb* DISCIPLINE, correct, castigate, chastise, beat, sentence, whip, lash, cane, flog, scourge, chasten, penalize, bring someone to book, slap someone's wrist, throw the book at, rap someone's knuckles, give someone the works (*slang*), give a lesson to

punishable *adjective* CULPABLE, criminal, chargeable, indictable, blameworthy, convictable

punishing *adjective* HARD, taxing, demanding, grinding, wearing, tiring, exhausting, uphill, gruelling, strenuous, arduous, burdensome, backbreaking

<< OPPOSITE easy

punishment *noun* 1 PENALIZING, discipline, correction, retribution, what for (*informal*), chastening, just deserts, chastisement, punitive measures

2 PENALTY, reward, sanction, penance, comeuppance (*slang*)

3 (*informal*) BEATING, abuse, torture, pain, victimization, manhandling, maltreatment, rough treatment

4 ROUGH TREATMENT, abuse, maltreatment

punitive *adjective* RETALIATORY, in retaliation, vindictive, in reprisal, revengeful, retaliative, punitory

punt *verb* BET, back, stake, gamble, lay, wager

▷ *noun* BET, stake, gamble, wager

punter *noun* 1 GAMBLER, better, backer, punt (*chiefly Brit*)

2 (*informal*) CUSTOMER, guest, client, patron, member of the audience

3 (*informal*) PERSON, guy (*informal*), fellow, bloke (*Brit informal*), man in the street

puny *adjective* 1 FEEBLE, weak, frail, little, tiny, weakly, stunted, diminutive, sickly, undeveloped, pint-sized (*informal*), undersized, underfed, dwarfish, pygmy *or* pigmy

<< OPPOSITE strong

2 INSIGNIFICANT, minor, petty, inferior, trivial, worthless, trifling, paltry, inconsequential, piddling (*informal*)

pup *or* **puppy** *noun* WHIPPERSNAPPER, braggart, whelp, jackanapes, popinjay

>> RELATED WORD *collective noun* litter

pupil *noun* 1 STUDENT, scholar, schoolboy *or* schoolgirl, schoolchild

<< OPPOSITE teacher

2 LEARNER, student, follower, trainee, novice, beginner, apprentice, disciple, protégé, neophyte, tyro, catechumen

<< OPPOSITE instructor

puppet *noun* 1 MARIONETTE, doll, glove puppet, finger puppet

2 PAWN, tool, instrument, creature, dupe, gull (*archaic*), figurehead, mouthpiece, stooge, cat's-paw

purchase *verb* BUY, pay for, obtain, get, score (*slang*), gain, pick up, secure, acquire, invest in, shop for, get hold of, come by, procure, make a purchase of

<< OPPOSITE sell

▷ *noun* 1 ACQUISITION, buy, investment, property, gain, asset, possession

2 GRIP, hold, support, footing, influence, edge, advantage, grasp, lever, leverage, foothold, toehold

purchaser *noun* BUYER, customer, consumer, vendee (*Law*)

<< OPPOSITE seller

pure *adjective* 1 UNMIXED, real, clear, true, simple, natural, straight, perfect, genuine, neat, authentic, flawless, unalloyed

<< OPPOSITE adulterated

2 CLEAN, immaculate, sterile, wholesome, sanitary, spotless, sterilized, squeaky-clean, unblemished, unadulterated, untainted, disinfected, uncontaminated, unpolluted, pasteurized, germ-free

<< OPPOSITE contaminated

3 THEORETICAL, abstract, philosophical, speculative, academic, conceptual, hypothetical, conjectural, non-practical

<< OPPOSITE practical

4 COMPLETE, total, perfect, absolute, mere, sheer, patent, utter, outright, thorough, downright, palpable, unqualified, out-and-out, unmitigated

<< OPPOSITE qualified

5 INNOCENT, virgin, modest, good, true, moral, maidenly, upright, honest, immaculate, impeccable, righteous, virtuous, squeaky-clean, blameless, chaste, virginal, unsullied, guileless, uncorrupted, unstained, undefiled, unspotted

<< OPPOSITE corrupt

purely *adverb* ABSOLUTELY, just, only, completely, simply, totally, entirely, exclusively, plainly, merely, solely, wholly

purgatory *noun* TORMENT, agony, murder (*informal*), hell (*informal*), torture, misery, hell on earth

purge *verb* 1 RID, clear, cleanse, strip, empty, void

2 GET RID OF, kill, remove, dismiss, axe (*informal*), expel, wipe out, oust, eradicate, eject, do away with, liquidate, exterminate, sweep out, rout out, wipe from the face of the earth, rid somewhere of

3 CLEANSE, clear, purify, wash, clean out, expiate

▷ *noun* REMOVAL, elimination, crushing, expulsion, suppression, liquidation, cleanup, witch hunt, eradication, ejection

purify *verb* 1 CLEAN, filter, cleanse, refine, clarify, disinfect, fumigate, decontaminate, sanitize

<< OPPOSITE contaminate

2 ABSOLVE, cleanse, redeem, exonerate, sanctify, exculpate, shrive, lustrate

<< OPPOSITE sully

purist *noun* STICKLER, traditionalist, perfectionist, classicist, pedant, formalist, literalist

puritan *noun* MORALIST, fanatic, zealot, prude,

pietist, rigorist
▷ *adjective* STRICT, austere, puritanical, narrow, severe, intolerant, ascetic, narrow-minded, moralistic, prudish, hidebound, strait-laced
puritanical *adjective* STRICT, forbidding, puritan, stuffy, narrow, severe, proper, stiff, rigid, disapproving, austere, fanatical, bigoted, prim, ascetic, narrow-minded, prudish, strait-laced
<< OPPOSITE liberal
puritanism *noun* STRICTNESS, austerity, severity, zeal, piety, rigidity, fanaticism, narrowness, asceticism, moralism, prudishness, rigorism, piousness
purity *noun* 1 CLEANNESS, clarity, cleanliness, brilliance, genuineness, wholesomeness, fineness, clearness, pureness, faultlessness, immaculateness, untaintedness
<< OPPOSITE impurity
2 INNOCENCE, virtue, integrity, honesty, decency, sincerity, virginity, piety, chastity, rectitude, guilelessness, virtuousness, chasteness, blamelessness
<< OPPOSITE immorality
purport *verb* CLAIM, allege, proclaim, maintain, declare, pretend, assert, pose as, profess
purpose *noun* 1 REASON, point, idea, goal, grounds, design, aim, basis, principle, function, object, intention, objective, motive, motivation, justification, impetus, the why and wherefore
2 AIM, end, plan, hope, view, goal, design, project, target, wish, scheme, desire, object, intention, objective, ambition, aspiration, Holy Grail (*informal*)
3 DETERMINATION, commitment, resolve, will, resolution, initiative, enterprise, ambition, conviction, motivation, persistence, tenacity, firmness, constancy, single-mindedness, steadfastness
4 USE, good, return, result, effect, value, benefit, profit, worth, gain, advantage, outcome, utility, merit, mileage (*informal*), avail, behoof (*archaic*)
▷▷ **on purpose** DELIBERATELY, purposely, consciously, intentionally, knowingly, wilfully, by design, wittingly, calculatedly, designedly

> The two concepts *purposeful* and *on purpose* should be carefully distinguished. *On purpose* and *purposely* have roughly the same meaning, and imply that a person's action is deliberate, rather than accidental. However, *purposeful* and its related adverb *purposefully* refer to the way that someone acts as being full of purpose or determination

purposeful *adjective* DETERMINED, resolved, resolute, decided, firm, settled, positive, fixed, deliberate, single-minded, tenacious, strong-willed, steadfast, immovable, unfaltering
<< OPPOSITE undecided ▷ see **purpose**
purposely *adverb* DELIBERATELY, expressly, consciously, intentionally, knowingly, with intent, on purpose, wilfully, by design, calculatedly, designedly
<< OPPOSITE accidentally ▷ see **purpose**
purse *noun* 1 POUCH, wallet, money-bag
2 (*US*) HANDBAG, bag, shoulder bag, pocket book, clutch bag
3 FUNDS, means, money, resources, treasury, wealth, exchequer, coffers, wherewithal
4 PRIZE, winnings, award, gift, reward
▷ *verb* PUCKER, close, contract, tighten, knit, wrinkle, pout, press together
pursue *verb* 1 ENGAGE IN, follow, perform, conduct, wage, tackle, take up, work at, carry on, practise, participate in, prosecute, ply, go in for, apply yourself to
2 TRY FOR, seek, desire, search for, aim for, aspire to, work towards, strive for, have as a goal
3 CONTINUE, maintain, carry on, keep on, hold to, see through, adhere to, persist in, proceed in, persevere in
4 FOLLOW, track, hunt, chase, dog, attend, shadow, accompany, harry, tail (*informal*), haunt, plague, hound, stalk, harass, go after, run after, hunt down, give chase to
<< OPPOSITE flee
5 COURT, woo, pay attention to, make up to (*informal*), chase after, pay court to, set your cap at
<< OPPOSITE fight shy of
pursuit *noun* 1 QUEST, seeking, search, aim of, aspiration for, striving towards
2 PURSUING, seeking, tracking, search, hunt, hunting, chase, trail, trailing
3 OCCUPATION, activity, interest, line, pleasure, hobby, pastime, vocation
push *verb* 1 SHOVE, force, press, thrust, drive, knock, sweep, plunge, elbow, bump, ram, poke, propel, nudge, prod, jostle, hustle, bulldoze, impel, manhandle
<< OPPOSITE pull
2 PRESS, operate, depress, squeeze, activate, hold down
3 MAKE *or* FORCE YOUR WAY, move, shoulder, inch, squeeze, thrust, elbow, shove, jostle, work your way, thread your way
4 URGE, encourage, persuade, spur, drive, press, influence, prod, constrain, incite, coerce, egg on, impel, browbeat, exert influence on
<< OPPOSITE discourage
5 PROMOTE, advertise, hype, publicize,

boost, plug (*informal*), puff, make known, propagandize, cry up
▷ *noun* 1 SHOVE, thrust, butt, elbow, poke, nudge, prod, jolt
<< OPPOSITE pull
2 (*informal*) EFFORT, charge, attack, campaign, advance, assault, raid, offensive, sally, thrust, blitz, onset
3 (*informal*) DRIVE, go (*informal*), energy, initiative, enterprise, ambition, determination, pep, vitality, vigour, dynamism, get-up-and-go (*informal*), gumption (*informal*)
▷▷ **push off** (*informal*) GO AWAY, leave, get lost (*informal*), clear off (*informal*), take off (*informal*), depart, beat it (*slang*), light out (*informal*), hit the road (*slang*), hook it (*slang*), slope off, pack your bags (*informal*), make tracks, buzz off (*informal*), hop it (*informal*), shove off (*informal*), skedaddle (*informal*), naff off (*informal*), be off with you, sling your hook (*informal*), make yourself scarce (*informal*), voetsek (*S African offensive*), rack off (*Austral & NZ slang*)
▷▷ **the push** (*informal, chiefly Brit*) DISMISSAL, the sack (*informal*), discharge, the boot (*slang*), your cards (*informal*), your books (*informal*), marching orders (*informal*), the kiss-off (*slang, chiefly US & Canad*), the (old) heave-ho (*informal*), the order of the boot (*slang*)

pushed *adjective often with* **for** (*informal*) SHORT OF, pressed, rushed, tight, hurried, under pressure, in difficulty, up against it (*informal*)

pushover *noun* 1 SUCKER (*slang*), mug (*Brit slang*), stooge (*slang*), soft touch (*slang*), chump (*informal*), walkover (*informal*), easy game (*informal*), easy *or* soft mark (*informal*)
2 (*informal*) PIECE OF CAKE (*Brit informal*), breeze (*US & Canad informal*), picnic (*informal*), child's play (*informal*), plain sailing, doddle (*Brit slang*), walkover (*informal*), cinch (*slang*), cakewalk (*informal*), duck soup (*US slang*)
<< OPPOSITE challenge

pushy *adjective* FORCEFUL, aggressive, assertive, brash, loud, offensive, ambitious, bold, obnoxious, presumptuous, obtrusive, officious, bumptious, self-assertive
<< OPPOSITE shy

put *verb* 1 PLACE, leave, set, position, rest, park (*informal*), plant, establish, lay, stick (*informal*), settle, fix, lean, deposit, dump (*informal*), prop, lay down, put down, situate, set down, stow, bung (*informal*), plonk (*informal*)
2 CONSIGN TO, place, commit to, doom to, condemn to
3 IMPOSE, subject, levy, inflict
4 EXPRESS, state, word, phrase, set, pose, utter
5 PRESENT, suggest, advance, propose, offer, forward, submit, tender, bring forward, proffer, posit, set before, lay before
▷▷ **put someone away** (*informal*) COMMIT, confine, cage (*informal*), imprison, certify, institutionalize, incarcerate, put in prison, put behind bars, lock up *or* away
▷▷ **put someone down** (*Slang*) HUMILIATE, shame, crush, show up, reject, dismiss, condemn, slight, criticize, snub, have a go at (*informal*), deflate, denigrate, belittle, disparage, deprecate, mortify, diss (*slang, chiefly US*)
▷▷ **put someone off** 1 DISCOURAGE, intimidate, deter, daunt, dissuade, demoralize, scare off, dishearten
2 DISCONCERT, confuse, unsettle, throw (*informal*), distress, rattle (*informal*), dismay, perturb, faze, discomfit, take the wind out of someone's sails, nonplus, abash
▷▷ **put someone out** 1 INCONVENIENCE, trouble, upset, bother, disturb, impose upon, discomfit, discommode, incommode
2 ANNOY, anger, provoke, irritate, disturb, harass, confound, exasperate, disconcert, nettle, vex, perturb, irk, put on the spot, take the wind out of someone's sails, discountenance, discompose
▷▷ **put someone up** 1 ACCOMMODATE, house, board, lodge, quarter, entertain, take someone in, billet, give someone lodging
2 NOMINATE, put forward, offer, present, propose, recommend, float, submit
▷▷ **put someone up to something** ENCOURAGE, urge, persuade, prompt, incite, egg on, goad, put the idea into someone's head
▷▷ **put something across** *or* **over** COMMUNICATE, explain, clarify, express, get through, convey, make clear, spell out, get across, make yourself understood
▷▷ **put something aside** *or* **by** 1 SAVE, store, stockpile, deposit, hoard, cache, lay by, stow away, salt away, keep in reserve, squirrel away
2 DISREGARD, forget, ignore, bury, discount, set aside, pay no heed to
▷▷ **put something away** 1 STORE AWAY, replace, put back, tidy up, clear away, tidy away, return to its place
2 SAVE, set aside, put aside, keep, deposit, put by, stash away, store away
3 (*informal*) CONSUME, devour, eat up, demolish (*informal*), gobble, guzzle, polish off (*informal*), gulp down, wolf down, pig out on (*informal*)
▷▷ **put something down** 1 RECORD, write down, list, enter, log, take down, inscribe, set down, transcribe, put in black and white
2 REPRESS, crush, suppress, check, silence, overthrow, squash, subdue, quash, quell, stamp out
3 PUT TO SLEEP, kill, destroy, do away with, put away, put out of its misery
▷▷ **put something down to something**

ATTRIBUTE, blame, ascribe, set down, impute, chalk up

▷▷ **put something forward** RECOMMEND, present, suggest, introduce, advance, propose, press, submit, tender, nominate, prescribe, move for, proffer

▷▷ **put something off** POSTPONE, delay, defer, adjourn, put back, hold over, reschedule, put on ice, put on the back burner (*informal*), take a rain check on (*US & Canad informal*)

▷▷ **put something on** 1 DON, dress in, slip into, pull on, climb into, change into, throw on, get dressed in, fling on, pour yourself into, doll yourself up in

2 PRESENT, stage, perform, do, show, produce, mount

3 ADD, gain, increase by

4 BET, back, place, chance, risk, lay, stake, hazard, wager

5 FAKE, affect, assume, simulate, feign, make believe, play-act

▷▷ **put something out** 1 ISSUE, release, publish, broadcast, bring out, circulate, make public, make known *verb*

2 EXTINGUISH, smother, blow out, stamp out, douse, snuff out, quench

▷▷ **put something up** 1 BUILD, raise, set up, construct, erect, fabricate

2 OFFER, present, mount, put forward

3 PROVIDE, advance, invest, contribute, give, pay up, supply, come up with, pledge, donate, furnish, fork out (*informal*), cough up (*informal*), shell out (*informal*)

▷▷ **put up with something** *or* **someone** (*informal*) STAND, suffer, bear, take, wear (*Brit informal*), stomach, endure, swallow, brook, stand for, lump (*informal*), tolerate, hack (*slang*), abide, countenance

▷▷ **put upon someone** TAKE ADVANTAGE OF, trouble, abuse, harry, exploit, saddle, take for granted, put someone out, inconvenience, beset, overwork, impose upon, take for a fool

putative *adjective* (*Formal*) SUPPOSED, reported, assumed, alleged, presumed, reputed, imputed, presumptive, commonly believed

putative *adjective* (*Formal*) SUPPOSED, reported, assumed, alleged, presumed, reputed, imputed, presumptive, commonly believed

put-down *noun* HUMILIATION, slight, snub, knock (*informal*), dig, sneer, rebuff, barb, sarcasm, kick in the teeth (*slang*), gibe, disparagement, one in the eye (*informal*)

puzzle *verb* PERPLEX, beat (*slang*), confuse, baffle, stump, bewilder, confound, mystify, faze, flummox, bemuse, nonplus

▷ *noun* 1 PROBLEM, riddle, maze, labyrinth, question, conundrum, teaser, poser, brain-teaser (*informal*)

2 MYSTERY, problem, paradox, enigma, conundrum

▷▷ **puzzle over something** THINK ABOUT, study, wonder about, mull over, muse on, think hard about, ponder on, brood over, ask yourself about, cudgel *or* rack your brains

▷▷ **puzzle something out** SOLVE, work out, figure out, unravel, see, get, crack, resolve, sort out, clear up, decipher, think through, suss (out) (*slang*), get the answer of, find the key to, crack the code of

puzzled *adjective* PERPLEXED, beaten, confused, baffled, lost, stuck, stumped, doubtful, at sea, bewildered, mixed up, at a loss, mystified, clueless, nonplussed, flummoxed, in a fog, without a clue

puzzlement *noun* PERPLEXITY, questioning, surprise, doubt, wonder, confusion, uncertainty, bewilderment, disorientation, bafflement, mystification, doubtfulness

puzzling *adjective* PERPLEXING, baffling, bewildering, hard, involved, misleading, unclear, ambiguous, enigmatic, incomprehensible, mystifying, inexplicable, unaccountable, knotty, unfathomable, labyrinthine, full of surprises, abstruse, beyond you, oracular

<< OPPOSITE simple

pygmy *or* **pigmy** *modifier* SMALL, miniature, dwarf, tiny, wee, stunted, diminutive, minuscule, midget, elfin, undersized, teeny-weeny, Lilliputian, dwarfish, teensy-weensy, pygmean

▷ *noun* 1 MIDGET, dwarf, shrimp (*informal*), Lilliputian, Tom Thumb, munchkin (*informal, chiefly US*), homunculus, manikin

2 NONENTITY, nobody, lightweight (*informal*), mediocrity, cipher, small fry, pipsqueak (*informal*)

Qq

quack *noun* CHARLATAN, fraud, fake, pretender, humbug, impostor, mountebank, phoney *or* phony (*informal*)
▷ *modifier* FAKE, fraudulent, phoney *or* phony (*informal*), pretended, sham, counterfeit

quaff *verb* DRINK, gulp, swig (*informal*), have, down, swallow, slug, guzzle, imbibe, partake of

quagmire *noun* 1 PREDICAMENT, difficulty, quandary, pass, fix (*informal*), jam (*informal*), dilemma, pinch, plight, scrape (*informal*), muddle, pickle (*informal*), impasse, entanglement, imbroglio
2 BOG, marsh, swamp, slough, fen, mire, morass, quicksand, muskeg (*Canad*)

quail *verb* SHRINK, cringe, flinch, shake, faint, tremble, quake, shudder, falter, droop, blanch, recoil, cower, blench, have cold feet (*informal*)

quaint *adjective* 1 UNUSUAL, odd, curious, original, strange, bizarre, fantastic, old-fashioned, peculiar, eccentric, queer, rum (*Brit slang*), singular, fanciful, whimsical, droll
<< OPPOSITE ordinary
2 OLD-FASHIONED, charming, picturesque, antique, gothic, old-world, antiquated
<< OPPOSITE modern

quake *verb* SHAKE, tremble, quiver, move, rock, shiver, throb, shudder, wobble, waver, vibrate, pulsate, quail, totter, convulse

qualification *noun* 1 ELIGIBILITY, quality, ability, skill, capacity, fitness, attribute, capability, endowment(s), accomplishment, achievement, aptitude, suitability, suitableness
2 CONDITION, restriction, proviso, requirement, rider, exception, criterion, reservation, allowance, objection, limitation, modification, exemption, prerequisite, caveat, stipulation

qualified *adjective* 1 CAPABLE, trained, experienced, seasoned, able, fit, expert, talented, chartered, efficient, practised, licensed, certificated, equipped, accomplished, eligible, competent, skilful, adept, knowledgeable, proficient
<< OPPOSITE untrained
2 RESTRICTED, limited, provisional, conditional, reserved, guarded, bounded, adjusted, moderated, adapted, confined, modified, tempered, cautious, refined, amended, contingent, tentative, hesitant, circumscribed, equivocal
<< OPPOSITE unconditional

qualify *verb* 1 CERTIFY, equip, empower, train, ground, condition, prepare, fit, commission, ready, permit, sanction, endow, capacitate
<< OPPOSITE disqualify
2 BE DESCRIBED, count, be considered as, be named, be counted, be eligible, be characterized, be designated, be distinguished
3 RESTRICT, limit, reduce, vary, ease, moderate, adapt, modify, regulate, diminish, temper, soften, restrain, lessen, mitigate, abate, tone down, assuage, modulate, circumscribe

quality *noun* 1 STANDARD, standing, class, condition, value, rank, grade, merit, classification, calibre
2 EXCELLENCE, status, merit, position, value, worth, distinction, virtue, superiority, calibre, eminence, pre-eminence
3 CHARACTERISTIC, feature, attribute, point, side, mark, property, aspect, streak, trait, facet, quirk, peculiarity, idiosyncrasy
4 NATURE, character, constitution, make, sort, kind, worth, description, essence

qualm *noun* MISGIVING, doubt, uneasiness, regret, anxiety, uncertainty, reluctance, hesitation, remorse, apprehension, disquiet, scruple, compunction, twinge *or* pang of conscience

quandary *noun* DIFFICULTY, dilemma, predicament, puzzle, uncertainty, embarrassment, plight, strait, impasse, bewilderment, perplexity, delicate situation, cleft stick

quantity *noun* 1 AMOUNT, lot, total, sum, part,

portion, quota, aggregate, number, allotment
2 SIZE, measure, mass, volume, length, capacity, extent, bulk, magnitude, greatness, expanse

> The use of a plural noun after *quantity of*, as in *a large quantity of bananas*, used to be considered incorrect, the objection being that the word *quantity* should only be used to refer to an uncountable amount, which was grammatically regarded as a singular concept. Nowadays, however, most people consider the use of *quantity* with a plural noun to be acceptable

quarrel *noun* DISAGREEMENT, fight, row, difference (of opinion), argument, dispute, controversy, breach, scrap (*informal*), disturbance, misunderstanding, contention, feud, fray, brawl, spat, squabble, strife, wrangle, skirmish, vendetta, discord, fracas, commotion, tiff, altercation, broil, tumult, dissension, affray, shindig (*informal*), disputation, dissidence, shindy (*informal*), bagarre (*French*), biffo (*Austral slang*)
<< OPPOSITE accord
▷ *verb* DISAGREE, fight, argue, row, clash, dispute, scrap (*informal*), differ, fall out (*informal*), brawl, squabble, spar, wrangle, bicker, be at odds, lock horns, cross swords, fight like cat and dog, go at it hammer and tongs, altercate
<< OPPOSITE get on *or* along (with)

quarrelsome *adjective* ARGUMENTATIVE, belligerent, pugnacious, cross, contentious, irritable, combative, fractious, petulant, ill-tempered, irascible, cantankerous, litigious, querulous, peevish, choleric, disputatious
<< OPPOSITE easy-going

quarry *noun* PREY, victim, game, goal, aim, prize, objective

quarter *noun* **1** DISTRICT, region, neighbourhood, place, point, part, side, area, position, station, spot, territory, zone, location, province, colony, locality
2 MERCY, pity, compassion, favour, charity, sympathy, tolerance, kindness, forgiveness, indulgence, clemency, leniency, forbearance, lenity
▷ *verb* ACCOMMODATE, house, lodge, place, board, post, station, install, put up, billet, give accommodation, provide with accommodation

quarters *plural noun* LODGINGS, rooms, accommodation, post, station, chambers, digs (*Brit informal*), shelter, lodging, residence, dwelling, barracks, abode, habitation, billet, domicile, cantonment (*Military*)

quash *verb* **1** ANNUL, overturn, reverse, cancel, overthrow, set aside, void, revoke, overrule, rescind, invalidate, nullify, declare null and void
2 SUPPRESS, crush, put down, beat, destroy, overthrow, squash, subdue, repress, quell, extinguish, quench, extirpate

quaver *verb* TREMBLE, shake, quiver, thrill, quake, shudder, flicker, flutter, waver, vibrate, pulsate, oscillate, trill, twitter

queasy *adjective* **1** SICK, ill, nauseous, squeamish, upset, uncomfortable, crook (*Austral & NZ informal*), queer, unwell, giddy, nauseated, groggy (*informal*), off colour, bilious, indisposed, green around the gills (*informal*), sickish
2 UNEASY, concerned, worried, troubled, disturbed, anxious, uncertain, restless, ill at ease, fidgety

queen *noun* **1** SOVEREIGN, ruler, monarch, leader, Crown, princess, majesty, head of state, Her Majesty, empress, crowned head
2 LEADING LIGHT, star, favourite, celebrity, darling, mistress, idol, big name, doyenne

queer *adjective* **1** STRANGE, odd, funny, unusual, extraordinary, remarkable, curious, weird, peculiar, abnormal, rum (*Brit slang*), uncommon, erratic, singular, eerie, unnatural, unconventional, uncanny, disquieting, unorthodox, outlandish, left-field (*informal*), anomalous, droll, atypical, outré
<< OPPOSITE normal
2 FAINT, dizzy, giddy, queasy, light-headed, reeling

> Although the term *queer* meaning 'gay' is still considered derogatory when used by non-gays, it is now being used by gay people themselves as a positive term in certain contexts, such as *queer politics*, *queer cinema*. Nevertheless, many gay people would not wish to have the term applied to them, nor would they use it of themselves

quell *verb* **1** SUPPRESS, crush, put down, defeat, overcome, conquer, subdue, stifle, overpower, quash, extinguish, stamp out, vanquish, squelch
2 CALM, quiet, silence, moderate, dull, soothe, alleviate, appease, allay, mitigate, assuage, pacify, mollify, deaden

quench *verb* **1** SATISFY, appease, allay, satiate, slake, sate
2 PUT OUT, extinguish, douse, end, check, destroy, crush, suppress, stifle, smother, snuff out, squelch

query *noun* **1** QUESTION, inquiry, problem, demand

2 DOUBT, suspicion, reservation, objection, hesitation, scepticism
▷ *verb* 1 QUESTION, challenge, doubt, suspect, dispute, object to, distrust, mistrust, call into question, disbelieve, feel uneasy about, throw doubt on, harbour reservations about
2 ASK, inquire *or* enquire, question

quest *noun* 1 SEARCH, hunt, mission, enterprise, undertaking, exploration, crusade
2 EXPEDITION, journey, adventure, voyage, pilgrimage

question *noun* 1 INQUIRY, enquiry, query, investigation, examination, interrogation
<< OPPOSITE answer
2 DIFFICULTY, problem, doubt, debate, argument, dispute, controversy, confusion, uncertainty, query, contention, misgiving, can of worms (*informal*), dubiety
3 ISSUE, point, matter, subject, problem, debate, proposal, theme, motion, topic, proposition, bone of contention, point at issue
▷ *verb* 1 INTERROGATE, cross-examine, interview, examine, investigate, pump (*informal*), probe, grill (*informal*), quiz, ask questions, sound out, catechize
2 DISPUTE, challenge, doubt, suspect, oppose, query, distrust, mistrust, call into question, disbelieve, impugn, cast aspersions on, cast doubt upon, controvert
<< OPPOSITE accept
▷▷ **in question** UNDER DISCUSSION, at issue, under consideration, in doubt, on the agenda, to be discussed, for debate, open to debate
▷▷ **out of the question** IMPOSSIBLE, unthinkable, inconceivable, not on (*informal*), hopeless, unimaginable, unworkable, unattainable, unobtainable, not feasible, impracticable, unachievable, unrealizable, not worth considering, not to be thought of

questionable *adjective* DUBIOUS, suspect, doubtful, controversial, uncertain, suspicious, dodgy (*Brit, Austral & NZ informal*), unreliable, shady (*informal*), debatable, unproven, fishy (*informal*), moot, arguable, iffy (*informal*), equivocal, problematical, disputable, controvertible, dubitable, shonky (*Austral & NZ informal*)
<< OPPOSITE indisputable

queue *noun* LINE, row, file, train, series, chain, string, column, sequence, succession, procession, crocodile (*Brit informal*), progression, cavalcade, concatenation

quibble *verb* SPLIT HAIRS, carp, cavil, prevaricate, beat about the bush, equivocate
▷ *noun* OBJECTION, complaint, niggle, protest, criticism, nicety, equivocation, prevarication, cavil, quiddity, sophism

quick *adjective* 1 FAST, swift, speedy, express, active, cracking (*Brit informal*), smart, rapid, fleet, brisk, hasty, headlong, nippy (*informal*), pdq (*slang*)
<< OPPOSITE slow
2 BRIEF, passing, hurried, flying, fleeting, summary, lightning, short-lived, hasty, cursory, perfunctory
<< OPPOSITE long
3 IMMEDIATE, instant, prompt, sudden, abrupt, instantaneous, expeditious
4 EXCITABLE, passionate, impatient, abrupt, hasty, irritable, touchy, curt, petulant, irascible, testy
<< OPPOSITE calm
5 INTELLIGENT, bright (*informal*), alert, sharp, acute, smart, clever, all there (*informal*), shrewd, discerning, astute, receptive, perceptive, quick-witted, quick on the uptake (*informal*), nimble-witted
<< OPPOSITE stupid

quicken *verb* 1 SPEED UP, hurry, accelerate, hasten, gee up
2 STIMULATE, inspire, arouse, excite, strengthen, revive, refresh, activate, animate, rouse, incite, resuscitate, energize, revitalize, kindle, galvanize, invigorate, reinvigorate, vitalize, vivify

quickly *adverb* 1 SWIFTLY, rapidly, hurriedly, speedily, fast, quick, hastily, briskly, at high speed, apace, at full speed, hell for leather (*informal*), like lightning, at the speed of light, at full tilt, hotfoot, at a rate of knots (*informal*), like the clappers (*Brit informal*), pdq (*slang*), like nobody's business (*informal*), with all speed, posthaste, lickety-split (*US informal*), like greased lightning (*informal*), at *or* on the double
<< OPPOSITE slowly
2 SOON, speedily, as soon as possible, momentarily (*US*), instantaneously, pronto (*informal*), a.s.a.p. (*informal*)
3 IMMEDIATELY, instantly, at once, directly, promptly, abruptly, without delay, expeditiously

quick-witted *adjective* CLEVER, bright (*informal*), sharp, keen, smart, alert, shrewd, astute, perceptive
<< OPPOSITE slow

quid pro quo *noun* EXCHANGE, interchange, tit for tat, equivalent, compensation, retaliation, reprisal, substitution

quiet *adjective* 1 SOFT, low, muted, lowered, whispered, faint, suppressed, stifled, hushed, muffled, inaudible, indistinct, low-pitched
<< OPPOSITE loud
2 PEACEFUL, silent, hushed, soundless, noiseless
<< OPPOSITE noisy
3 CALM, peaceful, tranquil, contented, gentle, mild, serene, pacific, placid, restful, untroubled

<< OPPOSITE exciting
4 STILL, motionless, calm, peaceful, tranquil, untroubled
<< OPPOSITE troubled
5 UNDISTURBED, isolated, secluded, private, secret, retired, sequestered, unfrequented
<< OPPOSITE crowded
6 SILENT, dumb
7 RESERVED, retiring, shy, collected, gentle, mild, composed, serene, sedate, meek, placid, docile, unflappable (*informal*), phlegmatic, peaceable, imperturbable, equable, even-tempered, unexcitable
<< OPPOSITE excitable
8 SUBDUED, conservative, plain, sober, simple, modest, restrained, unassuming, unpretentious, unobtrusive
<< OPPOSITE bright
▷ *noun* PEACE, rest, tranquillity, ease, silence, solitude, serenity, stillness, repose, calmness, quietness, peacefulness, restfulness
<< OPPOSITE noise

quieten *verb* 1 SILENCE, subdue, stifle, still, stop, quiet, mute, hush, quell, muffle, shush (*informal*)
2 SOOTHE, calm, allay, dull, blunt, alleviate, appease, lull, mitigate, assuage, mollify, deaden, tranquillize, palliate
<< OPPOSITE provoke

quietly *adverb* 1 NOISELESSLY, silently
2 SOFTLY, in hushed tones, in a low voice *or* whisper, inaudibly, in an undertone, under your breath
3 PRIVATELY, secretly, confidentially
4 CALMLY, serenely, placidly, patiently, mildly, meekly, contentedly, dispassionately, undemonstratively
5 SILENTLY, in silence, mutely, without talking, dumbly
6 MODESTLY, humbly, unobtrusively, diffidently, unpretentiously, unassumingly, unostentatiously

quilt *noun* BEDSPREAD, duvet, comforter (*US*), downie (*informal*), coverlet, eiderdown, counterpane, doona (*Austral*), continental quilt

quintessential *adjective* ULTIMATE, essential, typical, fundamental, definitive, archetypal, prototypical

quip *noun* JOKE, sally, jest, riposte, wisecrack (*informal*), retort, counterattack, pleasantry, repartee, gibe, witticism, bon mot, badinage

quirk *noun* PECULIARITY, eccentricity, mannerism, foible, idiosyncrasy, habit, fancy, characteristic, trait, whim, oddity, caprice, fetish, aberration, kink, vagary, singularity, idée fixe (*French*)

quirky *adjective* ODD, unusual, eccentric, idiosyncratic, curious, peculiar, unpredictable, rum (*Brit slang*), singular, fanciful, whimsical, capricious, offbeat

quit *verb* 1 RESIGN (FROM), leave, retire (from), pull out (of), surrender, chuck (*informal*), step down (from) (*informal*), relinquish, renounce, pack in (*informal*), abdicate
2 STOP, give up, cease, end, drop, abandon, suspend, halt, discontinue, belay (*Nautical*)
<< OPPOSITE continue
3 LEAVE, depart from, go out of, abandon, desert, exit, withdraw from, forsake, go away from, pull out from, decamp from

quite *adverb* 1 SOMEWHAT, rather, fairly, reasonably, kind of (*informal*), pretty (*informal*), relatively, moderately, to some extent, comparatively, to some degree, to a certain extent
2 ABSOLUTELY, perfectly, completely, totally, fully, entirely, precisely, considerably, wholly, in all respects, without reservation

quiver *verb* SHAKE, tremble, shiver, quake, shudder, agitate, vibrate, pulsate, quaver, convulse, palpitate
▷ *noun* SHAKE, tremble, shiver, throb, shudder, tremor, spasm, vibration, tic, convulsion, palpitation, pulsation

quixotic *adjective* UNREALISTIC, idealistic, romantic, absurd, imaginary, visionary, fanciful, impractical, dreamy, Utopian, impulsive, fantastical, impracticable, chivalrous, unworldly, chimerical

quiz *noun* EXAMINATION, questioning, interrogation, interview, investigation, grilling (*informal*), cross-examination, cross-questioning, the third degree (*informal*)
▷ *verb* QUESTION, ask, interrogate, examine, investigate, pump (*informal*), grill (*informal*), catechize

quizzical *adjective* MOCKING, questioning, inquiring, curious, arch, teasing, bantering, sardonic, derisive, supercilious

quota *noun* SHARE, allowance, ration, allocation, part, cut (*informal*), limit, proportion, slice, quantity, portion, assignment, whack (*informal*), dispensation

quotation *noun* 1 PASSAGE, quote (*informal*), excerpt, cutting, selection, reference, extract, citation
2 (*Commerce*) ESTIMATE, price, tender, rate, cost, charge, figure, quote (*informal*), bid price

quote *verb* 1 REPEAT, recite, reproduce, recall, echo, extract, excerpt, proclaim, parrot, paraphrase, retell
2 REFER TO, cite, give, name, detail, relate, mention, instance, specify, spell out, recount, recollect, make reference to, adduce

rabble *noun* 1 MOB, crowd, herd, swarm, horde, throng, canaille
2 (*Contemptuous*) COMMONERS, proletariat, common people, riffraff, crowd, masses, trash (*chiefly US & Canad*), scum, lower classes, populace, peasantry, dregs, hoi polloi, the great unwashed (*derogatory*), canaille, lumpenproletariat, commonalty
<< OPPOSITE upper classes

rabid *adjective* 1 FANATICAL, extreme, irrational, fervent, zealous, bigoted, intolerant, narrow-minded, intemperate
<< OPPOSITE moderate
2 CRAZED, wild, violent, mad, raging, furious, frantic, frenzied, infuriated, berserk, maniacal, berko (*Austral slang*)

race[1] *noun* 1 COMPETITION, contest, chase, dash, pursuit, contention
2 CONTEST, competition, rivalry, contention
▷ *verb* 1 COMPETE AGAINST, run against
2 COMPETE, run, contend, take part in a race
3 RUN, fly, career, speed, tear, dash, hurry, barrel (along) (*informal, chiefly US & Canad*), dart, gallop, zoom, hare (*Brit informal*), hasten, burn rubber (*informal*), go like a bomb (*Brit & NZ informal*), run like mad (*informal*)

race[2] *noun* PEOPLE, ethnic group, nation, blood, house, family, line, issue, stock, type, seed (*chiefly biblical*), breed, folk, tribe, offspring, clan, kin, lineage, progeny, kindred

racial *adjective* ETHNIC, ethnological, national, folk, genetic, tribal, genealogical

rack *noun* FRAME, stand, structure, framework
▷ *verb* TORTURE, distress, torment, harass, afflict, oppress, harrow, crucify, agonize, pain, excruciate

> The use of the spelling *wrack* rather than *rack* in sentences such as *she was wracked by grief* or *the country was wracked by civil war* is very common, but is thought by many people to be incorrect

racket *noun* 1 NOISE, row, shouting, fuss, disturbance, outcry, clamour, din, uproar, commotion, pandemonium, rumpus, babel, tumult, hubbub, hullabaloo, ballyhoo (*informal*)
2 FRAUD, scheme, criminal activity, illegal enterprise

racy *adjective* 1 RISQUÉ, naughty, indecent, bawdy, blue, broad, spicy (*informal*), suggestive, smutty, off colour, immodest, indelicate, near the knuckle (*informal*)
2 LIVELY, spirited, exciting, dramatic, entertaining, stimulating, sexy (*informal*), sparkling, vigorous, energetic, animated, heady, buoyant, exhilarating, zestful

radiance *noun* 1 HAPPINESS, delight, pleasure, joy, warmth, rapture, gaiety
2 BRIGHTNESS, light, shine, glow, glitter, glare, gleam, brilliance, lustre, luminosity, incandescence, resplendence, effulgence

radiant *adjective* 1 HAPPY, glowing, ecstatic, joyful, sent (*informal*), gay, delighted, beaming, joyous, blissful, rapturous, rapt, on cloud nine (*informal*), beatific, blissed out (*informal*), floating on air
<< OPPOSITE miserable
2 BRIGHT, brilliant, shining, glorious, beaming, glowing, sparkling, sunny, glittering, gleaming, luminous, resplendent, incandescent, lustrous, effulgent
<< OPPOSITE dull

radiate *verb* 1 EMIT, spread, send out, disseminate, pour, shed, scatter, glitter, gleam
2 SHINE, emanate, be diffused
3 SHOW, display, demonstrate, exhibit, emanate, give off *or* out
4 SPREAD OUT, diverge, branch out

radiation *noun* EMISSION, rays, emanation

radical *adjective* 1 EXTREME, complete, entire, sweeping, violent, severe, excessive, thorough, drastic
2 REVOLUTIONARY, extremist, fanatical
3 FUNDAMENTAL, natural, basic, essential, native, constitutional, organic, profound, innate, deep-seated, thoroughgoing

<< OPPOSITE superficial
▷ *noun* EXTREMIST, revolutionary, militant, fanatic
<< OPPOSITE conservative

raffle *noun* DRAW, lottery, sweepstake, sweep

rage *noun* 1 FURY, temper, frenzy, rampage, tantrum, foulie (*Austral slang*), hissy fit (*informal*)
<< OPPOSITE calmness
2 ANGER, violence, passion, obsession, madness, raving, wrath, mania, agitation, ire, vehemence, high dudgeon
3 CRAZE, fashion, enthusiasm, vogue, fad (*informal*), latest thing
▷ *verb* 1 BE AT ITS HEIGHT, surge, rampage, be uncontrollable, storm
2 BE FURIOUS, rave, blow up (*informal*), fume, lose it (*informal*), fret, seethe, crack up (*informal*), see red (*informal*), chafe, lose the plot (*informal*), go ballistic (*slang, chiefly US*), rant and rave, foam at the mouth, lose your temper, blow a fuse (*slang, chiefly US*), fly off the handle (*informal*), be incandescent, go off the deep end (*informal*), throw a fit (*informal*), wig out (*slang*), go up the wall (*slang*), blow your top, lose your rag (*slang*), be beside yourself, flip your lid (*slang*)
<< OPPOSITE stay calm

ragged *adjective* 1 TATTY, worn, poor, torn, rent, faded, neglected, run-down, frayed, shabby, worn-out, seedy, scruffy, in tatters, dilapidated, tattered, threadbare, unkempt, in rags, down at heel, the worse for wear, in holes, having seen better days, scraggy
<< OPPOSITE smart
2 ROUGH, fragmented, crude, rugged, notched, irregular, unfinished, uneven, jagged, serrated

raging *adjective* FURIOUS, mad, raving, fuming, frenzied, infuriated, incensed, enraged, seething, fizzing (*Scot*), incandescent, foaming at the mouth, fit to be tied (*slang*), boiling mad (*informal*), beside yourself, doing your nut (*Brit slang*), off the air (*Austral slang*)

raid *verb* 1 STEAL FROM, break into, plunder, pillage, sack
2 ATTACK, invade, assault, rifle, forage (*Military*), fall upon, swoop down upon, reive (*dialect*)
3 MAKE A SEARCH OF, search, bust (*informal*), descend on, make a raid on, make a swoop on
▷ *noun* 1 ATTACK, invasion, seizure, onset, foray, sortie, incursion, surprise attack, hit-and-run attack, sally, inroad, irruption
2 BUST (*informal*), swoop, descent, surprise search

raider *noun* ATTACKER, thief, robber, plunderer, invader, forager (*Military*), marauder, reiver (*dialect*)

rail *verb* COMPLAIN, attack, abuse, blast, put down, criticize, censure, scold, castigate, revile, tear into (*informal*), fulminate, inveigh, upbraid, lambast(e), vituperate, vociferate

railing *noun* FENCE, rails, barrier, paling, balustrade

rain *noun* 1 RAINFALL, fall, showers, deluge, drizzle, downpour, precipitation, raindrops, cloudburst
2 SHOWER, flood, stream, hail, volley, spate, torrent, deluge
▷ *verb* 1 POUR, pelt (down), teem, bucket down (*informal*), fall, shower, drizzle, rain cats and dogs (*informal*), come down in buckets (*informal*)
2 FALL, shower, be dropped, sprinkle, be deposited
3 BESTOW, pour, shower, lavish
>> RELATED WORDS *adjectives* pluvial, pluvious

rainy *adjective* WET, damp, drizzly, showery
<< OPPOSITE dry

raise *verb* 1 LIFT, move up, elevate, uplift, heave
2 SET UPRIGHT, lift, elevate
3 INCREASE, reinforce, intensify, heighten, advance, boost, strengthen, enhance, put up, exaggerate, hike (up) (*informal*), enlarge, escalate, inflate, aggravate, magnify, amplify, augment, jack up
<< OPPOSITE reduce
4 MAKE LOUDER, heighten, amplify, louden
5 COLLECT, get, gather, obtain
6 MOBILIZE, form, mass, rally, recruit, assemble, levy, muster
7 CAUSE, start, produce, create, occasion, provoke, bring about, originate, give rise to, engender
8 PUT FORWARD, suggest, introduce, advance, bring up, broach, moot
9 BRING UP, develop, rear, nurture
10 GROW, produce, rear, cultivate, propagate
11 BREED, keep
12 BUILD, construct, put up, erect
<< OPPOSITE demolish
13 PROMOTE, upgrade, elevate, advance, prefer, exalt, aggrandize
<< OPPOSITE demote

rake[1] *verb* 1 SCRAPE, break up, scratch, scour, harrow, hoe
2 GATHER, collect, scrape together, scrape up, remove
3 STRAFE, pepper, enfilade
4 GRAZE, scratch, scrape
5 *with* **through** SEARCH, hunt, examine, scan, comb, scour, ransack, forage, scrutinize, fossick (*Austral & NZ*)

rake[2] *noun* LIBERTINE, playboy, swinger (*slang*), profligate, lecher, roué, sensualist, voluptuary, debauchee, rakehell (*archaic*), dissolute man, lech *or* letch (*informal*)
<< OPPOSITE puritan

rakish *adjective* DASHING, smart, sporty, flashy,

breezy, jaunty, dapper, natty (*informal*), debonair, snazzy (*informal*), raffish, devil-may-care

rally *noun* 1 GATHERING, mass meeting, convention, convocation, meeting, conference, congress, assembly, congregation, muster, hui (NZ)
2 RECOVERY, improvement, comeback (*informal*), revival, renewal, resurgence, recuperation, turn for the better
<< OPPOSITE relapse
▷ *verb* 1 GATHER TOGETHER, unite, bring together, regroup, reorganize, reassemble, re-form
2 RECOVER, improve, pick up, revive, get better, come round, perk up, recuperate, turn the corner, pull through, take a turn for the better, regain your strength, get your second wind
<< OPPOSITE get worse

ram *verb* 1 HIT, force, drive into, strike, crash, impact, smash, slam, dash, run into, butt, collide with
2 CRAM, pound, force, stuff, pack, hammer, jam, thrust, tamp

ramble *noun* WALK, tour, trip, stroll, hike, roaming, excursion, roving, saunter, traipse (*informal*), peregrination, perambulation
▷ *verb* 1 WALK, range, drift, wander, stroll, stray, roam, rove, amble, saunter, straggle, traipse (*informal*), go walkabout (*Austral*), perambulate, stravaig (*Scot & Northern English dialect*), peregrinate
2 *often with* **on** BABBLE, wander, rabbit (on) (*Brit informal*), chatter, waffle (*informal, chiefly Brit*), digress, rattle on, maunder, witter on (*informal*), expatiate, run off at the mouth (*slang*)

rambler *noun* WALKER, roamer, wanderer, rover, hiker, drifter, stroller, wayfarer

rambling *adjective* 1 SPRAWLING, spreading, trailing, irregular, straggling
2 LONG-WINDED, incoherent, disjointed, prolix, irregular, diffuse, disconnected, desultory, wordy, circuitous, discursive, digressive, periphrastic
<< OPPOSITE concise

ramification *noun usually plural* CONSEQUENCES, results, developments, complications, sequel, upshot

ramp *noun* SLOPE, grade, incline, gradient, inclined plane, rise

rampage *verb* GO BERSERK, tear, storm, rage, run riot, run amok, run wild, go ballistic (*slang*), go ape (*slang*)
▷▷ **on the rampage** BERSERK, wild, violent, raging, destructive, out of control, rampant, amok, riotous, berko (*Austral slang*)

rampant *adjective* 1 WIDESPREAD, rank, epidemic, prevalent, rife, exuberant, uncontrolled, unchecked, unrestrained, luxuriant, profuse, spreading like wildfire
2 UNRESTRAINED, wild, violent, raging, aggressive, dominant, excessive, outrageous, out of control, rampaging, out of hand, uncontrollable, flagrant, unbridled, vehement, wanton, riotous, on the rampage, ungovernable
3 (*Heraldry*) UPRIGHT, standing, rearing, erect

rampart *noun* DEFENCE, wall, parapet, fortification, security, guard, fence, fort, barricade, stronghold, bastion, embankment, bulwark, earthwork, breastwork

ramshackle *adjective* RICKETY, broken-down, crumbling, shaky, unsafe, derelict, flimsy, tottering, dilapidated, decrepit, unsteady, tumbledown, jerry-built
<< OPPOSITE stable

rancid *adjective* ROTTEN, sour, foul, bad, off, rank, tainted, stale, musty, fetid, putrid, fusty, strong-smelling, frowsty
<< OPPOSITE fresh

rancour *noun* HATRED, hate, spite, hostility, resentment, bitterness, grudge, malice, animosity, venom, antipathy, spleen, enmity, ill feeling, bad blood, ill will, animus, malevolence, malignity, chip on your shoulder (*informal*), resentfulness

random *adjective* 1 CHANCE, spot, casual, stray, accidental, arbitrary, incidental, indiscriminate, haphazard, unplanned, fortuitous, aimless, desultory, hit or miss, purposeless, unpremeditated, adventitious
<< OPPOSITE planned
2 CASUAL, arbitrary, indiscriminate, unplanned, aimless, purposeless, unpremeditated
▷▷ **at random** HAPHAZARDLY, randomly, arbitrarily, casually, accidentally, irregularly, by chance, indiscriminately, aimlessly, willy-nilly, unsystematically, purposelessly, adventitiously

randy *adjective* (*informal*) LUSTFUL, hot, sexy (*informal*), turned-on (*slang*), aroused, raunchy (*slang*), horny (*slang*), amorous, lascivious, lecherous, sexually excited, concupiscent, satyric

range *noun* 1 SERIES, variety, selection, assortment, lot, collection, gamut
2 LIMITS, reach, distance, sweep, extent, pale, confines, parameters (*informal*), ambit
3 SCOPE, area, field, bounds, province, orbit, span, domain, compass, latitude, radius, amplitude, purview, sphere
4 ROW, series, line, file, rank, chain, string, sequence, tier
▷ *verb* 1 VARY, run, reach, extend, go, stretch, fluctuate
2 ARRANGE, order, line up, sequence, array,

dispose, draw up, align
3 ROAM, explore, wander, rove, sweep, cruise, stroll, ramble, traverse
4 GROUP, class, file, rank, arrange, grade, catalogue, classify, bracket, categorize, pigeonhole

rank[1] *noun* 1 STATUS, level, position, grade, order, standing, sort, quality, type, station, division, degree, classification, echelon
2 CLASS, dignity, caste, nobility, stratum
3 ROW, line, file, column, group, range, series, formation, tier
▷ *verb* 1 ORDER, class, grade, classify, dispose
2 ARRANGE, sort, position, range, line up, locate, sequence, array, marshal, align
▷▷ **rank and file** 1 GENERAL PUBLIC, body, majority, mass, masses, Joe (and Eileen) Public (*slang*), Joe Six-Pack (*US slang*)
2 LOWER RANKS, men, troops, soldiers, other ranks, private soldiers

rank[2] *adjective* 1 ABSOLUTE, complete, total, gross, sheer, excessive, utter, glaring, thorough, extravagant, rampant, blatant, downright, flagrant, egregious, unmitigated, undisguised, arrant
2 FOUL, off, bad, offensive, disgusting, revolting, stinking, stale, pungent, noxious, disagreeable, musty, rancid, fetid, putrid, fusty, strong-smelling, gamey, noisome, mephitic, olid, yucky *or* yukky (*slang*), festy (*Austral slang*)
3 ABUNDANT, flourishing, lush, luxuriant, productive, vigorous, dense, exuberant, profuse, strong-growing

rankle *verb* ANNOY, anger, irritate, gall, fester, embitter, chafe, irk, rile, get on your nerves (*informal*), get your goat (*slang*), hack you off (*informal*)

ransack *verb* 1 SEARCH, go through, rummage through, rake through, explore, comb, scour, forage, turn inside out, fossick (*Austral & NZ*)
2 PLUNDER, raid, loot, pillage, strip, sack, gut, rifle, ravage, despoil

ransom *noun* 1 PAYMENT, money, price, payoff
2 RELEASE, rescue, liberation, redemption, deliverance
▷ *verb* BUY THE FREEDOM OF, release, deliver, rescue, liberate, buy (someone) out (*informal*), redeem, set free, obtain *or* pay for the release of

rant *verb* SHOUT, roar, yell, rave, bellow, cry, spout (*informal*), bluster, declaim, vociferate
▷ *noun* TIRADE, rhetoric, bluster, diatribe, harangue, bombast, philippic, vociferation, fanfaronade (*rare*)

rap *verb* 1 HIT, strike, knock, crack, tap
2 REPRIMAND, knock (*informal*), blast, pan (*informal*), carpet (*informal*), criticize, censure, scold, tick off (*informal*), castigate, diss (*slang, chiefly US*), read the riot act, lambast(e), chew out (*US & Canad informal*), give a rocket (*Brit & NZ informal*)
3 (*Slang*) TALK, chat, discourse, converse, shoot the breeze (*slang, chiefly US*), confabulate
▷ *noun* 1 BLOW, knock, crack, tap, clout (*informal*)
2 (*Slang*) REBUKE, sentence, blame, responsibility, punishment, censure, chiding

rapacious *adjective* GREEDY, grasping, insatiable, ravenous, preying, plundering, predatory, voracious, marauding, extortionate, avaricious, wolfish, usurious

rape *verb* SEXUALLY ASSAULT, violate, abuse, ravish, force, outrage
▷ *noun* 1 SEXUAL ASSAULT, violation, ravishment, outrage
2 PLUNDERING, pillage, depredation, despoliation, rapine, spoliation, despoilment, sack

rapid *adjective* 1 SUDDEN, prompt, speedy, precipitate, express, fleet, swift, quickie (*informal*), expeditious
<< OPPOSITE gradual
2 QUICK, fast, hurried, swift, brisk, hasty, flying, pdq (*slang*)
<< OPPOSITE slow

rapidity *noun* SPEED, swiftness, promptness, speediness, rush, hurry, expedition, dispatch, velocity, haste, alacrity, quickness, briskness, fleetness, celerity, promptitude, precipitateness

rapidly *adverb* QUICKLY, fast, swiftly, briskly, promptly, hastily, precipitately, in a hurry, at speed, hurriedly, speedily, apace, in a rush, in haste, like a shot, pronto (*informal*), hell for leather, like lightning, expeditiously, hotfoot, like the clappers (*Brit informal*), pdq (*slang*), like nobody's business (*informal*), posthaste, with dispatch, like greased lightning (*informal*)

rapport *noun* BOND, understanding, relationship, link, tie, sympathy, harmony, affinity, empathy, interrelationship

rapprochement *noun* RECONCILIATION, softening, reunion, détente, reconcilement, restoration of harmony
<< OPPOSITE dissension

rapt *adjective* 1 SPELLBOUND, entranced, enthralled, engrossed, held, gripped, fascinated, absorbed, intent, preoccupied, carried away
<< OPPOSITE uninterested
2 RAPTUROUS, enchanted, captivated, bewitched, sent, transported, delighted, charmed, ecstatic, blissful, ravished, enraptured, blissed out

rapture *noun* ECSTASY, delight, enthusiasm, joy, transport, spell, happiness, bliss, euphoria, felicity, rhapsody, exaltation, cloud nine (*informal*), seventh heaven, delectation, beatitude, ravishment

rapturous *adjective* ECSTATIC, delighted, enthusiastic, rapt, sent (*informal*), happy, transported, joyous, exalted, joyful, over the moon (*informal*), overjoyed, blissful, ravished, euphoric, on cloud nine (*informal*), blissed out (*informal*), rhapsodic, in seventh heaven, floating on air

rare[1] *adjective* 1 PRICELESS, rich, precious, invaluable

2 UNCOMMON, unusual, exceptional, out of the ordinary, few, strange, scarce, singular, sporadic, sparse, infrequent, thin on the ground, recherché

<< OPPOSITE common

3 SUPERB, great, fine, excellent, extreme, exquisite, admirable, superlative, choice, incomparable, peerless

rare[2] *adjective* UNDERDONE, bloody, undercooked, half-cooked, half-raw

rarefied *adjective* EXCLUSIVE, select, esoteric, cliquish, private, occult, clannish

rarely *adverb* SELDOM, hardly, almost never, hardly ever, little, once in a while, infrequently, on rare occasions, once in a blue moon, only now and then, scarcely ever

<< OPPOSITE often

> Since the meaning of *rarely* is 'hardly ever', the combination *rarely ever* is repetitive and should be avoided in careful writing, even though you may sometimes hear this phrase used in informal speech

raring *adjective* (in construction *raring to do something*) EAGER, impatient, longing, yearning, willing, ready, keen, desperate, enthusiastic, avid, champing at the bit (*informal*), keen as mustard, athirst

rarity *noun* 1 CURIO, find, treasure, pearl, one-off, curiosity, gem, collector's item

2 UNCOMMONNESS, scarcity, infrequency, unusualness, shortage, strangeness, singularity, sparseness

rascal *noun* ROGUE, devil, villain, scoundrel, disgrace, rake, pickle (*Brit informal*), imp, scally (*Northwest English dialect*), wretch, knave (*archaic*), ne'er-do-well, reprobate, scallywag (*informal*), good-for-nothing, miscreant, scamp, wastrel, bad egg (*old-fashioned informal*), blackguard, varmint (*informal*), rapscallion, caitiff (*archaic*), wrong 'un (*Austral slang*), nointer (*Austral slang*)

rash[1] *adjective* RECKLESS, hasty, impulsive, imprudent, premature, adventurous, careless, precipitate, brash, audacious, headlong, madcap, ill-advised, foolhardy, unwary, thoughtless, unguarded, headstrong, impetuous, indiscreet, unthinking, helter-skelter, ill-considered, hot-headed, heedless, injudicious, incautious, venturesome, harebrained, harum-scarum

<< OPPOSITE cautious

rash[2] *noun* 1 OUTBREAK OF SPOTS, (skin) eruption

2 SPATE, series, wave, flood, succession, plague, outbreak, epidemic

rasp *verb* SCRAPE, grind, rub, scour, excoriate, abrade

▷ *noun* GRATING, grinding, scratch, scrape

rasping *or* **raspy** *adjective* HARSH, rough, hoarse, gravelly, jarring, grating, creaking, husky, croaking, gruff, croaky

rat (*informal*) *noun* 1 TRAITOR, grass (*Brit informal*), betrayer, deceiver, informer, defector, deserter, double-crosser, quisling, stool pigeon, nark (*Brit, Austral & NZ slang*), snake in the grass, two-timer (*informal*), fizgig (*Austral slang*)

2 ROGUE, scoundrel, heel (*slang*), cad (*old-fashioned informal, Brit*), bounder (*old-fashioned slang, Brit*), rotter (*slang, chiefly Brit*), bad lot, shyster (*informal, chiefly US*), ratfink (*slang, chiefly US & Canad*), wrong 'un (*Austral slang*)

▷▷ **rat on someone** BETRAY, denounce, tell on, shop (*slang, chiefly Brit*), grass (*Brit slang*), peach (*slang*), squeal (*slang*), incriminate (*informal*), blow the whistle on (*informal*), spill the beans (*informal*), snitch (*slang*), blab, let the cat out of the bag, blow the gaff (*Brit slang*), nark (*Brit, Austral & NZ slang*), put the finger on (*informal*), spill your guts (*slang*), inculpate, clype (*Scot*), dob in (*Austral slang*)

rate *noun* 1 SPEED, pace, tempo, velocity, time, measure, gait, frequency

2 DEGREE, standard, scale, proportion, percentage, ratio

3 CHARGE, price, cost, fee, tax, figure, dues, duty, hire, toll, tariff

▷ *verb* 1 EVALUATE, consider, rank, reckon, class, value, measure, regard, estimate, count, grade, assess, weigh, esteem, classify, appraise, adjudge

2 DESERVE, merit, be entitled to, be worthy of

▷▷ **at any rate** IN ANY CASE, anyway, nevertheless, anyhow, at all events

rather *adverb* 1 PREFERABLY, sooner, instead, more readily, more willingly

2 TO SOME EXTENT, quite, sort of (*informal*), kind of (*informal*), a little, a bit, pretty (*informal*), fairly, relatively, somewhat, slightly, moderately, to some degree

> It is acceptable to use either *would rather* or *had rather* in sentences such as *I would rather* (or *had rather*) *see a film than a play*. *Had rather*, however, is less common than *would rather*, and sounds a little old-fashioned nowadays

ratify *verb* APPROVE, sign, establish, confirm, bind, sanction, endorse, uphold, authorize, affirm, certify, consent to, validate, bear out, corroborate, authenticate
<< OPPOSITE annul

rating *noun* POSITION, evaluation, classification, placing, rate, order, standing, class, degree, estimate, rank, status, grade, designation

ratio *noun* PROPORTION, rate, relationship, relation, arrangement, percentage, equation, fraction, correspondence, correlation

ration *noun* ALLOWANCE, quota, allotment, provision, helping, part, share, measure, dole, portion
▷ *verb* 1 LIMIT, control, restrict, save, budget, conserve
2 DISTRIBUTE, issue, deal, dole, allocate, give out, allot, mete, apportion, measure out, parcel out

rational *adjective* 1 SENSIBLE, sound, wise, reasonable, intelligent, realistic, logical, enlightened, sane, lucid, judicious, sagacious
2 REASONING, thinking, cognitive, cerebral, ratiocinative
3 SANE, balanced, normal, all there (*informal*), lucid, of sound mind, compos mentis (*Latin*), in your right mind
<< OPPOSITE insane

rationale *noun* REASON, grounds, theory, principle, philosophy, logic, motivation, exposition, raison d'être (*French*)

rationalize *verb* 1 JUSTIFY, excuse, account for, vindicate, explain away, make allowances for, make excuses for, extenuate
2 REASON OUT, resolve, think through, elucidate, apply logic to
3 STREAMLINE, trim, make more efficient, make cuts in

rattle *verb* 1 CLATTER, bang, jangle
2 SHAKE, jiggle, jolt, vibrate, bounce, jar, jounce
3 (*informal*) FLUSTER, shake, upset, frighten, scare, disturb, disconcert, perturb, faze, discomfit, discountenance, put (someone) off his stride, discompose, put (someone) out of countenance
▷▷ **rattle on** PRATTLE, rabbit (on) (*Brit informal*), chatter, witter (*informal*), cackle, yak (away) (*slang*), gibber, jabber, gabble, blether, prate, run on, earbash (*Austral & NZ slang*)
▷▷ **rattle something off** RECITE, list, run through, rehearse, reel off, spiel off (*informal*)

ratty *adjective* IRRITABLE, cross, angry, annoyed, crabbed, impatient, snappy, touchy, tetchy, testy, short-tempered, tooshie (*Austral slang*)

raucous *adjective* HARSH, rough, loud, noisy, grating, strident, rasping, husky, hoarse
<< OPPOSITE quiet

raunchy *adjective* (*Slang*) SEXY, sexual, steamy (*informal*), earthy, suggestive, lewd, lusty, bawdy, salacious, smutty, lustful, lecherous, ribald, coarse

ravage *verb* DESTROY, ruin, devastate, wreck, shatter, gut, spoil, loot, demolish, plunder, desolate, sack, ransack, pillage, raze, lay waste, wreak havoc on, despoil, leave in ruins
▷ *noun often plural* DAMAGE, destruction, devastation, desolation, waste, ruin, havoc, demolition, plunder, pillage, depredation, ruination, rapine, spoliation

rave *verb* 1 RANT, rage, roar, thunder, fume, go mad (*informal*), babble, splutter, storm, be delirious, talk wildly
2 *usually with* **about** (*informal*) ENTHUSE, praise, gush, be delighted by, be mad about (*informal*), big up (*slang, chiefly Caribbean*), rhapsodize, be wild about (*informal*), cry up
▷ *noun* PARTY, rave-up (*Brit slang*), do (*informal*), affair, celebration, bash (*informal*), blow-out (*slang*), beano (*Brit slang*), hooley *or* hoolie (*chiefly Irish & NZ*)
▷ *modifier* (*informal*) ENTHUSIASTIC, excellent, favourable, ecstatic, laudatory

ravenous *adjective* 1 STARVING, starved, very hungry, famished, esurient
<< OPPOSITE sated
2 GREEDY, insatiable, avaricious, covetous, grasping, insatiate

ravine *noun* CANYON, pass, gap (*US*), gorge, clough (*dialect*), gully, defile, linn (*Scot*), gulch (*US & Canad*), flume

raving *adjective* MAD, wild, raging, crazy, furious, frantic, frenzied, hysterical, insane, irrational, crazed, berserk, delirious, rabid, out of your mind, gonzo (*slang*), berko (*Austral slang*), off the air (*Austral slang*)

ravish *verb* 1 (*Literary*) RAPE, sexually assault, violate, abuse, force, outrage
2 ENCHANT, transport, delight, charm, fascinate, entrance, captivate, enrapture, spellbind, overjoy

ravishing *adjective* ENCHANTING, beautiful, lovely, stunning (*informal*), charming, entrancing, gorgeous, dazzling, delightful, radiant, drop-dead (*slang*), bewitching

raw *adjective* 1 UNREFINED, natural, crude, unprocessed, basic, rough, organic, coarse, unfinished, untreated, unripe
<< OPPOSITE refined
2 UNCOOKED, natural, fresh, bloody (*of meat*), undressed, unprepared
<< OPPOSITE cooked
3 SORE, open, skinned, sensitive, tender, scratched, grazed, chafed, abraded
4 FRANK, plain, bare, naked, realistic, brutal, blunt, candid, unvarnished, unembellished
<< OPPOSITE embellished

5 INEXPERIENCED, new, green, ignorant, immature, unskilled, callow, untrained, untried, undisciplined, unseasoned, unpractised
<< OPPOSITE experienced
6 CHILLY, biting, cold, freezing, bitter, wet, chill, harsh, piercing, damp, unpleasant, bleak, parky (*Brit informal*)

ray *noun* 1 BEAM, bar, flash, shaft, gleam
2 TRACE, spark, flicker, glimmer, hint, indication, scintilla

raze *verb* DESTROY, level, remove, ruin, demolish, flatten, knock down, pull down, tear down, throw down, bulldoze, kennet (*Austral slang*), jeff (*Austral slang*)

re *preposition* CONCERNING, about, regarding, respecting, with regard to, on the subject of, in respect of, with reference to, apropos, anent (*Scot*)

> In contexts such as *re your letter, your remarks have been noted* or *he spoke to me re your complaint*, *re* is common in business or official correspondence. In spoken and in general written English *with reference to* is preferable in the former case and *about* or *concerning* in the latter. Even in business correspondence, the use of *re* is often restricted to the letter heading

reach *verb* 1 ARRIVE AT, get to, get as far as, make, attain, land at
2 ATTAIN, get to, amount to
3 TOUCH, grasp, extend to, get (a) hold of, stretch to, go as far as, contact
4 CONTACT, get in touch with, get through to, make contact with, get, find, communicate with, get hold of, establish contact with
5 COME TO, move to, rise to, fall to, drop to, sink to
6 ACHIEVE, come to, arrive at
▷ *noun* 1 GRASP, range, distance, stretch, sweep, capacity, extent, extension, scope
2 JURISDICTION, power, influence, command, compass, mastery, ambit

react *verb* RESPOND, act, proceed, behave, conduct yourself

reaction *noun* 1 RESPONSE, acknowledgment, feedback, answer, reply
2 COUNTERACTION, compensation, backlash, recoil, counterbalance, counterpoise
3 CONSERVATISM, the right, counter-revolution, obscurantism

> Some people say that *reaction* should always refer to an instant response to something (as in *his reaction was one of amazement*), and that this word should not be used to refer to a considered response given in the form of a statement (as in *the Minister gave his reaction to the court's decision*). Use *response* instead

reactionary *adjective* CONSERVATIVE, right-wing, counter-revolutionary, obscurantist, blimpish
<< OPPOSITE radical
▷ *noun* CONSERVATIVE, die-hard, right-winger, rightist, counter-revolutionary, obscurantist, Colonel Blimp
<< OPPOSITE radical

read *verb* 1 SCAN, study, look at, refer to, glance at, pore over, peruse, run your eye over
2 RECITE, deliver, utter, declaim, speak, announce
3 UNDERSTAND, interpret, comprehend, construe, decipher, perceive the meaning of, see, discover
4 REGISTER, show, record, display, indicate

readable *adjective* 1 ENJOYABLE, interesting, gripping, entertaining, pleasant, enthralling, easy to read, worth reading
<< OPPOSITE dull
2 LEGIBLE, clear, plain, understandable, comprehensible, intelligible, decipherable
<< OPPOSITE illegible

readily *adverb* 1 WILLINGLY, freely, quickly, gladly, eagerly, voluntarily, cheerfully, with pleasure, with good grace, lief (*rare*)
<< OPPOSITE reluctantly
2 PROMPTLY, quickly, easily, smoothly, at once, straight away, right away, effortlessly, in no time, speedily, without delay, without hesitation, without difficulty, unhesitatingly, hotfoot, without demur, pdq (*slang*)
<< OPPOSITE with difficulty

readiness *noun* 1 WILLINGNESS, inclination, eagerness, keenness, aptness, gameness (*informal*)
2 PREPAREDNESS, preparation, fitness, maturity, ripeness
3 PROMPTNESS, facility, ease, skill, dexterity, rapidity, quickness, adroitness, handiness, promptitude
▷▷ **in readiness** PREPARED, set, waiting, primed, ready, all set, waiting in the wings, at the ready, at *or* on hand, fit

reading *noun* 1 PERUSAL, study, review, examination, inspection, scrutiny
2 LEARNING, education, knowledge, scholarship, erudition, edification, book-learning
3 RECITAL, performance, rendering, rendition, lesson, lecture, sermon, homily
4 INTERPRETATION, take (*informal, chiefly US*), understanding, treatment, version, construction, impression, grasp, conception

ready *adjective* 1 PREPARED, set, primed, organized, all set, in readiness
<< OPPOSITE unprepared
2 COMPLETED, arranged
3 MATURE, ripe, mellow, ripened, fully developed, fully grown, seasoned
4 WILLING, happy, glad, disposed, game (*informal*), minded, keen, eager, inclined, prone, have-a-go (*informal*), apt, agreeable, predisposed
<< OPPOSITE reluctant
5 PROMPT, smart, quick, bright, sharp, keen, acute, rapid, alert, clever, intelligent, handy, apt, skilful, astute, perceptive, expert, deft, resourceful, adroit, quick-witted, dexterous
<< OPPOSITE slow
6 AVAILABLE, handy, at the ready, at your fingertips, present, near, accessible, convenient, on call, on tap (*informal*), close to hand, at *or* on hand
<< OPPOSITE unavailable
7 *with* **to** ON THE POINT OF, close to, about to, on the verge of, likely to, in danger of, liable to, on the brink of
▷ *verb* PREPARE, get set, organize, get ready, order, arrange, equip, fit out, make ready, jack up (*NZ informal*)

real *adjective* 1 TRUE, genuine, sincere, honest, factual, existent, dinkum (*Austral & NZ informal*), unfeigned
2 GENUINE, authentic, bona fide, dinkum (*Austral & NZ informal*)
<< OPPOSITE fake
3 PROPER, true, valid, legitimate
4 ACTUAL, true
5 TYPICAL, true, genuine, sincere, unaffected, dinkum (*Austral & NZ informal*), unfeigned
6 COMPLETE, right, total, perfect, positive, absolute, utter, thorough, veritable, out-and-out

realistic *adjective* 1 PRACTICAL, real, sensible, rational, common-sense, sober, pragmatic, down-to-earth, matter-of-fact, businesslike, level-headed, hard-headed, unsentimental, unromantic
<< OPPOSITE impractical
2 ATTAINABLE, reasonable, sensible
3 LIFELIKE, true to life, authentic, naturalistic, true, natural, genuine, graphic, faithful, truthful, representational, vérité

reality *noun* 1 FACT, truth, certainty, realism, validity, authenticity, verity, actuality, materiality, genuineness, verisimilitude, corporeality
2 TRUTH, fact, actuality
▷▷ **in reality** IN FACT, really, actually, in truth, as a matter of fact, in actuality, in point of fact

realization *noun* 1 AWARENESS, understanding, recognition, perception, imagination, consciousness, grasp, appreciation, conception, comprehension, apprehension, cognizance, aha moment, light bulb moment (*informal*)
2 ACHIEVEMENT, carrying-out, completion, accomplishment, fulfilment, consummation, effectuation

realize *verb* 1 BECOME AWARE OF, understand, recognize, appreciate, take in, grasp, conceive, catch on (*informal*), comprehend, twig (*Brit informal*), get the message, apprehend, become conscious of, be cognizant of
2 FULFIL, achieve, accomplish, make real
3 ACHIEVE, do, effect, complete, perform, fulfil, accomplish, bring about, consummate, incarnate, bring off, make concrete, bring to fruition, actualize, make happen, effectuate, reify, carry out *or* through
4 SELL FOR, go for, bring *or* take in, make, get, clear, produce, gain, net, earn, obtain, acquire

really *adverb* 1 CERTAINLY, absolutely, undoubtedly, genuinely, positively, categorically, without a doubt, assuredly, verily, surely
2 TRULY, actually, in fact, indeed, in reality, in actuality

realm *noun* 1 FIELD, world, area, province, sphere, department, region, branch, territory, zone, patch, orbit, turf (*US slang*)
2 KINGDOM, state, country, empire, monarchy, land, province, domain, dominion, principality

reap *verb* 1 GET, win, gain, obtain, acquire, derive
2 COLLECT, gather, bring in, harvest, garner, cut

rear[1] *noun* 1 BACK PART, back
<< OPPOSITE front
2 BACK, end, tail, rearguard, tail end, back end
▷ *modifier* BACK, aft, hind, hindmost, after (*Nautical*), last, following, trailing
<< OPPOSITE front

rear[2] *verb* 1 BRING UP, raise, educate, care for, train, nurse, foster, nurture
2 BREED, keep
3 *often with* **up** *or* **over** RISE, tower, soar, loom

reason *noun* 1 CAUSE, grounds, purpose, motive, end, goal, design, target, aim, basis, occasion, object, intention, incentive, warrant, impetus, inducement, why and wherefore (*informal*)
2 JUSTIFICATION, case, grounds, defence, argument, explanation, excuse, apology, rationale, exposition, vindication, apologia
3 SENSE, mind, reasoning, understanding, brains, judgment, logic, mentality, intellect, comprehension, apprehension, sanity, rationality, soundness, sound mind, ratiocination

<< OPPOSITE emotion

▷ *verb* DEDUCE, conclude, work out, solve, resolve, make out, infer, draw conclusions, think, ratiocinate, syllogize

▷▷ **in** *or* **within reason** WITHIN LIMITS, within reasonable limits, within bounds

▷▷ **reason with someone** PERSUADE, debate with, remonstrate with, bring round, urge, win over, argue with, dispute with, dissuade, prevail upon (*informal*), expostulate with, show (someone) the error of his ways, talk into *or* out of

Many people object to the expression *the reason is because*, on the grounds that it is repetitive. It is therefore advisable to use either *this is because* or *the reason is that*

reasonable *adjective* 1 SENSIBLE, reasoned, sound, practical, wise, intelligent, rational, logical, sober, credible, plausible, sane, judicious

<< OPPOSITE irrational

2 FAIR, just, right, acceptable, moderate, equitable, justifiable, well-advised, well-thought-out, tenable

<< OPPOSITE unfair

3 WITHIN REASON, fit, proper

<< OPPOSITE impossible

4 LOW, cheap, competitive, moderate, modest, inexpensive, tolerable

5 AVERAGE, fair, moderate, modest, tolerable, O.K. *or* okay (*informal*)

reasoned *adjective* SENSIBLE, clear, logical, systematic, judicious, well-thought-out, well-presented, well-expressed

reasoning *noun* 1 THINKING, thought, reason, analysis, logic, deduction, cogitation, ratiocination

2 CASE, argument, proof, interpretation, hypothesis, exposition, train of thought

reassure *verb* ENCOURAGE, comfort, bolster, hearten, cheer up, buoy up, gee up, restore confidence to, inspirit, relieve (someone) of anxiety, put *or* set your mind at rest

rebate *noun* REFUND, discount, reduction, bonus, allowance, deduction

rebel *noun* 1 REVOLUTIONARY, resistance fighter, insurgent, secessionist, mutineer, insurrectionary, revolutionist

2 NONCONFORMIST, dissenter, heretic, apostate, schismatic

▷ *verb* 1 REVOLT, resist, rise up, mutiny, take to the streets, take up arms, man the barricades

2 DEFY, dissent, disobey, come out against, refuse to obey, dig your heels in (*informal*)

3 RECOIL, shrink, shy away, flinch, show repugnance

▷ *modifier* REBELLIOUS, revolutionary, insurgent, mutinous, insubordinate, insurrectionary

rebellion *noun* 1 RESISTANCE, rising, revolution, revolt, uprising, mutiny, insurrection, insurgency, insurgence

2 NONCONFORMITY, dissent, defiance, heresy, disobedience, schism, insubordination, apostasy

rebellious *adjective* 1 DEFIANT, difficult, resistant, intractable, recalcitrant, obstinate, unmanageable, incorrigible, refractory, contumacious

<< OPPOSITE obedient

2 REVOLUTIONARY, rebel, disorderly, unruly, turbulent, disaffected, insurgent, recalcitrant, disloyal, seditious, mutinous, disobedient, ungovernable, insubordinate, insurrectionary

<< OPPOSITE obedient

rebirth *noun* REVIVAL, restoration, renaissance, renewal, resurrection, reincarnation, regeneration, resurgence, new beginning, revitalization, renascence

rebound *verb* 1 BOUNCE, ricochet, spring back, return, resound, recoil

2 MISFIRE, backfire, recoil, boomerang

rebuff *verb* REJECT, decline, refuse, turn down, cut, check, deny, resist, slight, discourage, put off, snub, spurn, knock back (*slang*), brush off (*slang*), repulse, cold-shoulder

<< OPPOSITE encourage

▷ *noun* REJECTION, defeat, snub, knock-back, check, opposition, slight, refusal, denial, brush-off (*slang*), repulse, thumbs down, cold shoulder, slap in the face (*informal*), kick in the teeth (*slang*), discouragement

<< OPPOSITE encouragement

rebuke *verb* SCOLD, censure, reprimand, reproach, blame, lecture, carpet (*informal*), berate, tick off (*informal*), castigate, chide, dress down (*informal*), admonish, tear into (*informal*), tell off (*informal*), take to task, read the riot act, reprove, upbraid, bawl out (*informal*), haul (someone) over the coals (*informal*), chew out (*US & Canad informal*), tear (someone) off a strip (*informal*), give a rocket (*Brit & NZ informal*), reprehend

<< OPPOSITE praise

▷ *noun* SCOLDING, censure, reprimand, reproach, blame, row, lecture, wigging (*Brit slang*), ticking-off (*informal*), dressing down (*informal*), telling-off (*informal*), admonition, tongue-lashing, reproof, castigation, reproval

<< OPPOSITE praise

rebut *verb* DISPROVE, defeat, overturn, quash, refute, negate, invalidate, prove wrong, confute

rebuttal *noun* DISPROOF, negation, refutation, invalidation, confutation, defeat

recalcitrant *adjective* DISOBEDIENT, contrary, unwilling, defiant, stubborn, wayward,

unruly, uncontrollable, intractable, wilful, obstinate, unmanageable, ungovernable, refractory, insubordinate, contumacious
<< OPPOSITE obedient

recall *verb* 1 RECOLLECT, remember, call up, evoke, reminisce about, call to mind, look *or* think back to, mind (*dialect*)
2 CALL BACK
3 ANNUL, withdraw, call in, take back, cancel, repeal, call back, revoke, retract, rescind, nullify, countermand, abjure
▷ *noun* 1 RECOLLECTION, memory, remembrance
2 ANNULMENT, withdrawal, repeal, cancellation, retraction, revocation, nullification, rescission, rescindment

recant *verb* WITHDRAW, take back, retract, disclaim, deny, recall, renounce, revoke, repudiate, renege, disown, disavow, forswear, abjure, unsay, apostatize
<< OPPOSITE maintain

recede *verb* 1 FALL BACK, withdraw, retreat, draw back, return, go back, retire, back off, regress, retrogress, retrocede
2 LESSEN, decline, subside, abate, sink, fade, shrink, diminish, dwindle, wane, ebb

receipt *noun* 1 SALES SLIP, proof of purchase, voucher, stub, acknowledgment, counterfoil
2 RECEIVING, delivery, reception, acceptance, recipience
▷ *plural noun* TAKINGS, return, profits, gains, income, gate, proceeds

receive *verb* 1 GET, accept, be given, pick up, collect, obtain, acquire, take, derive, be in receipt of, accept delivery of
2 EXPERIENCE, suffer, bear, go through, encounter, meet with, sustain, undergo, be subjected to
3 GREET, meet, admit, welcome, entertain, take in, accommodate, be at home to

recent *adjective* NEW, modern, contemporary, up-to-date, late, young, happening (*informal*), current, fresh, novel, latter, present-day, latter-day
<< OPPOSITE old

recently *adverb* NOT LONG AGO, newly, lately, currently, freshly, of late, latterly

receptacle *noun* CONTAINER, holder, repository

reception *noun* 1 PARTY, gathering, get-together, social gathering, do (*informal*), social, function, entertainment, celebration, bash (*informal*), festivity, knees-up (*Brit informal*), shindig (*informal*), soirée, levee, rave-up (*Brit slang*)
2 RESPONSE, reaction, acknowledgment, recognition, treatment, welcome, greeting
3 RECEIVING, admission, acceptance, receipt, recipience

receptive *adjective* OPEN, sympathetic, favourable, amenable, interested, welcoming, friendly, accessible, susceptible, open-minded, hospitable, approachable, open to suggestions
<< OPPOSITE narrow-minded

recess *noun* 1 BREAK, rest, holiday, closure, interval, vacation, respite, intermission, cessation of business, schoolie (*Austral*)
2 ALCOVE, corner, bay, depression, hollow, niche, cavity, nook, oriel, indentation
3 *often plural* DEPTHS, reaches, heart, retreats, bowels, innards (*informal*), secret places, innermost parts, penetralia

recession *noun* DEPRESSION, drop, decline, slump, downturn
<< OPPOSITE boom

recherché *adjective* REFINED, rare, exotic, esoteric, arcane, far-fetched, choice

recipe *noun* DIRECTIONS, instructions, ingredients, receipt (*obsolete*)
▷▷ **a recipe for something** METHOD, formula, prescription, process, programme, technique, procedure, modus operandi

reciprocal *adjective* MUTUAL, corresponding, reciprocative, reciprocatory, exchanged, equivalent, alternate, complementary, interchangeable, give-and-take, interdependent, correlative
<< OPPOSITE unilateral

reciprocate *verb* RETURN, requite, feel in return, match, respond, equal, return the compliment

recital *noun* 1 PERFORMANCE, rendering, rehearsal, reading
2 ACCOUNT, telling, story, detailing, statement, relation, tale, description, narrative, narration, enumeration, recapitulation
3 RECITATION, repetition

recitation *noun* RECITAL, reading, performance, piece, passage, lecture, rendering, narration, telling

recite *verb* PERFORM, relate, deliver, repeat, rehearse, declaim, recapitulate, do your party piece (*informal*)

reckless *adjective* CARELESS, wild, rash, irresponsible, precipitate, hasty, mindless, negligent, headlong, madcap, ill-advised, regardless, foolhardy, daredevil, thoughtless, indiscreet, imprudent, heedless, devil-may-care, inattentive, incautious, harebrained, harum-scarum, overventuresome
<< OPPOSITE cautious

reckon *verb* 1 (*informal*) THINK, believe, suppose, imagine, assume, guess (*informal, chiefly US & Canad*), fancy, conjecture, surmise, be of the opinion
2 CONSIDER, hold, rate, account, judge, think of, regard, estimate, count, evaluate, esteem, deem, gauge, look upon, appraise
3 COUNT, figure, total, calculate, compute, add

up, tally, number, enumerate
▷▷ **reckon on** *or* **upon something** RELY ON, count on, bank on, depend on, hope for, calculate, trust in, take for granted
▷▷ **reckon with something** *or* **someone** (usually in negative construction) TAKE INTO ACCOUNT, expect, plan for, anticipate, be prepared for, bear in mind, foresee, bargain for, take cognizance of
▷▷ **to be reckoned with** POWERFUL, important, strong, significant, considerable, influential, weighty, consequential, skookum (*Canad*)

reckoning *noun* 1 COUNT, working, estimate, calculation, adding, counting, addition, computation, summation
2 DAY OF RETRIBUTION, doom, judgment day, last judgment

reclaim *verb* 1 RETRIEVE, get *or* take back, rescue, regain, reinstate
2 REGAIN, restore, salvage, recapture, regenerate
3 RESCUE, reform, redeem

recline *verb* LEAN, lie (down), stretch out, rest, lounge, sprawl, loll, repose, be recumbent
<< OPPOSITE stand up

recluse *noun* HERMIT, solitary, ascetic, anchoress, monk, anchorite, eremite

reclusive *adjective* SOLITARY, retiring, withdrawn, isolated, secluded, cloistered, monastic, recluse, ascetic, sequestered, hermit-like, hermitic, eremitic
<< OPPOSITE sociable

recognition *noun* 1 IDENTIFICATION, recall, recollection, discovery, detection, remembrance
2 ACCEPTANCE, acknowledgement, understanding, admission, perception, awareness, concession, allowance, confession, realization, avowal
3 ACKNOWLEDGMENT, approval
4 APPROVAL, honour, appreciation, salute, gratitude, acknowledgment

recognize *verb* 1 IDENTIFY, know, place, remember, spot, notice, recall, make out, recollect, know again, put your finger on
2 ACKNOWLEDGE, see, allow, understand, accept, admit, grant, realize, concede, perceive, confess, be aware of, take on board, avow
<< OPPOSITE ignore
3 APPROVE, acknowledge, appreciate, greet, honour
4 APPRECIATE, respect, notice, salute

recoil *verb* 1 JERK BACK, kick, react, rebound, spring back, resile
2 DRAW BACK, shrink, falter, shy away, flinch, quail, balk at
▷ *noun* 1 JERKING BACK, reaction, springing back
2 KICKBACK, kick

recollect *verb* REMEMBER, mind (*dialect*), recall, reminisce, summon up, call to mind, place

recollection *noun* MEMORY, recall, impression, remembrance, reminiscence, mental image

recommend *verb* 1 ADVOCATE, suggest, propose, approve, endorse, commend
<< OPPOSITE disapprove of
2 PUT FORWARD, approve, endorse, commend, vouch for, praise, big up (*slang, chiefly Caribbean*), speak well of, put in a good word for
3 ADVISE, suggest, advance, propose, urge, counsel, advocate, prescribe, put forward, exhort, enjoin
4 MAKE ATTRACTIVE, make interesting, make appealing, make acceptable

recommendation *noun* 1 ADVICE, proposal, suggestion, counsel, urging
2 COMMENDATION, reference, praise, sanction, approval, blessing, plug (*informal*), endorsement, advocacy, testimonial, good word, approbation, favourable mention

recompense *noun* COMPENSATION, pay, payment, satisfaction, amends, repayment, remuneration, reparation, indemnity, restitution, damages, emolument, indemnification, requital
▷ *verb* COMPENSATE, reimburse, redress, repay, pay for, satisfy, make good, make up for, make amends for, indemnify, requite, make restitution for

reconcile *verb* 1 RESOLVE, settle, square, adjust, compose, rectify, patch up, harmonize, put to rights
2 REUNITE, bring back together, make peace between, pacify, conciliate
3 MAKE PEACE BETWEEN, reunite, propitiate, bring to terms, restore harmony between, re-establish friendly relations between
▷▷ **reconcile yourself to something** *often passive* ACCEPT, resign yourself to, get used to, put up with (*informal*), submit to, yield to, make the best of, accommodate yourself to

reconciliation *noun* 1 REUNION, conciliation, rapprochement (*French*), appeasement, détente, pacification, propitiation, understanding, reconcilement
<< OPPOSITE separation
2 ACCOMMODATION, settlement, compromise

reconnaissance *noun* INSPECTION, survey, investigation, observation, patrol, scan, exploration, scouting, scrutiny, recce (*slang*), reconnoitring

reconsider *verb* RETHINK, review, revise, think again, think twice, reassess, re-examine, have second thoughts, change your mind, re-evaluate, think over, think better of, take another look at

reconstruct *verb* 1 REBUILD, reform, restore,

recreate, remake, renovate, remodel, re-establish, regenerate, reorganize, reassemble
2 BUILD UP A PICTURE OF, build up, piece together, deduce

record *noun* 1 DOCUMENT, file, register, log, report, minute, account, entry, journal, diary, memorial, archives, memoir, chronicle, memorandum, annals
2 EVIDENCE, trace, documentation, testimony, witness, memorial, remembrance
3 DISC, recording, single, release, album, waxing (*informal*), LP, vinyl, EP, forty-five, platter (*US slang*), seventy-eight, gramophone record, black disc
4 BACKGROUND, history, performance, career, track record (*informal*), curriculum vitae
▷ *verb* 1 SET DOWN, report, minute, note, enter, document, register, preserve, log, put down, chronicle, write down, enrol, take down, inscribe, transcribe, chalk up (*informal*), put on record, put on file
2 MAKE A RECORDING OF, cut, video, tape, lay down (*slang*), wax (*informal*), video-tape, tape-record, put on wax (*informal*)
3 REGISTER, show, read, contain, indicate, give evidence of
▷▷ **off the record** 1 CONFIDENTIALLY, in private, in confidence, unofficially, sub rosa, under the rose
2 CONFIDENTIAL, private, unofficial, not for publication

recorder *noun* CHRONICLER, archivist, historian, scorer, clerk, registrar, scribe, diarist, scorekeeper, annalist

recording *noun* RECORD, video, tape, disc, gramophone record, cut (*informal*)

recount *verb* TELL, report, detail, describe, relate, repeat, portray, depict, rehearse, recite, tell the story of, narrate, delineate, enumerate, give an account of

recoup *verb* REGAIN, recover, make good, retrieve, redeem, win back

recourse *noun* OPTION, choice, alternative, resort, appeal, resource, remedy, way out, refuge, expedient

recover *verb* 1 GET BETTER, improve, get well, recuperate, pick up, heal, revive, come round, bounce back, mend, turn the corner, pull through, convalesce, be on the mend, take a turn for the better, get back on your feet, feel yourself again, regain your health *or* strength
<< OPPOSITE relapse
2 RALLY
3 SAVE, rescue, retrieve, salvage, reclaim
<< OPPOSITE abandon
4 RECOUP, restore, repair, get back, regain, make good, retrieve, reclaim, redeem, recapture, win back, take back, repossess, retake, find again
<< OPPOSITE lose

recovery *noun* 1 IMPROVEMENT, return to health, rally, healing, revival, mending, recuperation, convalescence, turn for the better
2 REVIVAL, improvement, rally, restoration, rehabilitation, upturn, betterment, amelioration
3 RETRIEVAL, repossession, reclamation, restoration, repair, redemption, recapture

recreation *noun* LEISURE, play, sport, exercise, fun, relief, pleasure, entertainment, relaxation, enjoyment, distraction, amusement, diversion, refreshment, beer and skittles (*informal*), me-time

recrimination *noun* BICKERING, retaliation, counterattack, mutual accusation, retort, quarrel, squabbling, name-calling, countercharge

recruit *verb* 1 GATHER, take on, obtain, engage, round up, enrol, procure, proselytize
2 ASSEMBLE, raise, levy, muster, mobilize
3 ENLIST, draft, impress, enrol
<< OPPOSITE dismiss
▷ *noun* BEGINNER, trainee, apprentice, novice, convert, initiate, rookie (*informal*), helper, learner, neophyte, tyro, greenhorn (*informal*), proselyte

rectify *verb* CORRECT, right, improve, reform, square, fix, repair, adjust, remedy, amend, make good, mend, redress, put right, set the record straight, emend

rectitude *noun* 1 MORALITY, principle, honour, virtue, decency, justice, equity, integrity, goodness, honesty, correctness, righteousness, probity, incorruptibility, scrupulousness, uprightness
<< OPPOSITE immorality
2 CORRECTNESS, justice, accuracy, precision, verity, rightness, soundness, exactness

recuperate *verb* RECOVER, improve, pick up, get better, mend, turn the corner, convalesce, be on the mend, get back on your feet, regain your health

recur *verb* HAPPEN AGAIN, return, come back, repeat, persist, revert, reappear, come and go, come again

recurrent *adjective* PERIODIC, continued, regular, repeated, frequent, recurring, repetitive, cyclical, habitual
<< OPPOSITE one-off

recycle *verb* REPROCESS, reuse, salvage, reclaim, save

red *noun* CRIMSON, scarlet, ruby, vermilion, rose, wine, pink, cherry, cardinal, coral, maroon, claret, carmine
▷ *adjective* 1 CRIMSON, scarlet, ruby, vermilion, rose, wine, pink, cherry, cardinal, coral, maroon, claret, carmine

2 FLUSHED, embarrassed, blushing, suffused, florid, shamefaced, rubicund
3 *(of hair)* CHESTNUT, flaming, reddish, flame-coloured, bay, sandy, foxy, Titian, carroty
4 BLOODSHOT, inflamed, red-rimmed
5 ROSY, healthy, glowing, blooming, ruddy, roseate
▷▷ **in the red** *(informal)* IN DEBT, bankrupt, on the rocks, insolvent, in arrears, overdrawn, owing money, in deficit, showing a loss, in debit
▷▷ **see red** *(informal)* LOSE YOUR TEMPER, boil, lose it *(informal)*, seethe, go mad *(informal)*, crack up *(informal)*, lose the plot *(informal)*, go ballistic *(slang, chiefly US)*, blow a fuse *(slang, chiefly US)*, fly off the handle *(informal)*, become enraged, go off the deep end *(informal)*, wig out *(slang)*, go up the wall *(slang)*, blow your top, lose your rag *(slang)*, be beside yourself with rage *(informal)*, be *or* get very angry, go off your head *(slang)*
>> RELATED WORDS *adjectives* rubicund, ruddy

red-blooded *adjective (informal)* VIGOROUS, manly, lusty, virile, strong, vital, robust, hearty

redden *verb* FLUSH, colour (up), blush, crimson, suffuse, go red, go beetroot *(informal)*

redeem *verb* 1 REINSTATE, absolve, restore to favour, rehabilitate
2 MAKE UP FOR, offset, make good, compensate for, outweigh, redress, atone for, make amends for, defray
3 TRADE IN, cash (in), exchange, change
4 BUY BACK, recover, regain, retrieve, reclaim, win back, repossess, repurchase, recover possession of
5 SAVE, free, deliver, rescue, liberate, ransom, set free, extricate, emancipate, buy the freedom of, pay the ransom of
6 FULFIL, meet, keep, carry out, satisfy, discharge, make good, hold to, acquit, adhere to, abide by, keep faith with, be faithful to, perform

redemption *noun* 1 COMPENSATION, amends, reparation, atonement, expiation
2 SALVATION, release, rescue, liberation, ransom, emancipation, deliverance
3 PAYING-OFF, paying back
4 TRADE-IN, recovery, retrieval, repurchase, repossession, reclamation, quid pro quo

red-handed *adjective* IN THE ACT, with your pants down *(US slang)*, (in) flagrante delicto, with your fingers *or* hand in the till *(informal)*, bang to rights *(slang)*

redolent *adjective* 1 REMINISCENT, evocative, suggestive, remindful
2 SCENTED, perfumed, fragrant, aromatic, sweet-smelling, odorous

redoubtable *adjective* FORMIDABLE, strong, powerful, terrible, awful, mighty, dreadful, fearful, fearsome, resolute, valiant, doughty

redress *verb* 1 MAKE AMENDS FOR, pay for, make up for, compensate for, put right, recompense for, make reparation for, make restitution for
2 PUT RIGHT, reform, balance, square, correct, ease, repair, relieve, adjust, regulate, remedy, amend, mend, rectify, even up, restore the balance
▷ *noun* AMENDS, payment, compensation, reparation, restitution, atonement, recompense, requital, quittance

reduce *verb* 1 LESSEN, cut, contract, lower, depress, moderate, weaken, diminish, turn down, decrease, slow down, cut down, shorten, dilute, impair, curtail, wind down, abate, tone down, debase, truncate, abridge, downsize, kennet *(Austral slang)*, jeff *(Austral slang)*
<< OPPOSITE increase
2 DEGRADE, downgrade, demote, lower in rank, break, humble, humiliate, bring low, take down a peg *(informal)*, lower the status of
<< OPPOSITE promote
3 DRIVE, force, bring, bring to the point of
4 CHEAPEN, cut, lower, discount, slash, mark down, bring down the price of
5 IMPOVERISH, ruin, bankrupt, pauperize
▷▷ **in reduced circumstances** IMPOVERISHED, broke *(informal)*, badly off, hard up *(informal)*, short, in need, needy, on the rocks, penniless, destitute, poverty-stricken, down and out, skint *(Brit slang)*, in want, indigent, down at heel, impecunious, dirt-poor *(informal)*, on the breadline, flat broke *(informal)*, penurious, on your uppers, stony-broke *(Brit slang)*, necessitous, in queer street, without two pennies to rub together *(informal)*, on your beam-ends

redundancy *noun* 1 LAYOFF, sacking, dismissal
2 UNEMPLOYMENT, the sack *(informal)*, the axe *(informal)*, joblessness
3 SUPERFLUITY, surplus, surfeit, superabundance

redundant *adjective* 1 SUPERFLUOUS, extra, surplus, excessive, unnecessary, unwanted, inordinate, inessential, supernumerary, de trop *(French)*, supererogatory
<< OPPOSITE essential
2 TAUTOLOGICAL, wordy, repetitious, verbose, padded, diffuse, prolix, iterative, periphrastic, pleonastic

reek *verb* 1 STINK, smell, pong *(Brit informal)*, smell to high heaven, hum *(slang)*
2 *with* **of** BE REDOLENT OF, suggest, smack of, testify to, be characterized by, bear the stamp of, be permeated by, be suggestive *or* indicative of
▷ *noun* STINK, smell, odour, stench, pong (*Brit*

informal), effluvium, niff (*Brit slang*), malodour, mephitis, fetor

reel *verb* 1 STAGGER, rock, roll, pitch, stumble, sway, falter, lurch, wobble, waver, totter
2 WHIRL, swim, spin, revolve, swirl, twirl, go round and round

refer *verb* 1 PASS ON, transfer, deliver, commit, hand over, submit, turn over, consign
2 DIRECT, point, send, guide, recommend
▷▷ **refer to something** *or* **someone** 1 ALLUDE TO, mention, cite, speak of, bring up, invoke, hint at, touch on, make reference to, make mention of
2 RELATE TO, concern, apply to, pertain to, be relevant to
3 CONSULT, go, apply, turn to, look up, have recourse to, seek information from

It is usually unnecessary to add *back* to the verb *refer*, since the sense of *back* is already contained in the *re-* part of this word. For example, you might say *This refers to* (not *refers back to*) *what has already been said*. *Refer back* is only considered acceptable when used to mean 'return a document or question to the person it came from for further consideration', as in *he referred the matter back to me*

referee *noun* UMPIRE, umpie (*Austral slang*), judge, ref (*informal*), arbiter, arbitrator, adjudicator
▷ *verb* UMPIRE, judge, mediate, adjudicate, arbitrate

reference *noun* 1 ALLUSION, note, mention, remark, quotation
2 CITATION
3 TESTIMONIAL, recommendation, credentials, endorsement, certification, good word, character reference

referendum *noun* PUBLIC VOTE, popular vote, plebiscite

refine *verb* 1 PURIFY, process, filter, cleanse, clarify, distil, rarefy
2 IMPROVE, perfect, polish, temper, elevate, hone

refined *adjective* 1 PURIFIED, processed, pure, filtered, clean, clarified, distilled
<< OPPOSITE unrefined
2 CULTURED, civil, polished, sophisticated, gentlemanly, elegant, polite, cultivated, gracious, civilized, genteel, urbane, courtly, well-bred, ladylike, well-mannered
<< OPPOSITE coarse
3 DISCERNING, fine, nice, sensitive, exact, subtle, delicate, precise, discriminating, sublime, fastidious, punctilious

refinement *noun* 1 SUBTLETY, nuance, nicety, fine point
2 SOPHISTICATION, finish, style, culture, taste, breeding, polish, grace, discrimination, courtesy, civilization, precision, elegance, delicacy, cultivation, finesse, politeness, good manners, civility, gentility, good breeding, graciousness, urbanity, fastidiousness, fineness, courtliness, politesse
3 PURIFICATION, processing, filtering, cleansing, clarification, distillation, rectification, rarefaction

reflect *verb* 1 SHOW, reveal, express, display, indicate, demonstrate, exhibit, communicate, manifest, bear out, bespeak, evince
2 THROW BACK, return, mirror, echo, reproduce, imitate, give back
3 *usually followed by* **on** CONSIDER, think, contemplate, deliberate, muse, ponder, meditate, mull over, ruminate, cogitate, wonder

reflection *noun* 1 IMAGE, echo, counterpart, mirror image
2 CRITICISM, censure, slur, reproach, imputation, derogation, aspersion
3 CONSIDERATION, thinking, pondering, deliberation, thought, idea, view, study, opinion, impression, observation, musing, meditation, contemplation, rumination, perusal, cogitation, cerebration

reflective *adjective* THOUGHTFUL, contemplative, meditative, pensive, reasoning, pondering, deliberative, ruminative, cogitating

reform *noun* IMPROVEMENT, amendment, correction, rehabilitation, renovation, betterment, rectification, amelioration
▷ *verb* 1 IMPROVE, better, correct, restore, repair, rebuild, amend, reclaim, mend, renovate, reconstruct, remodel, rectify, rehabilitate, regenerate, reorganize, reconstitute, revolutionize, ameliorate, emend
2 MEND YOUR WAYS, go straight (*informal*), shape up (*informal*), get it together (*informal*), turn over a new leaf, get your act together (*informal*), clean up your act (*informal*), pull your socks up (*Brit informal*), get back on the straight and narrow (*informal*)

refrain[1] *verb* STOP, avoid, give up, cease, do without, renounce, abstain, eschew, leave off, desist, forbear, kick (*informal*)

refrain[2] *noun* CHORUS, song, tune, melody

refresh *verb* 1 REVIVE, cool, freshen, revitalize, cheer, stimulate, brace, rejuvenate, kick-start (*informal*), enliven, breathe new life into, invigorate, revivify, reanimate, inspirit
2 REPLENISH, restore, repair, renew, top up, renovate
3 STIMULATE, prompt, renew, jog, prod, brush up (*informal*)

refreshing *adjective* 1 NEW, different, original,

novel
2 STIMULATING, fresh, cooling, bracing, invigorating, revivifying, thirst-quenching, inspiriting
<< OPPOSITE tiring

refreshment *noun* 1 REVIVAL, restoration, renewal, stimulation, renovation, freshening, reanimation, enlivenment, repair
2 *plural* FOOD AND DRINK, drinks, snacks, titbits, kai (*NZ informal*)

refrigerate *verb* COOL, freeze, chill, keep cold

refuge *noun* 1 PROTECTION, security, shelter, harbour, asylum
2 HAVEN, resort, retreat, sanctuary, hide-out, bolt hole

refugee *noun* EXILE, émigré, displaced person, runaway, fugitive, escapee

refund *noun* REPAYMENT, reimbursement, return
▷ *verb* REPAY, return, restore, make good, pay back, reimburse, give back

refurbish *verb* RENOVATE, restore, repair, clean up, overhaul, revamp, mend, remodel, do up (*informal*), refit, fix up (*informal, chiefly US & Canad*), spruce up, re-equip, set to rights

refusal *noun* REJECTION, denial, defiance, rebuff, knock-back (*slang*), thumbs down, repudiation, kick in the teeth (*slang*), negation, no
▷▷ **first refusal** OPTION, choice, opportunity, consideration

refuse[1] *verb* 1 DECLINE, reject, turn down, say no to, repudiate
2 DENY, decline, withhold
<< OPPOSITE allow

refuse[2] *noun* RUBBISH, waste, sweepings, junk (*informal*), litter, garbage, trash, sediment, scum, dross, dregs, leavings, dreck (*slang, chiefly US*), offscourings, lees

refute *verb* DISPROVE, counter, discredit, prove false, silence, overthrow, negate, rebut, give the lie to, blow out of the water (*slang*), confute
<< OPPOSITE prove

> The use of *refute* to mean *deny* as in *I'm not refuting the fact that* is thought by some people to be incorrect. In careful writing it may be advisable to use *refute* only where there is an element of disproving something through argument and evidence, as in *we haven't got evidence to refute their hypothesis*

regain *verb* 1 RECOVER, get back, retrieve, redeem, recapture, win back, take back, recoup, repossess, retake
2 GET BACK TO, return to, reach again, reattain

regal *adjective* ROYAL, majestic, kingly *or* queenly, noble, princely, proud, magnificent, sovereign, fit for a king *or* queen

regale *verb* 1 ENTERTAIN, delight, amuse, divert, gratify
2 SERVE, refresh, ply

regalia *plural noun* TRAPPINGS, gear, decorations, finery, apparatus, emblems, paraphernalia, garb, accoutrements, rigout (*informal*)

regard *verb* 1 CONSIDER, see, hold, rate, view, value, account, judge, treat, think of, esteem, deem, look upon, adjudge
2 LOOK AT, view, eye, watch, observe, check, notice, clock (*Brit slang*), remark, check out (*informal*), gaze at, behold, eyeball (*US slang*), scrutinize, get a load of (*informal*), take a dekko at (*Brit slang*)
▷ *noun* 1 RESPECT, esteem, deference, store, thought, love, concern, care, account, note, reputation, honour, consideration, sympathy, affection, attachment, repute
2 LOOK, gaze, scrutiny, stare, glance
3 *plural* GOOD WISHES, respects, greetings, compliments, best wishes, salutations, devoirs
▷▷ **as regards** CONCERNING, regarding, relating to, pertaining to
▷▷ **in this regard** ON THIS POINT, on this matter, on this detail, in this respect
▷▷ **with regard to** CONCERNING, regarding, relating to, with respect to, as regards

> The word *regard* in the expression *with regard to* is singular, and has no *s* at the end. People often make the mistake of saying *with regards to*, perhaps being influenced by the phrase *as regards*

regarding *preposition* CONCERNING, about, as to, on the subject of, re, respecting, in respect of, as regards, with reference to, in re, in the matter of, apropos, in *or* with regard to

regardless *adverb* IN SPITE OF EVERYTHING, anyway, nevertheless, nonetheless, in any case, no matter what, for all that, rain or shine, despite everything, come what may
▷ *adjective with* **of** IRRESPECTIVE OF, disregarding, unconcerned about, heedless of, unmindful of

regenerate *verb* RENEW, restore, revive, renovate, change, reproduce, uplift, reconstruct, re-establish, rejuvenate, kick-start (*informal*), breathe new life into, invigorate, reinvigorate, reawaken, revivify, give a shot in the arm, inspirit
<< OPPOSITE degenerate

regime *noun* 1 GOVERNMENT, rule, management, administration, leadership, establishment, reign
2 PLAN, course, system, policy, programme, scheme, regimen

region *noun* AREA, country, place, part, land,

quarter, division, section, sector, district, territory, zone, province, patch, turf (*US slang*), tract, expanse, locality

regional *adjective* LOCAL, district, provincial, parochial, sectional, zonal

register *noun* LIST, record, roll, file, schedule, diary, catalogue, log, archives, chronicle, memorandum, roster, ledger, annals
▷ *verb* 1 ENROL, sign on *or* up, enlist, list, note, enter, check in, inscribe, set down
2 RECORD, catalogue, chronicle, take down
3 INDICATE, show, record, read
4 SHOW, mark, record, reflect, indicate, betray, manifest, bespeak
5 EXPRESS, say, show, reveal, display, exhibit
6 (*informal*) HAVE AN EFFECT, get through, sink in, make an impression, tell, impress, come home, dawn on

regress *verb* REVERT, deteriorate, return, go back, retreat, lapse, fall back, wane, recede, ebb, degenerate, relapse, lose ground, turn the clock back, backslide, retrogress, retrocede, fall away *or* off
<< OPPOSITE progress

regret *verb* 1 BE *or* FEEL SORRY ABOUT, feel remorse about, be upset about, rue, deplore, bemoan, repent (of), weep over, bewail, cry over spilt milk
<< OPPOSITE be satisfied with
2 MOURN, miss, grieve for *or* over
▷ *noun* 1 REMORSE, compunction, self-reproach, pang of conscience, bitterness, repentance, contrition, penitence, ruefulness
2 SORROW, disappointment, grief, lamentation
<< OPPOSITE satisfaction

regretful *adjective* SORRY, disappointed, sad, ashamed, apologetic, mournful, rueful, contrite, sorrowful, repentant, remorseful, penitent

Regretful and *regretfully* are sometimes wrongly used where *regrettable* and *regrettably* are meant. A simple way of making the distinction is that when you regret something YOU have done, you are *regretful*: *he gave a regretful smile*; *he smiled regretfully*. In contrast, when you are sorry about an occurrence you did not yourself cause, you view the occurrence as *regrettable*: *this is a regrettable* (not *regretful*) *mistake*; *regrettably* (not *regretfully*, i.e. because of circumstances beyond my control) *I shall be unable to attend*

regrettable *adjective* UNFORTUNATE, wrong, disappointing, sad, distressing, unhappy, shameful, woeful, deplorable, ill-advised, lamentable, pitiable ▷ see **regretful**

regular *adjective* 1 FREQUENT, daily
2 NORMAL, common, established, usual, ordinary, typical, routine, everyday, customary, commonplace, habitual, unvarying
<< OPPOSITE infrequent
3 STEADY, consistent
4 EVEN, level, balanced, straight, flat, fixed, smooth, uniform, symmetrical
<< OPPOSITE uneven
5 METHODICAL, set, ordered, formal, steady, efficient, systematic, orderly, standardized, dependable, consistent
<< OPPOSITE inconsistent
6 OFFICIAL, standard, established, traditional, classic, correct, approved, formal, sanctioned, proper, prevailing, orthodox, time-honoured, bona fide

regulate *verb* 1 CONTROL, run, order, rule, manage, direct, guide, handle, conduct, arrange, monitor, organize, govern, administer, oversee, supervise, systematize, superintend
2 MODERATE, control, modulate, settle, fit, balance, tune, adjust

regulation *noun* 1 RULE, order, law, direction, procedure, requirement, dictate, decree, canon, statute, ordinance, commandment, edict, precept, standing order
2 CONTROL, government, management, administration, direction, arrangement, supervision, governance, rule
▷ *modifier* CONVENTIONAL, official, standard, required, normal, usual, prescribed, mandatory, customary

regurgitate *verb* DISGORGE, throw up (*informal*), chuck up (*slang, chiefly US*), puke up (*slang*), sick up (*informal*), spew out *or* up

rehabilitate *verb* 1 REINTEGRATE
2 RESTORE, convert, renew, adjust, rebuild, make good, mend, renovate, reconstruct, reinstate, re-establish, fix up (*informal, chiefly US & Canad*), reconstitute, recondition, reinvigorate

rehash *noun* REWORKING, rewrite, new version, rearrangement
▷ *verb* REWORK, rewrite, rearrange, change, alter, reshuffle, make over, reuse, rejig (*informal*), refashion

rehearsal *noun* PRACTICE, rehearsing, practice session, run-through, reading, preparation, drill, going-over (*informal*)

rehearse *verb* 1 PRACTISE, prepare, run through, go over, train, act, study, ready, repeat, drill, try out, recite
2 RECITE, practice, go over, run through, tell, list, detail, describe, review, relate, depict, spell out, recount, narrate, trot out (*informal*), delineate, enumerate

reign *verb* 1 BE SUPREME, prevail, predominate,

hold sway, be rife, be rampant
2 RULE, govern, be in power, occupy *or* sit on the throne, influence, command, administer, hold sway, wear the crown, wield the sceptre
▷ *noun* RULE, sovereignty, supremacy, power, control, influence, command, empire, monarchy, sway, dominion, hegemony, ascendancy

> The words *rein* and *reign* should not be confused; note the correct spellings in *he gave full rein to his feelings* (not *reign*); and *it will be necessary to rein in public spending* (not *reign in*)

reimburse *verb* PAY BACK, refund, repay, recompense, return, restore, compensate, indemnify, remunerate

rein *noun* CONTROL, harness, bridle, hold, check, restriction, brake, curb, restraint
▷▷ **give (a) free rein to something** *or* **someone** GIVE A FREE HAND (TO), give carte blanche (to), give a blank cheque (to), remove restraints (from), indulge, let go, give way to, give (someone) his *or* her head
▷▷ **rein something in** *or* **back** CHECK, control, limit, contain, master, curb, restrain, hold back, constrain, bridle, keep in check ▷ see **reign**

reincarnation *noun* REBIRTH, metempsychosis, transmigration of souls

reinforce *verb* 1 SUPPORT, strengthen, fortify, toughen, stress, prop, supplement, emphasize, underline, harden, bolster, stiffen, shore up, buttress
2 INCREASE, extend, add to, strengthen, supplement, augment

reinforcement *noun* 1 STRENGTHENING, increase, supplement, enlargement, fortification, amplification, augmentation
2 SUPPORT, stay, shore, prop, brace, buttress
3 *plural* RESERVES, support, auxiliaries, additional *or* fresh troops

reinstate *verb* RESTORE, recall, bring back, re-establish, return, rehabilitate

reiterate *verb* (*Formal*) REPEAT, restate, say again, retell, do again, recapitulate, iterate

reject *verb* 1 REBUFF, drop, jilt, desert, turn down, ditch (*slang*), break with, spurn, refuse, say no to, repulse, throw over
<< OPPOSITE accept
2 DENY, decline, abandon, exclude, veto, discard, relinquish, renounce, spurn, eschew, leave off, throw off, disallow, forsake, retract, repudiate, cast off, disown, forgo, disclaim, forswear, swear off, wash your hands of
<< OPPOSITE approve
3 DISCARD, decline, eliminate, scrap, bin, jettison, cast aside, throw away *or* out
<< OPPOSITE accept
▷ *noun* 1 CASTOFF, second, discard, flotsam, clunker (*informal*)
<< OPPOSITE treasure
2 FAILURE, loser, flop

rejection *noun* 1 DENIAL, veto, dismissal, exclusion, abandonment, spurning, casting off, disowning, thumbs down, renunciation, repudiation, eschewal
<< OPPOSITE approval
2 REBUFF, refusal, knock-back (*slang*), kick in the teeth (*slang*), bum's rush (*slang*), the (old) heave-ho (*informal*), brushoff (*slang*)
<< OPPOSITE acceptance

rejoice *verb* BE GLAD, celebrate, delight, be happy, joy, triumph, glory, revel, be overjoyed, exult, jump for joy, make merry
<< OPPOSITE lament

rejoicing *noun* HAPPINESS, delight, joy, triumph, celebration, cheer, festivity, elation, gaiety, jubilation, revelry, exultation, gladness, merrymaking

rejoin *verb* REPLY, answer, respond, retort, come back with, riposte, return

rejuvenate *verb* REVITALIZE, restore, renew, refresh, regenerate, breathe new life into, reinvigorate, revivify, give new life to, reanimate, make young again, restore vitality to

relapse *verb* 1 LAPSE, revert, degenerate, slip back, fail, weaken, fall back, regress, backslide, retrogress
2 WORSEN, deteriorate, sicken, weaken, fail, sink, fade
<< OPPOSITE recover
▷ *noun* 1 LAPSE, regression, fall from grace, reversion, backsliding, recidivism, retrogression
2 WORSENING, setback, deterioration, recurrence, turn for the worse, weakening
<< OPPOSITE recovery

relate *verb* 1 TELL, recount, report, present, detail, describe, chronicle, rehearse, recite, impart, narrate, set forth, give an account of
▷▷ **relate to something** *or* **someone**
1 CONCERN, refer to, apply to, have to do with, pertain to, be relevant to, bear upon, appertain to, have reference to
2 CONNECT WITH, associate with, link with, couple with, join with, ally with, correlate to, coordinate with

related *adjective* 1 ASSOCIATED, linked, allied, joint, accompanying, connected, affiliated, akin, correlated, interconnected, concomitant, cognate, agnate
<< OPPOSITE unconnected
2 AKIN, kin, kindred, cognate, consanguineous, agnate
<< OPPOSITE unrelated

relation *noun* 1 SIMILARITY, link, bearing,

bond, application, comparison, tie-in, correlation, interdependence, pertinence, connection
2 RELATIVE, kin, kinsman *or* kinswoman, rellie (*Austral slang*)
▷ *plural noun* 1 DEALINGS, relationship, rapport, communications, meetings, terms, associations, affairs, contact, connections, interaction, intercourse, liaison
2 FAMILY, relatives, tribe, clan, kin, kindred, kinsmen, kinsfolk, ainga (*NZ*), rellie (*Austral slang*)

relationship *noun* 1 ASSOCIATION, bond, communications, connection, conjunction, affinity, rapport, kinship
2 AFFAIR, romance, liaison, amour, intrigue
3 CONNECTION, link, proportion, parallel, ratio, similarity, tie-up, correlation

relative *noun* RELATION, connection, kinsman *or* kinswoman, member of your *or* the family, rellie (*Austral slang*)
▷ *adjective* 1 COMPARATIVE
2 CORRESPONDING, respective, reciprocal
3 *with* **to** IN PROPORTION TO, corresponding to, proportionate to, proportional to

relatively *adverb* COMPARATIVELY, rather, somewhat, to some extent, in *or* by comparison

relax *verb* 1 BE *or* FEEL AT EASE, chill out (*slang, chiefly US*), take it easy, loosen up, laze, lighten up (*slang*), put your feet up, hang loose (*slang*), let yourself go (*informal*), let your hair down (*informal*), mellow out (*informal*), make yourself at home, outspan (*S African*), take your ease
<< OPPOSITE be alarmed
2 CALM DOWN, calm, unwind, loosen up, tranquillize
3 MAKE LESS TENSE, soften, loosen up, unbend, rest
4 LESSEN, reduce, ease, relieve, weaken, loosen, let up, slacken
<< OPPOSITE tighten
5 MODERATE, ease, relieve, weaken, diminish, mitigate, slacken
<< OPPOSITE tighten up

relaxation *noun* 1 LEISURE, rest, fun, pleasure, entertainment, recreation, enjoyment, amusement, refreshment, beer and skittles (*informal*), me-time
2 LESSENING, easing, reduction, weakening, moderation, let-up (*informal*), slackening, diminution, abatement

relaxed *adjective* 1 EASY-GOING, easy, casual, informal, laid-back (*informal*), mellow, leisurely, downbeat (*informal*), unhurried, nonchalant, free and easy, mild, insouciant, untaxing
2 COMFORTABLE, easy-going, casual, laid-back (*informal*), informal

relay *verb* BROADCAST, carry, spread, communicate, transmit, send out

release *verb* 1 SET FREE, free, discharge, liberate, drop, deliver, loose, let go, undo, let out, extricate, untie, disengage, emancipate, unchain, unfasten, turn loose, unshackle, unloose, unfetter, unbridle, manumit
<< OPPOSITE imprison
2 ACQUIT, excuse, exempt, let go, dispense, let off, exonerate, absolve
3 ISSUE, publish, make public, make known, break, present, launch, distribute, unveil, put out, circulate, disseminate
<< OPPOSITE withhold
▷ *noun* 1 LIBERATION, freedom, delivery, liberty, discharge, emancipation, deliverance, manumission, relief
<< OPPOSITE imprisonment
2 ACQUITTAL, exemption, let-off (*informal*), dispensation, absolution, exoneration, acquittance
3 ISSUE, announcement, publication, proclamation, offering

relegate *verb* 1 DEMOTE, degrade, downgrade, declass
2 BANISH, exile, expel, throw out, oust, deport, eject, expatriate

relent *verb* 1 BE MERCIFUL, yield, give in, soften, give way, come round, capitulate, acquiesce, change your mind, unbend, forbear, show mercy, have pity, melt, give quarter
<< OPPOSITE show no mercy
2 EASE, die down, let up, fall, drop, slow, relax, weaken, slacken
<< OPPOSITE intensify

relentless *adjective* 1 MERCILESS, hard, fierce, harsh, cruel, grim, ruthless, uncompromising, unstoppable, inflexible, unrelenting, unforgiving, inexorable, implacable, unyielding, remorseless, pitiless, undeviating
<< OPPOSITE merciful
2 UNREMITTING, sustained, punishing, persistent, unstoppable, unbroken, unrelenting, incessant, unabated, nonstop, unrelieved, unflagging, unfaltering

relevant *adjective* SIGNIFICANT, appropriate, proper, related, fitting, material, suited, relative, to the point, apt, applicable, pertinent, apposite, admissible, germane, to the purpose, appurtenant, ad rem (*Latin*)
<< OPPOSITE irrelevant

reliable *adjective* 1 DEPENDABLE, trustworthy, honest, responsible, sure, sound, true, certain, regular, stable, faithful, predictable, upright, staunch, reputable, trusty, unfailing, tried and true
<< OPPOSITE unreliable
2 SAFE, dependable

3 DEFINITIVE, sound, dependable, trustworthy

reliance *noun* 1 DEPENDENCY, dependence
2 TRUST, confidence, belief, faith, assurance, credence, credit

relic *noun* REMNANT, vestige, memento, trace, survival, scrap, token, fragment, souvenir, remembrance, keepsake

relief *noun* 1 EASE, release, comfort, cure, remedy, solace, balm, deliverance, mitigation, abatement, alleviation, easement, palliation, assuagement
2 REST, respite, let-up, relaxation, break, diversion, refreshment (*informal*), remission, breather (*informal*)
3 AID, help, support, assistance, sustenance, succour

relieve *verb* 1 EASE, soothe, alleviate, allay, relax, comfort, calm, cure, dull, diminish, soften, console, appease, solace, mitigate, abate, assuage, mollify, salve, palliate
<< OPPOSITE intensify
2 FREE, release, deliver, discharge, exempt, unburden, disembarrass, disencumber
3 TAKE OVER FROM, substitute for, stand in for, take the place of, give (someone) a break *or* rest
4 HELP, support, aid, sustain, assist, succour, bring aid to

religion *noun* BELIEF, faith, theology, creed

religious *adjective* 1 SPIRITUAL, holy, sacred, divine, theological, righteous, sectarian, doctrinal, devotional, scriptural
2 CONSCIENTIOUS, exact, faithful, rigid, rigorous, meticulous, scrupulous, fastidious, unerring, unswerving, punctilious

relinquish *verb* (*Formal*) GIVE UP, leave, release, drop, abandon, resign, desert, quit, yield, hand over, surrender, withdraw from, let go, retire from, renounce, waive, vacate, say goodbye to, forsake, cede, repudiate, cast off, forgo, abdicate, kiss (something) goodbye, lay aside

relish *verb* 1 ENJOY, like, prefer, taste, appreciate, savour, revel in, luxuriate in
<< OPPOSITE dislike
2 LOOK FORWARD TO, fancy, delight in, lick your lips over
▷ *noun* 1 ENJOYMENT, liking, love, taste, fancy, stomach, appetite, appreciation, penchant, zest, fondness, gusto, predilection, zing (*informal*), partiality
<< OPPOSITE distaste
2 CONDIMENT, seasoning, sauce, appetizer

reluctance *noun* UNWILLINGNESS, dislike, loathing, distaste, aversion, backwardness, hesitancy, disinclination, repugnance, indisposition, disrelish

reluctant *adjective* UNWILLING, slow, backward, grudging, hesitant, averse, recalcitrant, loath, disinclined, unenthusiastic, indisposed
<< OPPOSITE willing

> *Reticent* is quite commonly used nowadays as a synonym of *reluctant* and followed by *to* and a verb. In careful writing it is advisable to avoid this use, since many people would regard it as mistaken

rely on *verb* 1 DEPEND ON, lean on
2 BE CONFIDENT OF, bank on, trust, count on, bet on, reckon on, lean on, be sure of, have confidence in, swear by, repose trust in

remain *verb* 1 STAY, continue, go on, stand, dwell, bide
2 STAY BEHIND, wait, delay, stay put (*informal*), tarry
<< OPPOSITE go
3 CONTINUE, be left, endure, persist, linger, hang in the air, stay

remainder *noun* REST, remains, balance, trace, excess, surplus, butt, remnant, relic, residue, stub, vestige(s), tail end, dregs, oddment, leavings, residuum

remaining *adjective* 1 LEFT-OVER, surviving, outstanding, lingering, unfinished, residual
2 SURVIVING, lasting, persisting, abiding, extant

remains *plural noun* 1 REMNANTS, leftovers, remainder, scraps, rest, pieces, balance, traces, fragments, debris, residue, crumbs, vestiges, detritus, dregs, odds and ends, oddments, leavings
2 RELICS
3 CORPSE, body, carcass, cadaver

remark *verb* 1 COMMENT, say, state, reflect, mention, declare, observe, pass comment, animadvert
2 NOTICE, note, observe, perceive, see, mark, regard, make out, heed, espy, take note *or* notice of
▷ *noun* 1 COMMENT, observation, reflection, statement, thought, word, opinion, declaration, assertion, utterance
2 NOTICE, thought, comment, attention, regard, mention, recognition, consideration, observation, heed, acknowledgment

remarkable *adjective* EXTRAORDINARY, striking, outstanding, famous, odd, strange, wonderful, signal, rare, unusual, impressive, surprising, distinguished, prominent, notable, phenomenal, uncommon, conspicuous, singular, miraculous, noteworthy, pre-eminent
<< OPPOSITE ordinary

remedy *noun* 1 SOLUTION, relief, redress, antidote, corrective, panacea, countermeasure
2 CURE, treatment, specific, medicine, therapy, antidote, panacea, restorative, relief, nostrum, physic (*rare*), medicament, counteractive

▷ *verb* 1 PUT RIGHT, redress, rectify, reform, fix, correct, solve, repair, relieve, ameliorate, set to rights
2 CURE, treat, heal, help, control, ease, restore, relieve, soothe, alleviate, mitigate, assuage, palliate

remember *verb* 1 RECALL, think back to, recollect, reminisce about, retain, recognize, call up, summon up, call to mind
<< OPPOSITE forget
2 BEAR IN MIND, keep in mind
3 LOOK BACK (ON), commemorate

remembrance *noun* 1 COMMEMORATION, memorial, testimonial
2 SOUVENIR, token, reminder, monument, relic, remembrancer (*archaic*), memento, keepsake
3 MEMORY, recollection, thought, recall, recognition, retrospect, reminiscence, anamnesis

remind *verb* JOG YOUR MEMORY, prompt, refresh your memory, make you remember
▷▷ **remind someone of something** *or* **someone** BRING TO MIND, call to mind, put in mind, awaken memories of, call up, bring back to

reminisce *verb* RECALL, remember, look back, hark back, review, think back, recollect, live in the past, go over in the memory

reminiscence *plural noun* RECOLLECTIONS, memories, reflections, retrospections, reviews, recalls, memoirs, anecdotes, remembrances

reminiscent *adjective* SUGGESTIVE, evocative, redolent, remindful, similar

remission *noun* 1 LESSENING, abatement, abeyance, lull, relaxation, ebb, respite, moderation, let-up (*informal*), alleviation, amelioration
2 REDUCTION, lessening, suspension, decrease, diminution
3 PARDON, release, discharge, amnesty, forgiveness, indulgence, exemption, reprieve, acquittal, absolution, exoneration, excuse

remit *noun* INSTRUCTIONS, brief, guidelines, authorization, terms of reference, orders
▷ *verb* 1 SEND, post, forward, mail, transmit, dispatch
2 CANCEL, stop, halt, repeal, rescind, desist, forbear
3 LESSEN, diminish, abate, ease up, reduce, relax, moderate, weaken, decrease, soften, dwindle, alleviate, wane, fall away, mitigate, slacken

remittance *noun* PAYMENT, fee, consideration, allowance

remnant *noun* REMAINDER, remains, trace, fragment, end, bit, rest, piece, balance, survival, scrap, butt, shred, hangover, residue, rump, leftovers, stub, vestige, tail end, oddment, residuum

remonstrate *verb* (*Formal*) PROTEST, challenge, argue, take issue, object, complain, dispute, dissent, take exception, expostulate

remorse *noun* REGRET, shame, guilt, pity, grief, compassion, sorrow, anguish, repentance, contrition, compunction, penitence, self-reproach, pangs of conscience, ruefulness, bad *or* guilty conscience

remorseless *adjective* PITILESS, hard, harsh, cruel, savage, ruthless, callous, merciless, unforgiving, implacable, inhumane, unmerciful, hardhearted, uncompassionate

remote *adjective* 1 DISTANT, far, isolated, lonely, out-of-the-way, far-off, secluded, inaccessible, faraway, outlying, in the middle of nowhere, off the beaten track, backwoods, godforsaken
<< OPPOSITE nearby
2 FAR, distant, obscure, far-off
<< OPPOSITE relevant
3 SLIGHT, small, outside, poor, unlikely, slim, faint, doubtful, dubious, slender, meagre, negligible, implausible, inconsiderable
<< OPPOSITE strong
4 ALOOF, cold, removed, reserved, withdrawn, distant, abstracted, detached, indifferent, faraway, introspective, uninterested, introverted, uninvolved, unapproachable, uncommunicative, standoffish
<< OPPOSITE outgoing

removal *noun* 1 EXTRACTION, stripping, withdrawal, purging, abstraction, uprooting, displacement, eradication, erasure, subtraction, dislodgment, expunction, taking away *or* off *or* out
2 DISMISSAL, expulsion, elimination, ejection, dispossession
3 MOVE, transfer, departure, relocation, flitting (*Scot & Northern English dialect*)

remove *verb* 1 TAKE OUT, withdraw, extract, abstract
<< OPPOSITE insert
2 TAKE OFF, doff
<< OPPOSITE put on
3 ERASE, eliminate, take out
4 DISMISS, eliminate, get rid of, discharge, abolish, expel, throw out, oust, relegate, purge, eject, do away with, depose, unseat, see the back of, dethrone, show someone the door, give the bum's rush (*slang*), throw out on your ear (*informal*)
<< OPPOSITE appoint
5 GET RID OF, wipe out, erase, eradicate, blow away (*slang, chiefly US*), blot out, expunge
6 TAKE AWAY, move, pull, transfer, detach, displace, do away with, dislodge, cart off (*slang*), carry off *or* away
<< OPPOSITE put back
7 DELETE, shed, get rid of, erase, excise, strike out, efface, expunge

<< OPPOSITE join
8 MOVE, transfer, transport, shift, quit, depart, move away, relocate, vacate, flit (*Scot & Northern English dialect*)
9 KILL, murder, do in (*slang*), eliminate, take out (*slang*), get rid of, execute, wipe out, dispose of, assassinate, do away with, liquidate, bump off (*slang*), wipe from the face of the earth

remuneration *noun* PAYMENT, income, earnings, salary, pay, return, profit, fee, wages, reward, compensation, repayment, reparation, indemnity, retainer, reimbursement, recompense, stipend, emolument, meed (*archaic*)

renaissance *or* **renascence** *noun* REBIRTH, revival, restoration, renewal, awakening, resurrection, regeneration, resurgence, reappearance, new dawn, re-emergence, reawakening, new birth

rend *verb* (*Literary*) TEAR, break, split, rip, pull, separate, divide, crack, burst, smash, disturb, shatter, pierce, fracture, sever, wrench, splinter, rupture, cleave, lacerate, rive, tear to pieces, sunder (*literary*), dissever

render *verb* 1 MAKE, cause to become, leave
2 PROVIDE, give, show, pay, present, supply, deliver, contribute, yield, submit, tender, hand out, furnish, turn over, make available
3 DELIVER, give, return, announce, pronounce
4 TRANSLATE, put, explain, interpret, reproduce, transcribe, construe, restate
5 *sometimes followed by* **up** GIVE UP, give, deliver, yield, hand over, surrender, turn over, relinquish, cede
6 REPRESENT, interpret, portray, depict, do, give, play, act, present, perform

rendezvous *noun* 1 APPOINTMENT, meeting, date, engagement, tryst (*archaic*), assignation
2 MEETING PLACE, venue, gathering point, place of assignation, trysting-place (*archaic*)
▷ *verb* MEET, assemble, get together, come together, collect, gather, rally, muster, converge, join up, be reunited

rendition *noun* (*Formal*) 1 PERFORMANCE, arrangement, interpretation, rendering, take (*informal, chiefly US*), reading, version, delivery, presentation, execution, portrayal, depiction
2 TRANSLATION, reading, version, construction, explanation, interpretation, transcription

renegade *noun* DESERTER, rebel, betrayer, dissident, outlaw, runaway, traitor, defector, mutineer, turncoat, apostate, backslider, recreant (*archaic*)
▷ *modifier* TRAITOROUS, rebel, dissident, outlaw, runaway, rebellious, unfaithful, disloyal, backsliding, mutinous, apostate, recreant (*archaic*)

renege *verb* BREAK YOUR WORD, go back, welsh (*slang*), default, back out, repudiate, break a promise

renew *verb* 1 RECOMMENCE, continue, extend, repeat, resume, prolong, reopen, recreate, reaffirm, re-establish, rejuvenate, regenerate, restate, begin again, revitalize, bring up to date
2 REAFFIRM, resume, breathe new life into, recommence
3 REPLACE, refresh, replenish, restock
4 RESTORE, repair, transform, overhaul, mend, refurbish, renovate, refit, fix up (*informal, chiefly US & Canad*), modernize

renounce *verb* 1 DISOWN, reject, abandon, quit, discard, spurn, eschew, leave off, throw off, forsake, retract, repudiate, cast off, abstain from, recant, forswear, abjure, swear off, wash your hands of
2 DISCLAIM, deny, decline, give up, resign, relinquish, waive, renege, forgo, abdicate, abjure, abnegate
<< OPPOSITE assert

renovate *verb* RESTORE, repair, refurbish, do up (*informal*), reform, renew, overhaul, revamp, recreate, remodel, rehabilitate, refit, fix up (*informal, chiefly US & Canad*), modernize, reconstitute, recondition

renown *noun* FAME, note, distinction, repute, mark, reputation, honour, glory, celebrity, acclaim, stardom, eminence, lustre, illustriousness

renowned *adjective* FAMOUS, noted, celebrated, well-known, distinguished, esteemed, acclaimed, notable, eminent, famed, illustrious
<< OPPOSITE unknown

rent[1] *verb* 1 HIRE, lease
2 LET, lease
▷ *noun* HIRE, rental, lease, tariff, fee, payment

rent[2] *noun* 1 TEAR, split, rip, slash, slit, gash, perforation, hole
2 OPENING, break, hole, crack, breach, flaw, chink

renunciation *noun* 1 REJECTION, giving up, denial, abandonment, spurning, abstention, repudiation, forswearing, disavowal, abnegation, eschewal, abjuration
2 GIVING UP, resignation, surrender, waiver, disclaimer, abdication, relinquishment, abjuration

repair[1] *verb* 1 MEND, fix, recover, restore, heal, renew, patch, make good, renovate, patch up, put back together, restore to working order
<< OPPOSITE damage
2 PUT RIGHT, make up for, compensate for, rectify, square, retrieve, redress
▷ *noun* 1 MEND, restoration, overhaul, adjustment
2 DARN, mend, patch

3 CONDITION, state, form, shape (*informal*), nick (*informal*), fettle

repair² *verb* GO, retire, withdraw, head for, move, remove, leave for, set off for, betake yourself

reparation *noun* COMPENSATION, damages, repair, satisfaction, amends, renewal, redress, indemnity, restitution, atonement, recompense, propitiation, requital

repay *verb* 1 PAY BACK, refund, settle up, return, square, restore, compensate, reimburse, recompense, requite, remunerate
2 REWARD, make restitution

repeal *verb* ABOLISH, reverse, revoke, annul, recall, withdraw, cancel, set aside, rescind, invalidate, nullify, obviate, abrogate, countermand, declare null and void
<< OPPOSITE pass
▷ *noun* ABOLITION, withdrawal, cancellation, rescinding, annulment, revocation, nullification, abrogation, rescission, invalidation, rescindment
<< OPPOSITE passing

repeat *verb* 1 REITERATE, restate, recapitulate, iterate
2 RETELL, relate, quote, renew, echo, replay, reproduce, rehearse, recite, duplicate, redo, rerun, reshow
▷ *noun* 1 REPETITION, echo, duplicate, reiteration, recapitulation
2 RERUN, replay, reproduction, reshowing

> Since the sense of *again* is already contained within the *re-* part of the word *repeat*, it is unnecessary to say that something is *repeated again*

repeatedly *adverb* OVER AND OVER, often, frequently, many times, again and again, time and (time) again, time after time, many a time and oft (*archaic* or *poetic*)

repel *verb* 1 DRIVE OFF, fight, refuse, check, decline, reject, oppose, resist, confront, parry, hold off, rebuff, ward off, beat off, repulse, keep at arm's length, put to flight
<< OPPOSITE submit to
2 DISGUST, offend, revolt, sicken, nauseate, put you off, make you sick, gross out (*US slang*), turn you off (*informal*), make you shudder, turn your stomach, give you the creeps (*informal*)
<< OPPOSITE delight ▷ see **repulse**

repellent *adjective* 1 DISGUSTING, offensive, revolting, obscene, sickening, distasteful, horrid, obnoxious, repulsive, noxious, nauseating, odious, hateful, repugnant, off-putting (*Brit informal*), loathsome, abhorrent, abominable, cringe-making (*Brit informal*), yucky *or* yukky (*slang*), yucko (*Austral slang*), discouraging
2 PROOF, resistant, repelling, impermeable

repent *verb* REGRET, lament, rue, sorrow, be sorry about, deplore, be ashamed of, relent, atone for, be contrite about, feel remorse about, reproach yourself for, see the error of your ways, show penitence

repentance *noun* REGRET, guilt, grief, sorrow, remorse, contrition, compunction, penitence, self-reproach, sackcloth and ashes, sorriness

repercussion *noun often plural* CONSEQUENCES, result, side effects, backlash, sequel

repertoire *noun* RANGE, list, stock, supply, store, collection, repertory, repository

repertory *noun* REPERTOIRE, list, range, stock, supply, store, collection, repository

repetition *noun* 1 RECURRENCE, repeating, reappearance, duplication, echo
2 REPEATING, redundancy, replication, duplication, restatement, iteration, reiteration, tautology, recapitulation, repetitiousness

repetitive *adjective* MONOTONOUS, boring, dull, mechanical, tedious, recurrent, unchanging, samey (*informal*), unvaried

replace *verb* 1 TAKE THE PLACE OF, follow, succeed, oust, take over from, supersede, supplant, stand in lieu of, fill (someone's) shoes *or* boots, step into (someone's) shoes *or* boots
2 SUBSTITUTE, change, exchange, switch, swap, commute
3 PUT BACK, restore

replacement *noun* 1 REPLACING
2 SUCCESSOR, double, substitute, stand-in, fill-in, proxy, surrogate, understudy

replenish *verb* 1 FILL, top up, refill, replace, renew, furnish
<< OPPOSITE empty
2 REFILL, provide, stock, supply, fill, make up, restore, top up, reload, restock

replete *adjective* 1 FILLED, stuffed, jammed, crammed, abounding, brimming, teeming, glutted, well-stocked, jam-packed, well-provided, chock-full, brimful, full to bursting, charged
<< OPPOSITE empty
2 SATED, full, gorged, full up, satiated
<< OPPOSITE hungry

replica *noun* 1 REPRODUCTION, model, copy, imitation, facsimile, carbon copy
<< OPPOSITE original
2 DUPLICATE, copy, carbon copy

replicate *verb* COPY, follow, repeat, reproduce, recreate, ape, mimic, duplicate, reduplicate

reply *verb* ANSWER, respond, retort, return, come back, counter, acknowledge, react, echo, rejoin, retaliate, write back, reciprocate, riposte, make answer
▷ *noun* ANSWER, response, reaction, counter, echo, comeback (*informal*), retort, retaliation,

acknowledgment, riposte, counterattack, return, rejoinder, reciprocation

report *verb* 1 INFORM OF, communicate, announce, mention, declare, recount, give an account of, bring word on
2 *often with* **on** COMMUNICATE, publish, record, announce, tell, state, air, detail, describe, note, cover, document, give an account of, relate, broadcast, pass on, proclaim, circulate, relay, recite, narrate, write up
3 PRESENT YOURSELF, come, appear, arrive, turn up, be present, show up (*informal*), clock in *or* on
▷ *noun* 1 ARTICLE, story, dispatch, piece, message, communiqué, write-up
2 ACCOUNT, record, detail, note, statement, relation, version, communication, tale, description, declaration, narrative, summary, recital
3 *often plural* NEWS, word, information, announcement, tidings
4 BANG, sound, crash, crack, noise, blast, boom, explosion, discharge, detonation, reverberation
5 RUMOUR, talk, buzz, gossip, goss (*informal*), hearsay, scuttlebutt (*US slang*)
6 REPUTE, character, regard, reputation, fame, esteem, eminence

reporter *noun* JOURNALIST, writer, correspondent, newscaster, hack (*derogatory*), announcer, pressman, journo (*slang*), newshound (*informal*), newspaperman *or* newspaperwoman

repose[1] *noun* 1 REST, relaxation, inactivity, restfulness
2 PEACE, rest, quiet, ease, relaxation, respite, tranquillity, stillness, inactivity, quietness, quietude, restfulness
3 COMPOSURE, dignity, peace of mind, poise, serenity, tranquillity, aplomb, calmness, equanimity, self-possession
▷ *verb* LIE, rest, sleep, relax, lie down, recline, take it easy, slumber, rest upon, lie upon, drowse, outspan (*S African*), take your ease

repose[2] *verb* PLACE, put, store, invest, deposit, lodge, confide, entrust

repository *noun* STORE, archive, storehouse, depository, magazine, treasury, warehouse, vault, depot, emporium, receptacle

reprehensible *adjective* BLAMEWORTHY, bad, disgraceful, shameful, delinquent, errant, unworthy, objectionable, culpable, ignoble, discreditable, remiss, erring, opprobrious, condemnable, censurable
<< OPPOSITE praiseworthy

represent *verb* 1 ACT FOR, speak for
2 STAND FOR, substitute for, play the part of, assume the role of, serve as
3 EXPRESS, equal, correspond to, symbolize, equate with, mean, betoken
4 EXEMPLIFY, embody, symbolize, typify, personify, epitomize
5 DEPICT, show, describe, picture, express, illustrate, outline, portray, sketch, render, designate, reproduce, evoke, denote, delineate
▷▷ **represent someone as something** *or* **someone** MAKE OUT TO BE, describe as

representation *noun* 1 BODY OF REPRESENTATIVES, committee, embassy, delegates, delegation
2 PICTURE, model, image, portrait, illustration, sketch, resemblance, likeness
3 PORTRAYAL, depiction, account, relation, description, narrative, narration, delineation
4 *often plural* STATEMENT, argument, explanation, exposition, remonstrance, expostulation, account

representative *noun* 1 DELEGATE, member, agent, deputy, commissioner, councillor, proxy, depute (*Scot*), spokesman *or* spokeswoman
2 MEMBER, congressman *or* congresswoman (*US*), member of parliament, Member of Congress (*US*), M.P.
3 AGENT, salesman, rep, traveller, commercial traveller
▷ *adjective* 1 CHOSEN, elected, delegated, elective
2 TYPICAL, characteristic, archetypal, exemplary, illustrative
<< OPPOSITE uncharacteristic
3 SYMBOLIC, evocative, emblematic, typical

repress *verb* 1 CONTROL, suppress, hold back, bottle up, check, master, hold in, overcome, curb, restrain, inhibit, overpower, keep in check
<< OPPOSITE release
2 HOLD BACK, suppress, stifle, smother, silence, swallow, muffle
3 SUBDUE, abuse, crush, quash, wrong, persecute, quell, subjugate, maltreat, trample underfoot, tyrannize over, rule with an iron hand
<< OPPOSITE liberate

repression *noun* 1 SUBJUGATION, control, constraint, domination, censorship, tyranny, coercion, authoritarianism, despotism
2 SUPPRESSION, crushing, prohibition, quashing, dissolution
3 INHIBITION, control, holding in, restraint, suppression, bottling up

repressive *adjective* OPPRESSIVE, tough, severe, absolute, harsh, authoritarian, dictatorial, coercive, tyrannical, despotic
<< OPPOSITE democratic

reprieve *verb* GRANT A STAY OF EXECUTION TO, pardon, let off the hook (*slang*), postpone *or* remit the punishment of

▷ *noun* STAY OF EXECUTION, suspension, amnesty, pardon, remission, abeyance, deferment, postponement of punishment

reprimand *verb* BLAME, censure, rebuke, reproach, check, lecture, carpet (*informal*), scold, tick off (*informal*), castigate, chide, dress down (*informal*), admonish, tear into (*informal*), tell off (*informal*), take to task, read the riot act, tongue-lash, reprove, upbraid, slap on the wrist (*informal*), bawl out (*informal*), rap over the knuckles, haul over the coals (*informal*), chew out (*US & Canad informal*), tear (someone) off a strip (*Brit informal*), give a rocket (*Brit & NZ informal*), reprehend, give (someone) a row (*informal*), send someone away with a flea in his *or* her ear (*informal*)

<< OPPOSITE praise

▷ *noun* BLAME, talking-to (*informal*), row, lecture, wigging (*Brit slang*), censure, rebuke, reproach, ticking-off (*informal*), dressing-down (*informal*), telling-off (*informal*), admonition, tongue-lashing, reproof, castigation, reprehension, flea in your ear (*informal*)

<< OPPOSITE praise

reprisal *noun* RETALIATION, revenge, vengeance, retribution, an eye for an eye, counterstroke, requital

reproach *verb* BLAME, criticize, rebuke, reprimand, abuse, blast, condemn, carpet (*informal*), discredit, censure, have a go at (*informal*), scold, disparage, chide, tear into (*informal*), diss (*slang, chiefly US*), defame, find fault with, take to task, read the riot act to, reprove, upbraid, lambast(e), bawl out (*informal*), chew out (*US & Canad informal*), tear (someone) off a strip (*Brit informal*), give a rocket (*Brit & NZ informal*), reprehend

▷ *noun* **1** REBUKE, lecture, wigging (*Brit slang*), censure, reprimand, scolding, ticking-off (*informal*), dressing down (*informal*), telling-off (*informal*), admonition, tongue-lashing, reproof, castigation, reproval

2 CENSURE, blame, abuse, contempt, condemnation, scorn, disapproval, opprobrium, odium, obloquy

3 DISGRACE, shame, slight, stain, discredit, stigma, slur, disrepute, blemish, indignity, ignominy, dishonour

reproduce *verb* **1** COPY, recreate, replicate, duplicate, match, represent, mirror, echo, parallel, imitate, emulate

2 PRINT, copy, transcribe

3 (*Biology*) BREED, produce young, procreate, generate, multiply, spawn, propagate, proliferate

reproduction *noun* **1** COPY, picture, print, replica, imitation, duplicate, facsimile

<< OPPOSITE original

2 (*Biology*) BREEDING, procreation, propagation, increase, generation, proliferation, multiplication

Republican *adjective* RIGHT-WING, Conservative

▷ *noun* RIGHT-WINGER, Conservative

repudiate *verb* **1** REJECT, renounce, retract, disown, abandon, desert, reverse, cut off, discard, revoke, forsake, cast off, rescind, disavow, turn your back on, abjure, wash your hands of

<< OPPOSITE assert

2 DENY, oppose, disagree with, rebuff, refute, disprove, rebut, disclaim, gainsay (*archaic or literary*)

repugnant *adjective* **1** DISTASTEFUL, offensive, foul, disgusting, revolting, sickening, vile, horrid, repellent, obnoxious, objectionable, nauseating, odious, hateful, loathsome, abhorrent, abominable, yucky *or* yukky (*slang*), yucko (*Austral slang*)

<< OPPOSITE pleasant

2 INCOMPATIBLE, opposed, hostile, adverse, contradictory, inconsistent, averse, antagonistic, inimical, antipathetic

<< OPPOSITE compatible

repulse *verb* **1** DRIVE BACK, check, defeat, fight off, repel, rebuff, ward off, beat off, throw back

2 REJECT, refuse, turn down, snub, disregard, disdain, spurn, rebuff, give the cold shoulder to

▷ *noun* **1** DEFEAT, check

2 REJECTION, refusal, snub, spurning, rebuff, knock-back (*slang*), cold shoulder, kick in the teeth (*slang*), the (old) heave-ho (*informal*)

Some people think that the use of *repulse* in sentences such as *he was repulsed by what he saw* is incorrect and that the correct word is *repel*

repulsive *adjective* DISGUSTING, offensive, foul, ugly, forbidding, unpleasant, revolting, obscene, sickening, hideous, vile, distasteful, horrid, repellent, obnoxious, objectionable, disagreeable, nauseating, odious, hateful, loathsome, abhorrent, abominable, yucky *or* yukky (*slang*), yucko (*Austral slang*)

<< OPPOSITE delightful

reputable *adjective* RESPECTABLE, good, excellent, reliable, worthy, legitimate, upright, honourable, honoured, trustworthy, creditable, estimable, well-thought-of, of good repute

<< OPPOSITE disreputable

reputation *noun* NAME, standing, credit, character, honour, fame, distinction, esteem, stature, eminence, renown, repute

repute *noun* **1** REPUTATION, standing, fame, celebrity, distinction, esteem, stature, eminence, estimation, renown

2 NAME, character, reputation

reputed *adjective* **1** SUPPOSED, said, seeming,

held, believed, thought, considered, accounted, regarded, estimated, alleged, reckoned, rumoured, deemed
2 APPARENT, supposed, putative, ostensible

reputedly *adverb* SUPPOSEDLY, apparently, allegedly, seemingly, ostensibly

request *verb* 1 ASK FOR, apply for, appeal for, put in for, demand, desire, pray for, beg for, requisition, beseech
2 INVITE, call for, beg, petition, beseech, entreat, supplicate
3 SEEK, ask (for), sue for, solicit
▷ *noun* 1 APPEAL, call, demand, plea, desire, application, prayer, petition, requisition, solicitation, entreaty, supplication, suit
2 ASKING, plea, begging

require *verb* 1 NEED, crave, depend upon, have need of, want, miss, lack, wish, desire, stand in need of
2 DEMAND, take, involve, call for, entail, necessitate
3 ORDER, demand, direct, command, compel, exact, oblige, instruct, call upon, constrain, insist upon
4 ASK, enjoin

> The use of *require to* as in *I require to see the manager* or *you require to complete a special form* is thought by many people to be incorrect. Useful alternatives are: *I need to see the manager* and *you are required to complete a special form*

required *adjective* OBLIGATORY, prescribed, compulsory, mandatory, needed, set, demanded, necessary, called for, essential, recommended, vital, unavoidable, requisite, de rigueur (*French*)
<< OPPOSITE optional

requirement *noun* NECESSITY, demand, specification, stipulation, want, need, must, essential, qualification, precondition, requisite, prerequisite, sine qua non (*Latin*), desideratum, must-have

requisite *adjective* NECESSARY, needed, required, called for, essential, vital, mandatory, indispensable, obligatory, prerequisite, needful
▷ *noun* NECESSITY, condition, requirement, precondition, need, must, essential, prerequisite, sine qua non (*Latin*), desideratum, must-have

requisition *verb* 1 TAKE OVER, appropriate, occupy, seize, commandeer, take possession of
2 DEMAND, call for, request, apply for, put in for
▷ *noun* 1 DEMAND, request, call, application, summons
2 TAKEOVER, occupation, seizure, appropriation, commandeering

rescind *verb* ANNUL, recall, reverse, cancel, overturn, set aside, void, repeal, quash, revoke, retract, invalidate, obviate, abrogate, countermand, declare null and void
<< OPPOSITE confirm

rescue *verb* 1 SAVE, get out, save the life of, extricate, free, release, deliver, recover, liberate, set free, save (someone's) bacon (*Brit informal*)
<< OPPOSITE desert
2 SALVAGE, deliver, redeem, come to the rescue of
▷ *noun* SAVING, salvage, deliverance, extrication, release, relief, recovery, liberation, salvation, redemption

research *noun* INVESTIGATION, study, inquiry, analysis, examination, probe, exploration, scrutiny, experimentation, delving, groundwork, fact-finding
▷ *verb* INVESTIGATE, study, examine, experiment, explore, probe, analyse, look into, work over, scrutinize, make inquiries, do tests, consult the archives

resemblance *noun* SIMILARITY, correspondence, conformity, semblance, image, comparison, parallel, counterpart, analogy, affinity, closeness, parity, likeness, kinship, facsimile, sameness, comparability, similitude
<< OPPOSITE dissimilarity

resemble *verb* BE LIKE, look like, favour (*informal*), mirror, echo, parallel, be similar to, duplicate, take after, remind you of, bear a resemblance to, put you in mind of

resent *verb* BE BITTER ABOUT, dislike, object to, grudge, begrudge, take exception to, be offended by, be angry about, take offence at, take umbrage at, harbour a grudge against, take as an insult, bear a grudge about, be in a huff about, take amiss to, have hard feelings about
<< OPPOSITE be content with

resentful *adjective* BITTER, hurt, wounded, angry, offended, put out, jealous, choked, incensed, grudging, exasperated, aggrieved, indignant, irate, miffed (*informal*), embittered, unforgiving, peeved (*informal*), in a huff, piqued, huffy, in high dudgeon, revengeful, huffish, tooshie (*Austral slang*)
<< OPPOSITE content

resentment *noun* BITTERNESS, indignation, ill feeling, ill will, hurt, anger, rage, fury, irritation, grudge, wrath, malice, animosity, huff, ire, displeasure, pique, rancour, bad blood, umbrage, vexation, chip on your shoulder (*informal*)

reservation *noun* 1 *often plural* DOUBT, scepticism, scruples, demur, hesitancy
2 RESERVE, territory, preserve, homeland, sanctuary, tract, enclave

reserve *verb* 1 BOOK, prearrange, pre-engage, engage, bespeak
2 PUT BY, secure, retain
3 KEEP, hold, save, husband, store, retain, preserve, set aside, withhold, hang on to, conserve, stockpile, hoard, lay up, put by, keep back
4 DELAY, postpone, withhold, put off, defer, keep back
▷ *noun* 1 STORE, fund, savings, stock, capital, supply, reservoir, fall-back, stockpile, hoard, backlog, cache
2 PARK, reservation, preserve, sanctuary, tract, forest park (NZ)
3 SHYNESS, silence, restraint, constraint, reluctance, formality, modesty, reticence, coolness, aloofness, secretiveness, taciturnity
4 RESERVATION, doubt, delay, uncertainty, indecision, hesitancy, vacillation, irresolution, dubiety
5 SUBSTITUTE, extra, spare, alternative, fall-back, auxiliary
reserved *adjective* 1 UNCOMMUNICATIVE, cold, cool, retiring, formal, silent, modest, shy, cautious, restrained, secretive, aloof, reticent, prim, demure, taciturn, unresponsive, unapproachable, unsociable, undemonstrative, standoffish, close-mouthed, unforthcoming
<< OPPOSITE uninhibited
2 SET ASIDE, taken, kept, held, booked, retained, engaged, restricted, spoken for
reservoir *noun* 1 LAKE, pond, basin
2 REPOSITORY, store, tank, holder, container, receptacle
3 STORE, stock, source, supply, reserves, fund, pool, accumulation, stockpile
reside *verb* 1 (*Formal*) LIVE, lodge, dwell, have your home, remain, stay, settle, abide, hang out (*informal*), sojourn
<< OPPOSITE visit
2 BE PRESENT, lie, exist, consist, dwell, abide, rest with, be intrinsic to, inhere, be vested
residence *noun* 1 HOME, house, household, dwelling, place, quarters, flat, lodging, pad (*slang*), abode, habitation, domicile
2 MANSION, seat, hall, palace, villa, manor
3 STAY, tenancy, occupancy, occupation, sojourn
resident *noun* 1 INHABITANT, citizen, denizen, indweller, local
<< OPPOSITE nonresident
2 TENANT, occupant, lodger
3 GUEST, lodger
▷ *adjective* 1 INHABITING, living, settled, dwelling
<< OPPOSITE nonresident
2 LOCAL, neighbourhood
residual *adjective* REMAINING, net, unused, leftover, vestigial, nett, unconsumed
residue *noun* REMAINDER, remains, remnant, leftovers, rest, extra, balance, excess, surplus, dregs, residuum
resign *verb* 1 QUIT, leave, step down (*informal*), vacate, abdicate, call it a day *or* night, give *or* hand in your notice
2 GIVE UP, abandon, yield, hand over, surrender, turn over, relinquish, renounce, forsake, cede, forgo
▷▷ **resign yourself to something** ACCEPT, reconcile yourself to, succumb to, submit to, bow to, give in to, yield to, acquiesce to
resignation *noun* 1 LEAVING, notice, retirement, departure, surrender, abandonment, abdication, renunciation, relinquishment
2 ACCEPTANCE, patience, submission, compliance, endurance, fortitude, passivity, acquiescence, forbearing, sufferance, nonresistance
<< OPPOSITE resistance
resigned *adjective* STOICAL, patient, subdued, long-suffering, compliant, submissive, acquiescent, unresisting, unprotesting
resilient *adjective* 1 FLEXIBLE, plastic, elastic, supple, bouncy, rubbery, pliable, springy, whippy
<< OPPOSITE rigid
2 TOUGH, strong, hardy, buoyant, feisty (*informal, chiefly US & Canad*), bouncy, irrepressible, quick to recover
<< OPPOSITE weak
resist *verb* 1 OPPOSE, fight, battle against, refuse, check, weather, dispute, confront, combat, defy, curb, thwart, stand up to, hinder, contend with, counteract, hold out against, put up a fight (against), countervail
<< OPPOSITE accept
2 FIGHT AGAINST, fight, struggle against, put up a fight (against)
3 REFRAIN FROM, refuse, avoid, turn down, leave alone, keep from, forgo, abstain from, forbear, prevent yourself from
<< OPPOSITE indulge in
4 WITHSTAND, repel, be proof against
resistance *noun* 1 OPPOSITION, hostility, aversion
2 FIGHTING, fight, battle, struggle, combat, contention, defiance, obstruction, impediment, intransigence, hindrance, counteraction
Resistance *noun* FREEDOM FIGHTERS, underground, guerrillas, partisans, irregulars, maquis
resistant *adjective* 1 OPPOSED, hostile, dissident, unwilling, defiant, intractable, combative, recalcitrant, antagonistic, intransigent

2 IMPERVIOUS, hard, strong, tough, unaffected, unyielding, insusceptible

resolute *adjective* DETERMINED, set, firm, dogged, fixed, constant, bold, relentless, stubborn, stalwart, staunch, persevering, inflexible, purposeful, tenacious, undaunted, strong-willed, steadfast, obstinate, unwavering, immovable, unflinching, unbending, unshakable, unshaken
<< OPPOSITE irresolute

resolution *noun* 1 DECLARATION, motion, verdict, judgment
2 DECISION, resolve, intention, aim, purpose, determination, intent
3 DETERMINATION, energy, purpose, resolve, courage, dedication, fortitude, sincerity, tenacity, perseverance, willpower, boldness, firmness, staying power, stubbornness, constancy, earnestness, obstinacy, steadfastness, doggedness, relentlessness, resoluteness, staunchness
4 SOLUTION, end, settlement, outcome, finding, answer, working out, solving, sorting out, unravelling, upshot

resolve *verb* 1 WORK OUT, answer, solve, find the solution to, clear up, crack, fathom, suss (out) (*slang*), elucidate
2 DECIDE, determine, undertake, make up your mind, agree, design, settle, purpose, intend, fix, conclude
3 CHANGE, convert, transform, alter, metamorphose, transmute
4 DISPEL, explain, remove, clear up, banish
▷ *noun* 1 DETERMINATION, resolution, courage, willpower, boldness, firmness, earnestness, steadfastness, resoluteness
<< OPPOSITE indecision
2 DECISION, resolution, undertaking, objective, design, project, purpose, conclusion, intention

resonant *adjective* 1 SONOROUS, full, rich, ringing, booming, vibrant
2 ECHOING, resounding, reverberating, reverberant

resort *noun* 1 HOLIDAY CENTRE, spot, retreat, haunt, refuge, tourist centre, watering place (*Brit*)
2 RECOURSE TO, reference to
▷▷ **resort to something** HAVE RECOURSE TO, turn to, fall back on, bring into play, use, exercise, employ, look to, make use of, utilize, avail yourself of

resound *verb* 1 ECHO, resonate, reverberate, fill the air, re-echo
2 RING

resounding *adjective* ECHOING, full, sounding, rich, ringing, powerful, booming, vibrant, reverberating, resonant, sonorous

resource *noun* 1 SUPPLY, source, reserve, stockpile, hoard
2 FACILITY
3 MEANS, course, resort, device, expedient
▷ *plural noun* 1 FUNDS, means, holdings, money, capital, wherewithal, riches, materials, assets, wealth, property
2 RESERVES, supplies, stocks

resourceful *adjective* INGENIOUS, able, bright, talented, sharp, capable, creative, clever, imaginative, inventive, quick-witted
<< OPPOSITE unimaginative

respect *verb* 1 THINK HIGHLY OF, value, regard, honour, recognize, appreciate, admire, esteem, adore, revere, reverence, look up to, defer to, venerate, set store by, have a good *or* high opinion of
2 SHOW CONSIDERATION FOR, regard, notice, honour, observe, heed, attend to, pay attention to
3 ABIDE BY, follow, observe, comply with, obey, heed, keep to, adhere to
<< OPPOSITE disregard
▷ *noun* 1 REGARD, honour, recognition, esteem, appreciation, admiration, reverence, estimation, veneration, approbation
<< OPPOSITE contempt
2 CONSIDERATION, kindness, deference, friendliness, tact, thoughtfulness, solicitude, kindliness, considerateness
3 PARTICULAR, way, point, matter, sense, detail, feature, aspect, characteristic, facet
▷ *plural noun* GREETINGS, regards, compliments, good wishes, salutations, devoirs
▷▷ **in respect of** *or* **with respect to** CONCERNING, in relation to, in connection with, with regard to, with reference to, apropos of

respectable *adjective* 1 HONOURABLE, good, respected, decent, proper, worthy, upright, admirable, honest, dignified, venerable, reputable, decorous, estimable
<< OPPOSITE disreputable
2 DECENT, neat, tidy (*informal*), spruce
3 REASONABLE, considerable, substantial, fair, tidy (*informal*), ample, tolerable, presentable, appreciable, fairly good, sizable *or* sizeable, goodly
<< OPPOSITE small

respectful *adjective* POLITE, civil, mannerly, humble, gracious, courteous, obedient, submissive, self-effacing, dutiful, courtly, deferential, reverential, solicitous, reverent, regardful, well-mannered

respective *adjective* SPECIFIC, own, several, individual, personal, particular, various, separate, relevant, corresponding

respite *noun* 1 PAUSE, break, rest, relief, halt, interval, relaxation, recess, interruption, lull, cessation, let-up (*informal*), breathing space,

breather (*informal*), hiatus, intermission
2 REPRIEVE, stay, delay, suspension, moratorium, postponement, adjournment
resplendent *adjective* BRILLIANT, radiant, splendid, glorious, bright, shining, beaming, glittering, dazzling, gleaming, luminous, lustrous, refulgent (*literary*), effulgent, irradiant
respond *verb* 1 ANSWER, return, reply, come back, counter, acknowledge, retort, rejoin
<< OPPOSITE remain silent
2 *often with* **to** REPLY TO, answer
3 REACT, retaliate, reciprocate, take the bait, rise to the bait, act in response
response *noun* ANSWER, return, reply, reaction, comeback (*informal*), feedback, retort, acknowledgment, riposte, counterattack, rejoinder, counterblast
responsibility *noun* 1 DUTY, business, job, role, task, accountability, answerability
2 FAULT, blame, liability, guilt, culpability, burden
3 OBLIGATION, duty, liability, charge, care
4 AUTHORITY, power, importance, mana (*NZ*)
5 JOB, task, function, role, pigeon (*informal*)
6 LEVEL-HEADEDNESS, stability, maturity, reliability, rationality, dependability, trustworthiness, conscientiousness, soberness, sensibleness
responsible *adjective* 1 TO BLAME, guilty, at fault, culpable
2 IN CHARGE, in control, at the helm, in authority, carrying the can (*informal*)
3 ACCOUNTABLE, subject, bound, liable, amenable, answerable, duty-bound, chargeable, under obligation
<< OPPOSITE unaccountable
4 SENSIBLE, sound, adult, stable, mature, reliable, rational, sober, conscientious, dependable, trustworthy, level-headed
<< OPPOSITE unreliable
5 AUTHORITATIVE, high, important, executive, decision-making
responsive *adjective* SENSITIVE, open, aware, sharp, alive, forthcoming, sympathetic, awake, susceptible, receptive, reactive, perceptive, impressionable, quick to react
<< OPPOSITE unresponsive
rest[1] *verb* 1 RELAX, sleep, take it easy, lie down, idle, nap, be calm, doze, sit down, slumber, kip (*Brit slang*), snooze (*informal*), laze, lie still, be at ease, put your feet up, take a nap, drowse, mellow out (*informal*), have a snooze (*informal*), refresh yourself, outspan (*S African*), zizz (*Brit informal*), have forty winks (*informal*), take your ease
<< OPPOSITE work
2 STOP, have a break, break off, take a breather (*informal*), stay, halt, cease, discontinue, knock off (*informal*), desist, come to a standstill
<< OPPOSITE keep going
3 DEPEND, turn, lie, be founded, hang, be based, rely, hinge, reside
4 PLACE, lay, repose, stretch out, stand, sit, lean, prop
5 BE PLACED, sit, lie, be supported, recline
▷ *noun* 1 SLEEP, snooze (*informal*), lie-down, nap, doze, slumber, kip (*Brit slang*), siesta, forty winks (*informal*), zizz (*Brit informal*)
2 RELAXATION, repose, leisure, idleness, me-time
<< OPPOSITE work
3 PAUSE, break, breather, time off, stop, holiday, halt, interval, vacation, respite, lull, interlude, cessation, breathing space (*informal*), intermission
4 REFRESHMENT, release, relief, ease, comfort, cure, remedy, solace, balm, deliverance, mitigation, abatement, alleviation, easement, palliation, assuagement
5 INACTIVITY, a halt, a stop, a standstill, motionlessness
6 SUPPORT, stand, base, holder, shelf, prop, trestle
7 CALM, tranquillity, stillness, somnolence
▷▷ **at rest** 1 MOTIONLESS, still, stopped, at a standstill, unmoving
2 CALM, still, cool, quiet, pacific, peaceful, composed, serene, tranquil, at peace, sedate, placid, undisturbed, restful, untroubled, unperturbed, unruffled, unexcited
3 ASLEEP, resting, sleeping, napping, dormant, crashed out (*slang*), dozing, slumbering, snoozing (*informal*), fast asleep, sound asleep, out for the count, dead to the world (*informal*)
rest[2] *noun* REMAINDER, remains, excess, remnants, others, balance, surplus, residue, rump, leftovers, residuum
▷ *verb* CONTINUE BEING, keep being, remain, stay, be left, go on being
restaurant *noun* CAFÉ, diner (*chiefly US & Canad*), bistro, cafeteria, trattoria, tearoom, eatery *or* eaterie
restful *adjective* RELAXING, quiet, relaxed, comfortable, pacific, calm, calming, peaceful, soothing, sleepy, serene, tranquil, placid, undisturbed, languid, unhurried, tranquillizing
<< OPPOSITE busy
restitution *noun* 1 (*Law*) COMPENSATION, satisfaction, amends, refund, repayment, redress, remuneration, reparation, indemnity, reimbursement, recompense, indemnification, requital
2 RETURN, replacement, restoration, reinstatement, re-establishment, reinstallation
restive *adjective* RESTLESS, nervous, uneasy,

impatient, agitated, unruly, edgy, jittery (*informal*), recalcitrant, on edge, fractious, ill at ease, jumpy, fretful, fidgety, refractory, unquiet, antsy (*informal*)

<< OPPOSITE calm

restless *adjective* **1** UNSETTLED, worried, troubled, nervous, disturbed, anxious, uneasy, agitated, unruly, edgy, fidgeting, on edge, ill at ease, restive, jumpy, fitful, fretful, fidgety, unquiet, antsy (*informal*)

<< OPPOSITE relaxed

2 SLEEPLESS, disturbed, wakeful, unsleeping, insomniac, tossing and turning

3 MOVING, active, wandering, unsettled, unstable, bustling, turbulent, hurried, roving, transient, nomadic, unsteady, changeable, footloose, irresolute, inconstant, having itchy feet

<< OPPOSITE settled

restlessness *noun* **1** MOVEMENT, activity, turmoil, unrest, instability, bustle, turbulence, hurry, transience, inconstancy, hurry-scurry, unsettledness

2 RESTIVENESS, anxiety, disturbance, nervousness, disquiet, agitation, insomnia, jitters (*informal*), uneasiness, edginess, heebie-jeebies (*slang*), jumpiness, fretfulness, ants in your pants (*slang*), fitfulness, inquietude, worriedness

restoration *noun* **1** REINSTATEMENT, return, revival, restitution, re-establishment, reinstallation, replacement

<< OPPOSITE abolition

2 REPAIR, recovery, reconstruction, renewal, rehabilitation, refurbishing, refreshment, renovation, rejuvenation, revitalization

<< OPPOSITE demolition

restore *verb* **1** REINSTATE, re-establish, reintroduce, reimpose, re-enforce, reconstitute

<< OPPOSITE abolish

2 REVIVE, build up, strengthen, bring back, refresh, rejuvenate, revitalize, revivify, reanimate

<< OPPOSITE make worse

3 RE-ESTABLISH, replace, reinstate, give back, reinstall, retrocede

4 REPAIR, refurbish, renovate, reconstruct, fix (up), recover, renew, rebuild, mend, rehabilitate, touch up, recondition, retouch, set to rights

<< OPPOSITE demolish

5 RETURN, replace, recover, bring back, send back, hand back

restrain *verb* **1** HOLD BACK, hold, control, check, contain, prevent, restrict, handicap, confine, curb, hamper, rein, harness, subdue, hinder, constrain, curtail, bridle, debar, keep under control, have on a tight leash, straiten

<< OPPOSITE encourage

2 CONTROL, keep in, limit, govern, suppress, inhibit, repress, muzzle, keep under control

3 IMPRISON, hold, arrest, jail, bind, chain, confine, detain, tie up, lock up, fetter, manacle, pinion

<< OPPOSITE release

restrained *adjective* **1** CONTROLLED, reasonable, moderate, self-controlled, soft, calm, steady, mild, muted, reticent, temperate, undemonstrative

<< OPPOSITE hot-headed

2 UNOBTRUSIVE, discreet, subdued, tasteful, quiet

<< OPPOSITE garish

restraint *noun* **1** LIMITATION, limit, check, ban, boycott, embargo, curb, rein, taboo, bridle, disqualification, interdict, restraining order (*US Law*)

<< OPPOSITE freedom

2 SELF-CONTROL, self-discipline, self-restraint, self-possession, pulling your punches

<< OPPOSITE self-indulgence

3 CONSTRAINT, limitation, inhibition, moderation, hold, control, restriction, prevention, suppression, hindrance, curtailment

restrict *verb* **1** LIMIT, fix, regulate, specify, curb, ration, keep within bounds *or* limits

<< OPPOSITE widen

2 HAMPER, impede, handicap, restrain, cramp, inhibit, straiten

restriction *noun* **1** CONTROL, rule, condition, check, regulation, curb, restraint, constraint, confinement, containment, demarcation, stipulation

2 LIMITATION, handicap, inhibition

result *noun* **1** CONSEQUENCE, effect, outcome, end result, issue, event, development, product, reaction, fruit, sequel, upshot

<< OPPOSITE cause

2 OUTCOME, conclusion, end, decision, termination

▷ *verb often followed by* **from** ARISE, follow, issue, happen, appear, develop, spring, flow, turn out, stem, derive, ensue, emanate, eventuate

▷▷ **result in something** END IN, bring about, cause, lead to, wind up, finish with, culminate in, terminate in

resume *verb* **1** BEGIN AGAIN, continue, go on with, proceed with, carry on, reopen, restart, recommence, reinstitute, take up *or* pick up where you left off

<< OPPOSITE discontinue

2 TAKE UP AGAIN, assume again

3 OCCUPY AGAIN, take back, reoccupy

résumé *noun* **1** SUMMARY, synopsis, abstract, précis, review, digest, epitome, rundown, recapitulation

2 (US) CURRICULUM VITAE, CV, career history, details, biography

resumption *noun* CONTINUATION, carrying on, reopening, renewal, restart, resurgence, new beginning, re-establishment, fresh outbreak

resurgence *noun* REVIVAL, return, renaissance, resurrection, resumption, rebirth, re-emergence, recrudescence, renascence

resurrect *verb* 1 REVIVE, renew, bring back, kick-start (*informal*), reintroduce, breathe new life into
2 RESTORE TO LIFE, raise from the dead

resurrection *noun* 1 REVIVAL, restoration, renewal, resurgence, return, comeback (*informal*), renaissance, rebirth, reappearance, resuscitation, renascence
<< OPPOSITE killing off
2 RAISING *or* RISING FROM THE DEAD, return from the dead
<< OPPOSITE demise

resuscitate *verb* 1 GIVE ARTIFICIAL RESPIRATION TO, save, quicken, bring to life, bring round, give the kiss of life to
2 REVIVE, rescue, restore, renew, resurrect, revitalize, breathe new life into, revivify, reanimate

retain *verb* 1 MAINTAIN, keep, reserve, preserve, keep up, uphold, nurture, continue to have, hang *or* hold onto
2 KEEP, keep possession of, hang *or* hold onto, save
<< OPPOSITE let go
3 REMEMBER, recall, bear in mind, keep in mind, memorize, recollect, impress on the memory
<< OPPOSITE forget

retainer *noun* 1 FEE, advance, deposit
2 SERVANT, domestic, attendant, valet, supporter, dependant, henchman, footman, lackey, vassal, flunky

retaliate *verb* PAY SOMEONE BACK, hit back, strike back, reciprocate, take revenge, get back at someone, get even with (*informal*), even the score, get your own back (*informal*), wreak vengeance, exact retribution, give as good as you get (*informal*), take an eye for an eye, make reprisal, give (someone) a taste of his *or* her own medicine, give tit for tat, return like for like
<< OPPOSITE turn the other cheek

retaliation *noun* REVENGE, repayment, vengeance, reprisal, retribution, tit for tat, an eye for an eye, reciprocation, counterstroke, requital, counterblow, a taste of your own medicine

retard *verb* SLOW DOWN, check, arrest, delay, handicap, stall, brake, detain, defer, clog, hinder, obstruct, impede, set back, encumber, decelerate, hold back *or* up
<< OPPOSITE speed up

retch *verb* GAG, be sick, vomit, regurgitate, chuck (*Austral & NZ informal*), throw up (*informal*), spew, heave, puke (*slang*), disgorge, barf (*US slang*), chunder (*slang, chiefly Austral*), upchuck (*US slang*), do a technicolour yawn (*slang*), toss your cookies (*US slang*)

reticence *noun* SILENCE, reserve, restraint, quietness, secretiveness, taciturnity, uncommunicativeness, unforthcomingness

reticent *adjective* UNCOMMUNICATIVE, reserved, secretive, unforthcoming, quiet, silent, restrained, taciturn, tight-lipped, unspeaking, close-lipped, mum
<< OPPOSITE communicative ▷ see **reluctant**

retinue *noun* ATTENDANTS, entourage, escort, servants, following, train, suite, aides, followers, cortege

retire *verb* 1 STOP WORKING, give up work, be pensioned off, (be) put out to grass (*informal*)
2 WITHDRAW, leave, remove, exit, go away, depart, absent yourself, betake yourself
3 GO TO BED, turn in (*informal*), go to sleep, hit the sack (*slang*), go to your room, kip down (*Brit slang*), hit the hay (*slang*)
4 RETREAT, withdraw, pull out, give way, recede, pull back, back off, decamp, give ground

retirement *noun* WITHDRAWAL, retreat, privacy, loneliness, obscurity, solitude, seclusion

retiring *adjective* SHY, reserved, quiet, modest, shrinking, humble, timid, coy, meek, reclusive, reticent, unassuming, self-effacing, demure, diffident, bashful, timorous, unassertive
<< OPPOSITE outgoing

retort *verb* REPLY, return, answer, respond, counter, rejoin, retaliate, come back with, riposte, answer back
▷ *noun* REPLY, answer, response, comeback, riposte, rejoinder

retract *verb* 1 WITHDRAW, take back, revoke, disown, deny, recall, reverse, cancel, repeal, renounce, go back on, repudiate, rescind, renege on, back out of, disavow, recant, disclaim, abjure, eat your words, unsay
2 DRAW IN, pull in, pull back, reel in, sheathe

retreat *verb* WITHDRAW, retire, back off, draw back, leave, go back, shrink, depart, fall back, recede, pull back, back away, recoil, give ground, turn tail
<< OPPOSITE advance
▷ *noun* 1 FLIGHT, retirement, departure, withdrawal, evacuation
<< OPPOSITE advance
2 REFUGE, haven, resort, retirement, shelter, haunt, asylum, privacy, den, sanctuary,

hideaway, seclusion

retrenchment *noun* CUTBACK, cuts, economy, reduction, pruning, contraction, cost-cutting, rundown, curtailment, tightening your belt
<< OPPOSITE expansion

retribution *noun* PUNISHMENT, retaliation, reprisal, redress, justice, reward, reckoning, compensation, satisfaction, revenge, repayment, vengeance, Nemesis, recompense, an eye for an eye, requital

retrieve *verb* 1 GET BACK, regain, repossess, fetch back, recall, recover, restore, recapture
2 REDEEM, save, rescue, repair, salvage, win back, recoup

retro *adjective* OLD-TIME, old, former, past, period, antique, old-fashioned, nostalgia, old-world, bygone, of yesteryear

retrograde *adjective* DETERIORATING, backward, regressive, retrogressive, declining, negative, reverse, retreating, worsening, downward, waning, relapsing, inverse, degenerative

retrospect *noun* HINDSIGHT, review, afterthought, re-examination, survey, recollection, remembrance, reminiscence
<< OPPOSITE foresight

return *verb* 1 COME BACK, go back, repair, retreat, turn back, revert, reappear
<< OPPOSITE depart
2 PUT BACK, replace, restore, render, transmit, convey, send back, reinstate, take back, give back, carry back, retrocede
<< OPPOSITE keep
3 GIVE BACK, repay, refund, pay back, remit, reimburse, recompense
<< OPPOSITE keep
4 RECIPROCATE, requite, feel in return, respond to
5 RECUR, come back, repeat, persist, revert, happen again, reappear, come and go, come again
6 ANNOUNCE, report, come to, deliver, arrive at, bring in, submit, render
7 EARN, make, net, yield, bring in, repay
<< OPPOSITE lose
8 ELECT, choose, pick, vote in
▷ *noun* 1 REAPPEARANCE
<< OPPOSITE departure
2 RESTORATION, replacement, reinstatement, re-establishment
<< OPPOSITE removal
3 RECURRENCE, repetition, reappearance, reversion, persistence
4 PROFIT, interest, benefit, gain, income, advantage, revenue, yield, proceeds, takings, boot (*dialect*)
5 REPAYMENT, reward, compensation, reparation, reimbursement, recompense, reciprocation, requital, retaliation, meed (*archaic*)
6 STATEMENT, report, form, list, account, summary

revamp *verb* RENOVATE, restore, overhaul, refurbish, rehabilitate, do up (*informal*), patch up, refit, repair, fix up (*informal, chiefly US & Canad*), recondition, give a face-lift to

reveal *verb* 1 MAKE KNOWN, disclose, give away, make public, tell, announce, publish, broadcast, leak, communicate, proclaim, betray, give out, let out, impart, divulge, let slip, let on, take the wraps off (*informal*), blow wide open (*slang*), get off your chest (*informal*)
<< OPPOSITE keep secret
2 SHOW, display, bare, exhibit, unveil, uncover, manifest, unearth, unmask, lay bare, bring to light, expose to view
<< OPPOSITE hide

revel *verb* CELEBRATE, rave (*Brit slang*), carouse, live it up (*informal*), push the boat out (*Brit informal*), whoop it up (*informal*), make merry, paint the town red (*informal*), go on a spree, roister
▷ *noun often plural* MERRYMAKING, party, celebration, rave (*Brit slang*), gala, spree, festivity, beano (*Brit slang*), debauch, saturnalia, bacchanal, rave-up (*Brit slang*), jollification, carousal, hooley *or* hoolie (*chiefly Irish & NZ*), carouse
▷▷ **revel in something** ENJOY, relish, indulge in, delight in, savour, thrive on, bask in, wallow in, lap up, take pleasure in, drool over, luxuriate in, crow about, rejoice over, gloat about, rub your hands about

revelation *noun* 1 DISCLOSURE, discovery, news, broadcast, exposé, announcement, publication, exposure, leak, uncovering, confession, divulgence
2 EXHIBITION, telling, communication, broadcasting, discovery, publication, exposure, leaking, unveiling, uncovering, manifestation, unearthing, giveaway, proclamation, exposition

reveller *noun* MERRYMAKER, carouser, pleasure-seeker, partygoer, roisterer, celebrator

revelry *noun* MERRYMAKING, partying, fun, celebration, rave (*Brit slang*), spree, festivity, beano (*Brit slang*), debauch, debauchery, carouse, jollity, saturnalia, roistering, rave-up (*Brit slang*), jollification, carousal, hooley *or* hoolie (*chiefly Irish & NZ*)

revenge *noun* RETALIATION, satisfaction, vengeance, reprisal, retribution, vindictiveness, an eye for an eye, requital
▷ *verb* AVENGE, repay, vindicate, pay (someone) back, take revenge for, requite, even the score for, get your own back for (*informal*), make reprisal for, take an eye for an eye for

revenue *noun* INCOME, interest, returns, profits, gain, rewards, yield, proceeds, receipts, takings
<< OPPOSITE expenditure

reverberate *verb* ECHO, ring, resound, vibrate, re-echo

reverberation *noun* ECHO, ringing, resonance, resounding, vibration, re-echoing

revere *verb* BE IN AWE OF, respect, honour, worship, adore, reverence, exalt, look up to, defer to, venerate, have a high opinion of, put on a pedestal, think highly of
<< OPPOSITE despise

reverence *noun* RESPECT, honour, worship, admiration, awe, devotion, homage, deference, adoration, veneration, high esteem
<< OPPOSITE contempt
▷ *verb* REVERE, respect, honour, admire, worship, adore, pay homage to, venerate, be in awe of, hold in awe

reverent *adjective* RESPECTFUL, awed, solemn, deferential, loving, humble, adoring, devout, pious, meek, submissive, reverential
<< OPPOSITE disrespectful

reverie *noun* DAYDREAM, musing, preoccupation, trance, abstraction, daydreaming, inattention, absent-mindedness, brown study, woolgathering, castles in the air *or* Spain

reverse *verb* 1 (*Law*) CHANGE, alter, cancel, overturn, overthrow, set aside, undo, repeal, quash, revoke, overrule, retract, negate, rescind, invalidate, annul, obviate, countermand, declare null and void, overset, upset
<< OPPOSITE implement
2 TURN ROUND, turn over, turn upside down, upend
3 TRANSPOSE, change, move, exchange, transfer, switch, shift, alter, swap, relocate, rearrange, invert, interchange, reorder
4 GO BACKWARDS, retreat, back up, turn back, backtrack, move backwards, back
<< OPPOSITE go forward
▷ *noun* 1 OPPOSITE, contrary, converse, antithesis, inverse, contradiction
2 MISFORTUNE, check, defeat, blow, failure, disappointment, setback, hardship, reversal, adversity, mishap, affliction, repulse, trial, misadventure, vicissitude
3 BACK, rear, other side, wrong side, underside, flip side, verso
<< OPPOSITE front
▷ *adjective* 1 OPPOSITE, contrary, converse, inverse
2 BACKWARD, inverted, back to front

revert *verb* 1 GO BACK, return, come back, resume, lapse, recur, relapse, regress, backslide, take up where you left off
2 RETURN

> Since the concept *back* is already contained in the *re-* part of the word *revert*, it is unnecessary to say that someone *reverts back* to a particular type of behaviour

review *noun* 1 RE-EXAMINATION, revision, rethink, retrospect, another look, reassessment, fresh look, second look, reconsideration, re-evaluation, recapitulation
2 SURVEY, report, study, analysis, examination, scrutiny, perusal
3 CRITIQUE, commentary, evaluation, critical assessment, study, notice, criticism, judgment
4 INSPECTION, display, parade, procession, march past
5 MAGAZINE, journal, periodical, zine (*informal*)
▷ *verb* 1 RECONSIDER, revise, rethink, run over, reassess, re-examine, re-evaluate, think over, take another look at, recapitulate, look at again, go over again
2 ASSESS, write a critique of, study, judge, discuss, weigh, evaluate, criticize, read through, give your opinion of
3 INSPECT, check, survey, examine, vet, check out (*informal*), scrutinize, give (something *or* someone) the once-over (*informal*)
4 LOOK BACK ON, remember, recall, reflect on, summon up, recollect, call to mind

reviewer *noun* CRITIC, judge, commentator, connoisseur, arbiter, essayist

revile *verb* MALIGN, abuse, knock (*informal*), rubbish (*informal*), run down, smear, libel, scorn, slag (off) (*slang*), reproach, denigrate, vilify, slander, defame, bad-mouth (*slang, chiefly US & Canad*), traduce, calumniate, vituperate, asperse

revise *verb* 1 CHANGE, review, modify, reconsider, re-examine
2 EDIT, correct, alter, update, amend, rewrite, revamp, rework, redo, emend
3 STUDY, go over, run through, cram (*informal*), memorize, reread, swot up on (*Brit informal*)

revision *noun* 1 EMENDATION, editing, updating, correction, rewriting
2 CHANGE, review, amendment, modification, alteration, re-examination
3 STUDYING, cramming (*informal*), memorizing, swotting (*Brit informal*), rereading, homework

revitalize *verb* REANIMATE, restore, renew, refresh, resurrect, rejuvenate, breathe new life into, bring back to life, revivify

revival *noun* 1 RESURGENCE
<< OPPOSITE decline
2 REAWAKENING, restoration, renaissance, renewal, awakening, resurrection, refreshment, quickening, rebirth, resuscitation, revitalization, recrudescence, reanimation, renascence, revivification

revive *verb* 1 REVITALIZE, restore, rally, renew, renovate, rekindle, kick-start (*informal*), breathe new life into, invigorate, reanimate
2 BRING ROUND, awaken, animate, rouse, resuscitate, bring back to life
3 COME ROUND, recover, quicken, spring up again
4 REFRESH, restore, comfort, cheer, renew, resurrect, rejuvenate, revivify
<< OPPOSITE exhaust

revoke *verb* CANCEL, recall, withdraw, reverse, abolish, set aside, repeal, renounce, quash, take back, call back, retract, repudiate, negate, renege, rescind, invalidate, annul, nullify, recant, obviate, disclaim, abrogate, countermand, declare null and void
<< OPPOSITE endorse

revolt *noun* UPRISING, rising, revolution, rebellion, mutiny, defection, insurrection, insurgency, putsch, sedition
▷ *verb* 1 REBEL, rise up, resist, defect, mutiny, take to the streets, take up arms (against)
2 DISGUST, offend, turn off (*informal*), sicken, repel, repulse, nauseate, gross out (*US slang*), shock, turn your stomach, make your flesh creep, give you the creeps (*informal*)

revolting *adjective* DISGUSTING, shocking, offensive, appalling, nasty, foul, horrible, obscene, sickening, distasteful, horrid, repellent, obnoxious, repulsive, nauseating, repugnant, loathsome, abhorrent, abominable, nauseous, cringe-making (*Brit informal*), noisome, yucky *or* yukky (*slang*), yucko (*Austral slang*)
<< OPPOSITE delightful

revolution *noun* 1 REVOLT, rising, coup, rebellion, uprising, mutiny, insurgency, coup d'état, putsch
2 TRANSFORMATION, shift, innovation, upheaval, reformation, metamorphosis, sea change, drastic *or* radical change
3 ROTATION, turn, cycle, circle, wheel, spin, lap, circuit, orbit, whirl, gyration, round

revolutionary *adjective* 1 REBEL, radical, extremist, subversive, insurgent, seditious, mutinous, insurrectionary
<< OPPOSITE reactionary
2 INNOVATIVE, new, different, novel, radical, fundamental, progressive, experimental, drastic, avant-garde, ground-breaking, thoroughgoing
<< OPPOSITE conventional
▷ *noun* REBEL, insurgent, mutineer, insurrectionary, revolutionist, insurrectionist
<< OPPOSITE reactionary

revolutionize *verb* TRANSFORM, reform, revamp, modernize, metamorphose, break with the past

revolve *verb* 1 GO ROUND, circle, orbit, gyrate
2 ROTATE, turn, wheel, spin, twist, whirl
3 CONSIDER, study, reflect, think about, deliberate, ponder, turn over (in your mind), meditate, mull over, think over, ruminate

revulsion *noun* DISGUST, loathing, distaste, aversion, recoil, abomination, repulsion, abhorrence, repugnance, odium, detestation
<< OPPOSITE liking

reward *noun* 1 PRIZE
2 PUNISHMENT, desert, retribution, comeuppance (*slang*), just deserts, requital
3 PAYMENT, return, benefit, profit, gain, prize, wages, honour, compensation, bonus, premium, merit, repayment, bounty, remuneration, recompense, meed (*archaic*), requital
<< OPPOSITE penalty
▷ *verb* COMPENSATE, pay, honour, repay, recompense, requite, remunerate, make it worth your while
<< OPPOSITE penalize

rewarding *adjective* SATISFYING, fulfilling, gratifying, edifying, economic, pleasing, valuable, profitable, productive, worthwhile, beneficial, enriching, fruitful, advantageous, gainful, remunerative
<< OPPOSITE unrewarding

rewrite *verb* REVISE, correct, edit, recast, touch up, redraft, emend

rhetoric *noun* 1 HYPERBOLE, rant, hot air (*informal*), pomposity, bombast, wordiness, verbosity, fustian, grandiloquence, magniloquence
2 ORATORY, eloquence, public speaking, speech-making, elocution, declamation, speechifying, grandiloquence, spieling (*informal*), whaikorero (*NZ*)

rhetorical *adjective* 1 ORATORICAL, verbal, linguistic, stylistic
2 HIGH-FLOWN, flamboyant, windy, flashy, pompous, pretentious, flowery, showy, florid, bombastic, hyperbolic, verbose, oratorical, grandiloquent, high-sounding, declamatory, arty-farty (*informal*), silver-tongued, magniloquent

rhyme *noun* POEM, song, verse, ode
▷▷ **rhyme or reason** (usually in negative construction) SENSE, meaning, plan, planning, system, method, pattern, logic

rhythm *noun* 1 BEAT, swing, accent, pulse, tempo, cadence, lilt
2 METRE, time, measure (*Prosody*)
3 PATTERN, movement, flow, periodicity

rhythmic *or* **rhythmical** *adjective* CADENCED, throbbing, periodic, pulsating, flowing, musical, harmonious, lilting, melodious, metrical

rich *adjective* 1 WEALTHY, affluent, well-off, opulent, propertied, rolling (*slang*), loaded

(*slang*), flush (*informal*), prosperous, well-heeled (*informal*), well-to-do, moneyed, filthy rich, stinking rich (*informal*), made of money (*informal*)
<< OPPOSITE poor
2 WELL-STOCKED, full, productive, ample, abundant, plentiful, copious, well-provided, well-supplied, plenteous
<< OPPOSITE scarce
3 FULL-BODIED, heavy, sweet, delicious, fatty, tasty, creamy, spicy, juicy, luscious, savoury, succulent, flavoursome, highly-flavoured
<< OPPOSITE bland
4 FRUITFUL, productive, fertile, prolific, fecund
<< OPPOSITE barren
5 ABOUNDING, full, luxurious, lush, abundant, exuberant, well-endowed
6 RESONANT, full, deep, mellow, mellifluous, dulcet
<< OPPOSITE high-pitched
7 VIVID, strong, deep, warm, bright, intense, vibrant, gay
<< OPPOSITE dull
8 COSTLY, fine, expensive, valuable, superb, elegant, precious, elaborate, splendid, gorgeous, lavish, exquisite, sumptuous, priceless, palatial, beyond price
<< OPPOSITE cheap
9 FUNNY, amusing, ridiculous, hilarious, ludicrous, humorous, laughable, comical, risible, side-splitting

riches *plural noun* 1 WEALTH, money, property, gold, assets, plenty, fortune, substance, treasure, abundance, richness, affluence, opulence, top whack (*informal*)
<< OPPOSITE poverty
2 RESOURCES, treasures

richly *adverb* 1 ELABORATELY, lavishly, elegantly, splendidly, exquisitely, expensively, luxuriously, gorgeously, sumptuously, opulently, palatially
2 FULLY, well, thoroughly, amply, appropriately, properly, suitably, in full measure

rickety *adjective* SHAKY, broken, weak, broken-down, frail, insecure, feeble, precarious, derelict, flimsy, wobbly, imperfect, tottering, ramshackle, dilapidated, decrepit, unsteady, unsound, infirm, jerry-built

rid *verb* FREE, clear, deliver, relieve, purge, lighten, unburden, disabuse, make free, disembarrass, disencumber, disburden
▷▷ **get rid of something** *or* **someone** DISPOSE OF, throw away *or* out, dispense with, dump, remove, eliminate, expel, unload, shake off, eject, do away with, jettison, weed out, see the back of, wipe from the face of the earth, give the bum's rush to (*slang*)

riddle¹ *noun* 1 PUZZLE, problem, conundrum, teaser, poser, rebus, brain-teaser (*informal*), Chinese puzzle
2 ENIGMA, question, secret, mystery, puzzle, conundrum, teaser, problem

riddle² *verb* 1 PIERCE, pepper, puncture, perforate, honeycomb
2 PERVADE, fill, spread through, mar, spoil, corrupt, impair, pervade, infest, permeate

ride *verb* 1 CONTROL, handle, sit on, manage
2 TRAVEL, be carried, be supported, be borne, go, move, sit, progress, journey
▷ *noun* JOURNEY, drive, trip, lift, spin (*informal*), outing, whirl (*informal*), jaunt

ridicule *verb* LAUGH AT, mock, make fun of, make a fool of, humiliate, taunt, sneer at, parody, caricature, jeer at, scoff at, deride, send up (*Brit informal*), lampoon, poke fun at, chaff, take the mickey out of (*informal*), satirize, pooh-pooh, laugh out of court, make a monkey out of, make someone a laughing stock, laugh to scorn
▷ *noun* MOCKERY, scorn, derision, laughter, irony, rib, taunting, sneer, satire, jeer, banter, sarcasm, chaff, gibe, raillery

ridiculous *adjective* LAUGHABLE, stupid, incredible, silly, outrageous, absurd, foolish, unbelievable, hilarious, ludicrous, preposterous, farcical, comical, zany, nonsensical, derisory, inane, risible, contemptible, cockamamie (*slang, chiefly US*)
<< OPPOSITE sensible

rife *adjective* 1 WIDESPREAD, abundant, plentiful, rampant, general, common, current, raging, universal, frequent, prevailing, epidemic, prevalent, ubiquitous
2 *usually with* **with** ABOUNDING, seething, teeming

rifle *verb* 1 RUMMAGE, go, rake, fossick (*Austral & NZ*)
2 RANSACK, rob, burgle, loot, strip, sack, gut, plunder, pillage, despoil

rift *noun* 1 BREACH, difference, division, split, separation, falling out (*informal*), disagreement, quarrel, alienation, schism, estrangement
2 SPLIT, opening, space, crack, gap, break, fault, breach, fracture, flaw, cleavage, cleft, chink, crevice, fissure, cranny

rig *verb* 1 FIX, doctor, engineer (*informal*), arrange, fake, manipulate, juggle, tamper with, fiddle with (*informal*), falsify, trump up, gerrymander
2 (*Nautical*) EQUIP, fit out, kit out, outfit, supply, turn out, provision, furnish, accoutre
▷▷ **rig something up** *verb* SET UP, build, construct, put up, arrange, assemble, put together, erect, improvise, fix up, throw together, cobble together

right *adjective* 1 CORRECT, true, genuine,

accurate, exact, precise, valid, authentic, satisfactory, spot-on (*Brit informal*), factual, on the money (*US*), unerring, admissible, dinkum (*Austral & NZ informal*), veracious, sound

<< OPPOSITE wrong

2 PROPER, done, becoming, seemly, fitting, fit, appropriate, suitable, desirable, comme il faut (*French*)

<< OPPOSITE inappropriate

3 FAVOURABLE, due, ideal, convenient, rightful, advantageous, opportune, propitious

<< OPPOSITE disadvantageous

4 JUST, good, fair, moral, proper, ethical, upright, honourable, honest, equitable, righteous, virtuous, lawful

<< OPPOSITE unfair

5 SANE, sound, balanced, normal, reasonable, rational, all there (*informal*), lucid, unimpaired, compos mentis (*Latin*)

6 HEALTHY, well, fine, fit, in good health, in the pink, up to par

<< OPPOSITE unwell

▷ *adverb* 1 CORRECTLY, truly, precisely, exactly, genuinely, accurately, factually, aright

<< OPPOSITE wrongly

2 SUITABLY, fittingly, appropriately, properly, aptly, satisfactorily, befittingly

<< OPPOSITE improperly

3 EXACTLY, squarely, precisely, bang, slap-bang (*informal*)

4 DIRECTLY, straight, precisely, exactly, unswervingly, without deviation, by the shortest route, in a beeline

5 ALL THE WAY, completely, totally, perfectly, entirely, absolutely, altogether, thoroughly, wholly, utterly, quite

6 STRAIGHT, directly, immediately, quickly, promptly, instantly, straightaway, without delay

<< OPPOSITE indirectly

7 PROPERLY, fittingly, fairly, morally, honestly, justly, ethically, honourably, righteously, virtuously

8 FAVOURABLY, well, fortunately, for the better, to advantage, beneficially, advantageously

<< OPPOSITE badly

▷ *noun* 1 PREROGATIVE, interest, business, power, claim, authority, title, due, freedom, licence, permission, liberty, privilege

2 JUSTICE, good, reason, truth, honour, equity, virtue, integrity, goodness, morality, fairness, legality, righteousness, propriety, rectitude, lawfulness, uprightness

<< OPPOSITE injustice

▷ *verb* RECTIFY, settle, fix, correct, repair, sort out, compensate for, straighten, redress, vindicate, put right

▷▷ **by rights** IN FAIRNESS, properly, justly, equitably

▷▷ **put something to rights** ORDER, arrange, straighten out

>> RELATED WORD *adjective* dextral

right away *adverb* IMMEDIATELY, now, directly, promptly, instantly, at once, right off, straightaway, without delay, without hesitation, straight off (*informal*), forthwith, pronto (*informal*), this instant, posthaste

righteous *adjective* VIRTUOUS, good, just, fair, moral, pure, ethical, upright, honourable, honest, equitable, law-abiding, squeaky-clean, blameless

<< OPPOSITE wicked

righteousness *noun* VIRTUE, justice, honour, equity, integrity, goodness, morality, honesty, purity, probity, rectitude, faithfulness, uprightness, blamelessness, ethicalness

rightful *adjective* LAWFUL, just, real, true, due, legal, suitable, proper, valid, legitimate, authorized, bona fide, de jure

right-wing *adjective* CONSERVATIVE, Tory, reactionary

<< OPPOSITE left-wing

rigid *adjective* 1 STRICT, set, fixed, exact, rigorous, stringent, austere, severe

<< OPPOSITE flexible

2 INFLEXIBLE, harsh, stern, adamant, uncompromising, unrelenting, unyielding, intransigent, unbending, invariable, unalterable, undeviating

3 STIFF, inflexible, inelastic

<< OPPOSITE pliable

rigorous *adjective* 1 STRICT, hard, firm, demanding, challenging, tough, severe, exacting, harsh, stern, rigid, stringent, austere, inflexible

<< OPPOSITE soft

2 THOROUGH, meticulous, painstaking, scrupulous, nice, accurate, exact, precise, conscientious, punctilious

<< OPPOSITE careless

rigour *noun* 1 *often plural* ORDEAL, suffering, trial, hardship, privation

2 STRICTNESS, austerity, rigidity, firmness, hardness, harshness, inflexibility, stringency, asperity, sternness

3 THOROUGHNESS, accuracy, precision, exactitude, exactness, conscientiousness, meticulousness, punctiliousness, preciseness

rile *verb* ANGER, upset, provoke, bug (*informal*), annoy, irritate, aggravate (*informal*), gall, nettle, vex, irk, pique, peeve (*informal*), get under your skin (*informal*), get on your nerves (*informal*), nark (*Brit, Austral & NZ slang*), get your goat (*slang*), try your patience, rub you up the wrong way, get *or* put your back up, hack you off (*informal*)

rim *noun* 1 EDGE, lip, brim, flange

2 BORDER, edge, trim, circumference

3 MARGIN, border, verge, brink
rind *noun* 1 SKIN, peel, outer layer, epicarp
2 CRUST, husk, integument
ring[1] *verb* 1 PHONE, call, telephone, buzz (*informal, chiefly Brit*)
2 CHIME, sound, toll, resound, resonate, reverberate, clang, peal
3 REVERBERATE, resound, resonate
▷ *noun* 1 CALL, phone call, buzz (*informal, chiefly Brit*)
2 CHIME, knell, peal

Rang is the past tense of the verb *ring*, as in *he rang the bell*. *Rung* is the past participle, as in *he has already rung the bell*, and care should be taken not to use it as if it were a variant form of the past tense

ring[2] *noun* 1 CIRCLE, round, band, circuit, loop, hoop, halo
2 ARENA, enclosure, circus, rink
3 GANG, group, association, band, cell, combine, organization, circle, crew (*informal*), knot, mob, syndicate, cartel, junta, clique, coterie, cabal
▷ *verb* ENCIRCLE, surround, enclose, encompass, seal off, girdle, circumscribe, hem in, gird
rinse *verb* WASH, clean, wet, dip, splash, cleanse, bathe, wash out
▷ *noun* WASH, wetting, dip, splash, bath
riot *noun* 1 DISTURBANCE, row, disorder, confusion, turmoil, quarrel, upheaval, fray, strife, uproar, turbulence, commotion, lawlessness, street fighting, tumult, donnybrook, mob violence
2 DISPLAY, show, splash, flourish, extravaganza, profusion
3 LAUGH, joke, scream (*informal*), blast (*US slang*), hoot (*informal*), lark
▷ *verb* RAMPAGE, take to the streets, run riot, go on the rampage, fight in the streets, raise an uproar
▷▷ **run riot** 1 RAMPAGE, go wild, be out of control, raise hell, let yourself go, break *or* cut loose, throw off all restraint
2 GROW PROFUSELY, luxuriate, spread like wildfire, grow like weeds
riotous *adjective* 1 RECKLESS, wild, outrageous, lavish, rash, luxurious, extravagant, wanton, unrestrained, intemperate, heedless, immoderate
2 UNRESTRAINED, wild, loud, noisy, boisterous, rollicking, uproarious, orgiastic, side-splitting, rambunctious (*informal*), saturnalian, roisterous
3 UNRULY, violent, disorderly, rebellious, rowdy, anarchic, tumultuous, lawless, mutinous, ungovernable, uproarious, refractory, insubordinate, rampageous
<< OPPOSITE orderly
rip *verb* 1 TEAR, cut, score, split, burst, rend, slash, hack, claw, slit, gash, lacerate
2 BE TORN, tear, split, burst, be rent
▷ *noun* TEAR, cut, hole, split, rent, slash, slit, cleavage, gash, laceration
▷▷ **rip someone off** (*slang*) CHEAT, trick, rob, con (*informal*), skin (*slang*), stiff (*slang*), steal from, fleece, defraud, dupe, swindle, diddle (*informal*), do the dirty on (*Brit informal*), gyp (*slang*), cozen
ripe *adjective* 1 RIPENED, seasoned, ready, mature, mellow, fully developed, fully grown
<< OPPOSITE unripe
2 RIGHT, suitable
3 MATURE
4 SUITABLE, timely, ideal, favourable, auspicious, opportune
<< OPPOSITE unsuitable
5 *with* **for** READY FOR, prepared for, eager for, in readiness for
ripen *verb* MATURE, season, develop, get ready, burgeon, come of age, come to fruition, grow ripe, make ripe
rip-off *or* **ripoff** *noun* (*slang*) CHEAT, con (*informal*), scam (*slang*), con trick (*informal*), fraud, theft, sting (*informal*), robbery, exploitation, swindle, daylight robbery (*informal*)
riposte *noun* RETORT, return, answer, response, reply, sally, comeback (*informal*), counterattack, repartee, rejoinder
▷ *verb* RETORT, return, answer, reply, respond, come back, rejoin, reciprocate
ripple *noun* 1 WAVE, tremor, oscillation, undulation
2 FLUTTER, thrill, tremor, tingle, vibration, frisson
rise *verb* 1 GET UP, stand up, get to your feet
2 ARISE, surface, get out of bed, rise and shine
3 GO UP, climb, move up, ascend
<< OPPOSITE descend
4 LOOM, tower
5 GET STEEPER, mount, climb, ascend, go uphill, slope upwards
<< OPPOSITE drop
6 INCREASE, mount, soar
<< OPPOSITE decrease
7 GROW, go up, intensify
8 REBEL, resist, revolt, mutiny, take up arms, mount the barricades
9 ADVANCE, progress, get on, be promoted, prosper, go places (*informal*), climb the ladder, work your way up
▷ *noun* 1 UPWARD SLOPE, incline, elevation, ascent, hillock, rising ground, acclivity, kopje *or* koppie (*S African*)
2 INCREASE, climb, upturn, upswing, advance, improvement, ascent, upsurge, upward turn
<< OPPOSITE decrease

3 PAY INCREASE, raise (*US*), increment
4 ADVANCEMENT, progress, climb, promotion, aggrandizement
▷▷ **give rise to something** CAUSE, produce, effect, result in, provoke, bring about, bring on

risible *adjective* (*Formal*) RIDICULOUS, ludicrous, laughable, farcical, funny, amusing, absurd, hilarious, humorous, comical, droll, side-splitting, rib-tickling (*informal*)

risk *noun* 1 DANGER, chance, possibility, speculation, uncertainty, hazard
2 GAMBLE, chance, venture, speculation, leap in the dark
3 PERIL, jeopardy
▷ *verb* 1 STAND A CHANCE OF
2 DARE, endanger, jeopardize, imperil, venture, gamble, hazard, take a chance on, put in jeopardy, expose to danger

risky *adjective* DANGEROUS, hazardous, unsafe, perilous, uncertain, tricky, dodgy (*Brit, Austral & NZ informal*), precarious, touch-and-go, dicey (*informal, chiefly Brit*), fraught with danger, chancy (*informal*), shonky (*Austral & NZ informal*)
<< OPPOSITE safe

risqué *adjective* SUGGESTIVE, blue, daring, naughty, improper, racy, bawdy, off colour, ribald, immodest, indelicate, near the knuckle (*informal*), Rabelaisian

rite *noun* CEREMONY, custom, ritual, act, service, form, practice, procedure, mystery, usage, formality, ceremonial, communion, ordinance, observance, sacrament, liturgy, solemnity

ritual *noun* 1 CEREMONY, rite, ceremonial, sacrament, service, mystery, communion, observance, liturgy, solemnity
2 CUSTOM, tradition, routine, convention, form, practice, procedure, habit, usage, protocol, formality, ordinance, tikanga (*NZ*)
▷ *adjective* CEREMONIAL, formal, conventional, routine, prescribed, stereotyped, customary, procedural, habitual, ceremonious

ritzy *adjective* (*Slang*) LUXURIOUS, grand, luxury, elegant, glittering, glamorous, stylish, posh (*informal, chiefly Brit*), sumptuous, plush (*informal*), high-class, opulent, swanky (*informal*), de luxe, schmick (*Austral informal*)

rival *noun* 1 OPPONENT, competitor, contender, challenger, contestant, adversary, antagonist, emulator
<< OPPOSITE supporter
2 EQUAL, match, fellow, equivalent, peer, compeer
▷ *verb* COMPETE WITH, match, equal, oppose, compare with, contend, come up to, emulate, vie with, measure up to, be a match for, bear comparison with, seek to displace
▷ *modifier* COMPETING, conflicting, opposed, opposing, competitive, emulating

rivalry *noun* COMPETITION, competitiveness, vying, opposition, struggle, conflict, contest, contention, duel, antagonism, emulation

river *noun* 1 STREAM, brook, creek, beck, waterway, tributary, rivulet, watercourse, burn (*Scot*)
2 FLOW, rush, flood, spate, torrent
>> RELATED WORD *adjective* fluvial

riveting *adjective* ENTHRALLING, arresting, gripping, fascinating, absorbing, captivating, hypnotic, engrossing, spellbinding

road *noun* 1 ROADWAY, street, highway, motorway, track, direction, route, path, lane, avenue, pathway, thoroughfare, course
2 WAY, path

roam *verb* WANDER, walk, range, travel, drift, stroll, stray, ramble, prowl, meander, rove, stravaig (*Scot & Northern English dialect*), peregrinate

roar *verb* 1 THUNDER, crash, rumble
2 GUFFAW, laugh heartily, hoot, crack up (*informal*), bust a gut (*informal*), split your sides (*informal*)
3 CRY, shout, yell, howl, bellow, clamour, bawl, bay, vociferate
▷ *noun* 1 RUMBLE, thunder
2 GUFFAW, hoot, belly laugh (*informal*)
3 CRY, crash, shout, yell, howl, outcry, bellow, clamour

rob *verb* 1 STEAL FROM, hold up, rifle, mug (*informal*), stiff (*slang*)
2 RAID, hold up, sack, loot, plunder, burgle, ransack, pillage
3 DISPOSSESS, con (*informal*), rip off (*slang*), skin (*slang*), cheat, defraud, swindle, despoil, gyp (*slang*)
4 DEPRIVE, strip, do out of (*informal*)

robber *noun* THIEF, raider, burglar, looter, stealer, fraud, cheat, pirate, bandit, plunderer, mugger (*informal*), highwayman, con man (*informal*), fraudster, swindler, brigand, grifter (*slang, chiefly US & Canad*), footpad (*archaic*), rogue trader

robbery *noun* 1 BURGLARY, raid, hold-up, rip-off (*slang*), stick-up (*slang, chiefly US*), home invasion (*Austral & NZ*)
2 THEFT, stealing, fraud, steaming (*informal*), mugging (*informal*), plunder, swindle, pillage, embezzlement, larceny, depredation, filching, thievery, rapine, spoliation

robe *noun* 1 GOWN, costume, vestment, habit
2 DRESSING GOWN, wrapper, bathrobe, negligée, housecoat, peignoir

robot *noun* MACHINE, automaton, android, mechanical man

robust *adjective* 1 STRONG, tough, powerful, athletic, well, sound, fit, healthy, strapping, hardy, rude, vigorous, rugged, muscular, sturdy, hale, stout, staunch, hearty, husky (*informal*), in good health, lusty, alive and kicking, fighting fit, sinewy, brawny, in fine fettle, thickset, fit as a fiddle (*informal*), able-bodied

<< OPPOSITE weak

2 ROUGH, raw, rude, coarse, raunchy (*slang*), earthy, boisterous, rollicking, unsubtle, indecorous, roisterous

<< OPPOSITE refined

3 STRAIGHTFORWARD, practical, sensible, realistic, pragmatic, down-to-earth, hard-headed, common-sensical

rock[1] *noun* 1 STONE, boulder

2 TOWER OF STRENGTH, foundation, cornerstone, mainstay, support, protection, anchor, bulwark

rock[2] *verb* 1 SWAY, pitch, swing, reel, toss, lurch, wobble, roll

2 SHOCK, surprise, shake, stun, astonish, stagger, jar, astound, daze, dumbfound, set you back on your heels (*informal*)

rocky[1] *adjective* ROUGH, rugged, stony, craggy, pebbly, boulder-strewn

rocky[2] *adjective* UNSTABLE, weak, uncertain, doubtful, shaky, unreliable, wobbly, rickety, unsteady, undependable

rod *noun* 1 STICK, bar, pole, shaft, switch, crook, cane, birch, dowel

2 STAFF, baton, mace, wand, sceptre

rogue *noun* 1 SCOUNDREL, crook (*informal*), villain, fraudster, sharper, fraud, cheat, devil, deceiver, charlatan, con man (*informal*), swindler, knave (*archaic*), ne'er-do-well, reprobate, scumbag (*slang*), blackguard, mountebank, grifter (*slang, chiefly US & Canad*), skelm (*S African*), rorter (*Austral slang*), wrong 'un (*Austral slang*)

2 SCAMP, rascal, scally (*Northwest English dialect*), rapscallion, nointer (*Austral slang*)

role *noun* 1 JOB, part, position, post, task, duty, function, capacity

2 PART, character, representation, portrayal, impersonation

roll *verb* 1 TURN, wheel, spin, reel, go round, revolve, rotate, whirl, swivel, pivot, twirl, gyrate

2 TRUNDLE, go, move

3 FLOW, run, course, slide, glide, purl

4 *often with* **up** WIND, bind, wrap, twist, curl, coil, swathe, envelop, entwine, furl, enfold

5 *often with* **out** LEVEL, even, press, spread, smooth, flatten

6 TOSS, rock, lurch, reel, tumble, sway, wallow, billow, swing, welter

7 RUMBLE, boom, echo, drum, roar, thunder, grumble, resound, reverberate

8 SWAY, reel, stagger, lurch, lumber, waddle, swagger

9 PASS, go past, elapse

▷ *noun* 1 REEL, ball, bobbin, cylinder

2 RUMBLE, boom, drumming, roar, thunder, grumble, resonance, growl, reverberation

3 REGISTER, record, list, table, schedule, index, catalogue, directory, inventory, census, chronicle, scroll, roster, annals

4 TOSSING, rocking, rolling, pitching, swell, lurching, wallowing

5 TURN, run, spin, rotation, cycle, wheel, revolution, reel, whirl, twirl, undulation, gyration

rollicking[1] *adjective* BOISTEROUS, spirited, lively, romping, merry, hearty, playful, exuberant, joyous, carefree, jaunty, cavorting, sprightly, jovial, swashbuckling, frisky, rip-roaring (*informal*), devil-may-care, full of beans (*informal*), frolicsome, sportive

<< OPPOSITE sedate

rollicking[2] *noun* (*Brit informal*) SCOLDING, lecture, reprimand, telling-off, roasting (*informal*), wigging (*Brit slang*), ticking off (*informal*), dressing-down (*informal*), tongue-lashing (*informal*)

romance *noun* 1 LOVE AFFAIR, relationship, affair, intrigue, attachment, liaison, amour, affair of the heart, affaire (du coeur) (*French*)

2 LOVE

3 EXCITEMENT, colour, charm, mystery, adventure, sentiment, glamour, fascination, nostalgia, exoticness

4 STORY, novel, tale, fantasy, legend, fiction, fairy tale, love story, melodrama, idyll, tear-jerker (*informal*)

romantic *adjective* 1 LOVING, tender, passionate, fond, sentimental, sloppy (*informal*), amorous, mushy (*informal*), soppy (*Brit informal*), lovey-dovey, icky (*informal*)

<< OPPOSITE unromantic

2 IDEALISTIC, unrealistic, visionary, high-flown, impractical, dreamy, utopian, whimsical, quixotic, starry-eyed

<< OPPOSITE realistic

3 EXCITING, charming, fascinating, exotic, mysterious, colourful, glamorous, picturesque, nostalgic

<< OPPOSITE unexciting

4 FICTITIOUS, made-up, fantastic, fabulous, legendary, exaggerated, imaginative, imaginary, extravagant, unrealistic, improbable, fairy-tale, idyllic, fanciful, wild, chimerical

<< OPPOSITE realistic

▷ *noun* IDEALIST, romancer, visionary, dreamer, utopian, Don Quixote, sentimentalist

romp *verb* FROLIC, sport, skip, have fun, revel, caper, cavort, frisk, gambol, make merry, rollick, roister, cut capers

▷ *noun* FROLIC, lark (*informal*), caper

▷▷ **romp home** *or* **in** WIN EASILY, walk it

(*informal*), win hands down, run away with it, win by a mile (*informal*)

room *noun* 1 CHAMBER, office, apartment
2 SPACE, area, territory, volume, capacity, extent, expanse, elbow room
3 OPPORTUNITY, scope, leeway, play, chance, range, occasion, margin, allowance, compass, latitude

roomy *adjective* SPACIOUS, large, wide, broad, extensive, generous, ample, capacious, commodious, sizable *or* sizeable
<< OPPOSITE cramped

root[1] *noun* 1 STEM, tuber, rhizome, radix, radicle
2 SOURCE, cause, heart, bottom, beginnings, base, seat, occasion, seed, foundation, origin, core, fundamental, essence, nucleus, starting point, germ, crux, nub, derivation, fountainhead, mainspring
▷ *plural noun* SENSE OF BELONGING, origins, heritage, birthplace, home, family, cradle
▷▷ **root and branch** 1 COMPLETE, total, entire, radical, thorough
2 COMPLETELY, finally, totally, entirely, radically, thoroughly, wholly, utterly, without exception, to the last man
▷▷ **root something** *or* **someone out** 1 GET RID OF, remove, destroy, eliminate, abolish, cut out, erase, eradicate, do away with, uproot, weed out, efface, exterminate, extirpate, wipe from the face of the earth
2 DISCOVER, find, expose, turn up, uncover, unearth, bring to light, ferret out
>> RELATED WORD *adjective* radical

root[2] *verb* DIG, hunt, nose, poke, burrow, delve, ferret, pry, rummage, forage, rootle

rooted *adjective* DEEP-SEATED, firm, deep, established, confirmed, fixed, radical, rigid, entrenched, ingrained, deeply felt

rootless *adjective* FOOTLOOSE, homeless, roving, transient, itinerant, vagabond

rope *noun* CORD, line, cable, strand, hawser
▷ *verb* TIE, bind, moor, lash, hitch, fasten, tether, pinion, lasso
▷▷ **know the ropes** BE EXPERIENCED, know the score (*informal*), be knowledgeable, know what's what, be an old hand, know your way around, know where it's at (*slang*), know all the ins and outs
▷▷ **rope someone in** *or* **into something** (*Brit*) PERSUADE, involve, engage, enlist, talk into, drag in, inveigle

roster *noun* ROTA, listing, list, table, roll, schedule, register, agenda, catalogue, inventory, scroll

rostrum *noun* STAGE, stand, platform, podium, dais

rosy *adjective* 1 GLOWING, fresh, blooming, flushed, blushing, radiant, reddish, ruddy, healthy-looking, roseate, rubicund
<< OPPOSITE pale
2 PROMISING, encouraging, bright, reassuring, optimistic, hopeful, sunny, cheerful, favourable, auspicious, rose-coloured, roseate
<< OPPOSITE gloomy
3 PINK, red, rose-coloured, roseate

rot *verb* 1 DECAY, break down, spoil, corrupt, deteriorate, taint, perish, degenerate, fester, decompose, corrode, moulder, go bad, putrefy
2 CRUMBLE, disintegrate, become rotten
3 DETERIORATE, decline, languish, degenerate, wither away, waste away
▷ *noun* 1 DECAY, disintegration, corrosion, decomposition, corruption, mould, blight, deterioration, canker, putrefaction, putrescence
2 (*informal*) NONSENSE, rubbish, drivel, twaddle, pants (*slang*), crap (*slang*), garbage (*chiefly US*), trash, bunk (*informal*), hot air (*informal*), tosh (*slang, chiefly Brit*), pap, bilge (*informal*), tripe (*informal*), guff (*slang*), moonshine, claptrap (*informal*), hogwash, hokum (*slang, chiefly US & Canad*), codswallop (*Brit slang*), piffle (*informal*), poppycock (*informal*), balderdash, bosh (*informal*), eyewash (*informal*), stuff and nonsense, flapdoodle (*slang*), tommyrot, horsefeathers (*US slang*), bunkum *or* buncombe (*chiefly US*), bizzo (*Austral slang*), bull's wool (*Austral & NZ slang*)
>> RELATED WORD *adjective* putrid

rotary *adjective* REVOLVING, turning, spinning, rotating, rotational, gyratory, rotatory

rotate *verb* 1 REVOLVE, turn, wheel, spin, reel, go round, swivel, pivot, gyrate, pirouette
2 FOLLOW IN SEQUENCE, switch, alternate, interchange, take turns

rotation *noun* 1 REVOLUTION, turning, turn, wheel, spin, spinning, reel, orbit, pirouette, gyration
2 SEQUENCE, switching, cycle, succession, interchanging, alternation

rotten *adjective* 1 DECAYING, bad, rank, foul, corrupt, sour, stinking, tainted, perished, festering, decomposed, decomposing, mouldy, mouldering, fetid, putrid, putrescent, festy (*Austral slang*)
<< OPPOSITE fresh
2 CRUMBLING, decayed, disintegrating, perished, corroded, unsound
3 (*informal*) BAD, disappointing, unfortunate, unlucky, regrettable, deplorable
4 (*informal*) DESPICABLE, mean, base, dirty, nasty, unpleasant, filthy, vile, wicked, disagreeable, contemptible, scurrilous
5 (*informal*) UNWELL, poorly (*informal*), ill, sick, rough (*informal*), bad, crook (*Austral & NZ informal*), below par, off colour, under the weather (*informal*), ropey *or* ropy (*Brit informal*)

6 (*informal*) INFERIOR, poor, sorry, inadequate, unacceptable, punk, duff (*Brit informal*), unsatisfactory, lousy (*slang*), low-grade, substandard, ill-considered, crummy (*slang*), ill-thought-out, poxy (*slang*), of a sort *or* of sorts, ropey *or* ropy (*Brit informal*), bodger *or* bodgie (*Austral slang*)
7 CORRUPT, immoral, deceitful, untrustworthy, bent (*slang*), crooked (*informal*), vicious, degenerate, mercenary, treacherous, dishonest, disloyal, faithless, venal, dishonourable, perfidious
<< OPPOSITE honourable

rotund *adjective* 1 PLUMP, rounded, heavy, fat, stout, chubby, obese, fleshy, tubby, portly, roly-poly, podgy, corpulent
<< OPPOSITE skinny
2 POMPOUS, orotund, magniloquent, full
3 ROUND, rounded, spherical, bulbous, globular, orbicular
4 SONOROUS, round, rich, resonant, orotund

rough *adjective* 1 UNEVEN, broken, rocky, rugged, irregular, jagged, bumpy, stony, craggy
<< OPPOSITE even
2 COARSE, disordered, tangled, hairy, fuzzy, bushy, shaggy, dishevelled, uncut, unshaven, tousled, bristly, unshorn
<< OPPOSITE smooth
3 BOISTEROUS, hard, tough, rugged, arduous
4 UNGRACIOUS, blunt, rude, coarse, bluff, curt, churlish, bearish, brusque, uncouth, unrefined, inconsiderate, impolite, loutish, untutored, discourteous, unpolished, indelicate, uncivil, uncultured, unceremonious, ill-bred, unmannerly, ill-mannered
<< OPPOSITE refined
5 UNPLEASANT, hard, difficult, tough, uncomfortable, drastic, unjust
<< OPPOSITE easy
6 (*informal*) UNWELL, poorly (*informal*), ill, upset, sick, crook (*Austral & NZ informal*), rotten (*informal*), below par, off colour, under the weather (*informal*), not a hundred per cent (*informal*), ropey *or* ropy (*Brit informal*)
7 APPROXIMATE, estimated
<< OPPOSITE exact
8 VAGUE, general, sketchy, imprecise, hazy, foggy, amorphous, inexact
9 BASIC, quick, raw, crude, unfinished, incomplete, hasty, imperfect, rudimentary, sketchy, cursory, shapeless, rough-and-ready, unrefined, formless, rough-hewn, untutored, unpolished
<< OPPOSITE complete
10 ROUGH-HEWN, crude, uncut, unpolished, raw, undressed, unprocessed, unhewn, unwrought
11 STORMY, wild, turbulent, agitated, choppy, tempestuous, inclement, squally
<< OPPOSITE calm
12 GRATING, harsh, jarring, raucous, rasping, husky, discordant, gruff, cacophonous, unmusical, inharmonious
<< OPPOSITE soft
13 HARSH, tough, sharp, severe, nasty, cruel, rowdy, curt, unfeeling
<< OPPOSITE gentle
▷ *noun* 1 OUTLINE, draft, mock-up, preliminary sketch, suggestion
2 (*informal*) THUG, tough, casual, rowdy, hoon (*Austral & NZ*), bully boy, bruiser, ruffian, lager lout, roughneck (*slang*), ned (*slang*), cougan (*Austral slang*), scozza (*Austral slang*), bogan (*Austral slang*)
▷▷ **rough and ready** 1 MAKESHIFT, adequate, crude, provisional, improvised, sketchy, thrown together, cobbled together, stopgap
2 UNREFINED, shabby, untidy, unkempt, unpolished, ungroomed, ill-groomed, daggy (*Austral & NZ informal*)
▷▷ **rough and tumble** 1 FIGHT, struggle, scrap (*informal*), brawl, scuffle, punch-up (*Brit informal*), fracas, affray (*Law*), dust-up (*informal*), shindig (*informal*), donnybrook, scrimmage, roughhouse (*slang*), shindy (*informal*), melee *or* mêlée, biffo (*Austral slang*)
2 DISORDERLY, rough, scrambled, scrambling, irregular, rowdy, boisterous, haphazard, indisciplined
▷▷ **rough someone up** (*informal*) BEAT UP, batter, thrash, do over (*Brit, Austral & NZ slang*), work over (*slang*), mistreat, manhandle, maltreat, bash up (*informal*), beat the living daylights out of (*informal*), knock about *or* around, beat *or* knock seven bells out of (*informal*)
▷▷ **rough something out** OUTLINE, plan, draft, sketch, suggest, block out, delineate, adumbrate

round *noun* 1 SERIES, session, cycle, sequence, succession, bout
2 STAGE, turn, level, period, division, session, lap
3 SPHERE, ball, band, ring, circle, disc, globe, orb
4 COURSE, turn, tour, circuit, beat, series, schedule, routine, compass, ambit
5 BULLET, shot, shell, discharge, cartridge
▷ *adjective* 1 SPHERICAL, rounded, bowed, curved, circular, cylindrical, bulbous, rotund, globular, curvilinear, ball-shaped, ring-shaped, disc-shaped, annular, discoid, orbicular
2 COMPLETE, full, whole, entire, solid, unbroken, undivided
3 PLUMP, full, rounded, ample, fleshy, roly-poly, rotund, full-fleshed
▷ *verb* GO ROUND, circle, skirt, flank, bypass, encircle, turn, circumnavigate
▷▷ **round on someone** ATTACK, abuse, turn

on, retaliate against, have a go at (*Brit slang*), snap at, wade into, lose your temper with, bite (someone's) head off (*informal*)
▷▷ **round something off** COMPLETE, close, settle, crown, cap, conclude, finish off, put the finishing touch to, bring to a close
▷▷ **round something** *or* **someone up** GATHER, assemble, bring together, muster, group, drive, collect, rally, herd, marshal

roundabout *adjective* 1 INDIRECT, meandering, devious, tortuous, circuitous, evasive, discursive, circumlocutory
<< OPPOSITE direct
2 OBLIQUE, implied, indirect, evasive, circuitous, circumlocutory, periphrastic

roundly *adverb* THOROUGHLY, sharply, severely, bitterly, fiercely, bluntly, intensely, violently, vehemently, rigorously, outspokenly, frankly

roundup *noun* 1 (*informal*) SUMMARY, survey, collation
2 MUSTER, collection, rally, assembly, herding

rouse *verb* 1 WAKE UP, call, wake, awaken
2 EXCITE, move, arouse, stir, disturb, provoke, anger, startle, animate, prod, exhilarate, get going, agitate, inflame, incite, whip up, galvanize, bestir
3 STIMULATE, provoke, arouse, incite, instigate

rousing *adjective* LIVELY, moving, spirited, exciting, inspiring, stirring, stimulating, vigorous, brisk, exhilarating, inflammatory, electrifying
<< OPPOSITE dull

rout *verb* DEFEAT, beat, overthrow, thrash, stuff (*slang*), worst, destroy, chase, tank (*slang*), crush, scatter, conquer, lick (*informal*), dispel, drive off, overpower, clobber (*slang*), wipe the floor with (*informal*), cut to pieces, put to flight, drub, put to rout, throw back in confusion
▷ *noun* DEFEAT, beating, hiding (*informal*), ruin, overthrow, thrashing, licking (*informal*), pasting (*slang*), shambles, debacle, drubbing, overwhelming defeat, headlong flight, disorderly retreat ▷ see **route**

route *noun* 1 WAY, course, road, direction, path, journey, passage, avenue, itinerary
2 BEAT, run, round, circuit
▷ *verb* 1 DIRECT, lead, guide, steer, convey
2 SEND, forward, dispatch

> When adding *-ing* to the verb *route* to form the present participle, it is more conventional, and clearer, to keep the final *e* from the end of the verb stem: *routeing*. The spelling *routing* in this sense is also possible, but keeping the *e* distinguishes it from *routing*, which is the participle formed from the verb *rout* meaning 'to defeat'

routine *noun* 1 PROCEDURE, programme, way, order, practice, method, pattern, formula, custom, usage, wont
2 GRIND (*informal*), monotony, banality, groove, boredom, chore, the doldrums, dullness, sameness, ennui, drabness, deadness, dreariness, tediousness, lifelessness
▷ *adjective* 1 USUAL, standard, normal, customary, ordinary, familiar, typical, conventional, everyday, habitual, workaday, wonted
<< OPPOSITE unusual
2 BORING, dull, predictable, tedious, tiresome, run-of-the-mill, humdrum, unimaginative, clichéd, uninspired, mind-numbing, hackneyed, unoriginal, shtick (*slang*)

rove *verb* WANDER, range, cruise, drift, stroll, stray, roam, ramble, meander, traipse (*informal*), gallivant, gad about, stravaig (*Scot & Northern English dialect*)

rover *noun* WANDERER, traveller, gypsy, rolling stone, rambler, transient, nomad, itinerant, ranger, drifter, vagrant, stroller, bird of passage, gadabout (*informal*)

row[1] *noun* LINE, bank, range, series, file, rank, string, column, sequence, queue, tier
▷▷ **in a row** CONSECUTIVELY, running, in turn, one after the other, successively, in sequence

row[2] *noun* 1 QUARREL, dispute, argument, squabble, tiff, trouble, controversy, scrap (*informal*), fuss, falling-out (*informal*), fray, brawl, fracas, altercation, slanging match (*Brit*), shouting match (*informal*), shindig (*informal*), ruction (*informal*), ruckus (*informal*), shindy (*informal*), bagarre (*French*)
2 DISTURBANCE, noise, racket, uproar, commotion, rumpus, tumult
3 TELLING-OFF, talking-to (*informal*), lecture, reprimand, ticking-off (*informal*), dressing-down (*informal*), rollicking (*Brit informal*) (*informal*), tongue-lashing, reproof, castigation, flea in your ear (*informal*)
▷ *verb* QUARREL, fight, argue, dispute, scrap (*informal*), brawl, squabble, spar, wrangle, go at it hammer and tongs

rowdy *adjective* DISORDERLY, rough, loud, noisy, unruly, boisterous, loutish, wild, uproarious, obstreperous
<< OPPOSITE orderly
▷ *noun* HOOLIGAN, tough, rough (*informal*), casual, ned (*Scot slang*), brawler, yahoo, lout, troublemaker, tearaway (*Brit*), ruffian, lager lout, yob *or* yobbo (*Brit slang*), cougan (*Austral slang*), scozza (*Austral slang*), bogan (*Austral slang*)

royal *adjective* 1 REGAL, kingly, queenly, princely, imperial, sovereign, monarchical, kinglike
2 SPLENDID, august, grand, impressive, superb, magnificent, superior, majestic,

stately

rub *verb* 1 STROKE, smooth, massage, caress, knead
2 POLISH, clean, shine, wipe, scour
3 SPREAD, put, apply, smear
4 CHAFE, scrape, grate, abrade
▷ *noun* 1 MASSAGE, caress, kneading
2 POLISH, stroke, shine, wipe
▷▷ **rub something out** ERASE, remove, cancel, wipe out, excise, delete, obliterate, efface, expunge
▷▷ **the rub** DIFFICULTY, problem, catch, trouble, obstacle, hazard, hitch, drawback, snag, uphill (*S African*), impediment, hindrance

rubbish *noun* 1 WASTE, refuse, scrap, junk (*informal*), litter, debris, crap (*slang*), garbage (*chiefly US*), trash, lumber, offal, dross, dregs, flotsam and jetsam, grot (*slang*), dreck (*slang, chiefly US*), offscourings
2 NONSENSE, garbage (*chiefly US*), drivel, twaddle, pants (*slang*), rot, crap (*slang*), trash, hot air (*informal*), tosh (*slang, chiefly Brit*), pap, bilge (*informal*), tripe (*informal*), gibberish, guff (*slang*), havers (*Scot*), moonshine, claptrap (*informal*), hogwash, hokum (*slang, chiefly US & Canad*), codswallop (*Brit slang*), piffle (*informal*), poppycock (*informal*), balderdash, bosh (*informal*), wack (*US slang*), eyewash (*informal*), stuff and nonsense, flapdoodle (*slang*), tommyrot, horsefeathers (*US slang*), bunkum *or* buncombe (*chiefly US*), bizzo (*Austral slang*), bull's wool (*Austral & NZ slang*)

ruddy *adjective* 1 ROSY, red, fresh, healthy, glowing, blooming, flushed, blushing, radiant, reddish, sanguine, florid, sunburnt, rosy-cheeked, rubicund
<< OPPOSITE pale
2 RED, pink, scarlet, ruby, crimson, reddish, roseate

rude *adjective* 1 IMPOLITE, insulting, cheeky, abrupt, short, blunt, abusive, curt, churlish, disrespectful, brusque, offhand, impertinent, insolent, inconsiderate, peremptory, impudent, discourteous, uncivil, unmannerly, ill-mannered
<< OPPOSITE polite
2 UNCIVILIZED, low, rough, savage, ignorant, coarse, illiterate, uneducated, brutish, barbarous, scurrilous, boorish, uncouth, unrefined, loutish, untutored, graceless, ungracious, unpolished, oafish, uncultured
3 VULGAR, gross, crude
<< OPPOSITE refined
4 UNPLEASANT, sharp, violent, sudden, harsh, startling, abrupt
5 ROUGHLY-MADE, simple, rough, raw, crude, primitive, makeshift, rough-hewn, artless, inelegant, inartistic
<< OPPOSITE well-made

rudiment *noun often plural* BASICS, elements, essentials, fundamentals, beginnings, foundation, nuts and bolts, first principles

rudimentary *adjective* 1 PRIMITIVE, undeveloped
2 BASIC, fundamental, elementary, early, primary, initial, introductory
3 UNDEVELOPED, embryonic, vestigial
<< OPPOSITE complete

rue *verb* (*Literary*) REGRET, mourn, grieve, lament, deplore, bemoan, repent, be sorry for, weep over, sorrow for, bewail, kick yourself for, reproach yourself for

rueful *adjective* REGRETFUL, sad, dismal, melancholy, grievous, pitiful, woeful, sorry, mournful, plaintive, lugubrious, contrite, sorrowful, repentant, doleful, remorseful, penitent, pitiable, woebegone, conscience-stricken, self-reproachful
<< OPPOSITE unrepentant

ruffle *verb* 1 DISARRANGE, disorder, wrinkle, mess up, rumple, tousle, derange, discompose, dishevel, muss (*US & Canad*)
2 ANNOY, worry, trouble, upset, confuse, stir, disturb, rattle (*informal*), irritate, put out, unsettle, shake up (*informal*), harass, hassle (*informal*), agitate, unnerve, disconcert, disquiet, nettle, vex, fluster, perturb, faze, peeve (*informal*), hack off (*informal*)
<< OPPOSITE calm

rugged *adjective* 1 ROCKY, broken, rough, craggy, difficult, ragged, stark, irregular, uneven, jagged, bumpy
<< OPPOSITE even
2 STRONG-FEATURED, lined, worn, weathered, wrinkled, furrowed, leathery, rough-hewn, weather-beaten
<< OPPOSITE delicate
3 WELL-BUILT, strong, tough, robust, sturdy
4 (*chiefly US & Canad*) TOUGH, strong, hardy, robust, vigorous, muscular, sturdy, hale, burly, husky (*informal*), beefy (*informal*), brawny
<< OPPOSITE delicate
5 STERN, hard, severe, rough, harsh, sour, rude, crabbed, austere, dour, surly, gruff

ruin *verb* 1 DESTROY, devastate, wreck, trash (*slang*), break, total (*slang*), defeat, smash, crush, overwhelm, shatter, overturn, overthrow, bring down, demolish, raze, lay waste, lay in ruins, wreak havoc upon, bring to ruin, bring to nothing, kennet (*Austral slang*), jeff (*Austral slang*)
<< OPPOSITE create
2 BANKRUPT, break, impoverish, beggar, pauperize
3 SPOIL, damage, mar, mess up, blow (*slang*), injure, undo, screw up (*informal*), botch, mangle, cock up (*Brit slang*), disfigure, make a mess of, bodge (*informal*), crool *or* cruel (*Austral*

slang)

<< OPPOSITE improve

▷ *noun* 1 BANKRUPTCY, insolvency, destitution

2 DISREPAIR, decay, disintegration, ruination, wreckage

3 DESTRUCTION, fall, the end, breakdown, damage, defeat, failure, crash, collapse, wreck, overthrow, undoing, havoc, Waterloo, downfall, devastation, dissolution, subversion, nemesis, crackup (*informal*)

<< OPPOSITE preservation

ruinous *adjective* 1 DESTRUCTIVE, devastating, shattering, fatal, deadly, disastrous, dire, withering, catastrophic, murderous, pernicious, noxious, calamitous, baleful, deleterious, injurious, baneful (*archaic*)

2 RUINED, broken-down, derelict, ramshackle, dilapidated, in ruins, decrepit

rule *noun* 1 REGULATION, order, law, ruling, guide, direction, guideline, decree, ordinance, dictum

2 PRECEPT, principle, criterion, canon, maxim, tenet, axiom

3 PROCEDURE, policy, standard, method, way, course, formula

4 CUSTOM, procedure, practice, routine, form, condition, tradition, habit, convention, wont, order *or* way of things

5 GOVERNMENT, power, control, authority, influence, administration, direction, leadership, command, regime, empire, reign, sway, domination, jurisdiction, supremacy, mastery, dominion, ascendancy, mana (NZ)

▷ *verb* 1 GOVERN, lead, control, manage, direct, guide, regulate, administer, oversee, preside over, have power over, reign over, command, have charge of

2 REIGN, govern, be in power, hold sway, wear the crown, be in authority, be number one (*informal*)

3 CONTROL, dominate, monopolize, tyrannize, be pre-eminent, have the upper hand over

4 DECREE, find, decide, judge, establish, determine, settle, resolve, pronounce, lay down, adjudge

5 BE PREVALENT, prevail, predominate, hold sway, be customary, preponderate, obtain

▷▷ **as a rule** USUALLY, generally, mainly, normally, on the whole, for the most part, ordinarily, customarily

▷▷ **rule someone out** EXCLUDE, eliminate, disqualify, ban, prevent, reject, dismiss, forbid, prohibit, leave out, preclude, proscribe, obviate, debar

▷▷ **rule something out** REJECT, exclude, eliminate

ruler *noun* 1 GOVERNOR, leader, lord, commander, controller, monarch, sovereign, head of state, potentate, crowned head, emperor *or* empress, king *or* queen, prince *or* princess

2 MEASURE, rule, yardstick, straight edge

ruling *adjective* 1 GOVERNING, upper, reigning, controlling, leading, commanding, dominant, regnant

2 PREDOMINANT, dominant, prevailing, preponderant, chief, main, current, supreme, principal, prevalent, pre-eminent, regnant

<< OPPOSITE minor

▷ *noun* DECISION, finding, resolution, verdict, judgment, decree, adjudication, pronouncement

rum *adjective* (*Brit slang*) STRANGE, odd, suspect, funny, unusual, curious, weird, suspicious, peculiar, dodgy (*Brit, Austral & NZ informal*), queer, singular, shonky (*Austral & NZ informal*)

ruminate *verb* PONDER, think, consider, reflect, contemplate, deliberate, muse, brood, meditate, mull over things, chew over things, cogitate, rack your brains, turn over in your mind

rummage *verb* SEARCH, hunt, root, explore, delve, examine, ransack, forage, fossick (*Austral & NZ*), rootle

rumour *noun* STORY, news, report, talk, word, whisper, buzz, gossip, dirt (*US slang*), goss (*informal*), hearsay, canard, tidings, scuttlebutt (*US slang*), bush telegraph, bruit (*archaic*)

▷▷ **be rumoured** BE SAID, be told, be reported, be published, be circulated, be whispered, be passed around, be put about, be noised abroad

rump *noun* BUTTOCKS, bottom, rear, backside (*informal*), tail (*informal*), seat, butt (*US & Canad informal*), bum (*Brit slang*), buns (*US slang*), rear end, posterior, haunch, hindquarters, derrière (*euphemistic*), croup, jacksy (*Brit slang*)

rumple *verb* RUFFLE, crush, disorder, dishevel, wrinkle, crease, crumple, screw up, mess up, pucker, crinkle, scrunch, tousle, derange, muss (*US & Canad*)

rumpus *noun* COMMOTION, row, noise, confusion, fuss, disturbance, disruption, furore, uproar, tumult, brouhaha, shindig (*informal*), hue and cry, kerfuffle (*informal*), shindy (*informal*)

run *verb* 1 RACE, speed, rush, dash, hurry, career, barrel (along) (*informal, chiefly US & Canad*), sprint, scramble, bolt, dart, gallop, hare (*Brit informal*), jog, scud, hasten, scurry, stampede, scamper, leg it (*informal*), lope, hie, hotfoot

<< OPPOSITE dawdle

2 FLEE, escape, take off (*informal*), depart, bolt, clear out, beat it (*slang*), leg it (*informal*), make off, abscond, decamp, take flight, do a runner (*slang*), scarper (*Brit slang*), slope off, cut and run (*informal*), make a run for it, fly the coop (*US & Canad informal*), beat a retreat, show a clean pair

of heels, skedaddle (*informal*), take a powder (*US & Canad slang*), take it on the lam (*US & Canad slang*), take to your heels
<< OPPOSITE stay
3 TAKE PART, compete
4 CONTINUE, go, stretch, last, reach, lie, range, extend, proceed
<< OPPOSITE stop
5 (*Chiefly US & Canad*) COMPETE, stand, contend, be a candidate, put yourself up for, take part, challenge
6 MANAGE, lead, direct, be in charge of, own, head, control, boss (*informal*), operate, handle, conduct, look after, carry on, regulate, take care of, administer, oversee, supervise, mastermind, coordinate, superintend
7 GO, work, operate, perform, function, be in business, be in action, tick over
8 PERFORM, carry out
9 WORK, go, operate, function
10 DRIVE
11 OPERATE, go
12 GIVE A LIFT TO, drive, carry, transport, convey, bear, manoeuvre, propel
13 PASS, go, move, roll, slide, glide, skim
14 FLOW, pour, stream, cascade, go, move, issue, proceed, leak, spill, discharge, gush, spout, course
15 SPREAD, mix, bleed, be diffused, lose colour
16 CIRCULATE, spread, creep, go round
17 PUBLISH, feature, display, print
18 MELT, dissolve, liquefy, go soft, turn to liquid
19 UNRAVEL, tear, ladder, come apart, come undone
20 SMUGGLE, deal in, traffic in, bootleg, ship, sneak
▷ *noun* **1** RACE, rush, dash, sprint, gallop, jog, spurt
2 RIDE, drive, trip, lift, journey, spin (*informal*), outing, excursion, jaunt, joy ride (*informal*)
3 SEQUENCE, period, stretch, spell, course, season, round, series, chain, cycle, string, passage, streak
4 TYPE, sort, kind, class, variety, category, order
5 TEAR, rip, ladder, snag
6 ENCLOSURE, pen, coop
7 DIRECTION, way, course, current, movement, progress, flow, path, trend, motion, passage, stream, tendency, drift, tide, tenor
8 *with* **on** SUDDEN DEMAND FOR, pressure for, rush for
▷▷ **in the long run** IN THE END, eventually, in time, ultimately, at the end of the day, in the final analysis, when all is said and done, in the fullness of time
▷▷ **on the run 1** ESCAPING, fugitive, in flight, at liberty, on the loose, on the lam (*US slang*)
2 IN RETREAT, defeated, fleeing, retreating, running away, falling back, in flight
3 HURRYING, hastily, in a hurry, at speed, hurriedly, in a rush, in haste
▷▷ **run across something** *or* **someone** MEET, encounter, meet with, come across, run into, bump into, come upon, chance upon
▷▷ **run away** *verb* FLEE, escape, take off, bolt, run off, clear out, beat it (*slang*), abscond, decamp, take flight, hook it (*slang*), do a runner (*slang*), scarper (*Brit slang*), cut and run (*informal*), make a run for it, turn tail, do a bunk (*Brit slang*), scram (*informal*), fly the coop (*US & Canad informal*), show a clean pair of heels, skedaddle (*informal*), take a powder (*US & Canad slang*), take it on the lam (*US & Canad slang*), take to your heels, do a Skase (*Austral informal*)
▷▷ **run away with something** *or* **someone**
1 ABSCOND WITH, run off with, elope with
2 WIN EASILY, walk it (*informal*), romp home, win hands down, win by a mile (*informal*)
▷▷ **run into someone** *verb* MEET, encounter, bump into, run across, chance upon, come across *or* upon
▷▷ **run into something 1** BE BESET BY, encounter, meet with, come across *or* upon, face, experience, be confronted by, happen on *or* upon
2 COLLIDE WITH, hit, strike, ram, bump into, crash into, dash against
▷▷ **run off** FLEE, escape, bolt, run away, clear out, make off, decamp, take flight, hook it (*slang*), do a runner (*slang*), scarper (*Brit slang*), cut and run (*informal*), turn tail, fly the coop (*US & Canad informal*), show a clean pair of heels, skedaddle (*informal*), take a powder (*US & Canad slang*), take it on the lam (*US & Canad slang*), take to your heels
▷▷ **run off with someone** RUN AWAY WITH, elope with, abscond with
▷▷ **run off with something** STEAL, take, lift (*informal*), nick (*slang, chiefly Brit*), pinch (*informal*), swipe (*slang*), run away with, make off with, embezzle, misappropriate, purloin, filch, walk *or* make off with
▷▷ **run out 1** BE USED UP, dry up, give out, peter out, fail, finish, cease, be exhausted
2 EXPIRE, end, terminate
▷▷ **run out of something** EXHAUST YOUR SUPPLY OF, be out of, be cleaned out, have no more, have none left, have no remaining
▷▷ **run out on someone** (*informal*) DESERT, abandon, strand, run away from, forsake, rat on (*informal*), leave high and dry, leave holding the baby, leave in the lurch
▷▷ **run over** OVERFLOW, spill over, brim over
▷▷ **run over something 1** EXCEED, overstep, go over the top of, go beyond the bounds of, go over the limit of
2 REVIEW, check, survey, examine, go through,

go over, run through, rehearse, reiterate
▷▷ **run over something** *or* **someone** KNOCK DOWN, hit, strike, run down, knock over
▷▷ **run someone in** (*informal*) ARREST, apprehend, pull in (*Brit slang*), take into custody, lift (*slang*), pick up, jail, nail (*informal*), bust (*informal*), collar (*informal*), pinch (*informal*), nab (*informal*), throw in jail, take to jail, feel your collar (*slang*)
▷▷ **run something in** BREAK IN GENTLY, run gently
▷▷ **run something off** PRODUCE, print, duplicate, churn out (*informal*)
▷▷ **run something** *or* **someone down**
1 CRITICIZE, denigrate, belittle, revile, knock (*informal*), rubbish (*informal*), put down, slag (off) (*slang*), disparage, decry, vilify, diss (*slang, chiefly US*), defame, bad-mouth (*slang, chiefly US & Canad*), speak ill of, asperse
2 DOWNSIZE, cut, drop, reduce, trim, decrease, cut back, curtail, pare down, kennet (*Austral slang*), jeff (*Austral slang*)
3 KNOCK DOWN, hit, strike, run into, run over, knock over
▷▷ **run through something** 1 REVIEW, check, survey, examine, go through, look over, run over
2 REHEARSE, read, practise, go over, run over
3 SQUANDER, waste, exhaust, throw away, dissipate, fritter away, spend like water, blow (*slang*)

runaway *adjective* 1 EASILY WON, easy, effortless
2 OUT OF CONTROL, uncontrolled
3 ESCAPED, wild, fleeing, loose, fugitive
▷ *noun* FUGITIVE, escaper, refugee, deserter, truant, escapee, absconder

run-down *or* **rundown** *adjective* 1 EXHAUSTED, weak, tired, drained, fatigued, weary, unhealthy, worn-out, debilitated, below par, under the weather (*informal*), enervated, out of condition, peaky
<< OPPOSITE fit
2 DILAPIDATED, broken-down, shabby, worn-out, seedy, ramshackle, dingy, decrepit, tumbledown
▷ *noun* SUMMARY, review, briefing, résumé, outline, sketch, run-through, synopsis, recap (*informal*), précis

run-in *noun* (*informal*) FIGHT, row, argument, dispute, set-to (*informal*), encounter, brush, confrontation, quarrel, skirmish, tussle, altercation, face-off (*slang*), dust-up (*informal*), contretemps, biffo (*Austral slang*)

runner *noun* 1 ATHLETE, miler, sprinter, harrier, jogger
2 MESSENGER, courier, errand boy, dispatch bearer
3 (*Botany*) STEM, shoot, sprout, sprig, offshoot, tendril, stolon (*Botany*)

running *noun* 1 MANAGEMENT, control, administration, direction, conduct, charge, leadership, organization, regulation, supervision, coordination, superintendency
2 WORKING, performance, operation, functioning, maintenance
▷ *adjective* 1 CONTINUOUS, constant, perpetual, uninterrupted, incessant, unceasing
2 IN SUCCESSION, together, unbroken, on the trot (*informal*)
3 FLOWING, moving, streaming, coursing

runny *adjective* FLOWING, liquid, melted, fluid, diluted, watery, streaming, liquefied

run-of-the-mill *adjective* ORDINARY, middling, average, fair, modest, commonplace, common, vanilla (*informal*), mediocre, banal, tolerable, passable, undistinguished, unimpressive, unexciting, unexceptional, bog-standard (*Brit & Irish slang*), no great shakes (*informal*), dime-a-dozen (*informal*)
<< OPPOSITE exceptional

run-up *noun* TIME LEADING UP TO, approach, build-up, preliminaries

rupture *noun* 1 HERNIA (*Medical*)
2 BREACH, split, hostility, falling-out (*informal*), disagreement, contention, feud, disruption, quarrel, rift, break, bust-up (*informal*), dissolution, altercation, schism, estrangement
3 BREAK, tear, split, crack, rent, burst, breach, fracture, cleavage, cleft, fissure
▷ *verb* 1 BREAK, separate, tear, split, crack, burst, rend, fracture, sever, puncture, cleave
2 CAUSE A BREACH, split, divide, disrupt, break off, come between, dissever

rural *adjective* 1 AGRICULTURAL, country, agrarian, upcountry, agrestic
2 RUSTIC, country, hick (*informal, chiefly US & Canad*), pastoral, bucolic, sylvan, Arcadian, countrified
<< OPPOSITE urban

ruse *noun* TRICK, deception, ploy, hoax, device, manoeuvre, dodge, sham, artifice, blind, subterfuge, stratagem, wile, imposture

rush *verb* 1 HURRY, run, race, shoot, fly, career, speed, tear, dash, sprint, scramble, bolt, dart, hasten, scurry, stampede, lose no time, make short work of, burn rubber (*informal*), make haste, hotfoot
<< OPPOSITE dawdle
2 PUSH, hurry, accelerate, dispatch, speed up, quicken, press, hustle, expedite
3 ATTACK, storm, capture, overcome, charge at, take by storm
▷ *noun* 1 DASH, charge, race, scramble, stampede, expedition, speed, dispatch
2 HURRY, urgency, bustle, haste, hustle, helter-skelter, hastiness
3 SURGE, flow, gush

4 ATTACK, charge, push, storm, assault, surge, onslaught
▷ *adjective* HASTY, fast, quick, hurried, emergency, prompt, rapid, urgent, swift, brisk, cursory, expeditious
<< OPPOSITE leisurely

rust *noun* **1** CORROSION, oxidation
2 MILDEW, must, mould, rot, blight
▷ *verb* **1** CORRODE, tarnish, oxidize
2 DETERIORATE, decline, decay, stagnate, atrophy, go stale

rustic *adjective* **1** RURAL, country, pastoral, bucolic, sylvan, Arcadian, countrified, upcountry, agrestic
<< OPPOSITE urban
2 SIMPLE, homely, plain, homespun, unsophisticated, unrefined, artless, unpolished
<< OPPOSITE grand
▷ *noun* YOKEL, peasant, hick (*informal, chiefly US & Canad*), bumpkin, swain (*archaic*), hillbilly, country boy, clod, boor, country cousin, hayseed (*US & Canad informal*), clodhopper (*informal*), son of the soil, clown, countryman *or* countrywoman
<< OPPOSITE sophisticate

rustle *verb* CRACKLE, whisper, swish, whoosh, crinkle, whish, crepitate, susurrate (*literary*)
▷ *noun* CRACKLE, whisper, rustling, crinkling, crepitation, susurration *or* susurrus (*literary*)

rusty *adjective* **1** CORRODED, rusted, oxidized, rust-covered
2 OUT OF PRACTICE, weak, impaired, sluggish, stale, deficient, not what it was, unpractised
3 REDDISH-BROWN, chestnut, reddish, russet, coppery, rust-coloured
4 CROAKING, cracked, creaking, hoarse, croaky

rut *noun* **1** HABIT, routine, dead end, humdrum existence, system, pattern, groove
2 GROOVE, score, track, trough, furrow, gouge, pothole, indentation, wheel mark

ruthless *adjective* MERCILESS, hard, severe, fierce, harsh, cruel, savage, brutal, stern, relentless, adamant, ferocious, callous, heartless, unrelenting, inhuman, inexorable, remorseless, barbarous, pitiless, unfeeling, hard-hearted, without pity, unmerciful, unpitying
<< OPPOSITE merciful

rutted *adjective* GROOVED, cut, marked, scored, holed, furrowed, gouged, indented

Ss

sable *adjective* 1 BLACK, jet, raven, jetty, ebony, ebon (*poetic*)
2 DARK, black, dim, gloomy, dismal, dreary, sombre, shadowy

sabotage *verb* 1 DAMAGE, destroy, wreck, undermine, disable, disrupt, cripple, subvert, incapacitate, vandalize, throw a spanner in the works (*Brit informal*)
2 DISRUPT, ruin, wreck, spoil, interrupt, interfere with, obstruct, intrude, crool *or* cruel (*Austral slang*)
▷ *noun* 1 DAMAGE, destruction, wrecking, vandalism, deliberate damage
2 DISRUPTION, ruining, wrecking, spoiling, interference, intrusion, interruption, obstruction

saboteur *noun* DEMONSTRATOR, rebel, dissident, hooligan, vandal, delinquent, dissenter, agitator, protest marcher

sac *noun* POUCH, bag, pocket, bladder, pod, cyst, vesicle

saccharine *adjective* SICKLY, honeyed, sentimental, sugary, nauseating, soppy (*Brit informal*), cloying, maudlin, syrupy (*informal*), mawkish, icky (*informal*), treacly, oversweet

sack[1] *noun* BAG, pocket, poke (*Scot*), sac, pouch, receptacle
▷ *verb* (*informal*) DISMISS, fire (*informal*), axe (*informal*), discharge, kick out (*informal*), give (someone) the boot (*slang*), give (someone) his marching orders, kiss off (*slang, chiefly US & Canad*), give (someone) the push (*informal*), give (someone) the bullet (*Brit slang*), give (someone) his books (*informal*), give (someone) the elbow, give (someone) his cards, kennet (*Austral slang*), jeff (*Austral slang*)
▷▷ **hit the sack** (*Slang*) GO TO BED, retire, turn in (*informal*), bed down, hit the hay (*slang*)
▷▷ **the sack** (*informal*) DISMISSAL, discharge, the boot (*slang*), the axe (*informal*), the chop (*Brit slang*), the push (*slang*), the (old) heave-ho (*informal*), termination of employment, the order of the boot (*slang*)

sack[2] *verb* PLUNDER, loot, pillage, destroy, strip, rob, raid, ruin, devastate, spoil, rifle, demolish, ravage, lay waste, despoil, maraud, depredate (*rare*)
▷ *noun* PLUNDERING, looting, pillage, waste, rape, ruin, destruction, ravage, plunder, devastation, depredation, despoliation, rapine

sacred *adjective* 1 HOLY, hallowed, consecrated, blessed, divine, revered, venerable, sanctified
<< OPPOSITE secular
2 RELIGIOUS, holy, ecclesiastical, hallowed, venerated
<< OPPOSITE unconsecrated
3 INVIOLABLE, protected, sacrosanct, secure, hallowed, inalienable, invulnerable, inviolate, unalterable

sacrifice *verb* 1 OFFER, offer up, immolate
2 GIVE UP, abandon, relinquish, lose, surrender, let go, do without, renounce, forfeit, forego, say goodbye to
▷ *noun* 1 OFFERING, immolation, oblation, hecatomb
2 SURRENDER, loss, giving up, resignation, rejection, waiver, abdication, renunciation, repudiation, forswearing, relinquishment, eschewal, self-denial

sacrificial *adjective* PROPITIATORY, atoning, reparative, expiatory, oblatory

sacrilege *noun* DESECRATION, violation, blasphemy, mockery, heresy, irreverence, profanity, impiety, profanation, profaneness
<< OPPOSITE reverence

sacrosanct *adjective* INVIOLABLE, sacred, inviolate, untouchable, hallowed, sanctified, set apart

sad *adjective* 1 UNHAPPY, down, low, blue, depressed, gloomy, grieved, dismal, melancholy, sombre, glum, wistful, mournful, dejected, downcast, grief-stricken, tearful, lugubrious, pensive, disconsolate, doleful, heavy-hearted, down in the dumps (*informal*), cheerless, lachrymose, woebegone, down in the mouth (*informal*), low-spirited, triste

(*archaic*), sick at heart
<< OPPOSITE happy
2 TRAGIC, moving, upsetting, dark, sorry, depressing, disastrous, dismal, pathetic, poignant, harrowing, grievous, pitiful, calamitous, heart-rending, pitiable
3 DEPLORABLE, bad, sorry, terrible, distressing, unfortunate, miserable, dismal, shabby, heartbreaking, regrettable, lamentable, wretched, to be deplored
<< OPPOSITE good
4 REGRETTABLE, disappointing, distressing, unhappy, unfortunate, unsatisfactory, woeful, deplorable, lamentable
<< OPPOSITE fortunate

sadden *verb* UPSET, depress, distress, grieve, desolate, cast down, bring tears to your eyes, make sad, dispirit, make your heart bleed, aggrieve, deject, cast a gloom upon

saddle *verb* BURDEN, load, lumber (*Brit informal*), charge, tax, task, encumber

sadism *noun* CRUELTY, savagery, brutality, severity, ferocity, spite, ruthlessness, depravity, harshness, inhumanity, barbarity, callousness, viciousness, bestiality, heartlessness, brutishness, spitefulness, bloodthirstiness, murderousness, mercilessness, fiendishness, hardheartedness

sadistic *adjective* CRUEL, savage, brutal, beastly, vicious, ruthless, perverted, perverse, inhuman, barbarous, fiendish

sadness *noun* UNHAPPINESS, sorrow, grief, tragedy, depression, the blues, misery, melancholy, poignancy, despondency, bleakness, heavy heart, dejection, wretchedness, gloominess, mournfulness, dolour (*poetic*), dolefulness, cheerlessness, sorrowfulness
<< OPPOSITE happiness

safe *adjective* 1 PROTECTED, secure, in safety, impregnable, out of danger, safe and sound, in safe hands, out of harm's way, free from harm
<< OPPOSITE endangered
2 ALL RIGHT, fine, intact, unscathed, unhurt, unharmed, undamaged, out of the woods, O.K. *or* okay (*informal*)
3 CAUTIOUS, prudent, sure, conservative, reliable, realistic, discreet, dependable, trustworthy, circumspect, on the safe side, unadventurous, tried and true
<< OPPOSITE risky
4 RISK-FREE, sound, secure, certain, impregnable, riskless
5 HARMLESS, wholesome, innocuous, pure, tame, unpolluted, nontoxic, nonpoisonous
<< OPPOSITE dangerous
▷ *noun* STRONGBOX, vault, coffer, repository, deposit box, safe-deposit box

safeguard *verb* PROTECT, guard, defend, save, screen, secure, preserve, look after, shield, watch over, keep safe
▷ *noun* PROTECTION, security, defence, guard, shield, armour, aegis, bulwark, surety

safely *adverb* IN SAFETY, securely, with impunity, without risk, with safety, safe and sound

safety *noun* 1 SECURITY, protection, safeguards, assurance, precautions, immunity, safety measures, impregnability
<< OPPOSITE risk
2 SHELTER, haven, protection, cover, retreat, asylum, refuge, sanctuary

sag *verb* 1 SINK, bag, droop, fall, drop, seat (*of skirts, etc*), settle, slump, dip, give way, bulge, swag, hang loosely, fall unevenly
2 DROP, sink, slump, flop, droop, loll
3 DECLINE, fall, slip, tire, slide, flag, slump, weaken, wilt, wane, cave in, droop

saga *noun* 1 CARRY-ON (*informal*), to-do, performance (*informal*), rigmarole, soap opera, pantomime (*informal*)
2 EPIC, story, tale, legend, adventure, romance, narrative, chronicle, yarn, fairy tale, folk tale, roman-fleuve (*French*)

sage *noun* WISE MAN, philosopher, guru, authority, expert, master, elder, pundit, Solomon, mahatma, Nestor, savant, Solon, man of learning, tohunga (*NZ*)
▷ *adjective* WISE, learned, intelligent, sensible, politic, acute, discerning, prudent, canny, judicious, perspicacious, sagacious, sapient

sail *noun* SHEET, canvas
▷ *verb* 1 GO BY WATER, cruise, voyage, ride the waves, go by sea
2 SET SAIL, embark, get under way, put to sea, put off, leave port, hoist sail, cast *or* weigh anchor
3 PILOT, steer, navigate, captain, skipper
4 GLIDE, sweep, float, shoot, fly, wing, soar, drift, skim, scud, skirr
▷▷ **sail through something** CRUISE THROUGH, walk through, romp through, pass easily, succeed easily at
▷▷ **set sail** PUT TO SEA, embark, get under way, put off, leave port, hoist sail, cast *or* weigh anchor

sailor *noun* MARINER, marine, seaman, salt, tar (*informal*), hearty (*informal*), navigator, sea dog, seafarer, matelot (*slang, chiefly Brit*), Jack Tar, seafaring man, lascar, leatherneck (*slang*)

saintly *adjective* VIRTUOUS, godly, holy, religious, sainted, blessed, worthy, righteous, devout, pious, angelic, blameless, god-fearing, beatific, sinless, saintlike, full of good works

sake *noun* PURPOSE, interest, cause, reason, end, aim, principle, objective, motive
▷▷ **for someone's sake** IN SOMEONE'S INTERESTS, to someone's advantage, on

someone's account, for the benefit of, for the good of, for the welfare of, out of respect for, out of consideration for, out of regard for

salacious *adjective* OBSCENE, indecent, pornographic, blue, erotic, steamy (*informal*), lewd, X-rated (*informal*), bawdy, smutty, lustful, ribald, ruttish

salary *noun* PAY, income, wage, fee, payment, wages, earnings, allowance, remuneration, recompense, stipend, emolument

sale *noun* 1 SELLING, marketing, dealing, trading, transaction, disposal, vending
2 AUCTION, fair, mart, bazaar

salient *adjective* PROMINENT, outstanding, important, marked, striking, arresting, signal, remarkable, pronounced, noticeable, conspicuous

saliva *noun* SPIT, dribble, drool, slaver, spittle, sputum

sallow *adjective* WAN, pale, sickly, pasty, pallid, unhealthy, yellowish, anaemic, bilious, jaundiced-looking, peely-wally (*Scot*)
<< OPPOSITE rosy

sally *noun* WITTICISM, joke, quip, crack (*informal*), retort, jest, riposte, wisecrack (*informal*), bon mot, smart remark
▷ *verb* GO FORTH, set out, rush, issue, surge, erupt

salon *noun* 1 SHOP, store, establishment, parlour, boutique
2 SITTING ROOM, lounge, living room, parlour, drawing room, front room, reception room, morning room

salt *noun* 1 SEASONING, sodium chloride, table salt, rock salt
2 SAILOR, marine, seaman, mariner, tar (*informal*), hearty (*informal*), navigator, sea dog, seafarer, matelot (*slang, chiefly Brit*), Jack Tar, seafaring man, lascar, leatherneck (*slang*)
▷ *adjective* SALTY, salted, saline, brackish, briny
▷▷ **rub salt into the wound** MAKE SOMETHING WORSE, add insult to injury, fan the flames, aggravate matters, magnify a problem
▷▷ **with a grain** *or* **pinch of salt** SCEPTICALLY, suspiciously, cynically, doubtfully, with reservations, disbelievingly, mistrustfully

salty *adjective* SALT, salted, saline, brackish, briny, over-salted, brak (*S African*)

salubrious *adjective* HEALTHY, beneficial, good for you, wholesome, invigorating, salutary, healthful, health-giving

salutary *adjective* BENEFICIAL, useful, valuable, helpful, profitable, good, practical, good for you, advantageous

salute *verb* 1 GREET, welcome, acknowledge, address, kiss, hail, salaam, accost, pay your respects to, doff your cap to, mihi (*NZ*)
2 HONOUR, acknowledge, recognize, take your hat off to (*informal*), pay tribute *or* homage to
▷ *noun* GREETING, recognition, salutation, address, kiss, salaam, obeisance

salvage *verb* SAVE, recover, rescue, restore, repair, get back, retrieve, redeem, glean, repossess, fetch back
▷ *noun* 1 RESCUE, saving, recovery, release, relief, liberation, salvation, deliverance, extrication
2 SCRAP, remains, waste, junk, offcuts

salvation *noun* 1 SAVING, rescue, recovery, restoration, salvage, redemption, deliverance
<< OPPOSITE ruin
2 LIFELINE, escape, relief, preservation

salve *verb* EASE, soothe, appease, still, allay, pacify, mollify, tranquillize, palliate
▷ *noun* BALM, cream, medication, lotion, lubricant, ointment, emollient, liniment, dressing, unguent

salvo *noun* BARRAGE, storm, bombardment, strafe, cannonade

same *adjective* 1 IDENTICAL, similar, alike, equal, twin, equivalent, corresponding, comparable, duplicate, indistinguishable, interchangeable
<< OPPOSITE different
2 THE VERY SAME, very, one and the same, selfsame
3 AFOREMENTIONED, aforesaid, selfsame
4 UNCHANGED, consistent, constant, uniform, unaltered, unfailing, invariable, unvarying, changeless
<< OPPOSITE altered
▷▷ **all the same** 1 NEVERTHELESS, still, regardless, nonetheless, after all, in any case, for all that, notwithstanding, in any event, anyhow, just the same, be that as it may
2 UNIMPORTANT, insignificant, immaterial, inconsequential, of no consequence, of little account, not worth mentioning

> The use of *same* as in *if you send us your order for the materials, we will deliver same tomorrow* is common in business and official English. In general English, however, this use of the word is best avoided, as it may sound rather stilted: *may I borrow your book? I will return it* (not *same*) *tomorrow*

sameness *noun* SIMILARITY, resemblance, uniformity, likeness, oneness, standardization, indistinguishability, identicalness

sample *noun* 1 SPECIMEN, example, model, pattern, instance, representative, indication, illustration, exemplification
2 CROSS SECTION, test, sampling
▷ *verb* TEST, try, check out (*informal*), experience, taste, examine, evaluate, inspect, experiment with, appraise, partake of

sanctify *verb* **1** CONSECRATE, bless, anoint, set apart, hallow, make sacred
2 CLEANSE, redeem, purify, absolve
sanctimonious *adjective* PIOUS, smug, hypocritical, pi (*Brit slang*), too good to be true, self-righteous, self-satisfied, goody-goody (*informal*), unctuous, holier-than-thou, priggish, pietistic, canting, pharisaical
sanction *verb* PERMIT, back, support, allow, approve, entitle, endorse, authorize, countenance, vouch for, lend your name to
<< OPPOSITE forbid
▷ *noun* **1** *often plural* BAN, restriction, boycott, embargo, exclusion, penalty, deterrent, prohibition, coercive measures
<< OPPOSITE permission
2 PERMISSION, backing, support, authority, approval, allowance, confirmation, endorsement, countenance, ratification, authorization, approbation, O.K. *or* okay (*informal*), stamp *or* seal of approval
<< OPPOSITE ban
sanctity *noun* SACREDNESS, inviolability, inalienability, hallowedness, sacrosanctness
sanctuary *noun* **1** PROTECTION, shelter, refuge, haven, retreat, asylum
2 RESERVE, park, preserve, reservation, national park, tract, nature reserve, conservation area
sanctum *noun* **1** REFUGE, retreat, den, private room
2 SANCTUARY, shrine, altar, holy place, Holy of Holies
sands *plural noun* BEACH, shore, strand (*literary*), dunes
sane *adjective* **1** RATIONAL, normal, all there (*informal*), lucid, of sound mind, compos mentis (*Latin*), in your right mind, mentally sound, in possession of all your faculties
<< OPPOSITE insane
2 SENSIBLE, sound, reasonable, balanced, moderate, sober, judicious, level-headed
<< OPPOSITE foolish
sanguine *adjective* CHEERFUL, confident, optimistic, assured, hopeful, buoyant, in good heart
<< OPPOSITE gloomy
sanitary *adjective* HYGIENIC, clean, healthy, wholesome, salubrious, unpolluted, germ-free
sanitation *noun* HYGIENE, cleanliness, sewerage
sanity *noun* **1** MENTAL HEALTH, reason, rationality, stability, normality, right mind (*informal*), saneness
<< OPPOSITE insanity
2 COMMON SENSE, sense, good sense, rationality, level-headedness, judiciousness, soundness of judgment
<< OPPOSITE stupidity
sap¹ *noun* **1** JUICE, essence, vital fluid, secretion, lifeblood, plant fluid
2 (*Slang*) FOOL, jerk (*slang, chiefly US & Canad*), idiot, noodle, wally (*slang*), wet (*Brit informal*), charlie (*Brit informal*), drip (*informal*), gull (*archaic*), prat (*slang*), plonker (*slang*), noddy, twit (*informal*), chump (*informal*), oaf, simpleton, nitwit (*informal*), ninny, nincompoop, dweeb (*US slang*), wuss (*slang*), Simple Simon, weenie (*US informal*), muggins (*Brit slang*), eejit (*Scot & Irish*), dumb-ass (*slang*), numpty (*Scot informal*), doofus (*slang, chiefly US*), nerd *or* nurd (*slang*), numskull *or* numbskull, dorba *or* dorb (*Austral slang*), bogan (*Austral slang*)
sap² *verb* WEAKEN, drain, undermine, rob, exhaust, bleed, erode, deplete, wear down, enervate, devitalize
sarcasm *noun* IRONY, satire, cynicism, contempt, ridicule, bitterness, scorn, sneering, mockery, venom, derision, vitriol, mordancy, causticness
sarcastic *adjective* IRONICAL, cynical, satirical, cutting, biting, sharp, acid, mocking, taunting, sneering, acrimonious, backhanded, contemptuous, disparaging, sardonic, caustic, bitchy (*informal*), vitriolic, acerbic, derisive, ironic, mordant, sarky (*Brit informal*), mordacious, acerb
sardonic *adjective* MOCKING, cynical, dry, bitter, sneering, jeering, malicious, wry, sarcastic, derisive, ironical, mordant, mordacious
sash *noun* BELT, girdle, waistband, cummerbund
Satan *noun* THE DEVIL, Lucifer, Prince of Darkness, Lord of the Flies, Mephistopheles, Beelzebub, Old Nick (*informal*), The Evil One, Apollyon, Old Scratch (*informal*)
satanic *adjective* EVIL, demonic, hellish, black, malignant, wicked, inhuman, malevolent, devilish, infernal, fiendish, accursed, iniquitous, diabolic, demoniac, demoniacal
<< OPPOSITE godly
sate *verb* SATISFY, satiate, slake, indulge to the full
satellite *noun* **1** SPACECRAFT, communications satellite, sputnik, space capsule
2 MOON, secondary planet
satire *noun* **1** MOCKERY, wit, irony, ridicule, sarcasm
2 PARODY, mockery, caricature, send-up (*Brit informal*), spoof (*informal*), travesty, takeoff (*informal*), lampoon, skit, burlesque
satirical *or* **satiric** *adjective* MOCKING, ironical, cynical, cutting, biting, bitter, taunting, pungent, incisive, sarcastic, sardonic, caustic, vitriolic, burlesque, mordant, Rabelaisian, mordacious
satisfaction *noun* **1** FULFILMENT, pleasure, achievement, joy, relish, glee, gratification,

pride, complacency
<< OPPOSITE dissatisfaction
2 COMPENSATION, damages, justice, amends, settlement, redress, remuneration, reparation, vindication, restitution, reimbursement, atonement, recompense, indemnification, requital
<< OPPOSITE injury
3 CONTENTMENT, content, comfort, ease, pleasure, well-being, happiness, enjoyment, peace of mind, gratification, satiety, repletion, contentedness
<< OPPOSITE discontent

satisfactory *adjective* ADEQUATE, acceptable, good enough, average, fair, all right, suitable, sufficient, competent, up to scratch, passable, up to standard, up to the mark
<< OPPOSITE unsatisfactory

satisfied *adjective* 1 CONTENTED, happy, content, pacified, pleased
<< OPPOSITE dissatisfied
2 SURE, smug, convinced, positive, easy in your mind

satisfy *verb* 1 CONTENT, please, indulge, fill, feed, appease, gratify, pander to, assuage, pacify, quench, mollify, surfeit, satiate, slake, sate
<< OPPOSITE dissatisfy
2 CONVINCE, persuade, assure, reassure, dispel (someone's) doubts, put (someone's) mind at rest
<< OPPOSITE dissuade
3 COMPLY WITH, meet, fulfil, answer, serve, fill, observe, obey, conform to
<< OPPOSITE fail to meet

satisfying *adjective* SATISFACTORY, pleasing, gratifying, pleasurable, cheering

saturate *verb* 1 FLOOD, overwhelm, swamp, overrun, deluge, glut
2 SOAK, steep, drench, seep, imbue, douse, impregnate, suffuse, ret (*used of flax, etc*), wet through, waterlog, souse, drouk (*Scot*)

saturated *adjective* SOAKED, soaking (wet), drenched, sodden, dripping, waterlogged, sopping (wet), wet through, soaked to the skin, wringing wet, droukit *or* drookit (*Scot*)

sauce *noun* DRESSING, dip, relish, condiment

saucy *adjective* IMPUDENT, cheeky (*informal*), impertinent, forward, fresh (*informal*), flip (*informal*), rude, sassy (*US informal*), pert, disrespectful, flippant, presumptuous, insolent, lippy (*US & Canad slang*), smart-alecky (*informal*)

saunter *verb* STROLL, wander, amble, roam, ramble, meander, rove, take a stroll, mosey (*informal*), stravaig (*Scot & Northern English dialect*)
▷ *noun* STROLL, walk, amble, turn, airing, constitutional, ramble, promenade, breather, perambulation

savage *adjective* 1 CRUEL, brutal, vicious, bloody, fierce, harsh, beastly, ruthless, ferocious, murderous, ravening, sadistic, inhuman, merciless, diabolical, brutish, devilish, bloodthirsty, barbarous, pitiless, bestial
<< OPPOSITE gentle
2 WILD, fierce, ferocious, unbroken, feral, untamed, undomesticated
<< OPPOSITE tame
3 PRIMITIVE, undeveloped, uncultivated, uncivilized, in a state of nature, nonliterate
4 UNCULTIVATED, rugged, unspoilt, uninhabited, waste, rough, uncivilized, unfrequented
<< OPPOSITE cultivated
▷ *noun* 1 NATIVE, barbarian, heathen, indigene, primitive person, autochthon
2 LOUT, yob (*Brit slang*), brute, bear, monster, beast, barbarian, fiend, yahoo, hoon (*Austral & NZ*), yobbo (*Brit slang*), roughneck (*slang*), boor, cougan (*Austral slang*), scozza (*Austral slang*), bogan (*Austral slang*)
▷ *verb* 1 MAUL, tear, claw, attack, mangle, lacerate, mangulate (*Austral slang*)
2 CRITICIZE, attack, knock (*informal*), blast, pan (*informal*), slam (*slang*), put down, slate (*informal*), have a go (at) (*informal*), disparage, tear into (*informal*), find fault with, lambast(e), pick holes in, pick to pieces, give (someone *or* something) a bad press
<< OPPOSITE praise

savagery *noun* CRUELTY, brutality, ferocity, ruthlessness, sadism, inhumanity, barbarity, viciousness, bestiality, fierceness, bloodthirstiness

save *verb* 1 RESCUE, free, release, deliver, recover, get out, liberate, salvage, redeem, bail out, come to someone's rescue, set free, save the life of, extricate, save someone's bacon (*Brit informal*)
<< OPPOSITE endanger
2 KEEP, reserve, set aside, store, collect, gather, hold, hoard, hide away, lay by, put by, salt away, treasure up, keep up your sleeve (*informal*), put aside for a rainy day
<< OPPOSITE spend
3 PROTECT, keep, guard, preserve, look after, take care of, safeguard, salvage, conserve, keep safe
4 BUDGET, be economical, economize, scrimp and save, retrench, be frugal, make economies, be thrifty, tighten your belt (*informal*)
5 PUT ASIDE, keep, reserve, collect, retain, set aside, amass, put by
6 PREVENT, avoid, spare, rule out, avert, obviate

saving *noun* ECONOMY, discount, reduction,

bargain, cut
▷ *plural noun* NEST EGG, fund, store, reserves, resources, fall-back, provision for a rainy day
saviour *noun* RESCUER, deliverer, defender, guardian, salvation, protector, liberator, Good Samaritan, redeemer, preserver, knight in shining armour, friend in need
Saviour *noun* CHRIST, Jesus, the Messiah, the Redeemer
savour *verb* 1 RELISH, like, delight in, revel in, luxuriate in, gloat over
2 ENJOY, appreciate, relish, delight in, revel in, partake of, drool over, luxuriate in, enjoy to the full, smack your lips over
▷ *noun* 1 FLAVOUR, taste, smell, relish, smack, zest, tang, zing (*informal*), piquancy
2 ZEST, interest, spice, excitement, salt, flavour
savoury *adjective* 1 SPICY, rich, delicious, tasty, luscious, palatable, tangy, dainty, delectable, mouthwatering, piquant, full-flavoured, scrumptious (*informal*), appetizing, toothsome, yummo (*Austral slang*)
<< OPPOSITE tasteless
2 WHOLESOME, decent, respectable, honest, reputable, apple-pie (*informal*)
<< OPPOSITE disreputable
▷ *plural noun* APPETIZERS, nibbles, apéritifs, canapés, titbits, hors d'oeuvres
savvy (*Slang*) *noun* UNDERSTANDING, perception, grasp, ken, comprehension, apprehension
▷ *adjective* SHREWD, sharp, astute, knowing, fly (*slang*), keen, smart, clever, intelligent, discriminating, discerning, canny, perceptive, artful, far-sighted, far-seeing, long-headed, perspicacious, sagacious
say *verb* 1 STATE, declare, remark, add, announce, maintain, mention, assert, affirm, asseverate
2 SPEAK, utter, voice, express, pronounce, come out with (*informal*), put into words, give voice *or* utterance to
3 MAKE KNOWN, reveal, disclose, divulge, answer, reply, respond, give as your opinion
4 SUGGEST, express, imply, communicate, disclose, give away, convey, divulge
5 SUPPOSE, supposing, imagine, assume, presume
6 ESTIMATE, suppose, guess, conjecture, surmise, dare say, hazard a guess
7 RECITE, perform, deliver, do, read, repeat, render, rehearse, orate
8 ALLEGE, report, claim, hold, suggest, insist, maintain, rumour, assert, uphold, profess, put about that
▷ *noun* 1 INFLUENCE, power, control, authority, weight, sway, clout (*informal*), predominance, mana (*NZ*)
2 CHANCE TO SPEAK, vote, voice, crack (*informal*), opportunity to speak, turn to speak
▷▷ **to say the least** AT THE VERY LEAST, without any exaggeration, to put it mildly
saying *noun* PROVERB, maxim, adage, saw, slogan, gnome, dictum, axiom, aphorism, byword, apophthegm
▷▷ **go without saying** BE OBVIOUS, be understood, be taken for granted, be accepted, be self-evident, be taken as read, be a matter of course
say-so *noun* (*informal*) ASSERTION, authority, agreement, word, guarantee, sanction, permission, consent, assurance, assent, authorization, dictum, asseveration, O.K. *or* okay (*informal*)
scalding *adjective* BURNING, boiling, searing, blistering, piping hot
scale[1] *noun* FLAKE, plate, layer, lamina
scale[2] *noun* 1 DEGREE, size, range, spread, extent, dimensions, scope, magnitude, breadth
2 SYSTEM OF MEASUREMENT, register, measuring system, graduated system, calibration, calibrated system
3 RANKING, ladder, spectrum, hierarchy, series, sequence, progression, pecking order (*informal*)
4 RATIO, proportion, relative size
▷ *verb* CLIMB UP, mount, go up, ascend, surmount, scramble up, clamber up, escalade
▷▷ **scale something down** REDUCE, cut, moderate, slow down, cut down, wind down, tone down, downsize, kennet (*Austral slang*), jeff (*Austral slang*)
▷▷ **scale something up** EXPAND, extend, blow up, enlarge, lengthen, magnify, amplify, augment
scaly *adjective* 1 SQUAMOUS, squamate, lamellose, lamelliform
2 FLAKY, scabrous, scurfy, furfuraceous (*Medical*), squamous *or* squamose (*Biology*), squamulose
scamper *verb* RUN, dash, dart, fly, hurry, sprint, romp, beetle, hasten, scuttle, scurry, scoot
scan *verb* 1 GLANCE OVER, skim, look over, eye, check, clock (*Brit slang*), examine, check out (*informal*), run over, eyeball (*slang*), size up (*informal*), get a load of (*informal*), look someone up and down, run your eye over, take a dekko at (*Brit slang*), surf (*Computing*)
2 SURVEY, search, investigate, sweep, con (*archaic*), scour, scrutinize, take stock of, recce (*slang*)
▷ *noun* 1 LOOK, glance, skim, browse, flick, squint, butcher's (*Brit slang*), brief look, dekko (*Brit slang*), shufti (*Brit slang*)
2 EXAMINATION, scanning, ultrasound
scandal *noun* 1 DISGRACE, crime, offence, sin, embarrassment, wrongdoing, skeleton in the cupboard, dishonourable behaviour, discreditable behaviour

2 GOSSIP, goss (*informal*), talk, rumours, dirt, slander, tattle, dirty linen (*informal*), calumny, backbiting, aspersion
3 SHAME, offence, disgrace, stigma, infamy, opprobrium, obloquy
4 OUTRAGE, shame, insult, disgrace, injustice, crying shame

scandalous *adjective* 1 SHOCKING, disgraceful, outrageous, offensive, appalling, foul, dreadful, horrifying, obscene, monstrous, unspeakable, atrocious, frightful, abominable
<< OPPOSITE decent
2 SLANDEROUS, gossiping, scurrilous, untrue, defamatory, libellous
<< OPPOSITE laudatory
3 OUTRAGEOUS, shocking, infamous, disgraceful, monstrous, shameful, atrocious, unseemly, odious, disreputable, opprobrious, highly improper
<< OPPOSITE proper

scant *adjective* 1 INADEQUATE, insufficient, meagre, sparse, little, limited, bare, minimal, deficient, barely sufficient
<< OPPOSITE adequate
2 SMALL, limited, inadequate, insufficient, meagre, measly, scanty, inconsiderable

scanty *adjective* 1 MEAGRE, sparse, poor, thin, narrow, sparing, restricted, bare, inadequate, pathetic, insufficient, slender, scant, deficient, exiguous
2 SKIMPY, short, brief, tight, thin

scapegoat *noun* FALL GUY, whipping boy

scar *noun* 1 MARK, injury, wound, trauma (*Pathology*), blemish, cicatrix
2 TRAUMA, suffering, pain, strain, torture, disturbance, anguish
▷ *verb* MARK, disfigure, damage, brand, mar, mutilate, maim, blemish, deface, traumatize, disfeature

scarce *adjective* 1 IN SHORT SUPPLY, wanting, insufficient, deficient, at a premium, thin on the ground
<< OPPOSITE plentiful
2 RARE, few, unusual, uncommon, few and far between, infrequent, thin on the ground
<< OPPOSITE common

scarcely *adverb* 1 HARDLY, barely, only just, scarce (*archaic*)
2 (*Often used ironically*) BY NO MEANS, hardly, not at all, definitely not, under no circumstances, on no account

Since *scarcely*, *hardly*, and *barely* already have negative force, it is unnecessary to use another negative word with them. Therefore, say *he had hardly had time to think* (not *he hadn't hardly had time to think*); and *there was scarcely any bread left* (not *there was scarcely no bread left*). When *scarcely*, *hardly*, and *barely* are used at the beginning of a sentence, as in *scarcely had I arrived*, the following clause should start with *when*: *scarcely had I arrived when I was asked to chair a meeting*. The word *before* can be used in place of *when* in this context, but the word *than* used in the same way is considered incorrect by many people, though this use is becoming increasingly common

scarcity *noun* SHORTAGE, lack, deficiency, poverty, want, dearth, paucity, insufficiency, infrequency, undersupply, rareness
<< OPPOSITE abundance

scare *verb* FRIGHTEN, alarm, terrify, panic, shock, startle, intimidate, dismay, daunt, terrorize, put the wind up (someone) (*informal*), give (someone) a fright, give (someone) a turn (*informal*), affright (*archaic*)
▷ *noun* 1 FRIGHT, shock, start
2 PANIC, hysteria
3 ALERT, warning, alarm

scared *adjective* AFRAID, alarmed, frightened, terrified, shaken, cowed, startled, fearful, unnerved, petrified, panicky, terrorized, panic-stricken, scared stiff, terror-stricken

scarf *noun* MUFFLER, stole, headscarf, comforter, cravat, neckerchief, headsquare

scary *adjective* (*informal*) FRIGHTENING, alarming, terrifying, shocking, chilling, horrifying, intimidating, horrendous, hairy (*slang*), unnerving, spooky (*informal*), creepy (*informal*), hair-raising, spine-chilling, bloodcurdling

scathing *adjective* CRITICAL, cutting, biting, harsh, savage, brutal, searing, withering, belittling, sarcastic, caustic, scornful, vitriolic, trenchant, mordant, mordacious

scatter *verb* 1 THROW ABOUT, spread, sprinkle, strew, broadcast, shower, fling, litter, sow, diffuse, disseminate
<< OPPOSITE gather
2 DISPERSE, separate, break up, dispel, disband, dissipate, disunite, put to flight
<< OPPOSITE assemble

scattering *noun* SPRINKLING, few, handful, scatter, smattering, smatter

scavenge *verb* SEARCH, hunt, forage, rummage, root about, fossick (*Austral* & NZ), scratch about

scenario *noun* 1 SITUATION, sequence of events, chain of events, course of events, series of developments
2 STORY LINE, résumé, outline, sketch, summary, rundown, synopsis

scene *noun* 1 ACT, part, division, episode

2 SETTING, set, background, location, backdrop, mise en scène (*French*)
3 INCIDENT, happening, event, episode
4 SITE, place, setting, area, position, stage, situation, spot, whereabouts, locality
5 (*informal*) WORLD, business, environment, preserve, arena, realm, domain, milieu, thing, field of interest
6 VIEW, prospect, panorama, vista, landscape, tableau, outlook
7 FUSS, to-do, row, performance, upset, drama, exhibition, carry-on (*informal, chiefly Brit*), confrontation, tantrum, commotion, hue and cry, display of emotion, hissy fit (*informal*)
8 SECTION, part, sequence, segment, clip

scenery *noun* 1 LANDSCAPE, view, surroundings, terrain, vista
2 (*Theatre*) SET, setting, backdrop, flats, décor, stage set

scenic *adjective* PICTURESQUE, beautiful, spectacular, striking, grand, impressive, breathtaking, panoramic

scent *noun* 1 FRAGRANCE, smell, perfume, bouquet, aroma, odour, niff (*Brit slang*), redolence
2 TRAIL, track, spoor
3 PERFUME, fragrance, cologne, eau de toilette (*French*), eau de cologne (*French*), toilet water
▷ *verb* SMELL, sense, recognize, detect, sniff, discern, sniff out, nose out, get wind of (*informal*), be on the track *or* trail of

scented *adjective* FRAGRANT, perfumed, aromatic, sweet-smelling, redolent, ambrosial, odoriferous

sceptic *noun* 1 DOUBTER, cynic, scoffer, disbeliever, Pyrrhonist
2 AGNOSTIC, doubter, unbeliever, doubting Thomas

sceptical *adjective* DOUBTFUL, cynical, dubious, questioning, doubting, hesitating, scoffing, unconvinced, disbelieving, incredulous, quizzical, mistrustful, unbelieving
<< OPPOSITE convinced

scepticism *noun* DOUBT, suspicion, disbelief, cynicism, incredulity

schedule *noun* 1 PLAN, programme, agenda, calendar, timetable, itinerary, list of appointments
2 LIST, catalogue, inventory, syllabus
▷ *verb* PLAN, set up, book, programme, arrange, organize, timetable

schematic *adjective* GRAPHIC, representational, illustrative, diagrammatic, diagrammatical

scheme *noun* 1 PLAN, programme, strategy, system, design, project, theory, proposal, device, tactics, course of action, contrivance
2 PLOT, dodge, ploy, ruse, game (*informal*), shift, intrigue, conspiracy, manoeuvre, machinations, subterfuge, stratagem
▷ *verb* PLOT, plan, intrigue, manoeuvre, conspire, contrive, collude, wheel and deal, machinate

scheming *adjective* CALCULATING, cunning, sly, designing, tricky, slippery, wily, artful, conniving, Machiavellian, foxy, deceitful, underhand, duplicitous
<< OPPOSITE straightforward

schism *noun* DIVISION, break, split, breach, separation, rift, splintering, rupture, discord, disunion

schmick *adjective* (*Austral slang*) 1 EXCELLENT, outstanding, good, great, fine, prime, capital, noted, choice, champion, cool (*informal*), select, brilliant, very good, cracking (*Brit informal*), crucial (*slang*), mean (*slang*), superb, distinguished, fantastic, magnificent, superior, sterling, worthy, first-class, marvellous, exceptional, terrific, splendid, notable, mega (*slang*), topping (*Brit slang*), sovereign, dope (*slang*), world-class, exquisite, admirable, exemplary, wicked (*slang*), first-rate, def (*slang*), superlative, top-notch (*informal*), brill (*informal*), pre-eminent, meritorious, estimable, tiptop, bodacious (*slang, chiefly US*), boffo (*slang*), jim-dandy (*slang*), A1 *or* A-one (*informal*), bitchin' (*US slang*), chillin' (*US slang*), booshit (*Austral slang*), exo (*Austral slang*), sik (*Austral slang*), rad (*informal*), phat (*slang*)
<< OPPOSITE terrible
2 STYLISH, smart, chic, polished, fashionable, trendy (*Brit informal*), classy (*slang*), in fashion, snappy, in vogue, dapper, natty (*informal*), snazzy (*informal*), modish, well turned-out, dressy (*informal*), à la mode, voguish
<< OPPOSITE scruffy

scholar *noun* 1 INTELLECTUAL, academic, man of letters, bookworm, egghead (*informal*), savant, bluestocking (*usually disparaging*), acca (*Austral slang*)
2 STUDENT, pupil, learner, schoolboy *or* schoolgirl

scholarly *adjective* LEARNED, academic, intellectual, lettered, erudite, scholastic, well-read, studious, bookish, swotty (*Brit informal*)
<< OPPOSITE uneducated

scholarship *noun* 1 GRANT, award, payment, exhibition, endowment, fellowship, bursary
2 LEARNING, education, culture, knowledge, wisdom, accomplishments, attainments, lore, erudition, academic study, book-learning

scholastic *adjective* LEARNED, academic, scholarly, lettered, literary, bookish

school *noun* 1 ACADEMY, college, institution, institute, discipline, seminary, educational institution, centre of learning, alma mater
2 GROUP, set, circle, following, class, faction, followers, disciples, sect, devotees,

denomination, clique, adherents, schism
3 WAY OF LIFE, creed, faith, outlook, persuasion, school of thought
▷ *verb* TRAIN, prime, coach, prepare, discipline, educate, drill, tutor, instruct, verse, indoctrinate

schooling *noun* 1 TEACHING, education, tuition, formal education, book-learning
2 TRAINING, coaching, instruction, grounding, preparation, drill, guidance

schoolteacher *noun* SCHOOLMASTER *or* SCHOOLMISTRESS, instructor, pedagogue, schoolmarm (*informal*), dominie (*Scot*)

science *noun* DISCIPLINE, body of knowledge, branch of knowledge

scientific *adjective* 1 TECHNOLOGICAL, technical, chemical, biological, empirical, factual
2 SYSTEMATIC, accurate, exact, precise, controlled, mathematical

scientist *noun* RESEARCHER, inventor, boffin (*informal*), technophile

scintillating *adjective* BRILLIANT, exciting, stimulating, lively, sparkling, bright, glittering, dazzling, witty, animated

scion *noun* DESCENDANT, child, offspring, successor, heir

scoff[1] *verb* SCORN, mock, laugh at, ridicule, knock (*informal*), taunt, despise, sneer, jeer, deride, slag (off) (*slang*), flout, belittle, revile, make light of, poke fun at, twit, gibe, pooh-pooh, make sport of

scoff[2] *verb* GOBBLE (UP), wolf, devour, bolt, cram, put away, guzzle, gulp down, gorge yourself on, gollop, stuff yourself with, cram yourself on, make a pig of yourself on (*informal*)

scold *verb* REPRIMAND, censure, rebuke, rate, blame, lecture, carpet (*informal*), slate (*informal, chiefly Brit*), nag, go on at, reproach, berate, tick off (*informal*), castigate, chide, tear into (*informal*), tell off (*informal*), find fault with, remonstrate with, bring (someone) to book, take (someone) to task, read the riot act, reprove, upbraid, bawl out (*informal*), give (someone) a talking-to (*informal*), haul (someone) over the coals (*informal*), chew out (*US & Canad informal*), give (someone) a dressing-down, tear (someone) off a strip (*Brit informal*), give a rocket (*Brit & NZ informal*), vituperate, give (someone) a row, have (someone) on the carpet (*informal*)
<< OPPOSITE praise

scolding *noun* TICKING-OFF, row, lecture, wigging (*Brit slang*), rebuke (*informal*), dressing-down (*informal*), telling-off (*informal*), tongue-lashing, piece of your mind, (good) talking-to (*informal*)

scoop *verb* WIN, get, receive, land, gain, achieve, net, earn, pick up, bag (*informal*), secure, collect, obtain, procure, come away with
▷ *noun* 1 LADLE, spoon, dipper
2 SPOONFUL, lump, dollop (*informal*), ball, ladleful
3 EXCLUSIVE, exposé, coup, revelation, sensation, inside story
▷▷ **scoop something out** 1 TAKE OUT, empty, dig out, scrape out, spoon out, bail *or* bale out
2 DIG, shovel, excavate, gouge, hollow out
▷▷ **scoop something** *or* **someone up** GATHER UP, lift, pick up, take up, sweep up *or* away

scoot *verb* DASH, run, dart, sprint, bolt, zip, scuttle, scurry, scamper, skitter, skedaddle (*informal*), skirr

scope *noun* 1 OPPORTUNITY, room, freedom, space, liberty, latitude, elbowroom, leeway
2 RANGE, capacity, reach, area, extent, outlook, orbit, span, sphere, ambit, purview, field of reference

scorch *verb* BURN, sear, char, roast, blister, wither, blacken, shrivel, parch, singe

scorching *adjective* BURNING, boiling, baking, flaming, tropical, roasting, searing, fiery, sizzling, red-hot, torrid, sweltering, broiling, unbearably hot

score *verb* 1 GAIN, win, achieve, make, get, net, bag, obtain, bring in, attain, amass, notch up (*informal*), chalk up (*informal*)
2 GO DOWN WELL WITH (SOMEONE), impress, triumph, make a hit (*informal*), make a point, gain an advantage, put yourself across, make an impact *or* impression
3 (*Music*) ARRANGE, set, orchestrate, adapt
4 CUT, scratch, nick, mark, mar, slash, scrape, notch, graze, gouge, deface, indent, crosshatch
▷ *noun* 1 RATING, mark, grade, percentage
2 POINTS, result, total, outcome
3 COMPOSITION, soundtrack, arrangement, orchestration
4 GRIEVANCE, wrong, injury, injustice, grudge, bone of contention, bone to pick
5 CHARGE, bill, account, total, debt, reckoning, tab (*US informal*), tally, amount due
▷ *plural noun* LOTS, loads, many, millions, gazillions (*informal*), hundreds, hosts, crowds, masses, droves, an army, legions, swarms, multitudes, myriads, very many, a flock, a throng, a great number
▷▷ **score something out** *or* **through** CROSS OUT, delete, strike out, cancel, obliterate, put a line through

scorn *noun* CONTEMPT, disdain, mockery, derision, despite, slight, sneer, sarcasm, disparagement, contumely, contemptuousness, scornfulness
<< OPPOSITE respect
▷ *verb* DESPISE, reject, disdain, slight, snub, shun, be above, spurn, rebuff, deride, flout,

look down on, scoff at, make fun of, sneer at, hold in contempt, turn up your nose at (*informal*), contemn, curl your lip at, consider beneath you
<< OPPOSITE respect
scornful *adjective* CONTEMPTUOUS, insulting, mocking, defiant, withering, sneering, slighting, jeering, scoffing, scathing, sarcastic, sardonic, haughty, disdainful, insolent, derisive, supercilious, contumelious
scornfully *adverb* CONTEMPTUOUSLY, with contempt, dismissively, disdainfully, with disdain, scathingly, witheringly, with a sneer, slightingly, with lip curled
scotch *verb* PUT AN END TO, destroy, smash, devastate, wreck, thwart, scupper, extinguish, put paid to, nip in the bud, bring to an end, put the lid on, put the kibosh on
scoundrel *noun* (*Old-fashioned*) ROGUE, villain, heel (*slang*), cheat, swine, rascal, son-of-a-bitch (*slang, chiefly US & Canad*), scally (*Northwest English dialect*), wretch, incorrigible, knave (*archaic*), rotter (*slang, chiefly Brit*), ne'er-do-well, reprobate, scumbag (*slang*), good-for-nothing, miscreant, scamp, bad egg (*old-fashioned informal*), blackguard, scapegrace, caitiff (*archaic*), dastard (*archaic*), skelm (*S African*), wrong 'un (*Austral slang*)
scour[1] *verb* SCRUB, clean, polish, rub, cleanse, buff, burnish, whiten, furbish, abrade
scour[2] *verb* SEARCH, hunt, comb, ransack, forage, look high and low, go over with a fine-tooth comb
scourge *noun* 1 AFFLICTION, plague, curse, terror, pest, torment, misfortune, visitation, bane, infliction
<< OPPOSITE benefit
2 WHIP, lash, thong, switch, strap, cat-o'-nine-tails
▷ *verb* 1 AFFLICT, plague, curse, torment, harass, terrorize, excoriate
2 WHIP, beat, lash, thrash, discipline, belt (*informal*), leather, punish, whale, cane, flog, trounce, castigate, wallop (*informal*), chastise, lather (*informal*), horsewhip, tan (someone's) hide (*slang*), take a strap to
scout *noun* VANGUARD, lookout, precursor, outrider, reconnoitrer, advance guard
▷ *verb* RECONNOITRE, investigate, check out, case (*slang*), watch, survey, observe, spy, probe, recce (*slang*), spy out, make a reconnaissance, see how the land lies
▷▷ **scout around** *or* **round** SEARCH, look for, hunt for, fossick (*Austral & NZ*), cast about *or* around, ferret about *or* around
scowl *verb* GLOWER, frown, look daggers, grimace, lour *or* lower
▷ *noun* GLOWER, frown, dirty look, black look, grimace
scrabble *verb* SCRAPE, scratch, scramble, dig, claw, paw, grope, clamber
scramble *verb* 1 STRUGGLE, climb, clamber, push, crawl, swarm, scrabble, move with difficulty
2 STRIVE, rush, contend, vie, run, push, hasten, jostle, jockey for position, make haste
3 JUMBLE, mix up, muddle, shuffle, entangle, disarrange
▷ *noun* 1 CLAMBER, ascent
2 RACE, competition, struggle, rush, confusion, hustle, free-for-all (*informal*), commotion, melee *or* mêlée
scrap[1] *noun* 1 PIECE, fragment, bit, trace, grain, particle, portion, snatch, part, atom, remnant, crumb, mite, bite, mouthful, snippet, sliver, morsel, modicum, iota
2 WASTE, junk, off cuts
▷ *plural noun* LEFTOVERS, remains, bits, scrapings, leavings
▷ *verb* GET RID OF, drop, abandon, shed, break up, ditch (*slang*), junk (*informal*), chuck (*informal*), discard, write off, demolish, trash (*slang*), dispense with, jettison, toss out, throw on the scrapheap, throw away *or* out
<< OPPOSITE bring back
scrap[2] (*informal*) *noun* FIGHT, battle, row, argument, dispute, set-to (*informal*), disagreement, quarrel, brawl, squabble, wrangle, scuffle, tiff, dust-up (*informal*), shindig (*informal*), scrimmage, shindy (*informal*), bagarre (*French*), biffo (*Austral slang*)
▷ *verb* FIGHT, argue, row, fall out (*informal*), barney (*informal*), squabble, spar, wrangle, bicker, have words, come to blows, have a shouting match (*informal*)
scrape *verb* 1 RAKE, sweep, drag, brush
2 GRATE, grind, scratch, screech, squeak, rasp
3 GRAZE, skin, scratch, bark, scuff, rub, abrade
4 CLEAN, remove, scour
▷ *noun* (*informal*) PREDICAMENT, trouble, difficulty, spot (*informal*), fix (*informal*), mess, distress, dilemma, plight, tight spot, awkward situation, pretty pickle (*informal*)
▷▷ **scrape something together** COLLECT, save, muster, get hold of, amass, hoard, glean, dredge up, rake up *or* together
scrapheap *noun* ▷▷ **on the scrapheap** DISCARDED, ditched (*slang*), redundant, written off, jettisoned, put out to grass (*informal*)
scrappy *adjective* INCOMPLETE, sketchy, piecemeal, disjointed, perfunctory, thrown together, fragmentary, bitty
scratch *verb* 1 RUB, scrape, claw at
2 MARK, cut, score, damage, grate, graze, etch, lacerate, incise, make a mark on
▷ *noun* MARK, scrape, graze, blemish, gash, laceration, claw mark
▷▷ **scratch something out** ERASE, eliminate,

delete, cancel, strike off, annul, cross out
▷▷ **not up to scratch** (*informal*) INADEQUATE, unacceptable, unsatisfactory, incapable, insufficient, incompetent, not up to standard, not up to snuff (*informal*)
scrawl *verb* SCRIBBLE, doodle, squiggle
▷ *noun* SCRIBBLE, doodle, squiggle
scrawny *adjective* THIN, lean, skinny, angular, gaunt, skeletal, bony, lanky, undernourished, skin-and-bones (*informal*), scraggy, rawboned, macilent (*rare*)
scream *verb* CRY, yell, shriek, screech, squeal, shrill, bawl, howl, holler (*informal*), sing out
▷ *noun* 1 CRY, yell, howl, wail, outcry, shriek, screech, yelp
2 (*informal*) LAUGH, card (*informal*), riot (*slang*), comic, character (*informal*), caution (*informal*), sensation, wit, comedian, entertainer, wag, joker, hoot (*informal*)
screech *verb* SHRIEK, scream, yell, howl, wail, squeal, holler
▷ *noun* CRY, scream, shriek, squeal, squawk, yelp
screen *noun* COVER, guard, shade, shelter, shield, hedge, partition, cloak, mantle, shroud, canopy, awning, concealment, room divider
▷ *verb* 1 BROADCAST, show, put on, present, air, cable, beam, transmit, relay, televise, put on the air
2 COVER, hide, conceal, shade, mask, veil, cloak, shroud, shut out
3 INVESTIGATE, test, check, examine, scan
4 PROCESS, sort, examine, grade, filter, scan, evaluate, gauge, sift
5 PROTECT, guard, shield, defend, shelter, safeguard
screw *noun* NAIL, pin, tack, rivet, fastener, spike
▷ *verb* 1 FASTEN, fix, attach, bolt, clamp, rivet
2 TURN, twist, tighten, work in
3 (*informal*) CONTORT, twist, distort, contract, wrinkle, warp, crumple, deform, pucker
4 (*informal*) CHEAT, do (*slang*), rip (someone) off (*slang*), skin (*slang*), trick, con, stiff (*slang*), sting (*informal*), deceive, fleece, dupe, overcharge, rook (*slang*), bamboozle (*informal*), diddle (*informal*), take (someone) for a ride (*informal*), put one over on (someone) (*informal*), pull a fast one (on someone) (*informal*), take to the cleaners (*informal*), sell a pup (to) (*slang*), hornswoggle (*slang*)
5 (*informal*) *often with* **out of** SQUEEZE, wring, extract, wrest, bleed someone of something
▷▷ **put the screws on someone** (*Slang*) COERCE, force, compel, drive, squeeze, intimidate, constrain, oppress, pressurize, browbeat, press-gang, bring pressure to bear on, hold a knife to someone's throat
▷▷ **screw something up** 1 CONTORT, contract, wrinkle, knot, knit, distort, crumple, pucker
2 (*informal*) BUNGLE, botch, mess up, spoil, bitch (up) (*slang*), queer (*informal*), cock up (*Brit slang*), mishandle, make a mess of (*slang*), mismanage, make a hash of (*informal*), make a nonsense of, bodge (*informal*), flub (*US slang*), louse up (*slang*), crool *or* cruel (*Austral slang*)
scribble *verb* SCRAWL, write, jot, pen, scratch, doodle, dash off
scribe *noun* SECRETARY, clerk, scrivener (*archaic*), notary (*archaic*), amanuensis, copyist
script *noun* 1 TEXT, lines, words, book, copy, dialogue, manuscript, libretto
2 HANDWRITING, writing, hand, letters, calligraphy, longhand, penmanship
▷ *verb* WRITE, draft, compose, author
scripture *noun* THE BIBLE, The Word, The Gospels, The Scriptures, The Word of God, The Good Book, Holy Scripture, Holy Writ, Holy Bible, The Book of Books
Scrooge *noun* MISER, penny-pincher (*informal*), skinflint, cheapskate (*informal*), tightwad (*US & Canad slang*), niggard, money-grubber (*informal*), meanie *or* meany (*informal, chiefly Brit*)
scrounge *verb* (*informal*) CADGE, beg, sponge (*informal*), bum (*informal*), touch (someone) for (*slang*), blag (*slang*), wheedle, mooch (*slang*), forage for, hunt around (for), sorn (*Scot*), freeload (*slang*), bludge (*Austral & NZ informal*)
scrounger *noun* PARASITE, freeloader (*slang*), sponger (*informal*), bum (*informal*), cadger, bludger (*Austral & NZ informal*), sorner (*Scot*), quandong (*Austral slang*)
scrub *verb* 1 SCOUR, clean, polish, rub, wash, cleanse, buff
2 (*informal*) CANCEL, drop, give up, abandon, abolish, forget about, call off, delete, do away with, discontinue
scruff *noun* NAPE, scrag (*informal*)
scruffy *adjective* SHABBY, untidy, ragged, run-down, messy, sloppy (*informal*), seedy, squalid, tattered, tatty, unkempt, disreputable, scrubby (*Brit informal*), grungy, slovenly, mangy, sluttish, slatternly, ungroomed, frowzy, ill-groomed, draggletailed (*archaic*), daggy (*Austral & NZ informal*)
<< OPPOSITE neat
scrumptious *adjective* (*informal*) DELICIOUS, delectable, inviting, magnificent, exquisite, luscious, succulent, mouthwatering, yummy (*slang*), appetizing, moreish (*informal*), yummo (*Austral slang*)
scrunch *verb* CRUMPLE, crush, squash, crunch, mash, ruck up
scruple *noun* MISGIVING, hesitation, qualm, doubt, difficulty, caution, reluctance, second thoughts, uneasiness, perplexity, compunction, squeamishness, twinge of conscience

scrupulous *adjective* 1 MORAL, principled, upright, honourable, conscientious
<< OPPOSITE unscrupulous
2 CAREFUL, strict, precise, minute, nice, exact, rigorous, meticulous, painstaking, fastidious, punctilious
<< OPPOSITE careless

scrutinize *verb* EXAMINE, study, inspect, research, search, investigate, explore, probe, analyse, scan, sift, dissect, work over, pore over, peruse, inquire into, go over with a fine-tooth comb

scrutiny *noun* EXAMINATION, study, investigation, search, inquiry, analysis, inspection, exploration, sifting, once-over (*informal*), perusal, close study

scud *verb* FLY, race, speed, shoot, blow, sail, skim

scuffle *noun* FIGHT, set-to (*informal*), scrap (*informal*), disturbance, fray, brawl, barney (*informal*), ruck (*slang*), skirmish, tussle, commotion, rumpus, affray (*Law*), shindig (*informal*), ruction (*informal*), ruckus (*informal*), scrimmage, shindy (*informal*), bagarre (*French*), biffo (*Austral slang*)
▷ *verb* FIGHT, struggle, clash, contend, grapple, jostle, tussle, come to blows, exchange blows

sculpture *noun* STATUE, figure, model, bust, effigy, figurine, statuette
▷ *verb* CARVE, form, cut, model, fashion, shape, mould, sculpt, chisel, hew, sculp

scum *noun* 1 RABBLE, trash (*chiefly US & Canad*), riffraff, rubbish, dross, lowest of the low, dregs of society, canaille (*French*), ragtag and bobtail
2 IMPURITIES, film, crust, froth, scruff, dross, offscourings

scungy *adjective* (*Austral & NZ slang*) SORDID, seedy, sleazy, squalid, mean, dirty, foul, filthy, unclean, wretched, seamy, slovenly, skanky (*slang*), slummy, festy (*Austral slang*)

scupper *verb* (*Brit slang*) DESTROY, ruin, wreck, defeat, overwhelm, disable, overthrow, demolish, undo, torpedo, put paid to, discomfit

scurrilous *adjective* SLANDEROUS, scandalous, defamatory, low, offensive, gross, foul, insulting, infamous, obscene, abusive, coarse, indecent, vulgar, foul-mouthed, salacious, ribald, vituperative, scabrous, Rabelaisian

scurry *verb* HURRY, race, dash, fly, sprint, dart, whisk, skim, beetle, scud, scuttle, scoot, scamper
<< OPPOSITE amble
▷ *noun* FLURRY, race, bustle, whirl, scampering

scuttle *verb* RUN, scurry, scamper, rush, hurry, scramble, hare (*Brit informal*), bustle, beetle, scud, hasten, scoot, scutter (*Brit informal*)

sea *noun* 1 OCEAN, the deep, the waves, the drink (*informal*), the briny (*informal*), main
2 MASS, lot, lots (*informal*), army, host, crowd, collection, sheet, assembly, mob, congregation, legion, abundance, swarm, horde, multitude, myriad, throng, expanse, plethora, profusion, concourse, assemblage, vast number, great number
▷ *modifier* MARINE, ocean, maritime, aquatic, oceanic, saltwater, ocean-going, seagoing, pelagic, briny, salt
▷▷ **at sea** BEWILDERED, lost, confused, puzzled, uncertain, baffled, adrift, perplexed, disconcerted, at a loss, mystified, disoriented, bamboozled (*informal*), flummoxed, at sixes and sevens
>> RELATED WORDS *adjectives* marine, maritime

seafaring *adjective* NAUTICAL, marine, naval, maritime, oceanic

seal *verb* SETTLE, clinch, conclude, consummate, finalize, shake hands on (*informal*)
▷ *noun* 1 SEALANT, sealer, adhesive
2 AUTHENTICATION, stamp, confirmation, assurance, ratification, notification, insignia, imprimatur, attestation
▷▷ **set the seal on something** CONFIRM, establish, assure, stamp, ratify, validate, attest, authenticate

seam *noun* 1 JOINT, closure, suture (*Surgery*)
2 LAYER, vein, stratum, lode

sear *verb* WITHER, burn, blight, brand, scorch, sizzle, shrivel, cauterize, desiccate, dry up *or* out

search *verb* EXAMINE, check, investigate, explore, probe, inspect, comb, inquire, sift, scour, ferret, pry, ransack, forage, scrutinize, turn upside down, rummage through, frisk (*informal*), cast around, rifle through, leave no stone unturned, turn inside out, fossick (*Austral & NZ*), go over with a fine-tooth comb
▷ *noun* HUNT, look, inquiry, investigation, examination, pursuit, quest, going-over (*informal*), inspection, exploration, scrutiny, rummage
▷▷ **search for something** *or* **someone** LOOK FOR, seek, hunt for, pursue, go in search of, cast around for, go in pursuit of, go in quest of, ferret around for, look high and low for

searching *adjective* KEEN, sharp, probing, close, severe, intent, piercing, penetrating, thorough, quizzical
<< OPPOSITE superficial

searing *adjective* 1 ACUTE, sharp, intense, shooting, violent, severe, painful, distressing, stabbing, fierce, stinging, piercing, sore, excruciating, gut-wrenching
2 CUTTING, biting, severe, bitter, harsh, scathing, acrimonious, barbed, hurtful, sarcastic, sardonic, caustic, vitriolic, trenchant, mordant, mordacious, acerb

season *noun* PERIOD, time, term, spell, time of year
▷ *verb* 1 FLAVOUR, salt, spice, lace, salt and pepper, enliven, pep up, leaven
2 MATURE, age, condition, prime, prepare, temper, mellow, ripen, acclimatize
3 MAKE EXPERIENCED, train, mature, prepare, discipline, harden, accustom, toughen, inure, habituate, acclimatize, anneal

seasoned *adjective* EXPERIENCED, veteran, mature, practised, old, weathered, hardened, long-serving, battle-scarred, time-served, well-versed
<< OPPOSITE inexperienced

seasoning *noun* FLAVOURING, spice, salt and pepper, condiment

seat *noun* 1 CHAIR, bench, stall, throne, stool, pew, settle
2 MEMBERSHIP, place, constituency, chair, incumbency
3 CENTRE, place, site, heart, capital, situation, source, station, location, headquarters, axis, cradle, hub
4 MANSION, house, residence, abode, ancestral hall
▷ *verb* 1 SIT, place, settle, set, fix, deposit, locate, install
2 HOLD, take, accommodate, sit, contain, cater for, have room *or* capacity for

seating *noun* ACCOMMODATION, room, places, seats, chairs

secede *verb* WITHDRAW, leave, resign, separate, retire, quit, pull out, break with, split from, disaffiliate, apostatize

secession *noun* WITHDRAWAL, break, split, defection, seceding, apostasy, disaffiliation

secluded *adjective* PRIVATE, sheltered, isolated, remote, lonely, cut off, solitary, out-of-the-way, tucked away, cloistered, sequestered, off the beaten track, unfrequented
<< OPPOSITE public

seclusion *noun* PRIVACY, isolation, solitude, hiding, retirement, shelter, retreat, remoteness, ivory tower, concealment, purdah

second[1] *adjective* 1 NEXT, following, succeeding, subsequent
2 ADDITIONAL, other, further, extra, alternative, repeated
3 SPARE, duplicate, alternative, additional, back-up
4 INFERIOR, secondary, subordinate, supporting, lower, lesser
▷ *noun* SUPPORTER, assistant, aide, partner, colleague, associate, backer, helper, collaborator, henchman, right-hand man, cooperator
▷ *verb* SUPPORT, back, endorse, forward, promote, approve, go along with, commend, give moral support to

second[2] *noun* MOMENT, minute, instant, flash, tick (*Brit informal*), sec (*informal*), twinkling, split second, jiffy (*informal*), trice, twinkling of an eye, two shakes of a lamb's tail (*informal*), bat of an eye (*informal*)

secondary *adjective* 1 SUBORDINATE, minor, lesser, lower, inferior, unimportant, second-rate
<< OPPOSITE main
2 RESULTANT, resulting, contingent, derived, derivative, indirect, second-hand, consequential
<< OPPOSITE original

second-class *adjective* 1 INFERIOR, lesser, second-best, unimportant, second-rate, low-class
2 MEDIOCRE, second-rate, mean, middling, ordinary, inferior, indifferent, commonplace, insignificant, so-so (*informal*), outclassed, uninspiring, undistinguished, uninspired, bog-standard (*Brit & Irish slang*), no great shakes (*informal*), déclassé, half-pie (*NZ informal*), fair to middling (*informal*)

second-hand *adjective* USED, old, handed down, hand-me-down (*informal*), nearly new, reach-me-down (*informal*), preloved (*Austral slang*)

secondly *adverb* NEXT, second, moreover, furthermore, also, in the second place

second-rate *adjective* INFERIOR, mediocre, poor, cheap, pants (*slang*), commonplace, tacky (*informal*), shoddy, low-grade, tawdry, low-quality, substandard, low-rent (*informal, chiefly US*), for the birds (*informal*), two-bit (*US & Canad slang*), end-of-the-pier (*Brit informal*), no great shakes (*informal*), cheap and nasty (*informal*), rubbishy, dime-a-dozen (*informal*), bush-league (*Austral & NZ informal*), not much cop (*Brit slang*), tinhorn (*US slang*), strictly for the birds (*informal*), bodger *or* bodgie (*Austral slang*)
<< OPPOSITE first-rate

secrecy *noun* 1 MYSTERY, stealth, concealment, furtiveness, cloak and dagger, secretiveness, huggermugger (*rare*), clandestineness, covertness
2 CONFIDENTIALITY, privacy
3 PRIVACY, silence, retirement, solitude, seclusion

secret *adjective* 1 UNDISCLOSED, unknown, confidential, underground, undercover, unpublished, under wraps, unrevealed
2 CONCEALED, hidden, disguised, covered, camouflaged, unseen
<< OPPOSITE unconcealed
3 UNDERCOVER, covert, furtive, shrouded, behind someone's back, conspiratorial, hush-hush (*informal*), surreptitious, cloak-and-dagger, backstairs
<< OPPOSITE open

4 SECRETIVE, reserved, withdrawn, close, deep, discreet, enigmatic, reticent, cagey (*informal*), unforthcoming
<< OPPOSITE frank
5 MYSTERIOUS, cryptic, abstruse, classified, esoteric, occult, clandestine, arcane, recondite, cabbalistic
<< OPPOSITE straightforward
▷ *noun* 1 PRIVATE AFFAIR, confidence, skeleton in the cupboard
2 KEY, answer, formula, recipe
▷▷ **in secret** SECRETLY, surreptitiously, slyly, behind closed doors, incognito, by stealth, in camera, huggermugger (*archaic*)
>> RELATED WORD *adjective* cryptic

secret agent *noun* SPY, undercover agent, spook (*US & Canad informal*), nark (*Brit, Austral & NZ slang*), cloak-and-dagger man

secrete[1] *verb* GIVE OFF, emit, emanate, exude, extrude

secrete[2] *verb* HIDE, conceal, stash (*informal*), cover, screen, secure, bury, harbour, disguise, veil, shroud, stow, cache, stash away (*informal*)
<< OPPOSITE display

secretion *noun* DISCHARGE, emission, excretion, exudation, extravasation (*Medical*)

secretive *adjective* RETICENT, reserved, withdrawn, close, deep, enigmatic, cryptic, cagey (*informal*), uncommunicative, unforthcoming, tight-lipped, playing your cards close to your chest, clamlike
<< OPPOSITE open

secretly *adverb* IN SECRET, privately, surreptitiously, quietly, covertly, behind closed doors, in confidence, in your heart, furtively, in camera, confidentially, on the fly (*slang, chiefly Brit*), stealthily, under the counter, clandestinely, unobserved, on the sly, in your heart of hearts, behind (someone's) back, in your innermost thoughts, on the q.t. (*informal*)

sect *noun* GROUP, division, faction, party, school, camp, wing, denomination, school of thought, schism, splinter group

sectarian *adjective* NARROW-MINDED, partisan, fanatic, fanatical, limited, exclusive, rigid, parochial, factional, bigoted, dogmatic, insular, doctrinaire, hidebound, clannish, cliquish
<< OPPOSITE tolerant
▷ *noun* BIGOT, extremist, partisan, disciple, fanatic, adherent, zealot, true believer, dogmatist

section *noun* 1 PART, piece, portion, division, sample, slice, passage, component, segment, fragment, fraction, instalment, cross section, subdivision
2 DISTRICT, area, region, sector, zone

sectional *adjective* REGIONAL, local, separate, divided, exclusive, partial, separatist, factional, localized

sector *noun* 1 PART, division, category, stratum, subdivision
2 AREA, part, region, district, zone, quarter

secular *adjective* WORLDLY, state, lay, earthly, civil, temporal, profane, laic, nonspiritual, laical
<< OPPOSITE religious

secure *verb* 1 OBTAIN, get, acquire, land (*informal*), score (*slang*), gain, pick up, get hold of, come by, procure, make sure of, win possession of
<< OPPOSITE lose
2 ATTACH, stick, fix, bind, pin, lash, glue, fasten, rivet
<< OPPOSITE detach
3 GUARANTEE, insure, ensure, assure
<< OPPOSITE endanger
▷ *adjective* 1 SAFE, protected, shielded, sheltered, immune, unassailable, impregnable
<< OPPOSITE unprotected
2 FAST, firm, fixed, tight, stable, steady, fortified, fastened, dependable, immovable
<< OPPOSITE insecure
3 RELIABLE, definite, solid, absolute, conclusive, in the bag (*informal*)
4 CONFIDENT, sure, easy, certain, assured, reassured
<< OPPOSITE uneasy

security *noun* 1 PRECAUTIONS, defence, safeguards, guards, protection, surveillance, safety measures
2 ASSURANCE, confidence, conviction, certainty, reliance, sureness, positiveness, ease of mind, freedom from doubt
<< OPPOSITE insecurity
3 PLEDGE, insurance, guarantee, hostage, collateral, pawn, gage, surety
4 PROTECTION, cover, safety, retreat, asylum, custody, refuge, sanctuary, immunity, preservation, safekeeping
<< OPPOSITE vulnerability

sedate *adjective* 1 CALM, collected, quiet, seemly, serious, earnest, cool, grave, proper, middle-aged, composed, sober, dignified, solemn, serene, tranquil, placid, staid, demure, unflappable (*informal*), unruffled, decorous, imperturbable
<< OPPOSITE wild
2 UNHURRIED, easy, relaxed, comfortable, steady, gentle, deliberate, leisurely, slow-moving

sedative *adjective* CALMING, relaxing, soothing, allaying, anodyne, soporific, sleep-inducing, tranquillizing, calmative, lenitive
▷ *noun* TRANQUILLIZER, narcotic, sleeping pill, opiate, anodyne, calmative, downer *or* down (*slang*)

sedentary *adjective* INACTIVE, sitting, seated, desk, motionless, torpid, desk-bound
<< OPPOSITE active

sediment *noun* DREGS, grounds, residue, lees, deposit, precipitate, settlings

sedition *noun* RABBLE-ROUSING, treason, subversion, agitation, disloyalty, incitement to riot

seduce *verb* **1** TEMPT, attract, lure, entice, mislead, deceive, beguile, allure, decoy, ensnare, lead astray, inveigle
2 CORRUPT, ruin (*archaic*), betray, deprave, dishonour, debauch, deflower

seduction *noun* **1** TEMPTATION, lure, snare, allure, enticement
2 CORRUPTION, ruin (*archaic*), defloration

seductive *adjective* TEMPTING, inviting, attractive, sexy (*informal*), irresistible, siren, enticing, provocative, captivating, beguiling, alluring, bewitching, ravishing, flirtatious, come-to-bed (*informal*), come-hither (*informal*)

see *verb* **1** PERCEIVE, note, spot, notice, mark, view, eye, check, regard, identify, sight, witness, clock (*Brit slang*), observe, recognize, distinguish, glimpse, check out (*informal*), make out, heed, discern, behold, eyeball (*slang*), catch a glimpse of, catch sight of, espy, get a load of (*slang*), descry, take a dekko at (*Brit slang*), lay *or* clap eyes on (*informal*)
2 UNDERSTAND, get, follow, realize, know, appreciate, take in, grasp, make out, catch on (*informal*), comprehend, fathom, get the hang of (*informal*), get the drift of
3 FORESEE, picture, imagine, anticipate, divine, envisage, visualize, foretell
4 FIND OUT, learn, discover, determine, investigate, verify, ascertain, make inquiries
5 CONSIDER, decide, judge, reflect, deliberate, mull over, think over, make up your mind, give some thought to
6 MAKE SURE, mind, ensure, guarantee, take care, make certain, see to it
7 ACCOMPANY, show, escort, lead, walk, attend, usher
8 SPEAK TO, receive, interview, consult, confer with
9 MEET, encounter, come across, run into, happen on, bump into, run across, chance on
10 GO OUT WITH, court, date (*informal, chiefly US*), walk out with (*obsolete*), keep company with, go steady with (*informal*), consort *or* associate with
▷▷ **see about something** TAKE CARE OF, deal with, look after, see to, attend to
▷▷ **see something through** PERSEVERE (WITH), keep at, persist, stick out (*informal*), see out, stay to the bitter end
▷▷ **see through something** *or* **someone** BE UNDECEIVED BY, penetrate, be wise to (*informal*), fathom, get to the bottom of, not fall for, have (someone's) number (*informal*), read (someone) like a book
▷▷ **see to something** *or* **someone** TAKE CARE OF, manage, arrange, look after, organize, be responsible for, sort out, attend to, take charge of, do
▷▷ **seeing as** SINCE, as, in view of the fact that, inasmuch as

> It is common to hear *seeing as how*, as in *seeing as how the bus is always late, I don't need to hurry*. However, the use of *how* here is considered incorrect or nonstandard, and should be avoided

seed *noun* **1** GRAIN, pip, germ, kernel, egg, embryo, spore, ovum, egg cell, ovule
2 BEGINNING, start, suspicion, germ, inkling
3 ORIGIN, source, nucleus
4 (*Chiefly Bible*) OFFSPRING, children, descendants, issue, race, successors, heirs, spawn, progeny, scions
▷▷ **go** *or* **run to seed** DECLINE, deteriorate, degenerate, decay, go downhill (*informal*), go to waste, go to pieces, let yourself go, go to pot, go to rack and ruin, retrogress

seedy *adjective* **1** SHABBY, run-down, scruffy, old, worn, faded, decaying, grubby, dilapidated, tatty, unkempt, grotty (*slang*), crummy (*slang*), down at heel, slovenly, mangy, manky (*Scot dialect*), scungy (*Austral & NZ*)
<< OPPOSITE smart
2 (*informal*) UNWELL, ill, poorly (*informal*), crook (*Austral & NZ informal*), ailing, sickly, out of sorts, off colour, under the weather (*informal*), peely-wally (*Scot*)

seek *verb* **1** LOOK FOR, pursue, search for, be after, hunt, go in search of, go in pursuit of, go gunning for, go in quest of
2 REQUEST, invite, ask for, petition, plead for, solicit, beg for, petition for
3 TRY, attempt, aim, strive, endeavour, essay, aspire to, have a go at (*informal*)

seem *verb* APPEAR, give the impression of being, look, look to be, sound as if you are, look as if you are, look like you are, strike you as being, have the *or* every appearance of being

seeming *adjective* APPARENT, appearing, outward, surface, illusory, ostensible, specious, quasi-

seemingly *adverb* APPARENTLY, outwardly, on the surface, ostensibly, on the face of it, to all intents and purposes, to all appearances, as far as anyone could tell

seep *verb* OOZE, well, leak, soak, bleed, weep, trickle, leach, exude, permeate, percolate

seer *noun* PROPHET, augur, predictor, soothsayer, sibyl

seesaw *verb* ALTERNATE, swing, fluctuate,

teeter, oscillate, go from one extreme to the other

seethe *verb* **1** BE FURIOUS, storm, rage, fume, simmer, be in a state (*informal*), see red (*informal*), be incensed, be livid, go ballistic (*slang, chiefly US*), foam at the mouth, be incandescent, get hot under the collar (*informal*), wig out (*slang*), breathe fire and slaughter
2 BOIL, bubble, foam, churn, fizz, ferment, froth

segment *noun* SECTION, part, piece, division, slice, portion, wedge, compartment

segregate *verb* SET APART, divide, separate, isolate, single out, discriminate against, dissociate
<< OPPOSITE unite

segregation *noun* SEPARATION, discrimination, apartheid, isolation

seize *verb* **1** GRAB, grip, grasp, take, snatch, clutch, snap up, pluck, fasten, latch on to, lay hands on, catch *or* take hold of
<< OPPOSITE let go
2 TAKE BY STORM, take over, acquire, occupy, conquer, annex, usurp
3 CONFISCATE, appropriate, commandeer, impound, take possession of, requisition, sequester, expropriate, sequestrate
<< OPPOSITE hand back
4 CAPTURE, catch, arrest, get, nail (*informal*), grasp, collar (*informal*), hijack, abduct, nab (*informal*), apprehend, take captive
<< OPPOSITE release

seizure *noun* **1** ATTACK, fit, spasm, convulsion, paroxysm
2 TAKING, grabbing, annexation, confiscation, commandeering
3 CAPTURE, arrest, apprehension, abduction

seldom *adverb* RARELY, occasionally, not often, infrequently, once in a blue moon (*informal*), hardly ever, scarcely ever
<< OPPOSITE often

select *verb* CHOOSE, take, pick, prefer, opt for, decide on, single out, adopt, single out, fix on, cherry-pick, settle upon
<< OPPOSITE reject
▷ *adjective* **1** CHOICE, special, prime, picked, selected, excellent, rare, superior, first-class, posh (*informal, chiefly Brit*), first-rate, hand-picked, top-notch (*informal*), recherché
<< OPPOSITE ordinary
2 EXCLUSIVE, elite, privileged, limited, cliquish
<< OPPOSITE indiscriminate

selection *noun* **1** CHOICE, choosing, pick, option, preference
2 ANTHOLOGY, collection, medley, choice, line-up, mixed bag (*informal*), potpourri, miscellany

selective *adjective* PARTICULAR, discriminating, critical, careful, discerning, astute, discriminatory, tasteful, fastidious
<< OPPOSITE indiscriminate

self-assurance *noun* CONFIDENCE, self-confidence, poise, nerve, assertiveness, self-possession, positiveness

self-centred *adjective* SELFISH, narcissistic, self-absorbed, inward looking, self-seeking, egotistic, wrapped up in yourself

self-confidence *noun* SELF-ASSURANCE, confidence, poise, nerve, self-respect, aplomb, self-reliance, high morale

self-confident *adjective* SELF-ASSURED, confident, assured, secure, poised, fearless, self-reliant, sure of yourself

self-conscious *adjective* EMBARRASSED, nervous, uncomfortable, awkward, insecure, diffident, ill at ease, sheepish, bashful, shamefaced, like a fish out of water, out of countenance

self-control *noun* WILLPOWER, restraint, self-discipline, cool, coolness, calmness, self-restraint, self-mastery, strength of mind *or* will

self-denial *noun* SELF-SACRIFICE, renunciation, asceticism, abstemiousness, selflessness, unselfishness, self-abnegation

self-esteem *noun* SELF-RESPECT, confidence, courage, vanity, boldness, self-reliance, self-assurance, self-regard, self-possession, amour-propre (*French*), faith in yourself, pride in yourself

self-evident *adjective* OBVIOUS, clear, undeniable, inescapable, written all over (something), cut-and-dried (*informal*), incontrovertible, axiomatic, manifestly *or* patently true

self-government *noun* INDEPENDENCE, democracy, sovereignty, autonomy, devolution, self-determination, self-rule, home rule

self-important *adjective* CONCEITED, arrogant, pompous, strutting, swaggering, cocky, pushy (*informal*), overbearing, presumptuous, bumptious, swollen-headed, bigheaded, full of yourself

self-indulgence *noun* EXTRAVAGANCE, excess, incontinence, dissipation, self-gratification, intemperance, sensualism

selfish *adjective* SELF-CENTRED, self-interested, greedy, mercenary, self-seeking, ungenerous, egoistic *or* egoistical, egotistic *or* egoistical, looking out for number one (*informal*)
<< OPPOSITE unselfish

selfless *adjective* UNSELFISH, generous, altruistic, self-sacrificing, magnanimous, self-denying, ungrudging

self-reliant *adjective* INDEPENDENT, capable, self-sufficient, self-supporting, able to stand on your own two feet (*informal*)
<< OPPOSITE dependent

self-respect *noun* PRIDE, dignity, self-esteem, morale, amour-propre (*French*), faith in yourself

self-restraint *noun* SELF-CONTROL, self-discipline, willpower, patience, forbearance, abstemiousness, self-command

self-righteous *adjective* SANCTIMONIOUS, smug, pious, superior, complacent, hypocritical, pi (*Brit slang*), too good to be true, self-satisfied, goody-goody (*informal*), holier-than-thou, priggish, pietistic, pharisaic

self-sacrifice *noun* SELFLESSNESS, altruism, self-denial, generosity, self-abnegation

self-satisfied *adjective* SMUG, complacent, proud of yourself, well-pleased, puffed up, self-congratulatory, flushed with success, pleased with yourself, like a cat that has swallowed the canary, too big for your boots *or* breeches

self-styled *adjective* SO-CALLED, would-be, professed, self-appointed, soi-disant (*French*), quasi-

sell *verb* 1 TRADE, dispose of, exchange, barter, put up for sale

<< OPPOSITE buy

2 DEAL IN, market, trade in, stock, handle, retail, hawk, merchandise, peddle, traffic in, vend, be in the business of

<< OPPOSITE buy

3 PROMOTE, put across, gain acceptance for

▷▷ **sell out of something** RUN OUT OF, be out of stock of

seller *noun* DEALER, merchant, vendor, agent, representative, rep, retailer, traveller, supplier, shopkeeper, purveyor, tradesman, salesman *or* saleswoman

semblance *noun* APPEARANCE, show, form, air, figure, front, image, bearing, aspect, mask, similarity, resemblance, guise, façade, pretence, veneer, likeness, mien

semen *noun* SPERM, seed (*archaic* or *dialect*), scum (*US slang*), seminal fluid, spermatic fluid

seminal *adjective* INFLUENTIAL, important, ground-breaking, original, creative, productive, innovative, imaginative, formative

send *verb* 1 DISPATCH, forward, direct, convey, consign, remit

2 TRANSMIT, broadcast, communicate

3 PROPEL, hurl, fling, shoot, fire, deliver, cast, let fly

▷▷ **send something** *or* **someone up** (*Brit informal*) MOCK, mimic, parody, spoof (*informal*), imitate, take off (*informal*), make fun of, lampoon, burlesque, take the mickey out of (*informal*), satirize

sendoff *noun* FAREWELL, departure, leave-taking, valediction, going-away party

send-up *noun* (*Brit informal*) PARODY, take-off (*informal*), satire, mockery, spoof (*informal*), imitation, skit, mickey-take (*informal*)

senile *adjective* DODDERING, doting, decrepit, failing, imbecile, gaga (*informal*), in your dotage, in your second childhood

Words such as *senile* and *geriatric* are only properly used as medical terms. They are very insulting when used loosely to describe a person of advanced years. Care should be taken when using *old* and its synonyms, as they can all potentially cause offence

senility *noun* DOTAGE, Alzheimer's disease, infirmity, senile dementia, decrepitude, senescence, second childhood, caducity, loss of your faculties

senior *adjective* 1 HIGHER RANKING, superior

<< OPPOSITE subordinate

2 THE ELDER, major (*Brit*)

<< OPPOSITE junior

senior citizen *noun* PENSIONER, retired person, old age pensioner, O.A.P., elder, old *or* elderly person

seniority *noun* SUPERIORITY, rank, priority, precedence, longer service

sensation *noun* 1 FEELING, sense, impression, perception, awareness, consciousness

2 EXCITEMENT, surprise, thrill, stir, scandal, furore, agitation, commotion

3 HIT, wow (*slang, chiefly US*), crowd puller (*informal*)

sensational *adjective* 1 AMAZING, dramatic, thrilling, revealing, spectacular, staggering, startling, horrifying, breathtaking, astounding, lurid, electrifying, hair-raising

<< OPPOSITE dull

2 SHOCKING, scandalous, exciting, yellow (*of the press*), melodramatic, shock-horror (*facetious*), sensationalistic

<< OPPOSITE unexciting

3 (*informal*) EXCELLENT, brilliant, superb, mean (*slang*), topping (*Brit slang*), cracking (*Brit informal*), crucial (*slang*), impressive, smashing (*informal*), fabulous (*informal*), first class, marvellous, exceptional, mega (*slang*), sovereign, awesome (*slang*), def (*slang*), brill (*informal*), out of this world (*informal*), mind-blowing (*informal*), bodacious (*slang, chiefly US*), boffo (*slang*), jim-dandy (*slang*), chillin' (*US slang*), booshit (*Austral slang*), exo (*Austral slang*), sik (*Austral slang*), rad (*informal*), phat (*slang*), schmick (*Austral informal*)

<< OPPOSITE ordinary

sense *noun* 1 FACULTY, sensibility

2 FEELING, impression, perception, awareness, consciousness, atmosphere, aura, intuition, premonition, presentiment

3 UNDERSTANDING, awareness, appreciation

4 *sometimes plural* INTELLIGENCE, reason, understanding, brains (*informal*), smarts (*slang, chiefly US*), judgment, discrimination, wisdom, wit(s), common sense, sanity, sharpness, tact, nous (*Brit slang*), cleverness, quickness, discernment, gumption (*Brit informal*), sagacity, clear-headedness, mother wit
<< OPPOSITE foolishness
5 POINT, good, use, reason, value, worth, advantage, purpose, logic
6 MEANING, definition, interpretation, significance, message, import, substance, implication, drift, purport, nuance, gist, signification, denotation
▷ *verb* PERCEIVE, feel, understand, notice, pick up, suspect, realize, observe, appreciate, grasp, be aware of, divine, discern, just know, have a (funny) feeling (*informal*), get the impression, apprehend, have a hunch
<< OPPOSITE be unaware of

senseless *adjective* 1 POINTLESS, mad, crazy, stupid, silly, ridiculous, absurd, foolish, daft (*informal*), ludicrous, meaningless, unreasonable, irrational, inconsistent, unwise, mindless, illogical, incongruous, idiotic, nonsensical, inane, fatuous, moronic, unintelligent, asinine, imbecilic, dumb-ass (*slang*), without rhyme or reason, halfwitted
<< OPPOSITE sensible
2 UNCONSCIOUS, stunned, insensible, out, cold, numb, numbed, deadened, unfeeling, out cold, anaesthetized, insensate
<< OPPOSITE conscious

sensibility *noun* 1 AWARENESS, insight, intuition, taste, appreciation, delicacy, discernment, perceptiveness
<< OPPOSITE lack of awareness
2 *often plural* FEELINGS, emotions, sentiments, susceptibilities, moral sense

sensible *adjective* 1 WISE, practical, prudent, shrewd, well-informed, judicious, well-advised
<< OPPOSITE foolish
2 INTELLIGENT, practical, reasonable, rational, sound, realistic, sober, discriminating, discreet, sage, shrewd, down-to-earth, matter-of-fact, prudent, sane, canny, judicious, far-sighted, sagacious
<< OPPOSITE senseless

sensitive *adjective* 1 THOUGHTFUL, kind, kindly, concerned, patient, attentive, tactful, unselfish
2 DELICATE, tender
3 SUSCEPTIBLE, responsive, reactive, easily affected
4 TOUCHY, oversensitive, easily upset, easily offended, easily hurt, umbrageous (*rare*)
<< OPPOSITE insensitive
5 PRECISE, fine, acute, keen, responsive, perceptive
<< OPPOSITE imprecise

sensitivity *noun* 1 SUSCEPTIBILITY, responsiveness, reactivity, receptiveness, sensitiveness, reactiveness
2 CONSIDERATION, patience, thoughtfulness
3 TOUCHINESS, oversensitivity
4 RESPONSIVENESS, precision, keenness, acuteness

sensual *adjective* 1 SEXUAL, sexy (*informal*), erotic, randy (*informal, chiefly Brit*), steamy (*informal*), raunchy (*slang*), lewd, lascivious, lustful, lecherous, libidinous, licentious, unchaste
2 PHYSICAL, bodily, voluptuous, animal, luxurious, fleshly, carnal, epicurean, unspiritual

sensuality *noun* EROTICISM, sexiness (*informal*), voluptuousness, prurience, licentiousness, carnality, lewdness, salaciousness, lasciviousness, animalism, libidinousness, lecherousness

sensuous *adjective* PLEASURABLE, pleasing, sensory, gratifying

sentence *noun* 1 PUNISHMENT, prison term, condemnation
2 VERDICT, order, ruling, decision, judgment, decree, pronouncement
▷ *verb* 1 CONDEMN, doom
2 CONVICT, condemn, penalize, pass judgment on, mete out justice to

sentient *adjective* FEELING, living, conscious, live, sensitive, reactive

sentiment *noun* 1 FEELING, thought, idea, view, opinion, attitude, belief, judgment, persuasion, way of thinking
2 SENTIMENTALITY, emotion, tenderness, romanticism, sensibility, slush (*informal*), emotionalism, tender feeling, mawkishness, soft-heartedness, overemotionalism

sentimental *adjective* ROMANTIC, touching, emotional, tender, pathetic, nostalgic, sloppy (*informal*), tearful, corny (*slang*), impressionable, mushy (*informal*), maudlin, simpering, weepy (*informal*), slushy (*informal*), mawkish, tear-jerking (*informal*), drippy (*informal*), schmaltzy (*slang*), icky (*informal*), gushy (*informal*), soft-hearted, overemotional, dewy-eyed, three-hankie (*informal*)
<< OPPOSITE unsentimental

sentimentality *noun* ROMANTICISM, nostalgia, tenderness, gush (*informal*), pathos, slush (*informal*), mush (*informal*), schmaltz (*slang*), sloppiness (*informal*), emotionalism, bathos, mawkishness, corniness (*slang*), play on the emotions, sob stuff (*informal*)

sentinel *noun* GUARD, watch, lookout, sentry, picket, watchman

separate *adjective* 1 UNCONNECTED, individual,

particular, divided, divorced, isolated, detached, disconnected, discrete, unattached, disjointed
<< OPPOSITE connected
2 INDIVIDUAL, independent, apart, distinct, autonomous
<< OPPOSITE joined
▷ *verb* 1 DIVIDE, detach, disconnect, come between, disentangle, keep apart, disjoin
<< OPPOSITE combine
2 COME APART, split, break off, come away
<< OPPOSITE connect
3 SEVER, disconnect, break apart, split in two, divide in two, uncouple, bifurcate
<< OPPOSITE join
4 SPLIT UP, part, divorce, break up, part company, get divorced, be estranged, go different ways
5 DISTINGUISH, mark, single out, set apart, make distinctive, set at variance *or* at odds
<< OPPOSITE link

separated *adjective* 1 ESTRANGED, parted, split up, separate, apart, broken up, disunited, living apart *or* separately
2 DISCONNECTED, parted, divided, separate, disassociated, disunited, sundered, put asunder

separately *adverb* 1 ALONE, independently, apart, personally, not together, severally
<< OPPOSITE together
2 INDIVIDUALLY, singly, one by one, one at a time

separation *noun* 1 DIVISION, break, segregation, detachment, severance, disengagement, dissociation, disconnection, disjunction, disunion
2 SPLIT-UP, parting, split, divorce, break-up, farewell, rift, estrangement, leave-taking

septic *adjective* INFECTED, poisoned, toxic, festering, pussy, putrid, putrefying, suppurating, putrefactive

sequel *noun* 1 FOLLOW-UP, continuation, development
2 CONSEQUENCE, result, outcome, conclusion, end, issue, payoff (*informal*), upshot

sequence *noun* 1 SUCCESSION, course, series, order, chain, cycle, arrangement, procession, progression
2 ORDER, structure, arrangement, ordering, placement, layout, progression

serene *adjective* CALM, peaceful, tranquil, composed, sedate, placid, undisturbed, untroubled, unruffled, imperturbable
<< OPPOSITE troubled

serenity *noun* CALM, peace, tranquillity, composure, peace of mind, stillness, calmness, quietness, peacefulness, quietude, placidity

serf *noun* VASSAL, servant, slave, thrall, bondsman, varlet (*archaic*), helot, villein, liegeman

series *noun* 1 SEQUENCE, course, chain, succession, run, set, line, order, train, arrangement, string, progression
2 DRAMA, serial, soap (*informal*), sitcom (*informal*), soap opera, soapie *or* soapie (*Austral slang*), situation comedy

serious *adjective* 1 GRAVE, bad, critical, worrying, dangerous, acute, alarming, severe, extreme, grievous
2 IMPORTANT, crucial, urgent, pressing, difficult, worrying, deep, significant, grim, far-reaching, momentous, fateful, weighty, no laughing matter, of moment *or* consequence
<< OPPOSITE unimportant
3 THOUGHTFUL, detailed, careful, deep, profound, in-depth
4 DEEP, sophisticated, highbrowed
5 SOLEMN, earnest, grave, stern, sober, thoughtful, sedate, glum, staid, humourless, long-faced, pensive, unsmiling
<< OPPOSITE light-hearted
6 SINCERE, determined, earnest, resolved, genuine, deliberate, honest, resolute, in earnest
<< OPPOSITE insincere

seriously *adverb* 1 TRULY, no joking (*informal*), in earnest, all joking aside
2 BADLY, severely, gravely, critically, acutely, sorely, dangerously, distressingly, grievously

seriousness *noun* 1 IMPORTANCE, gravity, urgency, moment, weight, danger, significance
2 SOLEMNITY, gravity, earnestness, sobriety, gravitas, sternness, humourlessness, staidness, sedateness

sermon *noun* HOMILY, address, exhortation

serpentine *adjective* TWISTING, winding, snaking, crooked, coiling, meandering, tortuous, sinuous, twisty, snaky

serrated *adjective* NOTCHED, toothed, sawtoothed, serrate, serrulate, sawlike, serriform (*Biology*)

servant *noun* ATTENDANT, domestic, slave, maid, help, helper, retainer, menial, drudge, lackey, vassal, skivvy (*chiefly Brit*), servitor (*archaic*), varlet (*archaic*), liegeman

serve *verb* 1 WORK FOR, help, aid, assist, be in the service of
2 PERFORM, do, complete, go through, fulfil, pass, discharge
3 BE ADEQUATE, do, suffice, answer, suit, content, satisfy, be good enough, be acceptable, fill the bill (*informal*), answer the purpose
4 PRESENT, provide, supply, deliver, arrange, set out, distribute, dish up, purvey
▷▷ **serve as something** *or* **someone** ACT AS, function as, do the work of, do duty as

service *noun* 1 FACILITY, system, resource, utility, amenity
2 CEREMONY, worship, rite, function, observance
3 WORK, labour, employment, business, office, duty, employ
4 CHECK, servicing, maintenance check
▷ *verb* OVERHAUL, check, maintain, tune (up), repair, go over, fine tune, recondition
serviceable *adjective* USEFUL, practical, efficient, helpful, profitable, convenient, operative, beneficial, functional, durable, usable, dependable, advantageous, utilitarian, hard-wearing
<< OPPOSITE useless
servile *adjective* SUBSERVIENT, cringing, grovelling, mean, low, base, humble, craven, fawning, abject, submissive, menial, sycophantic, slavish, unctuous, obsequious, toadying, bootlicking (*informal*), toadyish
serving *noun* PORTION, helping, plateful
servitude *noun* SLAVERY, bondage, enslavement, bonds, chains, obedience, thrall, subjugation, serfdom, vassalage, thraldom
session *noun* MEETING, hearing, sitting, term, period, conference, congress, discussion, assembly, seminar, get-together (*informal*)
set[1] *verb* 1 PUT, place, lay, park (*informal*), position, rest, plant, station, stick, deposit, locate, lodge, situate, plump, plonk
2 SWITCH ON, turn on, activate, programme
3 ADJUST, regulate, coordinate, rectify, synchronize
4 EMBED, fix, mount, install, fasten
5 ARRANGE, decide (upon), settle, name, establish, determine, fix, schedule, appoint, specify, allocate, designate, ordain, fix up, agree upon
6 ASSIGN, give, allot, prescribe
7 HARDEN, stiffen, condense, solidify, cake, thicken, crystallize, congeal, jell, gelatinize
8 GO DOWN, sink, dip, decline, disappear, vanish, subside
9 PREPARE, lay, spread, arrange, make ready
▷ *adjective* 1 ESTABLISHED, planned, decided, agreed, usual, arranged, rigid, definite, inflexible, hard and fast, immovable
2 STRICT, firm, rigid, hardened, stubborn, entrenched, inflexible, hidebound
<< OPPOSITE flexible
3 CONVENTIONAL, stock, standard, traditional, formal, routine, artificial, stereotyped, rehearsed, hackneyed, unspontaneous
▷ *noun* 1 SCENERY, setting, scene, stage setting, stage set, mise-en-scène (*French*)
2 POSITION, bearing, attitude, carriage, turn, fit, hang, posture
▷▷ **set about someone** ASSAULT, attack, mug (*informal*), assail, sail into (*informal*), lambast(e), belabour
▷▷ **set about something** BEGIN, start, get down to, attack, tackle, set to, get to work, sail into (*informal*), take the first step, wade into, get cracking (*informal*), make a start on, roll up your sleeves, get weaving (*informal*), address yourself to, put your shoulder to the wheel (*informal*)
▷▷ **set off** LEAVE, set out, depart, embark, start out, sally forth
▷▷ **set on** *or* **upon someone** ATTACK, beat up, assault, turn on, mug (*informal*), set about, ambush, go for, sic, pounce on, fly at, work over (*slang*), assail, sail into (*informal*), fall upon, lay into (*informal*), put the boot in (*slang*), pitch into (*informal*), let fly at, beat *or* knock seven bells out of (*informal*)
▷▷ **set on** *or* **upon something** DETERMINED TO, intent on, bent on, resolute about
▷▷ **set out** EMBARK, set off, start out, begin, get under way, hit the road (*slang*), take to the road, sally forth
▷▷ **set someone against someone** ALIENATE, oppose, divide, drive a wedge between, disunite, estrange, set at odds, make bad blood between, make mischief between, set at cross purposes, set by the ears (*informal*), sow dissension amongst
▷▷ **set someone up** 1 FINANCE, back, fund, establish, promote, build up, subsidize
2 PREPARE, prime, warm up, dispose, make ready, put in order, put in a good position
▷▷ **set something against something** BALANCE, compare, contrast, weigh, juxtapose
▷▷ **set something aside** 1 RESERVE, keep, save, separate, select, single out, earmark, keep back, set apart, put on one side
2 REJECT, dismiss, reverse, cancel, overturn, discard, quash, overrule, repudiate, annul, nullify, abrogate, render null and void
▷▷ **set something back** HOLD UP, slow, delay, hold back, hinder, obstruct, retard, impede, slow up
▷▷ **set something off** 1 DETONATE, trigger (off), explode, ignite, light, set in motion, touch off
2 CAUSE, start, produce, generate, prompt, trigger (off), provoke, bring about, give rise to, spark off, set in motion
3 ENHANCE, show off, throw into relief, bring out the highlights in
▷▷ **set something out** 1 ARRANGE, present, display, lay out, exhibit, array, dispose, set forth, expose to view
2 EXPLAIN, list, describe, detail, elaborate, recount, enumerate, elucidate, itemize, particularize
▷▷ **set something up** 1 ARRANGE, organize, prepare, make provision for, prearrange
2 ESTABLISH, begin, found, institute, install,

initiate
3 BUILD, raise, construct, put up, assemble, put together, erect, elevate
4 ASSEMBLE, put up

set² *noun* 1 SERIES, collection, assortment, kit, outfit, batch, compendium, assemblage, coordinated group, ensemble
2 GROUP, company, crowd, circle, class, band, crew (*informal*), gang, outfit, faction, sect, posse (*informal*), clique, coterie, schism

setback *noun* HOLD-UP, check, defeat, blow, upset, reverse, disappointment, hitch, misfortune, rebuff, whammy (*informal, chiefly US*), bummer (*slang*), bit of trouble

setting *noun* SURROUNDINGS, site, location, set, scene, surround, background, frame, context, perspective, backdrop, scenery, locale, mise en scène (*French*)

settle *verb* 1 RESOLVE, work out, put an end to, straighten out, set to rights
2 PAY, clear, square (up), discharge
3 MOVE TO, take up residence in, live in, dwell in, inhabit, reside in, set up home in, put down roots in, make your home in
4 COLONIZE, populate, people, pioneer
5 MAKE COMFORTABLE, bed down
6 SUBSIDE, fall, sink, decline
7 LAND, alight, descend, light, come to rest
8 CALM, quiet, relax, relieve, reassure, compose, soothe, lull, quell, allay, sedate, pacify, quieten, tranquillize
<< OPPOSITE disturb
▷▷ **settle on** *or* **upon something** *or* **someone** DECIDE ON, choose, pick, select, adopt, agree on, opt for, fix on, elect for

settlement *noun* 1 AGREEMENT, arrangement, resolution, working out, conclusion, establishment, adjustment, confirmation, completion, disposition, termination
2 PAYMENT, clearing, discharge, clearance, defrayal
3 COLONY, community, outpost, peopling, hamlet, encampment, colonization, kainga *or* kaika (NZ)

settler *noun* COLONIST, immigrant, pioneer, colonizer, frontiersman

setup *noun* (*informal*) ARRANGEMENT, system, structure, organization, conditions, circumstances, regime

sever *verb* 1 CUT, separate, split, part, divide, rend, detach, disconnect, cleave, bisect, disunite, cut in two, sunder, disjoin
<< OPPOSITE join
2 DISCONTINUE, terminate, break off, abandon, dissolve, put an end to, dissociate
<< OPPOSITE continue

several *adjective* VARIOUS, different, diverse, divers (*archaic*), assorted, disparate, indefinite, sundry

severe *adjective* 1 SERIOUS, critical, terrible, desperate, alarming, extreme, awful, distressing, appalling, drastic, catastrophic, woeful, ruinous
2 ACUTE, extreme, intense, burning, violent, piercing, racking, searing, tormenting, exquisite, harrowing, unbearable, agonizing, insufferable, torturous, unendurable
3 TOUGH, hard, difficult, taxing, demanding, fierce, punishing, exacting, rigorous, stringent, arduous, unrelenting
<< OPPOSITE easy
4 STRICT, hard, harsh, cruel, rigid, relentless, drastic, oppressive, austere, Draconian, unrelenting, inexorable, pitiless, unbending, iron-handed
<< OPPOSITE lenient
5 GRIM, serious, grave, cold, forbidding, stern, sober, disapproving, dour, unsmiling, flinty, strait-laced, tight-lipped
<< OPPOSITE genial
6 PLAIN, simple, austere, classic, restrained, functional, Spartan, ascetic, unadorned, unfussy, unembellished
<< OPPOSITE fancy
7 HARSH, cutting, biting, scathing, satirical, caustic, astringent, vitriolic, mordant, unsparing, mordacious
<< OPPOSITE kind

severely *adverb* 1 SERIOUSLY, badly, extremely, gravely, hard, sorely, dangerously, critically, acutely
2 STRICTLY, harshly, sternly, rigorously, sharply, like a ton of bricks (*informal*), with an iron hand, with a rod of iron

severity *noun* STRICTNESS, seriousness, harshness, austerity, rigour, toughness, hardness, stringency, sternness, severeness

sew *verb* STITCH, tack, seam, hem

sex *noun* 1 GENDER
2 FACTS OF LIFE, sexuality, reproduction, the birds and the bees (*informal*)
3 (*informal*) LOVEMAKING, sexual relations, copulation, the other (*informal*), screwing (*taboo slang*), intimacy, going to bed (with someone), shagging (*Brit taboo slang*), nookie (*slang*), fornication, coitus, rumpy-pumpy (*slang*), legover (*slang*), coition, rumpo (*slang*)

sex appeal *noun* DESIRABILITY, attractiveness, allure, glamour, sensuality, magnetism, sexiness (*informal*), oomph (*informal*), it (*informal*), voluptuousness, seductiveness

sexual *adjective* 1 CARNAL, erotic, intimate, of the flesh, coital
2 SEXY, erotic, sensual, inviting, bedroom, provoking, arousing, naughty, provocative, seductive, sensuous, suggestive, voluptuous, slinky, titillating, flirtatious, come-hither (*informal*), kissable, beddable

sexual intercourse *noun* COPULATION, sex (*informal*), the other (*informal*), union, coupling, congress, mating, commerce (*archaic*), screwing (*taboo slang*), intimacy, penetration, shagging (*Brit taboo slang*), nookie (*slang*), consummation, bonking (*informal*), coitus, carnal knowledge, rumpy-pumpy (*slang*), legover (*slang*), coition

sexuality *noun* DESIRE, lust, eroticism, sensuality, virility, sexiness (*informal*), voluptuousness, carnality, bodily appetites

sexy *adjective* EROTIC, sensual, seductive, inviting, bedroom, provoking, arousing, naughty, provocative, sensuous, suggestive, voluptuous, slinky, titillating, flirtatious, come-hither (*informal*), kissable, beddable

shabby *adjective* **1** TATTY, worn, ragged, scruffy, faded, frayed, worn-out, tattered, threadbare, down at heel, the worse for wear, having seen better days
<< OPPOSITE smart
2 RUN-DOWN, seedy, mean, neglected, dilapidated
3 MEAN, low, rotten (*informal*), cheap, dirty, shameful, low-down (*informal*), shoddy, unworthy, despicable, contemptible, scurvy, dishonourable, ignoble, ungentlemanly
<< OPPOSITE fair

shack *noun* HUT, cabin, shanty, lean-to, dump (*informal*), hovel, shiel (*Scot*), shieling (*Scot*), whare (NZ)

shackle *verb* **1** HAMPER, limit, restrict, restrain, hamstring, inhibit, constrain, obstruct, impede, encumber, tie (someone's) hands
2 FETTER, chain, handcuff, secure, bind, hobble, manacle, trammel, put in irons
▷ *noun often plural* FETTER, chain, iron, bond, handcuff, hobble, manacle, leg-iron, gyve (*archaic*)

shade *noun* **1** HUE, tone, colour, tint
2 SHADOW, screen, shadows, coolness, shadiness
3 DASH, trace, hint, suggestion, suspicion, small amount, semblance
4 NUANCE, difference, degree, graduation, subtlety
5 SCREEN, covering, cover, blind, curtain, shield, veil, canopy
6 (*Literary*) GHOST, spirit, shadow, phantom, spectre, manes, apparition, eidolon, kehua (NZ)
▷ *verb* **1** DARKEN, shadow, cloud, dim, cast a shadow over, shut out the light
2 COVER, protect, screen, hide, shield, conceal, obscure, veil, mute

shadow *noun* **1** SILHOUETTE, shape, outline, profile
2 SHADE, dimness, darkness, gloom, cover, protection, shelter, dusk, obscurity, gloaming (*Scot poetic*), gathering darkness
▷ *verb* **1** SHADE, screen, shield, darken, overhang, cast a shadow over
2 FOLLOW, dog, tail (*informal*), trail, stalk, spy on

shadowy *adjective* **1** DARK, shaded, dim, gloomy, shady, obscure, murky, dusky, funereal, crepuscular, tenebrous, tenebrious
2 VAGUE, indistinct, faint, ghostly, obscure, dim, phantom, imaginary, unreal, intangible, illusory, spectral, undefined, nebulous, dreamlike, impalpable, unsubstantial, wraithlike

shady *adjective* **1** SHADED, cool, shadowy, dim, leafy, bowery, bosky (*literary*), umbrageous
<< OPPOSITE sunny
2 (*informal*) CROOKED, dodgy (*Brit, Austral & NZ informal*), unethical, suspect, suspicious, dubious, slippery, questionable, unscrupulous, fishy (*informal*), shifty, disreputable, untrustworthy, shonky (*Austral & NZ informal*)
<< OPPOSITE honest

shaft *noun* **1** TUNNEL, hole, passage, burrow, passageway, channel
2 HANDLE, staff, pole, rod, stem, upright, baton, shank
3 RAY, beam, gleam, streak

shaggy *adjective* UNKEMPT, rough, tousled, hairy, long-haired, hirsute, unshorn
<< OPPOSITE smooth

shake *verb* **1** JIGGLE, agitate, joggle
2 TREMBLE, shiver, quake, shudder, quiver
3 ROCK, sway, shudder, wobble, waver, totter, oscillate
4 WAVE, wield, flourish, brandish
5 UPSET, shock, frighten, disturb, distress, move, rattle (*informal*), intimidate, unnerve, discompose, traumatize
6 UNDERMINE, threaten, disable, weaken, impair, sap, debilitate, subvert, pull the rug out from under (*informal*)
▷ *noun* VIBRATION, trembling, quaking, shock, jar, disturbance, jerk, shiver, shudder, jolt, tremor, agitation, convulsion, pulsation, jounce
▷▷ **shake someone off** LEAVE BEHIND, lose, get rid of, get away from, elude, get rid of, throw off, get shot of (*slang*), rid yourself of, give the slip
▷▷ **shake someone up** (*informal*) UPSET, shock, frighten, disturb, distress, rattle (*informal*), unsettle, unnerve, discompose
▷▷ **shake something off** GET RID OF, lose, recuperate from
▷▷ **shake something up** RESTRUCTURE, reorganize, mix, overturn, churn (up), turn upside down

shaky *adjective* **1** UNSTABLE, weak, precarious, tottering, rickety
<< OPPOSITE stable

2 UNSTEADY, faint, trembling, faltering, wobbly, tremulous, quivery, all of a quiver (*informal*)
3 UNCERTAIN, suspect, dubious, questionable, unreliable, unsound, iffy (*informal*), unsupported, undependable
<< OPPOSITE reliable

shallow *adjective* SUPERFICIAL, surface, empty, slight, foolish, idle, trivial, meaningless, flimsy, frivolous, skin-deep
<< OPPOSITE deep

sham *noun* FRAUD, imitation, hoax, pretence, forgery, counterfeit, pretender, humbug, impostor, feint, pseud (*informal*), wolf in sheep's clothing, imposture, phoney *or* phony (*informal*)
<< OPPOSITE the real thing
▷ *adjective* FALSE, artificial, bogus, pretended, mock, synthetic, imitation, simulated, pseudo (*informal*), counterfeit, feigned, spurious, ersatz, pseud (*informal*), phoney *or* phony (*informal*)
<< OPPOSITE real

shambles *noun* 1 CHAOS, mess, disorder, confusion, muddle, havoc, anarchy, disarray, madhouse, disorganization
2 MESS, state, jumble, untidiness

shambling *adjective* CLUMSY, awkward, shuffling, lurching, lumbering, unsteady, ungainly, unco (*Austral slang*)

shambolic *adjective* (*informal*) DISORGANIZED, disordered, chaotic, confused, muddled, inefficient, anarchic, topsy-turvy, at sixes and sevens, in total disarray, unsystematic

shame *noun* 1 EMBARRASSMENT, humiliation, chagrin, ignominy, compunction, mortification, loss of face, abashment
<< OPPOSITE shamelessness
2 DISGRACE, scandal, discredit, contempt, smear, degradation, disrepute, reproach, derision, dishonour, infamy, opprobrium, odium, ill repute, obloquy
<< OPPOSITE honour
▷ *verb* 1 EMBARRASS, disgrace, humiliate, humble, disconcert, mortify, take (someone) down a peg (*informal*), abash
<< OPPOSITE make proud
2 DISHONOUR, discredit, degrade, stain, smear, blot, debase, defile
<< OPPOSITE honour
▷▷ **put something** *or* **someone to shame** SHOW UP, disgrace, eclipse, surpass, outstrip, outclass

shameful *adjective* DISGRACEFUL, outrageous, scandalous, mean, low, base, infamous, indecent, degrading, vile, wicked, atrocious, unworthy, reprehensible, ignominious, dastardly, unbecoming, dishonourable
<< OPPOSITE admirable

shameless *adjective* BRAZEN, audacious, flagrant, abandoned, corrupt, hardened, indecent, brash, improper, depraved, wanton, unabashed, profligate, unashamed, incorrigible, insolent, unprincipled, impudent, dissolute, reprobate, immodest, barefaced, unblushing

shanty *noun* SHACK, shed, cabin, hut, lean-to, hovel, shiel (*Scot*), bothy (*Scot*), shieling (*Scot*)

shape *noun* 1 APPEARANCE, form, aspect, guise, likeness, semblance
2 FORM, profile, outline, lines, build, cut, figure, silhouette, configuration, contours
3 PATTERN, model, frame, mould
4 CONDITION, state, health, trim, kilter, fettle
▷ *verb* 1 FORM, make, produce, create, model, fashion, mould
2 MOULD, form, make, fashion, model, frame

shapeless *adjective* FORMLESS, irregular, amorphous, unstructured, misshapen, asymmetrical
<< OPPOSITE well-formed

shapely *adjective* WELL-FORMED, elegant, trim, neat, graceful, well-turned, curvaceous, sightly, comely, well-proportioned

share *noun* PART, portion, quota, ration, lot, cut (*informal*), due, division, contribution, proportion, allowance, whack (*informal*), allotment
▷ *verb* 1 DIVIDE, split, distribute, assign, apportion, parcel out, divvy up (*informal*)
2 GO HALVES ON, go fifty-fifty on (*informal*), go Dutch on (*informal*)

sharp *adjective* 1 KEEN, cutting, sharpened, honed, jagged, knife-edged, razor-sharp, serrated, knifelike
<< OPPOSITE blunt
2 QUICK-WITTED, clever, astute, knowing, ready, quick, bright, alert, subtle, penetrating, apt, discerning, on the ball (*informal*), perceptive, observant, long-headed
<< OPPOSITE dim
3 CUTTING, biting, severe, bitter, harsh, scathing, acrimonious, barbed, hurtful, sarcastic, sardonic, caustic, vitriolic, trenchant, mordant, mordacious, acerb
<< OPPOSITE gentle
4 SUDDEN, marked, abrupt, extreme, distinct
<< OPPOSITE gradual
5 CLEAR, distinct, clear-cut, well-defined, crisp
<< OPPOSITE indistinct
6 SOUR, tart, pungent, hot, burning, acid, acerbic, acrid, piquant, acetic, vinegary, acerb
<< OPPOSITE bland
7 (*informal*) STYLISH, smart, fashionable, trendy (*informal*), chic, classy (*slang*), snappy, natty (*informal*), dressy, schmick (*Austral informal*)
8 ACUTE, violent, severe, intense, painful, shooting, distressing, stabbing, fierce,

stinging, piercing, sore, excruciating, gut-wrenching
▷ *adverb* PROMPTLY, precisely, exactly, on time, on the dot, punctually
<< OPPOSITE approximately

sharpen *verb* MAKE SHARP, hone, whet, grind, edge, strop, put an edge on

shatter *verb* **1** SMASH, break, burst, split, crack, crush, explode, demolish, shiver, implode, pulverize, crush to smithereens
2 DESTROY, ruin, wreck, blast, disable, overturn, demolish, impair, blight, torpedo, bring to nought
3 DEVASTATE, shock, stun, crush, overwhelm, upset, break (someone's) heart, knock the stuffing out of (someone) (*informal*), traumatize

shattered *adjective* **1** DEVASTATED, crushed, upset, gutted (*slang*)
2 (*informal*) EXHAUSTED, drained, worn out, spent, done in (*informal*), all in (*slang*), wiped out (*informal*), weary, knackered (*slang*), clapped out (*Brit, Austral & NZ informal*), tired out, ready to drop, dog-tired (*informal*), zonked (*slang*), dead tired (*informal*), dead beat (*informal*), shagged out (*Brit slang*), jiggered (*informal*)

shattering *adjective* DEVASTATING, stunning, severe, crushing, overwhelming, paralysing

shave *verb* **1** TRIM, crop
2 SCRAPE, plane, trim, shear, pare
3 BRUSH PAST, touch, graze

shed[1] *noun* HUT, shack, lean-to, outhouse, lockup, bothy (*chiefly Scot*), whare (*NZ*)

shed[2] *verb* **1** DROP, spill, scatter
2 CAST OFF, discard, moult, slough off, exuviate
3 GIVE OUT, cast, emit, give, throw, afford, radiate, diffuse, pour forth

sheen *noun* SHINE, gleam, gloss, polish, brightness, lustre, burnish, patina, shininess

sheepish *adjective* EMBARRASSED, uncomfortable, ashamed, silly, foolish, self-conscious, chagrined, mortified, abashed, shamefaced
<< OPPOSITE unembarrassed

sheer *adjective* **1** TOTAL, complete, absolute, utter, rank, pure, downright, unqualified, out-and-out, unadulterated, unmitigated, thoroughgoing, unalloyed, arrant
<< OPPOSITE moderate
2 STEEP, abrupt, perpendicular, precipitous
<< OPPOSITE gradual
3 FINE, thin, transparent, see-through, gossamer, diaphanous, gauzy
<< OPPOSITE thick

sheet *noun* **1** PAGE, leaf, folio, piece of paper
2 PLATE, piece, panel, slab, pane
3 COAT, film, layer, membrane, surface, stratum, veneer, overlay, lamina
4 EXPANSE, area, stretch, sweep, covering, blanket

shell *noun* **1** HUSK, case, pod, shuck
2 CARAPACE, armour
3 FRAME, structure, hull, framework, skeleton, chassis
▷ *verb* **1** REMOVE THE SHELLS FROM, husk, shuck (*US*)
2 BOMB, barrage, bombard, attack, strike, blitz, strafe
▷▷ **shell something out** (*informal*) PAY OUT, fork out (*slang*), expend, give, hand over, lay out (*informal*), disburse, ante up (*informal, chiefly US*)

shelter *noun* **1** COVER, screen, awning, shiel (*Scot*)
2 PROTECTION, safety, refuge, cover, security, defence, sanctuary
3 REFUGE, haven, sanctuary, retreat, asylum
▷ *verb* **1** TAKE SHELTER, hide, seek refuge, take cover
2 PROTECT, shield, harbour, safeguard, cover, hide, guard, defend, take in
<< OPPOSITE endanger

sheltered *adjective* **1** SCREENED, covered, protected, shielded, secluded
<< OPPOSITE exposed
2 PROTECTED, screened, shielded, quiet, withdrawn, isolated, secluded, cloistered, reclusive, ensconced, hermitic, conventual

shelve *verb* POSTPONE, put off, defer, table (*US*), dismiss, freeze, suspend, put aside, hold over, mothball, pigeonhole, lay aside, put on ice, put on the back burner (*informal*), hold in abeyance, take a rain check on (*US & Canad informal*)

shepherd *noun* DROVER, stockman, herdsman, grazier
▷ *verb* GUIDE, conduct, steer, convoy, herd, marshal, usher
>> RELATED WORD *adjective* pastoral

sherang *noun* (*Austral & NZ*) BOSS, manager, head, leader, director, chief, executive, owner, master, governor (*informal*), employer, administrator, supervisor, superintendent, gaffer (*informal, chiefly Brit*), foreman, overseer, kingpin, big cheese (*old-fashioned slang*), baas (*S African*), numero uno (*informal*), Mister Big (*slang, chiefly US*)

shield *noun* **1** PROTECTION, cover, defence, screen, guard, ward (*archaic*), shelter, safeguard, aegis, rampart, bulwark
2 BUCKLER, escutcheon (*Heraldry*), targe (*archaic*)
▷ *verb* PROTECT, cover, screen, guard, defend, shelter, safeguard

shift *verb* **1** MOVE, drift, move around, veer, budge, swerve, change position
2 REMOVE, move, transfer, displace, relocate, rearrange, transpose, reposition
▷ *noun* **1** CHANGE, switch, shifting, modification, alteration, displacement, about-turn, permutation, fluctuation
2 MOVE, transfer, removal, veering,

rearrangement

shifty *adjective* (*informal*) UNTRUSTWORTHY, sly, devious, scheming, tricky, slippery, contriving, wily, crafty, evasive, furtive, deceitful, underhand, unprincipled, duplicitous, fly-by-night (*informal*)
<< OPPOSITE honest

shimmer *verb* GLEAM, twinkle, glimmer, dance, glisten, scintillate
▷ *noun* GLEAM, glimmer, iridescence, unsteady light

shine *verb* 1 GLEAM, flash, beam, glow, sparkle, glitter, glare, shimmer, radiate, twinkle, glimmer, glisten, emit light, give off light, scintillate
2 POLISH, buff, burnish, brush, rub up
3 BE OUTSTANDING, stand out, excel, star, be distinguished, steal the show, be conspicuous, be pre-eminent, stand out in a crowd
▷ *noun* 1 POLISH, gloss, sheen, glaze, lustre, patina
2 BRIGHTNESS, light, sparkle, radiance

shining *adjective* 1 OUTSTANDING, glorious, splendid, leading, celebrated, brilliant, distinguished, eminent, conspicuous, illustrious
2 BRIGHT, brilliant, gleaming, beaming, sparkling, glittering, shimmering, radiant, luminous, glistening, resplendent, aglow, effulgent, incandescent

shiny *adjective* BRIGHT, gleaming, glossy, glistening, polished, burnished, lustrous, satiny, sheeny, agleam

ship *noun* VESSEL, boat, craft

shirk *verb* 1 DODGE, avoid, evade, get out of, duck (out of) (*informal*), shun, sidestep, body-swerve (*Scot*), bob off (*Brit slang*), scrimshank (*Brit Military slang*)
2 SKIVE (*Brit slang*), slack, idle, malinger, swing the lead, gold-brick (*US slang*), bob off (*Brit slang*), bludge (*Austral & NZ informal*), scrimshank (*Brit Military slang*)

shiver *verb* SHUDDER, shake, tremble, quake, quiver, palpitate
▷ *noun* TREMBLE, shudder, quiver, thrill, trembling, flutter, tremor, frisson (*French*)
▷▷ **the shivers** THE SHAKES, a chill (*informal*), goose pimples, goose flesh, chattering teeth

shock *noun* 1 UPSET, blow, trauma, bombshell, turn (*informal*), distress, disturbance, consternation, whammy (*informal, chiefly US*), state of shock, rude awakening, bolt from the blue, prostration
2 IMPACT, blow, jolt, clash, encounter, jarring, collision
3 START, scare, fright, turn, jolt
▷ *verb* 1 SHAKE, stun, stagger, jar, shake up (*informal*), paralyse, numb, jolt, stupefy, shake out of your complacency
2 HORRIFY, appal, disgust, outrage, offend, revolt, unsettle, sicken, agitate, disquiet, nauseate, raise someone's eyebrows, scandalize, gross out (*US slang*), traumatize, give (someone) a turn (*informal*)

shocking *adjective* 1 (*informal*) TERRIBLE, appalling, dreadful, bad, fearful, dire, horrendous, ghastly, from hell (*informal*), deplorable, abysmal, frightful, godawful (*slang*)
2 APPALLING, outrageous, disgraceful, offensive, distressing, disgusting, horrible, dreadful, horrifying, revolting, obscene, sickening, ghastly, hideous, monstrous, scandalous, disquieting, unspeakable, atrocious, repulsive, nauseating, odious, loathsome, abominable, stupefying, hellacious (*US slang*)
<< OPPOSITE wonderful

shoddy *adjective* INFERIOR, poor, second-rate, cheap, tacky (*informal*), tawdry, tatty, trashy, low-rent (*informal, chiefly US*), slipshod, cheapo (*informal*), rubbishy, junky (*informal*), cheap-jack (*informal*), bodger or bodgie (*Austral slang*)
<< OPPOSITE excellent

shoemaker *noun* COBBLER, bootmaker, souter (*Scot*)

shoot *verb* 1 OPEN FIRE ON, blast (*slang*), hit, kill, bag, plug (*slang*), bring down, blow away (*slang, chiefly US*), zap (*slang*), pick off, pump full of lead (*slang*)
2 FIRE, launch, discharge, project, hurl, fling, propel, emit, let fly
3 SPEED, race, rush, charge, fly, spring, tear, flash, dash, barrel (along) (*informal, chiefly US & Canad*), bolt, streak, dart, whisk, whizz (*informal*), hurtle, scoot, burn rubber (*informal*)
▷ *noun* SPROUT, branch, bud, twig, sprig, offshoot, scion, slip

shop *noun* STORE, market, supermarket, mart, boutique, emporium, hypermarket, dairy (*NZ*)

shore *noun* BEACH, coast, sands, strand (*poetic*), lakeside, waterside, seaboard (*chiefly US*), foreshore, seashore

shore up *verb* SUPPORT, strengthen, reinforce, prop, brace, underpin, augment, buttress

short *adjective* 1 BRIEF, fleeting, short-term, short-lived, momentary
<< OPPOSITE long
2 CONCISE, brief, succinct, clipped, summary, compressed, curtailed, terse, laconic, pithy, abridged, compendious, sententious
<< OPPOSITE lengthy
3 SMALL, little, wee, squat, diminutive, petite, dumpy, knee high to a grasshopper, fubsy (*archaic or dialect*), knee high to a gnat
<< OPPOSITE tall
4 ABRUPT, sharp, terse, curt, blunt, crusty, gruff, brusque, offhand, testy, impolite,

discourteous, uncivil
<< OPPOSITE polite
5 (*of pastry*) CRUMBLY, crisp, brittle, friable
6 SCARCE, wanting, low, missing, limited, lacking, tight, slim, inadequate, insufficient, slender, scant, meagre, sparse, deficient, scanty
<< OPPOSITE plentiful
▷ *adverb* ABRUPTLY, suddenly, unaware, by surprise, without warning
<< OPPOSITE gradually

shortage *noun* DEFICIENCY, want, lack, failure, deficit, poverty, shortfall, inadequacy, scarcity, dearth, paucity, insufficiency
<< OPPOSITE abundance

shortcoming *noun* FAILING, fault, weakness, defect, flaw, drawback, imperfection, frailty, foible, weak point

shorten *verb* 1 CUT, reduce, decrease, cut down, trim, diminish, dock, cut back, prune, lessen, curtail, abbreviate, truncate, abridge, downsize
<< OPPOSITE increase
2 TURN UP, trim

short-lived *adjective* BRIEF, short, temporary, fleeting, passing, transient, ephemeral, transitory, impermanent

shortly *adverb* 1 SOON, presently, before long, anon (*archaic*), in a little while, any minute now, erelong (*archaic* or *poetic*)
2 CURTLY, sharply, abruptly, tartly, tersely, succinctly, briefly, concisely, in a few words

short-sighted *adjective* 1 NEAR-SIGHTED, myopic, blind as a bat
2 IMPRUDENT, injudicious, ill-advised, unthinking, careless, impractical, ill-considered, improvident, impolitic, seeing no further than (the end of) your nose

shot *noun* 1 DISCHARGE, report, gunfire, crack, blast, explosion, bang
2 AMMUNITION, bullet, slug, pellet, projectile, lead, ball
3 MARKSMAN, shooter, markswoman
4 STRIKE, throw, lob
5 (*informal*) ATTEMPT, go (*informal*), try, turn, chance, effort, opportunity, crack (*informal*), essay, stab (*informal*), endeavour
▷▷ **a shot in the arm** (*informal*) BOOST, lift, encouragement, stimulus, impetus, fillip, geeing-up
▷▷ **have a shot** (*informal*) MAKE AN ATTEMPT, have a go, try, have a crack (*informal*), try your luck, have a stab (*informal*), have a bash (*informal*), tackle
▷▷ **like a shot** AT ONCE, immediately, in a flash, quickly, eagerly, unhesitatingly, like a bat out of hell (*slang*)

shoulder *verb* 1 BEAR, carry, take on, accept, assume, be responsible for, take upon yourself
2 PUSH, thrust, elbow, shove, jostle, press
▷▷ **give someone the cold shoulder** (*informal*) SNUB, ignore, blank (*slang*), put down, shun, rebuff, kick in the teeth (*slang*), ostracize, send someone to Coventry, cut (*informal*)
▷▷ **rub shoulders with someone** (*informal*) MIX WITH, associate with, consort with, hobnob with, socialize with, fraternize with
▷▷ **shoulder to shoulder** 1 SIDE BY SIDE, abreast, next to each other
2 TOGETHER, united, jointly, as one, in partnership, in cooperation, in unity

shout *verb* CRY (OUT), call (out), yell, scream, roar, shriek, bellow, bawl, holler (*informal*), raise your voice
▷ *noun* CRY, call, yell, scream, roar, shriek, bellow
▷▷ **shout someone down** DROWN OUT, overwhelm, drown, silence

shove *verb* PUSH, shoulder, thrust, elbow, drive, press, crowd, propel, jostle, impel
▷ *noun* PUSH, knock, thrust, elbow, bump, nudge, jostle
▷▷ **shove off** (*informal*) GO AWAY, leave, clear off (*informal*), depart, go to hell (*informal*), push off (*informal*), slope off, pack your bags (*informal*), scram (*informal*), get on your bike (*Brit slang*), take yourself off, vamoose (*slang, chiefly US*), sling your hook (*Brit slang*), rack off (*Austral & NZ slang*)

shovel *noun* SPADE, scoop
▷ *verb* 1 MOVE, scoop, dredge, shift, load, heap
2 STUFF, spoon, ladle

show *verb* 1 INDICATE, demonstrate, prove, reveal, display, evidence, point out, manifest, testify to, evince
<< OPPOSITE disprove
2 DISPLAY, exhibit, put on display, present, put on show, put before the public
3 GUIDE, lead, conduct, accompany, direct, steer, escort
4 DEMONSTRATE, describe, explain, teach, illustrate, instruct
5 BE VISIBLE
<< OPPOSITE be invisible
6 EXPRESS, display, reveal, indicate, register, demonstrate, disclose, manifest, divulge, make known, evince
<< OPPOSITE hide
7 (*informal*) TURN UP, come, appear, arrive, attend, show up (*informal*), put in *or* make an appearance
8 BROADCAST, transmit, air, beam, relay, televise, put on the air
▷ *noun* 1 DISPLAY, view, sight, spectacle, array
2 EXHIBITION, fair, display, parade, expo (*informal*), exposition, pageant, pageantry
3 APPEARANCE, display, pose, profession, parade, ostentation

4 PRETENCE, appearance, semblance, illusion, pretext, likeness, affectation
5 PROGRAMME, broadcast, presentation, production
6 ENTERTAINMENT, performance, play, production, drama, musical, presentation, theatrical performance
▷▷ **show off** (*informal*) BOAST, brag, blow your own trumpet, swagger, hot-dog (*chiefly US*), strut your stuff (*chiefly US*), make a spectacle of yourself
▷▷ **show someone up** (*informal*) EMBARRASS, shame, let down, mortify, put to shame, show in a bad light
▷▷ **show something off** EXHIBIT, display, parade, advertise, demonstrate, spread out, flaunt
▷▷ **show something up** REVEAL, expose, highlight, pinpoint, unmask, lay bare, put the spotlight on

showdown *noun* (*informal*) CONFRONTATION, crisis, clash, moment of truth, face-off (*slang*)

shower *noun* 1 DELUGE, downpour
2 PROFUSION, plethora
▷ *verb* 1 COVER, dust, spray, sprinkle
2 INUNDATE, load, heap, lavish, pour, deluge

showing *noun* 1 DISPLAY, staging, presentation, exhibition, demonstration
2 PERFORMANCE, demonstration, track record, show, appearance, impression, account of yourself

showman *noun* PERFORMER, entertainer, artiste, player, Thespian, trouper, play-actor, actor *or* actress

show-off *noun* (*informal*) EXHIBITIONIST, boaster, swaggerer, hot dog (*chiefly US*), poseur, egotist, braggart, braggadocio, peacock, figjam (*Austral slang*)

showy *adjective* OSTENTATIOUS, flamboyant, flashy, flash (*informal*), loud, over the top (*informal*), brash, pompous, pretentious, gaudy, garish, tawdry, splashy (*informal*), tinselly
<< OPPOSITE tasteful

shred *noun* 1 STRIP, bit, piece, scrap, fragment, rag, ribbon, snippet, sliver, tatter
2 PARTICLE, trace, scrap, grain, atom, jot, whit, iota

shrew *noun* NAG, fury, dragon (*informal*), spitfire, virago, vixen, harpy, harridan, termagant (*rare*), scold, Xanthippe

shrewd *adjective* ASTUTE, clever, sharp, knowing, fly (*slang*), keen, acute, smart, calculated, calculating, intelligent, discriminating, cunning, discerning, sly, canny, perceptive, wily, crafty, artful, far-sighted, far-seeing, long-headed, perspicacious, sagacious
<< OPPOSITE naive

shrewdly *adverb* ASTUTELY, perceptively, cleverly, knowingly, artfully, cannily, with consummate skill, sagaciously, far-sightedly, perspicaciously, with all your wits about you

shriek *verb* SCREAM, cry, yell, howl, wail, whoop, screech, squeal, holler
▷ *noun* SCREAM, cry, yell, howl, wail, whoop, screech, squeal, holler

shrill *adjective* PIERCING, high, sharp, acute, piping, penetrating, screeching, high-pitched, ear-splitting, ear-piercing
<< OPPOSITE deep

shrink *verb* DECREASE, dwindle, lessen, grow *or* get smaller, contract, narrow, diminish, fall off, shorten, wrinkle, wither, drop off, deflate, shrivel, downsize
<< OPPOSITE grow

shrivel *verb* WITHER, dry (up), wilt, shrink, wrinkle, dwindle, dehydrate, desiccate, wizen

shrivelled *adjective* WITHERED, dry, dried up, wrinkled, shrunken, wizened, desiccated, sere (*archaic*)

shroud *noun* 1 WINDING SHEET, grave clothes, cerecloth, cerement
2 COVERING, veil, mantle, screen, cloud, pall
▷ *verb* CONCEAL, cover, screen, hide, blanket, veil, cloak, swathe, envelop

shudder *verb* SHIVER, shake, tremble, quake, quiver, convulse
▷ *noun* SHIVER, trembling, tremor, quiver, spasm, convulsion

shuffle *verb* 1 SHAMBLE, stagger, stumble, dodder
2 SCUFFLE, drag, scrape, scuff
3 REARRANGE, jumble, mix, shift, disorder, disarrange, intermix

shun *verb* AVOID, steer clear of, keep away from, evade, eschew, shy away from, cold-shoulder, have no part in, fight shy of, give (someone *or* something) a wide berth, body-swerve (*Scot*)

shut *verb* CLOSE, secure, fasten, bar, seal, slam, push to, draw to
<< OPPOSITE open
▷ *adjective* CLOSED, fastened, sealed, locked
<< OPPOSITE open
▷▷ **shut down** STOP WORK, halt work, cease operating, close down, cease trading, discontinue
▷▷ **shut someone out** EXCLUDE, bar, keep out, black, lock out, ostracize, debar, blackball
▷▷ **shut someone up** 1 (*informal*) SILENCE, gag, hush, muzzle, fall silent, button it (*slang*), pipe down (*slang*), hold your tongue, put a sock in it (*Brit slang*), keep your trap shut (*slang*), cut the cackle (*informal*), button your lip (*slang*)
2 CONFINE, cage, imprison, keep in, box in, intern, incarcerate, coop up, immure
▷▷ **shut something in** CONFINE, cage, enclose, imprison, impound, pound, wall off *or* up
▷▷ **shut something out** BLOCK OUT, screen,

hide, cover, mask, veil

shuttle *verb* GO BACK AND FORTH, commute, go to and fro, alternate, ply, shunt, seesaw

shy *adjective* 1 TIMID, self-conscious, bashful, reserved, retiring, nervous, modest, shrinking, backward, coy, reticent, self-effacing, diffident, mousy
<< OPPOSITE confident
2 CAUTIOUS, wary, hesitant, suspicious, reticent, distrustful, chary
<< OPPOSITE reckless
▷ *verb sometimes with* **off** *or* **away** RECOIL, flinch, draw back, start, rear, buck, wince, swerve, balk, quail, take fright

shyness *noun* TIMIDITY, self-consciousness, bashfulness, modesty, nervousness, lack of confidence, reticence, diffidence, timorousness, mousiness, timidness

sick *adjective* 1 UNWELL, ill, poorly (*informal*), diseased, weak, crook (*Austral & NZ informal*), under par (*informal*), ailing, feeble, laid up (*informal*), under the weather, indisposed, on the sick list (*informal*)
<< OPPOSITE well
2 NAUSEOUS, ill, queasy, nauseated, green about the gills (*informal*), qualmish
3 (*informal*) TIRED, bored, fed up, weary, jaded, blasé, satiated
4 (*informal*) MORBID, cruel, sadistic, black, macabre, ghoulish

sicken *verb* 1 DISGUST, revolt, nauseate, repel, gross out (*US slang*), turn your stomach, make your gorge rise
2 FALL ILL, take sick, ail, go down with something, contract something, be stricken by something

sickening *adjective* DISGUSTING, revolting, vile, offensive, foul, distasteful, repulsive, nauseating, loathsome, nauseous, gut-wrenching, putrid, stomach-turning (*informal*), cringe-making (*Brit informal*), noisome, yucky *or* yukky (*slang*), yucko (*Austral slang*)
<< OPPOSITE delightful

sickly *adjective* 1 UNHEALTHY, weak, delicate, ailing, feeble, infirm, in poor health, indisposed
2 PALE, wan, pasty, bloodless, pallid, sallow, ashen-faced, waxen, peaky
3 NAUSEATING, revolting (*informal*), cloying, icky (*informal*)
4 SENTIMENTAL, romantic, sloppy (*informal*), corny (*slang*), mushy (*informal*), weepy (*informal*), slushy (*informal*), mawkish, tear-jerking (*informal*), schmaltzy (*slang*), gushy (*informal*)

sickness *noun* 1 ILLNESS, disorder, ailment, disease, complaint, bug (*informal*), affliction, malady, infirmity, indisposition, lurgy (*informal*)
2 NAUSEA, queasiness
3 VOMITING, nausea, upset stomach, throwing up, puking (*slang*), retching, barfing (*US slang*)

side *noun* 1 BORDER, margin, boundary, verge, flank, rim, perimeter, periphery, edge
<< OPPOSITE middle
2 FACE, surface, facet
3 HALF, part
4 DISTRICT, area, region, quarter, sector, neighbourhood, vicinity, locality, locale, neck of the woods (*informal*)
5 PARTY, camp, faction, cause
6 POINT OF VIEW, viewpoint, position, opinion, angle, slant, standpoint
7 TEAM, squad, crew, line-up
8 ASPECT, feature, angle, facet
▷ *adjective* SUBORDINATE, minor, secondary, subsidiary, lesser, marginal, indirect, incidental, ancillary
<< OPPOSITE main
▷▷ **side with someone** SUPPORT, back, champion, agree with, stand up for, second, favour, defend, team up with (*informal*), go along with, befriend, join with, sympathize with, be loyal to, take the part of, associate yourself with, ally yourself with
>> RELATED WORD *adjective* lateral

sidestep *verb* AVOID, dodge, evade, duck (*informal*), skirt, skip, bypass, elude, circumvent, find a way round, body-swerve (*Scot*)

sidetrack *verb* DISTRACT, divert, lead off the subject, deflect

sidewalk *noun* (*US & Canad*) PAVEMENT, footpath (*Austral & NZ*)

sideways *adverb* 1 INDIRECTLY, obliquely
2 TO THE SIDE, laterally, crabwise
▷ *adjective* SIDELONG, side, slanted, oblique

sidle *verb* EDGE, steal, slink, inch, creep, sneak

siesta *noun* NAP, rest, sleep, doze, kip (*Brit slang*), snooze (*informal*), catnap, forty winks (*informal*), zizz (*Brit informal*)

sieve *noun* STRAINER, sifter, colander, screen, riddle, tammy cloth
▷ *verb* SIFT, filter, strain, separate, pan, bolt, riddle

sift *verb* 1 PART, filter, strain, separate, pan, bolt, riddle, sieve
2 EXAMINE, investigate, go through, research, screen, probe, analyse, work over, pore over, scrutinize

sigh *verb* 1 BREATHE OUT, exhale, moan, suspire (*archaic*)
2 MOAN, complain, groan, grieve, lament, sorrow
▷▷ **sigh for something** *or* **someone** LONG FOR, yearn for, pine for, mourn for, languish over, eat your heart out over

sight *noun* 1 VISION, eyes, eyesight, seeing, eye
2 SPECTACLE, show, scene, display, exhibition,

vista, pageant
3 VIEW, field of vision, range of vision, eyeshot, viewing, ken, visibility
4 (*informal*) EYESORE, mess, spectacle, fright (*informal*), monstrosity, blot on the landscape (*informal*)
▷ *verb* SPOT, see, observe, distinguish, perceive, make out, discern, behold
>> RELATED WORDS *adjectives* optical, visual

sign *noun* 1 SYMBOL, mark, character, figure, device, representation, logo, badge, emblem, ensign, cipher
2 FIGURE, form, shape, outline
3 GESTURE, signal, motion, indication, cue, gesticulation
4 NOTICE, board, warning, signpost, placard
5 INDICATION, evidence, trace, mark, note, signal, suggestion, symptom, hint, proof, gesture, clue, token, manifestation, giveaway, vestige, spoor
6 OMEN, warning, portent, foreboding, presage, forewarning, writing on the wall, augury, auspice, wake-up call
▷ *verb* 1 GESTURE, indicate, signal, wave, beckon, gesticulate, use sign language
2 AUTOGRAPH, initial, inscribe, subscribe, set your hand to
▷▷ **sign someone up** ENGAGE, recruit, employ, take on, hire, contract, take on board (*informal*), put on the payroll, take into service
▷▷ **sign something away** GIVE UP, relinquish, renounce, lose, transfer, abandon, surrender, dispose of, waive, forgo
▷▷ **sign up** ENLIST, join, volunteer, register, enrol, join up

signal *noun* 1 FLARE, rocket, beam, beacon, smoke signal, signal fire
2 CUE, sign, nod, prompting, go-ahead (*informal*), reminder, green light
3 SIGN, gesture, indication, mark, note, evidence, expression, proof, token, indicator, manifestation
▷ *verb* GESTURE, sign, wave, indicate, nod, motion, beckon, gesticulate, give a sign to

significance *noun* IMPORTANCE, import, consequence, matter, moment, weight, consideration, gravity, relevance, magnitude, impressiveness

significant *adjective* 1 IMPORTANT, notable, serious, material, vital, critical, considerable, momentous, weighty, noteworthy
<< OPPOSITE insignificant
2 MEANINGFUL, expressive, eloquent, knowing, meaning, expressing, pregnant, indicative, suggestive
<< OPPOSITE meaningless

signify *verb* INDICATE, show, mean, matter, suggest, announce, evidence, represent, express, imply, exhibit, communicate, intimate, stand for, proclaim, convey, be a sign of, symbolize, denote, connote, portend, betoken

silence *noun* 1 QUIET, peace, calm, hush, lull, stillness, quiescence, noiselessness
<< OPPOSITE noise
2 RETICENCE, dumbness, taciturnity, speechlessness, muteness, uncommunicativeness
<< OPPOSITE speech
▷ *verb* QUIETEN, still, quiet, cut off, subdue, stifle, cut short, quell, muffle, deaden, strike dumb
<< OPPOSITE make louder

silent *adjective* 1 MUTE, dumb, speechless, wordless, mum, struck dumb, voiceless, unspeaking
<< OPPOSITE noisy
2 UNCOMMUNICATIVE, quiet, taciturn, tongue-tied, unspeaking, nonvocal, not talkative
3 QUIET, still, hushed, soundless, noiseless, muted, stilly (*poetic*)
<< OPPOSITE loud
4 UNSPOKEN, implied, implicit, tacit, understood, unexpressed

silently *adverb* 1 QUIETLY, in silence, soundlessly, noiselessly, inaudibly, without a sound
2 MUTELY, dumbly, in silence, wordlessly, speechlessly

silhouette *noun* OUTLINE, form, shape, profile, delineation
▷ *verb* OUTLINE, delineate, etch

silky *adjective* SMOOTH, soft, sleek, velvety, silken

silly *adjective* 1 STUPID, ridiculous, absurd, daft, inane, childish, immature, senseless, frivolous, preposterous, giddy, goofy (*informal*), idiotic, dozy (*Brit informal*), fatuous, witless, puerile, brainless, asinine, dumb-ass (*slang*), dopy (*slang*)
<< OPPOSITE clever
2 FOOLISH, stupid, unwise, inappropriate, rash, irresponsible, reckless, foolhardy, idiotic, thoughtless, imprudent, inadvisable
<< OPPOSITE sensible
▷ *noun* (*informal*) FOOL, twit (*informal*), goose (*informal*), clot (*Brit informal*), wally (*slang*), prat (*slang*), plonker (*slang*), duffer (*informal*), simpleton, ignoramus, nitwit (*informal*), ninny, silly-billy (*informal*), dweeb (*US slang*), putz (*US slang*), eejit (*Scot & Irish*), doofus (*slang, chiefly US*), nerd *or* nurd (*slang*), dorba *or* dorb (*Austral slang*), bogan (*Austral slang*)

silt *noun* SEDIMENT, deposit, residue, ooze, sludge, alluvium
▷▷ **silt something up** CLOG UP, block up, choke up, obstruct, stop up, jam up, dam up, bung

up, occlude, congest
silver *noun* SILVERWARE, silver plate
▷ *adjective* SNOWY, white, grey, silvery, greyish-white, whitish-grey
similar *adjective* 1 ALIKE, uniform, resembling, corresponding, comparable, much the same, homogeneous, of a piece, homogenous, cut from the same cloth, congruous
<< OPPOSITE different
2 *with* **to** LIKE, much the same as, comparable to, analogous to, close to, cut from the same cloth as

> As should not be used after *similar* – so *Wilson held a similar position to Jones* is correct, but not *Wilson held a similar position as Jones*; and *the system is similar to the one in France* is correct, but not *the system is similar as in France*

similarity *noun* RESEMBLANCE, likeness, sameness, agreement, relation, correspondence, analogy, affinity, closeness, concordance, congruence, comparability, point of comparison, similitude
<< OPPOSITE difference
similarly *adverb* 1 IN THE SAME WAY, the same, identically, in a similar fashion, uniformly, homogeneously, undistinguishably
2 LIKEWISE, in the same way, by the same token, correspondingly, in like manner
simmer *verb* 1 BUBBLE, stew, boil gently, seethe, cook gently
2 FUME, seethe, smoulder, burn, smart, rage, boil, be angry, see red (*informal*), be tense, be agitated, be uptight (*informal*)
▷▷ **simmer down** (*informal*) CALM DOWN, grow quieter, control yourself, unwind (*informal*), contain yourself, collect yourself, cool off *or* down, get down off your high horse (*informal*)
simper *verb* SMILE COYLY, smirk, smile self-consciously, smile affectedly
simpering *adjective* COY, affected, flirtatious, coquettish, kittenish
simple *adjective* 1 UNCOMPLICATED, clear, plain, understandable, coherent, lucid, recognizable, unambiguous, comprehensible, intelligible, uninvolved
<< OPPOSITE complicated
2 EASY, straightforward, not difficult, light, elementary, manageable, effortless, painless, uncomplicated, undemanding, easy-peasy (*slang*)
3 PLAIN, natural, basic, classic, severe, Spartan, uncluttered, unadorned, unfussy, unembellished
<< OPPOSITE elaborate
4 PURE, mere, sheer, unalloyed
5 ARTLESS, innocent, naive, natural, frank, green, sincere, simplistic, unaffected, childlike, unpretentious, unsophisticated, ingenuous, guileless
<< OPPOSITE sophisticated
6 UNPRETENTIOUS, modest, humble, homely, lowly, rustic, uncluttered, unfussy, unembellished
<< OPPOSITE fancy
simple-minded *adjective* STUPID, simple, foolish, backward, idiot, retarded, idiotic, moronic, brainless, feeble-minded, addle-brained, dead from the neck up (*informal*), a bit lacking (*informal*), dim-witted
simplicity *noun* 1 STRAIGHTFORWARDNESS, ease, clarity, obviousness, easiness, clearness, absence of complications, elementariness
<< OPPOSITE complexity
2 PLAINNESS, restraint, purity, clean lines, naturalness, lack of adornment
<< OPPOSITE elaborateness
simplify *verb* MAKE SIMPLER, facilitate, streamline, disentangle, dumb down, make intelligible, reduce to essentials, declutter
simplistic *adjective* OVERSIMPLIFIED, shallow, facile, naive, oversimple

> Since *simplistic* already has 'too' as part of its meaning, some people object to something being referred to as *too simplistic* or *oversimplistic*, and it is best to avoid such uses in serious writing

simply *adverb* 1 JUST, only, merely, purely, solely
2 TOTALLY, really, completely, absolutely, altogether, wholly, utterly, unreservedly
3 CLEARLY, straightforwardly, directly, plainly, intelligibly, unaffectedly
4 PLAINLY, naturally, modestly, with restraint, unpretentiously, without any elaboration
5 WITHOUT DOUBT, surely, certainly, definitely, unquestionably, undeniably, unmistakably, beyond question, beyond a shadow of (a) doubt
simulate *verb* PRETEND, act, feign, affect, assume, put on, reproduce, imitate, sham, fabricate, counterfeit, make believe
simulated *adjective* 1 PRETENDED, put-on, feigned, assumed, artificial, make-believe, insincere, phoney *or* phony (*informal*)
2 SYNTHETIC, artificial, fake, substitute, mock, imitation, man-made, sham, pseudo (*informal*)
simultaneous *adjective* COINCIDING, concurrent, contemporaneous, coincident, synchronous, happening at the same time
simultaneously *adverb* AT THE SAME TIME, together, all together, in concert, in unison, concurrently, in the same breath, in chorus
sin *noun* 1 WICKEDNESS, wrong, evil, crime, error, trespass, immorality, transgression, iniquity, sinfulness, unrighteousness, ungodliness
2 CRIME, offence, misdemeanour, error,

wrongdoing, misdeed, transgression, act of evil, guilt
▷ *verb* TRANSGRESS, offend, lapse, err, trespass (*archaic*), fall from grace, go astray, commit a sin, do wrong

sincere *adjective* HONEST, genuine, real, true, serious, natural, earnest, frank, open, straightforward, candid, unaffected, no-nonsense, heartfelt, upfront (*informal*), bona fide, wholehearted, dinkum (*Austral* & *NZ informal*), artless, guileless, unfeigned
<< OPPOSITE false

sincerely *adverb* HONESTLY, really, truly, genuinely, seriously, earnestly, wholeheartedly, in good faith, in earnest, in all sincerity, from the bottom of your heart

sincerity *noun* HONESTY, truth, candour, frankness, seriousness, good faith, probity, bona fides, genuineness, straightforwardness, artlessness, guilelessness, wholeheartedness

sinewy *adjective* MUSCULAR, strong, powerful, athletic, robust, wiry, brawny

sinful *adjective* WICKED, bad, criminal, guilty, corrupt, immoral, erring, unholy, depraved, iniquitous, ungodly, irreligious, unrighteous, morally wrong
<< OPPOSITE virtuous

sing *verb* **1** CROON, carol, chant, warble, yodel, pipe, vocalize
2 TRILL, chirp, warble, make melody
▷▷ **sing out** CALL (OUT), cry (out), shout, yell, holler (*informal*), halloo

> *Sang* is the past tense of the verb *sing*, as in *she sang sweetly*. *Sung* is the past participle, as in *we have sung our song*, and care should be taken not to use it as if it were a variant form of the past tense

singe *verb* BURN, sear, scorch, char

singer *noun* VOCALIST, crooner, minstrel, soloist, cantor, troubadour, chorister, chanteuse (*fem*), balladeer, songster *or* songstress

single *adjective* **1** ONE, sole, lone, solitary, only, only one, unique, singular
2 INDIVIDUAL, particular, separate, distinct
3 UNMARRIED, free, unattached, a bachelor, unwed, a spinster
4 SEPARATE, individual, exclusive, undivided, unshared
5 SIMPLE, unmixed, unblended, uncompounded
▷▷ **single something** *or* **someone out** PICK, choose, select, separate, distinguish, fix on, set apart, winnow, put on one side, pick on *or* out

single-handed *adverb* UNAIDED, on your own, by yourself, alone, independently, solo, without help, unassisted, under your own steam

single-minded *adjective* DETERMINED, dogged, fixed, dedicated, stubborn, tireless, steadfast, unwavering, unswerving, hellbent (*informal*), undeviating, monomaniacal

singly *adverb* ONE BY ONE, individually, one at a time, separately, one after the other

singular *adjective* **1** SINGLE, individual
2 REMARKABLE, unique, extraordinary, outstanding, exceptional, rare, notable, eminent, uncommon, conspicuous, prodigious, unparalleled, noteworthy
<< OPPOSITE ordinary
3 UNUSUAL, odd, strange, extraordinary, puzzling, curious, peculiar, eccentric, out-of-the-way, queer, oddball (*informal*), atypical, wacko (*slang*), outré, daggy (*Austral* & *NZ informal*)
<< OPPOSITE conventional

singularity *noun* ODDITY, abnormality, eccentricity, peculiarity, strangeness, idiosyncrasy, irregularity, particularity, oddness, queerness, extraordinariness, curiousness

singularly *adverb* REMARKABLY, particularly, exceptionally, especially, seriously (*informal*), surprisingly, notably, unusually, extraordinarily, conspicuously, outstandingly, uncommonly, prodigiously

sinister *adjective* THREATENING, evil, menacing, forbidding, dire, ominous, malign, disquieting, malignant, malevolent, baleful, injurious, bodeful
<< OPPOSITE reassuring

sink *noun* BASIN, washbasin, hand basin, washhand basin
▷ *verb* **1** SCUPPER, scuttle
2 GO DOWN, founder, go under, submerge, capsize
3 SLUMP, drop, flop, collapse, droop
4 FALL, drop, decline, slip, plunge, plummet, subside, relapse, abate, retrogress
5 DROP, fall
6 STOOP, descend, be reduced to, succumb, lower yourself, debase yourself, demean yourself
7 DECLINE, die, fade, fail, flag, weaken, diminish, decrease, deteriorate, decay, worsen, dwindle, lessen, degenerate, depreciate, go downhill (*informal*)
<< OPPOSITE improve
8 DIG, bore, drill, drive, lay, put down, excavate

sinner *noun* WRONGDOER, offender, evildoer, trespasser (*archaic*), reprobate, miscreant, malefactor, transgressor

sinuous *adjective* CURVING, winding, meandering, crooked, coiling, tortuous, undulating, serpentine, curvy, lithe, twisty, mazy

sip *verb* DRINK, taste, sample, sup

▷ *noun* SWALLOW, mouthful, swig, drop, taste, thimbleful

siren *noun* 1 ALERT, warning, signal, alarm
2 SEDUCTRESS, vamp (*informal*), femme fatale (*French*), witch, charmer, temptress, Lorelei, Circe

sissy *or* **cissy** *noun* WIMP, softie (*informal*), weakling, baby, wet (*Brit informal*), coward (*informal*), jessie (*Scot slang*), pansy, pussy (*slang, chiefly US*), mummy's boy, mollycoddle, namby-pamby, wuss (*slang*), milksop, milquetoast (*US*), sisspot (*informal*)
▷ *adjective* WIMPISH *or* WIMPY (*informal*), soft (*informal*), weak, wet (*Brit informal*), cowardly, feeble, unmanly, effeminate, namby-pamby, wussy (*slang*), sissified (*informal*)

sit *verb* 1 TAKE A SEAT, perch, settle down, be seated, take the weight off your feet
2 PLACE, set, put, position, rest, lay, settle, deposit, situate
3 BE A MEMBER OF, serve on, have a seat on, preside on
4 CONVENE, meet, assemble, officiate, be in session

site *noun* 1 AREA, ground, plot, patch, tract
2 LOCATION, place, setting, point, position, situation, spot, whereabouts, locus
▷ *verb* LOCATE, put, place, set, position, establish, install, situate

sitting *noun* 1 SESSION, period
2 MEETING, hearing, session, congress, consultation, get-together (*informal*)

situation *noun* 1 POSITION, state, case, condition, circumstances, equation, plight, status quo, state of affairs, ball game (*informal*), kettle of fish (*informal*)
2 SCENARIO, the picture (*informal*), the score (*informal*), state of affairs, lie of the land
3 LOCATION, place, setting, position, seat, site, spot, locality, locale

> It is common to hear the word *situation* used in sentences such as *the company is in a crisis situation*. This use of *situation* is considered bad style and the word should be left out, since it adds nothing to the sentence's meaning

sixth sense *noun* INTUITION, second sight, clairvoyance

size *noun* DIMENSIONS, extent, measurement(s), range, amount, mass, length, volume, capacity, proportions, bulk, width, magnitude, greatness, vastness, immensity, bigness, largeness, hugeness
▷▷ **size something** *or* **someone up** (*informal*) ASSESS, evaluate, appraise, take stock of, eye up, get the measure of, get (something) taped (*Brit informal*)

sizeable *or* **sizable** *adjective* LARGE, considerable, substantial, goodly, decent, respectable, tidy (*informal*), decent-sized, largish

sizzle *verb* HISS, spit, crackle, sputter, fry, frizzle

skeletal *adjective* EMACIATED, wasted, gaunt, skin-and-bone (*informal*), cadaverous, hollow-cheeked, lantern-jawed, fleshless, worn to a shadow

skeleton *noun* 1 BONES, bare bones
2 FRAME, shell, framework, basic structure
3 PLAN, structure, frame, draft, outline, framework, sketch, abstract, blueprint, main points
▷ *modifier* MINIMUM, reduced, minimal, essential

sketch *noun* 1 DRAWING, design, draft, delineation
2 DRAFT, outline, framework, plan, frame, rough, skeleton, layout, lineament(s)
3 SKIT, piece, scene, turn, act, performance, item, routine, number
▷ *verb* DRAW, paint, outline, represent, draft, portray, depict, delineate, rough out

sketchy *adjective* INCOMPLETE, rough, vague, slight, outline, inadequate, crude, superficial, unfinished, skimpy, scrappy, cursory, perfunctory, cobbled together, bitty
<< OPPOSITE complete

skid *verb* SLIDE, slip, slither, coast, glide, skim, veer, toboggan

skilful *adjective* EXPERT, skilled, masterly, trained, experienced, able, professional, quick, clever, practised, accomplished, handy, competent, apt, adept, proficient, adroit, dexterous
<< OPPOSITE clumsy

skill *noun* EXPERTISE, ability, proficiency, experience, art, technique, facility, talent, intelligence, craft, competence, readiness, accomplishment, knack, ingenuity, finesse, aptitude, dexterity, cleverness, quickness, adroitness, expertness, handiness, skilfulness
<< OPPOSITE clumsiness

skilled *adjective* EXPERT, professional, accomplished, trained, experienced, able, masterly, practised, skilful, proficient, a dab hand at (*Brit informal*)
<< OPPOSITE unskilled

skim *verb* 1 REMOVE, separate, cream, take off
2 GLIDE, fly, coast, sail, float, brush, dart
3 *usually with* **over** *or* **through** SCAN, glance, run your eye over, thumb *or* leaf through

skimp *verb* STINT, scrimp, be sparing with, pinch, withhold, scant, cut corners, scamp, be mean with, be niggardly, tighten your belt
<< OPPOSITE be extravagant

skimpy *adjective* INADEQUATE, insufficient, scant, meagre, short, tight, thin, sparse, scanty, miserly, niggardly, exiguous

skin *noun* 1 COMPLEXION, colouring, skin tone
2 HIDE, fleece, pelt, fell, integument, tegument
3 PEEL, rind, husk, casing, outside, crust
4 FILM, coating, coat, membrane
▷ *verb* 1 PEEL, pare, hull
2 SCRAPE, graze, bark, flay, excoriate, abrade
▷▷ **by the skin of your teeth** NARROWLY, only just, by a whisker (*informal*), by a narrow margin, by a hair's-breadth
▷▷ **get under your skin** (*informal*) ANNOY, irritate, aggravate (*informal*), needle (*informal*), nettle, irk, grate on, get on your nerves (*informal*), get in your hair (*informal*), rub you up the wrong way, hack you off (*informal*)
skin-deep *adjective* SUPERFICIAL, surface, external, artificial, shallow, on the surface, meaningless
skinny *adjective* THIN, lean, scrawny, skeletal, emaciated, twiggy, undernourished, skin-and-bone (*informal*), scraggy
<< OPPOSITE fat
skip *verb* 1 HOP, dance, bob, trip, bounce, caper, prance, cavort, frisk, gambol
2 MISS OUT, omit, leave out, overlook, pass over, eschew, forego, skim over, give (something) a miss
3 (*informal*) MISS, cut (*informal*), bunk off (*slang*), play truant from, wag (*dialect*), dog it *or* dog off (*dialect*)
skirmish *noun* FIGHT, battle, conflict, incident, clash, contest, set-to (*informal*), encounter, brush, combat, scrap (*informal*), engagement, spat, tussle, fracas, affray (*Law*), dust-up (*informal*), scrimmage, biffo (*Austral slang*), boilover (*Austral*)
▷ *verb* FIGHT, clash, come to blows, scrap (*informal*), collide, grapple, wrangle, tussle, lock horns, cross swords
skirt *verb* 1 BORDER, edge, lie alongside, line, fringe, flank
2 *often with* **around** *or* **round** GO ROUND, bypass, walk round, circumvent
3 *often with* **around** *or* **round** AVOID, evade, steer clear of, sidestep, circumvent, detour, body-swerve (*Scot*)
▷ *noun often plural* BORDER, edge, margin, fringe, outskirts, rim, hem, periphery, purlieus
skit *noun* PARODY, spoof (*informal*), travesty, takeoff (*informal*), burlesque, turn, sketch
skittish *adjective* NERVOUS, lively, excitable, jumpy, restive, fidgety, highly strung, antsy (*informal*)
<< OPPOSITE calm
skookum *adjective* (*Canad*) POWERFUL, influential, big, dominant, controlling, commanding, supreme, prevailing, sovereign, authoritative, puissant

skulduggery *noun* (*informal*) TRICKERY, swindling, machinations, duplicity, double-dealing, fraudulence, shenanigan(s) (*informal*), unscrupulousness, underhandedness
skulk *verb* 1 CREEP, sneak, slink, pad, prowl
2 LURK, hide, lie in wait, loiter
sky *noun* HEAVENS, firmament, upper atmosphere, azure (*poetic*), welkin (*archaic*), vault of heaven, rangi (*NZ*)
>> RELATED WORD *adjective* celestial
slab *noun* PIECE, slice, lump, chunk, wedge, hunk, portion, nugget, wodge (*Brit informal*)
slack *adjective* 1 LIMP, relaxed, loose, lax, flaccid, not taut
2 LOOSE, hanging, flapping, baggy
<< OPPOSITE taut
3 SLOW, quiet, inactive, dull, sluggish, slow-moving
<< OPPOSITE busy
4 NEGLIGENT, lazy, lax, idle, easy-going, inactive, tardy, slapdash, neglectful, slipshod, inattentive, remiss, asleep on the job (*informal*)
<< OPPOSITE strict
▷ *noun* 1 SURPLUS, excess, overflow, leftover, glut, surfeit, overabundance, superabundance, superfluity
2 ROOM, excess, leeway, give (*informal*), play, looseness
▷ *verb* SHIRK, idle, relax, flag, neglect, dodge, skive (*Brit slang*), bob off (*Brit slang*), bludge (*Austral & NZ informal*)
slacken *verb often with* **off** LESSEN, reduce, decrease, ease (off), moderate, diminish, slow down, drop off, abate, let up, slack off
slacker *noun* LAYABOUT, shirker, loafer, skiver (*Brit slang*), idler, passenger, do-nothing, piker (*Austral & NZ slang*), dodger, good-for-nothing, bludger (*Austral & NZ informal*), gold brick (*US slang*), scrimshanker (*Brit Military slang*)
slag *noun* (*Brit slang*) TART (*informal*), scrubber (*Brit & Austral slang*), whore, pro (*slang*), brass (*slang*), prostitute, hooker (*US slang*), hustler (*US & Canad slang*), moll (*slang*), call girl, courtesan, working girl (*facetious slang*), harlot, slapper (*Brit informal*), streetwalker, camp follower, loose woman, fallen woman, strumpet, trollop, white slave, bawd (*archaic*), cocotte, fille de joie (*French*)
▷▷ **slag something** *or* **someone off** (*Slang*) CRITICIZE, abuse, malign, slam, insult, mock, slate, slang, deride, berate, slander, diss (*slang, chiefly US*), lambast(e), flame (*informal*)
slam *verb* 1 BANG, crash, smash, thump, shut with a bang, shut noisily
2 THROW, dash, hurl, fling
3 (*Slang*) CRITICIZE, attack, blast, pan (*informal*), damn, slate (*informal*), shoot down (*informal*), castigate, vilify, pillory, tear into (*informal*), diss (*slang, chiefly US*), lambast(e), excoriate

slander *noun* DEFAMATION, smear, libel, scandal, misrepresentation, calumny, backbiting, muckraking, obloquy, aspersion, detraction
<< OPPOSITE praise
▷ *verb* DEFAME, smear, libel, slur, malign, detract, disparage, decry, vilify, traduce, backbite, blacken (someone's) name, calumniate, muckrake
<< OPPOSITE praise

slang *noun* COLLOQUIALISMS, jargon, idioms, argot, informal language

slant *verb* 1 SLOPE, incline, tilt, list, bend, lean, heel, shelve, skew, cant, bevel, angle off
2 BIAS, colour, weight, twist, angle, distort
▷ *noun* 1 SLOPE, incline, tilt, gradient, pitch, ramp, diagonal, camber, declination
2 BIAS, emphasis, prejudice, angle, leaning, point of view, viewpoint, one-sidedness

slanting *adjective* SLOPING, angled, inclined, tilted, tilting, sideways, slanted, bent, diagonal, oblique, at an angle, canted, on the bias, aslant, slantwise, atilt, cater-cornered (*US informal*)

slap *verb* 1 SMACK, hit, strike, beat, bang, clap, clout (*informal*), cuff, whack, swipe, spank, clobber (*slang*), wallop (*informal*), lay one on (*slang*)
2 (*informal, chiefly Brit*) PLASTER, apply, spread, daub
▷ *noun* SMACK, blow, whack, wallop (*informal*), bang, clout (*informal*), cuff, swipe, spank
▷▷ **a slap in the face** INSULT, humiliation, snub, affront, blow, rejection, put-down, rebuke, rebuff, repulse

slapstick *noun* FARCE, horseplay, buffoonery, knockabout comedy

slap-up *adjective* (*Brit informal*) LUXURIOUS, lavish, sumptuous, princely, excellent, superb, magnificent, elaborate, splendid, first-rate, no-expense-spared, fit for a king

slash *verb* 1 CUT, slit, gash, lacerate, score, rend, rip, hack
2 REDUCE, cut, decrease, drop, lower, moderate, diminish, cut down, lessen, curtail
▷ *noun* CUT, slit, gash, rent, rip, incision, laceration

slate *verb* (*informal, chiefly Brit*) CRITICIZE, blast, pan (*informal*), slam (*slang*), blame, roast (*informal*), censure, rebuke, slang, scold, berate, castigate, rail against, tear into (*informal*), lay into (*informal*), pitch into (*informal*), take to task, lambast(e), flame (*informal*), excoriate, haul over the coals (*informal*), tear (someone) off a strip (*informal*), rap (someone's) knuckles

slaughter *verb* 1 KILL, murder, massacre, destroy, do in (*slang*), execute, dispatch, assassinate, blow away (*slang, chiefly US*), annihilate, bump off (*slang*)
2 BUTCHER, kill, slay, destroy, massacre, exterminate
3 DEFEAT, thrash, vanquish, stuff (*slang*), tank (*slang*), hammer (*informal*), crush, overwhelm, lick (*informal*), undo, rout, trounce, wipe the floor with (*informal*), blow out of the water (*slang*)
▷ *noun* SLAYING, killing, murder, massacre, holocaust, bloodshed, carnage, liquidation, extermination, butchery, blood bath

slaughterhouse *noun* ABATTOIR, butchery, shambles

slave *noun* 1 SERVANT, serf, vassal, bondsman, slavey (*Brit informal*), varlet (*archaic*), villein, bondservant
2 DRUDGE, skivvy (*chiefly Brit*), scullion (*archaic*)
▷ *verb* TOIL, labour, grind (*informal*), drudge, sweat, graft, slog, skivvy (*Brit*), work your fingers to the bone

slaver *verb* DRIBBLE, drool, salivate, slobber

slavery *noun* ENSLAVEMENT, servitude, subjugation, captivity, bondage, thrall, serfdom, vassalage, thraldom
<< OPPOSITE freedom

slavish *adjective* 1 IMITATIVE, unimaginative, unoriginal, conventional, second-hand, uninspired
<< OPPOSITE original
2 SERVILE, cringing, abject, submissive, grovelling, mean, low, base, fawning, despicable, menial, sycophantic, obsequious
<< OPPOSITE rebellious

slay *verb* 1 (*Archaic or literary*) KILL, destroy, slaughter, eliminate, massacre, butcher, dispatch, annihilate, exterminate
2 MURDER, kill, assassinate, do in (*slang*), eliminate, massacre, slaughter, do away with, exterminate, mow down, rub out (*US slang*)

sleaze *noun* (*informal*) CORRUPTION, fraud, dishonesty, fiddling (*informal*), bribery, extortion, venality, shady dealings (*informal*), crookedness (*informal*), unscrupulousness

sleazy *adjective* SQUALID, seedy, sordid, low, run-down, tacky (*informal*), disreputable, crummy, scungy (*Austral & NZ*)

sleek *adjective* GLOSSY, shiny, lustrous, smooth, silky, velvety, well-groomed
<< OPPOSITE shaggy

sleep *noun* SLUMBER(s), rest, nap, doze, kip (*Brit slang*), snooze (*informal*), repose, hibernation, siesta, dormancy, beauty sleep (*informal*), forty winks (*informal*), shuteye (*slang*), zizz (*Brit informal*)
▷ *verb* SLUMBER, drop off (*informal*), doze, kip (*Brit slang*), snooze (*informal*), snore, hibernate, nod off (*informal*), take a nap, catnap, drowse, go out like a light, take forty winks (*informal*), zizz (*Brit informal*), be in the land of Nod, rest in the arms of Morpheus

sleepless *adjective* 1 WAKEFUL, disturbed, restless, insomniac, unsleeping
2 ALERT, vigilant, watchful, wide awake, unsleeping

sleepwalking *noun* SOMNAMBULISM, noctambulation, noctambulism, somnambulation

sleepy *adjective* 1 DROWSY, sluggish, lethargic, heavy, dull, inactive, somnolent, torpid
<< OPPOSITE wide-awake
2 SOPORIFIC, hypnotic, somnolent, sleep-inducing, slumberous
3 QUIET, peaceful, dull, tranquil, inactive
<< OPPOSITE busy

slender *adjective* 1 SLIM, narrow, slight, lean, svelte, willowy, sylphlike
<< OPPOSITE chubby
2 FAINT, slight, remote, slim, thin, weak, fragile, feeble, flimsy, tenuous
<< OPPOSITE strong
3 MEAGRE, little, small, inadequate, insufficient, scant, scanty, inconsiderable
<< OPPOSITE large

sleuth *noun* (*informal*) DETECTIVE, private eye (*informal*), (private) investigator, tail (*informal*), dick (*slang, chiefly US*), gumshoe (*US slang*), sleuthhound (*informal*)

slice *noun* PIECE, segment, portion, wedge, sliver, helping, share, cut
▷ *verb* CUT, divide, carve, segment, sever, dissect, cleave, bisect

slick *adjective* 1 EFFICIENT, professional, smart, smooth, streamlined, masterly, sharp, deft, well-organized, adroit
2 SKILFUL, deft, adroit, dextrous, dexterous, professional, polished
<< OPPOSITE clumsy
3 GLIB, smooth, sophisticated, plausible, polished, specious, meretricious
▷ *verb* SMOOTH, oil, grease, sleek, plaster down, make glossy, smarm down (*Brit informal*)

slide *verb* SLIP, slither, glide, skim, coast, toboggan, glissade
▷▷ **let something slide** NEGLECT, forget, ignore, pass over, turn a blind eye to, gloss over, push to the back of your mind, let ride

slight *adjective* 1 SMALL, minor, insignificant, negligible, weak, modest, trivial, superficial, feeble, trifling, meagre, unimportant, paltry, measly, insubstantial, scanty, inconsiderable
<< OPPOSITE large
2 SLIM, small, delicate, spare, fragile, lightly-built
<< OPPOSITE sturdy
▷ *verb* SNUB, insult, ignore, rebuff, affront, neglect, put down, despise, scorn, disdain, disparage, cold-shoulder, treat with contempt, show disrespect for, give offence *or* umbrage to
<< OPPOSITE compliment
▷ *noun* INSULT, snub, affront, contempt, disregard, indifference, disdain, rebuff, disrespect, slap in the face (*informal*), inattention, discourtesy, (the) cold shoulder
<< OPPOSITE compliment

slightly *adverb* A LITTLE, a bit, somewhat, moderately, marginally, a shade, to some degree, on a small scale, to some extent *or* degree

slim *adjective* 1 SLENDER, slight, trim, thin, narrow, lean, svelte, willowy, sylphlike
<< OPPOSITE chubby
2 SLIGHT, remote, faint, distant, slender
<< OPPOSITE strong
▷ *verb* LOSE WEIGHT, diet, get thinner, get into shape, slenderize (*chiefly US*)
<< OPPOSITE put on weight

slimy *adjective* 1 VISCOUS, clammy, glutinous, muddy, mucous, gloopy (*informal*), oozy, miry
2 (*Chiefly Brit*) OBSEQUIOUS, creepy, unctuous, smarmy (*Brit informal*), oily, grovelling, soapy (*slang*), sycophantic, servile, toadying

sling *verb* 1 (*informal*) THROW, cast, toss, hurl, fling, chuck (*informal*), lob (*informal*), heave, shy
2 HANG, swing, suspend, string, drape, dangle
▷ *noun* HARNESS, support, bandage, strap

slink *verb* CREEP, steal, sneak, slip, prowl, skulk, pussyfoot (*informal*)

slinky *adjective* FIGURE-HUGGING, clinging, sleek, close-fitting, skintight

slip¹ *verb* 1 FALL, trip (over), slide, skid, lose your balance, miss *or* lose your footing
2 SLIDE, fall, drop, slither
3 SNEAK, creep, steal, insinuate yourself
▷ *noun* MISTAKE, failure, error, blunder, lapse, omission, boob (*Brit slang*), oversight, slip-up (*informal*), indiscretion, bloomer (*Brit informal*), faux pas, slip of the tongue, imprudence, barry *or* Barry Crocker (*Austral slang*)
▷▷ **give someone the slip** ESCAPE FROM, get away from, evade, shake (someone) off, elude, lose (someone), flee, dodge, outwit, slip through someone's fingers
▷▷ **let something slip** GIVE AWAY, reveal, disclose, divulge, leak, come out with (*informal*), let out (*informal*), blurt out, let the cat out of the bag
▷▷ **slip away** GET AWAY, escape, disappear, break away, break free, get clear of, take French leave
▷▷ **slip up** MAKE A MISTAKE, go wrong, blunder, mistake, boob (*Brit slang*), err, misjudge, miscalculate, drop a brick *or* clanger (*informal*)

slip² *noun* STRIP, piece, sliver

slippery *adjective* 1 SMOOTH, icy, greasy, glassy, slippy (*informal* or *dialect*), unsafe, lubricious (*rare*), skiddy (*informal*)
2 UNTRUSTWORTHY, tricky, cunning, false, treacherous, dishonest, devious, crafty,

evasive, sneaky, two-faced, shifty, foxy, duplicitous

slit *verb* CUT (OPEN), rip, slash, knife, pierce, lance, gash, split open
▷ *noun* 1 CUT, gash, incision, tear, rent, fissure
2 OPENING, split, crack, aperture, chink, space

slither *verb* SLIDE, slip, glide, snake, undulate, slink, skitter

sliver *noun* SHRED, fragment, splinter, slip, shaving, flake, paring

slob *noun* (*informal*) LAYABOUT, lounger, loafer, couch potato (*slang*), idler, good-for-nothing

slog *verb* 1 WORK, labour, toil, slave, plod, persevere, plough through, sweat blood (*informal*), apply yourself to, work your fingers to the bone, peg away at, keep your nose to the grindstone
2 TRUDGE, tramp, plod, trek, hike, traipse (*informal*), yomp, walk heavily, footslog
▷ *noun* 1 WORK, labour, toil, industry, grind (*informal*), effort, struggle, pains, sweat (*informal*), painstaking, exertion, donkey-work, blood, sweat, and tears (*informal*)
2 TRUDGE, tramp, trek, hike, traipse (*informal*), yomp, footslog

slogan *noun* CATCH PHRASE, motto, jingle, rallying cry, tag-line, catchword, catchcry (*Austral*)

slop *verb* SPILL, splash, overflow, splatter, spatter, slosh (*informal*)

slope *noun* INCLINATION, rise, incline, tilt, descent, downgrade (*chiefly US*), slant, ramp, gradient, brae (*Scot*), scarp, declination, declivity
▷ *verb* SLANT, incline, drop away, fall, rise, pitch, lean, tilt
▷▷ **slope off** SLINK AWAY, slip away, steal away, skulk, creep away, make yourself scarce

sloping *adjective* SLANTING, leaning, inclined, inclining, oblique, atilt

sloppy *adjective* 1 (*informal*) CARELESS, slovenly, slipshod, messy, clumsy, untidy, amateurish, hit-or-miss (*informal*), inattentive
2 (*informal*) SENTIMENTAL, mushy (*informal*), soppy (*Brit informal*), slushy (*informal*), wet (*Brit informal*), gushing, banal, trite, mawkish, icky (*informal*), overemotional, three-hankie (*informal*)
3 WET, watery, slushy, splashy, sludgy

slosh *verb* 1 SPLASH, wash, slop, break, plash
2 WADE, splash, flounder, paddle, dabble, wallow, swash

slot *noun* 1 OPENING, hole, groove, vent, slit, aperture, channel
2 (*informal*) PLACE, time, space, spot, opening, position, window, vacancy, niche
▷ *verb* FIT, slide, insert, put, place

sloth *noun* LAZINESS, inactivity, idleness, inertia, torpor, sluggishness, slackness, indolence

slouch *verb* LOUNGE, slump, flop, sprawl, stoop, droop, loll, lean

slouching *adjective* SHAMBLING, lumbering, ungainly, awkward, uncouth, loutish

slow *adjective* 1 UNHURRIED, sluggish, leisurely, easy, measured, creeping, deliberate, lagging, lazy, plodding, slow-moving, loitering, ponderous, leaden, dawdling, laggard, lackadaisical, tortoise-like, sluggardly
<< OPPOSITE quick
2 PROLONGED, time-consuming, protracted, long-drawn-out, lingering, gradual
3 UNWILLING, reluctant, loath, averse, hesitant, disinclined, indisposed
4 LATE, unpunctual, behindhand, behind, tardy
5 STUPID, dim, dense, thick, dull, dumb (*informal*), retarded, bovine, dozy (*Brit informal*), unresponsive, obtuse, slow on the uptake (*informal*), braindead (*informal*), dull-witted, blockish, slow-witted, intellectually handicapped (*Austral*)
<< OPPOSITE bright
6 DULL, quiet, boring, dead, tame, slack, sleepy, sluggish, tedious, stagnant, unproductive, inactive, one-horse (*informal*), uneventful, uninteresting, wearisome, dead-and-alive (*Brit*), unprogressive
<< OPPOSITE exciting
▷ *verb* 1 *often with* **down** DECELERATE, brake, lag
2 *often with* **down** DELAY, hold up, hinder, check, restrict, handicap, detain, curb, retard, rein in
<< OPPOSITE speed up

> While not as unkind as *thick* and *stupid*, words like *slow* and *backward*, when used to talk about a person's mental abilities, are both unhelpful and likely to cause offence. It is preferable to say that a person has *special educational needs* or *learning difficulties*

slowly *adverb* GRADUALLY, steadily, by degrees, unhurriedly, taking your time, at your leisure, at a snail's pace, in your own (good) time, ploddingly, inchmeal
<< OPPOSITE quickly

sludge *noun* SEDIMENT, ooze, silt, mud, muck, residue, slop, mire, slime, slush, slob (*Irish*), dregs, gloop (*informal*)

sluggish *adjective* INACTIVE, slow, lethargic, listless, heavy, dull, lifeless, inert, slow-moving, unresponsive, phlegmatic, indolent, torpid, slothful
<< OPPOSITE energetic

sluice *verb* DRAIN, cleanse, flush, drench, wash out, wash down

slum *noun* HOVEL, ghetto, shanty

slumber *noun* SLEEP, nap, doze, rest, kip (*Brit*

informal), snooze (*informal*), siesta, catnap, forty winks (*informal*)
▷ *verb* SLEEP, nap, doze, kip (*Brit slang*), snooze (*informal*), lie dormant, drowse, zizz (*Brit informal*)

slump *verb* 1 FALL, decline, sink, plunge, crash, collapse, slip, deteriorate, fall off, plummet, go downhill (*informal*)
<< OPPOSITE increase
2 SAG, bend, hunch, droop, slouch, loll
▷ *noun* 1 FALL, drop, decline, crash, collapse, reverse, lapse, falling-off, downturn, depreciation, trough, meltdown (*informal*)
<< OPPOSITE increase
2 RECESSION, depression, stagnation, inactivity, hard *or* bad times

slur *noun* INSULT, stain, smear, stigma, disgrace, discredit, blot, affront, innuendo, calumny, insinuation, aspersion
▷ *verb* MUMBLE, stammer, stutter, stumble over, falter, mispronounce, garble, speak unclearly

slut *noun* TART, slag (*Brit slang*), slapper (*Brit slang*), scrubber (*Brit & Austral slang*), trollop, drab (*archaic*), sloven, slattern, hornbag (*Austral slang*)

sly *adjective* 1 ROGUISH, knowing, arch, mischievous, impish
2 CUNNING, scheming, devious, secret, clever, subtle, tricky, covert, astute, wily, insidious, crafty, artful, furtive, conniving, Machiavellian, shifty, foxy, underhand, stealthy, guileful
<< OPPOSITE open
3 SECRET, furtive, surreptitious, stealthy, sneaking, covert, clandestine
▷▷ **on the sly** SECRETLY, privately, covertly, surreptitiously, under the counter (*informal*), on the quiet, behind (someone's) back, like a thief in the night, underhandedly, on the q.t. (*informal*)

smack *verb* 1 SLAP, hit, strike, pat, tap, sock (*slang*), clap, cuff, swipe, box, spank
2 DRIVE, hit, strike, thrust, impel
▷ *noun* SLAP, blow, whack, clout (*informal*), cuff, crack, swipe, spank, wallop (*informal*)
▷ *adverb* (*informal*) DIRECTLY, right, straight, squarely, precisely, exactly, slap (*informal*), plumb, point-blank
▷▷ **smack of something** BE SUGGESTIVE *or* INDICATIVE OF, suggest, smell of, testify to, reek of, have all the hallmarks of, betoken, be redolent of, bear the stamp of

small *adjective* 1 LITTLE, minute, tiny, slight, mini, miniature, minuscule, diminutive, petite, teeny, puny, pint-sized (*informal*), pocket-sized, undersized, teeny-weeny, Lilliputian, teensy-weensy, pygmy *or* pigmy
<< OPPOSITE big
2 INTIMATE, close, private
3 YOUNG, little, growing up, junior, wee, juvenile, youthful, immature, unfledged, in the springtime of life
4 UNIMPORTANT, minor, trivial, insignificant, little, lesser, petty, trifling, negligible, paltry, piddling (*informal*)
<< OPPOSITE important
5 MODEST, small-scale, humble, unpretentious
<< OPPOSITE grand
6 SOFT, low, inaudible, low-pitched, noiseless
7 MEAGRE, inadequate, insufficient, scant, measly, scanty, limited, inconsiderable
<< OPPOSITE ample

small-minded *adjective* PETTY, mean, rigid, grudging, envious, bigoted, intolerant, narrow-minded, hidebound, ungenerous
<< OPPOSITE broad-minded

small-time *adjective* (*informal*) MINOR, insignificant, unimportant, petty, no-account (*US informal*), piddling (*informal*), of no consequence, of no account

smart *adjective* 1 CHIC, trim, neat, fashionable, stylish, fine, elegant, trendy (*Brit informal*), spruce, snappy, natty (*informal*), modish, well turned-out, schmick (*Austral informal*)
<< OPPOSITE scruffy
2 CLEVER, bright, intelligent, quick, sharp, keen, acute, shrewd, apt, ingenious, astute, canny, quick-witted
<< OPPOSITE stupid
3 FASHIONABLE, stylish, chic, genteel, in vogue, voguish (*informal*)
4 BRISK, quick, lively, vigorous, spirited, cracking (*informal*), spanking, jaunty
▷ *verb* STING, burn, tingle, pain, hurt, throb

smarten *verb often with* **up** TIDY, spruce up, groom, beautify, put in order, put to rights, gussy up (*slang, chiefly US*)

smash *verb* 1 BREAK, crush, shatter, crack, demolish, shiver, disintegrate, pulverize, crush to smithereens
2 SHATTER, break, disintegrate, split, crack, explode, splinter
3 COLLIDE, crash, meet head-on, clash, come into collision
4 DESTROY, ruin, wreck, total (*slang*), defeat, overthrow, trash (*slang*), lay waste
▷ *noun* 1 (*informal*) SUCCESS, hit, winner, triumph (*informal*), belter (*slang*), sensation, smash hit, sellout
2 COLLISION, crash, accident, pile-up (*informal*), smash-up (*informal*)
3 CRASH, smashing, clatter, clash, bang, thunder, racket, din, clattering, clang

smashing *adjective* (*informal, chiefly Brit*) EXCELLENT, mean (*slang*), great (*informal*), wonderful, topping (*Brit slang*), brilliant

(*informal*), cracking (*Brit informal*), crucial (*slang*), superb, fantastic (*informal*), magnificent, fabulous (*informal*), first-class, marvellous, terrific (*informal*), sensational (*informal*), mega (*slang*), sovereign, awesome (*slang*), world-class, exhilarating, fab (*informal, chiefly Brit*), super (*informal*), first-rate, def (*slang*), superlative, brill (*informal*), stupendous, out of this world (*informal*), bodacious (*slang, chiefly US*), boffo (*slang*), jim-dandy (*slang*), chillin' (*US slang*), booshit (*Austral slang*), exo (*Austral slang*), sik (*Austral slang*), rad (*informal*), phat (*slang*), schmick (*Austral informal*)
<< OPPOSITE awful

smattering *noun* MODICUM, dash, rudiments, bit, elements, sprinkling, passing acquaintance, nodding acquaintance, smatter

smear *verb* 1 SPREAD OVER, daub, rub on, cover, coat, plaster, bedaub
2 SLANDER, tarnish, malign, vilify, blacken, sully, besmirch, traduce, calumniate, asperse, drag (someone's) name through the mud
3 SMUDGE, soil, dirty, stain, sully, besmirch, smirch
▷ *noun* 1 SMUDGE, daub, streak, blot, blotch, splotch, smirch
2 SLANDER, libel, defamation, vilification, whispering campaign, calumny, mudslinging

smell *noun* 1 ODOUR, scent, fragrance, perfume, bouquet, aroma, whiff, niff (*Brit slang*), redolence
2 STINK, stench, reek, pong (*Brit informal*), niff (*Brit slang*), malodour, fetor
▷ *verb* 1 STINK, reek, pong (*Brit informal*), hum (*slang*), whiff (*Brit slang*), stink to high heaven (*informal*), niff (*Brit slang*), be malodorous
2 SNIFF, scent, get a whiff of, nose
>> RELATED WORD *adjective* olfactory

smelly *adjective* STINKING, reeking, fetid, foul-smelling, high, strong, foul, putrid, strong-smelling, stinky (*informal*), malodorous, evil-smelling, noisome, whiffy (*Brit slang*), pongy (*Brit informal*), mephitic, niffy (*Brit slang*), olid, festy (*Austral slang*)
<< OPPOSITE fragrant

smile *verb* GRIN, beam, smirk, twinkle, grin from ear to ear
▷ *noun* GRIN, beam, smirk

smirk *noun* SMUG SMILE, grin, simper
▷ *verb* GIVE A SMUG LOOK, grin, simper

smitten *adjective* 1 INFATUATED, charmed, captivated, beguiled, bewitched, bowled over (*informal*), enamoured, swept off your feet
2 AFFLICTED, struck, beset, laid low, plagued

smoky *adjective* THICK, murky, hazy

smooth *adjective* 1 EVEN, level, flat, plane, plain, flush, horizontal, unwrinkled
<< OPPOSITE uneven
2 SLEEK, polished, shiny, glossy, silky, velvety, glassy, mirror-like
<< OPPOSITE rough
3 MELLOW, pleasant, mild, soothing, bland, agreeable
4 FLOWING, steady, fluent, regular, uniform, rhythmic
5 CALM, peaceful, serene, tranquil, undisturbed, unruffled, equable
<< OPPOSITE troubled
6 EASY, effortless, untroubled, well-ordered
7 SUAVE, slick, persuasive, urbane, silky, glib, facile, ingratiating, debonair, unctuous, smarmy (*Brit informal*)
▷ *verb* 1 FLATTEN, level, press, plane, iron
2 EASE, aid, assist, facilitate, pave the way, make easier, help along, iron out the difficulties of
<< OPPOSITE hinder

smoothness *noun* 1 EVENNESS, regularity, levelness, flushness, unbrokenness
2 FLUENCY, finish, flow, ease, polish, rhythm, efficiency, felicity, smooth running, slickness, effortlessness
3 SLEEKNESS, softness, smooth texture, silkiness, velvetiness
4 SUAVITY, urbanity, oiliness, glibness, smarminess (*Brit informal*)

smother *verb* 1 EXTINGUISH, put out, stifle, snuff
2 SUFFOCATE, choke, strangle, stifle
3 SUPPRESS, stifle, repress, hide, conceal, muffle, keep back
4 OVERWHELM, cover, shower, surround, heap, shroud, inundate, envelop, cocoon
5 STIFLE, suppress, hold in, restrain, hold back, repress, muffle, bottle up, keep in check
6 SMEAR, cover, spread

smoulder *verb* 1 SMOKE, burn slowly
2 SEETHE, rage, fume, burn, boil, simmer, fester, be resentful, smart

smudge *noun* SMEAR, blot, smut, smutch
▷ *verb* 1 SMEAR, blur, blot
2 MARK, soil, dirty, daub, smirch

smug *adjective* SELF-SATISFIED, superior, complacent, conceited, self-righteous, holier-than-thou, priggish, self-opinionated

smuggler *noun* TRAFFICKER, runner, bootlegger, moonshiner (*US*), rum-runner, contrabandist

snack *noun* LIGHT MEAL, bite, refreshment(s), nibble, titbit, bite to eat, elevenses (*Brit informal*)

snag *noun* DIFFICULTY, hitch, problem, obstacle, catch, hazard, disadvantage, complication, drawback, inconvenience, downside, stumbling block, the rub
▷ *verb* CATCH, tear, rip, hole

snake *noun* SERPENT
▷ *verb* WIND, twist, curve, turn, bend, ramble, meander, deviate, zigzag
>> RELATED WORD *adjective* serpentine

snap *verb* 1 BREAK, split, crack, separate, fracture, give way, come apart
2 POP, click, crackle
3 SPEAK SHARPLY, bark, lash out at, flash, retort, snarl, growl, fly off the handle at (*informal*), jump down (someone's) throat (*informal*)
4 BITE AT, bite, nip
▷ *noun* 1 CRACK, pop, crash, report, burst, explosion, clap
2 POP, crack, smack, whack
▷ *modifier* INSTANT, immediate, sudden, abrupt, spur-of-the-moment, unpremeditated
▷▷ **snap out of it** (*informal*) GET OVER IT, recover, cheer up, perk up, liven up, pull yourself together (*informal*), get a grip on yourself
▷▷ **snap something up** GRAB, seize, take advantage of, swoop down on, pounce upon, avail yourself of

snappy *adjective* 1 SMART, fashionable, stylish, trendy (*Brit informal*), chic, dapper, up-to-the-minute, natty (*informal*), modish, voguish, schmick (*Austral informal*)
2 IRRITABLE, cross, bad-tempered, tart, impatient, edgy, touchy, tetchy, ratty (*Brit & NZ informal*), testy, waspish, quick-tempered, snappish, like a bear with a sore head (*informal*), apt to fly off the handle (*informal*)
▷▷ **make it snappy** (*Slang*) HURRY (UP), be quick, get a move on (*informal*), buck up (*informal*), make haste, look lively, get your skates on

snare *noun* TRAP, net, wire, gin, pitfall, noose, springe
▷ *verb* TRAP, catch, net, wire, seize, entrap, springe

snarl[1] *verb* 1 GROWL, show your teeth (*of an animal*)
2 SNAP, bark, lash out, speak angrily, jump down someone's throat, speak roughly

snarl[2] ▷▷ **snarl something up** TANGLE, complicate, muddle, embroil, entangle, entwine, ravel, enmesh

snatch *verb* 1 GRAB, seize, wrench, wrest, take, grip, grasp, clutch, take hold of
2 STEAL, take, nick (*slang, chiefly Brit*), pinch (*informal*), swipe (*slang*), lift (*informal*), pilfer, filch, shoplift, thieve, walk *or* make off with
3 WIN, take, score, gain, secure, obtain
4 SAVE, free, rescue, pull, recover, get out, salvage, extricate
▷ *noun* BIT, part, fragment, piece, spell, snippet, smattering

snazzy *adjective* (*informal*) STYLISH, smart, dashing, with it (*informal*), attractive, sophisticated, flamboyant, sporty, flashy, jazzy (*informal*), showy, ritzy (*slang*), raffish, schmick (*Austral informal*)

sneak *verb* 1 SLINK, slip, steal, pad, sidle, skulk
2 SLIP, smuggle, spirit
▷ *noun* INFORMER, grass (*Brit slang*), betrayer, telltale, squealer (*slang*), Judas, accuser, stool pigeon, snake in the grass, nark (*Brit, Austral & NZ slang*), fizgig (*Austral slang*)
▷ *modifier* SECRET, quick, clandestine, furtive, stealthy

sneaking *adjective* 1 NAGGING, worrying, persistent, niggling, uncomfortable
2 SECRET, private, hidden, suppressed, unexpressed, unvoiced, unavowed, unconfessed, undivulged

sneaky *adjective* SLY, dishonest, devious, mean, low, base, nasty, cowardly, slippery, unreliable, malicious, unscrupulous, furtive, disingenuous, shifty, snide, deceitful, contemptible, untrustworthy, double-dealing

sneer *verb* 1 SCORN, mock, ridicule, laugh, jeer, disdain, scoff, deride, look down on, snigger, sniff at, gibe, hold in contempt, hold up to ridicule, turn up your nose (*informal*)
2 SAY CONTEMPTUOUSLY, snigger
▷ *noun* 1 SCORN, ridicule, mockery, derision, jeer, disdain, snigger, gibe, snidery
2 CONTEMPTUOUS SMILE, snigger, curl of the lip

snide *or* **snidey** *adjective* NASTY, sneering, malicious, mean, cynical, unkind, hurtful, sarcastic, disparaging, spiteful, insinuating, scornful, shrewish, ill-natured, snarky (*informal*)

sniff *verb* 1 BREATHE IN, inhale, snuffle, snuff
2 SMELL, nose, breathe in, scent, get a whiff of
3 INHALE, breathe in, suck in, draw in

sniffy *adjective* (*informal*) CONTEMPTUOUS, superior, condescending, haughty, scornful, disdainful, supercilious

snigger *verb* LAUGH, giggle, sneer, snicker, titter
▷ *noun* LAUGH, giggle, sneer, snicker, titter

snip *verb* CUT, nick, clip, crop, trim, dock, notch, nip off
▷ *noun* (*informal, chiefly Brit*) BARGAIN, steal (*informal*), good buy, giveaway

snipe *verb* CRITICIZE, knock (*informal*), put down, carp, bitch, have a go (at) (*informal*), jeer, denigrate, disparage

snippet *noun* PIECE, scrap, fragment, part, particle, snatch, shred

snob *noun* ELITIST, highbrow, social climber

snobbery *noun* ARROGANCE, airs, pride, pretension, condescension, snobbishness, snootiness (*informal*), side (*Brit slang*), uppishness (*Brit informal*)

snobbish *adjective* SUPERIOR, arrogant, stuck-up (*informal*), patronizing, condescending, snooty (*informal*), pretentious, uppity, high and mighty (*informal*), toffee-nosed (*slang, chiefly Brit*), hoity-toity (*informal*), high-hat (*informal, chiefly US*), uppish (*Brit informal*)
<< OPPOSITE humble

snoop *verb* 1 INVESTIGATE, explore, have a good look at, prowl around, nose around, peer into
2 SPY, poke your nose in, nose, interfere, pry (*informal*)
▷ *noun* LOOK, search, nose, prowl, investigation

snooty *adjective* (*informal*) SNOBBISH, superior, aloof, pretentious, stuck-up (*informal*), condescending, proud, haughty, disdainful, snotty, uppity, supercilious, high and mighty (*informal*), toffee-nosed (*slang, chiefly Brit*), hoity-toity (*informal*), high-hat (*informal, chiefly US*), uppish (*Brit informal*), toplofty (*informal*)
<< OPPOSITE humble

snooze (*informal*) *noun* DOZE, nap, kip (*Brit slang*), siesta, catnap, forty winks (*informal*)
▷ *verb* DOZE, drop off (*informal*), nap, kip (*Brit slang*), nod off (*informal*), catnap, drowse, take forty winks (*informal*)

snub *verb* INSULT, slight, put down, humiliate, cut (*informal*), shame, humble, rebuff, mortify, cold-shoulder, kick in the teeth (*slang*), give (someone) the cold shoulder, give (someone) the brush-off (*slang*), cut dead (*informal*)
▷ *noun* INSULT, put-down, humiliation, affront, slap in the face, brush-off (*slang*)

snug *adjective* 1 COSY, warm, comfortable, homely, sheltered, intimate, comfy (*informal*)
2 TIGHT, close, trim, neat

snuggle *verb* NESTLE, cuddle up

so *sentence connector* THEREFORE, thus, hence, consequently, then, as a result, accordingly, for that reason, whence, thence, ergo

soak *verb* 1 STEEP, immerse, submerge, infuse, marinate (*Cookery*), dunk, submerse
2 WET, damp, saturate, drench, douse, moisten, suffuse, wet through, waterlog, souse, drouk (*Scot*)
3 PENETRATE, pervade, permeate, enter, get in, infiltrate, diffuse, seep, suffuse, make inroads (into)
▷▷ **soak something up** ABSORB, suck up, take in *or* up, drink in, assimilate

soaking *adjective* SOAKED, dripping, saturated, drenched, sodden, waterlogged, streaming, sopping, wet through, soaked to the skin, wringing wet, like a drowned rat, droukit *or* drookit (*Scot*)

soar *verb* 1 RISE, increase, grow, mount, climb, go up, rocket, swell, escalate, shoot up
2 FLY, rise, wing, climb, ascend, fly up
<< OPPOSITE plunge
3 TOWER, rise, climb, go up

sob *verb* CRY, weep, blubber, greet (*Scot archaic*), howl, bawl, snivel, shed tears, boohoo
▷ *noun* CRY, whimper, howl

sober *adjective* 1 ABSTINENT, temperate, abstemious, moderate, on the wagon (*informal*)
<< OPPOSITE drunk
2 SERIOUS, practical, realistic, sound, cool, calm, grave, reasonable, steady, composed, rational, solemn, lucid, sedate, staid, level-headed, dispassionate, unruffled, clear-headed, unexcited
<< OPPOSITE frivolous
3 PLAIN, dark, sombre, quiet, severe, subdued, drab
<< OPPOSITE bright
▷ *verb* 1 *usually with* **up** COME TO YOUR SENSES
<< OPPOSITE get drunk
2 *usually with* **up** CLEAR YOUR HEAD

sobriety *noun* 1 ABSTINENCE, temperance, abstemiousness, moderation, self-restraint, soberness, nonindulgence
2 SERIOUSNESS, gravity, steadiness, restraint, composure, coolness, calmness, solemnity, reasonableness, level-headedness, staidness, sedateness

so-called *adjective* ALLEGED, supposed, professed, pretended, self-styled, ostensible, soi-disant (*French*)

sociability *noun* FRIENDLINESS, conviviality, cordiality, congeniality, neighbourliness, affability, gregariousness, companionability

sociable *adjective* FRIENDLY, social, outgoing, warm, neighbourly, accessible, cordial, genial, affable, approachable, gregarious, convivial, companionable, conversable
<< OPPOSITE unsociable

social *adjective* 1 COMMUNAL, community, collective, group, public, general, common, societal
2 SOCIABLE, friendly, companionable, neighbourly
3 ORGANIZED, gregarious
▷ *noun* GET-TOGETHER (*informal*), party, gathering, function, do (*informal*), reception, bash (*informal*), social gathering

socialize *verb* MIX, interact, mingle, be sociable, meet, go out, entertain, get together, fraternize, be a good mixer, get about *or* around

society *noun* 1 THE COMMUNITY, social order, people, the public, the population, humanity, civilization, mankind, the general public, the world at large
2 CULTURE, community, population
3 ORGANIZATION, group, club, union, league, association, institute, circle, corporation, guild, fellowship, fraternity, brotherhood *or* sisterhood
4 UPPER CLASSES, gentry, upper crust (*informal*), elite, the swells (*informal*), high society, the top drawer, polite society, the toffs (*Brit slang*), the smart set, beau monde, the nobs (*slang*), the country set, haut monde (*French*)
5 (*Old-fashioned*) COMPANIONSHIP, company, fellowship, friendship, camaraderie

sodden *adjective* SOAKED, saturated, sopping,

drenched, soggy, waterlogged, marshy, boggy, miry, droukit *or* drookit (*Scot*)

sodomy *noun* ANAL INTERCOURSE, anal sex, buggery

sofa *noun* COUCH, settee, divan, chaise longue, chesterfield, ottoman

soft *adjective* 1 VELVETY, smooth, silky, furry, feathery, downy, fleecy, like a baby's bottom (*informal*)
<< OPPOSITE rough
2 YIELDING, flexible, pliable, cushioned, elastic, malleable, spongy, springy, cushiony
<< OPPOSITE hard
3 SOGGY, swampy, marshy, boggy, squelchy, quaggy
4 SQUASHY, sloppy, mushy, spongy, squidgy (*Brit informal*), squishy, gelatinous, squelchy, pulpy, doughy
5 PLIABLE, flexible, supple, malleable, plastic, elastic, tensile, ductile (*of metals*), bendable, mouldable, impressible
6 QUIET, low, gentle, sweet, whispered, soothing, murmured, muted, subdued, mellow, understated, melodious, mellifluous, dulcet, soft-toned
<< OPPOSITE loud
7 LENIENT, easy-going, lax, liberal, weak, indulgent, permissive, spineless, boneless, overindulgent
<< OPPOSITE harsh
8 KIND, tender, sentimental, compassionate, sensitive, gentle, pitying, sympathetic, tenderhearted, touchy-feely (*informal*)
9 (*informal*) EASY, comfortable, undemanding, cushy (*informal*), easy-peasy (*slang*)
10 PALE, light, subdued, pastel, pleasing, bland, mellow
<< OPPOSITE bright
11 DIM, faint, dimmed
<< OPPOSITE bright
12 MILD, delicate, caressing, temperate, balmy
13 (*informal*) FEEBLE-MINDED, simple, silly, foolish, daft (*informal*), soft in the head (*informal*), a bit lacking (*informal*)

soften *verb* 1 MELT, tenderize
2 LESSEN, moderate, diminish, temper, lower, relax, ease, calm, modify, cushion, soothe, subdue, alleviate, lighten, quell, muffle, allay, mitigate, abate, tone down, assuage

soggy *adjective* SODDEN, saturated, moist, heavy, soaked, dripping, waterlogged, sopping, mushy, spongy, pulpy

soil[1] *noun* 1 EARTH, ground, clay, dust, dirt, loam
2 TERRITORY, country, land, region, turf (*US slang*), terrain

soil[2] *verb* DIRTY, foul, stain, smear, muddy, pollute, tarnish, spatter, sully, defile, besmirch, smirch, bedraggle, befoul, begrime
<< OPPOSITE clean

sojourn (*Literary*) *noun* STAY, visit, stop, rest, stopover

solace *noun* COMFORT, consolation, help, support, relief, succour, alleviation, assuagement
▷ *verb* COMFORT, console, soothe

soldier *noun* FIGHTER, serviceman, trooper, warrior, Tommy (*Brit informal*), GI (*US informal*), military man, redcoat, enlisted man (*US*), man-at-arms, squaddie *or* squaddy (*Brit slang*)

sole *adjective* ONLY, one, single, individual, alone, exclusive, solitary, singular, one and only

solely *adverb* ONLY, completely, entirely, exclusively, alone, singly, merely, single-handedly

solemn *adjective* 1 SERIOUS, earnest, grave, sober, thoughtful, sedate, glum, staid, portentous
<< OPPOSITE cheerful
2 FORMAL, august, grand, imposing, impressive, grave, majestic, dignified, ceremonial, stately, momentous, awe-inspiring, ceremonious
<< OPPOSITE informal
3 SACRED, religious, holy, ritual, venerable, hallowed, sanctified, devotional, reverential
<< OPPOSITE irreligious

solemnity *noun* 1 SERIOUSNESS, gravity, formality, grandeur, gravitas, earnestness, portentousness, momentousness, impressiveness
2 *often plural* RITUAL, proceedings, ceremony, rite, formalities, ceremonial, observance, celebration

solicit *verb* 1 REQUEST, seek, ask for, petition, crave, pray for, plead for, canvass, beg for
2 APPEAL TO, ask, call on, lobby, press, beg, petition, plead with, implore, beseech, entreat, importune, supplicate

solicitous *adjective* CONCERNED, caring, attentive, careful

solid *adjective* 1 FIRM, hard, compact, dense, massed, concrete
<< OPPOSITE unsubstantial
2 STRONG, stable, sturdy, sound, substantial, unshakable
<< OPPOSITE unstable
3 PURE, unalloyed, unmixed, complete
4 CONTINUOUS, unbroken, uninterrupted
5 RELIABLE, decent, dependable, upstanding, serious, constant, sensible, worthy, upright, sober, law-abiding, trusty, level-headed, estimable
<< OPPOSITE unreliable
6 SOUND, real, reliable, good, genuine, dinkum (*Austral & NZ informal*)
<< OPPOSITE unsound

solidarity *noun* UNITY, harmony, unification, accord, stability, cohesion, team spirit, camaraderie, unanimity, soundness, concordance, esprit de corps, community of interest, singleness of purpose, like-mindedness, kotahitanga (NZ)
solidify *verb* HARDEN, set, congeal, cake, jell, coagulate, cohere
soliloquy *noun* MONOLOGUE, address, speech, aside, oration, dramatic monologue

> Although *soliloquy* and *monologue* are close in meaning, you should take care when using one as a synonym of the other. Both words refer to a long speech by one person, but a *monologue* can be addressed to other people, whereas in a *soliloquy* the speaker is always talking to himself or herself

solitary *adjective* **1** UNSOCIABLE, retiring, reclusive, unsocial, isolated, lonely, cloistered, lonesome, friendless, companionless
<< OPPOSITE sociable
2 LONE, alone
3 ISOLATED, remote, out-of-the-way, desolate, hidden, sequestered, unvisited, unfrequented
<< OPPOSITE busy
solitude *noun* **1** ISOLATION, privacy, seclusion, retirement, loneliness, ivory tower, reclusiveness
2 (*Poetic*) WILDERNESS, waste, desert, emptiness, wasteland
solution *noun* **1** ANSWER, resolution, key, result, solving, explanation, unfolding, unravelling, clarification, explication, elucidation
2 (*Chemistry*) MIXTURE, mix, compound, blend, suspension, solvent, emulsion
solve *verb* ANSWER, work out, resolve, explain, crack, interpret, unfold, clarify, clear up, unravel, decipher, expound, suss (out) (*slang*), get to the bottom of, disentangle, elucidate
solvent *adjective* FINANCIALLY SOUND, secure, in the black, solid, profit-making, in credit, debt-free, unindebted
sombre *adjective* **1** GLOOMY, sad, sober, grave, dismal, melancholy, mournful, lugubrious, joyless, funereal, doleful, sepulchral
<< OPPOSITE cheerful
2 DARK, dull, gloomy, sober, drab
<< OPPOSITE bright
somebody *noun* CELEBRITY, big name, public figure, name, star, heavyweight (*informal*), notable, superstar, household name, dignitary, luminary, bigwig (*informal*), celeb (*informal*), big shot (*informal*), personage, megastar (*informal*), big wheel (*slang*), big noise (*informal*), big hitter (*informal*), heavy hitter (*informal*), person of note, V.I.P., someone
<< OPPOSITE nobody
someday *adverb* ONE DAY, eventually, ultimately, sooner or later, one of these (fine) days, in the fullness of time
somehow *adverb* ONE WAY OR ANOTHER, come what may, come hell or high water (*informal*), by fair means or foul, by hook or (by) crook, by some means or other
sometime *adverb* SOME DAY, one day, at some point in the future, sooner or later, one of these days, by and by
▷ *adjective* FORMER, one-time, erstwhile, ex-, late, past, previous

> *Sometime* as a single word should only be used to refer to an unspecified point in time. When referring to a considerable length of time, you should use *some time*. Compare: *it was some time after, that the rose garden was planted*, i.e. after a considerable period of time, with *it was sometime after the move that the rose garden was planted*, i.e. at some unspecified point after the move, but not necessarily a long time after

sometimes *adverb* OCCASIONALLY, at times, now and then, from time to time, on occasion, now and again, once in a while, every now and then, every so often, off and on
<< OPPOSITE always
son *noun* MALE CHILD, boy, lad (*informal*), descendant, son and heir
>> RELATED WORD *adjective* filial
song *noun* BALLAD, air, tune, lay, strain, carol, lyric, chant, chorus, melody, anthem, number, hymn, psalm, shanty, pop song, ditty, canticle, canzonet, waiata (NZ)
song and dance *noun* (*Brit informal*) FUSS, to-do, flap (*informal*), performance (*informal*), stir, pantomime (*informal*), commotion, ado, shindig (*informal*), kerfuffle (*informal*), hoo-ha, pother, shindy (*informal*)
soon *adverb* BEFORE LONG, shortly, in the near future, in a minute, anon (*archaic*), in a short time, in a little while, any minute now, betimes (*archaic*), in two shakes of a lamb's tail, erelong (*archaic* or *poetic*), in a couple of shakes
sooner *adverb* **1** EARLIER, before, already, beforehand, ahead of time
2 RATHER, more readily, by preference, more willingly

> *When* is sometimes used instead of *than* after *no sooner*, but this use is generally regarded as incorrect: *no sooner had he arrived than* (not *when*) *the telephone rang*

soothe *verb* **1** CALM, still, quiet, hush, settle, calm down, appease, lull, mitigate, pacify,

mollify, smooth down, tranquillize
<< OPPOSITE upset
2 RELIEVE, ease, alleviate, dull, diminish, assuage
<< OPPOSITE irritate

soothing *adjective* 1 CALMING, relaxing, peaceful, quiet, calm, restful
2 EMOLLIENT, palliative, balsamic, demulcent, easeful, lenitive

sophisticated *adjective* 1 COMPLEX, advanced, complicated, subtle, delicate, elaborate, refined, intricate, multifaceted, highly-developed
<< OPPOSITE simple
2 CULTURED, refined, cultivated, worldly, cosmopolitan, urbane, jet-set, world-weary, citified, worldly-wise
<< OPPOSITE unsophisticated

sophistication *noun* POISE, worldliness, savoir-faire, urbanity, finesse, savoir-vivre (*French*), worldly wisdom

soporific *adjective* SLEEP-INDUCING, hypnotic, sedative, sleepy, somnolent, tranquillizing, somniferous (*rare*)

soppy *adjective* (*Brit informal*) SENTIMENTAL, corny (*slang*), slushy (*informal*), soft (*informal*), silly, daft (*informal*), weepy (*informal*), mawkish, drippy (*informal*), lovey-dovey, schmaltzy (*slang*), icky (*informal*), gushy (*informal*), overemotional, three-hankie (*informal*)

sorcerer *or* **sorceress** *noun* MAGICIAN, witch, wizard, magus, warlock, mage (*archaic*), enchanter, necromancer

sorcery *noun* BLACK MAGIC, witchcraft, black art, necromancy, spell, magic, charm, wizardry, enchantment, divination, incantation, witchery

sordid *adjective* 1 BASE, degraded, shameful, low, vicious, shabby, vile, degenerate, despicable, disreputable, debauched
<< OPPOSITE honourable
2 DIRTY, seedy, sleazy, squalid, mean, foul, filthy, unclean, wretched, seamy, slovenly, slummy, scungy (*Austral & NZ*), festy (*Austral slang*)
<< OPPOSITE clean

sore *adjective* 1 PAINFUL, smarting, raw, tender, burning, angry, sensitive, irritated, inflamed, chafed, reddened
2 ANNOYED, cross, angry, pained, hurt, upset, stung, irritated, grieved, resentful, aggrieved, vexed, irked, peeved (*informal*), tooshie (*Austral slang*), hoha (*NZ*)
3 ANNOYING, distressing, troublesome, harrowing, grievous
4 URGENT, desperate, extreme, dire, pressing, critical, acute
▷ *noun* ABSCESS, boil, ulcer, inflammation, gathering

sorrow *noun* 1 GRIEF, sadness, woe, regret, distress, misery, mourning, anguish, unhappiness, heartache, heartbreak, affliction
<< OPPOSITE joy
2 HARDSHIP, trial, tribulation, affliction, worry, trouble, blow, woe, misfortune, bummer (*slang*)
<< OPPOSITE good fortune
▷ *verb* GRIEVE, mourn, lament, weep, moan, be sad, bemoan, agonize, eat your heart out, bewail
<< OPPOSITE rejoice

sorrowful *adjective* SAD, unhappy, miserable, sorry, depressed, painful, distressed, grieving, dismal, afflicted, melancholy, tearful, heartbroken, woeful, mournful, dejected, rueful, lugubrious, wretched, disconsolate, doleful, heavy-hearted, down in the dumps (*informal*), woebegone, piteous, sick at heart

sorry *adjective* 1 REGRETFUL, apologetic, contrite, repentant, guilt-ridden, remorseful, penitent, shamefaced, conscience-stricken, in sackcloth and ashes, self-reproachful
<< OPPOSITE unapologetic
2 SYMPATHETIC, moved, full of pity, pitying, compassionate, commiserative
<< OPPOSITE unsympathetic
3 SAD, distressed, unhappy, grieved, melancholy, mournful, sorrowful, disconsolate
<< OPPOSITE happy
4 WRETCHED, miserable, pathetic, mean, base, poor, sad, distressing, dismal, shabby, vile, paltry, pitiful, abject, deplorable, pitiable, piteous

sort *noun* KIND, type, class, make, group, family, order, race, style, quality, character, nature, variety, brand, species, breed, category, stamp, description, denomination, genus, ilk
▷ *verb* ARRANGE, group, order, class, separate, file, rank, divide, grade, distribute, catalogue, classify, categorize, tabulate, systematize, put in order
▷▷ **out of sorts** 1 IRRITABLE, cross, edgy, tense, crabbed, snarling, prickly, snappy, touchy, bad-tempered, petulant, ill-tempered, irascible, cantankerous, tetchy, ratty (*Brit & NZ informal*), testy, fretful, grouchy (*informal*), peevish, crabby, dyspeptic, choleric, crotchety, oversensitive, snappish, ill-humoured, narky (*Brit slang*), out of humour
2 DEPRESSED, miserable, in low spirits, down, low, blue, sad, unhappy, gloomy, melancholy, mournful, dejected, despondent, dispirited, downcast, long-faced, sorrowful, disconsolate, crestfallen, down in the dumps (*informal*), down in the mouth (*informal*), mopy
3 UNWELL, ill, sick, poorly (*informal*), funny

(*informal*), crook (*Austral & NZ informal*), ailing, queer, unhealthy, seedy (*informal*), laid up (*informal*), queasy, infirm, dicky (*Brit informal*), off colour, under the weather (*informal*), at death's door, indisposed, on the sick list (*informal*), not up to par, valetudinarian, green about the gills, not up to snuff (*informal*)
▷▷ **sort of** RATHER, somewhat, as it were, slightly, moderately, in part, reasonably

It is common in informal speech to combine singular and plural in sentences like *these sort of distinctions are becoming blurred*. This is not acceptable in careful writing, where the plural must be used consistently: *these sorts of distinctions are becoming blurred*

so-so *adjective* (*informal*) AVERAGE, middling, fair, ordinary, moderate, adequate, respectable, indifferent, not bad (*informal*), tolerable, run-of-the-mill, passable, undistinguished, fair to middling (*informal*), O.K. *or* okay (*informal*)

soul *noun* 1 SPIRIT, essence, psyche, life, mind, reason, intellect, vital force, animating principle, wairua (NZ)
2 EMBODIMENT, essence, incarnation, epitome, personification, quintessence, type
3 PERSON, being, human, individual, body, creature, mortal, man *or* woman
4 FEELING, force, energy, vitality, animation, fervour, ardour, vivacity

soulful *adjective* EXPRESSIVE, sensitive, eloquent, moving, profound, meaningful, heartfelt, mournful

soulless *adjective* 1 CHARACTERLESS, dull, bland, mundane, ordinary, grey, commonplace, dreary, mediocre, drab, uninspiring, colourless, featureless, unexceptional
2 UNFEELING, dead, cold, lifeless, inhuman, harsh, cruel, callous, unkind, unsympathetic, spiritless

sound[1] *noun* 1 NOISE, racket, din, report, tone, resonance, hubbub, reverberation
2 IDEA, impression, implication(s), drift
3 CRY, noise, peep, squeak
4 TONE, music, note, chord
5 EARSHOT, hearing, hearing distance
▷ *verb* 1 TOLL, set off
2 RESOUND, echo, go off, toll, set off, chime, resonate, reverberate, clang, peal
3 SEEM, seem to be, appear to be, give the impression of being, strike you as being
>> RELATED WORDS *adjectives* sonic, acoustic

sound[2] *adjective* 1 FIT, healthy, robust, firm, perfect, intact, vigorous, hale, unhurt, undamaged, uninjured, unimpaired, hale and hearty
<< OPPOSITE frail
2 STURDY, strong, solid, stable, substantial, durable, stout, well-constructed
3 SAFE, secure, reliable, proven, established, recognized, solid, stable, solvent, reputable, tried-and-true
<< OPPOSITE unreliable
4 SENSIBLE, wise, reasonable, right, true, responsible, correct, proper, reliable, valid, orthodox, rational, logical, prudent, trustworthy, well-founded, level-headed, right-thinking, well-grounded
<< OPPOSITE irresponsible
5 DEEP, peaceful, unbroken, undisturbed, untroubled
<< OPPOSITE troubled

sound[3] ▷▷ **sound someone out** QUESTION, interview, survey, poll, examine, investigate, pump (*informal*), inspect, canvass, test the opinion of
▷▷ **sound something out** INVESTIGATE, research, examine, probe, look into, test the water, put out feelers to, see how the land lies, carry out an investigation of

sound[4] *noun* CHANNEL, passage, strait, inlet, fjord, voe, arm of the sea

sour *adjective* 1 SHARP, acid, tart, bitter, unpleasant, pungent, acetic, acidulated, acerb
<< OPPOSITE sweet
2 RANCID, turned, gone off, fermented, unsavoury, curdled, unwholesome, gone bad, off
<< OPPOSITE fresh
3 BITTER, cynical, crabbed, tart, discontented, grudging, acrimonious, embittered, disagreeable, churlish, ill-tempered, jaundiced, waspish, grouchy (*informal*), ungenerous, peevish, ill-natured
<< OPPOSITE good-natured
▷ *verb* EMBITTER, disenchant, alienate, envenom

source *noun* 1 CAUSE, origin, derivation, beginning, author
2 INFORMANT, authority, documentation
3 ORIGIN, spring, fount, fountainhead, wellspring, rise

souvenir *noun* KEEPSAKE, token, reminder, relic, remembrancer (*archaic*), memento

sovereign *adjective* 1 SUPREME, ruling, absolute, chief, royal, principal, dominant, imperial, unlimited, paramount, regal, predominant, monarchal, kingly *or* queenly
2 EXCELLENT, efficient, efficacious, effectual
▷ *noun* MONARCH, ruler, king *or* queen, chief, shah, potentate, supreme ruler, emperor *or* empress, prince *or* princess, tsar *or* tsarina

sovereignty *noun* SUPREME POWER, domination, supremacy, primacy, sway, ascendancy, kingship, suzerainty, rangatiratanga (NZ)

sow *verb* SCATTER, plant, seed, lodge, implant, disseminate, broadcast, inseminate

space *noun* 1 ROOM, volume, capacity, extent, margin, extension, scope, play, expanse, leeway, amplitude, spaciousness, elbowroom
2 GAP, opening, interval, gulf, cavity, aperture
3 PERIOD, interval, time, while, span, duration, time frame, timeline
4 OUTER SPACE, the universe, the galaxy, the solar system, the cosmos
5 BLANK, gap, interval
>> RELATED WORD *adjective* spatial

spaceman *or* **spacewoman** *noun* ASTRONAUT, cosmonaut, space cadet, space traveller

spacious *adjective* ROOMY, large, huge, broad, vast, extensive, ample, expansive, capacious, uncrowded, commodious, comfortable, sizable *or* sizeable
<< OPPOSITE limited

span *noun* 1 PERIOD, term, duration, spell
2 EXTENT, reach, spread, length, distance, stretch
▷ *verb* EXTEND ACROSS, cross, bridge, cover, link, vault, traverse, range over, arch across

spank *verb* SMACK, slap, whack, belt (*informal*), tan (*slang*), slipper (*informal*), cuff, wallop (*informal*), give (someone) a hiding (*informal*), put (someone) over your knee

spanking *noun* SMACKING, hiding (*informal*), whacking, slapping, walloping (*informal*)

spanking *adjective* 1 (*informal*) SMART, brand-new, fine, gleaming
2 FAST, quick, brisk, lively, smart, vigorous, energetic, snappy

spar *verb* ARGUE, row, squabble, dispute, scrap (*informal*), fall out (*informal*), spat (*US*), wrangle, skirmish, bicker, have a tiff

spare *adjective* 1 BACK-UP, reserve, second, extra, relief, emergency, additional, substitute, fall-back, auxiliary, in reserve
2 EXTRA, surplus, leftover, over, free, odd, unwanted, in excess, unused, superfluous, supernumerary
<< OPPOSITE necessary
3 FREE, leisure, unoccupied
4 THIN, lean, slim, slender, slight, meagre, gaunt, wiry, lank
<< OPPOSITE plump
5 MEAGRE, sparing, modest, economical, frugal, scanty
▷ *verb* 1 AFFORD, give, grant, do without, relinquish, part with, allow, bestow, dispense with, manage without, let someone have
2 HAVE MERCY ON, pardon, have pity on, leave, release, excuse, let off (*informal*), go easy on (*informal*), be merciful to, grant pardon to, deal leniently with, refrain from hurting, save (from harm)
<< OPPOSITE show no mercy to

sparing *adjective* ECONOMICAL, frugal, thrifty, saving, careful, prudent, cost-conscious, chary, money-conscious
<< OPPOSITE lavish

spark *noun* 1 FLICKER, flash, gleam, glint, spit, flare, scintillation
2 TRACE, hint, scrap, atom, jot, vestige, scintilla
▷ *verb often with* **off** START, stimulate, provoke, excite, inspire, stir, trigger (off), set off, animate, rouse, prod, precipitate, kick-start, set in motion, kindle, touch off

sparkle *verb* GLITTER, flash, spark, shine, beam, glow, gleam, wink, shimmer, twinkle, dance, glint, glisten, glister (*archaic*), scintillate
▷ *noun* 1 GLITTER, flash, gleam, spark, dazzle, flicker, brilliance, twinkle, glint, radiance
2 VIVACITY, life, spirit, dash, zip (*informal*), vitality, animation, panache, gaiety, élan, brio, liveliness, vim (*slang*)

sparse *adjective* SCATTERED, scarce, meagre, sporadic, few and far between, scanty
<< OPPOSITE thick

Spartan *adjective* AUSTERE, severe, frugal, ascetic, plain, disciplined, extreme, strict, stern, bleak, rigorous, stringent, abstemious, self-denying

spasm *noun* 1 CONVULSION, contraction, paroxysm, twitch, throe (*rare*)
2 BURST, fit, outburst, seizure, frenzy, eruption, access

spasmodic *adjective* SPORADIC, irregular, erratic, intermittent, jerky, fitful, convulsive

spat *noun* QUARREL, dispute, squabble, controversy, contention, bickering, tiff, altercation

spate *noun* 1 FLOOD, flow, torrent, rush, deluge, outpouring
2 SERIES, sequence, course, chain, succession, run, train, string

spatter *verb* SPLASH, spray, sprinkle, soil, dirty, scatter, daub, speckle, splodge, bespatter, bestrew

spawn *verb* GENERATE, produce, give rise to, start, prompt, provoke, set off, bring about, spark off, set in motion

speak *verb* 1 TALK, say something
2 ARTICULATE, say, voice, pronounce, utter, tell, state, talk, express, communicate, make known, enunciate
3 CONVERSE, talk, chat, discourse, confer, commune, exchange views, shoot the breeze (*slang, chiefly US & Canad*)
4 LECTURE, talk, discourse, spout (*informal*), make a speech, pontificate, give a speech, declaim, hold forth, spiel (*informal*), address an audience, deliver an address, speechify
▷▷ **speak for something** *or* **someone**
1 REPRESENT, act for *or* on behalf of, appear for,

hold a brief for, hold a mandate for
2 SUPPORT, back, champion, defend, promote, advocate, fight for, uphold, commend, espouse, stick up for (*informal*)

speaker *noun* ORATOR, public speaker, lecturer, spokesperson, mouthpiece, spieler (*informal*), word-spinner, spokesman *or* spokeswoman

spearhead *verb* LEAD, head, pioneer, launch, set off, initiate, lead the way, set in motion, blaze the trail, be in the van, lay the first stone

special *adjective* 1 EXCEPTIONAL, important, significant, particular, unique, unusual, extraordinary, distinguished, memorable, gala, festive, uncommon, momentous, out of the ordinary, one in a million, red-letter, especial
<< OPPOSITE ordinary
2 MAJOR, chief, main, primary
3 SPECIFIC, particular, distinctive, certain, individual, appropriate, characteristic, precise, peculiar, specialized, especial
<< OPPOSITE general

specialist *noun* EXPERT, authority, professional, master, consultant, guru, buff (*informal*), whizz (*informal*), connoisseur, boffin (*Brit informal*), hotshot (*informal*), wonk (*informal*), maven (*US*), fundi (*S African*)

speciality *noun* 1 FORTE, strength, special talent, métier, specialty, bag (*slang*), claim to fame, pièce de résistance (*French*), distinctive *or* distinguishing feature
2 SPECIAL SUBJECT, specialty, field of study, branch of knowledge, area of specialization

species *noun* KIND, sort, type, group, class, variety, breed, category, description, genus

specific *adjective* 1 PARTICULAR, special, characteristic, distinguishing, peculiar, definite, especial
<< OPPOSITE general
2 PRECISE, exact, explicit, definite, limited, express, clear-cut, unequivocal, unambiguous
<< OPPOSITE vague
3 PECULIAR, appropriate, individual, particular, personal, unique, restricted, idiosyncratic, endemic

specification *noun* REQUIREMENT, detail, particular, stipulation, condition, qualification

specify *verb* STATE, designate, spell out, stipulate, name, detail, mention, indicate, define, cite, individualize, enumerate, itemize, be specific about, particularize

specimen *noun* 1 SAMPLE, example, individual, model, type, pattern, instance, representative, exemplar, exemplification
2 EXAMPLE, model, exhibit, embodiment, type

specious *adjective* FALLACIOUS, misleading, deceptive, plausible, unsound, sophistic, sophistical, casuistic

speck *noun* 1 MARK, spot, dot, stain, blot, fleck, speckle, mote
2 PARTICLE, bit, grain, dot, atom, shred, mite, jot, modicum, whit, tittle, iota

speckled *adjective* FLECKED, spotted, dotted, sprinkled, spotty, freckled, mottled, dappled, stippled, brindled, speckledy

spectacle *noun* 1 SHOW, display, exhibition, event, performance, sight, parade, extravaganza, pageant
2 SIGHT, wonder, scene, phenomenon, curiosity, marvel, laughing stock

spectacles *plural noun* GLASSES, specs (*informal*), eyeglasses (*US*), eyewear

spectacular *adjective* IMPRESSIVE, striking, dramatic, stunning (*informal*), marked, grand, remarkable, fantastic (*informal*), magnificent, staggering, splendid, dazzling, sensational, breathtaking, eye-catching
<< OPPOSITE unimpressive
▷ *noun* SHOW, display, spectacle, extravaganza

spectator *noun* ONLOOKER, observer, viewer, witness, looker-on, watcher, eyewitness, bystander, beholder
<< OPPOSITE participant

spectral *adjective* GHOSTLY, unearthly, eerie, supernatural, weird, phantom, shadowy, uncanny, spooky (*informal*), insubstantial, incorporeal, wraithlike

spectre *noun* GHOST, spirit, phantom, presence, vision, shadow, shade (*literary*), apparition, wraith, kehua (*NZ*)

speculate *verb* 1 CONJECTURE, consider, wonder, guess, contemplate, deliberate, muse, meditate, surmise, theorize, hypothesize, cogitate
2 GAMBLE, risk, venture, hazard, have a flutter (*informal*), take a chance with, play the market

speculation *noun* 1 THEORY, opinion, hypothesis, conjecture, guess, consideration, deliberation, contemplation, surmise, guesswork, supposition
2 GAMBLE, risk, gambling, hazard

speculative *adjective* 1 HYPOTHETICAL, academic, theoretical, abstract, tentative, notional, conjectural, suppositional
2 RISKY, uncertain, hazardous, unpredictable, dicey (*informal, chiefly Brit*), chancy (*informal*)

speech *noun* 1 COMMUNICATION, talk, conversation, articulation, discussion, dialogue, intercourse
2 DICTION, pronunciation, articulation, delivery, fluency, inflection, intonation, elocution, enunciation
3 LANGUAGE, tongue, utterance, jargon, dialect, idiom, parlance, articulation, diction, lingo (*informal*), enunciation
4 TALK, address, lecture, discourse, harangue, homily, oration, spiel (*informal*), disquisition,

whaikorero (NZ)

speechless *adjective* DUMB, dumbfounded, lost for words, dumbstruck, astounded, shocked, mum, amazed, silent, mute, dazed, aghast, inarticulate, tongue-tied, wordless, thunderstruck, unable to get a word out (*informal*)

speed *noun* 1 RATE, pace, momentum, tempo, velocity
2 VELOCITY, swiftness, acceleration, precipitation, rapidity, quickness, fastness, briskness, speediness, precipitateness
3 SWIFTNESS, rush, hurry, expedition, haste, rapidity, quickness, fleetness, celerity
<< OPPOSITE slowness
▷ *verb* 1 RACE, rush, hurry, zoom, career, bomb (along), tear, flash, belt (along) (*slang*), barrel (along) (*informal, chiefly US & Canad*), sprint, gallop, hasten, press on, quicken, lose no time, get a move on (*informal*), burn rubber (*informal*), bowl along, put your foot down (*informal*), step on it (*informal*), make haste, go hell for leather (*informal*), exceed the speed limit, go like a bomb (*Brit & NZ informal*), go like the wind, go like a bat out of hell
<< OPPOSITE crawl
2 HELP, further, advance, aid, promote, boost, assist, facilitate, impel, expedite
<< OPPOSITE hinder
▷▷ **speed something up** ACCELERATE, promote, hasten, help along, further, forward, advance

> The past tense of *speed up* is *speeded up* (not *sped up*), for example *I speeded up to overtake the lorry*. The past participle is also *speeded up*, for example *I had already speeded up when I spotted the police car*

speedy *adjective* QUICK, fast, rapid, swift, express, winged, immediate, prompt, fleet, hurried, summary, precipitate, hasty, headlong, quickie (*informal*), expeditious, fleet of foot, pdq (*slang*)
<< OPPOSITE slow

spell[1] *verb* INDICATE, mean, signify, suggest, promise, point to, imply, amount to, herald, augur, presage, portend
▷▷ **spell something out** MAKE CLEAR *or* PLAIN, specify, make explicit, clarify, elucidate, explicate

spell[2] *noun* 1 INCANTATION, charm, sorcery, exorcism, abracadabra, witchery, conjuration, makutu (NZ)
2 ENCHANTMENT, magic, fascination, glamour, allure, bewitchment

spell[3] *noun* PERIOD, time, term, stretch, turn, course, season, patch, interval, bout, stint

spellbound *adjective* ENTRANCED, gripped, fascinated, transported, charmed, hooked, possessed, bemused, captivated, enthralled, bewitched, transfixed, rapt, mesmerized, under a spell

spelling *noun* ORTHOGRAPHY

spend *verb* 1 PAY OUT, fork out (*slang*), expend, lay out, splash out (*Brit informal*), shell out (*informal*), disburse
<< OPPOSITE save
2 APPLY, use, employ, concentrate, invest, put in, devote, lavish, exert, bestow
3 PASS, fill, occupy, while away
4 USE UP, waste, squander, blow (*slang*), empty, drain, exhaust, consume, run through, deplete, dissipate, fritter away
<< OPPOSITE save

spendthrift *noun* SQUANDERER, spender, profligate, prodigal, big spender, waster, wastrel
<< OPPOSITE miser
▷ *adjective* WASTEFUL, extravagant, prodigal, profligate, improvident
<< OPPOSITE economical

spent *adjective* 1 USED UP, finished, gone, consumed, expended
2 EXHAUSTED, drained, worn out, bushed (*informal*), all in (*slang*), shattered (*informal*), weakened, wiped out (*informal*), wearied, weary, played out (*informal*), burnt out, fagged (out) (*informal*), whacked (*Brit informal*), debilitated, knackered (*slang*), prostrate, clapped out (*Brit, Austral & NZ informal*), tired out, ready to drop (*informal*), dog-tired (*informal*), zonked (*informal*), dead beat (*informal*), shagged out (*Brit slang*), done in *or* up (*informal*)

sperm *noun* 1 SPERMATOZOON, reproductive cell, male gamete
2 SEMEN, seed (*archaic* or *dialect*), spermatozoa, scum (*US slang*), come *or* cum (*taboo*), jism *or* jissom (*taboo*)

spew *verb* 1 SHED, discharge, send out, issue, throw out, eject, diffuse, emanate, exude, cast out
2 VOMIT, throw up (*informal*), puke (*slang*), chuck (*Austral & NZ informal*), spit out, regurgitate, disgorge, barf (*US slang*), chunder (*slang, chiefly Austral*), belch forth, upchuck (*US slang*), do a technicolour yawn (*slang*), toss your cookies (*US slang*)

sphere *noun* 1 BALL, globe, orb, globule, circle
2 FIELD, range, area, department, function, territory, capacity, province, patch, scope, turf (*US slang*), realm, domain, compass, walk of life
3 RANK, class, station, status, stratum

spherical *adjective* ROUND, globular, globe-shaped, rotund, orbicular

spice *noun* 1 SEASONING, condiment
2 EXCITEMENT, kick (*informal*), zest, colour, pep, zip (*informal*), tang, zap (*slang*), gusto, zing (*informal*), piquancy

spicy *adjective* 1 HOT, seasoned, pungent,

aromatic, savoury, tangy, piquant, flavoursome
2 (*informal*) RISQUÉ, racy, off-colour, ribald, hot (*informal*), broad, improper, suggestive, unseemly, titillating, indelicate, indecorous
spider *noun*
>> RELATED WORD *fear* arachnophobia
spiel *noun* PATTER, speech, pitch, recital, harangue, sales talk, sales patter
spike *noun* POINT, stake, spur, pin, nail, spine, barb, tine, prong
▷ *verb* 1 DRUG, lace, dope, cut, contaminate, adulterate
2 IMPALE, spit, spear, stick
spill *verb* 1 TIP OVER, upset, overturn, capsize, knock over, topple over
2 SHED, scatter, discharge, throw off, disgorge, spill *or* run over
3 SLOP, flow, pour, run, overflow, slosh, splosh
4 EMERGE, flood, pour, mill, stream, surge, swarm, crowd, teem
▷ *noun* SPILLAGE, flood, leak, leakage, overspill
spin *verb* 1 REVOLVE, turn, rotate, wheel, twist, reel, whirl, twirl, gyrate, pirouette, birl (*Scot*)
2 REEL, swim, whirl, be giddy, be in a whirl, grow dizzy
3 (*informal*) TELL, relate, recount, develop, invent, unfold, concoct, narrate
▷ *noun* 1 (*informal*) DRIVE, ride, turn, hurl (*Scot*), whirl, joy ride (*informal*)
2 REVOLUTION, roll, whirl, twist, gyration
▷▷ **spin something out** PROLONG, extend, lengthen, draw out, drag out, delay, amplify, pad out, protract, prolongate
spindly *adjective* LANKY, gangly, spidery, leggy, twiggy, attenuated, gangling, spindle-shanked
spine *noun* 1 BACKBONE, vertebrae, spinal column, vertebral column
2 BARB, spur, needle, spike, ray, quill
3 DETERMINATION, resolution, backbone, resolve, drive, conviction, fortitude, persistence, tenacity, perseverance, willpower, firmness, constancy, single-mindedness, steadfastness, doggedness, resoluteness, indomitability
spineless *adjective* WEAK, soft, cowardly, ineffective, feeble, yellow (*informal*), inadequate, pathetic, submissive, squeamish, vacillating, boneless, gutless (*informal*), weak-willed, weak-kneed (*informal*), faint-hearted, irresolute, spiritless, lily-livered, without a will of your own
<< OPPOSITE brave
spiral *adjective* COILED, winding, corkscrew, circular, scrolled, whorled, helical, cochlear, voluted, cochleate (*Biology*)
▷ *noun* COIL, helix, corkscrew, whorl, screw, curlicue
spirit *noun* 1 SOUL, life, psyche, essential being
2 LIFE FORCE, vital spark, breath, mauri (NZ)
3 GHOST, phantom, spectre, vision, shadow, shade (*literary*), spook (*informal*), apparition, sprite, atua (NZ), kehua (NZ)
4 COURAGE, guts (*informal*), grit, balls (*taboo slang*), backbone, spunk (*informal*), gameness, ballsiness (*taboo slang*), dauntlessness, stoutheartedness
5 LIVELINESS, energy, vigour, life, force, fire, resolution, enterprise, enthusiasm, sparkle, warmth, animation, zest, mettle, ardour, earnestness, brio
6 ATTITUDE, character, quality, humour, temper, outlook, temperament, complexion, disposition
7 HEART, sense, nature, soul, core, substance, essence, lifeblood, quintessence, fundamental nature
8 INTENTION, meaning, purpose, substance, intent, essence, purport, gist
9 FEELING, atmosphere, character, feel, quality, tone, mood, flavour, tenor, ambience, vibes (*slang*)
10 RESOLVE, will, drive, resolution, conviction, motivation, dedication, backbone, fortitude, persistence, tenacity, perseverance, willpower, firmness, constancy, single-mindedness, steadfastness, doggedness, resoluteness, indomitability
11 *plural* MOOD, feelings, morale, humour, temper, tenor, disposition, state of mind, frame of mind
spirited *adjective* LIVELY, vigorous, energetic, animated, game, active, bold, sparkling, have-a-go (*informal*), courageous, ardent, feisty (*informal, chiefly US & Canad*), plucky, high-spirited, sprightly, vivacious, spunky (*informal*), mettlesome, (as) game as Ned Kelly (*Austral slang*)
<< OPPOSITE lifeless
spirits *plural noun* STRONG ALCOHOL, liquor, the hard stuff (*informal*), firewater, strong liquor
spiritual *adjective* 1 NONMATERIAL, immaterial, incorporeal
<< OPPOSITE material
2 SACRED, religious, holy, divine, ethereal, devotional, otherworldly
spit *verb* 1 EXPECTORATE, sputter
2 EJECT, discharge, throw out
▷ *noun* SALIVA, dribble, spittle, drool, slaver, sputum
spite *noun* MALICE, malevolence, ill will, hate, hatred, gall, animosity, venom, spleen, pique, rancour, bitchiness (*slang*), malignity, spitefulness
<< OPPOSITE kindness
▷ *verb* ANNOY, hurt, injure, harm, provoke, offend, needle (*informal*), put out, gall, nettle,

vex, pique, discomfit, put someone's nose out of joint (*informal*), hack someone off (*informal*)

<< OPPOSITE benefit

▷▷ **in spite of** DESPITE, regardless of, notwithstanding, in defiance of, (even) though

spiteful *adjective* MALICIOUS, nasty, vindictive, cruel, malignant, barbed, malevolent, venomous, bitchy (*informal*), snide, rancorous, catty (*informal*), splenetic, shrewish, ill-disposed, ill-natured

spitting image *noun* DOUBLE, lookalike, (dead) ringer (*slang*), picture, spit (*informal, chiefly Brit*), clone, replica, likeness, living image, spit and image (*informal*)

splash *verb* 1 PADDLE, plunge, bathe, dabble, wade, wallow

2 SCATTER, shower, spray, sprinkle, spread, wet, strew, squirt, spatter, slop, slosh (*informal*)

3 SPATTER, mark, stain, smear, speck, speckle, blotch, splodge, bespatter

4 DASH, break, strike, wash, batter, surge, smack, buffet, plop, plash

▷ *noun* 1 SPLASHING, dashing, plash, beating, battering, swashing

2 DASH, touch, spattering, splodge

3 SPOT, burst, patch, stretch, spurt

4 BLOB, spot, smudge, stain, smear, fleck, speck

▷▷ **make a splash** (*informal*) CAUSE A STIR, make an impact, cause a sensation, cut a dash, be ostentatious

spleen *noun* SPITE, anger, bitterness, hostility, hatred, resentment, wrath, gall, malice, animosity, venom, bile, bad temper, acrimony, pique, rancour, ill will, animus, malevolence, vindictiveness, malignity, spitefulness, ill humour, peevishness

splendid *adjective* 1 EXCELLENT, wonderful, marvellous, mean (*slang*), great (*informal*), topping (*Brit slang*), fine, cracking (*Brit informal*), crucial (*slang*), fantastic (*informal*), first-class, glorious, mega (*slang*), sovereign, awesome (*slang*), def (*slang*), brill (*informal*), bodacious (*slang, chiefly US*), boffo (*slang*), chillin' (*US slang*), booshit (*Austral slang*), exo (*Austral slang*), sik (*Austral slang*), rad (*informal*), phat (*slang*), schmick (*Austral informal*)

<< OPPOSITE poor

2 MAGNIFICENT, grand, imposing, impressive, rich, superb, costly, gorgeous, dazzling, lavish, luxurious, sumptuous, ornate, resplendent, splendiferous (*facetious*)

<< OPPOSITE squalid

3 GLORIOUS, superb, magnificent, grand, brilliant, rare, supreme, outstanding, remarkable, sterling, exceptional, renowned, admirable, sublime, illustrious

<< OPPOSITE ignoble

splendour *noun* MAGNIFICENCE, glory, grandeur, show, display, ceremony, luxury, spectacle, majesty, richness, nobility, pomp, opulence, solemnity, éclat, gorgeousness, sumptuousness, stateliness, resplendence, luxuriousness

<< OPPOSITE squalor

splice *verb* JOIN, unite, graft, marry, wed, knit, mesh, braid, intertwine, interweave, yoke, plait, entwine, interlace, intertwist

splinter *noun* SLIVER, fragment, chip, needle, shaving, flake, paring

▷ *verb* SHATTER, split, fracture, shiver, disintegrate, break into fragments

split *verb* 1 BREAK, crack, burst, snap, break up, open, give way, splinter, gape, come apart, come undone

2 CUT, break, crack, snap, chop, cleave, hew

3 DIVIDE, separate, disunite, disrupt, disband, cleave, pull apart, set at odds, set at variance

4 DIVERGE, separate, branch, fork, part, go separate ways

5 TEAR, rend, rip, slash, slit

6 SHARE OUT, divide, distribute, halve, allocate, partition, allot, carve up, dole out, apportion, slice up, parcel out, divvy up (*informal*)

▷ *noun* 1 DIVISION, break, breach, rift, difference, disruption, rupture, discord, divergence, schism, estrangement, dissension, disunion

2 SEPARATION, break, divorce, break-up, split-up, disunion

3 CRACK, tear, rip, damage, gap, rent, breach, slash, slit, fissure

▷ *adjective* 1 DIVIDED, ambivalent, bisected

2 BROKEN, cracked, snapped, fractured, splintered, ruptured, cleft

▷▷ **split on someone** (*Slang*) BETRAY, tell on, shop (*slang, chiefly Brit*), sing (*slang, chiefly US*), grass (*Brit slang*), give away, squeal (*slang*), inform on, spill your guts (*slang*), dob in (*Austral slang*)

▷▷ **split up** BREAK UP, part, separate, divorce, disband, part company, go separate ways

spoil *verb* 1 RUIN, destroy, wreck, damage, total (*slang*), blow (*slang*), injure, upset, harm, mar, scar, undo, trash (*slang*), impair, mess up, blemish, disfigure, debase, deface, put a damper on, crool *or* cruel (*Austral slang*)

<< OPPOSITE improve

2 OVERINDULGE, indulge, pamper, baby, cosset, coddle, spoon-feed, mollycoddle, kill with kindness

<< OPPOSITE deprive

3 INDULGE, treat, pamper, satisfy, gratify, pander to, regale

4 GO BAD, turn, go off (*Brit informal*), rot, decay, decompose, curdle, mildew, addle, putrefy,

become tainted

spoils *plural noun* BOOTY, loot, plunder, gain, prizes, prey, pickings, pillage, swag (*slang*), boodle (*slang, chiefly US*), rapine

spoken *adjective* VERBAL, voiced, expressed, uttered, oral, said, told, unwritten, phonetic, by word of mouth, put into words, viva voce

▷▷ **spoken for** 1 RESERVED, booked, claimed, chosen, selected, set aside

2 ENGAGED, taken, going out with someone, betrothed (*archaic*), going steady

spokesperson *noun* SPEAKER, official, spokesman *or* spokeswoman, voice, spin doctor (*informal*), mouthpiece

spongy *adjective* POROUS, light, absorbent, springy, cushioned, elastic, cushiony

sponsor *verb* BACK, fund, finance, promote, subsidize, patronize, put up the money for, lend your name to

▷ *noun* BACKER, patron, promoter, angel (*informal*), guarantor

spontaneous *adjective* UNPLANNED, impromptu, unprompted, willing, free, natural, voluntary, instinctive, impulsive, unforced, unbidden, unconstrained, unpremeditated, extempore, uncompelled

<< OPPOSITE planned

spontaneously *adverb* VOLUNTARILY, freely, instinctively, impromptu, off the cuff (*informal*), on impulse, impulsively, in the heat of the moment, extempore, off your own bat, of your own accord, quite unprompted

spoof *noun* (*informal*) PARODY, take-off (*informal*), satire, caricature, mockery, send-up (*Brit informal*), travesty, lampoon, burlesque

spook (*informal*) *noun* GHOST, spirit, phantom, spectre, soul, shade (*literary*), manes, apparition, wraith, revenant, phantasm, eidolon, kehua (*NZ*)

▷ *verb* FRIGHTEN, alarm, scare, terrify, startle, intimidate, daunt, unnerve, petrify, scare (someone) stiff, put the wind up (someone) (*informal*), scare the living daylights out of (someone) (*informal*), make your hair stand on end (*informal*), get the wind up, make your blood run cold, throw into a panic, scare the bejesus out of (*informal*), affright (*archaic*), freeze your blood, make (someone) jump out of his skin (*informal*), throw into a fright

spooky *adjective* EERIE, frightening, chilling, ghostly, weird, mysterious, scary (*informal*), unearthly, supernatural, uncanny, creepy (*informal*), spine-chilling

sporadic *adjective* INTERMITTENT, occasional, scattered, isolated, random, on and off, irregular, infrequent, spasmodic, scattershot

<< OPPOSITE steady

sport *noun* 1 GAME, exercise, recreation, play, entertainment, amusement, diversion, pastime, physical activity

2 FUN, kidding (*informal*), joking, teasing, ridicule, joshing (*slang, chiefly US & Canad*), banter, frolic, jest, mirth, merriment, badinage, raillery

▷ *verb* (*informal*) WEAR, display, flaunt, boast, exhibit, flourish, show off, vaunt

sporting *adjective* FAIR, sportsmanlike, game (*informal*), gentlemanly

<< OPPOSITE unfair

sporty *adjective* 1 ATHLETIC, outdoor, energetic, hearty

2 CASUAL, stylish, jazzy (*informal*), loud, informal, trendy (*Brit informal*), flashy, jaunty, showy, snazzy (*informal*), raffish, rakish, gay, schmick (*Austral informal*)

spot *noun* 1 MARK, stain, speck, scar, flaw, taint, blot, smudge, blemish, daub, speckle, blotch, discoloration

2 PIMPLE, blackhead, pustule, zit (*slang*), plook (*Scot*), acne

3 (*informal, chiefly Brit*) BIT, little, drop, bite, splash, small amount, tad, morsel

4 PLACE, situation, site, point, position, scene, location, locality

5 (*informal*) PREDICAMENT, trouble, difficulty, mess, plight, hot water (*informal*), quandary, tight spot

▷ *verb* 1 SEE, observe, catch sight of, identify, sight, recognize, detect, make out, pick out, discern, behold (*archaic or literary*), espy, descry

2 MARK, stain, dot, soil, dirty, scar, taint, tarnish, blot, fleck, spatter, sully, speckle, besmirch, splodge, splotch, mottle, smirch

spotless *adjective* 1 CLEAN, immaculate, impeccable, white, pure, virgin, shining, gleaming, snowy, flawless, faultless, unblemished, virginal, unsullied, untarnished, unstained

<< OPPOSITE dirty

2 BLAMELESS, squeaky-clean, unimpeachable, innocent, chaste, irreproachable, above reproach

<< OPPOSITE reprehensible

spotlight *noun* 1 SEARCH LIGHT, headlight, floodlight, headlamp, foglamp

2 ATTENTION, limelight, public eye, interest, fame, notoriety, public attention

▷ *verb* HIGHLIGHT, feature, draw attention to, focus attention on, accentuate, point up, give prominence to, throw into relief

spot-on *adjective* (*British informal*) ACCURATE, exact, precise, right, correct, on the money (*US*), unerring, punctual (to the minute), hitting the nail on the head (*informal*), on the bull's-eye (*informal*)

spotted *adjective* SPECKLED, dotted, flecked, pied, specked, mottled, dappled, polka-dot

spotty *adjective* 1 PIMPLY, pimpled, blotchy,

poor-complexioned, plooky-faced (*Scot*)
2 INCONSISTENT, irregular, erratic, uneven, fluctuating, patchy, sporadic

spouse *noun* PARTNER, mate, husband *or* wife, companion, consort, significant other (*US informal*), better half (*humorous*), her indoors (*Brit slang*), helpmate

spout *verb* 1 STREAM, shoot, gush, spurt, jet, spray, surge, discharge, erupt, emit, squirt
2 (*informal*) HOLD FORTH, talk, rant, go on (*informal*), rabbit (on) (*Brit informal*), ramble (on), pontificate, declaim, spiel (*informal*), expatiate, orate, speechify

sprawl *verb* LOLL, slump, lounge, flop, slouch

spray[1] *noun* 1 DROPLETS, moisture, fine mist, drizzle, spindrift, spoondrift
2 AEROSOL, sprinkler, atomizer
▷ *verb* SCATTER, shower, sprinkle, diffuse

spray[2] *noun* SPRIG, floral arrangement, branch, bough, shoot, corsage

spread *verb* 1 OPEN (OUT), extend, stretch, unfold, sprawl, unfurl, fan out, unroll
2 EXTEND, open, stretch
3 COAT, cover, smear, smother
4 SMEAR, apply, rub, put, smooth, plaster, daub
5 GROW, increase, develop, expand, widen, mushroom, escalate, proliferate, multiply, broaden
6 SPACE OUT, stagger
7 CIRCULATE, publish, broadcast, advertise, distribute, scatter, proclaim, transmit, make public, publicize, propagate, disseminate, promulgate, make known, blazon, bruit
<< OPPOSITE suppress
8 DIFFUSE, cast, shed, radiate
▷ *noun* 1 INCREASE, development, advance, spreading, expansion, transmission, proliferation, advancement, escalation, diffusion, dissemination, dispersal, suffusion
2 EXTENT, reach, span, stretch, sweep, compass
3 (*informal*) FEAST, banquet, blowout (*slang*), repast, array

spree *noun* 1 FLING, binge (*informal*), orgy, splurge
2 BINGE, bender (*informal*), orgy, revel (*informal*), jag (*slang*), junketing, beano (*Brit slang*), debauch, carouse, bacchanalia, carousal

sprightly *adjective* LIVELY, spirited, active, energetic, animated, brisk, nimble, agile, jaunty, gay, perky, vivacious, spry, bright-eyed and bushy-tailed
<< OPPOSITE inactive

spring *noun* 1 SPRINGTIME, springtide (*literary*)
2 SOURCE, root, origin, well, beginning, cause, fount, fountainhead, wellspring
3 FLEXIBILITY, give (*informal*), bounce, resilience, elasticity, recoil, buoyancy, springiness, bounciness
▷ *verb* 1 JUMP, bound, leap, bounce, hop, rebound, vault, recoil
2 *usually followed by* **from** ORIGINATE, come, derive, start, issue, grow, emerge, proceed, arise, stem, descend, be derived, emanate, be descended
▷ *modifier* VERNAL, springlike
>> RELATED WORD *adjective* vernal

springy *adjective* FLEXIBLE, elastic, resilient, bouncy, rubbery, spongy

sprinkle *verb* SCATTER, dust, strew, pepper, shower, spray, powder, dredge

sprinkling *noun* SCATTERING, dusting, scatter, few, dash, handful, sprinkle, smattering, admixture

sprint *verb* RUN, race, shoot, tear, dash, barrel (along) (*informal, chiefly US & Canad*), dart, hare (*Brit informal*), whizz (*informal*), scamper, hotfoot, go like a bomb (*Brit & NZ informal*), put on a burst of speed, go at top speed

sprite *noun* SPIRIT, fairy, elf, nymph, brownie, pixie, apparition, imp, goblin, leprechaun, peri, dryad, naiad, sylph, Oceanid (*Greek myth*), atua (*NZ*)

sprout *verb* 1 GERMINATE, bud, shoot, push, spring, vegetate
2 GROW, develop, blossom, ripen

spruce *adjective* SMART, trim, neat, elegant, dainty, dapper, natty (*informal*), well-groomed, well turned out, trig (*archaic* or *dialect*), as if you had just stepped out of a bandbox, soigné *or* soignée
<< OPPOSITE untidy

spry *adjective* ACTIVE, sprightly, quick, brisk, supple, nimble, agile, nippy (*Brit informal*)
<< OPPOSITE inactive

spur *verb* INCITE, drive, prompt, press, urge, stimulate, animate, prod, prick, goad, impel
▷ *noun* STIMULUS, incentive, impetus, motive, impulse, inducement, incitement, kick up the backside (*informal*)
▷▷ **on the spur of the moment** ON IMPULSE, without thinking, impulsively, on the spot, impromptu, unthinkingly, without planning, impetuously, unpremeditatedly

spurious *adjective* FALSE, bogus, sham, pretended, artificial, forged, fake, mock, imitation, simulated, contrived, pseudo (*informal*), counterfeit, feigned, ersatz, specious, unauthentic, phoney *or* phony (*informal*)
<< OPPOSITE genuine

spurn *verb* REJECT, slight, scorn, rebuff, put down, snub, disregard, despise, disdain, repulse, cold-shoulder, kick in the teeth (*slang*), turn your nose up at (*informal*), contemn (*formal*)
<< OPPOSITE accept

spurt *verb* GUSH, shoot, burst, jet, surge, erupt, spew, squirt

▷ *noun* 1 GUSH, jet, burst, spray, surge, eruption, squirt
2 BURST, rush, surge, fit, access, spate

spy *noun* UNDERCOVER AGENT, secret agent, double agent, secret service agent, foreign agent, mole, fifth columnist, nark (*Brit, Austral & NZ slang*)
▷ *verb* 1 BE A SPY, snoop (*informal*), gather intelligence
2 *usually followed by* **on** WATCH, follow, shadow, tail (*informal*), trail, keep watch on, keep under surveillance
3 CATCH SIGHT OF, see, spot, notice, sight, observe, glimpse, behold (*archaic or literary*), set eyes on, espy, descry

spying *noun* ESPIONAGE, reconnaissance, infiltration, undercover work

squabble *verb* QUARREL, fight, argue, row, clash, dispute, scrap (*informal*), fall out (*informal*), brawl, spar, wrangle, bicker, have words, fight like cat and dog, go at it hammer and tongs
▷ *noun* QUARREL, fight, row, argument, dispute, set-to (*informal*), scrap (*informal*), disagreement, barney (*informal*), spat, difference of opinion, tiff, bagarre (*French*)

squad *noun* TEAM, group, band, company, force, troop, crew, gang

squalid *adjective* 1 DIRTY, filthy, seedy, sleazy, sordid, low, nasty, foul, disgusting, run-down, decayed, repulsive, poverty-stricken, unclean, fetid, slovenly, skanky (*slang*), slummy, yucky *or* yukky (*slang*), yucko (*Austral slang*), festy (*Austral slang*)
<< OPPOSITE hygienic
2 UNSEEMLY, sordid, inappropriate, unsuitable, out of place, improper, undignified, disreputable, unbecoming, unrefined, out of keeping, discreditable, indelicate, in poor taste, indecorous, unbefitting

squalor *noun* FILTH, wretchedness, sleaziness, decay, foulness, slumminess, squalidness, meanness
<< OPPOSITE luxury

squander *verb* WASTE, spend, fritter away, blow (*slang*), consume, scatter, run through, lavish, throw away, misuse, dissipate, expend, misspend, be prodigal with, frivol away, spend like water
<< OPPOSITE save

square *noun* 1 TOWN SQUARE, close, quad, market square, quadrangle, village square
2 (*informal*) CONSERVATIVE, dinosaur, traditionalist, die-hard, stick-in-the-mud (*informal*), fuddy-duddy (*informal*), old buffer (*Brit informal*), antediluvian, back number (*informal*), (old) fogey
▷ *adjective* 1 FAIR, just, straight, genuine, decent, ethical, straightforward, upright, honest, equitable, upfront (*informal*), on the level (*informal*), kosher (*informal*), dinkum (*Austral & NZ informal*), above board, fair and square, on the up and up
2 (*informal*) OLD-FASHIONED, straight (*slang*), conservative, conventional, dated, bourgeois, out of date, stuffy, behind the times, strait-laced, out of the ark (*informal*), Pooterish
<< OPPOSITE fashionable
▷ *verb often followed by* **with** AGREE, match, fit, accord, correspond, tally, conform, reconcile, harmonize

squash *verb* 1 CRUSH, press, flatten, mash, pound, smash, distort, pulp, compress, stamp on, trample down
2 SUPPRESS, put down (*slang*), quell, silence, sit on (*informal*), crush, quash, annihilate
3 EMBARRASS, put down, humiliate, shame, disgrace, degrade, mortify, debase, discomfit, take the wind out of someone's sails, put (someone) in his (*or* her) place, take down a peg (*informal*)

squawk *verb* 1 CRY, crow, screech, hoot, yelp, cackle
2 (*informal*) COMPLAIN, protest, squeal (*informal, chiefly Brit*), kick up a fuss (*informal*), raise Cain (*slang*)
▷ *noun* 1 CRY, crow, screech, hoot, yelp, cackle
2 SCREAM, cry, yell, wail, shriek, screech, squeal, yelp, yowl

squeak *verb* SQUEAL, pipe, peep, shrill, whine, yelp

squeal *verb* 1 SCREAM, yell, shriek, screech, yelp, wail, yowl
2 (*informal, chiefly Brit*) COMPLAIN, protest, moan, squawk (*informal*), kick up a fuss (*informal*)
3 (*Slang*) INFORM ON, grass (*Brit slang*), betray, shop (*slang, chiefly Brit*), sing (*slang, chiefly US*), peach (*slang*), tell all, spill the beans (*informal*), snitch (*slang*), blab, rat on (*informal*), sell (someone) down the river (*informal*), blow the gaff (*Brit slang*), spill your guts (*slang*), dob in (*Austral slang*)
▷ *noun* SCREAM, shriek, screech, yell, shriek, wail, yelp, yowl

squeamish *adjective* 1 QUEASY, sick, nauseous, queer, sickish, qualmish
<< OPPOSITE strong-stomached
2 FASTIDIOUS, particular, delicate, nice (*rare*), scrupulous, prudish, prissy (*informal*), finicky, strait-laced, punctilious
<< OPPOSITE coarse

squeeze *verb* 1 PRESS, crush, squash, pinch
2 CLUTCH, press, grip, crush, pinch, squash, nip, compress, wring
3 EXTRACT, force, press, express
4 CRAM, press, crowd, force, stuff, pack, jam, thrust, ram, wedge, jostle

5 PRESSURIZE, lean on (*informal*), bring pressure to bear on, milk, bleed (*informal*), oppress, wrest, extort, put the squeeze on (*informal*), put the screws on (*informal*)
6 HUG, embrace, cuddle, clasp, enfold, hold tight
▷ *noun* 1 PRESS, grip, clasp, crush, pinch, squash, nip, wring
2 CRUSH, jam, squash, press, crowd, congestion
3 HUG, embrace, cuddle, hold, clasp, handclasp

squint *verb* PEER, screw up your eyes, narrow your eyes, look through narrowed eyes
▷ *noun* CROSS EYES, strabismus

squirm *verb* WRIGGLE, twist, writhe, shift, flounder, wiggle, fidget

squirt *verb* SPURT, shoot, gush, burst, jet, surge, erupt, spew
▷ *noun* SPURT, jet, burst, gush, surge, eruption

stab *verb* PIERCE, cut, gore, run through, stick, injure, wound, knife, thrust, spear, jab, puncture, bayonet, transfix, impale, spill blood
▷ *noun* 1 (*informal*) ATTEMPT, go, try, shot (*informal*), crack (*informal*), essay (*informal*), endeavour
2 TWINGE, prick, pang, ache
▷▷ **stab someone in the back** BETRAY, double-cross (*informal*), sell out (*informal*), sell, let down, inform on, do the dirty on (*Brit slang*), break faith with, play false, give the Judas kiss to, dob in (*Austral slang*)

stability *noun* FIRMNESS, strength, soundness, durability, permanence, solidity, constancy, steadiness, steadfastness
<< OPPOSITE instability

stable *adjective* 1 SECURE, lasting, strong, sound, fast, sure, established, permanent, constant, steady, enduring, reliable, abiding, durable, deep-rooted, well-founded, steadfast, immutable, unwavering, invariable, unalterable, unchangeable
<< OPPOSITE insecure
2 WELL-BALANCED, balanced, sensible, reasonable, rational, mentally sound
3 SOLID, firm, secure, fixed, substantial, sturdy, durable, well-made, well-built, immovable, built to last
<< OPPOSITE unstable

stack *noun* 1 PILE, heap, mountain, mass, load, cock, rick, clamp (*Brit Agriculture*), mound
2 LOT, mass, load (*informal*), ton (*informal*), heap (*informal*), large quantity, great amount
▷ *verb* PILE, heap up, load, assemble, accumulate, amass, stockpile, bank up

staff *noun* 1 WORKERS, employees, personnel, workforce, team, organization
2 STICK, pole, rod, prop, crook, cane, stave, wand, sceptre

stage *noun* STEP, leg, phase, point, level, period, division, length, lap, juncture
▷ *verb* 1 PRESENT, produce, perform, put on, do, give, play
2 ORGANIZE, mount, arrange, lay on, orchestrate, engineer

stagger *verb* 1 TOTTER, reel, sway, falter, lurch, wobble, waver, teeter
2 ASTOUND, amaze, stun, surprise, shock, shake, overwhelm, astonish, confound, take (someone) aback, bowl (someone) over (*informal*), stupefy, strike (someone) dumb, throw (someone) off balance, give (someone) a shock, dumbfound, nonplus, flabbergast, take (someone's) breath away

stagnant *adjective* 1 STALE, still, standing, quiet, sluggish, motionless, brackish
<< OPPOSITE flowing
2 INACTIVE, declining, stagnating, slow, depressed, sluggish, slow-moving

stagnate *verb* VEGETATE, decline, deteriorate, rot, decay, idle, rust, languish, stand still, fester, go to seed, lie fallow

staid *adjective* SEDATE, serious, sober, quiet, calm, grave, steady, composed, solemn, demure, decorous, self-restrained, set in your ways
<< OPPOSITE wild

stain *noun* 1 MARK, spot, blot, blemish, discoloration, smirch
2 STIGMA, shame, disgrace, slur, reproach, blemish, dishonour, infamy, blot on the escutcheon
3 DYE, colour, tint
▷ *verb* 1 MARK, soil, discolour, dirty, tarnish, tinge, spot, blot, blemish, smirch
2 DYE, colour, tint
3 DISGRACE, taint, blacken, sully, corrupt, contaminate, deprave, defile, besmirch, drag through the mud

stake¹ *noun* POLE, post, spike, stick, pale, paling, picket, stave, palisade
▷ *verb* SUPPORT, secure, prop, brace, tie up, tether
▷▷ **stake something out** LAY CLAIM TO, define, outline, mark out, demarcate, delimit

stake² *noun* 1 BET, ante, wager, chance, risk, venture, hazard
2 INTEREST, share, involvement, claim, concern, investment
▷ *verb* BET, gamble, wager, chance, risk, venture, hazard, jeopardize, imperil, put on the line
▷▷ **at stake** TO LOSE, at risk, being risked

stale *adjective* 1 OLD, hard, dry, decayed, fetid
<< OPPOSITE fresh
2 MUSTY, stagnant, fusty
3 TASTELESS, flat, sour, insipid
4 UNORIGINAL, banal, trite, common,

flat, stereotyped, commonplace, worn-out, antiquated, threadbare, old hat, insipid, hackneyed, overused, repetitious, platitudinous, cliché-ridden
<< OPPOSITE original
stalemate *noun* DEADLOCK, draw, tie, impasse, standstill
stalk *verb* 1 PURSUE, follow, track, hunt, shadow, tail (*informal*), haunt, creep up on
2 MARCH, pace, stride, strut, flounce
stall[1] *verb* STOP DEAD, jam, seize up, catch, stick, stop short
▷ *noun* 1 STAND, table, counter, booth, kiosk
2 ENCLOSURE, pen, coop, corral, sty
stall[2] *verb* 1 HINDER, obstruct, impede, block, check, arrest, halt, slow down, hamper, thwart, sabotage
2 PLAY FOR TIME, delay, hedge, procrastinate, stonewall, beat about the bush (*informal*), temporize, drag your feet
3 HOLD UP, delay, detain, divert, distract
stalwart *adjective* 1 LOYAL, faithful, strong, firm, true, constant, resolute, dependable, steadfast, true-blue, tried and true
2 STRONG, strapping, robust, athletic, vigorous, rugged, manly, hefty (*informal*), muscular, sturdy, stout, husky (*informal*), beefy (*informal*), lusty, sinewy, brawny
<< OPPOSITE puny
stamina *noun* STAYING POWER, endurance, resilience, force, power, energy, strength, resistance, grit, vigour, tenacity, power of endurance, indefatigability, lustiness
stammer *verb* STUTTER, falter, splutter, pause, hesitate, hem and haw, stumble over your words
▷ *noun* SPEECH IMPEDIMENT, stutter, speech defect
stamp *noun* 1 IMPRINT, mark, brand, cast, mould, signature, earmark, hallmark
2 STOMP, stump, clump, tramp, clomp
3 TYPE, sort, kind, form, cut, character, fashion, cast, breed, description
▷ *verb* 1 PRINT, mark, fix, impress, mould, imprint, engrave, inscribe
2 STOMP, stump, clump, tramp, clomp
3 TRAMPLE, step, tread, crush
4 IDENTIFY, mark, brand, label, reveal, exhibit, betray, pronounce, show to be, categorize, typecast
▷▷ **stamp something out** ELIMINATE, destroy, eradicate, crush, suppress, put down, put out, scotch, quell, extinguish, quench, extirpate
stampede *noun* RUSH, charge, flight, scattering, rout
▷ *verb* BOLT, run, charge, race, career, rush, dash
stance *noun* 1 ATTITUDE, stand, position, viewpoint, standpoint
2 POSTURE, carriage, bearing, deportment
stand *verb* 1 BE UPRIGHT, be erect, be vertical
2 GET TO YOUR FEET, rise, stand up, straighten up
3 BE LOCATED, be, sit, perch, nestle, be positioned, be sited, be perched, be situated *or* located
4 BE VALID, be in force, continue, stay, exist, prevail, remain valid
5 PUT, place, position, set, mount
6 SIT, rest, mellow, maturate
7 RESIST, endure, withstand, wear (*Brit slang*), weather, undergo, defy, tolerate, stand up to, hold out against, stand firm against
8 TOLERATE, bear, abide, suffer, stomach, endure, brook, hack (*slang*), submit to, thole (*dialect*)
9 TAKE, bear, handle, cope with, experience, sustain, endure, undergo, put up with (*informal*), withstand, countenance
▷ *noun* 1 POSITION, attitude, stance, opinion, determination, standpoint, firm stand
2 STALL, booth, kiosk, table
3 GRANDSTAND
4 SUPPORT, base, platform, place, stage, frame, rack, bracket, tripod, dais, trivet
▷▷ **stand by** 1 BE PREPARED, wait, stand ready, prepare yourself, wait in the wings
2 LOOK ON, watch, not lift a finger, wait, turn a blind eye
▷▷ **stand by something** SUPPORT, maintain, defend, champion, justify, sustain, endorse, assert, uphold, vindicate, stand up for, espouse, speak up for, stick up for (*informal*)
▷▷ **stand by someone** SUPPORT, back, champion, defend, take (someone's) part, uphold, befriend, be loyal to, stick up for (*informal*)
▷▷ **stand for something** 1 REPRESENT, mean, signify, denote, indicate, exemplify, symbolize, betoken *verb*
2 (*informal*) TOLERATE, suffer, bear, endure, put up with, wear (*Brit informal*), brook, lie down under (*informal*)
▷▷ **stand in for someone** BE A SUBSTITUTE FOR, represent, cover for, take the place of, replace, understudy, hold the fort for, do duty for, deputize for
▷▷ **stand out** 1 BE CONSPICUOUS, be striking, be prominent, be obvious, be highlighted, attract attention, catch the eye, be distinct, stick out like a sore thumb (*informal*), stare you in the face (*informal*), be thrown into relief, bulk large, stick out a mile (*informal*), leap to the eye
2 PROJECT, protrude, bristle
▷▷ **stand up for something** *or* **someone** SUPPORT, champion, defend, uphold, side with, stick up for (*informal*), come to the defence of

▷▷ **stand up to something** *or* **someone**
1 WITHSTAND, take, bear, weather, cope with, resist, endure, tolerate, hold out against, stand firm against *verb*
2 RESIST, oppose, confront, tackle, brave, defy

standard *noun* 1 LEVEL, grade
2 CRITERION, measure, guideline, example, model, average, guide, pattern, sample, par, norm, gauge, benchmark, yardstick, touchstone
3 *often plural* PRINCIPLES, ideals, morals, rule, ethics, canon, moral principles, code of honour
4 FLAG, banner, pennant, colours, ensign, pennon
▷ *adjective* 1 USUAL, normal, customary, set, stock, average, popular, basic, regular, typical, prevailing, orthodox, staple, one-size-fits-all
<< OPPOSITE unusual
2 ACCEPTED, official, established, classic, approved, recognized, definitive, authoritative
<< OPPOSITE unofficial

standardize *verb* BRING INTO LINE, stereotype, regiment, assimilate, mass-produce, institutionalize

stand-in *noun* SUBSTITUTE, deputy, replacement, reserve, surrogate, understudy, locum, stopgap

standing *noun* 1 STATUS, position, station, footing, condition, credit, rank, reputation, eminence, estimation, repute
2 DURATION, existence, experience, continuance
▷ *adjective* 1 PERMANENT, lasting, fixed, regular, repeated, perpetual
2 UPRIGHT, erect, vertical, rampant (*Heraldry*), perpendicular, upended

standpoint *noun* POINT OF VIEW, position, angle, viewpoint, stance, vantage point

staple *adjective* PRINCIPAL, chief, main, key, basic, essential, primary, fundamental, predominant

star *noun* 1 HEAVENLY BODY, sun, celestial body
2 CELEBRITY, big name, celeb (*informal*), megastar (*informal*), name, draw, idol, luminary, leading man *or* lady, lead, hero *or* heroine, principal, main attraction
▷ *plural noun* HOROSCOPE, forecast, astrological chart
▷ *verb* PLAY THE LEAD, appear, feature, perform
>> RELATED WORDS *adjectives* astral, sidereal, stellar

starchy *adjective* FORMAL, stiff, stuffy, conventional, precise, prim, punctilious, ceremonious

stare *verb* GAZE, look, goggle, watch, gape, eyeball (*slang*), ogle, gawp (*Brit slang*), gawk, rubberneck (*slang*)

stark *adjective* 1 PLAIN, simple, harsh, basic, bare, grim, straightforward, blunt, bald
2 SHARP, clear, striking, distinct, clear-cut
3 AUSTERE, severe, plain, bare, harsh, unadorned
4 BLEAK, grim, barren, hard, cold, depressing, dreary, desolate, forsaken, godforsaken, drear (*literary*)
5 ABSOLUTE, pure, sheer, utter, downright, patent, consummate, palpable, out-and-out, flagrant, unmitigated, unalloyed, arrant
▷ *adverb* ABSOLUTELY, quite, completely, clean, entirely, altogether, wholly, utterly

start *verb* 1 SET ABOUT, begin, proceed, embark upon, take the plunge (*informal*), take the first step, make a beginning, put your hand to the plough (*informal*)
<< OPPOSITE stop
2 BEGIN, arise, originate, issue, appear, commence, get under way, come into being, come into existence, first see the light of day
<< OPPOSITE end
3 SET IN MOTION, initiate, instigate, open, trigger, kick off (*informal*), originate, get going, engender, kick-start, get (something) off the ground (*informal*), enter upon, get *or* set *or* start the ball rolling
<< OPPOSITE stop
4 ESTABLISH, begin, found, father, create, launch, set up, introduce, institute, pioneer, initiate, inaugurate, lay the foundations of
<< OPPOSITE terminate
5 START UP, activate, get something going
<< OPPOSITE turn off
6 JUMP, shy, jerk, twitch, flinch, recoil
▷ *noun* 1 BEGINNING, outset, opening, birth, foundation, dawn, first step(s), onset, initiation, inauguration, inception, commencement, kickoff (*informal*), opening move
<< OPPOSITE end
2 JUMP, jerk, twitch, spasm, convulsion

startle *verb* SURPRISE, shock, alarm, frighten, scare, agitate, take (someone) aback, make (someone) jump, give (someone) a turn (*informal*)

startling *adjective* SURPRISING, shocking, alarming, extraordinary, sudden, unexpected, staggering, unforeseen, jaw-dropping

starving *adjective* HUNGRY, starved, ravenous, famished, hungering, sharp-set, esurient, faint from lack of food, ready to eat a horse (*informal*)

stash (*informal*) *verb* STORE, stockpile, save up, hoard, hide, secrete, stow, cache, lay up, salt away, put aside for a rainy day
▷ *noun* HOARD, supply, store, stockpile, cache, collection

state *noun* 1 COUNTRY, nation, land, republic, territory, federation, commonwealth,

kingdom, body politic
2 PROVINCE, region, district, area, territory, federal state
3 GOVERNMENT, ministry, administration, executive, regime, powers-that-be
4 CONDITION, shape, state of affairs
5 FRAME OF MIND, condition, spirits, attitude, mood, humour
6 CEREMONY, glory, grandeur, splendour, dignity, majesty, pomp
7 CIRCUMSTANCES, situation, position, case, pass, mode, plight, predicament
▷ *verb* SAY, report, declare, specify, put, present, explain, voice, express, assert, utter, articulate, affirm, expound, enumerate, propound, aver, asseverate
▷▷ **in a state** (*informal*) 1 DISTRESSED, upset, agitated, disturbed, anxious, ruffled, uptight (*informal*), flustered, panic-stricken, het up, all steamed up (*slang*)
2 UNTIDY, disordered, messy, muddled, cluttered, jumbled, in disarray, topsy-turvy, higgledy-piggledy (*informal*)

stately *adjective* GRAND, majestic, dignified, royal, august, imposing, impressive, elegant, imperial, noble, regal, solemn, lofty, pompous, ceremonious
<< OPPOSITE lowly

statement *noun* 1 ANNOUNCEMENT, declaration, communication, explanation, communiqué, proclamation, utterance
2 ACCOUNT, report, testimony, evidence

state-of-the-art *adjective* LATEST, newest, up-to-date, up-to-the-minute
<< OPPOSITE old-fashioned

static *adjective* STATIONARY, still, motionless, fixed, constant, stagnant, inert, immobile, unmoving, stock-still, unvarying, changeless
<< OPPOSITE moving

station *noun* 1 RAILWAY STATION, stop, stage, halt, terminal, train station, terminus
2 HEADQUARTERS, base, depot
3 CHANNEL, wavelength, broadcasting company
4 POSITION, rank, status, standing, post, situation, grade, sphere
5 POST, place, location, position, situation, seat
▷ *verb* ASSIGN, post, locate, set, establish, fix, install, garrison

stationary *adjective* MOTIONLESS, standing, at a standstill, parked, fixed, moored, static, inert, unmoving, stock-still
<< OPPOSITE moving

This word, which is always an adjective, is occasionally wrongly used where 'paper products' are meant: *in the stationery* (not *stationary*) *cupboard*

statuesque *adjective* WELL-PROPORTIONED, stately, Junoesque, imposing, majestic, dignified, regal

stature *noun* 1 HEIGHT, build, size
2 IMPORTANCE, standing, prestige, size, rank, consequence, prominence, eminence, high station

status *noun* 1 POSITION, rank, grade, degree
2 PRESTIGE, standing, authority, influence, weight, reputation, honour, importance, consequence, fame, distinction, eminence, renown, mana (NZ)
3 STATE OF PLAY, development, progress, condition, evolution, progression

statute *noun* LAW, act, rule, regulation, decree, ordinance, enactment, edict

staunch *adjective* LOYAL, faithful, stalwart, sure, strong, firm, sound, true, constant, reliable, stout, resolute, dependable, trustworthy, trusty, steadfast, true-blue, immovable, tried and true

stay *verb* 1 REMAIN, continue to be, linger, stand, stop, wait, settle, delay, halt, pause, hover, abide, hang around (*informal*), reside, stay put, bide, loiter, hang in the air, tarry, put down roots, establish yourself
<< OPPOSITE go
2 *often with* **at** LODGE, visit, sojourn, put up at, be accommodated at
3 CONTINUE, remain, go on, survive, endure
4 SUSPEND, put off, defer, adjourn, hold over, hold in abeyance, prorogue
▷ *noun* 1 VISIT, stop, holiday, stopover, sojourn
2 POSTPONEMENT, delay, suspension, stopping, halt, pause, reprieve, remission, deferment

staying power *noun* ENDURANCE, strength, stamina, toughness

steadfast *adjective* 1 LOYAL, faithful, stalwart, staunch, constant, steady, dedicated, reliable, persevering, dependable
<< OPPOSITE undependable
2 RESOLUTE, firm, fast, fixed, stable, intent, single-minded, unwavering, immovable, unflinching, unswerving, unfaltering
<< OPPOSITE irresolute

steady *adjective* 1 CONTINUOUS, even, regular, constant, consistent, persistent, rhythmic, unbroken, habitual, uninterrupted, incessant, ceaseless, unremitting, unwavering, nonstop, unvarying, unfaltering, unfluctuating
<< OPPOSITE irregular
2 STABLE, fixed, secure, firm, safe, immovable, on an even keel
<< OPPOSITE unstable
3 REGULAR, established
4 DEPENDABLE, sensible, reliable, balanced, settled, secure, calm, supportive, sober, staunch, serene, sedate, staid, steadfast, level-headed, serious-minded, imperturbable, equable, unchangeable, having both feet on

the ground
<< OPPOSITE undependable

steal *verb* 1 TAKE, nick (*slang, chiefly Brit*), pinch (*informal*), lift (*informal*), cabbage (*Brit slang*), swipe (*slang*), half-inch (*old-fashioned slang*), heist (*US slang*), embezzle, blag (*slang*), pilfer, misappropriate, snitch (*slang*), purloin, filch, prig (*Brit slang*), shoplift, thieve, be light-fingered, peculate, walk *or* make off with
2 COPY, take, plagiarize, appropriate, pinch (*informal*), pirate, poach
3 SNEAK, slip, creep, flit, tiptoe, slink, insinuate yourself

stealth *noun* SECRECY, furtiveness, slyness, sneakiness, unobtrusiveness, stealthiness, surreptitiousness

stealthy *adjective* SECRET, secretive, furtive, sneaking, covert, sly, clandestine, sneaky, skulking, underhand, surreptitious

steamy *adjective* 1 (*informal*) EROTIC, hot (*slang*), sexy (*informal*), sensual, raunchy (*slang*), lewd, carnal, titillating, prurient, lascivious, lustful, lubricious (*formal* or *literary*)
2 MUGGY, damp, humid, sweaty, like a sauna

steep[1] *adjective* 1 SHEER, precipitous, perpendicular, abrupt, headlong, vertical
<< OPPOSITE gradual
2 SHARP, sudden, abrupt, marked, extreme, distinct
3 (*informal*) HIGH, excessive, exorbitant, extreme, stiff, unreasonable, overpriced, extortionate, uncalled-for
<< OPPOSITE reasonable

steep[2] *verb* SOAK, immerse, marinate (*Cookery*), damp, submerge, drench, moisten, macerate, souse, imbrue (*rare*)

steeped *adjective* SATURATED, pervaded, permeated, filled, infused, imbued, suffused

steer *verb* 1 DRIVE, control, direct, handle, conduct, pilot, govern, be in the driver's seat
2 DIRECT, lead, guide, conduct, escort, show in *or* out
▷▷ **steer clear of something** *or* **someone** AVOID, evade, fight shy of, shun, eschew, circumvent, body-swerve (*Scot*), give a wide berth to, sheer off

stem[1] *noun* STALK, branch, trunk, shoot, stock, axis, peduncle
▷▷ **stem from something** ORIGINATE FROM, be caused by, derive from, arise from, flow from, emanate from, develop from, be generated by, be brought about by, be bred by, issue forth from

stem[2] *verb* STOP, hold back, staunch, stay (*archaic*), check, contain, dam, curb, restrain, bring to a standstill, stanch

stench *noun* STINK, whiff (*Brit slang*), reek, pong (*Brit informal*), foul smell, niff (*Brit slang*), malodour, mephitis, noisomeness

step *noun* 1 PACE, stride, footstep
2 FOOTFALL
3 STAIR, tread, rung
4 MOVE, measure, action, means, act, proceeding, procedure, manoeuvre, deed, expedient
5 STAGE, point, phase
6 GAIT, walk
7 LEVEL, rank, remove, degree
▷ *verb* WALK, pace, tread, move
▷▷ **in step** (*informal*) IN AGREEMENT, in harmony, in unison, in line, coinciding, conforming, in conformity
▷▷ **mind** *or* **watch your step** (*informal*) BE CAREFUL, take care, look out, be cautious, be discreet, take heed, tread carefully, be canny, be on your guard, mind how you go, have your wits about you, mind your p's and q's
▷▷ **out of step** (*informal*) IN DISAGREEMENT, out of line, out of phase, out of harmony, incongruous, pulling different ways
▷▷ **step down** *or* **aside** (*informal*) RESIGN, retire, quit, leave, give up, pull out, bow out, abdicate
▷▷ **step in** (*informal*) INTERVENE, take action, become involved, chip in (*informal*), intercede, take a hand
▷▷ **step something up** INCREASE, boost, intensify, up, raise, accelerate, speed up, escalate, augment
▷▷ **take steps** TAKE ACTION, act, intervene, move in, take the initiative, take measures

stereotype *noun* FORMULA, cliché, pattern, mould, received idea
▷ *verb* CATEGORIZE, typecast, pigeonhole, dub, standardize, take to be, ghettoize, conventionalize

stereotyped *adjective* UNORIGINAL, stock, standard, tired, conventional, played out, stale, banal, standardized, mass-produced, corny (*slang*), threadbare, trite, hackneyed, overused, platitudinous, cliché-ridden

sterile *adjective* 1 GERM-FREE, antiseptic, sterilized, disinfected, aseptic
<< OPPOSITE unhygienic
2 BARREN, infertile, unproductive, childless, infecund
<< OPPOSITE fertile

sterilize *verb* DISINFECT, purify, fumigate, decontaminate, autoclave, sanitize

sterling *adjective* EXCELLENT, sound, fine, first-class, superlative

stern *adjective* 1 STRICT, harsh, rigorous, hard, cruel, grim, rigid, relentless, drastic, authoritarian, austere, inflexible, unrelenting, unyielding, unsparing
<< OPPOSITE lenient
2 SEVERE, serious, forbidding, steely, flinty
<< OPPOSITE friendly

stew *noun* HASH, goulash, ragout, olla, olio, olla

podrida
▷ *verb* BRAISE, boil, simmer, casserole
▷▷ **in a stew** (*informal*) TROUBLED, concerned, anxious, worried, fretting, in a panic, in a lather (*informal*)

stick[1] *noun* 1 TWIG, branch, birch, offshoot
2 CANE, staff, pole, rod, stake, switch, crook, baton, wand, sceptre
3 (*Slang*) ABUSE, criticism, flak (*informal*), blame, knocking (*informal*), hostility, slagging (*slang*), denigration, critical remarks, fault-finding

stick[2] *verb* 1 (*informal*) PUT, place, set, position, drop, plant, store, lay, stuff, fix, deposit, install, plonk
2 POKE, dig, stab, insert, thrust, pierce, penetrate, spear, prod, jab, transfix
3 FASTEN, fix, bind, hold, bond, attach, hold on, glue, fuse, paste, adhere, affix
4 ADHERE, cling, cleave, become joined, become cemented, become welded
5 STAY, remain, linger, persist
6 CATCH, lodge, jam, stop, clog, snag, be embedded, be bogged down, come to a standstill, become immobilized
7 (*Slang*) TOLERATE, take, stand, stomach, endure, hack (*slang*), abide, bear up under
▷▷ **stick out** PROTRUDE, stand out, jut out, show, project, bulge, obtrude
▷▷ **stick something out** 1 OFFER, present, extend, hold out, advance, reach out, stretch out, proffer
2 (*informal*) ENDURE, bear, put up with (*informal*), weather, take it (*informal*), see through, soldier on, last out, grin and bear it (*informal*)
▷▷ **stick to something** 1 KEEP TO, persevere in, cleave to
2 ADHERE TO, honour, hold to, keep to, abide by, stand by
▷▷ **stick up for someone** (*informal*) DEFEND, support, champion, uphold, stand up for, take the part *or* side of

stickler *noun* FANATIC, nut (*slang*), maniac (*informal*), purist, perfectionist, pedant, martinet, hard taskmaster, fusspot (*Brit informal*)

sticky *adjective* 1 ADHESIVE, gummed, adherent
2 GOOEY, tacky (*informal*), syrupy, viscous, glutinous, gummy, icky (*informal*), gluey, clinging, claggy (*dialect*), viscid
3 (*informal*) DIFFICULT, awkward, tricky, embarrassing, painful, nasty, delicate, unpleasant, discomforting, hairy (*slang*), thorny, barro (*Austral slang*)
4 HUMID, close, sultry, oppressive, sweltering, clammy, muggy

stiff *adjective* 1 INFLEXIBLE, rigid, unyielding, hard, firm, tight, solid, tense, hardened, brittle, taut, solidified, unbending, inelastic
<< OPPOSITE flexible
2 UNSUPPLE, arthritic, creaky (*informal*), rheumaticky
<< OPPOSITE supple
3 FORMAL, constrained, forced, laboured, cold, mannered, wooden, artificial, uneasy, chilly, unnatural, austere, pompous, prim, stilted, starchy (*informal*), punctilious, priggish, standoffish, ceremonious, unrelaxed
<< OPPOSITE informal
4 VIGOROUS, great, strong
5 SEVERE, strict, harsh, hard, heavy, sharp, extreme, cruel, drastic, rigorous, stringent, oppressive, austere, inexorable, pitiless
6 STRONG, fresh, powerful, vigorous, brisk
7 DIFFICULT, hard, tough, exacting, formidable, trying, fatiguing, uphill, arduous, laborious

stifle *verb* 1 SUPPRESS, repress, prevent, stop, check, silence, curb, restrain, cover up, gag, hush, smother, extinguish, muffle, choke back
2 RESTRAIN, suppress, repress, smother

stigma *noun* DISGRACE, shame, dishonour, mark, spot, brand, stain, slur, blot, reproach, imputation, smirch

stigmatize *verb* BRAND, label, denounce, mark, discredit, pillory, defame, cast a slur upon

still *adjective* 1 MOTIONLESS, stationary, at rest, calm, smooth, peaceful, serene, tranquil, lifeless, placid, undisturbed, inert, restful, unruffled, unstirring
<< OPPOSITE moving
2 SILENT, quiet, hushed, noiseless, stilly (*poetic*)
<< OPPOSITE noisy
▷ *verb* QUIETEN, calm, subdue, settle, quiet, silence, soothe, hush, alleviate, lull, tranquillize
<< OPPOSITE get louder
▷ *noun* (*Poetic*) STILLNESS, peace, quiet, silence, hush, tranquillity
<< OPPOSITE noise
▷ *adverb* YET, even now, up until now, up to this time
▷ *sentence connector* HOWEVER, but, yet, nevertheless, for all that, notwithstanding

stilted *adjective* STIFF, forced, wooden, laboured, artificial, inflated, constrained, unnatural, high-flown, pompous, pretentious, pedantic, bombastic, grandiloquent, high-sounding, arty-farty (*informal*), fustian
<< OPPOSITE natural

stimulant *noun* PICK-ME-UP, tonic, restorative, upper (*slang*), reviver, bracer (*informal or informal*), energizer, pep pill (*informal*), excitant, analeptic
<< OPPOSITE sedative

stimulate *verb* ENCOURAGE, inspire, prompt, fire, fan, urge, spur, provoke, turn on (*slang*), arouse, animate, rouse, prod, quicken, inflame, incite, instigate, goad, whet, impel, foment, gee up

stimulating *adjective* EXCITING, inspiring, stirring, provoking, intriguing, rousing, provocative, exhilarating, thought-provoking, galvanic

<< OPPOSITE boring

stimulus *noun* INCENTIVE, spur, encouragement, impetus, provocation, inducement, goad, incitement, fillip, shot in the arm (*informal*), clarion call, geeing-up

sting *verb* 1 HURT, burn, wound

2 SMART, burn, pain, hurt, tingle

3 ANGER, provoke, infuriate, incense, gall, inflame, nettle, rile, pique

▷ *noun* SMARTING, pain, stinging, pricking, soreness, prickling

stingy *adjective* 1 MEAN, penny-pinching (*informal*), miserly, near, parsimonious, scrimping, illiberal, avaricious, niggardly, ungenerous, penurious, tightfisted, close-fisted, mingy (*Brit informal*), cheeseparing, snoep (*S African informal*)

2 INSUFFICIENT, inadequate, meagre, small, pathetic, scant, skimpy, measly (*informal*), scanty, on the small side

stink *verb* 1 REEK, pong (*Brit informal*), whiff (*Brit slang*), stink to high heaven (*informal*), offend the nostrils

2 (*Slang*) BE BAD, be no good, be rotten, be offensive, be abhorrent, have a bad name, be detestable, be held in disrepute

▷ *noun* 1 STENCH, pong (*Brit informal*), foul smell, foulness, malodour, fetor, noisomeness

2 (*Slang*) FUSS, to-do, row, upset, scandal, stir, disturbance, uproar, commotion, rumpus, hubbub, brouhaha, deal of trouble (*informal*)

stinker *noun* (*Slang*) SCOUNDREL, heel, sod (*slang*), cad (*Brit informal*), swine, bounder (*Brit old-fashioned slang*), cur, rotter (*slang, chiefly Brit*), nasty piece of work (*informal*), dastard (*archaic*), wrong 'un (*Austral slang*)

stinking *adjective* 1 (*informal*) ROTTEN, disgusting, unpleasant, vile, contemptible, wretched

2 FOUL-SMELLING, smelly, reeking, fetid, malodorous, noisome, whiffy (*Brit slang*), pongy (*Brit informal*), mephitic, ill-smelling, niffy (*Brit slang*), olid, festy (*Austral slang*), yucko (*Austral slang*)

stint *noun* TERM, time, turn, bit, period, share, tour, shift, stretch, spell, quota, assignment

▷ *verb* BE MEAN, hold back, be sparing, scrimp, skimp on, save, withhold, begrudge, economize, be frugal, be parsimonious, be mingy (*Brit informal*), spoil the ship for a ha'porth of tar

stipulate *verb* SPECIFY, agree, require, promise, contract, settle, guarantee, engage, pledge, lay down, covenant, postulate, insist upon, lay down *or* impose conditions

stipulation *noun* CONDITION, requirement, provision, term, contract, agreement, settlement, rider, restriction, qualification, clause, engagement, specification, precondition, prerequisite, proviso, sine qua non (*Latin*)

stir *verb* 1 MIX, beat, agitate

2 MOVE, change position

3 GET MOVING, move, get a move on (*informal*), hasten, budge, make an effort, be up and about (*informal*), look lively (*informal*), shake a leg (*informal*), exert yourself, bestir yourself

4 STIMULATE, move, excite, fire, raise, touch, affect, urge, inspire, prompt, spur, thrill, provoke, arouse, awaken, animate, rouse, prod, quicken, inflame, incite, instigate, electrify, kindle

<< OPPOSITE inhibit

5 SPUR, drive, prompt, stimulate, prod, press, urge, animate, prick, incite, goad, impel

▷ *noun* COMMOTION, to-do, excitement, activity, movement, disorder, fuss, disturbance, bustle, flurry, uproar, ferment, agitation, ado, tumult

stirring *adjective* EXCITING, dramatic, thrilling, moving, spirited, inspiring, stimulating, lively, animating, rousing, heady, exhilarating, impassioned, emotive, intoxicating

stock *noun* 1 SHARES, holdings, securities, investments, bonds, equities

2 PROPERTY, capital, assets, funds

3 GOODS, merchandise, wares, range, choice, variety, selection, commodities, array, assortment

4 SUPPLY, store, reserve, fund, reservoir, stockpile, hoard, cache

5 LINEAGE, descent, extraction, ancestry, house, family, line, race, type, variety, background, breed, strain, pedigree, forebears, parentage, line of descent

6 LIVESTOCK, cattle, beasts, domestic animals

▷ *verb* 1 SELL, supply, handle, keep, trade in, deal in

2 FILL, supply, provide with, provision, equip, furnish, fit out, kit out

▷ *adjective* 1 HACKNEYED, standard, usual, set, routine, stereotyped, staple, commonplace, worn-out, banal, run-of-the-mill, trite, overused

2 REGULAR, traditional, usual, basic, ordinary, conventional, staple, customary

▷▷ **stock up with something** STORE (UP), lay in, hoard, save, gather, accumulate, amass, buy up, put away, replenish supplies of

▷▷ **take stock** REVIEW THE SITUATION, weigh up, appraise, estimate, size up (*informal*), see how the land lies

stocky *adjective* THICKSET, solid, sturdy, chunky, stubby, dumpy, stumpy, mesomorphic

stodgy *adjective* **1** HEAVY, filling, substantial, leaden, starchy
<< OPPOSITE light
2 DULL, boring, stuffy, formal, tedious, tiresome, staid, unimaginative, turgid, uninspired, unexciting, ho-hum, heavy going, fuddy-duddy (*informal*), dull as ditchwater
<< OPPOSITE exciting

stoical *adjective* RESIGNED, long-suffering, phlegmatic, philosophic, cool, calm, indifferent, stoic, dispassionate, impassive, stolid, imperturbable

stoicism *noun* RESIGNATION, acceptance, patience, indifference, fortitude, long-suffering, calmness, fatalism, forbearance, stolidity, dispassion, impassivity, imperturbability

stolen *adjective* HOT (*slang*), bent (*slang*), hooky (*slang*)

stolid *adjective* APATHETIC, unemotional, dull, heavy, slow, wooden, stupid, bovine, dozy (*Brit informal*), obtuse, lumpish, doltish
<< OPPOSITE lively

stomach *noun* **1** BELLY, inside(s) (*informal*), gut (*informal*), abdomen, tummy (*informal*), puku (NZ)
2 TUMMY, pot, spare tyre (*informal*), paunch, breadbasket (*slang*), potbelly
3 INCLINATION, taste, desire, appetite, relish, mind
▷ *verb* BEAR, take, tolerate, suffer, endure, swallow, hack (*slang*), abide, put up with (*informal*), submit to, reconcile *or* resign yourself to
>> RELATED WORD *adjective* gastric

stone *noun* **1** MASONRY, rock
2 ROCK, pebble
3 PIP, seed, pit, kernel

stony *adjective* **1** ROCKY, rough, gritty, gravelly, rock-strewn, pebble
2 COLD, icy, hostile, hard, harsh, blank, adamant, indifferent, chilly, callous, heartless, merciless, unforgiving, inexorable, frigid, expressionless, unresponsive, pitiless, unfeeling, obdurate

stooge *noun* (*Slang*) PAWN, puppet, fall guy (*informal*), butt, foil, patsy (*slang, chiefly US & Canad*), dupe, henchman, lackey

stoop *verb* **1** HUNCH, be bowed *or* round-shouldered
2 BEND, lean, bow, duck, descend, incline, kneel, crouch, squat
▷ *noun* SLOUCH, slump, droop, sag, bad posture, round-shoulderedness
▷▷ **stoop to something** RESORT TO, sink to, descend to, deign to, condescend to, demean yourself by, lower yourself by

stop *verb* **1** QUIT, cease, refrain, break off, put an end to, pack in (*Brit informal*), discontinue, leave off, call it a day (*informal*), desist, belay (*Nautical*), bring *or* come to a halt *or* standstill
<< OPPOSITE start
2 PREVENT, suspend, cut short, close, break, check, bar, arrest, silence, frustrate, axe (*informal*), interrupt, restrain, hold back, intercept, hinder, repress, impede, rein in, forestall, nip (something) in the bud
<< OPPOSITE facilitate
3 END, conclude, finish, be over, cut out (*informal*), terminate, come to an end, peter out
<< OPPOSITE continue
4 CEASE, shut down, discontinue, desist
<< OPPOSITE continue
5 HALT, pause, stall, draw up, pull up
<< OPPOSITE keep going
6 PAUSE, wait, rest, hesitate, deliberate, take a break, have a breather (*informal*), stop briefly
7 STAY, rest, put up, lodge, sojourn, tarry, break your journey
▷ *noun* **1** HALT, standstill
2 STATION, stage, halt, destination, depot, termination, terminus
3 STAY, break, visit, rest, stopover, sojourn

stopgap *noun* MAKESHIFT, improvisation, temporary expedient, shift, resort, substitute
▷ *modifier* MAKESHIFT, emergency, temporary, provisional, improvised, impromptu, rough-and-ready

stoppage *noun* **1** STOPPING, halt, standstill, close, arrest, lay-off, shutdown, cutoff, abeyance, discontinuance
2 BLOCKAGE, obstruction, stopping up, occlusion

store *noun* **1** SHOP, outlet, department store, market, supermarket, mart, emporium, chain store, hypermarket
2 SUPPLY, stock, reserve, lot, fund, mine, plenty, provision, wealth, quantity, reservoir, abundance, accumulation, stockpile, hoard, plethora, cache
3 REPOSITORY, warehouse, depot, storehouse, depository, storeroom
▷ *verb* **1** *often with* **away** *or* **up** PUT BY, save, hoard, keep, stock, husband, reserve, deposit, accumulate, garner, stockpile, put aside, stash (*informal*), salt away, keep in reserve, put aside for a rainy day, lay by *or* in
2 PUT AWAY, put in storage, put in store, lock away
3 KEEP, hold, preserve, maintain, retain, conserve
▷▷ **set great store by something** VALUE, prize, esteem, appreciate, hold in high regard, think highly of

storm *noun* **1** TEMPEST, blast, hurricane, gale, tornado, cyclone, blizzard, whirlwind, gust,

squall
2 OUTBURST, row, stir, outcry, furore, violence, anger, passion, outbreak, turmoil, disturbance, strife, clamour, agitation, commotion, rumpus, tumult, hubbub
3 ROAR, thunder, clamour, din
4 BARRAGE, volley, salvo, rain, shower, spray, discharge, fusillade
▷ *verb* 1 RUSH, stamp, flounce, fly, stalk, stomp (*informal*)
2 RAGE, fume, rant, complain, thunder, rave, scold, bluster, go ballistic (*slang, chiefly US*), fly off the handle (*informal*), wig out (*slang*)
3 ATTACK, charge, rush, assault, beset, assail, take by storm

stormy *adjective* 1 WILD, rough, tempestuous, raging, dirty, foul, turbulent, windy, blustering, blustery, gusty, inclement, squally
2 ROUGH, wild, turbulent, tempestuous, raging
3 ANGRY, heated, fierce, passionate, fiery, impassioned, tumultuous

story *noun* 1 TALE, romance, narrative, record, history, version, novel, legend, chronicle, yarn, recital, narration, urban myth, urban legend, fictional account
2 ANECDOTE, account, tale, report, detail, relation
3 (*informal*) LIE, falsehood, fib, fiction, untruth, porky (*Brit slang*), pork pie (*Brit slang*), white lie
4 REPORT, news, article, feature, scoop, news item

storyteller *noun* RACONTEUR, author, narrator, romancer, novelist, chronicler, bard, fabulist, spinner of yarns, anecdotist

stout *adjective* 1 FAT, big, heavy, overweight, plump, bulky, substantial, burly, obese, fleshy, tubby, portly, rotund, corpulent, on the large *or* heavy side
<< OPPOSITE slim
2 STRONG, strapping, muscular, tough, substantial, athletic, hardy, robust, vigorous, sturdy, stalwart, husky (*informal*), hulking, beefy (*informal*), lusty, brawny, thickset, able-bodied
<< OPPOSITE puny
3 BRAVE, bold, courageous, fearless, resolute, gallant, intrepid, valiant, plucky, doughty, indomitable, dauntless, lion-hearted, valorous
<< OPPOSITE timid

stow *verb* PACK, load, put away, store, stuff, deposit, jam, tuck, bundle, cram, stash (*informal*), secrete

straggle *verb* TRAIL, drift, wander, range, lag, stray, roam, ramble, rove, loiter, string out

straggly *adjective* SPREAD OUT, spreading, rambling, untidy, loose, drifting, random, straying, irregular, aimless, disorganized, straggling

straight *adjective* 1 DIRECT, unswerving, undeviating
<< OPPOSITE indirect
2 LEVEL, even, right, square, true, smooth, in line, aligned, horizontal
<< OPPOSITE crooked
3 FRANK, plain, straightforward, blunt, outright, honest, downright, candid, forthright, bold, point-blank, upfront (*informal*), unqualified
<< OPPOSITE evasive
4 SUCCESSIVE, consecutive, continuous, through, running, solid, sustained, uninterrupted, nonstop, unrelieved
<< OPPOSITE discontinuous
5 (*Slang*) CONVENTIONAL, conservative, orthodox, traditional, square (*informal*), bourgeois, Pooterish
<< OPPOSITE fashionable
6 HONEST, just, fair, decent, reliable, respectable, upright, honourable, equitable, law-abiding, trustworthy, above board, fair and square
<< OPPOSITE dishonest
7 UNDILUTED, pure, neat, unadulterated, unmixed
8 IN ORDER, organized, arranged, sorted out, neat, tidy, orderly, shipshape, put to rights
<< OPPOSITE untidy
▷ *adverb* 1 DIRECTLY, precisely, exactly, as the crow flies, unswervingly, by the shortest route, in a beeline
2 IMMEDIATELY, directly, promptly, instantly, at once, straight away, without delay, without hesitation, forthwith, unhesitatingly, before you could say Jack Robinson (*informal*)
3 FRANKLY, honestly, point-blank, candidly, pulling no punches (*informal*), in plain English, with no holds barred

straightaway *adverb* IMMEDIATELY, now, at once, directly, instantly, on the spot, right away, there and then, this minute, straightway (*archaic*), without more ado, without any delay

straighten *verb* NEATEN, arrange, tidy (up), order, spruce up, smarten up, put in order, set *or* put to rights
▷▷ **straighten something out** SORT OUT, resolve, put right, settle, correct, work out, clear up, rectify, disentangle, unsnarl

straightforward *adjective* 1 (*Chiefly Brit*) SIMPLE, easy, uncomplicated, routine, elementary, clear-cut, undemanding, easy-peasy (*slang*)
<< OPPOSITE complicated
2 HONEST, open, direct, genuine, sincere, candid, truthful, forthright, upfront (*informal*), dinkum (*Austral & NZ informal*), above board, guileless

<< OPPOSITE devious
strain[1] *noun* 1 PRESSURE, stress, difficulty, demands, burden, adversity
2 STRESS, pressure, anxiety, difficulty, distress, nervous tension
3 WORRY, effort, struggle, tension, hassle
<< OPPOSITE ease
4 BURDEN, tension
5 INJURY, wrench, sprain, pull, tension, tautness, tensity (*rare*)
6 TUNE, air, melody, measure (*poetic*), lay, song, theme
▷ *verb* 1 STRETCH, test, tax, overtax, push to the limit
2 INJURE, wrench, sprain, damage, pull, tear, hurt, twist, rick
3 STRIVE, struggle, endeavour, labour, go for it (*informal*), bend over backwards (*informal*), go for broke (*slang*), go all out for (*informal*), bust a gut (*informal*), give it your best shot (*informal*), make an all-out effort (*informal*), knock yourself out (*informal*), do your damnedest (*informal*), give it your all (*informal*), break your back *or* neck (*informal*), rupture yourself (*informal*)
<< OPPOSITE relax
4 SIEVE, filter, sift, screen, separate, riddle, purify
strain[2] *noun* 1 TRACE, suggestion, suspicion, tendency, streak, trait
2 BREED, type, stock, family, race, blood, descent, pedigree, extraction, ancestry, lineage
strained *adjective* 1 TENSE, difficult, uncomfortable, awkward, embarrassed, stiff, uneasy, constrained, self-conscious, unrelaxed
<< OPPOSITE relaxed
2 FORCED, put on, false, artificial, unnatural, laboured
<< OPPOSITE natural
strait *noun often plural* CHANNEL, sound, narrows, stretch of water, sea passage
▷ *plural noun* DIFFICULTY, crisis, mess, pass, hole (*slang*), emergency, distress, dilemma, embarrassment, plight, hardship, uphill (*S African*), predicament, extremity, perplexity, panic stations (*informal*), pretty *or* fine kettle of fish (*informal*)
strand *noun* FILAMENT, fibre, thread, length, lock, string, twist, rope, wisp, tress
stranded *adjective* 1 BEACHED, grounded, marooned, ashore, shipwrecked, aground, cast away
2 HELPLESS, abandoned, high and dry, left in the lurch
strange *adjective* 1 ODD, unusual, curious, weird, wonderful, rare, funny, extraordinary, remarkable, bizarre, fantastic, astonishing, marvellous, exceptional, peculiar, eccentric, abnormal, out-of-the-way, queer, irregular, rum (*Brit slang*), uncommon, singular, perplexing, uncanny, mystifying, unheard-of, off-the-wall (*slang*), oddball (*informal*), unaccountable, left-field (*informal*), outré, curiouser and curiouser, daggy (*Austral & NZ informal*)
<< OPPOSITE ordinary
2 OUT OF PLACE, lost, uncomfortable, awkward, bewildered, disoriented, ill at ease, like a fish out of water
<< OPPOSITE comfortable
3 UNFAMILIAR, new, unknown, foreign, novel, alien, exotic, untried, unexplored, outside your experience
<< OPPOSITE familiar
stranger *noun* 1 UNKNOWN PERSON
2 NEWCOMER, incomer, foreigner, guest, visitor, unknown, alien, new arrival, outlander
▷▷ **a stranger to something** UNACCUSTOMED TO, new to, unused to, ignorant of, inexperienced in, unversed in, unpractised in, unseasoned in
>> RELATED WORD *fear* xenophobia
strangle *verb* 1 THROTTLE, choke, asphyxiate, garrotte, strangulate, smother, suffocate
2 SUPPRESS, inhibit, subdue, stifle, gag, repress, overpower, quash, quell, quench
strap *noun* TIE, thong, leash, belt
▷ *verb* FASTEN, tie, secure, bind, lash, buckle, truss
strapping *adjective* WELL-BUILT, big, powerful, robust, hefty (*informal*), sturdy, stalwart, burly, husky (*informal*), hulking, beefy (*informal*), brawny, well set-up
stratagem *noun* TRICK, scheme, manoeuvre, plan, plot, device, intrigue, dodge, ploy, ruse, artifice, subterfuge, feint, wile
strategic *adjective* 1 TACTICAL, calculated, deliberate, planned, politic, diplomatic
2 CRUCIAL, important, key, vital, critical, decisive, cardinal
strategy *noun* 1 POLICY, procedure, planning, programme, approach, scheme, manoeuvring, grand design
2 PLAN, approach, scheme, manoeuvring, grand design
stratum *noun* 1 CLASS, group, level, station, estate, rank, grade, category, bracket, caste
2 LAYER, level, seam, table, bed, vein, tier, stratification, lode

The word *strata* is the plural form of *stratum*, and should not be used as if it is a singular form: so you would say *this stratum of society is often disregarded*, or *these strata of society are often disregarded*, but not *this strata of society is often disregarded*

stray *verb* 1 WANDER, roam, go astray, range, drift, meander, rove, straggle, lose your way, be

abandoned *or* lost
2 DRIFT, wander, roam, meander, rove
3 DIGRESS, diverge, deviate, ramble, get sidetracked, go off at a tangent, get off the point
▷ *adjective* 1 LOST, abandoned, homeless, roaming, vagrant
2 RANDOM, chance, freak, accidental, odd, scattered, erratic, scattershot

streak *noun* 1 BAND, line, strip, stroke, layer, slash, vein, stripe, smear
2 TRACE, touch, element, strain, dash, vein
▷ *verb* 1 FLECK, smear, daub, band, slash, stripe, striate
2 SPEED, fly, tear, sweep, flash, barrel (along) (*informal, chiefly US & Canad*), whistle, sprint, dart, zoom, whizz (*informal*), hurtle, burn rubber (*informal*), move like greased lightning (*informal*)

stream *noun* 1 RIVER, brook, creek (*US*), burn (*Scot*), beck, tributary, bayou, rivulet, rill, freshet
2 FLOW, current, rush, run, course, drift, surge, tide, torrent, outpouring, tideway
3 SUCCESSION, series, flood, chain, battery, volley, avalanche, barrage, torrent
▷ *verb* 1 FLOW, run, pour, course, issue, flood, shed, spill, emit, glide, cascade, gush, spout
2 RUSH, fly, speed, tear, flood, pour

streamer *noun* BANNER, flag, pennant, standard, colours, ribbon, ensign, pennon

streamlined *adjective* EFFICIENT, organized, modernized, rationalized, smooth, slick, sleek, well-run, time-saving, smooth-running

street *noun* ROAD, lane, avenue, terrace, row, boulevard, roadway, thoroughfare
▷▷ **up one's street** (*informal*) TO ONE'S LIKING, to one's taste, one's cup of tea (*informal*), pleasing, familiar, suitable, acceptable, compatible, congenial

strength *noun* 1 MIGHT, muscle, brawn, sinew, brawniness
<< OPPOSITE weakness
2 WILL, spirit, resolution, resolve, courage, character, nerve, determination, pluck, stamina, grit, backbone, fortitude, toughness, tenacity, willpower, mettle, firmness, strength of character, steadfastness, moral fibre
3 HEALTH, fitness, vigour, lustiness
4 MAINSTAY, anchor, tower of strength, security, succour
5 TOUGHNESS, soundness, robustness, sturdiness, stoutness
6 FORCE, power, intensity, energy, vehemence, intenseness
<< OPPOSITE weakness
7 POTENCY, effectiveness, concentration, efficacy
8 STRONG POINT, skill, asset, advantage, talent, forte, speciality, aptitude
<< OPPOSITE failing

strengthen *verb* 1 FORTIFY, encourage, harden, toughen, consolidate, stiffen, hearten, gee up, brace up, give new energy to
<< OPPOSITE weaken
2 REINFORCE, support, confirm, establish, justify, enhance, intensify, bolster, substantiate, buttress, corroborate, give a boost to
3 BOLSTER, harden, reinforce, give a boost to
4 HEIGHTEN, intensify
5 MAKE STRONGER, build up, invigorate, restore, nourish, rejuvenate, give strength to
6 SUPPORT, brace, steel, reinforce, consolidate, harden, bolster, augment, buttress
7 BECOME STRONGER, intensify, heighten, gain strength

strenuous *adjective* 1 DEMANDING, hard, tough, exhausting, taxing, uphill, arduous, laborious, Herculean, tough going, toilsome, unrelaxing
<< OPPOSITE easy
2 TIRELESS, determined, zealous, strong, earnest, spirited, active, eager, bold, persistent, vigorous, energetic, resolute

stress *verb* 1 EMPHASIZE, highlight, underline, repeat, draw attention to, dwell on, underscore, accentuate, point up, rub in, harp on, belabour
2 PLACE THE EMPHASIS ON, emphasize, give emphasis to, place the accent on, lay emphasis upon
▷ *noun* 1 EMPHASIS, importance, significance, force, weight, urgency
2 STRAIN, pressure, worry, tension, burden, anxiety, trauma, oppression, hassle (*informal*), nervous tension
3 ACCENT, beat, emphasis, accentuation, ictus

stressful *adjective* WORRYING, anxious, tense, taxing, demanding, tough, draining, exhausting, exacting, traumatic, agitating, nerve-racking

stretch *verb* 1 EXTEND, cover, spread, reach, unfold, put forth, unroll
2 LAST, continue, go on, extend, carry on, reach
3 EXPAND, lengthen, be elastic, be stretchy
4 PULL, distend, pull out of shape, strain, swell, tighten, rack, inflate, lengthen, draw out, elongate
5 HOLD OUT, offer, present, extend, proffer
▷ *noun* 1 EXPANSE, area, tract, spread, distance, sweep, extent
2 PERIOD, time, spell, stint, run, term, bit, space

strew *verb* SCATTER, spread, litter, toss, sprinkle, disperse, bestrew

stricken *adjective* AFFECTED, hit, afflicted,

struck, injured, struck down, smitten, laid low

strict *adjective* 1 SEVERE, harsh, stern, firm, rigid, rigorous, stringent, austere
<< OPPOSITE easy-going
2 STERN, firm, severe, harsh, authoritarian, austere, no-nonsense
3 EXACT, accurate, precise, close, true, particular, religious, faithful, meticulous, scrupulous
4 DEVOUT, religious, orthodox, pious, pure, reverent, prayerful
5 ABSOLUTE, complete, total, perfect, utter

stricture *noun* CRITICISM, censure, stick (*slang*), blame, rebuke, flak (*informal*), bad press, animadversion

strident *adjective* HARSH, jarring, grating, clashing, screeching, raucous, shrill, rasping, jangling, discordant, clamorous, unmusical, stridulant, stridulous
<< OPPOSITE soft

strife *noun* CONFLICT, battle, struggle, row, clash, clashes, contest, controversy, combat, warfare, rivalry, contention, quarrel, friction, squabbling, wrangling, bickering, animosity, discord, dissension

strike *noun* WALKOUT, industrial action, mutiny, revolt
▷ *verb* 1 WALK OUT, take industrial action, down tools, revolt, mutiny
2 HIT, smack, thump, pound, beat, box, knock, punch, hammer, deck (*slang*), slap, sock (*slang*), chin (*slang*), buffet, clout (*informal*), cuff, clump (*slang*), swipe, clobber (*slang*), smite, wallop (*informal*), lambast(e), lay a finger on (*informal*), lay one on (*slang*), beat *or* knock seven bells out of (*informal*)
3 DRIVE, propel, force, hit, smack, wallop (*informal*)
4 COLLIDE WITH, hit, run into, bump into, touch, smash into, come into contact with, knock into, be in collision with
5 KNOCK, bang, smack, thump, beat, smite
6 AFFECT, move, hit, touch, devastate, overwhelm, leave a mark on, make an impact *or* impression on
7 ATTACK, assault someone, fall upon someone, set upon someone, lay into someone (*informal*)
8 OCCUR TO, hit, come to, register (*informal*), come to the mind of, dawn on *or* upon
9 SEEM TO, appear to, look to, give the impression to
10 MOVE, touch, impress, hit, affect, overcome, stir, disturb, perturb, make an impact on
11 ACHIEVE, arrive at, attain, reach, effect, arrange
12 *sometimes with* **upon** DISCOVER, find, come upon *or* across, reach, encounter, turn up, uncover, unearth, hit upon, light upon, happen *or* chance upon, stumble upon *or* across
▷▷ **strike out** SET OUT, set off, start out, sally forth
▷▷ **strike someone down** KILL, destroy, slay, ruin, afflict, smite, bring low, deal a deathblow to
▷▷ **strike something out, off** *or* **through** SCORE OUT, delete, cross out, remove, cancel, erase, excise, efface, expunge

striking *adjective* 1 DISTINCT, noticeable, conspicuous, clear, obvious, evident, manifest, unmistakable, observable, perceptible, appreciable
2 IMPRESSIVE, dramatic, stunning (*informal*), wonderful, extraordinary, outstanding, astonishing, memorable, dazzling, noticeable, conspicuous, drop-dead (*slang*), out of the ordinary, forcible, jaw-dropping
<< OPPOSITE unimpressive

string *noun* 1 CORD, yarn, twine, strand, fibre, thread
2 SERIES, line, row, file, sequence, queue, succession, procession
3 SEQUENCE, run, series, chain, succession, streak
▷ *plural noun* 1 STRINGED INSTRUMENTS
2 CONDITIONS, catches (*informal*), provisos, stipulations, requirements, riders, obligations, qualifications, complications, prerequisites
▷ *verb* HANG, stretch, suspend, sling, thread, loop, festoon
▷▷ **string along with someone** ACCOMPANY, go with, go along with, chaperon
▷▷ **string someone along** DECEIVE, fool, take (someone) for a ride (*informal*), kid (*informal*), bluff, hoax, dupe, put one over on (someone) (*informal*), play fast and loose with (someone) (*informal*), play (someone) false

stringent *adjective* STRICT, tough, rigorous, demanding, binding, tight, severe, exacting, rigid, inflexible
<< OPPOSITE lax

stringy *adjective* FIBROUS, tough, chewy, sinewy, gristly, wiry

strip¹ *verb* 1 UNDRESS, disrobe, unclothe, uncover yourself
2 PLUNDER, rob, loot, empty, sack, deprive, ransack, pillage, divest, denude

strip² *noun* 1 PIECE, shred, bit, band, slip, belt, tongue, ribbon, fillet, swathe
2 STRETCH, area, tract, expanse, extent

striped *adjective* BANDED, stripy, barred, striated

stripy *or* **stripey** *adjective* BANDED, striped, streaky

strive *verb* TRY, labour, struggle, fight, attempt, compete, strain, contend, endeavour, go for it (*informal*), try hard, toil, make every effort, go all out (*informal*), bend over backwards (*informal*), do your best, go for broke (*slang*), leave no stone unturned, bust a gut (*informal*), do all you can, give it your best shot (*informal*), jump through hoops (*informal*), break your neck (*informal*), exert yourself, make an all-out effort (*informal*), knock yourself out (*informal*), do your utmost, do your damnedest (*informal*), give it your all (*informal*), rupture yourself (*informal*)

stroke *verb* CARESS, rub, fondle, pat, pet

▷ *noun* 1 APOPLEXY, fit, seizure, attack, shock, collapse

2 MARK, line, slash

3 MOVEMENT, action, motion

4 BLOW, hit, knock, pat, rap, thump, swipe

5 FEAT, move, achievement, accomplishment, movement

stroll *verb* WALK, ramble, amble, wander, promenade, saunter, stooge (*slang*), take a turn, toddle, make your way, mooch (*slang*), mosey (*informal*), stretch your legs

▷ *noun* WALK, promenade, turn, airing, constitutional, excursion, ramble, breath of air

strong *adjective* 1 POWERFUL, muscular, tough, capable, athletic, strapping, hardy, sturdy, stout, stalwart, burly, beefy (*informal*), virile, Herculean, sinewy, brawny

<< OPPOSITE weak

2 FIT, sound, healthy, robust, hale, in good shape, in good condition, lusty, fighting fit, fit as a fiddle

3 SELF-CONFIDENT, determined, tough, brave, aggressive, courageous, high-powered, forceful, resilient, feisty (*informal, chiefly US & Canad*), resolute, resourceful, tenacious, plucky, hard-nosed (*informal*), steadfast, unyielding, hard as nails, self-assertive, stouthearted, firm in spirit

<< OPPOSITE timid

4 DURABLE, substantial, sturdy, reinforced, heavy-duty, well-built, well-armed, hard-wearing, well-protected, on a firm foundation

<< OPPOSITE flimsy

5 FORCEFUL, powerful, intense, vigorous

6 EXTREME, radical, drastic, strict, harsh, rigid, forceful, uncompromising, Draconian, unbending

7 DECISIVE, firm, forceful, decided, determined, severe, resolute, incisive

8 PERSUASIVE, convincing, compelling, telling, great, clear, sound, effective, urgent, formidable, potent, well-established, clear-cut, overpowering, weighty, well-founded, redoubtable, trenchant, cogent

9 PUNGENT, powerful, concentrated, pure, undiluted

<< OPPOSITE bland

10 HIGHLY-FLAVOURED, hot, spicy, piquant, biting, sharp, heady, overpowering, intoxicating, highly-seasoned

11 KEEN, deep, acute, eager, fervent, zealous, vehement

12 INTENSE, deep, passionate, ardent, fierce, profound, forceful, fervent, deep-rooted, vehement, fervid

13 STAUNCH, firm, keen, dedicated, fierce, ardent, eager, enthusiastic, passionate, fervent

14 DISTINCT, marked, clear, unmistakable

<< OPPOSITE slight

15 BRIGHT, brilliant, dazzling, loud, bold, stark, glaring

<< OPPOSITE dull

strong-arm *modifier* (*informal*) BULLYING, threatening, aggressive, violent, terror, forceful, high-pressure, coercive, terrorizing, thuggish

stronghold *noun* 1 BASTION, fortress, bulwark, fastness

2 REFUGE, haven, retreat, sanctuary, hide-out, bolt hole

strong-minded *adjective* DETERMINED, resolute, strong-willed, firm, independent, uncompromising, iron-willed, unbending

strong point *noun* FORTE, strength, speciality, advantage, asset, strong suit, métier, long suit (*informal*)

stroppy *adjective* (*Brit informal*) AWKWARD, difficult, obstreperous, destructive, perverse, unhelpful, cantankerous, bloody-minded (*Brit informal*), quarrelsome, litigious, uncooperative

structure *noun* 1 ARRANGEMENT, form, make-up, make, design, organization, construction, fabric, formation, configuration, conformation, interrelation of parts

2 BUILDING, construction, erection, edifice, pile

▷ *verb* ARRANGE, organize, design, shape, build up, assemble, put together

struggle *verb* 1 STRIVE, labour, toil, work, strain, go for it (*informal*), make every effort, go all out (*informal*), bend over backwards (*informal*), go for broke (*slang*), bust a gut (*informal*), give it your best shot (*informal*), break your neck (*informal*), exert yourself, make an all-out effort (*informal*), work like a Trojan, knock yourself out (*informal*), do your damnedest (*informal*), give it your all (*informal*), rupture yourself (*informal*)

2 FIGHT, battle, wrestle, grapple, compete, contend, scuffle, lock horns

3 HAVE TROUBLE, have problems, have difficulties, fight, come unstuck

▷ *noun* 1 PROBLEM, battle, effort, trial, strain

2 EFFORT, labour, toil, work, grind (*informal*), pains, scramble, long haul, exertion

3 FIGHT, battle, conflict, clash, contest, encounter, brush, combat, hostilities, strife, skirmish, tussle, biffo (*Austral slang*)

strut *verb* SWAGGER, parade, stalk, peacock,

prance

stub *noun* 1 BUTT, end, stump, tail, remnant, tail end, fag end (*informal*), dog-end (*informal*)
2 COUNTERFOIL

stubborn *adjective* OBSTINATE, dogged, inflexible, fixed, persistent, intractable, wilful, tenacious, recalcitrant, unyielding, headstrong, unmanageable, unbending, obdurate, stiff-necked, unshakeable, self-willed, refractory, pig-headed, bull-headed, mulish, cross-grained, contumacious
<< OPPOSITE compliant

stubby *adjective* STUMPY, short, squat, stocky, chunky, dumpy, thickset, fubsy (*archaic* or *dialect*)

stuck *adjective* 1 FASTENED, fast, fixed, joined, glued, cemented
2 TRAPPED, caught, ensnared
3 BURDENED, saddled, lumbered, landed, loaded, encumbered
4 (*informal*) BAFFLED, stumped, at a loss, beaten, nonplussed, at a standstill, bereft of ideas, up against a brick wall (*informal*), at your wits' end
▷▷ **stuck on something** *or* **someone** (*Slang*) INFATUATED WITH, obsessed with, keen on, enthusiastic about, mad about, wild about (*informal*), hung up on (*slang*), crazy about, for, *or* over (*informal*)
▷▷ **get stuck into something** (*informal*) SET ABOUT, tackle, get down to, make a start on, take the bit between your teeth

stuck-up *adjective* (*informal*) SNOBBISH, arrogant, conceited, proud, patronizing, condescending, snooty (*informal*), haughty, uppity (*informal*), high and mighty (*informal*), toffee-nosed (*slang, chiefly Brit*), hoity-toity (*informal*), swollen-headed, bigheaded (*informal*), uppish (*Brit informal*)

student *noun* 1 UNDERGRADUATE, scholar
2 PUPIL, scholar, schoolchild, schoolboy *or* schoolgirl
3 LEARNER, observer, trainee, apprentice, disciple

studied *adjective* PLANNED, calculated, deliberate, conscious, intentional, wilful, purposeful, premeditated, well-considered
<< OPPOSITE unplanned

studio *noun* WORKSHOP, shop, workroom, atelier

studious *adjective* 1 SCHOLARLY, academic, intellectual, serious, earnest, hard-working, thoughtful, reflective, diligent, meditative, bookish, assiduous, sedulous
<< OPPOSITE unacademic
2 INTENT, attentive, watchful, listening, concentrating, careful, regardful
<< OPPOSITE careless
3 DELIBERATE, planned, conscious, calculated, considered, studied, designed, thoughtful, intentional, wilful, purposeful, premeditated, prearranged

study *verb* 1 LEARN, cram (*informal*), swot (up) (*Brit informal*), read up, hammer away at, bone up on (*informal*), burn the midnight oil, mug up (*Brit slang*)
2 EXAMINE, survey, look at, scrutinize, peruse
3 CONTEMPLATE, read, examine, consider, go into, con (*archaic*), pore over, apply yourself (to)
▷ *noun* 1 EXAMINATION, investigation, analysis, consideration, inspection, scrutiny, contemplation, perusal, cogitation
2 PIECE OF RESEARCH, survey, report, paper, review, article, inquiry, investigation
3 LEARNING, lessons, school work, academic work, reading, research, cramming (*informal*), swotting (*Brit informal*), book work
4 OFFICE, room, studio, workplace, den, place of work, workroom

stuff *noun* 1 THINGS, gear, possessions, effects, materials, equipment, objects, tackle, kit, junk, luggage, belongings, trappings, bits and pieces, paraphernalia, clobber (*Brit slang*), impedimenta, goods and chattels
2 NONSENSE, rubbish, rot, trash, bunk (*informal*), foolishness, humbug, twaddle, tripe (*informal*), baloney (*informal*), verbiage, claptrap (*informal*), bunkum, poppycock (*informal*), balderdash, pants (*slang*), bosh (*informal*), stuff and nonsense, tommyrot, bizzo (*Austral slang*), bull's wool (*Austral & NZ slang*)
3 SUBSTANCE, material, essence, matter, staple, pith, quintessence
▷ *verb* 1 SHOVE, force, push, squeeze, jam, ram, wedge, compress, stow
2 CRAM, fill, pack, load, crowd

stuffing *noun* 1 FILLING, forcemeat
2 WADDING, filling, packing, quilting, kapok

stuffy *adjective* 1 STAID, conventional, dull, old-fashioned, deadly, dreary, pompous, formal, prim, stilted, musty, stodgy, uninteresting, humourless, fusty, strait-laced, priggish, as dry as dust, old-fogeyish, niminy-piminy, prim and proper
2 AIRLESS, stifling, oppressive, close, heavy, stale, suffocating, sultry, fetid, muggy, unventilated, fuggy, frowsty
<< OPPOSITE airy

stumble *verb* 1 TRIP, fall, slip, reel, stagger, falter, flounder, lurch, come a cropper (*informal*), lose your balance, blunder about
2 TOTTER, reel, stagger, blunder, falter, lurch, wobble, teeter
3 FALTER, hesitate, stammer, stutter, fluff (*informal*)
▷▷ **stumble across, on** *or* **upon something** *or* **someone** DISCOVER, find, come across, encounter, run across, chance upon, happen upon, light upon, blunder upon

stumbling block *noun* OBSTACLE, difficulty, bar, barrier, hurdle, hazard, snag, uphill (*S African*), obstruction, impediment, hindrance

stump *noun* TAIL END, end, remnant, remainder

▷ *verb* 1 BAFFLE, confuse, puzzle, snooker, foil, bewilder, confound, perplex, mystify, outwit, stymie, flummox, bring (someone) up short, dumbfound, nonplus

2 STAMP, clump, stomp (*informal*), trudge, plod, clomp

▷▷ **stump something up** (*Brit informal*) (with money or a sum of money as object) PAY, fork out (*slang*), shell out (*informal*), contribute, hand over, donate, chip in (*informal*), cough up (*informal*), come across with (*informal*)

stumped *adjective* BAFFLED, perplexed, at a loss, floored (*informal*), at sea, stymied, nonplussed, flummoxed, brought to a standstill, uncertain which way to turn, at your wits' end

stun *verb* 1 OVERCOME, shock, amaze, confuse, astonish, stagger, bewilder, astound, overpower, confound, stupefy, strike (someone) dumb, knock (someone) for six (*informal*), dumbfound, flabbergast (*informal*), hit (someone) like a ton of bricks (*informal*), take (someone's) breath away

2 DAZE, knock out, stupefy, numb, benumb

stung *adjective* HURT, wounded, angered, roused, incensed, exasperated, resentful, nettled, goaded, piqued

stunned *adjective* STAGGERED, shocked, devastated, numb, astounded, bowled over (*informal*), gobsmacked (*Brit slang*), dumbfounded, flabbergasted (*informal*), struck dumb, at a loss for words

stunner *noun* (*informal*) BEAUTY, looker (*informal, chiefly US*), lovely (*slang*), dish (*informal*), sensation, honey (*informal*), good-looker, dazzler, peach (*informal*), wow (*slang, chiefly US*), dolly (*slang*), knockout (*informal*), heart-throb, charmer, eyeful (*informal*), smasher (*informal*), humdinger (*slang*), glamour puss, beaut (*Austral & NZ slang*)

stunning *adjective* (*informal*) WONDERFUL, beautiful, impressive, great (*informal*), striking, brilliant, dramatic, lovely, remarkable, smashing (*informal*), heavenly, devastating (*informal*), spectacular, marvellous, splendid, gorgeous, dazzling, sensational (*informal*), drop-dead (*slang*), ravishing, out of this world (*informal*), jaw-dropping

<< OPPOSITE unimpressive

stunt *noun* FEAT, act, trick, exploit, deed, tour de force (*French*)

stunted *adjective* UNDERSIZED, dwarfed, little, small, tiny, diminutive, dwarfish

stupefy *verb* ASTOUND, shock, amaze, stun, stagger, bewilder, numb, daze, confound, knock senseless, dumbfound

stupendous *adjective* 1 WONDERFUL, brilliant, amazing, stunning (*informal*), superb, overwhelming, fantastic (*informal*), tremendous (*informal*), fabulous (*informal*), surprising, staggering, marvellous, sensational (*informal*), breathtaking, phenomenal, astounding, prodigious, wondrous (*archaic or literary*), mind-boggling (*informal*), out of this world (*informal*), mind-blowing (*informal*), jaw-dropping, surpassing belief

<< OPPOSITE unremarkable

2 HUGE, vast, enormous, mega (*slang*), gigantic, colossal

<< OPPOSITE tiny

stupid *adjective* 1 UNINTELLIGENT, thick, dumb (*informal*), simple, slow, dull, dim, dense, sluggish, deficient, crass, gullible, simple-minded, dozy (*Brit informal*), witless, stolid, dopey (*informal*), moronic, obtuse, brainless, cretinous, half-witted, slow on the uptake (*informal*), braindead (*informal*), dumb-ass (*slang*), doltish, dead from the neck up, thickheaded, slow-witted, Boeotian, thick as mince (*Scot informal*), woodenheaded (*informal*)

<< OPPOSITE intelligent

2 SILLY, foolish, daft (*informal*), rash, trivial, ludicrous, meaningless, irresponsible, pointless, futile, senseless, mindless, laughable, short-sighted, ill-advised, idiotic, fatuous, nonsensical, half-baked (*informal*), inane, crackpot (*informal*), unthinking, puerile, unintelligent, asinine, imbecilic, crackbrained

<< OPPOSITE sensible

3 SENSELESS, dazed, groggy, punch-drunk, insensate, semiconscious, into a daze

stupidity *noun* 1 LACK OF INTELLIGENCE, imbecility, obtuseness, simplicity, thickness, slowness, dullness, dimness, dumbness (*informal*), feeble-mindedness, lack of brain, denseness, brainlessness, doziness (*Brit informal*), asininity, dopiness (*slang*), thickheadedness

2 SILLINESS, folly, foolishness, idiocy, madness, absurdity, futility, lunacy, irresponsibility, pointlessness, inanity, rashness, impracticality, foolhardiness, senselessness, bêtise (*rare*), ludicrousness, puerility, fatuousness, fatuity

stupor *noun* DAZE, numbness, unconsciousness, trance, coma, inertia, lethargy, torpor, stupefaction, insensibility

sturdy *adjective* 1 ROBUST, hardy, vigorous, powerful, athletic, muscular, stalwart, staunch, hearty, lusty, brawny, thickset

<< OPPOSITE puny

2 SUBSTANTIAL, secure, solid, durable, well-

made, well-built, built to last
<< OPPOSITE flimsy

stutter *noun* STAMMER, faltering, speech impediment, speech defect, hesitance
▷ *verb* STAMMER, stumble, falter, hesitate, splutter, speak haltingly

style *noun* 1 MANNER, way, method, approach, technique, custom, mode
2 ELEGANCE, taste, chic, flair, polish, grace, dash, sophistication, refinement, panache, élan, cosmopolitanism, savoir-faire, smartness, urbanity, stylishness, bon ton (*French*), fashionableness, dressiness (*informal*)
3 DESIGN, form, cut
4 TYPE, sort, kind, spirit, pattern, variety, appearance, tone, strain, category, characteristic, genre, tenor
5 FASHION, trend, mode, vogue, rage
6 LUXURY, ease, comfort, elegance, grandeur, affluence, gracious living
7 MODE OF EXPRESSION, phrasing, turn of phrase, wording, treatment, expression, vein, diction, phraseology
▷ *verb* 1 DESIGN, cut, tailor, fashion, shape, arrange, adapt
2 CALL, name, term, address, label, entitle, dub, designate, christen, denominate

stylish *adjective* SMART, chic, polished, fashionable, trendy (*Brit informal*), classy (*slang*), in fashion, snappy, in vogue, dapper, natty (*informal*), snazzy (*informal*), modish, well turned-out, dressy (*informal*), à la mode, voguish, schmick (*Austral informal*)
<< OPPOSITE scruffy

stymie *verb* FRUSTRATE, defeat, foil, thwart, puzzle, stump, snooker, hinder, confound, mystify, balk, flummox, throw a spanner in the works (*Brit informal*), nonplus, spike (someone's) guns

suave *adjective* SMOOTH, charming, urbane, debonair, worldly, cool (*informal*), sophisticated, polite, gracious, agreeable, courteous, affable, smooth-tongued

subconscious *noun* MIND, psyche
▷ *adjective* HIDDEN, inner, suppressed, repressed, intuitive, latent, innermost, subliminal
<< OPPOSITE conscious

subdue *verb* 1 OVERCOME, defeat, master, break, control, discipline, crush, humble, put down, conquer, tame, overpower, overrun, trample, quell, triumph over, get the better of, vanquish, beat down, get under control, get the upper hand over, gain ascendancy over
2 MODERATE, control, check, suppress, soften, repress, mellow, tone down, quieten down
<< OPPOSITE arouse

subdued *adjective* 1 QUIET, serious, sober, sad, grave, restrained, repressed, solemn, chastened, dejected, downcast, crestfallen, repentant, down in the mouth, sadder and wiser, out of spirits
<< OPPOSITE lively
2 HUSHED, soft, quiet, whispered, murmured, muted
<< OPPOSITE loud
3 DIM, soft, subtle, muted, shaded, low-key, understated, toned down, unobtrusive
<< OPPOSITE bright

subject *noun* 1 TOPIC, question, issue, matter, point, business, affair, object, theme, substance, subject matter, field of inquiry *or* reference
2 BRANCH OF STUDY, area, field, discipline, speciality, branch of knowledge
3 PARTICIPANT, case, patient, victim, client, guinea pig (*informal*)
4 CITIZEN, resident, native, inhabitant, national
5 DEPENDANT, subordinate, vassal, liegeman
▷ *adjective* SUBORDINATE, dependent, satellite, inferior, captive, obedient, enslaved, submissive, subservient, subjugated
▷ *verb* PUT THROUGH, expose, submit, lay open, make liable
▷▷ **subject to** 1 LIABLE TO, open to, exposed to, vulnerable to, prone to, susceptible to, disposed to
2 BOUND BY, under the control of, constrained by
3 DEPENDENT ON, contingent on, controlled by, conditional on

subjective *adjective* PERSONAL, emotional, prejudiced, biased, instinctive, intuitive, idiosyncratic, nonobjective
<< OPPOSITE objective

subjugate *verb* CONQUER, master, overcome, defeat, crush, suppress, put down, overthrow, tame, lick (*informal*), subdue, overpower, quell, rule over, enslave, vanquish, hold sway over, bring to heel, bring (someone) to his knees, bring under the yoke

sublimate *verb* CHANNEL, transfer, divert, redirect, turn

sublime *adjective* NOBLE, magnificent, glorious, high, great, grand, imposing, elevated, eminent, majestic, lofty, exalted, transcendent
<< OPPOSITE lowly

subliminal *adjective* SUBCONSCIOUS, unconscious

submerge *verb* 1 FLOOD, swamp, engulf, drown, overflow, inundate, deluge
2 IMMERSE, plunge, dip, duck, dunk
3 SINK, plunge, go under water
4 OVERWHELM, swamp, engulf, overload, inundate, deluge, snow under, overburden

submerged *adjective* IMMERSED, sunk, underwater, drowned, submarine, sunken, undersea, subaqueous, submersed, subaquatic

submission *noun* 1 SURRENDER, yielding, giving in, cave-in (*informal*), capitulation, acquiescence
2 PRESENTATION, submitting, handing in, entry, tendering
3 PROPOSAL, argument, contention
4 COMPLIANCE, obedience, submissiveness, meekness, resignation, deference, passivity, docility, tractability, unassertiveness

submissive *adjective* MEEK, passive, obedient, compliant, patient, resigned, yielding, accommodating, humble, subdued, lowly, abject, amenable, docile, dutiful, ingratiating, malleable, deferential, pliant, obsequious, uncomplaining, tractable, acquiescent, biddable, unresisting, bootlicking (*informal*), obeisant
<< OPPOSITE obstinate

submit *verb* 1 SURRENDER, yield, give in, agree, bend, bow, endure, tolerate, comply, put up with (*informal*), succumb, defer, stoop, cave in (*informal*), capitulate, accede, acquiesce, toe the line, knuckle under, resign yourself, lay down arms, hoist the white flag, throw in the sponge
2 PRESENT, hand in, tender, put forward, table, commit, refer, proffer
3 SUGGEST, claim, argue, propose, state, put, move, advance, volunteer, assert, contend, propound

subordinate *noun* INFERIOR, junior, assistant, aide, second, attendant, dependant, underling, subaltern
<< OPPOSITE superior
▷ *adjective* 1 INFERIOR, lesser, lower, junior, subject, minor, secondary, dependent, subservient
<< OPPOSITE superior
2 SUBSIDIARY, supplementary, auxiliary, ancillary

subordination *noun* INFERIORITY, servitude, subjection, inferior *or* secondary status

subscribe to *verb* 1 SUPPORT, agree with, advocate, consent to, endorse, countenance, acquiesce with
2 CONTRIBUTE TO, give to, donate to, chip in to (*informal*)

subscription *noun* (*Chiefly Brit*) MEMBERSHIP FEE, charge, dues, annual payment

subsequent *adjective* FOLLOWING, later, succeeding, after, successive, ensuing, consequent
<< OPPOSITE previous

subsequently *adverb* LATER, afterwards, in the end, consequently, in the aftermath (of), at a later date

subservient *adjective* 1 SERVILE, submissive, deferential, subject, inferior, abject, sycophantic, slavish, obsequious, truckling, bootlicking (*informal*)
<< OPPOSITE domineering
2 SUBORDINATE, subsidiary, accessory, auxiliary, conducive, ancillary

subside *verb* 1 DECREASE, diminish, lessen, ease, moderate, dwindle, wane, recede, ebb, abate, let up, peter out, slacken, melt away, quieten, level off, de-escalate
<< OPPOSITE increase
2 COLLAPSE, sink, cave in, drop, lower, settle
3 DROP, fall, decline, ebb, descend

subsidence *noun* SINKING, settling, collapse, settlement

subsidiary *noun* BRANCH, division, section, office, department, wing, subdivision, subsection, local office
▷ *adjective* SECONDARY, lesser, subordinate, minor, supplementary, auxiliary, supplemental, contributory, ancillary, subservient
<< OPPOSITE main

subsidize *verb* FUND, finance, support, promote, sponsor, underwrite, put up the money for

subsidy *noun* AID, help, support, grant, contribution, assistance, allowance, financial aid, stipend, subvention

subsist *verb* STAY ALIVE, survive, keep going, make ends meet, last, live, continue, exist, endure, eke out an existence, keep your head above water, sustain yourself

subsistence *noun* LIVING, maintenance, upkeep, keep, support, existence, survival, livelihood

substance *noun* 1 MATERIAL, body, stuff, element, fabric, texture
2 IMPORTANCE, significance, concreteness
3 MEANING, main point, gist, matter, subject, theme, import, significance, essence, pith, burden, sum and substance
4 TRUTH, fact, reality, certainty, validity, authenticity, verity, verisimilitude
5 WEALTH, means, property, assets, resources, estate, affluence

substandard *adjective* INFERIOR, inadequate, unacceptable, damaged, imperfect, second-rate, shoddy

substantial *adjective* 1 BIG, significant, considerable, goodly, large, important, generous, worthwhile, tidy (*informal*), ample, sizable *or* sizeable
<< OPPOSITE small
2 SOLID, sound, sturdy, strong, firm, massive, hefty, durable, bulky, well-built
<< OPPOSITE insubstantial

substantially *adverb* 1 CONSIDERABLY, significantly, very much, greatly, seriously (*informal*), remarkably, markedly, noticeably,

appreciably
2 ESSENTIALLY, largely, mainly, materially, in the main, in essence, to a large extent, in substance, in essentials

substantiate *verb* SUPPORT, prove, confirm, establish, affirm, verify, validate, bear out, corroborate, attest to, authenticate
<< OPPOSITE disprove

substitute *verb* 1 REPLACE, exchange, swap, change, switch, commute, interchange
2 *with* **for** STAND IN FOR, cover for, take over from, relieve, act for, double for, fill in for, hold the fort for, be in place of, deputize for
▷ *noun* REPLACEMENT, reserve, equivalent, surrogate, deputy, relief, representative, sub, temporary, stand-by, makeshift, proxy, temp (*informal*), expedient, locum, depute (*Scot*), stopgap, locum tenens

> Although *substitute* and *replace* have the same meaning, the structures they are used in are different. You replace A *with* B, while you substitute B *for* A. Accordingly, *he replaced the worn tyre with a new one*, and *he substituted a new tyre for the worn one* are both correct ways of saying the same thing

substitution *noun* REPLACEMENT, exchange, switch, swap, change, interchange

subterfuge *noun* TRICK, dodge, ploy, shift, manoeuvre, deception, evasion, pretence, pretext, ruse, artifice, duplicity, stratagem, deviousness, machination

subtle *adjective* 1 FAINT, slight, implied, delicate, indirect, understated, insinuated
<< OPPOSITE obvious
2 CRAFTY, cunning, sly, designing, scheming, intriguing, shrewd, ingenious, astute, devious, wily, artful, Machiavellian
<< OPPOSITE straightforward
3 MUTED, soft, subdued, low-key, toned down
4 FINE, minute, narrow, tenuous, hair-splitting

subtlety *noun* 1 FINE POINT, refinement, nicety, sophistication, delicacy, intricacy, discernment
2 SKILL, acumen, astuteness, ingenuity, guile, cleverness, deviousness, sagacity, acuteness, craftiness, artfulness, slyness, wiliness
3 SENSITIVITY, diplomacy, discretion, delicacy, understanding, skill, consideration, judgment, perception, finesse, thoughtfulness, discernment, savoir-faire, adroitness

subtract *verb* TAKE AWAY, take off, deduct, remove, withdraw, diminish, take from, detract
<< OPPOSITE add

suburb *noun* RESIDENTIAL AREA, neighbourhood, outskirts, precincts, suburbia, environs, purlieus, dormitory area (*Brit*), faubourgs

subversive *adjective* SEDITIOUS, inflammatory, incendiary, underground, undermining, destructive, overthrowing, riotous, insurrectionary, treasonous, perversive
▷ *noun* DISSIDENT, terrorist, saboteur, insurrectionary, quisling, fifth columnist, deviationist, seditionary, seditionist

subvert *verb* 1 OVERTURN, destroy, undermine, upset, ruin, wreck, demolish, sabotage
2 CORRUPT, pervert, deprave, poison, contaminate, confound, debase, demoralize, vitiate

succeed *verb* 1 TRIUMPH, win, prevail
2 WORK OUT, work, be successful, come off (*informal*), do the trick (*informal*), turn out well, go like a bomb (*Brit & NZ informal*), go down a bomb (*informal, chiefly Brit*), do the business (*informal*)
3 MAKE IT (*informal*), do well, be successful, arrive (*informal*), triumph, thrive, flourish, make good, prosper, cut it (*informal*), make the grade (*informal*), get to the top, crack it (*informal*), hit the jackpot (*informal*), bring home the bacon (*informal*), make your mark (*informal*), gain your end, carry all before you, do all right for yourself
<< OPPOSITE fail
4 TAKE OVER FROM, replace, assume the office of, fill (someone's) boots, step into (someone's) boots
5 *with* **to** TAKE OVER, assume, attain, acquire, come into, inherit, accede to, come into possession of
6 FOLLOW, come after, follow after, replace, be subsequent to, supervene
<< OPPOSITE precede

success *noun* 1 VICTORY, triumph, positive result, favourable outcome
<< OPPOSITE failure
2 PROSPERITY, fortune, luck, fame, eminence, ascendancy
3 HIT (*informal*), winner, smash (*informal*), triumph, sensation, wow (*slang*), best seller, market leader, smash hit (*informal*)
<< OPPOSITE flop (*informal*)
4 BIG NAME, star, hit (*informal*), somebody, celebrity, sensation, megastar (*informal*), V.I.P.
<< OPPOSITE nobody

successful *adjective* 1 TRIUMPHANT, victorious, lucky, fortunate
2 THRIVING, profitable, productive, paying, effective, rewarding, booming, efficient, flourishing, unbeaten, lucrative, favourable, fruitful, efficacious, moneymaking
<< OPPOSITE unprofitable
3 TOP, prosperous, acknowledged, wealthy,

out in front (*informal*), going places, at the top of the tree

successfully *adverb* WELL, favourably, in triumph, with flying colours, famously (*informal*), swimmingly, victoriously

succession *noun* 1 SERIES, run, sequence, course, order, train, flow, chain, cycle, procession, continuation, progression
2 TAKING OVER, assumption, inheritance, elevation, accession, entering upon
▷▷ **in succession** ONE AFTER THE OTHER, running, successively, consecutively, on the trot (*informal*), one behind the other

successive *adjective* CONSECUTIVE, following, succeeding, in a row, in succession, sequent

succinct *adjective* BRIEF, to the point, concise, compact, summary, condensed, terse, laconic, pithy, gnomic, compendious, in a few well-chosen words
<< OPPOSITE rambling

succour *noun* HELP, support, aid, relief, comfort, assistance
▷ *verb* HELP, support, aid, encourage, nurse, comfort, foster, assist, relieve, minister to, befriend, render assistance to, give aid and encouragement to

succulent *adjective* JUICY, moist, luscious, rich, lush, mellow, mouthwatering

succumb *verb* 1 *often with* **to** SURRENDER (TO), yield (to), submit (to), give in (to), give way (to), go under (to), cave in (to) (*informal*), capitulate (to), knuckle under (to)
<< OPPOSITE beat
2 *with* **to** (with an illness as object) CATCH, fall victim to, fall ill with

suck *verb* 1 DRINK, sip, draw
2 TAKE, draw, pull, extract
▷▷ **suck up to someone** (*informal*) INGRATIATE YOURSELF WITH, play up to (*informal*), curry favour with, flatter, pander to, toady, butter up, keep in with (*informal*), fawn on, truckle, lick someone's boots, dance attendance on, get on the right side of, worm yourself into (someone's) favour

sucker *noun* (*Slang*) FOOL, mug (*Brit slang*), dupe, victim, butt, sap (*slang*), pushover (*slang*), sitting duck (*informal*), sitting target, putz (*US slang*), cat's paw, easy game *or* mark (*informal*), nerd *or* nurd (*slang*), dorba *or* dorb (*Austral slang*), bogan (*Austral slang*)

sudden *adjective* QUICK, rapid, unexpected, swift, hurried, abrupt, hasty, impulsive, unforeseen
<< OPPOSITE gradual

suddenly *adverb* ABRUPTLY, all of a sudden, all at once, unexpectedly, out of the blue (*informal*), without warning, on the spur of the moment

sue *verb* 1 (*Law*) TAKE (SOMEONE) TO COURT, prosecute, bring an action against (someone), charge, summon, indict, have the law on (someone) (*informal*), prefer charges against (someone), institute legal proceedings against (someone)
2 APPEAL FOR, plead, beg, petition, solicit, beseech, entreat, supplicate

suffer *verb* 1 BE IN PAIN, hurt, ache, be racked, have a bad time, go through a lot (*informal*), go through the mill (*informal*), feel wretched
2 BE AFFECTED, have trouble with, be afflicted, be troubled with
3 UNDERGO, experience, sustain, feel, bear, go through, endure
4 DETERIORATE, decline, get worse, fall off, be impaired
5 TOLERATE, stand, put up with (*informal*), support, bear, endure, hack (*Brit informal*), abide

suffering *noun* PAIN, torture, distress, agony, misery, ordeal, discomfort, torment, hardship, anguish, affliction, martyrdom

suffice *verb* BE ENOUGH, do, be sufficient, be adequate, answer, serve, content, satisfy, fill the bill (*informal*), meet requirements

sufficient *adjective* ADEQUATE, enough, ample, satisfactory, enow (*archaic*)
<< OPPOSITE insufficient

suffocate *verb* 1 CHOKE, stifle, smother, asphyxiate
2 BE CHOKED, be stifled, be smothered, be asphyxiated

suffuse *verb* SPREAD THROUGH *or* OVER, flood, infuse, cover, steep, bathe, mantle, pervade, permeate, imbue, overspread, transfuse

suggest *verb* 1 RECOMMEND, propose, advise, move, advocate, prescribe, put forward, offer a suggestion
2 INDICATE, lead you to believe
3 HINT AT, imply, insinuate, intimate, get at, drive at (*informal*)
4 BRING TO MIND, evoke, remind you of, connote, make you think of, put you in mind of

suggestion *noun* 1 RECOMMENDATION, proposal, proposition, plan, motion
2 HINT, implication, insinuation, intimation
3 TRACE, touch, hint, breath, indication, whisper, suspicion, intimation

suggestive *adjective* SMUTTY, rude, indecent, improper, blue, provocative, spicy (*informal*), racy, unseemly, titillating, risqué, bawdy, prurient, off colour, ribald, immodest, indelicate
▷▷ **suggestive of** REMINISCENT OF, indicative of, redolent of, evocative of

suit *noun* 1 OUTFIT, costume, ensemble, dress, clothing, habit
2 LAWSUIT, case, trial, proceeding, cause, action, prosecution, industrial tribunal
▷ *verb* 1 BE ACCEPTABLE TO, please, satisfy, do,

answer, gratify
2 AGREE WITH, become, match, go with, correspond with, conform to, befit, harmonize with
▷▷ **follow suit** COPY SOMEONE, emulate someone, accord with someone, take your cue from someone, run with the herd

suitability *noun* APPROPRIATENESS, fitness, rightness, aptness

suitable *adjective* 1 APPROPRIATE, right, fitting, fit, suited, acceptable, becoming, satisfactory, apt, befitting
<< OPPOSITE inappropriate
2 SEEMLY, fitting, becoming, due, proper, correct
<< OPPOSITE unseemly
3 SUITED, appropriate, in keeping with, in character, cut out for
<< OPPOSITE out of keeping
4 PERTINENT, relevant, applicable, fitting, appropriate, to the point, apt, apposite, germane
<< OPPOSITE irrelevant
5 CONVENIENT, timely, appropriate, well-timed, opportune, commodious
<< OPPOSITE inopportune

suite *noun* 1 ROOMS, apartment, set of rooms, living quarters
2 SET, series, collection
3 ATTENDANTS, escorts, entourage, train, followers, retainers, retinue

suitor *noun* ADMIRER, young man, beau, follower (*obsolete*), swain (*archaic*), wooer

sulk *verb* BE SULLEN, brood, be in a huff, pout, be put out, have the hump (*Brit informal*)

sulky *adjective* HUFFY, sullen, petulant, cross, put out, moody, perverse, disgruntled, aloof, resentful, vexed, churlish, morose, querulous, ill-humoured, in the sulks

sullen *adjective* MOROSE, cross, moody, sour, gloomy, brooding, dour, surly, glowering, sulky, unsociable, out of humour
<< OPPOSITE cheerful

sully *verb* 1 DISHONOUR, ruin, disgrace, besmirch, smirch
2 DEFILE, dirty, stain, spot, spoil, contaminate, pollute, taint, tarnish, blemish, befoul

sultry *adjective* 1 HUMID, close, hot, sticky, stifling, oppressive, stuffy, sweltering, muggy
<< OPPOSITE cool
2 SEDUCTIVE, sexy (*informal*), sensual, voluptuous, passionate, erotic, provocative, amorous, come-hither (*informal*)

sum *noun* 1 AMOUNT, quantity, volume
2 CALCULATION, figures, arithmetic, problem, numbers, reckonings, mathematics, maths (*Brit informal*), tally, math (*US informal*), arithmetical problem
3 TOTAL, aggregate, entirety, sum total
4 TOTALITY, whole
▷▷ **sum something** *or* **someone up** SIZE UP, estimate (*informal*), get the measure of, form an opinion of

summarily *adverb* IMMEDIATELY, promptly, swiftly, on the spot, speedily, without delay, arbitrarily, at short notice, forthwith, expeditiously, peremptorily, without wasting words

summarize *verb* SUM UP, recap, review, outline, condense, encapsulate, epitomize, abridge, précis, recapitulate, give a rundown of, put in a nutshell, give the main points of

summary *noun* SYNOPSIS, résumé, précis, recapitulation, review, outline, extract, essence, abstract, summing-up, digest, epitome, rundown, compendium, abridgment
▷ *adjective* 1 HASTY, cursory, perfunctory, arbitrary
2 CONCISE, brief, compact, condensed, laconic, succinct, pithy, compendious

summit *noun* 1 MEETING, talks, conference, discussion, negotiation, dialogue
2 PEAK, top, tip, pinnacle, apex, head, crown, crest
<< OPPOSITE base
3 HEIGHT, pinnacle, culmination, peak, high point, zenith, acme, crowning point
<< OPPOSITE depths

summon *verb* 1 SEND FOR, call, bid, invite, rally, assemble, convene, call together, convoke
2 *often with* **up** GATHER, muster, draw on, invoke, mobilize, call into action

sumptuous *adjective* LUXURIOUS, rich, grand, expensive, superb, magnificent, costly, splendid, posh (*informal, chiefly Brit*), gorgeous, lavish, extravagant, plush (*informal*), opulent, palatial, ritzy (*slang*), de luxe, splendiferous (*facetious*)
<< OPPOSITE plain

sun *noun* SOL (*Roman myth*), Helios (*Greek myth*), Phoebus (*Greek myth*), daystar (*poetic*), eye of heaven, Phoebus Apollo (*Greek myth*)
▷▷ **sun yourself** SUNBATHE, tan, bask
>> RELATED WORD *adjective* solar

sundry *determiner* VARIOUS, several, varied, assorted, some, different, divers (*archaic*), miscellaneous

sunk *adjective* RUINED, lost, finished, done for (*informal*), on the rocks, all washed up (*informal*), up the creek without a paddle (*informal*)

sunken *adjective* 1 SUBMERGED, immersed, submersed
2 LOWERED, buried, depressed, recessed, below ground, at a lower level
3 HOLLOW, drawn, haggard, hollowed, concave

sunny *adjective* 1 BRIGHT, clear, fine, brilliant, radiant, luminous, sunlit, summery, unclouded, sunshiny, without a cloud in the sky

<< OPPOSITE dull

2 CHEERFUL, happy, cheery, smiling, beaming, pleasant, optimistic, buoyant, joyful, genial, chirpy (*informal*), blithe, light-hearted

<< OPPOSITE gloomy

sunrise *noun* DAWN, daybreak, break of day, daylight, aurora (*poetic*), sunup, cockcrow, dayspring (*poetic*)

sunset *noun* NIGHTFALL, dusk, sundown, eventide, gloaming (*Scot poetic*), close of (the) day

super *adjective* (*informal*) EXCELLENT, wonderful, marvellous, mean (*slang*), topping (*Brit slang*), cracking (*Brit informal*), crucial (*slang*), outstanding, smashing (*informal*), superb, magnificent, glorious, terrific (*informal*), sensational (*informal*), mega (*slang*), sovereign, awesome (*slang*), def (*slang*), top-notch (*informal*), brill (*informal*), incomparable, out of this world (*informal*), peerless, matchless, boffo (*slang*), jim-dandy (*slang*), chillin' (*US slang*), booshit (*Austral slang*), exo (*Austral slang*), sik (*Austral slang*), rad (*informal*), phat (*slang*), schmick (*Austral informal*)

superb *adjective* 1 SPLENDID, excellent, magnificent, topping (*Brit slang*), fine, choice, grand, superior, divine, marvellous, gorgeous, mega (*slang*), awesome (*slang*), world-class, exquisite, breathtaking, first-rate, superlative, unrivalled, brill (*informal*), bodacious (*slang, chiefly US*), boffo (*slang*), splendiferous (*facetious*), of the first water, chillin' (*US slang*), booshit (*Austral slang*), exo (*Austral slang*), sik (*Austral slang*), rad (*informal*), phat (*slang*), schmick (*Austral informal*)

<< OPPOSITE inferior

2 MAGNIFICENT, superior, marvellous, exquisite, breathtaking, admirable, superlative, unrivalled, splendiferous (*facetious*)

<< OPPOSITE terrible

superficial *adjective* 1 SHALLOW, frivolous, empty-headed, empty, silly, lightweight, trivial

<< OPPOSITE serious

2 HASTY, cursory, perfunctory, passing, nodding, hurried, casual, sketchy, facile, desultory, slapdash, inattentive

<< OPPOSITE thorough

3 SLIGHT, surface, external, cosmetic, on the surface, exterior, peripheral, skin-deep

<< OPPOSITE profound

superficially *adverb* AT FIRST GLANCE, apparently, on the surface, ostensibly, externally, at face value, to the casual eye

superfluous *adjective* EXCESS, surplus, redundant, remaining, extra, spare, excessive, unnecessary, in excess, needless, left over, on your hands, surplus to requirements, uncalled-for, unneeded, residuary, supernumerary, superabundant, pleonastic (*Rhetoric*), unrequired, supererogatory

<< OPPOSITE necessary

superhuman *adjective* HEROIC, phenomenal, prodigious, stupendous, herculean

superintend *verb* SUPERVISE, run, oversee, control, manage, direct, handle, look after, overlook, administer, inspect

superintendent *noun* 1 SUPERVISOR, director, manager, chief, governor, inspector, administrator, conductor, controller, overseer

2 (*US*) WARDEN, caretaker, curator, keeper, porter, custodian, watchman, janitor, concierge

superior *adjective* 1 BETTER, higher, greater, grander, preferred, prevailing, paramount, surpassing, more advanced, predominant, unrivalled, more extensive, more skilful, more expert, a cut above (*informal*), streets ahead (*informal*), running rings around (*informal*)

<< OPPOSITE inferior

2 FIRST-CLASS, excellent, first-rate, good, fine, choice, exclusive, distinguished, exceptional, world-class, good quality, admirable, high-class, high calibre, de luxe, of the first order, booshit (*Austral slang*), exo (*Austral slang*), sik (*Austral slang*), rad (*informal*), phat (*slang*), schmick (*Austral informal*)

<< OPPOSITE average

3 HIGHER-RANKING, senior, higher-level, upper-level

4 SUPERCILIOUS, patronizing, condescending, haughty, disdainful, lordly, lofty, airy, pretentious, stuck-up (*informal*), snobbish, on your high horse (*informal*)

▷ *noun* BOSS, senior, director, manager, chief (*informal*), principal, supervisor, baas (*S African*), sherang (*Austral & NZ*)

<< OPPOSITE subordinate

Superior should not be used with *than*: *he is a better* (not *a superior*) *poet than his brother*; *his poetry is superior to* (not *than*) *his brother's*

superiority *noun* SUPREMACY, lead, advantage, excellence, prevalence, ascendancy, pre-eminence, preponderance, predominance

superlative *adjective* SUPREME, excellent, outstanding, highest, greatest, crack (*slang*), magnificent, surpassing, consummate, stellar (*informal*), unparalleled, transcendent, unrivalled, peerless, unsurpassed, matchless, of the highest order, of the first water

<< OPPOSITE average

supernatural *adjective* PARANORMAL, mysterious, unearthly, uncanny, dark, hidden, ghostly, psychic, phantom, abnormal, mystic, miraculous, unnatural, occult, spectral, preternatural, supranatural

supersede *verb* REPLACE, displace, usurp, supplant, remove, take over, oust, take the place of, fill *or* step into (someone's) boots

supervise *verb* **1** OBSERVE, guide, monitor, oversee, keep an eye on
2 OVERSEE, run, manage, control, direct, handle, conduct, look after, be responsible for, administer, inspect, preside over, keep an eye on, be on duty at, superintend, have *or* be in charge of

supervision *noun* SUPERINTENDENCE, direction, instruction, control, charge, care, management, administration, guidance, surveillance, oversight, auspices, stewardship

supervisor *noun* BOSS (*informal*), manager, superintendent, chief, inspector, administrator, steward, gaffer (*informal, chiefly Brit*), foreman, overseer, baas (*S African*)

supervisory *adjective* MANAGERIAL, administrative, overseeing, superintendent, executive

supine *adjective* **1** FLAT ON YOUR BACK, flat, horizontal, recumbent
<< OPPOSITE prone
2 LETHARGIC, passive, lazy, idle, indifferent, careless, sluggish, negligent, inert, languid, uninterested, apathetic, lymphatic, listless, indolent, heedless, torpid, slothful, spiritless

supplant *verb* REPLACE, oust, displace, supersede, remove, take over, undermine, overthrow, unseat, take the place of

supple *adjective* **1** PLIANT, flexible, pliable, plastic, bending, elastic
<< OPPOSITE rigid
2 FLEXIBLE, lithe, limber, lissom(e), loose-limbed
<< OPPOSITE stiff

supplement *verb* ADD TO, reinforce, complement, augment, extend, top up, fill out
▷ *noun* **1** PULL-OUT, insert, magazine section, added feature
2 APPENDIX, sequel, add-on, complement, postscript, addendum, codicil
3 ADDITION, extra, surcharge

supplementary *adjective* ADDITIONAL, extra, complementary, accompanying, secondary, auxiliary, add-on, supplemental, ancillary

supply *verb* **1** PROVIDE, give, furnish, produce, stock, store, grant, afford, contribute, yield, come up with, outfit, endow, purvey, victual
2 FURNISH, provide, equip, endow
3 MEET, provide for, fill, satisfy, fulfil, be adequate for, cater to *or* for
▷ *noun* STORE, fund, stock, source, reserve, quantity, reservoir, stockpile, hoard, cache
▷ *plural noun* PROVISIONS, necessities, stores, food, materials, items, equipment, rations, foodstuff, provender

support *verb* **1** HELP, back, champion, second, aid, forward, encourage, defend, promote, take (someone's) part, strengthen, assist, advocate, uphold, side with, go along with, stand up for, espouse, stand behind, hold (someone's) hand, stick up for (*informal*), succour, buoy up, boost (someone's) morale, take up the cudgels for, be a source of strength to
<< OPPOSITE oppose
2 PROVIDE FOR, maintain, look after, keep, fund, finance, sustain, foster, take care of, subsidize
<< OPPOSITE live off
3 BEAR OUT, confirm, verify, substantiate, corroborate, document, endorse, attest to, authenticate, lend credence to
<< OPPOSITE refute
4 BEAR, hold up, carry, sustain, prop (up), reinforce, hold, brace, uphold, bolster, underpin, shore up, buttress
▷ *noun* **1** FURTHERANCE, backing, promotion, championship, approval, assistance, encouragement, espousal
2 HELP, protection, comfort, friendship, assistance, blessing, loyalty, patronage, moral support, succour
<< OPPOSITE opposition
3 AID, help, benefits, relief, assistance
4 PROP, post, foundation, back, lining, stay, shore, brace, pillar, underpinning, stanchion, stiffener, abutment
5 SUPPORTER, prop, mainstay, tower of strength, second, stay, backer, backbone, comforter
<< OPPOSITE antagonist
6 UPKEEP, maintenance, keep, livelihood, subsistence, sustenance

supporter *noun* FOLLOWER, fan, advocate, friend, champion, ally, defender, sponsor, patron, helper, protagonist, adherent, henchman, apologist, upholder, well-wisher
<< OPPOSITE opponent

supportive *adjective* HELPFUL, caring, encouraging, understanding, reassuring, sympathetic
>> RELATED WORD *prefix* pro-

suppose *verb* **1** IMAGINE, believe, consider, conclude, fancy, conceive, conjecture, postulate, hypothesize
2 THINK, imagine, expect, judge, assume, guess (*informal, chiefly US & Canad*), calculate (*US dialect*), presume, take for granted, infer, conjecture, surmise, dare say, opine, presuppose, take as read

supposed *adjective* **1** *usually with* **to** MEANT, expected, required, obliged
2 PRESUMED, alleged, professed, reputed, accepted, assumed, rumoured, hypothetical, putative, presupposed

supposedly *adverb* PRESUMABLY, allegedly, ostensibly, theoretically, by all accounts, purportedly, avowedly, hypothetically, at a guess, professedly
<< OPPOSITE actually

supposition *noun* BELIEF, idea, notion, view, theory, speculation, assumption, hypothesis, presumption, conjecture, surmise, guesswork

suppress *verb* 1 STAMP OUT, stop, check, crush, conquer, overthrow, subdue, put an end to, overpower, quash, crack down on, quell, extinguish, clamp down on, snuff out, quench, beat down, trample on, drive underground
<< OPPOSITE encourage
2 CHECK, inhibit, subdue, stop, quell, quench
3 RESTRAIN, cover up, withhold, stifle, contain, silence, conceal, curb, repress, smother, keep secret, muffle, muzzle, hold in check, hold in *or* back
4 CONCEAL, hide, keep secret, hush up, stonewall, sweep under the carpet, draw a veil over, keep silent about, keep dark, keep under your hat (*informal*)

suppression *noun* 1 ELIMINATION, crushing, crackdown, check, extinction, prohibition, quashing, dissolution, termination, clampdown
2 INHIBITION, blocking, restriction, restraint, smothering
3 CONCEALMENT, covering, hiding, disguising, camouflage
4 HIDING, hushing up, stonewalling

supremacy *noun* DOMINATION, dominance, ascendancy, sovereignty, sway, lordship, mastery, dominion, primacy, pre-eminence, predominance, supreme power, absolute rule, paramountcy

supreme *adjective* 1 PARAMOUNT, surpassing, superlative, prevailing, sovereign, predominant, incomparable, mother of all (*informal*), unsurpassed, matchless
<< OPPOSITE least
2 CHIEF, leading, principal, first, highest, head, top, prime, cardinal, foremost, pre-eminent, peerless
<< OPPOSITE lowest
3 ULTIMATE, highest, greatest, utmost, final, crowning, extreme, culminating

supremo *noun* (*Brit informal*) HEAD, leader, boss (*informal*), director, master, governor, commander, principal, ruler, baas (*S African*)

sure *adjective* 1 CERTAIN, positive, clear, decided, convinced, persuaded, confident, satisfied, assured, definite, free from doubt
<< OPPOSITE uncertain
2 INEVITABLE, guaranteed, bound, assured, in the bag (*slang*), inescapable, irrevocable, ineluctable, nailed-on (*slang*)
<< OPPOSITE unsure
3 RELIABLE, accurate, dependable, effective, precise, honest, unmistakable, undoubted, undeniable, trustworthy, never-failing, trusty, foolproof, infallible, indisputable, sure-fire (*informal*), unerring, well-proven, unfailing, tried and true
<< OPPOSITE unreliable
4 SECURE, firm, steady, fast, safe, solid, stable

surely *adverb* 1 IT MUST BE THE CASE THAT, assuredly
2 UNDOUBTEDLY, certainly, definitely, inevitably, doubtless, for certain, without doubt, unquestionably, inexorably, come what may, without fail, indubitably, doubtlessly, beyond the shadow of a doubt

surety *noun* 1 SECURITY, guarantee, deposit, insurance, bond, safety, pledge, bail, warranty, indemnity
2 GUARANTOR, sponsor, hostage, bondsman, mortgagor

surface *noun* 1 COVERING, face, exterior, side, top, skin, plane, facet, veneer
2 FAÇADE, outward appearance
▷ *modifier* SUPERFICIAL, external, outward, exterior
▷ *verb* 1 EMERGE, come up, come to the surface
2 APPEAR, emerge, arise, come to light, crop up (*informal*), transpire, materialize
▷▷ **on the surface** AT FIRST GLANCE, apparently, outwardly, seemingly, ostensibly, superficially, to all appearances, to the casual eye

surfeit *noun* EXCESS, plethora, glut, satiety, overindulgence, superabundance, superfluity
<< OPPOSITE shortage

surge *noun* 1 RUSH, flood, upsurge, sudden increase, uprush
2 FLOW, wave, rush, roller, breaker, gush, upsurge, outpouring, uprush
3 TIDE, roll, rolling, swell, swirling, billowing
4 WAVE, rush, storm, outburst, torrent, eruption
▷ *verb* 1 RUSH, pour, stream, rise, swell, spill, swarm, seethe, gush, well forth
2 ROLL, rush, billow, heave, swirl, eddy, undulate
3 SWEEP, rush, storm

surly *adjective* ILL-TEMPERED, cross, churlish, crabbed, perverse, crusty, sullen, gruff, bearish, sulky, morose, brusque, testy, grouchy (*informal*), curmudgeonly, ungracious, uncivil, shrewish
<< OPPOSITE cheerful

surmise *verb* GUESS, suppose, imagine, presume, consider, suspect, conclude, fancy, speculate, infer, deduce, come to the conclusion, conjecture, opine, hazard a guess
▷ *noun* GUESS, speculation, assumption, thought, idea, conclusion, notion,

suspicion, hypothesis, deduction, inference, presumption, conjecture, supposition

surmount *verb* OVERCOME, master, conquer, pass, exceed, surpass, overpower, triumph over, vanquish, prevail over

surpass *verb* OUTDO, top, beat, best, cap (*informal*), exceed, eclipse, overshadow, excel, transcend, outstrip, outshine, tower above, go one better than (*informal*), put in the shade

surpassing *adjective* SUPREME, extraordinary, outstanding, exceptional, rare, phenomenal, stellar (*informal*), transcendent, unrivalled, incomparable, matchless

surplus *noun* EXCESS, surfeit, superabundance, superfluity
 << OPPOSITE shortage
 ▷ *adjective* EXTRA, spare, excess, remaining, odd, in excess, left over, unused, superfluous
 << OPPOSITE insufficient

surprise *noun* **1** SHOCK, start (*informal*), revelation, jolt, bombshell, eye-opener (*informal*), bolt from the blue, turn-up for the books (*informal*)
 2 AMAZEMENT, astonishment, wonder, incredulity, stupefaction
 ▷ *verb* **1** AMAZE, astonish, astound, stun, startle, stagger, disconcert, take aback, bowl over (*informal*), leave open-mouthed, nonplus, flabbergast (*informal*), take (someone's) breath away
 2 CATCH UNAWARES *or* OFF-GUARD, catch napping, catch on the hop (*informal*), burst in on, spring upon, catch in the act *or* red-handed, come down on like a bolt from the blue

surprised *adjective* AMAZED, astonished, startled, disconcerted, at a loss, taken aback, speechless, incredulous, open-mouthed, nonplussed, thunderstruck, unable to believe your eyes

surprising *adjective* AMAZING, remarkable, incredible, astonishing, wonderful, unusual, extraordinary, unexpected, staggering, marvellous, startling, astounding, jaw-dropping, unlooked-for

surrender *verb* **1** GIVE IN, yield, submit, give way, quit, succumb, cave in (*informal*), capitulate, throw in the towel, lay down arms, give yourself up, show the white flag
 << OPPOSITE resist
 2 GIVE UP, abandon, relinquish, resign, yield, concede, part with, renounce, waive, forego, cede, deliver up
 ▷ *noun* SUBMISSION, yielding, cave-in (*informal*), capitulation, resignation, renunciation, relinquishment

surreptitious *adjective* SECRET, clandestine, furtive, sneaking, veiled, covert, sly, fraudulent, unauthorized, underhand, stealthy
 << OPPOSITE open

surrogate *noun* SUBSTITUTE, deputy, representative, stand-in, proxy

surround *verb* **1** ENCLOSE, ring, encircle, encompass, envelop, close in on, fence in, girdle, hem in, environ, enwreath
 2 BESIEGE, beset, lay siege to, invest (*rare*)

surrounding *adjective* NEARBY, neighbouring

surroundings *plural noun* ENVIRONMENT, setting, background, location, neighbourhood, milieu, environs

surveillance *noun* OBSERVATION, watch, scrutiny, supervision, control, care, direction, inspection, vigilance, superintendence

survey *noun* **1** POLL, study, research, review, inquiry, investigation, opinion poll, questionnaire, census
 2 EXAMINATION, inspection, scrutiny, overview, once-over (*informal*), perusal
 3 VALUATION, estimate, assessment, appraisal
 ▷ *verb* **1** INTERVIEW, question, poll, study, research, investigate, sample, canvass
 2 LOOK OVER, view, scan, examine, observe, contemplate, supervise, inspect, eyeball (*slang*), scrutinize, size up, take stock of, eye up, recce (*slang*), reconnoitre
 3 MEASURE, estimate, prospect, assess, appraise, triangulate

survive *verb* **1** REMAIN ALIVE, live, pull through, last, exist, live on, endure, hold out, subsist, keep body and soul together (*informal*), be extant, fight for your life, keep your head above water
 2 CONTINUE, last, live on, pull through
 3 LIVE LONGER THAN, outlive, outlast

susceptibility *noun* VULNERABILITY, weakness, liability, propensity, predisposition, proneness

susceptible *adjective* **1** RESPONSIVE, sensitive, receptive, alive to, impressionable, easily moved, suggestible
 << OPPOSITE unresponsive
 2 *usually with* **to** LIABLE, inclined, prone, given, open, subject, vulnerable, disposed, predisposed
 << OPPOSITE resistant

suspect *verb* **1** BELIEVE, feel, guess, consider, suppose, conclude, fancy, speculate, conjecture, surmise, hazard a guess, have a sneaking suspicion, think probable
 << OPPOSITE know
 2 DISTRUST, doubt, mistrust, smell a rat (*informal*), harbour suspicions about, have your doubts about
 << OPPOSITE trust
 ▷ *adjective* DUBIOUS, doubtful, dodgy (*Brit, Austral & NZ informal*), questionable, fishy (*informal*), iffy (*informal*), open to suspicion, shonky (*Austral & NZ informal*)
 << OPPOSITE innocent

suspend *verb* 1 POSTPONE, delay, put off, arrest, cease, interrupt, shelve, withhold, defer, adjourn, hold off, cut short, discontinue, lay aside, put in cold storage
<< OPPOSITE continue
2 REMOVE, expel, eject, debar
<< OPPOSITE reinstate
3 HANG, attach, dangle, swing, append

suspense *noun* UNCERTAINTY, doubt, tension, anticipation, expectation, anxiety, insecurity, expectancy, apprehension

suspension *noun* POSTPONEMENT, delay, break, stay, breaking off, interruption, moratorium, respite, remission, adjournment, abeyance, deferment, discontinuation, disbarment

suspicion *noun* 1 FEELING, theory, impression, intuition, conjecture, surmise, funny feeling (*informal*), presentiment
2 DISTRUST, scepticism, mistrust, doubt, misgiving, qualm, lack of confidence, wariness, bad vibes (*slang*), dubiety, chariness
3 IDEA, notion, hunch, guess, impression, conjecture, surmise, gut feeling (*informal*), supposition
4 TRACE, touch, hint, shadow, suggestion, strain, shade, streak, tinge, glimmer, soupçon (*French*)
▷▷ **above suspicion** BLAMELESS, unimpeachable, above reproach, pure, honourable, virtuous, sinless, like Caesar's wife

suspicious *adjective* 1 DISTRUSTFUL, suspecting, sceptical, doubtful, apprehensive, leery (*slang*), mistrustful, unbelieving, wary
<< OPPOSITE trusting
2 SUSPECT, dubious, questionable, funny, doubtful, dodgy (*Brit, Austral & NZ informal*), queer, irregular, shady (*informal*), fishy (*informal*), of doubtful honesty, open to doubt *or* misconstruction, shonky (*Austral & NZ informal*)
<< OPPOSITE beyond suspicion
3 ODD, strange, mysterious, dark, dubious, irregular, questionable, murky (*informal*), shady (*informal*), fishy

sustain *verb* 1 MAINTAIN, continue, keep up, prolong, keep going, keep alive, protract
2 SUFFER, experience, undergo, feel, bear, endure, withstand, bear up under
3 HELP, aid, comfort, foster, assist, relieve, nurture
4 KEEP ALIVE, nourish, provide for
5 SUPPORT, carry, bear, keep up, uphold, keep from falling
6 UPHOLD, confirm, endorse, approve, ratify, verify, validate

sustained *adjective* CONTINUOUS, constant, steady, prolonged, perpetual, unremitting, nonstop
<< OPPOSITE periodic

sustenance *noun* 1 NOURISHMENT, food, provisions, rations, refreshments, kai (*NZ informal*), daily bread, victuals, edibles, comestibles, provender, aliment, eatables, refection
2 SUPPORT, maintenance, livelihood, subsistence

svelte *adjective* SLENDER, lithe, willowy, graceful, slinky, lissom(e), sylphlike

swagger *verb* 1 STRIDE, parade, strut, prance
2 SHOW OFF, boast, brag, hot-dog (*chiefly US*), bluster, swank (*informal*), gasconade (*rare*)
▷ *noun* 1 STRUT
2 OSTENTATION, show, display, showing off (*informal*), bluster, swashbuckling, swank (*informal*), braggadocio, gasconade (*rare*)

swallow *verb* 1 EAT, down (*informal*), consume, devour, absorb, swig (*informal*), swill, wash down, ingest
2 GULP, drink
3 (*informal*) BELIEVE, accept, buy (*slang*), fall for, take (something) as gospel
4 SUPPRESS, hold in, restrain, contain, hold back, stifle, repress, bottle up, bite back, choke back
▷▷ **swallow something** *or* **someone up**
1 ENGULF, overwhelmed, overrun, consume
2 ABSORB, assimilate, envelop

swamp *noun* BOG, marsh, quagmire, moss (*Scot & Northern English dialect*), slough, fen, mire, morass, everglade(s) (*US*), pakihi (*NZ*), muskeg (*Canad*)
▷ *verb* 1 FLOOD, engulf, submerge, inundate, deluge
2 OVERLOAD, overwhelm, inundate, besiege, beset, snow under

swampy *adjective* BOGGY, waterlogged, marshy, wet, fenny, miry, quaggy, marish (*obsolete*)

swank (*informal*) *verb* SHOW OFF, swagger, give yourself airs, posture (*informal*), hot-dog (*chiefly US*), put on side (*Brit slang*)
▷ *noun* BOASTFULNESS, show, ostentation, display, swagger, vainglory

swanky *adjective* (*informal*) OSTENTATIOUS, grand, posh (*informal, chiefly Brit*), rich, expensive, exclusive, smart, fancy, flash, fashionable, glamorous, stylish, gorgeous, lavish, luxurious, sumptuous, plush (*informal*), flashy, swish (*informal, chiefly Brit*), glitzy (*slang*), showy, ritzy (*slang*), de luxe, swank (*informal*), plushy (*informal*), schmick (*Austral informal*)
<< OPPOSITE modest

swap *or* **swop** *verb* EXCHANGE, trade, switch, traffic, interchange, barter

swarm *noun* MULTITUDE, crowd, mass, army, host, drove, flock, herd, horde, myriad, throng, shoal, concourse, bevy
▷ *verb* 1 CROWD, flock, throng, mass, stream, congregate

2 TEEM, crawl, be alive, abound, bristle, be overrun, be infested
swarthy *adjective* DARK-SKINNED, black, brown, dark, tawny, dusky, swart (*archaic*), dark-complexioned
swashbuckling *adjective* DASHING, spirited, bold, flamboyant, swaggering, gallant, daredevil, mettlesome, roisterous
swastika *noun* CROOKED CROSS, fylfot
swath *or* **swathe** *noun* AREA, section, stretch, patch, tract
swathe *verb* WRAP, drape, envelop, bind, lap, fold, bandage, cloak, shroud, swaddle, furl, sheathe, enfold, bundle up, muffle up, enwrap
sway *verb* 1 MOVE FROM SIDE TO SIDE, rock, wave, roll, swing, bend, lean, incline, lurch, oscillate, move to and fro
2 INFLUENCE, control, direct, affect, guide, dominate, persuade, govern, win over, induce, prevail on
▷ *noun* POWER, control, influence, government, rule, authority, command, sovereignty, jurisdiction, clout (*informal*), dominion, predominance, ascendency
▷▷ **hold sway** PREVAIL, rule, predominate, reign
swear *verb* 1 CURSE, cuss (*informal*), blaspheme, turn the air blue (*informal*), be foul-mouthed, take the Lord's name in vain, utter profanities, imprecate
2 VOW, promise, take an oath, warrant, testify, depose, attest, avow, give your word, state under oath, pledge yourself
3 DECLARE, assert, affirm, swear blind, asseverate
▷▷ **swear by something** BELIEVE IN, trust, depend on, rely on, have confidence in
swearing *noun* BAD LANGUAGE, cursing, profanity, blasphemy, cussing (*informal*), foul language, imprecations, malediction
swearword *noun* OATH, curse, obscenity, expletive, four-letter word, cuss (*informal*), profanity
sweat *noun* 1 PERSPIRATION, moisture, dampness
2 (*informal*) PANIC, anxiety, state (*informal*), worry, distress, flap (*informal*), agitation, fluster, lather (*informal*), tizzy (*informal*), state of anxiety
▷ *verb* 1 PERSPIRE, swelter, break out in a sweat, exude moisture, glow
2 (*informal*) WORRY, fret, agonize, lose sleep over, be on tenterhooks, torture yourself, be on pins and needles (*informal*)
▷▷ **sweat something out** (*informal*) ENDURE, see (something) through, stick it out (*informal*), stay the course
sweaty *adjective* PERSPIRING, sweating, sticky, clammy, bathed *or* drenched *or* soaked in perspiration, glowing
sweep *verb* 1 BRUSH, clean
2 CLEAR, remove, brush, clean
3 SAIL, pass, fly, tear, zoom, glide, skim, scud, hurtle
4 SWAGGER, sail, breeze, stride, stroll, glide, flounce
▷ *noun* 1 MOVEMENT, move, swing, stroke, gesture
2 ARC, bend, curve
3 EXTENT, range, span, stretch, scope, compass
sweeping *adjective* 1 INDISCRIMINATE, blanket, across-the-board, wholesale, exaggerated, overstated, unqualified, overdrawn
2 WIDE-RANGING, global, comprehensive, wide, broad, radical, extensive, all-inclusive, all-embracing, overarching, thoroughgoing
<< OPPOSITE limited
sweet *adjective* 1 SUGARY, sweetened, cloying, honeyed, saccharine, syrupy, icky (*informal*), treacly
<< OPPOSITE sour
2 FRAGRANT, perfumed, aromatic, redolent, sweet-smelling
<< OPPOSITE stinking
3 FRESH, clean, pure, wholesome
4 MELODIOUS, musical, harmonious, soft, mellow, silvery, tuneful, dulcet, sweet-sounding, euphonious, silver-toned, euphonic
<< OPPOSITE harsh
5 CHARMING, kind, gentle, tender, affectionate, agreeable, amiable, sweet-tempered
<< OPPOSITE nasty
6 DELIGHTFUL, appealing, cute, taking, winning, fair, beautiful, attractive, engaging, lovable, winsome, cutesy (*informal, chiefly US*), likable *or* likeable
<< OPPOSITE unpleasant
7 (*Archaic*) BELOVED, dear, darling, dearest, pet, treasured, precious, cherished
▷ *noun* 1 *usually plural* (*Brit*) CONFECTIONERY, candy (*US*), sweetie, lolly (*Austral & NZ*), sweetmeat, bonbon
2 (*Brit*) DESSERT, pudding, afters (*Brit informal*), sweet course
▷▷ **sweet on** IN LOVE WITH, keen on, infatuated with, gone on (*slang*), fond of, taken with, enamoured of, head over heels in love with, obsessed *or* bewitched by, wild *or* mad about (*informal*)
sweeten *verb* 1 SUGAR
2 SOFTEN, ease, alleviate, relieve, temper, cushion, mellow, make less painful
3 MOLLIFY, appease, soothe, pacify, soften up, sugar the pill
sweetheart *noun* 1 DEAREST, beloved, sweet, angel, treasure, honey, dear, sweetie (*informal*)
2 LOVE, boyfriend *or* girlfriend, beloved, lover,

steady (*informal*), flame (*informal*), darling, follower (*obsolete*), valentine, admirer, suitor, beau, swain (*archaic*), truelove, leman (*archaic*), inamorata *or* inamorato

swell *verb* 1 INCREASE, rise, grow, mount, expand, accelerate, escalate, multiply, grow larger
<< OPPOSITE decrease
2 EXPAND, increase, grow, rise, extend, balloon, belly, enlarge, bulge, protrude, well up, billow, fatten, dilate, puff up, round out, be inflated, become larger, distend, bloat, tumefy, become bloated *or* distended
<< OPPOSITE shrink
▷ *noun* WAVE, rise, surge, billow

swelling *noun* ENLARGEMENT, lump, puffiness, bump, blister, bulge, inflammation, dilation, protuberance, distension, tumescence
>> RELATED WORD *adjective* tumescent

sweltering *adjective* HOT, burning, boiling, steaming, baking, roasting, stifling, scorching, oppressive, humid, torrid, sultry, airless

swerve *verb* VEER, turn, swing, shift, bend, incline, deflect, depart from, skew, diverge, deviate, turn aside, sheer off

swift *adjective* 1 QUICK, immediate, prompt, rapid, instant, abrupt, ready, expeditious
2 FAST, quick, rapid, flying, express, winged, sudden, fleet, hurried, speedy, spanking, nimble, quickie (*informal*), nippy (*Brit informal*), fleet-footed, pdq (*slang*)
<< OPPOSITE slow

swiftly *adverb* 1 QUICKLY, rapidly, speedily, without losing time
2 FAST, promptly, hurriedly, apace, pronto (*informal*), double-quick, hell for leather, like lightning, hotfoot, like the clappers (*Brit informal*), posthaste, like greased lightning (*informal*), nippily (*Brit informal*), in less than no time, as fast as your legs can carry you, (at) full tilt

swill *verb* 1 DRINK, gulp, swig (*informal*), guzzle, drain, consume, swallow, imbibe, quaff, bevvy (*dialect*), toss off, bend the elbow (*informal*), pour down your gullet
2 (*Chiefly Brit*) *often with* **out** RINSE, wash out, sluice, flush, drench, wash down
▷ *noun* WASTE, slops, mash, mush, hogwash, pigswill, scourings

swindle *verb* CHEAT, do (*slang*), con, skin (*slang*), trick, stiff (*slang*), sting (*informal*), rip (someone) off (*slang*), deceive, fleece, defraud, dupe, overcharge, rook (*slang*), bamboozle (*informal*), diddle (*informal*), take (someone) for a ride (*informal*), put one over on (someone) (*informal*), pull a fast one (on someone) (*informal*), bilk (of), take to the cleaners (*informal*), sell a pup (to) (*slang*), cozen, hornswoggle (*slang*)
▷ *noun* FRAUD, fiddle (*Brit informal*), rip-off (*slang*), racket, scam (*slang*), sting (*informal*), deception, imposition, deceit, trickery, double-dealing, con trick (*informal*), sharp practice, swizzle (*Brit informal*), knavery, swizz (*Brit informal*), roguery, fastie (*Austral slang*)

swing *verb* 1 BRANDISH, wave, shake, flourish, wield, dangle
2 SWAY, rock, wave, veer, vibrate, oscillate, move back and forth, move to and fro
3 *usually with* **round** TURN, veer, swivel, twist, curve, rotate, pivot, turn on your heel
4 HIT OUT, strike, swipe, lash out at, slap
5 HANG, dangle, be suspended, suspend, move back and forth
▷ *noun* 1 SWAYING, sway
2 FLUCTUATION, change, shift, switch, variation
▷▷ **in full swing** AT ITS HEIGHT, under way, on the go (*informal*)

swingeing *adjective* (*Chiefly Brit*) SEVERE, heavy, drastic, huge, punishing, harsh, excessive, daunting, stringent, oppressive, Draconian, exorbitant

swipe *verb* 1 (*informal*) HIT OUT, strike, slap, lash out at
2 (*Slang*) STEAL, nick (*slang, chiefly Brit*), pinch (*informal*), lift (*informal*), appropriate, cabbage (*Brit slang*), make off with, pilfer, purloin, filch, snaffle (*Brit informal*)
▷ *noun* (*informal*) BLOW, slap, smack, clip (*informal*), thump, clout (*informal*), cuff, clump (*slang*), wallop (*informal*)

swirl *verb* WHIRL, churn, spin, twist, boil, surge, agitate, eddy, twirl

swish *adjective* (*informal, chiefly Brit*) SMART, grand, posh (*informal, chiefly Brit*), exclusive, elegant, swell (*informal*), fashionable, sumptuous, ritzy (*slang*), de luxe, plush *or* plushy (*informal*)

switch *noun* 1 CONTROL, button, lever, on/off device
2 CHANGE, shift, transition, conversion, reversal, alteration, about-turn, change of direction
▷ *verb* 1 CHANGE, shift, convert, divert, deviate, change course
2 EXCHANGE, trade, swap, replace, substitute, rearrange, interchange
▷▷ **switch something off** TURN OFF, shut off, deactivate, cut
▷▷ **switch something on** TURN ON, put on, set off, activate, set in motion

swivel *verb* TURN, spin, revolve, rotate, pivot, pirouette, swing round

swollen *adjective* ENLARGED, bloated, puffy, inflamed, puffed up, distended, tumescent, oedematous, dropsical, tumid, edematous

swoop *verb* 1 POUNCE, attack, charge, rush,

descend
2 drop, plunge, dive, sweep, descend, plummet, pounce, stoop
▷ *noun* raid, attack, assault, surprise search

swop ▷ see **swap**

sword *noun* blade, brand (*archaic*), trusty steel

swot *verb* (*informal*) study, revise, cram (*informal*), work, get up (*informal*), pore over, bone up on (*informal*), burn the midnight oil, mug up (*Brit slang*), toil over, apply yourself to, lucubrate (*rare*)

sycophant *noun* crawler, yes man, toady, slave, parasite, cringer, fawner, hanger-on, sponger, flatterer, truckler, lickspittle, apple polisher (*US slang*), bootlicker (*informal*), toadeater (*rare*)

sycophantic *adjective* obsequious, grovelling, ingratiating, servile, crawling, flattering, cringing, fawning, slimy, slavish, unctuous, smarmy (*Brit informal*), toadying, parasitical, bootlicking (*informal*), timeserving

syllabus *noun* course of study, curriculum

symbol *noun* 1 metaphor, image, sign, representation, token
2 representation, sign, figure, mark, type, image, token, logo, badge, emblem, glyph

symbolic *adjective* 1 representative, token, emblematic, allegorical
2 figurative, representative

symbolize *verb* represent, signify, stand for, mean, exemplify, denote, typify, personify, connote, betoken, body forth

symmetrical *adjective* balanced, regular, proportional, in proportion, well-proportioned
<< opposite unbalanced

symmetry *noun* balance, proportion, regularity, form, order, harmony, correspondence, evenness

sympathetic *adjective* 1 caring, kind, understanding, concerned, feeling, interested, kindly, warm, tender, pitying, supportive, responsive, affectionate, compassionate, commiserating, warm-hearted, condoling
<< opposite uncaring
2 supportive, encouraging, pro, approving of, friendly to, in sympathy with, well-disposed towards, favourably disposed towards
3 like-minded, compatible, agreeable, friendly, responsive, appreciative, congenial, companionable, well-intentioned
<< opposite uncongenial

sympathetically *adverb* feelingly, kindly, understandingly, warmly, with interest, with feeling, sensitively, with compassion, appreciatively, perceptively, responsively, warm-heartedly

sympathize with *verb* 1 feel for, pity, empathize with, commiserate with, bleed for, have compassion for, grieve with, offer consolation for, condole with, share another's sorrow, feel your heart go out to
<< opposite have no feelings for
2 agree with, support, side with, understand, identify with, go along with, be in accord with, be in sympathy with
<< opposite disagree with

sympathizer *noun* supporter, partisan, protagonist, fellow traveller, well-wisher

sympathy *noun* 1 compassion, understanding, pity, empathy, tenderness, condolence(s), thoughtfulness, commiseration, aroha (*NZ*)
<< opposite indifference
2 affinity, agreement, rapport, union, harmony, warmth, correspondence, fellow feeling, congeniality
<< opposite opposition

symptom *noun* 1 sign, mark, indication, warning
2 manifestation, sign, indication, mark, evidence, expression, proof, token

symptomatic *adjective* indicative, characteristic, suggestive

synonymous with *adjective* equivalent to, the same as, identical to, similar to, identified with, equal to, tantamount to, interchangeable with, one and the same as

synopsis *noun* summary, review, résumé, outline, abstract, digest, epitome, rundown, condensation, compendium, précis, aperçu (*French*), abridgment, conspectus, outline sketch

synthesis *noun* combining, integration, amalgamation, unification, welding, coalescence

synthetic *adjective* artificial, manufactured, fake, man-made, mock, simulated, sham, pseudo (*informal*), ersatz
<< opposite real

system *noun* 1 arrangement, structure, organization, scheme, combination, classification, coordination, setup (*informal*)
2 network, organization, web, grid, set of channels
3 method, practice, technique, procedure, routine, theory, usage, methodology, frame of reference, modus operandi, fixed order

systematic *adjective* methodical, organized, efficient, precise, orderly, standardized, businesslike, well-ordered, systematized
<< opposite unmethodical

Tt

tab *noun* FLAP, tag, label, ticket, flag, marker, sticker

table *noun* **1** COUNTER, bench, stand, board, surface, slab, work surface
2 LIST, chart, tabulation, record, roll, index, register, digest, diagram, inventory, graph, synopsis, itemization
3 (*Formal*) FOOD, spread (*informal*), board, diet, fare, kai (*NZ informal*), victuals
▷ *verb* (*Brit*) SUBMIT, propose, put forward, move, suggest, enter, file, lodge, moot

tableau *noun* PICTURE, scene, representation, arrangement, spectacle

taboo *or* **tabu** *adjective* FORBIDDEN, banned, prohibited, ruled out, not allowed, unacceptable, outlawed, unthinkable, not permitted, disapproved of, anathema, off limits, frowned on, proscribed, beyond the pale, unmentionable
<< OPPOSITE permitted
▷ *noun* PROHIBITION, ban, restriction, disapproval, anathema, interdict, proscription, tapu (*NZ*)

tacit *adjective* IMPLIED, understood, implicit, silent, taken for granted, unspoken, inferred, undeclared, wordless, unstated, unexpressed
<< OPPOSITE stated

taciturn *adjective* UNCOMMUNICATIVE, reserved, reticent, unforthcoming, quiet, withdrawn, silent, distant, dumb, mute, aloof, antisocial, tight-lipped, close-lipped
<< OPPOSITE communicative

tack *noun* NAIL, pin, stud, staple, rivet, drawing pin, thumbtack (*US*), tintack
▷ *verb* **1** FASTEN, fix, attach, pin, nail, staple, affix
2 (*Brit*) STITCH, sew, hem, bind, baste
▷▷ **tack something on to something** APPEND, add, attach, tag, annex

tackle *noun* **1** (*Sport*) BLOCK, stop, challenge
2 RIG, rigging, apparatus
▷ *verb* **1** DEAL WITH, take on, set about, wade into, get stuck into (*informal*), sink your teeth into, apply yourself to, come *or* get to grips with
2 UNDERTAKE, deal with, attempt, try, begin, essay, engage in, embark upon, get stuck into (*informal*), turn your hand to, have a go *or* stab at (*informal*)
3 (*Sport*) INTERCEPT, block, bring down, stop, challenge

tacky[1] *adjective* STICKY, wet, adhesive, gummy, icky (*informal*), gluey

tacky[2] *adjective* (*informal*) **1** VULGAR, cheap, tasteless, nasty, sleazy, naff (*Brit slang*)
2 SEEDY, shabby, shoddy

tact *noun* DIPLOMACY, understanding, consideration, sensitivity, delicacy, skill, judgment, perception, discretion, finesse, thoughtfulness, savoir-faire, adroitness
<< OPPOSITE tactlessness

tactful *adjective* DIPLOMATIC, politic, discreet, prudent, understanding, sensitive, polished, careful, subtle, delicate, polite, thoughtful, perceptive, considerate, judicious
<< OPPOSITE tactless

tactic *noun* POLICY, approach, course, way, means, move, line, scheme, plans, method, trick, device, manoeuvre, tack, ploy, stratagem

tactical *adjective* STRATEGIC, politic, shrewd, smart, diplomatic, clever, cunning, skilful, artful, foxy, adroit
<< OPPOSITE impolitic

tactician *noun* STRATEGIST, campaigner, planner, mastermind, general, director, brain (*informal*), coordinator, schemer

tactics *plural noun* STRATEGY, campaigning, manoeuvres, generalship

tag *noun* LABEL, tab, sticker, note, ticket, slip, flag, identification, marker, flap, docket
▷ *verb* **1** LABEL, mark, flag, ticket, identify, earmark
2 NAME, call, label, term, style, dub, nickname, christen

tail *noun* **1** EXTREMITY, appendage, brush, rear end, hindquarters, hind part, empennage
2 (*Astronomy*) TRAIN, end, trail, tailpiece

3 (*informal*) BUTTOCKS, behind (*informal*), bottom, butt (*US & Canad informal*), bum (*Brit slang*), rear (*informal*), buns (*US slang*), backside (*informal*), rump, rear end, posterior, derrière (*euphemistic*), jacksy (*Brit slang*)
4 (used of hair) PONYTAIL, braid, plait, tress, pigtail
▷ *verb* (*informal*) FOLLOW, track, shadow, trail, stalk, keep an eye on, dog the footsteps of
▷▷ **turn tail** RUN AWAY, flee, run off, escape, take off (*informal*), retreat, make off, hook it (*slang*), run for it (*informal*), scarper (*Brit slang*), cut and run, show a clean pair of heels, skedaddle (*informal*), take to your heels
>> RELATED WORD *adjective* caudal

tailor *noun* OUTFITTER, couturier, dressmaker, seamstress, clothier, costumier, garment maker
▷ *verb* ADAPT, adjust, modify, cut, style, fit, fashion, shape, suit, convert, alter, accommodate, mould, customize
>> RELATED WORD *adjective* sartorial

tailor-made *adjective* 1 PERFECT, right, ideal, suitable, just right, right up your street (*informal*), up your alley
2 MADE-TO-MEASURE, fitted, cut to fit, made to order

taint *verb* 1 DISGRACE, shame, dishonour, brand, ruin, blacken, stigmatize
2 SPOIL, ruin, contaminate, damage, soil, dirty, poison, foul, infect, stain, corrupt, smear, muddy, pollute, blight, tarnish, blot, blemish, sully, defile, adulterate, besmirch, vitiate, smirch
<< OPPOSITE purify

take *verb* 1 GRIP, grab, seize, catch, grasp, clutch, get hold of, clasp, take hold of, lay hold of
2 CARRY, bring, bear, transport, ferry, haul, convey, fetch, cart, tote (*informal*)
<< OPPOSITE send
3 ACCOMPANY, lead, bring, guide, conduct, escort, convoy, usher
4 REMOVE, draw, pull, fish, withdraw, extract, abstract
5 STEAL, nick (*slang, chiefly Brit*), appropriate, pocket, pinch (*informal*), carry off, swipe (*slang*), run off with, blag (*slang*), walk off with, misappropriate, cart off (*slang*), purloin, filch, help yourself to, gain possession of
<< OPPOSITE return
6 CAPTURE, arrest, seize, abduct, take into custody, ensnare, entrap, lay hold of
<< OPPOSITE release
7 TOLERATE, stand, bear, suffer, weather, go through, brave, stomach, endure, undergo, swallow, brook, hack (*slang*), abide, put up with (*informal*), withstand, submit to, countenance, pocket, thole (*Scot*)
<< OPPOSITE avoid
8 REQUIRE, need, involve, demand, call for, entail, necessitate
9 ACCEPT, assume, take on, undertake, adopt, take up, enter upon
<< OPPOSITE reject
10 UNDERSTAND, follow, comprehend, get, see, grasp, apprehend
11 HIRE, book, rent, lease, reserve, pay for, engage, make a reservation for
12 PERFORM, have, do, make, effect, accomplish, execute
13 INGEST, consume, swallow, inhale
14 CONSUME, have, drink, eat, imbibe
15 HAVE ROOM FOR, hold, contain, accommodate, accept
16 WORK, succeed, do the trick (*informal*), have effect, be efficacious
<< OPPOSITE fail
▷ *noun* (*informal, chiefly US*) TAKINGS, profits, revenue, return, gate, yield, proceeds, haul, receipts
▷▷ **take it** ASSUME, suppose, presume, expect, imagine, guess (*informal, chiefly US & Canad*)
▷▷ **take off** 1 LIFT OFF, leave the ground, take to the air, become airborne
2 (*informal*) DEPART, go, leave, split (*slang*), disappear, set out, strike out, beat it (*slang*), hit the road (*slang*), abscond, decamp, hook it (*slang*), slope off, pack your bags (*informal*)
▷▷ **take on** (*informal*) GET UPSET, get excited, make a fuss, break down, give way
▷▷ **take someone for something** (*informal*) REGARD AS, see as, believe to be, consider to be, think of as, deem to be, perceive to be, hold to be, judge to be, reckon to be, presume to be, look on as
▷▷ **take someone in** 1 LET IN, receive, admit, board, welcome, harbour, accommodate, take care of, put up, billet
2 (*informal*) DECEIVE, fool, con (*informal*), do (*slang*), trick, cheat, mislead, dupe, gull (*archaic*), swindle, hoodwink, pull the wool over someone's eyes (*informal*), bilk, cozen
▷▷ **take someone off** (*informal*) PARODY, imitate, mimic, mock, ridicule, ape, caricature, send up (*Brit informal*), spoof (*informal*), travesty, impersonate, lampoon, burlesque, satirize
▷▷ **take someone on** 1 COMPETE AGAINST, face, contend with, fight, oppose, vie with, pit yourself against, enter the lists against, match yourself against
2 ENGAGE, employ, hire, retain, enlist, enrol
▷▷ **take something back** 1 RETURN, bring back, send back, hand back
2 RETRACT, withdraw, renounce, renege on, disavow, recant, disclaim, unsay
3 REGAIN, get back, reclaim, recapture, repossess, retake, reconquer

▷▷ **take something down** 1 REMOVE, take off, extract
2 DISMANTLE, demolish, take apart, disassemble, level, tear down, raze, take to pieces
3 MAKE A NOTE OF, record, write down, minute, note, set down, transcribe, put on record
▷▷ **take something in** 1 UNDERSTAND, absorb, grasp, digest, comprehend, assimilate, get the hang of (*informal*)
2 INCLUDE, contain, comprise, cover, embrace, encompass
▷▷ **take something off** REMOVE, discard, strip off, drop, peel off, doff, divest yourself of
▷▷ **take something on** 1 ACCEPT, tackle, undertake, shoulder, have a go at (*informal*), agree to do, address yourself to
2 (with a quality or identity as object) ACQUIRE, assume, come to have
▷▷ **take something over** GAIN CONTROL OF, take command of, assume control of, come to power in, become leader of
▷▷ **take something up** 1 START, begin, engage in, assume, adopt, become involved in
2 OCCUPY, absorb, consume, use up, cover, fill, waste, squander, extend over
3 RESUME, continue, go on with, pick up, proceed with, restart, carry on with, recommence, follow on with, begin something again
▷▷ **take to someone** LIKE, get on with, warm to, be taken with, be pleased by, become friendly with, conceive an affection for
▷▷ **take to something** 1 START, resort to, make a habit of, have recourse to
2 HEAD FOR, make for, run for, flee to

takeoff *noun* 1 DEPARTURE, launch, liftoff
2 (*informal*) PARODY, imitation, send-up (*Brit informal*), mocking, satire, caricature, spoof (*informal*), travesty, lampoon

takeover *noun* MERGER, coup, change of leadership, incorporation

tale *noun* 1 STORY, narrative, anecdote, account, relation, novel, legend, fiction, romance, saga, short story, yarn (*informal*), fable, narration, conte (*French*), spiel (*informal*), urban myth, urban legend
2 LIE, fabrication, falsehood, fib, untruth, spiel (*informal*), tall story (*informal*), rigmarole, cock-and-bull story (*informal*)

talent *noun* ABILITY, gift, aptitude, power, skill, facility, capacity, bent, genius, expertise, faculty, endowment, forte, flair, knack

talented *adjective* GIFTED, able, expert, master, masterly, brilliant, ace (*informal*), artistic, consummate, first-rate, top-notch (*informal*), adroit

talisman *noun* CHARM, mascot, amulet, lucky charm, fetish, juju

talk *verb* 1 SPEAK, chat, chatter, converse, communicate, rap (*slang*), articulate, witter (*informal*), gab (*informal*), express yourself, prattle, natter, shoot the breeze (*US slang*), prate, run off at the mouth (*slang*), earbash (*Austral & NZ slang*)
2 DISCUSS, confer, hold discussions, negotiate, palaver, parley, confabulate, have a confab (*informal*), chew the rag *or* fat (*slang*)
3 INFORM, shop (*slang, chiefly Brit*), grass (*Brit slang*), sing (*slang, chiefly US*), squeal (*slang*), squeak (*informal*), tell all, spill the beans (*informal*), give the game away, blab, let the cat out of the bag, reveal information, spill your guts (*slang*)
▷ *noun* 1 SPEECH, lecture, presentation, report, address, seminar, discourse, sermon, symposium, dissertation, harangue, oration, disquisition, whaikorero (*NZ*)
2 DISCUSSION, tête-à-tête, conference, dialogue, consultation, heart-to-heart, confabulation, confab (*informal*), powwow
3 CONVERSATION, chat, natter, crack (*Scot & Irish*), rap (*slang*), jaw (*slang*), chatter, gab (*informal*), chitchat, blether, blather
4 GOSSIP, rumour, hearsay, tittle-tattle, goss (*informal*)
5 LANGUAGE, words, speech, jargon, slang, dialect, lingo (*informal*), patois, argot
6 *often plural* MEETING, conference, discussions, negotiations, congress, summit, mediation, arbitration, conciliation, conclave, palaver, parley, hui (*NZ*)
▷▷ **talk big** BOAST, exaggerate, brag, crow, vaunt, bluster, blow your own trumpet
▷▷ **talk someone into something** PERSUADE, convince, win someone over, sway, bring round (*informal*), sweet-talk someone into, prevail on *or* upon

talkative *adjective* LOQUACIOUS, chatty, garrulous, long-winded, big-mouthed (*slang*), wordy, effusive, gabby (*informal*), voluble, gossipy, verbose, mouthy, prolix
<< OPPOSITE reserved

talker *noun* SPEAKER, lecturer, orator, conversationalist, chatterbox, speechmaker

talking-to *noun* (*informal*) REPRIMAND, lecture, rebuke, scolding, row, criticism, wigging (*Brit slang*), slating (*informal*), reproach, ticking-off (*informal*), dressing-down (*informal*), telling-off (*informal*), reproof, rap on the knuckles
<< OPPOSITE praise

tall *adjective* 1 LOFTY, big, giant, long-legged, lanky, leggy
2 HIGH, towering, soaring, steep, elevated, lofty
<< OPPOSITE short

tally *verb* 1 AGREE, match, accord, fit, suit, square, parallel, coincide, correspond,

conform, concur, harmonize
<< OPPOSITE disagree
2 COUNT UP, total, compute, keep score
▷ *noun* RECORD, score, total, count, reckoning, running total

tame *adjective* 1 DOMESTICATED, unafraid, docile, broken, gentle, fearless, obedient, amenable, tractable, used to human contact
<< OPPOSITE wild
2 SUBMISSIVE, meek, compliant, subdued, manageable, obedient, docile, spiritless, unresisting
<< OPPOSITE stubborn
3 UNEXCITING, boring, dull, bland, tedious, flat, tiresome, lifeless, prosaic, uninspiring, humdrum, uninteresting, insipid, vapid, wearisome
<< OPPOSITE exciting
▷ *verb* 1 DOMESTICATE, train, break in, gentle, pacify, house-train, make tame
<< OPPOSITE make fiercer
2 SUBDUE, suppress, master, discipline, curb, humble, conquer, repress, bridle, enslave, subjugate, bring to heel, break the spirit of
<< OPPOSITE arouse

tamper *verb usually with* **with** 1 INTERFERE WITH, tinker with, meddle with, alter, fiddle with (*informal*), mess about with, muck about with (*Brit slang*), monkey around with, fool about with (*informal*)
2 INFLUENCE, fix (*informal*), rig, corrupt, manipulate

tang *noun* 1 SCENT, smell, odour, perfume, fragrance, aroma, reek, redolence
2 TASTE, bite, flavour, edge, relish, smack, savour, zest, sharpness, piquancy, spiciness, zestiness
3 TRACE, touch, tinge, suggestion, hint, whiff, smattering

tangible *adjective* DEFINITE, real, positive, solid, material, physical, actual, substantial, objective, concrete, evident, manifest, palpable, discernible, tactile, perceptible, corporeal, touchable
<< OPPOSITE intangible

tangle *noun* 1 KNOT, mass, twist, web, jungle, mat, coil, snarl, mesh, ravel, entanglement
2 MESS, jam, fix (*informal*), confusion, complication, maze, mix-up, shambles, labyrinth, entanglement, imbroglio
▷ *verb* 1 TWIST, knot, mat, coil, snarl, mesh, entangle, interlock, kink, interweave, ravel, interlace, enmesh, intertwist
<< OPPOSITE disentangle
2 *sometimes with* **up** ENTANGLE, catch, ensnare, entrap
3 CONFUSE, mix up, muddle, jumble, scramble
▷▷ **tangle with someone** COME INTO CONFLICT WITH, come up against, cross swords with, dispute with, contend with, contest with, lock horns with

tangled *adjective* 1 KNOTTED, twisted, matted, messy, snarled, jumbled, entangled, knotty, tousled
2 COMPLICATED, involved, complex, confused, messy, mixed-up, convoluted, knotty

tangy *adjective* SHARP, tart, piquant, biting, fresh, spicy, pungent, briny, acerb

tantalize *or* **tantalise** *verb* TORMENT, tease, taunt, torture, provoke, entice, lead on, titillate, make someone's mouth water, keep someone hanging on

tantamount ▷▷ **tantamount to** EQUIVALENT TO, equal to, as good as, synonymous with, the same as, commensurate with

tantrum *noun* OUTBURST, temper, hysterics, fit, storm, paddy (*Brit informal*), wax (*informal, chiefly Brit*), flare-up, paroxysm, bate (*Brit slang*), ill humour, foulie (*Austral slang*), hissy fit (*informal*)

tap[1] *verb* KNOCK, strike, pat, rap, beat, touch, drum
▷ *noun* KNOCK, pat, rap, beat, touch, drumming, light blow

tap[2] *noun* 1 VALVE, spout, faucet (*US & Canad*), spigot, stopcock
2 BUG (*informal*), listening device, wiretap, bugging device, hidden microphone
▷ *verb* LISTEN IN ON, monitor, bug (*informal*), spy on, eavesdrop on, wiretap
▷▷ **on tap** 1 (*informal*) AVAILABLE, ready, standing by, to hand, on hand, at hand, in reserve
2 ON DRAUGHT, cask-conditioned, from barrels, not bottled *or* canned

tape *noun* BINDING, strip, band, string, ribbon
▷ *verb* 1 RECORD, video, tape-record, make a recording of
2 *sometimes with* **up** BIND, secure, stick, seal, wrap

taper *verb* NARROW, thin, attenuate, come to a point, become thinner, become narrow
▷▷ **taper off** DECREASE, dwindle, lessen, reduce, fade, weaken, wane, subside, wind down, die out, die away, thin out
<< OPPOSITE widen

tardy *adjective* 1 LATE, overdue, unpunctual, belated, dilatory, behindhand
2 SLOW, belated, delayed

target *noun* 1 MARK, goal, bull's-eye
2 GOAL, aim, objective, end, mark, object, intention, ambition, Holy Grail (*informal*)
3 VICTIM, butt, prey, quarry, scapegoat

tariff *noun* 1 TAX, rate, duty, toll, levy, excise, impost, assessment
2 PRICE LIST, charges, schedule

tarnish *verb* 1 STAIN, dull, discolour, spot, soil, dim, rust, darken, blot, blemish, befoul, lose lustre *or* shine

<< OPPOSITE brighten

2 DAMAGE, taint, blacken, sully, drag through the mud, smirch

<< OPPOSITE enhance

▷ *noun* STAIN, taint, discoloration, spot, rust, blot, blemish

tarry *verb* LINGER, remain, loiter, wait, delay, pause, hang around (*informal*), lose time, bide, dally, take your time, dawdle, drag your feet *or* heels

<< OPPOSITE hurry

tart[1] *noun* PIE, pastry, pasty, tartlet, patty

tart[2] *adjective* 1 SHARP, acid, sour, bitter, pungent, tangy, astringent, piquant, vinegary, acidulous, acerb

<< OPPOSITE sweet

2 CUTTING, biting, sharp, short, wounding, nasty, harsh, scathing, acrimonious, barbed, hurtful, caustic, astringent, vitriolic, trenchant, testy, mordant, snappish, mordacious

<< OPPOSITE kind

tart[3] *noun* (*informal*) SLUT, prostitute, hooker (*US slang*), whore, slag (*Brit slang*), call girl, working girl (*facetious slang*), harlot, streetwalker, loose woman, fallen woman, scrubber (*Brit & Austral slang*), strumpet, trollop, floozy (*slang*), woman of easy virtue, fille de joie (*French*), hornbag (*Austral slang*)

task *noun* JOB, duty, assignment, work, business, charge, labour, exercise, mission, employment, enterprise, undertaking, occupation, chore, toil

▷ *verb* CHARGE, assign to, entrust

▷▷ **take someone to task** CRITICIZE, blame, blast, lecture, carpet (*informal*), censure, rebuke, reprimand, reproach, scold, tear into (*informal*), tell off (*informal*), diss (*slang, chiefly US*), read the riot act, reprove, upbraid, lambast(e), bawl out (*informal*), chew out (*US & Canad informal*), tear (someone) off a strip (*Brit informal*), give a rocket (*Brit & NZ informal*)

taste *noun* 1 FLAVOUR, savour, relish, smack, tang

<< OPPOSITE blandness

2 BIT, bite, drop, swallow, sip, mouthful, touch, sample, dash, nip, spoonful, morsel, titbit, soupçon (*French*)

3 LIKING, preference, penchant, fondness, partiality, desire, fancy, leaning, bent, appetite, relish, inclination, palate, predilection

<< OPPOSITE dislike

4 REFINEMENT, style, judgment, culture, polish, grace, discrimination, perception, appreciation, elegance, sophistication, cultivation, discernment

<< OPPOSITE lack of judgment

5 PROPRIETY, discretion, correctness, delicacy, tact, politeness, nicety, decorum, tactfulness

<< OPPOSITE impropriety

▷ *verb* 1 *often with* **of** HAVE A FLAVOUR OF, smack of, savour of

2 SAMPLE, try, test, relish, sip, savour, nibble

3 DISTINGUISH, perceive, discern, differentiate

4 EXPERIENCE, know, undergo, partake of, feel, encounter, meet with, come up against, have knowledge of

<< OPPOSITE miss

>> RELATED WORD *noun* gustation

tasteful *adjective* REFINED, stylish, elegant, cultured, beautiful, smart, charming, polished, delicate, artistic, handsome, cultivated, discriminating, exquisite, graceful, harmonious, urbane, fastidious, aesthetically pleasing, in good taste

<< OPPOSITE tasteless

tasteless *adjective* 1 GAUDY, cheap, vulgar, tacky (*informal*), flashy, naff (*Brit slang*), garish, inelegant, tawdry

<< OPPOSITE tasteful

2 VULGAR, crude, improper, low, gross, rude, coarse, crass, unseemly, indiscreet, tactless, uncouth, impolite, graceless, indelicate, indecorous

3 INSIPID, bland, flat, boring, thin, weak, dull, mild, tame, watered-down, uninteresting, uninspired, vapid, flavourless

<< OPPOSITE tasty

tasty *adjective* DELICIOUS, luscious, palatable, delectable, good-tasting, savoury, full-flavoured, yummy (*slang*), flavoursome, scrumptious (*informal*), appetizing, toothsome, flavourful, sapid, lekker (*S African slang*), yummo (*Austral slang*)

<< OPPOSITE bland

tattletale *noun* (*chiefly US & Canad*) GOSSIP, busybody, babbler, prattler, chatterbox (*informal*), blether, chatterer, bigmouth (*slang*), scandalmonger, gossipmonger

tatty *adjective* (*Chiefly Brit*) SHABBY, seedy, scruffy, worn, poor, neglected, ragged, run-down, frayed, worn out, dilapidated, tattered, tawdry, threadbare, rumpled, bedraggled, unkempt, down at heel, the worse for wear, having seen better days

<< OPPOSITE smart

taunt *verb* JEER, mock, tease, ridicule, provoke, insult, torment, sneer, deride, revile, twit, guy (*informal*), gibe

▷ *noun* JEER, dig, insult, ridicule, cut, teasing, provocation, barb, derision, sarcasm, gibe

taut *adjective* 1 TENSE, rigid, tight, stressed, stretched, strained, flexed

<< OPPOSITE relaxed

2 TIGHT, stretched, rigid, tightly stretched

<< OPPOSITE slack

tavern *noun* INN, bar, pub (*informal, chiefly Brit*),

public house, watering hole (*facetious slang*), boozer (*Brit, Austral & NZ informal*), beer parlour (*Canad*), beverage room (*Canad*), hostelry, alehouse (*archaic*), taproom

tawdry *adjective* VULGAR, cheap, tacky (*informal*), flashy, tasteless, plastic (*slang*), glittering, naff (*Brit slang*), gaudy, tatty, showy, tinsel, raffish, gimcrack, meretricious, tinselly, cheap-jack (*informal*)
<< OPPOSITE stylish

tax *noun* 1 CHARGE, rate, duty, toll, levy, tariff, excise, contribution, assessment, customs, tribute, imposition, tithe, impost
2 STRAIN, demand, burden, pressure, weight, load, drain
▷ *verb* 1 CHARGE, impose a tax on, levy a tax on, rate, demand, assess, extract, exact, tithe
2 STRAIN, push, stretch, try, test, task, load, burden, drain, exhaust, weaken, weary, put pressure on, sap, wear out, weigh heavily on, overburden, make heavy demands on, enervate
3 ACCUSE, charge, blame, confront, impeach, incriminate, arraign, impugn, lay at your door
<< OPPOSITE acquit

taxing *adjective* DEMANDING, trying, wearing, heavy, tough, tiring, punishing, exacting, stressful, sapping, onerous, burdensome, wearisome, enervating
<< OPPOSITE easy

teach *verb* 1 INSTRUCT, train, coach, school, direct, advise, inform, discipline, educate, drill, tutor, enlighten, impart, instil, inculcate, edify, give lessons in
2 *often with* **how** SHOW, train, demonstrate

teacher *noun* INSTRUCTOR, coach, tutor, don, guide, professor, trainer, lecturer, guru, mentor, educator, handler, schoolteacher, pedagogue, dominie (*Scot*), master *or* mistress, schoolmaster *or* schoolmistress

team *noun* 1 SIDE, squad, troupe
2 GROUP, company, set, body, band, crew, gang, line-up, bunch, posse (*informal*)
3 PAIR, span, yoke
▷▷ **team up** JOIN, unite, work together, cooperate, couple, link up, get together, yoke, band together, collaborate, join forces ▷ see **family**

teamwork *noun* COOPERATION, collaboration, unity, concert, harmony, fellowship, coordination, joint action, esprit de corps

tear *verb* 1 RIP, split, rend, shred, rupture, sunder
2 RUN, rip, ladder, snag
3 SCRATCH, cut (open), gash, lacerate, injure, mangle, cut to pieces, cut to ribbons, mangulate (*Austral slang*)
4 PULL APART, claw, lacerate, sever, mutilate, mangle, mangulate (*Austral slang*)
5 RUSH, run, charge, race, shoot, fly, career, speed, belt (*slang*), dash, hurry, barrel (along) (*informal, chiefly US & Canad*), sprint, bolt, dart, gallop, zoom, burn rubber (*informal*)
6 *often with* **away** *or* **from** PULL, seize, rip, grab, snatch, pluck, yank, wrench, wrest
▷ *noun* HOLE, split, rip, run, rent, snag, rupture

tearaway *noun* (*Brit*) HOOLIGAN, delinquent, tough, rough (*informal*), rowdy, ruffian, roughneck (*slang*), good-for-nothing

tearful *adjective* 1 WEEPING, crying, sobbing, in tears, whimpering, blubbering, weepy (*informal*), lachrymose
2 SAD, pathetic, poignant, upsetting, distressing, harrowing, pitiful, woeful, mournful, lamentable, sorrowful, pitiable, dolorous

tears *plural noun* CRYING, weeping, sobbing, wailing, whimpering, blubbering, lamentation
▷▷ **in tears** WEEPING, crying, sobbing, whimpering, blubbering, visibly moved
>> RELATED WORDS *adjectives* lacrimal, lachrymal *or* lacrymal

tease *verb* 1 MOCK, bait, wind up (*Brit slang*), worry, bother, provoke, annoy, needle (*informal*), plague (*informal*), rag, rib (*informal*), torment, ridicule, taunt, aggravate (*informal*), badger, pester, vex, goad, bedevil, take the mickey out of (*informal*), twit, chaff, guy (*informal*), gibe, pull someone's leg (*informal*), make fun of
2 TANTALIZE, lead on, flirt with, titillate

technical *adjective* SCIENTIFIC, technological, skilled, specialist, specialized, hi-tech *or* high-tech

technique *noun* 1 METHOD, way, system, approach, means, course, style, fashion, manner, procedure, mode, MO, modus operandi
2 SKILL, art, performance, craft, touch, know-how (*informal*), facility, delivery, execution, knack, artistry, craftsmanship, proficiency, adroitness

tedious *adjective* BORING, dull, dreary, monotonous, tiring, annoying, fatiguing, drab, banal, tiresome, lifeless, prosaic, laborious, humdrum, uninteresting, long-drawn-out, mind-numbing, irksome, unexciting, soporific, ho-hum (*informal*), vapid, wearisome, deadly dull, prosy, dreich (*Scot*)
<< OPPOSITE exciting

tedium *noun* BOREDOM, monotony, dullness, routine, the doldrums, banality, sameness, ennui, drabness, deadness, dreariness, tediousness, lifelessness
<< OPPOSITE excitement

teem[1] *verb* BE FULL OF, abound, swarm, bristle, brim, overflow, be abundant, burst at the seams, be prolific, be crawling, pullulate

teem[2] *verb often with* **down** *or* **with rain** POUR, lash, pelt (down), sheet, stream, belt (*slang*), bucket down (*informal*), rain cats and dogs (*informal*)

teeming[1] *adjective* FULL, packed, crowded, alive, thick, bursting, numerous, crawling, swarming, abundant, bristling, brimming, overflowing, fruitful, replete, chock-full, brimful, chock-a-block

<< OPPOSITE lacking

teeming[2] *adjective* POURING, lashing, pelting, sheeting, streaming, belting (*slang*), bucketing down (*informal*)

teenage *adjective* YOUTHFUL, adolescent, juvenile, immature

teenager *noun* YOUTH, minor, adolescent, juvenile, girl, boy

teeny *adjective* (*informal*) TINY, minute, wee, miniature, microscopic, diminutive, minuscule, teeny-weeny, teensy-weensy

teeter *verb* WOBBLE, rock, totter, balance, stagger, sway, tremble, waver, pivot, seesaw

telegram *noun* CABLE, wire (*informal*), telegraph, telex, radiogram

telegraph *verb* CABLE, wire (*informal*), transmit, telex, send

telepathy *noun* MIND-READING, ESP, sixth sense, clairvoyance, extra sensory perception, psychometry, thought transference

telephone *noun* PHONE, blower (*informal*), mobile (phone), handset, dog and bone (*slang*)
▷ *verb* CALL, phone, ring (*chiefly Brit*), buzz (*informal*), dial, call up, give someone a call, give someone a ring (*informal, chiefly Brit*), give someone a buzz (*informal*), give someone a bell (*Brit slang*), put a call through to, give someone a tinkle (*Brit informal*), get on the blower to (*informal*)

telescope *noun* GLASS, scope (*informal*), spyglass
▷ *verb* SHORTEN, contract, compress, cut, trim, shrink, tighten, condense, abbreviate, abridge, capsulize

<< OPPOSITE lengthen

television *noun* TV, telly (*Brit informal*), small screen (*informal*), the box (*Brit informal*), receiver, the tube (*slang*), TV set, gogglebox (*Brit slang*), idiot box (*slang*)

tell *verb* **1** INFORM, notify, make aware, say to, state to, warn, reveal to, express to, brief, advise, disclose to, proclaim to, fill in, speak about to, confess to, impart, alert to, divulge, announce to, acquaint with, communicate to, mention to, make known to, apprise, utter to, get off your chest (*informal*), let know
2 DESCRIBE, relate, recount, report, portray, depict, chronicle, rehearse, narrate, give an account of
3 INSTRUCT, order, command, direct, bid, enjoin
4 SEE, make out, discern, understand, discover, be certain, comprehend
5 DISTINGUISH, discriminate, discern, differentiate, identify
6 HAVE *or* TAKE EFFECT, register, weigh, have force, count, take its toll, carry weight, make its presence felt
▷▷ **tell someone off** REPRIMAND, rebuke, scold, lecture, carpet (*informal*), censure, reproach, berate, chide, tear into (*informal*), read the riot act, reprove, upbraid, take to task, tick off (*informal*), bawl out (*informal*), chew out (*US & Canad informal*), tear off a strip (*Brit informal*), give a piece of your mind to, haul over the coals (*informal*), give a rocket to (*Brit & NZ informal*)

telling *adjective* EFFECTIVE, significant, considerable, marked, striking, powerful, solid, impressive, influential, decisive, potent, forceful, weighty, forcible, trenchant, effectual

<< OPPOSITE unimportant

temerity *noun* AUDACITY, nerve (*informal*), cheek, gall (*informal*), front, assurance, pluck, boldness, recklessness, chutzpah (*US & Canad informal*), impudence, effrontery, impulsiveness, rashness, brass neck (*Brit informal*), foolhardiness, sassiness (*US informal*), forwardness, heedlessness

temper *noun* **1** IRRITABILITY, anger, irascibility, passion, resentment, irritation, annoyance, petulance, surliness, ill humour, peevishness, hot-headedness

<< OPPOSITE good humour

2 FRAME OF MIND, character, nature, attitude, mind, mood, constitution, humour, vein, temperament, tenor, disposition
3 RAGE, fury, bad mood, passion, paddy (*Brit informal*), wax (*informal, chiefly Brit*), tantrum, bate (*Brit slang*), fit of pique, foulie (*Austral slang*), hissy fit (*informal*)
4 SELF-CONTROL, composure, cool (*slang*), calm, good humour, tranquillity, coolness, calmness, equanimity

<< OPPOSITE anger

▷ *verb* **1** MODERATE, restrain, tone down, calm, soften, soothe, lessen, allay, mitigate, abate, assuage, mollify, soft-pedal (*informal*), palliate, admix

<< OPPOSITE intensify

2 STRENGTHEN, harden, toughen, anneal

<< OPPOSITE soften

temperament *noun* NATURE, character, personality, quality, spirit, make-up, soul, constitution, bent, stamp, humour, tendencies, tendency, temper, outlook, complexion, disposition, frame of mind, mettle, cast of mind

temperamental *adjective* **1** MOODY, emotional, touchy, sensitive, explosive, passionate,

volatile, fiery, impatient, erratic, neurotic, irritable, mercurial, excitable, capricious, petulant, hot-headed, hypersensitive, highly strung, easily upset, unstable
<< OPPOSITE even-tempered
2 (*informal*) UNRELIABLE, unpredictable, undependable, inconsistent, erratic, inconstant, unstable
<< OPPOSITE reliable
3 NATURAL, inherent, innate, constitutional, ingrained, congenital, inborn

temperance *noun* 1 TEETOTALISM, abstinence, sobriety, abstemiousness
2 MODERATION, restraint, self-control, self-discipline, continence, self-restraint, forbearance
<< OPPOSITE excess

temperate *adjective* 1 MILD, moderate, balmy, fair, cool, soft, calm, gentle, pleasant, clement, agreeable
<< OPPOSITE extreme
2 MODERATE, dispassionate, self-controlled, calm, stable, reasonable, sensible, mild, composed, equable, even-tempered, self-restrained
<< OPPOSITE unrestrained

tempest *noun* 1 (*Literary*) STORM, hurricane, gale, tornado, cyclone, typhoon, squall
2 UPROAR, storm, furore, disturbance, upheaval, ferment, commotion, tumult
<< OPPOSITE calm

tempestuous *adjective* 1 PASSIONATE, intense, turbulent, heated, wild, excited, emotional, violent, flaming, hysterical, stormy, impassioned, uncontrolled, boisterous, feverish
<< OPPOSITE peaceful
2 STORMY, turbulent, inclement, raging, windy, boisterous, blustery, gusty, squally

temple *noun* SHRINE, church, sanctuary, holy place, place of worship, house of God

tempo *noun* PACE, time, rate, beat, measure (*Prosody*), speed, metre, rhythm, cadence, pulse

temporal *adjective* 1 SECULAR, worldly, lay, earthly, mundane, material, civil, fleshly, mortal, terrestrial, carnal, profane, sublunary
2 TEMPORARY, passing, transitory, fleeting, short-lived, fugitive, transient, momentary, evanescent, impermanent, fugacious

temporarily *adverb* BRIEFLY, for the moment, for the time being, momentarily, for a moment, for a short time, for a little while, fleetingly, for a short while, pro tem, for the nonce

temporary *adjective* 1 IMPERMANENT, passing, transitory, brief, fleeting, interim, short-lived, fugitive, transient, momentary, ephemeral, evanescent, pro tem, here today and gone tomorrow, pro tempore (*Latin*), fugacious
<< OPPOSITE permanent
2 SHORT-TERM, acting, interim, supply, stand-in, fill-in, caretaker, provisional, stopgap

tempt *verb* 1 ATTRACT, draw, appeal to, allure, whet the appetite of, make your mouth water
2 ENTICE, lure, lead on, invite, woo, seduce, coax, decoy, inveigle
<< OPPOSITE discourage
3 PROVOKE, try, test, risk, dare, bait, fly in the face of

temptation *noun* 1 ENTICEMENT, lure, inducement, pull, come-on (*informal*), invitation, bait, coaxing, snare, seduction, decoy, allurement, tantalization
2 APPEAL, draw, attraction, attractiveness

tempting *adjective* INVITING, enticing, seductive, alluring, attractive, mouthwatering, appetizing
<< OPPOSITE uninviting

tenacious *adjective* 1 STUBBORN, dogged, determined, persistent, sure, firm, adamant, staunch, resolute, inflexible, strong-willed, steadfast, unyielding, obstinate, intransigent, immovable, unswerving, obdurate, stiff-necked, pertinacious
<< OPPOSITE irresolute
2 FIRM, dogged, persistent, unyielding, unswerving
3 STRONG, firm, fast, iron, tight, clinging, forceful, immovable, unshakeable
4 RETENTIVE, good, photographic, unforgetful
5 ADHESIVE, clinging, sticky, glutinous, gluey, mucilaginous

tenacity *noun* PERSEVERANCE, resolution, determination, application, resolve, persistence, diligence, intransigence, firmness, stubbornness, inflexibility, obstinacy, steadfastness, obduracy, doggedness, strength of will, strength of purpose, resoluteness, pertinacity, staunchness

tenancy *noun* 1 LEASE, residence, occupancy, holding, renting, possession, occupation
2 PERIOD OF OFFICE, tenure, incumbency, time in office

tenant *noun* LEASEHOLDER, resident, renter, occupant, holder, inhabitant, occupier, lodger, boarder, lessee

tend[1] *verb* BE INCLINED, be likely, be liable, have a tendency, be apt, be prone, trend, lean, incline, be biased, be disposed, gravitate, have a leaning, have an inclination

tend[2] *verb* 1 TAKE CARE OF, look after, care for, keep, watch, serve, protect, feed, handle, attend, guard, nurse, see to, nurture, minister to, cater for, keep an eye on, wait on, watch over
<< OPPOSITE neglect
2 MAINTAIN, take care of, nurture, cultivate,

manage
<< OPPOSITE neglect
tendency *noun* 1 TREND, drift, movement, turning, heading, course, drive, bearing, direction, bias
2 INCLINATION, leaning, bent, liability, readiness, disposition, penchant, propensity, susceptibility, predisposition, predilection, proclivity, partiality, proneness
tender[1] *adjective* 1 GENTLE, loving, kind, caring, warm, sympathetic, fond, sentimental, humane, affectionate, compassionate, benevolent, considerate, merciful, amorous, warm-hearted, tenderhearted, softhearted, touchy-feely (*informal*)
<< OPPOSITE harsh
2 ROMANTIC, moving, touching, emotional, sentimental, poignant, evocative, soppy (*Brit informal*)
3 VULNERABLE, young, sensitive, new, green, raw, youthful, inexperienced, immature, callow, impressionable, unripe, wet behind the ears (*informal*)
<< OPPOSITE experienced
4 SENSITIVE, painful, sore, smarting, raw, bruised, irritated, aching, inflamed
5 FRAGILE, delicate, frail, soft, weak, feeble, breakable
6 DIFFICULT, sensitive, tricky, dangerous, complicated, risky, touchy, ticklish
tender[2] *verb* OFFER, present, submit, give, suggest, propose, extend, volunteer, hand in, put forward, proffer
▷ *noun* OFFER, bid, estimate, proposal, suggestion, submission, proffer
tenderness *noun* 1 GENTLENESS, love, affection, liking, care, consideration, sympathy, pity, humanity, warmth, mercy, attachment, compassion, devotion, kindness, fondness, sentimentality, benevolence, humaneness, amorousness, warm-heartedness, softheartedness, tenderheartedness
<< OPPOSITE harshness
2 SORENESS, pain, sensitivity, smart, bruising, ache, aching, irritation, inflammation, rawness, sensitiveness, painfulness
3 FRAGILITY, vulnerability, weakness, sensitivity, softness, feebleness, sensitiveness, frailness, delicateness
tenet *noun* PRINCIPLE, rule, doctrine, creed, view, teaching, opinion, belief, conviction, canon, thesis, maxim, dogma, precept, article of faith, kaupapa (*NZ*)
tenor *noun* MEANING, trend, drift, way, course, sense, aim, purpose, direction, path, theme, substance, burden, tendency, intent, purport
tense *adjective* 1 STRAINED, uneasy, stressful, fraught, charged, difficult, worrying, exciting, uncomfortable, knife-edge, nail-biting, nerve-racking
2 NERVOUS, wound up (*informal*), edgy, strained, wired (*slang*), anxious, under pressure, restless, apprehensive, jittery (*informal*), uptight (*informal*), on edge, jumpy, twitchy (*informal*), overwrought, strung up (*informal*), on tenterhooks, fidgety, keyed up, antsy (*informal*), wrought up, adrenalized
<< OPPOSITE calm
3 RIGID, strained, taut, stretched, tight
<< OPPOSITE relaxed
▷ *verb* TIGHTEN, strain, brace, tauten, stretch, flex, stiffen
<< OPPOSITE relax
tension *noun* 1 STRAIN, stress, nervousness, pressure, anxiety, unease, apprehension, suspense, restlessness, the jitters (*informal*), edginess
<< OPPOSITE calmness
2 FRICTION, hostility, unease, antagonism, antipathy, enmity, ill feeling
3 RIGIDITY, tightness, stiffness, pressure, stress, stretching, straining, tautness
tentative *adjective* 1 UNCONFIRMED, provisional, indefinite, test, trial, pilot, preliminary, experimental, unsettled, speculative, pencilled in, exploratory, to be confirmed, TBC, conjectural
<< OPPOSITE confirmed
2 HESITANT, cautious, uncertain, doubtful, backward, faltering, unsure, timid, undecided, diffident, iffy (*informal*)
<< OPPOSITE confident
tenuous *adjective* 1 SLIGHT, weak, dubious, shaky, doubtful, questionable, insignificant, flimsy, sketchy, insubstantial, nebulous
<< OPPOSITE strong
2 FINE, slim, delicate, attenuated, gossamer
tenure *noun* 1 OCCUPANCY, holding, occupation, residence, tenancy, possession, proprietorship
2 TERM OF OFFICE, term, incumbency, period in office, time
tepid *adjective* 1 LUKEWARM, warmish, slightly warm
2 UNENTHUSIASTIC, half-hearted, indifferent, cool, lukewarm, apathetic
<< OPPOSITE enthusiastic
term *noun* 1 WORD, name, expression, title, label, phrase, denomination, designation, appellation, locution
2 SESSION, course, quarter (*US*), semester, trimester (*US*)
3 PERIOD, time, spell, while, season, space, interval, span, duration, incumbency
4 CONCLUSION, end, close, finish, culmination, fruition
▷ *verb* CALL, name, label, style, entitle, tag, dub, designate, describe as, denominate

terminal *adjective* 1 FATAL, deadly, lethal, killing, mortal, incurable, inoperable, untreatable
2 FINAL, last, closing, finishing, concluding, ultimate, terminating
<< OPPOSITE initial
▷ *noun* TERMINUS, station, depot, end of the line

terminate *verb* 1 END, stop, conclude, finish, complete, axe (*informal*), cut off, wind up, put an end to, discontinue, pull the plug on (*informal*), belay (*Nautical*), bring to an end
<< OPPOSITE begin
2 CEASE, end, close, finish, run out, expire, lapse, come to an end
3 ABORT, end

termination *noun* 1 ENDING, end, close, finish, conclusion, wind-up, completion, cessation, expiry, cut-off point, finis, discontinuation
<< OPPOSITE beginning
2 ABORTION, ending, discontinuation

terminology *noun* LANGUAGE, terms, vocabulary, jargon, cant, lingo (*informal*), nomenclature, patois, phraseology, argot

terminus *noun* END OF THE LINE, terminal, station, depot, last stop, garage

terms *plural noun* 1 LANGUAGE, terminology, phraseology, manner of speaking
2 CONDITIONS, particulars, provisions, provisos, stipulations, qualifications, premises (*Law*), specifications
3 RELATIONSHIP, standing, footing, relations, position, status
4 PRICE, rates, charges, fee, payment
▷▷ **come to terms** COME TO AN AGREEMENT, reach agreement, come to an understanding, conclude agreement
▷▷ **come to terms with something** LEARN TO LIVE WITH, come to accept, be reconciled to, reach acceptance of

> Many people object to the use of *in terms of* as an all-purpose preposition replacing phrases such as 'as regards', 'about', and so forth in a context such as the following: *in terms of trends in smoking habits, there is good news*. They would maintain that in strict usage it should be used to specify a relationship, as in: *obesity is defined in terms of body mass index, which involves a bit of cumbersome maths*. Nevertheless, despite objections, it is very commonly used as a link phrase, particularly in speech

terrain *noun* GROUND, country, land, landscape, topography, going

terrestrial *adjective* EARTHLY, worldly, global, mundane, sublunary, tellurian, terrene

terrible *adjective* 1 AWFUL, shocking, appalling, terrifying, horrible, dreadful, horrifying, dread, dreaded, fearful, horrendous, monstrous, harrowing, gruesome, horrid, unspeakable, frightful, hellacious (*US slang*)
2 (*informal*) BAD, awful, dreadful, beastly (*informal*), dire, abysmal, abhorrent, poor, offensive, foul, unpleasant, revolting, rotten (*informal*), obscene, hideous, vile, from hell (*informal*), obnoxious, repulsive, frightful, odious, hateful, loathsome, godawful (*slang*)
<< OPPOSITE wonderful
3 SERIOUS, desperate, severe, extreme, bad, dangerous, insufferable
<< OPPOSITE mild

terribly *adverb* 1 VERY MUCH, greatly, very, much, dreadfully, seriously, extremely, gravely, desperately, thoroughly, decidedly, awfully (*informal*), exceedingly
2 EXTREMELY, very, much, greatly, dreadfully, seriously, desperately, thoroughly, decidedly, awfully (*informal*), exceedingly

terrific *adjective* 1 (*informal*) EXCELLENT, great (*informal*), wonderful, mean (*slang*), topping (*Brit slang*), fine, brilliant, very good, cracking (*Brit informal*), amazing, outstanding, smashing (*informal*), superb, fantastic (*informal*), ace (*informal*), magnificent, fabulous (*informal*), marvellous, sensational (*informal*), sovereign, awesome (*slang*), breathtaking, super (*informal*), brill (*informal*), stupendous, bodacious (*slang, chiefly US*), boffo (*slang*), jim-dandy (*slang*), chillin' (*US slang*), booshit (*Austral slang*), exo (*Austral slang*), sik (*Austral slang*), ka pai (*NZ*), rad (*informal*), phat (*slang*), schmick (*Austral informal*)
<< OPPOSITE awful
2 INTENSE, great, huge, terrible, enormous, severe, extreme, awful, tremendous, fierce, harsh, excessive, dreadful, horrific, fearful, awesome, gigantic, monstrous

terrified *adjective* FRIGHTENED, scared, petrified, alarmed, intimidated, awed, panic-stricken, scared to death, scared stiff, terror-stricken, horror-struck, frightened out of your wits

terrify *verb* FRIGHTEN, scare, petrify, alarm, intimidate, terrorize, scare to death, put the fear of God into, make your hair stand on end, fill with terror, make your flesh creep, make your blood run cold, frighten out of your wits

territory *noun* DISTRICT, area, land, region, state, country, sector, zone, province, patch, turf (*US slang*), domain, terrain, tract, bailiwick

terror *noun* 1 FEAR, alarm, dread, fright, panic, anxiety, intimidation, fear and trembling
2 NIGHTMARE, monster, bogeyman, devil, fiend, bugbear, scourge

terrorize *or* **terrorise** *verb* 1 BULLY, menace, intimidate, threaten, oppress, coerce, strong-arm (*informal*), browbeat

2 TERRIFY, alarm, frighten, scare, intimidate, petrify, scare to death, strike terror into, put the fear of God into, fill with terror, frighten out of your wits, inspire panic in

terse *adjective* 1 CURT, abrupt, brusque, short, rude, tart, snappy, gruff

<< OPPOSITE polite

2 CONCISE, short, brief, clipped, neat, to the point, crisp, compact, summary, condensed, incisive, elliptical, laconic, succinct, pithy, monosyllabic, gnomic, epigrammatic, aphoristic, sententious

<< OPPOSITE lengthy

test *verb* 1 CHECK, try, investigate, assess, research, prove, analyse, experiment with, try out, verify, assay, put something to the proof, put something to the test

2 EXAMINE, put someone to the test, put someone through their paces

▷ *noun* 1 TRIAL, research, check, investigation, attempt, analysis, assessment, proof, examination, evaluation, acid test

2 EXAMINATION, paper, assessment, evaluation

testament *noun* 1 PROOF, evidence, testimony, witness, demonstration, tribute, attestation, exemplification

2 (*Law*) WILL, last wishes

testify *verb* BEAR WITNESS, state, swear, certify, declare, witness, assert, affirm, depose (*Law*), attest, corroborate, vouch, evince, give testimony, asseverate

<< OPPOSITE disprove

testimonial *noun* REFERENCE, recommendation, credential, character, tribute, certificate, endorsement, commendation

> *Testimonial* is sometimes wrongly used where *testimony* is meant: *his re-election is a testimony* (not *a testimonial*) *to his popularity with his constituents*

testimony *noun* 1 (*Law*) EVIDENCE, information, statement, witness, profession, declaration, confirmation, submission, affirmation, affidavit, deposition, corroboration, avowal, attestation

2 PROOF, evidence, demonstration, indication, support, manifestation, verification, corroboration ▷ see **testimonial**

testing *adjective* DIFFICULT, trying, demanding, taxing, challenging, searching, tough, exacting, formidable, rigorous, strenuous, arduous

<< OPPOSITE undemanding

testy *adjective* IRRITABLE, cross, grumpy, crabbed, impatient, snappy, sullen, touchy, bad-tempered, petulant, irascible, cantankerous, peppery, tetchy, ratty (*Brit & NZ informal*), quarrelsome, fretful, short-tempered, waspish, peevish, quick-tempered, splenetic, snappish, liverish, captious

tetchy *adjective* IRRITABLE, cross, grumpy, crabbed, impatient, snappy, sullen, touchy, bad-tempered, petulant, irascible, cantankerous, peppery, ratty (*Brit & NZ informal*), testy, quarrelsome, fretful, short-tempered, waspish, peevish, quick-tempered, splenetic, snappish, liverish, captious

tether *noun* LEASH, rope, lead, bond, chain, restraint, fastening, shackle, fetter, halter

▷ *verb* TIE, secure, bind, chain, rope, restrain, fasten, shackle, leash, fetter, manacle

▷▷ **at the end of your tether** EXASPERATED, exhausted, at your wits' end, finished, out of patience, at the limit of your endurance

text *noun* 1 CONTENTS, words, content, wording, body, matter, subject matter, main body

2 WORDS, wording

3 TRANSCRIPT, script

4 REFERENCE BOOK, textbook, source, reader

5 PASSAGE, extract, line, sentence, paragraph, verse

6 SUBJECT, matter, topic, argument, theme, thesis, motif

texture *noun* FEEL, quality, character, consistency, structure, surface, constitution, fabric, tissue, grain, weave, composition

thank *verb* SAY THANK YOU TO, express gratitude to, show gratitude to, show your appreciation to

thankful *adjective* GRATEFUL, pleased, relieved, obliged, in (someone's) debt, indebted, appreciative, beholden

<< OPPOSITE ungrateful

thankless *adjective* UNREWARDING, unappreciated

<< OPPOSITE rewarding

thanks *plural noun* GRATITUDE, appreciation, thanksgiving, credit, recognition, acknowledgment, gratefulness

▷▷ **thanks to** BECAUSE OF, through, due to, as a result of, owing to, by reason of

thaw *verb* MELT, dissolve, soften, defrost, warm, liquefy, unfreeze

<< OPPOSITE freeze

theatrical *adjective* 1 DRAMATIC, stage, Thespian, dramaturgical

2 EXAGGERATED, dramatic, melodramatic, histrionic, affected, camp (*informal*), mannered, artificial, overdone, unreal, pompous, stilted, showy, ostentatious, hammy (*informal*), ceremonious, stagy, actorly *or* actressy

<< OPPOSITE natural

theft *noun* STEALING, robbery, thieving, fraud, rip-off (*slang*), swindling, embezzlement, pilfering, larceny, purloining, thievery

theme *noun* 1 MOTIF, leitmotif, recurrent image, unifying idea
2 SUBJECT, idea, topic, matter, argument, text, burden, essence, thesis, subject matter, keynote, gist
theological *adjective* RELIGIOUS, ecclesiastical, doctrinal, divine
theorem *noun* PROPOSITION, statement, formula, rule, principle, thesis, hypothesis, deduction, dictum
theoretical *or* **theoretic** *adjective* 1 ABSTRACT, pure, speculative, ideal, impractical
<< OPPOSITE practical
2 HYPOTHETICAL, academic, notional, unproven, conjectural, postulatory
theorize *or* **theorise** *verb* SPECULATE, conjecture, hypothesize, project, suppose, guess, formulate, propound
theory *noun* 1 HYPOTHESIS, philosophy, system of ideas, plan, system, science, scheme, proposal, principles, ideology, thesis
<< OPPOSITE fact
2 BELIEF, feeling, speculation, assumption, guess, hunch, presumption, conjecture, surmise, supposition
therapeutic *adjective* BENEFICIAL, healing, restorative, good, corrective, remedial, salutary, curative, salubrious, ameliorative, analeptic, sanative
<< OPPOSITE harmful
therapist *noun* PSYCHOLOGIST, analyst, psychiatrist, shrink (*informal*), counsellor, healer, psychotherapist, psychoanalyst, trick cyclist (*informal*)
therapy *noun* REMEDY, treatment, cure, healing, method of healing, remedial treatment
therefore *adverb* CONSEQUENTLY, so, thus, as a result, hence, accordingly, for that reason, whence, thence, ergo
thesaurus *noun* WORDBOOK, wordfinder
thesis *noun* 1 PROPOSITION, theory, hypothesis, idea, view, opinion, proposal, contention, line of argument
2 DISSERTATION, paper, treatise, essay, composition, monograph, disquisition
3 PREMISE, subject, statement, proposition, theme, topic, assumption, postulate, surmise, supposition
thick *adjective* 1 BULKY, broad, big, large, fat, solid, substantial, hefty, plump, sturdy, stout, chunky, stocky, meaty, beefy, thickset
<< OPPOSITE thin
2 WIDE, across, deep, broad, in extent *or* diameter
3 DENSE, close, heavy, deep, compact, impenetrable, lush
4 HEAVY, heavyweight, dense, chunky, bulky, woolly
5 OPAQUE, heavy, dense, impenetrable
6 VISCOUS, concentrated, stiff, condensed, clotted, coagulated, gelatinous, semi-solid, viscid
<< OPPOSITE runny
7 CROWDED, full, packed, covered, filled, bursting, jammed, crawling, choked, crammed, swarming, abundant, bristling, brimming, overflowing, seething, thronged, teeming, congested, replete, chock-full, bursting at the seams, chock-a-block
<< OPPOSITE empty
8 HUSKY, rough, hoarse, distorted, muffled, croaking, inarticulate, throaty, indistinct, gravelly, guttural, raspy, croaky
<< OPPOSITE clear
9 STRONG, marked, broad, decided, rich, distinct, pronounced
<< OPPOSITE slight
10 STUPID, slow, dull, dense, insensitive, dozy (*Brit informal*), dopey (*informal*), moronic, obtuse, brainless, blockheaded, braindead (*informal*), dumb-ass (*informal*), thickheaded, dim-witted (*informal*), slow-witted
<< OPPOSITE clever
11 (*informal*) FRIENDLY, close, intimate, familiar, pally (*informal*), devoted, well in (*informal*), confidential, inseparable, on good terms, chummy (*informal*), hand in glove, buddy-buddy (*slang, chiefly US & Canad*), palsy-walsy (*informal*), matey *or* maty (*Brit informal*)
<< OPPOSITE unfriendly
▷ *noun* MIDDLE, centre, heart, focus, core, midst, hub
thicken *verb* SET, condense, congeal, cake, gel, clot, jell, coagulate, inspissate (*archaic*)
<< OPPOSITE thin
thicket *noun* WOOD, grove, woodland, brake, clump, covert, hurst (*archaic*), copse, coppice, spinney (*Brit*)
thick-skinned *adjective* INSENSITIVE, tough, callous, hardened, hard-boiled (*informal*), impervious, stolid, unfeeling, case-hardened, unsusceptible
<< OPPOSITE sensitive
thief *noun* ROBBER, crook (*informal*), burglar, stealer, bandit, plunderer, mugger (*informal*), shoplifter, embezzler, pickpocket, pilferer, swindler, purloiner, housebreaker, footpad (*archaic*), cracksman (*slang*), larcenist
thin *adjective* 1 NARROW, fine, attenuate, attenuated, threadlike
<< OPPOSITE thick
2 SLIM, spare, lean, slight, slender, skinny, light, meagre, skeletal, bony, lanky, emaciated, spindly, underweight, scrawny, lank, undernourished, skin and bone, scraggy, thin as a rake
<< OPPOSITE fat

3 WATERY, weak, diluted, dilute, runny, rarefied, wishy-washy (*informal*)
<< OPPOSITE viscous
4 MEAGRE, sparse, scanty, poor, scattered, inadequate, insufficient, deficient, paltry
<< OPPOSITE plentiful
5 FINE, delicate, flimsy, sheer, transparent, see-through, translucent, skimpy, gossamer, diaphanous, filmy, unsubstantial
<< OPPOSITE thick
6 UNCONVINCING, inadequate, feeble, poor, weak, slight, shallow, insufficient, superficial, lame, scant, flimsy, scanty, unsubstantial
<< OPPOSITE convincing
7 WISPY, thinning, sparse, scarce, scanty
▷ *verb* 1 PRUNE, trim, cut back, weed out
2 DILUTE, water down, weaken, attenuate

thing *noun* 1 OBJECT, article, implement, machine, device, tool, instrument, mechanism, apparatus, gadget, gizmo (*informal*), contrivance, whatsit (*informal*), doo-dah (*informal*), thingummy (*informal*), thingummyjig (*informal*)
2 SUBSTANCE, stuff, element, being, body, material, fabric, texture, entity
3 CONCEPT, idea, notion, conception
4 MATTER, issue, subject, thought, concern, worry, topic, preoccupation
5 AFFAIR, situation, state of affairs, state, circumstance, scenario
6 FACT, detail, particular, point, factor, piece of information
7 FEATURE, point, detail, something, particular, factor, item, aspect, facet
8 HAPPENING, event, incident, proceeding, phenomenon, occurrence, eventuality
9 (*informal*) PHOBIA, fear, complex, horror, terror, hang-up (*informal*), aversion, neurosis, bee in your bonnet (*informal*)
10 (*informal*) OBSESSION, liking, preoccupation, mania, quirk, fetish, fixation, soft spot, predilection, idée fixe (*French*)
11 REMARK, comment, statement, observation, declaration, utterance, pronouncement
▷ *plural noun* 1 POSSESSIONS, stuff, gear, belongings, goods, effects, clothes, luggage, baggage, bits and pieces, paraphernalia, clobber (*Brit slang*), odds and ends, chattels, impedimenta
2 EQUIPMENT, gear, tool, stuff, tackle, implement, kit, apparatus, utensil, accoutrement
3 CIRCUMSTANCES, the situation, the state of affairs, matters, life, affairs

think *verb* 1 BELIEVE, hold that, be of the opinion, conclude, esteem, conceive, be of the view
2 ANTICIPATE, expect, figure (*US informal*), suppose, imagine, guess (*informal, chiefly US & Canad*), reckon (*informal*), presume, envisage, foresee, surmise
3 JUDGE, consider, estimate, reckon, deem, regard as
4 PONDER, reflect, contemplate, deliberate, brood, meditate, ruminate, cogitate, rack your brains, be lost in thought, cerebrate
5 REMEMBER, recall, recollect, review, think back to, bring to mind, call to mind
▷ *noun* (*informal*) PONDER, consideration, muse, assessment, reflection, deliberation, contemplation
▷▷ **think something over** CONSIDER, contemplate, ponder, reflect upon, give thought to, consider the pros and cons of, weigh up, rack your brains about, chew over (*informal*), mull over, turn over in your mind
▷▷ **think something up** DEVISE, create, imagine, manufacture, come up with, invent, contrive, improvise, visualize, concoct, dream up, trump up

thinker *noun* PHILOSOPHER, intellect (*informal*), wise man, sage, brain (*informal*), theorist, mastermind, mahatma

thinking *noun* REASONING, thoughts, philosophy, idea, view, position, theory, opinion, conclusions, assessment, judgment, outlook, conjecture
▷ *adjective* THOUGHTFUL, intelligent, cultured, reasoning, sophisticated, rational, philosophical, reflective, contemplative, meditative, ratiocinative

third-rate *adjective* MEDIOCRE, bad, inferior, indifferent, poor, duff (*Brit informal*), shoddy, poor-quality, low-grade, no great shakes (*informal*), not much cop (*informal*), cheap-jack, half-pie (*NZ informal*), of a sort *or* of sorts, ropey *or* ropy (*Brit informal*), bodger *or* bodgie (*Austral slang*)

thirst *noun* 1 DRYNESS, thirstiness, drought, craving to drink
2 CRAVING, hunger, appetite, longing, desire, passion, yen (*informal*), ache, lust, yearning, eagerness, hankering, keenness
<< OPPOSITE aversion

thirsty *adjective* 1 PARCHED, dry, dehydrated
2 *with* **for** EAGER FOR, longing for, hungry for, dying for, yearning for, lusting for, craving for, thirsting for, burning for, hankering for, itching for, greedy for, desirous of, avid for, athirst for

thorn *noun* PRICKLE, spike, spine, barb
▷▷ **thorn in your side** IRRITATION, nuisance, annoyance, trouble, bother, torture, plague, curse, pest, torment, hassle (*informal*), scourge, affliction, irritant, bane

thorny *adjective* 1 PRICKLY, spiky, spiny, pointed, sharp, barbed, bristly, spinous, bristling with thorns

2 TROUBLESOME, difficult, problematic(al), trying, hard, worrying, tough, upsetting, awkward, unpleasant, sticky (*informal*), harassing, irksome, ticklish, vexatious

thorough *adjective* 1 COMPREHENSIVE, full, complete, sweeping, intensive, in-depth, exhaustive, all-inclusive, all-embracing, leaving no stone unturned

<< OPPOSITE cursory

2 CAREFUL, conscientious, painstaking, efficient, meticulous, exhaustive, scrupulous, assiduous

<< OPPOSITE careless

3 COMPLETE, total, absolute, utter, perfect, entire, pure, sheer, outright, downright, unqualified, out-and-out, unmitigated, arrant, deep-dyed (*usually derogatory*)

<< OPPOSITE partial

thoroughbred *adjective* PUREBRED, pedigree, pure-blooded, blood, full-blooded, of unmixed stock

<< OPPOSITE mongrel

thoroughfare *noun* 1 ROAD, way, street, highway, roadway, passageway, avenue
2 ACCESS, way, passage

thoroughly *adverb* 1 CAREFULLY, completely, fully, comprehensively, sweepingly, efficiently, inside out, meticulously, painstakingly, scrupulously, assiduously, intensively, from top to bottom, conscientiously, exhaustively, leaving no stone unturned

<< OPPOSITE carelessly

2 FULLY, completely, throughout, inside out, through and through
3 COMPLETELY, quite, totally, perfectly, entirely, absolutely, utterly, to the full, downright, to the hilt, without reservation

<< OPPOSITE partly

though *conjunction* ALTHOUGH, while, even if, despite the fact that, allowing, granted, even though, albeit, notwithstanding, even supposing, tho' (*US poetic*)
▷ *adverb* NEVERTHELESS, still, however, yet, nonetheless, all the same, for all that, notwithstanding

thought *noun* 1 THINKING, consideration, reflection, deliberation, regard, musing, meditation, contemplation, introspection, rumination, navel-gazing (*slang*), cogitation, brainwork, cerebration
2 OPINION, view, belief, idea, thinking, concept, conclusion, assessment, notion, conviction, judgment, conception, conjecture, estimation
3 CONSIDERATION, study, attention, care, regard, scrutiny, heed
4 INTENTION, plan, idea, design, aim, purpose, object, notion
5 HOPE, expectation, dream, prospect, aspiration, anticipation
6 CONCERN, care, regard, anxiety, sympathy, compassion, thoughtfulness, solicitude, attentiveness

thoughtful *adjective* 1 REFLECTIVE, pensive, contemplative, meditative, thinking, serious, musing, wistful, introspective, rapt, studious, lost in thought, deliberative, ruminative, in a brown study

<< OPPOSITE shallow

2 CONSIDERATE, kind, caring, kindly, helpful, attentive, unselfish, solicitous

<< OPPOSITE inconsiderate

thoughtless *adjective* 1 INCONSIDERATE, rude, selfish, insensitive, unkind, uncaring, indiscreet, tactless, impolite, undiplomatic

<< OPPOSITE considerate

2 UNTHINKING, stupid, silly, careless, regardless, foolish, rash, reckless, mindless, negligent, inadvertent, ill-considered, tactless, absent-minded, imprudent, slapdash, neglectful, heedless, slipshod, inattentive, injudicious, remiss, unmindful, unobservant, ditsy *or* ditzy (*slang*)

<< OPPOSITE wise

thrall *noun* SLAVERY, bondage, servitude, enslavement, subjugation, serfdom, subjection, vassalage, thraldom

thrash *verb* 1 DEFEAT, beat, hammer (*informal*), stuff (*slang*), tank (*slang*), crush, overwhelm, slaughter (*informal*), lick (*informal*), paste (*slang*), rout, maul, trounce, clobber (*slang*), run rings around (*informal*), wipe the floor with (*informal*), make mincemeat of (*informal*), blow someone out of the water (*slang*), drub, beat someone hollow (*Brit informal*)
2 BEAT, wallop, whip, hide (*informal*), belt (*informal*), leather, tan (*slang*), cane, lick (*informal*), paste (*slang*), birch, flog, scourge, spank, clobber (*slang*), lambast(e), flagellate, horsewhip, give someone a (good) hiding (*informal*), drub, take a stick to, beat *or* knock seven bells out of (*informal*)
3 THRESH, flail, jerk, plunge, toss, squirm, writhe, heave, toss and turn
▷▷ **thrash something out** SETTLE, resolve, discuss, debate, solve, argue out, have out, talk over

thrashing *noun* 1 DEFEAT, beating, hammering (*informal*), hiding (*informal*), pasting (*slang*), rout, mauling, trouncing, drubbing
2 BEATING, hiding (*informal*), belting (*informal*), whipping, tanning (*slang*), lashing, caning, pasting (*slang*), flogging, drubbing, chastisement

thread *noun* 1 STRAND, fibre, yarn, filament, line, string, cotton, twine
2 THEME, motif, train of thought, course, direction, strain, plot, drift, tenor, story line

▷ *verb* MOVE, pass, inch, ease, thrust, meander, squeeze through, pick your way

threadbare *adjective* **1** SHABBY, worn, frayed, old, ragged, worn-out, scruffy, tattered, tatty, down at heel

<< OPPOSITE new

2 HACKNEYED, common, tired, stale, corny (*slang*), stock, familiar, conventional, stereotyped, commonplace, well-worn, trite, clichéd, overused, cliché-ridden

<< OPPOSITE original

threat *noun* **1** DANGER, risk, hazard, menace, peril

2 THREATENING REMARK, menace, commination, intimidatory remark

3 WARNING, foreshadowing, foreboding

threaten *verb* **1** INTIMIDATE, bully, menace, terrorize, warn, cow, lean on (*slang*), pressurize, browbeat, make threats to

<< OPPOSITE defend

2 ENDANGER, jeopardize, put at risk, imperil, put in jeopardy, put on the line

<< OPPOSITE protect

3 BE IMMINENT, hang over, be in the air, loom, be in the offing, hang over someone's head, impend

threatening *adjective* **1** MENACING, bullying, intimidatory, terrorizing, minatory, comminatory

2 OMINOUS, sinister, forbidding, grim, baleful, inauspicious, bodeful

<< OPPOSITE promising

threesome *noun* TRIO, trinity, trilogy, triplet, triad, triumvirate, troika, triptych, triplex, trine, triune

threshold *noun* **1** ENTRANCE, doorway, door, doorstep, sill, doorsill

2 START, beginning, opening, dawn, verge, brink, outset, starting point, inception

<< OPPOSITE end

3 LIMIT, margin, starting point, minimum

thrift *noun* ECONOMY, prudence, frugality, saving, parsimony, carefulness, good husbandry, thriftiness

<< OPPOSITE extravagance

thrifty *adjective* ECONOMICAL, prudent, provident, frugal, saving, sparing, careful, parsimonious

<< OPPOSITE extravagant

thrill *noun* **1** PLEASURE, charge (*slang*), kick (*informal*), glow, sensation, buzz (*slang*), high, stimulation, tingle, titillation, flush of excitement

<< OPPOSITE tedium

2 TREMBLING, throb, shudder, flutter, fluttering, tremor, quiver, vibration

▷ *verb* EXCITE, stimulate, arouse, move, send (*slang*), stir, flush, tingle, electrify, titillate, give someone a kick

thrilling *adjective* EXCITING, gripping, stimulating, stirring, sensational, rousing, riveting, electrifying, hair-raising, rip-roaring (*informal*)

<< OPPOSITE boring

thrive *verb* PROSPER, do well, flourish, increase, grow, develop, advance, succeed, get on, boom, bloom, wax, burgeon, grow rich

<< OPPOSITE decline

thriving *adjective* SUCCESSFUL, doing well, flourishing, growing, developing, healthy, booming, wealthy, blooming, prosperous, burgeoning, going strong

<< OPPOSITE unsuccessful

throaty *adjective* HOARSE, husky, gruff, low, deep, thick, guttural

throb *verb* **1** PULSATE, pound, beat, pulse, thump, palpitate

2 VIBRATE, pulse, resonate, pulsate, reverberate, shake, judder (*informal*)

▷ *noun* **1** PULSE, pounding, beat, thump, thumping, pulsating, palpitation

2 VIBRATION, pulse, throbbing, resonance, reverberation, judder (*informal*), pulsation

throes *plural noun* PAINS, spasms, pangs, fit, stabs, convulsions, paroxysm

▷▷ **in the throes of something** IN THE MIDST OF, in the process of, suffering from, struggling with, wrestling with, toiling with, anguished by, agonized by, in the pangs of

throng *noun* CROWD, mob, horde, press, host, pack, mass, crush, jam, congregation, swarm, multitude, concourse, assemblage

▷ *verb* **1** CROWD, flock, congregate, troop, bunch, herd, cram, converge, hem in, mill around, swarm around

<< OPPOSITE disperse

2 PACK, fill, crowd, press, jam

throttle *verb* **1** STRANGLE, choke, garrotte, strangulate

2 SUPPRESS, inhibit, stifle, control, silence, gag

through *preposition* **1** VIA, by way of, by, between, past, in and out of, from end to end of, from one side to the other of

2 BECAUSE OF, by way of, by means of, by virtue of, with the assistance of, as a consequence *or* result of

3 USING, via, by way of, by means of, by virtue of, with the assistance of

4 DURING, throughout, in the middle of, for the duration of, in

▷ *adjective* **1** *with* **with** FINISHED WITH, done with, having had enough of

2 COMPLETED, done, finished, ended, terminated

▷▷ **through and through** COMPLETELY, totally, fully, thoroughly, entirely, altogether, wholly, utterly, to the core, unreservedly

throughout *preposition* **1** RIGHT THROUGH, all

through, everywhere in, for the duration of, during the whole of, through the whole of, from end to end of
2 ALL OVER, all through, everywhere in, through the whole of, over the length and breadth of
▷ *adverb* 1 FROM START TO FINISH, right through, the whole time, all the time, from the start, all through, from beginning to end
2 ALL THROUGH, right through, in every nook and cranny

throw *verb* 1 HURL, toss, fling, send, project, launch, cast, pitch, shy, chuck (*informal*), propel, sling, lob (*informal*), heave, put
2 TOSS, fling, chuck (*informal*), cast, hurl, sling, heave, put
3 DISLODGE, unseat, upset, overturn, hurl to the ground
4 (*informal*) CONFUSE, baffle, faze, astonish, confound, unnerve, disconcert, perturb, throw you out, throw you off, dumbfound, discompose, put your off your stroke, throw you off your stride, unsettle
▷ *noun* TOSS, pitch, fling, put, cast, shy, sling, lob (*informal*), heave
▷▷ **throw someone off** 1 DISCONCERT, unsettle, faze, throw (*informal*), upset, confuse, disturb, put you off your stroke, throw you off your stride
2 ESCAPE FROM, lose, leave behind, get away from, evade, shake off, elude, outrun, outdistance, give someone the slip, show a clean pair of heels to
▷▷ **throw someone out** EXPEL, eject, evict, dismiss, get rid of, oust, kick out (*informal*), show the door to, turf out (*Brit informal*), give the bum's rush to (*slang*), kiss off (*slang, chiefly US & Canad*)
▷▷ **throw something away** 1 DISCARD, dump (*informal*), get rid of, reject, scrap, axe (*informal*), bin (*informal*), ditch (*slang*), junk (*informal*), chuck (*informal*), throw out, dispose of, dispense with, jettison, cast off
2 WASTE, lose, blow (*slang*), squander, fritter away, fail to make use of, make poor use of
▷▷ **throw something off** CAST OFF, shake off, rid yourself of, free yourself of, drop, abandon, discard
▷▷ **throw something out** 1 DISCARD, dump (*informal*), get rid of, reject, scrap, bin (*informal*), ditch (*slang*), junk (*informal*), chuck (*informal*), throw away, dispose of, dispense with, jettison, cast off
2 EMIT, radiate, give off, diffuse, disseminate, put forth
▷▷ **throw something up** 1 THROW TOGETHER, jerry-build, run up, slap together *verb*
2 PRODUCE, reveal, bring to light, bring forward, bring to the surface, bring to notice
3 GIVE UP, leave, abandon, quit, chuck (*informal*), resign from, relinquish, renounce, step down from (*informal*), jack in
▷▷ **throw up** (*informal*) VOMIT, be sick, spew, puke (*slang*), chuck (*Austral & NZ informal*), heave, regurgitate, disgorge, retch, barf (*US slang*), chunder (*slang, chiefly Austral*), upchuck (*US slang*), do a technicolour yawn (*slang*), toss your cookies (*US slang*)

throwaway *adjective* (*Chiefly Brit*) CASUAL, passing, offhand, careless, understated, unthinking, ill-considered

thrust *verb* 1 PUSH, force, shove, drive, press, plunge, jam, butt, ram, poke, propel, prod, impel
2 SHOVE, push, shoulder, lunge, jostle, elbow *or* shoulder your way
3 *often with* **through** *or* **into** STAB, stick, jab, pierce
▷ *noun* 1 STAB, pierce, lunge
2 PUSH, shove, poke, prod
3 MOMENTUM, impetus, drive, motive power, motive force, propulsive force

thud *noun* THUMP, crash, knock, smack, clump, wallop (*informal*), clunk, clonk
▷ *verb* THUMP, crash, knock, smack, clump, wallop (*informal*), clunk, clonk

thug *noun* RUFFIAN, hooligan, tough, heavy (*slang*), killer, murderer, robber, gangster, assassin, bandit, mugger (*informal*), cut-throat, bully boy, bruiser (*informal*), tsotsi (*S African*)

thumb *noun* DIGIT
▷ *verb* 1 HANDLE, finger, mark, soil, maul, mess up, dog-ear
2 HITCH, request (*informal*), signal for, hitchhike
▷▷ **all thumbs** CLUMSY, inept, cack-handed (*informal*), maladroit, butterfingered (*informal*), ham-fisted (*informal*), unco (*Austral slang*)
▷▷ **thumb through something** FLICK THROUGH, browse through, leaf through, glance at, turn over, flip through, skim through, riffle through, scan the pages of, run your eye over
▷▷ **thumbs down** DISAPPROVAL, refusal, rejection, no, rebuff, negation
▷▷ **thumbs up** APPROVAL, go-ahead (*informal*), acceptance, yes, encouragement, green light, affirmation, O.K. *or* okay (*informal*)

thumbnail *adjective* BRIEF, short, concise, quick, compact, succinct, pithy

thump *noun* 1 BLOW, knock, punch, rap, smack, clout (*informal*), whack, swipe, wallop (*informal*)
2 THUD, crash, bang, clunk, thwack
▷ *verb* 1 STRIKE, hit, punch, pound, beat, knock, deck (*slang*), batter, rap, chin (*slang*), smack, thrash, clout (*informal*), whack, swipe, clobber (*slang*), wallop (*informal*), lambast(e), belabour, lay one on (*slang*), beat *or* knock seven bells out of (*informal*)

2 THUD, crash, bang, thwack
3 THROB, pound, beat, pulse, pulsate, palpitate
thumping *adjective* (*Slang*) HUGE, massive, enormous, great, impressive, tremendous, excessive, terrific, thundering (*slang*), titanic, gigantic, monumental, mammoth, colossal, whopping (*informal*), stellar (*informal*), exorbitant, gargantuan, elephantine, humongous *or* humungous (*US slang*)
<< OPPOSITE insignificant
thunder *noun* RUMBLE, crash, crashing, boom, booming, explosion, rumbling, pealing, detonation, cracking
▷ *verb* 1 RUMBLE, crash, blast, boom, explode, roar, clap, resound, detonate, reverberate, crack, peal
2 SHOUT, roar, yell, bark, bellow, declaim
3 RAIL, curse, fulminate
thunderous *adjective* LOUD, noisy, deafening, booming, roaring, resounding, tumultuous, ear-splitting
thus *adverb* 1 IN THIS WAY, so, like this, as follows, like so, in this manner, in this fashion, to such a degree
2 THEREFORE, so, hence, consequently, accordingly, for this reason, ergo, on that account
thwart *verb* FRUSTRATE, stop, foil, check, defeat, prevent, oppose, snooker, baffle, hinder, obstruct, impede, balk, outwit, stymie, cook someone's goose (*informal*), put a spoke in someone's wheel (*informal*)
<< OPPOSITE assist
tic *noun* TWITCH, jerk, spasm
tick *noun* 1 CHECK MARK, mark, line, stroke, dash
2 CLICK, tap, tapping, clicking, clack, ticktock
3 (*Brit informal*) MOMENT, second, minute, shake (*informal*), flash, instant, sec (*informal*), twinkling, split second, jiffy (*informal*), trice, half a mo (*Brit informal*), two shakes of a lamb's tail (*informal*), bat of an eye (*informal*)
▷ *verb* 1 MARK, indicate, mark off, check off, choose, select
2 CLICK, tap, clack, ticktock
▷▷ **tick someone off** (*informal, chiefly Brit*) SCOLD, rebuke, tell off (*informal*), lecture, carpet (*informal*), censure, reprimand, reproach, berate, chide, tear into (*informal*), reprove, upbraid, take to task, read the riot act to, bawl out (*informal*), chew out (*US & Canad informal*), tear off a strip (*Brit informal*), haul over the coals (*informal*), give a rocket (*Brit & NZ informal*)
▷▷ **tick something off** MARK OFF, check off, put a tick at
ticket *noun* 1 VOUCHER, pass, coupon, card, slip, certificate, token, chit
2 LABEL, tag, marker, sticker, card, slip, tab, docket
tickle *verb* AMUSE, delight, entertain, please, divert, gratify, titillate
<< OPPOSITE bore
tide *noun* 1 CURRENT, flow, stream, course, ebb, undertow, tideway
2 COURSE, direction, trend, current, movement, tendency, drift
▷▷ **tide someone over** KEEP YOU GOING, see you through, keep the wolf from the door, keep your head above water, bridge the gap for
tidings *plural noun* NEWS, report, word, message, latest (*informal*), information, communication, intelligence, bulletin, gen (*Brit informal*)
tidy *adjective* 1 NEAT, orderly, ordered, clean, trim, systematic, spruce, businesslike, well-kept, well-ordered, shipshape, spick-and-span, trig (*archaic* or *dialect*), in apple-pie order (*informal*)
<< OPPOSITE untidy
2 ORGANIZED, neat, fastidious, methodical, smart, efficient, spruce, businesslike, well-groomed, well turned out
3 (*informal*) CONSIDERABLE, large, substantial, good, goodly, fair, healthy, generous, handsome, respectable, ample, largish, sizable *or* sizeable
<< OPPOSITE small
▷ *verb* NEATEN, straighten, put in order, order, clean, groom, spruce up, put to rights, put in trim
<< OPPOSITE disorder
tie *verb* 1 FASTEN, bind, join, unite, link, connect, attach, knot, truss, interlace
<< OPPOSITE unfasten
2 TETHER, secure, rope, moor, lash, make fast
3 RESTRICT, limit, confine, hold, bind, restrain, hamper, hinder
<< OPPOSITE free
4 DRAW, be even, be level, be neck and neck, match, equal
▷ *noun* 1 FASTENING, binding, link, band, bond, joint, connection, string, rope, knot, cord, fetter, ligature
2 BOND, relationship, connection, duty, commitment, obligation, liaison, allegiance, affinity, affiliation, kinship
3 DRAW, dead heat, deadlock, stalemate
4 (*Brit Sport*) MATCH, game, contest, fixture, meeting, event, trial, bout
5 ENCUMBRANCE, restriction, limitation, check, handicap, restraint, hindrance, bind (*informal*)
▷▷ **tie in with something** 1 LINK, relate to, connect, be relevant to, come in to, have a bearing on
2 FIT IN WITH, coincide with, coordinate with, harmonize with, occur simultaneously with
▷▷ **tie something up** 1 SECURE, lash, tether, make fast, moor, attach, rope

2 CONCLUDE, settle, wrap up (*informal*), end, wind up, terminate, finish off, bring to a close
▷▷ **tie something** *or* **someone up** BIND, restrain, pinion, truss up

tie in *or* **tie-in** *noun* LINK, connection, relation, relationship, association, tie-up, liaison, coordination, hook-up

tier *noun* ROW, bank, layer, line, order, level, series, file, rank, storey, stratum, echelon

tie-up *noun* LINK, association, connection, relationship, relation, liaison, tie-in, coordination, hook-up, linkup

tiff *noun* QUARREL, row, disagreement, words, difference, dispute, scrap (*informal*), falling-out (*informal*), squabble, petty quarrel

tight *adjective* 1 CLOSE-FITTING, narrow, cramped, snug, constricted, close
<< OPPOSITE loose
2 SECURE, firm, fast, fixed
3 TAUT, stretched, tense, rigid, stiff
<< OPPOSITE slack
4 STRICT, stringent, severe, tough, harsh, stern, rigid, rigorous, uncompromising, inflexible, unyielding
<< OPPOSITE easy-going
5 SEALED, watertight, impervious, sound, proof, hermetic
<< OPPOSITE open
6 CLOSE, even, well-matched, near, hard-fought, evenly-balanced
<< OPPOSITE uneven
7 (*informal*) MISERLY, mean, stingy, close, sparing, grasping, parsimonious, niggardly, penurious, tightfisted
<< OPPOSITE generous
8 DIFFICULT, tough, dangerous, tricky, sticky (*informal*), hazardous, troublesome, problematic, precarious, perilous, worrisome, ticklish
9 (*informal*) DRUNK, intoxicated, flying (*slang*), bombed (*slang*), stoned (*slang*), wasted (*slang*), smashed (*slang*), steaming (*slang*), wrecked (*slang*), out of it (*slang*), plastered (*slang*), blitzed (*slang*), lit up (*slang*), stewed (*slang*), pickled (*informal*), bladdered (*slang*), under the influence (*informal*), tipsy, legless (*informal*), paralytic (*informal*), sozzled (*informal*), steamboats (*Scot slang*), tiddly (*slang, chiefly Brit*), half cut (*Brit slang*), zonked (*slang*), blotto (*slang*), inebriated, out to it (*Austral & NZ slang*), three sheets to the wind (*slang*), in your cups, half seas over (*Brit informal*), bevvied (*dialect*), pie-eyed (*slang*)
<< OPPOSITE sober

tighten *verb* 1 CLOSE, narrow, strengthen, squeeze, harden, constrict
<< OPPOSITE slacken
2 STRETCH, strain, tense, tauten, stiffen, rigidify
<< OPPOSITE slacken
3 FASTEN, secure, screw, fix
<< OPPOSITE unfasten

tight-lipped *adjective* SECRETIVE, reticent, uncommunicative, reserved, quiet, silent, mute, taciturn, close-mouthed, unforthcoming, close-lipped

till[1] *verb* CULTIVATE, dig, plough, work, turn over

till[2] *noun* CASH REGISTER, cash box, cash drawer

tilt *verb* SLANT, tip, slope, list, lean, heel, incline, cant
▷ *noun* 1 SLOPE, angle, inclination, list, pitch, incline, slant, cant, camber, gradient
2 (*Medieval history*) JOUST, fight, tournament, lists, clash, set-to (*informal*), encounter, combat, duel, tourney

timber *noun* 1 BEAMS, boards, planks
2 WOOD, logs

timbre *noun* TONE, sound, ring, resonance, colour, tonality, tone colour, quality of sound

time *noun* 1 PERIOD, while, term, season, space, stretch, spell, phase, interval, span, period of time, stint, duration, length of time, time frame, timeline
2 OCCASION, point, moment, stage, instance, point in time, juncture
3 AGE, days, era, year, date, generation, duration, epoch, chronology, aeon
4 TEMPO, beat, rhythm, measure, metre
5 LIFETIME, day, life, season, duration, life span, allotted span
6 HEYDAY, prime, peak, hour, springtime, salad days, best years *or* days
▷ *verb* 1 MEASURE, judge, clock, count
2 SCHEDULE, set, plan, book, programme, set up, fix, arrange, line up, organize, timetable, slate (*US*), fix up, prearrange
3 REGULATE, control, calculate
▷▷ **at one time** ONCE, previously, formerly, for a while, hitherto, once upon a time
▷▷ **at times** SOMETIMES, occasionally, from time to time, now and then, on occasion, once in a while, every now and then, every so often
▷▷ **for the time being** FOR NOW, meanwhile, meantime, in the meantime, temporarily, for the moment, for the present, pro tem, for the nonce
▷▷ **from time to time** OCCASIONALLY, sometimes, now and then, at times, on occasion, once in a while, every now and then, every so often
▷▷ **in good time** 1 ON TIME, early, ahead of schedule, ahead of time, with time to spare
2 PROMPTLY, quickly, rapidly, swiftly, speedily, with dispatch
▷▷ **in no time** QUICKLY, rapidly, swiftly, in a moment, in a flash, speedily, in an instant, apace, before you know it, in a trice, in a jiffy (*informal*), in two shakes of a lamb's tail

(*informal*), before you can say Jack Robinson
▷▷ **in time** 1 ON TIME, on schedule, in good time, at the appointed time, early, with time to spare
2 EVENTUALLY, one day, ultimately, sooner or later, someday, in the fullness of time, by and by
▷▷ **on time** PUNCTUAL(LY), prompt(ly), on schedule, in good time, on the dot
▷▷ **time and again** OVER AND OVER AGAIN, repeatedly, time after time
>> RELATED WORD *adjective* temporal

time-honoured *adjective* LONG-ESTABLISHED, traditional, customary, old, established, fixed, usual, ancient, conventional, venerable, age-old

timeless *adjective* ETERNAL, lasting, permanent, enduring, abiding, immortal, everlasting, ceaseless, immutable, indestructible, undying, ageless, imperishable, deathless, changeless
<< OPPOSITE temporary

timely *adjective* OPPORTUNE, appropriate, well-timed, prompt, suitable, convenient, at the right time, judicious, punctual, propitious, seasonable
<< OPPOSITE untimely

timetable *noun* 1 SCHEDULE, programme, agenda, list, diary, calendar, order of the day
2 SYLLABUS, course, curriculum, programme, teaching programme

timid *adjective* NERVOUS, shy, retiring, modest, shrinking, fearful, cowardly, apprehensive, coy, diffident, bashful, mousy, timorous, pusillanimous, faint-hearted, irresolute
<< OPPOSITE bold

tincture *noun* TINGE, trace, hint, colour, touch, suggestion, shade, flavour, dash, stain, smack, aroma, tint, hue, soupçon (*French*)

tinge *noun* 1 TINT, colour, shade, cast, wash, stain, dye, tincture
2 TRACE, bit, drop, touch, suggestion, dash, pinch, smack, sprinkling, smattering, soupçon (*French*)
▷ *verb* TINT, colour, shade, stain, dye

tingle *verb* PRICKLE, sting, itch, tickle, have goose pimples
▷ *noun* PRICKLING, stinging, itch, itching, tickle, tickling, pins and needles (*informal*)

tinker *verb* MEDDLE, play, toy, monkey, potter, fiddle (*informal*), dabble, mess about, muck about (*Brit slang*)

tinsel *adjective* SHOWY, flashy, gaudy, cheap, plastic (*slang*), superficial, sham, tawdry, ostentatious, trashy, specious, gimcrack, meretricious, pinchbeck

tint *noun* 1 SHADE, colour, tone, hue, cast
2 DYE, wash, stain, rinse, tinge, tincture
3 HINT, touch, trace, suggestion, shade, tinge
▷ *verb* DYE, colour, stain, rinse, tinge, tincture

tiny *adjective* SMALL, little, minute, slight, mini, wee, miniature, trifling, insignificant, negligible, microscopic, diminutive, petite, puny, pint-sized (*informal*), infinitesimal, teeny-weeny, Lilliputian, dwarfish, teensy-weensy, pygmy *or* pigmy
<< OPPOSITE huge

tip[1] *noun* 1 END, point, head, extremity, sharp end, nib, prong
2 PEAK, top, summit, pinnacle, crown, cap, zenith, apex, spire, acme, vertex
▷ *verb* CAP, top, crown, surmount, finish

tip[2] *noun* 1 GRATUITY, gift, reward, present, sweetener (*informal*), perquisite, baksheesh, pourboire (*French*)
2 HINT, suggestion, piece of information, piece of advice, gen (*Brit informal*), pointer, piece of inside information
▷ *verb* 1 REWARD, remunerate, give a tip to, sweeten (*informal*)
2 PREDICT, back, recommend, think of

tip[3] *verb* 1 POUR, drop, empty, dump, drain, spill, discharge, unload, jettison, offload, slop (*informal*), slosh (*informal*), decant
2 (*Brit*) DUMP, empty, ditch (*slang*), unload, pour out
▷ *noun* (*Brit*) DUMP, midden, rubbish heap, refuse heap
▷▷ **tip off** ADVISE, warn, caution, forewarn, give a clue to, give a hint to, tip someone the wink (*Brit informal*)

tip-off *noun* HINT, word, information, warning, suggestion, clue, pointer, inside information, word of advice

tipple *verb* DRINK, imbibe, tope, indulge (*informal*), swig, quaff, take a drink, bevvy (*dialect*), bend the elbow (*informal*)
▷ *noun* ALCOHOL, drink, booze (*informal*), poison (*informal*), liquor, John Barleycorn

tipsy *adjective* TIDDLY (*slang, chiefly Brit*), fuddled, slightly drunk, happy (*informal*), merry (*Brit informal*), mellow, woozy (*slang, chiefly Brit*)

tirade *noun* OUTBURST, diatribe, harangue, abuse, lecture, denunciation, invective, fulmination, philippic

tire *verb* 1 EXHAUST, drain, fatigue, weary, fag (*informal*), whack (*Brit informal*), wear out, wear down, take it out of (*informal*), knacker (*slang*), enervate
<< OPPOSITE refresh
2 FLAG, become tired, fail, droop

tired *adjective* 1 EXHAUSTED, fatigued, weary, spent, done in (*informal*), flagging, all in (*slang*), drained, sleepy, fagged (*informal*), whacked (*Brit informal*), worn out, drooping, knackered (*slang*), drowsy, clapped out (*Brit, Austral & NZ informal*), enervated, ready to drop, dog-tired (*informal*), zonked (*slang*), dead beat (*informal*),

tuckered out (*Austral & NZ informal*), asleep *or* dead on your feet (*informal*)
<< OPPOSITE energetic
2 BORED, fed up, weary, sick, annoyed, irritated, exasperated, irked, hoha (*NZ*)
<< OPPOSITE enthusiastic about
3 HACKNEYED, stale, well-worn, old, stock, familiar, conventional, corny (*slang*), threadbare, trite, clichéd, outworn
<< OPPOSITE original

tireless *adjective* ENERGETIC, vigorous, industrious, determined, resolute, indefatigable, unflagging, untiring, unwearied
<< OPPOSITE exhausted

tiresome *adjective* BORING, annoying, irritating, trying, wearing, dull, tedious, exasperating, monotonous, laborious, uninteresting, irksome, wearisome, vexatious
<< OPPOSITE interesting

tiring *adjective* EXHAUSTING, demanding, wearing, tough, exacting, fatiguing, wearying, strenuous, arduous, laborious, enervative

tissue *noun* **1** MATTER, material, substance, stuff, structure
2 PAPER, wipe, paper handkerchief, wrapping paper
3 SERIES, pack, collection, mass, network, chain, combination, web, accumulation, fabrication, conglomeration, concatenation

titan *noun* GIANT, superman, colossus, leviathan

titanic *adjective* GIGANTIC, huge, giant, massive, towering, vast, enormous, mighty, immense, jumbo (*informal*), monstrous, mammoth, colossal, mountainous, stellar (*informal*), prodigious, stupendous, herculean, elephantine, humongous *or* humungous (*US slang*)

titbit *or esp US* **tidbit** *noun* DELICACY, goody, dainty, morsel, treat, snack, choice item, juicy bit, bonne bouche (*French*)

tit for tat *noun* RETALIATION, like for like, measure for measure, an eye for an eye, a tooth for a tooth, blow for blow, as good as you get

tithe *noun* TAX, levy, duty, assessment, tribute, toll, tariff, tenth, impost

titillate *verb* EXCITE, stimulate, arouse, interest, thrill, provoke, turn on (*slang*), tease, tickle, tantalize

titillating *adjective* EXCITING, stimulating, interesting, thrilling, arousing, sensational, teasing, provocative, lurid, suggestive, lewd

title *noun* **1** HEADING, name, caption, label, legend, inscription
2 NAME, designation, epithet, term, handle (*slang*), nickname, denomination, pseudonym, appellation, sobriquet, nom de plume, moniker *or* monicker (*slang*)
3 (*Sport*) CHAMPIONSHIP, trophy, laurels, bays, crown, honour
4 (*Law*) OWNERSHIP, right, claim, privilege, entitlement, tenure, prerogative, freehold
▷ *verb* NAME, call, term, style, label, tag, designate

titter *verb* SNIGGER, laugh, giggle, chuckle, chortle (*informal*), tee-hee, te-hee

toad *noun*
>> RELATED WORD *adjective* batrachian
>> RELATED WORD *young* tadpole

toast[1] *verb* **1** BROWN, grill, crisp, roast
2 WARM (UP), heat (up), thaw, bring back to life

toast[2] *noun* **1** TRIBUTE, drink, compliment, salute, health, pledge, salutation
2 FAVOURITE, celebrity, darling, talk, pet, focus of attention, hero *or* heroine, blue-eyed boy *or* girl (*Brit informal*)
▷ *verb* DRINK TO, honour, pledge to, salute, drink (to) the health of

to-do *noun* FUSS, performance (*informal*), disturbance, bother, stir, turmoil, unrest, flap (*informal*), quarrel, upheaval, bustle, furore, uproar, agitation, commotion, rumpus, tumult, brouhaha, ruction (*informal*), hue and cry, hoo-ha

together *adverb* **1** COLLECTIVELY, jointly, closely, as one, with each other, in conjunction, side by side, mutually, hand in hand, as a group, in partnership, in concert, in unison, shoulder to shoulder, cheek by jowl, in cooperation, in a body, hand in glove
<< OPPOSITE separately
2 AT THE SAME TIME, simultaneously, in unison, as one, (all) at once, en masse, concurrently, contemporaneously, with one accord, at one fell swoop
▷ *adjective* (*informal*) SELF-POSSESSED, calm, composed, well-balanced, cool, stable, well-organized, well-adjusted

toil *noun* HARD WORK, industry, labour, effort, pains, application, sweat, graft (*informal*), slog, exertion, drudgery, travail, donkey-work, elbow grease (*informal*), blood, sweat, and tears (*informal*)
<< OPPOSITE idleness
▷ *verb* **1** LABOUR, work, struggle, strive, grind (*informal*), sweat (*informal*), slave, graft (*informal*), go for it (*informal*), slog, grub, bend over backwards (*informal*), drudge, go for broke (*slang*), push yourself, bust a gut (*informal*), give it your best shot (*informal*), break your neck (*informal*), work like a dog, make an all-out effort (*informal*), work like a Trojan, knock yourself out (*informal*), do your damnedest (*informal*), give it your all (*informal*), work your fingers to the bone, rupture yourself (*informal*)
2 STRUGGLE, trek, slog, trudge, push yourself,

fight your way, drag yourself, footslog

toilet *noun* 1 LAVATORY, bathroom, loo (*Brit informal*), bog (*slang*), gents *or* ladies, can (*US & Canad slang*), john (*slang, chiefly US & Canad*), head(s) (*Nautical slang*), throne (*informal*), closet, privy, cloakroom (*Brit*), urinal, latrine, washroom, powder room, ablutions (*Military informal*), dunny (*Austral & NZ old-fashioned informal*), water closet, khazi (*slang*), pissoir (*French*), little boy's room *or* little girl's room (*informal*), (public) convenience, W.C., bogger (*Austral slang*), brasco (*Austral slang*)
2 BATHROOM, washroom, gents *or* ladies (*Brit informal*), privy, outhouse, latrine, powder room, water closet, pissoir (*French*), ladies' room, little boy's *or* little girl's room, W.C.

token *noun* SYMBOL, mark, sign, note, evidence, earnest, index, expression, demonstration, proof, indication, clue, representation, badge, manifestation
▷ *adjective* NOMINAL, symbolic, minimal, hollow, superficial, perfunctory

tolerable *adjective* 1 BEARABLE, acceptable, allowable, supportable, endurable, sufferable
<< OPPOSITE intolerable
2 (*informal*) FAIR, O.K. *or* okay (*informal*), middling, average, all right, ordinary, acceptable, reasonable, good enough, adequate, indifferent, not bad (*informal*), mediocre, so-so (*informal*), run-of-the-mill, passable, unexceptional, fairly good, fair to middling
<< OPPOSITE dreadful

tolerance *noun* 1 BROAD-MINDEDNESS, charity, sympathy, patience, indulgence, forbearance, permissiveness, magnanimity, open-mindedness, sufferance, lenity
<< OPPOSITE intolerance
2 ENDURANCE, resistance, stamina, fortitude, resilience, toughness, staying power, hardness, hardiness
3 RESISTANCE, immunity, resilience, non-susceptibility

tolerant *adjective* BROAD-MINDED, understanding, sympathetic, open-minded, patient, fair, soft, catholic, charitable, indulgent, easy-going, long-suffering, lax, lenient, permissive, magnanimous, free and easy, forbearing, kind-hearted, unprejudiced, complaisant, latitudinarian, unbigoted, easy-oasy (*slang*)
<< OPPOSITE intolerant

tolerate *verb* 1 ENDURE, stand, suffer, bear, take, stomach, undergo, swallow, hack (*slang*), abide, put up with (*informal*), submit to, thole (*Scot*)
2 ALLOW, accept, permit, sanction, take, receive, admit, brook, indulge, put up with (*informal*), condone, countenance, turn a blind eye to, wink at
<< OPPOSITE forbid

toleration *noun* 1 ACCEPTANCE, endurance, indulgence, sanction, allowance, permissiveness, sufferance, condonation
2 RELIGIOUS FREEDOM, freedom of conscience, freedom of worship

toll[1] *verb* 1 RING, sound, strike, chime, knell, clang, peal
2 ANNOUNCE, call, signal, warn of
▷ *noun* RINGING, ring, tolling, chime, knell, clang, peal

toll[2] *noun* 1 CHARGE, tax, fee, duty, rate, demand, payment, assessment, customs, tribute, levy, tariff, impost
2 DAMAGE, cost, loss, roll, penalty, sum, number, roster, inroad
3 ADVERSE EFFECTS, price, cost, suffering, damage, penalty, harm

tomb *noun* GRAVE, vault, crypt, mausoleum, sarcophagus, catacomb, sepulchre, burial chamber

tombstone *noun* GRAVESTONE, memorial, monument, marker, headstone

tome *noun* BOOK, work, title, volume, opus, publication

tone *noun* 1 PITCH, stress, volume, accent, force, strength, emphasis, inflection, intonation, timbre, modulation, tonality
2 VOLUME, timbre, tonality
3 CHARACTER, style, approach, feel, air, effect, note, quality, spirit, attitude, aspect, frame, manner, mood, drift, grain, temper, vein, tenor
4 COLOUR, cast, shade, tint, tinge, hue
▷ *verb* 1 HARMONIZE, match, blend, suit, go well with
▷▷ **tone something down** 1 MODERATE, temper, soften, restrain, subdue, play down, dampen, mitigate, modulate, soft-pedal (*informal*)
2 REDUCE, moderate, soften, lessen
▷▷ **tone something up** GET INTO CONDITION, trim, shape up, freshen, tune up, sharpen up, limber up, invigorate, get in shape

tongue *noun* 1 LANGUAGE, speech, vernacular, talk, dialect, idiom, parlance, lingo (*informal*), patois, argot
2 UTTERANCE, voice, speech, articulation, verbal expression
>> RELATED WORD *adjective* lingual

tongue-tied *adjective* SPEECHLESS, dumb, mute, inarticulate, dumbstruck, struck dumb, at a loss for words
<< OPPOSITE talkative

tonic *noun* STIMULANT, boost, bracer (*informal*), refresher, cordial, pick-me-up (*informal*), fillip, shot in the arm (*informal*), restorative, livener, analeptic, roborant

too *adverb* 1 ALSO, as well, further, in addition, moreover, besides, likewise, to boot, into the bargain
2 EXCESSIVELY, very, extremely, overly, unduly, unreasonably, inordinately, exorbitantly, immoderately, over- ▷ see **very**

tool *noun* 1 IMPLEMENT, device, appliance, apparatus, machine, instrument, gadget, utensil, contraption, contrivance
2 MEANS, agency, vehicle, medium, agent, intermediary, wherewithal
3 PUPPET, creature, pawn, dupe, stooge (*slang*), jackal, minion, lackey, flunkey, hireling, cat's-paw
▷ *verb* MAKE, work, cut, shape, chase, decorate, ornament

top *noun* 1 PEAK, summit, head, crown, height, ridge, brow, crest, high point, pinnacle, culmination, meridian, zenith, apex, apogee, acme, vertex
<< OPPOSITE bottom
2 LID, cover, cap, cork, plug, stopper, bung
3 FIRST PLACE, head, peak, lead, highest rank, high point
▷ *adjective* 1 HIGHEST, upper, loftiest, furthest up, uppermost, topmost
2 LEADING, best, first, highest, greatest, lead, head, prime, finest, crowning, crack (*informal*), elite, superior, dominant, foremost, pre-eminent
<< OPPOSITE lowest
3 CHIEF, most important, principal, most powerful, highest, lead, head, ruling, leading, main, commanding, prominent, notable, sovereign, eminent, high-ranking, illustrious
4 PRIME, best, select, first-class, capital, quality, choice, excellent, premier, superb, elite, superior, top-class, A1 (*informal*), top-quality, first-rate, top-notch (*informal*), grade A, top-grade
▷ *verb* 1 LEAD, head, command, be at the top of, be first in
2 COVER, coat, garnish, finish, crown, cap, overspread
3 SURPASS, better, beat, improve on, cap, exceed, best, eclipse, go beyond, excel, transcend, outstrip, outdo, outshine
<< OPPOSITE not be as good as
4 REACH THE TOP OF, scale, mount, climb, conquer, crest, ascend, surmount
▷▷ **over the top** EXCESSIVE, too much, going too far, inordinate, over the limit, a bit much (*informal*), uncalled-for, immoderate
▷▷ **top something up** 1 FILL (UP), refresh, recharge, refill, replenish, freshen
2 SUPPLEMENT, boost, add to, enhance, augment

topic *noun* SUBJECT, point, question, issue, matter, theme, text, thesis, subject matter

topical *adjective* CURRENT, popular, contemporary, up-to-date, up-to-the-minute, newsworthy

topple *verb* 1 FALL OVER, fall, collapse, tumble, overturn, capsize, totter, tip over, keel over, overbalance, fall headlong
2 KNOCK OVER, upset, knock down, tip over
3 OVERTHROW, overturn, bring down, oust, unseat, bring low

topsy-turvy *adjective* CONFUSED, upside-down, disorderly, chaotic, messy, mixed-up, jumbled, inside-out, untidy, disorganized, disarranged
<< OPPOSITE orderly

torment *verb* 1 TORTURE, pain, distress, afflict, rack, harrow, crucify, agonize, excruciate
<< OPPOSITE comfort
2 TEASE, annoy, worry, trouble, bother, provoke, devil (*informal*), harry, plague, irritate, hound, harass, hassle (*informal*), aggravate (*informal*), persecute, pester, vex, bedevil, chivvy, give someone grief (*Brit & S African*), lead someone a merry dance (*Brit informal*)
▷ *noun* 1 SUFFERING, distress, misery, pain, hell, torture, agony, anguish
<< OPPOSITE bliss
2 TROUBLE, worry, bother, plague, irritation, hassle (*informal*), nuisance, annoyance, bane, pain in the neck (*informal*)

torn *adjective* 1 CUT, split, rent, ripped, ragged, slit, lacerated
2 UNDECIDED, divided, uncertain, split, unsure, wavering, vacillating, in two minds (*informal*), irresolute

tornado *noun* WHIRLWIND, storm, hurricane, gale, cyclone, typhoon, tempest, squall, twister (*US informal*), windstorm

torpor *noun* INACTIVITY, apathy, inertia, lethargy, passivity, laziness, numbness, sloth, stupor, drowsiness, dullness, sluggishness, indolence, languor, listlessness, somnolence, inertness, stagnancy, accidie (*Theology*), inanition, torpidity
<< OPPOSITE vigour

torrent *noun* 1 STREAM, flow, rush, flood, tide, spate, cascade, gush, effusion, inundation
2 DOWNPOUR, flood, shower, deluge, rainstorm
3 OUTBURST, stream, barrage, hail, spate, outpouring, effusion

torrid *adjective* 1 HOT, tropical, burning, dry, boiling, flaming, blistering, stifling, fiery, scorched, scorching, sizzling, arid, sultry, sweltering, parched, parching, broiling
2 PASSIONATE, intense, sexy (*informal*), hot, flaming, erotic, ardent, steamy (*informal*), fervent

tortuous *adjective* 1 WINDING, twisting, meandering, bent, twisted, curved, crooked, indirect, convoluted, serpentine, zigzag, sinuous, circuitous, twisty, mazy

2 COMPLICATED, involved, misleading, tricky, indirect, ambiguous, roundabout, deceptive, devious, convoluted, mazy
<< OPPOSITE straightforward

The adjective *tortuous* is sometimes confused with *torturous*. A *tortuous* road is one that winds or twists, while a *torturous* experience is one that involves pain, suffering, or discomfort

torture *verb* 1 TORMENT, abuse, persecute, afflict, martyr, scourge, molest, crucify, mistreat, ill-treat, maltreat, put on the rack
<< OPPOSITE comfort
2 DISTRESS, torment, worry, trouble, pain, rack, afflict, harrow, agonize, give someone grief (*Brit & S African*), inflict anguish on
▷ *noun* 1 ILL-TREATMENT, abuse, torment, persecution, martyrdom, maltreatment, harsh treatment
2 AGONY, suffering, misery, anguish, hell, distress, torment, heartbreak
<< OPPOSITE bliss

toss *verb* 1 THROW, pitch, hurl, fling, project, launch, cast, shy, chuck (*informal*), flip, propel, sling, lob (*informal*)
2 SHAKE, turn, mix, stir, tumble, agitate, jiggle
3 HEAVE, labour, rock, roll, pitch, lurch, jolt, wallow
4 THRASH (ABOUT), twitch, wriggle, squirm, writhe
▷ *noun* THROW, cast, pitch, shy, fling, lob (*informal*)

tot *noun* 1 INFANT, child, baby, toddler, mite, wean (*Scot*), little one, sprog (*slang*), munchkin (*informal, chiefly US*), rug rat (*slang*), littlie (*Austral informal*), ankle-biter (*Austral slang*), tacker (*Austral slang*)
2 MEASURE, shot (*informal*), finger, nip, slug, dram, snifter (*informal*), toothful
▷▷ **tot something up** (*Chiefly Brit*) ADD UP, calculate, sum (up), total, reckon, compute, tally, enumerate, count up

total *noun* SUM, mass, entirety, grand total, whole, amount, aggregate, totality, full amount, sum total
<< OPPOSITE part
▷ *adjective* COMPLETE, absolute, utter, whole, perfect, entire, sheer, outright, all-out, thorough, unconditional, downright, undisputed, consummate, unqualified, out-and-out, undivided, overarching, unmitigated, thoroughgoing, arrant, deep-dyed (*usually derogatory*)
<< OPPOSITE partial
▷ *verb* 1 AMOUNT TO, make, come to, reach, equal, run to, number, add up to, correspond to, work out as, mount up to, tot up to
2 ADD UP, work out, sum up, compute, reckon, tot up
<< OPPOSITE subtract

totalitarian *adjective* DICTATORIAL, authoritarian, one-party, oppressive, undemocratic, monolithic, despotic, tyrannous
<< OPPOSITE democratic

totality *noun* 1 ENTIRETY, unity, fullness, wholeness, completeness, entireness
2 AGGREGATE, whole, entirety, all, total, sum, sum total

totally *adverb* COMPLETELY, entirely, absolutely, quite, perfectly, fully, comprehensively, thoroughly, wholly, utterly, consummately, wholeheartedly, unconditionally, to the hilt, one hundred per cent, unmitigatedly
<< OPPOSITE partly

totter *verb* 1 STAGGER, stumble, reel, sway, falter, lurch, wobble, walk unsteadily
2 SHAKE, sway, rock, tremble, quake, shudder, lurch, waver, quiver, vibrate, teeter, judder

touch *verb* 1 FEEL, handle, finger, stroke, brush, make contact with, graze, caress, fondle, lay a finger on, palpate
2 COME INTO CONTACT, meet, contact, border, brush, come together, graze, adjoin, converge, be in contact, abut, impinge upon
3 TAP, hit, strike, push, pat
4 AFFECT, mark, involve, strike, get to (*informal*), influence, inspire, impress, get through to, have an effect on, make an impression on
5 CONSUME, take, drink, eat, partake of
6 MOVE, upset, stir, disturb, melt, soften, tug at someone's heartstrings (*often facetious*), leave an impression on
7 MATCH, rival, equal, compare with, parallel, come up to, come near, be on a par with, be a match for, hold a candle to (*informal*), be in the same league as
8 GET INVOLVED IN, use, deal with, handle, have to do with, utilize, be a party to, concern yourself with
9 REACH, hit (*informal*), come to, rise to, arrive at, attain, get up to
▷ *noun* 1 CONTACT, push, stroke, brush, press, tap, poke, nudge, prod, caress, fondling
2 FEELING, feel, handling, physical contact, palpation, tactility
3 BIT, spot, trace, drop, taste, suggestion, hint, dash, suspicion, pinch, smack, small amount, tinge, whiff, jot, speck, smattering, intimation, tincture
4 STYLE, approach, method, technique, way, manner, characteristic, trademark, handiwork
5 AWARENESS, understanding, acquaintance, familiarity
6 COMMUNICATION, contact, association,

connection, correspondence
7 SKILL, ability, flair, art, facility, command, craft, mastery, knack, artistry, virtuosity, deftness, adroitness
8 INFLUENCE, hand, effect, management, direction
▷▷ **touch and go** RISKY, close, near, dangerous, critical, tricky, sticky (*informal*), hazardous, hairy (*slang*), precarious, perilous, nerve-racking, parlous
▷▷ **touch on** *or* **upon something** REFER TO, cover, raise, deal with, mention, bring in, speak of, hint at, allude to, broach, make allusions to
▷▷ **touch something off** 1 TRIGGER (OFF), start, begin, cause, provoke, set off, initiate, arouse, give rise to, ignite, stir up, instigate, spark off, set in motion, foment
2 IGNITE, light, fire, set off, detonate, put a match to
▷▷ **touch something up** 1 ENHANCE, revamp, renovate, patch up, brush up, gloss over, polish up, retouch, titivate, give a face-lift to
2 IMPROVE, perfect, round off, enhance, dress up, finish off, embellish, put the finishing touches to
>> RELATED WORDS *adjectives* haptic, tactile, tactual

touched *adjective* 1 MOVED, affected, upset, impressed, stirred, disturbed, melted, softened, swayed
2 MAD, crazy, nuts (*slang*), daft (*informal*), batty (*slang*), cuckoo (*informal*), barmy (*slang*), nutty (*slang*), bonkers (*slang, chiefly Brit*), loopy (*informal*), crackpot (*informal*), out to lunch (*informal*), gonzo (*slang*), not all there, doolally (*slang*), off your trolley (*slang*), up the pole (*informal*), soft in the head (*informal*), not right in the head, off your rocker (*slang*), nutty as a fruitcake (*slang*), wacko *or* whacko (*informal*), off the air (*Austral slang*)

touching *adjective* MOVING, affecting, sad, stirring, tender, melting, pathetic, poignant, heartbreaking, emotive, pitiful, pitiable, piteous

touchstone *noun* STANDARD, measure, par, criterion, norm, gauge, yardstick

touchy *adjective* 1 OVERSENSITIVE, irritable, bad-tempered, cross, crabbed, grumpy, surly, petulant, irascible, tetchy, ratty (*Brit & NZ informal*), testy, thin-skinned, grouchy (*informal*), querulous, peevish, quick-tempered, splenetic, easily offended, captious, pettish, toey (*NZ slang*)
<< OPPOSITE thick-skinned
2 DELICATE, sensitive, tricky, risky, sticky (*informal*), thorny, knotty, ticklish

tough *adjective* 1 STRONG, determined, aggressive, high-powered, feisty (*informal, chiefly US & Canad*), hard-nosed (*informal*), self-confident, unyielding, hard as nails, self-assertive, badass (*slang, chiefly US*)
<< OPPOSITE weak
2 HARDY, strong, seasoned, fit, strapping, hardened, vigorous, sturdy, stout, stalwart, resilient, brawny, hard as nails
3 VIOLENT, rough, vicious, ruthless, pugnacious, hard-bitten, ruffianly
4 STRICT, severe, stern, hard, firm, exacting, adamant, resolute, draconian, intractable, inflexible, merciless, unforgiving, unyielding, unbending
<< OPPOSITE lenient
5 HARD, difficult, exhausting, troublesome, uphill, strenuous, arduous, thorny, laborious, irksome
6 RESILIENT, hard, resistant, durable, strong, firm, solid, stiff, rigid, rugged, sturdy, inflexible, cohesive, tenacious, leathery, hard-wearing, robust
<< OPPOSITE fragile
▷ *noun* RUFFIAN, heavy (*slang*), rough (*informal*), bully, thug, hooligan, brute, rowdy, bravo, bully boy, bruiser (*informal*), roughneck (*slang*), tsotsi (*S African*)

tour *noun* 1 CIRCUIT, course, round
2 JOURNEY, expedition, excursion, trip, progress, outing, jaunt, junket, peregrination
▷ *verb* 1 TRAVEL ROUND, holiday in, travel through, journey round, trek round, go on a trip through
2 VISIT, explore, go round, inspect, walk round, drive round, sightsee

tourist *noun* TRAVELLER, journeyer, voyager, tripper, globetrotter, holiday-maker, sightseer, excursionist

tournament *noun* 1 COMPETITION, meeting, match, event, series, contest
2 (*Medieval history*) JOUST, the lists, tourney

tousled *adjective* DISHEVELLED, disordered, tangled, ruffled, messed up, rumpled, disarranged, disarrayed

tout *verb* 1 (*informal*) RECOMMEND, promote, endorse, support, tip, urge, approve, praise, commend, speak well of
2 SOLICIT, canvass, drum up, bark (*US informal*), spiel
▷ *noun* SELLER, solicitor, barker, canvasser, spieler

tow *verb* DRAG, draw, pull, trail, haul, tug, yank, hale, trawl, lug

towards *preposition* 1 IN THE DIRECTION OF, to, for, on the way to, on the road to, en route for
2 REGARDING, about, concerning, respecting, in relation to, with regard to, with respect to, apropos
3 JUST BEFORE, nearing, close to, coming up to, almost at, getting on for, shortly before

tower *noun* **1** COLUMN, pillar, turret, belfry, steeple, obelisk
2 STRONGHOLD, castle, fort, refuge, keep, fortress, citadel, fortification
▷ *verb often with* **over** RISE, dominate, loom, top, mount, rear, soar, overlook, surpass, transcend, ascend, be head and shoulders above, overtop

towering *adjective* **1** TALL, high, great, soaring, elevated, gigantic, lofty, colossal
2 IMPRESSIVE, imposing, supreme, striking, extraordinary, outstanding, magnificent, superior, paramount, surpassing, sublime, stellar (*informal*), prodigious, transcendent
3 INTENSE, violent, extreme, excessive, burning, passionate, mighty, fiery, vehement, inordinate, intemperate, immoderate

toxic *adjective* POISONOUS, deadly, lethal, harmful, pernicious, noxious, septic, pestilential, baneful (*archaic*)
<< OPPOSITE harmless

toy *noun* PLAYTHING, game, doll
▷▷ **toy with something** PLAY WITH, consider, trifle with, flirt with, dally with, entertain the possibility of, amuse yourself with, think idly of

trace *noun* **1** BIT, drop, touch, shadow, suggestion, hint, dash, suspicion, tinge, trifle, whiff, jot, tincture, iota
2 REMNANT, remains, sign, record, mark, evidence, indication, token, relic, vestige
3 TRACK, trail, footstep, path, slot, footprint, spoor, footmark
▷ *verb* **1** SEARCH FOR, follow, seek out, track, determine, pursue, unearth, ascertain, hunt down
2 FIND, track (down), discover, trail, detect, unearth, hunt down, ferret out, locate
3 OUTLINE, chart, sketch, draw, map out, depict, mark out, delineate
4 COPY, map, draft, outline, sketch, reproduce, draw over

track *noun* **1** PATH, way, road, route, trail, pathway, footpath
2 COURSE, line, path, orbit, trajectory, flight path
3 LINE, rail, tramline
▷ *verb* FOLLOW, pursue, chase, trace, tail (*informal*), dog, shadow, trail, stalk, hunt down, follow the trail of
▷▷ **keep track of something** *or* **someone** KEEP UP WITH, follow, monitor, watch, keep an eye on, keep in touch with, keep up to date with
▷▷ **lose track of something** *or* **someone** LOSE, lose sight of, misplace
▷▷ **track something** *or* **someone down** FIND, catch, capture, apprehend, discover, expose, trace, unearth, dig up, hunt down, sniff out, bring to light, ferret out, run to earth *or* ground

tracks *plural noun* TRAIL, marks, impressions, traces, imprints, prints

tract[1] *noun* AREA, lot, region, estate, district, stretch, quarter, territory, extent, zone, plot, expanse

tract[2] *noun* TREATISE, essay, leaflet, brochure, booklet, pamphlet, dissertation, monograph, homily, disquisition, tractate

traction *noun* GRIP, resistance, friction, adhesion, purchase

trade *noun* **1** COMMERCE, business, transactions, buying and selling, dealing, exchange, traffic, truck, barter
2 JOB, employment, calling, business, line, skill, craft, profession, occupation, pursuit, line of work, métier, avocation
3 EXCHANGE, deal, swap, interchange
▷ *verb* **1** DEAL, do business, buy and sell, exchange, traffic, truck, bargain, peddle, barter, transact, cut a deal, have dealings
2 EXCHANGE, switch, swap, barter
3 OPERATE, run, deal, do business
>> RELATED WORD *adjective* mercantile

trader *noun* DEALER, marketer, buyer, broker, supplier, merchant, seller, purveyor, merchandiser

tradesman *noun* CRAFTSMAN, workman, artisan, journeyman, skilled worker

tradition *noun* **1** CUSTOMS, institution, ritual, folklore, lore, praxis, tikanga (*NZ*)
2 ESTABLISHED PRACTICE, custom, convention, habit, ritual, unwritten law

traditional *adjective* **1** OLD-FASHIONED, old, established, conventional, fixed, usual, transmitted, accustomed, customary, ancestral, long-established, unwritten, time-honoured
<< OPPOSITE revolutionary
2 FOLK, old, historical

traffic *noun* **1** TRANSPORT, movement, vehicles, transportation, freight, coming and going
2 TRADE, dealing, commerce, buying and selling, business, exchange, truck, dealings, peddling, barter, doings
▷ *verb often with* **in** TRADE, market, deal, exchange, truck, bargain, do business, buy and sell, peddle, barter, cut a deal, have dealings, have transactions

tragedy *noun* DISASTER, catastrophe, misfortune, adversity, calamity, affliction, whammy (*informal, chiefly US*), bummer (*slang*), grievous blow
<< OPPOSITE fortune

tragic *or* **tragical** *adjective* **1** DISTRESSING, shocking, sad, awful, appalling, fatal, deadly, unfortunate, disastrous, dreadful, dire, catastrophic, grievous, woeful, lamentable, ruinous, calamitous, wretched, ill-starred,

ill-fated
<< OPPOSITE fortunate
2 SAD, miserable, dismal, pathetic, heartbreaking, anguished, mournful, heart-rending, sorrowful, doleful, pitiable
<< OPPOSITE happy

trail *noun* 1 PATH, track, route, way, course, road, pathway, footpath, beaten track
2 TRACKS, path, mark, marks, wake, trace, scent, footsteps, footprints, spoor
3 WAKE, stream, tail, slipstream
▷ *verb* 1 FOLLOW, track, chase, pursue, dog, hunt, shadow, trace, tail (*informal*), hound, stalk, keep an eye on, keep tabs on (*informal*), run to ground
2 DRAG, draw, pull, sweep, stream, haul, tow, dangle, droop
3 LAG, follow, drift, wander, linger, trudge, fall behind, plod, meander, amble, loiter, straggle, traipse (*informal*), dawdle, hang back, tag along (*informal*), bring up the rear, drag yourself
▷▷ **trail away** *or* **off** FADE AWAY *or* OUT, sink, weaken, diminish, decrease, dwindle, shrink, lessen, subside, fall away, peter out, die away, tail off, taper off, grow weak, grow faint

train *verb* 1 INSTRUCT, school, prepare, improve, coach, teach, guide, discipline, rear, educate, drill, tutor, rehearse
2 EXERCISE, prepare, work out, practise, do exercise, get into shape
3 AIM, point, level, position, direct, focus, sight, line up, turn on, fix on, zero in, bring to bear
▷ *noun* 1 CONVOY, file, rank, string, column, queue, succession, caravan, procession, progression, cavalcade
2 SEQUENCE, series, chain, string, set, course, order, cycle, trail, succession, progression, concatenation
3 TAIL, trail, appendage
4 RETINUE, following, entourage, court, staff, household, suite, cortège

trainer *noun* COACH, manager, guide, adviser, tutor, instructor, counsellor, guru, handler

training *noun* INSTRUCTION, practice, schooling, grounding, education, preparation, exercise, working out, body building, tutelage

traipse *or* **trapse** *verb* (*informal*) TRUDGE, trail, tramp, slouch, drag yourself, footslog
▷ *noun* TRUDGE, trek, tramp, slog, long walk

trait *noun* CHARACTERISTIC, feature, quality, attribute, quirk, peculiarity, mannerism, idiosyncrasy, lineament

traitor *noun* BETRAYER, deserter, turncoat, deceiver, informer, renegade, defector, Judas, double-crosser (*informal*), quisling, apostate, miscreant, fifth columnist, snake in the grass (*informal*), back-stabber, fizgig (*Austral slang*)
<< OPPOSITE loyalist

trajectory *noun* PATH, line, course, track, flight, route, flight path

tramp *verb* 1 TRUDGE, march, stamp, stump, toil, plod, traipse (*informal*), walk heavily
2 HIKE, walk, trek, roam, march, range, ramble, slog, rove, yomp, footslog
▷ *noun* 1 VAGRANT, bum (*informal*), derelict, drifter, down-and-out, hobo (*chiefly US*), vagabond, bag lady (*chiefly US*), dosser (*Brit slang*), derro (*Austral slang*)
2 TREAD, stamp, footstep, footfall
3 HIKE, march, trek, ramble, slog

trample *verb often with* **on, upon** *or* **over** STAMP, crush, squash, tread, flatten, run over, walk over

trance *noun* DAZE, dream, spell, ecstasy, muse, abstraction, rapture, reverie, stupor, unconsciousness, hypnotic state

tranquil *adjective* 1 PEACEFUL, quiet, calm, serene, still, cool, pacific, composed, at peace, sedate, placid, undisturbed, restful, untroubled, unperturbed, unruffled, unexcited
2 CALM, quiet, peaceful, serene, still, cool, pacific, composed, sedate, placid, undisturbed, restful, untroubled, unperturbed, unruffled, unexcited
<< OPPOSITE troubled

tranquillity *or (sometimes) US* **tranquility** *noun*
1 PEACE, calm, quiet, hush, composure, serenity, stillness, coolness, repose, rest, calmness, equanimity, quietness, peacefulness, quietude, placidity, restfulness, sedateness
2 CALM, peace, composure, serenity, stillness, coolness, repose, calmness, equanimity, quietness, peacefulness, quietude, placidity, imperturbability, restfulness, sedateness
<< OPPOSITE agitation

tranquillizer, tranquilliser *or US* **tranquilizer** *noun* SEDATIVE, opiate, barbiturate, downer (*slang*), red (*slang*), bromide

transact *verb* CARRY OUT, handle, conduct, do, manage, perform, settle, conclude, negotiate, carry on, accomplish, execute, take care of, discharge, see to, prosecute, enact

transaction *noun* 1 DEAL, matter, affair, negotiation, business, action, event, proceeding, enterprise, bargain, coup, undertaking, deed, occurrence
2 *plural* RECORDS, minutes, affairs, proceedings, goings-on (*informal*), annals, doings

transcend *verb* SURPASS, exceed, go beyond, rise above, leave behind, eclipse, excel, outstrip, outdo, outshine, overstep, go above, leave in the shade (*informal*), outrival, outvie

transcendence *or* **transcendency** *noun* GREATNESS, excellence, superiority, supremacy, ascendancy, pre-eminence, sublimity, paramountcy, incomparability, matchlessness

transcendent *adjective* UNPARALLELED, unique, extraordinary, superior, exceeding, sublime, consummate, unrivalled, second to none, pre-eminent, transcendental, incomparable, peerless, unequalled, matchless

transcribe *verb* 1 WRITE OUT, reproduce, take down, copy out, note, transfer, set out, rewrite
2 (*Music*) TRANSLATE, interpret, render, transliterate

transcript *noun* COPY, record, note, summary, notes, version, carbon, log, translation, manuscript, reproduction, duplicate, transcription, carbon copy, transliteration, written version

transfer *verb* MOVE, carry, remove, transport, shift, transplant, displace, relocate, transpose, change
▷ *noun* TRANSFERENCE, move, removal, handover, change, shift, transmission, translation, displacement, relocation, transposition

transfix *verb* STUN, hold, fascinate, paralyse, petrify, mesmerize, hypnotize, stop dead, root to the spot, engross, rivet the attention of, spellbind, halt *or* stop in your tracks
<< OPPOSITE bore

transform *verb* 1 CHANGE, convert, alter, translate, reconstruct, metamorphose, transmute, renew, transmogrify (*jocular*)
2 MAKE OVER, overhaul, revamp, remake, renovate, remodel, revolutionize, redo, transfigure, restyle

transformation *noun* 1 CHANGE, conversion, alteration, metamorphosis, transmutation, renewal, transmogrification (*jocular*)
2 REVOLUTION, radical change, sea change, revolutionary change, transfiguration

transgress *verb* 1 MISBEHAVE, sin, offend, break the law, err, lapse, fall from grace, go astray, be out of order, do *or* go wrong
2 GO BEYOND, exceed, infringe, overstep, break, defy, violate, trespass, contravene, disobey, encroach upon

transgression *noun* CRIME, wrong, fault, error, offence, breach, sin, lapse, violation, wrongdoing, infringement, trespass, misdemeanour, misdeed, encroachment, misbehaviour, contravention, iniquity, peccadillo, infraction

transient *adjective* BRIEF, passing, short-term, temporary, short, flying, fleeting, short-lived, fugitive, momentary, ephemeral, transitory, evanescent, impermanent, here today and gone tomorrow, fugacious
<< OPPOSITE lasting

transit *noun* MOVEMENT, transfer, transport, passage, travel, crossing, motion, transportation, carriage, shipment, traverse, conveyance, portage
▷ *verb* PASS, travel, cross, journey, traverse, move
▷▷ **in transit** EN ROUTE, on the way, on the road, on the move, in motion, on the go (*informal*), on the journey, while travelling, during transport, during passage

transition *noun* CHANGE, passing, development, shift, passage, conversion, evolution, transit, upheaval, alteration, progression, flux, metamorphosis, changeover, transmutation, metastasis

transitional *adjective* 1 CHANGING, passing, fluid, intermediate, unsettled, developmental, transitionary
2 TEMPORARY, working, acting, short-term, interim, fill-in, caretaker, provisional, makeshift, make-do, stopgap, pro tem

transitory *adjective* SHORT-LIVED, short, passing, brief, short-term, temporary, fleeting, transient, flying, momentary, ephemeral, evanescent, impermanent, here today and gone tomorrow, fugacious
<< OPPOSITE lasting

translate *verb* 1 RENDER, put, change, convert, interpret, decode, transcribe, construe, paraphrase, decipher, transliterate
2 PUT IN PLAIN ENGLISH, explain, make clear, clarify, spell out, simplify, gloss, unravel, decode, paraphrase, decipher, elucidate, rephrase, reword, state in layman's language
3 CONVERT, change, turn, transform, alter, render, metamorphose, transmute, transfigure
4 TRANSFER, move, send, relocate, carry, remove, transport, shift, convey, transplant, transpose

translation *noun* 1 INTERPRETATION, version, rendering, gloss, rendition, decoding, transcription, paraphrase, transliteration
2 CONVERSION, change, rendering, transformation, alteration, metamorphosis, transfiguration, transmutation

translator *noun* INTERPRETER, transcriber, paraphraser, decipherer, linguist, metaphrast, paraphrast, transliterator

translucent *adjective* SEMITRANSPARENT, clear, limpid, lucent, diaphanous, pellucid

transmission *noun* 1 TRANSFER, spread, spreading, communication, passing on, circulation, dispatch, relaying, mediation, imparting, diffusion, transference, dissemination, conveyance, channeling
2 BROADCASTING, showing, putting out, relaying, sending
3 PROGRAMME, broadcast, show, production, telecast

transmit *verb* 1 BROADCAST, put on the air,

televise, relay, send, air, radio, send out, disseminate, beam out
2 PASS ON, carry, spread, communicate, take, send, forward, bear, transfer, transport, hand on, convey, dispatch, hand down, diffuse, remit, impart, disseminate

transmute *verb* TRANSFORM, change, convert, alter, metamorphose, transfigure, alchemize

transparency *noun* 1 PHOTOGRAPH, slide, exposure, photo, picture, image, print, plate, still
2 CLARITY, translucency, translucence, clearness, limpidity, transparence, diaphaneity, filminess, diaphanousness, gauziness, limpidness, pellucidity, pellucidness, sheerness
<< OPPOSITE opacity
3 FRANKNESS, openness, candour, directness, forthrightness, straightforwardness
<< OPPOSITE ambiguity

transparent *adjective* 1 CLEAR, sheer, see-through, lucid, translucent, crystal clear, crystalline, limpid, lucent, diaphanous, gauzy, filmy, pellucid
<< OPPOSITE opaque
2 FRANK, open, direct, straight, straightforward, candid, forthright, unequivocal, unambiguous, plain-spoken
<< OPPOSITE unclear
3 OBVIOUS, plain, apparent, visible, bold, patent, evident, distinct, explicit, easy, understandable, manifest, recognizable, unambiguous, undisguised, as plain as the nose on your face (*informal*), perspicuous
<< OPPOSITE uncertain

transpire *verb* 1 BECOME KNOWN, emerge, come out, be discovered, come to light, be disclosed, be made public
2 (*informal*) HAPPEN, occur, take place, arise, turn up, come about, come to pass (*archaic*)

> It is sometimes maintained that *transpire* should not be used to mean 'happen' or 'occur', as in *the event transpired late in the evening*, and that the word is properly used to mean 'become known', as in *it transpired later that the thief had been caught*. The word is, however, widely used in this sense, especially in spoken English

transplant *verb* 1 (*Surgery*) IMPLANT, transfer, graft
2 TRANSFER, take, bring, carry, remove, transport, shift, convey, fetch, displace, relocate, uproot

transport *verb* 1 CONVEY, take, run, move, bring, send, carry, bear, remove, ship, transfer, deliver, conduct, shift, ferry, haul, fetch
2 ENRAPTURE, move, delight, entrance, enchant, carry away, captivate, electrify, ravish, spellbind
3 EXILE, banish, deport, sentence to transportation
▷ *noun* 1 VEHICLE, wheels (*informal*), transportation, conveyance
2 TRANSFERENCE, carrying, shipping, delivery, distribution, removal, transportation, carriage, shipment, freight, haulage, conveyance, freightage
3 *often plural* ECSTASY, delight, heaven, happiness, bliss, euphoria, rapture, enchantment, cloud nine (*informal*), seventh heaven, ravishment
<< OPPOSITE despondency

transpose *verb* 1 TRANSPLANT, move, transfer, shift, displace, relocate, reposition
2 INTERCHANGE, switch, swap, reorder, change, move, exchange, substitute, alter, rearrange

transverse *adjective* CROSSWAYS, diagonal, oblique, crosswise, athwart

trap *noun* 1 SNARE, net, booby trap, gin, toils (*old-fashioned*), pitfall, noose, springe
2 AMBUSH, set-up (*informal*), device, lure, bait, honey trap, ambuscade (*old-fashioned*)
3 TRICK, set-up (*informal*), deception, ploy, ruse, artifice, trickery, subterfuge, stratagem, wile, device
▷ *verb* 1 CATCH, snare, ensnare, entrap, take, corner, bag, lay hold of, enmesh, lay a trap for, run to earth *or* ground
2 TRICK, fool, cheat, lure, seduce, deceive, dupe, beguile, gull, cajole, ensnare, hoodwink, wheedle, inveigle
3 CAPTURE, catch, arrest, seize, take, lift (*slang*), secure, nail (*informal*), collar (*informal*), nab (*informal*), apprehend, take prisoner, take into custody

trapped *adjective* CAUGHT, cornered, snared, ensnared, stuck (*informal*), netted, surrounded, cut off, at bay, in a tight corner, in a tight spot, with your back to the wall

trappings *plural noun* ACCESSORIES, trimmings, paraphernalia, finery, things, fittings, dress, equipment, gear, fixtures, decorations, furnishings, ornaments, livery, adornments, panoply, accoutrements, fripperies, bells and whistles, raiment (*archaic* or *poetic*)

trash *noun* 1 NONSENSE, rubbish, garbage (*informal*), rot, pants (*slang*), crap (*slang*), hot air (*informal*), tosh (*slang, chiefly Brit*), pap, bilge (*informal*), drivel, twaddle, tripe (*informal*), guff (*slang*), moonshine, hogwash, hokum (*slang, chiefly US & Canad*), piffle (*informal*), poppycock (*informal*), inanity, balderdash, bosh (*informal*), eyewash (*informal*), kak (*S African taboo slang*), trumpery, tommyrot, foolish talk, horsefeathers (*US slang*), bunkum *or* buncombe (*chiefly US*), bizzo (*Austral slang*), bull's wool

(*Austral & NZ slang*)
<< OPPOSITE sense
2 (*Chiefly US & Canad*) LITTER, refuse, waste, rubbish, sweepings, junk (*informal*), garbage, dross, dregs, dreck (*slang, chiefly US*), offscourings

trashy *adjective* WORTHLESS, cheap, inferior, shabby, flimsy, shoddy, tawdry, tinsel, thrown together, crappy (*slang*), meretricious, rubbishy, poxy (*slang*), catchpenny, cheap-jack (*informal*), of a sort *or* of sorts
<< OPPOSITE excellent

trauma *noun* 1 SHOCK, suffering, worry, pain, stress, upset, strain, torture, distress, misery, disturbance, ordeal, anguish, upheaval, jolt
2 (*Pathology*) INJURY, damage, hurt, wound, agony

traumatic *adjective* SHOCKING, upsetting, alarming, awful, disturbing, devastating, painful, distressing, terrifying, scarring, harrowing
<< OPPOSITE calming

travel *verb* 1 GO, journey, proceed, make a journey, move, walk, cross, tour, progress, wander, trek, voyage, roam, ramble, traverse, rove, take a trip, make your way, wend your way
2 BE TRANSMITTED, move, advance, proceed, get through
▷ *noun usually plural* JOURNEY, wandering, expedition, globetrotting, walk, tour, touring, movement, trip, passage, voyage, excursion, ramble, peregrination
>> RELATED WORD *adjective* itinerant

traveller *noun* 1 VOYAGER, tourist, passenger, journeyer, explorer, hiker, tripper, globetrotter, holiday-maker, wayfarer, excursionist
2 TRAVELLING SALESMAN, representative, rep, salesman, sales rep, commercial traveller, agent

travelling *adjective* ITINERANT, moving, touring, mobile, wandering, unsettled, roaming, migrant, restless, roving, nomadic, migratory, peripatetic, wayfaring

traverse *verb* 1 CROSS, go across, travel over, make your way across, cover, range, bridge, negotiate, wander, go over, span, roam, ply
2 CUT ACROSS, pass over, stretch across, extend across, lie across

travesty *noun* MOCKERY, distortion, parody, caricature, sham, send-up (*Brit informal*), spoof (*informal*), perversion, takeoff (*informal*), lampoon, burlesque

treacherous *adjective* 1 DISLOYAL, deceitful, untrustworthy, duplicitous, false, untrue, unreliable, unfaithful, faithless, double-crossing (*informal*), double-dealing, perfidious, traitorous, treasonable, recreant (*archaic*)
<< OPPOSITE loyal
2 DANGEROUS, tricky, risky, unstable, hazardous, icy, slippery, unsafe, unreliable, precarious, deceptive, perilous, slippy (*informal or dialect*)
<< OPPOSITE safe

treachery *noun* BETRAYAL, infidelity, treason, duplicity, disloyalty, double-cross (*informal*), double-dealing, stab in the back, perfidy, faithlessness, perfidiousness
<< OPPOSITE loyalty

tread *verb* STEP, walk, march, pace, stamp, stride, hike, tramp, trudge, plod
▷ *noun* STEP, walk, pace, stride, footstep, gait, footfall
▷▷ **tread on something** 1 CRUSH UNDERFOOT, step on, stamp on, trample (on), stomp on, squash, flatten
2 REPRESS, crush, suppress, subdue, oppress, quell, bear down on, subjugate, ride roughshod over

treason *noun* DISLOYALTY, mutiny, treachery, subversion, disaffection, duplicity, sedition, perfidy, lese-majesty, traitorousness
<< OPPOSITE loyalty

treasure *noun* 1 RICHES, money, gold, fortune, wealth, valuables, jewels, funds, cash
2 ANGEL, darling, find, star (*informal*), prize, pearl, something else (*informal*), jewel, gem, paragon, one in a million (*informal*), one of a kind (*informal*), nonpareil
▷ *verb* PRIZE, value, worship, esteem, adore, cherish, revere, venerate, hold dear, love, idolize, set great store by, dote upon, place great value on

treasury *noun* 1 FUNDS, money, capital, finances, resources, assets, revenues, exchequer, coffers
2 STOREHOUSE, bank, store, vault, hoard, cache, repository

treat *verb* 1 BEHAVE TOWARDS, deal with, handle, act towards, use, consider, serve, manage, regard, look upon
2 TAKE CARE OF, minister to, attend to, give medical treatment to, doctor (*informal*), nurse, care for, medicate, prescribe medicine for, apply treatment to
3 *often with* **to** PROVIDE, give, buy, stand (*informal*), pay for, entertain, feast, lay on, regale, wine and dine, take out for, foot *or* pay the bill
4 NEGOTIATE, bargain, consult, have talks, confer, come to terms, parley, make a bargain, make terms
▷ *noun* 1 ENTERTAINMENT, party, surprise, gift, celebration, feast, outing, excursion, banquet, refreshment
2 PLEASURE, delight, joy, thrill, satisfaction, enjoyment, gratification, source of pleasure,

fun

▷▷ **treat of something** DEAL WITH, discuss, go into, be concerned with, touch upon, discourse upon

treatise *noun* PAPER, work, writing, study, essay, thesis, tract, pamphlet, exposition, dissertation, monograph, disquisition

treatment *noun* 1 CARE, medical care, nursing, medicine, surgery, therapy, healing, medication, therapeutics, ministrations
2 CURE, remedy, medication, medicine
3 *often with* **of** HANDLING, dealings with, behaviour towards, conduct towards, management, reception, usage, manipulation, action towards

treaty *noun* AGREEMENT, pact, contract, bond, alliance, bargain, convention, compact, covenant, entente, concordat

trek *noun* 1 SLOG, tramp, long haul, footslog
2 JOURNEY, hike, expedition, safari, march, odyssey
▷ *verb* 1 JOURNEY, march, range, hike, roam, tramp, rove, go walkabout (*Austral*)
2 TRUDGE, plod, traipse (*informal*), footslog, slog

tremble *verb* 1 SHAKE, shiver, quake, shudder, quiver, teeter, totter, quake in your boots, shake in your boots *or* shoes
2 VIBRATE, rock, shake, quake, wobble, oscillate
▷ *noun* SHAKE, shiver, quake, shudder, wobble, tremor, quiver, vibration, oscillation

tremendous *adjective* 1 HUGE, great, towering, vast, enormous, terrific, formidable, immense, awesome, titanic, gigantic, monstrous, mammoth, colossal, whopping (*informal*), stellar (*informal*), prodigious, stupendous, gargantuan
<< OPPOSITE tiny
2 (*informal*) EXCELLENT, great, wonderful, brilliant, mean (*slang*), topping (*Brit slang*), cracking (*Brit informal*), amazing, extraordinary, fantastic (*informal*), ace (*informal*), incredible, fabulous (*informal*), marvellous, exceptional, terrific (*informal*), sensational (*informal*), sovereign, awesome (*slang*), super (*informal*), brill (*informal*), bodacious (*slang, chiefly US*), boffo (*slang*), jim-dandy (*slang*), chillin' (*US slang*), booshit (*Austral slang*), exo (*Austral slang*), sik (*Austral slang*), rad (*informal*), phat (*slang*), schmick (*Austral informal*)
<< OPPOSITE terrible

tremor *noun* 1 SHAKE, shaking, tremble, trembling, shiver, quaking, wobble, quiver, quivering, agitation, vibration, quaver
2 EARTHQUAKE, shock, quake (*informal*), tremblor (*US informal*)

trench *noun* DITCH, cut, channel, drain, pit, waterway, gutter, trough, furrow, excavation, earthwork, fosse, entrenchment

trenchant *adjective* 1 SCATHING, pointed, cutting, biting, sharp, keen, acute, severe, acid, penetrating, tart, pungent, incisive, hurtful, sarcastic, caustic, astringent, vitriolic, acerbic, piquant, mordant, acidulous, mordacious
<< OPPOSITE kind
2 CLEAR, driving, strong, powerful, effective, distinct, crisp, explicit, vigorous, potent, energetic, clear-cut, forceful, emphatic, unequivocal, salient, well-defined, effectual, distinctly defined
<< OPPOSITE vague

trend *noun* 1 TENDENCY, swing, drift, inclination, current, direction, flow, leaning, bias
2 FASHION, craze, fad (*informal*), mode, look, thing, style, rage, vogue, mania
▷ *verb* TEND, turn, head, swing, flow, bend, lean, incline, veer, run

trendy (*Brit informal*) *adjective* FASHIONABLE, in (*slang*), now (*informal*), latest, with it (*informal*), flash (*informal*), stylish, in fashion, in vogue, up to the minute, modish, voguish, schmick (*Austral informal*)
▷ *noun* POSER (*informal*), pseud (*informal*)

trepidation *noun* (*Formal*) ANXIETY, fear, worry, alarm, emotion, excitement, dread, butterflies (*informal*), shaking, disturbance, dismay, trembling, fright, apprehension, tremor, quivering, nervousness, disquiet, agitation, consternation, jitters (*informal*), cold feet (*informal*), uneasiness, palpitation, cold sweat (*informal*), perturbation, the heebie-jeebies (*slang*)
<< OPPOSITE composure

trespass *verb* 1 INTRUDE, infringe, encroach, enter without permission, invade, poach, obtrude
2 *often with* **against** (*Archaic*) SIN, offend, transgress, commit a sin
▷ *noun* 1 INTRUSION, infringement, encroachment, unlawful entry, invasion, poaching, wrongful entry
2 SIN, crime, fault, error, offence, breach, misconduct, wrongdoing, misdemeanour, delinquency, misdeed, transgression, misbehaviour, iniquity, infraction, evildoing, injury

tress *noun often plural* HAIR, lock, curl, braid, plait, pigtail, ringlet

triad *noun* THREESOME, triple, trio, trinity, trilogy, triplet, triumvirate, triptych, trine, triune

trial *noun* 1 (*Law*) HEARING, case, court case, inquiry, contest, tribunal, lawsuit, appeal, litigation, industrial tribunal, court martial, legal proceedings, judicial proceedings, judicial examination
2 TEST, testing, experiment, evaluation, check, examination, audition, assay, dry

run (*informal*), assessment, proof, probation, appraisal, try-out, test-run, pilot study, dummy run
3 HARDSHIP, suffering, trouble, pain, load, burden, distress, grief, misery, ordeal, hard times, woe, unhappiness, adversity, affliction, tribulation, wretchedness, vexation, cross to bear
4 NUISANCE, drag (*informal*), bother, plague (*informal*), pest, irritation, hassle (*informal*), bane, pain in the neck (*informal*), vexation, thorn in your flesh *or* side
▷ *adjective* EXPERIMENTAL, probationary, testing, pilot, provisional, exploratory

tribe *noun* RACE, ethnic group, people, family, class, stock, house, division, blood, seed (*chiefly biblical*), sept, gens, clan, caste, dynasty, hapu (*NZ*), iwi (*NZ*)

tribulation *noun* TROUBLE, care, suffering, worry, trial, blow, pain, burden, distress, grief, misery, curse, ordeal, hardship, sorrow, woe, hassle (*informal*), misfortune, bad luck, unhappiness, heartache, adversity, affliction, bummer (*slang*), wretchedness, vexation, ill fortune, cross to bear
<< OPPOSITE joy

tribunal *noun* HEARING, court, trial, bar, bench, industrial tribunal, judgment seat, judicial examination

tribute *noun* ACCOLADE, testimonial, eulogy, recognition, respect, gift, honour, praise, esteem, applause, compliment, gratitude, acknowledgment, commendation, panegyric, encomium, laudation
<< OPPOSITE criticism

trick *noun* 1 JOKE, put-on (*slang*), gag (*informal*), stunt, spoof (*informal*), caper, prank, frolic, practical joke, antic, jape, leg-pull (*Brit informal*), cantrip (*Scot*)
2 DECEPTION, trap, fraud, con (*slang*), sting (*informal*), manoeuvre, dodge, ploy, scam (*slang*), imposition, gimmick, device, hoax, deceit, swindle, ruse, artifice, subterfuge, canard, feint, stratagem, wile, imposture, fastie (*Austral slang*)
3 SLEIGHT OF HAND, device, feat, stunt, juggle, legerdemain
4 SECRET, skill, device, knack, art, hang (*informal*), technique, know-how (*informal*), gift, command, craft, expertise
5 MANNERISM, habit, characteristic, trait, quirk, peculiarity, foible, idiosyncrasy, practice, crotchet
▷ *verb* DECEIVE, trap, have someone on, take someone in (*informal*), fool, cheat, con (*informal*), kid (*informal*), stiff (*slang*), sting (*informal*), mislead, hoax, defraud, dupe, gull (*archaic*), delude, swindle, impose upon, bamboozle (*informal*), hoodwink, put one over on (*informal*), pull the wool over someone's eyes, pull a fast one on (*informal*)
▷▷ **do the trick** (*informal*) WORK, fit the bill, have effect, achieve the desired result, produce the desired result, take care of the problem, be effective *or* effectual, do the business (*informal*)

trickery *noun* DECEPTION, fraud, cheating, con (*informal*), hoax, pretence, deceit, dishonesty, swindling, guile, double-dealing, skulduggery (*informal*), chicanery, hanky-panky (*informal*), hokum (*slang, chiefly US & Canad*), monkey business (*informal*), funny business, jiggery-pokery (*informal, chiefly Brit*), imposture
<< OPPOSITE honesty

trickle *verb* DRIBBLE, run, drop, stream, creep, crawl, drip, ooze, seep, exude, percolate
▷ *noun* DRIBBLE, drip, seepage, thin stream

trickster *noun* DECEIVER, fraud, cheat, joker, hoaxer, pretender, hustler (*US informal*), con man (*informal*), impostor, fraudster, swindler, practical joker, grifter (*slang, chiefly US & Canad*), chiseller (*informal*), rorter (*Austral slang*), rogue trader

tricky *adjective* 1 DIFFICULT, sensitive, complicated, delicate, risky, sticky (*informal*), hairy (*informal*), problematic, thorny, touch-and-go, knotty, dicey (*informal*), ticklish
<< OPPOSITE simple
2 CRAFTY, scheming, subtle, cunning, slippery, sly, deceptive, devious, wily, artful, foxy, deceitful
<< OPPOSITE open

trifle *noun* KNICK-KNACK, nothing, toy, plaything, bauble, triviality, bagatelle, gewgaw
▷▷ **a trifle** SLIGHTLY, a little, a bit, somewhat, rather, moderately, marginally, a shade, to some degree, on a small scale, to some extent

trifling *adjective* INSIGNIFICANT, small, tiny, empty, slight, silly, shallow, petty, idle, trivial, worthless, negligible, unimportant, frivolous, paltry, minuscule, puny, measly, piddling (*informal*), inconsiderable, valueless, nickel-and-dime (*US slang*), footling (*informal*)
<< OPPOSITE significant

trigger *verb* BRING ABOUT, start, cause, produce, generate, prompt, provoke, set off, activate, give rise to, elicit, spark off, set in motion
<< OPPOSITE prevent

trim *adjective* 1 NEAT, nice, smart, compact, tidy, orderly, spruce, dapper, natty (*informal*), well-groomed, well-ordered, well turned-out, shipshape, spick-and-span, trig (*archaic* or *dialect*), soigné *or* soignée
<< OPPOSITE untidy
2 SLENDER, fit, slim, sleek, streamlined, shapely, svelte, willowy, lissom
▷ *verb* 1 CUT, crop, clip, dock, shave, barber, tidy, prune, shear, pare, lop, even up, neaten

2 DECORATE, dress, array, adorn, embroider, garnish, ornament, embellish, deck out, bedeck, beautify, trick out
▷ *noun* 1 DECORATION, edging, border, piping, trimming, fringe, garnish, frill, embellishment, adornment, ornamentation
2 CONDITION, form, health, shape (*informal*), repair, fitness, wellness, order, fettle
3 CUT, crop, trimming, clipping, shave, pruning, shearing, tidying up

trimming *noun* DECORATION, edging, border, piping, fringe, garnish, braid, frill, festoon, embellishment, adornment, ornamentation
▷ *plural noun* 1 EXTRAS, accessories, garnish, ornaments, accompaniments, frills, trappings, paraphernalia, appurtenances
2 CLIPPINGS, ends, cuttings, shavings, brash, parings

trinity *noun* THREESOME, triple, trio, trilogy, triplet, triad, triumvirate, triptych, trine, triune

trinket *noun* ORNAMENT, bauble, knick-knack, piece of bric-a-brac, nothing, toy, trifle, bagatelle, gimcrack, gewgaw, bibelot, kickshaw

trio *noun* THREESOME, triple, trinity, trilogy, triplet, triad, triumvirate, triptych, trine, triune

trip *noun* 1 JOURNEY, outing, excursion, day out, run, drive, travel, tour, spin (*informal*), expedition, voyage, ramble, foray, jaunt, errand, junket (*informal*)
2 STUMBLE, fall, slip, blunder, false move, misstep, false step
▷ *verb* 1 *often with* **up** STUMBLE, fall, fall over, slip, tumble, topple, stagger, misstep, lose your balance, make a false move, lose your footing, take a spill
2 SKIP, dance, spring, hop, caper, flit, frisk, gambol, tread lightly
3 (*informal*) TAKE DRUGS, get high (*informal*), get stoned (*slang*), turn on (*slang*)
4 ACTIVATE, turn on, flip, release, pull, throw, engage, set off, switch on
▷▷ **trip someone up** CATCH OUT, trap, confuse, unsettle, disconcert, throw you off, wrongfoot, put you off your stride

tripe *noun* (*informal*) NONSENSE, rot, trash, twaddle, rubbish, pants (*slang*), crap (*slang*), garbage (*informal*), hot air (*informal*), tosh (*slang, chiefly Brit*), pap, bilge (*informal*), drivel, guff (*slang*), moonshine, claptrap (*informal*), hogwash, hokum (*slang, chiefly US & Canad*), piffle (*informal*), poppycock (*informal*), inanity, balderdash, bosh (*informal*), eyewash (*informal*), trumpery, tommyrot, foolish talk, horsefeathers (*US slang*), bunkum *or* buncombe (*chiefly US*), bizzo (*Austral slang*), bull's wool (*Austral & NZ slang*)

triple *adjective* 1 TREBLE, three times, three times as much as
2 THREE-WAY, threefold, tripartite
▷ *verb* TREBLE, triplicate, increase threefold

triplet *noun* THREESOME, triple, trio, trinity, trilogy, triad, triumvirate, trine, triune

tripper *noun* (*Chiefly Brit*) TOURIST, holiday-maker, sightseer, excursionist, journeyer, voyager

trite *adjective* UNORIGINAL, worn, common, stock, ordinary, tired, routine, dull, stereotyped, hack, pedestrian, commonplace, stale, banal, corny (*slang*), run-of-the-mill, threadbare, clichéd, uninspired, hackneyed, bromidic
<< OPPOSITE original

triumph *noun* 1 SUCCESS, victory, accomplishment, mastery, hit (*informal*), achievement, smash (*informal*), coup, sensation, feat, conquest, attainment, smash hit (*informal*), tour de force (*French*), walkover (*informal*), feather in your cap, smasheroo (*slang*)
<< OPPOSITE failure
2 JOY, pride, happiness, rejoicing, elation, jubilation, exultation
▷ *verb* 1 *often with* **over** SUCCEED, win, overcome, prevail, best, dominate, overwhelm, thrive, flourish, subdue, prosper, get the better of, vanquish, come out on top (*informal*), carry the day, take the honours
<< OPPOSITE fail
2 REJOICE, celebrate, glory, revel, swagger, drool, gloat, exult, jubilate, crow

triumphant *adjective* 1 VICTORIOUS, winning, successful, dominant, conquering, undefeated
<< OPPOSITE defeated
2 CELEBRATORY, rejoicing, jubilant, triumphal, proud, glorious, swaggering, elated, exultant, boastful, cock-a-hoop

trivia *noun* MINUTIAE, details, trifles, trivialities, petty details
<< OPPOSITE essentials

trivial *adjective* UNIMPORTANT, little, small, minor, slight, everyday, petty, meaningless, commonplace, worthless, trifling, insignificant, negligible, frivolous, paltry, incidental, puny, inconsequential, trite, inconsiderable, valueless, nickel-and-dime (*US slang*)
<< OPPOSITE important

triviality *noun* 1 INSIGNIFICANCE, frivolity, smallness, pettiness, worthlessness, meaninglessness, unimportance, littleness, slightness, triteness, paltriness, inconsequentiality, valuelessness, negligibility, much ado about nothing
<< OPPOSITE importance
2 TRIFLE, nothing, detail, technicality, petty detail, no big thing, no great matter

<< OPPOSITE essential

troop *noun* 1 GROUP, company, team, body, unit, band, crowd, pack, squad, gathering, crew (*informal*), drove, gang, bunch (*informal*), flock, herd, contingent, swarm, horde, multitude, throng, posse (*informal*), bevy, assemblage

2 *plural* SOLDIERS, men, armed forces, servicemen, fighting men, military, army, soldiery

▷ *verb* FLOCK, march, crowd, stream, parade, swarm, throng, traipse (*informal*)

trophy *noun* 1 PRIZE, cup, award, bays, laurels

2 SOUVENIR, spoils, relic, memento, booty, keepsake

tropical *adjective* HOT, stifling, lush, steamy, humid, torrid, sultry, sweltering

<< OPPOSITE cold

trot *verb* RUN, jog, scamper, lope, go briskly, canter

▷ *noun* RUN, jog, lope, brisk pace, canter

▷▷ **on the trot** (*informal*) ONE AFTER THE OTHER, in a row, in succession, without break, without interruption, consecutively

▷▷ **trot something out** (*informal*) REPEAT, relate, exhibit, bring up, reiterate, recite, come out with, bring forward, drag up

troubadour *noun* MINSTREL, singer, poet, balladeer, lyric poet, jongleur

trouble *noun* 1 BOTHER, problems, concern, worry, stress, difficulty (*informal*), anxiety, distress, grief (*Brit & S African*), irritation, hassle (*informal*), strife, inconvenience, unease, disquiet, annoyance, agitation, commotion, unpleasantness, vexation

2 *often plural* DISTRESS, problem, suffering, worry, pain, anxiety, grief, torment, hardship, sorrow, woe, irritation, hassle (*informal*), misfortune, heartache, disquiet, annoyance, agitation, tribulation, bummer (*slang*), vexation

<< OPPOSITE pleasure

3 AILMENT, disease, failure, complaint, upset, illness, disorder, disability, defect, malfunction

4 DISORDER, fighting, row, conflict, bother, grief (*Brit & S African*), unrest, disturbance, to-do (*informal*), discontent, dissatisfaction, furore, uproar, scuffling, discord, fracas, commotion, rumpus, breach of the peace, tumult, affray (*Law*), brouhaha, ructions, hullabaloo (*informal*), kerfuffle (*Brit informal*), hoo-ha (*informal*), biffo (*Austral slang*), boilover (*Austral*)

<< OPPOSITE peace

5 PROBLEM, bother, concern, pest, irritation, hassle (*informal*), nuisance, inconvenience, irritant, cause of annoyance

6 EFFORT, work, thought, care, labour, struggle, pains, bother, grief (*Brit & S African*), hassle (*informal*), inconvenience, exertion

<< OPPOSITE convenience

7 DIFFICULTY, hot water (*informal*), predicament, deep water (*informal*), spot (*informal*), danger, mess, dilemma, scrape (*informal*), pickle (*informal*), dire straits, tight spot

▷ *verb* 1 BOTHER, worry, upset, disturb, distress, annoy, plague, grieve, torment, harass, hassle (*informal*), afflict, pain, fret, agitate, sadden, perplex, disconcert, disquiet, pester, vex, perturb, faze, give someone grief (*Brit & S African*), discompose, put *or* get someone's back up, hack you off (*informal*)

<< OPPOSITE please

2 AFFLICT, hurt, bother, cause discomfort to, cause discomfort to, pain, grieve

3 INCONVENIENCE, disturb, burden, put out, impose upon, discommode, incommode

<< OPPOSITE relieve

4 TAKE PAINS, take the time, make an effort, go to the effort of, exert yourself

<< OPPOSITE avoid

troublemaker *noun* MISCHIEF-MAKER, firebrand, instigator, agitator, bad apple (*US informal*), rabble-rouser, agent provocateur (*French*), stirrer (*informal*), incendiary, rotten apple (*Brit informal*), meddler, stormy petrel

<< OPPOSITE peace-maker

troublesome *adjective* 1 BOTHERSOME, trying, taxing, demanding, difficult, worrying, upsetting, annoying, irritating, tricky, harassing, oppressive, arduous, tiresome, inconvenient, laborious, burdensome, hard, worrisome, irksome, wearisome, vexatious, importunate, pestilential, plaguy (*informal*)

<< OPPOSITE simple

2 DISORDERLY, violent, turbulent, rebellious, unruly, rowdy, recalcitrant, undisciplined, uncooperative, refractory, insubordinate

<< OPPOSITE well-behaved

trough *noun* MANGER, crib, water trough

trounce *verb* DEFEAT SOMEONE HEAVILY *or* UTTERLY, beat, thrash, slaughter (*informal*), stuff (*slang*), tank (*slang*), hammer (*informal*), crush, overwhelm, lick (*informal*), paste (*slang*), rout, walk over (*informal*), clobber (*slang*), run rings around (*informal*), wipe the floor with (*informal*), make mincemeat of, blow someone out of the water (*slang*), give someone a hiding (*informal*), drub, beat someone hollow (*Brit informal*), give someone a pasting (*slang*)

troupe *noun* COMPANY, group, band, cast, ensemble

truancy *noun* ABSENCE, shirking, skiving (*Brit slang*), malingering, absence without leave

truant *noun* ABSENTEE, skiver (*Brit slang*), shirker, dodger, runaway, delinquent,

deserter, straggler, malingerer
▷ *adjective* ABSENT, missing, skiving (*Brit slang*), absent without leave, A.W.O.L.
▷ *verb* ABSENT YOURSELF, play truant, skive (*Brit slang*), bunk off (*slang*), desert, run away, dodge, wag (*dialect*), go missing, shirk, malinger, bob off (*Brit slang*)

truce *noun* CEASEFIRE, break, stay, rest, peace, treaty, interval, moratorium, respite, lull, cessation, let-up (*informal*), armistice, intermission, cessation of hostilities

truculent *adjective* HOSTILE, defiant, belligerent, bad-tempered, cross, violent, aggressive, fierce, contentious, combative, sullen, scrappy (*informal*), antagonistic, pugnacious, ill-tempered, bellicose, obstreperous, itching *or* spoiling for a fight (*informal*), aggers (*Austral slang*)
<< OPPOSITE amiable

trudge *verb* PLOD, trek, tramp, traipse (*informal*), march, stump, hike, clump, lumber, slog, drag yourself, yomp, walk heavily, footslog
▷ *noun* TRAMP, march, haul, trek, hike, slog, traipse (*informal*), yomp, footslog

true *adjective* 1 CORRECT, right, accurate, exact, precise, valid, legitimate, factual, truthful, veritable, bona fide, veracious
<< OPPOSITE false
2 ACTUAL, real, natural, pure, genuine, proper, authentic, dinkum (*Austral & NZ informal*)
3 FAITHFUL, loyal, devoted, dedicated, firm, fast, constant, pure, steady, reliable, upright, sincere, honourable, honest, staunch, trustworthy, trusty, dutiful, true-blue, unswerving
<< OPPOSITE unfaithful
4 EXACT, perfect, correct, accurate, proper, precise, spot-on (*Brit informal*), on target, unerring
<< OPPOSITE inaccurate
▷ *adverb* 1 TRUTHFULLY, honestly, veritably, veraciously, rightly
2 PRECISELY, accurately, on target, perfectly, correctly, properly, unerringly

true-blue *adjective* STAUNCH, confirmed, constant, devoted, dedicated, loyal, faithful, orthodox, uncompromising, trusty, unwavering, dyed-in-the-wool

truism *noun* CLICHÉ, commonplace, platitude, axiom, stock phrase, trite saying

truly *adverb* 1 GENUINELY, really, correctly, truthfully, rightly, in fact, precisely, exactly, legitimately, accurately, in reality, in truth, beyond doubt, without a doubt, authentically, beyond question, factually, in actuality, veritably, veraciously
<< OPPOSITE falsely
2 REALLY, very, greatly, indeed, seriously (*informal*), extremely, to be sure, exceptionally, verily
3 FAITHFULLY, firmly, constantly, steadily, honestly, sincerely, staunchly, dutifully, loyally, honourably, devotedly, with all your heart, with dedication, with devotion, confirmedly

trump *verb* OUTDO, top, cap, surpass, score points off, excel
▷▷ **trump something up** INVENT, create, make up, manufacture, fake, contrive, fabricate, concoct, cook up (*informal*)

trumped up *adjective* INVENTED, made-up, manufactured, false, fake, contrived, untrue, fabricated, concocted, falsified, cooked-up (*informal*), phoney *or* phony (*informal*)
<< OPPOSITE genuine

trumpet *noun* HORN, clarion, bugle
▷ *verb* 1 PROCLAIM, advertise, extol, tout (*informal*), announce, publish, broadcast, crack up (*informal*), sound loudly, shout from the rooftops, noise abroad
<< OPPOSITE keep secret
2 ROAR, call, cry, bay, bellow
▷▷ **blow your own trumpet** BOAST, crow, brag, vaunt, sing your own praises, big yourself up (*slang, chiefly Caribbean*)

truncate *verb* SHORTEN, cut, crop, trim, clip, dock, prune, curtail, cut short, pare, lop, abbreviate
<< OPPOSITE lengthen

truncheon *noun* (*Chiefly Brit*) CLUB, staff, stick, baton, cudgel, mere (*NZ*), patu (*NZ*)

trunk *noun* 1 STEM, stock, stalk, bole
2 CHEST, case, box, crate, bin, suitcase, locker, coffer, casket, portmanteau, kist (*Scot & Northern English dialect*)
3 BODY, torso
4 SNOUT, nose, proboscis

truss *verb often with* **up** TIE, secure, bind, strap, fasten, tether, pinion, make fast
▷ *noun* 1 (*Medical*) SUPPORT, pad, bandage
2 JOIST, support, stay, shore, beam, prop, brace, strut, buttress, stanchion

trust *noun* 1 CONFIDENCE, credit, belief, faith, expectation, conviction, assurance, certainty, reliance, credence, certitude
<< OPPOSITE distrust
2 RESPONSIBILITY, duty, obligation
3 CUSTODY, care, guard, protection, guardianship, safekeeping, trusteeship
▷ *verb* 1 BELIEVE IN, have faith in, depend on, count on, bank on, lean on, rely upon, swear by, take at face value, take as gospel, place reliance on, place your trust in, pin your faith on, place *or* have confidence in
<< OPPOSITE distrust
2 ENTRUST, commit, assign, confide, consign, put into the hands of, allow to look after, hand over, turn over, sign over, delegate

3 EXPECT, believe, hope, suppose, assume, guess (*informal*), take it, presume, surmise, think likely

>> RELATED WORD *adjective* fiducial

trustful *or* **trusting** *adjective* UNSUSPECTING, simple, innocent, optimistic, naive, confiding, gullible, unwary, unguarded, credulous, unsuspicious

<< OPPOSITE suspicious

trustworthy *adjective* DEPENDABLE, responsible, principled, mature, sensible, reliable, ethical, upright, true, honourable, honest, staunch, righteous, reputable, truthful, trusty, steadfast, level-headed, to be trusted

<< OPPOSITE untrustworthy

trusty *adjective* RELIABLE, dependable, trustworthy, responsible, solid, strong, firm, true, steady, faithful, straightforward, upright, honest, staunch

<< OPPOSITE unreliable

truth *noun* 1 REALITY, fact(s), real life, actuality

<< OPPOSITE unreality

2 TRUTHFULNESS, fact, accuracy, honesty, precision, validity, legitimacy, authenticity, correctness, sincerity, verity, candour, veracity, rightness, genuineness, exactness, factuality, factualness

<< OPPOSITE inaccuracy

3 FACT, law, reality, certainty, maxim, verity, axiom, truism, proven principle

4 HONESTY, principle, honour, virtue, integrity, goodness, righteousness, candour, frankness, probity, rectitude, incorruptibility, uprightness

<< OPPOSITE dishonesty

>> RELATED WORDS *adjectives* veritable, veracious

truthful *adjective* 1 HONEST, frank, candid, upfront (*informal*), true, straight, reliable, faithful, straightforward, sincere, forthright, trustworthy, plain-spoken, veracious

<< OPPOSITE dishonest

2 TRUE, correct, accurate, exact, realistic, precise, literal, veritable, naturalistic

<< OPPOSITE untrue

try *verb* 1 ATTEMPT, seek, aim, undertake, essay, strive, struggle, endeavour, have a go, go for it (*informal*), make an effort, have a shot (*informal*), have a crack (*informal*), bend over backwards (*informal*), do your best, go for broke (*slang*), make an attempt, move heaven and earth, bust a gut (*informal*), give it your best shot (*informal*), have a stab (*informal*), break your neck (*informal*), exert yourself, make an all-out effort (*informal*), knock yourself out (*informal*), have a whack (*informal*), do your damnedest (*informal*), give it your all (*informal*), rupture yourself (*informal*)

2 EXPERIMENT WITH, try out, put to the test, test, taste, examine, investigate, sample, evaluate, check out, inspect, appraise

3 JUDGE, hear, consider, examine, adjudicate, adjudge, pass judgement on

4 TAX, test, trouble, pain, stress, upset, tire, strain, drain, exhaust, annoy, plague, irritate, weary, afflict, sap, inconvenience, wear out, vex, irk, make demands on, give someone grief (*Brit & S African*)

▷ *noun* ATTEMPT, go (*informal*), shot (*informal*), effort, crack (*informal*), essay, stab (*informal*), bash (*informal*), endeavour, whack (*informal*)

▷▷ **try something out** TEST, experiment with, appraise, put to the test, taste, sample, evaluate, check out, inspect, put into practice

trying *adjective* ANNOYING, hard, taxing, difficult, tough, upsetting, irritating, fatiguing, stressful, aggravating (*informal*), troublesome, exasperating, arduous, tiresome, vexing, irksome, wearisome, bothersome

<< OPPOSITE straightforward

tsar *or* **czar** *noun* (*informal*) HEAD, chief, boss, big cheese (*informal*), baas (*S African*), head honcho (*informal*), sherang (*Austral & NZ*)

tubby *adjective* FAT, overweight, plump, stout, chubby, obese, portly, roly-poly, podgy, corpulent, paunchy

tuck *verb* PUSH, stick, stuff, slip, ease, insert, pop (*informal*)

▷ *noun* 1 (*Brit informal*) FOOD, eats (*slang*), tack (*informal*), scoff (*slang*), grub (*slang*), kai (*NZ informal*), nosh (*slang*), victuals, comestibles, nosebag (*slang*), vittles (*obsolete or dialect*)

2 FOLD, gather, pleat, pinch

▷▷ **tuck in** (*informal*) EAT UP, get stuck in (*informal*), eat heartily, fall to, chow down (*slang*)

▷▷ **tuck someone in** MAKE SNUG, wrap up, put to bed, bed down, swaddle

tuft *noun* CLUMP, bunch, shock, collection, knot, cluster, tussock, topknot

tug *verb* 1 PULL, drag, pluck, jerk, yank, wrench, lug

2 DRAG, pull, haul, tow, lug, heave, draw

▷ *noun* PULL, jerk, yank, wrench, drag, haul, tow, traction, heave

tuition *noun* TRAINING, schooling, education, teaching, lessons, instruction, tutoring, tutelage

tumble *verb* FALL, drop, topple, plummet, roll, pitch, toss, stumble, flop, trip up, fall head over heels, fall headlong, fall end over end

▷ *noun* FALL, drop, roll, trip, collapse, plunge, spill, toss, stumble, flop, headlong fall

tummy *noun* (*informal*) STOMACH, belly, abdomen, corporation (*informal*), pot, gut (*informal*), paunch, tum (*informal*), spare tyre (*informal*), breadbasket (*slang*), potbelly

tumour *or US* **tumor** *noun* GROWTH, cancer,

swelling, lump, carcinoma (*Pathology*), sarcoma (*Medical*), neoplasm (*Medical*)

tumult *noun* 1 DISTURBANCE, trouble, chaos, turmoil, storms, upset, stir, disorder, excitement, unrest, upheaval, havoc, mayhem, strife, disarray, turbulence, ferment, agitation, convulsions, bedlam
2 CLAMOUR, row, outbreak, racket, din, uproar, fracas, commotion, pandemonium, babel, hubbub, hullabaloo
<< OPPOSITE silence

tumultuous *adjective* 1 TURBULENT, exciting, confused, disturbed, hectic, stormy, agitated
<< OPPOSITE quiet
2 WILD, excited, riotous, unrestrained, violent, raging, disorderly, fierce, passionate, noisy, restless, unruly, rowdy, boisterous, full-on (*informal*), lawless, vociferous, rumbustious, uproarious, obstreperous, clamorous

tune *noun* 1 MELODY, air, song, theme, strain(s), motif, jingle, ditty, melody line
2 HARMONY, pitch, euphony
▷ *verb* 1 TUNE UP, adjust, bring into harmony
2 REGULATE, adapt, modulate, harmonize, attune, pitch

tuneful *adjective* MELODIOUS, musical, pleasant, harmonious, melodic, catchy, consonant (*Music*), symphonic, mellifluous, easy on the ear (*informal*), euphonious, euphonic
<< OPPOSITE discordant

tunnel *noun* PASSAGE, underpass, passageway, subway, channel, hole, shaft
▷ *verb* DIG, dig your way, burrow, mine, bore, drill, excavate

turbulence *noun* CONFUSION, turmoil, unrest, instability, storm, boiling, disorder, upheaval, agitation, commotion, pandemonium, tumult, roughness
<< OPPOSITE peace

turbulent *adjective* 1 WILD, violent, disorderly, agitated, rebellious, unruly, rowdy, boisterous, anarchic, tumultuous, lawless, unbridled, riotous, undisciplined, seditious, mutinous, ungovernable, uproarious, refractory, obstreperous, insubordinate
2 STORMY, rough, raging, tempestuous, boiling, disordered, furious, unsettled, foaming, unstable, agitated, tumultuous, choppy, blustery
<< OPPOSITE calm

turf *noun* 1 GRASS, green, sward
2 SOD, divot, clod
▷▷ **the turf** HORSE-RACING, the flat, racecourse, racetrack, racing
▷▷ **turf someone out** (*Brit informal*) THROW OUT, evict, cast out, kick out (*informal*), fire (*informal*), dismiss, sack (*informal*), bounce (*slang*), discharge, expel, oust, relegate, banish, eject, dispossess, chuck out (*informal*), fling out, kiss off (*slang, chiefly US & Canad*), show someone the door, give someone the sack (*informal*), give someone the bum's rush (*slang*), kennet (*Austral slang*), jeff (*Austral slang*)

turgid *adjective* POMPOUS, inflated, windy, high-flown, pretentious, grandiose, flowery, overblown, stilted, ostentatious, fulsome, bombastic, grandiloquent, arty-farty (*informal*), fustian, orotund, magniloquent, sesquipedalian, tumid

turmoil *noun* CONFUSION, trouble, violence, row, noise, stir, disorder, chaos, disturbance, upheaval, bustle, flurry, strife, disarray, uproar, turbulence, ferment, agitation, commotion, pandemonium, bedlam, tumult, hubbub, brouhaha
<< OPPOSITE peace

turn *verb* 1 *sometimes with* **round** CHANGE COURSE, swing round, wheel round, veer, move, return, go back, switch, shift, reverse, swerve, change position
2 ROTATE, spin, go round (and round), revolve, roll, circle, wheel, twist, spiral, whirl, swivel, pivot, twirl, gyrate, go round in circles, move in a circle
3 GO ROUND, come round, negotiate, pass, corner, pass around, take a bend
4 *with* **into** CHANGE, transform, fashion, shape, convert, alter, adapt, mould, remodel, form, mutate, refit, metamorphose, transmute, transfigure
5 SHAPE, form, fashion, cast, frame, construct, execute, mould, make
6 SICKEN, upset, nauseate
7 GO BAD, go off (*Brit informal*), curdle, go sour, become rancid
8 MAKE RANCID, spoil, sour, taint
▷ *noun* 1 ROTATION, turning, cycle, circle, revolution, spin, twist, reversal, whirl, swivel, pivot, gyration
2 CHANGE OF DIRECTION, bend, curve, change of course, shift, departure, deviation
3 DIRECTION, course, tack, swing, tendency, drift, bias
4 OPPORTUNITY, go, spell, shot (*informal*), time, try, round, chance, period, shift, crack (*informal*), succession, fling, stint, whack (*informal*)
5 STROLL, airing, walk, drive, ride, spin (*informal*), circuit, constitutional, outing, excursion, promenade, jaunt, saunter
6 DEED, service, act, action, favour, gesture
7 (*informal*) SHOCK, start, surprise, scare, jolt, fright
8 INCLINATION, talent, gift, leaning, bent, bias, flair, affinity, knack, propensity, aptitude
▷▷ **by turns** ALTERNATELY, in succession, turn and turn about, reciprocally
▷▷ **to a turn** (*informal*) PERFECTLY, correctly,

precisely, exactly, just right
▷▷ **turn off** BRANCH OFF, leave, quit, depart from, deviate, change direction, take a side road, take another road
▷▷ **turn on someone** ATTACK, assault, fall on, round on, lash out at, assail, lay into (*informal*), let fly at, lose your temper with
▷▷ **turn on something** DEPEND ON, hang on, rest on, hinge on, be decided by, balance on, be contingent on, pivot on
▷▷ **turn out** 1 PROVE TO BE, transpire, become apparent, happen, emerge, become known, develop, come to light, crop up (*informal*)
2 END UP, happen, result, work out, evolve, come to be, come about, transpire, pan out (*informal*), eventuate
3 COME, be present, turn up, show up (*informal*), go, appear, attend, gather, assemble, put in an appearance
▷▷ **turn over** OVERTURN, tip over, flip over, upend, be upset, reverse, capsize, keel over
▷▷ **turn someone off** (*informal*) REPEL, bore, put someone off, disgust, offend, irritate, alienate, sicken, displease, nauseate, gross someone out (*US slang*), disenchant, lose your interest
▷▷ **turn someone on** (*Slang*) AROUSE, attract, excite, thrill, stimulate, please, press someone's buttons (*slang*), work someone up, titillate, ring someone's bell (*US slang*), arouse someone's desire
▷▷ **turn someone out** EXPEL, drive out, evict, throw out, fire (*informal*), dismiss, sack (*informal*), axe (*informal*), discharge, oust, relegate, banish, deport, put out, cashier, unseat, dispossess, kick out (*informal*), cast out, drum out, show the door, turf out (*Brit informal*), give someone the sack (*informal*), give someone the bum's rush (*slang*), kiss off (*slang, chiefly US & Canad*), kennet (*Austral slang*), jeff (*Austral slang*)
▷▷ **turn something down** 1 REFUSE, decline, reject, spurn, rebuff, say no to, repudiate, abstain from, throw something out
2 LOWER, soften, reduce the volume of, mute, lessen, muffle, quieten, diminish
▷▷ **turn something in** HAND IN, return, deliver, give back, give up, hand over, submit, surrender, tender
▷▷ **turn something off** SWITCH OFF, turn out, put out, stop, kill, cut out, shut down, unplug, flick off
▷▷ **turn something on** SWITCH ON, put on, activate, start, start up, ignite, kick-start, set in motion, energize
▷▷ **turn something out** 1 TURN OFF, put out, switch off, extinguish, disconnect, unplug, flick off
2 PRODUCE, make, process, finish, manufacture, assemble, put together, put out, bring out, fabricate, churn out
▷▷ **turn something over** 1 FLIP OVER, flick through, leaf through
2 CONSIDER, think about, contemplate, ponder, reflect on, wonder about, mull over, think over, deliberate on, give thought to, ruminate about, revolve
3 HAND OVER, transfer, deliver, commit, give up, yield, surrender, pass on, render, assign, commend, give over
4 START UP, warm up, activate, switch on, crank, set something in motion, set something going, switch on the ignition of
▷▷ **turn something up** 1 FIND, reveal, discover, expose, come up with, disclose, unearth, dig up, bring to light
2 INCREASE, raise, boost, enhance, intensify, amplify, increase the volume of, make louder
▷▷ **turn up** 1 ARRIVE, come, appear, show up (*informal*), show (*informal*), attend, put in an appearance, show your face
2 COME TO LIGHT, be found, show up, pop up, materialize, appear

turning *noun* 1 TURN-OFF, turn, junction, crossroads, side road, exit
2 BEND, turn, curve

turning point *noun* CROSSROADS, critical moment, decisive moment, change, crisis, crux, moment of truth, point of no return, moment of decision, climacteric, tipping point

turn-off *noun* TURNING, turn, branch, exit, side road

turnout *noun* ATTENDANCE, crowd, audience, gate, assembly, congregation, number, throng, assemblage

turnover *noun* 1 OUTPUT, business, production, flow, volume, yield, productivity, outturn (*rare*)
2 MOVEMENT, replacement, coming and going, change

tussle *verb* FIGHT, battle, struggle, scrap (*informal*), contend, wrestle, vie, brawl, grapple, scuffle
▷ *noun* FIGHT, scrap (*informal*), brawl, scuffle, battle, competition, struggle, conflict, contest, set-to (*informal*), bout, contention, fray, punch-up (*Brit informal*), fracas, shindig (*informal*), scrimmage, shindy (*informal*), bagarre (*French*), biffo (*Austral slang*)

tutelage *noun* (*Formal*) GUIDANCE, education, instruction, preparation, schooling, charge, care, teaching, protection, custody, tuition, dependence, patronage, guardianship, wardship

tutor *noun* TEACHER, coach, instructor, educator, guide, governor, guardian, lecturer, guru, mentor, preceptor, master *or* mistress, schoolmaster *or* schoolmistress
▷ *verb* TEACH, educate, school, train, coach, guide, discipline, lecture, drill, instruct, edify,

direct

tutorial *noun* SEMINAR, lesson, individual instruction
▷ *adjective* TEACHING, coaching, guiding, instructional

TV *noun* TELEVISION, telly (*Brit informal*), the box (*Brit informal*), receiver, the tube (*slang*), television set, TV set, small screen (*informal*), gogglebox (*Brit slang*), idiot box (*slang*)

twaddle *noun* NONSENSE, rubbish, rot, garbage (*informal*), pants (*slang*), gossip, crap (*slang*), trash, hot air (*informal*), tosh (*slang, chiefly Brit*), waffle (*informal, chiefly Brit*), pap, bilge (*informal*), drivel, tripe (*informal*), guff (*slang*), tattle, moonshine, verbiage, gabble, claptrap (*informal*), gobbledegook (*informal*), hogwash, hokum (*slang, chiefly US & Canad*), rigmarole, blather, piffle (*informal*), poppycock (*informal*), inanity, balderdash, bosh (*informal*), eyewash (*informal*), trumpery, tommyrot, foolish talk, horsefeathers (*US slang*), bunkum *or* buncombe (*chiefly US*), bizzo (*Austral slang*), bull's wool (*Austral & NZ slang*)

tweak *verb* TWIST, pull, pinch, jerk, squeeze, nip, twitch
▷ *noun* TWIST, pull, squeeze, pinch, jerk, nip, twitch

twee *adjective* (*Brit*) **1** SWEET, pretty, cute, sentimental, quaint, dainty, cutesy (*informal, chiefly US*), bijou, precious
2 SENTIMENTAL, over-sentimental, soppy (*Brit informal*), mawkish, affected, precious

twiddle *verb* FIDDLE WITH, adjust, finger, play with, juggle, wiggle (*informal*), twirl, jiggle, monkey with (*informal*)

twig[1] *noun* BRANCH, stick, sprig, offshoot, shoot, spray, withe

twig[2] *verb* (*Brit informal*) UNDERSTAND, get, see, find out, grasp, make out, rumble (*Brit informal*), catch on (*informal*), comprehend, fathom, tumble to (*informal*)

twilight *noun* **1** DUSK, evening, sunset, early evening, nightfall, sundown, gloaming (*Scot poetic*), close of day, evo (*Austral slang*)
<< OPPOSITE dawn
2 HALF-LIGHT, gloom, dimness, semi-darkness
3 DECLINE, last years, final years, closing years, autumn, downturn, ebb, last phase
<< OPPOSITE height
▷ *adjective* **1** EVENING, dim, darkening, evo (*Austral slang*)
2 DECLINING, last, final, dying, ebbing

twin *noun* DOUBLE, counterpart, mate, match, fellow, clone, duplicate, lookalike, likeness, ringer (*slang*), corollary
▷ *verb* PAIR, match, join, couple, link, yoke
▷ *adjective* IDENTICAL, matched, matching, double, paired, parallel, corresponding, dual, duplicate, twofold, geminate

twine *noun* STRING, cord, yarn, strong thread
▷ *verb* **1** TWIST TOGETHER, weave, knit, braid, splice, interweave, plait, entwine, interlace, twist
2 COIL, wind, surround, bend, wrap, twist, curl, loop, spiral, meander, encircle, wreathe

twinge *noun* **1** PANG, twitch, tweak, throe (*rare*), twist
2 PAIN, sharp pain, gripe, stab, bite, twist, stitch, pinch, throb, twitch, prick, spasm, tweak, tic

twinkle *verb* SPARKLE, flash, shine, glitter, gleam, blink, flicker, wink, shimmer, glint, glisten, scintillate, coruscate
▷ *noun* **1** SPARKLE, light, flash, spark, shine, glittering, gleam, blink, flicker, wink, shimmer, glimmer, glistening, scintillation, coruscation
2 MOMENT, second, shake (*informal*), flash, instant, tick (*Brit informal*), twinkling, split second, jiffy (*informal*), trice, two shakes of a lamb's tail (*informal*)

twinkling *or* **twink** *noun* MOMENT, second, flash, instant, tick (*Brit informal*), twinkle, split second, jiffy (*informal*), trice, two shakes of a lamb's tail (*informal*), shake (*informal*), bat of an eye (*informal*)

twirl *verb* **1** TWIDDLE, turn, rotate, wind, spin, twist, revolve, whirl
2 TURN, whirl, wheel, spin, twist, pivot, gyrate, pirouette, turn on your heel
▷ *noun* TURN, spin, rotation, whirl, wheel, revolution, twist, pirouette, gyration

twist *verb* **1** COIL, curl, wind, plait, wrap, screw, twirl
2 INTERTWINE, wind, weave, braid, interweave, plait, entwine, twine, wreathe, interlace
3 DISTORT, screw up, contort, mangle, mangulate (*Austral slang*)
<< OPPOSITE straighten
4 SPRAIN, turn, rick, wrench
5 MISREPRESENT, distort, misquote, alter, change, pervert, warp, falsify, garble
6 SQUIRM, wriggle, writhe
▷ *noun* **1** SURPRISE, change, turn, development, revelation
2 DEVELOPMENT, emphasis, variation, slant
3 WIND, turn, spin, swivel, twirl
4 COIL, roll, curl, hank, twine
5 CURVE, turn, bend, loop, arc, kink, zigzag, convolution, dog-leg, undulation
6 TRAIT, fault, defect, peculiarity, bent, characteristic, flaw, deviation, quirk, eccentricity, oddity, aberration, imperfection, kink, foible, idiosyncrasy, proclivity, crotchet
7 SPRAIN, turn, pull, jerk, wrench

twit *noun* (*informal, chiefly Brit*) FOOL, idiot, jerk (*slang, chiefly US & Canad*), charlie (*Brit informal*), dope (*informal*), clown, ass, plank (*Brit slang*), berk (*Brit slang*), wally (*slang*), prat (*slang*), plonker (*slang*), geek (*slang*), chump (*informal*), oaf, simpleton, airhead (*slang*), dipstick (*Brit slang*), gonzo (*slang*), schmuck (*US slang*), dork (*slang*), nitwit (*informal*), blockhead, ninny, divvy (*Brit slang*), pillock (*Brit slang*), halfwit, silly-billy (*informal*), nincompoop, dweeb (*US slang*), putz (*US slang*), weenie (*US informal*), eejit (*Scot & Irish*), dumb-ass (*slang*), numpty (*Scot informal*), doofus (*slang, chiefly US*), juggins (*Brit informal*), dickwit (*slang*), nerd *or* nurd (*slang*), numbskull *or* numskull, twerp *or* twirp (*informal*), dorba *or* dorb (*Austral slang*), bogan (*Austral slang*)

twitch *verb* 1 JERK, blink, flutter, jump, squirm
2 PULL (AT), snatch (at), tug (at), pluck (at), yank (at)
▷ *noun* JERK, tic, spasm, twinge, jump, blink, flutter, tremor

twitter *verb* 1 CHIRRUP, whistle, chatter, trill, chirp, warble, cheep, tweet
2 CHATTER, chat, rabbit (on) (*Brit informal*), gossip, babble, gab (*informal*), prattle, natter, jabber, blather, prate
▷ *noun* CHIRRUP, call, song, cry, whistle, chatter, trill, chirp, warble, cheep, tweet

two-faced *adjective* HYPOCRITICAL, false, deceiving, treacherous, deceitful, untrustworthy, insincere, double-dealing, duplicitous, dissembling, perfidious, Janus-faced
<< OPPOSITE honest

tycoon *noun* MAGNATE, capitalist, baron, industrialist, financier, fat cat (*slang, chiefly US*), mogul, captain of industry, potentate, wealthy businessman, big cheese (*slang* or *old-fashioned*), plutocrat, big noise (*informal*), merchant prince

type *noun* 1 KIND, sort, class, variety, group, form, order, style, species, breed, strain, category, stamp, kidney, genre, classification, ilk, subdivision
2 PRINT, printing, face, case, characters, font, fount

typhoon *noun* STORM, tornado, cyclone, tempest, squall, tropical storm

typical *adjective* 1 ARCHETYPAL, standard, model, normal, classic, stock, essential, representative, usual, conventional, regular, characteristic, orthodox, indicative, illustrative, archetypical, stereotypical
<< OPPOSITE unusual
2 CHARACTERISTIC, in keeping, in character, true to type
3 AVERAGE, normal, usual, conventional, routine, regular, orthodox, predictable, run-of-the-mill, bog-standard (*Brit & Irish slang*)

typify *verb* REPRESENT, illustrate, sum up, characterize, embody, exemplify, personify, incarnate, epitomize

tyrannical *or* **tyrannic** *adjective* OPPRESSIVE, cruel, authoritarian, dictatorial, severe, absolute, unreasonable, arbitrary, unjust, autocratic, inhuman, coercive, imperious, domineering, overbearing, magisterial, despotic, high-handed, peremptory, overweening, tyrannous
<< OPPOSITE liberal

tyranny *noun* OPPRESSION, cruelty, dictatorship, authoritarianism, reign of terror, despotism, autocracy, absolutism, coercion, high-handedness, harsh discipline, unreasonableness, imperiousness, peremptoriness
<< OPPOSITE liberality

tyrant *noun* DICTATOR, bully, authoritarian, oppressor, despot, autocrat, absolutist, martinet, slave-driver, Hitler

tyro *or* **tiro** *noun* BEGINNER, novice, apprentice, learner, neophyte, rookie (*informal*), greenhorn (*informal*), catechumen

Uu

ubiquitous *adjective* EVER-PRESENT, pervasive, omnipresent, all-over, everywhere, universal
ugly *adjective* 1 UNATTRACTIVE, homely (*chiefly US*), plain, unsightly, unlovely, unprepossessing, not much to look at, no oil painting (*informal*), ill-favoured, hard-featured, hard-favoured
<< OPPOSITE beautiful
2 UNPLEASANT, shocking, terrible, offensive, nasty, disgusting, revolting, obscene, hideous, monstrous, vile, distasteful, horrid, repulsive, frightful, objectionable, disagreeable, repugnant
<< OPPOSITE pleasant
3 BAD-TEMPERED, nasty, sullen, surly, threatening, dangerous, angry, forbidding, menacing, sinister, ominous, malevolent, spiteful, baleful, bodeful
<< OPPOSITE good-natured
ulcer *noun* SORE, abscess, gathering, peptic ulcer, gumboil
ulterior *adjective* HIDDEN, secret, concealed, personal, secondary, selfish, covert, undisclosed, unexpressed
<< OPPOSITE obvious
ultimate *adjective* 1 FINAL, eventual, conclusive, last, end, furthest, extreme, terminal, decisive
2 FUNDAMENTAL, basic, primary, radical, elemental
3 SUPREME, highest, greatest, maximum, paramount, most significant, superlative, topmost
4 WORST, greatest, utmost, extreme
5 BEST, greatest, supreme, optimum, quintessential
▷ *noun* EPITOME, height, greatest, summit, peak, extreme, perfection, the last word
ultimately *adverb* 1 FINALLY, eventually, in the end, after all, at last, at the end of the day, sooner or later, in the fullness of time, in due time
2 FUNDAMENTALLY, essentially, basically, primarily, at heart, deep down
ultra-modern *adjective* ADVANCED, progressive, avant-garde, futuristic, ahead of its time, modernistic, neoteric (*rare*)
umbrella *noun* 1 BROLLY (*Brit informal*), parasol, sunshade, gamp
2 COVER, protection, guardianship, backing, support, charge, care, agency, responsibility, guidance, patronage, auspices, aegis, safe keeping, protectorship
umpire *noun* REFEREE, judge, ref (*informal*), arbiter, arbitrator, moderator, adjudicator, umpie (*Austral slang*)
▷ *verb* REFEREE, judge, adjudicate, arbitrate, call (*Sport*), moderate, mediate
umpteen *adjective* (*informal*) VERY MANY, numerous, countless, millions, gazillions (*informal*), considerable, a good many, a thousand and one, ever so many
unable *adjective with* **to** INCAPABLE, inadequate, powerless, unfit, unfitted, not able, impotent, not up to, unqualified, ineffectual, not equal to
<< OPPOSITE able
unaccountable *adjective* 1 INEXPLICABLE, mysterious, baffling, odd, strange, puzzling, peculiar, incomprehensible, inscrutable, unfathomable, unexplainable
<< OPPOSITE understandable
2 NOT ANSWERABLE, exempt, not responsible, free, unliable
unaccustomed *adjective* 1 UNFAMILIAR, unusual, unexpected, new, special, surprising, strange, remarkable, unprecedented, uncommon, out of the ordinary, unwonted
<< OPPOSITE familiar
2 *with* **to** NOT USED TO, unfamiliar with, unused to, not given to, a newcomer to, a novice at, inexperienced at, unversed in, unpractised in
<< OPPOSITE used to
unaffected[1] *adjective* NATURAL, genuine, unpretentious, simple, plain, straightforward, naive, sincere, honest, unassuming, unspoilt, unsophisticated, dinkum (*Austral & NZ informal*),

artless, ingenuous, without airs, unstudied
<< OPPOSITE pretentious

unaffected² *adjective often with* **by** IMPERVIOUS TO, unchanged, untouched, unimpressed, unmoved, unaltered, not influenced, unresponsive to, unstirred
<< OPPOSITE affected

unanimity *noun* AGREEMENT, accord, consensus, concert, unity, harmony, chorus, unison, assent, concord, one mind, concurrence, like-mindedness
<< OPPOSITE disagreement

unanimous *adjective* 1 AGREED, united, in agreement, agreeing, at one, harmonious, like-minded, concordant, of one mind, of the same mind, in complete accord
<< OPPOSITE divided
2 UNITED, common, concerted, solid, consistent, harmonious, undivided, congruent, concordant, unopposed
<< OPPOSITE split

unanimously *adverb* WITHOUT EXCEPTION, by common consent, without opposition, with one accord, unitedly, nem. con.

unarmed *adjective* DEFENCELESS, helpless, unprotected, without arms, unarmoured, weaponless
<< OPPOSITE armed

unassailable *adjective* UNDENIABLE, indisputable, irrefutable, sound, proven, positive, absolute, conclusive, incontrovertible, incontestable
<< OPPOSITE doubtful

unassuming *adjective* MODEST, quiet, humble, meek, simple, reserved, retiring, unpretentious, unobtrusive, self-effacing, diffident, unassertive, unostentatious
<< OPPOSITE conceited

unattached *adjective* 1 SINGLE, available, unmarried, on your own, by yourself, a free agent, not spoken for, left on the shelf, footloose and fancy-free, unengaged
2 *often with* **to** INDEPENDENT (FROM), unaffiliated (to), nonaligned (to), free (from), autonomous (from), uncommitted (to)
<< OPPOSITE attached (to)

unavoidable *adjective* INEVITABLE, inescapable, inexorable, sure, certain, necessary, fated, compulsory, obligatory, bound to happen, ineluctable

unaware *adjective* IGNORANT, unconscious, oblivious, in the dark (*informal*), unsuspecting, uninformed, unknowing, heedless, unenlightened, unmindful, not in the loop (*informal*), incognizant
<< OPPOSITE aware

unawares *adverb* 1 BY SURPRISE, unprepared, off guard, suddenly, unexpectedly, abruptly, aback, without warning, on the hop (*Brit informal*), caught napping
<< OPPOSITE prepared
2 UNKNOWINGLY, unwittingly, unconsciously
<< OPPOSITE knowingly

unbalanced *adjective* 1 DERANGED, disturbed, unstable, touched, mad, crazy, barking (*slang*), eccentric, insane, irrational, erratic, lunatic, demented, unsound, unhinged, loopy (*informal*), out to lunch (*informal*), barking mad (*slang*), gonzo (*slang*), not all there, doolally (*slang*), off your trolley (*slang*), up the pole (*informal*), non compos mentis (*Latin*), not the full shilling (*informal*), wacko *or* whacko (*informal*), off the air (*Austral slang*), daggy (*Austral & NZ informal*)
2 BIASED, one-sided, prejudiced, unfair, partial, partisan, unjust, inequitable
3 IRREGULAR, not balanced, lacking
4 SHAKY, unstable, wobbly
<< OPPOSITE stable

unbearable *adjective* INTOLERABLE, insufferable, unendurable, too much (*informal*), unacceptable, oppressive, insupportable
<< OPPOSITE tolerable

unbeatable *adjective* 1 UNSURPASSED, matchless, unsurpassable
2 INVINCIBLE, unstoppable, indomitable, unconquerable

unbeaten *adjective* UNDEFEATED, winning, triumphant, victorious, unsurpassed, unbowed, unvanquished, unsubdued

unbelievable *adjective* 1 WONDERFUL, excellent, superb, fantastic (*informal*), mean (*slang*), great (*informal*), topping (*Brit slang*), bad (*slang*), cracking (*Brit informal*), crucial (*slang*), smashing (*informal*), magnificent, fabulous (*informal*), divine (*informal*), glorious, terrific (*informal*), splendid, sensational (*informal*), mega (*slang*), sovereign, awesome (*slang*), colossal, super (*informal*), wicked (*informal*), def (*slang*), brill (*informal*), stupendous, bodacious (*slang, chiefly US*), boffo (*slang*), jim-dandy (*slang*), chillin' (*US slang*), booshit (*Austral slang*), exo (*Austral slang*), sik (*Austral slang*), rad (*informal*), phat (*slang*), schmick (*Austral informal*)
<< OPPOSITE terrible
2 INCREDIBLE, impossible, unthinkable, astonishing, staggering, questionable, improbable, inconceivable, preposterous, unconvincing, unimaginable, outlandish, far-fetched, implausible, beyond belief, jaw-dropping, cock-and-bull (*informal*)
<< OPPOSITE believable

unbeliever *noun* ATHEIST, sceptic, disbeliever, agnostic, infidel, doubting Thomas

unborn *adjective* EXPECTED, awaited, embryonic, in utero (*Latin*)

unbridled *adjective* UNRESTRAINED, uncontrolled, unchecked, violent, excessive, rampant, unruly, full-on (*informal*), wanton, riotous, intemperate, ungovernable, unconstrained, licentious, ungoverned, uncurbed

unbroken *adjective* 1 INTACT, whole, undamaged, complete, total, entire, solid, untouched, unscathed, unspoiled, unimpaired
<< OPPOSITE broken
2 CONTINUOUS, uninterrupted, constant, successive, endless, progressive, incessant, ceaseless, unremitting
<< OPPOSITE interrupted
3 UNDISTURBED, uninterrupted, sound, fast, deep, profound, untroubled, unruffled
4 UNTAMED, wild, undomesticated

unburden *verb* 1 REVEAL, confide, disclose, lay bare, unbosom
2 UNLOAD, relieve, discharge, lighten, disencumber, disburden, ease the load of
▷▷ **unburden yourself** CONFESS, come clean about (*informal*), get something off your chest (*informal*), tell all about, empty yourself, spill your guts about (*slang*), make a clean breast of something

uncanny *adjective* 1 WEIRD, strange, mysterious, queer, unearthly, eerie, supernatural, unnatural, spooky (*informal*), creepy (*informal*), eldritch (*poetic*), preternatural
2 EXTRAORDINARY, remarkable, incredible, unusual, fantastic, astonishing, exceptional, astounding, singular, miraculous, unheard-of, prodigious

uncertain *adjective* 1 UNSURE, undecided, at a loss, vague, unclear, doubtful, dubious, ambivalent, hazy, hesitant, vacillating, in two minds, undetermined, irresolute
<< OPPOSITE sure
2 DOUBTFUL, undetermined, unpredictable, insecure, questionable, ambiguous, unreliable, precarious, indefinite, indeterminate, incalculable, iffy (*informal*), changeable, indistinct, chancy, unforeseeable, unsettled, unresolved, in the balance, unconfirmed, up in the air, unfixed, conjectural
<< OPPOSITE decided

uncertainty *noun* 1 UNPREDICTABILITY, precariousness, state of suspense, ambiguity, unreliability, fickleness, inconclusiveness, chanciness, changeableness
<< OPPOSITE predictability
2 DOUBT, confusion, dilemma, misgiving, qualm, bewilderment, quandary, puzzlement, perplexity, mystification
<< OPPOSITE confidence
3 HESITANCY, hesitation, indecision, lack of confidence, vagueness, irresolution

uncharted *adjective* UNEXPLORED, unknown, undiscovered, strange, virgin, unfamiliar, unplumbed, not mapped

> *Unchartered* is sometimes mistakenly used where *uncharted* is meant: *We did not want to pioneer in completely uncharted* (not *unchartered*) *territory*

unclean *adjective* 1 DIRTY, soiled, foul, contaminated, polluted, nasty, filthy, defiled, impure, scuzzy (*slang, chiefly US*)
<< OPPOSITE clean
2 IMMORAL, corrupt, impure, evil, dirty, nasty, foul, polluted, filthy, scuzzy (*slang, chiefly US*)

uncomfortable *adjective* 1 UNEASY, troubled, disturbed, embarrassed, distressed, awkward, out of place, self-conscious, disquieted, ill at ease, discomfited, like a fish out of water
<< OPPOSITE comfortable
2 PAINFUL, awkward, irritating, hard, rough, troublesome, disagreeable, causing discomfort

uncommitted *adjective* UNDECIDED, uninvolved, nonpartisan, nonaligned, free, floating, neutral, not involved, unattached, free-floating, (sitting) on the fence

uncommon *adjective* 1 RARE, unusual, odd, novel, strange, bizarre, curious, peculiar, unfamiliar, scarce, queer, singular, few and far between, out of the ordinary, infrequent, thin on the ground
<< OPPOSITE common
2 EXTRAORDINARY, rare, remarkable, special, outstanding, superior, distinctive, exceptional, unprecedented, notable, singular, unparalleled, noteworthy, inimitable, incomparable
<< OPPOSITE ordinary

uncommonly *adverb* 1 EXCEPTIONALLY, very, extremely, remarkably, particularly, strangely, seriously (*informal*), unusually, peculiarly, to the nth degree
2 (always used in a negative construction) RARELY, occasionally, seldom, not often, infrequently, hardly ever, only now and then, scarcely ever

uncompromising *adjective* INFLEXIBLE, strict, rigid, decided, firm, tough, stubborn, hardline, die-hard, inexorable, steadfast, unyielding, obstinate, intransigent, unbending, obdurate, stiff-necked

unconcerned *adjective* UNTROUBLED, relaxed, unperturbed, nonchalant, easy, careless, not bothered, serene, callous, carefree, unruffled, blithe, insouciant, unworried, not giving a toss (*informal*)
<< OPPOSITE concerned

unconditional *adjective* ABSOLUTE, full, complete, total, positive, entire, utter, explicit, outright, unlimited, downright, unqualified, unrestricted, out-and-out, plenary, categorical, unreserved

<< OPPOSITE qualified

unconscious *adjective* 1 SENSELESS, knocked out, out cold (*informal*), out, stunned, numb, dazed, blacked out (*informal*), in a coma, comatose, stupefied, asleep, out for the count (*informal*), insensible, dead to the world (*informal*)

<< OPPOSITE awake

2 UNAWARE, ignorant, oblivious, unsuspecting, lost to, blind to, in ignorance, unknowing

<< OPPOSITE aware

3 UNINTENTIONAL, unwitting, unintended, inadvertent, accidental, unpremeditated

<< OPPOSITE intentional

4 SUBCONSCIOUS, automatic, suppressed, repressed, inherent, reflex, instinctive, innate, involuntary, latent, subliminal, unrealized, gut (*informal*)

unconventional *adjective* 1 UNUSUAL, unorthodox, odd, eccentric, different, individual, original, bizarre, way-out (*informal*), informal, irregular, bohemian, far-out (*slang*), idiosyncratic, off-the-wall (*slang*), oddball (*informal*), individualistic, out of the ordinary, offbeat, left-field (*informal*), freakish, atypical, nonconformist, wacko (*slang*), outré, uncustomary, daggy (*Austral & NZ informal*)

<< OPPOSITE conventional

2 UNORTHODOX, original, unusual, irregular, atypical, different, uncustomary

<< OPPOSITE normal

uncover *verb* 1 REVEAL, find, discover, expose, encounter, turn up, detect, disclose, unveil, come across, unearth, dig up, divulge, chance on, root out, unmask, lay bare, make known, blow the whistle on (*informal*), bring to light, smoke out, take the wraps off, blow wide open (*slang*), stumble on *or* across

<< OPPOSITE conceal

2 OPEN, unveil, unwrap, show, strip, expose, bare, lay bare, lift the lid, lay open

undaunted *adjective* UNDETERRED, unflinching, not discouraged, not put off, brave, bold, courageous, gritty, fearless, resolute, gallant, intrepid, steadfast, indomitable, dauntless, undismayed, unfaltering, nothing daunted, undiscouraged, unshrinking

undecided *adjective* 1 UNSURE, uncertain, uncommitted, torn, doubtful, dubious, wavering, hesitant, ambivalent, dithering (*chiefly Brit*), in two minds, irresolute, swithering (*Scot*)

<< OPPOSITE sure

2 UNSETTLED, open, undetermined, vague, pending, tentative, in the balance, indefinite, debatable, up in the air, moot, iffy (*informal*), unconcluded

<< OPPOSITE settled

undeniable *adjective* CERTAIN, evident, undoubted, incontrovertible, clear, sure, sound, proven, obvious, patent, manifest, beyond (a) doubt, unassailable, indisputable, irrefutable, unquestionable, beyond question, incontestable, indubitable

<< OPPOSITE doubtful

under *preposition* 1 BELOW, beneath, underneath, on the bottom of

<< OPPOSITE over

2 SUBORDINATE TO, subject to, reporting to, directed by, governed by, inferior to, secondary to, subservient to, junior to

3 INCLUDED IN, belonging to, subsumed under, comprised in

▷ *adverb* BELOW, down, beneath, downward, to the bottom

<< OPPOSITE up

>> RELATED WORD *prefix* sub-

undercover *adjective* SECRET, covert, clandestine, private, hidden, intelligence, underground, spy, concealed, confidential, hush-hush (*informal*), surreptitious

<< OPPOSITE open

undercurrent *noun* 1 UNDERTONE, feeling, atmosphere, sense, suggestion, trend, hint, flavour, tendency, drift, murmur, tenor, aura, tinge, vibes (*slang*), vibrations, overtone, hidden feeling

2 UNDERTOW, tideway, riptide, rip, rip current, crosscurrent, underflow

undercut *verb* UNDERPRICE, sell cheaply, sell at a loss, undersell, sacrifice, undercharge

underdog *noun* WEAKER PARTY, victim, loser, little fellow (*informal*), outsider, fall guy (*informal*)

underestimate *verb* 1 UNDERVALUE, understate, underrate, diminish, play down, minimize, downgrade, miscalculate, trivialize, rate too low, underemphasize, hold cheap, misprize

<< OPPOSITE overestimate

2 UNDERRATE, undervalue, belittle, sell short (*informal*), not do justice to, rate too low, set no store by, hold cheap, think too little of

<< OPPOSITE overrate

Underestimate is sometimes wrongly used where *overestimate* is meant: *the importance of his work cannot be overestimated* (not *cannot be underestimated*)

undergo *verb* EXPERIENCE, go through, be subjected to, stand, suffer, bear, weather, sustain, endure, withstand, submit to

underground *adjective* 1 SUBTERRANEAN, basement, lower-level, sunken, covered, buried, below the surface, below ground, subterrestrial

2 SECRET, undercover, covert, hidden, guerrilla, revolutionary, concealed, confidential, dissident, closet, subversive, clandestine, renegade, insurgent, hush-hush (*informal*), surreptitious, cloak-and-dagger, hugger-mugger, insurrectionist, hole-and-corner, radical

▷▷**the underground** 1 THE TUBE (*Brit*), the subway, the metro

2 THE RESISTANCE, partisans, freedom fighters, the Maquis

undergrowth *noun* SCRUB, brush, underwood, bracken, brambles, briars, underbrush, brushwood, underbush

underhand *adjective* SLY, secret, crooked (*informal*), devious, sneaky, secretive, fraudulent, treacherous, dishonest, deceptive, clandestine, unscrupulous, crafty, unethical, furtive, deceitful, surreptitious, stealthy, dishonourable, below the belt (*informal*), underhanded

<< OPPOSITE honest

underline *verb* 1 EMPHASIZE, stress, highlight, bring home, accentuate, point up, give emphasis to, call *or* draw attention to

<< OPPOSITE minimize

2 UNDERSCORE, mark, italicize, rule a line under

underling *noun* (*Derogatory*) SUBORDINATE, inferior, minion, servant, slave, cohort (*chiefly US*), retainer, menial, nonentity, lackey, hireling, flunky, understrapper

underlying *adjective* 1 FUNDAMENTAL, basic, essential, root, prime, primary, radical, elementary, intrinsic, basal

2 HIDDEN, concealed, lurking, veiled, latent

undermine *verb* WEAKEN, sabotage, subvert, compromise, disable, debilitate

<< OPPOSITE reinforce

underpinning *noun* SUPPORT, base, foundation, footing, groundwork, substructure

underprivileged *adjective* DISADVANTAGED, poor, deprived, in need, impoverished, needy, badly off, destitute, in want, on the breadline

underrate *verb* UNDERESTIMATE, discount, undervalue, belittle, disparage, fail to appreciate, not do justice to, set (too) little store by, misprize

<< OPPOSITE overestimate

understand *verb* 1 COMPREHEND, get, take in, perceive, grasp, know, see, follow, realize, recognize, appreciate, be aware of, penetrate, make out, discern, twig (*Brit informal*), fathom, savvy (*slang*), apprehend, conceive of, suss (*Brit informal*), get to the bottom of, get the hang of (*informal*), tumble to (*informal*), catch on to (*informal*), cotton on to (*informal*), make head or tail of (*informal*), get your head round

2 SYMPATHIZE WITH, appreciate, be aware of, be able to see, take on board (*informal*), empathize with, commiserate with, show compassion for

3 BELIEVE, hear, learn, gather, think, see, suppose, notice, assume, take it, conclude, fancy, presume, be informed, infer, surmise, hear tell, draw the inference

understandable *adjective* REASONABLE, natural, normal, justified, expected, inevitable, legitimate, logical, predictable, accountable, on the cards (*informal*), foreseeable, to be expected, justifiable, unsurprising, excusable, pardonable

understanding *noun* 1 PERCEPTION, knowledge, grasp, sense, know-how (*informal*), intelligence, judgment, awareness, appreciation, insight, skill, penetration, mastery, comprehension, familiarity with, discernment, proficiency

<< OPPOSITE ignorance

2 AGREEMENT, deal, promise, arrangement, accord, contract, bond, pledge, bargain, pact, compact, concord, gentlemen's agreement

<< OPPOSITE disagreement

3 BELIEF, view, opinion, impression, interpretation, feeling, idea, conclusion, notion, conviction, judgment, assumption, point of view, perception, suspicion, viewpoint, hunch, way of thinking, estimation, supposition, sneaking suspicion, funny feeling

▷ *adjective* SYMPATHETIC, kind, compassionate, considerate, kindly, accepting, patient, sensitive, forgiving, discerning, tolerant, responsive, perceptive, forbearing

<< OPPOSITE unsympathetic

understood *adjective* 1 ASSUMED, presumed, accepted, taken for granted

2 IMPLIED, implicit, unspoken, inferred, tacit, unstated

understudy *noun* STAND-IN, reserve, substitute, double, sub, replacement, fill-in

undertake *verb* 1 TAKE ON, embark on, set about, commence, try, begin, attempt, tackle, enter upon, endeavour to do

2 AGREE, promise, contract, guarantee, engage, pledge, covenant, commit yourself, take upon yourself

undertaker *noun* FUNERAL DIRECTOR, mortician (*US*)

undertaking *noun* 1 TASK, business, operation, project, game, attempt, effort, affair, venture, enterprise, endeavour

2 PROMISE, commitment, pledge, word, vow, assurance, word of honour, solemn word

undertone *noun* 1 MURMUR, whisper, low tone, subdued voice

2 UNDERCURRENT, suggestion, trace, hint, feeling, touch, atmosphere, flavour, tinge, vibes (*slang*)

undervalue *verb* UNDERRATE, underestimate, minimize, look down on, misjudge, depreciate, make light of, set no store by, hold cheap, misprize

<< OPPOSITE overrate

underwater *adjective* SUBMERGED, submarine, immersed, sunken, undersea, subaqueous, subaquatic

under way *adjective* IN PROGRESS, going on, started, begun, in business, in motion, in operation, afoot

underwear *noun* UNDERCLOTHES, lingerie, undies (*informal*), smalls (*informal*), undergarments, unmentionables (*humorous*), underclothing, underthings, underlinen, broekies (*S African informal*), underdaks (*Austral slang*)

underweight *adjective* SKINNY, puny, emaciated, undernourished, skin and bone (*informal*), undersized, half-starved, underfed

underworld *noun* 1 CRIMINALS, gangsters, organized crime, gangland (*informal*), criminal element

2 NETHER WORLD, hell, Hades, the inferno, nether regions, infernal region, abode of the dead

underwrite *verb* FINANCE, back, fund, guarantee, sponsor, insure, ratify, subsidize, bankroll (*US informal*), provide security, provide capital for

undesirable *adjective* UNWANTED, unwelcome, disagreeable, objectionable, offensive, disliked, unacceptable, dreaded, unpopular, unsuitable, out of place, unattractive, distasteful, unsavoury, obnoxious, repugnant, unpleasing, unwished-for

<< OPPOSITE desirable

undo *verb* 1 OPEN, unfasten, loose, loosen, unlock, unwrap, untie, disengage, unbutton, disentangle, unstrap, unclasp

2 REVERSE, cancel, offset, wipe out, neutralize, invalidate, annul, nullify

3 RUIN, defeat, destroy, wreck, shatter, upset, mar, undermine, overturn, quash, subvert, bring to naught

undoing *noun* DOWNFALL, weakness, curse, trouble, trial, misfortune, blight, affliction, the last straw, fatal flaw

undone[1] *adjective* UNFINISHED, left, outstanding, not done, neglected, omitted, incomplete, passed over, unfulfilled, not completed, unperformed, unattended to

<< OPPOSITE finished

undone[2] *adjective* (*Literary*) RUINED, destroyed, overcome, hapless, forlorn, prostrate, wretched

undoubted *adjective* CERTAIN, sure, definite, confirmed, positive, obvious, acknowledged, patent, evident, manifest, transparent, clear-cut, undisputed, indisputable, unquestioned, unquestionable, incontrovertible, indubitable, nailed-on (*slang*)

undoubtedly *adverb* CERTAINLY, definitely, undeniably, surely, of course, doubtless, without doubt, unquestionably, unmistakably, assuredly, beyond question, beyond a shadow of (a) doubt

undress *verb* STRIP, strip naked, disrobe, take off your clothes, peel off, doff your clothes

▷ *noun* NAKEDNESS, nudity, disarray, deshabille

undue *adjective* EXCESSIVE, too much, inappropriate, extreme, unnecessary, extravagant, needless, unsuitable, improper, too great, disproportionate, unjustified, unwarranted, unseemly, inordinate, undeserved, intemperate, uncalled-for, overmuch, immoderate

<< OPPOSITE appropriate

undulate *verb* WAVE, roll, surge, swell, ripple, rise and fall, billow, heave

unduly *adverb* EXCESSIVELY, overly, too much, unnecessarily, disproportionately, improperly, unreasonably, extravagantly, out of all proportion, inordinately, unjustifiably, overmuch, immoderately

<< OPPOSITE reasonably

undying *adjective* ETERNAL, everlasting, perpetual, continuing, permanent, constant, perennial, infinite, unending, indestructible, undiminished, imperishable, deathless, inextinguishable, unfading, sempiternal (*literary*)

<< OPPOSITE short-lived

unearth *verb* 1 DISCOVER, find, reveal, expose, turn up, uncover, bring to light, ferret out, root up

2 DIG UP, excavate, exhume, dredge up, disinter

unearthly *adjective* 1 EERIE, strange, supernatural, ghostly, weird, phantom, uncanny, spooky (*informal*), nightmarish, spectral, eldritch (*poetic*), preternatural

2 UNREASONABLE, ridiculous, absurd, strange, extraordinary, abnormal, unholy (*informal*), ungodly (*informal*)

uneasiness *noun* ANXIETY, apprehension, misgiving, worry, doubt, alarm, suspicion, nervousness, disquiet, agitation, qualms, trepidation, perturbation, apprehensiveness, dubiety

<< OPPOSITE ease

uneasy *adjective* 1 ANXIOUS, worried, troubled, upset, wired (*slang*), nervous, disturbed, uncomfortable, unsettled, impatient, restless, agitated, apprehensive, edgy, jittery (*informal*), perturbed, on edge, ill at ease, restive, twitchy (*informal*), like a fish out of water, antsy

(*informal*), discomposed
<< OPPOSITE relaxed
2 PRECARIOUS, strained, uncomfortable, tense, awkward, unstable, shaky, insecure, constrained
3 DISTURBING, upsetting, disquieting, worrying, troubling, bothering, dismaying

uneconomic *adjective* UNPROFITABLE, loss-making, non-profit-making, nonpaying, nonviable
<< OPPOSITE profitable

unemployed *adjective* OUT OF WORK, redundant, laid off, jobless, idle, on the dole (*Brit informal*), out of a job, workless, resting (*of an actor*)
<< OPPOSITE working

unequal *adjective* 1 DISPROPORTIONATE, uneven, unbalanced, unfair, irregular, unjust, inequitable, ill-matched
2 DIFFERENT, differing, dissimilar, unlike, varying, variable, disparate, unmatched, not uniform
<< OPPOSITE identical
3 *with* **to** NOT UP TO, not qualified for, inadequate for, insufficient for, found wanting in, not cut out for (*informal*), incompetent at

unequalled *or US* **unequaled** *adjective* INCOMPARABLE, supreme, unparalleled, paramount, transcendent, unrivalled, second to none, pre-eminent, inimitable, unmatched, peerless, unsurpassed, matchless, beyond compare, without equal, nonpareil

unequivocal *adjective* CLEAR, absolute, definite, certain, direct, straight, positive, plain, evident, black-and-white, decisive, explicit, manifest, clear-cut, unmistakable, unambiguous, cut-and-dried (*informal*), incontrovertible, indubitable, uncontestable, nailed-on (*slang*)
<< OPPOSITE vague

unerring *adjective* ACCURATE, sure, certain, perfect, exact, impeccable, faultless, infallible, unfailing

uneven *adjective* 1 ROUGH, bumpy, not flat, not level, not smooth
<< OPPOSITE level
2 IRREGULAR, unsteady, fitful, variable, broken, fluctuating, patchy, intermittent, jerky, changeable, spasmodic, inconsistent
3 UNEQUAL, unfair, one-sided, ill-matched
4 LOPSIDED, unbalanced, asymmetrical, odd, out of true, not parallel

uneventful *adjective* HUMDRUM, ordinary, routine, quiet, boring, dull, commonplace, tedious, monotonous, unremarkable, uninteresting, unexciting, unexceptional, ho-hum (*informal*), unmemorable, unvaried
<< OPPOSITE exciting

unexpected *adjective* UNFORESEEN, surprising, unanticipated, chance, sudden, astonishing, startling, unpredictable, accidental, abrupt, out of the blue, unannounced, fortuitous, unheralded, unlooked-for, not bargained for
<< OPPOSITE expected

unfailing *adjective* 1 CONTINUOUS, endless, persistent, unlimited, continual, never-failing, boundless, bottomless, ceaseless, inexhaustible, unflagging
2 RELIABLE, constant, dependable, sure, true, certain, loyal, faithful, staunch, infallible, steadfast, tried and true
<< OPPOSITE unreliable

unfair *adjective* 1 BIASED, prejudiced, unjust, one-sided, partial, partisan, arbitrary, discriminatory, bigoted, inequitable
2 UNSCRUPULOUS, crooked (*informal*), dishonest, unethical, wrongful, unprincipled, dishonourable, unsporting
<< OPPOSITE ethical

unfaithful *adjective* 1 FAITHLESS, untrue, two-timing (*informal*), adulterous, fickle, inconstant, unchaste
<< OPPOSITE faithful
2 DISLOYAL, false, treacherous, deceitful, faithless, perfidious, traitorous, treasonable, false-hearted, recreant (*archaic*)
<< OPPOSITE loyal

unfamiliar *adjective* 1 STRANGE, new, unknown, different, novel, unusual, curious, alien, out-of-the-way, uncommon, little known, unaccustomed, beyond your ken
<< OPPOSITE familiar
2 *with* **with** UNACQUAINTED WITH, a stranger to, unaccustomed to, inexperienced in, uninformed about, unversed in, uninitiated in, unskilled at, unpractised in, unconversant with
<< OPPOSITE acquainted with

unfathomable *adjective* 1 BAFFLING, incomprehensible, inexplicable, deep, profound, esoteric, impenetrable, unknowable, abstruse, indecipherable
2 IMMEASURABLE, bottomless, unmeasured, unplumbed, unsounded

unfavourable *or US* **unfavorable** *adjective* ADVERSE, bad, unfortunate, disadvantageous, threatening, contrary, unlucky, ominous, untimely, untoward, unpromising, unsuited, inauspicious, ill-suited, inopportune, unseasonable, unpropitious, infelicitous
<< OPPOSITE positive

unfinished *adjective* 1 INCOMPLETE, uncompleted, half-done, lacking, undone, in the making, imperfect, unfulfilled, unaccomplished
2 NATURAL, rough, raw, bare, crude, unrefined, unvarnished, unpolished
<< OPPOSITE polished

unfit *adjective* 1 OUT OF SHAPE, feeble,

unhealthy, debilitated, flabby, decrepit, in poor condition, out of trim, out of kilter
<< OPPOSITE healthy
2 INCAPABLE, inadequate, incompetent, no good, useless, not up to, unprepared, ineligible, unqualified, untrained, ill-equipped, not equal, not cut out
<< OPPOSITE capable
3 UNSUITABLE, inadequate, inappropriate, useless, not fit, not designed, unsuited, ill-adapted
<< OPPOSITE suitable

unflappable *adjective* (*informal*) IMPERTURBABLE, cool, collected, calm, composed, level-headed, unfazed (*informal*), impassive, unruffled, self-possessed, not given to worry
<< OPPOSITE excitable

unflinching *adjective* DETERMINED, firm, steady, constant, bold, stalwart, staunch, resolute, steadfast, unwavering, immovable, unswerving, unshaken, unfaltering, unshrinking
<< OPPOSITE wavering

unfold *verb* 1 DEVELOP, happen, progress, grow, emerge, occur, take place, expand, work out, mature, evolve, blossom, transpire, bear fruit
2 REVEAL, tell, present, show, describe, explain, illustrate, disclose, uncover, clarify, divulge, narrate, make known
3 OPEN, spread out, undo, expand, flatten, straighten, stretch out, unfurl, unwrap, unroll

unfortunate *adjective* 1 DISASTROUS, calamitous, inopportune, adverse, untimely, unfavourable, untoward, ruinous, ill-starred, infelicitous, ill-fated
<< OPPOSITE opportune
2 REGRETTABLE, deplorable, lamentable, inappropriate, unsuitable, ill-advised, unbecoming
<< OPPOSITE becoming
3 UNLUCKY, poor, unhappy, doomed, cursed, hopeless, unsuccessful, hapless, luckless, out of luck, wretched, star-crossed, unprosperous
<< OPPOSITE fortunate

unfounded *adjective* GROUNDLESS, false, unjustified, unproven, unsubstantiated, idle, fabricated, spurious, trumped up, baseless, without foundation, without basis
<< OPPOSITE justified

unfriendly *adjective* 1 HOSTILE, cold, distant, sour, chilly, aloof, surly, antagonistic, disagreeable, quarrelsome, unsociable, ill-disposed, unneighbourly
<< OPPOSITE friendly
2 UNFAVOURABLE, hostile, inhospitable, alien, inauspicious, inimical, uncongenial, unpropitious, unkind
<< OPPOSITE congenial

ungainly *adjective* AWKWARD, clumsy, inelegant, lumbering, slouching, gawky, uncouth, gangling, loutish, uncoordinated, ungraceful, lubberly, unco (*Austral slang*)
<< OPPOSITE graceful

unguarded *adjective* 1 UNPROTECTED, vulnerable, defenceless, undefended, open to attack, unpatrolled
2 CARELESS, rash, unwary, foolhardy, thoughtless, indiscreet, unthinking, ill-considered, imprudent, heedless, incautious, undiplomatic, impolitic, uncircumspect
<< OPPOSITE cautious

unhappiness *noun* SADNESS, depression, misery, gloom, sorrow, melancholy, heartache, despondency, blues, dejection, wretchedness, low spirits

unhappy *adjective* 1 SAD, depressed, miserable, down, low, blue, gloomy, melancholy, mournful, dejected, despondent, dispirited, downcast, long-faced, sorrowful, disconsolate, crestfallen, down in the dumps (*informal*)
<< OPPOSITE happy
2 UNLUCKY, unfortunate, hapless, luckless, cursed, wretched, ill-omened, ill-fated
<< OPPOSITE fortunate
3 INAPPROPRIATE, awkward, clumsy, unsuitable, inept, ill-advised, tactless, ill-timed, injudicious, infelicitous, malapropos, untactful
<< OPPOSITE apt

unhealthy *adjective* 1 HARMFUL, detrimental, unwholesome, noxious, deleterious, insanitary, noisome, insalubrious
<< OPPOSITE beneficial
2 SICK, sickly, unwell, poorly (*informal*), weak, delicate, crook (*Austral & NZ informal*), ailing, frail, feeble, invalid, unsound, infirm, in poor health
<< OPPOSITE well
3 WEAK, unsound, ailing
<< OPPOSITE strong
4 UNWHOLESOME, morbid, bad, negative, corrupt, corrupting, degrading, undesirable, demoralizing, baneful (*archaic*)
<< OPPOSITE wholesome

unheard-of *adjective* 1 UNPRECEDENTED, inconceivable, undreamed-of, new, novel, unique, unusual, unbelievable, singular, ground-breaking, never before encountered, unexampled
2 SHOCKING, extreme, outrageous, offensive, unacceptable, unthinkable, disgraceful, preposterous, outlandish
3 OBSCURE, unknown, undiscovered, unfamiliar, little known, unsung, unremarked, unregarded

unhinge *verb* UNBALANCE, confuse, derange, disorder, unsettle, madden, craze, confound, distemper (*archaic*), dement, drive you out of your mind

unholy *adjective* 1 (*informal*) SHOCKING, awful, appalling, dreadful, outrageous, horrendous, unearthly, ungodly (*informal*)
2 EVIL, vile, wicked, base, corrupt, immoral, dishonest, sinful, heinous, depraved, profane, iniquitous, ungodly, irreligious
<< OPPOSITE holy

unification *noun* UNION, uniting, alliance, combination, coalition, merger, federation, confederation, fusion, amalgamation, coalescence

uniform *noun* 1 REGALIA, suit, livery, colours, habit, regimentals
2 OUTFIT, dress, costume, attire, gear (*informal*), get-up (*informal*), ensemble, garb
▷ *adjective* 1 CONSISTENT, unvarying, similar, even, same, matching, regular, constant, equivalent, identical, homogeneous, unchanging, equable, undeviating
<< OPPOSITE varying
2 ALIKE, similar, identical, like, same, equal, selfsame

uniformity *noun* 1 REGULARITY, similarity, sameness, constancy, homogeneity, evenness, invariability
2 MONOTONY, sameness, tedium, dullness, flatness, drabness, lack of diversity

unify *verb* UNITE, join, combine, merge, consolidate, bring together, fuse, confederate, amalgamate, federate
<< OPPOSITE divide

uninterested *adjective* INDIFFERENT, unconcerned, apathetic, bored, distant, listless, impassive, blasé, unresponsive, uninvolved, incurious
<< OPPOSITE concerned ▷ see **disinterested**

union *noun* 1 JOINING, uniting, unification, combination, coalition, merger, mixture, blend, merging, integration, conjunction, fusion, synthesis, amalgamating, amalgam, amalgamation
2 ALLIANCE, league, association, coalition, federation, confederation, confederacy, Bund
3 MARRIAGE, match, wedlock, matrimony
4 INTERCOURSE, coupling, copulation, the other (*informal*), nookie (*slang*), coitus, rumpy-pumpy (*slang*), coition

unique *adjective* 1 DISTINCT, special, exclusive, peculiar, only, single, lone, solitary, one and only, sui generis
2 UNPARALLELED, unrivalled, incomparable, inimitable, unmatched, peerless, unequalled, matchless, without equal, nonpareil, unexampled

> *Unique* with the meaning 'being the only one' or 'having no equal' describes an absolute state: *a case unique in British law*. In this use it cannot therefore be qualified; something is either *unique* or *not unique*. However, *unique* is also very commonly used in the sense of 'remarkable' or 'exceptional', particularly in the language of advertising, and in this meaning it can be used with qualifying words such as *rather*, *quite*, etc. Since many people object to this use, it is best avoided in formal and serious writing

unit *noun* 1 ENTITY, whole, item, feature, piece, portion, module
2 SECTION, company, group, force, detail, division, cell, squad, crew, outfit, faction, corps, brigade, regiment, battalion, legion, contingent, squadron, garrison, detachment, platoon
3 MEASURE, quantity, measurement
4 PART, section, segment, class, element, component, constituent, tutorial

unite *verb* 1 JOIN, link, combine, couple, marry, wed, blend, incorporate, merge, consolidate, unify, fuse, amalgamate, coalesce, meld
<< OPPOSITE separate
2 COOPERATE, ally, join forces, league, band, associate, pool, collaborate, confederate, pull together, join together, close ranks, club together
<< OPPOSITE split

united *adjective* 1 IN AGREEMENT, agreed, unanimous, one, like-minded, in accord, of like mind, of one mind, of the same opinion
2 COMBINED, leagued, allied, unified, pooled, concerted, collective, affiliated, in partnership, banded together

unity *noun* 1 UNION, unification, coalition, federation, integration, confederation, amalgamation
2 WHOLENESS, integrity, oneness, union, unification, entity, singleness, undividedness
<< OPPOSITE disunity
3 AGREEMENT, accord, consensus, peace, harmony, solidarity, unison, assent, unanimity, concord, concurrence
<< OPPOSITE disagreement

universal *adjective* 1 WIDESPREAD, general, common, whole, total, entire, catholic, unlimited, ecumenical, omnipresent, all-embracing, overarching, one-size-fits-all
2 GLOBAL, worldwide, international, pandemic

> The use of *more universal* as in *his writings have long been admired by fellow scientists, but his latest book should have more universal appeal* is acceptable in modern English usage

universality *noun* COMPREHENSIVENESS, generalization, generality, totality, completeness, ubiquity, all-inclusiveness

universally *adverb* WITHOUT EXCEPTION, uniformly, everywhere, always, invariably, across the board, in all cases, in every instance

universe *noun* COSMOS, space, creation, everything, nature, heavens, the natural world, macrocosm, all existence

unjust *adjective* UNFAIR, prejudiced, biased, wrong, one-sided, partial, partisan, unjustified, wrongful, undeserved, inequitable, unmerited

<< OPPOSITE fair

unkempt *adjective* 1 UNCOMBED, tousled, shaggy, ungroomed

2 UNTIDY, scruffy, dishevelled, disordered, messy, sloppy (*informal*), shabby, rumpled, bedraggled, slovenly, blowsy, sluttish, slatternly, disarranged, ungroomed, disarrayed, frowzy, daggy (*Austral & NZ informal*)

<< OPPOSITE tidy

unkind *adjective* CRUEL, mean, nasty, spiteful, harsh, malicious, insensitive, unfriendly, inhuman, unsympathetic, uncaring, thoughtless, unfeeling, inconsiderate, uncharitable, unchristian, hardhearted

<< OPPOSITE kind

unknown *adjective* 1 STRANGE, new, undiscovered, uncharted, unexplored, virgin, remote, alien, exotic, outlandish, unmapped, untravelled, beyond your ken

2 UNIDENTIFIED, mysterious, anonymous, unnamed, nameless, incognito

3 OBSCURE, little known, minor, humble, unfamiliar, insignificant, lowly, unimportant, unheard-of, unsung, inconsequential, undistinguished, unrenowned

<< OPPOSITE famous

unleash *verb* RELEASE, let go, let loose, free, untie, unloose, unbridle

unlike *preposition* 1 DIFFERENT FROM, dissimilar to, not resembling, far from, not like, distinct from, incompatible with, unrelated to, distant from, unequal to, far apart from, divergent from, not similar to, as different as chalk and cheese from (*informal*)

<< OPPOSITE similar to

2 CONTRASTED WITH, not like, in contradiction to, in contrast with *or* to, as opposed to, differently from, opposite to

unlikely *adjective* 1 IMPROBABLE, doubtful, remote, slight, faint, not likely, unimaginable

<< OPPOSITE probable

2 UNBELIEVABLE, incredible, unconvincing, implausible, questionable, cock-and-bull (*informal*)

<< OPPOSITE believable

unlimited *adjective* 1 INFINITE, endless, countless, great, vast, extensive, immense, stellar (*informal*), limitless, boundless, incalculable, immeasurable, unbounded, illimitable

<< OPPOSITE finite

2 TOTAL, full, complete, absolute, unconditional, unqualified, unfettered, unrestricted, all-encompassing, unconstrained

<< OPPOSITE restricted

unload *verb* 1 EMPTY, clear, unpack, dump, discharge, off-load, disburden, unlade

2 UNBURDEN, relieve, lighten, disburden

unlock *verb* OPEN, undo, unfasten, release, unbolt, unlatch, unbar

unlucky *adjective* 1 UNFORTUNATE, unhappy, disastrous

<< OPPOSITE fortunate

2 ILL-FATED, doomed, inauspicious, ominous, untimely, unfavourable, cursed, ill-starred, ill-omened

unmask *verb* REVEAL, expose, uncover, discover, disclose, unveil, show up, lay bare, bring to light, uncloak

unmistakable *adjective* CLEAR, certain, positive, decided, sure, obvious, plain, patent, evident, distinct, pronounced, glaring, manifest, blatant, conspicuous, palpable, unequivocal, unambiguous, indisputable

<< OPPOSITE doubtful

unmitigated *adjective* 1 UNRELIEVED, relentless, unalleviated, intense, harsh, grim, persistent, oppressive, unbroken, unqualified, unabated, undiminished, unmodified, unredeemed

2 COMPLETE, absolute, utter, perfect, rank, sheer, total, outright, thorough, downright, consummate, out-and-out, thoroughgoing, arrant, deep-dyed (*usually derogatory*)

unnatural *adjective* 1 ABNORMAL, odd, strange, unusual, extraordinary, bizarre, perverted, queer, irregular, perverse, supernatural, uncanny, outlandish, unaccountable, anomalous, freakish, aberrant

<< OPPOSITE normal

2 FALSE, forced, artificial, studied, laboured, affected, assumed, mannered, strained, stiff, theatrical, contrived, self-conscious, feigned, stilted, insincere, factitious, stagy, phoney *or* phony (*informal*)

<< OPPOSITE genuine

3 INHUMAN, evil, monstrous, wicked, savage, brutal, ruthless, callous, heartless, cold-blooded, fiendish, unfeeling

<< OPPOSITE humane

unnecessary *adjective* NEEDLESS, excessive, unwarranted, useless, pointless, not needed, redundant, wasteful, gratuitous, superfluous, wanton, expendable, surplus to requirements, uncalled-for, dispensable, unneeded, nonessential, inessential, unmerited, to no

purpose, unrequired, supererogatory
<< OPPOSITE essential

unnerve *verb* SHAKE, upset, disconcert, disturb, intimidate, frighten, rattle (*informal*), discourage, dismay, daunt, disarm, confound, fluster, faze, unman, demoralize, unhinge, psych out (*informal*), throw off balance, dishearten, dispirit
<< OPPOSITE strengthen

unoccupied *adjective* 1 EMPTY, vacant, uninhabited, untenanted, tenantless
2 IDLE, unemployed, inactive, disengaged, at leisure, at a loose end

unofficial *adjective* 1 UNCONFIRMED, off the record, unsubstantiated, private, personal, unauthorized, undocumented, uncorroborated
2 UNAUTHORIZED, informal, unsanctioned, casual, wildcat

unparalleled *adjective* UNEQUALLED, exceptional, unprecedented, rare, unique, singular, consummate, superlative, unrivalled, incomparable, unmatched, peerless, unsurpassed, matchless, beyond compare, without equal

unpleasant *adjective* 1 NASTY, bad, horrid, distressing, annoying, irritating, miserable, troublesome, distasteful, obnoxious, unpalatable, displeasing, repulsive, objectionable, disagreeable, abhorrent, irksome, unlovely, execrable
<< OPPOSITE nice
2 OBNOXIOUS, disagreeable, vicious, malicious, rude, mean, cruel, poisonous, unattractive, unfriendly, vindictive, venomous, mean-spirited, inconsiderate, impolite, unloveable, ill-natured, unlikable *or* unlikeable
<< OPPOSITE likable *or* likeable

unpleasantness *noun* 1 HOSTILITY, animosity, antagonism, bad feeling, malice, rudeness, offensiveness, abrasiveness, argumentativeness, unfriendliness, quarrelsomeness, ill humour *or* will
<< OPPOSITE friendliness
2 NASTINESS, awfulness, grimness, trouble, misery, woe, ugliness, unacceptability, dreadfulness, disagreeableness, horridness
<< OPPOSITE pleasantness

unpopular *adjective* DISLIKED, rejected, unwanted, avoided, shunned, unwelcome, undesirable, unattractive, detested, out of favour, unloved, out in the cold, cold-shouldered, not sought out, sent to Coventry (*Brit*)
<< OPPOSITE popular

unprecedented *adjective* 1 UNPARALLELED, unheard-of, exceptional, new, original, novel, unusual, abnormal, singular, ground-breaking, unrivalled, freakish, unexampled
2 EXTRAORDINARY, amazing, remarkable, outstanding, fantastic, marvellous, exceptional, phenomenal, uncommon

unprofessional *adjective* 1 UNETHICAL, unfitting, improper, lax, negligent, unworthy, unseemly, unprincipled
2 AMATEURISH, amateur, incompetent, inefficient, cowboy (*informal*), inexperienced, untrained, slapdash, slipshod, inexpert
<< OPPOSITE skilful

unqualified *adjective* 1 UNFIT, incapable, incompetent, not up to, unprepared, ineligible, ill-equipped, not equal to
2 UNCONDITIONAL, complete, total, absolute, utter, outright, thorough, downright, consummate, unrestricted, out-and-out, categorical, unmitigated, unreserved, thoroughgoing, without reservation, arrant, deep-dyed (*usually derogatory*)

unquestionable *adjective* CERTAIN, undeniable, indisputable, clear, sure, perfect, absolute, patent, definite, manifest, unmistakable, conclusive, flawless, unequivocal, faultless, self-evident, irrefutable, incontrovertible, incontestable, indubitable, beyond a shadow of doubt, nailed-on (*slang*)
<< OPPOSITE doubtful

unravel *verb* 1 SOLVE, explain, work out, resolve, interpret, figure out (*informal*), make out, clear up, suss (out) (*slang*), get to the bottom of, get straight, puzzle out
2 UNDO, separate, disentangle, free, unwind, extricate, straighten out, untangle, unknot

unreadable *adjective* 1 TURGID, heavy going, badly written, dry as dust
2 ILLEGIBLE, undecipherable, crabbed

unreal *adjective* IMAGINARY, make-believe, illusory, fabulous, visionary, mythical, fanciful, fictitious, intangible, immaterial, storybook, insubstantial, nebulous, dreamlike, impalpable, chimerical, phantasmagoric

unreasonable *adjective* 1 BIASED, arbitrary, irrational, illogical, blinkered, opinionated, headstrong
<< OPPOSITE open-minded
2 EXCESSIVE, steep (*informal*), exorbitant, unfair, absurd, extravagant, unjust, too great, undue, preposterous, unwarranted, far-fetched, extortionate, uncalled-for, immoderate
<< OPPOSITE moderate

unrelenting *adjective* 1 MERCILESS, tough, ruthless, relentless, cruel, stern, inexorable, implacable, intransigent, remorseless, pitiless, unsparing
2 STEADY, constant, continuous, endless, perpetual, continual, unbroken, incessant, unabated, ceaseless, unremitting, unwavering

unremitting *adjective* CONSTANT, continuous,

relentless, perpetual, continual, unbroken, incessant, diligent, unabated, unwavering, indefatigable, remorseless, assiduous, unceasing, sedulous, unwearied

unrest *noun* DISCONTENT, rebellion, dissatisfaction, protest, turmoil, upheaval, strife, agitation, discord, disaffection, sedition, tumult, dissension

<< OPPOSITE peace

unrivalled *adjective* UNPARALLELED, incomparable, unsurpassed, supreme, unmatched, peerless, unequalled, matchless, beyond compare, without equal, nonpareil, unexcelled

unruffled *adjective* 1 CALM, cool, collected, peaceful, composed, serene, tranquil, sedate, placid, undisturbed, unmoved, unfazed (*informal*), unperturbed, unflustered

2 SMOOTH, even, level, flat, unbroken

unruly *adjective* UNCONTROLLABLE, wild, unmanageable, disorderly, turbulent, rebellious, wayward, rowdy, intractable, wilful, lawless, fractious, riotous, headstrong, mutinous, disobedient, ungovernable, refractory, obstreperous, insubordinate

<< OPPOSITE manageable

unsafe *adjective* DANGEROUS, risky, hazardous, threatening, uncertain, unstable, insecure, unreliable, precarious, treacherous, perilous, unsound

<< OPPOSITE safe

unsavoury *adjective* 1 UNPLEASANT, nasty, obnoxious, offensive, revolting, distasteful, repellent, repulsive, objectionable, repugnant

2 UNAPPETIZING, unpalatable, distasteful, sickening, disagreeable, nauseating

<< OPPOSITE appetizing

unscathed *adjective* UNHARMED, unhurt, uninjured, whole, sound, safe, untouched, unmarked, in one piece, unscarred, unscratched

unscrupulous *adjective* UNPRINCIPLED, corrupt, crooked (*informal*), ruthless, improper, immoral, dishonest, unethical, exploitative, dishonourable, roguish, unconscionable, knavish, conscienceless, unconscientious

<< OPPOSITE honourable

unseat *verb* 1 DEPOSE, overthrow, oust, remove, dismiss, discharge, displace, dethrone

2 THROW, unsaddle, unhorse

unseemly *adjective* IMPROPER, inappropriate, unsuitable, out of place, undignified, disreputable, unbecoming, unrefined, out of keeping, discreditable, indelicate, in poor taste, indecorous, unbefitting

<< OPPOSITE proper

unseen *adjective* 1 UNOBSERVED, undetected, unperceived, lurking, unnoticed, unobtrusive

2 HIDDEN, concealed, invisible, veiled, obscure

unselfish *adjective* GENEROUS, selfless, noble, kind, liberal, devoted, humanitarian, charitable, disinterested, altruistic, self-sacrificing, magnanimous, self-denying

unsettle *verb* DISTURB, trouble, upset, throw (*informal*), bother, confuse, disorder, rattle (*informal*), agitate, ruffle, unnerve, disconcert, unbalance, fluster, perturb, faze, throw into confusion, throw off balance, discompose, throw into disorder, throw into uproar

unsettled *adjective* 1 UNSTABLE, shaky, insecure, disorderly, unsteady

2 RESTLESS, tense, uneasy, troubled, shaken, confused, wired (*slang*), disturbed, anxious, agitated, unnerved, flustered, perturbed, on edge, restive, adrenalized

3 UNRESOLVED, undecided, undetermined, open, doubtful, debatable, up in the air, moot

4 INCONSTANT, changing, unpredictable, variable, uncertain, changeable

5 OWING, due, outstanding, pending, payable, in arrears

unsightly *adjective* UGLY, unattractive, repulsive, unpleasant, revolting (*informal*), hideous, horrid, disagreeable, unprepossessing

<< OPPOSITE attractive

unskilled *adjective* UNPROFESSIONAL, inexperienced, unqualified, untrained, uneducated, amateurish, cowboy (*informal*), untalented

<< OPPOSITE skilled

unsophisticated *adjective* 1 SIMPLE, plain, uncomplicated, straightforward, unrefined, uninvolved, unspecialized, uncomplex

<< OPPOSITE advanced

2 NAIVE, innocent, inexperienced, unworldly, unaffected, childlike, natural, artless, ingenuous, guileless

unsound *adjective* 1 FLAWED, faulty, weak, false, shaky, unreliable, invalid, defective, illogical, erroneous, specious, fallacious, ill-founded

2 UNSTABLE, shaky, insecure, unsafe, unreliable, flimsy, wobbly, tottering, rickety, unsteady, not solid

<< OPPOSITE stable

3 UNHEALTHY, unstable, unbalanced, diseased, ill, weak, delicate, ailing, frail, defective, unwell, deranged, unhinged

unspeakable *adjective* DREADFUL, shocking, appalling, evil, awful, overwhelming, horrible, unbelievable, monstrous, from hell (*informal*), inconceivable, unimaginable, repellent, abysmal, frightful, heinous, odious, indescribable, loathsome, abominable, ineffable, beyond words, execrable, unutterable, inexpressible, beyond description, hellacious (*US slang*), too horrible for words

unstable *adjective* 1 CHANGEABLE, volatile, unpredictable, variable, fluctuating, unsteady, fitful, inconstant
<< OPPOSITE constant
2 INSECURE, shaky, precarious, unsettled, wobbly, tottering, rickety, unsteady, not fixed
3 UNPREDICTABLE, irrational, erratic, inconsistent, unreliable, temperamental, capricious, changeable, untrustworthy, vacillating
<< OPPOSITE level-headed

unsteady *adjective* 1 UNSTABLE, shaky, insecure, unsafe, precarious, treacherous, rickety, infirm
2 REELING, wobbly, tottering
3 ERRATIC, unpredictable, volatile, unsettled, wavering, unreliable, temperamental, changeable, vacillating, flighty, inconstant

unsung *adjective* UNACKNOWLEDGED, unrecognized, unappreciated, unknown, neglected, anonymous, disregarded, unnamed, uncelebrated, unhonoured, unacclaimed, unhailed

unswerving *adjective* FIRM, staunch, steadfast, constant, true, direct, devoted, steady, dedicated, resolute, single-minded, unwavering, unflagging, untiring, unfaltering, undeviating

untangle *verb* 1 DISENTANGLE, unravel, sort out, extricate, straighten out, untwist, unsnarl
<< OPPOSITE entangle
2 SOLVE, clear up, straighten out, understand, explain, figure out (*informal*), clarify, unravel, fathom, get to the bottom of, elucidate, suss out (*informal*), puzzle out
<< OPPOSITE complicate

untenable *adjective* UNSUSTAINABLE, indefensible, unsound, groundless, weak, flawed, shaky, unreasonable, illogical, fallacious, insupportable
<< OPPOSITE justified

unthinkable *adjective* 1 IMPOSSIBLE, out of the question, inconceivable, unlikely, not on (*informal*), absurd, unreasonable, improbable, preposterous, illogical
2 INCONCEIVABLE, incredible, unbelievable, unimaginable, beyond belief, beyond the bounds of possibility

unthinking *adjective* 1 THOUGHTLESS, insensitive, tactless, rude, blundering, inconsiderate, undiplomatic
2 IMPULSIVE, senseless, unconscious, mechanical, rash, careless, instinctive, oblivious, negligent, unwitting, witless, inadvertent, heedless, unmindful
<< OPPOSITE deliberate

untidy *adjective* 1 MESSY, disordered, chaotic, littered, muddled, cluttered, jumbled, rumpled, shambolic, bedraggled, unkempt, topsy-turvy, higgledy-piggledy (*informal*), mussy (*US informal*), muddly, disarrayed
<< OPPOSITE neat
2 UNKEMPT, dishevelled, tousled, disordered, messy, ruffled, scruffy, rumpled, bedraggled, ratty (*informal*), straggly, windblown, disarranged, mussed up (*informal*), daggy (*Austral & NZ informal*)
3 SLOPPY, messy (*informal*), slovenly, slipshod, slatternly
<< OPPOSITE methodical

untie *verb* UNDO, free, release, loosen, unfasten, unbind, unstrap, unclasp, unlace, unknot, unmoor, unbridle

untimely *adjective* 1 EARLY, premature, before time, unseasonable
<< OPPOSITE timely
2 ILL-TIMED, inappropriate, badly timed, inopportune, unfortunate, awkward, unsuitable, inconvenient, mistimed, inauspicious
<< OPPOSITE well-timed

untold *adjective* 1 INDESCRIBABLE, unthinkable, unimaginable, unspeakable, undreamed of, unutterable, inexpressible
2 COUNTLESS, incalculable, innumerable, myriad, numberless, uncounted, uncountable, unnumbered, measureless
3 UNDISCLOSED, unknown, unrevealed, private, secret, hidden, unrelated, unpublished, unrecounted

untoward *adjective* UNFAVOURABLE, unfortunate, disastrous, adverse, contrary, annoying, awkward, irritating, unlucky, inconvenient, untimely, inauspicious, inimical, ill-timed, vexatious, inopportune

untrue *adjective* 1 FALSE, lying, wrong, mistaken, misleading, incorrect, inaccurate, sham, dishonest, deceptive, spurious, erroneous, fallacious, untruthful
<< OPPOSITE true
2 UNFAITHFUL, disloyal, deceitful, treacherous, two-faced, faithless, false, untrustworthy, perfidious, forsworn, traitorous, inconstant
<< OPPOSITE faithful

untruth *noun* LIE, fabrication, falsehood, fib, story, tale, fiction, deceit, whopper (*informal*), porky (*Brit slang*), pork pie (*Brit slang*), falsification, prevarication

unused *adjective* 1 NEW, untouched, remaining, fresh, intact, immaculate, pristine
2 REMAINING, leftover, unconsumed, left, available, extra, unutilized
3 *with* **to** UNACCUSTOMED TO, new to, unfamiliar with, not up to, not ready for, a stranger to, inexperienced in, unhabituated to

unusual *adjective* 1 RARE, odd, strange, extraordinary, different, surprising, novel, bizarre, unexpected, curious, weird (*informal*), unfamiliar, abnormal, queer, phenomenal, uncommon, out of the ordinary, left-field (*informal*), unwonted

<< OPPOSITE common

2 EXTRAORDINARY, unique, remarkable, exceptional, notable, phenomenal, uncommon, singular, unconventional, out of the ordinary, atypical

<< OPPOSITE average

unveil *verb* REVEAL, publish, launch, introduce, release, display, broadcast, demonstrate, expose, bare, parade, exhibit, disclose, uncover, bring out, make public, flaunt, divulge, lay bare, make known, bring to light, put on display, lay open, put on show, put on view

<< OPPOSITE conceal

unwarranted *adjective* UNNECESSARY, unjustified, indefensible, wrong, unreasonable, unjust, gratuitous, unprovoked, inexcusable, groundless, uncalled-for

unwary *adjective* CARELESS, rash, reckless, hasty, thoughtless, unguarded, indiscreet, imprudent, heedless, incautious, uncircumspect, unwatchful

<< OPPOSITE cautious

unwell *adjective* ILL, poorly (*informal*), sick, crook (*Austral & NZ informal*), ailing, unhealthy, sickly, out of sorts, off colour, under the weather (*informal*), in poor health, at death's door, indisposed, green about the gills

<< OPPOSITE well

unwieldy *adjective* 1 BULKY, massive, hefty, clumsy, weighty, ponderous, ungainly, clunky (*informal*)

2 AWKWARD, cumbersome, inconvenient, burdensome, unmanageable, unhandy

unwilling *adjective* 1 DISINCLINED, reluctant, averse, loath, slow, opposed, resistant, not about, not in the mood, indisposed

<< OPPOSITE willing

2 RELUCTANT, grudging, unenthusiastic, resistant, involuntary, averse, demurring, laggard (*rare*)

<< OPPOSITE eager

unwind *verb* 1 RELAX, wind down, take it easy, slow down, sit back, calm down, take a break, loosen up, quieten down, let yourself go, mellow out (*informal*), make yourself at home, outspan (*S African*)

2 UNRAVEL, undo, uncoil, slacken, disentangle, unroll, unreel, untwist, untwine

unwise *adjective* FOOLISH, stupid, silly, rash, irresponsible, reckless, senseless, short-sighted, ill-advised, foolhardy, inane, indiscreet, ill-judged, ill-considered, imprudent, inadvisable, asinine, injudicious, improvident, impolitic

<< OPPOSITE wise

unwitting *adjective* 1 UNINTENTIONAL, involuntary, inadvertent, chance, accidental, unintended, unplanned, undesigned, unmeant

<< OPPOSITE deliberate

2 UNKNOWING, innocent, unsuspecting, unconscious, unaware, ignorant

<< OPPOSITE knowing

unworthy *adjective* 1 UNDESERVING, not good enough, not fit, not worth, ineligible, not deserving

<< OPPOSITE deserving

2 DISHONOURABLE, base, contemptible, degrading, disgraceful, shameful, disreputable, ignoble, discreditable

<< OPPOSITE commendable

3 *with* **of** UNBEFITTING, beneath, unfitting to, unsuitable for, inappropriate to, improper to, out of character with, out of place with, unbecoming to

unwritten *adjective* 1 ORAL, word-of-mouth, unrecorded, vocal

2 UNDERSTOOD, accepted, tacit, traditional, conventional, silent, customary, implicit, unformulated

up ▷▷ **ups and downs** FLUCTUATIONS, changes, vicissitudes, moods, ebb and flow

up-and-coming *adjective* PROMISING, ambitious, go-getting (*informal*), pushing, eager

upbeat *adjective* (*informal*) CHEERFUL, positive, optimistic, promising, encouraging, looking up, hopeful, favourable, rosy, buoyant, heartening, cheery, forward-looking

upbringing *noun* EDUCATION, training, breeding, rearing, care, raising, tending, bringing-up, nurture, cultivation

update *verb* BRING UP TO DATE, improve, correct, renew, revise, upgrade, amend, overhaul, streamline, modernize, rebrand

upgrade *verb* 1 IMPROVE, better, update, reform, add to, enhance, refurbish, renovate, remodel, make better, modernize, spruce up, ameliorate

2 PROMOTE, raise, advance, boost, move up, elevate, kick upstairs (*informal*), give promotion to

<< OPPOSITE demote

upheaval *noun* DISTURBANCE, revolution, disorder, turmoil, overthrow, disruption, eruption, cataclysm, violent change

uphill *adjective* 1 ASCENDING, rising, upward, mounting, climbing

<< OPPOSITE descending

2 ARDUOUS, hard, taxing, difficult, tough, exhausting, punishing, gruelling, strenuous, laborious, wearisome, Sisyphean

uphold *verb* 1 SUPPORT, back, defend, aid,

champion, encourage, maintain, promote, sustain, advocate, stand by, stick up for (*informal*)
2 CONFIRM, support, sustain, endorse, approve, justify, hold to, ratify, vindicate, validate
upkeep *noun* 1 MAINTENANCE, running, keep, subsistence, support, repair, conservation, preservation, sustenance
2 RUNNING COSTS, expenses, overheads, expenditure, outlay, operating costs, oncosts (*Brit*)
uplift *verb* IMPROVE, better, raise, advance, inspire, upgrade, refine, cultivate, civilize, ameliorate, edify
▷ *noun* IMPROVEMENT, enlightenment, advancement, cultivation, refinement, enhancement, enrichment, betterment, edification
upper *adjective* 1 TOPMOST, top
<< OPPOSITE bottom
2 HIGHER, high
<< OPPOSITE lower
3 SUPERIOR, senior, higher-level, greater, top, important, chief, most important, elevated, eminent, higher-ranking
<< OPPOSITE inferior
upper class *adjective* ARISTOCRATIC, upper-class, noble, high-class, patrician, top-drawer, blue-blooded, highborn
uppermost *adjective* 1 TOP, highest, topmost, upmost, loftiest, most elevated
<< OPPOSITE bottom
2 SUPREME, greatest, chief, leading, main, primary, principal, dominant, paramount, foremost, predominant, pre-eminent
<< OPPOSITE least
upright *adjective* 1 VERTICAL, straight, standing up, erect, on end, perpendicular, bolt upright
<< OPPOSITE horizontal
2 HONEST, good, principled, just, true, faithful, ethical, straightforward, honourable, righteous, conscientious, virtuous, trustworthy, high-minded, above board, incorruptible, unimpeachable
<< OPPOSITE dishonourable
uprising *noun* REBELLION, rising, revolution, outbreak, revolt, disturbance, upheaval, mutiny, insurrection, putsch, insurgence
uproar *noun* 1 COMMOTION, noise, racket, riot, confusion, turmoil, brawl, mayhem, clamour, din, turbulence, pandemonium, rumpus, hubbub, hurly-burly, brouhaha, ruction (*informal*), hullabaloo, ruckus (*informal*), bagarre (*French*)
2 PROTEST, outrage, complaint, objection, fuss, stink (*informal*), outcry, furore, hue and cry
uproot *verb* 1 DISPLACE, remove, exile, disorient, deracinate
2 PULL UP, dig up, root out, weed out, rip up, grub up, extirpate, deracinate, pull out by the roots
upset *adjective* 1 DISTRESSED, shaken, disturbed, worried, troubled, hurt, bothered, confused, unhappy, gutted (*Brit informal*), put out, dismayed, choked (*informal*), grieved, frantic, hassled (*informal*), agitated, ruffled, cut up (*informal*), disconcerted, disquieted, overwrought, discomposed
2 SICK, queasy, bad, poorly (*informal*), ill, gippy (*slang*)
▷ *verb* 1 DISTRESS, trouble, disturb, worry, alarm, bother, dismay, grieve, hassle (*informal*), agitate, ruffle, unnerve, disconcert, disquiet, fluster, perturb, faze, throw someone off balance, give someone grief (*Brit & S African*), discompose
2 TIP OVER, overturn, capsize, knock over, spill, topple over
3 MESS UP, spoil, disturb, change, confuse, disorder, unsettle, mix up, disorganize, turn topsy-turvy, put out of order, throw into disorder
▷ *noun* 1 DISTRESS, worry, trouble, shock, bother, disturbance, hassle (*informal*), disquiet, agitation, discomposure
2 REVERSAL, surprise, shake-up (*informal*), defeat, sudden change
3 ILLNESS, complaint, disorder, bug (*informal*), disturbance, sickness, malady, queasiness, indisposition
upshot *noun* RESULT, consequence, outcome, end, issue, event, conclusion, sequel, finale, culmination, end result, payoff (*informal*)
upside down *or* **upside-down** *adverb* WRONG SIDE UP, bottom up, on its head
▷ *adjective* 1 INVERTED, overturned, upturned, on its head, bottom up, wrong side up
2 (*informal*) CONFUSED, disordered, chaotic, muddled, jumbled, in disarray, in chaos, topsy-turvy, in confusion, higgledy-piggledy (*informal*), in disorder
upstanding *adjective* HONEST, principled, upright, honourable, good, moral, ethical, trustworthy, incorruptible, true
<< OPPOSITE immoral
upstart *noun* SOCIAL CLIMBER, nobody, nouveau riche (*French*), parvenu, arriviste, status seeker
uptight *adjective* (*informal*) TENSE, wired (*slang*), anxious, neurotic, uneasy, prickly, edgy, on the defensive, on edge, nervy (*Brit informal*), adrenalized
up-to-date *adjective* MODERN, fashionable, trendy (*Brit informal*), in, newest, now (*informal*), happening (*informal*), current, with it (*informal*), stylish, in vogue, all the rage, up-to-the-minute, having your finger on the pulse
<< OPPOSITE out of date
upturn *noun* RISE, increase, boost,

improvement, recovery, revival, advancement, upsurge, upswing

urban *adjective* CIVIC, city, town, metropolitan, municipal, dorp (*S African*), inner-city

urbane *adjective* SOPHISTICATED, cultured, polished, civil, mannerly, smooth, elegant, refined, cultivated, cosmopolitan, civilized, courteous, suave, well-bred, debonair, well-mannered

<< OPPOSITE boorish

urchin *noun* (*Old-fashioned*) RAGAMUFFIN, waif, guttersnipe, brat, mudlark (*slang*), gamin, street Arab (*offensive*), young rogue

urge *verb* 1 BEG, appeal to, exhort, press, prompt, plead, put pressure on, lean on, solicit, goad, implore, enjoin, beseech, pressurize, entreat, twist someone's arm (*informal*), put the heat on (*informal*), put the screws on (*informal*)

2 ADVOCATE, suggest, recommend, advise, back, support, champion, counsel, insist on, endorse, push for

<< OPPOSITE discourage

▷ *noun* IMPULSE, longing, wish, desire, fancy, drive, yen (*informal*), hunger, appetite, craving, yearning, itch (*informal*), thirst, compulsion, hankering

<< OPPOSITE reluctance

▷▷ **urge someone on** DRIVE ON, push, encourage, force, press, prompt, stimulate, compel, induce, propel, hasten, constrain, incite, egg on, goad, spur on, impel, gee up

urgency *noun* IMPORTANCE, need, necessity, gravity, pressure, hurry, seriousness, extremity, exigency, imperativeness

urgent *adjective* 1 CRUCIAL, desperate, pressing, great, important, crying, critical, immediate, acute, grave, instant, compelling, imperative, top-priority, now or never, exigent, not to be delayed

<< OPPOSITE unimportant

2 INSISTENT, earnest, determined, intense, persistent, persuasive, resolute, clamorous, importunate

<< OPPOSITE casual

urinate *verb* PEE, wee, leak (*slang* or *slang*), tinkle (*Brit informal*), piddle (*informal*), spend a penny (*Brit informal*), make water, pass water, wee-wee (*informal*), micturate, take a whizz (*slang, chiefly US*)

usable *adjective* SERVICEABLE, working, functional, available, current, practical, valid, at your disposal, ready for use, in running order, fit for use, utilizable

usage *noun* 1 USE, operation, employment, running, control, management, treatment, handling

2 PRACTICE, method, procedure, form, rule, tradition, habit, regime, custom, routine, convention, mode, matter of course, wont

use *verb* 1 EMPLOY, utilize, make use of, work, apply, operate, exercise, practise, resort to, exert, wield, ply, put to use, bring into play, find a use for, avail yourself of, turn to account

2 *sometimes with* **up** CONSUME, go through, exhaust, spend, waste, get through, run through, deplete, dissipate, expend, fritter away

3 TAKE ADVANTAGE OF, exploit, manipulate, abuse, milk, profit from, impose on, misuse, make use of, cash in on (*informal*), walk all over (*informal*), take liberties with

▷ *noun* 1 USAGE, employment, utilization, operation, application

2 SERVICE, handling, wear and tear, treatment, practice, exercise

3 PURPOSE, call, need, end, point, cause, reason, occasion, object, necessity

4 GOOD, point, help, service, value, benefit, profit, worth, advantage, utility, mileage (*informal*), avail, usefulness

▷▷ **use something up** CONSUME, drain, exhaust, finish, waste, absorb, run through, deplete, squander, devour, swallow up, burn up, fritter away

used *adjective* SECOND-HAND, worn, not new, cast-off, hand-me-down (*informal*), nearly new, shopsoiled, reach-me-down (*informal*), preloved (*Austral slang*)

<< OPPOSITE new

used to *adjective* ACCUSTOMED TO, familiar with, in the habit of, given to, at home in, attuned to, tolerant of, wont to, inured to, hardened to, habituated to

useful *adjective* HELPFUL, effective, valuable, practical, of use, profitable, of service, worthwhile, beneficial, of help, fruitful, advantageous, all-purpose, salutary, general-purpose, serviceable

<< OPPOSITE useless

usefulness *noun* HELPFULNESS, value, worth, use, help, service, benefit, profit, utility, effectiveness, convenience, practicality, efficacy

useless *adjective* 1 WORTHLESS, of no use, valueless, pants (*slang*), ineffective, impractical, fruitless, unproductive, ineffectual, unworkable, disadvantageous, unavailing, bootless, unsuitable

<< OPPOSITE useful

2 POINTLESS, hopeless, futile, vain, idle, profitless

<< OPPOSITE worthwhile

3 (*informal*) INEPT, no good, hopeless, weak, stupid, pants (*slang*), incompetent, ineffectual

usher *verb* ESCORT, lead, direct, guide, conduct, pilot, steer, show

▷ *noun* ATTENDANT, guide, doorman,

usherette, escort, doorkeeper
▷▷ **usher something in** INTRODUCE, launch, bring in, precede, initiate, herald, pave the way for, ring in, open the door to, inaugurate

usual *adjective* NORMAL, customary, regular, expected, general, common, stock, standard, fixed, ordinary, familiar, typical, constant, routine, everyday, accustomed, habitual, bog-standard (*Brit & Irish slang*), wonted
<< OPPOSITE unusual

usually *adverb* NORMALLY, generally, mainly, commonly, regularly, mostly, routinely, on the whole, in the main, for the most part, by and large, most often, ordinarily, as a rule, habitually, as is usual, as is the custom

usurp *verb* SEIZE, take over, assume, take, appropriate, wrest, commandeer, arrogate, infringe upon, lay hold of

utility *noun* USEFULNESS, use, point, benefit, service, profit, fitness, convenience, mileage (*informal*), avail, practicality, efficacy, advantageousness, serviceableness

utilize *verb* USE, employ, deploy, take advantage of, resort to, make the most of, make use of, put to use, bring into play, have recourse to, avail yourself of, turn to account

utmost *adjective* **1** GREATEST, highest, maximum, supreme, extreme, paramount, pre-eminent
2 FARTHEST, extreme, last, final, outermost, uttermost, farthermost
▷ *noun* BEST, greatest, maximum, most, highest, hardest

utopia *noun* PARADISE, heaven, Eden, bliss, perfect place, Garden of Eden, Shangri-la, Happy Valley, seventh heaven, ideal life, Erewhon

utopian *adjective* PERFECT, ideal, romantic, dream, fantasy, imaginary, visionary, airy, idealistic, fanciful, impractical, illusory, chimerical
▷ *noun* DREAMER, visionary, idealist, Don Quixote, romanticist

utter[1] *verb* SAY, state, speak, voice, express, deliver, declare, mouth, breathe, pronounce, articulate, enunciate, put into words, verbalize, vocalize

utter[2] *adjective* ABSOLUTE, complete, total, perfect, positive, pure, sheer, stark, outright, all-out, thorough, downright, real, consummate, veritable, unqualified, out-and-out, unadulterated, unmitigated, thoroughgoing, arrant, deep-dyed (*usually derogatory*)

utterance *noun* **1** SPEECH, words, statement, comment, opinion, remark, expression, announcement, observation, declaration, reflection, pronouncement
2 SPEAKING, voicing, expression, breathing, delivery, ejaculation, articulation, enunciation, vocalization, verbalization, vociferation

utterly *adverb* TOTALLY, completely, absolutely, just, really, quite, perfectly, fully, entirely, extremely, altogether, thoroughly, wholly, downright, categorically, to the core, one hundred per cent, in all respects, to the nth degree, unqualifiedly

Vv

vacancy *noun* **1** OPENING, job, post, place, position, role, situation, opportunity, slot, berth (*informal*), niche, job opportunity, vacant position, situation vacant
2 ROOM, space, available accommodation, unoccupied room

vacant *adjective* **1** EMPTY, free, available, abandoned, deserted, to let, for sale, on the market, void, up for grabs, disengaged, uninhabited, unoccupied, not in use, unfilled, untenanted
<< OPPOSITE occupied
2 UNFILLED, unoccupied
<< OPPOSITE taken
3 BLANK, vague, dreamy, dreaming, empty, abstracted, idle, thoughtless, vacuous, inane, expressionless, unthinking, absent-minded, incurious, ditzy *or* ditsy (*slang*)
<< OPPOSITE thoughtful

vacate *verb* **1** LEAVE, quit, move out of, give up, withdraw from, evacuate, depart from, go away from, leave empty, relinquish possession of
2 QUIT, leave, resign from, give up, withdraw from, chuck (*informal*), retire from, relinquish, renounce, walk out on, pack in (*informal*), abdicate, step down from (*informal*), stand down from

vacuous *adjective* VAPID, stupid, inane, blank, vacant, unintelligent

vacuum *noun* **1** GAP, lack, absence, space, deficiency, void
2 EMPTINESS, space, void, gap, empty space, nothingness, vacuity

vagabond *noun* TRAMP, bum (*informal*), drifter, vagrant, migrant, rolling stone, wanderer, beggar, outcast, rover, nomad, itinerant, down-and-out, hobo (*US*), bag lady (*chiefly US*), wayfarer, dosser (*Brit slang*), knight of the road, person of no fixed address, derro (*Austral slang*)
▷ *modifier* VAGRANT, drifting, wandering, homeless, journeying, unsettled, roaming, idle, roving, nomadic, destitute, itinerant, down and out, rootless, footloose, fly-by-night (*informal*), shiftless

vagary *noun usually plural* WHIM, caprice, unpredictability, sport, urge, fancy, notion, humour, impulse, quirk, conceit, whimsy, crotchet, sudden notion

vagrant *noun* TRAMP, bum (*informal*), drifter, vagabond, rolling stone, wanderer, beggar, derelict, itinerant, down-and-out, hobo (*US*), bag lady (*chiefly US*), dosser (*Brit slang*), person of no fixed address, derro (*Austral slang*)
▷ *adjective* VAGABOND, drifting, wandering, homeless, journeying, unsettled, roaming, idle, roving, nomadic, destitute, itinerant, down and out, rootless, footloose, fly-by-night (*informal*), shiftless
<< OPPOSITE settled

vague *adjective* **1** UNCLEAR, indefinite, hazy, confused, loose, uncertain, doubtful, unsure, superficial, incomplete, woolly, imperfect, sketchy, cursory
<< OPPOSITE clear
2 IMPRECISE, unspecified, generalized, rough, loose, ambiguous, hazy, equivocal, ill-defined, non-specific, inexact, obfuscatory, inexplicit
3 ABSENT-MINDED, absorbed, abstracted, distracted, unaware, musing, vacant, preoccupied, bemused, oblivious, dreamy, daydreaming, faraway, unthinking, heedless, inattentive, unheeding
4 INDISTINCT, blurred, unclear, dim, fuzzy, unknown, obscure, faint, shadowy, indefinite, misty, hazy, indistinguishable, amorphous, indeterminate, bleary, nebulous, out of focus, ill-defined, indiscernible
<< OPPOSITE distinct

vaguely *adverb* **1** SLIGHTLY, rather, sort of (*informal*), kind of (*informal*), a little, a bit, somewhat, moderately, faintly, dimly, to some extent, kinda (*informal*)
2 ABSENT-MINDEDLY, evasively, abstractedly, obscurely, vacantly, inattentively
3 ROUGHLY, loosely, indefinitely, carelessly, in a

general way, imprecisely

vagueness *noun* 1 IMPRECISENESS, ambiguity, obscurity, looseness, inexactitude, woolliness, undecidedness, lack of preciseness
<< OPPOSITE preciseness
2 ABSENT-MINDEDNESS, abstraction, forgetfulness, confusion, inattention, disorganization, giddiness, dreaminess, befuddlement, empty-headedness

vain *adjective* 1 FUTILE, useless, pointless, unsuccessful, empty, hollow, idle, trivial, worthless, trifling, senseless, unimportant, fruitless, unproductive, abortive, unprofitable, time-wasting, unavailing, nugatory
<< OPPOSITE successful
2 CONCEITED, narcissistic, proud, arrogant, inflated, swaggering, stuck-up (*informal*), cocky, swanky (*informal*), ostentatious, egotistical, self-important, overweening, vainglorious, swollen-headed (*informal*), pleased with yourself, bigheaded (*informal*), peacockish
<< OPPOSITE modest
▷▷ **in vain** 1 USELESS, to no avail, unsuccessful, fruitless, wasted, vain, ineffectual, without success, to no purpose, bootless
2 USELESSLY, to no avail, unsuccessfully, fruitlessly, vainly, ineffectually, without success, to no purpose, bootlessly

valiant *adjective* BRAVE, heroic, courageous, bold, worthy, fearless, gallant, intrepid, plucky, doughty, indomitable, redoubtable, dauntless, lion-hearted, valorous, stouthearted
<< OPPOSITE cowardly

valid *adjective* 1 SOUND, good, reasonable, just, telling, powerful, convincing, substantial, acceptable, sensible, rational, logical, viable, credible, sustainable, plausible, conclusive, weighty, well-founded, cogent, well-grounded
<< OPPOSITE unfounded
2 LEGAL, official, legitimate, correct, genuine, proper, in effect, authentic, in force, lawful, bona fide, legally binding, signed and sealed
<< OPPOSITE invalid

validate *verb* 1 CONFIRM, prove, certify, substantiate, corroborate
2 AUTHORIZE, endorse, ratify, legalize, authenticate, make legally binding, set your seal on *or* to

validity *noun* 1 SOUNDNESS, force, power, grounds, weight, strength, foundation, substance, point, cogency
2 LEGALITY, authority, legitimacy, right, lawfulness

valley *noun* HOLLOW, dale, glen, vale, depression, dell, dingle, strath (*Scot*), cwm (*Welsh*), coomb

valour *or US* **valor** *noun* BRAVERY, courage, heroism, spirit, boldness, gallantry, derring-do (*archaic*), fearlessness, intrepidity, doughtiness, lion-heartedness
<< OPPOSITE cowardice

valuable *adjective* 1 USEFUL, important, profitable, worthwhile, beneficial, valued, helpful, worthy, of use, of help, invaluable, serviceable, worth its weight in gold
<< OPPOSITE useless
2 TREASURED, esteemed, cherished, prized, precious, held dear, estimable, worth your weight in gold
3 PRECIOUS, expensive, costly, dear, high-priced, priceless, irreplaceable
<< OPPOSITE worthless
▷ *plural noun* TREASURES, prized possessions, precious items, heirlooms, personal effects, costly article

value *noun* 1 IMPORTANCE, use, benefit, worth, merit, point, help, service, sense, profit, advantage, utility, significance, effectiveness, mileage (*informal*), practicality, usefulness, efficacy, desirability, serviceableness
<< OPPOSITE worthlessness
2 COST, price, worth, rate, equivalent, market price, face value, asking price, selling price, monetary worth
▷ *plural noun* PRINCIPLES, morals, ethics, mores, standards of behaviour, code of behaviour, (moral) standards
▷ *verb* 1 APPRECIATE, rate, prize, regard highly, respect, admire, treasure, esteem, cherish, think much of, hold dear, have a high opinion of, set store by, hold in high regard *or* esteem
<< OPPOSITE undervalue
2 *with* **at** EVALUATE, price, estimate, rate, cost, survey, assess, set at, appraise, put a price on

valued *adjective* APPRECIATED, prized, esteemed, highly regarded, loved, dear, treasured, cherished

vandal *noun* HOOLIGAN, ned (*Scot slang*), delinquent, rowdy, lager lout, graffiti artist, yob *or* yobbo (*Brit slang*), cougan (*Austral slang*), scozza (*Austral slang*), bogan (*Austral slang*)

vanguard *noun* FOREFRONT, front line, cutting edge, leaders, front, van, spearhead, forerunners, front rank, trailblazers, advance guard, trendsetters
<< OPPOSITE rearguard

vanish *verb* 1 DISAPPEAR, become invisible, be lost to sight, dissolve, evaporate, fade away, melt away, disappear from sight, exit, evanesce
<< OPPOSITE appear
2 DIE OUT, disappear, pass away, end, fade, dwindle, cease to exist, become extinct, disappear from the face of the earth

vanity *noun* 1 PRIDE, arrogance, conceit, airs, showing off (*informal*), pretension, narcissism, egotism, self-love, ostentation, vainglory, self-admiration, affected ways, bigheadedness

(*informal*), conceitedness, swollen-headedness (*informal*)
<< OPPOSITE modesty
2 FUTILITY, uselessness, worthlessness, emptiness, frivolity, unreality, triviality, hollowness, pointlessness, inanity, unproductiveness, fruitlessness, unsubstantiality, profitlessness
<< OPPOSITE value

vanquish *verb* (*Literary*) DEFEAT, beat, conquer, reduce, stuff (*slang*), master, tank (*slang*), overcome, crush, overwhelm, put down, lick (*informal*), undo, subdue, rout, repress, overpower, quell, triumph over, clobber (*slang*), subjugate, run rings around (*informal*), wipe the floor with (*informal*), blow out of the water (*slang*), put to flight, get the upper hand over, put to rout

vapour *or US* **vapor** *noun* MIST, fog, haze, smoke, breath, steam, fumes, dampness, miasma, exhalation

variable *adjective* CHANGEABLE, unstable, fluctuating, shifting, flexible, wavering, uneven, fickle, temperamental, mercurial, capricious, unsteady, protean, vacillating, fitful, mutable, inconstant, chameleonic
<< OPPOSITE constant

variance ▷▷ **at variance** IN DISAGREEMENT, conflicting, at odds, in opposition, out of line, at loggerheads, at sixes and sevens (*informal*), out of harmony

variant *adjective* DIFFERENT, alternative, modified, derived, exceptional, divergent
▷ *noun* VARIATION, form, version, development, alternative, adaptation, revision, modification, permutation, transfiguration, aberration, derived form

variation *noun* 1 ALTERNATIVE, variety, modification, departure, innovation, variant
2 VARIETY, change, deviation, difference, diversity, diversion, novelty, alteration, discrepancy, diversification, departure from the norm, break in routine
<< OPPOSITE uniformity

varied *adjective* DIFFERENT, mixed, various, diverse, assorted, miscellaneous, sundry, motley, manifold, heterogeneous
<< OPPOSITE unvarying

variegated *adjective* MOTTLED, pied, streaked, motley, many-coloured, parti-coloured, varicoloured

variety *noun* 1 DIVERSITY, change, variation, difference, diversification, heterogeneity, many-sidedness, multifariousness
<< OPPOSITE uniformity
2 RANGE, selection, assortment, mix, collection, line-up, mixture, array, cross section, medley, multiplicity, mixed bag (*informal*), miscellany, motley collection, intermixture
3 TYPE, sort, kind, make, order, class, brand, species, breed, strain, category

various *adjective* 1 DIFFERENT, assorted, miscellaneous, varied, differing, distinct, diverse, divers (*archaic*), diversified, disparate, sundry, heterogeneous
<< OPPOSITE similar
2 MANY, numerous, countless, several, abundant, innumerable, sundry, manifold, profuse

> The use of *different* after *various*, which seems to be most common in speech, is unnecessary and should be avoided in serious writing: *the disease exists in various forms* (not *in various different forms*)

varnish *noun* LACQUER, polish, glaze, japan, gloss, shellac
▷ *verb* 1 LACQUER, polish, glaze, japan, gloss, shellac
2 POLISH, decorate, glaze, adorn, gild, lacquer, embellish

vary *verb* 1 DIFFER, be different, be dissimilar, disagree, diverge, be unlike
2 CHANGE, shift, swing, transform, alter, fluctuate, oscillate, see-saw
3 ALTERNATE, mix, diversify, reorder, intermix, bring variety to, permutate, variegate
4 MODIFY, change, alter, adjust

varying *adjective* 1 DIFFERENT, contrasting, inconsistent, varied, distinct, diverse, assorted, disparate, dissimilar, distinguishable, discrepant, streets apart
2 CHANGING, variable, irregular, inconsistent, fluctuating
<< OPPOSITE unchanging

vassal *noun* SERF, slave, bondsman, subject, retainer, thrall, varlet (*archaic*), bondservant, liegeman

vast *adjective* HUGE, massive, enormous, great, wide, sweeping, extensive, tremendous, immense, mega (*slang*), unlimited, gigantic, astronomical, monumental, monstrous, mammoth, colossal, never-ending, prodigious, limitless, boundless, voluminous, immeasurable, unbounded, elephantine, ginormous (*informal*), vasty (*archaic*), measureless, illimitable, humongous *or* humungous (*US slang*)
<< OPPOSITE tiny

vault[1] *noun* 1 STRONGROOM, repository, depository
2 CRYPT, tomb, catacomb, cellar, mausoleum, charnel house, undercroft
3 ARCH, roof, ceiling, span

vault[2] *verb* JUMP, spring, leap, clear, bound, hurdle

vaunted *adjective* BOASTED ABOUT, flaunted,

paraded, shown off, made much of, bragged about, crowed about, exulted in, made a display of, prated about

veer *verb* CHANGE DIRECTION, turn, swerve, shift, sheer, tack, be deflected, change course

vehemence *noun* FORCEFULNESS, force, violence, fire, energy, heat, passion, emphasis, enthusiasm, intensity, warmth, vigour, zeal, verve, fervour, eagerness, ardour, earnestness, keenness, fervency
<< OPPOSITE indifference

vehement *adjective* STRONG, fierce, forceful, earnest, powerful, violent, intense, flaming, eager, enthusiastic, passionate, ardent, emphatic, fervent, impassioned, zealous, forcible, fervid
<< OPPOSITE half-hearted

vehicle *noun* **1** CONVEYANCE, machine, motor vehicle, means of transport
2 MEDIUM, means, channel, mechanism, organ, apparatus, means of expression

veil *noun* **1** MASK, cover, shroud, film, shade, curtain, cloak
2 SCREEN, mask, disguise, blind
3 FILM, cover, curtain, cloak, shroud
▷ *verb* COVER, screen, hide, mask, shield, disguise, conceal, obscure, dim, cloak, mantle
<< OPPOSITE reveal

veiled *adjective* DISGUISED, implied, hinted at, covert, masked, concealed, suppressed

vein *noun* **1** BLOOD VESSEL
2 MOOD, style, spirit, way, turn, note, key, character, attitude, atmosphere, tone, manner, bent, stamp, humour, tendency, mode, temper, temperament, tenor, inclination, disposition, frame of mind
3 STREAK, element, thread, suggestion, strain, trace, hint, dash, trait, sprinkling, nuance, smattering
4 SEAM, layer, stratum, course, current, bed, deposit, streak, stripe, lode
>> RELATED WORD *adjective* venous

velocity *noun* SPEED, pace, rapidity, quickness, swiftness, fleetness, celerity

velvety *adjective* SOFT, smooth, downy, delicate, mossy, velvet-like

venal *adjective* CORRUPT, bent (*slang*), crooked (*informal*), prostituted, grafting (*informal*), mercenary, sordid, rapacious, unprincipled, dishonourable, corruptible, purchasable
<< OPPOSITE honest

vendetta *noun* FEUD, dispute, quarrel, enmity, bad blood, blood feud

veneer *noun* **1** MASK, show, façade, front, appearance, guise, pretence, semblance, false front
2 LAYER, covering, finish, facing, film, gloss, patina, laminate, cladding, lamination

venerable *adjective* RESPECTED, august, sage, revered, honoured, wise, esteemed, reverenced

venerate *verb* RESPECT, honour, esteem, revere, worship, adore, reverence, look up to, hold in awe
<< OPPOSITE scorn

veneration *noun* RESPECT, esteem, reverence, worship, awe, deference, adoration

vengeance *noun* REVENGE, retaliation, reprisal, retribution, avenging, an eye for an eye, settling of scores, requital, lex talionis
<< OPPOSITE forgiveness
▷▷ **with a vengeance** TO THE UTMOST, greatly, extremely, to the full, and no mistake, to the nth degree, with no holds barred

vengeful *adjective* UNFORGIVING, relentless, avenging, vindictive, punitive, implacable, spiteful, retaliatory, rancorous, thirsting for revenge, revengeful

venom *noun* **1** MALICE, hate, spite, bitterness, grudge, gall, acidity, spleen, acrimony, rancour, ill will, malevolence, virulence, pungency, malignity, spitefulness, maliciousness
<< OPPOSITE benevolence
2 POISON, toxin, bane

venomous *adjective* **1** MALICIOUS, vindictive, spiteful, hostile, savage, vicious, malignant, virulent, baleful, rancorous
<< OPPOSITE benevolent
2 POISONOUS, poison, toxic, virulent, noxious, baneful (*archaic*), envenomed, mephitic
<< OPPOSITE harmless

vent *noun* OUTLET, opening, hole, split, aperture, duct, orifice
▷ *verb* EXPRESS, release, voice, air, empty, discharge, utter, emit, come out with, pour out, give vent to, give expression to
<< OPPOSITE hold back

ventilate *verb* **1** AERATE, fan, cool, refresh, air-condition, freshen, oxygenate
2 DISCUSS, air, bring out into the open, talk about, debate, examine, broadcast, sift, scrutinize, make known

venture *verb* **1** GO, travel, journey, set out, wander, stray, plunge into, rove, set forth
2 DARE, presume, have the courage to, be brave enough, hazard, go out on a limb (*informal*), take the liberty, stick your neck out (*informal*), go so far as, make so bold as, have the temerity *or* effrontery *or* nerve
3 PUT FORWARD, offer, suggest, present, air, table, advance, propose, volunteer, submit, bring up, postulate, proffer, broach, posit, moot, propound, dare to say
▷ *noun* UNDERTAKING, project, enterprise, chance, campaign, risk, operation, activity, scheme, task, mission, speculation, gamble, adventure, exploit, pursuit, fling, hazard, crusade, endeavour

veracity *noun* 1 ACCURACY, truth, credibility, precision, exactitude
2 TRUTHFULNESS, integrity, honesty, candour, frankness, probity, rectitude, trustworthiness, uprightness
verbal *adjective* 1 SPOKEN, oral, word-of-mouth, unwritten
2 VERBATIM, literal
verbally *adverb* ORALLY, vocally, in words, in speech, by word of mouth
verbatim *adverb* EXACTLY, to the letter, word for word, closely, precisely, literally, faithfully, rigorously, in every detail, letter for letter
▷ *adjective* WORD FOR WORD, exact, literal, close, precise, faithful, line by line, unabridged, unvarnished, undeviating, unembellished
verdant *adjective* (*Literary*) GREEN, lush, leafy, grassy, fresh, flourishing
verdict *noun* DECISION, finding, judgment, opinion, sentence, conclusion, conviction, adjudication, pronouncement
verge *noun* 1 BRINK, point, edge, threshold
2 (*Brit*) BORDER, edge, margin, limit, extreme, lip, boundary, threshold, roadside, brim
▷▷ **verge on something** COME NEAR TO, approach, border on, resemble, incline to, be similar to, touch on, be more or less, be tantamount to, tend towards, be not far from, incline towards
verification *noun* PROOF, confirmation, validation, corroboration, authentication, substantiation
verify *verb* 1 CHECK, confirm, make sure, examine, monitor, check out (*informal*), inspect
2 CONFIRM, prove, substantiate, support, validate, bear out, attest, corroborate, attest to, authenticate
<< OPPOSITE disprove
vernacular *noun with* **the** SPEECH, jargon, idiom, parlance, cant, native language, dialect, patois, argot, vulgar tongue
▷ *adjective* COLLOQUIAL, popular, informal, local, common, native, indigenous, vulgar
versatile *adjective* 1 ADAPTABLE, flexible, all-round, resourceful, protean, multifaceted, many-sided, all-singing, all-dancing
<< OPPOSITE unadaptable
2 ALL-PURPOSE, handy, functional, variable, adjustable, all-singing, all-dancing
<< OPPOSITE limited
versed *adjective with* **in** KNOWLEDGEABLE, experienced, skilled, seasoned, qualified, familiar, practised, accomplished, competent, acquainted, well-informed, proficient, well up (*informal*), conversant
<< OPPOSITE ignorant
version *noun* 1 FORM, variety, variant, sort, kind, class, design, style, model, type, brand, genre
2 ADAPTATION, edition, interpretation, form, reading, copy, rendering, translation, reproduction, portrayal
3 ACCOUNT, report, side, description, record, reading, story, view, understanding, history, statement, analysis, take (*informal, chiefly US*), construction, tale, impression, explanation, interpretation, rendering, narrative, chronicle, rendition, narration, construal
vertical *adjective* UPRIGHT, sheer, perpendicular, straight (up and down), erect, plumb, on end, precipitous, vertiginous, bolt upright
<< OPPOSITE horizontal
vertigo *noun* DIZZINESS, giddiness, light-headedness, fear of heights, loss of balance, acrophobia, loss of equilibrium, swimming of the head
verve *noun* ENTHUSIASM, energy, spirit, life, force, punch (*informal*), dash, pep, sparkle, zip (*informal*), vitality, animation, vigour, zeal, gusto, get-up-and-go (*informal*), élan, brio, vivacity, liveliness, vim (*slang*)
<< OPPOSITE indifference
very *adverb* EXTREMELY, highly, greatly, really, deeply, particularly, seriously (*informal*), truly, absolutely, terribly, remarkably, unusually, jolly (*Brit*), wonderfully, profoundly, decidedly, awfully (*informal*), acutely, exceedingly, excessively, noticeably, eminently, superlatively, uncommonly, surpassingly
▷ *adjective* 1 EXACT, actual, precise, same, real, express, identical, unqualified, selfsame
2 IDEAL, perfect, right, fitting, appropriate, suitable, spot on (*Brit informal*), apt, just the job (*Brit informal*)

> In strict usage, adverbs of degree such as *very*, *too*, *quite*, *really*, and *extremely* are used only to qualify adjectives: *he is very happy*; *she is too sad*. By this rule, these words should not be used to qualify past participles that follow the verb *to be*, since they would then be technically qualifying verbs. With the exception of certain participles, such as *tired* or *disappointed*, that have come to be regarded as adjectives, all other past participles are qualified by adverbs such as *much*, *greatly*, *seriously*, or *excessively*: *he has been much* (not *very*) *inconvenienced*; *she has been excessively* (not *too*) *criticized*

vessel *noun* 1 SHIP, boat, craft, barque (*poetic*)
2 CONTAINER, receptacle, can, bowl, tank, pot, drum, barrel, butt, vat, bin, jar, basin, tub, jug, pitcher, urn, canister, repository, cask
vest ▷▷ **vest in something** *or* **someone** *usually*

passive PLACE, invest, entrust, settle, lodge, confer, endow, bestow, consign, put in the hands of, be devolved upon
▷▷ **vest with something** *usually passive* ENDOW WITH, furnish with, entrust with, empower with, authorize with
vestibule *noun* HALL, lobby, foyer, porch, entrance hall, portico, anteroom
vestige *noun* TRACE, sign, hint, scrap, evidence, indication, suspicion, glimmer
vet *verb* CHECK, examine, investigate, check out, review, scan, look over, appraise, scrutinize, size up (*informal*), give the once-over (*informal*), pass under review
veteran *noun* OLD HAND, master, pro (*informal*), old-timer, past master, trouper, warhorse (*informal*), old stager
<< OPPOSITE novice
▷ *modifier* LONG-SERVING, seasoned, experienced, old, established, expert, qualified, mature, practised, hardened, adept, proficient, well trained, battle-scarred, worldly-wise
veto *noun* BAN, dismissal, rejection, vetoing, boycott, embargo, prohibiting, prohibition, suppression, knock-back (*informal*), interdict, declination, preclusion, nonconsent
<< OPPOSITE ratification
▷ *verb* BAN, block, reject, rule out, kill (*informal*), negative, turn down, forbid, boycott, prohibit, disallow, put a stop to, refuse permission to, interdict, give the thumbs down to, put the kibosh on (*slang*)
<< OPPOSITE pass
vex *verb* ANNOY, bother, irritate, worry, trouble, upset, disturb, distress, provoke, bug (*informal*), offend, needle (*informal*), plague, put out, tease, torment, harass, hassle (*informal*), aggravate (*informal*), afflict, fret, gall, agitate, exasperate, nettle, pester, displease, rile, pique, peeve (*informal*), grate on, get on your nerves (*informal*), nark (*Brit, Austral & NZ slang*), give someone grief (*Brit & S African*), get your back up, put your back up, hack you off (*informal*)
<< OPPOSITE soothe
vexed *adjective* 1 ANNOYED, upset, irritated, worried, troubled, bothered, confused, disturbed, distressed, provoked, put out, fed up, tormented, harassed, aggravated (*informal*), afflicted, agitated, ruffled, exasperated, perplexed, nettled, miffed (*informal*), displeased, riled, peeved (*informal*), hacked off (*US slang*), out of countenance, tooshie (*Austral slang*), hoha (*NZ*)
2 CONTROVERSIAL, disputed, contested, moot, much debated
viable *adjective* WORKABLE, practical, feasible, suitable, realistic, operational, applicable, usable, practicable, serviceable, operable, within the bounds of possibility
<< OPPOSITE unworkable
vibes *plural noun sometimes singular* (*Slang*)
1 FEELINGS, emotions, response, reaction
2 ATMOSPHERE, aura, vibrations, feeling, emanation
vibrant *adjective* 1 ENERGETIC, dynamic, sparkling, vivid, spirited, storming, alive, sensitive, colourful, vigorous, animated, responsive, electrifying, vivacious, full of pep (*informal*)
2 VIVID, bright, brilliant, intense, clear, rich, glowing, colourful, highly-coloured
vibrate *verb* 1 SHAKE, tremble, shiver, fluctuate, quiver, oscillate, judder (*informal*)
2 THROB, pulse, resonate, pulsate, reverberate
vibration *noun* 1 SHAKING, shake, trembling, quake, quaking, shudder, shuddering, quiver, oscillation, judder (*informal*)
2 THROBBING, pulse, thumping, hum, humming, throb, resonance, tremor, drone, droning, reverberation, pulsation
vicarious *adjective* INDIRECT, substitute, surrogate, by proxy, empathetic, at one remove
vice *noun* 1 FAULT, failing, weakness, limitation, defect, deficiency, flaw, shortcoming, blemish, imperfection, frailty, foible, weak point, infirmity
<< OPPOSITE good point
2 WICKEDNESS, evil, corruption, sin, depravity, immorality, iniquity, profligacy, degeneracy, venality, turpitude, evildoing
<< OPPOSITE virtue
vice versa *adverb* THE OTHER WAY ROUND, conversely, in reverse, contrariwise
vicinity *noun* NEIGHBOURHOOD, area, district, precincts, locality, environs, neck of the woods (*informal*), purlieus
vicious *adjective* 1 SAVAGE, brutal, violent, bad, dangerous, foul, cruel, ferocious, monstrous, vile, atrocious, diabolical, heinous, abhorrent, barbarous, fiendish
<< OPPOSITE gentle
2 DEPRAVED, corrupt, wicked, infamous, degraded, worthless, degenerate, immoral, sinful, debased, profligate, unprincipled
<< OPPOSITE virtuous
3 MALICIOUS, vindictive, spiteful, mean, cruel, venomous, bitchy (*informal*), defamatory, rancorous, backbiting, slanderous
<< OPPOSITE complimentary
vicissitude *noun often plural* VARIATION, change, shift, change of fortune, life's ups and downs (*informal*)
victim *noun* 1 CASUALTY, sufferer, injured party, fatality
<< OPPOSITE survivor
2 PREY, patsy (*slang, chiefly US & Canad*), sucker (*slang*), dupe, gull (*archaic*), stooge, sitting duck

(*informal*), sitting target, innocent
<< OPPOSITE culprit
3 SCAPEGOAT, sacrifice, martyr, fall guy (*informal*), whipping boy

victimize *or* **victimise** *verb* PERSECUTE, bully, pick on, abuse, harass, discriminate against, lean on, have it in for (*informal*), push around, give a hard time, demonize, have a down on (*informal*), have your knife into

victor *noun* WINNER, champion, conqueror, first, champ (*informal*), vanquisher, top dog (*informal*), prizewinner, conquering hero
<< OPPOSITE loser

victorious *adjective* WINNING, successful, triumphant, first, champion, conquering, vanquishing, prizewinning
<< OPPOSITE losing

victory *noun* WIN, success, triumph, the prize, superiority, conquest, laurels, mastery, walkover (*informal*)
<< OPPOSITE defeat

vie *verb with* **with** *or* **for** COMPETE, struggle, contend, contest, strive, be rivals, match yourself against

view *noun* 1 *sometimes plural* OPINION, thought, idea, belief, thinking, feeling, attitude, reckoning, impression, notion, conviction, judgment, point of view, sentiment, viewpoint, persuasion, way of thinking, standpoint
2 SCENE, picture, sight, prospect, aspect, perspective, landscape, outlook, spectacle, panorama, vista
3 VISION, sight, visibility, perspective, eyeshot, range *or* field of vision
4 STUDY, review, survey, assessment, examination, scan, inspection, look, scrutiny, contemplation
▷ *verb* 1 REGARD, see, consider, judge, perceive, treat, estimate, reckon, deem, look on, adjudge, think about *or* of
2 LOOK AT, see, inspect, gaze at, eye, watch, check, regard, survey, witness, clock (*Brit slang*), examine, observe, explore, stare at, scan, contemplate, check out (*informal*), behold, eyeball (*slang*), gawp at, recce (*slang*), get a load of (*informal*), spectate, take a dekko at (*Brit slang*)
▷▷ **with a view to** WITH THE AIM *or* INTENTION OF, in order to, so as to, in the hope of

viewer *noun* WATCHER, observer, spectator, onlooker, couch potato (*informal*), TV watcher, one of an audience

viewpoint *noun* POINT OF VIEW, perspective, angle, position, attitude, stance, slant, belief, conviction, feeling, opinion, way of thinking, standpoint, vantage point, frame of reference

vigilance *noun* WATCHFULNESS, alertness, caution, observance, circumspection, attentiveness, carefulness

vigilant *adjective* WATCHFUL, alert, on the lookout, careful, cautious, attentive, circumspect, wide awake, on the alert, on your toes, wakeful, on your guard, on the watch, on the qui vive, keeping your eyes peeled *or* skinned (*informal*)
<< OPPOSITE inattentive

vigorous *adjective* 1 STRENUOUS, energetic, arduous, hard, taxing, active, intense, exhausting, rigorous, brisk
2 SPIRITED, lively, energetic, active, intense, dynamic, sparkling, animated, forceful, feisty (*informal*), spanking, high-spirited, sprightly, vivacious, forcible, effervescent, full of energy, zippy (*informal*), spunky (*informal*)
<< OPPOSITE lethargic
3 STRONG, powerful, robust, sound, healthy, vital, lively, flourishing, hardy, hale, hearty, lusty, virile, alive and kicking, red-blooded, fighting fit, full of energy, full of beans (*informal*), hale and hearty, fit as a fiddle (*informal*)
<< OPPOSITE weak

vigorously *adverb* 1 ENERGETICALLY, hard, forcefully, strongly, all out, eagerly, with a vengeance, strenuously, like mad (*slang*), lustily, hammer and tongs, with might and main
2 FORCEFULLY, strongly, vehemently, strenuously

vigour *or US* **vigor** *noun* ENERGY, might, force, vitality, power, activity, spirit, strength, snap (*informal*), punch (*informal*), dash, pep, zip (*informal*), animation, verve, gusto, dynamism, oomph (*informal*), brio, robustness, liveliness, vim (*slang*), forcefulness
<< OPPOSITE weakness

vile *adjective* 1 WICKED, base, evil, mean, bad, low, shocking, appalling, ugly, corrupt, miserable, vicious, humiliating, perverted, coarse, degrading, worthless, disgraceful, vulgar, degenerate, abject, sinful, despicable, depraved, debased, loathsome, contemptible, impure, wretched, nefarious, ignoble
<< OPPOSITE honourable
2 DISGUSTING, foul, revolting, offensive, nasty, obscene, sickening, horrid, repellent, repulsive, noxious, nauseating, repugnant, loathsome, yucky *or* yukky (*slang*), yucko (*Austral slang*)
<< OPPOSITE pleasant

vilification *noun* DENIGRATION, abuse, defamation, invective, calumny, mudslinging, disparagement, vituperation, contumely, aspersion, scurrility, calumniation

vilify *verb* MALIGN, abuse, denigrate, knock (*informal*), rubbish (*informal*), run down, smear, slag (off) (*slang*), berate, disparage, decry, revile, slander, dump on (*slang, chiefly US*),

debase, defame, bad-mouth (*slang, chiefly US & Canad*), traduce, speak ill of, pull to pieces (*informal*), calumniate, vituperate, asperse
<< OPPOSITE praise

villain *noun* 1 EVILDOER, criminal, rogue, profligate, scoundrel, wretch, libertine, knave (*archaic*), reprobate, miscreant, malefactor, blackguard, rapscallion, caitiff (*archaic*), wrong 'un (*Austral slang*)
2 BADDY (*informal*), antihero
<< OPPOSITE hero

villainous *adjective* WICKED, evil, depraved, mean, bad, base, criminal, terrible, cruel, vicious, outrageous, infamous, vile, degenerate, atrocious, inhuman, sinful, diabolical, heinous, debased, hateful, scoundrelly, fiendish, ruffianly, nefarious, ignoble, detestable, blackguardly, thievish
<< OPPOSITE virtuous

vindicate *verb* 1 CLEAR, acquit, exonerate, absolve, let off the hook, exculpate, free from blame
<< OPPOSITE condemn
2 SUPPORT, uphold, ratify, defend, excuse, justify, substantiate

vindication *noun* 1 EXONERATION, pardon, acquittal, dismissal, discharge, amnesty, absolution, exculpating, exculpation
2 SUPPORT, defence, ratification, excuse, apology, justification, assertion, substantiation

vindictive *adjective* VENGEFUL, malicious, spiteful, relentless, resentful, malignant, unrelenting, unforgiving, implacable, venomous, rancorous, revengeful, full of spleen
<< OPPOSITE merciful

vintage *noun* 1 (always used of wines) HARVEST, year, crop, yield
2 ERA, period, origin, sort, type, generation, stamp, epoch, ilk, time of origin
▷ *adjective* 1 (always used of wines) HIGH-QUALITY, best, prime, quality, choice, select, rare, superior
2 CLASSIC, old, veteran, historic, heritage, enduring, antique, timeless, old-world, age-old, ageless

violate *verb* 1 BREAK, infringe, disobey, transgress, ignore, defy, disregard, flout, rebel against, contravene, fly in the face of, overstep, not comply with, take no notice of, encroach upon, pay no heed to, infract
<< OPPOSITE obey
2 INVADE, infringe on, disturb, upset, shatter, disrupt, impinge on, encroach on, intrude on, trespass on, obtrude on
3 DESECRATE, profane, defile, abuse, outrage, pollute, deface, dishonour, vandalize, treat with disrespect, befoul
<< OPPOSITE honour
4 RAPE, molest, sexually assault, ravish, abuse, assault, interfere with, sexually abuse, indecently assault, force yourself on

violation *noun* 1 BREACH, abuse, infringement, contravention, abuse, trespass, transgression, infraction
2 INVASION, intrusion, trespass, breach, disturbance, disruption, interruption, encroachment
3 DESECRATION, sacrilege, defilement, profanation, spoliation
4 RAPE, sexual assault, molesting, ravishing (*old-fashioned*), abuse, sexual abuse, indecent assault, molestation

violence *noun* 1 BRUTALITY, bloodshed, savagery, fighting, terrorism, frenzy, thuggery, destructiveness, bestiality, strong-arm tactics (*informal*), rough handling, bloodthirstiness, murderousness
2 FORCE, power, strength, might, ferocity, brute force, fierceness, forcefulness, powerfulness
3 INTENSITY, passion, fury, force, cruelty, severity, fervour, sharpness, harshness, vehemence
4 POWER, turbulence, wildness, raging, tumult, roughness, boisterousness, storminess

violent *adjective* 1 BRUTAL, aggressive, savage, wild, rough, fierce, bullying, cruel, vicious, destructive, ruthless, murderous, maddened, berserk, merciless, bloodthirsty, homicidal, pitiless, hot-headed, thuggish, maniacal, hot-tempered
<< OPPOSITE gentle
2 SHARP, hard, powerful, forceful, strong, fierce, fatal, savage, deadly, brutal, vicious, lethal, hefty, ferocious, death-dealing
3 INTENSE, acute, severe, biting, sharp, extreme, painful, harsh, excruciating, agonizing, inordinate
4 PASSIONATE, intense, extreme, strong, wild, consuming, uncontrollable, vehement, unrestrained, tempestuous, ungovernable
5 FIERY, raging, fierce, flaming, furious, passionate, peppery, ungovernable
6 POWERFUL, wild, devastating, strong, storming, raging, turbulent, tumultuous, tempestuous, gale force, blustery, ruinous, full of force
<< OPPOSITE mild

VIP *noun* CELEBRITY, big name, public figure, star, somebody, lion, notable, luminary, bigwig (*informal*), leading light (*informal*), big shot (*informal*), personage, big noise (*informal*), big hitter (*informal*), heavy hitter (*informal*), man *or* woman of the hour

virago *noun* HARRIDAN, fury, shrew, vixen,

scold, battle-axe (*informal*), termagant (*rare*)

virgin *noun* MAIDEN, maid (*archaic*), damsel (*archaic*), girl (*archaic*), celibate, vestal, virgo intacta

▷ *adjective* 1 UNTOUCHED, immaculate, fresh, new, pure, unused, pristine, flawless, unblemished, unadulterated, unsullied

<< OPPOSITE spoiled

2 PURE, maidenly, chaste, immaculate, virginal, unsullied, vestal, uncorrupted, undefiled

<< OPPOSITE corrupted

virginal *adjective* 1 CHASTE, pure, maidenly, virgin, immaculate, celibate, uncorrupted, undefiled

2 IMMACULATE, fresh, pristine, white, pure, untouched, snowy, undisturbed, spotless

virginity *noun* CHASTITY, maidenhead, maidenhood

virile *adjective* MANLY, masculine, macho, strong, male, robust, vigorous, potent, forceful, lusty, red-blooded, manlike

<< OPPOSITE effeminate

virility *noun* MASCULINITY, manhood, potency, vigour, machismo

<< OPPOSITE effeminacy

virtual *adjective* PRACTICAL, near, essential, implied, indirect, implicit, tacit, near enough, unacknowledged, in all but name

virtually *adverb* PRACTICALLY, almost, nearly, in effect, in essence, as good as, to all intents and purposes, in all but name, for all practical purposes, effectually

virtue *noun* 1 GOODNESS, honour, integrity, worth, dignity, excellence, morality, honesty, decency, respectability, nobility, righteousness, propriety, probity, rectitude, worthiness, high-mindedness, incorruptibility, uprightness, virtuousness, ethicalness

<< OPPOSITE vice

2 MERIT, strength, asset, plus (*informal*), attribute, good quality, good point, strong point

<< OPPOSITE failing

3 ADVANTAGE, benefit, merit, credit, usefulness, efficacy

4 CHASTITY, honour, virginity, innocence, purity, maidenhood, chasteness

<< OPPOSITE unchastity

▷▷ **by virtue of** BECAUSE OF, in view of, on account of, based on, thanks to, as a result of, owing to, by reason of, by dint of

virtuosity *noun* MASTERY, skill, brilliance, polish, craft, expertise, flair, panache, éclat

virtuoso *noun* MASTER, artist, genius, maestro, magician, grandmaster, maven (*US*), master hand

▷ *modifier* MASTERLY, brilliant, dazzling, bravura (*Music*)

virtuous *adjective* 1 GOOD, moral, ethical, upright, honourable, excellent, pure, worthy, honest, righteous, exemplary, squeaky-clean, blameless, praiseworthy, incorruptible, high-principled

<< OPPOSITE corrupt

2 CHASTE, pure, innocent, celibate, spotless, virginal, clean-living

<< OPPOSITE promiscuous

virulent *adjective* 1 VICIOUS, vindictive, bitter, hostile, malicious, resentful, acrimonious, malevolent, spiteful, venomous, rancorous, splenetic, envenomed

<< OPPOSITE benign

2 DEADLY, lethal, toxic, poisonous, malignant, pernicious, venomous, septic, infective, injurious, baneful (*archaic*)

<< OPPOSITE harmless

viscous *adjective* THICK, sticky, gooey (*informal*), adhesive, tenacious, clammy, syrupy, glutinous, gummy, gelatinous, icky (*informal*), gluey, treacly, mucilaginous, viscid

visible *adjective* PERCEPTIBLE, noticeable, observable, clear, obvious, plain, apparent, bold, patent, to be seen, evident, manifest, in sight, in view, conspicuous, unmistakable, palpable, discernible, salient, detectable, not hidden, distinguishable, unconcealed, perceivable, discoverable, anywhere to be seen

<< OPPOSITE invisible

vision *noun* 1 IMAGE, idea, dream, plans, hopes, prospect, ideal, concept, fancy, fantasy, conception, delusion, daydream, reverie, flight of fancy, mental picture, pipe dream, imago (*Psychoanalysis*), castle in the air, fanciful notion

2 HALLUCINATION, illusion, apparition, revelation, ghost, phantom, delusion, spectre, mirage, wraith, chimera, phantasm, eidolon

3 SIGHT, seeing, eyesight, view, eyes, perception

4 FORESIGHT, imagination, perception, insight, awareness, inspiration, innovation, creativity, intuition, penetration, inventiveness, shrewdness, discernment, prescience, perceptiveness, farsightedness, breadth of view

5 PICTURE, dream, sight, delight, beauty, joy, sensation, spectacle, knockout (*informal*), beautiful sight, perfect picture, feast for the eyes, sight for sore eyes, pearler (*Austral slang*), beaut (*Austral & NZ slang*)

visionary *adjective* 1 IDEALISTIC, romantic, unrealistic, utopian, dreaming, speculative, impractical, dreamy, unworkable, quixotic, starry-eyed, with your head in the clouds

<< OPPOSITE realistic

2 PROPHETIC, mystical, divinatory, predictive,

oracular, sibylline, mantic, vatic (*rare*), fatidic (*rare*)
3 IMAGINARY, fantastic, unreal, fanciful, ideal, idealized, illusory, imaginal (*Psychoanalysis*), chimerical, delusory
<< OPPOSITE real
▷ *noun* 1 IDEALIST, romantic, dreamer, daydreamer, utopian, enthusiast (*archaic*), theorist, zealot, Don Quixote
<< OPPOSITE realist
2 PROPHET, diviner, mystic, seer, soothsayer, sibyl, scryer, spaewife (*Scot*)

visit *verb* 1 CALL ON, go to see, drop in on (*informal*), stop by, look up, call in on, pop in on (*informal*), pay a call on, go see (US)
2 STAY AT, stay with, spend time with, pay a visit to, be the guest of
3 STAY IN, see, tour, explore, take in (*informal*), holiday in, go to see, stop by, spend time in, vacation in (US), stop over in
▷ *noun* 1 CALL, social call
2 TRIP, stop, stay, break, tour, holiday, vacation (*informal*), stopover, sojourn

visitation *noun* 1 APPARITION, vision, manifestation, appearance, materialization
2 INSPECTION, survey, examination, visit, review, scrutiny

visitor *noun* GUEST, caller, company, visitant, manu(w)hiri (NZ)

vista *noun* VIEW, scene, prospect, landscape, panorama, perspective

visual *adjective* 1 OPTICAL, optic, ocular
2 OBSERVABLE, visible, perceptible, discernible
<< OPPOSITE imperceptible

visualize *or* **visualise** *verb* PICTURE, imagine, think about, envisage, contemplate, conceive of, see in the mind's eye, conjure up a mental picture of

vital *adjective* 1 ESSENTIAL, important, necessary, key, basic, significant, critical, radical, crucial, fundamental, urgent, decisive, cardinal, imperative, indispensable, requisite, life-or-death, must-have
<< OPPOSITE unnecessary
2 LIVELY, vigorous, energetic, spirited, dynamic, animated, vibrant, forceful, sparky, vivacious, full of beans (*informal*), zestful, full of the joy of living
<< OPPOSITE lethargic

vitality *noun* ENERGY, vivacity, sparkle, go (*informal*), life, strength, pep, stamina, animation, vigour, exuberance, brio, robustness, liveliness, vim (*slang*), lustiness, vivaciousness
<< OPPOSITE lethargy

vitriolic *adjective* VENOMOUS, scathing, malicious, acid, bitter, destructive, withering, virulent, sardonic, caustic, bitchy (*informal*), acerbic, envenomed, dripping with malice

vivacious *adjective* LIVELY, spirited, vital, gay, bubbling, sparkling, cheerful, jolly, animated, merry, upbeat (*informal*), high-spirited, ebullient, chirpy (*informal*), sparky, scintillating, sprightly, effervescent, full of life, full of beans (*informal*), frolicsome, sportive, light-hearted
<< OPPOSITE dull

vivid *adjective* 1 CLEAR, detailed, realistic, telling, moving, strong, affecting, arresting, powerful, sharp, dramatic, stirring, stimulating, haunting, graphic, distinct, lively, memorable, unforgettable, evocative, lucid, lifelike, true to life, sharply-etched
<< OPPOSITE vague
2 BRIGHT, brilliant, intense, clear, rich, glowing, colourful, highly-coloured
<< OPPOSITE dull
3 LIVELY, strong, dynamic, striking, spirited, powerful, quick, storming, active, vigorous, energetic, animated, vibrant, fiery, flamboyant, expressive, vivacious, zestful
<< OPPOSITE quiet

vixen *noun* SHREW, fury, spitfire, virago, harpy, scold, harridan, termagant (*rare*), hellcat

viz *adverb* NAMELY, that is to say, to wit, videlicet

vocabulary *noun* 1 LANGUAGE, words, lexicon, word stock, word hoard
2 WORDBOOK, dictionary, glossary, lexicon

vocal *adjective* 1 OUTSPOKEN, frank, blunt, forthright, strident, vociferous, noisy, articulate, expressive, eloquent, plain-spoken, clamorous, free-spoken
<< OPPOSITE quiet
2 SPOKEN, voiced, uttered, oral, said, articulate, articulated, put into words

vocation *noun* PROFESSION, calling, job, business, office, trade, role, post, career, mission, employment, pursuit, life work, métier

vociferous *adjective* OUTSPOKEN, vocal, strident, noisy, shouting, loud, ranting, vehement, loudmouthed (*informal*), uproarious, obstreperous, clamorous
<< OPPOSITE quiet

vogue *noun* FASHION, trend, craze, style, the latest, the thing (*informal*), mode, last word, the rage, passing fancy, dernier cri (*French*)
▷ *adjective* FASHIONABLE, trendy (*Brit informal*), in, now (*informal*), popular, with it (*informal*), prevalent, up-to-the-minute, modish, voguish
▷▷ **in vogue** POPULAR, big, fashionable, all the rage, happening, accepted, current, cool, in favour, stylish, up to date, in use, prevalent, up to the minute, modish, trendsetting, schmick (*Austral informal*)

voice *noun* 1 TONE, sound, language, articulation, power of speech
2 UTTERANCE, expression, words, airing,

vocalization, verbalization
3 OPINION, will, feeling, wish, desire
4 SAY, part, view, decision, vote, comment, input
5 INSTRUMENT, medium, spokesman *or* spokeswoman, agency, channel, vehicle, organ, spokesperson, intermediary, mouthpiece
▷ *verb* EXPRESS, say, declare, air, raise, table, reveal, mention, mouth, assert, pronounce, utter, articulate, come out with (*informal*), divulge, ventilate, enunciate, put into words, vocalize, give expression *or* utterance to
>> RELATED WORD *adjective* vocal

void *adjective* 1 INVALID, null and void, inoperative, useless, ineffective, worthless, ineffectual, unenforceable, nonviable
2 *with* **of** DEVOID OF, without, lacking, free from, wanting, bereft of, empty of, bare of, destitute of, vacant of
▷ *noun* 1 GAP, space, lack, want, hole, blank, emptiness
2 EMPTINESS, space, vacuum, oblivion, blankness, nullity, vacuity
▷ *verb* INVALIDATE, nullify, cancel, withdraw, reverse, undo, repeal, quash, revoke, disallow, retract, repudiate, negate, rescind, annul, abrogate, countermand, render invalid, abnegate

volatile *adjective* 1 CHANGEABLE, shifting, variable, unsettled, unstable, explosive, unreliable, unsteady, inconstant
<< OPPOSITE stable
2 TEMPERAMENTAL, erratic, mercurial, up and down (*informal*), fickle, whimsical, giddy, flighty, over-emotional, inconstant
<< OPPOSITE calm

volition *noun* FREE WILL, will, choice, election, choosing, option, purpose, resolution, determination, preference, discretion

volley *noun* BARRAGE, blast, burst, explosion, shower, hail, discharge, bombardment, salvo, fusillade, cannonade

voluble *adjective* TALKATIVE, garrulous, loquacious, forthcoming, articulate, fluent, glib, blessed with the gift of the gab
<< OPPOSITE reticent

volume *noun* 1 AMOUNT, quantity, level, body, total, measure, degree, mass, proportion, bulk, aggregate
2 CAPACITY, size, mass, extent, proportions, dimensions, bulk, measurements, magnitude, compass, largeness, cubic content
3 BOOK, work, title, opus, publication, manual, tome, treatise, almanac, compendium
4 LOUDNESS, sound, amplification
>> RELATED WORD *adjective* cubical

voluminous *adjective* 1 LARGE, big, full, massive, vast, ample, bulky, billowing, roomy, cavernous, capacious
<< OPPOSITE small
2 COPIOUS, extensive, prolific, abundant, plentiful, profuse
<< OPPOSITE scanty

voluntarily *adverb* WILLINGLY, freely, by choice, without being asked, without prompting, lief (*rare*), on your own initiative, of your own free will, off your own bat, of your own accord, of your own volition

voluntary *adjective* 1 INTENTIONAL, intended, deliberate, planned, studied, purposed, calculated, wilful, done on purpose
<< OPPOSITE unintentional
2 OPTIONAL, discretionary, up to the individual, open, unforced, unconstrained, unenforced, at your discretion, discretional, open to choice, uncompelled
<< OPPOSITE obligatory
3 UNPAID, volunteer, free, willing, honorary, gratuitous, pro bono (*Law*)

volunteer *verb* 1 OFFER, step forward, offer your services, propose, let yourself in for (*informal*), need no invitation, present your services, proffer your services, put yourself at someone's disposal
<< OPPOSITE refuse
2 SUGGEST, advance, put forward, venture, tender

voluptuous *adjective* 1 BUXOM, shapely, curvaceous, erotic, ample, enticing, provocative, seductive (*informal*), well-stacked (*Brit slang*), full-bosomed
2 SENSUAL, luxurious, self-indulgent, hedonistic, sybaritic, epicurean, licentious, bacchanalian, pleasure-loving
<< OPPOSITE abstemious

vomit *verb* 1 BE SICK, throw up (*informal*), spew, chuck (*Austral & NZ informal*), heave (*slang*), puke (*slang*), retch, barf (*US slang*), chunder (*slang, chiefly Austral*), belch forth, upchuck (*US slang*), do a technicolour yawn, toss your cookies (*US slang*)
2 *often with* **up** BRING UP, throw up, regurgitate, chuck (up) (*slang, chiefly US*), emit (*informal*), eject, puke (*slang*), disgorge, sick up (*informal*), spew out *or* up

voracious *adjective* 1 GLUTTONOUS, insatiable, ravenous, hungry, greedy, ravening, devouring
2 AVID, prodigious, insatiable, uncontrolled, rapacious, unquenchable
<< OPPOSITE moderate

vortex *noun* WHIRLPOOL, eddy, maelstrom, gyre, countercurrent

vote *noun* 1 POLL, election, ballot, referendum, popular vote, plebiscite, straw poll, show of hands
2 RIGHT TO VOTE, franchise, voting rights, suffrage, say, voice, enfranchisement

▷ *verb* 1 CAST YOUR VOTE, go to the polls, mark your ballot paper
2 JUDGE, declare, pronounce, decree, adjudge
▷▷ **vote someone in** ELECT, choose, select, appoint, return, pick, opt for, designate, decide on, settle on, fix on, plump for, put in power

voucher *noun* TICKET, token, coupon, pass, slip, chit, chitty (*Brit informal*), docket

vouch for *verb* 1 GUARANTEE, back, certify, answer for, swear to, stick up for (*informal*), stand witness, give assurance of, asseverate, go bail for
2 CONFIRM, support, affirm, attest to, assert, uphold

vow *noun* PROMISE, commitment, pledge, oath, profession, troth (*archaic*), avowal
▷ *verb* PROMISE, pledge, swear, commit, engage, affirm, avow, bind yourself, undertake solemnly

voyage *noun* JOURNEY, travels, trip, passage, expedition, crossing, sail, cruise, excursion
▷ *verb* TRAVEL, journey, tour, cruise, steam, take a trip, go on an expedition

vulgar *adjective* 1 TASTELESS, common, flashy, low, gross, nasty, gaudy, tawdry, cheap and nasty, common as muck
<< OPPOSITE tasteful
2 CRUDE, dirty, rude, low, blue, nasty, naughty, coarse, indecent, improper, suggestive, tasteless, risqué, off colour, ribald, indelicate, indecorous
3 UNCOUTH, boorish, unrefined, impolite, ill-bred, unmannerly
<< OPPOSITE refined
4 VERNACULAR, native, common, general, ordinary

vulgarity *noun* 1 TASTELESSNESS, bad taste, grossness, tawdriness, gaudiness, lack of refinement
<< OPPOSITE tastefulness
2 CRUDENESS, rudeness, coarseness, crudity, ribaldry, suggestiveness, indelicacy, indecorum
<< OPPOSITE decorum
3 COARSENESS, roughness, boorishness, rudeness, loutishness, oafishness, uncouthness
<< OPPOSITE refinement

vulnerable *adjective* 1 SUSCEPTIBLE, helpless, unprotected, defenceless, exposed, weak, sensitive, tender, unguarded, thin-skinned
<< OPPOSITE immune
2 (*Military*) EXPOSED, open, unprotected, defenceless, accessible, wide open, open to attack, assailable
<< OPPOSITE well-protected

Ww

wacky *adjective* UNUSUAL, odd, wild, strange, crazy, silly, weird, way-out (*informal*), eccentric, unpredictable, daft (*informal*), irrational, erratic, Bohemian, unconventional, far-out (*slang*), loony (*slang*), kinky (*informal*), off-the-wall (*slang*), unorthodox, nutty (*slang*), oddball, zany, goofy (*informal*), offbeat (*informal*), freaky (*slang*), outré, gonzo (*slang*), screwy (*informal*), wacko *or* whacko (*informal*), off the air (*Austral slang*)

wad *noun* **1** BUNDLE, roll, bankroll (*US & Canad*), pocketful
2 MASS, ball, lump, hunk, piece, block, plug, chunk

waddle *verb* SHUFFLE, shamble, totter, toddle, rock, stagger, sway, wobble

wade *verb* **1** PADDLE, splash, splash about, slop
2 WALK THROUGH, cross, ford, pass through, go across, travel across, make your way across
▷▷ **wade in** MOVE IN, pitch in, dive in (*informal*), set to work, advance, set to, get stuck in (*informal*), buckle down
▷▷ **wade into someone** LAUNCH YOURSELF AT, charge at, attack, rush, storm, tackle, go for, set about, strike at, assail, tear into (*informal*), fall upon, set upon, lay into (*informal*), light into (*informal*)
▷▷ **wade into something** GET INVOLVED IN, tackle, pitch in, interfere in, dive in, plunge in, get stuck into
▷▷ **wade through something** PLOUGH THROUGH, trawl through, labour at, work your way through, toil at, drudge at, peg away at

waffle *verb often followed by* **on** CHATTER, rabbit (on) (*Brit informal*), babble, drivel, prattle, jabber, gabble, rattle on, verbalize, blather, witter on (*informal*), blether, run off at the mouth (*slang*), prate, earbash (*Austral & NZ slang*)
▷ *noun* PRATTLE, nonsense, hot air (*informal*), twaddle, padding, prating, gibberish, jabber, verbiage, blather, wordiness, verbosity, prolixity, bunkum *or* buncombe (*chiefly US*), bizzo (*Austral slang*), bull's wool (*Austral & NZ slang*)

waft *verb* **1** DRIFT, float, be carried, be transported, coast, flow, stray, glide, be borne, be conveyed
2 TRANSPORT, bring, carry, bear, guide, conduct, transmit, convey
▷ *noun* CURRENT, breath, puff, whiff, draught, breeze

wag¹ *verb* **1** WAVE, shake, swing, waggle, stir, sway, flutter, waver, quiver, vibrate, wiggle, oscillate
2 WAGGLE, wave, shake, flourish, brandish, wobble, wiggle
3 SHAKE, bob, nod
▷ *noun* **1** WAVE, shake, swing, toss, sway, flutter, waver, quiver, vibration, wiggle, oscillation, waggle
2 NOD, bob, shake

wag² *noun* JOKER, comic, wit, comedian, clown, card (*informal*), kidder (*informal*), jester, dag (*NZ informal*), prankster, buffoon, trickster, humorist, joculator *or (fem.)* joculatrix

wage *noun often plural* PAYMENT, pay, earnings, remuneration, fee, reward, compensation, income, allowance, recompense, stipend, emolument
▷ *verb* ENGAGE IN, conduct, pursue, carry on, undertake, practise, prosecute, proceed with

wager *verb* BET, chance, risk, stake, lay, venture, put on, pledge, gamble, hazard, speculate, punt (*chiefly Brit*)
▷ *noun* BET, stake, pledge, gamble, risk, flutter (*Brit informal*), ante, punt (*chiefly Brit*), long shot

waggle *verb* WAG, wiggle, wave, shake, flutter, wobble, oscillate

waif *noun* STRAY, orphan, outcast, urchin, foundling

wail *verb* CRY, weep, grieve, lament, keen, greet (*Scot archaic*), howl, whine, deplore, bemoan, bawl, bewail, yowl, ululate
▷ *noun* CRY, moan, sob, howl, keening, lament, bawl, lamentation, yowl, ululation

wait *verb* **1** STAY, remain, stop, pause, rest,

delay, linger, hover, hang around (*informal*), dally, loiter, tarry
<< OPPOSITE go
2 STAND BY, delay, hold on (*informal*), hold back, wait in the wings, mark time, hang fire, bide your time, kick your heels, cool your heels
3 BE POSTPONED, be suspended, be delayed, be put off, be put back, be deferred, be put on hold (*informal*), be shelved, be tabled, be held over, be put on ice (*informal*), be put on the back burner (*informal*)
▷ *noun* DELAY, gap, pause, interval, stay, rest, halt, hold-up, lull, stoppage, hindrance, hiatus, entr'acte
▷▷ **wait for** *or* **on something** *or* **someone** AWAIT, expect, look forward to, hope for, anticipate, look for
▷▷ **wait on** *or* **upon someone** SERVE, tend to, look after, take care of, minister to, attend to, cater to
▷▷ **wait up** STAY AWAKE, stay up, keep vigil

waiter *noun* ATTENDANT, server, flunkey, steward, servant

waitress *noun* ATTENDANT, server, stewardess, servant

waive *verb* 1 GIVE UP, relinquish, renounce, forsake, drop, abandon, resign, yield, surrender, set aside, dispense with, cede, forgo
<< OPPOSITE claim
2 DISREGARD, ignore, discount, overlook, set aside, pass over, dispense with, brush aside, turn a blind eye to, forgo

waiver *noun* RENUNCIATION, surrender, remission, abdication, giving up, resignation, denial, setting aside, abandonment, disclaimer, disavowal, relinquishment, eschewal, abjuration

wake¹ *verb* 1 AWAKE, stir, awaken, come to, arise, get up, rouse, get out of bed, waken, bestir, rouse from sleep, bestir yourself
<< OPPOSITE fall asleep
2 AWAKEN, arouse, rouse, waken, rouse someone from sleep
3 EVOKE, recall, excite, renew, stimulate, revive, induce, arouse, call up, awaken, rouse, give rise to, conjure up, stir up, rekindle, summon up, reignite
▷ *noun* VIGIL, watch, funeral, deathwatch, tangi (NZ)
▷▷ **wake someone up** ACTIVATE, stimulate, enliven, galvanize, fire, excite, provoke, motivate, arouse, awaken, animate, rouse, mobilize, energize, kindle, switch someone on, stir someone up

> Both *wake* and its synonym *waken* can be used either with or without an object: *I woke/wakened my sister*, and also *I woke/wakened (up) at noon*. *Wake*, *wake up*, and occasionally *waken*, can also be used in a figurative sense, for example *seeing him again woke painful memories*; and *it's time he woke up to his responsibilities*. The verbs *awake* and *awaken* are more commonly used in the figurative than the literal sense, for example *he awoke to the danger he was in*

wake² *noun* SLIPSTREAM, wash, trail, backwash, train, track, waves, path
▷▷ **in the wake of** IN THE AFTERMATH OF, following, because of, as a result of, on account of, as a consequence of

waken *verb* 1 AWAKEN, wake, stir, wake up, stimulate, revive, awake, arouse, activate, animate, rouse, enliven, galvanize
2 WAKE UP, come to, get up, awake, awaken, be roused, come awake
<< OPPOSITE fall asleep
▷ see **wake**1

Wales *noun* CYMRU (*Welsh*), Cambria (*Latin*)

walk *verb* 1 STRIDE, wander, stroll, trudge, go, move, step, march, advance, pace, trek, hike, tread, ramble, tramp, promenade, amble, saunter, take a turn, traipse (*informal*), toddle, make your way, mosey (*informal*), plod on, perambulate, footslog
2 TRAVEL ON FOOT, go on foot, hoof it (*slang*), foot it, go by shanks's pony (*informal*)
3 ESCORT, take, see, show, partner, guide, conduct, accompany, shepherd, convoy, usher, chaperon
▷ *noun* 1 STROLL, hike, ramble, tramp, turn, march, constitutional, trek, outing, trudge, promenade, amble, saunter, traipse (*informal*), breath of air, perambulation
2 GAIT, manner of walking, step, bearing, pace, stride, carriage, tread
3 PATH, pathway, footpath, track, way, road, lane, trail, avenue, pavement, alley, aisle, sidewalk (*chiefly US*), walkway (*chiefly US*), promenade, towpath, esplanade, footway, berm (NZ)
▷▷ **walk of life** AREA, calling, business, line, course, trade, class, field, career, rank, employment, province, profession, occupation, arena, sphere, realm, domain, caste, vocation, line of work, métier
▷▷ **walk out** 1 LEAVE SUDDENLY, storm out, get up and go, flounce out, vote with your feet, make a sudden departure, take off (*informal*)
2 GO ON STRIKE, strike, revolt, mutiny, stop work, take industrial action, down tools, withdraw your labour
▷▷ **walk out on someone** ABANDON, leave, desert, strand, betray, chuck (*informal*), run away from, forsake, jilt, run out on (*informal*), throw over, leave high and dry, leave in the

lurch

walker *noun* HIKER, rambler, backpacker, wayfarer, footslogger, pedestrian

walkout *noun* STRIKE, protest, revolt, stoppage, industrial action

wall *noun* 1 PARTITION, divider, room divider, screen, panel, barrier, enclosure

2 BARRICADE, rampart, fortification, bulwark, blockade, embankment, parapet, palisade, stockade, breastwork

3 BARRIER, obstacle, barricade, obstruction, check, bar, block, fence, impediment, hindrance

▷▷ **drive someone up the wall** (*informal*) INFURIATE, madden, exasperate, get on your nerves (*informal*), anger, provoke, annoy, irritate, aggravate (*informal*), incense, enrage, gall, rile, drive you crazy (*informal*), nark (*Brit, Austral & NZ slang*), be like a red rag to a bull, make your blood boil, get your goat (*slang*), drive you insane, make your hackles rise, raise your hackles, send you off your head (*slang*), get your back up, make you see red (*informal*), put your back up, hack you off (*informal*)

▷▷ **go to the wall** (*informal*) FAIL, close down, go under, go out of business, fall, crash, collapse, fold (*informal*), be ruined, go bust (*informal*), go bankrupt, go broke (*informal*), go into receivership, become insolvent

>> RELATED WORD *adjective* mural

wallet *noun* PURSE, pocketbook, notecase, pouch, case, holder, money-bag

wallop (*informal*) *verb* 1 HIT, beat, strike, knock, belt (*informal*), deck (*slang*), bang, batter, bash (*informal*), pound, chin (*slang*), smack, thrash, thump, paste (*slang*), buffet, clout (*informal*), slug, whack, swipe, clobber (*slang*), pummel, tonk (*slang*), lambast(e), lay one on (*slang*), beat *or* knock seven bells out of (*informal*)

2 BEAT, defeat, slaughter, thrash, best, stuff (*slang*), worst, tank, hammer (*informal*), crush, overwhelm, lick (*informal*), paste (*slang*), rout, walk over (*informal*), trounce, clobber (*slang*), vanquish, run rings around (*informal*), wipe the floor with (*informal*), make mincemeat of, blow out of the water (*slang*), drub, beat hollow (*Brit informal*), defeat heavily *or* utterly

▷ *noun* BLOW, strike, punch, thump, belt (*informal*), bash, sock (*slang*), smack, clout (*informal*), slug, whack, swipe, thwack, haymaker (*slang*)

wallow *verb* 1 REVEL, indulge, relish, savour, delight, glory, thrive, bask, take pleasure, luxuriate, indulge yourself

<< OPPOSITE refrain from

2 ROLL ABOUT, lie, tumble, wade, slosh, welter, splash around

wan *adjective* 1 PALE, white, washed out, pasty, faded, bleached, ghastly, sickly, bloodless, colourless, pallid, anaemic, discoloured, ashen, sallow, whitish, cadaverous, waxen, like death warmed up (*informal*), wheyfaced

<< OPPOSITE glowing

2 DIM, weak, pale, faint, feeble

wand *noun* STICK, rod, cane, baton, stake, switch, birch, twig, sprig, withe, withy

wander *verb* ROAM, walk, drift, stroll, range, cruise, stray, ramble, prowl, meander, rove, straggle, traipse (*informal*), mooch around (*slang*), stravaig (*Scot & Northern English dialect*), knock about *or* around, peregrinate

▷ *noun* EXCURSION, turn, walk, stroll, cruise, ramble, meander, promenade, traipse (*informal*), mosey (*informal*), peregrination

▷▷ **wander off** STRAY, roam, go astray, lose your way, drift, depart, rove, straggle

▷▷ **wander off something** DEVIATE, diverge, veer, swerve, digress, go off at a tangent, go off course, lapse

wanderer *noun* TRAVELLER, rover, nomad, drifter, ranger, journeyer, gypsy, explorer, migrant, rolling stone, rambler, voyager, tripper, itinerant, globetrotter, vagrant, stroller, vagabond, wayfarer, bird of passage

wandering *adjective* ITINERANT, travelling, journeying, roving, drifting, homeless, strolling, voyaging, unsettled, roaming, rambling, nomadic, migratory, vagrant, peripatetic, vagabond, rootless, wayfaring

wane *verb* 1 DECLINE, flag, weaken, diminish, fall, fail, drop, sink, fade, decrease, dim, dwindle, wither, lessen, subside, ebb, wind down, die out, fade away, abate, draw to a close, atrophy, taper off

<< OPPOSITE grow

2 DIMINISH, decrease, dwindle

<< OPPOSITE wax

▷▷ **on the wane** DECLINING, dropping, fading, weakening, dwindling, withering, lessening, subsiding, ebbing, dying out, on the way out, on the decline, tapering off, obsolescent, on its last legs, at its lowest ebb

want *verb* 1 WISH FOR, desire, fancy, long for, crave, covet, hope for, yearn for, thirst for, hunger for, pine for, hanker after, set your heart on, feel a need for, have a yen for (*informal*), have a fancy for, eat your heart out over, would give your eyeteeth for

<< OPPOSITE have

2 NEED, demand, require, call for, have need of, stand in need of

3 SHOULD, need, must, ought

4 DESIRE, fancy, long for, crave, wish for, yearn for, thirst for, hanker after, burn for

5 LACK, need, require, be short of, miss, be deficient in, be without, fall short in

▷ *noun* 1 LACK, need, absence, shortage, deficiency, famine, default, shortfall,

inadequacy, scarcity, dearth, paucity, shortness, insufficiency, non-existence, scantiness
<< OPPOSITE abundance
2 POVERTY, need, hardship, privation, penury, destitution, neediness, hand-to-mouth existence, indigence, pauperism, pennilessness, distress
<< OPPOSITE wealth
3 WISH, will, need, demand, desire, requirement, fancy, yen (*informal*), longing, hunger, necessity, appetite, craving, yearning, thirst, whim, hankering

wanting *adjective* 1 DEFICIENT, poor, disappointing, inadequate, pathetic, inferior, insufficient, faulty, not good enough, defective, patchy, imperfect, sketchy, unsound, substandard, leaving much to be desired, not much cop (*Brit slang*), not up to par, not up to expectations, bodger *or* bodgie (*Austral slang*)
<< OPPOSITE adequate
2 LACKING, missing, absent, incomplete, needing, short, shy
<< OPPOSITE complete

wanton *adjective* 1 WILFUL, needless, senseless, unjustified, willed, evil, cruel, vicious, deliberate, arbitrary, malicious, wicked, purposeful, gratuitous, malevolent, spiteful, unprovoked, groundless, unjustifiable, uncalled-for, motiveless
<< OPPOSITE justified
2 PROMISCUOUS, immoral, shameless, licentious, fast, wild, abandoned, loose, dissipated, lewd, profligate, debauched, lustful, lecherous, dissolute, libertine, libidinous, of easy virtue, unchaste
<< OPPOSITE puritanical

war *noun* 1 CONFLICT, drive, attack, fighting, fight, operation, battle, movement, push, struggle, clash, combat, offensive, hostilities, hostility, warfare, expedition, crusade, strife, bloodshed, jihad, enmity, armed conflict
<< OPPOSITE peace
2 CAMPAIGN, drive, attack, operation, movement, push, mission, offensive, crusade
▷ *verb* FIGHT, battle, clash, wage war, campaign, struggle, combat, contend, go to war, do battle, make war, take up arms, bear arms, cross swords, conduct a war, engage in hostilities, carry on hostilities
<< OPPOSITE make peace
>> RELATED WORDS *adjectives* belligerent, martial

warble *verb* SING, trill, chirp, twitter, chirrup, make melody, pipe, quaver
▷ *noun* SONG, trill, quaver, twitter, call, cry, chirp, chirrup

ward *noun* 1 ROOM, department, unit, quarter, division, section, apartment, cubicle
2 DISTRICT, constituency, area, division, zone, parish, precinct
3 DEPENDANT, charge, pupil, minor, protégé
▷▷ **ward someone off** DRIVE OFF, resist, confront, fight off, block, oppose, thwart, hold off, repel, fend off, beat off, keep someone at bay, keep someone at arm's length
▷▷ **ward something off** 1 AVERT, turn away, fend off, stave off, avoid, block, frustrate, deflect, repel, forestall
2 PARRY, avert, deflect, fend off, avoid, block, repel, turn aside

warden *noun* 1 STEWARD, guardian, administrator, superintendent, caretaker, curator, warder, custodian, watchman, janitor
2 (*chiefly US & Canadian*) JAILER, prison officer, guard, screw (*slang*), keeper, captor, turnkey (*archaic*), gaoler
3 (*Brit*) GOVERNOR, head, leader, director, manager, chief, executive, boss (*informal*), commander, ruler, controller, overseer, baas (*S African*)
4 RANGER, keeper, guardian, protector, custodian, official

warder *or* **wardress** *noun* (*Chiefly Brit*) JAILER, guard, screw (*slang*), warden, prison officer, keeper, captor, custodian, turnkey (*archaic*), gaoler

wardrobe *noun* 1 CLOTHES CUPBOARD, cupboard, closet (*US*), clothes-press, cabinet
2 CLOTHES, outfit, apparel, clobber (*Brit slang*), attire, collection of clothes

warehouse *noun* STORE, depot, storehouse, repository, depository, stockroom

wares *plural noun* GOODS, produce, stock, products, stuff, commodities, merchandise, lines

warfare *noun* WAR, fighting, campaigning, battle, struggle, conflict, combat, hostilities, strife, bloodshed, jihad, armed struggle, discord, enmity, armed conflict, clash of arms, passage of arms
<< OPPOSITE peace

warily *adverb* 1 CAUTIOUSLY, carefully, discreetly, with care, tentatively, gingerly, guardedly, circumspectly, watchfully, vigilantly, cagily (*informal*), heedfully
<< OPPOSITE carelessly
2 SUSPICIOUSLY, uneasily, guardedly, sceptically, cagily (*informal*), distrustfully, mistrustfully, charily

wariness *noun* 1 CAUTION, care, attention, prudence, discretion, deliberation, foresight, vigilance, alertness, forethought, circumspection, mindfulness, watchfulness, carefulness, caginess (*informal*), heedfulness
<< OPPOSITE carelessness
2 SUSPICION, scepticism, distrust, mistrust

warlike *adjective* BELLIGERENT, military,

aggressive, hostile, martial, combative, unfriendly, antagonistic, pugnacious, argumentative, bloodthirsty, hawkish, bellicose, quarrelsome, militaristic, inimical, sabre-rattling, jingoistic, warmongering, aggers (*Austral slang*), biffo (*Austral slang*)
<< OPPOSITE peaceful

warm *adjective* 1 BALMY, mild, temperate, pleasant, fine, bright, sunny, agreeable, sultry, summery, moderately hot
<< OPPOSITE cool
2 COSY, snug, toasty (*informal*), comfortable, homely, comfy (*informal*)
3 MODERATELY HOT, heated
<< OPPOSITE cool
4 THERMAL, winter, thick, chunky, woolly
<< OPPOSITE cool
5 MELLOW, relaxing, pleasant, agreeable, restful
6 AFFABLE, kindly, friendly, affectionate, loving, happy, tender, pleasant, cheerful, hearty, good-humoured, amiable, amicable, cordial, sociable, genial, congenial, hospitable, approachable, amorous, good-natured, likable *or* likeable
<< OPPOSITE unfriendly
7 NEAR, close, hot, near to the truth
▷ *verb* WARM UP, heat, thaw (out), heat up
<< OPPOSITE cool down
▷▷ **warm something** *or* **someone up** 1 HEAT, thaw, heat up
2 ROUSE, stimulate, stir up, animate, interest, excite, provoke, turn on (*slang*), arouse, awaken, exhilarate, incite, whip up, galvanize, put some life into, get something *or* someone going, make something *or* someone enthusiastic

warm-hearted *adjective* KINDLY, loving, kind, warm, gentle, generous, tender, pleasant, mild, sympathetic, affectionate, compassionate, hearty, cordial, genial, affable, good-natured, kind-hearted, tender-hearted
<< OPPOSITE cold-hearted

warmth *noun* 1 HEAT, snugness, warmness, comfort, homeliness, hotness
<< OPPOSITE coolness
2 AFFECTION, feeling, love, goodwill, kindness, tenderness, friendliness, cheerfulness, amity, cordiality, affability, kindliness, heartiness, amorousness, hospitableness, fondness
<< OPPOSITE hostility

warn *verb* 1 NOTIFY, tell, remind, inform, alert, tip off, give notice, make someone aware, forewarn, apprise, give fair warning
2 ADVISE, urge, recommend, counsel, caution, commend, exhort, admonish, put someone on his *or* her guard

warning *noun* 1 CAUTION, information, advice, injunction, notification, caveat, word to the wise
2 NOTICE, notification, word, sign, threat, tip, signal, alarm, announcement, hint, alert, tip-off (*informal*)
3 OMEN, sign, forecast, indication, token, prediction, prophecy, premonition, foreboding, portent, presage, augury, foretoken, rahui (NZ)
4 REPRIMAND, talking-to (*informal*), caution, censure, counsel, carpeting (*Brit informal*), rebuke, reproach, scolding, berating, ticking-off (*informal*), chiding, dressing down (*informal*), telling-off (*informal*), admonition, upbraiding, reproof, remonstrance
▷ *adjective* CAUTIONARY, threatening, ominous, premonitory, admonitory, monitory, bodeful

warp *verb* 1 DISTORT, bend, twist, buckle, deform, disfigure, contort, misshape, malform
2 BECOME DISTORTED, bend, twist, contort, become deformed, become misshapen
3 PERVERT, twist, corrupt, degrade, deprave, debase, desecrate, debauch, lead astray
▷ *noun* TWIST, turn, bend, defect, flaw, distortion, deviation, quirk, imperfection, kink, contortion, deformation

warrant *verb* CALL FOR, demand, require, merit, rate, commission, earn, deserve, permit, sanction, excuse, justify, license, authorize, entail, necessitate, be worthy of, give grounds for
▷ *noun* AUTHORIZATION, permit, licence, permission, security, authority, commission, sanction, pledge, warranty, carte blanche

warranty *noun* GUARANTEE, promise, contract, bond, pledge, certificate, assurance, covenant

warring *adjective* HOSTILE, fighting, conflicting, opposed, contending, at war, embattled, belligerent, combatant, antagonistic, warlike, bellicose, ill-disposed

warrior *noun* SOLDIER, combatant, fighter, gladiator, champion, brave, trooper, military man, fighting man, man-at-arms

wary *adjective* 1 SUSPICIOUS, sceptical, mistrustful, suspecting, guarded, apprehensive, cagey (*informal*), leery (*slang*), distrustful, on your guard, chary, heedful
2 WATCHFUL, careful, alert, cautious, prudent, attentive, vigilant, circumspect, heedful
<< OPPOSITE careless

wash *verb* 1 CLEAN, scrub, sponge, rinse, scour, cleanse
2 LAUNDER, clean, wet, rinse, dry-clean, moisten
3 RINSE, clean, scrub, lather
4 BATHE, bath, shower, take a bath *or* shower, clean yourself, soak, sponge, douse, freshen up, lave (*archaic*), soap, scrub yourself down
5 LAP, break, dash, roll, flow, surge, splash,

slap, ripple, swish, splosh
6 MOVE, overcome, touch, upset, stir, disturb, perturb, surge through, tug at someone's heartstrings (*often facetious*)
7 (*informal*) (always used in negative constructions) BE PLAUSIBLE, stand up, hold up, pass muster, hold water, stick, carry weight, be convincing, bear scrutiny
▷ *noun* 1 LAUNDERING, cleaning, clean, cleansing
2 BATHE, bath, shower, dip, soak, scrub, shampoo, rinse, ablution
3 BACKWASH, slipstream, path, trail, train, track, waves, aftermath
4 SPLASH, roll, flow, sweep, surge, swell, rise and fall, ebb and flow, undulation
5 COAT, film, covering, layer, screen, coating, stain, overlay, suffusion
▷▷ **wash something away** ERODE, corrode, eat into, wear something away, eat something away
▷▷ **wash something** *or* **someone away** SWEEP AWAY, carry off, bear away

washed out *adjective* 1 PALE, light, flat, mat, muted, drab, lacklustre, watery, lustreless
2 WAN, drawn, pale, pinched, blanched, haggard, bloodless, colourless, pallid, anaemic, ashen, chalky, peaky, deathly pale
3 FADED, bleached, blanched, colourless, stonewashed
4 EXHAUSTED, drained, worn-out, tired-out, spent, drawn, done in (*informal*), all in (*slang*), fatigued, wiped out (*informal*), weary, knackered (*slang*), clapped out (*Austral & NZ informal*), dog-tired (*informal*), zonked (*slang*), dead on your feet (*informal*)
<< OPPOSITE lively

washout *noun* 1 FAILURE, disaster, disappointment, flop (*informal*), mess, fiasco, dud (*informal*), clunker (*informal*)
<< OPPOSITE success
2 LOSER, failure, incompetent, no-hoper

waste *verb* 1 SQUANDER, throw away, blow (*slang*), run through, lavish, misuse, dissipate, fritter away, frivol away (*informal*)
<< OPPOSITE save
2 *followed by* **away** WEAR OUT, wither, deplete, debilitate, drain, undermine, exhaust, disable, consume, gnaw, eat away, corrode, enfeeble, sap the strength of, emaciate
▷ *noun* 1 SQUANDERING, misuse, loss, expenditure, extravagance, frittering away, lost opportunity, dissipation, wastefulness, misapplication, prodigality, unthriftiness
<< OPPOSITE saving
2 RUBBISH, refuse, debris, sweepings, scrap, litter, garbage, trash, leftovers, offal, dross, dregs, leavings, offscourings
3 *usually plural* DESERT, wilds, wilderness, void, solitude, wasteland
▷ *adjective* 1 UNWANTED, useless, worthless, unused, leftover, superfluous, unusable, supernumerary
<< OPPOSITE necessary
2 UNCULTIVATED, wild, bare, barren, empty, devastated, dismal, dreary, desolate, unproductive, uninhabited
<< OPPOSITE cultivated
▷▷ **lay something waste** DEVASTATE, destroy, ruin, spoil, total (*slang*), sack, undo, trash (*slang*), ravage, raze, kennet (*Austral slang*), jeff (*Austral slang*), despoil, wreak havoc upon, depredate (*rare*)
▷▷ **waste away** DECLINE, dwindle, wither, perish, sink, fade, crumble, decay, wane, ebb, wear out, atrophy

Waste and *wastage* are to some extent interchangeable, but many people think that *wastage* should not be used to refer to loss resulting from human carelessness, inefficiency, etc.: *a waste* (not *a wastage*) *of time, money, effort*, etc

wasteful *adjective* EXTRAVAGANT, lavish, prodigal, profligate, ruinous, spendthrift, uneconomical, improvident, unthrifty, thriftless
<< OPPOSITE thrifty

wasteland *noun* WILDERNESS, waste, wild, desert, void

waster *noun* LAYABOUT, loser, good-for-nothing, shirker, piker (*Austral & NZ slang*), drone, loafer, skiver (*Brit slang*), idler, ne'er-do-well, wastrel, malingerer, bludger (*Austral & NZ informal*)

watch *verb* 1 LOOK AT, observe, regard, eye, see, mark, view, note, check, clock (*Brit slang*), stare at, contemplate, check out (*informal*), look on, gaze at, pay attention to, eyeball (*slang*), peer at, leer at, get a load of (*informal*), feast your eyes on, take a butcher's at (*Brit informal*), take a dekko at (*Brit slang*)
2 SPY ON, follow, track, monitor, keep an eye on, stake out, keep tabs on (*informal*), keep watch on, keep under observation, keep under surveillance
3 GUARD, keep, mind, protect, tend, look after, shelter, take care of, safeguard, superintend
▷ *noun* 1 WRISTWATCH, timepiece, pocket watch, clock, chronometer
2 GUARD, eye, attention, supervision, surveillance, notice, observation, inspection, vigil, lookout, vigilance
▷▷ **watch out for something** *or* **someone** KEEP A SHARP LOOKOUT FOR, look out for, be alert for, be on the alert for, keep your eyes open for, be on your guard for, be on (the) watch for, be vigilant for, keep a weather eye open for, be

watchful for, keep your eyes peeled *or* skinned for (*informal*)

▷▷ **watch out** *or* **watch it** *or* **watch yourself** BE CAREFUL, look out, be wary, be alert, be on the lookout, be vigilant, take heed, have a care, be on the alert, watch yourself, keep your eyes open, be watchful, be on your guard, mind out, be on (the) watch, keep a sharp lookout, keep a weather eye open, keep your eyes peeled *or* skinned (*informal*), pay attention

watchdog *noun* 1 GUARDIAN, monitor, inspector, protector, custodian, scrutineer

2 GUARD DOG

watchful *adjective* ALERT, attentive, vigilant, observant, guarded, suspicious, wary, on the lookout, circumspect, wide awake, on your toes, on your guard, on the watch, on the qui vive, heedful

<< OPPOSITE careless

watchman *noun* GUARD, security guard, security man, custodian, caretaker

watchword *noun* MOTTO, slogan, maxim, byword, rallying cry, battle cry, catch phrase, tag-line, catchword, catchcry (*Austral*)

water *noun* 1 LIQUID, aqua, Adam's ale *or* wine, H_2O, wai (NZ)

2 *often plural* SEA, main, waves, ocean, depths, briny

▷ *verb* 1 SPRINKLE, spray, soak, irrigate, damp, hose, dampen, drench, douse, moisten, souse, fertigate (*Austral*)

2 GET WET, cry, weep, become wet, exude water

▷▷ **hold water** BE SOUND, work, stand up, be convincing, hold up, make sense, be logical, ring true, be credible, pass the test, be plausible, be tenable, bear examination *or* scrutiny

▷▷ **water something down** 1 DILUTE, add water to, put water in, weaken, water, doctor, thin, adulterate

2 MODERATE, weaken, temper, curb, soften, qualify, tame, mute, play down, mitigate, tone down, downplay, adulterate, soft-pedal

>> RELATED WORDS *adjectives* aquatic, aqueous

>> RELATED WORD *combining form* hydro-

>> RELATED WORD *fear* hydrophobia

waterfall *noun* CASCADE, fall, cataract, chute, linn (*Scot*), force (*Northern English dialect*)

waterlogged *adjective* SOAKED, saturated, drenched, sodden, streaming, dripping, sopping, wet through, wringing wet, droukit *or* drookit (*Scot*)

watertight *adjective* 1 WATERPROOF, hermetically sealed, sealed, water-resistant, sound, coated, impermeable, weatherproof, water-repellent, damp-proof, rubberized

<< OPPOSITE leaky

2 FOOLPROOF, firm, sound, perfect, conclusive, flawless, undeniable, unassailable, airtight, indisputable, impregnable, irrefutable, unquestionable, incontrovertible

<< OPPOSITE weak

watery *adjective* 1 PALE, thin, weak, faint, feeble, washed-out, wan, colourless, anaemic, insipid, wishy-washy (*informal*)

2 DILUTED, thin, weak, dilute, watered-down, tasteless, runny, insipid, washy, adulterated, wishy-washy (*informal*), flavourless, waterish

<< OPPOSITE concentrated

3 WET, damp, moist, soggy, humid, marshy, squelchy

4 LIQUID, fluid, aqueous, hydrous

5 TEARFUL, moist, weepy, lachrymose (*formal*), tear-filled, rheumy

wave *verb* 1 SIGNAL, sign, gesture, gesticulate

2 GUIDE, point, direct, indicate, signal, motion, gesture, nod, beckon, point in the direction

3 BRANDISH, swing, flourish, wield, wag, move something to and fro, shake

4 FLUTTER, flap, stir, waver, shake, swing, sway, ripple, wag, quiver, undulate, oscillate, move to and fro

▷ *noun* 1 GESTURE, sign, signal, indication, gesticulation

2 RIPPLE, breaker, sea surf, swell, ridge, roller, comber, billow

3 OUTBREAK, trend, rash, upsurge, sweep, flood, tendency, surge, ground swell

4 STREAM, flood, surge, spate, current, movement, flow, rush, tide, torrent, deluge, upsurge

waver *verb* 1 HESITATE, dither (*chiefly Brit*), vacillate, be irresolute, falter, fluctuate, seesaw, blow hot and cold (*informal*), be indecisive, hum and haw, be unable to decide, shillyshally (*informal*), be unable to make up your mind, swither (*Scot*)

<< OPPOSITE be decisive

2 FLICKER, wave, shake, vary, reel, weave, sway, tremble, wobble, fluctuate, quiver, undulate, totter

wax *verb* 1 INCREASE, rise, grow, develop, mount, expand, swell, enlarge, fill out, magnify, get bigger, dilate, become larger

<< OPPOSITE wane

2 BECOME FULLER, become larger, enlarge, get bigger

way *noun* 1 METHOD, means, system, process, approach, practice, scheme, technique, manner, plan, procedure, mode, course of action

2 MANNER, style, fashion, mode

3 ASPECT, point, sense, detail, feature, particular, regard, respect, characteristic, facet

4 *often plural* CUSTOM, manner, habit,

idiosyncrasy, style, practice, nature, conduct, personality, characteristic, trait, usage, wont, tikanga (*NZ*)
5 ROUTE, direction, course, road, path
6 ACCESS, street, road, track, channel, route, path, lane, trail, avenue, highway, pathway, thoroughfare
7 JOURNEY, approach, advance, progress, passage
8 ROOM, opening, space, elbowroom
9 DISTANCE, length, stretch, journey, trail
10 (*informal*) CONDITION, state, shape (*informal*), situation, status, circumstances, plight, predicament, fettle
11 WILL, demand, wish, desire, choice, aim, pleasure, ambition
▷▷ **by the way** INCIDENTALLY, in passing, in parenthesis, en passant, by the bye
▷▷ **give way** 1 COLLAPSE, give, fall, crack, break down, subside, cave in, crumple, fall to pieces, go to pieces
2 CONCEDE, yield, back down, make concessions, accede, acquiesce, acknowledge defeat
▷▷ **give way to something** BE REPLACED BY, be succeeded by, be supplanted by
▷▷ **under way** IN PROGRESS, going, started, moving, begun, on the move, in motion, afoot, on the go (*informal*)
▷▷ **ways and means** CAPABILITY, methods, procedure, way, course, ability, resources, capacity, tools, wherewithal

way-out *adjective* OUTLANDISH, eccentric, unconventional, unorthodox, advanced, wild, crazy, bizarre, weird, progressive, experimental, avant-garde, far-out (*slang*), off-the-wall (*slang*), oddball (*informal*), offbeat, freaky (*slang*), outré, wacko *or* whacko (*informal*), off the air (*Austral slang*)

wayward *adjective* ERRATIC, unruly, wilful, unmanageable, disobedient, contrary, unpredictable, stubborn, perverse, rebellious, fickle, intractable, capricious, obstinate, headstrong, changeable, flighty, incorrigible, obdurate, ungovernable, self-willed, refractory, insubordinate, undependable, inconstant, mulish, cross-grained, contumacious, froward (*archaic*)
<< OPPOSITE obedient

weak *adjective* 1 FEEBLE, exhausted, frail, debilitated, spent, wasted, weakly, tender, delicate, faint, fragile, shaky, sickly, languid, puny, decrepit, unsteady, infirm, anaemic, effete, enervated
<< OPPOSITE strong
2 DEFICIENT, wanting, poor, lacking, inadequate, pathetic, faulty, substandard, under-strength
<< OPPOSITE effective
3 INEFFECTUAL, pathetic, cowardly, powerless, soft, impotent, indecisive, infirm, spineless, boneless, timorous, weak-kneed (*informal*), namby-pamby, irresolute
<< OPPOSITE firm
4 SLIGHT, faint, feeble, pathetic, shallow, hollow
5 FAINT, soft, quiet, slight, small, low, poor, distant, dull, muffled, imperceptible
<< OPPOSITE loud
6 FRAGILE, brittle, flimsy, unsound, fine, delicate, frail, dainty, breakable
7 UNSAFE, exposed, vulnerable, helpless, wide open, unprotected, untenable, defenceless, unguarded
<< OPPOSITE secure
8 UNCONVINCING, unsatisfactory, lame, invalid, flimsy, inconclusive, pathetic
<< OPPOSITE convincing
9 TASTELESS, thin, diluted, watery, runny, insipid, wishy-washy (*informal*), under-strength, milk-and-water, waterish
<< OPPOSITE strong

weaken *verb* 1 REDUCE, undermine, moderate, diminish, temper, impair, lessen, sap, mitigate, invalidate, soften up, take the edge off
<< OPPOSITE boost
2 WANE, fail, diminish, dwindle, lower, flag, fade, give way, lessen, abate, droop, ease up
<< OPPOSITE grow
3 SAP THE STRENGTH OF, tire, exhaust, debilitate, depress, disable, cripple, incapacitate, enfeeble, enervate
<< OPPOSITE strengthen

weakness *noun* 1 FRAILTY, fatigue, exhaustion, fragility, infirmity, debility, feebleness, faintness, decrepitude, enervation
<< OPPOSITE strength
2 LIKING, appetite, penchant, soft spot, passion, inclination, fondness, predilection, proclivity, partiality, proneness
<< OPPOSITE aversion
3 POWERLESSNESS, vulnerability, impotence, meekness, irresolution, spinelessness, ineffectuality, timorousness, cravenness, cowardliness
4 INADEQUACY, deficiency, transparency, lameness, hollowness, implausibility, flimsiness, unsoundness, tenuousness
5 FAILING, fault, defect, deficiency, flaw, shortcoming, blemish, imperfection, Achilles' heel, chink in your armour, lack
<< OPPOSITE strong point

wealth *noun* 1 RICHES, fortune, prosperity, affluence, goods, means, money, funds, property, cash, resources, substance, possessions, big money, big bucks (*informal, chiefly US*), opulence, megabucks (*US & Canad*

slang), lucre, pelf
<< OPPOSITE poverty
2 PROPERTY, funds, capital, estate, assets, fortune, possessions
3 ABUNDANCE, store, plenty, richness, bounty, profusion, fullness, cornucopia, plenitude, copiousness
<< OPPOSITE lack
>> RELATED WORD *like* plutomania

wealthy *adjective* RICH, prosperous, affluent, well-off, loaded (*slang*), comfortable, flush (*informal*), in the money (*informal*), opulent, well-heeled (*informal*), well-to-do, moneyed, quids in (*slang*), filthy rich, rolling in it (*slang*), on Easy Street (*informal*), stinking rich (*slang*), made of money (*informal*)
<< OPPOSITE poor

wear *verb* 1 BE DRESSED IN, have on, dress in, be clothed in, carry, sport (*informal*), bear, put on, clothe yourself in
2 SHOW, present, bear, display, assume, put on, exhibit
3 DETERIORATE, fray, wear thin, become threadbare
4 ACCEPT (*Brit informal*), take, allow, permit, stomach, swallow (*informal*), brook, stand for, fall for, put up with (*informal*), countenance
▷ *noun* 1 CLOTHES, things, dress, gear (*informal*), attire, habit, outfit, costume, threads (*slang*), garments, apparel, garb, raiments
2 USEFULNESS, use, service, employment, utility, mileage (*informal*)
3 DAMAGE, wear and tear, use, erosion, friction, deterioration, depreciation, attrition, corrosion, abrasion
<< OPPOSITE repair
▷▷ **wear down** BE ERODED, erode, be consumed, wear away
▷▷ **wear off** 1 SUBSIDE, disappear, fade, weaken, diminish, decrease, dwindle, wane, ebb, abate, peter out, lose strength, lose effect
2 RUB AWAY, disappear, fade, abrade
▷▷ **wear out** DETERIORATE, become worn, become useless, wear through, fray
▷▷ **wear someone down** UNDERMINE, reduce, chip away at (*informal*), fight a war of attrition against, overcome gradually
▷▷ **wear someone out** (*informal*) EXHAUST, tire, fatigue, weary, impair, sap, prostrate, knacker (*slang*), frazzle (*informal*), fag someone out (*informal*), enervate
▷▷ **wear something down** ERODE, grind down, consume, impair, corrode, grind down, rub away, abrade
▷▷ **wear something out** ERODE, go through, consume, use up, wear holes in, make worn

weariness *noun* TIREDNESS, fatigue, exhaustion, lethargy, drowsiness, lassitude, languor, listlessness, prostration, enervation
<< OPPOSITE energy

wearing *adjective* TIRESOME, trying, taxing, tiring, exhausting, fatiguing, oppressive, exasperating, irksome, wearisome
<< OPPOSITE refreshing

weary *adjective* 1 TIRED, exhausted, drained, worn out, spent, done in (*informal*), flagging, all in (*slang*), fatigued, wearied, sleepy, fagged (*informal*), whacked (*Brit informal*), jaded, drooping, knackered (*slang*), drowsy, clapped out (*Austral & NZ informal*), enervated, ready to drop, dog-tired (*informal*), zonked (*slang*), dead beat (*informal*), asleep *or* dead on your feet (*informal*)
<< OPPOSITE energetic
2 FED UP, bored, sick (*informal*), discontented, impatient, indifferent, jaded, sick and tired (*informal*), browned-off (*informal*)
<< OPPOSITE excited
3 TIRING, taxing, wearing, arduous, tiresome, laborious, irksome, wearisome, enervative
<< OPPOSITE refreshing
▷ *verb* 1 GROW TIRED, tire, sicken, have had enough, become bored
2 BORE, annoy, plague, sicken, jade, exasperate, vex, irk, try the patience of, make discontented
<< OPPOSITE excite
3 TIRE, tax, burden, drain, fatigue, fag (*informal*), sap, wear out, debilitate, take it out of (*informal*), tire out, enervate
<< OPPOSITE invigorate

weather *noun* CLIMATE, conditions, temperature, forecast, outlook, meteorological conditions, elements
▷ *verb* 1 TOUGHEN, season, wear, expose, harden
2 WITHSTAND, stand, suffer, survive, overcome, resist, brave, endure, come through, get through, rise above, live through, ride out, make it through (*informal*), surmount, pull through, stick it out (*informal*), bear up against
<< OPPOSITE surrender to
▷▷ **under the weather** ILL, unwell, poorly (*informal*), sick, rough (*informal*), crook (*Austral & NZ informal*), ailing, not well, seedy (*informal*), below par, queasy, out of sorts, nauseous, off-colour (*Brit*), indisposed, peaky, ropy (*Brit informal*), wabbit (*Scot informal*)

weave *verb* 1 KNIT, twist, intertwine, plait, unite, introduce, blend, incorporate, merge, mat, fuse, braid, entwine, intermingle, interlace
2 ZIGZAG, wind, move in and out, crisscross, weave your way
3 CREATE, tell, recount, narrate, make, build, relate, make up, spin, construct, invent, put together, unfold, contrive, fabricate

web *noun* 1 COBWEB, spider's web

2 MESH, net, netting, screen, webbing, weave, lattice, latticework, interlacing, lacework
3 TANGLE, series, network, mass, chain, knot, maze, toils, nexus

wed *verb* 1 GET MARRIED TO, espouse, get hitched to (*slang*), be united to, plight your troth to (*old-fashioned*), get spliced to (*informal*), take as your husband *or* wife
<< OPPOSITE divorce
2 GET MARRIED, marry, be united, tie the knot (*informal*), take the plunge (*informal*), get hitched (*slang*), get spliced (*informal*), become man and wife, plight your troth (*old-fashioned*)
<< OPPOSITE divorce
3 UNITE, combine, bring together, amalgamate, join, link, marry, ally, connect, blend, integrate, merge, unify, make one, fuse, weld, interweave, yoke, coalesce, commingle
<< OPPOSITE divide

wedding *noun* MARRIAGE, nuptials, wedding ceremony, marriage ceremony, marriage service, wedding service, nuptial rite, espousals

wedge *verb* SQUEEZE, force, lodge, jam, crowd, block, stuff, pack, thrust, ram, cram, stow
▷ *noun* BLOCK, segment, lump, chunk, triangle, slab, hunk, chock, wodge (*Brit informal*)

wedlock *noun* MARRIAGE, matrimony, holy matrimony, married state, conjugal bond

wee *adjective* LITTLE, small, minute, tiny, miniature, insignificant, negligible, microscopic, diminutive, minuscule, teeny, itsy-bitsy (*informal*), teeny-weeny, titchy (*Brit informal*), teensy-weensy, pygmy *or* pigmy

weedy *adjective* WEAK, thin, frail, skinny, feeble, ineffectual, puny, undersized, weak-kneed (*informal*), namby-pamby, nerdy *or* nurdy (*slang*)

weekly *adjective* ONCE A WEEK, hebdomadal, hebdomadary
▷ *adverb* EVERY WEEK, once a week, by the week, hebdomadally

weep *verb* CRY, shed tears, sob, whimper, complain, keen, greet (*Scot archaic*), moan, mourn, grieve, lament, whinge (*informal*), blubber, snivel, ululate, blub (*slang*), boohoo
<< OPPOSITE rejoice

weepy *adjective* TEARFUL, crying, weeping, sobbing, whimpering, close to tears, blubbering, lachrymose, on the verge of tears
▷ *noun* TEAR-JERKER (*informal*)

weigh *verb* 1 HAVE A WEIGHT OF, tip the scales at (*informal*)
2 MEASURE THE WEIGHT OF, put someone *or* something on the scales, measure how heavy someone *or* something is
3 CONSIDER, study, examine, contemplate, evaluate, ponder, mull over, think over, eye up, reflect upon, give thought to, meditate upon, deliberate upon
4 COMPARE, balance, contrast, juxtapose, place side by side
5 MATTER, carry weight, cut any ice (*informal*), impress, tell, count, have influence, be influential
▷▷ **weigh on someone** OPPRESS, burden, depress, distress, plague, prey, torment, hang over, bear down, gnaw at, cast down, take over
▷▷ **weigh someone down** 1 BURDEN, overload, encumber, overburden, tax, weight, strain, handicap, saddle, hamper
2 OPPRESS, worry, trouble, burden, depress, haunt, plague, get down, torment, take control of, hang over, beset, prey on, bear down, gnaw at, cast down, press down on, overburden, weigh upon, lie heavy on
▷▷ **weigh someone up** ASSESS, judge, gauge, appraise, eye someone up, size someone up (*informal*)
▷▷ **weigh something out** MEASURE, dole out, apportion, deal out

weight *noun* 1 HEAVINESS, mass, burden, poundage, pressure, load, gravity, tonnage, heft (*informal*), avoirdupois
2 LOAD, mass, ballast, heavy object
3 IMPORTANCE, force, power, moment, value, authority, influence, bottom, impact, import, muscle, consequence, substance, consideration, emphasis, significance, sway, clout (*informal*), leverage, efficacy, mana (*NZ*), persuasiveness
4 BURDEN, pressure, load, strain, oppression, albatross, millstone, encumbrance
5 PREPONDERANCE, mass, bulk, main body, most, majority, onus, lion's share, greatest force, main force, best *or* better part
▷ *verb* 1 *often with* **down** LOAD, ballast, make heavier
2 BIAS, load, slant, unbalance
3 BURDEN, handicap, oppress, impede, weigh down, encumber, overburden

weighty *adjective* 1 IMPORTANT, serious, significant, critical, crucial, considerable, substantial, grave, solemn, momentous, forcible, consequential, portentous
<< OPPOSITE unimportant
2 HEAVY, massive, dense, hefty (*informal*), cumbersome, ponderous, burdensome
3 ONEROUS, taxing, demanding, difficult, worrying, crushing, exacting, oppressive, burdensome, worrisome, backbreaking

weird *adjective* 1 STRANGE, odd, unusual, bizarre, ghostly, mysterious, queer, unearthly, eerie, grotesque, supernatural, unnatural, far-out (*slang*), uncanny, spooky (*informal*), creepy (*informal*), eldritch (*poetic*)
<< OPPOSITE normal
2 BIZARRE, odd, strange, unusual, queer, grotesque, unnatural, creepy (*informal*),

outlandish, freakish
<< OPPOSITE ordinary

weirdo *or* **weirdie** *noun* ECCENTRIC, nut (*slang*), freak (*informal*), crank (*informal*), loony (*slang*), nutter (*Brit slang*), oddball (*informal*), crackpot (*informal*), nutcase (*slang*), headcase (*informal*), headbanger (*informal*), queer fish (*Brit informal*)

welcome *verb* 1 GREET, meet, receive, embrace, hail, usher in, say hello to, roll out the red carpet for, offer hospitality to, receive with open arms, bid welcome, karanga (NZ), mihi (NZ)
<< OPPOSITE reject
2 ACCEPT GLADLY, appreciate, embrace, approve of, be pleased by, give the thumbs up to (*informal*), be glad about, express pleasure *or* satisfaction at
▷ *noun* GREETING, welcoming, entertainment, reception, acceptance, hail, hospitality, salutation
<< OPPOSITE rejection
▷ *adjective* 1 PLEASING, wanted, accepted, appreciated, acceptable, pleasant, desirable, refreshing, delightful, gratifying, agreeable, pleasurable, gladly received
<< OPPOSITE unpleasant
2 WANTED, at home, invited
<< OPPOSITE unwanted
3 FREE, invited

weld *verb* 1 JOIN, link, bond, bind, connect, cement, fuse, solder, braze
2 UNITE, combine, blend, consolidate, unify, fuse, meld
▷ *noun* JOINT, bond, seam, juncture

welfare *noun* 1 WELLBEING, good, interest, health, security, benefit, success, profit, safety, protection, fortune, comfort, happiness, prosperity, prosperousness
2 STATE BENEFIT, support, benefits, pensions, dole (*slang*), social security, unemployment benefit, state benefits, pogey (*Canad*)

well[1] *adverb* 1 SKILFULLY, expertly, adeptly, with skill, professionally, correctly, properly, effectively, efficiently, adequately, admirably, ably, conscientiously, proficiently
<< OPPOSITE badly
2 SATISFACTORILY, nicely, smoothly, successfully, capitally, pleasantly, happily, famously (*informal*), splendidly, agreeably, like nobody's business (*informal*), in a satisfactory manner
<< OPPOSITE badly
3 THOROUGHLY, completely, fully, carefully, effectively, efficiently, rigorously
4 INTIMATELY, closely, completely, deeply, fully, personally, profoundly
<< OPPOSITE slightly
5 CAREFULLY, closely, minutely, fully, comprehensively, accurately, in detail, in depth, extensively, meticulously, painstakingly, rigorously, scrupulously, assiduously, intensively, from top to bottom, methodically, attentively, conscientiously, exhaustively
6 FAVOURABLY, highly, kindly, warmly, enthusiastically, graciously, approvingly, admiringly, with admiration, appreciatively, with praise, glowingly, with approbation
<< OPPOSITE unfavourably
7 CONSIDERABLY, easily, very much, significantly, substantially, markedly
8 FULLY, highly, greatly, completely, amply, very much, thoroughly, considerably, sufficiently, substantially, heartily, abundantly
9 POSSIBLY, probably, certainly, reasonably, conceivably, justifiably
10 DECENTLY, right, kindly, fittingly, fairly, easily, correctly, properly, readily, politely, suitably, generously, justly, in all fairness, genially, civilly, hospitably
<< OPPOSITE unfairly
11 PROSPEROUSLY, comfortably, splendidly, in comfort, in (the lap of) luxury, flourishingly, without hardship
▷ *adjective* 1 HEALTHY, strong, sound, fit, blooming, robust, hale, hearty, in good health, alive and kicking, fighting fit (*informal*), in fine fettle, up to par, fit as a fiddle, able-bodied, in good condition
<< OPPOSITE ill
2 SATISFACTORY, good, right, fine, happy, fitting, pleasing, bright, useful, lucky, proper, thriving, flourishing, profitable, fortunate
<< OPPOSITE unsatisfactory
3 ADVISABLE, useful, proper, prudent, agreeable
<< OPPOSITE inadvisable
▷▷ **as well** ALSO, too, in addition, moreover, besides, to boot, into the bargain
▷▷ **as well as** INCLUDING, along with, in addition to, not to mention, at the same time as, over and above

well[2] *noun* 1 HOLE, bore, pit, shaft
2 WATERHOLE, source, spring, pool, fountain, fount
3 SOURCE, fund, mine, treasury, reservoir, storehouse, repository, fount, wellspring
▷ *verb* 1 FLOW, trickle, seep, run, issue, spring, pour, jet, burst, stream, surge, discharge, trickle, gush, ooze, seep, exude, spurt, spout
2 RISE, increase, grow, mount, surge, swell, intensify

well-balanced *adjective* 1 SENSIBLE, rational, level-headed, well-adjusted, together (*slang*), sound, reasonable, sober, sane, judicious
<< OPPOSITE unbalanced
2 WELL-PROPORTIONED, proportional, graceful,

harmonious, symmetrical

well-bred *adjective* 1 POLITE, ladylike, well-brought-up, well-mannered, cultured, civil, mannerly, polished, sophisticated, gentlemanly, refined, cultivated, courteous, gallant, genteel, urbane, courtly

<< OPPOSITE ill-bred

2 ARISTOCRATIC, gentle, noble, patrician, blue-blooded, well-born, highborn

well-groomed *adjective* SMART, trim, neat, tidy, spruce, well-dressed, dapper, well turned out, soigné *or* soignée

well-heeled *adjective* (*informal*) PROSPEROUS, rich, wealthy, affluent, loaded (*slang*), comfortable, flush (*informal*), well-off, in the money (*informal*), opulent, well-to-do, moneyed, well-situated, in clover (*informal*)

well-informed *adjective* EDUCATED, aware, informed, acquainted, knowledgeable *or* knowledgable, understanding, well-educated, in the know (*informal*), well-read, conversant, au fait (*French*), in the loop (*informal*), well-grounded, au courant (*French*), clued-up (*informal*), cognizant *or* cognisant, well-versed

well-known *adjective* 1 FAMOUS, important, celebrated, prominent, great, leading, noted, august, popular, familiar, distinguished, esteemed, acclaimed, notable, renowned, eminent, famed, illustrious, on the map, widely known

2 FAMILIAR, common, established, popular, everyday, widely known

well-mannered *adjective* POLITE, civil, mannerly, gentlemanly, gracious, respectful, courteous, genteel, well-bred, ladylike

well-nigh *adverb* ALMOST, nearly, virtually, practically, next to, all but, just about, more or less

well-off *adjective* 1 RICH, wealthy, comfortable, affluent, loaded (*slang*), flush (*informal*), prosperous, well-heeled (*informal*), well-to-do, moneyed

<< OPPOSITE poor

2 FORTUNATE, lucky, comfortable, thriving, flourishing, successful

well-to-do *adjective* RICH, wealthy, affluent, well-off, loaded (*slang*), comfortable, flush (*informal*), prosperous, well-heeled (*informal*), moneyed

<< OPPOSITE poor

well-worn *adjective* 1 STALE, tired, stereotyped, commonplace, banal, trite, hackneyed, overused, timeworn

2 SHABBY, worn, faded, ragged, frayed, worn-out, scruffy, tattered, tatty, threadbare

welter *noun* JUMBLE, confusion, muddle, hotchpotch, web, mess, tangle

wend ▷▷ **wend your way** GO, move, travel, progress, proceed, make for, direct your course

wet *adjective* 1 DAMP, soaked, soaking, dripping, saturated, moist, drenched, watery, soggy, sodden, waterlogged, moistened, dank, sopping, aqueous, wringing wet

<< OPPOSITE dry

2 RAINY, damp, drizzly, showery, raining, pouring, drizzling, misty, teeming, humid, dank, clammy

<< OPPOSITE sunny

3 (*informal*) FEEBLE, soft, weak, silly, foolish, ineffectual, weedy (*informal*), spineless, effete, boneless, timorous, namby-pamby, irresolute, wussy (*slang*), nerdy *or* nurdy (*slang*)

▷ *verb* MOISTEN, spray, damp, dampen, water, dip, splash, soak, steep, sprinkle, saturate, drench, douse, irrigate, humidify, fertigate (*Austral*)

<< OPPOSITE dry

▷ *noun* 1 RAIN, rains, damp, drizzle, wet weather, rainy season, rainy weather, damp weather

<< OPPOSITE fine weather

2 MOISTURE, water, liquid, damp, humidity, condensation, dampness, wetness, clamminess

<< OPPOSITE dryness

whack (*informal*) *verb* STRIKE, hit, beat, box, belt (*informal*), deck (*slang*), bang, rap, slap, bash (*informal*), sock (*slang*), chin (*slang*), smack, thrash, thump, buffet, clout (*informal*), slug, cuff, swipe, clobber (*slang*), wallop (*informal*), thwack, lambast(e), lay one on (*slang*), beat *or* knock seven bells out of (*informal*)

▷ *noun* 1 BLOW, hit, box, stroke, belt (*informal*), bang, rap, slap, bash (*informal*), sock (*slang*), smack, thump, buffet, clout (*informal*), slug, cuff, swipe, wallop (*informal*), wham, thwack

2 SHARE, part, cut (*informal*), bit, portion, quota, allotment

3 ATTEMPT, go (*informal*), try, turn, shot (*informal*), crack (*informal*), stab (*informal*), bash (*informal*)

whacking *adjective* (*informal*) HUGE, big, large, giant, enormous, extraordinary, tremendous, gigantic, great, monstrous, mammoth, whopping (*informal*), prodigious, elephantine, humongous *or* humungous (*US slang*)

whale *noun*

>> RELATED WORD *adjective* cetacean

>> RELATED WORD *male* bull

>> RELATED WORD *female* cow

>> RELATED WORD *young* calf

>> RELATED WORDS *collective nouns* school, gam, run

wharf *noun* DOCK, pier, berth, quay, jetty, landing stage

wheedle *verb* COAX, talk, court, draw, persuade, charm, worm, flatter, entice, cajole, inveigle

wheel *noun* DISC, ring, hoop

▷ *verb* 1 PUSH, trundle, roll
2 TURN, swing, spin, revolve, rotate, whirl, swivel
3 CIRCLE, orbit, go round, twirl, gyrate
▷▷ **at** *or* **behind the wheel** DRIVING, steering, in the driving seat, in the driver's seat

wheeze *verb* GASP, whistle, cough, hiss, rasp, catch your breath, breathe roughly
▷ *noun* 1 GASP, whistle, cough, hiss, rasp
2 (*Brit slang*) TRICK, plan, idea, scheme, stunt, ploy, expedient, ruse

whereabouts *plural noun* POSITION, situation, site, location

wherewithal *noun* RESOURCES, means, money, funds, capital, supplies, ready (*informal*), essentials, ready money

whet *verb* STIMULATE, increase, excite, stir, enhance, provoke, arouse, awaken, animate, rouse, quicken, incite, kindle, pique
<< OPPOSITE suppress

whiff *noun* 1 SMELL, hint, scent, sniff, aroma, odour, draught, niff (*Brit slang*)
2 (*Brit slang*) STINK, stench, reek, pong (*Brit informal*), niff (*Brit slang*), malodour, hum (*slang*)
3 TRACE, suggestion, hint, suspicion, bit, drop, note, breath, whisper, shred, crumb, tinge, jot, smidgen (*informal*), soupçon
4 PUFF, breath, flurry, waft, rush, blast, draught, gust
▷ *verb* (*Brit slang*) STINK, stench, reek, pong (*Brit informal*), niff (*Brit slang*), hum (*slang*)

whim *noun* IMPULSE, sudden notion, caprice, fancy, sport, urge, notion, humour, freak, craze, fad (*informal*), quirk, conceit, vagary, whimsy, passing thought, crotchet

whimper *verb* CRY, moan, sob, weep, whine, whinge (*informal*), grizzle (*informal, chiefly Brit*), blubber, snivel, blub (*slang*), mewl
▷ *noun* SOB, moan, whine, snivel

whimsical *adjective* FANCIFUL, odd, funny, unusual, fantastic, curious, weird, peculiar, eccentric, queer, flaky (*slang, chiefly US*), singular, quaint, playful, mischievous, capricious, droll, freakish, fantastical, crotchety, chimerical, waggish

whine *verb* 1 CRY, sob, wail, whimper, sniffle, snivel, moan
2 COMPLAIN, grumble, gripe (*informal*), whinge (*informal*), moan, cry, beef (*slang*), carp, sob, wail, grouse, whimper, bleat, grizzle (*informal, chiefly Brit*), grouch (*informal*), bellyache (*slang*), kvetch (*US slang*)
▷ *noun* 1 CRY, moan, sob, wail, whimper, plaintive cry
2 DRONE, note, hum
3 COMPLAINT, moan, grumble, grouse, gripe (*informal*), whinge (*informal*), grouch (*informal*), beef (*slang*)

whinge (*informal*) *verb* COMPLAIN, moan, grumble, grouse, gripe (*informal*), beef (*slang*), carp, bleat, grizzle (*informal, chiefly Brit*), grouch (*informal*), bellyache (*slang*), kvetch (*US slang*)
▷ *noun* COMPLAINT, moan, grumble, whine, grouse, gripe (*informal*), grouch, beef (*slang*)

whip *noun* LASH, cane, birch, switch, crop, scourge, thong, rawhide, riding crop, horsewhip, bullwhip, knout, cat-o'-nine-tails
▷ *verb* 1 LASH, cane, flog, beat, switch, leather, punish, strap, tan (*slang*), thrash, lick (*informal*), birch, scourge, spank, castigate, lambast(e), flagellate, give a hiding (*informal*)
2 (*informal*) DASH, shoot, fly, tear, rush, dive, dart, whisk, flit
3 WHISK, beat, mix vigorously, stir vigorously
4 INCITE, drive, push, urge, stir, spur, provoke, compel, hound, prod, work up, get going, agitate, prick, inflame, instigate, goad, foment
5 (*informal*) BEAT, thrash, trounce, wipe the floor with (*informal*), best, defeat, stuff (*slang*), worst, overcome, hammer (*informal*), overwhelm, conquer, lick (*informal*), rout, overpower, outdo, clobber (*slang*), take apart (*slang*), run rings around (*informal*), blow out of the water (*slang*), make mincemeat out of (*informal*), drub
▷▷ **whip someone up** ROUSE, excite, provoke, arouse, stir up, work up, agitate, inflame
▷▷ **whip something out** PULL OUT, produce, remove, jerk out, show, flash, seize, whisk out, snatch out

whipping *noun* BEATING, lashing, thrashing, caning, hiding (*informal*), punishment, tanning (*slang*), birching, flogging, spanking, the strap, flagellation, castigation, leathering

whirl *verb* 1 SPIN, turn, circle, wheel, twist, reel, rotate, pivot, twirl
2 ROTATE, roll, twist, revolve, swirl, twirl, gyrate, pirouette
3 FEEL DIZZY, swim, spin, reel, go round
▷ *noun* 1 REVOLUTION, turn, roll, circle, wheel, spin, twist, reel, swirl, rotation, twirl, pirouette, gyration, birl (*Scot*)
2 BUSTLE, round, series, succession, flurry, merry-go-round
3 CONFUSION, daze, dither (*chiefly Brit*), giddiness
4 TUMULT, spin, stir, agitation, commotion, hurly-burly
▷▷ **give something a whirl** (*informal*) ATTEMPT, try, have a go at (*informal*), have a crack at (*informal*), have a shot at (*informal*), have a stab at (*informal*), have a bash at, have a whack at (*informal*)

whirlwind *noun* 1 TORNADO, hurricane, cyclone, typhoon, twister (*US*), dust devil, waterspout
2 TURMOIL, chaos, swirl, mayhem, uproar,

maelstrom, welter, bedlam, tumult, hurly-burly, madhouse
▷ *modifier* RAPID, short, quick, swift, lightning, rash, speedy, hasty, impulsive, headlong, impetuous
<< OPPOSITE unhurried

whisk *verb* 1 RUSH, sweep, hurry
2 PULL, whip (*informal*), snatch, take
3 SPEED, race, shoot, fly, career, tear, rush, sweep, dash, hurry, barrel (along) (*informal, chiefly US & Canad*), sprint, dart, hasten, burn rubber (*informal*), go like the clappers (*Brit informal*), hightail it (*US informal*), wheech (*Scot informal*)
4 FLICK, whip, sweep, brush, wipe, twitch
5 BEAT, mix vigorously, stir vigorously, whip, fluff up
▷ *noun* 1 FLICK, sweep, brush, whip, wipe
2 BEATER, mixer, blender

whisky *noun* SCOTCH, malt, rye, bourbon, firewater, John Barleycorn, usquebaugh (*Gaelic*), barley-bree (*Scot*)

whisper *verb* 1 MURMUR, breathe, mutter, mumble, purr, speak in hushed tones, say softly, say sotto voce, utter under the breath
<< OPPOSITE shout
2 GOSSIP, hint, intimate, murmur, insinuate, spread rumours
3 RUSTLE, sigh, moan, murmur, hiss, swish, sough, susurrate (*literary*)
▷ *noun* 1 MURMUR, mutter, mumble, undertone, low voice, soft voice, hushed tone
2 (*informal*) RUMOUR, report, word, story, hint, buzz, gossip, dirt (*US slang*), goss (*informal*), innuendo, insinuation, scuttlebutt (*US slang*)
3 RUSTLE, sigh, sighing, murmur, hiss, swish, soughing, susurration *or* susurrus (*literary*)
4 HINT, shadow, suggestion, trace, breath, suspicion, fraction, tinge, whiff

whit *noun* BIT, drop, piece, trace, scrap, dash, grain, particle, fragment, atom, pinch, shred, crumb, mite, jot, speck, modicum, least bit, iota

white *adjective* 1 PALE, grey, ghastly, wan, pasty, bloodless, pallid, ashen, waxen, like death warmed up (*informal*), wheyfaced
2 (only used of *hair*) SILVER, grey, snowy, grizzled, hoary

white-collar *adjective* CLERICAL, office, executive, professional, salaried, nonmanual

whiten *verb* 1 PALE, blanch, go white, turn pale, blench, fade, etiolate
<< OPPOSITE darken
2 BLEACH, lighten
<< OPPOSITE darken

whitewash *verb* COVER UP, conceal, suppress, camouflage, make light of, gloss over, extenuate
<< OPPOSITE expose
▷ *noun* COVER-UP, deception, camouflage, concealment, extenuation

whittle *verb* CARVE, cut, hew, shape, trim, shave, pare
▷▷ **whittle something away** UNDERMINE, reduce, destroy, consume, erode, eat away, wear away, cut down, cut, decrease, prune, scale down

whole *noun* 1 TOTAL, all, lot, everything, aggregate, sum total, the entire amount
2 UNIT, body, piece, object, combination, unity, entity, ensemble, entirety, fullness, totality
<< OPPOSITE part
▷ *adjective* 1 COMPLETE, full, total, entire, integral, uncut, undivided, unabridged, unexpurgated, uncondensed
<< OPPOSITE partial
2 UNDAMAGED, intact, unscathed, unbroken, good, sound, perfect, mint, untouched, flawless, unhurt, faultless, unharmed, in one piece, uninjured, inviolate, unimpaired, unmutilated
<< OPPOSITE damaged
▷ *adverb* IN ONE PIECE, in one
▷▷ **on the whole** 1 ALL IN ALL, altogether, all things considered, by and large, taking everything into consideration
2 GENERALLY, in general, for the most part, as a rule, chiefly, mainly, mostly, principally, on average, predominantly, in the main, to a large extent, as a general rule, generally speaking

wholehearted *adjective* SINCERE, complete, committed, genuine, real, true, determined, earnest, warm, devoted, dedicated, enthusiastic, emphatic, hearty, heartfelt, zealous, unqualified, unstinting, unreserved, unfeigned
<< OPPOSITE half-hearted

wholesale *adjective* EXTENSIVE, total, mass, sweeping, broad, comprehensive, wide-ranging, blanket, outright, far-reaching, indiscriminate, all-inclusive
<< OPPOSITE limited
▷ *adverb* EXTENSIVELY, comprehensively, across the board, all at once, indiscriminately, without exception, on a large scale

wholesome *adjective* 1 MORAL, nice, clean, pure, decent, innocent, worthy, ethical, respectable, honourable, uplifting, righteous, exemplary, virtuous, apple-pie (*informal*), squeaky-clean, edifying
<< OPPOSITE corrupt
2 HEALTHY, good, strengthening, beneficial, nourishing, nutritious, sanitary, invigorating, salutary, hygienic, healthful, health-giving
<< OPPOSITE unhealthy

wholly *adverb* 1 COMPLETELY, totally, perfectly, fully, entirely, comprehensively, altogether, thoroughly, utterly, heart and soul, one

hundred per cent (*informal*), in every respect
<< OPPOSITE partly
2 SOLELY, only, exclusively, without exception, to the exclusion of everything else

whoop *verb* CRY, shout, scream, cheer, yell, shriek, hoot, holler (*informal*)
▷ *noun* CRY, shout, scream, cheer, yell, shriek, hoot, holler (*informal*), hurrah, halloo

whopper *noun* 1 BIG LIE, fabrication, falsehood, untruth, tall story (*informal*), fable
2 GIANT, monster, jumbo (*informal*), mammoth, colossus, leviathan, crackerjack (*informal*)

whopping *adjective* GIGANTIC, great, big, large, huge, giant, massive, enormous, extraordinary, tremendous, monstrous, whacking (*informal*), mammoth, prodigious, elephantine, humongous *or* humungous (*US slang*)

whore *noun* PROSTITUTE, hooker (*US slang*), tart (*informal*), streetwalker, tom (*Brit slang*), brass (*slang*), slag (*Brit slang*), hustler (*US & Canad slang*), call girl, courtesan, working girl (*facetious slang*), harlot, loose woman, fallen woman, scrubber (*Brit & Austral slang*), strumpet, trollop, lady of the night, cocotte, woman of easy virtue, demimondaine, woman of ill repute, fille de joie (*French*), demirep (*rare*)
▷ *verb* SLEEP AROUND, womanize, wanton (*informal*), wench (*archaic*), fornicate, lech *or* letch (*informal*)

whorl *noun* SWIRL, spiral, coil, twist, vortex, helix, corkscrew

wicked *adjective* 1 BAD, evil, corrupt, vile, guilty, abandoned, foul, vicious, worthless, shameful, immoral, scandalous, atrocious, sinful, heinous, depraved, debased, devilish, amoral, egregious, abominable, fiendish, villainous, unprincipled, nefarious, dissolute, iniquitous, irreligious, black-hearted, impious, unrighteous, maleficent, flagitious
<< OPPOSITE virtuous
2 MISCHIEVOUS, playful, impish, devilish, arch, teasing, naughty, cheeky, rascally, incorrigible, raffish, roguish, rakish, tricksy, puckish, waggish
<< OPPOSITE well-behaved
3 AGONIZING, terrible, acute, severe, intense, awful, painful, fierce, mighty, dreadful, fearful, gut-wrenching
4 HARMFUL, terrible, intense, mighty, crashing, dreadful, destructive, injurious
<< OPPOSITE harmless
5 (*Slang*) EXPERT, great (*informal*), strong, powerful, masterly, wonderful, outstanding, remarkable, ace (*informal*), first-class, marvellous, mighty, dazzling, skilful, A1 (*informal*), adept, deft, adroit

wide *adjective* 1 SPACIOUS, broad, extensive, ample, roomy, commodious
<< OPPOSITE confined
2 BAGGY, full, loose, ample, billowing, roomy, voluminous, capacious, oversize, generously cut
3 EXPANDED, dilated, fully open, distended
<< OPPOSITE shut
4 BROAD, comprehensive, extensive, wide-ranging, large, catholic, expanded, sweeping, vast, immense, ample, inclusive, expansive, exhaustive, encyclopedic, far-ranging, compendious
<< OPPOSITE restricted
5 EXTENSIVE, general, far-reaching, overarching
6 LARGE, broad, vast, immense
7 DISTANT, off, away, remote, off course, off target
▷ *adverb* 1 FULLY, completely, right out, as far as possible, to the furthest extent
<< OPPOSITE partly
2 OFF TARGET, nowhere near, astray, off course, off the mark

wide-eyed *adjective* 1 NAIVE, green, trusting, credulous, simple, innocent, impressionable, unsophisticated, ingenuous, wet behind the ears (*informal*), unsuspicious, as green as grass
2 STARING, spellbound, gobsmacked (*Brit slang*), dumbfounded, agog, agape, thunderstruck, goggle-eyed, awe-stricken

widen *verb* 1 BROADEN, expand, enlarge, dilate, spread, extend, stretch, open wide, open out *or* up
<< OPPOSITE narrow
2 GET WIDER, spread, extend, expand, broaden, open wide, open out *or* up
<< OPPOSITE narrow

wide open *adjective* 1 OUTSPREAD, spread, outstretched, splayed, fully open, fully extended, gaping
2 UNPROTECTED, open, exposed, vulnerable, at risk, in danger, susceptible, defenceless, in peril
3 UNCERTAIN, unsettled, unpredictable, up for grabs (*informal*), indeterminate, anybody's guess (*informal*)

widespread *adjective* COMMON, general, popular, sweeping, broad, extensive, universal, epidemic, wholesale, far-reaching, prevalent, rife, pervasive, far-flung
<< OPPOSITE limited

width *noun* BREADTH, extent, span, wideness, reach, range, measure, scope, diameter, compass, thickness, girth

wield *verb* 1 BRANDISH, flourish, manipulate, swing, use, manage, handle, employ, ply
2 EXERT, hold, maintain, exercise, have, control, manage, apply, command, possess, make use of, utilize, put to use, be possessed

of, have at your disposal

wife *noun* SPOUSE, woman (*informal*), partner, mate, bride, old woman (*informal*), old lady (*informal*), little woman (*informal*), significant other (*US informal*), better half (*humorous*), her indoors (*Brit slang*), helpmate, helpmeet, (the) missis *or* missus (*informal*), vrou (*S African*), wahine (NZ), wifey (*informal*)
>> RELATED WORD *adjective* uxorial

wiggle *verb* 1 JERK, shake, twitch, wag, jiggle, waggle
2 SQUIRM, twitch, writhe, shimmy
▷ *noun* JERK, shake, twitch, wag, squirm, writhe, jiggle, waggle, shimmy

wild *adjective* 1 UNTAMED, fierce, savage, ferocious, unbroken, feral, undomesticated, free, warrigal (*Austral literary*)
<< OPPOSITE tame
2 UNCULTIVATED, natural, native, indigenous
<< OPPOSITE cultivated
3 DESOLATE, empty, desert, deserted, virgin, lonely, uninhabited, godforsaken, uncultivated, uncivilized, trackless, unpopulated
<< OPPOSITE inhabited
4 STORMY, violent, rough, intense, raging, furious, howling, choppy, tempestuous, blustery
5 EXCITED, mad (*informal*), crazy (*informal*), eager, nuts (*slang*), enthusiastic, raving, frantic, daft (*informal*), frenzied, hysterical, avid, potty (*Brit informal*), delirious, agog
<< OPPOSITE unenthusiastic
6 UNCONTROLLED, violent, rough, disorderly, noisy, chaotic, turbulent, wayward, unruly, rowdy, boisterous, lawless, unfettered, unbridled, riotous, unrestrained, unmanageable, impetuous, undisciplined, ungovernable, self-willed, uproarious
<< OPPOSITE calm
7 MAD (*informal*), furious, fuming, infuriated, incensed, enraged, very angry, irate, livid (*informal*), in a rage, on the warpath (*informal*), hot under the collar (*informal*), beside yourself, tooshie (*Austral slang*), off the air (*Austral slang*)
8 OUTRAGEOUS, fantastic, foolish, rash, extravagant, reckless, preposterous, giddy, madcap, foolhardy, flighty, ill-considered, imprudent, impracticable
<< OPPOSITE practical
9 DISHEVELLED, disordered, untidy, unkempt, tousled, straggly, windblown, daggy (*Austral & NZ informal*)
10 PASSIONATE, mad (*informal*), ardent, fervent, zealous, fervid
11 UNCIVILIZED, fierce, savage, primitive, rude, ferocious, barbaric, brutish, barbarous
<< OPPOSITE civilized
▷▷ **the wilds** WILDERNESS, desert, wasteland, middle of nowhere (*informal*), backwoods, back of beyond (*informal*), uninhabited area
▷▷ **run wild** 1 GROW UNCHECKED, spread, ramble, straggle
2 GO ON THE RAMPAGE, stray, rampage, run riot, cut loose, run free, kick over the traces, be undisciplined, abandon all restraint

wilderness *noun* 1 WILDS, waste, desert, wasteland, uncultivated region
2 TANGLE, confusion, maze, muddle, clutter, jumble, welter, congeries, confused mass

wildlife *noun* FLORA AND FAUNA, animals, fauna

wile *noun* CUNNING, craft, fraud, cheating, guile, artifice, trickery, chicanery, craftiness, artfulness, slyness
▷ *plural noun* PLOYS, tricks, devices, lures, manoeuvres, dodges, ruses, artifices, subterfuges, stratagems, contrivances, impositions

wilful *or* **willful** *adjective* 1 INTENTIONAL, willed, intended, conscious, voluntary, deliberate, purposeful, volitional
<< OPPOSITE unintentional
2 OBSTINATE, dogged, determined, persistent, adamant, stubborn, perverse, uncompromising, intractable, inflexible, unyielding, intransigent, headstrong, obdurate, stiff-necked, self-willed, refractory, pig-headed, bull-headed, mulish, froward (*archaic*)
<< OPPOSITE obedient

will *noun* 1 DETERMINATION, drive, aim, purpose, commitment, resolution, resolve, intention, spine, backbone, tenacity, willpower, single-mindedness, doggedness, firmness of purpose
2 WISH, mind, desire, pleasure, intention, fancy, preference, inclination
3 CHOICE, decision, option, prerogative, volition
4 DECREE, wish, desire, command, dictate, ordinance
5 TESTAMENT, declaration, bequest(s), last wishes, last will and testament
▷ *verb* 1 DECREE, order, cause, effect, direct, determine, bid, intend, command, resolve, bring about, ordain
2 WISH, want, choose, prefer, desire, elect, opt, see fit
3 BEQUEATH, give, leave, transfer, gift, hand on, pass on, confer, hand down, settle on
▷▷ **at will** AS YOU PLEASE, at your discretion, as you think fit, at your pleasure, at your desire, at your whim, at your inclination, at your wish
>> RELATED WORDS *adjectives* voluntary, volitive

willing *adjective* 1 INCLINED, prepared, happy, pleased, content, in favour, consenting, disposed, favourable, agreeable, in the mood, compliant, amenable, desirous, so minded, nothing loath

<< OPPOSITE unwilling

2 READY, game (*informal*), eager, enthusiastic

<< OPPOSITE reluctant

willingly *adverb* READILY, freely, gladly, happily, eagerly, voluntarily, cheerfully, with pleasure, without hesitation, by choice, with all your heart, lief (*rare*), of your own free will, of your own accord

<< OPPOSITE unwillingly

willingness *noun* INCLINATION, will, agreement, wish, favour, desire, enthusiasm, consent, goodwill, disposition, volition, agreeableness

<< OPPOSITE reluctance

willowy *adjective* SLENDER, slim, graceful, supple, lithe, limber, svelte, lissom(e), sylphlike

willpower *noun* SELF-CONTROL, drive, resolution, resolve, determination, grit, self-discipline, single-mindedness, fixity of purpose, firmness of purpose *or* will, force *or* strength of will

<< OPPOSITE weakness

willy-nilly *adverb* 1 WHETHER YOU LIKE IT OR NOT, necessarily, of necessity, perforce, whether or no, whether desired or not, nolens volens (*Latin*)

2 HAPHAZARDLY, at random, randomly, without order, without method, without planning, any old how (*informal*)

wilt *verb* 1 DROOP, wither, sag, shrivel, become limp *or* flaccid

2 WEAKEN, sag, languish, droop

3 WANE, fail, sink, flag, fade, diminish, dwindle, wither, ebb, melt away, lose courage

wily *adjective* CUNNING, designing, scheming, sharp, intriguing, arch, tricky, crooked, shrewd, sly, astute, deceptive, crafty, artful, shifty, foxy, cagey (*informal*), deceitful, underhand, guileful, fly (*slang*)

<< OPPOSITE straightforward

wimp *noun* (*informal*) WEAKLING, wet (*Brit slang*), mouse, drip (*informal*), coward, jessie (*Scot slang*), pussy (*slang, chiefly US*), jellyfish (*informal*), sissy, doormat (*slang*), wuss (*slang*), milksop, softy *or* softie

win *verb* 1 BE VICTORIOUS IN, succeed in, prevail in, come first in, finish first in, be the victor in, gain victory in, achieve first place in

<< OPPOSITE lose

2 BE VICTORIOUS, succeed, triumph, overcome, prevail, conquer, come first, finish first, carry the day, sweep the board, take the prize, gain victory, achieve mastery, achieve first place, carry all before you

<< OPPOSITE lose

3 GAIN, get, receive, land, catch, achieve, net, earn, pick up, bag (*informal*), secure, collect, obtain, acquire, accomplish, attain, procure, come away with

<< OPPOSITE forfeit

▷ *noun* VICTORY, success, triumph, conquest

<< OPPOSITE defeat

▷▷ **win someone over** *or* **round** CONVINCE, influence, attract, persuade, convert, charm, sway, disarm, allure, prevail upon, bring *or* talk round

wince *verb* FLINCH, start, shrink, cringe, quail, recoil, cower, draw back, blench

▷ *noun* FLINCH, start, cringe

wind[1] *noun* 1 AIR, blast, breath, hurricane, breeze, draught, gust, zephyr, air-current, current of air

2 FLATULENCE, gas, flatus

3 BREATH, puff, respiration

4 NONSENSE, talk, boasting, hot air, babble, bluster, humbug, twaddle (*informal*), gab (*informal*), verbalizing, blather, codswallop (*informal*), eyewash (*informal*), idle talk, empty talk, bizzo (*Austral slang*), bull's wool (*Austral & NZ slang*)

▷▷ **get wind of something** HEAR ABOUT, learn of, find out about, become aware of, be told about, be informed of, be made aware of, hear tell of, have brought to your notice, hear on the grapevine (*informal*)

▷▷ **in the wind** IMMINENT, coming, near, approaching, on the way, looming, brewing, impending, on the cards (*informal*), in the offing, about to happen, close at hand

▷▷ **put the wind up someone** (*informal*) SCARE, alarm, frighten, panic, discourage, unnerve, scare off, frighten off

wind[2] *verb* 1 MEANDER, turn, bend, twist, curve, snake, ramble, twist and turn, deviate, zigzag

2 WRAP, twist, reel, curl, loop, coil, twine, furl, wreathe

3 COIL, curl, spiral, encircle, twine

▷▷ **wind down** 1 CALM DOWN, unwind, take it easy, unbutton (*informal*), put your feet up, de-stress (*informal*), outspan (*S African*), cool down *or* off

2 SUBSIDE, decline, diminish, come to an end, dwindle, tail off, taper off, slacken off

▷▷ **wind someone up** (*informal*) 1 IRRITATE, excite, anger, annoy, exasperate, nettle, work someone up, pique, make someone nervous, put someone on edge, make someone tense, hack you off (*informal*)

2 TEASE, kid (*informal*), have someone on (*informal*), annoy, rag (*informal*), rib (*informal*), josh (*informal*), vex, make fun of, take the mickey out of (*informal*), send someone up (*informal*), pull someone's leg (*informal*), jerk *or* yank someone's chain (*informal*)

▷▷ **wind something up** 1 END, finish, settle, conclude, tie up, wrap up, finalize, bring to a close, tie up the loose ends of (*informal*)
2 CLOSE DOWN, close, dissolve, terminate, liquidate, put something into liquidation
▷▷ **wind up** END UP, be left, find yourself, finish up, fetch up (*informal*), land up, end your days

winded *adjective* OUT OF BREATH, panting, puffed, breathless, gasping for breath, puffed out, out of puff, out of whack (*informal*)

windfall *noun* GODSEND, find, jackpot, bonanza, stroke of luck, manna from heaven, pot of gold at the end of the rainbow
<< OPPOSITE misfortune

winding *adjective* TWISTING, turning, bending, curving, crooked, spiral, indirect, roundabout, meandering, tortuous, convoluted, serpentine, sinuous, circuitous, twisty, anfractuous, flexuous
<< OPPOSITE straight

windy *adjective* BREEZY, wild, stormy, boisterous, blustering, windswept, tempestuous, blustery, gusty, inclement, squally, blowy
<< OPPOSITE calm

wing *noun* 1 ORGAN OF FLIGHT, pinion (*poetic*), pennon (*poetic*)
2 ANNEXE, part, side, section, extension, adjunct, ell (*US*)
3 FACTION, grouping, group, set, side, arm, section, camp, branch, circle, lobby, segment, caucus, clique, coterie, schism, cabal
▷ *verb* 1 FLY, soar, glide, take wing
2 HURRY, fly, race, speed, streak, zoom, hasten, hurtle
3 WOUND, hit, nick, clip, graze

wink *verb* 1 BLINK, bat, flutter, nictate, nictitate
2 TWINKLE, flash, shine, sparkle, gleam, shimmer, glimmer
▷ *noun* 1 BLINK, flutter, nictation, nictitation
2 TWINKLE, flash, sparkle, gleam, blink, glimmering, glimmer
▷▷ **wink at something** CONDONE, allow, ignore, overlook, tolerate, put up with (*informal*), disregard, turn a blind eye to, blink at, connive at, pretend not to notice, shut your eyes to

winner *noun* VICTOR, first, champion, master, champ (*informal*), conqueror, vanquisher, prizewinner, conquering hero
<< OPPOSITE loser

winning *adjective* 1 VICTORIOUS, first, top, successful, unbeaten, conquering, triumphant, undefeated, vanquishing, top-scoring, unvanquished
2 CHARMING, taking, pleasing, sweet, attractive, engaging, lovely, fascinating, fetching, delightful, cute, disarming, enchanting, endearing, captivating, amiable, alluring, bewitching, delectable, winsome, prepossessing, likable *or* likeable
<< OPPOSITE unpleasant
▷ *plural noun* SPOILS, profits, gains, prize, proceeds, takings, booty

winsome *adjective* CHARMING, taking, winning, pleasing, pretty, fair, sweet, attractive, engaging, fascinating, pleasant, fetching, cute, disarming, enchanting, endearing, captivating, agreeable, amiable, alluring, bewitching, delectable, comely, likable *or* likeable

wintry *adjective* 1 COLD, freezing, frozen, harsh, icy, chilly, snowy, frosty, hibernal
<< OPPOSITE warm
2 UNFRIENDLY, cold, cool, remote, distant, bleak, chilly, frigid, cheerless

wipe *verb* 1 CLEAN, dry, polish, brush, dust, rub, sponge, mop, swab
2 ERASE, remove, take off, get rid of, take away, rub off, efface, clean off, sponge off
▷ *noun* RUB, clean, polish, brush, lick, sponge, mop, swab
▷▷ **wipe something *or* someone out** DESTROY, eliminate, take out (*slang*), massacre, slaughter, erase, eradicate, blow away (*slang, chiefly US*), obliterate, liquidate (*informal*), annihilate, efface, exterminate, expunge, extirpate, wipe from the face of the earth (*informal*), kill to the last man, kennet (*Austral slang*), jeff (*Austral slang*)

wiry *adjective* 1 LEAN, strong, tough, thin, spare, skinny, stringy, sinewy
<< OPPOSITE flabby
2 STIFF, rough, coarse, curly, kinky, bristly

wisdom *noun* 1 UNDERSTANDING, learning, knowledge, intelligence, smarts (*slang, chiefly US*), judgment, insight, enlightenment, penetration, comprehension, foresight, erudition, discernment, sagacity, sound judgment, sapience
<< OPPOSITE foolishness
2 PRUDENCE, reason, circumspection, judiciousness
>> RELATED WORD *adjective* sagacious

wise *adjective* 1 SAGE, knowing, understanding, aware, informed, clever, intelligent, sensible, enlightened, shrewd, discerning, perceptive, well-informed, erudite, sagacious, sapient, clued-up (*informal*)
<< OPPOSITE foolish
2 SENSIBLE, sound, politic, informed, reasonable, clever, intelligent, rational, logical, shrewd, prudent, judicious, well-advised
<< OPPOSITE unwise

wisecrack *noun* JOKE, sally, gag (*informal*), quip, jibe, barb, jest, witticism, smart remark, pithy remark, sardonic remark

wish *noun* 1 DESIRE, liking, want, longing,

hope, urge, intention, fancy (*informal*), ambition, yen (*informal*), hunger, aspiration, craving, lust, yearning, inclination, itch (*informal*), thirst, whim, hankering
<< OPPOSITE aversion
2 REQUEST, will, want, order, demand, desire, command, bidding, behest (*literary*)
▷ *verb* 1 WANT, feel, choose, please, desire, think fit
2 REQUIRE, ask, order, direct, bid, desire, command, instruct
3 BID, greet with
▷▷ **wish for** DESIRE, want, need, hope for, long for, crave, covet, aspire to, yearn for, thirst for, hunger for, hanker for, sigh for, set your heart on, desiderate

wisp *noun* PIECE, twist, strand, thread, shred, snippet

wispy *adjective* 1 STRAGGLY, fine, thin, frail, wisplike
2 THIN, light, fine, delicate, fragile, flimsy, ethereal, insubstantial, gossamer, diaphanous, wisplike

wistful *adjective* MELANCHOLY, longing, dreaming, sad, musing, yearning, thoughtful, reflective, dreamy, forlorn, mournful, contemplative, meditative, pensive, disconsolate

wit *noun* 1 HUMOUR, fun, quips, banter, puns, pleasantry, repartee, wordplay, levity, witticisms, badinage, jocularity, facetiousness, drollery, raillery, waggishness, wittiness
<< OPPOSITE seriousness
2 HUMORIST, card (*informal*), comedian, wag, joker, dag (*NZ informal*), punster, epigrammatist
3 CLEVERNESS, mind, reason, understanding, sense, brains, smarts (*slang, chiefly US*), judgment, perception, wisdom, insight, common sense, intellect, comprehension, ingenuity, acumen, nous (*Brit slang*), discernment, practical intelligence
<< OPPOSITE stupidity

witch *noun* ENCHANTRESS, magician, hag, crone, occultist, sorceress, Wiccan, necromancer

witchcraft *noun* MAGIC, spell, witching, voodoo, the occult, wizardry, black magic, enchantment, occultism, sorcery, incantation, Wicca, the black art, witchery, necromancy, sortilege, makutu (*NZ*)

withdraw *verb* 1 REMOVE, pull, take off, pull out, extract, take away, pull back, draw out, draw back
2 TAKE OUT, extract, draw out
3 RETREAT, go, leave (*informal*), retire, depart, pull out, fall back, pull back, back out, back off, cop out (*slang*), disengage from
<< OPPOSITE advance
4 GO, leave, retire, retreat, depart, make yourself scarce, absent yourself
5 PULL OUT, leave, drop out, secede, disengage, detach yourself, absent yourself
6 RETRACT, recall, take back, revoke, rescind, disavow, recant, disclaim, abjure, unsay

withdrawal *noun* 1 REMOVAL, ending, stopping, taking away, abolition, elimination, cancellation, termination, extraction, discontinuation
2 EXIT, retirement, departure, pull-out, retreat, exodus, evacuation, disengagement
3 DEPARTURE, retirement, exit, secession
4 RETRACTION, recall, disclaimer, repudiation, revocation, disavowal, recantation, rescission, abjuration

withdrawn *adjective* UNCOMMUNICATIVE, reserved, retiring, quiet, silent, distant, shy, shrinking, detached, aloof, taciturn, introverted, timorous, unforthcoming
<< OPPOSITE outgoing

wither *verb* 1 WILT, dry, decline, shrink, decay, disintegrate, perish, languish, droop, shrivel, desiccate
<< OPPOSITE flourish
2 WASTE, decline, shrink, shrivel, atrophy
3 FADE, decline, wane, perish
<< OPPOSITE increase
4 HUMILIATE, blast, shame, put down, snub, mortify, abash

withering *adjective* SCORNFUL, blasting, devastating, humiliating, snubbing, blighting, hurtful, mortifying

withhold *verb* 1 KEEP SECRET, keep, refuse, hide, reserve, retain, sit on (*informal*), conceal, suppress, hold back, keep back
<< OPPOSITE reveal
2 HOLD BACK, check, resist, suppress, restrain, repress, keep back
<< OPPOSITE release

withstand *verb* RESIST, take, face, suffer, bear, weather, oppose, take on, cope with, brave, confront, combat, endure, defy, tolerate, put up with (*informal*), thwart, stand up to, hold off, grapple with, hold out against, stand firm against
<< OPPOSITE give in to

witless *adjective* FOOLISH, crazy, stupid, silly, dull, daft (*informal*), senseless, goofy (*informal*), idiotic, dozy (*Brit informal*), inane, loopy (*informal*), crackpot (*informal*), moronic, obtuse, unintelligent, empty-headed, asinine, imbecilic, braindead (*informal*), dumb-ass (*slang*), halfwitted, rattlebrained (*slang*)

witness *noun* 1 OBSERVER, viewer, spectator, looker-on, watcher, onlooker, eyewitness, bystander, beholder
2 TESTIFIER, deponent, attestant

▷ *verb* 1 SEE, mark, view, watch, note, notice, attend, observe, perceive, look on, be present at, behold (*archaic* or *literary*)
2 COUNTERSIGN, sign, endorse, validate
▷▷ **bear witness** 1 CONFIRM, show, prove, demonstrate, bear out, testify to, be evidence of, corroborate, attest to, be proof of, vouch for, evince, betoken, be a monument to, constitute proof of
2 GIVE EVIDENCE, testify, depose, give testimony, depone
>> RELATED WORD *adjective* testimonial

witter *verb* CHATTER, chat, rabbit (on) (*Brit informal*), babble, waffle (*informal, chiefly Brit*), cackle, twaddle, clack, burble, gab (*informal*), prattle, tattle, jabber, blab, gabble, blather, blether, prate, earbash (*Austral & NZ slang*)

witty *adjective* HUMOROUS, gay, original, brilliant, funny, clever, amusing, lively, sparkling, ingenious, fanciful, whimsical, droll, piquant, facetious, jocular, epigrammatic, waggish
<< OPPOSITE dull

wizard *noun* 1 MAGICIAN, witch, shaman, sorcerer, occultist, magus, conjuror, warlock, mage (*archaic*), enchanter, necromancer, thaumaturge (*rare*), tohunga (*NZ*)
2 GENIUS, star, expert, master, ace (*informal*), guru, buff (*informal*), adept, whizz (*informal*), prodigy, maestro, virtuoso, hotshot (*informal*), rocket scientist (*informal, chiefly US*), wiz (*informal*), whizz kid (*informal*), wonk (*informal*), maven (*US*), fundi (*S African*), up-and-comer (*informal*)

wizardry *noun* 1 EXPERTISE, skill, know-how (*informal*), craft, mastery, cleverness, expertness
2 MAGIC, witching, witchcraft, voodoo, enchantment, occultism, sorcery, the black art, witchery, necromancy, conjuration, sortilege

wizened *adjective* WRINKLED, lined, worn, withered, dried up, shrivelled, gnarled, shrunken, sere (*archaic*)
<< OPPOSITE rounded

wobble *verb* 1 SHAKE, rock, sway, tremble, quake, waver, teeter, totter, seesaw
2 TREMBLE, shake, vibrate
3 HESITATE, waver, fluctuate, dither (*chiefly Brit*), be undecided, vacillate, shillyshally (*informal*), be unable to make up your mind, swither (*Scot*)
▷ *noun* 1 UNSTEADINESS, shake, tremble, quaking
2 SHAKE, unsteadiness, tremor, vibration

wobbly *adjective* 1 UNSTABLE, shaky, unsafe, uneven, teetering, unbalanced, tottering, rickety, unsteady, wonky (*Brit slang*)
2 UNSTEADY, weak, unstable, shaky, quivery, all of a quiver (*informal*)
3 SHAKY, unsteady, tremulous

woe *noun* 1 MISERY, suffering, trouble, pain, disaster, depression, distress, grief, agony, gloom, sadness, hardship, sorrow, anguish, misfortune, unhappiness, heartache, heartbreak, adversity, dejection, wretchedness
<< OPPOSITE happiness
2 PROBLEM, trouble, trial, burden, grief, misery, curse, hardship, sorrow, misfortune, heartache, heartbreak, affliction, tribulation

woeful *adjective* 1 WRETCHED, sad, unhappy, tragic, miserable, gloomy, grieving, dismal, pathetic, afflicted, pitiful, anguished, agonized, disconsolate, doleful, pitiable
<< OPPOSITE happy
2 SAD, distressing, tragic, miserable, gloomy, dismal, pathetic, harrowing, heartbreaking, grievous, mournful, plaintive, heart-rending, sorrowful, doleful, piteous
<< OPPOSITE happy
3 PITIFUL, mean, bad, poor, shocking, sorry, disappointing, terrible, awful, appalling, disastrous, inadequate, dreadful, miserable, hopeless, rotten (*informal*), pathetic, catastrophic, duff (*Brit informal*), feeble, disgraceful, lousy (*slang*), grievous, paltry, deplorable, abysmal, lamentable, calamitous, wretched, pitiable, godawful (*slang*), not much cop (*Brit slang*)

wolf *verb often with* **down** DEVOUR, stuff, bolt, cram, scoff (*slang*), gulp, gobble, pack away (*informal*), gorge on, gollop
<< OPPOSITE nibble
▷ *noun* (*informal*) WOMANIZER, seducer, Don Juan, Casanova, philanderer, Lothario, lecher, lady-killer, lech *or* letch (*informal*)
>> RELATED WORD *adjective* lupine
>> RELATED WORD *female* bitch
>> RELATED WORDS *young* cub, whelp
>> RELATED WORDS *collective nouns* pack, rout, herd

woman *noun* 1 LADY, girl, miss, female, bird (*slang*), dame (*slang*), ho (*US derogatory slang*), sheila (*Austral & NZ informal*), vrou (*S African*), maiden (*archaic*), chick (*slang*), maid (*archaic*), gal (*slang*), lass, lassie (*informal*), wench (*facetious*), adult female, she, charlie (*Austral slang*), chook (*Austral slang*), wahine (*NZ*)
<< OPPOSITE man
2 (*informal*) GIRLFRIEND, girl, wife, partner, mate, lover, bride, mistress, spouse, old lady (*informal*), sweetheart, significant other (*US informal*), ladylove, wifey (*informal*)
3 MAID, domestic, char (*informal*), housekeeper, lady-in-waiting, chambermaid, handmaiden, charwoman, maidservant, female servant
>> RELATED WORDS *combining forms* gyn(o)-, gynaeco-

womanly *adjective* 1 FEMININE, motherly, female, warm, tender, matronly, ladylike

2 CURVACEOUS, ample, voluptuous, shapely, curvy (*informal*), busty (*informal*), buxom, full-figured, Rubenesque, Junoesque

wonder *verb* 1 THINK, question, doubt, puzzle, speculate, query, ponder, inquire, ask yourself, meditate, be curious, conjecture, be inquisitive

2 BE AMAZED, stare, marvel, be astonished, gape, boggle, be awed, be flabbergasted (*informal*), gawk, be dumbstruck, stand amazed

▷ *noun* 1 AMAZEMENT, surprise, curiosity, admiration, awe, fascination, astonishment, bewilderment, wonderment, stupefaction

2 PHENOMENON, sight, miracle, spectacle, curiosity, marvel, prodigy, rarity, portent, wonderment, nonpareil

wonderful *adjective* 1 EXCELLENT, mean (*slang*), great (*informal*), topping (*Brit slang*), brilliant, cracking (*Brit informal*), outstanding, smashing (*informal*), superb, fantastic (*informal*), tremendous, ace (*informal*), magnificent, fabulous (*informal*), marvellous, terrific, sensational (*informal*), sovereign, awesome (*slang*), admirable, super (*informal*), brill (*informal*), stupendous, out of this world (*informal*), tiptop, bodacious (*slang, chiefly US*), boffo (*slang*), jim-dandy (*slang*), chillin' (*US slang*), booshit (*Austral slang*), exo (*Austral slang*), sik (*Austral slang*), rad (*informal*), phat (*slang*), schmick (*Austral informal*)

<< OPPOSITE terrible

2 REMARKABLE, surprising, odd, strange, amazing, extraordinary, fantastic, incredible, astonishing, staggering, marvellous, startling, peculiar, awesome, phenomenal, astounding, miraculous, unheard-of, wondrous (*archaic* or *literary*), awe-inspiring, jaw-dropping

<< OPPOSITE ordinary

wonky *adjective* 1 ASKEW, squint (*informal*), awry, out of alignment, skewwhiff (*Brit informal*)

2 SHAKY, weak, wobbly, unsteady, infirm

wont *adjective* ACCUSTOMED, used, given, in the habit of

▷ *noun* HABIT, use, way, rule, practice, custom

woo *verb* 1 SEEK, cultivate, try to attract, curry favour with, seek to win, solicit the goodwill of

2 COURT, chase, pursue, spark (*rare*), importune, seek to win, pay court to, seek the hand of, set your cap at (*old-fashioned*), pay your addresses to, pay suit to, press your suit with

wood *noun* 1 TIMBER, planks, planking, lumber (*US*)

2 Also woods WOODLAND, trees, forest, grove, hurst (*archaic*), thicket, copse, coppice, bushland

3 FIREWOOD, fuel, logs, kindling

▷▷ **out of the wood(s)** (usually used in a negative construction) SAFE, clear, secure, in the clear, out of danger, home and dry (*Brit slang*), safe and sound

>> RELATED WORDS *adjectives* ligneous, sylvan

wooded *adjective* TREE-COVERED, forested, timbered, woody, sylvan (*poetic*), tree-clad

wooden *adjective* 1 MADE OF WOOD, timber, woody, of wood, ligneous

2 AWKWARD, stiff, rigid, clumsy, lifeless, stilted, ungainly, gauche, gawky, inelegant, graceless, maladroit

<< OPPOSITE graceful

3 EXPRESSIONLESS, empty, dull, blank, vacant, lifeless, deadpan, colourless, glassy, unresponsive, unemotional, emotionless, spiritless

wool *noun* 1 FLEECE, hair, coat

2 YARN

▷▷ **pull the wool over someone's eyes** DECEIVE, kid (*informal*), trick, fool, take in (*informal*), con (*slang*), dupe, delude, bamboozle (*informal*), hoodwink, put one over on (*slang*), pull a fast one on someone (*informal*), lead someone up the garden path (*informal*)

woolly *or (sometimes) US* **wooly** *adjective*

1 WOOLLEN, fleecy, made of wool

2 VAGUE, confused, clouded, blurred, unclear, muddled, fuzzy, indefinite, hazy, foggy, nebulous, ill-defined, indistinct

<< OPPOSITE precise

3 DOWNY, hairy, shaggy, flocculent

▷ *noun* SWEATER, jersey, jumper, pullover

word *noun* 1 TERM, name, expression, designation, appellation (*formal*), locution, vocable

2 CHAT, tête-à-tête, talk, discussion, consultation, chitchat, brief conversation, colloquy, confabulation, confab (*informal*), heart-to-heart, powwow (*informal*)

3 COMMENT, remark, expression, declaration, utterance, brief statement

4 MESSAGE, news, latest (*informal*), report, information, account, notice, advice, communication, intelligence, bulletin, dispatch, gen (*Brit informal*), communiqué, intimation, tidings

5 PROMISE, guarantee, pledge, undertaking, vow, assurance, oath, parole, word of honour, solemn oath, solemn word

6 COMMAND, will, order, go-ahead (*informal*), decree, bidding, mandate, commandment, edict, ukase (*rare*)

▷ *verb* EXPRESS, say, state, put, phrase, utter, couch, formulate

▷▷ **in a word** BRIEFLY, in short, in a nutshell, to sum up, succinctly, concisely, not to put too fine a point on it, to put it briefly

▷▷ **the last word** 1 FINAL SAY, ultimatum

2 SUMMATION, finis
▷▷ **the last word in something** EPITOME, newest, best, latest, crown, cream, rage, ultimate, vogue, perfection, mother of all (*informal*), quintessence, crème de la crème (*French*), ne plus ultra (*French*), dernier cri (*French*)
>> RELATED WORDS *adjectives* lexical, verbal

wording *noun* PHRASEOLOGY, words, language, phrasing, terminology, choice of words, mode of expression

wordy *adjective* LONG-WINDED, rambling, windy, diffuse, garrulous, discursive, loquacious, verbose, prolix, pleonastic (*rare*)
<< OPPOSITE brief

work *verb* 1 BE EMPLOYED, do business, have a job, earn a living, be in work, hold down a job
2 LABOUR, sweat, slave, toil, slog (away), drudge, peg away, exert yourself, break your back
<< OPPOSITE relax
3 FUNCTION, go, run, operate, perform, be in working order
<< OPPOSITE be out of order
4 SUCCEED, work out, pay off (*informal*), be successful, be effective, do the trick (*informal*), do the business (*informal*), get results, turn out well, have the desired result, go as planned
5 ACCOMPLISH, cause, create, effect, achieve, carry out, implement, execute, bring about, encompass, contrive
6 HANDLE, move, excite, manipulate, rouse, stir up, agitate, incite, whip up, galvanize
7 CULTIVATE, farm, dig, till, plough
8 OPERATE, use, move, control, drive, manage, direct, handle, manipulate, wield, ply
9 MANIPULATE, make, form, process, fashion, shape, handle, mould, knead
10 PROGRESS, move, force, manoeuvre, make your way
11 MOVE, twitch, writhe, convulse, be agitated
12 (*informal*) CONTRIVE, handle, fix (*informal*), swing (*informal*), arrange, exploit, manipulate, pull off, fiddle (*informal*), bring off
▷ *noun* 1 EMPLOYMENT, calling, business, job, line, office, trade, duty, craft, profession, occupation, pursuit, livelihood, métier
<< OPPOSITE play
2 EFFORT, industry, labour, grind (*informal*), sweat, toil, slog, exertion, drudgery, travail (*literary*), elbow grease (*facetious*)
<< OPPOSITE leisure
3 TASK, jobs, projects, commissions, duties, assignments, chores, yakka (*Austral & NZ informal*)
4 HANDIWORK, doing, act, feat, deed
5 CREATION, performance, piece, production, opus, achievement, composition, oeuvre (*French*), handiwork
▷▷ **work out** 1 HAPPEN, go, result, develop, come out, turn out, evolve, pan out (*informal*)
2 SUCCEED, flourish, go well, be effective, prosper, go as planned, prove satisfactory, do the business (*informal*)
3 EXERCISE, train, practise, drill, warm up, do exercises
▷▷ **work out at something** AMOUNT TO, come to, reach, add up to, reach a total of
▷▷ **work someone up** *verb* EXCITE, move, spur, wind up (*informal*), arouse, animate, rouse, stir up, agitate, inflame, incite, instigate, get someone all steamed up (*slang*)
▷▷ **work something out** 1 SOLVE, find out, resolve, calculate, figure out, clear up, suss (out) (*slang*), puzzle out
2 PLAN, form, develop, arrange, construct, evolve, devise, elaborate, put together, formulate, contrive
▷▷ **work something up** GENERATE, rouse, instigate, foment, enkindle

workable *adjective* VIABLE, possible, practical, feasible, practicable, doable
<< OPPOSITE unworkable

workaday *adjective* ORDINARY, common, familiar, practical, routine, everyday, commonplace, mundane, prosaic, run-of-the-mill, humdrum, bog-standard (*Brit & Irish slang*)
<< OPPOSITE extraordinary

worker *noun* EMPLOYEE, hand, labourer, workman, craftsman, artisan, tradesman, wage earner, proletarian, working man *or* working woman

working *adjective* 1 EMPLOYED, labouring, in work, in a job
2 FUNCTIONING, going, running, operating, active, operative, operational, functional, usable, serviceable, in working order
3 EFFECTIVE, useful, practical, sufficient, adequate
▷ *noun* OPERATION, running, action, method, functioning, manner, mode of operation
▷ *plural noun* MINE, pit, shaft, quarry, excavations, diggings

workman *noun* LABOURER, hand, worker, employee, mechanic, operative, craftsman, artisan, tradesman, journeyman, artificer (*rare*)

workmanlike *adjective* EFFICIENT, professional, skilled, expert, masterly, careful, satisfactory, thorough, skilful, adept, painstaking, proficient
<< OPPOSITE amateurish

workmanship *noun* SKILL, work, art, technique, manufacture, craft, expertise, execution, artistry, craftsmanship, handiwork, handicraft

workout *noun* EXERCISE, training, drill, warm-up, training session, practice session, exercise session

works *plural noun* 1 FACTORY, shop, plant, mill, workshop
2 WRITINGS, productions, output, canon, oeuvre (*French*)
3 DEEDS, acts, actions, doings
4 MECHANISM, workings, parts, action, insides (*informal*), movement, guts (*informal*), machinery, moving parts, innards (*informal*)

workshop *noun* 1 SEMINAR, class, discussion group, study group, masterclass
2 FACTORY, works, shop, plant, mill
3 WORKROOM, studio, atelier

world *noun* 1 EARTH, planet, globe, earthly sphere
2 MANKIND, man, men, everyone, the public, everybody, humanity, human race, humankind, the race of man
3 SPHERE, system, area, field, environment, province, kingdom, realm, domain
4 LIFE, nature, existence, creation, universe, cosmos
5 PLANET, star, orb, heavenly body
6 PERIOD, times, days, age, era, epoch
7 (usually used in phrase *a world of difference*) HUGE AMOUNT, mountain, wealth, great deal, good deal, abundance, enormous amount, vast amount
▷▷ **for all the world** EXACTLY, just like, precisely, in every way, to all intents and purposes, just as if, in every respect
▷▷ **on top of the world** (*informal*) OVERJOYED, happy, ecstatic, elated, over the moon (*informal*), exultant, on cloud nine (*informal*), cock-a-hoop, in raptures, beside yourself with joy, stoked (*Austral & NZ informal*)
▷▷ **out of this world** (*informal*) WONDERFUL, great (*informal*), excellent, superb, fantastic (*informal*), incredible, fabulous (*informal*), marvellous, unbelievable, awesome (*slang*), indescribable, bodacious (*slang, chiefly US*), booshit (*Austral slang*), exo (*Austral slang*), sik (*Austral slang*), rad (*informal*), phat (*slang*), schmick (*Austral informal*)

worldly *adjective* 1 EARTHLY, lay, physical, fleshly, secular, mundane, terrestrial, temporal, carnal, profane, sublunary
<< OPPOSITE spiritual
2 MATERIALISTIC, grasping, selfish, greedy, avaricious, covetous, worldly-minded
<< OPPOSITE nonmaterialistic
3 WORLDLY-WISE, knowing, experienced, politic, sophisticated, cosmopolitan, urbane, blasé, well versed in the ways of the world
<< OPPOSITE naive

worldwide *adjective* GLOBAL, general, international, universal, ubiquitous, omnipresent, pandemic
<< OPPOSITE limited

worn *adjective* 1 RAGGED, shiny, frayed, shabby, tattered, tatty, threadbare, the worse for wear
2 HAGGARD, lined, drawn, pinched, wizened, careworn
3 EXHAUSTED, spent, tired, fatigued, wearied, weary, played-out (*informal*), worn-out, jaded, tired out

worn out *adjective* 1 WORN, done, used, broken-down, ragged, useless, run-down, frayed, used-up, shabby, tattered, tatty, threadbare, decrepit, clapped out (*Brit, Austral & NZ informal*), moth-eaten
2 EXHAUSTED, spent, done in (*informal*), tired, all in (*slang*), fatigued, wiped out (*informal*), weary, played-out, knackered (*slang*), prostrate, clapped out (*Austral & NZ informal*), tired out, dog-tired (*informal*), zonked (*slang*), shagged out (*Brit slang*), fit to drop, jiggered (*dialect*), dead *or* out on your feet (*informal*)
<< OPPOSITE refreshed

worried *adjective* ANXIOUS, concerned, troubled, upset, afraid, bothered, frightened, wired (*slang*), nervous, disturbed, distressed, tense, distracted, uneasy, fearful, tormented, distraught, apprehensive, perturbed, on edge, ill at ease, overwrought, fretful, hot and bothered, unquiet, antsy (*informal*)
<< OPPOSITE unworried

worrisome *adjective* DISTURBING, worrying, upsetting, distressing, troublesome, disquieting, vexing, perturbing, irksome, bothersome

worry *verb* 1 BE ANXIOUS, be concerned, be worried, obsess, brood, fret, agonize, feel uneasy, get in a lather (*informal*), get in a sweat (*informal*), get in a tizzy (*informal*), get overwrought
<< OPPOSITE be unconcerned
2 TROUBLE, upset, harry, bother, disturb, distress, annoy, plague, irritate, tease, unsettle, torment, harass, hassle (*informal*), badger, hector, disquiet, pester, vex, perturb, tantalize, importune, make anxious
<< OPPOSITE soothe
▷ *noun* 1 ANXIETY, concern, care, fear, trouble, misery, disturbance, torment, woe, irritation, unease, apprehension, misgiving, annoyance, trepidation, perplexity, vexation
<< OPPOSITE peace of mind
2 PROBLEM, care, trouble, trial, bother, plague, pest, torment, irritation, hassle (*informal*), annoyance, vexation

worsen *verb* 1 DETERIORATE, decline, sink, decay, get worse, degenerate, go downhill (*informal*), go from bad to worse, take a turn for the worse, retrogress
<< OPPOSITE improve
2 AGGRAVATE, damage, exacerbate, make worse

<< OPPOSITE improve

worship *verb* 1 REVERE, praise, respect, honour, adore, glorify, reverence, exalt, laud, pray to, venerate, deify, adulate
<< OPPOSITE dishonour
2 LOVE, adore, idolize, put on a pedestal
<< OPPOSITE despise
▷ *noun* REVERENCE, praise, love, regard, respect, honour, glory, prayer(s), devotion, homage, adulation, adoration, admiration, exaltation, glorification, deification, laudation

worth *noun* 1 VALUE, price, rate, cost, estimate, valuation
<< OPPOSITE worthlessness
2 MERIT, value, quality, importance, desert(s), virtue, excellence, goodness, estimation, worthiness
<< OPPOSITE unworthiness
3 USEFULNESS, value, benefit, quality, importance, utility, excellence, goodness
<< OPPOSITE uselessness

worthless *adjective* 1 VALUELESS, poor, miserable, trivial, trifling, paltry, trashy, measly, wretched, two a penny (*informal*), rubbishy, poxy (*slang*), nickel-and-dime (*US slang*), wanky (*taboo slang*), a dime a dozen, nugatory, negligible
<< OPPOSITE valuable
2 USELESS, meaningless, pointless, futile, no use, insignificant, unimportant, ineffectual, unusable, unavailing, not much cop (*Brit slang*), inutile, not worth a hill of beans (*chiefly US*), negligible, pants (*slang*)
<< OPPOSITE useful
3 GOOD-FOR-NOTHING, base, abandoned, useless, vile, abject, despicable, depraved, contemptible, ignoble
<< OPPOSITE honourable

worthwhile *adjective* USEFUL, good, valuable, helpful, worthy, profitable, productive, beneficial, meaningful, constructive, justifiable, expedient, gainful
<< OPPOSITE useless

worthy *adjective* PRAISEWORTHY, good, excellent, deserving, valuable, decent, reliable, worthwhile, respectable, upright, admirable, honourable, honest, righteous, reputable, virtuous, dependable, commendable, creditable, laudable, meritorious, estimable
<< OPPOSITE disreputable
▷ *noun* DIGNITARY, notable, luminary, bigwig (*informal*), big shot (*informal*), personage, big hitter (*informal*), heavy hitter (*informal*)
<< OPPOSITE nobody

would-be *adjective* BUDDING, potential, so-called, professed, dormant, self-styled, latent, wannabe (*informal*), unfulfilled, undeveloped, self-appointed, unrealized, manqué, soi-disant (*French*), quasi-

wound *noun* 1 INJURY, cut, damage, hurt, harm, slash, trauma (*Pathology*), gash, lesion, laceration
2 *often plural* TRAUMA, injury, shock, pain, offence, slight, torture, distress, insult, grief, torment, anguish, heartbreak, pang, sense of loss
▷ *verb* 1 INJURE, cut, hit, damage, wing, hurt, harm, slash, pierce, irritate, gash, lacerate
2 OFFEND, shock, pain, hurt, distress, annoy, sting, grieve, mortify, cut to the quick, hurt the feelings of, traumatize

wounding *adjective* HURTFUL, pointed, cutting, damaging, acid, bitter, slighting, offensive, distressing, insulting, cruel, savage, stinging, destructive, harmful, malicious, scathing, grievous, barbed, unkind, pernicious, caustic, spiteful, vitriolic, trenchant, injurious, maleficent

wrangle *verb* ARGUE, fight, row, dispute, scrap, disagree, fall out (*informal*), contend, quarrel, brawl, squabble, spar, bicker, have words, altercate
▷ *noun* ARGUMENT, row, clash, dispute, contest, set-to (*informal*), controversy, falling-out (*informal*), quarrel, brawl, barney (*informal*), squabble, bickering, tiff, altercation, slanging match (*Brit*), angry exchange, argy-bargy (*Brit informal*), bagarre (*French*)

wrap *verb* 1 COVER, surround, fold, enclose, roll up, cloak, shroud, swathe, muffle, envelop, encase, sheathe, enfold, bundle up
<< OPPOSITE uncover
2 PACK, package, parcel (up), tie up, gift-wrap
<< OPPOSITE unpack
3 BIND, wind, fold, swathe
<< OPPOSITE unwind
▷ *noun* CLOAK, cape, stole, mantle, shawl
▷▷ **wrap something up** 1 GIFTWRAP, pack, package, enclose, bundle up, enwrap
2 (*informal*) END, conclude, wind up, terminate, finish off, round off, tidy up, polish off, bring to a close
▷▷ **wrap up** DRESS WARMLY, muffle up, wear something warm, put warm clothes on

wrapper *noun* COVER, case, paper, packaging, wrapping, jacket, envelope, sleeve, sheath

wrath *noun* ANGER, passion, rage, temper, fury, resentment, irritation, indignation, ire, displeasure, exasperation, choler
<< OPPOSITE satisfaction

wreak *verb* 1 CREATE, work, cause, visit, effect, exercise, carry out, execute, inflict, bring about
2 UNLEASH, express, indulge, vent, gratify, give vent to, give free rein to

wreath *noun* GARLAND, band, ring, crown, loop, festoon, coronet, chaplet

wreathe *verb* 1 SURROUND, envelop, encircle, enfold, coil around, writhe around, enwrap
2 FESTOON, wind, crown, wrap, twist, coil, adorn, intertwine, interweave, entwine, twine, engarland
wreck *verb* 1 DESTROY, break, total (*slang*), smash, ruin, devastate, mar, shatter, spoil, demolish, sabotage, trash (*slang*), ravage, dash to pieces, kennet (*Austral slang*), jeff (*Austral slang*)
<< OPPOSITE build
2 SPOIL, blow (*slang*), ruin, devastate, shatter, undo, screw up (*informal*), cock up (*Brit slang*), play havoc with, crool *or* cruel (*Austral slang*)
<< OPPOSITE save
3 RUN AGROUND, strand, shipwreck, run onto the rocks
▷ *noun* 1 SHIPWRECK, derelict, hulk, sunken vessel
2 RUIN, mess, destruction, overthrow, undoing, disruption, devastation, desolation
<< OPPOSITE preservation
3 Also wreckage REMAINS, pieces, ruin, fragments, debris, rubble, hulk, wrack
4 ACCIDENT, smash, pile-up
wrench *verb* 1 TWIST, force, pull, tear, rip, tug, jerk, yank, wring, wrest
2 SPRAIN, strain, rick, distort
▷ *noun* 1 TWIST, pull, rip, tug, jerk, yank
2 SPRAIN, strain, twist
3 BLOW, shock, pain, ache, upheaval, uprooting, pang
4 SPANNER, adjustable spanner, shifting spanner
wrest *verb* 1 SEIZE, take, win, extract
2 PULL, force, strain, seize, twist, extract, wrench, wring
wrestle *verb* FIGHT, battle, struggle, combat, contend, strive, grapple, tussle, scuffle
wretch *noun* 1 POOR THING, unfortunate, poor soul, poor devil (*informal*), miserable creature
2 SCOUNDREL, rat (*informal*), worm, villain, rogue, outcast, swine, rascal, son-of-a-bitch (*slang, chiefly US & Canad*), profligate, vagabond, ruffian, cur, rotter (*slang, chiefly Brit*), scumbag (*slang*), good-for-nothing, miscreant, bad egg (*old-fashioned informal*), blackguard, wrong 'un (*Austral slang*)
wretched *adjective* 1 UNFORTUNATE, poor, sorry, hapless, pitiful, luckless, star-crossed, pitiable
<< OPPOSITE happy
2 WORTHLESS, poor, sorry, miserable, pathetic, inferior, paltry, deplorable
<< OPPOSITE excellent
3 SHAMEFUL, mean, low, base, shabby, vile, low-down (*informal*), paltry, despicable, contemptible, scurvy, crappy (*slang*), poxy (*slang*)
<< OPPOSITE admirable
4 ILL, poorly, sick, crook (*Austral & NZ informal*), sickly, unwell, off colour (*Brit informal*), under the weather (*informal*)
wriggle *verb* 1 JIGGLE, turn, twist, jerk, squirm, writhe
2 WIGGLE, jerk, wag, jiggle, waggle
3 CRAWL, snake, worm, twist and turn, zigzag, slink
▷ *noun* TWIST, turn, jerk, wag, squirm, wiggle, jiggle, waggle
▷▷ **wriggle out of something** AVOID, duck, dodge, extricate yourself from, talk your way out of, worm your way out of
wring *verb* TWIST, force, squeeze, extract, screw, wrench, coerce, wrest, extort
wrinkle *noun* 1 LINE, fold, crease, furrow, pucker, crow's-foot, corrugation
2 CREASE, gather, fold, crumple, furrow, rumple, pucker, crinkle, corrugation
▷ *verb* CREASE, line, gather, fold, crumple, ruck, furrow, rumple, pucker, crinkle, corrugate
<< OPPOSITE smooth
writ *noun* SUMMONS, document, decree, indictment, court order, subpoena, arraignment
write *verb* 1 RECORD, copy, scribble, take down, inscribe, set down, transcribe, jot down, put in writing, commit to paper, indite, put down in black and white
2 COMPOSE, create, author, draft, pen, draw up
3 CORRESPOND, get in touch, keep in touch, write a letter, drop a line, drop a note
▷▷ **write something off** 1 (*informal*) WRECK, total (*slang*), crash, destroy, trash (*slang*), smash up, damage beyond repair
2 (*Accounting*) CANCEL, shelve, forget about, cross out, score out, give up for lost
▷▷ **write something** *or* **someone off** DISREGARD, ignore, dismiss, regard something *or* someone as finished, consider something *or* someone as unimportant
writer *noun* AUTHOR, novelist, hack, columnist, scribbler, scribe, essayist, penman, wordsmith, man of letters, penpusher, littérateur, penny-a-liner (*rare*)
writhe *verb* SQUIRM, struggle, twist, toss, distort, thrash, jerk, wriggle, wiggle, contort, convulse, thresh
writing *noun* 1 SCRIPT, hand, print, printing, fist (*informal*), scribble, handwriting, scrawl, calligraphy, longhand, penmanship, chirography
2 DOCUMENT, work, book, letter, title, opus, publication, literature, composition, belle-lettre
wrong *adjective* 1 AMISS, faulty, unsatisfactory, not right, defective, awry
2 INCORRECT, mistaken, false, faulty, inaccurate, untrue, erroneous, off target,

unsound, in error, wide of the mark, fallacious, off base (*US & Canad informal*), off beam (*informal*), way off beam (*informal*)
3 INAPPROPRIATE, incorrect, unfitting, unsuitable, unhappy, not done, unacceptable, undesirable, improper, unconventional, incongruous, unseemly, unbecoming, indecorous, inapt, infelicitous, malapropos
 << OPPOSITE correct
4 BAD, criminal, illegal, evil, unfair, crooked, unlawful, illicit, immoral, unjust, dishonest, wicked, sinful, unethical, wrongful, under-the-table, reprehensible, dishonourable, iniquitous, not cricket (*informal*), felonious, blameworthy
 << OPPOSITE moral
5 DEFECTIVE, not working, faulty, out of order, awry, askew, out of commission
6 OPPOSITE, inside, reverse, inverse
▷ *adverb* 1 INCORRECTLY, badly, wrongly, mistakenly, erroneously, inaccurately
 << OPPOSITE correctly
2 AMISS, astray, awry, askew
▷ *noun* 1 WICKEDNESS, injustice, unfairness, inequity, immorality, iniquity, sinfulness
 << OPPOSITE morality
2 OFFENCE, injury, crime, abuse, error, sin, injustice, grievance, infringement, trespass, misdeed, transgression, infraction, bad *or* evil deed
 << OPPOSITE good deed
▷ *verb* MISTREAT, abuse, hurt, injure, harm, cheat, take advantage of, discredit, oppress, malign, misrepresent, dump on (*slang, chiefly US*), impose upon, dishonour, ill-treat, maltreat, ill-use
 << OPPOSITE treat well
▷▷ **go wrong** 1 FAIL, flop (*informal*), fall through, come to nothing, miscarry, misfire, come to grief (*informal*), go pear-shaped (*informal*)
2 MAKE A MISTAKE, boob (*Brit slang*), err, slip up (*informal*), go astray
3 BREAK DOWN, fail, malfunction, misfire, cease to function, conk out (*informal*), go on the blink (*slang*), go kaput (*informal*), go phut (*informal*)
4 LAPSE, sin, err, fall from grace, go astray, go to the bad, go off the straight and narrow (*informal*)

wrongful *adjective* IMPROPER, illegal, unfair, inappropriate, unlawful, illicit, immoral, unjust, illegitimate, unethical, groundless
 << OPPOSITE rightful

wry *adjective* 1 IRONIC, dry, mocking, sarcastic, sardonic, droll, pawky (*Scot*), mordacious
2 CONTORTED, twisted, crooked, distorted, warped, uneven, deformed, awry, askew, aslant, skewwhiff (*Brit informal*)
 << OPPOSITE straight

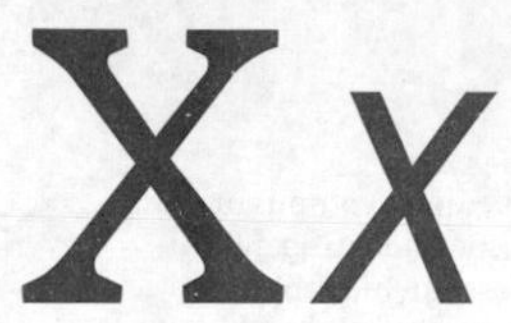

Xmas *noun* CHRISTMAS, Noel, festive season, Yule (*archaic*), Yuletide (*archaic*), Christmastime, Christmastide, Crimbo (*Brit informal*)

X-ray *noun* RADIOGRAPH, x-ray image

Yy

yahoo *noun* PHILISTINE, savage, lout, beast, barbarian, brute, rowdy, hoon (*Austral & NZ*), roughneck (*slang*), boor, churl, yob *or* yobbo (*Brit slang*), cougan (*Austral slang*), scozza (*Austral slang*), bogan (*Austral slang*)

yak *verb* GOSSIP, go on, gab (*informal*), rabbit (on) (*Brit informal*), run on, jaw (*slang*), chatter, spout, waffle (*informal, chiefly Brit*), yap (*informal*), tattle, jabber, blather, chew the fat (*slang*), witter on (*informal*), run off at the mouth

yank *verb* PULL, tug, jerk, seize, snatch, pluck, hitch, wrench

▷ *noun* PULL, tug, jerk, snatch, hitch, wrench, tweak

yap *verb* **1** YELP, bark, woof, yip (*chiefly US*)
2 (*informal*) TALK, go on, rabbit (on) (*Brit informal*), gossip, jaw (*slang*), chatter, spout, babble, waffle (*informal, chiefly Brit*), prattle, jabber, blather, run off at the mouth (*slang*), earbash (*Austral & NZ slang*)

yardstick *noun* STANDARD, measure, criterion, gauge, benchmark, touchstone, par

yarn *noun* **1** THREAD, fibre, cotton, wool
2 (*informal*) STORY, tale, anecdote, account, narrative, fable, reminiscence, urban myth, tall story, urban legend, cock-and-bull story (*informal*)

yawning *adjective* GAPING, wide, huge, vast, wide-open, cavernous

yearly *adjective* ANNUAL, each year, every year, once a year

▷ *adverb* ANNUALLY, every year, by the year, once a year, per annum

yearn *verb often with* **for** LONG, desire, pine, pant, hunger, ache, lust, crave, covet, itch, languish, hanker after, have a yen for (*informal*), eat your heart out over, set your heart upon, suspire (*archaic* or *poetic*), would give your eyeteeth for

yell *verb* SCREAM, shout, cry out, howl, call out, wail, shriek, screech, squeal, bawl, holler (*informal*), yelp, call at the top of your voice
<< OPPOSITE whisper
▷ *noun* SCREAM, cry, shout, roar, howl, shriek, whoop, screech, squeal, holler (*informal*), yelp, yowl
<< OPPOSITE whisper

yellow *noun* LEMON, gold, amber

yelp *verb* BARK, howl, yap, yip (*chiefly US*), yowl
▷ *noun* CRY, squeal

yen *noun* LONGING, desire, craving, yearning, passion, hunger, ache, itch, thirst, hankering

yet *adverb* 1 SO FAR, until now, up to now, still, as yet, even now, thus far, up till now, up to the present time
2 NOW, right now, just now, so soon, already
3 STILL, further, in addition, as well, moreover, besides, to boot, additionally, over and above, into the bargain
▷ *conjunction* NEVERTHELESS, still, however, for all that, notwithstanding, just the same, be that as it may

yield *verb* 1 BOW, submit, give in, surrender, give way, succumb, cave in (*informal*), capitulate, knuckle under, resign yourself
2 RELINQUISH, resign, hand over, surrender, turn over, part with, make over, cede, give over, bequeath, abdicate, deliver up
<< OPPOSITE retain
3 SURRENDER, give up, give in, concede defeat, cave in (*informal*), throw in the towel, admit defeat, accept defeat, give up the struggle, knuckle under, raise the white flag, lay down your arms, cry quits
4 PRODUCE, give, provide, pay, return, supply, bear, net, earn, afford, generate, bring in, furnish, bring forth
<< OPPOSITE use up
▷ *noun* 1 PRODUCE, crop, harvest, output
2 PROFIT, return, income, revenue, earnings, takings
<< OPPOSITE loss
▷▷ **yield to something** COMPLY WITH, agree to, concede, allow, grant, permit, go along with, bow to, consent to, accede to
<< OPPOSITE resist

yielding *adjective* 1 SOFT, pliable, springy, elastic, resilient, supple, spongy, unresisting, quaggy
2 SUBMISSIVE, obedient, compliant, docile, easy, flexible, accommodating, pliant, tractable, acquiescent, biddable
<< OPPOSITE obstinate

yob *or* **yobbo** *noun* THUG, hooligan, lout, heavy (*slang*), tough, rough (*informal*), rowdy, yahoo, hoon (*Austral & NZ slang*), hoodlum, ruffian, roughneck (*slang*), tsotsi (*S African*), cougan (*Austral slang*), scozza (*Austral slang*), bogan (*Austral slang*)

yoke *noun* 1 OPPRESSION, slavery, bondage, servitude, service, burden, enslavement, serfdom, servility, vassalage, thraldom
2 HARNESS, coupling, tackle, chain, collar, tack
▷ *verb* 1 UNITE, join, link, tie, bond, bind, connect
2 HARNESS, join, couple, link, tie, connect, bracket, hitch

young *adjective* 1 IMMATURE, juvenile, youthful, little, growing, green, junior, infant, adolescent, callow, unfledged, in the springtime of life
<< OPPOSITE old
2 EARLY, new, undeveloped, fledgling, newish, not far advanced
<< OPPOSITE advanced
▷ *noun* OFFSPRING, baby, litter, family, issue, brood, little onesy, progeny
<< OPPOSITE parent

youngster *noun* YOUTH, girl, boy, kid (*informal*), lad, teenager, juvenile, cub, young person, lass, young adult, pup (*informal, chiefly Brit*), urchin, teenybopper (*slang*), young shaver (*informal*), young 'un (*informal*)

youth *noun* 1 IMMATURITY, adolescence, early life, young days, boyhood *or* girlhood, salad days, juvenescence
<< OPPOSITE old age
2 BOY, lad, youngster, kid (*informal*), teenager, young man, adolescent, teen (*informal*), stripling, young shaver (*informal*)
<< OPPOSITE adult
3 YOUNG PEOPLE, the young, the younger generation, teenagers, the rising generation
<< OPPOSITE old people

youthful *adjective* 1 YOUNG, juvenile, childish, immature, boyish, pubescent, girlish, puerile
<< OPPOSITE elderly
2 VIGOROUS, fresh, active, young looking, young at heart, spry
<< OPPOSITE tired

Zz

zany *adjective* COMICAL, crazy, nutty (*slang*), funny, eccentric, wacky (*slang*), loony (*slang*), oddball (*informal*), madcap, goofy (*informal*), kooky (*US informal*), clownish, wacko *or* whacko (*informal*), off the air (*Austral slang*)

zeal *noun* ENTHUSIASM, passion, zest, fire, spirit, warmth, devotion, verve, fervour, eagerness, gusto, militancy, fanaticism, ardour, earnestness, keenness, fervency
<< OPPOSITE apathy

zealot *noun* FANATIC, enthusiast, extremist, militant, maniac, fiend (*informal*), bigot

zealous *adjective* ENTHUSIASTIC, passionate, earnest, burning, spirited, keen, devoted, eager, militant, ardent, fanatical, fervent, impassioned, rabid, fervid
<< OPPOSITE apathetic

zenith *noun* HEIGHT, summit, peak, top, climax, crest, high point, pinnacle, meridian, apex, high noon, apogee, acme, vertex
<< OPPOSITE lowest point

zero *noun* 1 NOUGHT, nothing, nil, naught, cipher
2 ROCK BOTTOM, the bottom, an all-time low, a nadir, as low as you can get, the lowest point *or* ebb
▷▷ **zero in on something** 1 ZOOM IN ON, focus on, aim at, train on, home in on
2 FOCUS ON, concentrate on, home in on, pinpoint on, converge

zest *noun* 1 ENJOYMENT, love, appetite, relish, interest, joy, excitement, zeal, gusto, keenness, zing (*informal*), delectation
<< OPPOSITE aversion
2 FLAVOUR, taste, savour, kick (*informal*), spice, relish, smack, tang, piquancy, pungency
3 RIND, skin, peel, outer layer

zip *verb* SPEED, shoot, fly, tear, rush, flash, dash, hurry, barrel (along) (*informal, chiefly US & Canad*), buzz, streak, hare (*Brit informal*), zoom, whizz (*informal*), hurtle, pelt, burn rubber (*informal*)
▷ *noun* (*informal*) ENERGY, go (*informal*), life, drive, spirit, punch (*informal*), pep, sparkle, vitality, vigour, verve, zest, gusto, get-up-and-go (*informal*), oomph (*informal*), brio, zing (*informal*), liveliness, vim (*slang*), pizzazz *or* pizazz (*informal*)
<< OPPOSITE lethargy

zone *noun* AREA, region, section, sector, district, territory, belt, sphere, tract

zoom *verb* SPEED, shoot, fly, tear, rush, flash, dash, barrel (along) (*informal, chiefly US & Canad*), buzz, streak, hare (*Brit informal*), zip (*informal*), whizz (*informal*), hurtle, pelt, burn rubber (*informal*)

Supplement

World in Action

Contents

The Solar System

Mercury

DISTANCE FROM THE SUN = 57,909,175 km
VOLUME (Earth = 1) = 0.054
SIDEREAL ROTATION PERIOD = 58.646225 earth days
SIDEREAL ORBIT PERIOD = 0.2408467 sidereal years
MASS = 0.3302 X 10²⁷ g
INCLINATION OF EQUATOR TO ORBIT = 0.0 degrees
NUMBER OF MOONS = 0

Venus

DISTANCE FROM THE SUN = 108,208,930 km
VOLUME (Earth = 1) = 0.88
SIDEREAL ROTATION PERIOD = 243.0187 earth days (retrograde)
SIDEREAL ORBIT PERIOD = 0.61519726 sidereal years
MASS = 4.8690 X 10²⁷ g
INCLINATION OF EQUATOR TO ORBIT = 177.3 degrees
NUMBER OF MOONS = 0

Earth

DISTANCE FROM THE SUN = 149,597,890 km
SIDEREAL ROTATION PERIOD = 0.99726968 earth day
SIDEREAL ORBIT PERIOD = 1.0000174 sidereal years
MASS = 5.9742 X 10²⁷ g
INCLINATION OF EQUATOR TO ORBIT = 23.45 degrees
NUMBER OF MOONS = 1
NAMES OF MOON:
The Moon

Mars

DISTANCE FROM THE SUN = 227,936,640 km
VOLUME (Earth = 1) = 0.149
SIDEREAL ROTATION PERIOD = 1.02595675earth days
SIDEREAL ORBIT PERIOD = 1.8808476 sidereal years
MASS = 0.64191 X 10²⁷ g
INCLINATION OF EQUATOR TO ORBIT =25.19 degrees
NUMBER OF MOONS = 2
NAMES OF MOONS:
Phobos
Deimos

Jupiter

DISTANCE FROM THE SUN = 778,412,010 km
VOLUME (Earth = 1) = 1316
SIDEREAL ROTATION PERIOD = 0.41354 earth day
SIDEREAL ORBIT PERIOD = 11.862615 sidereal years
MASS = 1,898.7 X 10²⁷ g
INCLINATION OF EQUATOR TO ORBIT = 3.12 degrees
NUMBER OF MOONS = 61
NAMES OF MOONS:
Metis
Adrastea
Amalthea
Thebe
Io
Europa
Ganymede
Callisto
Themisto
Leda
Himalia
Lysithea
Elara
S/2000 J11
Iocaste
Praxidike
Harpalyke
Ananke
Isonoe
Erinome
Taygete
Chaldene
Carme
Pasiphae
S/2002 J1
Kalkyke
Megaclite
Sinope
Callirhoe
Euporie
Kale
Orthosie
Thyone
Euanthe
Hermippe
Pasithee
Eurydome
Aitne
Sponde
Autonoe
S/2003 J1
S/2003 J2
S/2003 J3
S/2003 J4
S/2003 J5
S/2003 J6
S/2003 J7
S/2003 J8
S/2003 J9
S/2003 J10
S/2003 J11
S/2003 J12
S/2003 J13
S/2003 J14
S/2003 J15
S/2003 J16
S/2003 J17
S/2003 J18
S/2003 J19
S/2003 J20
S/2003 J21

Saturn
DISTANCE FROM THE SUN = 1,426,725,400 km
VOLUME (Earth = 1) = 755
SIDEREAL ROTATION PERIOD = 0.44401 earth day
SIDEREAL ORBIT PERIOD = 29.447498 sidereal years
MASS = 568.51 x 10²⁷ g
INCLINATION OF EQUATOR TO ORBIT = 26.73 degrees
NUMBER OF MOONS = 30
NAMES OF MOONS:
Pan
Atlas
Prometheus
Pandora
Epimetheus
Janus
Mimas
Enceladus
Tethys
Telesto
Calypso
Dione
Helene
Rhea
Titan
Hyperion
Iapetus
Phoebe
Ymir
Paaliaq
Siarnaq
Tarvos
Kiviuq
Ijiraq
Thrym
Skadi
Mundilfari
Erriapo
Albiorix
Suttung
S/2003 S1

Uranus
DISTANCE FROM THE SUN = 2,870,972,200 km
VOLUME (Earth = 1) = 52
SIDEREAL ROTATION PERIOD = 0.71833 earth day
SIDEREAL ORBIT PERIOD = 84.016846 sidereal years
MASS = 86.849 x 10²⁷ g
INCLINATION OF EQUATOR TO ORBIT = 97.86 degrees
NUMBER OF MOONS = 21
NAMES OF MOONS:
Cordelia
Ophelia
Bianca
Cressida
Desdemona
Juliet
Portia
Rosalind
Belinda
Puck
Miranda
Ariel
Umbriel
Titania
Oberon
Caliban
Stephano
Trinculo
Sycorax
Prospero
Setebos

Neptune
DISTANCE FROM THE SUN = 4,498,252,900 km
VOLUME (Earth = 1) = 44
SIDEREAL ROTATION PERIOD = 0.67125 earth day
SIDEREAL ORBIT PERIOD = 164.79132 sidereal years
MASS = 102.44 x 10²⁷ g
INCLINATION OF EQUATOR TO ORBIT = 29.58 degrees
NUMBER OF MOONS = 11
NAMES OF MOONS:
Naiad
Thalassa
Despina
Galatea
Larissa
Proteus
Triton
Nereid
S/2002 N1
S/2002 N2
S/2002 N3

Pluto
DISTANCE FROM THE SUN = 5,906,376,200 km
VOLUME (Earth = 1) = 0.005
SIDEREAL ROTATION PERIOD = 6.38718 earth days (retrograde)
SIDEREAL ORBIT PERIOD = 247.92065 sidereal years
MASS = 0.013 x 10²⁷ g
EQUATORIAL INCLINATION = 119.61 degrees
NUMBER OF MOONS = 1
NAME OF MOON:
Charon

▸ http://solarsystem.nasa.gov/features/planets

Winds

Wind	Location
berg wind	South Africa
bise	Switzerland
bora	Adriatic Sea
buran *or* bura	central Asia
Cape doctor	Cape Town, South Africa
chinook	Washington & Oregon coasts
föhn *or* foehn	N slopes of the Alps
harmattan	W African coast
khamsin, kamseen *or* kamsin	Egypt
levanter	W Mediterranean
libeccio *or* libecchio	Corsica
meltemi *or* etesian wind	NE Mediterranean
mistral	S France to Mediterranean
monsoon	S Asia
nor'wester	Southern Alps, New Zealand
pampero	S America
simoom *or* simoon	Arabia & N Africa
sirocco	N Africa to S Europe
tramontane *or* tramontana	W coast of Italy

- ▹ www.spc.ncep.noaa.gov/faq/tornado
- ▹ www.aoml.noaa.gov/hrd/tcfaq/tcfaqHED.html
- ▹ http://sciencepolicy.colorado.edu/socasp/toc_img.html
- ▹ http://personal.cmich.edu/~francim/homepage.htm
- ▹ www.wmo.ch
- ▹ www.worldweather.org

SI Units

Base and Supplementary SI Units

Physical quantity	*Name of SI unit*	*Symbol for SI unit*
length	metre	m
mass	kilogram	kg
time	second	s
electric current	ampere	A
thermodynamic temperature	kelvin	K
luminous intensity	candela	cd
amount of substance	mole	mol
*plane angle	radian	rad
*solid angle	steradian	sr

*supplementary units

Derived SI Units with Special Names

Physical quantity	*Name of SI unit*	*Symbol for SI unit*
frequency	hertz	Hz
energy	joule	J
force	newton	N
power	watt	W
pressure	pascal	Pa
electric charge	coulomb	C
electric potential difference	volt	V
electrical resistance	ohm	W
electric conductance	siemens	S
electric capacitance	farad	F
magnetic flux	weber	Wb
inductance	henry	H
magnetic flux density	tesla	T
luminous flux	lumen	lm
illuminance (illumination)	lux	lx
absorbed dose	gray	Gy
activity	becquerel	Bq
dose equivalent	sievert	Sv

Decimal Multiples and Submultiples used with SI Units

Sub-multiple	*Prefix*	*Symbol*	*Multiple*	*Prefix*	*Symbol*
10^{-1}	deci-	d	101	deca-	da
10^{-2}	centi-	c	102	hecto-	h
10^{-3}	milli-	m	103	kilo-	k
10^{-6}	micro-	m	106	mega-	M
10^{-9}	nano-	n	109	giga-	G
10^{-12}	pico-	p	1012	tera-	T
10^{-15}	femto-	f	1015	peta-	P
10^{-18}	atto-	a	1018	exa-	E
10^{-21}	zepto-	z	1021	zetta-	Z
10^{-24}	yocto-	y	1024	yotta-	Y

Tables of Weights and Measures

The Metric System

linear measure

1 millimetre	=	0.039 37 inch		
10 millimetre	=	1 centimetre	=	0.3937 inch
10 decimetres	=	1 metre	=	39.37 inches or 3.2808 feet
1 kilometre	=	0.621 mile or 3280.8 feet		

square measure

1 square millimetre	=	0.001 55 square inch		
100 square millimetres	=	1 square centimetre	=	0.154 99 square inch
100 square decimetres	=	1 square metre	=	1549.9 square inches or 1.196 square yards
100 square hectometres	=	1 square kilometre	=	0.386 square mile or 247.1 acres

land measure

100 centiares	=	1 are	=	119.6 square yards
100 ares	=	1 hectare	=	2.471 acres
100 hectares	=	1 square kilometre	=	0.386 square mile or 247.1 acres

volume measure

1000 cubic millimetres	=	1 cubic centimetre	=	0.061 02 cubic inch
1000 cubic centimetres	=	1 cubic decimetre (1 litre)	=	61.023 cubic inches or 0.0353 cubic foot
1000 cubic decimetres	=	1 cubic metre	=	35.314 cubic feet or 1.308 cubic yards

weights

10 decigrammes	=	1 gram	=	15.432 grains or 0.035 274 ounce (avdp.)
10 hectogrammes	=	1 kilogram	=	2.2046 pounds
10 quintals	=	1 metric ton	=	2204.6 pounds

The Imperial System

linear measure

1 mil	=	0.001 inch	=	0.0254 mm
1 inch	=	1000 mils	=	2.54 cm
12 inches	=	1 foot	=	0.3048 metre
3 feet	=	1 yard	=	0.9144 metre
5½ yards or 16½ feet	=	1 rod (or pole or perch)	=	5.029 metres
40 rods	=	1 furlong	=	201.168 metres
8 furlongs or 1760 yards or 5280 feet	=	1 (statute) mile	=	1.6093 kilometres

square measure

1 square inch	=	6.452 square centimetres		
144 square inches	=	1 square foot	=	929.03 square centimetres
9 square feet	=	1 square yard	=	0.8361 square metre
30¼ square yards	=	1 square rod	=	25.292 square metres (or square pole or square perch)

160 square rods or 4840 square yards or 43560 square feet	=	1 acre	=	0.4047 hectare
640 acres	=	1 square mile	=	259.00 hectares or 2.590 square kilometres

CUBIC MEASURE

1 cubic inch	=	16.387 cubic centimetre		
1728 cubic inches	=	1 cubic foot	=	0.0283 cubic metre
27 cubic feet	=	1 cubic yard	=	0.7646 cubic metre

NAUTICAL MEASURE

6 feet	=	1 fathom	=	1.829 metres
100 fathoms	=	1 cable's length		
(in the Royal Navy, 608 feet, or 185.329 metres	=	1 cable's length)		
10 cables' length	=	1 international nautical mile	=	1.852 kilometres (exactly)
1 international nautical mile	=	1.150779 statute miles (the length of a minute of latitude at the equator)		
60 nautical miles	=	1 degree of a great circle of the earth	=	69.047 statute miles

LIQUID AND DRY MEASURE

1 gill	=	5 fluid ounces	=	9.0235 cubic inches	=	0.1480 litre
4 gills	=	1 pint	=	34.68 cubic inches	=	0.568 litre
2 pints	=	1 quart	=	69.36 cubic inches	=	1.136 litres
4 quarts	=	1 gallon	=	277.4 cubic inches	=	4.546 litres
2 gallons	=	1 peck	=	554.8 cubic inches	=	9.092 litres
4 pecks	=	1 bushel	=	2219.2 cubic inches	=	36.37 litres
The US gallon (4 US quarts)	=	231 cubic inches	=	3.7854 litres		

APOTHECARIES' FLUID MEASURE

1 minim	=	0.0038 cubic inch	=	0.0616 millilitre		
60 minims	=	1 fluid dram	=	0.2256 cubic inch	=	3.6966 millilitres
8 fluid drams	=	1 fluid ounce	=	1.8047 cubic inches	=	0.0296 litre
20 fluid ounces	=	1 pint	=	34.68 cubic inches	=	0.568 litre
The US pint	=	16 fluid ounces				

AVOIRDUPOIS WEIGHT

(The grain, equal to 0.0648 gram, is the same in all three tables of weight.)

1 dram or 27.34 grains	=	1.722 grams		
16 drams or 437.5 grains	=	1 ounce	=	28.3495 grams
16 ounces or 7000 grains	=	1 pound	=	453.59 grams
14 pounds	=	1 stone	=	6.35 kilograms
112 pounds	=	1 hundredweight	=	50.80 kilograms
2240 pounds	=	1 (long) ton	=	1016.05 kilograms
2000 pounds	=	1 (short) ton	=	907.18 kilograms

TROY WEIGHT

(The grain, equal to 0.0648 gram, is the same in all three tables of weight.)

3.086 grains	=	1 carat	=	200.00 milligrams
24 grains	=	1 pennyweight	=	2.5552 grams
20 pennyweights or 480 grains	=	1 ounce	=	31.1035 grams
12 ounces or 5760 grains	=	1 pound	=	373.24 grams

APOTHECARIES' WEIGHT

(The grain, equal to 0.0648 gram, is the same in all three tables of weight.)

20 grains	=	1 scruple	=	1.296 grams
3 scruples	=	1 dram	=	3.888 grams
8 drams or 480 grains	=	1 ounce	=	31.1035 grams

▹ www.ex.ac.uk/cimt/dictunit/dictunit.htm
▹ www.unc.edu/-rowlett/units/metric.html
▹ www.unc.edu/-rowlett/units/usmetric.html
▹ http://scienceworld.wolfram.com/physics/AvoirdupoisSystemofUnits.html
▹ http://scienceworld.wolfram.com/physics/ApothecariesSystemofWeights.html

Communications code words for the alphabet

Alpha
Bravo
Charlie
Delta
Echo
Foxtrot
Golf
Hotel
India
Juliet
Kilo
Lima
Mike
November
Oscar
Papa
Quebec
Romeo
Sierra
Tango
Uniform
Victor
Whiskey
X-Ray
Yankee
Zulu

▹ http://en.wikipedia.org/wiki/Nato_phonetic_alphabet
▹ www.canadiansoldiers.com/phonetics.htm

Australian States and Territories

Australian Capital Territory

New South Wales
▹ www.nsw.gov.au
▹ www.tourism.nsw.gov.au

Northern Territory
▹ www.nt.gov.au
▹ www.nttc.com.au

Queensland
▹ www.qld.gov.au
▹ www.qttc.com.au

South Australia
▹ www.sa.gov.au
▹ www.tourism.sa.gov.au

Tasmania
▹ www.parliament.tas.gov.au
▹ www.discovertasmania.com.au

Victoria
▹ www.vic.gov.au www.victoria-australia.
▹ worldweb.com

Western Australia
▹ www.wa.gov.au www.westernaustralia.net

▹ http://www.gov.au/sites/

Canadian provinces

Province	Abbreviation
Alberta ▹ www.gov.ab.ca ▹ www.discoveralberta.com	AB
British Columbia ▹ www.gov.bc.ca ▹ www.bc-tourism.com	BC
Manitoba ▹ www.gov.mb.ca ▹ www.travelmanitoba.com	MB
New Brunswick ▹ www.gnb.ca ▹ www.tourismenouveau-brunswick.ca/ ▹ Cultures/en-CA/welcome.htm	NB
Newfoundland ▹ www.gov.nf.ca ▹ www.gov.nf.ca/tourism	NF
Northwest Territories ▹ www.gov.nt.com ▹ www.nwttravel.nt.ca	NWT
Nova Scotia ▹ www.gov.ns.ca ▹ www.gov.ns.ca/tourism.htm	NS
Nunavut ▹ www.gov.nu.ca ▹ www.nunavuttourism.com	NU
Ontario ▹ www.gov.on.ca ▹ www.tourism.gov.on.ca/english	ON
Prince Edward Island ▹ www.gov.pe.ca ▹ www.gov.pe.ca/visitorsguide/index.php3	PE
Quebec ▹ www.gouv.qc.ca/index_en.html ▹ www.tourisme.gouv.qc.ca/anglais	PQ
Saskatchewan ▹ www.gov.sk.ca ▹ www.sasktourism.com	SK
Yukon Territory ▹ www.gov.yk.ca ▹ www.yukonweb.com/tourism	YT

▹ http://canada.gc.ca/othergov/prov_e.html
▹ http://canada.gc.ca
▹ www.travelcanada.org
▹ http://canada.gc.ca/othergov/prov_e.html

English counties

Bedfordshire
Berkshire
Bristol
Buckinghamshire
Cambridgeshire
Cheshire
Cornwall
Cumbria
Derbyshire
Devon
Dorset
Durham
East Riding of Yorkshire
East Sussex
Essex
Gloucestershire
Greater London
Greater Manchester
Hampshire
Herefordshire
Hertfordshire
Isle of Wight
Kent
Lancashire
Leicestershire
Lincolnshire
Merseyside
Norfolk
Northamptonshire
Northumberland
North Yorkshire
Nottinghamshire
Oxfordshire
Rutland
Shropshire
Somerset
South Yorkshire
Staffordshire
Suffolk
Surrey
Tyne and Wear
Warwickshire
West Midlands
West Sussex
West Yorkshire
Wiltshire
Worcestershire

▹ www.ukwebstart.com/listdepartments.html
▹ www.travelengland.org.uk
▹ http://www.peak.org/~jeremy/dictionary/tables/counties.php

Member states of the EU

1958 Belgium
- www.belgium.be
- www.visitbelgium.com

1958 France
- www.assemblee-nationale.com/english/index.asp
- www.francetourism.com

1958 Germany
- http://eng.bundesregierung.de/frameset/index.jsp
- www.visits-to-germany.com

1958 Italy
- www.italiantourism.com
- www.governo.it

1958 Luxembourg
- www.ont.lu
- www.luxembourg.co.uk

1958 The Netherlands
- www.overheid.nl/guest
- www.nbt.nl

1973 Denmark
- www.denmark.dk
- www.visitdenmark.com

1973 Republic of Ireland
- www.irlgov.ie
- www.ireland.travel.ie

1973 United Kingdom
- www.ukonline.gov.uk
- www.visitbritain.com

1981 Greece
- www.parliament.gr/english/default.asp
- www.gnto.gr

1986 Portugal
- www.portugal.gov.pt
- www.portugalinsite.pt

1986 Spain
- www.tourspain.es
- tizz.com/spain
- www.spaintour.com

1995 Finland
- www.valtioneuvosto.fi/vn/liston/base.lsp?k=en
- www.finland-tourism.com

1995 Sweden
- www.sweden.gov.se
- www.visit-sweden.com

1995 Austria
- www.austria.org
- www.austria-tourism.at

2004 Cyprus
- www.pio.gov.cy
- www.cyprustourism.org

2004 Czech Republic
- http://wtd.vlada.cz/eng/aktuality.htm
- www.czech.cz
- www.visitczech.cz
- www.lonelyplanet.com/destinations/europe/czech_republic/

2004 Estonia
- www.riik.ee/en/valitsus
- http://visitestonia.com
- www.estonia.org/

2004 Hungary
- www.fsz.bme.hu/hungary/homepage.html
- www.gotohungary.com/
- www.lonelyplanet.com/destinations/europe/hungary/
- www.mkogy.hu
- www.lonelyplanet.com/destinations/europe/hungary/

2004 Latvia
- www.saeima.lv/index_eng.html
- www.latviatourism.com
- www.lv/
- www.lonelyplanet.com/destinations/europe/latvia/

2004 Lithuania
- www.lrv.lt/main_en.php
- www.tourism.lt
- www.on.lt/travel.htm
- neris.mii/lt/homepage/lietuva.html

2004 Malta
- www.malta.co.uk/malta/geninfo.htm
- www.visitmalta.com
- www.aboutmalta.com

2004 Poland
- www.poland.pl
- www.nto-poland.gov.pl/wyd_dwlnd.asp
- www.polandonline.com

2004 Slovakia
- www.slovak.com/
- www.sacr.sk
- www.slovakia.org/

2004 Slovenia
- www.sigov.si
- www.slovenia-tourism.si; www.tourist-board.si
- www.matkurja.com/eng/country-info
- www.lonelyplanet.com/destinations/europe/slovenia/

- www.europa.eu.int/index_en.htm
- www.eia.org.uk/websites.htm

Indian states and territories

Indian states
Andhra Pradesh
Arunachal Pradesh
Assam
Bihar
Chhattisgarh
Goa
Gujarat
Haryana
Himachal Pradesh
Jammu and Kashmir
Jharkand
Karnataka
Kerala
Madhya Pradesh
Maharashtra
Manipur
Meghalaya
Mizoram
Nagaland
Orissa
Punjab
Rajasthan
Sikkim
Tamil Nadu
Tripura
Uttaranchal
Uttar Pradesh
West Bengal

Indian Union territories
Andaman and Nicobar Islands
Chandigarh
Dadra and Nagar Haveli
Daman and Diu
Delhi
▹ http://delhigovt.nic.in
Lakshadweep
Pondicherry

▹ http://www.mapsofindia.com/maps/india/indiastateandunion.htm
▹ http://www.indiaonestop.com/stategovetlist.htm

Irish counties

Northern Irish counties
Antrim
Armagh
Belfast City
Down
Fermanagh
Londonderry
Londonderry City
Tyrone

Republic of Ireland counties
Carlow
Cavan
Clare
Cork
Donegal
Dublin
▹ www.visitdublin.com
Galway
Kerry
Kildare
Kilkenny
Laois
Leitrim
Limerick
Longford
Louth
Mayo
Meath
Monaghan
Offaly
Roscommon
Sligo
Tipperary
Waterford
Westmeath
Wexford
Wicklow

▹ http://www.genuki.org.uk/big/irl/counties.html
▹ www.irlgov.ie
▹ www.ireland.travel.ie

New Zealand Territories

Cook Islands
Niue
the Ross Dependency
Tokelau *or* Union Islands

▹ www.govt.nz/en/aboutnz
▹ www.purenz.com
▹ www.newzealandnz.co.nz

South African provinces and provincial capitals

Province	Capital
Eastern Cape	Bisho
▹ www.ecprov.gov.za	
▹ www.ectourism.co.za	
Free State	Bloemfontein
▹ www.fs.gov.za	
▹ www.fstourism.co.za	
Gauteng	Johannesburg
KwaZulu-Natal	Pietermaritzburg
▹ www.kwazulunatal.gov.za	
▹ www.kzn.org.za	
Limpopo	Pietersburg
▹ www.limpopo.gov.za	
▹ www.tourismboard.org.za	
Mpumalanga	Nelspruit
▹ http://mpulanga.mpu.gov.za	
▹ www.mpulanga.com	
North-West	Mafikeng
▹ www.nwpg.gov.za	
▹ www.tourismnorthwest.co.za	
Northern Cape	Kimberley
▹ www.northern-cape.gov.za	
▹ www.northerncape.org.za	
Western Cape	Cape Town
▹ www.westerncape.gov/za	
▹ www.capetourism.org	

▹ www.gov.za
▹ www.southafrica.net
▹ www.satour.org

Scottish counties

Aberdeen City
Aberdeenshire
Angus
Argyll and Bute
City of Edinburgh
Clackmannanshire
Dumfries and Galloway
Dundee City
East Ayrshire
East Dunbartonshire
East Lothian
East Renfrewshire
Falkirk
Fife
Glasgow City
Highland
Inverclyde
Midlothian
Moray
North Ayrshire
North Lanarkshire
Orkney
Perth and Kinross
Renfrewshire
Scottish Borders
Shetland
South Ayrshire
South Lanarkshire
Stirling
West Dunbartonshire
Western Isles (Eilean Siar)
West Lothian

▹ www.scotland.gov.uk
▹ www.visitscotland.com
▹ http://www.peak.org/~jeremy/dictionary/tables/counties.php

US States

State	Abbreviation	Zip code
Alabama	Ala.	AL
Alaska	Alas.	AK
Arizona	Ariz.	AZ
Arkansas	Ark.	AR
California	Cal.	CA
Colorado	Colo.	CO
Connecticut	Conn.	CT
Delaware	Del.	DE
District of Columbia	D.C.	DC
Florida	Fla.	FL
Georgia	Ga.	GA
Hawaii	Haw.	HI
Idaho	Id. *or* Ida.	ID
Illinois	Ill.	IL
Indiana	Ind.	IN
Iowa	Ia. *or* Io.	IA
Kansas	Kan. *or* Kans.	KS
Kentucky	Ken.	KY
Louisiana	La.	LA
Maine	Me.	ME
Maryland	Md.	MD
Massachusetts	Mass.	MA
Michigan	Mich.	MI
Minnesota	Minn.	MN
Mississippi	Miss.	MS
Missouri	Mo.	MO
Montana	Mont.	MT
Nebraska	Neb.	NE
Nevada	Nev.	NV
New Hampshire	N.H.	NH
New Jersey	N.J.	NJ
New Mexico	N.M. *or* N.Mex.	NM
New York	N.Y.	NY
North Carolina	N.C.	NC
North Dakota	N.D. *or* N.Dak.	ND
Ohio	O.	OH
Oklahoma	Okla.	OK
Oregon	Oreg.	OR
Pennsylvania	Pa., Penn., *or* Penna.	PA
Rhode Island	R.I.	RI
South Carolina	S.C.	SC
South Dakota	S.Dak.	SD
Tennessee	Tenn.	TN
Texas	Tex.	TX
Utah	Ut.	UT
Vermont	Vt.	VT
Virginia	Va.	VA
Washington	Wash.	WA
▹ about.dc.gov ▹ www.washington.org ▹ dcpages.com/Tourism		
West Virginia	W.Va.	WV
Wisconsin	Wis.	WI
Wyoming	Wyo.	WY

▹ www.whitehouse.gov/government
▹ www.usinfo.state.gov/usa/infousa/travel
▹ www.usatourism.com
▹ http://www.50states.com/

Welsh counties

Anglesey
Blaenau Gwent
Bridgend
Caerphilly
Cardiff
Carmarthenshire
Ceredigion
Conwy
Denbighshire
Flintshire
Gwynedd
Merthyr Tydfil
Monmouthshire
Neath Port Talbot
Newport
Pembrokeshire
Powys
Rhondda, Cynon, Taff
Swansea
Torfaen
Vale of Glamorgan
Wrexham

▹ www.wales.gov.uk
▹ www.visitwales.com
▹ http://www.peak.org/~jeremy/dictionary/tables/counties.php

Australian Prime Ministers

Prime minister	Party	Term of office
Edmund Barton	Protectionist	1901-03
Alfred Deakin	Protectionist	1903-04
John Christian Watson	Labor	1904
George Houston Reid	Free Trade	1904-05
Alfred Deakin	Protectionist	1905-08
Andrew Fisher	Labor	1908-09
Alfred Deakin	Fusion	1909-10
Andrew Fisher	Labor	1910-13
Joseph Cook	Liberal	1913-14
Andrew Fisher	Labor	1914-15
William Morris Hughes	National Labor	1915-17
William Morris Hughes	Nationalist	1917-23
Stanley Melbourne Bruce	Nationalist	1923-29
James Henry Scullin	Labor	1929-31
Joseph Aloysius Lyons	United	1931-39
Earle Christmas Page	Country	1939
Robert Gordon Menzies	United	1939-41
Arthur William Fadden	Country	1941
John Joseph Curtin	Labor	1941-45
Joseph Benedict Chifley	Labor	1945-49
Robert Gordon Menzies	Liberal	1949-66
Harold Edward Holt	Liberal	1966-67
John McEwen	Country	1967-68
John Grey Gorton	Liberal	1968-71
William McMahon	Liberal	1971-72
Edward Gough Whitlam	Labor	1972-75
John Malcolm Fraser	Liberal	1975-83
Robert James Lee Hawke	Labor	1983-91
Paul Keating	Labor	1991-96
John Howard	Liberal	1996-

▹ http://www.pm.gov.au/your_pm/prime_ministers.html

British Prime Ministers

Prime Minister	Party	Term of office
Robert Walpol	Whig	1721-42
Earl of Wilmington	Whig	1742-43
Henry Pelham	Whig	1743-54
Duke of Newcastle	Whig	1754-56
Duke of Devonshire	Whig	1756-57
Duke of Newcastle	Whig	1757-62
Earl of Bute	Tory	1762-63
George Grenville	Whig	1763-65
Marquess of Rockingham	Whig	1765-66
Duke of Grafton	Whig	1766-70
Lord North	Tory	1770-82
Marquess of Rockingham	Whig	1782
Earl of Shelburne	Whig	1782-83
Duke of Portland	Coalition	1783
William Pitt	Tory	1783-1801
Henry Addington	Tory	1801-04
William Pitt	Tory	1804-06
Lord Grenville	Whig	1806-7
Duke of Portland	Tory	1807-09

Prime Minister	Party	Term of office
Spencer Perceval	Tory	1809-12
Earl of Liverpool	Tory	1812-27
George Canning	Tory	1827
Viscount Goderich	Tory	1827-28
Duke of Wellington	Tory	1828-30
Earl Grey	Whig	1830-34
Viscount Melbourne	Whig	1834
Robert Peel	Conservative	1834-35
Viscount Melbourne	Whig	1835-41
Robert Peel	Conservative	1841-46
Lord John Russell	Liberal	1846-52
Earl of Derby	Conservative	1852
Lord Aberdeen	Peelite	1852-55
Viscount Palmerston	Liberal	1855-58
Earl of Derby	Conservative	1858-59
Viscount Palmerston	Liberal	1859-65
Lord John Russell	Liberal	1865-66
Earl of Derby	Conservative	1866-68
Benjamin Disraeli	Conservative	1868
William Gladstone	Liberal	1868-74
Benjamin Disraeli	Conservative	1874-80
William Gladstone	Liberal	1880-85
Marquess of Salisbury	Conservative	1885-86
William Gladstone	Liberal	1886
Marquess of Salisbury	Conservative	1886-92
William Gladstone	Liberal	1892-94
Earl of Rosebery	Liberal	1894-95
Marquess of Salisbury	Conservative	1895-1902
Arthur James Balfour	Conservative	1902-05
Henry Campbell-Bannerman	Liberal	1905-08
Herbert Henry Asquith	Liberal	1908-15
Herbert Henry Asquith	Coalition	1915-16
David Lloyd George	Coalition	1916-22
Andrew Bonar Law	Conservative	1922-23
Stanley Baldwin	Conservative	1923-24
James Ramsay MacDonald	Labour	1924
Stanley Baldwin	Conservative	1924-29
James Ramsay MacDonald	Labour	1929-31
James Ramsay MacDonald	Nationalist	1931-35
Stanley Baldwin	Nationalist	1935-37
Arthur Neville Chamberlain	Nationalist	1937-40
Winston Churchill	Coalition	1940-45
Clement Attlee	Labour	1945-51
Winston Churchill	Conservative	1951-55
Anthony Eden	Conservative	1955-57
Harold Macmillan	Conservative	1957-63
Alec Douglas-Home	Conservative	1963-64
Harold Wilson	Labour	1964-70
Edward Heath	Conservative	1970-74
Harold Wilson	Labour	1974-76
James Callaghan	Labour	1976-79
Margaret Thatcher	Conservative	1979-90
John Major	Conservative	1990-97
Tony Blair	Labour	1997-

▹ http://www.number-10.gov.uk/output/Page123.asp
▹ http://www.psr.keele.ac.uk/areea/uk/pm.htm

Canadian Prime Ministers

Prime Minister	Party	Term of office
John A. MacDonald	Conservative	1867-73
Alexander Mackenzie	Liberal	1873-78
John A. MacDonald	Conservative	1878-91
John J.C. Abbot	Conservative	1891-92
John S.D. Thompson	Conservative	1892-94
Mackenzie Bowell	Conservative	1894-96
Charles Tupper	Conservative	1896
Wilfrid Laurier	Liberal	1896-1911
Robert Borden	Conservative	1911-20
Arthur Meighen	Conservative	1920-21
William Lyon Mackenzie King	Liberal	1921-26
Arthur Meighen	Conservative	1926
William Lyon Mackenzie King	Liberal	1926-30
Richard Bedford Bennet	Conservative	1930-35
William Lyon Mackenzie King	Liberal	1935-48
Louis St. Laurent	Liberal	1948-57
John George Diefenbaker	Conservative	1957-63
Lester Bowles Pearson	Liberal	1963-68
Pierre Elliott Trudeau	Liberal	1968-79
Joseph Clark	Conservative	1979-80
Pierre Elliott Trudeau	Liberal	1980-84
John Turner	Liberal	1984
Brian Mulroney	Conservative	1984-93
Kim Campbell	Conservative	1993
Joseph Jacques Jean Chrétien	Liberal	1993-

▹ http://www.parl.gc.ca/information/about/people/key/PrimeMinister.asp?Language=E
▹ http://www.primeministers.ca

New Zealand Prime Ministers

Prime Minister	Party	Term of office
Henry Sewell	-	1856
William Fox	-	1856
Edward William Stafford	-	1856-61
William Fox	-	1861-62
Alfred Domett	-	1862-63
Frederick Whitaker	-	1863-64
Frederick Aloysius Weld	-	1864-65
Edward William Stafford	-	1865-69
William Fox	-	1869-72
Edward William Stafford	-	1872
William Fox	-	1873
Julius Vogel	-	1873-75
Daniel Pollen	-	1875-76
Julius Vogel	-	1876
Harry Albert Atkinson	-	1876-77
George Grey	-	1877-79
John Hall	-	1879-82
Frederick Whitaker	-	1882-83
Harry Albert Atkinson	-	1883-84
Robert Stout	-	1884
Harry Albert Atkinson	-	1884
Robert Stout	-	1884-87
Harry Albert Atkinson	-	1887-91

Prime Minister	Party	Term of office
John Ballance	-	1891-93
Richard John Seddon	Liberal	1893-1906
William Hall-Jones	Liberal	1906
Joseph George Ward	Liberal/National	1906-12
Thomas Mackenzie	National	1912
William Ferguson Massey	Reform	1912-25
Francis Henry Dillon Bell	Reform	1925
Joseph Gordon Coates	Reform	1925-28
Joseph George Ward	Liberal/National	1928-30
George William Forbes	United	1930-35
Michael Joseph Savage	Labour	1935-40
Peter Fraser	Labour	1940-49
Sidney George Holland	National	1949-57
Keith Jacka Holyoake	National	1957
Walter Nash	Labour	1957-60
Keith Jacka Holyoake	National	1960-72
John Ross Marshall	National	1972
Norman Eric Kirk	Labour	1972-74
Wallace Edward Rowling	Labour	1974-75
Robert David Muldoon	National	1975-84
David Russell Lange	Labour	1984-89
Geoffrey Palmer	Labour	1989-90
Mike Moore	Labour	1990
Jim Bolger	National	1990-97
Jenny Shipley	National	1997-99
Helen Clark	Labour	1999-

▹ http://www.atonz.com/new_zealand/nz_prime-ministers.html
▹ http://history-nz.org/ministers.html

U.S. Presidents

President	Party	Term of office
1. George Washington	Federalist	1789-97
2. John Adams	Federalist	1797-1801
3. Thomas Jefferson	Democratic Republican	1801-1809
4. James Madison	Democratic Republican	1809-1817
5. James Monroe	Democratic Republican	1817-25
6. John Quincy Adams	Democratic Republican	1825-29
7. Andrew Jackson	Democrat	1829-37
8. Martin Van Buren	Democrat	1837-41
9. William Henry Harrison	Whig	1841
10. John Tyler	Whig	1841-45
11. James K. Polk	Democrat	1845-49
12. Zachary Taylor	Whig	1849-50
13. Millard Fillmore	Whig	1850-53
14. Franklin Pierce	Democrat	1853-57
15. James Buchanan	Democrat	1857-61
16. Abraham Lincoln	Republican	1861-65
17. Andrew Johnson	Republican	1865-69
18. Ulysses S. Grant	Republican	1869-77
19. Rutherford B. Hayes	Republican	1877-81
20. James A. Garfield	Republican	1881
21. Chester A. Arthur	Republican	1881-85
22. Grover Cleveland	Democrat	1885-89
23. Benjamin Harrison	Republican	1889-93
24. Grover Cleveland	Democrat	1893-97

President	Party	Term of office
25. William McKinley	Republican	1897-1901
26. Theodore Roosevelt	Republican	1901-1909
27. William Howard Taft	Republican	1909-13
28. Woodrow Wilson	Democrat	1913-21
29. Warren G. Harding	Republican	1921-23
30. Calvin Coolidge	Republican	1923-29
31. Herbert C. Hoover	Republican	1929-33
32. Franklin D. Roosevelt	Democrat	1933-45
33. Harry S. Truman	Democrat	1945-53
34. Dwight D. Eisenhower	Republican	1953-61
35. John F. Kennedy	Democrat	1961-63
36. Lyndon B. Johnson	Democrat	1963-69
37. Richard M. Nixon	Republican	1969-74
38. Gerald R. Ford	Republican	1974-77
39. James E. Carter, Jr	Democrat	1977-81
40. Ronald W. Reagan	Republican	1981-89
41. George H. W. Bush	Republican	1989-93
42. William J. Clinton	Democrat	1993-2001
43. George W. Bush	Republican	2001-

▹ http://www.whitehouse.gov/history/presidents
▹ http://www.ipl.org/div/potus/
▹ http://www.heptune.com/preslist.html

Capital cities

City	Country
Abu Dhabi	United Arab Emirates
Abuja	Nigeria
Accra	Ghana
Addis Ababa	Ethiopia
▹ www.tourethio.com/capital	
Astana	Kazakhstan
Algiers	Algeria
Amman	Jordan
▹ www.access2arabia.com/moga	
Amsterdam	Netherlands
▹ www.visitamsterdam.nl	
Andorra la Vella	Andorra
Ankara	Turkey
▹ www.visitturkeynow.com/cities/c_ankara.htm	
Antananarivo	Madagascar
Apia	Samoa
www.go-samoa.com/apia.html	
Ashkhabad	Turkmenistan
Asmara	Eritrea
Asunción	Paraguay
Athens	Greece
▹ www.cityofathens.gr/et/en/index.html	
Baghdad	Iraq
▹ www.iraqioasis.com/baghdad.html	
Baku	Azerbaijan
▹ www.baku.com	
Bamako	Mali
Bandar Seri Begawan	Brunei
▹ www.municipal-bsb.gov.bn	
Bangkok	Thailand
▹ www.tourismthailand.org	
▹ www.guidetothailand.com/bangkok-thailand	
Bangui	Central African Republic
Banjul	Gambia
Basseterre	St. Kitts and Nevis
▹ www.geographia.com/stkitts-nevis/knpnto2.htm	
Beijing	People's Republic of China
▹ www.beijing.gov.cn	
Beirut *or* **Beyrouth**	Lebanon
▹ www.middleeast.com/beirut.htm	
Belfast	Northern Ireland
Belgrade	Yugoslavia (Serbia and Montenegro)
▹ www.beograd.org.yu	
▹ www.belgradetourism.org.yu	
Belmopan	Belize
▹ www.travel-belize.com/belmopan.htm	
Berlin	Germany
▹ www.btm.de	
Bern	Switzerland
▹ www.berne.ch	
▹ www.tripadvisor.com/Tourism-g188052-Bern-Vacations.html	
Bishkek	Kyrgyzstan
Bissau	Guinea-Bissau
Bloemfontein	judicial capital of South Africa
Bogotá	Colombia
▹ www.bogota-dc.com	
Brasília	Brazil
▹ www.infobrasilia.com.br	
Bratislava	Slovakia
▹ www.bratislava.sk	
▹ slovakia.eunet.sk	
Brazzaville	Congo (Republic of)
▹ www.brazzaville.i-p.cm	
Bridgetown	Barbados
▹ www.barbados.org/btown.htm	
Brussels	Belgium
▹ www.brussels.org	
▹ www.bruxelles.irisnet.be/En/Homeen.htm	
Bucharest	Romania
▹ www.romaniatourism.com/main.html	
▹ www.explore-bucharest.com	
▹ www.rotravel.com/romania/sites/tour	
Budapest	Hungary
▹ www.budapest.hu	
Buenos Aires	Argentina
▹ www.buenosaires.gov.ar	
Bujumbura	Burundi
Cairo	Egypt
▹ www.cairotourist.com	
Canberra	Australia
▹ www.act.gov.au	
▹ www.nationalcapital.gov.au	
Cape Town	legislative capital of South Africa
Caracas	Venezuela
▹ www.discovervenezuela.com/caracas.cfm	
Cardiff	Wales
Castries	St. Lucia
▹ stlucia.rezrez.com/whattoseedo/attractions/castries/index.htm	
Cayenne	French Guiana
Colombo	Sri Lanka
▹ www.atsrilanka.com/cityofcolombo.htm	
▹ www.explorelanka.com/places/colombo.htm	
Conakry *or* **Konakry**	Guinea
▹ www.gn.refer.org	
Copenhagen	Denmark
▹ www.copenhagen.com	
Dakar	Senegal
Damascus	Syria
▹ www.syriatourism.org/new/index.html	
▹ www.made-in-syria.com/damascus.htm	
Delhi	India
▹ http://delhigovt.nic.in	
Dhaka *or* **Dacca**	Bangladesh
▹ www.dhaka-bangladesh.com	
Dili	East Timor
Djibouti *or* **Jibouti**	Djibouti *or* Jibouti
▹ www.republique-djibouti.com/gouvernement.htm	
Dodoma	Tanzania
▹ www.itanzania.info/Dodoma_Region.htm	

City	Country
Doha	Qatar
▹ www.qatartourism.org/edo.asp?ID=185	
Douglas	Isle of Man
Dublin	Republic of Ireland
▹ www.visitdublin.com	
Dushanbe	Tajikistan
Edinburgh	Scotland
Fort-de-France	Martinique
Freetown	Sierra Leone
Funafuti	Tuvalu
▹ www.southpacific.org/text/tuvalu.html	
Gaborone	Botswana
▹ www.gov.bw/tourism/attractions/gaborone. html	
Georgetown	Guyana
Guatemala City	Guatemala
Hanoi	Vietnam
▹ www.thudo.gov.vn/Hanoi_Tourism	
Harare	Zimbabwe
▹ www.zimbabwetourism.co.zw/destzim/index.html	
Havana	Cuba
Helsinki	Finland
▹ www.hel.fi/English	
Honiara	Solomon Islands
Islamabad	Pakistan
Jakarta *or* **Djakarta**	Indonesia
▹ www.jakarta.go.id	
Jerusalem	Israel
▹ www.jerusalem.muni.il	
Kabul	Afghanistan
Kampala	Uganda
▹ www.visituganda.com/uganda/cities_n_towns/index.htm	
▹ www.destinationplanner.com/africa/uganda/kampala.html	
Katmandu *or* **Kathmandu**	Nepal
▹ www.welcomenepal.com/destinationKTM.asp?ID=1	
Khartoum *or* **Khartum**	Sudan
Kiev	Ukraine
▹ www.uazone.net/Kiev.html; also	
▹ www.kiev.info	
Kigali	Rwanda
Kingston	Jamaica
▹ www.jamaicatravelnet.com/info/kingston.html	
Kingstown	St. Vincent and the Grenadines
Kinshasa	Congo (Democratic Republic of)
Kishinev	Moldova
▹ www.chisinau.md/pmc/en/home.htm	
▹ www.turism.md/eng/content/42	
Koror	Palau
▹ www.visit-palau.com/kor.html	
Kuala Lumpur	Malaysia
▹ www.visitmalaysia.com/kualalumpur.html	
Kuwait	Kuwait
La Paz	administrative capital of Bolivia

City	Country
Libreville	Gabon
Lilongwe	Malawi
▹ www.tourismmalawi.com	
Lima	Peru
▹ www.peru-travel.net/lima/lima.html	
Lisbon	Portugal
▹ www.atl-turismolisboa.pt	
▹ www.explore-lisbon.com	
Ljubljana	Slovenia
▹ www.ljubljana.si/generalinformation	
▹ www.slovenia-tourism.si	
Lomé	Togo
London	United Kingdom
▹ www.cityoflondon.gov.uk	
▹ www.londontourist.org	
Luanda	Angola
▹ www.angola.org/referenc/luanda.html	
Lusaka	Zambia
▹ www.zambiatourism.com	
Luxembourg	Luxembourg
▹ www.luxembourg-city.lu/touristinfo	
Madrid	Spain
▹ www.madridtourism.org	
▹ www.europeanrailguide.com/destinationguides/madrid	
Majuro	Marshall Islands
Malabo	Equatorial Guinea
Malé	Maldives
▹ www.visitmaldives.com/thecapital/index. html	
Managua	Nicaragua
▹ www.edicioneslupita.com/paseo/managuai.html	
Manama	Bahrain
▹ www.bahraintourism.com/manama_map	
Manila	Philippines
▹ www.tourism.gov.ph/top_25/manilam.htm	
Maputo	Mozambique
▹ www.mozambique.mz/turismo/emaputo.htm	
▹ www.go2africa.com/mozambique/maputo/	
Maseru	Lesotho
▹ www.go2africa.com/Lesotho/Lesotho/Maseru	
Mbabane	Swaziland
▹ www.mbabane.org.sz	
Mexico City	Mexico
▹ www.mexicocity.gob.mx	
Minsk	Belarus
▹ www.belarustourist.minsk.by/english/city	
Mogadishu	Somalia
Monaco-Ville	Monaco
Monrovia	Liberia
Montevideo	Uruguay
▹ www.visit-uruguay.com/montevideo.htm	
Moroni	Comoros
Moscow	Russia
▹ www.intourist.com/ENG/MOSCOW/info.shtml	
▹ www.all-moscow.ru	
Muscat	Oman
▹ www.omanet.com	
Nairobi	Kenya
▹ www.kenyaweb.com/vnairobi	

City	Country
Nassau	Bahamas
▹ www.bahamas.com/islands/nassau	
Ndjamena	Chad
Niamey	Niger
Nicosia	Cyprus
▹ www.kypros.org/Cyprus/nicosia.html	
Nouakchott	Mauritania
lexicorient.com/mauritania/nouakch.htm	
Nuku'alofa	Tonga
Nuuk	Greenland
Oslo	Norway
▹ www.a-zoftourism.com/Shopping-in-Oslo.htm	
▹ www.bugbog.com/european_cities/oslo_travel.html	
Ottawa	Canada
▹ www.city.ottawa.on.ca	
Ouagadougou	Burkina-Faso
Palikir	Micronesia
▹ www.thebusinesstravelreport.com	
Panama City	Panama
Paramaribo	Suriname
▹ www.sr.net/srnet/InfoSurinam/paramaribo.html	
Paris	France
▹ www.paris.org	
Phnom Penh	Cambodia
Pishpek	Kirghizia
Port-au-Prince	Haiti
▹ www.haiti-reference.com/geographie/villes/pap.html	
Port Louis	Mauritius
▹ www.mauritius.net/whattovisit/historical.places_main.htm	
Port Moresby	Papua New Guinea
▹ portmoresby.com	
Port of Spain	Trinidad and Tobago
▹ www.discover-tt.com/trinidad/port-of-spa-novo.org	
Port Vila	Vanuatu
▹ www.vanuatutourism.com	
Prague	Czech Republic
▹ www.pis.cz	
Praia	Cape Verde
Pretoria	administrative capital of South Africa
▹ www.sa-venues.com/gauteng_pretoria.htm	
Pristina	Kosovo (Federal Republic of Yugoslavia)
Pyongyang	North Korea
Quito	Ecuador
▹ www.quito.gov.ec	
Rabat	Morocco
▹ www.mincom.gov.ma/english/reg_cit/cities/rabat/rabat.html	
▹ www.cyber.net.ma/chadiatours/images/rabat2.htm	
Reykjavik	Iceland
▹ www.rvk.is	

City	Country
Riga	Latvia
▹ www.virtualriga.com/default.asp	
Riyadh	Saudi Arabia
▹ www.vvtel.com/vvtravels/saudi_arabia-su/007_guides/02_cities	
Rome	Italy
▹ www.comune.roma.it/eng/index.asp	
Roseau	Dominica
San`a	Yemen
▹ members.aol.com/yalnet/sanaa.htm	
San José	Costa Rica
▹ www.msj.co.cr	
San Juan	Puerto Rico
San Marino	San Marino
San Salvador	El Salvador
Santiago	Chile
▹ www.ciudad.cl	
Santo Domingo	Dominican Republic
▹ www.sdq.com	
São Tomé	São Tomé and Principe
Sarajevo	Bosnia and Herzegovina
Seoul	South Korea
▹ welcome.seoul.go.kr	
▹ english.seoul.go.kr	
Singapore	Singapore
▹ www.gov.sg	
▹ www.visitsingapore.com	
Skopje	Macedonia
▹ www.skopjeonline.com.mk	
▹ www.b-info.com/places/Macedonia	
Sofia	Bulgaria
▹ www.sofia.bg	
St. George's	Grenada
St. John's	Antigua and Barbuda
▹ www.antigua-barbuda.org/Agjohn01.htm	
Stockholm	Sweden
▹ www.sverigeturism.se/smorgasbord/index. html	
Sucre	legislative and judicial capital of Bolivia
Suva	Fiji
Taipei	Taiwan
▹ www.taipei.gov.tw/English	
Tallinn	Estonia
▹ http://tallinn.ee	
Tarawa	Kiribati
Tashkent	Uzbekistan
▹ www.tashkent.org	
▹ www.advantour.com/uzbekistan/tashkent.htm	
▹ www.uzbekistanembassy.uk.net/main/uzbe	
Tbilisi	Georgia
▹ www.parliament.ge/~nino/tbilisi.html	
Tegucigalpa	Honduras
Tehran	Iran
▹ www.farsinet.com/tehran	
Tel Aviv	Israel
▹ www.tel-aviv.gov.il	

City	Country
Thimphu	Bhutan
Tirana	Albania
▹ www.tirana-online	
Tokyo	Japan
▹ www.chijihonbu.metro.tokyo.jp/english/index.htm	
Tripoli	Libya
▹ www.libyaonline.com/libya/cities/tripoli.php	
Tunis	Tunisia
▹ www.tourismtunisia.com/togo/tunis/tunis.html	
Ulan Bator	Mongolia
▹ www.niislel.com	
ulaanbaatar.net	
Vaduz	Liechtenstein
Valletta	Malta
▹ www.visitmalta.com	
▹ web.idirect.com/~malta/valletta.htm	
Vatican City	Vatican City
▹ www.vatican.va	
Victoria	Seychelles
Vienna	Austria
▹ www.wien.gv.at	
▹ http://info.wien.at	
Vientiane	Laos
▹ www.visit-laos.com/where/vientiane	
Vilnius	Lithuania
▹ www.vilnius.lt	
▹ www.turizmas.vilnius.lt	
▹ neris.mii.lt/homepage/liet1-1.html	
Warsaw	Poland
▹ www.explorewarsaw.com	
Washington DC	United States of America
▹ about.dc.gov	
▹ www.washington.org	
▹ dcpages.com/Tourism	
Wellington	New Zealand
▹ www.wellingtonnz.com	
▹ www.wellingtonnewzealand.co.nz/wellington	
▹ www.wrc.govt.nz	
Windhoek	Namibia
▹ www.windhoekcc.org.na	
▹ www.grnnet.gov.na/Nav_frames/Nutshell_launch.htm	
Yamoussoukro	Côte d'Ivoire
▹ http://yamoussoukro.org	
Yangon (Rangoon)	Myanmar (Burma)
▹ www.yangoncity.com.mm	
▹ www.myanmar-tourism.com/yangon.htm	
Yaoundé *or* **Yaunde**	Cameroon
Yaren	Nauru
Yerevan	Armenia
Zagreb	Croatia
▹ www.zagreb-touristinfo.hr	

Currencies

Country	Currency	Code
Afghanistan	afghani	AFA
Albania	lek	ALL
Algeria	dinar	DZD
American Samoa	US dollarUSD	
Andorra	euro	EUR
Angola	kwanza	KWA
Anguilla	East Caribbean dollar	XCD
Antarctica	Norwegian krone	NOK
Antigua and Barbuda	East Caribbean dollar	XCD
Argentina	Argentine peso	ARS
Armenia	dram	AMD
Aruba	Arubian guilder	AWG
Australia	Australian dollar	AUD
Austria	euro	EUR
Azerbaijan	manat	AZM
Bahamas	Bahamanian dollar	BSD
Bahrain	Bahraini dinar	BHD
Bangladesh	taka	BDT
Barbados	Barbados dollar	BBD
Belarus	Belarussian rouble	BYR
Belgium	euro	EUR
Belize	Belize dollar	BZD
Benin	CFA franc BCEAO	XOF
Bermuda	Bermudian dollar	BMD
Bhutan	ngultrum	BTN
Bolivia	boliviano	BOB
Bosnia-Herzegovina	convertible marka	BAM
Botswana	pula	BWP
Brazil	real	BRL
British Virgin Islands	US dollar	USD
Brunei	Bruneian dollar	BND
Bulgaria	lev	BGN
Burkina Faso	CFA franc BCEAO	XOF
Burundi	Burundi franc	BIF
Cambodia	riel	KHR
Cameroon	CFA franc BEAC	XAF
Canada	Canadian dollar	CAD
Cape Verde	Cape Verde escudo	CVE
Cayman Islands	Cayman Islands dollar	KYD
Central African Republic	CFA franc BEAC	XAF
Chad	CFA franc BEAC	XAF
Chile	Chilean peso	CLP
China	yuan renminbi	CNY
Christmas Island	Australian dollar	AUD
Cocos (Keeling) Islands	Australian dollar	AUD
Colombia	Colombian peso	COP
Comoros	Comoro franc	KMF

Country	Currency	Code
Congo	CFA franc BEAC	XAF
Congo, Democratic Republic of	Congolese franc	CDF
Cook Islands	New Zealand dollar	NZD
Costa Rica	Costa Rican colon	CRC
Côte d'Ivoire	CFA franc BCEAO	XOF
Croatia	kuna	HRK
Cuba	Cuban peso	CUP
Cyprus	Cyprus pound	CYP
Czech Republic	Czech koruna	CZK
Denmark	Danish krone	DKK
Djibouti	Djibouti franc	DJF
Dominica	East Caribbean dollar	XCD
Dominican Republic	Dominican peso	DOP
East Timor	Timor escudo	TPE
Ecuador	US dollar	USD
Egypt	Egyptian pound	EGP
El Salvador	El Salvador colon	SVC
Equatorial Guinea	CFA franc BEAC	XAF
Eritrea	nakfa	ERN
Estonia	kroon	EEK
Ethiopia	Ethiopian birr	ETB
Falkland Islands	Falkland Islands pound	FKP
Faroe Islands	Danish krone	DKK
Fiji	Fiji dollar	FJD
Finland	euro	EUR
France	euro	EUR
French Guiana	euro	EUR
French Polynesia	CFP franc	XPF
French Southern and Antarctic Territories	euro	EUR
Gabon	CFA franc BEAC	XAF
Gambia	dalasi	GMD
Georgia	lari	GEL
Germany	euro	EUR
Ghana	cedi	GHC
Gibraltar	Gibraltar pound	GIP
Greece	euro	EUR
Greenland	Danish krone	DKK
Grenada	East Caribbean dollar	XCD
Guadeloupe	euro	EUR
Guam	US dollar	USD
Guatemala	Quetzal	GTQ
Guinea	Guinea franc	GNF
Guinea-Bissau	Guinea-Bissau peso	GWP
Guyana	Guyana dollar	GYD
Haiti	gourde	HTG
Heard and McDonald Islands	Australian dollar	AUD
Honduras	lempira	HNL
Hong Kong	Hong Kong dollar	HKD

Country	Currency	Code
Hungary	forint	FOR
Iceland	Iceland krona	ISK
India	Indian rupee	INR
Indonesia	rupiah	IDR
Iran	Iranian rial	IRR
Iraq	Iraqi dinar	IQD
Ireland	euro	EUR
Israel	Israeli sheqel	ILS
Italy	euro	EUR
Jamaica	Jamaican dollar	JMD
Japan	yen	JPY
Jordan	Jordanian dinar	JOD
Kazakhstan	tenge	KZT
Kenya	Kenyan shilling	KES
Kiribati	Australian dollar	AUD
Korea (North)	North Korean won	KPW
Korea (South)	won	KRW
Kuwait	Kuwaiti dinar	KWD
Kyrgyzstan	som	KGS
Lao People's Democratic Republic	kip	LAK
Latvia	lats	LVL
Lebanon	Lebanese pound	LBP
Lesotho	loti	LSL
Liberia	Liberian dollar	LRD
Libya	Libyan dinar	LYD
Liechtenstein	Swiss franc	CHF
Lithuania	litus	LTL
Luxembourg	euro	EUR
Macau	pataca	MOP
Macedonia, FYR of	denar	MKD
Madagascar	Malagasy franc	MGF
Malawi	kwacha	MWK
Malaysia	Malaysian ringgit	MYR
Maldives	rufiyaa	MVR
Mali	CFA franc BCEAO	XOF
Malta	Maltese lira	MTL
Marshall Islands	US dollar	USD
Martinique	euro	EUR
Mauritania	ouguiya	MRO
Mauritius	Mauritius rupee	MUR
Mayotte	euro	EUR
Mexico	Mexican peso	MXN
Micronesia (Federated States of)	US dollar	USD
Moldova	Moldovan leu	MDL
Monaco	euro	EUR
Mongolia	tugrik	MNT
Montserrat	East Caribbean dollar	XCD
Morocco	Moroccan dirham	MAD
Mozambique	metical	MZM
Myanmar	kyat	MMK
Namibia	rand;	ZAR;
Nauru	Australian dollar	AUD

Country	Currency	Code
Nepal	Nepalese rupee	NPR
Netherlands	euro	EUR
Netherlands Antilles	Netherlands Antillian guilder	ANG
New Caledonia	CFP franc	XPF
New Zealand	New Zealand dollar	NZD
Nicaragua	cordoba oro	NIO
Niger	CFA franc BCEAO	XOF
Nigeria	naira	NGN
Niue	New Zealand dollar	NZD
Norfolk Island	Australian dollar	AUD
Northern Mariana Islands	US dollar	USD
Norway	Norwegian krone	NOK
Oman	rial Omani	OMR
Pakistan	Pakistan rupee	PKR
Palau	US dollar	USD
Panama	balboa;	PAB;
Papua New Guinea	kina	PGK
Paraguay	guarani	PYG
Peru	new sol	PEN
Philippine	Philippine peso	PHP
Pitcairn Island	New Zealand dollar	NZD
Poland	zloty	PLN
Portugal	euro	EUR
Puerto Rico	US dollar	USD
Qatar	Qatari rial	QAR
Réunion	euro	EUR
Romania	leu	ROL
Russian Federation	Russian ruble	RUR
Rwanda	Rwanda franc	RWF
Saint Helena	Saint Helena pound	SHP
Saint Kitts and Nevis	East Caribbean dollar	XCD
Saint Lucia	East Caribbean dollar	XCD
Saint Pierre and Miquelon	euro	EUR
Saint Vincent and the Grenadines	East Caribbean dollar	XCD
Samoa	tala	WST
San Marino	euro	EUR
São Tomé and Príncipe	dobra	STD
Saudi Arabia	Saudi riyal	SAR
Senegal	Senegal franc BCEAO	XOF
Serbia and Montenegro	euro	EUR
Seychelles	Seychelles rupee	SCR
Sierra Leone	leone	SLL
Singapore	Singapore dollar	SGD

Country	Currency	Code
Slovakia	Slovak koruna	SKK
Slovenia	tolar	SIT
Soloman Islands	Soloman Islands dollar	SBD
Somalia	Somali shilling	SOS
South Africa	rand	ZAR
Spain	euro	EUR
Sri Lanka	Sri Lanka rupee	LKR
Sudan	Sudanese dinar	SDD
Suriname	Suriname guilder	SRG
Svalbard and Jan Mayen	Norwegian krone	NOK
Swaziland	lilangeni	SZL
Sweden	Swedish krona	SEK
Switzerland	Swiss franc	CHF
Syria	Syrian pound	SYP
Taiwan	New Taiwan dollar	TWD
Tajikistan	somoni	TJS
Tanzania	Tanzanian shilling	TZS
Thailand	baht	THB
Togo	CFA franc BCEAO	XOF
Tokelau	New Zealand dollar	NZD
Tonga	pa'anga	TOP
Trinidad and Tobago	Trinidad and Tobago dollar	TTD
Tunisia	Tunisian dinar	TND
Turkey	Turkish lira	TRL
Turkmenistan	manat	TMM
Turks and Caicos Islands	US dollar	USD
Tuvalu	Australian dollar	AUD
Uganda	Ugandan shilling	UGX
Ukraine	hryvnia	UAH
United Arab Emirates	UAE dirham	AED
United Kingdom	pound sterling	GBP
United States	US dollar	USD
Uruguay	Uruguayan peso	UYU
Uzbekistan	Uzbekistan sum	UZS
Vanuatu	vatu	VUV
Vatican City	euro	EUR
Venezuela	bolivar	VEB
Vietnam	dong	VND
Virgin Islands (UK)	US dollar	USD
Virgin Islands (US)	US dollar	USD
Wallis and Futuna	CFP franc	XPF
Western Sahara	Moroccan dirham	MAD
Yemen	Yemeni rial	YER
Zambia	kwacha	ZMK
Zimbabwe	Zimbabwe dollar	ZWD

▹www.exchangerate.com/indication_rates.html

▹ http://www.xe.com/ucc

▹ www.uta.fi/~ktmatu/rate-symbols.html